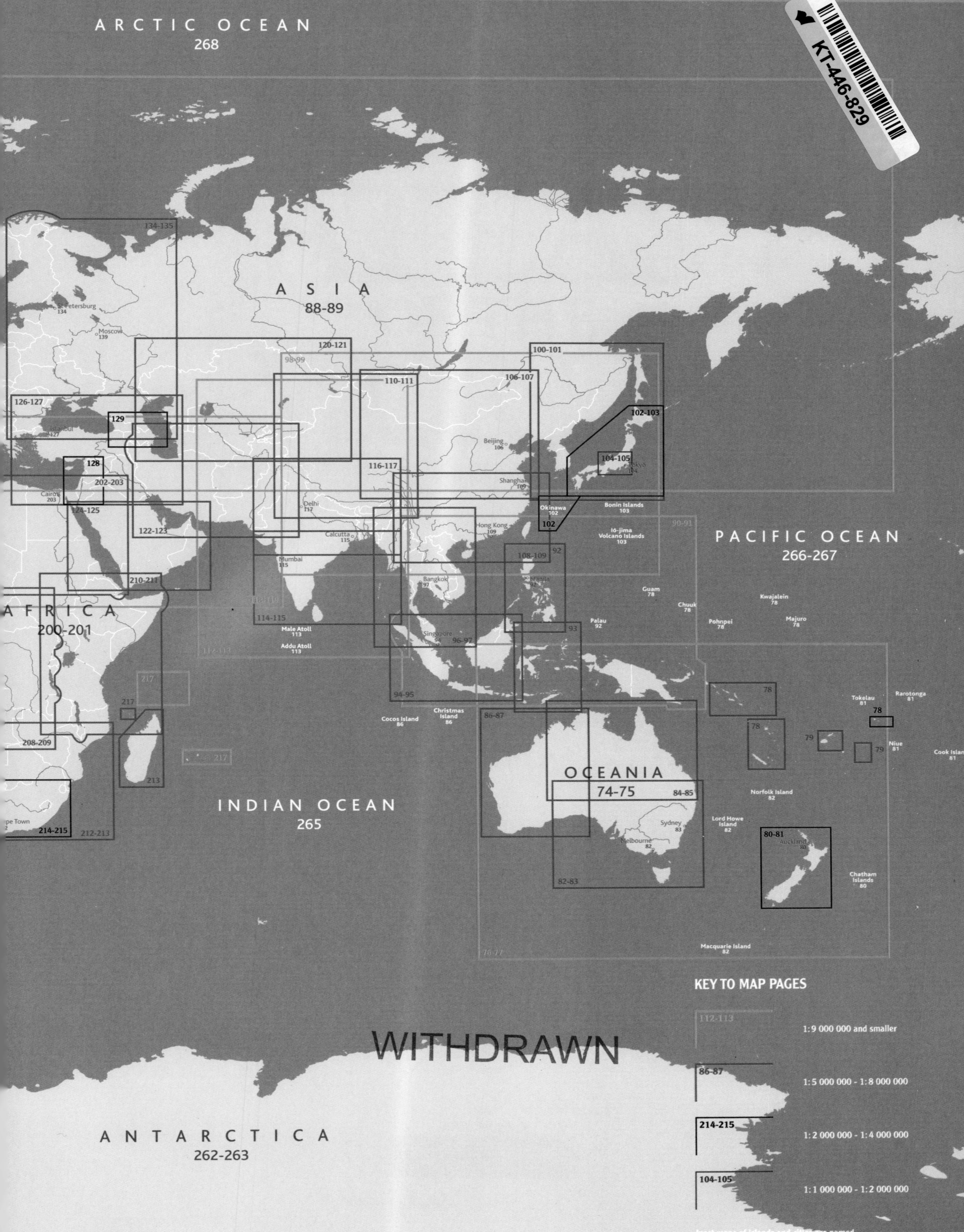

ARCTIC OCEAN
268
ASIA
88-89
134-135
St Petersburg
134
Moscow
139
120-121
98-99
100-101
110-111
106-107
126-127
129
Istanbul
127
102-103
Beijing
106
104-105
Tokyo
104
128
202-203
Cairo
203
116-117
Shanghai
109
Okinawa
102
102
Bonin Islands
103
124-125
Delhi
117
122-123
Calcutta
115
Hong Kong
109
Iō-jima
Volcano Islands
103
90-91
PACIFIC OCEAN
266-267
Mumbai
115
108-109
92
Manila
210-211
118-119
Bangkok
97
Guam
78
Kwajalein
78
Chuuk
78
AFRICA
200-201
114-115
Male Atoll
113
Addu Atoll
113
Singapore
94
96-97
93
Palau
92
Pohnpei
78
Majuro
78
112-113
217
94-95
78
Tokelau
81
Rarotonga
81
217
Cocos Island
86
Christmas
Island
86
86-87
78
78
79
79
Niue
81
Cook Islands
81
208-209
213
217
OCEANIA
74-75
84-85
Norfolk Island
82
INDIAN OCEAN
265
Cape Town
214-215
212-213
Lord Howe
Island
82
Sydney
83
80-81
Auckland
80
Melbourne
82
82-83
Chatham
Islands
80
Macquarie Island
82
76-77
KEY TO MAP PAGES
112-113
1:9 000 000 and smaller
86-87
1:5 000 000 - 1:8 000 000
214-215
1:2 000 000 - 1:4 000 000
104-105
1:1 000 000 - 1:2 000 000
ANTARCTICA
262-263
Inset maps of islands and cities are named.
See back endpapers for detailed keys to North America and Europe.

Times Books, 77-85 Fulham Palace Road, London W6 8JB

First Edition 1972
Second Edition 1975
Third Edition 1978
Fourth Edition 1980
Fifth Edition 1986
Sixth Edition 1992
Seventh Edition 1995

Eighth Edition 2000
Reprinted 2001

Printed and bound in the UK

British Library Cataloguing in Publication Data
A catalogue record for this book is available from the British Library

ISBN 0 7230 1084 6

OH10986 Imp 002

The maps in this product are also available for
purchase in digital format from Bartholomew Data Sales
Tel: +44 (0) 141 306 3155, Fax: +44 (0) 141 306 3130
www.bartholomewmaps.com

THE TIMES

CONCISE

ATLAS

OF THE

WORLD

TIMES BOOKS

London

CONTENTS

THE WORLD TODAY

GEOGRAPHICAL INFORMATION

ATLAS OF THE WORLD

WORLD

OCEANIA

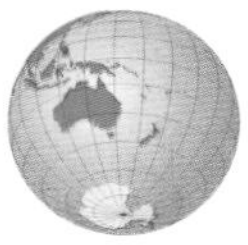

CONTENTS

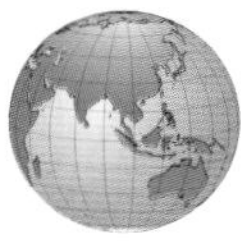

ASIA

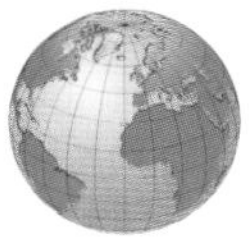

EUROPE

CONTENTS

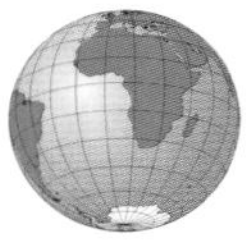

AFRICA

CONTENTS

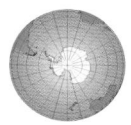

OCEANIA

Australia and the vast expanse of the Pacific Ocean dominate this satellite image of Oceania. The islands of Indonesia lie to the northwest of Australia and New Guinea lies to the north, with the islands of the Solomon Island chain, Vanuatu and New Caledonia stretching southeast from New Guinea towards New Zealand. The Hawaiian Islands appear in the top right of the image.

The different colours on these images reveal a great variety of vegetation. This is particularly evident here in the contrasts between the highlands and lowlands of New Guinea and between the east coast, the Great Dividing Range and the complex interior of Australia.

See pages 74–75 for a map of Oceania.

Data from the 1km AVHRR Global Land dataset project by ESA, CEOS, IGBP, NASA, NOAA, USGS, IONIA processed by ESA/ESRIN distributed by Eurimage S.p.A

ASIA

This image shows the continent of
Asia from the Mediterranean Sea
and the distinctive shape of
The Gulf in the west, to Japan in
the east, and from snow-covered
Siberia in the north to the tropical
islands of Indonesia in the south.
The shapes of the Caspian and Aral Seas
appear in the northwest.

The image illustrates a wide range of land cover –
particularly in China, with great variation
between the intricate patterns of vegetation in
the southeast and the large, relatively featureless
areas of the Tarim Pendi basin in the northwest,
in the centre of the image. The snow covered
Himalaya form a dominating feature of the
image, stretching in a gentle white arc between
the Indian sub-continent and China.

See pages 88–89 for a map of Asia.

Data from the 1km AVHRR Global Land dataset project by ESA, CEOS,
IGBP, NASA, NOAA, USGS, IONIA processed by ESA/ESRIN distributed
by Eurimage S.p.A

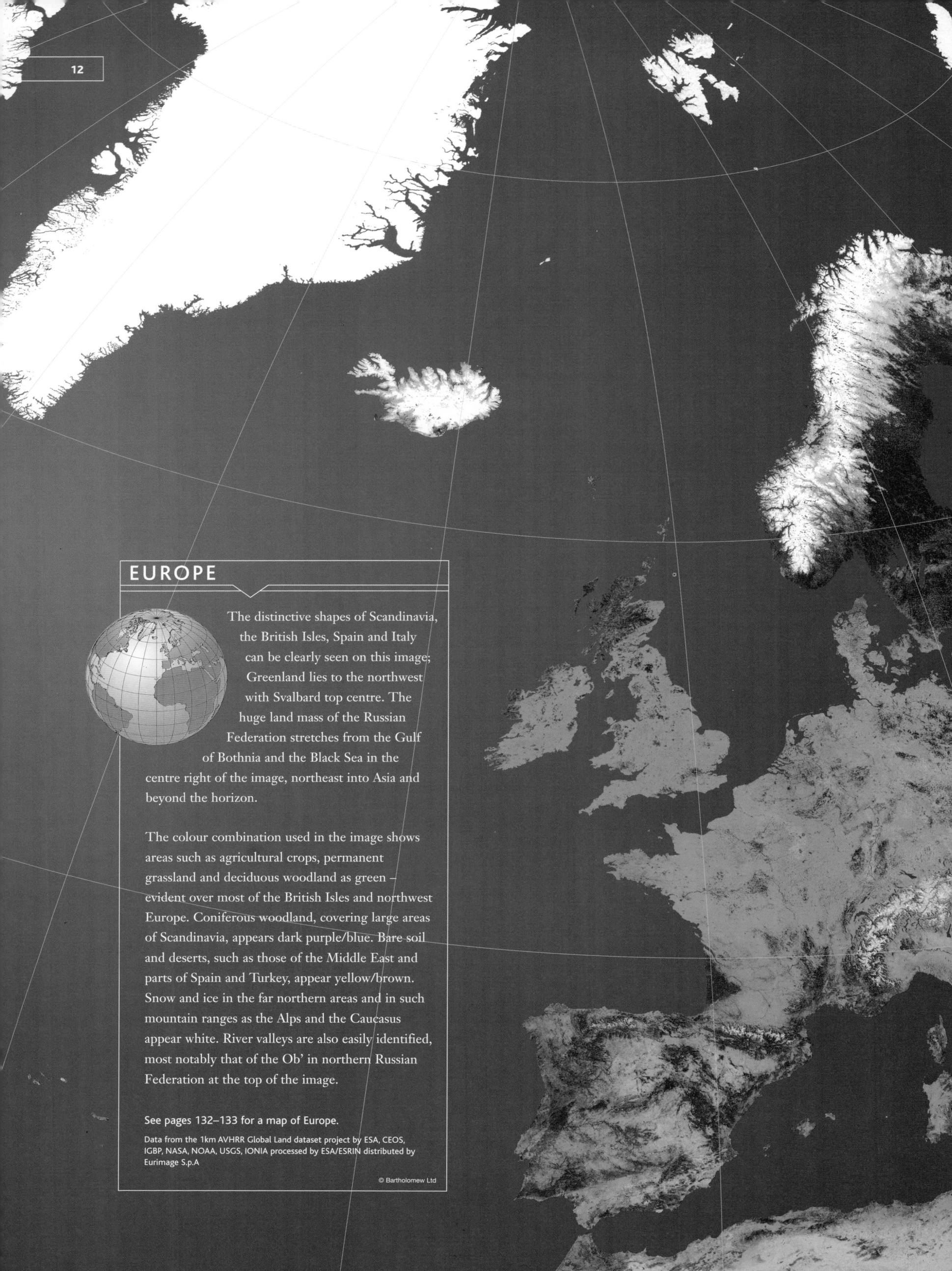

EUROPE

The distinctive shapes of Scandinavia, the British Isles, Spain and Italy can be clearly seen on this image; Greenland lies to the northwest with Svalbard top centre. The huge land mass of the Russian Federation stretches from the Gulf of Bothnia and the Black Sea in the centre right of the image, northeast into Asia and beyond the horizon.

The colour combination used in the image shows areas such as agricultural crops, permanent grassland and deciduous woodland as green – evident over most of the British Isles and northwest Europe. Coniferous woodland, covering large areas of Scandinavia, appears dark purple/blue. Bare soil and deserts, such as those of the Middle East and parts of Spain and Turkey, appear yellow/brown. Snow and ice in the far northern areas and in such mountain ranges as the Alps and the Caucasus appear white. River valleys are also easily identified, most notably that of the Ob' in northern Russian Federation at the top of the image.

See pages 132–133 for a map of Europe.

Data from the 1km AVHRR Global Land dataset project by ESA, CEOS, IGBP, NASA, NOAA, USGS, IONIA processed by ESA/ESRIN distributed by Eurimage S.p.A

AFRICA

This view of Africa looks north, with South America just appearing in the southwest, the island of Madagascar to the southeast and Arabia and Asia to the northeast.

Subtle variations in vegetation are evident, particularly across the north of the continent and in the Sahara – an area of desert that could be expected to be more uniform in appearance. Also clearly shown are the variations in basic land cover with latitude. The gradations in colour southwards from the Sahara indicate a steady change in vegetation type through the equatorial regions. Sharp contrasts in land use are also clear along the northern coast of Africa with the cultivated area of the Nile valley and delta particularly impressive.

See pages 200–201 for a map of Africa.

Data from the 1km AVHRR Global Land dataset project by ESA, CEOS, IGBP, NASA, NOAA, USGS, IONIA processed by ESA/ESRIN distributed by Eurimage S.p.A

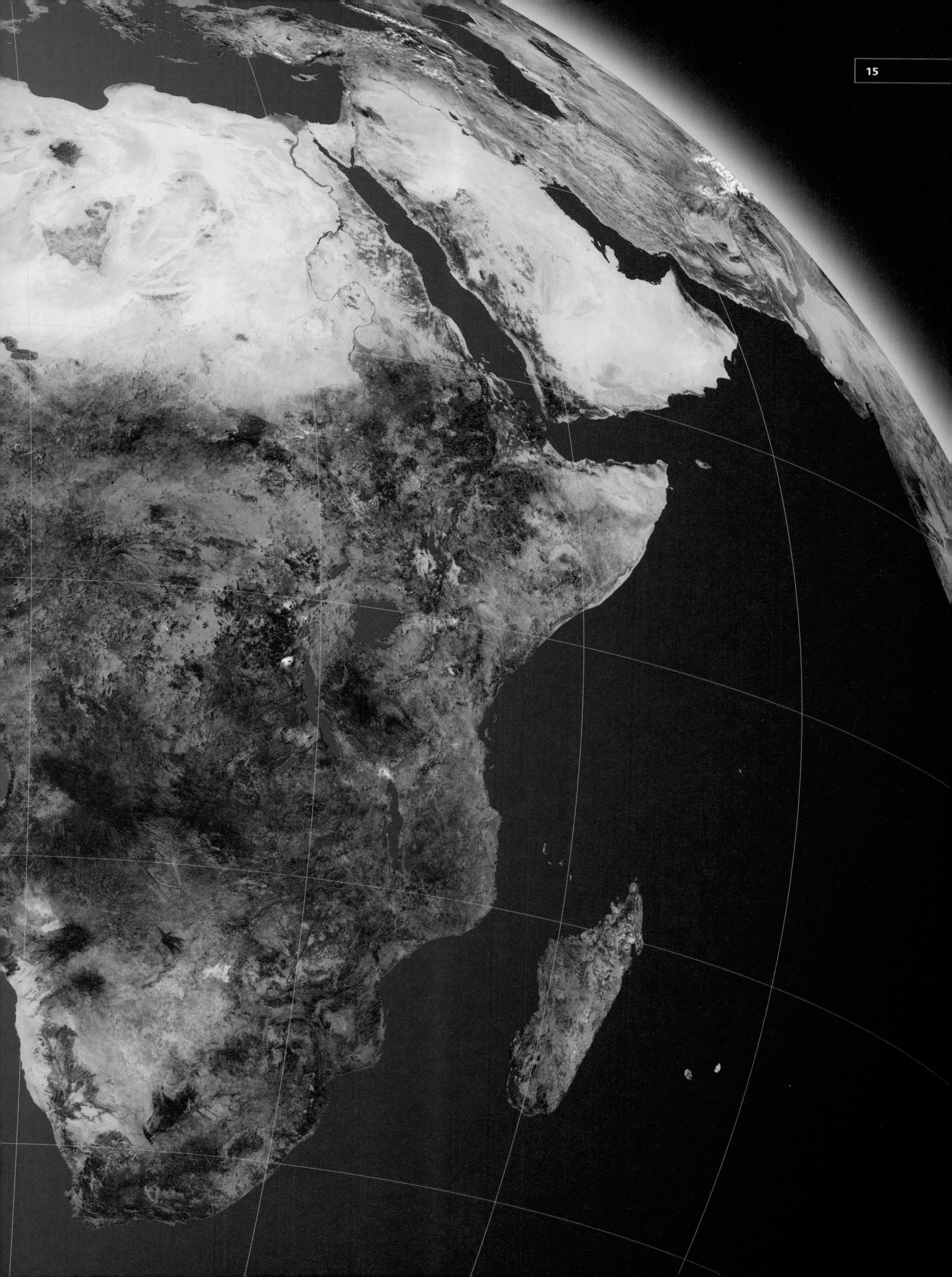

NORTH AMERICA

This image views North America from above the centre of the continent and includes most of the Arctic Ocean. The Aleutian Islands in the northwest stretch in an arc toward the Kamchatka Peninsula in eastern Asia, and western Europe and northwest Africa appear to the northeast. The islands of the Caribbean lie east and south of Florida in the bottom right of the image.

The contrast between land and water areas is very clear, with the complex drainage patterns and coastlines of Alaska, northern Canada and Greenland shown in great detail. In northwest Canada the Great Slave Lake, Great Bear Lake and thousands of others in the far north are clearly visible, as is the Mackenzie river in northwest Canada. The outlines of the Great Lakes are also impressively clear. The easy identification of specific variations in vegetation and land cover is also illustrated by the prominence of such features as the Mississippi river valley, and the San Joaquin and Sacramento valleys of California. The dominance of coniferous forest (dark purple/blue) across large areas of Canada, stretching in a wide band virtually across the whole continent, is also clearly seen.

See pages 218–219 for a map of North America.

Data from the 1km AVHRR Global Land dataset project by ESA, CEOS, IGBP, NASA, NOAA, USGS, IONIA processed by ESA/ESRIN distributed by Eurimage S.p.A

SOUTH AMERICA

South and Central America appear in the centre of this image with the Pacific Ocean to the west and the Atlantic Ocean to the east, and Africa appearing on the northeast and southeast horizons. The Galapagos Islands lie off the coast of Ecuador and the Falkland Islands, South Georgia and the Antarctic Peninsula off the southern tip of the continent.

The great range of green and blue tones represent different types and conditions of vegetation across the Amazon basin. Although the data contains no indication of surface height, it can indicate the underlying structure of the land. Here, the mountain ranges of the northern Andes and western Colombia are clearly evident. The small red areas on the east coast of Brazil, representing the major urban areas of São Paulo and Rio de Janeiro, illustrate the impressive level of detail available from this type of imagery.

See pages 248–249 for a map of South America.

Data from the 1km AVHRR Global Land dataset project by ESA, CEOS, IGBP, NASA, NOAA, USGS, IONIA processed by ESA/ESRIN distributed by Eurimage S.p.A

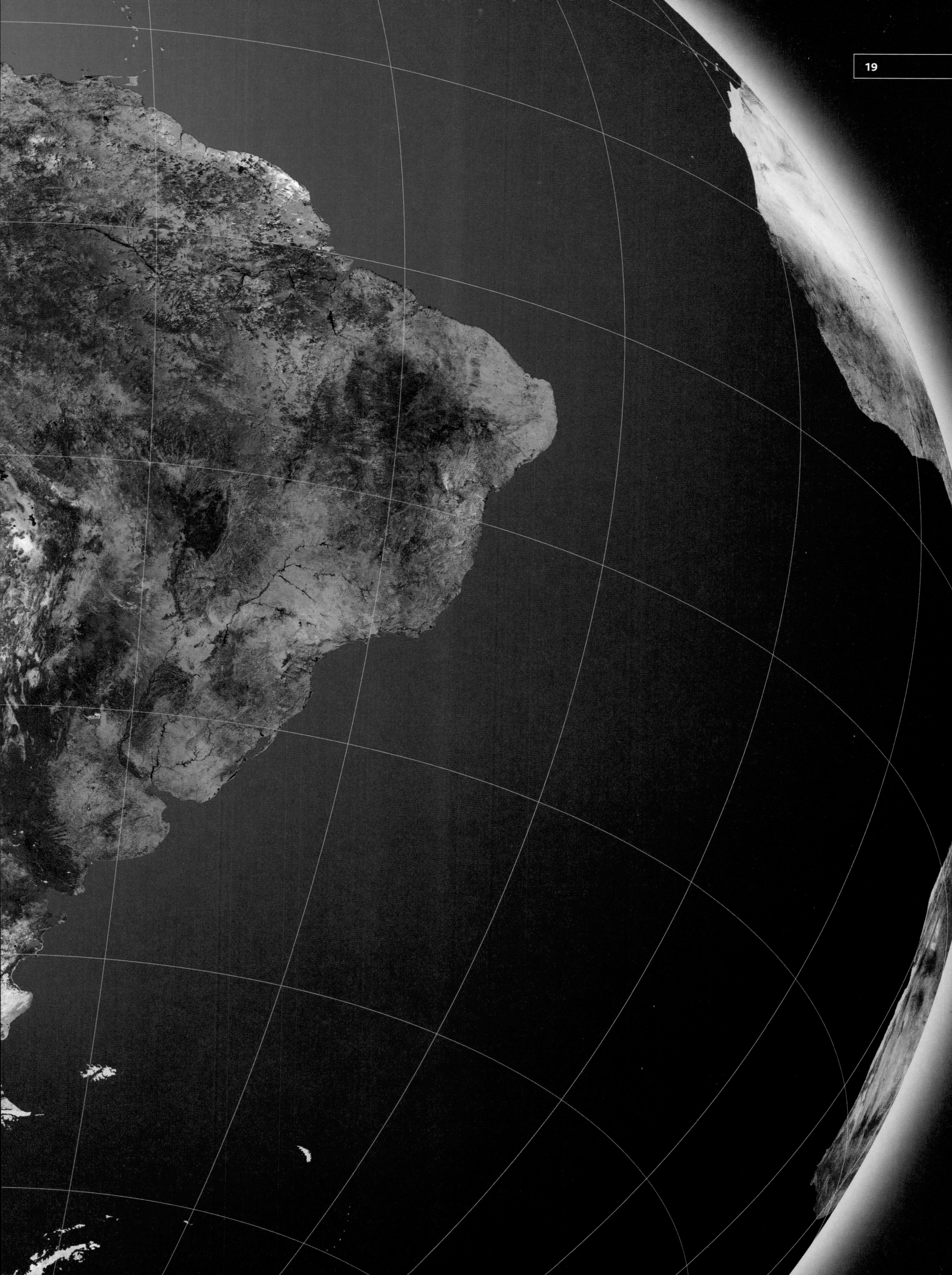

ANTARCTICA

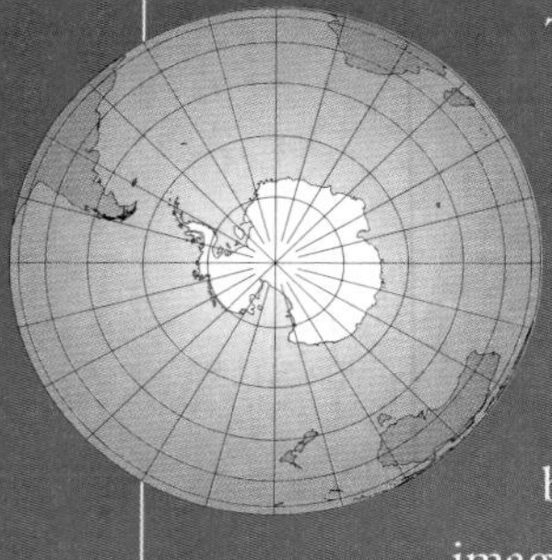

This image positions the Antarctic continent with the Greenwich meridian to the top centre. The distinctive shape of the Antarctic Peninsula lies to the top left and the prominent Ross Ice Shelf can be identified to the bottom of the image, below the Transantarctic Mountains range.

Although not completely cloud-free – there is some cloud cover in the eastern area to the right of the image – the image is impressive in its depiction of the physical features of the continent. The Ronne Ice Shelf, including Berkner Island, and the Transantarctic Mountains are particularly spectacular. Floating ice is excluded from the image, resulting in a clear definition of the extent of the continental ice sheet in an austral summer.

See pages 262–263 for a continental map of Antarctica.

NEPTUNE

ORIGINS OF THE SOLAR SYSTEM

The nature and origin of our Solar System has been a subject of much debate. Early ideas of an Earth-centred system took many hundreds of years to be discarded in favour of Copernicus' heliocentric, or sun-centred model. More refined theories followed with Kepler's laws of orbital motion, and Newton's laws of gravity. The question of origin remained unanswered, and was regarded more as a philosophical matter.

The fact that the Sun and the planets rotate in a similar direction suggests a common formation mechanism - that of a large collapsing cloud or nebula. It is now believed that this did happen, about 4 600 million years ago. The nebula consisted of predominantly hydrogen and helium, but with a small amount of heavier elements. Over time, the cloud collapsed to form a rotating disk around a dense core. As core collapse continued and pressure in the core increased, material was heated enough to allow the nuclear fusion of hydrogen. Meanwhile as the disk cooled, the heavier elements began to condense and agglomerate. Larger bodies grew rapidly by sweeping up much of the remaining smaller material. As the core began to shine, its radiation pushed back much of the nearby volatile disk material into the outer Solar System, where it condensed and accumulated on the more distant planetary cores. This left the Inner Planets as small rocky bodies, and produced the Gas Giants of the outer system. Bombardment of the planets by a decreasing number of small bodies continued for several hundred million years, causing the craters now seen on many of the planets and moons.

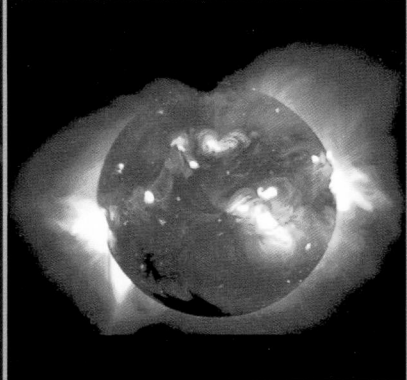

The Sun

The Sun is a typical star. It accounts for 99.85 per cent of the total mass contained within the Solar System, ensuring that it provides a dominating gravitational hold on its orbiting planets. The tremendous amount of heat and light produced by the Sun is the result of nuclear fusion reactions which occur in its core. In this process, hydrogen is converted into helium to produce a core temperature of roughly 15 million°C. Intense magnetic fields can induce cooling zones seen as dark sun spots on the Sun's surface. The Sun constantly emits a stream of charged particles which form the solar wind and cause auroral activity which can be seen on Earth.

	Sun	Mercury	Venus	Earth	Mars	Jupiter	Saturn	Uranus	Neptune	Pluto
Mass (Earth=1)	332 830	0.055	0.815	1(6 x 10²⁴)	0.107	317.9	95.2	14.5	17.1	0.002
Volume (Earth=1)	1 306 000	0.06	0.89	1	0.157	1 323	752	64	54	0.006
Density (Water=1)	1.41	5.43	5.25	5.52	3.95	1.33	0.69	1.29	1.64	2.03
Equatorial diameter (km)	1 392 000	4 879	12 104	12 756	6 794	142 984	120 536	51 118	49 492	2 320
Polar flattening	0	0	0	0.003	0.005	0.065	0.108	0.03	0.021	0
Surface gravity (Earth=1)	27.5	0.38	0.902	1	0.382	0.248	1.02	0.9	1.13	0.4
Number of satellites > 100 km	-	0	0	1	0	7	13	8	6	1
Total number of satellites	-	0	0	1	2	16	20	17	8	1
Rotation period (Earth days)	25 - 36	58.65	-243	23hr 56m 4s	1.03	0.414	0.444	-0.71	0.67	-6.39
Year (Earth days/years)	-	88 days	224.7 days	365.26 days	687 days	11.86 years	29.46 years	84.01 years	164.8 years	248.6 years
Mean orbital distance (million km)	-	57.9	108.2	149.6	227.9	778.3	1 249	2 871	4 504	5 914
Orbital eccentricity	-	0.2056	0.0068	0.0167	0.0934	0.0483	0.056	0.0461	0.0097	0.2482
Mean orbital velocity (km/s)	-	47.88	35.02	29.79	24.13	13.06	9.65	6.81	5.44	4.74
Inclination of equator to orbit	7.25	0	177.3	23.45	25.19	3.12	26.73	97.86	29.56	122.46
Orbital inclination (w.r.t. ecliptic)	-	7.01	3.4	0	1.85	1.31	2.49	0.77	1.77	17.13
Mean surface temperature (°C)	5 700	427(d), -173(n)	482	15	-63	-153	-185	-215	-225	-235
Atmospheric pressure (bars)	-	10^{-15}	92	1.013	0.007	-	-	-	-	3×10^{-6}
Atmospheric composition	H_2 92.1% He 7.8% O_2 0.061%	He 42% Na 42% O_2 15%	CO_2 96% N_2 3%	N_2 77% O_2 21% Ar 1.6%	CO_2 95.3% N_2 2.7%	H_2 90% He 10%	H_2 97% He 3%	H_2 83% He 15% CH_4 2%	H_2 85% He 13% CH_4 2%	N_2 CO CH_4

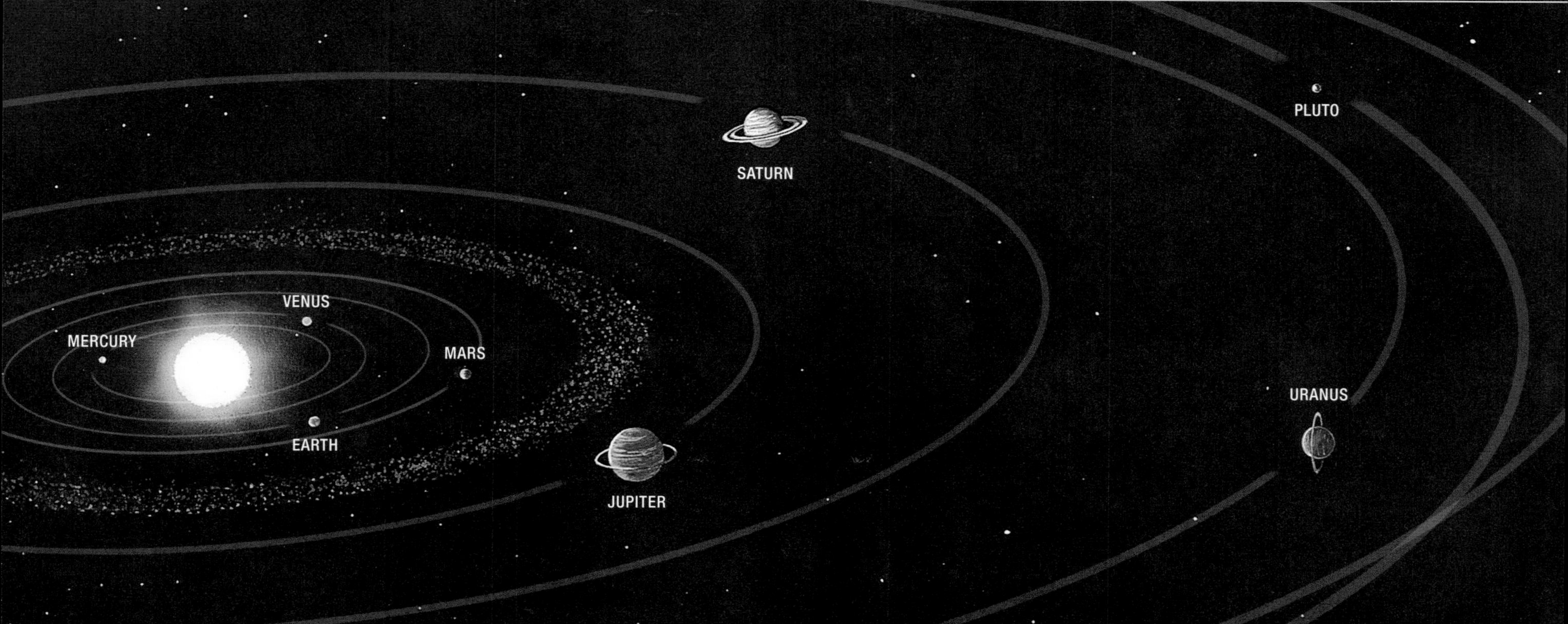

MERCURY VENUS EARTH MARS

JUPITER SATURN

URANUS

PLUTO

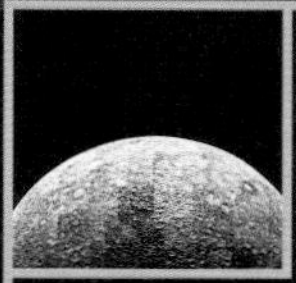

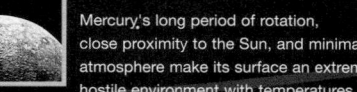

Mercury

Mercury's long period of rotation, close proximity to the Sun, and minimal atmosphere make its surface an extremely hostile environment with temperatures ranging from 427 to minus 173°C between its day and night side. Mercury is similar to Earth's Moon in size and appearance; its cratered surface was first photographed in detail in the mid-1970s by the Mariner 10 space probe. However the internal structure differs from the Moon; analysis of its magnetic field suggests that the core consists of molten iron, believed to be 40 per cent of the planet's volume. Mercury has a very eccentric orbit with its orbital distance varying from 46 to 70 million km.

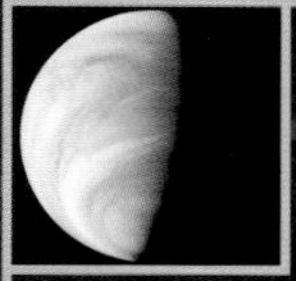

Venus

Venus' thick atmosphere of carbon dioxide and nitrogen creates not only a huge surface pressure of over ninety times that on Earth but also a greenhouse effect producing temperatures in excess of 480°C. Traces of sulphur dioxide and water vapour form clouds of dilute sulphuric acid, making the atmosphere extremely corrosive. This atmosphere reflects almost all incident visible radiation and prevents direct observation of surface features. In 1990 use of radar imaging enabled the Magellan space probe to see through the cloud. Magellan mapped 98 per cent of the planet during three years to find a surface covered in craters, volcanoes, mountains and solidified lava flows. Venus is the brightest object in the sky after the Sun and Moon and is unusual in that its year is less than its rotation period.

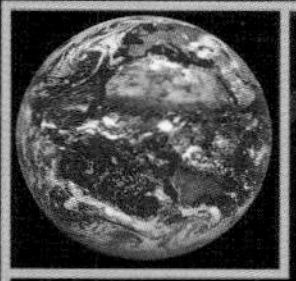

Earth

Earth is the largest and densest of the Inner Planets. Created some 4 500 million years ago, the core, rocky mantle and crust are similar in structure to Venus. The Earth's core is composed almost entirely of iron and oxygen compounds which exist in a molten state at temperatures of around 5 000°C. Earth is the only planet with vast quantities of life-sustaining water, with the oceans covering 70.8 per cent of its surface. The action of plate tectonics has created vast mountain ranges and is responsible for volcanic activity. The Moon is Earth's only natural satellite and with a diameter of over one quarter that of the Earth's, makes the Earth-Moon system a near double-planet.

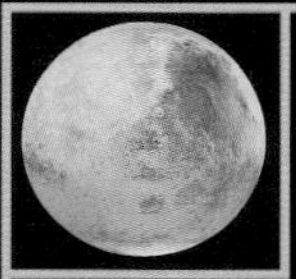

Mars

Named after the Roman god of war because of its blood-red appearance, Mars is the last of the Inner Planets. The red colour comes from the high concentration of iron-oxides on its surface. Mars has impressive surface features, including the highest known peak in the Solar System, Olympus Mons, an inactive volcano reaching a height of 23 km above the surrounding plains, and Marineris, a 2 500 km long canyon four times as deep as the Grand Canyon. The Pathfinder mission in 1997 has shown that much of the Martian surface is shaped by intense dust storms which often engulf the entire planet. Mars has polar caps composed of water and carbon dioxide ice which partially evaporate during its summer.

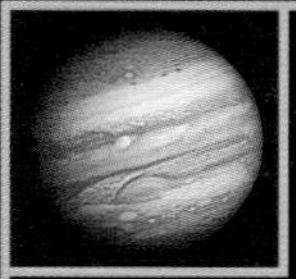

Jupiter

Jupiter is by far the most massive of all the planets and is the dominant body in the Solar System after the Sun. It is the innermost of the Gas Giants. The dense surface atmosphere is predominantly hydrogen, with helium, water vapour, and methane. Below this is a layer of liquid hydrogen, then an even deeper layer of metallic hydrogen. Unlike solid bodies, Jupiter's rotation period is somewhat ill-defined, with equatorial regions rotating faster than the polar caps; this, combined with convection currents in lower layers, cause intense magnetic fields and rapidly varying surface features. Most notable of these is the Great Red Spot, a giant circular storm visible since the first observations of Jupiter's surface, which shows no signs of abating.

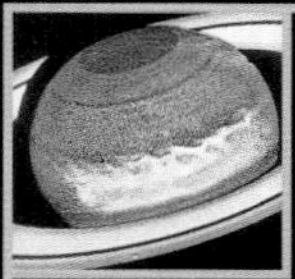

Saturn

Although only slightly smaller that Jupiter, Saturn is a mere one third of Jupiter's mass, and the least dense of all the planets - less dense than water. The low mass, combined with a fast rotation rate, leads to the planet's significant polar flattening. Saturn exhibits a striking ring system, more than twice the diameter of the planet; the rings consist of countless small rock and ice clumps which vary in size from a grain of sand to tens of metres in diameter. It is believed that the rings were formed from a stray moon coming too close to, and being ripped apart by Saturn. Distinct bands and gaps in the rings are the result of complex interactions between Saturn and its closer moons. Recent rare opportunities to view Saturn's rings edge ways have yielded the discovery of at least two other moons.

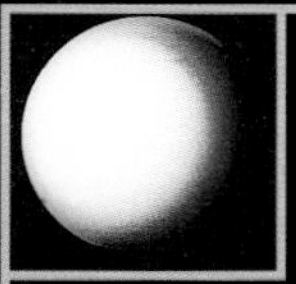

Uranus

Uranus has many surprising features; the most prominent of these is the tilt of its rotation axis by over 90 degrees caused by a series of large collisions in its early history. Like the other Gas Giants, Uranus is predominantly hydrogen and helium with a small proportion of methane and other gases. However, because Uranus is colder than Jupiter and Saturn, the methane forms ice crystals which give Uranus a featureless blue-green colour. The interior is also different from that expected. Instead of having a gaseous atmosphere above liquid and metallic hydrogen layers, Uranus has a super dense gaseous atmosphere extending down to its core. Uranus' magnetic field is inclined at 60 degrees to the rotation axis, and is off centre by one third of the planet's radius, which suggests that it is not generated by the core. The system of eleven narrow rings around Uranus is prevented from spreading by the interaction of nearby 'shepherd' moons. Two new moons, Caliban and Sycorax, were discovered in 1997 although their large orbits indicate they are probably captured asteroids.

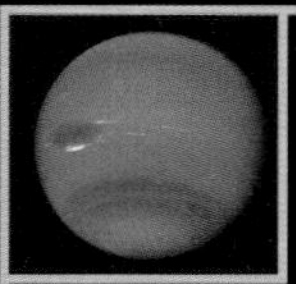

Neptune

Neptune has always been associated with Uranus because of its similar size, composition and appearance, but, unexpectedly, Neptune's atmosphere is more active than that of Uranus. This was shown by Voyager 2 in 1989 with the observation of the Great Dark Spot, Neptune's equivalent to Jupiter's Great Red Spot. Voyager 2 recorded the fastest winds ever seen in the Solar System, 2 000 km per hour, around the Dark Spot. This feature disappeared in 1994, but has been replaced by a similar storm in the northern polar cap. Like Uranus, Neptune has a magnetic field highly inclined to the planet's axis of rotation and off-centre by more than half of the planet's radius. The cause of this magnetic field is convection currents in conducting fluid layers outside the core. Neptune's largest moon, Triton, is in an inclined retrograde orbit, indicating that it was captured by Neptune rather than formed alongside it. The slowly decaying orbit will one day bring Triton too close to Neptune, and it will be torn apart forming a spectacular ring.

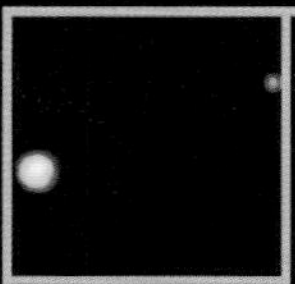

Pluto

Pluto's existence was predicted before its discovery in 1930, from perturbations in Neptune's orbital motion. Pluto's orbit is highly eccentric and tilted with respect to the solar plane, unusually so for a planet. Its only moon, Charon, is abnormally large, and orbits Pluto at 90 degrees to the solar plane. Both Pluto and Charon have an uncharacteristically high proportion of rock, 70 per cent, with only 30 per cent water ice. All these anomalies bring Pluto's planetary status into question. It is likely that Pluto is a large planetesimal formed farther out of the Solar System, and is now in a stable orbit. Pluto, unlike Charon, possesses a methane ice surface layer, which forms a tenuous yet deep atmosphere when close to the Sun.

THE EARTH'S STRUCTURE

The interior of the Earth can be divided into three principal regions (see 1). The outermost region is known as the crust, which is extremely thin compared to the Earth as a whole. Under the continents the crust is about 33 km thick on average, only 0.5 per cent of the total radius of the Earth (6 370 km). Under the oceans the crust is even thinner: perhaps a third of its continental thickness. Over the course of geological time the Earth's crust has broken up into large fragments, which are known as lithospheric plates. These plates are slowly moving relative to one another at rates of a few centimetres per year – a process know as continental drift.

The next layer down is known as the mantle which is about 2 850 km thick. The distinction between the mantle and crust is made on the basis of composition and strength. There is a zone of the upper mantle, at depths between about 100 and 700 km, which behaves like a fluid when under stress. This weak zone is called the asthenosphere. The outermost 70 km or so of the mantle, together with the crust, is known as the lithosphere and is much stronger. The transition between the lithosphere and asthenosphere is due to variation in temperature, and is therefore gradual rather than being a distinct boundary.

Below the mantle is the Earth's core, which is about 3 470 km in radius, and is mainly made up of iron. The greater part of the core is completely liquid; however, there is a solid inner core, about 1 220 km in radius.

It is the dynamic processes operating in the upper parts of the Earth's interior which give rise to very dramatic and violent expressions of the huge energies involved: earthquakes and volcanoes. Both of these can be very destructive, even disastrous, in terms of both loss of life and economic impact. Consequently, study of these phenomena is very important if the natural disasters arising from them are to be mitigated.

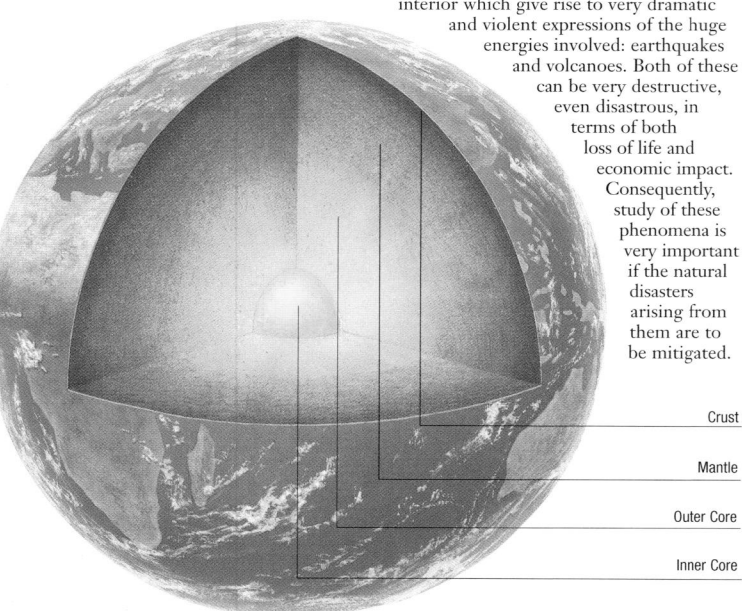

Crust

Mantle

Outer Core

Inner Core

1. THE EARTH'S INTERIOR

DISTRIBUTION OF EARTHQUAKES AND VOLCANOES

Any map showing the distribution of earthquakes and volcanoes (see 2) will inevitably look very similar to a map showing the boundaries of the tectonic plates (see 3). This is because both phenomena are largely controlled by the processes of plate tectonics. The vast majority of the world's earthquakes occur at plate boundaries as a result of one plate pushing past another along what is known as a constructive boundary, or under another at a destructive boundary, creating a subduction zone. Even those earthquakes which occur away from

plate margins (intraplate earthquakes) are still mostly due to stresses in the rocks that result indirectly from plate movements.

Most major volcanoes occur along lines parallel to subduction zones, as for example, in the Andes. Other volcanoes can form along mid-ocean ridges where the asthenosphere is close to the surface; such volcanoes can produce what are known as fissure eruptions, where vast amounts of basaltic lava suddenly erupt on the surface, inundating huge areas.

3. PLATE BOUNDARIES

scale 1:270 000 000

| Constructive - mid ocean ridge | | Destructive | | Conservative |

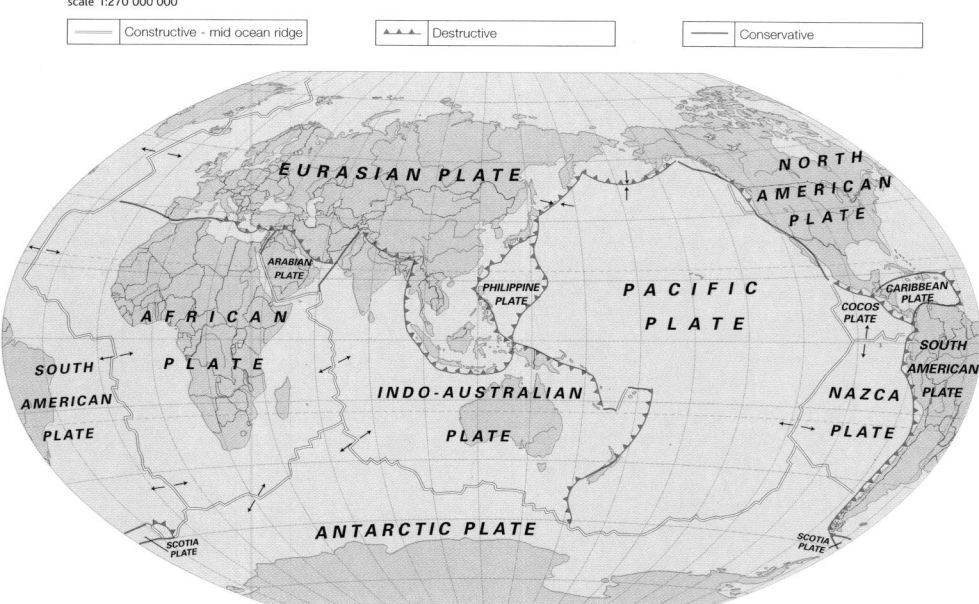

EURASIAN PLATE

NORTH AMERICAN PLATE

ARABIAN PLATE

PHILIPPINE PLATE

PACIFIC PLATE

CARIBBEAN PLATE

COCOS PLATE

AFRICAN PLATE

SOUTH AMERICAN PLATE

INDO-AUSTRALIAN PLATE

NAZCA PLATE

SOUTH AMERICAN PLATE

SCOTIA PLATE

ANTARCTIC PLATE

SCOTIA PLATE

2. DISTRIBUTION OF MAJOR EARTHQUAKES AND VOLCANOES

Winkel Tripel Projection
scale 1:90 000 000

Key

▲ Volcanoes active between 1900 and 2000

● Earthquakes between 1900 and 2000 causing over 10 000 deaths.

Arctic Circle

EUROPE

AFRICA

ATLANTIC

Tropic of Cancer

Equator

SOUTH AMERICA

OCEAN

Tropic of Capricorn

IN

OC

SOUTHERN OCE

Antarctic Circle

A

EARTHQUAKES

An earthquake is produced by a sudden breaking of rock in the Earth's crust as the stresses become too great for the strength of the rock to withstand. Naturally, this is most likely to happen where the rock is weakest. Where the rock breaks, a fracture line, known as a fault is left, and because there is now a break, future movements are likely to happen along the same weakness. The forces involved derive mostly from the movements of the tectonic plates; for example, between the upper surface of a subducting plate and the lower surface of the plate under which it is sliding – conditions which have caused some of the world's largest earthquakes.

The force with which the rock breaks releases a large amount of energy in the form of waves that travel through the Earth. These radiate outwards from where the fault has ruptured. The point on the fault at which the rupture begins is known as the hypocentre; this is usually at a depth of 10 to 30 km for shallow earthquakes; earthquakes in subduction zones can be as deep as 600 km below the Earth's surface. The point on the Earth's surface directly above the hypocentre is called the epicentre; this is what can be shown on a map. The magnitude of an earthquake, the so-call Richter scale, is a logarithmic approximation of the total amount of energy released. A large earthquake which may be severely damaging at the epicentre, is less strongly felt by people at greater distances. The strength of shaking at any point is known as the intensity, and this decreases with distance from the epicentre.

The earthquake off the southern coast of Honshū, Japan in January 1995 caused over 5 500 deaths and extensive damage in the Köbe area and on Awaji-shima; the photo shows damage in Köbe.

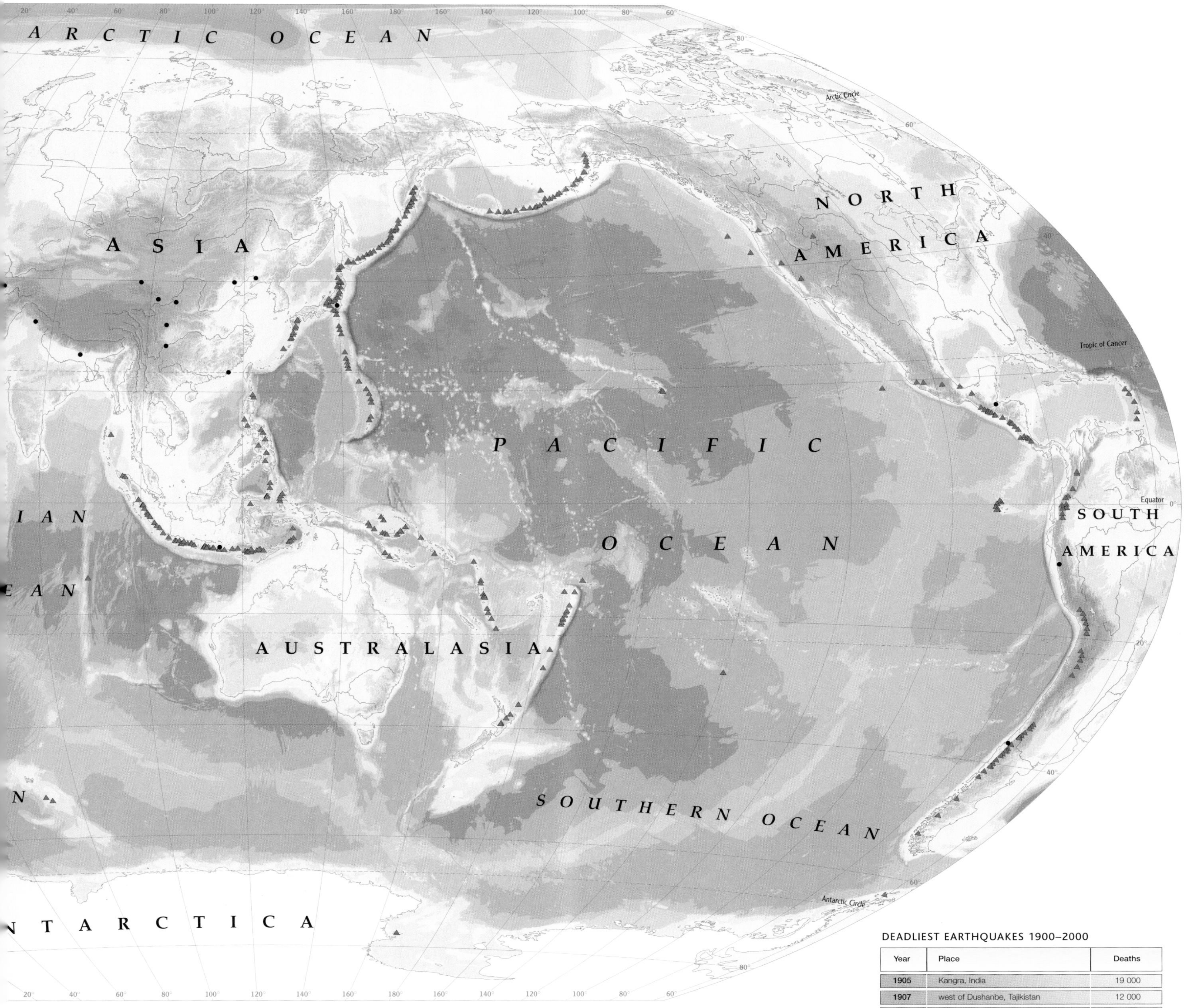

VOLCANOES

In the simplest terms, a volcano is a vent at the surface of the Earth where molten rock (magma) from the interior can reach the surface. The magma originates ultimately in the Earth's mantle. It then erupts either as a stream of liquid rock (called lava when it appears at the surface) or as fine particles of ash or cinder. The erupted material builds up over time into a mountain, typically conical in shape. The exact shape of the volcano is controlled by the type of material erupted. Volcanoes in oceanic locations (such as Hawaii) tend to erupt very basic (non-acidic) lava which flows relatively easily. Because it can run quite far before cooling, this produces a very flat volcano with gentle slopes, known as a shield volcano. Continental volcanoes produce more acidic lava which flows more slowly, and they produce more ash, and therefore have steeper-sided cones. Such volcanoes also tend to erupt more explosively, because of the greater amount of steam or gas in the lava, and are generally more dangerous. They can produce what is know as a pyroclastic flow, a fast-moving cloud of super-heated ash and gases, which is what destroyed Pompeii in AD79.

Volcanoes can also be classified according to their eruptive history. Active volcanoes are those that are currently erupting; an eruption can go on intermittently for years, and some volcanoes, such as Stromboli in Italy, are almost permanently active. However, most volcanoes erupt much less frequently, and those that have not erupted for tens or hundreds of years, but may be expected to erupt again, are said to be dormant. Volcanoes which were once active in response to the tectonic situation as it was millions of years ago, and which cannot possibly erupt again today are said to be extinct.

Kilauea volcano, Hawaii, showing lava flows

DEADLIEST EARTHQUAKES 1900–2000

Year	Place	Deaths
1905	Kangra, India	19 000
1907	west of Dushanbe, Tajikistan	12 000
1908	Messina, Italy	110 000
1915	Abruzzo, Italy	35 000
1917	Bali, Indonesia	15 000
1918	Guangdong Province, China	10 000
1920	Ningxia Province, China	200 000
1923	Tokyo, Japan	142 807
1927	Qinghai Province, China	200 000
1932	Gansu Province, China	70 000
1933	Sichuan Province, China	10 000
1934	Nepal/India	10 700
1935	Quetta, Pakistan	30 000
1939	Chillán, Chile	28 000
1939	Erzincan, Turkey	32 700
1948	Ashgabat, Turkmenistan	19 800
1960	Agadir, Morocco	12 000
1962	northwest Iran	12 225
1968	Dasht-e-Bayaz, Iran	12 100
1970	Huánuco Province, Peru	66 794
1974	Yunnan and Sichuan Provinces, China	20 000
1975	Liaoning Province, China	10 000
1976	central Guatemala	22 778
1976	Hebei Province, China	242 000
1978	Khorāsān Province, Iran	20 000
1980	Ech Chélif, Algeria	11 000
1988	Spitak, Armenia	25 000
1990	Manjil, Iran	50 000
1999	Kocaeli (İzmit), Turkey	17 000

OBSERVING THE OCEANS

The oceans cover 70.8 per cent of the surface of the Earth and exert an extraordinary influence on the physical processes of the Earth and its atmosphere. The circulation of water throughout the oceans is critical to world climate and climate change. Any study of these relationships relies upon a clear understanding of the role of the oceans and of the complex processes within them. Methods of direct and indirect observation of the oceans, particularly by sampling and through the application of satellite remote sensing, have developed enormously over the last forty years and continue to provide the data required to develop this understanding.

Until the advent of Earth-observation satellites in the late 1970s all ocean observations were made from ships. The first global survey of the oceans, their bathymetry and their physical and biological characteristics, was made by HMS Challenger between 1872 and 1876. Throughout the 20th century, comprehensive descriptions of the distributions of temperature and salinity were made through numerous regional and global expeditions. Analysis of the temperature and salinity characteristics of a water sample allowed its origins to be determined, and enabled overall patterns of water circulation to be deduced.

Until the 1960s there was no means of directly measuring currents below the ocean surface. Parallel developments produced two solutions to this problem. In the USA, current-recording meters were designed which returned records of current speed and direction, and water temperature. In the UK, devices were produced which could be made to drift with the currents at a predetermined depth and which could be tracked from an attendant ship. Such floats can now be used globally, independent of ships.

Earth observation satellites have become increasingly important in observing the oceans. Radiometers allow sea surface temperatures to be monitored and radar altimeters permit ocean surface currents to be inferred from measurements of sea surface height. Such developments meant that by the early 1990s routine monitoring of ocean surface currents was possible. The combination of satellite altimetry and other observation methods has also allowed a detailed picture of the ocean floor to be established (see 1).

1. GLOBAL SEAFLOOR TOPOGRAPHY

This image has been produced from a combination of shipboard depth soundings and gravity data derived from satellite altimetry from the ERS-1 and Geosat satellites. The range of colours represents different depths of the ocean – from orange and yellow on the shallow continental shelves to dark blues in the deepest ocean trenches. The heavily fractured mid-ocean ridges (ranging from green to yellow) are particularly prominent.

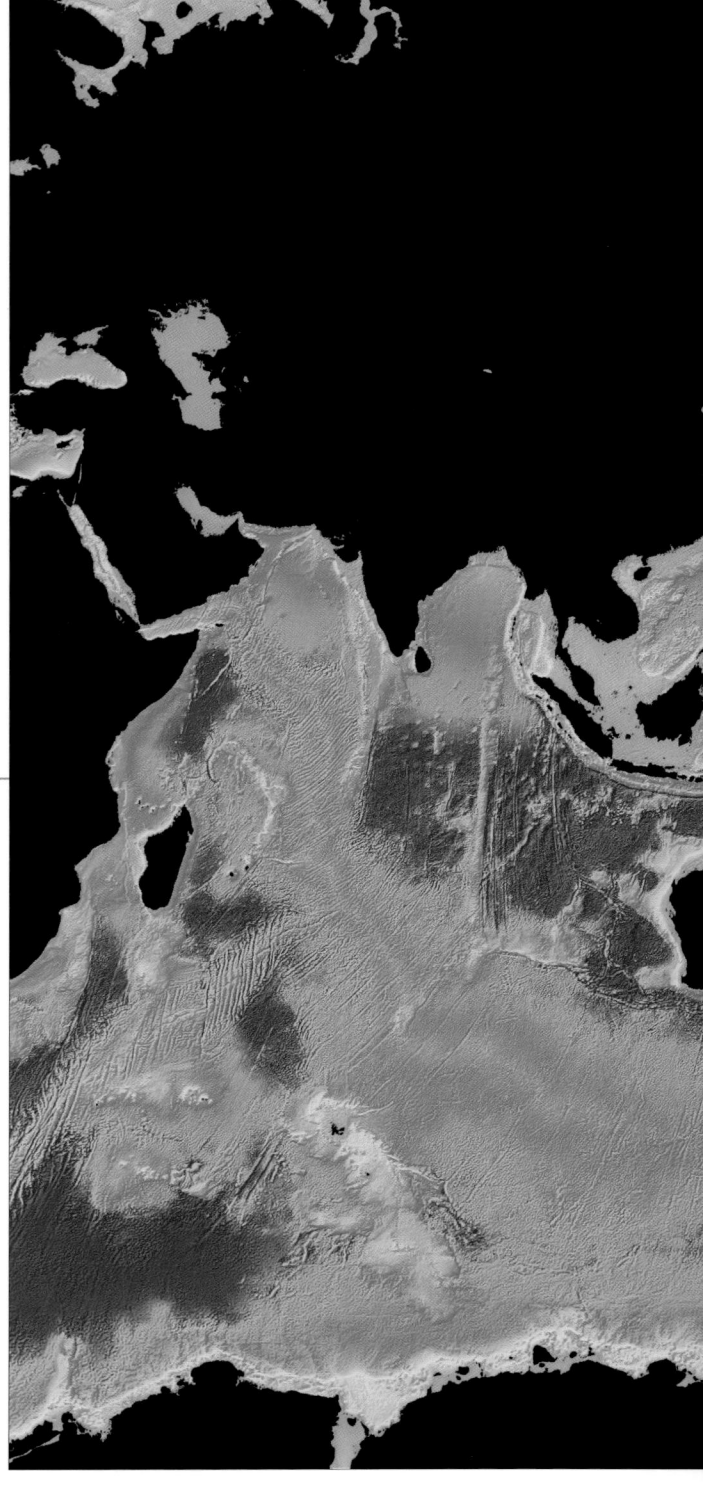

OCEAN CIRCULATION

Most of the Earth's incoming solar radiation is absorbed in the top few tens of metres of the ocean. Thus the upper ocean is warmed, the warming being greatest around the equator. Sea water has a high thermal capacity in comparison with the atmosphere or lithosphere and as a consequence, the ocean is an extremely effective store of thermal energy. Slow ocean currents play a major role in redistributing this heat around the globe and the oceans and their circulation are thus key elements in the climate system.

Estimates of the global transport of heat by the oceans (see 2) show a pattern of heat flow in the Indian and North Pacific Oceans away from the equator and towards the poles. However, the Atlantic Ocean has a clear northward flow throughout, decreasing from a maximum value of 1.4 petawatts (PW) at 24°N to effectively zero in the Arctic Ocean. This decrease is indicative of the heat loss to the atmosphere which is responsible for the temperate climate of western Europe.

Ocean currents are influenced by winds, by density gradients and by the Earth's rotation. They are also constrained by the topography of the seafloor. Surface currents are usually strong, narrow, western-boundary currents flowing towards the poles. Some of these are well known, for example the Gulf Stream in the North Atlantic Ocean, the Kuroshio Current in the northwest Pacific, and the Brazil Current (see 3). These poleward flows are returned towards the equator in broad, slow, interior flows which complete a gyre in each hemisphere basin. Sea surface circulation is reflected in variations in sea surface height which can vary greatly across currents (see 4). For example, differences in sea surface height of over 1m are evident across the Kuroshio Current. At high latitudes, winter cooling produces high density water which sinks towards the ocean floor and flows towards the equator, being constrained by the sea floor topography (see 5). This fills the deep ocean basins with water at temperatures close to 0°C.

2. OCEAN TRANSPORT OF HEAT

In petawatts (PW) (10^{15} watts). 1 PW is about sixty times the global consumption of energy.

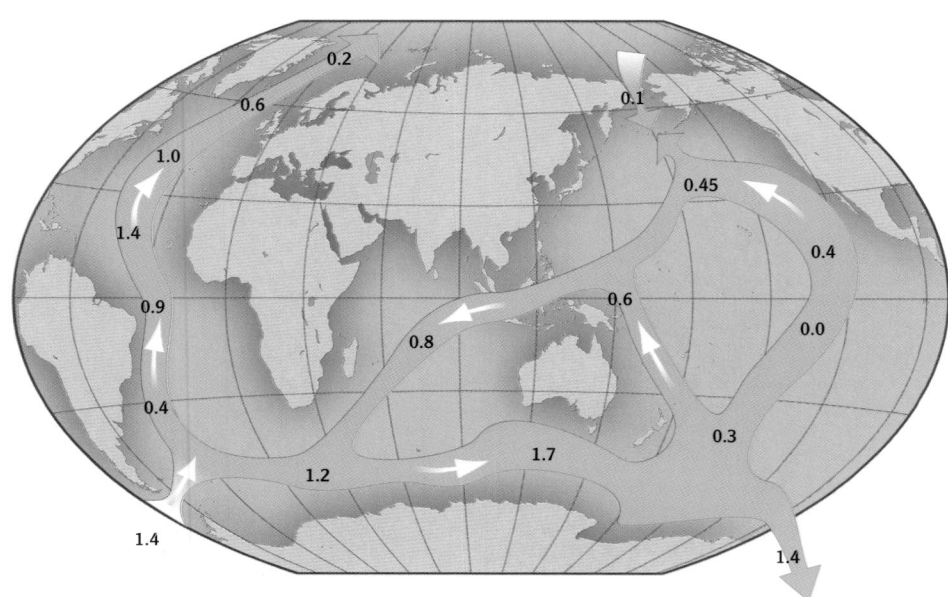

3. OCEAN SURFACE CURRENTS

scale 1 : 200 000 000

→	Warm current
→	Cold current
→	Seasonal drift during northern winter

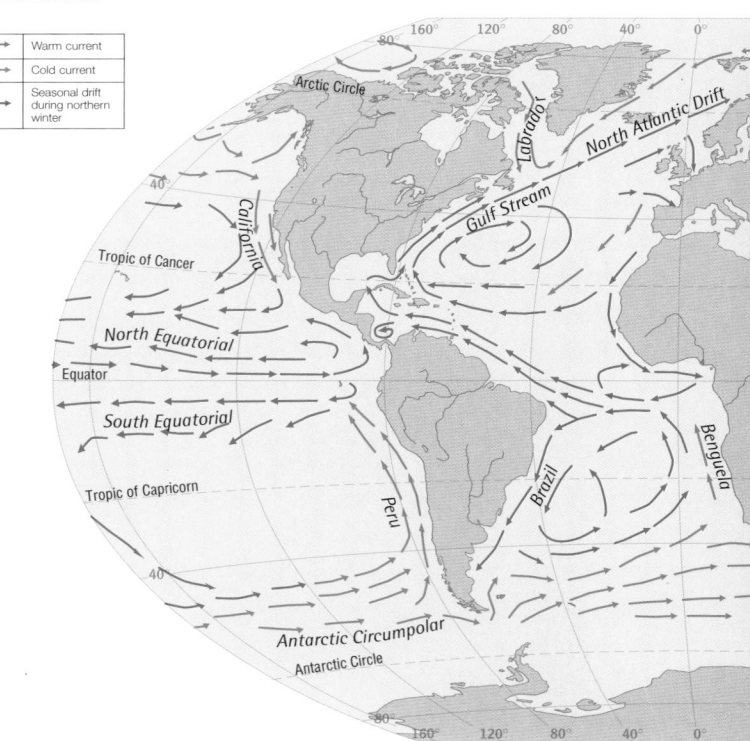

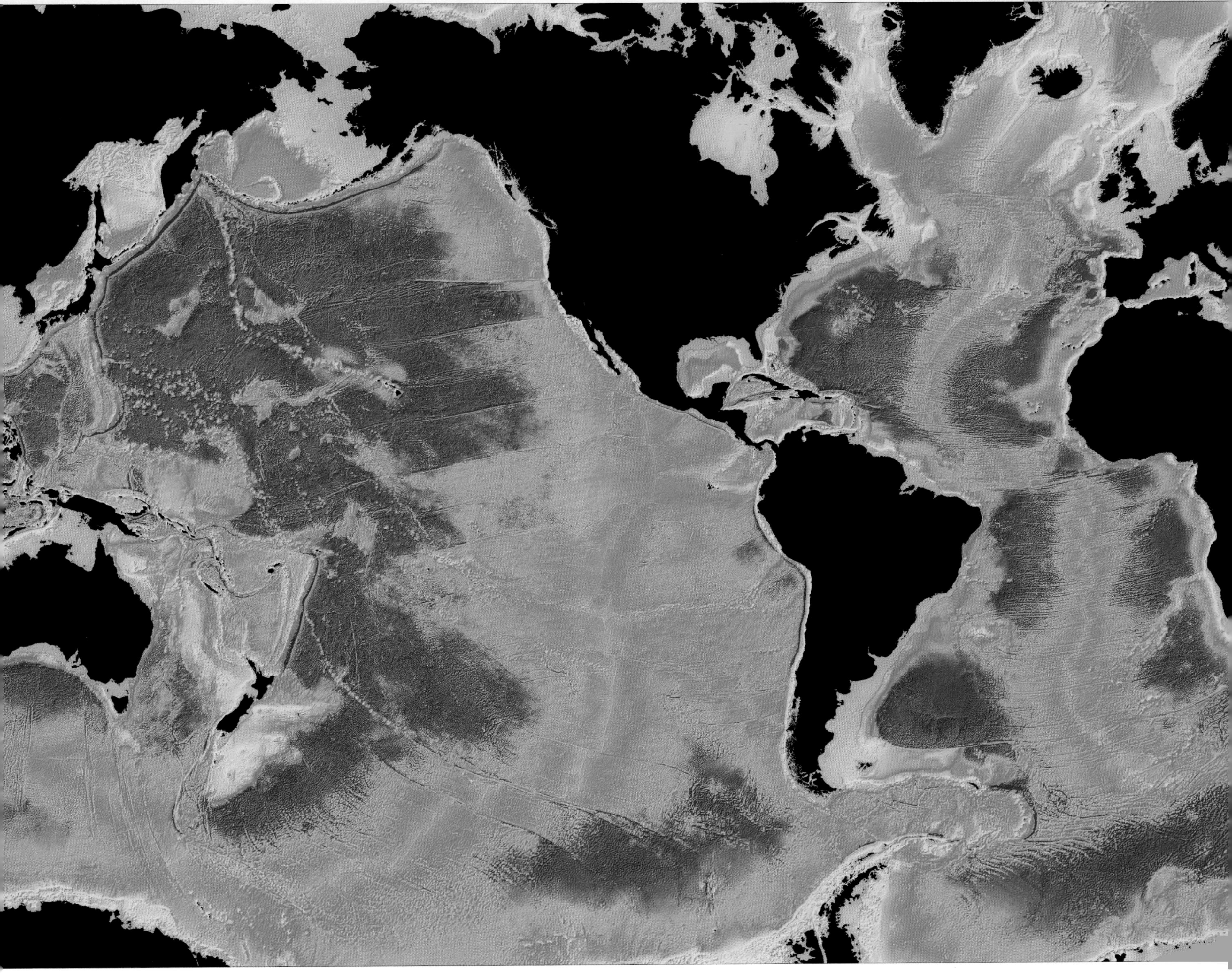

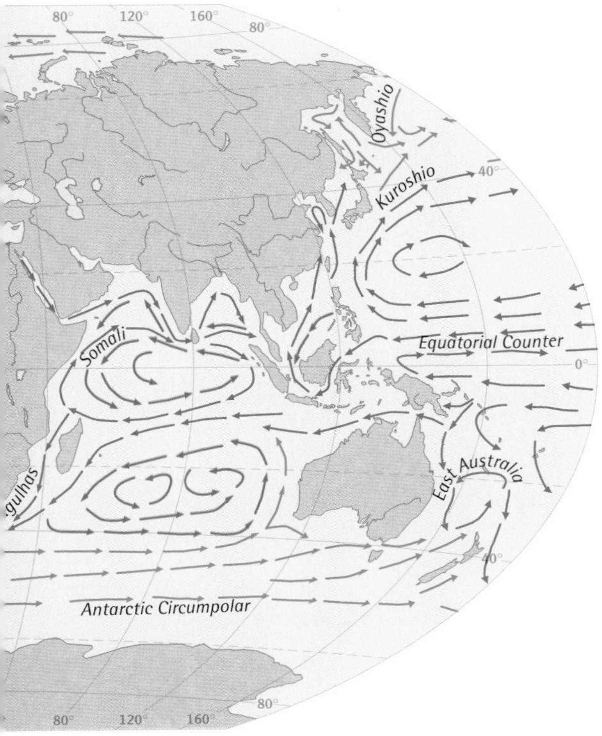

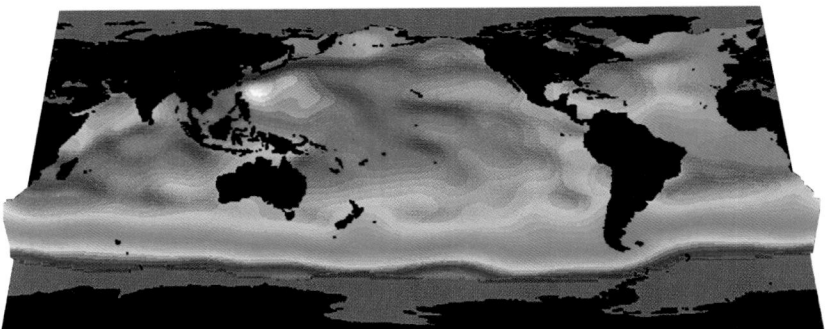

4. SEA SURFACE HEIGHT

From the TOPEX/POSEIDON satellite. Currents flow along the slopes and are strongest where the slopes are greatest.

5. CROSS-SECTION OF SALINITY AND THE OCEAN FLOOR

Stretching 12 000 km across the Pacific Ocean from Antarctica (left) to Alaska (right) approximately along longitude 150°W. It shows water modified in the Antarctic descending to the ocean floor and into the ocean interior.

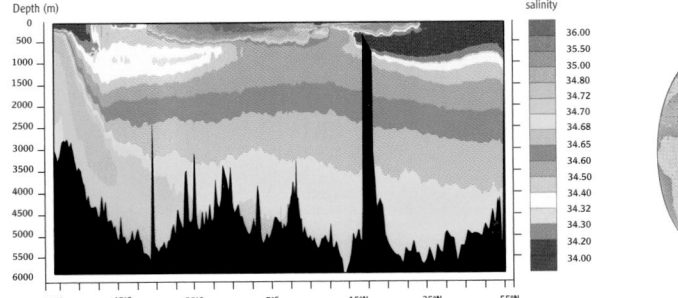

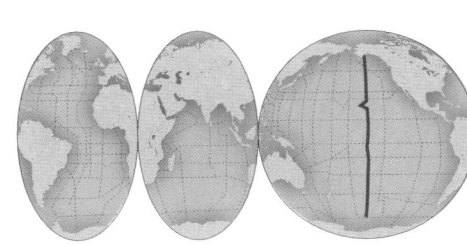

THE CLIMATE SYSTEM

The Earth's climate system is a highly complex interactive system involving the atmosphere, hydrosphere (oceans, lakes and rivers), cryosphere (particularly sea ice and polar ice caps), biosphere (the Earth's living resources), and lithosphere (the Earth's crust and upper mantle). This results in a great variety of climate types (*see 1*). Man's activities are affecting this system, and the monitoring of climate change, and of human influences upon it, is now a major issue.

Greenhouse gases such as carbon dioxide, methane and chlorofluorocarbons (CFCs) act to trap outgoing long-wave radiation, keeping the Earth's surface and lower atmosphere warmer than it would be otherwise. This is the phenomenon usually referred to as the greenhouse effect. Human activity has increased the atmospheric concentration of some of these gases and has therefore contributed to the effect. As a result of this, the world is about 0.6°C warmer than it was a hundred years ago with the three warmest years globally (in decreasing order) being 1998, 1997 and 1995 (*see 2*).

CLIMATE GRAPHS

These graphs relate by number, name and colour to the selected stations on the map and present mean temperature and precipitation values for each month. Red bars show average daily maximum and minimum temperatures for each month in degrees centigrade and fahrenheit. Vertical blue columns depict precipitation in millimetres and inches, with the total mean annual precipitation shown under the graph. The altitude of each station above sea level is given in metres and feet.

1. MAJOR CLIMATIC REGIONS AND SUB-TYPES

Köppen classification system
Winkel Tripel Projection
scale 1:110 000 000

● Climate graph location   ○ Weather extreme location

Polar		Cooler humid		Warmer humid		Dry		Tropical humid	
EF	Ice cap	Dc Dd	Subarctic	Cb Cc	Temperate	BS	Steppe	Aw As	Savanna
ET	Tundra	Db	Continental cool summer	Ca	Humid subtropical	BW	Desert	Af Am	Rain forest
		Da	Continental warm summer	Cs	Mediterranean				

A   Rainy climate with no winter: coolest month above 18°C (64.4°F).

B   Dry climates; limits are defined by formulae based on rainfall effectiveness:
  BS Steppe or semi-arid climate.
  BW Desert or arid climate.

*C   Rainy climates with mild winters: coolest month above 0°C (32°F), but below 18°C (64.4°F); warmest month above 10°C (50°F).

*D   Rainy climates with severe winters: coldest month below 0°C (32°F); warmest month above 10°C (50°F).

E   Polar climates with no warm season: warmest month below 10°C (50°F).
  ET Tundra climate: warmest month below 10°C (50°F) but above 0°C (32°F).
  EF Perpetual frost: all months below 0°C (32°F).

* Modification of Köppen definition

a   Warmest month above 22°C (71.6°F).

b   Warmest month below 22°C (71.6°F).

c   Less than four months over 10°C (50°F).

d   As 'c', but with severe cold: coldest month below -38°C (-36.4°F).

f   Constantly moist rainfall throughout the year.

*h   Warmer dry: all months above 0°C (32°F).

*k   Cooler dry: at least one month below 0°C (32°F).

m   Monsoon rain: short dry season, but is compensated by heavy rains during rest of the year.

n   Frequent fog.

s   Dry season in summer.

w   Dry season in winter.

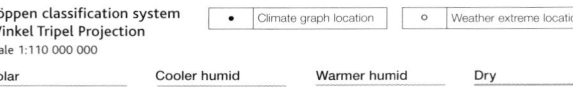

■ Precipitation (average monthly total)   ■ Temperature (average daily maximum and minimum)

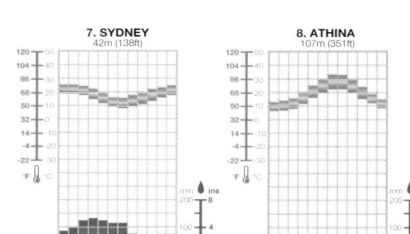
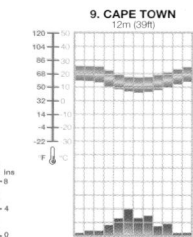
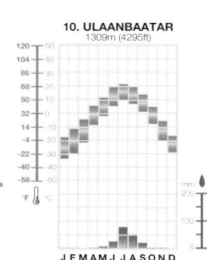
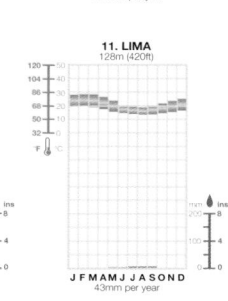
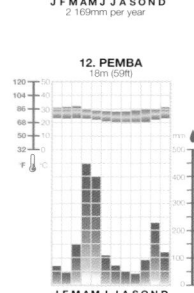
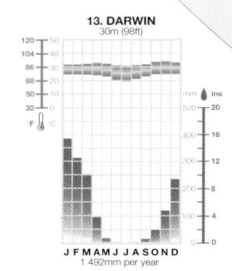
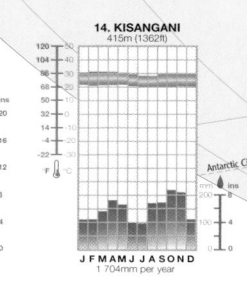

1. NOME 7m (23ft)	2. ARKHANGEL'SK 3m (10ft)	3. MOSKVA 167m (548ft)	4. KÁBUL 1799m (5902ft)	5. VICTORIA 26m (85ft)	6. HONG KONG 33m (108ft)
454mm per year	530mm per year	624mm per year	339mm per year	696mm per year	2 169mm per year

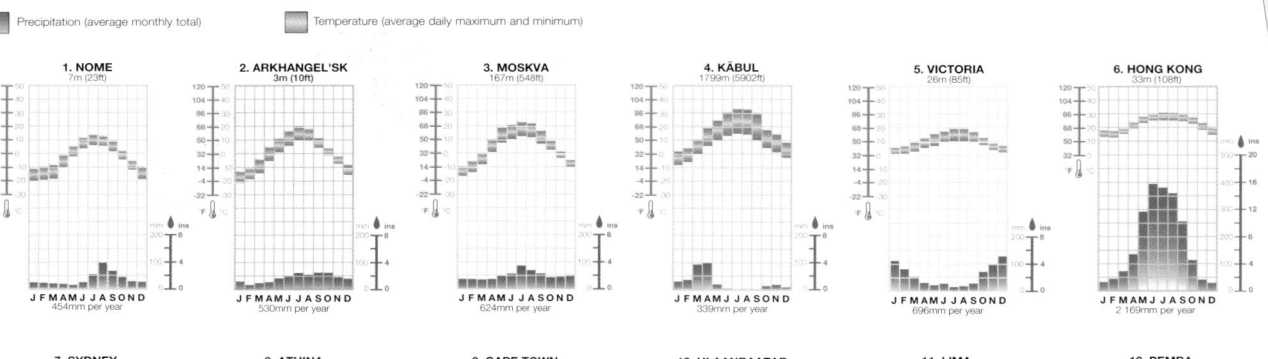

7. SYDNEY 42m (138ft)	8. ATHINA 107m (351ft)	9. CAPE TOWN 12m (39ft)	10. ULAANBAATAR 1309m (4295ft)	11. LIMA 128m (420ft)	12. PEMBA 18m (59ft)	13. DARWIN 30m (98ft)	14. KISANGANI 415m (1362ft)
1 181mm per year	402mm (16ins)	509mm per year	209mm per year	43mm per year	1 819mm per year	1 492mm per year	1 704mm per year

CLIMATE CHANGE

Future climate change depends on how quickly and to what extent the concentration of greenhouse gases and aerosols in the atmosphere increases. If we assume that no action is taken to limit future greenhouse gas emissions, then a warming during the 21st century of 0.2 to 0.3°C per decade is likely. Such a rate of warming would be greater than anything that has occurred over the last 10 000 years.

The detailed climatic response to the increase in carbon dioxide and other greenhouse gases is predicted using complex mathematical models of the climate. One of the most advanced climate models in the world is that produced by the Hadley Centre of the UK Meteorological Office. This model has produced predictions of climatic change, including changes in temperature and precipitation (*see 3 and 4*). According to this model, some regions of the world will warm more quickly than others and precipitation will increase in some areas and decrease in others. Such changes are likely to have significant impacts on sea-level which could rise by as much as 50 cm over the next century. Human impacts would also be through the effects on water resources, food production and health.

2. COMBINED GLOBAL LAND, AIR AND SEA SURFACE TEMPERATURES 1860-1999

Relative to 1961-1990 average. The black line is a smoothing of the annual values to suppress sub-decadal time-scale variations.

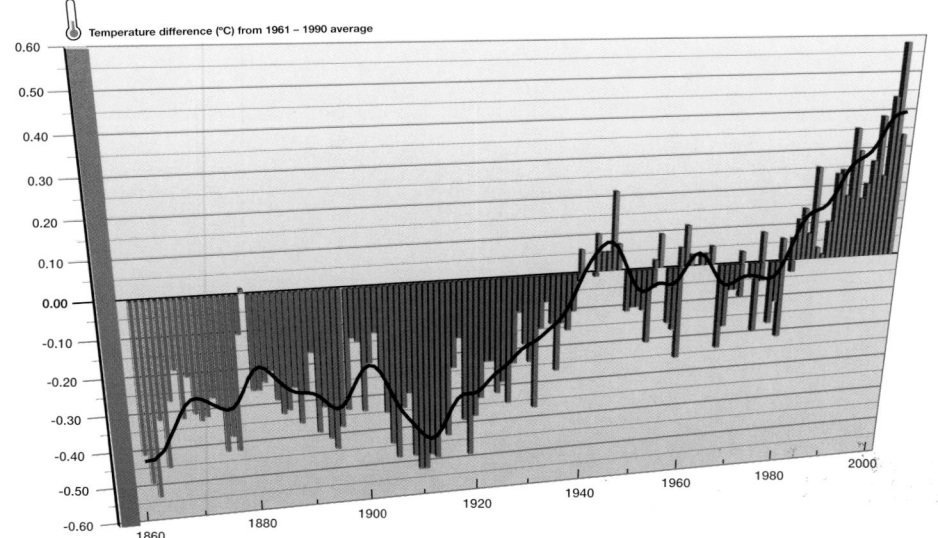

3. TEMPERATURE IN THE 2050s

Predicted annual mean temperature change

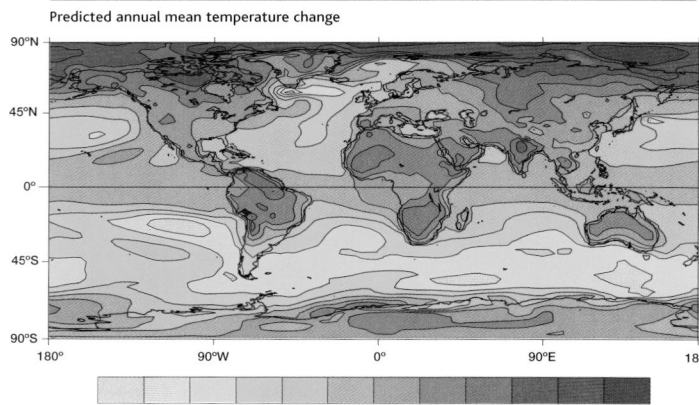

Annual mean temperature change (°C)

4. PRECIPITATION IN THE 2050s

Predicted average precipitation change

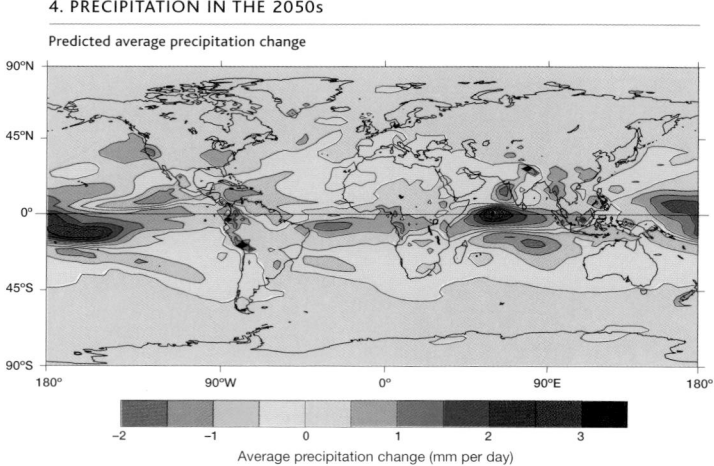

Average precipitation change (mm per day)

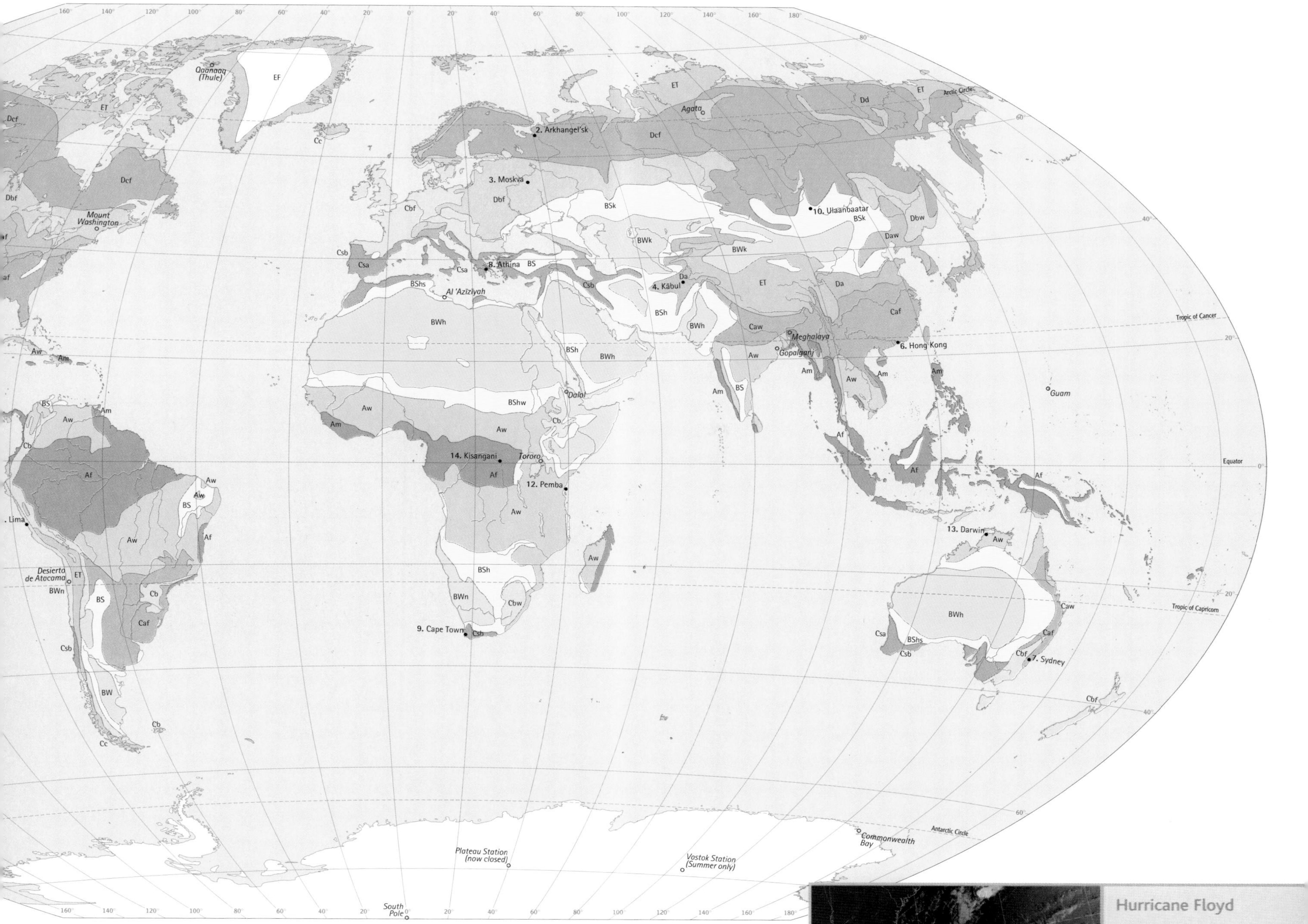

(Map labels — Köppen climate zones and locations)

Qaanaaq (Thule) · EF · ET · Dcf · ET · Dd · ET · Arctic Circle · 2. Arkhangel'sk · Agata · Dcf · Cc · Dbf · Cbf · 3. Moskva · Dbf · 10. Ulaanbaatar · BSk · Dbw · Daw · Mount Washington · af · Csb · Csa · Csa · 8. Athina · BS · BWk · Da · 4. Kâbul · BWk · Da · Al 'Azīzīyah · BShs · Da · BSh · Caf · Tropic of Cancer · BWh · BSh · BWh · Caw · Meghalaya · 6. Hong Kong · Aw · Gopalgonj · Am · Am · Am · Aw · Am · Am · Guam · Aw · Am · BShw · Cb · BSh · BWh · Dolol · Equator · Aw · Aw · 14. Kisangani · Tororo · Af · Af · Af · 12. Pemba · Aw · Am · Cb · Af · BS · Aw · Af · Aw · 13. Darwin · Aw · Lima · Aw · Desierto de Atacama · ET · BWn · BS · Caf · BSh · BWn · Caw · Tropic of Capricorn · Csb · Af · Cbw · 9. Cape Town · Csb · BWh · BSh · Csa · BSh · Cbf · 7. Sydney · BW · Csb · Cb · Cbf · Cc · Cbf · South Pole · Plateau Station (now closed) · Vostok Station (Summer only) · Commonwealth Bay · Antarctic Circle

TROPICAL STORMS

Tropical storms develop, and have different names, in different parts of the world: hurricanes in the north Atlantic and east Pacific; typhoons in the northwest Pacific; and cyclones in the Indian Ocean region. There are also many local names for these events – those affecting the northern coast of Australia are known colloquially as the 'Willy-willies' (*see 5*).

Tropical storms are among the most powerful and destructive weather systems on Earth. Of the eighty to one hundred which develop annually over the tropical oceans, many make landfall and cause considerable damage to property and loss of life as a result of high winds and heavy rain.

The majority of tropical storms originate in the northwest Pacific, where as typhoons they commonly affect areas from

the Philippines through to China and Japan. They are also found as cyclones in the Bay of Bengal, either developing locally or on occasion being the remnants of typhoons which have moved westwards across Thailand. These storms bring heavy rains to eastern India or to the Ganges Delta in Bangladesh. In these places the land is so close to sea level that the rise in water levels has great potential for heavy loss of life.

The conditions required for the development of tropical storms – warm (over 26.5°C) ocean waters to a depth of at least 50 m; pre-existing cyclonic (low pressure) systems; thunderstorm activity; and moist layers of air in the mid-troposphere (around 5 km above the Earth's surface) – mean that most occur in mid- to late-summer in the areas concerned.

Hurricane Floyd

Hurricane Floyd developed in the northern Atlantic during early September 1999. It increased in intensity to maximum wind speeds of 249 km per hour – a high category 4 hurricane – on 13 September just west of The Bahamas. From here, it turned to the north and made landfall near Cape Fear, North Carolina, USA early on the 16th. Although wind speeds had dropped to around 166 km per hour, it had a devastating effect. Serious flooding affected several states, in particular North Carolina. 57 deaths were directly attributed to the hurricane, making it the deadliest US hurricane since Hurricane Agnes in 1972.

Image from the National Climatic Data Center, NOAA.

5. TRACKS OF TROPICAL STORMS

Wind speeds often over 160 km per hour
scale 1:295 000 000

→ Cyclone track
→ Typhoon track
→ Willy-willies

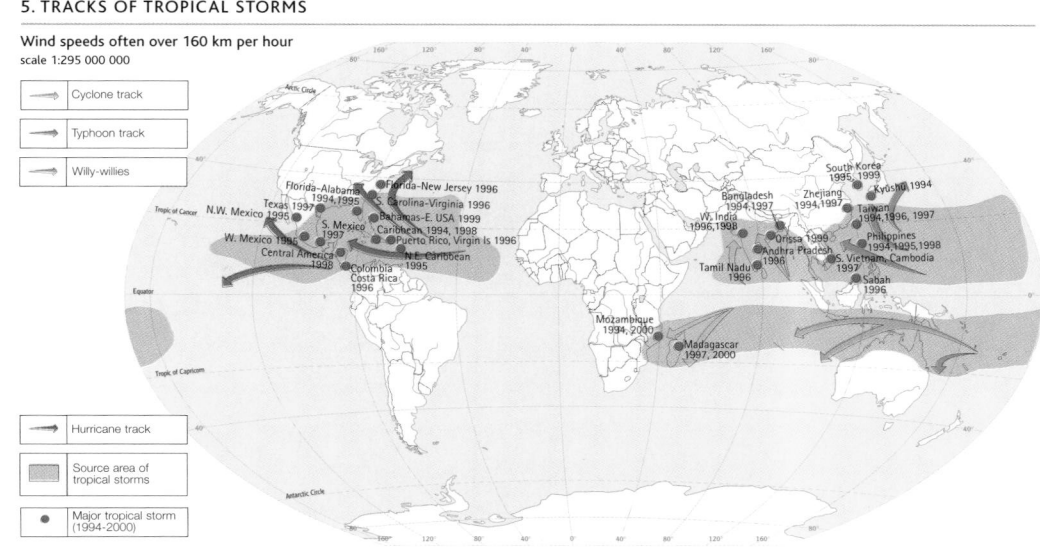

→ Hurricane track

▨ Source area of tropical storms

● Major tropical storm (1994-2000)

(Map labels) Florida-Alabama 1994,1995 · S. Carolina-Virginia 1996 · N.-New Jersey 1996 · Texas 1999 · N.W. Mexico 1999 · Bahamas-E USA 1999 · 5. Mexico 1997 · Caribbean 1994, 1998 · Puerto Rico, Virgin Is 1996 · W. Mexico 1996 · Central America 1998 · Colombia 1995 · Costa Rica 1996 · South Korea 1995, 1999 · Kyūshū 1999 · Japan 1994 · Zhejiang 1994,1997 · Kyūshū 1994,1996, 1997 · Bangladesh 1994,1997 · W. India 1996,1998 · Orissa 1999 · Andhra Pradesh 1996 · Tamil Nadu 1996 · Philippines 1994,1995,1998 · S. Vietnam, Cambodia 1997 · Sabah 1996 · Mozambique 1994, 2000 · Madagascar 1997, 2000

WORLD WEATHER EXTREMES

Highest shade temperature	57.8°C/136°F Al 'Azīzīyah, Libya (13th September 1922)
Hottest place — Annual mean	34.4°C/93.9°F Dalol, Ethiopia
Driest place — Annual mean	0.1 mm/0.004 inches Desierto de Atacama, Chile
Most sunshine — Annual mean	90% Yuma, Arizona, USA (over 4 000 hours)
Least sunshine	Nil for 182 days each year, South Pole
Lowest screen temperature	-89.2°C/-128.6°F Vostok Station, Antarctica (21st July 1983)
Coldest place — Annual mean	-56.6°C/-69.9°F Plateau Station, Antarctica
Wettest place — Annual mean	11 873 mm/467.4 inches Meghalaya, India
Most rainy days	Up to 350 per year Mount Waialeale, Hawaii, USA
Windiest place	322 km per hour/200 miles per hour in gales, Commonwealth Bay, Antarctica
Highest surface wind speed — High altitude	372 km per hour/231 miles per hour Mount Washington, New Hampshire, USA, (12th April 1934)
Low altitude	333 km per hour/207 miles per hour Qaanaaq (Thule), Greenland 8th March 1972
Tornado	512 km per hour/318 miles per hour Oklahoma City, Oklahoma, USA (3rd May 1999)
Greatest snowfall	31 102 mm/1 224.5 inches Mount Rainier, Washington, USA (19th February 1971 — 18th February 1972)
Heaviest hailstones	1 kg/2.21 lb Gopalganj, Bangladesh (14th April 1986)
Thunder-days Average	251 days per year Tororo, Uganda
Highest barometric pressure	1 083.8 mb Agata, Siberia, Russian Federation (31st December 1968)
Lowest barometric pressure	870 mb 483 km/300 miles west of Guam, Pacific Ocean (12th October 1979)

THE DISCover PROJECT

Most existing global land cover maps show only a general idea of the actual conditions on the Earth's surface. They tend to be fairly coarse, of unknown accuracy, and are derived from a variety of primary data sources. Most also contain a climate element in the class definitions which leads to a mixture of potential versus actual land cover. Since 1992 the International Geosphere Biosphere Programme's (IGBP) Data and Information System (DIS) has been working towards the completion of a new global land cover data set without these shortcomings. The resulting land cover map as shown here – known as DISCover – was completed in June 1997 and shows the Earth's land cover as it was in 1992/1993 at a ground resolution of 1 km (see 1).

The final data set has been created from over 4.4 terabytes of data from the Advanced Very High Resolution Radiometer (AVHRR) sensor on board the polar orbiting satellites of the US National Oceanic and Atmospheric Administration (NOAA). These satellites provide images of the entire Earth's surface every day at a ground resolution of 1 km (see also the continental satellite images on pages 8–21). Development of the data set used to create DISCover was endorsed by the G7 Committee on Earth Observation Satellites, and implemented by the United States Geological Survey (USGS), the National Aeronautics and Space Administration (NASA), NOAA, and the European Space Agency (ESA).

Collecting the data involved the collaborative efforts of twenty-three satellite receiving stations around the world.

The subsequent classification of the data was performed at the USGS Earth Resources Observation Systems (EROS) Data Center in Sioux Falls, South Dakota, at the University of Nebraska–Lincoln, USA and at the European Commission's Joint Research Centre (JRC) in Italy. The accuracy of the map classification is currently being assessed by specialists in the USA, comparing it with a sample of more than 400 high resolution satellite images from US Landsat (see 2) and French SPOT (see 3) satellites.

The land cover classes shown on the map are not the typical vegetation classes often found in world vegetation maps. For example, there are no tundra or tropical rainforest classes. This is because the philosophy for DISCover was to describe land cover in terms of structure – in particular the three components of above-ground biomass, leaf longevity and leaf type – mainly for the science community interested in global change, and not in terms of traditional climate/vegetation distinctions.

4. GLOBAL LAND COVER COMPOSITION

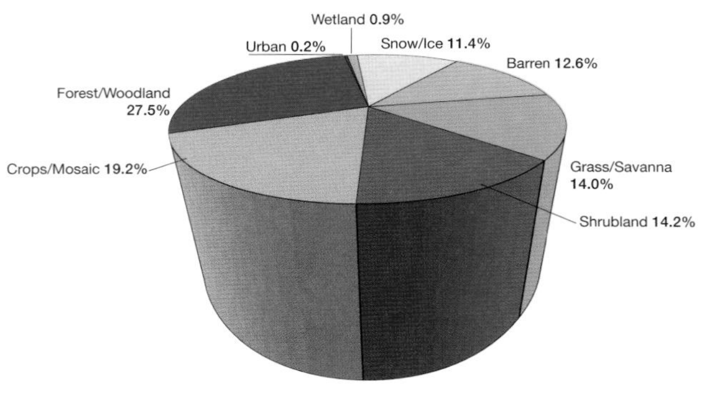

Wetland 0.9%
Urban 0.2%
Snow/Ice 11.4%
Barren 12.6%
Forest/Woodland 27.5%
Grass/Savanna 14.0%
Crops/Mosaic 19.2%
Shrubland 14.2%

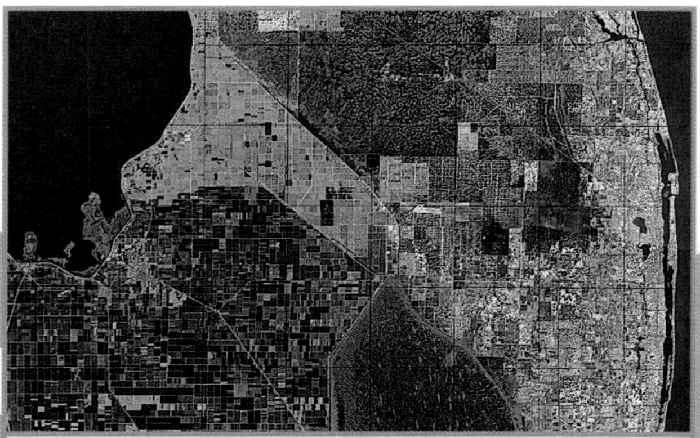

2. Agricultural land use in Florida, USA

This example of high resolution Landsat satellite imagery illustrates the level of land cover detail available from such images. It shows part of Florida, USA with Lake Okeechobee to the top left and the city of West Palm Beach to the far right. The regular field pattern shows crops at different stages of growth and the dark green, mottled areas (top centre and bottom centre) are parts of the Everglades swamp.

1. WORLD LAND COVER

Goode Interrupted Homolosine Projection
scale approximately 1:75 000 000
Map courtesy of IGBP, JRC and USGS

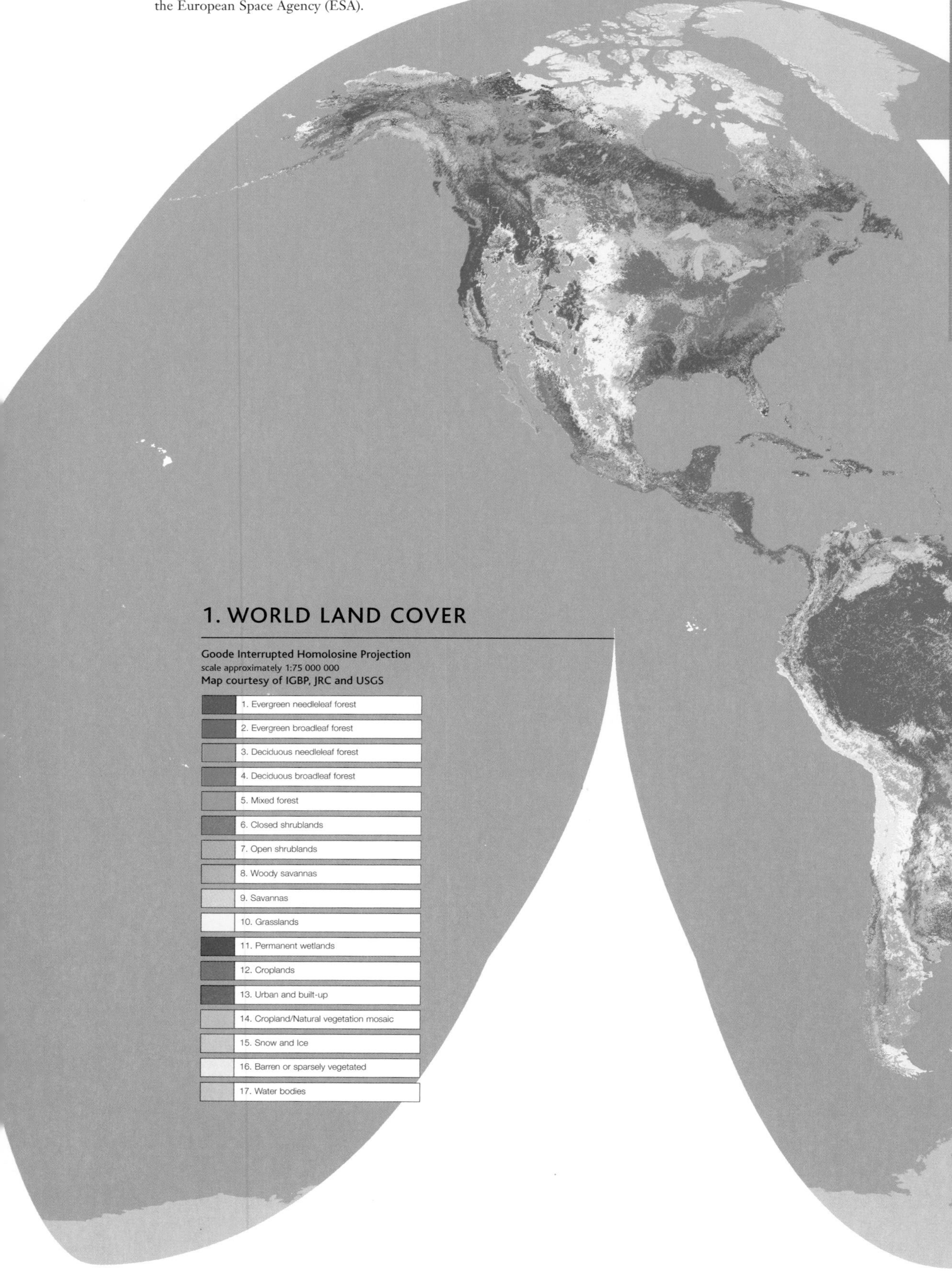

1. Evergreen needleleaf forest
2. Evergreen broadleaf forest
3. Deciduous needleleaf forest
4. Deciduous broadleaf forest
5. Mixed forest
6. Closed shrublands
7. Open shrublands
8. Woody savannas
9. Savannas
10. Grasslands
11. Permanent wetlands
12. Croplands
13. Urban and built-up
14. Cropland/Natural vegetation mosaic
15. Snow and Ice
16. Barren or sparsely vegetated
17. Water bodies

LANDCOVER GRAPHS - CLASSIFICATION

Class description	IGBP/DISCover classes
Forest/Woodland	1 Evergreen needleleaf forest 2 Evergreen broadleaf forest 3 Deciduous needleleaf forest 4 Deciduous broadleaf forest 5 Mixed forest
Shrubland	6 Closed shrublands 7 Open shrublands
Grass/Savanna	8 Woody savannas 9 Savannas 10 Grasslands
Wetland	11 Permanent wetlands
Crops/Mosaic	12 Croplands 14 Cropland/Natural vegetation mosaic
Urban	13 Urban and built-up
Snow/Ice	15 Snow and Ice
Barren	16 Barren or sparsely vegetated

5. CONTINENTAL LAND COVER COMPOSITION

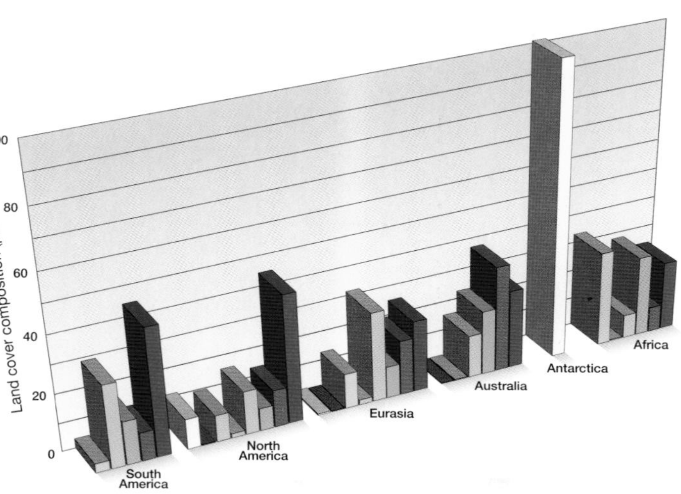

Land cover composition (per cent)

South America · North America · Eurasia · Australia · Antarctica · Africa

INTERPRETATION AND USES

The high resolution of the imagery used to compile the data set and map allows detailed interpretation of land cover patterns across the world. An additional benefit of holding the data in digital form is the ease with which land cover on global and continental scales can be extracted and analysed (*see 4 and 5*).

The small areas of permanent wetlands show just how rare these fragile ecosystems are. Apart from those in Sudan and the Okavango Delta in Botswana, only the swamp areas of Siberia are really evident on the global scale. In contrast, the concentration the world's extensive croplands in the northern hemisphere is obvious with the cereal belt in North America clearly visible. This contrasts with western Europe where the smaller field sizes and more common mixed farming lead to much of this region being classified as cropland/natural vegetation mosaics. The cereal belts of eastern Europe show the transition once again to extensive agriculture.

One of the most striking agricultural features on the Earth's surface is the heavily cultivated Nile valley and delta. In fact, humankind's influence on the Earth's vegetation is apparent throughout the map. Tropical forest cover is far from the uniform, unbroken swath so often depicted on world vegetation maps. In all areas of the world the tropical forest margins show encroachment of cropland or savanna in the wake of human activity (*see 3*), although parts of their interiors still remain largely untouched. In the light of such patterns, the global figures for tropical deforestation rates (typically around 0.5–1 per cent per year) become even more alarming. Deforestation is not uniform, so such figures hide far more rapid rates of loss in the forest margins.

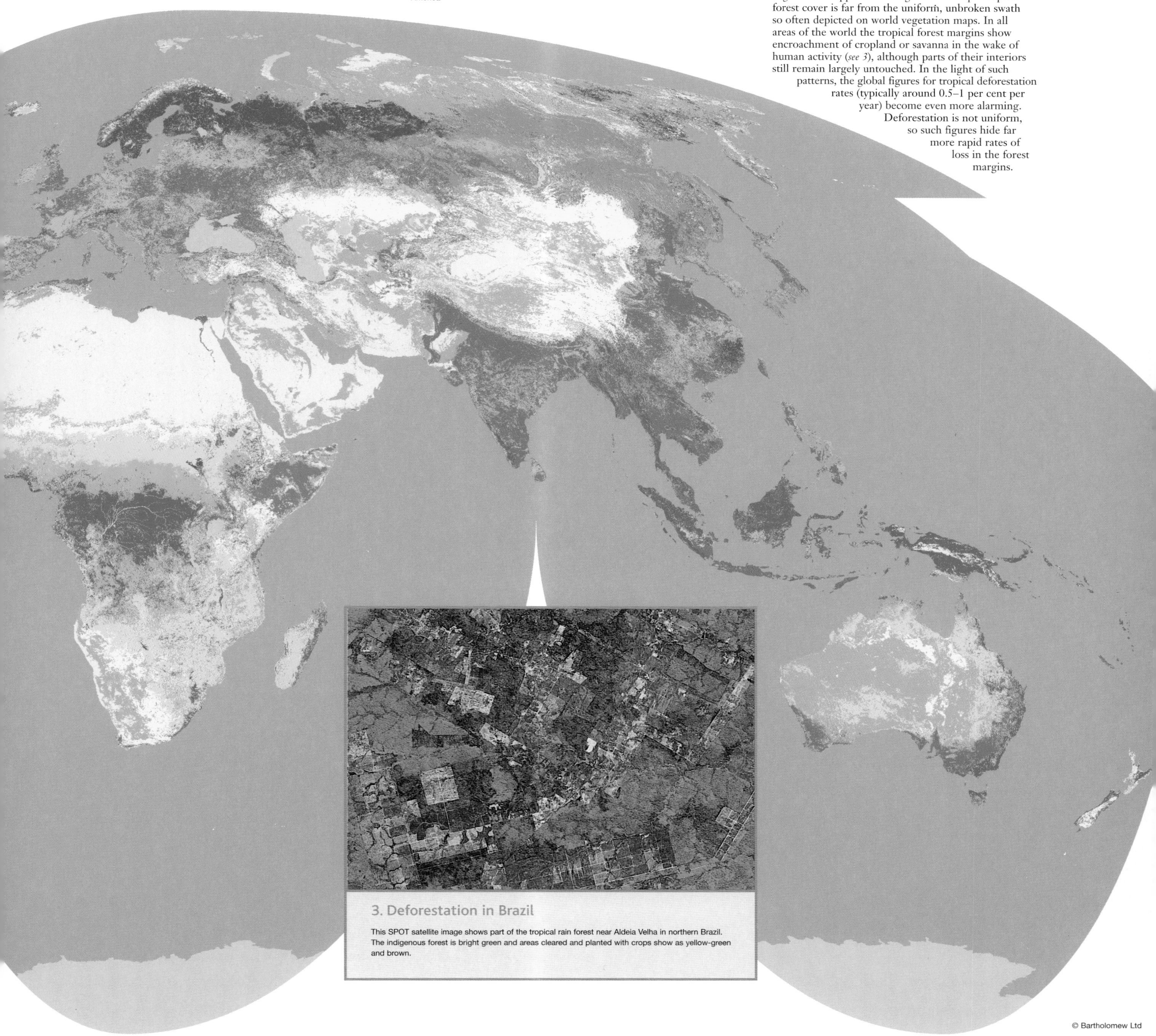

3. Deforestation in Brazil

This SPOT satellite image shows part of the tropical rain forest near Aldeia Velha in northern Brazil. The indigenous forest is bright green and areas cleared and planted with crops show as yellow-green and brown.

POPULATION DISTRIBUTION AND GROWTH

People are distributed very unevenly over the Earth. As shown on the population distribution map *(see 1)*, over a quarter of the land area is uninhabited or has extremely low population density. Barely a quarter of the land area is occupied at densities of 10 or more persons per square km, with the three largest concentrations in east Asia, the Indian subcontinent and Europe accounting for over half the world total. China and India dominate the scene, together accounting for nearly two-fifths of world population *(see 2)*.

Over the past half century world population has been growing faster than it has ever done before. Whereas world population did not pass the one billion mark until 1804 and took another 123 years to reach two billion in 1927, it then added the third billion in 33 years, the fourth in 14 years and the fifth in 13 years, with the 6 billion mark being passed only 12 years after this in 1999. It is expected that another three billion people will have been added to the world population by 2050 *(see 3)*.

Population growth since 1950 has been spread very unevenly between the continents. While overall numbers have been growing extremely rapidly since 1950, a massive 89 per cent increase has taken place in the less developed regions, especially southern and eastern Asia, while Europe's population is now almost stationary and ageing rapidly. India and China alone are responsible for over one-third of current growth, but most of the highest percentage rates of growth are to be found in Sub-Saharan Africa. The latest trends in population growth at country level *(see 4)* emphasize the continuing contrast between the more and less developed regions. Annual growth rates of 1.5 per cent or more are very common in Latin America, Africa and the southern half of Asia. A number of countries have rates in excess of 3.0 per cent, which if continued would lead to the doubling of their populations in 23 years or less.

2. TOP TEN COUNTRIES BY POPULATION AND POPULATION DENSITY

TOTAL POPULATION 1998	COUNTRY	RANK	COUNTRY	POPULATION DENSITY 1998 (countries with populations over 10 million)	
				per sq mile	per sq km
1 262 817 000	China	1	Bangladesh	2 244	866
982 223 000	India	2	Taiwan	1 568	606
274 028 000	USA	3	South Korea	1 203	465
206 338 000	Indonesia	4	Netherlands	978	378
165 851 000	Brazil	5	Japan	866	334
148 166 000	Pakistan	6	Belgium	861	332
147 434 000	Russian Federation	7	India	830	320
126 281 000	Japan	8	Sri Lanka	729	281
124 774 000	Bangladesh	9	Philippines	630	243
106 409 000	Nigeria	10	UK	622	240

3. WORLD POPULATION GROWTH BY CONTINENT 1750–2050

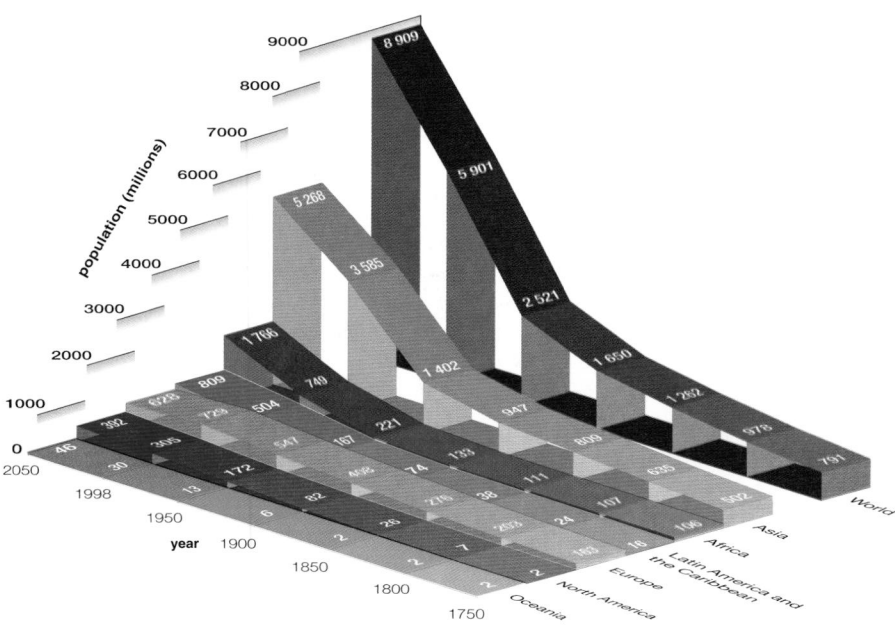

4. POPULATION CHANGE 1995–2000

Average annual rate of population change (per cent) and the top ten contributors to world population growth (net annual addition)
scale 1:255 000 000

increase decrease	
	>5.6
	2.9 – 5.6
	1.5 – 2.8
	0.8 – 1.4
	0.0 – 0.7
	-0.7 – -0.1
	< -0.7
	no data

1. WORLD POPULATION DISTRIBUTION

Winkel Tripel Projection
scale 1:93 000 000

Population density

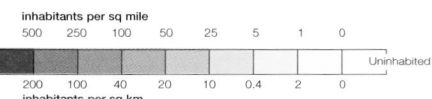

inhabitants per sq mile
500 250 100 50 25 5 1 0

Uninhabited

200 100 40 20 10 0.4 2 0
inhabitants per sq km

5. KEY POPULATION STATISTICS FOR MAJOR REGIONS

	Population 1998 (millions)	Growth (per cent)	Infant mortality rate	Total fertility rate	Life expectancy (years)
World	5 901	1.33	57	2.7	65
More developed regions[1]	1 182	0.28	9	1.6	75
Less developed regions[2]	4 719	1.59	63	3.0	63
Africa	749	2.37	87	5.1	51
Asia	3 585	1.38	57	2.6	66
Europe[3]	729	0.03	12	1.4	73
Latin America and the Caribbean[4]	504	1.57	36	2.7	69
North America	305	0.85	7	1.9	77
Oceania	30	1.30	24	2.4	74

Except for population (1998), the data are annual averages projected for the period 1995-2000.

1. Europe, North America, Australia, New Zealand and Japan.

2. Africa, Asia (excluding Japan), Latin America and the Caribbean, and Oceania (excluding Australia and New Zealand).

3. Includes Russian Federation.

4. South America, Central America (including Mexico) and all Carribean Islands.

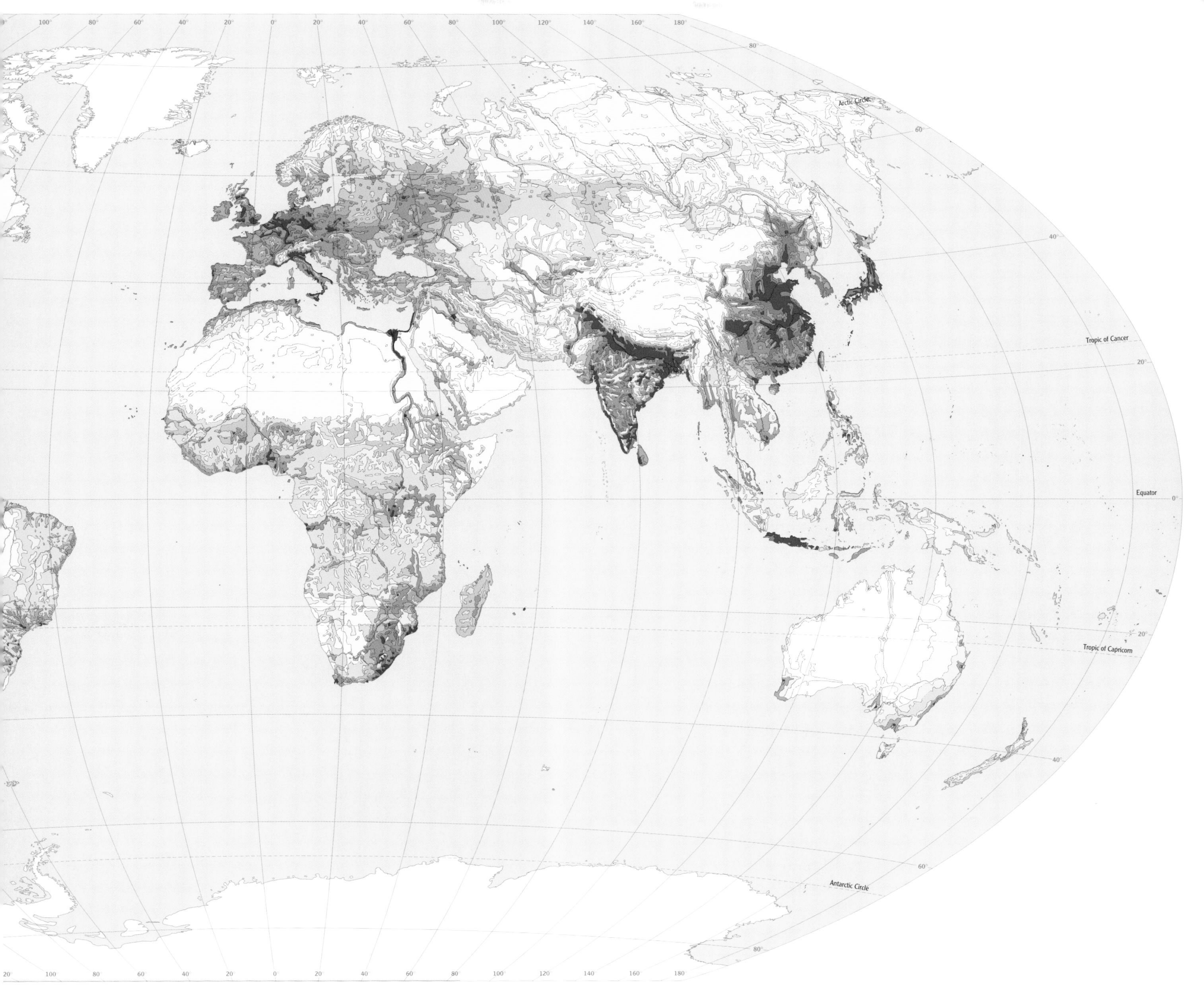

DEMOGRAPHIC TRANSITION

Behind patterns of population growth lies the 'demographic transition' process, where countries pass through a phase of falling death rates and then a phase of falling fertility. Most parts of the world have passed through the first phase, with the average life expectancy of 63 years in the less developed world now not far behind that of 75 years in the more developed regions (see 5). Even so, infant mortality – a very

good indicator of human development levels – remains a major challenge in the less developed regions (see 6). Here, an average of sixty-three out of every one thousand babies die before their first birthday, compared to only nine out of every one thousand in the more developed regions. Sub-Saharan Africa started this transitional phase later than most other parts of the world and has so far seen life expectancy rise

to only 48 years, with progress being hampered by continuing high levels of infant mortality and by rising numbers of AIDS-related deaths.

Reductions in fertility rate (see 7) hold the key to the successful completion of the transition and the future stabilization of population growth. Much of the more developed world is well advanced in this process. In particular,

Europe's total fertility rate (broadly the average number of babies born to each woman) is now down to 1.4 – well below the 'replacement rate' of 2.1 needed to give a constant population in the long term. By contrast, the average for less developed regions, excluding China, is 3.8 and it is as high as 6.5 in Sub-Saharan Africa.

6. INFANT MORTALITY RATE 1995–2000

Deaths of infants less than one year old per 1000 live births
scale 1:315 000 000

	0 – 10
	11 – 28
	29 – 70
	71 – 130
	>130
	no data

7. TOTAL FERTILITY RATE 1995–2000

Estimate of the number of children a woman will bear during her child-bearing years.
scale 1:315 000 000

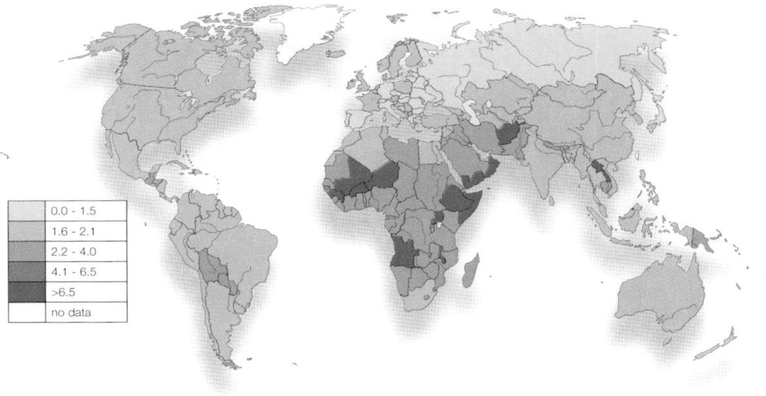

	0.0 - 1.5
	1.6 - 2.1
	2.2 - 4.0
	4.1 - 6.5
	>6.5
	no data

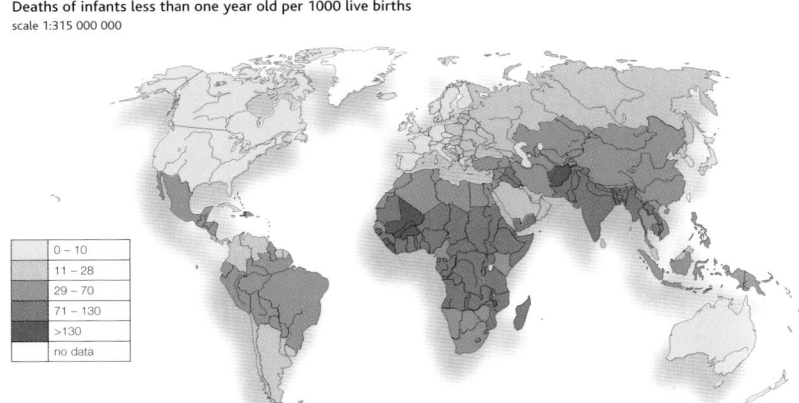

© Bartholomew Ltd

TOWARDS AN URBANIZED WORLD

World population is urbanizing rapidly but the current level of urbanization – the proportion of the population living in urban conditions – varies greatly across the world, as does its rate of increase. In the hundred years up to 1950 the greatest changes in urban population patterns took place in Europe and North America. Relatively few large cities developed elsewhere and most of these were in coastal locations with good trading connections with the imperial and industrial nations. This legacy is still highly visible on the world map of major cities (see 1). The main feature of the past half century has been the massive growth in the numbers of urban dwellers in the less developed regions. This process is still accelerating, posing an even greater logistical challenge during the next few decades than it did in the closing decades of the twentieth century.

The year 2006 is likely to be a momentous point in world history, when for the first time urban dwellers will outnumber those living in traditionally rural areas, according to UN projections. The annual rise in the percentage of the world's population living in cities has been accelerating steadily since the 1970s and will be running at unprecedentedly high levels for the next three decades. As a result, by 2030, 61.1 per cent of the world's population will be urbanites compared to 36.7 per cent in 1970 and 47.4 per cent in 2000 (see 2). In absolute terms, the global urban population more than doubled between 1970 and 2000 and is expected to grow by a further 2.2 billion by 2030 (see 3).

1. THE WORLD'S MAJOR CITIES

Urban agglomerations with over 1 million inhabitants
Winkel Tripel Projection
scale 1:106 000 000

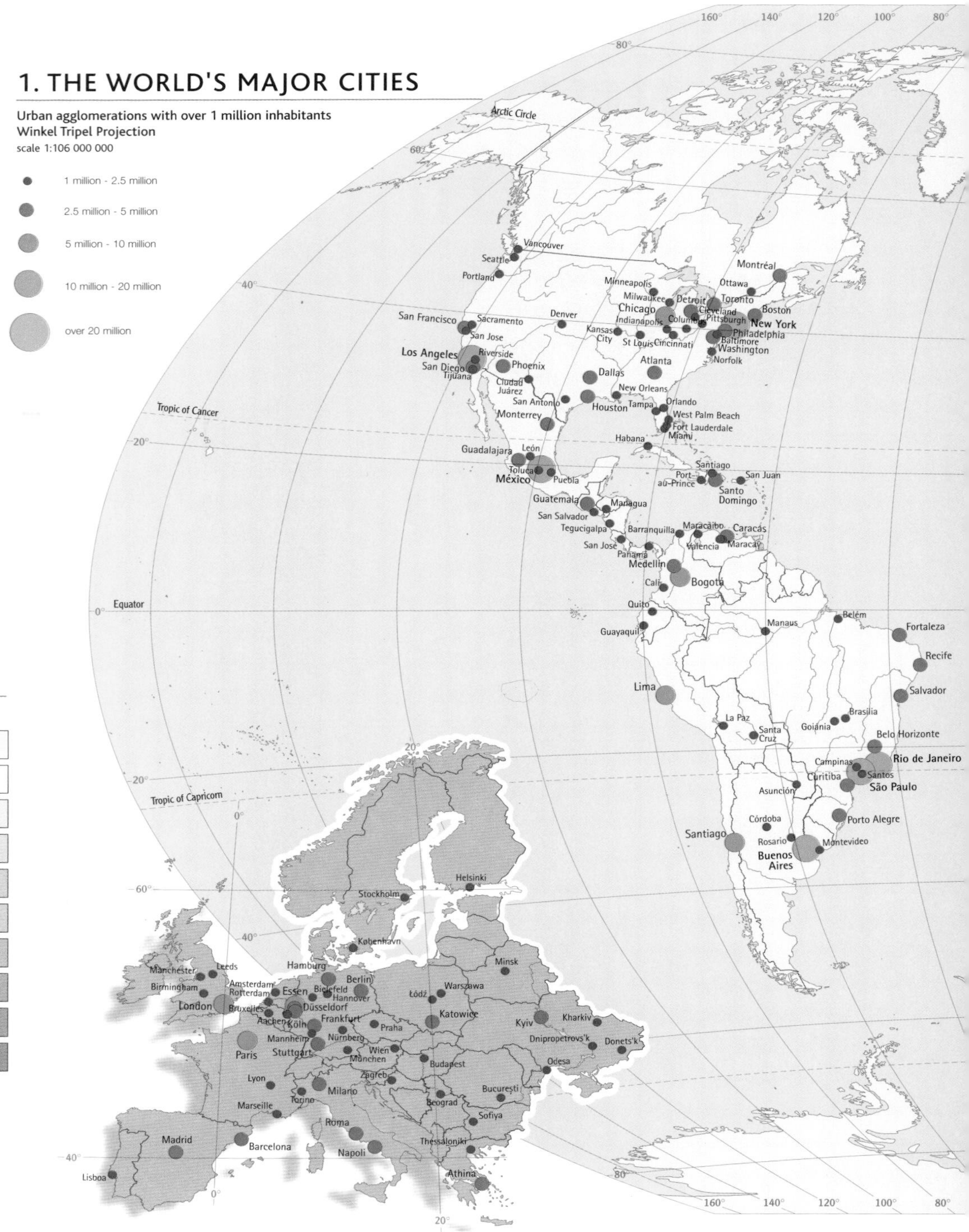

- 1 million - 2.5 million
- 2.5 million - 5 million
- 5 million - 10 million
- 10 million - 20 million
- over 20 million

2. LEVEL OF URBANIZATION BY MAJOR REGION 1970–2030

Urban population as a percentage of total population

	1970	2000	2030
World	36.7	47.4	61.1
More developed regions[1]	67.7	76.1	83.7
Less developed regions[2]	25.1	40.5	57.3
Africa	23.0	37.8	54.4
Asia	23.4	37.6	55.2
Europe[3]	64.5	74.9	82.9
Latin America and the Caribbean[4]	57.4	75.4	83.2
North America	73.8	77.2	84.4
Oceania	70.8	70.0	74.5

1. Europe, North America, Australia, New Zealand and Japan.
2. Africa, Asia (excluding Japan), Latin America and the Caribbean, and Oceania (excluding Australia and New Zealand).
3. Includes Russian Federation.
4. South America, Central America (including Mexico) and all Caribbean Islands.

3. TOTAL URBAN POPULATION OF MAJOR REGIONS 1950–2030

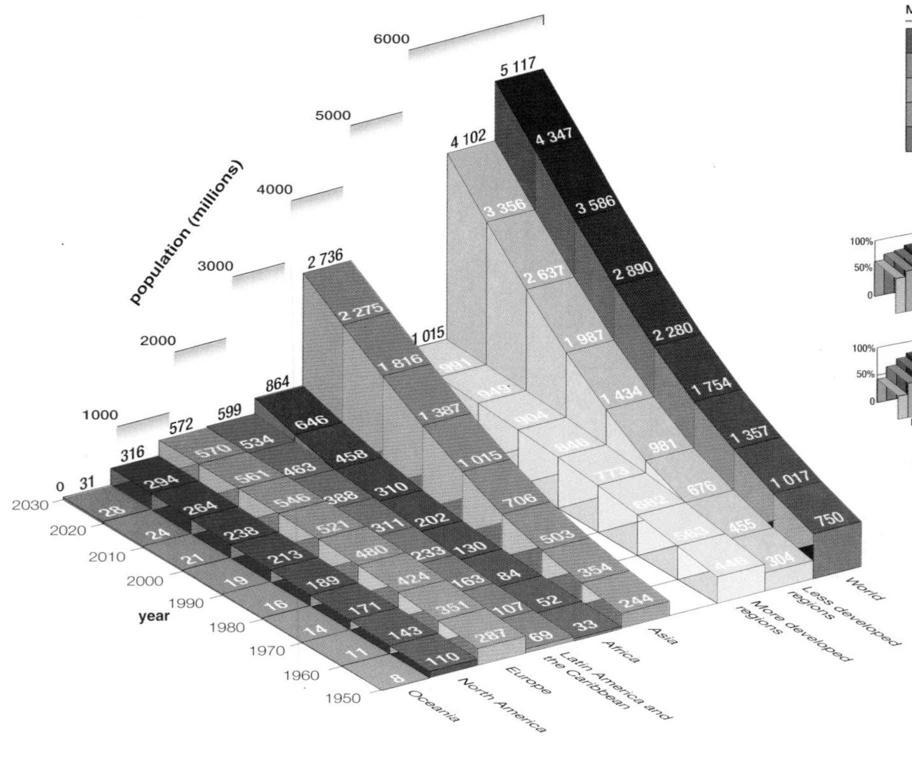

4. LEVEL OF URBANIZATION

Percentage of total population living in urban areas 2000 and growth in urbanization 1950-2025 (selected countries)
scale 1:250 000 000

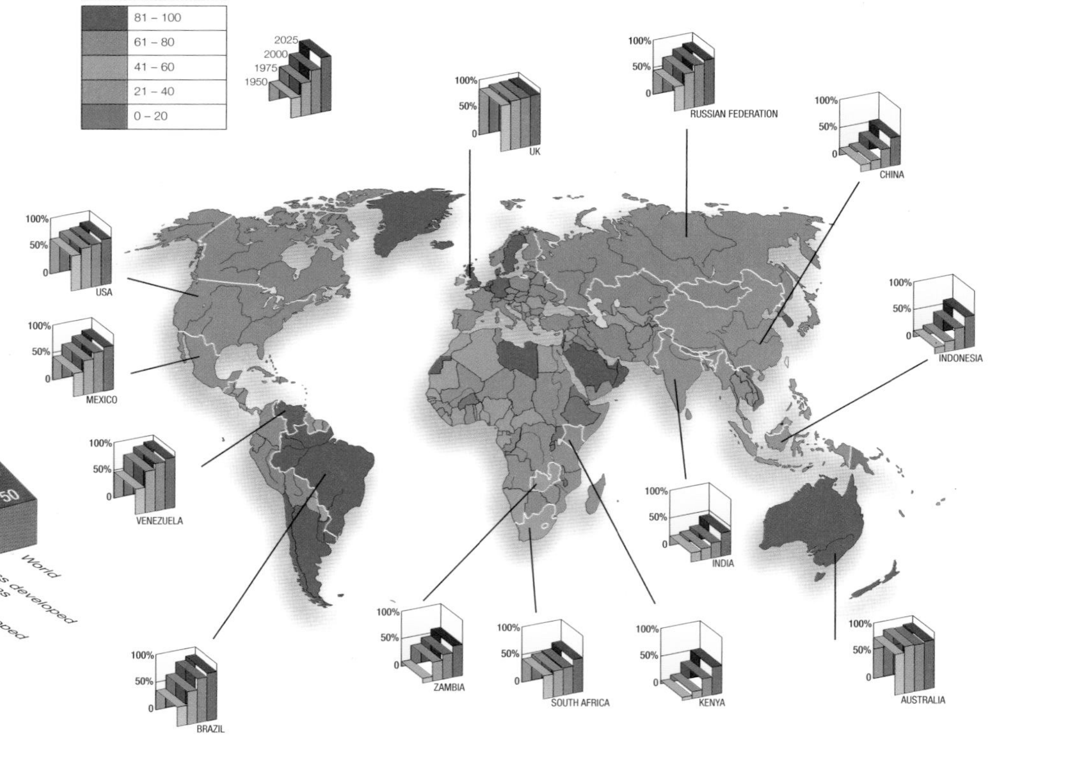

Map Key – per cent

- 81 – 100
- 61 – 80
- 41 – 60
- 21 – 40
- 0 – 20

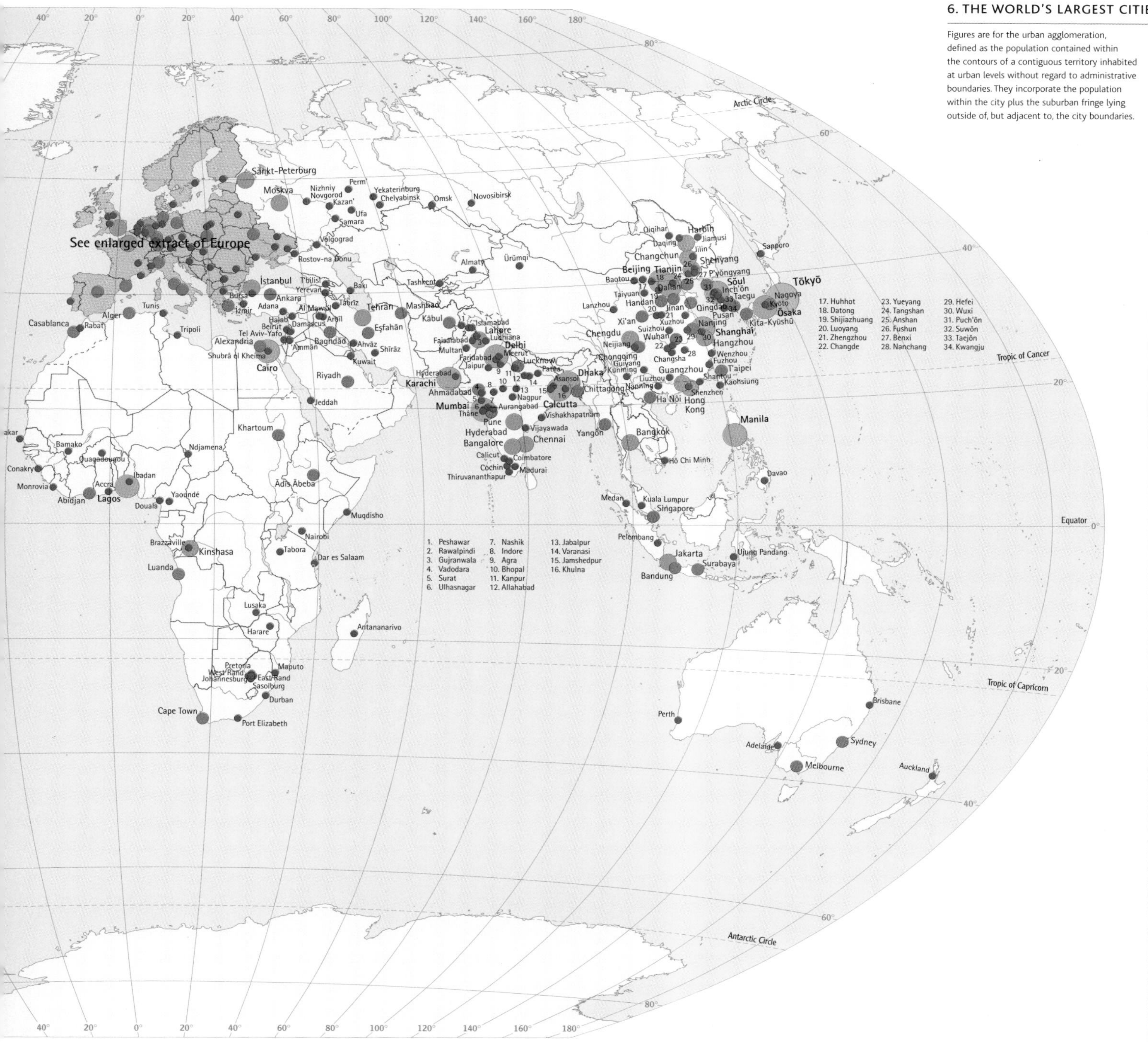

6. THE WORLD'S LARGEST CITIES 2000

Figures are for the urban agglomeration, defined as the population contained within the contours of a contiguous territory inhabited at urban levels without regard to administrative boundaries. They incorporate the population within the city plus the suburban fringe lying outside of, but adjacent to, the city boundaries.

City	Population
Tōkyō Japan	28 025 000
México Mexico	18 131 000
Mumbai India	18 042 000
São Paulo Brazil	17 711 000
New York USA	16 626 000
Shanghai China	14 173 000
Lagos Nigeria	13 488 000
Los Angeles USA	13 129 000
Calcutta India	12 900 000
Buenos Aires Argentina	12 431 000
Sŏul South Korea	12 215 000
Beijing China	12 033 000
Karachi Pakistan	11 774 000
Delhi India	11 680 000
Dhaka Bangladesh	10 979 000
Manila Philippines	10 818 000
Cairo Egypt	10 772 000
Ōsaka Japan	10 609 000
Rio de Janeiro Brazil	10 556 000
Tianjin China	10 239 000
Jakarta Indonesia	9 815 000
Paris France	9 638 000
İstanbul Turkey	9 413 000
Moskva Russian Federation	9 299 000
London United Kingdom	7 640 000
Lima Peru	7 443 000
Tehrān Iran	7 380 000
Bangkok Thailand	7 221 000
Chicago USA	6 945 000
Bogotá Colombia	6 834 000
Hyderabad India	6 833 000
Chennai India	6 639 000
Essen Germany	6 559 000
Hangzhou China	6 389 000
Hong Kong China	6 097 000
Lahore Pakistan	6 030 000
Shenyang China	5 681 000
Changchun China	5 566 000
Bangalore India	5 544 000
Harbin China	5 475 000
Chengdu China	5 293 000
Santiago Chile	5 261 000
Guangzhou China	5 162 000
Sankt-Peterburg Russian Federation	5 132 000
Kinshasa Dem. Rep. Congo	5 068 000
Baghdād Iraq	4 796 000
Jinan China	4 789 000
Wuhan China	4 750 000
Toronto Canada	4 657 000
Yangôn Myanmar	4 458 000
Alger Algeria	4 447 000
Philadelphia USA	4 398 000
Qingdao China	4 376 000
Milano Italy	4 251 000
Pusan South Korea	4 239 000
Belo Horizonte Brazil	4 160 000
Ahmadabad India	4 154 000
Madrid Spain	4 072 000
San Francisco USA	4 051 000
Alexandria Egypt	3 995 000
Washington USA	3 927 000
Dallas USA	3 912 000
Guadalajara Mexico	3 908 000
Chongqing China	3 896 000
Medellín Colombia	3 831 000
Detroit USA	3 785 000
Handan China	3 763 000
Frankfurt Germany	3 700 000
Porto Alegre Brazil	3 699 000
Ha Nôi Vietnam	3 678 000
Sydney Australia	3 665 000
Santo Domingo Dominican Republic	3 601 000
Singapore Singapore	3 587 000
Casablanca Morocco	3 535 000
Katowice Poland	3 488 000
Pune India	3 485 000
Bandung Indonesia	3 420 000
Monterrey Mexico	3 416 000
Montréal Canada	3 401 000
Nagoya Japan	3 377 000
Nanjing China	3 375 000
Houston USA	3 365 000
Abidjan Côte d'Ivoire	3 359 000
Xi'an China	3 352 000
Berlin Germany	3 337 000
Riyadh Saudi Arabia	3 328 000
Recife Brazil	3 307 000
Düsseldorf Germany	3 251 000
Ankara Turkey	3 190 000
Melbourne Australia	3 188 000
Salvador Brazil	3 180 000
Dalian China	3 153 000
Caracas Venezuela	3 153 000
Ādīs Ābeba Ethiopia	3 112 000
Athina Greece	3 103 000
Cape Town South Africa	3 092 000
Köln Germany	3 067 000
Maputo Mozambique	3 017 000
Napoli Italy	3 012 000
Fortaleza Brazil	3 007 000
San Diego USA	2 983 000
Boston USA	2 915 000
Chittagong Bangladesh	2 906 000
Kita-Kyūshū Japan	2 898 000
Kyiv Ukraine	2 897 000
T'aipei Taiwan	2 880 000
Inch'ŏn South Korea	2 837 000
Barcelona Spain	2 819 000
Khartoum Sudan	2 748 000
P'yŏngyang North Korea	2 726 000
Kābul Afghanistan	2 716 000
Guatemala Guatemala	2 697 000
Atlanta USA	2 689 000
Stuttgart Germany	2 688 000
Roma Italy	2 688 000
Hamburg Germany	2 680 000
Luanda Angola	2 665 000
Eşfahān Iran	2 644 000
Phoenix USA	2 607 000
Lucknow India	2 565 000
Taegu South Korea	2 559 000
Curitiba Brazil	2 519 000
Surabaya Indonesia	2 507 000
Tashkent Uzbekistan	2 495 000
Kanpur India	2 447 000
Johannesburg South Africa	2 412 000
Izmir Turkey	2 399 000
Mashhad Iran	2 378 000
Arbil Iraq	2 368 000
Minneapolis USA	2 363 000
Surat India	2 341 000
Damascus Syria	2 335 000
Nairobi Kenya	2 320 000
München Germany	2 306 000
Habana Cuba	2 302 000
Taiyuan China	2 280 000
Zhengzhou China	2 275 000
Birmingham United Kingdom	2 271 000
Warszawa Poland	2 269 000
Manchester United Kingdom	2 252 000
Guiyang China	2 230 000
Faisalabad Pakistan	2 228 000
Miami USA	2 210 000
Halab Syria	2 173 000
Tel Aviv-Yafo Israel	2 170 000
Jaipur India	2 143 000
București Romania	2 130 000
Guayaquil Ecuador	2 127 000
Peshawar Pakistan	2 094 000
Seattle USA	2 084 000
Cali Colombia	2 082 000
Dakar Senegal	2 077 000
Wien Austria	2 072 000
St Louis USA	2 071 000
Nagpur India	2 060 000

REGIONAL PATTERNS OF URBANIZATION

There is a broad contrast in the levels of urbanization between the more and less developed regions (*see 4*). In the more developed regions as a whole, three-quarters of the population now live in urban places. Excluding city states, levels range from 97 per cent for Belgium to under 40 per cent for Albania, Bosnia-Herzegovina and Portugal. Many countries have seen very little increase in their level of urbanization over the last few decades, with some reporting renewed population growth in rural areas. Only 40.5 per cent of the population in the less developed regions are urbanites, but this represents a big jump from the 25.1 per cent figure for 1970. Africa and Asia both currently average less than this, but will be seeing the greatest changes in the future, with their urban proportions likely to pass the 50 per cent mark by 2025. Between 2000 and 2030, Africa and Asia are expected to account for 86 per cent of the world's new urbanites – around 550 and 1 350 million people in absolute terms.

Alongside the rise in the world's urban population has occurred a massive increase in the number and size of cities. In 1950, New York was the only urban agglomeration with over 10 million inhabitants, but the number of cities of this size had grown to five by 1975 and to fourteen by 1995. There are expected to be twenty-six such cities by 2015, according to UN figures (*see 5*). This increase is principally an Asian phenomenon. Asia's total of cities of this size has grown from two to seven between 1975 and 1995, and today Asia dominates any list of the world's largest cities (*see 6*). Even more impressively, eleven of the additional twelve megacities that are expected to emerge by 2015 are in Asian countries, nine of them in south and east Asia. This massive growth is due to a combination of in-migration and natural increase, together with the physical outward expansion of their built-up areas and the incorporation of nearby settlements.

5. CITIES OF OVER 10 MILLION INHABITANTS 1975–2015

Figures are for urban agglomerations as defined in Table 6.

Africa   Asia   Latin America and the Caribbean   North America

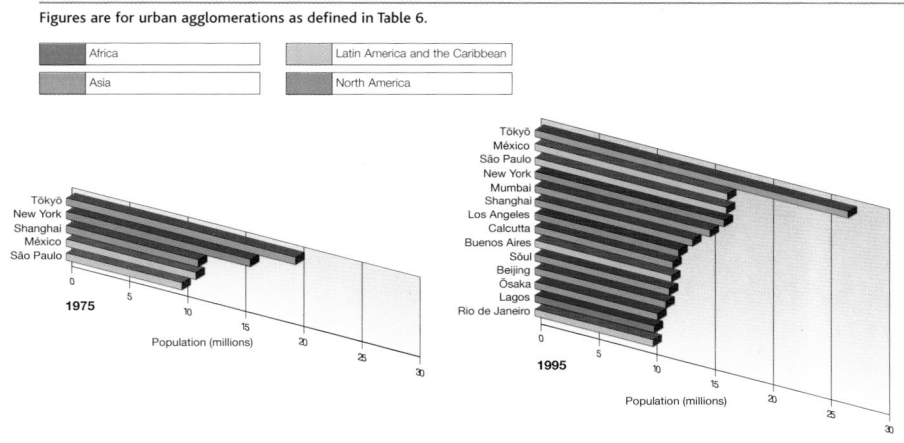

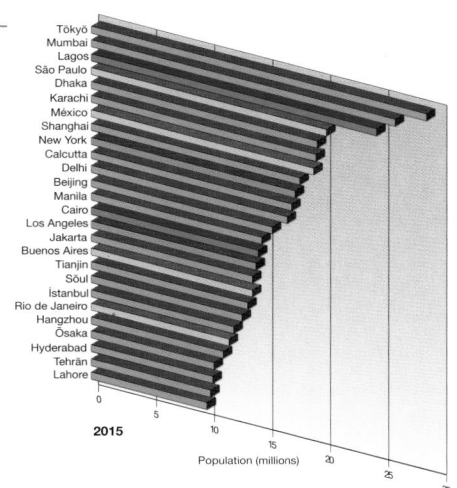

© Bartholomew Ltd

THE DISTRIBUTION OF MINERALS

Geological processes have determined the distribution of mineral resources but the location of productive mines is the result of geological, economic and political factors. The map *(see 1)* shows the locations of the most important mines producing industrial and metallic minerals. The bulk of world reserves – those resources which can be extracted economically at a particular time – are located at the mines shown.

Many aspects of the distribution of mineral resources are related to the Earth's tectonic structure. For example, the numerous large copper mines around parts of the Pacific rim are related to the destructive plate margins in these areas *(see pages 24-25)*. Most iron ore now comes from giant sedimentary deposits which have been naturally enriched by near-surface processes. These occur in ancient 'cratons' which are areas of the crust which have been internally stable for more than half a billion years and are typified by western Australia, eastern Brazil and the Canadian and Eurasian 'shields'. Output from the main iron ore producers has varied over time, with China becoming the leading world producer in the 1990s *(see 2)*.

Another striking relationship of mineral resources to geography and climate is provided by the distribution of bauxite, the main ore of aluminium. With few exceptions, major bauxite deposits are situated in the tropics, because bauxite is formed by the weathering of rocks at the Earth's surface under tropical climatic conditions *(see 3)*.

1. LOCATION OF SIGNIFICANT MINES

Producing mines or major deposits in active development, 1999
See table below for index to sites
Winkel Tripel Projection
scale 1:100 000 000

◯ ▭ ◇ >5% of world production

○ ▫ ◇ 1-5% of world production

∘ ▫ ◊ Other selected deposits (<1% of world production)

METALLIC MINERALS

- ● Iron **Fe**
- ● Copper **Cu**
- ● Gold **Au**
- ● Uranium **U**
- ● Aluminium **Al**
- ● Manganese **Mn**
- ● Lead **Pb**, Zinc **Zn**, Cadmium **Cd**, Silver **Ag**
- ● Tin **Sn**, Tantalum **Ta**, Beryllium **Be**, Antimony **Sb**, Mercury **Hg**, Bismuth **Bi**, Caesium **Cs**, Rubidium **Rb**
- ● Nickel **Ni**, Molybdenum **Mo**, Niobium **Nb**, Cobalt **Co**, Chromium **Cr**, Platinum **Pt**, Palladium **Pd**, Vanadium **V**, Tungsten **W**

INDUSTRIAL (NON METALLIC) MINERALS

- ▭ Potash **K**, Phosphate **P**, Borates **B**, Sulphur **S**, Lithium **Li**
- ▭ Baryte **Ba**, Fluorspar **F**, Asbestos **Asb**
- ■ Titanium minerals (ilmenite, rutile) **Ti**, Zircon **Zr**
- ◆ Diamonds **Diam.**

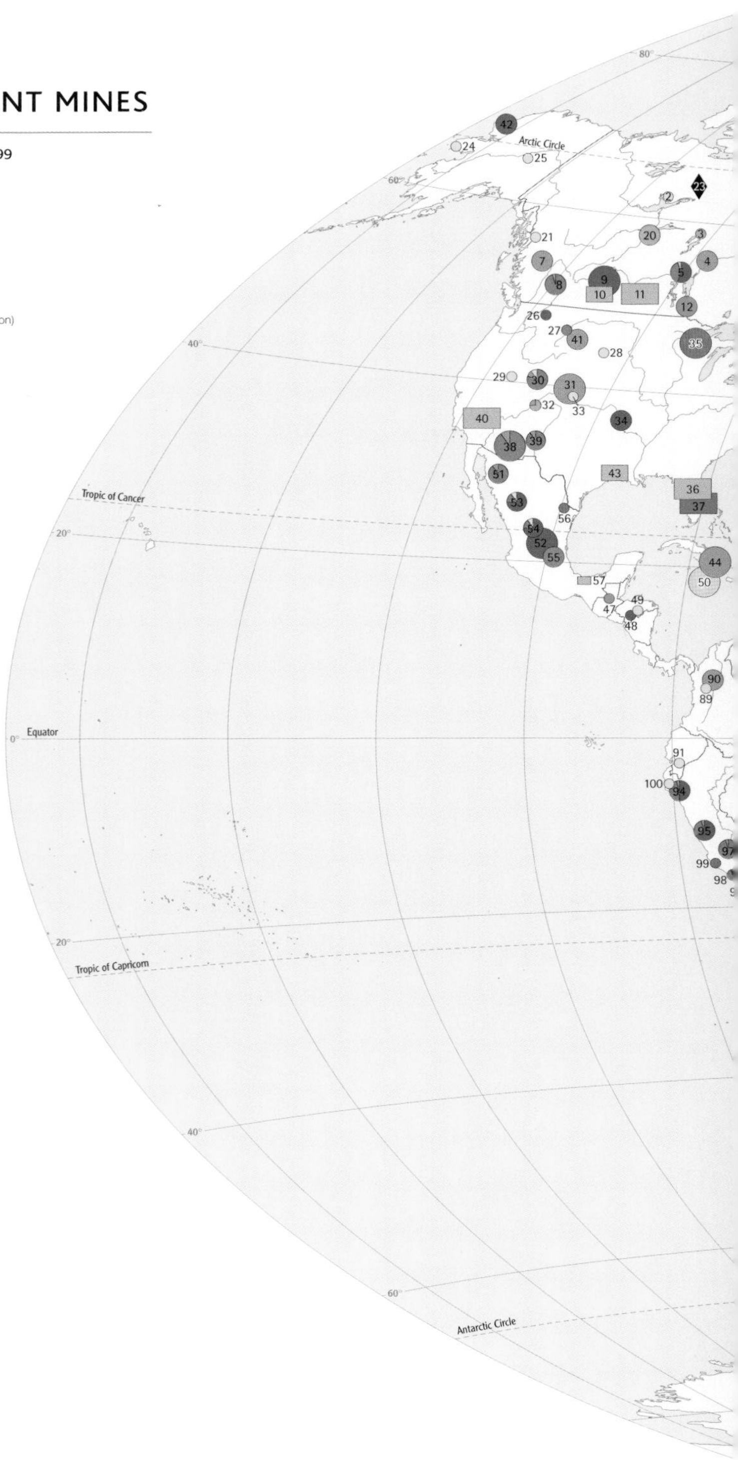

Arctic Circle
Tropic of Cancer
Equator
Tropic of Capricorn
Antarctic Circle

TYPES OF MINERAL

Minerals are usually grouped into four classes defined chiefly by their use:

Industrial minerals are minerals such as salt, fluorspar, barytes and sulphur, which are used in their natural state in industrial processes, and phosphate rock and potash which are vital constituents of fertilizers in addition to other uses. Gemstones are a special case in that, with the exception of industrial diamonds which are used as an abrasive, they are valued only for their aesthetic appearance.

Metallic minerals are mined to extract the metals they contain. Deposits of metallic minerals are evaluated chiefly on the costs of mining the ore and of extracting the metal from it.

Construction minerals such as sand, gravel, clay and gypsum, are used to make building materials. Their production costs are relatively low, but because their transport costs are high, they are normally used close to where they are produced. They are produced in most countries and are not shown on the map.

Energy minerals comprise coal, oil and natural gas, collectively known as 'fossil fuels', and uranium, the raw material for nuclear power. In terms of mass they are the most important traded minerals. Uranium is shown on the map; the others are shown on pages 38-39.

MINERAL PRODUCTION

Economies of scale have always been a strong influence on the geographic patterns of mineral production: a very large orebody is able to supply a significant proportion of world demand and can often be worked at a lower unit cost than a smaller deposit. Thus, for example, only a handful of giant mines in the Americas dominate the world supply of copper *(see 4)*. Similar geographical concentration of supply are marked also in other minerals, including chromium and nickel *(see 5 and 6)*. Production of gold *(see 7)* and diamonds was until fairly recently dominated by southern African countries but advances in exploration and processing technology have led to many new discoveries of both of these commodities in other continents, notably Australia and North America. China is the dominant producer of tungsten, antimony and fluorspar *(see 8)*, having a large number of small to medium sized mines. The absence of mines of these materials elsewhere indicates not a lack of resources, but a lack of economic reserves.

2. IRON ORE PRODUCERS 1972-1998

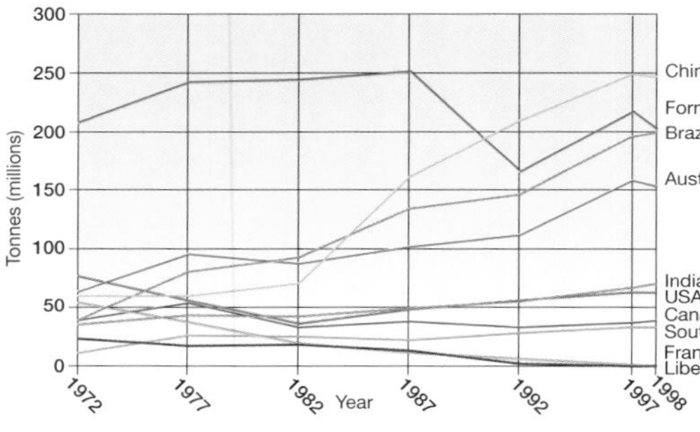

300
250
200
150
100
50
0
Tonnes (millions)
1972
1977
1982
Year
1987
1992
1997
1998
China
Former Soviet Union¹
Brazil
Australia
India
USA
Canada
South Africa
France
Liberia

¹Ukraine: 111.8
Russian Federation: 72.3
Kazakhstan: 18.0

3. ALUMINIUM ORE PRODUCTION 1998

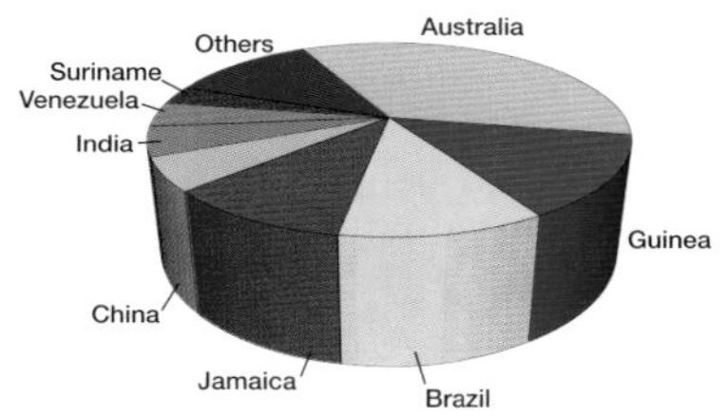

Others
Australia
Suriname
Venezuela
India
Guinea
China
Jamaica
Brazil

4. COPPER PRODUCTION 1998

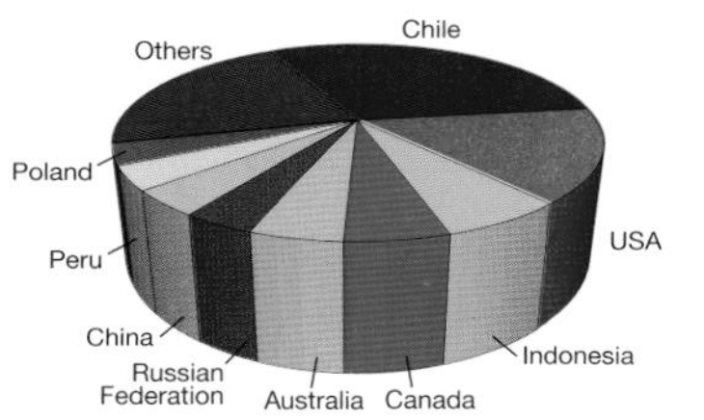

Others
Chile
Poland
Peru
USA
China
Russian Federation
Australia
Canada
Indonesia

INDEX TO SITES ON THE MAP

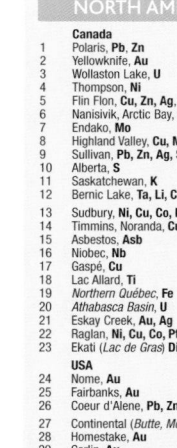

KEY: SITE NUMBER, MINE/*PROVINCE/ DISTRICT/ AREA*, **MINERALS**

NORTH AMERICA

Canada
1 Polaris, **Pb, Zn**
2 Yellowknife, **Au**
3 Wollaston Lake, **U**
4 Thompson, **Ni**
5 Flin Flon, **Cu, Zn, Ag, Au**
6 Nanisivik, Arctic Bay, **Pb, Zn, Ag**
7 Endako, **Mo**
8 Highland Valley, **Cu, Mo**
9 Sullivan, **Pb, Zn, Ag, Sb**
10 Alberta, **S**
11 Saskatchewan, **K**
12 Bernic Lake, **Ta, Li, Cs, Rb**
13 Sudbury, **Ni, Cu, Co, Pt**
14 Timmins, Noranda, **Cu, Pb, Zn, Au**
15 Asbestos, **Asb**
16 Niobec, **Nb**
17 Gaspé, **Cu**
18 Lac Allard, **Ti**
19 *Northern Québec*, **Fe**
20 *Athabasca Basin*, **U**
21 Eskay Creek, **Au, Ag**
22 Raglan, **Ni, Cu, Co, Pt**
23 Ekati (*Lac de Gras*) **Diam.**

USA
24 Nome, **Au**
25 Fairbanks, **Au**
26 Coeur d'Alene, **Pb, Zn, Ag**
27 Continental (*Butte, Montana*), **Cu**
28 Homestake, **Au**
29 Carlin, **Au**
30 Bingham Canyon, **Cu, Mo, Au**
31 Henderson, **Mo, W**
32 *Colorado Plateau*, **U, V**
33 Cresson (*Cripple Creek*), **Au**
34 *Viburnum Trend*, **Pb, Zn, Ag**
35 *Lake Superior, Minnesota*, **Fe**
36 *Florida*, **P**
37 *Florida, East Coast*, **Ti, Zr**
38 *Arizona*, **Cu, Mo**
39 *New Mexico*, **Cu, Mo**
40 Boron, Searles Lake, **B**
41 Stillwater, **Pt, Pd**
42 Red Dog, **Zn, Pb, Ag**
43 *Texas, Louisiana*, **S**

CENTRAL AMERICA

Cuba
44 *Eastern Cuba*, **Ni, Co**

Dominican Republic
45 Pueblo Viejo, **Au**
46 Bonao, **Ni**

Guatemala
47 *Ixtahuacan*, **Sb**

Honduras
48 El Mochito, **Zn, Pb, Ag**
49 San Andres, **Au**

Jamaica
50 *Jamaica*, **Al**

Mexico
51 *Sonora*, **Cu, Mo**
52 *San Luis Potosí*, **Pb, Zn, Ag, Sb**
53 Chihuahua, *Northern Durango*, **Pb, Zn, Ag, Cu, Au**
54 *Zacatecas*, **Pb, Zn, Ag, Cu, Au**
55 *Hidalgo*, **Mn**
56 Hercules, **Fe**
57 Coatzacoalcos, **S**

SOUTH AMERICA

Argentina
58 Aguilar, **Pb, Zn, Ag**
59 Bajo de la Alumbrera, **Cu, Mo, Au**
60 El Pachon, **Cu, Mo, Au**
61 *Northern Provinces*, **B**

Bolivia
62 Potosí, Oruro, **Sn, Sb, Pb, Zn, Ag, W**

Brazil
63 Trombetas, **Al**
64 *Rondônia*, **Sn**
65 Carajás,
66 Igarape Azul, Carajás, **Mn**
67 Caraiba, **Cu**
68 Campo Formoso, **Cr**
69 Cana Brava, **Cr**
70 Niquelândia, **Ni**
71 Morro do Niquel, **Ni**
72 Tocantins, **Ni**
73 Urucum, **Mn, Fe**
74 Vazante, **Pb, Zn**
75 Boquira, **Pb, Zn**
76 Jequitinhonha, **Diam.**
77 *Araxá*, **Nb, P**
78 Morro Velho, **Au**
79 *Iron Quadrilateral*, **Fe**
80 Morro da Fumaça, **F**
81 *Roraima*, **Diam.**

Chile
82 Chuquicamata, Abra, **Cu, Mo**
83 Escondida, El Salvador, **Cu, Mo, Au**
84 Disputada, Andina, Pelambres, **Cu, Mo**
85 El Teniente, **Cu, Mo**
86 Cerro Colorado, Quebrada Blanca, **Cu, Mo**
87 La Candelaria, **Cu, Mo, Au**
88 *Atacama*, **Fe**

Colombia
89 Titiribi, **Au**
90 Cerro Matoso, **Ni**

Ecuador
91 Portovelo, **Au**

Guyana
92 *Guyana*, **Al**
93 Omai, **Au**

Peru
94 *Northern Peru*, **Pb, Zn, Ag, Cu, Mo**
95 Cerro de Pasco, *central Peru*, **Pb, Zn, Ag, Cu, Mo**
96 Cuajone, Toquepala, **Cu, Mo**
97 Tintaya, **Cu, Mo**
98 Cerro Verde, **Cu, Mo**
99 Marcona, **Fe**
100 Yanacocha, **Au**

Suriname
101 *Suriname*, **Al**

Venezuela
102 Cedeno, **Al**
103 Cerro Bolivar, San Isidro, **Fe**
104 Cristinas, **Au, Cu**

EUROPE

Albania
1 *Kukës*, **Cr**

Austria
2 Mittersill, **W**

Belarus
3 Soligorsk, **K**

Belgium
4 Fleurus, **Ba**

Bulgaria
5 Chleopech, **Cu, Au**

Czech Republic
6 Erzgebirge, **U**

Finland
7 Kemi, **Cr**
8 Siilinjärvi, **P**
9 *Outokumpu Area*, **Cu, Ni, Co, Zn, Ag**

France
10 Chaillac, **Ba, F**
11 *South of Massif Central*, **F**
12 Lodève, **U**
13 Vendée, **U**
14 Salsigne, **Au, Bi, Ag, Cu**
15 Lacq, **S**
16 *Alsace*, **K**

Germany
17 *Stassfurt*, **K**
18 Mechernich, **Ba**

Greece
19 Parnasse, **Al**
20 Evvoia, **Ni**

Hungary
21 *Danube Region*, **Al**

Ireland
22 Navan, Lisheen, Galmoy, **Zn, Pb, Ag**

Italy
23 *Iglesiente*, **Pb, Zn, Ag, Ba, F**
24 Furtei, **Au**

Norway
25 Tellnes, **Ti**

Poland
26 *Lubin Region*, **Cu, Ag, Au**
27 *Upper Silesia* (*Kraków*), **Pb, Zn, Ag**
28 Tarnobrzeg, **S**

Portugal
29 Neves Corvo, **Cu, Sn, Zn**
30 *Iberian Pyrite Belt*, **Cu, Ag, Pb, Zn, S**
31 *Panasqueira*, **W, Cu, Sn**

Romania
32 *Apuseni Mountains*, **Au, Zn, Pb, Ag**

Russian Federation (in Europe)
33 Pechenga, **Ni, Cu, Pt, Co**
34 Monchegorsk, **Ni, Cu, Pt, Co**
35 Lovozero, Khibiny, **P, Nb**
36 Berezniki, Solikamsk, **K**
37 Kotshkanav, **Cr, Pt**
38 Kursk, **Fe**
39 Tyrnyauz, **W, Mo**
40 Sadan, **Pb, Zn, Ag**

Spain
30 *Iberian Pyrite Belt*, **Cu, Ag, Pb, Zn, S**
41 El Valle (Río Narcea), **Au**
42 Almaden, **Hg**
43 Reocin, **Zn, Pb, Ag**
44 La Collada, **F**

Sweden
45 Kiruna, **Fe**
46 *Skellefteå*, **Cu, Zn, Pb, Au, Ag**
47 Aitik, **Cu, Ag, Au**
48 Bjorkdal, **Au**
49 Laisvall, **Pb, Zn, Ag**
50 Falun, **Pb, Zn, Ag, Cu**
51 Zinkgruvan, **Zn, Pb, Ag**
52 Grängesberg, **Fe**
53 Malmberget, **Fe**

Ukraine
54 Kalush, **K**
55 *Krivoy Rog*, **Fe**
56 Nikopol, **Mn**

United Kingdom
57 Boulby, **K**
58 Foss, **Ba**
59 *Southern Pennines*, **F, Ba**

Yugoslavia
60 Bor, **Cu, Au**
61 Trepča, **Pb, Zn, Ag**

AFRICA

Algeria
1 *Annaba*, **Hg**
2 *Djebel Onk and Gafsa Region*, **P**

Angola
3 *Lunda Norte*, **Diam.**

Botswana
4 Orapa, **Diam.**
5 Jwaneng, **Diam.**
6 Selebi-Phikwe, **Ni, Cu**

Central African Republic
7 Berbérati, **Diam.**
8 Kotto, **Diam.**

Democratic Republic of Congo
9 Kasai, **Diam.**
10 Bakwanga, **Diam.**
11 *Copperbelt*, **Cu, Co**

Gabon
12 Mounana, **U**
13 Moanda, **Mn**

Ghana
14 Nsuta, **Mn**
15 *Ashanti, Western*, **Au**
16 Birim, **Diam.**

Guinea
17 Boké, Kindia, **Al**
18 Kono, Sanniquellie, Macenta, **Diam.**

Ivory Coast (Côte d'Ivoire)
19 Tortiya Segala, **Diam.**

Kenya
20 Kerio Valley, **F**

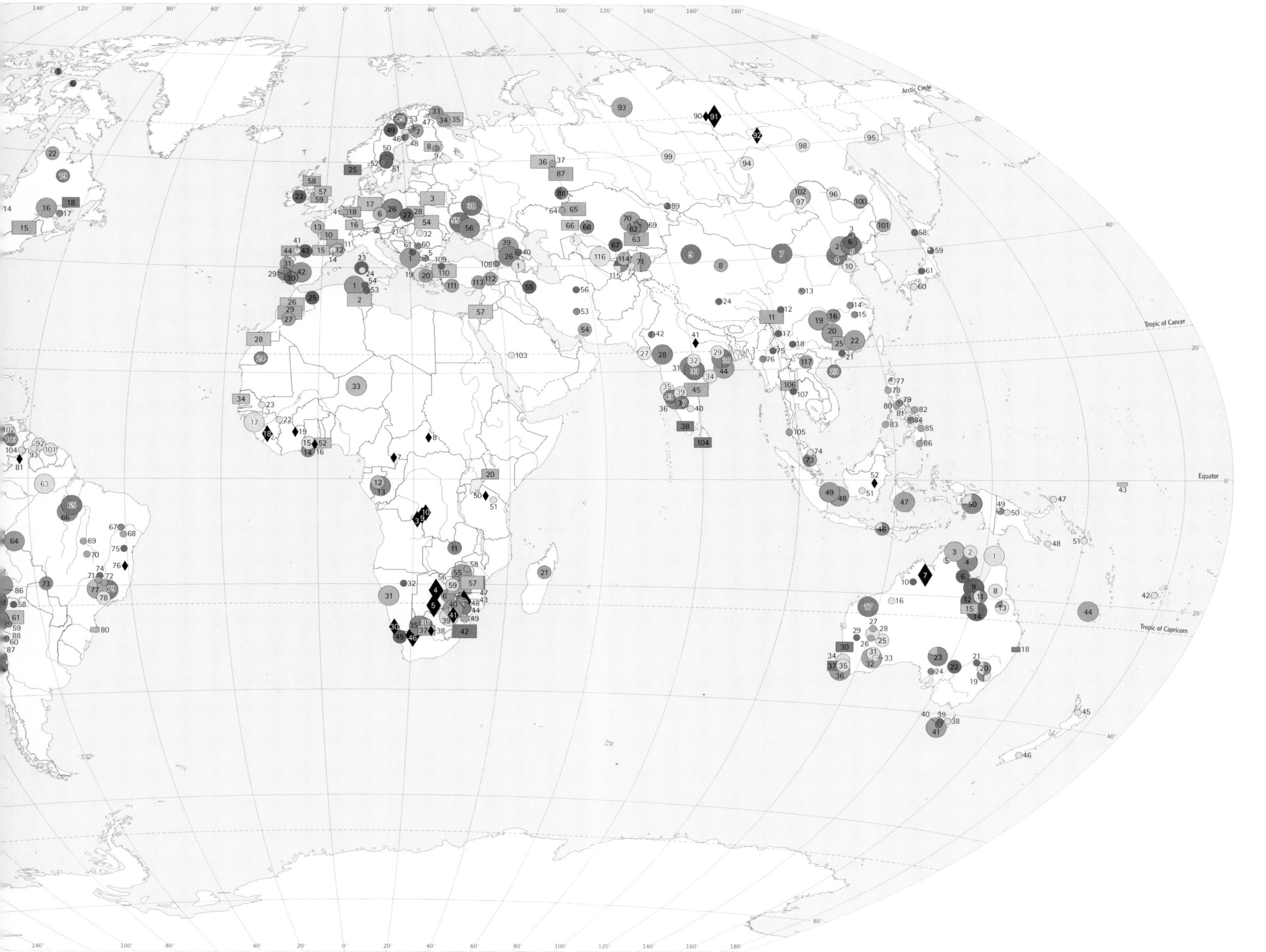

5. CHROMIUM ORE PRODUCTION 1998

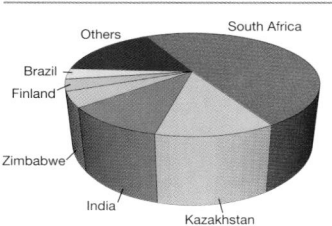

Others · South Africa · Brazil · Finland · Zimbabwe · India · Kazakhstan

6. NICKEL PRODUCTION 1998

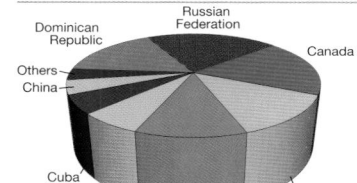

Dominican Republic · Russian Federation · Canada · Others · China · Australia · Cuba · Indonesia · New Caledonia

7. GOLD PRODUCTION 1972–1998

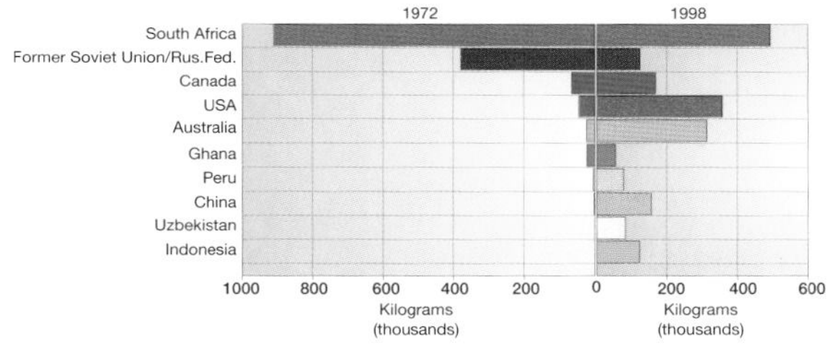

	1972	1998
South Africa		
Former Soviet Union/Rus.Fed.		
Canada		
USA		
Australia		
Ghana		
Peru		
China		
Uzbekistan		
Indonesia		

1000 800 600 400 200 0 200 400 600
Kilograms (thousands)   Kilograms (thousands)

8. FLUORSPAR PRODUCTION 1998

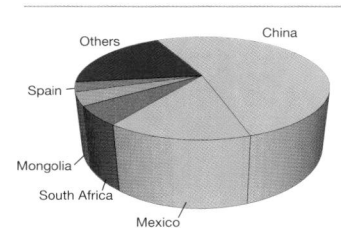

Others · China · Spain · Mongolia · South Africa · Mexico

Liberia
18 Kono, Sanniquellie, Macenta, **Diam.**

Madagascar
21 Andriamena, **Cr**

Mali
22 Syama, **Au**
23 Sadiola, **Au**

Mauritania
24 Fdérik, **Fe**

Morocco
25 Touissit, Boubeker, **Pb, Zn, Ag**
26 Central Morocco, **P**
27 Bou Azzer, **Co**
28 Boukra, **P**
29 Jebel Irhoud, Jebel Zelmou, **Ba, F**

Namibia
30 Oranjemund, **Diam.**
31 Rossing, **U**
32 Kombat, **Pb, Zn, Ag**

Niger
33 Agadez, **U**

Senegal
34 Taiba, **P**

Sierra Leone
35 Kono, Sanniquellie, Macenta, **Diam.**

South Africa, Republic of
35 Northern Cape, **Mn**
36 Sishen, **Fe**
37 Griqualand, **Asb**
38 Kimberley, **Diam.**
39 Witwatersrand, **Au, U**
40 Bushveld, **Cr, Pt, Ni, V, F**
41 Premier Mine, **Diam.**
42 Richards Bay, **Ti, Zr**
43 Murchison Range, **Sb**
44 Phalaborwa, **Cu, P**

45 Black Mountain, **Pb, Zn, Ag**
46 Finsch, **Diam.**
47 Messina, **Cu**
48 Venetia, **Diam.**

Swaziland
49 Swaziland, **Asb**

Tanzania
50 Northern Tanzania, **Diam.**
51 Golden Pride, **Au**

Togo
52 Hahotoé, Akoumapé, **P**

Tunisia
2 Djebel Onk and Gafsa Region, **P**
53 Northern Tunisia, **Pb, F**
54 Bou Grine, **Zn, Pb**

Zambia
11 Copperbelt, **Cu, Co**

Zimbabwe
55 Great Dyke, **Cr, Pt, Pd**
56 Zvishavane, **Asb**
57 Bikita, **Li, Be**
58 Bindura, **Ni, Cu**
59 Bulawayo, **Au**

ASIA

Armenia
1 Armenia, **Cu, Mo, Au**

China
2 Jinzhou, **Mo**
3 Hongtoushan, **Cu, Au**
4 Shijiaying, Shuicheng, **Fe**
5 Nanfen, **Fe**
6 Bayan Obo Kuanggu, **Fe**
7 Jinchuan, **Ni, Cu**
8 Xinjiang Uygur Zizhiqu (Sinkiang), **Fe**

9
10 Penglai, **Au**
11 Sichuan, **Asb**
12 Cheng Xian, **Pb, Zn**
13 Changduicheng, **Cu, Mo**
14 Shinchao, **Cu**
15 Tongshankou, **Cu**
16 Dexing, **Cu, Ag, Au**
17 Lanping, **Pb, Zn**
18 Zhehai, **Pb, Zn**
19 Hunan-Sichuan, **Hg, Sb**
20 Hunan-Guangxi, **Sn, W**
21 Fankou, **Pb, Zn**
22 South Jiangxi, Guangdong, **W**
23 Hainan, **Fe**
24 Xitieshan, **Pb, Zn**
25 South China, **Ba, F**

Georgia
26 Chiatura, **Mn**

India
27 Bhuj, **Al**
28 Panch Mahals, **Mn**
29 Ranchi, **Al**
30 Bihar, Orissa, **Fe, Mn**
31 Nagpur, Balaghat, **Mn**
32 Madhya Pradesh, **Al**
33 Rowghat, Bailadila, **Fe**
34 Koraput, **Al**
35 Maharashtra, **Al**
36 Supa, **Mn**
37 Karnataka, **Fe, Mn**
38 Southeast Kerala (Travancore), **Ti, Zr**
39 Hutti, **Al**
40 Kolar, **Au**
41 Majhgawan, **Diam.**
42 Rajasthan, **Cu, Zn, Pb, Ag**
43 Goa, **Fe**
44 Cuttack, **Sn**
45 Mangampet, **Ba**

Indonesia
46 Batu Hijau, **Cu, Au**
47 Pomalaa, **Ni**
48 Belitung, **Sn**
49 Bangka, **Sn**
50 Grasberg, **Cu, Au**
51 Kelian, **Au**
52 Kalimantan, **Diam.**

Iran
53 Sar Cheshmeh, **Cu, Ag, Au, Mo**
54 Faryab Area, **Cr**
55 Angorhan, **Pb, Zn**
56 Nakhlak, **Pb, Zn**

Israel
57 Dead Sea Region, **K, P**

Japan
58 Toyoha, **Pb, Zn, Ag**
59 Hokuroko District, **Pb, Zn, Ag, Cu**
60 Hishikari, **Au, Ag**
61 Kamioka, **Pb, Zn, Ag**

Jordan
57 Dead Sea Region, **K, P**

Kazakhstan
62 Balkhash, **Cu, Mo**
63 Chiganak, Baikanour, **Ba**
64 Khrom Tau, **Cr**
65 Kiembay, **Asb**
66 Kara Tau, **P**
67 Achisay, **Pb, Zn, Ag**
68 Dzhezkazgan, **Cu, Mo**
69 Kounrad, **Cu, Mo**
70 Akchatau, **W, Mo**

Kyrgystan
71 Kyrgystan, **Hg, Sb, U**
72 Kumtor, **Au**

Malaysia
73 Malaya, **Sn, Ti**
74 Penjom, **Au**

Myanmar
75 Bawdwin, **Zn, Pb, Ag**
76 Monywa, **Cu**

Philippines
77 Luzon, **Au, Cu**
78 Zambales Mountains, **Cr**
79 Marinduque, **Cu, Mo, Au**
80 Mindoro, **Ni, Co**
81 Masbate, **Au**
82 Samar, **Cr**
83 Palawan, **Ni, Co**
84 Cebu, **Cu, Mo, Au**
85 Northern Mindanao, **Ni, Co**
86 Southern Mindanao, **Ni, Co**

Russian Federation (in Asia)
87 Bazhenovskoye, **Asb**
88 Central Urals, **Cu, Au**
89 Altay, **Pb, Zn, Ag, Cu**
90 Alakit, **Diam.**
91 Daldyn, **Diam.**
92 Noril'sk, **Ni, Cu, Pt, Co**
93 Udachnaya, **Diam.**
94 Lena, Vitim, **Au**
95 Magadan Region, **Au**
96 Amur, **Au**
97 Zabaykal'sk, **Sn**
98 Yakutsk, **Au**
99 Yenisey, **Au**
100 Birobidzhan, **Sn**
101 Primorskiy Kray, **Sn, W**
102 Chitinskaya, **Ni, Sn**

Saudi Arabia
103 Madh adh Dhahab, **Au, Ag, Cu, Zn**

Sri Lanka
104 Southern Sri Lanka, **Ti, Zr**

Thailand
105 Southern Thailand, Phuket, **Sn, W**
106 Northern Thailand, **Ba, F**

107 Mae Sod, **Zn, Cd**

Turkey
108 Murgul, **Cu**
109 Biga Region, **Pb, Zn, Ag, Ba**
110 Balikesir, Emet, **B**
111 Fethiye, **Cr**
112 Malatya, Guleman, **Cr, Fe**
113 Karsanti, **Cr**

Uzbekistan/Tajikistan
114 Almalyk, **U, F**
115 Southeast Uzbekistan/Tajikistan, **Cu, Au, Pb, Zn, Ag**
    Muruntau, Zarafshan, **Au**

Vietnam
117 Vietnam, **Sn**

OCEANIA

Australia
1 Weipa, **Al**
2 Gove, **Al**
3 Ranger, **U**
4 Groote Eylandt, **Mn**
5 Mount Todd, **Au**
6 McArthur River, **Pb, Zn, Ag**
7 Argyll, **Diam.**
8 Kidston, **Au, Ag**
9 Century, **Zn, Pb, Ag**
10 Lennard Shelf, **Zn, Pb, Ag**
11 Ernest Henry, **Cu**
12 Mount Isa Region, **Cu, Pb, Zn, Ag**
13 Mount Leyshon, **Au, Ag**
14 Cannington, **Pb, Ag, Zn**
15 Phosphate Hill, **P**
16 Telfer, **Au**
17 Hamersley Range, **Fe**
18 Sydney, Brisbane, **Ti, Zr**
19 Cadia, **Au, Cu**
20 North Parkes, **Cu, Au, Ag**

21 Elura, **Zn, Pb**
22 Broken Hill, **Pb, Zn, Ag**
23 Olympic Dam, **Cu, U**
24 Middleback Ranges, **Fe**
25 Granny Smith, **Au**
26 Leinster, **Ni, Cu**
27 Mount Keith, **Ni, Cu**
28 Agnew, **Au**
29 Golden Grove, **Zn, Ag, Au, Cu**
30 Eneabba, **Ti, Zr**
31 Kalgoorlie Region, **Au, Ag**
32 Kambalda, **Ni, Cu, Co, Pt**
33 St Ives, **Au**
34 Darling Ranges, **Al**
35 Boddington, **Au, Cu**
36 Greenbushes, **Ta, Li**
37 Capel, **Ti, Zr**
38 Beaconsfield, **Au**
39 Hellyer, **Zn, Pb, Ag**
40 Rosebery, **Zn, Pb, Ag**
41 Renison Bell, **Sn**

Fiji
42 Viti Levu, Emperor, **Au**

Nauru
43 Nauru, **P**

New Caledonia
44 New Caledonia, **Ni, Co**

New Zealand
45 Martha Hill, **Au, Ag**
46 Macraes, **Au, Ag**

Papua New Guinea
47 Lihir, **Au**
48 Misima, **Au, Ag**
49 Ok Tedi, **Cu, Au**
50 Porgera, **Au**

Solomon Islands
51 Gold Ridge, **Au**

© Bartholomew Ltd

ENERGY PRODUCTION AND CONSUMPTION

The world's energy resources are unevenly distributed (*see 1*). Similarly, the geography of energy production and consumption is highly uneven, with three countries, the USA, Russian Federation and China, dominating both the production and consumption of energy (*see 2*). Some countries – typically the oil-exporting states, such as Saudi Arabia, Nigeria, Venezuela, Mexico and Indonesia – produce much more than they consume, but many of the most advanced industrial economies, such as the USA and Japan, consume vastly more energy than they produce. The USA is the largest single energy consumer, using over a quarter of the world's energy despite having only 5 per cent of its population.

As a result of the uneven geography of production and consumption, energy sources are the largest single item in international trade (*see 3*). Taking the example of oil, some regions are net exporters, such as the Middle East and West Africa. Others rely heavily upon imported oil and so have to generate wealth by other means to be able to pay for their imports. These include the USA, Central and Western Europe and Japan (*see 4*).

2. WORLD'S TOP 10 ENERGY PRODUCERS AND CONSUMERS 1998

Million tonnes of oil equivalent

Producers		Consumers	
USA	1 835	USA	2 389
Russian Federation	1 034	China	855
China	835	Russian Federation	655
Saudi Arabia	529	Japan	536
Canada	433	Germany	349
UK	293	India	315
India	251	Canada	299
Iran	249	France	252
Mexico	234	UK	246
Australia	209	Brazil	204
World total	9 631	World total	9 519

3. THE ENERGY TRADE

Major trade flows between trading regions 1999
scale 1:217 000 000

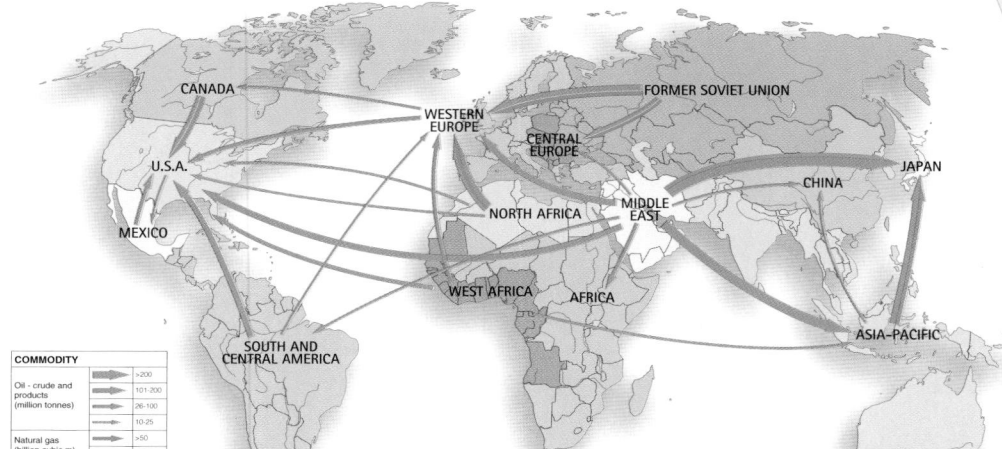

COMMODITY	
Oil - crude and products (million tonnes)	>200
	101-200
	26-100
	10-25
Natural gas (billion cubic m)	>50
	20-50
Liquefied Natural Gas (LNG) (billion cubic m)	>50
	11-50
	2-10

1. DISTRIBUTION OF RESOURCES

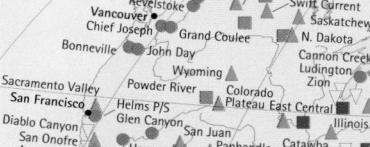

Winkel Tripel Projection
scale 1:94 000 000

▲	Major oil fields
▲	Major gas fields
■	Major coal deposits
■	Major lignite deposits
▽	Major nuclear reactors
●	Major hydro plants

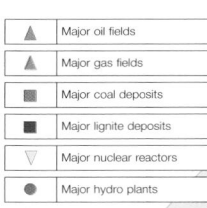

4. OIL IMPORTS AND EXPORTS 1999

Movements within the regions indicated are not included in the figures.

	Crude Exports (million tonnes)	Crude Imports (million tonnes)	Balance of Trade (million tonnes)
USA	6.6	427.6	-421.0
Canada	58.4	40.6	17.8
Mexico	81.2	-	81.2
South and Central America	110.2	54.3	55.9
Western Europe	60.5	393.5	-333.0
Former Soviet Union[1]	135.8	-	135.8
Central Europe	0.1	48.6	-48.5
Middle East	794.1	4.2	789.9
North Africa	99.3	7.7	91.6
West Africa	145.1	3.8	141.6
Eastern and Southern Africa	2.2	23.6	-21.4
Australasia	10.4	28.6	-18.2
China	7.9	36.6	-28.7
Japan	0.2	214.9	-214.7
Other Asia-Pacific	53.6	294.1	-240.5
Unidentified	12.2	-	12.2
Total World	1578.1	1578.1	0.0
1. Comprises: Russian Federation, Estonia, Latvia, Lithuania, Belarus, Ukraine, Moldova, Georgia, Armenia, Azerbaijan, Kazakhstan, Uzbekistan, Turkmenistan, Tajikistan and Kyrgyzstan			

ENERGY RESERVES AND RATES OF CONSUMPTION

Proven energy reserves are also unevenly distributed (*see 5*). Nearly two-thirds of proven oil reserves are concentrated in the Middle East. Reserves in the USA and Russian Federation have declined and Europe's reserves are expected to dry up early this century. Central America and Africa are expected to cease oil exports around 2025. Proven reserves of natural gas are dominated by the Former Soviet Union and the Middle East while coal reserves are more evenly distributed between the Asia-Pacific region, North America and the Former Soviet Union.

Between 1989 and 1999 the world level of primary energy consumption increased by 11 per cent (*see 6*). This change was led by the Middle East with a 52 per cent increase, followed by South and Central America with a 38 per cent rise. Relatively costly energy in Europe depressed consumption to the comparatively low growth level of 2 per cent, while the dissolution of the Soviet Union led to the collapse in consumption there by over a third. If rates of energy consumption were to remain constant, then it has been estimated that proven oil reserves would last forty years, natural gas sixty years and coal three hundred years. However, because energy consumption rates are increasing these estimates may need revision.

5. PROVEN ENERGY RESERVES 1999

	🜄	%	⚒	%	⬛	%
North America[1]	8.4	6.0	7.31	5.0	256 477	26.1
South & Central America	12.9	9.2	6.31	4.3	21 574	2.2
Europe	2.7	1.9	5.15	3.5	122 032	12.4
Former Soviet Union[2]	9.0	6.4	56.70	38.7	230 178	23.4
Middle East	91.5	65.2	49.52	33.8	193	-
Africa	10.0	7.1	11.16	7.7	61 412	6.2
Asia-Pacific	5.9	4.2	10.28	7.0	292 345	29.7
World	140.4	100	146.43	100	984.211	100

1. Canada, USA and Mexico 2. See footnote for table 4

🜄 Oil (thousand million barrels)   ⚒ Natural Gas (trillion cubic metres)   ⬛ Coal (million tonnes)

6. PRIMARY ENERGY CONSUMPTION

Million tonnes of oil equivalent

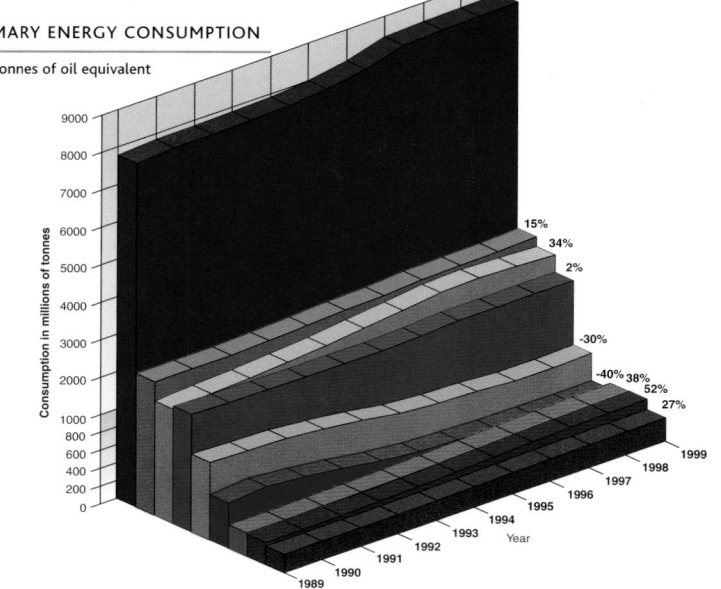

■	World
	North America
	Europe
	Middle East
	Russian Federation
	Other Former Soviet Union
	South and Central America
	Africa
	Asia-Pacific

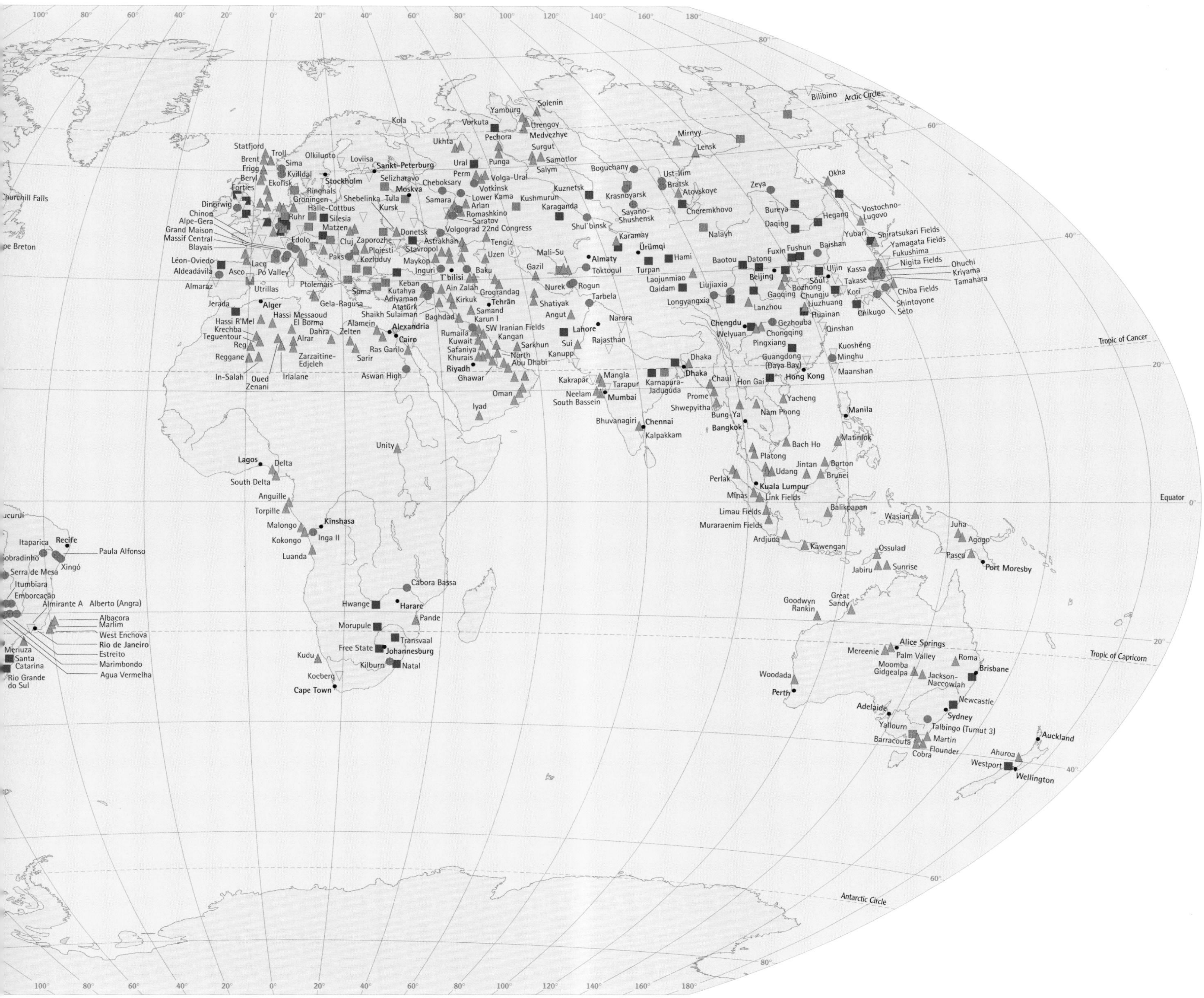

Map labels (selection):

Churchill Falls · Cape Breton · Statfjord · Brent · Frigg · Beryl · Forties · Troll · Sima · Kvilldal · Olkiluoto · Loviisa · Sankt-Peterburg · Ukhta · Vorkuta · Yamburg · Solenin · Bilibino · Arctic Circle · Mirnyy · Lensk · Okha · Kola · Pechora · Medvezhye · Surgut · Samotlor · Urengoy · Boguchany · Ust-Ilim · Zeya · Bureya · Hegang · Vostochno-Lugovo

Dinorwig · Chinon · Alpe-Gera · Grand Maison · Massif Central · Blayais · Léon-Oviedo · Aldeadávila · Almaraz · Ekofisk · Ringhals · Stockholm · Groningen · Halle-Cottbus · Ruhr · Silesia · Edolo · Matzen · Cluj · Zaporozhe · Donetsk · Selizharovo · Cheboksary · Moskva · Tula · Kursk · Samara · Lower Kama · Saratov · Volgograd 22nd Congress · Ural · Perm · Volga-Ural · Kuznetsk · Krasnoyarsk · Sayano-Shushensk · Cheremkhovo · Nalayh · Karaganda · Kushmurun · Karamay · Ürümqi · Hami · Daqing · Fuxin · Fushun · Baishan · Yubari · Shiratsukari Fields · Yamagata Fields · Fukushima · Nigita Fields · Ohuchi · Kriyama · Tamahara

Jerada · Hassi R'Mel · Krechba · Teguentour · Reg · Reggane · In-Salah · Oued Zenani · Irlalane · Zarzaitine-Edjeleh · Alger · Utrillas · Ptolemais · Soma · Kutahya · Adiyaman · Atatürk · Kirkuk · Keban · Gela-Ragusa · T'bilisi · Baku · Gazil · Mali-Su · Almaty · Toktogul · Nurek · Rogun · Shatiyak · Tengiz · Uzen · Angut · Tarbela · Narora · Rajasthan · Laojunmiao · Qaidam · Baotou · Datong · Beijing · Uljin · Kassa · Sŏul · Takase · Kori · Chiba Fields · Shintoyone · Seto · Chikugo

Alexandria · Cairo · Shaikh Sulaiman · Alamein · Zelten · El Borma · Dahra · Alrar · Sarir · Aswan High · Baghdad · Samand · Karun 1 · SW Iranian Fields · Kangan · Sarkhun · Sui · Kanupp · Kanpura · Rumaila · Kuwait · Safaniya · Khurais · North Abu Dhabi · Riyadh · Ghawar · Oman · Iyad · Neelam · South Bassein · Mumbai · Bhuvanagiri · Chennai · Kalpakkam · Lahore · Narora · Tehrān · Shaikh

Lanzhou · Longyangxia · Chengdu · Welyuan · Chongqing · Pingxiang · Guangdong (Daya Bay) · Minghu · Kuosheng · Maanshan · Qinshan · Yacheng · Hong Kong · Hon Gai · Chaul · Dhaka · Prome · Shwepyitha · Bung-Ya · Nam Phong · Bangkok · Manila · Kakrapar · Mangla · Tarapur · Karnapura-Jaduguda

Lagos · Delta · South Delta · Anguille · Torpille · Malongo · Kokongo · Kinshasa · Inga II · Luanda · Unity · Cabora Bassa · Hwange · Pande · Harare · Morupule · Free State · Transvaal · Johannesburg · Kudu · Kilburn · Natal · Koeberg · Cape Town

Perlak · Minas · Limau Fields · Muraraenim Fields · Ardjuna · Kawengan · Balikpapan · Wasian · Ossulad · Jabiru · Sunrise · Pasca · Juha · Agogo · Port Moresby · Platong · Jintan · Barton · Brunei · Udang · Kuala Lumpur · Link Fields · Bach Ho · Matinlok · Goodwyn Rankin · Great Sandy

Woodada · Perth · Mereenie · Moomba · Gidgealpa · Palm Valley · Alice Springs · Jackson-Naccowlah · Roma · Brisbane · Newcastle · Adelaide · Yallourn · Sydney · Barracouta · Martin · Talbingo (Tumut 3) · Cobra · Flounder · Westport · Ahuroa · Auckland · Wellington

Ucuruí · Itaparica · Recife · Paula Alfonso · Sobradinho · Serra de Mesa · Xingó · Itumbiara · Emborcação · Almirante A · Alberto (Angra) · Albacora · Marlim · West Enchova · Rio de Janeiro · Estreito · Meriuza · Marimbondo · Santa Catarina · Agua Vermelha · Rio Grande do Sul

Tropic of Cancer · Equator · Tropic of Capricorn · Antarctic Circle

ALTERNATIVE ENERGY SOURCES

Alternatives to traditional energy sources are nuclear power and renewable resources. Consumption of nuclear power (*see 7*) has been at relatively low levels and has grown more slowly than traditional energy sources. Asia-Pacific and South and Central America have experienced the highest growth in the past decade, led by Japan, which generates two-thirds of its electricity from nuclear sources. The question of sustainability has underpinned the search for new sources of energy which are less detrimental to the environment than traditional sources and nuclear power. One proposed solution is conservation through increased energy efficiency, i.e. increasing the ratio of useful energy input to output. Other solutions lie in energy resources which are renewable, such as geothermal, wind, solar, biomass and hydropower. Around 5 per cent of total primary energy requirements in Australia, Austria, Canada, Denmark, Sweden and Switzerland are currently met by renewables. The most successful form of renewable energy has been hydroelectric power, consumption of which has risen over 20 per cent in world terms between 1989 and 1999 (*see 8*), with South and Central America showing the largest rise (52 per cent), followed by Asia-Pacific (31 per cent).

7. NUCLEAR ENERGY CONSUMPTION

Million tonnes of oil equivalent

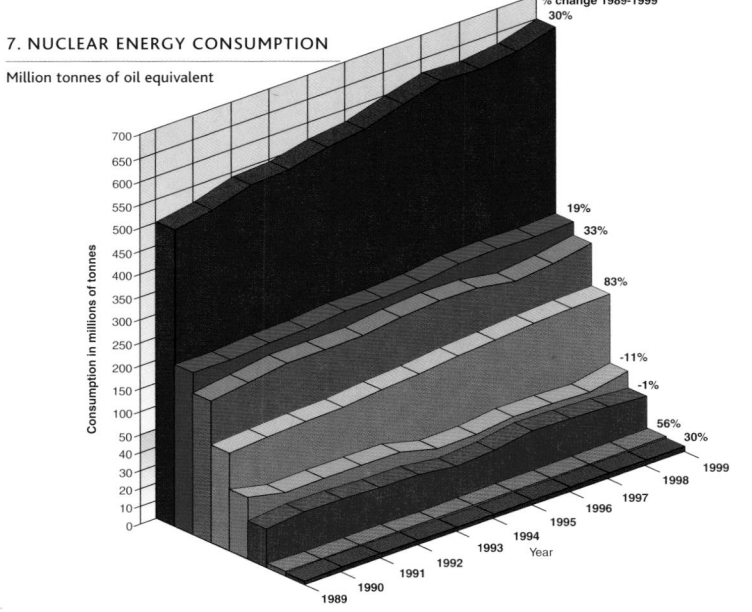

8. HYDROELECRICITY CONSUMPTION

Million tonnes of oil equivalent

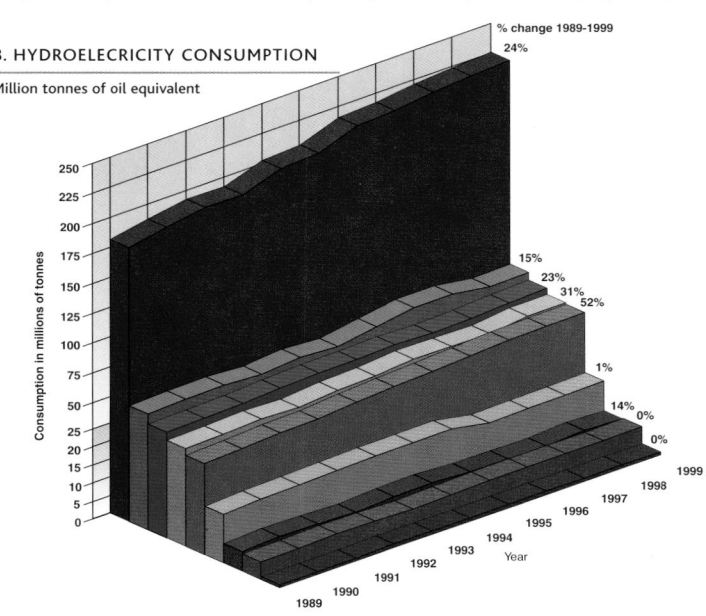

© Bartholomew Ltd

GLOBAL TOURISM AND AIR TRAVEL

The globalization of the world's social, economic and financial markets, whereby physical and political boundaries are no longer obstacles to movement between countries, has been made possible by improved transport and telecommunications networks. The growth of international air travel has meant that more people can move between countries with greater frequency and more cheaply.

International tourism grew throughout the world in the latter part of the 20th century. Between 1989-1999 the average annual growth rate for international tourist arrivals worldwide was nearly 5 per cent (over 230 million people – see 1). This global figure masks wide regional variations, however (see 2). Europe contributes the most to worldwide figures in terms of volume, but the rate of growth there has slowed, due mainly to the growing accessibility of East Asian and Pacific destinations. The regional share of tourist arrivals in this region has grown significantly in the last thirty years.

Improvements in air transport technology, an increasing number of air carriers and favourable economic conditions have combined to produce large increases in worldwide air travel. Passenger and freight traffic grew steadily in the latter half of the 20th century and this pattern is expected to continue. The largest proportion of international travel today occurs between the USA and Europe, and within the East Asia and Pacific region (see 3). Routes between the Middle East and both Africa and Europe – carrying high numbers of passengers in the 1980s – have been overtaken by routes within the East Asia and Pacific region and by long haul flights from Europe to East Asia and western USA. The pattern is reinforced by airport statistics (see 4). Airports in the USA – where air travel is used as much for internal as for international travel – and Europe dominate. However, as Far Eastern economies have developed, these countries have become more popular destinations for both business and leisure travellers.

1. INTERNATIONAL TOURIST ARRIVALS 1989 – 1999

'Tourist' refers to a visitor (visiting for either leisure or business) who stays for at least one night in the country visited

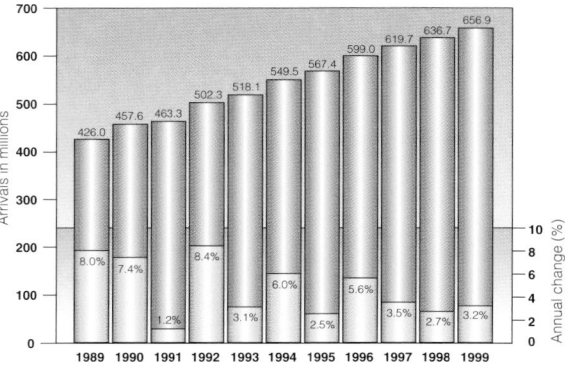

2. REGIONAL SHARE OF INTERNATIONAL TOURIST ARRIVALS 1970–1999

Height of each chart relates to total worldwide tourist arrivals

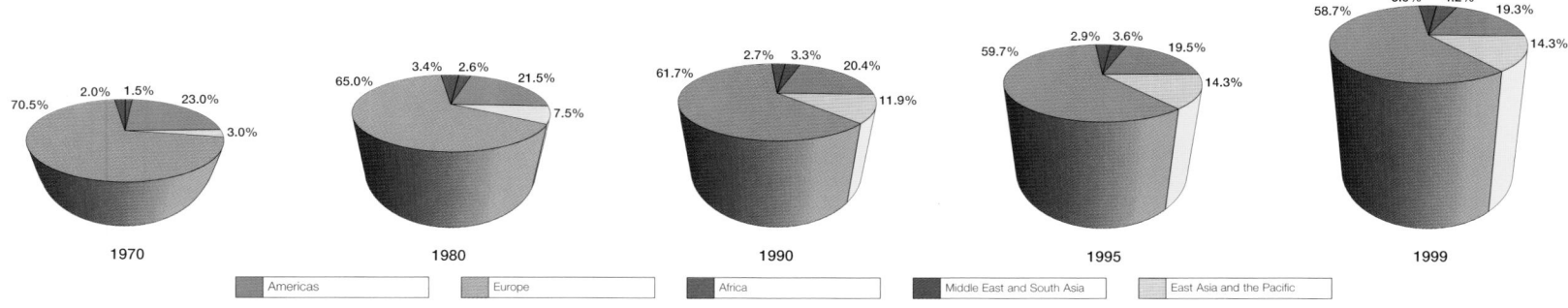

| | 1970 | 1980 | 1990 | 1995 | 1999 |

Americas | Europe | Africa | Middle East and South Asia | East Asia and the Pacific

3. BUSIEST SCHEDULED INTERNATIONAL AIR PASSENGER ROUTES 1999

Figures are for scheduled international passenger traffic in both directions. Land colours represent World Tourism Organization regions
Briesemeister Projection
scale 1:129 500 000

thickness of line symbolizes volume of international passenger traffic

• World's busiest airports

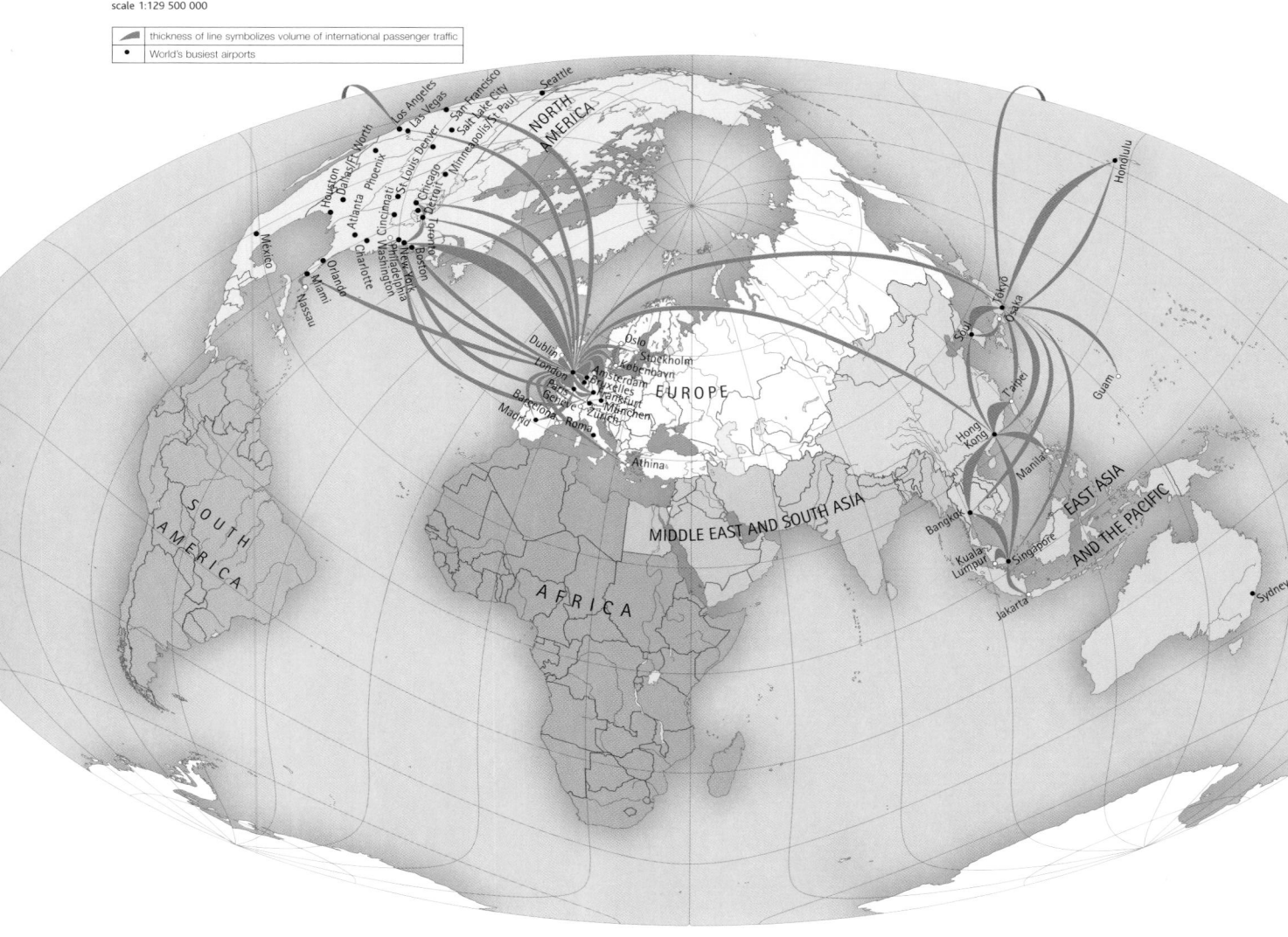

Route	Number of passengers
London–New York	3 793 405
Amsterdam–London	2 992 447
London–Paris	2 449 049
Hong Kong–T'aipei	2 381 710
Sŏul–Tōkyō	2 154 211
Kuala Lumpur–Singapore	2 073 874
Bangkok–Hong Kong	1 975 228
Frankfurt–London	1 928 209
Honolulu–Tōkyō	1 890 343
Bangkok–Singapore	1 798 607
Hong Kong–Tōkyō	1 678 542
Hong Kong–Manila	1 463 014
Hong Kong–Singapore	1 456 021
Dublin–London	1 387 477
Bangkok–Tōkyō	1 286 850
London–Madrid	1 264 659
New York–Toronto	1 262 157
New York–Paris	1 253 899
Los Angeles–London	1 244 180
Bruxelles–London	1 223 334
Jakarta–Singapore	1 181 580
Ōsaka–Sŏul	1 157 984
Hong Kong–Sŏul	1 146 669
Los Angeles–Tōkyō	1 142 747
Chicago–London	1 110 305
London–Zürich	1 083 403
Singapore–Tōkyō	1 071 597
Boston–London	1 055 978
London–Stockholm	1 055 828
Barcelona–London	1 028 320
Madrid–Paris	1 021 285
London–San Francisco	1 016 824
Chicago–Toronto	991 529
T'aipei–Tōkyō	986 424
London–München	975 606
Frankfurt–New York	965 365
Frankfurt–Paris	965 231
London–Toronto	945 283
Genève–London	945 223
London–Washington	925 481
London–Tōkyō	924 232
København–London	884 971
London–Miami	882 245
Hong Kong–London	881 924
Honolulu–Ōsaka	871 907
København–Oslo	870 994
Guam–Tōkyō	867 245
Miami–Nassau	858 866
Athína–London	850 610

4. THE WORLD'S BUSIEST AIRPORTS 1999

Figures given are total passenger arrivals and departures.
See map 3 for airport locations

Atlanta Hartsfield USA	Chicago O'Hare USA	Los Angeles USA	London Heathrow UK	Dallas/Ft Worth USA	Tōkyō Haneda Japan	Frankfurt Germany	Paris Charles de Gaulle France	San Francisco USA	Denver USA	Amsterdam Netherlands	Minneapolis/St Paul USA	Detroit Wayne County USA	Miami USA	New York Newark USA	Las Vegas McCarran USA	Phoenix Sky Harbor USA	Sŏul Kimpo South Korea	Houston USA	New York JFK USA	London Gatwick UK	St Louis Lambert USA
77 939 536	72 568 076	63 876 561	62 263 710	60 000 125	54 338 212	45 858 315	43 596 943	40 387 422	38 034 231	36 781 015	34 216 331	34 038 381	33 899 246	33 814 000	33 669 185	33 533 353	33 371 074	33 089 333	32 003 000	30 559 461	30 188 973

INTERNATIONAL TELECOMMUNICATIONS

Increased availability and ownership of telecommunications equipment over the last thirty years (see 5) has aided the globalization of the world economy. Over half of the world's fixed telephone lines have been installed since 1987, and the majority of the world's Internet hosts have come on-line since 1997. Network access is uneven, however. Over half of existing telephone lines and cellular phones are in North America and Europe, and over 70 per cent of Internet host computers are located in North America (see 6).

One measure of the perceived 'death of distance' is the steady rise in international telephone calls, which has increased nearly 400 per cent since 1988. The map (see 8) shows telephone and fax traffic between countries in different continents for routes using at least 100 million minutes of telecommunications time in 1998. In that year, these streams totalled 27.3 billion minutes, which accounted for approximately 29 per cent of global international traffic.

Growing volumes of data traffic, particularly from the Internet, have boosted demand for international transmission capacity. Most traffic is routed over fibre-optic cables which encode electronic signals into beams of laser light, which are sent down fine fibres of coated glass. In 1999, the world's trans-oceanic cables could carry approximately 250 gigabits per second (Gbps), which is equivalent to 17.5 million simultaneous phone calls. By 2001, international cable capacity will have grown by close to 400 per cent, although the largest cable systems will still only link a relative handful of countries (see 7).

5. WORLD COMMUNICATIONS EQUIPMENT 1970–2000

Source: TeleGeography, Inc and International Telecommunications Union

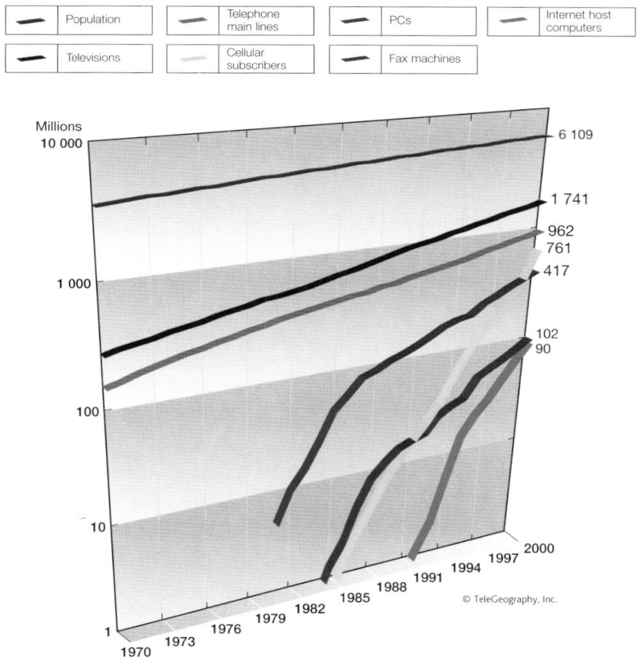

Population	Telephone main lines	PCs	Internet host computers
Televisions	Cellular subscribers	Fax machines	

© TeleGeography, Inc.

6. INTERNATIONAL TELECOMMUNICATIONS INDICATORS BY REGION 1998

Source: TeleGeography, Inc and International Telecommunications Union

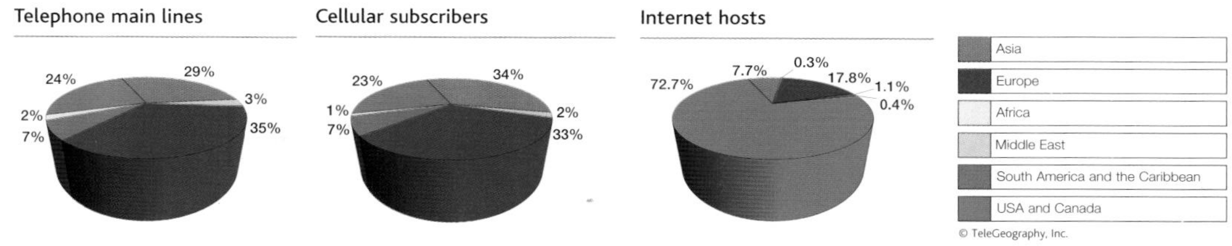

Telephone main lines — 24% 29% 3% 35% 7% 2%

Cellular subscribers — 23% 34% 2% 33% 7% 1%

Internet hosts — 72.7% 7.7% 0.3% 17.8% 1.1% 0.4%

- Asia
- Europe
- Africa
- Middle East
- South America and the Caribbean
- USA and Canada

© TeleGeography, Inc.

7. CAPACITY OF MAJOR INTERNATIONAL SUBMARINE CABLES 1999 AND 2001

Each 10 Gbps of cable capacity can carry approximately 700 000 simultaneous calls

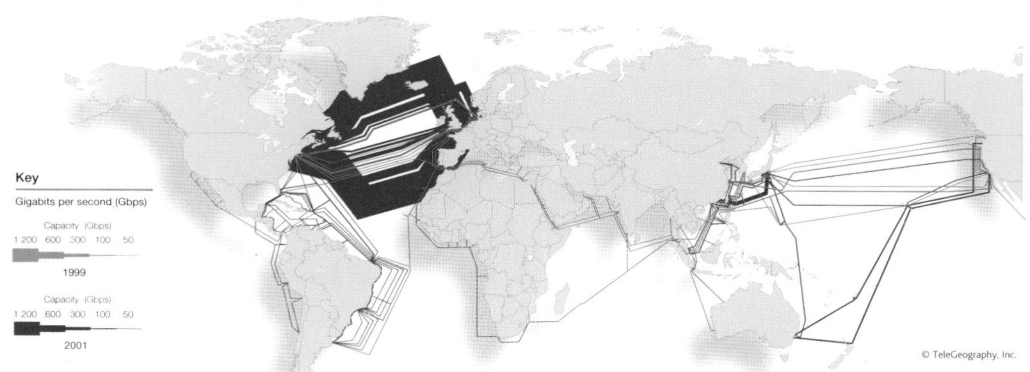

Key

Gigabits per second (Gbps)

Capacity (Gbps) 1 200 600 300 100 50
1999

Capacity (Gbps) 1 200 600 300 100 50
2001

© TeleGeography, Inc.

8. INTERNATIONAL TELECOMMUNICATIONS TRAFFIC 1998

Each band is proportional to the total annual traffic on the public telephone network in both directions between each pair of countries
Robinson Projection
scale 1:144 000 000

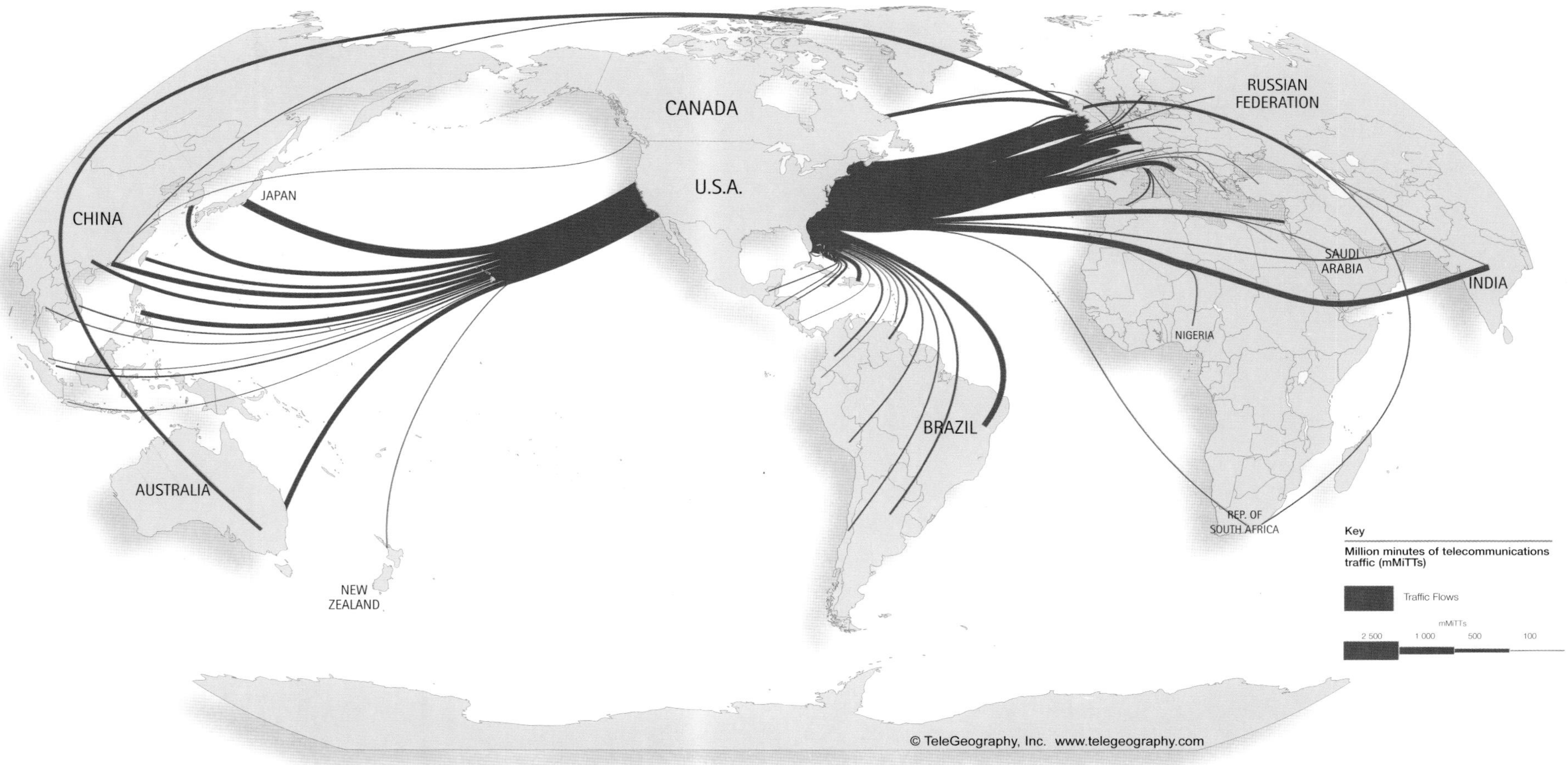

RUSSIAN FEDERATION

CANADA

CHINA

JAPAN

U.S.A.

SAUDI ARABIA

INDIA

NIGERIA

BRAZIL

AUSTRALIA

REP. OF SOUTH AFRICA

NEW ZEALAND

Key

Million minutes of telecommunications traffic (mMiTTs)

Traffic Flows

mMiTTs
2 500 1 000 500 100

© TeleGeography, Inc. www.telegeography.com

Hong Kong China 29 733 470
Orlando USA 29 173 491
Toronto Lester B. Pearson Canada 27 771 473
Seattle/Tacoma USA 27 698 733
Madrid Spain 27 532 237
Bangkok Thailand 27 289 863
Boston USA 26 964 984
Singapore Changi Singapore 26 064 645
Tokyo Narita Japan 25 667 634
Paris Orly France 25 349 270
Roma Leonardo da Vinci Italy 24 023 952
Philadelphia USA 23 786 285
New York La Guardia USA 23 756 000
Honolulu USA 22 640 670
Cincinnati USA 21 771 689
Sydney Kingsford Smith Australia 21 542 000
Charlotte USA 21 449 392
München Franz Josef Strauss Germany 21 282 906
Zürich Switzerland 20 990 179
México México 20 453 568
Salt Lake City USA 20 033 241
Bruxelles Belgium 20 025 014

© Bartholomew Ltd

PREHISTORIC AND CLASSICAL CARTOGRAPHY (500 BC – AD 500)

The evolution of mapping has been inextricably linked to people's knowledge of the world and to related scientific and technological developments. Mapping skills have been influenced by factors such as way of life and the nature of the physical environment, and maps can therefore provide an excellent insight into cultures and civilizations. Surviving examples of ancient maps are rare. Their limits of coverage tended to be the extent of the producers' accurate geographical knowledge. Beyond the local area, maps appeared to reflect a speculative or cosmological approach *(see 1)*.

The most significant contribution of the Greeks to cartography was theoretical rather than practical. It is primarily the work of Claudius Ptolemy, a Greek mathematician, astronomer and geographer living in the 2nd century AD, which provides us with information about the level of geographical knowledge at this time. Ptolemy's work *Geographia* included theoretical principles of cartography, lists of place names and computed co-ordinates. Later maps, based on this work, show how he believed the world to look at that time *(see 2)*.

1. MAP OF THE WORLD

Carved on a Babylonian clay tablet, c. 600 BC. Babylon is shown as a rectangle intersected by vertical lines representing the Euphrates river. Small circles show other cities and countries, and the world is encircled by an ocean – the 'Bitter River'.
British Museum, Department of Western Asiatic Antiquities, London, UK.

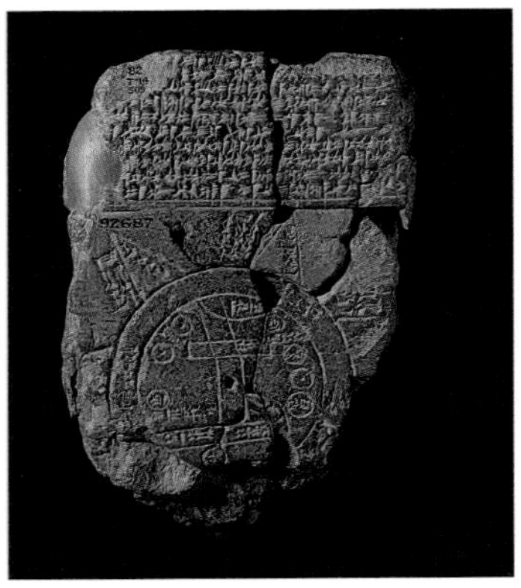

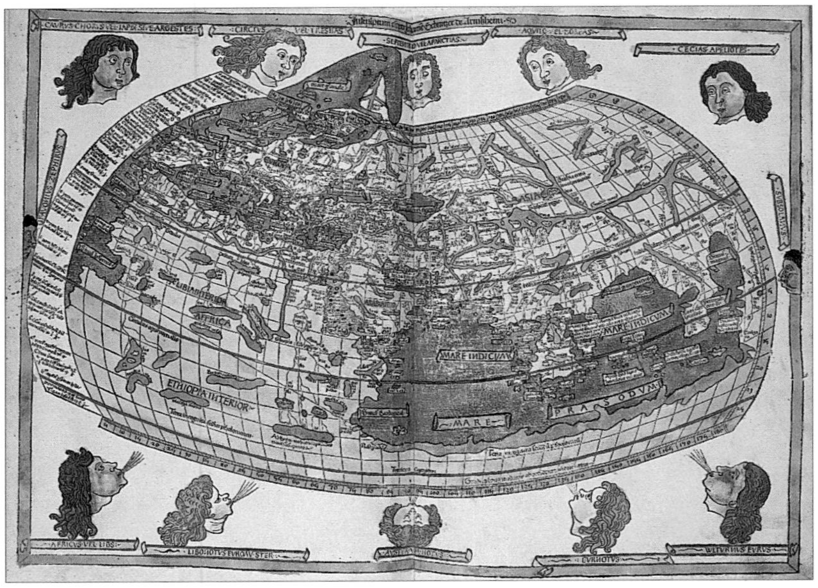

2. PTOLEMAIC WORLD MAP

Based on the work of Claudius Ptolemy, produced by Donis Nicolaus in Ulm, Germany, 1630. The map includes lines of latitude and longitude which give a sense of accuracy. The figures represent different wind directions.
British Library, London, UK.

AD 500–1600

During this period, maps originating in the classical tradition were overlain with later Christian elements. Such maps were usually oval or circular in shape, schematic in content, and centred on Jerusalem. These world maps (*mappæmundi*) conveyed a Christian perspective of the world, and their detail ranged from the virtually diagrammatic to the highly complex *(see 3)*.

Maps from the later medieval period include sea charts, town plans and local, district and route maps. Of these, portolan charts – sea charts designed primarily for navigation – were by far the most significant *(see 4)*. Providing impressively detailed and accurate information on coastlines, harbours and related navigational matters, the charts appear to have been regularly updated. Route maps, for the use of pilgrims and merchants travelling overland, also developed over this period, as exemplified by Matthew Paris's map of the route from London to Otranto, Italy produced around AD 1250 *(see 5)*.

The 15th and 16th centuries were essentially the age of exploration and discovery, a period which witnessed an explosion of global knowledge and a veritable renaissance in cartography. The period saw a great development of world maps, many of which began to include the coastal detail of the earlier portolan charts and to show the latest geographical information resulting from the voyages of discovery. Rome and Venice dominated European map production from 1550 to 1570, but later in the period dominance in mapmaking passed to the Low Countries. This 'Golden Age' of Dutch cartography is exemplified by the first printed 'atlas' of map sheets by Abraham Ortelius in 1570 – the *Theatrum Orbis Terrarum*. The term 'atlas' was coined by Gerard Mercator the Flemish cartographer – perhaps the most widely known figure in the history of cartography. His work, in particular his map projection published in 1569, make him the geographical colossus of the period.

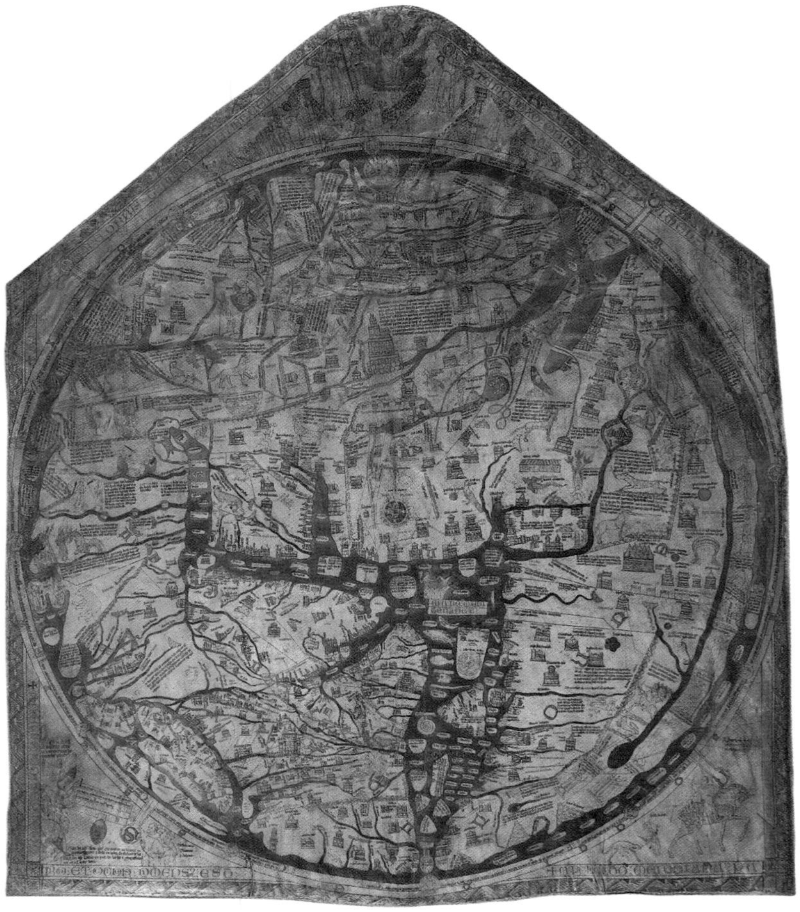

3. THE HEREFORD MAPPAMUNDI

Produced on vellum, and attributed to Richard of Haldingham and Lafford, c. 1290. The map follows the form of a T-O map, centred on Jerusalem, with east to the top. The continents of Asia (top), Africa (lower right) and Europe (lower left) are separated by the Mediterranean Sea and the Nile and Don rivers.
Hereford Cathedral, Hereford, UK.

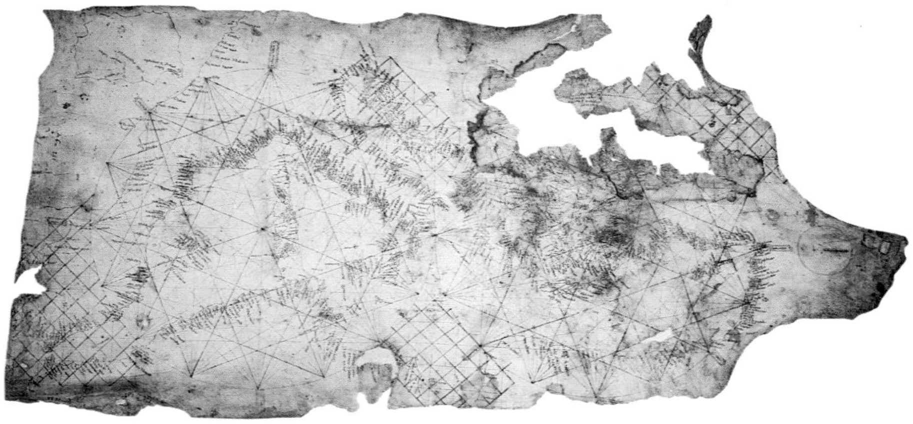

4. THE CARTE PISANE

The oldest surviving portolan chart, c. 1290. It shows most of Europe, with a remarkably detailed coastline of the Mediterranean Sea with Italy and Sicily in the centre.
Bibliothèque Nationale, Paris, France.

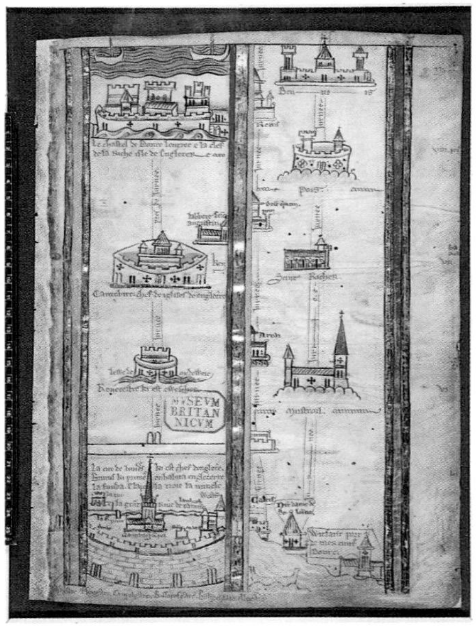

5. ITINERARY MAP OF A ROUTE FROM LONDON TO ITALY

Produced by Matthew Paris, c. 1250. This is a fine, early example of a road map in strip form. This extract includes Rochester, Canterbury and Dover.
British Library, London, UK.

1600–1900

Cartography in the earlier years of the 17th century was dominated by the Low Countries, epitomized by the Blaeu publishing house *(see 6)* but, by the late 17th century, the world centre for cartographic production had shifted from Amsterdam to Paris. France was one of the first countries to recognize the importance of establishing a national survey and mapping programme. There, the Cassini family established the national survey of France well ahead of other such surveys in western Europe *(see 7)*.

The colonial scramble for North America, and the American War of Independence (1775–1783), drove the development of cartography in North America, and it was an age, too, when the exploration of Australia, Tasmania and New Zealand resulted in their appearance on world maps. Such exploration was aided by great developments in navigation and particularly the ability to establish longitude more precisely.

During the 19th century special maps appeared in greater numbers reflecting scientific and social observation and analysis. One significant example of this development of thematic mapping was the *Physikalischer Atlas* of Heinrich Berghaus, published in two volumes in 1845 and 1848 *(see 8)*. Lithographic printing of maps was developed in the early years of the century allowing the production of multiple copies of maps very much more cheaply, stimulating a proliferation of maps for mass consumption and for educational purposes.

As the 19th century progressed, factors such as exploration and emigration were reflected in extended world coverage of maps and charts. Work on national surveys proceeded, one particularly notable national cartographic achievement being the Great Trigonometrical Survey (GTS) of India which facilitated the creation of extensive and detailed topographic maps of the sub-continent.

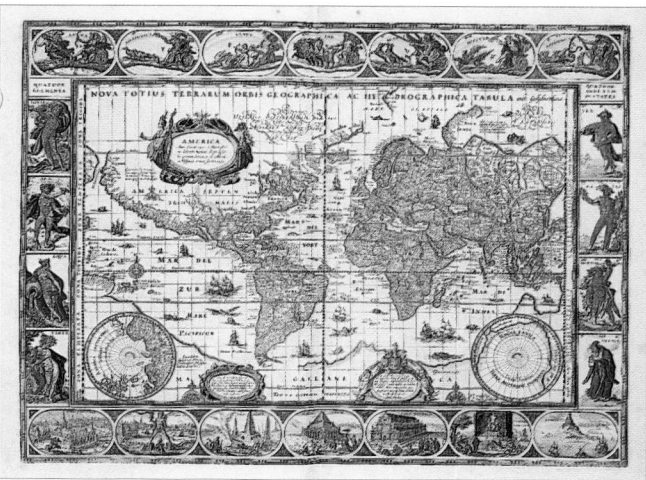

6. WORLD MAP

Produced in Amsterdam by Willem Blaeu, 1630. This is one of the finest examples of early maps on Mercator's projection. British Library, London, UK.

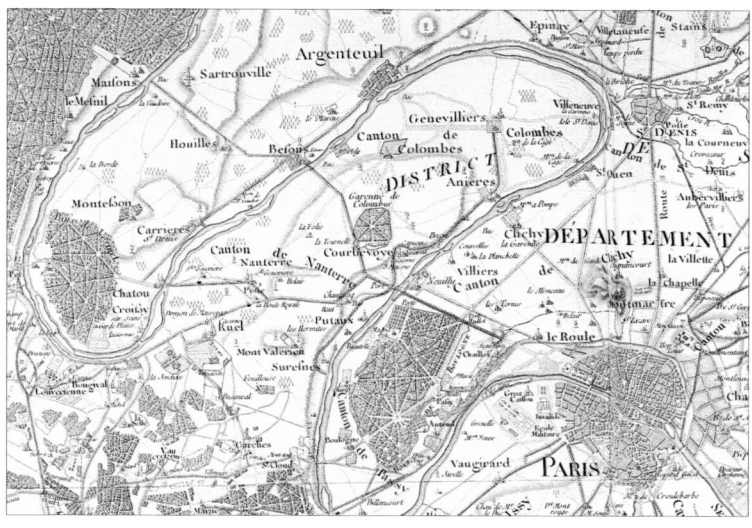

7. CARTE DE FRANCE

Detail from the first sheet – Sheet No. 1 Paris – by Cassini de Thury, 1736. Original scale 1:86 400. National Library of Scotland, Edinburgh, UK.

20TH CENTURY

War, politics and technological development were instrumental in prompting the expansion of map and chart coverage throughout the 20th century. The development of aviation and, in turn, space exploration, and photography and imagery possible through them, have been particularly significant in recent developments in cartography and have spawned a new age in cartography. The development of the computer has led to the production of digital maps and the consequent development of Geographical Information Systems (GIS) which allow users to combine and manipulate geographical data sets of many kinds.

There has been a significant increase in map coverage throughout the world, and yet the fact that comprehensive national topographic mapping has been produced, does not mean that it is readily available *(see 9)*. Many countries, particularly in Africa and Asia, impose strict restrictions on the release of their mapping. The question of national map coverage and availability is complicated by the activities of external mapping organizations. The former USSR had extensive programmes producing topographic mapping of countries throughout the world *(see 10)*. Easy access to this previously classified military mapping has recently served to extend map availability.

8. THEMATIC ATLAS MAP

Extract from a map of the *Survey of the geographical distribution and cultivation of the most important plants which are used as food for man: with indications of the isotheres and isokhimenes*, 1842. Published in the *Physikalischer Atlas* by Heinrich Berghaus, 1845 and 1848. This English language version appeared as Plate 44 in W & A K Johnston's *National Atlas of Historical, Commercial and Political Geography*, 1847. National Library of Scotland, Edinburgh, UK.

10. GROZNYY, RUSSIAN FEDERATION

Extract from a Russian military topographic map 1:500 000, 1988.

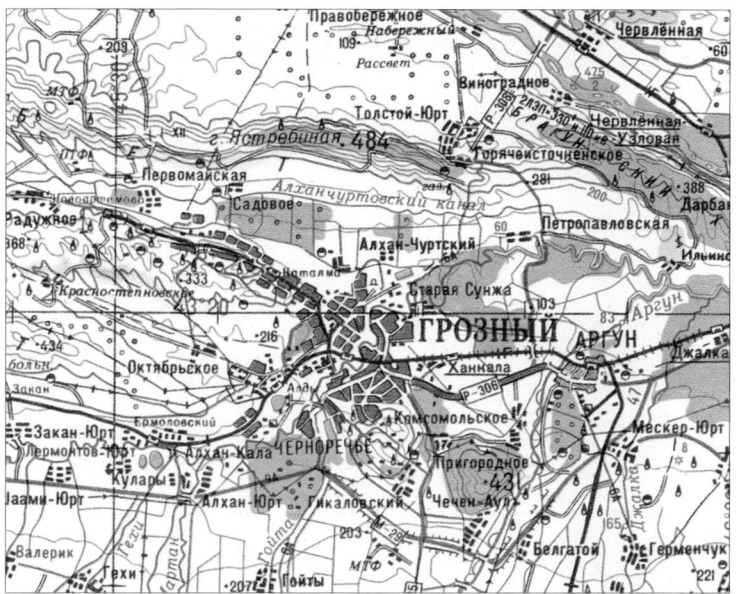

9. AVAILABILITY OF TOPOGRAPHIC MAPPING

Degree of access to topographic mapping of scales 1:100 000 or larger

Readily available	Not available locally for public distribution
Some restrictions on availability	no data

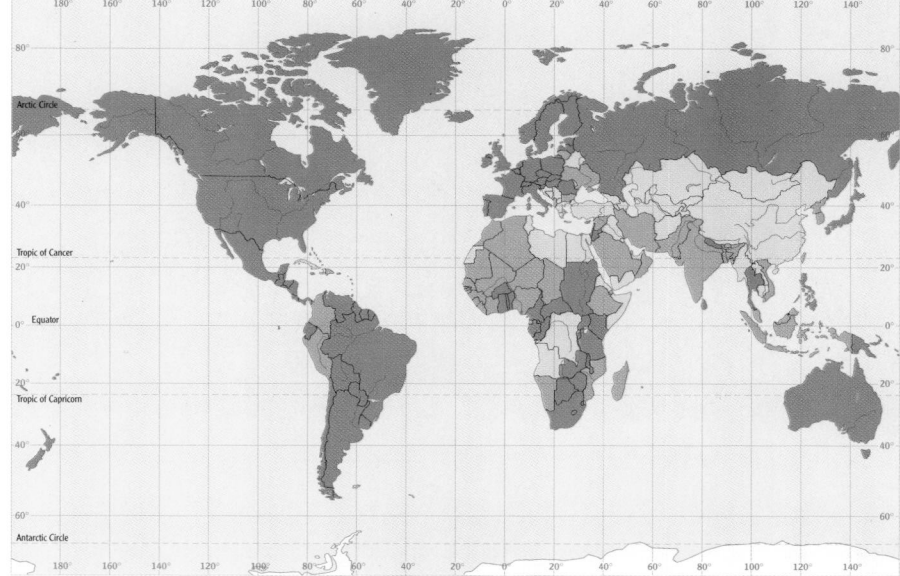

MEASURING THE EARTH

Speculation on the form of the universe and the place of the known world in it, and the attempts to express these graphically, constituted an important influence on mapmakers from earliest times. The Greeks inherited from the Babylonians such beliefs that the Earth was stationary, flat, the centre of the universe, and surrounded by water. Pythagoras in the 6th century BC and Aristotle in the 4th century BC proposed that the Earth was a sphere, revolving on its own axis. In Alexandria, Egypt, Eratosthenes (c. 276–194 BC) measured the circumference of the Earth using elementary geometric techniques. His value proved to be only 320 kilometres less than the true value, an error of less than 1 per cent.

One of the principal challenges of cartography is how to depict the spherical world on a flat map surface. It is essentially an impossible task without distorting the map in terms of either shape, azimuth (angles or bearings), area or distance. The problem assumed greater importance with the development of sea charts and the need to navigate in safety, preferably in straight lines (to reflect constant compass bearing) over considerable distances while simultaneously compensating for the curvature of the Earth. Mercator achieved this in the 16th century with his map projection in which the distance between the lines of latitude increases away from the equator. This projection, in modified form, still serves navigators well but has also resulted in distorted perceptions of the relative sizes of land areas, as those in high latitudes (eg Greenland) appear relatively too large, and those in low latitudes (eg India) appear relatively too small.

As far as establishing position on the Earth in terms of latitude and longitude is concerned, the concept of the tropics and the equator was established in early times through astronomical observation of the sun, moon and planets. The concept was later refined by Hipparchus and incorporated by Ptolemy into his *Geographia* (see page 42). The development of navigational instruments allowed latitude to be determined relatively easily. However, the establishment of longitude proved more problematic. In the 17th century Galileo established a method of determining longitude based on observations of the movement of Jupiter's moons, which served reasonably well on land. But the ability to establish longitude correctly at sea was believed to be so crucial that a Board of Longitude was established by the UK government in 1714 offering a prize of £20 000 for any method of defining longitude to within half a degree. In the search for a mechanical means of establishing longitude which could be used both on land and at sea, the principal difficulty was the lack of an accurate timepiece: the longitudinal value of a position being the distance reflected by the difference between local time and the time of a known position, with 15° of longitude equivalent to a time difference of one hour. The prize was eventually awarded to the Englishman John Harrison *(see 1)* whose marine chronometers, culminating in the one known as H4 which won the prize *(see 2)*, were remarkably accurate and also highly reliable at sea.

Any longitudinal position needs to be defined with reference to a standard position. Such a line of zero longitude, usually referred to as the prime meridian, could, in theory, be placed anywhere. Separate prime meridians were established in, for example, Paris, Cadiz, Naples, Pulkova and Stockholm, as well as London. The universal acceptance, in 1884, of a single prime meridian – the Greenwich Meridian – was an early example of international standardization in cartography.

(see page 42)

1. JOHN HARRISON (1693–1776)

2. JOHN HARRISON'S FOURTH MARINE CHRONOMETER, H4.

Made c. 1760. This was the first truly accurate chronometer and won Harrison the Board of Longitude prize in 1772.

SURVEYING

Surveying is the initial data collection stage in the mapmaking process and it was the Greeks who established the first systematic approach. Astronomy underpinned its development and instruments such as the gnomon, a sundial device, and the astrolabe, a navigational instrument, were adopted by land surveyors to establish position. Major advances took place during the 16th, 17th and 18th centuries with the development of increasingly accurate surveying instruments which improved the precision of measurements and allowed the introduction of greater topographical detail into maps. The systematic surveying of entire countries, and the subsequent production of detailed, large scale maps, began in earnest in the 18th century, notably in France (see page 43). It was James Cook (1728–1779) who combined the traditional approach to marine surveying with newer land surveying techniques and laid the foundations of modern nautical charting *(see 3)*.

In the 20th century, technological developments have been reflected in related advances in surveying. The availability of aerial photography and satellite imagery allowed cartography to extend to formerly inaccessible parts of the world and have provided a vast amount of data for numerous mapping applications. Aerial photography and high resolution satellite imagery *(see 4,* and also pages 8-21) are important for the production of large-scale topographic mapping, while lower resolution imagery from a variety of sensors provides data on a global scale. The accurate coverage provided by the Global Positioning System (GPS), a satellite navigation system designed in the USA primarily for military use, is now widely used by surveyors for position fixing and also for navigation.

(see page 43)

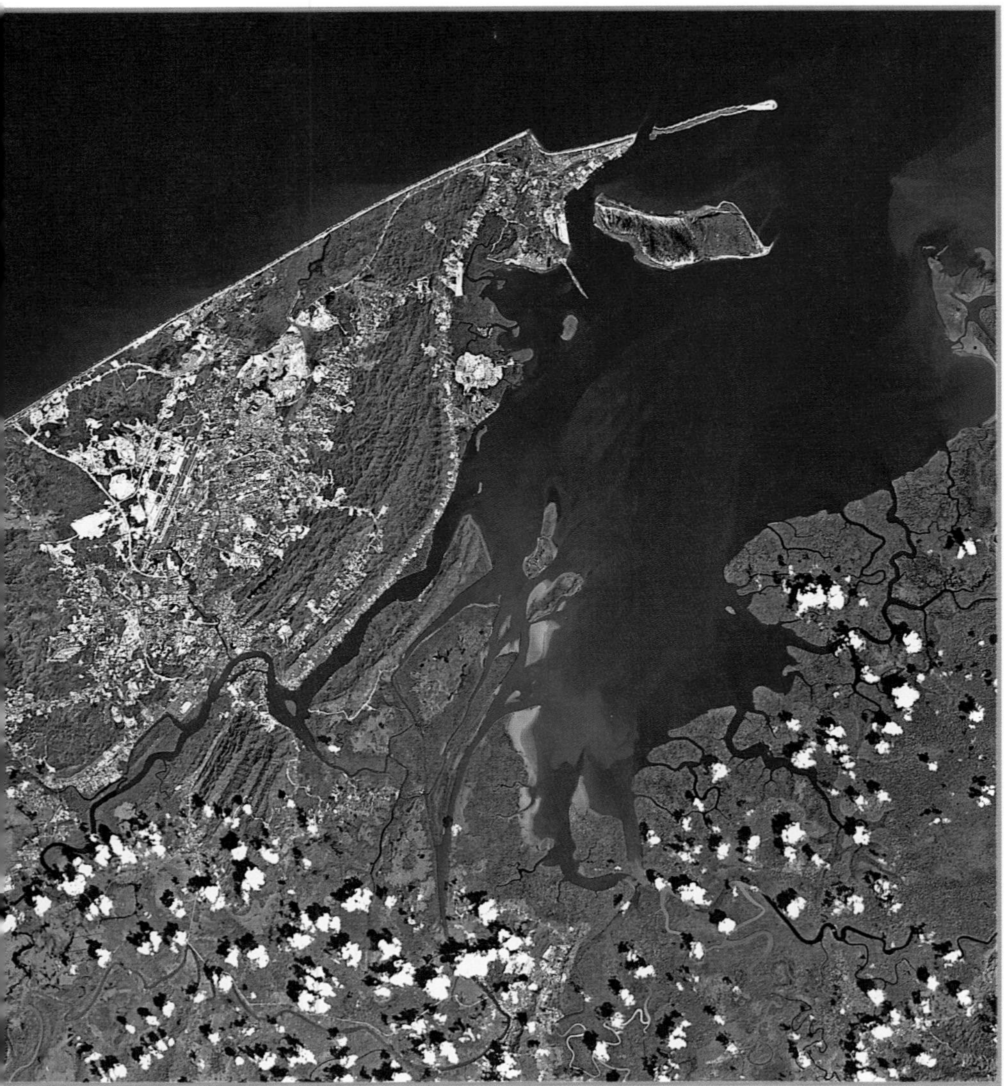

4. SPOT satellite image.

Showing Bandar Seri Begawan, Brunei. A high level of detail is visible within the built-up area and also along the coast within Brunei Bay. Variations in sediments and currents produce the variety of colours within the bay itself.

6. TERRAIN MODEL OF SOUTH AMERICA

A 3-D relief view of the continent of South America generated from a 1 km resolution digital elevation – or terrain – model.

3. CAPTAIN COOK'S CHART OF NEW ZEALAND 1772

This chart was published following Cook's explorations in 1769 and 1770. The chart is remarkably accurate in terms of the shape of the islands and in terms of latitude. However, the coloured overlays representing the coastline from a later survey in 1788 (green) and from British Admiralty charts up to 1968 (red), illustrate well the problems of establishing longitude at the time of Cook's voyages.

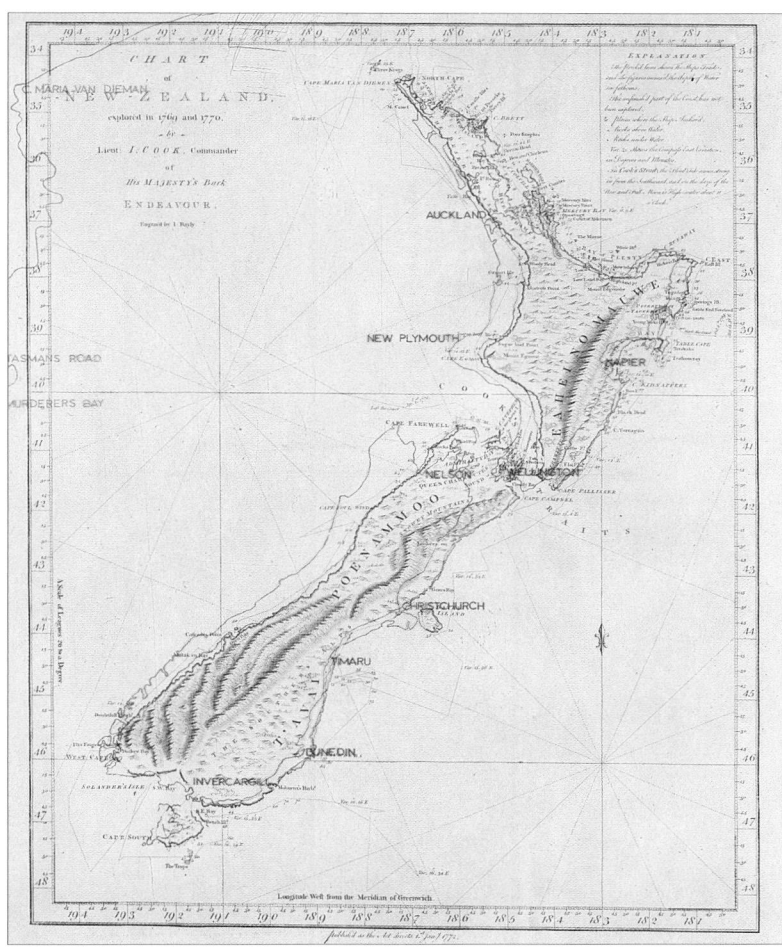

MAP PRODUCTION TECHNIQUES

For centuries, the only method of producing maps was to draw and copy them by hand. Production was, therefore, time-consuming and labour-intensive. As a result, few maps were produced and even fewer survived. In the 15th century, the invention of printing prompted a veritable revolution in mapmaking. It allowed the production of repeat copies and in a form consistent with the original, thus eliminating human error likely in hand copying. Early relief woodcut prints gave way during the 16th century to printing from engraved copper plates *(see 5)*. This allowed greater versatility and continued to be the principal method of map reproduction until the introduction of the much faster process of lithographic printing in the early 19th century. Later in the 19th century the development of photographic techniques was applied to mapmaking, eventually becoming an integral part of the process and facilitating the greater use of colour.

The most significant revolution in cartographic production, since the introduction of printing, dates from the late 1950s with the increasing use of the computer. This accelerated map production processes and allowed the generation of digital data, the manipulation of which supports new forms of output and visualization *(see 6)*. Maps can now be produced from scale-free and seamless databases, allowing individual customization of the output, and the ability to produce digital images of early maps by scanning allows their increased copying and wider dissemination. Digital maps are also now widely available on the Internet and the World Wide Web.

5. Copper Engraving

The highly skilled task of engraving a map on a copper plate. The image had to be drawn in reverse, for the map to appear correct when printed.

EUROPE total land area: 9 908 599 sq km / 3 825 731 sq miles

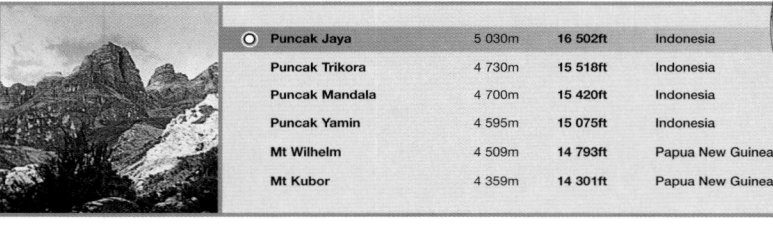

Elbrus	5 642m	18 510ft	Russian Federation
Gora Dykh-Tau	5 204m	17 073ft	Russian Federation
Shkhara	5 201m	17 063ft	Georgia/ Russian Federation
Kazbek	5 047m	16 558ft	Georgia/ Russian Federation
Mont Blanc	4 808m	15 774ft	France/Italy
Dufourspitze	4 634m	15 203ft	Italy/Switzerland

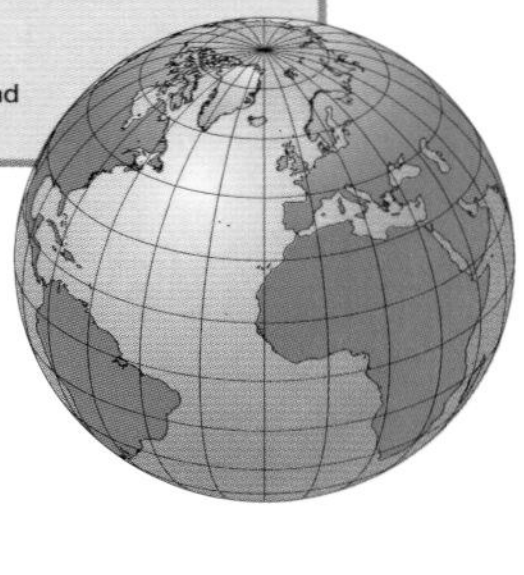

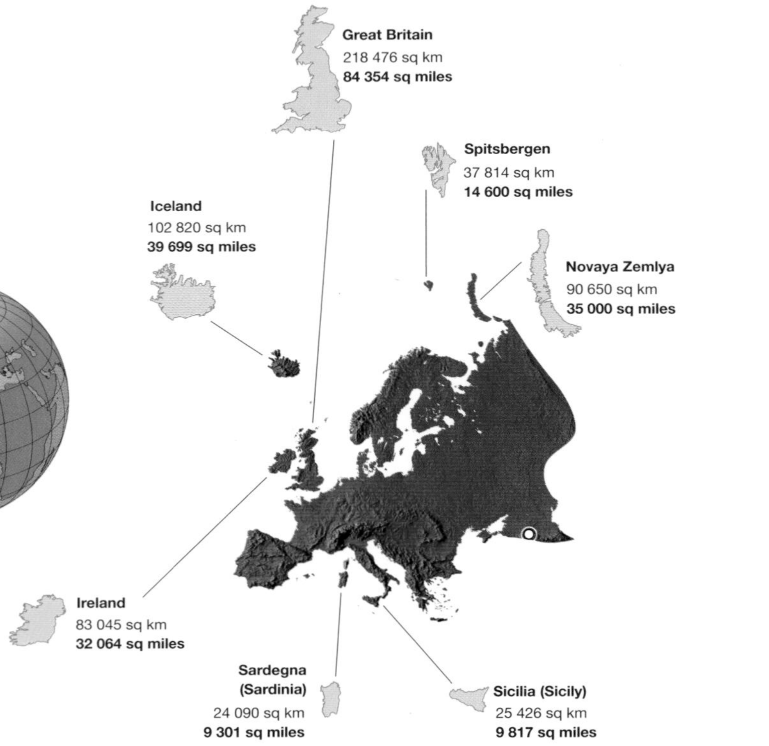

Great Britain
218 476 sq km
84 354 sq miles

Spitsbergen
37 814 sq km
14 600 sq miles

Iceland
102 820 sq km
39 699 sq miles

Novaya Zemlya
90 650 sq km
35 000 sq miles

Ireland
83 045 sq km
32 064 sq miles

Sardegna (Sardinia)
24 090 sq km
9 301 sq miles

Sicilia (Sicily)
25 426 sq km
9 817 sq miles

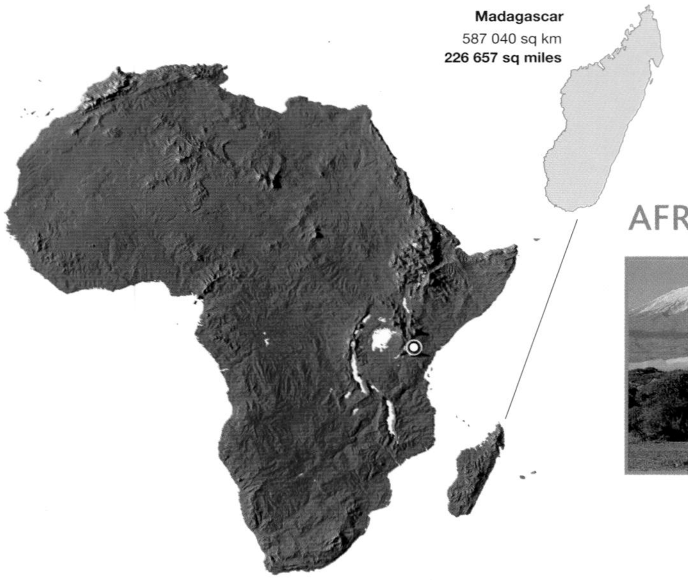

Madagascar
587 040 sq km
226 657 sq miles

AFRICA total land area: 30 343 578 sq km / 11 715 721 sq miles

Kilimanjaro	5 892m	19 331ft	Tanzania
Kirinyaga (Mt Kenya)	5 199m	17 057ft	Kenya
Margherita Peak (Mt Stanley)	5 110m	16 765ft	Democratic Republic of Congo/Uganda
Meru	4 565m	14 977ft	Tanzania
Ras Dashen	4 533m	14 872ft	Ethiopia
Mt Karisimbi	4 510m	14 796ft	Rwanda

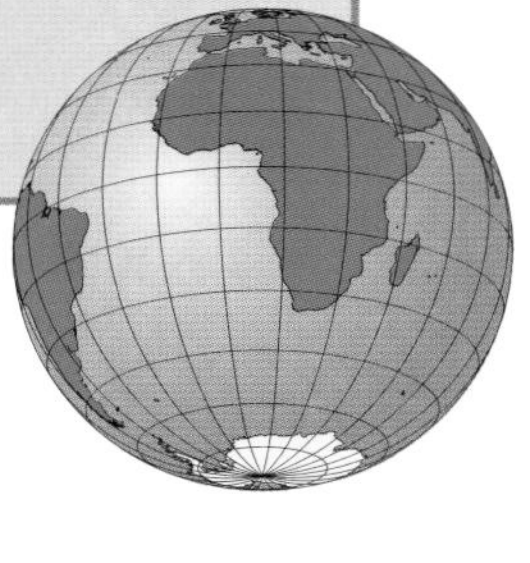

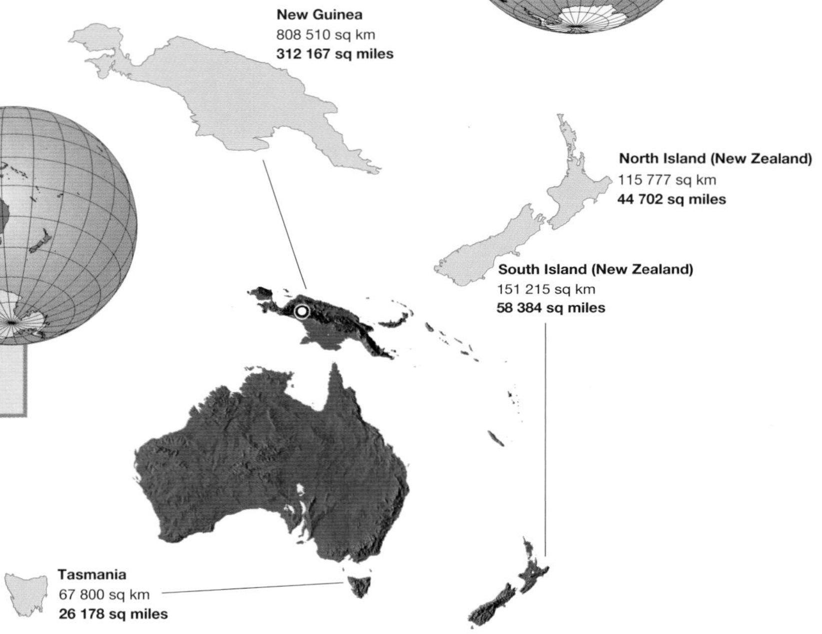

New Guinea
808 510 sq km
312 167 sq miles

North Island (New Zealand)
115 777 sq km
44 702 sq miles

South Island (New Zealand)
151 215 sq km
58 384 sq miles

AUSTRALASIA total land area: 8 820 962 sq km / 3 405 792 sq miles

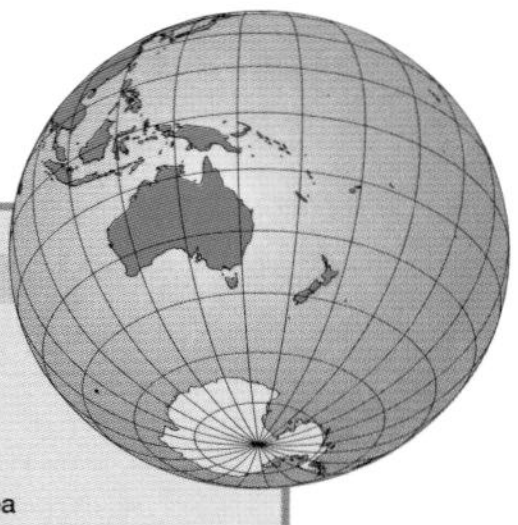

Puncak Jaya	5 030m	16 502ft	Indonesia
Puncak Trikora	4 730m	15 518ft	Indonesia
Puncak Mandala	4 700m	15 420ft	Indonesia
Puncak Yamin	4 595m	15 075ft	Indonesia
Mt Wilhelm	4 509m	14 793ft	Papua New Guinea
Mt Kubor	4 359m	14 301ft	Papua New Guinea

Tasmania
67 800 sq km
26 178 sq miles

ANTARCTICA total land area: 12 093 000 sq km * / 4 669 133 sq miles *
*excluding ice shelves

Vinson Massif	4 897m	16 066ft
Mt Tyree	4 852m	15 918ft
Mt Kirkpatrick	4 528m	14 855ft
Mt Markham	4 351m	14 275ft
Mt Jackson	4 190m	13 747ft
Mt Sidley	4 181m	13 717ft

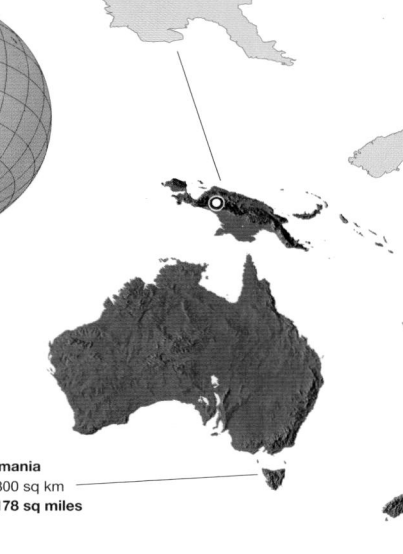
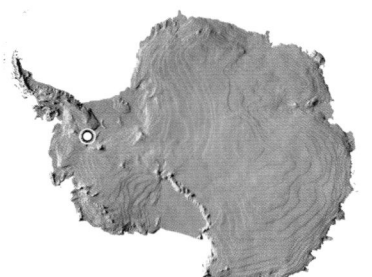
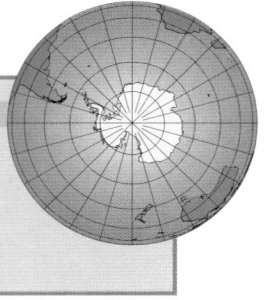

HIGHEST MOUNTAINS IN THE WORLD

Mt Everest
China/Nepal / 8 848m / 29 028ft

K2
China/Jammu and Kashmir / 8 611m / 28 251ft

Kangchenjunga
India/Nepal / 8 586m / 28 169ft

Lhotse
China/Nepal / 8 516m / 27 939ft

Makalu
China/Nepal / 8 463m / 27 765ft

Cho Oyu
China/Nepal / 8 201m / 26 906ft

Dhaulagiri
Nepal / 8 167m / 26 794ft

Manaslu
Nepal / 8 163m / 26 781ft

Nanga Parbat
Jammu and Kashmir / 8 126m / 26 660ft

Annapurna I
Nepal / 8 091m / 26 545ft

Gasherbrum I
China/Jammu and Kashmir / 8 068m / 26 469ft

Broad Peak
China/Jammu and Kashmir / 8 047m / 26 401ft

Gasherbrum II
China/Jammu and Kashmir / 8 035m / 26 361ft

Xixabangma Feng
China / 8 012m / 26 286ft

Annapurna II
Nepal / 7 937m / 26 040ft

Nuptse
Nepal / 7 885m / 25 869ft

Himalchul
Nepal / 7 864m / 25 800ft

Masherbrum
Jammu and Kashmir / 7 821m / 25 659ft

Nanda Devi
India / 7 816m / 25 643ft

Rakaposhi
Jammu and Kashmir / 7 788m / 25 551ft

Namjagbarwa Feng
China / 7 756m / 25 446ft

Kamet
China / 7 756m / 25 446ft

Hokkaidō
78 073 sq km
30 144 sq miles

Sakhalin
76 400 sq km
29 498 sq miles

Honshū
227 414 sq km
87 805 sq miles

Shikoku
18 256 sq km
7 049 sq miles

Kyūshū
36 554 sq km
14 114 sq miles

Taiwan
35 873 sq km
13 851 sq miles

Luzon
104 690 sq km
40 421 sq miles

Mindanao
94 630 sq km
36 537 sq miles

ASIA total land area: 45 036 492 sq km / **17 388 686 sq miles**

	Name			Location
⊙	**Mt Everest** (Sagarmatha/Qomolangma Feng)	8 848m	**29 028ft**	China/Nepal
	K2 (Qogir Feng)	8 611m	**28 251ft**	China/Jammu and Kashmir
	Kangchenjunga	8 586m	**28 169ft**	India/Nepal
	Lhotse	8 516m	**27 939ft**	China/Nepal
	Makalu	8 463m	**27 765ft**	China/Nepal
	Cho Oyu	8 201m	**26 906ft**	China/Nepal

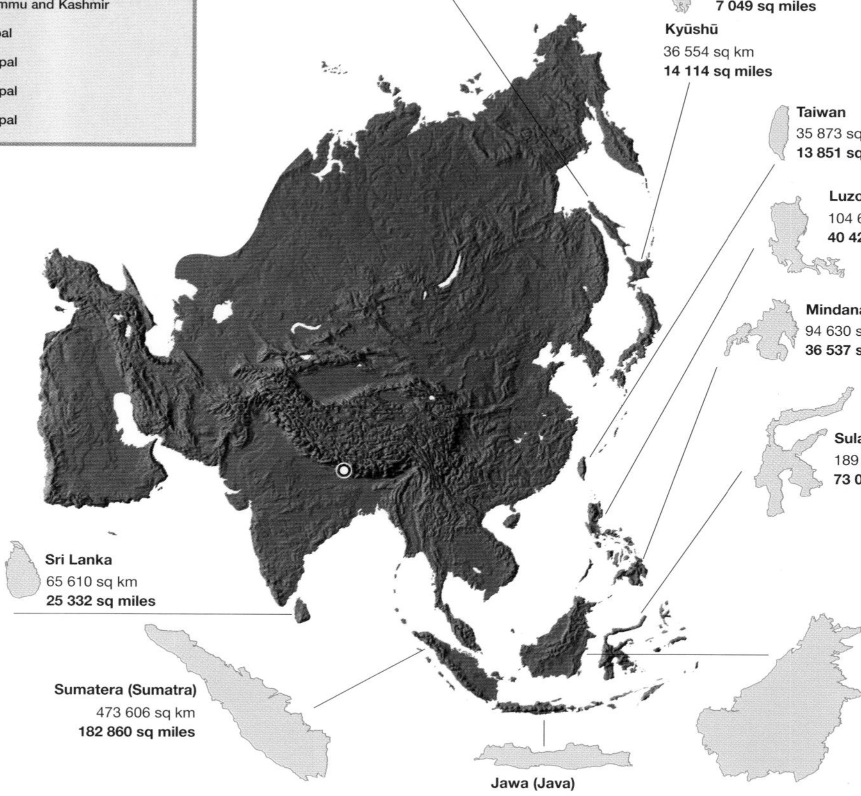

Sulawesi (Celebes)
189 216 sq km
73 057 sq miles

Greenland
2 175 600 sq km
840 004 sq miles

Ellesmere Island
196 236 sq km
75 767 sq miles

Borneo
745 561 sq km
287 863 sq miles

Sri Lanka
65 610 sq km
25 332 sq miles

Victoria Island
217 291 sq km
83 897 sq miles

Sumatera (Sumatra)
473 606 sq km
182 860 sq miles

Baffin Island
507 451 sq km
195 927 sq miles

Jawa (Java)
132 188 sq km
51 038 sq miles

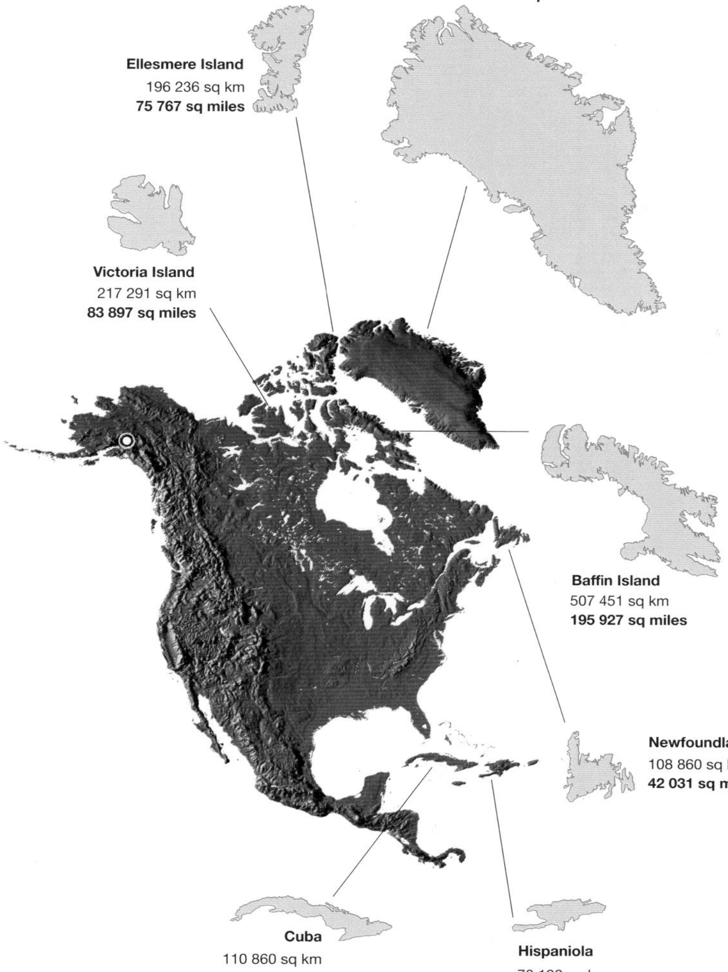

NORTH AMERICA total land area: 24 680 331 sq km / **9 529 129 sq miles**

	Name			Location
⊙	**Mt McKinley**	6 194m	**20 321ft**	USA
	Mt Logan	5 959m	**19 550ft**	Canada
	Pico de Orizaba	5 747m	**18 855ft**	Mexico
	Mt St Elias	5 489m	**18 008ft**	USA
	Volcán Popocatépetl	5 452m	**17 887ft**	Mexico
	Mt Foraker	5 303m	**17 398ft**	USA

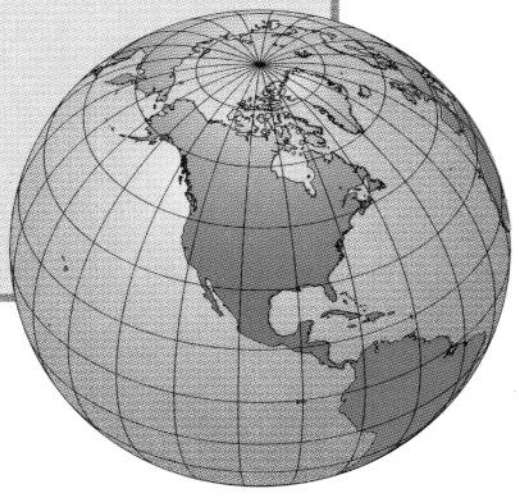

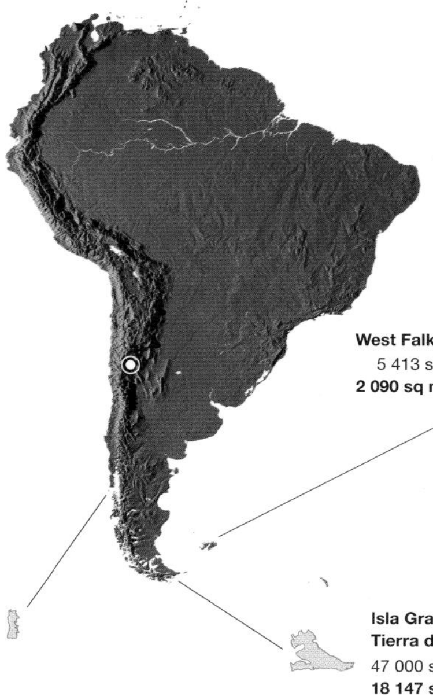

Newfoundland
108 860 sq km
42 031 sq miles

Cuba
110 860 sq km
42 803 sq miles

Hispaniola
76 192 sq km
29 418 sq miles

SOUTH AMERICA total land area: 17 815 420 sq km / **6 878 572 sq miles**

	Name			Location
⊙	**Cerro Aconcagua**	6 960m	**22 834ft**	Argentina
	Nevado Ojos del Salado	6 908m	**22 664ft**	Argentina/Chile
	Cerro Bonete	6 872m	**22 546ft**	Argentina
	Cerro Pissis	6 858m	**22 500ft**	Argentina
	Cerro Tupungato	6 800m	**22 309ft**	Argentina/Chile
	Cerro Mercedario	6 770m	**22 211ft**	Argentina

West Falkland
5 413 sq km
2 090 sq miles

East Falkland
6 760 sq km
2 610 sq miles

Isla de Chiloé
8 394 sq km
3 240 sq miles

Isla Grande de Tierra del Fuego
47 000 sq km
18 147 sq miles

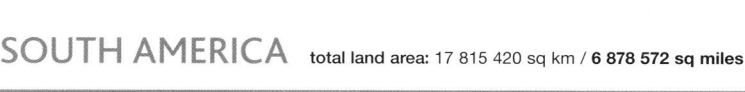
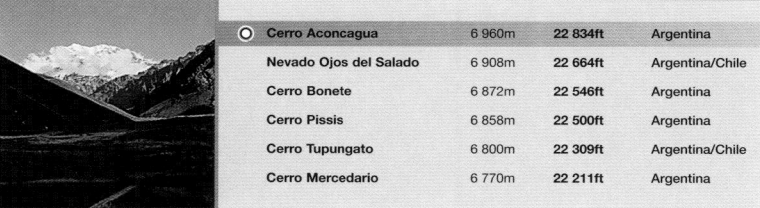

Gurla Mandhata China 7 739m / 25 390ft	**Muztag** China 7 723m / 25 338ft	**Kongur Shan** China 7 719m / 25 324ft	**Tirich Mir** Pakistan 7 690m / 25 229ft	**Kula Kangri** Bhutan 7 554m / 24 783ft	**Muztagata** China 7 546m / 24 757ft	**Gongga Shan** China 7 514m / 24 652ft	**Qullai Garmo** Tajikistan 7 495m / 24 590ft	**Jongsang** India/Nepal 7 483m / 24 550ft	**Teram Kangri** China/Jammu and Kashmir 7 470m / 24 508ft	**Pik Pobedy** China/Kyrgyzstan 7 439m / 24 406ft	**Ganesh I** China/Nepal 7 429m / 24 327ft	**Churen Himal** Nepal 7 371m / 24 183ft	**Sad Istragh** Afghanistan/Pakistan 7 367m / 24 170ft	**Kabru** India/Nepal 7 353m / 24 124ft	**Chamlang** Nepal 7 319m / 24 012ft	**Choksiam** China 7 316m / 24 002ft	**Chomo Lhari** Bhutan 7 313m / 23 992ft	**Muztag** China 7 282m / 23 891ft	**Langtang Lirung** Nepal 7 225m / 23 799ft	**Gankar Punsum** Bhutan 7 239m / 23 750ft	**Nagarzé** China 7 223m / 23 697ft

OCEANS AND SEAS

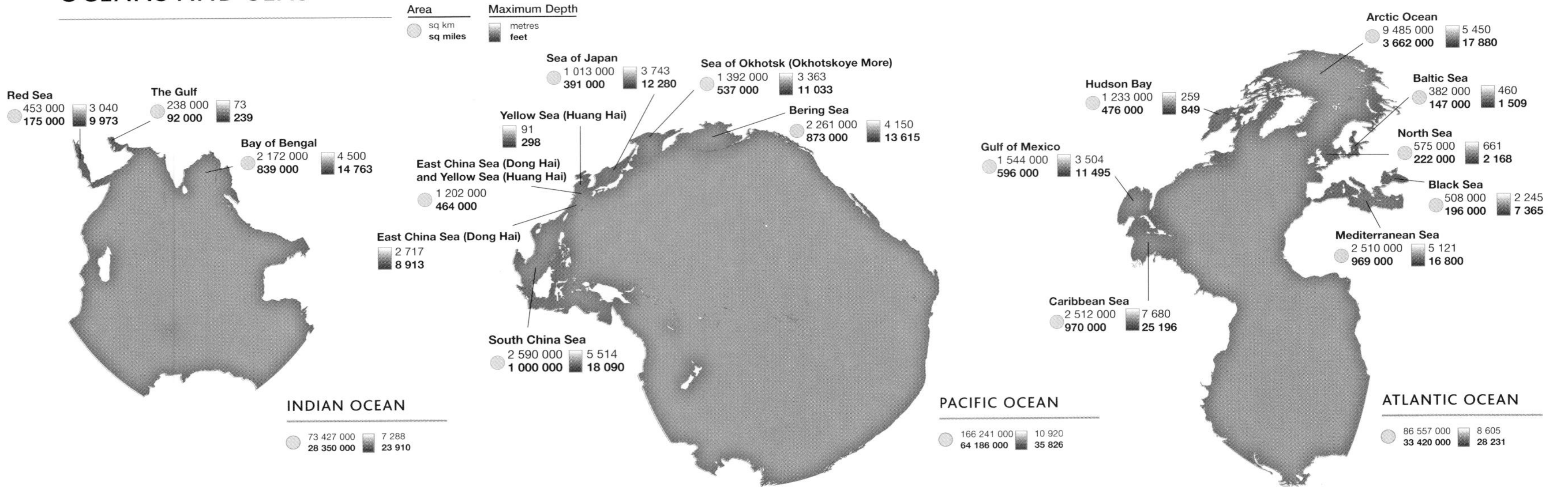

Area
○ sq km
sq miles

Maximum Depth
▮ metres
feet

Red Sea
○ 453 000
175 000
▮ 3 040
9 973

The Gulf
○ 238 000
92 000
▮ 73
239

Bay of Bengal
○ 2 172 000
839 000
▮ 4 500
14 763

Sea of Japan
○ 1 013 000
391 000
▮ 3 743
12 280

Sea of Okhotsk (Okhotskoye More)
○ 1 392 000
537 000
▮ 3 363
11 033

Yellow Sea (Huang Hai)
▮ 91
298

East China Sea (Dong Hai) and Yellow Sea (Huang Hai)
○ 1 202 000
464 000

East China Sea (Dong Hai)
▮ 2 717
8 913

Bering Sea
○ 2 261 000
873 000
▮ 4 150
13 615

South China Sea
○ 2 590 000
1 000 000
▮ 5 514
18 090

Arctic Ocean
○ 9 485 000
3 662 000
▮ 5 450
17 880

Baltic Sea
○ 382 000
147 000
▮ 460
1 509

North Sea
○ 575 000
222 000
▮ 661
2 168

Black Sea
○ 508 000
196 000
▮ 2 245
7 365

Mediterranean Sea
○ 2 510 000
969 000
▮ 5 121
16 800

Hudson Bay
○ 1 233 000
476 000
▮ 259
849

Gulf of Mexico
○ 1 544 000
596 000
▮ 3 504
11 495

Caribbean Sea
○ 2 512 000
970 000
▮ 7 680
25 196

INDIAN OCEAN
○ 73 427 000
28 350 000
▮ 7 288
23 910

PACIFIC OCEAN
○ 166 241 000
64 186 000
▮ 10 920
35 826

ATLANTIC OCEAN
○ 86 557 000
33 420 000
▮ 8 605
28 231

EUROPE

Volga	3 688 km	2 291 miles
Danube	2 850 km	1 770 miles
Dnieper	2 285 km	1 419 miles
Kama	2 028 km	1 260 miles
Don	1 931 km	1 199 miles
Pechora	1 802 km	1 119 miles

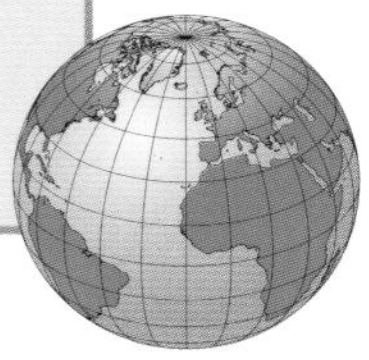

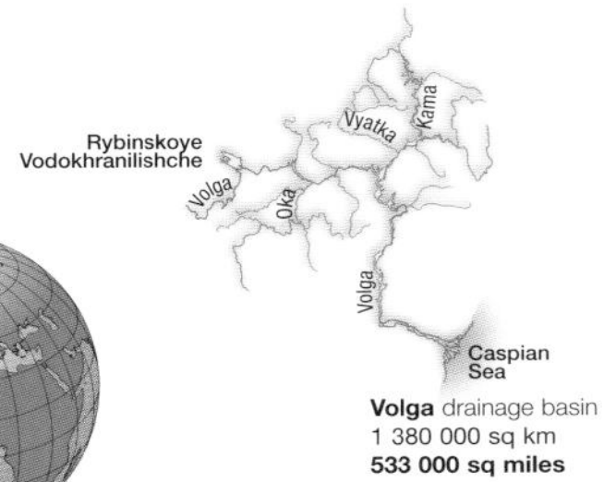

Rybinskoye Vodokhranilishche
Vyatka · Kama · Oka · Volga · Caspian Sea

Volga drainage basin
1 380 000 sq km
533 000 sq miles

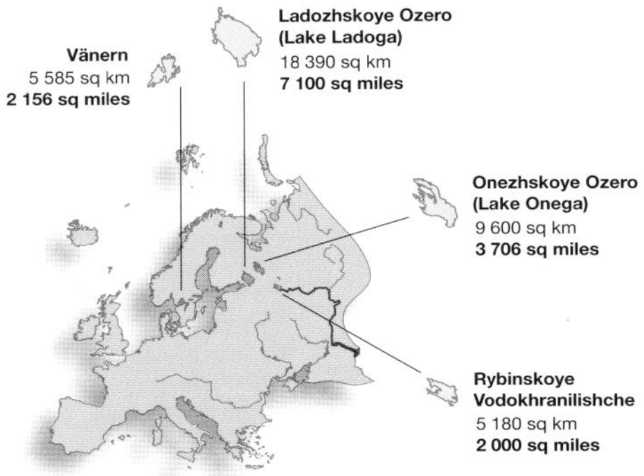

Vänern
5 585 sq km
2 156 sq miles

Ladozhskoye Ozero (Lake Ladoga)
18 390 sq km
7 100 sq miles

Onezhskoye Ozero (Lake Onega)
9 600 sq km
3 706 sq miles

Rybinskoye Vodokhranilishche
5 180 sq km
2 000 sq miles

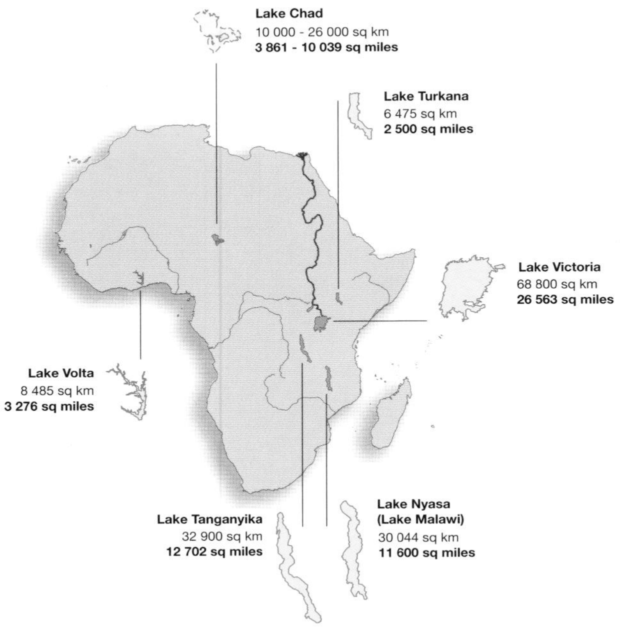

AFRICA

Lake Chad
10 000 - 26 000 sq km
3 861 - 10 039 sq miles

Lake Turkana
6 475 sq km
2 500 sq miles

Lake Victoria
68 800 sq km
26 563 sq miles

Lake Volta
8 485 sq km
3 276 sq miles

Lake Tanganyika
32 900 sq km
12 702 sq miles

Lake Nyasa (Lake Malawi)
30 044 sq km
11 600 sq miles

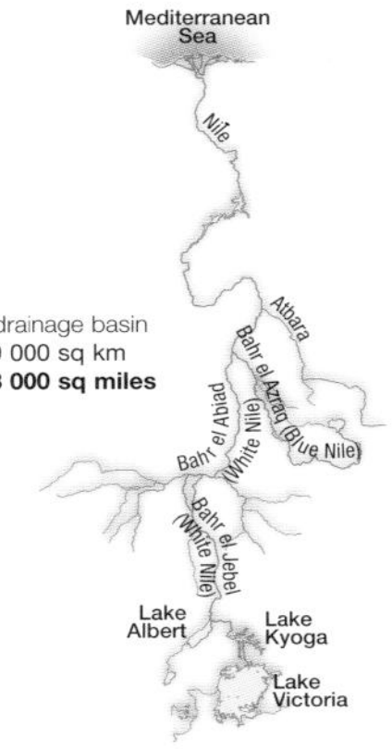

Mediterranean Sea · Nile · Atbara · Blue Nile (Bahr el Azraq) · White Nile (Bahr el Jebel) · Lake Albert · Lake Kyoga · Lake Victoria

Nile drainage basin
3 349 000 sq km
1 293 000 sq miles

Lungwebungu · Kafue · Cuando · Zambezi · Luangwa · Lake Nyasa (Lake Malawi) · Zambezi · Lake Kariba · Indian Ocean

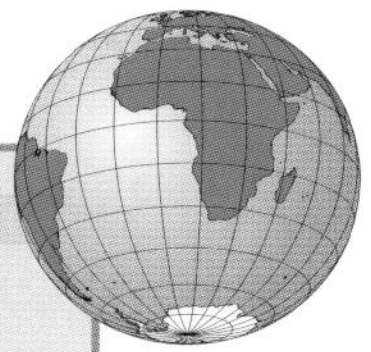

Zambezi (Zambeze) drainage basin
1 330 000 sq km
514 000 sq miles

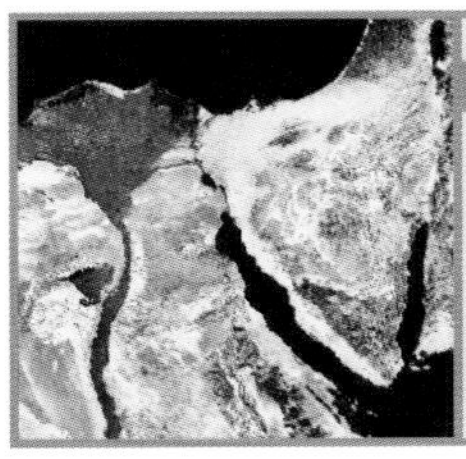

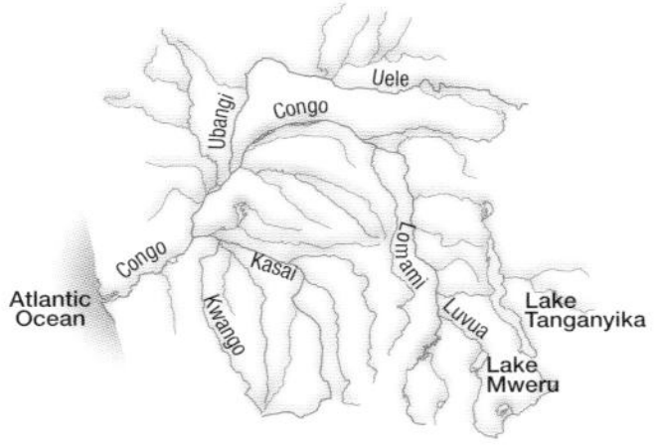

Nile	6 695 km	4 160 miles
Congo	4 667 km	2 900 miles
Niger	4 184 km	2 599 miles
Zambezi (Zambeze)	2 736 km	1 700 miles
Webi Shabeelle	2 490 km	1 547 miles
Ubangi	2 250 km	1 398 miles

Ubangi · Uele · Congo · Kasai · Kwango · Congo · Lomami · Lualaba · Lake Tanganyika · Lake Mweru · Atlantic Ocean

Congo drainage basin
3 700 000 sq km
1 429 000 sq miles

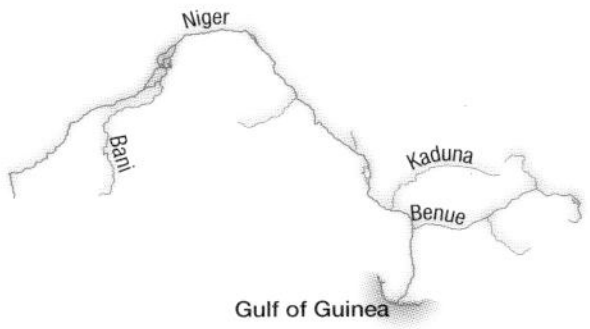

Niger · Kaduna · Benue · Bani · Gulf of Guinea

Niger drainage basin
1 890 000 sq km
730 000 sq miles

AUSTRALASIA

Murray-Darling	3 750 km	2 330 miles
Darling	2 739 km	1 702 miles
Murray	2 589 km	1 608 miles
Murrumbidgee	1 690 km	1 050 miles
Lachlan	1 480 km	919 miles
Macquarie	950 km	590 miles

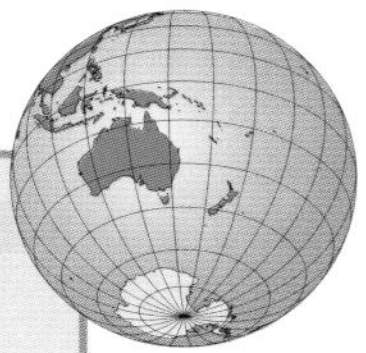

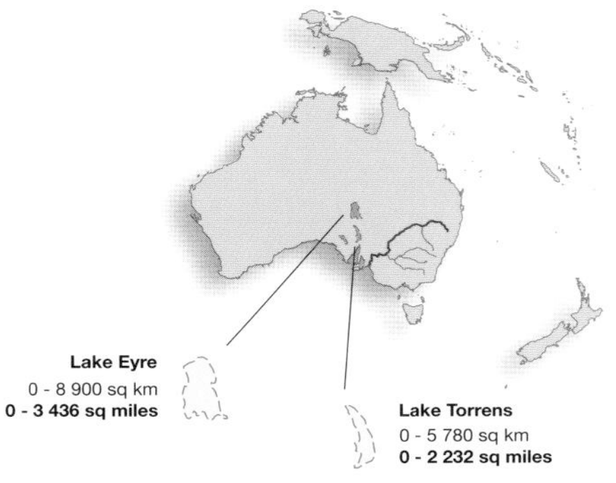

Lake Eyre
0 - 8 900 sq km
0 - 3 436 sq miles

Lake Torrens
0 - 5 780 sq km
0 - 2 232 sq miles

Darling · Bwgo · Lachlan · Murray · Encounter Bay

Murray-Darling drainage basin
1 058 000 sq km
408 000 sq miles

LONGEST RIVERS IN THE WORLD

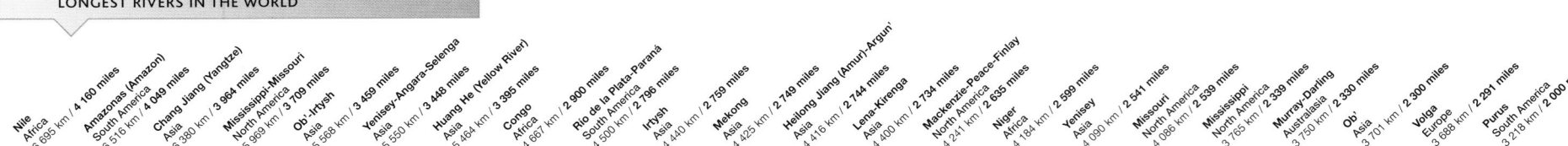

Nile
Africa
6 695 km / 4 160 miles

Amazonas (Amazon)
South America
6 516 km / 4 049 miles

Chang Jiang (Yangtze)
Asia
6 380 km / 3 964 miles

Mississippi-Missouri
North America
5 969 km / 3 709 miles

Ob'-Irtysh
Asia
5 568 km / 3 459 miles

Yenisey-Angara-Selenga
Asia
5 550 km / 3 448 miles

Huang He (Yellow River)
Asia
5 464 km / 3 395 miles

Congo
Africa
4 667 km / 2 900 miles

Rio de la Plata-Paraná
South America
4 500 km / 2 796 miles

Irtysh
Asia
4 440 km / 2 759 miles

Mekong
Asia
4 425 km / 2 749 miles

Heilong Jiang (Amur)-Argun'
Asia
4 416 km / 2 744 miles

Lena-Kirenga
Asia
4 400 km / 2 734 miles

Mackenzie-Peace-Finlay
North America
4 241 km / 2 635 miles

Niger
Africa
4 184 km / 2 599 miles

Yenisey
Asia
4 090 km / 2 541 miles

Missouri
North America
4 086 km / 2 539 miles

Mississippi
North America
3 765 km / 2 339 miles

Murray-Darling
Australasia
3 750 km / 2 330 miles

Ob'
Asia
3 701 km / 2 300 miles

Volga
Europe
3 688 km / 2 291 miles

Purus
South America
3 218 km / 2 000 miles

ASIA

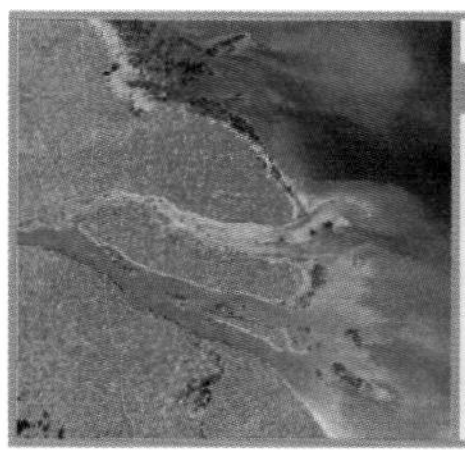

Chang Jiang (Yangtze)	6 380 km	**3 964 miles**
Ob'-Irtysh	5 568 km	**3 459 miles**
Yenisey-Angara-Selenga	5 550 km	**3 448 miles**
Huang He (Yellow River)	5 464 km	**3 395 miles**
Mekong	4 425 km	**2 749 miles**
Heilong Jiang (Amur)-**Argun'**	4 416 km	**2 744 miles**

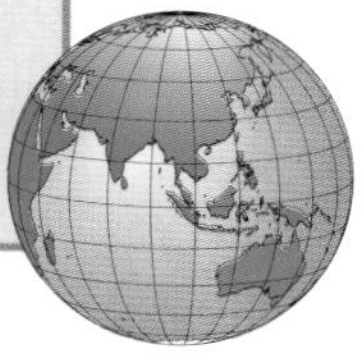

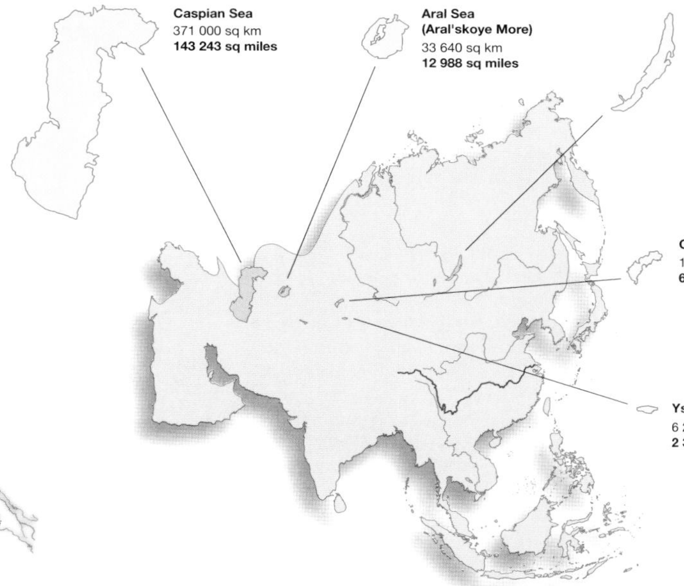

Caspian Sea
371 000 sq km
143 243 sq miles

Aral Sea
(Aral'skoye More)
33 640 sq km
12 988 sq miles

Ozero Baykal
(Lake Baikal)
30 500 sq km
11 776 sq miles

Ozero Balkhash
17 400 sq km
6 718 sq miles

Ysyk-Köl
6 200 sq km
2 393 sq miles

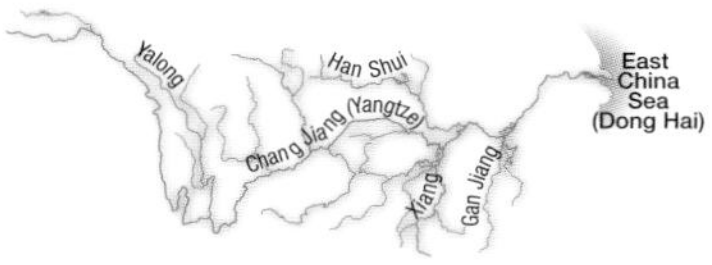

Chang Jiang (Yangtze) drainage basin
1 959 000 sq km
756 000 sq miles

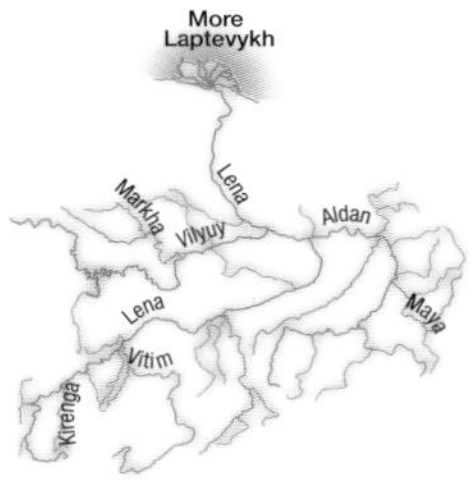

Lena-Kirenga drainage basin
2 490 000 sq km
961 000 sq miles

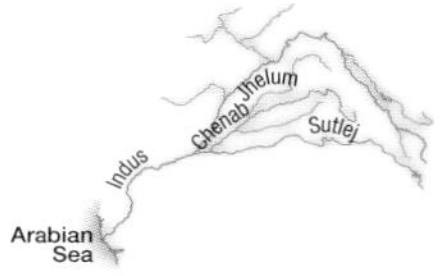

Indus drainage basin
1 166 000 sq km
450 000 sq miles

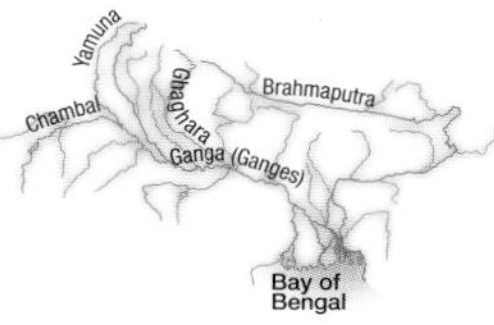

Ganga (Ganges)-Brahmaputra drainage basin
1 621 000 sq km
626 000 sq miles

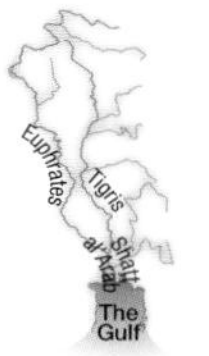

Shatt al'Arab drainage basin
1 114 000 sq km
430 000 sq miles

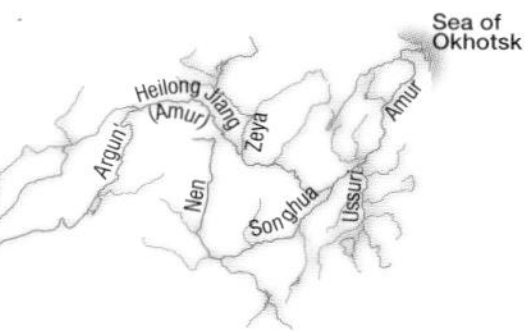

Heilong Jiang (Amur)-Argun' drainage basin
1 855 000 sq km
716 000 sq miles

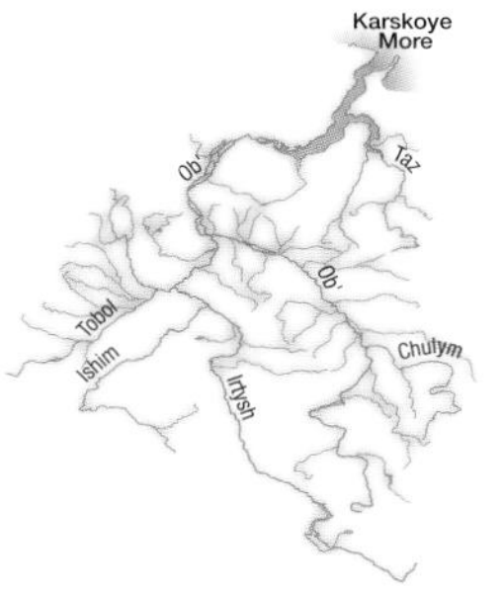

Ob'-Irtysh drainage basin
2 990 000 sq km
1 154 000 sq miles

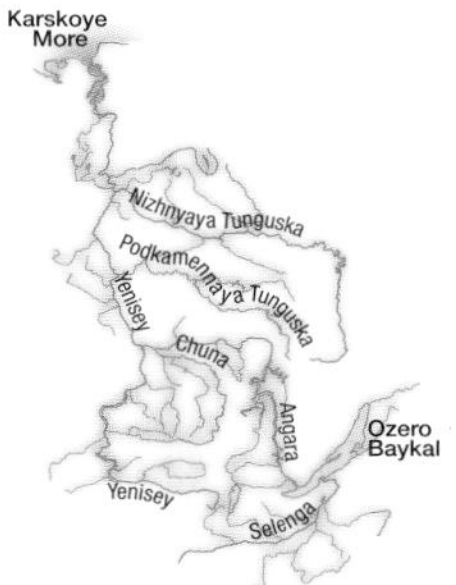

Yenisey-Angara-Selenga drainage basin
2 580 000 sq km
996 000 sq miles

NORTH AMERICA

Mississippi-Missouri	5 969 km	**3 709 miles**
Mackenzie-Peace-Finlay	4 241 km	**2 635 miles**
Missouri	4 086 km	**2 539 miles**
Mississippi	3 765 km	**2 339 miles**
Yukon	3 185 km	**1 979 miles**
Rio Grande (Rio Bravo del Norte)	3 057 km	**1 899 miles**

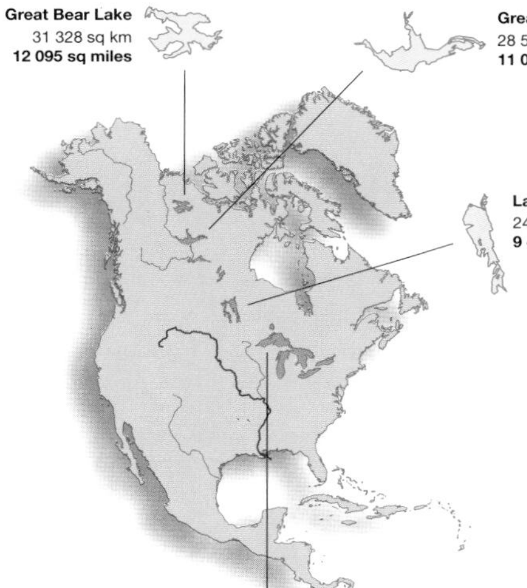

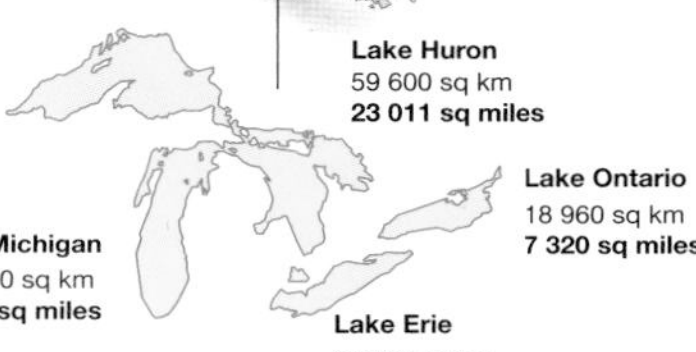

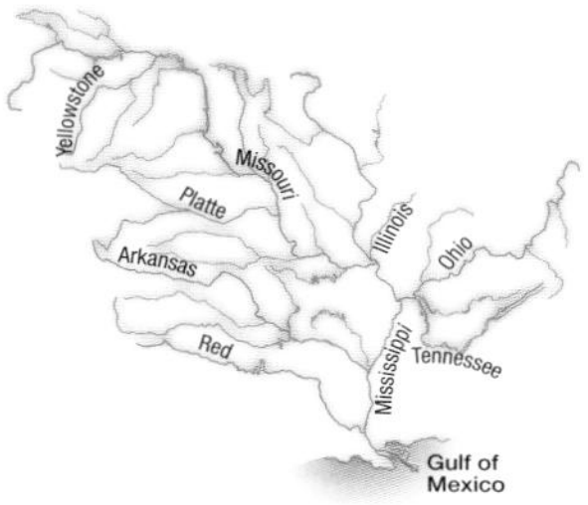

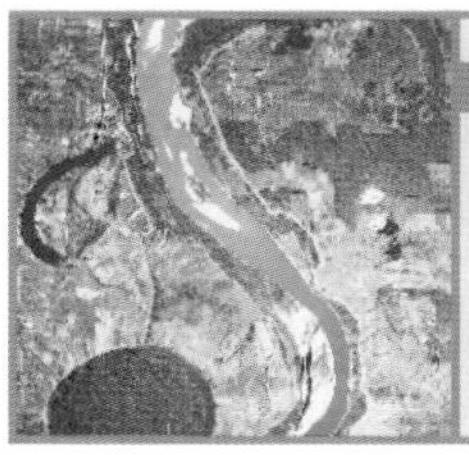

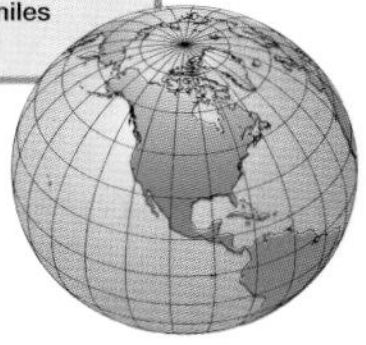

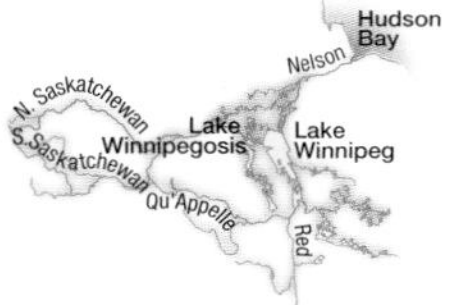

Great Bear Lake
31 328 sq km
12 095 sq miles

Great Slave Lake
28 568 sq km
11 030 sq miles

Lake Winnipeg
24 387 sq km
9 415 sq miles

Lake Superior
82 100 sq km
31 698 sq miles

Lake Huron
59 600 sq km
23 011 sq miles

Lake Ontario
18 960 sq km
7 320 sq miles

Lake Michigan
57 800 sq km
22 316 sq miles

Lake Erie
25 700 sq km
9 922 sq miles

Mississippi-Missouri drainage basin
3 250 000 sq km
1 255 000 sq miles

Nelson-Saskatchewan drainage basin
1 150 000 sq km
444 000 sq miles

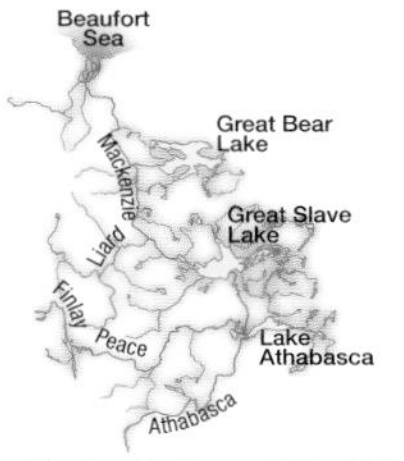

Mackenzie-Peace-Finlay drainage basin
1 805 000 sq km
697 000 sq miles

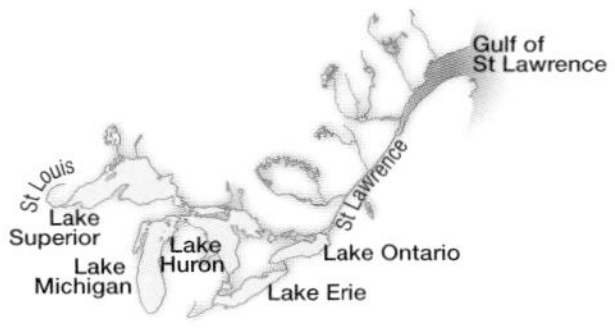

St Lawrence-St Louis drainage basin
1 463 000 sq km
565 000 sq miles

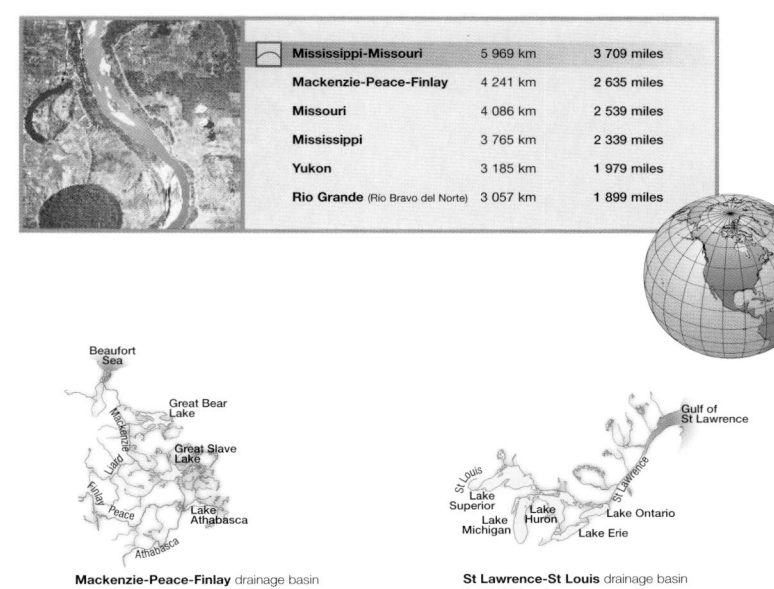

SOUTH AMERICA

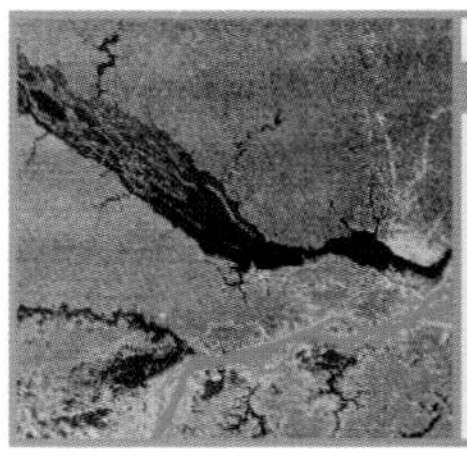

Amazonas (Amazon)	6 516 km	**4 049 miles**
Río de la Plata-Paraná	4 500 km	**2 796 miles**
Purus	3 218 km	**1 999 miles**
Madeira	3 200 km	**1 988 miles**
São Francisco	2 900 km	**1 802 miles**
Tocantins	2 750 km	**1 708 miles**

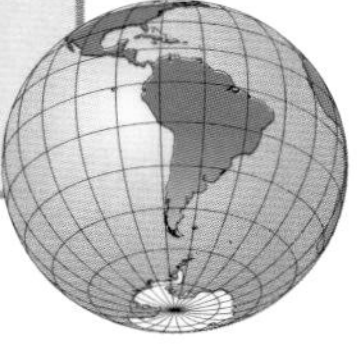

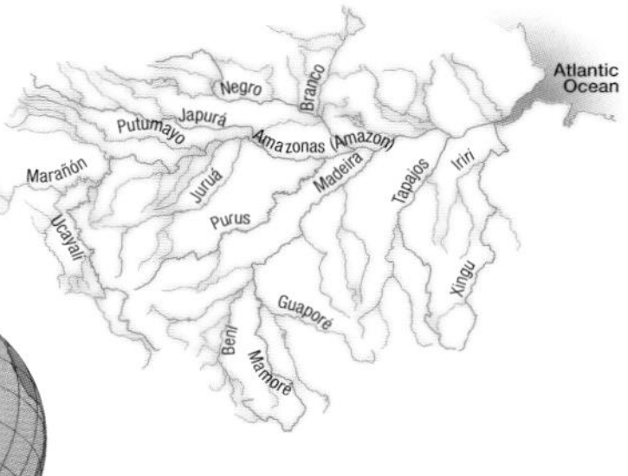

Amazonas (Amazon) drainage basin
7 050 000 sq km
2 722 000 sq miles

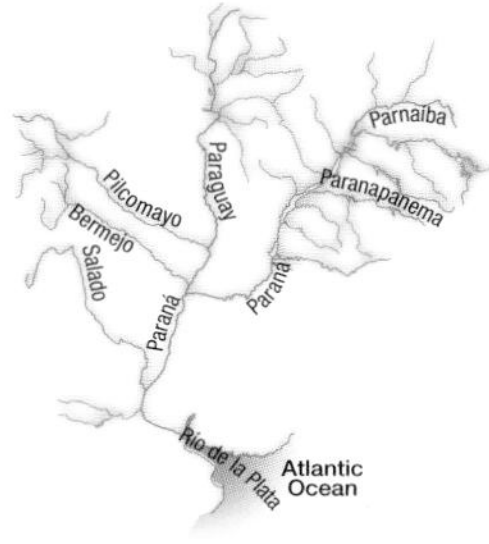

Río de la Plata-Paraná drainage basin
3 100 000 sq km
1 197 000 sq miles

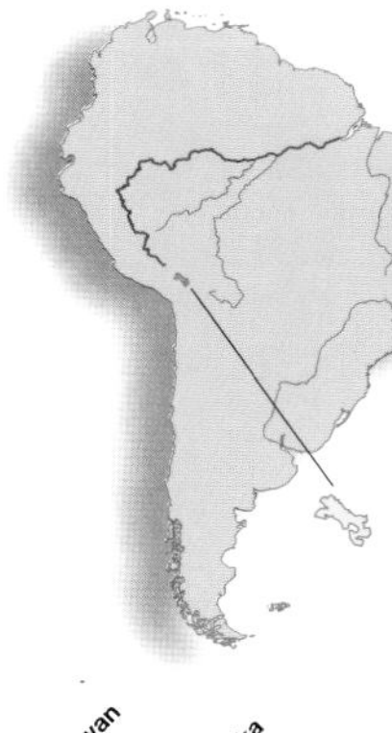

Lago Titicaca
8 340 sq km
3 220 sq miles

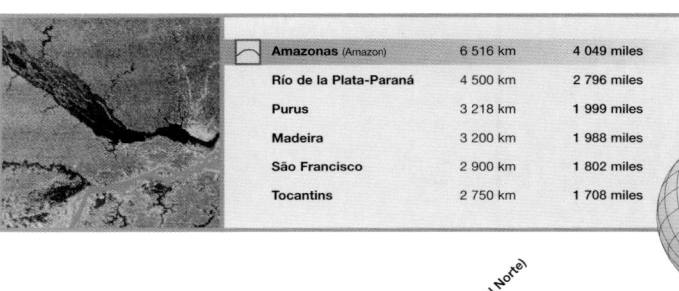

Madeira South America 3 200 km / **1 988 miles** · **Yukon** North America 3 185 km / **1 979 miles** · **Indus** Asia 3 180 km / **1 976 miles** · **Syrdar'ya** 3 078 km / **1 913 miles** · **St Lawrence** North America 3 058 km / **1 900 miles** · **Rio Grande** (Rio Bravo del Norte) North America 3 057 km / **1 899 miles** · **São Francisco** South America 2 900 km / **1 802 miles** · **Danube** Europe 2 850 km / **1 770 miles** · **Brahmaputra** Asia 2 840 km / **1 765 miles** · **Salween** Asia 2 816 km / **1 750 miles** · **Euphrates** Asia 2 815 km / **1 749 miles** · **Tocantins** South America 2 750 km / **1 708 miles** · **Tarim He** Asia 2 750 km / **1 708 miles** · **Darling** Australasia 2 739 km / **1 702 miles** · **Zambezi (Zambeze)** Africa 2 736 km / **1 700 miles** · **Araguaia** South America 2 627 km / **1 632 miles** · **Paraguay** South America 2 600 km / **1 615 miles** · **Murray** Australasia 2 589 km / **1 608 miles** · **Nelson-Saskatchewan** North America 2 570 km / **1 597 miles** · **Nizhnyaya Tunguska** Asia 2 559 km / **1 590 miles** · **Amudar'ya** Asia 2 540 km / **1 578 miles** · **Ural** Europe / Asia 2 534 km / **1 575 miles**

© Bartholomew Ltd

All independent countries and populated dependent and disputed territories are included in this list of the states and territories of the world; the list is arranged in alphabetical order by the conventional name form. For independent states, the full name is given below the conventional name, if this is different; for territories, the status is given. The capital city name is given in the local form as shown on the reference maps.

The statistics used for the area and population are the latest available and include estimates. The information on languages and religions is based on the latest information on 'de facto' speakers of the language or 'de facto' adherents of the religion. The information available on languages and religions varies greatly from country to country, some countries include questions in census others do not, in which case best estimates are used. The order of the languages and religions reflect their relative importance within the country; generally, languages or religions are included when more than one per cent of the population are estimated to be speakers or adherents.

Membership of the following international organizations is shown by the abbreviations below; territories are not shown as having separate memberships of these organizations.

APEC	Asia-Pacific Economic Cooperation
ASEAN	Association of Southeast Asian Nations
CARICOM	Caribbean Community
CIS	Commonwealth of Independent States
Comm.	The Commonwealth
EU	European Union
OECD	Organization of Economic Cooperation and Development
OPEC	Organization of Petroleum Exporting Countries
SADC	Southern African Development Community
UN	United Nations

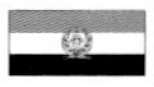

AFGHANISTAN
Islamic Emirate of Afghanistan

Area Sq Km	652 225	Currency	Afghani
Area Sq Miles	251 825	Languages	Dari, Pushtu, Uzbek, Turkmen
Population	21 354 000	Religions	Sunni Muslim, Shi'a Muslim
Capital	Kābul	Organizations	UN

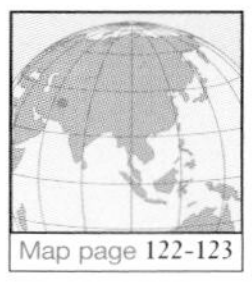

Map page 122-123

A landlocked country in central Asia, Afghanistan borders Pakistan, Iran, Turkmenistan, Uzbekistan, Tajikistan and China. The central highlands are bordered by plains in the north and southwest, and by the Hindu Kush to the northeast. The climate is dry with cold winters and hot summers. Over the last twenty years war has disrupted the economy which was highly dependent on farming and livestock rearing.

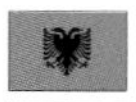

ALBANIA
Republic of Albania

Area Sq Km	28 748	Currency	Lek
Area Sq Miles	11 100	Languages	Albanian, Greek
Population	3 119 000	Religions	Sunni Muslim, Orthodox, Roman Catholic
Capital	Tiranë	Organizations	UN

Albania lies in the western Balkans in southeast Europe, on the Adriatic Sea. It is mountainous, with coastal plains where half the population lives. The economy is based on agriculture and mining, mainly chromium. The fall of communism brought foreign aid for the ailing economy, but Albania remains one of the poorest countries in Europe.

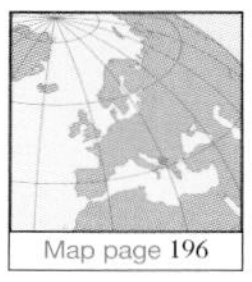

Map page 196

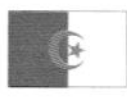

ALGERIA
Democratic and Popular Republic of Algeria

Area Sq Km	2 381 741	Currency	Dinar
Area Sq Miles	919 595	Languages	Arabic, French, Berber
Population	30 081 000	Religions	Sunni Muslim
Capital	Alger	Organizations	OPEC, UN

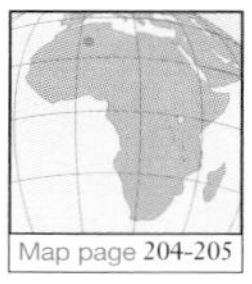

Map page 204-205

Algeria is on the Mediterranean coast of northwest Africa. The second largest country in Africa, it extends southwards from the coastal plain to the Atlas Mountains and to the Sahara which is dry sandstone plateau and desert, cut by valleys and rocky mountains, including the Hoggar in the southeast. The climate is Mediterranean on the coast, but dry inland. Most people live on the coastal plain and on the fertile northern slopes of the Atlas Mountains. Oil, natural gas and related products are the mainstay of the economy and account for over ninety five per cent of export earnings. Agriculture employs about a quarter of the workforce, producing mainly food crops; attempts are being made to diversify the economy, but unemployment remains high, as do social tensions.

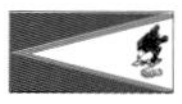

American Samoa
United States Unincorporated Territory

Area Sq Km	197	Currency	US dollar
Area Sq Miles	76	Languages	Samoan, English
Population	63 000	Religions	Protestant, Roman Catholic
Capital	Fagatogo		

Lying in the south Pacific Ocean, American Samoa consists of five main islands and two coral atolls. The main island is Tutuila. The economy is strongly linked to the USA, tuna and tuna products are the main export.

Map page 78

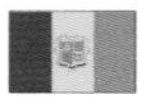

ANDORRA
Principality of Andorra

Area Sq Km	465	Currency	French franc, Spanish peseta
Area Sq Miles	180	Languages	Spanish, Catalan, French
Population	72 000	Religions	Roman Catholic
Capital	Andorra la Vella	Organizations	UN

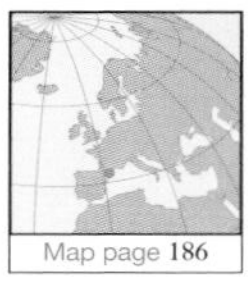

Map page 186

A landlocked state in southwest Europe, Andorra nestles in the Pyrenees between France and Spain. It consists of deep valleys and gorges, surrounded by mountains. Tourism (there are about ten million visitors a year) is the mainstay of the economy, banking is also important.

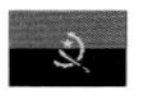

ANGOLA
Republic of Angola

Area Sq Km	1 246 700	Currency	Kwanza
Area Sq Miles	481 354	Languages	Portuguese, Bantu, local languages
Population	12 092 000	Religions	Roman Catholic, Protestant, traditional beliefs
Capital	Luanda	Organizations	SADC, UN

Angola lies on the Atlantic coast of southern central Africa. Its small northern province, Cabinda, is separated from the rest of the country by part of Democratic Republic of Congo. Much of Angola is high plateau, with a narrow coastal plain where most people live. The climate is equatorial in the north but desert in the south. Over eighty per cent of the population rely on subsistence agriculture. Angola is rich in minerals, and oil accounts for around seventy five per cent of exports earnings. Continued civil war for the last twenty years has restricted economic development.

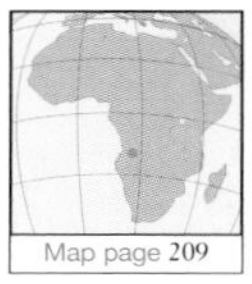

Map page 209

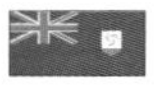

Anguilla
United Kingdom Overseas Territory

Area Sq Km	155	Currency	E. Carib. dollar
Area Sq Miles	60	Languages	English
Population	8 000	Religions	Protestant, Roman Catholic
Capital	The Valley		

Anguilla lies at the northern end of the Leeward Islands in the Caribbean. Tourism and fishing are the basis of the economy

Map page 247

ANTIGUA AND BARBUDA

Area Sq Km	442	Currency	E. Carib. dollar
Area Sq Miles	171	Languages	English, creole
Population	67 000	Religions	Protestant, Roman Catholic
Capital	St John's	Organizations	CARICOM, Comm., UN

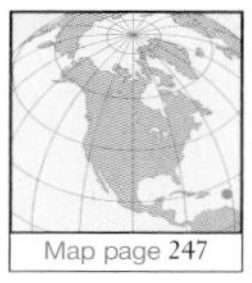

Map page 247

The state comprises Antigua, Barbuda and the tiny island of Redonda, in the Leeward Islands in the eastern Caribbean. Antigua, the largest and most populous, is mainly hilly scrubland, with many beaches and a warm, dry climate. The economy relies heavily on tourism with about half the tourists coming from the USA.

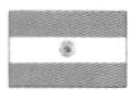

ARGENTINA
Argentine Republic

Area Sq Km	2 766 889	Currency	Peso
Area Sq Miles	1 068 302	Languages	Spanish, Italian, Amerindian languages
Population	36 123 000	Religions	Roman Catholic, Protestant
Capital	Buenos Aires	Organizations	UN

Argentina occupies almost the whole of the southern part of South America, from Bolivia to Cape Horn and from the Andes to the Atlantic Ocean. The second largest South American state has four geographical regions: the subtropical forests and swampland in the northeast; the temperate fertile plains or Pampas in the centre, which support most of the farming and the bulk of the population; the wooded foothills and valleys of the Andes in the west; and the cold, semi-arid plateaus of Patagonia, in the south. The highest mountain in South America, Cerro Aconcagua is in Argentina. Nearly ninety per cent of the population live in towns and cities. Though declining as a percentage of the GDP, agricultural products still dominate exports, which include motor vehicles and crude oil. Most trade is with Brazil and the USA.

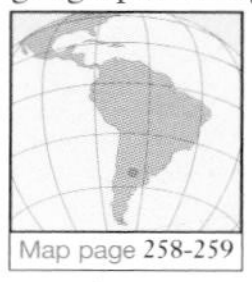

Map page 258-259

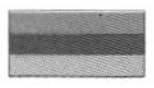

ARMENIA
Republic of Armenia

Area Sq Km	29 800	Currency	Dram
Area Sq Miles	11 506	Languages	Armenian, Azeri
Population	3 536 000	Religions	Armenian Orthodox
Capital	Yerevan	Organizations	CIS, UN

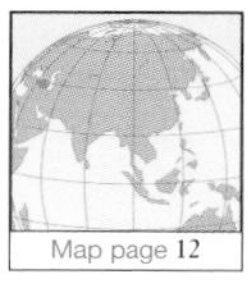

Map page 12

A landlocked state in southwest Asia, Armenia is in the south of the Lesser Caucasus and borders Georgia, Azerbaijan, Iran and Turkey. It is mountainous, with a central plateau-basin, and dry, with warm summers and cold winters. One third of the population lives in Yerevan. Armenia supports the ethnic Armenians in Nagorno-Karabkh in their separatist dispute with Azerbaijan. Economic growth has been slow; gold, jewellery and precious stones are important exports; many Armenians depend on remittances from abroad.

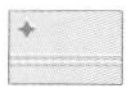

Aruba
Self-governing Netherlands Territory

Area Sq Km	193	Currency	Florin
Area Sq Miles	75	Languages	Papiamento, Dutch, English
Population	94 000	Religions	Roman Catholic, Protestant
Capital	Oranjestad		

The most southwesterly of the islands in the Lesser Antilles in the Caribbean, Aruba lies just off the coast of Venezuela. Tourism and offshore finance are the most important sectors of the economy.

Map page 247

Ascension Dependency of St Helena

Area Sq Km (Miles) 88 (34) | Population 1 100 | Capital Georgetown

A volcanic island in the south Atlantic Ocean about 1300 kilometres (800 miles) northwest of St Helena.

Map page 216

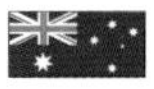

AUSTRALIA
Commonwealth of Australia

Area Sq Km	7 682 395	Currency	Dollar
Area Sq Miles	2 966 189	Languages	English, Italian, Greek
Population	18 520 000	Religions	Protestant, Roman Catholic, Orthodox
Capital	Canberra	Organizations	APEC, Comm., OECD, UN

Australia, the world's sixth largest country, occupies the smallest, flattest and driest continent. The western half of the continent is mostly arid plateaus, ridges and vast deserts. The central-eastern area comprises the lowlands of river systems draining into Lake Eyre, while to the east is the Great Dividing Range, a belt of ridges and plateaus running from Queensland to Tasmania. Climatically more than two-thirds of the country is arid or semi-arid. The north is tropical monsoon, the east subtropical, and the southwest and southeast temperate. A majority of Australia's highly urbanized population lives in cities along on the east, southeast and southwest coasts. Australia is rich in natural resources. It has vast mineral deposits and various sources of energy. It is among the world's leading producers of iron ore, bauxite, nickel, copper and uranium, and other minerals include lead, gold, silver, zinc, manganese, tungsten and gems. It is a major producer of coal; oil and natural gas are also being exploited. Although accounting for only five per cent of the workforce, agriculture continues to be an important sector of the economy with food and agricultural raw materials making up around one third of exports by value; fuel, ores and metals, and manufactures account for the remainder of exports. Japan and the USA are Australia's main trading partners.

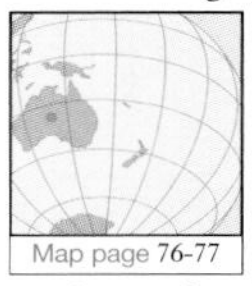

Map page 76-77

Australian Capital Territory (Federal territory)
Area Sq Km (Miles) 2 400 (927) | Population 299 243 | Capital Canberra

New South Wales (State)
Area Sq Km (Miles) 801 600 (309 499) | Population 6 038 696 | Capital Sydney

Northern Territory (Territory)
Area Sq Km (Miles) 1 346 200 (519 771) | Population 195 101 | Capital Darwin

Queensland (State)
Area Sq Km (Miles) 1 727 200 (666 876) | Population 3 368 850 | Capital Brisbane

South Australia (State)
Area Sq Km (Miles) 984 000 (379 925) | Population 1 427 936 | Capital Adelaide

Tasmania (State)
Area Sq Km (Miles) 67 800 (26 178) | Population 459 659 | Capital Hobart

Victoria (State)
Area Sq Km (Miles) 227 600 (87 877) | Population 4 373 520 | Capital Melbourne

Western Australia (State)
Area Sq Km (Miles) 2 525 500 (975 101) | Population 1 726 095 | Capital Perth

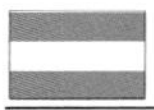

AUSTRIA
Republic of Austria

Area Sq Km	83 855	Currency	Schilling, Euro
Area Sq Miles	32 377	Languages	German, Croatian, Turkish
Population	8 140 000	Religions	Roman Catholic, Protestant
Capital	Wien (Vienna)	Organizations	EU, OECD, UN

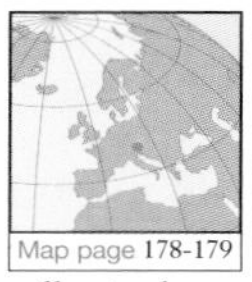

Map page 178-179

A landlocked state in central Europe, Austria borders the Czech Republic, Hungary, Slovenia, Switzerland, Italy, Germany and Liechtenstein. Two-thirds of the country, from the Swiss border to eastern Austria, lies within the Alps, with low mountains to the north. The only lowlands are in the east. The Danube river valley in the northeast contains almost all the agricultural land and most of the population. Though the climate varies with altitude, in general summers are warm and winters cold with heavy snowfalls. Manufacturing industry and tourism are the most important sectors of the economy. Exports are dominated by manufactured goods of which machinery and transport equipment make up over one third; Germany is Austria's main trading partner.

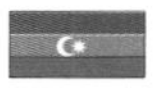

AZERBAIJAN
Azerbaijani Republic

Area Sq Km	86 600	Currency	Manat
Area Sq Miles	33 436	Languages	Azeri, Armenian, Russian, Lezgian
Population	7 669 000	Religions	Shi'a Muslim, Sunni Muslim, Orthodox
Capital	Bakı	Organizations	CIS, UN

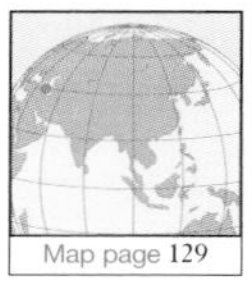

Map page 129

Azerbaijan lies to the southeast of the Caucasus, on the Caspian Sea. Its region of NaxÁivan is separated from the rest of the country by part of Armenia. It has mountains in the northeast and west, valleys in the centre and a low coastal plain. The climate is continental. It is rich in energy and mineral resources. Oil production, onshore and offshore, is the main industry and the basis of heavy industries. Agriculture is still important, with cotton and tobacco the main cash crops. War with Armenia has reduced output.

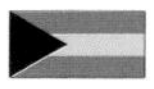

THE BAHAMAS
Commonwealth of The Bahamas

Area Sq Km	13 939	Currency	Dollar
Area Sq Miles	5 382	Languages	English, creole
Population	296 000	Religions	Protestant, Roman Catholic
Capital	Nassau	Organizations	CARICOM, Comm., UN

The Bahamas is an archipelago of about seven hundred islands and over two thousand cays, to the northeast of Cuba and east of the Florida coast of the USA. Twenty-two islands are inhabited, and two

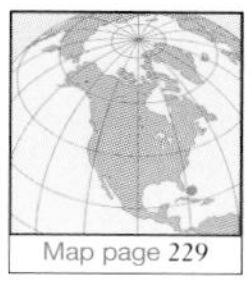
Map page 229

thirds of the population live on the main island of New Providence. The climate is warm for much of the year, with heavy rainfall in the summer. Tourism is the islands' main industry. Offshore banking, insurance and ship registration are also major foreign exchange earners.

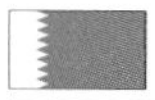

BAHRAIN
State of Bahrain

Area Sq Km	691	Currency	Dinar
Area Sq Miles	267	Languages	Arabic, English
Population	595 000	Religions	Shi'a Muslim, Sunni Muslim, Christian
Capital	Manama	Organizations	UN

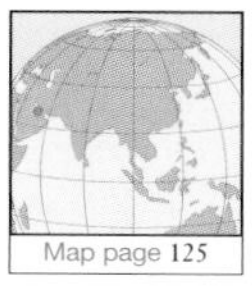
Map page 125

Bahrain consists of more than thirty islands lying in a bay in The Gulf, off the coasts of Saudi Arabia and Qatar. Bahrain Island, the largest island is connected to Muharraq and Sitrah islands by causeways. Oil production and processing are the main sectors of the economy.

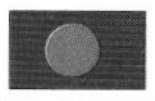

BANGLADESH
People's Republic of Bangladesh

Area Sq Km	143 998	Currency	Taka
Area Sq Miles	55 598	Languages	Bengali, English
Population	124 774 000	Religions	Sunni Muslim, Hindu
Capital	Dhaka	Organizations	Comm., UN

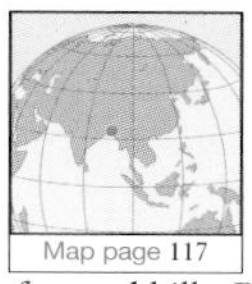
Map page 117

The south Asian state of Bangladesh is in the northeast of the Indian subcontinent, on the Bay of Bengal. It consists almost entirely of the low-lying alluvial plains and deltas of the Ganges and Brahmaputra rivers. The southwest is swampy, with mangrove forests in the delta area. The north, northeast and southeast have low forested hills. Bangladesh is one of the world's most densely populated and least developed countries. The economy is agriculture based, though the garment industry is the main export sector. Floods and cyclones during the summer monsoon season often cause devastating flooding and destroy crops. The country relies on large scale foreign aid and remittances from workers abroad.

BARBADOS

Area Sq Km	430	Currency	Dollar
Area Sq Miles	166	Languages	English, creole
Population	268 000	Religions	Protestant, Roman Catholic
Capital	Bridgetown	Organizations	CARICOM, Comm, UN

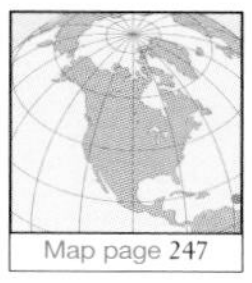
Map page 247

The most easterly of the Caribbean islands, Barbados is small and densely populated, with white-sand beaches and a tropical climate. The economy is based on tourism, financial services, light industries and sugar production.

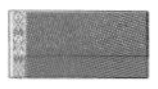

BELARUS
Republic of Belarus

Area Sq Km	207 600	Currency	Rouble
Area Sq Miles	80 155	Languages	Belorussian, Russian
Population	10 315 000	Religions	Belorussian Orthodox, Roman Catholic
Capital	Minsk	Organizations	CIS, UN

Belarus is a landlocked state in east Europe, bounded by Lithuania, Latvia, Russia, Ukraine and Poland. Belarus consists of low hills and plains, with many lakes, rivers and, in the south, extensive marshes; forests cover around a third of the country. It has a continental climate. Agriculture contributes a third of national income, with beef cattle and grains as the major products. Manufacturing industries produce a range of items, from construction equipment to textiles. Belarus remains closely tied economically to Russia.

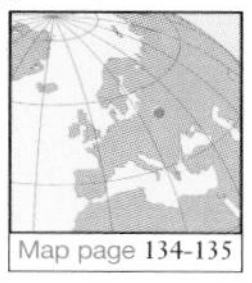
Map page 134-135

BELGIUM
Kingdom of Belgium

Area Sq Km	30 520	Currency	Franc, Euro
Area Sq Miles	11 784	Languages	Dutch (Flemish), French (Walloon), German
Population	10 141 000	Religions	Roman Catholic, Protestant
Capital	Bruxelles	Organizations	EU, OECD, UN

Belgium lies on the North Sea coast of western Europe. Beyond low sand dunes and a narrow belt of reclaimed land are fertile plains which extend to the Sambre-Meuse river valley from where the land rises to the forested Ardennes plateau in the southeast. Belgium has mild winters and cool summers. It is densely populated and has a highly urbanized population. The economy is based on trade, industry and services. With few mineral resources, Belgium imports raw materials for processing and manufacture. The agricultural sector is small, but provides for most food needs and a tenth of exports. A large services sector reflects Belgium's position as the home base for over eight hundred international institutions. The headquarters of the EU are in Bruxelles.

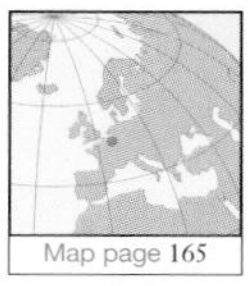
Map page 165

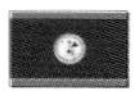

BELIZE

Area Sq Km	22 965	Currency	Dollar
Area Sq Miles	8 867	Languages	English, Spanish, Mayan, creole
Population	230 000	Religions	Roman Catholic, Protestant
Capital	Belmopan	Organizations	CARICOM, Comm., UN

Belize is on the Caribbean coast of central America and includes cays and a large barrier reef offshore. Belize's coastal areas are flat and swampy; the north and west are hilly, to the southwest are the Maya Mountains. Forests cover about half of the country. The climate is humid tropical, but tempered by sea breezes. A third of the population lives in the capital. The economy is based primarily on agriculture, forestry and fishing. Exports include raw sugar, orange concentrate and bananas.

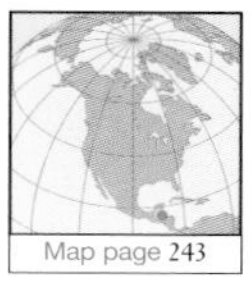
Map page 243

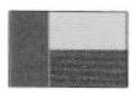

BENIN
Republic of Benin

Area Sq Km	112 620	Currency	CFA franc
Area Sq Miles	43 483	Languages	French, Fon, Yoruba, Adja, local languages
Population	5 781 000	Religions	Traditional beliefs, Roman Catholic, Sunni Muslim
Capital	Porto-Novo	Organizations	UN

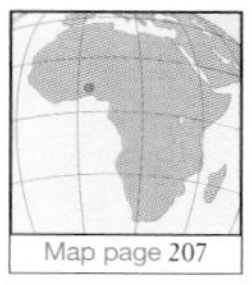
Map page 207

Benin is in west Africa, on the Gulf of Guinea. The climate is tropical in the north, but equatorial in the south. The economy is based mainly on agriculture and transit trade. Agricultural products account for two thirds of export earnings. Oil, produced offshore, is also a major export.

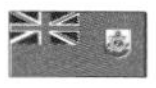

Bermuda
United Kingdom Overseas Territory

Area Sq Km	54	Currency	Dollar
Area Sq Miles	21	Languages	English
Population	64 000	Religions	Protestant, Roman Catholic
Capital	Hamilton		

In the Atlantic Ocean to the east of the USA, Bermuda is a group of small islands. The climate is warm and humid. The economy is based on tourism, insurance and shipping.

Map page 231

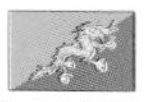

BHUTAN
Kingdom of Bhutan

Area Sq Km	46 620	Currency	Ngultrum
Area Sq Miles	18 000	Languages	Dzongkha, Nepali, Assamese
Population	2 004 000	Religions	Buddhist, Hindu
Capital	Thimphu	Organizations	UN

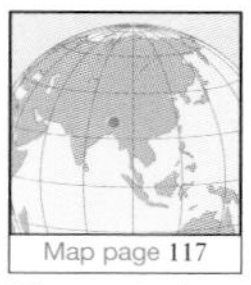
Map page 117

Bhutan is in the eastern Himalaya, between China and India. It is mountainous in the north, with fertile valleys where most people live. The climate ranges between permanently cold in the far north and subtropical in the south. Most of the population is involved in livestock raising and subsistence farming. Bhutan is the world's largest producer of cardamom. Tourism is an increasingly important foreign currency earner.

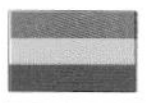

BOLIVIA
Republic of Bolivia

Area Sq Km	1 098 581	Currency	Boliviano
Area Sq Miles	424 164	Languages	Spanish, Quechua, Aymara
Population	7 957 000	Religions	Roman Catholic, Protestant, Baha'i
Capital	La Paz/Sucre	Organizations	UN

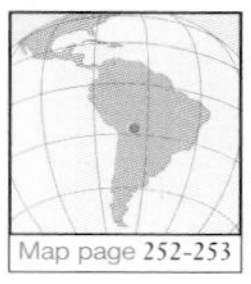
Map page 252-253

A landlocked state in central South America, Bolivia borders Brazil, Paraguay, Argentina, Chile and Peru. Most Bolivians live in the high plateau within the Andes ranges. The lowlands range between dense rainforest in the northeast and semi-arid grasslands in the southeast. Bolivia is rich in minerals (zinc, tin and silver) and sales generate around half of export income. Natural gas and timber are also exported. Subsistence farming predominates, though soya beans and, unofficially, coca are exported. USA is the main trading partner.

Bonaire part of Netherlands Antilles

Area Sq Km (Miles) 288 (111) Population 14 218

An island in the Caribbean Sea off the north coast of Venezuela; known for its fine beaches; tourism is the mainstay of the economy.

Map page 247

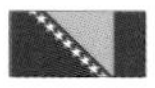

BOSNIA-HERZEGOVINA
Republic of Bosnia and Herzegovina

Area Sq Km	51 130	Currency	Marka
Area Sq Miles	19 741	Languages	Bosnian, Serbian, Croatian
Population	3 675 000	Religions	Sunni Muslim, Orthodox, Roman Catholic, Protestant
Capital	Sarajevo	Organizations	UN

Bosnia-Herzegovina lies in the western Balkans of southern Europe, on the Adriatic Sea. It is mountainous, with ridges running northwest-southeast. The main lowlands are around the Sava valley in the north. Summers are warm, but winters can be very cold. The Dayton Accord split the country into Republika Srpska and Federacija Bosna i Hercegovina. Much of the population relies on UN aid.

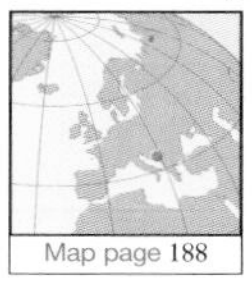
Map page 188

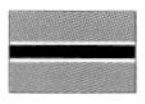

BOTSWANA
Republic of Botswana

Area Sq Km	581 370	Currency	Pula
Area Sq Miles	224 468	Languages	English, Setswana, Shona, local languages
Population	1 570 000	Religions	Traditional beliefs, Protestant, Roman Catholic
Capital	Gaborone	Organizations	Comm., SADC, UN

Botswana, a landlocked state in southern Africa, borders South Africa, Namibia, and Zimbabwe. Over half of the country lies within the Kalahari Desert, with swamps to the north and salt-pans to the northeast. Most people live near the eastern border. As a result of the AIDS epidemic, life expectancy has fallen by fourteen per cent since 1975. The climate is subtropical, but drought-prone. The economy was founded on cattle rearing, and though beef remains an important export, the economy is now based on mining. Diamonds account for eighty per cent of export earnings. Copper-nickel matte is also exported.

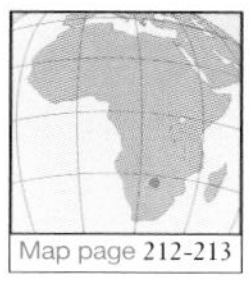
Map page 212-213

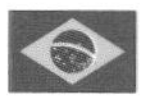

BRAZIL
Federative Republic of Brazil

Area Sq Km	8 547 379	Currency	Real
Area Sq Miles	3 300 161	Languages	Portuguese
Population	165 851 000	Religions	Roman Catholic, Protestant
Capital	Brasília	Organizations	UN

Brazil, in eastern South America, covers almost half of the continent - making it the world's fifth largest country - and borders ten countries and the Atlantic Ocean. The northwest contains the vast basin of the Amazon. The centre west is largely a vast plateau of savanna and rock escarpments. The northeast is mostly semi-arid plateaus, while to the east and south are rugged mountains, fertile valleys and narrow, fertile coastal plains. The Amazon basin is hot, humid and wet; the rest of Brazil is cooler and drier, with seasonal variations. The northeast is drought-prone. Most Brazilians live in urban areas along the coast and on the central plateau. Brazil has large and well developed agricultural, mining, and service sectors and the economy is larger than that of all other South American countries combined. Brazil is the world's largest producer of coffee, other agricultural crops include grains and sugar cane; mineral production includes iron, aluminium, and gold. Manufactured goods include food products, transport equipment, machinery and industrial chemicals. The main trading partners are USA and Argentina. Despite its natural wealth and being one of the largest economies in the world, Brazil has a large external debt and growing poverty gap.

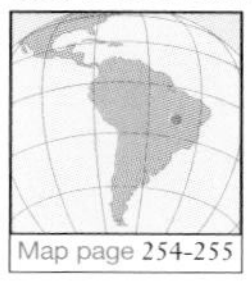
Map page 254-255

British Indian Ocean Territory
United Kingdom Overseas Territory

Area Sq Km (Miles) 60 (23) Population *uninhabited*

The territory consists of the Chagos Archipelago in central Indian Ocean. The islands are uninhabited apart from the joint British-US military base on Diego Garcia.

Map page 88

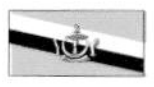

BRUNEI
State of Brunei Darussalam

Area Sq Km	5 765	Currency	Dollar
Area Sq Miles	2 226	Languages	Malay, English, Chinese
Population	315 000	Religions	Sunni Muslim, Buddhist, Christian
Capital	Bandar Seri Begawan	Organizations	APEC, ASEAN, Comm., UN

The southeast Asian state of Brunei lies on the northwest coast of the island of Borneo, on the South China Sea. Its two enclaves are surrounded inland by the Malaysian state of Sarawak. Tropical rainforest covers over two thirds of Brunei. The narrow coastal plain supports some crops and most of the population. The economy is dominated by the oil and gas industries.

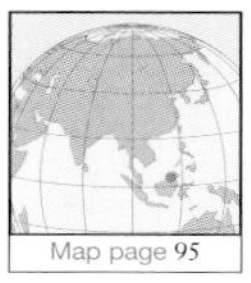
Map page 95

BULGARIA
Republic of Bulgaria

Area Sq Km	110 994	Currency	Lev
Area Sq Miles	42 855	Languages	Bulgarian, Turkish, Romany, Macedonian
Population	8 336 000	Religions	Bulgarian Orthodox, Sunni Muslim
Capital	Sofiya	Organizations	UN

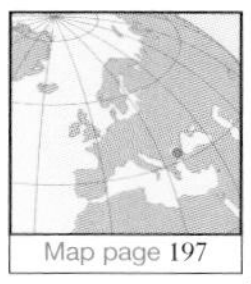
Map page 197

Bulgaria, in south Europe, borders Romania, Yugoslavia, Macedonia, Greece, Turkey and the Black Sea. The Balkan Mountains separate the Danube plains in the north from the Rhodope Mountains and the lowlands in the south. The economy is based on agriculture and manufacturing, chiefly machinery, consumer goods, chemicals and metals. Recent fiscal reforms have reduced inflation and helped economic recovery. Bulgaria is negotiating to join the EU.

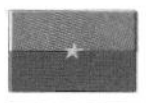

BURKINA
Democratic Republic of Burkina Faso

Area Sq Km	274 200	Currency	CFA franc
Area Sq Miles	105 869	Languages	French, Moore (Mossi), Fulani, local languages
Population	11 305 000	Religions	Sunni Muslim, traditional beliefs, Roman Catholic
Capital	Ouagadougou	Organizations	UN

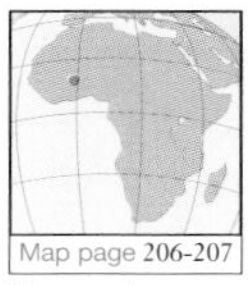
Map page 206-207

Burkina, a landlocked country in west Africa, borders Mali, Niger, Benin, Togo, Ghana and Côte d'Ivoire. The north of Burkina lies within the Sahara and is arid. The south is mainly semi-arid savanna. Rainfall is erratic and droughts are common. Livestock rearing and farming are the main activities. Cotton, livestock, groundnuts and some minerals are exported. Burkina relies heavily on aid, and is amongst the poorest and least developed countries in the world.

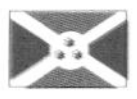

BURUNDI
Republic of Burundi

Area Sq Km	27 835	Currency	Franc
Area Sq Miles	10 747	Languages	Kirundi (Hutu, Tutsi), French
Population	6 457 000	Religions	Roman Catholic, traditional beliefs, Protestant
Capital	Bujumbura	Organizations	UN

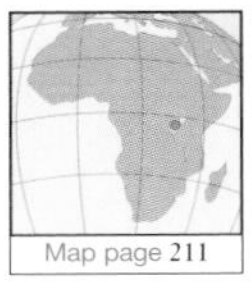

Map page 211

The densely populated east African state of Burundi borders Rwanda, Democratic Republic of Congo, Tanzania and Lake Tanganyika. It is hilly with high plateaus and a tropical climate. Burundi depends upon subsistence farming, coffee exports; ethnic violence in the mid 1990s increased dependence on foreign aid.

CAMBODIA
Kingdom of Cambodia

Area Sq Km	181 000	Currency	Riel
Area Sq Miles	69 884	Languages	Khmer, Vietnamese
Population	10 716 000	Religions	Buddhist, Roman Catholic, Sunni Muslim
Capital	Phnum Pénh	Organizations	ASEAN, UN

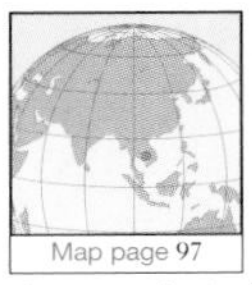

Map page 97

Cambodia lies in southeast Asia, on the Gulf of Thailand and occupies the Mekong river basin, with the Tônlé Sap at its centre; there are mountains in the southwest and north. The climate is tropical monsoon, forests cover half the land. Most people live on the plains and are engaged in farming (chiefly rice growing), fishing and forestry. Devastated by decades of civil war, continued political instability hampers development.

CAMEROON
Republic of Cameroon

Area Sq Km	475 442	Currency	CFA franc
Area Sq Miles	183 569	Languages	French, English, Fang, Bamileke, local languages
Population	14 305 000	Religions	Roman Catholic, Sunni Muslim, Protestant
Capital	Yaoundé	Organizations	Comm., UN

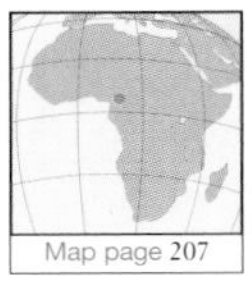

Map page 207

Cameroon is in west Africa, on the Gulf of Guinea. The coastal plains, southern and central plateaus are covered with tropical forest. Despite oil resources and favourable agricultural conditions Cameroon still faces problems of underdevelopment. Oil, timber and cocoa are the main exports. France is the main trading partner.

CANADA

Area Sq Km	9 970 610	Currency	Dollar
Area Sq Miles	3 849 674	Languages	English, French
Population	30 563 000	Religions	Roman Catholic, Protestant, Orthodox, Jewish
Capital	Ottawa	Organizations	APEC, Comm., OECD, UN

The world's second largest country, Canada covers the northern two-fifths of North America and has coastlines on the Atlantic, Arctic and Pacific Oceans. On the west coast, the mountain ranges include the Coast Mountains, interior plateaus and the Rocky Mountains. In the centre lie the fertile prairies. Further east, covering about half the total land area, is the Canadian Shield, fairly flat lowlands around the Hudson Bay extending to Labrador. The Shield is bordered to the south by the fertile Great Lakes-St Lawrence lowlands. In the far north climatic conditions are polar, the rest of Canada has a continental climate. Winters are long and cold with heavy snowfalls, while summers are hot with light to moderate rainfall. Most Canadians live in the south, chiefly in the southeast, in the urban areas of the Great Lakes-St Lawrence basin. Canada is rich in mineral and energy resources. Only five per cent of land is as arable, but that is still a large area. Canada is among the world's leading producers of wheat, a leading exporter of wood from its vast coniferous forests, and fish and seafood from its rich Atlantic and Pacific fishing grounds. It is a top producer of nickel, uranium, copper, iron ore, zinc and other minerals, as well as oil and natural gas. Its abundant raw materials are the basis for manufacturing industries. Main exports are machinery, motor vehicles, oil, timber, newsprint and paper, wood pulp and wheat. Since the 1989 free trade agreement with USA and the 1994 North America Free Trade Agreement (which includes Mexico), trade with the USA has grown and now accounts for around eighty per cent of imports and around seventy five per cent of exports.

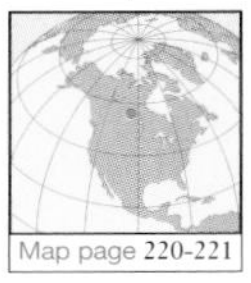

Map page 220-221

	Area Sq Km (Miles)	Population	Capital
Alberta (Province)	661 190 (255 287)	2 914 900	Edmonton
British Columbia (Province)	947 800 (365 948)	4 009 900	Victoria
Manitoba (Province)	649 950 (250 947)	1 138 000	Winnipeg
New Brunswick (Province)	73 440 (28 355)	753 000	Fredericton
Newfoundland (Province)	405 720 (156 649)	544 400	St John's
Northwest Territories (Province)	1 432 320 (553 022)	45 500	Yellowknife
Nova Scotia (Province)	55 490 (21 425)	934 600	Halifax
Nunavut (Territory)	1 994 000 (769 888)	22 000	Iqaluit
Ontario (Province)	1 068 580 (412 581)	11 411 500	Toronto
Prince Edward Island (Province)	5 660 (2 185)	136 400	Charlottetown
Québec (Province)	1 540 680 (594 860)	7 333 300	Québec
Saskatchewan (Province)	652 330 (251 866)	1 024 400	Regina
Yukon Territory (Territory)	483 450 (186 661)	31 700	Whitehorse

CAPE VERDE
Republic of Cape Verde

Area Sq Km	4 033	Currency	Escudo
Area Sq Miles	1 557	Languages	Portuguese, creole
Population	408 000	Religions	Roman Catholic, Protestant
Capital	Praia	Organizations	UN

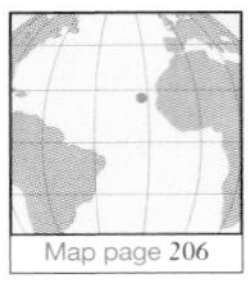

Map page 206

Cape Verde is a group of ten semi-arid volcanic islands off the coast of west Africa. The economy is based on fishing and subsistence farming, but relies on emigrant workers' remittances and foreign aid.

Cayman Islands
United Kingdom Overseas Territory

Area Sq Km	259	Currency	Dollar
Area Sq Miles	100	Languages	English
Population	36 000	Religions	Roman Catholic, Protestant
Capital	George Town	Organizations	UN

A group of islands in the Caribbean, northwest of Jamaica; there are three main islands: Grand Cayman, Little Cayman and Cayman Brac. They form one of the world's major offshore financial centres, tourism is also important and is aimed at the luxury market.

Map page 246

CENTRAL AFRICAN REPUBLIC

Area Sq Km	622 436	Currency	CFA franc
Area Sq Miles	240 324	Languages	French, Sango, Banda, Baya, local languages
Population	3 485 000	Religions	Protestant, Roman Catholic, trad. beliefs, Muslim
Capital	Bangui	Organizations	UN

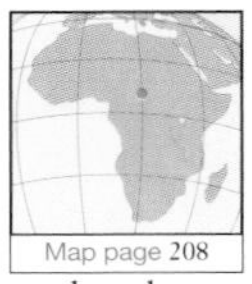

Map page 208

The landlocked Central African Republic borders Chad, Sudan, Democratic Republic of Congo, Congo and Cameroon. Most of the country is savanna plateau, drained by the Ubangi and Chari river systems, with mountains to the east and west. The climate is tropical with high rainfall. Most of the population live in the south and west, and a majority of the workforce is involved in subsistence farming. Some cotton, coffee, tobacco and timber are exported, but diamonds account for around half of export earnings.

CHAD
Republic of Chad

Area Sq Km	1 284 000	Currency	CFA franc
Area Sq Miles	495 755	Languages	Arabic, French, Sara, local languages
Population	7 270 000	Religions	Sunni Muslim, Roman Catholic, Protestant
Capital	Ndjamena	Organizations	UN

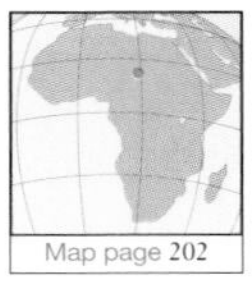

Map page 202

Chad is a landlocked state of central Africa, bordered by Libya, Sudan, Central African Republic, Niger, Nigeria and Cameroon. It consists of plateaus, the Tibesti mountains in the north and Lake Chad basin in the west. Climatic conditions range between desert in the north and tropical forest in the southwest. The largely rural population live in the south and near Lake Chad. Farming, cattle herding and fishing are the main activities; raw cotton is the main export. Chad relies heavily on foreign aid.

CHILE
Republic of Chile

Area Sq Km	756 945	Currency	Peso
Area Sq Miles	292 258	Languages	Spanish, Amerindian languages
Population	14 824 000	Religions	Roman Catholic, Protestant
Capital	Santiago	Organizations	APEC, UN

Chile lies along the Pacific coast of the southern half of South America. Between the Andes in the east and the lower coastal ranges, is a central valley, with a mild climate, where most Chileans live. To the north is the arid Atacama Desert, to the south is cold, wet forested grassland. Chile is the world's leading exporter of copper; nitrates, molybdenum, gold, iron are also important. Agriculture, forestry and fishing are important activities. Copper accounts for a third of the value of exports, other minerals, timber and fish production are also important.

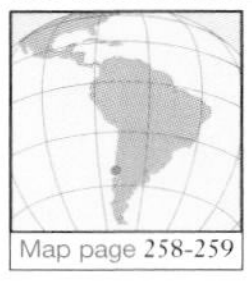

Map page 258-259

CHINA
People's Republic of China

Area Sq Km	9 584 492	Currency	Yuan
Area Sq Miles	3 700 593	Languages	Mandarin, Wu, Cantonese, Hsiang, regional languages
Population	1 262 817 000		
Capital	Beijing	Religions	Confucian, Taoist, Buddhist, Christian, Muslim
		Organizations	APEC, UN

China, the world's most populous and third largest country, occupies almost the whole of east Asia, borders fourteen states and has coastlines on the Yellow, East China and South China Seas. It has an amazing variety of landscapes. The southwest contains the high Plateau of Tibet, flanked by the Himalaya and Kunlun Shan. The north is mountainous with arid basins and extends from the Tien Shan and Altai Mountains and vast Taklimakan Shamo in the west to the plateau and Gobi desert in the centre-east. Eastern China is predominantly lowland and is divided broadly into the basins of the Huang He (Yellow River) in the north, Chang Jiang (Yangtze) in the centre and Xi Jiang (Pearl River) in the southeast. Climatic conditions and vegetation are as diverse as the topography: much of the country experiences temperate conditions, while southwest China has an extreme mountain climate, and the southeast enjoys a moist, warm subtropical climate. Nearly seventy per cent of China's huge population live in rural areas, chiefly in the northern part of the eastern lowlands, in the Red Basin and along the coast. Agriculture employs around half of the working population. The main crops are rice, wheat, soya beans, peanuts, cotton, tobacco and hemp. China is rich in coal, oil and natural gas and has the world's largest potential in hydroelectric power; it is a major world producer of iron ore, molybdenum, copper, asbestos and gold. Economic reforms from the early 1980's onward led to an explosion in manufacturing development concentrated on the 'coastal economic open region'. The main exports are machinery, textiles, footwear, toy and sports goods. Japan and the USA are the main trading partners.

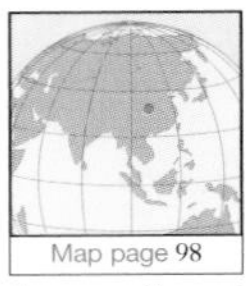

Map page 98

	Area Sq Km (Miles)	Population	Capital
Anhui (Province)	139 000 (53 668)	60 130 000	Hefei
Beijing (Municipality)	16 800 (6 487)	12 510 000	Beijing
Chongqing (Municipality)	23 000 (8 880)	14 600 000	Chongqing
Fujian (Province)	121 400 (46 873)	32 370 000	Fuzhou
Gansu (Province)	453 700 (175 175)	24 380 000	Lanzhou
Guangdong (Province)	178 000 (68 726)	68 680 000	Guangzhou
Guangxi Zhuangzu Zizhiqu (Autonomous Region)	236 000 (91 120)	45 430 000	Nanning
Guizhou (Province)	176 000 (67 954)	35 080 000	Guiyang
Hainan (Province)	34 000 (13 127)	7 240 000	Haikou
Hebei (Province)	187 700 (72 471)	64 370 000	Shijiazhuang
Heilongjiang (Province)	454 600 (175 522)	37 010 000	Harbin
Henan (Province)	167 000 (64 479)	91 000 000	Zhengzhou
Hong Kong (Special Administrative Region)	1 075 (415)	6 706 965	Hong Kong
Hubei (Province)	185 900 (71 776)	57 720 000	Wuhan
Hunan (Province)	210 000 (81 081)	63 920 000	Changsha
Jiangsu (Province)	102 600 (39 614)	70 660 000	Nanjing
Jiangxi (Province)	166 900 (64 440)	40 630 000	Nanchang
Jilin (Province)	187 000 (72 201)	25 920 000	Changchun
Liaoning (Province)	147 400 (56 911)	40 920 000	Shenyang
Macau (Special Administrative Region)	17 (7)	459 000	Macau
Nei Mongol Zizhiqu (Inner Mongolia) (Autonomous Region)	1 183 000 (456 759)	22 840 000	Huhhot
Ningxia Huizu Zizhiqu (Autonomous Region)	66 400 (25 637)	5 130 000	Yinchuan
Qinghai (Province)	721 000 (278 380)	4 810 000	Xining
Shaanxi (Province)	205 600 (79 383)	35 140 000	Xi'an
Shandong (Province)	153 300 (59 189)	87 050 000	Jinan
Shanghai (Municipality)	6 300 (2 432)	14 150 000	Shanghai
Shanxi (Province)	156 300 (60 348)	30 770 000	Taiyuan
Sichaun (Province)	569 000 (219 692)	98 650 000	Chengdu
Tianjin (Municipality)	11 300 (4 363)	9 420 000	Tianjin
Xinjiang Uygur Zizhiqu (Sinkiang) (Autonomous Region)	1 600 000 (617 763)	16 610 000	Ürümqi
Xizang Zizhiqu (Tibet) (Autonomous Region)	1 228 400 (474 288)	2 400 000	Lhasa
Yunnan (Province)	394 000 (152 124)	39 900 000	Kunming
Zhejiang (Province)	101 800 (39 305)	43 190 000	Hangzhou

Christmas Island
Australian External Territory

Area Sq Km	135	Currency	Austr. dollar
Area Sq Miles	52	Languages	English
Population	2 195	Religions	Buddhist, Sunni Muslim, Protestant, Roman Catholic
Capital	The Settlement		

The island is situated in the east of the Indian Ocean, to the south of Indonesia. The economy is based on phosphate extraction, though reserves are nearing depletion; tourism is developing and is the major employer.

Map page 86

Cocos Islands (Keeling Islands)
Australian External Territory

Area Sq Km	14	Currency	Austr. dollar
Area Sq Miles	5	Languages	English
Population	637	Religions	Sunni Muslim, Christian
Capital	West Island		

The Cocos Islands are two separate coral atolls in the east of the Indian Ocean between Sri Lanka and Australia. Most of the population live on West Island and Home Island. Coconuts are the only cash crop and the economy is based on these and on tourism.

Map page 86

COLOMBIA
Republic of Colombia

Area Sq Km	1 141 748	Currency	Peso
Area Sq Miles	440 831	Languages	Spanish, Amerindian languages
Population	40 803 000	Religions	Roman Catholic, Protestant
Capital	Bogotá	Organizations	APEC, UN

A state in northwest South America, Colombia has coastlines on the Pacific Ocean and the Caribbean Sea. Behind coastal plains lie three ranges of the Andes, separated by high valleys and plateaus where most Colombians live. To the southeast are grasslands and then the forests of the Amazon. Colombia has a tropical climate, though temperatures vary with altitude. Only five per cent of land can be cultivated, but a range of crops are grown. Coffee (Colombia is the world's second largest producer), sugar, bananas, cotton and flowers are exported. Coal, nickel, gold, silver, platinum and emeralds (Colombia is the world's largest producer) are mined. Oil and its products are the main export. Industry involves processing minerals and agricultural produce. The main trade partner is the USA. In spite of government efforts to stop the drugs trade, coca growing and cocaine smuggling are rife.

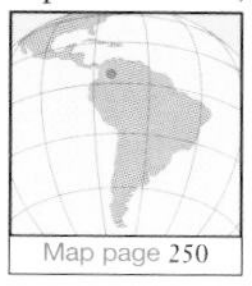

Map page 250

COMOROS
Federal Islamic Republic of the Comoros

Area Sq Km	1 862	Currency	Franc
Area Sq Miles	719	Languages	Comorian, French, Arabic
Population	658 000	Religions	Sunni Muslim, Roman Catholic
Capital	Moroni	Organizations	UN

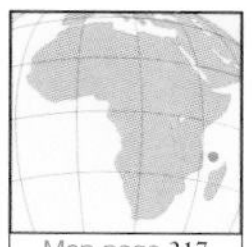

Map page 217

The state comprises three volcanic islands: Grande Comore, Anjouan and Mohéil, and some coral atolls in the Indian Ocean, off the east African coast. The tropical islands are mountainous, with poor soil. Subsistence farming predominates, but vanilla, cloves and ylang-ylang (an essential oil) are exported.

CONGO
Republic of the Congo

Area Sq Km	342 000	Currency	CFA franc
Area Sq Miles	132 047	Languages	French, Kongo, Monokutuba, local languages
Population	2 785 000	Religions	Roman Catholic, Protestant, trad. beliefs, Muslim
Capital	Brazzaville	Organizations	UN

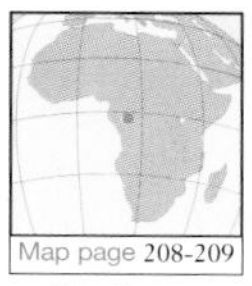

Map page 208-209

Congo, in central Africa, is mostly forest or savanna-covered plateaus drained by the Ubangi-Congo river systems. Sand dunes and lagoons line the short Atlantic coast. The climate is hot and tropical. Most Congolese live in the southern third of the country. Half of the workforce are farmers, growing food crops and cash crops including sugar, coffee, cocoa and oil palms. Oil makes up over three quarters of export revenues, hardwoods are the second biggest export earner.

CONGO, DEMOCRATIC REPUBLIC OF

Area Sq Km	2 345 410	Currency	Franc
Area Sq Miles	905 568	Languages	French, Lingala, Swahili, Kongo, local languages
Population	49 139 000	Religions	Christian, Sunni Muslim
Capital	Kinshasa	Organizations	SADC, UN

The central African state consists of the basin of the Congo river flanked by plateaus, with high mountain ranges to the east and a short Atlantic coastline to the west. The climate is tropical with rainforest close to the Equator and savannas to the north and south. Congo has fertile land that grows a range of food crops and cash crops, chiefly coffee. It has vast mineral resources, copper, cobalt and diamonds being the most important. Continued political instability inhibits development.

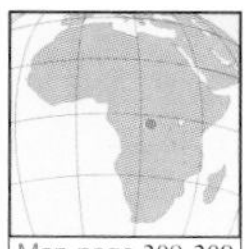

Map page 208-209

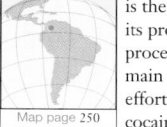

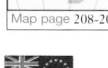

Cook Islands
Self-governing New Zealand Territory

Area Sq Km	293	Currency	Dollar
Area Sq Miles	113	Languages	English, Maori
Population	19 000	Religions	Protestant, Roman Catholic
Capital	Avarua		

Groups of coral atolls and volcanic islands in the southwest Pacific Ocean. The main island is Rarotonga. Distance from foreign markets and few natural resources hinder development and there were severe economic problems in the late 1990s.

Map page 81

COSTA RICA
Republic of Costa Rica

Area Sq Km	51 100	Currency	Colón
Area Sq Miles	19 730	Languages	Spanish
Population	3 841 000	Religions	Roman Catholic, Protestant
Capital	San José	Organizations	UN

Costa Rica has coastlines on the Caribbean Sea and Pacific Ocean. From the tropical coastal plains, the land rises to mountains and a temperate central plateau where most people live. The economy depends on tourism, with ecotourism becoming increasingly important, and agriculture; main exports are textiles, coffee and bananas; almost half of all trade is with USA.

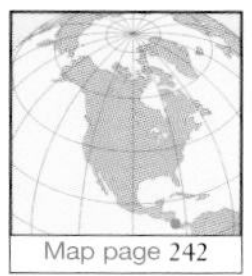

Map page 242

CÔTE D'IVOIRE
Republic of Côte d'Ivoire

Area Sq Km	322 463	Currency	CFA franc
Area Sq Miles	124 504	Languages	French, creole, Akan, local languages
Population	14 292 000	Religions	Muslim, Roman Catholic, trad. beliefs, Protestant
Capital	Yamoussoukro	Organizations	UN

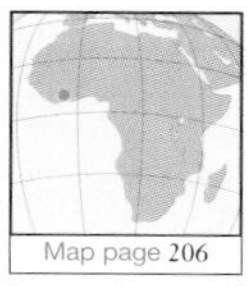

Map page 206

Côte d'Ivoire is in west Africa, on the Gulf of Guinea. In the north are plateaus and savanna, in the south are low undulating plains and rainforest, with sand-bars and lagoons on the coast. Temperatures are warm, and rainfall is heavier in the south. Most of the workforce is engaged in farming. Côte d'Ivoire is a major producer of cocoa and coffee, and agricultural products (including cotton and timber) are the main export. Oil and gas have begun to be exploited.

CROATIA
Republic of Croatia

Area Sq Km	56 538	Currency	Kuna
Area Sq Miles	21 829	Languages	Croatian, Serbian
Population	4 481 000	Religions	Roman Catholic, Serbian Orthodox, Sunni Muslim
Capital	Zagreb	Organizations	UN

The south European state of Croatia has a long coastline on the Adriatic Sea and many offshore islands. Coastal areas have a Mediterranean climate, inland is colder and wetter. Croatia was strong agriculturally and industrially, but conflict in 1991-1992, the loss of markets and tourist revenue have caused economic difficulties; recovery has been slow.

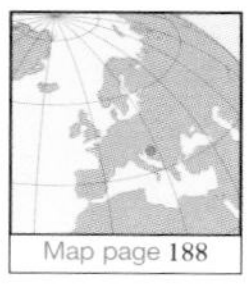

Map page 188

CUBA
Republic of Cuba

Area Sq Km	110 860	Currency	Peso
Area Sq Miles	42 803	Languages	Spanish
Population	110 860	Religions	Roman Catholic, Protestant
Capital	La Habana	Organizations	UN

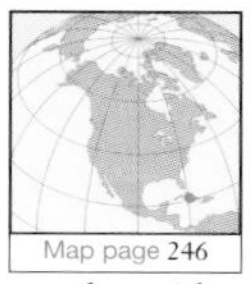

Map page 246

Cuba comprises the island of Cuba, the largest island in the Caribbean, and many islets and cays. A fifth of Cubans live in and around La Habana. Cuba is slowly recovering from the withdrawal of aid and subsidies from the former USSR. Sugar remains the basis of the economy, though tourism is developing and is, together with remittances from workers abroad, an important source of foreign currency.

Curaçao part of Netherlands Antilles

Area Sq Km (Miles) 444 (171) Population 151 448 Capital Willemstad

An island in the Caribbean Sea off the north coast of Venezuela, it is the largest and most populous island of the Netherlands Antilles. Oil refining and tourism form the basis of the economy.

Map page 247

CYPRUS
Republic of Cyprus

Area Sq Km	9 251	Currency	Pound
Area Sq Miles	3 572	Languages	Greek, Turkish, English
Population	771 000	Religions	Greek Orthodox, Sunni Muslim
Capital	Lefkosia	Organizations	Comm., UN

The eastern Mediterranean island of Cyprus has hot dry summers and mild winters. The economy of the Greek south is based mainly on specialist agriculture and tourism, though shipping and offshore banking are also major sources of income. The Turkish north depends upon agriculture, tourism and aid from Turkey. Cyprus is negotiating to join the EU.

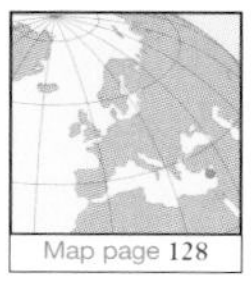

Map page 128

CZECH REPUBLIC

Area Sq Km	78 864	Currency	Koruna
Area Sq Miles	30 450	Languages	Czech, Moravian, Slovak
Population	10 282 000	Religions	Roman Catholic, Protestant
Capital	Praha	Organizations	UN

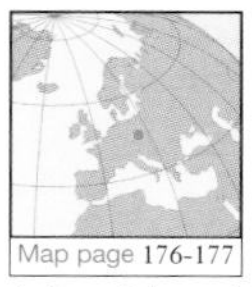

Map page 176-177

The landlocked Czech Republic in central Europe consists of rolling countryside, wooded hills and fertile valleys. The climate is temperate, but winters are fairly cold. The country has substantial reserves of coal and lignite, timber and some minerals, chiefly iron ore. It is highly industrialized and major manufactures include industrial machinery, consumer goods, cars, iron and steel, chemicals and glass. Germany is the main trading partner. The Czech Republic began formal talks on EU accession in 1998.

DENMARK
Kingdom of Denmark

Area Sq Km	43 075	Currency	Krone
Area Sq Miles	16 631	Languages	Danish
Population	5 270 000	Religions	Protestant
Capital	København	Organizations	EU, OECD, UN

In north Europe, Denmark occupies the Jylland (Jutland) peninsula and nearly five hundred islands in and between the North and Baltic Seas. The country is low-lying, with long, indented coastlines. The climate is cool and temperate, with rainfall throughout the year. A fifth of the population lives around København on the largest of the islands, Sjaelland (Zealand). Denmark's main natural resource is its agricultural potential; two thirds of the total area is fertile farmland or pasture. But agriculture is now high-tech and with forestry and fishing employs only around six per cent of the workforce. Denmark is self-sufficient in oil and natural gas, produced from fields in the North Sea. Manufacturing, largely based on imported raw materials, now accounts for over half of exports which include machinery, food, furniture, and pharmaceuticals. The main trading partners are Germany and Sweden.

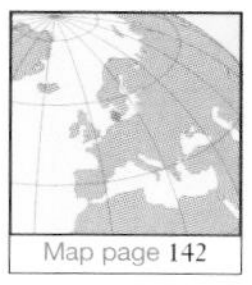

Map page 142

DJIBOUTI
Republic of Djibouti

Area Sq Km	23 200	Currency	Franc
Area Sq Miles	8 958	Languages	Somali, Afar, French, Arabic
Population	623 000	Religions	Sunni Muslim, Christian
Capital	Djibouti	Organizations	UN

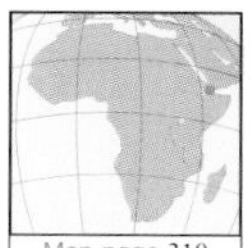

Map page 210

Djibouti lies in northeast Africa, on the Gulf of Aden at the entrance to the Red Sea. Most of the country is semi-arid desert with high temperatures and low rainfall. More than half of the population live in the capital. There is some camel, sheep and goat herding but with few natural resources, the economy is based on services and trade. The deep-water port and the railway line to Ādīs Ābeba in Ethiopia account for about two thirds of national income.

DOMINICA
Commonwealth of Dominica

Area Sq Km	750	Currency	E. Carib.dollar
Area Sq Miles	290	Languages	English, creole
Population	71 000	Religions	Roman Catholic, Protestant
Capital	Roseau	Organizations	CARICOM, Comm., UN

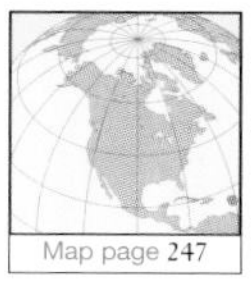

Map page 247

Dominica is the most northerly of the Windward Islands in the eastern Caribbean. It is very mountainous and forested, with a coastline of steep cliffs. The climate is tropical and rainfall abundant. Around a quarter of Dominicans live in the capital. The economy is based on agriculture, with bananas (the major export), coconuts and citrus fruits the most important crops. Tourism is developing, but is hindered by the rugged coastline and lack of sandy beaches.

DOMINICAN REPUBLIC

Area Sq Km	48 442	Currency	Peso
Area Sq Miles	18 704	Languages	Spanish, creole
Population	8 232 000	Religions	Roman Catholic, Protestant
Capital	Santo Domingo	Organizations	UN

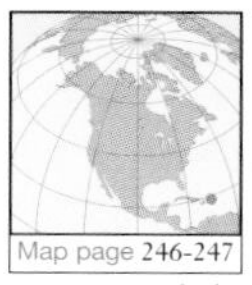

Map page 246-247

The state occupies the eastern two thirds of the Caribbean island of Hispaniola (the western third is Haiti). The frontier with Haiti is closed. It has a series of mountain ranges, fertile valleys and a large coastal plain in the east. The climate is hot tropical, with heavy rainfall. Sugar, coffee and cocoa are the main cash crops. Nickel (the main export), and gold are mined, and there is some light industry. USA is the main trading partner. Tourism is the main foreign exchange earner.

East Timor
under UN Transitional Administration

Area Sq Km	14 874	Languages	Portuguese, Tetun, English
Area Sq Miles	5 743	Religions	Roman Catholic
Population	857 000		
Capital	Dili		

The eastern part, and a small coastal enclave to the west, of the island Timor, which is part of Indonesian archipelago to the north of Western Australia. A referendum in 1999 officially ended Indonesia's occupation; East Timor is under a UN transitional administration.

Map page 93

ECUADOR
Republic of Ecuador

Area Sq Km	272 045	Currency	Sucre
Area Sq Miles	105 037	Languages	Spanish, Quechua, and other Amerindian languages
Population	12 175 000	Religions	Roman Catholic
Capital	Quito	Organizations	APEC, UN

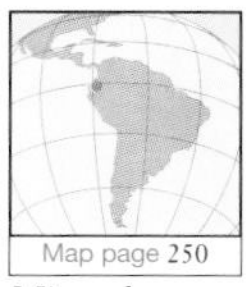

Map page 250

Ecuador is in northwest South America, on the Pacific coast. It consists of a broad coastal plain, the high ranges of the Andes and the forested upper Amazon basin to the east. The climate is tropical, moderated by altitude. Most people live on the coast or in the mountain valleys. Ecuador is one of South America's main oil producers. Mineral reserves include gold. Most of the workforce depends on agriculture; bananas, shrimps, coffee and cocoa are exported; USA is the main trading partner.

EGYPT
Arab Republic of Egypt

Area Sq Km	1 000 250	Currency	Pound
Area Sq Miles	386 199	Languages	Arabic
Population	65 978 000	Religions	Sunni Muslim, Coptic Christian
Capital	Cairo	Organizations	UN

Egypt, on the eastern Mediterranean coast of North Africa, is low-lying, with areas below sea level in the Qattâra depression, and mountain ranges along the Red Sea coast and in the Sinai peninsula. It is a land of desert and semi-desert, except for the Nile valley, where ninety nine per cent of Egyptians live, nearly half of them in towns and cities. A project for the development of Sinai aims to resettle over three million people in the area by 2017. The summers are hot, the winters mild and rainfall is negligible. Less than four per cent of land (chiefly around the Nile floodplain and delta) is cultivated, but farming employs about one third of the workforce; cotton is the main cash crop, rice, fruit and vegetables are exported, but Egypt imports

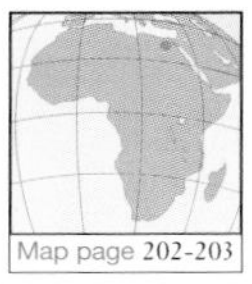
Map page 202-203

over half its food needs. There are oil and natural gas reserves, though nearly a quarter of electricity comes from hydro-electric power. Main exports are oil and oil products, cotton, textiles and clothing.

EL SALVADOR
Republic of El Salvador

Area Sq Km	21 041	Currency	Colón
Area Sq Miles	8 124	Languages	Spanish
Population	6 032 000	Religions	Roman Catholic, Protestant
Capital	San Salvador	Organizations	UN

A densely populated state on the Pacific coast of central America, El Salvador has a coastal plain and volcanic mountain ranges that enclose a plateau where most people live. The coast is hot, with heavy summer rainfall, the highlands are cooler. Coffee (the chief export), sugar and cotton are main cash crops. The main trading partners are USA and Guatemala.

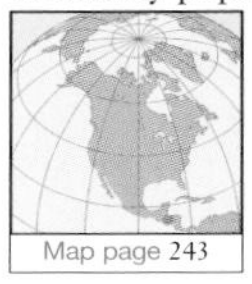
Map page 243

EQUATORIAL GUINEA
Republic of Equatorial Guinea

Area Sq Km	28 051	Currency	CFA franc
Area Sq Miles	10 831	Languages	Spanish, French, Fang
Population	431 000	Religions	Roman Catholic, traditional beliefs
Capital	Malabo	Organizations	UN

The state consists of Rio Muni, an enclave on the Atlantic coast of central Africa, and the islands of Bioco, Annobón and the Corisco group. Most people live on the coastal plain and upland plateau of Rio Muni; the capital is on the fertile volcanic island of Bioco. The climate is hot, humid and wet. Oil production started in 1992 and oil is now the main export along with timber, but the economy depends heavily upon foreign aid.

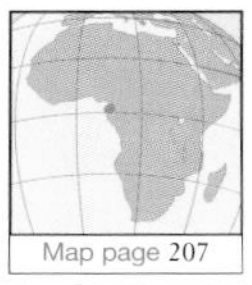
Map page 207

ERITREA
State of Eritrea

Area Sq Km	117 400	Currency	Nakfa
Area Sq Miles	45 328	Languages	Tigrinya, Tigre
Population	3 577 000	Religions	Sunni Muslim, Coptic Christian
Capital	Asmara	Organizations	UN

Eritrea, on the Red Sea coast of northeast Africa, consists of high plateau in the north and a coastal plain that widens to the south. The coast is hot, inland is cooler. Rainfall is unreliable. The agricultural-based economy has suffered from over thirty years of war and occasional poor rains. Eritrea is one of the least developed countries in the world.

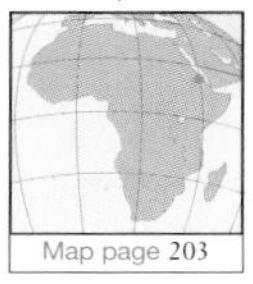
Map page 203

ESTONIA
Republic of Estonia

Area Sq Km	45 200	Currency	Kroon
Area Sq Miles	17 452	Languages	Estonian, Russian
Population	1 429 000	Religions	Protestant, Estonian and Russian Orthodox
Capital	Tallinn	Organizations	UN

Estonia is in north Europe, on the Gulf of Finland and Baltic Sea. The land, over one third of which is forested, is generally low-lying, with many lakes. The climate is temperate. About one third of Estonians live in Tallinn. Industries and exported goods include timber, furniture production, shipbuilding, leather, fur and food processing. The main trading partners are Russia, Finland and Sweden. Estonia is negotiating to join the EU.

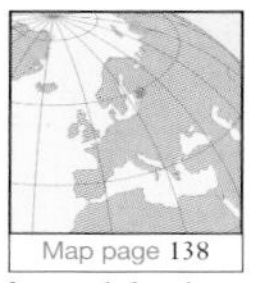
Map page 138

ETHIOPIA
Federal Democratic Republic of Ethiopia

Area Sq Km	1 133 880	Currency	Birr
Area Sq Miles	437 794	Languages	Oromo, Amharic, Tigrinya, local languages
Population	59 649 000	Religions	Ethiopian Orthodox, Muslim, trad. beliefs
Capital	Ādīs Ābeba	Organizations	UN

A landlocked country in northeast Africa, Ethiopia borders Eritrea, Djibouti, Somalia, Kenya and Sudan. The western half is a mountainous region traversed by the Great Rift Valley. To the east is mostly arid plateaus. The highlands are warm with summer rainfall, though droughts occur; the east is hot and dry. Most people live in the centre-north. Civil war, continued conflict with Eritrea and poor infrastructure hamper economic development. Subsistence farming is the main activity, though droughts have led to famine. Coffee is the main export and there is some light industry; Ethiopia remains one of the least developed countries in the world.

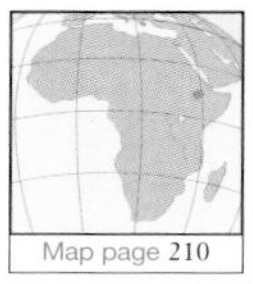
Map page 210

Falkland Islands
United Kingdom Overseas Territory

Area Sq Km	12 170	Currency	Pound
Area Sq Miles	4 699	Languages	English
Population	2 000	Religions	Protestant, Roman Catholic
Capital	Stanley		

Lying in the southwest Atlantic Ocean, northeast of Cape Horn, there are two main islands, West Falkland and East Falkland, where most of the population live, and many smaller islands. The economy is based on sheep farming and the sale of fishing licences, though oil has been discovered off-shore.

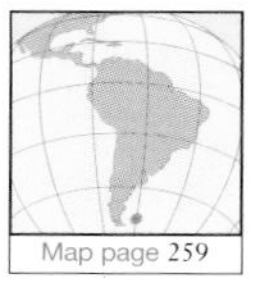
Map page 259

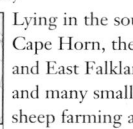

Faroe Islands
Self-governing Danish Territory

Area Sq Km	1 399	Currency	Danish krone
Area Sq Miles	540	Languages	Faroese, Danish
Population	43 000	Religions	Protestant
Capital	Tórshavn	Organizations	UN

A self governing territory, lying in the north Atlantic Ocean between the UK and Iceland. The islands benefit from the North Atlantic Drift which has a moderating effect on the climate. The economy is based on deep-sea fishing.

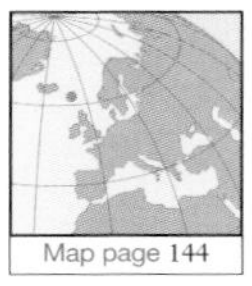
Map page 144

FIJI
Sovereign Democratic Republic of Fiji

Area Sq Km	18 330	Currency	Dollar
Area Sq Miles	7 077	Languages	English, Fijian, Hindi
Population	796 000	Religions	Christian, Hindu, Sunni Muslim
Capital	Suva	Organizations	Comm., UN

Fiji comprises two main islands, Vanua Levu and Viti Levu of volcanic origin and mountainous, and over three hundred smaller islands in the south Pacific Ocean. The climate is tropical and the economy is based on agriculture (chiefly sugar, the main export), fishing, forestry, gold mining and tourism.

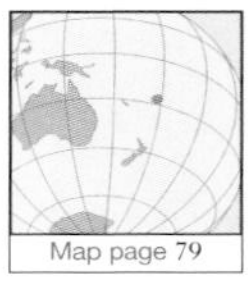
Map page 79

FINLAND
Republic of Finland

Area Sq Km	338 145	Currency	Markka, Euro
Area Sq Miles	130 559	Languages	Finnish, Swedish
Population	5 154 000	Religions	Protestant, Greek Orthodox
Capital	Helsinki	Organizations	EU, OECD, UN

Finland is in north Europe, on the Gulf of Bothnia and the Gulf of Finland. It is low-lying, forests cover over seventy per cent of the land area, only about eight per cent is cultivated, though Finland is self-sufficient in cereals and dairy products. Summers are short and warm, and winters are long and severe, particularly in the north. Most people live in the southern third of the country, along the coast or near the many lakes. Timber is a major resource and there are important mineral resources, chiefly chromium. Main industries include metal working, electronics, paper and paper products, and chemicals; these account for most of the exports. The main trading partners are Germany, Sweden and the UK.

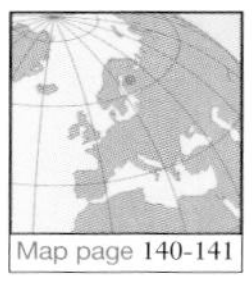
Map page 140-141

FRANCE
French Republic

Area Sq Km	543 965	Currency	Franc, Euro
Area Sq Miles	210 026	Languages	French, Arabic
Population	58 683 000	Religions	Roman Catholic, Protestant, Sunni Muslim
Capital	Paris	Organizations	EU, OECD, UN

France lies in southwest Europe, with coastlines on the Atlantic Ocean and Mediterranean Sea; it includes the Mediterranean island of Corsica. Northern and western regions consist mostly of flat or rolling countryside, and include the major lowlands of the Paris basin, the Loire valley and the Aquitaine basin, drained by the Seine, Loire and Garonne river systems respectively. The centre-south is dominated by the Massif Central. Eastwards, are the Vosges and Jura mountains and the Alps. In the southwest, the Pyrenees form a natural border with Spain. The climate is temperate with warm summers and cool winters, apart from the Mediterranean coast which has hot, dry summers and mild winters with some rainfall. Over seventy per cent of the population live in towns, but Greater Paris is the only major conurbation, with almost a sixth of the French population. Rich soil, a large cultivable area and contrasts in temperature and relief have given France a substantial and varied agricultural base; it is a major producer of both fresh and processed food. Major agricultural exports include cereals (chiefly wheat), dairy products, wines and sugar. France has relatively few mineral resources; it has coal reserves, some oil and natural gas, but it relies heavily on nuclear and hydroelectric power and imported fuels. France is one of the world's major industrial countries. Main industries include food processing, iron, steel and aluminium production, chemicals, cars, electronics and oil refining. The main exports are machinery, agricultural products, cars and other transport equipment. France has a strong services sector and tourism is a major source of revenue and employment. Trade is predominantly with other EU countries.

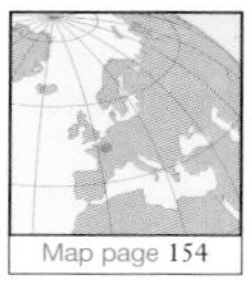
Map page 154

French Guiana
French Overseas Department

Area Sq Km	90 000	Currency	French franc
Area Sq Miles	34 749	Languages	French, creole
Population	167 000	Religions	Roman Catholic
Capital	Cayenne		

French Guiana, on the northeast coast of South America, is densely forested. The climate is tropical with high rainfall. Most people live in the coastal strip; agriculture is mostly subsistence farming; forestry and fishing are important, though timber and mineral resources are largely unexploited and industry is limited. French Guiana depends upon French aid. The European Space Agency (ESA) base is near Kourou.

Map page 251

FRENCH POLYNESIA
French Overseas Territory

Area Sq Km	3 265	Currency	Pacific franc
Area Sq Miles	1 261	Languages	French, Tahitian, Polynesian languages
Population	227 000	Religions	Protestant, Roman Catholic
Capital	Papeete		

Extending over a vast area of the southeast Pacific Ocean, French Polynesia comprises more than one hundred and thirty islands and coral atolls. The main island groups are the Marquesas Islands, the Tuamotu Archipelago and the Society Islands. The capital, Papeete, is on Tahiti in the Society Islands. The climate is subtropical and the economy is based on tourism.

Map page 79

French Southern and Antarctic Lands
French Overseas Territory

Area Sq Km (Miles) 439 580 (169 723) Population *uninhabited*

This territory includes Crozet Island, Kerguelen, Amsterdam Island and St Paul Island. All are uninhabited apart from scientific research staff. In accordance with the Antarctic Treaty, French territorial claims in Antarctica have been suspended.

Map page 73

GABON
Gabonese Republic

Area Sq Km	267 667	Currency	CFA franc
Area Sq Miles	103 347	Languages	French, Fang, local languages
Population	1 167 000	Religions	Roman Catholic, Protestant, traditional beliefs
Capital	Libreville	Organizations	UN

Gabon, on the Atlantic coast of central Africa consists of low plateaus, with a coastal plain lined by lagoons and mangrove swamps. The climate is tropical and rainforests cover over three quarters of the land area. Over seventy per cent of the population lives in towns. The economy is heavily dependent on oil, which accounts for around eighty per cent of exports; manganese, uranium and timber are the other exports. Agriculture is mainly at subsistence level.

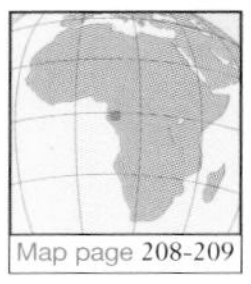
Map page 208-209

THE GAMBIA
Republic of The Gambia

Area Sq Km	11 295	Currency	Dalasi
Area Sq Miles	4 361	Languages	English, Malinke, Fulani, Wolof
Population	1 229 000	Religions	Sunni Muslim, Protestant
Capital	Banjul	Organizations	Comm., UN

The Gambia, on the coast of west Africa, occupies a strip of land along the lower Gambia river. Sandy beaches are backed by mangrove swamps, beyond which is savanna. The climate is tropical, with rainfall in the summer. Over seventy per cent of Gambians are farmers, growing chiefly groundnuts (the main export) but also cotton, oil palms and food crops. Livestock rearing and fishing are important, while manufacturing is limited. Re-exports, mainly from Senegal, and tourism are major sources of income.

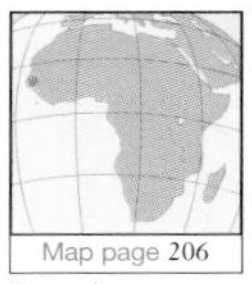
Map page 206

Gaza semi-autonomous region

Area Sq Km	363	Currency	Israeli shekel
Area Sq Miles	140	Languages	Arabic
Population	1 036 000	Religions	Sunni Muslim, Shi'a Muslim
Capital	Gaza		

Gaza is a narrow strip of land on the southeast corner of the Mediterranean Sea, between Egypt and Israel. The Palestinian territory has limited autonomy from Israel.

Map page 128

GEORGIA
Republic of Georgia

Area Sq Km	69 700	Currency	Lari
Area Sq Miles	26 911	Languages	Georgian, Russian, Armenian, Azeri, Ossetian, Abkhaz
Population	5 059 000	Religions	Georgian Orthodox, Russian Orthodox, Sunni Muslim
Capital	T'bilisi	Organizations	CIS, UN

Georgia is in the northwest Caucasus, in southwest Asia, on the Black Sea. Mountain ranges in the north and south flank the Kura and Rioni valleys. The climate is generally mild, but subtropical along the coast. Agriculture is important, with tea, grapes, and citrus fruits the main crops. Mineral resources include manganese, coal and oil, and the main industries are steel, oil refining and machine building. Economic development remains slow.

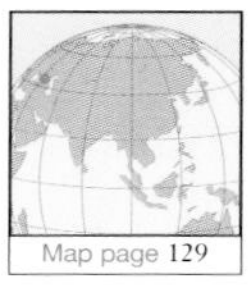
Map page 129

GERMANY
Federal Republic of Germany

Area Sq Km	357 028	Currency	Mark, Euro
Area Sq Miles	137 849	Languages	German, Turkish
Population	82 133 000	Religions	Protestant, Roman Catholic
Capital	Berlin	Organizations	EU, OECD, UN

The west European state of Germany borders nine countries and has coastlines on the North and Baltic Seas. Behind the indented coastline, and covering about one third of the country, is the north German plain, a region of fertile farmland and sandy heaths drained by the country's major rivers. The central highlands are a belt of forested hills and plateaus which stretches from the Eifel region in the west to the Erzgebirge along the border with the Czech Republic. Farther south the land rises to the Schwäbische Alb, with the high rugged and forested Schwarzald (Black Forest) in the southwest and the Alps in the far south. The climate is temperate, with continental conditions in eastern areas where

Map page 166-167

winters are colder. The population is highly urbanized with over eighty-five per cent living in cities and towns. With the exception of coal, lignite, potash and baryte, Germany lacks minerals and other industrial raw materials. It has a small agricultural base, though a few products (chiefly wines and beers) enjoy an international reputation. Germany is the world's third ranking economy after that of USA and Japan. It's industries are amongst the world's most technologically advanced, producing machinery, motor vehicles, electrical equipment, chemicals and pharmaceuticals. The majority of trade is with other countries in the EU.

Baden-Württemberg (State)

Area Sq Km (Miles) 35 751 (13 804)	Population 10 374 505	Capital Stuttgart

Bayern (State)

Area Sq Km (Miles) 70 552 (27 240)	Population 12 043 869	Capital München

Berlin(State)

Area Sq Km (Miles) 891 (344)	Population 3 467 322	Capital Berlin

Brandenburg(State)

Area Sq Km (Miles) 29 476 (11 381)	Population 2 554 441	Capital Potsdam

Bremen(State)

Area Sq Km (Miles) 404 (156)	Population 678 731	Capital Bremen

Hamburg(State)

Area Sq Km (Miles) 755 (292)	Population 1 708 528	Capital Hamburg

Hessen(State)

Area Sq Km (Miles) 21 114 (8 152)	Population 6 027 284	Capital Wiesbaden

Mecklenburg-Vorpommern(State)

Area Sq Km (Miles) 23 170 (8 946)	Population 1 817 196	Capital Schwerin

Niedersachsen(State)

Area Sq Km (Miles) 47 612 (18 383)	Population 7 795 149	Capital Hannover

Nordrhein-Westfalen(State)

Area Sq Km (Miles) 34 079 (13 158)	Population 17 947 715	Capital Düsseldorf

Rheinland-Pfalz(State)

Area Sq Km (Miles) 19 853 (7 665)	Population 4 009 753	Capital Mainz

Saarland(State)

Area Sq Km (Miles) 2 570 (992)	Population 1 084 184	Capital Saarbrücken

Sachsen(State)

Area Sq Km (Miles) 18 413 (7 109)	Population 4 545 702	Capital Dresden

Sachsen-Anhalt(State)

Area Sq Km (Miles) 20 446 (7 894)	Population 2 731 463	Capital Magdeburg

Schleswig-Holstein(State)

Area Sq Km (Miles) 15 771 (6 089)	Population 2 742 293	Capital Kiel

Thüringen(State)

Area Sq Km (Miles) 16 171 (6 244)	Population 2 491 119	Capital Erfurt

GHANA
Republic of Ghana

Area Sq Km	238 537	Currency	Cedi
Area Sq Miles	92 100	Languages	English, Hausa, Akan, local languages
Population	19 162 000	Religions	Christian, Sunni Muslim, traditional beliefs
Capital	Accra	Organizations	Comm., UN

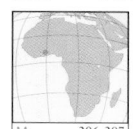
Map page 206-207

A west African state on the Gulf of Guinea, Ghana is a land of plains and low plateaus covered with savanna and rainforest. In the east is the Volta basin. The climate is tropical, with high rainfall in the south, where most people live. Agriculture employs around sixty per-cent of the workforce, main exports are gold, timber, cocoa and manganese ore.

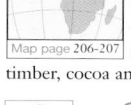
Gibraltar
United Kingdom Overseas Territory

Area Sq Km	7	Currency	Pound
Area Sq Miles	3	Languages	English, Spanish
Population	25 000	Religions	Roman Catholic, Protestant, Sunni Muslim
Capital	Gibraltar		

Gibraltar lies on the south coast of Spain at the western entrance to the Mediterranean Sea. The economy depends on tourism, offshore banking and shipping services.

Map page 185

GREECE
Hellenic Republic

Area Sq Km	131 957	Currency	Drachma
Area Sq Miles	50 949	Languages	Greek
Population	10 600 000	Religions	Greek Orthodox, Sunni Muslim
Capital	Athina	Organizations	EU, OECD, UN

Map page 198-199

Greece occupies the southern Balkans in south Europe and many islands in the Ionian, Aegean and Mediterranean Seas. The islands make up over one fifth of its area. Mountains and hills cover much of the country. The most important lowlands are the plains of Thessalia in the centre-east and around Thessalonika in the northeast. Summers are hot and dry. Winters are mild and wet, but colder in the north with heavy snowfalls in the mountains. One third of Greeks live in the Athina area. Employment in agriculture is decreasing, but still accounts for around twenty per cent of the workforce and exports include citrus fruits, raisins, wine, olives and olive oil. Aluminium and nickel are mined and a wide range of manufactures are produced including food and tobacco, textiles, clothing, and chemicals. Tourism is an important industry and there is a large services sector. Most trade is with other EU countries.

GREENLAND
Self-governing Danish Territory

Area Sq Km	2 175 600	Currency	Danish krone
Area Sq Miles	840 004	Languages	Greenlandic, Danish
Population	56 000	Religions	Protestant
Capital	Nuuk		

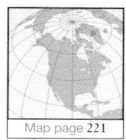
Map page 221

Situated to the northeast of North America between the Atlantic and Arctic Oceans, Greenland is the largest island in the world. It has a polar climate and over eighty per cent of the land area is permanent ice cap. The economy is based on fishing and fish processing.

GRENADA

Area Sq Km	378	Currency	E. Carib. dollar
Area Sq Miles	146	Languages	English, creole
Population	93 000	Religions	Roman Catholic, Protestant
Capital	St George's	Organizations	CARICOM, Comm., UN

The Caribbean state comprises Grenada, the most southerly of the Windward Islands, and the southern islands of The Grenadines. Grenada has wooded hills, beaches in the southwest, a warm climate and good rainfall. Agriculture is the main activity, with bananas, nutmeg and cocoa the main exports. Tourism is the main foreign exchange earner.

Map page 247

Guadeloupe
French Overseas Department

Area Sq Km	1 780	Currency	French franc
Area Sq Miles	687	Languages	French, creole
Population	443 000	Religions	Roman Catholic
Capital	Basse-Terre		

Guadeloupe, in the Leeward Islands in the Caribbean, consists of two main islands, Basse-Terre and Grande Terre, connected by a bridge, Marie Galante and a few outer islands. The climate is tropical, but moderated by trade winds. Bananas, sugar and rum, tourism and French aid are the main sources of foreign exchange.

Map page 247

Guam
United States Unincorporated Territory

Area Sq Km	541	Currency	US dollar
Area Sq Miles	209	Languages	Chamorro, English, Tagalog
Population	161 000	Religions	Roman Catholic
Capital	Agana		

Lying at the south end of the North Mariana Islands in the western Pacific Ocean, Guam has a humid tropical climate. The island has a large US military base and the economy relies on that and on tourism, which has grown rapidly.

Map page 91

GUATEMALA
Republic of Guatemala

Area Sq Km	108 890	Currency	Quetzal
Area Sq Miles	42 043	Languages	Spanish, Mayan languages
Population	10 801 000	Religions	Roman Catholic, Protestant
Capital	Guatemala		

Map page 243

The most populous country in Central America after Mexico, Guatemala has a long Pacific and a short Caribbean coastline. Northern areas are lowland tropical forests. To the south lie the mountain ranges with some active volcanoes, then the Pacific coastal plain. The climate is hot tropical in the lowlands, cooler in the highlands, where most people live. Farming is the main activity, coffee, sugar and bananas are the main exports. There is some manufacturing (chiefly clothing and textiles). Most trade is with USA.

GUERNSEY
United Kingdom Crown Dependency

Area Sq Km	78	Currency	Pound
Area Sq Miles	30	Languages	English, French
Population	64 555	Religions	Protestant, Roman Catholic
Capital	St Peter Port		

One of the Channel Islands lying off the west coast of the Cherbourg peninsula in northern France.

Map page 158

GUINEA
Republic of Guinea

Area Sq Km	245 857	Currency	Franc
Area Sq Miles	94 926	Languages	French, Fulani, Malinke, local languages
Population	7 337 000	Religions	Sunni Muslim, traditional beliefs, Christian
Capital	Conakry	Organizations	UN

Map page 206

Guinea is in west Africa, on the Atlantic Ocean. There are mangrove swamps along the coast, inland are lowlands and then the Fouta Djallon mountains and plateaus. To the east are savanna plains drained by the upper Niger river system, while to the southeast are mountains. The climate is tropical, with high coastal rainfall. Agriculture is the main activity employing nearly eighty per cent of the workforce, with coffee, bananas and pineapples the chief cash crops. There are huge reserves of bauxite; bauxite, alumina, gold, coffee and diamonds are the main exports.

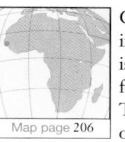
GUINEA-BISSAU
Republic of Guinea-Bissau

Area Sq Km	36 125	Currency	CFA franc
Area Sq Miles	13 948	Languages	Portuguese, crioulo, local languages
Population	1 161 000	Religions	Traditional beliefs, Sunni Muslim, Christian
Capital	Bissau	Organizations	UN

Map page 206

Guinea-Bissau, on the Atlantic coast of west Africa, includes the Bijagos Archipelago. The mainland coast is swampy and contains many estuaries. Inland are forested plains and to the east are savanna plateaus. The climate is tropical. The economy is based mainly on subsistence farming, there is little industry and timber and mineral resources are largely unexploited. Cashews make up over eighty per cent of exports. Guinea-Bissau is one of the least developed countries in the world.

GUYANA
Co-operative Republic of Guyana

Area Sq Km	214 969	Currency	Dollar
Area Sq Miles	83 000	Languages	English, creole, Amerindian languages
Population	850 000	Religions	Protestant, Hindu, Roman Catholic, Sunni Muslim
Capital	Georgetown	Organizations	CARICOM, Comm., UN

Map page 251

Guyana, on the northeast coast of South America, consists of the highlands in the west, and the savanna uplands of the southwest. Most of the country is densely forested; a lowland coastal belt supports crops and most of the population. The generally hot, humid and wet conditions are modified along the coast by sea breezes. The economy is based on agriculture, mining and forestry. Sugar, bauxite, gold, rice and timber are the main exports.

HAITI
Republic of Haiti

Area Sq Km	27 750	Currency	Gourde
Area Sq Miles	10 714	Languages	French, creole
Population	7 952 000	Religions	Roman Catholic, Protestant, Voodoo
Capital	Port-au-Prince	Organizations	CARICOM, Comm., UN

Haiti, occupying the western third of the Caribbean island of Hispaniola, is a mountainous state, with small coastal plains and a central valley. The Dominican Republic occupies the rest of the island. The climate is tropical, hottest in coastal areas. Haiti has few natural resources, is overpopulated and relies on exports of local crafts and coffee, and remittances from workers abroad.

Map page 246

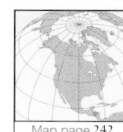
HONDURAS
Republic of Honduras

Area Sq Km	112 088	Currency	Lempira
Area Sq Miles	43 277	Languages	Spanish, Amerindian languages
Population	6 147 000	Religions	Roman Catholic, Protestant
Capital	Tegucigalpa	Organizations	UN

Map page 242

Honduras, in central America, is a mountainous and forested country with lowland areas along its long Caribbean and short Pacific coasts. Coastal areas are hot and humid with heavy summer rainfall, inland is cooler and drier. Most people live in the central valleys. Coffee and bananas are the main exports, along with shrimps and zinc. Industry involves mainly agricultural processing. Honduras was the country hardest hit by hurricane Mitch in 1998 but has received significant aid for reconstruction.

HUNGARY
Republic of Hungary

Area Sq Km	93 030	Currency	Forint
Area Sq Miles	35 919	Languages	Hungarian
Population	10 116 000	Religions	Roman Catholic, Protestant
Capital	Budapest	Organizations	OECD, UN

Map page 176-177

A landlocked country in central Europe, Hungary borders Austria, Slovakia, Ukraine, Romania, Yugoslavia, Croatia and Slovenia. The Danube river flows north-south through central Hungary. To the east lies a great plain, flanked by highlands in the north. To the west low mountains and Lake Balaton separate a small plain and southern uplands. The climate is continental, with warm summers and cold winters. Sixty per cent of the population live in urban areas, and one fifth lives in Budapest. Some minerals and energy resources are exploited, chiefly bauxite, coal and natural gas. Hungary has an industrial economy. The main industries produce metals, machinery, transport equipment, chemicals and food products. The main trading partners are Germany and Austria. Hungary is negotiating to join the EU.

ICELAND
Republic of Iceland

Area Sq Km	102 820	Currency	Króna
Area Sq Miles	39 699	Languages	Icelandic
Population	276 000	Religions	Protestant
Capital	Reykjavik	Organizations	OECD, UN

Map page 140

Iceland lies in the Atlantic Ocean, near the Arctic Circle to the northwest of Scandinavia. It consists mainly of a plateau of basalt lava flows. Some of its two hundred volcanoes are active, and there are geysers and hot springs; one tenth of the country is covered by ice caps. Only coastal lowlands can be cultivated and settled, and over half the population lives in the Reykjavik area. The climate is mild, moderated by the North Atlantic Drift and southwesterly winds. The mainstay of the economy is fishing and fish processing, which account for seventy per cent of exports. Agriculture involves mainly sheep and dairy farming. Hydro-electric and geothermal energy resources are considerable. The main industries produce aluminium, ferro-silicon and fertilizers. Tourism, including ecotourism, is growing in importance.

INDIA
Republic of India

Area Sq Km	3 065 027	Currency	Rupee
Area Sq Miles	1 183 414	Languages	Hindi, English, many regional languages
Population	982 223 000	Religions	Hindu, Sunni Muslim, Shi'a Muslim, Sikh, Christian
Capital	New Delhi	Organizations	Comm., UN

The south Asian state of India occupies a peninsula that juts out into the Indian Ocean between the Arabian Sea and Bay of Bengal. The heart of the peninsula is the Deccan plateau, bordered on either side by ranges of hills, the Western Ghats and the lower Eastern Ghats, which fall away to narrow coastal plains. To the north is a broad plain, drained by the Indus, Ganges and Brahmaputra rivers and their tributaries. The plain is intensively farmed and is the most populous region. In the west is the Thar Desert. The Himalaya form India's northern border, together with parts of the Karakoram and Hindu Kush ranges in the northwest. The climate shows marked seasonal variation: the hot season from March to June; the monsoon season from June to October; and the cold season from November to

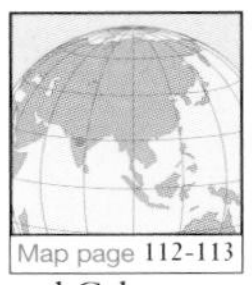
Map page 112-113

February. Rainfall ranges between very high in the northeast Assam region to negligible in the Thar Desert, while temperatures range from very cold in the Himayalas to tropical heat over much of the south. Over seventy per cent of the huge population – the second largest in the world – is rural, though Mumbai and Calcutta rank among the ten largest cities in the world. Agriculture, forestry and fishing account for a quarter of national output and two thirds of employment. Much of the farming is on a subsistence basis and involves mainly rice and wheat growing. India is a major world producer of tea, sugar, jute, cotton and tobacco. Livestock is raised mainly for dairy products and hides. India has major reserves of coal, reserves of oil and natural gas and many minerals, including iron, manganese, bauxite, diamonds and gold. The manufacturing sector is large and diverse. The main manufactures are chemicals and chemical products, textiles, iron and steel, food products, electrical goods and transport equipment; software and pharmaceuticals are also important. All the main manufactured products are exported, together with diamonds and jewellery. The USA, Germany, Japan and the UK are the main trading partners.

INDONESIA
Republic of Indonesia

Area Sq Km	1 919 445	Currency	Rupiah
Area Sq Miles	741 102	Languages	Indonesian, local languages
Population	206 338 000	Religions	Sunni Muslim, Protestant, Roman Catholic
Capital	Jakarta	Organizations	APEC, ASEAN, OPEC, UN

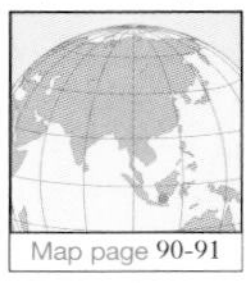
Map page 90-91

Indonesia, the largest and most populous country in southeast Asia, consists of over thirteen thousand islands extending along the equator between the Pacific and Indian Oceans. Sumatera, Jawa, Sulawesi, Kalimantan (two thirds of Borneo) and Irian Jaya (western New Guinea) make up ninety per cent of the land area. Most of Indonesia is mountainous and covered with rainforest or mangrove swamps, and there are over three hundred volcanoes, many active. Two thirds of the population live in the lowland areas of Jawa and Madura. The climate is tropical monsoon. Agriculture is the largest sector of the economy and Indonesia is among the world's top producers of rice, palm oil, tea, coffee, rubber and tobacco. It is the world's leading exporter of natural gas, a major exporter of oil and timber, and a major producer of tin. A range of goods are produced including textiles, clothing, cement, fertilizer and vehicles. Main exports are oil, natural gas, timber products and clothing. The main trading partner is Japan. However, Indonesia remains a relatively poor country, and ethnic tensions and civil unrest are hindering economic development.

IRAN
Islamic Republic of Iran

Area Sq Km	1 648 000	Currency	Rial
Area Sq Miles	636 296	Languages	Farsi, Azeri, Kurdish, regional languages
Population	65 758 000	Religions	Shi'a Muslim, Sunni Muslim
Capital	Tehrān	Organizations	OPEC, UN

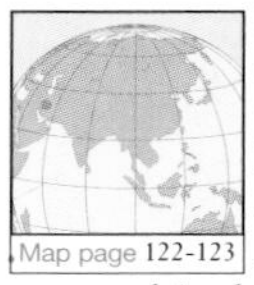
Map page 122-123

Iran is in southwest Asia, on The Gulf, the Gulf of Oman and Caspian Sea. Eastern Iran is high plateau, with large salt pans and a vast sand desert. In the west the Zagros Mountains form a series of ridges, while to the north lie the Elburz Mountains. Most farming and settlement is on the narrow plain along the Caspian Sea and the foothills of the north and west. The climate is one of extremes, with hot summers and very cold winters. Most of the light rainfall is in the winter months. Agriculture involves about a third of the workforce. Wheat is the main crop but fruit (chiefly dates) and pistachio nuts are grown for export. Petroleum (the main export) and natural gas are Iran's leading natural resources. Manufactures include carpets, clothing, food products and construction materials.

IRAQ
Republic of Iraq

Area Sq Km	438 317	Currency	Dinar
Area Sq Miles	169 235	Languages	Arabic, Kurdish, Turkmen
Population	21 800 000	Religions	Shi'a Muslim, Sunni Muslim, Christian
Capital	Baghdād	Organizations	OPEC, UN

Iraq, which lies on the northwest shores of The Gulf in southwest Asia, has at its heart the lowland valley of the Tigris and Euphrates rivers. In the southeast where the two rivers join are marshes and the Shatt al Arab waterway. Northern Iraq is hilly, while western Iraq is desert. Summers are hot and dry, while winters are mild with light, unreliable

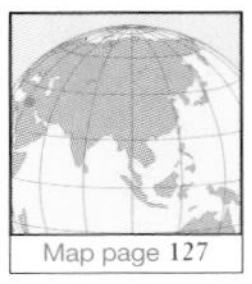
Map page 127

rainfall. The Tigris-Euphrates valley contains most of the arable land and population, including one in five who live in Baghdād. Defeat in the 1991 Gulf war and continued international sanctions have ruined the economy and caused considerable hardship. Oil is exported, almost all to Japan.

IRELAND, REPUBLIC OF

Area Sq Km	70 282	Currency	Punt, Euro
Area Sq Miles	27 136	Languages	English, Irish
Population	3 681 000	Religions	Roman Catholic, Protestant
Capital	Dublin	Organizations	EU, OECD, UN

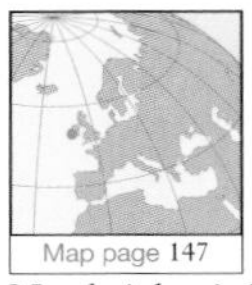
Map page 147

A state in northwest Europe, the Irish Republic occupies some eighty per cent of the island of Ireland. It is a lowland country of wide valleys, lakes and peat bogs, with isolated mountain ranges around the coast. The west coast is rugged and indented with many bays. The climate is mild due to the North Atlantic Drift and rainfall is plentiful, though highest in the west. Nearly sixty per cent of people live in urban areas, Dublin and Cork being the main cities. Resources include natural gas, peat, lead and zinc. Agriculture, the traditional mainstay, now employs less than ten per cent of the workforce, while industry employs nearly thirty per cent. The main industries are electronics, pharmaceuticals and engineering as well as food processing, brewing and textiles. Service industries are expanding, with tourism a major foreign exchange earner. The UK is the main trading partner.

Isle of Man
United Kingdom Crown Dependency

Area Sq Km	572	Currency	Pound
Area Sq Miles	221	Languages	English
Population	77 000	Religions	Protestant, Roman Catholic
Capital	Douglas		

In the Irish Sea, the island is self governing while the UK is responsible for defense and foreign affairs. The island is not part of the EU, but has a special relationship with the EU which allows for free trade.

Map page 148

ISRAEL
State of Israel

Area Sq Km	20 770	Currency	Shekel
Area Sq Miles	8 019	Languages	Hebrew, Arabic
Population	5 984 000	Religions	Jewish, Sunni Muslim, Christian, Druze
Capital	Jerusalem	Organizations	UN

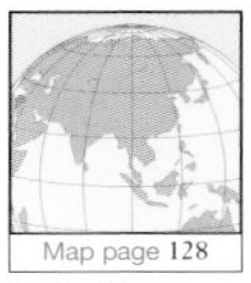
Map page 128

Israel lies on the Mediterranean coast of southwest Asia. Beyond the coastal Plain of Sharon are the hills and valleys of Samaria with the Galilee highlands to the north. In the east is the rift valley, which extends from Lake Tiberias to the Gulf of Aqaba and contains the Jordan river and Dead Sea. In the south is the Negev, a triangular semi-desert plateau. Most people live on the coastal plain or in northern and central areas. Much of Israel has warm summers and mild, wet winters. Southern Israel is hot and dry. Agricultural production was boosted by the inclusion of the West Bank in 1967. Mineral resources are few, and manufacturing makes the largest contribution to the economy. Israel exports machinery and transport equipment, diamonds, clothing, fruit and vegetables. Tourism and foreign aid are important to the economy.

ITALY
Italian Republic

Area Sq Km	301 245	Currency	Lira, Euro
Area Sq Miles	116 311	Languages	Italian
Population	57 369 000	Religions	Roman Catholic
Capital	Roma	Organizations	EU, OECD, UN

Most of the south European state of Italy occupies a peninsula that juts out into the Mediterranean Sea. It includes the islands of Sicily and Sardinia and about seventy much smaller islands in the surrounding seas. Italy is mountainous and dominated by two high ranges: the Alps, which form its northern border; and the various ranges of the Apennines, which run almost the full length of the peninsula. Many of Italy's mountains are of volcanic origin and its active volcanoes are

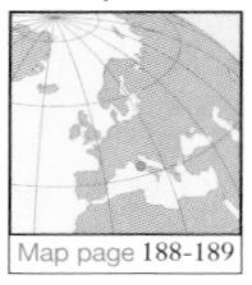
Map page 188-189

Vesuvio, near Naples, Etna and Stromboli. The main lowland area, the Po river valley in the northeast, is the main agricultural and industrial area and is the most populous region. Italy has a Mediterranean climate with warm, dry summers and mild winters. Northern Italy experiences colder, wetter winters, with heavy snow in the Alps. Italy's natural resources are limited. Only about twenty per cent of the land is suitable for cultivation. Some oil, natural gas and coal are produced, but most fuels and minerals used by industry must be imported. Italy has a fairly diversified economy. Agriculture is important, with cereals, vines, fruit and vegetables the main crops; Italy is the world's largest wine producer. The north is the centre of Italian industry, especially around Turin, Milan and Genoa. Italy's leading manufactures include industrial and office equipment, domestic appliances, cars, textiles, clothing, leather goods, chemicals and metal products. Italy has a strong service sector. With over twenty-five million visitors a year, tourism is a major employer and accounts for five per cent of the national income. Finance and banking are also important. Most trade is with other EU countries.

JAMAICA

Area Sq Km	10 991	Currency	Dollar
Area Sq Miles	4 244	Languages	English, creole
Population	2 538 000	Religions	Protestant, Roman Catholic
Capital	Kingston	Organizations	CARICOM, Comm., UN

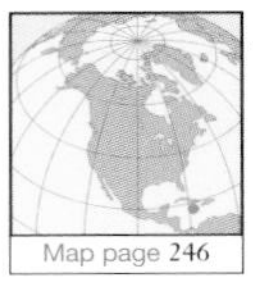
Map page 246

Jamaica, the third largest Caribbean island, has beaches and densely populated coastal plains traversed by hills and plateaus rising to the forested Blue Mountains in the east. The climate is tropical, but cooler and wetter on high ground. The economy is based on tourism, agriculture, mining and light manufacturing. Bauxite, alumina, sugar and bananas are the main exports. The USA is the main trading partner. Jamaica receives foreign aid.

Jammu and Kashmir Disputed territory (India,Pakistan)

Area Sq Km (Miles)	222 236 (85 806)	Population	13 000 000	Capital	Srinagar

A region in the north of Pakistan and India to the west of the Karakoram and Himalaya. The 'Line of control' separates the northern, Pakistani controlled area and the southern, Indian controlled area.

Map page 116

JAPAN

Area Sq Km	377 727	Currency	Yen
Area Sq Miles	145 841	Languages	Japanese
Population	126 281 000	Religions	Shintoist, Buddhist, Christian
Capital	Tōkyō	Organizations	APEC, OECD, UN

Japan, lies in the Pacific Ocean off the coast of east Asia and consists of four main islands - Hokkaidō, Honshū, Shikoku and Kyūshū - and more than three thousand smaller islands in the surrounding Sea of

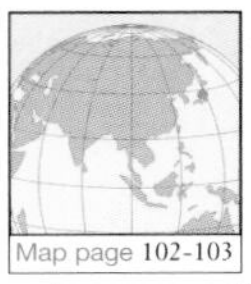
Map page 102-103

Japan, East China Sea and Pacific Ocean. The central island of Honshū accounts for sixty per cent of the total land area and contains eighty per cent of the population. Behind the long and deeply indented coastline, nearly three quarters of Japan is mountainous and heavily forested. Japan has over sixty active volcanoes, and is subject to frequent earthquakes, typhoons and tidal waves. The climate is generally temperate maritime, with warm summers and mild winters, except in western Hokkaidō and northwest Honshū, where the winters are very cold with heavy snow. Japan has few natural resources. It has a limited land area of which only fourteen per cent is suitable for cultivation, and production of its few industrial raw materials: coal, oil, natural gas, lead, zinc and copper is insufficient for its industry. Most raw materials must be imported, including about ninety per cent of energy requirements. Yet Japan is the world's second largest industrial economy, with a range of modern heavy and light industries centred mainly around the major ports of Yokohama, Ōsaka and Tōkyō. It is the world's largest manufacturer of cars, motorcycles and merchant ships, and a major producer of steel, textiles, chemicals and cement. It is a leading producer of many consumer durables, such as washing machines, and electronic equipment, chiefly office equipment and computers. Japan has a strong service sector, banking and finance are particularly important and Tōkyō is one of the world's major stock exchanges. Owing to intensive agricultural production, Japan is seventy per cent self-sufficient in food. The main food crops are rice, barley, fruit, wheat and soya beans. Livestock raising (chiefly cattle, pigs and chickens) and fishing are also important. Japan has one of the largest fishing fleets in the world. A major trading nation, Japan has trade links with many countries in southeast Asia and in Europe, though the main trading partner is USA.

Jersey
United Kingdom Crown Dependency

Area Sq Km	116	Currency	Pound
Area Sq Miles	45	Languages	English, French
Population	89 136	Religions	Protestant, Roman Catholic
Capital	St Helier		

One of the Channel Islands lying off the west coast of the Cherbourg peninsula in northern France.

Map page 148

JORDAN
Hashemite Kingdom of Jordan

Area Sq Km	89 206	Currency	Dinar
Area Sq Miles	34 443	Languages	Arabic
Population	6 304 000	Religions	Sunni Muslim, Christian
Capital	'Ammān	Organizations	UN

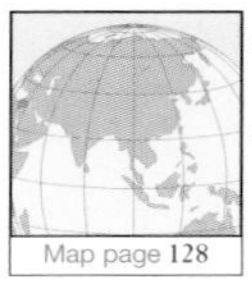
Map page 128

Jordan, in southwest Asia, is landlocked apart from a short coastline on the Gulf of Aqaba. Much of Jordan is rocky desert plateaus. To the west of the mountains, the land falls below sea level to the Dead Sea and Jordan river. Much of Jordan is hot and dry, the west is cooler and wetter; most people live in the northwest. Phosphates, potash, pharmaceuticals, fruit and vegetables are the main exports. Jordan's economy relies upon tourism, workers' remittances and foreign aid.

KAZAKHSTAN
Republic of Kazakhstan

Area Sq Km	2 717 300	Currency	Tenge
Area Sq Miles	1 049 155	Languages	Kazakh, Russian, Ukrainian, German, Uzbek, Tatar
Population	16 319 000	Religions	Sunni Muslim, Russian Orthodox, Protestant
Capital	Astana	Organizations	CIS, UN

Stretching across central Asia, Kazakhstan covers a vast area of steppe land and semi-desert. The land is flat in the west rising to mountains in

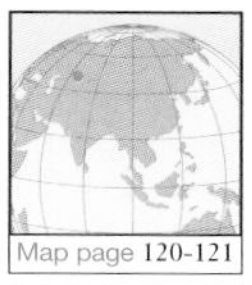
Map page 120-121

the southeast. The climate is continental and mainly dry. Agriculture and livestock rearing are important, with cotton and tobacco the main cash crops. Kazakhstan is very rich in minerals, including coal, chromium, gold, molybdenum, lead and zinc and has substantial reserves of oil and gas; oil pipelines to the Black Sea are planned. Mining, metallurgy, machine building and food processing are major industries. Oil and gas, and minerals are the main exports and Russia is the dominant trading partner.

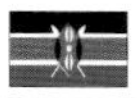

KENYA
Republic of Kenya

Area Sq Km	582 646	Currency	Shilling
Area Sq Miles	224 961	Languages	Swahili, English, local languages
Population	29 008 000	Religions	Christian, traditional beliefs
Capital	Nairobi	Organizations	Comm., UN

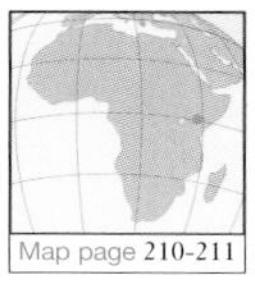
Map page 210-211

Kenya is in east Africa, on the Indian Ocean. Inland beyond the coastal plains the land rises to plateaus interrupted by volcanic mountains. The Great Rift Valley runs north-south to the west of Nairobi. Most people live in central Kenya. Conditions are tropical on the coast, semi-desert in the north and savanna in the south. Hydro-electric power from the Upper Tana river provides most of the electricity requirement. Agricultural products, mainly tea, coffee, fruit and vegetables are the main exports. Light industry is important. Tourism is the main foreign exchange earner; oil refining and re-exports for landlocked neighbours are others.

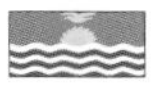

KIRIBATI
Republic of Kiribati

Area Sq Km	717	Currency	Australian dollar
Area Sq Miles	277	Languages	Gilbertese, English
Population	81 000	Religions	Roman Catholic, Protestant
Capital	Bairiki	Organizations	Comm., UN

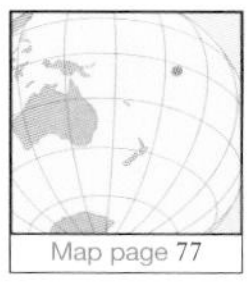
Map page 77

Kiribati comprises coral islands in the Gilbert, Phoenix and Line groups and the volcanic island of Banaba, straddling the equator in the Pacific Ocean. Most people live on the Gilbert Islands, and the capital, Bairiki, is on Tarawa, one of the Gilbert Islands. The climate is hot, wetter in the north. Copra and fish are exported, but Kiribati relies on remittances from workers abroad and foreign aid.

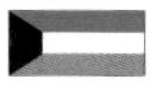

KUWAIT
State of Kuwait

Area Sq Km	17 818	Currency	Dinar
Area Sq Miles	6 880	Languages	Arabic
Population	1 811 000	Religions	Sunni Muslim, Shi'a Muslim, Christian, Hindu
Capital	Kuwait	Organizations	OPEC, UN

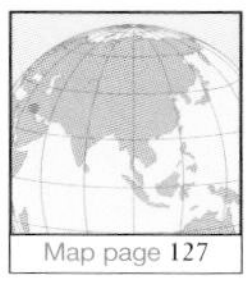
Map page 127

Kuwait lies on the northwest shores of The Gulf in southwest Asia. It is mainly low-lying desert, with irrigated areas along the bay, Kuwait Jun, where most people live. Summers are hot and dry, winters are cool with some rainfall. The oil industry, which accounts for eighty per cent of exports, has largely recovered from the damage caused by Iraq in 1991. Income is also derived from extensive overseas investments.

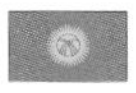

KYRGYZSTAN
Kyrgyz Republic

Area Sq Km	198 500	Currency	Som
Area Sq Miles	76 641	Languages	Kyrgyz, Russian, Uzbek
Population	4 643 000	Religions	Sunni Muslim, Russian Orthodox
Capital	Bishkek	Organizations	CIS, UN

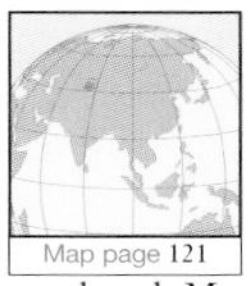
Map page 121

A landlocked central Asian state, Kyrgyzstan is rugged and mountainous, lying to the west of the Tien Shan range. Most people live in the valleys of the north and west. Summers are hot and winters cold. Agriculture (chiefly livestock farming) is the main activity. Some oil and gas, coal, gold, antimony and mercury are produced. Manufactures include machinery, metals and products, which are the main exports. Most trade is with the Russian Federation, Kazakhstan and Uzbekistan.

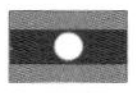

LAOS
Lao People's Democratic Republic

Area Sq Km	236 800	Currency	Kip
Area Sq Miles	91 429	Languages	Lao, local languages
Population	5 163 000	Religions	Buddhist, traditional beliefs
Capital	Viangchan	Organizations	ASEAN, UN

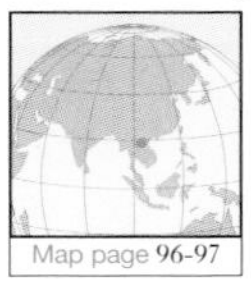
Map page 96-97

A landlocked country in southeast Asia, Laos borders Vietnam, Cambodia, Thailand, Myanmar and China. The land is mostly forested mountains and plateaus. The climate is tropical monsoon. Most people live in the Mekong valley and the low plateau in the south, and grow food crops, chiefly rice. Hydro-electricity from a plant on the Mekong, timber, coffee and tin are exported, but Laos depends on aid.

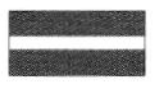

LATVIA
Republic of Latvia

Area Sq Km	63 700	Currency	Lat
Area Sq Miles	24 595	Languages	Latvian, Russian
Population	2 424 000	Religions	Protestant, Roman Catholic, Russian Orthodox
Capital	Riga	Organizations	UN

Latvia is in north Europe, on the Baltic Sea and Gulf of Riga. The land is flat near the coast but hilly with woods and lakes inland. Latvia has a modified continental climate. One third of the people live in Riga.

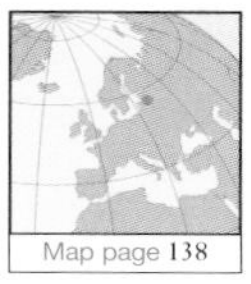
Map page 138

Crop and livestock farming are important. Latvia has few natural resources. Industries include food products, transport equipment, wood and wood products and textiles; these form most of the exports. The main trading partners are Russia and Germany. Latvia is negotiating to join the EU.

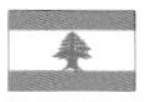

LEBANON
Republic of Lebanon

Area Sq Km	10 452	Currency	Pound
Area Sq Miles	4 036	Languages	Arabic, Armenian, French
Population	3 191 000	Religions	Shi'a Muslim, Sunni Muslim, Christian
Capital	Beirut	Organizations	UN

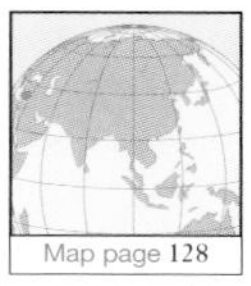
Map page 128

Lebanon lies on the Mediterranean coast of southwest Asia. Beyond the coastal strip, where most people live, are two parallel mountain ranges, separated by the El Beq'a valley. The 1975-1991 civil war crippled the traditional sectors of banking, commerce and tourism; some fruit production and light industry survived; reconstruction of the infrastructure is under way, and financial service companies are beginning to return.

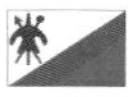

LESOTHO
Kingdom of Lesotho

Area Sq Km	30 355	Currency	Loti
Area Sq Miles	11 720	Languages	Sesotho, English, Zulu
Population	2 062 000	Religions	Christian, traditional beliefs
Capital	Maseru	Organizations	Comm., SADC, UN

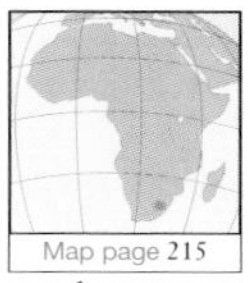
Map page 215

Lesotho is a landlocked state surrounded by the Republic of South Africa. It is a mountainous country lying within the Drakensberg range. Farming and herding are the main activities. Exports include livestock, vegetables, wool and mohair. The economy depends heavily on South Africa for transport links and employment; a major hydro-electric plant completed in 1998 will allow the sale of water to South Africa.

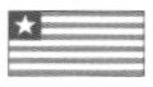

LIBERIA
Republic of Liberia

Area Sq Km	111 369	Currency	Dollar
Area Sq Miles	43 000	Languages	English, creole, local languages
Population	2 666 000	Religions	Traditional beliefs, Christian, Sunni Muslim
Capital	Monrovia	Organizations	UN

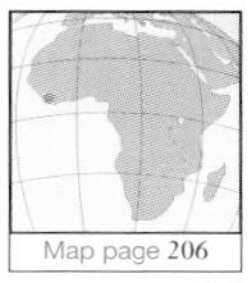
Map page 206

Liberia is on the Atlantic coast of west Africa. Beyond the coastal belt of sandy beaches and mangrove swamps the land rises to a forested plateau, with highlands along the Guinea border. A quarter of the population lives along the coast. The climate is hot with heavy rainfall. Sporadic civil war throughout the 1990's has ruined the economy and destroyed much of the infrastructure especially around Monrovia; Liberia relies on foreign aid.

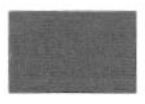

LIBYA
Socialist People's Libyan Arab Jamahiriya

Area Sq Km	1 759 540	Currency	Dinar
Area Sq Miles	679 362	Languages	Arabic, Berber
Population	5 339 000	Religions	Sunni Muslim
Capital	Tripoli	Organizations	OPEC, UN

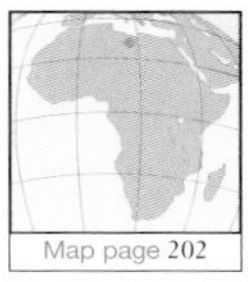
Map page 202

Libya lies on the Mediterranean coast of north Africa. The desert plains and hills of the Sahara dominate the landscape and the climate is hot and dry. Most people live in cities near the coast, where the climate is cooler with moderate rainfall. Farming and herding, chiefly in the northwest, are important but the main industry is oil. Libya is a major oil producer and oil accounts for virtually all of export earnings. Italy and Germany are the main trading partners.

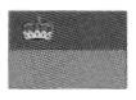

LIECHTENSTEIN
Principality of Liechtenstein

Area Sq Km	160	Currency	Swiss franc
Area Sq Miles	62	Languages	German
Population	32 000	Religions	Roman Catholic, Protestant
Capital	Vaduz	Organizations	UN

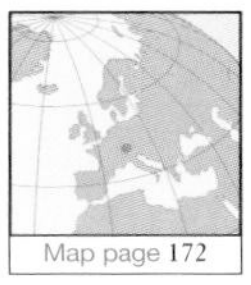
Map page 172

A landlocked state between Switzerland and Austria Liechtenstein has an industrialized, free-enterprize economy. Low business taxes have attracted companies to establish nominal offices providing about a third of state revenues. Banking is also important. Major products include precision instruments, ceramics and textiles.

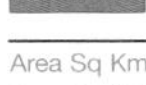

LITHUANIA
Republic of Lithuania

Area Sq Km	65 200	Currency	Litas
Area Sq Miles	25 174	Languages	Lithuanian, Russian, Polish
Population	3 694 000	Religions	Roman Catholic, Protestant, Russian Orthodox
Capital	Vilnius	Organizations	UN

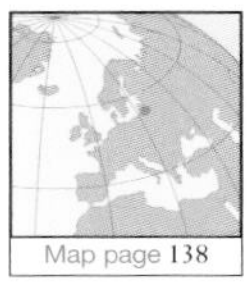
Map page 138

Lithuania is in north Europe, on the eastern shores of the Baltic Sea. It is mainly lowland with many lakes, rivers and marshes. The climate is generally temperate. Agriculture, fishing and forestry are important, but manufacturing dominates the economy. The main products are processed foods, textiles, chemicals, wood and wood products. Russia and Germany are the main trading partners. Lithuania is negotiating to join the EU.

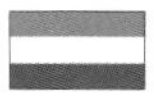

LUXEMBOURG
Grand Duchy of Luxembourg

Area Sq Km	2 586	Currency	Franc, Euro
Area Sq Miles	998	Languages	Letzeburgish, German, French
Population	422 000	Religions	Roman Catholic
Capital	Luxembourg	Organizations	EU, OECD, UN

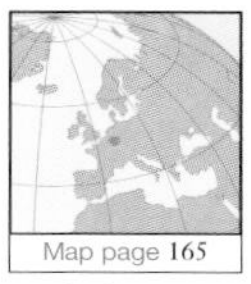
Map page 165

Luxembourg, a small landlocked country in west Europe, borders Belgium, France and Germany. The hills and forests of the Ardennes dominate the north, with rolling pasture to the south, where the main towns, farms and industries are found. The iron and steel industry is still important, but light industries (including textiles, chemicals and food products) are growing. Luxembourg is a major banking centre and the home base of key European Union institutions.

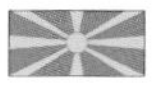

MACEDONIA (F.Y.R.O.M.)
Republic of Macedonia

Area Sq Km	25 713	Currency	Denar
Area Sq Miles	9 928	Languages	Macedonian, Albanian, Turkish
Population	1 999 000	Religions	Macedonian Orthodox, Sunni Muslim
Capital	Skopje	Organizations	UN

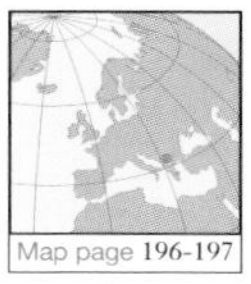
Map page 196-197

The Former Yugoslav Republic of Macedonia, is a landlocked state in southern Europe, bordered by Yugoslavia, Bulgaria, Greece and Albania. Lying within the south Balkans, it is a mountainous country, traversed northwest-southeast by the Vardar valley. It has hot summers, but very cold winters. The economy is based on industry, mining and agriculture. But the conflicts in the region have reduced trade and caused economic difficulties. Aid and loans are now assisting in modernization and development.

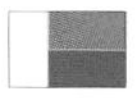

MADAGASCAR
Republic of Madagascar

Area Sq Km	587 041	Currency	Franc
Area Sq Miles	226 658	Languages	Malagasy, French
Population	15 057 000	Religions	Traditional beliefs, Christian, Sunni Muslim
Capital	Antananarivo	Organizations	UN

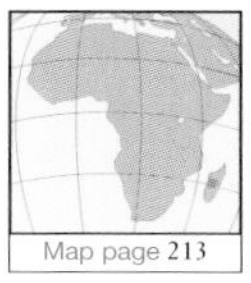
Map page 213

Madagascar lies off the east coast of southern Africa. The world's fourth largest island, it is mainly a high plateau with a coastal strip to the east and scrubby plain to the west. The climate is tropical with heavy rainfall in the north and east. Most people live on the plateau. Though the amount of arable land is limited the economy is based on agriculture. The main industries are agricultural processing, textile manufacturing and oil refining, foreign aid is important. Exports include coffee, vanilla, cloves, cloth, sugar and shrimps. France is the main trading partner.

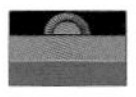

MALAWI
Republic of Malawi

Area Sq Km	118 484	Currency	Kwacha
Area Sq Miles	45 747	Languages	Chichewa, English, local languages
Population	10 346 000	Religions	Christian, traditional beliefs, Sunni Muslim
Capital	Lilongwe	Organizations	Comm., SADC, UN

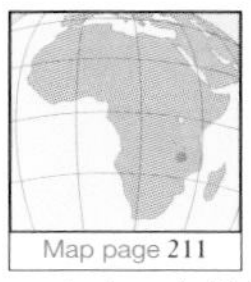
Map page 211

Landlocked Malawi in central Africa is a narrow hilly country at the southern end of the Great Rift Valley. One fifth of the country is covered by Lake Malawi, which lies above sea level. Most people live in the southern regions. The climate is mainly subtropical with varying rainfall. The economy is predominantly agricultural. Tobacco, tea and sugar are the main exports. The small manufacturing sector involves mainly chemicals, textiles and agricultural products. Malawi relies heavily on foreign aid.

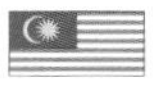

MALAYSIA
Federation of Malaysia

Area Sq Km	332 965	Currency	Ringgit
Area Sq Miles	128 559	Languages	Malay, English, Chinese, Tamil, local languages
Population	21 410 000	Religions	Sunni Muslim, Buddhist, Hindu, Christian
Capital	Kuala Lumpur	Organizations	APEC, ASEAN, Comm., UN

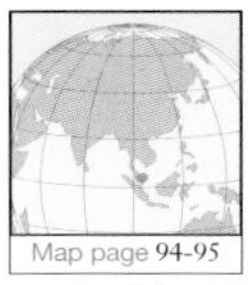
Map page 94-95

The Federation of Malaysia, in southeast Asia, comprises two regions, separated by the South China Sea. The western region occupies the southern Malay Peninsula, which has a chain of mountains dividing the eastern coastal strip from the wider plains to the west. To the east, the states of Sabah and Sarawak in the north of the island of Borneo are mainly rainforest-covered hills and mountains with mangrove swamps along the coast. Both regions have a tropical climate with heavy rainfall. About eighty per cent of the population live in the western part of the country, Peninsular Malaysia, mainly on the coasts. The country is rich in natural resources and has reserves of minerals and fuels. It is an important producer of tin, oil, natural gas and tropical hardwoods. Agriculture remains a substantial part of the economy, but industry has become the most important sector. The main exports are transport and electronic equipment, oil, palm oil, wood and rubber. The main trading partners are Japan, USA and Singapore.

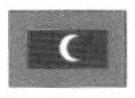

MALDIVES
Republic of the Maldives

Area Sq Km	298	Currency	Rufiyaa
Area Sq Miles	115	Languages	Divehi (Maldivian)
Population	271 000	Religions	Sunni Muslim
Capital	Male	Organizations	Comm., UN

The Maldive archipelago comprises over a thousand coral atolls (around two hundred of which are inhabited), in the Indian Ocean, southwest of India. Over eighty per cent of the land area is less than one metre above sea level. The main atolls are North and South Male

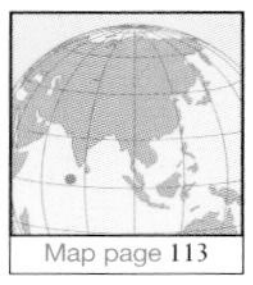
Map page 113

and Addu. The climate is hot, humid and monsoonal. There is little cultivation and almost all food is imported. Tourism has expanded rapidly and is the most important sector of the economy.

MALI
Republic of Mali

Area Sq Km	1 240 140	Currency	CFA franc
Area Sq Miles	478 821	Languages	French, Bambara, local languages
Population	10 694 000	Religions	Sunni Muslim, traditional beliefs, Christian
Capital	Bamako	Organizations	UN

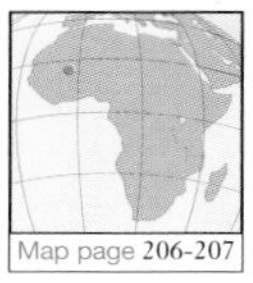
Map page 206-207

A landlocked state in west Africa, Mali is low-lying, rising to mountains in the northeast. Northern regions lie within the Sahara desert. To the south, around the Niger river, are marshes and savanna grassland. Rainfall is unreliable. Most people live along the Niger and Sénégal rivers. Exports include cotton, livestock and gold. Mali is one of the least developed countries in the world and relies heavily on foreign aid.

MALTA
Republic of Malta

Area Sq Km	316	Currency	Lira
Area Sq Miles	122	Languages	Maltese, English
Population	384 000	Religions	Roman Catholic
Capital	Valletta	Organizations	Comm., UN

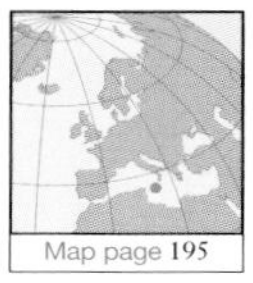
Map page 195

The islands of Malta and Gozo lie in the Mediterranean Sea, off the coast of south Italy. Malta, the main island, has low hills and an indented coastline. The islands have hot, dry summers and mild winters. The main industries are tourism, ship building and repair, electronics and textiles, which are the main exports. Malta is negotiating to join the EU.

MARSHALL ISLANDS
Republic of the Marshall Islands

Area Sq Km	181	Currency	US dollar
Area Sq Miles	70	Languages	English, Marshallese
Population	60 000	Religions	Protestant, Roman Catholic
Capital	Dalap-Uliga-Darrit	Organizations	UN

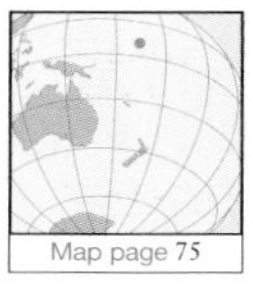
Map page 75

The Marshall Islands consist of over a thousand atolls, islands and islets, within two chains, in the north of the Pacific Ocean. The main atolls are Majuro (home to half the population), Kwajalein, Jaluit, Enewetak and Bikini. The climate is tropical with heavy autumn rainfall. About half the workforce are employed in farming or fishing but the islands depend heavily on US aid.

Martinique
French Overseas Department

Area Sq Km	1 079	Currency	French franc
Area Sq Miles	417	Languages	French, creole
Population	389 000	Religions	Roman Catholic, traditional beliefs
Capital	Fort-de-France		

Martinique, one of the Caribbean Windward Islands, has volcanic peaks in the north, a populous central plain, and hills and beaches in the south. The economy is based on sugar cane, bananas, oil refining, rum distilling, tourism and French aid.

Map page 247

MAURITANIA
Islamic Arab and African Republic of Mauritania

Area Sq Km	1 030 700	Currency	Ouguiya
Area Sq Miles	397 955	Languages	Arabic, French, local languages
Population	2 529 000	Religions	Sunni Muslim
Capital	Nouakchott	Organizations	UN

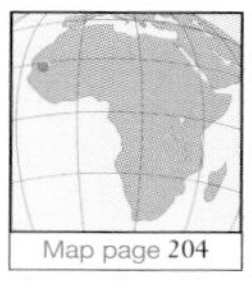
Map page 204

Mauritania is on the Atlantic coast of northwest Africa and lies almost entirely within the Sahara desert. Oases and a fertile strip along the Sénégal river to the south are the only areas suitable for cultivation. The climate is generally hot and dry. About a quarter of Mauritanians live in Nouakchott. Though most of the workforce depend on livestock rearing and subsistence farming, the economy is heavily dependent on iron ore mining and fishing, which together account for ninety per cent of export earnings, and foreign aid.

MAURITIUS
Republic of Mauritius

Area Sq Km	2 040	Currency	Rupee
Area Sq Miles	788	Languages	English, creole, Hindi, Bhojpuri, French
Population	1 141 000	Religions	Hindu, Roman Catholic, Sunni Muslim
Capital	Port Louis	Organizations	Comm., SADC, UN

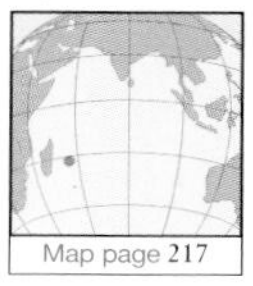
Map page 217

The state comprises Mauritius, Rodrigues and some twenty small islands in the Indian Ocean, east of Madagascar. The main island of Mauritius is volcanic in origin and has a coral coast rising to a central plateau. Most people live in the north and west side of the island. The climate is warm and humid. The economy is based on sugar production, light manufacturing (chiefly clothing) and tourism.

Mayotte
French Territorial Collectivity

Area Sq Km	373	Currency	French franc
Area Sq Miles	144	Languages	French, Mahorian
Population	144 944	Religions	Sunni Muslim, Christian
Capital	Dzaoudzi		

Lying in the Indian Ocean off the east coast of central Africa, Mayotte is geographically part of the Comoros archipelago. The economy is based on agriculture, but Mayotte depends heavily on aid from France.

Map page 217

MEXICO
United Mexican States

Area Sq Km	1 972 545	Currency	Peso
Area Sq Miles	761 604	Languages	Spanish, Amerindian languages
Population	95 831 000	Religions	Roman Catholic, Protestant
Capital	México	Organizations	APEC, OECD, UN

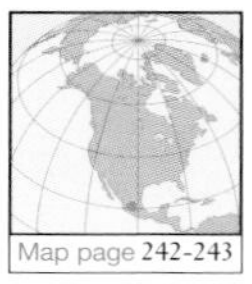
Map page 242-243

The largest country in Central America, Mexico extends south from the USA to Guatemala and Belize, and from the Pacific Ocean to the Gulf of Mexico. The greater part of the country is high plateau flanked by the western and eastern ranges of the Sierra Madre mountains. The principal lowland is the Yucatán peninsula in the southeast. The climate varies with latitude and altitude: hot and humid in the lowlands, warm on the plateau and cool with cold winters in the mountains. The north is arid, while the far south has heavy rainfall. México is one of the world's largest conurbations and the centre of trade and industry. Agriculture involves a quarter of the workforce, crops include grains, sugar cane, coffee, cotton and vegetables. Mexico is rich in minerals, including copper, zinc, lead, tin, sulphur, and silver. It is one of the world's largest producers of oil, from vast oil and gas reserves in the Gulf of Mexico. The oil and petrochemical industries still dominate, but a variety of manufactures are now produced including iron and steel, motor vehicles, textiles, chemicals and food and tobacco products. Tourism is growing in importance. Around three-quarters of all trade is with USA.

MICRONESIA, FEDERATED STATES OF

Area Sq Km	701	Currency	US dollar
Area Sq Miles	271	Languages	English, Chuukese, Pohnpeian, local languages
Population	114 000	Religions	Roman Catholic, Protestant
Capital	Palikir	Organizations	UN

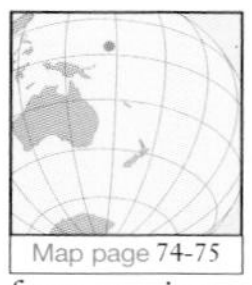
Map page 74-75

Micronesia comprises over six hundred atolls and islands of the Caroline Islands in the north Pacific Ocean. A third of the population lives on Pohnpei. The climate is tropical with heavy rainfall. Fishing and subsistence farming are the main activities. Copra and fish are the main exports. Income also derives from tourism and the licensing of foreign fishing fleets. The islands depend heavily on US aid.

MOLDOVA
Republic of Moldova

Area Sq Km	33 700	Currency	Leu
Area Sq Miles	13 012	Languages	Romanian, Ukrainian, Gagauz, Russian
Population	4 378 000	Religions	Romanian Orthodox, Russian Orthodox
Capital	Chişinău	Organizations	CIS, UN

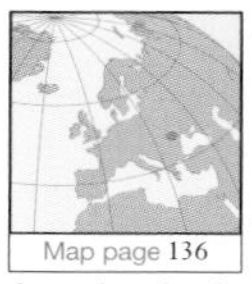
Map page 136

Moldova is in east Europe, between Romania and Ukraine. It consists of hilly steppe land, drained by the Prut and Nistru (Dniester) rivers; the latter provides access to the Black Sea through Ukrainian territory. Moldova has no mineral resources and the economy is mainly agricultural, with sugar beet, tobacco, wine and fruit the chief products. Food processing and textiles are the main industries. Russia is the main trading partner.

MONACO
Principality of Monaco

Area Sq Km	2	Currency	French franc
Area Sq Miles	1	Languages	French, Monegasque, Italian
Population	33 000	Religions	Roman Catholic
Capital	Monaco-Ville	Organizations	UN

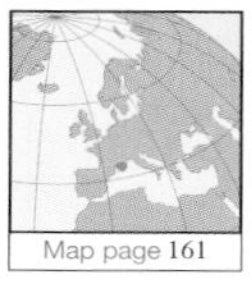
Map page 161

The principality occupies a rocky peninsula and a strip of land on France's Mediterranean coast. It depends on service industries (chiefly tourism, banking and finance) and light industry.

MONGOLIA

Area Sq Km	1 565 000	Currency	Tugrik
Area Sq Miles	604 250	Languages	Khalka (Mongolian), Kazakh, local languages
Population	2 579 000	Religions	Buddhist, Sunni Muslim
Capital	Ulaanbaatar	Organizations	UN

Mongolia is a landlocked country in east Asia between Russia and China. Much of it is high steppe land, with mountains and lakes in the west and the north. In the south is the Gobi desert. Mongolia has long, cold winters and short, mild summers. A quarter of the population lives in the capital. Livestock breeding and agricultural processing are important; there are some mineral resources. Copper and textiles are the main exports.

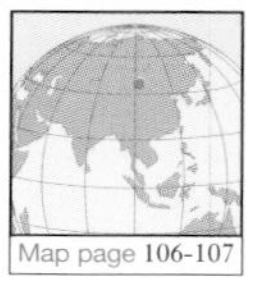
Map page 106-107

Montserrat
United Kingdom Overseas Territory

Area Sq Km	100	Currency	E. Carib. dollar
Area Sq Miles	39	Languages	English
Population	11 000	Religions	Protestant, Roman Catholic
Capital	Plymouth	Organizations	CARICOM

An island in the Leeward Island group in the Lesser Antilles in the Caribbean. From 1995 to 1997 the volcanoes in the Soufrière Hills erupted for the first time since 1630, over sixty per cent of the island was covered in volcanic ash, the capital town was destroyed, many people emigrated and the remaining population moved to the north of the island. Reconstruction, funded by aid from the UK has begun.

Map page 247

MOROCCO
Kingdom of Morocco

Area Sq Km	446 550	Currency	Dirham
Area Sq Miles	172 414	Languages	Arabic, Berber, French
Population	27 377 000	Religions	Sunni Muslim
Capital	Rabat	Organizations	UN

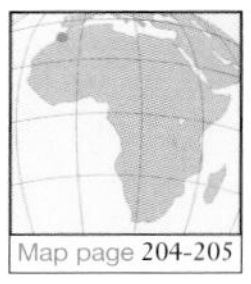
Map page 204-205

Lying in the northwest corner of Africa, Morocco has both Atlantic and Mediterranean coasts. The Atlas Mountains separate the arid south and disputed region of Western Sahara from the fertile regions of the west and north, which have a milder climate. Most Moroccans live on the Atlantic coastal plain. The economy is based mainly on agriculture, phosphate mining and tourism, the main industries are food processing, textiles and chemicals. France is the main trading partner.

MOZAMBIQUE
Republic of Mozambique

Area Sq Km	799 380	Currency	Metical
Area Sq Miles	308 642	Languages	Portuguese, Makua, Tsonga, local languages
Population	18 880 000	Religions	Traditional beliefs, Roman Catholic, Sunni Muslim
Capital	Maputo	Organizations	Comm., SADC, UN

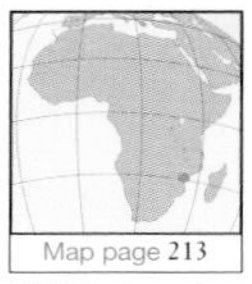
Map page 213

Mozambique lies on the east coast of southern Africa. The land is mainly a savanna plateau drained by the Zambezi and Limpopo rivers, with highlands to the north. Most people live on the coast or in the river valleys. In general the climate is tropical with winter rainfall, but droughts occur. Reconstruction began in 1992 after sixteen years of civil war. The economy is based on subsistence agriculture. Exports include shrimps, cashews, cotton and sugar, but Mozambique relies heavily on aid, and remains one of the least developed countries in the world.

MYANMAR
Union of Myanmar

Area Sq Km	676 577	Currency	Kyat
Area Sq Miles	261 228	Languages	Burmese, Shan, Karen, local languages
Population	44 497 000	Religions	Buddhist, Christian, Sunni Muslim
Capital	Yangôn	Organizations	ASEAN, UN

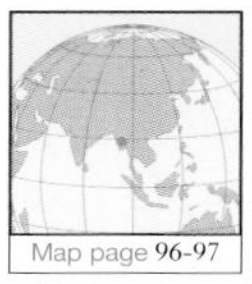
Map page 96-97

Myanmar is in southeast Asia, on the Bay of Bengal and Andaman Sea. Most people live in the valley and delta of the Irrawaddy river, which is flanked on three sides by mountains and high plateaus. The climate is hot and monsoonal, and rainforest covers much of the land. Most people are employed in agriculture. Myanmar is rich in minerals, including zinc, lead, copper and silver. Political and social unrest and lack of foreign investment have affected economic development.

NAMIBIA
Republic of Namibia

Area Sq Km	824 292	Currency	Dollar
Area Sq Miles	318 261	Languages	English, Afrikaans, German, Ovambo, local languages
Population	1 660 000	Religions	Protestant, Roman Catholic
Capital	Windhoek	Organizations	Comm., SADC, UN

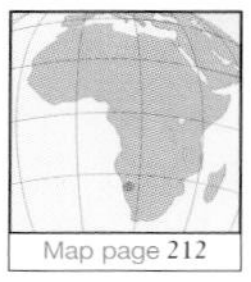
Map page 212

Namibia lies on the Atlantic coast of southern Africa. Mountain ranges separate the coastal Namib Desert from the interior plateau, bordered to the south and east by the Kalahari Desert. Namibia is hot and dry, but some summer rain falls in the north which supports crops and livestock; most of the population live in this area. Most of the workforce are employed in agriculture though the economy is based on mineral extraction, predominantly diamonds, but also uranium, lead, zinc and silver. Fishing is increasingly important. The economy is closely linked to that of South Africa.

NAURU
Republic of Nauru

Area Sq Km	21	Currency	Australian dollar
Area Sq Miles	8	Languages	Nauruan, English
Population	11 000	Religions	Protestant, Roman Catholic
Capital	Yaren	Organizations	Comm., UN

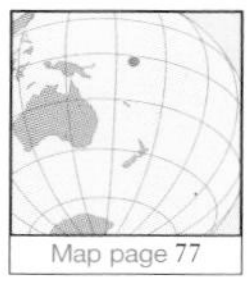
Map page 77

Nauru is a coral island near the equator in the Pacific Ocean, it has a fertile coastal strip, a barren central plateau and a tropical climate. The economy is based on phosphate mining, but reserves are near exhaustion and replacement of this income is a serious long-term problem.

NEPAL
Kingdom of Nepal

Area Sq Km	147 181	Currency	Rupee
Area Sq Miles	56 827	Languages	Nepali, Maithili, Bhojpuri, English, local languages
Population	22 847 000	Religions	Hindu, Buddhist, Sunni Muslim
Capital	Kathmandu	Organizations	UN

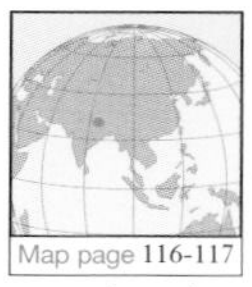
Map page 116-117

The south Asian country of Nepal lies in the eastern Himalaya between India and China. High mountains (including Everest) dominate northern Nepal. Most people live in the temperate central valleys and subtropical southern plains. The economy is based largely on agriculture and forestry; there is some manufacturing, chiefly textiles and carpets, and tourism is important. Nepal relies heavily on foreign aid.

NETHERLANDS
Kingdom of the Netherlands

Area Sq Km	41 526	Currency	Guilder, Euro
Area Sq Miles	16 033	Languages	Dutch, Frisian
Population	15 678 000	Religions	Roman Catholic, Protestant, Sunni Muslim
Capital	Amsterdam/ 's-Gravenhage	Organizations	EU, OECD, UN

The Netherlands lie on the North Sea coast of western Europe. Apart from low hills in the far southeast, the land is flat and low-lying, much of it below sea level. The coastal region includes the delta of five rivers and polders (reclaimed land), protected by sand dunes, dikes and canals. The climate is temperate, with cool summers and mild winters. Rainfall is spread evenly throughout the year. The Netherlands is a densely populated and highly urbanized country, with the majority of people living in the western Amsterdam-Rotterdam-s'Gravenhage area. Horticulture and dairy farming are important activities, though they employ less than four per cent of the workforce. The Netherlands rank as the world's third agricultural exporter, and is a leading producer and exporter of natural gas from reserves in the North Sea, but otherwise lacks raw materials. The economy is based mainly on international trade and manufacturing industry. The main industries produce food products, chemicals, machinery, electric and electronic goods and transport equipment. Germany is the main trading partner followed by other EU countries.

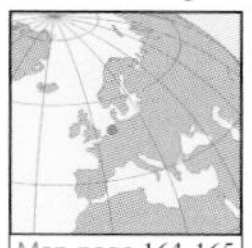
Map page 164-165

Netherlands Antilles
Self-governing NetherlandsTerritory

Area Sq Km	800	Currency	NA guilder
Area Sq Miles	309	Languages	Dutch, Papiamento, English
Population	213 000	Religions	Roman Catholic, Protestant
Capital	Willemstad		

The territory comprises two separate island groups: Curaçao and Bonaire off the northern coast of Venezuela, and Saba, Sint Eustatius and the southern part of Sint Maarten in the northern Lesser Antilles.

Map page 247

New Caledonia
French Overseas Territory

Area Sq Km	19 058	Currency	Pacific franc
Area Sq Miles	7 358	Languages	French, local languages
Population	206 000	Religions	Roman Catholic, Protestant, Sunni Muslim
Capital	Nouméa		

An island group, lying in the southwest Pacific, with a sub-tropical climate. The economy is based on nickel mining and tourism, and aid from France.

Map page 78

NEW ZEALAND

Area Sq Km	270 534	Currency	Dollar
Area Sq Miles	104 454	Languages	English, Maori
Population	3 796 000	Religions	Protestant, Roman Catholic
Capital	Wellington	Organizations	APEC, Comm., OECD, UN

New Zealand comprises two main islands separated by the narrow Cook Strait, and a number of smaller islands. North Island, where three quarters of the population live, has mountain ranges, broad fertile valleys and a central plateau with hot springs and active volcanoes. South Island is also mountainous with the Southern Alps running its entire length. The only major lowland area is the Canterbury Plains in the centre east. The climate is generally temperate, though South Island has colder winters. Farming is the mainstay of the economy. New Zealand is one of the world's leading producers of meat (beef, lamb and mutton), wool and dairy products; fruit and fish are also important. Coal, oil and natural gas are produced, but hydroelectric and geothermal power provide much of the country's energy needs. Other industries produce timber, wood pulp, iron, aluminium, machinery and chemicals. Tourism is the fastest growing sector of the economy. The main trading partners are Australia, USA and Japan.

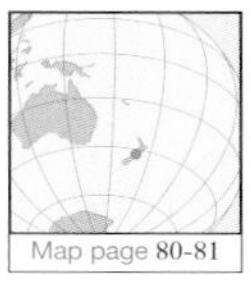
Map page 80-81

NICARAGUA
Republic of Nicaragua

Area Sq Km	130 000	Currency	Córdoba
Area Sq Miles	50 193	Languages	Spanish, Amerindian languages
Population	4 807 000	Religions	Roman Catholic, Protestant
Capital	Managua	Organizations	UN

Nicaragua lies at the heart of Central America, with both Pacific and Caribbean coasts. Mountain ranges separate the east, which is largely rainforest, from the more developed western regions, which include Lake Nicaragua and some active volcanoes. The highest land is in the north. The climate is tropical. The economy is largely agricultural. Exports include coffee, seafood and bananas. Nicaragua relies heavily on aid and was one of the countries worse hit by hurricane Mitch in 1998; though it has received significant relief to help reconstruction, development has been seriously affected.

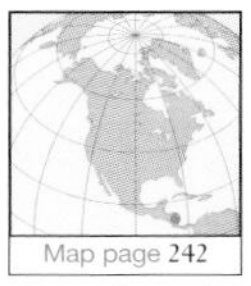
Map page 242

NIGER
Republic of Niger

Area Sq Km	1 267 000	Currency	CFA franc
Area Sq Miles	489 191	Languages	French, Hausa, Fulani, local languages
Population	10 078 000	Religions	Sunni Muslim, traditional beliefs
Capital	Niamey	Organizations	UN

A landlocked state of west Africa, Niger lies mostly within the Sahara desert, but with savanna in the south and Niger valley. The mountains of the Air massif dominate central regions. Much of the country is hot and dry. The south has some summer rainfall, though droughts occur. The economy depends on subsistence farming and herding, and uranium exports, but Niger is one of the world's least developed countries and relies heavily on foreign aid.

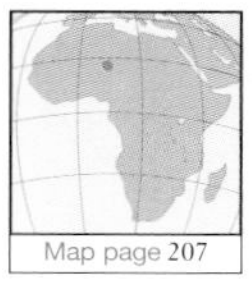
Map page 207

NIGERIA
Federal Republic of Nigeria

Area Sq Km	923 768	Currency	Naira
Area Sq Miles	356 669	Languages	English, Hausa, Yoruba, Ibo, Fulani, local languages
Population	106 409 000	Religions	Sunni Muslim, Christian, traditional beliefs
Capital	Abuja	Organizations	Comm., OPEC, UN

Nigeria is in west Africa, on the Gulf of Guinea, and is the most populous country in Africa. The Niger delta dominates coastal areas, fringed with sandy beaches, mangrove swamps and lagoons. Inland is a belt of rainforest that gives way to woodland or savanna on high plateaus. The far north is the semi-desert edge of the Sahara. The climate is tropical with heavy summer rainfall in the south but low rainfall in the north. Most people live in the coastal lowlands or in western Nigeria. About half the workforce is involved in agriculture, mainly growing subsistence crops, but agricultural production has failed to keep up with the rapid population growth and Nigeria is now a net importer of food. Cocoa and rubber are the only significant export crops. The economy is heavily dependent on vast oil resources in the Niger delta and shallow offshore waters, which account for over ninety per cent of export earnings. Nigeria also has natural gas reserves and some mineral deposits, but these are largely undeveloped. Industry involves mainly oil refining, chemicals (chiefly fertilizer), agricultural processing, textiles, steel manufacture and vehicle assembly. Political instability has left Nigeria with heavy debts, poverty and unemployment.

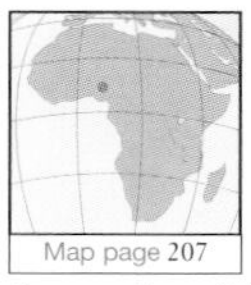
Map page 207

Niue
Self-governing New Zealand Overseas Territory

Area Sq Km	258	Currency	NZ dollar
Area Sq Miles	100	Languages	English, Polynesian
Population	2 000	Religions	Christian
Capital	Alofi		

One of the largest coral islands in the world, in the south Pacific Ocean about 500 kilometres (300 miles) east of Tonga. The economy depends on aid and remittances from New Zealand. The population is declining because of migration to New Zealand.

Map page 81

Norfolk Island
Australian External Territory

Area Sq Km	35	Currency	Australian dollar
Area Sq Miles	14	Languages	English
Population	2 000	Religions	Protestant, Roman Catholic
Capital	Kingston		

In the south Pacific Ocean, between Vanuatu and New Zealand; tourism has increased steadily and is the mainstay of the economy, providing revenues for agricultural development.

Map page 82

Northern Mariana Islands
United States Commonwealth

Area Sq Km	477	Currency	US dollar
Area Sq Miles	184	Languages	English, Chamorro, local languages
Population	70 000	Religions	Roman Catholic
Capital	Saipan		

A chain of islands in the northwest Pacific Ocean, extending over 550 kilometres (350 miles) north to south; the main island is Saipan; tourism is a major industry employing around half the workforce, the majority of tourists are from Japan.

Map page 74

NORTH KOREA
People's Democratic Republic of Korea

Area Sq Km	120 538	Currency	Won
Area Sq Miles	46 540	Languages	Korean
Population	23 348 000	Religions	Traditional beliefs, Chondoist, Buddhist
Capital	P'yŏngyang	Organizations	UN

Occupying the northern half of the Korean peninsula in east Asia, North Korea is a rugged and mountainous country. The principal lowlands and the main agricultural areas are the plains in the southwest. More than half the population lives in urban areas, mainly on the coastal plains. North Korea has a continental climate, with cold, dry winters and hot, wet summers. About a third of the workforce is involved in agriculture, mainly growing food crops on cooperative farms. A variety of minerals and ores, chiefly iron ore, are mined and are the basis of the country's heavy industry. Exports include minerals (lead, magnesite and zinc) and metal products (chiefly iron and steel). The economy has declined since 1991 when ties to the former USSR and eastern bloc collapsed, and there were serious food shortages between 1994 and 1998. North Korea receives some foreign aid.

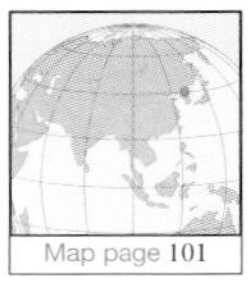
Map page 101

NORWAY
Kingdom of Norway

Area Sq Km	323 878	Currency	Krone
Area Sq Miles	125 050	Languages	Norwegian
Population	4 419 000	Religions	Protestant, Roman Catholic
Capital	Oslo	Organizations	OECD, UN

Norway stretches along the north and west coasts of Scandinavia, from the Arctic Ocean to the southern North Sea. Its extensive coastline is indented with fjords and fringed with many islands. Inland, the terrain is mountainous, with coniferous forests and lakes in the south. The only major lowland areas are along the southern North Sea and Skagerrak coasts, where most people live. The climate is modified by the North Atlantic Drift. Norway has vast petroleum and natural gas resources in the North Sea. It is west one of Europe's leading producers of oil and gas, which account for around half of export earnings. Related industries include engineering (oil and gas platforms) and petrochemicals. More traditional industries process local raw materials: fish, timber and minerals. Agriculture is limited, but fishing and fish farming are important. Norway is the world's leading exporter of farmed salmon. Merchant shipping and tourism are major sources of foreign exchange.

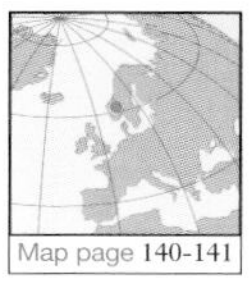
Map page 140-141

OMAN
Sultanate of Oman

Area Sq Km	309 500	Currency	Rial
Area Sq Miles	119 499	Languages	Arabic, Baluchi, Indian languages
Population	2 382 000	Religions	Ibadhi Muslim, Sunni Muslim
Capital	Muscat	Organizations	UN

In southwest Asia, Oman occupies the east and southeast coasts of the Arabian Peninsula and an enclave north of the United Arab Emirates. Most of the land is desert, with mountains in the north and south. The climate is hot and mainly dry. Most people live on the coastal strip on the Gulf of Oman. The majority depend on farming and fishing, but the oil and gas industries dominate the economy, with around eighty per cent of export revenues from oil.

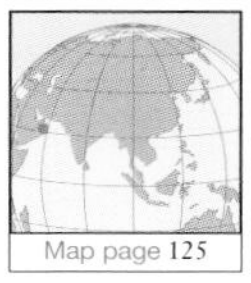
Map page 125

PAKISTAN
Islamic Republic of Pakistan

Area Sq Km	803 940	Currency	Rupee
Area Sq Miles	310 403	Languages	Urdu, Punjabi, Sindhi, Pushtu, English
Population	148 166 000	Religions	Sunni Muslim, Shi'a Muslim, Christian, Hindu
Capital	Islamabad	Organizations	Comm., UN

Pakistan is in the northwest part of the Indian subcontinent in south Asia, on the Arabian Sea. Eastern and southern Pakistan are dominated by the great basin drained by the Indus river system. It is the main agricultural area and contains most of the predominantly rural population. To the north the land rises to the mountains of the Karakoram, Hindu Kush and Himalaya. The west is semi-desert plateaus and mountain ranges. The climate ranges between dry desert and tundra on the mountain tops. However, temperatures are generally warm and rainfall is monsoonal. Agriculture is the main sector of the economy, employing about half the workforce; cultivation is based on extensive irrigation schemes. Pakistan is one of the world's leading producers of cotton and an important exporter of rice. However, much of the country's food needs must be imported. Pakistan produces natural gas and has a variety of mineral deposits including coal and gold, but they are little developed. The main industries are textiles and clothing manufacture and food processing, with fabrics and ready-made clothing the leading exports. Pakistan also produces leather goods, fertilizers, chemicals, paper and precision instruments. The country depends heavily upon foreign aid and remittances from Pakistanis working abroad.

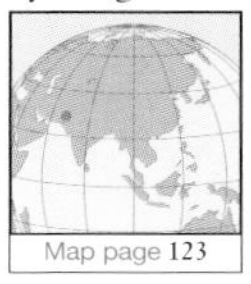
Map page 123

PALAU
Republic of Palau

Area Sq Km	497	Currency	US dollar
Area Sq Miles	192	Languages	Palauan, English
Population	19 000	Religions	Roman Catholic, Protestant, traditional beliefs
Capital	Koror	Organizations	UN

Palau comprises over three hundred islands in the western Caroline Islands in the west Pacific Ocean. The climate is tropical. The economy is based on farming, fishing and tourism; Palau is heavily dependent on US aid.

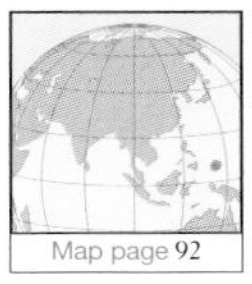
Map page 92

PANAMA
Republic of Panama

Area Sq Km	77 082	Currency	Balboa
Area Sq Miles	29 762	Languages	Spanish, English, Amerindian languages
Population	2 767 000	Religions	Roman Catholic, Protestant, Sunni Muslim
Capital	Panamá	Organizations	UN

Panama is the most southerly state in central America and has Pacific and Caribbean coasts. It is hilly, with mountains in the west and jungle near the Colombian border. The climate is tropical. Most people live on the drier Pacific side. The economy is based mainly on services related to the canal: shipping, banking and tourism. Exports include bananas, shrimps, coffee, clothing and fish products. USA is the main trading partner.

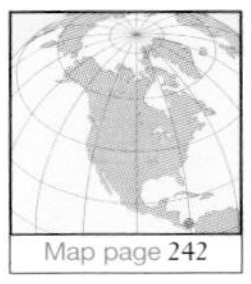
Map page 242

PAPUA NEW GUINEA
Independent State of Papua New Guinea

Area Sq Km	462 840	Currency	Kina
Area Sq Miles	178 704	Languages	English, Tok Pisin (creole), local languages
Population	4 600 000	Religions	Protestant, Roman Catholic, traditional beliefs
Capital	Port Moresby	Organizations	Comm., UN

Papua New Guinea, in Australasia, occupies the eastern half of the island of New Guinea and includes many island groups. Papua New Guinea has a forested and mountainous interior, bordered by swampy plains, and a tropical monsoon climate. Most of the workforce are farmers. Timber, copra, coffee and cocoa are important, but exports are dominated by minerals, chiefly gold and copper. The country depends on foreign aid. Australia and Japan are the main trading partners.

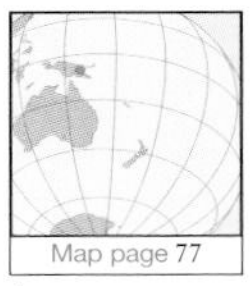
Map page 77

© Bartholomew Ltd

PARAGUAY
Republic of Paraguay

Area Sq Km	406 752	Currency	Guaraní
Area Sq Miles	157 048	Languages	Spanish, Guaraní
Population	5 222 000	Religions	Roman Catholic, Protestant
Capital	Asunción	Organizations	UN

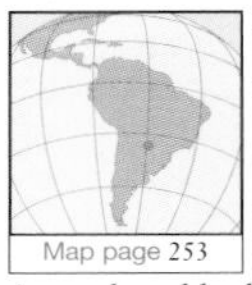
Map page 253

Paraguay is a landlocked country in central South America, bordering Bolivia, Brazil and Argentina. The river Paraguay separates a sparsely populated western zone of marsh and flat alluvial plains from a more developed, hilly and forested region to the east and south. The climate is subtropical. Virtually all electricity is produced by hydro plants and surplus power is exported to Brazil and Argentina. The hydroelectric dam at Itaipu is the largest in the world. The mainstay of the economy is agriculture and agricultural industries. Exports include cotton, soya bean and edible oil products, timber and meat. Brazil and Argentina are the main trading partners.

PERU
Republic of Peru

Area Sq Km	1 285 216	Currency	Sol
Area Sq Miles	496 225	Languages	Spanish, Quechua, Aymara
Population	24 797 000	Religions	Roman Catholic, Protestant
Capital	Lima	Organizations	APEC, UN

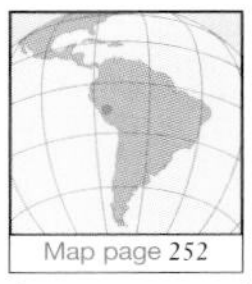
Map page 252

Peru lies on the Pacific coast of South America. Most people live on the coastal strip and the plateaus of the high Andes. East of the Andes is the Amazon rainforest. The coast is temperate with low rainfall, while the east is hot, humid and wet. Agriculture involves one third of the workforce, fishing is also important; agriculture and fishing were both disrupted by the El Nino effect in the 1990s. Sugar, cotton, coffee and, illegally, coca are the main cash crops. Copper and copper products, fishmeal, zinc products, coffee, petroleum and its products, and textiles are the main exports. America is the main trading partner.

PHILIPPINES
Republic of the Philippines

Area Sq Km	300 000	Currency	Peso
Area Sq Miles	115 831	Languages	English, Pilipino, Cebuano, local languages
Population	72 944 000	Religions	Roman Catholic, Protestant, Sunni Muslim
Capital	Manila	Organizations	APEC, ASEAN, UN

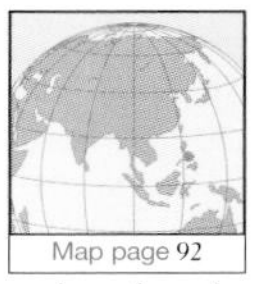
Map page 92

The Philippines, in southeast Asia, consists of over seven thousand islands and atolls lying between the South China Sea and the Pacific Ocean. The islands of Luzon and Mindanao account for two thirds of the land area. They and nine other fairly large islands are mountainous and forested. There are active volcanoes, and earthquakes are common. Most people live in the plains on the larger islands or on the coastal strips. The climate is hot and humid with heavy monsoonal rainfall. Coconuts, sugar, pineapples and bananas are the main agricultural crops; fish and timber are also important. The Philippines produces copper, gold, chromium, cobalt and nickel as well as oil, though geothermal power is also used. The main industries process raw materials and produce electrical and electronic equipment and components, footwear and clothing, textiles and furniture. These manufactured goods are the main exports. Foreign aid and remittances from workers abroad are important to the economy, which faces problems of high population growth rate and high unemployment. USA is the main trading partner.

Pitcairn Islands
United Kingdom Overseas Territory

Area Sq Km	45	Currency	NZ dollar
Area Sq Miles	17	Languages	English
Population	46	Religions	Protestant
Capital	Adamstown		

An island group in the southeast Pacific Ocean consisting of Pitcairn Island and three uninhabited islands. It was originally settled by mutineers from HMS Bounty.

Map page 75

POLAND
Polish Republic

Area Sq Km	312 683	Currency	Zloty
Area Sq Miles	120 728	Languages	Polish, German
Population	38 718 000	Religions	Roman Catholic, Polish Orthodox
Capital	Warszawa	Organizations	OECD, UN

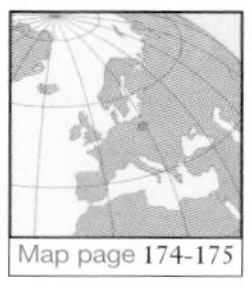
Map page 174-175

Poland lies on the Baltic coast of central Europe. The Odra (Oder) and Wisla (Vistula) deltas dominate the coast. Inland, much of Poland is low-lying with woods and lakes. In the south the land rises to the Sudety and western part of the Carpathian Mountains which form the borders with the Czech Republic and Slovakia respectively. The climate is continental, with warm summers and cold winters. Around a quarter of the workforce is involved in agriculture, and exports include livestock products and sugar. The economy is heavily industrialized, with mining and manufacturing accounting for forty per cent of national income. Poland is one of the world's major producers of coal, and also produces copper, zinc, lead, sulphur and natural gas. The main industries are machinery and transport equipment, ship building, metal and chemical production. Germany is the main trading partner. Poland is negotiating to join the EU.

PORTUGAL
Portuguese Republic

Area Sq Km	88 940	Currency	Escudo, Euro
Area Sq Miles	34 340	Languages	Portuguese
Population	9 869 000	Religions	Roman Catholic, Protestant
Capital	Lisboa	Organizations	EU, OECD, UN

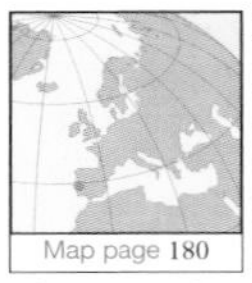
Map page 180

Portugal lies in the western part of the Iberian peninsula in southwest Europe, has an Atlantic coastline and is bordered by Spain to the north and east. The land north of the river Tejo (Tagus) is mostly highland with extensive forests of pine and cork. South of the river is undulating lowland. The climate in the north is cool and moist, the south is warmer, with dry, mild winters. Most Portuguese live near the coast, with one third of the total population in Lisbon (Lisboa) and Oporto. Agriculture, fishing and forestry involve about twelve per cent of the workforce. Mining and manufacturing are the main sectors of the economy. Portugal produces kaolin, coppet, tin, zinc, tungsten and salt. Export manufactures include textiles, clothing and footwear, electrical machinery and transport equipment, cork and wood products, and chemicals. Service industries, chiefly tourism and banking, are important to the economy as are remittances from workers abroad. Most trade is with other EU countries.

PUERTO RICO
United States Commonwealth

Area Sq Km	9 104	Currency	US dollar
Area Sq Miles	3 515	Languages	Spanish, English
Population	3 810 000	Religions	Roman Catholic, Protestant
Capital	San Juan		

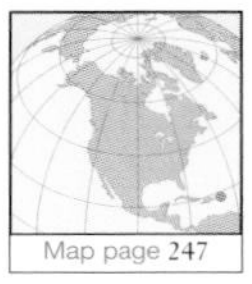
Map page 247

The Caribbean island of Puerto Rico has a forested, hilly interior, coastal plains and a tropical climate. Half the population lives in the San Juan area. The economy is based on manufacturing (chiefly chemicals, electronics and food), tourism and agriculture. USA is the predominant trading partner.

QATAR
State of Qatar

Area Sq Km	11 437	Currency	Riyal
Area Sq Miles	4 416	Languages	Arabic
Population	579 000	Religions	Sunni Muslim
Capital	Doha	Organizations	OPEC, UN

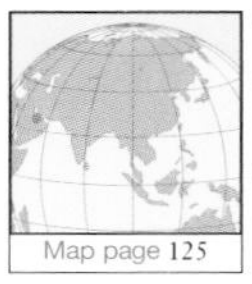
Map page 125

The emirate occupies a peninsula that extends northwards from east-central Saudi Arabia into The Gulf in southwest Asia. The land is flat and barren with sand dunes and salt pans. The climate is hot and mainly dry. Most people live in the Doha area. The economy is heavily dependent on oil and natural gas production and the oil-refining industry. Income also comes from overseas investment. Japan is the largest trading partner.

Réunion
French Overseas Department

Area Sq Km	2 551	Currency	French franc
Area Sq Miles	985	Languages	French, creole
Population	682 000	Religions	Roman Catholic
Capital	St-Denis		

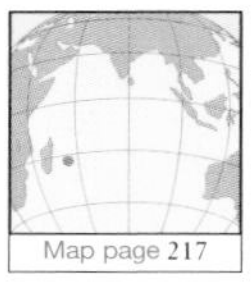
Map page 217

The Indian Ocean island of Réunion is mountainous, with coastal lowlands and a warm climate. It depends heavily on sugar, tourism and French aid. Some uninhabited islets to the east are administered from Réunion.

ROMANIA

Area Sq Km	237 500	Currency	Leu
Area Sq Miles	91 699	Languages	Romanian, Hungarian
Population	22 474 000	Religions	Romanian Orthodox, Protestant, Roman Catholic
Capital	București	Organizations	UN

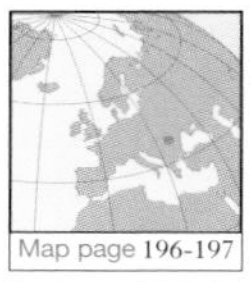
Map page 196-197

Romania lies on the Black Sea coast of east Europe. Mountains separate the Transylvanian Basin at the centre of the country from the populous plains of the east and south and the Danube delta. The climate is continental. Romania has mineral resources (zinc, lead, silver and gold), and oil and natural gas reserves. Economic reform has been slow and sporadic, but measures to accelerate change were introduced in 1999. Agriculture still employs over a quarter of the workforce. The main exports are textiles, mineral products, chemicals, machinery and footwear. The most important trading partners are Germany and Italy. Negotiations to join the EU have been started.

RUSSIAN FEDERATION

Area Sq Km	17 075 400	Currency	Rouble
Area Sq Miles	6 592 849	Languages	Russian, Tatar, Ukrainian, local languages
Population	147 434 000	Religions	Russian Orthodox, Sunni Muslim, Protestant
Capital	Moskva	Organizations	APEC, CIS, UN

Russia occupies much of east Europe and all of north Asia, and is the world's largest state, nearly twice the size of the USA. It borders thirteen countries to the west and south and has long coastlines on the Arctic and Pacific Oceans to the north and east. European Russia lies west of the Ural mountains. To the south the land rises to uplands and the Caucasus on the border with Georgia and Azerbaijan. East of the Urals lies the flat West Siberian Plain; much of central Siberia is plateau. In the south is Lake Baikal, the world's deepest lake, and the Sayan ranges on the border with Kazakhstan and Mongolia. Eastern Siberia is rugged and mountainous with many active volcanoes in the Kamchatka Peninsula. Russia's major rivers are the Volga in the west and the Ob', Yenisey, Lena and Amur in Siberia. The climate and vegetation range between arctic tundra in the north and semi-arid steppe towards the Black and Caspian Sea coasts in the south. In general, the climate is continental

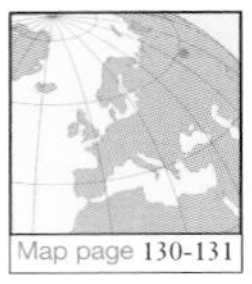
Map page 130-131

with extreme temperatures. The majority of the population (the seventh largest in the world), and industry and agriculture are concentrated in European Russia, but there has been increased migration to Siberia to exploit its vast natural resources. The economy is heavily dependent on exploitation of raw materials and on heavy industry. Russia has a wealth of mineral resources, though they are often difficult to exploit because of the climate and remote locations. It is one of the world's leading producers of petroleum, natural gas and coal as well as iron ore, nickel, copper and bauxite, and many precious and rare metals. Forests cover over forty per cent of the land area and supply an important timber, paper and pulp industry; around eight per cent of land is suitable for cultivation, but farming is generally inefficient and food, especially grains, must be imported. Fishing is important and Russia has a large fleet operating around the world. The transition to a market economy has been slow and difficult, with high unemployment and considerable underemployment. As well as mining and extractive industries there is a wide range of manufacturing industry from steel mills to aircraft and space vehicles, shipbuilding, synthetic fabrics, plastics, cotton fabrics, consumer durable, chemicals and fertilizers. Exports include fuels, metals, machinery, chemicals and forest products. The most important trading partners include Germany, Italy, USA, China and Switzerland.

RWANDA
Republic of Rwanda

Area Sq Km	26 338	Currency	Franc
Area Sq Miles	10 169	Languages	Kinyarwanda, French, English
Population	6 604 000	Religions	Roman Catholic, traditional beliefs, Protestant
Capital	Kigali	Organizations	UN

A densely populated and landlocked state in east Africa, Rwanda

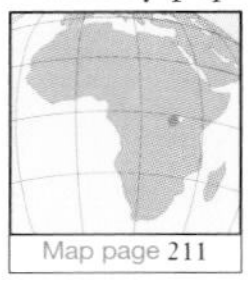
Map page 211

is situated in the mountains and plateaus to the east of the Great Rift Valley. The climate is warm with a summer dry season. Rwanda depends upon subsistence farming, coffee and tea exports, light industry and foreign aid, but in the 1990s civil war and ethnic conflict devastated the country.

Saba part of Netherlands Antilles

Area Sq Km (Miles) 13 (5) | Population 1 200 | Capital Bottom

An island in the Leeward Islands in the Lesser Antilles in the Caribbean, to the south of Sint Maarten.

Map page 247

St-Barthélémy Dependency of Guadeloupe

Area Sq Km (Miles) 21 (8) | Population 5 038 | Capital Gustavia

An island in the Leeward Islands in the Lesser Antilles in the Caribbean south of Sint Maarten. Tourism is the main economic activity.

Map page 247

St Helena
United Kingdom Overseas Territory

Area Sq Km	121	Currency	Pound sterling
Area Sq Miles	47	Languages	English
Population	5 644	Religions	Protestant, Roman Catholic
Capital	Jamestown		

St Helena and its dependencies, Ascension and Tristan da Cunha are isolated island groups lying in the south Atlantic Ocean. St Helena is a rugged island of volcanic origin; the main activity is fishing but the island depends on financial aid from the UK.

Map page 216

ST KITTS AND NEVIS
Federation of St Kitts and Nevis

Area Sq Km	261	Currency	E. Carib. dollar
Area Sq Miles	101	Languages	English, creole
Population	39 000	Religions	Protestant, Roman Catholic
Capital	Basseterre	Organizations	CARICOM, Comm., UN

St Kitts and Nevis are in the Leeward Islands in the Caribbean Sea.

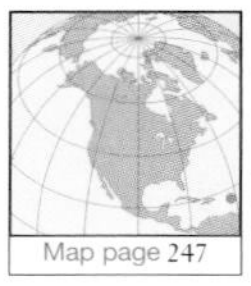
Map page 247

Both volcanic islands are mountainous and forested with sandy beaches and a warm, wet climate. About three-quarters of the population live on St Kitts. Agriculture is the main activity, with sugar the main product. Tourism and manufacturing (chiefly garments and electronic components) are important.

ST LUCIA

Area Sq Km	616	Currency	E. Carib. dollar
Area Sq Miles	238	Languages	English, creole
Population	150 000	Religions	Roman Catholic, Protestant
Capital	Castries	Organizations	CARICOM, Comm., UN

St Lucia, one of the Windward Islands in the Caribbean Sea, is a

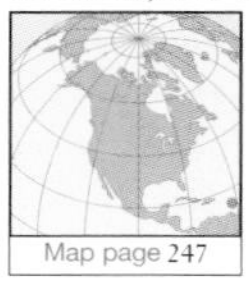
Map page 247

volcanic island with forested mountains, hot springs, sandy beaches and a wet tropical climate. Agriculture is the main activity, with bananas accounting for about forty per cent of export earnings. Tourism, agricultural processing and light manufacturing are increasingly important.

St Martin Dependency of Guadeloupe

Area Sq Km (Miles) 54 (21) | Population 28 518 | Capital Marigot

The northern part of one of the Leeward Islands is in the Caribbean, the other part of the island is part of the Netherlands Antilles. Tourism is the main source of income.

Map page 247

St Pierre and Miquelon
French Territorial Collectivity

Area Sq Km	242	Currency	French franc
Area Sq Miles	93	Languages	French
Population	7 000	Religions	Roman Catholic
Capital	St-Pierre		

A group of islands off the south coast of Newfoundland in eastern Canada. The islands are unsuitable for agriculture; fishing and fish processing are still important, though the islands rely heavily on assistance from France.

Map page 225

ST VINCENT AND THE GRENADINES

Area Sq Km	389	Currency	E. Carib. dollar
Area Sq Miles	150	Languages	English, creole
Population	112 000	Religions	Protestant, Roman Catholic
Capital	Kingstown	Organizations	CARICOM, Comm., UN

St Vincent, whose territory includes islets and cays in The Grenadines, is in the Windward Islands in the Caribbean Sea. St Vincent is forested and mountainous, with an active volcano, Soufrière. The climate is tropical and wet. The economy is based mainly on agriculture and tourism. Bananas account for around a third of export earnings, arrowroot is also important.

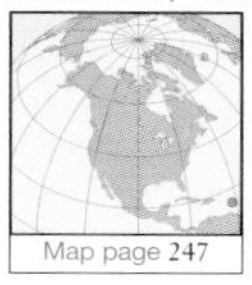
Map page 247

SAMOA
Independent State of Samoa

Area Sq Km	2 831	Currency	Tala
Area Sq Miles	1 093	Languages	Samoan, English
Population	174 000	Religions	Protestant, Roman Catholic
Capital	Apia	Organizations	Comm., UN

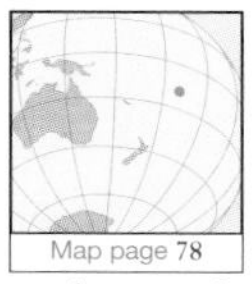
Map page 78

Samoa consists of two larger mountainous and forested islands, Savai'i and Upolu, and seven smaller islands in the south Pacific Ocean. Over half the population live on Upolu. The climate is tropical. The economy is based on agriculture, with some fishing and light manufacturing. Traditional exports are coconut products, timber, taro, cocoa and fruit. Tourism is increasing, but the islands depend upon workers' remittances and foreign aid.

SAN MARINO
Republic of San Marino

Area Sq Km	61	Currency	Ital. lira
Area Sq Miles	24	Languages	Italian
Population	26 000	Religions	Roman Catholic
Capital	San Marino	Organizations	UN

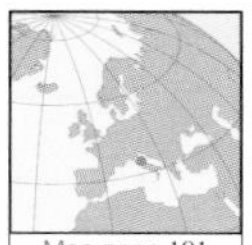
Map page 191

Landlocked San Marino lies in northeast Italy. A third of the people live in the capital. There is some agriculture and light industry, but most income comes from tourism. Most trade is with Italy.

SÃO TOMÉ AND PRÍNCIPE
Democratic Republic of São Tomé and Príncipe

Area Sq Km	964	Currency	Dobra
Area Sq Miles	372	Languages	Portuguese, creole
Population	141 000	Religions	Roman Catholic, Protestant
Capital	São Tomé	Organizations	UN

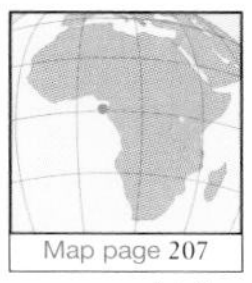
Map page 207

The two main islands and adjacent islets lie off the coast of west Africa in the Gulf of Guinea. São Tomé is the larger island with over ninety per cent of the population. Both São Tomé and Príncipe are mountainous and tree-covered, and have a hot and humid climate. The economy is heavily dependent on cocoa, which accounts for around ninety per cent of export earnings.

SAUDI ARABIA
Kingdom of Saudi Arabia

Area Sq Km	2 200 000	Currency	Riyal
Area Sq Miles	849 425	Languages	Arabic
Population	20 181 000	Religions	Sunni Muslim, Shi'a Muslim
Capital	Riyadh	Organizations	OPEC, UN

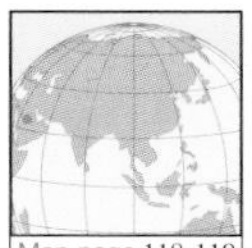
Map page 118-119

Saudi Arabia occupies most of the Arabian Peninsula in southwest Asia. The terrain is desert or semi-desert plateaus, which rise to mountains running parallel to the Red Sea in the west and slope down to plains in the southeast and along The Gulf in the east. Over eighty per cent of the population live in urban areas. There are around four million foreign workers in Saudi Arabia employed mainly in the oil and service industries. Summers are hot, winters are warm and rainfall is low. Saudi Arabia has the world's largest reserves of oil and significant natural gas reserves, located in the northeast, both onshore and in The Gulf. Crude oil and refined products account for over ninety per cent of export earnings. Other industries and irrigated agriculture are being encouraged, but most food and raw materials are imported. Saudi Arabia has important banking and commercial interests. Each year around two million pilgrims visit Islam's holiest cities, Mecca and Medina, in the west. Japan, USA, South Korea and Singapore are the main export trading partners.

SENEGAL
Republic of Senegal

Area Sq Km	196 720	Currency	CFA franc
Area Sq Miles	75 954	Languages	French, Wolof, Fulani, local languages
Population	9 003 000	Religions	Sunni Muslim, Roman Catholic, traditional beliefs
Capital	Dakar	Organizations	UN

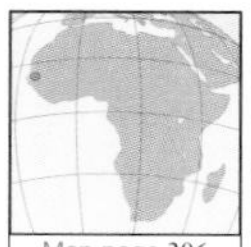
Map page 206

Senegal lies on the Atlantic coast of west Africa. The north is arid semi-desert, while the south is mainly fertile savanna bushland. The climate is tropical with summer rains, though droughts occur. One fifth of the population lives in and around Dakar. Fish, chemical products, groundnuts and phosphates are the main exports. Dakar is a major port and tourism is developing. France is the main trading partner.

SEYCHELLES
Republic of the Seychelles

Area Sq Km	455	Currency	Rupee
Area Sq Miles	176	Languages	English, French, creole
Population	76 000	Religions	Roman Catholic, Protestant
Capital	Victoria	Organizations	Comm., SADC, UN

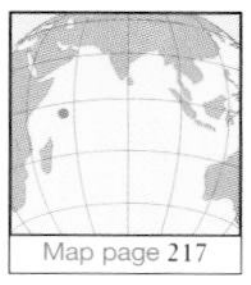
Map page 217

The Seychelles comprises an archipelago of over one hundred granitic and coral islands in the western Indian Ocean. Over ninety per cent of the population live on the main island, Mahé. The climate is hot and humid with heavy rainfall. The economy is based mainly on tourism, fishing and light manufacturing.

SIERRA LEONE
Republic of Sierra Leone

Area Sq Km	71 740	Currency	Leone
Area Sq Miles	27 699	Languages	English, creole, Mende, Temne, local languages
Population	4 568 000	Religions	Sunni Muslim, traditional beliefs
Capital	Freetown	Organizations	Comm., UN

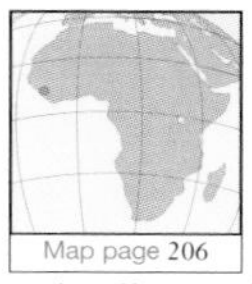
Map page 206

Sierra Leone lies on the Atlantic coast of west Africa. Its coast is heavily indented and lined with mangrove swamps. Inland is a forested area rising to savanna plateaus, with the mountains to the northeast. The climate is tropical and rainfall is heavy. Most of the workforce is involved in subsistence farming. Cocoa and coffee are the main cash crops, but diamonds and rutile (titanium ore) are the main exports, though a substantial amount of diamonds are smuggled out of the country. Civil war and economic decline have caused serious difficulties.

SINGAPORE
Republic of Singapore

Area Sq Km	639	Currency	Dollar
Area Sq Miles	247	Languages	Chinese, English, Malay, Tamil
Population	3 476 000	Religions	Buddhist, Taoist, Sunni Muslim, Christian, Hindu
Capital	Singapore	Organizations	APEC, ASEAN, Comm., UN

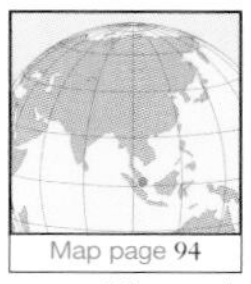
Map page 94

The state comprises the main island of Singapore and over fifty other islands, lying off the southern tip of the Malay Peninsula in southeast Asia. Singapore is generally low-lying and includes land reclaimed from swamps and the sea. It is hot and humid, with heavy rainfall throughout the year. There are fish farms and vegetable gardens in the north and east of the island, but most food needs must be imported. Singapore also lacks mineral and energy resources. Manufacturing industries and services are the main sectors of the economy. Their rapid development has fuelled the nation's impressive economic growth over the last three decades. The main industries include electronics, oil refining, chemicals, pharmaceuticals, ship repair, food processing and textiles. Singapore is a major financial centre. Its port is one of the world's largest and busiest and acts as an entrepôt for neighbouring states. Tourism is also important. Japan, USA and Malaysia are the main trading partners.

Sint Eustatius part of Netherlands Antilles

Area Sq Km (Miles) 21 (8) | Population 1 900 | Capital Oranjestad

An island in the Leeward Islands in the Lesser Antilles in the Caribbean south of Sint Maarten; there is a developing tourism industry.

Map page 247

Sint Maarten part of Netherlands Antilles

Area Sq Km (Miles) 34 (13) | Population 38 567 | Capital Philipsburg

The southern part of one of the Leeward Islands is in the Caribbean, the other part of the island is a dependency of Guadeloupe. Tourism and fishing are the most important industries.

Map page 247

SLOVAKIA
Slovak Republic

Area Sq Km	49 035	Currency	Koruna
Area Sq Miles	18 933	Languages	Slovak, Hungarian, Czech
Population	5 377 000	Religions	Roman Catholic, Protestant, Orthodox
Capital	Bratislava	Organizations	UN

A landlocked country in central Europe, Slovakia borders the Czech Republic, Poland, Ukraine, Hungary and Austria. Slovakia is mountainous along the border with Poland in the north, but low-lying in the southwest. The climate is continental. There are a range of manufacturing industries and the main exports are machinery and transport equipment, but during the 1990s there were continued economic difficulties and economic growth has been slow. Most trade is with EU countries and the Czech Republic and negotiations to join the EU have begun.

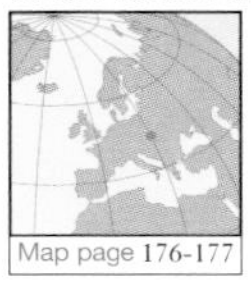
Map page 176-177

SLOVENIA
Republic of Slovenia

Area Sq Km	20 251	Currency	Tólar
Area Sq Miles	7 819	Languages	Slovene, Croatian, Serbian
Population	1 993 000	Religions	Roman Catholic, Protestant
Capital	Ljubljana	Organizations	UN

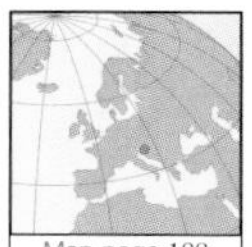
Map page 188

Slovenia lies in the northwest Balkans of south Europe and has a short coastline on the Adriatic Sea. It is mountainous and hilly, with lowlands on the coast and in the Sava and Drava river valleys. The climate is generally continental, but Mediterranean nearer the coast. The main agricultural products are potatoes, grains and sugar beet; the main industries include metal processing, electronics and consumer goods. Trade has been re-orientated towards western markets, the main trading partners are Germany and Italy. Negotiations to join the EU have begun.

SOLOMON ISLANDS

Area Sq Km	28 370	Currency	Dollar
Area Sq Miles	10 954	Languages	English, creole, local languages
Population	417 000	Religions	Protestant, Roman Catholic
Capital	Honiara	Organizations	Comm., UN

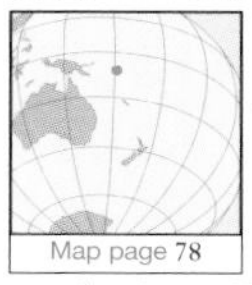
Map page 78

The state consists of the Solomon, Santa Cruz and Shortland Islands in the southwest Pacific Ocean. The six main islands are volcanic, mountainous and forested, though Guadalcanal, the most populous, has a large lowland area. The climate is generally hot and humid. Subsistence farming, forestry and fishing predominate. Exports include timber products, fish, copra and palm oil. The islands depend on foreign aid.

SOMALIA
Somali Democratic Republic

Area Sq Km	637 657	Currency	Shilling
Area Sq Miles	246 201	Languages	Somali, Arabic
Population	9 237 000	Religions	Sunni Muslim
Capital	Muqdisho	Organizations	UN

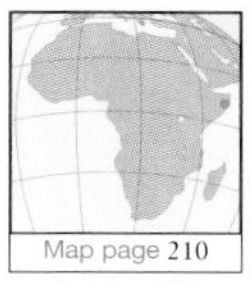
Map page 210

Somalia is in the northeast Africa, on the Gulf of Aden and Indian Ocean. It consists of a dry scrubby plateau, rising to highlands in the north. The climate is hot and dry, but coastal areas and the Jubba and Webi Shabeelle river valleys support crops and most of the population. Subsistence farming and livestock rearing are the main activities. Exports include livestock and bananas. Frequent drought and civil war have prevented economic development. Somalia is one of the poorest and least developed countries in the world.

SOUTH AFRICA, REPUBLIC OF

Area Sq Km	1 219 090	Currency	Rand
Area Sq Miles	470 693	Languages	Afrikaans, English, nine official local languages
Population	39 357 000	Religions	Protestant, Roman Catholic, Sunni Muslim, Hindu
Capital	Pretoria/ Cape Town	Organizations	Comm., SADC, UN

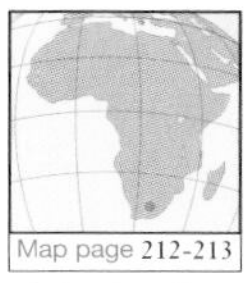
Map page 212-213

South Africa occupies most of the southern part of Africa. It borders five states, surrounds Lesotho and has a long coastline stretching from the Atlantic to the Indian Ocean. Much of the land is a vast plateau, covered with grassland or bush and drained by the Orange and Limpopo river systems. A fertile coastal plain rises to mountain ridges in the south and east, including Table Mountain near Cape Town and the Drakensberg range in the east. Gauteng is the most populous province, with Johannesburg and Pretoria its main cities. South Africa has warm summers and mild winters. Most of the country has rainfall in summer, but the coast around Cape Town has winter rains. South Africa is the largest and most developed economy in Africa, though wealth and economic control is unevenly distributed and unemployment is very high. Agriculture employs about a third of the workforce, crops include fruit, wine, wool and maize. South Africa is rich in minerals. It is the world's leading producer of gold and chromium and an important producer of diamonds; many other minerals are also mined. The main industries process minerals and agricultural produce, manufacture chemical products, electrical equipment and textiles, and assemble motor vehicles. Financial services are also important.

SOUTH KOREA
Republic of Korea

Area Sq Km	99 274	Currency	Won
Area Sq Miles	38 330	Languages	Korean
Population	46 109 000	Religions	Buddhist, Protestant, Roman Catholic
Capital	Sŏul	Organizations	APEC, UN

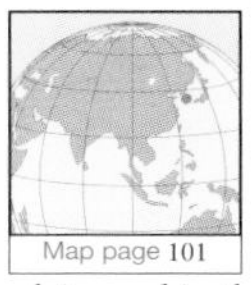
Map page 101

The state consists of the southern half of the Korean Peninsula in east Asia and many islands lying off the western and southern coasts in the Yellow Sea. The terrain is mountainous, though less rugged than that of North Korea. Population density is high and highly urbanized; most people live on the western coastal plains and in the basins of the Han-gang in the northwest and the Naktong-gang in the southeast. South Korea has a continental climate, with hot, wet summers and dry, cold winters. Arable land is limited by the mountainous terrain, but because of intensive farming South Korea is nearly self-sufficient in food. Sericulture is important as is fishing, which contributes to exports. South Korea has few mineral resources, except for coal and tungsten. It has achieved high economic growth based mainly on export manufacturing. The main manufactures are cars, electronic and electrical goods, ships, steel, chemicals, and toys as well as textiles, clothing, footwear and food products. USA and Japan are the main trading partners.

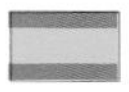

SPAIN
Kingdom of Spain

Area Sq Km	504 782	Currency	Peseta, Euro
Area Sq Miles	194 897	Languages	Castilian, Catalan, Galician, Basque
Population	39 628 000	Religions	Roman Catholic
Capital	Madrid	Organizations	EU, OECD, UN

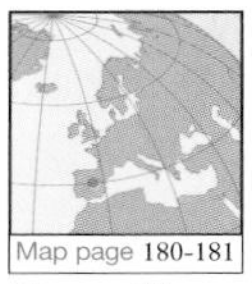

Map page 180-181

Spain occupies the greater part of the Iberian peninsula in southwest Europe, with coastlines on the Atlantic Ocean and Mediterranean Sea. It includes the Balearic and Canary Islands in the Mediterranean and Atlantic, and two enclaves in north Africa, Ceuta and Melilla. Much of the mainland is a high plateau drained by the Duero, Tagus and Guadiana rivers. The plateau is interrupted by a low mountain range and bounded to the east and north also by mountains, including the Pyrenees which form the border with France and Andorra. The main lowland areas are the Ebro basin in the northeast, the eastern coastal plains and the Guadalquivir basin in the southwest. Over three quarters of the population live in urban areas. The plateau experiences hot summers and cold winters. Conditions are cooler and wetter to the north, though warmer and drier to the south. Agriculture involves about ten per cent of the workforce and fruit, vegetables and wine are exported. Fishing is an important industry and Spain has a large fishing fleet. Mineral resources include lead, copper, mercury and fluorspar. Some oil is produced, but Spain has to import most energy needs. The economy is based on manufacturing and services. The principal products are machinery, transport equipment, and motor vehicles; other manufactures are agricultural products, chemicals, steel and other metals, paper products, wood and cork products, clothing and footwear, and textiles. With around fifty million visitors a year, tourism is a major industry, banking and commerce are also important. Around seventy per cent of trade is with other EU countries.

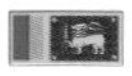

SRI LANKA
Democratic Socialist Republic of Sri Lanka

Area Sq Km	65 610	Currency	Rupee
Area Sq Miles	25 332	Languages	Sinhalese, Tamil, English
Population	18 455 000	Religions	Buddhist, Hindu, Sunni Muslim, Roman Catholic
Capital	Sri Jayewardenepura Kotte	Organizations	Comm., UN

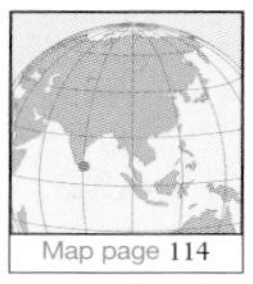

Map page 114

Sri Lanka lies in the Indian Ocean off the southeast coast of India in south Asia. It has rolling coastal plains with mountains in the centre-south. The climate is hot and monsoonal and most people live on the west coast. Manufactures (chiefly textiles and clothing), tea, rubber, copra and gems are exported. The economy relies on aid and workers' remittances. Tourism has been damaged by separatist activities.

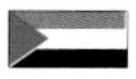

SUDAN
Republic of the Sudan

Area Sq Km	2 505 813	Currency	Dinar
Area Sq Miles	967 500	Languages	Arabic, Dinka, Nubian, Beja, Nuer, local languages
Population	28 292 000	Religions	Sunni Muslim, traditional beliefs, Christian
Capital	Khartoum	Organizations	UN

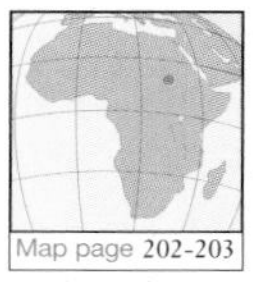

Map page 202-203

Africa's largest country, Sudan is in the northeast, on the Red Sea. It lies within the upper Nile basin, much of which is arid plain but with swamps to the south. Mountains lie to the northeast, west and south. The climate is hot and arid with light summer rainfall, though droughts occur. Most people live along the Nile and are farmers and herders. Cotton, gum arabic, livestock and other agricultural products are exported. The government is working with foreign investors to develop oil resources; but civil war in the south of Sudan continues to restrict growth of the economy.

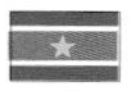

SURINAME
Republic of Suriname

Area Sq Km	163 820	Currency	Guilder
Area Sq Miles	63 251	Languages	Dutch, Surinamese, English, Hindi
Population	414 000	Religions	Hindu, Roman Catholic, Protestant, Sunni Muslim
Capital	Paramaribo	Organizations	CARICOM, UN

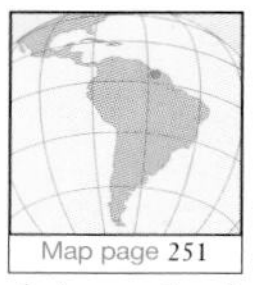

Map page 251

Suriname, on the Atlantic coast of northern South America, consists of a swampy coastal plain (where most people live), central plateaus and highlands in the south. The climate is tropical and rainforest covers much of the land. Bauxite mining is the main industry, and alumina and aluminium are the chief exports, with shrimps, rice, bananas and timber also exported. The main trading partners are The Netherlands, Norway and USA.

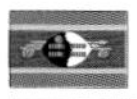

SWAZILAND
Kingdom of Swaziland

Area Sq Km	17 364	Currency	Lilangeni
Area Sq Miles	6 704	Languages	Swazi, English
Population	952 000	Religions	Christian, traditional beliefs
Capital	Mbabane	Organizations	Comm., SADC, UN

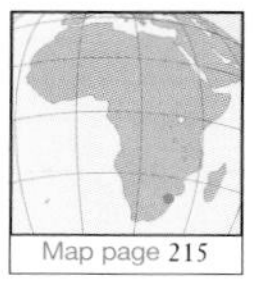

Map page 215

Landlocked Swaziland in southern Africa lies between Mozambique and South Africa. Savanna plateaus descend from mountains in the west towards hill country in the east. The climate is subtropical, but temperate in the mountains. Subsistence farming predominates. Asbestos and some diamonds are mined. Exports include sugar, fruit and wood pulp. Tourism and workers' remittances are important to the economy. Most trade is with South Africa.

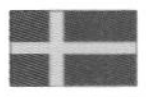

SWEDEN
Kingdom of Sweden

Area Sq Km	449 964	Currency	Krona
Area Sq Miles	173 732	Languages	Swedish
Population	8 875 000	Religions	Protestant, Roman Catholic
Capital	Stockholm	Organizations	EU, OECD, UN

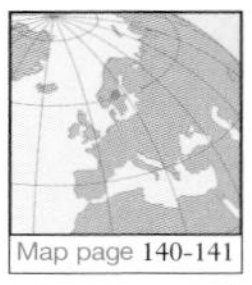

Map page 140-141

Sweden, the largest and most populous of the Scandinavian countries, occupies the eastern part of the peninsula in north Europe and borders the North and Baltic Seas and Gulf of Bothnia. Forested mountains cover the northern half of the country, part of which lies within the Arctic Circle. Southwards is a lowland lake region, where most of the population lives. Farther south is an upland region, and then a fertile plain at the tip of the peninsula. Sweden has warm summers and cold winters, though the latter are longer and more severe in the north. Natural resources include coniferous forests, mineral deposits and water resources. There is little agriculture, though some dairy products, meat, cereals and vegetables are produced in the south. The forests supply timber for export and for the important pulp, paper and furniture industries. Sweden is an important producer of iron ore and copper; zinc, lead, silver and gold are also mined. Machinery and transport equipment, chemicals, electrical goods and telecommunications equipment are the main industries. The majority of trade is with other EU countries.

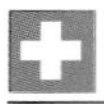

SWITZERLAND
Swiss Confederation

Area Sq Km	41 293	Currency	Franc
Area Sq Miles	15 943	Languages	German, French, Italian, Romansch
Population	7 299 000	Religions	Roman Catholic, Protestant
Capital	Bern	Organizations	OECD

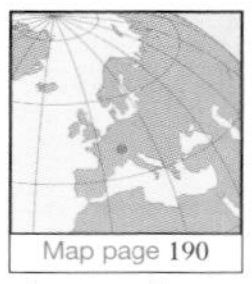

Map page 190

Switzerland is a landlocked country of west central Europe that is surrounded by France, Germany, Austria, Liechtenstein and Italy. It is also Europe's most mountainous country. The southern half lies within the Alps, while the northwest is dominated by the Jura mountains. The rest of the land is a high plateau where most people live. The climate varies greatly, depending on altitude and relief, but in general summers are mild and winters are cold with heavy snowfalls. Switzerland has one of the highest standards of living in the world. Yet it has few mineral resources and most food and industrial raw materials have to be imported. Manufacturing makes the largest contribution to the economy and though varied is specialist in certain products. Engineering is the most important industry, producing precision instruments and heavy machinery, other important industries are chemicals and pharmaceuticals. Banking and financial services are very important and Zurich is one of the world's leading banking cities. Tourism, and international organizations based in Switzerland are also major foreign currency earners. Germany is the main trading partner.

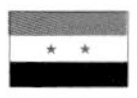

SYRIA
Syrian Arab Republic

Area Sq Km	185 180	Currency	Pound
Area Sq Miles	71 498	Languages	Arabic, Kurdish, Armenian
Population	15 333 000	Religions	Sunni Muslim, Shi'a Muslim, Christian
Capital	Damascus	Organizations	UN

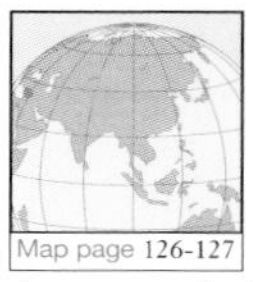

Map page 126-127

Syria is in southwest Asia, on the Mediterranean Sea. Behind the coastal plain lies a range of hills and then a plateau cut by the Euphrates river. Mountains flank the southwest borders with Lebanon and Israel, east of which is desert. The climate is Mediterranean in coastal regions, hotter and drier inland. Most Syrians live on the coast or in the river valleys. Cotton, cereals and fruit are important, but the main exports are petroleum and its products, and textiles.

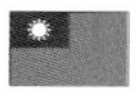

TAIWAN

Area Sq Km	36 179	Currency	Dollar
Area Sq Miles	13 969	Languages	Mandarin, Min, Hakka, local languages
Population	21 908 135	Religions	Buddhist, Taoist, Confucian, Christian
Capital	T'aipei	Organizations	APEC

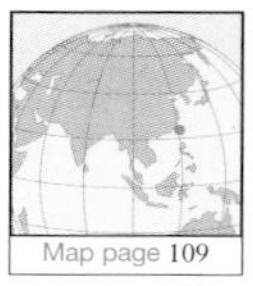

Map page 109

The east Asian state consists of the island of Taiwan, separated from mainland China by the Taiwan Strait, and several much smaller islands. Much of Taiwan is mountainous and forested. Densely populated coastal plains in the west contain the bulk of the population and most economic activity. Taiwan has a tropical monsoon climate, with warm, wet summers and mild winters. Agriculture is highly productive. Taiwan is virtually self-sufficient in food and exports some products. Coal, oil and natural gas are produced and a few minerals are mined but none of them are of great significance to the economy. Taiwan depends heavily on imports of raw materials and exports of manufactured goods. The main manufactures are electrical and electronic goods, including television sets, personal computers and calculators, textiles, fertilizers, clothing, footwear and toys. The main trading partners are USA, Japan and Germany.

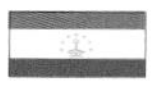

TAJIKISTAN
Republic of Tajikistan

Area Sq Km	143 100	Currency	Rouble
Area Sq Miles	55 251	Languages	Tajik, Uzbek, Russian
Population	6 015 000	Religions	Sunni Muslim
Capital	Dushanbe	Organizations	CIS, UN

Landlocked Tajikistan in central Asia is a mountainous country, occupying the Alai Range and the Pamir. In less mountainous western areas summers are warm though winters are cold. Agriculture is the main sector of the economy, chiefly cotton growing and cattle breeding. Mineral deposits include lead, zinc, and uranium. Metal processing, textiles and clothing are the main manufactures; the main exports are aluminium and cotton. Russia, Kazakhstan and Uzbekistan are the main trading partners.

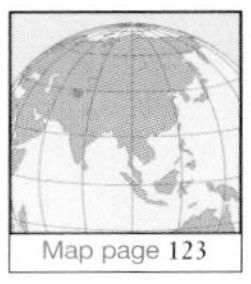

Map page 123

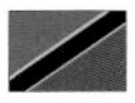

TANZANIA
United Republic of Tanzania

Area Sq Km	945 087	Currency	Shilling
Area Sq Miles	364 900	Languages	Swahili, English, Nyamwezi, local languages
Population	32 102 000	Religions	Muslim, traditional beliefs, Christian
Capital	Dodoma	Organizations	Comm., SADC, UN

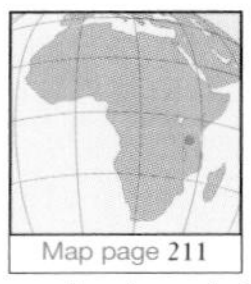

Map page 211

Tanzania lies on the coast of east Africa and includes the island of Zanzibar in the Indian Ocean. Most of the mainland is a savanna plateau lying east of the Great Rift Valley. In the north are Kilimanjaro, the highest mountain in Africa, and the Serangeti National Park. The climate is tropical. The economy is predominantly based on agriculture which employs an estimated ninety per cent of the workforce. Coffee, cotton, cashew nuts and tobacco are the main exports, with cloves from Zanzibar. Agricultural processing and gold and diamond mining are the main industries, though tourism is growing. Tanzania is one of the least developed countries in the world and depends heavily on aid.

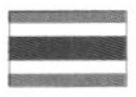

THAILAND
Kingdom of Thailand

Area Sq Km	513 115	Currency	Baht
Area Sq Miles	198 115	Languages	Thai, Lao, Chinese, Malay, Mon-Khmer languages
Population	60 300 000	Religions	Buddhist, Sunni Muslim
Capital	Bangkok	Organizations	APEC, ASEAN, ÙN

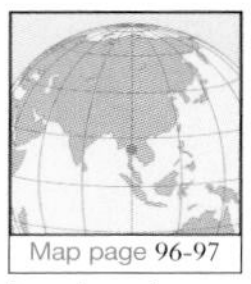

Map page 96-97

A country in southeast Asia, Thailand borders Myanmar, Laos, Cambodia and Malaysia and has coastlines on the Gulf of Thailand and Andaman Sea. Central Thailand is dominated by the Chao Phraya river basin, which contains Bangkok, the only major urban centre, and most economic activity. To the east is a dry plateau drained by tributaries of the Mekong river, while to the north, west and south, extending halfway down the Malay peninsula, are forested hills and mountains. Many small islands line the coast. The climate is hot, humid and monsoonal. About half the workforce is involved in agriculture. Thailand is one of the world's leading exporters of rice and rubber, and a major exporter of maize and tapioca. Fish and fish processing are important. Thailand produces natural gas, some oil and lignite, minerals (chiefly tin, tungsten and baryte) and gemstones. Manufacturing is the largest contributor to national income, with electronics, textiles, clothing and footwear, and food processing the main industries. With around seven million visitors a year, tourism is the major source of foreign exchange. Japan and USA are the main trading partners.

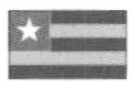

TOGO
Republic of Togo

Area Sq Km	56 785	Currency	CFA franc
Area Sq Miles	21 925	Languages	French, Ewe, Kabre, local languages
Population	4 397 000	Religions	Traditional beliefs, Christian, Sunni Muslim
Capital	Lomé	Organizations	UN

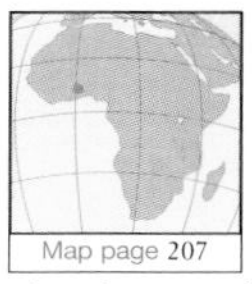

Map page 207

Togo is a long narrow country in west Africa with a short coastline on the Gulf of Guinea. The interior consists of plateaus rising to mountainous areas. The climate is tropical, drier inland. Agriculture is the mainstay of the economy. Phosphate mining and food processing are the main industries. Cotton, phosphates, coffee and cocoa are the main exports. Lomé is an entrepôt trade centre.

Tokelau New Zealand Overseas Territory

Area Sq Km (Miles)	10 (4)	Population	1 000

Tokelau consists of three atolls, Atafu, Nukunonu and Fakaofa, in the Pacific Ocean north of Samoa. Subsistence agriculture is the main activity, and the islands rely on aid and remittances from New Zealand.

Map page 81

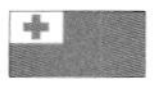

TONGA
Kingdom of Tonga

Area Sq Km	748	Currency	Pa'anga
Area Sq Miles	289	Languages	Tongan, English
Population	98 000	Religions	Protestant, Roman Catholic
Capital	Nuku'alofa	Organizations	Comm., UN

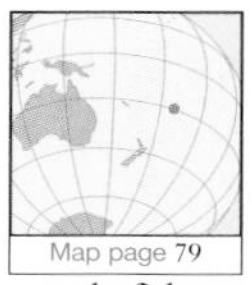

Map page 79

Tonga comprises some one hundred and seventy islands in the south Pacific Ocean, northeast of New Zealand. The three main groups are Tongatapu (where sixty per cent of Tongans live), Ha'apai and Vava'u. The climate is warm with good rainfall and the economy relies heavily on agriculture. Exports include squash, fish, vanilla beans and root crops. Tourism and light industry are increasingly important.

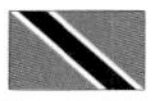

TRINIDAD AND TOBAGO
Republic of Trinidad and Tobago

Area Sq Km	5 130	Currency	Dollar
Area Sq Miles	1 981	Languages	English, creole, Hindi
Population	1 283 000	Religions	Roman Catholic, Hindu, Protestant, Sunni Muslim
Capital	Port of Spain	Organizations	CARICOM, Comm., UN

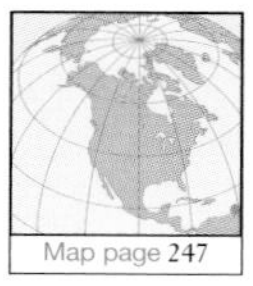
Map page 247

Trinidad, the most southerly Caribbean island, lies off the Venezuelan coast. It is hilly in the north, with a central plain. Tobago, to the northeast, is smaller, more mountainous and less developed. The climate is tropical. Oil and petrochemicals industries dominate the economy. The main crops are cocoa, sugar cane, coffee and fruit and vegetables. Tourism is also important.USA is the main trading partner.

Tristan da Cunha Dependency of St Helena

Area Sq Km (Miles) 98 (38) Population 300 Capital Settlement of Edinburgh

A group of volcanic islands in the south Atlantic Ocean, the other main islands in the group are Nightingale Island and Inaccessible Island; the group is over 2000 kilometres (1250 miles) south of St Helena. The economy is based on fishing, fish processing and agriculture, and ecotourism is increasing.

Map page 216

TUNISIA
Republic of Tunisia

Area Sq Km	164 150	Currency	Dinar
Area Sq Miles	63 379	Languages	Arabic, French
Population	9 335 000	Religions	Sunni Muslim
Capital	Tunis	Organizations	UN

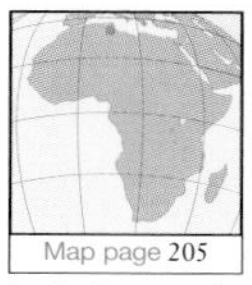
Map page 205

Tunisia is on the Mediterranean coast of north Africa. The north is mountainous with valleys and coastal plains, where most people live. The north has a Mediterranean climate, the south is hot and arid. Oil and phosphates are the main resources. The main crops are olives and citrus fruit. Exports include petroleum products, textiles, fruit and phosphorus; tourism is important with around five million visitors a year. Most trade is with EU countries; Tunisia has an agreement with the EU to create a free trade zone.

TURKEY
Republic of Turkey

Area Sq Km	779 452	Currency	Lira
Area Sq Miles	300 948	Languages	Turkish, Kurdish
Population	64 479 000	Religions	Sunni Muslim, Shi'a Muslim
Capital	Ankara	Organizations	OECD, UN

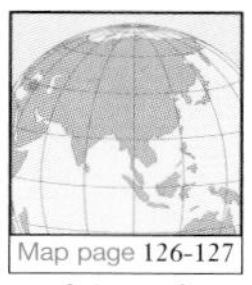
Map page 126-127

Turkey occupies the Asia Minor peninsula of southwest Asia and has coastlines on the Black, Mediterranean and Aegean Seas. It includes eastern Thrace, which is in south Europe and separated from the rest of the country by the Bosporus, Sea of Marmara and Dardanelles. The Asian mainland consists of the semi-arid Anatolian plateau, flanked to the north, south and east by mountains. Over forty per cent of Turks live in central Anatolia and the Marmara and Aegean coastal plains. The coast has a Mediterranean climate, but inland conditions are more extreme with hot, dry summers and cold, snowy winters. Agriculture involves about forty per cent of the workforce and products include cotton, grain, tobacco, fruit, nuts and livestock. Turkey is a leading producer of chrome, iron ore, lead, tin, borates, and baryte; coal is also mined. The main manufactures are textiles (the chief export), food processing, steel, vehicles and chemicals; tourism is a major industry with nine million visitors a year. Germany and USA are the main trading partners. Remittances by workers aboard are important.

TURKMENISTAN
Republic of Turkmenistan

Area Sq Km	488 100	Currency	Manat
Area Sq Miles	188 456	Languages	Turkmen, Uzbek, Russian
Population	4 309 000	Religions	Sunni Muslim, Russian Orthodox
Capital	Ashgabat	Organizations	CIS, UN

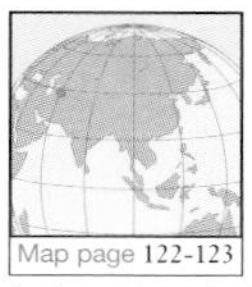
Map page 122-123

Turkmenistan, in central Asia, lies mainly within the plains of the Karakum Desert; most people live on the desert fringes: the foothills of the Kopet Dag in the south, Amudar'ya valley in the north and Caspian Sea plains in the west. The climate is dry with extreme temperatures. The economy is based mainly on irrigated agriculture, chiefly cotton growing, and the production of natural gas; there are also reserves of oil. Development of the natural gas and oil resources depend on building further pipelines. Russia is the main trading partner.

Turks and Caicos Islands
United Kingdom Overseas Territory

Area Sq Km (Miles) 430 (166) Population 16 000 Capital Grand Turk

The state consists of forty or so low-lying islands and cays in the northern Caribbean. Only eight islands are inhabited; two fifths of the people live on Grand Turk and Salt Cay. The climate is tropical. The economy is based on tourism, fishing and offshore banking.

Map page 246

TUVALU

Area Sq Km	25	Currency	Dollar
Area Sq Miles	10	Languages	Tuvaluan, English
Population	11 000	Religions	Protestant
Capital	Vaiaku	Organizations	Comm.

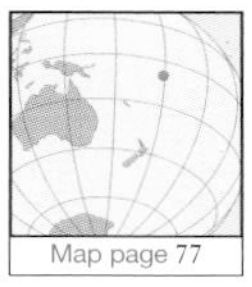
Map page 77

Tuvalu comprises nine low lying coral atolls in the south Pacific Ocean. One third of the population lives on Funafuti and most people depend on subsistence farming and fishing. The islands export copra, stamps and clothing, but rely heavily on foreign aid. Tuvalu is a special member of the Commonwealth.

UGANDA
Republic of Uganda

Area Sq Km	241 038	Currency	Shilling
Area Sq Miles	93 065	Languages	English, Swahili, Luganda, local languages
Population	20 554 000	Religions	Roman Catholic, Protestant, Muslim, trad. beliefs
Capital	Kampala	Organizations	Comm., UN

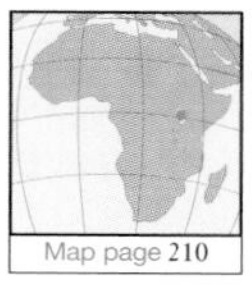
Map page 210

A landlocked country in east Africa, Uganda consists of a savanna plateau with mountains and lakes. The climate is warm and wet. Most people live in the southern half of the country; life expectancy in Uganda has fallen by fifteen per cent since 1975 because of AIDS. Agriculture employs around eighty per cent of the workforce and dominates the economy. Coffee, cotton and tea are the main exports. Uganda relies heavily on aid.

UKRAINE

Area Sq Km	603 700	Currency	Hryvnia
Area Sq Miles	233 090	Languages	Ukrainian, Russian
Population	50 861 000	Religions	Orthodox, Ukrainian Catholic, Roman Catholic
Capital	Kyiv	Organizations	CIS, UN

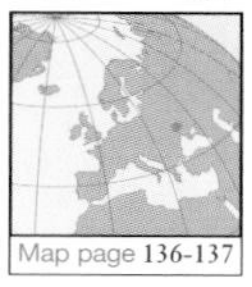
Map page 136-137

Ukraine lies on the Black Sea coast of east Europe. Much of the land is steppe, generally flat and treeless, but with rich black soil and drained by the river Dnieper. Along the border with Belarus are forested, marshy plains. The only uplands are the Carpathian Mountains in the west and smaller ranges on the Crimea peninsula. Summers are warm and winters are cold, with milder conditions in the Crimea. About a quarter of the population lives in the mainly industrial areas around Donets'k, Kyiv and Dnipropetrovs'k. The Ukraine is rich in natural resources: fertile soil, substantial mineral and natural gas deposits, and forests. Agriculture and livestock raising are important, but mining and manufacturing are the most important sectors of the economy. Coal, iron and manganese mining, steel and metal production, machinery, chemicals and food processing are the main industries. Russia is the main trading partner.

UNITED ARAB EMIRATES
Federation of Emirates

Area Sq Km	83 600	Currency	Dirham
Area Sq Miles	32 278	Languages	Arabic,English
Population	2 377 453	Religions	Sunni Muslim, Shi'a Muslim
Capital	Abu Dhabi	Organizations	OPEC, UN

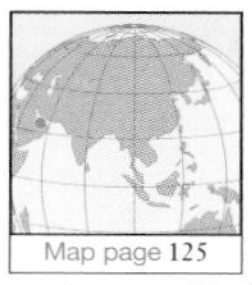
Map page 125

The UAE lies on the northeast of the Arabian Peninsula, in southwest Asia. Six emirates lie on The Gulf while the seventh, Fujairah, lies on the Gulf of Oman. Most of the land is flat desert with sand dunes and salt pans. The only hilly area is in the northeast. Over eighty per cent of the population live in three emirates - Abu Dhabi, Dubai and Sharjah. Summers are hot and winters are mild with occasional rainfall in coastal areas. Fruit and vegetables are grown in oases and irrigated areas, but the Emirates wealth is based on hydrocarbons, mainly within Abu Dhabi, but with smaller supplies in Dubai, Sharjah and Ras al Khaimah. The UAE is the third largest oil producer in the Middle East after Saudi Arabia and Iran. Dubai is an important entrepôt trade centre; tourism is increasing in importance.

Abu Dhabi (Emirate)
Area Sq Km (Miles) 73 060 (28 209) Population 928 360 Capital Abu Dhabi

Ajman (Emirate)
Area Sq Km (Miles) 260 (100) Population 118 812 Capital Ajman

Dubai (Emirate)
Area Sq Km (Miles) 3 900 (1 506) Population 674 101 Capital Dubai

Fujairah (Emirate)
Area Sq Km (Miles) 1 300 (502) Population 76 254 Capital Fujairah

Ras al Khaimah (Emirate)
Area Sq Km (Miles) 1 700 (656) Population 144 430 Capital Ras al Khaimah

Sharjah (Emirate)
Area Sq Km (Miles) 2 600 (1 004) Population 400 339 Capital Sharjah

Umm al Qaiwain (Emirate)
Area Sq Km (Miles) 780 (301) Population 35 157 Capital Umm al Qaiwain

UNITED KINGDOM
United Kingdom of Great Britain and Northern Ireland

Area Sq Km	244 082	Currency	Pound
Area Sq Miles	94 241	Languages	English, Welsh, Gaelic
Population	58 649 000	Religions	Protestant, Roman Catholic, Muslim
Capital	London	Organizations	Comm., EU, OECD, UN

A country in northwest Europe, the United Kingdom occupies the island of Great Britain, part of Ireland and many small adjacent islands. Great Britain comprises the countries of England, Scotland and Wales. England covers over half the land area and supports over four-fifths of the population, chiefly in the southeast region. The landscape is flat or rolling with some uplands, notably the Cheviot Hills on the Scottish border, the Pennines in the centre-north and the hills of the Lake District in the northwest. Scotland consists of southern uplands, central lowlands, highlands (which include the UK's highest peak) and islands. Wales is a land of mountains and river valleys. Northern Ireland contains uplands, plains and the UK's largest lake, Lough Neagh. The climate is mild, wet and variable. The UK has few mineral deposits, but has important energy resources. Over forty per cent of land is suitable for grazing, about twenty five per cent is cultivated, and ten per cent is forested. Agriculture involves mainly sheep and cattle raising and dairy farming, with crop and fruit growing in the east and southeast. Productivity is high, but about one third of food needs must be imported. The UK produces petroleum and natural gas from reserves in the North Sea and is self-sufficient in energy in net terms. It also has

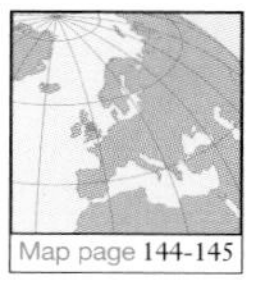
Map page 144-145

reserves of coal, though the coal industry has contracted. Major manufactures are food and drinks, motor vehicles and parts, aerospace equipment, machinery, electronic and electrical equipment, and chemicals and chemical products. However, the economy is dominated by service industries, including banking, insurance, finance and business services. London is one of the world's major financial centres. Tourism is a major industry, with around twenty five million visitors a year. International trade is also important, equivalent to a third of national income; over half of trade is with other EU countries.

England (Constituent country)
Area Sq Km (Miles) 130 423 (50 357) Population 49 284 200 Capital London

Northern Ireland (Province)
Area Sq Km (Miles) 14 121 (5 452) Population 1 675 000 Capital Belfast

Scotland (Constituent country)
Area Sq Km (Miles) 78 772 (30 414) Population 5 122 500 Capital Edinburgh

Wales (Principality)
Area Sq Km (Miles) 20 766 (8 018) Population 2 926 900 Capital Cardiff

UNITED STATES OF AMERICA
Federal Republic

Area Sq Km	9 809 378	Currency	Dollar
Area Sq Miles	3 787 422	Languages	English, Spanish
Population	274 028 000	Religions	Protestant, Roman Catholic, Sunni Muslim, Jewish
Capital	Washington	Organizations	APEC, OECD, UN

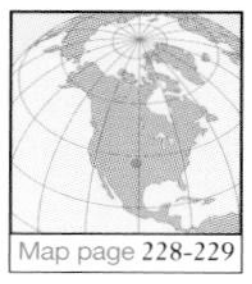
Map page 228-229

The USA comprises forty eight contiguous states in North America, bounded by Canada and Mexico, and the states of Alaska, to the northwest of Canada, and Hawaii, in the Pacific Ocean. The populous eastern states consist of the Atlantic coastal plain (which includes the Florida peninsula and the Gulf of Mexico coast) and the Appalachian Mountains. The central states form a vast interior plain drained by the Mississippi-Missouri river system. To the west lie the Rocky Mountains, separated from the Pacific coastal ranges by the intermontane plateaus. The coastal ranges are prone to earthquakes. Hawaii is a group of some twenty volcanic islands. Climatic conditions range between arctic in Alaska to desert in the intermontane plateaus. Most of the USA is temperate, though the interior has continental conditions. The USA has abundant natural resources. It has major reserves minerals and energy resources. About twenty per cent of the land can be used for crops, over twenty five per cent is suitable for livestock rearing and over thirty per cent is forested. The USA has the largest and most technologically advanced economy in the world, based on manufacturing and services. Though agriculture accounts for only about two per cent national income, productivity is high and the USA is a net exporter of food, chiefly grains and fruit. Cotton is the major industrial crop; livestock rearing, forestry and fishing are also important. The USA produces iron ore, copper, lead, zinc, and many other minerals. It is a major producer of coal, petroleum and natural gas, though being the world's biggest energy user it imports significant quantities of petroleum and its products. Manufacturing is well diversified. The main industries are: petroleum, steel, motor vehicles, aerospace, telecommunications, electrics, food processing, chemicals and consumer goods. Tourism is a major foreign currency earner with around forty-five million visitors a year. Other important service industries are banking and finance, and Wall Street in New York is a major stock exchange.

Alabama (State)
Area Sq Km (Miles) 135 775 (52 423) Population 4 351 999 Capital Montgomery

Alaska (State)
Area Sq Km (Miles) 1 700 130 (656 424) Population 614 010 Capital Juneau

Arizona (State)
Area Sq Km (Miles) 295 274 (114 006) Population 4 668 631 Capital Phoenix

Arkansas (State)
Area Sq Km (Miles) 137 741 (53 182) Population 2 538 303 Capital Little Rock

California (State)
Area Sq Km (Miles) 423 999 (163 707) Population 32 666 550 Capital Sacramento

Colorado (State)
Area Sq Km (Miles) 269 618 (104 100) Population 3 970 971 Capital Denver

Connecticut (State)
Area Sq Km (Miles) 14 359 (5 544) Population 3 274 069 Capital Hartford

Delaware (State)
Area Sq Km (Miles) 6 446 (2 489) Population 743 603 Capital Dover

District of Columbia (District)
Area Sq Km (Miles) 176 (68) Population 523 124 Capital Washington

Florida (State)
Area Sq Km (Miles) 170 312 (65 758) Population 14 915 980 Capital Tallahassee

Georgia (State)
Area Sq Km (Miles) 153 951 (59 441) Population 7 642 207 Capital Atlanta

Hawaii (State)
Area Sq Km (Miles) 28 314 (10 932) Population 1 193 001 Capital Honolulu

Idaho (State)
Area Sq Km (Miles) 216 456 (83 574) Population 1 228 684 Capital Boise

Illinois (State)
Area Sq Km (Miles) 150 007 (57 918) Population 13 045 326 Capital Springfield

Indiana (State)
Area Sq Km (Miles) 94 327 (36 420) Population 5 899 195 Capital Indianapolis

Iowa (State)
Area Sq Km (Miles) 145 754 (56 276) Population 2 862 447 Capital Des Moines

Kansas (State)
Area Sq Km (Miles) 213 109 (82 282) Population 2 629 067 Capital Topeka

Kentucky (State)
Area Sq Km (Miles) 104 664 (40 411) Population 3 936 499 Capital Frankfort

Louisiana (State)
Area Sq Km (Miles) 134 273(51 843) Population 4 368 967 Capital Baton Rouge

Maine (State)
Area Sq Km (Miles) 91 652(35 387) Population 1 244 250 Capital Augusta

State	Area Sq Km (Miles)	Population	Capital
Maryland (State)	32 134(12 407)	5 134 808	Annapolis
Massachusetts (State)	27 337 (10 555)	6 147 132	Boston
Michigan (State)	250 737 (96 810)	9 817 242	Lansing
Minnesota (State)	225 181 (86 943)	4 725 419	St Paul
Mississippi (State)	125 443 (48 434)	2 752 092	Jackson
Missouri (State)	180 545 (69 709)	5 438 559	Jefferson City
Montana (State)	380 847 (147 046)	880 453	Helena
Nebraska (State)	200 356 (77 358)	1 662 719	Lincoln
Nevada (State)	286 367 (110 567)	1 746 898	Carson City
New Hampshire (State)	24 219 (9 351)	1 185 048	Concord
New Jersey (State)	22 590 (8 722)	8 115 011	Trenton
New Mexico (State)	314 937(121 598)	1 736 931	Santa Fe
New York (State)	141 090 (54 475)	18 175 301	Albany
North Carolina (State)	139 396 (53 821)	7 546 493	Raleigh
North Dakota (State)	183 123 (70 704)	638 244	Bismarck
Ohio (State)	116 104 (44 828)	11 209 493	Columbus
Oklahoma (State)	181 048 (69 903)	3 346 713	Oklahoma City
Oregon (State)	254 819 (98 386)	3 281 974	Salem
Pennsylvania (State)	119 290 (46 058)	12 001 451	Harrisburg
Rhode Island (State)	4 002 (1 545)	988 480	Providence
South Carolina (State)	82 898 (32 007)	3 835 962	Columbia
South Dakota (State)	199 742 (77 121)	738 171	Pierre
Tennessee (State)	109 158 (42 146)	5 430 621	Nashville
Texas (State)	695 673 (268 601)	19 759 614	Austin
Utah (State)	219 900 (84 904)	2 099 758	Salt Lake City
Vermont (State)	24 903 (9 615)	590 883	Montpelier
Virginia (State)	110 771 (42 769)	6 791 345	Richmond
Washington (State)	184 674 (71 303)	5 689 263	Olympia
West Virginia (State)	62 758 (24 231)	1 811 156	Charleston
Wisconsin (State)	169 652 (65 503)	5 223 500	Madison
Wyoming (State)	253 347 (97 818)	480 907	Cheyenne

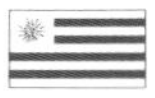

URUGUAY
Oriental Republic of Uruguay

Area Sq Km	176 215	Currency	Peso
Area Sq Miles	68 037	Languages	Spanish
Population	3 289 000	Religions	Roman Catholic, Protestant, Jewish
Capital	Montevideo	Organizations	UN

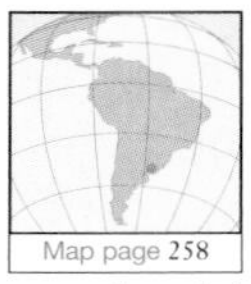
Map page 258

Uruguay, on the Atlantic coast of central South America, is a low-lying land of prairies. The coast and the River Plate estuary in the south are fringed with lagoons and sand dunes. Almost half the population lives in Montevideo. Uruguay has warm summers and mild winters. The economy is based on cattle and sheep ranching, and the main industries produce food products, textiles, and petroleum products. Meat, wool, hides, textiles and agricultural products are the main exports. Brazil and Argentina are the main trading partners.

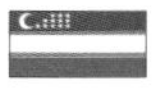

UZBEKISTAN
Republic of Uzbekistan

Area Sq Km	447 400	Currency	Sum
Area Sq Miles	172 742	Languages	Uzbek, Russian, Tajik, Kazakh
Population	23 574 000	Religions	Sunni Muslim, Russian Orthodox
Capital	Tashkent	Organizations	CIS, UN

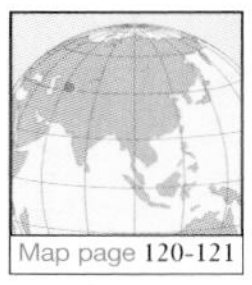
Map page 120-121

A landlocked country of central Asia, Uzbekistan borders the Aral Sea and five countries. It consists mainly of the flat Kyzylkum Desert, which rises eastwards towards the mountains. Most settlement is in the basin around Fergana. The climate is dry and arid. The economy is based mainly on irrigated agriculture, chiefly cotton production. Uzbekistan is rich in minerals including gold, copper, lead, zinc and uranium and has the largest gold mine in the world. Industry specializes in fertilizers and machinery for cotton harvesting and textile manufacture. Russia is the main trading partner.

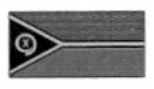

VANUATU
Republic of Vanuatu

Area Sq Km	12 190	Currency	Vatu
Area Sq Miles	4 707	Languages	English, Bislama (creole), French
Population	182 000	Religions	Protestant, Roman Catholic, traditional beliefs
Capital	Port Vila	Organizations	Comm., UN

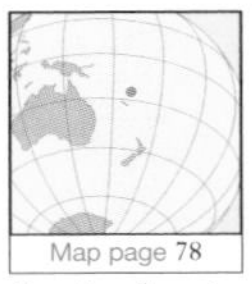
Map page 78

Vanuatu occupies an archipelago of some eighty islands in the southwest Pacific. Many of the islands are mountainous, of volcanic origin and densely forested. The climate is tropical with heavy rainfall. Half the population lives on the main islands of Éfaté and Espíritu Santo, and the majority of people live by farming. Copra, beef, timber, vegetables, and cocoa are the main exports; tourism is growing. Australia and Japan are the main trading partners.

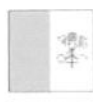

VATICAN CITY
Vatican City State

Area Sq Km	0.5	Currency	Italian lira
Area Sq Miles	0.2	Languages	Italian
Population	480	Religions	Roman Catholic
Capital	Vatican City		

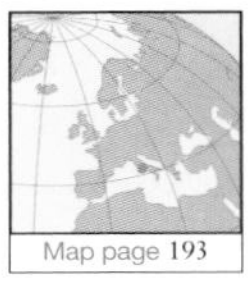
Map page 193

The world's smallest sovereign state, the Vatican City occupies a hill to the west of the river Tiber in the Italian capital, Rome. It is the headquarters of the Roman Catholic church and income comes from investments, voluntary contributions and tourism.

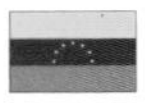

VENEZUELA
Republic of Venezuela

Area Sq Km	912 050	Currency	Bolívar
Area Sq Miles	352 144	Languages	Spanish, Amerindian languages
Population	23 242 000	Religions	Roman Catholic, Protestant
Capital	Caracas	Organizations	OPEC, UN

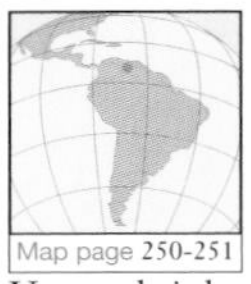
Map page 250-251

Venezuela is in northern South America, on the Caribbean Sea. Its coast is much indented, with the oil-rich area of Lago de Maracaibo at the western end and the swampy Orinoco Delta in the east. Mountain ranges run parallel to the coast then turn southwestwards to form the northern extension of the Andes. Central Venezuela is lowland grasslands drained by the Orinoco river system, while to the south are the Guiana Highlands which contain the Angel Falls, the world's highest waterfall. Over eighty per cent of the population live in towns, mostly in the coastal mountain areas. The climate is tropical, with summer rainfall. Temperatures are lower in the mountains. Farming is important, particularly cattle ranching and dairy farming; coffee, maize, rice and sugar cane are the main crops. Venezuela is a major oil producer, and sales account for about seventy five per cent of export earnings. Aluminium, iron ore, copper and gold are also mined and manufactures include petrochemicals, aluminium, steel, textiles and food products. USA is the dominant trading partner.

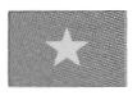

VIETNAM
Socialist Republic of Vietnam

Area Sq Km	329 565	Currency	Dong
Area Sq Miles	127 246	Languages	Vietnamese, Thai, Khmer, Chinese, local languages
Population	77 562 000	Religions	Buddhist, Taoist, Roman Catholic
Capital	Ha Nôi	Organizations	APEC, ASEAN, UN

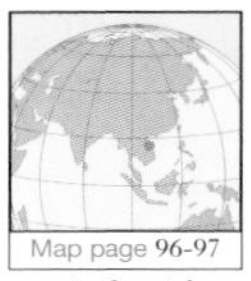
Map page 96-97

Vietnam is in southeast Asia, with the South China Sea to the east and south. The Red River delta lowlands in the north are separated from the huge Mekong delta in the south by long, narrow coastal plains backed by the mountainous and forested terrain of the Annam Plateau. Most people live in the river deltas. The climate is tropical, with summer monsoon rains. Over three quarters of the workforce is involved in agriculture, forestry and fishing. Rice is the main crop; coffee, tea and rubber are important cash crops. Vietnam is the world's third largest rice exporter, after the USA and Thailand. Oil, coal and copper are produced; the main industries are food processing, clothing and footwear, cement and fertilizers. Exports include oil, coffee, rice, clothing, fish and fish products. Japan and Singapore are the main trading partners.

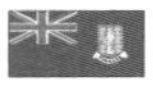

Virgin Islands (U.K.)
United Kingdom Overseas Territory

Area Sq Km	153	Currency	US dollar
Area Sq Miles	59	Languages	English
Population	20 000	Religions	Protestant, Roman Catholic
Capital	Road Town		

The Caribbean territory comprises four main islands and over thirty islets at the eastern end of the Virgin Islands group. Apart from the flat coral atoll of Anegada, the islands are volcanic in origin and hilly. The climate is subtropical and tourism is the main industry.

Map page 247

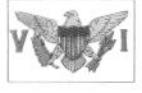

Virgin Islands (U.S.A.)
United States Unincorporated Territory

Area Sq Km	352	Currency	US dollar
Area Sq Miles	136	Languages	English, Spanish
Population	94 000	Religions	Protestant, Roman Catholic
Capital	Charlotte Amalie		

The territory consists of three main islands and over fifty islets in the Caribbean's western Virgin Islands. The islands are mostly hilly and of volcanic origin and the climate is subtropical. The economy is based on tourism, with some manufacturing, including a major oil refinery, on St Croix.

Map page 247

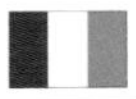

Wallis and Futuna Islands
French Overseas Territory

Area Sq Km	274	Currency	Pacific franc
Area Sq Miles	106	Languages	French, Wallisian, Futunian
Population	14 000	Religions	Roman Catholic
Capital	Matā'utu		

The south Pacific territory comprises the volcanic islands of the Wallis archipelago and Hoorn Islands. The climate is tropical. The islands depend upon subsistence farming, the sale of licences to foreign fishing fleets, workers' remittances and French aid.

Map page 75

West Bank
Territory Occupied by Israel

Area Sq Km	5 860	Languages	Arabic, Hebrew
Area Sq Miles	2 263	Religions	Sunni Muslim, Jewish, Shi'a Muslim, Christian

The territory consists of the west bank of the river Jordan and parts of Judea and Samaria. The land was annexed by Israel in 1967, but the Jericho area was granted self-government under an agreement between Israel and the PLO in 1993.

Map page 128

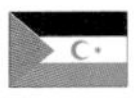

WESTERN SAHARA
Disputed territory (Morocco)

Area Sq Km	266 000	Currency	Moroccan dirhamr
Area Sq Miles	102 703	Languages	Arabic
Population	275 000	Religions	Sunni Muslim
Capital	Laâyoune		

Situated on the northwest coast of Africa, the territory of Western Sahara is controlled by Morocco. The land is low, flat desert with higher land in the northeast. There is little cultivation and only about twenty per cent of the land is pasture. Livestock herding, fishing and phosphate mining are the main activities. All trade is controlled by Morocco.

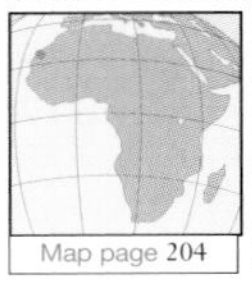
Map page 204

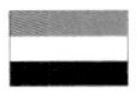

YEMEN
Republic of Yemen

Area Sq Km	527 968	Currency	Rial
Area Sq Miles	203 850	Languages	Arabic
Population	16 887 000	Religions	Sunni Muslim, Shi'a Muslim
Capital	Şan'ā'	Organizations	UN

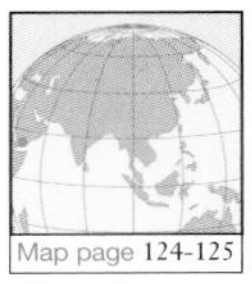
Map page 124-125

Yemen occupies the southwestern Arabian Peninsula, on the Red Sea and Gulf of Aden. Beyond the Red Sea coastal plain the land rises to a mountain range then descends to desert plateaus. Much of Yemen is hot and arid, but rainfall in the west supports crops and most settlement. Farming and fishing are the main activities, with cotton the main cash crop. The main exports are crude oil, cotton, coffee and dried fruit. Despite its oil resources Yemen is one of the poorest countries in the Arab World.

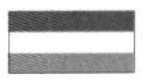

YUGOSLAVIA
Federal Republic of Yugoslavia

Area Sq Km	102 173	Currency	Dinar
Area Sq Miles	39 449	Languages	Serbian, Albanian, Hungarian
Population	10 635 000	Religions	Serbian and Montenegrin Orthodox, Muslim
Capital	Beograd	Organizations	UN

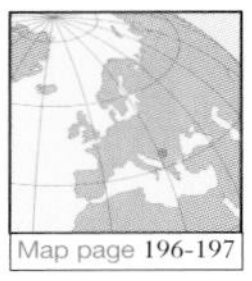
Map page 196-197

The south European state comprises two of the former Yugoslav republics: Serbia and the much smaller Montenegro. The landscape is for the most part rugged, mountainous and forested. Northern Serbia is low-lying, drained by the Danube river system. The climate is Mediterranean on the coast, continental inland. Since 1991 the economy has been seriously affected by war, trade embargoes and economic sanctions.

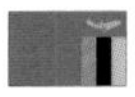

ZAMBIA
Republic of Zambia

Area Sq Km	752 614	Currency	Kwacha
Area Sq Miles	290 586	Languages	English, Bemba, Nyanja, Tonga, local languages
Population	8 781 000	Religions	Christian, traditional beliefs
Capital	Lusaka	Organizations	Comm., SADC, UN

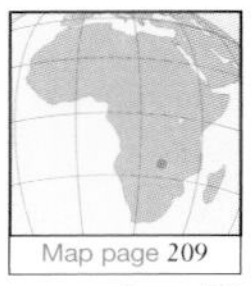
Map page 209

A landlocked state in central Africa, Zambia borders seven countries. It is dominated by high savanna plateaus and bordered by the Zambezi river in the south. Most people live in the Copperbelt area. Life expectancy has dropped by seventeen per cent because of AIDS, compared to 1975. The climate is tropical with a rainy season from November to May. Agriculture employs around eighty per cent of the workforce, but is mainly at subsistence level. Copper mining is the mainstay of the economy, though reserves are declining. Copper and cobalt are the main exports.

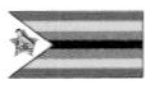

ZIMBABWE
Republic of Zimbabwe

Area Sq Km	390 759	Currency	Dollar
Area Sq Miles	150 873	Languages	English, Shona, Ndebele
Population	11 377 000	Religions	Christian, traditional beliefs
Capital	Harare	Organizations	Comm., SADC, UN

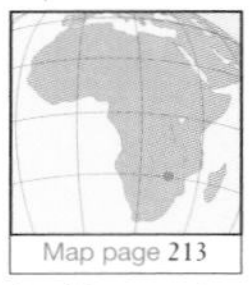
Map page 213

Zimbabwe, a landlocked state in southern central Africa, consists of high plateaus flanked by the Zambezi river valley and Lake Kariba in the north and the Limpopo in the south. Most people live in central Zimbabwe. The effect of AIDS has reduced life expectancy by seventeen per cent compared to 1975. There are significant mineral resources including gold, nickel, copper, asbestos, platinum and chromium. Agriculture is a major sector of the economy, crops include tobacco, maize, sugar cane, and cotton, and beef cattle are important. Exports include tobacco, gold, ferroalloys, nickel and cotton. South Africa is the main trading partner.

ATLAS OF THE WORLD

ATLAS MAPPING

The Atlas of the World includes a variety of styles and scales of mapping which together provide comprehensive coverage of all parts of the world; the map styles and editorial policies followed are introduced here. The area covered by each map is shown on the front and back endpapers.

Each continent is introduced by a politically coloured map followed by reference maps of sub-continental regions and then more detailed reference mapping of regions and individual countries. Scales for continental maps (*see 1*) range between 1:15 000 000 and 1:27 000 000 and regional maps (*see 2*) are in the range 1:11 000 000 to 1:13 000 000. Mapping for most countries is at scales between 1:3 000 000 and 1:7 500 000 (*see 3*) although selected, more densely populated areas of Europe, North America

and Asia are mapped at larger scales, up to 1:1 000 000 (*see 4*). Large-scale city plans of a selection of the world's major cities (*see 5*), are included on the appropriate map pages. A suite of maps covering the world's oceans and poles (*see 6*) at a variety of scales, concludes the main reference map section.

The symbols and place name abbreviations used on the maps are fully explained on pages 68–69 and a glossary of geographical terms is included at the back of the atlas on pages 269–272. The alphanumeric reference system used in the index is based on latitude and longitude, and the number and letter for each graticule square are shown within each map frame, in red. The numbers of adjoining or overlapping pages are shown by arrows in the page frame and accompanying numbers in the margin.

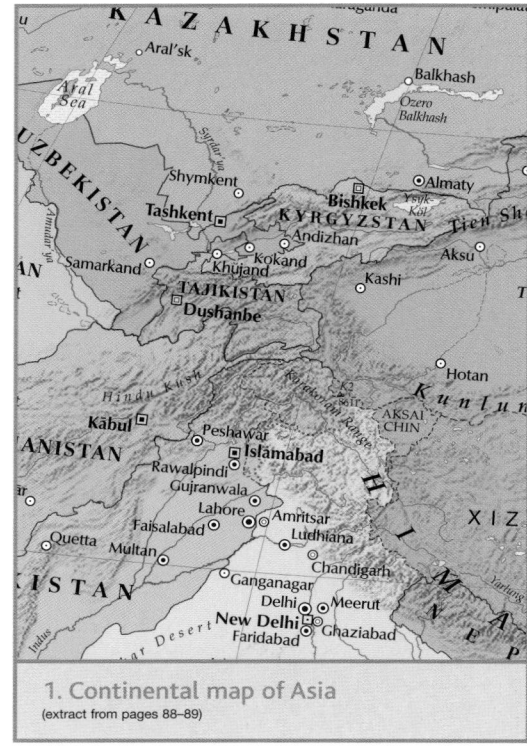

1. Continental map of Asia
(extract from pages 88–89)

BOUNDARIES

The status, names and boundaries of nations are shown in this atlas as they are at the time of going to press, as far as can be ascertained. Where an international boundary symbol appears in the sea or ocean it does not necessarily infer a legal maritime boundary, but shows which off-shore islands belong to which country.

Where international boundaries are the subject of dispute it may be that no portrayal of them will meet with the approval of any of the countries involved, but it is not seen as the function of this atlas to try to adjudicate between the rights and wrongs of political issues. The atlas aims to take a neutral viewpoint of all such cases. Although reference mapping at atlas scales is not the ideal medium for indicating territorial claims, every reasonable attempt is made to show where an active territorial dispute exists, and where there is an important difference between 'de facto' (existing in fact, on the ground) and 'de jure' (according to law) boundaries. This is done by the use of a different symbol where international boundaries are disputed, or where the alignment is unconfirmed, to that used for settled international boundaries. Cease-fire lines are also shown by a separate symbol. For clarity, disputed boundaries and areas are annotated where this is considered necessary.

The latest internal administrative division boundaries are shown on the maps for selected countries where the combination of map scale and the number of divisions permits, with recent changes to local government systems being taken into account as far as possible. Towns which are first-order and second-order administrative centres are also symbolized where scale permits.

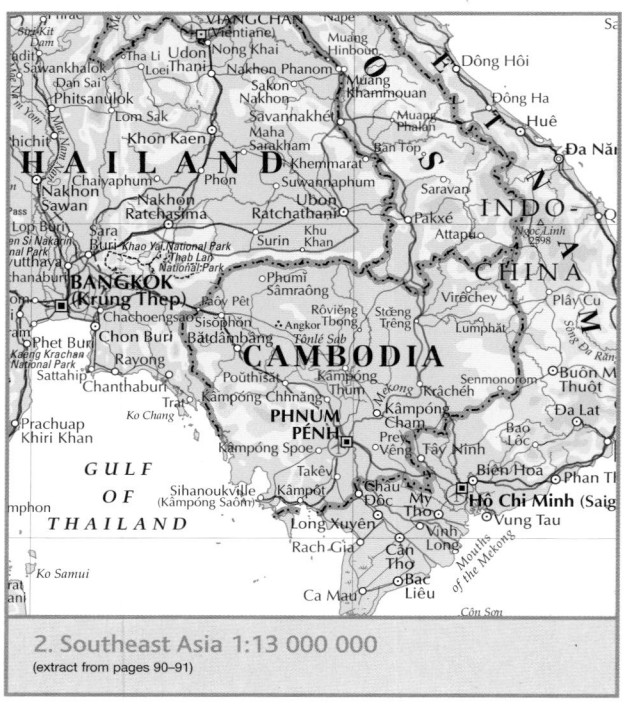

2. Southeast Asia 1:13 000 000
(extract from pages 90–91)

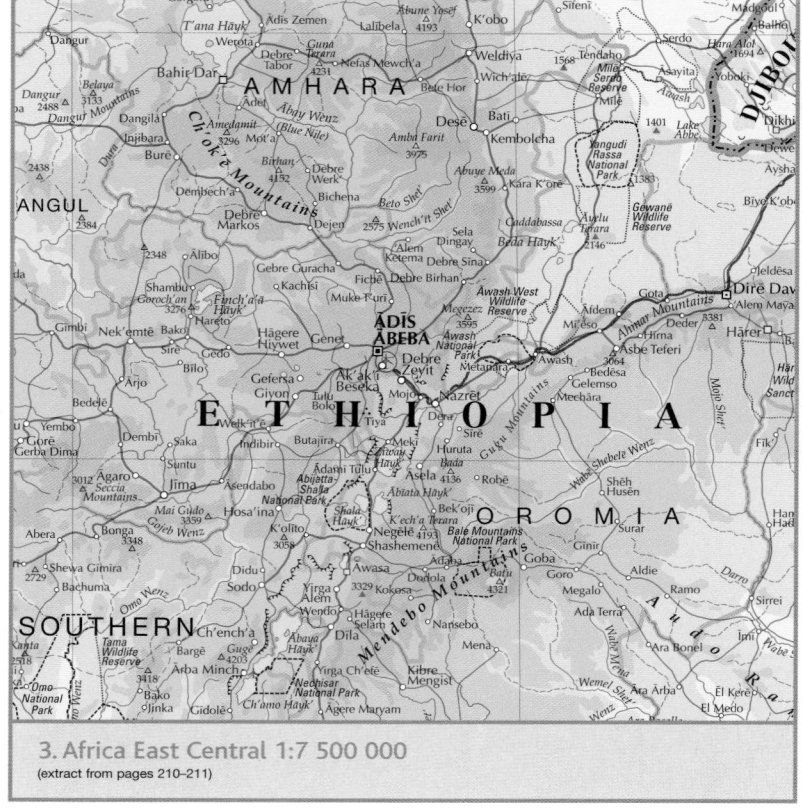

3. Africa East Central 1:7 500 000
(extract from pages 210–211)

PLACE NAMES

The spelling of place names on maps has always been a matter of great complexity, because of the variety of the world's languages and the systems used to write them down. Continuing changes in official languages, and in writing systems, also have to be taken into account. In many countries different languages are in use in different regions, or side-by-side in the same region. Sometimes the problem is dealt with by the use of a 'lingua franca' such as English to provide a mutually intelligible standard. In many cases the most spoken language takes precedence, but there is still the potential for widely varying name forms even within a single country. A worldwide trend towards national, regional and ethnic self-determination is operating at the same time as pressure towards increased international standardization of name forms.

There is no standard way of spelling names or of converting them from one alphabet, or symbol set, to another. Instead, conventional ways of spelling have evolved in each of the world's major languages, and the results often differ significantly from the name as it is spelled in the original language. Familiar examples of English conventional names include Munich (München), Florence (Firenze) and Moscow (from the transliterated form, Moskva).

In this atlas, local name forms are used where these are in the Roman alphabet. Such a policy results in mapping which

is internally consistent and which closely reflects name forms found in the country itself. These local forms are those which are officially recognized by the government of the country concerned, usually as represented by its official mapping agency. This is a basic principle laid down by the United Kingdom government's Permanent Committee on Geographical Names (PCGN) and the equivalent United States Board on Geographic Names (BGN).

For languages in non-Roman alphabets and syllabaries, the atlas generally follows BGN/PCGN romanization principles. For example, Russian-language names are spelled using the standard BGN/PCGN system, which gives names such as Lipetsk and Yoshkar-Ola as opposed to a system used in eastern Europe which gives Lipeck and Joškar-Ola.

Although local forms are preferred, prominent English-language conventional names and historic names are not neglected. Together with significant superseded names and other alternate spellings, they are included in brackets on the maps where space permits, and are cross-referenced in the index. The names of continents, oceans, seas and under-water features in international waters appear in English throughout the atlas, as do those of other international features – features crossing one or more

international boundary – where such an English form exists and is in common use.

Country names are shown in conventional English form, and include changes promulgated by national governments and adopted by the United Nations – Myanmar (replacing Burma), Belarus (replacing Belorussia and a variety of other versions including the traditional White Russia), Kyrgyzstan (for Kirghizia or Kirgizia), Moldova (Moldavia), and Côte d'Ivoire (Ivory Coast). In the adoption of these name forms for country names, and for certain city names, such as Beijing (replacing Peking), the gradual incorporation of local forms into common English usage can be seen at work. This atlas reflects that process.

CHANGES IN NAME FORMS

Place names are, to an extent, a mirror for the changes that continue to transform the political world. Predictably, changes of territorial control have an effect on name forms. Yet even in countries where name forms could be expected to have been standardized, there are continuing issues for the cartographer to address. In the UK, for example, the increased prominence given to the use of Gaelic and Welsh has meant that more consideration has been given to the use of Gaelic and Welsh name forms in relation to the English form. Name spelling

PROJECTIONS

The creation of computer-generated maps presents the opportunity to select projections specifically for the area and scale of each map. As the only way to show the Earth with absolute accuracy is on a globe, all map projections are compromises. Some projections seek to maintain correct area relationships (equal area projections), true distances and bearings from a point (equidistant projections) or correct angles and shapes (conformal projections); others attempt to achieve a balance between these properties. The choice of projections used in this atlas has been made on an individual continental and regional basis. Projections used, and their individual parameters, have been defined to minimize distortion and to reduce scale errors as much as possible.

For world maps, the Bartholomew version of the Winkel Tripel Projection is used. This projection combines elements of conformality with that of equal area, and shows, over the world as a whole, relatively true shapes and reasonably equal areas. The Mercator Projection (see 7) has been selected for the regional maps of southeast Asia along the Equator , while in higher latitudes, particularly in Europe and to some extent in North America, the Conic Equidistant Projection (see 8) has been used extensively for regional mapping. The Lambert Azimuthal Equal Area Projection (see 9) has been employed in both South America and Australia.

7. MERCATOR PROJECTION

This rectangular or cylindrical projection is constructed on the basis of a cylinder in contact with the globe, in this case around the Equator. Scale is correct along the Equator and distortion increases away from it in both directions.

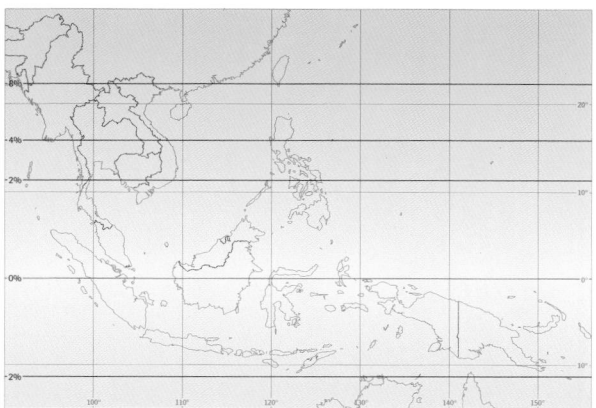

8. CONIC EQUIDISTANT PROJECTION

Constructed on the basis of a cone intersecting the globe along two standard parallels (55°N and 75°N in this illustration), along both of which scale is correct. Lines of equal scale error are parallel to the standard lines, with distortion increasing away from each.

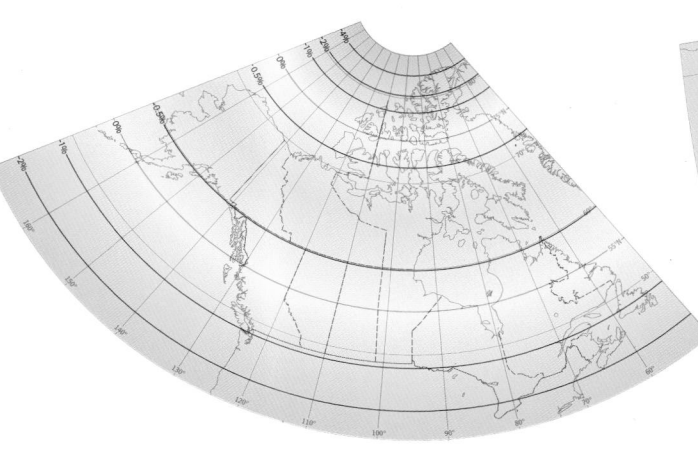

9. LAMBERT AZIMUTHAL EQUAL AREA PROJECTION

Points are projected onto a plane in contact with the globe at the centre point (25°S, 135°E in this illustration). Scale is correct at the centre, and scale errors increase in concentric circles away from it. Areas are true in relation to the corresponding areas on the globe.

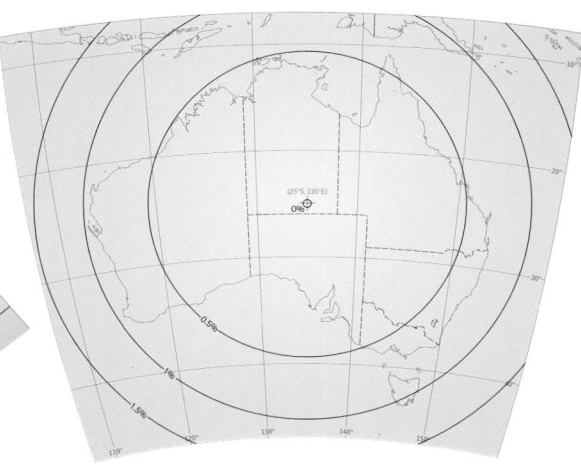

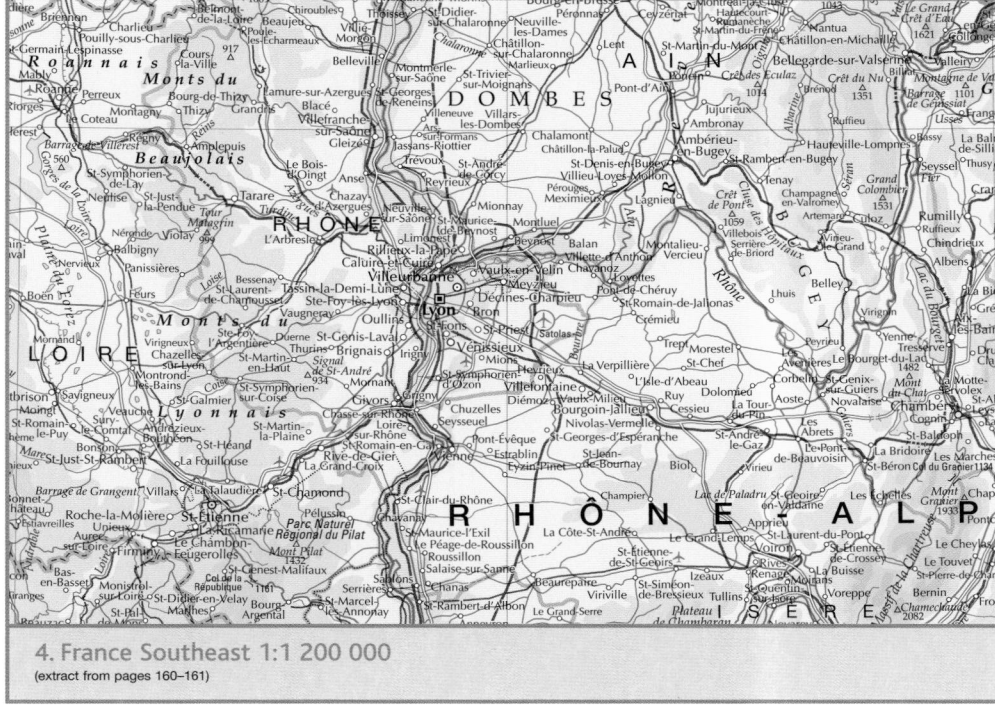

4. France Southeast 1:1 200 000
(extract from pages 160–161)

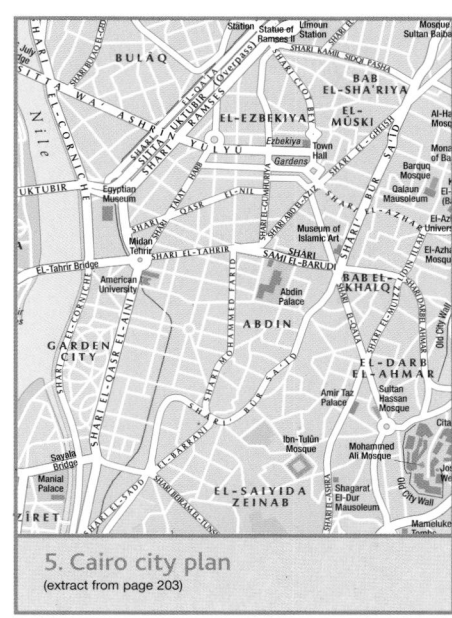

5. Cairo city plan
(extract from page 203)

issues are, in fact, likely to emerge in any part of the world. A close watch is kept on areas where changes might be expected, although sometimes they crop up in unexpected places.

The dissolution of the former USSR gave rise to many changes in name forms. Names were converted from Russian to the main national language in Belarus, Ukraine, Moldova, Armenia, Georgia, Azerbaijan, Kyrgyzstan and Tajikistan. On the maps, where space permits, the main Russian-language forms for significant places are shown as alternatives in such cases. Russian naturally continues to be used as the main form in the Russian Federation, although in Chechnia main Chechen alternative forms have been included in the index as cross-references. Russian also continues to be used as the prime language on maps of Kazakhstan, Turkmenistan and Uzbekistan. In Kazakhstan, both Russian and Kazakh are recognized as joint official languages, and Russian is maintained as the first form, while Kazakh alternatives (derived from Kazakh cyrillic), are included for main place names where space permits on the maps, with additional alternatives in the index.

In Spain, account is taken of the official prominence now given to Catalan, Galician and some Basque names, which results in name forms such as Eivissa for Ibiza; A Coruña for La Coruña; and San Sebastián amended to Donostia-San Sebastián.

Chinese name forms, which use the official Pinyin romanization system continue to change. Name forms have been brought into line with the latest official sources resulting in a more rigorous and updated use of the principle whereby numerous towns, which are the centres of administrative units such as the county or 'xian', officially take the name of the county itself. The alternative place name in common local use is shown in brackets where possible.

As well as the above-mentioned systematic changes in name forms, which mostly involve official modifications in the way all names in a country are rendered in the Roman alphabet, the atlas also aims to account for entirely new names being adopted. Such name changes can happen for a variety of reasons – one example is the move away from communist-inspired names in the former Soviet Union. Changes can be a result of official policy changes, such as those in India when Bombay was changed to Mumbai, and Madras to Chennai. Although particularly prominent, these in fact represent the continuation of a long process of name amendments in India since independence.

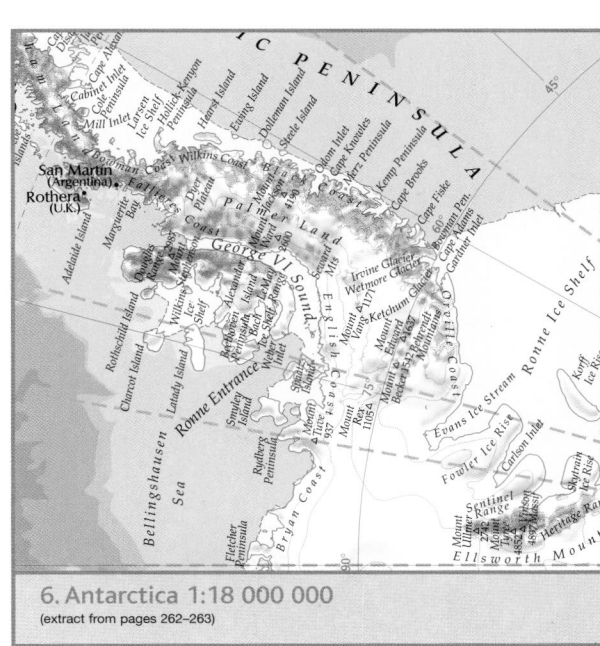

6. Antarctica 1:18 000 000
(extract from pages 262–263)

REFERENCE MAPS

CITIES AND TOWNS

Population	National Capital	Administrative Capital Shown for selected countries only		Other City or Town
		First order	Second order Scales larger than 1:9 000 000.	
over 5 million	**BEIJING** ▣	**Tianjin** ▣	**Los Angeles** ◉	**New York** ◉
1 million to 5 million	**KĀBUL** ▣	**Sydney** ▣	**Tangshan** ◉	**Kaohsiung** ◉
500 000 to 1 million	BANGUI ▣	Trujillo ▣	Agra ◎	Jeddah ◎
100 000 to 500 000	WELLINGTON ▢	Mansa ▢	Naogaon ◎	Apucarana ◎
50 000 to 100 000	PORT OF SPAIN ▢	Potenza ▢	Trier ○	Arecibo ○
10 000 to 50 000	MALABO ▫	Chinhoyi ▫	Willimantic ◌	Ceres ○
1 000 to 10 000	VALLETTA ▫	Ati ▫	Nepalganj ◌	Abla ○
under 1000 Scales 1: 4 000 000 and larger		Chhukha ▫	Carmel ◌	Lopigna ○

▢ Built-up area

MISCELLANEOUS FEATURES

---------- National park   ·············· Regional park   ·············· Reserve or special land area   ∴ Site of specific interest   ∿∿∿∿∿ Wall

RELIEF

Contour intervals used in layer-colouring for land height and sea depth

Scales 1:4 000 000 and larger	Scales 1:4 000 000 and larger (Europe only)	Scales smaller than 1:4 000 000	Oceans and Antarctica (Pages 262-268)
METRES / FEET	METRES / FEET	METRES / FEET	METRES / FEET
6000 / 19686	6000 / 19686	6000 / 19686	4000 / 13124
5000 / 16404	5000 / 16404	5000 / 16404	2000 / 6562
4000 / 13124	4000 / 13124	4000 / 13124	1000 / 3281
3000 / 9843	3000 / 9843	3000 / 9843	500 / 1640
2000 / 6562	2000 / 6562	2000 / 6562	200 / 656
1500 / 4921	1500 / 4921	1000 / 3281	0 / 0
1000 / 3281	1000 / 3281	500 / 1640	LAND BELOW SEA LEVEL
500 / 1640	500 / 1640	200 / 656	200 / 656
200 / 656	200 / 656	0 / 0	2000 / 6562
100 / 328	100 / 328	LAND BELOW SEA LEVEL	3000 / 9843
0 / 0	0 / 0	200 / 656	4000 / 13124
LAND BELOW SEA LEVEL	LAND BELOW SEA LEVEL	2000 / 6562	5000 / 16409
200 / 656	50 / 164	4000 / 13124	6000 / 19686
1000 / 3281	200 / 656	6000 / 19686	7000 / 22967
2000 / 6562	1000 / 3281		9000 / 29529
	2000 / 6562		

1234 △ Summit
Height in metres

-123 • Spot height
Surface height in metres for depressions and areas below sea level.

5678 • Ocean deep
In metres. Ocean pages only.

LAND AND SEA FEATURES

Rock desert

Sand desert / Dunes

⌣ Oasis

Lava field

1234 ▲ Volcano
height in metres

Marsh

Ice cap / Glacier

Nunatak

········ Coral reef

·············· Escarpment

·············· Flood dyke

] [123 Pass
height in metres

········ Ice shelf

STYLES OF LETTERING

Cities and towns are explained separately

Country	**FRANCE**
Overseas Territory/Dependency	**Guadeloupe**
Disputed Territory	AKSAI CHIN
Administrative name, first order internal division Shown for selected countries only.	**SCOTLAND**
Administrative name, second order internal division Scales 1:4 000 000 and larger. Shown for selected countries only.	**MANCHE**
Area name	ARTOIS

Physical features

Island	*Gran Canaria*
Lake	*LAKE ERIE*
Mountain	*Mt Blanc*
River	*Thames*
Region	*PAMPAS*

BOUNDARIES

International boundary

Disputed international boundary or alignment unconfirmed

Undefined international boundary in the sea.
All land within this boundary is part of state or territory named.

Administrative boundary, first order internal division.
Scales 1:4 000 000 and larger.
Shown for selected countries only.

Administrative boundary, first order internal division.
Scales smaller than 1:4 000 000.
Shown for selected countries only.

Administrative boundary, second order internal division.
Scales 1:4 000 000 and larger.
Shown for selected countries only.

Disputed administrative boundary
Scales 1:4 000 000 and larger.
Shown for selected countries only.

Ceasefire line or other boundary described on the map

LAKES AND RIVERS

Lake

Impermanent lake

Salt lake or lagoon

Impermanent salt lake

Dry salt lake or salt pan

123 Lake height
surface height above sea level, in metres

———— River

-------- Impermanent river

-------- Wadi or watercourse

Waterfall

— Dam

Barrage

TRANSPORT

═══ Motorway Scales 1:4 000 000 and larger.		━━━ Main railway	
─── Main road		─── Secondary railway	
─── Secondary road		─•─•─ Railway tunnel	
═•═•═ Motorway tunnel		········ Canal	
─•─•─ Road tunnel		─── Minor canal	
----- Track		✈ Main airport	
		✈ Regional airport	

CITY PLANS

- Built-up area
- Cemetery
- Park
- Place of worship
- General place of interest
- Transport location
- Academic / municipal building

CONTINENTAL MAPS

BOUNDARIES

———	International boundary
- - - - -	Disputed international boundary or alignment unconfirmed
╱	Undefined international boundary in the sea. All land within this boundary is part of state or territory named.
••••••••	Ceasefire line
- - - - -	Administrative boundary Shown for selected countries only.

CITIES AND TOWNS

Population	National Capital	Other City or Town
over 5 million	**Beijing** ▣	New York ◉
1 million to 5 million	**Kabul** ▣	Kaohsiung ◉
500 000 to 1 million	**Bangui** ▣	Khulna ◉
100 000 to 500 000	**Wellington** ▣	Iquitos ◉
50 000 to 100 000	**Port of Spain** ▢	Naga ◦
10 000 to 50 000	**Malabo** ▫	Ushuaia ◦
under 10 000	**Valletta** ▫	Arviat ◦

ABBREVIATIONS

A.C.T.	Australian Capital Territory		
Arch.	Archipelago		
	Archipiélago	Spanish	archipelago
B.	Bay		
	Bahia, Baía	Portuguese	bay
	Bahía	Spanish	bay
	Baie	French	bay
Bol.	Bol'shaya, Bol'shoy, Bol'shoye	Russian	big
C.	Cape		
	Cabo	Portuguese, Spanish	cape, headland
	Cap	Catalan, French	cape, headland
Cach.	Cachoeira	Portuguese	waterfall, rapids
Can.	Canal	French, Portuguese, Spanish	canal, channel
Cd	Ciudad	Spanish	city, town
Chan.	Channel		
Co	Cerro	Spanish	hill, mountain, peak
Cord.	Cordillera	Spanish	mountain range
Cr.	Creek		
Cuch.	Cuchilla	Spanish	hills, mountain range
D.	Dağ, Dağı	Turkish	mountain
	Dāgh	Farsi	mountain, mountains
	Dağları	Turkish	mountain range
	Danau	Indonesian, Malay	lake
Div.	Division		
Dr	Doctor		
E.	East, Eastern		
Emb.	Embalse	Spanish	reservoir
Est.	Estero	Spanish	estuary, inlet
	Estrecho	Spanish	strait
Fj.	Fjörður	Icelandic	fjord, inlet
Ft	Fort		
G.	Gebel	Arabic	hill, mountain
	Golfo	Italian, Spanish	gulf, bay
	Gora	Russian	mountain
	Gunung	Indonesian, Malay	hill, mountain
Gd	Grand	French	big
Gde	Grande	French, Italian, Portuguese, Spanish	big
Geb.	Gebergte	Afrikaans, Dutch	mountain range
Gen.	General		
Gl.	Glacier		
Gp	Group		
Gt	Great		
Harb.	Harbour		
Hd	Head		
I.	Island, Isle		
	Ilha	Portuguese	island
	Isla	Spanish	island
Î.	Île	French	island
im.	imeni	Russian	'in the name of'
Ind. Res.	Indian Reservation		
Ing.	Ingeniero	Spanish	engineer
Is	Islands, Isles		
	Islas	Spanish	islands
Îs	Îles	French	islands
J.	Jabal, Jebel	Arabic	mountain, mountains
Kep.	Kepulauan	Indonesian, Malay	archipelago, islands
Khr.	Khrebet	Russian	mountain range
L.	Lake		
	Loch	(Scotland)	lake
	Lough	(Ireland)	lake
	Lac	French	lake
	Lago	Portuguese, Spanish	lake
Lag.	Laguna	Spanish	lagoon
M.	Mys	Russian	cape, point
Mt	Mount		
	Mont	French	hill, mountain
Mt.	Mountain		
Mte	Monte	Portuguese, Spanish	hill, mountain

Mts	Mountains		
	Monts	French	hills, mountains
N.	North, Northern		
Nev.	Nevado	Spanish	peak
Nat.	National		
Nat. Park	National Park		
Nat. Res.	Nature Reserve		
Nizh.	Nizhniy, Nizhnyaya	Russian	lower
N.E.	Northeast, Northeastern		
N.H.S.	National Heritage Site		
N.W.	Northwest, Northwestern		
O.	Ostrov	Russian	island
O-va	Ostrova	Russian	islands
Oz.	Ozero	Russian, Ukrainian	lake
P.	Paso	Spanish	pass
	Pulau	Indonesian, Malay	island
Pass.	Passage		
Peg.	Pegunungan	Indonesian, Malay	mountain range
Pen.	Peninsula		
	Península	Spanish	peninsula
Pk	Peak		
	Puncak	Indonesian	mountain, peak
P-ov	Poluostrov	Russian	peninsula
P. P.	Pulau-pulau	Indonesian	islands
Psa	Presa	Spanish	reservoir
Pt	Point		
Pta	Punta	Italian, Spanish	cape, point
Pte	Pointe	French	cape, point
Pto	Porto	Portuguese	harbour, port
	Puerto	Spanish	harbour, port
R.	River		
	Rio	Portuguese	river
	Río	Spanish	river
	Rivière	French	river
	Rūd	Farsi	river
Ra.	Range		
Rec.	Recreation		
Res.	Reservation, Reserve		
Resr	Reservoir		
S.	South, Southern		
	Salar, Salina, Salinas	Spanish	salt pan, salt pans
Sa	Serra	Portuguese	mountain range
	Sierra	Spanish	mountain range
Sd	Sound		
S.E.	Southeast, Southeastern		
Serr.	Serranía	Spanish	mountain range
Sk.	Shuiku	Chinese	reservoir
Sr.	Sredniy, Srednyaya	Russian	middle, central
St	Saint		
	Sankt	German, Russian	saint
	Sint	Dutch	saint
Sta	Santa	Italian, Portuguese, Spanish	saint
Ste	Sainte	French	saint
Sto	Santo	Italian, Portuguese, Spanish	saint
Str.	Strait		
S.W.	Southwest, Southwestern		
Tg	Tanjong, Tanjung	Indonesian, Malay	cape, point
Tk	Teluk, Telukan	Indonesian, Malay	bay, gulf
Tte	Teniente	Spanish	lieutenant
Va	Villa	Spanish	town
Vdkhr.	Vodokhranilishche	Russian	reservoir
Verkh.	Verkhniy, Verkhnyaya	Russian	upper
Vol.	Volcano		
	Volcan	French	volcano
	Volcán	Spanish	volcano
Vozv.	Vozvyshennost'	Russian	hills, upland
W.	West, Western		
	Wadi, Wâdi, Wādī	Arabic	watercourse

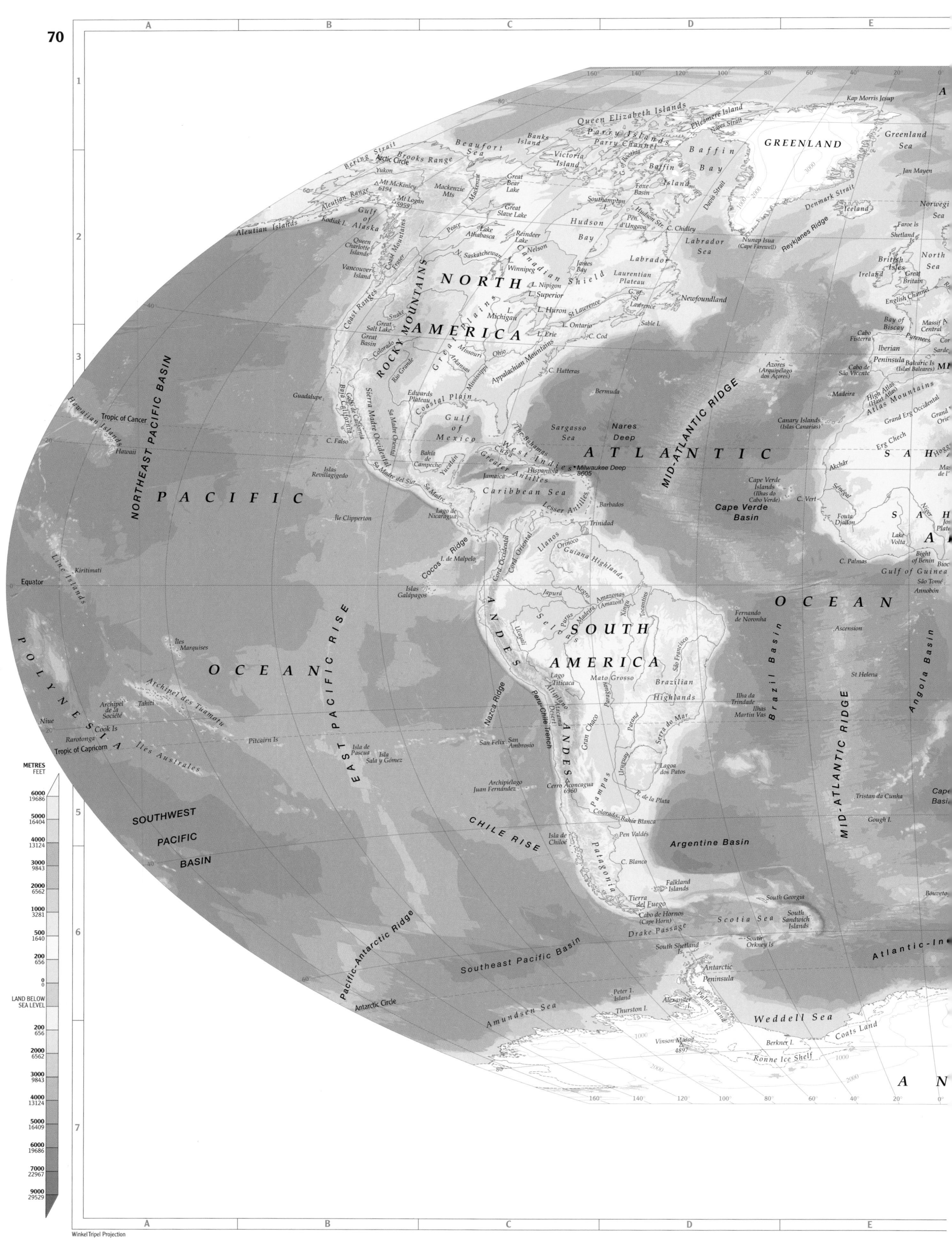

METRES / FEET

6000	19686
5000	16404
4000	13124
3000	9843
2000	6562
1000	3281
500	1640
200	656
0	0
LAND BELOW SEA LEVEL	
200	656
2000	6562
3000	9843
4000	13124
5000	16409
6000	19686
7000	22967
9000	29529

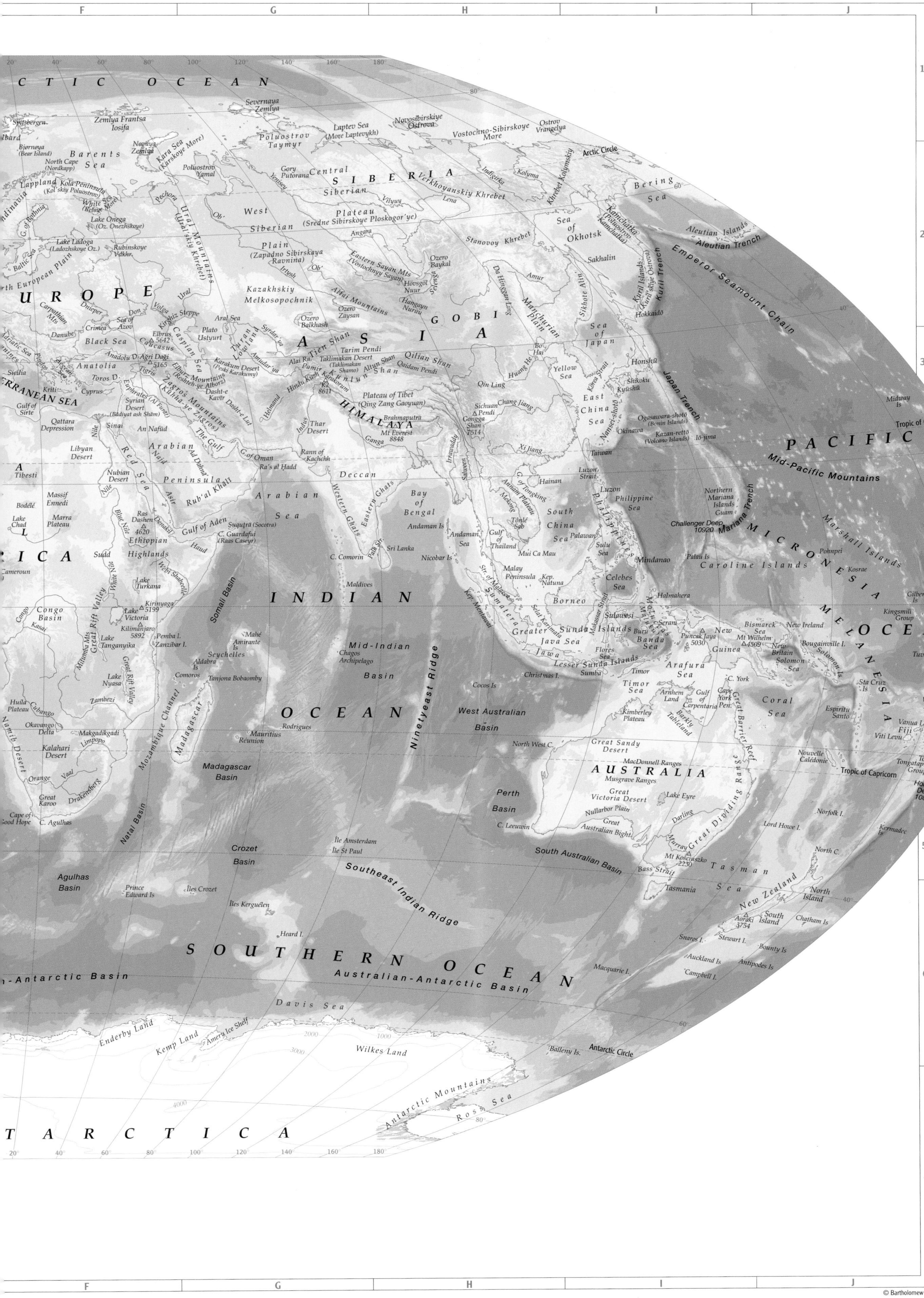

CTIC OCEAN

Spitsbergen
Bjørnøya
(Bear Island)
North Cape (Nordkapp)
Svalbard
Zemlya Frantsa Iosifa
Novaya Zemlya
Kara Sea (Karskoye More)
Severnaya Zemlya
Poluostrov Taymyr
Laptev Sea (More Laptevykh)
Novosibirskiye Ostrova
Vostochno-Sibirskoye More
Ostrov Vrangelya
Arctic Circle

Barents Sea
Lappland
Kola Peninsula (Kol'skiy Poluostrov)
White Sea (Beloye More)
Pechora
Poluostrov Yamal
Gory Putorana
Central Siberian Plateau (Sredne Sibirskoye Ploskogor'ye)
Vilyuy
Verkhoyanskiy Khrebet
Lena
Indigirka
Kolyma
Khrebet Kolymskiy
Bering Sea

SIBERIA

Lake Onega (Oz. Onezhskoye)
West Siberian Plain (Zapadno Sibirskaya Ravnina)
Ob'
Angara
Stanovoy Khrebet
Amur
Sea of Okhotsk
Kamchatka (Poluostrov Kamchatka)
Aleutian Islands
Aleutian Trench

Lake Ladoga (Ladozhskoye Oz.)
Rubinskoye Vdkhr.
Ural Mountains (Ural'skiy Khrebet)
Irtysh
Ob'
Eastern Sayan Mts (Vostochnyy Sayany)
Ozero Baykal
Hövsgöl Nuur
Hangayn Nuruu
Da Hinggan Ling
Sakhalin
Hokkaidō
Kuril Islands (Kuril'skiye Ostrova)
Kuril Trench
Emperor Seamount Chain

EUROPE
North European Plain
Kazakhskiy Melkosopochnik
Aral Sea
Syrdar'ya
Ozero Balkhash
Ozero Zaysan
Altai Mountains
Sea of Japan
Honshū
Shikoku
Kyūshū
Korea Strait
Sikhote Alin'
Manchurian Plain
Bo Hai
Yellow Sea
East China Sea
Midway Is
Tropic of Cancer

Carpathian Mts
Dnieper
Don
Volga
Sea of Azov
Crimea
Danube
Black Sea
Caucasus
Elbrus 5642
Caspian Sea
Kirghiz Steppe
Turan Lowland
Amudar'ya
Plato Ustyurt
ASIA
Alai Ra (Tien Shan)
Pamir
Hindu Kush
Tien Shan
Kunlun Shan
Taklimakan Desert (Taklimakan Shamo)
Tarim Pendi
Altun Shan
Qaidam Pendi
Qilian Shan
GOBI
Huang He
Qin Ling
Chang Jiang
Sichuan Pendi
Gongga Shan 7514
Taiwan
Luzon Strait
Ogasawara-shoto (Bonin Islands)
Kazan-retto (Volcano Islands)
Io-jima

PACIFIC
Mid-Pacific Mountains

MEDITERRANEAN SEA
Siella
Kriti
Cyprus
Anadolu D-Ağrı Dağı 5165
Toros D.
Anatolia
Zagros Mountains (Kühhā-ye Zāgros)
Euphrates (Al Furāt)
Tigris
Elburz Mountains (Reshteh-ye Alborz)
Syrian Desert (Bādiyat ash Shām)
Dasht-e Kavīr
Dasht-e Lūt
Himalaya
Helmand
Hindu Kush 8611
Plateau of Tibet (Qing Zang Gaoyuan)
Brahmaputra
Mt Everest 8848
Ganga
HIMALAYA
Chang Jiang
Xi Jiang
G. of Tongking
Hainan
Anhui Plateau
South China Sea
Palawan
Philippine Sea
Northern Mariana Islands
Guam
Marshall Islands
MICRONESIA

Gulf of Sirte
Qattara Depression
Nile
Sinai
An Nafūd
Arabian Peninsula
Najd
Ad Dahnā'
The Gulf
G. of Oman
Ra's al Hadd
Thar Desert
Indus
Rann of Kachchh
Deccan
Salween
Irrawaddy
Western Ghats
Eastern Ghats
Bay of Bengal
Nam Co
Mekong
Tônlé Sab
Gulf of Thailand
Mui Ca Mau
Luzon
PHILIPPINES
Mindanao
Palau Is
Caroline Islands
Pohnpei
Kosrae
Gilbert Is
Equator
Kingsmill Group
Phoenix Islands

Libyan Desert
A Tibesti
Bodélé
Massif Ennedi
Lake Chad
Marra Plateau
Nubian Desert
Red Sea
Ras Dashen 4620
Denakil
Ethiopian Highlands
Wenji Shebelle
Asir
Rub' al Khali
Arabian Sea
Gulf of Aden
C. Guardafui (Raas Caseyr)
Suqutra (Socotra)
Haud
Sri Lanka
Pak Str.
Andaman Is
Andaman Sea
Nicobar Is
Str. of Malacca
Malay Peninsula
Kep. Natuna
Sulu Sea
Celebes Sea
Halmahera
Seram
New Guinea
Bismarck Sea
New Ireland
New Britain
Bougainville I.
Solomon Is
Nauru
Tuvalu
Tokelau

Cameroun
Sudd
White Nile
Lake Turkana
Maldives
Mid-Indian Basin
Gulf of Thailand
Kuala Lumpur
Sumatera
Borneo
Greater Sunda Islands
Sulawesi
Banda Sea
Buru
Puncak Jaya 5030
Mt Wilhelm 4509
New Britain
Espíritu Santo
Wallis and Futuna Is
Savai'i
Upolu

Congo Basin
Kasai
Mitumba Mts
Great Rift Valley
Lake Victoria
Kirinyaga 5199
Kilimanjaro 5892
Pemba I.
Zanzibar I.
Lake Tanganyika
Seychelles
Amirante Is
Mahé
Aldabra Is
Comoros
Tanjona Bobaomby
INDIAN OCEAN
Chagos Archipelago
Java
Lesser Sunda Islands
Jawa
Flores Sea
Flores
Timor
Timor Sea
Arafura Sea
C. York
Cape York Pen.
Gulf of Carpentaria
Solomon Sea
Coral Sea
Sta Cruz Is
Viti Levu
Fiji
Vanua Levu

Huíla Plateau
Cabinda
Lake Nyasa
Somali Basin
Mahé
Seychelles
Mauritius
Réunion
Rodrigues
West Australian Basin
Cocos Is
Christmas I.
Sumba
Arnhem Land
Kimberley Plateau
Great Sandy Desert
MacDonnell Ranges
Barkly Tableland
Great Dividing Range
Nouvelle Calédonie
Tropic of Capricorn
Norfolk I.
Lord Howe I.

Okavango Delta
Makgadikgadi
Limpopo
Zambezi
Madagascar
Mozambique Channel
Madagascar Basin
North West C.
AUSTRALIA
Musgrave Ranges
Great Victoria Desert
Lake Eyre
Darling
Tasman Sea
Kermadec Is

Namib Desert
Kalahari Desert
Orange
Vaal
Seberg
Natal Basin
'Mauritius
Réunion
Crozet Basin
Ile Amsterdam
Ile St Paul
Perth Basin
Nullarbor Plain
C. Leeuwin
Great Australian Bight
South Australian Basin
Bass Strait
Mt Kosciuszko 2229
Murray
Tasmania
New Zealand
North Island
North C.
Chatham Is
Aoraki 3754
South Island

Great Karoo
Drakensberg
Cape of Good Hope
C. Agulhas
Agulhas Basin
Prince Edward Is
Îles Crozet
Îles Kerguélen
Heard I.
Southeast Indian Ridge
Ninetyeast Ridge
Snares I.
Stewart I.
Auckland Is
Bounty Is
Antipodes Is
Campbell I.
Horizon Deep 10800
Tonga Trench
Tongatapu Group

SOUTHERN OCEAN
Australian-Antarctic Basin

-Antarctic Basin
Davis Sea

Enderby Land
Kemp Land
Amery Ice Shelf
Wilkes Land
Antarctic Circle
Balleny Is

ANTARCTICA
Antarctic Mountains
Ross Sea

Challenger Deep 10920
Mariana Trench
Japan Trench

MILES   KILOMETRES

2400   4200
        3600
1800   3000
        2400
1200   1800
        1200
600   600
0   0

1:70 000 000

© Bartholomew Ltd

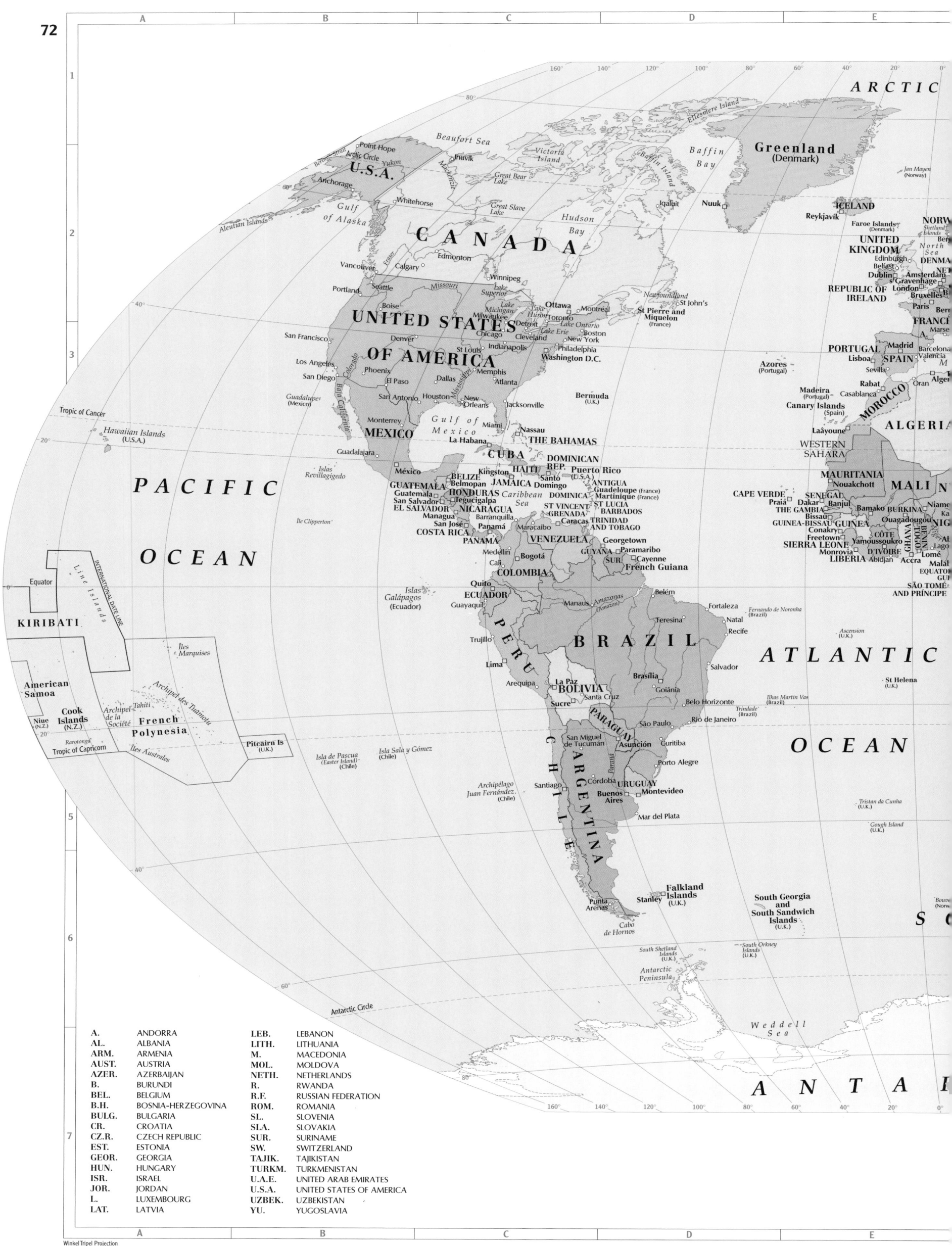

A. ANDORRA
AL. ALBANIA
ARM. ARMENIA
AUST. AUSTRIA
AZER. AZERBAIJAN
B. BURUNDI
BEL. BELGIUM
B.H. BOSNIA-HERZEGOVINA
BULG. BULGARIA
CR. CROATIA
CZ.R. CZECH REPUBLIC
EST. ESTONIA
GEOR. GEORGIA
HUN. HUNGARY
ISR. ISRAEL
JOR. JORDAN
L. LUXEMBOURG
LAT. LATVIA

LEB. LEBANON
LITH. LITHUANIA
M. MACEDONIA
MOL. MOLDOVA
NETH. NETHERLANDS
R. RWANDA
R.F. RUSSIAN FEDERATION
ROM. ROMANIA
SL. SLOVENIA
SLA. SLOVAKIA
SUR. SURINAME
SW. SWITZERLAND
TAJIK. TAJIKISTAN
TURKM. TURKMENISTAN
U.A.E. UNITED ARAB EMIRATES
U.S.A. UNITED STATES OF AMERICA
UZBEK. UZBEKISTAN
YU. YUGOSLAVIA

Winkel Tripel Projection

20° 40° 60° 80° 100° 120° 140° 160° 180°

OCEAN

Svalbard (Norway)

Barents Sea

Zemlya Frantsa-Iosifa

Bjørnøya (Norway)

Novaya Zemlya

Severnaya Zemlya

Arctic Circle

SWEDEN
FINLAND
Stockholm Helsinki
Oslo EST. Tallinn
København Riga LAT.
Hamburg R.F. LITH. Moskva
Berlin Vilnius
ANY POLAND BELARUS Minsk
Warszawa Kyïv Khar'kiv
Praha UKRAINE
Wien Budapest MOL. Chişinău
jubljana HUN. ROM.
Zagreb B.H. Beograd Bucureşti Rostov-na-Donu Krasnodar
Sarajevo YU. Sofiya BULG. Black Sea
Roma ITALY Skopje istanbul
Tiranë GREECE TURKEY Ankara
Palermo Athina CYPRUS LEB.
UNISIA Lefkosia SYRIA Damascus
Tripoli Jerusalem IRAQ
Alexandria Amman JOR. Baghdād
El Giza Cairo KUWAIT Kuwait

Murmansk
Arkhangel'sk

RUSSIAN FEDERATION

Yenisey Ob' Lena Yakutsk
Sankt-Peterburg
Nizhniy Novgorod
Perm' Yekaterinburg
Kazan' Novosibirsk Krasnoyarsk
Samara Omsk Novokuznetsk Irkutsk
Volgograd Astana Karaganda

Komsomol'sk-na-Amure
Khabarovsk

Sea of Okhotsk

Bering Sea

Aleutian Islands

KAZAKHSTAN
Aral Sea
Bishkek Almaty
Tashkent KYRGYZSTAN
UZBEK. Ürümqi
T'bilisi TURKM. TAJIK.
GEOR. ARM. Ashgabat Dushanbe
Bakı Caspian Sea
AZER. Tehrān Mashhad Kābul
Tabrīz IRAN AFGHANISTAN Islamabad
Al Mawsil Esfahān Lahore
Shīrāz PAKISTAN New Delhi
BAHRAIN Faisalabad Delhi
Riyadh QATAR Karachi Jaipur
Abu Dhabi Ahmadabad Indore
U.A.E. Muscat Bhopal Nagpur
Mecca OMAN Mumbai Pune
Jeddah SAUDI ARABIA

MONGOLIA Ulaanbaatar

Yichun
Qiqihar Harbin
Changchun Shenyang Vladivostok
Beijing N. KOREA P'yŏngyang Sapporo
Lanzhou Tianjin Dalian Sŏul
Xi'an Jinan S. KOREA JAPAN Sendai
CHINA Nanjing Pusan Kyōto Tōkyō
Chengdu Chongqing Shanghai Kōbe Ōsaka Yokohama
Chang Jiang Wuhan Nagoya
Lhasa Huang He Fukuoka
Kunming Fuzhou Kagoshima
NEPAL Kathmandu Nanning Guangzhou East China Sea
BHUTAN Hong Kong
Lucknow BANGLADESH Zhanjiang Macau TAIWAN
Patna Dhaka Hainan T'aipei
Calcutta Chittagong Kaohsiung
INDIA MYANMAR Mandalay South China Sea
Hyderabad Ha Nôi
Vijayawada LAOS Luzon
Yangon Viangchan Quezon City
Bangalore Chennai THAILAND VIETNAM Manila
Bangkok CAMBODIA PHILIPPINES
Phnum Pénh
Trivandrum Hô Chi Minh
Andaman Islands (India)
Mindanao

Sea of Japan

Komsomol'sk

JAPAN

PACIFIC

OCEAN

Midway Islands (U.S.A.)
Tropic of Cancer

Ogasawara-shotō (Bonin Islands) (Japan)
Kazan-rettō (Volcano Islands) (Japan)

Northern Mariana Islands (U.S.A.)
Guam (U.S.A.)

MARSHALL ISLANDS
Delap-Uliga-Djarrit

Koror PALAU Caroline Islands Palikir
FEDERATED STATES OF MICRONESIA

Bairiki Gilbert Islands

LIBYA EGYPT

CHAD Khartoum Asmara San'ā'
SUDAN ERITREA YEMEN Aden
Ndjamena ʿĀdis Ābeba DJIBOUTI Djibouti
CENTRAL AFRICAN REPUBLIC ETHIOPIA
CAMEROON Bangui
Yaoundé UGANDA Kampala
ABON DEM. REP. Kigali KENYA Nairobi
breville OF R. Bujumbura B. Lake Victoria Dodoma
CONGO CONGO TANZANIA Dar es Salaam
Brazzaville Kinshasa

Suquṭrā (Yemen)

Arabian Sea

MALDIVES Male

Muqdisho

SOMALIA

Red Sea

Sri Jayewardenepura Kotte SRI LANKA

British Indian Ocean Territory

SEYCHELLES

Victoria

Medan BRUNEI Bandar Seri Begawan
Kuala Lumpur
MALAYSIA Borneo
SINGAPORE
Padang Sumatera Sulawesi
Palembang
Jakarta INDONESIA
Jawa Surabaya

Yaren NAURU Kingsmill Group KIRIBATI
Phoenix Islands
Equator

New PAPUA
Irian Jaya Guinea NEW GUINEA
Port Moresby SOLOMON TUVALU Tokelau (N.Z.)
EAST TIMOR Timor Honiara ISLANDS Vaiaku
Darwin Coral Sea

Wallis and Futuna Islands (France) SAMOA
VANUATU Apia
Port Vila FIJI
Nouméa New Caledonia (France) Suva TONGA

Luanda Lilongwe COMOROS Mayotte (France)
ANGOLA Moroni
ZAMBIA MALAWI
Lusaka MOZAMBIQUE
ZIMBABWE Harare
NAMIBIA Bulawayo Antananarivo
Windhoek MADAGASCAR Port Louis
BOTSWANA Réunion (France) MAURITIUS
Gaborone Pretoria Maputo
Johannesburg SWAZILAND Mbabane
Maseru LESOTHO
REPUBLIC OF SOUTH AFRICA Durban
Cape Town Cape Agulhas

INDIAN

OCEAN

Cocos Islands (Australia)

Christmas Island (Australia)

INDONESIA

AUSTRALIA

Alice Springs
Cairns
Brisbane

Perth Darling Lord Howe Island (Australia) Norfolk Island (Australia)
Adelaide Sydney Kermadec Islands (N.Z.)
Canberra NEW ZEALAND
Melbourne Tasman Sea Auckland North Island
Tasmania Wellington
Hobart South Island Chatham Islands (N.Z.)
Christchurch Dunedin

French Southern and Antarctic Lands

Prince Edward Island (South Africa)
Îles Crozet
Île Amsterdam
Île St Paul
Îles Kerguélen

Heard Island (Australia)

Snares Islands (N.Z.)
Bounty Islands (N.Z.)
Antipodes Islands (N.Z.)
Macquarie Island (Australia)
Auckland Islands (N.Z.)
Campbell Island (N.Z.)

UTHERN OCEAN

Antarctic Circle

Ross Sea

CTICA

20° 40° 60° 80° 100° 120° 140° 160° 180°

MILES KILOMETRES
4200
2400 3600
3000
1800 2400
1800
1200 1200
600 600
0 0

1:70 000 000

© Bartholomew Ltd

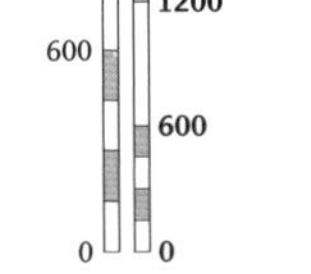

A   B   C   D   E

1

2

3

4

5

6

7

150°

Kuril'skiye Ostrova

Hokkaido

Sea of Japan

Honshū

East China Sea

Nansei-shotō

Kyūshū

Shikoku

Ogasawara-shotō

Kazan-rettō

Pagan

Tinian   Saipan   **Northern Mariana Islands**
Rota   (U.S.A.)

Guam □ **Hagåtña**
(U.S.A.)

A S I A

Chang Jiang

Luzon Strait

Luzon

Samar

Ulithi   Fais
Yap   Sorol   Faraulep   Pikelot   Hall Islands
Ngulu   C a r o l i n e   I s l a n d s   Chuuk
Palau Islands   Eauripik

Mortlock Islands

FEDERATED STATES

Hainan

Tropic of Cancer

90°

Bay of Bengal

Gulf of Thailand

South China Sea

Palawan

Negros

Panay

Mindanao

Sulu Sea

Celebes Sea

Molucca Sea

Halmahera

Mussau Island
Admiralty Islands   New Hanover
   B i s m a r c k   New Ireland
Vanimo   Wewak   S e a
Sepik   Madang   Rabaul
New   Mt Wilhelm   Goroka   New Britain
Guinea   4509   Lae   **PAPUA**
Balimo   Kerema   **NEW GUINEA**
Daru   Gulf of Papua   Woodlark Island
    Port   D'Entrecasteaux
    Moresby   Islands
Torres Strait   Cape York   Louisiade Archipelago

Solomon Islands

Bougainville Island

Madura

A

Strait of Malacca

Kepulauan Mentawai

Sumatera

Borneo

Sulawesi

Makassar Strait

Java Sea

Bali

Java (Jawa)

Sumbawa

Flores Sea

Timor

Sumba

Flores

Banda Sea

Arafura Sea

15°

Christmas Island
(Australia)

Equator

75°

Cocos Islands
(Australia)

INDIAN OCEAN

Timor Sea

Cape Londonderry

Ashmore and Cartier
Islands
(Australia)

Cape Lévêque

Broome

Melville Island

Bathurst Island

Darwin

Arnhem Land

Cape Arnhem

Wessel Islands

Gulf of Carpentaria

Groote Eylandt

Wellesley Islands

Cape York Peninsula

Cape York

Coral Sea Islands Territory
(Australia)

Great Barrier Reef

Cooktown

Cairns

Mitchell

Gilbert

Normanton

Townsville

Mackay

Coral Sea

Wyndham

Halls Creek

NORTHERN TERRITORY

QUEENSLAND

Cloncurry

Mount Isa

Great Dividing Range

Great Sandy Desert

Port Hedland

Karratha

Barrow Island

North West Cape

Newman

Paraburdoo

Lake Mackay

Mount Liebig
1524

Alice Springs

Lake Amadeus

Diamantina

Longreach

Charleville

Cooper Creek

Rockhampton

Gladstone

Fraser Island

Maryborough

Brisbane ⊙

Toowoomba

Gold Coast

Grafton

AUSTRALIA

WESTERN AUSTRALIA

Lake Disappointment

Meekatharra

Mount Magnet

Geraldton

Lake Moore

Leonora

Kalgoorlie

Great Victoria Desert

Oodnadatta

Lake Eyre (North)

SOUTH AUSTRALIA

Woomera

Ceduna

Whyalla

Port Augusta   Broken Hill

Port Pirie

NEW SOUTH WALES

Balonne

Darling

Orange

Lachlan

Tamworth

Newcastle

Lithgow

Sydney ⊙

Wollongong

A.C.T. **Canberra**

Perth ⊙
Fremantle

Bunbury

Albany

Cape Leeuwin

Esperance

Great Australian Bight

Port Lincoln

Cape Carnot

Adelaide ⊙

Kangaroo Island

Wagga Wagga

Murray

Murrumbidgee

Bendigo

Albury

Mount Gambier

VICTORIA

Melbourne ⊙

Geelong

Bass Strait

Flinders Island

King Island

Devonport

Launceston

TASMANIA

Hobart

South East Cape

SOUTHERN OCEAN

Tropic of Capricorn

60°   *30°*   *75°*   *90°*   *45°*   *105°*   *120°*   *135°*   *150°*

A   B   C   D   E

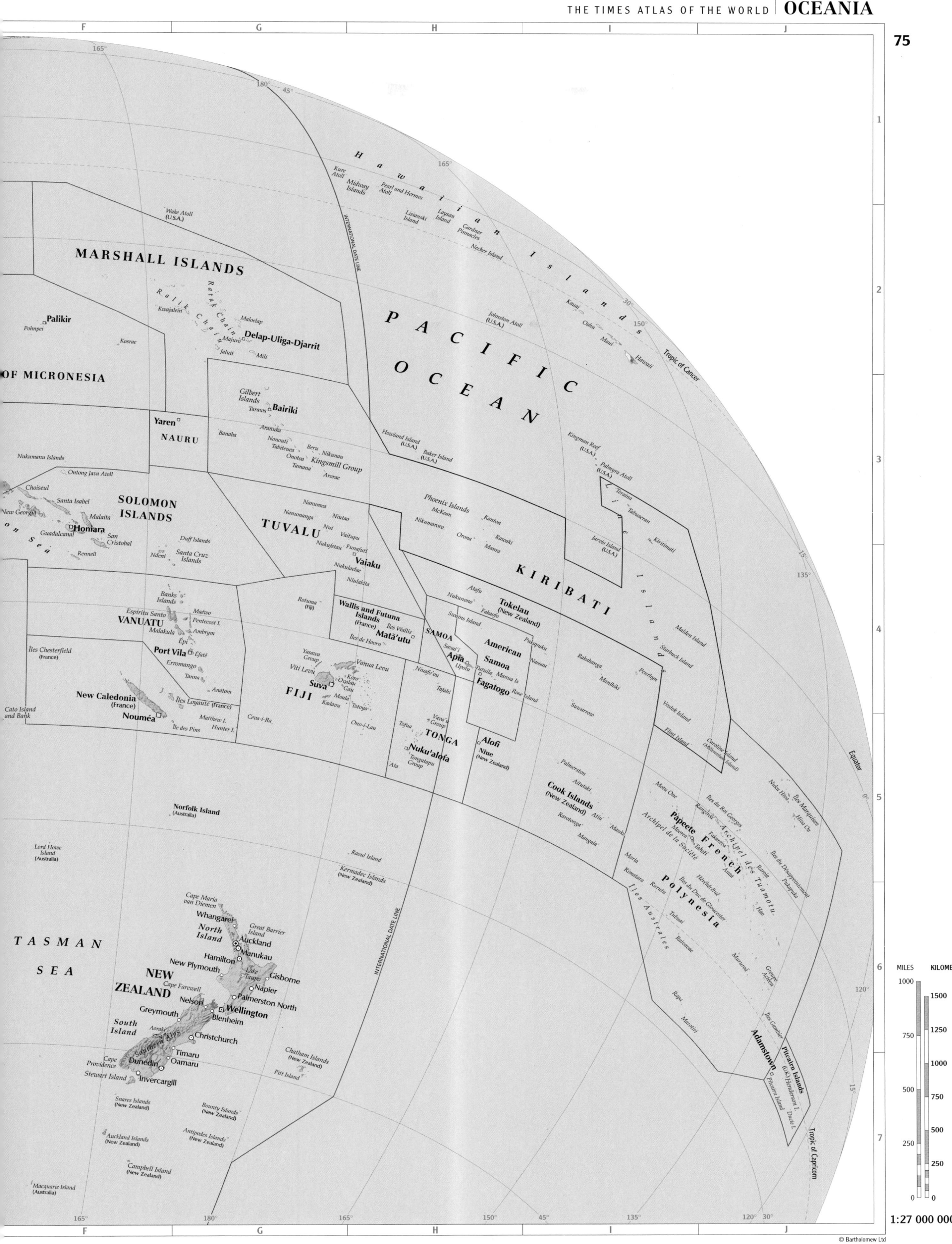

Kure Atoll

Midway Islands *Pearl and Hermes Atoll*

H a w a i i a n   I s l a n d s

Lisianski Island *Laysan Island* *Gardner Pinnacles* *Necker Island*

MARSHALL ISLANDS

Wake Atoll (U.S.A.)

Ratak Chain *Ralik Chain* *Kwajalein* *Maloelap*

Palikir *Pohnpei* *Kosrae*

OF MICRONESIA

Majuro **Delap-Uliga-Djarrit** *Jaluit* *Mili*

P A C I F I C

Johnston Atoll (U.S.A.) *Kauai* *Oahu* *Maui* *Hawaii*

Tropic of Cancer

Yaren □ **NAURU** *Banaba* *Aranuka*

Gilbert Islands *Tarawa* **Bairiki** *Nonouti* *Beru* *Nikunau* *Tabiteuea* *Onotoa* *Tamana* *Arorae* *Kingsmill Group*

Howland Island (U.S.A.) *Baker Island (U.S.A.)*

O C E A N

Kingman Reef (U.S.A.) *Palmyra Atoll (U.S.A.)*

Nukumanu Islands *Ontong Java Atoll*

SOLOMON ISLANDS *Choiseul* *Santa Isabel* *New Georgia* *Malaita*

Nanumea *Niutao* *Nanumanga* *Nui* *Vaitupu* *Nukufetau*

TUVALU

Phoenix Islands *McKean* *Nikumaroro* *Kanton* *Orona* *Rawaki* *Manra*

Teraina *Tabuaeran* *Kiritimati*

on SEA **Honiara** *Guadalcanal* *San Cristobal* *Rennell* *Ndeni* *Duff Islands* *Santa Cruz Islands* *Funafuti* **Vaiaku** *Nukulaelae*

Niulakita

K I R I B A T I

Maiden Island *Starbuck Island*

Banks Islands *Maéwo* *Pentecost I.* *Espíritu Santo* *Malakula* *Ambrym* *Épi*

VANUATU

Rotuma (Fiji) **Wallis and Futuna Islands (France)** *Îles Wallis* **Mata'utu** *Îles de Hoorn*

Nukunono *Atafu* *Fakaofo* **Tokelau (New Zealand)** *Swains Island*

SAMOA *Savai'i* **American Samoa**

Pukapuka *Nassau* *Rakahanga* *Manihiki* *Penrhyn*

Port Vila *Éfaté* *Erromango* *Tanna*

Yasawa Group *Viti Levu* *Vanua Levu* *Koro* *Ovalau* *Gau* **Suva** *Kadavu*

Apia *Upolu* *Niuafo'ou* *Tutuila* *Manua Is* **Fagatogo** *Rose Island*

Vostok Island

Suwarrow

New Caledonia (France) *Îles Loyauté (France)* **Nouméa** *Île des Pins*

FIJI *Cera-i-Ra* *Moala* *Totoya* *Ono-i-Lau* *Matthew I.* *Hunter I.*

Tafahi *Vava'u Group* *Tofua*

TONGA **Nuku'alofa** *Tongatapu Group* *Ata*

Alofi *Niue (New Zealand)*

Palmerston **Cook Islands (New Zealand)** *Aitutaki* *Atiu* *Rarotonga* *Mangaia* *Mauke* *Maria*

Caroline Island (Millennium Island)

Filippi Islands

Equator

Cato Island and Bank

Norfolk Island (Australia)

Lord Howe Island (Australia)

Raoul Island

Kermadec Islands (New Zealand)

Motu One *Rangiroa* *Tikehau* **Papeete** *Moorea* *Tahiti* **French** *Île du Duc de Gloucester* *Hao* *Anaa*

Îles du Roi Georges *Archipel des Tuamotu* *Îles Marquises* *Nuku Hiva* *Hiva Oa* *Îles du Désappointement* *Pukarua*

Archipel de la Société *Hereheretue*

Polynesia *Rurutu* *Rimatara* *Tubuai* *Îles Australes* *Raivavae*

Marutea

Mangareva *Groupe Actéon*

Rapa

Marotiri

Cape Maria van Diemen *Whangarei* *Great Barrier Island* *North Island* **Auckland** ○ **Manukau** *Hamilton*

T A S M A N

S E A

New Plymouth *Gisborne* *Lake Taupo* *Napier*

NEW **ZEALAND** *Cape Farewell* *Palmerston North* *Nelson* **Wellington** *Greymouth* *Blenheim*

Chatham Islands (New Zealand) *Pitt Island*

Adamstown *Pitcairn Islands (U.K.)* *Henderson I.* *Ducie I.* *Pitcairn Island*

South Island *Aoraki 3754* *Christchurch*

Cape Providence *Southern Alps* *Timaru* *Oamaru* **Dunedin** *Stewart Island* **Invercargill**

Snares Islands (New Zealand) *Bounty Islands (New Zealand)*

Auckland Islands (New Zealand) *Antipodes Islands (New Zealand)*

Tropic of Capricorn

Campbell Island (New Zealand)

Macquarie Island (Australia)

MILES KILOMETRES

1000 1500

750 1250

1000

500 750

500

250 250

0 0

1:27 000 000

© Bartholomew Ltd

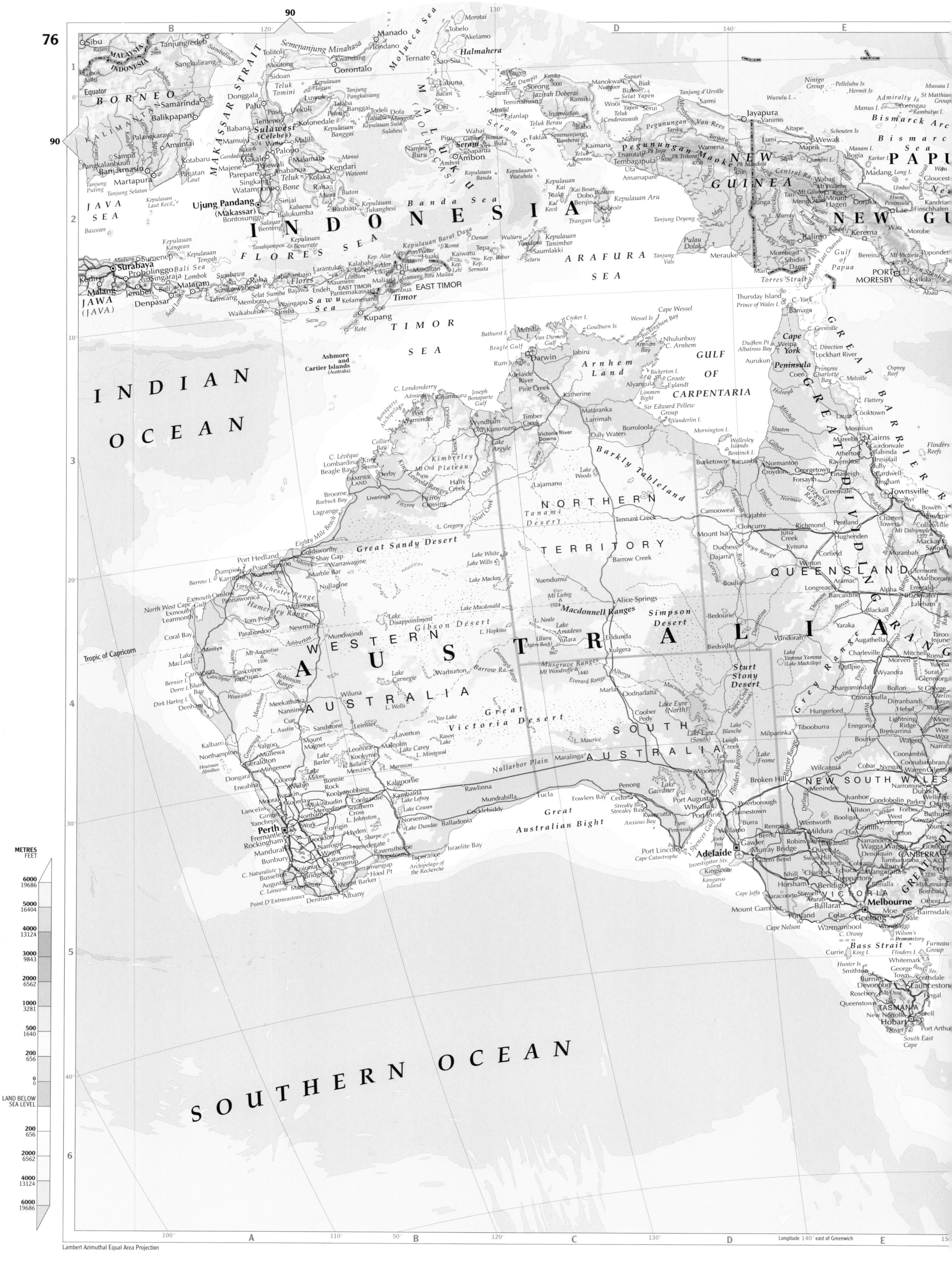

INDONESIA

BORNEO

KALIMANTAN

Sibu
Rajang
Anjang
Tanjungredeb
MALAYSIA
INDONESIA
Equator
Sangkulirang
Samarinda
Balikpapan
Banjarmasin
Pangkalanbuun
Martapura
Amuntai
Kotabaru

JAVA SEA

Sulawesi (Celebes)
Makassar Strait
Palu
Poso
Kendari
Ujung Pandang (Makassar)
Sinjai
Bulukumba

MOLUCCAS

Manado
Tolitoli
Gorontalo
Ternate
Halmahera
Morotai
Tobelo

Molucca Sea
Ceram Sea
Seram
Ambon
Buru
Banda Sea

INDONESIA

JAWA (JAVA)
Surabaya
Malang
Jember
Denpasar
Bali
Lombok
Mataram

Flores Sea
Flores
Sumbawa
Komodo

TIMOR SEA

Sumba
Savu Sea
Kupang
Timor
EAST TIMOR
Dili

ARAFURA SEA

NEW GUINEA
Jayapura
Vanimo
PAPUA NEW GUINEA

Pegunungan Maoke

Merauke

Torres Strait
PORT MORESBY

Gulf of Papua

INDIAN OCEAN

TIMOR SEA

Darwin
Arnhem Land
GULF OF CARPENTARIA

Bathurst I.
Melville I.
C. Arnhem

Katherine
Kununurra
Wyndham
Kimberley
Halls Creek
Derby
Broome
Ord Plateau

Cape York Peninsula
Weipa
Cooktown
Cairns
Townsville

NORTHERN TERRITORY

Tanami Desert
Great Sandy Desert
Tennant Creek
Barrow Creek
Alice Springs
Macdonnell Ranges
Simpson Desert

QUEENSLAND

Mount Isa
Cloncurry
Longreach

Port Hedland
Marble Bar
Newman
Nullagine

WESTERN AUSTRALIA

Gibson Desert
Lake Disappointment
Lake Mackay
Great Victoria Desert

Tropic of Capricorn

Carnarvon
Geraldton

Uluru (Ayers Rock)
Musgrave Ranges
Everard Range

SOUTH AUSTRALIA

Lake Eyre
Sturt Stony Desert
Coober Pedy
Oodnadatta
Birdsville

Kalgoorlie
Norseman
Nullarbor Plain
Great Australian Bight

Perth
Fremantle
Rockingham
Mandurah
Bunbury
Busselton
Augusta
Albany

NEW SOUTH WALES
Broken Hill
Port Augusta
Whyalla
Port Pirie
Adelaide
Port Lincoln
Kangaroo Island

CANBERRA

VICTORIA
Mildura
Bendigo
Ballarat
Geelong
Melbourne
Warrnambool
Portland

Bass Strait
King I.
Flinders I.

TASMANIA
Devonport
Launceston
Queenstown
Hobart
Port Arthur

SOUTHERN OCEAN

Lambert Azimuthal Equal Area Projection

Longitude 140° east of Greenwich

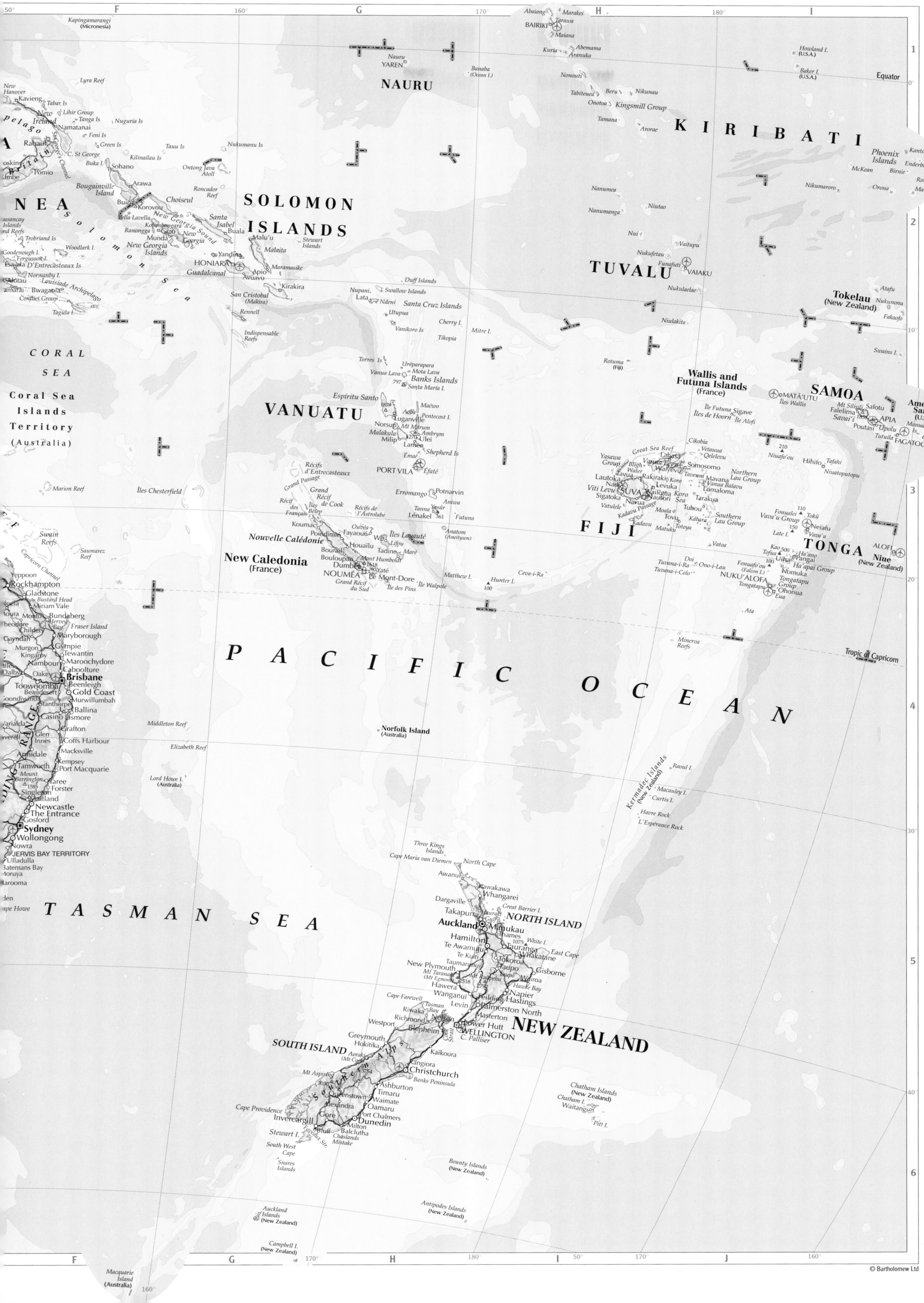

NAURU
YAREN

KIRIBATI

BAIRIKI

Phoenix
Islands

Equator

SOLOMON
ISLANDS

HONIARA
Guadalcanal

TUVALU

VAIAKU

Tokelau
(New Zealand)

CORAL
SEA

Coral Sea
Islands
Territory
(Australia)

VANUATU

Wallis and
Futuna Islands
(France)

SAMOA

APIA

American
Samoa
(U.S.A.)

FAGATOGO

PORT VILA

FIJI

SUVA

TONGA

New Caledonia
(France)

NOUMÉA

NUKU'ALOFA

Niue
(New Zealand)

Norfolk Island
(Australia)

PACIFIC OCEAN

Tropic of Capricorn

Brisbane
Gold Coast

Sydney
Wollongong

JERVIS BAY TERRITORY

Newcastle

Kermadec Islands
(New Zealand)

TASMAN SEA

Three Kings
Islands
Cape Maria van Diemen
North Cape

NORTH ISLAND

Auckland
Hamilton
Tauranga

New Plymouth

Wanganui

Napier
Hastings
Palmerston North

NEW ZEALAND

Nelson
Lower Hutt
WELLINGTON

Chatham Islands
(New Zealand)

SOUTH ISLAND

Greymouth

Christchurch
Timaru

Invercargill
Dunedin
Stewart I.

Bounty Islands
(New Zealand)

Snares
Islands

Antipodes Islands
(New Zealand)

Auckland
Islands
(New Zealand)

Campbell I.
(New Zealand)

Macquarie
Island
(Australia)

MILES   KILOMETRES

800   1200

600   1000

400   800

400

200   200

0

1:18 000 000

© Bartholomew Ltd

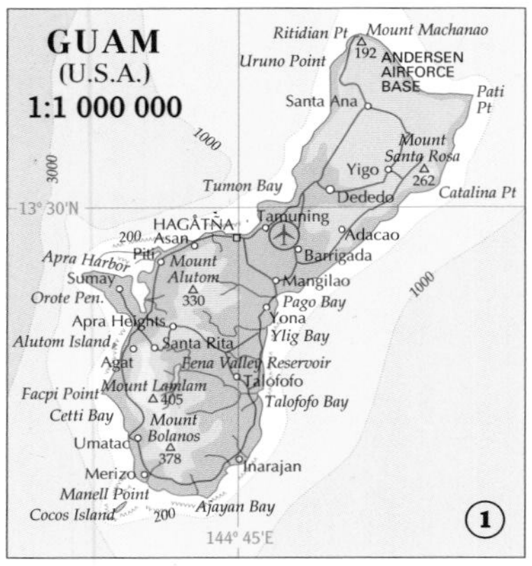

GUAM (U.S.A.)
1:1 000 000

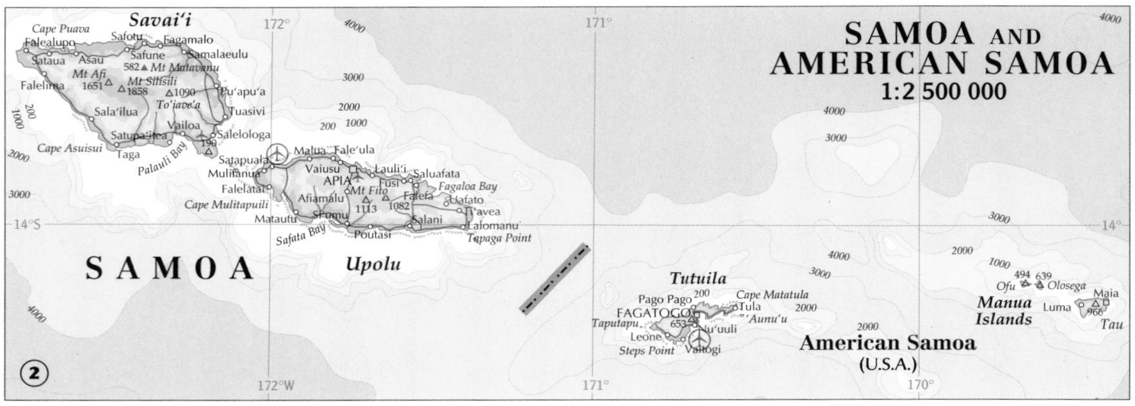

SAMOA AND AMERICAN SAMOA
1:2 500 000

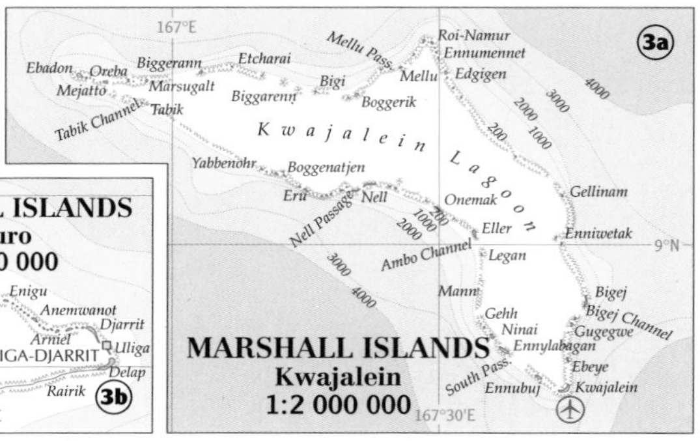

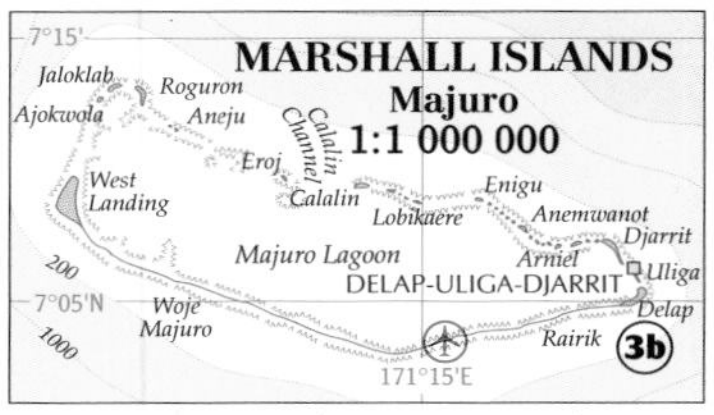

MARSHALL ISLANDS
Majuro
1:1 000 000

MARSHALL ISLANDS
Kwajalein
1:2 000 000

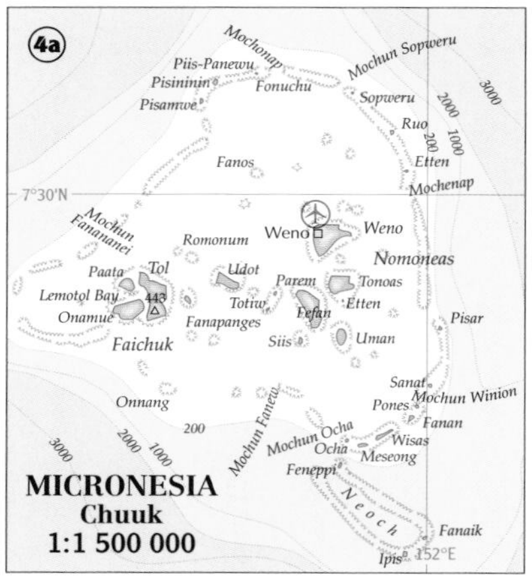

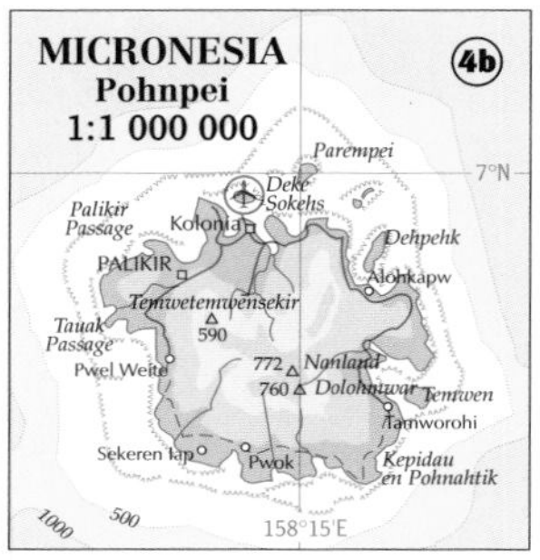

MICRONESIA
Pohnpei
1:1 000 000

MICRONESIA
Chuuk
1:1 500 000

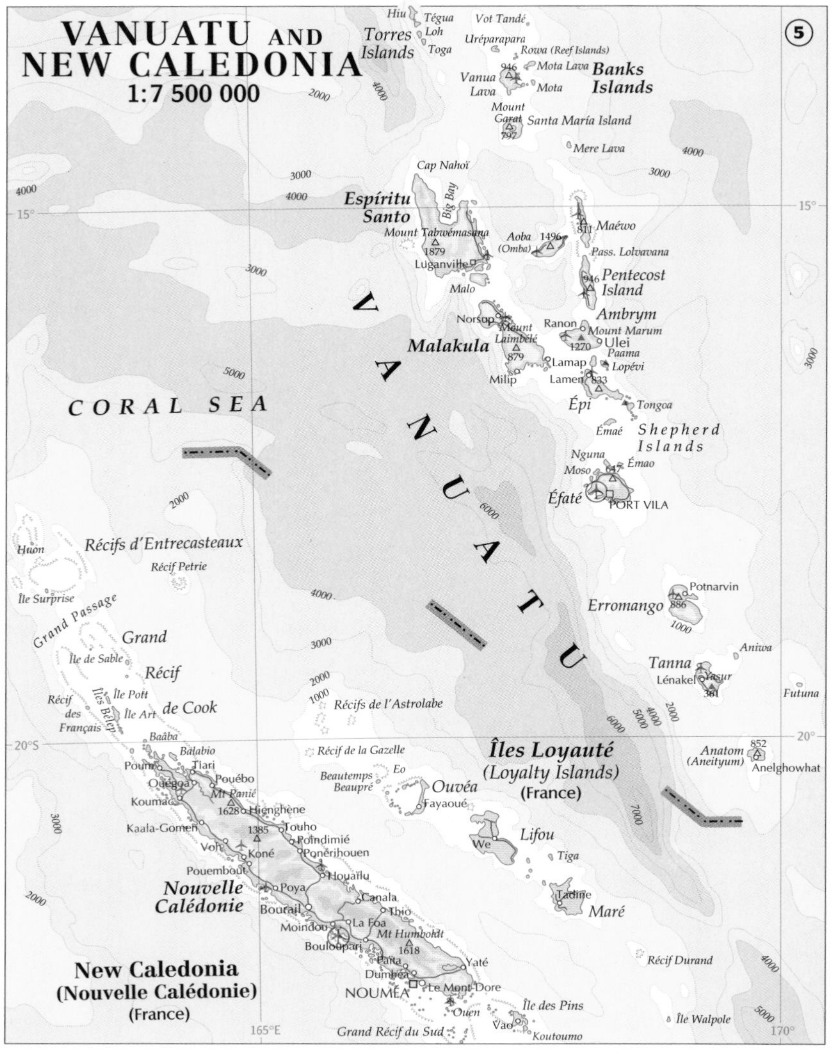

VANUATU AND NEW CALEDONIA
1:7 500 000

New Caledonia (Nouvelle Calédonie) (France)

PAPUA NEW GUINEA

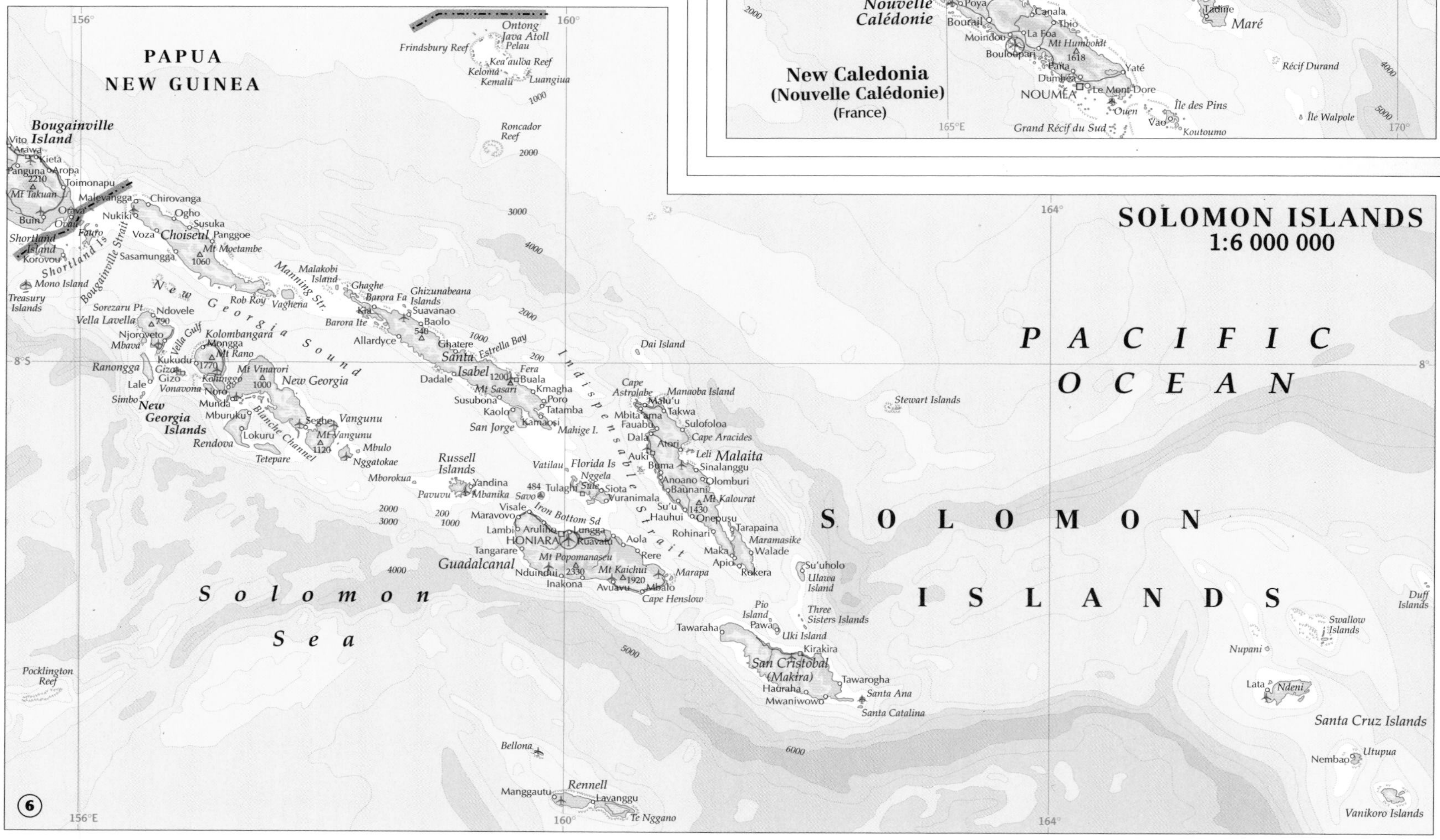

SOLOMON ISLANDS
1:6 000 000

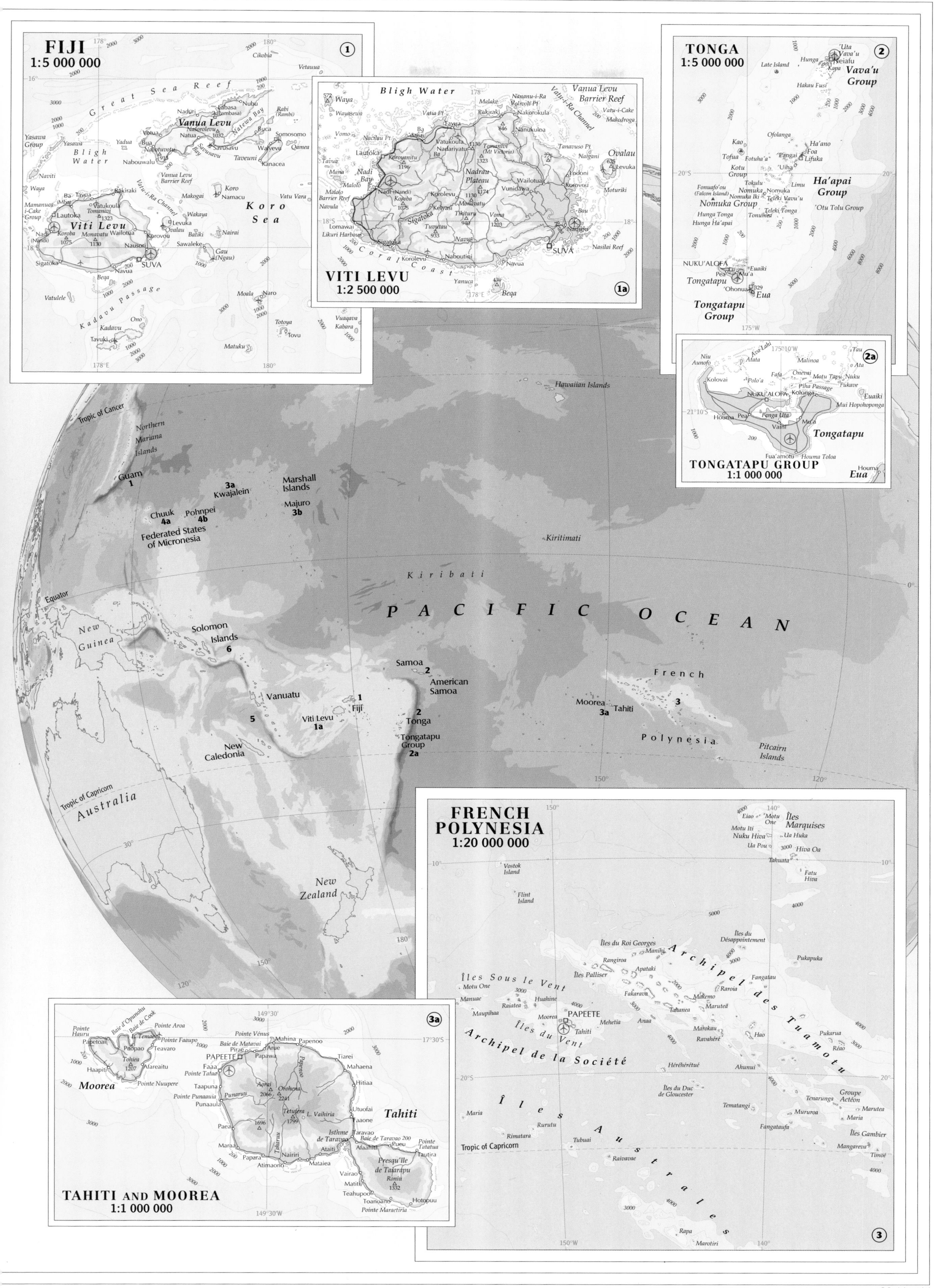
FIJI
1:5 000 000
Great Sea Reef
Vanua Levu
Bligh Water
Viti Levu
Koro Sea
Kadavu Passage
Kadavu
Taveuni
Lautoka
Nadi
Sigatoka
SUVA
Labasa
Savusavu
VITI LEVU
1:2 500 000
Bligh Water
Vanua Levu Barrier Reef
Vatu-i-Ra Channel
Coral Coast
Nadrau Plateau
Ovalau
Levuka
Nausori
Navua
Beqa
TONGA
1:5 000 000
Vava'u Group
Ha'apai Group
Nomuka Group
Tongatapu Group
'Otu Tolu Group
NUKU'ALOFA
Tongatapu
'Eua
Late Island
Kao
Tofua
TONGATAPU GROUP
1:1 000 000
Tongatapu
Eua
NUKU'ALOFA
Kolovai
Houma
Pea
Vaini
Mu'a
Hawaiian Islands
Tropic of Cancer
Northern Mariana Islands
Guam 1
Chuuk 4a
Pohnpei 4b
Federated States of Micronesia
Kwajalein 3a
Marshall Islands
Majuro 3b
Kiritimati
Kiribati
Equator
PACIFIC OCEAN
New Guinea
Solomon Islands 6
Samoa 2
American Samoa
Vanuatu
5
Viti Levu 1a
Fiji 1
Tonga 2
Tongatapu Group 2a
New Caledonia
Moorea 3a
Tahiti
French Polynesia 3
Pitcairn Islands
Tropic of Capricorn
Australia
New Zealand
FRENCH POLYNESIA
1:20 000 000
Îles Marquises
Nuku Hiva
Hiva Oa
Vostok Island
Flint Island
Îles du Roi Georges
Îles du Désappointement
Rangiroa
Îles Palliser
Îles Sous le Vent
Archipel des Tuamotu
PAPEETE
Tahiti
Îles du Vent
Archipel de la Société
Îles du Duc de Gloucester
Mururoa
Fangataufa
Îles Gambier
Mangareva
Tropic of Capricorn
Îles Australes
Rurutu
Tubuai
Raivavae
Rimatara
Rapa
Marotiri
TAHITI AND MOOREA
1:1 000 000
Moorea
Tahiti
PAPEETE
Faaa
Mahina
Papenoo
Tiarei
Hitiaa
Taravao
Isthme de Taravao
Presqu'île de Taiarapu
Mataiea
Papara
Paea
Punaauia
Teahupoo
Pointe Venus
Orohena 2241
Aorai 2066

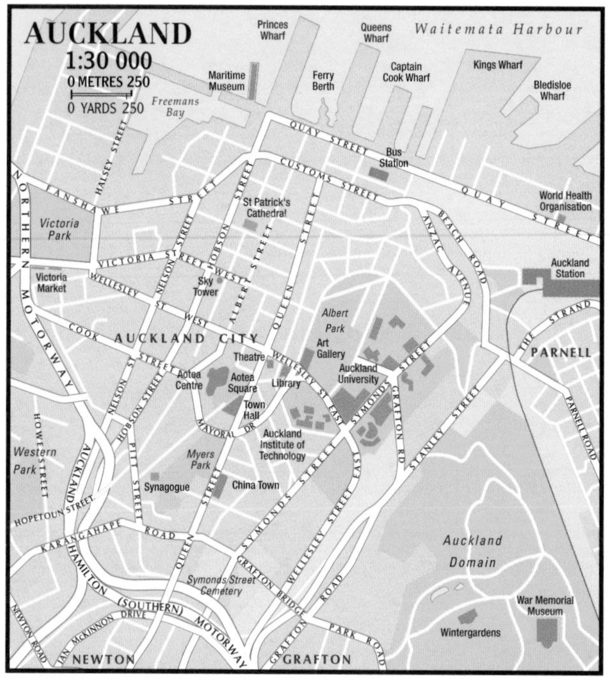

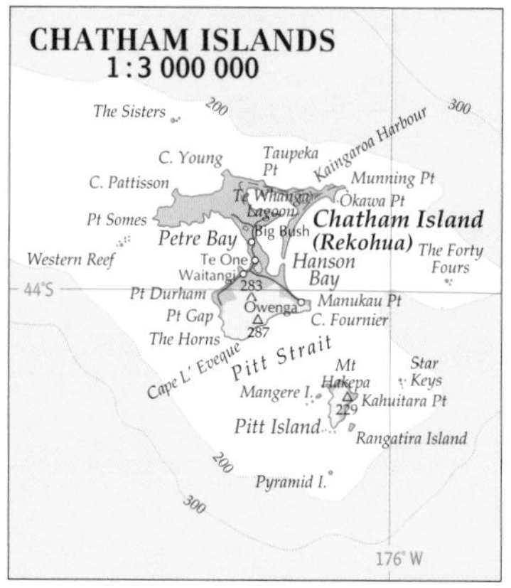

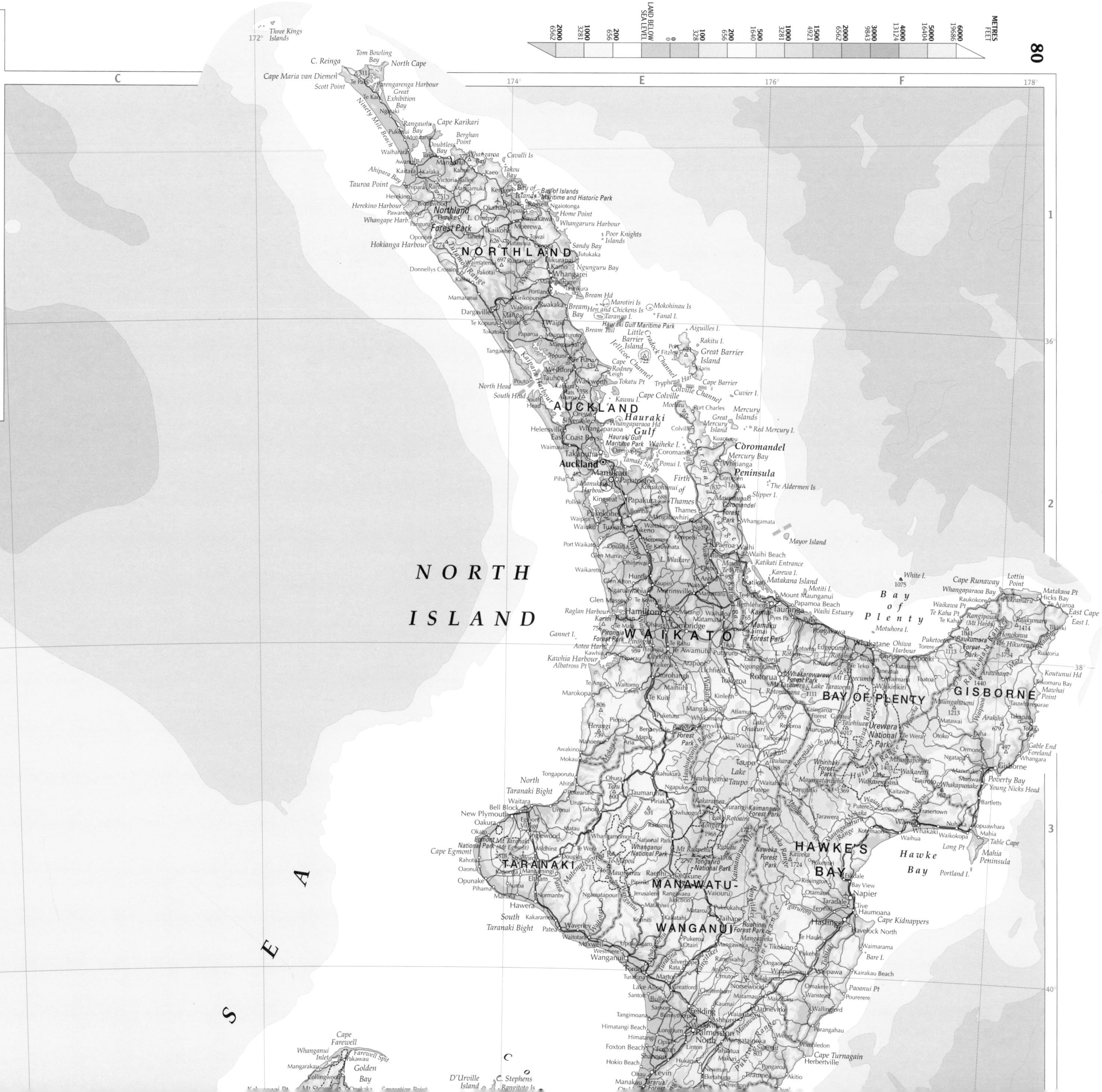

METRES
FEET

6000
19686

5000
16404

4000
13124

3000
9843

2000
6562

1500
4921

1000
3281

500
1640

200
656

100
328

0
0

LAND BELOW
SEA LEVEL

200
656

1000
3281

2000
6562

AUCKLAND
1:30 000
0 METRES 250
0 YARDS 250

Waitemata Harbour

Bledisloe Wharf
Princes Wharf
Kings Wharf
Queens Wharf
Captain Cook Wharf
Ferry Berth
Maritime Museum
Freemans Bay
Viaduct Basin

World Health Organisation
Auckland Station

PARNELL
PARNELL ROAD

War Memorial Museum
Auckland Domain
Wintergardens

Auckland University
Albert Park
Art Gallery
St Patrick's Cathedral
Aotea Centre
Town Hall
Library
Sky Tower
Myers Park
Synagogue
Auckland Institute of Technology

Victoria Park
NEWTON

SOUTHERN MOTORWAY
NORTHERN MOTORWAY

CHATHAM ISLANDS
1:3 000 000

Chatham Island
(Rekohu)
The Forty Fours

Hanson Bay
Petre Bay
Pitt Strait
Pitt Island
Rangatira Island
Pyramid I.

C. Young
C. Pattisson
Pt Somes

The Sisters

Western Reef

N O R T H

I S L A N D

NORTHLAND

Cape Reinga
North Cape
Three Kings Islands
Cape Maria van Diemen
Scott Point
Ninety Mile Beach
Tom Bowling Bay
Doubtless Bay
Cape Karikari
Bay of Islands
Whangaroa Harbour
Kaitaia
Kaikohe
Hokianga Harbour
Dargaville
Whangarei
Kaipara Harbour

AUCKLAND
Auckland
Manukau
Hauraki Gulf

Coromandel
Peninsula
Thames
Firth of Thames

WAIKATO
Hamilton
Waikato

BAY OF PLENTY
Bay of Plenty
White I.
Mayor Island

GISBORNE
Gisborne
Cape Runaway
East Cape
Poverty Bay

HAWKE'S BAY
Hawke Bay
Napier
Cape Kidnappers

TARANAKI
New Plymouth
Mt Egmont
South Taranaki Bight
North Taranaki Bight

WANGANUI
Wanganui

MANAWATU-WANGANUI

Cape Farewell
Golden Bay
D'Urville Island

T A S M A N

S E A

Conic Equidistant Projection

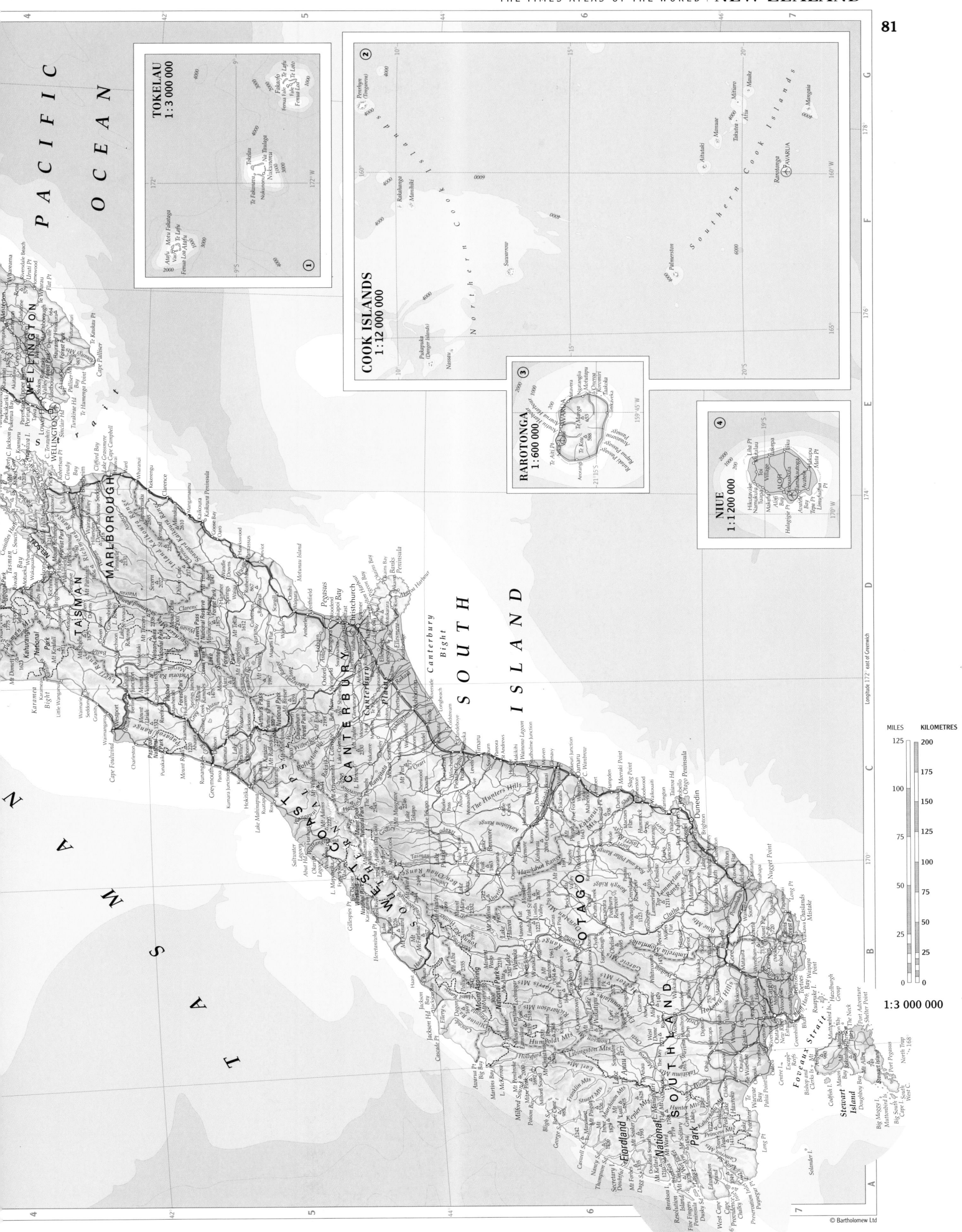

TOKELAU
1:3 000 000

COOK ISLANDS
1:12 000 000

RAROTONGA
1:600 000

NIUE
1:1 200 000

PACIFIC

OCEAN

TASMAN

SEA

WELLINGTON

MARLBOROUGH

TASMAN

SOUTH

ISLAND

CANTERBURY

Canterbury Bight

Christchurch

WEST COAST

SOUTHERN ALPS

OTAGO

Dunedin

SOUTHLAND

Fiordland
National
Park

Stewart
Island

Foveaux Strait

MILES   KILOMETRES

1:3 000 000

© Bartholomew Ltd

METRES FEET

6000 19686
5000 16404
4000 13124
3000 9843
2000 6562
1000 3281
500 1640
200 656
0 0
LAND BELOW SEA LEVEL
200 656
2000 6562
4000 13124
6000 19686

WESTERN AUSTRALIA

GREAT VICTORIA DESERT

SOUTH AUSTRALIA

Musgrave Ranges

Anangu Pitjantjatjara Aboriginal Lands

Warakurna-Wingellina-Irrunytju Aboriginal Reserve

Great Victoria Desert Conservation Park

Great Victoria Desert Nature Reserve

Maralinga-Tjarutja Aboriginal Lands

Woomera Prohibited Area

Nullarbor Plain

Simpson Desert Conservation Park

Simpson Desert Regional Reserve

Sturt Stony Desert

Lake Eyre (North)

Lake Eyre National Park

Strzelecki Regional Reserve

Lake Torrens National Park

Lake Gairdner National Park

FLINDERS RANGES

Flinders Ranges National Park

GREAT AUSTRALIAN BIGHT

NORFOLK ISLAND ①
1 : 900 000

Pt Vincent
Anson Bay
Burnt Pine
Rocky Pt
Sydney Bay
Mt Bates 321
Cascade Bay
Steel's Pt
Pt Blackbourne
Ball Bay
Hunter
Nepean Island
Philip Island

29°S
168°E

LORD HOWE ISLAND ②
1 : 900 000

North Rock
Admiralty Is
Malabar
Phillip Pt
Prince William Henry Bay
Middle Beach
Mutton Bird I.
Mt East Pt
Gower
Lord Howe I.
King Pt

31°30'S
31°45'S

Observatory Rock
Ball's Pyramid
Wheatsheaf I.
South East Rock

159°15'E

GREAT AUSTRALIAN BIGHT

Eyre Peninsula

Yorke Peninsula

Kangaroo Island

Adelaide

Spencer Gulf

Gulf St Vincent

S O U T H E R N

O C E A N

MELBOURNE 1:30 000
0 METRES 250
0 YARDS 250

St James Cathedral
Flagstaff Gardens
Royal Melbourne Institute of Technology
National Museum
St Patrick's Cathedral
Parliament House
Fitzroy Gardens
Treasury Gardens
Cook's Cottage
Town Hall
St Paul's Cathedral
Flinders Street Station
Princes Bridge Station
Jolimont Station
Australian Gallery of Sport
Melbourne Cricket Ground
Spencer Street Station
World Trade Centre
Maritime Museum
Melbourne Casino Complex
Melbourne Exhibition Centre
Batman Park
Melbourne Concert Hall
National Gallery of Victoria
Alexandra Gardens
Floral Clock
Old Scotch Oval
National Tennis Centre
Myer Music Bowl
Kings Domain
Olympic Park
Ground No.1
Ground No.2
Government House
Shrine Of Remembrance
La Trobe Cottage
Royal Botanic Gardens
SOUTH MELBOURNE
Yarra

MACQUARIE ISLAND ③
1 : 900 000

Hasselborough Bay
Elliot Reef
North Hd
Anare Station
Buckles Bay
Nuggetts Pt
Handspike Pt
Half Moon Bay
Eagle Pt
Langdon Pt
Bauer Bay
Mt Elder
Sandy Bay
Brothers Pt
Prion Lake
Aurora Pt
Mt Waite
Victoria Pt
Sandell Bay
Cape Toutcher
Mt Hamilton
Major L.
Lusitania Bay
Caroline Cove
Waterfall L.
Green Pt
Hurd Pt
South Reef
South East Reef

54°30'S
54°45'S
158°45'E
159°

Lambert Azimuthal Equal Area Projection

QUEENSLAND

NEW SOUTH WALES

VICTORIA

TASMANIA

Darling Downs

GREAT DIVIDING RANGE

GREY RANGE

RIVERINA

Brisbane
Gold Coast
Tweed Heads

Newcastle
Sydney
Parramatta
Liverpool
Sutherland
Campbelltown
Wollongong
Port Kembla
Shellharbour
Kiama

CANBERRA
AUSTRALIAN CAPITAL TERRITORY
JERVIS BAY TERRITORY

Melbourne
Geelong
Frankston

Hobart
Launceston

Fraser Island
Fraser Island National Park

TASMAN SEA

Bass Strait

King Island

Flinders Island
Furneaux Group

Hunter Islands

MILES / KILOMETRES
250 — 400
200 — 350
— 300
150 — 250
— 200
100 — 150
— 100
50 — 50
0 — 0

1:6 000 000

SYDNEY inset

SYDNEY
1:45 000
0 METRES 500
0 YARDS 500

Sydney Harbour
Sydney Opera House
THE ROCKS
MILLERS POINT
Darling Harbour
Royal Botanic Gardens
The Domain
WOOLLOOMOOLOO
KINGS CROSS
DARLINGHURST
PADDINGTON
SURRY HILLS
ULTIMO
Central Station
Walsh Bay
Dawes Point
Bennelong Point
Fort Denison
Mrs Macquarie's Point
Elizabeth Bay
Garden Island
PARK STREET
WILLIAM STREET
OXFORD STREET
GEORGE STREET
BROADWAY

© Bartholomew Ltd

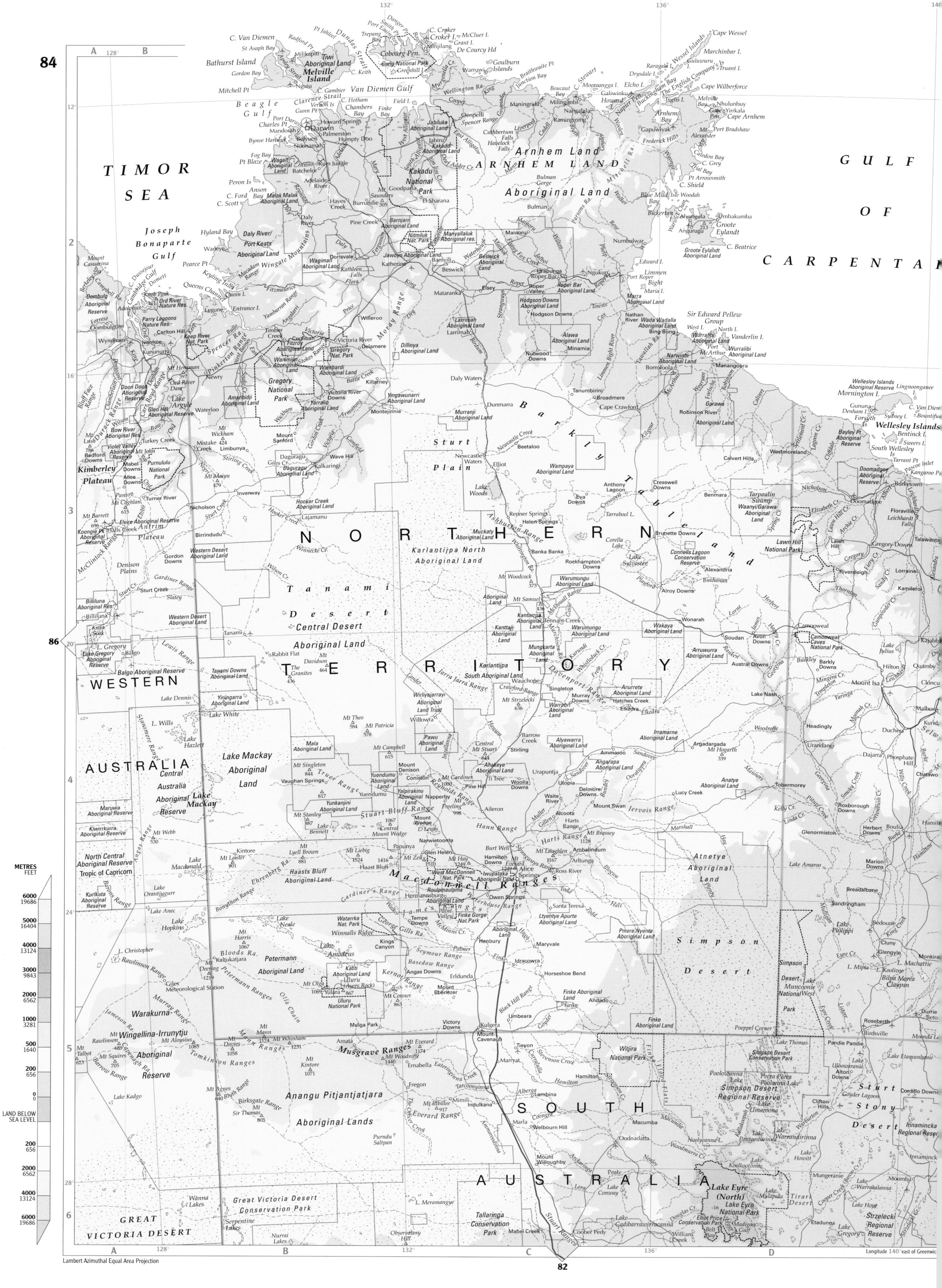

TIMOR SEA

GULF OF CARPENTARIA

NORTHERN TERRITORY

WESTERN AUSTRALIA

SOUTH AUSTRALIA

Arnhem Land
ARNHEM LAND
Aboriginal Land

Bathurst Island
Melville Island
Tiwi Aboriginal Land

Beagle Gulf
Van Diemen Gulf

Darwin
Palmerston
Howard Springs
Humpty Doo

Kakadu National Park
Jabiru
Jabiluka

Joseph Bonaparte Gulf

Daly River/Port Keats Aboriginal Land
Wadeye

Katherine
Pine Creek

Wingate Mountains
Macadam Range

Victoria River
Gregory National Park
Timber Creek

Kununurra
Lake Argyle

Kimberley Plateau

Purnululu National Park
Halls Creek

Antrim Plateau

Tanami Desert

Central Desert Aboriginal Land

Lake Mackay
Lake Mackay Aboriginal Land

Central Australia Aboriginal Reserve

Lake White

Tropic of Capricorn

Rabbit Flat
The Granites

Tanami Downs Aboriginal Land

Lander
Willowra

South Tanami Aboriginal Land

Yuendumu
Papunya

Haasts Bluff Aboriginal Land

MacDonnell Ranges
Alice Springs
Hermannsburg

Barkly Tableland

Sturt Plain

Newcastle Waters
Elliott

Lake Woods

Daly Waters
Dunmarra

Brunette Downs

Tennant Creek

Warumungu Aboriginal Land

Barkly Downs

Mount Isa

Camooweal

Kintore

Petermann Aboriginal Land
Petermann Ranges

Uluru-Kata Tjuta National Park
Yulara
Uluru (Ayers Rock)
Mount Olga

Lake Amadeus

Musgrave Ranges
Mann Ranges
Tomkinson Ranges

Anangu Pitjantjatjara Aboriginal Lands

Warakurna
Wingellina-Irruntytju Aboriginal Reserve

Great Victoria Desert

Great Victoria Desert Conservation Park

Simpson Desert

Simpson Desert Regional Reserve
Simpson Desert National Park

Simpson Desert Conservation Park

Witjira National Park

Lake Eyre (North)
Lake Eyre National Park

Sturt Stony Desert

Strzelecki Regional Reserve

Coober Pedy
Oodnadatta
Marla

METRES / FEET
6000 / 19686
5000 / 16404
4000 / 13124
3000 / 9843
2000 / 6562
1000 / 3281
500 / 1640
200 / 656
0
LAND BELOW SEA LEVEL
200 / 656
2000 / 6562
4000 / 13124
6000 / 19686

Lambert Azimuthal Equal Area Projection

Longitude 140° east of Greenwich

© Bartholomew Ltd

1:6 000 000

PAPUA
NEW GUINEA
CORAL SEA
Coral Sea Islands Territory
GREAT BARRIER REEF
Great Barrier Reef Marine Park (Far North Section)
Great Barrier Reef Marine Park (Cairns Section)
Great Barrier Reef Marine Park (Central Section)
Great Barrier Reef Marine Park (Capricorn Section)
Capricorn Channel
Tropic of Capricorn
CAPE YORK PENINSULA
GREAT DIVIDING RANGE
QUEENSLAND
Gregory Range
Grey Range
Darling Downs
Swain Reefs
Whitsunday Group
Fraser Island
Cape York
Cairns
Townsville
Mackay
Rockhampton
Gladstone
Bundaberg
Maryborough
Gympie
Toowoomba
Brisbane
Charters Towers
Hughenden
Longreach
Emerald
Roma
Charleville
Cunnamulla
Winton
Quilpie
Cooktown
Weipa
MILES | KILOMETRES

84

INDONESIA

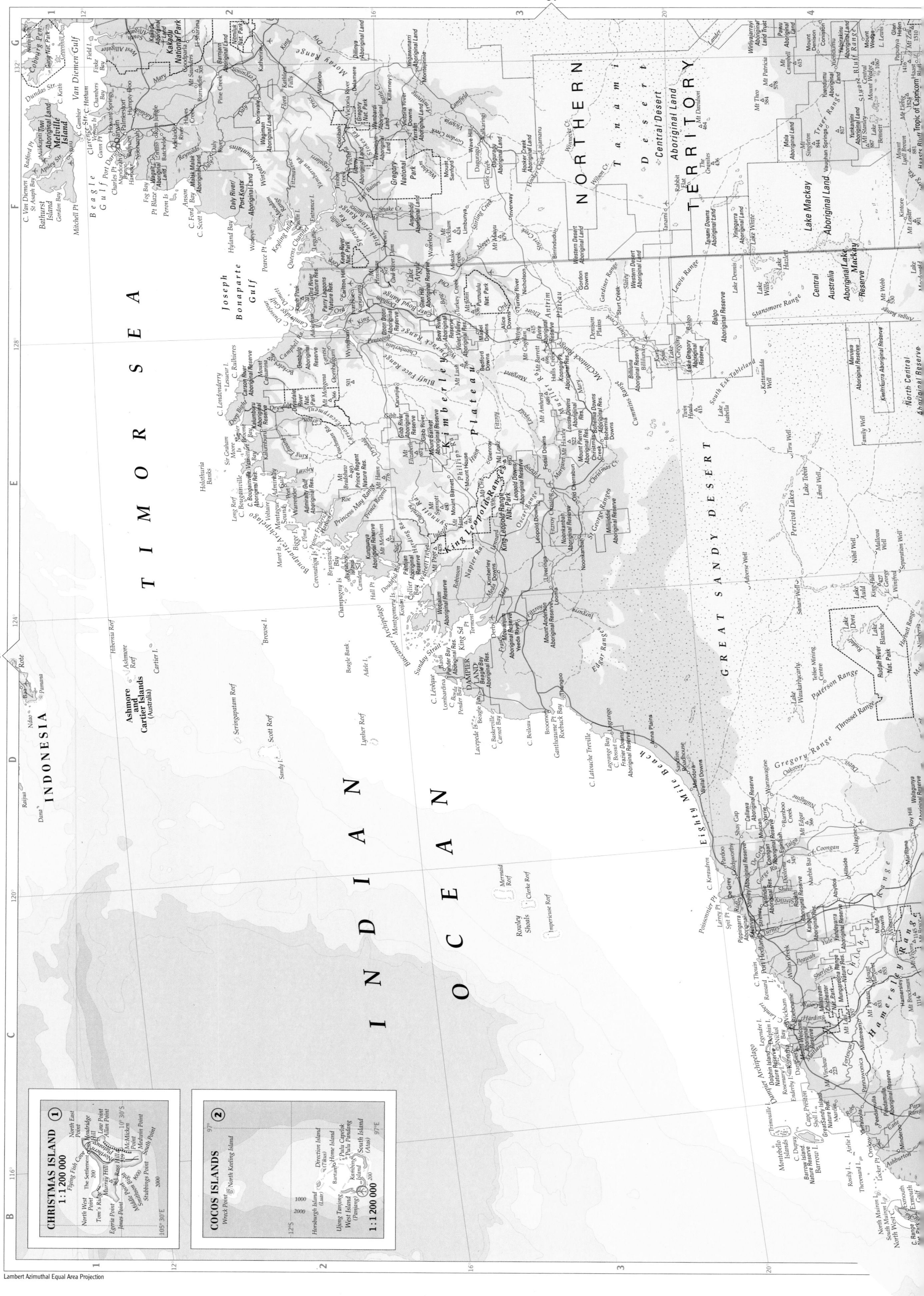

TIMOR SEA

INDIAN OCEAN

NORTHERN TERRITORY

Kakadu National Park

Bathurst Island

Melville Island

Van Diemen Gulf

Beagle Gulf

Joseph Bonaparte Gulf

Ashmore and Cartier Islands (Australia)

Kimberley Plateau

King Leopold Ranges

Bluff Face Range

GREAT SANDY DESERT

Tanami Desert

Central Desert

Aboriginal Land

Lake Mackay

Central Australia Aboriginal Land

Lake Mackay Reserve

Eighty Mile Beach

Hamersley Range

Gregory Range

Dampier Archipelago

CHRISTMAS ISLAND ①
1:1 200 000

North East Point
Flying Fish Cove
The Settlement
North West Point
Egeria Point
South Point
105°30'E

COCOS ISLANDS ②
1:1 200 000

North Keeling Island
Direction Island
West Island
Home Island
South Island (Atas)
1:1 200 000
97°E

Lambert Azimuthal Equal Area Projection

GREAT AUSTRALIAN BIGHT

SOUTH AUSTRALIA

WESTERN AUSTRALIA

GIBSON DESERT

GREAT VICTORIA DESERT

Nullarbor Plain

Great Victoria Desert Conservation Park

Great Victoria Desert Nature Reserve

Nullarbor Regional Reserve

Nullarbor National Park

Anangu Pitjantjatjara Aboriginal Lands

Aboriginal Lands

Musgrave Ranges

Petermann Ranges

Warakurna-Irrunytju Wingellina Aboriginal Lands

Maralinga-Tjarutja Aboriginal Lands

Woomera Prohibited Area

Little Sandy Desert

Perth
Fremantle
Mandurah
Geraldton
Kalgoorlie
Esperance
Albany
Bunbury

Shark Bay

Dirk Hartog Island

Houtman Abrolhos

Tropic of Capricorn

Longitude 120 east of Greenwich

1:6 000 000

MILES | KILOMETRES
250 | 400
200 | 350
150 | 300
| 250
100 | 200
| 150
50 | 100
| 50

© Bartholomew Ltd

A B C D E

ARCTIC

1

Baltic Sea
Gulf of Bothnia
Beloye More
Arctic Circle
Nordvik
Karskoye More
R U S S I A N
Urengoy
Noril'sk
Ozero Onezhskoye
Ob'
Obskaya Guba
30° 45° 60° 75°
E U R O P E
Ural'skiy Khrebet (Ural Mountains)
Surgut
Yekaterinburg
Tobol'sk
Irtysh
Chelyabinsk
Tomsk
Krasnoyarsk
Omsk
Novosibirsk
Novokuznetsk
Volga
Pavlodar
Barnaul

2

Alps
Carpathian Mountains
Sea of Azov
Don
Ural'sk
Aktyubinsk
K A Z A K H S T A N
Astana
Karaganda
Semipalatinsk
Ust'-Kamenogorsk
Ulaangom
Kyzy
Altai Mountains
Altay
Tacheng
Adriatic Sea
Black Sea
Caucasus
Kura
Volga
Atyrau
Aktau
Aral'sk
Aral Sea
Ozero Zaysan
Ozero Balkhash
Balkhash

3

Bursa
Samsun
T'bilisi
GEORGIA
Ankara
Yerevan
ARMENIA AZERBAIJAN
Izmir
Sivas
Erzurum
Baku
Konya
Kayseri
Caspian Sea
Shymkent
U Z B E K I S T A N
Almaty
Yining
Ürümqi
T U R K E Y
Malatya
Tabriz
Zaliv Kara-Bogaz-Gol
Tashkent
Bishkek
Turpan
Antalya
Adana
Gaziantep
Turkmenbashi
Syr Darya
KYRGYZSTAN
Andizhan
Korla
XINJIANG UYGUR ZIZHIQU
Kizil
Lefkosia
Halab
Al Mawsil
TURKMENISTAN
Ashgabat
Samarkand
Khujand
Kokand
Kashi
(SINKIANG)
CYPRUS
LEBANON
SYRIA
Nahr Dijlah
Arbil
Gorgān
TAJIKISTAN
Dushanbe
Tien Shan
Tarim Pendi
Beirut
Damascus
Kirkūk
Mashhad
Hindu Kush
Kunlun Shan
Lop Nur
ISRAEL
Tel Aviv-Yafo
Baghdad
Kermānshāh
Tehrān
Hotan
AKSAI CHIN
Qaidam Pen
Gaza
Amman
IRAQ
An Najaf
Qom
Borūjerd
Esfahān
Herāt
Kābul
Peshawar
Islamabad
XIZANG ZIZHIQU
Golmud
Jerusalem
JORDAN
Al Furāt (Euphrates)
I R A N
Birjand
AFGHANISTAN
Rawalpindi
Gujranwala
(TIBET)
Siling Co
Al Basrah
Ahvāz
Ābādān
Kermān
Kandahar
Lahore
Amritsar
HIMALAYA
Lhasa
Xigazē
Nam Co

4

An Nafud
Kuwait
KUWAIT
The Gulf
Būshehr
Shirāz
Zāhedān
P A K I S T A N
Quetta
Multan
Faisalabad
Ludhiana
Chandigarh
Ganganagar
Delhi
Meerut
Kathmandu
Thimphu
Dibrugarh
Xizang
Ad Dammām
BAHRAIN
Bandar-e 'Abbās
Thar Desert
New Delhi
Ghaziabad
BHUTAN
Guwahati
Shillong
Al Manāmah
Al Hufūf
QATAR
Dubai
Faridabad
Jaipur
Agra
Lucknow
Gorakhpur
Darjiling
Brahmaputra
Al Madīnah
Riyadh
Doha
Abu Dhabi
UNITED ARAB EMIRATES
Muscat
Pasni
Jodhpur
Kanpur
Patna
BANGLADESH
Jeddah
Mecca
S A U D I
Ibrā'
Gulf of Oman
Karachi
Hyderabad
Beawar
Gwalior
Allahabad
Varanasi
Asansol
Dhaka
Şūr
Kota
Ganga (Ganges)
Ranchi
Jamshedpur
Calcutta (Kolkata)
Khulna
Chittagong

5

A R A B I A
Şalālah
Rub' al Khālī
OMAN
Maşīrah
Ahmadabad
Vadodara
Indore
Bhopal
Jabalpur
Mouths of the Ganges
MYA
Mandalay
Meiktila
Sittwe
Al Hudaydah
San'ā'
Baiyuda Desert
Red Sea
Nile
Libyan Desert
Tropic of Cancer
Surat
I N D I A
Nagpur
Nashik
Aurangabad
Deccan
Cuttack
YEMEN
Ta'izz
Al Mukallā
A R A B I A N
Thane
Mumbai
Ulhasnagar
Pune
Solapur
Hyderabad
Vishakhapatnam
BAY
OF BENGAL
Yangon
Aden
Gulf of Aden
S E A
Dharwad
Kurnool
Vijayawada
Bassein
Pyu

6

Suquţra
Mangalore
Bangalore
Mysore
Nellore
Chennai
Andaman Islands (India)
Andaman Sea
Salem
Calicut
Coimbatore
Tiruchchirappalli
Laccadive Islands (India)
Cochin
Madurai
Trivandrum
Jaffna
Trincomalee
Gulf of Mannar
Kandy
SRI LANKA
Colombo
Sri Jayewardenepura Kotte
Nicobar Islands (India)
Male
MALDIVES
Banda Aceh
Simeulue
Mahé

7

A F R I C A
Equator
Lake Victoria
Lake Nyasa
Njuzidja
Comoros
Mayotte
Aldabra Islands (Seychelles)
Farquhar Islands (Seychelles)
Agalega Islands (Mauritius)
Seychelles
Coëtivy
I N D I A N   O C E A N
British Indian Territory
Chagos Archipelago
Diego Garcia

A B C D E
30° 45° 60° 75° 90°

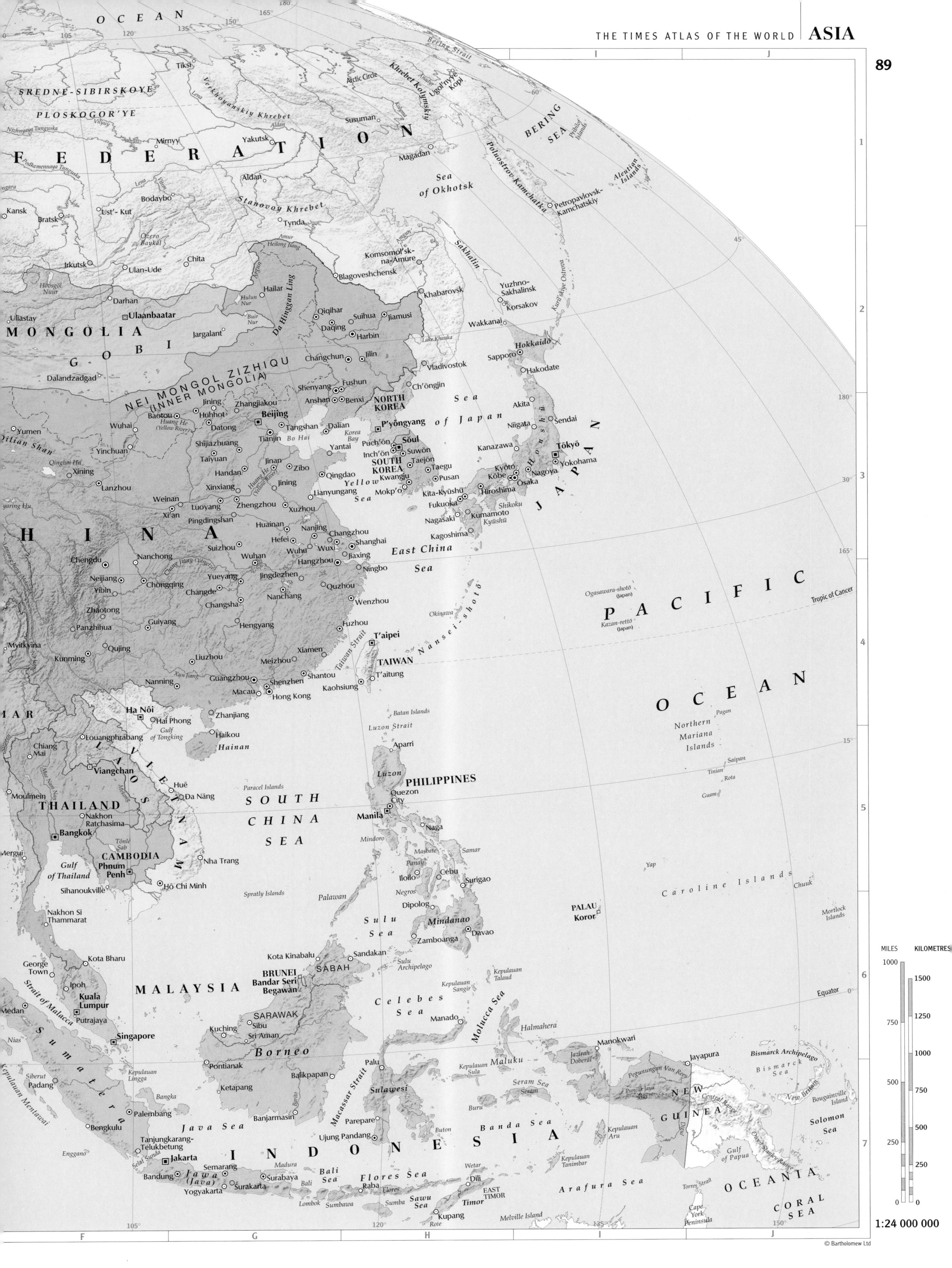

OCEAN

SREDNE-SIBIRSKOYE
PLOSKOGOR'YE

FEDERATION

Tiksi
Arctic Circle
Khrebet Kolymskiy
Ugol'nyye Kopi
Bering Strait

Verkhoyanskiy Khrebet
Susuman
BERING SEA
Pevek
Komandorskiye Ostrova

Nizhnyaya Tunguska
Mirnyy
Yakutsk
Aldan
Magadan

Kansk
Bratsk
Bodaybo
Ust'-Kut
Chita
Tynda
Stanovoy Khrebet
Amur
Heilong Jiang
Komsomol'sk-na-Amure
Blagoveshchensk
Sea of Okhotsk
Poluostrov Kamchatka
Petropavlovsk-Kamchatskiy
Aleutian Islands

Irkutsk
Ulan-Ude
Darhan
Hailar
Hulun Nur
Qiqihar
Suihua
Jiamusi
Khabarovsk
Sakhalin
Yuzhno-Sakhalinsk
Korsakov
Kuril'skiye Ostrova

Uliastay
Ozero Baykal
Hövsgöl Nuur
Ulaanbaatar
Jargalant
Da Hinggan Ling
Buir Nur
Daqing
Harbin
Vladivostok
Wakkanai
Hokkaidō
Sapporo
Hakodate

MONGOLIA
GOBI
Dalandzadgad
NEI MONGOL ZIZHIQU (INNER MONGOLIA)
Changchun
Jilin
Shenyang
Fushun
Ch'ŏngjin
Sea of Japan
Akita
Niigata
Sendai

Yumen
Baotou
Jining
Huhhot
Zhangjiakou
Beijing
Datong
NORTH KOREA
Anshan
Benxi
P'yŏngyang
Honshū
Kanazawa
Tōkyō
Yokohama

Qilian Shan
Yinchuan
Wuhai
Huang He (Yellow River)
Tangshan
Dalian
Korea Bay
Puch'ŏn
Sŏul
Suwŏn
Kyōto
Nagoya
Osaka
Kōbe

Qinghai Hu
Xining
Lanzhou
Taiyuan
Shijiazhuang
Tianjin
Bo Hai
Yantai
Inch'ŏn
SOUTH KOREA
Taejŏn
Pusan
Hiroshima
Kyūshū
Shikoku

Weinan
Xi'an
Handan
Jinan
Zibo
Qingdao
Yellow Sea
Kwangju
Taegu
Kita-kyūshū
Fukuoka
Kumamoto
Kagoshima

Luoyang
Xinxiang
Zhengzhou
Xuzhou
Jining
Huang He (Yellow River)
Lianyungang
Mokp'o
Nagasaki

CHINA
Pingdingshan
Chengdu
Nanchong
Suizhou
Huainan
Nanjing
Hefei
Changzhou
Wuxi
Shanghai
Jiaxing

Neijiang
Yibin
Chongqing
Changde
Yueyang
Wuhan
Wuhu
Hangzhou
Ningbo
East China Sea

Zhaotong
Panzhihua
Chang Jiang (Yangtze)
Nanchang
Jingdezhen
Quzhou
Wenzhou

Guiyang
Changsha
Hengyang
Fuzhou
Ogasawara-shotō (Japan)
Kazan-rettō (Japan)
PACIFIC
Tropic of Cancer

Myitkyina
Kunming
Qujing
Liuzhou
Meizhou
Xiamen
T'aipei
Nansei-shotō
TAIWAN
T'aitung
Okinawa

Nanning
Guangzhou
Shenzhen
Shantou
Kaohsiung
Taiwan Strait

Macau
Hong Kong
Xun Jiang
Zhanjiang

Ha Nôi
Hai Phong
Gulf of Tongking
Haikou
Hainan

OCEAN

Chiang Mai
Louangphrabang
Viangchan
LAOS
VIETNAM
Huế
Đa Nẵng
Paracel Islands
SOUTH CHINA SEA
Batan Islands
Luzon Strait
Aparri
Northern Mariana Islands
Pagan

Moulmein
THAILAND
Nakhon Ratchasima
Bangkok
Tônlé Sab
CAMBODIA
Phnum Penh
Nha Trang
Hô Chi Minh
Luzon
PHILIPPINES
Quezon City
Manila
Naga
Saipan
Tinian
Rota
Guam

Mergui
Gulf of Thailand
Sihanoukville
Mindoro
Masbate
Samar
Yap

Nakhon Si Thammarat
Spratly Islands
Palawan
Iloilo
Panay
Cebu
Surigao
Negros
Dipolog
Caroline Islands
Chuuk

George Town
Kota Bharu
PALAU
Koror
Sulu Sea
Mindanao
Davao
Zamboanga
Mortlock Islands

Ipoh
Kota Kinabalu
Sandakan
Sulu Archipelago
Kepulauan Talaud

Medan
Kuala Lumpur
Putrajaya
BRUNEI
Bandar Seri Begawan
SABAH
Kepulauan Sangir
Equator

Nias
Singapore
SARAWAK
Kuching
Sibu
Sri Aman
Celebes Sea
Manado
Molucca Sea
Halmahera
Manokwari

Siberut
Kepulauan Lingga
Pontianak
Borneo
Palu
Kepulauan Sula
Jazirah Doberai
Pegunungan Van Rees
Jayapura
Bismarck Archipelago

Padang
Bangka
Balikpapan
Macassar Strait
Sulawesi
Kepulauan Maluku
Seram Sea
Seram
NEW GUINEA
Bismarck Sea

Palembang
Ketapang
Banjarmasin
Parepare
Buru
Banda Sea
Kepulauan Aru
Central Range
Bougainville Island
Solomon Sea

Bengkulu
Java Sea
Ujung Pandang
Buton
Kepulauan Tanimbar
Puncak Jaya
New Britain

Tanjungkarang-Telukbetung
MALAYSIA
Jakarta
Semarang
Surabaya
Bali
Flores Sea
Wetar
EAST TIMOR
Dili
Arafura Sea
Gulf of Papua
OCEANIA

Enggano
Selat Sunda
Bandung
Jawa (Java)
Surakarta
Yogyakarta
INDONESIA
Lombok
Sumbawa
Sumba
Sawu Sea
Flores
Raba
Timor
Kupang
Rote
Melville Island
Torres Strait
Cape York Peninsula
CORAL SEA

MILES
1000
750
500
250

KILOMETRES
1500
1250
1000
750
500
250
0

1:24 000 000

© Bartholomew Ltd

98

112

CHINA

YUNNAN
GUIZHOU
HUNAN
JIANGXI
FUJIAN
GUANGXI ZHUANGZU ZIZHIQU
GUANGDONG
HAINAN

Panzhihua
Dukou
Kuanwei
Guiyang
Duyun
Sanming
Fuzhou
Matsu Tao (Taiwan)
Dali
Xiaguan
Dongehuan
Qujing
Anshun
Panxian
Rong'an (Chang'an)
Guilin
Ganzhou
Yong'an
Zhanping
Putian
Hsinchu
Chilung
Kunming
Chuxiong
Yuxi
Kaiyuan (Fengqing)
Yuanjiang
Gejiu
Wenshan (Kaihua)
Bose
Litang
Liuzhou
Hechi
Lipu (Licheng)
Yigde
Zhangzhou
Quanzhou (Taiwan)
Chinmen (Quemoy)
Xiamen (Amoy)
T'aichung
T'aipei
Nanning
Hengxian (Hengzhou)
Yulin
Luoding
Zhaoqing
Huizhou
Meizhou
Chaozhou
Shantou
T'ainan
Kaohsiung
T'aitung
Qinzhou
Maoming
Zhanjiang
Zhuhai
Shenzhen
Macau
Kowloon
Hong Kong
Guangzhou (Canton)
Tropic of Cancer

MYANMAR
Myitkyina
Baoshan
Lashio
Namtu
Mong Pawk
Kengtung
Mawkmai
Chiang Rai
Chiang Mai
Lampang
Chiang Kham
Lamphun
Phrae
Nan
Tak
Phitsanulok
Kamphaeng Phet
Phayao
Moulmein
Thaton
Thanbyuzayat
Ye
Tavoy
Mergui
Tenasserim
Bokpyin
Kawthaung
MYANMAR

LAOS
VIANGCHAN (Vientiane)
Louangphrabang
Louang Namtha
Ban Houayxay
Viangphoukha
Muang Xaignabouri
Muang Vangviang
Phou Bia
Muang Khammouan
Savannakhet
Pakxé
Attapu

VIETNAM
HA NOI
Hai Phong
Nam Dinh
Thai Binh
Thanh Hoa
Vinh
Ha Tinh
Dong Hoi
Dong Ha
Huê
Da Nang
Quang Ngai
Qui Nhon
Tuy Hoa
Nha Trang
Da Lat
Buôn Me Thuot
Phan Rang
Phan Thiet
Vung Tau
Hô Chi Minh (Saigon)
Biên Hoa
Tây Ninh
My Tho
Can Tho
Long Xuyên
Rach Gia
Ca Mau
Bac Liêu
Côn Son
Mui Ca Mau
Mouths of the Mekong
Hông Gai
Cao Bang
Thai Nguyên
Son La
Yên Bai
Lao Cai
Ha Giang
Lang Son

THAILAND
BANGKOK (Krung Thep)
Nakhon Sawan
Nakhon Ratchasima
Ubon Ratchathani
Udon Thani
Nong Khai
Nakhon Phanom
Sakon Nakhon
Maha Sarakham
Khon Kaen
Loei
Uttaradit
Sukhothai
Lop Buri
Ayutthaya
Chon Buri
Rayong
Chanthaburi
Sattahip
Chachoengsao
Samut Songkhram
Ratchaburi
Phet Buri
Prachuap Khiri Khan
Chumphon
Surat Thani
Nakhon Si Thammarat
Phatthalung
Songkhla
Hat Yai
Yala
Pattani
Narathiwat
Phuket
Krabi
Phangnga
Ranong
Takua Pa
Ko Samui
Nakhon Pathom
Kanchanaburi
Three Pagodas Pass
Khao Yai National Park
Khao Sok National Park
Phitsanulok
Phrae

CAMBODIA
PHNUM PÉNH
Bátdâmbâng
Siĕmréab
Kâmpóng Cham
Kâmpóng Thum
Kâmpóng Chhnang
Kâmpóng Spœ
Kâmpôt
Takêv
Krâchéh
Stœng Trêng
Rôviĕng
Sênmônoŭrôm
Pouthisat
Sihanoukville (Kâmpóng Saôm)
Tônlé Sab
Poŭthĭsăt

GULF OF THAILAND

SOUTH CHINA SEA

INDO-CHINA

Paracel Islands (Xisha Qundao)
Amphitrite Group
Crescent Group
Lincoln Island
Triton Island
Macclesfield Bank
Scarborough Shoal
Dongsha Qundao

Itu Aba Island
Namyit Island
Spratly Island
Spratly Islands
Flat Island Nanshan Island

PHILIPPINE SEA
Luzon Strait
Batan Islands
Babuyan Islands
Balintang Channel
Camiguin
Fuga
Babuyan Channel
Calayan
LUZON
Laoag
Vigan
Tuguegarao
Ilagan
Aparri
Bontoc
San Fernando
Dagupan
Lingayen
Tarlac
Cabanatuan
Baguio
Mount Pulog
Mount Pinatubo
Olongapo
Balanga
Quezon City
MANILA
San Pablo
Batangas
Lucena
Calapan
Naga
Legaspi
Boac
Sorsogon
Catanduanes
Daet
Lopez
Mindoro
Calamian Group
Culion
Cuyo Islands
Roxas
Romblon
Masbate
Panay
Iloilo
Bacolod
Cebu
Negros
Dumaguete
Tagbilaran
Bohol
Dipolog
Oroquieta
Ozamiz
Pagadian
Iligan
MINDANAO
Cotabato
Zamboanga
Isabela
Jolo
Sulu Archipelago
Tawitawi
Sibutu

Calamian Group
Cuyo Islands
Taytay
San Jose de Buenavista
Roxas Sea
Visayan Sea
Sibuyan Sea
Palawan
Puerto Princesa
Brooke's Point
Balabac
Balabac Strait
Banggi
Bugsuk

SULU SEA
CELEBES SEA

MALAYSIA
KUALA LUMPUR
Kelang
Seremban
Melaka
Muar
Batu Pahat
Johor Bahru
SINGAPORE
Kota Bharu
Kuala Terengganu
Dungun
Kuantan
Temerloh
Bahau
Segamat
Mersing
Keluang
Taiping
Ipoh
Butterworth
George Town
Sungei Petani
Alor Setar
Kangar
Taman Negara National Park
Semenanjung Malaysia
Pasir Putih

SARAWAK
SABAH
BRUNEI
BANDAR SERI BEGAWAN
Kuching
Sibu
Bintulu
Miri
Kota Kinabalu
Sandakan
Tawau
Lahad Datu
Labuan
Beaufort
Crocker Range National Park
Gunung Kinabalu
Niah National Park
Sri Aman
Sibuti
Lumbis
Serian
Simanggang
Mukah
Debak
Saratok
Sematan
Sambas

BORNEO
KALIMANTAN
Pontianak
Singkawang
Sukadana
Ketapang
Palangkaraya
Banjarmasin
Martapura
Muaralaung
Sampit
Amuntai
Kotabaru
Pagatan
Samarinda
Balikpapan
Tarakan
Tanjungselor
Tanjungredeb
Kelandis
Nangahpinoh
Sintang
Putussibau
Muaratewe
Muarateweh
Kandangan
Kendawangan
Pangkalanbuun
Kumai
Gunung Palung National Park
Bukit Baka Bukit Raya National Park
Tanjung Puting National Park

SUMATERA
Medan
Banda Aceh
Sigli
Bireun
Lhokseumawe
Langsa
Pangkalansusu
Binjai
Tebingtinggi
Pematangsiantar
Kisaran
Labuhanbilik
Rantauprapat
Sibolga
Gunungsitoli
Padangsidimpuan
Pekanbaru
Dumai
Bengkalis
Bagansiapiapi
Bukittinggi
Payakumbuh
Padangpanjang
Sawahlunto
Sijunjung
Padang
Solok
Muarabungo
Jambi
Sarolangun
Muaratembesi
Bangko
Lubuklinggau
Curup
Bengkulu
Lahat
Muaradua
Martapura
Palembang
Prabumulih
Metro
Kotabumi
Tanjungkarang-Telukbetung
Menggala
Kotaagung
Gunung Leuser National Park
Danau Toba
Baligé
Kerinci Seblat National Park
Gunung Kerinci
Siberut
Sipura
Pagai Utara
Pagai Selatan
Enggano
Nias
Batu
Simeulue
Sinabang

SINGAPORE
Tanjungpinang
Kepulauan Riau
Kepulauan Lingga
Daik
Rengat
Bangka
Muntok
Pangkalpinang
Sungailiat
Belinyu
Toboali
Tanjungpandan
Belitung
Manggar
Kepulauan Karimata

INDONESIA
JAKARTA
Karawang
Serang
Merak
Bogor
Sukabumi
Bandung
Purwakarta
Cirebon
Tasikmalaya
Garut
Cilacap
Kebumen
Yogyakarta
Semarang
Kudus
Purwodadi
Surakarta
Madiun
Kediri
Malang
Surabaya
Pasuruan
Probolinggo
Situbondo
Banyuwangi
Jember
JAWA (JAVA)
Madura
Bangkalan
Sumenep
Pamekasan
Tuban
Gresik
Mojokerto
Blitar
Pacitan
Magelang
Temanggung
Tegal
Pekalongan
Lumajang

JAVA SEA
Pulau-pulau Karimunjawa
Bawean
Kepulauan Laut Kecil

BALI SEA
Bali
Denpasar
Singaraja
Bali Barat National Park
Komodo National Park
Lombok
Mataram
Sumbawa
Sumbawabesar
Raba
Dompu
Bima
Selat Lombok
Selat Sumbawa

FLORES SEA
Flores
Ruteng
Ende
Maumere
Larantuka
Reo
Kepulauan Solor
Lomblen
Alor
Kalabahi
Pantar
Kepulauan Alor

SAWU SEA
Sumba
Waingapu
Waikabubak
Savu
Rote
Kupang

SULAWESI (CELEBES)
Ujung Pandang (Makassar)
Palu
Donggala
Poso
Luwuk
Gorontalo
Toli-toli
Kwandang
Moutong
Kotamobagu
Tolitoli
Watampone
Parepare
Pare
Majene
Mamuju
Palopo
Malili
Kolaka
Kendari
Raha
Bau-bau
Buton
Muna
Sinjai
Bulukumba
Bantaeng
Jeneponto
Takalar
Bontosunggu
Selayar
Tenteno
Kolonedale
Ampana
Bungku
Uekuli
Makale
Rantepao
Masamba
Enrekang
Pinrang
Sidrap
Soppeng
Barru
Pangkajene
Maros
Teluk Bone
Teluk Tolo
Teluk Tomini
Semenanjung Minahasa

Kepulauan Sula
Kepulauan Banggai
Banggai
Peleng
Taliabu
Mangole
Sanana

Kepulauan Tukangbesi
Tanahjampea
Kalaotoa
Kalao

Natuna Besar
Kepulauan Natuna
Kepulauan Anambas
Kepulauan Tambelan
Serasan
Subi Besar
Subi

Makassar Strait
Sabalana

INDIAN OCEAN

Christmas Island (Australia)

Equator

METRES / FEET
6000 / 19686
5000 / 16404
4000 / 13124
3000 / 9843
2000 / 6562
1000 / 3281
500 / 1640
200 / 656
0
LAND BELOW SEA LEVEL
200 / 656
2000 / 6562
4000 / 13124
6000 / 19686

Mercator Projection

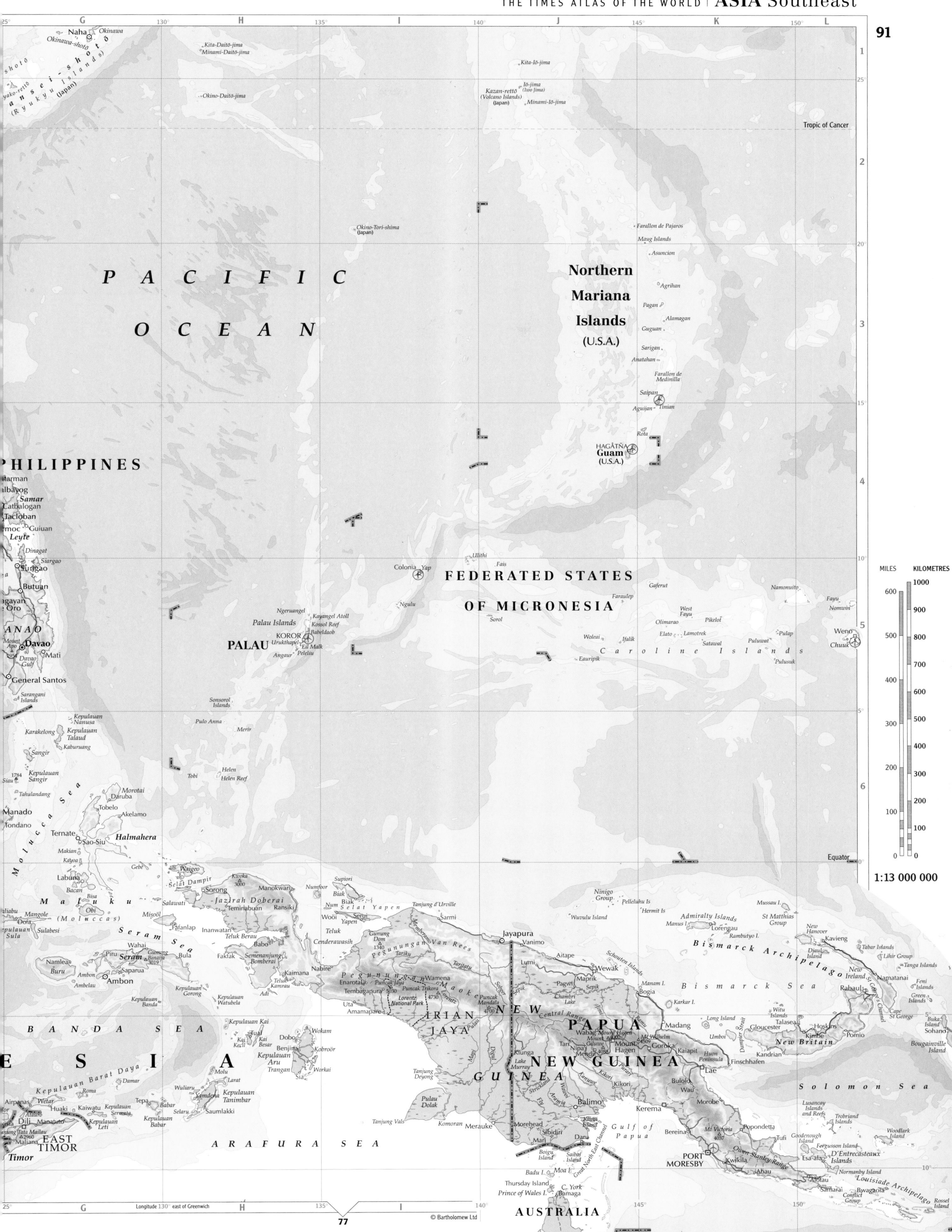

Naha · Okinawa

Okinawa-shotō

Kita-Daitō-jima
Minami-Daitō-jima

Okino-Daitō-jima

Kita-Iō-jima

Iō-jima
(Iwo Jima)
(Japan)

Kazan-rettō
(Volcano Islands)
(Japan)

Minami-Iō-jima

Tropic of Cancer

P A C I F I C

Okino-Tori-shima
(Japan)

Farallon de Pajaros

Maug Islands

Asuncion

Northern

Mariana

Islands

(U.S.A.)

Agrihan

Pagan

Alamagan

Guguan

O C E A N

Sarigan

Anatahan

Farallon de
Medinilla

Saipan

Aguijan · Tinian

Rota

HAGÅTÑA
Guam
(U.S.A.)

PHILIPPINES

Matarman

Calbayog

Catbalogan

Tacloban

Ormoc · Guiuan

Leyte

Dinagat

Siargao

Surigao

Butuan

Cagayan
de Oro

ANAO

Davao

Apo

Davao
Gulf

Mati

General Santos

Sarangani
Islands

Colonia · Yap

Ulithi

Fais

FEDERATED STATES

OF MICRONESIA

Gaferut

Namonuito

Ngulu

Faraulep

Ngeruangel

Sorol

Olimarao

West
Fayu

Pikelot

Fayu
Nomwin

Palau Islands

Kayangel Atoll

Kossol Reef

Babeldaob

PALAU

KOROR

Urukthapel · Eil Malk

Angaur · Peleliu

Woleai

Ifalik

Elato

Lamotrek

Satawal

Puluwat

Pulap

Weno

Chuuk

C a r o l i n e   I s l a n d s

Eauripik

Pulusuk

Sonsorol
Islands

Pulo Anna

Merir

Kepulauan
Nanusa

Karakelong

Kepulauan
Talaud

Kaburuang

1784

Kepulauan
Sangir

Siau

Tobi

Helen

Helen Reef

Tahulandang

Sangir

Molucca Sea

Morotai
Daruba

Manado

Tondano

Tobelo

Akelamo

Ternate

Sao-Siu

Halmahera

Makian

Kayoa

Equator

MILES   KILOMETRES

1000

600   900

800

500   700

400   600

500

300   400

200   300

200

100   100

0   0

1:13 000 000

Waigeo

Selat Dampir

Kwoka

3000

Manokwari

Numfoor

Supiori

Ninigo
Group

Pelleluhu Is

Hermit Is

Mussau I.

Bismarck Archipelago

New
Hanover

M a l u k u

Bisa

Obi

Salawati

Jazirah Doberai

Temirabuan

Ransiki

Num

Biak

Selat Yapen

Wooi

Serui

Tanjung d'Urville

Sarmi

Wuvulu Island

Admiralty Islands

Manus I.

Lorengau

Rambutyo I.

St Matthias
Group

Kavieng

Djaul
Island

Lihir Group

Tabar Islands

Mangole
(Moluccas)

Misool

Inanwatan

Teluk Berau

Babo

Fakfak

Semenanjung
Bomberai

Gunung
Dom
1340

Tariku

Pegunungan Van Rees

Taritatu

Jayapura

Vanimo

Lumi

Aitape

Wewak

Maprik

Pagwi

Sepik

**New
Ireland**

Namatanai

Feni
Islands

S e r a m

Seram

Gunung
Binaia
3019

Bula

*Teluk
Cenderawasih*

Nabire

P e g u n u n g a n

Wamena

M a o k e

Puncak
Mandala
4730

Chambri
Lake

Manam I.

Bogia

Karkar I.

Witu
Islands

Rabaul

Green
Islands

Buka
Island

Sohano

Namlea

Piru

Wahai

Ambon

Kaimana

Uta

Enarotali

Puncak Trikora
5030

Puncak Jaya

Tembagapura

Lorentz
National Park

**IRIAN
JAYA**

NEW

PAPUA

Wabag

Mount Hagen

Goroka

Mount
Hagen

Madang

Long Island

Gloucester

New Britain

Hoskins

Kimbe

Pomio

Bougainville
Island

Buru

Ambelau

*Kepulauan
Gorong*

*Kepulauan
Watubela*

Adi

Amamapare

GUINEA

NEW GUINEA

Wabo

Nipa

Kundiawa

Tari

Mendi

Menyamya

Kerema

Bulolo

Wau

Morobe

Lae

Finschhafen

Kandrian

S o l o m o n   S e a

B A N D A   S E A

Kepulauan Barat Daya

Kepulauan
Banda

Kepulauan Kai

Jual

Kai
Kecil

Kai
Besar

Dobo

Benjina

Kobroör

*Kepulauan
Aru*

Trangan

Workai

Sia

Tanjung
Deyong

Klunga

Fly

Mount
Murray

Kikori

Kikori

Balimo

Kerema

Mt Victoria
4037

Popondetta

Tufi

Lusancay
Islands
and Reefs

Trobriand
Islands

Woodlark
Island

Goodenough
Island

Fergusson Island

Esa-ala

I N D O N E S I A

Damar

Roma

Kepulauan
Serniata

Kepulauan Babar

Wetar

Huaki

Kaiwatu

Leti

Kepulauan
Leti

Tepa

Wuliaru

Yamdena

Selaru

Saumlakki

Kepulauan Tanimbar

Larat

Molu

Tanjung Vals

Komoran

Merauke

Morehead

Sibidiri

Daru

Balimo

*Gulf of
Papua*

Bereina

**PORT
MORESBY**

Kwikila

Owen Stanley Range

Abau

Samarai

Louisiade Archipelago

Rossel
Island

Airpanas

Dili

Manatuto

**EAST
TIMOR**

Timor

Maliana

A R A F U R A   S E A

Pulau
Dolak

Kimaam

Mari

Boigu
Island

Saibai
Island

Badu I.

Moa I.

Thursday Island

Prince of Wales I.

C. York

Bamaga

AUSTRALIA

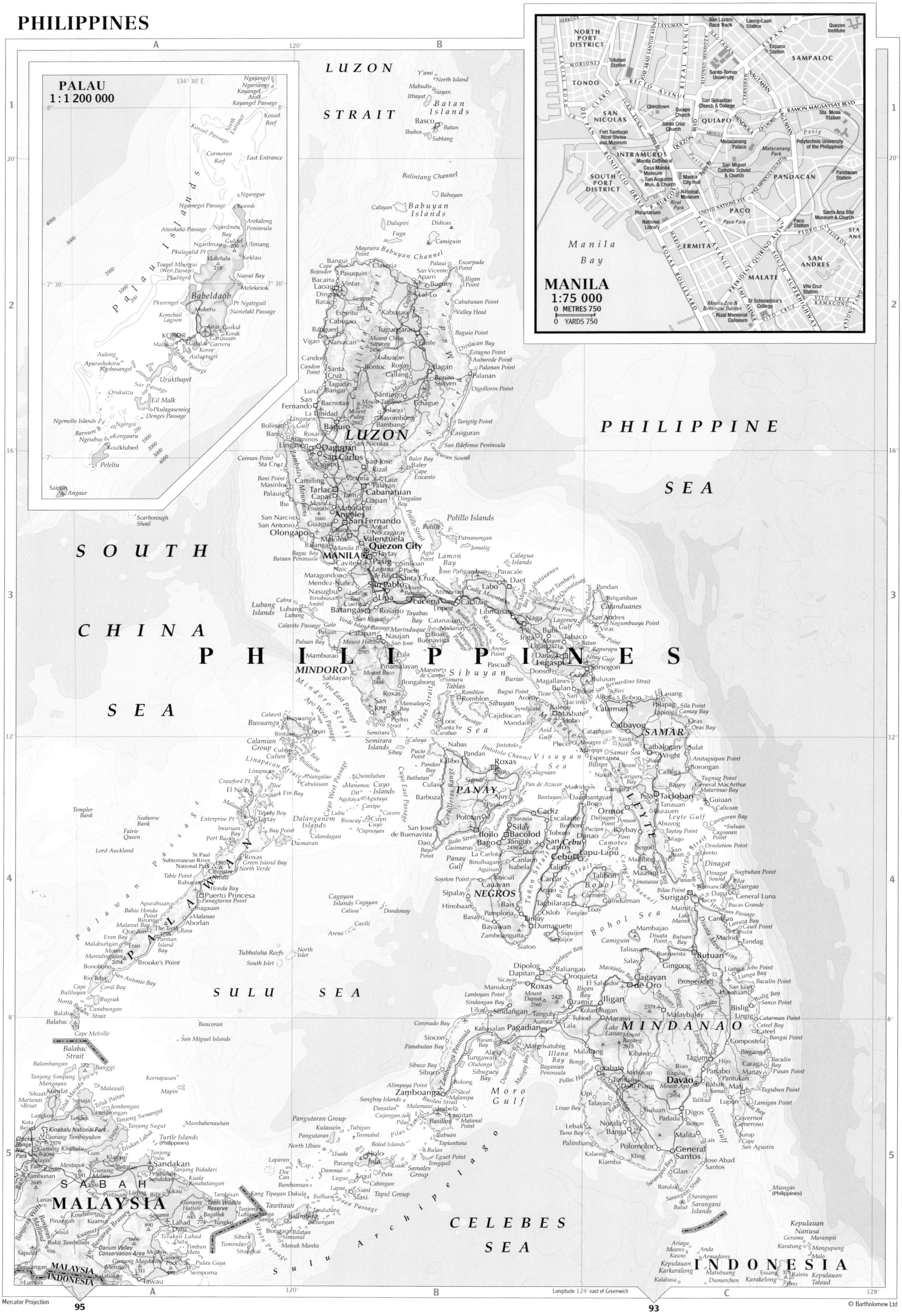

PALAU
1 : 1 200 000

MANILA
1 : 75 000

0 METRES 750
0 YARDS 750

LUZON STRAIT

Batan Islands

Babuyan Islands

PHILIPPINE SEA

LUZON

MANILA
Quezon City

SOUTH CHINA SEA

PHILIPPINES

MINDORO

PANAY

SAMAR

LEYTE

NEGROS

CEBU

BOHOL

Bohol Sea

PALAWAN

SULU SEA

MINDANAO

Moro Gulf

Davao

General Santos

CELEBES SEA

SABAH

MALAYSIA

Sulu Archipelago

INDONESIA

Manila Bay

METRES / FEET
6000 / 19686
5000 / 16404
4000 / 13124
3000 / 9843
2000 / 6562
1000 / 3281
500 / 1640
200 / 656
0
LAND BELOW SEA LEVEL
200 / 656
2000 / 6562
4000 / 13124
6000 / 19686

Mercator Projection

95

93

Longitude 124° east of Greenwich

© Bartholomew Ltd

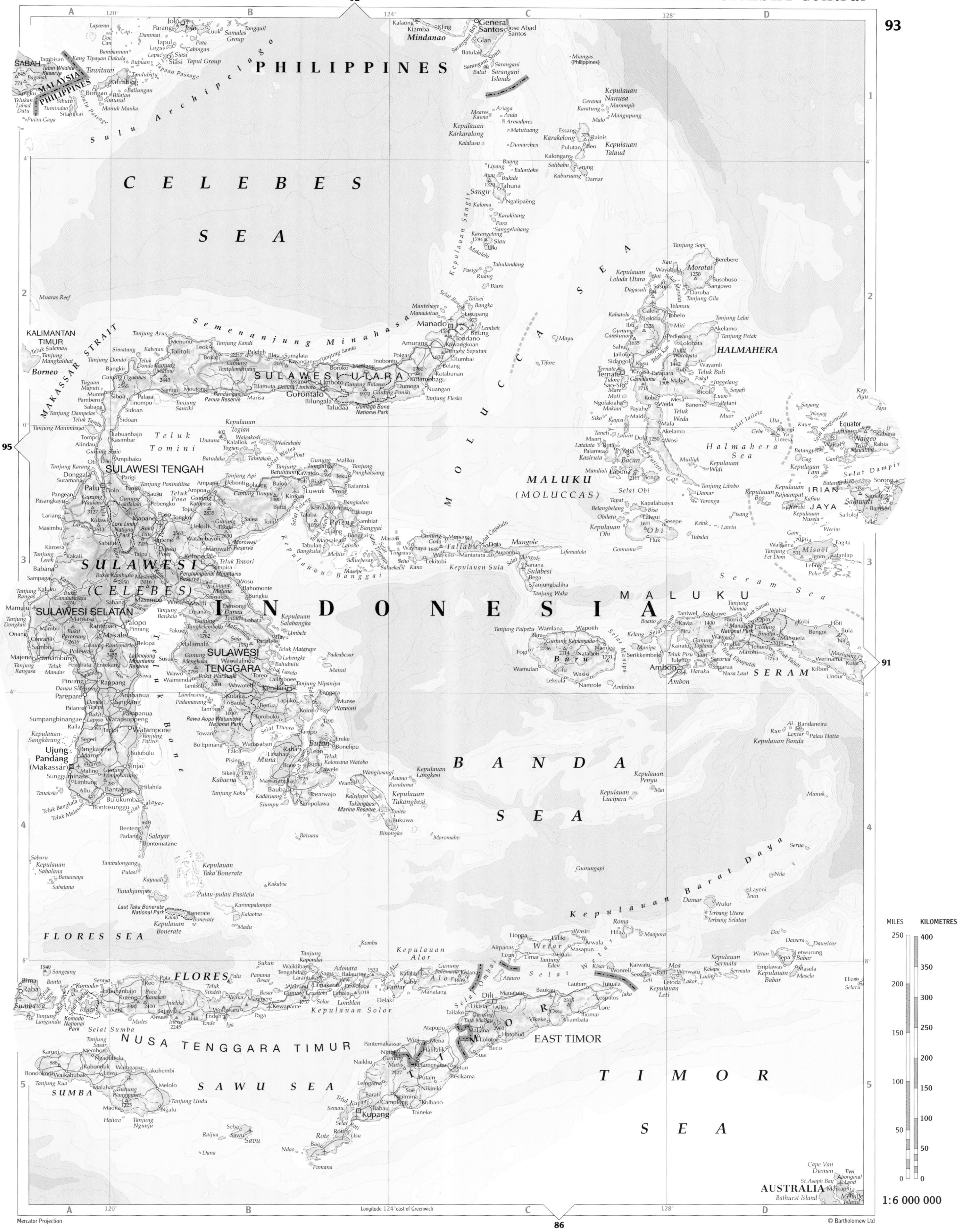
92
A
B
C
D
120°
124°
128°
PHILIPPINES
Mindanao
General Santos
Jolo
Sulu Archipelago
SABAH
MALAYSIA
PHILIPPINES
Tawitawi
CELEBES SEA
Kepulauan Nanusa
Kepulauan Talaud
Karakelong
Sangir
Siau
Kepulauan Sangir
Miangas (Philippines)
Muaras Reef
KALIMANTAN TIMUR
Borneo
MAKASSAR STRAIT
Semenanjung Minahasa
Manado
SULAWESI UTARA
Gorontalo
Teluk Tomini
Kepulauan Togian
SULAWESI TENGAH
Palu
Donggala
SULAWESI (CELEBES)
SULAWESI SELATAN
Mamuju
Palopo
Pare-pare
Watampone
Teluk Bone
Ujung Pandang (Makassar)
Bulukumba
Salayar
SULAWESI TENGGARA
Kendari
Kabaena
Muna
Buton
Bau-Bau
Peleng
Banggai
Kepulauan Banggai
Taliabu
Mangole
Kepulauan Sula
Sanana
Sulabesi
MOLUCCA SEA
Morotai
Halmahera
HALMAHERA
Ternate
Tidore
Bacan
Obi
Kepulauan Obi
MALUKU (MOLUCCAS)
Halmahera Sea
Waigeo
Salawati
Misool
Sorong
IRIAN JAYA
Equator
Seram Sea
MALUKU
INDONESIA
Buru
Ambon
SERAM
Kepulauan Banda
BANDA SEA
Kepulauan Tukangbesi
Kepulauan Lucipara
Kepulauan Penyu
Kepulauan Barat Daya
Damar
Wetar
Alor
Kepulauan Alor
Kisar
Leti
Kepulauan Leti
Moa
Kepulauan Sermata
Kepulauan Babar
Kepulauan Taka'Bonerate
Kepulauan Bonerate
Tanahjampea
Kepulauan Sabalana
FLORES SEA
FLORES
Sumbawa
Bima
Komodo
Komodo National Park
Ende
Maumere
Lomblen
Kepulauan Solor
Pantar
Selat Ombai
Dili
EAST TIMOR
TIMOR
Kupang
Rote
Savu
Sawu Sea
SUMBA
Waingapu
Selat Sumba
NUSA TENGGARA TIMUR
TIMOR SEA
AUSTRALIA
Bathurst Island
Melville Island
Cape Van Diemen
95
91
86
1
2
3
4
5
MILES
KILOMETRES
250
200
150
100
50
0
400
350
300
250
200
150
100
50
0
1:6 000 000
Longitude 124° east of Greenwich
Mercator Projection
© Bartholomew Ltd

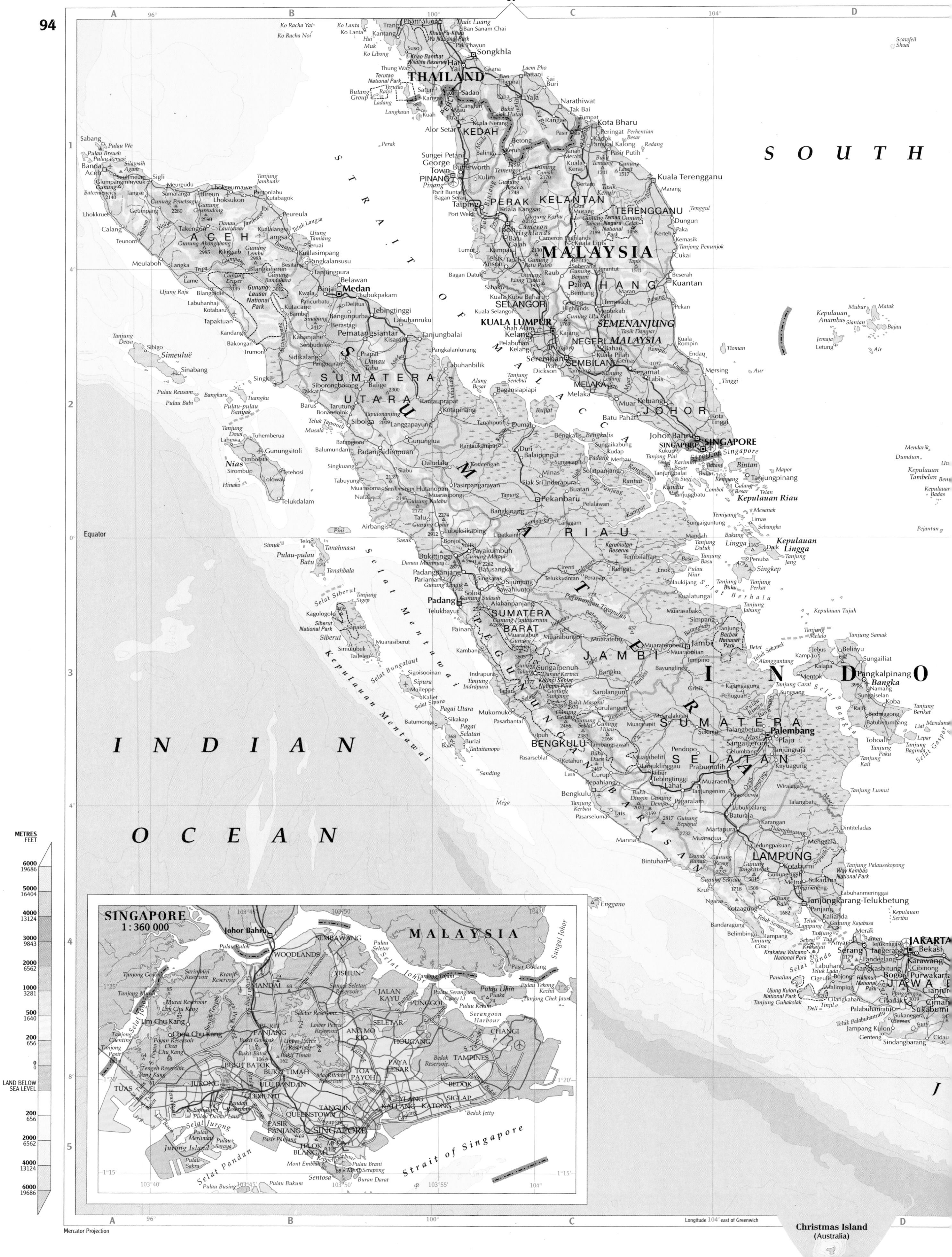

THAILAND

MALAYSIA

KEDAH

PERAK · KELANTAN

TERENGGANU

PAHANG

SELANGOR

KUALA LUMPUR

NEGERI SEMBILAN

SEMENANJUNG MALAYSIA

MELAKA

JOHOR

SINGAPORE

ACEH

SUMATERA UTARA

SUMATERA BARAT

RIAU

JAMBI

BENGKULU

SUMATERA SELATAN

LAMPUNG

PEGUNUNGAN BARISAN

INDONESIA

Bangka

Palembang

JAKARTA

JAWA

S O U T H

I N D I A N

O C E A N

Strait of Malacca

Kepulauan Riau

Kepulauan Lingga

Kepulauan Anambas

Simeulue

Nias

Siberut

Kepulauan Mentawai

Banda Aceh

Medan

Pekanbaru

Padang

Kuala Terengganu

Kota Bharu

George Town

PINANG

Ipoh

Kuantan

Johor Bahru

SINGAPORE

Pangkalpinang

Christmas Island (Australia)

METRES / FEET
6000 / 19686
5000 / 16404
4000 / 13124
3000 / 9843
2000 / 6562
1000 / 3281
500 / 1640
200 / 656
0
LAND BELOW SEA LEVEL
200 / 656
2000 / 6562
4000 / 13124
6000 / 19686

SINGAPORE
1 : 360 000

MALAYSIA

Johor Bahru

WOODLANDS

SEMBAWANG

YISHUN

MANDAI

PUNGGOL

SELETAR

ANG MO KIO

HOUGANG

CHANGI

TAMPINES

BEDOK

JURONG

BUKIT BATOK

BUKIT PANJANG

CHOA CHU KANG

LIM CHU KANG

CLEMENTI

QUEENSTOWN

PASIR PANJANG

SINGAPORE

GEYLANG

KALLANG

PAYA LEBAR

TOA PAYOH

BUKIT TIMAH

ULU PANDAN

TUAS

Sentosa

Strait of Singapore

Selat Johor

Mercator Projection

Longitude 104° east of Greenwich

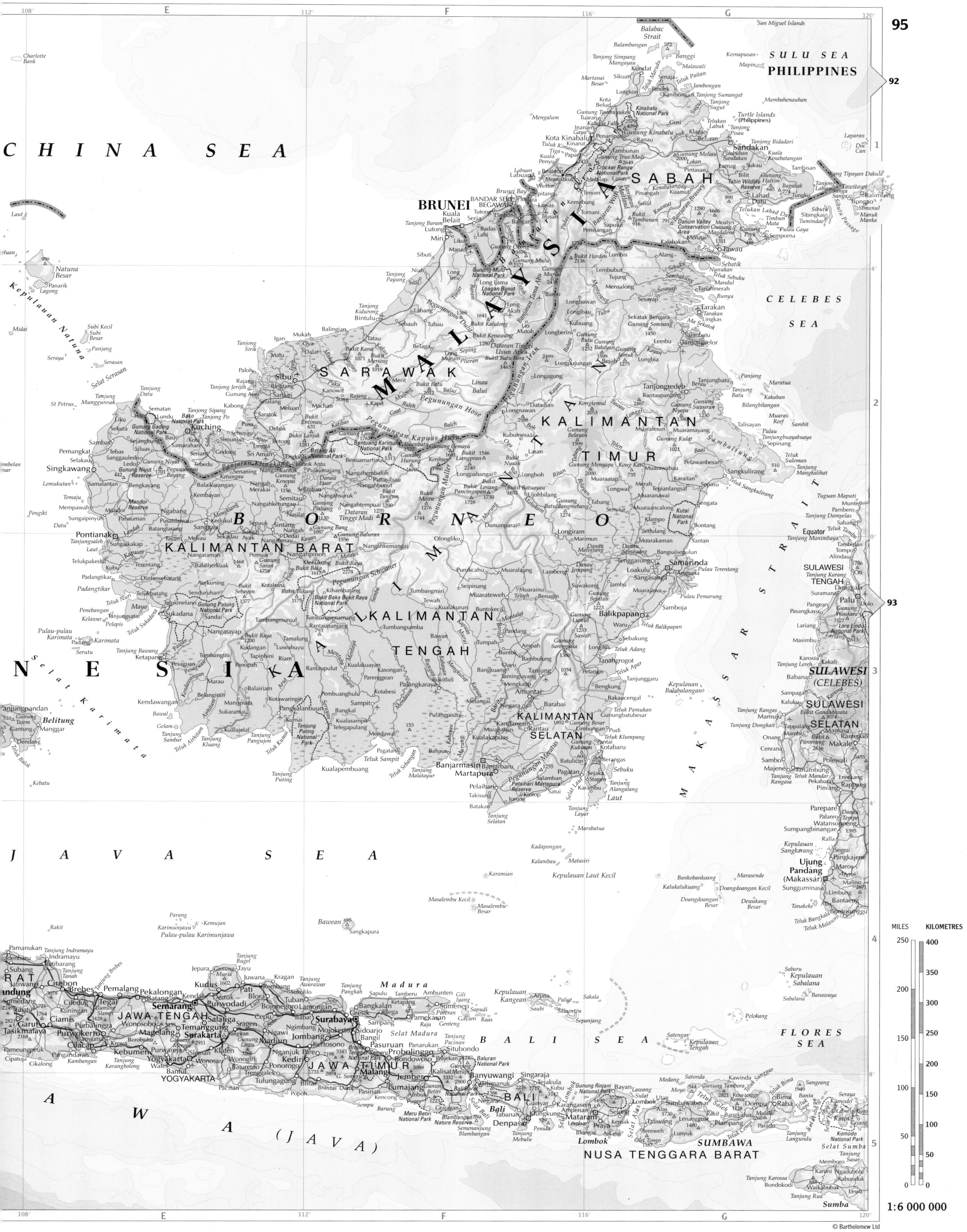

PHILIPPINES

SULU SEA

CHINA SEA

CELEBES SEA

SABAH

BRUNEI
BANDAR SERI BEGAWAN

MALAYSIA

SARAWAK

Kuching

Gunung Mulu National Park

KALIMANTAN TIMUR

BORNEO

KALIMANTAN BARAT

Pontianak

KALIMANTAN TENGAH

KALIMANTAN SELATAN

Samarinda

Balikpapan

Banjarmasin
Martapura

MAKASSAR STRAIT

Equator

SULAWESI TENGAH

Palu

SULAWESI (CELEBES)

SULAWESI SELATAN

Ujung Pandang (Makassar)

Parepare

Natuna Besar

Kepulauan Natuna

Belitung

Manggar

JAVA SEA

Singkawang

Bawean

J A V A   S E A

Semarang
Surakarta
YOGYAKARTA
Surabaya

JAWA TENGAH

JAWA TIMUR

Malang

Madura

BALI SEA

BALI
Denpasar

Mataram
Lombok

SUMBAWA

FLORES SEA

NUSA TENGGARA BARAT

A   W   A   (J A V A)

I N D O N E S I A

93

92

95

1

2

3

4

5

MILES   KILOMETRES
250   400
200   300
150   250
100   150
50   50
0   0

1:6 000 000

© Bartholomew Ltd

108°   112°   116°   120°
E   F   G

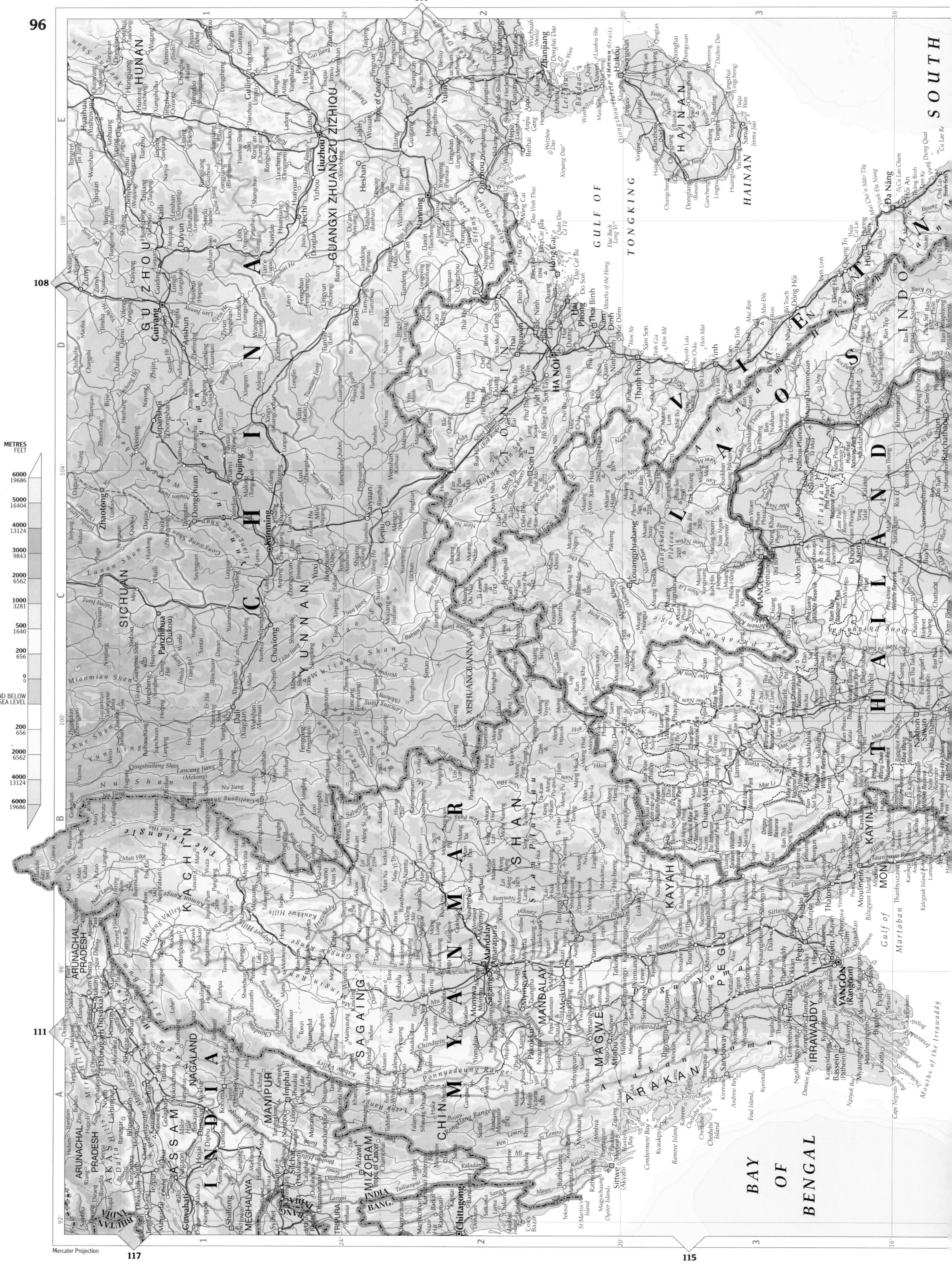

109

108

108

111

117

115

Mercator Projection

METRES / FEET

6000 / 19686
5000 / 16404
4000 / 13124
3000 / 9843
2000 / 6562
1000 / 3281
500 / 1640
200 / 656
0 / 0
LAND BELOW SEA LEVEL
200 / 656
2000 / 6562
4000 / 13124
6000 / 19686

CHINA

HUNAN

GUIZHOU

Guiyang

GUANGXI ZHUANGZU ZIZHIQU

Nanning

SICHUAN

Panzhihua (Dukou)

Zhaotong

YUNNAN

Kunming

Tropic of Cancer

HAINAN

Haikou

GULF OF TONGKING

VIETNAM

HANOI

Hải Phòng

LAOS

Louangphabang

Vientiane

THAILAND

Đà Nẵng

MYANMAR

MANDALAY

Mandalay

SAGAING

MAGWE

PEGU

YANGON (Rangoon)

IRRAWADDY

ARAKAN

CHIN

KAYAH

KAYIN

MON

Moulmein

Gulf of Martaban

SHAN

Shan Plateau

INDIA

ARUNACHAL PRADESH

ASSAM

NAGALAND

MANIPUR

Imphal

MIZORAM

TRIPURA

MEGHALAYA

Shillong

BHUTAN

BANG.

Chittagong

BAY OF BENGAL

Mouths of the Irrawaddy

SOUTH

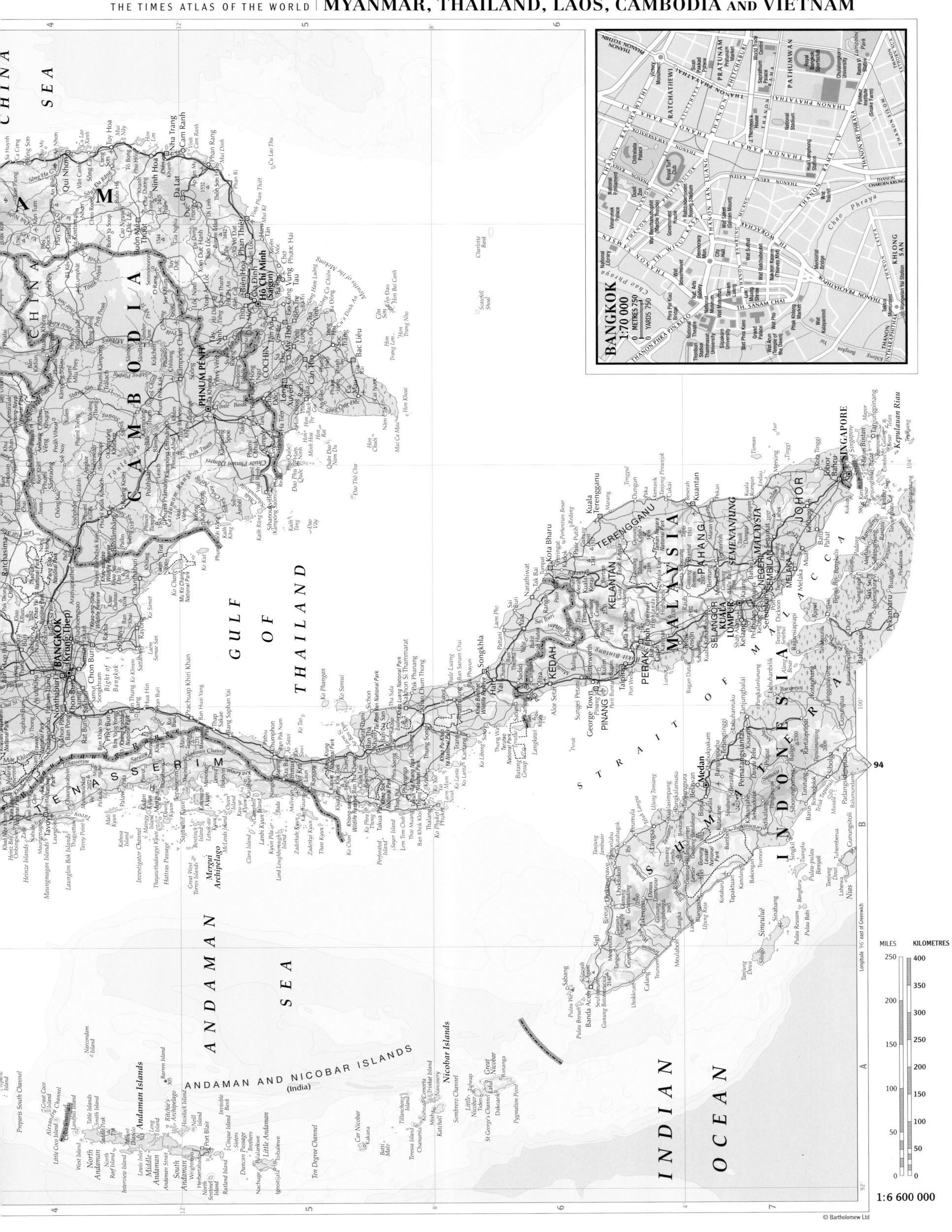

CHINA SEA

VIETNAM

CHINA

CAMBODIA

PHNUM PENH

GULF OF THAILAND

BANGKOK (Krung Thep)

TENASSERIM

ANDAMAN SEA

ANDAMAN AND NICOBAR ISLANDS
(India)

Nicobar Islands

Andaman Islands

MALAYSIA

PAHANG

TERENGGANU

KELANTAN

PERAK

SELANGOR

NEGERI SEMBILAN

JOHOR

SINGAPORE

STRAIT OF MALACCA

SUMATERA

INDONESIA

INDIAN OCEAN

BANGKOK 1:70 000

1:6 600 000

MILES   KILOMETRES

© Bartholomew Ltd

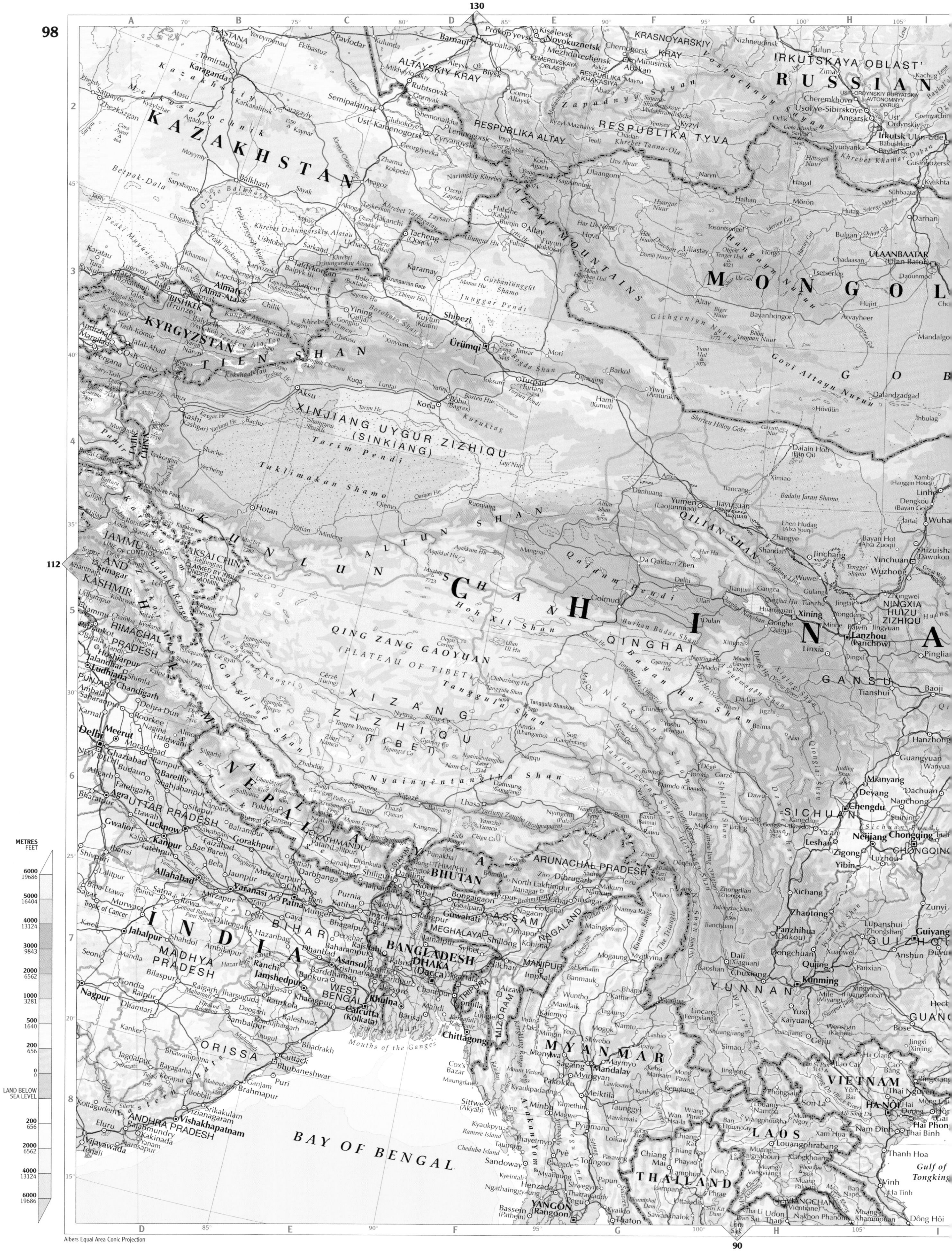

130

KAZAKHSTAN

RUSSIAN

IRKUTSKAYA OBLAST'

KRASNOYARSKIY KRAY

KEMEROVSKAYA OBLAST'

ALTAYSKIY KRAY

RESPUBLIKA ALTAY

RESPUBLIKA KHAKASIYA

RESPUBLIKA TYVA

MONGOLIA

GOBI

Govi Altayn Nuruu

ULAANBAATAR (Ulan Bator)

KYRGYZSTAN

TIEN SHAN

BISHKEK (Frunze)

Alma-Ata (Almaty)

XINJIANG UYGUR ZIZHIQU (SINKIANG)

Taklimakan Shamo

Tarim Pendi

Ürümqi

Junggar Pendi

Gurbantünggüt Shamo

KUN LUN SHAN

ALTUN SHAN

QILIAN SHAN

CHINA

QINGHAI

GANSU

Xining

Lanzhou (Lanchow)

NINGXIA HUIZU ZIZHIQU

SICHUAN

Chengdu

CHONGQING

GUIZHOU

Guiyang

YUNNAN

Kunming

GUANGXI

JAMMU AND KASHMIR

Srinagar

HIMACHAL PRADESH

PUNJAB

Chandigarh

Ludhiana

Delhi

NEW DELHI

UTTAR PRADESH

Lucknow

Kanpur

Agra

Gwalior

RAJASTHAN

MADHYA PRADESH

Jabalpur

Nagpur

Raipur

ORISSA

Bhubaneshwar

ANDHRA PRADESH

Vishakhapatnam

Vijayawada

INDIA

NEPAL

KATHMANDU

BHUTAN

THIMPHU

Mount Everest

SIKKIM

Darjiling

Gangtok

BANGLADESH

DHAKA (Dacca)

WEST BENGAL

Calcutta (Kolkata)

Khulna

Chittagong

BIHAR

Patna

Varanasi

Allahabad

JHARKHAND

Ranchi

Jamshedpur

Asansol

ASSAM

Guwahati

MEGHALAYA

Shillong

NAGALAND

MANIPUR

Imphal

TRIPURA

MIZORAM

ARUNACHAL PRADESH

XIZANG ZIZHIQU (TIBET)

QING ZANG GAOYUAN (PLATEAU OF TIBET)

Lhasa (Quxar)

Xigazê

Nyainqêntanglha Shan

Tanggula Shan

Nam Co

MYANMAR

Mandalay

Sagaing

YANGON (Rangoon)

THAILAND

LAOS

VIETNAM

HANOI

Gulf of Tongking

BAY OF BENGAL

Mouths of the Ganges

Cox's Bazar

Sittwe (Akyab)

Tropic of Cancer

Albers Equal Area Conic Projection

METRES FEET
6000 19686
5000 16404
4000 13124
3000 9843
2000 6562
1000 3281
500 1640
200 656
0 0
LAND BELOW SEA LEVEL
200 656
2000 6562
4000 13124
6000 19686

112

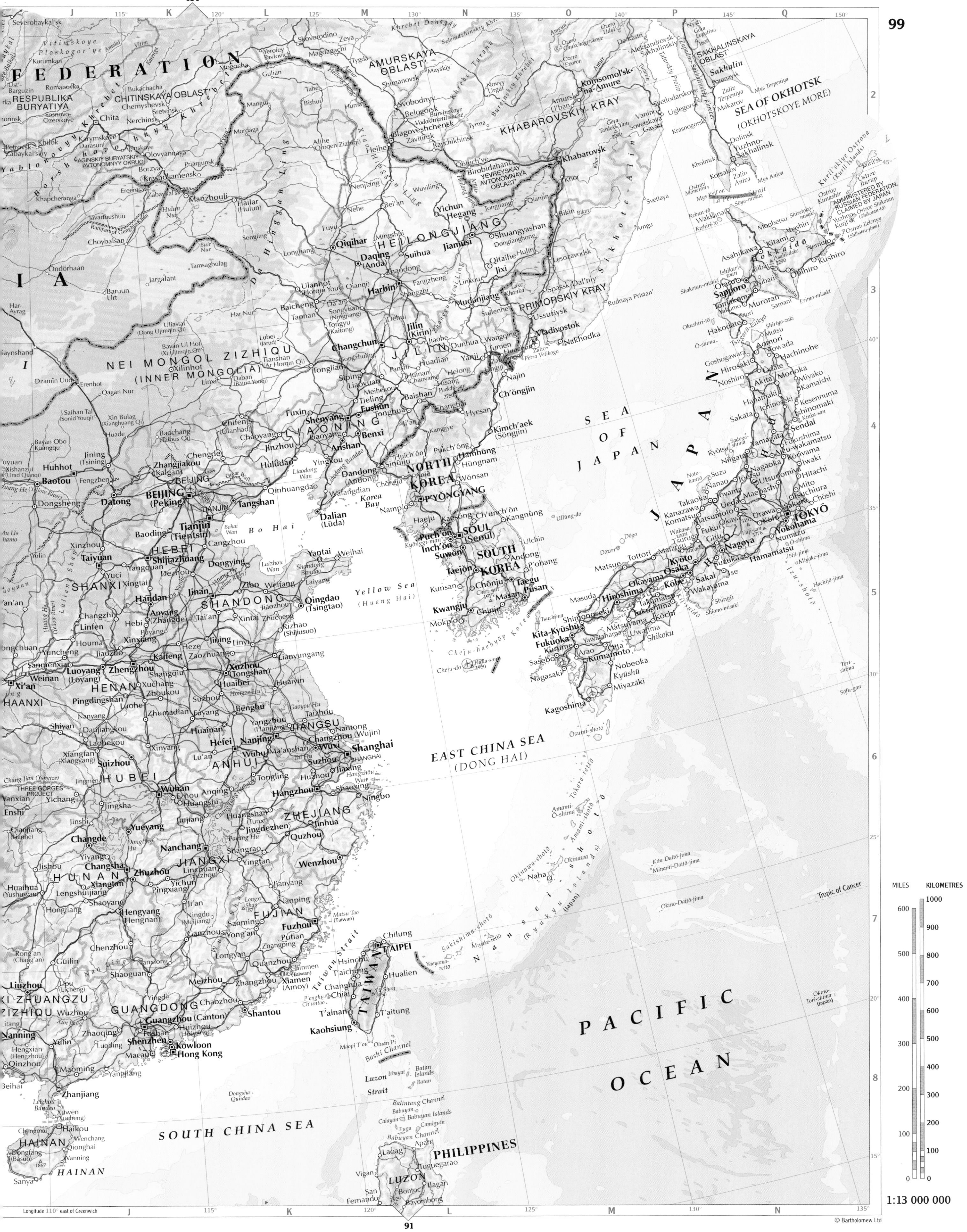

FEDERATION

RESPUBLIKA
BURYATIYA

CHITINSKAYA OBLAST'

AMURSKAYA
OBLAST'

KHABAROVSKIY KRAY

SEA OF OKHOTSK
(OKHOTSKOYE MORE)

SAKHALINSKAYA
OBLAST'

Sakhalin

HEILONGJIANG

Qiqihar

Harbin

Mudanjiang

PRIMORSKIY KRAY

Vladivostok

HOKKAIDO

Sapporo

Hakodate

NEI MONGOL ZIZHIQU
(INNER MONGOLIA)

JILIN

Changchun

Jilin (Kirin)

Shenyang

LIAONING

Anshan

Benxi

NORTH
KOREA

P'YONGYANG

SEA
OF
JAPAN

J A P A N

Aomori

Akita

Sendai

Baotou

Huhhot

Zhangjiakou

BEIJING (Peking)

Datong

Dalian (Lüda)

Tangshan

Bo Hai

Dandong (Andong)

SOUTH
KOREA

SOUL (Seoul)

Inch'on

Taejon

Taegu

Pusan

TOKYO

Yokohama

Nagoya

Kyoto

Osaka

Kobe

TIANJIN (Tientsin)

Tianjin

HEBEI

Taiyuan

Shijiazhuang

SHANXI

Jinan

SHANDONG

Qingdao (Tsingtao)

Yellow Sea
(Huang Hai)

Hiroshima

Kita-Kyushu

Fukuoka

Nagasaki

Kagoshima

Kyūshū

Shikoku

Xi'an

SHAANXI

Luoyang

Zhengzhou

HENAN

Xuzhou (Tongshan)

Nanjing

JIANGSU

Shanghai

Hefei

ANHUI

Wuhan

HUBEI

Hangzhou

ZHEJIANG

Nanchang

JIANGXI

Wenzhou

EAST CHINA SEA
(DONG HAI)

Changsha

Zhuzhou

HUNAN

FUJIAN

Fuzhou

Xiamen (Amoy)

TAIWAN

T'AIPEI

Kaohsiung

GUANGDONG

Guangzhou (Canton)

Shenzhen

Kowloon

Hong Kong

Macau

Shantou

GUANGXI ZHUANGZU ZIZHIQU

Nanning

HAINAN

Haikou

SOUTH CHINA SEA

PACIFIC

OCEAN

Nansei-shotō (Ryukyu Islands)

Naha

Okinawa-shotō

Tropic of Cancer

PHILIPPINES

LUZON

MILES | KILOMETRES

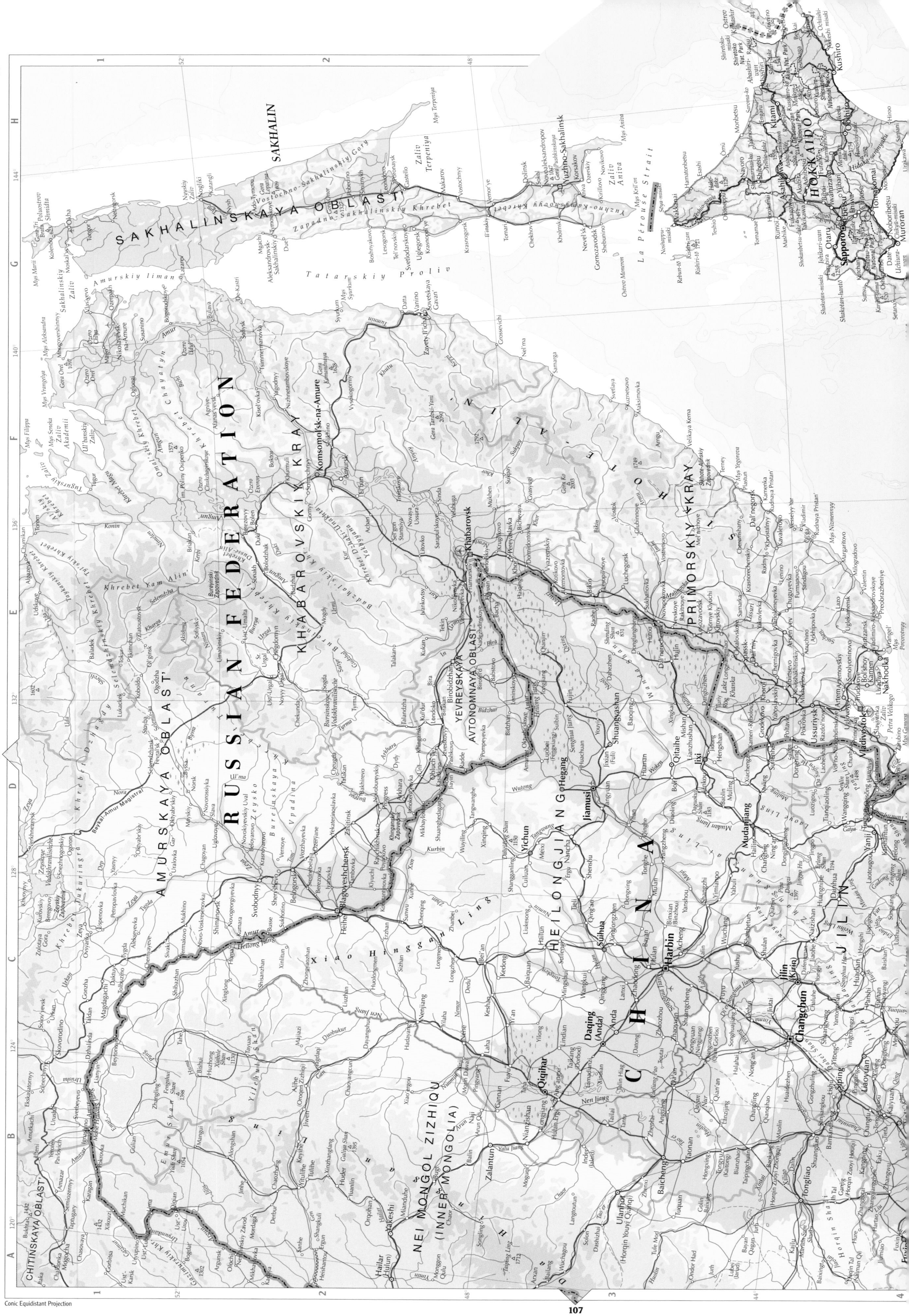

Conic Equidistant Projection

131

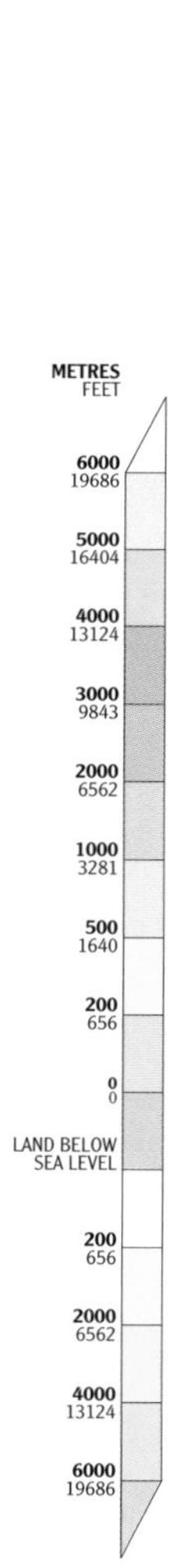

METRES / FEET

6000 / 19686
5000 / 16404
4000 / 13124
3000 / 9843
2000 / 6562
1000 / 3281
500 / 1640
200 / 656
0 / 0
LAND BELOW SEA LEVEL
200 / 656
2000 / 6562
4000 / 13124
6000 / 19686

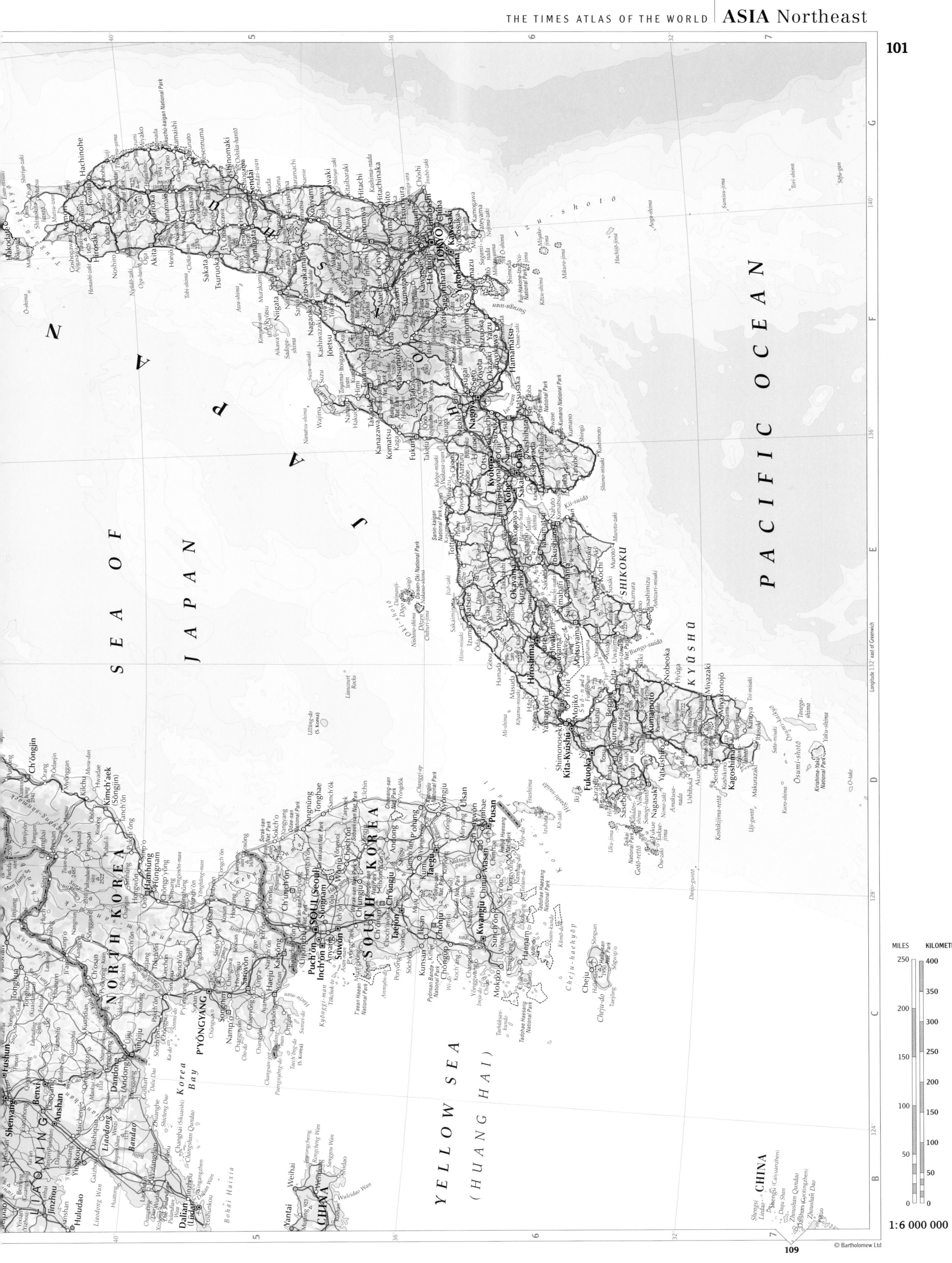

PACIFIC OCEAN

SEA OF JAPAN

YELLOW SEA (HUANG HAI)

NORTH KOREA

SOUTH KOREA

CHINA

LIAONING

SHIKOKU

KYŪSHŪ

P'YŎNGYANG

SŎUL (Seoul)

Pusan

Tōkyō

Sendai

Hiroshima

Nagoya

Kyōto

Ōsaka

Fukuoka

Kagoshima

Kumamoto

MILES	KILOMETRES
250	400
200	350
200	300
150	250
150	200
100	150
50	100
50	50
0	0

1:6 000 000

HOKKAIDŌ

Sea of Okhotsk
(Okhotskoye More)

La Pérouse Strait

142 *Strait*

J A P A N

E A S T   C H I N A   S E A
(DONG HAI)

RYUKYU ISLANDS
CONTINUATION AT THE SAME SCALE

Okinawa

1:1 200 000

METRES
FEET

METRES	FEET
6000	19686
5000	16404
4000	13124
3000	9843
2000	6562
1500	4921
1000	3281
500	1640
200	656
100	328
0	0
LAND BELOW SEA LEVEL	
200	656
4000	13124
6000	19686

Polyconic Projection

Administrative divisions
numbered on the map:
1. CHIBA (J6)
2. KANAGAWA (I6)
3. OSAKA (G6)
4. SAITAMA (I6)
5. TŌKYŌ (I6)
6. YAMANASHI (I6)

PACIFIC OCEAN

SEA OF JAPAN

SOUTH KOREA

Korea Strait

TŌKYŌ

FUKUSHIMA

NIIGATA

TOCHIGI

GUMMA

NAGANO

TOYAMA

ISHIKAWA

FUKUI

GIFU

AICHI

SHIZUOKA

MIE

NARA

WAKAYAMA

KYŌTO

HYŌGO

OKAYAMA

TOTTORI

SHIMANE

HIROSHIMA

YAMAGUCHI

SHIKOKU

KŌCHI

TOKUSHIMA

KYŪSHŪ

FUKUOKA

SAGA

NAGASAKI

KUMAMOTO

OITA

MIYAZAKI

KAGOSHIMA

Osaka

Hiroshima

Kita-Kyūshū

Fukuoka

Kagoshima

Pusan

Iō-jima (Iwō-jima)
1:300 000

**BONIN ISLANDS AND
VOLCANO ISLANDS**
1:3 600 000

Ogasawara-shotō
(Bonin Islands)

Kazan-rettō
(Volcano Islands)

PACIFIC OCEAN

Izu-shotō

Longitude 134 east of Greenwich

MILES   KILOMETRES
125   200
         175
100   150
         125
75   100
50   75
         50
25   25
0   0

1:3 600 000

© Bartholomew Ltd

101

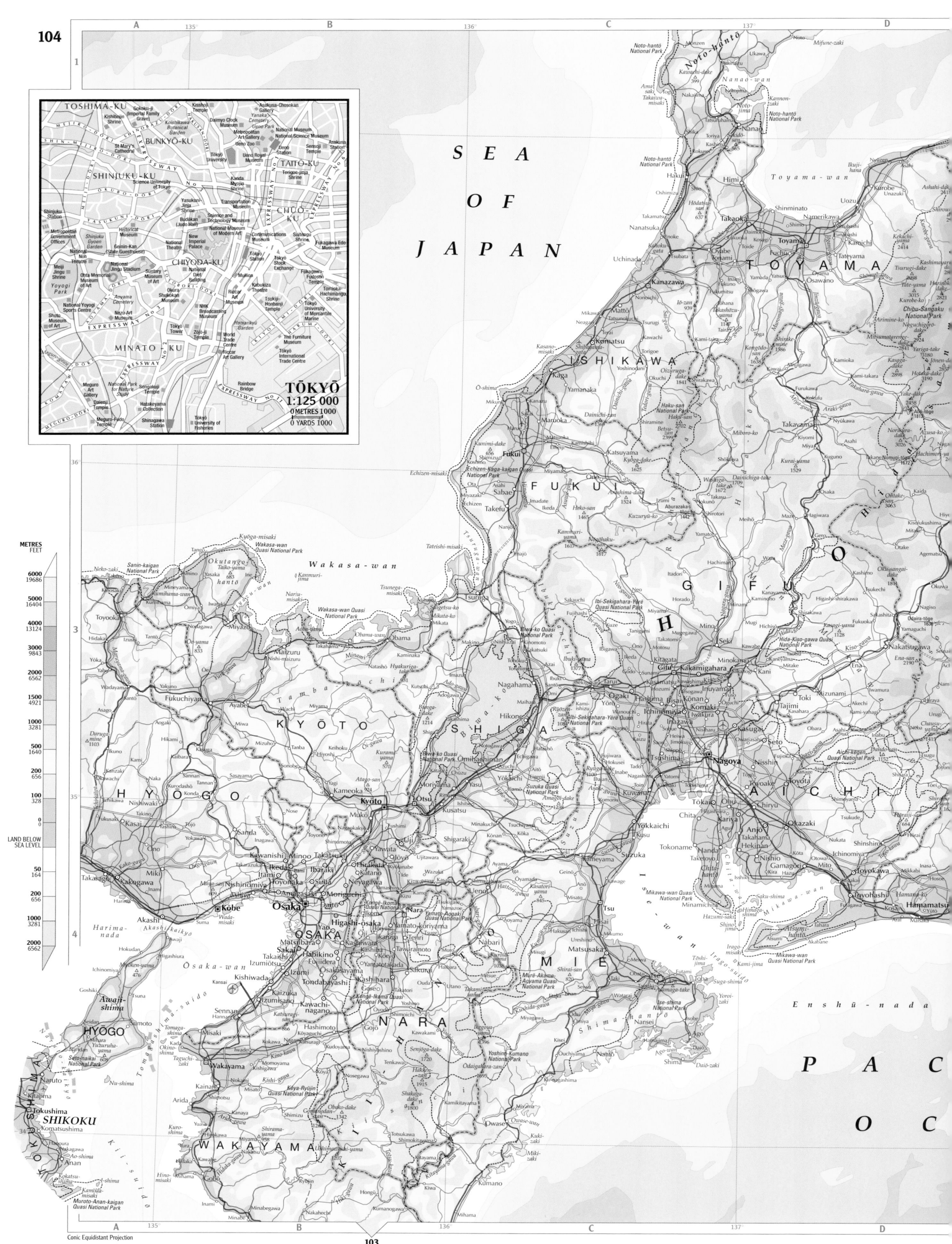

SEA

OF

JAPAN

PACIFIC OCEAN

TŌKYŌ
1:125 000

0 METRES 1000

0 YARDS 1000

TOSHIMA-KU
BUNKYŌ-KU
SHINJUKU-KU
CHIYODA-KU
CHŪŌ-KU
TAITO-KU
MINATO-KU

METRES FEET

6000 19686
5000 16404
4000 13124
3000 9843
2000 6562
1500 4921
1000 3281
500 1640
200 656
100 328
0 0
LAND BELOW SEA LEVEL
50 164
200 656
1000 3281
2000 6562

TOYAMA

ISHIKAWA

FUKUI

GIFU

KYŌTO

SHIGA

HYŌGO

AICHI

MIE

NARA

WAKAYAMA

HYŌGO

SHIKOKU

Nagoya

Ōsaka

Kyōto

Kōbe

Conic Equidistant Projection

1:1 200 000

© Bartholomew Ltd

102
NIIGATA
FUKUSHIMA
TOCHIGI
GUMMA
IBARAKI
NAGANO
SAITAMA
TŌKYŌ
YAMANASHI
KANAGAWA
CHIBA
SHIZUOKA
TOKYO
Yokohama
Kawasaki
Chiba
Utsunomiya
Maebashi
Mito
Nagano
Kōfu
Shizuoka
Tōkyō-wan
Sagami-wan
Sagami-nada
Suruga-wan
Kashima-nada
Bōsō-hantō
Izu-hantō
Ō-shima
Nii-jima
Kōzu-shima
Miyake-jima
Mikura-jima
IFIC
EAN
MILES
KILOMETRES
Longitude 138° east of Greenwich

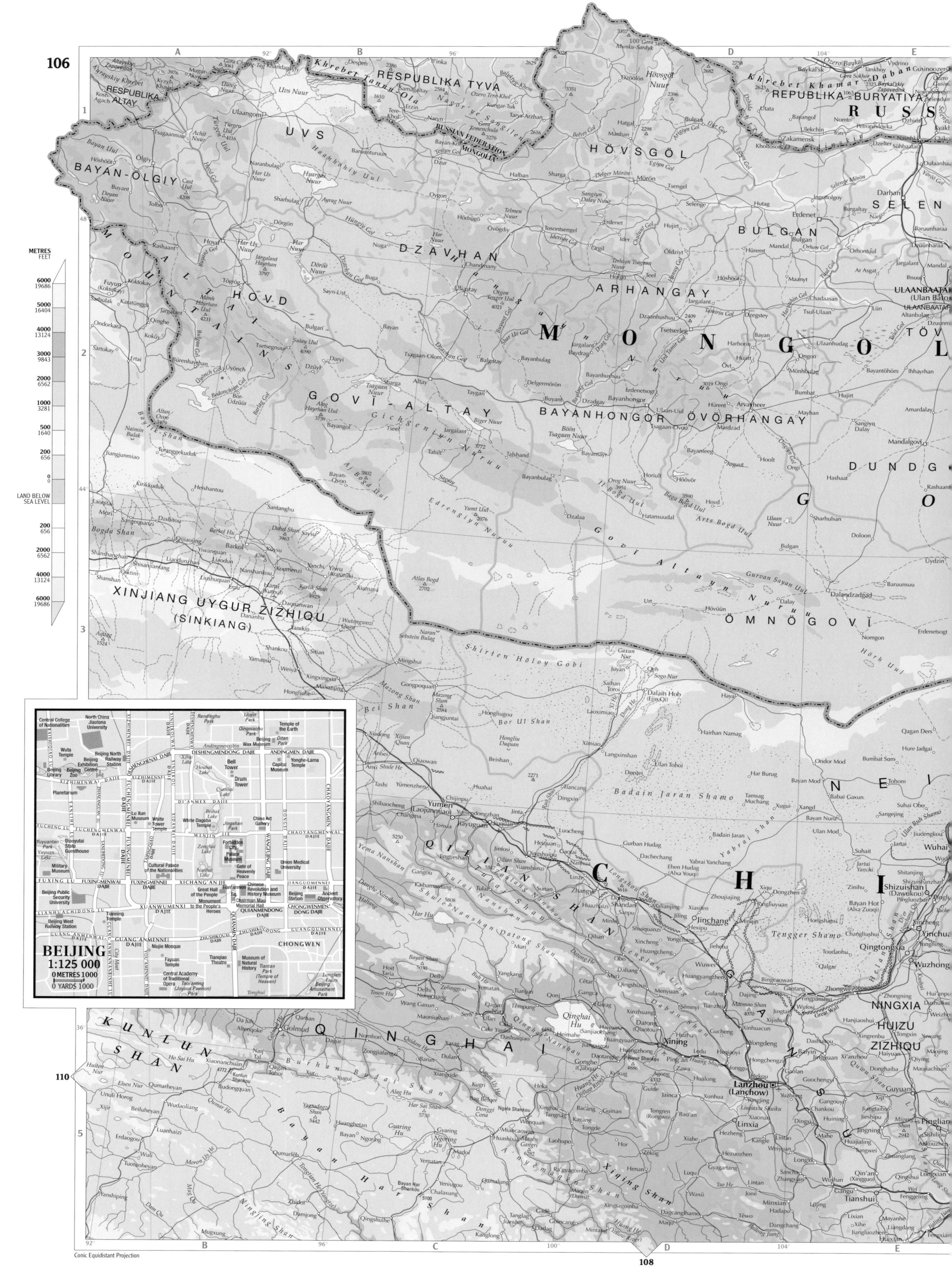
METRES
FEET
6000 19686
5000 16404
4000 13124
3000 9843
2000 6562
1000 3281
500 1640
200 656
0 0
LAND BELOW SEA LEVEL
200 656
2000 6562
4000 13124
6000 19686
RESPUBLIKA ALTAY
RESPUBLIKA TYVA
RUSSIAN FEDERATION
MONGOLIA
REPUBLIKA BURYATIYA
RUSS
UVS
Uvs Nuur
BAYAN-ÖLGIY
HÖVSGÖL
Hövsgöl Nuur
BULGAN
SELEN
DZAVHAN
ARHANGAY
HOVD
MONGOLIA
MONGOL ALTAI MOUNTAINS
GOVĬ-ALTAY
BAYANHONGOR
ÖVÖRHANGAY
DUNDG
ÖMNÖGOVĬ
Gobi Altayn Nuruu
Shirten Höloy Gobi
ULAANBAATAR (Ulan Bator)
TÖV
Ulaangom
Ölgiy
Hovd
Altay
Uliastay
Mörön
Erdenet
Bayanhongor
Arvayheer
Dalandzadgad
Mandalgovĭ
Tsetserleg
XINJIANG UYGUR ZIZHIQU (SINKIANG)
Bogda Shan
Barkol Hu
Hami (Kumul)
Bei Shan
Badain Jaran Shamo
Tengger Shamo
NEI
GO
CHINA
QILIAN SHAN
Yumen (Laojunmiao)
Jiuquan
Zhangye
Jinchang
Wuwei
Lanzhou (Lanchow)
Xining
Qinghai Hu
QINGHAI
KUNLUN SHAN
Golmud
Bayan Har Shan
Xiqing Shan
Tianshui
NINGXIA HUIZU ZIZHIQU
Yinchuan
Shizuishan (Dawukou)
Wuhai
Guyuan
Linxia
Central College of Nationalities
North China Jiaotona University
Temple of the Earth
Ditan Park
Beijing Wax Museum
DESHENGMENDONG DAJIE
ANDINGMEN DAJIE
Bell Tower
Drum Tower
Capital Museum
Yonghe-Lama Temple
Beijing North Railway Station
Beijing Exhibition Centre
Beijing Zoo
Beijing Library
Wuta Temple
XIZHIMENWAI DAJIE
XIZHIMENNEI DAJIE
Planetarium
Lu Xun Museum
White Tower Temple
White Dagoba Temple
Beihai Lake
Jingshan Park
China Art Gallery
Forbidden City
Palace Museum
Gate of Heavenly Peace
Diaoyutai State Guesthouse
Yuyuantan Park
Military Museum
Cultural Palace of the Nationalities
Union Medical University
FUXING LU
FUXINGMENWAI DAJIE
FUXINGMENNEI DAJIE
XICHANG'AN JIE
Tian'anmen Sq.
Chinese Revolution and History Museum
Great Hall of the People
Monument to the People's Heroes
Chairman Mao Memorial Hall
Beijing Station
Ancient Observatory
JIANGUOMENNEI DAJIE
Beijing Public Security University
XUANWUMENXI DAJIE
QIANMENDONG DAJIE
CHONGWENMEN DONG DAJIE
Tianning Temple
Beijing West Railway Station
GUANG'ANMENNEI DAJIE
Niujie Mosque
CHONGWEN
Fayuan Temple
Tianqiao Theatre
Museum of Natural History
Tiantan Park (Temple of Heaven)
Central Academy of Traditional Opera
Taoranting (Joyous Pavilion) Park
Beijing Amusement Park
BEIJING
1:125 000
0 METRES 1000
0 YARDS 1000

110
108

Conic Equidistant Projection

RUSSIAN FEDERATION

CHITINSKAYA OBLAST
AGINSKIY BURYATSKIY AVT. OKRUG

MONGOLIA

HENTIY
SÜHBAATAR
DORNOD
DORNOGOVI

INNER MONGOLIA
(NEI MONGOL ZIZHIQU)

CHINA

HEILONGJIANG
Qiqihar

JILIN

Zalantun
Ulanhot

Manzhouli
Hailar (Hulun)
Yakeshi

Xilinhot
(Abag Qi)

Chifeng (Ulanhad)

LIAONING
Shenyang   Fushun
Fuxin
Chaoyang
Jinzhou
Anshan   Benxi
Huludao   Yingkou
Dalian (Lüda)

Tongliao

Hohhot
Baotou
Dongsheng

Zhangjiakou (Kalgan)
Xuanhua
Datong

BEIJING
BEIJING (Peking)
Langfang
TIANJIN
Tianjin (Tientsin)
Hangu
Tangshan
Qinhuangdao

HEBEI
Baoding
Xinzhou (Xinxian)
Taiyuan
Shijiazhuang
Yangquan
Hengshui
Dezhou
Cangzhou

BO HAI
Bohai Wan
Laizhou Wan

SHANXI
Yuci

Yantai
Weihai

SHANDONG
Jinan
Zibo   Weifang
Qingdao (Tsingtao)
Laiwu
Xintai

Handan
Anyang

Linfen

Liaocheng
Jining
Heze
Xinxiang
Kaifeng
Zhengzhou

HENAN
Luoyang (Loyang)
Pingdingshan

Xuzhou (Tongshan)
Lianyungang
Huaibei

JIANGSU
Huaiyin (Wangying)
Huai'an
Yancheng

YELLOW SEA
(HUANG HAI)

ANHUI

Tongchuan
Xianyang
Xi'an
Weinan

SHAANXI
Yan'an

MILES   KILOMETRES
250   400
200   350
        300
150   250
        200
100   150
        100
50   50
0   0

1:6 000 000

Longitude 108° east of Greenwich

© Bartholomew Ltd

106

96

111

96

METRES
FEET
6000 19686
5000 16404
4000 13124
3000 9843
2000 6562
1000 3281
500 1640
200 656
0
LAND BELOW SEA LEVEL
200 656
2000 6562
4000 13124
6000 19686

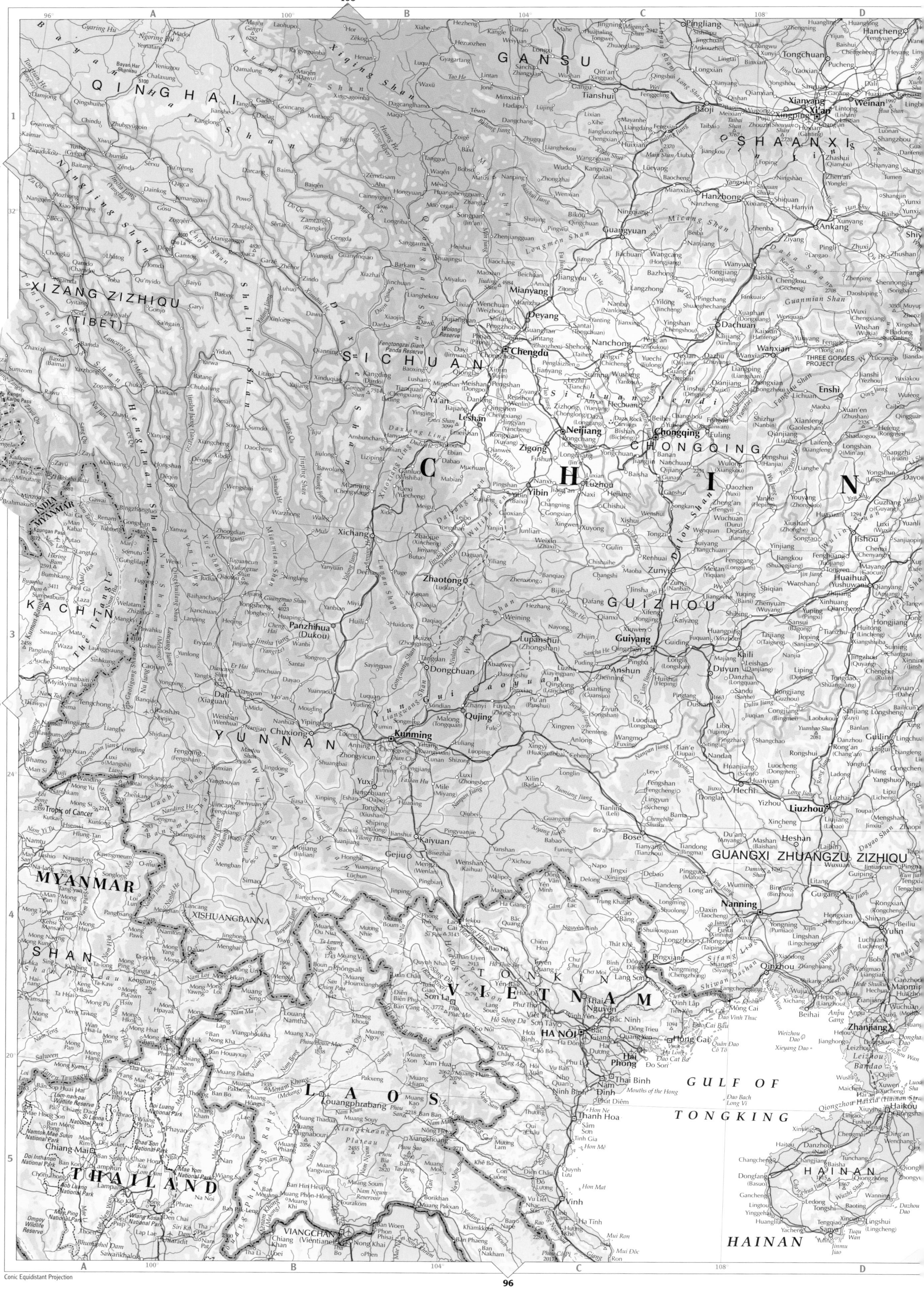

QINGHAI

GANSU

SHAANXI

XIZANG ZIZHIQU
(TIBET)

SICHUAN

CHONGQING

C H I N A

GUIZHOU

YUNNAN

GUANGXI ZHUANGZU ZIZHIQU

MYANMAR

KACHIN

SHAN

XISHUANGBANNA

THAILAND

LAOS

VIETNAM

TONKIN

HAINAN

GULF OF
TONGKING

Chengdu
Mianyang
Deyang
Neijiang
Zigong
Chongqing
Guiyang
Kunming
Guilin
Liuzhou
Nanning
Zhanjiang
Haikou
Xi'an
Xianyang
Weinan
Guangyuan
Dachuan
Wanxian
Enshi
Zhaotong
Panzhihua
(Dukou)
Xichang
Dali
(Xiaguan)
Dongchuan
Qujing
Yuxi
Gejiu
Kaiyuan
Baoji
Tongchuan
Nanchong
Zunyi
Duyun
Dongchuan
HA NÔI
Hai Phong
Hong Gai
Thanh Hoa
Vinh
Ha Tinh
Chiang Mai
Lampang
Louangphrabang
VIANGCHAN
(Vientiane)
Nong Khai

Tropic of Cancer

THREE GORGES PROJECT

Conic Equidistant Projection

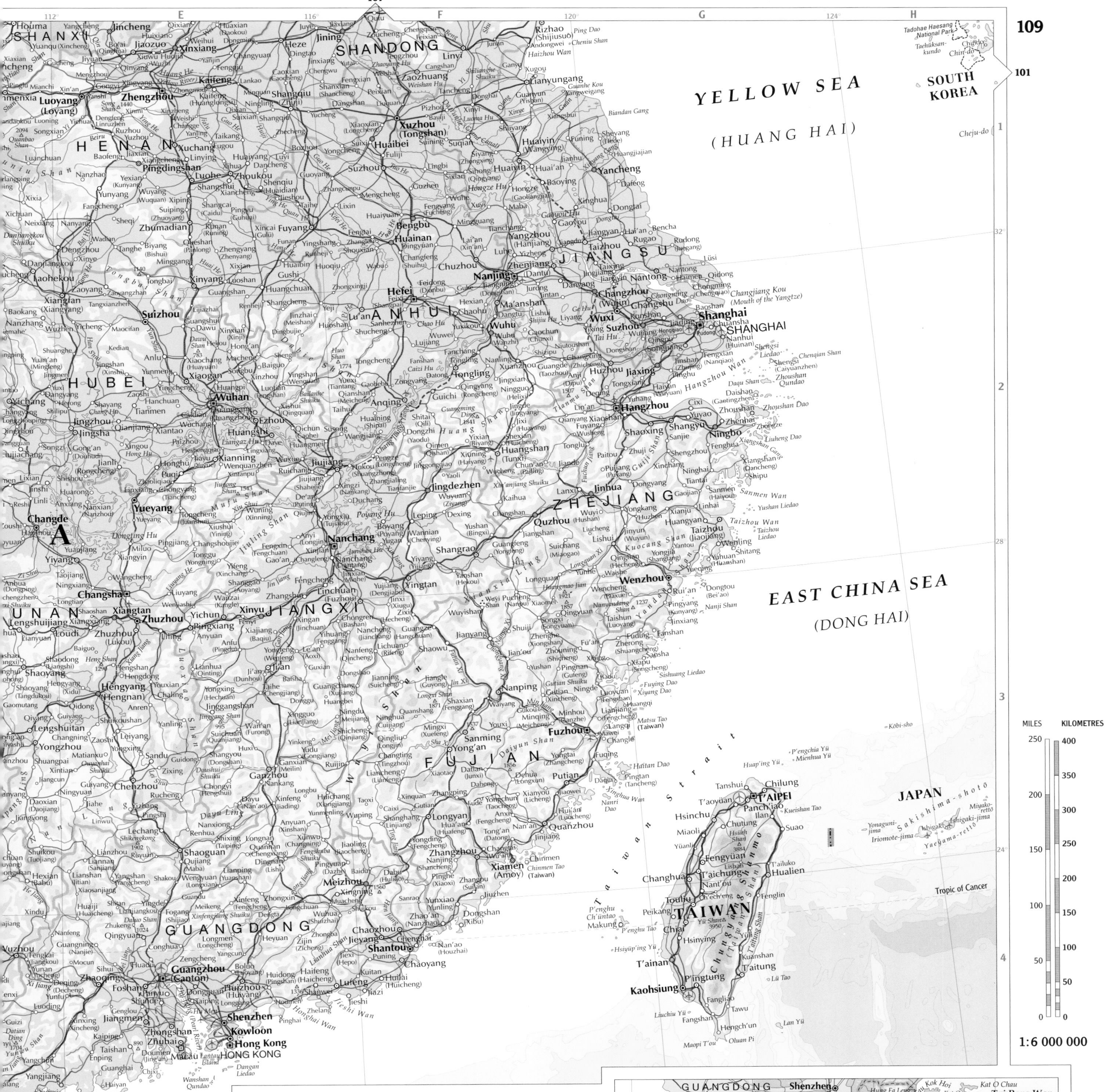

YELLOW SEA

(HUANG HAI)

SOUTH KOREA

EAST CHINA SEA

(DONG HAI)

JAPAN

SHANXI

HENAN

HUBEI

ANHUI

JIANGSU

Shanghai

SHANGHAI

ZHEJIANG

HUNAN

JIANGXI

FUJIAN

GUANGDONG

TAIWAN

Tropic of Cancer

Guangzhou (Canton)

Kowloon
HONG KONG

Macau

MILES / KILOMETRES

250 / 400
350
200 / 300
250
150 / 200
100 / 150
100
50 / 50
0 / 0

1:6 000 000

JINGAN

HUANGPU

NANSHI

LUWAN

PUDONG AREA

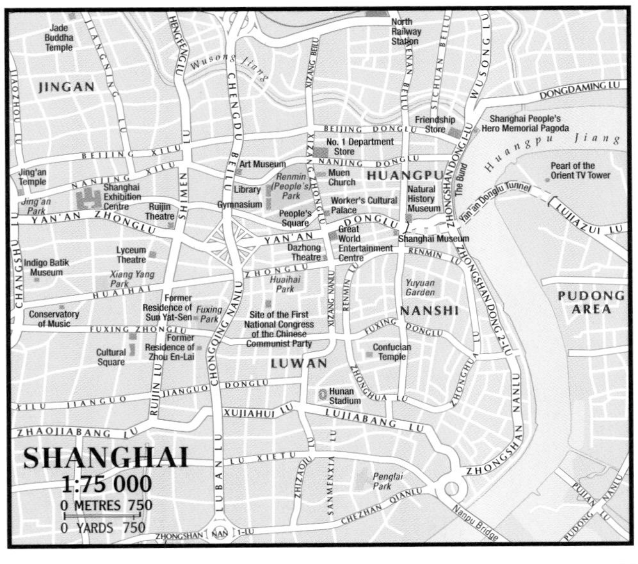

SHANGHAI
1:75 000

0 METRES 750
0 YARDS 750

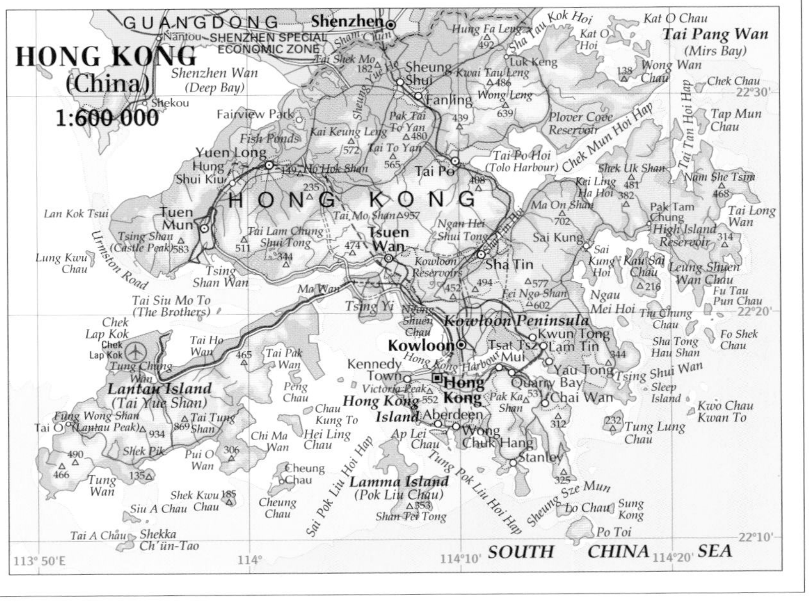

HONG KONG
(China)
1:600 000

GUANGDONG   Shenzhen

SHENZHEN SPECIAL ECONOMIC ZONE

Tai Pang Wan
(Mirs Bay)

HONG KONG

Kowloon Peninsula

Kowloon

Hong Kong Island

Lantau Island
(Tai Yue Shan)

Lamma Island
(Pok Liu Chau)

SOUTH CHINA SEA

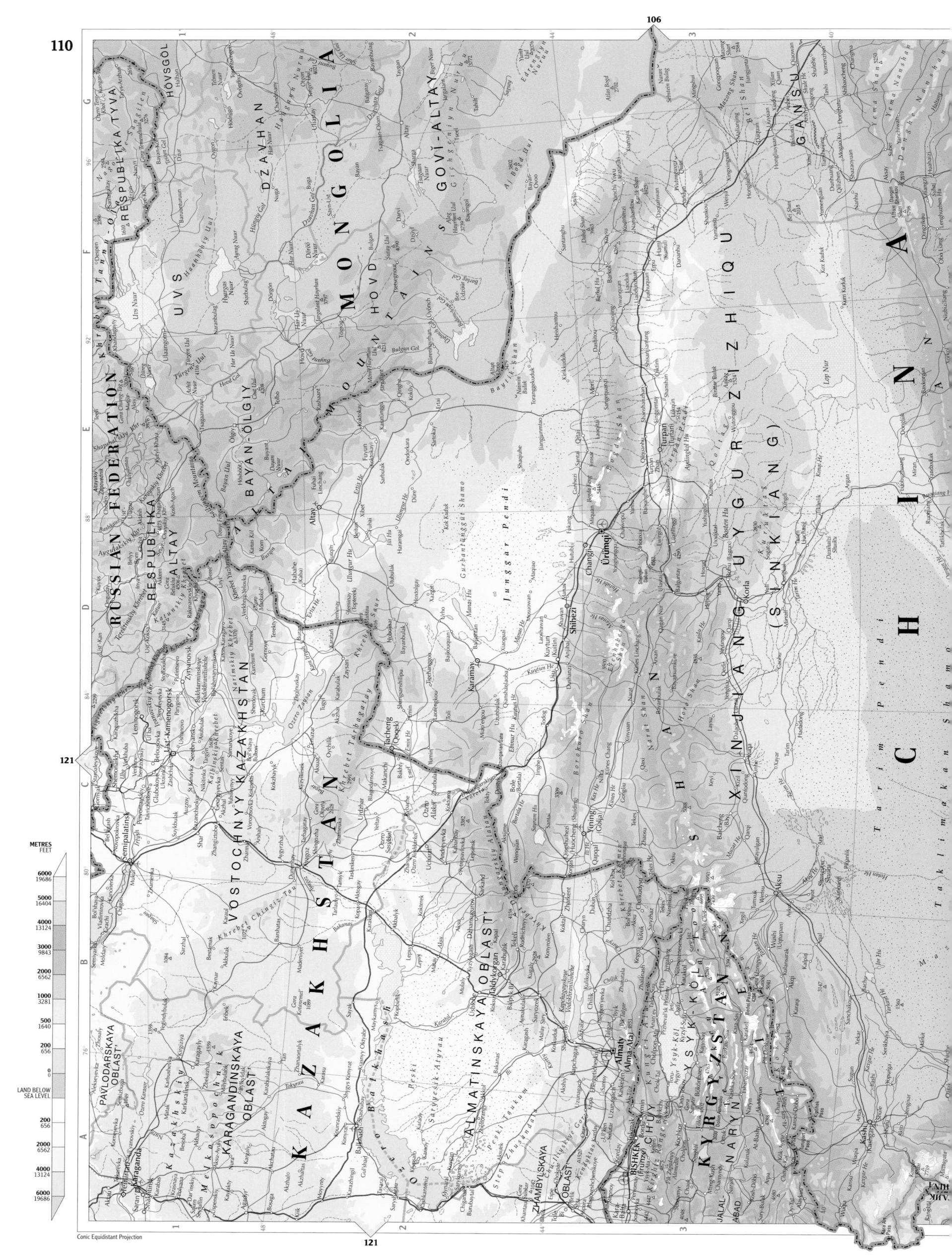

METRES
FEET

6000
19686

5000
16404

4000
13124

3000
9843

2000
6562

1000
3281

500
1640

200
656

0

LAND BELOW
SEA LEVEL

200
656

2000
6562

4000
13124

6000
19686

Conic Equidistant Projection

QINGHAI

XIZANG (TIBET)

Qingzang Gaoyuan
(PLATEAU OF TIBET)

KUNLUN

NEPAL

BHUTAN

BANGLADESH

MYANMAR

ASSAM

ARUNACHAL PRADESH

NAGALAND

SAGAING

SIKKIM

WEST BENGAL

BIHAR

INDIA

UTTAR PRADESH

HARYANA

RAJASTHAN

MADHYA PRADESH

PUNJAB

HIMACHAL PRADESH

JAMMU & KASHMIR

LADAKH

ZASKAR

AKSAI CHIN
CLAIMED BY INDIA
UNDER CHINESE
ADMINISTRATION

NORTHERN AREAS

BALTISTAN

HUNZA

Kunlun Shan

Karakoram Range

Qaidam Pendi

Bayan Har Shan

Delhi

New Delhi

Kathmandu

Srinagar

Lucknow

Kanpur

Longitude 88 east of Greenwich

117

116

123

MILES   KILOMETRES

250   400
         350
200   300
         250
150   200
100   150
         100
50   50
0   0

1:6 000 000

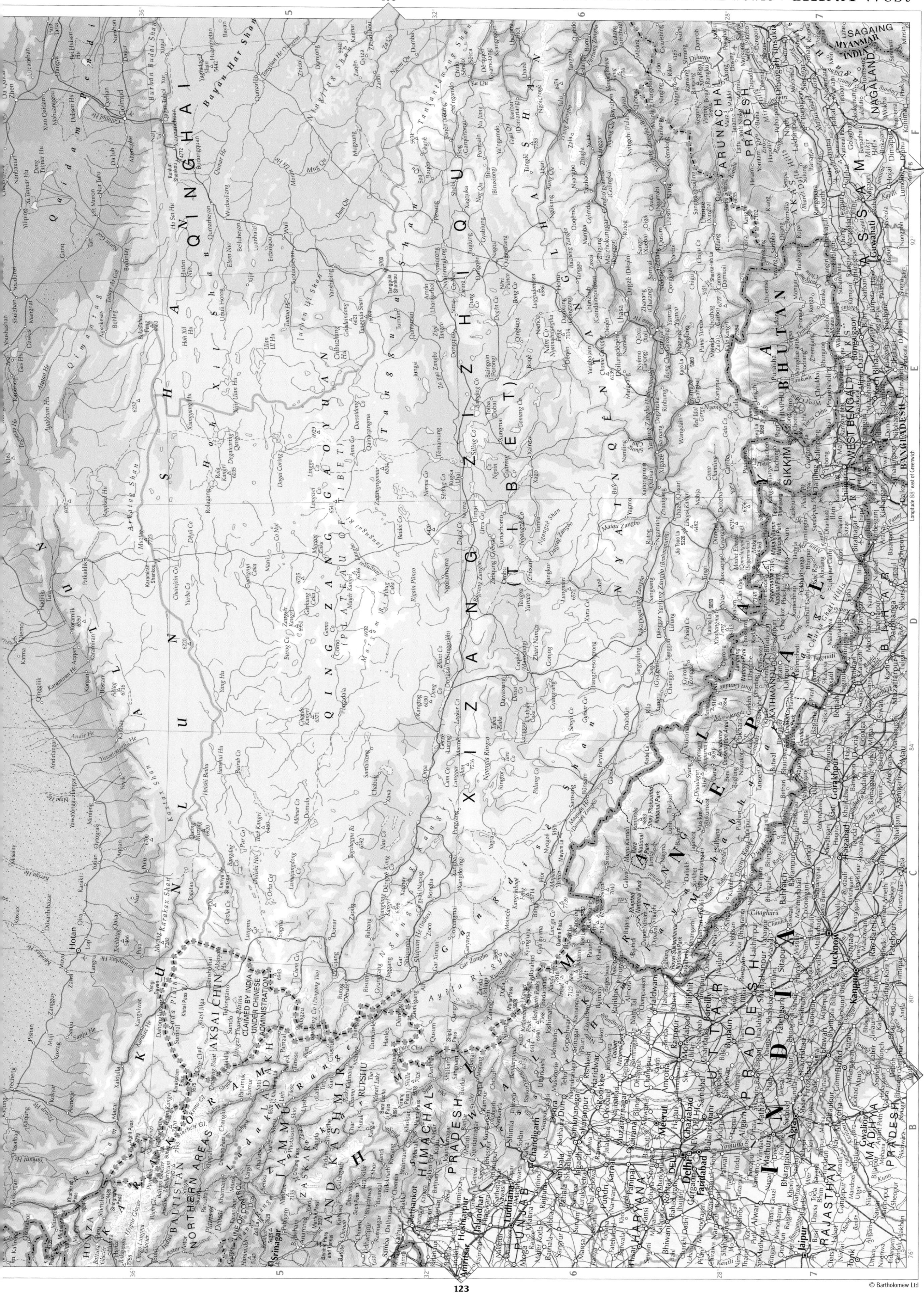

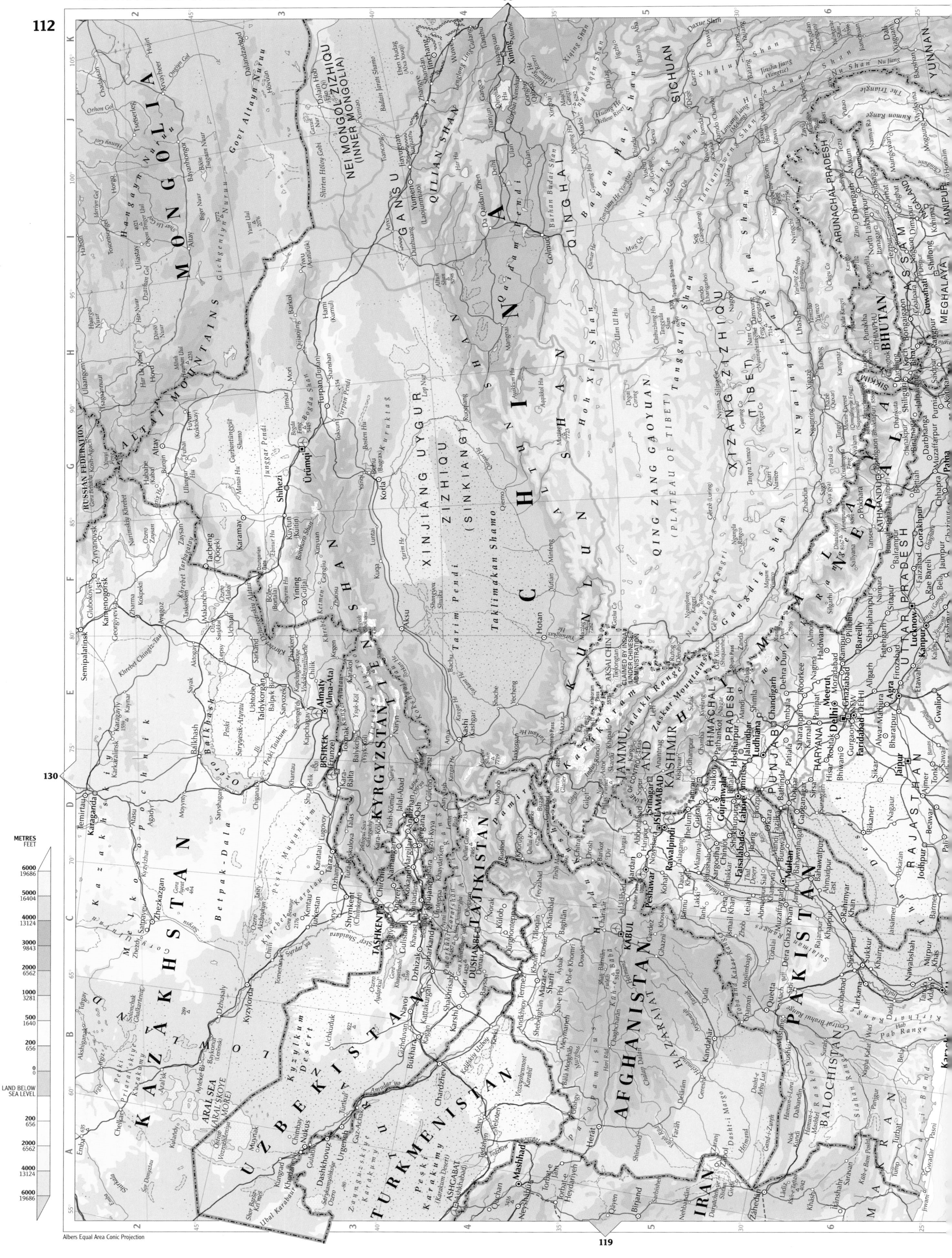

MONGOLIA

NEI MONGOL ZIZHIQU (INNER MONGOLIA)

RUSSIAN FEDERATION

ALTAI MOUNTAINS

KAZAKHSTAN

UZBEKISTAN

TURKMENISTAN

KYRGYZSTAN

TAJIKISTAN

AFGHANISTAN

IRAN

PAKISTAN

XINJIANG UYGUR ZIZHIQU (SINKIANG)

Taklimakan Shamo

TIAN SHAN

GANSU

QINGHAI

QING ZANG GAOYUAN (PLATEAU OF TIBET)

XIZANG ZIZHIQU (TIBET)

KUN LUN SHAN

SICHUAN

YUNNAN

NEPAL

BHUTAN

ASSAM

ARUNACHAL PRADESH

MEGHALAYA

MANIPUR

SIKKIM

UTTAR PRADESH

RAJASTHAN

HARYANA

PUNJAB

HIMACHAL PRADESH

JAMMU AND KASHMIR

BALOCHISTAN

Delhi

NEW DELHI

Almaty (Alma-Ata)

BISHKEK Frunze

TASHKENT

DUSHANBE

ASHGABAT

KABUL

ISLAMABAD

Rawalpindi

Lahore

KATHMANDU

Lucknow

Kanpur

Jaipur

Ürümqi

Mashhad

Herat

Kandahar

Quetta

ARAL SEA (ARAL'SKOYE MORE)

Betpak-Dala

Balkhash

Albers Equal Area Conic Projection

METRES / FEET
6000 19686
5000 16404
4000 13124
3000 9843
2000 6562
1000 3281
500 1640
200 656
0
LAND BELOW SEA LEVEL
200 656
2000 6562
4000 13124
6000 19686

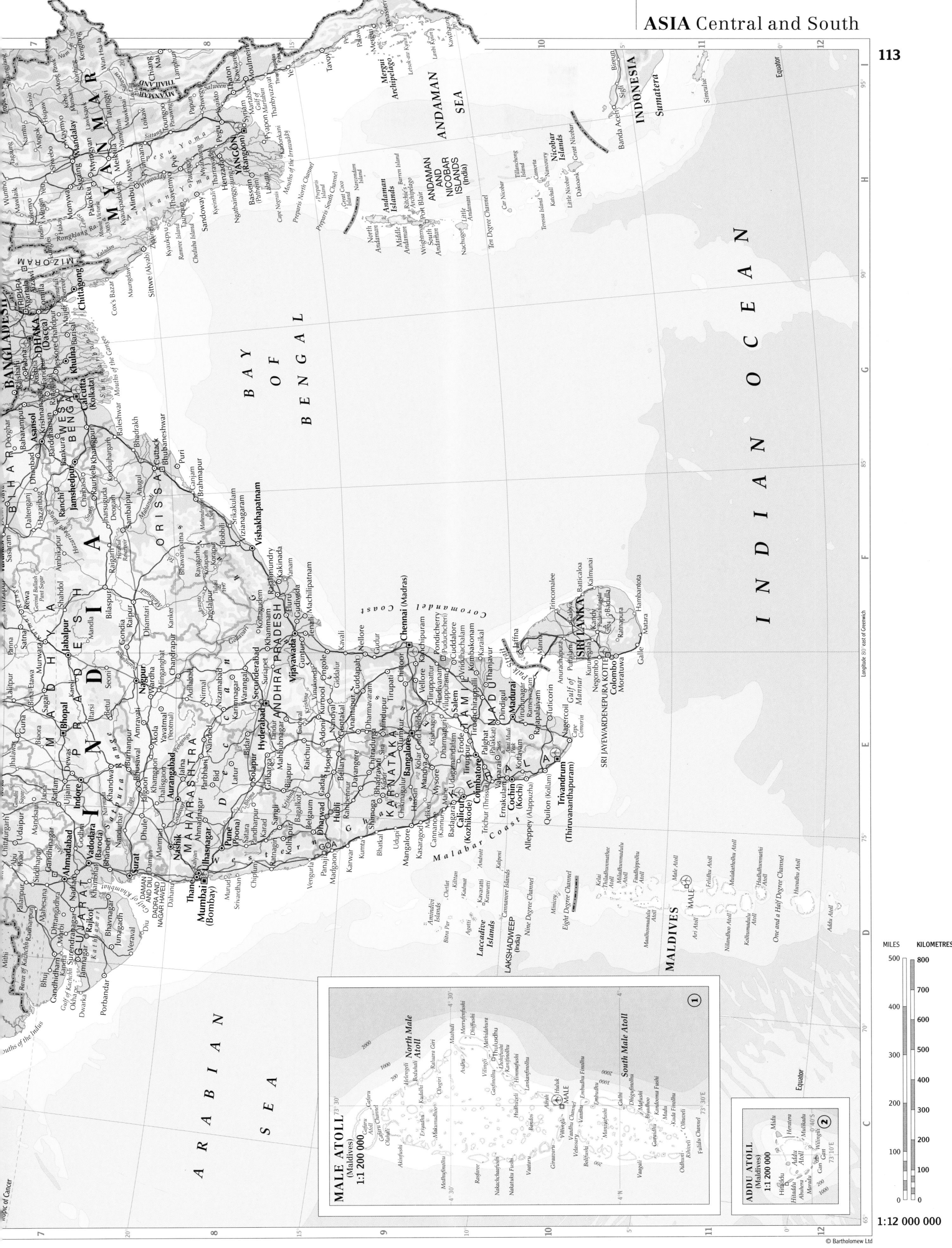

MYANMAR

THAILAND

ANDAMAN SEA

INDONESIA
Sumatera

ANDAMAN AND NICOBAR ISLANDS (India)

Andaman Islands

Nicobar Islands

BANGLADESH

DHAKA

Calcutta (Kolkata)

Chittagong

BAY OF BENGAL

INDIAN OCEAN

I N D I A

MADHYA PRADESH

ORISSA

MAHARASHTRA

ANDHRA PRADESH

KARNATAKA

TAMIL NADU

KERALA

GOA

GUJARAT

Mumbai (Bombay)

Hyderabad

Bangalore

Chennai (Madras)

Vishakhapatnam

Nagpur

Bhopal

Pune (Poona)

Ahmadabad

Vadodara (Baroda)

Surat

Indore

SRI LANKA

Colombo

SRI JAYEWARDENEPURA KOTTE

Coimbatore

Cochin (Kochi)

Madurai

Trivandrum (Thiruvananthapuram)

ARABIAN SEA

MALDIVES

LAKSHADWEEP (India)

Laccadive Islands

Amindivi Islands

MALE

MALE ATOLL (Maldives)
1:1 200 000
North Male Atoll
South Male Atoll
MALE
①

ADDU ATOLL
1:1 200 000
Addu Atoll
Gan
②

Tropic of Cancer

Equator

MILES	KILOMETRES
500	800
400	700
	600
300	500
	400
200	300
	200
100	100
0	0

1:12 000 000

© Bartholomew Ltd

116
ARABIAN SEA
INDIA
GUJARAT
MADHYA PRADESH
MAHARASHTRA
ANDHRA PRADESH
KARNATAKA
TAMIL NADU
KERALA
GOA
DECCAN
WESTERN GHATS
EASTERN GHATS
SRI LANKA
MALDIVES
LAKSHADWEEP (India)
Laccadive Islands
Amindivi Islands
Cannanore Islands
Nine Degree Channel
Eight Degree Channel
Gulf of Kachchh
Gulf of Khambhat
Gulf of Mannar
Palk Strait
Coromandel Coast
Malabar Coast
Tropic of Cancer
Ahmadabad
Vadodara (Baroda)
Surat
Bhopal
Indore
Jabalpur
Nagpur
Mumbai (Bombay)
Pune (Poona)
Nashik
Aurangabad
Solapur
Hyderabad
Secunderabad
Vijayawada
Bangalore
Mysore
Mangalore
Chennai (Madras)
Pondicherry (Puducherri)
Madurai
Coimbatore
Calicut (Kozhikode)
Cochin (Kochi)
Trivandrum (Thiruvananthapuram)
Jaffna
Colombo
SRI JAYEWARDENEPURA KOTTE
METRES
FEET
6000 19686
5000 16404
4000 13124
3000 9843
2000 6562
1000 3281
500 1640
200 656
0 0
LAND BELOW SEA LEVEL
200 656
2000 6562
4000 13124
6000 19686

Conic Equidistant Projection

MYANMAR

BANGLADESH

BAY

OF

BENGAL

Administrative areas not named on the map:
INDIA
1. DADRA AND NAGAR HAVELI (B1)
2. DAMAN AND DIU (A1,B1)
3. PONDICHERRY (D2,C4)

CALCUTTA
1:70 000
0 METRES 750
0 YARDS 750

MUMBAI
1:90 000
0 METRES 1000
0 YARDS 1000

Arabian Sea

INDIAN

OCEAN

ANDAMAN

AND

NICOBAR

ISLANDS

(India)

MILES   KILOMETRES

250   400

200   350

300

150   250

200

100   150

100

50   50

0   0

© Bartholomew Ltd

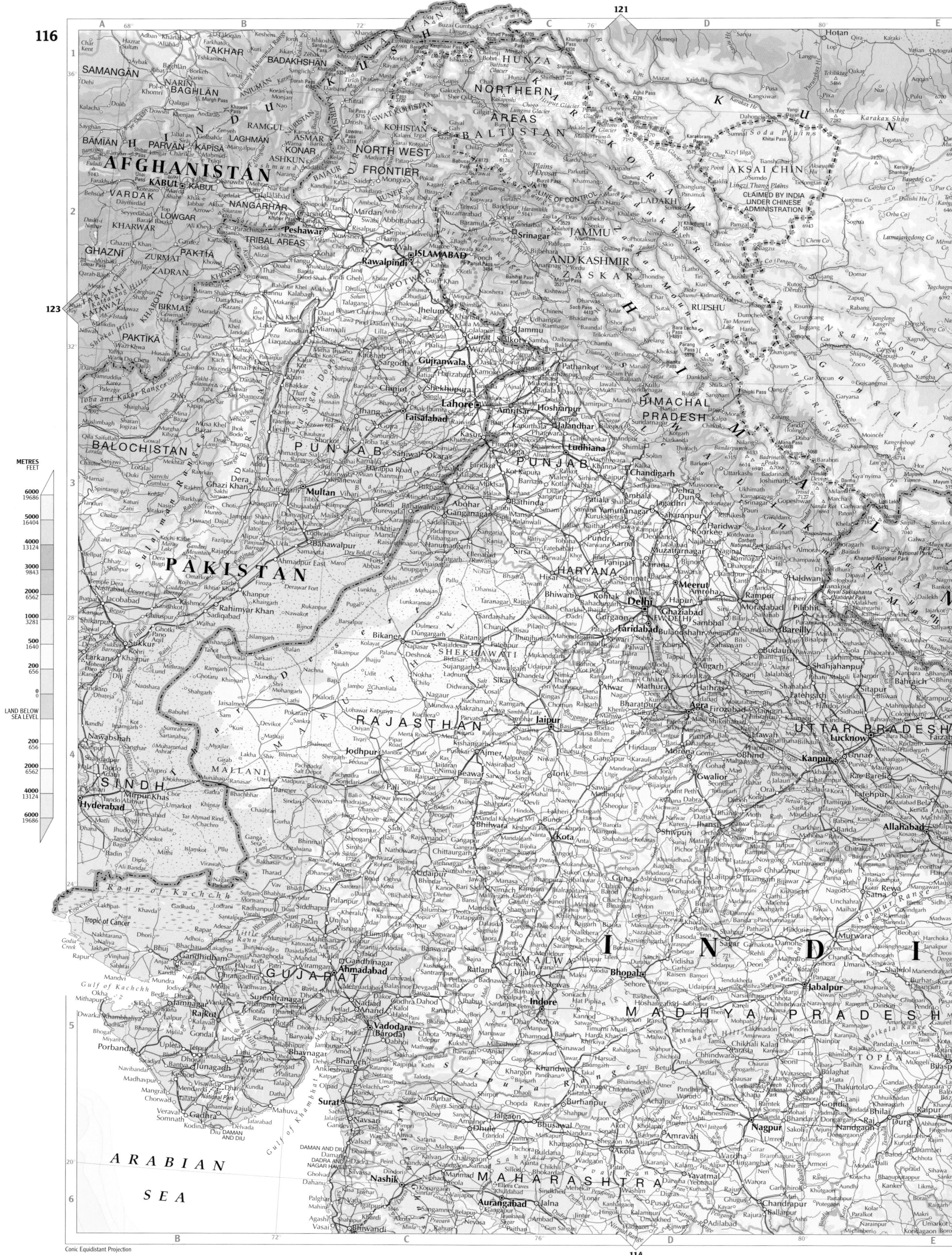

121
123
114
METRES
FEET
6000
19686
5000
16404
4000
13124
3000
9843
2000
6562
1000
3281
500
1640
200
656
0
0
LAND BELOW SEA LEVEL
200
656
2000
6562
4000
13124
6000
19686
AFGHANISTAN
PAKISTAN
INDIA
KABUL
ISLAMABAD
NEW DELHI
Delhi
Lahore
Peshawar
Rawalpindi
Srinagar
Jammu
Amritsar
Multan
Faisalabad
Karachi
Hyderabad
Jaipur
Jodhpur
Ahmadabad
Gandhinagar
Vadodara (Baroda)
Surat
Indore
Bhopal
Nagpur
Jabalpur
Kanpur
Lucknow
Agra
Gwalior
Allahabad
Nashik
Aurangabad
Chandigarh
Shimla
Bikaner
Kota
Ajmer
Rajkot
Jamnagar
Bhavnagar
NORTHERN AREAS
NORTH WEST FRONTIER
TRIBAL AREAS
BALOCHISTAN
PUNJAB
SINDH
JAMMU AND KASHMIR
HIMACHAL PRADESH
HARYANA
RAJASTHAN
GUJARAT
MADHYA PRADESH
MAHARASHTRA
UTTAR PRADESH
LADAKH
AKSAI CHIN
CLAIMED BY INDIA UNDER CHINESE ADMINISTRATION
LINE OF CONTROL
BALTISTAN
HUNZA
KARAKORAM RANGE
HINDU KUSH
THAR DESERT
ARABIAN SEA
Gulf of Kachchh
Gulf of Khambhat
Rann of Kachchh
Tropic of Cancer
DAMAN AND DIU
DADRA AND NAGAR HAVELI

Conic Equidistant Projection

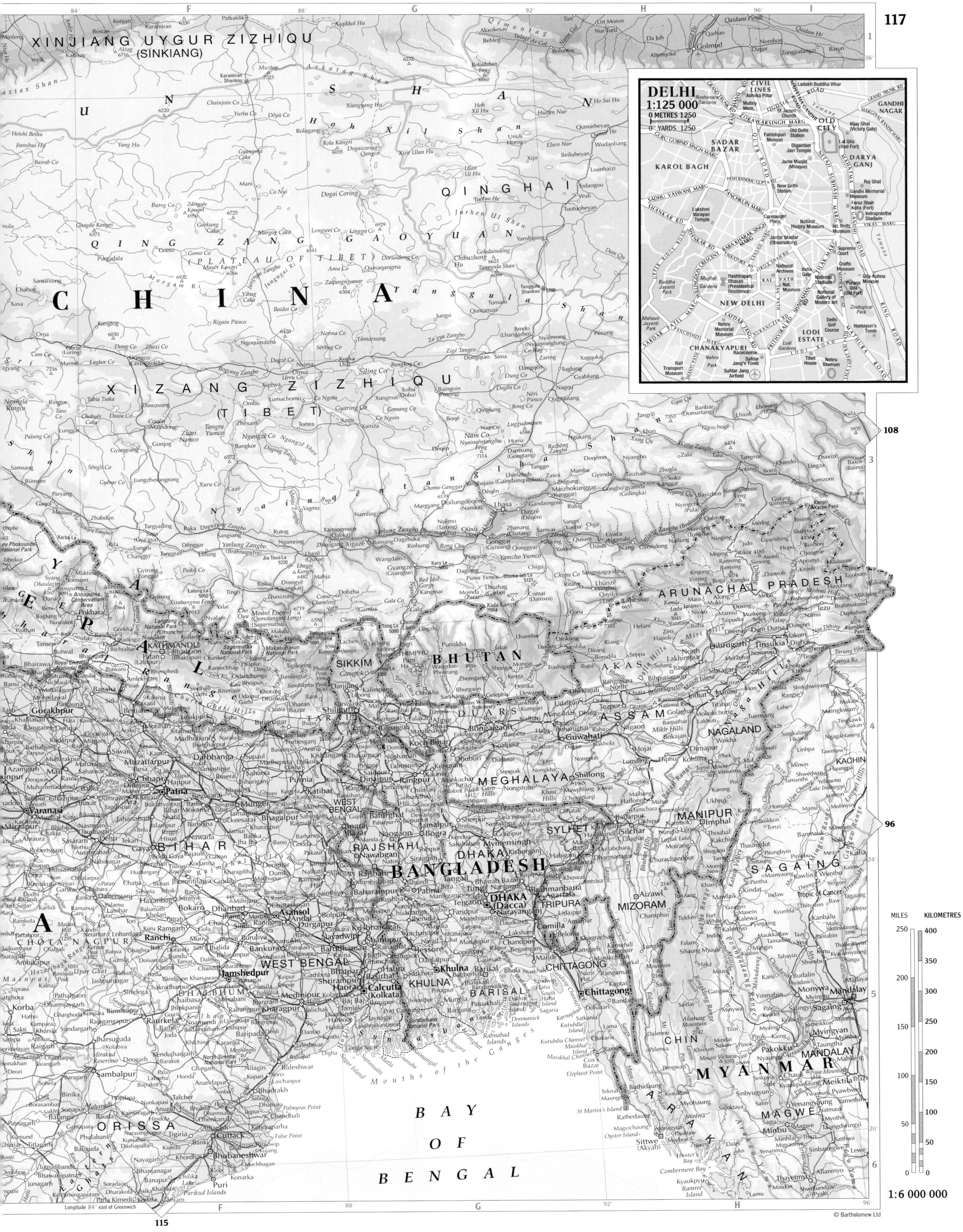

XINJIANG UYGUR ZIZHIQU
(SINKIANG)

QINGHAI

C H I N A

XIZANG ZIZHIQU
(TIBET)

QING ZANG GAOYUAN
(PLATEAU OF TIBET)

DELHI
1:125 000
0 METRES 1250
0 YARDS 1250

CIVIL LINES
OLD CITY
SADAR BAZAR
KAROL BAGH
NEW DELHI
CHANAKYAPURI
LODI ESTATE
GANDHI NAGAR
DARYA GANJ

N E P A L

KATHMANDU

SIKKIM
THIMPHU
BHUTAN
ARUNACHAL PRADESH

ASSAM
MEGHALAYA
NAGALAND
Shillong
Guwahati

WEST BENGAL
BIHAR
Patna
Varanasi
Gorakhpur
Muzaffarpur
Darbhanga

SYLHET
MANIPUR
Imphal
TRIPURA
DHAKA
BANGLADESH
DHAKA
Dacca
Narayanganj
RAJSHAHI
MIZORAM

CHOTA NAGPUR
Ranchi
Jamshedpur
Asansol
Durgapur
WEST BENGAL
Calcutta (Kolkata)
Khulna
KHULNA
BARISAL
CHITTAGONG
Chittagong

SAGAING
Mandalay
Sagaing
MYANMAR
CHIN
MAGWE
ARAKAN

ORISSA
Cuttack
Bhubaneshwar
Puri

B A Y
O F
B E N G A L

Mouths of the Ganges

MILES   KILOMETRES
250   400
           350
200   300
           250
150   200
100   150
50   100
           50

© Bartholomew Ltd

1:6 000 000

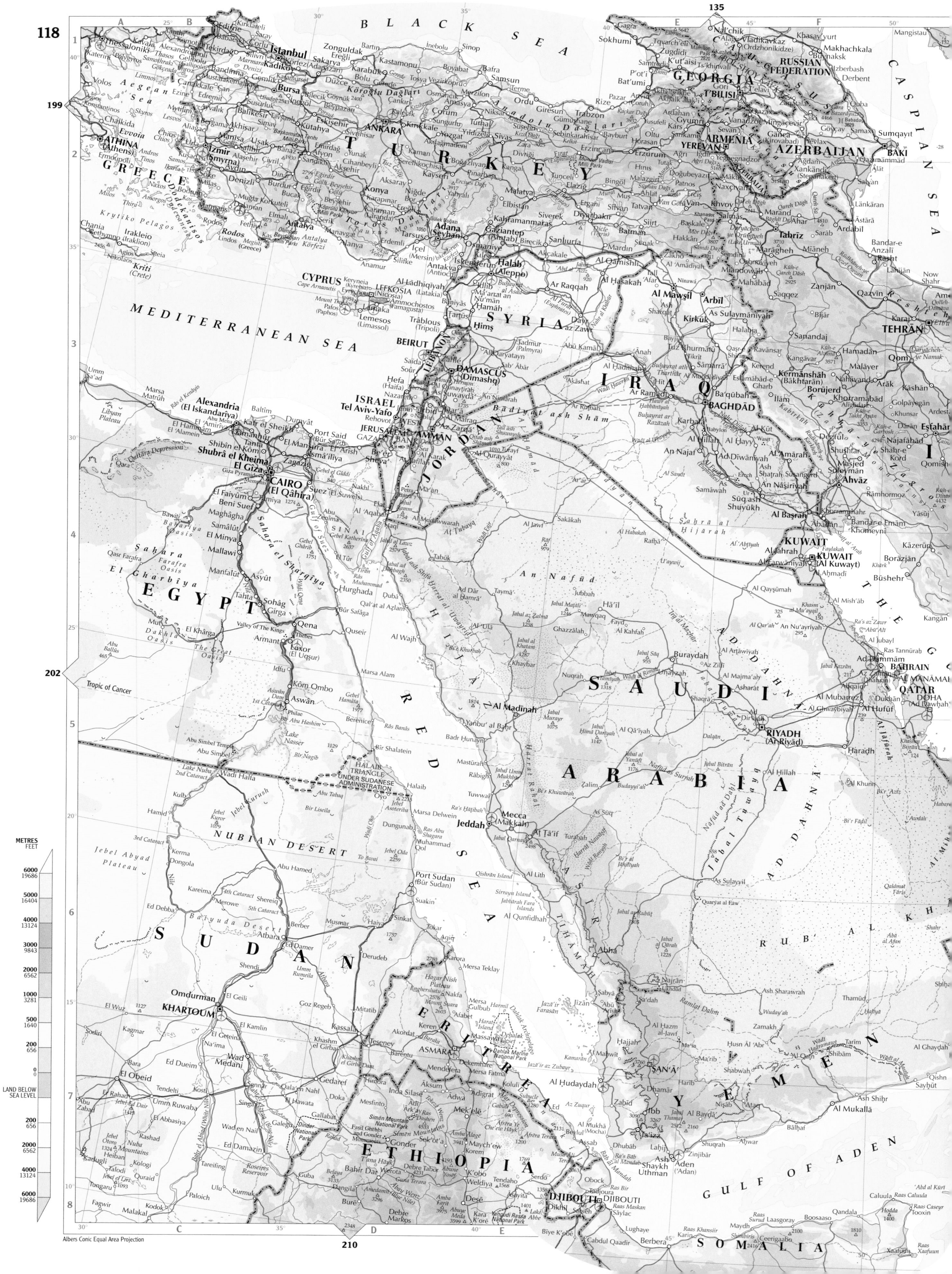

BLACK SEA

CASPIAN SEA

RUSSIAN FEDERATION

GEORGIA
T'BILISI

ARMENIA
YEREVAN

AZERBAIJAN
BAKI

GREECE
ATHINA (Athens)

Istanbul

TURKEY
ANKARA

Aegean Sea

CYPRUS
LEFKOSIA (Nicosia)

MEDITERRANEAN SEA

SYRIA
DAMASCUS (Dimashq)
Aleppo (Halab)
Hims

LEBANON
BEIRUT

ISRAEL
Tel Aviv-Yafo
JERUSALEM

IRAQ
BAGHDAD
Al Mawsil
Arbil
Kirkuk
As Sulaymaniyah
Al Basrah

TEHRAN

JORDAN
AMMAN

EGYPT
CAIRO (El Qâhira)
El Gîza
Alexandria (El Iskandariya)
Suez (El Suweis)
Asyût
Luxor (El Uqsur)
Aswân

SINAI

RED SEA

KUWAIT
KUWAIT (Al Kuwayt)

BAHRAIN
AL MANAMAH

QATAR
DOHA

SAUDI ARABIA
RIYADH (Ar Riyâd)
Al Madinah
Mecca (Makkah)
Jeddah
Ad Dammâm

AN NAFUD

RUB' AL KHALI

AD DAHNA

SUDAN
KHARTOUM
Omdurman
Port Sudan (Bûr Sudan)
Atbara

NUBIAN DESERT

ERITREA
ASMARA
Massawa

YEMEN
SAN'A'
Aden ('Adan)
Al Hudaydah
Ta'izz
Al Mukallā

GULF OF ADEN

ETHIOPIA
Mek'ele
Gonder

DJIBOUTI
DJIBOUTI

SOMALIA

Tropic of Cancer

METRES / FEET

METRES	FEET
6000	19686
5000	16404
4000	13124
3000	9843
2000	6562
1000	3281
500	1640
200	656
0	0

LAND BELOW SEA LEVEL

200	656
2000	6562
4000	13124
6000	19686

Albers Conic Equal Area Projection

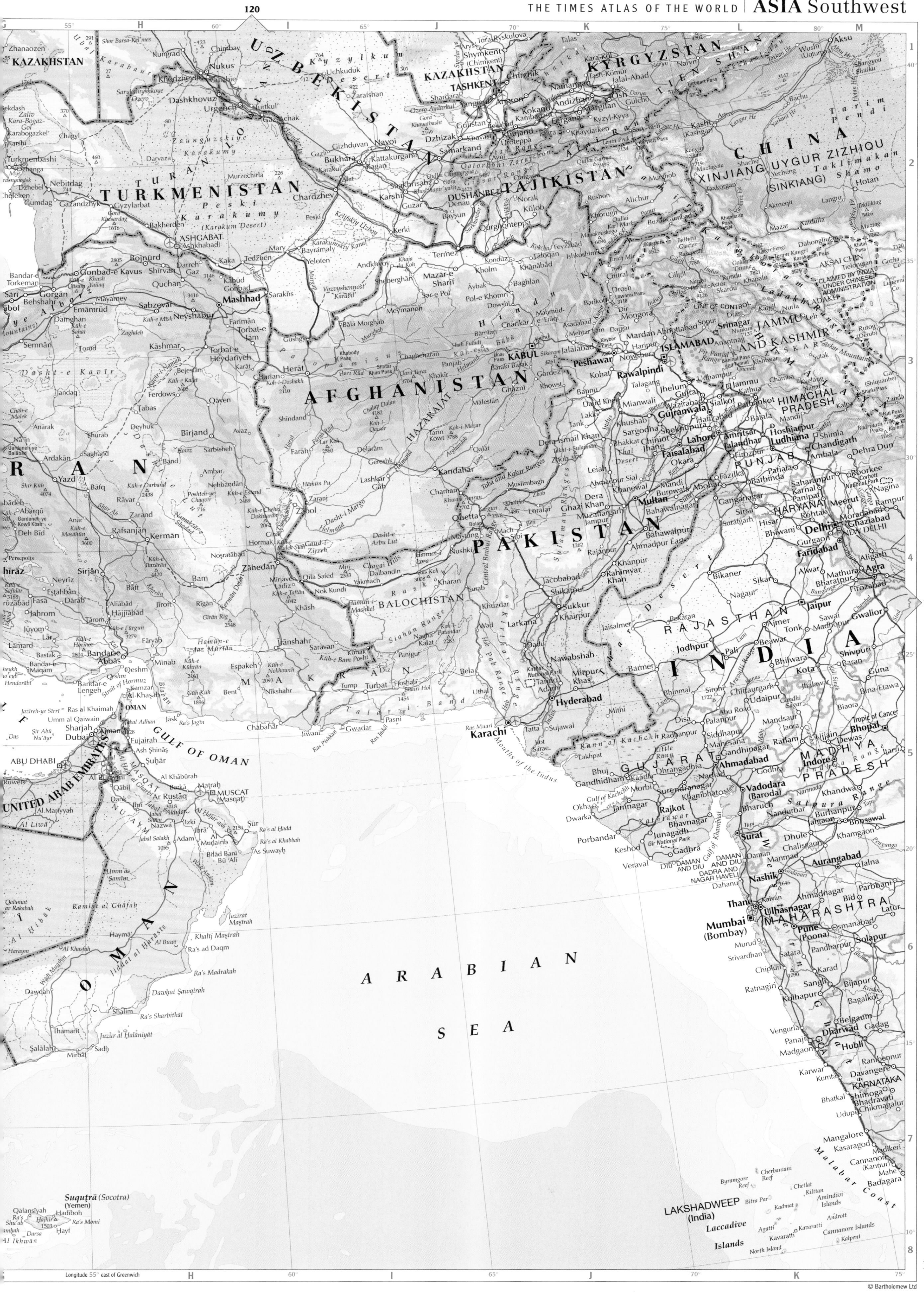

KAZAKHSTAN

UZBEKISTAN

KYRGYZSTAN

TURKMENISTAN

TASHKENT

DUSHANBE

TAJIKISTAN

CHINA

XINJIANG UYGUR ZIZHIQU
(SINKIANG)

Taklimakan
Shamo

ASHGABAT
Ashkhabad

Karakumy
(Karakum Desert)

Mashhad

I R A N

AFGHANISTAN

HAZARAJAT

HINDU KUSH

KĀBUL

Peshawar

ISLAMABAD

Rawalpindi

JAMMU AND KASHMIR

Srinagar

Jammu

HIMACHAL PRADESH

Herāt

Ghaznī

Kandahār

Quetta

Lahore

Amritsar

Jalandhar

Ludhiana

Chandigarh

PUNJAB

Faisalabad

Multan

Dera Ghazi Khan

Bahawalpur

HARYANA

Delhi

NEW DELHI

Faridabad

Zāhedān

Kermān

Bam

PAKISTAN

BALOCHISTAN

Sukkur

Khairpur

Bikaner

RAJASTHAN

Jaipur

Gwalior

Agra

Aligarh

Bandar-e Abbas

Dubai

UNITED ARAB EMIRATES

ABU DHABI

OMAN

Jodhpur

Ajmer

Kota

I N D I A

Muslimbagh

Hyderabad

Karachi

Mouths of the Indus

GUJARAT

Ahmadabad

MADHYA PRADESH

Bhopal

Indore

MUSCAT
(Masqat)

GULF OF OMAN

Rajkot

Jamnagar

Vadodara
(Baroda)

Surat

Bharuch

Porbandar

Junagadh

Nashik

Thane

Mumbai
(Bombay)

Ulhasnagar

MAHARASHTRA

Pune
(Poona)

Solapur

Aurangabad

A R A B I A N

S E A

Salālah

Kolhapur

Bijapur

Belgaum

Dharwad

Hubli

KARNATAKA

Davangere

LAKSHADWEEP
(India)

Laccadive
Islands

Mangalore

MILES   KILOMETRES
700
400   600
        500
300   400
        300
200
        200
100   100

0   0

Administrative regions numbered on the map:

UZBEKISTAN

1. ANDIZHANSKAYA OBLAST' (H4)
2. DZHIZAKSKAYA OBLAST' (F5)
3. FERGANSKAYA OBLAST' (G4)
4. KASHKADAR'INSKAYA OBLAST' (F5)
5. NAMANGANSKAYA OBLAST' (G4)
6. SAMARKANDSKAYA OBLAST' (F5)
7. SYRDAR'INSKAYA OBLAST' (G4)
8. TASHKENTSKAYA OBLAST' (G4)

METRES
FEET

6000
19686

5000
16404

4000
13124

3000
9843

2000
6562

1000
3281

500
1640

200
656

0

LAND BELOW
SEA LEVEL

200
656

2000
6562

4000
13124

6000
19686

Conic Equidistant Projection

1 : 6 000 000

© Bartholomew Ltd

KAZAKHSTAN
UZBEKISTAN
KYRGYZSTAN
TAJIKISTAN
RUSSIAN FEDERATION
CHINA
XINJIANG UYGUR ZIZHIQU (SINKIANG)
SEVERNYY KAZAKHSTAN
AKMOLINSKAYA OBLAST'
PAVLODARSKAYA OBLAST'
KARAGANDINSKAYA OBLAST'
VOSTOCHNYY KAZAKHSTAN
ALMATINSKAYA OBLAST'
ZHAMBYLSKAYA OBLAST
YUZHNYY KAZAKHSTAN
ALTAYSKIY KRAY
RESPUBLIKA ALTAY
JALAL-ABAD
NARYN
OSH
CHÜY
TALAS
YSYK-KÖL
LENINOBOD
KHATLON
KUHISTONI BADAKHSHON
SURKHANDAR'INSKAYA OBLAST
BADAKHSHAN
TAKHAR
KONDUZ
BALKH
AFGHANISTAN
PAKISTAN
JAMMU AND KASHMIR
ASTANA (Akmola)
Karaganda
Pavlodar
Semipalatinsk
Ust'-Kamenogorsk
Almaty (Alma-Ata)
BISHKEK (Frunze)
TASHKENT
DUSHANBE
Samarkand
Petropavlovsk
Kokshetau
Zhezkazgan
Balkhash
Taldykorgan
Taraz (Dzhambul)
Shymkent (Chimkent)
Kashi (Kashgar)
Aksu
Hotan
Ozero Balkhash
Betpak-Dala
Melkosopochnik
Taklimakan Shamo
Tarim Pendi
Kunlun Shan
Tien Shan
Longitude 68° east of Greenwich
MILES
KILOMETRES
110
123

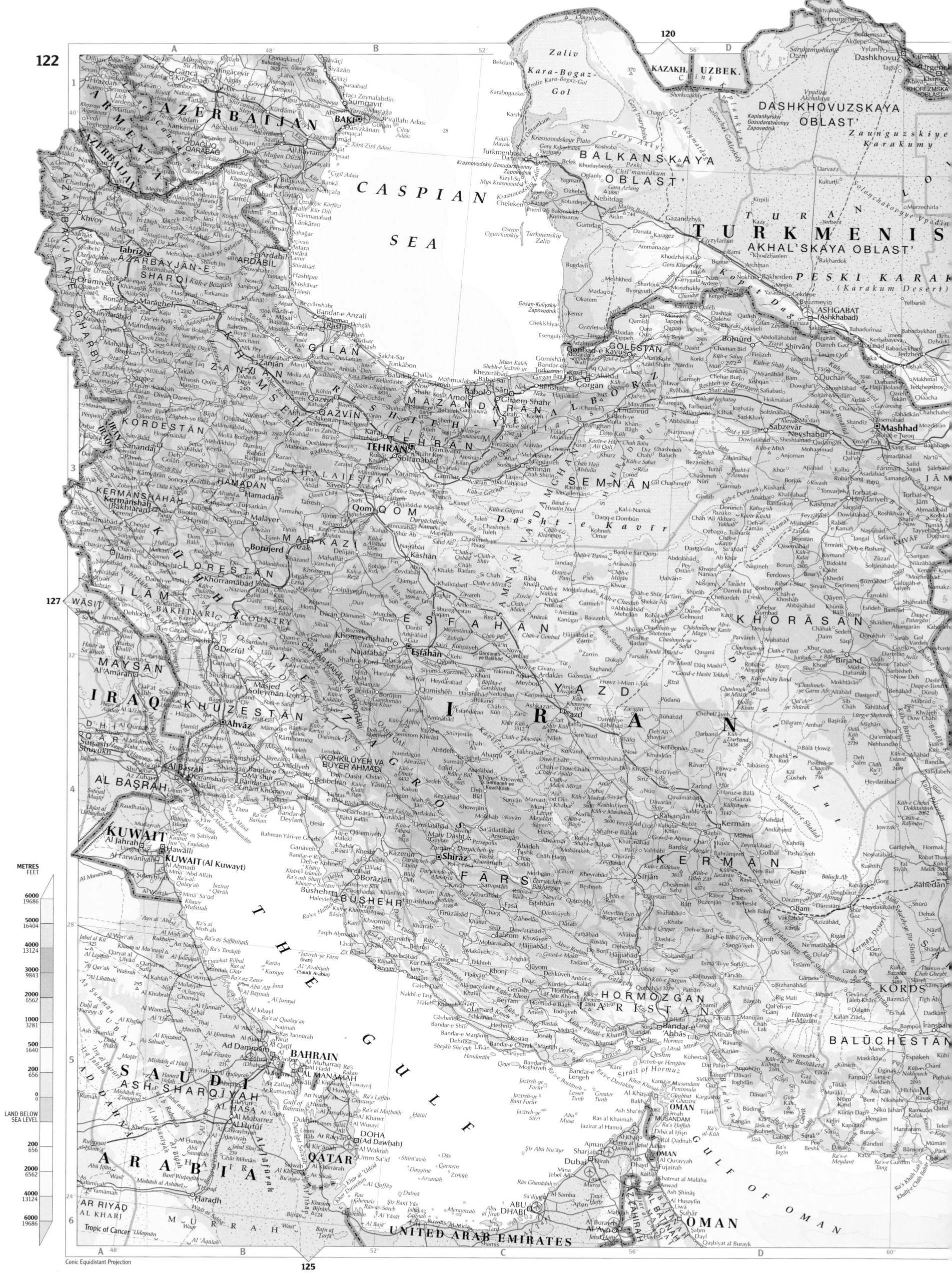
120
125
127
KAZAKH.
UZBEK.
AZERBAIJAN
ARMENIA
CASPIAN
SEA
TURKMENIS
DASHKHOVUZSKAYA OBLAST'
BALKANSKAYA OBLAST'
AKHAL'SKAYA OBLAST'
ASHGABAT (Ashkhabad)
BAKI
Tabrīz
TEHRĀN
Mashhad
Qom
Eşfahān
Yazd
Kermān
Shīrāz
Ahvāz
Zāhedān
Bandar-e 'Abbās
I R A N
IRAQ
KUWAIT
KUWAIT (Al Kuwayt)
AL BAŞRAH
MAYSĀN
WĀSIT
SAUDI ARABIA
ASH SHARQĪYAH
AR RIYĀD
BAHRAIN
AL MANĀMAH
QATAR
DOHA (Ad Dawhah)
UNITED ARAB EMIRATES
ABU DHABI
Dubai
Sharjah
OMAN
GULF OF OMAN
THE GULF
Strait of Hormuz
KHORĀSĀN
KERMĀN
FĀRS
BŪSHEHR
HORMOZGĀN
KHŪZESTĀN
SEMNĀN
MĀZANDARĀN
GOLESTĀN
GĪLĀN
ZANJĀN
QAZVĪN
HAMADĀN
KORDESTĀN
KERMĀNSHĀH
ĪLĀM
LORESTĀN
MARKAZĪ
ESFAHĀN
YAZD
BALŪCHESTĀN
Dasht-e Kavīr
Dasht-e Lūt
ZAGROS MOUNTAINS
Tropic of Cancer
METRES
FEET
6000
19686
5000
16404
4000
13124
3000
9843
2000
6562
1000
3281
500
1640
200
656
0
LAND BELOW SEA LEVEL
200
656
2000
6562
4000
13124
6000
19686
Conic Equidistant Projection

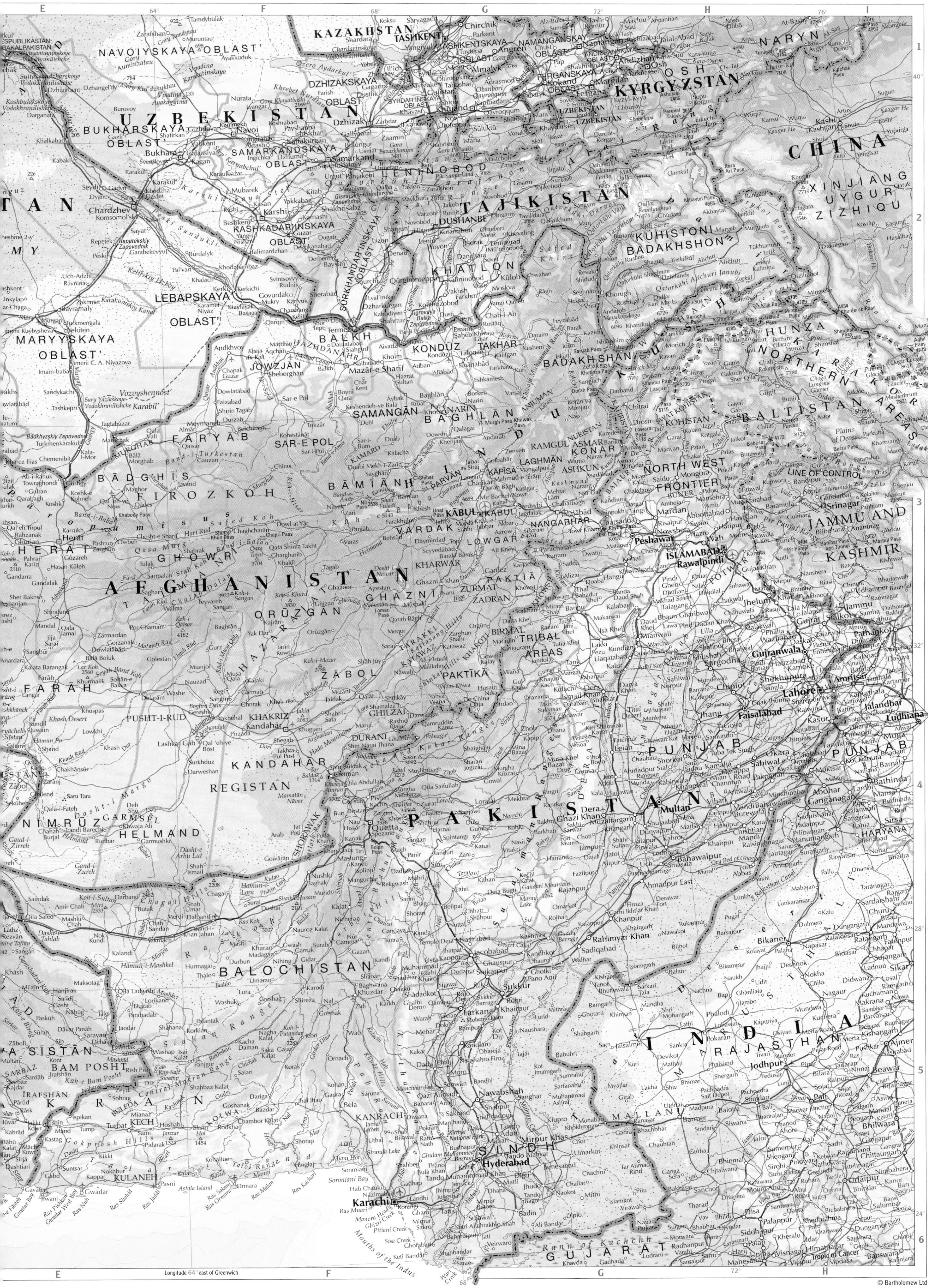

1:6 000 000

MILES / KILOMETRES

© Bartholomew Ltd

KAZAKHSTAN
UZBEKISTAN
KYRGYZSTAN
TAJIKISTAN
CHINA
XINJIANG UYGUR ZIZHIQU
AFGHANISTAN
PAKISTAN
INDIA
JAMMU AND KASHMIR
NORTHERN AREAS
NORTH WEST FRONTIER
TRIBAL AREAS
PUNJAB
SINDH
BALOCHISTAN
RAJASTHAN
HARYANA
GUJARAT
NAVOIYSKAYA OBLAST'
BUKHARSKAYA OBLAST'
SAMARKANDSKAYA OBLAST'
KASHKADAR'INSKAYA OBLAST'
LEBAPSKAYA OBLAST'
MARYYSKAYA OBLAST'
KÜHISTONI BADAKHSHON
KHATLON
BADAKHSHAN
HERAT
KANDAHAR
HELMAND
NIMRUZ
FARAH
REGISTAN
TASHKENT
DUSHANBE
KĀBUL
ISLAMABAD
Rawalpindi
Peshawar
Lahore
Karachi
Hyderabad
Multan
Quetta
Faisalabad
Srinagar
Kandahār
Herāt
Mazār-e Sharif
Samarkand
Bukhara
Kashi (Kashgar)
Jodhpur
Bikaner
Amritsar
Ludhiana
LINE OF CONTROL
Mouths of the Indus
Rann of Kachchh
Longitude 64° east of Greenwich
116

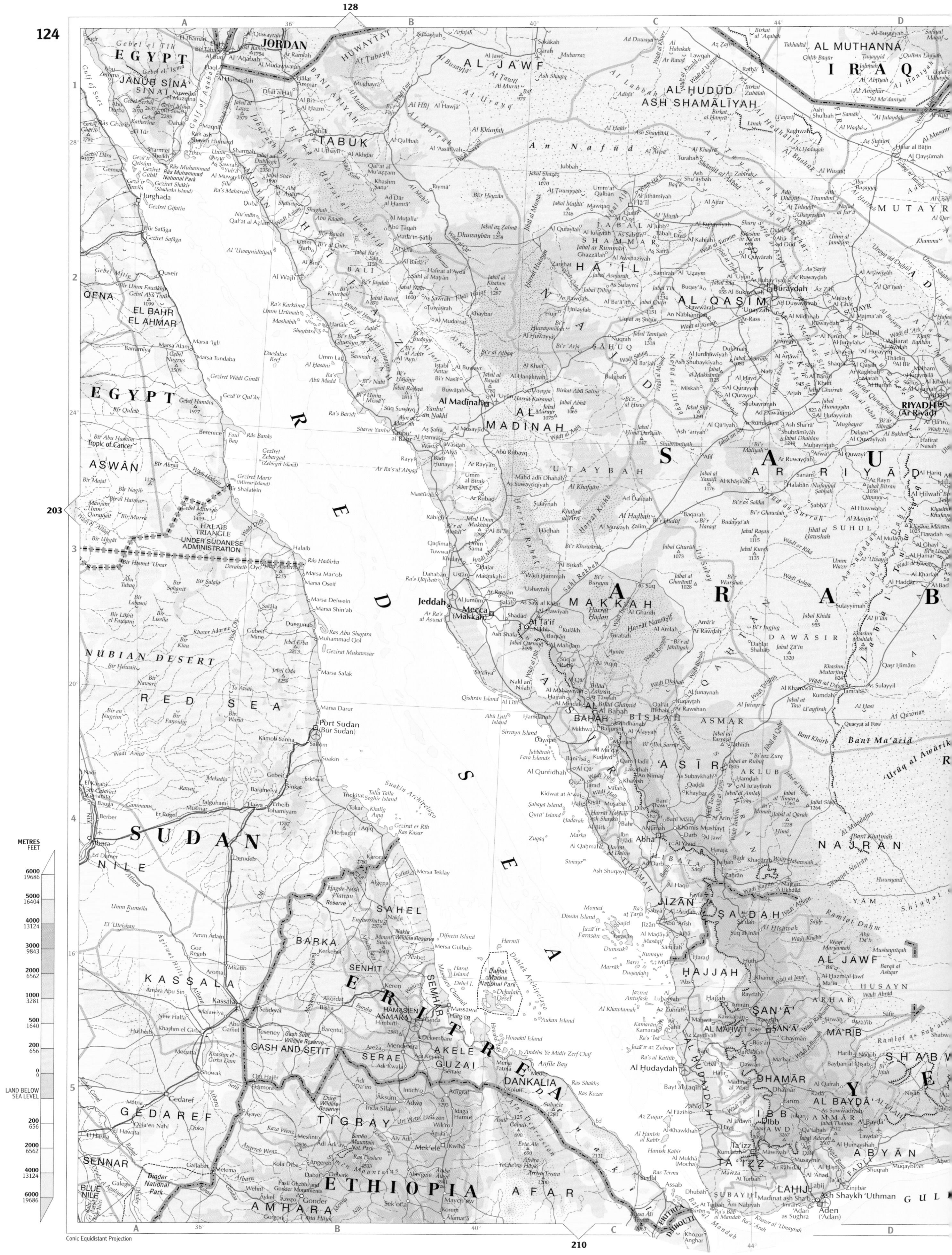

A B C D

EGYPT

JORDAN

JANŪB SĪNĀʾ
SĪNAĪ

AL JAWF

AL HUDŪD
ASH SHAMĀLIYAH

IRAQ

AL MUTHANNĀ

TABŪK

An Nafūd

HĀʾIL

MUTAYR

QENA

EL BAHR
EL AHMAR

BALI

HIJAZ

JABAL
SHAMMAR

AL QASIM

Al Madīnah

AL
MADĪNAH

ʿUTAYBAH

ʿĀNIZAH

RIYADH
(Ar Riyāḍ)

AR RIYĀD

ASWĀN

Tropic of Cancer

HALAIB
TRIANGLE
UNDER SUDANESE
ADMINISTRATION

R E D   S E A

Jeddah
Mecca
(Makkah)

MAKKAH

Aṭ Ṭāʾif

S A U D I   A R A B I A

DAWĀSIR

NUBIAN DESERT

BAHAH

BISHAH

ʿASĪR

ASMAR

Banī Maʿāriḍ

Port Sudan
(Bûr Sudan)

Suakin Archipelago

Al Qunfidhah

NAJRĀN

S U D A N

NILE

Abha

TIHĀMAH

ṢAʿDAH

AL JAWF

ERITREA

HAJJAH

HUSAYN

Jīzān

ḤAJJAH

AL
MAHWIT

ṢANʿĀʾ

MAʿRIB

KASSALA

BARKA

SENHIT

Asmara

AKELE
GUZAI

DANKALIA

Al Ḥudaydah

DHAMĀR

SHABW

GASH AND SETIT

SERAE

YEMEN

GEDAREF

TIGRAY

AL BAYDĀ

IBB

AMMĀR

SENNAR

BLUE
NILE

ETHIOPIA

AMHARA

AFAR

TAʿIZZ

LAHIJ

ABYĀN

DJIBOUTI

Aden
(ʿAdan)

GUL

METRES / FEET

6000	19686
5000	16404
4000	13124
3000	9843
2000	6562
1000	3281
500	1640
200	656
0	0

LAND BELOW
SEA LEVEL

200	656
2000	6562
4000	13124
6000	19686

Conic Equidistant Projection

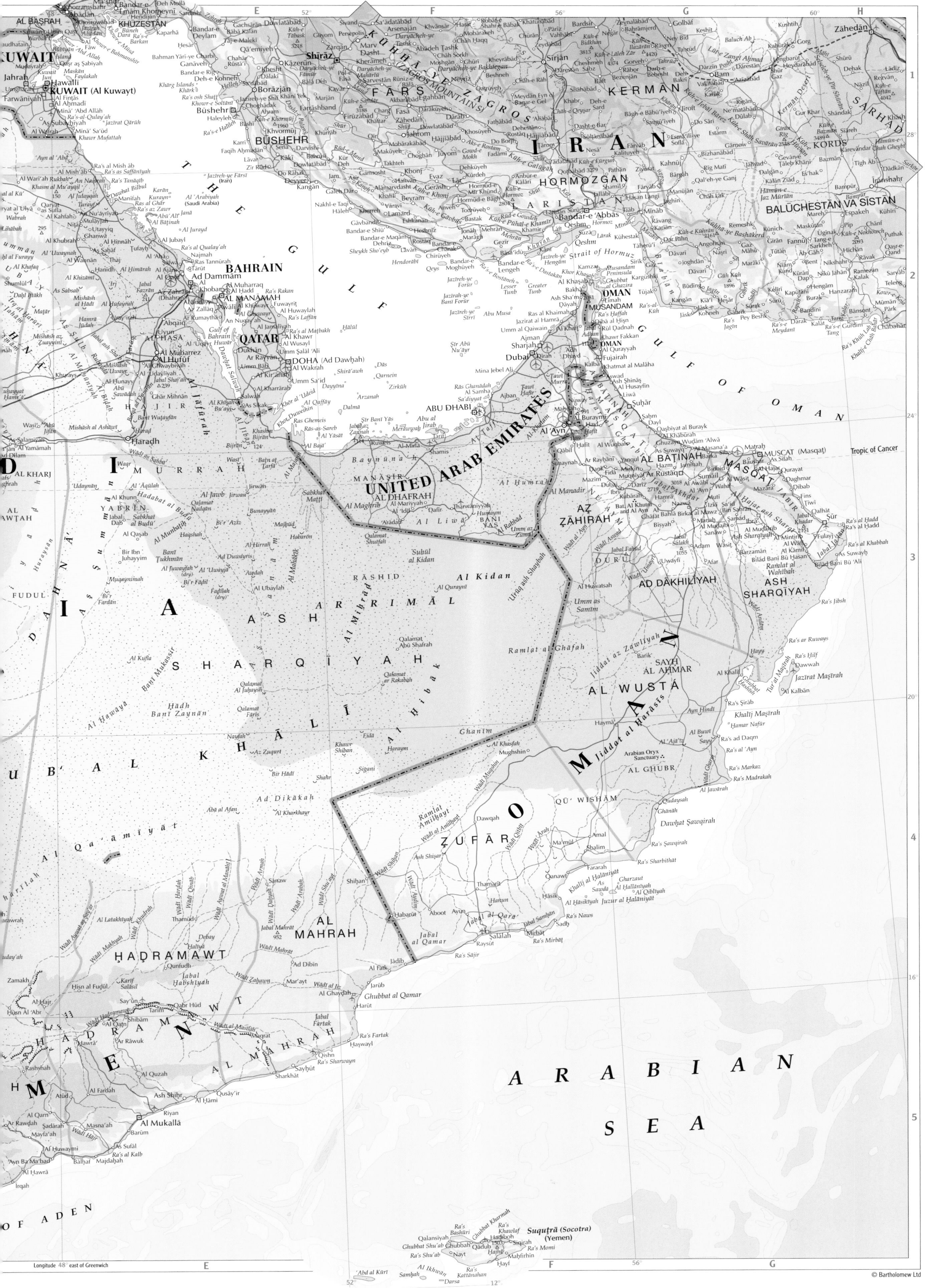
122
IRAN
KUWAIT
KUWAIT (Al Kuwayt)
BAHRAIN
AL MANAMAH
QATAR
DOHA (Ad Dawḩah)
UNITED ARAB EMIRATES
ABU DHABI
Dubai
Sharjah
OMAN
MUSANDAM
MUSCAT (Masqaţ)
AL BAŢINAH
AZ ZĀHIRAH
AD DĀKHILIYAH
ASH SHARQĪYAH
AL WUSŢÁ
ZUFĀR
AL MAHRAH
HAḐRAMAWT
FĀRS
KERMĀN
HORMOZGĀN
BŪSHEHR
KHUZESTĀN
BALŪCHESTĀN VA SĪSTĀN
AL BAŞRAH
Shīrāz
Bandar-e 'Abbās
Strait of Hormuz
THE GULF
GULF OF OMAN
ARABIAN SEA
GULF OF ADEN
AR RUB' AL KHĀLĪ
ASH SHARQĪYAH
RIMĀL
Tropic of Cancer
Al Hufūf
Ad Dammām
Al Mukallā
Şalālah
Suquţrā (Socotra) (Yemen)
Longitude 48° east of Greenwich

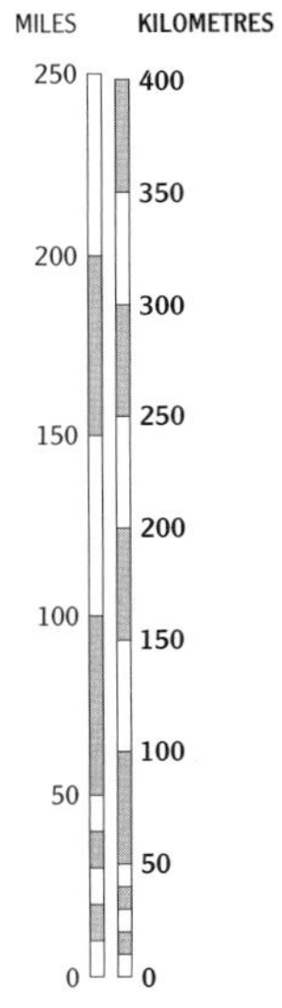
MILES
KILOMETRES
250
200
150
100
50
0
400
350
300
250
200
150
100
50
0

1:6 000 000

Major features

BLACK SEA

ROMANIA
BUCUREŞTI (Bucharest)

BULGARIA
SOFIYA

UKRAINE
Simferopol'
Sevastopol'

KRASNODARSKI
Krasnodar
Novorossiysk

GREECE
AEGEAN SEA
ATHINA (Athens)

TURKEY
ANKARA
Istanbul
Izmir (Smyrna)
Konya
Adana (Seyhan)
Gaziantep ('Aintab)

TOROS DAĞLARI (TAURUS MOUNTAINS)

ANATOLIA

PISIDIA

CYPRUS
LEFKOSIA (Nicosia)

SYRIA
Halab (Aleppo)
Hamāh
Himş

LEBANON
BEIRUT (Beyrouth)

DAMASCUS (Dimashq)

MEDITERRANEAN SEA

KRITI (CRETE)
Irakleio (Iraklion)

RODOS (RHODES)

KYKLADES (CYCLADES)

ISRAEL
Tel Aviv-Yafo (Jaffa)
JERUSALEM
GAZA

JORDAN
AMMAN

EGYPT
CAIRO (El Qâhira)
Alexandria (El Iskandarîya)
El Giza
Shubra el Kheima
Helwân
Port Said (Bûr Sa'îd)
El Mansûra

MATRÛH

SINAI

Qattâra Depression

Great Sand Sea

Libyan Plateau

Gulf of Suez

Administrative divisions numbered on the map:

RUSSIAN FEDERATION
1. CHECHENSKAYA RESPUBLIKA (G2)
2. INGUSHSKAYA RESPUBLIKA (G2)
3. RESPUBLIKA SEVERNAYA OSETIYA (G2)
4. KABARDINO-BALKARSKAYA RESPUBLIKA (F2)
5. KARACHAYEVO-CHERKESSKAYA RESPUBLIKA (F2)
6. RESPUBLIKA ADYGEYA (F1)

GEORGIA
7. AP'KHAZET'I (F2)
8. SAMKHRET' OSET'I (G2)
9. ACH'ARA (F2)

Administrative divisions numbered on the map:

EGYPT
10. EL ISKANDARÎYA (C5)
11. BEHEIRA (C5)
12. EL QÂHIRA (C5)
13. DAQAHLÎYA (C5)
14. DUMYÂT (C5)
15. GHARBÎYA (C5)
16. ISMÂ'ILÎYA (D5)
17. KAFR EL SHEIKH (C5)
18. MINÛFÎYA (C5)
19. BÛR SA'ÎD (D5)
20. QALYÛBÎYA (C5)
21. SHARQÎYA (C5)
22. EL SUWEIS (D5)

METRES / FEET
6000 / 19686
5000 / 16404
4000 / 13124
3000 / 9843
2000 / 6562
1000 / 3281
500 / 1640
200 / 656
0 / 0
LAND BELOW SEA LEVEL
200 / 656
2000 / 6562
4000 / 13124
6000 / 19686

Conic Equidistant Projection

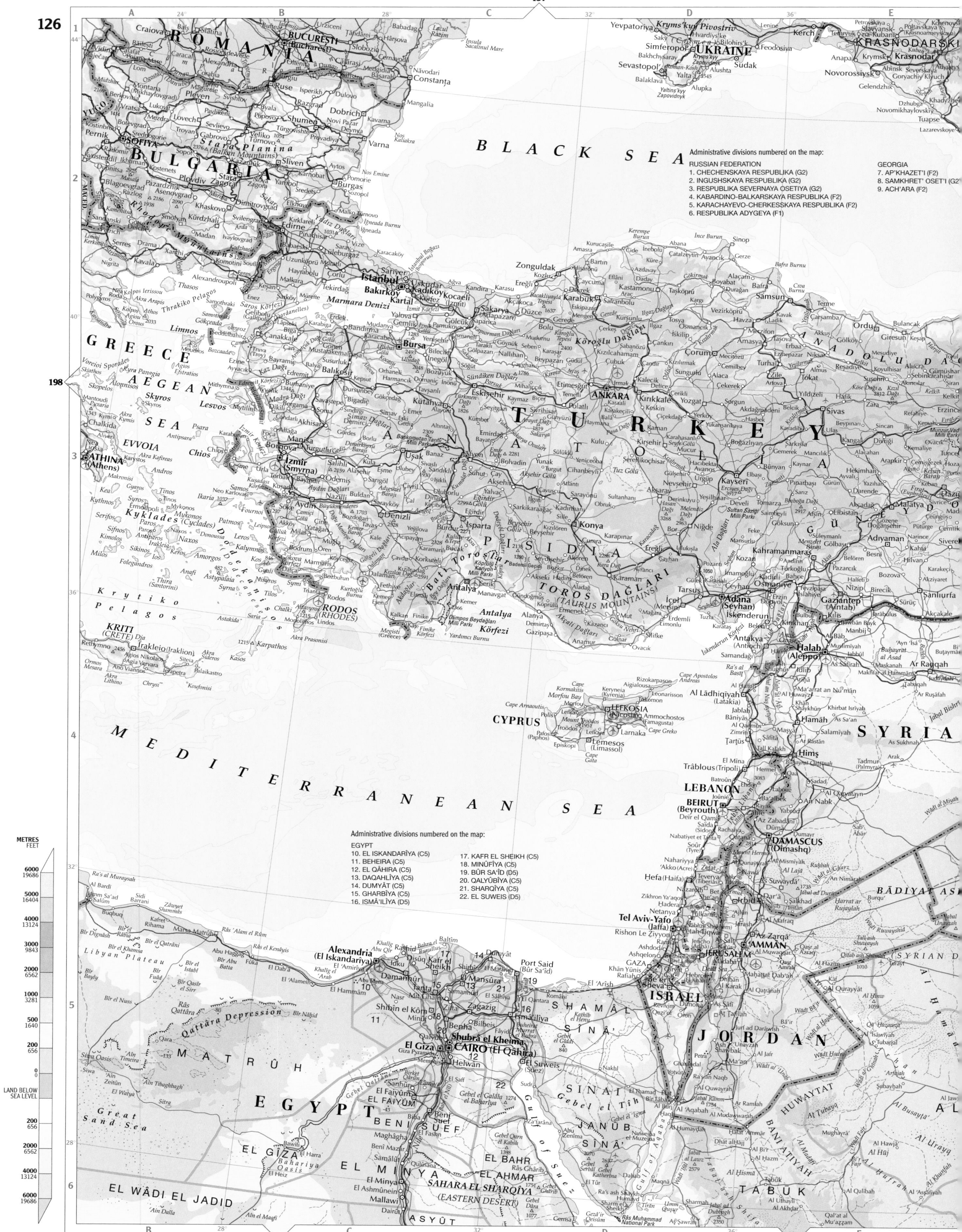

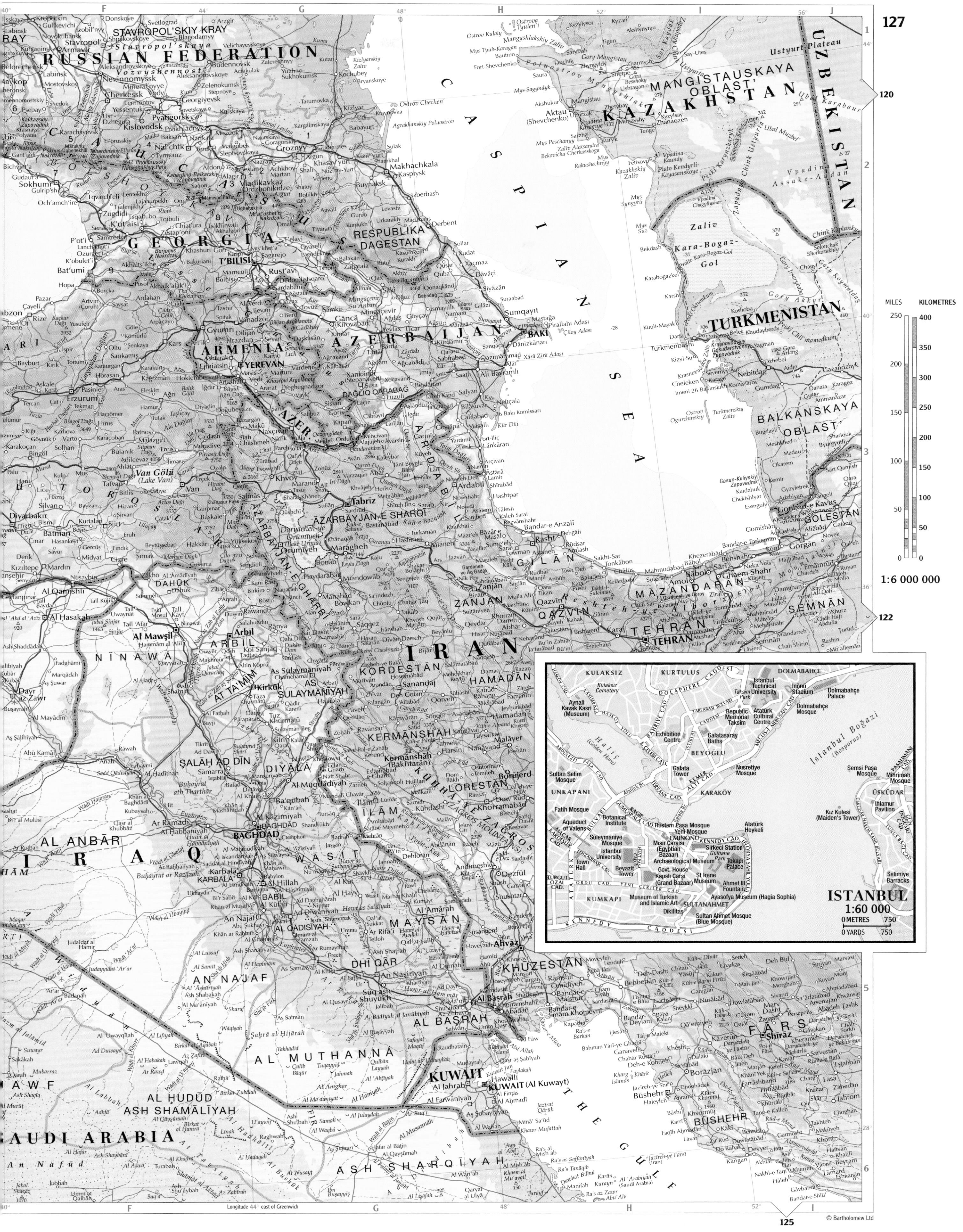

RUSSIAN FEDERATION

STAVROPOL'SKIY KRAY

KAZAKHSTAN

MANGISTAUSKAYA OBLAST'

UZBEKISTAN

GEORGIA

RESPUBLIKA DAGESTAN

ARMENIA

AZERBAIJAN

AZER.

TURKMENISTAN

BALKANSKAYA OBLAST

C A S P I A N   S E A

T'BILISI

BAKI

YEREVAN

Tabriz

ĀZARBĀYJĀN-E SHARQĪ

ĀZARBĀYJĀN-E GHARB

GĪLĀN

MĀZANDARĀN

GOLESTĀN

ZANJĀN

QAZVĪN

SEMNĀN

TEHRĀN

TEHRĀN

I R A N

KORDESTĀN

HAMADĀN

KERMĀNSHĀH

KHORĀSĀN

LORESTĀN

ĪLĀM

KHŪZESTĀN

FĀRS

BŪSHEHR

Shīrāz

Al Başrah

KUWAIT (Al Kuwayt)

KUWAIT

NĪNAWĀ

Al Mawşil

Arbil

AT TA'MĪM

Kirkūk

AS SULAYMĀNĪYAH

ŞALĀḤ AD DĪN

DIYĀLĀ

BAGHDAD

I R A Q

AL ANBĀR

WĀSIŢ

KARBALĀ

BĀBIL

AN NAJAF

AL QĀDISĪYAH

MAYSĀN

DHĪ QĀR

AL MUTHANNĀ

SAUDI ARABIA

AL ḤUDŪD ASH SHAMĀLĪYAH

ASH SHARQĪYAH

T H E   G U L F

MILES   KILOMETRES

250   400

1:6 000 000

ISTANBUL
1:60 000

KULAKSIZ   **KURTULUS**   **DOLMABAHCE**

BEYOĞLU

KARAKÖY

UNKAPANI

ÜSKÜDAR

EMINÖNÜ

KUMKAPI

SULTANAHMET

Galata Tower

Aynalı Kavak Kasrı (Museum)

Istanbul Technical University

İnönü Stadium

Dolmabahçe Palace

Dolmabahçe Mosque

Galatasaray Baths

Nusretiye Mosque

Şemsi Paşa Mosque

Mihrimah Mosque

Kız Kulesi (Maiden's Tower)

İhlamur Pavilion

Fatih Mosque

Aqueduct of Valens

Botanical Institute

Süleymaniye Mosque

Istanbul University

Town Hall

Beyazit Tower

Govt. House

Mısır Çarşısı (Egyptian Bazaar)

Kapalı Çarşı (Grand Bazaar)

Museum of Turkish and Islamic Art

Dikilitaş

Sultan Ahmet Mosque (Blue Mosque)

Sirkeci Station

Topkapi Palace

St Irene Museum

Ahmet III Fountain

Ayasofya Museum (Hagia Sophia)

Selimiye Barracks

Atatürk Heykeli

Yeni Mosque

Rüstem Paşa Mosque

Archaeological Museum

Istanbul Boğazi (Bosporus)

Halic (Golden Horn)

0 METRES 750

0 YARDS 750

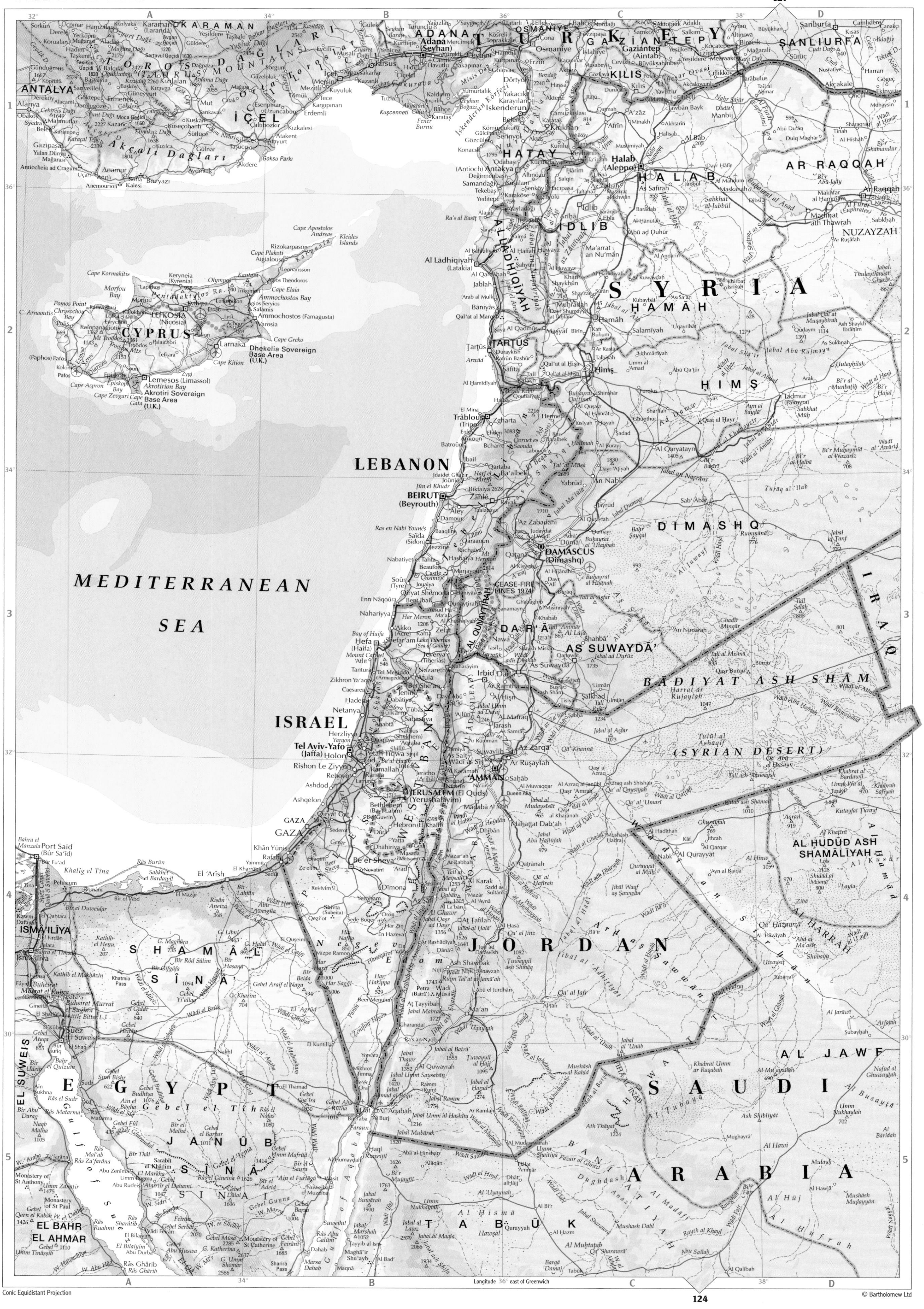

TURKEY

KARAMAN
ADANA
GAZİANTEP
ŞANLIURFA
İÇEL
ANTALYA
HATAY
KILIS
AR RAQQAH

Adana (Seyhan)
Antakya (Antioch)
Gaziantep (Aintab)
İskenderun
Halab (Aleppo)
Ar Raqqah

TOROS DAĞLARI
TAURUS MOUNTAINS

SYRIA

HALAB
IDLIB
HAMĀH
HIMŞ
DIMASHQ
DARʻĀ
AS SUWAYDĀʼ

Al Lādhiqīyah (Latakia)
TARTŪS
Ḥimş
Ḥamāh
DAMASCUS (Dimashq)

CYPRUS

LEFKOŞA (Nicosia)
Larnaka
Lemesos (Limassol)
Akrotiri Sovereign Base Area (U.K.)
Dhekelia Sovereign Base Area (U.K.)

MEDITERRANEAN SEA

LEBANON

BEIRUT (Beyrouth)
Trâblous (Tripoli)
Saïda (Sidon)
Sûr (Tyre)

ISRAEL

Tel Aviv-Yafo (Jaffa)
Hefa (Haifa)
Nazareth
JERUSALEM (El Quds / Yerushalayim)
Bethlehem
Hebron
Ashdod
Ashqelon

WEST BANK
GAZA

Lake Tiberias (Sea of Galilee)

CEASE-FIRE LINES 1974
AL QUNAYTIRAH

JORDAN

AMMAN
Az Zarqaʼ
Irbid
Al Karak
Maʻān
Petra Wâdi (Batra)

AL HUDŪD ASH SHAMĀLIYAH

IRAQ

BADIYAT ASH SHĀM
(SYRIAN DESERT)

EGYPT

SHAMĀL SĪNĀʼ
JANŪB SĪNĀʼ
Port Said (Bûr Saʻîd)
ISMAʻĪLĪYA
EL SUWEIS (Suez)
El ʻArîsh
El Bahr El Ahmar

Monastery of St Anthony
Monastery of St Catherine
Monastery of St Paul

SAUDI ARABIA

AL JAWF
TABŪK

Al ʻAqabah

Gulf of Suez
Gulf of Aqaba

1:3 000 000

Conic Equidistant Projection

Longitude 36° east of Greenwich

© Bartholomew Ltd

METRES / FEET
6000 / 19686
5000 / 16404
4000 / 13124
3000 / 9843
2000 / 6562
1500 / 4921
1000 / 3281
500 / 1640
200 / 656
100 / 328
0 / 0
LAND BELOW SEA LEVEL
200 / 164
1000 / 656
2000 / 3281

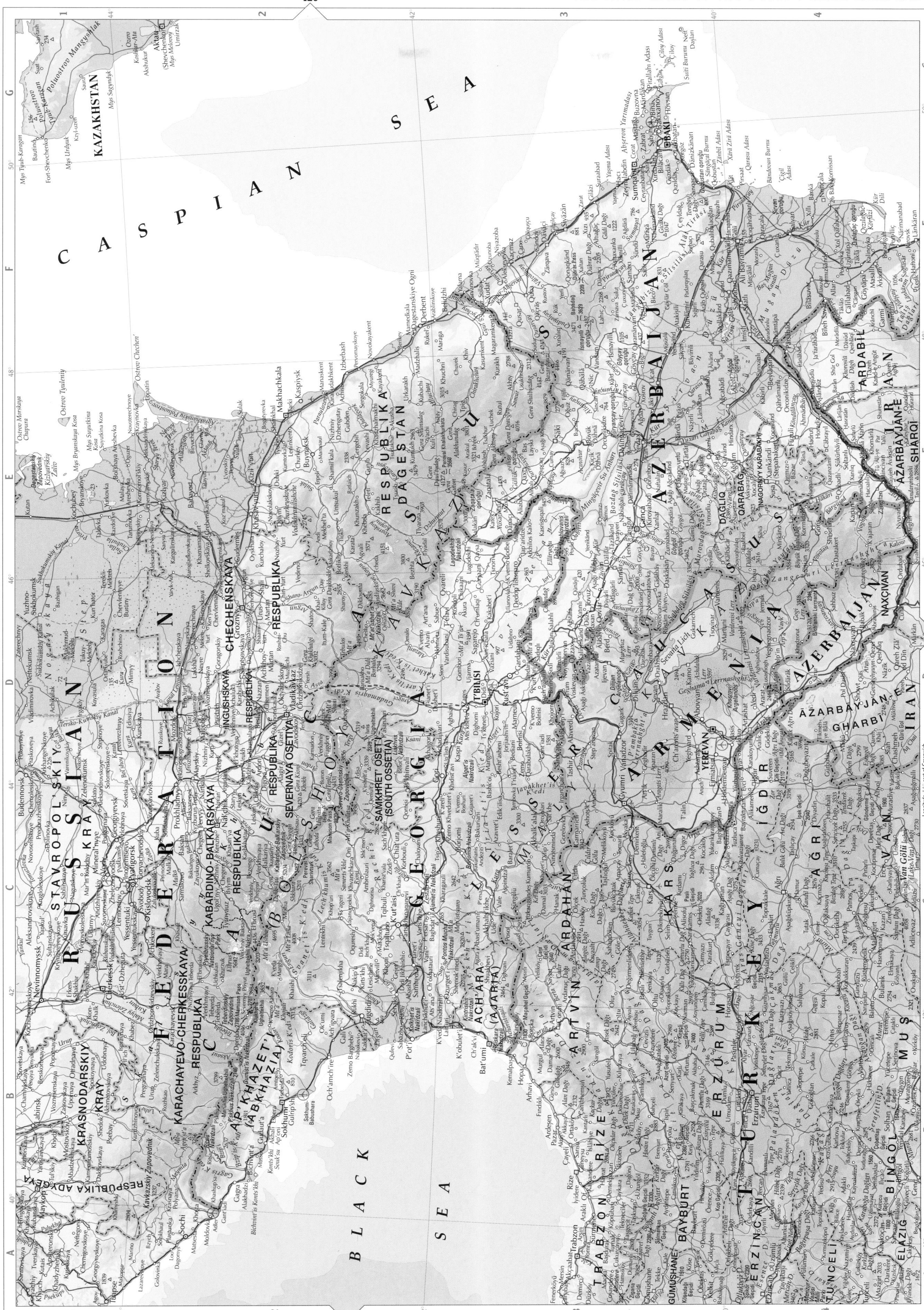

CASPIAN SEA

BLACK SEA

KAZAKHSTAN

RUSSIAN FEDERATION

STAVROPOL'SKIY KRAY

KRASNODARSKIY KRAY

RESPUBLIKA ADYGEYA

KARACHAYEVO-CHERKESSKAYA RESPUBLIKA

KABARDINO-BALKARSKAYA RESPUBLIKA

RESPUBLIKA SEVERNAYA OSETIYA

INGUSHSKAYA RESPUBLIKA

CHECHENSKAYA RESPUBLIKA

RESPUBLIKA DAGESTAN

SAMKHRET OSETI (SOUTH OSSETIA)

AP. KHAZET' (ABKHAZIYA)

GEORGIA

ACH'ARA (AJARIA)

K A V K A Z

B O L S H O Y   K A V K A Z

M A L Y Y   K A V K A Z

L E S S E R   C A U C A S U S

TBILISI

ARMENIA

YEREVAN

AZERBAIJAN

AZƏRBAYCAN

BAKI

SUMQAYIT

NAXÇIVAN

DAĞLIQ QARABAĞ / NAGORNY KARABAKH

IRAN

AZARBAYJAN-E SHARQI

AZARBAYJAN-E GHARBI

ARDABIL

TURKEY

ERZURUM

KARS

ARDAHAN

ARTVIN

RIZE

TRABZON

GÜMÜSHANE

BAYBURT

ERZINCAN

TUNCELI

BINGÖL

MUŞ

VAN

AĞRI

IĞDIR

ELAZIĞ

Longitude 44 east of Greenwich

Conic Equidistant Projection

© Bartholomew Ltd

1:3 000 000

MILES   KILOMETRES
125   200
100   175
75   150
50   125
25   100
         75
         50
         25
0   0

120
126
127

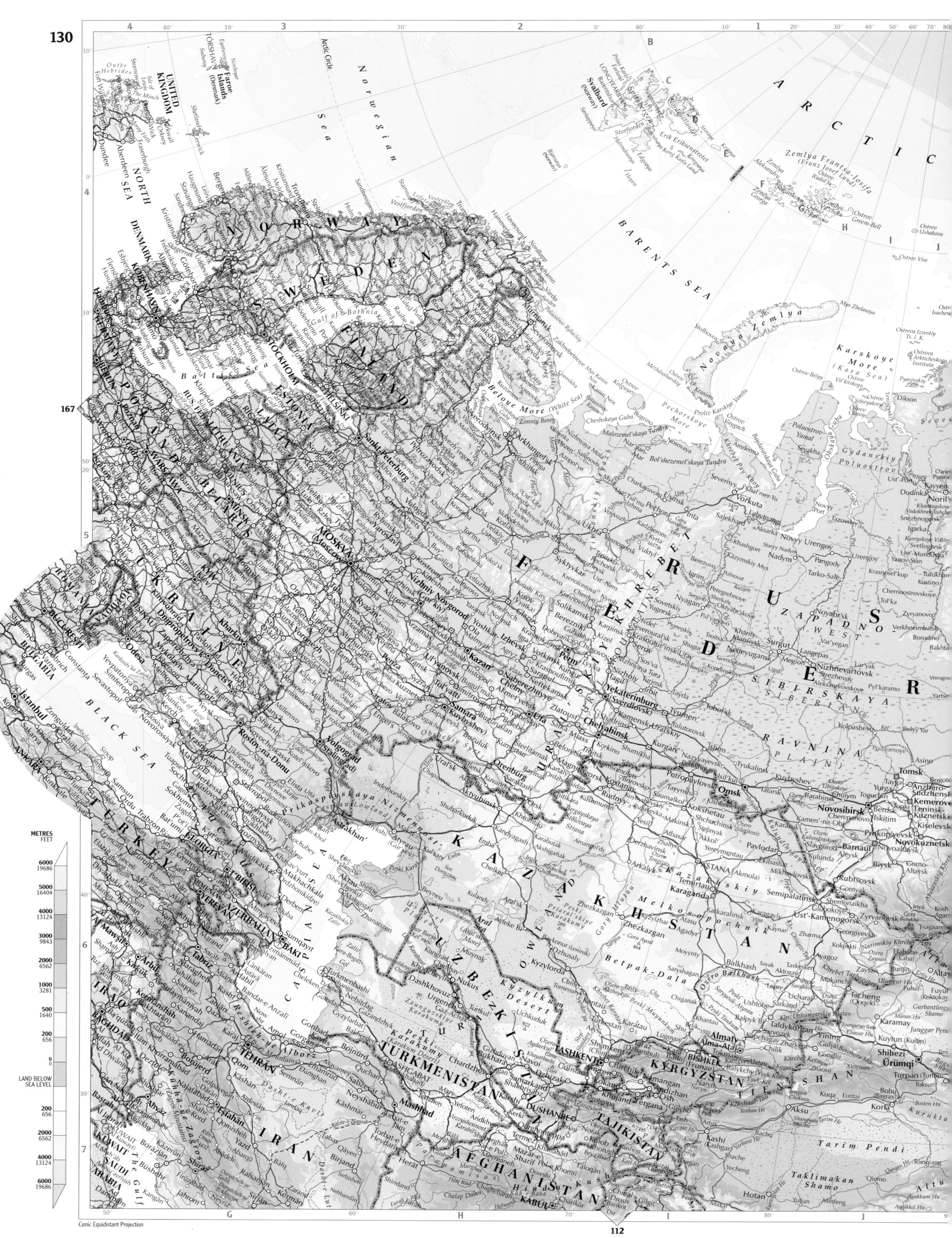
METRES
FEET
6000
19686
5000
16404
4000
13124
3000
9843
2000
6562
1000
3281
500
1640
200
656
0
0
LAND BELOW SEA LEVEL
200
656
2000
6562
4000
13124
6000
19686
ARCTIC
BARENTS SEA
Norwegian Sea
NORTH SEA
Arctic Circle
Svalbard (Norway)
Zemlya Frantsa-Iosifa (Franz Josef Land)
Novaya Zemlya
Karskoye More (Kara Sea)
Pechorskoye More
Beloye More (White Sea)
Baltic Sea
Gulf of Bothnia
NORWAY
SWEDEN
FINLAND
DENMARK
UNITED KINGDOM
Faroe Islands (Denmark)
ESTONIA
LATVIA
LITHUANIA
POLAND
BELARUS
UKRAINE
MOLDOVA
ROMANIA
BULGARIA
TURKEY
GEORGIA
ARMENIA
AZERBAIJAN
IRAQ
IRAN
KUWAIT
SAUDI ARABIA
TURKMENISTAN
UZBEKISTAN
KAZAKHSTAN
KYRGYZSTAN
TAJIKISTAN
AFGHANISTAN
RUSSIAN FEDERATION
BLACK SEA
CASPIAN SEA
Sea of Azov
Aral Sea
The Gulf
STOCKHOLM
HELSINKI
Sankt-Peterburg
MOSKVA (Moscow)
MINSK
KYIV
WARSZAWA
BUCUREȘTI
CHIȘINĂU
ANKARA
İstanbul
TBILISI
YEREVAN
BAKI
TEHRAN
BAGHDAD
KABUL
TASHKENT
DUSHANBE
BISHKEK
ASTANA (Akmola)
Almaty (Alma-Ata)
Novosibirsk
Omsk
Yekaterinburg (Sverdlovsk)
Chelyabinsk
Volgograd (Stalingrad)
Rostov-na-Donu
Samara (Kuybyshev)
Nizhniy Novgorod (Gor'kiy)
Kazan'
Perm'
Ufa
Arkhangel'sk
Murmansk
Ürümqi
Zapadno-Sibirskaya Ravnina (West Siberian Plain)
Kazakhskiy Melkosopochnik
Prikaspiyskaya Nizmennost' (Caspian Lowland)
Kyzylkum Desert
Karakumy
Tien Shan
Tarim Pendi
Taklimakan Shamo
Betpak-Dala
Ural'skiy Khrebet
Poluostrov Yamal
Gydanskiy Poluostrov
167
112

Conic Equidistant Projection

112

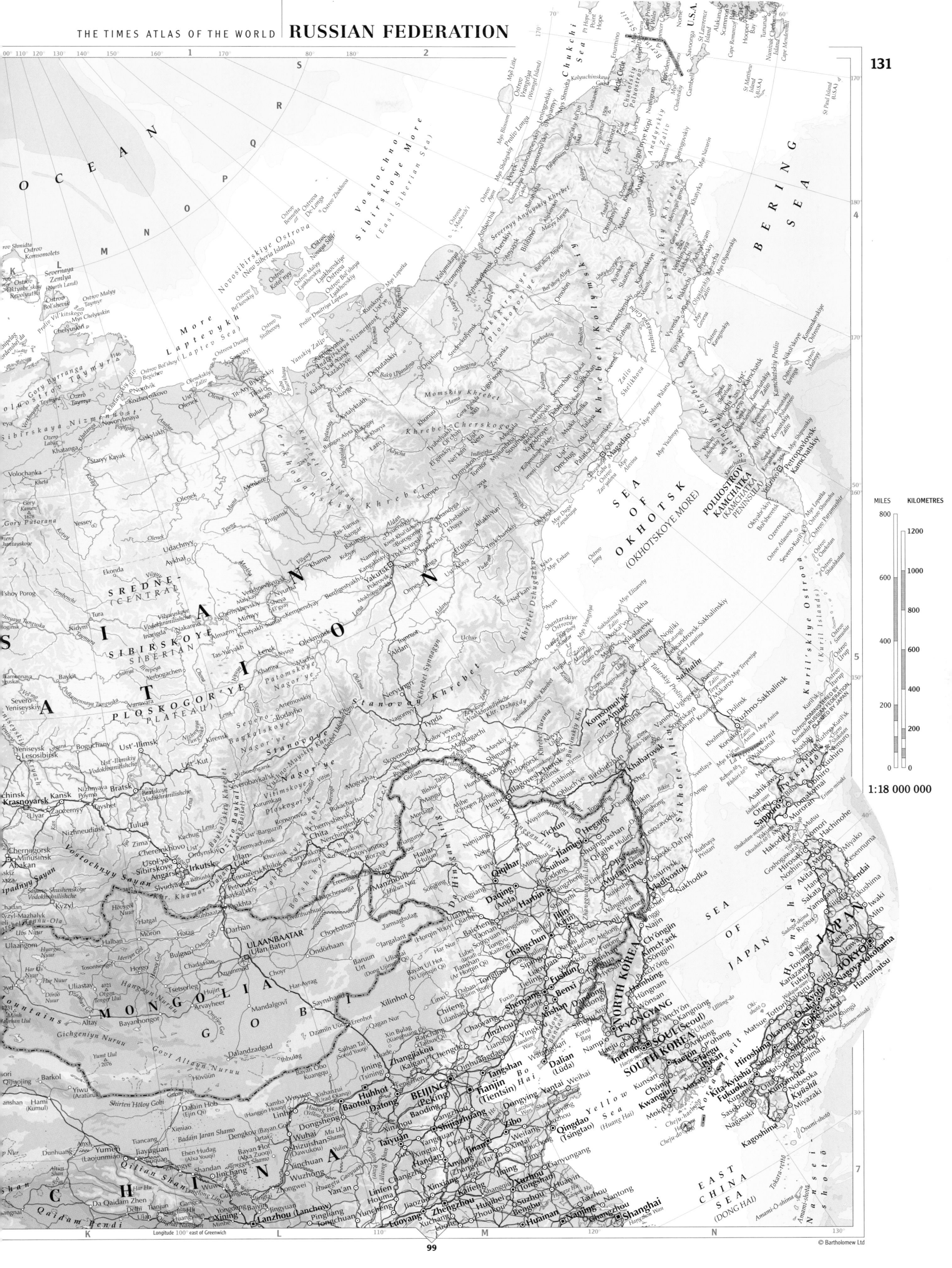
SEA OF OKHOTSK (OKHOTSKOYE MORE)
BERING SEA
SEA OF JAPAN
EAST CHINA SEA (DONG HAI)
Yellow Sea (Huang Hai)
Bo Hai
More Laptevykh (Laptev Sea)
Vostochno-Sibirskoye More (East Siberian Sea)
Chukchi Sea
Novosibirskiye Ostrova (New Siberia Islands)
Severnaya Zemlya (North Land)
SREDNE-SIBIRSKOYE PLOSKOGOR'YE (CENTRAL SIBERIAN PLATEAU)
POLUOSTROV KAMCHATKA (KAMCHATKA PENINSULA)
Kuril'skiye Ostrova (Kuril Islands)
Khrebet Cherskogo
Verkhoyanskiy Khrebet
Stanovoy Khrebet
Khrebet Kolymskiy
MONGOLIA
GOBI
CHINA
NORTH KOREA
SOUTH KOREA
JAPAN
U.S.A.
Yakutsk
Magadan
Khabarovsk
Vladivostok
Irkutsk
Krasnoyarsk
Chita
Petropavlovsk-Kamchatskiy
Yuzhno-Sakhalinsk
Sakhalin
Hokkaido
Honshu
Kyushu
Sapporo
Sendai
TOKYO
Yokohama
Nagoya
Kyoto
Osaka
Kobe
Hiroshima
Fukuoka
Kagoshima
ULAANBAATAR (Ulan Bator)
BEIJING (Peking)
Tianjin (Tientsin)
Shenyang
Harbin
Changchun
Dalian (Lüda)
Qingdao (Tsingtao)
Shanghai
Nanjing
Zhengzhou
Lanzhou (Lanchow)
Xining
Taiyuan
Shijiazhuang
Baotou
Hohhot
Datong
Jinan
Qiqihar
PYONGYANG
SOUL (Seoul)
Pusan
Taegu
Taejon
Kwangju
Komsomol'sk-na-Amure
Blagoveshchensk
Bratsk
Anadyr'
Norilsk
1:18 000 000
MILES
KILOMETRES
Longitude 100° east of Greenwich

NORTH AMERICA

Baffin Bay

Greenland

Arctic Circle

Greenland Sea

Nordaustlandet

Spitsbergen

Longyearbyen

Svalbard (Norway)

Zemlja Frantsa-Iosifa

BARENTS SEA

Bjørnøya (Norway)

Jan Mayen (Norway)

Denmark Strait

ICELAND

Reykjavík

NORWEGIAN SEA

Nordkapp

N O R W A Y

Trondheim

Faroe Islands (Denmark)

Tórshavn

Shetland Islands

Bergen

Oslo

S W E D E N

Gulf of Bothnia

Vänern

Göteborg

Stockholm

Vättern

Orkney Islands

Outer Hebrides

SCOTLAND

Glasgow Edinburgh

NORTHERN IRELAND

Belfast

Dublin

REPUBLIC OF IRELAND

UNITED KINGDOM

Manchester Leeds

Liverpool

WALES

Birmingham

Cardiff

ENGLAND

London

Skagerrak *Kattegat*

Ålborg

D E N M A R K

København Malmö

Odense

Bornholm

N O R T H

S E A

Hamburg

NETHERLANDS

Amsterdam

's-Gravenhage

Rotterdam

Bremen

Hannover

Bielefeld

Essen

Berlin

G E R M A N Y

Leipzig

Bruxelles

Aachen Düsseldorf

Köln

Bonn

BELGIUM

Lille

Frankfurt am Main

Nürnberg

LUXEMBOURG

Luxembourg

Mannheim

Stuttgart

English Channel

Channel Islands

Brest

Paris

Rennes

Orléans

Loire

Dijon

Strasbourg

München

Zürich LIECHTEN-STEIN

Bern Innsbruck

SWITZERLAND

A T L A N T I C

O C E A N

Nantes

F R A N C E

Genève

Lyon

Milano

Bay of Biscay

Bordeaux

Torino

Genova

MONACO

Nice

Toulouse

Marseille

Corse

A Coruña

Bilbao

Pyrenees

Andorra la Vella **ANDORRA**

Ebro

Corvo

Flores

Arquipélago dos Açores

São Jorge

Faial *Terceira*

Pico

Azores (Portugal)

São Miguel

Ponta Delgada

Santa Maria

Porto

Salamanca

Zaragoza

Barcelona

Madrid

Tajo

S P A I N

Valencia

Islas Baleares

Menorca

Sardegna

Mallorca

Eivissa

Lisboa

P O R T U G A L

Córdoba

Cartagena

M E D

Sevilla

Málaga

Cádiz

Gibraltar (U.K.)

Ceuta (Spain)

Melilla (Spain)

Arquipélago da Madeira

Madeira (Portugal)

Ilha de Porto Santo

Funchal

A

F

RUSSIAN FEDERATION

A S I A

Karskoye More

Novaya Zemlya

Ostrov Kolguyev

Arctic Circle

Yenisey

Vorkuta

Ural'skiy Khrebet (Ural Mountains)

Ob'

Pechora

Urals

Atau Mountains

Murmansk

Beloye More

Arkhangel'sk

Severnaya Dvina

Petrozavodsk

Onezhskoye Ozero

Syktyvkar

Kirov

Perm'

Izhevsk

Naberezhnyye Chelny

Ufa

Ozero Balkhash

FINLAND

Tampere

Turku

Helsinki

Sankt-Peterburg

Ladozhskoye Ozero

Vologda

Rybinskoye Vodokhranilishche

Yaroslavl'

Nizhniy Novgorod

Moskva

Kazan'

Samara

Orenburg

Ysyk

ESTONIA

Tallinn

Lake Peipus

Smolensk

Tula

Ul'yanovsk

Penza

Saratov

Aral Sea

Aral'sk

Baltic Sea

Gotland

LATVIA

Riga

Voronezh

Belgorod

Don

Volgograd

Volga

Astrakhan'

Caspian Sea

LITHUANIA

Vilnius

Vitsyebsk

Mahilyow

Chernihiv

Sumy

Kharkiv

Rostov-na-Donu

Zaliv Kara-Bogaz-Gol

Kaliningrad RUS. FED.

Minsk

Homyel'

Kyiv

Donets'k

Dnipropetrovs'k

Hindu Kush

Gdańsk

Hrodna

BELARUS

Brest

U K R A I N E

Stavropol'

Elbrus

Groznyy

Bydgoszcz

Białystok

Rivne

Kirovohrad

Krasnodar

Caucasus

Warszawa

P O L A N D

Wisła

L'viv

Dnister (Dniester)

Mykolayiv

Novorossiysk

Poznań

Łódź

Odra

Wrocław

Katowice

Kraków

MOLDOVA

Iaşi

Chişinău

Odesa

Dnipro (Dnieper)

Sea of Azov

Simferopol'

Black Sea

Praha

CZECH REPUBLIC

Brno

SLOVAKIA

Košice

Carpathian Mountains

R O M A N I A

Danube

Wien

Bratislava

Budapest

Debrecen

Oradea

Brašov

AUSTRIA

HUNGARY

Szeged

Timişoara

Bucureşti

Craiova

Salzburg

SLOVENIA

Ljubljana

Trieste

Zagreb

CROATIA

Pleven

Varna

Venezia

Beograd

BOSNIA-HERZEGOVINA

Sarajevo

Niš

Burgas

SAN MARINO

Split

YUGOSLAVIA

Podgorica

BULGARIA

Sofiya

Edirne

İstanbul

Marmara Denizi

Bologna

Firenze

Adriatic Sea

Skopje

MACEDONIA

Tiranë

ALBANIA

Thessaloniki

T U R K E Y

I T A L Y

VATICAN CITY

Roma

Napoli

Bari

Aegean Sea

Larisa

G R E E C E

Al Furat (Euphrates)

Nahr Dijlah (Tigris)

Zagros Mountains

Kuhha-ye Zagros

Tyrrhenian Sea

Cosenza

Ionian Sea

Athina

Dodekanisos

Rodos

Palermo

Messina

Sicilia

Siracusa

Cyprus

The Gulf

Kriti

MALTA

Valletta

M E D I T E R R A N E A N S E A

A F R I C A

A S I A

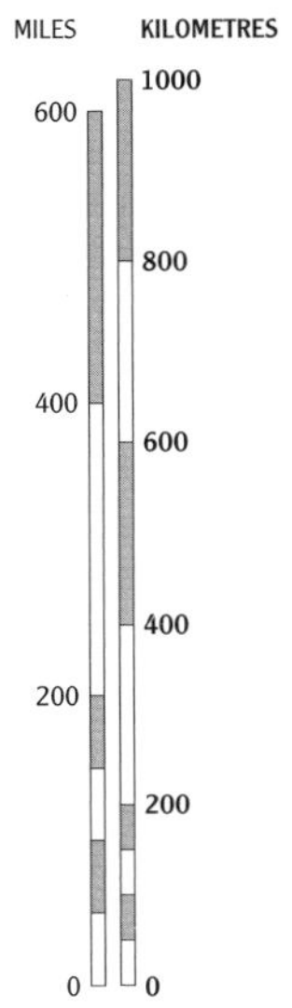

MILES KILOMETRES

600 — 1000
     — 800
400 — 600
     — 400
200 — 200
0 — 0

1:15 000 000

© Bartholomew Ltd

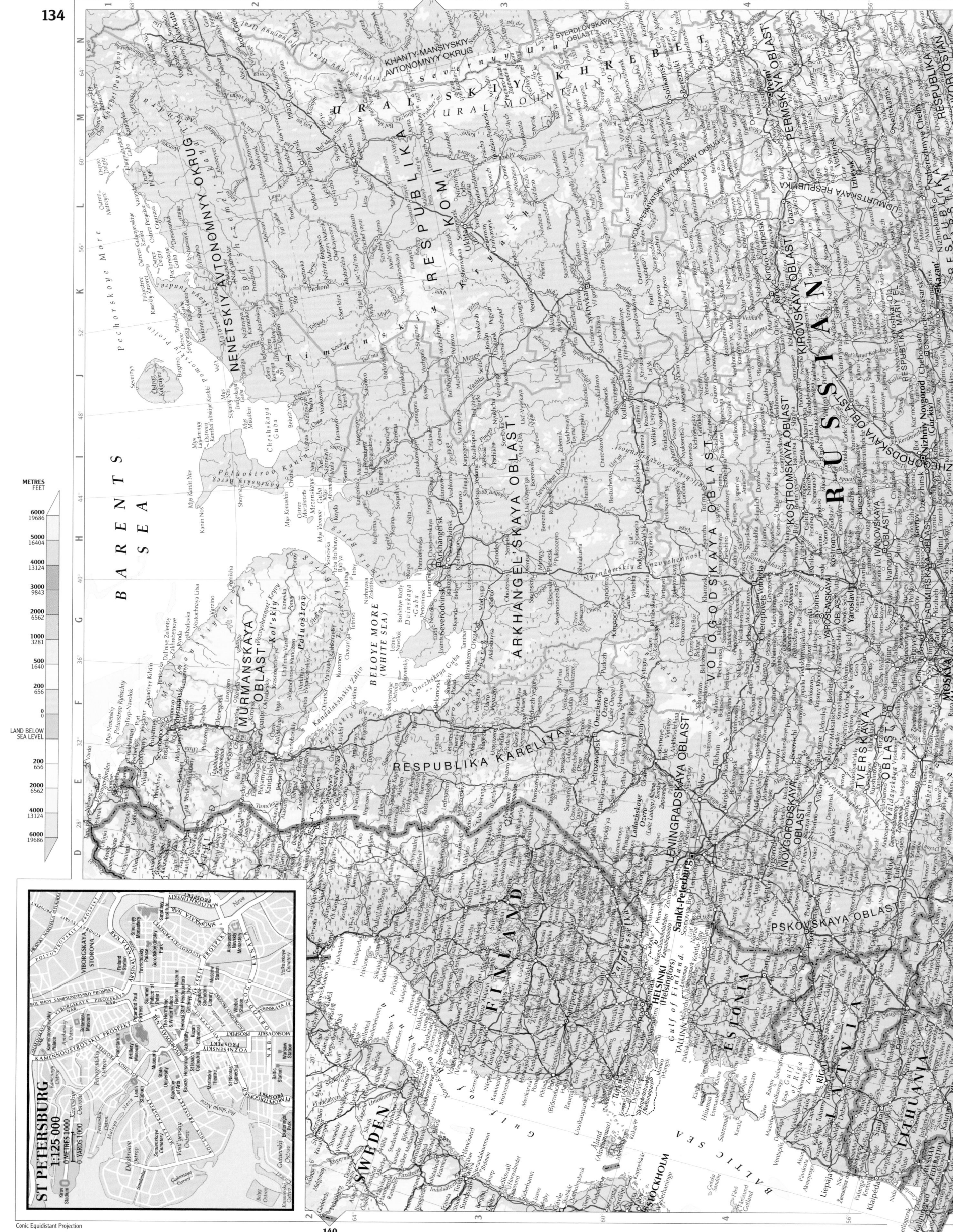

METRES
FEET

6000
19686

5000
16404

4000
13124

3000
9843

2000
6562

1000
3281

500
1640

200
656

0
0

LAND BELOW
SEA LEVEL

200
656

2000
6562

4000
13124

6000
19686

Conic Equidistant Projection

B A R E N T S   S E A

NENETSKIY AVTONOMNYY OKRUG

RESPUBLIKA KOMI

URAL MOUNTAINS

URAL'SKIY KHREBET

KHANTY-MANSIYSKIY
AVTONOMNYY OKRUG

SVERDLOVSKAYA
OBLAST'

PERMSKAYA OBLAST'

UDMURTSKAYA RESPUBLIKA

KIROVSKAYA OBLAST'

RESPUBLIKA TATARSTAN

R U S S I A

ARKHANGEL'SKAYA OBLAST'

VOLOGODSKAYA OBLAST'

KOSTROMSKAYA OBLAST'

IVANOVSKAYA
OBLAST'

VLADIMIRSKAYA
OBLAST'

MOSKVA

MURMANSKAYA
OBLAST'

Kol'skiy Poluostrov

BELOYE MORE
(WHITE SEA)

RESPUBLIKA KARELIYA

LENINGRADSKAYA OBLAST'

Sankt-Peterburg

TVERSKAYA OBLAST'

NOVGORODSKAYA
OBLAST'

PSKOVSKAYA OBLAST'

FINLAND

HELSINKI
(Helsingfors)

Gulf of Finland

TALLINN

ESTONIA

LATVIA

RIGA

LITHUANIA

SWEDEN

STOCKHOLM

B A L T I C   S E A

Gulf of Riga

ST PETERSBURG
1:125 000

Nizhniy Novgorod

Kazan'

NIZHEGORODSKAYA OBLAST'

122

126

MILES   KILOMETRES

300   500

400

200   300

200
100
100

0   0

1:7 200 000

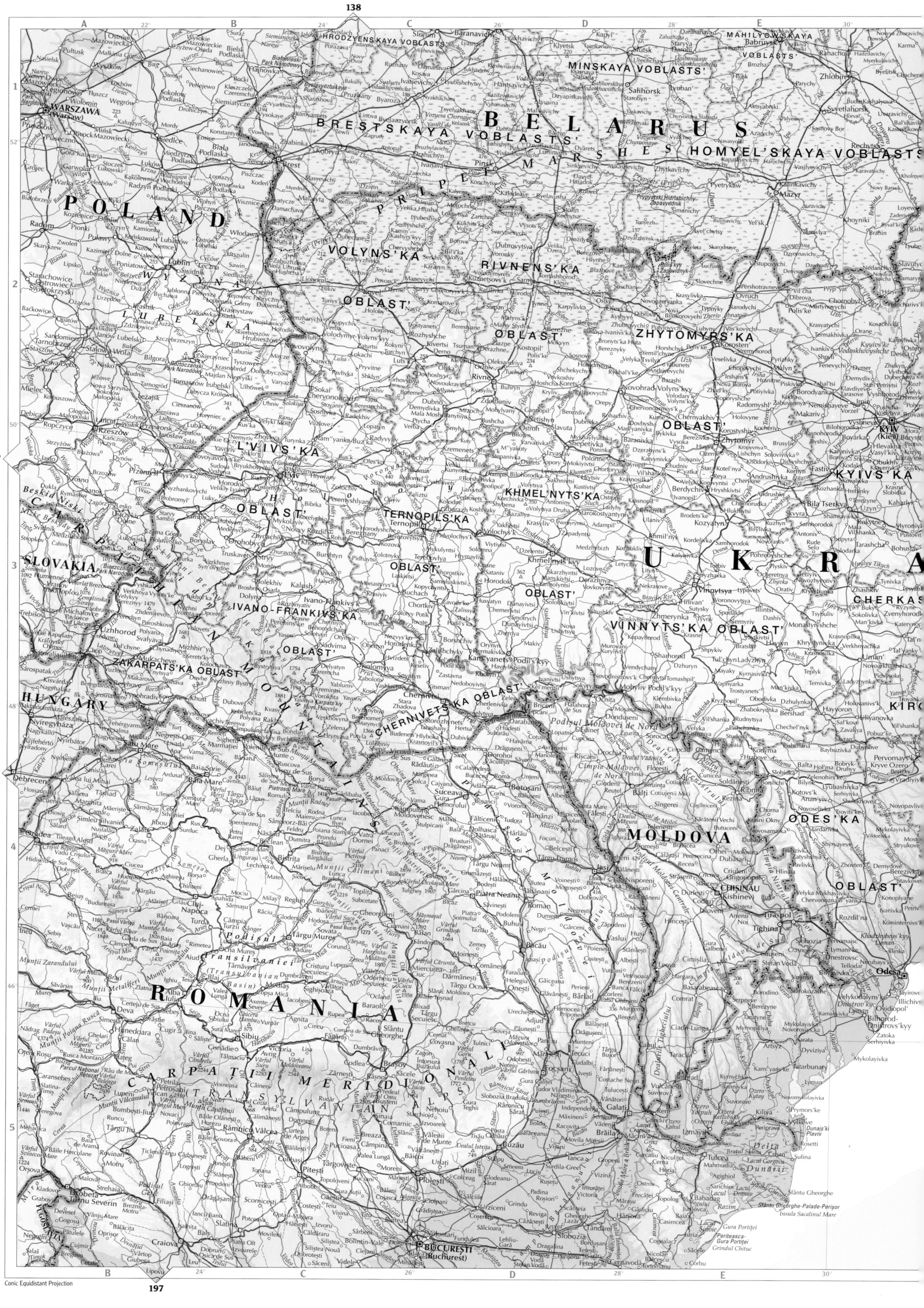

POLAND

BELARUS

BRESTSKAYA VOBLASTS'

MINSKAYA VOBLASTS'

HOMYEL'SKAYA VOBLASTS'

HRODZYENSKAYA VOBLASTS'

PRIPET MARSHES

WARSZAWA (Warsaw)

VOLYNS'KA OBLAST'

RIVNENS'KA OBLAST'

ZHYTOMYRS'KA OBLAST'

L'VIVS'KA OBLAST'

TERNOPIL'S'KA OBLAST'

KHMEL'NYTS'KA OBLAST'

UKRA...

KYIV (Kiev)

KYIVS'KA

SLOVAKIA

IVANO-FRANKIVS'KA OBLAST'

ZAKARPATS'KA OBLAST'

VINNYTS'KA OBLAST'

CHERKAS

CHERNIVTS'KA OBLAST'

VINNYTSYA

KIRO...

HUNGARY

ODES'KA

MOLDOVA

CHISINAU (Kishinev)

OBLAST'

Odesa

ROMANIA

CARPATHIAN MOUNTAINS

CARPAȚII MERIDIONALI

TRANSYLVANIAN ALPS

Podișul Transilvaniei (Transylvanian Basin)

Cluj-Napoca

Târgu Mureș

Sibiu

Brașov

BUCUREȘTI (Bucharest)

Craiova

Iași

Galați

Brăila

Tulcea

Delta Dunării

METRES / FEET

METRES	FEET
6000	19686
5000	16404
4000	13124
3000	9843
2000	6562
1500	4921
1000	3281
500	1640
200	656
100	328
0	0

LAND BELOW SEA LEVEL

50	164
200	656
1000	3281
2000	6562

Conic Equidistant Projection

167
197

RUSSIAN

FEDERATION

BRYANSKAYA OBLAST'

ORLOVSKAYA OBLAST'

LIPETSKAYA OBLAST'

TAMBOVSKAYA OBLAST'

KURSKAYA OBLAST'

VORONEZHSKAYA OBLAST'

CHERNIHIVS'KA OBLAST'

SUMS'KA OBLAST'

BELGORODSKAYA OBLAST'

Kharkiv

KHARKIVS'KA OBLAST'

POLTAVS'KA OBLAST'

Poltava

LUHANS'KA OBLAST'

CHERKAS'KA OBLAST'

UKRAINE

KIROVOHRAD'SKA OBLAST'

Kirovohrad

DNIPROPETROVS'KA OBLAST'

Dnipropetrovs'k

DONETS'KA OBLAST'

Donets'k

ROSTOVSKAYA OBLAST'

Rostov-na-Donu

MYKOLAYIVS'KA OBLAST'

Kryvyy Rih

ZAPORIZ'KA OBLAST'

Zaporizhzhya

Mariupol'

Mykolayiv

Kherson

KHERSONS'KA OBLAST'

Melitopol'

Berdyans'k

Gulf of Taganrog

Sea of Azov

KRASNODARSKIY KRAY

Prikubanskaya Nizmennost'

RESPUBLIKA KRYM

Simferopol'

Sevastopol'

Yalta

Kerch

Novorossiysk

Krasnodar

BLACK SEA

Longitude 32 east of Greenwich

MILES | KILOMETRES

125 | 200

100 | 150

75 | 125

50 | 75

25 | 50

0 | 0

1:3 000 000

© Bartholomew Ltd

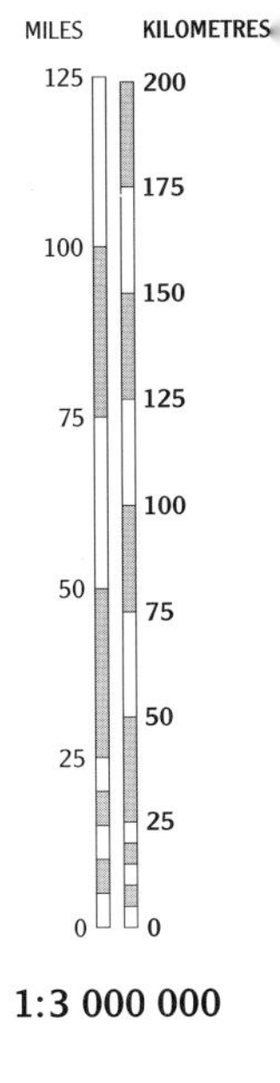

GULF OF BOTHNIA

FINLAND

ETELÄ-SUOMI

LÄNSI-SUOMI

VARSINAIS-SUOMI

SWEDEN

UPPSALA

STOCKHOLM

Åland (Ahvenanmaa)

HELSINKI (Helsingfors)

143

GULF OF FINLAND

TALLINN

ESTONIA

Hiiumaa

Saaremaa

Lake Peipus

Lake Pskov

BALTIC SEA

GULF OF RIGA

GOTLAND

Gotland (Sweden)

LATVIA

RIGA

PSKOVSKAYA OBL

Liepāja

Ventspils

LITHUANIA

VILNIUS

Klaipėda

VITSYEBSKAYA VOBLASTS

RUSSIAN FEDERATION

KALININGRADSKAYA OBLAST'

Kaliningrad

Gulf of Gdańsk

MINSKAYA VOBLASTS'

MINSK

BELARUS

HRODZYENSKAYA VOBLASTS

POLAND

POJEZIERZE MAZURSKIE

NIZINA MAZOWIECKA

WARSZAWA (Warsaw)

BRESTSKAYA VOBLASTS

METRES / FEET

6000 / 19686
5000 / 16404
4000 / 13124
3000 / 9843
2000 / 6562
1500 / 4921
1000 / 3281
500 / 1640
200 / 656
100 / 328
0 / 0
LAND BELOW SEA LEVEL
50 / 164
200 / 656
1000 / 3281
2000 / 6562

Conic Equidistant Projection

167

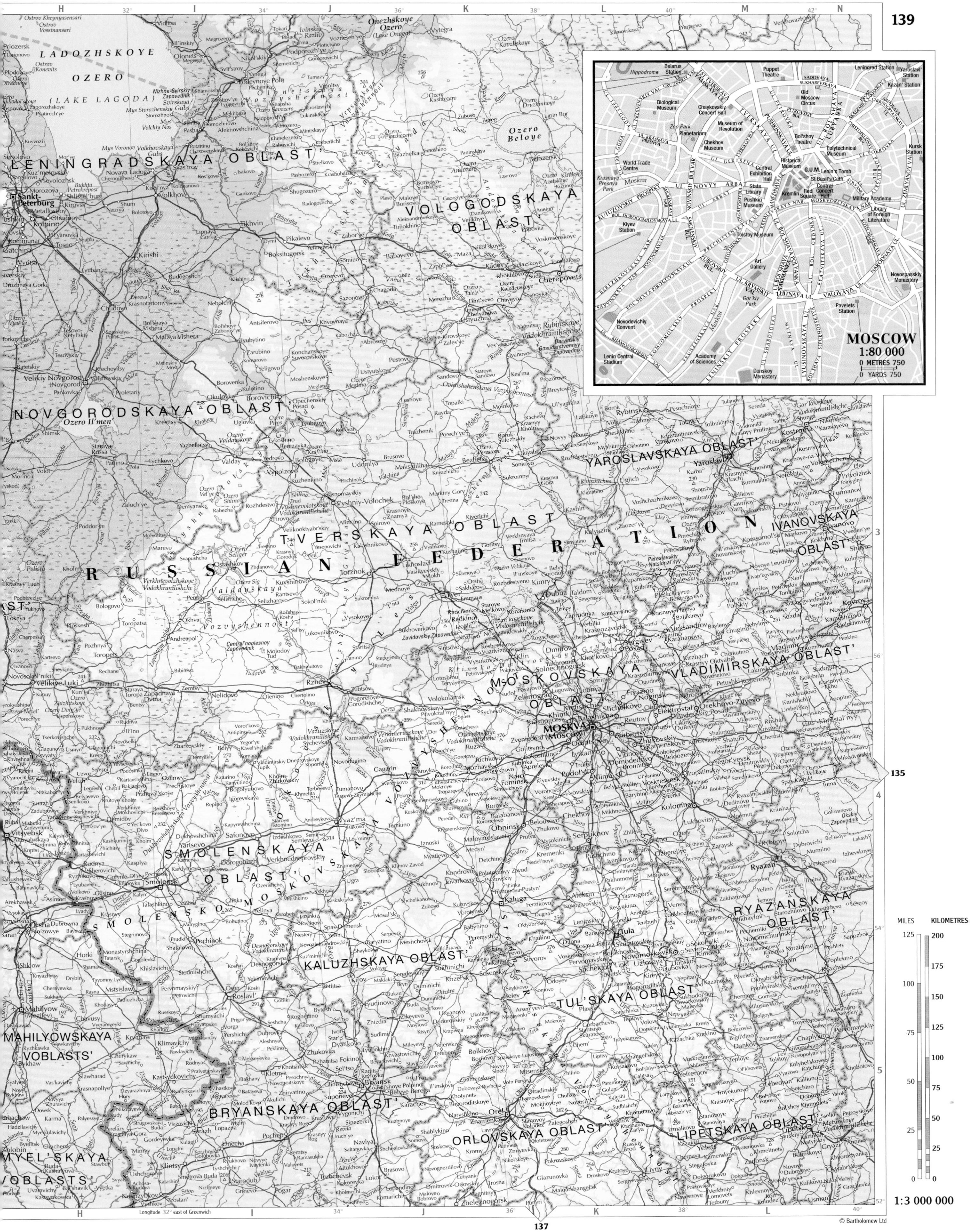

MOSCOW

1:80 000

0 METRES 750
0 YARDS 750

LADOZHSKOYE OZERO (LAKE LADOGA)

LENINGRADSKAYA OBLAST'

Sankt-Peterburg

VOLOGODSKAYA OBLAST'

Ozero Beloye

NOVGORODSKAYA OBLAST

Ozero Il'men

YAROSLAVSKAYA OBLAST

TVERSKAYA OBLAST

R U S S I A N   F E D E R A T I O N

IVANOVSKAYA OBLAST

VLADIMIRSKAYA OBLAST'

MOSKOVSKAYA OBLAST'

MOSKVA (Moscow)

SMOLENSKAYA OBLAST'

KALUZHSKAYA OBLAST

TUL'SKAYA OBLAST'

RYAZANSKAYA OBLAST'

Tula

Ryazan'

Kaluga

MAHILYOWSKAYA VOBLASTS'

BRYANSKAYA OBLAST'

ORLOVSKAYA OBLAST'

LIPETSKAYA OBLAST'

Smolensk

Velikiye Luki

MILES KILOMETRES

125 200
100 175
      150
75   125
      100
50   75
25   50
      25
0   0

1:3 000 000

© Bartholomew Ltd

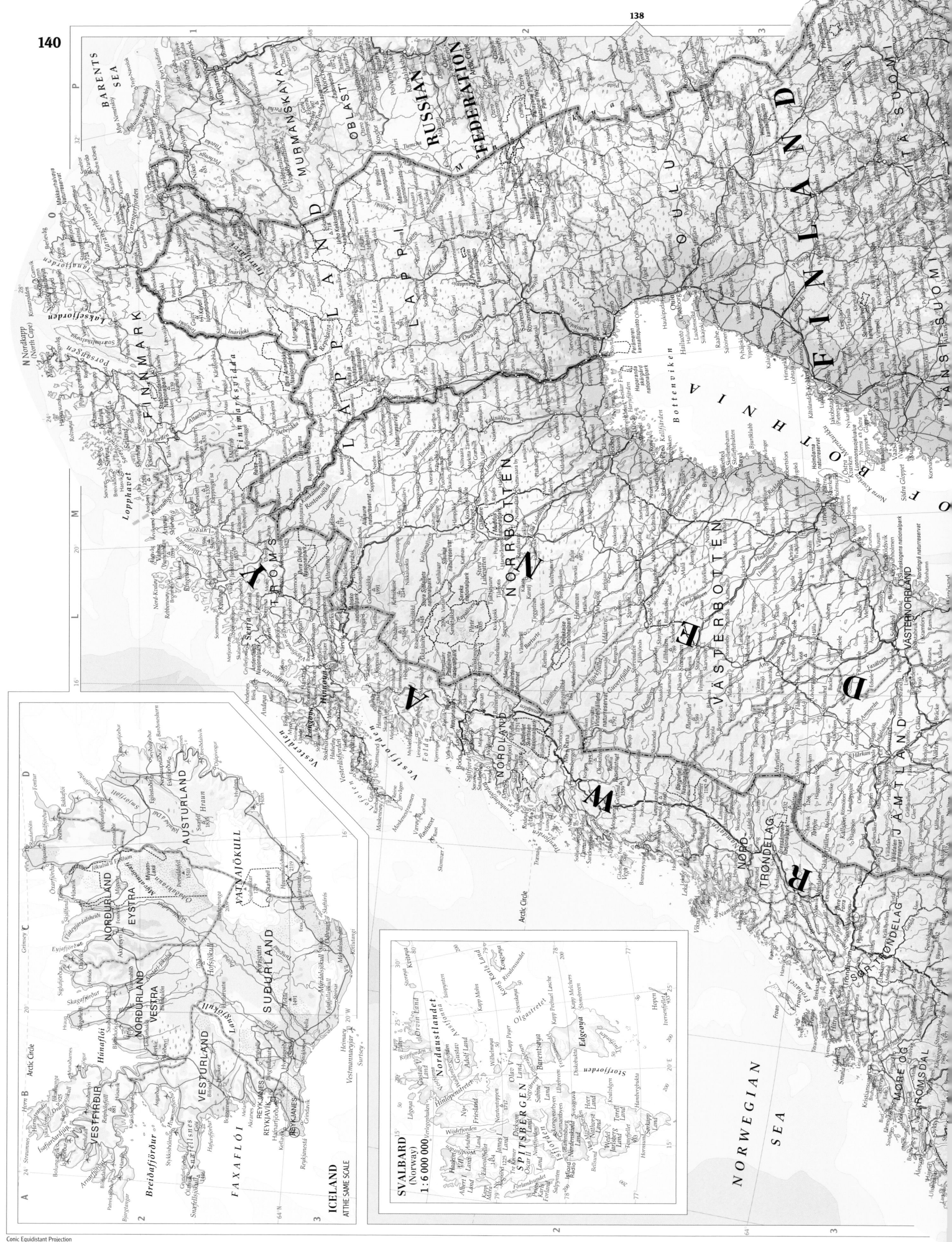

BARENTS SEA

N Nordkapp
(North Cape)

MURMANSKAYA OBLAST'

RUSSIAN FEDERATION

FINNMARK

LAPPLAND

LAPPI

OULU

FINLAND

ITÄ-SUOMI

TROMS

NORRBOTTEN

POHJOIS

Bottenviken

Arctic Circle

NORDLAND

VÄSTERBOTTEN

JÄMTLAND

VÄSTERNORRLAND

NORD-TRØNDELAG

SØR-TRØNDELAG

Trondheim

MØRE OG ROMSDAL

NORWEGIAN SEA

Arctic Circle

VESTFIRÐIR

NORÐURLAND VESTRA

NORÐURLAND EYSTRA

AUSTURLAND

VESTURLAND

VATNAJÖKULL

SUÐURLAND

REYKJAVÍK

FAXAFLÓI

ICELAND
ATTHE SAME SCALE

SVALBARD
(Norway)
1:6 000 000

Nordaustlandet

SPITSBERGEN

Edgeøya

Barentsøya

Conic Equidistant Projection

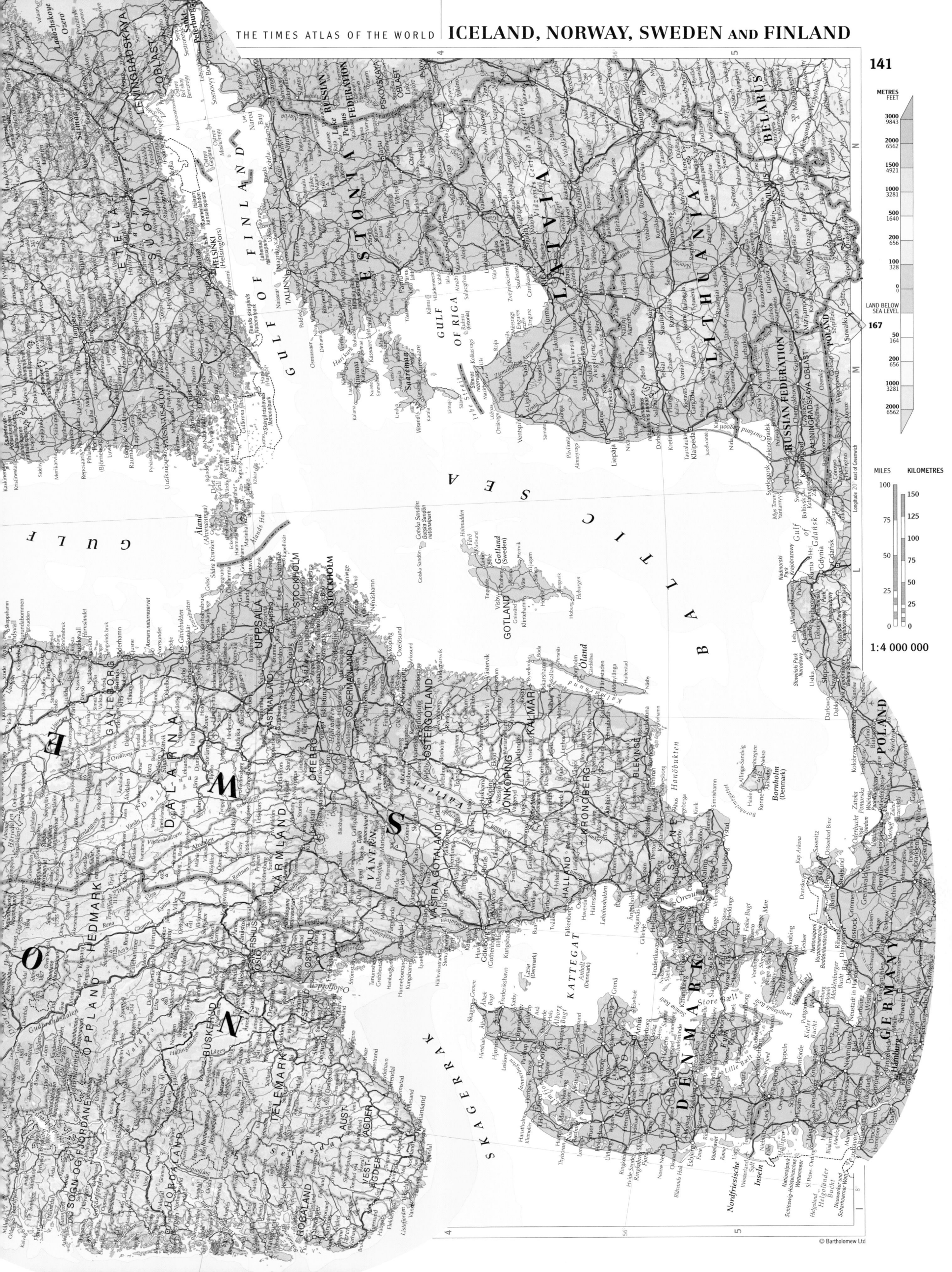
METRES
FEET
3000 9843
2000 6562
1500 4921
1000 3281
500 1640
200 656
100 328
0 0
LAND BELOW SEA LEVEL
50 164
200 656
1000 3281
2000 6562
167
MILES
KILOMETRES
1:4 000 000
GULF OF FINLAND
GULF OF RIGA
BALTIC SEA
SKAGERRAK
KATTEGAT
ESTONIA
LATVIA
LITHUANIA
BELARUS
RUSSIAN FEDERATION
POLAND
GERMANY
DENMARK
SWEDEN
NORWAY
SUOMI
HELSINKI (Helsingfors)
TALLINN
RIGA
VILNIUS
STOCKHOLM
OSLO
KØBENHAVN
Gotland (Sweden)
Öland
Bornholm (Denmark)
Saaremaa
Åland (Ahvenanmaa)
© Bartholomew Ltd

140

NORWAY

HORDALAND BUSKERUD HEDMARK

Bergen

TELEMARK AKERSHUS VÄRML

OSLO

VESTFOLD ØSTFOLD

ROGALAND

Stavanger

Sandnes

AUST-AGDER

VEST-AGDER

Kristiansand

SW

VÄST-
GÖTALA

S K A G E R R A K

Skagen

HALLAND

Frederikshavn

Læsø
(Denmark)

Thy Limfjorden Ålborg

NORDJYLLAND Älborg
Bugt

Mors K A T T E G A T

Salling

VIBORG Anholt
(Denmark)

RINGKØBING ÅRHUS

Halmstad

Århus

D E N M A R K

Randers

Grenå

SKÅ

Helsingborg

FREDERIKSBORG

Ringkøbing Fjord

VEJLE KØBENHAVN

Vejle ROSKILDE København
Copenhagen

RIBE Malmö

Esbjerg VESTSJÆLLAND

Odense SJÆLLAND

Kolding

FYN

SØNDERJYLLAND STORSTRØM

Falster

Lolland

Nykøbing

Flensburg

Kiel Femern

G E R M A N Y

Mecklenburger
Bucht

Helgoland Rügen

Helgoländer
Bucht

METRES / FEET

6000 / 19686
5000 / 16404
4000 / 13124
3000 / 9843
2000 / 6562
1500 / 4921
1000 / 3281
500 / 1640
200 / 656
100 / 328
0 / 0

LAND BELOW
SEA LEVEL

50 / 164
200 / 656
1000 / 3281
2000 / 6562

Conic Equidistant Projection

1:2 250 000

© Bartholomew Ltd

DALARNA
GÄVLEBORG
UPPSALA
VÄSTMANLAND
ÖREBRO
SÖDERMANLAND
STOCKHOLM
ÖSTERGOTLAND
JÖNKÖPING
KALMAR
KRONOBERG
BLEKINGE
GOTLAND
Gotland (Sweden)
Öland
Gotska Sandön (Sweden)
Åland (Ahvenanmaa)
FINLAND
LÄNSI-SUOMI
ESTONIA
Hiiumaa
Saaremaa
LATVIA
LITHUANIA
RUSSIAN FEDERATION
POLAND
Bornholm (Denmark)
BALTIC SEA
Ålands Hav
Södra Kvarken
Irbe Strait
Gulf of Gdańsk
Hanöbukten
Kalmarsund
Courland Lagoon
Bornholmsgattet
Gävle
Uppsala
Västerås
Örebro
Norrköping
Linköping
Jönköping
Kalmar
Karlskrona
Visby
Liepāja
Klaipėda
Kaliningrad
Gdańsk
Gdynia
Słupsk
Koszalin
Elbląg
Turku (Åbo)
Ventspils
Ystad
Rønne
Longitude 14° east of Greenwich
138
MILES | KILOMETRES

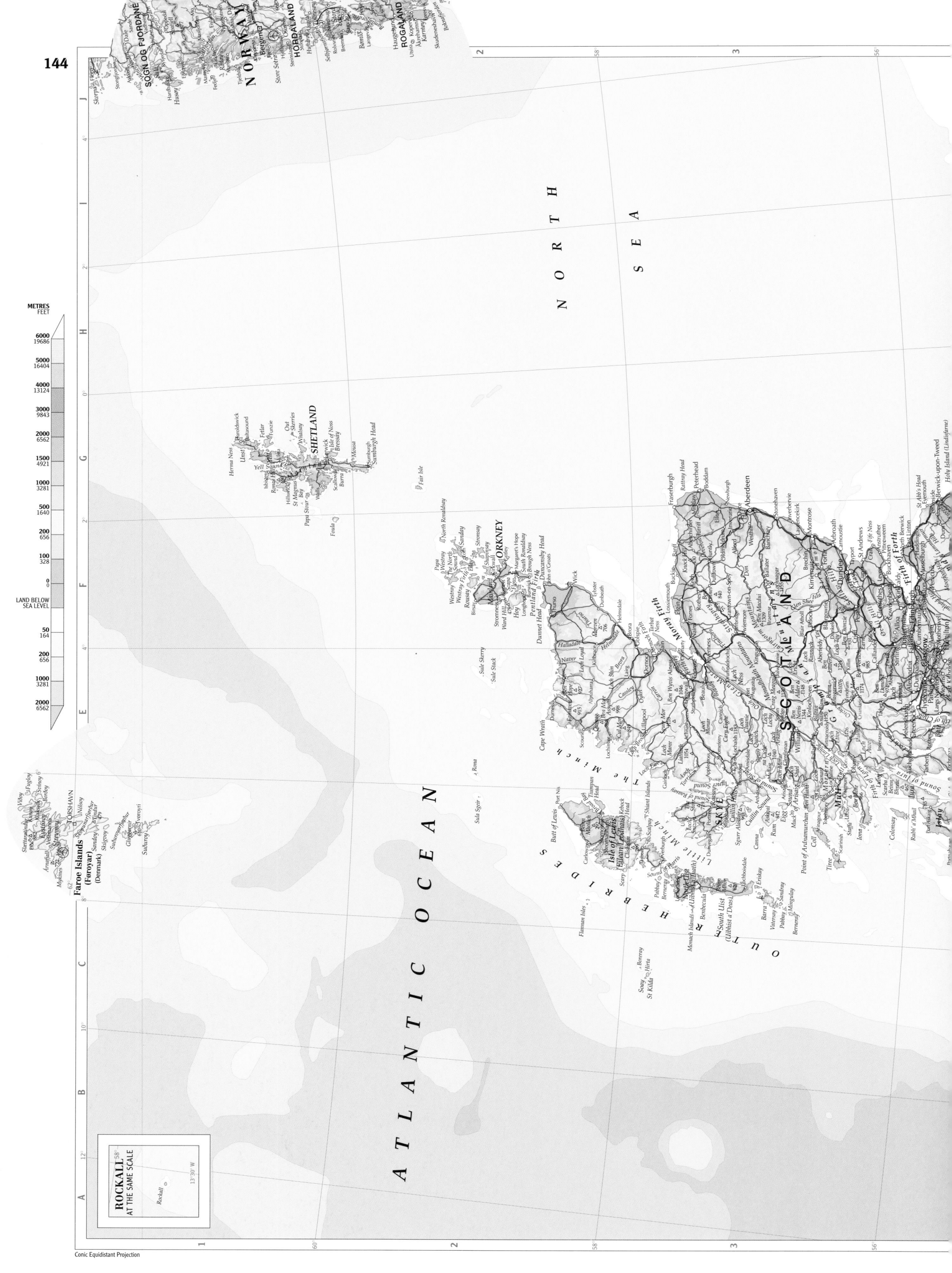
METRES
FEET
6000
19686
5000
16404
4000
13124
3000
9843
2000
6562
1500
4921
1000
3281
500
1640
200
656
100
328
0
0
LAND BELOW
SEA LEVEL
50
164
200
656
1000
3281
2000
6562
NORTH SEA
ATLANTIC OCEAN
NORWAY
SOGN OG FJORDANE
HORDALAND
ROGALAND
Bergen
Haugesund
SHETLAND
Fair Isle
Foula
ORKNEY
Kirkwall
Pentland Firth
SCOTLAND
Aberdeen
Dundee
Firth of Forth
Glasgow
Inverness
Moray Firth
Fraserburgh
Peterhead
St Andrews
Thurso
Wick
Cape Wrath
The Minch
Little Minch
Isle of Lewis
SKYE
North Uist
South Uist
OUTER HEBRIDES
St Kilda
Sula Sgeir
Sule Skerry
Sule Stack
Rona
Flannan Isles
Faroe Islands
(Føroyar)
(Denmark)
TÓRSHAVN
Streymoy
Eysturoy
Vágar
Sandoy
Suðuroy
ROCKALL
AT THE SAME SCALE
Rockall
13°30' W

Conic Equidistant Projection

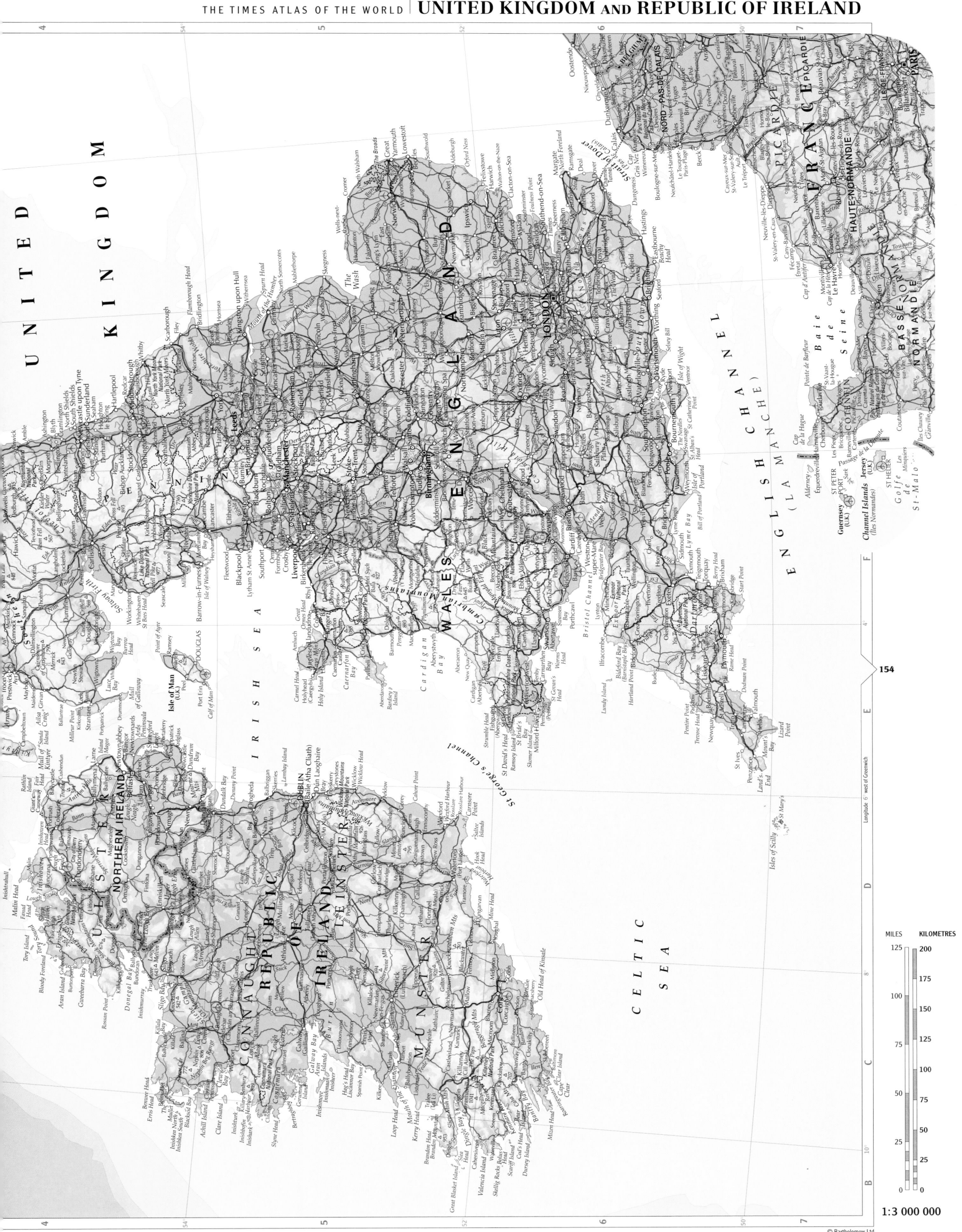

154

1:3 000 000

MILES   KILOMETRES
125   200
100   175
        150
75   125
        100
50   75
        50
25   25
0   0

© Bartholomew Ltd

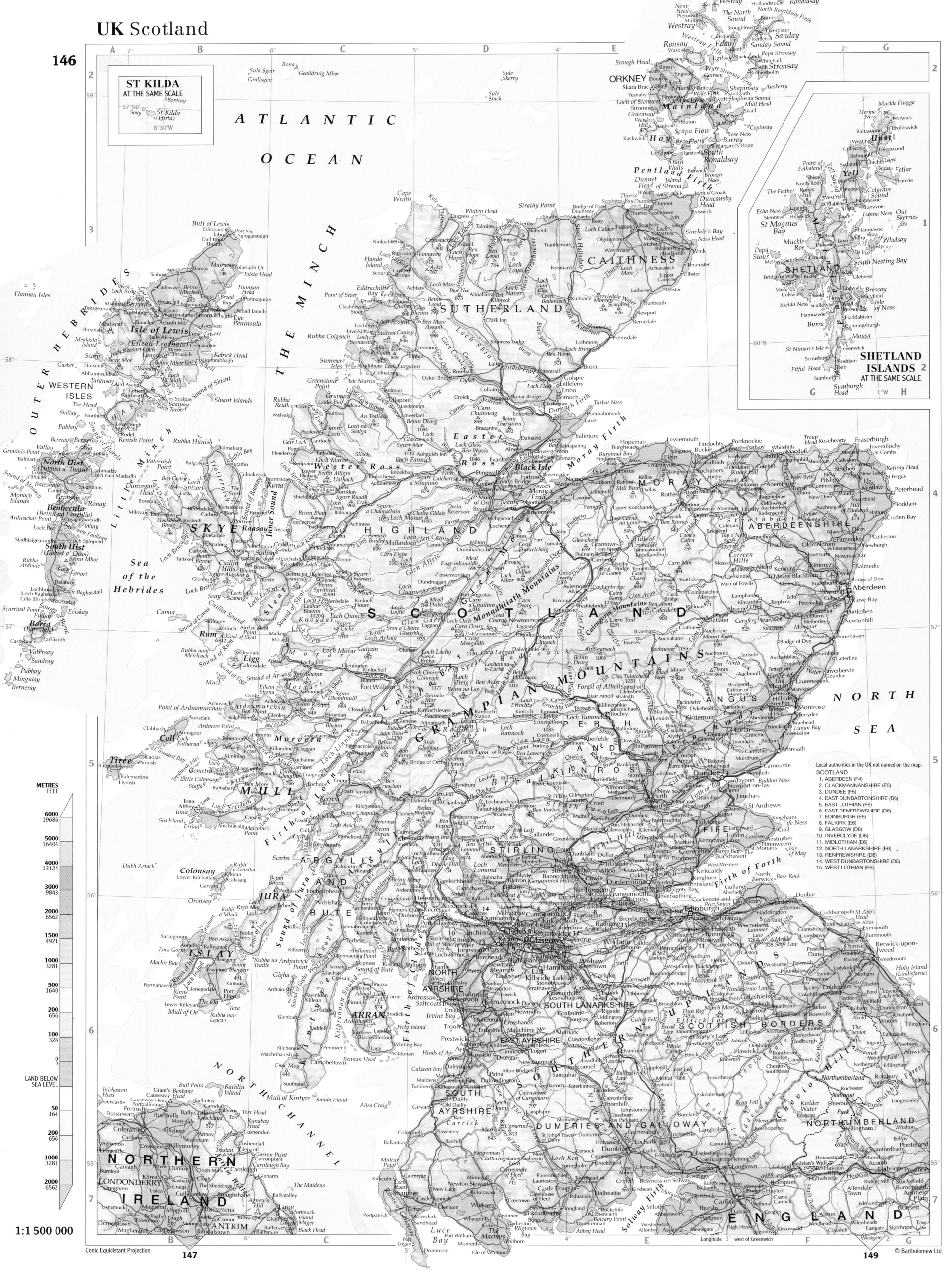

1:1 500 000

Conic Equidistant Projection

147

149

© Bartholomew Ltd

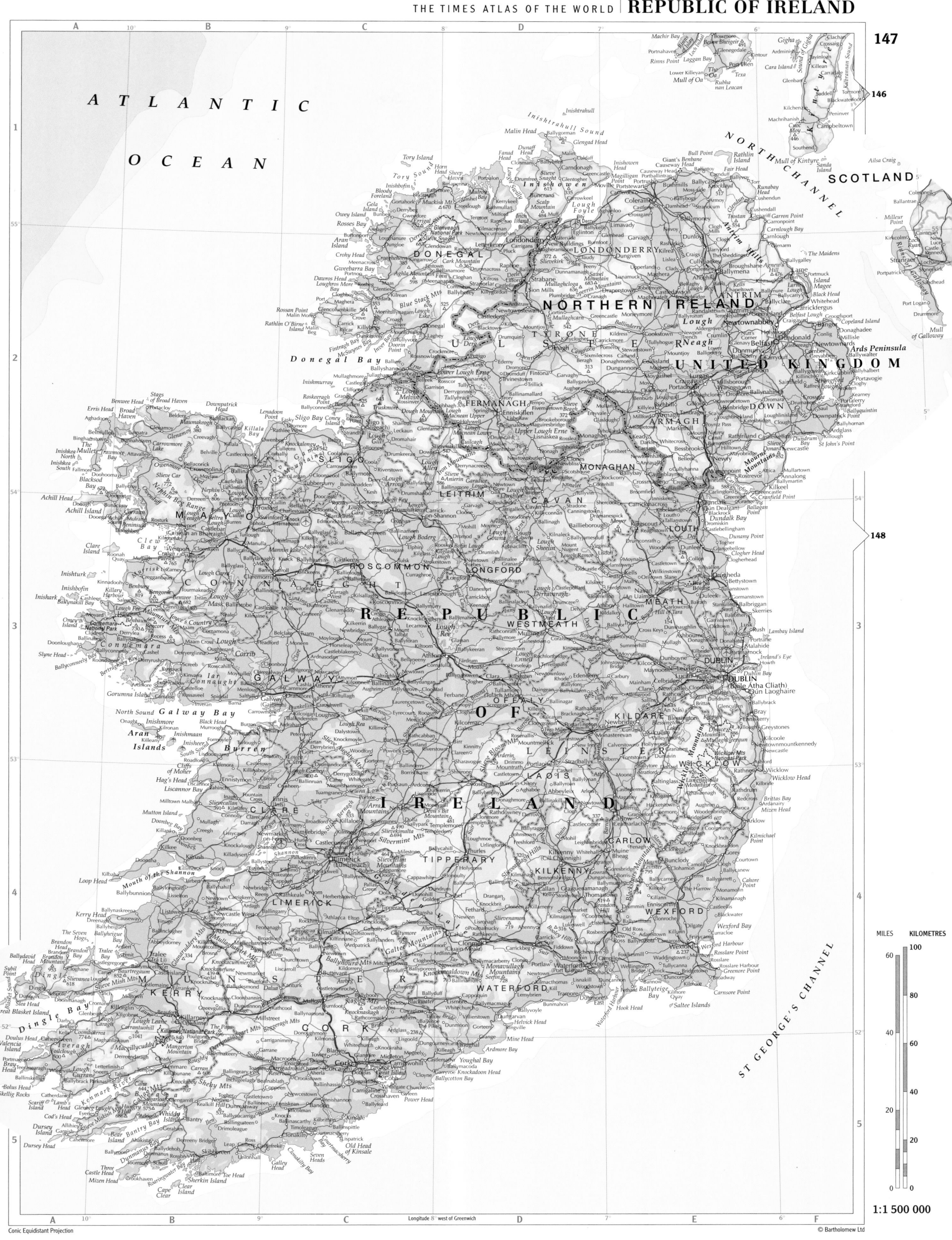

1:1 500 000

Conic Equidistant Projection

Longitude 8° west of Greenwich

© Bartholomew Ltd

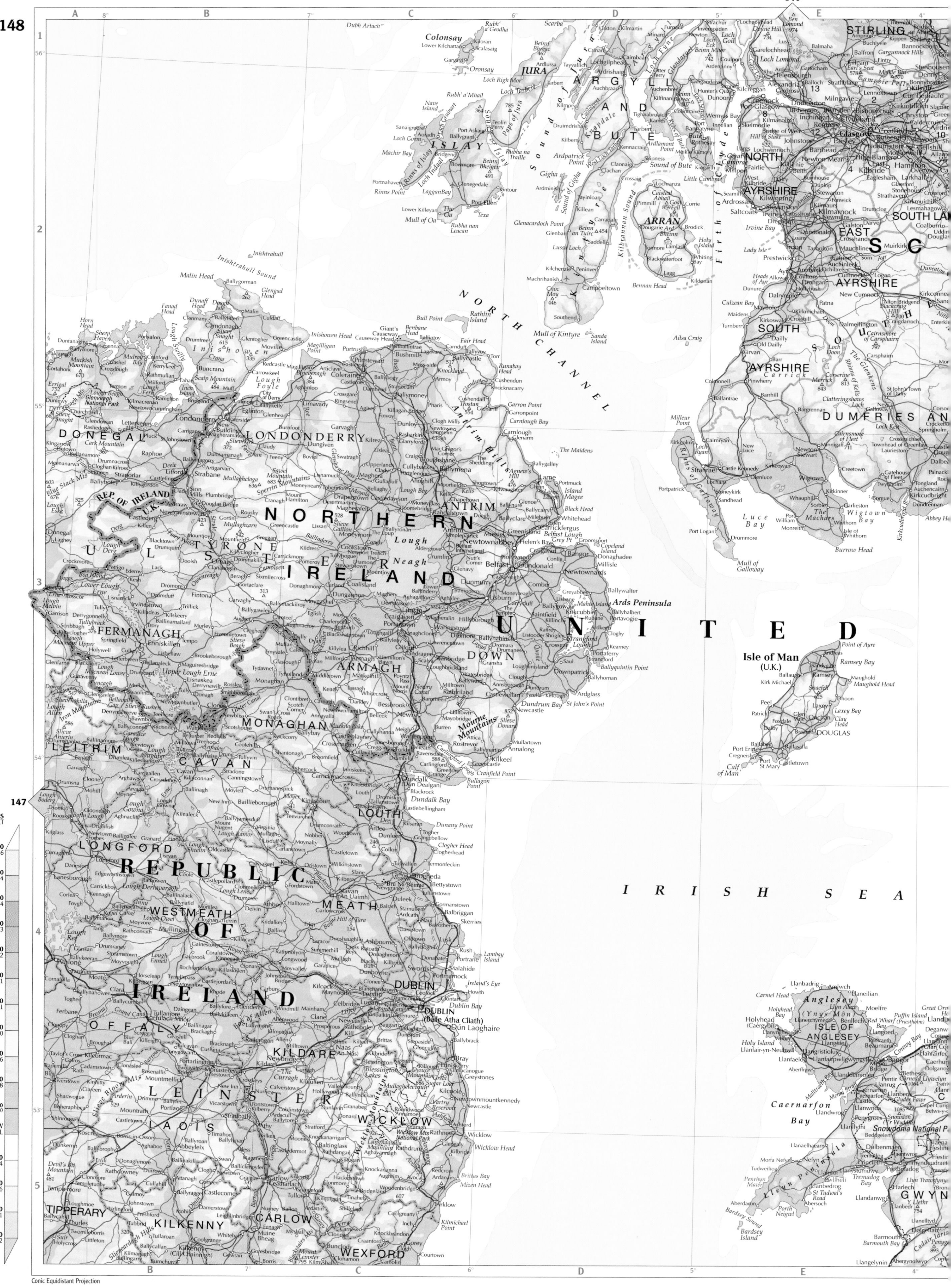

METRES FEET

6000	19686
5000	16404
4000	13124
3000	9843
2000	6562
1500	4921
1000	3281
500	1640
200	656
100	328
0	0

LAND BELOW SEA LEVEL

50	164
200	656
1000	3281
2000	6562

Conic Equidistant Projection

NORTH CHANNEL

IRISH SEA

NORTHERN IRELAND

ULSTER

UNITED

REPUBLIC OF IRELAND

LEINSTER

DONEGAL

LONDONDERRY

ANTRIM

TYRONE

FERMANAGH

ARMAGH

DOWN

MONAGHAN

LEITRIM

CAVAN

LONGFORD

WESTMEATH

MEATH

LOUTH

OFFALY

KILDARE

DUBLIN

WICKLOW

LAOIS

CARLOW

KILKENNY

WEXFORD

TIPPERARY

Lough Neagh

Lough Foyle

Lough Swilly

Upper Lough Erne

Lower Lough Erne

Strangford Lough

Mourne Mountains

Isle of Man (U.K.)

DOUGLAS

Ramsey Bay

Maughold Head

Calf of Man

ARGYLL AND BUTE

Firth of Clyde

JURA

ISLAY

ARRAN

Mull of Kintyre

Rathlin Island

North Channel

STIRLING

GLASGOW

NORTH AYRSHIRE

EAST AYRSHIRE

SOUTH AYRSHIRE

DUMFRIES AN

SOUTH LA

Anglesey (Ynys Môn)

ISLE OF ANGLESEY

Caernarfon Bay

Snowdonia National P.

GWYN

Lleyn Peninsula

Malin Head

Horn Head

Giant's Causeway

Belfast

Belfast Lough

Londonderry

Dublin (Baile Átha Cliath)

Dublin Bay

Dundalk Bay

Wicklow Head

Carnsore Point

Irish Sea

Local authorities in the UK not named on the map:

SCOTLAND
1. CLACKMANNANSHIRE (F1)
2. EAST DUNBARTONSHIRE (E2)
3. EAST LOTHIAN (G2)
4. EAST RENFREWSHIRE (E2)
5. EDINBURGH (F2)
6. FALKIRK (F2)
7. GLASGOW (E2)
8. INVERCLYDE (E2)
9. MIDLOTHIAN (F2)
10. NORTH LANARKSHIRE (F2)
11. PERTH AND KINROSS (F1)
12. RENFREWSHIRE (E2)
13. WEST DUNBARTONSHIRE (E2)
14. WEST LOTHIAN (F2)

ENGLAND
15. BLACKPOOL (F4)
16. DARLINGTON (H3)
17. HARTLEPOOL (H3)
18. KINGSTON UPON HULL (I4)
19. MIDDLESBROUGH (H3)
20. NORTH EAST LINCOLNSHIRE (I4)
21. STOCKTON-ON-TEES (H3)
22. STOKE-ON-TRENT (G4)

NORTH

SEA

MILES   KILOMETRES

1:1 200 000

Greenwich 0° meridian

© Bartholomew Ltd

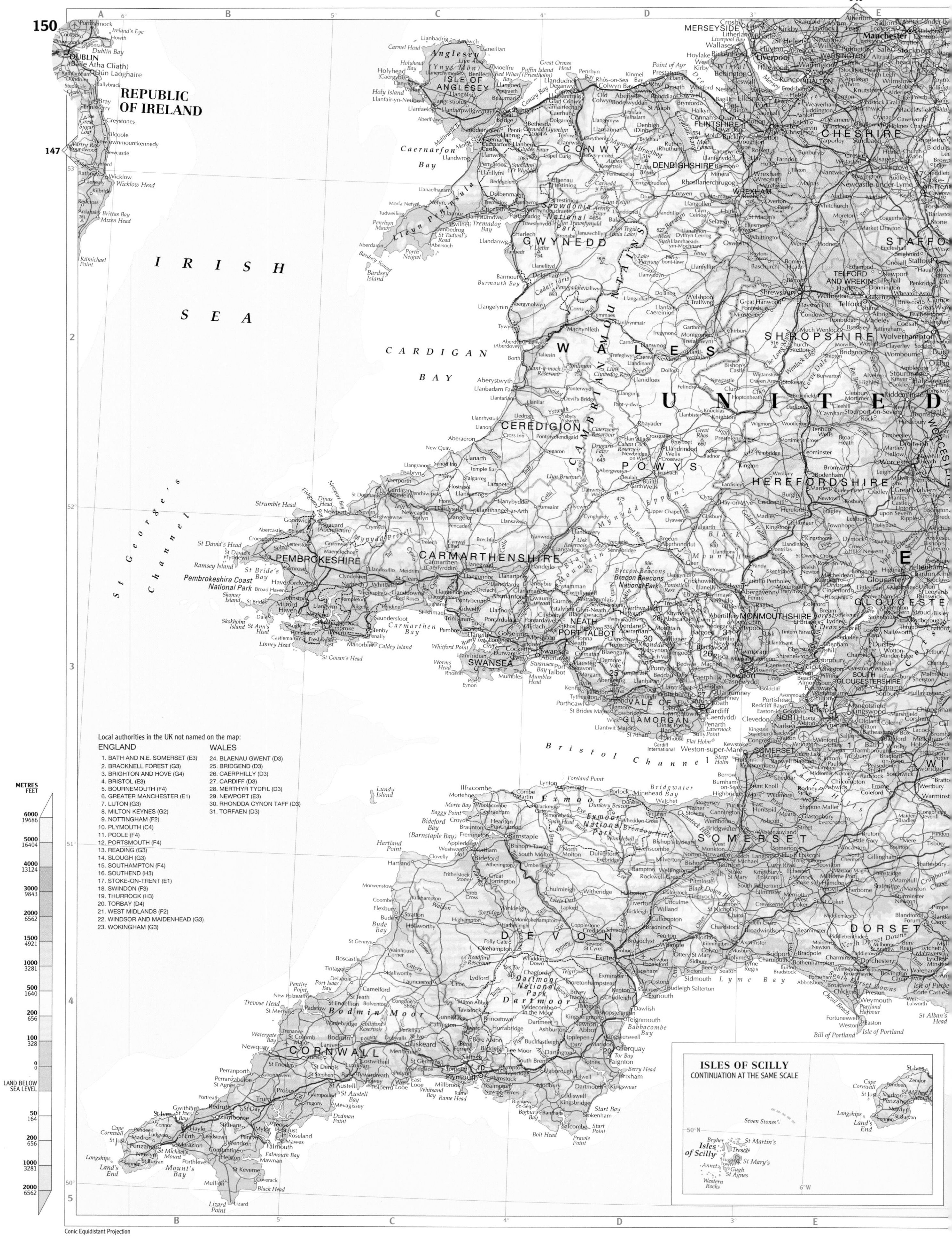

REPUBLIC OF IRELAND

IRISH SEA

CARDIGAN BAY

WALES

UNITED

GWYNEDD

CONWY

DENBIGHSHIRE

WREXHAM

SHROPSHIRE

CHESHIRE

STAFFO

MERSEYSIDE

Manchester

Liverpool

CEREDIGION

POWYS

HEREFORDSHIRE

PEMBROKESHIRE

CARMARTHENSHIRE

Pembrokeshire Coast National Park

Brecon Beacons National Park

MONMOUTHSHIRE

NEATH

PORT TALBOT

SWANSEA

GLAMORGAN

VALE OF GLAMORGAN

Cardiff (Caerdydd)

GLOUCESTERSHIRE

GLOUCESTE

SOMERSET

NORTH

Bristol Channel

Bristol

DEVON

Exmoor National Park

SOMERSET

DORSET

CORNWALL

Dartmoor National Park

Bodmin Moor

Plymouth

St George's Channel

ISLE OF ANGLESEY

METRES / FEET

METRES	FEET
6000	19686
5000	16404
4000	13124
3000	9843
2000	6562
1500	4921
1000	3281
500	1640
200	656
100	328
0	0

LAND BELOW SEA LEVEL

50	164
200	656
1000	3281
2000	6562

Local authorities in the UK not named on the map:

ENGLAND
1. BATH AND N.E. SOMERSET (E3)
2. BRACKNELL FOREST (G3)
3. BRIGHTON AND HOVE (G4)
4. BRISTOL (E3)
5. BOURNEMOUTH (F4)
6. GREATER MANCHESTER (E1)
7. LUTON (G3)
8. MILTON KEYNES (G2)
9. NOTTINGHAM (F2)
10. PLYMOUTH (C4)
11. POOLE (F4)
12. PORTSMOUTH (F4)
13. READING (G3)
14. SLOUGH (G3)
15. SOUTHAMPTON (F4)
16. SOUTHEND (H3)
17. STOKE-ON-TRENT (E1)
18. SWINDON (F3)
19. THURROCK (H3)
20. TORBAY (D4)
21. WEST MIDLANDS (F2)
22. WINDSOR AND MAIDENHEAD (G3)
23. WOKINGHAM (G3)

WALES
24. BLAENAU GWENT (D3)
25. BRIDGEND (D3)
26. CAERPHILLY (D3)
27. CARDIFF (D3)
28. MERTHYR TYDFIL (D3)
29. NEWPORT (E3)
30. RHONDDA CYNON TAFF (D3)
31. TORFAEN (D3)

ISLES OF SCILLY
CONTINUATION AT THE SAME SCALE

Isles of Scilly
St Martin's
Tresco
St Mary's
St Agnes
Western Rocks
Seven Stones

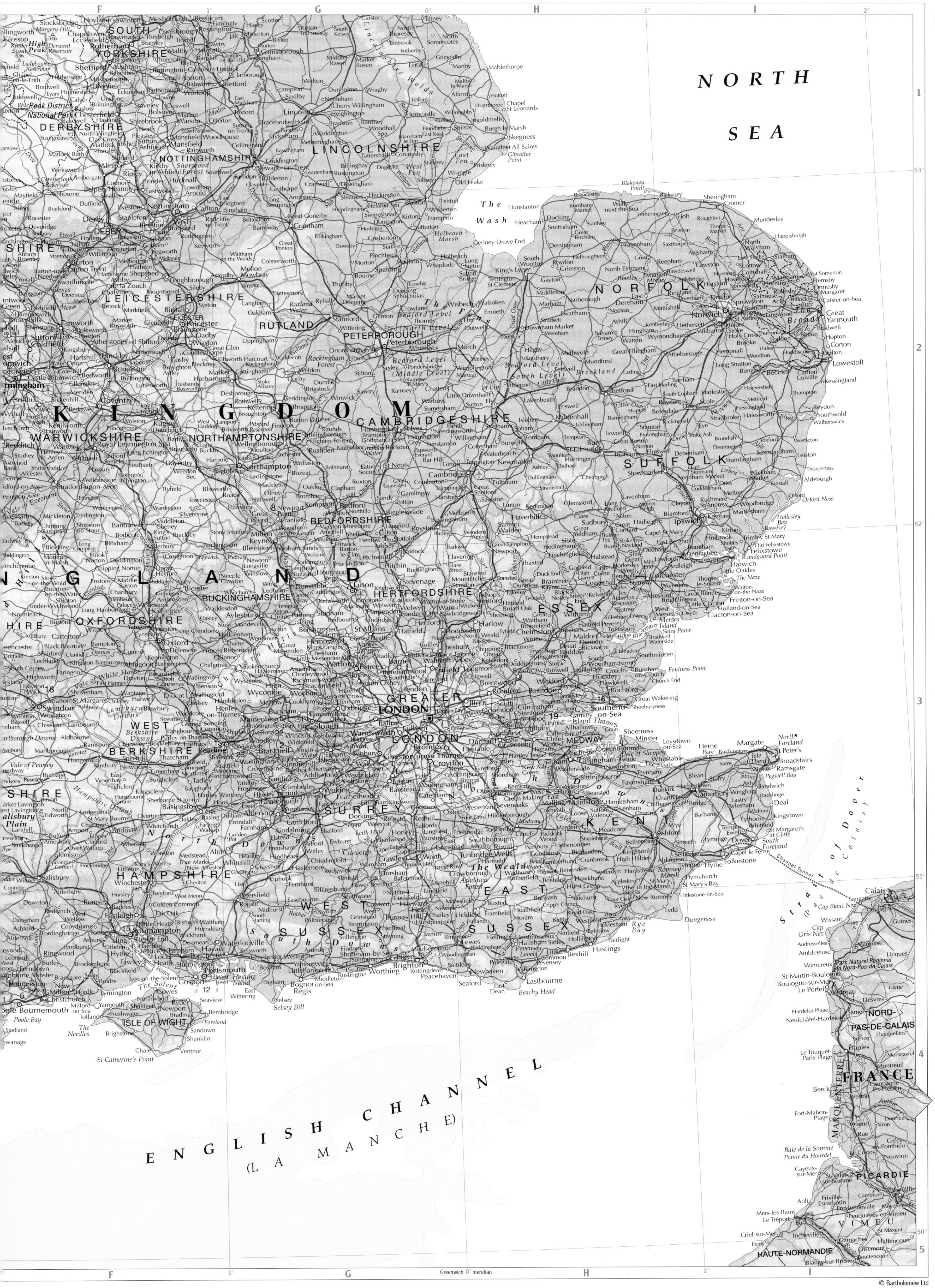

NORTH SEA

The Wash

NORFOLK

The Broads

LINCOLNSHIRE

SOUTH YORKSHIRE

DERBYSHIRE

NOTTINGHAMSHIRE

LEICESTERSHIRE

RUTLAND

PETERBOROUGH

CAMBRIDGESHIRE

SUFFOLK

KINGDOM

WARWICKSHIRE

NORTHAMPTONSHIRE

BEDFORDSHIRE

ENGLAND

OXFORDSHIRE

BUCKINGHAMSHIRE

HERTFORDSHIRE

ESSEX

WEST BERKSHIRE

GREATER LONDON

LONDON

MEDWAY

KENT

SURREY

HAMPSHIRE

WEST SUSSEX

EAST SUSSEX

The Weald

Strait of Dover (Pas de Calais)

Channel Tunnel

ISLE OF WIGHT

The Solent

The Needles

St Catherine's Point

ENGLISH CHANNEL

(LA MANCHE)

FRANCE

NORD-PAS-DE-CALAIS

PICARDIE

HAUTE-NORMANDIE

VIMEU

1:1 200 000

MILES	KILOMETRES
60	100
	90
50	80
	70
40	60
30	50
	40
20	30
	20
10	
	10
0	0

156

© Bartholomew Ltd

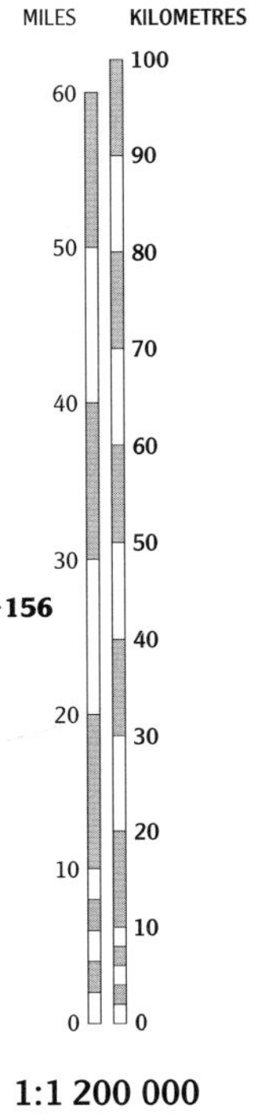

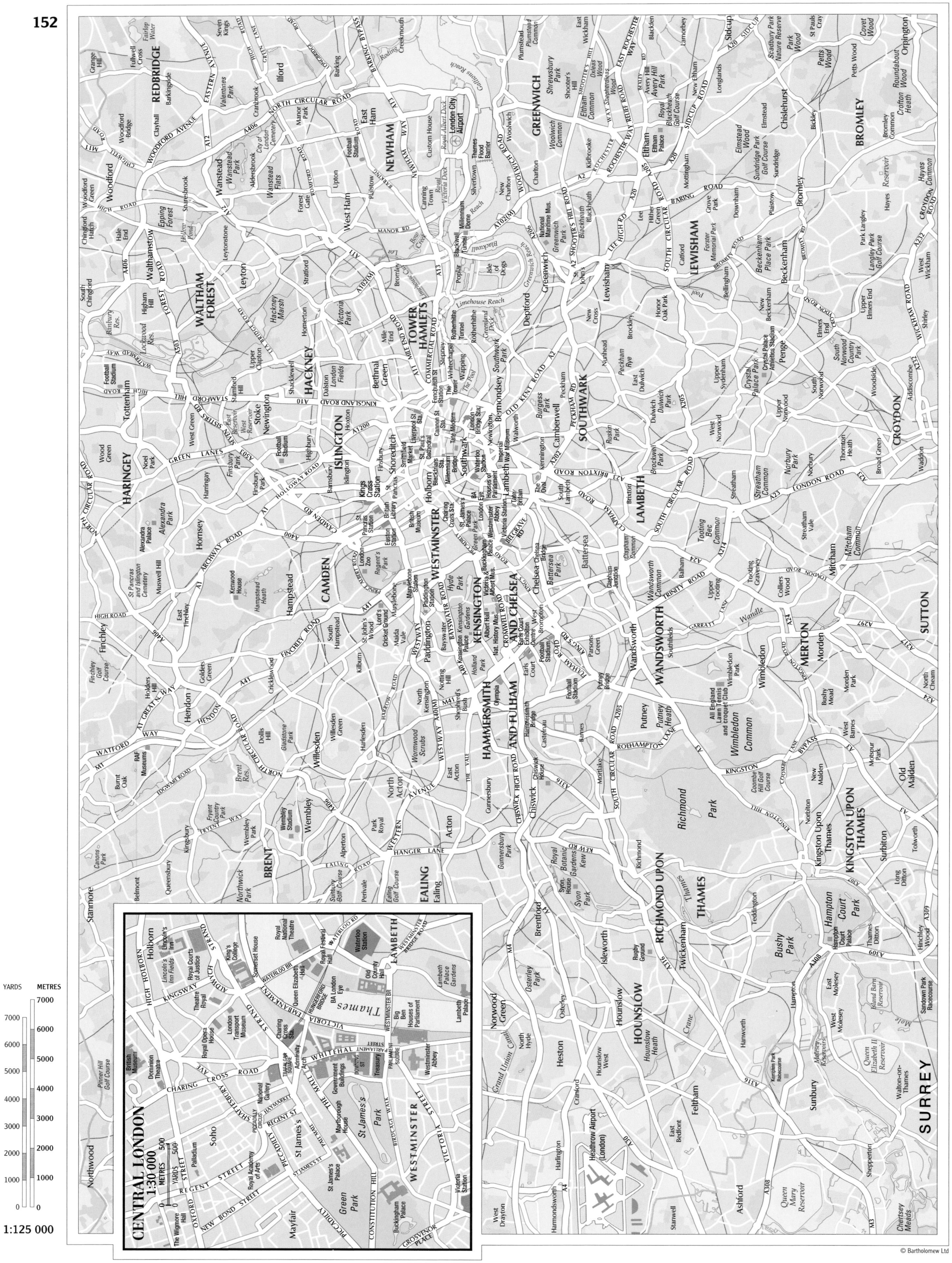
REDBRIDGE
WALTHAM FOREST
HARINGEY
HACKNEY
ISLINGTON
CAMDEN
TOWER HAMLETS
NEWHAM
GREENWICH
LEWISHAM
BROMLEY
SOUTHWARK
LAMBETH
WESTMINSTER
KENSINGTON AND CHELSEA
HAMMERSMITH AND FULHAM
WANDSWORTH
MERTON
SUTTON
CROYDON
BRENT
EALING
HOUNSLOW
RICHMOND UPON THAMES
KINGSTON UPON THAMES
SURREY
Thames
Richmond Park
Heathrow Airport (London)
CENTRAL LONDON
1:30 000
YARDS
METRES
1:125 000

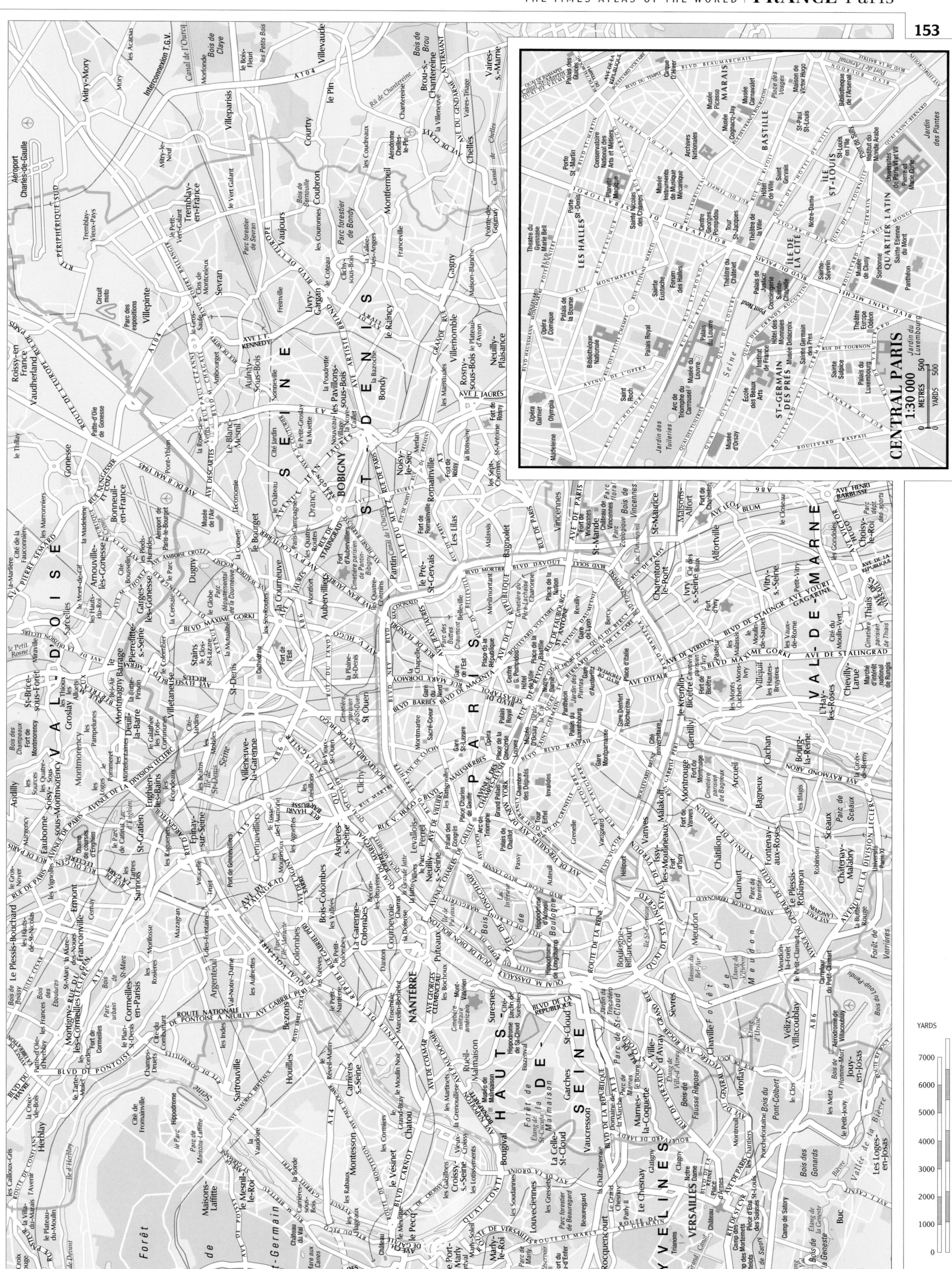

CENTRAL PARIS
1:30 000

1:125 000

© Bartholomew Ltd

METRES 0 500
YARDS 0 500
S E I N E - S T - D E N I S
V A L - D E - M A R N E
H A U T S - D E - S E I N E
Y V E L I N E S
V A L - D ' O I S E
ÎLE DE LA CITÉ
ÎLE ST-LOUIS
QUARTIER LATIN
LES HALLES
MARAIS
BASTILLE
ST-GERMAIN DES PRÉS
Seine
Aéroport Charles-de-Gaulle
Aéroport de Paris-le-Bourget
St-Denis
Versailles
Nanterre
Vincennes
Bois de Boulogne
Bois de Vincennes
Forêt de St-Germain
Forêt de Meudon
YARDS
METRES
7000
6000
4000
2000
1000

Major labels

ENGLAND
U.K.

ENGLISH CHANNEL
(LA MANCHE)

BAY OF BISCAY

Golfe de Gascogne

Mar Cantábrico

FRANCE

SPAIN

BRETAGNE

BASSE-NORMANDIE
HAUTE-NORMANDIE
PICARDIE
NORD-PAS-DE
ÎLE-DE-FRANCE
PARIS

PAYS DE LA LOIRE
CENTRE
BERRY
TOURAINE
ANJOU

POITOU-CHARENTES
LIMOUSIN
MARCHE

AQUITAINE
GUYENNE
MÉDOC
GASCOGNE

MIDI-PYRÉNÉES
PYRÉNÉES
LANGUEDOC

ASTURIAS
CANTABRIA
PAÍS VASCO
NAVARRA
LA RIOJA
CASTILLA Y LEÓN
ARAGÓN
CATALUÑA
ANDORRA LA VELLA

Channel Islands
(Îles Normandes)
Guernsey (U.K.)
ST PETER PORT
Jersey (U.K.)
ST HELIER
Alderney

Cordillera Cantábrica

Scale legend

METRES / FEET

6000	19686
5000	16404
4000	13124
3000	9843
2000	6562
1500	4921
1000	3281
500	1640
200	656
100	328
0	0

LAND BELOW SEA LEVEL

50	164
200	656
1000	3281
2000	6562

Conic Equidistant Projection

BELGIUM

GERMANY

RHEINLAND-PFALZ

HESSEN

Frankfurt am Main

SAARLAND

BADEN-WÜRTTEMBERG

BAYERN

Stuttgart

München (Munich)

Nürnberg

LUXEMBOURG

LORRAINE

Nancy

Strasbourg

ALSACE

Mulhouse

CHAMPAGNE

ARDENNE

Reims

VOSGES

BOURGOGNE

FRANCHE-COMTÉ

Dijon

Besançon

SWITZERLAND

JURA

BERN

AUSTRIA

LIECHTENSTEIN

VADUZ

ALPS

TRENTINO-ALTO ADIGE

VALLE D'AOSTA

Lyon

RHÔNE-ALPES

Grenoble

PIEMONTE

LOMBARDIA

Milano (Milan)

VENETO

Torino (Turin)

ITALY

EMILIA-ROMAGNA

MASSIF CENTRAL

St-Étienne

Clermont-Ferrand

LIGURIA

Genova (Genoa)

TOSCANA

PROVENCE-ALPES-CÔTE-D'AZUR

Monte-Carlo MONACO

Nice

Cannes

Marseille

Toulon

Aix-en-Provence

Avignon

Nîmes

Montpellier

Arles

GOLFE DU LION

ROUSSILLON

LIGURIAN SEA

Cap Corse

Bastia

CORSE (CORSICA) (France)

Ajaccio

MEDITERRANEAN SEA

1:3 000 000

MILES
125
100
75
50
25

KILOMETRES
200
175
150
125
100
75
50
25
0

© Bartholomew Ltd

151
159

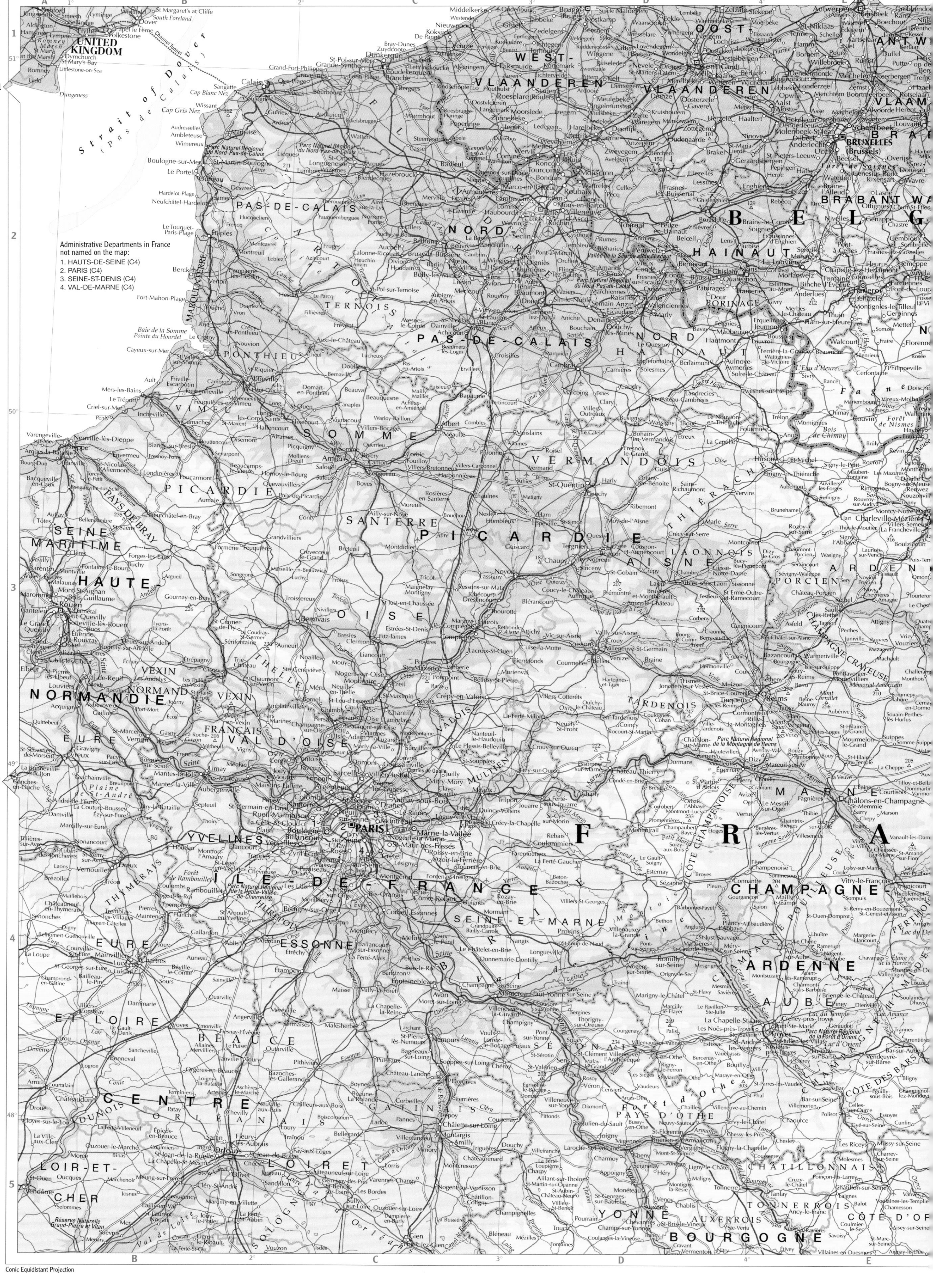

Administrative Departments in France
not named on the map:
1. HAUTS-DE-SEINE (C4)
2. PARIS (C4)
3. SEINE-ST-DENIS (C4)
4. VAL-DE-MARNE (C4)

UNITED KINGDOM

Strait of Dover
(Pas de Calais)

PAS-DE-CALAIS

NORD

WEST-VLAANDEREN

OOST-VLAANDEREN

VLAANDEREN

VLAAM

BELG

HAINAUT

BORINAGE

BRABANT W

BRUXELLES
(Brussel)

PONTHIEU

SOMME

SANTERRE

PICARDIE

VERMANDOIS

AISNE

LAONNOIS

ARDEN

PORCIEN

CHAMPAGNE CRAYEUSE

VIMEU

TERNOISS

ARTOIS

SEINE-MARITIME

HAUTE-

PAYS DE BRAY

NORMANDIE

NORMAND

VEXIN

VEXIN FRANÇAIS

OISE

THELLE

VAL-D'OISE

EURE

VALOIS

TARDENOIS

MULIEN

MARNE

CHAMPAGNE

ARDENNE

PARIS

ÎLE-DE-FRANCE

YVELINES

ESSONNE

SEINE-ET-MARNE

AUBE

THYMERAIS

EURE-ET-LOIRE

BEAUCE

GATINAIS

CÔTE DES BARS

CENTRE

ORLEANAIS

DUNOIS

LOIRET

SÉNONAIS

PAYS D'OTHE

CHATILLONNAIS

LOIR-ET-CHER

SOLOGNE

YONNE

AUXERROIS

TONNERROIS

CÔTE-D'OR

BOURGOGNE

FRA

METRES / FEET
6000 19686
5000 16404
4000 13124
3000 9843
2000 6562
1500 4921
1000 3281
500 1640
200 656
100 328
0 0
LAND BELOW SEA LEVEL
50 164
200 656
1000 3281
2000 6562

Conic Equidistant Projection

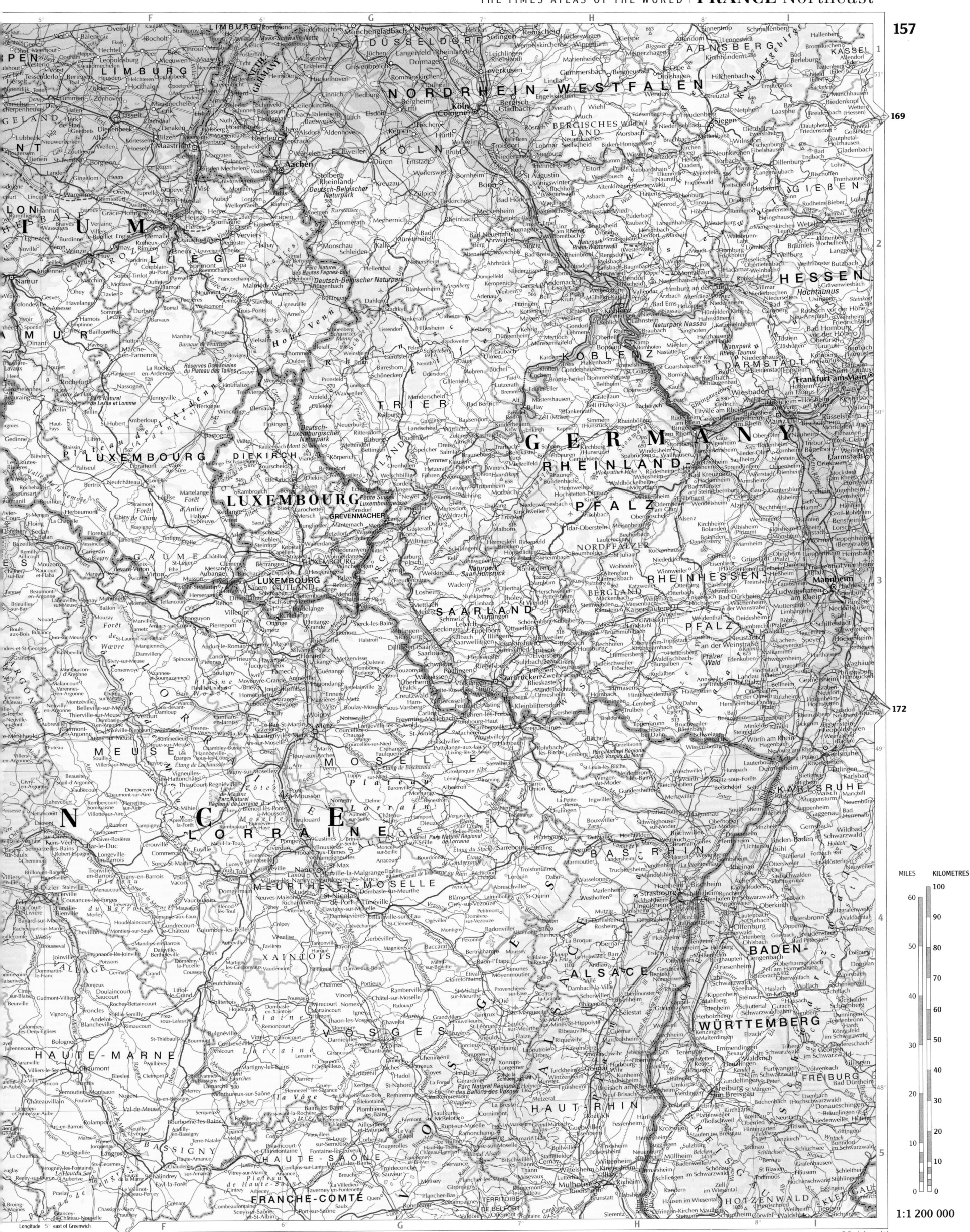
NORDRHEIN-WESTFALEN
DÜSSELDORF
KÖLN
ARNSBERG
KASSEL
LIMBURG
BERGISCHES LAND
GIESSEN
HESSEN
KOBLENZ
DARMSTADT
TRIER
GERMANY
RHEINLAND-PFALZ
LUXEMBOURG
DIEKIRCH
GREVENMACHER
LIÈGE
NAMUR
RHEINHESSEN-PFALZ
SAARLAND
KARLSRUHE
MOSELLE
MEUSE
LORRAINE
MEURTHE-ET-MOSELLE
BAS-RHIN
ALSACE
BADEN-WÜRTTEMBERG
FREIBURG
VOSGES
HAUT-RHIN
HAUTE-MARNE
HAUTE-SAÔNE
FRANCHE-COMTÉ
TERRITOIRE DE BELFORT
HOTZENWALD
1:1 200 000
MILES
KILOMETRES

169
172
160

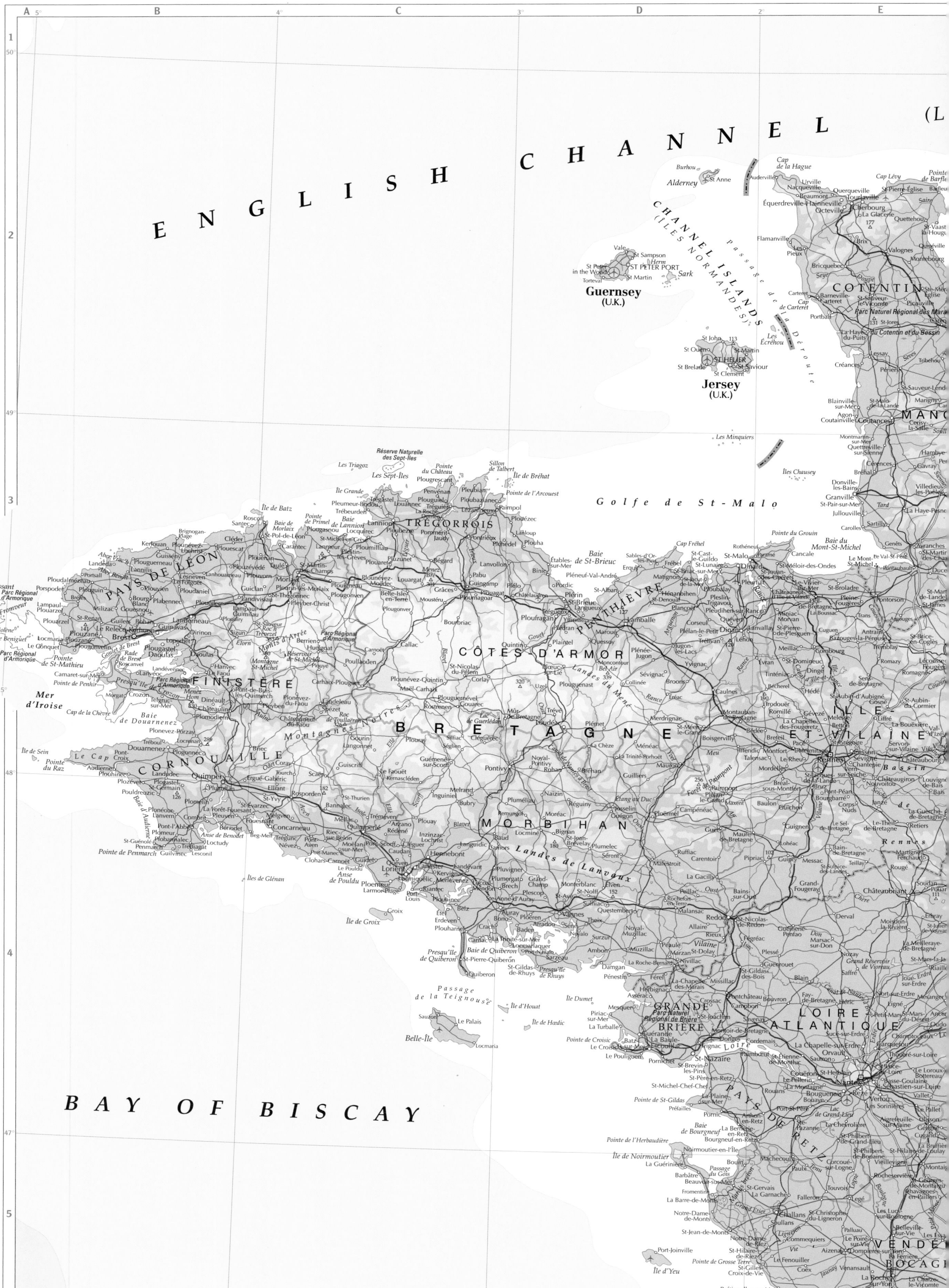

ENGLISH CHANNEL (L

BAY OF BISCAY

Mer d'Iroise

Golfe de St-Malo

Passage de la Déroute

CHANNEL ISLANDS (ÎLES NORMANDES)

Guernsey (U.K.)

Jersey (U.K.)

COTENTIN

MANC

PAYS DE LÉON

FINISTÈRE

CORNOUAILLE

TRÉGORROIS

CÔTES D'ARMOR

PENTHIÈVRE

BRETAGNE

ILLE ET VILAINE

MORBIHAN

Landes de Lanvaux

GRANDE BRIÈRE

LOIRE ATLANTIQUE

PAYS DE RETZ

VENDÉE BOCAGE

Conic Equidistant Projection

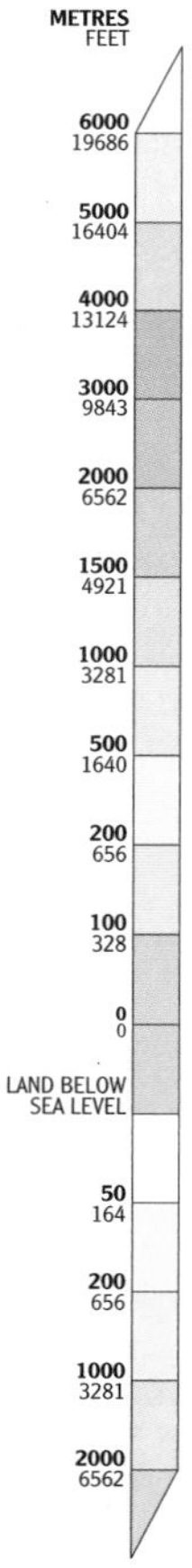

METRES / FEET

6000 / 19686
5000 / 16404
4000 / 13124
3000 / 9843
2000 / 6562
1500 / 4921
1000 / 3281
500 / 1640
200 / 656
100 / 328
0

LAND BELOW SEA LEVEL

50 / 164
200 / 656
1000 / 3281
2000 / 6562

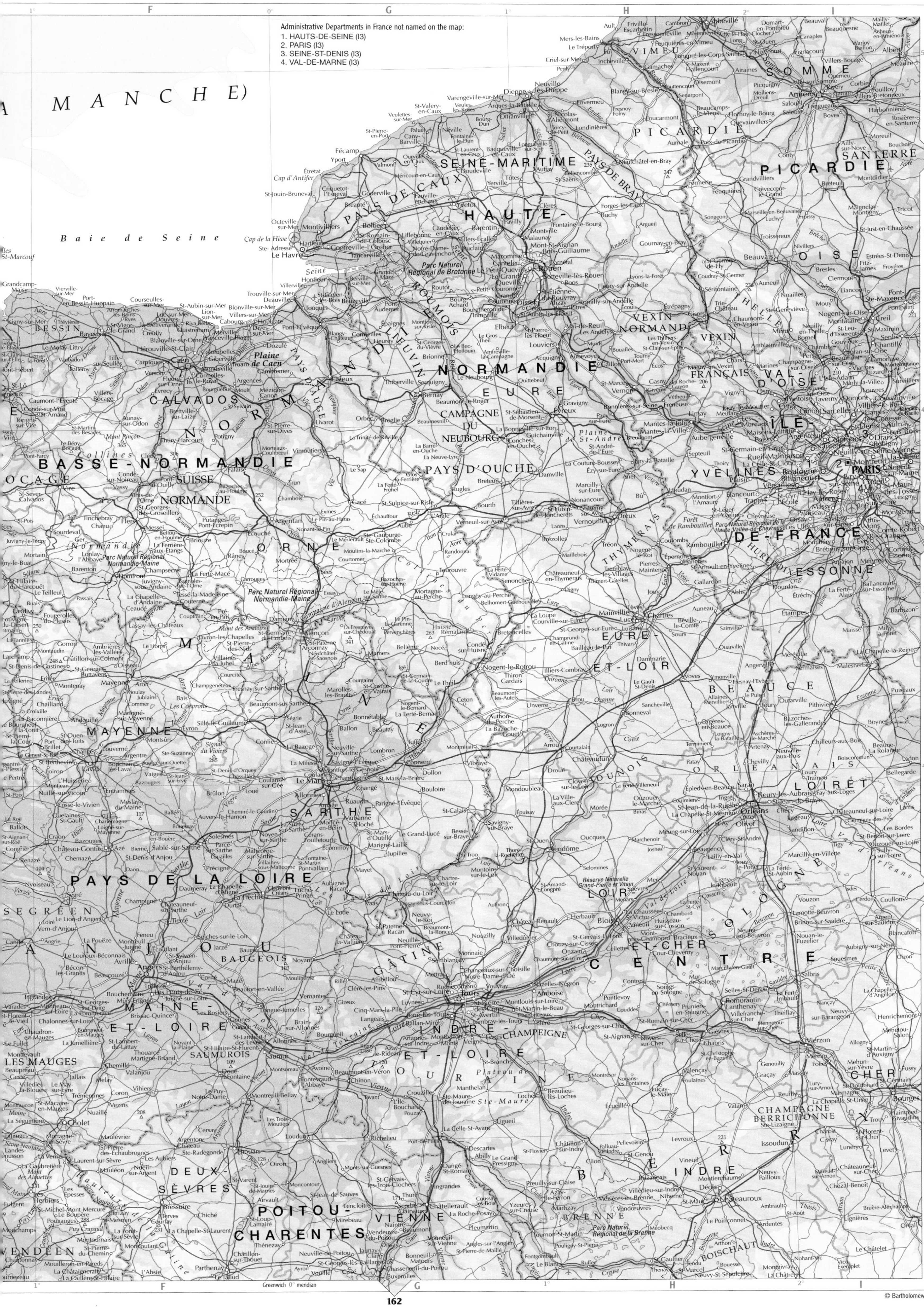

Administrative Departments in France not named on the map:
1. HAUTS-DE-SEINE (I3)
2. PARIS (I3)
3. SEINE-ST-DENIS (I3)
4. VAL-DE-MARNE (I3)

LA MANCHE (ENGLISH CHANNEL)

Baie de Seine

MILES   KILOMETRES

100

90

80

70

60   60

50

50   80

40   70

60

30   50

40

20   30

20

10   10

10

0   0

1:1 200 000

© Bartholomew Ltd

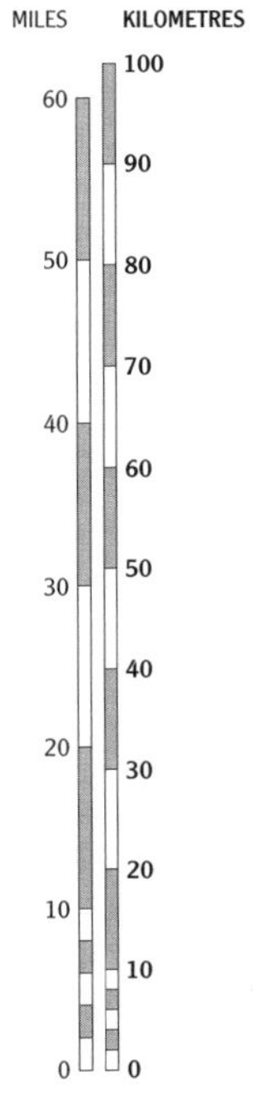

172

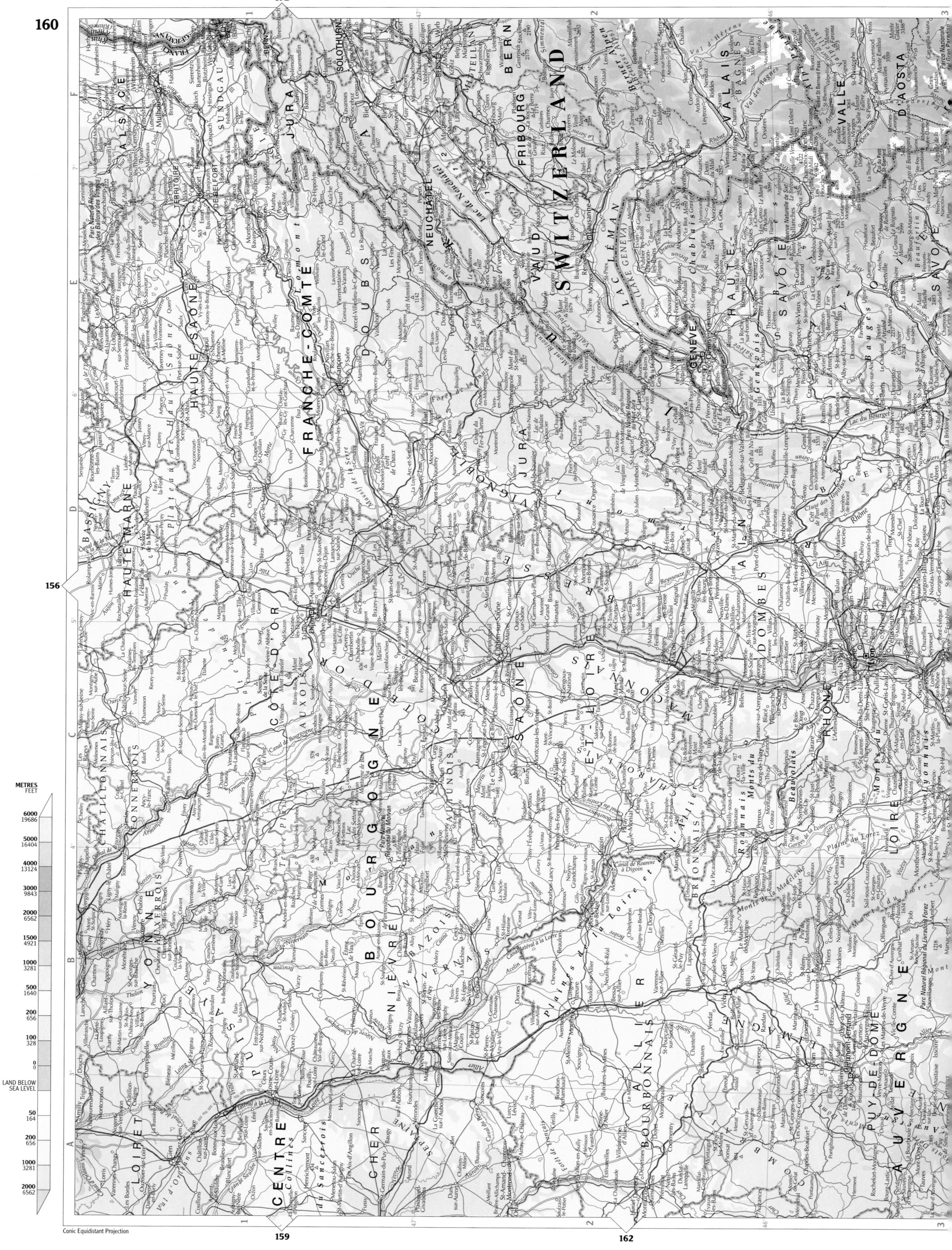

159

162

156

SWITZERLAND

FRANCE
ALSACE
SUNDGAU
TERRITOIRE
DE BELFORT
JURA
HAUTE-SAÔNE
HAUTE-MARNE
BASSIGNY
FRANCHE-COMTÉ
DOUBS
NEUCHÂTEL
Lac de Neuchâtel
SOLOTHURN
BERN
MITTELLAND
FRIBOURG
VAUD
LAC LÉMAN (LAKE GENEVA)
GENÈVE
HAUTE-SAVOIE
VALAIS
VALLE D'AOSTA
SAVOIE
CÔTE-D'OR
BOURGOGNE
AUXOIS
SAÔNE-ET-LOIRE
AIN
BRESSE
DOMBES
BUGEY
JURA
BUGEY
CHÂTILLONNAIS
YONNE
AUXERROIS
PUISAYE
NIÈVRE
MORVAN
AUTUNOIS
CHAROLAIS
BEAUJOLAIS
RHÔNE
LYON
MÂCONNAIS
BRIONNAIS
LOIRE
FOREZ
BOURBONNAIS
ALLIER
NIVERNAIS
BAZOIS
CENTRE
LOIRET
CHER
SOLOGNE
Sancerrois
Collines du Sancerrois
Val de Sancerre
AUVERGNE
PUY-DE-DÔME
Clermont-Ferrand
LIMAGNE

Dijon
Besançon
Lyon
Vichy
Moulins
Nevers
Mâcon
Bourg-en-Bresse
Annecy
Chambéry
Genève
Neuchâtel
Bern

Parc Naturel Régional des Ballons des Vosges
Parc Naturel Régional du Morvan
Parc Naturel Régional du Livradois Forez

Canal de Bourgogne
Canal du Nivernais
Canal de Roanne à Digoin
Canal latéral à la Loire

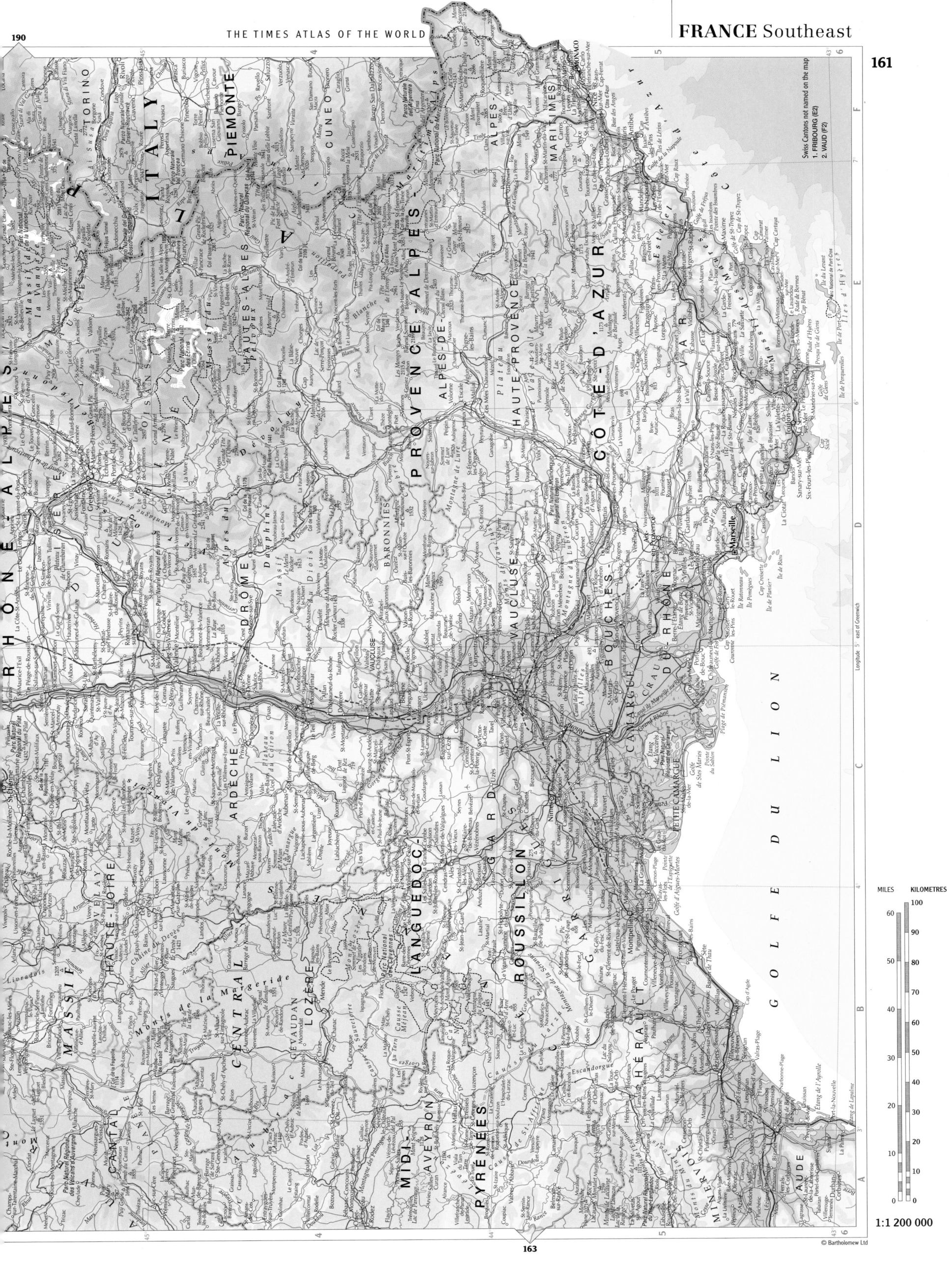

Swiss Cantons not named on the map
1. FRIBOURG (E2)
2. VAUD (F2)

MILES   KILOMETRES

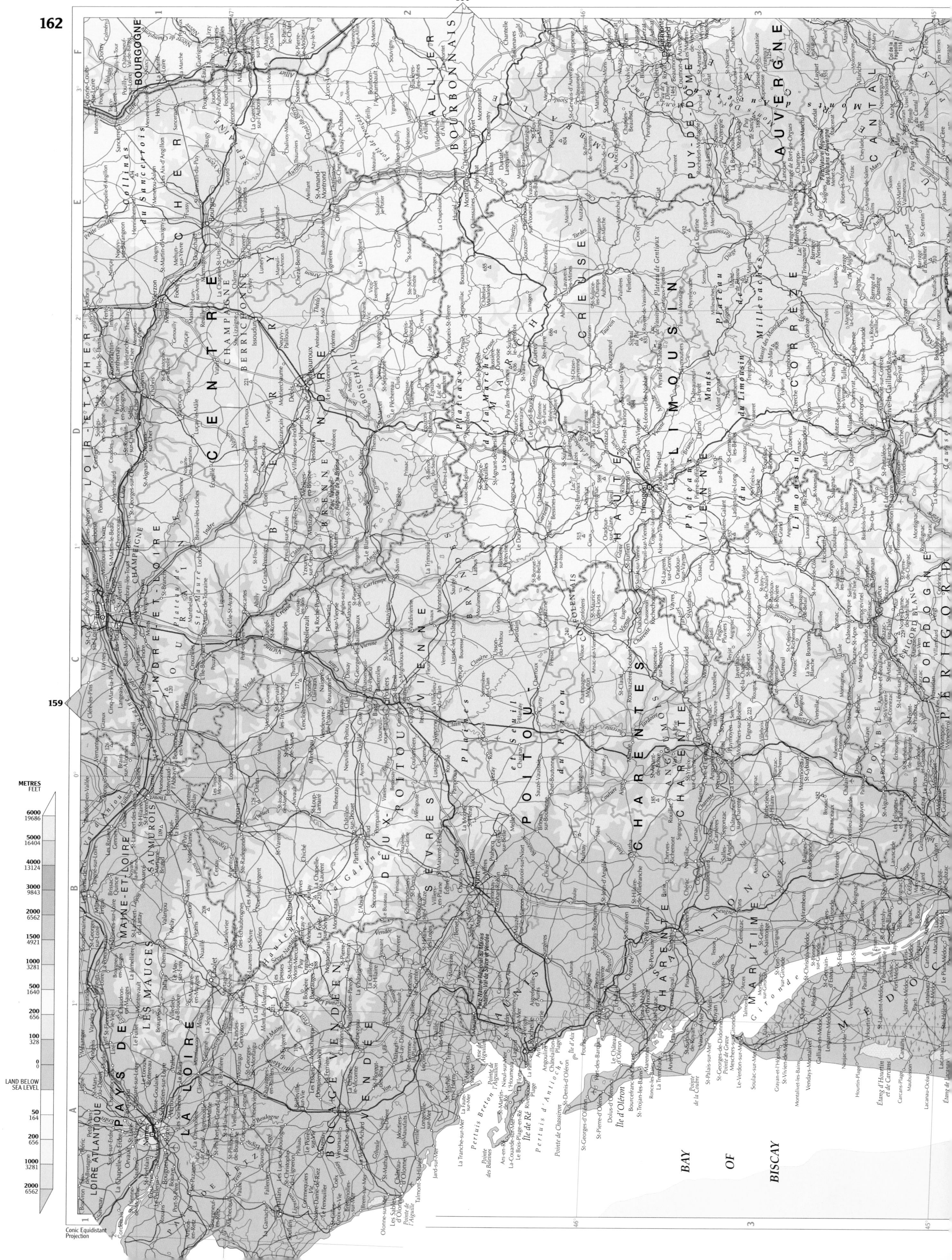

160

159

BOURGOGNE

CENTRE

LOIR-ET-CHER

CHER

INDRE

BERRICHONNE

CHAMPAGNE

ALLIER

BOURBONNAIS

AUVERGNE

PUY-DE-DÔME

CANTAL

CREUSE

HAUTE-VIENNE

LIMOUSIN

CORRÈZE

INDRE-ET-LOIRE

TOURAINE

BRENNE

VIENNE

POITOU-CHARENTES

DEUX-SÈVRES

CHARENTE

ANGOUMOIS

CHARENTE-MARITIME

SAINTONGE

AUNIS

MÉDOC

PÉRIGORD BLANC

DORDOGNE

PAYS DE LA LOIRE

MAINE-ET-LOIRE

ANJOU

SAUMUROIS

LES MAUGES

BOCAGE VENDÉEN

VENDÉE

LOIRE-ATLANTIQUE

Île de Ré

Île d'Oléron

Pertuis Breton

Pertuis d'Antioche

Gironde

BAY OF BISCAY

METRES / FEET
6000 / 19686
5000 / 16404
4000 / 13124
3000 / 9843
2000 / 6562
1500 / 4921
1000 / 3281
500 / 1640
200 / 656
100 / 328
0 / 0
LAND BELOW SEA LEVEL
50 / 164
200 / 656
1000 / 3281
2000 / 6562

Conic Equidistant Projection

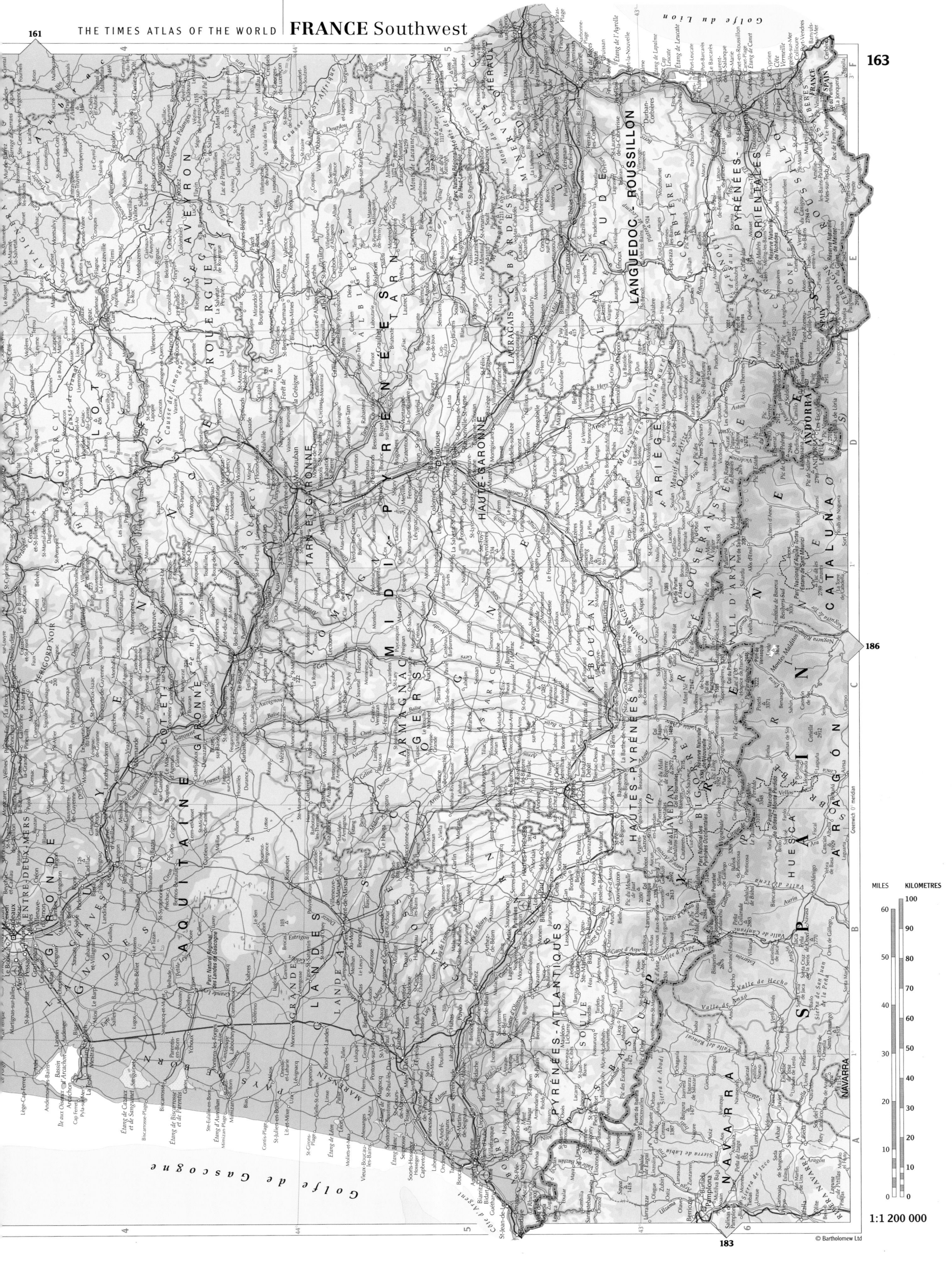
161
186
183
Golfe de Gascogne
Golfe du Lion
AQUITAINE
MIDI-PYRÉNÉES
LANGUEDOC-ROUSSILLON
PYRÉNÉES-ATLANTIQUES
HAUTES-PYRÉNÉES
HAUTE-GARONNE
PYRÉNÉES-ORIENTALES
TARN-ET-GARONNE
LOT-ET-GARONNE
GIRONDE
LANDES
GERS
TARN
AVEYRON
LOT
ARIÈGE
AUDE
HÉRAULT
ANDORRA
NAVARRA
HUESCA
ARAGÓN
CATALUÑA
SPAIN
FRANCE
Toulouse
Bordeaux
Pamplona
MILES
KILOMETRES
1:1 200 000
© Bartholomew Ltd

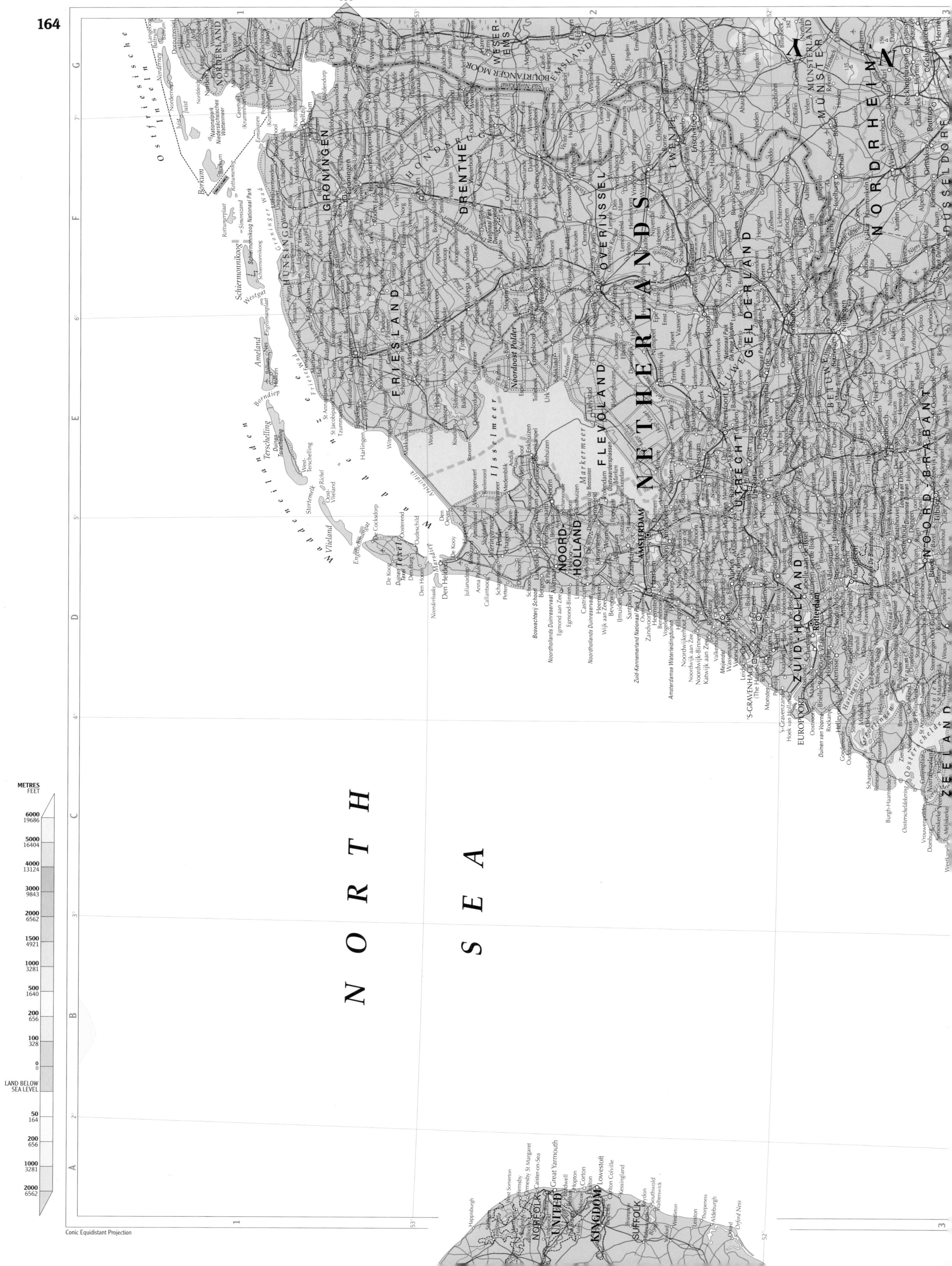

168

NORTH SEA

NETHERLANDS

NORDERLAND
GRONINGEN
FRIESLAND
DRENTHE
OVERIJSSEL
FLEVOLAND
NOORD-HOLLAND
ZUID-HOLLAND
UTRECHT
GELDERLAND
NOORD-BRABANT
ZEELAND
WESER-EMS
MÜNSTERLAND
MÜNSTER
NORDRHEIN
DÜSSEL-

Ostfriesische Inseln

Waddeneilanden
Vlieland
Terschelling
Ameland
Schiermonnikoog
Borkum

IJsselmeer
Markermeer
Noordoost Polder

Nationalpark Niedersächsisches Wattenmeer

AMSTERDAM
Rotterdam
'S-GRAVENHAGE (The Hague)
EUROPOORT

UNITED KINGDOM
NORFOLK
SUFFOLK
Great Yarmouth
Lowestoft

Conic Equidistant Projection

METRES	FEET
6000	19686
5000	16404
4000	13124
3000	9843
2000	6562
1500	4921
1000	3281
500	1640
200	656
100	328
0	0

LAND BELOW SEA LEVEL

50	164
200	656
1000	3281
2000	6562

157

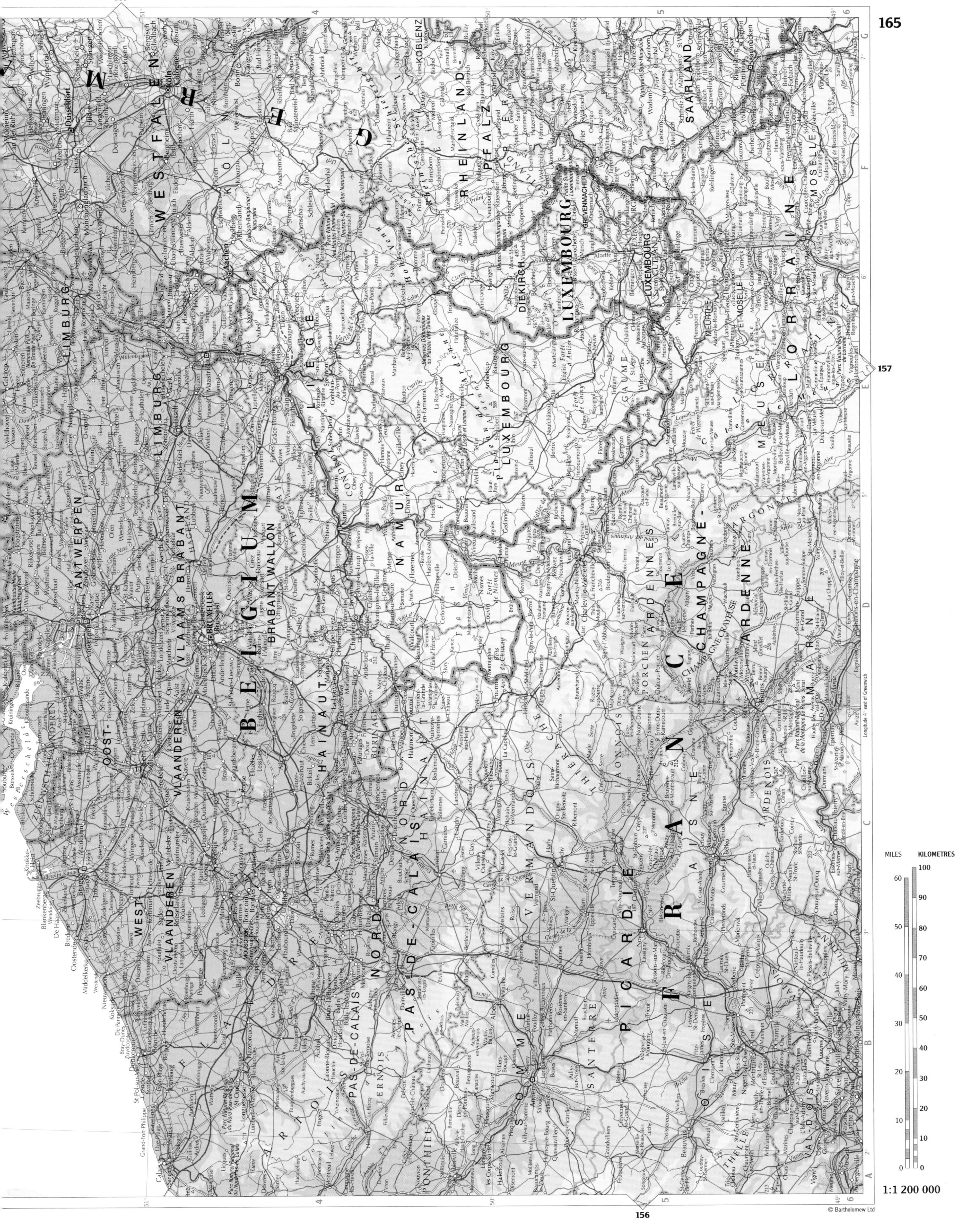

BELGIUM

LUXEMBOURG

FRANCE

WESTFALEN

RHEINLAND-PFALZ

LIMBURG

ANTWERPEN

VLAAMS BRABANT

BRABANT WALLON

OOST-VLAANDEREN

WEST-VLAANDEREN

HAINAUT

NAMUR

LIÈGE

LUXEMBOURG

DIEKIRCH

LUXEMBOURG

GRÉVENMACHER

MEUSE-ET-MOSELLE

MEURTHE-ET-MOSELLE

LORRAINE

ARDENNES

CHAMPAGNE-ARDENNE

MARNE

AISNE

PICARDIE

SOMME

PAS-DE-CALAIS

NORD

ZEEUWSCH-VLAANDEREN

GAUME

BRUXELLES (Brussel)

Maastricht

Aachen

KÖLN

KOBLENZ

MILES   KILOMETRES
60   100
50   90
          80
40   70
          60
30   50
          40
20   30
          20
10   10
0   0

Longitude 4° east of Greenwich

142

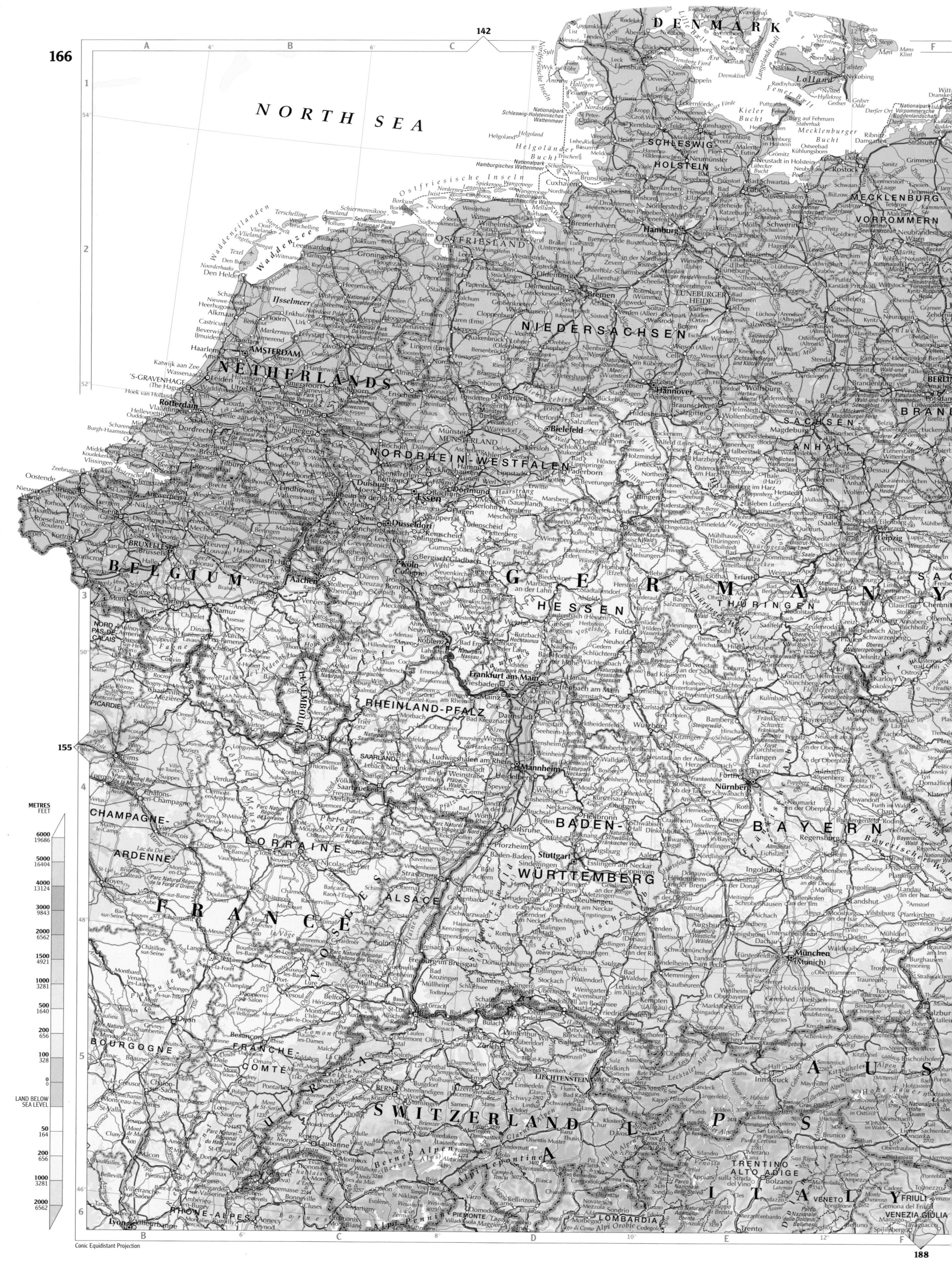
NORTH SEA
DENMARK
NETHERLANDS
BELGIUM
GERMANY
FRANCE
SWITZERLAND
AUSTRIA
ITALY
ALPS
SCHLESWIG-HOLSTEIN
MECKLENBURG-VORPOMMERN
NIEDERSACHSEN
SACHSEN-ANHALT
NORDRHEIN-WESTFALEN
HESSEN
THÜRINGEN
RHEINLAND-PFALZ
SAARLAND
BADEN-WÜRTTEMBERG
BAYERN
LORRAINE
ALSACE
CHAMPAGNE-ARDENNE
BOURGOGNE
FRANCHE-COMTÉ
RHÔNE-ALPES
PICARDIE
NORD PAS-DE-CALAIS
LOMBARDIA
TRENTINO ALTO ADIGE
VENETO
FRIULI VENEZIA GIULIA
PIEMONTE
LIECHTENSTEIN
LUXEMBOURG
AMSTERDAM
BRUXELLES (Brussel)
Hamburg
Bremen
Hannover
Köln (Cologne)
Frankfurt am Main
Stuttgart
München (Munich)
Nürnberg
Zürich
BERN
Genève
Lyon
Strasbourg
METRES
FEET
6000
19686
5000
16404
4000
13124
3000
9843
2000
6562
1500
4921
1000
3281
500
1640
200
656
100
328
0
0
LAND BELOW SEA LEVEL
50
164
200
656
1000
3281
2000
6562

155

Conic Equidistant Projection

188

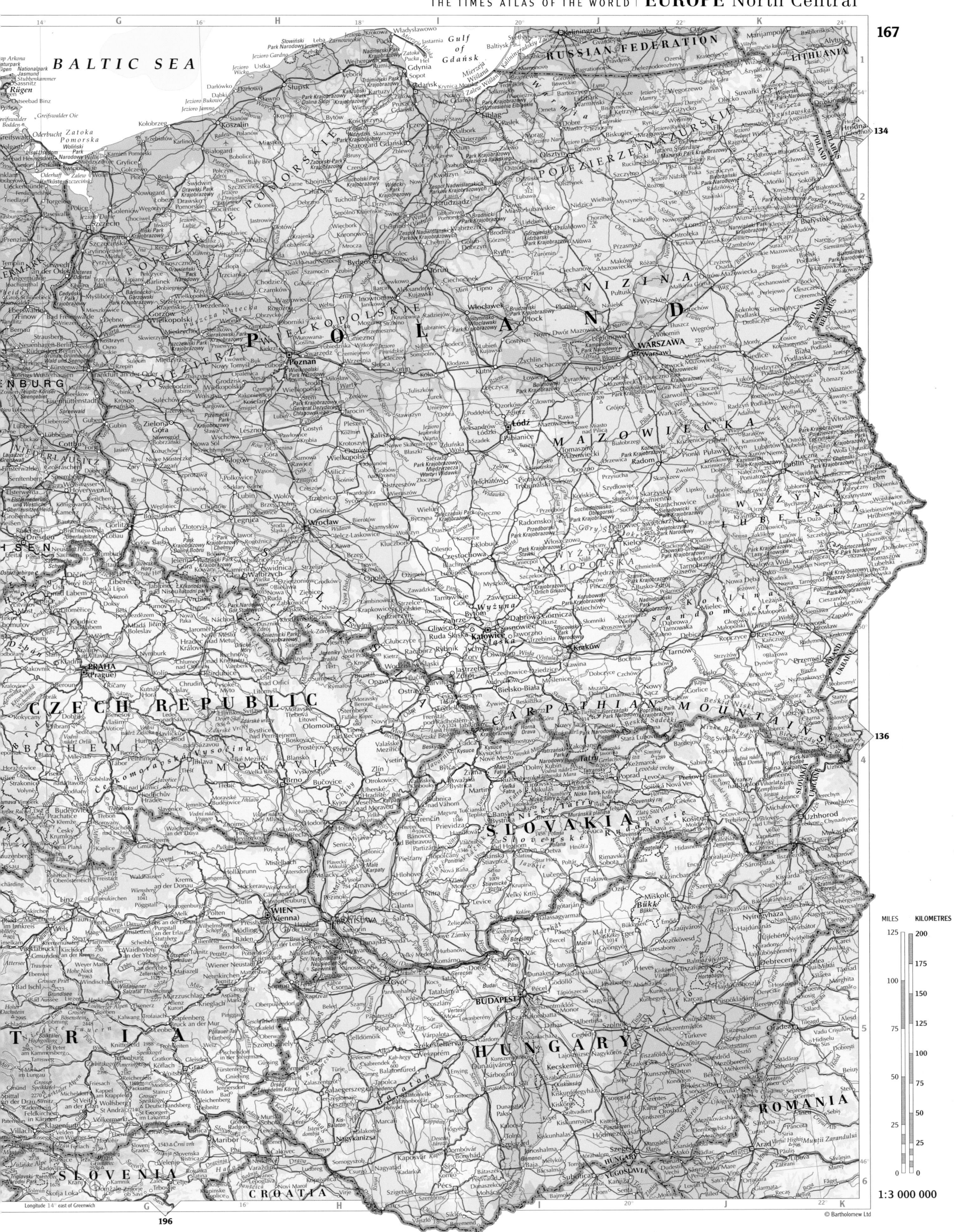
BALTIC SEA
Gulf of Gdańsk
RUSSIAN FEDERATION
LITHUANIA
BELARUS
POLAND
UKRAINE
CZECH REPUBLIC
SLOVAKIA
HUNGARY
ROMANIA
SLOVENIA
CROATIA
YUGOSLAVIA
BOHEMIA
MORAVIA
CARPATHIAN MOUNTAINS
POJEZIERZE POMORSKIE
POJEZIERZE MAZURSKIE
POJEZIERZE WIELKOPOLSKIE
NIZINA MAZOWIECKA
WYŻYNA LUBELSKA
WYŻYNA MAŁOPOLSKA
WARSZAWA (Warsaw)
PRAHA (Prague)
WIEN (Vienna)
BRATISLAVA
BUDAPEST
Gdańsk
Poznań
Łódź
Kraków
Wrocław
Katowice
Kaliningrad
134
136
196
MILES
KILOMETRES
1:3 000 000
Longitude 14° east of Greenwich
© Bartholomew Ltd

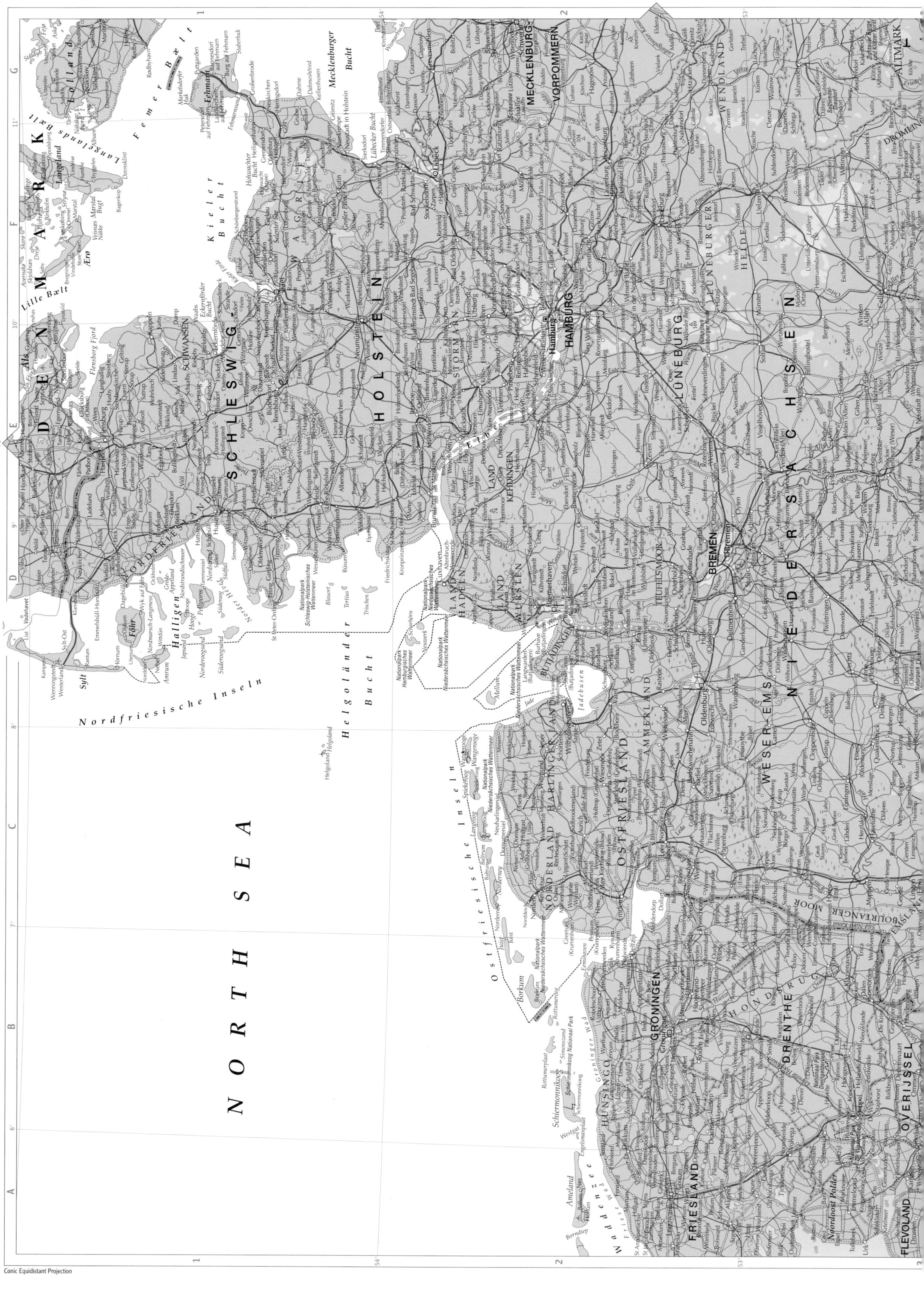

171

173

172

164

157

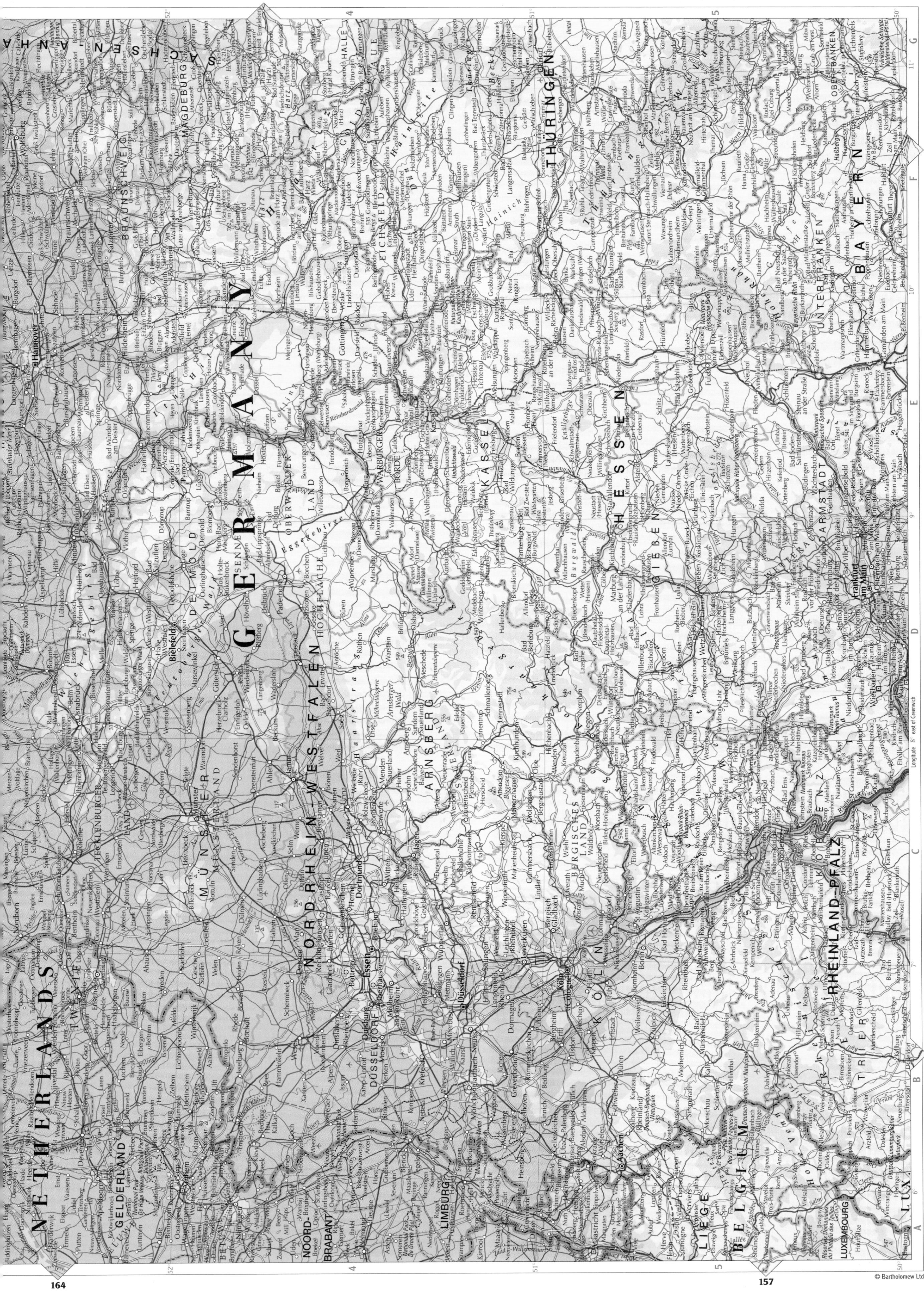

GERMANY

NETHERLANDS

BELGIUM

LUXEMBOURG

NORDRHEIN-WESTFALEN

NIEDERSACHSEN

SACHSEN-ANHALT

THÜRINGEN

BAYERN

HESSEN

RHEINLAND-PFALZ

BRAUNSCHWEIG

MAGDEBURG

MÜNSTERLAND

TECKLENBURGER LAND

OBERWESER HOCHFLÄCHE

DETMOLD

BIELEFELD

ARNSBERG

BERGISCHES LAND

KASSEL

GIESSEN

DARMSTADT

KOBLENZ

TRIER

UNTERFRANKEN

OBERFRANKEN

LIÈGE

LIMBURG

NOORD-BRABANT

GELDERLAND

TWENTE

Hannover

Bielefeld

Dortmund

Essen

Duisburg

Düsseldorf

KÖLN

Göttingen

Frankfurt am Main

Longitude 8 east of Greenwich

MILES	KILOMETRES
60	100
	90
50	80
	70
40	60
	50
30	40
20	30
	20
10	10
0	0

1:1 200 000

© Bartholomew Ltd

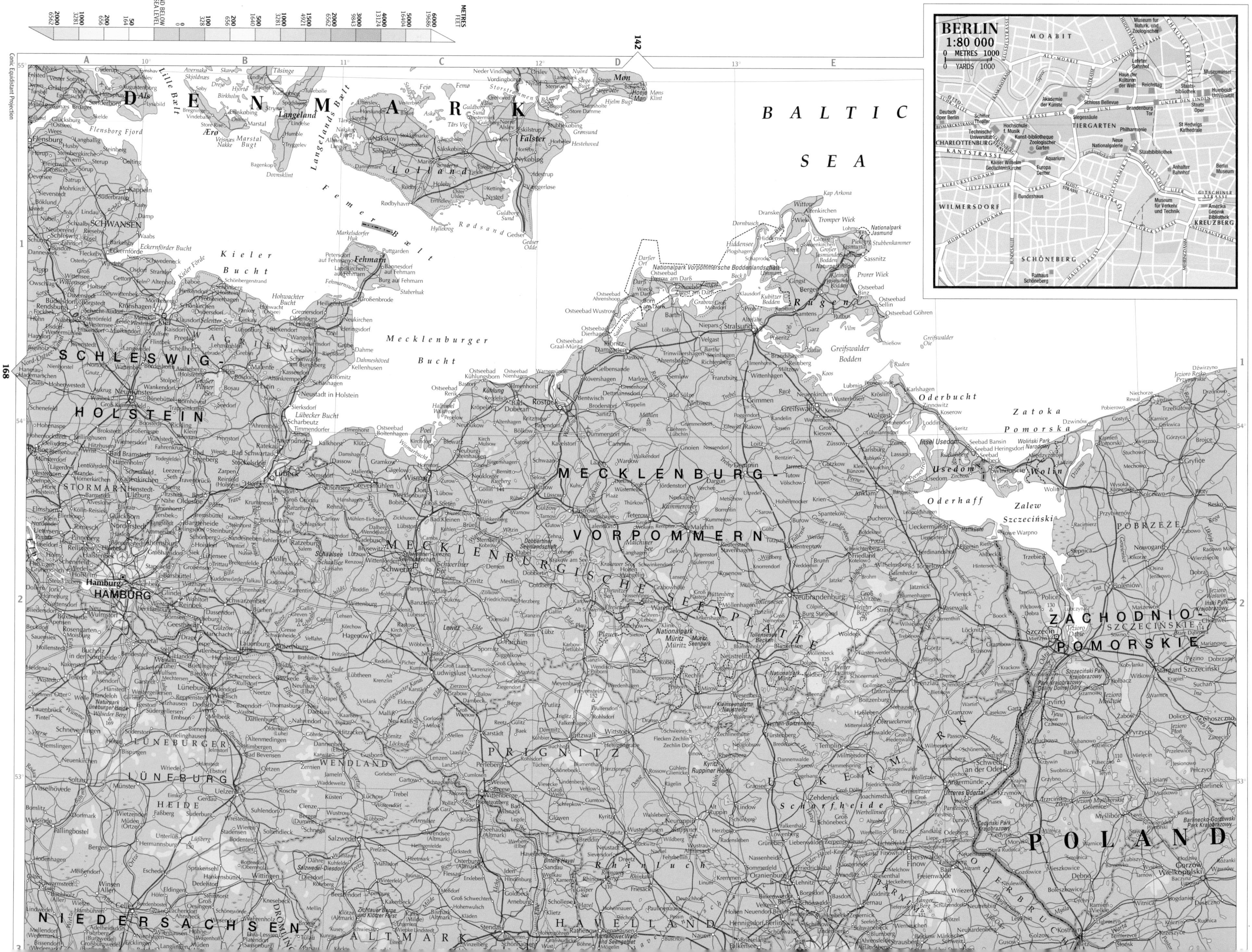
BERLIN
1:80 000
METRES 1000
YARDS 1000
MOABIT
TIERGARTEN
CHARLOTTENBURG
WILMERSDORF
SCHÖNEBERG
KREUZBERG
BALTIC
SEA
DENMARK
SCHLESWIG-HOLSTEIN
MECKLENBURG-VORPOMMERN
MECKLENBURGISCHE SEENPLATTE
NIEDERSACHSEN
LÜNEBURGER HEIDE
ZACHODNIOPOMORSKIE
POLAND
Mecklenburger Bucht
Kieler Bucht
Zatoka Pomorska
Zalew Szczeciński
Oderhaff
Hamburg
HAMBURG
Lübeck
Kiel
Rostock
Stralsund
Szczecin
METRES
FEET
LAND BELOW SEA LEVEL
Conic Equidistant Projection
142
168

1:1 200 000

MILES   KILOMETRES

© Bartholomew Ltd

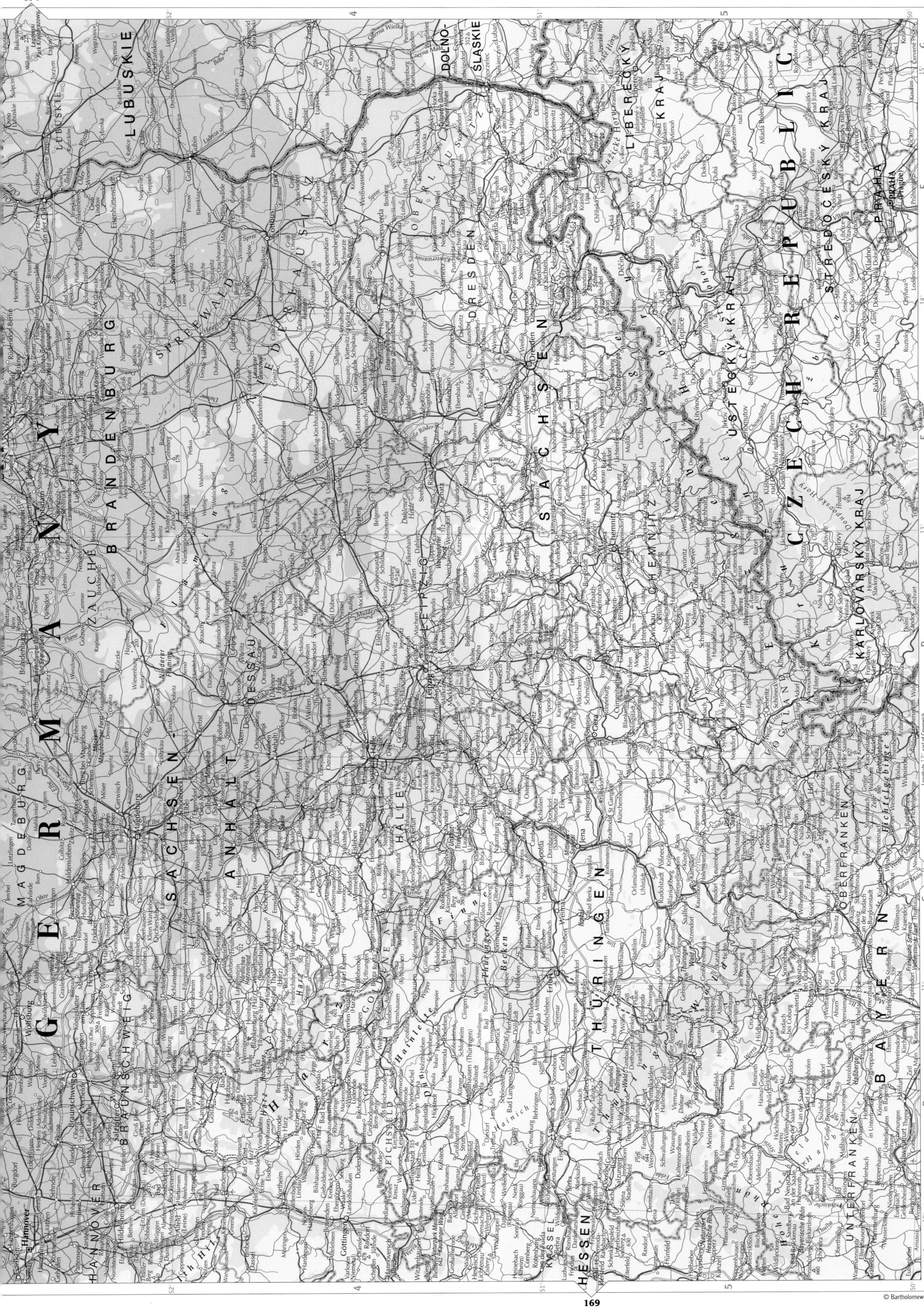

174
GERMANY
CZECH REPUBLIC
BRANDENBURG
SACHSEN
SACHSEN-ANHALT
THÜRINGEN
BAYERN
HESSEN
LUBUSKIE
DOLNOŚLĄSKIE
MAGDEBURG
DESSAU
HALLE
LEIPZIG
CHEMNITZ
DRESDEN
KASSEL
BRAUNSCHWEIG
HANNOVER
OBERFRANKEN
UNTERFRANKEN
LIBERECKÝ KRAJ
ÚSTECKÝ KRAJ
KARLOVARSKÝ KRAJ
STŘEDOČESKÝ KRAJ
PRAHA (Prague)
SPREEWALD
ZAUCHE
Longitude 12° east of Greenwich
176
173
169

157

BELGIUM

LIÈGE

LUXEMBOURG

KÖLN

KOBLENZ

RHEINLAND

PFALZ

NORDPFÄLZER

BERGLAND

SAARLAND

HESSEN

DARMSTADT

Frankfurt am Main

Wiesbaden

Mainz

Mannheim

Ludwigshafen am Rhein

Heidelberg

RHEINHESSEN-PFALZ

KARLSRUHE

Pforzheim

STUTTGART

Stuttgart

BADEN-WÜRTTEMBERG

MOSELLE

LORRAINE

MEURTHE-ET-MOSELLE

FRANCE

ALSACE

BAS-RHIN

Strasbourg

FREIBURG

Freiburg im Breisgau

TÜBINGEN

VOSGES

HAUT-RHIN

Mulhouse

HAUTE-SAÔNE

FRANCHE-COMTÉ

TERRITOIRE DE BELFORT

SUNDGAU

HOTZENWALD

SCHAFFHAUSEN

THURGAU

ZÜRICH

AARGAU

SOLOTHURN

BERN

JURA

DOUBS

NEUCHÂTEL

VAUD

SWITZERLAND

LUZERN

ZUG

SCHWYZ

GLARUS

SANKT GALLEN

APPENZELL AUSSER RHODEN

APPENZELL INNER RHODEN

NIDWALDEN

LIECHTENSTEIN

METRES / FEET

6000 / 19686
5000 / 16404
4000 / 13124
3000 / 9843
2000 / 6562
1500 / 4921
1000 / 3281
500 / 1640
200 / 656
100 / 328
0

LAND BELOW SEA LEVEL

50 / 164
200 / 656
1000 / 3281
2000 / 6562

Conic Equidistant Projection

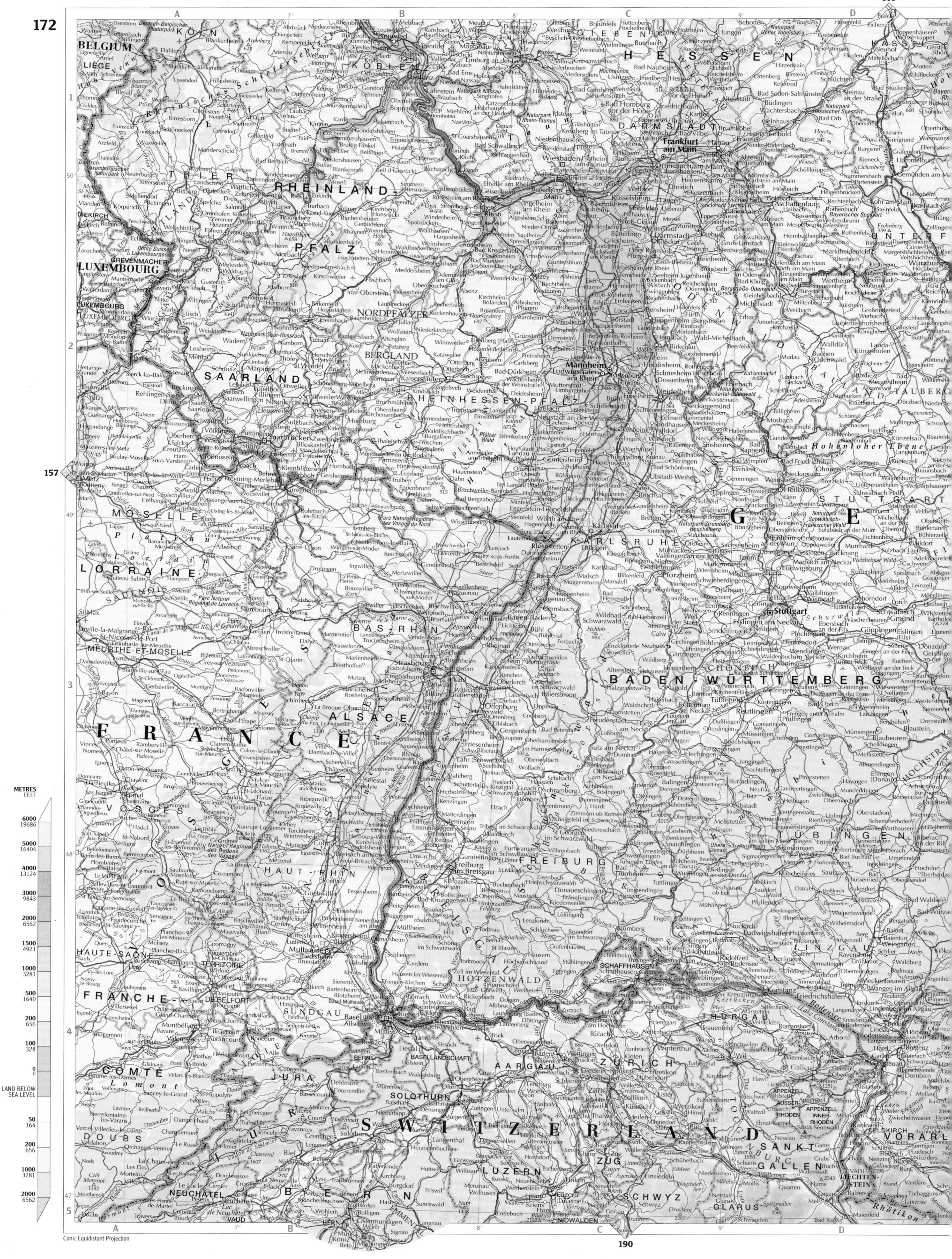

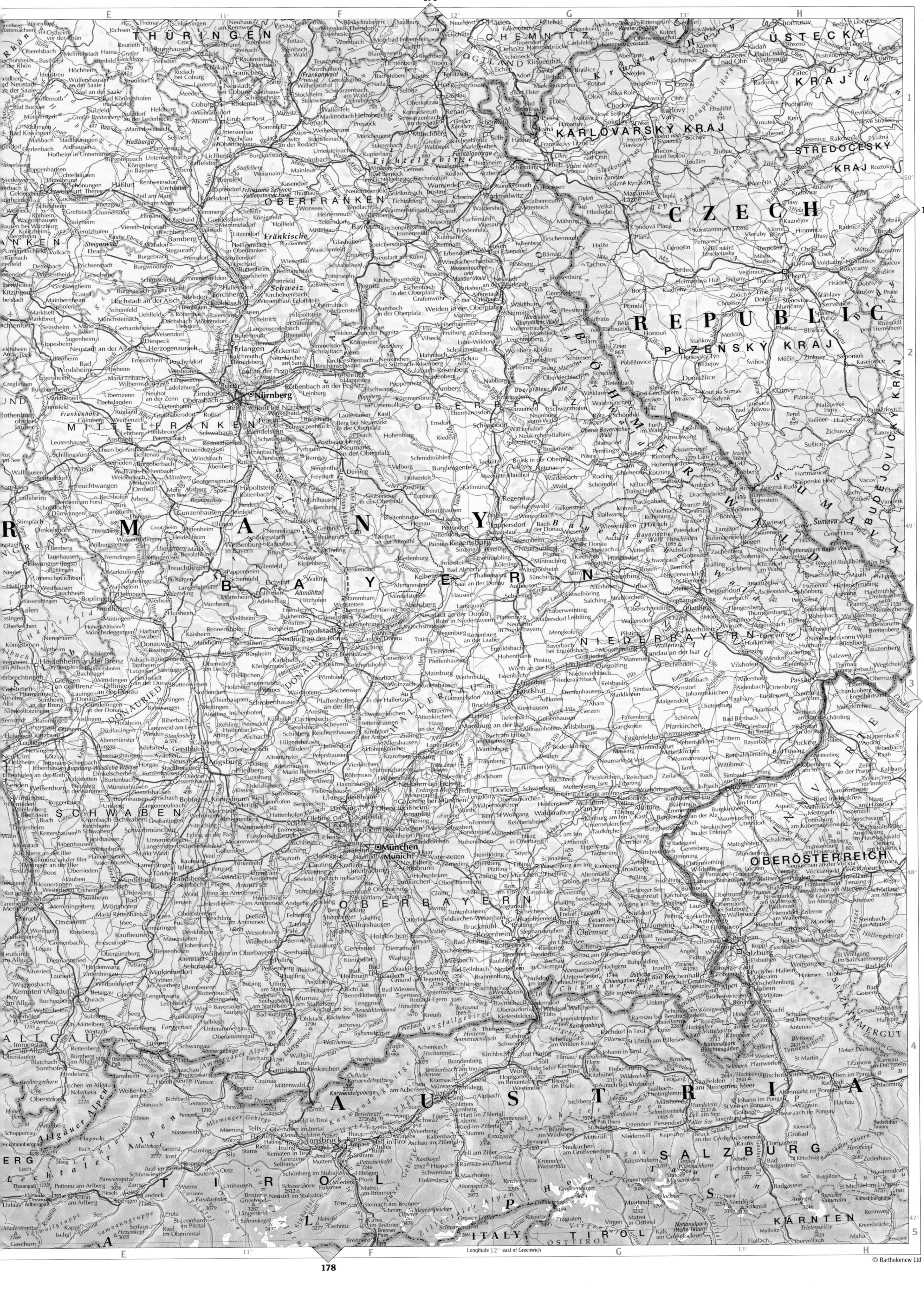

THÜRINGEN

CHEMNITZ

ÜSTECKÝ KRAJ

KARLOVARSKÝ KRAJ

STREDOČESKÝ KRAJ

OBERFRANKEN

Fichtelgebirge

Fränkische Schweiz

C Z E C H   R E P U B L I C

PLZEŇSKÝ KRAJ

Bamberg

MITTELFRANKEN

Erlangen

Nürnberg

OBERPFALZ

B Ö H M E R W A L D

Bayerischer Wald

G E R M A N Y

B A Y E R N

Regensburg

Ingolstadt

NIEDERBAYERN

Passau

DONAURIED

Donauwörth

Landshut

SCHWABEN

Augsburg

OBERBAYERN

München
Munich

Chiemsee

OBERÖSTERREICH

Salzburg

ALLGÄU

SALZBURG

Allgäuer Alpen

A U S T R I A

KÄRNTEN

T I R O L

Innsbruck

A L P S

ITALY

OSTTIROL

Brenner

Longitude 12° east of Greenwich

1:1 200 000

© Bartholomew Ltd

MILES   KILOMETRES
60   100
        90
50   80
        70
40   60
30   50
        40
20   30
10   20
        10
0   0

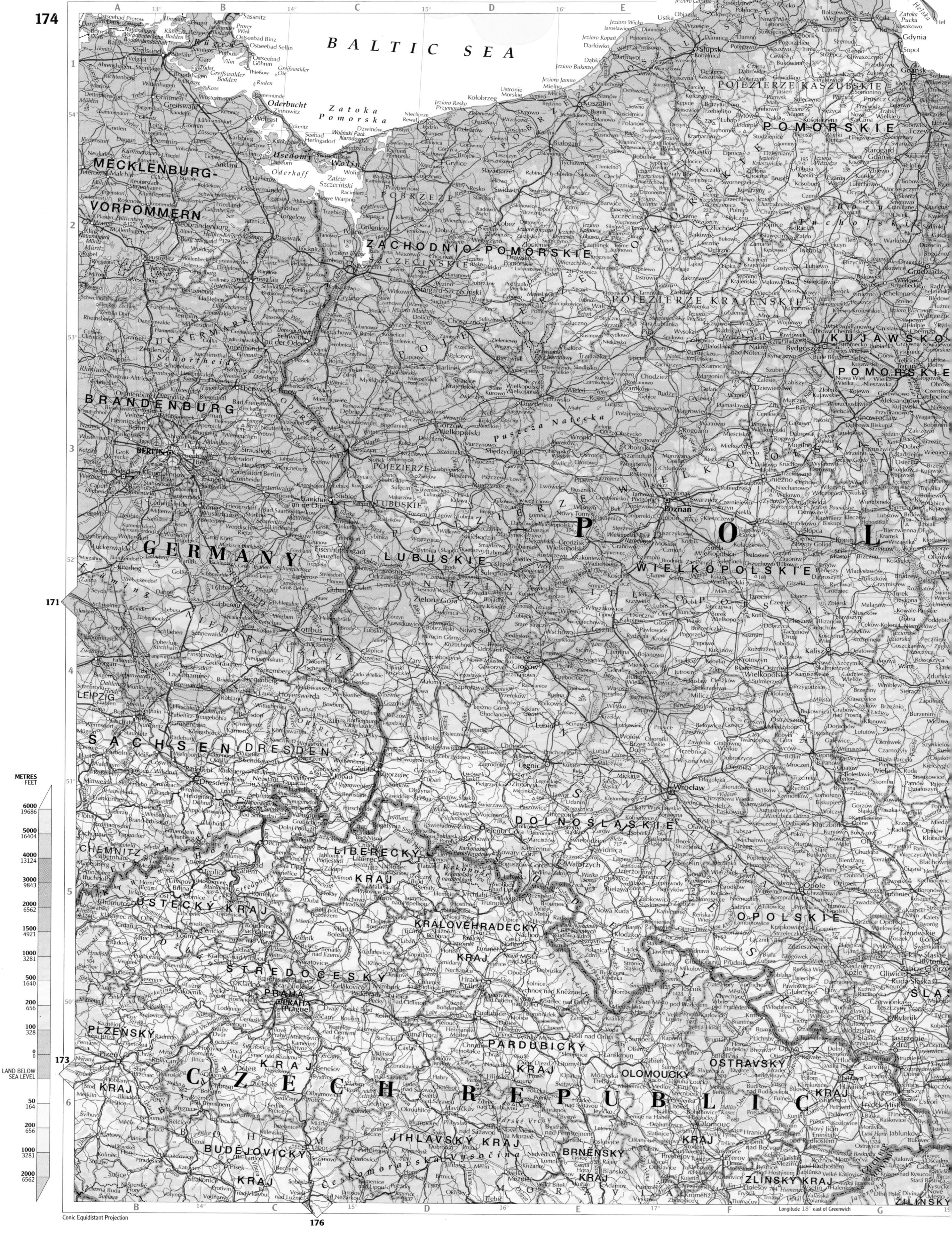

BALTIC SEA

Zatoka
Pomorska

MECKLENBURG-
VORPOMMERN

POMORSKIE

POJEZIERZE KASZUBSKIE

ZACHODNIO-POMORSKIE

POJEZIERZE KRAJEŃSKIE

KUJAWSKO-
POMORSKIE

BRANDENBURG

Berlin

POJEZIERZE

LUBUSKIE

WIELKOPOLSKIE

Poznań

POLSKA

WIELKOPOLSKA

GERMANY

LUBUSKIE

Zielona Góra

Cottbus

Głogów

DOLNOŚLĄSKIE

Wrocław

OPOLSKIE

Opole

SACHSEN   DRESDEN

LEIPZIG

Dresden

CHEMNITZ

LIBERECKÝ
KRAJ

Legnica

ŚLĄSKIE

ÚSTECKÝ KRAJ

KRÁLOVÉHRADECKÝ
KRAJ

STŘEDOČESKÝ

PLZEŇSKÝ

PRAHA
PRAHA
Prague

PARDUBICKÝ
KRAJ

OLOMOUCKÝ
KRAJ

OSTRAVSKÝ
KRAJ

KRAJ

CZECH   REPUBLIC

KRAJ

BUDĚJOVICKÝ

JIHLAVSKÝ KRAJ

BRNĚNSKÝ
KRAJ

ZLÍNSKÝ KRAJ

KRAJ

ZLÍNSKÝ

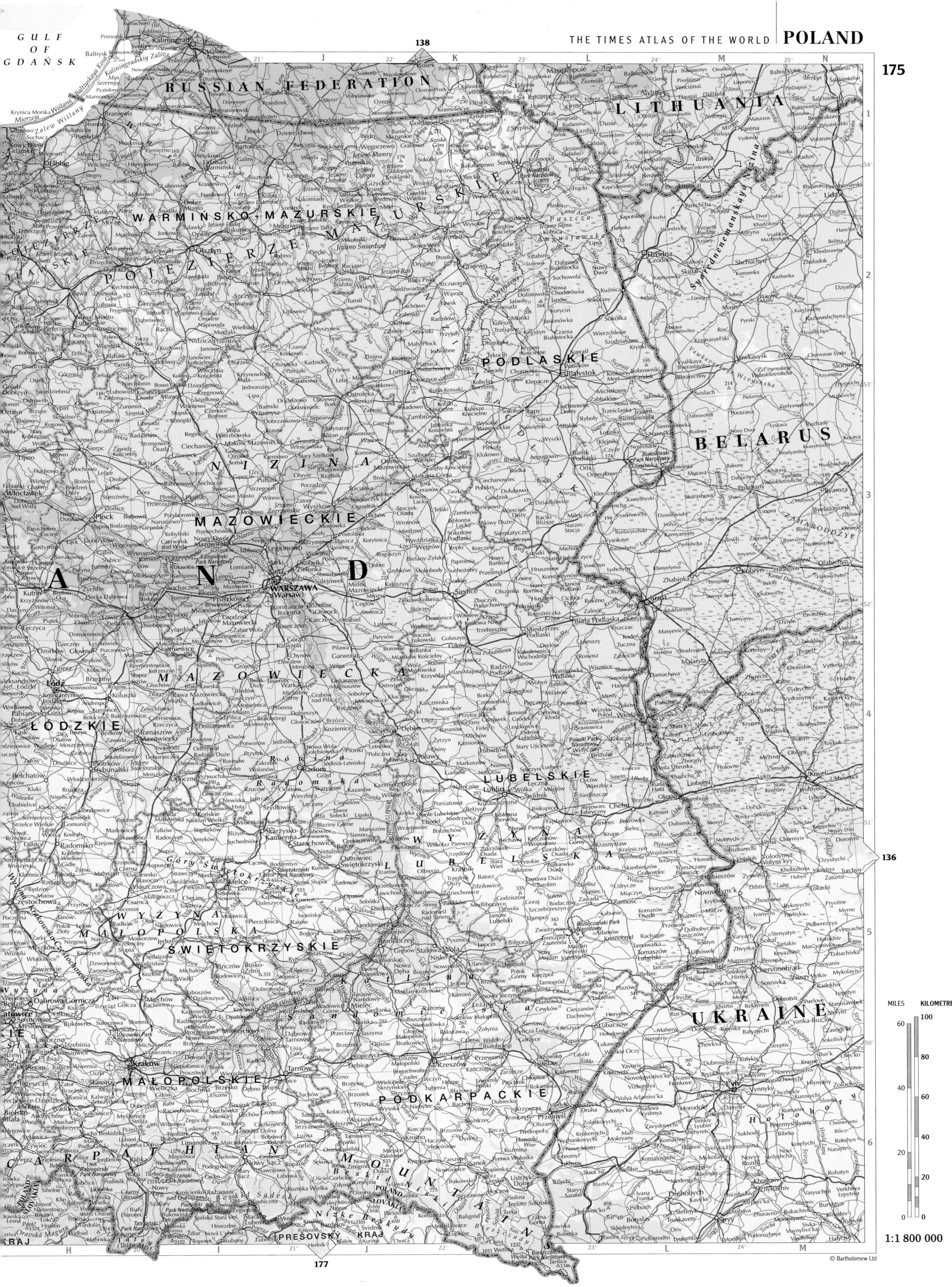

GULF
OF
GDAŃSK

RUSSIAN FEDERATION

LITHUANIA

WARMIŃSKO-MAZURSKIE

POJEZIERZE MAZURSKIE

PODLASKIE

Białystok

BELARUS

NIZINA

MAZOWIECKIE

WARSZAWA
(Warsaw)

P O L A N D

MAZOWIECKA

ŁÓDZKIE

Łódź

Radom

LUBELSKIE

Lublin

WYŻYNA
MAŁOPOLSKA

ŚWIĘTOKRZYSKIE

W Y Ż Y N A   L U B E L S K A

Brest

Biała Podlaska

Częstochowa

Kraków

MAŁOPOLSKIE

PODKARPACKIE

Rzeszów

CARPATHIAN

MOUNTAINS

UKRAINE

Lviv

PREŠOVSKÝ KRAJ

MILES   KILOMETRES
60   100
         80
40   60
20   40
         20
0   0

171

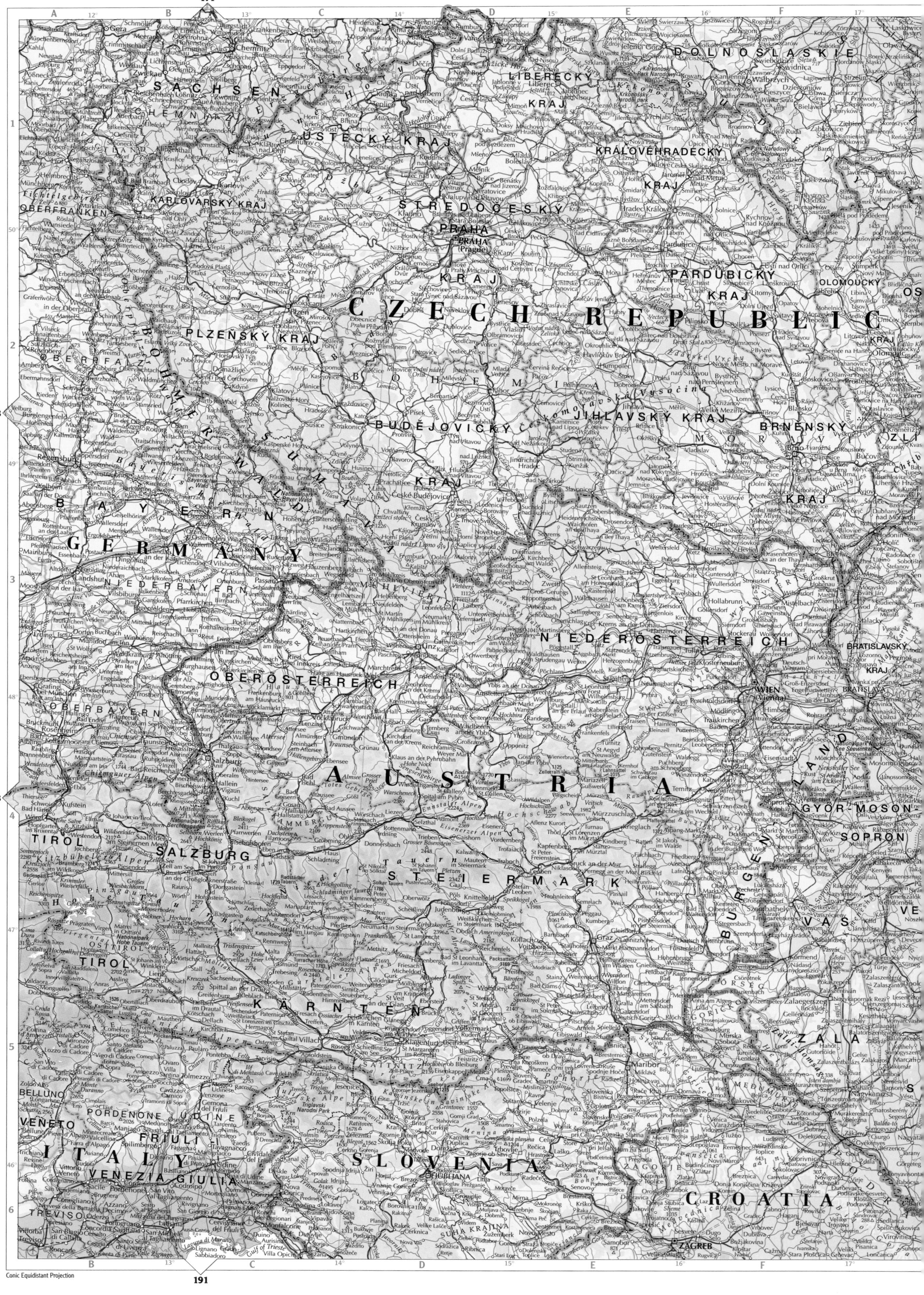

CZECH REPUBLIC

GERMANY

AUSTRIA

ITALY

SLOVENIA

CROATIA

SACHSEN

CHEMNITZ

OBERFRANKEN

KARLOVARSKÝ KRAJ

ÚSTECKÝ KRAJ

LIBERECKÝ KRAJ

KRÁLOVÉHRADECKÝ KRAJ

DOLNOŚLĄSKIE

STŘEDOČESKÝ KRAJ

PRAHA (PRAGUE)

PARDUBICKÝ KRAJ

OLOMOUCKÝ KRAJ

PLZEŇSKÝ KRAJ

OBERPFALZ

JIHLAVSKÝ KRAJ

BRNĚNSKÝ KRAJ

BUDĚJOVICKÝ KRAJ

BAYERN

NIEDERBAYERN

MÜHLVIERTEL

NIEDERÖSTERREICH

BRATISLAVSKÝ KRAJ

BRATISLAVA

OBERBAYERN

OBERÖSTERREICH

WIEN (Vienna)

BURGENLAND

GYŐR-MOSON

SOPRON

TIROL

SALZBURG

STEIERMARK

VAS

KÄRNTEN

ZALA

VENETO

PORDENONE

UDINE

FRIUL

VENEZIA GIULIA

TREVISO

BELLUNO

LJUBLJANA

MARIBOR

ZAGREB

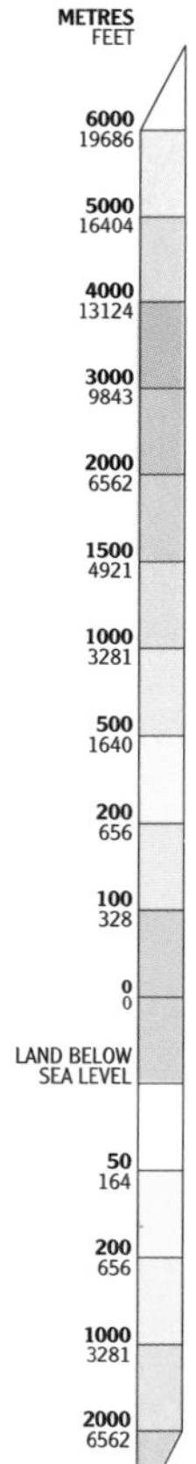

METRES / FEET

6000 19686
5000 16404
4000 13124
3000 9843
2000 6562
1500 4921
1000 3281
500 1640
200 656
100 328
0 0
LAND BELOW SEA LEVEL
50 164
200 656
1000 3281
2000 6562

Conic Equidistant Projection

173

178

191

POLAND

OPOLSKIE · ŚLĄSKIE · MAŁOPOLSKIE · ŚWIĘTOKRZYSKIE · PODKARPACKIE · LUBELSKIE

MORAVSKÝ KRAJ

CARPATHIAN MOUNTAINS

ŽILINSKÝ KRAJ · PREŠOVSKÝ KRAJ

SLOVAKIA

TRENČIANSKY KRAJ · BANSKOBYSTRICKÝ KRAJ · KOŠICKÝ KRAJ

TRNAVSKÝ · NITRIANSKY KRAJ

Tatry (Tatra Mountains)

UKRAINE

BORSOD-ABAÚJ-ZEMPLÉN · SZABOLCS-SZATMÁR-BEREG

NÓGRÁD · HEVES · SATU MARE

KOMÁROM-ESZTERGOM · PEST · JÁSZ-NAGYKUN-SZOLNOK · HAJDÚ-BIHAR

BUDAPEST

HUNGARY

FEJÉR · SZOLNOK · SĂLAJ

BÁCS-KISKUN · BÉKÉS · BIHOR

TOLNA · CSONGRÁD

ROMANIA

BARANYA · ARAD

VOJVODINA · TIMIŞ

YUGOSLAVIA

MILES   KILOMETRES

1:1 800 000

© Bartholomew Ltd

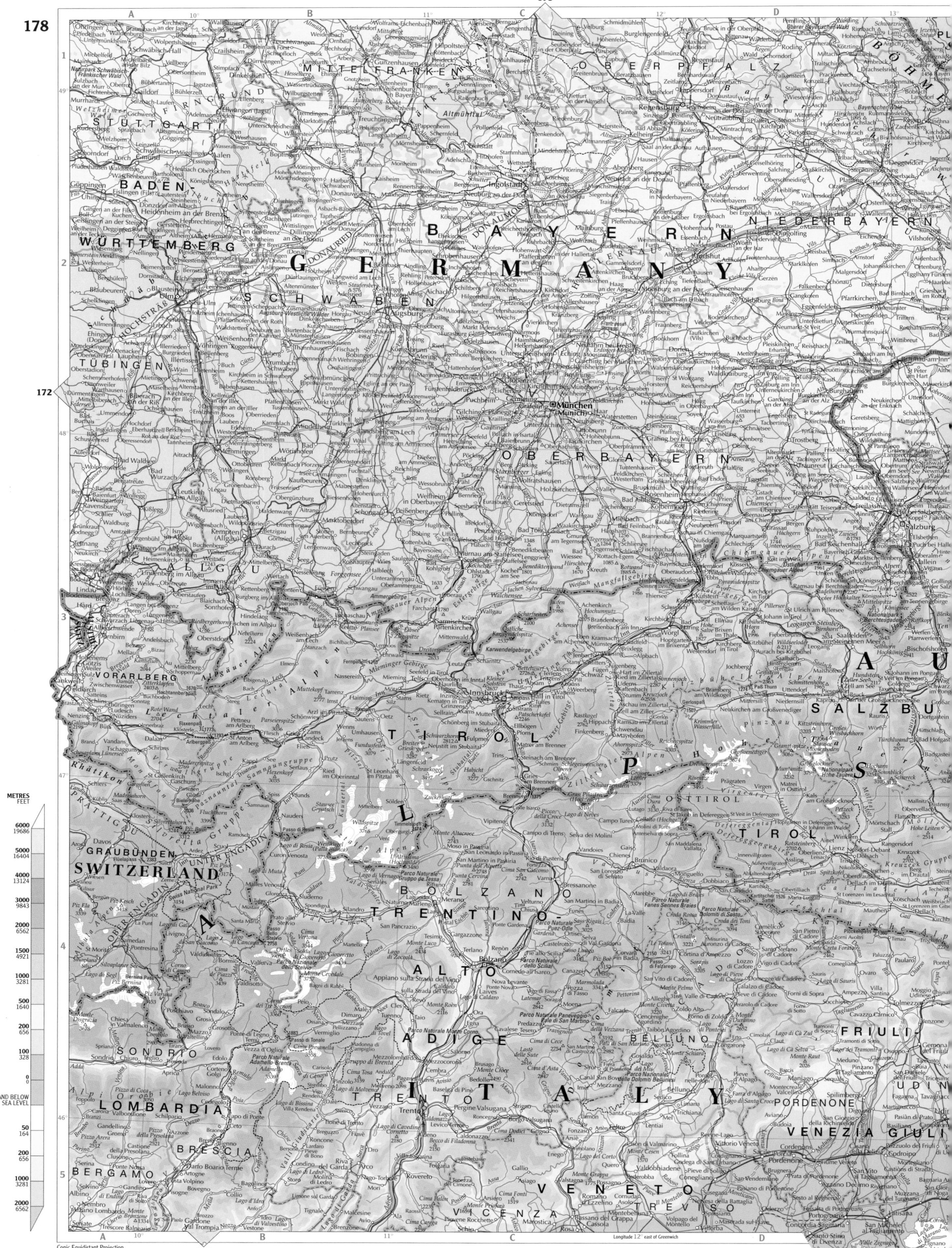
173
172
190
A
B
C
D
1
2
3
4
5
10°
11°
12°
13°
49°
48°
47°
46°
GERMANY
BAYERN
NIEDERBAYERN
OBERPFALZ
MITTELFRANKEN
SCHWABEN
OBERBAYERN
BADEN
WÜRTTEMBERG
STUTTGART
TÜBINGEN
ALLGÄU
München (Munich)
Augsburg
Ingolstadt
Regensburg
Salzburg
Innsbruck
Bolzano
Trento
AUSTRIA
SALZBURG
TIROL
OSTTIROL
VORARLBERG
ALPS
SWITZERLAND
GRAUBÜNDEN
ITALY
BOLZANO
ALTO ADIGE
TRENTINO-
TRENTO
LOMBARDIA
SONDRIO
BRESCIA
BERGAMO
VENETO
BELLUNO
TREVISO
VICENZA
FRIULI-
VENEZIA GIULIA
UDINE
PORDENONE
Bodensee
METRES
FEET
6000 19686
5000 16404
4000 13124
3000 9843
2000 6562
1500 4921
1000 3281
500 1640
200 656
100 328
0 0
LAND BELOW SEA LEVEL
50 164
200 656
1000 3281
2000 6562
Longitude 12° east of Greenwich

Conic Equidistant Projection

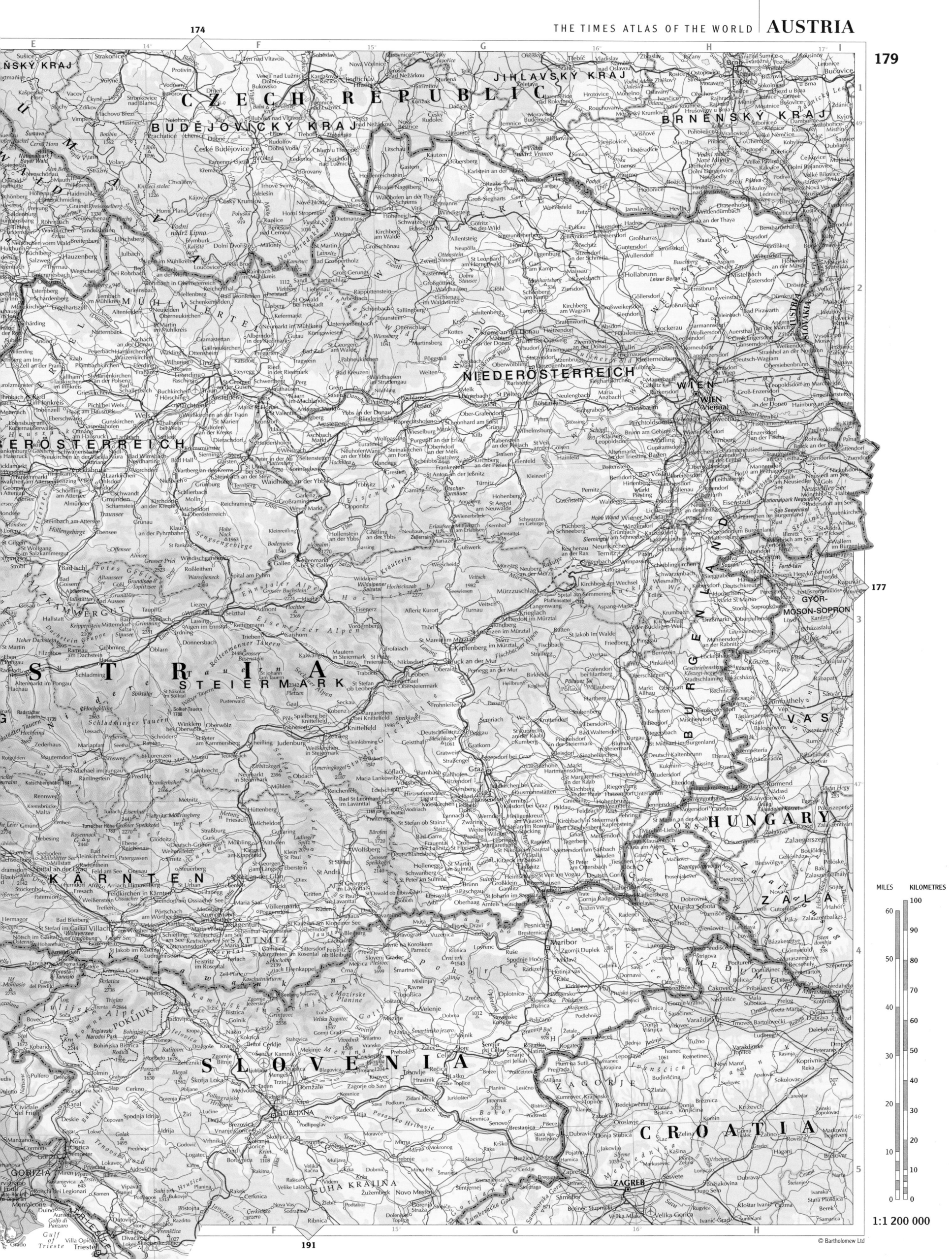
174
177
191
CZECH REPUBLIC
JIHLAVSKÝ KRAJ
BUDĚJOVICKÝ KRAJ
BRNĚNSKÝ KRAJ
NIEDERÖSTERREICH
WIEN
WIEN (Vienna)
STEIERMARK
KÄRNTEN
BURGENLAND
GYŐR-MOSON-SOPRON
VAS
ZALA
HUNGARY
SLOVENIA
CROATIA
ZAGORJE
MEDJIMURJE
SLOVAKIA
AUSTRIA
Linz
Graz
Maribor
LJUBLJANA
ZAGREB
Sopron
Szombathely
Zalaegerszeg
Klagenfurt
Villach
St Pölten
České Budějovice
Gulf of Trieste
Trieste
GORIZIA
MILES
KILOMETRES
1:1 200 000

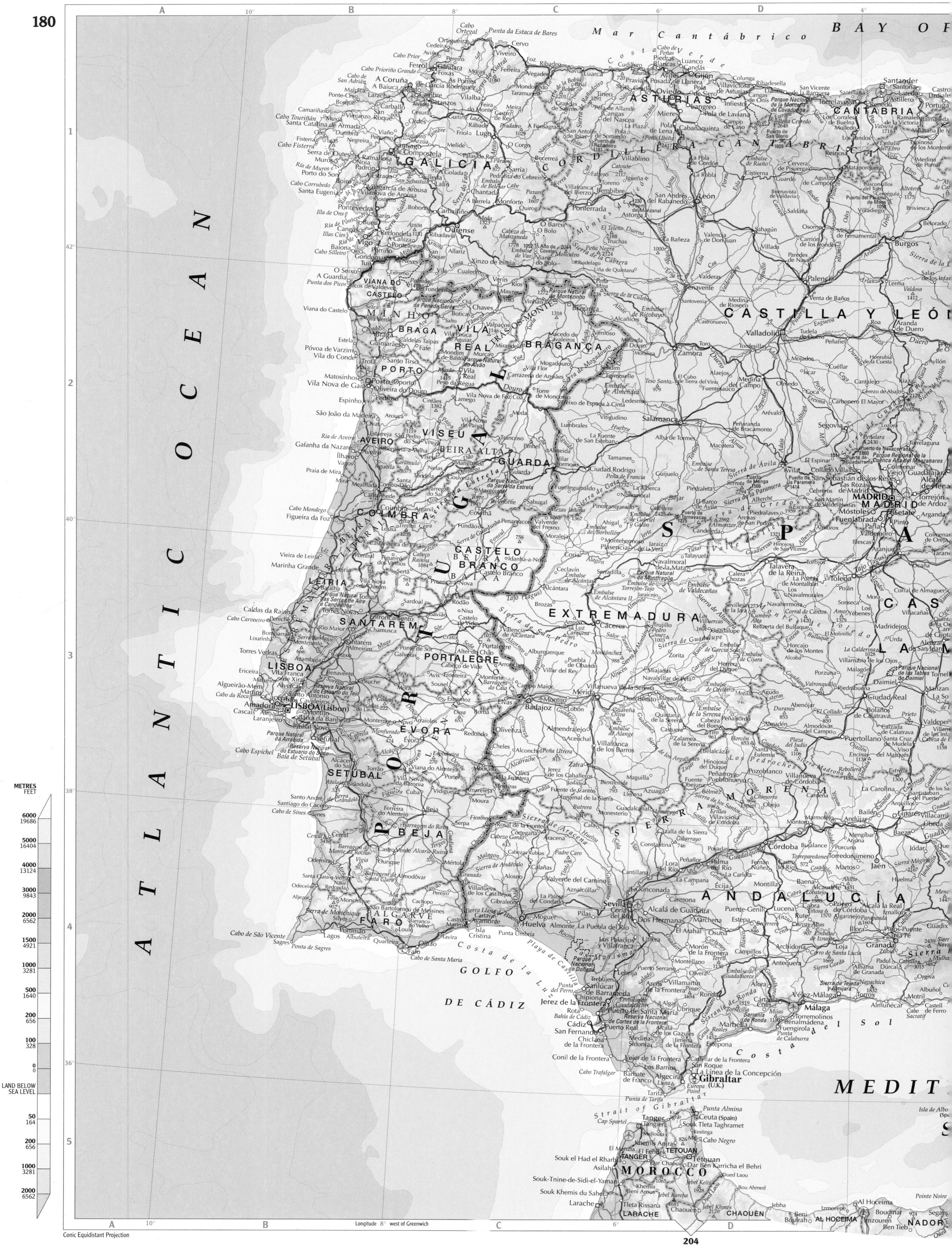

Map of Portugal and Spain (Iberian Peninsula)

A T L A N T I C   O C E A N

Mar Cantábrico   **BAY OF**

GALICIA   **ASTURIAS**   **CANTABRIA**

CORDILLERA CANTÁBRICA

CASTILLA Y LEÓN

MINHO   **VILA REAL**   **BRAGANÇA**   **TRÁS-OS-MONTES**

BRAGA

PORTO

VISEU   **BEIRA ALTA**   **GUARDA**

AVEIRO

COIMBRA   **BEIRA BAIXA**

P O R T U G A L   **E S P A Ñ A**

CASTELO BRANCO

LEIRIA   **MADRID**

SANTARÉM   **EXTREMADURA**

LISBOA   **Lisboa (Lisbon)**

ÉVORA

SETÚBAL   **PORTALEGRE**

BEJA

ALGARVE   **FARO**

ANDALUCÍA

Sevilla   **Córdoba**

GOLFO DE CÁDIZ

Cádiz

Gibraltar (U.K.)

Strait of Gibraltar

Ceuta (Spain)

TÁNGER   **TETOUAN**

MOROCCO

MEDIT

Principal cities: A Coruña, Ferrol, Santiago de Compostela, Vigo, Pontevedra, Ourense, Lugo, León, Ponferrada, Zamora, Valladolid, Salamanca, Segovia, Ávila, Madrid, Toledo, Cáceres, Badajoz, Mérida, Ciudad Real, Córdoba, Sevilla, Huelva, Cádiz, Jerez de la Frontera, Málaga, Granada, Jaén, Marbella, Algeciras

SIERRA MORENA

Metres / Feet scale

METRES	FEET
6000	19686
5000	16404
4000	13124
3000	9843
2000	6562
1500	4921
1000	3281
500	1640
200	656
100	328
0	0
LAND BELOW SEA LEVEL	
50	164
200	656
1000	3281
2000	6562

Conic Equidistant Projection

Longitude 8° west of Greenwich

B I S C A Y

F R A N C E

AQUITAINE

MIDI-PYRÉNÉES

LANGUEDOC

ROUSSILLON

GOLFE DU LION

Marseille

PAÍS VASCO

NAVARRA

LA RIOJA

CASTILLA Y LEÓN

P Y R É N É E S

ANDORRA

CATALUÑA

Zaragoza

ARAGÓN

Barcelona

Costa Brava

Costa Dorada

Tarragona

Costa del Azahar

VALENCIA

Valencia

Golfo de Valencia

Menorca (Minorca)

Mahón (Maó)

Mallorca (Majorca)

Palma de Mallorca

Eivissa (Ibiza)

Formentera

ISLAS BALEARES (BALEARIC ISLANDS)

M E D I T E R R A N E A N S E A

Costa Blanca

Alicante

Elche

MURCIA

Murcia

Cartagena

Cabo de Palos

Almería

Golfo de Almería

Cabo de Gata

ALGERIA

Melilla (Spain)

CANARY ISLANDS (Spain) AT THE SAME SCALE

A T L A N T I C O C E A N

I S L A S C A N A R I A S

Lanzarote

Fuerteventura

La Palma

Tenerife

Santa Cruz de Tenerife

La Gomera

Gran Canaria

Las Palmas de Gran Canaria

El Hierro

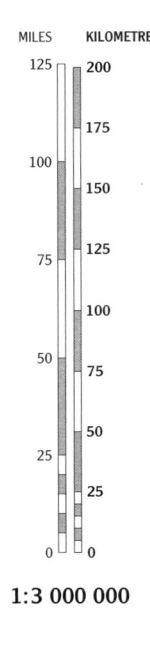

MILES KILOMETRES

125 200

100 175

150

75 125

100

50 75

25 50

25

0 0

1:3 000 000

A
B
C
D
9°
8°
7°
6°
1
2
3
4
5
43°
42°
41°
40°
ATLANTIC OCEAN
Mar Ca
Costa Ver
GALICIA
A CORUÑA
LUGO
PONTEVEDRA
OURENSE
A LIMIA
BERGANTIÑOS
AS MARIÑAS
PORTUGAL
VIANA DO CASTELO
MINHO
BRAGA
VILA REAL
BRAGANÇA
PORTO
DOURO
AVEIRO
VISEU
GUARDA
BEIRA ALTA
COIMBRA
CASTELO BRANCO
BEIRA BAIXA
LEIRIA
ASTURIAS
OVIEDO
BABIA
EL BIERZO
MARAGATERÍA
SANABRIA
ZAMORA
SAYAGO
TIERRA DEL VINO
TIERRA DEL PAN
SALAMANCA
ABADENGO
LAS HURDES
CÁCERES
EXTREMADURA
CAMPO
LA VERA
CORDILLERA CANTÁBRICA
CAST
S
METRES
FEET
6000
19686
5000
16404
4000
13124
3000
9843
2000
6562
1500
4921
1000
3281
500
1640
200
656
100
328
0
0
LAND BELOW SEA LEVEL
50
164
200
656
1000
3281
2000
6562

Conic Equidistant Projection

184

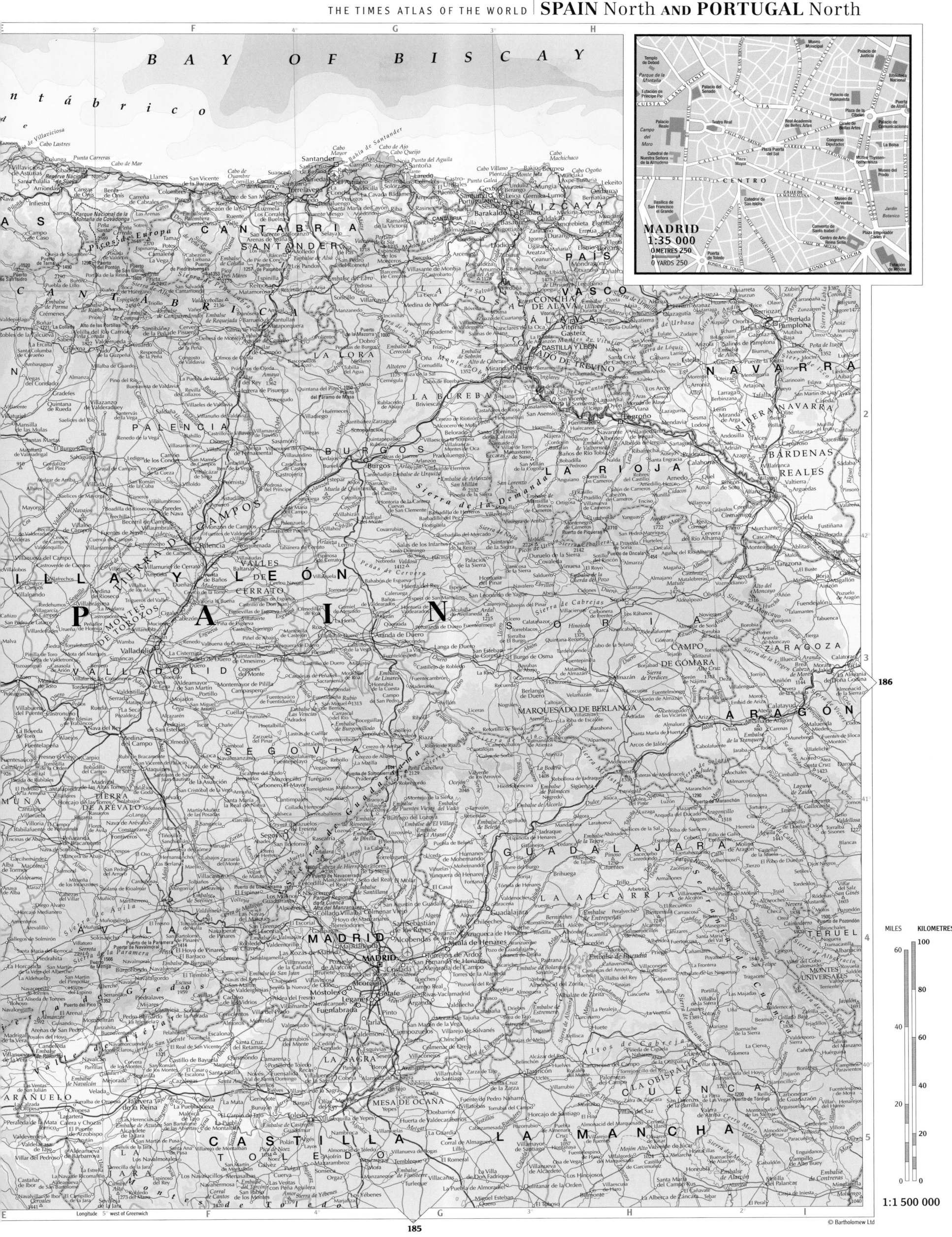

BAY OF BISCAY

186

MILES   KILOMETRES

1:1 500 000

© Bartholomew Ltd

PORTUGAL

LEIRIA

CASTELO BRANCO

BEIRA BAIXA

CÁCERES

EXTREMADURA

SANTARÉM

PORTALEGRE

RIBATEJO

LISBOA

LISBOA (Lisbon)

ÉVORA

BADAJOZ

TIERRA DE BARROS

PLANOS DE OLIVENZA

Mérida

Badajoz

SETÚBAL

Baía de Setúbal

Costa Belga

BEJA

SIERRA ARACENA

HUELVA

EL ANDÉVALO

EL ALJARAFE

CONDADO DE NIEBLA

SEVILLA

Sevilla

ALGARVE

FARO

Cabo de São Vicente

Ponta de Sagres

Cabo de Santa Maria

Costa de la Luz

GOLFO DE CÁDIZ

CÁDIZ

Cádiz

Jerez de la Frontera

Playa de Castilla

MOROCCO

TANGER (Tanger)

Strait of

Cap Spartel

MADEIRA
(Portugal)
1:1 250 000

Arquipélago da Madeira

Ilha de Porto Santo

Ilha da Madeira

FUNCHAL

Ilhas Desertas

Deserta Grande

Bugio

Ponta de São Lourenço

METRES FEET	
6000	19686
5000	16404
4000	13124
3000	9843
2000	6562
1500	4921
1000	3281
500	1640
200	656
100	328
0	0
LAND BELOW SEA LEVEL	
50	164
200	656
1000	3281
2000	6562

Conic Equidistant Projection

CASTILLA-LA MANCHA

SPAIN

TOLEDO

CIUDAD REAL

CUENCA

ALBACETE

MURCIA

JAÉN

CÓRDOBA

ANDALUCÍA

GRANADA

ALMERÍA

MÁLAGA

SERENA

SIERRA MORENA

CAMPO DE CALATRAVA

VALLE DE ALCUDIA

LOMA DE ÚBEDA

SIERRA NEVADA

Costa del Sol

Golfo de Almería

Gibraltar (U.K.)

Ceuta (Spain)

MEDITERRANEAN SEA

Gibraltar Harbour

North Mole

Detached Mole

Gibraltar (Caleta)

Catalan Bay (Caleta)

St Abb's Hd

Shirley Cove

Eastern Beach

The Rock

Middle Hill

Signal Hill

Sandy Bay

Bay of Gibraltar

South Mole

Rosia Bay

Camp Bay

Buena

Little Bay

Europa Flats

Europa Pt

36° 08' N

5° 21' E

GIBRALTAR
(U.K.)
1:100 000

MILES | KILOMETRES
60 | 100
 | 80
40 | 60
 | 40
20 |
 | 20
0 | 0

© Bartholomew Ltd

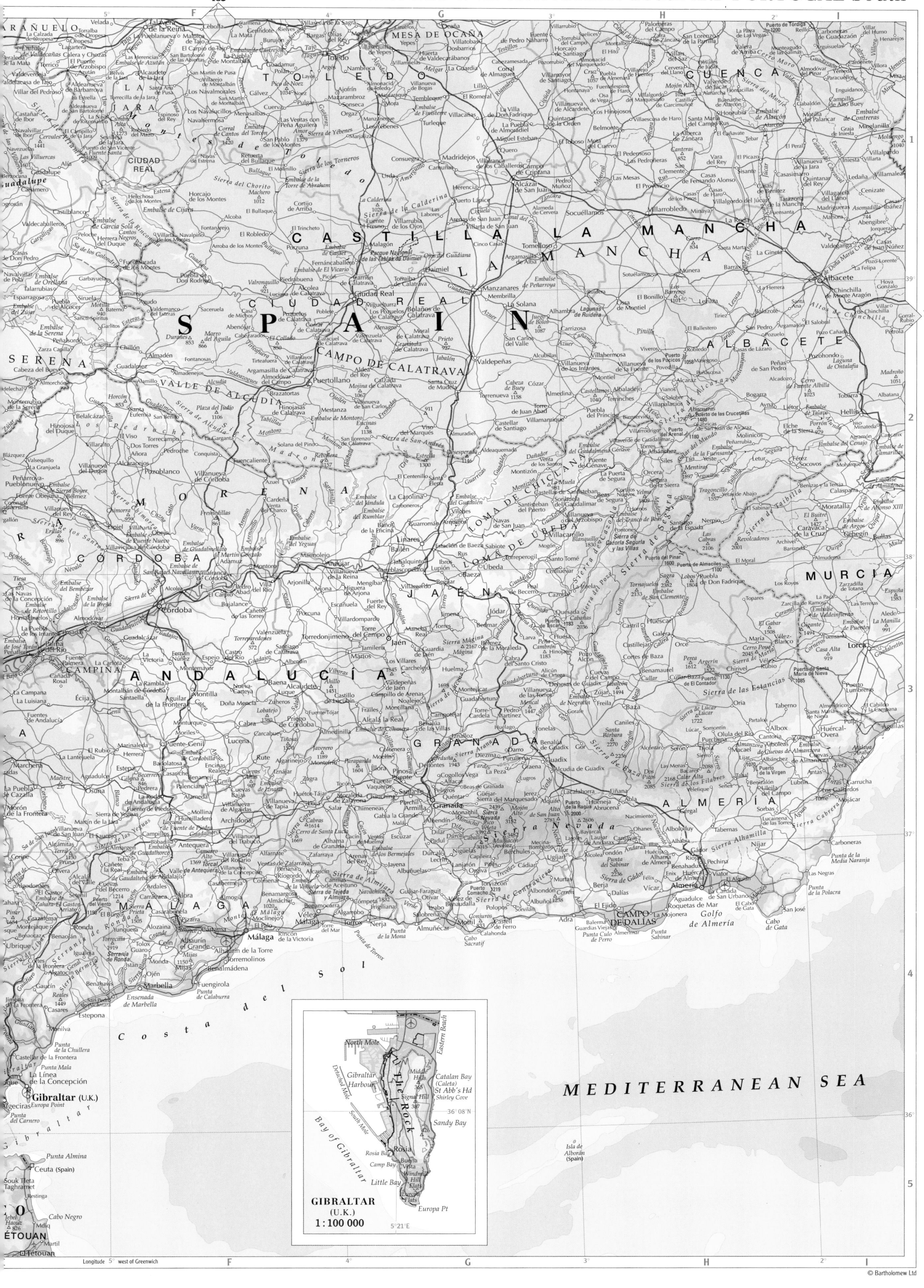

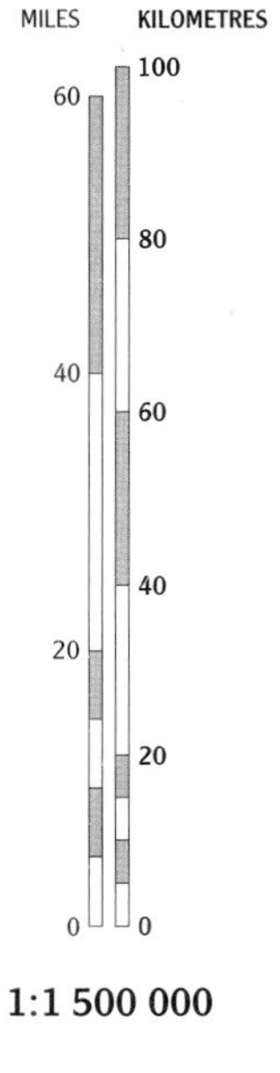

1:1 500 000

FRANCE

SPAIN

MIDI-PYRÉNÉES
LANGUEDOC
ROUSSILLON
AQUITAINE
CATALUÑA
ARAGÓN
NAVARRA
LA RIOJA
CASTILLA Y LEÓN
GUADALAJARA
ANDORRA
PYRÉNÉES
HAUTES-PYRÉNÉES
ARIÈGE
HAUTE-GARONNE
GERS
TARN
CORBIÈRES
ROUSSILLON
PAYS BASQUE
PAÍS VASCO
GUIPÚZCOA
VIZCAYA
ÁLAVA
HUESCA
LLEIDA
GIRONA
BARCELONA
TARRAGONA
ZARAGOZA
TERUEL

Barcelona
Zaragoza
Pamplona
Donostia-San Sebastián
Andorra la Vella

MENORCA
(Spain)
MENORCA
(MINORCA)
AT THE SAME SCALE

Golfe du Lion
Côte Vermeille
Costa Brava
Costa Dorada

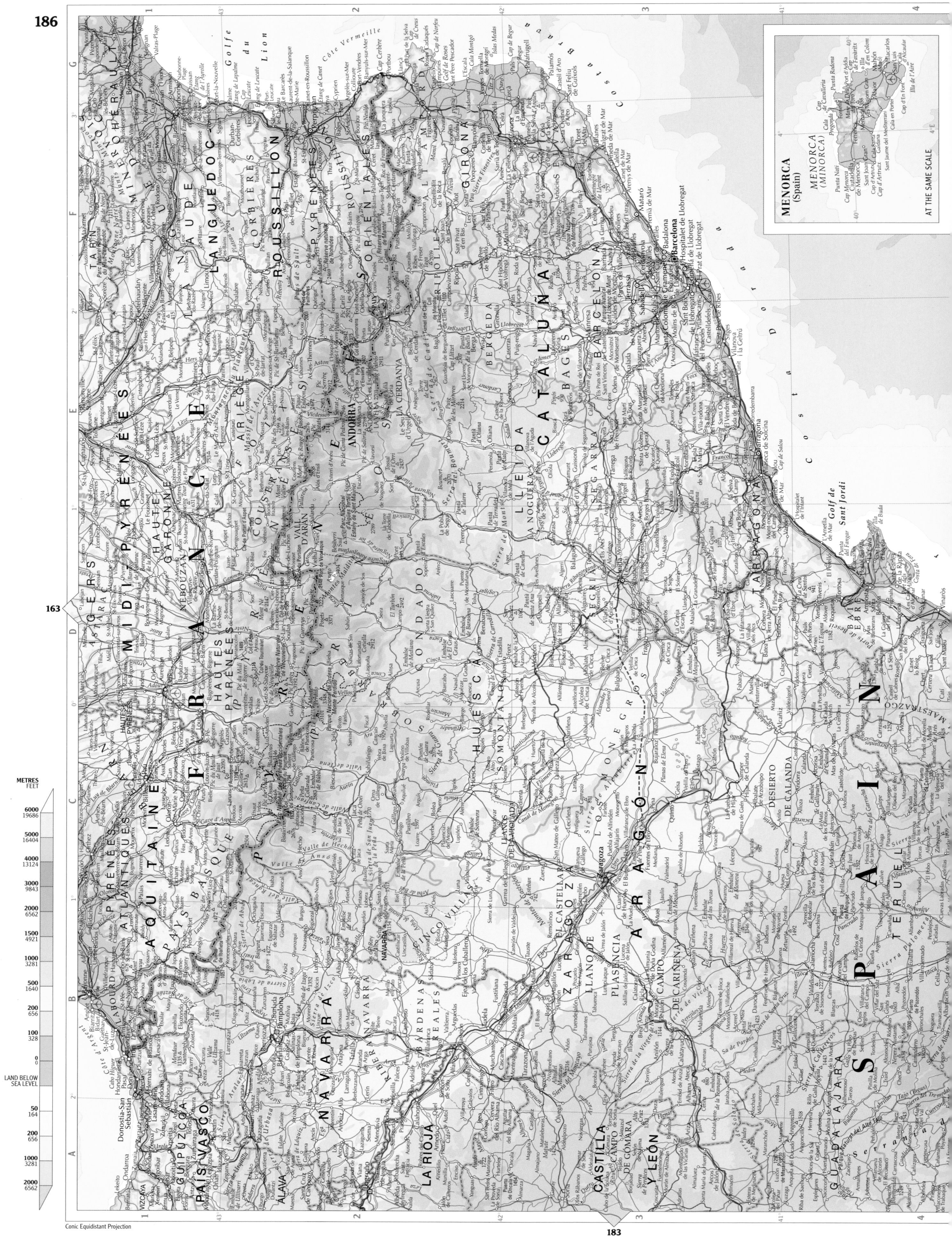

METRES / FEET
6000 / 19686
5000 / 16404
4000 / 13124
3000 / 9843
2000 / 6562
1500 / 4921
1000 / 3281
500 / 1640
200 / 656
100 / 328
0 / 0
LAND BELOW SEA LEVEL
50 / 164
200 / 656
1000 / 3281
2000 / 6562

Conic Equidistant Projection

163

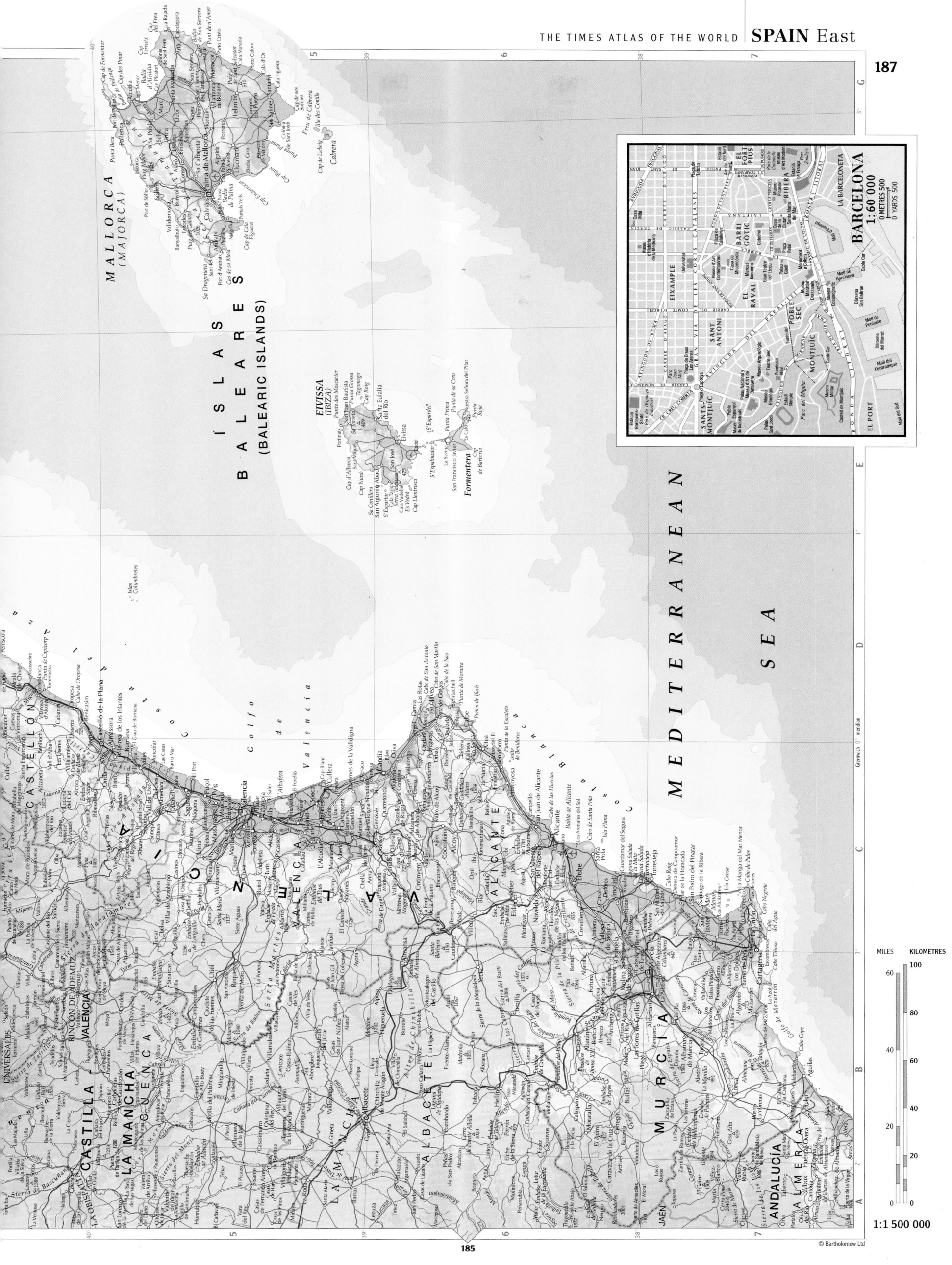

MALLORCA
(MAJORCA)

I S L A S   B A L E A R E S
(BALEARIC ISLANDS)

EIVISSA
(IBIZA)

Formentera

M E D I T E R R A N E A N

S E A

BARCELONA 1:60 000

CASTILLA-LA MANCHA

CUENCA

VALENCIA

CASTELLÓN

Valencia

Alicante

ALICANTE

MURCIA

ALBACETE

ANDALUCÍA

ALMERÍA

JAÉN

Cabrera

1:1 500 000

MILES   KILOMETRES

© Bartholomew Ltd

185

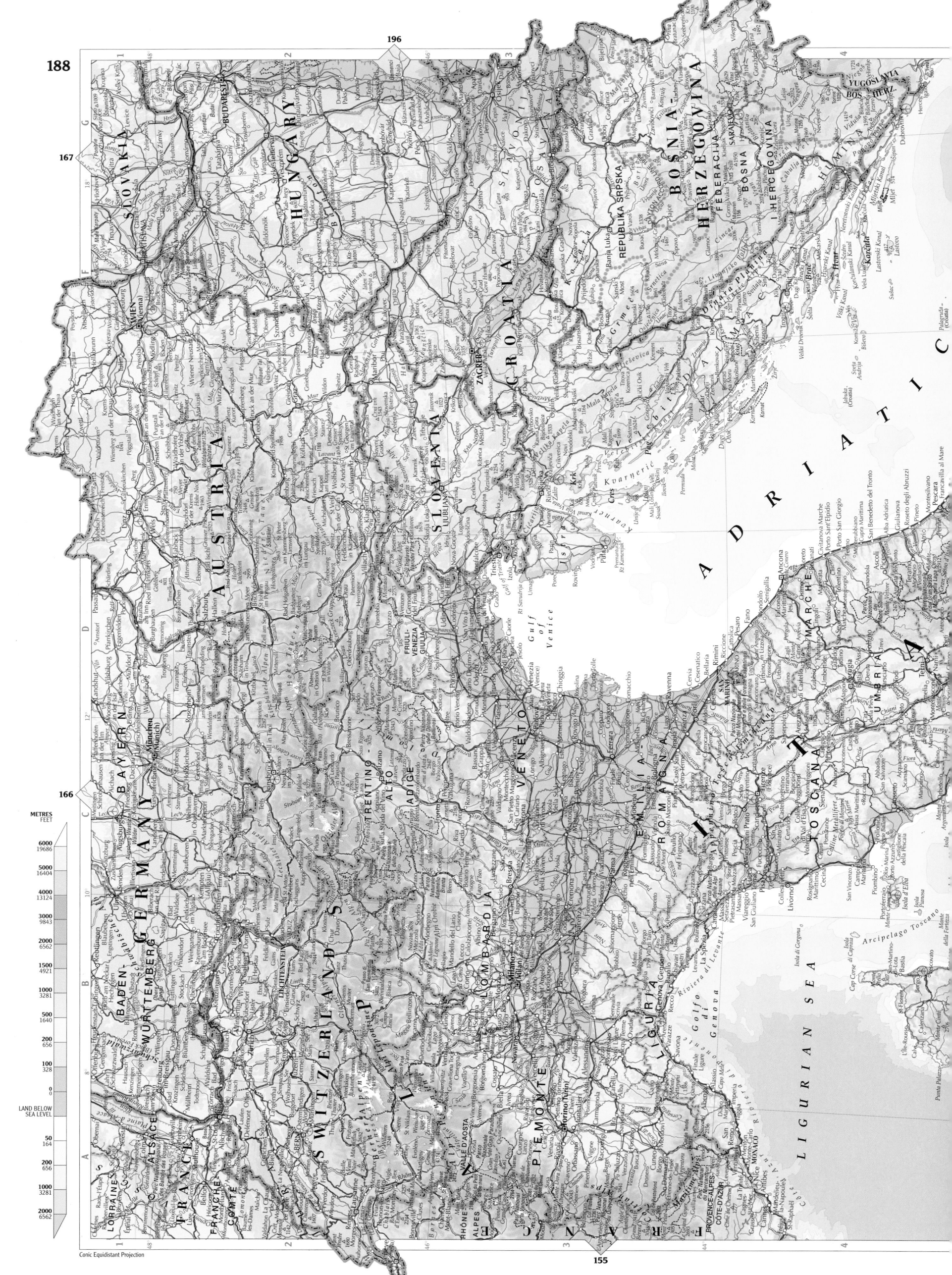

167

166

METRES
FEET

6000
19686

5000
16404

4000
13124

3000
9843

2000
6562

1500
4921

1000
3281

500
1640

200
656

100
328

0
0

LAND BELOW
SEA LEVEL

50
164

200
656

1000
3281

2000
6562

Conic Equidistant Projection

SLOVAKIA

HUNGARY

GERMANY

BAYERN

BADEN-
WÜRTTEMBERG

AUSTRIA

SWITZERLAND

LIECHTENSTEIN

FRANCE

ALSACE

LORRAINE

FRANCHE-
COMTÉ

RHÔNE-
ALPES

PROVENCE-ALPES-
CÔTE-D'AZUR

PIEMONTE

VALLE D'AOSTA

LIGURIA

LOMBARDIA

TRENTINO-
ALTO
ADIGE

VENETO

FRIULI-
VENEZIA
GIULIA

SLOVENIA

CROATIA

BOSNIA-
HERZEGOVINA

REPUBLIKA SRPSKA

FEDERACIJA
BOSNA I HERCEGOVINA

YUGOSLAVIA
BOS.-HERZ.

DALMACIJA

EMILIA-
ROMAGNA

TOSCANA

UMBRIA

MARCHE

ITALY

ADRIATIC
SEA

Gulf
of
Venice

LIGURIAN SEA

Arcipelago Toscano

WIEN
Vienna

BUDAPEST

ZAGREB

SARAJEVO

LJUBLJANA

Venezia
(Venice)

Milano
(Milan)

München
Munich

Salzburg

Torino (Turin)

Nice
Nice

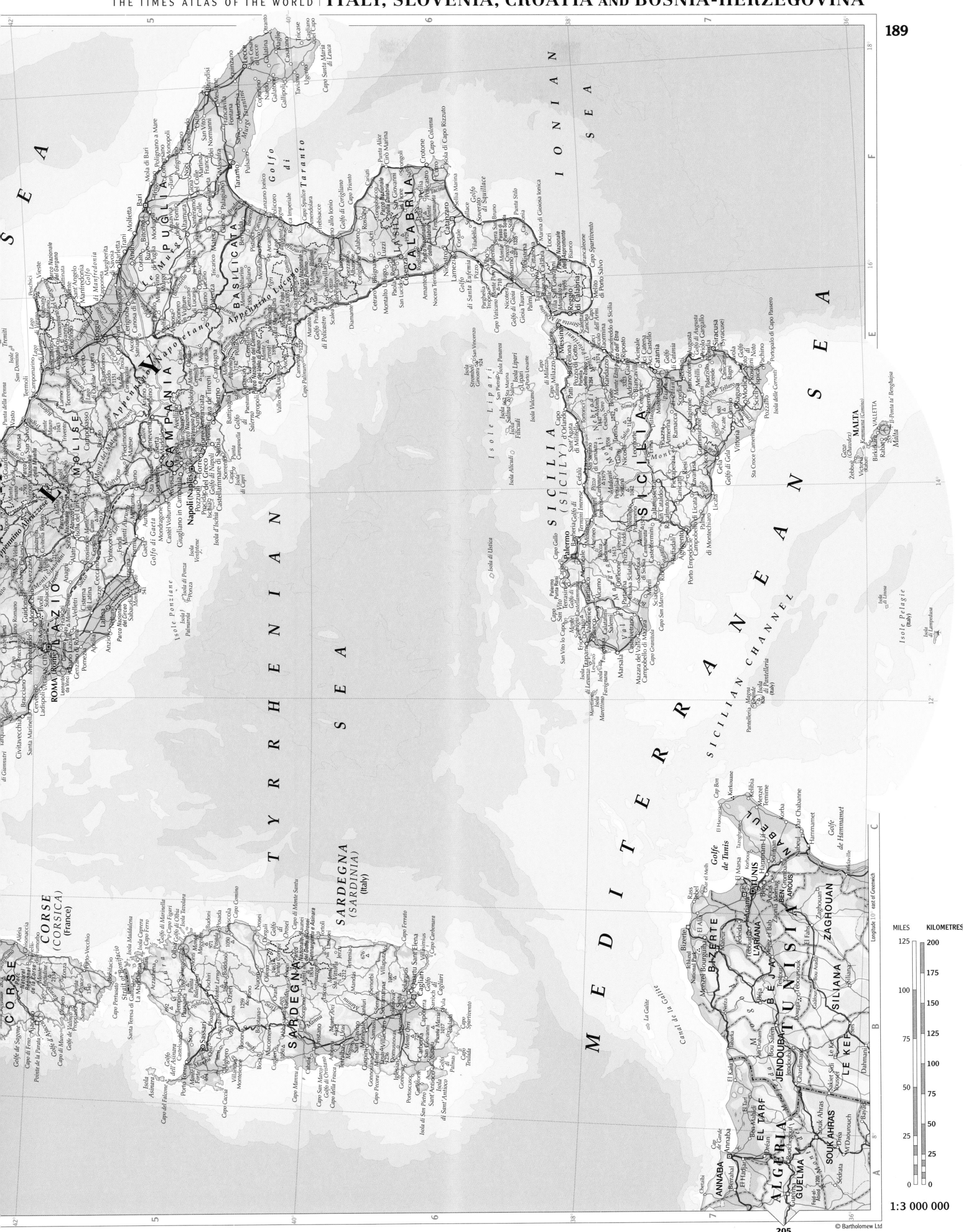

1:3 000 000

MILES   KILOMETRES

205

© Bartholomew Ltd

TYRRHENIAN SEA
IONIAN SEA
MEDITERRANEAN SEA
SICILIAN CHANNEL
SARDEGNA (SARDINIA) (Italy)
CORSE (CORSICA) (France)
SICILIA (SICILY)
MALTA
VALLETTA
TUNISIA
ALGERIA
Roma (Rome)
Napoli (Naples)
Palermo
Cagliari
TUNIS
Isole Pelagie (Italy)
Isole Lipari
LAZIO
CAMPANIA
MOLISE
PUGLIA
BASILICATA
CALABRIA
Longitude 10° east of Greenwich

LIGURIAN SEA

Swiss Cantons not named on the map
1. APPENZELL AUSSER-RHODEN (E1)
2. APPENZELL INNER-RHODEN (E1)
3. FRIBOURG (B2)
4. VAUD (C2)

METRES
FEET
6000
19686
5000
16404
4000
13124
3000
9843
2000
6562
1500
4921
1000
3281
500
1640
200
656
100
328
0
LAND BELOW
SEA LEVEL
50
164
200
656
1000
3281
2000
6562

Conic Equidistant Projection

GERMANY
BAYERN
TIROL
AUSTRIA
SALZBURG
STEIERMARK
OSTTIROL
TIROL
KÄRNTEN
BOLZANO
TRENTINO-
ALTO ADIGE
TRENTO
BELLUNO
FRIULI-
UDINE
PORDENONE
VENEZIA GIULIA
SLOVENIA
GORIZIA
VICENZA
TREVISO
VENETO
VERONA
VENEZIA (Venice)
PADOVA
Gulf of Trieste
Trieste
CROATIA
Istra
ITALY
MANTOVA
ROVIGO
POLESINE
Gulf of
Venice
FERRARA
EMILIA-ROMAGNA
MODENA
BOLOGNA
RAVENNA
ADRIATIC SEA
Rijeka
GORSKI KOTAR
Cres
Lošinj
Pag
PISTOIA
PRATO
FIRENZE
FORLÌ
Rimini
RIMINI
San Marino
SAN MARINO
TOSCANA
PESARO
URBINO
ANCONA
MARCHE
AREZZO
PERUGIA
UMBRIA
MACERATA

Longitude 11° east of Greenwich

G   193   H   I   J

193

196

1:1 500 000

© Bartholomew Ltd

MILES   KILOMETRES
100
60
80
60
40
40
20
20
0   0

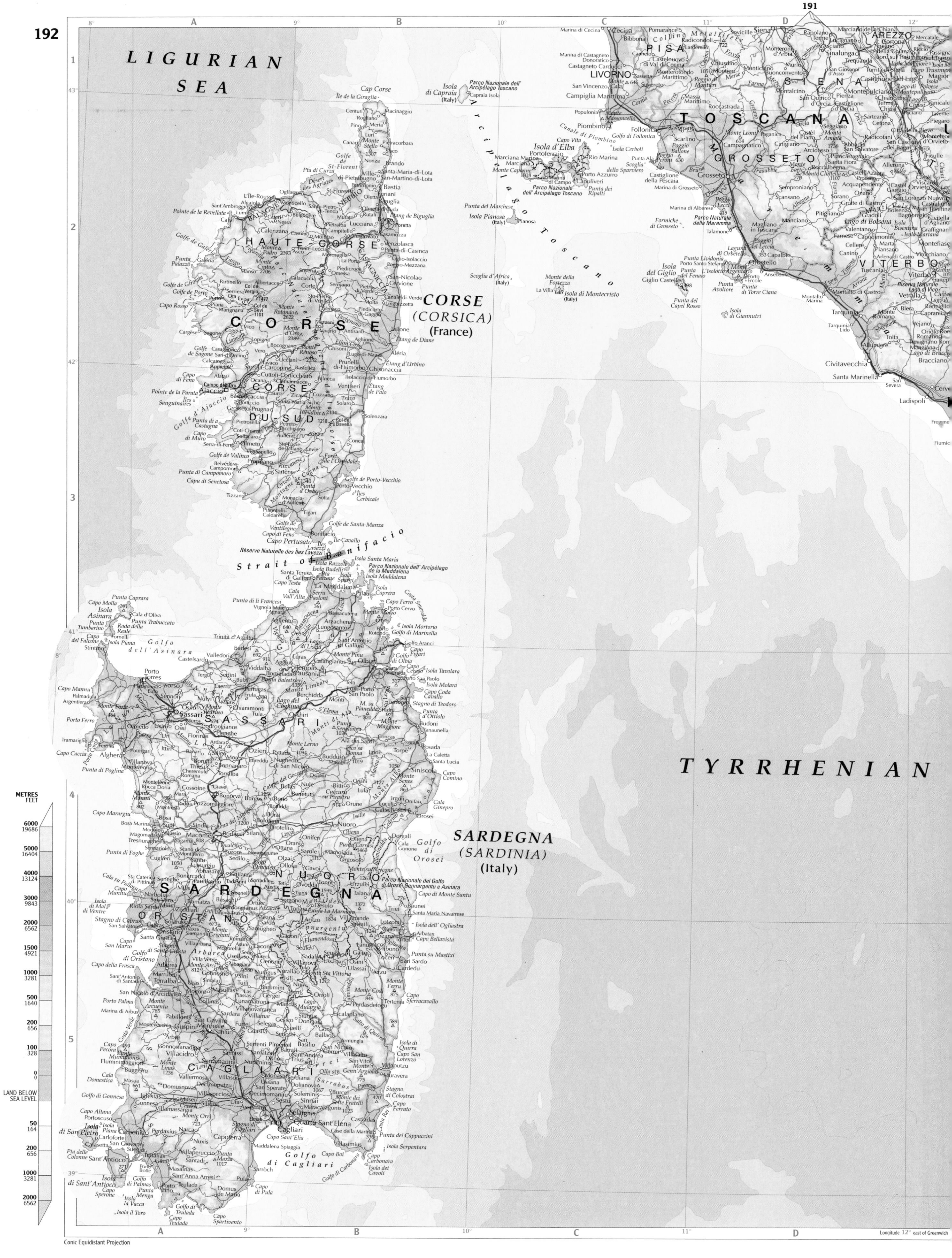

LIGURIAN
SEA

CORSE
(CORSICA)
(France)

HAUTE-CORSE

CORSE

CORSE
DU-SUD

Strait of Bonifacio

SARDEGNA
(SARDINIA)
(Italy)

SASSARI

NUORO

ORISTANO

CAGLIARI

SARDEGNA

TYRRHENIAN

PISA
LIVORNO
TOSCANA
GROSSETO
SIENA
AREZZO
VITERBO

Golfo
dell' Asinara

Golfo
di
Orosei

Golfo di
Cagliari

METRES
FEET

6000 / 19686
5000 / 16404
4000 / 13124
3000 / 9843
2000 / 6562
1500 / 4921
1000 / 3281
500 / 1640
200 / 656
100 / 328
0 / 0
LAND BELOW
SEA LEVEL
50 / 164
200 / 656
1000 / 3281
2000 / 6562

Conic Equidistant Projection

Longitude 12° east of Greenwich

CROATIA

ADRIATIC SEA

SEA

ITALY

MARCHE
MACERATA
ASCOLI PICENO
ABRUZZO
TERAMO
PESCARA
CHIETI
L'AQUILA
LAZIO
ROMA (Rome)
FROSINONE
LATINA
CAMPOBASSO
ISERNIA
MOLISE
FOGGIA
CASERTA
BENEVENTO
PUGLIA
AVELLINO
NAPOLI (Naples)
CAMPANIA
BARI
SALERNO
POTENZA
BASILICATA
MATERA
COSENZA
CALABRIA

Golfo di Manfredonia
Golfo di Gaeta
Golfo di Napoli
Golfo di Salerno
Golfo di Policastro
Golfo di Santa Eufemia

Isole Tremiti (Italy)
Isola di Capri
Isola d'Ischia
Isole Ponziane
Promontorio del Gargano
Parco Nazionale del Gargano

ROME
1:50 000
0 METRES 500
0 YARDS 500

TRIONFALE
SALARIO
Villa Borghese
VATICAN CITY
Musei Vaticani
Basilica di San Pietro
Castel Sant'Angelo
Piazza del Popolo
Palazzo del Quirinale
Pantheon
TRASTEVERE
Villa Doria Pamphili

MILES   KILOMETRES
60   100
        80
40   60
        40
20
        20
0   0

1:1 500 000

© Bartholomew Ltd

1

A   11°   12°   B   13°   C   14°   D

41°

T Y R R H E N I A N   S E A

CASERTA   BENEVENTO

Mondragone

San Cipriano   Aversa
Giugliano in Campania
Marano di Napoli   NAPOLI   NAPOLI (Naples)

Isola
Palmarola   Isola di Gavi
Isola di Ponza   Ponza   Pozzuoli   Bacoli
Isola Zannone   Miseno   del Greco
Isole Ponziane   Lacco Ameno   Isola di Procida   Procida   Capo
Forio   Ischia   Torre
Monte Epomeo   Ischia   Castellammare di Stabia
Isola d'Ischia   Barano   Vico Equense   Meta
d'Ischia   Sorrento   CAMP
Isola Ventotene   Massa Lubrense   Piano

C A M P

Anacapri   Capri
Isola di Capri   Punta
Campanella

**Golfo
di Salerno**

Salerno

Sta Maria di Castellab
Isola Licosa
Oligastro Mari

2

40°

3

Isola di Ustica   Ustica

Isole Lipari
Isola Salina
Filicudi   Malfa
Isola Alicudi   Isola Filicudi   Rinella   Is del Mar
Acquacalda
Isola Lipari
Lipari
Porto di Levante
Isola Vulcano

39°

4

**S I C I L I A
(SICILY)**   Capo d'Orlando

Capo San Vito   Capo Gallo
Punta   Mondello
San Vito lo Capo   Raisi   Isola delle   **Golfo**   Capo Zafferano   **Golfo**   Cefalù   Sto Stefano   MESS
Punta   Femmine   **di Palermo**   **di Termini**   Finale   di Camastra   Nebrodi
del Saraceno   **Palermo**   Bagheria   **Imerese**   Sant'Agata di Militello   San
Isola   Erice   Castellammare   Monreale   Termini   Campofelice   Polizzi   Reitano   Mistretta
Marettimo   Trapani   del Golfo   Imerese   Mont
Isola di Levanzo   Monte   Misilmeri   Gangi   Cesarò
Levanzo   Paceco   Partinico   Monte   Petralia Sottana   Troina   Randazzo
Marsala   **TRAPANI**   Alcamo   **PALERMO**   Caccamo   Gangi   Leonforte   Bronte
Favignana   Salemi   Corleone   Caltavuturo   Gagliano   Parco dell'E
Isola   Calatafimi   Bisacquino   Roccapalumba   Alimena   Castiglione
Favignana   Vita   Alia   Nicosia   Adr
Val   Gibellina   Prizzi   Caltanissetta
Mazara del Vallo   Salaparuta   Contessa   Castel di Iudica   Monte
Campobello   Partanna   Entellina   Lercara Friddi   **ENNA**   Enna   **CATANIA**
di Mazara   Castelvetrano   Menfi   Sambuca   Villarosa
Granitola   Sciacca   Santa Caterina   Agira   **SICILIA**
Torretta   **AGRIGENTO**   Ribera   Casteltermini   Piazza Armerina
Capo Granitola   Raffadali   Serradifalco   Caltagirone
Capo San Marco   Montallegro   Aragona   **CALTANISSETTA**   Mazzarino
Capo   **Agrigento**   Favara   Mirabella
Bianco   Porto   Canicattì   Gela
Empedocle   Campobello   Niscemi
Punta   Palma   di Licata   **Golfo di Gela**   Vittoria   **RAGUSA**
Bianca   di Montechiaro   Licata   Gela   Scoglitti   Sta Croce Camerina
Marina
di Ragusa   Modica

5

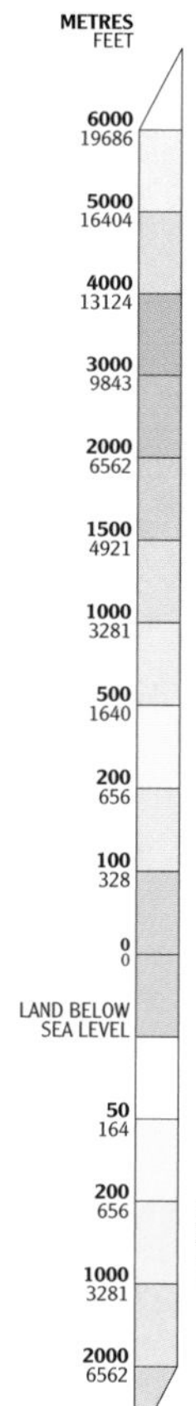

METRES
FEET

6000   19686
5000   16404
4000   13124
3000   9843
2000   6562
1500   4921
1000   3281
500   1640
200   656
100   328
0   0

LAND BELOW
SEA LEVEL

50   164
200   656
1000   3281
2000   6562

Cap Bon
El Haouaria
Kerkouane

TUNISIA
Kelibia

S I C I L I A N   C H A N N E L

Pantelleria   Isola
di Pantelleria
(Italy)
Madonna   Scauri
Grande   Tracino

Conic Equidistant Projection

6

A   12°   B   13°   C   14°   D

ADRIATIC SEA

PUGLIA

BASILICATA

POTENZA

MATERA

BARI

BRINDISI

TARANTO

LECCE

Strait of Otranto

GOLFO DI TARANTO

COSENZA

LA SILA

CROTONE

CALABRIA

CATANZARO

VIBO VALENTIA

REGGIO DI CALABRIA

Golfo di Santa Eufemia

Golfo di Gioia

Golfo di Squillace

IONIAN SEA

Golfo di Catania

Golfo di Augusta

Golfo di Noto

SIRACUSA (Syracuse)

MALTA
1:500 000

Gozo (Ghawdex)

Kemmuna (Comino)

Malta

Valletta

MILES   KILOMETRES

METRES
FEET

6000
19686

5000
16404

4000
13124

3000
9843

2000
6562

1500
4921

1000
3281

500
1640

200
656

100
328

0
0

LAND BELOW
SEA LEVEL

50
164

200
656

1000
3281

2000
6562

Conic Equidistant Projection

1:3 000 000

© Bartholomew Ltd

MILES   KILOMETRES

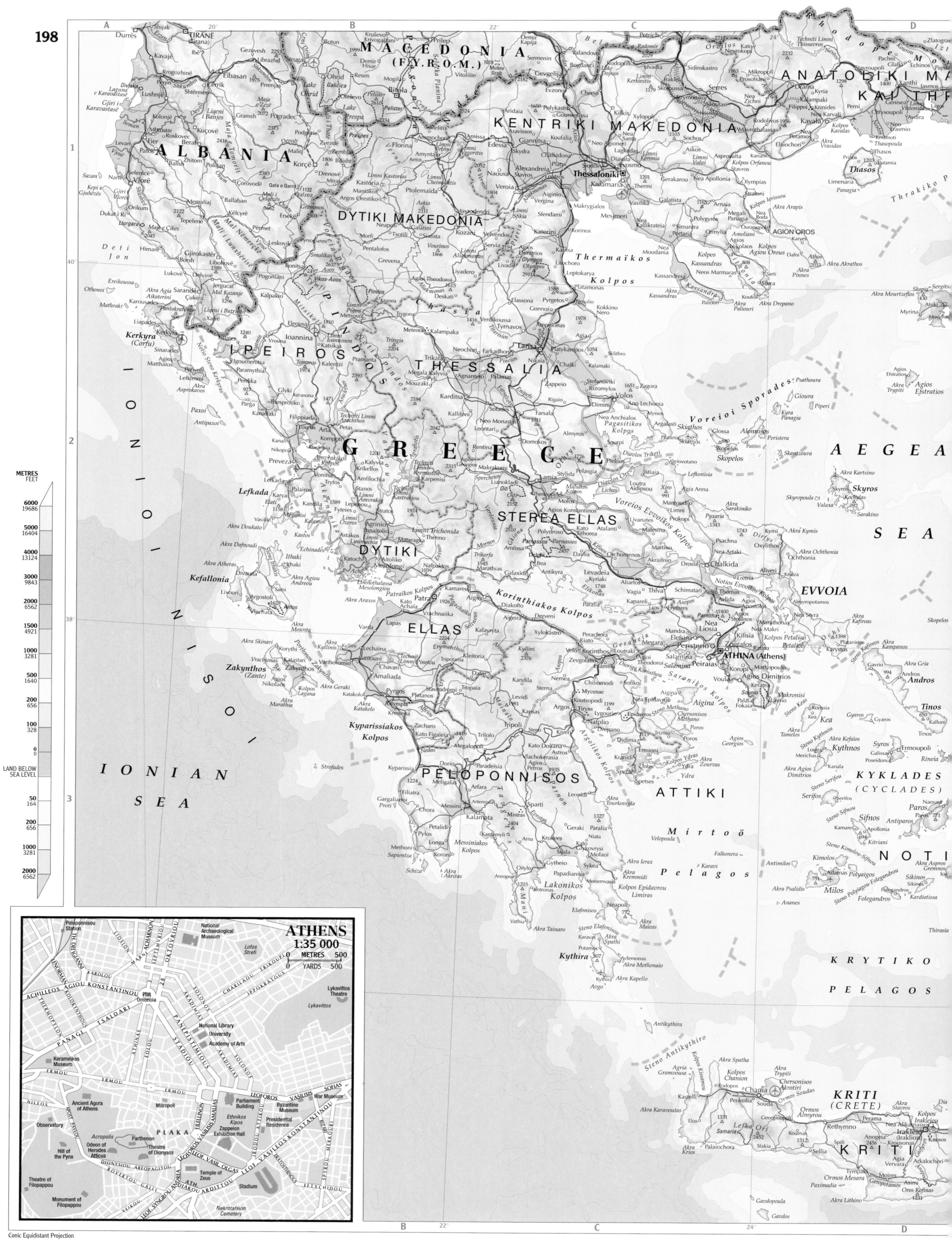
ALBANIA
MACEDONIA (F.Y.R.O.M.)
KENTRIKI MAKEDONIA
DYTIKI MAKEDONIA
ANATOLIKI MA KAI THR
IPEIROS
THESSALIA
GREECE
STEREA ELLAS
DYTIKI ELLAS
PELOPONNISOS
ATTIKI
EVVOIA
KYKLADES (CYCLADES)
KRITI (CRETE)
IONIAN SEA
IONIOI NISOI
AEGEAN SEA
Thermaïkos Kolpos
Voreioi Sporades
Mirtoö Pelagos
KRYTIKO PELAGOS
Thessaloniki
ATHINA (Athens)
METRES FEET
6000 19686
5000 16404
4000 13124
3000 9843
2000 6562
1500 4921
1000 3281
500 1640
200 656
100 328
0 0
LAND BELOW SEA LEVEL
50 164
200 656
1000 3281
2000 6562
ATHENS
1:35 000
METRES 0 500
YARDS 0 500

Conic Equidistant Projection

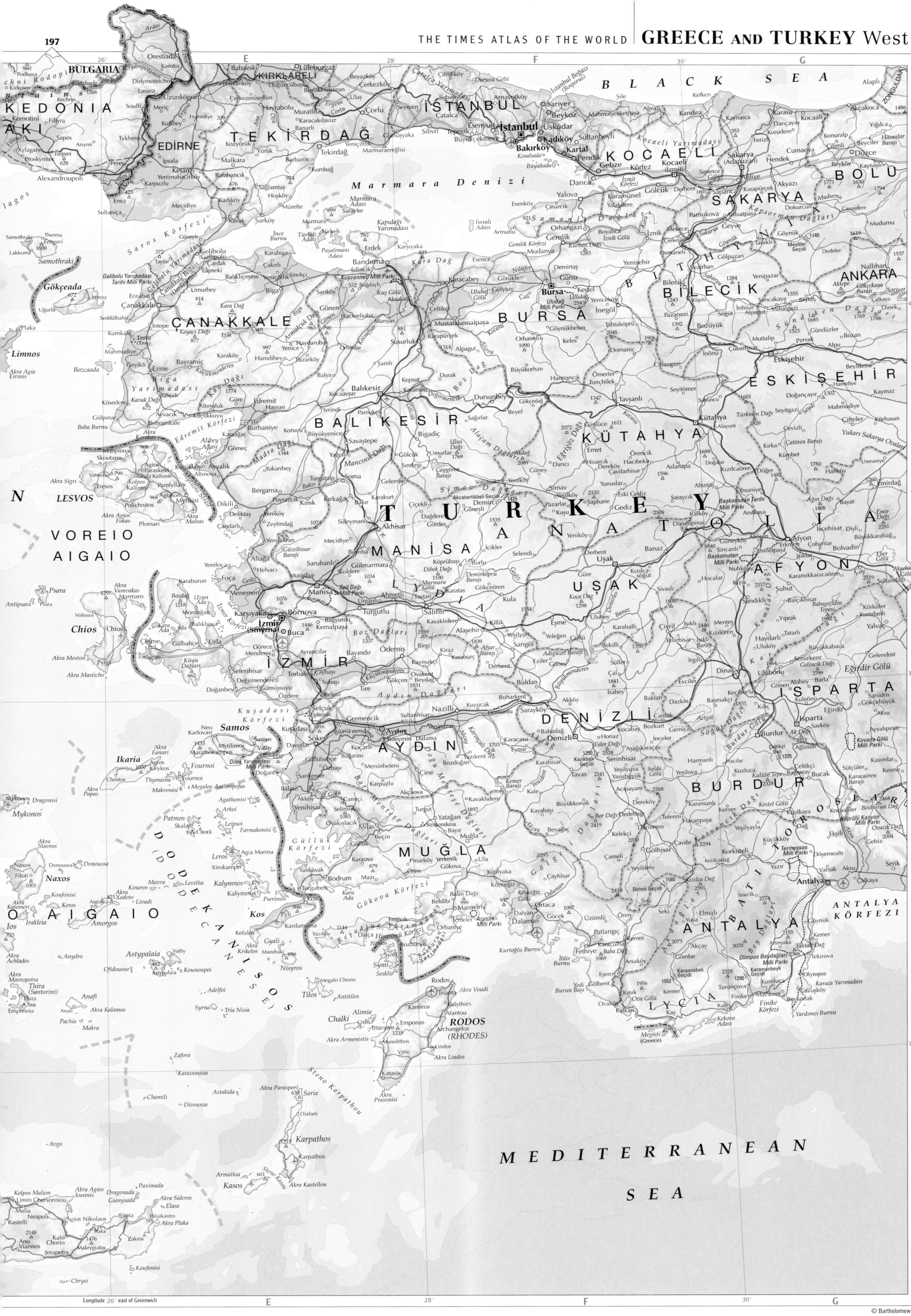
BLACK SEA
Marmara Denizi
MEDITERRANEAN SEA
TURKEY
ANATOLIA
VOREIO AIGAIO
DODEKANISOS (DODECANESE)
BULGARIA
İSTANBUL
TEKİRDAĞ
EDİRNE
KIRKLARELİ
KOCAELİ
SAKARYA
BOLU
BİLECİK
ANKARA
ESKİŞEHİR
BURSA
ÇANAKKALE
BALIKESİR
KÜTAHYA
MANİSA
UŞAK
AFYON
İZMİR
AYDIN
DENİZLİ
ISPARTA
BURDUR
MUĞLA
ANTALYA
ANTALYA KÖRFEZİ
LYCIA
LYDIA
BITHYNIA
TOROSLAR
Lesvos
Chios
Samos
Ikaria
Limnos
Gökçeada
Kos
Kalymnos
Tilos
RODOS (RHODES)
Karpathos
Kasos
Naxos
Mykonos
Thira (Santorini)
Astypalaia
Saros Körfezi
Edremit Körfezi
Kuşadası Körfezi
Güllük Körfezi
Gökova Körfezi
Steno Karpathou
İstanbul
Bursa
İzmir (Smyrna)
Manisa
Balıkesir
Kütahya
Eskişehir
Afyon
Uşak
Denizli
Aydın
Muğla
Isparta
Burdur
Antalya
Çanakkale
Tekirdağ
Edirne
Bodrum
Marmaris
Fethiye
Kaş
Alexandroupoli
Komotini
Longitude 26° east of Greenwich
E
F
G
26°
28°
30°
36°
38°
40°
1
2
3
4
126

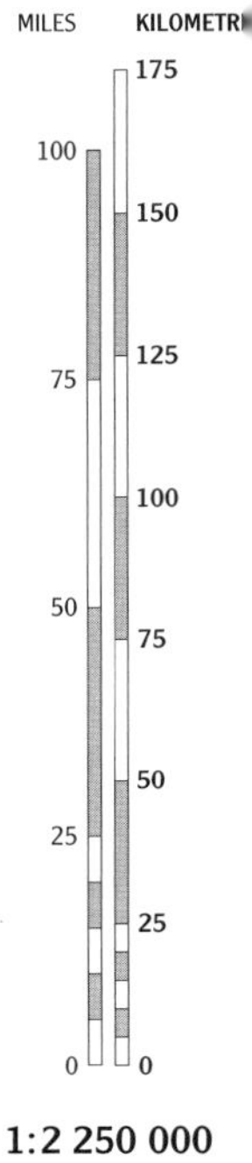
MILES
KILOMETRES
0
25
50
75
100
125
150
175

1:2 250 000

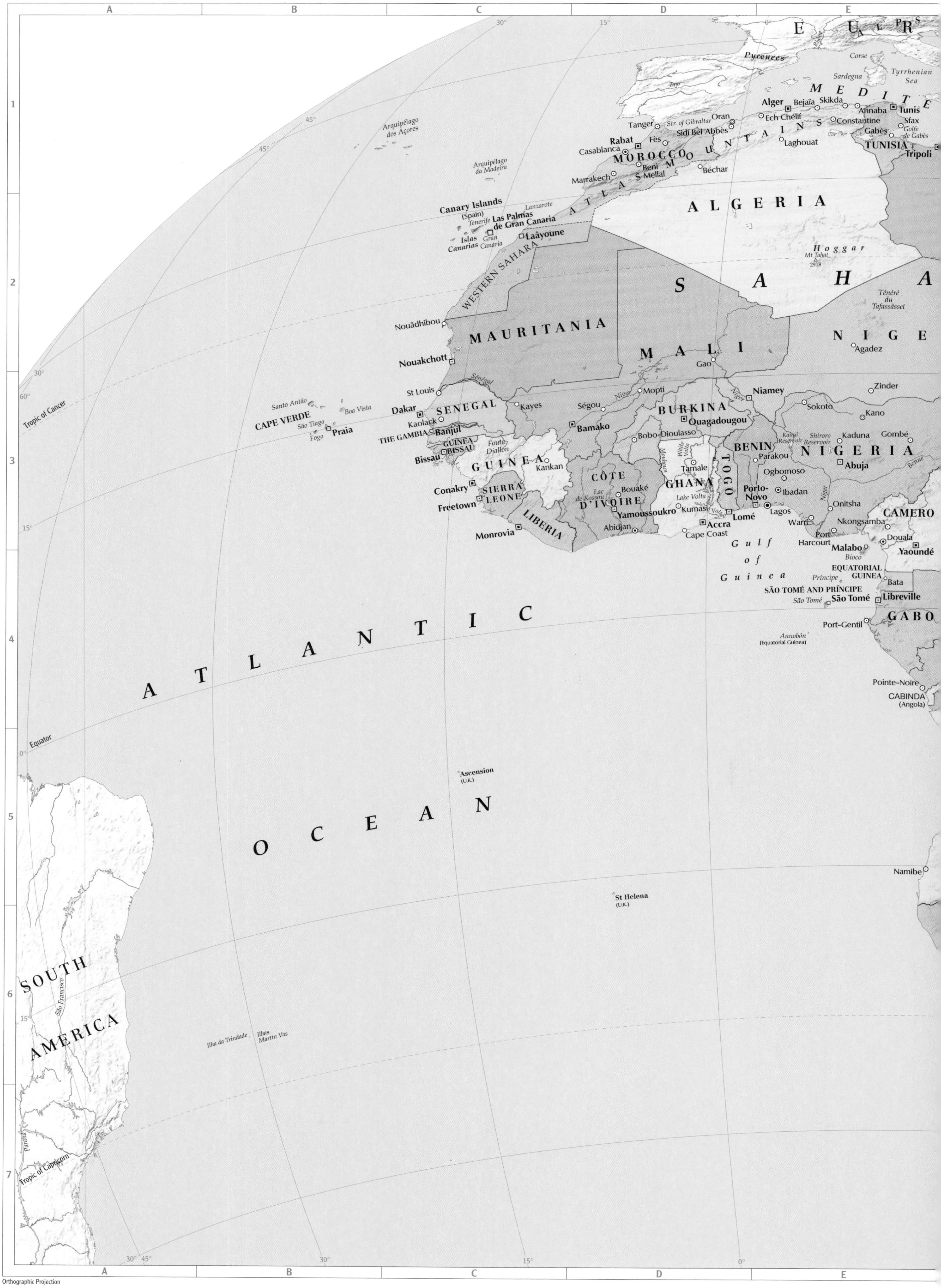

E U R O P E

Pyrenees

Corse

MEDITE

Sardegna

Tyrrhenian Sea

Tanger
Str. of Gibraltar
Oran
Alger
Bejaïa
Skikda
Annaba
Tunis
Ech Chélif
Constantine
Sfax
Gabès
Golfe de Gabès
TUNISIA
Tripoli

Rabat
Casablanca
Fès
Sidi Bel Abbès
MOROCCO
Beni Mellal
Marrakech
Béchar
Laghouat

Arquipélago dos Açores

Arquipélago da Madeira

ATLAS

MOUNTAINS

ALGERIA

Hoggar
Mt Tahat
2918

SAHA

Canary Islands
(Spain)
Lanzarote
Tenerife
Las Palmas de Gran Canaria
Islas Canarias
Gran Canaria
Laâyoune

WESTERN SAHARA

Ténéré du Tafassâsset

Nouâdhibou

MAURITANIA

MALI

NIGE

Agadez

Nouakchott

Gao

Senegal

St Louis

Zinder

Santo Antão
Boa Vista
Dakar
Kayes
Ségou
Niger
Mopti
Niamey
Sokoto
Kano

CAPE VERDE
São Tiago
Fogo
Praia
SENEGAL
Kaolack
Banjul
THE GAMBIA
GUINEA-BISSAU
Bissau
Fouta Djallon
Kankan
GUINEA
Bamako
BURKINA
Ouagadougou
Bobo-Dioulasso
Kainji Reservoir
Shiroro Reservoir
Kaduna
Gombé
BENIN
Parakou
NIGERIA
Abuja
Benue

Conakry
SIERRA LEONE
Freetown
CÔTE D'IVOIRE
Bouaké
Lac de Kossou
GHANA
Tamale
Lake Volta
TOGO
Ogbomoso
Ibadan

Monrovia
LIBERIA
Yamoussoukro
Kumasi
Abidjan
Accra
Cape Coast
Porto-Novo
Lomé
Lagos
Warri
Onitsha
Nkongsamba
CAMERO
Port Harcourt
Douala
Malabo
Bioco
Yaoundé

Gulf of Guinea

EQUATORIAL GUINEA
Bata
SÃO TOMÉ AND PRÍNCIPE
Príncipe
São Tomé
São Tomé
Libreville
GABO

Annobón
(Equatorial Guinea)
Port-Gentil

ATLANTIC

OCEAN

Tropic of Cancer

Ascension
(U.K.)

Pointe-Noire
CABINDA
(Angola)

Equator

Namibe

St Helena
(U.K.)

SOUTH

San Francisco

AMERICA

Ilha da Trindade
Ilhas Martin Vas

Paraná

Tropic of Capricorn

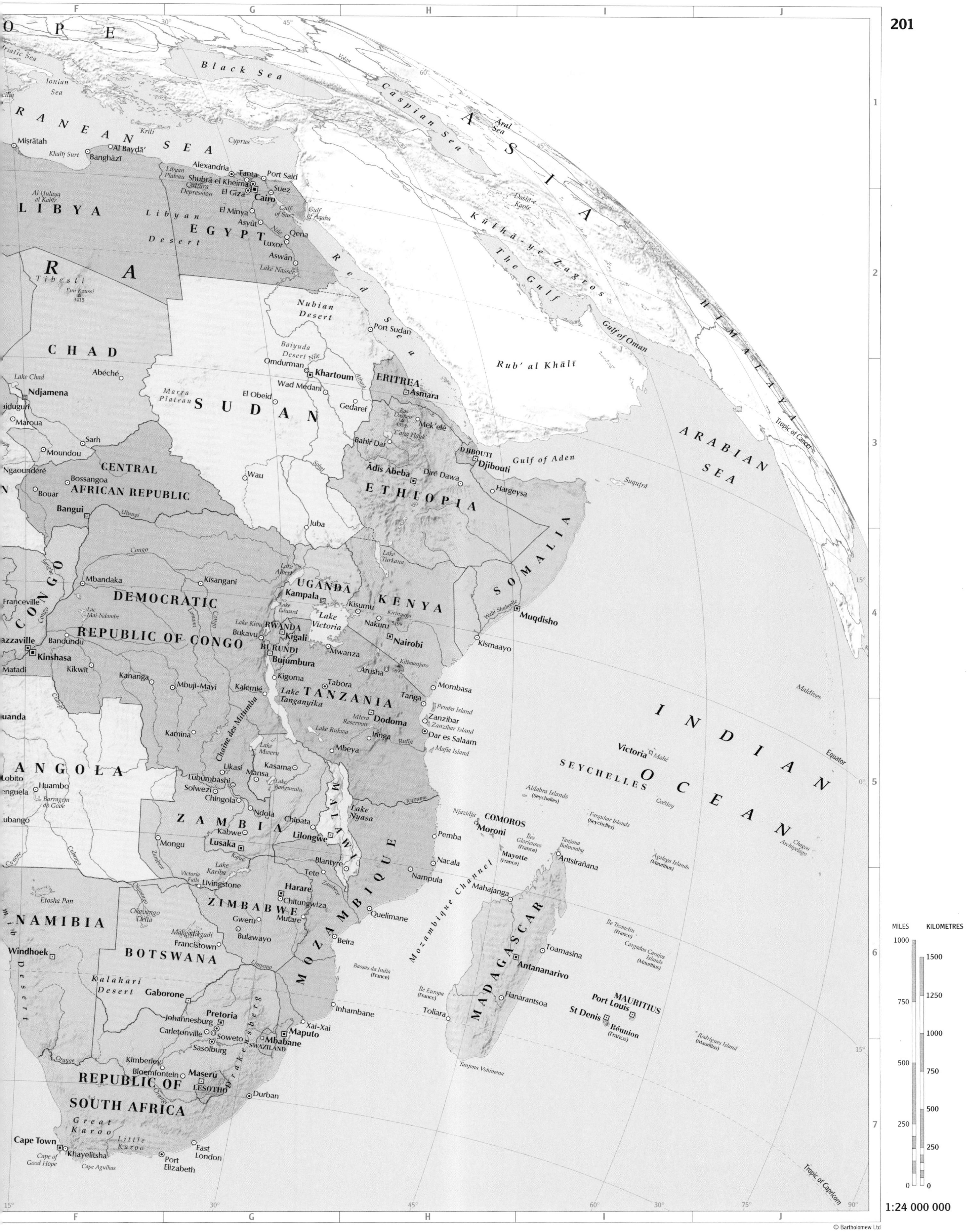
ASIA
Black Sea
Caspian Sea
Aral Sea
Ionian Sea
MEDITERRANEAN SEA
Kriti
Cyprus
Volga
Mişrātah
Khalīj Surt
Banghāzī
Al Bayḑā'
Alexandria
Tanta
Port Said
Shubrā el Kheima
Qattara Depression
Libyan Plateau
El Gîza
Cairo
Suez
Gulf of Suez
Gulf of Aqaba
El Minya
Asyût
Qena
Luxor
Aswân
Lake Nasser
Nile
Al Hulayq al Kabīr
LIBYA
Libyan Desert
EGYPT
Tibesti
Emi Koussi 3415
CHAD
Lake Chad
Abéché
Ndjamena
Maroua
Sarh
Moundou
Ngaoundéré
Red Sea
Nubian Desert
Port Sudan
Bayuda Desert
Omdurman
Khartoum
Wad Medani
El Obeid
Marra Plateau
SUDAN
Gedaref
ERITREA
Asmara
Ras Dashen 4533
Mek'elē
T'ana Hāyk'
Bahir Dar
DJIBOUTI
Djibouti
Gulf of Aden
Adīs Ābeba
Dirē Dawa
Hargeysa
ETHIOPIA
Wau
Juba
Sobat
Suquţrā
Rub' al Khālī
Dasht-e Kavīr
Kūhhā-ye Zagros
The Gulf
Gulf of Oman
HIMALAYA
Tropic of Cancer
ARABIAN SEA
CENTRAL AFRICAN REPUBLIC
Bossangoa
Bouar
Bangui
Ubangi
Congo
SOMALIA
Lake Turkana
Lake Albert
UGANDA
Kampala
Kisumu
KENYA
Mbandaka
Kisangani
DEMOCRATIC REPUBLIC OF CONGO
Lac Mai-Ndombe
Franceville
CONGO
Lake Edward
Lake Victoria
Kirinyaga 5199
Nakuru
Nairobi
Webi Shabeelle
Muqdisho
Kismaayo
Lake Kivu
RWANDA
Kigali
BURUNDI
Bukavu
Bujumbura
Mwanza
Brazzaville
Kinshasa
Bandundu
Kikwit
Matadi
Lomami
Kilimanjaro 5892
Arusha
Kigoma
Tabora
Kananga
Mbuji-Mayi
Kalémié
Lake Tanganyika
TANZANIA
Tanga
Mombasa
Pemba Island
Zanzibar
Zanzibar Island
Dar es Salaam
Mafia Island
Mtera Reservoir
Dodoma
Lake Rukwa
Iringa
Rufiji
Chaîne des Mitumba
Kamina
Mbeya
Lake Mweru
Kasama
Luanda
Maldives
INDIAN OCEAN
Victoria
Mahé
SEYCHELLES
Equator
Aldabra Islands (Seychelles)
Farquhar Islands (Seychelles)
Coëtivy
Chagos Archipelago
Agalega Islands (Mauritius)
ANGOLA
Lobito
Benguela
Huambo
Barragem do Gove
Lubango
Likasi
Lubumbashi
Mansa
Lake Bangweulu
Solwezi
Chingola
Ndola
MALAWI
Lake Nyasa
Ruvuma
ZAMBIA
Chipata
Kabwe
Lilongwe
Mongu
Lusaka
Kafue
Zambeze
Cunene
Cubango
Lake Kariba
Blantyre
Victoria Falls
Livingstone
Tete
Etosha Pan
Okavango
Okavango Delta
Harare
Chitungwiza
ZIMBABWE
Mutare
Gweru
Bulawayo
Makgadikgadi
Francistown
MOZAMBIQUE
Pemba
Nacala
Nampula
Quelimane
Beira
Njazidja
COMOROS
Moroni
Îles Glorieuses (France)
Mayotte (France)
Tanjona Bobaomby
Antsirañana
Mozambique Channel
Mahajanga
NAMIBIA
Windhoek
BOTSWANA
Kalahari Desert
Namib Desert
Gaborone
Limpopo
Bassas da India (France)
Île Europa (France)
Toliara
MADAGASCAR
Antananarivo
Toamasina
Fianarantsoa
Île Tromelin (France)
Cargados Carajos Islands (Mauritius)
MAURITIUS
Port Louis
St Denis
Réunion (France)
Rodrigues Island (Mauritius)
Tanjona Vohimena
Pretoria
Johannesburg
Carletonville
Soweto
Sasolburg
Inhambane
Xai-Xai
Maputo
Mbabane
SWAZILAND
Drakensberg
Orange
Kimberley
Bloemfontein
Maseru
LESOTHO
REPUBLIC OF SOUTH AFRICA
Durban
Great Karoo
Little Karoo
Cape Town
Khayelitsha
Cape of Good Hope
Cape Agulhas
Port Elizabeth
East London
Tropic of Capricorn
F G H I J
1 2 3 4 5 6 7
MILES
KILOMETRES
1:24 000 000

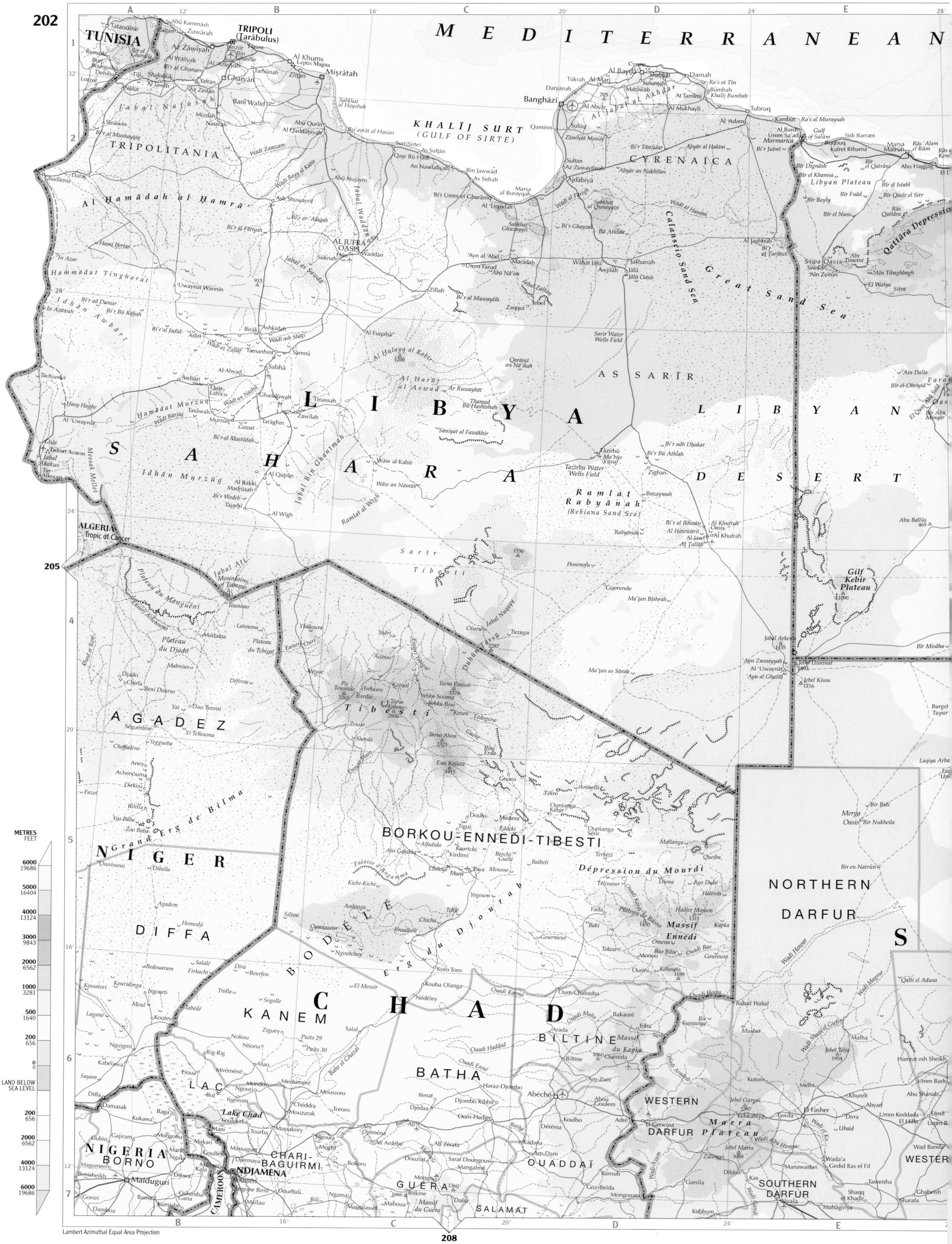
MEDITERRANEAN
TUNISIA
TRIPOLI (Ṭarābulus)
Az Zāwiyah
Gharyān
Al Khums
Leptis Magna
Miṣrātah
Zliṭan
Tarhūnah
Banī Walīd
Nālūt
Mizdah
Nasmah
Sinawin
TRIPOLITANIA
Ghadāmis
Darāj
Al Ḥamādah al Ḥamrā'
KHALĪJ SURT
(GULF OF SIRTE)
Surt (Sirte)
Banghāzī
Al Bayḍā'
Cyrene
Shaḥḥāt
Darnah
Ṭubruq
Al Marj
Ajdābiyā
Al Jabal al Akhḍar
CYRENAICA
Calanscio Sand Sea
Great Sand Sea
Al Jaghbūb
Jālū
Awjilah
Marādah
Zillah
AL JUFRA OASIS
Hūn
Waddān
Sūknah
Jabal as Sawdā'
Hammādat Tingharat
Idhān Awbārī
Sabhā
Awbārī
Ghāt
Murzuq
Idhān Murzūq
Al Qaṭrūn
Tmassah
Al Harūj al Aswad
LIBYA
SAHARA
AS SARĪR
LIBYAN DESERT
Ramlat Rabyānah
(Rebiana Sand Sea)
Al Kufrah
Al Jawf
Al Khufrah Oasis
Sarīr Tibesti
Jabal Arkenū
Jabal 'Uwaynāt
Jebel Uweinat
Gilf Kebir Plateau
Abu Ballâs
Siwa Oasis
Qattâra Depression
Libyan Plateau
Salûm
Marsa Matrûh
ALGERIA
Tropic of Cancer
Plateau du Manguéni
Plateau du Djado
Djado
Chirfa
AGADEZ
Séguédine
Bilma
Grand Erg de Bilma
NIGER
DIFFA
Tibesti
Emi Koussi
Tarso Emissi
Pic Toussidé
Bardaï
Zouar
Aozou
Yebbi-Bou
BORKOU-ENNEDI-TIBESTI
Faya
Ounianga Kebir
Dépression du Mourdi
Plateau de Basso
Massif Ennedi
Fada
BODÉLÉ
Erg du Djourab
Koro Toro
KANEM
CHAD
Mao
BILTINE
Massif du Kapka
BATHA
Abéché
Ati
OUADDAÏ
LAC
Lake Chad
Bol
NIGERIA
BORNO
Maiduguri
CHARI-BAGUIRMI
NDJAMENA
CAMEROON
GUÉRA
SALAMAT
Massif du Guéra
NORTHERN DARFUR
WESTERN DARFUR
SOUTHERN DARFUR
Marra Plateau
Jebel Marra
El Fasher
El Geneina
Nyala
Wadi Howar
Merga Oasis
METRES
FEET
6000 19686
5000 16404
4000 13124
3000 9843
2000 6562
1000 3281
500 1640
200 656
0 0
LAND BELOW SEA LEVEL
200 656
2000 6562
4000 13124
6000 19686
Lambert Azimuthal Equal Area Projection

205

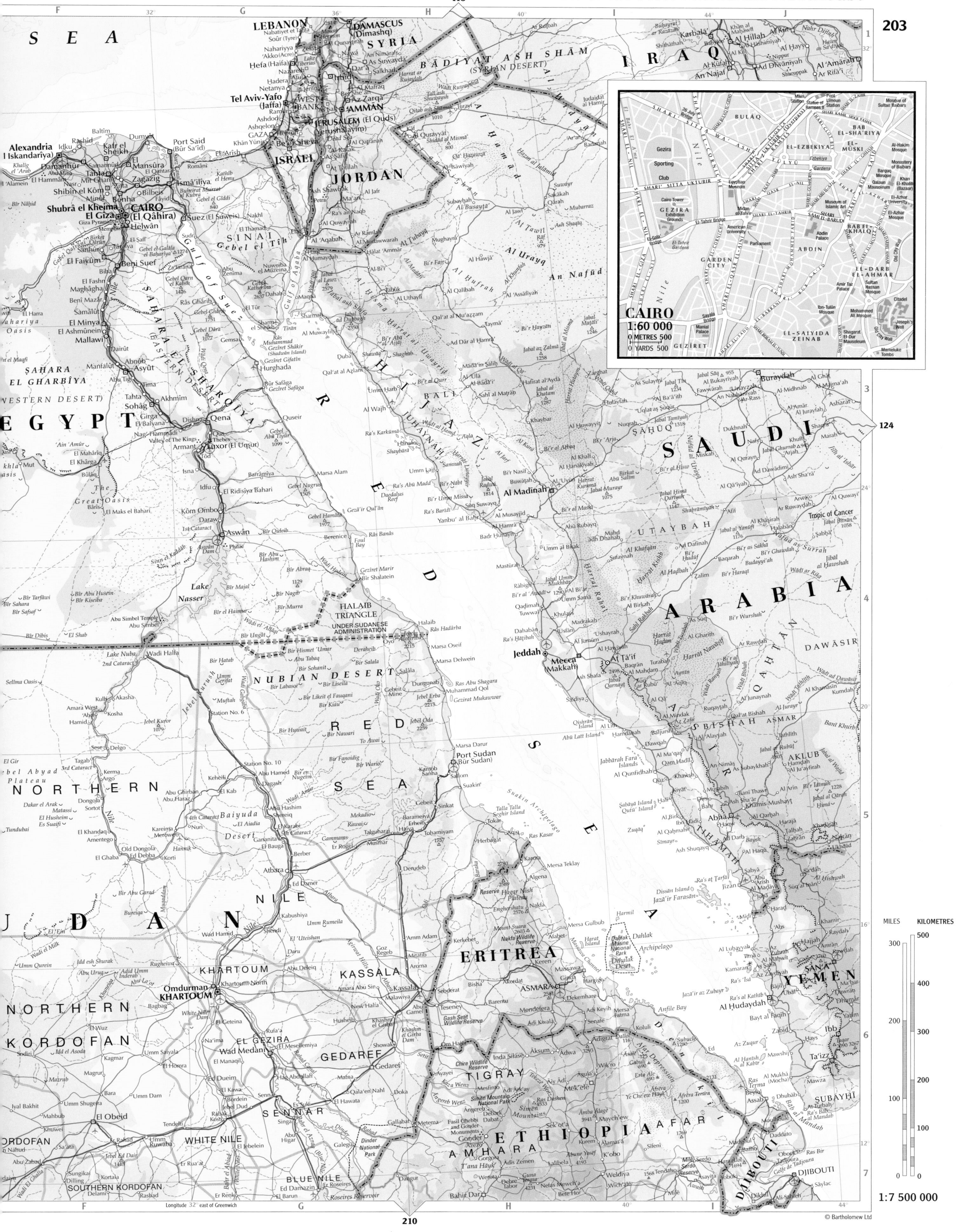

124

Country/region labels:

SEA

LEBANON
SYRIA · DAMASCUS (Dimashq)
IRAQ
ISRAEL
JORDAN
BÂDIYAT ASH SHÂM (SYRIAN DESERT)

EGYPT
ṢAHARA EL GHARBÎYA (WESTERN DESERT)
SAHARA EL SHARQÎYA (EASTERN DESERT)
SINAI
HIJAZ
SAUDI ARABIA
NUBIAN DESERT
RED SEA
NORTHERN
SUDAN
NILE
KHARTOUM
KASSALA
GEDAREF
SENNAR
BLUE NILE
WHITE NILE
KORDOFAN
SOUTHERN KORDOFAN
ERITREA
ASMARA
TIGRAY
AMHARA
ETHIOPIA
AFAR
DJIBOUTI
YEMEN
SANA'
Mecca (Makkah)
Jeddah

HALAIB TRIANGLE
UNDER SUDANESE ADMINISTRATION

Lake Nasser

Cities:
Alexandria (El Iskandarîya), Cairo (El Qâhira), El Giza (El Qâhira), Port Said (Bûr Sa'îd), Suez (El Suweis), Luxor (El Uqsur), Aswân, Jerusalem (Yerushalayim / El Quds), Tel Aviv-Yafo (Jaffa), AMMÂN, Port Sudan (Bûr Sudan), Al Madinah, Omdurman, Khartoum North

CAIRO 1:60 000
0 METRES 500
0 YARDS 500

BULÂQ · EL-EZBEKIYA · EL-MUSKI · BAB EL-SHA'RIYA
GEZIRA · Sporting Club · GARDEN CITY · ABDIN · EL-DARB EL-AHMAR · EL-SAIYIDA ZEINAB · GEZIRET
Cairo Tower · Egyptian Museum · Nile · American University · Parliament · Citadel

Scale bars:

MILES   KILOMETRES
300   500
        400
200   300
        200
100   100
0   0

1:7 500 000

Longitude 32° east of Greenwich

ATLANTIC

OCEAN

SPAIN

PORTUGAL
LISBOA
Lisbon

MOROCCO

RABAT

Casablanca

Marrakech

Agadir

HAUT ATLAS

ANTI ATLAS

Arquipélago de Madeira
MADEIRA
(Portugal)
FUNCHAL

Canary Islands
(Spain)
Islas Canarias

La Palma
Tenerife
Santa Cruz de Tenerife
La Gomera
El Hierro
Gran Canaria
Las Palmas de Gran Canaria
Fuerteventura
Lanzarote
Arrecife
Puerto del Rosario

LAÂYOUNE

WESTERN
SAHARA

Ad Dakhla

Tropic of Cancer

TIRIS
ZEMMOUR

Nouâdhibou
DAKHLET
NOUÂDHIBOU

AZZEFFÂL
AKTIIRÎT
INCHIRI

ADRAR

OUARÂNE

TOMBOUCTOU

S A H

MAURITANIA

NOUAKCHOTT

TRARZA
BRÂKNA

TAGANT

EL MREYYÉ

HODH ECH
CHARGUI

HODH EL GHARBI
ASSABA

M A

METRES / FEET

6000 / 19686
5000 / 16404
4000 / 13124
3000 / 9843
2000 / 6562
1000 / 3281
500 / 1640
200 / 656
0
LAND BELOW SEA LEVEL
200 / 656
2000 / 6562
4000 / 13124
6000 / 19686

Lambert Azimuthal Equal Area Projection

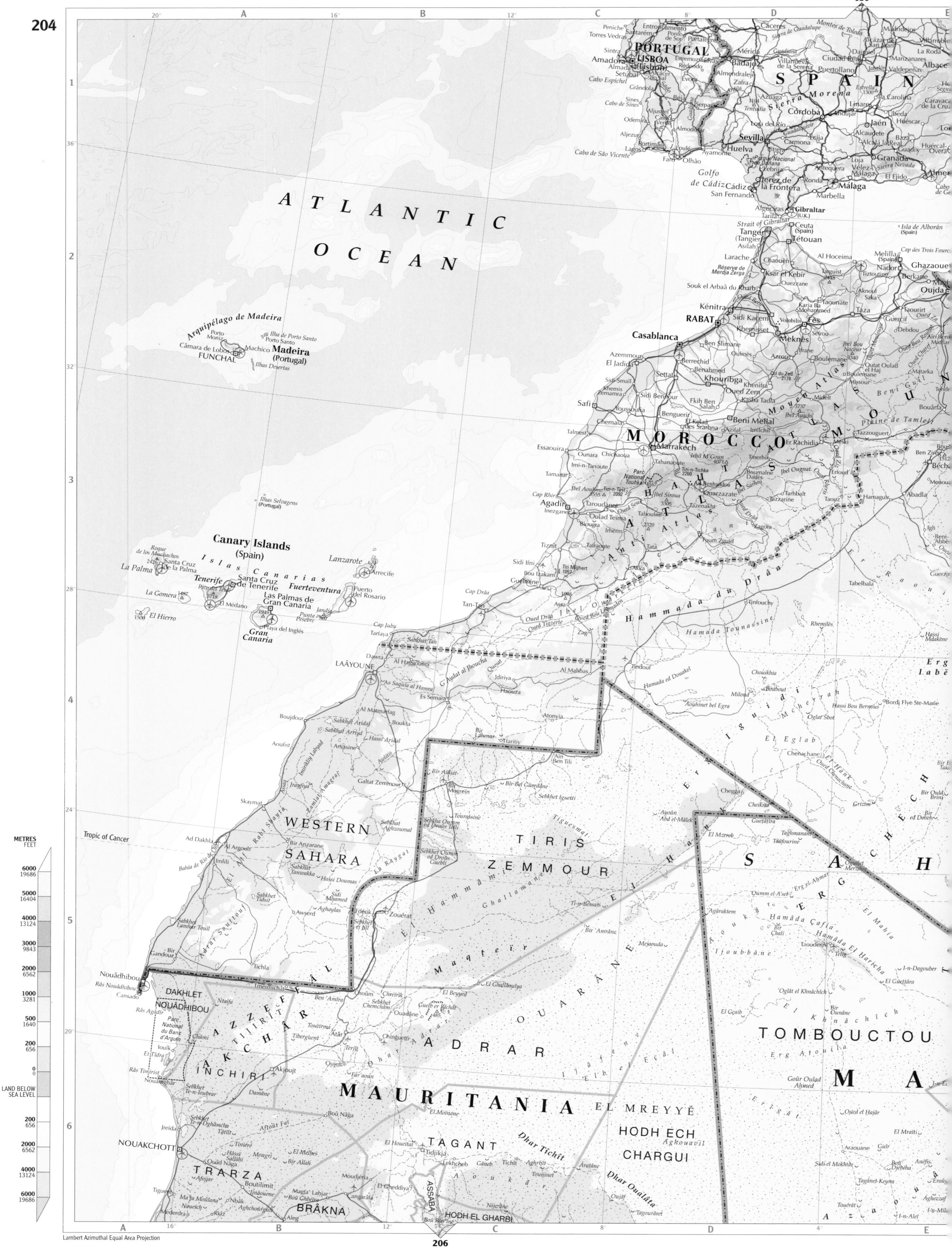

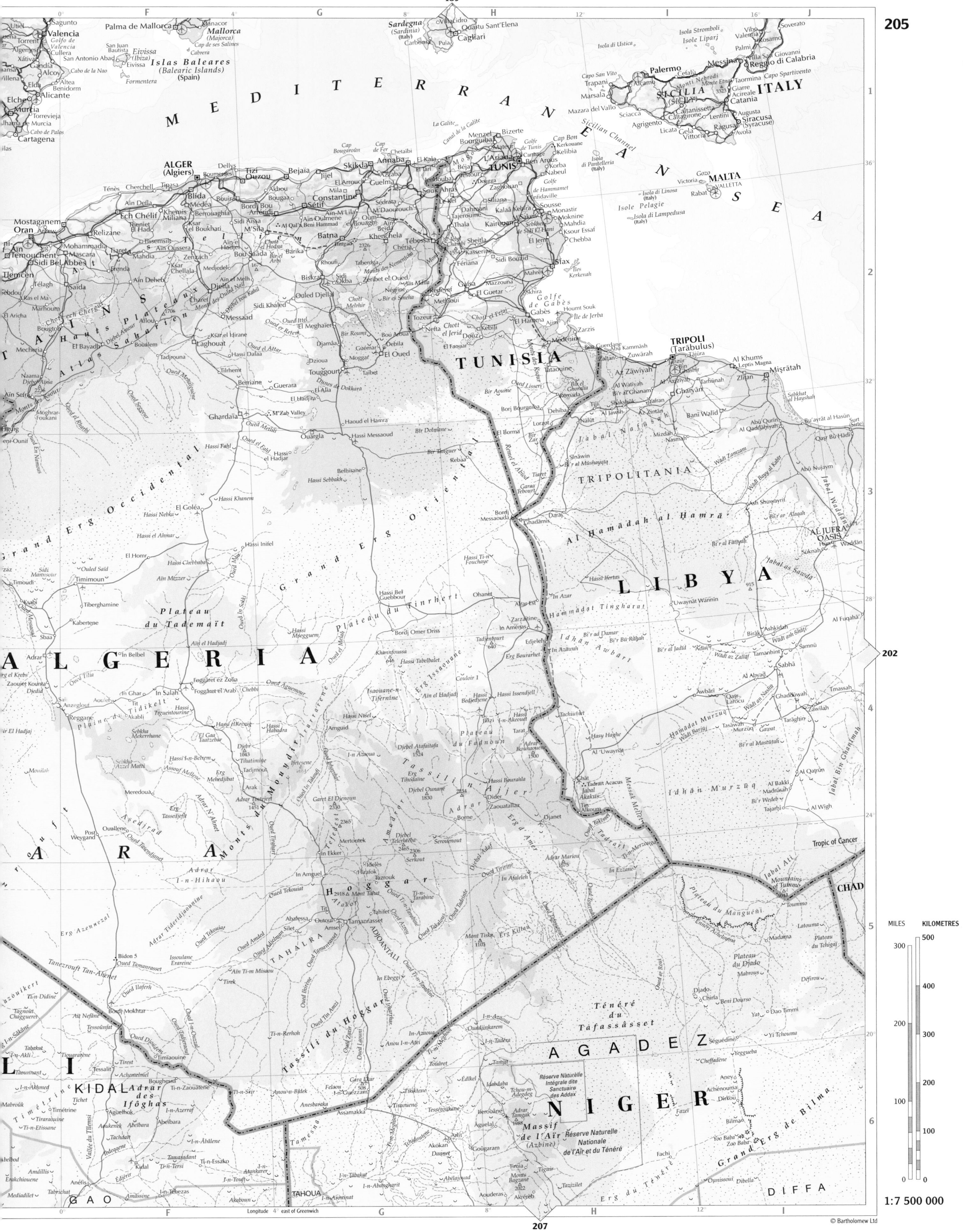

MEDITERRANEAN SEA

ITALY

SICILIA (SICILY)

MALTA

ALGER (Algiers)

TUNIS

TRIPOLI (Tarābulus)

TUNISIA

TRIPOLITANIA

LIBYA

ALGERIA

NIGER

CHAD

Tropic of Cancer

Grand Erg Occidental

Grand Erg Oriental

Plateau du Tademaït

Plateau du Tinrhert

Plateau du Fadnoun

Tassili-n-Ajjer

Idhān Murzūq

Al Hamādah al Hamrā'

Hoggar

TAHALTA

ADRAR DES IFOGHAS

KIDAL

GAO

TAHOUA

AGADEZ

DIFFA

Massif de l'Aïr (Azbine)

Ténéré du Tafassâsset

Réserve Naturelle Nationale de l'Aïr et du Ténéré

MILES   KILOMETRES

300   500

200   300

100   200

   100

0   0

202

1:7 500 000

© Bartholomew Ltd

A   B   C   D   E

MAURITANIA

INCHIRI
ADRAR
DAKHLET
NOUÂDHIBOU
AKCHÂR
Parc National
du Banc
d'Arguin
TRARZA
TAGANT
BRAKNA
ASSABA
GORGOL
GUIDIMAKA

HODH
ECH CHARGUI
EL MREYYÉ
Dhar Tichît
Dhar Oualâta
HODH
EL GHARBI
HODH

SAHARA
Erg Atouila
TOMBOUCTOU

MALI

NOUAKCHOTT
St-Louis
DAKAR
Thiès
Rufisque
Cap Vert

SENEGAL

THE GAMBIA
BANJUL
Parc National
du Delta du Saloum

KAYES
KOULIKORO
BAMAKO
SÉGOU
MOPTI

GUINEA-BISSAU
BISSAU

MOYENNE-GUINÉE
GUINÉE-
MARITIME
GUINEA
HAUTE-
GUINÉE
SIKASSO

BURKINA
OUAGADOUGOU

CONAKRY

NORTHERN
SIERRA
LEONE
FREETOWN
WESTERN AREA
EASTERN
SOUTHERN

GUINÉE-FORESTIÈRE

Bobo-
Dioulasso

UPPER
WEST
UPPER EAST
NORTHERN

CÔTE
D'IVOIRE

GHANA
BRONG-AHAFO

LIBERIA
MONROVIA

YAMOUSSOUKRO
Bouaké

ASHANTI
Kumasi
WESTERN
CENTRAL
ACCRA
Abidjan

ATLANTIC

OCEAN

Equator

CAPE VERDE
AT THE SAME SCALE

Santo
Antão
São
Vicente
Mindelo
São
Luzia
Branco
Raso
São
Nicolau
Sal
Pedra Lume
Santa Maria
Boa
Vista

Ilhas do Cabo Verde

São
Tiago
Maio
PRAIA
Fogo
Brava

METRES
FEET
6000
19686
5000
16404
4000
13124
3000
9843
2000
6562
1000
3281
500
1640
200
656
0
0
LAND BELOW
SEA LEVEL
200
656
2000
6562
4000
13124
6000
19686

Lambert Azimuthal Equal Area Projection

Longitude 4 west of Greenwich

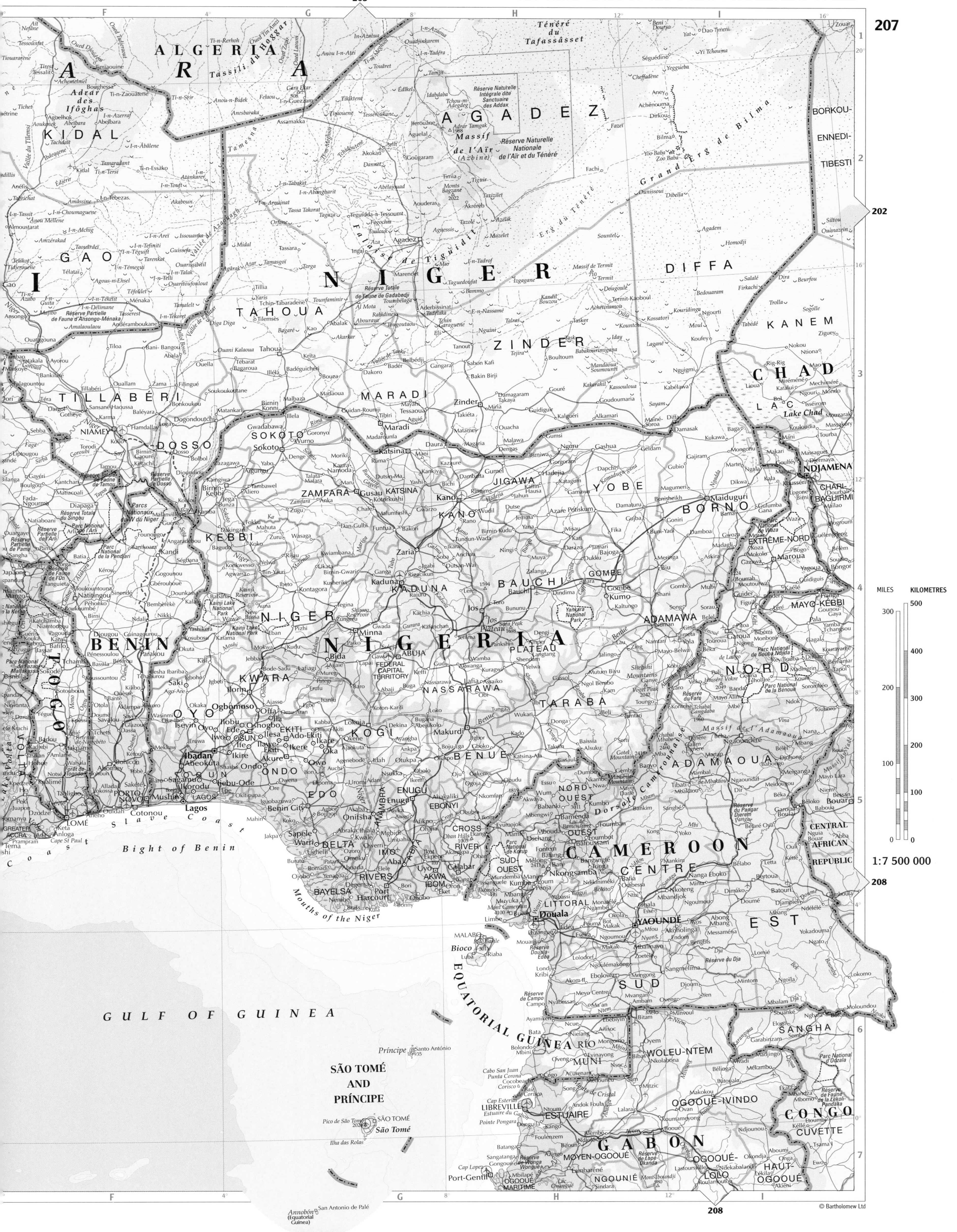
205
202
208
208
ALGERIA
KIDAL
GAO
TILLABÉRI
TAHOUA
AGADEZ
NIGER
DIFFA
ZINDER
MARADI
DOSSO
NIAMEY
KANEM
CHAD
LAC
Lake Chad
BORKOU-ENNEDI-TIBESTI
NDJAMENA
CHARI-BAGUIRMI
MAYO-KEBBI
EXTRÊME-NORD
NORD
ADAMAOUA
CENTRAL AFRICAN REPUBLIC
CAMEROON
CENTRE
EST
LITTORAL
SUD
SUD-OUEST
NORD-OUEST
OUEST
YAOUNDÉ
Douala
BENIN
TOGO
NIGERIA
SOKOTO
ZAMFARA
KATSINA
KANO
JIGAWA
YOBE
BORNO
KEBBI
NIGER
KADUNA
BAUCHI
GOMBE
ADAMAWA
PLATEAU
NASSARAWA
TARABA
KWARA
OYO
OSUN
EKITI
KOGI
BENUE
ONDO
OGUN
LAGOS
EDO
ENUGU
EBONYI
ANAMBRA
IMO
ABIA
CROSS RIVER
AKWA IBOM
RIVERS
BAYELSA
DELTA
FEDERAL CAPITAL TERRITORY
ABUJA
Lagos
PORTO-NOVO
Cotonou
LOMÉ
Bight of Benin
Slave Coast
Mouths of the Niger
GULF OF GUINEA
EQUATORIAL GUINEA
MALABO
Bioco
RÍO MUNI
SÃO TOMÉ AND PRÍNCIPE
Príncipe
SÃO TOMÉ
São Tomé
Annobón (Equatorial Guinea)
GABON
ESTUAIRE
LIBREVILLE
WOLEU-NTEM
OGOOUÉ-IVINDO
MOYEN-OGOOUÉ
OGOOUÉ-MARITIME
NGOUNIÉ
OGOOUÉ-LOLO
HAUT-OGOOUÉ
Port-Gentil
CONGO
CUVETTE
SANGHA
Ténéré du Tafassâsset
Grand Erg de Bilma
Massif de l'Aïr (Azbine)
Adrar des Ifôghas
Tassili du Hoggar
MILES
KILOMETRES
1:7 500 000
© Bartholomew Ltd

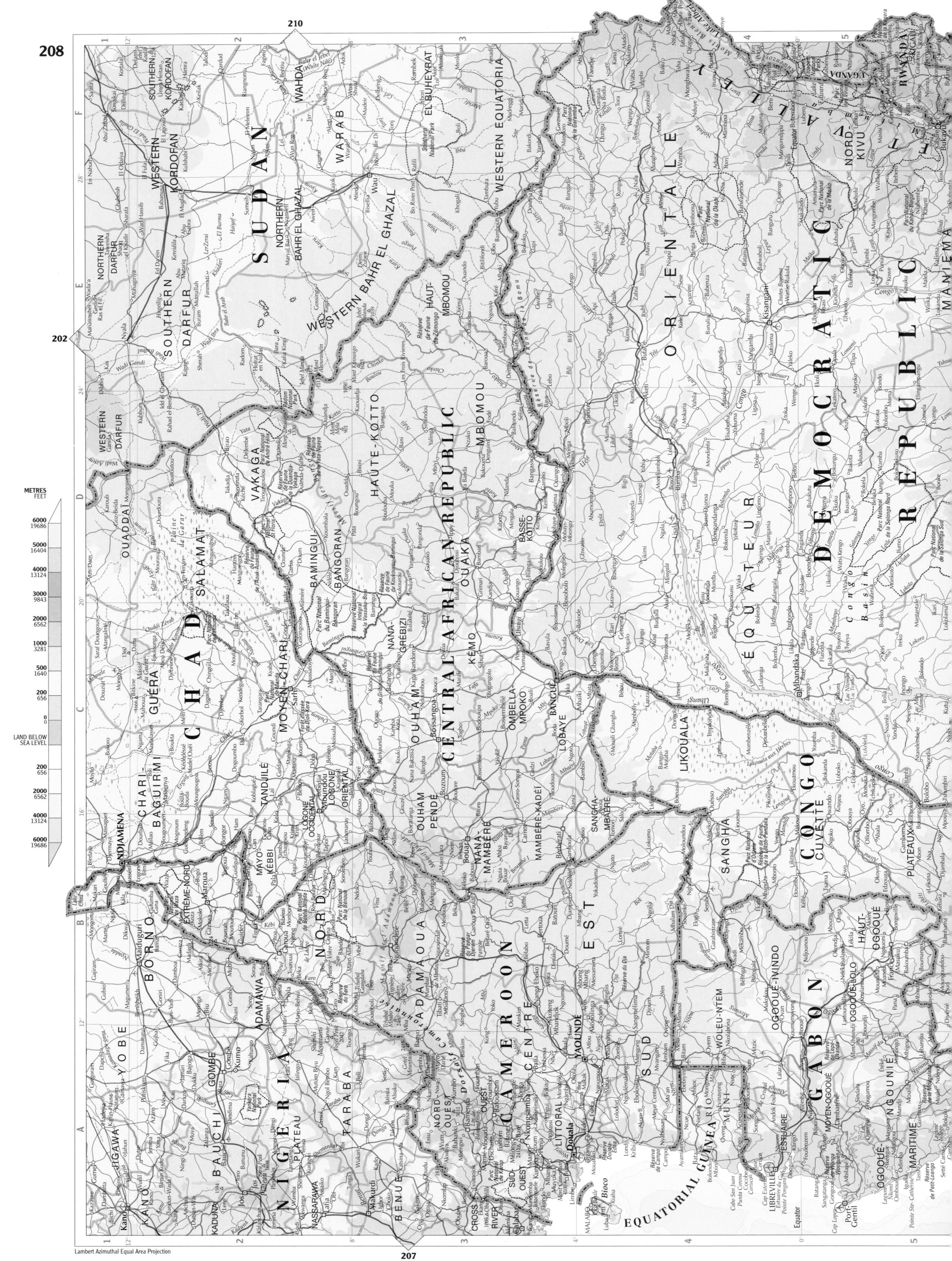

METRES
FEET

6000
19686

5000
16404

4000
13124

3000
9843

2000
6562

1000
3281

500
1640

200
656

0
0

LAND BELOW
SEA LEVEL

200
656

2000
6562

4000
13124

6000
19686

202

Lambert Azimuthal Equal Area Projection

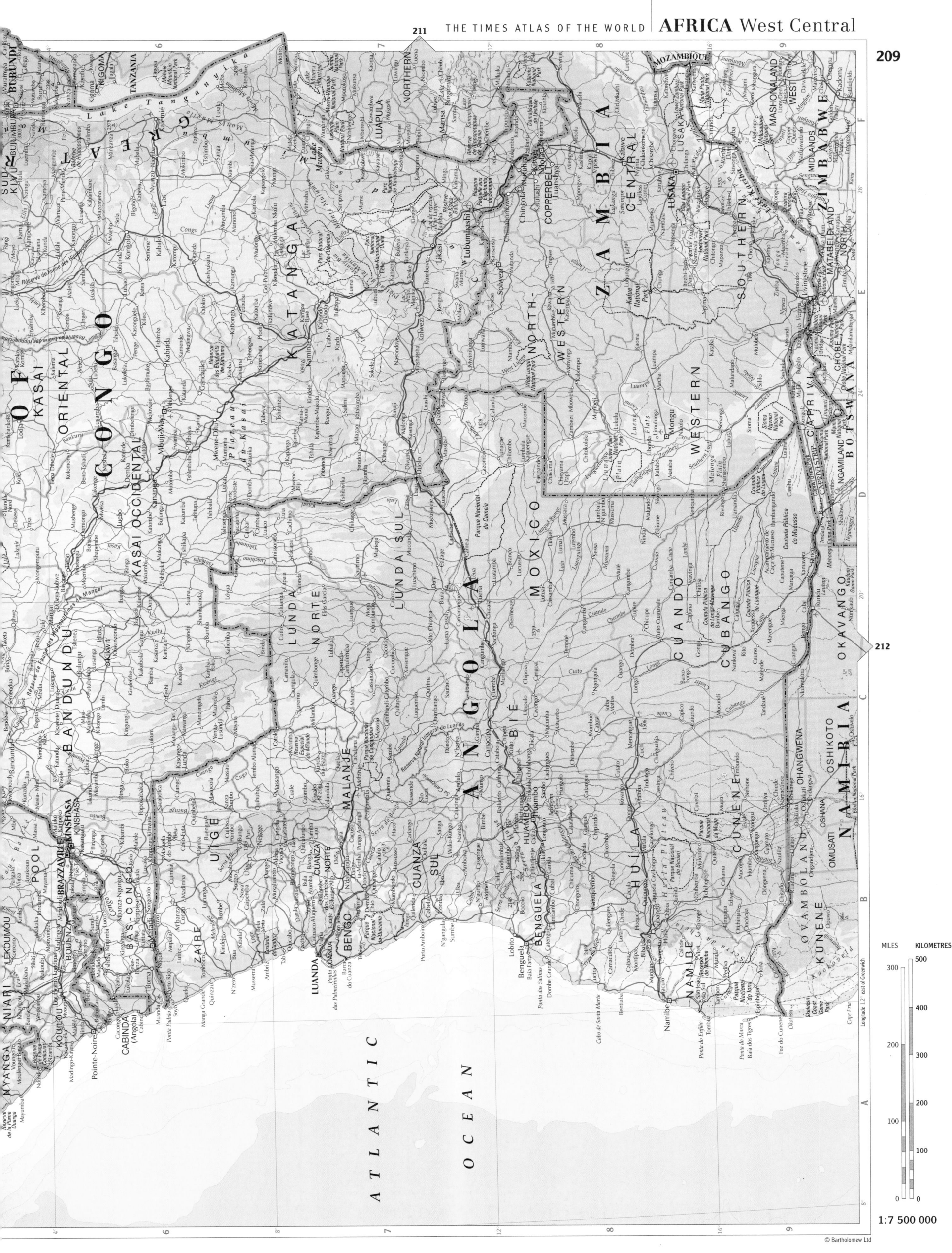

212

ATLANTIC

OCEAN

MILES   KILOMETRES

1:7 500 000

© Bartholomew Ltd

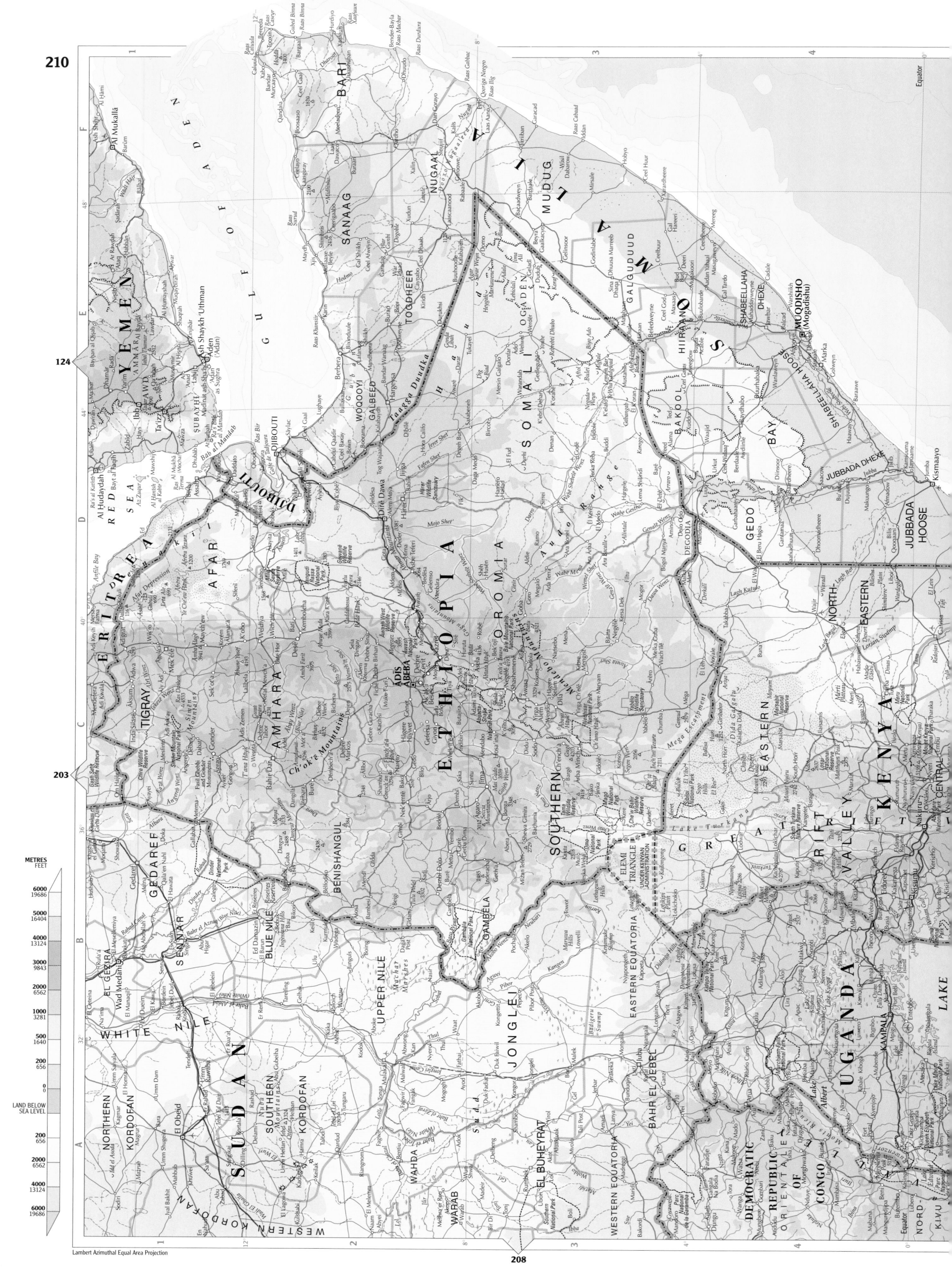

124

203

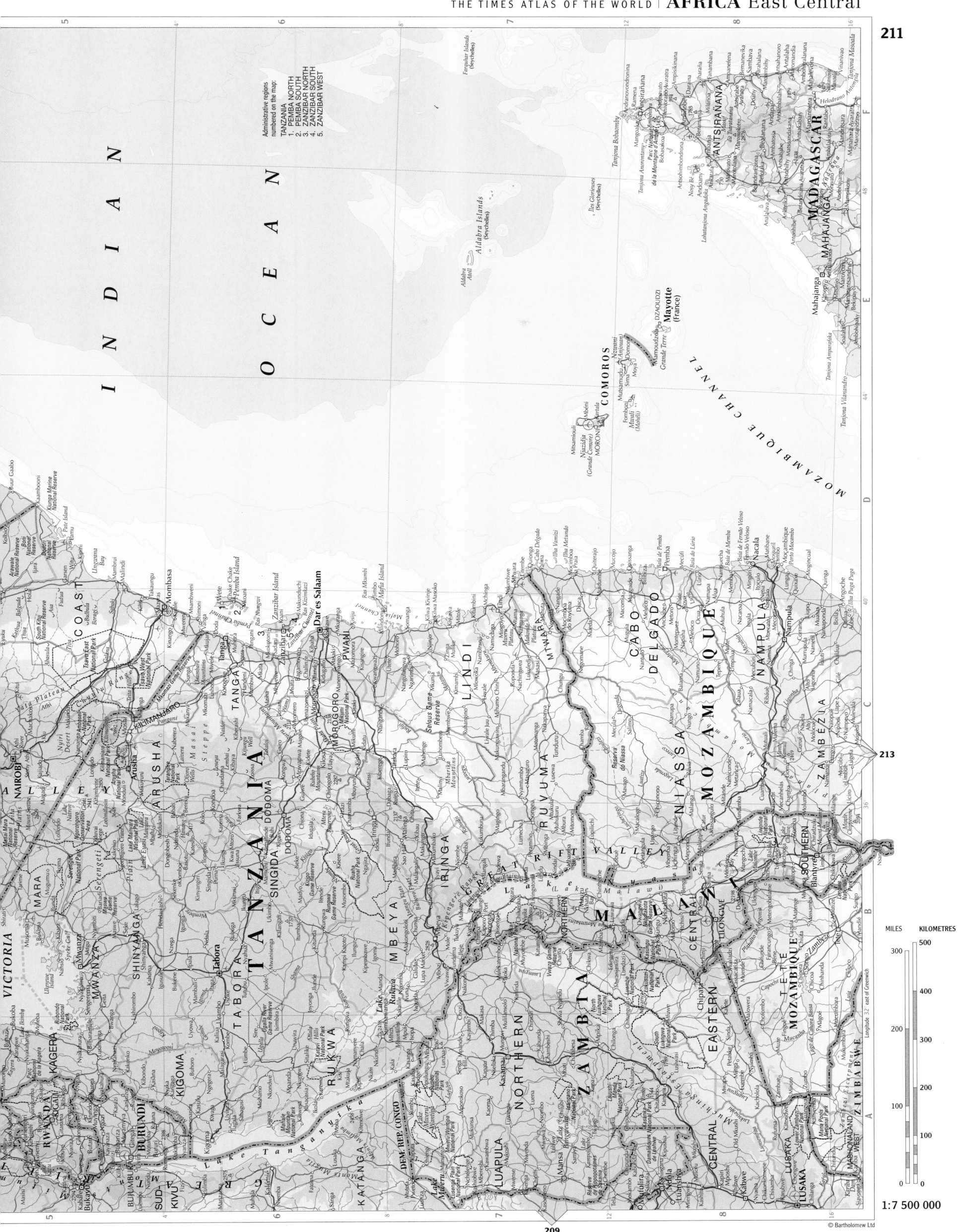

Administrative regions
numbered on the map:
TANZANIA
1. PEMBA NORTH
2. PEMBA SOUTH
3. ZANZIBAR NORTH
4. ZANZIBAR SOUTH
5. ZANZIBAR WEST

I N D I A N

O C E A N

MOZAMBIQUE CHANNEL

MADAGASCAR

COMOROS

Mayotte
(France)

Aldabra Islands
(Seychelles)

213

TANZANIA

MOZAMBIQUE

ZAMBIA

MALAWI

MILES   KILOMETRES
300   500

            400

200   300

            200
100
            100

0   0

1:7 500 000

209

© Bartholomew Ltd

ANGOLA

BENGUELA

HUILA

NAMIBE

CUNENE

CUBANGO

CUANDO

MOXICO

WESTERN

Z

OVAMBOLAND

OHANGWENA

OMUSATI

OSHANA

OSHIKOTO

OKAVANGO

CAPRIVI STRIP CAPRIVI

CHOBE

KUNENE

Etosha Pan

Etosha National Park

NGAMILAND

Okavango Delta

Makgadikgadi

NAMIBIA

OTJOZONDJUPA

OMAHEKE

BOTSWANA

CENT

GHANZI

Central Kalahari Game Reserve

ERONGO

WINDHOEK

KHOMAS

KALAHARI

KWENENG

NGWAKETSE

GABORONE

KGATLE

DESERT

HARDAP

Kgalagadi

KGALAGADI

Gemsbok National Park

Kalahari Gemsbok National Park

NORTH

WEST

NAMAQUALAND

KARAS

Fish River Canyon Park

REPUBLIC OF

GRIQUALAND WEST

FRE

NORTHERN CAPE

SOUTH AFRICA

EASTER

ATLANTIC

OCEAN

Tropic of Capricorn

Walvis Bay

Swakopmund

Namib-Naukluft Game Park

Great Karoo

Little Karoo

WESTERN CAPE

CAPE TOWN

Khayelitsha

Cape of Good Hope

Cape Agulhas

Port Elizabeth

Cape Recife

METRES / FEET

6000 / 19686
5000 / 16404
4000 / 13124
3000 / 9843
2000 / 6562
1000 / 3281
500 / 1640
200 / 656
0 / 0

LAND BELOW SEA LEVEL

200 / 656
2000 / 6562
4000 / 13124
6000 / 19686

CAPE TOWN

1:30 000

FORESHORE

CENTRAL

Cape Town Railway Station

Civic Centre

Nico Malan Opera House

The Castle of Good Hope

Houses of Parliament

SCHOTSCHE KLOOF

TAMBOERSKLOOF

VREDEHOEK

Malay Quarter

Botanical Gardens

South African National Gallery

0 METRES 250

0 YARDS 250

Lambert Azimuthal Equal Area Projection

MILES KILOMETRE

1:7 500 000

ZAMBIA
LUSAKA
CENTRAL
SOUTHERN

MALAWI
LILONGWE
CENTRAL
EASTERN
SOUTHERN
NIASSA
TETE
CABO DELGADO
Nampula
NAMPULA

ZIMBABWE
HARARE
MASHONALAND WEST
MASHONALAND CENTRAL
MASHONALAND EAST
MANICALAND
MASVINGO
MIDLANDS
MATABELELAND NORTH
MATABELELAND SOUTH
Bulawayo

MOZAMBIQUE
ZAMBÉZIA
Quelimane
SOFALA
Beira
MANICA
GAZA
INHAMBANE
Inhambane
MAPUTO

MOZAMBIQUE CHANNEL

NORTHERN
GAUTENG
PRETORIA
Johannesburg
Soweto
MPUMALANGA
Sasolburg
MBABANE
SWAZILAND

FREE STATE

LESOTHO
MASERU

KWAZULU-NATAL
Pietermaritzburg
Durban
KwaMashu
Umlazi

EASTERN CAPE
Umtata
East London
Mdantsane

Tropic of Capricorn

INDIAN OCEAN

MADAGASCAR
ANTSIRANANA
MAHAJANGA
Mahajanga
ANTANANARIVO
TOAMASINA
Toamasina
ANTSIRABE
FIANARANTSOA
Fianarantsoa
TOLIARA
Toliara

Tropic of Capricorn

MADAGASCAR
AT THE SAME SCALE

Longitude 28° east of Greenwich

© Bartholomew Ltd

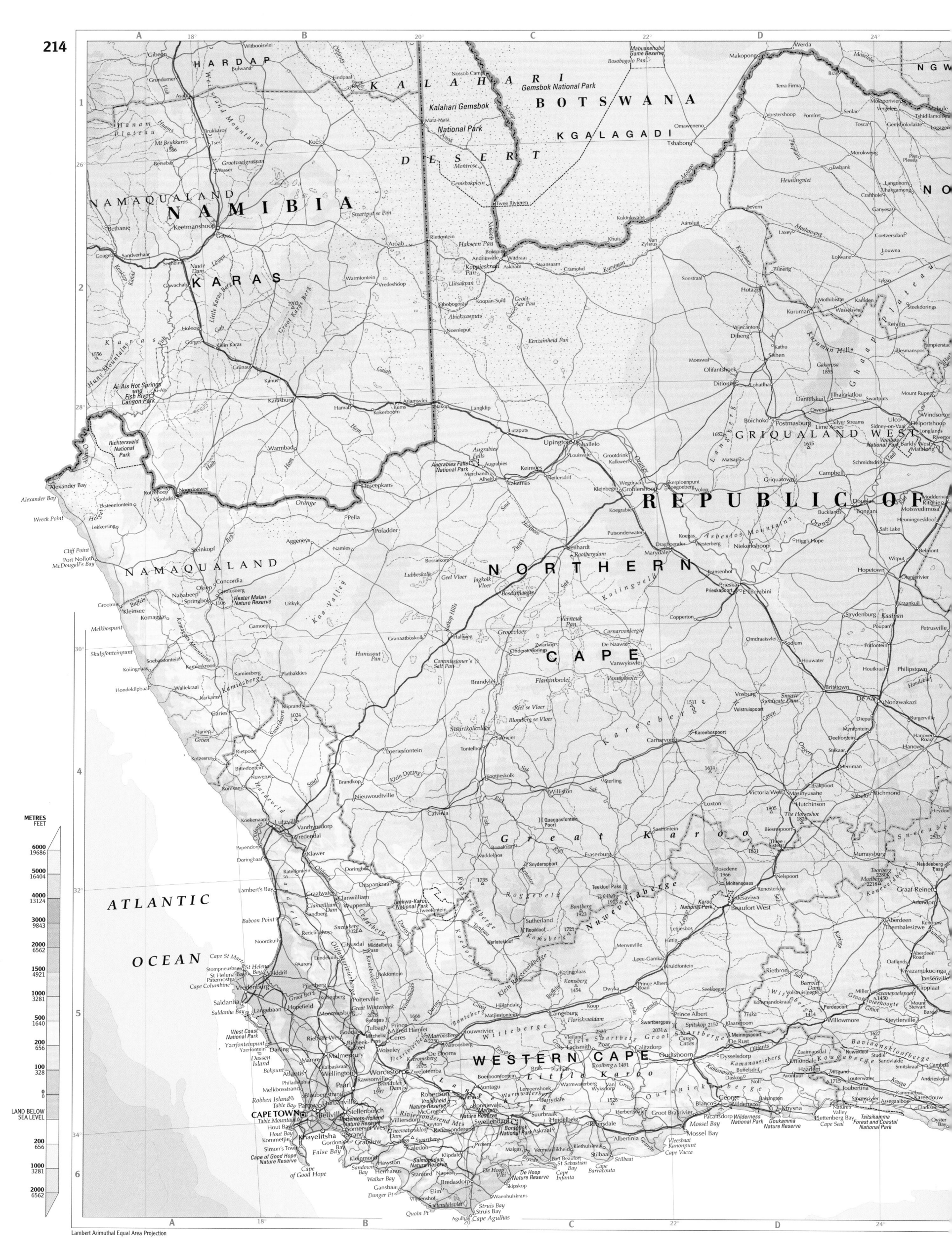

Lambert Azimuthal Equal Area Projection

D
18°
20°
22°
24°
1
2
4
5
6
26°
28°
30°
32°
34°
HARDAP
KALAHARI
Gemsbok National Park
BOTSWANA
KGALAGADI
Kalahari Gemsbok National Park
DESERT
NAMAQUALAND
NAMIBIA
KARAS
Mabuasehube Game Reserve
NGW
NO
Richtersveld National Park
Ai-Ais Hot Springs and Fish River Canyon Park
Augrabies Falls National Park
GRIQUALAND WEST
Vaalbos National Park
REPUBLIC OF
NAMAQUALAND
Hester Malan Nature Reserve
NORTHERN
CAPE
Great Karoo
Tankwa-Karoo National Park
Karoo National Park
WESTERN CAPE
Little Karoo
West Coast National Park
Table Mountain National Park
Cape of Good Hope Nature Reserve
Wilderness National Park
Goukamma Nature Reserve
Tsitsikamma Forest and Coastal National Park
De Hoop Nature Reserve
Bontebok National Park
ATLANTIC
OCEAN
Keetmanshoop
Upington
Kuruman
Kimberley
Springbok
Calvinia
Beaufort West
De Aar
Vredenburg
Saldanha
CAPE TOWN
Bellville
Stellenbosch
Paarl
Worcester
Oudtshoorn
George
Knysna
Mossel Bay
Plettenberg Bay
Cape Agulhas
Alexander Bay
Port Nolloth
METRES
FEET
6000
19686
5000
16404
4000
13124
3000
9843
2000
6562
1500
4921
1000
3281
500
1640
200
656
100
328
0
0
LAND BELOW SEA LEVEL
200
656
1000
3281
2000
6562

SOUTH AFRICA

NORTH WEST

GAUTENG

PRETORIA

Johannesburg

Soweto

MPUMALANGA

FREE STATE

LESOTHO

MASERU

SWAZILAND

MBABANE

MANZINI

HHOHHO

LUBOMBO

MANZINI

SHISELWENI

MAPUTO

MOZAMBIQUE

MAPUTO

KWAZULU-NATAL

Pietermaritzburg

KwaMashu

Durban

Pinetown

EASTERN CAPE

GRIQUALAND EAST

Umtata

Pondoland

Tembuland

Mdantsane

East London

Port Elizabeth

Algoa Bay

I N D I A N

O C E A N

Kruger National Park

Drakensberg

Maluti Mountains

MILES | KILOMETRES

125 — 200

100 — 150

75 — 125

50 — 75

25 — 50

0 — 0

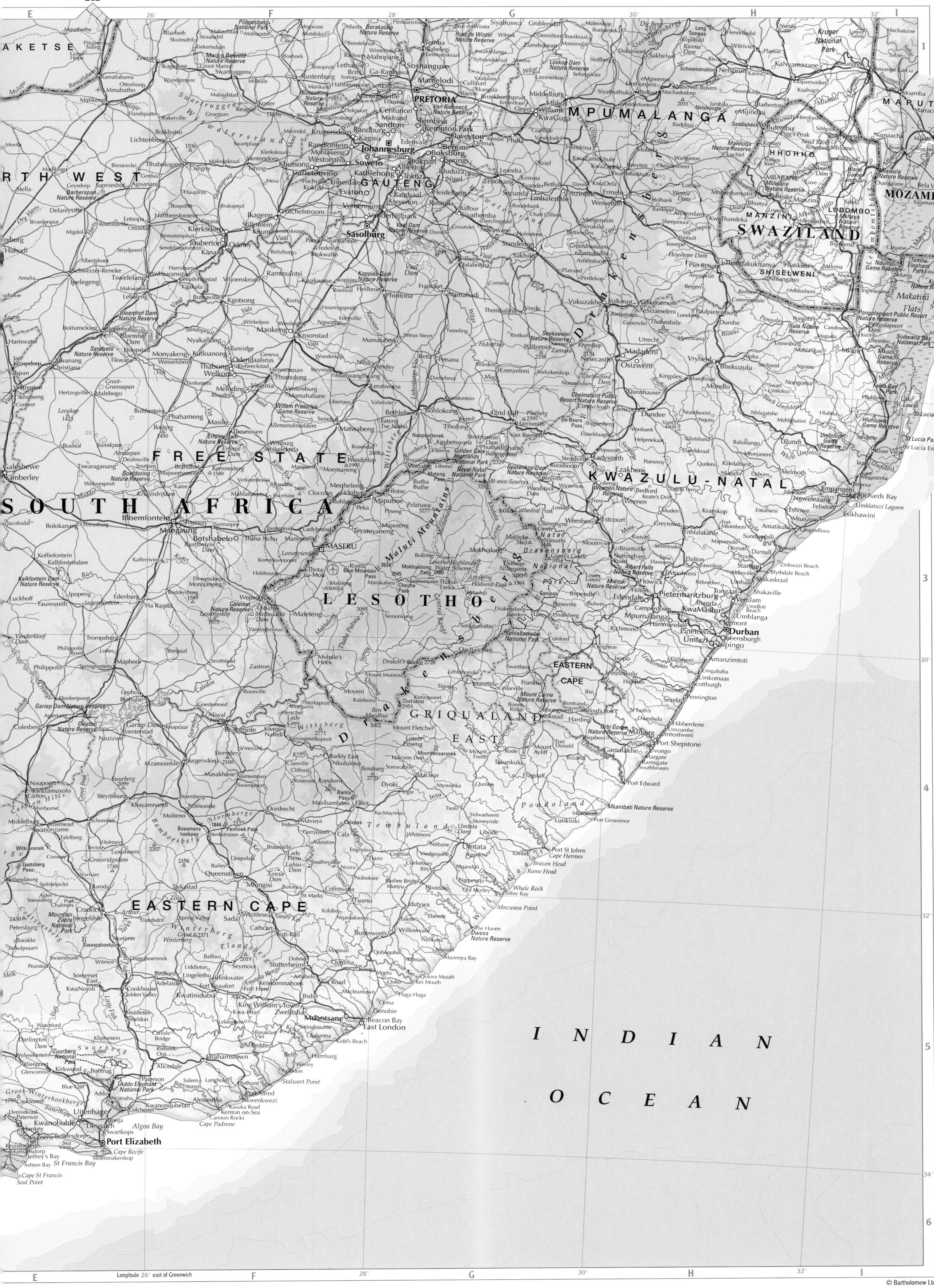

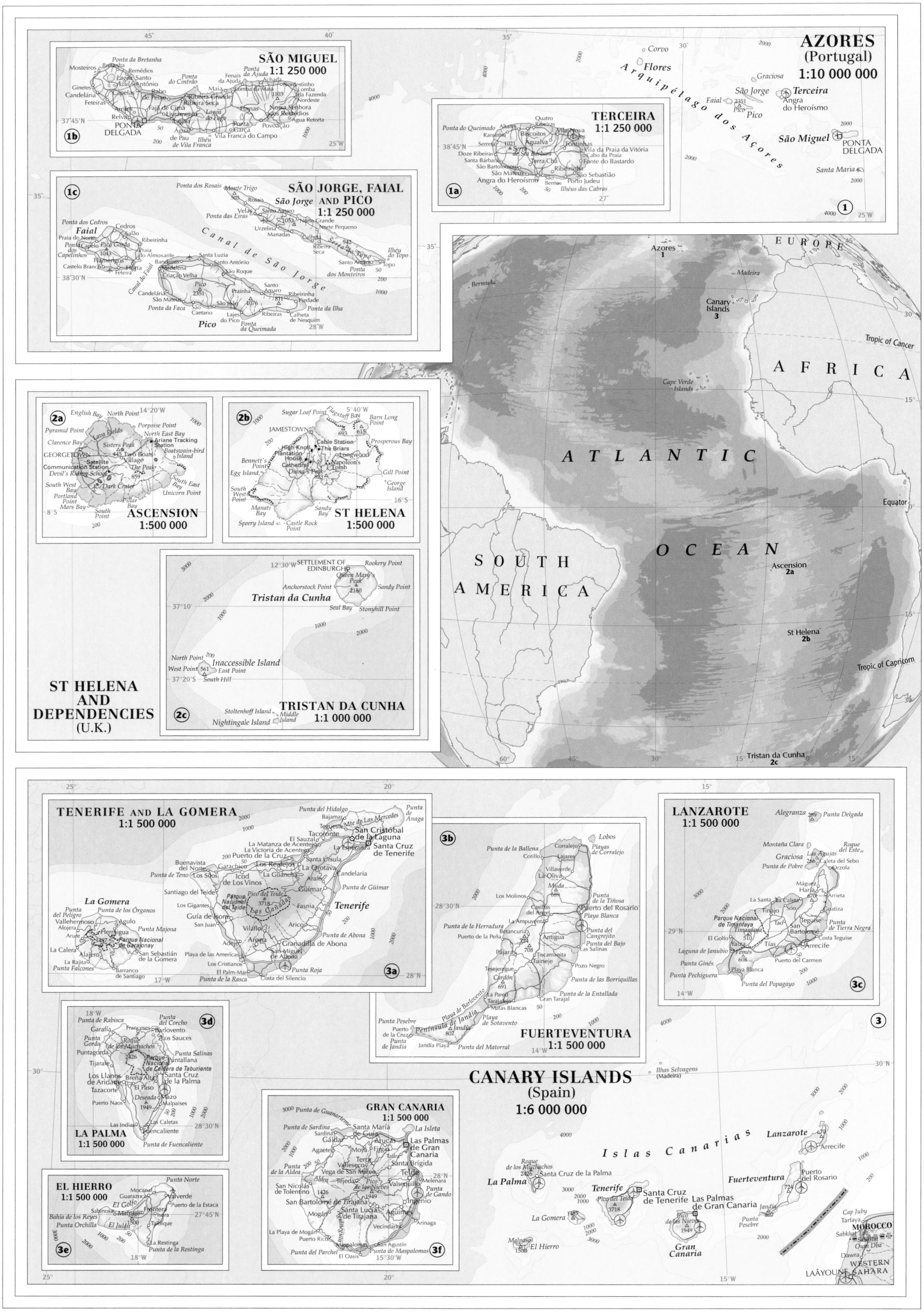
AZORES
(Portugal)
1:10 000 000
Arquipélago dos Açores
Corvo
Flores
Graciosa
São Jorge
Terceira
Angra do Heroísmo
Faial
Pico
São Miguel
PONTA DELGADA
Santa Maria
SÃO MIGUEL
1:1 250 000
TERCEIRA
1:1 250 000
SÃO JORGE, FAIAL AND PICO
1:1 250 000
Canal de São Jorge
ASCENSION
1:500 000
GEORGETOWN
Two Boats Village
ST HELENA
1:500 000
JAMESTOWN
TRISTAN DA CUNHA
1:1 000 000
SETTLEMENT OF EDINBURGH
Tristan da Cunha
Inaccessible Island
Nightingale Island
ST HELENA AND DEPENDENCIES
(U.K.)
EUROPE
AFRICA
ATLANTIC
OCEAN
SOUTH AMERICA
Azores
Madeira
Bermuda
Canary Islands
Cape Verde Islands
Tropic of Cancer
Equator
Ascension
St Helena
Tropic of Capricorn
Tristan da Cunha
TENERIFE AND LA GOMERA
1:1 500 000
San Cristóbal de la Laguna
Santa Cruz de Tenerife
Tenerife
La Gomera
San Sebastián de la Gomera
FUERTEVENTURA
1:1 500 000
Puerto del Rosario
LANZAROTE
1:1 500 000
Arrecife
LA PALMA
1:1 500 000
Santa Cruz de la Palma
EL HIERRO
1:1 500 000
Valverde
GRAN CANARIA
1:1 500 000
Las Palmas de Gran Canaria
CANARY ISLANDS
(Spain)
1:6 000 000
Islas Canarias
Ilhas Selvagens (Madeira)
La Palma
Tenerife
La Gomera
El Hierro
Gran Canaria
Fuerteventura
Lanzarote
MOROCCO
WESTERN SAHARA
LAÂYOUNE

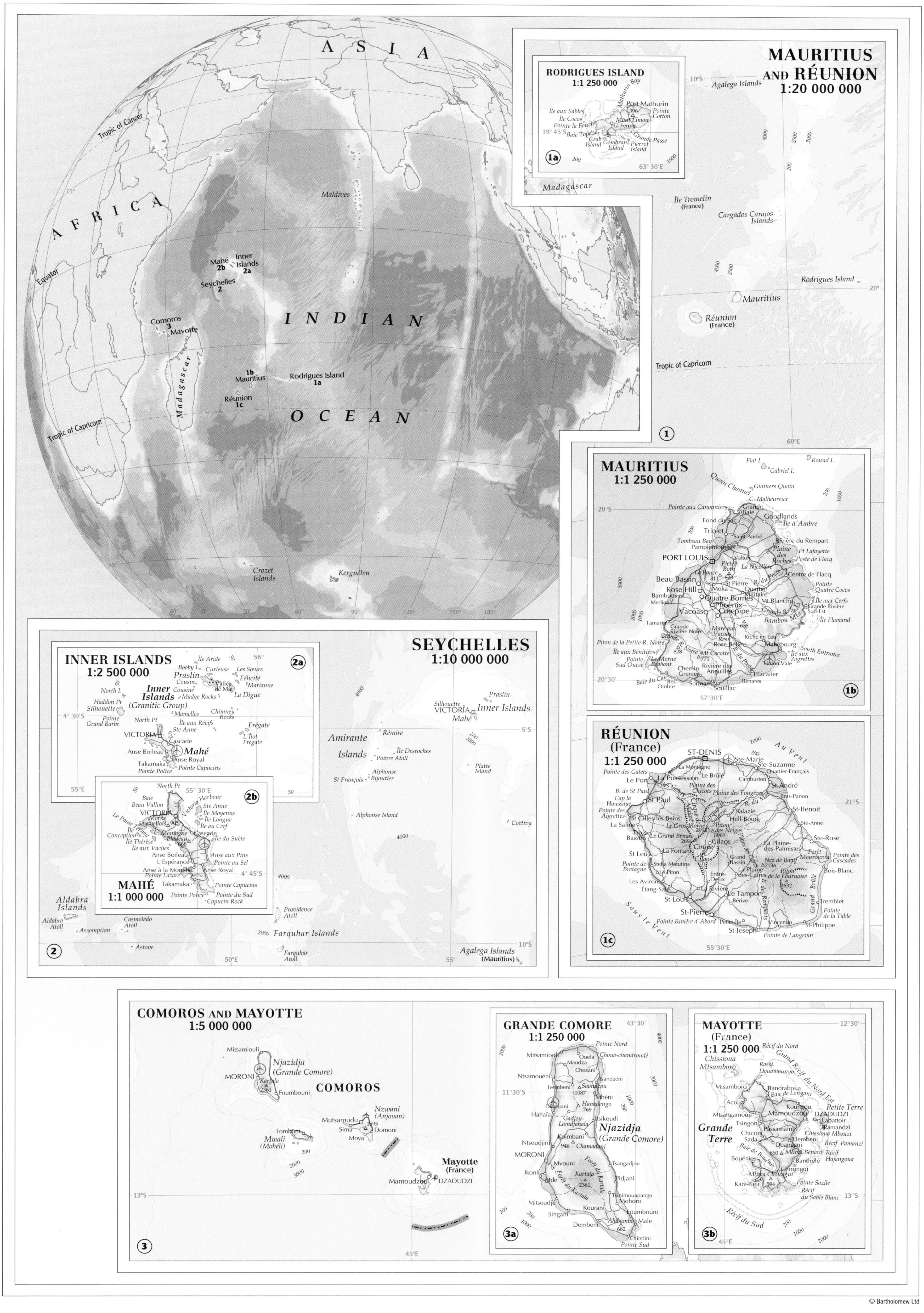

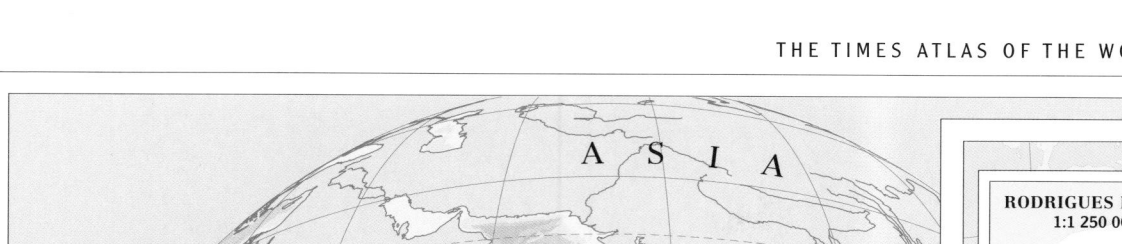

RODRIGUES ISLAND
1:1 250 000

MAURITIUS
AND **RÉUNION**
1:20 000 000

MAURITIUS
1:1 250 000

INNER ISLANDS
1:2 500 000

SEYCHELLES
1:10 000 000

RÉUNION
(France)
1:1 250 000

MAHÉ
1:1 000 000

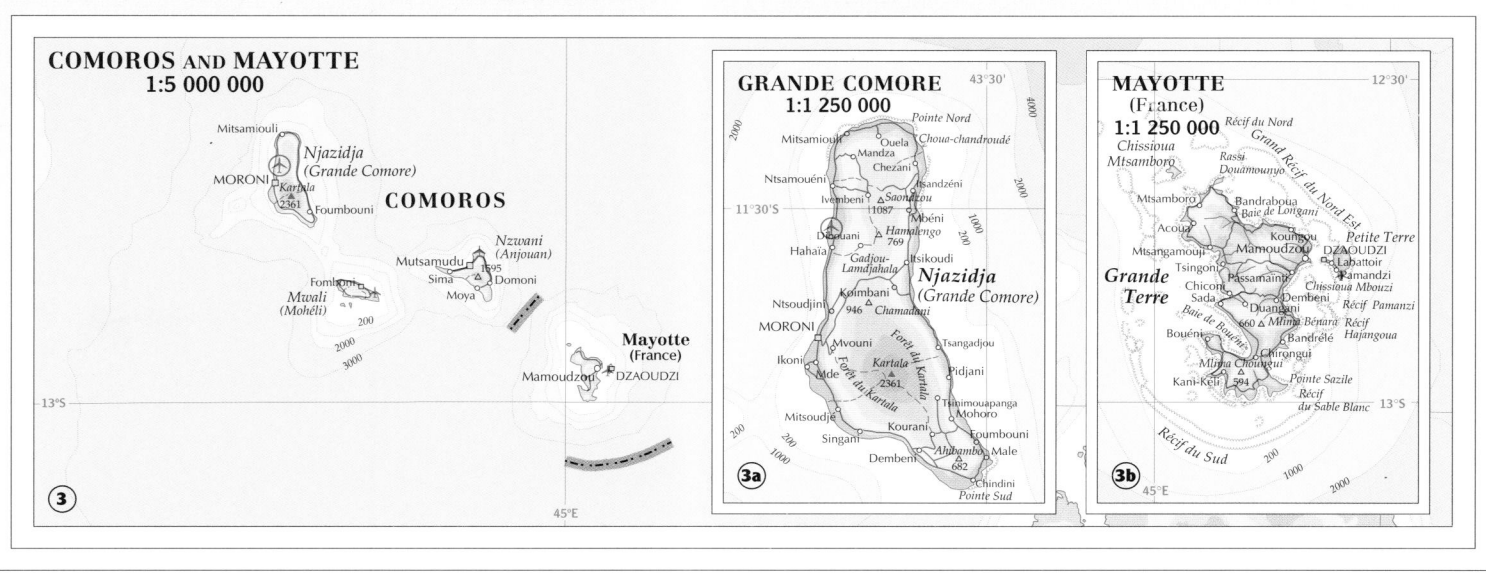

COMOROS AND **MAYOTTE**
1:5 000 000

GRANDE COMORE
1:1 250 000

MAYOTTE
(France)
1:1 250 000

© Bartholomew Ltd

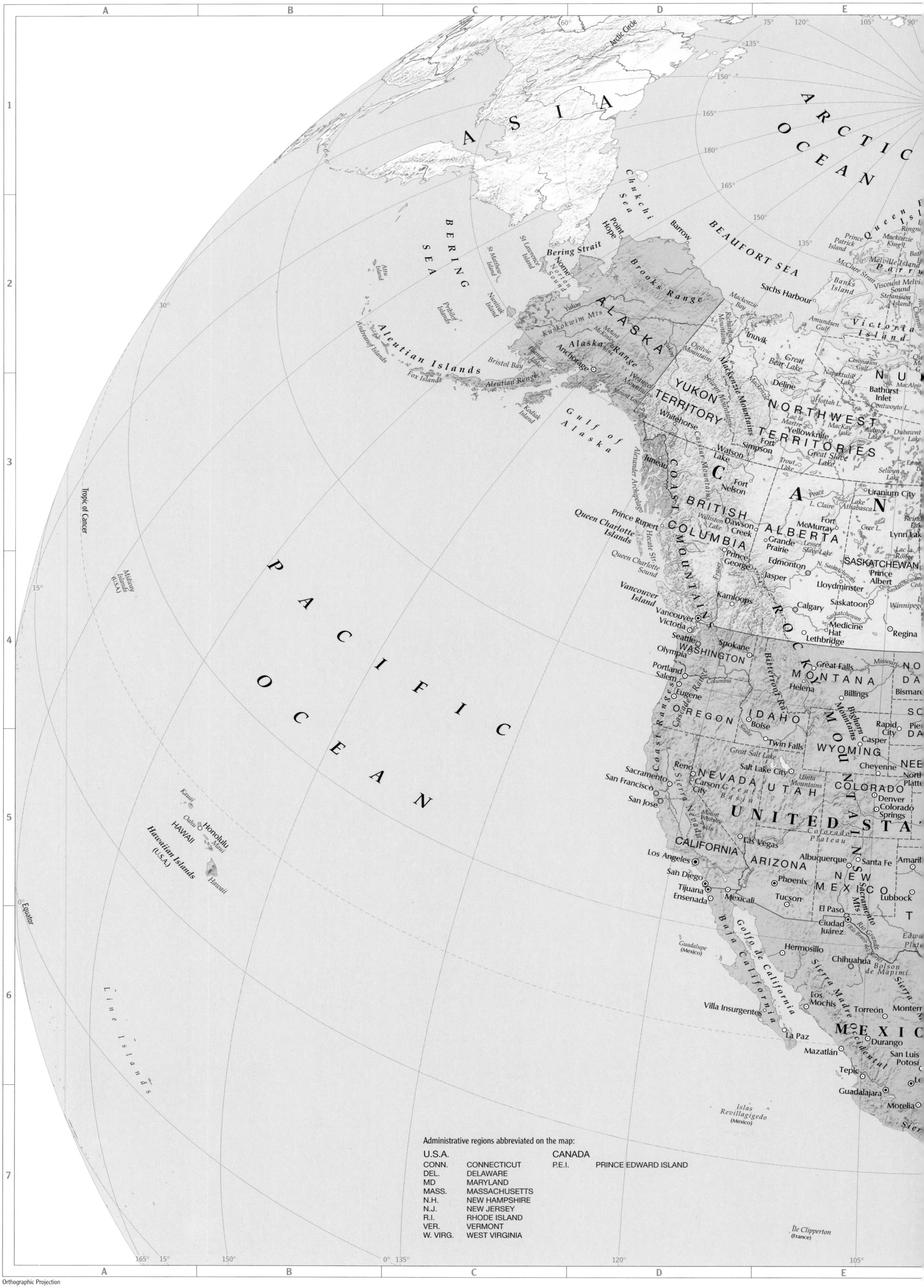

A B C D E

1

2

3

4

5

6

7

A S I A

A R C T I C
O C E A N

60°

Arctic Circle

75° 120°

135°

105°

90°

165°

180°

165°

150°

135°

Chukchi
Sea

Point
Hope

Barrow

BEAUFORT SEA

Queen
Is

Prince
Patrick
Island

Ringne

Mackenzie
King I.

Bath

BERING
SEA

St Matthew
Island

St Lawrence
Island

Bering Strait

Nome

Norton
Sound

Kotzebue
Sound

Brooks Range

ALASKA

YUKON

Sachs Harbour

Banks
Island

McClure Strait
Viscount Melvi
Sound

Parry

Melville Island

Stefansson
Island

Pribilof
Islands

30°

Attu
Island

Andreanof Islands

Aleutian Islands

Fox Islands

Bristol Bay

Kuskokwim Mts

Alaska
Range

Mount
Foraker

Mount McKinley

Anchorage

Aleutian Range

Kodiak
Island

Gulf of
Alaska

Yukon

Inuvik

Amundsen
Gulf

Victoria
Island

Great
Bear Lake

Déline

Napaktulik
Lake

Coronation
Gulf

Qu
Ma

NU

Bathurst
Inlet

Contwoyto L.

MacAlp

Richardson
Mountains

Mackenzie
Bay

Mackenzie
Mountains

Ogilvie
Mountains

Selwyn Mountains

NORTHWEST

TERRITORIES

Whitehorse

YUKON
TERRITORY

Watson
Lake

Fort
Simpson

Yellowknife

Fort

Great Slave
Lake

Trout
Lake

Selw
Lak

Hottah L.

MacKay
Lake

Aylmer
Lake

Dubawnt
Lake

Erie

Juneau

Alexander Archipelago

Cassiar Mountains

C A N

Fort
Nelson

Uranium City

Peace

L. Claire

Lake
Athabasca

Reind
L

Gree L.

Lynn Lak

Prince Rupert

Queen Charlotte
Islands

BRITISH

COLUMBIA

Williston
Lake

Dawson
Creek

Fort
McMurray

Tropic of Cancer

Hecate St.

Prince
George

Queen Charlotte
Sound

ALBERTA

Grande
Prairie

Lesser
Slave Lake

N. Saskatchewan

Lac la
Ronge

Lac la
B

15°

Midway
Islands
(U.S.A.)

Vancouver
Island

Vancouver

Kamloops

Jasper

Edmonton

Prince
Albert

SASKATCHEWAN

Lloydminster

Saskatoon

Saskatchewan

Winnipeg

Cedi

Victoria

Seattle

Olympia

Spokane

COAST MOUNTAINS

R O C

Calgary

Medicine
Hat

Lethbridge

Regina

WASHINGTON

Portland

Salem

Eugene

Columbia

Coast Ranges

Cascade Ranges

Bitterroot Mountains

Snake

Great Falls

MONTANA

Helena

Billings

Missouri

NO

DA

Bismarc

OREGON

IDAHO

Boise

Twin Falls

WYOMING

Bighorn
Mountains

Rapid
City

Casper

SC

DA

Pie

4

PACIFIC

OCEAN

Great Salt Lake

Salt Lake City

Cheyenne

North
Platte

NEB

Kauai

Oahu

Honolulu

Maui

HAWAII

Hawaiian Islands
(U.S.A.)

Hawaii

Sacramento

San Francisco

San Jose

Reno

Carson
City

NEVADA

Sierra Nevada

Great
Basin

Mount
Whitney

UTAH

Uinta
Mountains

Colorado

Colorado
Plateau

COLORADO

Denver

Colorado
Springs

5

UNITED STA

Las Vegas

CALIFORNIA

Los Angeles

San Diego

Tijuana

Ensenada

ARIZONA

Albuquerque

Santa Fe

Amaril

NEW
MEXICO

Sacramento Mts

Phoenix

Tucson

Mexicali

El Paso

Lubbock

Rio Grande

T

Guadalupe
(Mexico)

Ciudad
Juárez

Edwa
Plate

Hermosillo

Baja California

Chihuahua

Sierra Madre Occidental

Bolsón
de Mapimí

Sierra

6

Line Islands

Villa Insurgentes

Los
Mochis

La Paz

Golfo de California

Torreón

Monte

MÉXIC

Equator

Mazatlán

Durango

San Luis
Potosí

Le

Tepic

Guadalajara

Morelia

Islas
Revillagigedo
(Mexico)

Sier

7

Administrative regions abbreviated on the map:

U.S.A.		CANADA	
CONN.	CONNECTICUT	P.E.I.	PRINCE EDWARD ISLAND
DEL.	DELAWARE		
MD	MARYLAND		
MASS.	MASSACHUSETTS		
N.H.	NEW HAMPSHIRE		
N.J.	NEW JERSEY		
R.I.	RHODE ISLAND		
VER.	VERMONT		
W. VIRG.	WEST VIRGINIA		

Île Clipperton
(France)

165° 15°

150°

0° 135°

120°

105°

A B C D E

Orthographic Projection

EUROPE

AFRICA

ATLANTIC OCEAN

SOUTH AMERICA

Greenland (Kalaallit Nunaat) (Denmark)

Greenland Sea

Denmark Strait

Davis Strait

Baffin Bay

Baffin Island

Station Nord
Daneborg
Kong Wilhelm Land
Dronning Louise Land
Kong Oscars Fjord
Kangerlussuaq
Iceland

Uummannaq
Nuussuaq
Sigguup Nunaa
Qeqertarsuaq
Ilulissat
Ammassalik
Nuuk
Kong Frederik VI Kyst
Nanortalik

Ellesmere Island
Jones Sd
Devon Island
Prince Regent Inlet
Lancaster Sd
Somerset Island
Boothia Pen.
Gulf of Boothia
Melville Peninsula
Foxe Basin
Prince Charles I.
Nettilling Lake
Amadjuak Lake
Iqaluit
Frobisher Bay
Resolution I.

Clyde River
Cumberland Peninsula
Cumberland Sound
Cape Mercy

Labrador Sea

Repulse Bay
Southampton Island
Coral Harbour
Cape Dorset
Coats I.
Mansel I.
Arviat
Baker Lake

HUDSON BAY

Péninsule d'Ungava
Ungava Bay
Torngat Mts
Nain

CANADA

NEWFOUNDLAND

LABRADOR

Gander
St John's
Cape Race
Cape Spear
Newfoundland

Belcher Islands
Big Trout Lake
James Bay
Fort George
Akimiski Island
Lac Bienville
Réservoir La Grande 3
Réservoir La Grande 2
Mistassini
Lac St-Jean

St Pierre and Miquelon (France)

QUÉBEC
ONTARIO
MANITOBA
Thompson
Southern Indian Lake
Lake Winnipeg
Lake Manitoba
Winnipeg
Lake of the Woods
International Falls
Grand Forks

Moosonee
Sept-Îles
Réservoir Manicouagan
Île d'Anticosti
Gulf of St Lawrence
Cabot Str.
Cape Breton Island
Sable Island

Timmins
Rouyn
North Bay
Chicoutimi
Québec
Sudbury
Lake Nipissing
Ottawa
Montréal
NEW BRUNSWICK
Fredericton
P.E.I.
Charlottetown
NOVA SCOTIA
Halifax
Cape Sable
MAINE

Thunder Bay
Sault Ste Marie
Lake Superior
Lake Huron
Toronto
Lake Ontario
Lake Erie
MICHIGAN
Lansing
Detroit
Erie
Buffalo
Montpelier
N.H.
VT.
Concord
Augusta
Boston
MASS.
Providence
CONN.
R.I.
Cape Cod

Duluth
MINNESOTA
Minneapolis
St Paul
WISCONSIN
Rochester
Milwaukee
Madison
Grand Rapids
Sioux Falls
Chicago
Fort Wayne
Cleveland
Toledo
PENNSYLVANIA
Harrisburg
Trenton
New York
Philadelphia

IOWA
Des Moines
Omaha
Lincoln
ILLINOIS
INDIANA
Springfield
Indianapolis
Columbus
OHIO
Pittsburgh
W. VIRG.
MD.
DEL.
Dover
Baltimore
Annapolis
Washington

Topeka
Kansas City
St Louis
Cincinnati
Frankfort
Charleston
VIRGINIA
Richmond
Raleigh
NORTH CAROLINA

UNITED STATES OF AMERICA

Jefferson City
MISSOURI
Springfield
KENTUCKY
Nashville
Knoxville
TENNESSEE
Chattanooga
Charlotte
Columbia
SOUTH CAROLINA
Cape Hatteras

Wichita
Ozark Plateau
ARKANSAS
Memphis
Huntsville
Atlanta
Appalachian Mountains

OKLAHOMA
Tulsa
Oklahoma City
Little Rock
MISSISSIPPI
ALABAMA
Birmingham
Montgomery
Macon
GEORGIA
Savannah

Fort Worth
Dallas
Shreveport
Jackson
Baton Rouge
LOUISIANA
Mobile
Tallahassee
Jacksonville

Austin
San Antonio
Houston
New Orleans
Apalachee Bay

GULF OF MEXICO

TEXAS

Corpus Christi
Matamoros
Ciudad Victoria

Tampico
Poza Rica
Veracruz
MÉXICO
Puebla
Villahermosa
Oaxaca
Golfo de Tehuantepec
Acapulco del Sur
Mérida
Yucatán
Bahía de Campeche

Orlando
Tampa
FLORIDA
Cape Canaveral
West Palm Beach
Miami
Key West
Straits of Florida
Florida Keys

Grand Bahama
Great Abaco
THE BAHAMAS
Nassau
Andros
Acklins Island
Great Inagua
Turks and Caicos Is (U.K.)

La Habana
Santa Clara
CUBA
Holguín
Santiago
Cayman Is (U.K.)
Montego Bay
JAMAICA
Kingston

Greater Antilles

Hispaniola
HAITI
Port-au-Prince
DOMINICAN REPUBLIC
Santo Domingo
San Juan
Puerto Rico (U.S.A.)

Virgin Is (U.K.)
Virgin Is (U.S.A.)
Anguilla (U.K.)
ST KITTS AND NEVIS
ANTIGUA AND BARBUDA
Montserrat (U.K.)
Guadeloupe (France)
DOMINICA
Martinique (France)
ST LUCIA
BARBADOS
ST VINCENT AND THE GRENADINES
GRENADA

Leeward Islands
Lesser Antilles
Windward Islands

BELIZE
Belmopan
GUATEMALA
Guatemala
San Pedro Sula
HONDURAS
Tegucigalpa
San Salvador
EL SALVADOR
NICARAGUA
Managua
Lago de Nicaragua
COSTA RICA
San José
PANAMA
Panamá
Colón
Golfo de Panamá
Cordillera Oriental

CARIBBEAN SEA

Netherlands Antilles
Aruba (Neth.)
Bonaire
Curaçao
Port of Spain
TRINIDAD AND TOBAGO

Bermuda (U.K.)

Arquipélago da Madeira
Arquipélago dos Açores
Islas Canarias
Ilhas do Cabo Verde

Tropic of Cancer
Equator

1:27 000 000

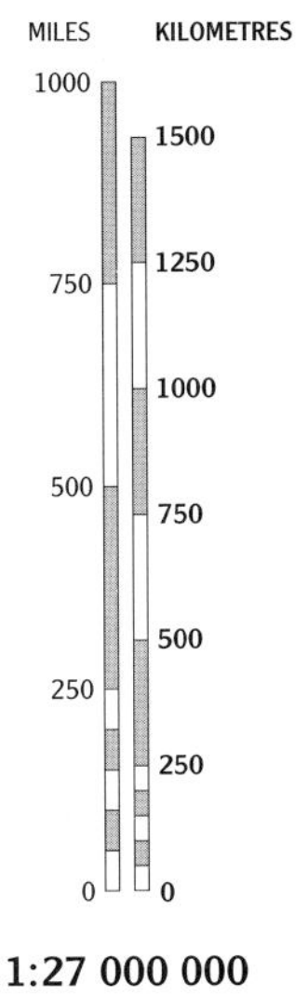

MILES | KILOMETRES
1000 | 1500
750 | 1250
 | 1000
500 | 750
250 | 500
 | 250
0 | 0

© Bartholomew Ltd

131
228
BERING SEA
ARCTIC OCEAN
BEAUFORT SEA
Chukchi Sea
RUSSIAN FEDERATION
ALEUTIAN ISLANDS
U.S.A.
ALASKA
Brooks Range
Philip Smith Mountains
Kuskokwim Mountains
Bering Strait
Norton Sound
Bristol Bay
Shelikof Strait
Anchorage
Fairbanks
Juneau
GULF OF ALASKA
PACIFIC OCEAN
YUKON TERRITORY
NORTHWEST TERRITORIES
BRITISH COLUMBIA
ALBERTA
SASKATCHEWAN
CANADA
ROCKY MOUNTAINS
COAST MOUNTAINS
Queen Charlotte Islands
Vancouver Island
Vancouver
Victoria
Edmonton
Calgary
Saskatoon
Regina
Yellowknife
Great Slave Lake
Great Bear Lake
Banks Island
Victoria Island
Mackenzie Mountains
WASHINGTON
Seattle
Tacoma
Spokane
OREGON
Portland
Salem
Eugene
IDAHO
Boise
MONTANA
Helena
Billings
Great Falls
WYOMING
Casper
Cheyenne
NORTH DAKOTA
SOUTH DAKOTA
NEBRASKA
NEVADA
Reno
UTAH
Salt Lake City
CALIFORNIA
Sacramento
San Francisco
Oakland
San Jose
Fresno
UNITED STATES OF AMERICA
METRES
FEET
6000 19686
5000 16404
4000 13124
3000 9843
2000 6562
1000 3281
500 1640
200 656
0 0
LAND BELOW SEA LEVEL
200 656
2000 6562
4000 13124
6000 19686
E
F
G
H
4
5
6
A
B
C
D
130°
120°
110°
100°
170°
180°
150°
60°
70°
80°
50°
40°

Greenland
(Kalaallit Nunaat)
(Denmark)

ICELAND

GREENLAND SEA

BAFFIN BAY

LABRADOR SEA

NUNAVUT

CANADA

HUDSON BAY

JAMES BAY

MANITOBA

ONTARIO

QUÉBEC

NEWFOUNDLAND

NEW BRUNSWICK

NOVA SCOTIA

PRINCE EDWARD ISLAND

MAINE

MINNESOTA

WISCONSIN

MICHIGAN

IOWA

NEW YORK

PENNSYLVANIA

VERMONT

NEW HAMPSHIRE

MASSACHUSETTS

ATLANTIC OCEAN

QUEEN ELIZABETH ISLANDS

MILES   KILOMETRES

600 — 1000
        — 800
400 — 600
200 — 400
        — 200
0 — 0

1:15 000 000

Longitude 70° west of Greenwich

© Bartholomew Ltd

220

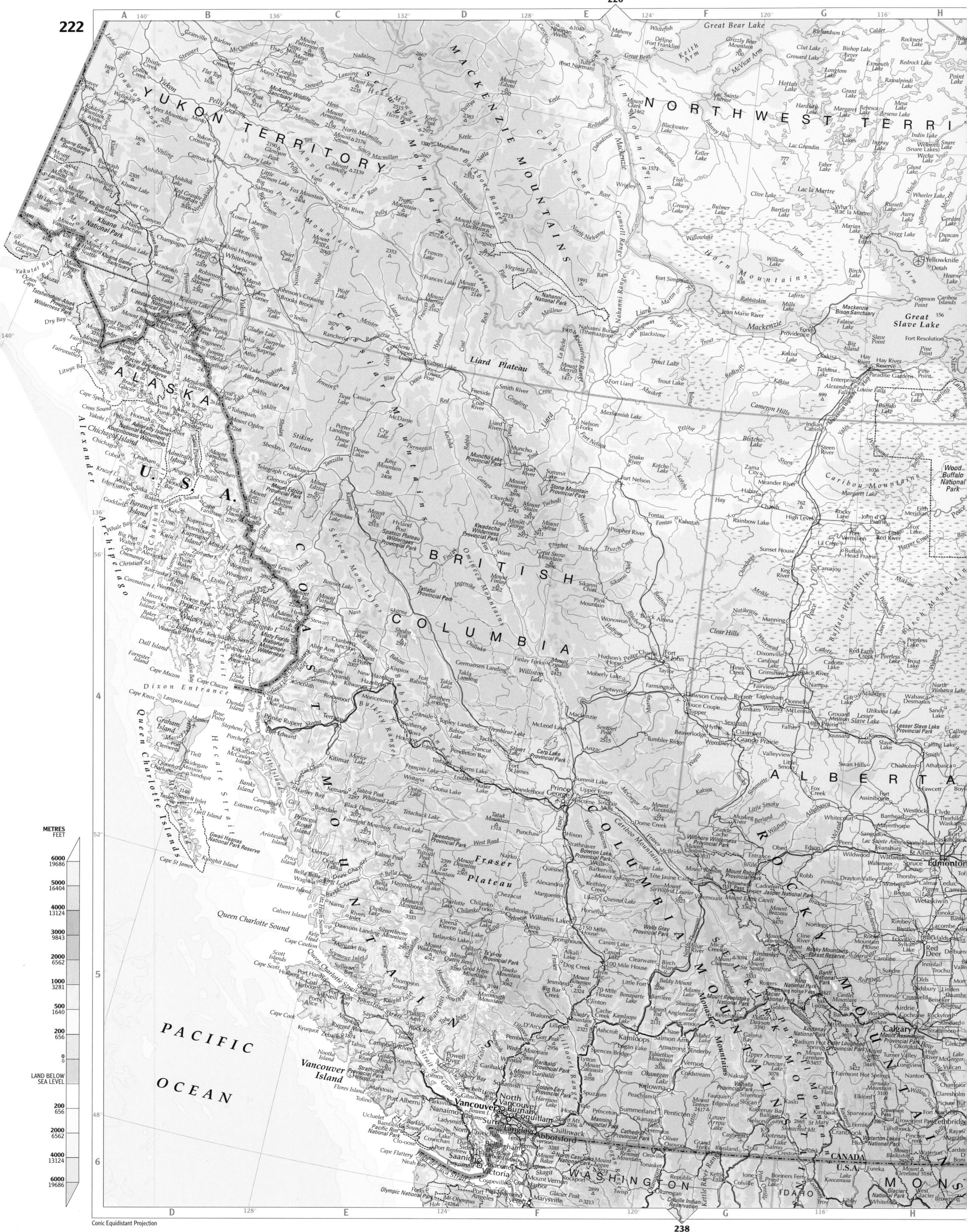

YUKON TERRITORY
NORTHWEST TERRI
BRITISH COLUMBIA
ALBERTA
ALASKA
U.S.A.
WASHINGTON
IDAHO
MONT.
CANADA
U.S.A.
PACIFIC OCEAN
COAST MOUNTAINS
MACKENZIE MOUNTAINS
ROCKY MOUNTAINS
COLUMBIA MOUNTAINS
Selwyn Mountains
Cassiar Mountains
Skeena Mountains
Omineca Mountains
Pelly Mountains
Logan Mountains
Franklin Mountains
Horn Mountains
Caribou Mountains
Cariboo Mountains
Selkirk Mountains
Monashee Mountains
Purcell Mountains
Fraser Plateau
Liard Plateau
Stikine Plateau
Great Bear Lake
Great Slave Lake
Lesser Slave Lake
Vancouver Island
Queen Charlotte Islands
Alexander Archipelago
Queen Charlotte Sound
Hecate Strait
Dixon Entrance
Juan de Fuca Strait
Strait of Georgia
Whitehorse
Yellowknife
Edmonton
Calgary
Vancouver
Victoria
Prince George
Prince Rupert
Kamloops
Kelowna
Juneau
Dawson Creek
Fort Nelson
Fort St John
Peace River
Grande Prairie
Red Deer
Lethbridge
Kluane National Park
Wood Buffalo National Park
Nahanni National Park
METRES
FEET
6000 19686
5000 16404
4000 13124
3000 9843
2000 6562
1000 3281
500 1640
200 656
0 0
LAND BELOW SEA LEVEL
200 656
2000 6562
4000 13124
6000 19686

Conic Equidistant Projection

238

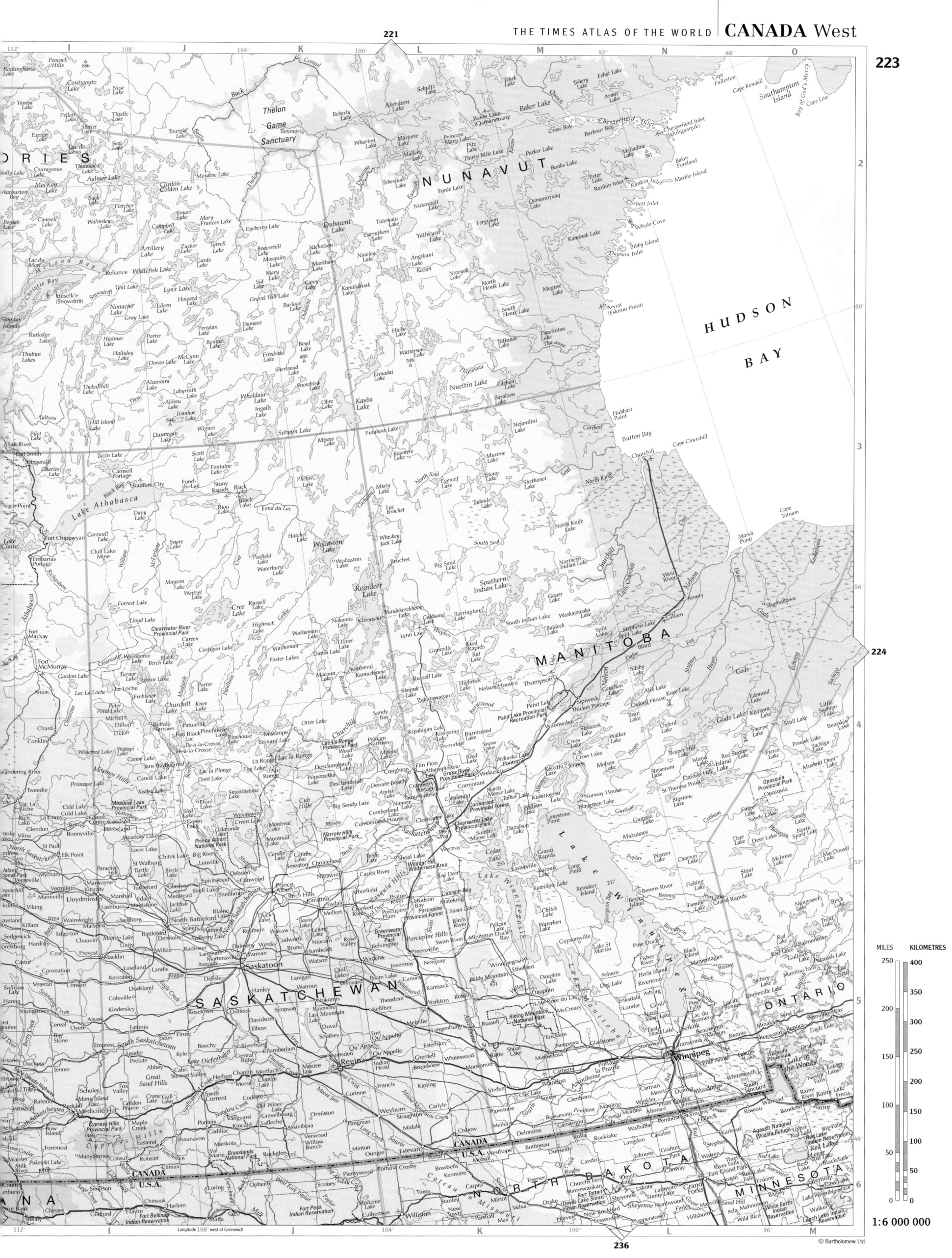

MILES   KILOMETRES

1:6 000 000

© Bartholomew Ltd

221
NUNAVUT
HUDSON BAY
MANITOBA
SASKATCHEWAN
ONTARIO
NORTH DAKOTA
MINNESOTA
CANADA
U.S.A.
Thelon Game Sanctuary
Lake Athabasca
Reindeer Lake
Wollaston Lake
Southern Indian Lake
Lake Winnipeg
Lake Winnipegosis
Lake Manitoba
Lake of the Woods
Southampton Island
Chesterfield Inlet
Baker Lake
Churchill
Thompson
Flin Flon
The Pas
Prince Albert
Saskatoon
Regina
Moose Jaw
Brandon
Winnipeg
Medicine Hat
Lloydminster
Fort McMurray
Fort Smith
Uranium City
Arviat (Eskimo Point)
Rankin Inlet
224
236
Longitude 108° west of Greenwich

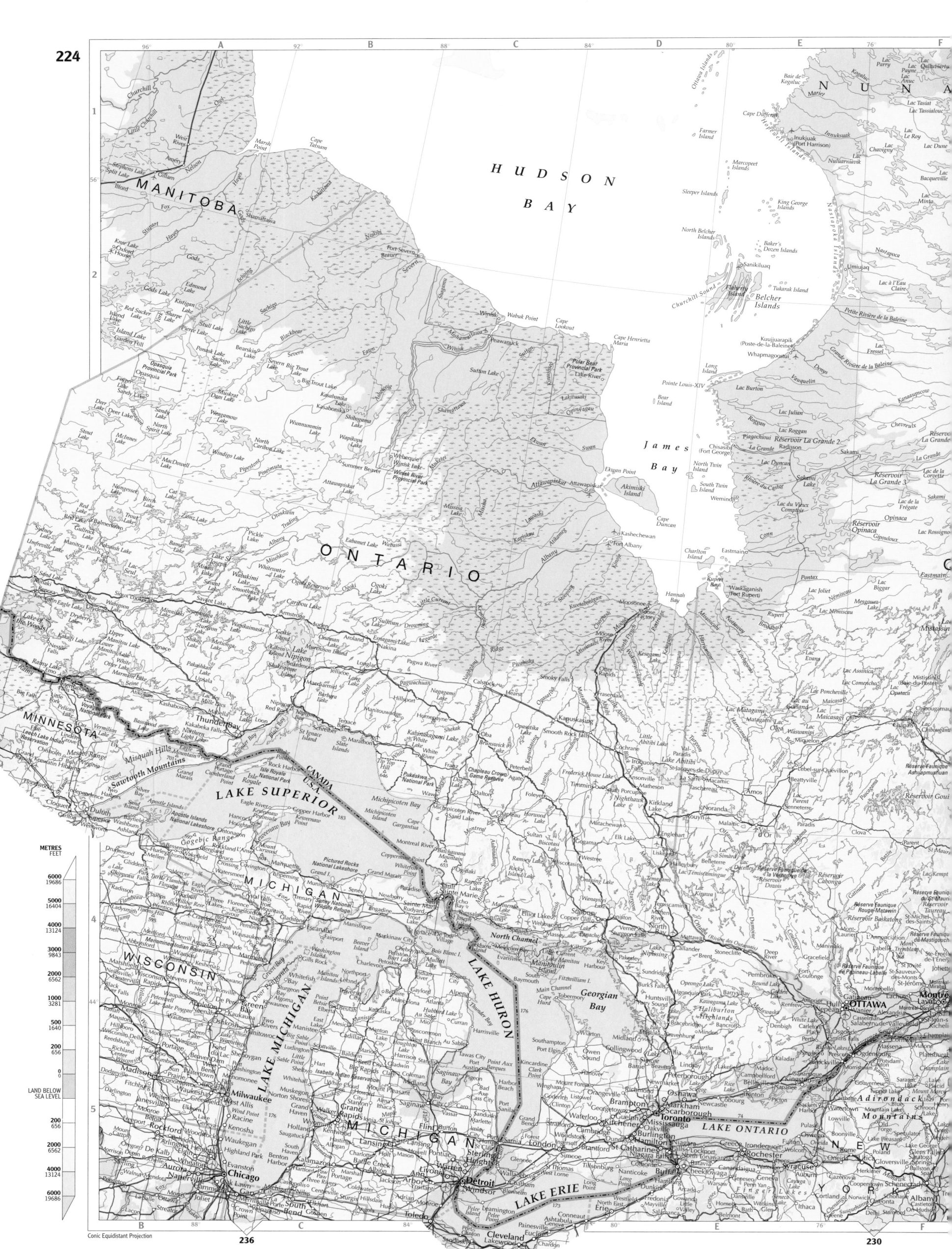
HUDSON BAY
James Bay
MANITOBA
ONTARIO
MINNESOTA
MICHIGAN
WISCONSIN
NEW YORK
NUNA
LAKE SUPERIOR
LAKE MICHIGAN
LAKE HURON
LAKE ONTARIO
LAKE ERIE
Georgian Bay
North Channel
Belcher Islands
Akimiski Island
Sleeper Islands
Ottawa Islands
Polar Bear Provincial Park
Opasquia Provincial Park
Woodland Caribou Provincial Park
Wabakimi Lake
Lake Nipigon
Lake of the Woods
Lake Nipissing
Lake Abitibi
Lake Simcoe
CANADA
U.S.A.
Thunder Bay
Sault Sainte Marie
Sudbury
Timmins
Moosonee
Kapuskasing
Hearst
North Bay
Kuujjuarapik (Poste-de-la-Baleine)
Chisasibi (Fort George)
Inukjuak (Port Harrison)
Sanikiluaq
Waskaganish (Fort Rupert)
Réservoir La Grande 2
Réservoir La Grande 3
Réservoir Opinaca
OTTAWA
Montréal
Kingston
Toronto
Mississauga
Hamilton
London
Windsor
Detroit
Cleveland
Toledo
Buffalo
Rochester
Syracuse
Erie
Chicago
Milwaukee
Madison
Green Bay
Duluth
Grand Rapids
Lansing
Flint
Saginaw
Adirondack Mountains
Sawtooth Mountains
Gogebic Range
Mesabi Range
Misquah Hills
METRES
FEET
6000
19686
5000
16404
4000
13124
3000
9843
2000
6562
1000
3281
500
1640
200
656
0
0
LAND BELOW SEA LEVEL
200
656
2000
6562
4000
13124
6000
19686
A
B
C
D
E
F
1
2
3
4
5
96°
92°
88°
84°
80°
76°
56°
52°
44°

Conic Equidistant Projection

236

230

LABRADOR SEA

LABRADOR

NEWFOUNDLAND

Ungava Bay

QUÉBEC

JÉBEC

GULF OF ST LAWRENCE

NEWFOUNDLAND
Newfoundland

Péninsule de Gaspé

Monts Notre Dame

Détroit d'Honguedo

Île d'Anticosti

St Pierre and Miquelon (France)

Cabot Strait

MAINE

NEW BRUNSWICK

PRINCE EDWARD ISLAND

Cape Breton Island

NOVA SCOTIA

Bay of Fundy

Halifax

Québec

Boston

NEW HAMPSHIRE

VERMONT

White Mountains

Green Mountains

Gulf of Maine

Massachusetts Bay

ATLANTIC OCEAN

Sable Island

Smallwood Reservoir

Lake Melville

Happy Valley-Goose Bay

Churchill Falls

Réservoir Manicouagan

Gros Morne National Park

1:6 000 000

MILES / KILOMETRES
250 / 400
350
200 / 300
250
150 / 200
150
100 / 150
100
50 / 50
0 / 0

Longitude 72° west of Greenwich

© Bartholomew Ltd

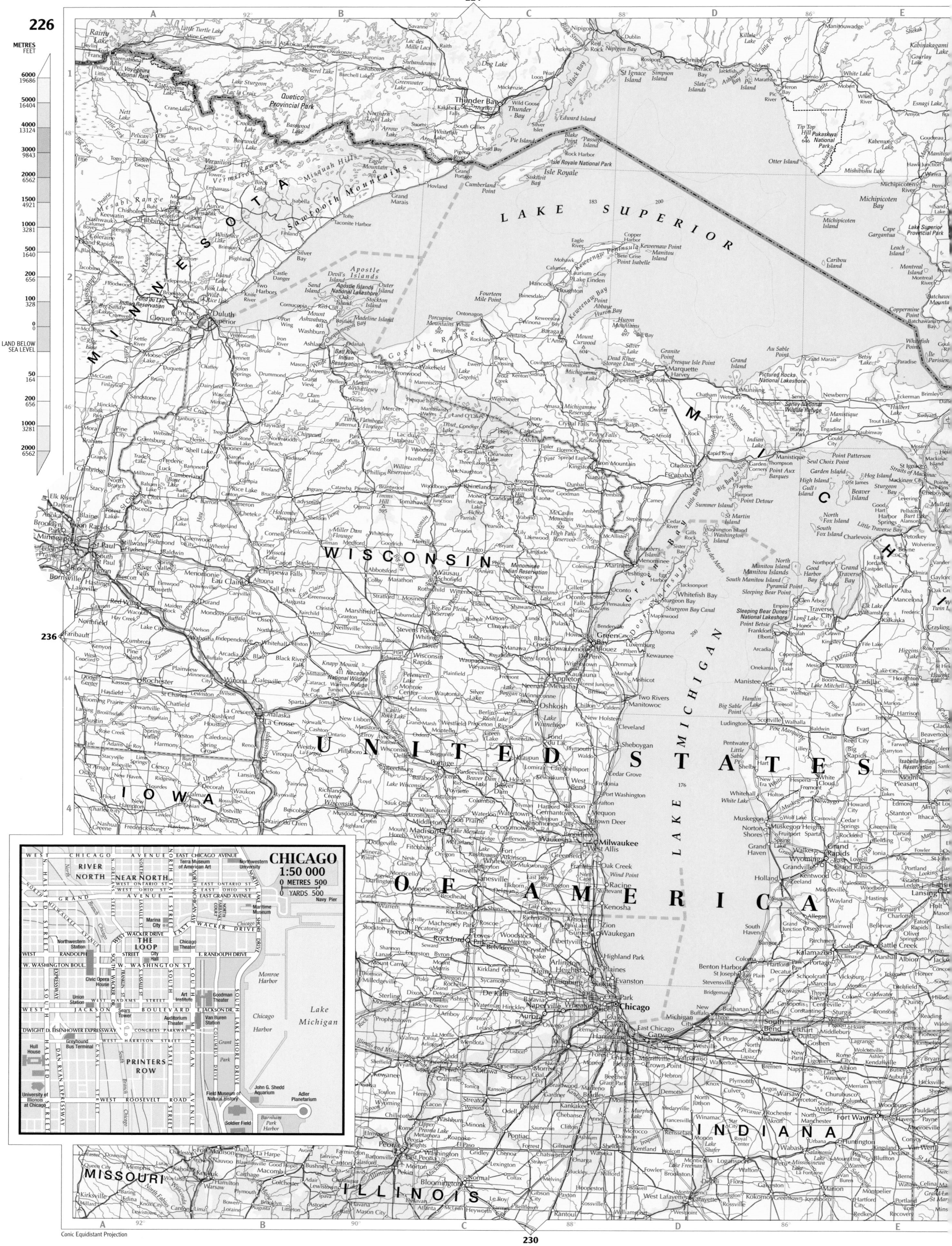

METRES FEET

6000 19686
5000 16404
4000 13124
3000 9843
2000 6562
1500 4921
1000 3281
500 1640
200 656
100 328
0 0

LAND BELOW SEA LEVEL

50 164
200 656
1000 3281
2000 6562

236

MINNESOTA

WISCONSIN

IOWA

UNITED STATES

OF AMERICA

ILLINOIS

MISSOURI

INDIANA

MICHIGAN

LAKE SUPERIOR

LAKE MICHIGAN

Isle Royale National Park

Apostle Islands National Lakeshore

Quetico Provincial Park

Voyageurs National Park

Duluth

Minneapolis
St Paul

Milwaukee

Chicago

Green Bay

Lake Michigan

CHICAGO 1:50 000

0 METRES 500
0 YARDS 500

RIVER NORTH

NEAR NORTH

THE LOOP

PRINTERS ROW

WEST CHICAGO AVENUE   EAST CHICAGO AVENUE

Northwestern University

Terra Museum of American Art

WEST ONTARIO ST   EAST ONTARIO ST

WEST GRAND AVENUE   EAST GRAND AVENUE

Marina City

Chicago Theater

WACKER DRIVE

WEST WACKER DRIVE

Northwestern Station

WEST RANDOLPH STREET   E. RANDOLPH DRIVE

City Hall

Civic Opera House

WEST WASHINGTON ST

Goodman Theater

Monroe Harbor

Union Station

WEST ADAMS STREET   E. JACKSON DR.

Sears Tower

Art Institute

WEST JACKSON BOULEVARD

Auditorium Theater

Van Buren Station

DWIGHT D. EISENHOWER EXPRESSWAY   CONGRESS PARKWAY

Chicago Harbor

Greyhound Bus Terminal

WEST HARRISON STREET

Grant Park

Hull House

John G. Shedd Aquarium

Adler Planetarium

University of Illinois at Chicago

WEST ROOSEVELT ROAD

Field Museum of Natural History

Soldier Field

Burnham Park Harbor

Navy Pier

Maritime Museum

Lake Michigan

DAN RYAN EXPRESSWAY

Conic Equidistant Projection

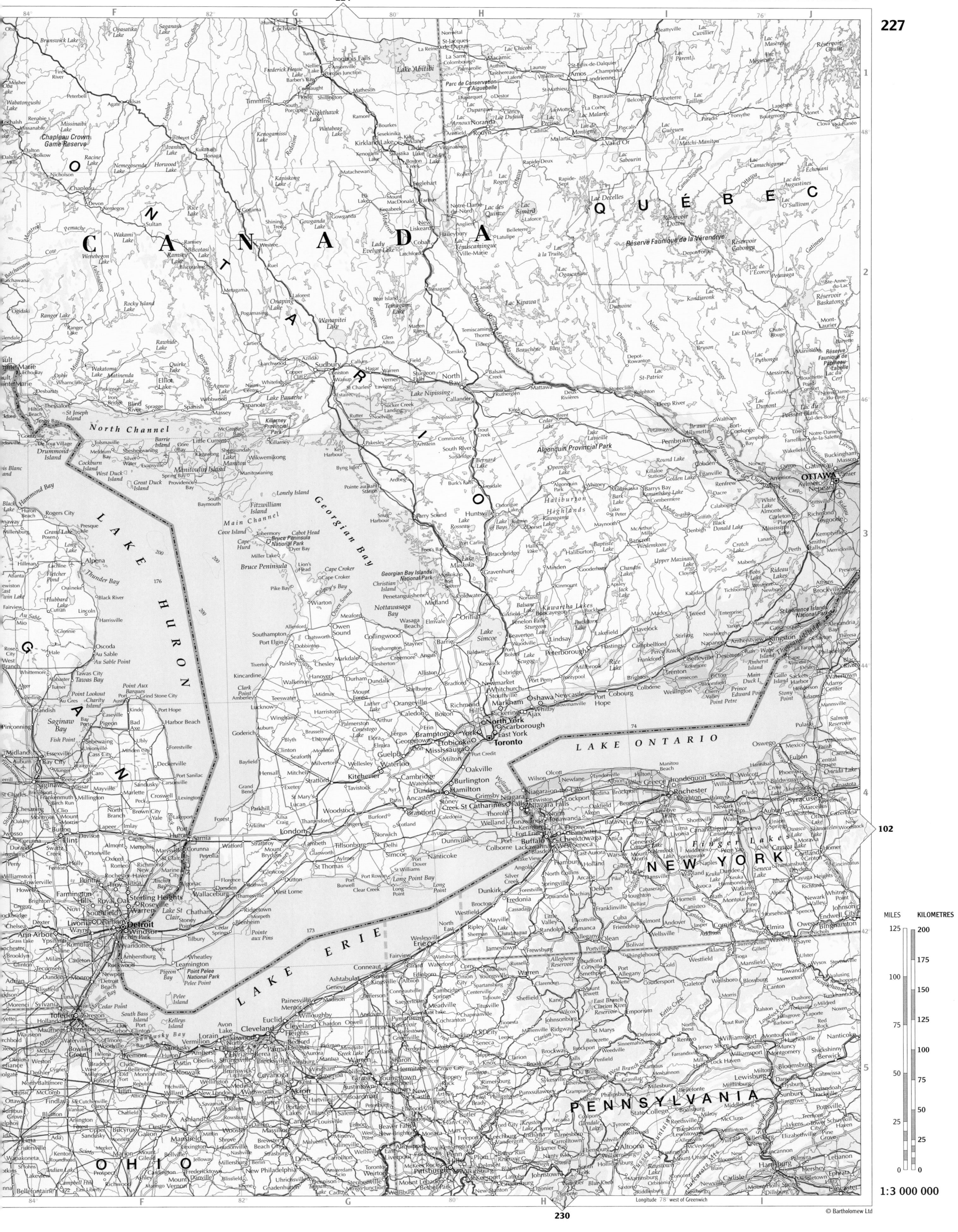

CANADA

QUÉBEC

ONTARIO

LAKE HURON

Georgian Bay

North Channel

Manitoulin Island

Bruce Peninsula

MICHIGAN

LAKE ONTARIO

LAKE ERIE

NEW YORK

Finger Lakes

PENNSYLVANIA

OHIO

OTTAWA

Toronto

Detroit

Cleveland

Algonquin Provincial Park

Haliburton Highlands

MILES   KILOMETRES

1:3 000 000

© Bartholomew Ltd

Lambert Conformal Conic Projection

METRES
FEET

6000 / 19686
5000 / 16404
4000 / 13124
3000 / 9843
2000 / 6562
1000 / 3281
500 / 1640
200 / 656
0
LAND BELOW SEA LEVEL
200 / 656
2000 / 6562
4000 / 13124
6000 / 19686

CANADA

ONTARIO

QUÉBEC

NEW BRUNSWICK

NOVA SCOTIA

MAINE

VERMONT

NEW HAMPSHIRE

MASSACHUSETTS

Lake Superior

MICHIGAN

WISCONSIN

Lake Michigan

Lake Huron

Lake Ontario

Lake Erie

NEW YORK

MINNESOTA

Minneapolis
St Paul

Milwaukee

Chicago

Detroit

ILLINOIS

INDIANA

OHIO

Indianapolis

Columbus

Cincinnati

PENNSYLVANIA

Pittsburgh

NEW JERSEY

New York

Philadelphia

Baltimore

WASHINGTON

MARYLAND

DELAWARE

WEST VIRGINIA

VIRGINIA

Richmond

KENTUCKY

Louisville

Lexington

Norfolk
Virginia Beach
Chesapeake

IOWA

MISSOURI

St Louis

Ozark plateau

ARKANSAS

Memphis

TENNESSEE

Nashville

Knoxville

APPALACHIAN MOUNTAINS

NORTH CAROLINA

Charlotte

Raleigh

SOUTH CAROLINA

Columbia

MISSISSIPPI

ALABAMA

Birmingham

Montgomery

GEORGIA

Atlanta

Savannah

Charleston

LOUISIANA

Shreveport

Baton Rouge

New Orleans

Mobile

Jacksonville

FLORIDA

Orlando

Tampa

St Petersburg

Miami

Fort Lauderdale

Hollywood

Everglades

Key West

Florida Keys

GULF OF MEXICO

Bermuda
(U.K.)
HAMILTON

ATLANTIC

OCEAN

Cape Hatteras

Cape Fear

Cape Canaveral

Cape Sable

Straits of Florida

THE BAHAMAS

NASSAU

New Providence

Andros

Great Bahama Bank

Grand Bahama

Great Abaco

Eleuthera

Cat Island

San Salvador

Rum Cay

Long Island

Great Exuma

Crooked Island

Acklins Island

Mayaguana

Turks and Caicos Islands (U.K.)
GRAND TURK
(Cockburn Town)

Tropic of Cancer

WEST INDIES

LA HABANA (Havana)

Matanzas

Santa Clara

Cienfuegos

CUBA

Camagüey

Holguín

Santiago de Cuba

Guantánamo

Cayman Islands (U.K.)
GEORGE TOWN
Grand Cayman

Isla de la Juventud

GREATER ANTILLES

JAMAICA

KINGSTON

Montego Bay

HISPANIOLA

HAITI

PORT-AU-PRINCE

DOMINICAN REPUBLIC

SANTO DOMINGO

Santiago

Puerto Rico (U.S.A.)

CARIBBEAN SEA

YUCATÁN

Mérida

Campeche

Cancún

Cozumel

GUATEMALA

BELIZE

BELMOPAN

Gulf of Honduras

MILES KILOMETRES
500 — 800
700
400 — 600
500
300 — 400
200 — 300
200
100 — 100
0 — 0

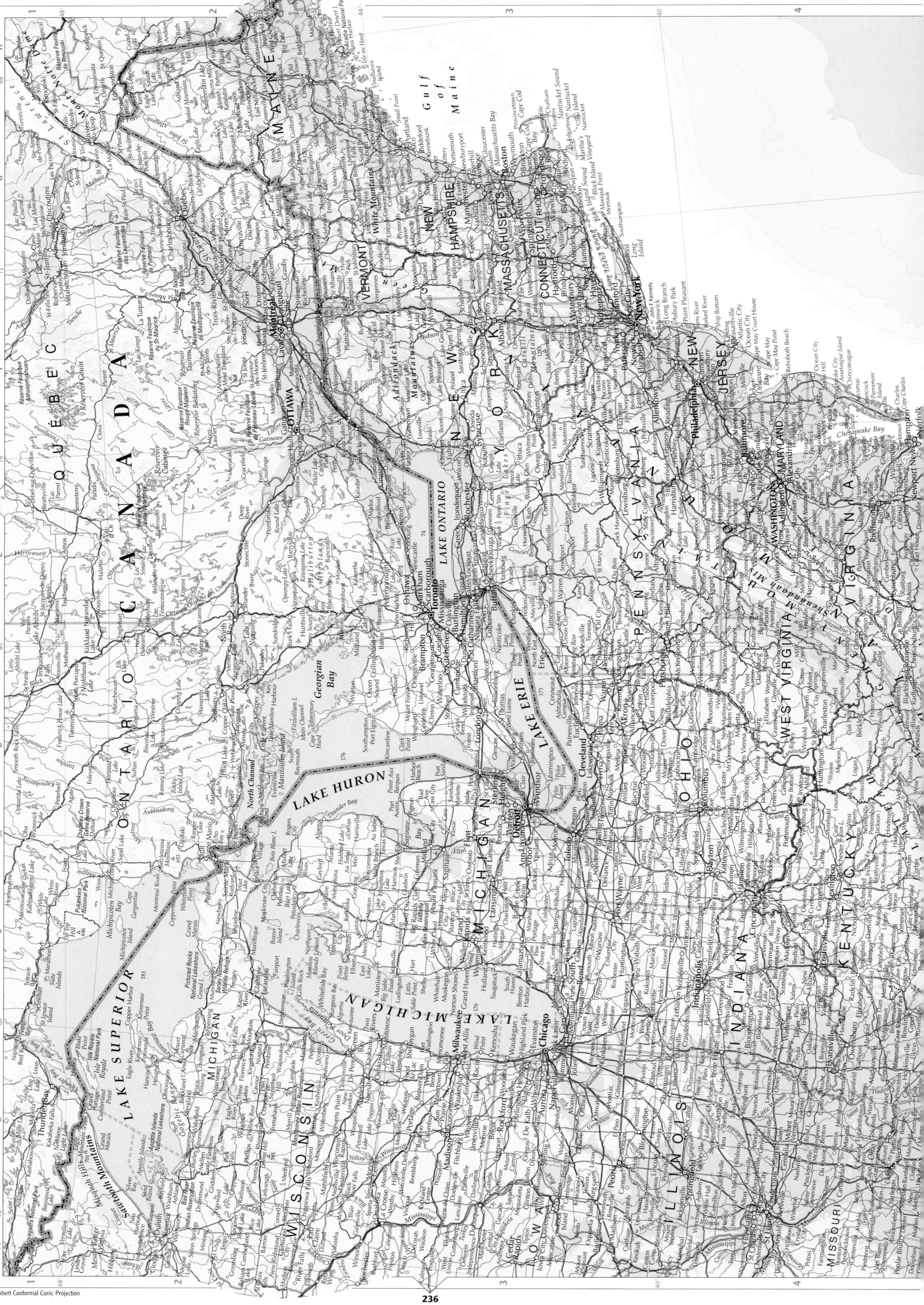

224

236

BERMUDA
(U.K.)
1:500 000
NEW PROVIDENCE
(The Bahamas)
1: 500 000
NASSAU
HAMILTON
ATLANTIC OCEAN
THE BAHAMAS
Great Abaco
Grand Bahama
Andros
Eleuthera
Cat Island
Long Island
Great Exuma
San Salvador
Tropic of Cancer
Great Bahama Bank
Straits of Florida
GULF OF MEXICO
TENNESSEE
NORTH CAROLINA
SOUTH CAROLINA
GEORGIA
ALABAMA
MISSISSIPPI
FLORIDA
Nashville
Knoxville
Memphis
Atlanta
Birmingham
Montgomery
Jackson
Mobile
Charlotte
Raleigh
Durham
Columbia
Charleston
Savannah
Jacksonville
Tallahassee
Orlando
Tampa
St Petersburg
West Palm Beach
Fort Lauderdale
Miami
246
237
MILES
KILOMETRES
1:6 000 000
Longitude 88° west of Greenwich

96

226

231

ONTARIO

LAKE HURON

CANADA
U.S.A.

Georgian Bay

LAKE ONTARIO

Toronto

MICHIGAN

LAKE ERIE

NEW YORK

Detroit

OHIO

PENNSYLVANIA

Cleveland

Pittsburgh

Columbus

Dayton

Cincinnati

WEST VIRGINIA

KENTUCKY

VIRGINIA

ALLEGHENY MOUNTAINS

APPALACHIAN MOUNTAINS

Baltimore

WASHINGTON

Richmond

Cumberland Mountains

TENNESSEE

NORTH CAROLINA

Legend

METRES
FEET

6000 / 19686
5000 / 16404
4000 / 13124
3000 / 9843
2000 / 6562
1500 / 4921
1000 / 3281
500 / 1640
200 / 656
100 / 328
0 / 0

LAND BELOW SEA LEVEL

200 / 656
1000 / 3281
2000 / 6562

Lambert Conformal Conic Projection

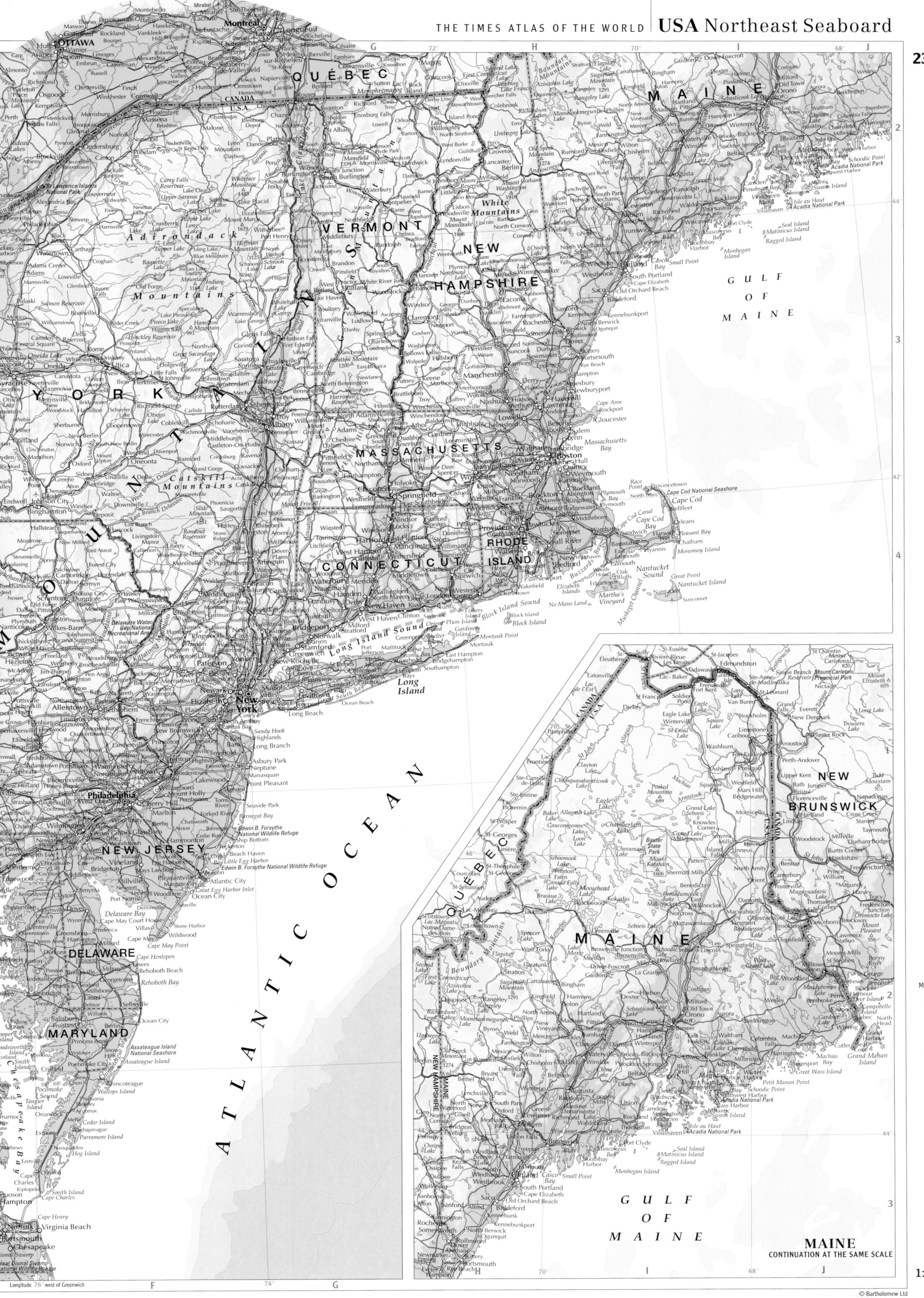

GULF
OF
MAINE

ATLANTIC OCEAN

MAINE
CONTINUATION AT THE SAME SCALE

MILES   KILOMETRES

1:3 000 000

© Bartholomew Ltd

233

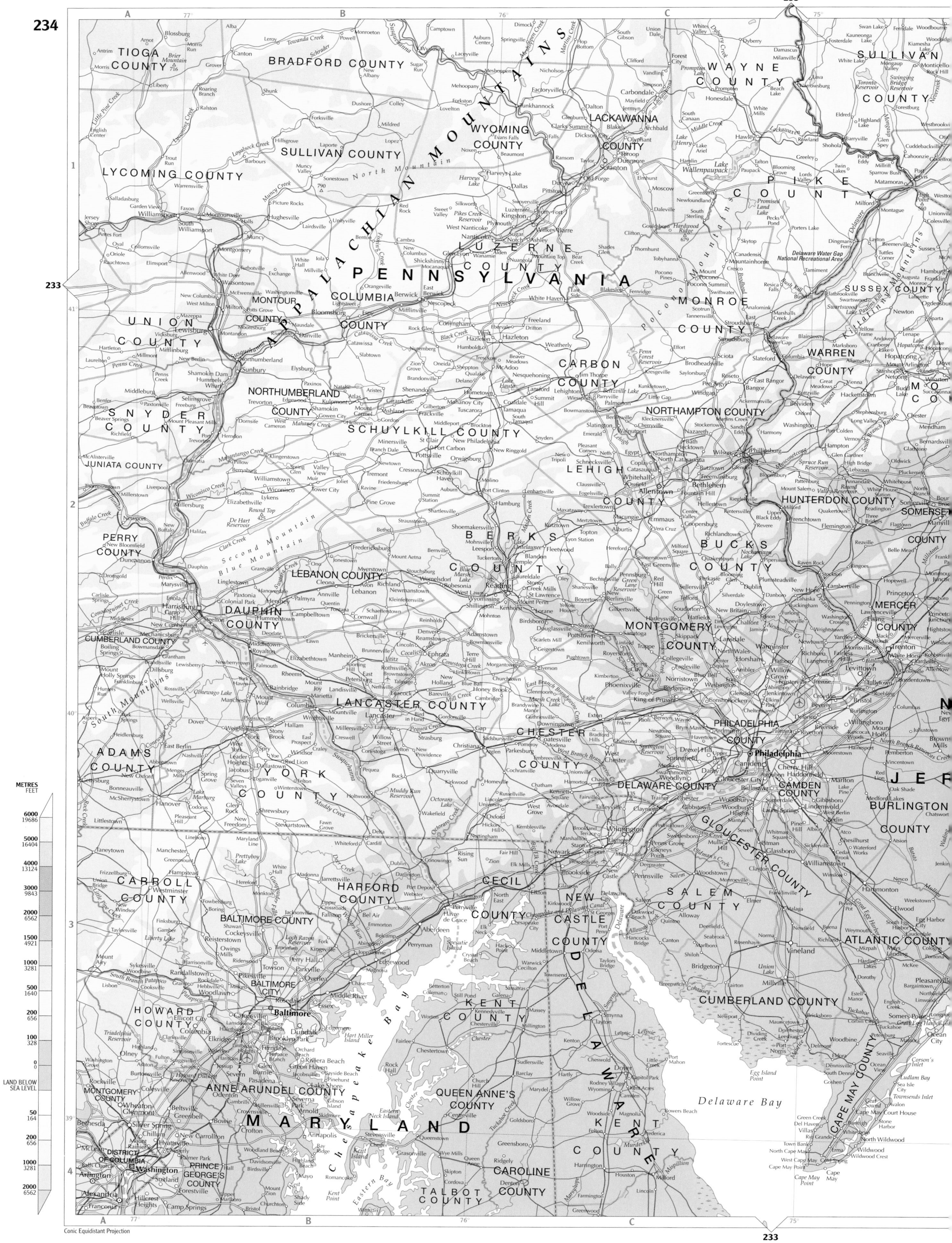
A
B
C
77°
76°
75°
1
2
3
4
41°
40°
39°
APPALACHIAN MOUNTAINS
PENNSYLVANIA
MARYLAND
DELAWARE
TIOGA COUNTY
BRADFORD COUNTY
WAYNE COUNTY
SULLIVAN COUNTY
LYCOMING COUNTY
WYOMING COUNTY
LACKAWANNA COUNTY
PIKE COUNTY
LUZERNE COUNTY
MONTOUR COUNTY
COLUMBIA COUNTY
UNION COUNTY
MONROE COUNTY
CARBON COUNTY
NORTHUMBERLAND COUNTY
SNYDER COUNTY
SCHUYLKILL COUNTY
NORTHAMPTON COUNTY
WARREN COUNTY
JUNIATA COUNTY
LEHIGH COUNTY
HUNTERDON COUNTY
PERRY COUNTY
BERKS COUNTY
BUCKS COUNTY
LEBANON COUNTY
DAUPHIN COUNTY
MONTGOMERY COUNTY
MERCER COUNTY
CUMBERLAND COUNTY
LANCASTER COUNTY
CHESTER COUNTY
PHILADELPHIA COUNTY
ADAMS COUNTY
YORK COUNTY
DELAWARE COUNTY
CAMDEN COUNTY
BURLINGTON COUNTY
GLOUCESTER COUNTY
CARROLL COUNTY
HARFORD COUNTY
CECIL COUNTY
NEW CASTLE COUNTY
SALEM COUNTY
BALTIMORE COUNTY
BALTIMORE CITY
ATLANTIC COUNTY
HOWARD COUNTY
KENT COUNTY
CUMBERLAND COUNTY
ANNE ARUNDEL COUNTY
QUEEN ANNE'S COUNTY
MONTGOMERY COUNTY
CAPE MAY COUNTY
DISTRICT OF COLUMBIA
PRINCE GEORGE'S COUNTY
CAROLINE COUNTY
TALBOT COUNTY
Philadelphia
Baltimore
Washington
Chesapeake Bay
Delaware Bay
Pocono Mountains
Kittatinny Mountains
Second Mountain
Blue Mountain
South Mountains
North Mountain
Delaware Water Gap National Recreational Area
METRES FEET
6000 19686
5000 16404
4000 13124
3000 9843
2000 6562
1500 4921
1000 3281
500 1640
200 656
100 328
0 0
LAND BELOW SEA LEVEL
50 164
200 656
1000 3281
2000 6562

Conic Equidistant Projection

233

CONNECTICUT

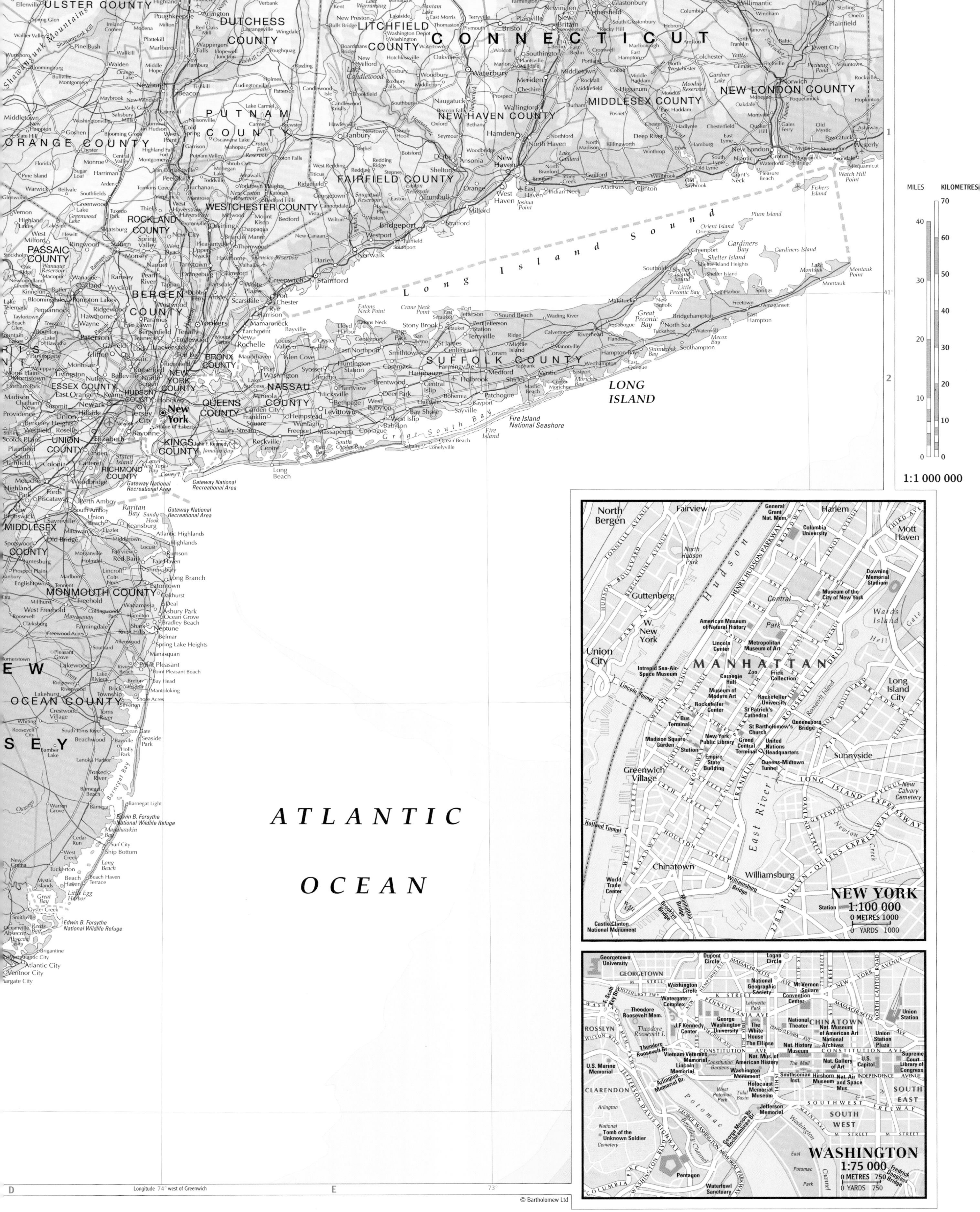

ULSTER COUNTY
DUTCHESS COUNTY
LITCHFIELD COUNTY
PUTNAM COUNTY
ORANGE COUNTY
NEW HAVEN COUNTY
MIDDLESEX COUNTY
NEW LONDON COUNTY
FAIRFIELD COUNTY
WESTCHESTER COUNTY
ROCKLAND COUNTY
PASSAIC COUNTY
BERGEN COUNTY
ESSEX COUNTY
HUDSON COUNTY
BRONX COUNTY
NEW YORK COUNTY
QUEENS COUNTY
NASSAU COUNTY
SUFFOLK COUNTY
KINGS COUNTY
RICHMOND COUNTY
UNION COUNTY
MIDDLESEX COUNTY
MONMOUTH COUNTY
OCEAN COUNTY
MORRIS
NEW JERSEY

New York

Long Island Sound

LONG ISLAND

Great South Bay

Gateway National Recreational Area

Edwin B. Forsythe National Wildlife Refuge

Fire Island National Seashore

ATLANTIC OCEAN

MILES KILOMETRES

1:1 000 000

NEW YORK
1:100 000
0 METRES 1000
0 YARDS 1000

MANHATTAN

North Bergen, Fairview, General Grant Nat. Mem., Harlem, Columbia University, Mott Haven, Guttenberg, North Hudson Park, Central Park, Museum of the City of New York, American Museum of Natural History, Ward's Island, Union City, W. New York, Lincoln Center, Metropolitan Museum of Art, Hell Gate, Intrepid Sea-Air-Space Museum, Carnegie Hall, Zoo, Frick Collection, Long Island City, Museum of Modern Art, Rockefeller University, Rockefeller Center, St Patrick's Cathedral, Queensboro Bridge, Roosevelt Island, Bus Terminal, St Bartholomew's Church, United Nations Headquarters, Sunnyside, Madison Square Garden, New York Public Library, Grand Central Terminal, Queens-Midtown Tunnel, Empire State Building, New Calvary Cemetery, Greenwich Village, Holland Tunnel, Chinatown, Williamsburg, Williamsburg Bridge, World Trade Center, Manhattan Bridge, Brooklyn Bridge, Castle Clinton National Monument

Hudson River
East River

WASHINGTON
1:75 000
0 METRES 750
0 YARDS 750

Georgetown University, GEORGETOWN, Dupont Circle, Logan Circle, National Geographic Society, Mt Vernon Square, Convention Center, Washington Circle, Watergate Complex, Rosslyn, Theodore Roosevelt Mem., J.F. Kennedy Center, George Washington University, Lafayette Park, The White House, National Theater, CHINATOWN, Nat. Museum of American Art, National Archives, Union Station Plaza, U.S. Marine Memorial, Vietnam Veterans Memorial, Lincoln Memorial, The Ellipse, Nat. History Museum, Nat. Mus. of American History, Washington Monument, Smithsonian Inst., The Mall, Holocaust Museum, Hirshhorn Museum, Nat. Air and Space Mus., Nat. Gallery of Art, U.S. Capitol, Supreme Court, Library of Congress, CLARENDON, Arlington Memorial Br., Jefferson Memorial, SOUTH WEST, SOUTH EAST, National Cemetery, Tomb of the Unknown Soldier, Pentagon, Waterfront Park, Waterside Park

Potomac River

© Bartholomew Ltd

230

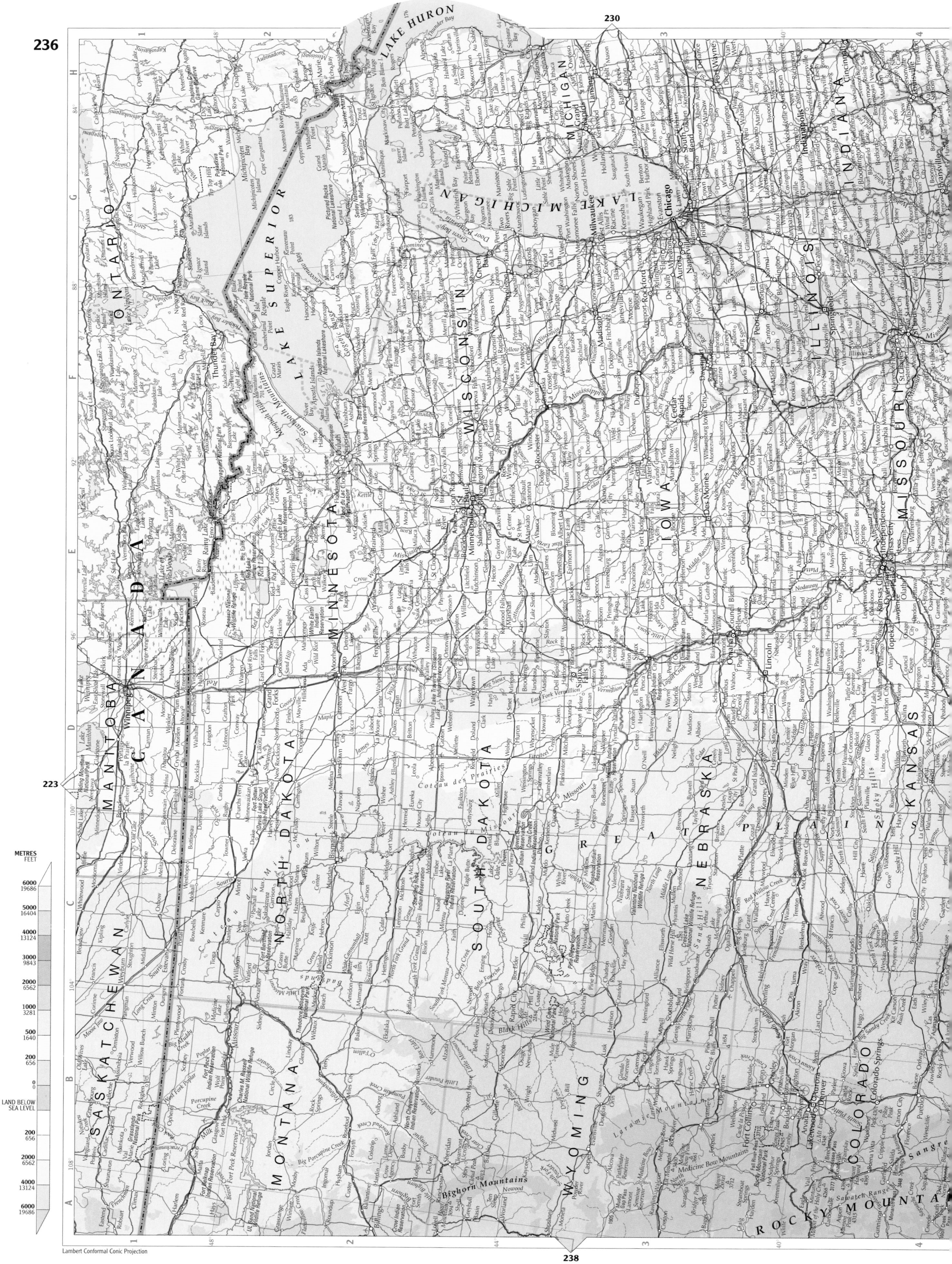

LAKE HURON

L A K E   S U P E R I O R

LAKE MICHIGAN

O N T A R I O

C A N A D A

M A N I T O B A

S A S K A T C H E W A N

M O N T A N A

W Y O M I N G

N O R T H   D A K O T A

S O U T H   D A K O T A

M I N N E S O T A

W I S C O N S I N

M I C H I G A N

I O W A

N E B R A S K A

K A N S A S

M I S S O U R I

I L L I N O I S

I N D I A N A

C O L O R A D O

G R E A T   P L A I N S

R O C K Y   M O U N T A I N S

Bighorn Mountains

Black Hills

Medicine Bow Mountains

Sangre

Sawatch Range

Chicago

Milwaukee

Duluth

Thunder Bay

Winnipeg

Des Moines

Omaha

Council Bluffs

Lincoln

Kansas City

Independence

St Joseph

Topeka

Denver

Colorado Springs

Pueblo

Fort Collins

Billings

Bismarck

Sioux Falls

Fargo

Minneapolis

St Paul

Rochester

Springfield

Peoria

Rockford

Aurora

Joliet

Cedar Rapids

Isle Royale National Park

Pictured Rocks National Lakeshore

Apostle Islands National Lakeshore

Theodore Roosevelt National Park

Badlands National Park

Wind Cave National Park

Rocky Mountain National Park

223

Lambert Conformal Conic Projection

METRES
FEET

6000	19686
5000	16404
4000	13124
3000	9843
2000	6562
1000	3281
500	1640
200	656
0	0

LAND BELOW SEA LEVEL

200	656
2000	6562
4000	13124
6000	19686

231

239

243

GULF OF MEXICO

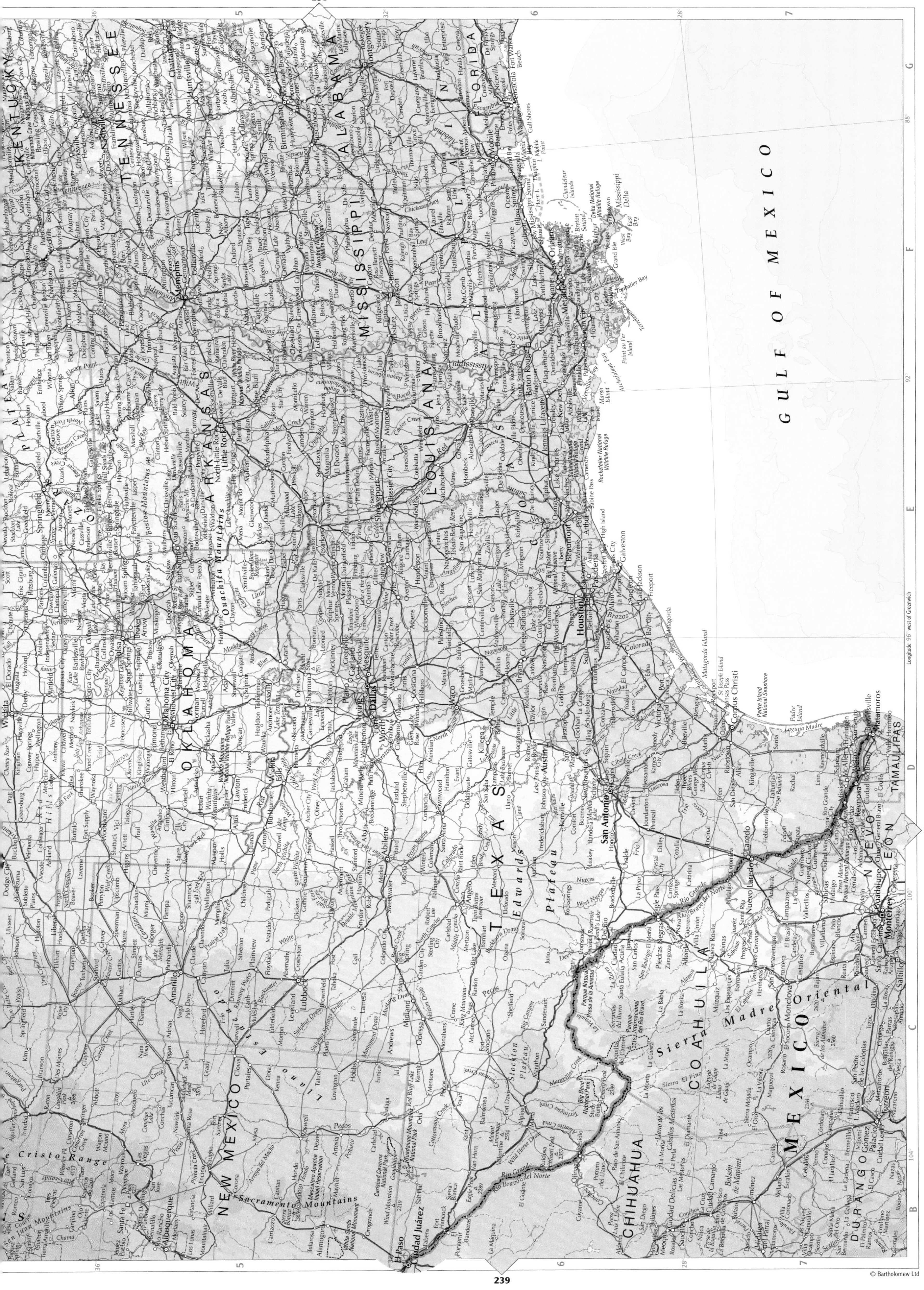

KENTUCKY

TENNESSEE

ALABAMA

FLORIDA

MISSISSIPPI

ARKANSAS

LOUISIANA

OKLAHOMA

TEXAS

NEW MEXICO

Ouachita Mountains

Boston Mountains

Edwards Plateau

Stockton Plateau

Sacramento Mountains

Sierra Madre Oriental

COAHUILA

CHIHUAHUA

NUEVO LEÓN

TAMAULIPAS

DURANGO

MEXICO

Memphis

Nashville

Chattanooga

Birmingham

Montgomery

Mobile

New Orleans

Baton Rouge

Jackson

Little Rock

North Little Rock

Springfield

Tulsa

Oklahoma City

Wichita

Amarillo

Lubbock

Midland

Odessa

El Paso

Ciudad Juárez

Dallas

Fort Worth

Plano

Mesquite

Waco

Austin

San Antonio

Houston

Pasadena

Beaumont

Galveston

Corpus Christi

Laredo

Nuevo Laredo

Reynosa

Matamoros

Monterrey

Saltillo

Rio Grande

Longitude 96 west of Greenwich

MILES

KILOMETRES

250 — 400

350

200 — 300

250

150 — 200

100 — 150

100

50 — 50

0 — 0

1 : 6 000 000

236

222

CANADA

SASKATCHEWAN

ALBERTA

BRITISH COLUMBIA

NORTH DAKOTA

SOUTH DAKOTA

NEBRASKA

MONTANA

WYOMING

IDAHO

WASHINGTON

OREGON

ROCKY MOUNTAINS

ROCKY MO

COLUMBIA MOUNTAINS

SELKIRK MOUNTAINS

PURCELL MOUNTAINS

COAST MOUNTAINS

Lewis Range

Bighorn Mountains

Absaroka Range

Wind River Range

Wyoming Range

Teton Range

Medicine Bow Mountains

Laramie Mountains

BITTERROOT RANGE

Salmon River Mountains

Beaverhead Mountains

Bitterroot Range

Cabinet Mountains

COLUMBIA PLATEAU

Snake River Plain

Great Salt Lake

Great Salt Lake Desert

Harney Basin

CASCADE RANGE

COAST RANGE

Klamath Mountains

Vancouver Island

Regina

Saskatoon

Calgary

Red Deer

Lethbridge

Billings

Casper

Cheyenne

Fort Collins

Salt Lake City

West Valley City

Ogden

Boise

Nampa

Idaho Falls

Pocatello

Spokane

Seattle

Tacoma

Bellevue

Everett

Vancouver

North Vancouver

Burnaby

Victoria

Nanaimo

Kelowna

Kamloops

Bend

Salem

Portland

Eugene

Medford

Redding

Sacramento

Missouri

Columbia

Snake River

Yellowstone

Fraser

Bitterroot

Lambert Conformal Conic Projection

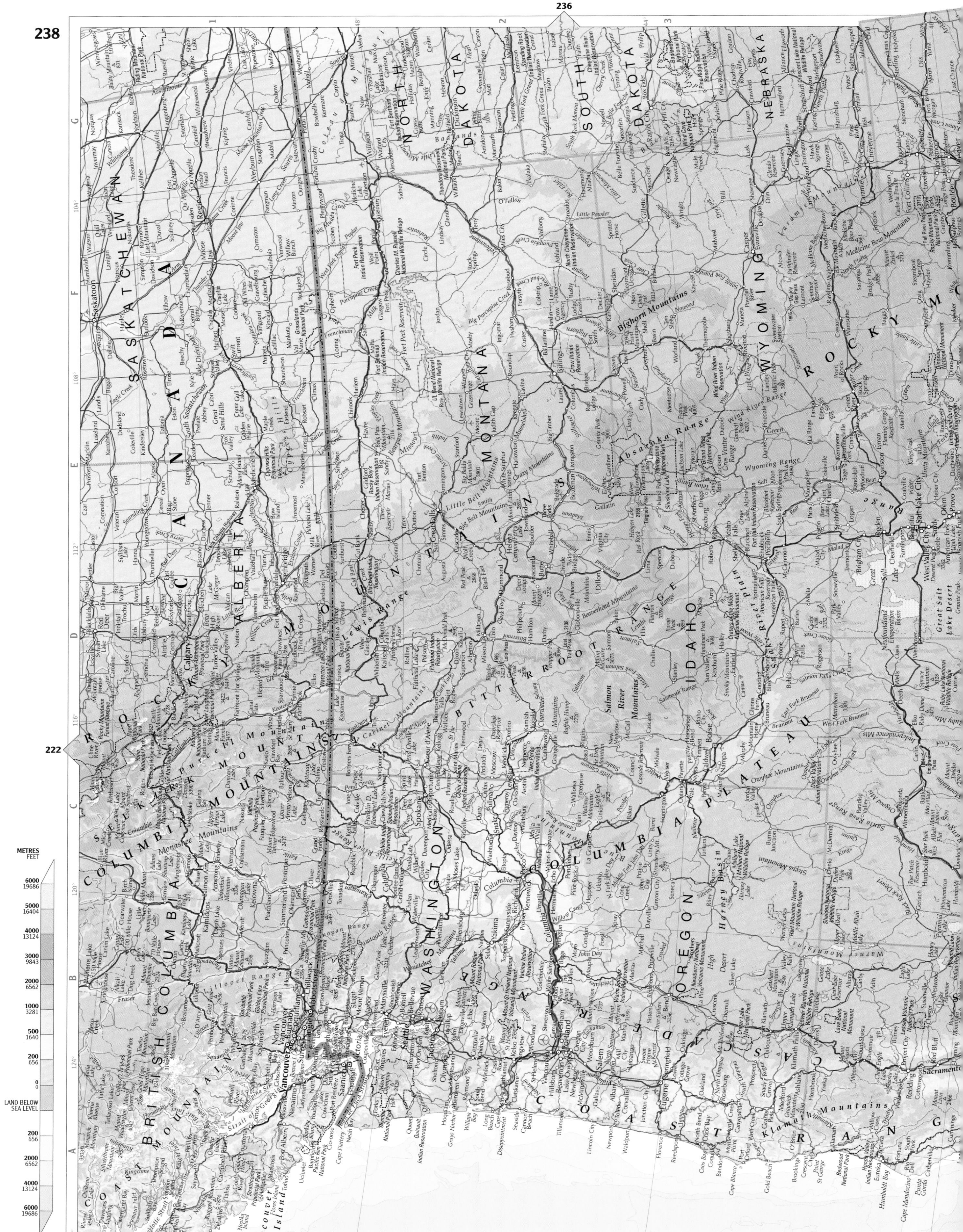

METRES
FEET

6000 19686
5000 16404
4000 13124
3000 9843
2000 6562
1000 3281
500 1640
200 656
0
LAND BELOW
SEA LEVEL
200 656
2000 6562
4000 13124
6000 19686

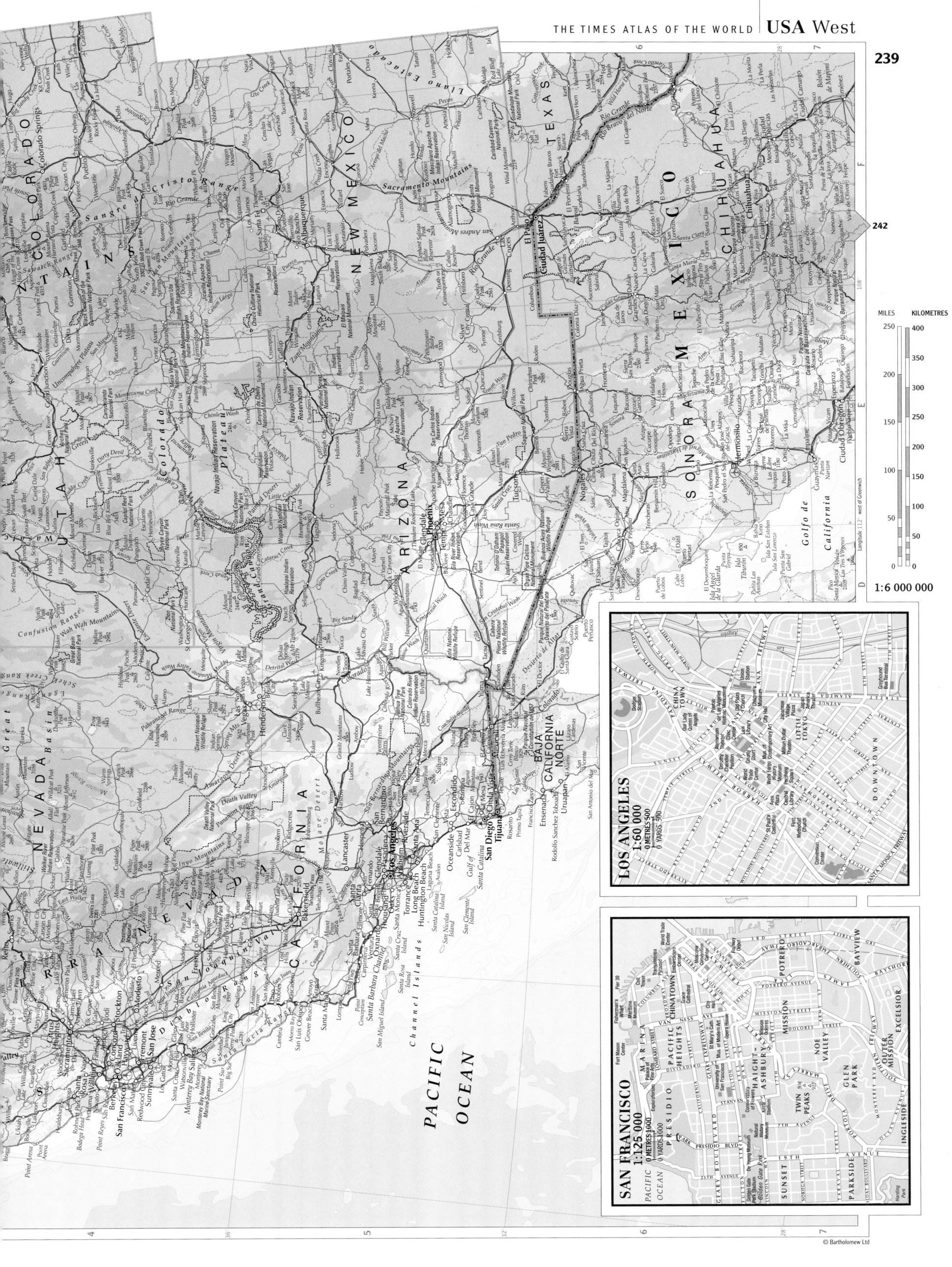

LOS ANGELES 1:60 000
0 METRES 500
0 YARDS 500

SAN FRANCISCO 1:125 000
0 METRES 1000
0 YARDS 1000

MILES KILOMETRES
250   400
       350
200   300
       250
150   200
100   150
       100
50   50
       0

1:6 000 000

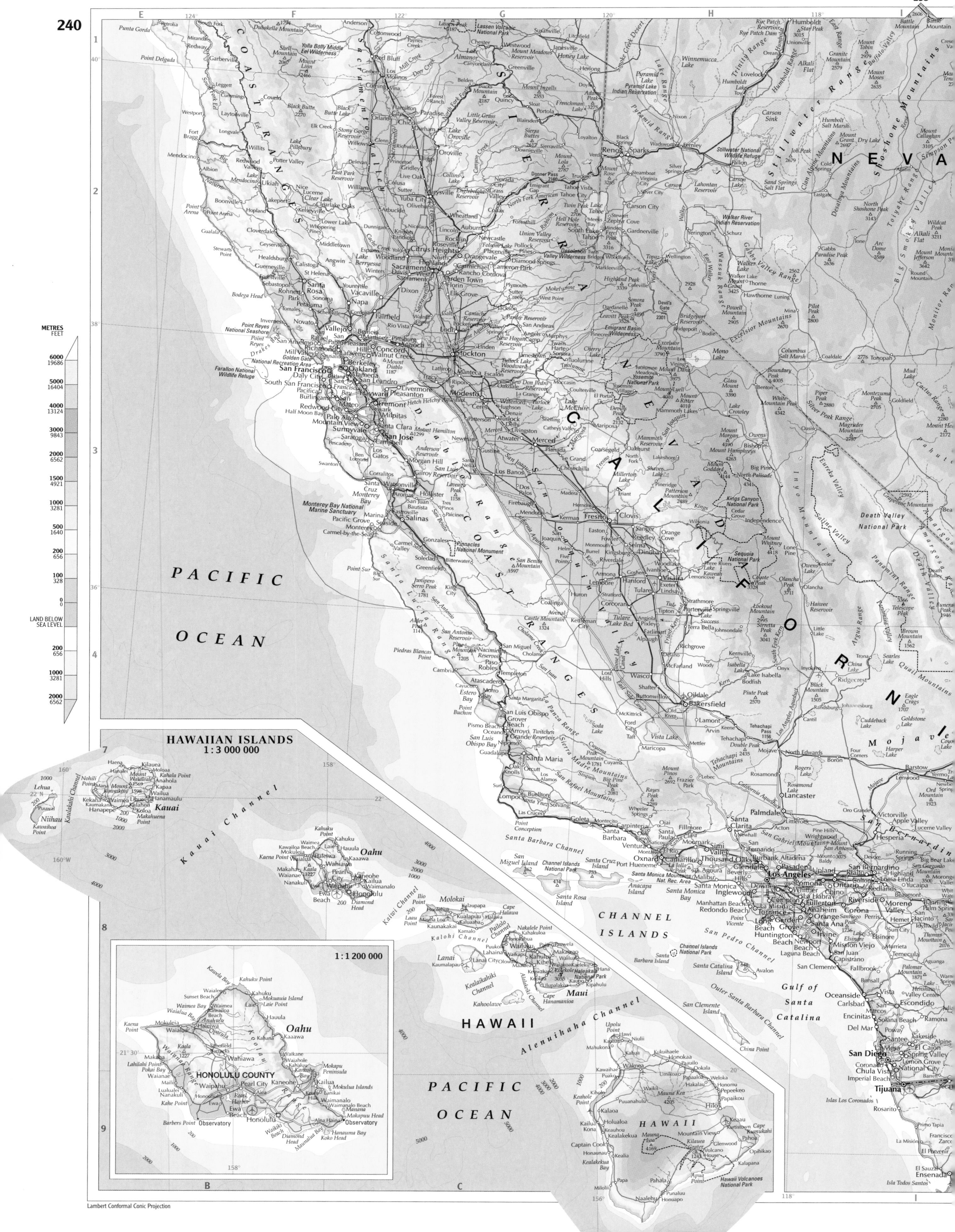

METRES
FEET

6000 19686
5000 16404
4000 13124
3000 9843
2000 6562
1500 4921
1000 3281
500 1640
200 656
100 328
0 0

LAND BELOW
SEA LEVEL

200 656
1000 3281
2000 6562

PACIFIC

OCEAN

N E V A D A

C A L I F O R N I A

HAWAIIAN ISLANDS
1 : 3 000 000

Kauai

Oahu

Molokai

Lanai

Maui

Kahoolawe

HAWAII

PACIFIC

OCEAN

CHANNEL

ISLANDS

1 : 1 200 000

Oahu

HONOLULU COUNTY

Pearl
Harbor

Honolulu

Lambert Conformal Conic Projection

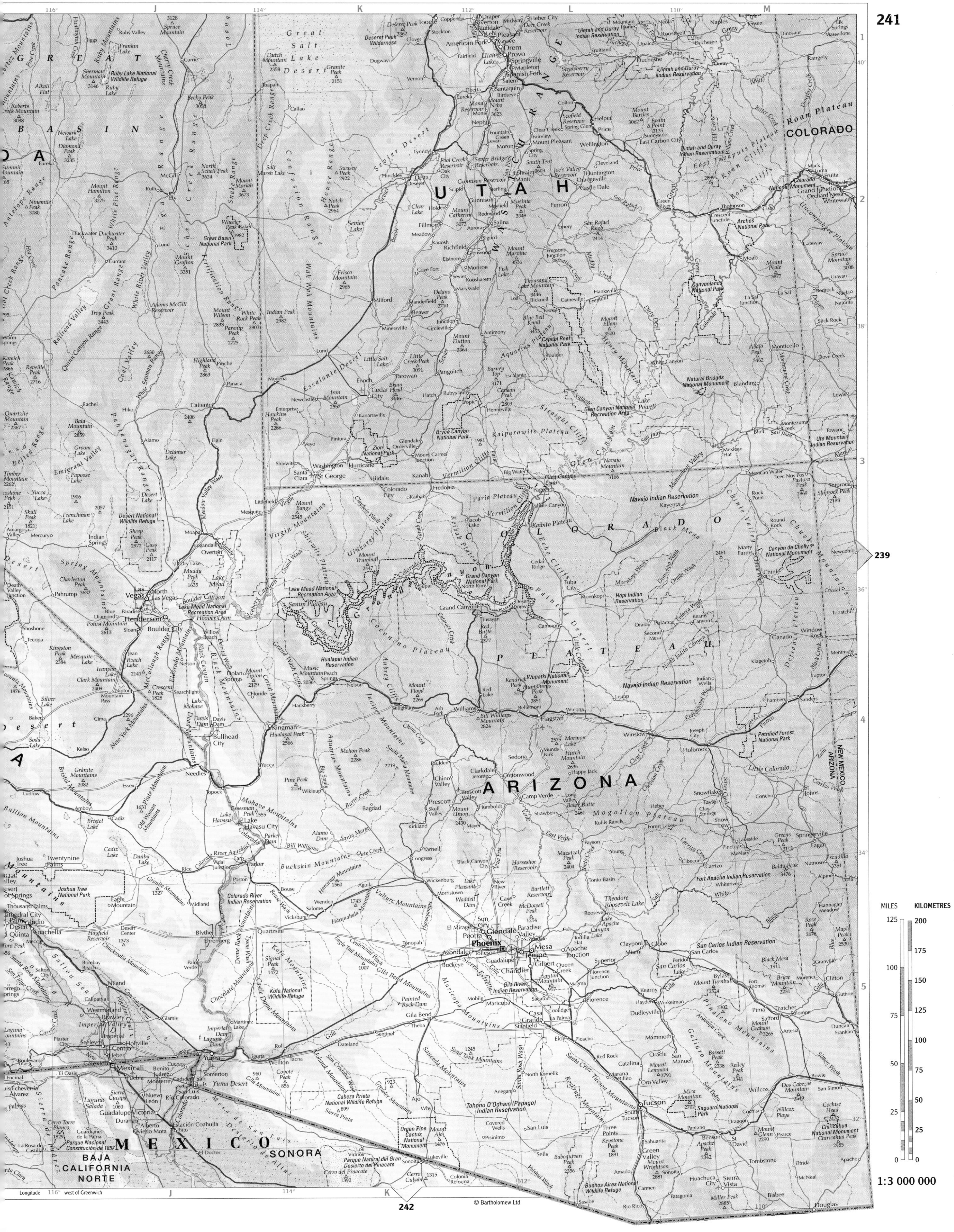
UTAH
ARIZONA
COLORADO
NEW MEXICO
ARIZONA
MEXICO
BAJA CALIFORNIA NORTE
SONORA
G R E A T   B A S I N
C O L O R A D O   P L A T E A U
Great Salt Lake Desert
Sevier Desert
Escalante Desert
Wasatch Range
Mogollon Plateau
Grand Canyon
Lake Powell
Lake Mead
Provo
Salt Lake City
St George
Las Vegas
Henderson
Flagstaff
Kingman
Phoenix
Mesa
Tempe
Tucson
Yuma
Mexicali
Grand Junction
Moab
Prescott
Winslow
Holbrook
Nogales
Douglas
Grand Canyon National Park
Zion National Park
Bryce Canyon National Park
Capitol Reef National Park
Arches National Park
Canyonlands National Park
Great Basin National Park
Petrified Forest National Park
Joshua Tree National Park
Navajo Indian Reservation
Hopi Indian Reservation
Fort Apache Indian Reservation
San Carlos Indian Reservation
Tohono O'Odham (Papago) Indian Reservation
Organ Pipe Cactus National Monument
Saguaro National Park
Kofa National Wildlife Refuge
Cabeza Prieta National Wildlife Refuge
Desert National Wildlife Refuge
MILES
KILOMETRES
1:3 000 000
239
242
Longitude 116° west of Greenwich
© Bartholomew Ltd

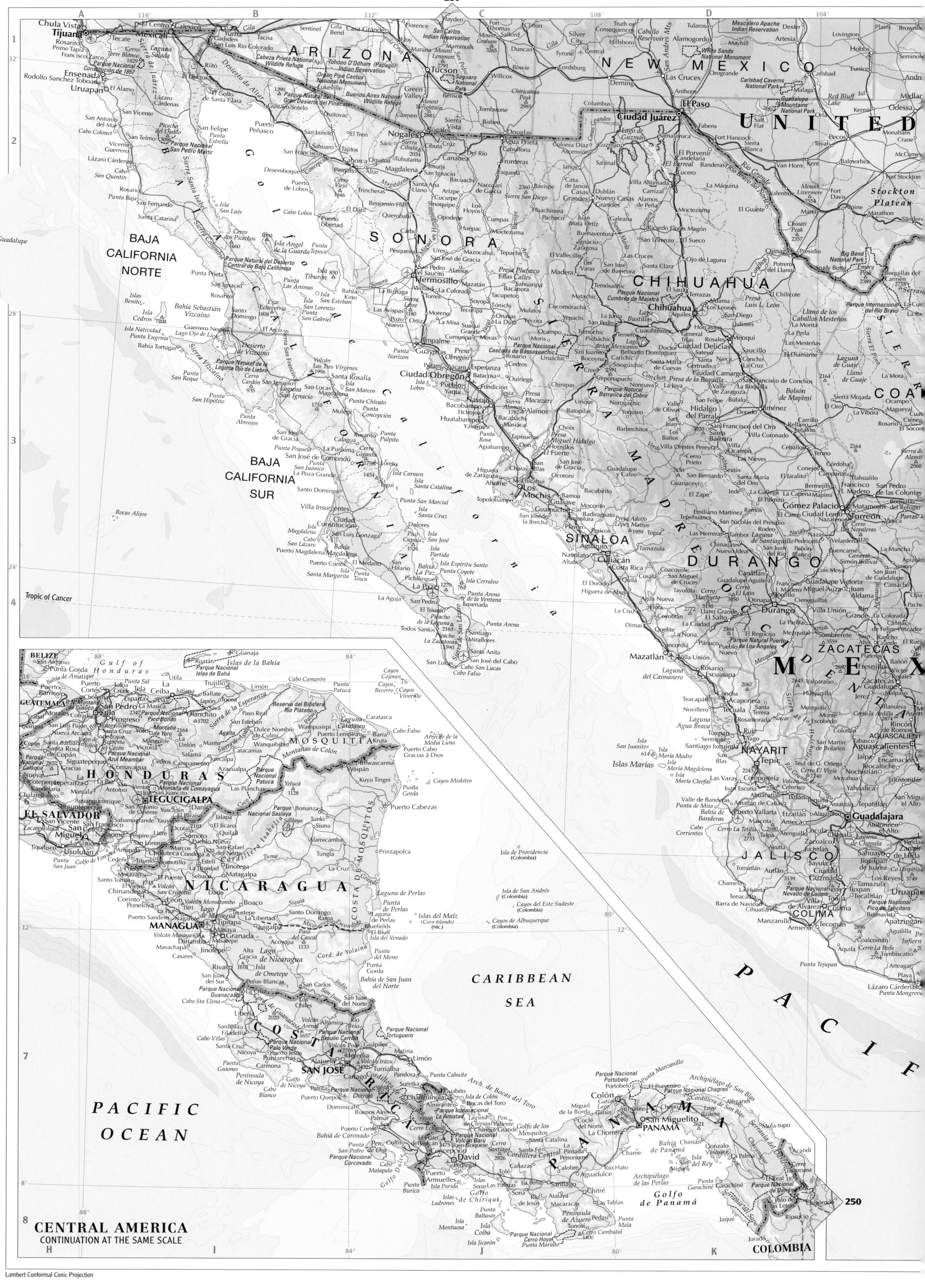

ARIZONA

NEW MEXICO

UNITED

SONORA

CHIHUAHUA

BAJA
CALIFORNIA
NORTE

BAJA
CALIFORNIA
SUR

SINALOA

DURANGO

ZACATECAS

COAH

M E X

NAYARIT

JALISCO

COLIMA

Ciudad Juárez

El Paso

Tijuana

Chihuahua

Hermosillo

Ciudad Obregón

Los Mochis

Culiacán

Durango

Mazatlán

Gómez Palacio

Torreón

Tepic

Guadalajara

Tropic of Cancer

METRES / FEET

METRES	FEET
6000	19686
5000	16404
4000	13124
3000	9843
2000	6562
1000	3281
500	1640
200	656
0	0

LAND BELOW
SEA LEVEL

200	656
2000	6562
4000	13124
6000	19686

BELIZE

GUATEMALA

HONDURAS

EL SALVADOR

NICARAGUA

COSTA RICA

PANAMA

COLOMBIA

TEGUCIGALPA

MANAGUA

SAN JOSÉ

PANAMÁ

Gulf of
Honduras

MOSQUITIA

CARIBBEAN
SEA

PACIFIC
OCEAN

PACIF

Golfo
de Panamá

CENTRAL AMERICA
CONTINUATION AT THE SAME SCALE

Lambert Conformal Conic Projection

250

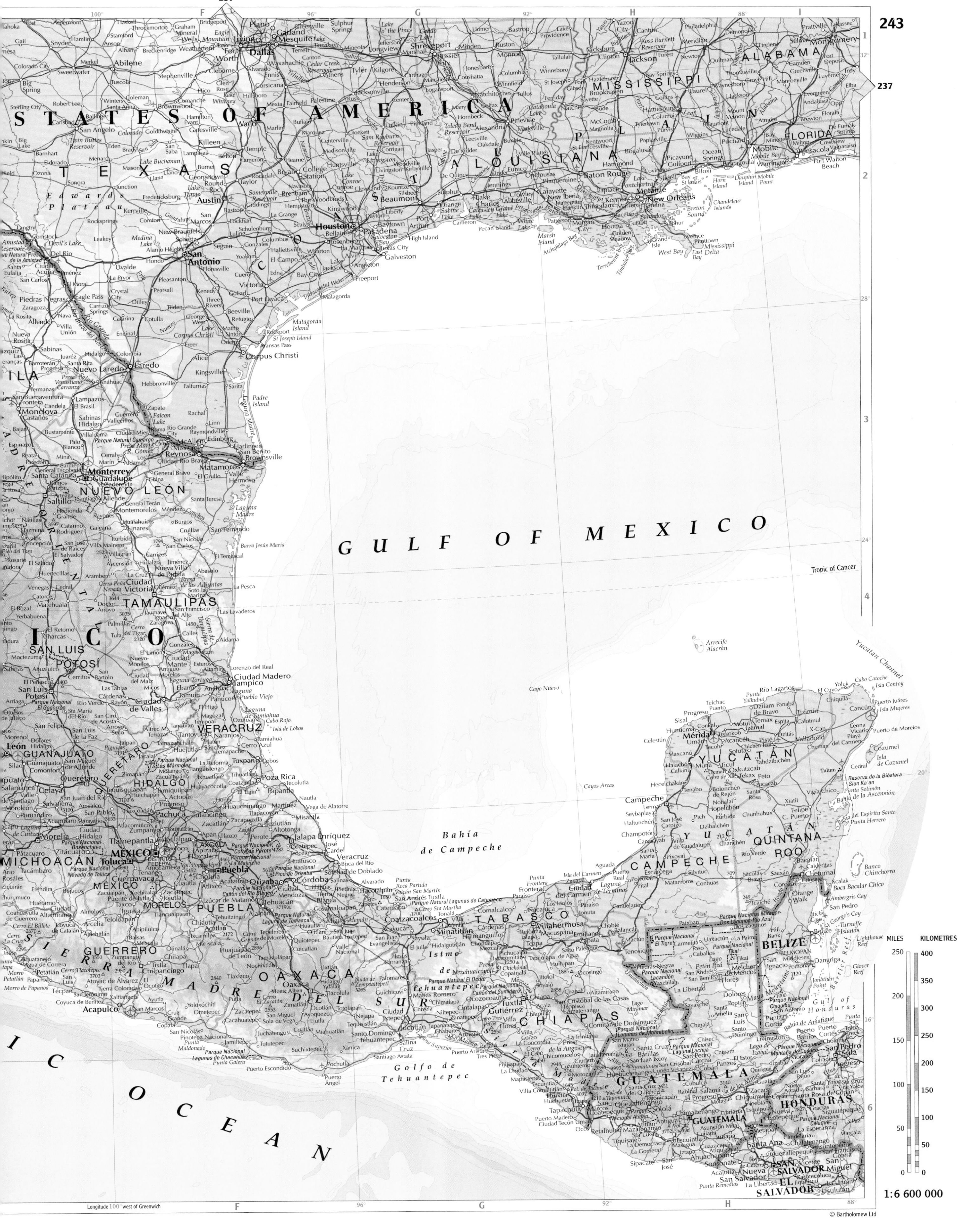

GULF OF MEXICO

STATES OF AMERICA

TEXAS

LOUISIANA

MISSISSIPPI

ALABAMA

FLORIDA

COASTAL PLAIN

TAMAULIPAS

NUEVO LEÓN

SAN LUIS POTOSÍ

GUANAJUATO

QUERÉTARO

HIDALGO

VERACRUZ

MÉXICO

MICHOACÁN

MORELOS

PUEBLA

TLAXCALA

GUERRERO

OAXACA

SIERRA MADRE DEL SUR

CHIAPAS

TABASCO

CAMPECHE

YUCATÁN

QUINTANA ROO

Bahía de Campeche

Istmo de Tehuantepec

Golfo de Tehuantepec

GUATEMALA

BELIZE

HONDURAS

EL SALVADOR

PACIFIC OCEAN

Tropic of Cancer

Yucatan Channel

Major cities / places:
Dallas, Fort Worth, Austin, San Antonio, Houston, Pasadena, Galveston, Corpus Christi, Nuevo Laredo, Laredo, Monterrey, Guadalupe, Saltillo, Matamoros, Reynosa, Ciudad Victoria, Tampico, Ciudad Madero, Veracruz, Poza Rica, Pachuca, MÉXICO, Toluca, Cuernavaca, Puebla, Orizaba, Córdoba, Acapulco, Oaxaca, Tuxtla Gutiérrez, Villahermosa, Coatzacoalcos, Minatitlán, Campeche, Mérida, Cancún, Cozumel, Chetumal, Belize, GUATEMALA, Quezaltenango, San Salvador, SAN SALVADOR

Shreveport, Jackson, Baton Rouge, New Orleans, Mobile, Biloxi, Gulfport, Montgomery

Longitude 100° west of Greenwich

© Bartholomew Ltd

MILES   KILOMETRES
250   400
        350
200   300
        250
150   200
100   150
        100
50   50
        0

1:6 600 000

242

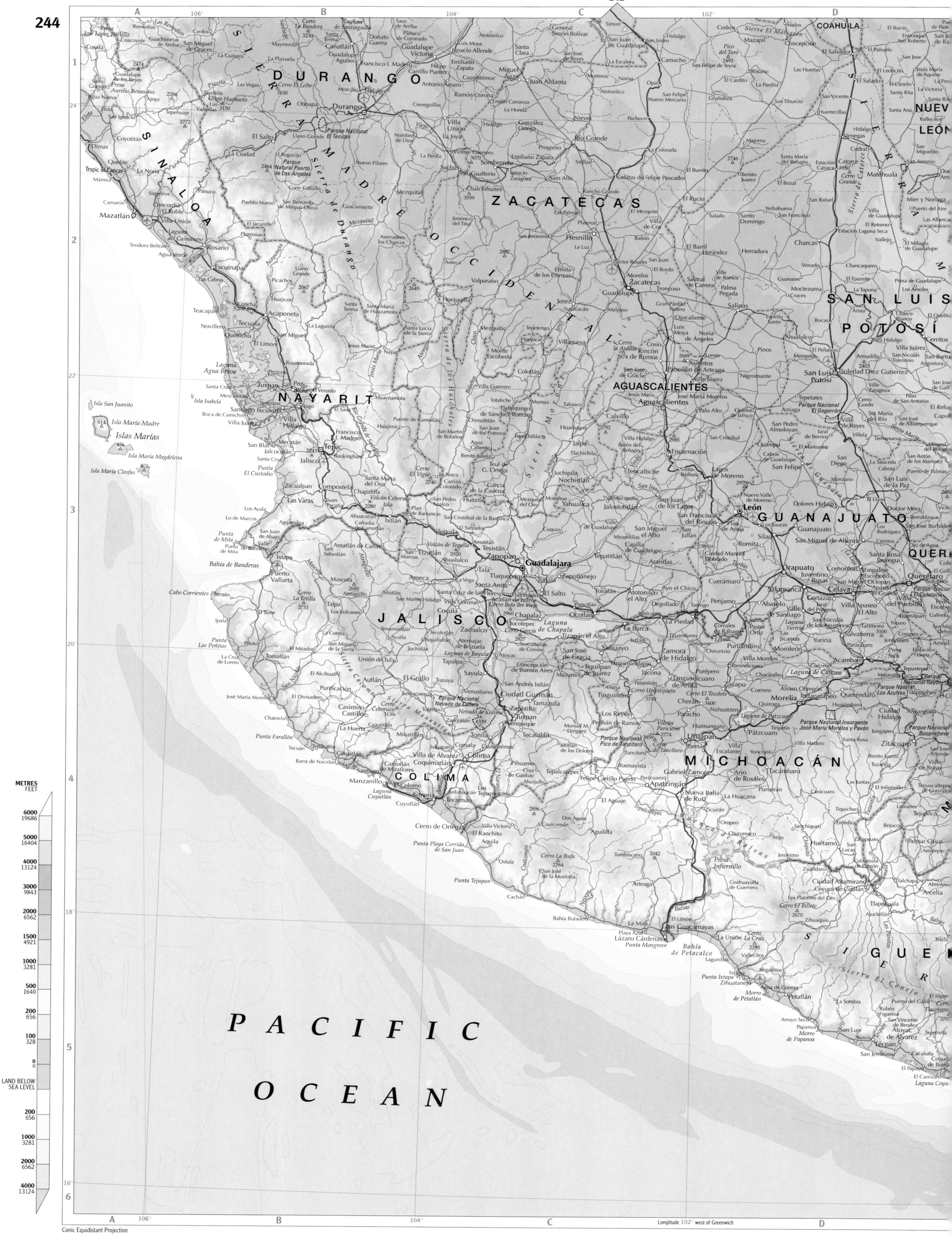

PACIFIC OCEAN

DURANGO

SINALOA

ZACATECAS

NAYARIT

AGUASCALIENTES

SAN LUIS POTOSÍ

JALISCO

COLIMA

GUANAJUATO

MICHOACÁN

COAHUILA

NUEVO LEÓN

QUERÉTARO

SIERRA MADRE OCCIDENTAL

SIERRA DE DURANGO

Sierra de los Huicholes

Islas Marías

Isla San Juanito

Isla María Madre

Isla María Magdalena

Isla María Cleofas

Isla Isabela

Bahía de Banderas

Cabo Corrientes

Laguna de Chapala

Presa Infiernillo

Tropic of Cancer

Mazatlán

Durango

Zacatecas

Guadalupe

Aguascalientes

San Luis Potosí

León

Guanajuato

Querétaro

Irapuato

Celaya

Salamanca

Guadalajara

Zapopan

Tepic

Colima

Manzanillo

Morelia

Uruapan

Pátzcuaro

Lázaro Cárdenas

Puerto Vallarta

Zihuatanejo

METRES / FEET

6000 / 19686
5000 / 16404
4000 / 13124
3000 / 9843
2000 / 6562
1500 / 4921
1000 / 3281
500 / 1640
200 / 656
100 / 328
0 / 0

LAND BELOW SEA LEVEL

200 / 656
1000 / 3281
2000 / 6562
4000 / 13124

Longitude 102° west of Greenwich

106° · 104° · 102°

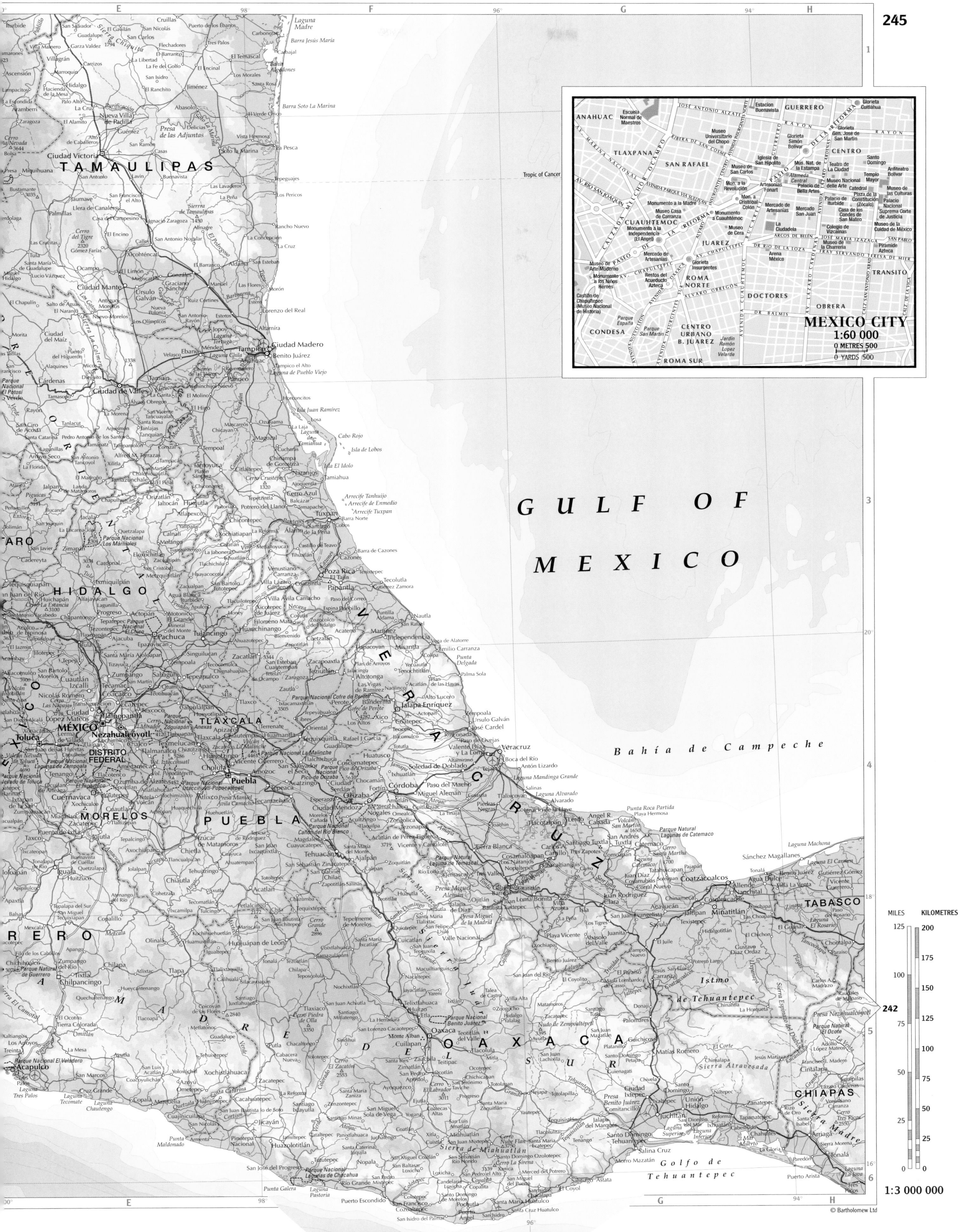

TAMAULIPAS

Ciudad Victoria

Tropic of Cancer

Ciudad Mante

Ciudad Madero
Tampico

HIDALGO

GULF OF MEXICO

VERACRUZ

Pachuca

MEXICO

TLAXCALA

Nezahualcóyotl

Toluca

DISTRITO FEDERAL

Puebla

Cuernavaca

MORELOS

PUEBLA

Orizaba
Córdoba

Veracruz

Bahía de Campeche

GUERRERO

Chilpancingo

Acapulco

SIERRA MADRE DEL SUR

Oaxaca

OAXACA

Coatzacoalcos

TABASCO

Istmo de Tehuantepec

CHIAPAS

Golfo de Tehuantepec

MEXICO CITY 1:60 000

0 METRES 500
0 YARDS 500

ANAHUAC

GUERRERO

TLAXPANA

SAN RAFAEL

CUAUHTEMOC

JUAREZ

CENTRO
URBANO
B. JUAREZ

ROMA
NORTE

CONDESA

DOCTORES

OBRERA

ROMA SUR

CENTRO

TRANSITO

242

MILES KILOMETRES

125 200
      175
100 150
      125
75   100
      75
50
      50
25
      25
0   0

1:3 000 000

© Bartholomew Ltd

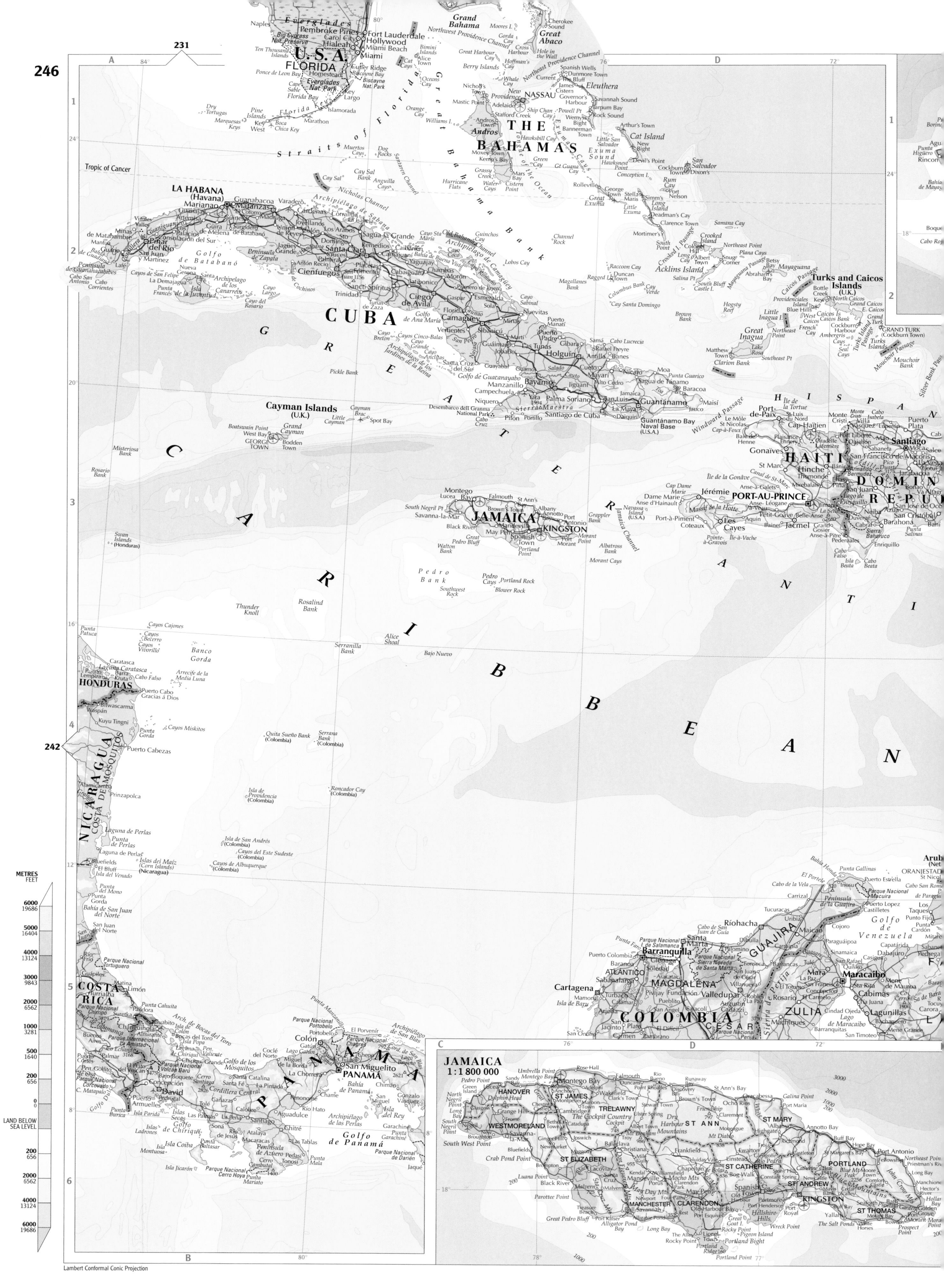

231

Countries / Regions
U.S.A. — FLORIDA
THE BAHAMAS
Grand Bahama
Great Abaco
CUBA
Cayman Islands (U.K.)
JAMAICA
HAITI
DOMINICAN REPUBLIC
Turks and Caicos Islands (U.K.)
HONDURAS
NICARAGUA
COSTA RICA
PANAMA
COLOMBIA
VENEZUELA

Major places / labels
Naples, Pembroke Pines, Hollywood, Fort Lauderdale, Miami Beach, Hialeah, Miami, Cutler Ridge, Key Largo, Homestead, Everglades Nat. Park, Florida Bay, Marathon, Key West, Dry Tortugas, Pine Islands

Straits of Florida
Tropic of Cancer

LA HABANA (Havana), Guanabacoa, Marianao, Matanzas, Varadero, Cárdenas, Pinar del Río, San Juan y Martínez, Cienfuegos, Santa Clara, Sancti Spíritus, Trinidad, Ciego de Ávila, Camagüey, Las Tunas, Holguín, Bayamo, Manzanillo, Palma Soriano, Santiago de Cuba, Guantánamo, Guantánamo Bay Naval Base (U.S.A.), Baracoa

GREATER ANTILLES
CARIBBEAN SEA

NASSAU, Andros Town, Eleuthera, Cat Island, San Salvador, Rum Cay, Long Island, Great Exuma, Crooked Island, Acklins Island, Mayaguana, Great Inagua, Little Inagua

GRAND TURK (Cockburn Town)

GEORGE TOWN, Grand Cayman, Bodden Town, Cayman Brac, Spot Bay

Montego Bay, Savanna-la-Mar, KINGSTON, Spanish Town, Port Antonio

Pedro Bank
Morant Cays

Port-de-Paix, Cap-Haïtien, Gonaïves, PORT-AU-PRINCE, Jérémie, Les Cayes, Jacmel
Santiago, San Francisco de Macorís, San José de Ocoa, San Cristóbal, Barahona, Enriquillo

Punta Patuca, Puerto Cabezas, Bluefields, El Bluff, San Juan del Norte
Tegucigalpa
MANAGUA, León, Granada

Banco Gorda
Serranilla Bank
Alice Shoal
Bajo Nuevo

Isla de Providencia (Colombia)
Isla de San Andrés (Colombia)
Quita Sueño Bank (Colombia)
Serrana Bank (Colombia)
Roncador Cay (Colombia)
Islas del Maíz (Corn Islands) (Nicaragua)

Colón, PANAMÁ, San Miguelito, David, Chitré, Las Tablas

Barranquilla, Cartagena, Santa Marta, Ríohacha, Maicao, Maracaibo, Valledupar, Cabimas, Lagunillas

Golfo de Venezuela
Lago de Maracaibo
Península de la Guajira

ORANJESTAD, Aruba (Net.)

Scale / elevation key
METRES / FEET
6000 / 19686
5000 / 16404
4000 / 13124
3000 / 9843
2000 / 6562
1000 / 3281
500 / 1640
200 / 656
0 / 0
LAND BELOW SEA LEVEL
200 / 656
2000 / 6562
4000 / 13124
6000 / 19686

Lambert Conformal Conic Projection

JAMAICA inset
JAMAICA 1:1 800 000
HANOVER, ST JAMES, TRELAWNY, ST ANN, ST MARY, WESTMORELAND, ST ELIZABETH, MANCHESTER, CLARENDON, ST CATHERINE, ST ANDREW, PORTLAND, ST THOMAS
Montego Bay, Falmouth, Runaway Bay, Ocho Rios, Port Maria, Port Antonio, Mandeville, May Pen, Spanish Town, KINGSTON, Morant Bay
The Cockpit Country
Blue Mountains

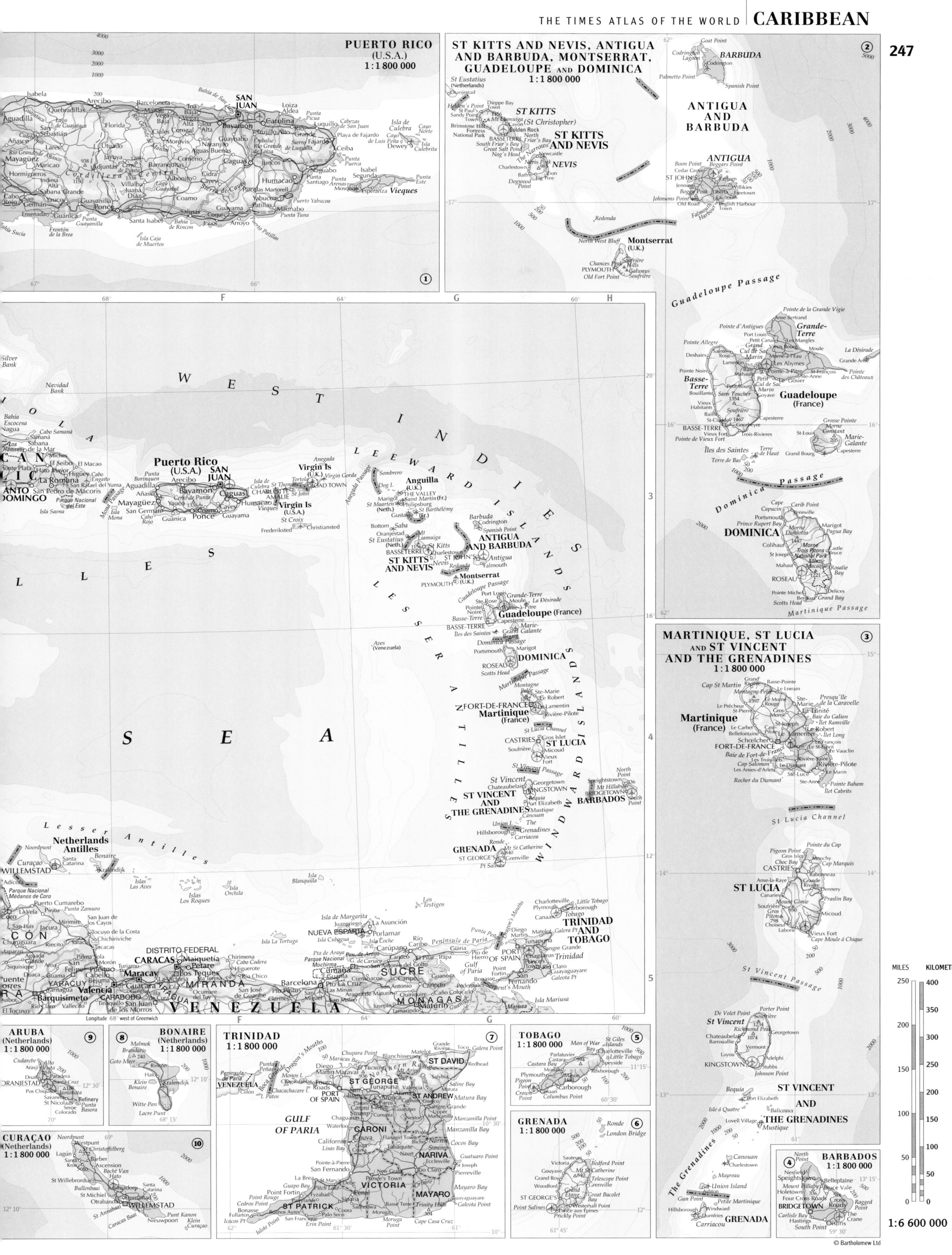

PUERTO RICO (U.S.A.)
1:1 800 000

ST KITTS AND NEVIS, ANTIGUA AND BARBUDA, MONTSERRAT, GUADELOUPE AND DOMINICA
1:1 800 000

ANTIGUA AND BARBUDA

MARTINIQUE, ST LUCIA AND ST VINCENT AND THE GRENADINES
1:1 800 000

ARUBA
(Netherlands)
1:1 800 000

BONAIRE
(Netherlands)
1:1 800 000

TRINIDAD
1:1 800 000

TOBAGO
1:1 800 000

CURAÇAO
(Netherlands)
1:1 800 000

GRENADA
1:1 800 000

BARBADOS
1:1 800 000

MILES   KILOMETRES

1:6 600 000

© Bartholomew Ltd

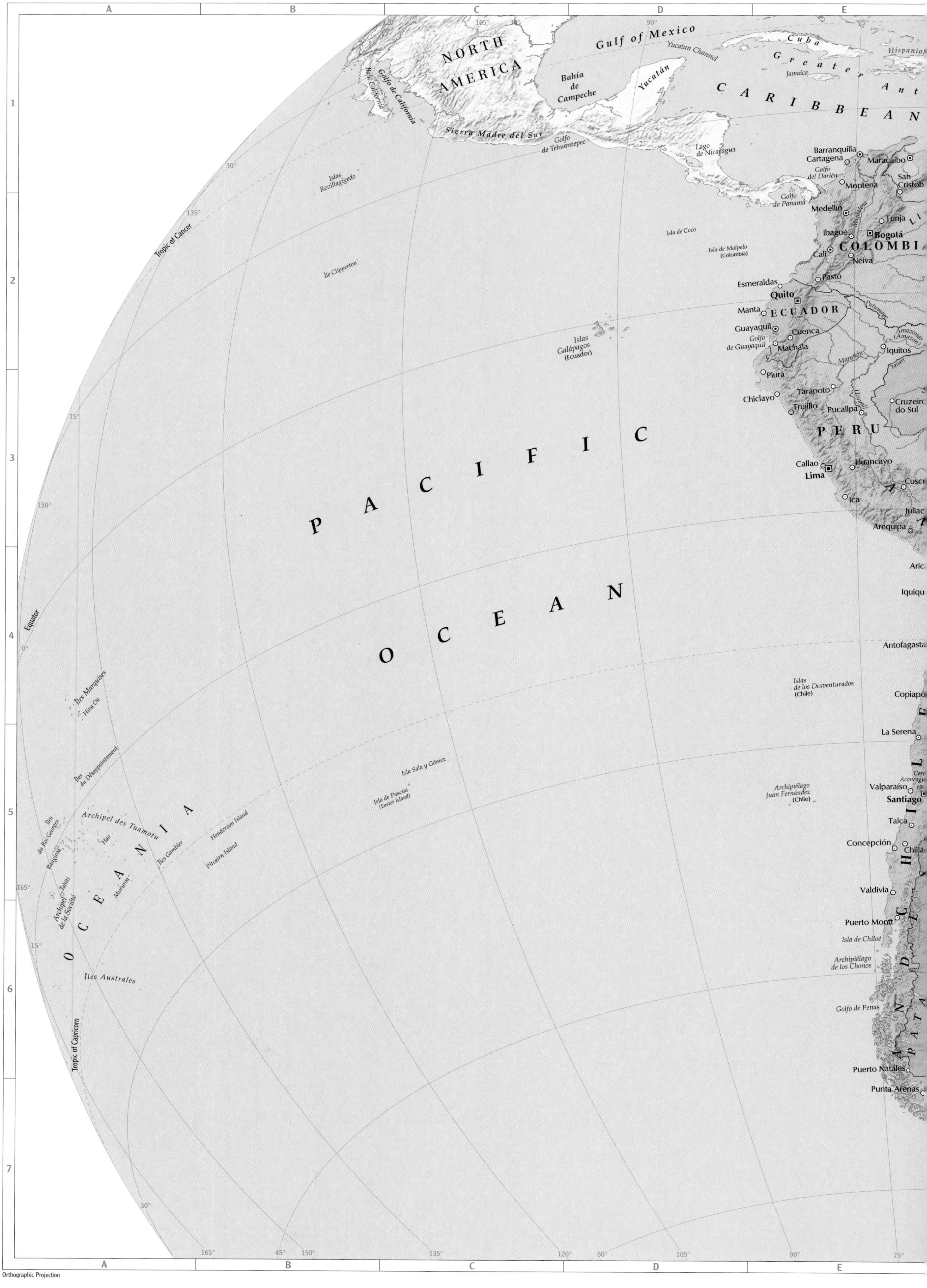

A   B   C   D   E

1

2

3

4

5

6

7

NORTH AMERICA

Gulf of Mexico

Yucatan Channel

Cuba

Hispaniol

Greater

Jamaica

Ant

C A R I B B E A N

Barranquilla

Cartagena

Maracaibo

Golfo del Darién

Montería

San Cristób

Bahía de Campeche

Yucatán

Sierra Madre del Sur

Golfo de Tehuantepec

Lago de Nicaragua

Medellín

Tunja

Ibagué

Bogotá

Cali

COLOMBIA

Neiva

Pasto

Isla de Coco

Isla de Malpelo (Colombia)

Esmeraldas

Quito

Manta

E C U A D O R

Guayaquil

Cuenca

Golfo de Guayaquil

Machala

Iquitos

Amazonas (Amazon)

Piura

Marañón

Tarapoto

Chiclayo

Trujillo

Pucallpa

Cruzeiro do Sul

P E R U

Islas Revillagigedo

Islas Galápagos (Ecuador)

Ucayali

Callao

Lima

Huancayo

Cusco

Ica

Juliac

Arequipa

Aric

Iquiqu

Antofagasta

Copiapó

Islas de los Desventurados (Chile)

La Serena

Cerr Aconcagu

Valparaíso

Santiago

C H I L E

Talca

Concepción

Chillá

Valdivia

Puerto Montt

Isla de Chiloé

Archipiélago de los Chonos

Golfo de Penas

P A T A G O N I A

Puerto Natales

Punta Arenas

Île Clipperton

P A C I F I C

O C E A N

Isla Sala y Gómez

Isla de Pascua (Easter Island)

Archipiélago Juan Fernández (Chile)

Îles Marquises

Hiva Oa

Îles du Désappointement

Îles Gambier

Henderson Island

Pitcairn Island

Archipel des Tuamotu

Hao

Mangareva

O C E A N I A

Îles du Roi Georges

Îles

Tahiti

Archipel de la Société

Îles Australes

Tropic of Cancer

Equator

Tropic of Capricorn

Golfo de California

Baja California

105°

90°

75°

30°

135°

30°

150°

15°

150°

0°

15°

165°

15°

30°

Orthographic Projection

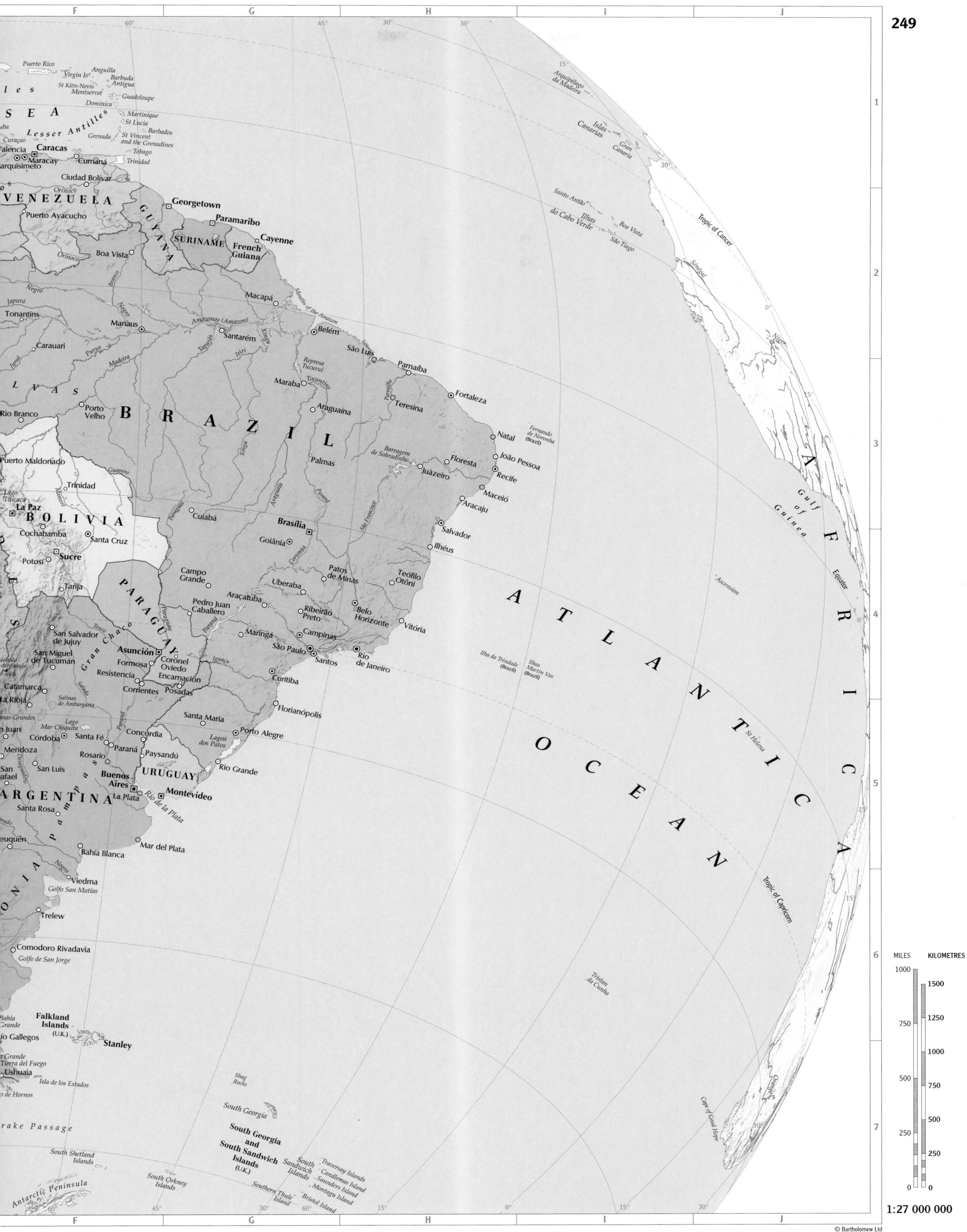

F G 45° 30° H 30° I J

Puerto Rico
Virgin Is Anguilla
St Kitts-Nevis Barbuda
Montserrat Antigua
les Dominica
Guadeloupe Arquipélago
da Madeira

S E A Martinique
St Lucia
Lesser Antilles Barbados
St Vincent Tobago
Grenada and the Grenadines
Curaçao Trinidad
valencia **Caracas** Cumaná
Maracay
arquisimeto *Orinoco*

V E N E Z U E L A **Georgetown**

Puerto Ayacucho **Paramaribo**
SURINAME **Cayenne**
Boa Vista **GUIANA** **French**
Guiana

Orinoco Macapá *Mouths of the Amazon*

Tonantins *Negro* Manaus *Amazonas (Amazon)* Belém
Japurá Santarém São Luís Parnaíba
Branco *Tapajós* *Iriri* *Xingu* Marabá Teresina Fortaleza
Carauari *Purus* *Madeira* *Represa* *Tocantins*
Tucurui Araguaína

L V A S Rio Branco Porto
Velho Natal *Fernando*
de Noronha
(Brazil)

B R A Z I L Palmas Floresta João Pessoa
Puerto Maldonado *Barragem* Juàzeiro Recife
de Sobradinho Maceió
Trinidad Cuiabá Aracaju
Lago
Titicaca **Brasília** Salvador
La Paz Goiânia Ilhéus
B O L I V I A
Cochabamba Santa Cruz Campo Patos
Grande de Minas Teófilo
Potosí **Sucre** Uberaba Otôni
Araçatuba Ribeirão Belo
Preto Horizonte
Tarija Pedro Juan Vitória
P A R A G U A Y Caballero Campinas
San Salvador Maringá São Paulo
de Jujuy *Gran Chaco* Santos
San Miguel Asunción **Rio**
de Tucumán Formosa Coronel **de Janeiro**
Oviedo Curitiba
Resistencia Encarnación *Ilha da Trindade*
Catamarca Corrientes Posadas *(Brazil)*
Rioja *Salinas*
de Ambargasta Santa Maria Florianópolis
Lago
Mar Chiquita Concordia Porto Alegre
Juan Córdoba Santa Fé *Lagoa*
dos Patos
Mendoza Paraná Paysandú Rio Grande
Rosario **URUGUAY**
San San Luis **Buenos**
afael **Aires** **Montevideo**
A R G E N T I N A **La Plata** *Río de la Plata*
Santa Rosa
endo Bahía Blanca Mar del Plata

A T L A N T I C

Santo Antão *Ilhas*
do Cabo Verde Boa Vista
São Tiago

Tropic of Cancer

Senegal

A F R I C A

Equator

Niger

Gulf
of
Guinea

Ascension

O C E A N

St Helena

Ilhas Martin Vas
(Brazil)

Tristan
da Cunha

Tropic of Capricorn

Cape of Good Hope
Orange

Negro Viedma
Golfo San Matías

Trelew

Comodoro Rivadavia
Golfo de San Jorge

Bahía **Falkland**
Grande **Islands**
o Gallegos (U.K.) **Stanley**
t Grande
Tierra del Fuego
Ushuaia
Isla de los Estados
o de Hornos

rake Passage *Shag*
Rocks

South Georgia

South Georgia
and
South Shetland **South Sandwich**
Islands **Islands**
South (U.K.) *Traversay Islands*
Sandwich *Candlemas Island*
Antarctic Peninsula *South Orkney* *Islands* *Saunders Island*
Islands *Montagu Island*
Southern Thule *Bristol Island*
Island

F 45° G 60° H 15° I 30° J

1

2

3

4

5

6

7

MILES KILOMETRES

1000 1500

750 1250

1000

500 750

500

250 250

0 0

1:27 000 000

© Bartholomew Ltd

CARIBBEAN SEA

Administrative regions numbered on the map:

COLOMBIA
1. SANTAFÉ DE BOGOTÁ (C3)

ECUADOR
2. BOLÍVAR (B5)
3. CHIMBORAZO (B5)
4. TUNGURAHUA (B5)
5. ZAMORA-CHINCHIPE (B5)

GALAPAGOS ISLANDS
(Ecuador)
AT THE SAME SCALE

ISLAS GALÁPAGOS Equator

Isla Culpepper
Isla Wenman
Isla Pinta Isla Marchena Isla Genovesa
Roca Redonda
Volcán Wolf Isla San Salvador
Volcán Darwin Isla Santa Cruz
Isla Fernandina Isla Isabela Puerto Ayora Isla San Cristóbal
Cerro Azul Puerto Villamil Isla Santa Fé Baquerizo Moreno
Isla Santa María Isla Española

92° W

PACIFIC OCEAN

PANAMA

COLOMBIA

ECUADOR

PERU

VENEZUELA

METRES / FEET

6000 / 19686
5000 / 16404
4000 / 13124
3000 / 9843
2000 / 6562
1000 / 3281
500 / 1640
200 / 656
0
LAND BELOW SEA LEVEL
200 / 656
2000 / 6562
4000 / 13124
6000 / 19686

Major cities and regions:

Barranquilla, Cartagena, Santa Marta, MAGDALENA, ATLÁNTICO, CÉSAR, BOLÍVAR, SUCRE, CÓRDOBA, ANTIOQUIA, Medellín, CHOCÓ, Quibdó, RISARALDA, CALDAS, Manizales, Pereira, Armenia, QUINDÍO, VALLE DEL CAUCA, Cali, Palmira, Buenaventura, CAUCA, Popayán, HUILA, Neiva, NARIÑO, Pasto, Tumaco, PUTUMAYO, CAQUETÁ, Florencia

SANTANDER, NORTE DE SANTANDER, Cúcuta, Bucaramanga, BOYACÁ, Tunja, CUNDINAMARCA, BOGOTÁ, TOLIMA, Ibagué, META, Villavicencio, CASANARE, Yopal, ARAUCA, VICHADA, GUAINÍA, GUAVIARE, VAUPÉS, AMAZONAS

ZULIA, Maracaibo, Cabimas, FALCÓN, LARA, Barquisimeto, TRUJILLO, MÉRIDA, TÁCHIRA, San Cristóbal, BARINAS, APURE, PORTUGUESA, COJEDES, ARAGUA, Maracay, CARACAS, Valencia, DISTRITO FEDERAL, WILLEMSTAD, ORANJESTAD, Aruba (Netherlands), Netherlands Antilles, Bonaire, Curaçao

Lago de Maracaibo, Golfo de Venezuela

ESMERALDAS, CARCHI, IMBABURA, Ibarra, PICHINCHA, QUITO, NAPO, COTOPAXI, Latacunga, MANABÍ, Manta, Portoviejo, LOS RÍOS, Babahoyo, Ambato, PASTAZA, Riobamba, Guayaquil, GUAYAS, CAÑAR, Cuenca, AZUAY, MORONA-SANTIAGO, Machala, EL ORO, LOJA, Loja, ZAMORA

Golfo de Guayaquil, Equator

TUMBES, PIURA, Piura, Sullana, Chiclayo, LAMBAYEQUE, CAJAMARCA, Cajamarca, LA LIBERTAD, Trujillo, AMAZONAS, SAN MARTÍN, LORETO, Iquitos, Leticia, UCAYALI, Pucallpa, HUÁNUCO, ANCASH

AMAZONAS (Brazil), ACRE, Cruzeiro do Sul, Benjamim Constant, Tabatinga

Lambert Azimuthal Equal Area Projection

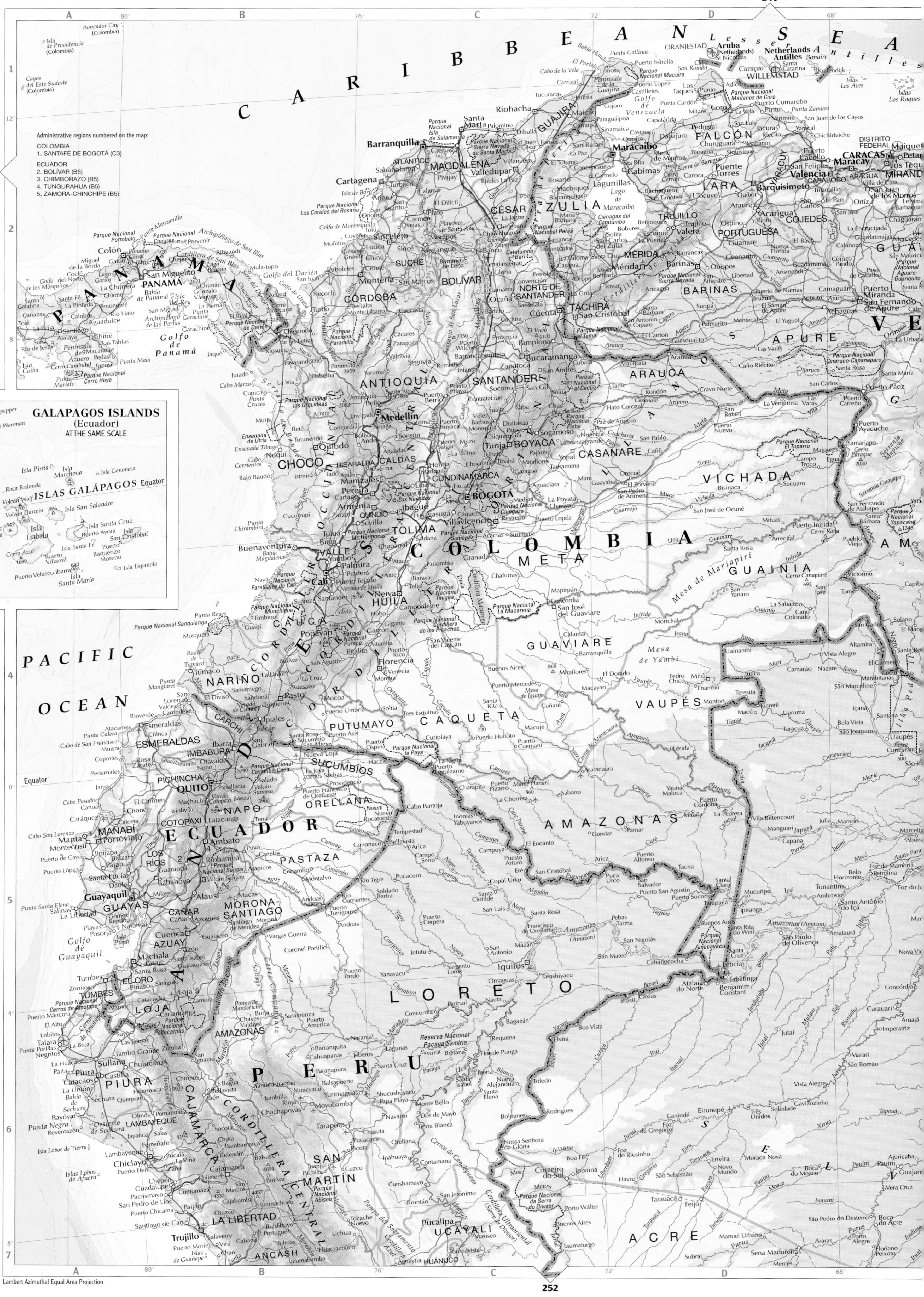

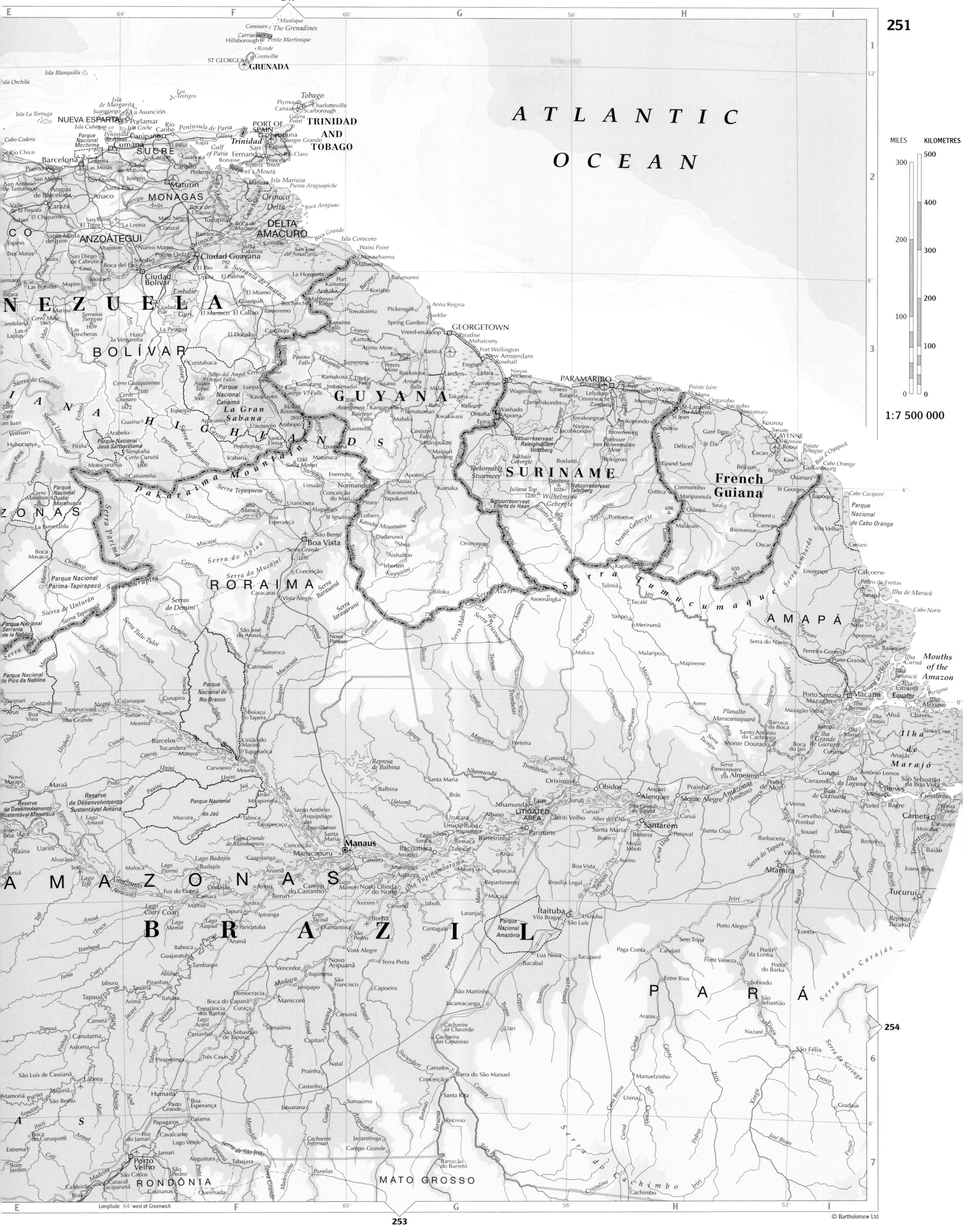

A T L A N T I C O C E A N

GRENADA

TRINIDAD AND TOBAGO

PORT OF SPAIN

NUEVA ESPARTA

SUCRE

MONAGAS

ANZOÁTEGUI

DELTA AMACURO

VENEZUELA

BOLÍVAR

GUIANA HIGHLANDS

GUYANA

GEORGETOWN

PARAMARIBO

SURINAME

French Guiana

CAYENNE

La Gran Sabana

Pakaraima Mountains

Mount Roraima

Boa Vista

RORAIMA

AMAZONAS

AMAPÁ

Mouths of the Amazon

Macapá Equator

Ilha de Marajó

Manaus

B R A Z I L

Parque Nacional Amazônia

PARÁ

Santarém

Altamira

Tucuruí

RONDÔNIA

Porto Velho

MATO GROSSO

Serra dos Carajás

Serra do Cachimbo

MILES KILOMETRES
300 500
400
200 300
200
100
100
0 0

1:7 500 000

© Bartholomew Ltd

PACIFIC

OCEAN

Tropic of Capricorn

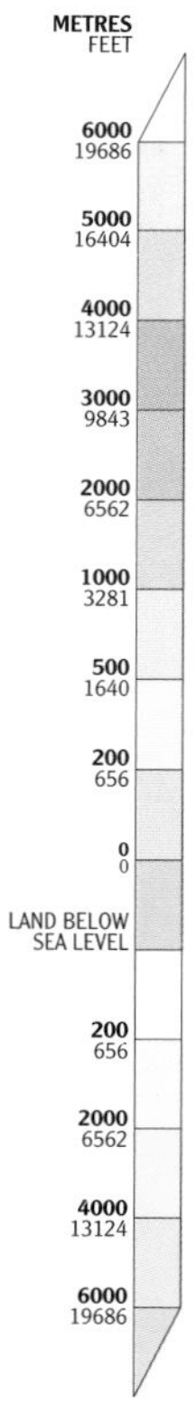

METRES
FEET

6000	19686
5000	16404
4000	13124
3000	9843
2000	6562
1000	3281
500	1640
200	656
0	0

LAND BELOW
SEA LEVEL

200	656
2000	6562
4000	13124
6000	19686

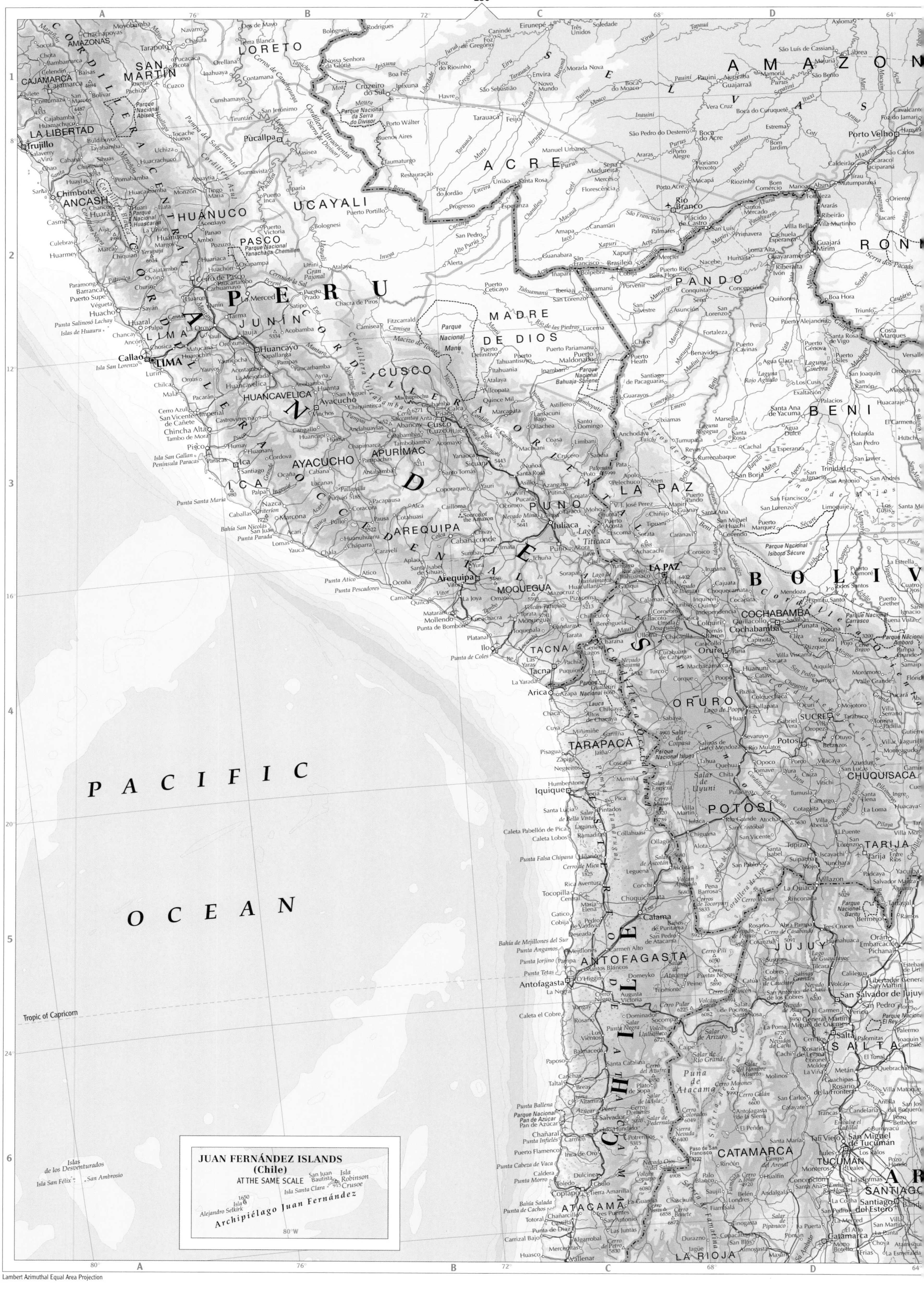

Lambert Azimuthal Equal Area Projection

PARÁ

TOCANTINS

MATO GROSSO

B R A Z I L

GOIÁS

DISTRITO FEDERAL
BRASÍLIA

Goiânia

MINAS GERAIS

Uberlândia

SANTA CRUZ

Santa Cruz

BOLIVIA

MATO GROSSO DO SUL

Campo Grande

SÃO PAULO

São Paulo
Santo André
Santos

Tropic of Capricorn

PARAGUAY

ASUNCIÓN

FORMOSA

CHACO

PARANÁ

Curitiba

ARGENTINA

MISIONES

SANTA CATARINA

RIO GRANDE DO SUL

ATLANTIC OCEAN

CORRIENTES

SANTA FÉ

SANTIAGO DEL ESTERO

MILES / KILOMETRES

1:7 500 000

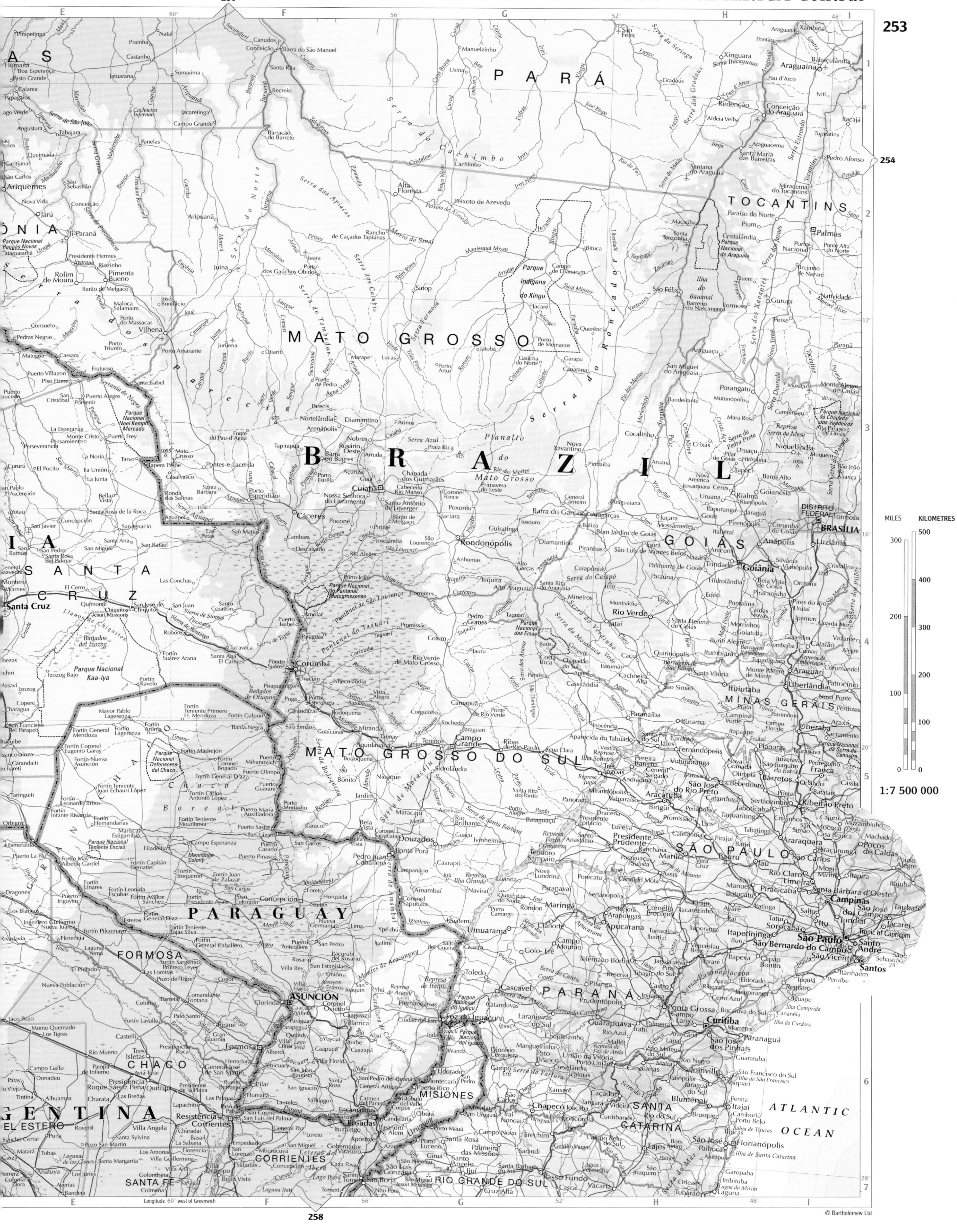

ATLANTIC OCEAN

METRES / FEET scale:

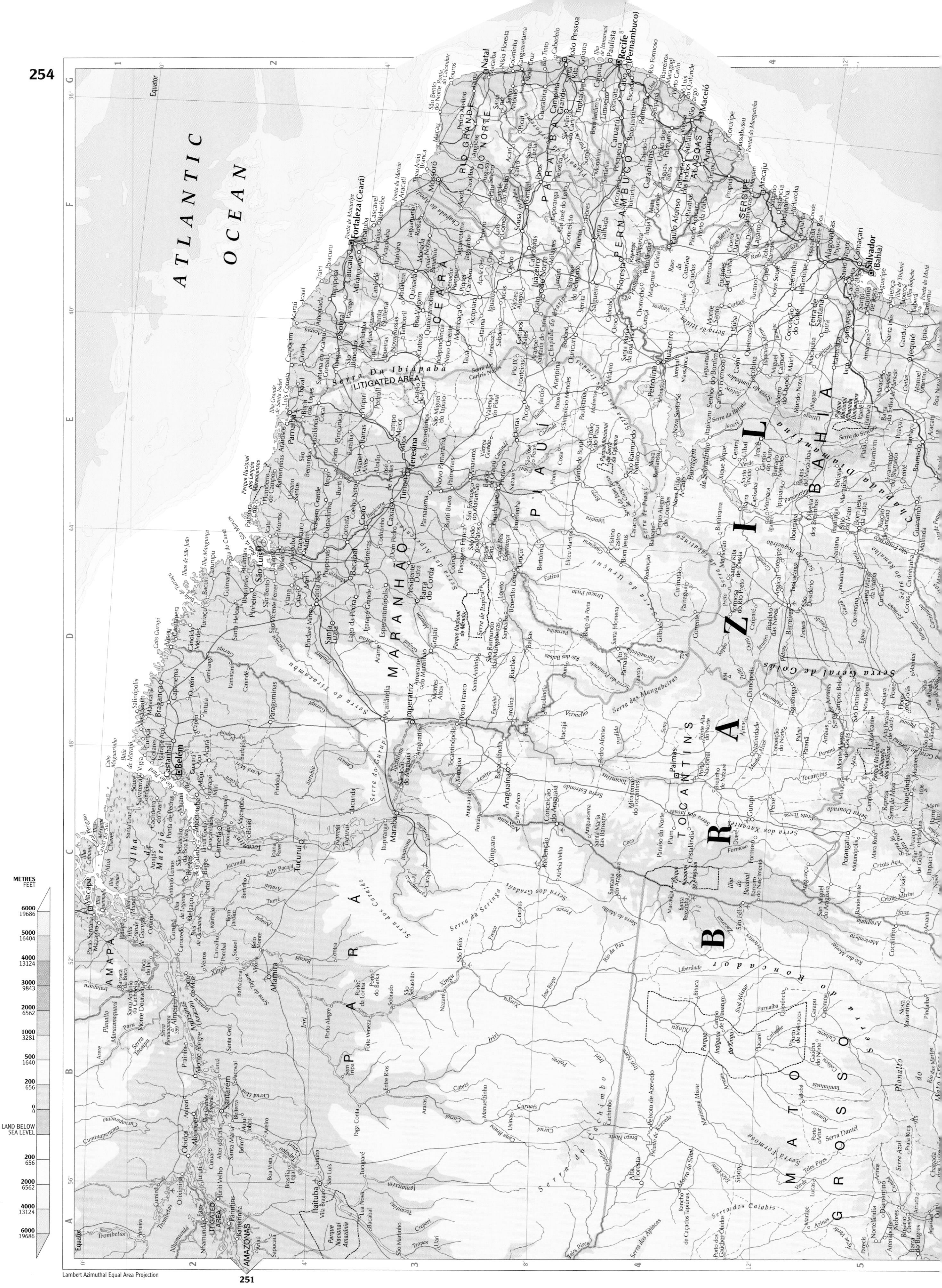

METRES	FEET
6000	19686
5000	16404
4000	13124
3000	9843
2000	6562
1000	3281
500	1640
200	656
0	0
LAND BELOW SEA LEVEL	
200	656
2000	6562
4000	13124
6000	19686

BRAZIL

Major states and labels: AMAZONAS, AMAPÁ, PARÁ, MARANHÃO, PIAUÍ, CEARÁ, RIO GRANDE DO NORTE, PARAÍBA, PERNAMBUCO, ALAGOAS, SERGIPE, BAHIA, TOCANTINS, MATO GROSSO, GOIÁS

Cities: Fortaleza (Ceará), Natal, Recife (Pernambuco), Maceió, Salvador (Bahia), Aracaju, João Pessoa, Campina Grande, Mossoró, Sobral, Parnaíba, Teresina, São Luís, Belém, Macapá, Santarém, Imperatriz, Marabá, Palmas, Juazeiro, Petrolina, Barreiras

LITIGATED AREA

Serra Da Ibiapaba, Serra Geral de Goiás, Serra das Mangabeiras, Serra do Roncador, Chapada Diamantina

Lambert Azimuthal Equal Area Projection

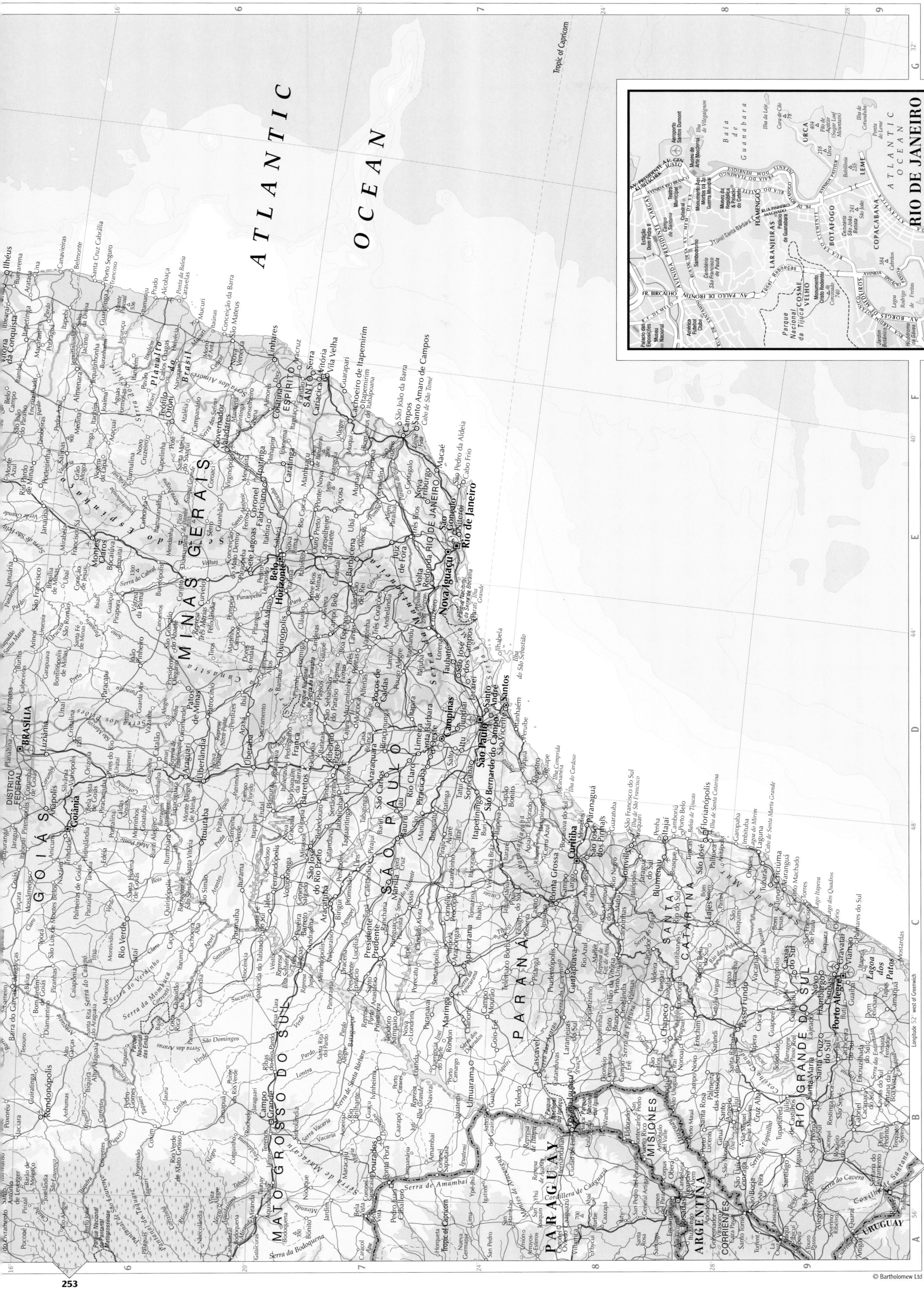

ATLANTIC

OCEAN

MINAS GERAIS

ESPÍRITO SANTO

GOIÁS

DISTRITO FEDERAL

BRASÍLIA

Belo Horizonte

Rio de Janeiro

São Paulo

SÃO PAULO

PARANÁ

Curitiba

SANTA CATARINA

Florianópolis

RIO GRANDE DO SUL

Porto Alegre

MATO GROSSO DO SUL

PARAGUAY

ARGENTINA

CORRIENTES

MISIONES

URUGUAY

Tropic of Capricorn

Longitude 52 west of Greenwich

© Bartholomew Ltd

RIO DE JANEIRO
1:125 000
0 METRES 1000
0 YARDS 1000
ATLANTIC OCEAN

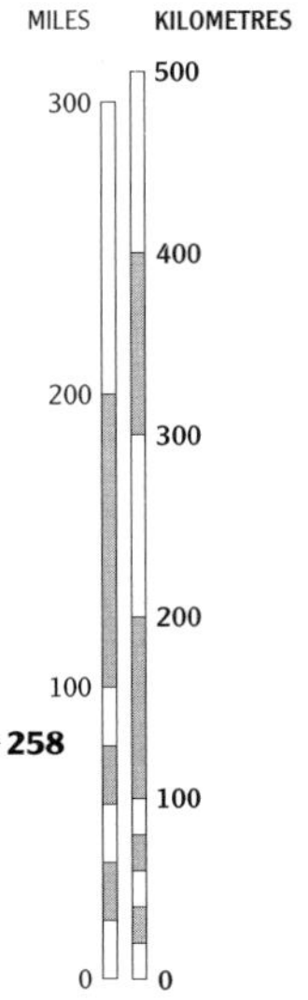

MILES   KILOMETRES
300   500
         400
200   300
100   200
         100
0   0

1:7 500 000

253

258

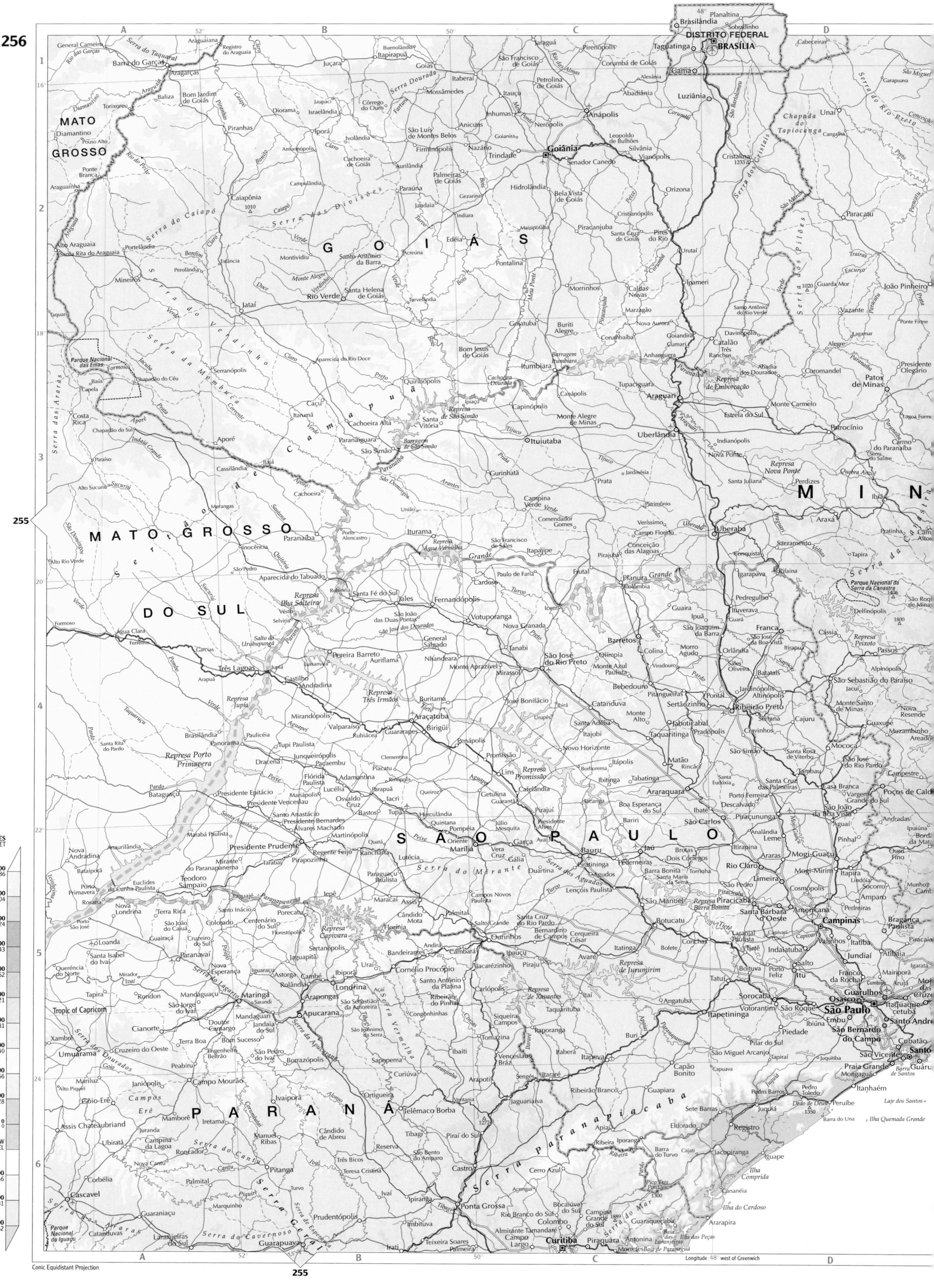

A   52   B   50   C   48   D

Conic Equidistant Projection

MATO GROSSO

GOIÁS

DISTRITO FEDERAL
BRASÍLIA

MATO GROSSO DO SUL

SÃO PAULO

MIN

PARANÁ

Tropic of Capricorn

METRES
FEET

6000 19686
5000 16404
4000 13124
3000 9843
2000 6562
1500 4921
1000 3281
500 1640
200 656
100 328
0
LAND BELOW SEA LEVEL
200 656
1000 3281
2000 6562

Longitude 48 west of Greenwich

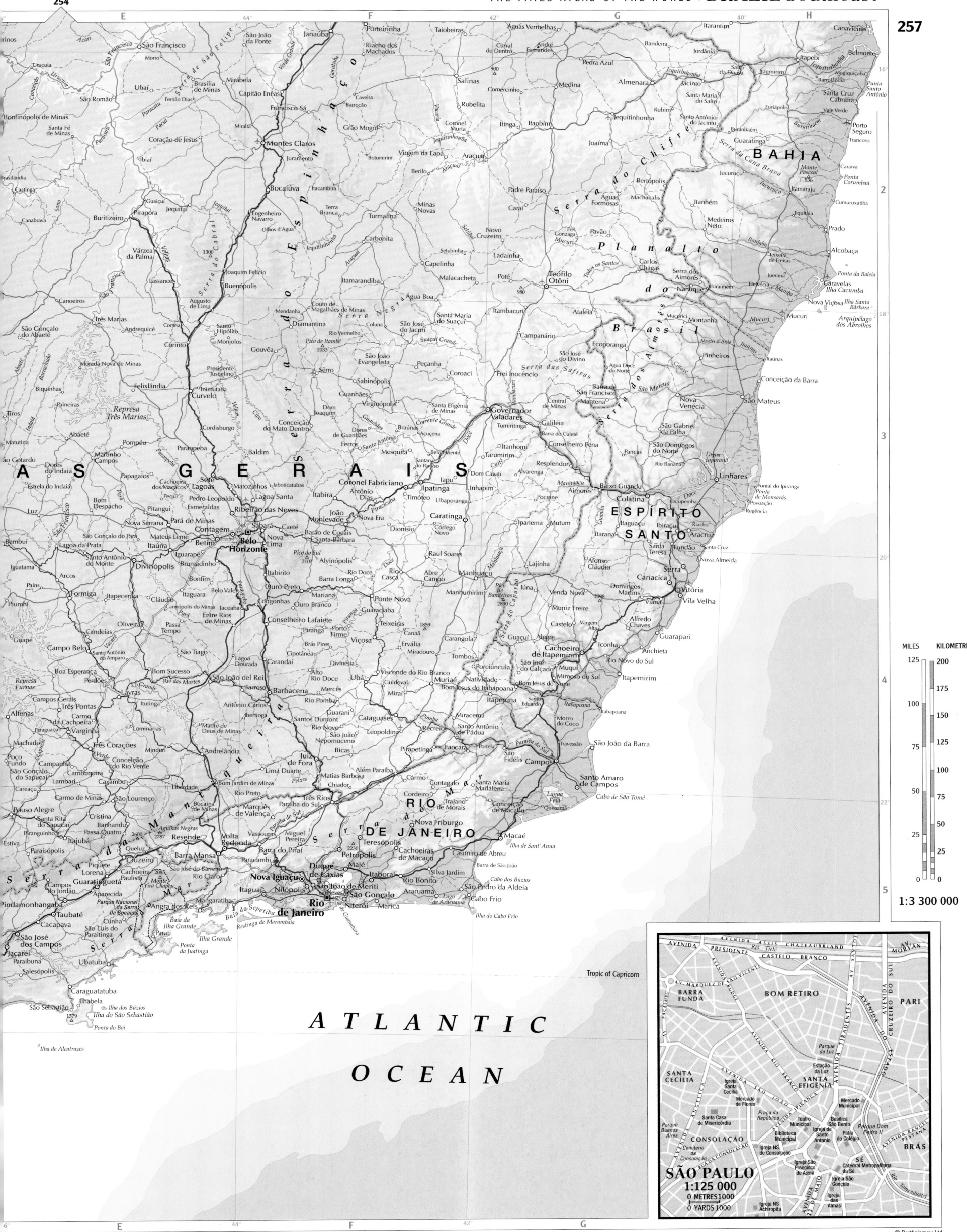

BAHIA

Planalto

Brasil

MINAS GERAIS

ESPÍRITO SANTO

RIO DE JANEIRO

Belo Horizonte

Vitória

Rio de Janeiro

Tropic of Capricorn

ATLANTIC

OCEAN

MILES   KILOMETRES

125   200

         175

100   150

         125

75   100

         75

50   50

25   25

0   0

1:3 300 000

SÃO PAULO
1:125 000

BARRA FUNDA   BOM RETIRO   PARI

SANTA CECILIA   SANTA EFIGÊNIA

CONSOLAÇÃO   SÉ   BRÁS

0 METRES 1000
0 YARDS 1000

© Bartholomew Ltd

Scale / Legend

METRES / FEET

6000 / 19686
4000 / 13124
3000 / 9843
2000 / 6562
1000 / 3281
500 / 1640
200 / 656
0 / 0
LAND BELOW SEA LEVEL
200 / 656
2000 / 6562
4000 / 13124
6000 / 19686

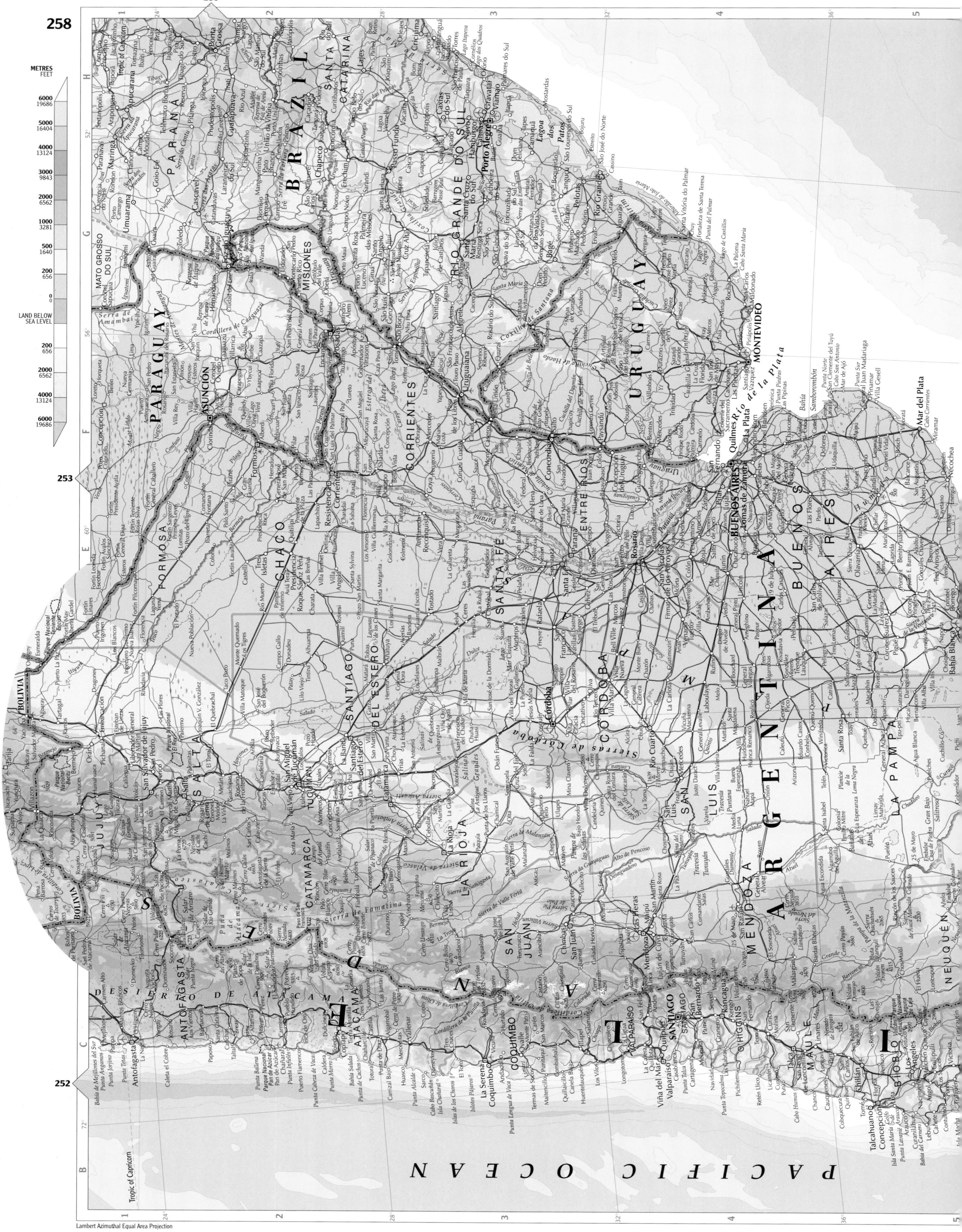

Major labels

BRAZIL

PARANÁ

SANTA CATARINA

RIO GRANDE DO SUL

MATO GROSSO DO SUL

MISIONES

PARAGUAY

ASUNCIÓN

CORRIENTES

URUGUAY

MONTEVIDEO

FORMOSA

CHACO

SANTA FE

ENTRE RÍOS

BUENOS AIRES

BUENOS AIRES

Rosario

Río de la Plata

Mar del Plata

BOLIVIA

JUJUY

SALTA

TUCUMÁN

SANTIAGO DEL ESTERO

CATAMARCA

LA RIOJA

CÓRDOBA

Sierras de Córdoba

SAN LUIS

LA PAMPA

A R G E N T I N A

DESIERTO DE ATACAMA

ANTOFAGASTA

ATACAMA

COQUIMBO

SAN JUAN

MENDOZA

NEUQUÉN

C H I L E

SANTIAGO

VALPARAÍSO

MAULE

BÍO BÍO

PACIFIC OCEAN

Tropic of Capricorn

Lambert Azimuthal Equal Area Projection

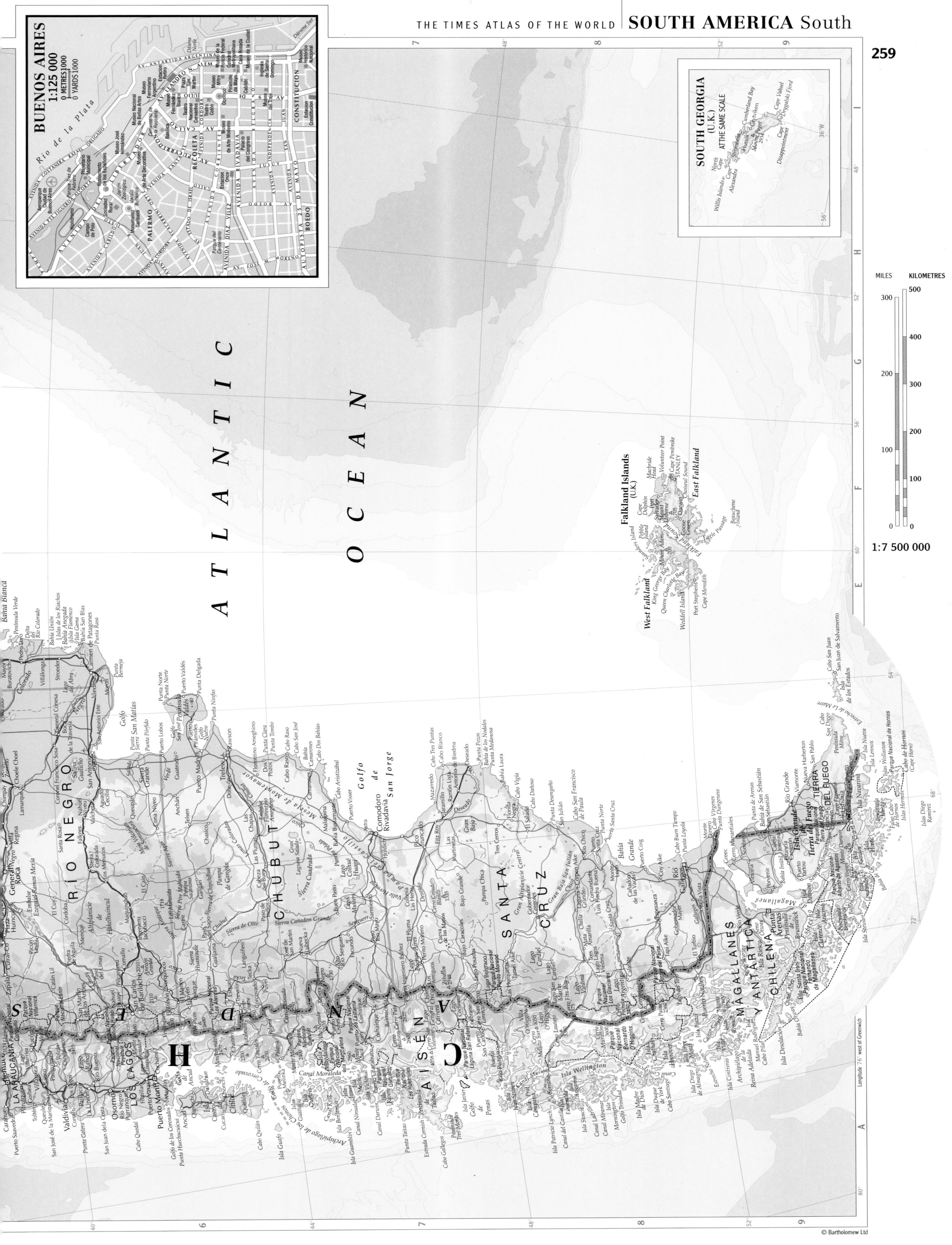
BUENOS AIRES
1:125 000
0 METRES 1000
0 YARDS 1000
Río de la Plata
SOUTH GEORGIA
(U.K.)
AT THE SAME SCALE
ATLANTIC
OCEAN
Falkland Islands
(U.K.)
West Falkland
East Falkland
STANLEY
MILES
KILOMETRES
1:7 500 000
RÍO NEGRO
CHUBUT
SANTA CRUZ
AISÉN
LOS LAGOS
LA ARAUCANÍA
MAGALLANES Y ANTÁRTICA CHILENA
TIERRA DEL FUEGO
Golfo San Jorge
Comodoro Rivadavia
Punta Arenas
Isla Grande de Tierra del Fuego
Longitude 76° west of Greenwich

A | B | 70° | C | 68° | D | 66° | E

PACIFIC OCEAN

COQUIMBO

SAN JUAN

LA RIOJA

CÓRDOBA

VALPARAÍSO

SANTIAGO

O'HIGGINS

SAN LUIS

MENDOZA

ARGEN

C H I L E

A N D E S

C O R D I L L E R A

MAULE

PAMPA SECA

BÍOBÍO

LA PAMPA

NEUQUÉN

LA ARAUCANÍA

RÍO NEGRO

La Serena · Coquimbo · Ovalle · Illapel · San Felipe · Los Andes · Viña del Mar · Valparaíso · Santiago · San Bernardo · Rancagua · San Fernando · Curicó · Talca · Linares · Chillán · Los Ángeles · Angol · Temuco

San Juan · Mendoza · Godoy Cruz · Maipú · San Martín · San Rafael · Malargüe · Neuquén · Cipolletti · General Roca

METRES / FEET

METRES	FEET
6000	19686
5000	16404
4000	13124
3000	9843
2000	6562
1500	4921
1000	3281
500	1640
200	656
100	328
0	0
LAND BELOW SEA LEVEL	
200	656
1000	3281
2000	6562

Conic Equidistant Projection

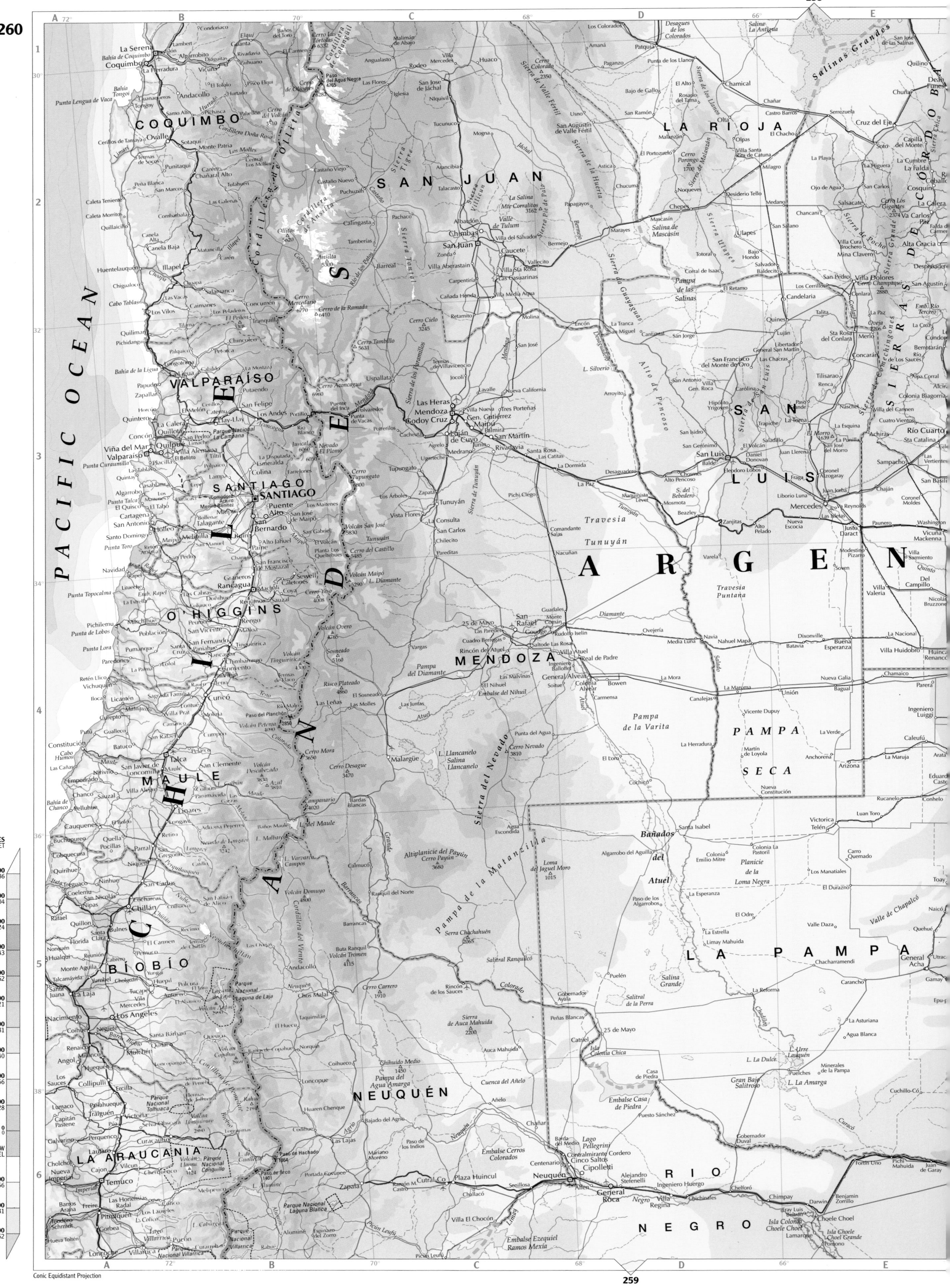

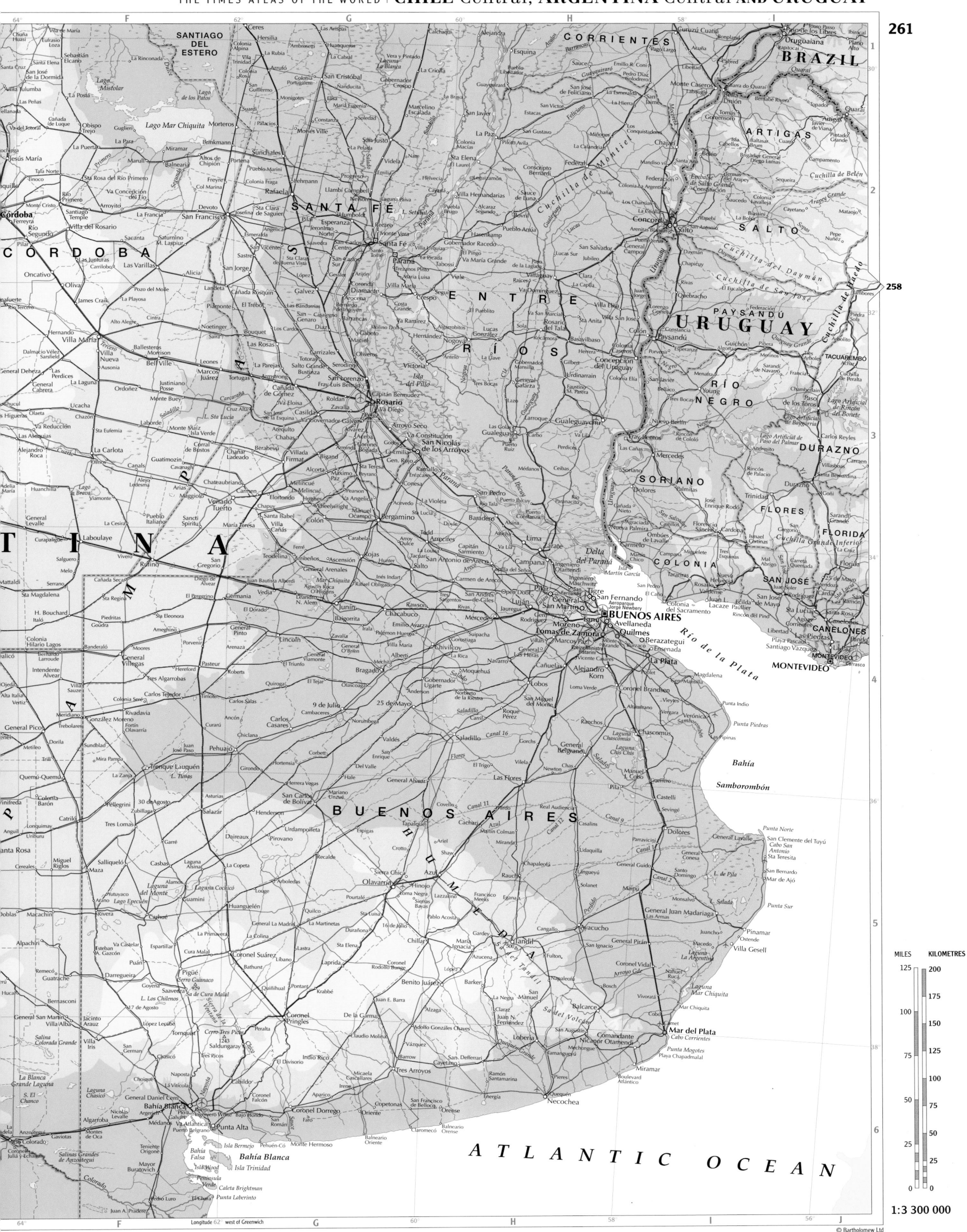
SANTIAGO DEL ESTERO
CORRIENTES
BRAZIL
ARTIGAS
SALTO
CÓRDOBA
SANTA FÉ
ENTRE RÍOS
PAYSANDÚ
URUGUAY
TACUAREMBÓ
RÍO NEGRO
DURAZNO
SORIANO
FLORES
FLORIDA
COLONIA
SAN JOSÉ
CANELONES
MONTEVIDEO
BUENOS AIRES
La Plata
Río de la Plata
Bahía Samborombón
Mar del Plata
Bahía Blanca
Rosario
Córdoba
Santa Fé
Paraná
Concordia
Tandil
Necochea
Lago Mar Chiquita
ATLANTIC OCEAN
258
MILES
KILOMETRES
1:3 300 000
Longitude 62° west of Greenwich

ATLA

QUE

SCOTIA RIDGE

SCOTIA SEA

SCOTIA RIDGE

ARGENTINE CLAIM

BRITISH ANTARCTIC TERRITORY

WEDDELL ABYSSAL PLAIN

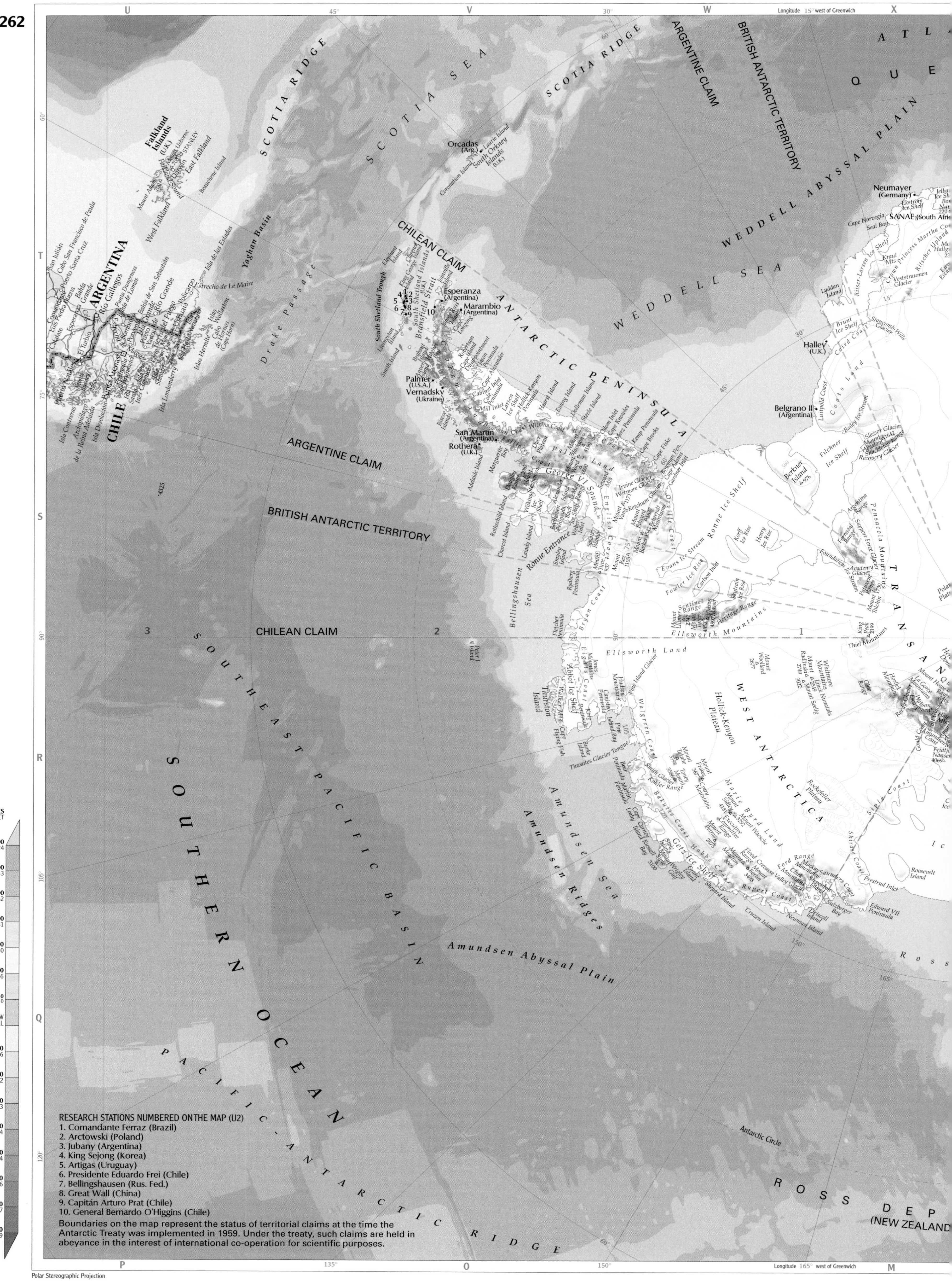

Longitude 15° west of Greenwich

Falkland Islands (U.K.)

PORT STANLEY
West Falkland
East Falkland
Beauchene Island
Mount Adam

Orcadas (Arg.)
Coronation Island
Laurie Island
South Orkney Islands (U.K.)

Neumayer (Germany)
Ekström Ice Shelf
SANAE (South Africa)

CHILEAN CLAIM

Esperanza (Argentina)
Marambio (Argentina)

Cape Norvegia
Seal Bay

Riiser-Larsen Ice Shelf

Kraul Mts
Princess Martha Coast

ARGENTINA

San Julián
Cabo San Francisco de Paula
Puerto Santa Cruz
Río Gallegos
Bahía Grande
Punta Dúngeness
Bahía de San Sebastián
Río Grande
Estrecho de Le Maire
Isla de los Estados
Tierra del Fuego

CHILE

Puerto Williams
Punta Arenas
Archipiélago de la Reina Adelaida
Isla Contreras
Isla Desolación
Isla Londonderry

Drake Passage

South Shetland Islands

South Shetland Trough

Yaghan Basin

King George Island
Elephant Island
Bransfield Strait

ANTARCTIC PENINSULA

Palmer (U.S.A.)
Vernadsky (Ukraine)

Larsen Ice Shelf

WEDDELL SEA

Halley (U.K.)

Brunt Ice Shelf
Caird Coast

Lyddan Island

Coats Land

Luitpold Coast

Belgrano II (Argentina)

Filchner Ice Shelf

Slessor Glacier
Recovery Glacier

ARGENTINE CLAIM

San Martín (Argentina)
Rothera (U.K.)

Palmer Land

George VI Sound

English Coast

Orville Coast

Ronne Ice Shelf

Berkner Island

Pensacola Mountains

BRITISH ANTARCTIC TERRITORY

Ronne Entrance

Ronne Ice Shelf

Evans Ice Stream

Fowler Ice Rise

Ellsworth Mountains

Henry Ice Rise
Korff Ice Rise

Bellingshausen Sea

Bryan Coast

Fletcher Peninsula

Sentinel Range
Heritage Range

Ellsworth Land

Mount Woollard

Thiel Mountains

TRANS

CHILEAN CLAIM

Abbot Ice Shelf

Thurston Island

Walgreen Coast

Ellsworth Land

WEST ANTARCTICA

Hollick-Kenyon Plateau

Whitmore Mountains

Rockefeller Plateau

Thwaites Glacier Tongue

Amundsen Sea

Pine Island Bay

Bakutis Coast

MARIE BYRD LAND

Amundsen Ridges

Getz Ice Shelf

Hobbs Coast

Ruppert Coast

Ford Range

Ross Ice Shelf

METRES / FEET

SOUTHEAST PACIFIC BASIN

SOUTHERN OCEAN

Amundsen Abyssal Plain

Antarctic Circle

Saunders Coast

Siple Coast

Sulzberger Bay

Edward VII Peninsula

Roosevelt Island

Prestrud Inlet

PACIFIC-ANTARCTIC RIDGE

ROSS DEP (NEW ZEALAND)

4000 / 13124
3000 / 9843
2000 / 6562
1000 / 3281
500 / 1640
200 / 656
0
LAND BELOW SEA LEVEL
200 / 656
2000 / 6562
3000 / 9843
4000 / 13124
5000 / 16404
6000 / 19686
7000 / 22967
9000 / 29529

RESEARCH STATIONS NUMBERED ON THE MAP (U2)
1. Comandante Ferraz (Brazil)
2. Arctowski (Poland)
3. Jubany (Argentina)
4. King Sejong (Korea)
5. Artigas (Uruguay)
6. Presidente Eduardo Frei (Chile)
7. Bellingshausen (Rus. Fed.)
8. Great Wall (China)
9. Capitán Arturo Prat (Chile)
10. General Bernardo O'Higgins (Chile)

Boundaries on the map represent the status of territorial claims at the time the Antarctic Treaty was implemented in 1959. Under the treaty, such claims are held in abeyance in the interest of international co-operation for scientific purposes.

Polar Stereographic Projection

Longitude 165° west of Greenwich

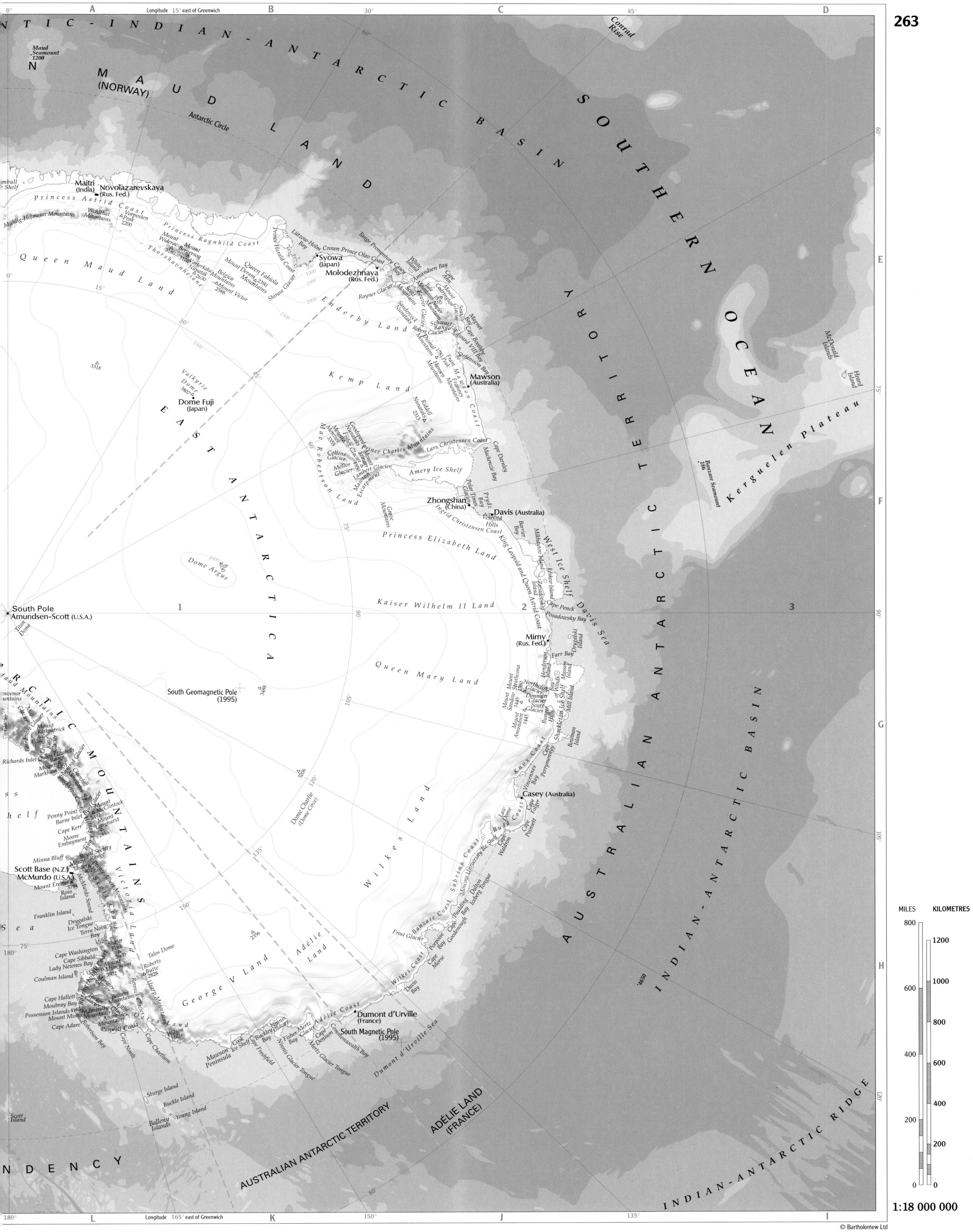
Longitude 15° east of Greenwich
Longitude 165° east of Greenwich
SOUTHERN OCEAN
ATLANTIC-INDIAN-ANTARCTIC BASIN
QUEEN MAUD LAND (NORWAY)
Antarctic Circle
Maud Seamount 1200
Maitri (India)
Novolazarevskaya (Rus. Fed.)
Princess Astrid Coast
Princess Ragnhild Coast
Queen Maud Land
Syowa (Japan)
Molodezhnaya (Rus. Fed.)
Enderby Land
Kemp Land
Mawson (Australia)
Mawson Coast
Dome Fuji (Japan)
Valkyrie Dome
EAST ANTARCTICA
Prince Charles Mountains
Lars Christensen Coast
Amery Ice Shelf
Mac Robertson Land
Zhongshan (China)
Davis (Australia)
Ingrid Christensen Coast
Princess Elizabeth Land
Dome Argus
Kaiser Wilhelm II Land
West Ice Shelf
Davis Sea
Mirny (Rus. Fed.)
Queen Mary Land
Shackleton Ice Shelf
South Pole
Amundsen-Scott (U.S.A.)
South Geomagnetic Pole (1995)
Knox Coast
Casey (Australia)
Dome Charlie (Dome Circe)
Wilkes Land
Sabrina Coast
Banzare Coast
Adélie Land
George V Land
Dumont d'Urville (France)
South Magnetic Pole (1995)
Dumont d'Urville Sea
TRANSANTARCTIC MOUNTAINS
Scott Base (N.Z.)
McMurdo (U.S.A.)
Ross Island
Victoria Land
Cape Adare
Balleny Islands
Scott Island
AUSTRALIAN ANTARCTIC TERRITORY
ADÉLIE LAND (FRANCE)
AUSTRALIAN ANTARCTIC BASIN
INDIAN-ANTARCTIC BASIN
INDIAN-ANTARCTIC RIDGE
Kerguelen Plateau
Banzare Seamount
McDonald Islands
Heard Island
Conrad Rise
MILES
KILOMETRES
1:18 000 000

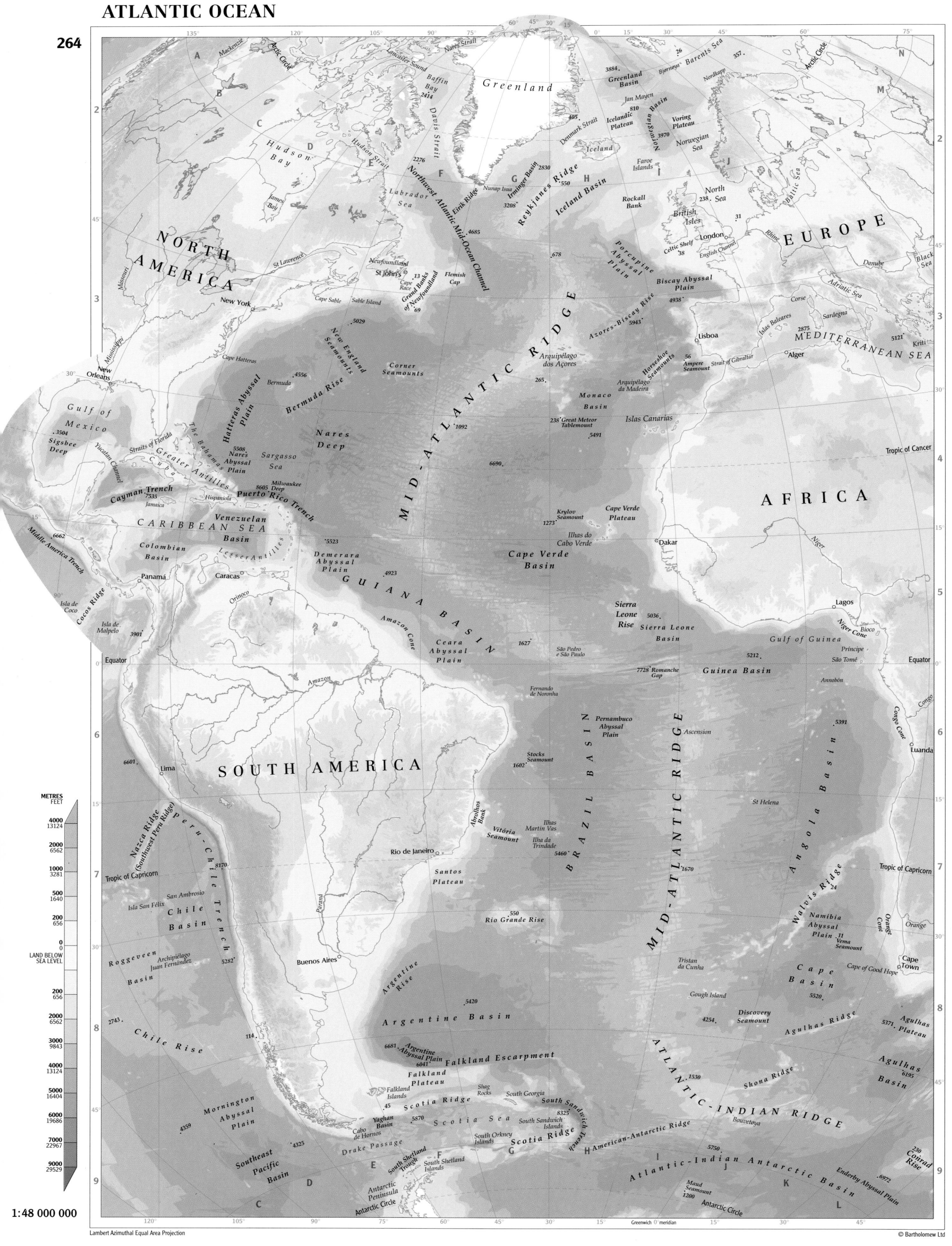

Lambert Azimuthal Equal Area Projection

© Bartholomew Ltd

ASIA

Black Sea 2210
Caspian Sea 1025
Aral Sea
Mediterranean Sea
Tigris
Euphrates
The Gulf
Strait of Hormuz
Gulf of Oman 3694
Mashtah
Indus
Karachi
Indus Cone
Ganges
Calcutta
Ganges Cone
Mumbai
Gulf of Khambhat
.3954
Bay of Bengal
Yangon
Andaman Islands
Andaman Basin 4267
Gulf of Thailand
Mui Ca Mau
22'
Strait of Malacca
Huang He
Bo Hai
Korea Bay
Yellow Sea .67
Sea of Japan
Japan Basin 3510
Hokkaido
Honshu
Tokyo
Shikoku
Kyushu
Chang Jiang
Shanghai
Guangzhou
Gulf of Tongking
Hainan
Taiwan Strait
Taiwan
Kyushu–Palau Ridge
Ryukyu Trench 7460
.7181
Nansei-shoto
Tropic of Cancer
South China Sea 5560
Luzon Strait
Batan Islands
Cape Engaño
Luzon
Palawan
Palawan Trough
Sulu Sea
Philippines
Philippine Basin .6745
Philippine Trench .10057
Mindanao
Celebes Sea .5484
Halmahera
Molucca Sea
Seram Sea
Seram
Banda Sea 7288
Weber .7258
Buru
Sulawesi
Makassar Strait
Borneo
Bangka
Java Sea
Jakarta
Java
Flores Sea
Flores
Sumba
Sumbawa
Bali
Timor
Timor Sea
Melville Island
Arafura Sea
Arafura Shelf
New Guinea
Gulf of Papua
Torres Strait
Cape York
Cape Arnhem
Gulf of Carpentaria
Cape Lévêque
Exmouth Plateau
North West Cape
.1924
North Australian Basin
WEST AUSTRALIAN BASIN
COCOS BASIN 2302
Cocos Islands
Investigator Ridge .6360
Christmas Island
Java Trench (Sunda Trench) 7125
Java Ridge
Kepulauan Mentawai
Sunda Shelf
Singapore
Sumatera
NINETYEAST RIDGE .549
East Indiaman Ridge
Broken Plateau 2067
.3745
MID-INDIAN BASIN .5421
.4735
Maldives
Chagos-Laccadive Ridge
.5406
Diego Garcia
Chagos Archipelago
Chagos Trench
Laccadive Islands
Cape Comorin
Sri Lanka
Gulf of Mannar
Nicobar Islands
Carlsberg Ridge .1682
.5803
Gulf of Aden
Aden
Suqutra
Red Sea 3039
Tropic of Cancer
Arabian Basin
Arabian Sea
.1481
Somali Basin 5060
Mombasa
Pemba Island
Zanzibar Island
Mafia Island
Njazidja
Comoros
Mayotte
AFRICA
Amirante Islands
Amirante Trench
Seychelles 5273
Aldabra Islands
Farquhar Islands
Agalega Islands
Mascarene Ridge
Vema Trench 6402
Mascarene Plain
Mascarene Basin
Ile Tromelin
Cargados Carajos Islands
Mauritius 5194
Réunion
Rodrigues Island
Madagascar
Madagascar Basin 6400
Madagascar Ridge
Mozambique Channel
Bassas da India
Europa
Tropic of Capricorn
Durban 1207
Natal Basin 6291
Mozambique Ridge
Agulhas Plateau 5371
Agulhas Basin 6195
MID-INDIAN RIDGE
SOUTHWEST INDIAN RIDGE
Crozet Basin 5195
Ile Amsterdam
Ile St Paul 4181
Crozet Plateau
Prince Edward Islands
Iles Crozet 4590
Iles Kerguelen
Kerguelen Plateau
Heard Island
McDonald Islands
230 Conrad Rise
Banzare Seamount .186
SOUTHEAST INDIAN RIDGE
SOUTHERN OCEAN
Indian-Antarctic Basin .3650
INDIAN-ANTARCTIC RIDGE 1646
.3902
Perth Basin 5746
Perth
Naturaliste Plateau
Cape Leeuwin
Diamantina Deep 6602
7102
South Australian Basin .3670
Great Australian Bight
AUSTRALIA
Darling
Murray
Sydney
Melbourne
Tasmania
Bass Strait
South East Cape .770
South Tasman Rise
Tasman Abyssal Plain
Tasman Sea
Tasman Basin 5576
Lord Howe Rise
Lord Howe Island
North Island
Auckland
Wellington
New Zealand
South Island
Stewart Island
Snares Islands
Campbell Plateau
Bounty Islands
Auckland Islands
Campbell Island
Antipodes Islands .6096
.60
Macquarie Ridge
Macquarie Island
Atlantic-Indian Ridge
Shona Ridge
Bouvetoya
5750
American-Antarctic Ridge
Atlantic-Indian Antarctic Basin
Enderby Abyssal Plain 6972
Weddell Abyssal Plain
Weddell Sea
Maud Seamount 1200
Cape Norvegia
Lützow-Holm Bay
Cape Darnley
Davis Sea
Vincennes Bay
Cape Poinsett
Cape Penck
Faber Bay
Balleny Islands
956
Cape North
Cape Adare
Coulman Island
Ross Sea
ANTARCTICA
South Pole
Antarctic Circle
Antarctic Peninsula
South Shetland Islands
South Orkney Islands
South Georgia
Shag Rocks
South Sandwich Islands
South Sandwich Trench 8125
Scotia Sea
Scotia Ridge
Pacific-Antarctic Ridge

Equator

Tropic of Capricorn

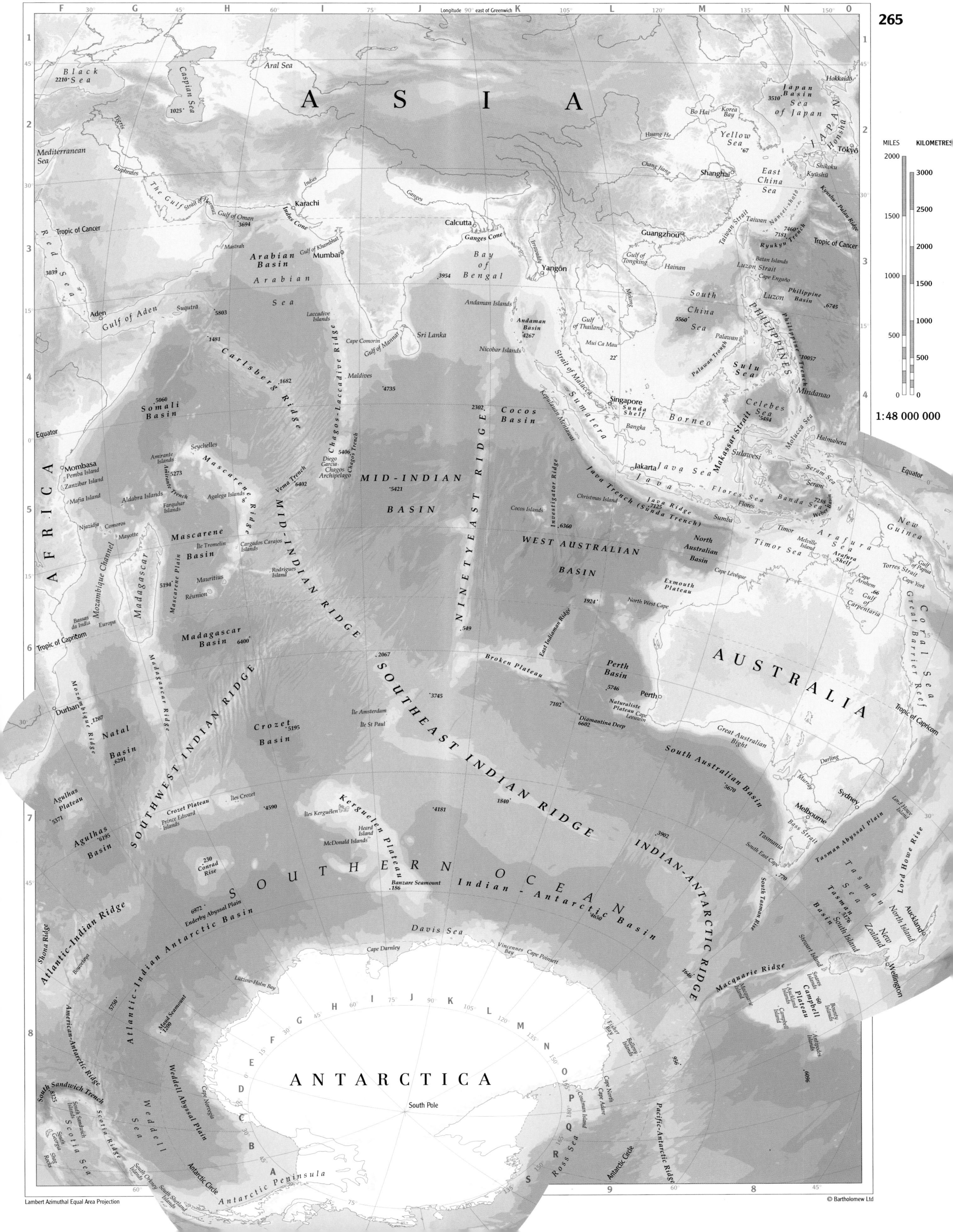

Longitude 90° east of Greenwich

Lambert Azimuthal Equal Area Projection
© Bartholomew Ltd

MILES 2000 1500 1000 500 0
KILOMETRES 3000 2500 2000 1500 1000 500 0

1:48 000 000

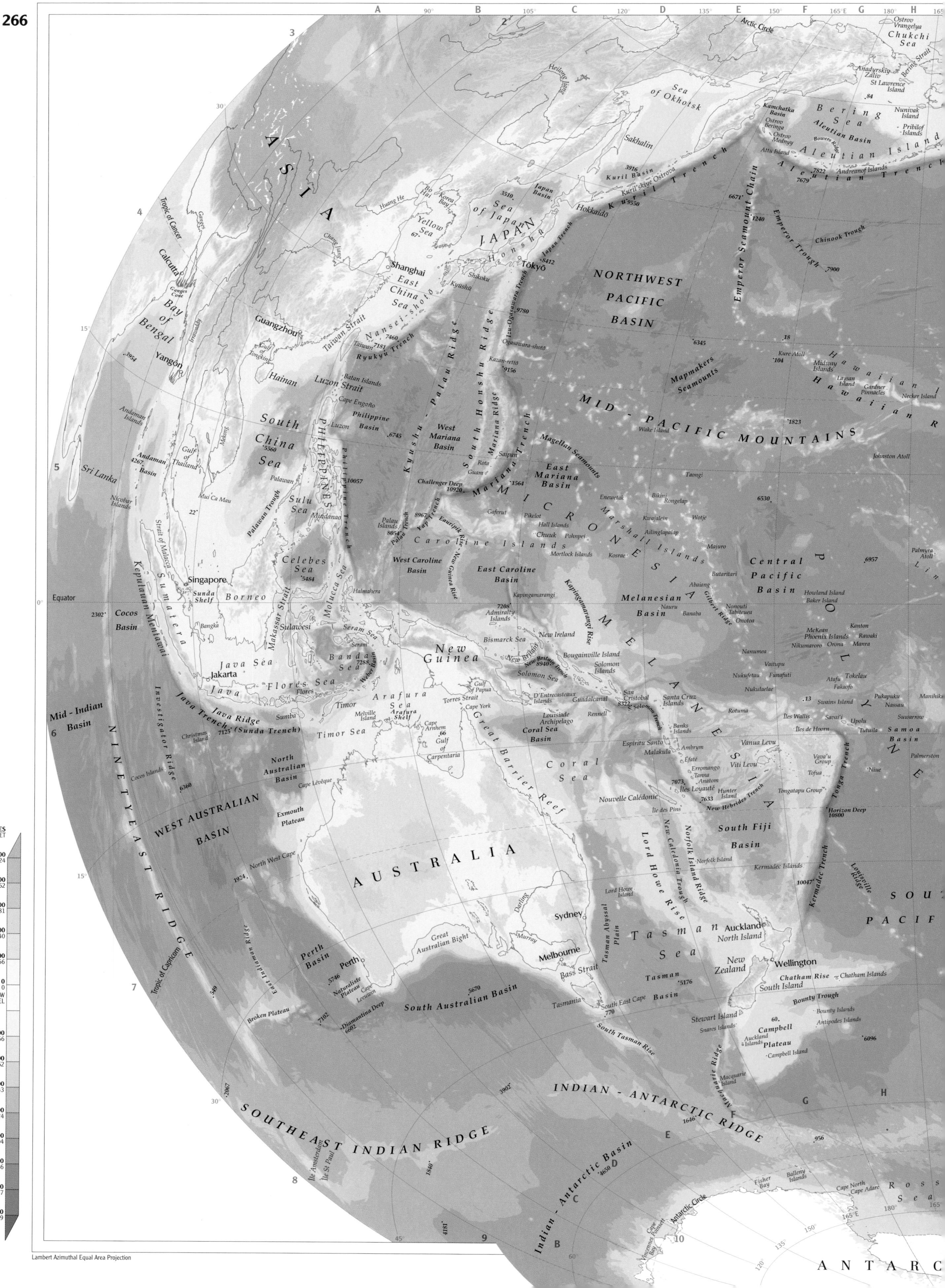

A S I A
Arctic Circle
Ostrov Vrangelya
Chukchi Sea
Bering Strait
Anadyrskiy Zaliv
St Lawrence Island
Nunivak Island
Pribilof Islands
Bering Sea
Kamchatka Basin
Ostrov Beringa
Ostrov Mednyy
Bowers Ridge
Aleutian Basin
Aleutian Islands
Aleutian Trench
Attu Island
Andreanof Islands
Sea of Okhotsk
Heilong Jiang
Sakhalin
Kuril Basin
Kuril'skiye Ostrova
Kuril Trench
Hokkaidō
Emperor Seamount Chain
Emperor Trough
Chinook Trough
Japan Basin
Sea of Japan
JAPAN
Honshu
Japan Trench
Tōkyō
Bo Hai
Korea Bay
Huang He
Yellow Sea
Chang Jiang
Shanghai
East China Sea
Nansei-shotō
Kyūshū
Shikoku
Izu-Ogasawara Trench
Ogasawara-shotō
Kazan-rettō
NORTHWEST PACIFIC BASIN
Tropic of Cancer
Ganges
Calcutta
Ganges Cone
Bay of Bengal
Irrawaddy
Yangôn
Guangzhou
Taiwan Strait
Taiwan
Ryukyu Trench
Gulf of Tongking
Hainan
Luzon Strait
Batan Islands
Cape Engaño
Luzon
Philippine Basin
PHILIPPINES
Philippine Trench
Kyushu - Palau Ridge
South Honshu Ridge
Mariana Ridge
Mariana Trench
West Mariana Basin
Mapmakers Seamounts
Kure Atoll
Midway Islands
Laysan Island
Gardner Pinnacles
Necker Island
Hawaiian Islands
Hawaiian Ridge
MID - PACIFIC MOUNTAINS
Wake Island
Johnston Atoll
Andaman Islands
Andaman Basin
Sri Lanka
Nicobar Islands
Mekong
Gulf of Thailand
Mui Ca Mau
South China Sea
Palawan
Palawan Trough
Sulu Sea
Mindanao
Magellan Seamounts
Saipan
Rota
Guam
Challenger Deep
East Mariana Basin
M I C R O N E S I A
Taongi
Enewetak
Bikini
Rongelap
Marshall Islands
Kwajalein
Wotje
Ailinglapalap
Majuro
Gaferut
Pikelot
Hall Islands
Chuuk
Pohnpei
Mortlock Islands
Kosrae
Palau Islands
Yap Trench
Palau Trench
Eauripik Rise
Caroline Islands
West Caroline Basin
New Guinea Rise
East Caroline Basin
Strait of Malacca
Singapore
Celebes Sea
Molucca Sea
Halmahera
Central Pacific Basin
Palmyra Atoll
Line Islands
POLYNESIA
Kepulauan Mentawai
Sumatera
Sunda Shelf
Borneo
Equator
Cocos Basin
Bangka
Makassar Strait
Sulawesi
Seram
Seram Sea
Banda Sea
Weber Basin
Kapingamarangi
Admiralty Islands
Kapingamarangi Rise
Butaritari
Abaiang
Gilbert Ridge
Melanesian Basin
Nauru
Banaba
Nonouti
Tabiteuea
Onotoa
Howland Island
Baker Island
Java Sea
Jakarta
Java
Flores Sea
Flores
Timor
Sumba
Bismarck Sea
New Ireland
New Britain
New Britain Trench
Bougainville Island
Solomon Islands
Solomon Sea
New Guinea
Gulf of Papua
Torres Strait
Cape York
Arafura Sea
Arafura Shelf
Melville Island
Cape Arnhem
Gulf of Carpentaria
D'Entrecasteaux Islands
Guadalcanal
Rennell
San Cristobal
Solomon Trench
Santa Cruz Islands
McKean
Phoenix Islands
Kanton
Rawaki
Nikumaroro
Orona
Manra
Nanumea
Vaitupu
Nukufetau
Funafuti
Nukulaelae
Atafu
Tokelau
Fakaofo
Pukapuka
Nassau
Manihiki
Swains Island
Suwarrow
Rotuma
Îles Wallis
Savai'i
Upolu
Tutuila
Îles de Hoorn
Samoa Basin
Palmerston
Niue
Tonga Trench
Mid - Indian Basin
Investigator Ridge
Java Ridge
Java Trench (Sunda Trench)
Christmas Island
Timor Sea
North Australian Basin
Cape Lévêque
Cocos Islands
NINETYEAST RIDGE
WEST AUSTRALIAN BASIN
Exmouth Plateau
Great Barrier Reef
Louisiade Archipelago
Coral Sea Basin
Coral Sea
Espiritu Santo
Malakula
Ambrym
Éfaté
Erromango
Tanna
Anatom
Îles Loyauté
Hunter Island
New Hebrides Trench
Banks Islands
Vanua Levu
Viti Levu
Vava'u Group
Tofua
Tongatapu Group
Horizon Deep
Nouvelle Calédonie
Île des Pins
South Fiji Basin
North West Cape
AUSTRALIA
New Caledonia Trough
Norfolk Island Ridge
Norfolk Island
Lord Howe Rise
Lord Howe Island
Kermadec Islands
Kermadec Trench
Louisville Ridge
SOUTH PACIFIC
Darling
Sydney
Tasman Abyssal Plain
Tasman Sea
Auckland
North Island
New Zealand
Wellington
Chatham Rise
Chatham Islands
South Island
Bounty Trough
Bounty Islands
Antipodes Islands
Great Australian Bight
Murray
Melbourne
Bass Strait
Tasmania
South East Cape
Tasman Basin
Perth Basin
Perth
Naturaliste Plateau
Cape Leeuwin
East Indiaman Ridge
Tropic of Capricorn
Broken Plateau
Diamantina Deep
South Australian Basin
South Tasman Rise
Stewart Island
Snares Islands
Campbell Plateau
Auckland Islands
Campbell Island
Macquarie Ridge
Macquarie Island
INDIAN - ANTARCTIC RIDGE
SOUTHEAST INDIAN RIDGE
Île Amsterdam
Île St Paul
Indian - Antarctic Basin
Antarctic Circle
Fisher Bay
Balleny Islands
Cape North
Cape Adare
Ross Sea
Vincennes Bay
Cape Poinsett
ANTARCTICA
METRES
FEET
4000 13124
2000 6562
1000 3281
500 1640
200 656
0 0
LAND BELOW SEA LEVEL
200 656
2000 6562
3000 9843
4000 13124
5000 16404
6000 19686
7000 22967
9000 29529

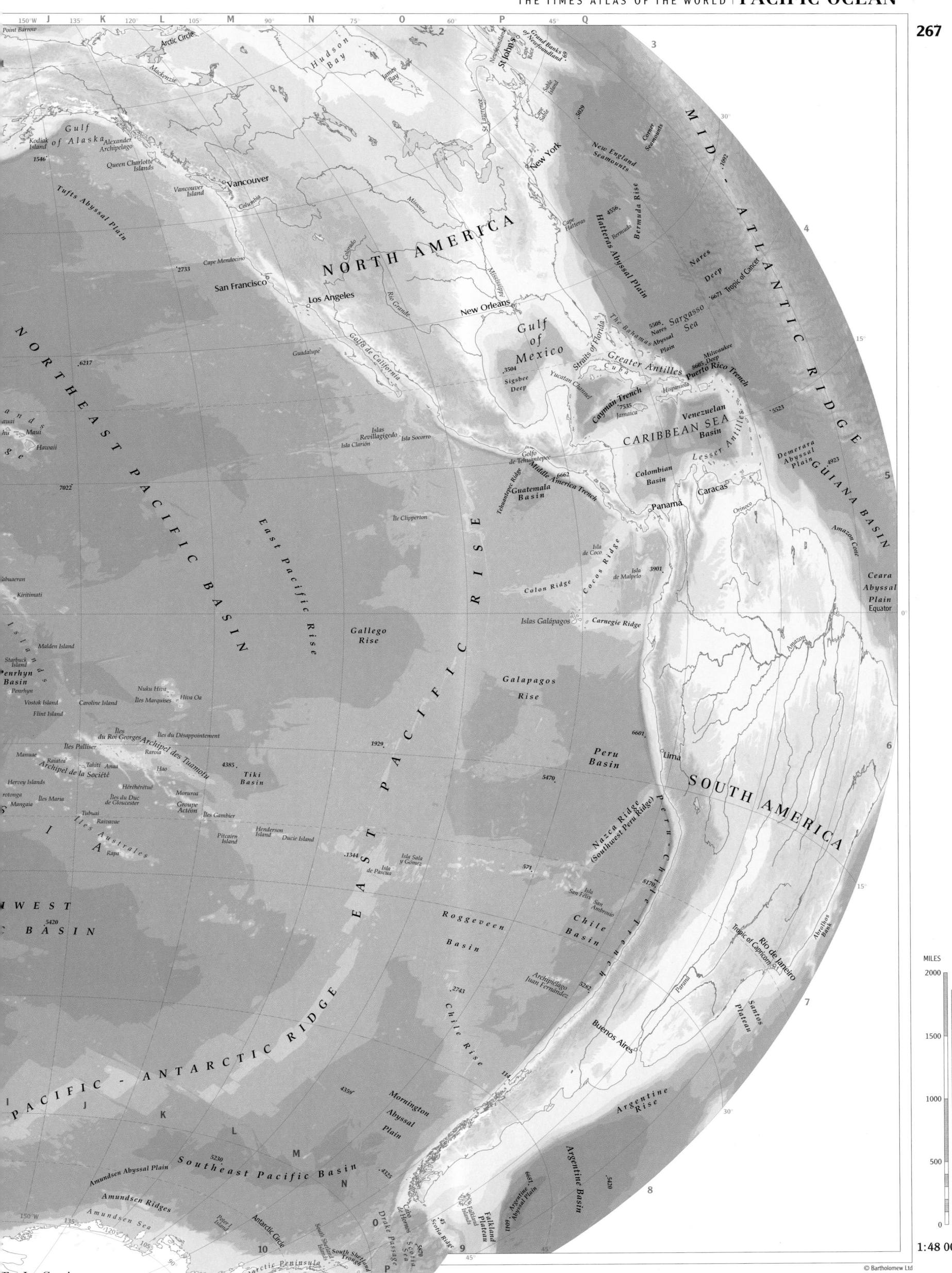

Point Barrow

Arctic Circle

Hudson Bay

James Bay

Mackenzie

Gulf of Alaska

Kodiak Island

1546

Alexander Archipelago

Queen Charlotte Islands

Vancouver Island

Vancouver

Columbia

Tufts Abyssal Plain

Cape Mendocino

2733

San Francisco

Los Angeles

Colorado

Rio Grande

Gulf of Mexico

New Orleans

Mississippi

Missouri

NORTH AMERICA

St John's

Grand Banks of Newfoundland

Cape Race

Cape Sable

New York

Cape Hatteras

New England Seamounts

Corner Seamounts

MID - ATLANTIC RIDGE

Hatteras Abyssal Plain

Bermuda

Bermuda Rise

4556

5225

Nares Deep

6677 Tropic of Cancer

1102

Sargasso Sea

The Bahamas

Nares Abyssal Plain

5508

Straits of Florida

Greater Antilles

Cuba

Milwaukee 8605 Deep

Puerto Rico Trench

Sigsbee Deep

Yucatan Channel

Yucatan Channel

Cayman Trench

7535

Jamaica

Hispaniola

5523

3504

Guadalupe

Golfo de California

Islas Revillagigedo

Isla Socorro

Isla Clarión

6217

NORTHEAST PACIFIC BASIN

7022

ḥū

Kauai

Maui

Hawaii

Île Clipperton

East Pacific Rise

Golfo de Tehuantepec

Tehuantepec Ridge

Middle America Trench

6662

Guatemala Basin

CARIBBEAN SEA

Colombian Basin

Venezuelan Basin

Caracas

Panamá

Lesser Antilles

5523

Demerara Abyssal Plain

4923

GUIANA BASIN

Amazon Cone

Isla de Coco

Cocos Ridge

Colon Ridge

3901

Isla de Malpelo

Ceara Abyssal Plain Equator

0°

Islas Galápagos

Carnegie Ridge

Orinoco

Amazon

abuaeran

Kiritimati

Malden Island

Starbuck Island

Penrhyn Basin

Penrhyn

Vostok Island

Caroline Island

Flint Island

Nuku Hiva

Hiva Oa

Îles Marquises

Islands

Gallego Rise

Galapagos Rise

Peru Basin

6601

Lima

SOUTH AMERICA

Manuae

Raiatea

Tahiti Anaa

Îles Palliser

Hao

Raroia

Îles du Roi Georges

Îles du Désappointement

Archipel des Tuamotu

4385

Tiki Basin

1929

5470

Hervey Islands

Archipel de la Société

Hérehérétué

rotonga

Mangaia

Îles Maria

Îles du Duc de Gloucester

Moruroa

Groupe Actéon

Îles Gambier

Nazca Ridge (Southwest Peru Ridge)

Tubuai

Raivavae

Îles Australes

Rapa

Henderson Island

Ducie Island

Pitcairn Island

1344

Isla Sala y Gómez

Isla de Pascua

571

8170

Chile Basin

Isla San Félix

Isla San Ambrosio

EAST PACIFIC RISE

Roggeveen Basin

WEST

BASIN

5420

Chile Rise

2743

Archipiélago Juan Fernández

5282

Rio de Janeiro

Tropic of Capricorn

Abrolhos Bank

Santos Plateau

Buenos Aires

4359

Mornington Abyssal Plain

Panamá

Argentine Rise

PACIFIC - ANTARCTIC RIDGE

5230

4325

Amundsen Abyssal Plain

Southeast Pacific Basin

Amundsen Ridges

Amundsen Sea

150° W

Antarctic Circle

Pitcairr Island

Antarctic Peninsula

P I C A

Drake Passage

South Orkney Islands

South Shetland Islands

South Sandwich Trench

Scotia Sea

Scotia Ridge

Falkland Islands

Falkland Plateau

Argentine Abyssal Plain

Argentine Basin

5420

MILES

2000

1500

1000

500

0

KILOMETRES

3000

2500

2000

1500

1000

500

0

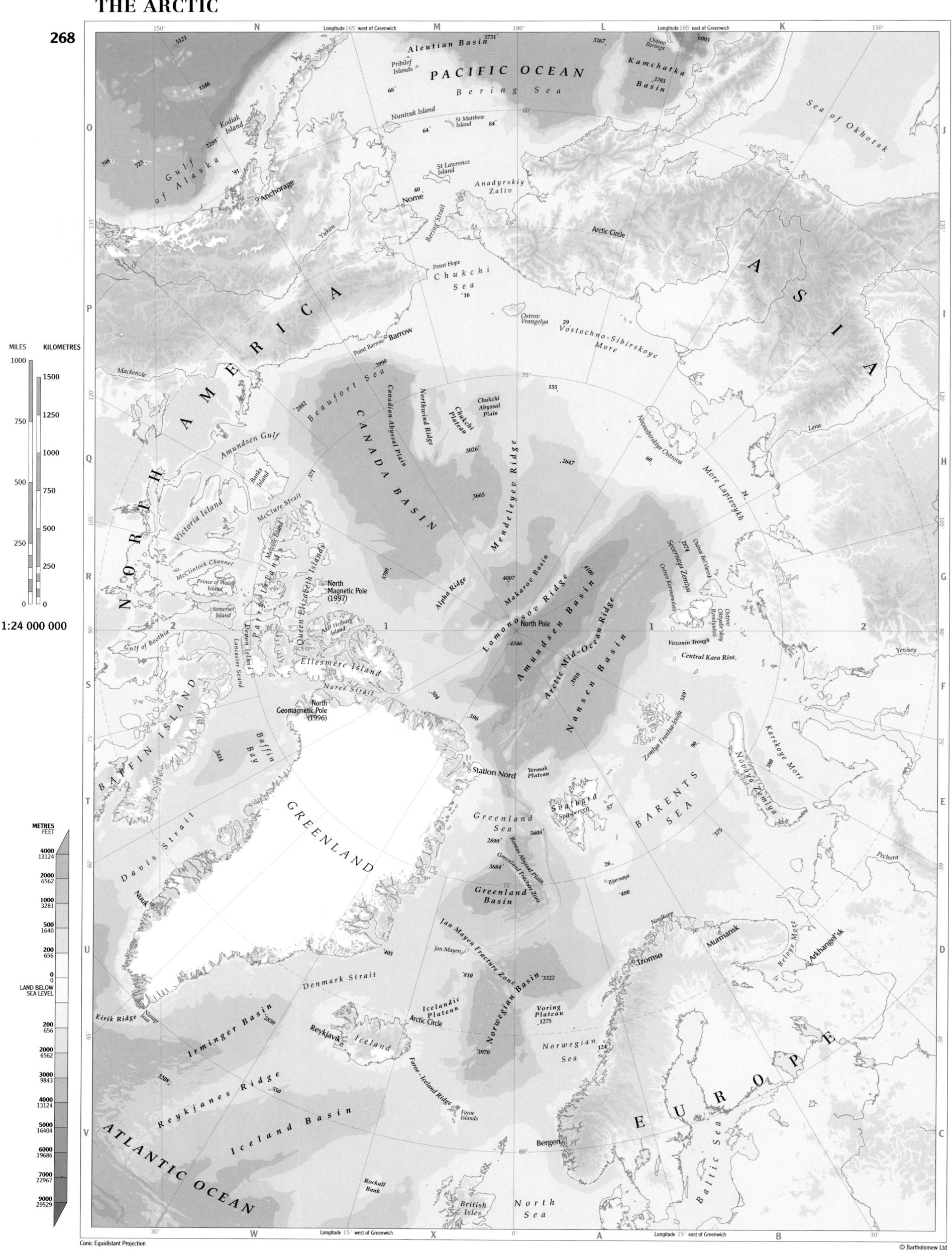

MILES / KILOMETRES

1000 / 1500
750 / 1250
1000
500 / 750
250 / 500
250
0 / 0

1:24 000 000

METRES / FEET

4000 / 13124
2000 / 6562
1000 / 3281
500 / 1640
200 / 656
0 / 0
LAND BELOW
SEA LEVEL
200 / 656
2000 / 6562
3000 / 9843
4000 / 13124
5000 / 16404
6000 / 19686
7000 / 22967
9000 / 29529

Longitude 165° west of Greenwich
Longitude 165° east of Greenwich

PACIFIC OCEAN

Aleutian Basin
Pribilof Islands
Bering Sea
Kamchatka Basin
Sea of Okhotsk
Nunivak Island
St Matthew Island
St Lawrence Island
Anadyrskiy Zaliv
Nome
Anchorage
Kodiak Island
Gulf of Alaska
Yukon
Bering Strait
Arctic Circle
Point Hope
Chukchi Sea
Ostrov Vrangelya
Vostochno-Sibirskoye More
ASIA
Barrow
Point Barrow
Mackenzie
Beaufort Sea
Canadian Abyssal Plain
Northwind Ridge
Chukchi Plateau
Chukchi Abyssal Plain
Lena
NORTH AMERICA
Amundsen Gulf
CANADA BASIN
Mendeleyev Ridge
More Laptevykh
Banks Island
Victoria Island
McClure Strait
Melville Island
Parry Islands
Makarov Basin
Lomonosov Ridge
North Pole
Amundsen Basin
Arctic Mid-Ocean Ridge
Nansen Basin
Ostrov Bol'shevik
Severnaya Zemlya
Ostrov Oktyabr'skoy Revolyutsii
Ostrov Komsomolets
McClintock Channel
Prince of Wales Island
Somerset Island
Gulf of Boothia
North Magnetic Pole (1997)
Alpha Ridge
Axel Heiberg Island
Devon Island
Lancaster Sound
Queen Elizabeth Islands
Ellesmere Island
Nares Strait
North Geomagnetic Pole (1996)
Vozonin Trough
Central Kara Rise
Yenisey
BAFFIN ISLAND
Baffin Bay
Station Nord
Yermak Plateau
Svalbard
Spitsbergen
Zemlya Frantsa-Iosifa
BARENTS SEA
Karskoye More
Novaya Zemlya
Davis Strait
GREENLAND
Greenland Sea
Bjørnøya
Pechora
Nuuk
Denmark Strait
Greenland Fracture Zone
Boreas Abyssal Plain
Greenland Basin
Nordkapp
Murmansk
Belove More
Arkhangel'sk
Jan Mayen Fracture Zone
Jan Mayen
Tromsø
Eirik Ridge
Nunap
Norwegian Basin
Voring Plateau
Norwegian Sea
Baltic Sea
Irminger Basin
Icelandic Plateau
Arctic Circle
Reykjavik
Iceland
EUROPE
Bergen
Reykjanes Ridge
Faroe-Iceland Ridge
Faroe Islands
Rockall Bank
British Isles
North Sea
Iceland Basin
ATLANTIC OCEAN

Longitude 15° west of Greenwich
Longitude 0°
Longitude 15° east of Greenwich

Conic Equidistant Projection

© Bartholomew Ltd

GLOSSARY

Geographical term	Language	Meaning
A		
-á	Icelandic	river
-å	Danish	river
Āb	Farsi	river
Abajo	Spanish	lower
Abbaye	French	abbey
Abhainn	Gaelic	river
Abyār	Arabic	wells
Açude	Portuguese	reservoir
Adası	Azeri, Turkish	island
Adrar	Berber	hills, mountains
Agia, Agios	Greek	saint
Agioi	Greek	saints
Aiguille	French	peak
Ain, 'Ain, 'Aïn, Aïn, 'Aïn	Arabic	spring, well
Akra	Greek	cape, point
Ala-	Finnish	lower
Allt	Gaelic	river
Alpi	Italian	mountain range
Alpe	Slovene	mountain range
Alpen	German	mountain range
Alpes	French	mountain range
Alt-	German	old
Alta	Italian, Portuguese, Spanish	upper
Altiplanicie	Spanish	high plain
Alto	Italian, Portuguese, Spanish	upper
Alto	Spanish	summit
-älv, -älven	Swedish	river
Ano	Greek	upper
Anou, Ânou	Berber	well
Anse	French	bay
Ao	Thai	bay
Archipel	French	archipelago
Archipiélago	Spanish	archipelago
Arenas	Spanish	sands
Argelanots'	Armenian	reserve
Arkhipelag	Russian	archipelago
Arquipélago	Portuguese	archipelago
Arrecife	Spanish	reef
Arriba	Spanish	upper
Arroio	Portuguese	watercourse
Arroyo	Spanish	watercourse
Augstiene	Latvian	hill region
Aust-	Norwegian	east, eastern
Austur-	Icelandic	east, eastern
Avtonomnaya, Avtonomnyy	Russian	autonomous
Āw	Kurdish	river
'Ayn	Arabic	spring, waterhole, well
B		
Baai, -baai	Afrikaans, Dutch	bay
Bāb	Arabic	strait
Bad	German	spa
Badia	Catalan	bay
Bādiyah	Arabic	desert
Bælt	Danish	strait
Bagh	Gaelic	bay
Bahia	Portuguese	bay
Bahía	Spanish	bay
Bahr, Baḥr, Baḩr	Arabic	bay, lake, canal, river, watercourse
Bahra, Baḩra	Arabic	lagoon, lake
Baía	Portuguese	bay
Baie	French	bay
Baixa, Baixo	Portuguese	lower
Baja	Spanish	lower
Bajja	Maltese	bay
Bajo	Spanish	depression, lower
Bālā	Farsi	upper
Ban	Laotian, Thai	village
Banc	Welsh	hill
Banco	Spanish	shoal
Bandao	Chinese	peninsula
Bandar	Arabic, Farsi, Somali	anchorage, inlet, port, harbour
Bandar	Malay	port, town
Banī	Arabic	desert
Banjaran	Malay	mountain range
Baraj, Barajı	Turkish	dam
Barat	Indonesian, Malay	west, western
Barra	Portuguese, Spanish	sandbank, sandbar, spit
Barrage	French	dam
Barragem	Portuguese	dam, reservoir
Barranco	Spanish	gorge, ravine
Baruun	Mongolian	west, western
Bas, Basse	French	lower
Bassin	French	basin
Bāţin, Baţn	Arabic	depression
-beek	Afrikaans, Dutch	river
Beg, Beag	Gaelic, Irish	small
Bei	Chinese	north, northern

Geographical term	Language	Meaning
bei	German	at, near
Beinn	Gaelic	mountain
Belogor'ye	Russian	mountain range
Ben	Gaelic	mountain
Bereg	Russian	coastal area
-berg, -berge	German, Norwegian, Swedish, Afrikaans	mountain, mountains
Besar	Indonesian, Malay	big
Bi'ār	Arabic	wells
Bir, Bi'r, Bīr	Arabic	waterhole, well
Birkat	Arabic	waterhole, well
-bjerg	Danish	hill
Boca	Portuguese, Spanish	mouth
Bodden	German	bay
Boğazı	Turkish	strait, pass
Bois	French	forest, wood
Boloto	Russian	marsh
Bol'shaya, Bol'shiye, Bol'shoy, Bol'shoye	Russian	big
-bong	Korean	mountain
Boquerón	Spanish	pass
Bory	Polish	woods
-botn	Norwegian	valley floor
-botten	Swedish	valley floor
Böyük	Azeri	big
Braţul	Romanian	arm, branch
-bre, -breen	Norwegian	glacier
Bredning	Danish	bay
Breg	Croatian, Serbian	hill
-bron	Afrikaans	spring, well
Brücke	German	bridge
Bucht	German	bay
Bugt	Danish	bay
-bugten	Danish	bay
Bukhta	Russian	bay
Bukit	Indonesian, Malay	hill, mountain
-bukt, -bukta	Norwegian	bay
-bukten	Swedish	bay
Bulag	Mongolian	spring
Bulak	Russian, Uighur	spring
Bum	Burmese	mountain
Burnu, Burun	Turkish	cape, point
Büyük	Turkish	big
Bwlch	Welsh	pass
C		
Cabo	Portuguese, Spanish	cape, point
Cachoeira	Portuguese	waterfall
Caka	Tibetan	salt lake
Cala	Catalan, Italian	bay
Caleta	Spanish	inlet
Câmpia	Romanian	plain
Campo	Italian, Spanish	plain
Cañada, Cañadón	Spanish	ravine, gorge
Canal	French, Portuguese, Spanish	canal, channel
Caño	Spanish	river
Cañon	Spanish	canyon
Caol	Gaelic	hill
Cap	Catalan, French	cape, point
Capo	Italian	cape, point
Carn	Welsh	hill
Castell	Catalan	castle
Causse	French	limestone plateau
Çay, -çay, Çayı, -çayı	Azeri, Turkish	river
Cayo	Spanish	island
Cefn	Welsh	hill, ridge
Cerro	Spanish	hill, mountain, peak
Česká, České, Český	Czech	Czech
Chaco	Spanish	plain
Chāh	Farsi	river
Chaîne	French	mountain range
Cham	Kurdish	river
Chapada	Portuguese	hills, uplands
Château	French	castle, palace
Chau	Chinese	island
Chaung	Burmese	river
Chāy	Kurdish	river
Chhu	Dzongkha (Bhutan)	river
Chiang	Thai	town
Chink	Russian	hill range
Chiyā	Kurdish	mountain, hill range
Chott	Arabic	salt lake
Chuan	Chinese	river
Chuŏr Phnum	Cambodian	mountain range
Ci	Indonesian	river
Ciénaga	Spanish	marshy lake
Cima	Italian	peak
Cime	French	peak
Città	Italian	city
Ciudad	Spanish	town, city
Cnoc	Gaelic	hill
Co	Tibetan	lake
Col	French	pass
Collado	Spanish	mountain
Colle	Italian	pass
Colline	French	hill
Cona	Tibetan	lake
Cordillera	Spanish	mountain range

Geographical term	Language	Meaning
Corno	Italian	peak
Coronel	Spanish	colonel
Costa	Catalan, Italian, Portuguese, Spanish	coastal area
Côte	French	coast, hill region, slope
Coutada	Portuguese	reserve
Coxilha	Portuguese	mountain pasture
Cratère	French	crater
Creag	Gaelic	mountain
Cruz	Spanish	cross
Cu Lao	Vietnamese	island
Cuchilla	Spanish	mountain range
Cuenca	Spanish	deep valley, river basin
Cueva	Spanish	cave
Cumbre	Spanish	mountain
-cun	Chinese	village
D		
Da	Chinese	big
Da	Vietnamese	river
Dağ, Dağı	Azeri, Turkish	hill(s), mountain(s)
Dāgh	Farsi	mountain(s)
Dağları	Turkish	mountains
-dake	Japanese	hill, mountain
-dal	Afrikaans, Danish, Swedish	valley
-dal, -dalen	Norwegian	valley
-dalur	Icelandic	valley
-dan	Korean	cape, point
Danau	Indonesian, Malay	lake
Dao	Chinese	island
Đao	Vietnamese	island
Daqq	Farsi	salt flat, salt lake
-dara	Tajik	river
Darreh	Farsi	valley
Dar'ya	Russian	river
Daryācheh	Farsi	lake
Dashan	Chinese	mountain
Dasht	Farsi	desert
Dataran Tinggi	Malay	plateau
Davan	Kazakh	pass
Dawḩat	Arabic	bay
Dayr	Arabic	monastery
Dealul	Romanian	hill, mountain
Dealurile	Romanian	hills
Deh	Farsi	village
Deir	Arabic	monastery
Denizi	Turkish	sea
Deresi	Turkish	river
Desierto	Spanish	desert
Détroit	French	channel
-diep	Dutch	channel
Dingzi	Chinese	hill, small mountain
Djebel	Arabic	mountain
-do	Korean	island
Dolna, Dolni	Bulgarian	lower
Dolna, Dolne, Dolny	Polish	lower
Dolní	Czech	lower
Dong	Chinese	east, eastern
-dong	Korean	village
Donja, Donji	Croatian, Serbian	lower
Dorf	German	village
-dorp	Afrikaans, Dutch	village
Druim	Gaelic	hill, mountain
Dund	Mongolian	middle, central
Düzü	Azeri	plain
-dyngja	Icelandic	hill, mountain
Dzüün	Mongolian	east, eastern
E		
Eilean	Gaelic	island
-elv, -elva	Norwegian	river
Embalse	Spanish	reservoir
'Emeq	Hebrew	plain
Ensenada	Spanish	bay
Erg, 'Erg, 'Erg	Arabic	sand dunes
Eski	Turkish	old
Estany	Catalan	pond
Estero	Spanish	estuary, inlet, lagoon
Estrada	Spanish	bay
Estrecho	Spanish	strait
Étang	French	lagoon, lake
-ey, -eyjar	Icelandic	island, islands
-eyri	Icelandic	sandbar
ežeras	Lithuanian	lake
ezers	Latvian	lake
F		
Falaise	French	cliff, escarpment
Farihy	Malagasy	lake
Fayḑat	Arabic	waterhole
-fell	Icelandic	hill, mountain
Fels	German	rock
Feng	Chinese	mountain
Fiume	Italian	river

Geographical term	Language	Meaning
-fjäll, -fjällen, -fjället	Swedish	hill(s), mountain(s)
-fjallgarður	Icelandic	mountains
-fjara	Icelandic	beach
-fjell, -fjellet	Norwegian	mountain
-fjöll	Icelandic	hill(s), mountain(s)
Fjord, -fjord, -fjorden	Danish, Norwegian, Swedish	fjord
-fjörður	Icelandic	fjord
Fliegu	Maltese	channel
-fljót	Icelandic	river
-flói	Icelandic	bay
-főcsatorna	Hungarian	canal
Foel	Welsh	hill
Förde	German	inlet
Forêt	French	forest
Forst	German	forest
-foss	Icelandic	waterfall
-foss, -fossen	Norwegian	rapids, waterfall
Fuente	Spanish	source, well
Fulayj	Arabic	watercourse

G

-gan	Japanese	rock
Gang	Dzongkha (Bhutan)	mountain
Gang	Chinese	bay, river
-gang	Korean	river
Gaoyuan	Chinese	plateau
Gardaneh	Farsi	pass
-gat	Dutch	channel
-gata	Japanese	inlet, lagoon, lake
Gau	German	district
Gave	French	torrent
-gawa	Japanese	river
Gebel	Arabic	mountain
Gebergte	Dutch	mountain range
Gebiet	German	district, region
Gebirge	German	mountains
Geodha	Gaelic	inlet
Gezâ'ir	Arabic	islands
Gezirat	Arabic	island
Ghard	Arabic	sand dunes
Ghubba	Arabic	bay
Gjiri	Albanian	bay
Gletscher	German	glacier
Gobernador	Spanish	governor
Gobi	Mongolian	desert
Gol	Mongolian	river
Göl	Azeri	lake
Golets	Russian	mountain
Golf	Catalan	gulf
Golfe	French	bay, gulf
Golfo	Italian, Spanish	bay, gulf
Gölü	Azeri, Turkish	lake
Gora	Bulgarian, Croatian, Russian, Serbian	mountain(s)
Gorges	French	gorge
Górka	Polish	hill
Gornja, Gornje, Gornji	Croatian, Serbian	upper
Gorno-	Russian	mountainous
Gory	Russian	mountains
Góry	Polish	mountains
Gou	Chinese	river
Graben	German	trench
-grad	Bulgarian, Croatian, Russian, Serbian	town
Grand, Grande	French	big
-gród	Polish	town
Groot	Afrikaans, Dutch	big
Gross, Grosse, Grossen, Grosser (also Groß-)	German	big
Grotta	Italian	cave
Grotte	French	cave
Grotte	Italian	caves
Groupe	French	group
Grund	German	ground, valley
Gruppo	Italian	group
Gryada	Russian	mountains
Guan	Chinese	pass
Guba	Russian	bay, gulf
Gubed	Somali	bay
-guntō	Japanese	islands
Gunung	Indonesian, Malay	mountain
Guri	Albanian	peak

H

Ḥafar	Arabic	wells
Hafen	German	port, harbour
Haff	German	bay
Hai	Chinese	lake, sea
Haixia	Chinese	channel, strait
-háls	Icelandic	ridge
-halvøya	Norwegian	peninsula
Hamada, Hammada	Arabic	plateau
-hamn	Norwegian, Swedish	port, harbour
-hamrar	Icelandic	cliffs
Hämün	Farsi	marsh, salt pan
-hantō	Japanese	peninsula
Har	Hebrew	mountain
Hara	Belorussian	hill
Hardt	German	wooded hills
Ḥarrat, Ḥarrät	Arabic	lava field
Hassi	Arabic	well
-haug, -haugen	Norwegian	hill
-havn	Danish, Faroese, Norwegian	bay, harbour, port
Hawr	Arabic	lake, impermanent lake, marsh
Häyk'	Amharic	lake
He	Chinese	river
-hegység	Hungarian	hills, mountains
-hei	Norwegian	heath, moor
-heide	Dutch	heath, marsh
Heide	German	heath, moor
-heiði	Icelandic	heath

Geographical term	Language	Meaning
Helodrano	Malagasy	bay
Higashi-	Japanese	east, eastern
-hisar	Turkish	castle
Ḥiṣn	Arabic	fort
Hka	Burmese	river
-hnjúkur	Icelandic	hill
-ho	Korean	lake
-hø	Norwegian	peak
Hoch	German	high
Hoek	Dutch	cape, point
-höfði	Icelandic	hill, mountain
-höfn	Icelandic	cove
Hög	Swedish	height, high
-högda	Norwegian	height
Höhe	German	height
Hohen-	German	high
Hoi, Hoi Hap	Chinese	bay, channel, harbour, inlet
-høj, -høje	Danish	hill, hills
Hon	Vietnamese	island
Hoog	Dutch	high
Hora, Hory	Czech, Ukrainian	mountain(s)
-horn	Icelandic	cape, point, peak
Horn, -horn	German	mountain, peak
Horná, Horné, Horní, Horný	Czech	upper
Ḥorvot	Hebrew	ruins
-hot	Mongolian	town
-hrad	Czech	town
-hraun	Icelandic	lava field
Hu	Chinese	lake

I

Idd	Arabic	well
Île	French	island
Ilha, Ilhéu	Portuguese	island
Illa	Catalan	island
im	German	in
imeni	Russian	in the name of
Inish	Irish	island
Insel, Inseln	German	island, islands
Insula	Romanian	island
Irq, 'Irq	Arabic	hill, sand dune, sand dunes
Isla	Spanish	island
Iso-	Finnish	big
Isola, Isole	Italian	island, islands
Isolte	Catalan	island
Isthme	French	isthmus
Istmo	Spanish	isthmus
-iwa	Japanese	island

J

Jabal	Arabic	mountain
järv	Estonian	lake
-järvi	Finnish	lake
Jasiired	Somali	island
Jaun-	Latvian	new
-jaure	Lappish	lake
Jazirah, Jazireh, Jazirat	Arabic	island
Jbel, Jebel	Arabic	mountain
Jezero, jezero	Croatian, Serbian, Slovene	lake
Jezioro	Polish	lake
Jiang	Chinese	river
Jiao	Chinese	cape, point
Jibāl	Arabic	mountains
-jima	Japanese	island
Jing	Chinese	well
-jōgi	Estonian	river
-joki	Finnish	river
-jokka	Lappish	river
-jökull, jökullen	Icelandic, Norwegian	glacier, ice cap

K

Kaap	Afrikaans	cape, point
-kai	Japanese	bay, channel
-kaigan	Japanese	coastal area
-kaikyō	Japanese	channel, strait
Kali	Indonesian, Malay	river
kalnas, kalnis	Lithuanian	hill
Kalns	Latvian	hill
Kamen'	Russian	rock
Kamm	German	ridge, crest
Kâmpóng	Cambodian	town, village
-kanaal	Dutch	canal
Kanal	German, Russian	canal
Kanał	Polish	canal
Kanalı	Azeri	canal
Kaôh	Cambodian	island
Kap	Danish	cape, point
Kapp	Norwegian	cape, point
Karang	Indonesian, Malay	reef
Kato	Greek	lower
Kavīr	Farsi	salt desert
-kawa	Japanese	river
Kecil	Indonesian, Malay	small
K'edi	Georgian	hills
Kefar	Hebrew	village
Kepi	Albanian	cape, point
Kepulauan	Indonesian	islands
Keski-	Finnish	middle, central
Khabrah, Khabrat	Arabic	impermanent lake
Khalīg, Khalīj	Arabic	bay, gulf
Khao	Thai	peak
Khashm	Arabic	hill
Khawr	Arabic	bay, channel
Khor, Khōr	Arabic	bay
Khowr	Farsi	bay, inlet
Khrebet	Russian	mountain range
Kis-	Hungarian	small
Kita-	Japanese	north, northern
Klein	Afrikaans	small
Klein, Kleine, Kleiner	German	small

Geographical term	Language	Meaning
Klint	Danish	cliff
-kloof	Afrikaans	pass
Knock	Irish	hill
-ko	Japanese	lake
Ko	Thai	island
-kōchi, -kōgen	Japanese	plateau
Koh	Farsi	mountain
Kok	Chinese	cape, point
Köl	Kazakh, Kyrgyz	lake
Kolpos	Greek	gulf
Koog	German	polder (reclaimed land)
-kop	Afrikaans	hill, mountain
Kopf	German	hill
Körfezi	Turkish	bay, gulf
körgustik	Estonian	upland
Kosa	Russian, Ukrainian	spit
Kou	Chinese	river mouth
-köy	Turkish	village
Kraj	Croatian, Czech, Polish, Serbian	region
Krajobrazowy	Polish	regional
Kray	Russian	territory
Kryazh	Russian	hills, ridge
Kuala	Malay	river mouth
Küçük	Turkish	small
Kuduk	Uighur	well
Küh	Farsi	mountain
Kühhä	Farsi	mountain range
Kul'	Russian	lake
-kül	Tajik	lake
-küla	Estonian	village
Kum	Russian	sandy desert
-kundo	Korean	islands
Kuppe	German	hill top
kurk	Estonian	channel, strait
K'vemo	Georgian	upper
-kvísl, kvislar	Icelandic	river, rivers
-kylä	Finnish	village
Kyun	Burmese	island

L

La	Tibetan	pass
Lac	French	lake
Lacul	Romanian	lake
Laem	Thai	cape, point
Lago	Italian, Portuguese, Spanish	lake
Lagoa	Portuguese	lagoon
Laguna	Spanish	lagoon, lake
Lagune	French	lagoon
laht	Estonian	bay
-laid	Estonian	island
Lam	Thai	river
Län	Swedish	county
Land	German	province
Lande	French	heath, sandy moor
Las	Polish	wood, forest
Laut	Indonesian, Malay	sea
Lerr	Armenian	mountain
Lerrnashght'a	Armenian	mountains
Lich	Armenian	lake
Liedao	Chinese	islands
Liel-	Latvian	big
Lille	Danish, Norwegian	small
Liman	Russian	bay, lagoon, lake
Limni	Greek	lagoon, lake
Limnothalassa	Greek	inlet, lagoon
Ling	Chinese	mountain range
Liqeni	Albanian	lake
Llano	Spanish	plain, prairie
Llyn	Welsh	lake
Loch, Lochan	Gaelic	lake, small lake
Lohatanjona	Malagasy	cape, point
Loi	Burmese	mountain
looduskaitseala	Estonian	reserve
Luonnonpuisto	Finnish	nature reserve
-luoto	Finnish	rocky island
Lyman	Ukrainian	bay, lake

M

Macizo	Spanish	mountain range
Madh	Albanian	big
Madīnat	Arabic	town
Mae, Mae Nam	Thai	river
mägi	Estonian	hill
Măgura	Romanian	hill, mountain
Maḥaṭṭat	Arabic	station
Maja	Albanian	mountain
Mal	Albanian	mountain(s)
Mala	Croatian, Serbian	small
Malá	Czech, Slovak	small
Mali	Albanian	mountain
Mali	Croatian, Serbian, Ukrainian	small
Malo	Croatian, Serbian	small
Maloye	Russian	small
Maly, Malyya	Belorussian	small
-man	Korean	bay
Mar	Spanish	lagoon, lake
Marais	French	marsh, swamp
Mare	Italian	sea
Mare	Romanian	big
marios	Lithuanian	lake
Marsa	Arabic	anchorage, bay, inlet
Marsch	German	fen, marsh
Masabb	Arabic	estuary
Massif	French	mountains, upland
Ma'ṭan	Arabic	well
Mayor	Spanish	higher, larger
Maz-	Latvian	small
Meall	Gaelic	hill, mountain
Meer	Dutch, German	lake
Mega, Megalo-	Greek	big
Men	Chinese	gate

Geographical term	Language	Meaning
Menor	Portuguese, Spanish	smaller, lesser
Mersa	Arabic	anchorage, inlet
Mesa, Meseta	Spanish	tableland
Mesto	Croatia, Serbian	town
Město	Czech	town
Mets	Armenian	big
Mezzo	Italian	middle, central
Miao	Chinese	temple
Miasto	Polish	town
Mic, Mica	Romanian	small
Mikra, Mikri	Greek	small
Minā'	Arabic	port, harbour
Minami-	Japanese	south, southern
-mine	Japanese	mountain
-misaki	Japanese	cape, point
Mishāsh	Arabic	well
Mittel-, Mitten-	German	middle, central
Moel	Welsh	hill
Monasterio	Spanish	monastery
Moni	Greek	monastery
Mont	French	hill, mountain
Montagna	Italian	mountain
Montagne	French	mountain
Monte	Italian, Portuguese, Spanish	hill, mountain
Monti	Italian	mountains
Moor	German	marsh, moor, swamp
Moos	German	marsh, moss
More	Russian	sea
Mörön	Mongolian	river
Morro	Portuguese	hill
Morro	Spanish	cape, point
-mose	Danish	marsh, moor
Moyen	French	middle, central
Mt'a	Georgian	mountain
Muang	Laotian, Thai	town
Muara	Indonesian, Malay	estuary
Mui	Vietnamese	cape, point
Mun	Chinese	channel
Munţii	Romanian	mountains
Mynydd	Welsh	mountain
-mýri	Icelandic	marsh
Mys	Russian	cape, point

N

Geographical term	Language	Meaning
na	Croatian, Czech, Russian, Serbian, Slovak, Slovene	on
Nacional	Portuguese, Spanish	national
nacionalinis	Lithuanian	national
nad	Czech, Polish, Slovak	above, over
-nada	Japanese	bay, gulf
Nafūd	Arabic	desert, sand dunes
Nagor'ye	Russian	mountains, plateau
Nagy-	Hungarian	big
Nahr	Arabic	river
Nakhon	Thai	town
Nakrdzali	Georgian	reserve
Nam	Burmese, Laotian	river
Nam	Korean, Vietnamese	south, southern
Nan	Chinese	south, southern
Nanshan	Chinese	mountain range
Narodowy	Polish	national
Nationaal	Dutch	national
Naturreservat	Norwegian, Swedish	nature reserve
Natuurreservaat	Dutch	nature reserve
Naviglio	Italian	canal
Nawa-	Urdu	new
Nazionale	Italian	national
Neder-	Dutch	lower
Nehri	Turkish	river
Nei	Chinese	inner
Nek	Afrikaans	pass
-nes	Icelandic	cape, point
Neu-	German	new
Neuf, Neuve	French	new
Nevado, Nevada	Spanish	snow-covered mountain(s)
Nieder-	German	lower
Nieuw, Nieuwe, Nieuwer	Dutch	new
nina	Estonian	cape, point
Nishi-	Japanese	west, western
Nizhneye, Nizhniy, Nizhniye, Nizhnyaya	Russian	lower
Nizina	Belorussian	lowland
Nizke	Slovak	low
Nizmennost'	Russian	lowland
Nižní	Czech	lower
Nižný	Slovak	lower
Noguera	Catalan	river
Noord	Dutch	north, northern
Nord	French, German	north, northern
Nord-, Nordre	Danish	north, northern
Norður	Icelandic	north, northern
Norra	Swedish	north, northern
Norre	Danish	north, northern
Norte	Portuguese, Spanish	north, northern
Nos	Bulgarian, Russian	cape, point, spit
Nosy	Malagasy	island
Nou	Romanian	new
Nouveau, Nouvelle	French	new
Nova	Bulgarian, Croatian, Portuguese, Serbian, Slovene, Ukrainian	new
Nová	Czech	new
Novaya	Russian	new
Nové	Czech, Slovak	new
Novi	Bulgarian, Croatian, Serbian, Ukrainian	new
Novo	Portuguese, Slovene	new
Novo-, Novoye	Russian	new
Novy	Belorussian	new
Nový	Czech	new
Novyy, Novyye	Russian, Ukrainian	new
Novyya	Belorussian	new
Nowa, Nowe, Nowy	Polish	new
Nueva, Nuevo	Spanish	new
-numa	Japanese	lake

Geographical term	Language	Meaning
-núpur	Icelandic	hill
Nur	Chinese, Mongolian	lake
Nuruu	Mongolian	mountain range
Nuur	Mongolian	lake
Ny-	Danish, Norwegian, Swedish	new

O

Geographical term	Language	Meaning
-ø	Danish	island
-ö	Swedish	island
oaivi, oaivve	Lappish	hill, mountain
Obanbari	Tajik	reservoir
Ober-	German	upper
Oblast'	Russian, Ukrainian	administrative division
-odde	Danish, Norwegian	cape, point
Oeste	Spanish	west, western
Okrug	Russian	administrative district
-ön	Swedish	island
Öndör-	Mongolian	upper
-oog	German	island
Oost, Ooster	Dutch	east, eastern
-öræfi	Icelandic	lava field
Oriental	Spanish	east, eastern
Ormos	Greek	bay
Oros	Greek	mountain
-ós	Icelandic	river mouth
Ost-	German	east, eastern
Øster-	Danish, Norwegian	east, eastern
Östra-	Swedish	east, eastern
Ostriv	Ukrainian	island
Ostrov, Ostrova	Russian	island, islands
Oud, Oude, Ouden, Ouder	Dutch	old
Oued	Arabic	watercourse
Ovası	Turkish	plain
Over-	Danish, Dutch	upper
Över-, Övre-	Norwegian, Swedish	upper
-oy	Faroese	island
Ozero	Russian, Ukrainian	lake

P

Geographical term	Language	Meaning
-pää	Finnish	hill
Pampa	Spanish	plain
Pantà	Catalan	reservoir
Pantanal	Portuguese	marsh
Pao	Chinese	small lake
Parbat	Urdu	mountain
Parc	French	park
Parc Naturel	French	nature reserve
Parco	Italian	park
parkas	Lithuanian	park
Parque	Portuguese, Spanish	park
-pas	Afrikaans	pass
Paso	Spanish	pass
Paß	German	pass
Passage	French	channel
Passe	French	channel
Passo	Italian	pass
Pasul	Romanian	pass
Pegunungan	Indonesian, Malay	mountain range
Pelabuhan	Malay	port, harbour
Pen	Welsh	hill
Peña	Spanish	cliff, rock
Pendi	Chinese	basin
Peninsula	Spanish	peninsula
Péninsule	French	peninsula
Penisola	Italian	peninsula
Pereval	Russian	pass
Pervo-, Pervyy	Russian	first
Peski	Russian	desert
Petit, Petite	French	small
Phou	Laotian	mountain
Phu	Thai, Vietnamese	mountain
Phumĭ	Cambodian	town, village
Pic	Catalan, French	peak
Picacho	Spanish	peak
Pico	Spanish	peak
Pik	Russian	peak
Pingyuan	Chinese	plain
Pivostriv	Ukrainian	peninsula
Pizzo	Italian	peak
-plaat	Dutch	flat, sandbank, shoal
Plage	French	beach
Plaine	French	plain
Planalto	Portuguese	plateau
Planina	Bulgarian, Croatian, Serbian	mountain(s)
Platforma	Romanian	plateau
Plato	Bulgarian, Russian	plateau
Playa	Spanish	beach
Plaza	Spanish	market-place, square
Ploskogor'ye	Russian	plateau
Po	Chinese	lake
pod	Czech, Russian, Slovak	under, sub-, near
Podişul	Romanian	plateau
Pointe	French	cape, point
Pojezierze	Polish	area of lakes
Polje	Croatian, Serbian	plain
Poluostrov	Russian	peninsula
Pont	French	bridge
Ponta	Maltese, Portuguese	cape, point
Ponte	Portuguese	bridge
poolsaar	Estonian	peninsula
Porogi	Russian	rapids
Port	Catalan, French, Maltese, Russian	port, harbour
Portella	Italian	pass
Portillo	Spanish	gap, pass
Porto	Italian, Portuguese, Spanish	bay, port, harbour, pass
Pradesh	Hindi	state

Geographical term	Language	Meaning
Praia	Portuguese	beach, shore
Prêk	Cambodian	lake, river
près	French	near, beside
Presa	Spanish	reservoir
Presqu'île	French	peninsula
Pri-	Russian	near, by
Proliv	Russian	channel, strait
Protoka	Russian	channel, watercourse
Pueblo	Spanish	village
Puente	Spanish	bridge
Puerta	Spanish	narrow pass
Puerto	Spanish	pass, port, harbour
Puig	Catalan	hill, mountain
Puk-	Korean	north, northern
Pulau	Indonesian, Malay	island
Pulau-pulau	Indonesian, Malay	islands
Puncak	Indonesian, Malay	hill, mountain, summit
Punta	Italian, Spanish	cape, point
Punta	Italian	hill, mountain
Puntan	Marshallese	cape, point
Puy	French	peak

Q

Geographical term	Language	Meaning
Qā'	Arabic	depression, salt flat, impermanent lake
Qabr	Arabic	tomb
Qafa	Albanian	pass
Qala	Maltese	bay
Qalamat	Arabic	well
Qalti	Arabic	well
Qâret	Arabic	hill
Qatorkŭhi	Tajik	mountain range
Qi	Chinese	banner (administrative division)
Qiao	Chinese	bridge
Qiryat	Hebrew	town
Qolleh	Farsi	mountain
Qoor, Qooriga	Somali	bay
qoruğu	Azeri	reserve
Qu	Tibetan	river
Quan	Chinese	spring, well
Quebrada	Spanish	ravine, river
Qullai	Tajik	mountain
Qundao	Chinese	islands

R

Geographical term	Language	Meaning
Raas	Somali	cape, point
Rade	French	harbour
rags	Latvian	cape, point
Rambla	Catalan	river
Ramla	Maltese	bay, harbour
Ramlat	Arabic	sandy desert
-rani	Icelandic	spur
Ras	Arabic, Maltese	cape, point
Ra's	Arabic, Farsi	cape, point
Rās, Rãs	Arabic	cape, point
Ravnina	Russian	plain
Récif	French	reef
Represa	Portuguese, Spanish	reservoir
Reserva	Portuguese, Spanish	reserve
Réserve de Faune, Réserve Faunique	French	wildlife reserve
Réserve Naturelle	French	nature reserve
Reshteh	Farsi	mountain range
Respublika	Russian	republic
-rettō	Japanese	island chain, island group
rezervatas	Lithuanian	reserve
-ri	Korean	village
Ri	Tibetan	mountain
Ría	Spanish	estuary, inlet, river mouth
Ribeirão, Ribeiro	Portuguese	river
Rio	Portuguese	river
Río	Spanish	river
Riserva	Italian	reserve
-rivier	Afrikaans	river
Riviera	Italian	coastal area
Rivière	French	river
Roca	Spanish	rock
Rocher	French	rock
Rt	Croatian, Serbian	cape, point
Rū, Rūbār	Kurdish	river
Rubh', Rubha	Gaelic	cape, point
Rūd, Rūdkhāneh	Farsi	river
Rujm	Arabic	hill

S

Geographical term	Language	Meaning
-saar	Estonian	island
-saari	Finnish	island
Sabkhat, Sabkhet	Arabic	impermanent lake, salt flat, salt marsh
Sadd, Saddat	Arabic	dam
Sagar, Sagara	Hindi	lake
Şaghīr, Şaghīr	Arabic	small
Şaḥrā'	Arabic	desert
-saki	Japanese	cape, point
Salar, Salina	Spanish	salt pan
Salto	Portuguese, Spanish	waterfall
San	Italian, Maltese, Portuguese, Spanish	saint
San	Laotian	mountain
-san	Japanese, Korean	mountain
-sanchi	Japanese	mountain range
-sandur	Icelandic	sandy area
Sankt	German, Russian	saint
-sanmaek	Korean	mountain range
-sanmyaku	Japanese	mountain range
Sant	Catalan	saint
Sant'	Italian	saint

Geographical term	Language	Meaning
Santa	Italian, Portuguese, Spanish	saint
Santo	Italian, Portuguese, Spanish	saint
São	Portuguese	saint
Sar	Kurdish	mountain
Sarīr	Arabic	desert
Satu	Romanian	village
Say	Kyrgyz	river
Schloß	German	castle, mansion
Şcoglio	Italian	reef, rock
Sebkha, Sebkhet	Arabic	salt flat, salt marsh
See, -see	German	lake
-şehir	Turkish	town
Selat	Indonesian, Malay	channel, strait
Selatan	Indonesian, Malay	south, southern
-selkä	Finnish	lake, open water, ridge
Selo	Croatian, Russian, Serbian	village
Selva	Portuguese, Spanish	forest
Semenanjung	Indonesian, Malay	peninsula
Seno	Spanish	bay, sound
Serra	Catalan, Portuguese	hills, mountains
Serranía	Spanish	mountain range
-seter	Norwegian	mountain pasture
-seto	Japanese	channel, strait
Severnaya, Severnoye, Severnyy, Severo-	Russian	north, northern
Sfântu	Romanian	saint
Sgeir	Gaelic	island
Sgor, Sgorach, Sgorr, Sgurr	Gaelic	hill
Shahr	Farsi	town
Sha'ib, Sha'iān	Arabic	watercourse
Shamo	Chinese	desert
Shan	Chinese	hill(s), mountain(s)
Shang	Chinese	next to, upper
Shankou	Chinese	pass
Sharm	Arabic	bay
Shaţţ	Arabic	estuary, river mouth, watercourse
Shën-	Albanian	saint
Shet'	Amharic	watercourse
Shi	Chinese	city
-shima	Japanese	island
-sho	Japanese	island
-shotō	Japanese	islands
Shui	Chinese	river
Shui Tong	Chinese	reservoir
Shuiku	Chinese	reservoir
Sierra	Spanish	mountain range
Silsiläsi	Azeri	hills
-sjø	Norwegian	lake
-sjö, -sjön	Swedish	lake
-sjór	Icelandic	lake
-sker	Icelandic	island
-skog	Norwegian	wood
Slieau	Manx	hill, mountain
Slieve	Irish	hill, mountain
Sloboda	Russian	large village
Sø	Danish, Norwegian	lake
Söder, Södra	Swedish	south, southern
Solonchak	Russian	salt lake
Sommet	French	peak, summit
Sønder-, Søndre	Danish	south, southern
Sông	Vietnamese	river
Sopka	Russian	hill, mountain, volcano
Sør-	Norwegian	south, southern
Sor	Russian	salt pan
sous	French	under
Sovkhoz	Russian	state farm
Spitze	German	peak
Sredna, Sredno	Bulgarian	middle, central
Sredne-, Sredneye, Sredniy, Srednyaya	Russian	middle, central
Sron	Gaelic	hill
Stac	Gaelic	hill, stack
-stad	Afrikaans, Norwegian, Swedish	town
-stadt	German	town
-staður	Icelandic	town
Stagno	Italian	lagoon, lake
Stara, Stari	Croatian, Serbian, Ukrainian	old
Stará, Staré, Starý	Czech	old
Staraya, Stary, Staryya	Belorussian	old
Staraya, Staroye, Staryy, Staryye	Russian	old
Stare, Staro-, Staryy	Ukrainian	old
Stausee	German	reservoir
Steno	Greek	strait
Step'	Russian	plain, steppe
Stob	Gaelic	hill, mountain
Stœng	Cambodian	river
Stór-, Stóra, Stóri	Icelandic	big
Stor, Stora	Swedish	big
Store	Danish	big
Strand	Danish, German	beach
-strand	Norwegian, Swedish	beach
Straße	German	street
Stretta	Italian	strait
-strönd	Icelandic	beach
Sud	French	south, southern
Süd-, Süder-	German	south, southern
Suður-	Icelandic	south, southern
Suid	Afrikaans	south, southern
-suidō	Japanese	channel, strait
Sul	Portuguese	south, southern
sul, sull'	Italian	on
Sund	Swedish	strait, sound
Sungai	Indonesian, Malay	river
-suo	Finnish	marsh, swamp
Superior	Spanish	upper
Süq	Arabic	market
Sur	Spanish	south, southern
sur	French	on
Suur	Estonian	big
Sveti	Croatian, Serbian	saint
Syðra, Syðri	Icelandic	south, southern
sýsla	Icelandic	county
Szent-	Hungarian	saint
-sziget	Hungarian	island

T

Geographical term	Language	Meaning
-tag	Uighur	mountain
-take	Japanese	hill, mountain
Tal	German	valley
Tall	Arabic	hill
Tanjona	Malagasy	cape, point
Tanjong, Tanjung	Indonesian, Malay	cape, point
Tao	Chinese	island
Tassili	Berber	plateau
Tau	Russian	mountain(s)
Taung	Burmese	mountain
Tba	Georgian	lake
Techniti Limni	Greek	reservoir
tekojärvi	Finnish	reservoir
Tell	Arabic	hill, mountain
Teluk, Telukan	Indonesian, Malay	bay, gulf
Tengah	Indonesian, Malay	middle, central
Teniente	Spanish	lieutenant
Tepe, Tepesi	Turkish	hill, mountain
Terara	Amharic	mountain
Terre	French	land
Thale	Thai	lake
Thamad	Arabic	well
Tierra	Spanish	land
Timur	Indonesian, Malay	east, eastern
-tind, -tinden	Norwegian	peak
-tindar	Icelandic	peak
-tindur	Faroese, Icelandic	peak
Tir'at	Arabic	canal, river, watercourse
Tizi	Berber	pass
-tjåkkå	Lappish	mountain
-tjärro	Lappish	mountain
-tó	Hungarian	lake
-tō	Japanese	island
-to	Korean	island
-töge	Japanese	pass
-tong	Korean	village
Tônlé	Cambodian	lake, river
Too	Kyrgyz	mountain range
-topp, -toppen	Norwegian	peak
T'ou	Chinese	cape, point
Tsentral'nyy	Russian	central
Tso	Tibetan	lake
Tsqalsats'avi	Georgian	reservoir
Tsui	Chinese	cape, point
Túnel	Spanish	tunnel
-tunturi	Finnish	treeless mountain

U

Geographical term	Language	Meaning
Über-	German	upper
-udden	Swedish	cape, point
Ugheltekhili	Georgian	pass
Új-	Hungarian	new
Ujung	Indonesian	cape, point
Unter-, unter	German	below, lower
'Uqlat	Arabic	well
-ura	Japanese	inlet
'Urayq, 'Urūq	Arabic	sand dunes
Ust'-, Ust'ye	Russian	river mouth
Utara	Indonesian, Malay	north, northern
Uttar	Hindi	north, northern
Uul	Mongolian	mountain range
Uval	Russian	hills
'Uyūn	Arabic	springs

V

Geographical term	Language	Meaning
v	Czech	in
-vaara, -vaarat	Finnish	hill(s), mountain(s)
Vaart, -vaart	Dutch	canal
-vaðall	Icelandic	inlet
-våg	Norwegian	bay
-vágur	Faroese	bay
Väike-	Estonian	small
väin	Estonian	bay, channel, strait
Val	French, Portuguese, Spanish	valley
Vale	Portuguese, Romanian	valley
Vall	Catalan, Spanish	valley
Valle	Italian, Spanish	valley
Vallée	French	valley
Valli	Italian	valleys
Vallon	French	small valley
Vârful	Romanian	hill, mountain
-város	Hungarian	town
-varre	Norwegian	mountain
Väster, Västra	Swedish	west, western
-vatn	Icelandic	lake
-vatn, -vatnet	Norwegian	lake
-vatten, -vattnet	Swedish	lake
Vaux	French	valleys
Vechi	Romanian	old
veehoidla	Estonian	lake
-veld	Afrikaans	field
Velha, Velho	Portuguese	old
Velika	Croatian, Slovene, Serbian	big
Velikaya, Velikiy, Velikiye	Russian	big
Velike	Slovene	big
Veliki	Croatian, Serbian	big
Velká, Velké, Velký	Czech	big
Veľká, Veľké, Veľký	Slovak	big
-vellir	Icelandic	plain
Velyka	Ukrainian	big
Verkhne-, Verkhneye, Verkhniy, Verkhnyaya	Russian	upper
-vesi	Finnish	lake, water
Viaduc	French	viaduct
-vidda	Norwegian	plateau
Vieja, Viejo	Spanish	old
Vieux	French	old
Vig	Danish	bay
-vík	Icelandic	bay
-vik	Norwegian	bay, inlet
Vila	Portuguese	small town
Ville	French	town
Vinh	Vietnamese	bay
-víz	Hungarian	river
-víztároló	Hungarian	reservoir
-vlei	Afrikaans	lake, salt pan
-vloer	Afrikaans	salt pan
Voblasts'	Belorussian	province
Vodaskhovishcha	Belorussian	reservoir
Vodná nádrž	Slovak	reservoir
Vodní nádrž	Czech	reservoir
Vodokhranilishche	Russian	reservoir
Vodoskhovyshche	Ukrainian	reservoir
-vogur	Icelandic	bay
Volcán	Spanish	volcano
Vostochno-, Vostochnyy	Russian	east, eastern
-vötn	Icelandic	lakes
Vozvyshennost'	Russian	hills, upland
Vozyera	Belorussian	lake
Vpadina	Russian	depression
Vrchovina	Czech	hills, mountain region
Vrükh	Bulgarian	hill, mountain
Vulkan	Russian	volcano
Vyalikaya, Vyalikaye, Vyaliki, Vyalikiya	Belorussian	big
Vyerkhnya	Belorussian	upper
Vysokaya, Vysokoye	Russian	upper

W

Geographical term	Language	Meaning
-waard	Dutch	polder (reclaimed land)
Wad	Dutch	sandflat
Wadi, Wâdi, Wâdī	Arabic	watercourse
Wai	Chinese	outer
Wald	German	forest
Wan	Chinese	bay
-wan	Japanese	bay
Wand	German	cliff
Wasser	German	water
Wāw	Arabic	well
Webi	Somali	river
Wenz	Amharic	river, watercourse
Wielka, Wielki, Wielkie, Wielko-	Polish	big
-woud	Dutch	wood, forest
Wysoka, Wysoki, Wysokie	Polish	upper
Wyżna	Polish	lowland
Wzvyshsha	Belorussian	upland

X

Geographical term	Language	Meaning
Xé	Vietnamese	river
Xi	Chinese	river, west, western
Xia	Chinese	gorge, lower
Xian	Chinese	county
Xiao	Chinese	small

Y

Geographical term	Language	Meaning
Yam	Hebrew	lake, sea
-yama	Japanese	mountain
Yang	Chinese	channel
Yangi	Russian	new
Yarımadası	Azeri, Turkish	peninsula
Yazovir	Bulgarian	reservoir
Ye	Burmese	island
Yeni	Turkish	new
Yli-	Finnish	upper
Ynys	Welsh	island
Yoma	Burmese	mountain range
You	Chinese	right
Ytra-, Ytri-	Icelandic	outer
Ytre-	Norwegian	outer
Ytter-	Norwegian, Swedish	outer
Yuan	Chinese	spring
Yumco	Tibetan	lake
Yunhe	Chinese	canal
Yuzhno-, Yuzhnyy	Russian	south, southern

Z

Geographical term	Language	Meaning
Za-	Russian	behind, beyond
-zaki	Japanese	cape, point
Zalew	Polish	bay
Zaliv	Russian	bay, gulf, inlet
-zan	Japanese	mountain
Zand	Dutch	sandbank, sandhill
Zangbo	Tibetan	river
Zapadnaya, Zapadno-, Zapadnyy	Russian	west, western
Zapavyednik	Belorussian	reserve
Zapovednik	Russian	reserve
Zapovidnyk	Ukrainian	reserve
Zatoka	Polish, Ukrainian	bay, gulf, lagoon
-zee	Dutch	lake, sea
Zemlya	Russian	land
Zemo	Georgian	upper
Zhen	Chinese	town
Zhong	Chinese	middle, central
Zhou	Chinese	island
Zizhiqu	Chinese	autonomous region
Zuid, Zuider	Dutch	south, southern
Zuo	Chinese	left

INTRODUCTION TO THE INDEX

The index includes names shown on the maps in the Atlas of the World. Each entry includes the country or geographical area in which the feature is located, a page number and an alphanumeric reference. Additional details within the entries are explained below. Abbreviations used in the index are explained in the table below.

REFERENCING

Names are referenced by page number, the first element of each entry, and by a grid reference. The grid reference correlates to the alphanumeric values which appear within each map frame. These reflect the graticule on the map – the letter relates to longitude divisions, the number to latitude divisions.

Names are generally referenced to the largest scale map page on which they appear. For large geographical features, including countries, the reference is to the largest scale map on which the feature appears in its entirety, or on which the majority of it appears.

Rivers are referenced to their lowest downstream point – either their mouth or their confluence with another river. The river name will generally be positioned as close to this point as possible, but may not necessarily be in the same grid square.

ALTERNATIVE NAMES

Alternative names or name forms appear as cross-references and refer the user to the entry for the map form of the name.

For rivers with multiple names – for example those which flow through several countries – all alternative name forms are included within the main index entries, with details of the countries in which each form applies. Different types of name used are: alternative forms or spellings currently in use (alt.); English conventional name forms normally used in English-language contexts (conv.); and long names – full forms of names which are most commonly used in the abbreviated form.

ADMINISTRATIVE QUALIFIERS

Entries within the following countries include the main administrative division in which they occur: Australia, Canada, China, India, U.K., U.S.A. and Yugoslavia. Administrative divisions are also included to differentiate duplicate names – entries of exactly the same name and feature type within the one country – where these division names are shown on the maps. In such cases, duplicate names are alphabetized in the order of the administrative division names.

Additional qualifiers are included for names within selected geographical areas, to indicate more clearly their location. In particular, this has been applied to island nations to indicate the island group, or individual island, on which a feature occurs.

DESCRIPTORS

Entries, other than those for towns and cities, include a descriptor indicating the type of geographical feature. Descriptors are not included where the type of feature is implicit in the name itself, unless there is a town or city of exactly the same name.

INSETS

Entries relating to names appearing on insets are indicated by a small box symbol: □, followed by an index number if there is more than one inset on the page, or by a grid reference if the inset has its own alphanumeric values.

NAME FORMS AND ALPHABETICAL ORDER

Name forms are as they appear on the maps, with additional alternative forms included as cross-references. Names appear in full in the index, although they may appear in abbreviated form on the maps.

The Icelandic characters Þ and þ are transliterated and alphabetized as 'Th' and 'th'. The German character ß is alphabetized as 'ss'. Names beginning with Mac or Mc are alphabetized exactly as they appear. The terms Saint, Sainte, etc, are abbreviated to St, Ste, etc, but alphabetized as if in the full form.

Name form policies are explained in the Introduction to the Atlas (pp 66-67).

NUMERICAL ENTRIES

Entries beginning with numerals appear at the beginning of the index, in numerical order. Elsewhere, numerals appear before 'a'.

PERMUTED TERMS

Names beginning with generic, geographical terms are permuted – the descriptive term is placed after, and the index alphabetized by, the main part of the name. For example, Lake Superior is indexed as Superior, Lake; Mount Everest as Everest, Mount. This policy is applied to all languages. Permuting has not been applied to names of towns, cities or administrative divisions beginning with such geographical terms. These remain in their full form, for example, Lake Isabella, California, USA.

The definite article is not permuted in any language.

INDEX ABBREVIATIONS

A.C.T.	Australian Capital Territory	est.	estuary	Moz.	Mozambique	rf	reef
admin. dist.	administrative district	Eth.	Ethiopia	MS	Mississippi	RI	Rhode Island
admin. div.	administrative division	Fin.	Finland	MT	Montana	Rus. Fed.	Russian Federation
admin. reg.	administrative region	FL	Florida	mt.	mountain	S.	South
Afgh.	Afghanistan	for.	forest	mts	mountains	S.A.	South Australia
AK	Alaska	Fr. Guiana	French Guiana	mun.	municipality	Sask.	Saskatchewan
AL	Alabama	Fr. Polynesia	French Polynesia	N.	North	SC	South Carolina
Alg.	Algeria	g.	gulf	N.B.	New Brunswick	SD	South Dakota
alt.	alternative name form	GA	Georgia	NC	North Carolina	sea chan.	sea channel
Alta	Alberta	Gd Bahama	Grand Bahama	ND	North Dakota	Sing.	Singapore
Andhra Prad.	Andhra Pradesh	Ger.	Germany	NE	Nebraska	str.	strait
AR	Arkansas	Guat.	Guatemala	Neth.	Netherlands	Switz.	Switzerland
Arg.	Argentina	hd	headland	Nfld.	Newfoundland	Tajik.	Tajikistan
Arun. Prad.	Arunachal Pradesh	Heilong.	Heilongjiang	NH	New Hampshire	Tanz.	Tanzania
Austr.	Australia	HI	Hawaii	Nic.	Nicaragua	Tas.	Tasmania
aut. comm.	autonomous community	Hima. Prad.	Himachal Pradesh	NJ	New Jersey	terr.	territory
aut. div.	autonomous division	H.K.	Hong Kong	NM	New Mexico	Thai.	Thailand
aut. prov.	autonomous province	Hond.	Honduras	N.S.	Nova Scotia	TN	Tennessee
aut. reg.	autonomous region	i.	island	N.S.W.	New South Wales	Trin. and Tob.	Trinidad and Tobago
aut. rep.	autonomous republic	is	islands	N.T.	Northern Territory	tun.	tunnel
AZ	Arizona	IA	Iowa	NV	Nevada	Turkm.	Turkmenistan
Azer.	Azerbaijan	ID	Idaho	N.W.T.	Northwest Territories	TX	Texas
b.	bay	IL	Illinois	NY	New York	U.A.E.	United Arab Emirates
Bangl.	Bangladesh	imp. l.	impermanent lake	N.Z.	New Zealand	U.K.	United Kingdom
B.C.	British Columbia	IN	Indiana	OH	Ohio	Ukr.	Ukraine
B.I.O.T.	British Indian Ocean Territory	Indon.	Indonesia	OK	Oklahoma	Uru.	Uruguay
Bol.	Bolivia	isth.	isthmus	Ont.	Ontario	U.S.A.	United States of America
Bos.-Herz.	Bosnia-Herzegovina	Kazakh.	Kazakhstan	OR	Oregon	UT	Utah
Bulg.	Bulgaria	KS	Kansas	PA	Pennsylvania	Uttar Prad.	Uttar Pradesh
c.	cape	KY	Kentucky	Pak.	Pakistan	Uzbek.	Uzbekistan
CA	California	Kyrg.	Kyrgyzstan	Para.	Paraguay	VA	Virginia
Can.	Canada	l.	lake	P.E.I.	Prince Edward Island	val.	valley
C.A.R.	Central African Republic	LA	Louisiana	pen.	peninsula	Venez.	Venezuela
CO	Colorado	lag.	lagoon	Phil.	Philippines	Vic.	Victoria
Col.	Colombia	Lith.	Lithuania	plat.	plateau	vol.	volcano
conv.	conventional name form	Lux.	Luxembourg	P.N.G.	Papua New Guinea	vol. crater	volcanic crater
CT	Connecticut	MA	Massachusetts	Pol.	Poland	VT	Vermont
Czech Rep.	Czech Republic	Madag.	Madagascar	Port.	Portugal	W.	West, Western
DC	District of Columbia	Madh. Prad.	Madhya Pradesh	pref.	prefecture	W.A.	Western Australia
DE	Delaware	Mahar.	Maharashtra	prov.	province	WA	Washington
Dem. Rep. Congo	Democratic Republic of Congo	Man.	Manitoba	Qld	Queensland	WI	Wisconsin
depr.	depression	Maur.	Mauritania	Que.	Québec	WV	West Virginia
dept	department	MD	Maryland	r.	river	WY	Wyoming
des.	desert	ME	Maine	r. mouth	river mouth	Y.T.	Yukon Territory
Dom. Rep.	Dominican Republic	Mex.	Mexico	reg.	region	Yugo.	Yugoslavia
E.	East, Eastern	MI	Michigan	Rep.	Republic		
Equat. Guinea	Equatorial Guinea	MN	Minnesota	research stn	research station		
esc.	escarpment	MO	Missouri	resr	reservoir		

9 de Julio to Ahaura

274

1

261 G4 9 de Julio Arg.
261 G4 25 de Mayo Buenos Aires Arg.
260 D5 25 de Mayo La Pampa Arg.
260 C4 25 de Mayo Mendoza Arg.
261 I4 25 de Mayo Uru.
129 F4 26 Bakı Komissarı Azer.
261 F5 30 de Agosto Arg.
215 G3 42nd Hill S. Africa
222 F5 70 Mile House B.C. Can.
222 F5 100 Mile House B.C. Can.
222 F4 150 Mile House B.C. Can.

A

156 C1 Aa r. France
169 B4 Aa r. Ger.
169 C4 Aa r. Ger.
Aabenraa Denmark see Åbenrå
172 C4 Aach Ger.
172 D4 Aach r. Ger.
169 B5 Aachen Ger.
190 D1 Aadorf Switz.
Aalborg Denmark see Ålborg
173 E3 Aalen Ger.
Aalesund Norway see Ålesund
Aaley Lebanon see 'Āley
164 D2 Aalsmeer Neth.
165 D4 Aalst Belgium
165 E3 Aalst Neth.
164 F3 Aalten Neth.
165 C3 Aalter Belgium
Aanaar Fin. see Inari
140 N3 Äänekoski Fin.
214 D2 Aansluit S. Africa
Aar r. Switz. see Aare
113 □1 Aarah i. N. Male Maldives
190 D1 Aarau Switz.
190 C1 Aarberg Switz.
190 C1 Aarburg Switz.
165 C3 Aardenburg Neth.
190 D1 Aare r. Switz.
140 M2 Aareavaara Sweden
190 D1 Aargau canton Switz.
Aarhus Denmark see Århus
164 E3 Aarle Neth.
Aarlen Belgium see Arlon
165 D4 Aarschot Belgium
165 D3 Aartselaar Belgium
172 B4 Aarwangen Switz.
221 M3 Aasiaat Greenland
Aath Belgium see Ath
108 B1 Aba Sichuan China
208 F4 Aba Dem. Rep. Congo
177 H4 Aba Hungary
207 G5 Aba Nigeria
124 D2 Abā ad Dūd Saudi Arabia
251 G6 Abacaxis r. Brazil
122 B4 Ābādān Iran
122 B4 Ābādān, Jazīrah i. Iran/Iraq
122 C4 Ābādeh Iran
122 C4 Ābādeh Ţashk Iran
183 F4 Abades Spain
256 D3 Abadia dos Dourados Brazil
256 C2 Abadiânia Brazil
182 C1 Abadín Spain
204 E3 Abadla Alg.
177 J4 Abádszalók Hungary
129 B1 Abadzekhskaya Rus. Fed.
257 E3 Abaeté Brazil
257 E3 Abaeté r. Brazil
254 C2 Abaetetuba Brazil
Abagnar Qi Nei Mongol China see Xilinhot
Abag Qi Nei Mongol China see Xin Hot
253 G6 Abaí Para.
77 H1 Abaiang atoll Kiribati
182 B1 A Baiuca Spain
241 M3 Abajo Peak UT U.S.A.
207 H5 Abakaliki Nigeria
98 F1 Abakan Rus. Fed.
98 E1 Abakanskiy Khrebet mts Rus. Fed.
208 B5 Abala Congo
207 F3 Abala Niger
207 G3 Abalak Niger
138 H4 Abalyanka r. Belarus
126 D2 Abana Turkey
183 H4 Abánades Spain
252 B3 Abancay Peru
208 A5 Abanga r. Gabon
187 B6 Abanilla Spain
191 G3 Abano Terme Italy
252 E4 Abapó Bol.
187 B6 Abarán Spain
Abariringa i. Phoenix Is Kiribati see Kanton
122 C4 Abarqū Iran
182 C2 A Barrela Spain
Abarshahr Iran see Neyshābūr
177 J4 Abasár Hungary
129 C2 Abasha Georgia
102 L1 Abashiri Japan
102 L2 Abashiri-ko l. Japan
102 L1 Abashiri-wan b. Japan
244 D3 Abasolo Guanajuato Mex.
245 E1 Abasolo Tamaulipas Mex.
245 G5 Abasolo del Valle Mex.
129 C3 Abast'umani Georgia
177 K3 Abaújszántó Hungary
138 C3 Abava r. Latvia
121 H2 Abay Karagandinskaya Oblast' Kazakh.
Abay Vostochnyy Kazakhstan Kazakh. see Karaul
Abay Bazar Karagandinskaya Oblast' Kazakh. see Abay
210 B2 Ābay Wenz r. Eth. alt. Azraq, Bahr el (Sudan), conv. Blue Nile
98 F1 Abaza Rus. Fed.
208 B3 Abba C.A.R.
192 D2 Abbadia San Salvatore Italy
122 D3 Abbāsābād Iran
192 A4 Abbasanta Sardegna Italy
Abbatis Villa France see Abbeville
156 B2 Abbeville France
231 C6 Abbeville AL U.S.A.
231 D6 Abbeville GA U.S.A.
237 E6 Abbeville LA U.S.A.
231 D5 Abbeville SC U.S.A.
223 I5 Abbey Sask. Can.
147 B4 Abbeydorney Rep. of Ireland
147 B4 Abbeyfeale Rep. of Ireland
147 D4 Abbeyleix Rep. of Ireland
149 F3 Abbeytown Cumbria, England U.K.
190 D3 Abbiategrasso Italy
140 L2 Abborrträsk Sweden
85 F4 Abbot, Mount Qld Austr.
85 F3 Abbot Bay Qld Austr.
151 F2 Abbots Bromley Staffordshire, England U.K.
150 E4 Abbotsbury Dorset, England U.K.
222 F5 Abbotsford B.C. Can.
226 B3 Abbotsford WI U.S.A.
151 G3 Abbots Langley Hertfordshire, England U.K.
234 B3 Abbotstown PA U.S.A.
239 F4 Abbott NM U.S.A.
232 C6 Abbott VA U.S.A.
232 C5 Abbott WV U.S.A.
123 H3 Abbottabad Pak.
262 R2 Abbott Ice Shelf Antarctica
164 D2 Abcoude Neth.
177 G4 Abda Hungary
127 F3 'Abd al 'Azīz, Jabal hill Syria
122 A3 Ābdānān Iran
120 C1 Abdulino Rus. Fed.
202 D6 Abéché Chad
105 E4 Abe-gawa r. Japan
183 H3 Abejar Spain
187 C5 Abejuela Spain
207 G5 Abejukolo Nigeria
184 B2 Abela Port.
165 B4 Abele Belgium
Abellinum Italy see Avellino
77 H1 Abemama atoll Gilbert Is Kiribati
173 E2 Abenberg Ger.
185 I1 Abengibre Spain
206 E5 Abengourou Côte d'Ivoire
185 F2 Abenójar Spain
142 C4 Åbenrå Denmark
173 F3 Abens r. Ger.
173 F3 Abensberg Ger.
207 F5 Abeokuta Nigeria
150 C2 Aberaeron Ceredigion, Wales U.K.
150 D3 Aberaman Rhondda Cynon Taff, Wales U.K.
150 D3 Aberavon Neath Port Talbot, Wales U.K.
150 D3 Abercanaid Merthyr Tydfil, Wales U.K.
150 B3 Abercastle Pembrokeshire, Wales U.K.
146 F4 Aberchirder Aberdeenshire, Scotland U.K.
Abercorn Zambia see Mbala
83 G3 Abercrombie r. N.S.W. Austr.
150 D3 Abercynon Rhondda Cynon Taff, Wales U.K.
150 D3 Aberdare Rhondda Cynon Taff, Wales U.K.
210 C5 Aberdare National Park Kenya
150 C2 Aberdaron Gwynedd, Wales U.K.
Aberdaugleddau Pembrokeshire, Wales U.K. see Milford Haven
83 G3 Aberdeen N.S.W. Austr.
109 □ Aberdeen H.K. China
214 E5 Aberdeen S. Africa
146 F4 Aberdeen Aberdeen, Scotland U.K.
146 F4 Aberdeen admin. div. Scotland U.K.
234 B3 Aberdeen MD U.S.A.
237 F5 Aberdeen MS U.S.A.
232 B5 Aberdeen OH U.S.A.
236 D2 Aberdeen SD U.S.A.
238 B2 Aberdeen WA U.S.A.
223 L1 Aberdeen Lake Nunavut Can.
214 E5 Aberdeen Road S. Africa
146 F4 Aberdeenshire admin. div. Scotland U.K.
146 E5 Aberdour Fife, Scotland U.K.
Aberdovey Gwynedd, Wales U.K. see Aberdyfi
150 C2 Aberdyfi Gwynedd, Wales U.K.
146 E5 Aberfeldy Perth and Kinross, Scotland U.K.
150 C1 Aberffraw Isle of Anglesey, Wales U.K.
149 H4 Aberford West Yorkshire, England U.K.
146 D5 Aberfoyle Stirling, Scotland U.K.
150 D3 Abergavenny Monmouthshire, Wales U.K.
150 D1 Abergele Conwy, Wales U.K.
Abergwaun Pembrokeshire, Wales U.K. see Fishguard
150 D2 Abergwesyn Powys, Wales U.K.
150 D2 Abergynolwyn Gwynedd, Wales U.K.
Aberhonddu Powys, Wales U.K. see Brecon
150 D3 Aberkenfig Bridgend, Wales U.K.
146 F5 Aberlady East Lothian, Scotland U.K.
146 F5 Aberlemno Angus, Scotland U.K.
146 E5 Aberlour Moray, Scotland U.K.
Abermaw Gwynedd, Wales U.K. see Barmouth
237 C5 Abernathy TX U.S.A.
146 E5 Abernethy Perth and Kinross, Scotland U.K.
150 C2 Aberporth Ceredigion, Wales U.K.
150 C2 Abersoch Gwynedd, Wales U.K.
150 D3 Abersychan Torfaen, Wales U.K.
176 B1 Abertamy Czech Rep.
Abertawe Swansea, Wales U.K. see Swansea
Aberteifi Ceredigion, Wales U.K. see Cardigan
150 D3 Abertillery Blaenau Gwent, Wales U.K.
184 E1 Abertura Spain
146 E5 Aberuthven Perth and Kinross, Scotland U.K.
150 C2 Aberystwyth Ceredigion, Wales U.K.
Abeshr Chad see Abéché
134 M2 Abez' Rus. Fed.
124 C4 Abhā Saudi Arabia
124 C2 Abhā, Jabal hill Saudi Arabia
146 A4 Abhainnsuidhe Western Isles, Scotland U.K.
116 E5 Abhanpur Madh. Prad. India
122 B2 Abhar Iran
122 B2 Abhar Rūd r. Iran
207 G5 Abia state Nigeria
203 G6 Abiad, Bahr el r. Sudan/Uganda alt. Jebel, Bahr el, conv. White Nile
183 H4 Abia de la Obispalía Spain
210 C3 Ābīata Hāyk' l. Eth.
122 B4 Ab-i-Bazuft r. Iran
250 B2 Abibe, Serranía de mts Col.
206 D5 Abidjan Côte d'Ivoire
186 C2 Abiego Spain
105 G3 Abiko Japan
168 D1 Abild Denmark
236 D4 Abilene KS U.S.A.
237 D5 Abilene TX U.S.A.
159 G5 Abilly France
151 F3 Abingdon Oxfordshire, England U.K.
234 B3 Abingdon MD U.S.A.
232 B6 Abingdon VA U.S.A.
Abingdon Island Islas Galápagos Ecuador see Pinta, Isla
146 E6 Abington South Lanarkshire, Scotland U.K.
233 H3 Abington MA U.S.A.
234 C2 Abington PA U.S.A.
85 G3 Abington Reef Coral Sea Is Terr. Austr.
135 G7 Abinsk Rus. Fed.
183 G3 Abión r. Spain
Ab-i-Panja r. Afgh./Tajik. see Pyandzh
123 F2 Ab-i-Safed r. Afgh.
223 J2 Abitau Lake N.W.T. Can.
224 D3 Abitibi r. Ont. Can.
224 D3 Abitibi, Lake Ont./Que. Can.
Abkhazia aut. rep. Georgia see Ap'khazet'i
185 H3 Abla Spain
156 B4 Ablis France
183 I3 Ablitas Spain
127 G4 Āb Naft r. Iraq
203 F3 Abnūb Egypt
Åbo Fin. see Turku
116 C3 Abohar Punjab India
182 B3 Aboim das Choças Port.
206 E5 Aboisso Côte d'Ivoire
207 F5 Abomey Benin
160 E2 Abondance France
94 B1 Abongabong, Gunung mt. Indon.
207 I6 Abong Mbang Cameroon
177 J4 Abony Hungary
206 E5 Abooso Ghana
125 F4 Aboot Oman
92 A4 Aborlan Phil.
208 B5 Aboumi Gabon
208 E2 Abourasséin, Mont mt. C.A.R.
129 D3 Abovyan Armenia
146 F4 Aboyne Aberdeenshire, Scotland U.K.
125 E2 Abqaiq Saudi Arabia
182 B3 Abragão Port.
246 D2 Abraham's Bay Mayaguana Bahamas
207 G5 Abraka Nigeria
177 L4 Abram Romania
149 G4 Abram Greater Manchester, England U.K.
137 K2 Abramovka Rus. Fed.
226 C3 Abrams WI U.S.A.
177 L4 Abrămuţ Romania
184 B1 Abrantes Port.
258 D1 Abra Pampa Arg.
137 I5 Abrau Dyurso Rus. Fed.
182 C4 Abraveses Port.
257 F4 Abre Campo Brazil
182 C3 Abreiro Port.
186 E3 Abrera Spain
157 H4 Abreschviller France
160 B2 Abrest France
203 F4 'Abri Sudan
161 E4 Abriès France
257 H3 Abrolhos, Arquipélago dos is Brazil
264 G7 Abrolhos Bank sea feature S. Atlantic Ocean
139 J2 Abrosovo Rus. Fed.
185 H3 Abrucena Spain
197 F2 Abrud Romania
Abruzzi admin. reg. Italy see Abruzzo
193 F2 Abruzzo admin. reg. Italy
124 C4 'Abs Yemen
262 W1 Absalom, Mount Antarctica
178 C3 Absam Austria
238 E2 Absaroka Range mts WY U.S.A.
173 E2 Absberg Ger.
179 G2 Absdorf Austria
235 D3 Absecon NJ U.S.A.
129 F3 Abşeron Yarımadası pen. Azer.
179 E3 Abtenau Austria
172 D3 Abtsgmünd Ger.
128 C2 Abū aḑ Ḑuhūr Syria
128 D3 Abū al Ḩusayn, Qā' imp. l. Jordan
124 C4 Abū 'Arīsh Saudi Arabia
202 E3 Abu Ballûs hill Egypt
125 F2 Abu Dhabi U.A.E.
128 C4 Abū Ḩallūfah, Jabal hill Jordan
203 G5 Abu Hamed Sudan
113 □2 Abuhera i. Addu Atoll Maldives
128 A5 Abu Huswa, Gebel hill Egypt
207 G4 Abuja Nigeria
127 F4 Abū Kamāl Syria
105 G1 Abukuma-gawa r. Japan
105 G2 Abukuma-kōchi plat. Japan
126 C5 Abu Mena tourist site Egypt
125 F2 Abu Musa i. The Gulf
Abū Mūsá, Jazīreh-ye i. The Gulf see Abu Musa
252 D2 Abunã r. Bol.
210 C1 Ābune Yosēf mt. Eth.
126 C5 Abu Qîr, Khalîg b. Egypt
208 F4 Aburo mt. Dem. Rep. Congo
116 C4 Abu Road Rajasthan India
128 B5 Abu Rûtha, Gebel mt. Egypt
203 F4 Abu Simbel Temple tourist site Egypt
203 F3 Abu Tig Egypt
203 G3 Abû Tiyûr, Gebel mt. Egypt
210 C2 Abuye Meda mt. Eth.
92 C4 Abuyog Phil.
203 F6 Abu Zabad Sudan
Abū Ẓabī U.A.E. see Abu Dhabi
143 G2 Åby Sweden
124 D5 Abyān governorate Yemen
86 C4 Abydos W.A. Austr.
140 M2 Åbyn Sweden
Abyssinia country Africa see Ethiopia
120 D1 Abzakovo Rus. Fed.
120 D2 Abzanovo Rus. Fed.
250 C4 Acacias Col.
Acacus, Jabal mts Libya see Akakus, Jabal
Academician Vernadskiy research stn Antarctica see Vernadsky
Acadia prov. Can. see Nova Scotia
254 D3 Açailândia Brazil
254 F4 Acajutiba Brazil
243 H6 Acajutla El Salvador
243 G5 Acala Mex.
Acamarachi mt. Chile see Pili, Cerro
244 D3 Acámbaro Mex.
245 E4 Acambay Mex.
209 D9 Acampamento de Caça do Mucusso Angola
243 H4 Acancéh Mex.
250 B2 Acandí Col.
182 B2 A Cañiza Spain
244 B2 Acaponeta Mex.
244 B2 Acaponeta r. Mex.
245 E5 Acapulco Mex.
Acapulco de Juárez Mex. see Acapulco
254 C2 Acará Brazil
254 C2 Acará r. Brazil
254 C2 Acará Miri r. Brazil
254 E2 Acaraú Brazil
254 E2 Acaraú r. Brazil
253 G6 Acaray, Represa de resr Para.
254 F3 Acarí Brazil
257 E1 Acari r. Brazil
252 B3 Acarí Peru
252 B3 Acarí r. Peru
251 G4 Acari, Serra hills Brazil/Guyana
250 D2 Acarigua Venez.
197 F2 Acâş Romania
194 D5 Acate Sicilia Italy
245 F3 Acateno Mex.
245 E4 Acatlan Mex.
244 C3 Acatlán de Juárez Mex.
245 F4 Acatlán de Pérez Figueroa Mex.
245 F4 Acatzingo Mex.
258 D2 Acay, Nevado de mt. Arg.
245 G5 Acayucán Mex.
193 H3 Accadia Italy
190 B4 Acceglio Italy
193 I4 Accettura Italy
Accho Israel see 'Akko
193 F2 Acciano Italy
233 F6 Accomac VA U.S.A.
Accomack VA U.S.A. see Accomac
163 B6 Accous France
206 E5 Accra Ghana
149 G4 Accrington Lancashire, England U.K.
193 F2 Accumoli Italy
261 G3 Aceba Arg.
182 D4 Acebo Spain
184 E1 Acedera Spain
183 H2 Acedo Spain
258 G3 Aceguá Brazil
94 B1 Aceh admin. dist. Indon.
182 D5 Acehuche Spain
182 D4 Aceituna Spain
183 I3 Acered Spain
193 H4 Acerenza Italy
193 H4 Acerno Italy
193 G4 Acerra Italy
184 D2 Aceuchal Spain
178 D2 Ach Austria
173 F3 Ach r. Ger.
173 F4 Ach r. Ger.
216 □1b Achada São Miguel Azores
184 □ Achadas da Cruz Madeira
146 B3 Achadh Mór Western Isles, Scotland U.K.
250 D3 Achaguas Venez.
116 D5 Achalpur Mahar. India
114 C2 Achampet Andhra Prad. India
100 F2 Achan Rus. Fed.
182 B2 A Chán Spain
114 D2 Achanta Andhra Prad. India
129 C3 Ach'ara aut. rep. Georgia
146 C5 Acharacle Highland, Scotland U.K.
129 B3 Acharistsqali r. Georgia
146 E3 Achavanich Highland, Scotland U.K.
Acheh admin. dist. Indon. see Aceh
165 E3 Achel Belgium
198 B2 Acheloös r. Greece
100 C3 Acheng Heilong. China
178 C3 Achenkirch Austria
178 C3 Achensee l. Austria
172 C3 Achern Ger.
156 C2 Acheux-en-Amiénois France
146 D3 Achfary Highland, Scotland U.K.
116 E5 Achhota Madh. Prad. India
156 C2 Achicourt France
129 B2 Ach'igvara Georgia
129 D1 Achikulak Rus. Fed.
147 A3 Achill Head hd Rep. of Ireland
147 A3 Achill Island Rep. of Ireland
147 B3 Achill Sound Rep. of Ireland
146 C3 Achiltibuie Highland, Scotland U.K.
168 E2 Achim Ger.
Achin admin. dist. Indon. see Aceh
131 K4 Achinsk Rus. Fed.
146 C4 Achintee Highland, Scotland U.K.
260 E3 Achiras Arg.
121 G4 Achisay Kazakh.
129 E2 Achisu Rus. Fed.
134 L4 Achit Rus. Fed.
129 D2 Achkhoy-Martan Rus. Fed.
146 C4 Achnasheen Highland, Scotland U.K.
146 B5 Achosnich Highland, Scotland U.K.
173 G3 Achslach Ger.
172 D3 Achstetten Ger.
168 E1 Achtrup Ger.
195 E5 Aci Castello Sicilia Italy
195 E5 Aci Catena Sicilia Italy
199 F3 Acıpayam Turkey
195 E5 Acireale Sicilia Italy
195 E5 Aci St Antonio Sicilia Italy
237 F5 Ackerman MS U.S.A.
234 C2 Ackermanville PA U.S.A.
236 E3 Ackley IA U.S.A.
246 D2 Acklins Island Bahamas
149 H4 Ackworth Moor Top West Yorkshire, England U.K.
151 I2 Acle Norfolk, England U.K.
252 B3 Acobamba Peru
160 B2 Acolin r. France
252 C3 Acomayo Cusco Peru
252 A2 Acomayo Huánuco Peru
149 G3 Acomb Northumberland, England U.K.
260 B3 Aconcagua r. Chile
260 B3 Aconcagua, Cerro mt. Arg.
254 F3 Acopiara Brazil
252 C3 Acora Peru
216 □1 Açores, Arquipélago dos is N. Atlantic Ocean
182 B1 A Coruña Spain
182 B1 A Coruña prov. Galicia Spain
217 □3b Acoua Mayotte
242 □I7 Acoyapa Nic.
194 D4 Acquacalda Isole Lipari Italy
191 H5 Acqualagna Italy
195 F3 Acquaniti r. Italy
192 D2 Acquapendente Italy
193 H5 Acquappesa Italy
195 F4 Acquaro Italy
190 D2 Acquarossa Switz.
193 F2 Acquasanta Terme Italy
193 E2 Acquasparta Italy
193 F2 Acquaviva Picena Italy
194 D4 Acquedolci Sicilia Italy
156 B3 Acquigny France
190 D4 Acqui Terme Italy
233 F3 Acra NY U.S.A.
Acragas Sicilia Italy see Agrigento
82 C3 Acraman, Lake salt flat S.A. Austr.
252 D2 Acre r. Brazil
252 C2 Acre state Brazil
Acre Israel see 'Akko
256 B2 Acreúna Brazil
195 F3 Acri Italy
182 C2 A Cruz de Incio Spain
177 H4 Ács Hungary
177 I4 Acsa Hungary
Actaeon Group is Arch. des Tuamotu Fr. Polynesia see Actéon, Groupe
79 □3 Actéon, Groupe is Arch. des Tuamotu Fr. Polynesia
227 G4 Acton Ont. Can.
151 H2 Acton Suffolk, England U.K.
240 H4 Acton CA U.S.A.
245 E3 Actopán Mex.
252 D1 Açuã r. Brazil
257 F3 Açuçena Brazil
245 E3 Aculco de Espinosa Mex.
245 F4 Acultzingo Mex.
Acunum Acusio France see Montélimar
207 H6 Acurenam Equat. Guinea
253 F3 Açurizal Brazil
193 F3 Acuto Italy
207 F5 Ada Ghana
236 D2 Ada MN U.S.A.
232 B4 Ada OH U.S.A.
237 D5 Ada OK U.S.A.
196 E3 Ada Vojvodina, Srbija Yugo.
210 C3 Ādaba Eth.
Adabazar Turkey see Sakarya
137 I5 Adagum r. Rus. Fed.
186 C2 Adahuesca Spain
226 B5 Adair IL U.S.A.
183 F3 Adaja r. Spain
140 L2 Adak Sweden
220 A4 Adak AK U.S.A.
220 A4 Adak Island AK U.S.A.
129 B4 Adaklı Turkey
128 C1 Adaklı Turkey
Adalia Turkey see Antalya
125 G3 Adam Oman
259 F8 Adam, Mount hill Falkland Is
256 B4 Adamantina Brazil
207 I5 Adamaoua prov. Cameroon
198 D3 Adamas Notio Aigaio Greece
207 H4 Adamawa state Nigeria
197 H3 Adamclisi Romania
190 F2 Adamello mt. Italy
83 G4 Adaminaby N.S.W. Austr.
210 C3 Ādamī Tulu Eth.
174 E6 Adamov Czech Rep.
120 D2 Adamovka Rus. Fed.
175 K4 Adamów Pol.
175 L5 Adamów Pol.
175 K5 Adamówka Pol.
136 D3 Adampil' Ukr.
232 B5 Adams KY U.S.A.
233 G3 Adams MA U.S.A.
226 A4 Adams MN U.S.A.
233 E3 Adams NY U.S.A.
226 C4 Adams WI U.S.A.
262 T2 Adams, Cape Antarctica
81 C5 Adams, Mount South I. N.Z.
233 E3 Adams Center NY U.S.A.
234 A3 Adams County county PA U.S.A.
222 D4 Adams Mountain AK U.S.A.
Adam's Peak Sri Lanka see Sri Pada
240 G2 Adams Peak CA U.S.A.
147 E4 Adamstown Rep. of Ireland
234 B2 Adamstown PA U.S.A.
185 F2 Adamuz Spain
'Adan Yemen see Aden
126 D3 Adana Turkey
128 B1 Adana prov. Turkey
Adana Yemen see Aden
124 D5 'Adan as Sughra Yemen
197 H2 Adâncata Romania
177 H5 Ádánd Hungary
183 F4 Adanero Spain
207 G5 Adani Nigeria
182 C4 Adão Port.
Adapazari Turkey see Sakarya
124 D5 Adaran, Jabal mt. Yemen
147 C4 Adare Rep. of Ireland
263 L2 Adare, Cape Antarctica
102 J5 Adatara-san vol. Japan
85 F5 Adavale Qld Austr.
138 E3 Ādaži Latvia
190 E3 Adda r. Italy
Ad Dabbah Sudan see Ed Debba
124 C3 Ad Dafinah Saudi Arabia
124 D3 Ad Dahnā' des. Saudi Arabia
125 G3 Ad Dākhilīyah admin. reg. Oman
204 B5 Ad Dakhla Western Sahara
124 D5 Aḑ Ḑāli' Yemen
Ad Damir Sudan see Ed Damer
125 E2 Ad Dammām Saudi Arabia
114 C3 Addanki Andhra Prad. India
124 B2 Ad Dār al Ḩamrā' Saudi Arabia
124 C4 Ad Darb Saudi Arabia
114 D2 Addatigala Andhra Prad. India
124 D2 Ad Dawādimī Saudi Arabia
Ad Dawḩah Qatar see Doha
128 C2 Ad Daww plain Syria
151 F2 Adderbury Oxfordshire, England U.K.
124 D2 Ad Dibdibah plain Saudi Arabia
125 E4 Ad Dikākah des. Saudi Arabia
125 D3 Ad Dilam Saudi Arabia
149 H4 Addingham West Yorkshire, England U.K.
124 D2 Ad Dir'īyah Saudi Arabia
Addis Ababa Eth. see Ādīs Ābeba
232 E3 Addison NY U.S.A.
127 G5 Ad Dīwānīyah Iraq
Ad Dīwānīyah governorate Iraq see Al Qādisīyah
151 G3 Addlestone Surrey, England U.K.
215 E5 Addo S. Africa
Addoo Atoll Maldives see Addu Atoll
113 □2 Addu Atoll Maldives
Ad Duwaym Sudan see Ed Dueim
216 □3a Adeje Tenerife Canary Is
231 D6 Adel GA U.S.A.
236 E3 Adel IA U.S.A.
82 D3 Adelaide S.A. Austr.
84 B2 Adelaide r. N.T. Austr.
246 C1 Adelaide New Prov. Bahamas
215 F5 Adelaide S. Africa
262 T2 Adelaide Island Antarctica
84 B2 Adelaide River N.T. Austr.
190 C2 Adelboden Switz.
169 E4 Adelebsen Ger.
86 D2 Adele Island W.A. Austr.
195 F1 Adelfia Italy
168 F3 Adelheidsdorf Ger.
Adélie Coast reg. Antarctica see Adélie Land
263 J2 Adélie Land reg. Antarctica
172 D3 Adelmannsfelden Ger.
83 G3 Adelong N.S.W. Austr.
173 F3 Adelschlag Ger.
173 E2 Adelsdorf Ger.
172 D2 Adelsheim Ger.
173 E3 Adelsried Ger.
173 F3 Adelzhausen Ger.
187 B4 Ademuz Spain
124 D5 Aden Yemen
118 F7 Aden, Gulf of Somalia/Yemen
232 C4 Adena OH U.S.A.
169 B5 Adenau Ger.
168 F2 Adendorf Ger.
214 E5 Adendorp S. Africa
169 E4 Adenstedt Ger.
207 G3 Aderbissinat Niger
Aderno Sicilia Italy see Adrano
116 B5 Adesar Gujarat India
Adhámas Notio Aigaio Greece see Adamas
125 G2 Adhan, Jabal mt. U.A.E.
124 D5 Adhanah, Wādī watercourse Yemen
125 F2 Adh Dhayd U.A.E.
128 C4 'Ādhirīyāt, Jibāl al mts Jordan
116 B5 Adhoi Gujarat India
206 E5 Adiaké Côte d'Ivoire
210 C1 Ādī Ārk'ay Eth.
184 C2 Adiça, Serra da hills Port.
124 B5 Ādī Da'iro Eth.
191 H3 Adige r. Italy
Adigey Autonomous Oblast aut. rep. Rus. Fed. see Adygeya, Respublika
210 C1 Ādīgrat Eth.
203 H6 Adi Keyih Eritrea
203 H6 Adi Kwala Eritrea
114 C2 Adilabad Andhra Prad. India
127 F3 Adilcevaz Turkey
238 B3 Adin CA U.S.A.
Adîncata Romania see Adâncata
165 B3 Adinkerke Belgium
202 B3 Adīrī Libya
233 F2 Adirondack Mountains NY U.S.A.
210 C2 Ādīs Ābeba Eth.
210 C1 Ādīs Zemen Eth.
Adi Ugri Eritrea see Mendefera
126 E3 Adıyaman Turkey
Adjaria aut. rep. Georgia see Ach'ara
197 H2 Adjud Romania
210 A4 Adjumani Uganda
247 □1 Adjuntas Puerto Rico
149 G4 Adlington Lancashire, England U.K.
190 D1 Adliswil Switz.
173 G3 Adlkofen Ger.
86 E2 Admiralty Gulf W.A. Austr.
220 E4 Admiralty Island AK U.S.A.
91 K7 Admiralty Islands P.N.G.
263 L2 Admiralty Mountains Antarctica
179 F3 Admont Austria
207 G5 Ado-Ekiti Nigeria
104 C3 Ado-gawa r. Japan
140 L2 Adolfsström Sweden
86 F2 Adolphus Island W.A. Austr.
114 C3 Adoni Andhra Prad. India
177 H4 Adony Hungary
171 D5 Adorf Sachsen Ger.
171 D5 Adorf Sachsen Ger.
169 D4 Adorf (Diemelsee) Ger.
184 A1 A-dos-Cunhados Port.
182 C3 Adoufe Port.
163 A5 Adour r. France
117 F5 Adra W. Bengal India
185 G4 Adra Spain
185 H4 Adra r. Spain
183 H3 Adradas Spain
183 F3 Adrados Spain
Adramyttium Turkey see Edremit
Adramyttium, Gulf of Turkey see Edremit Körfezi
194 D5 Adrano Sicilia Italy
205 E4 Adrar Alg.
205 G4 Adrar mts Alg.
Adrar hills Mali see Ifôghas, Adrar des
204 C5 Adrar admin. reg. Maur.
Adrar des Iforas hills Mali see Ifôghas, Adrar des
123 E3 Adraskand r. Afgh.
123 G1 Adrasmon Tajik.
191 H3 Adria Italy
227 E5 Adrian MI U.S.A.
237 C5 Adrian TX U.S.A.
Adrianople Turkey see Edirne
Adrianopolis Turkey see Edirne
188 D3 Adriatic Sea Europe
162 C2 Adriers France
147 B5 Adrigole Rep. of Ireland
Adua Eth. see Ādwa
260 B5 Aduana Pejerrey Chile
164 F1 Aduard Neth.
190 E2 Adula Gruppe mts Switz.
114 C4 Adur Kerala India
138 F4 Adutiškis Lith.
Aduwa Eth. see Ādwa
86 D4 Adverse Well W.A. Austr.
210 C1 Ādwa Eth.
149 H4 Adwick le Street South Yorkshire, England U.K.
206 E5 Adwufia Ghana
131 O3 Adycha r. Rus. Fed.
129 B1 Adyge-Khabl' Rus. Fed.
Adygeya aut. rep. Rus. Fed. see Adygeya, Respublika
129 A1 Adygeya, Respublika aut. rep. Rus. Fed.
135 G7 Adygeysk Rus. Fed.
Adygeyskaya Avtonomnaya Oblast' aut. rep. Rus. Fed. see Adygeya, Respublika
135 I7 Adyk Respublika Kalmykiya - Khalm'g-Tangch Rus. Fed.
187 C4 Adzaneta Spain
187 C6 Adzaneta de Albaida Spain
137 G3 Adzhamka Ukr.
Adzharia aut. rep. Georgia see Ach'ara
122 C2 Adzhiyan Turkm.
206 E5 Adzopé Côte d'Ivoire
134 M2 Adz'va r. Rus. Fed.
199 D2 Aegean Sea Greece/Turkey
Aegina i. Greece see Aigina
138 E2 Aegviidu Estonia
Aegyptus country Africa see Egypt
Aela Jordan see Al 'Aqabah
Aelana Jordan see Al 'Aqabah
Aelia Capitolina Israel/West Bank see Jerusalem
Aelōnlaplap atoll Marshall Is see Ailinglapalap
Aenus Turkey see Enez
142 D4 Ærø i. Denmark
137 H5 Aeroflots'kyy Ukr.
150 C2 Aeron r. Wales U.K.
168 F1 Ærøskøbing Denmark
169 E3 Aerzen Ger.
Aesernia Italy see Isernia
182 B2 A Estrada Spain
141 M3 Äetsä Fin.
137 J2 Afanas'yevka Rus. Fed.
134 K4 Afanas'yevo Rus. Fed.
Afándou Notio Aigaio Greece see Afantou
199 F3 Afantou Notio Aigaio Greece
210 D1 Afar admin. reg. Eth.
203 I6 Afar Depression Eritrea/Eth.
158 D4 Aff r. France
206 E5 Afféri Côte d'Ivoire
193 F3 Affile Italy
173 E3 Affing Ger.
190 D1 Affoltern am Albis Switz.
Affreville Alg. see Khemis Miliana
Afghānestān country Asia see Afghanistan
123 F3 Afghanistan country Asia
210 E4 Afgooye Somalia
124 C3 'Afīf Saudi Arabia
182 B3 Afife Port.
207 G5 Afikpo Nigeria
139 J3 Afim'ino Rus. Fed.
137 J5 Afipskiy Rus. Fed.
Afiun Karahissar Turkey see Afyon
140 J3 Åfjord Norway
179 G3 Aflenz Kurort Austria
205 F2 Aflou Alg.
210 D4 Afmadow Somalia
182 C1 A Fonsagrada Spain
257 G4 Afonso Cláudio Brazil
182 C2 A Forxa Galicia Spain
182 C2 A Forxa Galicia Spain
191 H5 Afra r. Italy
193 G4 Afragola Italy
254 E4 Afrânio Brazil
210 D1 Āfrēra Terara vol. Eth.
210 D1 Āfrēra YeChe'ew Hāyk' l. Eth.
200 Africa continent
Africa Nova country Africa see Tunisia
128 C1 'Afrīn Syria
128 C1 'Afrīn, Nahr r. Syria/Turkey
179 E4 Afritz Austria
126 E3 Afşin Turkey
233 F3 Afton NY U.S.A.
238 E3 Afton WY U.S.A.
146 D6 Afton Bridgend East Ayrshire, Scotland U.K.
251 I5 Afuá Brazil
128 B3 'Afula Israel
199 G2 Afyon Turkey
199 G2 Afyon prov. Turkey
Afyonkarahisar Turkey see Afyon
171 D5 Aga Ger.
107 G1 Aga r. Rus. Fed.
Aga-Buryat Autonomous Okrug admin. div. Rus. Fed. see Aginskiy Buryatskiy Avtonomnyy Okrug
Agadès Niger see Agadez
207 G2 Agadez Niger
207 H2 Agadez dept Niger
204 C3 Agadir Morocco
121 H2 Agadyr' Kazakh.
216 □3f Agaete Gran Canaria Canary Is
207 G4 Agaie Nigeria
217 □1 Agalega Islands Mauritius
182 D4 Agallas Spain
Agana Guam see Hagåtña
120 D1 Agapovka Rus. Fed.
116 D5 Agar Madh. Prad. India
210 C3 Āgaro Eth.
117 G5 Agartala Tripura India
177 I5 Ágasegyháza Hungary
114 B2 Agashi Mahar. India
224 D3 Agate Ont. Can.
Agathe France see Agde
199 E3 Agathonisi i. Greece
105 F2 Agatsuma-gawa r. Japan
226 E2 Agawa r. Ont. Can.
Agayani Georgia see Aghaiani
207 G5 Agbor Bojiboji Nigeria
206 D5 Agboville Côte d'Ivoire
129 E3 Ağcabädi Azer.
129 E4 Ağdam Azer.
129 E3 Ağdärä Azer.
129 E3 Ağdaş Azer.
Agdash Azer. see Ağdaş
161 B5 Agde France
Agdzhabedi Azer. see Ağcabädi
Agedabia Libya see Ajdābiyā
163 C4 Agen France
163 C4 Agenais reg. France
207 G5 Agenebode Nigeria
Agenois reg. France see Agenais
105 F3 Ageo Japan
129 B2 Agep'st'a, Mt'a Georgia/Rus. Fed.
186 D2 Àger Spain
142 C4 Agerbæk Denmark
210 C3 Āgere Maryam Eth.
139 K4 Ageyevo Rus. Fed.
176 F4 Ágfalva Hungary
214 B3 Aggeneys S. Africa
169 C5 Agger r. Ger.
Aggershus county Norway see Akershus
192 B4 Aggius Sardegna Italy
147 D4 Aghaboe Rep. of Ireland
147 A2 Aghadoon Rep. of Ireland
148 C3 Aghagallon Northern Ireland U.K.
129 D3 Aghaiani Georgia
148 C3 Aghalee Northern Ireland U.K.
147 C3 Aghamore Rep. of Ireland
147 E1 Aghanloo Northern Ireland U.K.
147 E4 Aghavannagh Rep. of Ireland
147 C4 Aghern Rep. of Ireland
192 B2 Aghione Corse France
197 F2 Aghireşu Romania
147 C2 Aghla Mountain hill Rep. of Ireland
147 D3 Aghnacliff Rep. of Ireland
206 D2 Aghouavil des. Maur.
198 C2 Agia Greece
198 C2 Agia Anna Sterea Ellas Greece
242 C3 Agiabampo Mex.
199 E3 Agia Marina Greece
199 E2 Agiasos Voreio Aigaio Greece
198 D4 Agia Vervara Kriti Greece
197 I3 Agigea Romania
197 I3 Agighiol Romania
Agiguan i. N. Mariana Is see Aguijan
126 E3 Ağın Turkey
Agincourt France see Azincourt
199 G2 Ağın Dağı mt. Turkey
107 G1 Aginskiy Buryatskiy Avtonomnyy Okrug admin. div. Rus. Fed.
107 G1 Aginskoye Rus. Fed.
Aginum France see Agen
198 C2 Agioi Apostoloi Greece
198 C3 Agioi Theodoroi Greece
198 C1 Agion Oros admin. div. Greece
198 C3 Agios Dimitrios Attiki Greece
198 C1 Agios Dimitrios Kentriki Makedonia Greece
198 D2 Agios Efstratios i. Greece
199 E3 Agios Kirykos Voreio Aigaio Greece
198 C2 Agios Konstantinos Greece
198 A2 Agios Matthaios Ionioi Nisoi Greece
198 C1 Agios Nikolaos Kentriki Makedonia Greece
199 D4 Agios Nikolaos Kriti Greece
199 E2 Agios Paraskevi Voreio Aigaio Greece
198 C3 Agios Petros Greece
198 C2 Agios Stefanos Attiki Greece
198 C2 Agios Thomas Sterea Ellas Greece
198 C1 Agiou Orous, Kolpos b. Greece
194 D5 Agira Sicilia Italy
215 E2 Agisanang S. Africa
148 C2 Agivey Northern Ireland U.K.
172 C2 Aglasterhausen Ger.
199 G3 Ağlasun Turkey
191 G5 Agliana Italy
192 B3 Aglientu Sardegna Italy
163 F6 Agly r. France
190 E3 Agnadello Italy
198 B2 Agnantero Greece
159 E2 Agneaux France
193 F3 Agnena r. Italy
82 B1 Agnes, Mount hill S.A. Austr.
87 D6 Agnew W.A. Austr.
147 F2 Agnew's Hill hill Northern Ireland U.K.
206 E5 Agnibilékrou Côte d'Ivoire
197 G3 Agnita Romania
190 D2 Agno Switz.
193 G3 Agnone Italy
104 C4 Ago Japan
207 F4 Ago-Are Nigeria
190 D3 Agogna r. Italy
206 E5 Agogo Ghana
Agoitz Spain see Aoiz
182 B2 A Golada Spain
206 E5 Agona Ghana
162 C3 Agonac France
206 E5 Agona Junction Ghana
158 E2 Agon-Coutainville France
106 D4 Agong Qinghai China
191 H2 Agordo Italy
187 C6 Agost Spain
163 B5 Agos-Vidalos France
240 H4 Agoura CA U.S.A.
163 D5 Agout r. France
116 D4 Agra Uttar Prad. India
198 B2 Agrafiotis r. Greece
Agram Croatia see Zagreb
185 I2 Agramón Spain
186 E3 Agramunt Spain
190 E3 Agrate Brianza Italy
183 I3 Agreda Spain
187 C6 Agres Spain
195 F4 Agri r. Italy
127 F3 Ağrı Turkey
129 C4 Ağrı prov. Turkey
129 D4 Ağrı Dağı mt. Turkey
Agrigan i. N. Mariana Is see Agrihan
194 C5 Agrigento Sicilia Italy
194 C5 Agrigento prov. Sicilia Italy
Agrigentum Sicilia Italy see Agrigento
91 K3 Agrihan i. N. Mariana Is
197 F2 Agrij r. Romania
198 B2 Agrinio Greece
260 C6 Agrio r. Arg.
182 C3 Agrochão Port.
193 G4 Agropoli Italy
134 K4 Agryz Rus. Fed.
129 D3 Ağstafa Azer.
129 D3 Agstev r. Armenia
129 F3 Ağsu Azer.
215 E5 Agter Sneeuberg S. Africa
215 E4 Agtertang S. Africa
260 C6 Agua Amarga, Pampa del plain Arg.
245 E3 Agua Blanca Iturbide Mex.
257 F2 Água Boa Brazil
244 B2 Agua Brava, Laguna lag. Mex.
256 A4 Água Clara Brazil
243 H5 Aguada Mex.
247 □1 Aguada Puerto Rico
250 C3 Aguadas Col.
216 □1b Agua de Pau São Miguel Azores
247 □1 Aguadilla Puerto Rico
257 G3 Agua Doce do Norte Brazil
256 C5 Aguados, Serra dos mts Brazil
245 G4 Agua Dulce Mex.
242 □J7 Aguadulce Panama
185 F3 Aguadulce Andalucía Spain
185 H4 Aguadulce Andalucía Spain
241 K5 Agua Fria r. AZ U.S.A.
256 D5 Aguaí Brazil
216 □1a Agualva Terceira Azores
244 C1 Aguanaval r. Mex.
184 C3 Água Negra hill Port.
240 I5 Aguanga CA U.S.A.
242 □I6 Aguanqueterique Hond.
225 I3 Aguanus r. Que. Can.
256 B4 Aguapeí r. Brazil
253 F3 Aguapeí r. Brazil
253 F4 Aguapeí, Serra hills Brazil
242 C2 Agua Prieta Mex.
252 E5 Aguaragüe, Cordillera de mts Bol.
258 E1 Aguaray Arg.
182 B3 A Guardia Galicia Spain
216 □1b Agua Retorta São Miguel Azores
186 B3 Aguarón Spain
242 D3 Aguaruto Mex.
186 C2 Aguas Spain
185 I3 Aguas r. Spain
254 F4 Águas Belas Brazil
182 B5 Águas Belas Port.
247 □1 Aguas Buenas Puerto Rico
244 C3 Aguascalientes Mex.
244 C3 Aguascalientes state Mex.
261 I4 Aguas Corrientes Uru.
187 C6 Aguas de Busot Spain
257 G2 Águas Formosas Brazil
182 C3 Águas Frias Port.
257 G1 Águas Vermelhas Brazil
186 C3 Aguasvivas r. Spain
253 F3 Água Verde r. Brazil
244 B2 Agua Verde Mex.
186 C4 Aguaviva Spain
182 C2 A Gudiña Spain
185 F2 Agudo Spain
256 C5 Agudos Brazil
182 B4 Águeda Port.
182 D3 Águeda r. Port./Spain
183 G1 Agüera r. Spain
161 B1 Aguessac France
191 I5 Agugliano Italy
184 C2 Aguiar Port.
182 C4 Aguiar da Beira Port.
207 G3 Aguié Niger
182 B4 Aguieira, Barragem da resr Port.
91 K4 Aguijan i. N. Mariana Is
183 I4 Aguila mt. Spain
241 K5 Aguila AZ U.S.A.
183 F3 Aguilafuente Spain
239 F4 Aguilar CO U.S.A.
186 C4 Aguilar de Alfambra Spain
183 F2 Aguilar de Campóo Spain
185 F3 Aguilar de la Frontera Spain
183 I3 Aguilar del Rio Alhama Spain
185 I3 Águilas Spain
244 C4 Aguililla Mex.
182 B4 Aguim Port.
216 □3f Agüimes Gran Canaria Canary Is
216 □3f Aguineguín r. Gran Canaria Canary Is
92 B4 Aguisan Phil.
183 G3 Aguisejo r. Spain
210 C1 Āgula'i Eth.
214 C6 Agulhas S. Africa
214 C6 Agulhas, Cape S. Africa
264 K9 Agulhas Basin sea feature Southern Ocean
257 E4 Agulhas Negras mt. Brazil
265 F7 Agulhas Plateau sea feature Southern Ocean
264 J8 Agulhas Ridge sea feature S. Atlantic Ocean
186 F2 Agullana Spain
187 C6 Agullent Spain
216 □3a Agulo La Gomera Canary Is
102 □1 Aguni-jima i. Japan
Aguntum Italy see San Candido
92 C4 Agusan r. Phil.
92 B4 Agutaya Phil.
199 F1 Ağva Turkey
129 E2 Agvali Rus. Fed.
207 G4 Agwarra Nigeria
210 B3 Agwei r. Sudan
Agyrium Sicilia Italy see Agira
Ahaggar plat. Alg. see Hoggar
147 B5 Ahakista Rep. of Ireland
173 G3 Aham Ger.
122 A2 Ahar Iran
81 C5 Ahaura South I. N.Z.
81 C5 Ahaura r. South I. N.Z.

Ahaus to Aleshki
275

169 C3 Ahaus Ger.
168 E2 Ahausen Ger.
147 D4 Ahenny Rep. of Ireland
147 C5 Aherla Rep. of Ireland
147 D4 Aherlow r. Rep. of Ireland
217 □3a Ahibambo mt. Njazidja Comoros
182 D4 Ahigal Spain
182 D3 Ahigal de Villarino Spain
185 F3 Ahillo mt. Spain
184 E2 Ahillones Spain
80 F3 Ahimanawa Range mts North I. N.Z.
80 D1 Ahipara North I. N.Z.
114 D2 Ahiri Mahar. India
80 E3 Ahititi North I. N.Z.
138 F2 Ahja r. Estonia
220 B4 Ahklun Mountains AK U.S.A.
127 F3 Ahlat Turkey
170 F2 Ahlbeck Ger.
168 E3 Ahlden (Aller) Ger.
169 C4 Ahlen Ger.
168 E2 Ahlerstedt Ger.
168 D3 Ahlhorn Ger.
171 C4 Ahlsdorf Ger.
116 C5 Ahmadabad Gujarat India
128 B5 Aḥmad al Bāqir, Jabal mt. Jordan
129 E4 Āhmädbäyli Azer.
114 B2 Ahmadnagar Mahar. India
114 C2 Ahmadpur Mahar. India
123 G4 Ahmadpur East Pak.
123 G4 Ahmadpur Sial Pak.
210 D2 Ahmar Mountains Eth.
Ahmedabad Gujarat India see Ahmadabad
Ahmednagar Mahar. India see Ahmadnagar
199 E2 Ahmetli Turkey
199 G2 Ahmetpaşa Turkey
168 F3 Ahnsbeck Ger.
207 G5 Ahoada Nigeria
147 E2 Ahoghill Northern Ireland U.K.
242 C3 Ahome Mex.
116 C4 Ahore Rajasthan India
169 F5 Ahorn Ger.
178 C3 Ahornspitze mt. Austria
231 E4 Ahoskie NC U.S.A.
169 C5 Ahr r. Ger.
122 B4 Ahram Iran
Ahrâmât el Jîzah tourist site Egypt see Giza Pyramids
137 H5 Ahrarne Ukr.
117 E4 Ahraura Uttar Prad. India
169 B5 Ahrbrück Ger.
168 F1 Ahrensbök Ger.
168 F2 Ahrensburg Ger.
170 E3 Ahrensfelde Ger.
170 D1 Ahrenshagen Ger.
169 C4 Ahse r. Ger.
134 D3 Āhtäri Fin.
138 F2 Ahtme Estonia
243 H6 Ahuachapán El Salvador
244 C3 Ahualulco Jalisco Mex.
244 D2 Ahualulco San Luis Potosí Mex.
162 E2 Ahun France
79 □3 Ahunui atoll Arch. des Tuamotu Fr. Polynesia
81 C6 Ahuriri r. South I. N.Z.
143 F4 Åhus Sweden
122 B4 Ahvāz Iran
Ahvenanmaa is Fin. see Åland
116 C5 Ahwa Gujarat India
124 D5 Aḥwar Yemen
Ahwāz Iran see Ahvāz
101 C4 Ai r. China
250 D4 Aiari r. Brazil
107 F3 Aibag Gol r. China
183 I2 Aibar Spain
179 G4 Aibl Austria
247 □1 Aibonito Puerto Rico
173 F3 Aichach Ger.
172 C3 Aichhalden Ger.
104 D4 Aichi pref. Japan
173 E4 Aichstetten Ger.
232 B5 Aid OH U.S.A.
173 H3 Aidenbach Ger.
169 F5 Aidhausen Ger.
194 D5 Aidone Sicilia Italy
240 □ Aiea HI U.S.A.
193 I5 Aiello Calabro Italy
193 H5 Aieta Italy
162 B2 Aiffres France
198 C2 Aigeira Greece
179 F3 Aigen im Ennstal Austria
179 E2 Aigen im Mühlkreis Austria
128 B2 Aigialousa Cyprus
198 C3 Aigina Greece
198 C3 Aigina i. Greece
198 C1 Aiginio Greece
198 C2 Aigio Greece
190 B2 Aigle Switz.
161 E4 Aigle de Chambeyron mt. France
161 E4 Aiglun France
163 C5 Aignan France
156 E5 Aignay-le-Duc France
161 B4 Aigoual, Mont mt. France
162 C3 Aigre France
162 B2 Aigrefeuille-d'Aunis France
158 E4 Aigrefeuille-sur-Maine France
258 G4 Aiguá Uru.
160 C1 Aigue, Mont hill France
160 E3 Aiguebelle France
160 E3 Aigueblanche France
160 B2 Aigueperse France
161 C4 Aigues r. France
161 C5 Aigues-Mortes France
161 B5 Aigues-Mortes, Golfe d' b. France
161 A5 Aigues-Vives France
161 C5 Aigues-Vives France
163 D6 Aigues-Vives France
161 D4 Aiguille, Mont mt. France
160 F3 Aiguille d'Argentière mt. France/Switz.
160 F3 Aiguille de la Grande Sassière mt. France
161 E3 Aiguille de Péclet mt. France
161 E3 Aiguille de Scolette mt. France/Italy
160 E3 Aiguille du Midi mt. France
161 E4 Aiguilles France
161 E3 Aiguilles d'Arves mts France
160 E3 Aiguilles des Glaciers mts France
160 E3 Aiguille Verte mt. France
163 C4 Aiguillon France
162 D2 Aigurande France
Aihua Yunnan China see Yunxian
Aihui Heilong. China see Heihe
252 A2 Aija Peru
Aijal Mizoram India see Aizawl
105 F3 Aikawa Japan
231 D5 Aiken SC U.S.A.
108 B3 Ailao Shan mts Yunnan China
84 C4 Aileron N.T. Austr.
108 D3 Ailing Guangxi China
Ailinglabelab atoll Marshall Is see Ailinglapalap
266 G6 Ailinglapalap atoll Marshall Is
156 D5 Aillant-sur-Tholon France
163 B4 Aillas France
161 E5 Aille r. France
157 G5 Aillevillers-et-Lyaumont France
156 B2 Ailly-le-Haut-Clocher France
156 C3 Ailly-sur-Noye France
156 C3 Ailly-sur-Somme France
227 G4 Ailsa Craig Ont. Can.
146 C6 Ailsa Craig i. Scotland U.K.
161 C5 Aimargues France
160 E3 Aime France
Aimeo i. Fr. Polynesia see Moorea
258 D3 Aimogasta Arg.
257 G3 Aimorés Brazil
257 G2 Aimorés, Serra dos hills Brazil
160 D2 Ain dept Rhône-Alpes France
160 D3 Ain r. France
160 A2 Ainay-le-Château France
138 E3 Ainaži Latvia
205 G2 Aïn Beïda Alg.
204 E2 Aïn Beni Mathar Morocco
204 C4 'Aïn Ben Tili Maur.
205 F1 Aïn Defla Alg.
205 F2 Aïn Deheb Alg.
173 E3 Aindling Ger.
205 F2 Aïn el Hadjel Alg.
205 G2 Aïn el Melh Alg.
178 D4 Ainet Austria
163 A5 Ainhoa France
205 G1 Aïn-M'Lila Alg.
Aïn Mokra Alg. see Berrahal
205 G2 Aïn Oulmene Alg.
205 F2 Aïn Oussera Alg.
173 G4 Ainring Ger.
186 D2 Ainsa Spain
Ain Salah Alg. see In Salah
149 F4 Ainsdale Merseyside, England U.K.
205 E2 Aïn Sefra Alg.
236 D3 Ainsworth NE U.S.A.
Aintab Turkey see Gaziantep
205 E2 Aïn Temouchent Alg.
149 G4 Aintree Merseyside, England U.K.
183 I3 Ainzón Spain
103 G6 Aioi Japan
250 C4 Aipe Col.
252 D4 Aiquile Bol.
156 B3 Airaines France
190 C4 Airasca Italy
94 B2 Airbangis Sumatera Indon.
146 B4 Aird Asaig Western Isles, Scotland U.K.
146 C4 Aird of Sleat Highland, Scotland U.K.
222 H5 Airdrie Alta Can.
146 E6 Airdrie North Lanarkshire, Scotland U.K.
157 E3 Aire r. France
149 H4 Airedale val. England U.K.
163 B5 Aire-sur-l'Adour France
156 C2 Aire-sur-la-Lys France
95 E3 Airhitam r. Indon.
146 B3 Airidh a'Bhruaich Western Isles, Scotland U.K.
85 G4 Airlie Beach Qld Austr.
86 B4 Airlie Island W.A. Austr.
193 G3 Airola Italy
190 D2 Airolo Switz.
223 J4 Air Ronge Sask. Can.
146 E5 Airth Falkirk, Scotland U.K.
149 G3 Airton North Yorkshire, England U.K.
162 B2 Airvault France
96 A2 Aisatung Mountain Myanmar
173 F2 Aisch r. Ger.
259 B7 Aisén admin. reg. Chile
156 E5 Aisey-sur-Seine France
107 I4 Ai Shan hill Shandong China
222 B2 Aishihik Y.T. Can.
173 E3 Aislingen Ger.
156 D3 Aisne dept Picardie France
157 C3 Aisne r. France
205 E2 Aïssa, Djebel mt. Alg.
160 E1 Aïssey France
160 C1 Aisy-sur-Armançon France
187 C6 Aitana mt. Spain
204 D3 Aït Benhaddou tourist site Morocco
173 G3 Aiterach r. Ger.
173 G3 Aiterhofen Ger.
146 F2 Aith Orkney, Scotland U.K.
236 E2 Aitkin MN U.S.A.
198 B2 Aitoliko Greece
186 D3 Aitona Spain
120 C1 Aitova Rus. Fed.
173 E4 Aitrach Ger.
173 E4 Aitrang Ger.
81 □2 Aitutaki i. Cook Is
197 F2 Aiud Romania
138 E3 Aiviekste r. Latvia
Aix France see Aix-en-Provence
160 C3 Aix r. France
156 D4 Aix-en-Othe France
161 D5 Aix-en-Provence France
162 D3 Aixe-sur-Vienne France
Aix-la-Chapelle Ger. see Aachen
160 D3 Aix-les-Bains France
210 C1 Āīy Ādī Eth.
Aíyina i. Greece see Aigina
Aiyínion Greece see Aiginio
Aíyion Greece see Aigio
Aíyira Greece see Aigeira
117 H5 Aizawl Mizoram India
158 E5 Aizenay France
138 E3 Aizkraukle Latvia
183 I2 Aizpun Spain
138 C3 Aizpute Latvia
103 I5 Aizu-wakamatsu Japan
124 C2 Ajā, Jibāl mts Saudi Arabia
192 A3 Ajaccio Corse France
Ajaccio airport Corse France see Campo dell'Oro
192 A3 Ajaccio, Golfe d' b. Corse France
245 E3 Ajacuba Mex.
116 E4 Ajaigarh Madh. Prad. India
250 C4 Ajajú r. Col.
177 L3 Ajak Hungary
245 F4 Ajalpán Mex.
116 C5 Ajanta Mahar. India
Ajanta Range hills India see Sahyadriparvat Range
207 G5 Ajaokuta Nigeria
Ajaria aut. rep. Georgia see Ach'ara
207 G4 Ajasse Nigeria
162 D3 Ajat France
227 H4 Ajax Ont. Can.
81 D5 Ajax, Mount South I. N.Z.
Ajayameru Rajasthan India see Ajmer
106 B2 Aj Bogd Uul mts Mongolia
202 D2 Ajdābiyā Libya
188 D3 Ajdovščina Slovenia
a-Jiddét des. Oman see Ḥarāsīs, Jiddat al
117 G4 Ajimganj W. Bengal India
177 G4 Ajka Hungary
128 B3 'Ajlūn Jordan
125 F2 Ajman U.A.E.
116 C4 Ajmer Rajasthan India
Ajmer-Merwara Rajasthan India see Ajmer
183 G1 Ajo Spain
241 K5 Ajo AZ U.S.A.
241 K5 Ajo, Mount AZ U.S.A.
183 G5 Ajofrín Spain
78 □3b Ajokwola i. Majuro Marshall Is
114 B2 Ajra Mahar. India
92 B4 Ajuy Phil.
102 K2 Akabira Japan
Akademii Nauk, Khrebet mt. Tajik. see Akademiyai Fanho, Qatorkŭhi
123 G2 Akademiyai Fanho, Qatorkŭhi mt. Tajik.
102 I4 Aka-gawa r. Japan
103 F6 Akagi Japan
105 F2 Akagi-yama vol. Japan
105 E3 Akaishi-dake mt. Japan
105 D4 Akaishi-sanmyaku mts Japan
210 C2 Āk'ak'ī Beseka Eth.
202 A3 Akakus, Jabal mts Libya
114 C2 Akalkot Mahar. India
Akamagaseki Japan see Shimonoseki
207 H5 Akamkpa Nigeria
198 B2 Akarnanika mts Greece
81 D5 Akaroa South I. N.Z.
81 D5 Akaroa Harbour South I. N.Z.
127 E4 Akāshat Iraq
104 A4 Akashi Japan
215 G1 Akasia S. Africa
140 M2 Äkäsjoki r. Fin.
177 I5 Akasztó Hungary
81 E4 Akatarawa North I. N.Z.
121 H3 Akbakay Kazakh.
116 E4 Akbarpur Uttar Prad. India
117 E4 Akbarpur Uttar Prad. India
121 G2 Akbeit Kazakh.
128 C1 Akbez Turkey
205 G1 Akbou Alg.
120 C2 Akbulak Rus. Fed.
129 A3 Akçaabat Turkey
126 E3 Akçadağ Turkey
129 C4 Akça Dağ mt. Turkey
126 E3 Akçakale Turkey
199 G1 Akçakoca Turkey
128 A1 Akçalı Dağları mts Turkey
199 E3 Akçaova Turkey
199 F3 Akçay Antalya Turkey
199 F3 Akçay r. Turkey
122 D1 Akchakaya, Vpadina depr. Turkm.
206 B2 Akchâr reg. Maur.
121 H3 Akchatau Kazakh.
Akchi Kazakh. see Akshiy
129 B4 Akdağ mt. Turkey
199 F2 Akdağ mt. Turkey
199 F3 Akdağ mts Turkey
199 G3 Ak Dağı mt. Turkey
199 F3 Akdağlar mts Turkey
126 D3 Akdağmadeni Turkey
129 C3 Akdam Turkey
122 D1 Akdepe Turkm.
128 A1 Akdere Turkey
129 B4 Akdoğan Dağı mts Turkey
149 G2 Akeld Northumberland, England U.K.
124 B5 Akele Guzai prov. Eritrea
171 D4 Aken Ger.
143 H2 Åkersberga Sweden
142 D1 Akershus county Norway
164 D2 Akersloot Neth.
143 G2 Åkers styckebruk Sweden
208 D4 Aketi Dem. Rep. Congo
Akgyr Erezi hills Turkm. see Akkyr, Gory
129 D2 Akhalgori Georgia
Akhali-Afoni Georgia see Akhali Ap'oni
129 B2 Akhali Ap'oni Georgia
129 C3 Akhalk'alak'i Georgia
Akhal Oblast admin. div. Turkm. see Akhal'skaya Oblast'
122 D2 Akhal'skaya Oblast' admin. div. Turkm.
129 C3 Akhalts'ikhe Georgia
202 D2 Akhḍar, Al Jabal al mts Libya
125 G3 Akhḍar, Jabal mts Oman
Akhelóös r. Greece see Acheloös
197 H4 Akheloy Bulg.
199 E2 Akhisar Turkey
129 D3 Akhk'erp'i Georgia
129 D2 Akhmeta Georgia
129 B1 Akhmetovskaya Rus. Fed.
203 F3 Akhmîm Egypt
116 C2 Akhnoor Jammu and Kashmir
Akhsu Azer. see Ağsu
Akhta Armenia see Hrazdan
127 I6 Akhtar Iran
128 C1 Akhtarīn Syria
135 I6 Akhtubinsk Rus. Fed.
129 E3 Akhty Rus. Fed.
Akhtyrka Ukr. see Okhtyrka
137 J5 Akhtyrskiy Rus. Fed.
120 D1 Akhunovo Rus. Fed.
129 E3 Akhvay, Gora mt. Azer./Rus. Fed.
103 F7 Aki Japan
208 B5 Akiéni Gabon
Akıncılar Turkey see Selçuk
126 E2 Akıncılar Turkey
113 □1 Akinfushi i. N. Male Maldives
143 F4 Åkirkeby Bornholm Denmark
105 F3 Akiruno Japan
105 F3 Akishima Japan
100 E1 Akishma r. Rus. Fed.
102 J4 Akita Japan
102 J4 Akita pref. Japan
80 F4 Akitio North I. N.Z.
105 F2 Akiyama-gawa r. Japan
206 B2 Akjoujt Maur.
204 C3 Akka Morocco
140 L2 Akkajaure l. Sweden
Akkerman Ukr. see Bilhorod-Dnistrovs'kyy
120 D2 Akkermanovka Rus. Fed.
128 B3 'Akko Israel
121 G1 Akkol' Akmolinskaya Oblast' Kazakh.
135 J7 Akkol' Kazakh.
121 G4 Akkol' Kazakh.
199 E3 Akköy Turkey
199 F3 Akköy Turkey
164 E1 Akkrum Neth.
121 I2 Akku Kazakh.
Akkul' Kazakh. see Akkol'
120 F3 Akkum Kazakh.
126 E2 Akkuş Turkey
122 C1 Akkyr, Gory hills Turkm.
120 B3 Akkystau Kazakh.
207 F4 Aklampa Benin
220 E3 Aklavik N.W.T. Can.
116 D4 Aklera Rajasthan India
Ak-Mechet Kazakh. see Kyzylorda
138 D4 Akmena r. Lith.
138 D3 Akmenė Lith.
Akmola Kazakh. see Astana
Akmola Oblast admin. div. Kazakh. see Akmolinskaya Oblast'
Akmolinsk Kazakh. see Astana
121 G2 Akmolinskaya Oblast' admin. div. Kazakh.
138 E3 Aknīste Latvia
204 E2 Aknoul Morocco
103 G6 Akō Japan
210 B3 Akobo Wenz r. Eth./Sudan
116 D5 Akodia Madh. Prad. India
114 B2 Akola Mahar. India
116 D5 Akola Mahar. India
207 H6 Akom II Cameroon
207 I6 Akonolinga Cameroon
203 H6 Akordat Eritrea
199 G2 Akören Afyon Turkey
126 D3 Akören Turkey
116 D5 Akot Mahar. India
206 E5 Akoupé Côte d'Ivoire
221 L3 Akpatok Island Nunavut Can.
110 B3 Akqi Xinjiang China
198 C2 Akraifnio Greece
140 □B2 Akranes Iceland
142 A2 Åkrehamn Norway
236 C3 Akron CO U.S.A.
226 D5 Akron IN U.S.A.
232 D3 Akron NY U.S.A.
232 C4 Akron OH U.S.A.
234 B2 Akron PA U.S.A.
Akrotiri Bay Cyprus see Akrotirion Bay
128 A2 Akrotirion Bay Cyprus
Akrotiriou, Kolpos b. Cyprus see Akrotirion Bay
128 A2 Akrotiri Sovereign Base Area military base Cyprus
111 B5 Aksai Chin terr. Asia
199 F1 Aksakal Turkey
197 H4 Aksakovo Bulg.
135 K5 Aksakovo Rus. Fed.
126 D3 Aksaray Turkey
130 H3 Aksarka Rus. Fed.
129 B2 Aksaut r. Rus. Fed.
110 F4 Aksay Gansu China
120 C2 Aksay Kazakh.
121 H4 Ak-Say r. Kyrg.
135 G7 Aksay Rostovskaya Oblast' Rus. Fed.
135 I7 Aksay Volgogradskaya Oblast' Rus. Fed.
137 J4 Aksay r. Rus. Fed.
126 C3 Akşehir Turkey
199 G2 Akşehir Gölü l. Turkey
126 C3 Akseki Turkey
120 C1 Aksenovo Rus. Fed.
122 C4 Aks-e Rostam r. Iran
107 G1 Aksha Rus. Fed.
120 C2 Akshatau Kazakh.
120 E2 Akshiganak Kazakh.
121 I4 Akshiy Kazakh.
120 B4 Akshukur Kazakh.
110 C3 Aksu Xinjiang China
121 I3 Aksu Almatinskaya Oblast' Kazakh.
121 I1 Aksu Pavlodarskaya Oblast' Kazakh.
121 G1 Aksu Severnyy Kazakhstan Kazakh.
120 C2 Aksu Zapadnyy Kazakhstan Kazakh.
121 I3 Aksu r. Kazakh.
Aksu r. Tajik. see Oksu
199 G3 Aksu Antalya Turkey
199 G3 Aksu Isparta Turkey
199 G3 Aksu r. Turkey
120 F2 Aksuat Kustanayskaya Oblast' Kazakh.
121 J3 Aksuat Vostochnyy Kazakhstan Kazakh.
121 H2 Aksu-Ayuly Kazakh.
135 J5 Aksubayevo Rus. Fed.
121 H3 Aksuek Kazakh.
110 C3 Aksu He r. China
210 C1 Āksum Eth.
111 D4 Aktag mt. Xinjiang China
134 K5 Aktanysh Rus. Fed.
128 C1 Aktaş Turkey
127 G3 Aktaş Dağı mt. Turkey
129 E2 Aktash r. Rus. Fed.
120 F5 Aktash Uzbek.
121 G3 Aktau Karagandinskaya Oblast' Kazakh.
121 H2 Aktau Karagandinskaya Oblast' Kazakh.
120 B4 Aktau Mangistauskaya Oblast' Kazakh.
128 C1 Aktepe Turkey
199 G1 Aktepe hill Turkey
110 B4 Akto Xinjiang China
121 H2 Aktogay Karagandinskaya Oblast' Kazakh.
121 H1 Aktogay Pavlodarskaya Oblast' Kazakh.
121 I3 Aktogay Vostochnyy Kazakhstan Kazakh.
128 C1 Aktoprak Turkey
139 H4 Aktsyabrskaya Belarus
138 G5 Aktsyabrski Homyel'skaya Voblasts' Belarus
138 G4 Aktsyabrski Vitsyebskaya Voblasts' Belarus
121 H4 Ak-Tüz Kyrg.
120 D2 Aktyubinsk Kazakh.
120 D2 Aktyubinskaya Oblast' admin. div. Kazakh.
Aktyubinsk Oblast admin. div. Kazakh. see Aktyubinskaya Oblast'
Aktyuz Kyrg. see Ak-Tüz
221 K3 Akulivik Que. Can.
206 E5 Akumadan Ghana
103 E7 Akune Japan
210 B4 Akur mt. Uganda
129 D3 Akura Georgia
207 G5 Akure Nigeria
140 □C2 Akureyri Iceland
80 E2 Akuroa North I. N.Z.
102 □1 Akuseki-jima i. Japan
129 E2 Akusha Rus. Fed.
220 B4 Akutan AK U.S.A.
207 G5 Akwa Ibom state Nigeria
207 H4 Akwanga Nigeria
207 H5 Akwaya Cameroon
Akyab Myanmar see Sittwe
129 C3 Akyaka Turkey
120 D2 Ak"yar Rus. Fed.
199 G1 Akyazı Turkey
121 H3 Akzhal Karagandinskaya Oblast' Kazakh.
121 J2 Akzhal Vostochnyy Kazakhstan Kazakh.
120 F3 Akzhar Kzyl-Ordinskaya Oblast' Kazakh.
121 J3 Akzhar Vostochnyy Kazakhstan Kazakh.
121 G4 Akzhar Zhambylskaya Oblast' Kazakh.
121 F3 Akzhaykyn, Ozero salt l. Kazakh.
142 C1 Ål Norway
138 G5 Ala r. Belarus
191 G3 Ala Italy
231 C6 Alabama r. AL U.S.A.
231 C5 Alabama state U.S.A.
231 C5 Alabaster AL U.S.A.
227 F3 Alabaster MI U.S.A.
121 G4 Ala-Buka Kyrg.
202 D1 Al Abyār Libya
195 F4 Alaca r. Italy
126 D2 Alaca Turkey
129 B3 Alaca Dağı mt. Turkey
126 E3 Alacahan Turkey
126 D2 Alaçam Turkey
199 F2 Alaçam Dağları mts Turkey
Alacant Spain see Alicante
199 E2 Alaçatı Turkey
243 H4 Alacrán, Arrecife rf Mex.
197 G5 Aladag mt. Bulg.
126 D3 Aladağ Turkey
129 C3 Aladağ mt. Turkey
127 F3 Ala Dağlar mts Turkey
126 D3 Ala Dağları mts Turkey
192 B4 Alà dei Sardi Sardegna Italy
190 C3 Ala di Stura Italy
183 E3 Alaejos Spain
114 C4 Alagapuram Tamil Nadu India
Alagez mt. Armenia see Aragats Lerr
106 B2 Alag Hayrhan Uul mt. Mongolia
129 D2 Alagir Rus. Fed.
190 C3 Alagna Valsesia Italy
161 B3 Alagnon r. France
254 F4 Alagoas state Brazil
254 F5 Alagoinhas Brazil
186 B3 Alagón Spain
182 D5 Alagón r. Spain
129 C3 Alagöz Dağı mt. Turkey
92 C5 Alah r. Phil.
94 C3 Alahanpanjang Sumatera Indon.
140 M3 Alahärmä Fin.
127 H5 Al Aḥmadī Kuwait
163 E5 Alaigne France
186 □ Alaior Spain
123 G2 Alai Range mts Asia
122 C3 Ālaivān Iran
184 D3 Alájar Spain
140 M3 Alajärvi Fin.
216 □3a Alajero La Gomera Canary Is
124 C2 Al Ajfar Saudi Arabia
138 F2 Alajõgi r. Estonia
242 □I7 Alajuela Costa Rica
213 □J4 Alak Ambohimaha Madag.
220 B3 Alakanuk AK U.S.A.
129 B2 Alakhadzi Georgia
129 E3 Alakhundag, Gora mt. Rus. Fed.
116 D3 Alaknanda r. India
121 J3 Alakol', Ozero salt l. Kazakh.
Ala Kul salt l. Kazakh. see Alakol', Ozero
140 O2 Alakurtti Rus. Fed.
251 F5 Alalaú r. Brazil
124 C4 Al 'Alayyah Saudi Arabia
Alalia Corse France see Aléria
182 B2 A Lama Spain
127 F3 Al 'Amādīyah Iraq
91 K3 Alamagan i. N. Mariana Is
Alamaguan i. N. Mariana Is see Alamagan
127 G5 Al 'Amārah Iraq
210 C1 Ālamat'ā Eth.
185 F3 Alameda Spain
240 F3 Alameda CA U.S.A.
185 G1 Alameda de Cervera Spain
183 G4 Alameda de la Sagra Spain
127 G5 Al Amghar waterhole Iraq
185 F2 Alamillo Spain
92 A2 Alaminos Phil.
239 F6 Alamito Creek r. TX U.S.A.
124 C3 Al Amlah Saudi Arabia
245 F3 Álamo Mex.
184 C2 Álamo r. Port.
184 E4 Alamo r. Spain
231 D5 Alamo GA U.S.A.
241 J3 Alamo NV U.S.A.
237 F5 Alamo TN U.S.A.
239 F5 Alamogordo NM U.S.A.
237 D6 Alamo Heights TX U.S.A.
250 A6 Alamor Ecuador
242 C2 Alamos Sonora Mex.
242 C3 Alamos Sonora Mex.
243 E3 Alamos r. Mex.
242 C3 Alamos, Sierra mts Mex.
239 F4 Alamosa CO U.S.A.
239 F5 Alamosa Creek r. NM U.S.A.
114 C3 Alampur Andhra Prad. India
124 D5 Al 'Anad Yemen
140 K2 Alanäs Sweden
127 F4 Al Anbār governorate Iraq
141 L3 Åland is Fin.
170 C2 Aland r. Ger.
114 C2 Aland Karnataka India
122 A2 Aland r. Iran
129 B3 Alan Dağı mt. Turkey
Åland Islands Fin. see Åland
184 C2 Alandroal Port.
141 L4 Ålands Hav sea chan. Fin./Sweden
114 D3 Alandur Tamil Nadu India
184 D2 Alange Spain
184 D2 Alange, Embalse de resr Spain
Alania aut. reg. Georgia see Samkhret' Oset'i
184 E2 Alanís Spain
226 E3 Alanson MI U.S.A.
126 D3 Alanya Turkey
177 H5 Alap Hungary
231 D6 Alapaha r. GA U.S.A.
114 C4 Alapakam Tamil Nadu India
199 G1 Alaplı Turkey
Alappuzha Kerala India see Alleppey
116 D4 Alapur Uttar Prad. India
128 B5 Al 'Aqabah Jordan
124 C3 Al 'Aqīq Saudi Arabia
125 E2 Al 'Arabīyah i. Saudi Arabia
Al 'Arabīyah as Sa'ūdīyah country Asia see Saudi Arabia
183 E4 Alaraz Spain
183 H5 Alarcón Spain
183 H5 Alarcón, Embalse de resr Spain
183 F2 Alar del Rey Spain
187 F5 Alaró Spain
124 D2 Al Arṭāwīyah Saudi Arabia
95 G5 Alas, Selat sea chan. Indon.
199 F2 Alaşehir Turkey
129 D3 Äläsgärli Azer.
Alashiya country Asia see Cyprus
220 D3 Alaska state U.S.A.
213 F3 Alaska Zimbabwe
220 D4 Alaska, Gulf of AK U.S.A.
222 A2 Alaska Highway Can./U.S.A.
220 B4 Alaska Peninsula AK U.S.A.
220 D3 Alaska Range mts AK U.S.A.
190 D4 Alassio Italy
141 M3 Alastaro Fin.
129 F4 Älät Azer.
120 E5 Alat Uzbek.
192 A3 Alata Corse France
187 B5 Alatoz Spain
193 F3 Alatri Italy
129 F3 Älät Tiräsi plat. Azer.
177 J4 Alattyán Hungary
135 I5 Alatyr' Rus. Fed.
135 I5 Alatyr' r. Rus. Fed.
250 B5 Alausí Ecuador
183 H2 Álava prov. País Vasco Spain
129 D3 Alaverdi Armenia
140 N2 Alavieska Fin.
140 M3 Alavus Fin.
125 G3 Al Awābī Oman
82 E3 Alawoona S.A. Austr.
Alay Kyrka Toosu mts Asia see Alai Range
125 F2 Al 'Ayn U.A.E.
Alayskiy Khrebet mts Asia see Alai Range
129 E3 Alazani r. Azer./Georgia
131 Q2 Alazeya r. Rus. Fed.
202 B1 Al 'Azīzīyah Libya
172 C4 Alb r. Ger.
190 D4 Alba Italy
186 B4 Alba Spain
226 E3 Alba MI U.S.A.
234 B1 Alba PA U.S.A.
81 B6 Alba, Mount South I. N.Z.
193 F2 Alba Adriatica Italy
128 C1 Al Bāb Syria
185 I1 Albacete Spain
185 I2 Albacete prov. Castilla - La Mancha Spain
124 B2 Al Badā'i' Saudi Arabia
183 E4 Alba de Tormes Spain
124 D3 Al Badī' Saudi Arabia
127 G5 Al Bādiyah al Janūbīyah hill Iraq
142 D3 Ålbæk Denmark
142 D3 Ålbæk Bugt b. Denmark
192 A5 Albagiara Sardegna Italy
124 C3 Al Bāḥah Egypt
124 C3 Al Bāḥah prov. Saudi Arabia
128 B2 Al Bahlūlīyah Syria
Al Bahrayn country Asia see Bahrain
187 C6 Albaida Spain
197 F2 Alba Iulia Romania
185 H2 Albaladejo Spain
184 D1 Albalá del Caudillo Spain
161 C4 Alba-la-Romaine France
186 C3 Albalate de Arzobispo Spain
186 D3 Albalate de Cinca Spain
183 H4 Albalate de las Nogueras Spain
183 H4 Albalate de Zorita Spain
186 C3 Albalatillo Spain
163 E5 Alban France
185 H3 Albánchez Spain
193 H4 Albanella Italy
196 D5 Albania country Europe
193 I4 Albano di Lucania Italy
193 E3 Albano Laziale Italy
87 C7 Albany W.A. Austr.
224 D2 Albany r. Ont. Can.
246 □ Albany Jamaica
231 C6 Albany GA U.S.A.
236 E3 Albany MO U.S.A.
233 G3 Albany NY U.S.A.
232 B5 Albany OH U.S.A.
238 B2 Albany OR U.S.A.
237 D5 Albany TX U.S.A.
186 F2 Albanyà Spain
85 G5 Albany Downs Qld Austr.
258 G4 Albardão do João Maria coastal area Brazil
202 E2 Al Bardī Libya
260 C2 Albardón Arg.
190 E2 Albaredo per San Marco Italy
161 B4 Albaret-le-Comtal France
190 E4 Albareto Italy
161 B4 Albaret-Ste-Marie France
160 D3 Albarine r. France
161 C5 Albaron France
183 I4 Albarracín Spain
184 D1 Albarragena r. Spain
137 J4 Albasi r. Rus. Fed.
127 G5 Al Başrah Iraq
127 G5 Al Başrah governorate Iraq
150 C4 Albaston Cornwall, England U.K.
185 I2 Albatana Spain
186 D3 Albatàrrec Spain
187 C6 Albatera Spain
125 G3 Al Bāṭinah admin. reg. Oman
85 E2 Albatross Bay Qld Austr.
83 F5 Albatross Island Tas. Austr.
202 D1 Al Bayḍā' Libya
124 D5 Al Bayḍā' Yemen
124 D5 Al Bayḍā' governorate Yemen
172 C4 Albbruck Ger.
157 H4 Albe r. France
192 D2 Albegna r. Italy
186 D3 Albelda Spain
183 H2 Albelda de Iregua Spain
186 C2 Albella Spain
231 D5 Albemarle NC U.S.A.
Albemarle Island Islas Galápagos Ecuador see Isabela, Isla
231 E5 Albemarle Sound sea chan. NC U.S.A.
183 H4 Albendea Spain
185 F3 Albendín Spain
190 D4 Albenga Italy
160 D3 Albens France
187 C4 Albentosa Spain
183 F5 Alberche r. Spain
253 F6 Alberdi Para.
182 B4 Albergaria-a-Velha Port.
182 B5 Albergaria dos Doze Port.
190 B3 Albergian, Monte mt. Italy
187 C5 Alberic Spain
183 H2 Alberite Spain
179 F2 Alberndorf in der Riedmark Austria
184 C3 Albernoa Port.
186 C2 Albero Alto Spain
195 G2 Alberobello Italy
191 H3 Alberoni Italy
178 A3 Alberschwende Austria
168 E1 Albersdorf Ger.
83 F3 Albert N.S.W. Austr.
84 D3 Albert r. Qld Austr.
156 C3 Albert France
82 D3 Albert, Lake S.A. Austr.
210 A4 Albert, Lake Dem. Rep. Congo/Uganda
222 H4 Alberta prov. Can.
232 E6 Alberta VA U.S.A.
192 A2 Albertacce Corse France
190 E4 Alberta Ligure Italy
261 G4 Alberti Arg.
140 □ Albert I Land reg. Svalbard
214 C6 Albertinia S. Africa
177 I4 Albertirsa Hungary
236 E3 Albert Lea MN U.S.A.
210 B4 Albert Nile r. Sudan/Uganda
225 H4 Alberton P.E.I. Can.
215 G2 Alberton S. Africa
238 D2 Alberton MT U.S.A.
241 J5 Alberto Oviedo Mota Mex.
215 E2 Albertshoek S. Africa
173 E2 Albertshofen Ger.
246 □ Albert Town Jamaica
81 B6 Albert Town South I. N.Z.
Albertville Dem. Rep. Congo see Kalémié
160 E3 Albertville France
231 C5 Albertville AL U.S.A.
186 C3 Alberuela de Tubo Spain
186 D3 Albesa Spain
197 H2 Albeşti Romania
197 H2 Albeşti Romania
157 G4 Albestroff France
163 E5 Albi France
236 E3 Albia IA U.S.A.
163 D4 Albias France
125 E2 Al Bīḍah des. Saudi Arabia
195 F3 Albidona Italy
191 G3 Albignasego Italy
251 H3 Albina Suriname
190 E3 Albino Italy
240 F2 Albion CA U.S.A.
230 C3 Albion IN U.S.A.
226 E4 Albion MI U.S.A.
236 D3 Albion NE U.S.A.
234 D3 Albion NJ U.S.A.
232 D3 Albion NY U.S.A.
232 C4 Albion PA U.S.A.
183 E2 Albires Spain
124 C4 Al Birk Saudi Arabia
172 C2 Albisheim (Pfrimm) Ger.
190 D4 Albisola Marina Italy
190 D4 Albisola Superiore Italy
124 D3 Al Biyāḍh reg. Saudi Arabia
164 D3 Alblasserdam Neth.
187 D4 Albocácer Spain
185 H3 Alboloduy Spain
161 C3 Albon France
185 G4 Albondón Spain
187 B5 Alborea Spain
142 C3 Ålborg Denmark
142 D3 Ålborg Bugt b. Denmark
122 B2 Alborz, Reshteh-ye mts Iran
197 G3 Albota Romania
185 H3 Albox Spain
177 H2 Albrechtice Czech Rep.
150 E2 Albrighton Shropshire, England U.K.
85 F4 Albro Qld Austr.
172 D3 Albstadt Ger.
173 D3 Albuch hills Ger.
125 E2 Al Budayyi Bahrain
184 B3 Albufeira Port.
187 B7 Albujón Spain
124 C2 Al Bukayrīyah Saudi Arabia
190 E2 Albula r. Switz.
190 E2 Albula Alpen mts Switz.
185 G4 Albuñol Spain
185 G4 Albuñuelas Spain
239 F5 Albuquerque NM U.S.A.
246 B4 Albuquerque, Cayos de is Caribbean Sea
125 F2 Al Buraymī Oman
233 G2 Alburg VT U.S.A.
128 B5 Al Burj Jordan
193 H4 Alburno, Monte mt. Italy
184 D1 Alburquerque Spain
234 C2 Alburtis PA U.S.A.
83 F4 Albury N.S.W. Austr.
81 C6 Albury South I. N.Z.
127 F4 Al Buşayrah Syria
128 D4 Al Busayṭā' plain Saudi Arabia
126 E5 Al Busayṭā' plain Saudi Arabia
124 D1 Al Bushūk well Saudi Arabia
160 E3 Alby-sur-Chéran France
252 B3 Alca Peru
184 A2 Alcabideche Port.
187 C5 Alcácer Spain
184 B2 Alcácer do Sal Port.
184 B2 Alcáçovas Port.
184 B2 Alcáçovas r. Port.
185 I2 Alcadozo Spain
186 C4 Alcaine Spain
182 C5 Alcains Port.
187 D4 Alcalá de Chivert Spain
184 E3 Alcalá de Guadaira Spain
186 C2 Alcalá de Gurrea Spain
183 G4 Alcalá de Henares Spain
187 C4 Alcalá de la Selva Spain
187 B5 Alcalá del Júcar Spain
184 E4 Alcalá de los Gazules Spain
184 E3 Alcalá del Río Spain
185 E4 Alcalá del Valle Spain
185 G3 Alcalá la Real Spain
194 B5 Alcamo Sicilia Italy
186 D3 Alcampell Spain
186 D3 Alcanadre r. Spain
186 D4 Alcanar Spain
184 B1 Alcanede Port.
184 B1 Alcanena Port.
184 B1 Alcanhões Port.
182 D3 Alcañices Spain
186 C3 Alcañiz Spain
254 D2 Alcântara Brazil
182 D5 Alcántara Spain
182 D5 Alcántara, Embalse de resr Spain
187 B7 Alcantarilla Spain
183 H4 Alcantud Spain
185 F2 Alcaracejos Spain
194 D4 Alcara li Fusi Sicilia Italy
185 H2 Alcaraz Spain
184 C3 Alcaria do Cume hill Port.
184 C3 Alcaria Ruiva Port.
180 C4 Alcaria Ruiva hill Port.
184 C2 Alcarrache r. Port./Spain
186 D3 Alcarràs Spain
185 F4 Alcaucín Spain
185 F3 Alcaudete Spain
183 F5 Alcaudete de la Jara Spain
163 B5 Alçay-Alçabéhéty-Sunharette France
184 D2 Alcazaba r. Spain
183 H4 Alcázar del Rey Spain
185 G1 Alcázar de San Juan Spain
183 F3 Alcazarén Spain
Alcazarquivir Morocco see Ksar el Kebir
151 F2 Alcester Warwickshire, England U.K.
137 J3 Alchevs'k Ukr.
260 E3 Alcira Arg.
Alcira Spain see Alzira
185 F1 Alcoba Spain
257 H2 Alcobaça Brazil
182 B5 Alcobaça Port.
183 G4 Alcobendas Spain
184 B1 Alcobertas Port.
Alcocebre Spain see Alcossebre
183 H4 Alcocer Spain
183 G2 Alcocero de Mola Spain
184 B2 Alcochete Port.
184 B1 Alcoentre Port.
182 B4 Alcofra Port.
185 F3 Alcolea Andalucía Spain
185 H4 Alcolea Andalucía Spain
185 F2 Alcolea de Calatrava Spain
186 D3 Alcolea de Cinca Spain
183 H3 Alcolea del Pinar Spain
184 E3 Alcolea del Río Spain
186 D3 Alcoletge Spain
184 E1 Alcollarín Spain
184 C2 Alconchel Spain
184 D2 Alconera Spain
185 H3 Alcóntar Spain
84 C4 Alcoota N.T. Austr.
187 C4 Alcora Spain
183 G4 Alcorcón Spain
186 C4 Alcorisa Spain
184 D1 Alcorneo r. Port./Spain
183 I4 Alcoroches Spain
261 G3 Alcorta Arg.
187 D4 Alcossebre Spain
184 C3 Alcoutim Port.
238 F3 Alcova WY U.S.A.
186 E3 Alcover Spain
187 C6 Alcoy Spain
177 H4 Alcsútdobos Hungary
186 C3 Alcubierre Spain
183 G3 Alcubilla de Avellaneda Spain
185 G2 Alcubillas Spain
187 C5 Alcublas Spain
187 G5 Alcúdia Spain
185 F2 Alcudia r. Spain
Alcudia de Carlet Spain see L'Alcudia
185 G3 Alcudia de Guadix Spain
181 E4 Alcudia de Monteagud Spain
184 D1 Alcuéscar Spain
217 □2 Aldabra Atoll Aldabra Is Seychelles
217 □2 Aldabra Islands Seychelles
242 D2 Aldama Chihuahua Mex.
245 E2 Aldama Tamaulipas Mex.
131 N4 Aldan Rus. Fed.
131 N3 Aldan r. Rus. Fed.
151 F3 Aldbourne Wiltshire, England U.K.
149 I4 Aldbrough East Riding of Yorkshire, England U.K.
151 I2 Alde r. England U.K.
216 □3f Aldea r. Gran Canaria Canary Is
184 E1 Aldeacentenera Spain
182 D3 Aldeadávila de la Ribera Spain
184 D1 Aldea del Cano Spain
183 F4 Aldea del Fresno Spain
182 D4 Aldea del Obispo Spain
185 G2 Aldea del Rey Spain
182 E5 Aldea de Trujillo Spain
183 H3 Aldealafuente Spain
183 H3 Aldealpozo Spain
183 F3 Aldeamayor de San Martín Spain
183 E5 Aldeanueva de Barbarroya Spain
182 E3 Aldeanueva de Figueroa Spain
182 E4 Aldeanueva del Camino Spain
183 E5 Aldeanueva de San Bartolomé Spain
185 G2 Aldeaquemada Spain
182 E3 Aldearrodrigo Spain
183 F3 Aldeaseca Spain
182 E4 Aldeatejada Spain
183 F4 Aldeavieja Spain
151 I2 Aldeburgh Suffolk, England U.K.
182 D4 Aldehuela de la Bóveda Spain
182 D4 Aldehuela de Yeltes Spain
184 C1 Aldeia da Mata Port.
182 D4 Aldeia da Ponte Port.
184 C2 Aldeia de Ferreira Port.
182 C4 Aldeia do Bispo Port.
184 B3 Aldeia dos Elvas Port.
184 B3 Aldeia dos Palheiros Port.
182 D4 Aldeia Velha Guarda Port.
184 B1 Aldeia Velha Portalegre Port.
234 B1 Alden PA U.S.A.
151 G3 Aldenham Hertfordshire, England U.K.
169 B5 Aldenhoven Ger.
191 G3 Aldeno Italy
151 F3 Alderbury Wiltshire, England U.K.
233 F3 Alder Creek NY U.S.A.
147 E2 Aldergrove Northern Ireland U.K.
151 F4 Alderholt Dorset, England U.K.
149 G4 Alderley Edge Cheshire, England U.K.
158 D2 Alderney i. Channel Is
240 G4 Alder Peak CA U.S.A.
173 H3 Aldersbach Ger.
151 G3 Aldershot Hampshire, England U.K.
232 C6 Alderson WV U.S.A.
196 E5 Aldinci Macedonia
172 C3 Aldingen Ger.
149 F3 Aldingham Cumbria, England U.K.
151 H3 Aldington Kent, England U.K.
215 H3 Aldinville S. Africa
186 D4 Aldover Spain
151 F2 Aldridge West Midlands, England U.K.
163 A5 Aldudes France
142 E3 Åled Sweden
185 I3 Aledo Spain
236 F3 Aledo IL U.S.A.
206 B2 Aleg Maur.
216 □3c Alegranza i. Canary Is
257 G4 Alegre Espírito Santo Brazil
256 D3 Alegre Minas Gerais Brazil
255 B9 Alegrete Brazil
184 C1 Alegrete Port.
183 H2 Alegría-Dulantzi Spain
239 E5 Alegros Mountain NM U.S.A.
261 H1 Alejandra Arg.
261 H4 Alejandro Korn Arg.
261 F3 Alejandro Roca Arg.
252 □ Alejandro Selkirk, Isla i. S. Pacific Ocean
260 D6 Alejandro Stefenelli Arg.
139 I1 Alekhovshchina Rus. Fed.
Aleksandriya Kirovohrads'ka Oblast' Ukr. see Oleksandriya
139 M5 Aleksandro-Nevskiy Rus. Fed.
Aleksandropol Armenia see Gyumri
139 L3 Aleksandrov Rus. Fed.
196 E4 Aleksandrovac Srbija Yugo.
Aleksandrov Dar Ukr. see Rakhmanivka
120 B2 Aleksandrov Gay Rus. Fed.
135 K5 Aleksandrovka Orenburgskaya Oblast' Rus. Fed.
137 J4 Aleksandrovka Rostovskaya Oblast' Rus. Fed.
197 G4 Aleksandrovo Khaskovo Bulg.
197 G4 Aleksandrovo Lovech Bulg.
134 L4 Aleksandrovsk Rus. Fed.
Aleksandrovsk Ukr. see Zaporizhzhya
Aleksandrovskiy Rus. Fed. see Aleksandrovsk
129 C1 Aleksandrovskoye Stavropol'skiy Kray Rus. Fed.
127 G1 Aleksandrovskoye Stavropol'skiy Kray Rus. Fed.
130 I3 Aleksandrovskoye Tomskaya Oblast' Rus. Fed.
100 G2 Aleksandrovsk-Sakhalinskiy Sakhalin Rus. Fed.
175 I3 Aleksandrów Pol.
174 G3 Aleksandrów Kujawski Pol.
175 H4 Aleksandrów Łódzki Pol.
177 I6 Aleksa Šantić Vojvodina, Srbija Yugo.
129 F3 Alekseyevka Azer.
Alekseyevka Akmolinskaya Oblast' Kazakh. see Akkol'
121 H2 Alekseyevka Pavlodarskaya Oblast' Kazakh.
Alekseyevka Vostochnyy Kazakhstan Kazakh. see Terekty
135 G6 Alekseyevka Belgorodskaya Oblast' Rus. Fed.
135 G6 Alekseyevka Belgorodskaya Oblast' Rus. Fed.
137 K3 Alekseyevo-Lozovskoye Rus. Fed.
135 H6 Alekseyevskaya Rus. Fed.
139 K4 Aleksin Rus. Fed.
197 E4 Aleksinac Srbija Yugo.
143 G3 Ålem Sweden
208 A5 Alèmbé Gabon
210 D2 'Alem Maya Eth.
257 F4 Além Paraíba Brazil
140 J3 Ålen Norway
159 G3 Alençon France
160 B2 Alène r. France
251 H5 Alenquer Brazil
184 B1 Alenquer Port.
184 B1 Alenquer r. Port.
240 □C9 Alenuihaha Channel HI U.S.A.
163 E6 Alénya France
Alep Syria see Ḥalab
206 E5 Alépé Côte d'Ivoire
Aleppo Syria see Ḥalab
114 C2 Aler r. India
173 E3 Alerheim Ger.
192 B2 Aléria Corse France
186 C2 Alerre Spain
221 L1 Alert Nunavut Can.
222 E5 Alert Bay B.C. Can.
161 C4 Alès France
192 A5 Ales Sardegna Italy
197 F2 Aleşd Romania
Aleshki Ukr. see Tsyurupyns'k

Alesia to Amakazari-yama

276

Alesia France see Alise-Ste-Reine
Aleşkirt Turkey see Eleşkirt
183 H2 Alesón Spain
190 D4 Alessandria Italy
190 D4 Alessandria prov. Piemonte Italy
195 F3 Alessandria del Carretto Italy
195 H3 Alessano Italy
Alessio Albania see Lezhë
142 C3 Ålestrup Denmark
140 I3 Ålesund Norway
163 E5 Alet-les-Bains France
Aletrium Italy see Alatri
190 C2 Aletschhorn mt. Switz.
266 G2 Aleutian Basin sea feature Bering Sea
220 A4 Aleutian Islands AK U.S.A.
220 C4 Aleutian Range mts AK U.S.A.
266 H2 Aleutian Trench sea feature N. Pacific Ocean
Alevişik Turkey see Samandağı
236 C2 Alexander ND U.S.A.
262 T2 Alexander, Cape Antarctica
84 D2 Alexander, Mount hill N.T. Austr.
87 B4 Alexander, Mount hill W.A. Austr.
220 E4 Alexander Archipelago is AK U.S.A.
214 A3 Alexander Bay b. Namibia/S. Africa
214 A3 Alexander Bay S. Africa
231 C5 Alexander City AL U.S.A.
262 T2 Alexander Island Antarctica
122 C2 Alexander's Wall tourist site Iran
83 F4 Alexandra Vic. Austr.
84 D3 Alexandra r. Qld Austr.
81 B6 Alexandra South I. N.Z.
259 □ Alexandra, Cape S. Georgia
Alexandra Land i. Zemlya Frantsa-Iosifa Rus. Fed. see Zemlya Aleksandry
198 C1 Alexandreia Greece
Alexandretta Turkey see İskenderun
Alexandria Afgh. see Ghaznī
84 D3 Alexandria N.T. Austr.
222 F4 Alexandria B.C. Can.
224 F4 Alexandria Ont. Can.
203 F2 Alexandria Egypt
197 G4 Alexandria Romania
215 F5 Alexandria S. Africa
Alexandria Turkm. see Mary
146 D6 Alexandria West Dunbartonshire, Scotland U.K.
232 A5 Alexandria KY U.S.A.
237 E6 Alexandria LA U.S.A.
236 E2 Alexandria MN U.S.A.
236 D3 Alexandria SD U.S.A.
234 A4 Alexandria VA U.S.A.
Alexandria Arachoton Afgh. see Kandahār
Alexandria Areion Afgh. see Herāt
233 F2 Alexandria Bay NY U.S.A.
Alexandria Prophthasia Afgh. see Farāh
82 D3 Alexandrina, Lake S.A. Austr.
199 D1 Alexandroupoli Greece
256 C2 Alexânia Brazil
225 J2 Alexis r. Nfld. Can.
222 F4 Alexis Creek B.C. Can.
128 B3 'Āley Lebanon
121 J1 Aley r. Rus. Fed.
121 J1 Aleysk Rus. Fed.
195 H2 Alezio Italy
169 C5 Alf Ger.
185 G3 Alfacar Spain
187 C5 Alfafar Spain
182 D4 Alfaiates Port.
186 C3 Alfajarín Spain
245 E3 Alfajayucan Mex.
186 B4 Alfambra Spain
186 B4 Alfambra r. Spain
184 B3 Alfambras Port.
186 B3 Alfamén Spain
182 D3 Alfândega da Fé Port.
186 D3 Alfántega Spain
125 E5 Al Fardah Yemen
182 B4 Alfarelos Port.
185 F3 Alfarnate Spain
183 I2 Alfaro Spain
186 D3 Alfarràs Spain
125 E2 Al Farūq reg. Saudi Arabia
127 G5 Al Farwānīyah Kuwait
Al Fas Morocco see Fès
197 H4 Alfatar Bulg.
127 F4 Al Fatḩah Iraq
Al Fayyūm Egypt see El Faiyûm
187 C6 Alfaz del Pi Spain
124 C5 Al Fāzih Yemen
172 D3 Alfdorf Ger.
193 G3 Alfedena Italy
198 B3 Alfeios r. Greece
182 A5 Alfeizerão Port.
169 E4 Alfeld (Leine) Ger.
182 B3 Alfena Port.
257 E4 Alfenas Brazil
184 B3 Alferce Port.
184 B1 Alferrarede Port.
169 C3 Alfhausen Ger.
Alfíos r. Greece see Alfeios
177 J5 Alföld plain Hungary
191 H4 Alfonsine Italy
146 F4 Alford Aberdeenshire, Scotland U.K.
149 J4 Alford Lincolnshire, England U.K.
186 D3 Alforja Spain
233 F2 Alfred Ont. Can.
233 □H3 Alfred ME U.S.A.
87 E5 Alfred and Marie Range hills W.A. Austr.
245 E3 Alfred M. Terrazas Mex.
257 G4 Alfredo Chaves Brazil
80 E4 Alfredton North I. N.Z.
149 H4 Alfreton Derbyshire, England U.K.
141 L3 Alfta Sweden
Al Fujayrah U.A.E. see Fujairah
184B2 Alfundão Port.
118 D2 Al Furāt r. Iraq/Syria alt. Fırat (Turkey), conv. Euphrates
120 D2 Alga Kazakh.
120 C2 Algabas Kazakh.
187 F5 Algaida Spain
192 A2 Algajola Corse France
185 E3 Algámitas Spain
184 E4 Algar Spain
142 A2 Ålgård Norway
185 F3 Algarinejo Spain
261 F6 Algarroba Arg.
260 B1 Algarrobito Chile
260 B3 Algarrobo Chile
185 F4 Algarrobo Spain
187 B7 Algarrobo hill Spain
184 B3 Algarve reg. Port.
135 H5 Algasovo Rus. Fed.
185 E4 Algatocín Spain
185 E4 Algeciras Spain
Algeciras, Bahía de b. Gibraltar/Spain see Gibraltar, Bay of
187 C5 Algemesí Spain
205 F1 Alger Alg.
227 E3 Alger MI U.S.A.
205 F3 Algeria country Africa
169 E3 Algermissen Ger.
186 D3 Algerri Spain
183 G4 Algete Spain
129 D3 Alget'i r. Georgia
Algha Kazakh. see Alga
125 G3 Al Ghāfāt Oman
Al Ghardaqah Egypt see Hurghada
124 C3 Al Gharīth Saudi Arabia
128 B4 Al Ghawr plain Jordan/West Bank
125 F4 Al Ghayḑah Yemen
124 D3 Al Ghayl Saudi Arabia
192 A4 Alghero Sardegna Italy
125 G4 Al Ghubr reg. Oman
125 E2 Al Ghwaybiyah Saudi Arabia
184 B3 Algibre r. Port.
Algiers Alg. see Alger
187 C5 Alginet Spain
215 E5 Algoa Bay S. Africa
250 D5 Algodón r. Peru
185 E4 Algodonales Spain
183 G5 Algodor r. Spain
226 D3 Algoma WI U.S.A.
236 E3 Algona IA U.S.A.
227 F4 Algonac MI U.S.A.
224 E4 Algonquin Park Ont. Can.
183 H4 Algora Spain
182 D3 Algoso Port.
184 B3 Algoz Port.
157 G3 Algrange France
140 L2 Älgsjö Sweden
186 D3 Alguaire Spain
187 B6 Alguazas Spain
Algueirao Moz. see Hacufera
184 A2 Algueirão-Mem Martins Port.
187 C6 Algueña Spain
127 F4 Al Ḩabbānīyah Iraq
185 H4 Alhabia Spain
182 B4 Alhadas Port.
124 C3 Al Ḩadbah reg. Saudi Arabia
125 E2 Al Ḩadd Bahrain
124 D3 Al Ḩaddār Saudi Arabia
127 F5 Al Hadhālīl plat. Saudi Arabia
127 F4 Al Ḩadīthah Iraq
127 F4 Al Ḩaḑr Iraq
128 C2 Al Ḩaffah Syria
124 D2 Al Ḩā'ir Saudi Arabia
125 G3 Al Ḩajar Oman
125 G2 Al Ḩajar al Gharbī mts Oman
125 G3 Al Ḩajar ash Sharqī mts Oman
185 G3 Alhama r. Spain
183 I2 Alhama r. Spain
128 D4 Al Ḩamād plain Asia
202 A2 Al Ḩamādah al Ḩamrā' plat. Libya
185 H4 Alhama de Almería Spain
183 I3 Alhama de Aragón Spain
185 G3 Alhama de Granada Spain
187 B7 Alhama de Murcia Spain
124 D3 Al Ḩamar Saudi Arabia
185 G2 Alhambra Spain
125 E5 Al Ḩāmī Yemen
124 B3 Al Ḩamrā' Saudi Arabia
124 C2 Al Ḩanākīyah Saudi Arabia
184 A2 Alhandra Port.
124 C5 Al Ḩanīsh al Kabīr i. Yemen
127 G5 Al Ḩaniyah esc. Iraq
124 D3 Al Ḩariq Saudi Arabia
202 C3 Al Ḩarūj al Aswad hills Libya
127 F3 Al Ḩasakah Syria
127 G4 Al Hāshimīyah Iraq
185 F4 Alhaurín de la Torre Spain
185 F4 Alhaurín el Grande Spain
125 E3 Al Ḩawāyā des. Saudi Arabia
128 D5 Al Hawi salt pan Saudi Arabia
124 C3 Al Ḩawīyah Saudi Arabia
127 G4 Al Ḩayy Iraq
124 D4 Al Ḩazm al-Jawf Yemen
214 C3 Alheit S. Africa
185 G3 Alhendín Spain
125 F4 Al Ḩibāk des. Saudi Arabia
127 G4 Al Ḩillah Iraq
Al Ḩillah governorate Iraq see Bābil
124 D3 Al Ḩillah Saudi Arabia
124 D3 Al Ḩilwah Saudi Arabia
127 G4 Al Hindīyah Iraq
125 E2 Al Ḩinnāh Saudi Arabia
126 E5 Al Ḩinw mt. Saudi Arabia
124 D4 Al Ḩishwah hills Yemen
124 A1 Al Ḩismā plain Saudi Arabia
128 B3 Al Ḩişn Jordan
124 D5 Al Ḩişn Yemen
204 E2 Al Hoceima Morocco
180 D5 Al Hoceima prov. Morocco
182 C4 Alhões Port.
183 H4 Alhóndiga Spain
124 C5 Al Ḩudaydah Yemen
124 C5 Al Ḩudaydah governorate Yemen
124 C1 Al Ḩudūd ash Shamālīyah prov. Saudi Arabia
124 B1 Al Ḩufrah reg. Saudi Arabia
125 E2 Al Hufūf Saudi Arabia
124 B1 Al Hūj hills Saudi Arabia
202 C3 Al Ḩulayq al Kabīr hills Libya
124 D5 Al Ḩumayshah Yemen
125 E2 Al Ḩunayy Saudi Arabia
125 G2 Al Husayfin Oman
125 G3 Al Huwatsah Oman
125 D5 Al Ḩuwaymī Yemen
128 C2 Al Ḩuwayz Syria
195 E4 Alì Sicilia Italy
194 C5 Alia Sicilia Italy
185 E1 Alía Spain
129 E3 Äliabad Azer.
122 C2 'Alīābād Iran
122 C4 'Alīābād Iran
122 D3 'Alīābād Iran
122 A2 'Alīābād Iran
122 A3 'Alīābād Iran
122 B3 'Alīābād Iran
122 B3 Alīābād, Kūh-e mt. Iran
186 C4 Aliaga Spain
199 E2 Aliağa Turkey
187 B5 Aliaguilla Spain
198 C1 Aliakmonas r. Greece
198 B1 Aliakmonas, Limni l. Greece
122 A3 'Alī al Gharbī Iraq
193 I4 Aliano Italy
198 C2 Aliartos Greece
114 B2 Alibag Mahar. India
129 D3 Älibäyli Azer.
129 F4 Äli Bayramlı Azer.
199 E2 Alibey Adası i. Turkey
196 E3 Alibunar Vojvodina, Srbija Yugo.
129 E3 Älicançay r. Azer.
187 C6 Alicante Spain
187 C6 Alicante prov. Valencia Spain
85 F4 Alice Qld Austr.
85 E2 Alice r. Qld Austr.
215 F5 Alice S. Africa
237 D7 Alice TX U.S.A.
222 D4 Alice Arm B.C. Can.
215 F5 Alicedale S. Africa
86 E3 Alice Downs W.A. Austr.
246 C3 Alice Shoal sea feature Caribbean Sea
84 C4 Alice Springs N.T. Austr.
237 F5 Aliceville AL U.S.A.
129 C3 Aliçeyrek Turkey
123 H2 Alichur Tajik.
123 H2 Alichur r. Tajik.
261 F2 Alicia Arg.
92 B5 Alicia Phil.
85 E4 Alick Creek r. Qld Austr.
194 D4 Alicudi, Isola i. Isole Lipari Italy
185 G3 Alicún de Ortega Spain
207 G3 Aliero Nigeria
193 G3 Alife Italy
199 G1 Alifuatpaşa Sakarya Turkey
116 D4 Aligarh Uttar Prad. India
122 B3 Alīgūdarz Iran
107 I1 Alihe Nei Mongol China
182 E2 Alija del Infantado Spain
Alija de los Melones Spain see Alija del Infantado
182 C3 Alijó Port.
122 B4 Alījūq, Kūh-e mt. Iran
129 C4 Alikamerli Turkey
129 E2 Alikazgan r. Rus. Fed.
134 I5 Alikovo Rus. Fed.
208 C5 Alima r. Congo
Al Imārāt al 'Arabīyah at Muttaḩidah country Asia see United Arab Emirates
194 D5 Alimena Sicilia Italy
199 E3 Alimia i. Greece
194 C5 Aliminusa Sicilia Italy
208 D3 Alindao C.A.R.
123 G3 Alinghar r. Afgh.
142 E3 Alingsås Sweden
199 F2 Aliova r. Turkey
116 D5 Alipur Mahar. India
123 G4 Alipur Pak.
117 G4 Alipur Duar W. Bengal India
232 C4 Aliquippa PA U.S.A.
116 C5 Alirajpur Madh. Prad. India
210 D2 Ali Sabieh Djibouti
184 D1 Aliseda Spain
160 C1 Alise-Ste-Reine France
Al Iskandarīyah Egypt see Alexandria
127 G4 Al Iskandarīyah Iraq
131 R3 Aliskerovo Rus. Fed.
Al Ismā'īlīyah Egypt see Ismâ'ilîya
129 C3 Alisofu Turkey
182 D3 Aliste r. Spain
140 L2 Alitåive mt. Sweden
195 E4 Alì Terme Sicilia Italy
Al Ittihab Yemen see Madīnat ash Sha'b
198 D2 Aliveri Greece
215 F4 Aliwal North S. Africa
222 H4 Alix Alta Can.
136 E5 Aliyaha r. Ukr.
156 B3 Alizay France
125 E2 Al Jāfūrah des. Saudi Arabia
202 E2 Al Jaghbūb Libya
127 G5 Al Jahrah Kuwait
125 E2 Al Jamalīyah Qatar
184 C3 Aljaraque Spain
Al Jauf Saudi Arabia see Al Jawf
125 E3 Al Jawb reg. Saudi Arabia
202 D3 Al Jawf Libya
118 D4 Al Jawf Al Jawf Saudi Arabia
126 E5 Al Jawf Al Jawf Saudi Arabia
124 B1 Al Jawf prov. Saudi Arabia
124 D4 Al Jawf governorate Yemen
Al Jawlān hills Syria see Golan
Al Jaza'ir Alg. see Alger
122 C2 Alj Beyk Iran
184 B3 Aljezur Port.
125 E2 Al Jībān reg. Saudi Arabia
184 E4 Aljibe mt. Spain
124 D2 Al Jilh esc. Saudi Arabia
Al Jīzah Egypt see El Gîza
182 B5 Aljubarrota Port.
125 E2 Al Jubayl Saudi Arabia
125 D2 Al Jubayl hills Saudi Arabia
124 D2 Al Jubaylah Saudi Arabia
184 D1 Aljucén Spain
184 D2 Aljucén r. Spain
202 B2 Al Jufra Oasis Libya
124 B3 Al Jumūm Saudi Arabia
124 C3 Al Junaynah Saudi Arabia
124 D2 Al Jurayfah Saudi Arabia
124 C2 Al Jurdhāwīyah Saudi Arabia
184 B3 Aljustrel Port.
124 C2 Al Kahfah Saudi Arabia
125 G3 Al Kalbān Oman
222 F5 Alkali Lake B.C. Can.
136 F5 Alkaliya r. Ukr.
125 G3 Al Kāmil Oman
128 B4 Al Karak Jordan
128 B4 Al Karāmah Jordan
127 G4 Al Kāẓimīyah Iraq
165 E4 Alken Belgium
125 G3 Al Khābūrah Oman
124 C3 Al Khafqān salt pan Saudi Arabia
Al Khalīl West Bank see Hebron
127 G4 Al Khāliş Iraq
124 D3 Al Khamāsīn Saudi Arabia
124 D3 Al Kharfah Saudi Arabia
Al Khārijah Egypt see El Khârga
125 G2 Al Khaşab Oman
124 C3 Al Khāşirah Saudi Arabia
125 F2 Al-Khatam reg. U.A.E.
128 D4 Al Khaţīnī vol. Saudi Arabia
125 E2 Al Khawr Qatar
125 E2 Al Khobar Saudi Arabia
202 D3 Al Khufrah Oasis Libya
202 B1 Al Khums Libya
124 B1 Al Khunfah sand area Saudi Arabia
125 E3 Al Khunn Saudi Arabia
125 E2 Al Khuwayr Qatar
127 G4 Al Kifl Iraq
125 E2 Al Kir'ānah Qatar
164 D2 Alkmaar Neth.
179 F2 Alkoven Austria
127 G4 Al Kūfah Iraq
127 G4 Al Kumayt Iraq
128 D4 Al Kusūr hills Saudi Arabia
127 G4 Al Kūt Iraq
Al Kuwayt country Asia see Kuwait
127 G5 Al Kuwayt Kuwait
127 F5 Al Labbah plain Saudi Arabia
207 F5 Allada Benin
128 B2 Al Lādhiqīyah Syria
128 B2 Al Lādhiqīyah governorate Syria
114 C3 Allagadda Andhra Prad. India
233 □I1 Allagash r. ME U.S.A.
116 E4 Allahabad Uttar Prad. India
129 C3 Allahüekber Dağları mts Turkey
129 C3 Allahüekber Tepe mt. Turkey
192 A5 Allai Sardegna Italy
156 C3 Allaines France
156 B4 Allaines-Mervilliers France
158 D4 Allaire France
128 C3 Al Lajā lava field Syria
220 C3 Allakaket AK U.S.A.
131 O3 Allakh-Yun' Rus. Fed.
234 D2 Allamuchy NJ U.S.A.
161 C4 Allan France
161 A3 Allanche France
215 F3 Allandale S. Africa
96 A3 Allanmyo Myanmar
215 F2 Allanridge S. Africa
148 F2 Allanton North Lanarkshire, Scotland U.K.
114 D2 Allapalli Mahar. India
129 F4 Allar Azer.
225 H4 Allardville N.B. Can.
182 C2 Allariz Spain
157 H4 Allarmont France
162 D3 Allassac France
161 D5 Allauch France
213 F4 Alldays S. Africa
190 C1 Alle Switz.
226 E4 Allegan MI U.S.A.
232 D3 Allegany NY U.S.A.
191 H2 Alleghe Italy
232 D4 Allegheny r. PA U.S.A.
232 B6 Allegheny Mountains U.S.A.
232 D4 Allegheny Reservoir PA U.S.A.
161 B3 Allègre France
161 D5 Alleins France
161 E3 Allemond France
260 D6 Allen Arg.
92 C3 Allen Phil.
148 C4 Allen Rep. of Ireland
232 A4 Allen MI U.S.A.
147 C2 Allen, Lough l. Rep. of Ireland
81 A7 Allen, Mount hill Stewart I. N.Z.
231 D5 Allendale SC U.S.A.
149 G3 Allendale Town Northumberland, England U.K.
243 E2 Allende Coahuila Mex.
243 E3 Allende Nuevo León Mex.
245 G4 Allende Veracruz Mex.
169 D4 Allendorf (Eder) Ger.
169 D5 Allendorf (Lumda) Ger.
227 G3 Allenford Ont. Can.
149 G3 Allenheads Northumberland, England U.K.
172 D4 Allensbach Ger.
Allenstein Warmińsko-Mazurskie Pol. see Olsztyn
232 B5 Allensville OH U.S.A.
232 E4 Allensville PA U.S.A.
234 D2 Allentown NJ U.S.A.
234 C2 Allentown PA U.S.A.
179 G2 Allentsteig Austria
147 E3 Allenwood Rep. of Ireland
235 D2 Allenwood NJ U.S.A.
234 B1 Allenwood PA U.S.A.
114 C4 Alleppey Kerala India
186 C4 Allepuz Spain
168 E3 Aller r. Ger.
160 C2 Allerey-sur-Saône France
192 D2 Allerona Italy
173 F2 Allersberg Ger.
173 F3 Allershausen Ger.
161 E3 Allevard France
161 C4 Allex France
151 H3 Allhallows Medway, England U.K.
236 C3 Alliance NE U.S.A.
232 C4 Alliance OH U.S.A.
156 E4 Allibaudières France
Al Lībīyah country Africa see Libya
160 B2 Allier dept Auvergne France
160 B2 Allier r. France
85 E3 Alligator Point Qld Austr.
246 □ Alligator Pond Jamaica
160 C1 Alligny-en-Morvan France
147 A5 Allihies Rep. of Ireland
114 C2 Allikher Karnataka India
160 E2 Allinges France
143 F4 Allinge-Sandvig Bornholm Denmark
236 E3 Allison IA U.S.A.
195 H3 Alliste Italy
227 H3 Alliston Ont. Can.
124 C3 Al Līth Saudi Arabia
125 F3 Al Liwā' oasis U.A.E.
172 D3 Allmendingen Ger.
183 H2 Allo Spain
146 E5 Alloa Clackmannanshire, Scotland U.K.
159 I4 Allogny France
149 F3 Allonby Cumbria, England U.K.
162 C1 Allonnes Pays de la Loire France
159 G4 Allonnes Pays de la Loire France
163 B4 Allons France
83 H2 Allora Qld Austr.
161 E4 Allos France
162 C2 Alloue France
226 C3 Allouez WI U.S.A.
147 C4 Allow r. Rep. of Ireland
146 D6 Alloway South Ayrshire, Scotland U.K.
234 C3 Alloway NJ U.S.A.
234 C3 Alloway Creek r. NJ U.S.A.
186 C4 Alloza Spain
190 C1 Allschwil Switz.
171 C4 Allstedt Ger.
124 C5 Al Luḩayyah Yemen
192 D2 Allumiere Italy
114 D3 Allur Andhra Prad. India
114 D3 Alluru Kottapatnam Andhra Prad. India
160 B1 Alluy France
225 G3 Alma Que. Can.
231 D6 Alma GA U.S.A.
236 D4 Alma KS U.S.A.
226 E4 Alma MI U.S.A.
236 D3 Alma NE U.S.A.
Alma-Ata Kazakh. see Almaty
Alma-Ata Oblast admin. div. Kazakh. see Almatinskaya Oblast'
186 D3 Almacelles Spain
185 F4 Almáchar Spain
184 A2 Almada Port.
124 B1 Al Madāfi' plat. Saudi Arabia
85 F3 Almaden Qld Austr.
185 F2 Almadén Spain
184 D3 Almadén de la Plata Spain
185 F2 Almadenejos Spain
122 A4 Al Madīnah Iraq
124 B2 Al Madīnah Saudi Arabia
124 C2 Al Madīnah prov. Saudi Arabia
128 C3 Al Mafraq Jordan
261 E3 Almafuerte Arg.
125 F3 Al Maghrib reg. U.A.E.
185 G2 Almagro Spain
125 E3 Al Mahākīk reg. Saudi Arabia
204 C4 Al Mahbas Western Sahara
127 G4 Al Maḩmūdīyah Iraq
125 E4 Al Mahrah governorate Yemen
125 E5 Al Mahrah reg. Yemen
124 C5 Al Maḩwīt Yemen
124 C5 Al Maḩwīt governorate Yemen
183 H3 Almajano Spain
124 D2 Al Majma'ah Saudi Arabia
197 F3 Almăjului, Munţii mts Romania
125 E2 Al Malsūnīyah reg. Saudi Arabia
183 H3 Almaluez Spain
121 G4 Almalyk Uzbek.
125 F3 Al Manadir reg. Oman
125 E2 Al Manāmah Bahrain
187 B6 Almansa Spain
184 B3 Almansil Port.
184 B2 Almansor r. Port.
Al Manşūrah Egypt see El Mansûra
183 E2 Almanza Spain
183 E4 Almanzor mt. Spain
185 I3 Almanzora r. Spain
127 G5 Al Ma'qil Iraq
183 E4 Almar r. Spain
182 E5 Almaraz Spain
185 E3 Almargen Spain
125 F3 Al Mariyyah U.A.E.
202 D1 Al Marj Libya
183 H3 Almarza Spain
254 D4 Almas Brazil
177 L5 Almaş Romania
197 F2 Almaş r. Romania
256 C1 Almas, Rio das r. Brazil
125 G3 Al Masana'a Oman
177 H4 Almásfüzitő Hungary
177 G6 Almás-patak r. Hungary
187 C5 Almassora Spain
121 I3 Almatinskaya Oblast' admin. div. Kazakh.
121 I4 Almaty Kazakh.
Almaty Oblast admin. div. Kazakh. see Almatinskaya Oblast'
Almaty Oblysy admin. div. Kazakh. see Almatinskaya Oblast'
127 F3 Al Mawşil Iraq
127 F4 Al Mayādīn Syria
183 H3 Almazán Spain
131 M3 Almaznyy Rus. Fed.
Almazora Spain see Almassora
183 H3 Almazul Spain
173 H3 Alm Berg mt. Ger.
169 D4 Alme r. Ger.
187 B6 Almeces mt. Spain
185 H2 Almedina Spain
185 F3 Almedinilla Spain
182 D4 Almeida Port.
182 D3 Almeida de Sayago Spain
251 H5 Almeirim Brazil
184 B1 Almeirim Port.
164 F2 Almelo Neth.
186 D3 Almenar Spain
257 G2 Almenara Brazil
187 C5 Almenara Spain
187 B7 Almenara hill Spain
185 H2 Almenaras mt. Spain
183 H3 Almenar de Soria Spain
182 C3 Almendra Port.
182 D3 Almendra Spain
182 D3 Almendra, Embalse de resr Spain
184 D2 Almendral Spain
184 D2 Almendralejo Spain
185 I3 Almendricos Spain
164 E2 Almere Neth.
185 H4 Almería Spain
185 H3 Almería prov. Andalucía Spain
185 H4 Almería, Golfo de b. Spain
185 H4 Almerimar Spain
Almetievsk Rus. Fed. see Al'met'yevsk
135 K5 Al'met'yevsk Rus. Fed.
143 F3 Älmhult Sweden
124 D2 Al Midhnab Saudi Arabia
125 F3 Al Miḩrāḑ reg. Saudi Arabia
185 E5 Almina, Punta pt Ceuta Spain
124 C3 Al Mindak Saudi Arabia
125 G3 Al Mintirib Oman
242 □J7 Almirante Panama
256 C6 Almirante Tamandaré Brazil
125 F2 Al-Mirfa U.A.E.
Almirós Greece see Almyros
164 D3 Almkerk Neth.
184 B3 Almodôvar Port.
183 G4 Almodóvar hill Spain
184 E4 Almodóvar r. Spain
185 F2 Almodóvar del Campo Spain
183 I5 Almodóvar del Pinar Spain
185 E3 Almodóvar del Río Spain
182 C4 Almofala Port.
185 F4 Almogía Spain
184 B3 Almograve Port.
183 H4 Almoguera Spain
184 D1 Almoharín Spain
183 I3 Almonacid de la Sierra Spain
183 H5 Almonacid del Marquesado Spain
183 H4 Almonacid del Zorita Spain
183 G5 Almonacid de Toledo Spain
184 D3 Almonaster la Real Spain
146 E5 Almond r. Scotland U.K.
146 E5 Almondbank Perth and Kinross, Scotland U.K.
150 E3 Almondsbury South Gloucestershire, England U.K.
227 F4 Almont MI U.S.A.
227 I3 Almonte Ont. Can.
184 D3 Almonte Spain
182 D5 Almonte r. Spain
116 D3 Almora Uttar Prad. India
187 C6 Almoradí Spain
185 E2 Almorchón Spain
183 F4 Almorox Spain
177 K4 Álmosd Hungary
182 B5 Almoster Port.
184 B1 Almoster r. Port.
169 E3 Almstedt Ger.
128 D5 Al Mu'ayzīlah hill Saudi Arabia
125 E2 Al Mubarrez Saudi Arabia
125 G3 Al Muḑairib Oman
185 I2 Almudema Spain
186 C2 Almudévar Spain
125 E2 Al Muharraq Bahrain
128 C5 Al Muḩtaţab depr. Saudi Arabia
125 E5 Al Mukallā Yemen
124 C5 Al Mukhā Yemen
125 E3 Al Munbaţiḩ des. Saudi Arabia
124 D4 Al Mundafan pass Saudi Arabia
185 G4 Almuñécar Spain
186 C3 Almuniente Spain
179 E3 Almünster Austria
127 G4 Al Muqdādīyah Iraq
185 G2 Álmuradiel Spain
Al Mūrītānīyah country Africa see Mauritania
184 C1 Almuro r. Port.
126 E2 Almus Turkey
124 D1 Al Musannāh ridge Saudi Arabia
124 B2 Al Musayjīd Saudi Arabia
187 C5 Almussafes Spain
127 G5 Al Muthanná governorate Iraq
124 C3 Al Muwayh Saudi Arabia
124 A2 Al Muwayliḩ Saudi Arabia
198 C2 Almyros Greece
198 D4 Almyrou, Ormos b. Kriti Greece
235 G1 Almyville CT U.S.A.
146 D4 Alness Highland, Scotland U.K.
Alness r. Scotland U.K. see Averon
149 H2 Alnmouth Northumberland, England U.K.
149 H2 Alnwick Northumberland, England U.K.
187 B4 Alobras Spain
183 H4 Alocén Spain
81 □4 Alofi Niue
77 I3 Alofi, Île i. Wallis and Futuna Is
138 E3 Aloja Latvia
138 G3 Alolya r. Rus. Fed.
117 H3 Along Arun. Prad. India
100 B2 Alongshan Nei Mongol China
198 C2 Alonnisos i. Greece
256 B6 Alonso r. Brazil
93 C5 Alor i. Indon.
93 C5 Alor, Kepulauan is Indon.
185 F4 Álora Spain
94 C1 Alor Setar Malaysia
Alor Star Malaysia see Alor Setar
186 E2 Alós d'Ensil Spain
184 C3 Alosno Spain
Alost Belgium see Aalst
116 C5 Alot Madh. Prad. India
91 L9 Alotau P.N.G.
159 F5 Alouettes, Mont des hill France
183 G4 Alovera Spain
160 C1 Aloxe-Corton France
87 F5 Aloysius, Mount W.A. Austr.
185 F4 Alozaina Spain
186 E2 Alp Spain
261 F5 Alpachiri Arg.
199 F2 Alpagut Bursa Turkey
199 G1 Alpagut Eskişehir Turkey
184 C1 Alpalhão Port.
183 H3 Alpanseque Spain
240 H4 Alpaugh CA U.S.A.
178 C3 Alpbach Austria
183 F4 Alpedrete Spain
182 C4 Alpedrinha Port.
182 B5 Alpedriz Port.
169 B4 Alpen Ger.
227 F3 Alpena MI U.S.A.
169 C5 Alpenrod Ger.
186 F2 Alpens Spain
187 B6 Alpera Spain
254 D3 Alpercatas, Serra das hills Brazil
161 E4 Alpes-de-Haute-Provence dept Provence-Alpes-Côte-d'Azur France
161 F5 Alpes-Maritimes dept Provence-Alpes-Côte-d'Azur France
Alpes Maritimes mts France/Italy see Maritime Alps
178 C4 Alpetta, Punta dell' mt. Italy
85 F4 Alpha Qld Austr.
215 H2 Alpha S. Africa
85 F4 Alpha Creek r. Qld Austr.
268 P1 Alpha Ridge sea feature Arctic Ocean
164 D3 Alphen Neth.
164 D2 Alphen aan den Rijn Neth.
217 □2 Alphonse i. Seychelles
217 □2 Alphonse Island Seychelles
184 B1 Alpiarça Port.
Alpi Dolomitiche mts Italy see Dolomiti
161 C5 Alpilles hills France
Alpi Marittime mts France/Italy see Maritime Alps
241 M5 Alpine AZ U.S.A.
240 I5 Alpine CA U.S.A.
227 I4 Alpine NY U.S.A.
237 C6 Alpine TX U.S.A.
238 E3 Alpine WY U.S.A.
256 D4 Alpinópolis Brazil
172 C3 Alpirsbach Ger.
190 D2 Alpnach Switz.
179 H3 Alpokalja mts Hungary
191 G3 Alpone r. Italy
184 C3 Alportel r. Port.
190 B3 Alps mts Europe
199 G2 Alpu Turkey
187 C5 Alpuente Spain
125 D4 Al Qa'āmīyāt reg. Saudi Arabia
127 G5 Al Qādisīyah governorate Iraq
128 C2 Al Qadmūs Syria
Al Qāhirah Egypt see Cairo
124 C2 Al Qā'īyah Saudi Arabia
205 G2 Al Qal'a Beni Hammad tourist site Alg.
127 F3 Al Qāmishlī Syria
128 C2 Al Qardāḩah Syria
128 C2 Al Qaryatayn Syria
124 C2 Al Qaşīm prov. Saudi Arabia
125 E2 Al Qaţīf Saudi Arabia
125 E5 Al Qaţn Yemen
128 C4 Al Qaţrānah Jordan
124 D3 Al Qawnas reg. Saudi Arabia
124 D1 Al Qayşūmah Saudi Arabia
187 C6 Alquería de la Condesa Spain
184 C2 Alqueva Port.
186 D2 Alquézar Spain
185 G3 Alquife Spain
Al Qumur country Africa see Comoros
128 B3 Al Qunayţirah Syria
128 B3 Al Qunayţirah governorate Syria
124 C4 Al Qunfidhah Saudi Arabia
124 C2 Al Qurayn Saudi Arabia
124 C2 Al Qurayyah Saudi Arabia
125 G2 Al Qurayyah U.A.E.
126 E5 Al Qurayyāt Saudi Arabia
127 G5 Al Qurnah Iraq
124 C2 Al Quwārah Saudi Arabia
124 D3 Al Quwayi' Saudi Arabia
124 D2 Al Quwayīyah Saudi Arabia
128 B5 Al Quwayrah Jordan
125 E5 Al Quzah Yemen
125 F3 Al Rabbād reg. U.A.E.
161 A4 Alrance France
151 I3 Alresford Essex, England U.K.
151 F2 Alrewas Staffordshire, England U.K.
84 D3 Alroy Downs N.T. Austr.
142 C4 Als i. Denmark
157 H4 Alsace admin. reg. France
157 H4 Alsace reg. France
157 H5 Alsace, Plaine d' val. France
149 G4 Alsager Cheshire, England U.K.
223 I5 Alsask Sask. Can.
183 H2 Alsasua Spain
Alsatia reg. France see Alsace
172 C2 Alsbach Ger.
169 B5 Alsdorf Ger.
222 B3 Alsek r. AK U.S.A.
172 B2 Alsenborn Ger.
190 E4 Alseno Italy
172 B2 Alsenz Ger.
169 E5 Alsfeld Ger.
146 C4 Alsh, Loch sea chan. Scotland U.K.
172 C2 Alsheim Ger.
171 C4 Alsleben (Saale) Ger.
177 I4 Alsónémedi Hungary
177 G4 Alsóörs Hungary
177 J3 Alsóvadász Hungary
177 J3 Alsózsolca Hungary
143 G3 Alsterån r. Sweden
143 F3 Alstermo Sweden
157 G3 Alsting France
149 G3 Alston Cumbria, England U.K.
83 H2 Alstonville N.S.W. Austr.
138 C3 Alsunga Latvia
140 M1 Alta Norway
143 H2 Älta Sweden
81 B6 Alta, Mount South I. N.Z.
190 E1 Altach Austria
191 G2 Altacroce, Monte mt. Italy
240 H4 Altadena CA U.S.A.
140 M1 Altaelva r. Norway
140 M1 Altafjorden sea chan. Norway
253 F2 Alta Floresta Brazil
186 E3 Altafulla Spain
260 E2 Alta Gracia Arg.
110 D1 Altai Mountains Asia
231 D6 Altamaha r. GA U.S.A.
251 H5 Altamira Brazil
242 □I7 Altamira Costa Rica
245 F2 Altamíra Mex.
183 F1 Altamira, Cuevas de tourist site Spain
185 E1 Altamira, Sierra de mts Spain
231 D6 Altamonte Springs City FL U.S.A.
193 I4 Altamura Italy
107 F1 Altan Rus. Fed.
106 E2 Altanbulag Mongolia
107 H1 Altan Emel Nei Mongol China
106 A2 Altan Ovoo mt. China/Mongolia
107 F4 Altan Shiret Nei Mongol China
Altan Xiret Nei Mongol China see Altan Shiret
254 D5 Alta Paraiso de Goiás Brazil
242 C2 Altar Mex.
239 E6 Altar r. Mex.
242 B1 Altar, Desierto de des. Mex.
190 D4 Altare Italy
216 □1a Altares Terceira Azores
242 D3 Altata Mex.
179 E3 Altaussee Austria
194 D2 Altavilla Irpina Italy
193 H4 Altavilla Silentina Italy
232 D6 Altavista VA U.S.A.
110 E2 Altay Xinjiang China
106 C2 Altay Mongolia
106 A1 Altay, Respublika aut. rep. Rus. Fed.
Altay Kray admin. div. Rus. Fed. see Altayskiy Kray
121 K2 Altayskiy Rus. Fed.
Altayskiy Khrebet mts Asia see Altai Mountains
121 J2 Altayskiy Kray admin. div. Rus. Fed.
171 F4 Altdöbern Ger.
173 G3 Altdorf Ger.
190 D2 Altdorf Switz.
173 F2 Altdorf bei Nürnberg Ger.
168 E1 Alt Duvenstedt Ger.
184 B3 Alte Port.
187 C6 Altea Spain
170 C2 Alte Elde r. Ger.
170 E1 Altefähr Ger.
173 G3 Alteglofsheim Ger.
140 M1 Alteidet Norway
169 C4 Altena Ger.
169 B5 Altenahr Ger.
169 F4 Altenau Ger.
169 D4 Altenbeken Ger.
171 E5 Altenberg Ger.
169 C3 Altenberge Ger.
168 D2 Altenbruch-Westerende Ger.
172 D2 Altenbuch Ger.
171 D5 Altenburg Ger.
169 C5 Altendiez Ger.
169 F5 Altenfeld Ger.
179 E2 Altenfelden Austria
172 B2 Altenglan Ger.
169 F4 Altengottern Ger.
170 C1 Altenhagen Ger.
172 B3 Altenheim Ger.
170 E3 Altenhof Ger.
168 F1 Altenholz Ger.
170 E1 Altenkirchen Ger.
169 C5 Altenkirchen (Westerwald) Ger.
168 F1 Altenkrempe Ger.
173 G3 Altenmarkt an der Alz Ger.
179 G2 Altenmarkt an der Triesting Austria
179 F3 Altenmarkt bei St Gallen Austria
179 E3 Altenmarkt im Pongau Austria
168 F2 Altenmedingen Ger.
173 E3 Altenmünster Ger.
106 B4 Altenqoke Qinghai China
173 E3 Altenstadt Bayern Ger.
173 E4 Altenstadt Bayern Ger.
169 D5 Altenstadt Hessen Ger.
173 G2 Altenstadt an der Waldnaab Ger.
172 C3 Altensteig Ger.
170 E2 Altentreptow Ger.
171 C4 Altenweddingen Ger.
170 F3 Alte Oder r. Ger.
184 C1 Alter do Chão Port.
184 C1 Alter Pedroso hill Port.
171 E3 Altes Lager Ger.
140 L1 Altevatnet l. Norway
173 G3 Altfraunhofen Ger.
173 F3 Althegnenberg Ger.
178 E2 Altheim Austria
172 D3 Altheim Ger.
173 E3 Altheim (Alb) Ger.
172 C3 Althengstett Ger.
179 F4 Althofen Austria
129 F3 Altıağaç Azer.
161 B4 Altier France
161 B4 Altier r. France
129 A4 Altınbasak Turkey
127 G4 Altin Köprü Iraq
199 E2 Altınoluk Turkey
256 D4 Altinópolis Brazil
199 E2 Altınova Turkey
128 C1 Altınova Turkey
128 C1 Altınözü Turkey
199 G2 Altıntaş Turkey
199 G3 Altınyaka Turkey
252 C4 Altiplano plain Bol.
129 C4 Altıyol Turkey
160 F1 Altkirch France
171 D5 Altkirchen Ger.
170 C2 Alt Krenzlin Ger.
170 E3 Altlandsberg Ger.
173 F3 Altmannstein Ger.
171 D5 Altmittweida Ger.
173 F3 Altmühl r. Ger.
146 D5 Altnafeadh Highland, Scotland U.K.
146 D3 Altnaharra Highland, Scotland U.K.
226 E4 Alto MI U.S.A.
191 G3 Alto, Monte hill Italy
256 A2 Alto Araguaia Brazil
246 D2 Alto Cedro Cuba
209 C7 Alto Chicapa Angola
183 H3 Alto Cruz mt. Spain
183 G2 Alto de Cabezas mt. Spain
183 I3 Alto del Moncayo mt. Spain
260 D3 Alto de Pencoso hills Arg.
185 G3 Alto de San Juan mt. Spain
182 B4 Alto do Trevim mt. Port.
194 C4 Altofonte Sicilia Italy
255 B6 Alto Garças Brazil
260 B3 Alto Jahuel Chile
213 H2 Alto Ligonha Moz.
245 F4 Alto Lucero Mex.
213 H2 Alto Molócuè Moz.
193 I5 Altomonte Italy
173 F3 Altomünster Ger.
151 G3 Alton Hampshire, England U.K.
151 F2 Alton Staffordshire, England U.K.
236 F4 Alton IL U.S.A.
237 F4 Alton MO U.S.A.
233 □H3 Alton NH U.S.A.
222 F3 Altona B.C. Can.
223 L5 Altona Man. Can.
82 D1 Alton Downs S.A. Austr.
259 B7 Alto Nevado mt. Chile
232 D4 Altoona PA U.S.A.
226 B3 Altoona WI U.S.A.
251 I5 Alto Pacajá r. Brazil
254 D4 Alto Parnaíba Brazil
191 F5 Altopascio Italy
256 A6 Alto Piquiri Brazil
252 C2 Alto Purús r. Peru
182 C3 Alto Rabagão, Barragem do resr Port.
257 F4 Alto Rio Doce Brazil
259 C7 Alto Río Senguerr Arg.
186 D3 Altorricón Spain
254 E3 Altos Brazil
183 H4 Altos de Cabrejas mts Spain
261 F2 Altos de Chipión Arg.
183 G2 Altotero mt. Spain
245 F4 Altotonga Mex.
173 G3 Altötting Ger.
170 F3 Altranft Ger.
172 A2 Altrich Ger.
149 G4 Altrincham Greater Manchester, England U.K.
170 D3 Alt Ruppin Ger.
Altsasu Spain see Alsasua
170 D2 Alt Schwerin Ger.
172 D4 Altshausen Ger.
190 E1 Altstätten Switz.
129 C2 Altud Rus. Fed.
139 J5 Altukhovo Rus. Fed.
129 B4 Altunkent Turkey
110 F4 Altun Shan mt. Qinghai China
111 D4 Altun Shan mts China
187 C5 Altura Spain
238 B3 Alturas CA U.S.A.
237 D5 Altus OK U.S.A.
173 E4 Altusried Ger.
169 F3 Alt Wallmoden Ger.
137 G2 Altynivka Ukr.
120 D4 Altynkul' Uzbek.
Altyn-Topkan Tajik. see Oltintopkan
138 E2 Alu Estonia
213 H2 Alua Moz.
126 E2 Alucra Turkey
125 E2 Al 'Uḑaylīyah Saudi Arabia
138 F3 Alūksne Latvia
138 F3 Alūksnes l. Latvia
124 B2 Al 'Ulā Saudi Arabia
122 B3 Alūm Iran
232 C5 Alum Bridge WV U.S.A.
260 B6 Aluminé Arg.
260 B6 Aluminé r. Arg.
143 H1 Alunda Sweden
197 G2 Aluniş Romania
137 H5 Alupka Ukr.
202 C2 Al 'Uqaylah Libya
Al 'Uqaylah Saudi Arabia see An Nabk
125 E2 Al 'Uqayr Saudi Arabia
Al Uqşur Egypt see El Uqşur
114 C3 Alur Andhra Prad. India
126 E5 Al Urayq des. Saudi Arabia
Al 'Urdun country Asia see Jordan
Alur Setar Malaysia see Alor Setar
137 H5 Alushta Ukr.
183 I4 Alustante Spain
Aluva Kerala India see Alwaye
127 F5 Al 'Uwayqīlah Saudi Arabia
124 D2 Al Uyainah Saudi Arabia
127 G5 Al 'Uzayr Iraq
182 B4 Alva r. Port.
146 E5 Alva Clackmannanshire, Scotland U.K.
237 D4 Alva OK U.S.A.
182 B5 Alvaiázere Port.
184 B3 Alvalade Port.
122 B3 Alvand, Kūh-e mt. Iran
190 E2 Alvaneu Switz.
182 C3 Alvão, Serra de mts Spain
129 B4 Alvar Turkey
245 G4 Alvarado Mex.
237 D5 Alvarado TX U.S.A.
251 E5 Alvarães Brazil
182 B3 Alvarães Port.
257 G3 Alvarenga Brazil
182 B4 Alvarenga Port.
182 B4 Álvares Port.
256 B5 Álvares Machado Brazil
261 G3 Alvarez Arg.
182 C5 Álvaro Port.
244 D4 Álvaro Obregón Mex.
141 K3 Älvdalen Sweden
141 E1 Alvdalen val. Sweden
151 F2 Alvechurch Worcestershire, England U.K.
182 B1 Alvedro airport Spain
184 B1 Alvega Port.
150 E2 Alveley Shropshire, England U.K.
182 B5 Alvelos, Serra de mts Port.
184 A2 Alverca Port.
182 C4 Alverca da Beira Port.
165 B3 Alveringem Belgium
146 E4 Alves Moray, Scotland U.K.
168 E2 Alveslohe Ger.
143 F3 Alvesta Sweden
150 E3 Alveston South Gloucestershire, England U.K.
193 E2 Alviano Italy
146 E4 Alvie Highland, Scotland U.K.
163 D4 Alvignac France
142 B1 Ålvik Norway
141 L3 Alvik Sweden
237 E6 Alvin TX U.S.A.
226 C3 Alvin WI U.S.A.
257 F4 Alvinópolis Brazil
182 C4 Alvite Port.
193 F3 Alvito Italy
184 C2 Alvito Port.
143 G1 Älvkarleby Sweden
193 H4 Alvo r. Italy
182 C4 Alvoco da Serra Port.
184 B3 Alvor Port.
140 M2 Älvsbyn Sweden
124 B2 Al Wajh Saudi Arabia
125 E2 Al Wakrah Qatar
116 D4 Alwar Rajasthan India
114 C4 Alwaye Kerala India
175 H5 Alwernia Pol.
127 F4 Al Widyān plat. Iraq/Saudi Arabia
202 C3 Al Wīgh, Ramlat des. Libya
125 G3 Al Wustá admin. reg. Oman
Alxa Youqi Nei Mongol China see Ehen Hudag
Alxa Zuoqi Nei Mongol China see Bayan Hot
84 D2 Alyangula N.T. Austr.
146 E5 Alyth Perth and Kinross, Scotland U.K.
138 E4 Alytus Lith.
173 G3 Alz r. Ger.
238 F2 Alzada MT U.S.A.
190 E3 Alzano Lombardo Italy
169 E5 Alzenau in Unterfranken Ger.
165 F5 Alzette r. Lux.
172 C2 Alzey Ger.
187 C5 Alzira Spain
161 B5 Alzon France
163 E5 Alzonne France
215 F5 Amabele S. Africa
245 E5 Amacuzac r. Mex.
141 K3 Ämådalen Sweden
84 B5 Amadeus, Lake salt flat N.T. Austr.
221 K3 Amadjuak Lake Nunavut Can.
241 L6 Amado AZ U.S.A.
184 A2 Amadora Port.
205 G4 Amadror plain Alg.
250 C3 Amaga Col.
105 E3 Amaga-dake mt. Japan
235 F2 Amagansett NY U.S.A.
104 B4 Amagasaki Japan
142 E4 Amager i. Denmark
103 E7 Amagi Japan
105 E4 Amagi-san vol. Japan
156 E3 Amagne France
104 C3 Amagoi-dake mt. Japan
245 E3 Amajac r. Mex.
105 D2 Amakazari-yama mt. Japan

103 D7 Amakusa-nada b. Japan
125 F4 Amal Oman
142 E2 Åmal Sweden
114 D2 Amalapuram Andhra Prad. India
99 K1 Amalat r. Rus. Fed.
193 G4 Amalfi Italy
215 E2 Amalia S. Africa
198 B3 Amaliada Greece
116 C5 Amalner Mahar. India
253 G5 Amambaí Brazil
253 G5 Amambaí, Serra de hills Brazil/Para.
102 □1 Amami-Ō-shima i. Japan
102 □1 Amami-shotō is Japan
141 K3 Åmån r. Sweden
157 G5 Amance France
157 F5 Amance r. France
160 E1 Amancey France
232 B5 Amanda OH U.S.A.
193 F2 Amandola Italy
120 D2 Amangel'dy Aktyubinskaya Oblast' Kazakh.
120 F2 Amangel'dy Kustanayskaya Oblast' Kazakh.
120 F1 Amankaragay Kazakh.
Amankeldi Aktyubinskaya Oblast' Kazakh. see Amangel'dy
Amankeldi Kustanayskaya Oblast' Kazakh. see Amangel'dy
120 E3 Amanotkel' Kazakh.
Amanqaraghay Kazakh. see Amankaragay
193 I5 Amantea Italy
215 H4 Amanzimtoti S. Africa
251 I4 Amapá Brazil
251 I4 Amapá state Brazil
245 F4 Amapa r. Mex.
242 □I6 Amapala Hond.
251 I4 Amapari r. Brazil
197 F3 Amaradia r. Romania
255 B9 Amaral Ferrador Brazil
254 E3 Amarante Brazil
182 B3 Amarante Port.
254 D3 Amarante do Maranhão Brazil
96 B2 Amarapura Myanmar
114 C4 Amaravati r. India
106 E2 Amardalay Mongolia
182 B3 Amarela, Serra mts Port.
184 C2 Amareleja Port.
182 B3 Amares Port.
254 F5 Amargosa Brazil
241 I3 Amargosa Desert NV U.S.A.
240 I3 Amargosa Range mts CA U.S.A.
241 I3 Amargosa Valley NV U.S.A.
185 G1 Amarguillo r. Spain
Amargura Island Tonga see Fonualei
237 C5 Amarillo TX U.S.A.
258 C4 Amarillo, Cerro mt. Arg.
116 E5 Amarkantak Madh. Prad. India
193 G2 Amaro, Monte mt. Italy
195 F4 Amaroni Italy
84 D4 Amaroo, Lake salt flat Qld Austr.
117 G5 Amarpur Tripura India
116 D5 Amarwara Madh. Prad. India
226 C2 Amasa MI U.S.A.
193 F3 Amaseno Italy
193 F3 Amaseno r. Italy
129 C3 Amasia Armenia
Amasia Turkey see Amasya
204 B4 Amasine Western Sahara
126 D2 Amasra Turkey
126 D2 Amasya Turkey
82 B1 Amata S.A. Austr.
250 D5 Amataurá Brazil
243 G5 Amatenango Mex.
215 H3 Amatikulu S. Africa
245 F4 Amatlán Mex.
244 B3 Amatlán de Cañas Mex.
195 F4 Amato r. Italy
193 F2 Amatrice Italy
235 E1 Amawalk NY U.S.A.
165 E4 Amay Belgium
183 F2 Amaya mt. Spain
100 B1 Amazar Rus. Fed.
100 B1 Amazar r. Rus. Fed.
251 I4 Amazon r. S. America alt. Amazonas
251 I4 Amazon, Mouths of the Brazil
252 C3 Amazon, Source of the Peru
251 E6 Amazonas state Brazil
250 D5 Amazonas dept Col.
250 B6 Amazonas dept Peru
251 I4 Amazonas r. S. America conv. Amazon
251 E4 Amazonas state Venez.
264 F5 Amazon Cone sea feature S. Atlantic Ocean
210 C1 Āmba Ālagē mt. Eth.
114 B2 Ambad Mahar. India
210 C2 Āmba Farit mt. Eth.
213 □I4 Ambahikily Madag.
114 C2 Ambajogai Mahar. India
116 D3 Ambala Haryana India
213 □J3 Ambalajanakomby Madag.
114 D5 Ambalangoda Sri Lanka
213 □J4 Ambalatany Madag.
213 □J4 Ambalavao Madag.
84 C4 Ambalindum N.T. Austr.
207 H6 Ambam Cameroon
213 □K2 Ambanja Madag.
162 B4 Ambarès-et-Lagarve France
258 D3 Ambargasta, Salinas de salt pan Arg.
134 F2 Ambarnyy Rus. Fed.
117 G5 Ambasa Tripura India
183 E2 Ambasaguas Spain
114 C4 Ambasamudram Tamil Nadu India
85 F5 Ambathala Qld Austr.
250 B5 Ambato Ecuador
258 D3 Ambato, Sierra mts Arg.
213 □J3 Ambato Boeny Madag.
213 □J4 Ambato Finandrahana Madag.
213 □J3 Ambatolampy Madag.
213 □J3 Ambatomainty Madag.
213 □J3 Ambatomanoina Madag.
213 □K3 Ambatondrazaka Madag.
213 □K2 Ambatosia Madag.
213 □K3 Ambatosoratra Madag.
162 D3 Ambazac France
Ambejogai Mahar. India see Ambajogai
Ambelón Greece see Ampelonas
Amber Rajasthan India see Amer
173 F2 Amberg Ger.
226 D3 Amberg WI U.S.A.
149 H4 Ambergate Derbyshire, England U.K.
246 E2 Ambergris Cays is Turks and Caicos Is
160 D3 Ambérieu-en-Bugey France
227 G3 Amberley Ont. Can.
81 D5 Amberley South I. N.Z.
165 E4 Amberloup Belgium
160 B3 Ambert France
162 B3 Ambès France
116 E5 Ambgaon Mahar. India
163 E5 Ambialet France
Ambianum France see Amiens
206 C3 Ambidédi Mali
160 B2 Ambierle France
116 C5 Ambika r. India
117 E5 Ambikapur Madh. Prad. India
213 □J4 Ambila Madag.
159 G4 Ambillou France
213 □K2 Ambilobe Madag.
222 D3 Ambition, Mount B.C. Can.
156 C3 Amblainville France
149 H2 Amble Northumberland, England U.K.
150 E2 Amblecote West Midlands, England U.K.
220 C3 Ambler AK U.S.A.
234 C2 Ambler PA U.S.A.
149 G3 Ambleside Cumbria, England U.K.
156 B2 Ambleteuse France
165 E4 Amblève r. Belgium
117 F5 Ambo Orissa India
252 A2 Ambo Peru
213 □J5 Amboasary Madag.
213 □K3 Amboasary Gara Madag.
213 □K3 Amboavory Madag.
213 □K3 Ambodifotatra Madag.
213 □K4 Ambodiharina Madag.
213 □J3 Ambohidratrimo Madag.
213 □K3 Ambohijanahary Madag.
213 □J4 Ambohimahasoa Madag.
213 □I4 Ambohimahavelona Madag.
213 □K2 Ambohitra mt. Madag.
213 □K2 Ambohitralanana Madag.
Amboina Maluku Indon. see Ambon
162 C1 Amboise France
158 D4 Ambon France
93 D3 Ambon Maluku Indon.
93 C3 Ambon i. Maluku Indon.
213 □J5 Ambondro Madag.
156 E3 Ambonnay France
211 C5 Amboseli National Park Kenya
213 □J4 Ambositra Madag.
213 □J5 Ambovombe Madag.
241 J4 Amboy CA U.S.A.
226 C5 Amboy IL U.S.A.
159 H5 Ambrault France
Ambre, Cap d' c. Madag. see Bobaomby, Tanjona
159 F3 Ambrières-les-Vallées France
Ambrim i. Vanuatu see Ambrym
209 B6 Ambriz Angola
Ambrizete Angola see N'zeto
129 C2 Ambrolauri Georgia
160 D2 Ambronay France
151 F3 Ambrosden Oxfordshire, England U.K.
78 □5 Ambrym i. Vanuatu
95 F4 Ambunten Jawa Timur Indon.
114 C3 Ambur Tamil Nadu India
85 G5 Amby Qld Austr.
220 A4 Amchitka Island AK U.S.A.
202 D6 Am-Dam Chad
130 H3 Amderma Rus. Fed.
111 E5 Amdo Xizang China
244 D3 Amealco Mex.
244 B3 Ameca Mex.
244 B3 Ameca r. Mex.
245 E4 Amecameca Mex.
210 C2 Amedamit mt. Eth.
190 E4 Ameglia Italy
179 E2 Ameisberg hill Austria
184 C3 Ameixial Port.
165 F4 Amel Belgium
164 E1 Ameland i. Neth.
193 E2 Amelia Italy
232 E6 Amelia Court House VA U.S.A.
163 E6 Amélie-les-Bains-Palalda France
168 F2 Amelinghausen Ger.
116 E4 Amellu Uttar Prad. India
182 B5 Amêndoa Port.
184 C3 Amendoeira Port.
195 F3 Amendolara Italy
195 E5 Amendolea r. Italy
233 G4 Amenia NY U.S.A.
111 A7 Amer Rajasthan India
186 F2 Amer Spain
173 G4 Amerang Ger.
182 C2 A Merca Spain
240 G2 American, North Fork r. CA U.S.A.
256 D5 Americana Brazil
264 H9 American-Antarctic Ridge sea feature S. Atlantic Ocean
238 D3 American Falls ID U.S.A.
241 L1 American Fork UT U.S.A.
78 □2 American Samoa terr. S. Pacific Ocean
231 C5 Americus GA U.S.A.
179 F3 Ameringkogel mt. Austria
164 E3 Amerongen Neth.
164 E2 Amersfoort Neth.
215 G2 Amersfoort S. Africa
151 G3 Amersham Buckinghamshire, England U.K.
223 M3 Amery Man. Can.
236 E3 Ames IA U.S.A.
151 F3 Amesbury Wiltshire, England U.K.
233 H3 Amesbury MA U.S.A.
116 C4 Amet Rajasthan India
116 E4 Amethi Uttar Prad. India
186 A1 Amezketa Spain
182 C2 A Mezquita Spain
198 B2 Amfilochia Greece
198 C2 Amfissa Greece
159 G2 Amfreville-la-Campagne France
131 O3 Amga Rus. Fed.
107 H1 Amgalang Nei Mongol China
131 T3 Amguema Rus. Fed.
99 O1 Amgun' r. Rus. Fed.
210 C2 Amhara admin. reg. Eth.
225 H4 Amherst N.S. Can.
233 G3 Amherst MA U.S.A.
232 B4 Amherst OH U.S.A.
232 D6 Amherst VA U.S.A.
86 E3 Amherst, Mount hill W.A. Austr.
227 F4 Amherstburg Ont. Can.
232 C6 Amherstdale WV U.S.A.
227 I3 Amherstview Ont. Can.
184 B1 Amiais de Baixo Port.
192 D2 Amiata, Monte mt. Italy
Amida Turkey see Diyarbakır
236 C2 Amidon ND U.S.A.
184 C2 Amieira Port.
182 C5 Amieira do Tejo Port.
156 C3 Amiens France
126 E3 Amik Ovası marsh Turkey
125 F4 Amilḩayt, Wādī al r. Oman
156 C5 Amilly France
Amíndhaion Greece see Amyntaio
114 B4 Amindivi Islands Lakshadweep India
128 B2 Amioun Lebanon
116 D3 Amipshahr Uttar Prad. India
Amirabad Iran see Fūlād Maïalleh
217 □2 Amirante Islands Seychelles
265 H5 Amirante Trench sea feature Indian Ocean
Amistad, Represa de resr Mex./U.S.A. see Amistad Reservoir
243 E2 Amistad Reservoir Mex./U.S.A.
Amisus Turkey see Samsun
237 F6 Amite LA U.S.A.
237 F6 Amite Creek r. MS U.S.A.
85 H5 Amity Point Qld Austr.
116 D5 Amla Madh. Prad. India
124 C4 Amlaḩ, Jabal al hill Saudi Arabia
207 F5 Amlamé Togo
122 B2 Amlash Iran
142 C2 Åmli Norway
220 A4 Amlia Island AK U.S.A.
150 C1 Amlwch Isle of Anglesey, Wales U.K.
128 B4 'Ammān Jordan
150 D3 Ammanford Carmarthenshire, Wales U.K.
134 E2 Ämmänsaari Fin.
128 C3 'Ammār, Tall hill Syria
140 L2 Ammarnäs Sweden
84 C4 Ammaroo N.T. Austr.
221 O3 Ammassalik Greenland
173 F4 Ammer r. Ger.
140 L3 Ammerån r. Sweden
172 C3 Ammerbuch Ger.
178 B3 Ammergauer Alpen mts Austria/Ger.
169 F4 Ammern Ger.
168 F2 Ammersbek Ger.
157 H4 Ammerschwihr France
173 F4 Ammersee l. Ger.
198 B1 Ammochori Dytiki Makedonia Greece
128 A2 Ammochostos Cyprus
128 B2 Ammochostos Bay Cyprus
124 C5 Am Nābiyah Yemen
Amne Machin Range mts China see A'nyêmaqên Shan
157 G3 Amnéville France
Amnok-kang r. China/N. Korea see Yalu Jiang
116 C5 Amod Gujarat India
182 C2 Amoeiro Spain
108 B4 Amo Jiang r. Yunnan China
122 C2 Amol Iran
137 H2 Amon' Rus. Fed.
182 B3 Amonde Port.
169 D5 Amöneburg Ger.
254 F2 Amontada Brazil
183 F5 Amor mt. Spain
172 D2 Amorbach Ger.
183 H1 Amorebieta Spain
258 F3 Amores r. Arg.
199 D3 Amorgos i. Greece
256 B2 Amorinópolis Brazil
237 F5 Amory MS U.S.A.
224 E3 Amos Que. Can.
142 D4 Åmose r. Denmark
142 C2 Åmot Buskerud Norway
142 B2 Åmot Telemark Norway
141 L3 Åmot Sweden
Amota i. Vanuatu see Mota
250 A6 Amotape, Cerros de mts Peru
142 E2 Åmotfors Sweden
163 B5 Amou France
205 F2 Amour, Djebel mts Alg.
206 D2 Amourj Maur.
Amoy Fujian China see Xiamen
245 E4 Amozoc Mex.
213 □K2 Ampanefena Madag.
115 D2 Ampani Orissa India
213 □J5 Ampanihy Madag.
213 □K3 Amparafaravola Madag.
114 D5 Amparai Sri Lanka
256 D5 Amparo Brazil
213 □K3 Ampasimanolotra Madag.
213 □K3 Ampasimbe Madag.
178 C3 Ampass Austria
198 C2 Ampelonas Greece
95 G5 Ampenan Lombok Indon.
173 F3 Amper r. Ger.
207 H4 Amper Nigeria
264 I3 Ampere Seamount sea feature N. Atlantic Ocean
191 H2 Ampezzo Italy
173 G3 Ampfing Ger.
173 H3 Ampflwang im Hausruckwald Austria
90 D3 Amphitrite Group is Paracel Is
160 C3 Amplepuis France
151 F3 Amport Hampshire, England U.K.
186 D4 Amposta Spain
151 G2 Ampthill Bedfordshire, England U.K.
183 F3 Ampudia Spain
183 G1 Ampuero Spain
161 E5 Ampus France
225 H3 Amqui Que. Can.
114 C2 Amrabad Andhra Prad. India
124 C2 'Amrah, Jabal hill Saudi Arabia
124 C5 Amrān Yemen
Amraoti Mahar. India see Amravati
116 D5 Amravati Mahar. India
116 B5 Amreli Gujarat India
190 E1 Amriswil Switz.
116 C3 Amritsar Punjab India
116 D3 Amroha Uttar Prad. India
168 D1 Amrum i. Ger.
140 L2 Åmsele Sweden
Amselfeld prov. Yugo. see Kosovo
164 D2 Amstelveen Neth.
164 D2 Amsterdam Neth.
215 H2 Amsterdam S. Africa
233 F3 Amsterdam NY U.S.A.
232 C4 Amsterdam OH U.S.A.
265 J7 Amsterdam, Île i. Indian Ocean
179 F2 Amstetten Austria
172 D3 Amstetten Ger.
235 F1 Amston CT U.S.A.
208 D2 Am Timan Chad
172 D4 Amtzell Ger.
250 C4 Amú r. Col.
120 D3 Amudar'ya r. Asia
Amudaryo r. Asia see Amudar'ya
221 I2 Amund Ringnes Island Nunavut Can.
263 G2 Amundsen, Mount Antarctica
267 K10 Amundsen Abyssal Plain sea feature Southern Ocean
268 B1 Amundsen Basin sea feature Arctic Ocean
262 O1 Amundsen Coast Antarctica
220 F2 Amundsen Gulf N.W.T. Can.
267 K10 Amundsen Ridge sea feature Southern Ocean
263 A1 Amundsen-Scott research stn Antarctica
95 F3 Amuntai Kalimantan Selatan Indon.
100 E2 Amur r. China/Rus. Fed. alt. Heilong Jiang
93 C2 Amurang Sulawesi Utara Indon.
Amur Oblast admin. div. Rus. Fed. see Amurskaya Oblast'
183 H1 Amurrio Spain
100 F2 Amursk Rus. Fed.
100 D1 Amurskaya Oblast' admin. div. Rus. Fed.
100 D3 Amurzet Rus. Fed.
195 F4 Amusa r. Italy
183 F2 Amusco Spain
198 B2 Amvrakia, Limni l. Greece
198 B2 Amvrakikos Kolpos b. Greece
137 J4 Amvrosiyivka Ukr.
Amyderya r. Asia see Amudar'ya
198 B1 Amyntaio Greece
226 E1 Amyot Ont. Can.
197 I4 Amzacea Romania
202 D6 Am-Zoer Chad
199 E1 Ana r. Turkey
79 □3 Anaa atoll Arch. des Tuamotu Fr. Polynesia
93 B3 Anabanua Sulawesi Selatan Indon.
131 M2 Anabar r. Rus. Fed.
83 E3 Ana Branch r. N.S.W. Austr.
128 B3 Anabtā West Bank
240 H4 Anacapa Islands CA U.S.A.
193 G4 Anacapri Italy
251 E2 Anaco Venez.
238 D2 Anaconda MT U.S.A.
238 B1 Anacortes WA U.S.A.
237 D5 Anadarko OK U.S.A.
182 B4 Anadia Port.
126 E2 Anadolu Dağları mts Turkey
131 S3 Anadyr' Rus. Fed.
131 S3 Anadyr' r. Rus. Fed.
Anadyr, Gulf of Rus. Fed. see Anadyrskiy Zaliv
131 T3 Anadyrskiy Zaliv b. Rus. Fed.
199 D3 Anafi i. Greece
254 E5 Anagé Brazil
193 F3 Anagni Italy
Anagnia Italy see Anagni
127 F4 'Ānah Iraq
240 I5 Anaheim CA U.S.A.
222 E4 Anahim Lake B.C. Can.
240 □B7 Anahola HI U.S.A.
243 E3 Anáhuac Mex.
245 F2 Anáhuac Mex.
237 E6 Anahuac TX U.S.A.
114 C4 Anaimalai Hills India
114 C4 Anai Mudi Peak Kerala India
Anaiteum i. Vanuatu see Anatom
251 I5 Anajás Brazil
251 I5 Anajás, Ilha i. Brazil
254 D2 Anajatuba Brazil
213 □I4 Anakao Madag.
115 D2 Anakapalle Andhra Prad. India
85 F4 Anakie Qld Austr.
213 □J2 Analalava Madag.
256 D5 Analândia Brazil
213 □I4 Analavelona mts Madag.
234 C1 Analomink PA U.S.A.
251 F5 Anamã Brazil
94 D2 Anambas, Kepulauan is Indon.
207 G5 Anambra state Nigeria
Anamooka i. Tonga see Nomuka
236 F3 Anamosa IA U.S.A.
251 G4 Anamu r. Brazil
126 D3 Anamur Turkey
104 A5 Anan Japan
116 C5 Anand Gujarat India
117 F5 Anandapur Orissa India
116 D3 Anandpur Punjab India
117 F5 Anandpur r. W. Bengal India
121 I4 Anan'ev Kyrg.
114 C3 Anantapur Andhra Prad. India
116 C2 Anantnag Jammu and Kashmir
116 D4 Anant Peth Madh. Prad. India
Ananyev Ukr. see Anan'yiv
Anan'yevo Kyrg. see Anan'ev
136 E4 Anan'yiv Ukr.
135 G7 Anapa Rus. Fed.
195 E5 Anapo r. Sicilia Italy
198 D4 Anapodaris r. Kriti Greece
256 C2 Anápolis Brazil
251 I5 Anapú r. Brazil
Anár Fin. see Inari
122 C4 Anār Iran
122 C3 Anārak Iran
122 B3 Anarbar r. Iran
177 L3 Anarcs Hungary
263 L2 Anare Mountains Antarctica
147 A4 Anascaul Rep. of Ireland
247 □1 Añasco Puerto Rico
247 □1 Añasco, Río Grande de r. Puerto Rico
140 M2 Ånäset Sweden
137 J4 Anastasiyevka Rus. Fed.
137 I5 Anastasiyevskaya Rus. Fed.
91 K3 Anatahan i. N. Mariana Is
Anatajan i. N. Mariana Is see Anatahan
199 G2 Anatolia reg. Turkey
198 D1 Anatoliki Makedonia kai Thraki admin. reg. Greece
78 □5 Anatom i. Vanuatu
258 E3 Añatuya Arg.
251 F4 Anauá r. Brazil
256 A5 Anaurilândia Brazil
251 F5 Anavilhanas, Arquipélago das is Brazil
183 E4 Anaya de Alba Spain
Anaypazari Turkey see Gülnar
106 C3 Anbei Gansu China
101 C5 Anbyon N. Korea
182 B4 Ançã Port.
182 C2 Ancares, Serra dos mts Spain
252 A2 Ancash dept Peru
227 H4 Ancaster Ont. Can.
151 G2 Ancaster Lincolnshire, England U.K.
258 D3 Ancasti, Sierra mts Arg.
161 B4 Ance r. France
161 E4 Ancelle France
158 E4 Ancenis France
157 F4 Ancerville France
Anchang Sichuan China see Anxian
207 H4 Anchau Nigeria
257 G4 Anchieta Brazil
220 D3 Anchorage AK U.S.A.
Anchorage Island atoll Cook Is see Suwarrow
Anchuthengu Kerala India see Anjengo
Anci Hebei China see Langfang
138 D4 Ančia r. Lith.
183 H2 Ancín Spain
An Cóbh Rep. of Ireland see Cóbh
252 A2 Ancón Peru
191 I5 Ancona Italy
191 H5 Ancona prov. Marche Italy
156 C3 Ancre r. France
146 F6 Ancrum Scottish Borders, Scotland U.K.
211 C8 Ancuabe Moz.
259 B6 Ancud Chile
259 B6 Ancud, Golfo de g. Chile
156 E5 Ancy-le-Franc France
Ancyra Turkey see Ankara
Anda Heilong. China see Daqing
100 C3 Anda Heilong. China
260 B5 Andacollo Arg.
260 B2 Andacollo Chile
84 C5 Andado N.T. Austr.
252 B3 Andahuaylas Peru
213 □K3 Andaingo Gara Madag.
117 F5 Andal W. Bengal India
Andalaly Rus. Fed. see Nozhay-Yurt
258 D2 Andalgalá Arg.
191 G2 Andalo Italy
140 I3 Åndalsnes Norway
185 F3 Andalucía aut. comm. Spain
Andalusia S. Africa see Jan Kempdorp
Andalusia aut. comm. Spain see Andalucía
231 C6 Andalusia AL U.S.A.
125 G3 Andām, Wādī r. Oman
97 A5 Andaman and Nicobar Islands union terr. India
265 K4 Andaman Basin sea feature Indian Ocean
115 G3 Andaman Islands Andaman & Nicobar Is India
97 A5 Andaman Sea Indian Ocean
82 D2 Andamooka S.A. Austr.
161 C3 Andance France
213 □K2 Andapa Madag.
185 H4 Andarax r. Spain
179 I3 Andau Austria
182 E3 Andavías Spain
173 F4 Andechs Ger.
190 E2 Andeer Switz.
Andegavum France see Angers
190 D1 Andelfingen Switz.
156 B3 Andelle r. France
157 F4 Andelot-Blancheville France
160 D2 Andelot-en-Montagne France
178 A3 Andelsbuch Austria
164 E3 Andelst Neth.
140 L1 Andenes Norway
165 E4 Andenne Belgium
207 F3 Andéramboukane Mali
165 D4 Anderlecht Belgium
165 D4 Anderlues Belgium
190 D2 Andermatt Switz.
169 C5 Andernach Ger.
163 A4 Andernos-les-Bains France
143 G1 Andersbo Sweden
220 F3 Anderson r. N.W.T. Can.
220 D3 Anderson AK U.S.A.
240 F1 Anderson CA U.S.A.
230 C3 Anderson IN U.S.A.
237 E4 Anderson MO U.S.A.
231 D5 Anderson SC U.S.A.
83 F5 Anderson Bay Tas. Austr.
232 B5 Andersonville OH U.S.A.
169 C3 Andervenne Ger.
250 C3 Andes Col.
252 B3 Andes mts S. America
140 L1 Andfjorden sea chan. Norway
Andhíparos i. Greece see Antiparos
114 C2 Andhra Pradesh state India
164 E2 Andijk Neth.
Andijon Uzbek. see Andizhan
Andijon Wiloyati admin. div. Uzbek. see Andizhanskaya Oblast'
Andikíra Greece see Antikyra
213 □K3 Andilamena Madag.
213 □K3 Andilanatoby Madag.
157 F5 Andilly-en-Bassigny France
122 B3 Andīmeshk Iran
Andímilos i. Greece see Antimilos
Andípsara i. Greece see Antipsara
256 B5 Andirá Brazil
111 C4 Andir He r. China
126 E3 Andırın Turkey
129 E2 Andiyskoye Koysu r. Rus. Fed.
114 C4 Andiyur Tamil Nadu India
121 H4 Andizhan Uzbek.
Andizhan Oblast admin. div. Uzbek. see Andizhanskaya Oblast'
121 H4 Andizhanskaya Oblast' admin. div. Uzbek.
123 F2 Andkhui r. Afgh.
123 F2 Andkhvoy Afgh.
157 H4 Andlau France
157 H4 Andlau r. France
186 A1 Andoain Spain
213 □K2 Andoany Madag.
250 B5 Andoas Peru
177 G5 Andocs Hungary
139 K2 Andoga r. Rus. Fed.
139 K2 Andogskaya Gryada hills Rus. Fed.
213 □K2 Andohajango Madag.
114 C2 Andol Andhra Prad. India
114 C2 Andola Karnataka India
157 H4 Andolsheim France
Andong Liaoning China see Dandong
101 D5 Andong S. Korea
85 E2 Andoom Qld Austr.
179 E2 Andorf Austria
177 J4 Andornaktálya Hungary
190 D3 Andorno Micca Italy
186 E2 Andorra country Europe
186 C4 Andorra Spain
186 E2 Andorra la Vella Andorra
Andorra la Vieja Andorra see Andorra la Vella
183 I2 Andosilla Spain
159 F3 Andouillé France
177 H4 Andovce Slovakia
151 F3 Andover Hampshire, England U.K.
235 F1 Andover CT U.S.A.
233 H3 Andover MA U.S.A.
233 H3 Andover NH U.S.A.
234 D2 Andover NJ U.S.A.
232 E3 Andover NY U.S.A.
232 C4 Andover OH U.S.A.
140 K1 Andøya i. Norway
139 K2 Andozero, Ozero l. Rus. Fed.
161 C3 Andrable r. France
256 D5 Andradas Brazil
241 J5 Andrade CA U.S.A.
256 B4 Andradina Brazil
Andraitx Spain see Andratx
213 □J3 Andramasina Madag.
195 H3 Andrano Italy
213 □I4 Andranopasy Madag.
187 F5 Andratx Spain
220 A4 Andreanof Islands AK U.S.A.
139 I3 Andreapol' Rus. Fed.
140 □ Andrée Land reg. Svalbard
257 G1 André Fernandes Brazil
257 E4 Andrelândia Brazil
257 E3 Andrequicé Brazil
175 H4 Andrespol Pol.
163 C5 Andrest France
223 H4 Andrew Alta Can.
231 E5 Andrews SC U.S.A.
237 C5 Andrews TX U.S.A.
121 J3 Andreyevka Almatinskaya Oblast' Kazakh.
121 F1 Andreyevka Severnyy Kazakhstan Kazakh.
120 B1 Andreyevka Rus. Fed.
137 G1 Andreykovichi Rus. Fed.
160 C3 Andrézieux-Bouthéon France
193 I3 Andria Italy
213 □J3 Andriamena Madag.
213 □J3 Andriba Madag.
177 L4 Andrid Romania
214 E5 Andrieskraal S. Africa
214 C2 Andriesvale S. Africa
213 □J4 Andringitra mts Madag.
137 I4 Andrivka Ukr.
136 D2 Andriyevychi Ukr.
137 I4 Andriyivka Donets'ka Oblast' Ukr.
137 I3 Andriyivka Kharkivs'ka Oblast' Ukr.
137 G5 Andriyivka Respublika Krym Ukr.
137 I4 Andriyivka Zaporiz'ka Oblast' Ukr.
213 □J5 Androka Madag.
213 □K2 Androna reg. Madag.
Andropov Rus. Fed. see Rybinsk
246 C1 Andros i. Bahamas
198 D3 Andros Notio Aigaio Greece
198 D3 Andros i. Greece
233 I3 Androscoggin r. ME/NH U.S.A.
120 B1 Androsovka Rus. Fed.
246 C1 Andros Town Andros Bahamas
Andrushevka Ukr. see Andrushivka
136 E2 Andrushivka Ukr.
136 E3 Andrushky Ukr.
175 H6 Andrychów Pol.
175 K3 Andrzejewo Pol.
140 L1 Andselv Norway
185 F2 Andújar Spain
209 C7 Andulo Angola
161 B4 Anduze France
129 C1 Andzhiyevskiy Rus. Fed.
87 F4 Anec, Lake salt flat W.A. Austr.
259 C6 Anecón Grande mt. Arg.
Āneen-Kio N. Pacific Ocean see Wake Atoll
247 F3 Anegada i. Virgin Is (U.K.)
259 E6 Anegada, Bahía b. Arg.
247 G3 Anegada Passage Virgin Is (U.K.)
241 K5 Anegam AZ U.S.A.
207 F5 Aného Togo
Aneityum i. Vanuatu see Anatom
'Aneiza, Jabal hill Iraq see 'Unayzah, Jabal
78 □3b Aneju i. Majuro Marshall Is
114 C3 Anekal Karnataka India
128 A1 Anemourion tourist site Turkey
78 □3b Anemwanot i. Majuro Marshall Is
136 E4 Anenii Noi Moldova
156 B4 Anet France
Anetchom, Île i. Vanuatu see Anatom
186 D2 Aneto mt. Spain
Ānewetak atoll Marshall Is see Enewetak
Aneytioum, Île i. Vanuatu see Anatom
203 I6 Anfile Bay Eritrea
178 B5 Anfo Italy
109 E3 Anfu Jiangxi China
114 C4 Angadippuram Kerala India
84 B2 Angalarri r. N.T. Austr.
244 D4 Angangueo Mex.
107 I2 Ang'angxi Heilong. China
98 H1 Angara r. Rus. Fed.
207 F4 Angaradébou Benin
98 H1 Angarsk Rus. Fed.
84 C5 Angas Downs N.T. Austr.
86 F4 Angas Range hills W.A. Austr.
82 D3 Angaston S.A. Austr.
92 B3 Angat Phil.
Angatau atoll Arch. des Tuamotu Fr. Polynesia see Fangatau
256 C5 Angatuba Brazil
92 □ Angaur i. Palau
141 K3 Ånge Sweden
182 B4 Angeja Port.
251 F3 Angel, Salto del waterfall Venez.
242 B2 Angel de la Guarda, Isla i. Mex.
92 B3 Angeles Phil.
Angel Falls Venez. see Angel, Salto del
142 E3 Ängelholm Sweden
237 E6 Angelina r. TX U.S.A.
85 F5 Angellala Creek r. Qld Austr.
87 C4 Angelo r. W.A. Austr.
245 G4 Angel R. Cabada Mex.
240 G2 Angels Camp CA U.S.A.
143 E3 Angelstad Sweden
160 C1 Angely France
173 G4 Anger Ger.
210 C1 Āngereb Wenz r. Eth.
140 L3 Ångermanälven r. Sweden
170 F2 Angermünde Ger.
171 C3 Angern Ger.
179 H2 Angern an der March Austria
159 F4 Angers France
156 C4 Angerville France
191 H5 Anghiari Italy
254 D4 Angical Brazil
254 F3 Angicos Brazil
240 H4 Angiola CA U.S.A.
198 C1 Angitis r. Greece
97 C4 Angkor tourist site Cambodia
162 B3 Anglade France
162 E3 Anglards-de-Salers France
150 B3 Angle Pembrokeshire, Wales U.K.
81 A7 Anglem, Mount hill Stewart I. N.Z.
222 G5 Anglemont B.C. Can.
163 E5 Anglès France
186 F3 Anglès Spain
150 C1 Anglesey i. Wales U.K.
186 E3 Anglesona Spain
159 G5 Angles-sur-l'Anglin France
163 A5 Anglet France
237 E6 Angleton TX U.S.A.
227 H2 Angliers Que. Can.
159 G5 Angliers France
162 C2 Anglin r. France
Anglo-Egyptian Sudan country Africa see Sudan
192 A4 Anglona reg. Sardegna Italy
156 D4 Anglure France
Angmagssalik Greenland see Ammassalik
213 H3 Angoche Moz.
122 D5 Angohrān Iran
162 D3 Angoisse France
260 A5 Angol Chile
209 C7 Angola country Africa
230 C3 Angola IN U.S.A.
232 D3 Angola NY U.S.A.
264 I7 Angola Basin sea feature S. Atlantic Ocean
220 E4 Angoon AK U.S.A.
Angora Turkey see Ankara
242 C3 Angostura Mex.
162 C3 Angoulême France
162 A2 Angoulins France
216 □1a Angra do Heroísmo Terceira Azores
257 E5 Angra dos Reis Brazil
121 G4 Angren Uzbek.
193 G4 Angri Italy
159 F4 Angrie France
97 C4 Ang Thong Thai.
107 I2 Anguang Jilin China
186 C2 Angüés Spain
183 H2 Anguiano Spain
247 G3 Anguilla terr. West Indies
246 C2 Anguilla Cays is Bahamas
193 E2 Anguillara Sabazia Italy
191 G3 Anguillara Veneta Italy
183 H3 Anguita Spain
107 G4 Anguo Hebei China
84 D2 Angurugu N.T. Austr.
227 H3 Angus Ont. Can.
146 F5 Angus admin. div. Scotland U.K.
240 F2 Angwin CA U.S.A.
256 C3 Anhanguera Brazil
165 D4 Anhée Belgium
142 D3 Anholt i. Denmark
109 D2 Anhua Hunan China
109 F1 Anhui prov. China
Anhwei prov. China see Anhui
129 C3 Ani tourist site Turkey
191 F4 Ania r. Italy
220 C3 Aniak AK U.S.A.
161 B5 Aniane France
156 D2 Aniche France
256 C2 Anicuns Brazil
207 F5 Anié Togo
163 B6 Anie, Pic d' mt. France
193 E3 Aniene r. Italy
178 E3 Anif Austria
103 □3 Ani-jima i. Japan
120 E2 Anikhovka Rus. Fed.
134 H4 Anikovo Rus. Fed.
105 G2 Animaki-san hill Japan
239 E4 Animas r. CO U.S.A.
197 E3 Anina Romania
183 I3 Aniñón Spain
207 H6 Añisoc Equat. Guinea
255 C8 Anitápolis Brazil
199 G2 Anıtkaya Afyon Turkey
128 A1 Anıtlı Turkey
100 G3 Aniva Sakhalin Rus. Fed.
100 G3 Aniva, Zaliv b. Sakhalin Rus. Fed.
213 □K3 Anivorano Madag.
213 □K2 Anivorano Avaratra Madag.
226 C3 Aniwa WI U.S.A.
78 □5 Aniwa i. Vanuatu
156 D3 Anizy-le-Château France
116 C5 Anjad Madh. Prad. India
213 □J3 Anjafy mt. Madag.
141 N3 Anjalankoski Fin.
116 D5 Anjangaon Mahar. India
116 B5 Anjar Gujarat India
114 C4 Anjengo Kerala India
109 F2 Anji Zhejiang China
116 D5 Anji Mahar. India
Anjiang Hunan China see Qianyang
104 D4 Anjō Japan
122 D3 Anjoman Iran
162 B1 Anjou, Val d' val. France
Anjouan i. Comoros see Nzwani
213 □J3 Anjozorobe Madag.
99 M4 Anjŭ N. Korea
164 F1 Anjum Neth.
207 G3 Anka Nigeria
213 □I4 Ankaboa, Tanjona pt Madag.
108 D1 Ankang Shaanxi China
126 D3 Ankara Turkey
199 G1 Ankara prov. Turkey
191 I3 Ankaran Slovenia
143 G3 Ankarsrum Sweden
140 L2 Ankarsund Sweden
213 □K2 Ankatafa Madag.
213 □J3 Ankavandra Madag.
213 □J4 Ankazoabo Madag.
213 □J3 Ankazobe Madag.
213 □J3 Ankazomiriotra Madag.
236 E3 Ankeny IA U.S.A.
170 D2 Ankershagen Ger.
213 □I4 Ankiliabo Madag.
170 E2 Anklam Ger.
116 C5 Ankleshwar Gujarat India
Anklesvar Gujarat India see Ankleshwar
213 □K3 Ankofa mt. Madag.
178 E3 Ankogel mt. Austria
114 B3 Ankola Karnataka India
207 G5 Ankpa Nigeria
168 C3 Ankum Ger.
149 I4 Anlaby East Riding of Yorkshire, England U.K.
173 F3 Anlauter r. Ger.
160 B2 Anlezy France
165 E5 Anlier, Forêt d' for. Belgium
Anling Henan China see Yanling
207 F5 Anloga Ghana
108 C3 Anlong Guizhou China
97 D4 Ânlong Vêng Cambodia
109 E2 Anlu Hubei China
232 C5 Anmoore WV U.S.A.
An Muileann gCearr Rep. of Ireland see Mullingar
263 D2 Ann, Cape Antarctica
135 H6 Anna Rus. Fed.
187 C5 Anna Spain
232 A4 Anna OH U.S.A.
205 G1 Annaba Alg.
189 A7 Annaba prov. Alg.
171 E5 Annaberg-Buchholtz Ger.
128 C4 An Nabk Saudi Arabia
128 C2 An Nabk Syria
171 E4 Annaburg Ger.
147 C4 Annacotty Rep. of Ireland
124 C1 An Nafūd des. Saudi Arabia
147 C1 Annagry Rep. of Ireland
171 E4 Annahütte Ger.
251 G4 Annai Guyana
127 G5 An Najaf Iraq
127 F5 An Najaf governorate Iraq
105 E2 Annaka Japan
147 D2 Annalee r. Rep. of Ireland
147 F2 Annalong Northern Ireland U.K.
96 D3 Annam Highlands mts Laos/Vietnam
148 C4 Annamoe Rep. of Ireland
146 E7 Annan Dumfries and Galloway, Scotland U.K.
146 E7 Annan r. Scotland U.K.
234 D2 Annandale NJ U.S.A.
232 E5 Annandale VA U.S.A.
164 D2 Anna Paulowna Neth.
86 D3 Anna Plains W.A. Austr.
234 B4 Annapolis MD U.S.A.
225 H4 Annapolis Royal N.S. Can.
117 E3 Annapurna I mt. Nepal
227 F4 Ann Arbor MI U.S.A.
251 G3 Anna Regina Guyana
171 C4 Annarode Ger.
An Nás Rep. of Ireland see Naas
127 G5 An Nāṣirīyah Iraq
147 E2 Annayalla Rep. of Ireland
146 D6 Annbank South Ayrshire, Scotland U.K.
193 I5 Annea r. Italy
87 C5 Annean, Lake salt flat W.A. Austr.
234 B4 Anne Arundel County county MD U.S.A.
Anne Arundel Town MD U.S.A. see Annapolis
160 E3 Annecy France
160 E3 Annecy, Lac d' l. France
160 E3 Annecy-le-Vieux France
160 E2 Annemasse France
164 F1 Annen Neth.
162 C3 Annesse-et-Beaulieu France
161 C3 Anneyron France
149 H3 Annfield Plain Durham, England U.K.
148 E2 Annick r. Scotland U.K.
85 E2 Annie r. Qld Austr.
128 C3 An Nimārah Syria
124 C4 An Nimāṣ Saudi Arabia
108 B3 Anning Yunnan China
108 B3 Anning He r. Sichuan China
139 M5 Annino Rus. Fed.
231 C5 Anniston AL U.S.A.
207 G7 Annobón i. Equat. Guinea
156 C2 Annœullin France
161 C3 Annonay France
161 E5 Annot France
246 □ Annotto Bay Jamaica
148 D3 Annsborough Northern Ireland U.K.
125 E2 An Nu'ayrīyah Saudi Arabia
125 E2 An Nuqay'ah Qatar
232 B6 Annville KY U.S.A.
234 B2 Annville PA U.S.A.
172 B2 Annweiler am Trifels Ger.
186 A1 Anoeta Spain
198 D4 Anogeia Kriti Greece
226 A3 Anoka MN U.S.A.
198 C2 Ano Lechonia Thessalia Greece
183 I3 Añón Spain
Anonima atoll Micronesia see Namonuito
139 M4 Anopino Rus. Fed.
156 E3 Anor France
185 F2 Añora Spain
251 F5 Anori Brazil
213 □K3 Anosibe An'Ala Madag.
157 G4 Anould France
183 G5 Añover de Tajo Spain
199 D4 Ano Viannos Kriti Greece
Anóyia Kriti Greece see Anogeia
108 D4 Anpu Guangdong China
108 D4 Anpu Gang b. China
109 F2 Anqing Anhui China
107 H4 Anqiu Shandong China
183 H4 Anquela del Ducado Spain
178 D4 Anras Austria
109 E3 Anren Hunan China
169 D4 Anröchte Ger.
An Rubha pen. Scotland U.K. see Eye Peninsula
165 E4 Ans Belgium
142 C3 Ans Denmark
162 C3 Ansac-sur-Vienne France
107 F4 Ansai Shaanxi China
173 E2 Ansbach Ger.
160 C3 Anse France
246 D3 Anse-à-Galets Haiti
246 E3 Anse-à-Pitre Haiti
246 D3 Anse-à-Veau Haiti
247 □2 Anse Bertrand Guadeloupe
192 D2 Ansedonia Italy
165 D4 Anseremme Belgium
83 F4 Anser Group is Tas. Austr.
179 F2 Ansfelden Austria
146 E5 An Sgarsoch mt. Scotland U.K.
107 I3 Anshan Liaoning China
108 C3 Anshun Guizhou China
108 B2 Anshunchang Sichuan China
182 B5 Ansião Port.
191 H2 Ansiei r. Italy
260 C2 Ansilta mt. Arg.
260 C2 Ansilta, Cordillera de mts Arg.
258 G3 Ansina Uru.
126 E5 An Sirhān, Wādī watercourse Saudi Arabia
140 L3 Ansjö Sweden
236 D3 Ansley NE U.S.A.
186 C2 Ansó Spain
237 D5 Anson TX U.S.A.
84 B2 Anson Bay N.T. Austr.
207 F3 Ansongo Mali
235 E1 Ansonia CT U.S.A.
232 A4 Ansonia OH U.S.A.
224 D3 Ansonville Ont. Can.
171 E5 Ansprung Ger.
232 C5 Ansted WV U.S.A.
146 F5 Anstruther Fife, Scotland U.K.
Ansu Hebei China see Xushui
151 I2 Ant r. England U.K.
116 D4 Anta Rajasthan India
252 B3 Anta Peru
252 B3 Antabamba Peru
126 E3 Antakya Turkey
213 □K2 Antalaha Madag.
199 G3 Antalya Turkey
199 G3 Antalya prov. Turkey
199 G3 Antalya Körfezi g. Turkey
213 □K3 Antanambao Manampotsy Madag.
213 □J3 Antananarivo Madag.
213 □J3 Antananarivo prov. Madag.
213 □J3 Antanifotsy Madag.
213 □J5 Antanimora Atsimo Madag.
An tAonach Rep. of Ireland see Nenagh
262 Antarctica continent
262 T2 Antarctic Peninsula Antarctica
182 C4 Antas Port.
185 I3 Antas Spain
185 I3 Antas r. Spain
182 C2 Antas de Ulla Spain
146 C4 An Teallach mt. Scotland U.K.
241 I2 Antelope Range mts NV U.S.A.
162 B3 Antenne r. France
185 F3 Antequera Spain
178 D4 Anterselva di Sopra Italy
234 A1 Antes Fort PA U.S.A.
161 E5 Anthéor France
178 E3 Anthering Austria
160 B1 Anthien France
237 D4 Anthony KS U.S.A.
239 F5 Anthony NM U.S.A.
82 C2 Anthony, Lake salt flat S.A. Austr.
84 C3 Anthony Lagoon N.T. Austr.
204 C3 Anti Atlas mts Morocco
161 F5 Antibes France
225 I3 Anticosti, Île d' i. Que. Can.
Anticosti Island Que. Can. see Anticosti, Île d'
159 G2 Antifer, Cap d' c. France
226 C3 Antigo WI U.S.A.
225 I4 Antigonish N.S. Can.
247 □2 Antigua i. Antigua and Barbuda
216 □3b Antigua Fuerteventura Canary Is
243 H6 Antigua Guat.
Antigua country West Indies see Antigua and Barbuda
247 □2 Antigua and Barbuda country West Indies
Antigua Guatemala Guat. see Antigua
245 E2 Antiguo-Morelos Mex.
198 C2 Antikyra Greece
198 C4 Antikythiro, Steno sea chan. Greece
Anti Lebanon mts Lebanon/Syria see Sharqī, Jabal ash
246 D2 Antilla Cuba
195 E5 Antillo Sicilia Italy
198 D3 Antimilos i. Greece
241 L2 Antimony UT U.S.A.
An tInbhear Mór Rep. of Ireland see Arklow
Antioch Turkey see Antakya
240 G2 Antioch CA U.S.A.
226 C4 Antioch IL U.S.A.
128 A1 Antiocheia ad Cragum tourist site Turkey
Antiochia Turkey see Antakya
250 C3 Antioquia Col.
250 C3 Antioquia dept Col.
198 D3 Antiparos i. Greece
77 H6 Antipodes Islands N.Z.
199 D2 Antipsara i. Greece
192 B2 Antisanti Corse France
Antium Italy see Anzio
237 E5 Antlers OK U.S.A.

An t-Ob Western Isles, Scotland U.K. see Leverburgh
252 C5 Antofagasta Chile
252 C5 Antofagasta admin. reg. Chile
165 C4 Antoing Belgium
177 H3 Antol Slovakia
190 E4 Antola, Monte mt. Italy
213 □J2 Antonhibe Madag.
256 C6 Antonina Brazil
136 D3 Antoniny Ukr.
195 F3 Antonio r. Italy
244 B1 Antonio Amaro Mex.
257 F4 Antônio Carlos Brazil
257 F3 Antônio Dias Brazil
António Enes Moz. see Angoche
136 E3 Antoniv Ukr.
137 G2 Antonivka Chernihivs'ka Oblast' Ukr.
137 G4 Antonivka Khersons'ka Oblast' Ukr.
177 L3 Antonivka Zakarpats'ka Oblast' Ukr.
245 G4 Antón Lizardo Mex.
162 C3 Antonne-et-Trigonant France
246 B2 Antón Recio Cuba
156 C4 Antony France
136 C1 Antopal' Belarus
161 C4 Antraigues-sur-Volane France
158 E3 Antrain France
137 J3 Antratsyt Ukr.
147 E2 Antrim Northern Ireland U.K.
147 E2 Antrim county Northern Ireland U.K.
234 A1 Antrim PA U.S.A.
147 E1 Antrim Hills Northern Ireland U.K.
86 F3 Antrim Plateau W.A. Austr.
193 F2 Antrodoco Italy
134 H4 Antropovo Rus. Fed.
213 □K2 Antsahanoro Madag.
213 □K2 Antsakabary Madag.
213 □J3 Antsalova Madag.
213 □K2 Antsambalahy Madag.
Antseranana Madag. see Antsirañana
139 I2 Antsiferovo Rus. Fed.
213 □J3 Antsirabe Madag.
213 □K2 Antsirabe Avaratra Madag.
213 □K2 Antsirañana Madag.
213 □K2 Antsirañana prov. Madag.
138 F3 Antsla Estonia
213 □J2 Antsohihy Madag.
140 M2 Anttis Sweden
141 N3 Anttola Fin.
Antu Jilin China see Songjiang
260 B5 Antuco Chile
260 B5 Antuco, Volcán vol. Chile
160 C2 Antully France
Antunnacum Ger. see Andernach
Antwerp Belgium see Antwerpen
233 F2 Antwerp NY U.S.A.
165 D3 Antwerpen Belgium
165 D3 Antwerpen prov. Belgium
186 A1 Antzuola Spain
An Uaimh Rep. of Ireland see Navan
100 E4 Anuchino Rus. Fed.
259 C6 Anueque, Sierra mts Arg.
117 F5 Anugul Orissa India
116 C3 Anupgarh Rajasthan India
114 D4 Anuradhapura Sri Lanka
Anvers Belgium see Antwerpen
262 T2 Anvers Island Antarctica
222 C2 Anvil Range mts Y.T. Can.
156 C2 Anvin France
109 F3 Anxi Fujian China
106 B3 Anxi Gansu China
108 C2 Anxian Sichuan China
109 E2 Anxiang Hunan China
107 G4 Anxin Hebei China
82 C3 Anxious Bay S.A. Austr.
Anxur Italy see Terracina
206 D5 Anyama Côte d'Ivoire
Anyang Guangxi China see Du'an
107 G4 Anyang Henan China
101 C5 Anyang S. Korea
94 D4 Anyar Jawa Barat Indon.
106 C5 A'nyêmaqên Shan mts China
109 E2 Anyi Jiangxi China
138 E4 Anykščiai Lith.
215 H2 Anysspruit S. Africa
109 E3 Anyuan Jiangxi China
109 E3 Anyuan Jiangxi China
108 C2 Anyue Sichuan China
100 F2 Anyuy r. Rus. Fed.
131 R3 Anyuysk Rus. Fed.
190 D2 Anza r. Italy
223 I3 Anzac Alta Can.
222 F4 Anzac B.C. Can.
186 C2 Anzánigo Spain
193 H3 Anzano di Puglia Italy
161 B3 Anzat-le-Luguet France
107 G4 Anze Shanxi China
165 C4 Anzegem Belgium
173 F2 Anzelberg hill Ger.
130 J4 Anzhero-Sudzhensk Rus. Fed.
193 H4 Anzi Italy
156 D2 Anzin France
176 A3 Anzing Ger.
193 E3 Anzio Italy
251 E2 Anzoátegui state Venez.
185 F3 Anzur r. Spain
78 □5 Aoba i. Vanuatu
104 B3 Aoba-yama hill Japan
103 I7 Aoga-shima i. Japan
Aohan Qi Nei Mongol China see Xinhui
183 I2 Aoiz Spain
78 □6 Aola Guadalcanal Solomon Is
Aomen Macau China see Macau
102 J3 Aomori Japan
102 J3 Aomori pref. Japan
146 C4 Aonach Buidhe hill Scotland U.K.
198 B1 Aoos r. Greece
146 B6 Aoradh Argyll and Bute, Scotland U.K.
81 C5 Aoraki mt. South I. N.Z.
97 D4 Aôral, Phnum mt. Cambodia
Aorangi mt. South I. N.Z. see Aoraki
81 C5 Aoraki mt. South I. N.Z.
81 E4 Aorangi Mountains North I. N.Z.
81 D4 Aorere r. South I. N.Z.
183 I2 Aos Spain
190 C3 Aosta Italy
160 D3 Aoste France
Aotearoa country Oceania see New Zealand
208 C2 Aouk, Bahr r. C.A.R./Chad
208 D2 Aoukalé r. C.A.R./Chad
204 D5 Aoukâr reg. Mali/Maur.
205 F4 Aoulef Alg.
204 C3 Aoulime, Jbel mt. Morocco
206 C3 Aourou Mali
161 D4 Aouste-sur-Sye France
Aoxi Jiangxi China see Le'an
Aoyang Jiangxi China see Shanggao
253 F5 Apa r. Brazil
197 F2 Apa Romania
210 B4 Apac Uganda
241 M6 Apache AZ U.S.A.
237 D5 Apache OK U.S.A.
241 L5 Apache Junction AZ U.S.A.
241 L6 Apache Peak AZ U.S.A.
252 D5 Apagado, Volcán vol. Bol.
177 K4 Apagy Hungary
197 F2 Apahida Romania
256 C5 Apaiaí r. Brazil
Apaiang atoll Kiribati see Abaiang
177 I4 Apaj Hungary
231 C6 Apalachee Bay FL U.S.A.
231 C6 Apalachicola FL U.S.A.
231 C6 Apalachicola r. FL U.S.A.
206 E5 Apam Ghana
Apamama atoll Gilbert Is Kiribati see Abemama
Apamea Turkey see Dinar
245 E4 Apan Mex.
157 G5 Apance r. France
250 D5 Apaporis r. Col.
129 D3 Aparan Armenia
257 E5 Áparecida Brazil
256 B4 Aparecida do Tabuado Brazil
177 H5 Aparhant Hungary
Aparima South I. N.Z. see Riverton
81 B7 Aparima r. South I. N.Z.
92 B2 Aparri Phil.
138 E3 Apaščia r. Lith.
244 D3 Apaseo El Grande Mex.
79 □3 Apataki atoll Arch. des Tuamotu Fr. Polynesia
177 K5 Apateu Romania
177 J5 Apátfalva Hungary
196 D3 Apatin Vojvodina, Srbija Yugo.
134 F2 Apatity Rus. Fed.
251 H3 Apatou Fr. Guiana
244 C4 Apatzingán Mex.
245 E4 Apaxtla Mex.
138 F3 Ape Latvia
191 H5 Apecchio Italy
253 E2 Apediá r. Brazil
164 E2 Apeldoorn Neth.
169 E3 Apelern Ger.
168 C2 Apen Ger.
170 C3 Apenburg Ger.
168 E2 Apensen Ger.
252 D3 Apere r. Bol.
182 C2 A Peroxa Spain
222 B2 Apex Mountain Y.T. Can.
116 E3 Api mt. Nepal
Api i. Vanuatu see Épi
Apia atoll Kiribati see Abaiang
78 □2 Apia Samoa
253 F2 Apiacas, Serra dos hills Brazil
256 C6 Apiaí Brazil
251 F4 Apiaú, Serra do mts Brazil
193 G3 Apice Italy
182 B2 A Picota Spain
191 I5 Apiro Italy
237 C4 Apishapa r. CO U.S.A.
80 E3 Apiti North I. N.Z.
245 E4 Apizaco Mex.
129 B2 Ap'khazet'i aut. rep. Georgia
252 B4 Aplao Peru
92 C5 Apo, Mount vol. Mindanao Phil.
137 I2 Apochka r. Rus. Fed.
254 F3 Apodi Brazil
254 F3 Apodi, Chapada do hills Brazil
92 B3 Apo East Passage Phil.
171 C4 Apolda Ger.
Apollinopolis Magna Egypt see Idfu
83 E4 Apollo Bay Vic. Austr.
Apollonia Bulg. see Sozopol
182 C1 A Pontenova Spain
231 D6 Apopka FL U.S.A.
255 B6 Aporé Brazil
256 B3 Aporé Brazil
256 B3 Aporé r. Brazil
177 H5 Apostag Hungary
221 N3 Apostolens Tommelfinger mt. Greenland
258 G2 Apóstoles Arg.
137 G4 Apostolove Ukr.
251 G3 Apoteri Guyana
Apoucaroua atoll Arch. des Tuamotu Fr. Polynesia see Pukarua
92 B3 Apo West Passage Phil.
232 B6 Appalachia VA U.S.A.
232 B6 Appalachian Mountains U.S.A.
Appalla i. Fiji see Kabara
164 F2 Appelscha Neth.
193 F2 Appennino Abruzzese mts Italy
193 H4 Appennino Lucano mts Italy
193 H3 Appennino Napoletano mts Italy
191 F5 Appennino Tosco-Emiliano mts Italy
191 H5 Appennino Umbro-Marchigiano mts Italy
172 B3 Appenweier Ger.
190 E1 Appenzell Switz.
190 E1 Appenzell Ausser-Rhoden canton Switz.
190 E1 Appenzell Inner-Rhoden canton Switz.
191 G2 Appiano sulla Strada del Vino Italy
192 A2 Appietto Corse France
191 I5 Appignano Italy
164 F1 Appingedam Neth.
149 G3 Appleby-in-Westmorland Cumbria, England U.K.
146 C4 Applecross Highland, Scotland U.K.
150 C3 Appledore Devon, England U.K.
151 H3 Appledore Kent, England U.K.
236 D2 Appleton MN U.S.A.
226 C3 Appleton WI U.S.A.
149 G4 Appleton Thorn Warrington, England U.K.
240 I4 Apple Valley CA U.S.A.
156 D5 Appoigny France
232 D6 Appomattox VA U.S.A.
161 D3 Apprieu France
139 K4 Aprelevka Rus. Fed.
160 D1 Apremont France
157 F4 Apremont-la-Forêt France
190 F2 Aprica Italy
193 H3 Apricena Italy
195 F3 Aprigliano Italy
193 E3 Aprilia Italy
129 A1 Apsheronsk Rus. Fed.
Apsheronskaya Rus. Fed. see Apsheronsk
Apsheronskiy Poluostrov pen. Azer. see Abşeron Yarımadası
82 E4 Apsley Vic. Austr.
227 H3 Apsley Ont. Can.
161 D5 Apt France
256 B5 Apucarana Brazil
256 B5 Apucarana, Serra da hills Brazil
182 B3 Apúlia Port.
Apulum Romania see Alba Iulia
92 A4 Apurahuan Phil.
250 E3 Apure r. Venez.
250 D3 Apure state Venez.
252 B3 Apurímac dept Peru
252 B3 Apurimac r. Peru
Aq"a Georgia see Sokhumi
'Aqaba Jordan see Al 'Aqabah
124 A1 Aqaba, Gulf of Asia
Aqadyr Kazakh. see Agadyr'
110 B3 Aqal Xinjiang China
Aqbeyit Kazakh. see Akbeit
123 F2 Āqchah Afgh.
127 G3 Aq Chai r. Iran
122 C3 Āqdā Iran
122 A2 Aqdoghmish r. Iran
106 A3 Aqitag mt. Xinjiang China
Aqköl Akmolinskaya Oblast' Kazakh. see Akkol'
Aqköl Kazakh. see Akkol'
Aqmola Kazakh. see Astana
Aqmola Oblysy admin. div. Kazakh. see Akmolinskaya Oblast'
Aqqystaū Kazakh. see Akkystau
128 B3 'Aqraba West Bank
127 F3 'Aqrah Iraq
128 D4 'Aqran hill Saudi Arabia
Aqsay Kazakh. see Aksay
Aqsayqin Hit terr. Asia see Aksai Chin
Aqshataū Kazakh. see Akchatau
Aqshī Kazakh. see Akshiy
Aqshuqyr Kazakh. see Akshukur
Aqsū Almatinskaya Oblast' Kazakh. see Aksu
Aqsū Pavlodarskaya Oblast' Kazakh. see Aksu
Aqsū Severnyy Kazakhstan Kazakh. see Aksu
Aqsūat Vostochnyy Kazakhstan Kazakh. see Aksuat
Aqsū-Ayuly Kazakh. see Aksu-Ayuly
Aqtaū Mangistauskaya Oblast' Kazakh. see Aktau
Aqtöbe Kazakh. see Aktyubinsk
Aqtöbe Oblysy admin. div. Kazakh. see Aktyubinskaya Oblast'
Aqtoghay Karagandinskaya Oblast' Kazakh. see Aktogay
Aqtoghay Pavlodarskaya Oblast' Kazakh. see Aktogay
Aquae Grani Ger. see Aachen
Aquae Gratianae France see Aix-les-Bains
Aquae Mortuae France see Aigues-Mortes
Aquae Sextiae France see Aix-en-Provence
Aquae Statiellae Italy see Acqui Terme
241 K4 Aquarius Mountains AZ U.S.A.
241 L3 Aquarius Plateau UT U.S.A.
195 F2 Aquaviva delle Fonti Italy
235 F2 Aquebogue NY U.S.A.
253 F5 Aquidabánmi r. Para.
253 G5 Aquidauana Brazil
253 F4 Aquidauana r. Brazil
244 C4 Aquila Mex.
242 D2 Aquiles Mex.
193 H4 Aquilonia Italy
186 C2 Aquilué Spain
246 D3 Aquin Haiti
Aquincum Hungary see Budapest
193 F3 Aquino Italy
Aquinum Italy see Aquino
Aquiry r. Brazil see Acre
Aquisgranum Ger. see Aachen
163 B4 Aquitaine admin. reg. France
Aqzhal Vostochnyy Kazakhstan Kazakh. see Akzhal
Aqzhar Vostochnyy Kazakhstan Kazakh. see Akzhar
Aqzhayqyn Köli salt l. Kazakh. see Akzhaykyn, Ozero
117 F4 Ara Bihar India
186 D2 Ara r. Spain
231 C5 Arab AL U.S.A.
208 F2 Arab, Bahr el watercourse Sudan
125 E4 'Arabah, Wādī r. Yemen
128 B5 'Arabah, Wādī al watercourse Israel/Jordan
137 H5 Arabats'ka Strilka, Kosa spit Ukr.
Arabatskaya Strelka spit Ukr. see Arabats'ka Strilka, Kosa
187 B6 Arabí mt. Spain
265 I4 Arabian Basin sea feature Indian Ocean
Arabian Gulf Asia see The Gulf
125 G4 Arabian Oryx Sanctuary tourist site Saudi Arabia
119 J6 Arabian Sea Indian Ocean
129 F3 Äräb Qubalı Azer.
163 D6 Arac r. France
126 D2 Araç Turkey
251 F5 Araça r. Brazil
254 F4 Aracaju Brazil
253 G6 Aracanguy, Montes de hills Para.
258 D2 Aracar, Volcán vol. Arg.
246 D5 Aracataca Col.
254 F3 Aracati Brazil
254 E5 Aracatu Brazil
256 B4 Araçatuba Brazil
184 D3 Aracena Spain
259 C9 Aracena, Isla i. Chile
184 C3 Aracena, Sierra de hills Spain
198 B2 Arachthos r. Greece
198 B2 Arachthos, Techniti Limni resr Greece
197 E4 Aračinovo Macedonia
254 F3 Aracoiaba Brazil
257 G3 Aracruz Brazil
257 F2 Araçuaí Brazil
257 F2 Araçuaí r. Brazil
128 B4 'Arad Israel
196 E2 Arad Romania
177 K5 Arad county Romania
202 D6 Arada Chad
182 B4 Arada, Serra de mts Port.
125 F3 'Arādah U.A.E.
122 C3 Arādān Iran
184 B3 Arade r. Port.
195 H2 Aradeo Italy
177 J5 Aradului, Câmpia plain Romania
216 □3a Arafo Tenerife Canary Is
105 E2 Arafune-yama mt. Japan
76 D2 Arafura Sea Austr./Indon.
266 D6 Arafura Shelf sea feature Austr./Indon.
256 A1 Aragarças Brazil
129 D3 Aragats Lerr mt. Armenia
105 E1 Ara-gawa r. Japan
105 F3 Ara-gawa r. Japan
163 C6 Aragnouet France
183 3 Aragón aut. comm. Spain
183 I2 Aragón r. Spain
194 C5 Aragona Sicilia Italy
183 H4 Aragoncillo Spain
183 H4 Aragoncillo mt. Spain
250 E2 Aragua state Venez.
254 C4 Araguacema Brazil
254 C5 Araguaçu Brazil
251 E2 Aragua de Barcelona Venez.
256 C Araguaia r. Brazil
256 B1 Araguaiana Brazil
254 C3 Araguaína Brazil
256 A2 Araguainha Brazil
251 F2 Araguao, Boca r. mouth Venez.
256 C3 Araguari Brazil
256 C3 Araguari r. Minas Gerais Brazil
251 I4 Araguari r. Amápa Brazil
254 C3 Araguatins Brazil
129 D3 Aragvi r. Georgia
125 F4 'Ārah, Wādī r. Oman
105 E2 Arai Japan
183 H2 Araia Spain
128 B4 Araif el Naga, Gebel hill Egypt
254 E2 Araiosos Brazil
205 F4 Arak Alg.
122 B3 Arāk Iran
105 F1 Arakai-yama mt. Japan
96 A2 Arakan state Myanmar
96 A2 Arakan Yoma mts Myanmar
Arakhthos r. Greece see Arachthos
104 D2 Araki-gawa r. Japan
80 G3 Arakihi hill North I. N.Z.
114 C3 Arakkonam Tamil Nadu India
129 B3 Araklı Turkey
129 D4 Araks r. Armenia/Turkey alt. Aras (Turkey), alt. Araz (Azerbaijan)
110 C3 Aral Xinjiang China
Aral Kazakh. see Aral'sk
Aral Tajik. see Vose
129 D4 Aralık Turkey
120 E3 Aral Sea salt l. Kazakh./Uzbek.
120 E3 Aral'sk Kazakh.
120 B2 Aralsor, Ozero l. Kazakh.
120 E3 Aralsul'fat Kazakh.
Aral Tengizi salt l. Kazakh./Uzbek. see Aral Sea
85 F4 Aramac Qld Austr.
124 D2 Aramah plat. Saudi Arabia
182 B2 A Ramallosa Spain
245 E1 Aramberri Mex.
254 D3 Arame Brazil
91 J8 Aramia r. P.N.G.
163 B5 Aramits France
161 C5 Aramon France
129 E3 Aran Azer.
114 C2 Aran r. India
183 I3 Aranda r. Spain
183 G3 Aranda de Duero Spain
183 I3 Aranda de Moncayo Spain
244 C3 Arandas Mex.
196 E3 Aranđelovac Srbija Yugo.
116 E5 Arang Madh. Prad. India
182 C4 Aranhas Port.
114 C3 Arani Tamil Nadu India
147 C2 Aran Island Rep. of Ireland
147 B3 Aran Islands Rep. of Ireland
183 G4 Aranjuez Spain
212 C5 Aranos Namibia
237 D7 Aransas Pass TX U.S.A.
114 C4 Arantangi Tamil Nadu India
256 B3 Arantes r. Brazil
77 H1 Aranuka atoll Gilbert Is Kiribati
97 C4 Aranyaprathet Thai.
177 L3 Aranyosapáti Hungary
183 G4 Aranzueque Spain
103 E7 Arao Japan
237 D5 Arapaho OK U.S.A.
236 D3 Arapahoe NE U.S.A.
81 E4 Arapawa Island South I. N.Z.
261 I2 Arapey Grande r. Uru.
182 E4 Arapiles Spain
254 F4 Arapiraca Brazil
126 E3 Arapkir Turkey
256 B5 Arapongas Brazil
256 C6 Arapoti Brazil
Arapsun Turkey see Gülşehir
80 E3 Arapuni North I. N.Z.
255 C8 Araquari Brazil
127 F5 'Ar'ar Saudi Arabia
251 F5 Arara r. Brazil
250 C5 Araracuara Col.
250 C5 Araracuara, Cerros de hills Col.
255 C9 Araranguá Brazil
256 C6 Ararapira Brazil
256 C4 Araraquara Brazil
256 D5 Araras Brazil
254 E3 Araras, Açude resr Brazil
256 A3 Araras, Serra das hills Brazil
256 A6 Araras, Serra das mts Brazil
129 D4 Ararat Armenia
83 E4 Ararat Vic. Austr.
Ararat, Mount Turkey see Ağrı Dağı
254 D2 Arari Brazil
117 F4 Araria Bihar India
254 E3 Araripe Brazil
254 E3 Araripe, Chapada do hills Brazil
254 E3 Araripina Brazil
257 F5 Araruama Brazil
183 H2 Aras Spain
127 F3 Aras Turkey
127 G3 Aras r. Turkey alt. Araks (Armenia/Turkey), alt. Araz (Azerbaijan)
187 B5 Aras de Alpuente Spain
106 E1 Ar Asgat Mongolia
129 C4 Aras Güneyi Dağları mts Turkey
104 C3 Arashima-dake mt. Japan
129 B4 Aras Nehri r. Turkey
255 F5 Arataca Brazil
251 I5 Arataú r. Brazil
Aratürük Xinjiang China see Yiwu
252 D2 Arauã r. Brazil
251 F6 Arauá r. Brazil
251 F6 Arauá r. Brazil
250 D3 Arauca Col.
250 D3 Arauca dept Col.
250 E3 Arauca r. Venez.
255 C8 Araucária Brazil
258 B5 Arauco Chile
258 B5 Arauco, Golfo de b. Chile
161 C3 Araules France
250 D3 Arauquita Col.
250 D2 Araure Venez.
116 C4 Aravalli Range mts India
138 E2 Aravete Estonia
183 H3 Araviana r. Spain
160 E3 Aravis mts France
198 C1 Aravissos Greece
78 □6 Arawa P.N.G.
81 B6 Arawata r. South I. N.Z.
80 F3 Arawhana mt. North I. N.Z.
Arawhata r. South I. N.Z. see Arawata
256 D3 Araxá Brazil
Araya Spain see Araia
251 E2 Araya, Península de pen. Venez.
126 C3 Arayıt Dağı mt. Turkey
129 F3 Araz r. Azer. alt. Araks (Armenia/Turkey), alt. Aras (Turkey)
182 B4 Arazede Port.
186 B3 Arba r. Spain
186 B2 Arba de Biel r. Spain
186 B2 Arba de Luesia r. Spain
Arbailu Iraq see Arbīl
210 C3 Ārba Minch Eth.
163 C6 Arbas France
192 B5 Arbatax Sardegna Italy
134 J4 Arbazh Rus. Fed.
186 D3 Arbeca Spain
157 F5 Arbecey France
190 E2 Arbedo Switz.
Arbela Iraq see Arbīl
160 D2 Arbent France
163 B6 Arbéost France
173 E2 Arberg Ger.
Arberth Pembrokeshire, Wales U.K. see Narberth
179 F2 Arbesbach Austria
183 H4 Arbeteta Spain
191 G5 Arbia r. Italy
127 G3 Arbīl Iraq
127 F4 Arbīl governorate Iraq
183 H2 Arbizu Spain
143 F2 Arboga Sweden
160 D2 Arbois France
185 H3 Arboleas Spain
250 B2 Arboletes Col.
190 E1 Arbon Switz.
192 A5 Arborea Sardegna Italy
192 A5 Arborea reg. Sardegna Italy
223 K4 Arborfield Sask. Can.
223 L5 Arborg Man. Can.
190 D3 Arborio Italy
141 L3 Arbrå Sweden
146 F5 Arbroath Angus, Scotland U.K.
186 F3 Arbúcies Spain
240 F2 Arbuckle CA U.S.A.
123 E4 Arbu Lut, Dasht-e des. Afgh.
163 B5 Arbus France
192 A5 Arbus Sardegna Italy
137 F4 Arbuzynka Ukr.
161 D5 Arc r. France
161 E3 Arc r. France
163 A4 Arcachon France
163 A4 Arcachon, Bassin d' inlet France
232 D3 Arcade NY U.S.A.
231 D7 Arcadia FL U.S.A.
237 E5 Arcadia LA U.S.A.
226 D3 Arcadia MI U.S.A.
232 D4 Arcadia PA U.S.A.
226 B3 Arcadia WI U.S.A.
160 E3 Arcalod, Pointe d' mt. France
232 A5 Arcanum OH U.S.A.
243 H4 Arcas, Cayos is Mex.
238 A3 Arcata CA U.S.A.
240 I2 Arc Dome mt. NV U.S.A.
193 F3 Arce Italy
244 D4 Arcelia Mex.
164 F3 Arcen Neth.
157 F5 Arc-en-Barrois France
183 G1 Arceniega Spain
162 B3 Arces France
156 D4 Arces-Dilo France
160 D1 Arc-et-Senans France
191 H5 Arcevia Italy
Archangel Rus. Fed. see Arkhangel'sk
Archangel Oblast admin. div. Rus. Fed. see Arkhangel'skaya Oblast'
199 F3 Archangelos Notio Aigaio Greece
197 F4 Archar r. Bulg.
234 C1 Archbald PA U.S.A.
232 A4 Archbold OH U.S.A.
187 B6 Archena Spain
85 E2 Archer r. Qld Austr.
237 D5 Archer City TX U.S.A.
157 G4 Arches France
162 B3 Archiac France
185 F3 Archidona Spain
84 D3 Archie Creek r. Qld Austr.
177 L5 Archiș Romania
185 I2 Archivel Spain
122 D2 Archman Turkm.
192 A5 Arci, Monte hill Sardegna Italy
192 D2 Arcidosso Italy
156 E4 Arcis-sur-Aube France
122 B2 Ärçivan Azer.
160 D1 Arc-lès-Gray France
191 F3 Arco Italy
238 D3 Arco ID U.S.A.
184 □ Arco da Calheta Madeira
182 C3 Arco de Baúlhe Port.
190 E4 Arcola Italy
232 E5 Arcola VA U.S.A.
160 E2 Arçon France
160 B2 Arconce r. France
159 G3 Arconnay France
257 E4 Arcos Brazil
184 C2 Arcos Port.
183 G2 Arcos Spain
183 H3 Arcos de Jalón Spain
184 E4 Arcos de la Frontera Spain
187 B5 Arcos de las Salinas Spain
182 B3 Arcos de Valdevez Port.
114 C3 Arcot Tamil Nadu India
254 F4 Arcoverde Brazil
182 B3 Arcozelo Braga Port.
182 C4 Arcozelo Guarda Port.
182 B3 Arcozelo Porto Port.
182 B3 Arcozelo Viana do Castelo Port.
160 D1 Arc-sur-Tille France
221 J2 Arctic Bay Nunavut Can.
268 B1 Arctic Mid-Ocean Ridge sea feature Arctic Ocean
268 Arctic Ocean
220 E3 Arctic Red r. N.W.T. Can.
Arctic Red River N.W.T. Can. see Tsiigehtchic
262 N8 Arctowski research stn Antarctica
192 A5 Arcuentu, Monte hill Sardegna Italy
186 D2 Arcusa Spain
160 B1 Arcy-sur-Cure France
126 B2 Arda r. Bulg. alt. Ardas (Greece)
190 F3 Arda r. Italy
122 B2 Ardabīl Iran
122 A2 Ardabīl prov. Iran
179 F2 Ardagger Markt Austria
147 B4 Ardagh Rep. of Ireland
127 F2 Ardahan Turkey
129 C3 Ardahan prov. Turkey
122 D2 Ardāk Iran
122 C4 Ardakān Iran
122 C3 Ardakān Iran
122 B4 Ardal Iran
141 I3 Årdal Norway
183 G3 Ardal mt. Spain
185 F4 Ardales Spain
142 B2 Ardalsknapen hill Norway
141 I3 Årdalstangen Norway
147 E4 Ardanairy Rep. of Ireland
163 A6 Ardanaz Spain
129 C3 Ardanuç Turkey
192 A4 Ardara Sardegna Italy
147 C2 Ardara Rep. of Ireland
126 B2 Ardas r. Greece alt. Arda (Bulgaria)
128 C4 Ard aş Şawwān plain Jordan
135 H5 Ardatov Nizhegorodskaya Oblast' Rus. Fed.
135 I5 Ardatov Respublika Mordoviya Rus. Fed.
148 C5 Ardattin Rep. of Ireland
227 G3 Ardbeg Ont. Can.
146 C6 Ard Bheinn hill Scotland U.K.
148 C4 Ardcath Rep. of Ireland
146 B5 Ardchiavaig Argyll and Bute, Scotland U.K.
147 C4 Ardconry Rep. of Ireland
193 E3 Ardea Italy
161 C4 Ardèche dept Rhône-Alpes France
161 C4 Ardèche r. France
147 E3 Ardee Rep. of Ireland
146 D5 Arden Argyll and Bute, Scotland U.K.
235 D1 Arden NY U.S.A.
82 D3 Arden, Mount hill S.A. Austr.
156 E3 Ardennes dept Champagne-Ardenne France
156 E3 Ardennes r. France
162 D2 Ardentes France
146 D5 Ardentinny Argyll and Bute, Scotland U.K.
240 G2 Arden Town CA U.S.A.
147 D3 Arderin hill Rep. of Ireland
146 D4 Ardersier Highland, Scotland U.K.
161 B3 Ardes France
129 B3 Ardeşen Turkey
122 C3 Ardestān Iran
190 F2 Ardez Switz.
147 B4 Ardfert Rep. of Ireland
147 D4 Ardfinnan Rep. of Ireland
146 D4 Ardgay Highland, Scotland U.K.
147 C4 Ardglass Rep. of Ireland
147 F2 Ardglass Northern Ireland U.K.
129 B4 Ardıcın Dağı mt. Turkey
184 C2 Ardila r. Port.
197 G5 Ardino Bulg.
80 F3 Ardkeen North I. N.Z.
147 F2 Ardkeen Northern Ireland U.K.
151 H3 Ardleigh Essex, England U.K.
83 F3 Ardlethan N.S.W. Austr.
146 D5 Ardlui Argyll and Bute, Scotland U.K.
146 C5 Ardlussa Argyll and Bute, Scotland U.K.
146 C4 Ardmair Highland, Scotland U.K.
146 C6 Ardminish Argyll and Bute, Scotland U.K.
146 C5 Ardmolich Highland, Scotland U.K.
147 B3 Ardmore Rep. of Ireland
237 D5 Ardmore OK U.S.A.
234 C2 Ardmore PA U.S.A.
147 C4 Ardnacrusha Rep. of Ireland
146 B5 Ardnamurchan pen. Scotland U.K.
146 B5 Ardnamurchan, Point of Scotland U.K.
147 C3 Ardnasodan Rep. of Ireland
137 G1 Ardon' Rus. Fed.
129 D2 Ardon Respublika Severnaya Osetiya Rus. Fed.
129 D2 Ardon r. Rus. Fed.
190 C2 Ardon Switz.
165 C4 Ardooie Belgium
195 F4 Ardore Italy
147 C4 Ardpatrick Rep. of Ireland
146 C6 Ardpatrick Point Scotland U.K.
147 C3 Ardrahan Rep. of Ireland
156 B2 Ardres France
146 C5 Ardrishaig Argyll and Bute, Scotland U.K.
82 D3 Ardrossan S.A. Austr.
146 D6 Ardrossan North Ayrshire, Scotland U.K.
148 C4 Ardscull Rep. of Ireland
235 E1 Ardsley NY U.S.A.
147 F2 Ards Peninsula Northern Ireland U.K.
147 D2 Ardstraw Northern Ireland U.K.
197 F2 Ardusat Romania
146 C4 Ardvasar Highland, Scotland U.K.
140 K3 Åre Sweden
256 D4 Areado Brazil
183 H1 Areatza Spain
160 E3 Arèches France
247 □1 Arecibo Puerto Rico
261 H3 Areco r. Arg.
197 G3 Arefu Romania
254 F3 Areia Branca Brazil
182 B5 Areias Port.
139 H4 Arekhawsk Belarus
Arel Belgium see Arlon
Arelas France see Arles
Arelate France see Arles
142 D2 Aremark Norway
169 B5 Aremberg hill Ger.
186 D2 Arén Spain
240 F2 Arena, Point CA U.S.A.
258 D2 Arenal, Campo del plain Arg.
242 □I7 Arenal, Volcán vol. Costa Rica
253 F3 Arenápolis Brazil
183 F1 Arenas de Iguña Spain
185 G4 Arenas del Rey Spain
185 G1 Arenas de San Juan Spain
183 E4 Arenas de San Pedro Spain
142 C2 Arendal Norway
165 E3 Arendonk Belgium
170 C3 Arendsee l. Ger.
170 C3 Arendsee (Altmark) Ger.
163 B4 Arengosse France
150 D2 Arenig Fawr hill Wales U.K.
183 H3 Arenillas Spain
185 F2 Arenosillo r. Spain
185 F2 Arenoso r. Spain
169 E4 Arenshausen Ger.
195 F3 Arente r. Italy
186 F3 Arenys de Mar Spain
190 D4 Arenzano Italy
182 B3 Areosa Port.
252 C4 Arequipa Peru
252 B3 Arequipa dept Peru
261 G3 Arequlto Arg.
163 A4 Arès France
182 B1 Ares Spain
138 G5 Aresa r. Belarus
173 F3 Aresing Ger.
163 B5 Arette France
163 B6 Arette-Pierre-St-Martin France
183 E4 Arevalillo Spain
183 F3 Arevalillo r. Spain
183 F3 Arévalo Spain
184 C1 Arez Port.
191 G5 Arezzo Italy
191 G5 Arezzo prov. Toscana Italy
198 C3 Arfara Greece
163 E5 Arfons France
183 I2 Arga r. Spain
84 D4 Argadargada N.T. Austr.
198 C2 Argalasti Greece
185 E2 Argallón Spain
185 G1 Argamasilla de Alba Spain
185 F2 Argamasilla de Calatrava Spain
185 H2 Argamasón Spain
110 E3 Argan Xinjiang China
183 G4 Arganda Spain
182 B4 Arganil Port.
182 D2 Arganza Spain
92 B4 Argao Phil.
193 F3 Argatone, Monte mt. Italy
190 E3 Argegno Italy
Argel Alg. see Alger
163 B5 Argelès-Gazost France
163 F6 Argelès-sur-Mer France
161 A5 Argeliers France
187 C4 Argelita Spain
172 D4 Argen r. Ger.
172 D4 Argenbühl Ger.
159 F2 Argences France
161 E5 Argens r. France
191 G4 Argenta Italy
159 F3 Argentan France
192 D2 Argentario, Monte hill Italy
162 D3 Argentat France
186 B4 Argente Spain
190 B4 Argentera Italy
190 C4 Argentera, Cima dell' mt. Italy
156 C4 Argenteuil France
172 B2 Argenthal Ger.
192 A4 Argentiera Sardegna Italy
160 E3 Argentière France
190 C5 Argentina r. Italy
258 D4 Argentina country S. America
262 V1 Argentina Range mts Antarctica
160 E3 Argentine France
264 F9 Argentine Abyssal Plain sea feature S. Atlantic Ocean
264 G8 Argentine Basin sea feature S. Atlantic Ocean
Argentine Republic country S. America see Argentina
264 F8 Argentine Rise sea feature S. Atlantic Ocean
259 B8 Argentino, Lago l. Arg.
162 B1 Argenton r. France
159 F5 Argenton-Château France
Argentoratum France see Strasbourg
159 F3 Argentre France
159 E3 Argentré-du-Plessis France
159 I4 Argent-sur-Sauldre France
185 H3 Argerín mt. Spain
197 H3 Argeș r. Romania
183 F5 Argés Spain
197 G3 Argeșel r. Romania
123 F4 Arghandab r. Afgh.
123 F4 Arghastan r. Afgh.
148 B4 Arghavas Rep. of Ireland
198 C3 Argolikos Kolpos b. Greece
160 E3 Argonay France
226 C3 Argonne WI U.S.A.
198 C3 Argos Greece
185 I2 Argos r. Spain
226 D5 Argos IN U.S.A.
198 B1 Argos Orestiko Greece
198 B2 Argostoli Ionioi Nisoi Greece
158 E3 Argouges France
Argovie canton Switz. see Aargau
129 C2 Argudan Rus. Fed.
183 I2 Arguedas Spain
156 B3 Argueil France
185 H2 Arguellite Spain
158 D3 Arguenon r. France
186 C2 Arguís Spain
183 I5 Arguisuelas Spain
182 E3 Argujillo Spain
100 B1 Argun' r. China/Rus. Fed.
129 E2 Argun r. Georgia/Rus. Fed.
129 D2 Argun Rus. Fed.
207 G3 Argungu Nigeria
240 I4 Argus Range mts CA U.S.A.
106 D2 Arguut Mongolia
225 H5 Argyle N.S. Can.
226 B5 Argyle IA U.S.A.
226 C4 Argyle WI U.S.A.
86 F3 Argyle, Lake W.A. Austr.
146 C5 Argyll reg. Scotland U.K.
146 C6 Argyll and Bute admin. div. Scotland U.K.
Argyrokastron Albania see Gjirokastër
106 D2 Arhangay prov. Mongolia
129 B3 Arhavi Turkey
Ar Horqin Qi Nei Mongol China see Tianshan
142 D3 Århus Denmark
142 D3 Århus county Denmark
142 D3 Århus Bugt b. Denmark
142 D3 Århus-Tirstrup airport Denmark
80 E3 Aria North I. N.Z.
195 D4 Ária, Monte hill Isole Lipari Italy
83 F3 Ariah Park N.S.W. Austr.
103 E7 Ariake-kai b. Japan
193 H3 Ariano Irpino Italy
191 H4 Ariano nel Polesine Italy
261 F3 Arias Arg.
113 D11 Ari Atoll Maldives
251 F2 Aribí r. Venez.
206 E3 Aribinda Burkina
252 C4 Arica Chile
250 D2 Aricagua Venez.
193 E3 Ariccia Italy
216 □3a Arico Tenerife Canary Is
87 D7 Arid, Cape W.A. Austr.
104 B4 Arida Japan
104 B4 Arida-gawa r. Japan
129 C4 Arı Dağı mt. Turkey
198 C1 Aridaia Greece
163 D6 Ariège dept Midi-Pyrénées France
163 D5 Ariège r. France
197 F2 Arieș r. Romania
177 L5 Arieșeni Romania
197 F2 Arieșul Mic r. Romania
199 G1 Arifiye Turkey
106 D1 Arigiyn Gol r. Mongolia
128 C2 Arīḩā Syria
Arīḩā West Bank see Jericho
183 G2 Arija Spain
236 C3 Arikaree r. CO U.S.A.
196 E4 Arilje Srbija Yugo.
247 □7 Arima Trin. and Tob.
Ariminum Italy see Rimini
146 B5 Arinagour Argyll and Bute, Scotland U.K.
186 C3 Ariño Spain
257 D1 Arinos Brazil
253 F2 Arinos r. Brazil
160 D2 Arinthod France
244 D4 Ario de Rosáles Mex.
138 D4 Ariogala Lith.
250 D3 Ariporo r. Col.
253 F2 Aripuanã Brazil
251 F6 Aripuanã r. Brazil
253 E2 Ariquemes Brazil
255 B6 Ariranhá r. Brazil
146 C5 Arisaig Highland, Scotland U.K.
146 C5 Arisaig, Sound of sea chan. Scotland U.K.
234 B2 Aristes PA U.S.A.
258 G2 Aristóbulo del Valle Arg.
123 H4 Aritwala Pak.
192 B5 Aritzo Sardegna Italy
186 B2 Arive Spain
213 □J3 Arivonimamo Madag.
Arixang Xinjiang China see Wenquan
114 C4 Ariyalur Tamil Nadu India
182 C4 Ariz Port.
183 H3 Ariza Spain
258 D2 Arizaro, Salar de salt flat Arg.
163 D5 Arize r. France
183 I2 Arizola Spain
260 E4 Arizona Arg.
241 L4 Arizona state U.S.A.
242 C2 Arizpe Mex.
124 D2 'Arjah Saudi Arabia
142 E2 Årjäng Sweden
140 L2 Arjeplog Sweden
250 C2 Arjona Col.
185 F3 Arjona Spain
185 F3 Arjonilla Spain
116 E5 Arjuni Mahar. India
135 H6 Arkadak Rus. Fed.
237 E5 Arkadelphia AR U.S.A.
137 I3 Arkadivka Ukr.
146 C5 Arkaig, Loch l. Scotland U.K.
114 C3 Arkalgud Karnataka India
198 D4 Arkalochori Kriti Greece
121 F2 Arkalyk Kazakh.
237 F5 Arkansas r. AR U.S.A.
237 E5 Arkansas state U.S.A.
237 F5 Arkansas City AR U.S.A.
237 D4 Arkansas City KS U.S.A.
197 F4 Arkata r. Bulg.
111 E4 Arkatag Shan mts China
222 C2 Arkell, Mount Y.T. Can.
202 E4 Arkenu, Jabal mt. Libya
134 H2 Arkhangel'sk Rus. Fed.
134 H3 Arkhangel'skaya Oblast' admin. div. Rus. Fed.
135 L5 Arkhangel'skoye Rus. Fed.
129 D1 Arkhangel'skoye Rus. Fed.
139 K5 Arkhangel'skoye Rus. Fed.
137 K2 Arkhangel'skoye Rus. Fed.
137 G4 Arkhanhel's'ke Ukr.
100 D2 Arkhara Rus. Fed.
100 D2 Arkhara r. Rus. Fed.
129 E3 Arkhilos Kalo Georgia
137 J5 Arkhipo-Osipovka Rus. Fed.
139 M3 Arkhipovka Rus. Fed.
129 D2 Arkhonskaya Rus. Fed.
129 B2 Arkhyz Rus. Fed.
Árki i. Greece see Arkoi
129 F4 Ärkivan Azer.
146 D3 Arkle hill Scotland U.K.
147 E4 Arklow Rep. of Ireland
199 E3 Arkoi i. Greece
227 G4 Arkona Ont. Can.
Arkonam Tamil Nadu India see Arakkonam
143 G2 Årkosund Sweden
134 J4 Arkul' Rus. Fed.
143 G2 Ärla Sweden
161 B3 Arlanc France
122 C2 Arlang, Gora mt. Turkm.
183 F2 Arlanza r. Spain
183 G2 Arlanzón Spain
183 F2 Arlanzón r. Spain
183 H4 Arlas r. Spain
168 C2 Arle (Großheide) Ger.
161 B4 Arlempdes France
192 D2 Arlena di Castro Italy
161 C5 Arles France
151 G2 Arlesey Bedfordshire, England U.K.
147 D4 Arless Rep. of Ireland
163 E6 Arles-sur-Tech France
160 C1 Arleuf France
156 D2 Arleux France
226 C5 Arlington IL U.S.A.
235 E1 Arlington NY U.S.A.
232 B4 Arlington OH U.S.A.
238 B2 Arlington OR U.S.A.
236 D2 Arlington SD U.S.A.
234 A4 Arlington VA U.S.A.
226 C4 Arlington WI U.S.A.
226 C4 Arlington Heights IL U.S.A.
207 G2 Arlit Niger
165 E5 Arlon Belgium
84 C4 Arltunga N.T. Austr.
190 D3 Arluno Italy
160 E3 Arly r. France
223 J5 Arm r. Sask. Can.
184 B3 Armação de Pêra Port.
182 B1 Armada Spain
232 B3 Armada MI U.S.A.
87 B7 Armadale W.A. Austr.
146 E6 Armadale West Lothian, Scotland U.K.
Armageddon tourist site Israel see Tel Megiddo
147 E2 Armagh Northern Ireland U.K.
147 E2 Armagh county Northern Ireland U.K.
125 E4 Armah, Wādī r. Yemen
183 H4 Armallones Spain
182 C3 Armamar Port.
156 D5 Armance r. France
156 D5 Armançon r. France
203 G3 Armant Egypt
140 M2 Armasjärvi Sweden
135 H7 Armavir Rus. Fed.
163 A5 Armendarits France
129 D3 Armenia country Asia
250 C3 Armenia Col.
190 D3 Armeno Italy
Armenopolis Romania see Gherla
183 E4 Armenteros Spain
156 C2 Armentières France
193 I4 Armento Italy
244 C4 Armeria Mex.
244 C4 Armería r. Mex.
83 G2 Armidale N.S.W. Austr.
185 G3 Armilla Spain
238 E2 Armington MT U.S.A.
161 B5 Armissan France
149 H5 Armitage Staffordshire, England U.K.
240 H3 Armona CA U.S.A.
116 E5 Armori Mahar. India
236 D3 Armour SD U.S.A.
147 E1 Armoy Northern Ireland U.K.
172 C2 Armsheim Ger.
261 G3 Armstrong Arg.
84 B3 Armstrong r. N.T. Austr.
222 G5 Armstrong B.C. Can.
224 B3 Armstrong Ont. Can.
222 C2 Armstrong, Mount Y.T. Can.
Armstrong Island Cook Is see Rarotonga
232 C5 Armstrong Mills OH U.S.A.
100 F3 Armu r. Rus. Fed.
183 F3 Armuña Spain
192 B5 Armungia Sardegna Italy
182 E2 Armunia Spain
114 C2 Armur Andhra Prad. India
199 E2 Armutçuk Dağı mts Turkey
199 F1 Armutlu Turkey
Armutova Turkey see Gömeç
137 G4 Armyans'k Ukr.
Armyanskaya S.S.R. country Asia see Armenia
142 C4 Arnå r. Denmark
162 D3 Arnac-Pompadour France
190 C3 Arnad Italy
144 D1 Árnafjall hill Faroe Is
159 G4 Arnage France
198 C1 Arnaia Greece
140 □B2 Arnarfjörður inlet Iceland
225 G1 Arnaud r. Que. Can.
199 F1 Arnavutköy Turkey
160 C1 Arnay-le-Duc France
173 G2 Arnbruck Ger.
149 G3 Arncliffe North Yorkshire, England U.K.
150 E4 Arne Dorset, England U.K.
170 D3 Arneburg Ger.
183 H2 Arnedillo Spain
183 H2 Arnedo Spain
182 B2 Arnego r. Spain
163 A5 Arnéguy France
254 E3 Arneiroz Brazil
140 M2 Arnemark Sweden
164 C3 Arnemuiden Neth.
142 D1 Årnes Norway
186 D4 Arnes Spain
237 D4 Arnett OK U.S.A.
179 G4 Arnfels Austria
164 E3 Arnhem Neth.
84 D2 Arnhem, Cape N.T. Austr.
84 D2 Arnhem Bay N.T. Austr.
84 C2 Arnhem Land reg. N.T. Austr.
78 □3b Arniel i. Majuro Marshall Is
146 C4 Arnisdale Highland, Scotland U.K.
198 B1 Arnissa Greece

Arno to Auckland Islands
279

191 F5 Arno r. Italy
82 D3 Arno Bay S.A. Austr.
182 B2 Arnoia r. Spain
146 B3 Arnol Western Isles, Scotland U.K.
149 H4 Arnold Nottinghamshire, England U.K.
234 B3 Arnold MD U.S.A.
226 D2 Arnold MI U.S.A.
236 F4 Arnold MO U.S.A.
225 K4 Arnold's Cove Nfld. Can.
179 E4 Arnoldstein Austria
162 E1 Arnon r. France
Arnon r. Jordan see Mawjib, Wādī al
177 J3 Arnót Hungary
234 A1 Arnot PA U.S.A.
140 M1 Arnøya i. Norway
Arnoya r. Spain see Arnoia
224 E4 Arnprior Ont. Can.
148 E1 Arnprior Stirling, Scotland U.K.
169 D4 Arnsberg Ger.
169 D4 Arnsberg admin. reg. Nordrhein-Westfalen Ger.
169 D4 Arnsberger Wald hills Ger.
173 G2 Arnschwang Ger.
171 E4 Arnsdorf bei Dresden Ger.
169 F5 Arnstadt Ger.
227 H3 Arnstein Ont. Can.
171 A5 Arnstein Ger.
173 G3 Arnstorf Ger.
227 H1 Arntfield Que. Can.
183 G1 Arnuero Spain
251 E3 Aro r. Venez.
212 C5 Aroab Namibia
261 G3 Arocena Arg.
184 D3 Aroche Spain
182 B4 Arões Port.
182 B3 Arões Port.
177 J4 Ároktő Hungary
224 C3 Aroland Ont. Can.
169 E4 Arolsen Ger.
203 H6 Aroma Sudan
240 G3 Aromas CA U.S.A.
159 F3 Aron France
160 B2 Aron r. France
159 F3 Aron r. France
116 D4 Aron Madh. Prad. India
216 □3a Arona Tenerife Canary Is
190 D3 Arona Italy
233 □J1 Aroostook N.B. Can.
233 □J1 Aroostook r. ME U.S.A.
77 H2 Arorae i. Gilbert Is Kiribati
Arore i. Gilbert Is Kiribati see Arorae
92 B3 Aroroy Phil.
242 C2 Aros r. Mex.
182 B3 Arosa Port.
190 E2 Arosa Switz.
Arossi i. Solomon Is see San Cristobal
182 B4 Arouca Port.
129 D4 Arp'a r. Armenia
129 C3 Arpa r. Armenia/Turkey
127 F2 Arpaçay Turkey
128 B1 Arpaçsakarlar Turkey
156 C4 Arpajon France
163 E4 Arpajon-sur-Cère France
193 F3 Arpino Italy
Arpinum Italy see Arpino
Arqalyq Kazakh. see Arkalyk
193 F2 Arquata del Tronto Italy
190 D4 Arquata Scrivia Italy
163 E6 Arques Languedoc-Roussillon France
156 C2 Arques Nord - Pas-de-Calais France
156 B3 Arques-la-Bataille France
185 G2 Arquillos Spain
123 F5 Arra r. Pak.
182 B2 Arrabal Spain
85 E5 Arrabury Qld Austr.
173 G2 Arrach Ger.
157 G4 Arracourt France
158 D4 Arradon France
206 E5 Arrah Côte d'Ivoire
Arrah Bihar India see Ara
124 D5 Ar Rāhidah Yemen
254 D5 Arraias Brazil
254 B4 Arraias r. Brazil
254 D5 Arraias, Serra de hills Brazil
184 C2 Arraiolos Port.
127 F4 Ar Ramādī Iraq
147 C4 Arra Mountains hills Rep. of Ireland
128 C3 Ar Ramthā Jordan
146 C6 Arran i. Scotland U.K.
157 F3 Arrancy-sur-Crusne France
184 A2 Arranhó Port.
128 D2 Ar Raqqah Syria
128 D1 Ar Raqqah governorate Syria
156 C2 Arras France
Arrasate Spain see Mondragón
163 B6 Arras-en-Lavedan France
124 C2 Ar-Rass Saudi Arabia
163 C4 Arrats r. France
163 A5 Arraute-Charritte France
124 C3 Ar Rawḍah Saudi Arabia
125 D5 Ar Rawḍah Yemen
124 D3 Ar Rayn Saudi Arabia
125 E2 Ar Rayyān Qatar
163 C6 Arreau France
250 D4 Arrecifal Col.
216 □3c Arrecife Lanzarote Canary Is
261 G4 Arrecifes Arg.
183 G1 Arredondo Spain
158 B3 Arrée, Monts d' hills France
156 E4 Arrentières France
Arretium Italy see Arezzo
179 E4 Arriach Austria
245 H5 Arriagá Mex.
244 D3 Arriaga San Luis Potosí Mex.
185 E4 Arriate Spain
261 G4 Arribeños Arg.
127 G5 Ar Rifā'ī Iraq
182 B4 Arrifana Aveiro Port.
182 B4 Arrifana Coimbra Port.
182 C4 Arrifana Guarda Port.
216 □1b Arrifes São Miguel Azores
156 E4 Arrigny France
183 H1 Arrigorriaga Spain
127 G5 Ar Rihāb salt flat Iraq
125 F3 Ar Rimāl des. Saudi Arabia
232 D6 Arrington VA U.S.A.
87 B6 Arrino W.A. Austr.
183 E1 Arriondas Spain
Ar Riyāḍ Saudi Arabia see Riyadh
124 D2 Ar Riyāḍ prov. Saudi Arabia
185 F1 Arroba de los Montes Spain
182 D4 Arrobuey mt. Spain
146 D5 Arrochar Argyll and Bute, Scotland U.K.
258 G4 Arroio Grande Brazil
159 F2 Arromanches-les-Bains France
184 C1 Arronches Port.
193 E2 Arrone Italy
192 D2 Arrone r. Italy
193 E3 Arrone r. Italy
183 H2 Arroniz Spain
163 B5 Arros r. France
190 D4 Arroscia r. Italy
156 B4 Arrou France
160 B2 Arroux r. France
226 C1 Arrow r. Ont. Can.
150 E2 Arrow r. England U.K.
147 C2 Arrow, Lough l. Rep. of Ireland
238 E2 Arrow Creek r. MT U.S.A.
81 C5 Arrowsmith, Mount South I. N.Z.
81 B6 Arrowtown South I. N.Z.
183 F2 Arroyal Spain
261 F2 Arroyito Arg.
247 □1 Arroyo Puerto Rico
184 D1 Arroyo de la Luz Spain
184 D2 Arroyo de San Serván Spain
261 I5 Arroyo Grande r. Arg.
240 G4 Arroyo Grande CA U.S.A.
184 D2 Arroyomolinos de León Spain
261 G3 Arroyo Seco Arg.
245 E3 Arroyo Seco Mex.
184 A2 Arruda dos Vinhos Port.
261 G2 Arrufó Arg.
127 G5 Ar Rumaythah Iraq
128 C3 Ar Ruşayfah Jordan
125 G3 Ar Rustāq Oman
127 F4 Ar Ruṭbah Iraq
124 D3 Ar Ruwayḍah Saudi Arabia
157 G3 Arry France
142 C3 Års Denmark
122 A2 Ars Iran
199 F3 Arsaköy Turkey
Ärsarybaba Erezi hills Turkm. see Irsarybaba, Gory
186 E2 Arsèguel Spain
122 C4 Arsenajān Iran
162 A2 Ars-en-Ré France
100 E3 Arsen'yev Rus. Fed.
139 K5 Arsen'yevo Rus. Fed.
138 G4 Arshanskaye Wzvyshsha hills Belarus
191 G3 Arsiè Italy
191 G3 Arsiero Italy
114 C3 Arsikere Karnataka India
129 A3 Arsin Turkey
134 J4 Arsk Rus. Fed.
193 F2 Arsoli Italy
160 C3 Ars-sur-Formans France
157 G3 Ars-sur-Moselle France
78 □5 Art, Île i. New Caledonia
198 B2 Arta Greece
187 G5 Artà Spain
183 I2 Artajona Spain
129 D2 Art'ana Georgia
187 C5 Artana Spain
190 C3 Artanavaz r. Italy
159 G4 Artannes-sur-Indre France
129 D4 Artashat Armenia
243 E3 Arteaga Coahuila Mex.
244 C4 Arteaga Michoacán Mex.
187 C5 Arteas de Abajo mt. Spain
100 E4 Artem Rus. Fed.
160 D3 Artemare France
246 B2 Artemisa Cuba
137 I3 Artemivka Kharkivs'ka Oblast' Ukr.
137 H3 Artemivka Poltavs'ka Oblast' Ukr.
137 J3 Artemivs'k Ukr.
137 J3 Artemivs'k Ukr.
Artemovsk Ukr. see Artemivs'k
131 M4 Artemovskiy Irkutskaya Oblast' Rus. Fed.
100 E4 Artemovskiy Primorskiy Kray Rus. Fed.
191 G2 Artèn Italy
193 E3 Artena Italy
156 B4 Artenay France
171 C4 Artern (Unstrut) Ger.
186 E3 Artés Spain
186 E3 Artesa de Segre Spain
241 M5 Artesia AZ U.S.A.
239 F5 Artesia NM U.S.A.
190 D1 Arth Switz.
163 E5 Arthès France
163 B5 Arthez-d'Asson France
163 B5 Arthez-de-Béarn France
159 H5 Arthon France
158 E4 Arthon-en-Retz France
87 B5 Arthur r. W.A. Austr.
227 G4 Arthur Ont. Can.
236 C3 Arthur NE U.S.A.
232 B6 Arthur TN U.S.A.
82 D2 Arthur, Lake salt flat S.A. Austr.
232 C4 Arthur, Lake PA U.S.A.
83 F5 Arthur Lake Tas. Austr.
85 G4 Arthur Point Qld Austr.
81 C5 Arthur's Pass South I. N.Z.
246 D1 Arthur's Town Cat I. Bahamas
148 C2 Articlave Northern Ireland U.K.
186 C2 Artieda Spain
186 D2 Arties Spain
148 B3 Artigarvan Northern Ireland U.K.
262 U2 Artigas research stn Antarctica
261 I2 Artigas Uru.
261 I2 Artigas dept Uru.
163 D5 Artigat France
129 C3 Art'ik Armenia
223 I2 Artillery Lake N.W.T. Can.
163 B5 Artix France
138 F1 Artjärvi Fin.
168 F2 Artlenburg Ger.
190 F3 Artogne Italy
127 F3 Artos Dağı mt. Turkey
126 E2 Artova Turkey
Artsakh aut. reg. Azer. see Dağlıq Qarabağ
106 D2 Arts Bogd Uul mts Mongolia
Artsiz Ukr. see Artsyz
136 E5 Artsyz Ukr.
161 E5 Artuby r. France
Artur de Paiva Angola see Kuvango
110 B4 Artux Xinjiang China
127 F2 Artvin Turkey
129 B3 Artvin prov. Turkey
91 H8 Aru, Kepulauan is Indon.
182 C2 A Rúa Spain
210 A4 Arua Uganda
254 C5 Aruanã Brazil
247 □9 Aruba terr. West Indies
216 □3f Arucas Gran Canaria Canary Is
163 B5 Arudy France
256 D5 Arujá Brazil
107 J2 Arun r. China
117 F4 Arun r. Nepal
117 H4 Arunachal Pradesh state India
81 C5 Arundel South I. N.Z.
151 G4 Arundel West Sussex, England U.K.
Arun Qi Nei Mongol China see Naji
142 D4 Årup Denmark
114 C4 Aruppukkottai Tamil Nadu India
211 C5 Arusha Tanz.
211 C5 Arusha admin. reg. Tanz.
211 C5 Arusha National Park Tanz.
95 E3 Arut r. Indon.
208 D4 Aruwimi r. Dem. Rep. Congo
236 B4 Arvada CO U.S.A.
147 D3 Arvagh Rep. of Ireland
161 E3 Arvan r. France
106 D2 Arvayheer Mongolia
160 E2 Arve r. France
162 A3 Arvert France
163 B4 Arveyres France
116 D5 Arvi Mahar. India
223 M2 Arviat Nunavut Can.
230 G1 Arvida Que. Can.
140 L2 Arvidsjaur Sweden
161 A4 Arvieu France
161 E4 Arvieux France
142 E2 Arvika Sweden
240 H4 Arvin CA U.S.A.
195 F3 Arvo, Lago l. Italy
232 D6 Arvonia VA U.S.A.
124 D3 Arwā' Saudi Arabia
107 H2 Arxan Nei Mongol China
Aryanah Tunisia see L'Ariana
134 K4 Aryazh Rus. Fed.
121 G1 Arykbalyk Kazakh.
Aryqbayq Kazakh. see Arykbalyk
121 G4 Arys' Kazakh.
121 G4 Arys' r. Kazakh.
192 B3 Arzachena Sardegna Italy
163 B5 Arzacq-Arraziguet France
135 H5 Arzamas Rus. Fed.
192 B5 Arzana Sardegna Italy
158 C4 Arzano France
169 C5 Arzbach Ger.
171 D5 Arzberg Bayern Ger.
171 E4 Arzberg Sachsen Ger.
163 E5 Arzens France
205 E2 Arzew Alg.
169 B5 Arzfeld Ger.
135 I7 Arzgir Rus. Fed.
191 G3 Arzignano Italy
Arzila Morocco see Asilah
178 B3 Arzl im Pitztal Austria
161 B3 Arzon r. France
182 B2 Arzúa Spain
165 E3 As Belgium
176 B1 Aš Czech Rep.
142 D3 Aså Denmark
142 E3 Åsa Sweden
207 G5 Asaba Nigeria
128 D1 Asad, Buḥayrat al resr Syria
123 G3 Asadābād Afgh.
122 B3 Asadābād Iran
129 E3 Aşağı Ağcakänd Azer.
129 D3 Aşağı Äskipara Azer.
129 D3 Aşağı Ayıblı Azer.
129 C3 Aşağı Dağ mt. Turkey
199 F3 Aşağıkaraçay Turkey
129 B3 Aşağıkatıklı Turkey
129 C4 Aşağıküpkıran Turkey
129 E3 Aşağı Oratağ Azer.
129 D4 Aşağısağmallı Turkey
129 B4 Aşağısöylemez Turkey
94 B2 Asahan r. Indon.
105 G3 Asahi Japan
102 I4 Asahi-dake mt. Japan
102 K2 Asahi-dake vol. Japan
103 F6 Asahi-gawa r. Japan
102 K2 Asahikawa Japan
105 F1 Asahi-take mt. Japan
105 F3 Asaka Japan
121 H4 Asaka Uzbek.
104 C3 Asake-gawa r. Japan
104 C4 Asamaga-take hill Japan
206 E5 Asamankese Ghana
105 E2 Asama-yama vol. Japan
206 E5 Asankranguaa Ghana
117 F5 Asansol W. Bengal India
206 E5 Asanwenso Ghana
163 B5 Asasp-Arros France
Asava i. Fiji see Yasawa
210 D2 Āsayita Eth.
169 C5 Asbach Ger.
173 E3 Asbach-Bäumenheim Ger.
230 G2 Asbestos Que. Can.
Asbestos Hill Que. Can. see Purtuniq
214 D3 Asbestos Mountains S. Africa
210 D2 Āsbe Teferi Eth.
143 F2 Åsbro Sweden
233 F4 Asbury Park NJ U.S.A.
163 A5 Ascain France
Ascalon Israel see Ashqelon
193 H4 Ascea Italy
261 G4 Ascensión Arg.
253 E3 Ascensión Bol.
245 E1 Ascensión Mex.
Ascension atoll Micronesia see Pohnpei
216 □2a Ascension i. S. Atlantic Ocean
173 G2 Ascha Ger.
173 G2 Ascha r. Ger.
179 F2 Aschach an der Donau Austria
172 D2 Aschaffenburg Ger.
178 C3 Aschau im Zillertal Austria
173 G4 Aschau in Chiemgau Ger.
179 F2 Aschbach Markt Austria
169 C4 Ascheberg Ger.
168 F1 Ascheberg (Holstein) Ger.
173 H3 Aschenstein hill Ger.
156 C4 Aschères-le-Marché France
171 C4 Aschersleben Ger.
173 F3 Aschheim Ger.
191 G5 Asciano Italy
192 B2 Asco Corse France
193 F2 Ascoli Piceno Italy
193 F2 Ascoli Piceno prov. Marche Italy
193 H3 Ascoli Satriano Italy
190 D2 Ascona Switz.
151 G3 Ascot Windsor and Maidenhead, England U.K.
252 C5 Ascotán, Salar de salt flat Chile
163 D6 Ascou France
182 B2 As Covas Spain
Asculum Italy see Ascoli Piceno
Asculum Picenum Italy see Ascoli Piceno
233 G3 Ascutney VT U.S.A.
113 □1 Asdhu i. N. Male Maldives
Asdu i. N. Male Maldives see Asdhu
Āseb Eritrea see Assab
143 F3 Åseda Sweden
205 F4 Asedjrad plat. Alg.
120 C1 Asekeyevo Rus. Fed.
210 C3 Āsela Eth.
140 L2 Åsele Sweden
141 K3 Åsen Sweden
168 E2 Asendorf Niedersachsen Ger.
168 E3 Asendorf Niedersachsen Ger.
197 G4 Asenovgrad Bulg.
142 B2 Åseral Norway
138 F2 Aseri Estonia
122 D3 Aşfāk Iran
128 C3 Aşfar, Jabal al mt. Jordan
128 C3 Aşfar, Tall al hill Syria
156 E3 Asfeld France
151 G2 Asfordby Leicestershire, England U.K.
151 I3 Ash Kent, England U.K.
151 G3 Ash Surrey, England U.K.
134 L5 Asha Rus. Fed.
104 D2 Ashahi-dake mt. Japan
206 E5 Ashanti admin. reg. Ghana
134 L4 Ashap Rus. Fed.
124 D2 Asharat Saudi Arabia
235 G1 Ashaway RI U.S.A.
147 E3 Ashbourne Rep. of Ireland
149 H4 Ashbourne Derbyshire, England U.K.
231 D6 Ashburn GA U.S.A.
87 B4 Ashburton watercourse W.A. Austr.
81 C5 Ashburton South I. N.Z.
81 C6 Ashburton r. South I. N.Z.
150 D4 Ashburton Devon, England U.K.
84 C3 Ashburton Range hills N.T. Austr.
151 F3 Ashbury Oxfordshire, England U.K.
151 F2 Ashby de la Zouch Leicestershire, England U.K.
150 E3 Ashchurch Gloucestershire, England U.K.
Ashchysay Kazakh. see Achisay
150 E3 Ashcott Somerset, England U.K.
222 F5 Ashcroft B.C. Can.
128 B4 Ashdod Israel
237 E5 Ashdown AR U.S.A.
151 H3 Ashdown Forest reg. England U.K.
231 E5 Asheboro NC U.S.A.
237 D5 Asher OK U.S.A.
223 L5 Ashern Man. Can.
231 D5 Asheville NC U.S.A.
224 C2 Asheweig r. Ont. Can.
83 G2 Ashford N.S.W. Austr.
147 E3 Ashford Rep. of Ireland
148 C5 Ashford r. Rep. of Ireland
151 F4 Ashford Hampshire, England U.K.
151 H3 Ashford Kent, England U.K.
151 G3 Ashford Surrey, England U.K.
241 K4 Ash Fork AZ U.S.A.
122 D2 Ashgabat Turkm.
80 E4 Ashhurst North I. N.Z.
102 K2 Ashibetsu Japan
105 F2 Ashikaga Japan
151 H2 Ashill Norfolk, England U.K.
149 H2 Ashington Northumberland, England U.K.
226 C4 Ashippun WI U.S.A.
104 B4 Ashiya Japan
122 C4 Ashkazar Iran
Ashkelon Israel see Ashqelon
Ashkhabad Turkm. see Ashgabat
Ashkhabadskaya Oblast' admin. div. Turkm. see Akhal'skaya Oblast'
146 F6 Ashkirk Scottish Borders, Scotland U.K.
226 D5 Ashkum IL U.S.A.
231 C5 Ashland AL U.S.A.
237 D4 Ashland KS U.S.A.
232 B5 Ashland KY U.S.A.
233 □I1 Ashland ME U.S.A.
237 F5 Ashland MS U.S.A.
238 F2 Ashland MT U.S.A.
236 D3 Ashland NE U.S.A.
233 H3 Ashland NH U.S.A.
232 B4 Ashland OH U.S.A.
238 B3 Ashland OR U.S.A.
234 B2 Ashland PA U.S.A.
232 E6 Ashland VA U.S.A.
226 B2 Ashland WI U.S.A.
231 C4 Ashland City TN U.S.A.
83 G2 Ashley N.S.W. Austr.
81 D5 Ashley r. South I. N.Z.
151 H2 Ashley Cambridgeshire, England U.K.
226 E5 Ashley IN U.S.A.
226 E4 Ashley MI U.S.A.
236 D2 Ashley ND U.S.A.
232 B4 Ashley OH U.S.A.
234 C1 Ashley PA U.S.A.
86 D2 Ashmore and Cartier Islands terr. Austr.
86 D2 Ashmore Reef Ashmore & Cartier Is Austr.
138 E4 Ashmyanskaye Wzvyshsha hills Belarus
138 E4 Ashmyany Hrodzyenskaya Voblasts' Belarus
138 F4 Ashmyany Hrodzyenskaya Voblasts' Belarus
116 D4 Ashoknagar Madh. Prad. India
129 C3 Ashots'k' Armenia
128 B4 Ashqelon Israel
127 F5 Ash Shabakah Iraq
127 F3 Ash Shaddādah Syria
124 C3 Ash Shafa Saudi Arabia
Ash Sham Syria see Damascus
125 G2 Ash Sha'm U.A.E.
127 G5 Ash Shanāfiyah Iraq
124 D2 Ash Sha'rā' Saudi Arabia
125 D4 Ash Sharawrah Saudi Arabia
Ash Shāriqah U.A.E. see Sharjah
127 F4 Ash Sharqāṭ Iraq
125 G3 Ash Sharqīyah admin. reg. Oman
125 G3 Ash Sharqīyah reg. Oman
125 E3 Ash Sharqīyah prov. Saudi Arabia
127 G5 Ash Shaṭrah Iraq
128 B4 Ash Shawbak Jordan
124 D5 Ash Shaykh 'Uthman Yemen
128 C5 Ash Shiblīyāt hill Saudi Arabia
125 E5 Ash Shiḥr Yemen
125 G2 Ash Shināş Oman
124 C2 Ash Shubaykīyah Saudi Arabia
125 D2 Ash Shumlūl Saudi Arabia
124 C4 Ash Shuqayq Saudi Arabia
Ash Shurayf Saudi Arabia see Khaybar
116 D5 Ashta Madh. Prad. India
114 B2 Ashta Mahar. India
232 C4 Ashtabula OH U.S.A.
129 D3 Ashtarak Armenia
114 B2 Ashti Mahar. India
114 C2 Ashti Mahar. India
116 D5 Ashti Mahar. India
214 C5 Ashton S. Africa
149 G4 Ashton Cheshire, England U.K.
238 E2 Ashton ID U.S.A.
226 C5 Ashton IL U.S.A.
234 A3 Ashton MD U.S.A.
215 E6 Ashton Bay S. Africa
149 G4 Ashton-under-Lyne Greater Manchester, England U.K.
225 H2 Ashuanipi r. Nfld. Can.
230 F1 Ashuapmushuan r. Que. Can.
Ashur Iraq see Ash Sharqāṭ
151 F4 Ashurst Hampshire, England U.K.
151 H3 Ashurst Kent, England U.K.
231 C5 Ashville AL U.S.A.
233 □I2 Ashville ME U.S.A.
232 D4 Ashville PA U.S.A.
226 B2 Ashwabay, Mount hill WI U.S.A.
226 C3 Ashwaubenon WI U.S.A.
150 E3 Ashwick Somerset, England U.K.
128 C2 'Āṣī r. Lebanon/Syria
128 C1 Asi r. Turkey
alt. 'Āṣī, Nahr al (Asia), conv. Orontes (Lebanon/Syria)
128 C1 'Āṣī, Nahr al r. Asia
alt. Asi (Turkey), conv. Orontes (Lebanon/Syria)
88 Asia continent
191 G3 Asiago Italy
244 C2 Asientos Mex.
114 C2 Asifabad Andhra Prad. India
115 E2 Asika Orissa India
141 N3 Asikkala Fin.
204 D2 Asilah Morocco
252 C3 Asillo Peru
198 D4 Asimi Kriti Greece
186 B2 Asín Spain
192 A4 Asinara, Golfo dell' b. Sardegna Italy
192 A3 Asinara, Isola i. Sardegna Italy
116 C4 Asind Rajasthan India
130 J4 Asino Rus. Fed.
139 H4 Asintorf Belarus
138 G5 Asipovichy Belarus
124 C4 'Asīr prov. Saudi Arabia
124 C3 'Asīr reg. Saudi Arabia
Asisium Italy see Assisi
138 C1 Askainen Fin.
127 F3 Aşkale Turkey
137 G4 Askaniya Nova Ukr.
120 D1 Askarovo Rus. Fed.
147 C4 Askeaton Rep. of Ireland
215 F4 Askeaton S. Africa
142 D2 Asker Norway
129 A4 Asker Dağı mt. Turkey
149 H4 Askern South Yorkshire, England U.K.
143 F2 Askersund Sweden
214 C2 Askham S. Africa
147 C2 Askill Rep. of Ireland
142 D2 Askim Norway
134 L4 Askino Rus. Fed.
198 B1 Askio mt. Greece
207 I4 Askira Nigeria
146 B5 Askival hill Scotland U.K.
98 F1 Askiz Rus. Fed.
141 N3 Askola Fin.
143 G2 Äsköping Sweden
198 C1 Askos Kentriki Makedonia Greece
116 E3 Askot Uttar Prad. India
142 A1 Askøy i. Norway
214 C6 Askraal S. Africa
141 I3 Askvoll Norway
129 E4 Askyaran Azer.
199 F2 Aslanapa Turkey
122 A2 Aşlāndūz Iran
138 G5 Aslik r. Belarus
Aslóközpont Hungary see Mórahalom
203 H6 Asmara Eritrea
Āsmera Eritrea see Asmara
143 F3 Åsnen l. Sweden
182 B1 As Neves Galicia Spain
182 B2 As Neves Galicia Spain
182 C2 As Nogais Spain
193 F1 Aso r. Italy
190 F3 Asola Italy
191 G3 Asolo Italy
185 I1 Asomadilla hill Spain
198 C2 Asopos r. Greece
198 C3 Asopos r. Greece
210 B2 Āsosa Eth.
103 E7 Aso-san vol. Japan
203 H4 Asoteriba, Jebel mt. Sudan
238 C2 Asotin WA U.S.A.
177 I5 Ásotthalom Hungary
134 L4 Aspa Rus. Fed.
179 E2 Aspach Austria
179 H3 Aspang-Markt Austria
122 B2 Aspar Iran
121 H4 Aspara Kazakh.
179 H2 Asparn an der Zaya Austria
197 H4 Asparukhovo Bulg.
140 K3 Aspås Sweden
149 F3 Aspatria Cumbria, England U.K.
187 C6 Aspe Spain
140 L3 Äspea Sweden
239 F4 Aspen CO U.S.A.
164 E3 Asperen Neth.
172 D3 Asperg Ger.
237 C5 Aspermont TX U.S.A.
234 A3 Aspers PA U.S.A.
163 C5 Aspet France
129 C3 Aspindza Georgia
161 B5 Aspiran France
81 B6 Aspiring, Mount South I. N.Z.
182 C1 As Pontes de García Rodríguez Spain
161 D4 Aspremont France
161 D4 Aspres-sur-Buëch France
163 E4 Asprières France
Aspropotamos r. Greece see Acheloös
198 C1 Asprovalta Greece
116 C5 Aspur Rajasthan India
223 J4 Asquith Sask. Can.
191 G3 Assa r. Italy
204 C3 Assa Morocco
129 D2 Assa r. Rus. Fed.
128 C2 As Sa'an Syria
203 I6 Assab Eritrea
206 C2 Assaba admin. reg. Maur.
124 C2 Aš Sab'ān Saudi Arabia
128 D2 As Sabkhah Syria
128 C3 Aş Şafā lava field Syria
Aş Şafāqis Tunisia see Sfax
128 B4 Aş Şāfī Jordan
128 C1 As Safīrah Syria
124 C5 Aş Şahīf Yemen
Assake Uzbek. see Asaka
120 D4 Assake-Audan, Vpadina depr. Uzbek.
125 D2 As Salamiyah Saudi Arabia
127 F4 Aş Şālihīyah Syria
128 B3 As Salṭ Jordan
117 G4 Assam state India
127 G5 As Samāwah Iraq
172 D2 Assamstadt Ger.
125 E3 Aş Şanām reg. Saudi Arabia
163 B5 Assat France
124 D3 As Sawādah reg. Saudi Arabia
165 D4 Asse Belgium
161 D5 Asse r. France
214 E5 Assegaaibos S. Africa
192 B5 Assemini Sardegna Italy
164 F1 Assen Neth.
164 D2 Assendelft Neth.
165 C3 Assenede Belgium
142 C4 Assens Denmark
158 D4 Assérac France
193 F2 Assergi Italy
165 E4 Assesse Belgium
163 D4 Assier France
223 J5 Assiniboia Sask. Can.
223 L5 Assiniboine r. Man./Sask. Can.
222 H5 Assiniboine, Mount Alta/B.C. Can.
256 B5 Assis Brazil
256 A6 Assis Chateaubriand Brazil
193 E1 Assisi Italy
169 D5 Aßlar Ger.
178 D4 Assling Austria
173 G4 Aßling Ger.
190 E3 Asso Italy
206 □ Assomada São Tiago Cape Verde
217 □2 Assomption i. Seychelles
163 B5 Asson France
194 D5 Assoro Sicilia Italy
127 G5 Aş Şubayḩīyah Kuwait
124 C4 As Subaykhah Saudi Arabia
125 E5 As Sufāl Yemen
127 G4 As Sulaymānīyah Iraq
127 G4 As Sulaymānīyah governorate Iraq
124 C2 As Sulaymī Saudi Arabia
124 D3 As Sulayyil Saudi Arabia
125 E2 Aş Şulb reg. Saudi Arabia
184 C1 Assumar Port.
124 D2 Aş Şummān plat. Saudi Arabia
125 E3 Aş Şummān plat. Saudi Arabia
As Sūrīyah country Asia see Syria
127 F4 Aş Şuwar Syria
128 C3 As Suwaydā' Syria
128 C3 As Suwaydā' governorate Syria
125 G3 As Suwayḩ Oman
125 G3 As Suwayq Oman
124 C3 As Suwayriqīyah Saudi Arabia
As Suways Egypt see El Suweis
124 D5 As Suwwādīyah Yemen
146 C3 Assynt, Loch l. Scotland U.K.
141 J3 Asta r. Norway
191 G2 Asta, Cima d' mt. Italy
Astacus Turkey see Kocaeli
163 C4 Astaffort France
198 B2 Astakos Greece
121 G2 Astana Kazakh.
122 B2 Astaneh Iran
122 B2 Āstārā Iran
142 E1 Åsteby Sweden
179 F2 Asten Austria
165 E3 Asten Neth.
Asterabad Iran see Gorgān
190 D4 Asti Italy
190 D4 Asti prov. Piemonte Italy
191 G3 Astico r. Italy
177 L4 Aştileu Romania
252 C3 Astillero Peru
Astin Tag mts China see Altun Shan
Astipálaia i. Greece see Astypalaia
163 D6 Aston r. France
151 G3 Aston Clinton Buckinghamshire, England U.K.
116 C2 Astor Jammu and Kashmir
123 H3 Astor r. Pak.
256 B5 Astorga Brazil
182 D2 Astorga Spain
226 B5 Astoria IL U.S.A.
238 B2 Astoria OR U.S.A.
142 E3 Åstorp Sweden
217 □2 Astove i. Seychelles
Astrabad Iran see Gorgān
Astrakhan' Kazakh. see Astrakhanka
120 B3 Astrakhan' Rus. Fed.
Astrakhan' Bazar Azer. see Cälilabad
121 G2 Astrakhanka Kazakh.
137 H4 Astrakhanka Ukr.
Astrakhan Oblast admin. div. Rus. Fed. see Astrakhanskaya Oblast'
120 A3 Astrakhanskaya Oblast' admin. div. Rus. Fed.
138 E4 Astravyets Belarus
129 F3 Astraxanka Azer.
Astrida Rwanda see Butare
78 □5 Astrolabe, Récifs de l' rf New Caledonia
198 C3 Astros Greece
138 E5 Astryna Belarus
139 H5 Astsyer r. Belarus
183 F2 Astudillo Spain
193 E3 Astura r. Italy
182 D1 Asturias airport Spain
182 D1 Asturias aut. comm. Spain
Asturica Augusta Spain see Astorga
151 F2 Astwood Bank Worcestershire, England U.K.
199 E3 Astypalaia i. Greece
121 J2 Asubulak Kazakh.
Asūbulaq Kazakh. see Asubulak
239 D6 Asunción r. Mex.
91 K3 Asuncion i. N. Mariana Is
253 F6 Asunción Para.
243 H6 Asunción Mita Guat.
192 A5 Asuni Sardegna Italy
104 C2 Asuwa-gawa r. Japan
138 G3 Asvyeya Belarus
138 G3 Asvyeyskaye, Vozyera l. Belarus
210 A4 Aswa r. Uganda
125 G2 Aswad Oman
203 G3 Aswân Egypt
124 A2 Aswân governorate Egypt
203 F3 Asyût Egypt
126 C6 Asyût governorate Egypt
177 J3 Aszaló Hungary
79 □2a Ata i. Tonga
250 E3 Atabapo r. Col./Venez.
121 G4 Atabay Kazakh.
199 G3 Atabey Turkey
258 C2 Atacama admin. reg. Chile
258 C2 Atacama, Desierto de des. Chile
252 C5 Atacama, Salar de salt flat Chile
250 B4 Atacames Ecuador
205 G4 Atafaitafa, Djebel mt. Alg.
81 □1 Atafu atoll Tokelau
81 □1 Atafu i. Tokelau
104 B3 Atago-san hill Japan
105 F3 Atago-yama hill Japan
128 A5 Atairtîr el Dahami, Gebel mt. Egypt
128 B1 Atakent Turkey
129 F3 Atakişili Azer.
205 G5 Atakor mts Alg.
207 F5 Atakpamé Togo
254 G4 Atalaia Brazil
184 B2 Atalaia hill Port.
250 D6 Atalaia do Norte Brazil
Atalándi Greece see Atalanti
198 C2 Atalanti Greece
242 □J7 Atalaya Panama
252 B2 Atalaya Peru
185 I3 Atalaya Arabe hill Spain
257 G3 Ataléia Brazil
105 F3 Atami Japan
Ataniya Turkey see Adana
177 J4 Átány Hungary
124 D5 'Ataq Yemen
128 A5 'Ataqa, Gebel hill Egypt
183 F3 Ataquines Spain
204 B5 Atâr Maur.
96 B3 Ataran r. Myanmar
Atas i. Cocos Is see South Island
240 G4 Atascadero CA U.S.A.
121 G2 Atasu Kazakh.
111 E4 Atatan He r. China
Atáviros mt. Notio Aigaio Greece see Attavyros
122 D1 Atayab Turkm.
128 A1 Atayurt Turkey
203 G5 Atbara Sudan
203 G5 Atbara r. Sudan
121 G2 Atbasar Kazakh.
121 H4 At-Bashy Kyrg.
236 E4 Atchison KS U.S.A.
234 D3 Atco NJ U.S.A.
183 I3 Atea Spain
206 E5 Atebubu Ghana
183 I3 Ateca Spain
182 C3 Atei Port.
182 C2 A Teixeira Spain
193 G3 Ateleta Italy
193 H4 Atella Italy
193 H4 Atella r. Italy
244 C3 Atemajac de Brizuela Mex.
105 E1 Atema-yama mt. Japan
252 C3 Aten Bol.
193 H4 Atena Lucana Italy
244 B3 Atengo r. Mex.
244 B3 Atenguillo r. Mex.
244 C4 Atenquique Mex.
Ateransk Kazakh. see Atyrau
193 F2 Aterno r. Italy
123 E3 Āteshkhāneh, Kūh-e hill Afgh.
193 G2 Atessa Italy
234 C3 Atglen PA U.S.A.
165 C4 Ath Belgium
222 H4 Athabasca Alta Can.
222 I3 Athabasca r. Alta Can.
223 I3 Athabasca, Lake Alberta/Saskatchewan Can.
117 F5 Athagarh Orissa India
232 B5 Athalia OH U.S.A.
147 E3 Athboy Rep. of Ireland
147 B4 Athea Rep. of Ireland
Athenae Greece see Athina
147 C3 Athenry Rep. of Ireland
227 J3 Athens Ont. Can.
Athens Greece see Athina
231 C5 Athens AL U.S.A.
231 D5 Athens GA U.S.A.
233 G3 Athens NY U.S.A.
232 B5 Athens OH U.S.A.
232 E4 Athens PA U.S.A.
231 C5 Athens TN U.S.A.
237 E5 Athens TX U.S.A.
169 F4 Athenstedt Ger.
150 C4 Atherington Devon, England U.K.
151 F2 Atherstone Warwickshire, England U.K.
85 F3 Atherton Qld Austr.
149 G4 Atherton Greater Manchester, England U.K.
211 C5 Athi r. Kenya
156 C3 Athies France
156 D3 Athies-sous-Laon France
198 C3 Athina Greece
Athínai Greece see Athina
211 C5 Athi River Kenya
159 F3 Athis-de-l'Orne France
156 C4 Athis-Mons France
147 C4 Athlacca Rep. of Ireland
147 C3 Athleague Rep. of Ireland
147 D3 Athlone Rep. of Ireland
114 B2 Athni Karnataka India
81 B6 Athol South I. N.Z.
233 G3 Athol MA U.S.A.
146 D5 Atholl, Forest of reg. Scotland U.K.
198 D1 Athos mt. Greece
Athos, Mount admin. div. Greece see Agion Oros
127 F4 Ath Tharthār, Wādī r. Iraq
128 C5 Ath Thāyat mt. Saudi Arabia
147 E4 Athy Rep. of Ireland
202 C6 Ati Chad
202 B4 Ati, Jabal mts Libya
80 F3 Atiamuri North I. N.Z.
256 D5 Atibaia Brazil
252 B4 Atico Peru
183 H3 Atienza Spain
222 H4 Atikameg Alta Can.
224 D2 Atikameg r. Ont. Can.
224 B3 Atikokan Ont. Can.
92 B3 Atimonan Phil.
193 F3 Atina Italy
114 C4 Atirampattinam Tamil Nadu India
243 H6 Atitlán Guat.
81 □2 Atiu i. Cook Is
Atjeh admin. dist. Indon. see Aceh
131 Q3 Atka Rus. Fed.
220 A4 Atka AK U.S.A.
220 A4 Atka Island AK U.S.A.
177 I4 Atkár Hungary
135 I6 Atkarsk Rus. Fed.
237 E5 Atkins AR U.S.A.
245 E4 Atlacomulco Mex.
215 F1 Atlanta S. Africa
231 C5 Atlanta GA U.S.A.
226 C5 Atlanta IL U.S.A.
227 E3 Atlanta MI U.S.A.
237 E5 Atlanta TX U.S.A.
126 D3 Atlantı Turkey
236 E3 Atlantic IA U.S.A.
233 □I2 Atlantic ME U.S.A.
231 E5 Atlantic NC U.S.A.
233 F5 Atlantic City NJ U.S.A.
234 D3 Atlantic County county NJ U.S.A.
235 D2 Atlantic Highlands NJ U.S.A.
263 H3 Atlantic-Indian-Antarctic Basin sea feature S. Atlantic Ocean
265 D8 Atlantic-Indian Ridge sea feature Southern Ocean
250 C2 Atlántico dept Col.
264 Atlantic Ocean
238 E3 Atlantic Peak WY U.S.A.
214 B5 Atlantis S. Africa
245 E3 Atlapexco Mex.
234 B2 Atlas PA U.S.A.
106 C3 Atlas Bogd mt. Mongolia
Atlas Méditerranéen mts Alg. see Atlas Tellien
204 D3 Atlas Mountains Africa
205 F2 Atlas Saharien mts Alg.
205 F2 Atlas Tellien mts Alg.
245 E4 Atlatlahucan Mex.
222 C3 Atlin B.C. Can.
128 B3 'Atlit Israel
245 E4 Atlixco Mex.
114 C3 Atmakur Andhra Prad. India
114 C3 Atmakur Andhra Prad. India
231 C6 Atmore AL U.S.A.
116 D5 Atner Madh. Prad. India
114 C2 Atnur Karnataka India
252 D5 Atocha Bol.
237 D5 Atoka OK U.S.A.
245 E3 Atotonico El Grande Mex.
244 C3 Atotonilco el Alto Mex.
96 D3 Atouat mt. Laos
184 A1 Atouguia da Baleia Port.
244 C3 Atoyac Mex.
245 F5 Atoyac r. Oaxaca Mex.
245 E4 Atoyac r. Puebla Mex.
245 F4 Atoyac r. Veracruz Mex.
244 D5 Atoyac de Álvarez Mex.
114 B2 Atpadi Mahar. India
220 C2 Atqasuk AK U.S.A.
117 G4 Atrai r. India
122 C2 Atrak, Rūd-e r. Iran/Turkm.
alt. Atrek, alt. Etrek
142 E3 Ätran r. Sweden
116 D4 Atranh Uttar Prad. India
250 B2 Atrato r. Col.
245 G5 Atravesada, Sierra mts Mex.
122 C2 Atrek r. Iran/Turkm.
alt. Atrak, Rūd-e, alt. Etrek
193 F2 Atri Italy
Atria Italy see Adria
193 G4 Atripalda Italy
Atropatene country Asia see Azerbaijan
129 C2 Ats'ana Georgia
234 D3 Atsion NJ U.S.A.
105 F3 Atsugi Japan
128 B4 Aţ Ţafīlah Jordan
124 C3 Aţ Ţā'if Saudi Arabia
177 H5 Attala Hungary
Attalea Turkey see Antalya
Attalia Turkey see Antalya
231 C5 Attalla AL U.S.A.
127 F4 At Ta'mīm governorate Iraq
202 D1 At Tamīmī Libya
148 B5 Attanagh Rep. of Ireland
97 D4 Attapu Laos
147 B2 Attavalley Rep. of Ireland
199 E3 Attavyros mt. Notio Aigaio Greece
224 D2 Attawapiskat Ont. Can.
224 D2 Attawapiskat r. Ont. Can.
203 H2 Aţ Ţawīl mts Saudi Arabia
124 C1 At Taysīyah plat. Saudi Arabia
128 B4 Aţ Ţayyibah Jordan
80 D4 Attempt Hill hill South I. N.Z.
169 C4 Attendorn Ger.
173 F3 Attenkirchen Ger.
215 G1 Atteridgeville S. Africa
179 E3 Attersee Austria
179 E3 Attersee l. Austria
165 E5 Attert Belgium
165 F5 Attert r. Lux.
147 E2 Attica Northern Ireland U.K.
230 C3 Attica IN U.S.A.
232 D3 Attica NY U.S.A.
232 B4 Attica OH U.S.A.
156 D3 Attichy France
193 E2 Attigliano Italy
160 D2 Attignat France
156 E3 Attigny France
198 C3 Attiki admin. reg. Greece
114 C4 Attingal Kerala India
233 H4 Attleboro MA U.S.A.
151 I2 Attleborough Norfolk, England U.K.
151 I2 Attlebridge Norfolk, England U.K.
179 E2 Attnang Austria
123 H3 Attock City Pak.
Attopeu Laos see Attapu
126 E5 Aţ Ţubayq reg. Saudi Arabia
266 G2 Attu Island AK U.S.A.
83 G2 Attunga N.S.W. Austr.
At Tūnisīyah country Africa see Tunisia
114 C4 Attur Tamil Nadu India
114 C4 Attur Tamil Nadu India
124 C5 At Turbah Yemen
124 D5 At Turbah Yemen
147 C3 Attymon Rep. of Ireland
125 E5 Atūd Yemen
260 D5 Atuel r. Arg.
162 C3 Atur France
143 F2 Åtvidaberg Sweden
117 G4 Atwari Bangl.
240 G3 Atwater CA U.S.A.
236 C4 Atwood KS U.S.A.
135 I5 Atyashevo Rus. Fed.
120 B3 Atyrau Kazakh.
Atyrau Oblast admin. div. Kazakh. see Atyrauskaya Oblast'
Atyraū Oblysy admin. div. Kazakh. see Atyrauskaya Oblast'
120 B3 Atyrauskaya Oblast' admin. div. Kazakh.
135 H5 Atyur'yevo Rus. Fed.
137 G2 Atyusha Ukr.
192 B5 Atzara Sardegna Italy
179 G2 Atzenbrugg Austria
171 C4 Atzendorf Ger.
178 A3 Au Austria
190 E1 Au Switz.
250 E5 Auati-Paraná r. Brazil
173 E2 Aub Ger.
169 E5 Aubach r. Ger.
161 D5 Aubagne France
161 C5 Aubais France
165 E5 Aubange Belgium
162 D3 Aubazines France
159 G3 Aube France
156 E4 Aube dept Champagne-Ardenne France
156 D4 Aube r. France
213 H3 Aúbe Moz.
165 E4 Aubel Belgium
161 C4 Aubenas France
156 E3 Aubenton France
156 B4 Aubergenville France
156 E3 Aubérive France
157 F5 Auberive Champagne-Ardenne France
162 C3 Aubeterre-sur-Dronne France
156 D4 Aubetin r. France
156 B3 Aubevoye France
163 C5 Aubiet France
161 D4 Aubignan France
159 G4 Aubigné-Racan France
161 D4 Aubignosc France
156 C2 Aubigny-en-Artois France
159 I4 Aubigny-sur-Nère France
163 E4 Aubin France
224 D4 Aubinadong r. Ont. Can.
190 B2 Aubonne Switz.
161 C5 Aubord France
157 F3 Auboué France
161 A4 Aubrac mts France
157 F3 Aubreville France
241 K4 Aubrey Cliffs mts AZ U.S.A.
220 F3 Aubry Lake N.W.T. Can.
85 G5 Auburn r. Qld Austr.
227 G4 Auburn Ont. Can.
231 C5 Auburn AL U.S.A.
240 G2 Auburn CA U.S.A.
236 F4 Auburn IL U.S.A.
230 C3 Auburn IN U.S.A.
233 H3 Auburn MA U.S.A.
233 □H2 Auburn ME U.S.A.
227 E4 Auburn MI U.S.A.
236 E3 Auburn NE U.S.A.
232 E3 Auburn NY U.S.A.
234 B2 Auburn PA U.S.A.
238 B2 Auburn WA U.S.A.
234 B1 Auburn Center PA U.S.A.
226 B3 Auburndale WI U.S.A.
85 G5 Auburn Range hills Qld Austr.
162 E3 Aubusson France
156 D2 Auby France
260 C5 Auca Mahuida, Sierra de mt. Arg.
163 D5 Aucamville France
138 D3 Auce Latvia
163 C5 Auch France
146 E5 Auchallater Aberdeenshire, Scotland U.K.
148 D2 Auchbraad Argyll and Bute, Scotland U.K.
156 C2 Auchel France
146 F5 Auchenblae Aberdeenshire, Scotland U.K.
146 C6 Auchenbreck Argyll and Bute, Scotland U.K.
146 E7 Auchencairn Dumfries and Galloway, Scotland U.K.
146 F6 Auchencrow Scottish Borders, Scotland U.K.
207 G5 Auchi Nigeria
146 D6 Auchinleck East Ayrshire, Scotland U.K.
146 F5 Auchmull Angus, Scotland U.K.
146 F4 Auchnagatt Aberdeenshire, Scotland U.K.
146 E4 Aucholzie Aberdeenshire, Scotland U.K.
146 F5 Auchronie Angus, Scotland U.K.
146 E5 Auchterarder Perth and Kinross, Scotland U.K.
146 E5 Auchtermuchty Fife, Scotland U.K.
156 C2 Auchy-au-Bois France
80 E2 Auckland North I. N.Z.
80 E2 Auckland admin. reg. North I. N.Z.
77 G6 Auckland Islands N.Z.

Aucun to Bagni di Rabbi
280

163 B6 Aucun France
161 A5 Aude dept Languedoc-Roussillon France
161 B5 Aude r. France
224 C3 Auden Ont. Can.
Audenarde Belgium see Oudenaarde
163 A4 Audenge France
158 E2 Auderville France
233 □H2 Audet Que. Can.
160 D1 Audeux France
158 B3 Audierne France
160 E1 Audincourt France
150 E2 Audlem Cheshire, England U.K.
149 G4 Audley Staffordshire, England U.K.
163 B5 Audon France
210 D3 Audo Range mts Eth.
156 B2 Audresselles France
138 E2 Audru Estonia
156 C2 Audruicq France
236 E3 Audubon IA U.S.A.
234 C3 Audubon NJ U.S.A.
157 F3 Audun-le-Roman France
171 D5 Aue Ger.
168 C2 Aue r. Ger.
169 E3 Aue r. Ger.
169 F3 Aue r. Ger.
173 H3 Auerbach Bayern Ger.
171 D5 Auerbach Sachsen Ger.
171 D5 Auerbach Sachsen Ger.
173 F2 Auerbach in der Oberpfalz Ger.
171 D5 Auersberg mt. Ger.
179 H2 Auersthal Austria
171 D5 Auerswalde Ger.
156 B3 Auffay France
173 G3 Aufhausen Ger.
85 F5 Augathella Qld Austr.
147 D2 Augher Northern Ireland U.K.
147 E2 Aughnacloy Northern Ireland U.K.
147 C3 Aughrim Galway Rep. of Ireland
147 E4 Aughrim Wicklow Rep. of Ireland
149 G4 Aughton Lancashire, England U.K.
149 H4 Aughton South Yorkshire, England U.K.
162 C3 Augignac France
214 C3 Augrabies S. Africa
214 C3 Augrabies Falls S. Africa
227 F3 Au Gres MI U.S.A.
173 E3 Augsburg Ger.
178 B2 Augsburg airport Ger.
138 E3 Augšligatne Latvia
138 F3 Augšzemes augstiene hills Latvia
87 B7 Augusta W.A. Austr.
195 E5 Augusta Sicilia Italy
237 F5 Augusta AR U.S.A.
231 D5 Augusta GA U.S.A.
226 B5 Augusta IL U.S.A.
237 D4 Augusta KS U.S.A.
232 A5 Augusta KY U.S.A.
233 □I2 Augusta ME U.S.A.
238 D2 Augusta MT U.S.A.
234 D1 Augusta NJ U.S.A.
226 B3 Augusta WI U.S.A.
232 D5 Augusta WV U.S.A.
195 E5 Augusta, Golfo di b. Sicilia Italy
Augusta Auscorum France see Auch
Augusta Taurinorum Italy see Torino
Augusta Treverorum Ger. see Trier
Augusta Vindelicorum Ger. see Augsburg
168 E1 Augustenborg Denmark
246 D5 Augustin Cadazzi Col.
Augusto Cardosa Moz. see Metangula
257 E3 Augusto de Lima Brazil
Augustodunum France see Autun
254 F3 Augusto Severo Brazil
175 K2 Augustów Pol.
175 L3 Augustowo Pol.
87 C5 Augustus, Mount W.A. Austr.
171 E5 Augustusburg Ger.
86 E2 Augustus Island W.A. Austr.
169 E3 Auhagen Ger.
173 F3 Au in der Hallertau Ger.
157 E4 Aujon r. France
222 C3 Auke Bay AK U.S.A.
78 □6 Auki Malaita Solomon Is
168 E1 Aukrug Ger.
138 D4 Aukštelkai Lith.
140 L2 Auktsjaur Sweden
86 D4 Auld, Lake salt flat W.A. Austr.
146 E4 Auldearn Highland, Scotland U.K.
169 F4 Auleben Ger.
190 E4 Aulella r. Italy
172 D4 Aulendorf Ger.
193 H4 Auletta Italy
Auliye Ata Zhambylskaya Oblast' Kazakh. see Taraz
190 E4 Aulla Italy
192 B3 Aullène Corse France
160 B3 Aulnat France
160 B3 Aulnat airport France
162 B2 Aulnay France
156 C4 Aulnay-sous-Bois France
158 B3 Aulne r. France
157 G4 Aulnois sur-Seille France
156 D2 Aulnoye-Aymeries France
Aulon Albania see Vlorë
163 C5 Aulon France
170 C3 Aulosen Ger.
156 B2 Ault France
146 C4 Aultbea Highland, Scotland U.K.
146 D4 Aultguish Inn Highland, Scotland U.K.
163 D6 Aulus-les-Bains France
171 C5 Auma Ger.
156 B3 Aumale France
160 A2 Aumance r. France
157 F3 Aumetz France
120 E4 Auminzatau, Gory hills Uzbek.
160 D2 Aumont France
161 B4 Aumont-Aubrac France
168 F2 Aumühle Ger.
207 G4 Auna Nigeria
160 B1 Aunay-en-Bazois France
159 F2 Aunay-sur-Odon France
156 B4 Auneau France
156 C3 Auneuil France
142 D3 Auning Denmark
183 H4 Auñón Spain
191 I2 Aupa r. Italy
225 G1 Aupaluk Que. Can.
161 E5 Aups France
141 M3 Aura Fin.
173 E2 Aurach Ger.
178 D3 Aurach bei Kitzbühel Austria
114 C2 Aurad Karnataka India
163 D5 Auradé France
169 E5 Aura im Singrund Ger.
116 D4 Auraiya Uttar Prad. India
138 D1 Aurajoki r. Fin.
117 F4 Aurangabad Bihar India
114 B2 Aurangabad Mahar. India
158 D4 Auray France
159 E2 Aure r. France
140 J3 Aure Norway
161 C3 Aurec-sur-Loire France
163 C5 Aureilhan France
161 C5 Aureille France
161 D4 Aurel Provence-Alpes-Côte-d'Azur France
161 D4 Aurel Rhône-Alpes France
244 A1 Aurelio Benassini, Presa resr Mex.
163 B5 Aurensan France
168 C2 Aurich Ger.
256 B4 Auriflama Brazil
163 C5 Aurignac France
Aurigny i. Channel Is see Alderney
256 B2 Aurilândia Brazil
162 E4 Aurillac France
186 C2 Aurín r. Spain
191 G2 Aurino r. Italy
161 D5 Auriol France
191 I3 Aurisina Italy
80 E3 Auroa North I. N.Z.
179 E2 Aurolzmünster Austria
161 E4 Auron France
160 A1 Auron r. France
191 H2 Auronzo di Cadore Italy
92 B5 Aurora Phil.
214 B5 Aurora S. Africa
238 F4 Aurora CO U.S.A.
226 C5 Aurora IL U.S.A.
233 □I2 Aurora ME U.S.A.
226 A2 Aurora MN U.S.A.
237 E4 Aurora MO U.S.A.
236 D3 Aurora NE U.S.A.
232 C4 Aurora OH U.S.A.
241 L2 Aurora UT U.S.A.
Aurora Island Vanuatu see Maéwo
163 B4 Auros France
161 B4 Auroux France
85 E2 Aurukun Qld Austr.
193 F3 Aurunci, Monti mts Italy
114 C2 Ausa Mahar. India
191 I3 Ausa r. Italy
227 F3 Au Sable MI U.S.A.
227 F3 Au Sable r. MI U.S.A.
233 G2 Ausable r. NY U.S.A.
233 G2 Ausable Forks NY U.S.A.
191 I3 Ausa-Corno Italy
Auschwitz Pol. see Oświęcim
Ausculum Italy see Ascoli Satriano
Ausculum Apulum Italy see Ascoli Satriano
183 H2 Ausejo Spain
193 F3 Ausente r. Italy
177 L4 Auşeu Romania
146 F2 Auskerry i. Scotland U.K.
171 C3 Ausleben Ger.
193 F3 Ausoni, Monti mts Italy
193 F3 Ausonia Italy
163 D5 Ausseing Tour hill France
163 E5 Aussillon France
161 E3 Aussois France
163 D5 Aussonne France
163 B5 Aussurucq France
142 C2 Aust-Agder county Norway
140 □C2 Austari-Jökulsá r. Iceland
140 □ Austfonna ice cap Svalbard
226 A4 Austin MN U.S.A.
240 I2 Austin NV U.S.A.
237 D6 Austin TX U.S.A.
87 C5 Austin, Lake salt flat W.A. Austr.
232 C4 Austintown OH U.S.A.
192 B4 Austis Sardegna Italy
84 D4 Austral Downs N.T. Austr.
79 □3 Australes, Îles is Fr. Polynesia
76 C4 Australia country Oceania
263 J2 Australian Antarctic Territory Antarctica
83 G3 Australian Capital Territory admin. div. Austr.
87 B7 Australind W.A. Austr.
179 E3 Austria country Europe
138 D3 Austrumkursas augstiene hills Latvia
140 □D2 Austurland constituency Iceland
140 K1 Austvågøy i. Norway
251 G5 Autazes Brazil
163 D5 Auterive France
Autesiodorum France see Auxerre
160 D1 Autet France
156 B2 Authie r. France
227 H1 Authier Que. Can.
159 F4 Authion r. France
159 G4 Authon Centre France
161 E4 Authon Provence-Alpes-Côte-d'Azur France
159 G3 Authon-du-Perche France
244 B4 Autlán Mex.
183 H2 Autol Spain
161 D3 Autrans France
157 F4 Autreville France
160 D1 Autrey-lès-Gray France
157 E3 Autry France
160 C2 Autun France
156 E3 Auve France
165 D4 Auvelais Belgium
160 B3 Auvergne admin. reg. France
161 A4 Auvergne reg. France
160 A3 Auvergne, Monts d' mts France
159 F4 Auvers-le-Hamon France
156 C3 Auvers-sur-Oise France
162 C3 Auvézère r. France
163 C4 Auvignon r. France
163 C4 Auvillar France
156 E3 Auvillers-les-Forges France
156 D5 Auxerre France
156 C2 Auxi-le-Château France
160 D1 Auxonne France
160 C2 Auxy France
251 F3 Auyan Tepuí plat. Venez.
160 A2 Auzances France
163 D6 Auzat France
161 B3 Auzat-sur-Allier France
162 E3 Auze r. France
163 E4 Auzits France
161 B3 Auzon France
163 C4 Auzoue r. France
121 J2 Auzzov Kazakh.
96 A2 Ava Myanmar
237 E4 Ava MO U.S.A.
233 F3 Ava NY U.S.A.
256 C5 Avaí Brazil
162 C2 Availles-Limouzine France
160 B1 Avallon France
159 F3 Avaloirs, Mont des hill France
240 H5 Avalon CA U.S.A.
234 D3 Avalon NJ U.S.A.
225 K4 Avalon Peninsula Nfld. Can.
261 H2 Avalos r. Arg.
122 A2 Avān Iran
114 C4 Avanashi Tamil Nadu India
182 B4 Avanca Port.
163 C4 Avance r. France
161 E4 Avançon France
251 G3 Avanganna mt. Guyana
114 D2 Avanigadda Andhra Prad. India
126 D3 Avanos Turkey
156 E4 Avant-lès-Ramerupt France
Avarau atoll Cook Is see Palmerston
256 C5 Avaré Brazil
Avaricum France see Bourges
127 G3 Āvārsin Iran
129 E2 Avarskoye Koysu r. Rus. Fed.
81 □3 Avarua Rarotonga Cook Is
140 L2 Avaträsk Sweden
140 L2 Avaviken Sweden
232 B6 Avawam KY U.S.A.
Avdeyevka Ukr. see Avdiyivka
198 D1 Avdira Anatoliki Makedonia kai Thraki Greece
137 I3 Avdiyivka Ukr.
182 B3 Ave r. Port.
151 F3 Avebury Wiltshire, England U.K.
182 D2 A Veiga Galicia Spain
184 B1 Aveiras de Cima Port.
182 B4 Aveiro Port.
182 B4 Aveiro admin. dist. Port.
182 B4 Aveiro, Ria de est. Port.
182 B5 Avelar Port.
182 B3 Aveleda Braga Port.
182 D3 Aveleda Bragança Port.
151 H3 Aveley Thurrock, England U.K.
165 C4 Avelgem Belgium
261 H4 Avellaneda Buenos Aires Arg.
258 F3 Avellaneda Santa Fé Arg.
193 G4 Avellino Italy
193 H4 Avellino prov. Campania Italy
158 C4 Aven r. France
240 G3 Avenal CA U.S.A.
156 E3 Avenay-Val-d'Or France
190 C2 Avenches Switz.
161 B5 Avène France
164 D2 Avenhorn Neth.
182 B1 Avenida do Marqués de Figueroa Spain
Avenio France see Avignon
Aventicum Switz. see Avenches
160 B2 Avermes France
146 D4 Averon r. Scotland U.K.
140 I3 Averøya i. Norway
190 E2 Avers Switz.
193 G4 Aversa Italy
247 G4 Aves i. West Indies
Aves is West Indies see Las Aves, Islas
156 C2 Avesnes-le-Comte France
156 D2 Avesnes-sur-Helpe France
143 G1 Avesta Sweden
190 E4 Aveto r. Italy
195 G2 Avetrano Italy
161 A4 Aveyron dept Midi-Pyrénées France
163 D4 Aveyron r. France
193 F2 Avezzano Italy
186 E2 Avia Spain
182 B2 Avia r. Spain
191 H2 Aviano Italy
258 E2 Aviá Terai Arg.
146 E4 Aviemore Highland, Scotland U.K.
81 C6 Aviemore, Lake South I. N.Z.
190 C3 Avigliana Italy
193 H4 Avigliano Italy
193 E2 Avigliano Umbro Italy
161 C5 Avignon France
163 D5 Avignonet-Lauragais France
183 F4 Ávila Spain
183 F4 Ávila prov. Castilla y León Spain
183 E4 Ávila, Sierra de mts Spain
182 E1 Avilés Spain
160 E1 Avilley France
137 J4 Avilo-Uspenka Rus. Fed.
182 B1 Aviño Spain
182 B3 Avintes Port.
186 E3 Avinyó Spain
191 F3 Avio Italy
156 C2 Avion France
182 B2 Avión mt. Spain
157 F3 Avioth France
184 C1 Avis Port.
191 G2 Avisio r. Italy
156 E4 Avize France
128 A1 Avlama Dağı mt. Turkey
198 C2 Avlida Greece
Avlona Albania see Vlorë
142 C3 Avlum Denmark
134 I3 Avnyugskiy Rus. Fed.
83 F5 Avoca Tas. Austr.
83 E4 Avoca Vic. Austr.
83 E3 Avoca r. Vic. Austr.
147 E4 Avoca Rep. of Ireland
215 H1 Avoca S. Africa
236 E3 Avoca IA U.S.A.
232 E3 Avoca NY U.S.A.
146 D4 Avoch Highland, Scotland U.K.
159 G4 Avoine France
195 E6 Avola Sicilia Italy
87 C6 Avon r. W.A. Austr.
156 C4 Avon France
150 D4 Avon r. Devon, England U.K.
150 E3 Avon r. England U.K.
151 E2 Avon r. England U.K.
151 F4 Avon r. England U.K.
226 B5 Avon IL U.S.A.
232 E3 Avon NY U.S.A.
234 B2 Avon PA U.S.A.
147 E4 Avonbeg r. Rep. of Ireland
149 F2 Avonbridge Falkirk, Scotland U.K.
241 K5 Avondale AZ U.S.A.
234 C3 Avondale PA U.S.A.
235 G1 Avondale RI U.S.A.
84 D4 Avon Downs N.T. Austr.
85 F4 Avon Downs Qld Austr.
232 B4 Avon Lake OH U.S.A.
147 E4 Avonmore r. Rep. of Ireland
150 E3 Avonmouth Bristol, England U.K.
231 D7 Avon Park FL U.S.A.
214 D5 Avontuur S. Africa
160 A1 Avord France
160 E2 Avoriaz France
138 E3 Avoti Latvia
160 E1 Avoudrey France
197 H1 Avrămeni Romania
197 E2 Avram Iancu Romania
158 E3 Avranches France
156 C3 Avre r. France
159 H3 Avre r. France
157 G4 Avricourt France
197 G3 Avrig Romania
157 F3 Avril France
162 A2 Avrillé France
159 F4 Avrillé France
129 B3 Avsek Dağı mt. Turkey
Avveel Fin. see Ivalo
Avvil Fin. see Ivalo
128 B3 A'waj r. Syria
104 A4 Awaji-shima i. Japan
80 F3 Awakeri North I. N.Z.
80 E3 Awakino North I. N.Z.
125 E2 Awālī Bahrain
165 E4 Awans Belgium
80 D1 Awanui North I. N.Z.
210 E2 Āwarē Eth.
81 B7 Awarua South I. N.Z.
210 C3 Āwasa Eth.
210 D2 Āwash Eth.
210 D2 Āwash r. Eth.
110 C3 Awat Xinjiang China
210 C3 Āwatā Shet' r. Eth.
81 E4 Awatere r. South I. N.Z.
202 B3 Awbārī Libya
147 C4 Awbeg r. Rep. of Ireland
146 C5 Awe, Loch l. Scotland U.K.
208 E2 Aweil Sudan
207 G5 Awgu Nigeria
207 G5 Awka Nigeria
204 B4 Awlitis watercourse Western Sahara
93 B3 Awo r. Indon.
150 E3 Awre Gloucestershire, England U.K.
93 C2 Awu vol. Indon.
178 C3 Axams Austria
163 E6 Axat France
150 D4 Axe r. Devon/Dorset, England U.K.
150 E3 Axe r. North Somerset/Somerset, England U.K.
83 F4 Axedale Vic. Austr.
165 C3 Axel Neth.
221 I2 Axel Heiberg Island Nunavut Can.
197 G2 Axente Sever Romania
206 E5 Axim Ghana
198 C1 Axios r. Greece
163 D6 Ax-les-Thermes France
150 E4 Axminster Devon, England U.K.
245 E4 Axochiapan Mex.
183 H1 Axpe-Busturia Spain
168 D2 Axstedt Ger.
Axum Eth. see Āksum
156 E3 Ay France
104 B3 Ayabe Japan
204 D2 Ayachi, Jbel mt. Morocco
261 H5 Ayacucho Arg.
252 B3 Ayacucho Peru
252 B3 Ayacucho dept Peru
121 J3 Ayagoz Kazakh.
Ayaguz Kazakh. see Ayagoz
120 F4 Ayakagytma, Vpadina depr. Uzbek.
120 F4 Ayakkuduk Uzbek.
Ayaköz Kazakh. see Ayagoz
206 E5 Ayamé Côte d'Ivoire
184 C3 Ayamonte Spain
131 O4 Ayan Rus. Fed.
126 D2 Ayancık Turkey
101 C5 Ayang N. Korea
207 G5 Ayangba Nigeria
250 C3 Ayapel, Serranía de mts Col.
126 D2 Ayaş Turkey
105 F3 Ayase Japan
252 C3 Ayaviri Peru
210 C1 Ayayei Eth.
123 G2 Āybak Afgh.
149 H3 Aycliffe Durham, England U.K.
121 G1 Aydabul Kazakh.
137 J2 Aydar Rus. Fed.
137 J3 Aydar r. Ukr.
121 F4 Aydarkul', Ozero l. Uzbek.
120 F3 Aydarly Kazakh.
160 A3 Aydat France
125 F4 'Aydim, Wādī r. Oman
199 E3 Aydın Turkey
199 F3 Aydın prov. Turkey
128 A1 Aydıncık Turkey
199 E2 Aydın Dağları mts Turkey
129 C4 Aydınlar Turkey
129 B3 Aydıntepe Turkey
121 G3 Ayeat, Gora hill Kazakh.
183 H2 Ayedo mt. Spain
210 D2 Āyelu Terara vol. Eth.
162 D3 Ayen France
233 H3 Ayer MA U.S.A.
186 C2 Ayerbe Spain
Ayers Rock hill N.T. Austr. see Uluru
Ayeyarwady r. Myanmar see Irrawaddy
110 D1 Aygulakskiy Khrebet mts Rus. Fed.
Ayiá Greece see Agia
Ayiásos Voreio Aigaio Greece see Agiasos
173 F4 Aying Ger.
Áyion Óros admin. div. Greece see Agion Oros
Áyios Dhimítrios Attiki Greece see Agios Dimitrios
Áyios Evstrátios i. Greece see Agios Efstratios
Áyios Nikólaos Kriti Greece see Agios Nikolaos
210 C1 Āykel Eth.
131 M3 Aykhal Rus. Fed.
134 J3 Aykino Rus. Fed.
81 D5 Aylesbury South I. N.Z.
151 G3 Aylesbury Buckinghamshire, England U.K.
151 H3 Aylesford Kent, England U.K.
151 I3 Aylesham Kent, England U.K.
232 E6 Aylett VA U.S.A.
183 G3 Ayllón Spain
227 G4 Aylmer Ont. Can.
227 J3 Aylmer Que. Can.
223 I1 Aylmer Lake N.W.T. Can.
151 I2 Aylsham Norfolk, England U.K.
120 E2 Aymagambetov Kazakh.
190 C3 Aymavilles Italy
252 B3 Ayna Peru
185 H2 Ayna Spain
121 I3 Aynabulak Kazakh.
163 D4 Aynac France
125 D5 'Ayn Ba Ma'bad Yemen
123 G2 Ayní Tajik.
126 E3 'Ayn 'Īsá Syria
244 C3 Ayo el Chico Mex.
131 R3 Ayon, Ostrov i. Rus. Fed.
182 D2 Ayoo de Vidriales Spain
245 F5 Ayoquezco Mex.
187 B5 Ayora Spain
207 F3 Ayorou Niger
207 I6 Ayos Cameroon
206 C2 'Ayoûn el 'Atroûs Maur.
85 F3 Ayr Qld Austr.
227 G4 Ayr Ont. Can.
146 D6 Ayr South Ayrshire, Scotland U.K.
146 D6 Ayr r. Scotland U.K.
150 D1 Ayr, Point of Wales U.K.
128 C1 Ayran Turkey
126 D3 Ayrancı Turkey
199 E2 Ayrancılar Turkey
129 E3 Āyriçay r. Azer.
159 G5 Ayron France
129 D3 Ayrum Armenia
149 H3 Aysgarth North Yorkshire, England U.K.
210 D2 Āysha Eth.
173 E3 Aystetten Ger.
120 E3 Ayteke Bi Kazakh.
197 H4 Aytos Bulg.
197 H4 Aytoska Reka r. Bulg.
162 A2 Aytré France
93 D2 Ayu, Kepulauan atoll Irian Jaya Indon.
183 H2 Ayuda r. Spain
184 D1 Ayuela r. Spain
125 F4 Ayun Oman
Ayuthia Thai. see Ayutthaya
137 K4 Ayutinskiy Rus. Fed.
245 E5 Ayutla Mex.
97 C4 Ayutthaya Thai.
199 E2 Ayvacık Turkey
126 E3 Ayvalı Turkey
199 E2 Ayvalık Turkey
199 G3 Ayvalıpınar Turkey
165 E4 Aywaille Belgium
125 E4 Aywat al Manāhīl, Wādī r. Yemen
125 E4 Aywat aş Şay'ar, Wādī r. Yemen
242 □I6 Azacualpa Hond.
183 I2 Azagra Spain
186 C3 Azaila Spain
Azak Rus. Fed. see Azov
184 B1 Azambuja Port.
184 C2 Azambuja r. Port.
117 E4 Azamgarh Uttar Prad. India
252 C3 Azangaro Peru
196 E3 Azanja Srbija Yugo.
157 F3 Azannes-et-Soumazannes France
186 D3 Azanúy Spain
206 E2 Azaouâd reg. Mali
207 F2 Azaouagh, Vallée de watercourse Mali/Niger
252 C4 Azapa Chile
258 G3 Azara Arg.
Azaran Iran see Hashtrud
Azārbayjan country Asia see Azerbaijan
122 A2 Āžarbāyjān-e Gharbī prov. Iran
122 A2 Āžarbāyjān-e Sharqī prov. Iran
207 H4 Azare Nigeria
184 C2 Azaruja Port.
138 G5 Azarychy Belarus
129 D3 Azatamut Armenia
139 K2 Azatskoye, Ozero l. Rus. Fed.
129 C3 Azavret'i Georgia
159 H5 Azay-le-Ferron France
159 G4 Azay-le-Rideau France
128 C1 A'zāz Syria
Azbine mts Niger see L'Aïr, Massif de
126 D2 Azdavay Turkey
159 F4 Azé France
204 C2 Azemmour Morocco
162 D2 Azerables France
129 F3 Azerbaijan country Asia
Azerbaydzhanskaya S.S.R. country Asia see Azerbaijan
160 C3 Azergues r. France
184 C2 Azevel r. Port.
210 C1 Āzezo Eth.
129 D3 Azhdahak Lerr mt. Armenia
204 D2 Azilal Morocco
227 G2 Azilda Ont. Can.
161 A5 Azille France
156 C2 Azincourt France
184 B1 Azinhaga Port.
184 C3 Azinhal Port.
182 D3 Azinhoso Port.
Azizbekov Armenia see Vayk'
Aziziye Turkey see Pınarbaşı
186 A1 Azkoitia Spain
135 K5 Aznakayevo Rus. Fed.
184 D3 Aznalcázar Spain
184 D3 Aznalcóllar Spain
250 B5 Azogues Ecuador
184 A2 Azóia Port.
216 □1 Azores aut. reg. N. Atlantic Ocean
264 H3 Azores-Biscay Rise sea feature N. Atlantic Ocean
Azotus Israel see Ashdod
135 G7 Azov Rus. Fed.
137 I4 Azov, Sea of Rus. Fed./Ukr.
Azovs'ke More sea Rus. Fed./Ukr. see Azov, Sea of
Azovskoye More sea Rus. Fed./Ukr. see Azov, Sea of
245 E5 Azoyú Mex.
186 A1 Azpeitia Spain
203 G6 Azraq, Bahr el r. Sudan alt. Abay Wenz (Ethiopia), conv. Blue Nile
204 D2 Azrou Morocco
239 E4 Aztec NM U.S.A.
246 E3 Azua Dom. Rep.
184 E2 Azuaga Spain
186 C3 Azuara Spain
250 B5 Azuay prov. Ecuador
258 C2 Azúcar r. Chile
185 F2 Azuel Spain
183 H2 Azuelo Spain
185 G1 Azuer r. Spain
242 □J8 Azuero, Península de pen. Panama
258 C2 Azufre, Cerro del mt. Chile
261 H5 Azul Arg.
261 H5 Azul r. Arg.
260 B4 Azul vol. Chile
243 H5 Azul r. Mex.
250 □ Azul, Cerro vol. Islas Galápagos Ecuador
252 B2 Azul, Cordillera mts Peru
253 G3 Azul, Serra hills Brazil
102 J5 Azuma-san vol. Japan
105 E2 Azumaya-san mt. Japan
183 G4 Azuqueca de Henares Spain
163 A5 Azur France
182 B3 Azurara Port.
252 D5 Azurduy Bol.
183 E5 Azután Spain
160 B2 Azy-le-Vif France
'Azza Gaza see Gaza
205 G1 Azzaba Alg.
128 C3 Az Zabadānī Syria
125 G3 Aẓ Ẓāhirah admin. reg. Oman
125 E2 Aẓ Ẓahrān Saudi Arabia
125 E2 Az Zallāq Bahrain
191 H3 Azzano Decimo Italy
Az Zaqāzīq Egypt see Zagazig
128 C1 Az Zarbah Syria
128 C3 Az Zarqā' Jordan
202 B1 Az Zāwiyah Libya
124 C5 Az Zaydīyah Yemen
204 B5 Azzeffâl hills Maur./W. Sahara
124 D2 Az Zilfī Saudi Arabia
190 F3 Azzone Italy
127 G5 Az Zubayr Iraq
124 C5 Az Zuhrah Yemen
124 C5 Az Zuqur i. Yemen

B

79 □1a Ba Viti Levu Fiji
78 □5 Baâba i. New Caledonia
95 G2 Baai r. Indon.
128 C2 Ba'albek Lebanon
171 C4 Baalberge Ger.
164 F2 Baalder Neth.
128 B4 Ba'al Hazor mt. West Bank
157 F3 Baâlon France
190 D1 Baar Switz.
210 D4 Baardheere Somalia
173 F3 Baar-Ebenhausen Ger.
165 D3 Baarle-Hertog Belgium
165 D3 Baarle-Nassau Neth.
164 E2 Baarn Neth.
116 D4 Bab Uttar Prad. India
197 F4 Baba mt. Bulg.
179 F1 Baba hill Czech Rep.
123 G3 Bābā, Kūh-e mts Afgh.
206 B2 Bababé Maur.
254 D3 Babaçulândia Brazil
197 I3 Babadag Romania
199 F3 Babadağ Turkey
199 F3 Baba Dağ mt. Turkey
197 I3 Babadagului, Podişul plat. Romania
122 E2 Babadaykhan Akhal'skaya Oblast' Turkm.
122 E2 Babadaykhan Akhal'skaya Oblast' Turkm.
199 E1 Babaeski Turkey
199 G2 Babageçidin Tepesi mt. Turkey
250 B5 Babahoyo Ecuador
116 E3 Babai r. Nepal
106 E3 Babai Gaxun Nei Mongol China
127 G3 Bābā Jān Iran
129 D4 Babāk Azer.
92 C5 Babak Phil.
203 I6 Bāb al Mandab str. Africa/Asia
124 C5 Bāb al Mandab, Ra's c. Yemen
93 A3 Babana Sulawesi Selatan Indon.
215 H3 Babanango S. Africa
215 G3 Babangiboni mt. S. Africa
207 H5 Babanki Cameroon
208 E2 Babanusa Sudan
Babao Qinghai China see Qilian
108 C4 Babao Yunnan China
95 F4 Babat Jawa Timur Indon.
211 B6 Babati Tanz.
139 J2 Babayevo Rus. Fed.
137 H3 Babaykivka Ukr.
129 E2 Babayurt Rus. Fed.
150 D4 Babbacombe Bay England U.K.
87 B5 Babbage Island W.A. Austr.
164 F3 Babberich Neth.
92 □ Babeldaob i. Palau
215 G1 Babelegi S. Africa
Babelthuap i. Palau see Babeldaob
173 E3 Babenhausen Bayern Ger.
172 C2 Babenhausen Hessen Ger.
197 G3 Băbeni Romania
116 E4 Baberu Uttar Prad. India
175 H6 Babia Góra mt. Pol.
175 I1 Babiak Warmińsko-Mazurskie Pol.
174 G3 Babiak Wielkopolskie Pol.
108 B4 Babian Jiang r. Yunnan China
176 G2 Babice Czech Rep.
175 H5 Babice Pol.
127 G4 Bābil governorate Iraq
183 E4 Babilafuente Spain
174 D3 Babimost Pol.
85 F3 Babinda Qld Austr.
220 F4 Babine r. B.C. Can.
222 E4 Babine r. B.C. Can.
222 E4 Babine Range mts B.C. Can.
176 G5 Babócsa Hungary
122 C2 Bābol Iran
177 G4 Bábolna Hungary
122 C2 Bābol Sar Iran
214 B5 Baboon Point S. Africa
241 L6 Baboquivari Peak AZ U.S.A.
174 F5 Baborów Pol.
175 I3 Baboszewo Pol.
208 B3 Baboua C.A.R.
138 G5 Babruysk Belarus
138 D4 Babtai Lith.
Babu Guangxi China see Hexian
197 E5 Babuna Planina mts Macedonia
98 I1 Babushkin Rus. Fed.
197 F4 Babušnica Srbija Yugo.
92 A4 Babuyan Phil.
92 B2 Babuyan Channel Phil.
92 B2 Babuyan Islands Phil.
149 I4 Babworth Nottinghamshire, England U.K.
127 G4 Babylon tourist site Iraq
235 E2 Babylon NY U.S.A.
139 J4 Babynino Rus. Fed.
196 D3 Bač Vojvodina, Srbija Yugo.
210 E3 Bacaadweyn Somalia
250 D5 Bacaba r. Brazil
242 C3 Bacabáchi Mex.
254 D3 Bacabal Brazil
251 I5 Bacajá r. Brazil
126 C2 Bacakliyayla Tepesi mt. Turkey
243 H5 Bacalar Mex.
93 C3 Bacan i. Maluku Indon.
163 C6 Bacanère, Pic de mt. France
185 H3 Bacares Spain
92 B2 Bacarra Phil.
197 H2 Bacău Romania
157 G4 Baccarat France
191 H3 Bacchiglione r. Italy
190 D2 Baceno Italy
96 D2 Băc Giang Vietnam
173 G2 Bach an der Donau Ger.
169 C5 Bacharach Ger.
138 G4 Bacheykava Belarus
173 E3 Bachhagel Ger.
239 F6 Bachiniva Mex.
175 K6 Bachórz Pol.
110 B4 Bachu Xinjiang China
175 K3 Baciki Bliższe Pol.
85 E3 Back r. Qld Austr.
223 M1 Back r. N.W.T./Nunavut Can.
146 F2 Backaland Orkney, Scotland U.K.
196 D3 Bačka Palanka Vojvodina, Srbija Yugo.
196 D3 Bačka Topola Vojvodina, Srbija Yugo.
232 D5 Backbone Mountain MD U.S.A.
222 D2 Backbone Ranges mts N.W.T. Can.
140 L3 Backe Sweden
142 E2 Bäckefors Sweden
143 F2 Bäckhammar Sweden
177 H6 Bački Breg Vojvodina, Srbija Yugo.
177 H6 Bački Monoštor Vojvodina, Srbija Yugo.
196 D3 Bački Petrovac Vojvodina, Srbija Yugo.
172 D3 Backnang Ger.
196 E3 Bačko Gradište Vojvodina, Srbija Yugo.
175 J5 Baćkowice Pol.
82 D3 Backstairs Passage S.A. Austr.
150 E3 Backwell North Somerset, England U.K.
97 D5 Bac Liêu Vietnam
96 D2 Băc Ninh Vietnam
92 B2 Bacnotan Phil.
92 B3 Baco, Mount Mindoro Phil.
242 C2 Bacoachi Mex.
242 C3 Bacobampo Mex.
193 G4 Bacoli Italy
92 B4 Bacolod Phil.
Bacou, Pic de mt. France see Guerreys, Pic de
156 A3 Bacqueville-en-Caux France
177 I5 Bácsalmás Hungary
177 I5 Bácsbokod Hungary
177 I5 Bácsborsód Hungary
177 I5 Bács-Kiskun county Hungary
Bactra Afgh. see Balkh
177 I3 Bacúch Slovakia
149 G4 Bacup Lancashire, England U.K.
254 D2 Bacuri Brazil
236 C2 Bad r. SD U.S.A.
Bada Guangxi China see Xilin
210 C3 Bada mt. Eth.
173 G3 Bad Abbach Ger.
114 B4 Badagara Kerala India
173 G4 Bad Aibling Ger.
106 D3 Badain Jaran Shamo des. Nei Mongol China
251 F5 Badajós, Lago l. Brazil
184 D2 Badajoz Spain
184 D2 Badajoz prov. Extremadura Spain
123 G2 Badakhshān prov. Afgh.
Badakhshan aut. rep. Tajik. see Kŭhistoni Badakhshon
Badakhshoni Kŭhí aut. rep. Tajik. see Kŭhistoni Badakhshon
186 F3 Badalona Spain
190 C5 Badalucco Italy
183 G1 Bádames Spain
114 B3 Badami Karnataka India
127 F5 Badanah Saudi Arabia
Badaojiang Jilin China see Baishan
183 H2 Badarán Spain
Badarinath mts India see Badrinath Peaks
117 H4 Badarpur Assam India
179 E3 Bad Aussee Austria
227 F4 Bad Axe MI U.S.A.
169 C3 Bad Bentheim Ger.
168 C3 Badbergen Ger.
172 B2 Bad Bergzabern Ger.
171 C5 Bad Berka Ger.
169 D4 Bad Berleburg Ger.
171 C5 Bad Berneck im Fichtelgebirge Ger.
169 C5 Bad Bertrich Ger.
168 F2 Bad Bevensen Ger.
171 C4 Bad Bibra Ger.
173 H3 Bad Birnbach Ger.
171 C5 Bad Blankenburg Ger.
179 E4 Bad Bleiberg Austria
169 F5 Bad Bocklet Ger.
171 D5 Bad Brambach Ger.
168 E2 Bad Bramstedt Ger.
169 C5 Bad Breisig Ger.
169 E5 Bad Brückenau Ger.
172 D3 Bad Buchau Ger.
169 D5 Bad Camberg Ger.
146 C4 Badcaul Highland, Scotland U.K.
225 I4 Baddeck N.S. Can.
169 F3 Baddeckenstedt Ger.
123 F4 Baddo r. Pak.
170 C1 Bad Doberan Ger.
169 E4 Bad Driburg Ger.
171 D4 Bad Düben Ger.
172 C2 Bad Dürkheim Ger.
171 D4 Bad Dürrenberg Ger.
172 C3 Bad Dürrheim Ger.
171 C4 Badeborn Ger.
162 D3 Badefols-d'Ans France
169 E3 Bad Eilsen Ger.
171 D5 Bad Elster Ger.
Bademli Turkey see Aladağ
169 C5 Bad Ems Ger.
179 H2 Baden Austria
158 D4 Baden France
190 D1 Baden Switz.
186 B3 Badenas Spain
172 C3 Baden-Baden Ger.
169 D5 Bad Endbach Ger.
173 G4 Bad Endorf Ger.
169 F4 Badenhausen Ger.
146 D5 Badenoch reg. Scotland U.K.
146 F4 Badenscoth Aberdeenshire, Scotland U.K.
172 B4 Badenweiler Ger.
172 C3 Baden-Württemberg land Ger.
207 G3 Badér Niger
169 F4 Badersleben Ger.
192 A4 Badesi Sardegna Italy
169 D3 Bad Essen Ger.
173 G4 Bad Feilnbach Ger.
170 F3 Bad Freienwalde Ger.
172 D2 Bad Friedrichshall Ger.
173 H3 Bad Füssing Ger.
179 G4 Bad Gams Austria
169 F4 Bad Gandersheim Ger.
178 E3 Badgastein Austria
225 K3 Badger Nfld. Can.
123 E3 Bādghīs prov. Afgh.
179 G4 Bad Gleichenberg Austria
179 E3 Bad Goisern Austria
179 F2 Bad Großpertholz Austria
169 F4 Bad Grund (Harz) Ger.
179 F2 Bad Hall Austria
178 D3 Bad Häring Austria
169 F4 Bad Harzburg Ger.
173 F4 Bad Heilbrunn Ger.
172 C3 Bad Herrenalb Ger.
169 E5 Bad Hersfeld Ger.
164 D2 Badhoevedorp Neth.
178 E3 Bad Hofgastein Austria
169 D5 Bad Homburg vor der Höhe Ger.
169 C5 Bad Honnef Ger.
206 B4 Badi r. Guinea
191 G2 Badia Italy
191 G3 Badia Calavena Italy
187 F5 Badia Gran Spain
191 G3 Badia Polesine Italy
191 H5 Badia Tedalda Italy
169 D3 Bad Iburg Ger.
183 G4 Badiel r. Spain
210 B3 Badigeru Swamp Sudan
123 G5 Badin Pak.
177 I3 Badín Slovakia
242 D3 Badiraguato Mex.
179 E3 Bad Ischl Austria
126 E4 Bādiyat ash Shām des. Asia
Badje-Sohppar Sweden see Övre Soppero
169 E4 Bad Karlshafen Ger.
169 F5 Bad Kissingen Ger.
170 C2 Bad Kleinen Ger.
179 E4 Bad Kleinkirchheim Austria
171 C5 Bad Klosterlausnitz Ger.
173 F4 Bad Kohlgrub Ger.
172 D2 Bad König Ger.
Bad Königsdorff Pol. see Jastrzębie-Zdrój
169 F5 Bad Königshofen im Grabfeld Ger.
171 C4 Bad Kösen Ger.
179 F2 Bad Kreuzen Austria
172 B2 Bad Kreuznach Ger.
172 B4 Bad Krozingen Ger.
169 D5 Bad Laasphe Ger.
169 D3 Bad Laer Ger.
236 C2 Badlands reg. ND U.S.A.
236 C3 Badlands reg. SD U.S.A.
169 F4 Bad Langensalza Ger.
171 C4 Bad Lauchstädt Ger.
171 D4 Bad Lausick Ger.
169 F4 Bad Lauterberg im Harz Ger.
179 F2 Bad Leonfelden Austria
171 E4 Bad Liebenwerda Ger.
172 C3 Bad Liebenzell Ger.
169 D4 Bad Lippspringe Ger.
146 E3 Badlipster Highland, Scotland U.K.
172 D2 Bad Mergentheim Ger.
179 E3 Bad Mitterndorf Austria
169 E3 Bad Münder am Deister Ger.
172 B2 Bad Münster am Stein-Ebernburg Ger.
169 B5 Bad Münstereifel Ger.
171 F4 Bad Muskau Ger.
169 D5 Bad Nauheim Ger.
116 C5 Badnawar Madh. Prad. India
169 E3 Bad Nenndorf Ger.
169 C5 Bad Neuenahr-Ahrweiler Ger.
169 F5 Bad Neustadt an der Saale Ger.
169 D3 Bad Oeynhausen Ger.
195 F4 Badolato Italy
185 F3 Badolatosa Spain
168 F2 Bad Oldesloe Ger.
108 D2 Badong Hubei China
157 G4 Badonviller France
169 E5 Bad Orb Ger.
207 F5 Badou Togo
196 D3 Badovinci Srbija Yugo.
172 C3 Bad Peterstal Ger.
179 H2 Bad Pirawarth Austria
215 H1 Badplaas S. Africa
169 E4 Bad Pyrmont Ger.
179 G4 Bad Radkersburg Austria
190 E1 Bad Ragaz Switz.
172 D2 Bad Rappenau Ger.
173 G4 Bad Reichenhall Ger.
124 B3 Badr Hunayn Saudi Arabia
116 D3 Badrinath Peaks India
169 D3 Bad Rothenfelde Ger.
171 F3 Bad Saarow-Pieskow Ger.
169 F4 Bad Sachsa Ger.
172 B4 Bad Säckingen Ger.
179 F4 Bad St Leonhard im Lavanttal Austria
169 F3 Bad Salzdetfurth Ger.
169 E5 Bad Salzschlirf Ger.
169 D3 Bad Salzuflen Ger.
169 F5 Bad Salzungen Ger.
169 D4 Bad Sassendorf Ger.
179 E2 Bad Schallerbach Austria
171 F5 Bad Schandau Ger.
171 D4 Bad Schmiedeberg Ger.
172 C2 Bad Schönborn Ger.
172 D3 Bad Schussenried Ger.
169 D5 Bad Schwalbach Ger.
168 F2 Bad Schwartau Ger.
168 F2 Bad Segeberg Ger.
151 F2 Badsey Worcestershire, England U.K.
169 E5 Bad Soden-Salmünster Ger.
169 E4 Bad Sooden-Allendorf Ger.
171 C5 Bad Steben Ger.
171 C4 Bad Suderode Ger.
171 C4 Bad Sulza Ger.
170 D1 Bad Sülze Ger.
169 F4 Bad Tennstedt Ger.
173 F4 Bad Tölz Ger.
109 F3 Badu Fujian China
172 D3 Bad Überkingen Ger.
91 J9 Badu Island Qld Austr.
186 B3 Badules Spain
114 D5 Badulla Sri Lanka
172 D3 Bad Urach Ger.
114 C3 Badvel Andhra Prad. India
169 D5 Bad Vilbel Ger.
179 H3 Bad Vöslau Austria
172 D4 Bad Waldsee Ger.
179 H3 Bad Waltersdorf Austria
173 F4 Bad Wiessee Ger.
169 E4 Bad Wildungen Ger.
170 C3 Bad Wilsnack Ger.
172 D2 Bad Wimpfen Ger.
179 E2 Bad Wimsbach-Neydharting Austria
173 E2 Bad Windsheim Ger.
173 E4 Bad Wörishofen Ger.
172 D4 Bad Wurzach Ger.
179 F2 Bad Zell Austria
169 E4 Bad Zwesten Ger.
168 D2 Bad Zwischenahn Ger.
Bae Cinmel Conwy, Wales U.K. see Kinmel Bay
Bae Colwyn Conwy, Wales U.K. see Colwyn Bay
170 C2 Baek Ger.
142 C4 Bække Denmark
142 C3 Bækmarksbro Denmark
165 E4 Baelen Belgium
185 F3 Baena Spain
Bae Penrhyn Conwy, Wales U.K. see Penrhyn Bay
169 B5 Baesweiler Ger.
185 G3 Baeza Spain
207 H5 Bafang Cameroon
206 B3 Bafatá Guinea-Bissau
123 H3 Baffa Pak.
221 L2 Baffin Bay sea Can./Greenland
221 L3 Baffin Island Nunavut Can.
207 H5 Bafia Cameroon
207 F4 Bafilo Togo
206 C3 Bafing r. Guinea/Mali
164 F1 Baflo Neth.
206 C3 Bafoulabé Mali
207 H5 Bafoussam Cameroon
122 C4 Bāfq Iran
126 D2 Bafra Turkey
122 D4 Bāft Iran
208 E4 Bafwasende Dem. Rep. Congo
177 I4 Bag Hungary
186 E2 Bagà Spain
106 D2 Baga Bogd Uul mts Mongolia
117 F4 Bagaha Bihar India
95 G1 Bagahak hill Sabah Malaysia
195 E4 Bagaladi Italy
114 B2 Bagalkot Karnataka India
177 K4 Bagamér Hungary
211 C6 Bagamoyo Tanz.
121 I1 Bagan Rus. Fed.
92 C5 Baganga Phil.
94 C2 Bagansiapiapi Sumatera Indon.
190 F4 Baganza r. Italy
199 E3 Bağarası Turkey
161 C4 Bagard France
207 G3 Bagaroua Niger
209 C5 Bagata Dem. Rep. Congo
241 K4 Bagdad AZ U.S.A.
Bagdadi Georgia see Baghdat'i
258 G3 Bagé Brazil
160 C2 Bâgé-le-Châtel France
168 F1 Bagenkop Denmark
114 C3 Bagepalli Karnataka India
Bagerhat Bangl. see Bagherhat
163 E6 Bages France
116 D3 Bageshwar Uttar Prad. India
114 C2 Bagevadi Karnataka India
143 F2 Baggå Sweden
238 F3 Baggs WY U.S.A.
116 C5 Bagh Madh. Prad. India
Bagh a'Chaisteil Western Isles, Scotland U.K. see Castlebay
122 E2 Baghbaghū Iran
127 G4 Baghdād Iraq
127 G4 Baghdād governorate Iraq
129 C2 Baghdat'i Georgia
117 G5 Bagherhat Bangl.
194 C4 Bagheria Sicilia Italy
122 D4 Bāghīn Iran
123 G2 Baghlān Afgh.
123 G3 Baghlān prov. Afgh.
122 A2 Bāghlī Da hill Iran
129 C3 Baghramyan Armenia
150 D1 Bagillt Flintshire, Wales U.K.
129 A4 Bağırpaşa Dağı mts Turkey
Bağırsak Deresi r. Syria/Turkey see Sājūr, Nahr
129 B4 Bağlar Turkey
236 E2 Bagley MN U.S.A.
117 E3 Baglung Nepal
141 J3 Bagn Norway
191 G4 Bagnacavallo Italy
163 E4 Bagnac-sur-Célé France
195 E4 Bagnara Calabra Italy
190 E4 Bagnaria Italy
191 I3 Bagnaria Arsa Italy
190 D4 Bagnasco Italy
156 C4 Bagneaux-sur-Loing France
163 C5 Bagnères-de-Bigorre France
163 C6 Bagnères-de-Luchon France
190 E2 Bagni di Masino Italy
191 F2 Bagni di Rabbi Italy

191 G5 Bagno di Romagna Italy
159 F3 Bagnoles-de-l'Orne France
193 G3 Bagnoli del Trigno Italy
191 G3 Bagnoli di Sopra Italy
193 H4 Bagnoli Irpino Italy
191 F4 Bagnolo in Piano Italy
190 F3 Bagnolo Mella Italy
161 F3 Bagnolo Piemonte Italy
161 F3 Bagnolo San Vito Italy
161 E5 Bagnols-en-Forêt France
161 E5 Bagnols-les-Bains France
161 C4 Bagnols-sur-Cèze France
190 F4 Bagnone Italy
192 E2 Bagnoregio Italy
117 F4 Bagnuti r. Nepal
Bago Myanmar see Pegu
Bago admin. div. Myanmar see Pegu
92 B4 Bago Phil.
176 F5 Bago Hungary
206 D3 Bagoé r. Côte d'Ivoire/Mali
190 F3 Bagolino Italy
Bagong Guizhou China see Sansui
138 C4 Bagrationovsk Rus. Fed.
251 I5 Bagre Brazil
199 G3 Bağsaray Burdur Turkey
151 G3 Bagshot Surrey, England U.K.
254 C4 Baguelo Nigeria
186 B3 Baguena Spain
92 C5 Baguio Luzon Phil.
92 C5 Baguio Mindanao Phil.
Baguio see Begur
176 G4 Bágyogszovát Hungary
199 E2 Bağyurdu Turkey
207 H2 Bagzane, Monts mts Niger
183 G3 Bahabón de Esgueva Spain
111 C7 Bahadurganj Nepal
116 D3 Bahadurgarh Haryana India
Bahāmābād Iran see Rafsanjān
Bahamas country West Indies see The Bahamas
117 G4 Baharampur W. Bengal India
203 F3 Bahariya Oasis Egypt
137 I4 Bahatyr Ukr.
94 C2 Bahau r. Indon.
123 H4 Bahawalnagar Pak.
123 G4 Bahawalpur Pak.
128 B1 Bahçe Turkey
126 E3 Bahçe Turkey
108 C2 Ba He r. China
Bāherden Turkm. see Bakherden
116 D3 Bahi Tanz.
211 B6 Bahi Tanz.
Bahia Brazil see Salvador
257 G1 Bahia state Brazil
261 F6 Bahía Blanca Arg.
242 C2 Bahía Kino Mex.
253 F5 Bahía Negra Para.
242 B3 Bahía Tortugas Mex.
183 F2 Bahillo Spain
125 G3 Bahla Oman
197 H2 Bahlui r. Romania
122 B4 Bahmanshir, Khowr-e r. Iran
176 G3 Báhoň Slovakia
116 E4 Bahraich Uttar Prad. India
125 C2 Bahrain country Asia
125 E2 Bahrain, Gulf of Asia
122 B2 Bahrāmābād Iran
129 E4 Bahrāmtāpā Azer.
171 C3 Bahrdorf Ger.
210 A3 Bahr el Jebel state Sudan
116 D4 Bahrenborstel Ger.
116 D4 Bahror Rajasthan India
123 E5 Bāhū Kālāt Iran
139 H4 Bahushewsk Belarus
197 H2 Baia Suceava Romania
197 I3 Baia Tulcea Romania
197 F3 Baia de Aramă Romania
197 F2 Baia de Arieş Romania
177 L5 Baia de Criş Romania
193 I3 Baia della Zagare Italy
209 A9 Baía dos Tigres Angola
194 B3 Baia Farta Angola
197 F2 Baia Mare Romania
251 I5 Baião Brazil
182 B3 Baião Port.
197 F2 Baia Sprie Romania
194 B3 Baiata r. Sicilia Italy
208 B3 Baïbokoum Chad
Baicheng Henan China see Xiping
107 I2 Baicheng Jilin China
110 C3 Baicheng Xinjiang China
197 G3 Baicoi Romania
Baidoa Somalia see Baydhabo
109 F3 Baidu Guangdong China
Baie-aux-Feuilles Que. Can. see Tasiujaq
225 G2 Baie-Comeau Que. Can.
246 D3 Baie de Henne Haiti
Baie-du-Poste Que. Can. see Mistissini
225 I3 Baie-Johan-Beetz Que. Can.
172 D4 Baienfurt Ger.
173 C3 Baiersbronn Ger.
173 F2 Baiersdorf Ger.
225 G4 Baie-St-Paul Que. Can.
225 H3 Baie-Trinite Que. Can.
225 J3 Baie Verte Nfld. Can.
162 B3 Baigneux-Ste-Radegonde France
160 C1 Baigorrita Arg.
261 G4 Baigorria Arg.
107 H4 Baigou r. China
Baiguan Zhejiang China see Shangyu
109 E2 Baiguo Hubei China
183 I2 Baigura mt. Spain
108 A3 Baihanchang Yunnan China
116 C5 Baihar Madh. Prad. India
100 D4 Baihe Jilin China
109 E1 Bai He r. China
Baiji Iraq see Bayjī
116 D2 Baijnath Hima. Prad. India
116 D3 Baijnath Uttar Prad. India
111 E7 Baikunthpur Madh. Prad. India
117 E5 Baikunthpur Bihar India
107 I2 Bailang Nei Mongol China
149 H4 Baildon West Yorkshire, England U.K.
146 B3 Baile Ailein Western Isles, Scotland U.K.
Baile Átha Cliath Rep. of Ireland see Dublin
Baile Átha Luain Rep. of Ireland see Athlone
197 G3 Băile Govora Romania
197 F3 Băile Herculane Romania
Baile Mhártainn Western Isles, Scotland U.K. see Balmartin
185 G2 Băile Olăneşti Romania
197 G3 Băileşti Romania
197 F3 Băileştilor, Câmpia plain Romania
215 F4 Bailey S. Africa
87 D6 Bailey Range hills W.A. Austr.
232 B6 Baileyton TN U.S.A.
158 B3 Bailleau-le-Pin France
156 C2 Bailleul France
223 J1 Baillie r. Nunavut Can.
147 E3 Baillieborough Rep. of Ireland
155 E5 Baillonville Belgium
108 C2 Bailong Spain
108 C1 Bailong Jiang r. Gansu China
209 B8 Bailundo Angola
108 B1 Baima Qinghai China
Baima Xizang China see Baxoi
149 I4 Bainbridge North Yorkshire, England U.K.
111 E6 Bainang Xizang China
121 G4 Bairkum Kazakh.
231 G11 Bainbridge GA U.S.A.
233 F3 Bainbridge NY U.S.A.
234 B2 Bainbridge PA U.S.A.
172 E4 Baindt Ger.
114 B3 Bainduru Karnataka India

246 D3 Bainet Haiti
111 E6 Baingoin Xizang China
Baini Guizhou China see Yuqing
161 B3 Bains France
157 G4 Bains-les-Bains France
158 D4 Bains-sur-Oust France
149 I4 Bainton East Riding of Yorkshire, England U.K.
182 B1 Baio Grande Spain
182 B2 Baiona Spain
108 B1 Baiqên Qinghai China
100 C3 Baiquan Heilong. China
117 F4 Bairagnia Bihar India
237 D5 Baird TX U.S.A.
220 C3 Baird Mountains AK U.S.A.
77 H1 Bairiki Kiribati
107 H3 Bairin Youqi Nei Mongol China see Daban
Bairin Zuoqi Nei Mongol China see Lindong
83 F4 Bairnsdale Vic. Austr.
184 C2 Bairro dos Canaviais Port.
158 E3 Bais Bretagne France
159 F3 Bais Pays de la Loire France
92 B4 Bais Phil.
163 C4 Baïse r. France
108 C2 Baisha Chongqing China
108 D5 Baisha Hainan China
109 E3 Baisha Jiangxi China
108 D2 Baisha Sichuan China
Baishan Guangxi China see Mashan
100 C4 Baishan Jilin China
101 C4 Baishan Jilin China
107 F5 Baishui Shaanxi China
108 C3 Baishui Jiang r. Sichuan China
191 F4 Baiso Italy
197 F2 Băişoara Romania
138 D4 Baisogala Lith.
197 G2 Băiuţ Romania
161 C4 Baix France
184 A2 Baixa da Banheira Port.
163 E6 Baixas France
Baixi Sichuan China see Yibin
107 G4 Baixing Hebei China
107 I3 Baixing Nei Mongol China
257 G3 Baixo Guandu Brazil
209 C8 Baixo-Longa Angola
107 H4 Baiyang Dian resr China
110 E3 Baiyanghe Xinjiang China
Baiyashi Hunan China see Dong'an
106 E4 Baiyin Gansu China
108 A2 Baiyü Sichuan China
203 G5 Baiyuda Desert Sudan
242 B2 Baja Hungary
242 B2 Baja California pen. Mex.
242 B2 Baja California Norte state Mex.
242 B3 Baja California Sur state Mex.
122 B2 Bājalān Iran
243 E3 Bajan Mex.
117 G5 Baj Baj W. Bengal India
177 H4 Bajč Slovakia
124 C5 Bājil Yemen
196 D4 Bajina Bašta Srbija Yugo.
117 G4 Bajitpur Bangl.
196 C3 Bajmok Vojvodina, Srbija Yugo.
177 H4 Bajna Hungary
116 C5 Bajna Madh. Prad. India
242 J7 Bajo Boquete Panama
207 H4 Bajoga Nigeria
85 G4 Bajool Qld Austr.
163 F7 Bajou Hungary
163 E5 Bajoz r. Spain
117 F5 Bajrakot Orissa India
196 E4 Bajram Curri Albania
177 I6 Bajša Vojvodina, Srbija Yugo.
177 G4 Baka Slovakia
95 F3 Baka, Bukit mt. Indon.
208 D3 Baka C.A.R.
175 K1 Bakałarzewo Pol.
134 K5 Bakaly Rus. Fed.
121 I3 Bakanas Kazakh.
193 J3 Bakar Croatia
206 A3 Bakau Gambia
95 G2 Bakayan, Gunung mt. Indon.
137 G2 Bakayivka Ukr.
164 E3 Bakel Neth.
206 B3 Bakel Senegal
241 I4 Baker CA U.S.A.
238 D2 Baker ID U.S.A.
237 F6 Baker LA U.S.A.
238 F2 Baker MT U.S.A.
241 I2 Baker OR U.S.A.
238 C2 Baker OR U.S.A.
232 D5 Baker WV U.S.A.
238 B1 Baker, Mount vol. WA U.S.A.
241 L4 Baker Butte mt. AZ U.S.A.
77 I1 Baker Island N. Pacific Ocean
223 M1 Baker Lake salt flat W.A. Austr.
223 M1 Baker Lake Nunavut Can.
223 M1 Baker Lake l. Nunavut Can.
233 O11 Baker Lake l. ME U.S.A.
107 I7 Bal'dzhikan Rus. Fed.
85 G4 Bakers Creek Qld Austr.
240 H4 Bakersfield CA U.S.A.
231 D8 Bakersville NC U.S.A.
215 F1 Bakerville S. Africa
149 H4 Bakewell Derbyshire, England U.K.
125 G2 Bakhā Oman
122 D2 Bākhārz mts Iran
Bakhchisaray Ukr. see Bakhchysaray
137 G5 Bakhchysaray Ukr.
122 D2 Bakherden Turkm.
100 D2 Bakhirevo Rus. Fed.
137 G2 Bakhmach Ukr.
Bakhmut r. Ukr. see Artemivs'k
Bākhtarān Iran see Kermānshāh
Bākhtarān prov. Iran see Kermānshāh
122 C4 Bakhtegan, Daryācheh-ye l. Iran
117 F4 Bakhtiyarpur Bihar India
121 J3 Bakhty Kazakh.
251 G2 Bakhuis Gebergte mts Suriname
129 E3 Bakı Azer.
183 H1 Bakio Spain
199 E2 Bakır r. Manisa Turkey
199 E2 Bakır r. Turkey
199 F1 Bakırköy Turkey
129 F3 Bakıxanov Azer.
140 D2 Bakkaflói b. Iceland
159 F3 Baconnière France
116 C4 Bako Côte d'Ivoire
210 B3 Bako Oromia Eth.
210 C3 Bako S. Nations Eth.
177 H4 Bakonszeg Hungary
176 F4 Bakony hills Hungary
176 F5 Bakonynána Hungary
177 G4 Bakonyszentkirály Hungary
177 G4 Bakonyszentlászló Hungary
176 F4 Bakonyszombathely Hungary
210 D4 Bakool admin. reg. Somalia
207 G4 Bakori Nigeria
208 D3 Bakouma C.A.R.
208 B3 Bakoumba Gabon
179 H1 Bakov nad Jizerou Czech Rep.
206 C3 Bakoy r. Mali
129 C2 Baksan Rus. Fed.
129 C2 Baksanenok Rus. Fed.
177 H4 Baktalórántháza Hungary
Baku Azer. see Bakı
168 D3 Bakum Ger.
129 C3 Bakuriani Georgia
262 P2 Bakutis Coast Antarctica
131 P3 Baky Uyandino r. Rus. Fed.
126 E3 Balâ Turkey
150 D2 Bala Gwynedd, Wales U.K.
252 C3 Bala, Cerros de mts Bol.

92 A5 Balabac i. Phil.
95 G1 Balabac Strait Malaysia/Phil.
95 G3 Balabalangan, Kepulauan atolls Indon.
199 E1 Balabanık Turkey
139 K4 Balabanovo Rus. Fed.
78 □5 Balabio i. New Caledonia
137 H4 Balabyne Ukr.
197 H3 Bălăceanu Romania
197 F3 Bălăciţa Romania
246 □ Balaclava Jamaica
127 G4 Balad Iraq
122 B2 Baladeh Iran
116 E5 Balaghat Madh. Prad. India
116 D4 Balaghat Range hills India
186 D3 Balaguer Spain
122 D4 Balā Howz Iran
94 C2 Balaipungut Sumatera Indon.
163 B6 Balaïtous mt. France
211 B8 Balaka Malawi
138 ? Balaka Azer.
134 H4 Balakhna Rus. Fed.
139 I4 Balakirevo Rus. Fed.
82 D3 Balaklava S.A. Austr.
137 G5 Balaklava Ukr.
Balakleya Ukr. see Balakliya
137 I3 Balakliya Ukr.
120 A1 Balakovo Rus. Fed.
213 H2 Balama Moz.
157 J3 Balan Champagne-Ardenne France
160 D3 Balan Rhône-Alpes France
116 B4 Baladoran India
197 G2 Bălan Romania
243 H5 Balancán Mex.
Balanda Rus. Fed. see Kalininsk
199 F3 Balan Dağı hill Turkey
137 F3 Balandyne Ukr.
136 E4 Bălăneşti Moldova
92 B3 Balanga Phil.
117 E5 Balangir Orissa India
114 D5 Balangoda Sri Lanka
83 F4 Balaram W. Bengal India
161 B5 Baruc-les-Bains France
93 B3 Balase r. Indon.
197 H2 Bălăşeşti Romania
120 B2 Balashi Rus. Fed.
139 I6 Balashov Rus. Fed.
135 H5 Balashov Rus. Fed.
116 C5 Balasinor Gujarat India
177 I3 Balassagyarmat Hungary
77 J5 Balástya Hungary
199 E3 Balat l. Hungary
177 G5 Balaton l. Hungary
Balaton, Lake Hungary see Balaton
177 H4 Balatonalmádi Hungary
177 G5 Balatonboglár Hungary
177 G5 Balatonföldvár Hungary
177 G5 Balatonfüred Hungary
177 G5 Balatonfűzfő Hungary
177 G5 Balatonkenese Hungary
177 G5 Balatonkeresztúr Hungary
177 G5 Balatonlelle Hungary
177 G5 Balatonszabadi Hungary
177 G5 Balatonszemes Hungary
177 G5 Balatonszentgyörgy Hungary
177 H5 Balatonvilágos Hungary
185 H2 Balazote Spain
138 D4 Balbieriškis Lith.
160 C3 Balbigny France
251 G5 Balbina, Represa de resr Brazil
146 D4 Balblair Highland, Scotland U.K.
147 E3 Balbriggan Rep. of Ireland
147 E2 Balc Romania
210 E4 Balcad Somalia
82 D2 Balcanoona S.A. Austr.
261 H5 Balcarce Arg.
197 I4 Balchik Bulg.
199 E2 Balçıkhisar Turkey
128 A1 Balcis Turkey
81 B7 Balclutha South I. N.Z.
149 I4 Balcombe West Sussex, England U.K.
149 I4 Balderton Nottinghamshire, England U.K.
87 C7 Bald Head hd W.A. Austr.
257 F3 Baldim Brazil
237 F5 Bald Knob AR U.S.A.
232 C6 Bald Knob WV U.S.A.
241 J3 Bald Mountain NV U.S.A.
151 G3 Baldock Hertfordshire, England U.K.
179 H4 Baldramsdorf Austria
151 H4 Baldslow East Sussex, England U.K.
192 B3 Baldu r. Sardegna Italy
221 H3 Baldwin Can.
221 G4 Baldwin FL U.S.A.
226 C4 Baldwin MI U.S.A.
226 A3 Baldwin WI U.S.A.
233 F3 Baldwinsville NY U.S.A.
233 G3 Baldwinville MA U.S.A.
223 G5 Baldy Mountain hill Man. Can.
241 M5 Baldy Peak AZ U.S.A.
Bâle Switz. see Basel
206 C3 Baléa Mali
187 E5 Baleares, Islas is Spain
Baleares Insulae is Spain see Baleares, Islas
Balearic Islands is Spain see Baleares, Islas
82 □1 Ball's Pyramid i. Lord Howe I. Austr.
169 F2 Balge Ger.
206 C3 Bali Mali
92 □ Baler Phil.
184 C2 Baleizão Port.
146 B5 Balemartine Argyll and Bute, Scotland U.K.
165 E3 Balen Belgium
197 G3 Băleni Romania
92 B3 Baler Phil.
185 J4 Balerma Spain
146 E3 Baleshare i. Scotland U.K.
117 F5 Baleshwar Orissa India
142 B1 Balestrand Norway
194 E4 Balestrate Sicilia Italy
134 H4 Balezino Rus. Fed.
242 □16 Balfate Hond.
85 F4 Balfe's Creek Qld Austr.
222 □ Balfour Can.
215 H3 Balfour S. Africa
146 F1 Balfour Orkney, Scotland U.K.
146 D5 Balfron Stirling, Scotland U.K.
106 C2 Balgatay Mongolia
168 D2 Balge Ger.
86 C3 Balgo W.A. Austr.
146 B2 Balgown Highland, Scotland U.K.
193 K4 Balgy Croatia
125 C2 Bali Rajasthan India
95 F5 Bali i. Indon.
95 F5 Bali, Laut sea chan. Indon.
207 I4 Bali Cameroon
116 D4 Baliapal Orissa India
199 E3 Balıbey Turkey
95 F3 Balıkesir Turkey
199 E2 Balıkesir Turkey
126 E3 Balıkesir prov. Turkey
127 H5 Balıkh r. Syria/Turkey
199 E1 Balıklıçeşme Turkey
199 E2 Balıklıova Turkey
95 G3 Balikpapan Kalimantan Timur Indon.
197 G3 Bâlileşti Romania
92 A1 Balili Phil.
91 J8 Balimo P.N.G.
107 I1 Balin Nei Mongol China
143 M2 Bälinge Sweden
172 E3 Balingen Ger.
95 F2 Balingian Sarawak Malaysia
95 F2 Balingian r. Sarawak Malaysia
147 F3 Balinoe Phil.
92 B2 Balintang Channel Phil.

146 E4 Balintore Highland, Scotland U.K.
95 F4 Bali Sea Indon.
256 A2 Baliza Brazil
168 D2 Balje Ger.
124 C4 Baljurshi Saudi Arabia
164 E2 Balk Neth.
Balkan Mountains Bulg./Yugo. see Stara Planina
Balkan Oblast admin. div. Turkm. see Balkanskaya Oblast'
122 C2 Balkanabat Turkm.
122 C2 Balkanskaya Oblast' admin. div. Turkm.
177 K4 Balkány Hungary
121 G5 Balkashino Kazakh.
164 F2 Balkbrug Neth.
123 F2 Balkh Afgh.
123 F2 Balkh prov. Afgh.
123 F2 Balkh r. Afgh.
121 H3 Balkhash Kazakh.
Balkhash, Lake Kazakh. see Balkhash, Ozero
121 H3 Balkhash, Ozero l. Kazakh.
114 C2 Balkonda Andhra Prad. India
120 A3 Balkuduk Kazakh.
190 E3 Ballabio Italy
146 D5 Ballachulish Highland, Scotland U.K.
87 D7 Balladonia W.A. Austr.
83 G2 Balladoran N.S.W. Austr.
147 C3 Ballaghaderreen Rep. of Ireland
156 C4 Ballancourt-sur-Essonne France
140 L1 Ballangen Norway
159 G4 Ballan-Miré France
238 E2 Ballantine MT U.S.A.
146 D6 Ballantrae South Ayrshire, Scotland U.K.
199 F3 Ballangir Orissa India
83 E2 Ballandean N.S.W. Austr.
82 B5 Ballarat Vic. Austr.
87 D6 Ballard, Lake salt flat W.A. Austr.
114 C2 Ballarpur Mahar. India
146 E4 Ballater Aberdeenshire, Scotland U.K.
206 C3 Ballé Mali
159 F4 Ballée France
146 E5 Ballenleuch Law hill Scotland U.K.
263 K2 Balleny Islands Antarctica
159 F2 Balleroy France
261 E3 Ballesteros Arg.
117 F4 Ballia Uttar Prad. India
148 B5 Ballickmoyler Rep. of Ireland
83 H2 Ballina N.S.W. Austr.
147 B2 Ballina Rep. of Ireland
147 D3 Ballinaboy Rep. of Ireland
147 D3 Ballinafad Rep. of Ireland
147 D3 Ballinagh Rep. of Ireland
147 E5 Ballinakill Rep. of Ireland
147 E3 Ballinalack Rep. of Ireland
147 E3 Ballinalee Rep. of Ireland
147 D4 Ballinamallard Northern Ireland U.K.
147 D3 Ballinameen Rep. of Ireland
147 D3 Ballinamore Rep. of Ireland
147 D4 Ballinamuck Rep. of Ireland
147 E3 Ballinascarthy Rep. of Ireland
147 C3 Ballinasloe Rep. of Ireland
147 D4 Ballincollig Rep. of Ireland
147 E2 Ballinderreen Rep. of Ireland
147 E2 Ballinderry r. Northern Ireland U.K.
147 E2 Ballinderry Northern Ireland U.K.
259 C7 Balmaceda Chile
147 D3 Ballindine Rep. of Ireland
147 D3 Ballindooly Rep. of Ireland
147 D3 Ballineen Rep. of Ireland
147 C4 Ballingarry Limerick Rep. of Ireland
147 E4 Ballingarry Tipperary Rep. of Ireland
147 C4 Ballingeary Rep. of Ireland
237 D6 Ballinger TX U.S.A.
146 E5 Ballingry Fife, Scotland U.K.
147 E4 Ballingurteen Rep. of Ireland
147 D3 Ballinhassig Rep. of Ireland
147 D4 Ballinlough Rep. of Ireland
190 D3 Ballino Italy
147 C3 Ballinrobe Rep. of Ireland
147 B4 Ballinruan Rep. of Ireland
147 D5 Ballinskelligs Rep. of Ireland
147 B5 Ballinskelligs Bay Rep. of Ireland
147 E5 Ballintober Rep. of Ireland
146 D5 Ballintoy Northern Ireland U.K.
147 E4 Ballintra Rep. of Ireland
147 D3 Ballon France
159 F3 Ballon France
147 D5 Ballon d'Alsace mt. France
177 L5 Ballószög Hungary
159 E4 Ballots France
198 B1 Ballsh Albania
82 □ Ball's Pyramid i. Lord Howe I. Austr.
169 F4 Ballstadt Ger.
233 G3 Ballston Spa NY U.S.A.
164 E1 Ballum Neth.
147 C2 Ballure Rep. of Ireland
234 E4 Bally PA U.S.A.
146 D5 Ballybay Rep. of Ireland
147 D2 Ballybofey Rep. of Ireland
147 E2 Ballyboghill Northern Ireland U.K.
147 E3 Ballybogy Northern Ireland U.K.
147 E4 Ballybrack Dublin Rep. of Ireland
147 A5 Ballybrack Kerry Rep. of Ireland
147 D4 Ballybrophy Rep. of Ireland
147 E4 Ballybunnion Rep. of Ireland
147 E5 Ballycahill Rep. of Ireland
147 E2 Ballycallan Rep. of Ireland
147 E2 Ballycanew Rep. of Ireland
147 D4 Ballycarney Rep. of Ireland
147 F2 Ballycarry Northern Ireland U.K.
147 E2 Ballycastle Rep. of Ireland
147 E1 Ballycastle Northern Ireland U.K.
147 F2 Ballyclare Northern Ireland U.K.
147 E2 Ballyconneely Rep. of Ireland
147 F3 Ballyconnell Cavan Rep. of Ireland
147 E2 Ballyconnell Sligo Rep. of Ireland
147 E4 Ballycotton Rep. of Ireland
134 J4 Ballycroy Rep. of Ireland
147 B3 Ballycumber Rep. of Ireland
147 E2 Ballydangan Rep. of Ireland
147 D4 Ballydavid Rep. of Ireland
147 E4 Ballydehob Rep. of Ireland
147 E4 Ballydesmond Rep. of Ireland
147 D4 Ballyduff Kerry Rep. of Ireland
147 D5 Ballyduff Waterford Rep. of Ireland
147 B4 Ballyfarnan Rep. of Ireland
147 E2 Ballyfeard Rep. of Ireland
147 E4 Ballyfin Rep. of Ireland
147 E2 Ballygalley Northern Ireland U.K.
147 D4 Ballygar Rep. of Ireland
147 D3 Ballygawley Northern Ireland U.K.
147 D2 Ballyglass Mayo Rep. of Ireland
147 B3 Ballyglass Mayo Rep. of Ireland
147 F2 Ballygowan Northern Ireland U.K.
147 E2 Ballygrant Argyll and Bute, Scotland U.K.
146 B5 Ballygrant Argyll and Bute, Scotland U.K.
147 D3 Ballyhack Rep. of Ireland
147 E4 Ballyhahill Rep. of Ireland
147 C4 Ballyhaise Rep. of Ireland
147 D3 Ballyhalbert Northern Ireland U.K.
147 F2 Ballyhaunis Rep. of Ireland

147 B4 Ballyheigue Rep. of Ireland
147 C4 Ballyhooly Rep. of Ireland
147 F2 Ballyhornan U.K.
147 C4 Ballyhoura Mountains hills Rep. of Ireland
147 E5 Ballyjamesduff Rep. of Ireland
147 D3 Ballykeeran Rep. of Ireland
147 D2 Ballykelly Northern Ireland U.K.
147 C3 Ballylanders Rep. of Ireland
147 E2 Ballyleague Rep. of Ireland
148 C3 Ballyleny Northern Ireland U.K.
147 D3 Ballyliffen Rep. of Ireland
147 B4 Ballylongford Rep. of Ireland
147 D4 Ballylynan Rep. of Ireland
147 D4 Ballymacarbry Rep. of Ireland
147 E5 Ballymacelligott Rep. of Ireland
147 B4 Ballymack Rep. of Ireland
148 D3 Ballymackilroy Northern Ireland U.K.
147 D4 Ballymacmague Rep. of Ireland
147 D2 Ballymacoda Rep. of Ireland
147 D2 Ballymagorry Rep. of Ireland
147 D4 Ballymahon Rep. of Ireland
147 B4 Ballymakeery Rep. of Ireland
147 F2 Ballymartin Northern Ireland U.K.
147 E2 Ballymena Northern Ireland U.K.
147 E1 Ballymoe Rep. of Ireland
147 D1 Ballymoney Rep. of Ireland
147 D1 Ballymore Donegal Rep. of Ireland
147 E3 Ballymore Westmeath Rep. of Ireland
147 D3 Ballymote Rep. of Ireland
147 E5 Ballymurphy Rep. of Ireland
147 F2 Ballymurray Rep. of Ireland
147 E4 Ballynacarriga Rep. of Ireland
147 B3 Ballynacarrigy Rep. of Ireland
148 D3 Ballynafid Rep. of Ireland
147 D3 Ballynahinch Rep. of Ireland
147 F3 Ballynahinch Northern Ireland U.K.
147 E4 Ballynahow Rep. of Ireland
147 C4 Ballynahown Rep. of Ireland
147 D3 Ballynamona Rep. of Ireland
147 C4 Ballynaskreena Rep. of Ireland
147 E2 Ballyneety Rep. of Ireland
147 E2 Ballynockan Rep. of Ireland
147 D3 Ballynoe Rep. of Ireland
147 E2 Ballynure Northern Ireland U.K.
147 C4 Ballyporeen Rep. of Ireland
147 E4 Ballyragget Rep. of Ireland
147 E2 Ballyronan Northern Ireland U.K.
259 C7 Balmaceda Chile
147 D3 Ballyroon Rep. of Ireland
147 B4 Ballyshannon Rep. of Ireland
147 C2 Ballysteen Rep. of Ireland
147 B4 Ballyteige Bay Rep. of Ireland
147 E4 Ballytore Rep. of Ireland
147 E4 Ballyvaughan Rep. of Ireland
147 B3 Ballyvoy Northern Ireland U.K.
147 E1 Ballyvoyle Rep. of Ireland
147 D5 Ballywalter Northern Ireland U.K.
147 F3 Ballyward Northern Ireland U.K.
147 E3 Ballywilliam Rep. of Ireland
146 C4 Balmacara Highland, Scotland U.K.
146 D5 Balmaha Stirling, Scotland U.K.
146 A3 Balmartin Western Isles, Scotland U.K.
183 P3 Balmaseda Spain
177 K4 Balmazújváros Hungary
146 F3 Balmedie Aberdeenshire, Scotland U.K.
261 F2 Balnearia Arg.
190 D3 Balocco Italy
123 F4 Balochistan prov. Pak.
119 H4 Balochistan prov. Pak.
116 E5 Balod Madh. Prad. India
117 E5 Baloda Madh. Prad. India
116 E5 Baloda Bazar Madh. Prad. India
176 F4 Balogunyom Hungary
209 B8 Balombo Angola
83 G2 Balonne r. Qld Austr.
116 C4 Balotra Rajasthan India
129 Balow Ger.
121 I3 Balpyk Bi Kazakh.
Balqash Kazakh. see Balkhash
Balqash Köli l. Kazakh. see Balkhash, Ozero
146 D5 Balquhidder Stirling, Scotland U.K.
234 D5 Bally PA U.S.A.
116 E4 Balrampur Uttar Prad. India
83 F3 Balranald N.S.W. Austr.
116 E5 Balrath Rep. of Ireland
147 E2 Balrothery Rep. of Ireland
197 G3 Balş Romania
185 Balsa de Ves Spain
227 I2 Balsam Creek Ont. Can.
226 A2 Balsam Lake WI U.S.A.
187 B7 Balsa Pintada Spain
250 B6 Balsapuerto Peru
186 C3 Balsareny Spain
254 C5 Balsas Brazil
254 D5 Balsas, Rio das r. Brazil
139 H5 Bal'shavik Belarus
187 B7 Balsicas Spain
193 Q6 Balsorano Italy
143 N3 Bålsta Sweden
141 L6 Balsthal Switz.
136 H1 Balta Ukr.
197 H2 Balta Berilovac Srbija Yugo.
183 R3 Baltanás Spain
197 Bălteni Romania
146 H1 Baltasound Shetland, Scotland U.K.
120 A1 Baltay Rus. Fed.
136 E1 Bălţi Moldova
143 L5 Baltic Sea g. Europe
203 F2 Baltîm Egypt
147 C5 Baltimore Rep. of Ireland
215 G3 Baltimore S. Africa
234 B6 Baltimore MD U.S.A.
234 B6 Baltimore City county MD U.S.A.
234 A5 Baltimore County county MD U.S.A.
234 A6 Baltimore Highlands MD U.S.A.
116 D2 Baltit Jammu and Kashmir
175 K1 Baltiysk Rus. Fed.
175 L1 Baltiyskaya Kosa spit Rus. Fed.
138 F6 Baltoji Vokė Lith.
175 L5 Baltów Pol.
116 C2 Baltoro Glacier Jammu and Kashmir
175 J4 Bałtów Pol.
197 Bălușeni Romania
174 E4 Balve Ger.
244 A2 Baluarte r. Mex.
123 I9 Baluch Ab well Iran
122 B4 Baluchestan va Sīstān prov. Iran
Baluchistan reg. Pak. see Balochistan

117 F5 Balumath Bihar India
82 D3 Balumbah S.A. Austr.
138 F3 Balupe r. Latvia
95 Baluran, Gunung mt. Indon.
121 G4 Balughat W. Bengal India
122 C3 Baluţ i. Iran
193 H4 Balvano Italy
140 Balvatnet l. Norway
199 G3 Balya Turkey
107 I1 Balyaga Rus. Fed.
120 B3 Balykchy Kyrg.
106 C1 Balykshi Kazakh.
250 D5 Balza Ecuador
172 A4 Balzers Liechtenstein
122 D4 Bam Kermān Iran
122 D2 Bām Iran
108 C2 Bama Guangxi China
207 I4 Bama Nigeria
85 F4 Bamaga Qld Austr.
206 D3 Bamako Mali
208 C3 Bamba r. C.A.R.
206 D3 Bamba Mali
208 B5 Bamba Congo
92 B2 Bambang Phil.
209 D9 Bambangando Angola
208 D3 Bambari C.A.R.
173 K2 Bamberg Ger.
231 D6 Bamberg SC U.S.A.
235 I2 Bamber Lake NJ U.S.A.
206 A3 Bambey Senegal
208 C4 Bambio C.A.R.
215 H4 Bamboesberg mts S. Africa
86 D4 Bamboo Creek W.A. Austr.
206 C4 Bambouk reg. Mali
208 B2 Bambouti C.A.R.
149 H2 Bamburgh Northumberland, England U.K.
209 D6 Bambuí Brazil
207 H5 Bamenda Cameroon
222 E5 Bamfield B.C. Can.
123 F3 Bāmīān Afgh.
123 F3 Bāmīān prov. Afgh.
208 C2 Bamingui C.A.R.
208 C2 Bamingui r. C.A.R.
208 C2 Bamingui-Bangoran pref. C.A.R.
123 F2 Bamiyan r. Afgh.
172 E2 Bammental Ger.
208 C2 Bamori Mex.
116 D4 Bamor Madh. Prad. India
123 E5 Bam Posht, Kûh-e mts Iran
150 C4 Bampton Devon, England U.K.
151 F3 Bampton Oxfordshire, England U.K.
122 E5 Bampûr Iran
122 E3 Bamrûd Iran
84 C2 Bamyili N.T. Austr.
206 E3 Ban Burkina
132 G3 Bana Hungary
77 P2 Banaba i. Kiribati
254 F3 Banabuiu, Açude resr Brazil
260 C3 Bañados del Atuel marsh Arg.
253 E4 Bañados del Izozog swamp Bol.
253 F4 Bañados de Otuquis marsh Bol.
92 B3 Banahao, Mount vol. Luzon Phil.
206 D3 Banamba Mali
108 C2 Banan Chongqing China
85 G5 Banana Qld Austr.
254 C4 Bananal, Ilha do i. Brazil
115 B2 Banapur Orissa India
192 A4 Banari Sardegna Italy
199 E1 Banarlı Turkey
161 B4 Banassac France
196 E3 Banatski Karlovac Vojvodina, Srbija Yugo.
177 J5 Banatsko Aranđelovac Vojvodina, Srbija Yugo.
196 D3 Banatsko Veliko Selo Vojvodina, Srbija Yugo.
199 F3 Banaz Turkey
199 F3 Banaz r. Turkey
111 H5 Banbar Xizang China
147 E2 Banbridge Northern Ireland U.K.
151 F2 Banbury Oxfordshire, England U.K.
197 H2 Banca Romania
191 G5 Ban Chiang tourist site Thai.
146 F3 Banchory Aberdeenshire, Scotland U.K.
224 E4 Bancroft Ont. Can.
Bancroft Zambia see Chililabombwe
207 I4 Banda Cameroon
116 D4 Banda Madh. Prad. India
116 E4 Banda Uttar Prad. India
94 A1 Banda Aceh Sumatera Indon.
93 B5 Banda, Kepulauan is Indon.
94 B2 Bandahara, Gunung mt. Indon.
206 D3 Bandama r. Côte d'Ivoire
206 D4 Bandama Blanc r. Côte d'Ivoire
123 E3 Bandān Kūh mts Iran
116 E5 Bandanwara Rajasthan India
116 E5 Bāndarban Bangl.
122 D5 Bandar-e ‘Abbās Iran
122 B3 Bandar-e Anzalī Iran
122 C4 Bandar-e Deylam Iran
122 C4 Bandar-e Emām Khomeynī Iran
122 C4 Bandar-e Lengeh Iran
122 C4 Bandar-e Maqām Iran
122 C4 Bandar-e Ma'shur Iran
122 D5 Bandar-e Moghūyeh Iran
Bandar-e Pahlavī Iran see Bandar-e Anzalī
122 D5 Bandar-e Rig Iran
122 C4 Bandar-e Torkeman Iran
Bandar Lampung Sumatera Indon. see Tanjungkarang-Telukbetung
116 E3 Bandarpunch mt. Uttar Prad. India
95 F1 Bandar Seri Begawan Brunei
93 C5 Banda Sea Indon.
256 D2 Bandeira Brazil
216 Bandeiras, Pico Azores
261 Bandera Arg.
244 D5 Banderas, Bahía b. Mex.
245 I7 Banderilla Mex.
116 C4 Bandi r. Rajasthan India
116 D3 Bandikui Rajasthan India
123 F4 Bandīni Jammu and Kashmir
122 D2 Band-e Amīr r. Afgh.
123 F3 Band-i-Baba mts Afgh.
114 C4 Bandipur Karnataka India
199 E1 Bandırma Turkey
147 C5 Bandon r. Rep. of Ireland

147 C5 Bandon r. Rep. of Ireland
238 A3 Bandon OR U.S.A.
113 □1 Bandos i. N. Male Maldives
217 □3b Bandraboua Mayotte
217 □3b Bandrélé Mayotte
209 C6 Bandundu Dem. Rep. Congo
209 C6 Bandundu prov. Dem. Rep. Congo
95 D4 Bandung Jawa Barat Indon.
87 B6 Bandya W.A. Austr.
197 G3 Băneasa Romania
197 H3 Băneasa Romania
122 A2 Bāneh Iran
246 D2 Banes Cuba
222 G4 Banff Alta. Can.
146 F4 Banff Aberdeenshire, Scotland U.K.
206 D3 Banfora Burkina
95 G4 Banga, Gunung mt. Indon.
209 B7 Banga Angola
209 D6 Banga Dem. Rep. Congo
92 C5 Banga Phil.
92 C5 Banga r. Phil.
114 C3 Bangalore Karnataka India
83 H2 Bangalow N.S.W. Austr.
114 C3 Banganapalle Andhra Prad. India
116 D4 Banganga r. India
207 H5 Bangangté Cameroon
117 G4 Bangaon W. Bengal India
95 F1 Bangar Brunei
92 B2 Bangar Phil.
117 G5 Bangara r. Bangl.
114 C3 Bangarapet Karnataka India
208 D3 Bangassou C.A.R.
96 C3 Bangfai, Xé r. Laos
95 H2 Banggai, Kepulauan is Indon.
95 G3 Banggai Sulawesi Indon.
95 G1 Banggi i. Sabah Malaysia
202 D1 Banghāzī Libya
96 D3 Banghiang, Xé r. Laos
95 E3 Bangka i. Indon.
94 D3 Bangka i. Indon.
95 F4 Bangka, Selat sea chan. Indon.
95 G2 Bangkalan Jawa Timur Indon.
94 D4 Bangkinang Sumatera Indon.
95 E3 Bangko Sumatera Indon.
97 C4 Bangkok Thai.
97 C4 Bangkok, Bight of b. Thai.
Bangla state India see West Bengal
117 G5 Bangladesh country Asia
108 A4 Bangma Shan mts Yunnan China
96 B2 Bang Mun Nak Thai.
140 K2 Bångnäs Sweden
206 D3 Bangolo Côte d'Ivoire
150 C1 Bangor Gwynedd, Wales U.K.
147 F2 Bangor Northern Ireland U.K.
233 O2 Bangor ME U.S.A.
226 C4 Bangor MI U.S.A.
234 D2 Bangor PA U.S.A.
117 F5 Bangriposi Orissa India
241 L5 Bangs, Mount AZ U.S.A.
96 B2 Bang Saphan Yai Thai.
92 B2 Bangued Phil.
208 C3 Bangui C.A.R.
92 B1 Bangui Phil.
211 B8 Bangula Malawi
94 B2 Banguru Sumatera Indon.
209 F7 Bangweulu, Lake Zambia
Banhā Egypt see Benha
151 I2 Banham Norfolk, England U.K.
96 C2 Ban Houayxay Laos
Ban Houei Sai Laos see Ban Houayxay
246 E3 Baní Dom. Rep.
206 D3 Bani r. Mali
207 H3 Bani C.A.R.
204 C3 Bani, Jbel ridge Morocco
208 C3 Bania C.A.R.
207 F3 Bani-Bangou Niger
246 E3 Bánica Dom. Rep.
175 J3 Banie Pol.
175 K3 Banie Mazurskie Pol.
206 D3 Banifing r. Mali
122 C3 Bani Forūr, Jazīreh-ye i. Iran
124 D4 Bani Khaṭmah reg. Saudi Arabia
124 D4 Banī Ma'ārid des. Saudi Arabia
125 D3 Banī Mukassir des. Saudi Arabia
Banī Suwayf Egypt see Beni Suef
197 F2 Băniţa Romania
232 D6 Banister r. VA U.S.A.
196 B3 Banja Srbija Yugo.
196 C3 Banja Luka Bos.-Herz.
95 F3 Banjarbaru Kalimantan Selatan Indon.
95 F3 Banjarmasin Kalimantan Selatan Indon.
206 A3 Banjul Gambia
129 A3 Bank Azer.
116 E4 Banka Bihar India
84 B3 Banka Banka N.T. Austr.
114 C2 Bankapur Karnataka India
143 M3 Bankeryd Sweden
146 E4 Bankfoot Perth and Kinross, Scotland U.K.
97 B4 Ban Khai Thai.
97 C4 Ban Khao Yoi Thai.
117 F5 Bānki Orissa India
206 E3 Bankilaré Niger
215 G2 Bankkop S. Africa
114 C2 Bankot Mahar. India
222 D4 Banks Island B.C. Can.
220 F2 Banks Island N.W.T. Can.
81 □2 Banks Islands Vanuatu
81 C6 Banks Peninsula South I. N.Z.
83 □ Banks Strait Tas. Austr.
117 G4 Bankura W. Bengal India
196 B2 Bankya Sofiya Bulg.
96 C4 Ban Lamduan Thai.
108 C3 Banluo Guangxi China
197 Banloc Romania
158 C4 Bannalec France
147 F3 Bann r. Northern Ireland U.K.
160 Banne France
172 Bannesdorf auf Fehmarn Ger.
240 I5 Banning CA U.S.A.
Banningville Dem. Rep. Congo
136 Bannivka Ukr.
81 A6 Bannockburn South I. N.Z.
146 E5 Bannockburn Stirling, Scotland U.K.
123 Bannu Pak.
182 Bañobárez Spain
Bañoles see Banyoles
161 Banon France
250 Bañon Ecuador
185 Baños de la Encina Spain
186 Baños de Molgas Spain
182 Baños de Montemayor Spain
183 Baños de Río Tobía Spain
183 Baños de Valdearados Spain
177 Bánov Czech Rep.
177 H3 Bánov Slovakia

Baygakum to Benito Juárez

283

121 F3 Baygakum Kazakh.
120 C2 Bayganin Kazakh.
120 E1 Baygora Kazakh.
137 J1 Baygora r. Rus. Fed.
261 I3 Baygorria, Lago Artificial de resr Uru.
124 D5 Bayḩan al Qişab Yemen
235 D2 Bay Head NJ U.S.A.
129 E3 Bäyimli Azer.
199 E2 Bayındır Turkey
199 F3 Bayır Turkey
Bay Islands is Hond. see La Bahía, Islas de
111 F6 Bayizhen Xizang China
127 F4 Bayjī Iraq
Baykadam Kazakh. see Saudakent
106 E1 Baykal, Ozero l. Rus. Fed.
100 D1 Baykal-Amur Magistral Rus. Fed.
Baykal Range mts Rus. Fed. see Baykal'skiy Khrebet
106 E1 Baykal'sk Rus. Fed.
98 I1 Baykal'skiy Khrebet mts Rus. Fed.
127 F3 Baykan Turkey
134 L5 Baykibashevo Rus. Fed.
131 K3 Baykit Rus. Fed.
120 D1 Baymak Rus. Fed.
231 C6 Bay Minette AL U.S.A.
125 F3 Baynūna'h reg. U.A.E.
Bayo Spain see Baio Grande
80 F2 Bay of Plenty admin. reg. North I. N.Z.
92 B2 Bayombong Phil.
157 G4 Bayon France
Bayona Spain see Baiona
163 A5 Bayonne France
235 D2 Bayonne NJ U.S.A.
250 A6 Bayóvar Peru
227 F4 Bay Port MI U.S.A.
235 E2 Bayport NY U.S.A.
Bayqadam Kazakh. see Saudakent
129 C3 Bayraktutan Turkey
123 E2 Bayramaly Turkm.
199 E2 Bayramiç Turkey
173 F2 Bayreuth Ger.
234 B4 Bay Ridge MD U.S.A.
173 G4 Bayrischzell Ger.
Bayrūt Lebanon see Beirut
237 F6 Bay St Louis MS U.S.A.
Bayshonas Kazakh. see Baychunas
235 E2 Bay Shore NY U.S.A.
234 B3 Bayside Beach MD U.S.A.
237 F6 Bay Springs MS U.S.A.
150 E2 Bayston Hill Shropshire, England U.K.
121 F5 Baysun Uzbek.
121 F5 Baysuntau, Gory mts Uzbek.
124 C5 Bayt al Faqīh Yemen
106 A2 Baytik-Shan mts China
Bayt Lahm West Bank see Bethlehem
237 E6 Baytown TX U.S.A.
183 H3 Bayubas de Abajo Spain
80 F3 Bay View North I. N.Z.
235 D3 Bayville NJ U.S.A.
235 E2 Bayville NY U.S.A.
Bayyrqum Kazakh. see Bairkum
121 G4 Bayzhansay Kazakh.
185 H3 Baza Spain
185 H3 Baza r. Spain
185 H3 Baza, Sierra de mts Spain
176 F5 Bázakerettye Hungary
136 D3 Bazaliya Ukr.
156 E3 Bazancourt France
136 E2 Bazar Ukr.
120 B2 Bazarchulan Kazakh.
129 E3 Bazardyuzi, Gora mt. Azer./Rus. Fed.
122 B2 Bāzār-e Māsāl Iran
127 G3 Bāzārgān Iran
121 G5 Bazarkhanym, Gora mt. Uzbek.
121 H4 Bazar-Korgon Kyrg.
Bazar Kurgan Kyrg. see Bazar-Korgon
120 A1 Bazarnyy Karabulak Rus. Fed.
135 I5 Bazarnyy Syzgan Rus. Fed.
Bazarshulan Kazakh. see Bazarchulan
120 B2 Bazartobe Kazakh.
163 B4 Bazas France
137 H4 Bazavluk r. Ukr.
157 E3 Bazeilles France
163 C5 Bazet France
108 C2 Bazhong Sichuan China
107 H4 Bazhou Hebei China
163 D5 Baziège France
163 C5 Bazillac France
224 F4 Bazin r. Que. Can.
206 C4 Baziwehn Liberia
122 E5 Bazmān Iran
122 E4 Bazmān, Kūh-e mt. Iran
160 B1 Bazoches France
159 F3 Bazoches-au-Houlme France
156 C4 Bazoches-les-Gallerandes France
159 G3 Bazoches-sur-Hoëne France
159 F3 Bazougers France
159 F4 Bazouges France
158 E3 Bazouges-la-Pérouse France
128 C2 Bcharre Lebanon
97 D5 Be r. Vietnam
236 C2 Beach ND U.S.A.
227 I3 Beachburg Ont. Can.
232 C4 Beach City OH U.S.A.
235 D2 Beach Glen NJ U.S.A.
235 D3 Beach Haven NJ U.S.A.
235 D3 Beach Haven Terrace NJ U.S.A.
234 C1 Beach Lake PA U.S.A.
82 E4 Beachport S.A. Austr.
235 D3 Beachwood NJ U.S.A.
151 H4 Beachy Head hd England U.K.
87 C6 Beacon W.A. Austr.
233 G4 Beacon NY U.S.A.
215 F5 Beacon Bay S. Africa
235 E1 Beacon Falls CT U.S.A.
83 F5 Beaconsfield Tas. Austr.
151 G3 Beaconsfield Buckinghamshire, England U.K.
149 H2 Beadnell Northumberland, England U.K.
259 C9 Beagle, Canal sea chan. Arg.
86 D2 Beagle Bank rf W.A. Austr.
86 D3 Beagle Bay W.A. Austr.
84 B2 Beagle Gulf N.T. Austr.
87 B6 Beagle Island W.A. Austr.
213 □K2 Bealanana Madag.
Béal an Átha Rep. of Ireland see Ballina
Béal Átha na Sluaighe Rep. of Ireland see Ballinasloe
147 C5 Bealnablath Rep. of Ireland
237 C5 Beals Creek r. TX U.S.A.
150 E4 Beaminster Dorset, England U.K.
213 □J5 Beampingaratra mts Madag.
183 I4 Beamub Spain
213 □K2 Beandrarezona Madag.
238 D3 Bear r. ID U.S.A.
147 B5 Beara reg. Rep. of Ireland
Bearalváhki Norway see Berlevåg
234 C1 Bear Creek PA U.S.A.
237 C4 Bear Creek r. KS U.S.A.
224 C3 Beardmore Ont. Can.
236 F3 Beardstown IL U.S.A.
Bear Island i. Arctic Ocean see Bjørnøya
227 G2 Bear Island Ont. Can.
147 B5 Bear Island i. Rep. of Ireland
182 B2 Beariz Spain
226 D3 Bear Lake MI U.S.A.
238 E3 Bear Lake l. ID U.S.A.
116 D4 Bearma r. Madh. Prad. India
236 C3 Bear Mountain SD U.S.A.
Bearnaraigh i. Western Isles, Scotland U.K. see Berneray
238 E1 Bear Paw Mountain MT U.S.A.
238 E1 Bearpaw Mountains MT U.S.A.
262 Q2 Bear Peninsula Antarctica
146 D6 Bearsden East Dunbartonshire, Scotland U.K.
223 N4 Bearskin Lake Ont. Can.
151 H3 Bearsted Kent, England U.K.
116 C3 Beas r. India
184 D3 Beas Spain
186 A1 Beasain Spain
185 G3 Beas de Granada Spain
185 H2 Beas de Segura Spain
236 D3 Beatrice NE U.S.A.
213 F3 Beatrice Zimbabwe
84 D2 Beatrice, Cape N.T. Austr.
146 E6 Beattock Dumfries and Galloway, Scotland U.K.
222 F3 Beatton r. B.C. Can.
240 I3 Beatty NV U.S.A.
224 E3 Beattyville Que. Can.
232 B6 Beattyville KY U.S.A.
161 C5 Beaucaire France
156 B3 Beaucamps-le-Vieux France
161 C4 Beauchastel France
160 E1 Beaucourt France
159 F4 Beaucouzé France
163 C5 Beaudéan France
85 H5 Beaudesert Qld Austr.
Beauduc, Golfe de b. France see Stes Maries, Golfe des
159 G3 Beaufay France
83 E4 Beaufort Vic. Austr.
160 D2 Beaufort Franche-Comté France
160 E3 Beaufort Rhône-Alpes France
147 B4 Beaufort Rep. of Ireland
231 E5 Beaufort NC U.S.A.
231 D5 Beaufort SC U.S.A.
128 B3 Beaufort Castle tourist site Lebanon
162 B1 Beaufort-en-Vallée France
160 E3 Beaufortin mts France
220 F2 Beaufort Sea Can./U.S.A.
214 D5 Beaufort West S. Africa
156 B5 Beaugency France
233 G2 Beauharnois Que. Can.
161 E4 Beaujeu Provence-Alpes-Côte-d'Azur France
160 C2 Beaujeu Rhône-Alpes France
160 C2 Beaujolais, Monts du hills France
161 C5 Beaulieu France
159 H4 Beaulieu-lès-Loches France
162 D4 Beaulieu-sur-Dordogne France
160 A1 Beaulieu-sur-Loire France
160 B2 Beaulon France
146 D4 Beauly Highland, Scotland U.K.
146 D4 Beauly r. Scotland U.K.
146 D4 Beauly Firth est. Scotland U.K.
163 C5 Beaumarchés France
150 C1 Beaumaris Isle of Anglesey, Wales U.K.
161 D4 Beaumes-de-Venise France
159 G2 Beaumesnil France
156 C2 Beaumetz-lès-Loges France
165 D4 Beaumont Belgium
163 C4 Beaumont Aquitaine France
160 B3 Beaumont Auvergne France
158 E2 Beaumont Basse-Normandie France
159 G5 Beaumont Poitou-Charentes France
81 B6 Beaumont South I. N.Z.
240 I5 Beaumont CA U.S.A.
237 F6 Beaumont MS U.S.A.
234 C1 Beaumont PA U.S.A.
237 E6 Beaumont TX U.S.A.
163 C5 Beaumont-de-Lomagne France
161 D5 Beaumont-de-Pertuis France
157 F3 Beaumont-en-Argonne France
159 G4 Beaumont-en-Véron France
159 G4 Beaumont-la-Ronce France
159 G2 Beaumont-le-Roger France
159 G3 Beaumont-les-Autels France
161 C4 Beaumont-lès-Valence France
156 C3 Beaumont-sur-Oise France
159 G3 Beaumont-sur-Sarthe France
160 C1 Beaune France
156 C4 Beaune-La Rolande France
159 F4 Beaupréau France
156 C2 Beauquesne France
165 D4 Beauraing Belgium
161 D3 Beaurepaire France
160 D2 Beaurepaire-en-Bresse France
161 D4 Beaurières France
223 L5 Beauséjour Man. Can.
157 F4 Beausite France
161 F5 Beausoleil France
156 D3 Beautor France
156 C3 Beauvais France
223 J4 Beauval Sask. Can.
156 C2 Beauval France
161 E4 Beauvezer France
163 C4 Beauville France
158 D5 Beauvoir-sur-Mer France
162 B2 Beauvoir-sur-Niort France
161 C5 Beauvoisin France
161 C3 Beauzac France
163 D5 Beauzelle France
223 J4 Beaver r. Alberta/Saskatchewan Can.
224 C2 Beaver r. Ont. Can.
222 C2 Beaver r. Y.T. Can.
222 E3 Beaver r. Y.T. Can.
237 C4 Beaver OK U.S.A.
241 K2 Beaver UT U.S.A.
237 C4 Beaver r. OK U.S.A.
241 K2 Beaver r. UT U.S.A.
236 D3 Beaver City NE U.S.A.
222 A2 Beaver Creek Y.T. Can.
237 E4 Beaver Creek r. MO U.S.A.
238 F1 Beaver Creek r. MT U.S.A.
236 C2 Beaver Creek r. ND U.S.A.
236 D3 Beaver Creek r. NE U.S.A.
230 C4 Beaver Dam KY U.S.A.
226 C4 Beaver Dam WI U.S.A.
232 C4 Beaver Falls PA U.S.A.
263 D2 Beaver Glacier Antarctica
238 D2 Beaverhead r. MT U.S.A.
238 D2 Beaverhead Mountains MT U.S.A.
237 E4 Beaver Lake resr AR U.S.A.
222 G4 Beaverlodge Alta Can.
234 C2 Beaver Meadows PA U.S.A.
234 A2 Beaver Springs PA U.S.A.
224 E4 Beaverton Ont. Can.
226 E4 Beaverton MI U.S.A.
238 B2 Beaverton OR U.S.A.
234 A2 Beavertown PA U.S.A.
116 C4 Beawar Rajasthan India
177 J5 Beba Veche Romania
208 C2 Bébédjia Chad
256 C4 Bebedouro Brazil
254 F3 Beberibe Brazil
171 C3 Bebertal Ger.
149 F4 Bebington Merseyside, England U.K.
208 C2 Béboto Chad
169 E5 Bebra Ger.
108 A2 Bêca Qinghai China
160 E3 Becca du Lac mt. France
151 I2 Beccles Suffolk, England U.K.
191 G3 Becco di Filadonna mt. Italy
182 E4 Becedas Spain
186 D4 Beceite Spain
196 E3 Bečej Vojvodina, Srbija Yugo.
182 C2 Becerreá Spain
185 F3 Becerrero hill Spain
183 F2 Becerril de Campos Spain
204 E3 Béchar Alg.
172 B2 Becherbach Ger.
158 E3 Bécherel France
134 G4 Bechevinka Rus. Fed.
173 E2 Bechhofen Bayern Ger.
172 B2 Bechhofen Rheinland-Pfalz Ger.
171 F5 Bechlín Czech Rep.
234 C2 Bechtelsville PA U.S.A.
172 C2 Bechtheim Ger.
Bechuanaland country Africa see Botswana
176 D2 Bechyně Czech Rep.
177 K6 Becicherecu Mic Romania
183 E2 Becilla de Valderaduey Spain
199 E3 Beçin Turkey
168 E2 Beckdorf Ger.
169 E3 Beckedorf Ger.
168 D3 Beckeln Ger.
262 T1 Becker, Mount Antarctica
172 A2 Beckingen Ger.
149 I4 Beckingham Nottinghamshire, England U.K.
232 C6 Beckley WV U.S.A.
177 G3 Beckov Slovakia
81 B6 Becks South I. N.Z.
169 D4 Beckum Ger.
241 J2 Becky Peak NV U.S.A.
197 G2 Beclean Romania
159 F4 Bécon-les-Granits France
171 E5 Bečov Czech Rep.
176 B1 Bečov nad Teplou Czech Rep.
176 F5 Becsehely Hungary
176 F5 Becsvölgye Hungary
177 G2 Bečva r. Czech Rep.
210 D2 Beda Hāyk' l. Eth.
149 H3 Bedale North Yorkshire, England U.K.
161 B5 Bédarieux France
161 C4 Bédarrides France
169 B5 Bedburg Ger.
169 B4 Bedburg-Hau Ger.
150 D3 Beddau Rhondda Cynon Taff, Wales U.K.
150 C1 Beddgelert Gwynedd, Wales U.K.
151 H4 Beddingham East Sussex, England U.K.
233 □I2 Beddington ME U.S.A.
158 E3 Bédée France
179 G4 Bedekovčina Croatia
210 C2 Bedelē Eth.
168 D2 Bederkesa Ger.
210 D2 Bedēsa Eth.
134 L5 Bedeyeva Polyana Rus. Fed.
225 I4 Bedford N.S. Can.
233 G2 Bedford Que. Can.
215 F5 Bedford E. Cape S. Africa
215 H3 Bedford Kwazulu-Natal S. Africa
151 G2 Bedford Bedfordshire, England U.K.
236 E3 Bedford IA U.S.A.
230 C4 Bedford IN U.S.A.
230 C4 Bedford KY U.S.A.
235 E1 Bedford NY U.S.A.
232 D4 Bedford PA U.S.A.
232 D6 Bedford VA U.S.A.
85 F2 Bedford, Cape Qld Austr.
86 E3 Bedford Downs W.A. Austr.
232 C4 Bedford Heights OH U.S.A.
235 E1 Bedford Hills NY U.S.A.
151 G2 Bedford Level (Middle Level) lowland England U.K.
151 G2 Bedford Level (North Level) lowland England U.K.
151 H2 Bedford Level (South Level) lowland England U.K.
151 G2 Bedfordshire admin. div. England U.K.
83 F3 Bedgerebong N.S.W. Austr.
116 B5 Bedi Gujarat India
129 D3 Bediani Georgia
175 H4 Będków Pol.
149 H2 Bedlington Northumberland, England U.K.
175 H3 Bedlno Pol.
185 G3 Bedmar Spain
188 F2 Bednja r. Croatia
135 H5 Bednodem'yanovsk Rus. Fed.
161 D4 Bédoin France
191 G2 Bedollo Italy
190 E4 Bedonia Italy
84 D5 Bedourie Qld Austr.
163 B5 Bedous France
241 M2 Bedrock CO U.S.A.
163 D4 Béduer France
164 F1 Bedum Neth.
150 D3 Bedwas Caerphilly, Wales U.K.
151 F2 Bedworth Warwickshire, England U.K.
175 H5 Będzin Pol.
174 D1 Będzino Pol.
226 D5 Beecher IL U.S.A.
233 H2 Beecher Falls VT U.S.A.
83 F4 Beechworth Vic. Austr.
223 J5 Beechy Sask. Can.
168 F3 Beedenbostel Ger.
149 I4 Beeford East Riding of Yorkshire, England U.K.
164 E3 Beek Gelderland Neth.
164 E3 Beek Noord-Brabant Neth.
164 E2 Beekbergen Neth.
171 D3 Beelitz Ger.
234 D1 Beemerville NJ U.S.A.
171 C3 Beendorf Ger.
85 H5 Beenleigh Qld Austr.
170 E2 Beenz Ger.
150 D4 Beer Devon, England U.K.
172 C2 Beerfelden Ger.
87 C6 Beeringgnurding, Mount hill W.A. Austr.
165 C3 Beernem Belgium
164 E3 Beers Neth.
165 D3 Beerse Belgium
165 D4 Beersel Belgium
Beersheba Israel see Be'ér Sheva'
128 B4 Be'ér Sheva' Israel
165 B3 Beerst Belgium
164 G1 Beerta Neth.
171 C4 Beesenstedt Ger.
171 F3 Beeskow Ger.
215 F1 Beestekraal S. Africa
169 C3 Beesten Ger.
151 F2 Beeston Nottinghamshire, England U.K.
84 C3 Beetaloo N.T. Austr.
262 T2 Beethoven Peninsula Antarctica
151 H2 Beetley Norfolk, England U.K.
164 F1 Beetsterzwaag Neth.
170 C3 Beetzendorf Ger.
237 D6 Beeville TX U.S.A.
213 □I4 Befandriana Atsimo Madag.
213 □K2 Befandriana Avaratra Madag.
213 □J4 Befasy Madag.
213 □J4 Befotaka Madag.
83 G4 Bega N.S.W. Austr.
197 E3 Bega r. Romania
163 B5 Bégaar France
162 B3 Bégadan France
117 G5 Begamganj Bangl.
158 C3 Bégard France
123 G4 Begari r. Pak.
Begicheva, Ostrov i. Rus. Fed. see Bol'shoy Begichev, Ostrov
185 G3 Begíjar Spain
165 D3 Begijnendijk Belgium
163 B4 Bègles France
158 C4 Beg-Meil France
142 D1 Begna r. Norway
182 C1 Begonte Spain
206 E5 Begoro Ghana
Begovat Uzbek. see Bekabad
116 C4 Begun Rajasthan India
186 G3 Begur Spain
117 F4 Begusarai Bihar India
213 □J5 Behara Madag.
122 B4 Behbehān Iran
126 C5 Beheira governorate Egypt
168 F2 Behlendorf Ger.
262 T2 Behrendt Mountains Antarctica
157 G3 Behren-lès-Forbach France
170 D1 Behren-Lübchin Ger.
169 F4 Behringen Ger.
122 C2 Behshahr Iran
215 E5 Behulpsaam S. Africa
100 C2 Bei'an Heilong. China
Bei'ao Zhejiang China see Dongtou
108 C1 Beiba Shaanxi China
108 C2 Beibei Chongqing China
108 C2 Beichuan Sichuan China
Beida Libya see Al Bayḑā'
171 D5 Beierfeld Ger.
Beigang Taiwan see Peikang
149 H4 Beighton South Yorkshire, England U.K.
190 D4 Beigua, Monte mt. Italy
108 D4 Beihai Guangxi China
109 E4 Bei Jiang r. China
107 H4 Beijing Beijing China
107 H3 Beijing mun. China
164 F2 Beilen Neth.
108 D4 Beiliu Guangxi China
173 F2 Beilngries Ger.
171 E4 Beilrode Ger.
172 D2 Beilstein Ger.
172 D3 Beimerstetten Ger.
208 B2 Béinamar Chad
190 C3 Beinasco Italy
156 E3 Beine-Nauroy France
190 C4 Beinette Italy
107 I3 Beining Liaoning China
146 C4 Beinn Alligin hill Scotland U.K.
148 D2 Beinn an Tuirc hill Scotland U.K.
146 C4 Beinn Bhan hill Scotland U.K.
146 B6 Beinn Bheigeir hill Scotland U.K.
146 C5 Beinn Bhreac hill Argyll and Bute, Scotland U.K.
146 C5 Beinn Bhreac hill Argyll and Bute, Scotland U.K.
146 C6 Beinn Bhreac hill Argyll and Bute, Scotland U.K.
146 B4 Beinn Bhreac hill Highland, Scotland U.K.
146 D5 Beinn Bhuidhe hill Scotland U.K.
146 C5 Beinn Chapull hill Scotland U.K.
146 D4 Beinn Dearg mt. Highland, Scotland U.K.
146 E5 Beinn Dearg mt. Perth and Kinross, Scotland U.K.
146 D5 Beinn Dorain mt. Scotland U.K.
144 E3 Beinn Heasgarnich mt. Scotland U.K.
146 D5 Beinn Ime mt. Scotland U.K.
146 D3 Beinn Leoid hill Scotland U.K.
146 B3 Beinn Mholach hill Scotland U.K.
146 C5 Beinn Mhor hill Scotland U.K.
146 A4 Beinn Mhòr hill Western Isles, Scotland U.K.
146 B4 Beinn Mhòr hill Western Isles, Scotland U.K.
Beinn na Faoghlia i. Scotland U.K. see Benbecula
146 D5 Beinn na Lap hill Scotland U.K.
146 C4 Beinn na Seamraig hill Scotland U.K.
146 C5 Beinn Resipol hill Scotland U.K.
146 C4 Beinn Sgritheall hill Scotland U.K.
146 C5 Beinn Sgulaird hill Scotland U.K.
146 D4 Beinn Tharsuinn hill Scotland U.K.
146 D5 Beinn Udlamain mt. Scotland U.K.
190 D1 Beinwil Switz.
107 I3 Beipiao Liaoning China
213 G3 Beira Moz.
Beira prov. Moz. see Sofala
184 C1 Beirã Port.
183 I2 Beire Spain
109 E1 Beiru r. China
128 B3 Beirut Lebanon
222 H5 Beiseker Alta Can.
106 C3 Beishan Nei Mongol China
110 F3 Bei Shan mt. Gansu China
106 B3 Bei Shan mts China
213 F4 Beitbridge Zimbabwe
146 D6 Beith North Ayrshire, Scotland U.K.
128 B4 Beit Jālā West Bank
197 F2 Beiuş Romania
Beizhen Liaoning China see Beining
184 C2 Beja Port.
184 B3 Beja admin. dist. Port.
205 H1 Béja Tunisia
189 B7 Béja admin. div. Tunisia
205 G1 Bejaïa Alg.
182 E4 Béjar Spain
122 D3 Bejestān Iran
123 G4 Beji r. Pak.
187 C5 Bejís Spain
247 E5 Bejuma Venez.
207 I6 Bek r. Cameroon
119 J1 Bekabad Uzbek.
213 □J3 Bekapaika Madag.
94 D4 Bekasi Jawa Barat Indon.
122 C1 Bekdash Turkm.
177 K5 Békés Hungary
177 K5 Békés county Hungary
177 K5 Békéscsaba Hungary
177 J5 Békéssámson Hungary
177 J5 Békésszentandrás Hungary
137 G4 Bekhtery Ukr.
199 F2 Bekilli Turkey
213 □J5 Bekily Madag.
Bekobod Uzbek. see Bekabad
213 □I4 Bekoropoka-Antongo Madag.
135 H5 Bekovo Rus. Fed.
206 E5 Bekwai Ghana
206 E5 Bekyem Ghana
117 F4 Bela Bihar India
116 E4 Bela Uttar Prad. India
123 F5 Bela Pak.
177 H2 Belá Slovakia
123 G4 Belab r. Pak.
213 F5 Bela-Bela S. Africa
207 I5 Bélabo Cameroon
162 D2 Bélâbre France
196 E3 Bela Crkva Vojvodina, Srbija Yugo.
177 H3 Beladice Slovakia
177 H2 Belá-Dulice Slovakia
121 J2 Bel'agash Kazakh.
158 D3 Bel Air hill France
234 B3 Bel Air MD U.S.A.
185 E2 Belalcázar Spain
176 B2 Bělá nad Radbuzou Czech Rep.
197 F4 Bela Palanka Srbija Yugo.
177 J3 Bélapátfalva Hungary
176 D1 Bělá pod Bezdězem Czech Rep.
176 G1 Bělá pod Pradědem Czech Rep.
114 B2 Belapur Mahar. India
135 E5 Belarus country Europe
183 I2 Belascoáin Spain
197 F5 Belasica mts Bulg./Macedonia
Belasitsa mts Bulg./Macedonia see Belasica
Belau country N. Pacific Ocean see Palau
209 B6 Bela Vista Bengo Angola
Bela Vista Huambo Angola see Katchiungo
253 F5 Bela Vista Brazil
213 G5 Bela Vista Moz.
256 C2 Bela Vista de Goiás Brazil
94 B2 Belawan Sumatera Indon.
210 C2 Belaya mt. Eth.
137 H2 Belaya Rus. Fed.
137 J5 Belaya r. Rus. Fed.
131 S3 Belaya r. Rus. Fed.
137 G1 Belaya Berezka Rus. Fed.
135 H7 Belaya Glina Rus. Fed.
135 H6 Belaya Kalitva Rus. Fed.
134 J4 Belaya Kholunitsa Rus. Fed.
95 G3 Belayan r. Indon.
95 F2 Belayan, Gunung mt. Indon.
139 L3 Belaya Rechka Rus. Fed.
Belaya Tserkva Ukr. see Bila Tserkva
182 B4 Belazaima do Chão Port.
190 D4 Belbo r. Italy
163 D6 Belcaire France
234 B3 Belcamp MD U.S.A.
163 E4 Belcastel France
197 H2 Belceşti Romania
175 H4 Bełchatów Pol.
172 B4 Belchen mt. Ger.
232 B6 Belcher KY U.S.A.
224 E1 Belcher Islands Nunavut Can.
186 C3 Belchite Spain
176 C2 Bělčice Czech Rep.
147 C3 Belclare Rep. of Ireland
227 I1 Belcourt Que. Can.
117 G5 Beldanga W. Bengal India
240 G1 Belden CA U.S.A.
147 B2 Belderg Rep. of Ireland
199 F3 Beldibi Turkey
226 E4 Belding MI U.S.A.
120 C1 Belebey Rus. Fed.
176 G4 Beled Hungary
210 E3 Beledweyne Somalia
206 C5 Belefuanai Liberia
122 C2 Belek Turkm.
206 D3 Béléko Mali
207 I5 Bélèl Cameroon
207 I4 Belel Nigeria
254 C2 Belém Brazil
258 D2 Belén Arg.
128 A1 Belen Antalya Turkey
126 E3 Belen Hatay Turkey
261 I2 Belén Uru.
239 F5 Belen NM U.S.A.
261 I2 Belén, Cuchilla de hills Uru.
197 G4 Belene Bulg.
78 □5 Bélep, Îles is New Caledonia
163 D6 Bélesta France
139 K5 Belev Rus. Fed.
199 E2 Belevi Turkey
176 F5 Belezna Hungary
81 D5 Belfast South I. N.Z.
215 H1 Belfast S. Africa
147 F2 Belfast Northern Ireland U.K.
233 □I2 Belfast ME U.S.A.
232 D3 Belfast NY U.S.A.
148 C3 Belfast International airport Northern Ireland U.K.
147 F2 Belfast Lough inlet Northern Ireland U.K.
165 F3 Belfeld Neth.
236 C2 Belfield ND U.S.A.
210 B2 Bēlfodiyo Eth.
149 H2 Belford Northumberland, England U.K.
160 E1 Belfort France
163 D4 Belfort-du-Quercy France
193 F1 Belforte del Chienti Italy
114 B3 Belgaum Karnataka India
161 E5 Belgentier France
171 E4 Belgern Ger.
171 D4 Belgershain Ger.
Belgian Congo country Africa see Congo, Democratic Republic of
Belgicafjella mts Antarctica see Belgica Mountains
263 C2 Belgica Mountains Antarctica
België country Europe see Belgium
190 E3 Belgioioso Italy
Belgique country Europe see Belgium
165 D4 Belgium country Europe
192 B2 Belgodère Corse France
135 G6 Belgorod Rus. Fed.
Belgorod-Dnestrovskyy Ukr. see Bilhorod-Dnistrovs'kyy
Belgorod Oblast admin. div. Rus. Fed. see Belgorodskaya Oblast'
135 G6 Belgorodskaya Oblast' admin. div. Rus. Fed.
233 □I2 Belgrade ME U.S.A.
238 E2 Belgrade MT U.S.A.
Belgrade Srbija Yugo. see Beograd
262 V1 Belgrano II research stn Antarctica
81 D4 Belgrove South I. N.Z.
163 B4 Belhade France
156 B4 Belhomert-Guéhouville France
206 B4 Béli Guinea-Bissau
207 H5 Beli Nigeria
186 E3 Belianes Spain
179 H4 Belica Croatia
194 B5 Belice r. Sicilia Italy
184 C3 Beliche r. Port.
194 C5 Belici r. Sicilia Italy
196 E4 Beli Drim r. Yugo.
129 F3 Belidzhi Rus. Fed.
Beliliou i. Palau see Peleliu
197 H4 Beli Lom r. Bulg.
188 G3 Beli Manastir Croatia
163 B4 Belin-Béliet France
183 G4 Belinchón Spain
232 D5 Belington WV U.S.A.
Belingwe Zimbabwe see Mberengwa
135 H5 Belinskiy Rus. Fed.
197 E3 Belinţ Romania
94 D3 Belinyu Indon.
197 F3 Beli Timok r. Yugo.
197 F5 Belitsa Bulg.
137 H2 Belitsa Rus. Fed.
95 E3 Belitung i. Indon.
177 L5 Beliu Romania
209 B6 Belize Angola
243 H5 Belize Belize
243 H5 Belize country Central America
251 H3 Bélizon Fr. Guiana
Beljak Austria see Villach
197 E3 Beljanica mt. Yugo.
85 G5 Bell Qld Austr.
83 G3 Bell r. N.S.W. Austr.
224 E3 Bell r. Que. Can.
169 C5 Bell Ger.
215 F5 Bell S. Africa
169 C5 Bell (Hunsrück) Ger.
82 C3 Bell, Point S.A. Austr.
193 H4 Bella Italy
222 D4 Bella Bella B.C. Can.
162 D2 Bellac France
160 E3 Bellacha, Mont mt. France
222 E4 Bella Coola B.C. Can.
222 E4 Bella Coola r. B.C. Can.
147 B2 Bellacorick Rep. of Ireland
147 E2 Bellaghy Northern Ireland U.K.
190 E3 Bellagio Italy
147 C3 Bellahy Rep. of Ireland
226 E3 Bellaire MI U.S.A.
237 E6 Bellaire TX U.S.A.
147 C3 Bellanagare Rep. of Ireland
147 D2 Bellanaleck Northern Ireland U.K.
147 C2 Bellanamore Rep. of Ireland
147 C3 Bellaneeny Rep. of Ireland
190 E2 Bellano Italy
193 F2 Bellante Italy
191 H4 Bellaria Italy
114 C3 Bellary Karnataka India
83 G2 Bellata N.S.W. Austr.
261 I2 Bella Unión Uru.
147 B3 Bellavary Rep. of Ireland
258 F3 Bella Vista Arg.
253 F5 Bella Vista Para.
250 B6 Bellavista Peru
80 E3 Bell Block North I. N.Z.
85 G4 Bell Cay rf Qld Austr.
186 D3 Bellclaire d'Urgell Spain
232 C5 Belle WV U.S.A.
246 D3 Belle-Anse Haiti
171 C4 Belleben Ger.
161 D3 Belledonne mts France
147 C2 Belleek Northern Ireland U.K.
147 E2 Belleek Northern Ireland U.K.
157 G4 Bellefontaine France
247 □3 Bellefontaine Martinique
232 B4 Bellefontaine OH U.S.A.
232 E4 Bellefonte PA U.S.A.
236 C2 Belle Fourche SD U.S.A.
236 C2 Belle Fourche r. SD U.S.A.
156 C5 Bellegarde Centre France
161 C5 Bellegarde Languedoc-Roussillon France
162 E3 Bellegarde-en-Marche France
160 D2 Bellegarde-sur-Valserine France
231 D7 Belle Glade FL U.S.A.
158 C4 Belle-Île i. France
225 K3 Belle Isle i. Nfld. Can.
225 J3 Belle Isle, Strait of Nfld. Can.
158 C3 Belle-Isle-en-Terre France
159 G3 Bellême France
234 D2 Belle Mead NJ U.S.A.
241 L4 Bellemont AZ U.S.A.
160 B2 Bellenaves France
173 E3 Bellenberg Ger.
156 B3 Bellencombre France
160 B2 Bellerive-sur-Allier France
157 G4 Belles-Forêts France
224 E4 Belleterre Que. Can.
156 D3 Belleu France
160 E2 Bellevaux France
160 D2 Bellevesvre France
224 E4 Belleville Ont. Can.
160 C2 Belleville France
236 D4 Belleville KS U.S.A.
235 D2 Belleville NJ U.S.A.
160 A1 Belleville-sur-Loire France
157 F3 Belleville-sur-Meuse France
158 E5 Belleville-sur-Vie France
230 B3 Bellevue IA U.S.A.
226 E4 Bellevue MI U.S.A.
236 E3 Bellevue NE U.S.A.
232 B4 Bellevue OH U.S.A.
238 B2 Bellevue WA U.S.A.
161 B3 Bellevue-la-Montagne France
160 D3 Belley France
226 C5 Bellflower IL U.S.A.
172 C2 Bellheim Ger.
160 E1 Bellherbe France
160 D2 Bellignat France
Bellin Que. Can. see Kangirsuk
83 H2 Bellingen N.S.W. Austr.
149 G2 Bellingham Northumberland, England U.K.
238 B1 Bellingham WA U.S.A.
262 U2 Bellingshausen research stn Antarctica
Bellingshausen Island atoll Arch. de la Société Fr. Polynesia see Motu One
164 G1 Bellingwolde Neth.
190 D3 Bellinzago Novarese Italy
190 E2 Bellinzona Switz.
222 D4 Bell Island Hot Springs AK U.S.A.
193 G4 Bellizzi Italy
234 C3 Bellmawr NJ U.S.A.
250 C3 Bello Col.
183 I4 Bello Spain
163 B5 Bellocq France
78 □6 Bellona i. Solomon Is
159 F3 Bellou-en-Houlme France
233 G3 Bellows Falls VT U.S.A.
186 E3 Bellpuig d'Urgell Spain
146 D6 Bellshill North Lanarkshire, Scotland U.K.
191 H2 Belluno Italy
191 H2 Belluno prov. Veneto Italy
114 C3 Belluru Karnataka India
235 D1 Bellvale NY U.S.A.
186 E2 Bellver de Cerdanya Spain
261 F3 Bell Ville Arg.
214 B5 Bellville S. Africa
232 B4 Bellville OH U.S.A.
237 D6 Bellville TX U.S.A.
232 D4 Bellwood PA U.S.A.
222 H5 Belly r. Alta Can.
169 D3 Belm Ger.
235 D2 Belmar NJ U.S.A.
177 K5 Bélmegyer Hungary
185 E2 Bélmez Spain
185 G3 Bélmez de la Moraleda Spain
83 G3 Belmont N.S.W. Austr.
163 C5 Belmont France
214 E3 Belmont S. Africa
146 □H1 Belmont Shetland, Scotland U.K.
233 H3 Belmont NH U.S.A.
232 D3 Belmont NY U.S.A.
160 C2 Belmont-de-la-Loire France
257 H1 Belmonte Brazil
182 C4 Belmonte Port.
182 D1 Belmonte Asturias Spain
183 H5 Belmonte Castilla - La Mancha Spain
193 I5 Belmonte Calabro Italy
193 G3 Belmonte del Sannio Italy
193 E2 Belmonte in Sabina Italy
194 C4 Belmonte Mezzagno Sicilia Italy
161 A5 Belmont-sur-Rance France
243 H5 Belmopan Belize
85 E3 Belmore Creek r. Qld Austr.
147 B2 Belmullet Rep. of Ireland
213 □J4 Belo Madag.
255 E5 Belo Campo Brazil
165 C4 Belœil Belgium
Beloe More sea Rus. Fed. see Beloye More
Beloevo Rus. Fed. see Beloyevo
100 D2 Belogorsk Rus. Fed.
Belogorsk Ukr. see Bilohirs'k
121 I2 Belogor'ye Kazakh.
137 K2 Belogor'ye Rus. Fed.
197 F4 Belogradchik Bulg.
213 □J5 Beloha Madag.
257 F3 Belo Horizonte Brazil
236 D4 Beloit KS U.S.A.
226 C4 Beloit WI U.S.A.
254 F4 Belo Jardim Brazil
Belokamensk Ukr. see Inkerman
121 K2 Belokurikha Rus. Fed.
Belo Monte Brazil see Batalha
134 F2 Belomorsk Rus. Fed.
117 G5 Belonia Tripura India
139 L4 Beloomut Rus. Fed.
257 F3 Belo Oriente Brazil
Beloozersk Belarus see Byelaazyorsk
139 L4 Beloozerskiy Rus. Fed.
Belopol'ye Ukr. see Bilopillya
183 G2 Belorado Spain
135 G7 Belorechensk Rus. Fed.
Belorechenskaya Rus. Fed. see Belorechensk
126 E3 Belören Turkey
126 D3 Belören Turkey
120 D1 Beloretsk Rus. Fed.
Belorussia country Europe see Belarus
Belorusskaya S.S.R. country Europe see Belarus
197 H4 Beloslav Bulg.
Belostok Pol. see Białystok
177 G2 Bělotín Czech Rep.
197 F4 Belotintsi Bulg.
213 □J3 Belo Tsiribihina Madag.
121 J2 Belousovka Kazakh.
139 K4 Belousovo Rus. Fed.
257 E4 Belo Vale Brazil
197 G4 Belovo Bulg.
100 D2 Beloyarovo Rus. Fed.
139 K1 Beloye, Ozero l. Rus. Fed.
134 G2 Beloye More sea Rus. Fed.
134 K4 Beloyevo Rus. Fed.
120 C1 Belozerka Rus. Fed.
139 K1 Belozersk Rus. Fed.
Belozerskoye Ukr. see Bilozers'ke
190 C2 Belp Switz.
172 B5 Belp airport Switz.
194 D5 Belpasso Sicilia Italy
163 D5 Belpech France
149 H4 Belper Derbyshire, England U.K.
232 C5 Belpre OH U.S.A.
149 H2 Belsay Northumberland, England U.K.
175 I4 Belsk Duży Pol.
82 D2 Beltana S.A. Austr.
82 D2 Belt Bay salt flat S.A. Austr.
241 I3 Belted Range mts NV U.S.A.
106 C1 Beltes Gol r. Mongolia
169 C5 Beltheim Ger.
179 H4 Beltinci Slovenia
177 L4 Beltiug Romania
151 I2 Belton Norfolk, England U.K.
236 E4 Belton MO U.S.A.
237 D6 Belton TX U.S.A.
147 B3 Beltra Mayo Rep. of Ireland
147 C2 Beltra Sligo Rep. of Ireland
164 F2 Beltrum Neth.
Bel'ts' Moldova see Bălţi
234 B3 Beltsville MD U.S.A.
Bel'tsy Moldova see Bălţi
147 D2 Belturbet Rep. of Ireland
192 A5 Belu r. Sardegna Italy
112 G2 Belukha, Gora mt. Kazakh./Rus. Fed.
114 B3 Belur Karnataka India
177 H2 Beluša Slovakia
232 C5 Belva WV U.S.A.
192 A3 Belvédère-Campomoro Corse France
193 H5 Belvedere Marittimo Italy
184 C1 Belver Port.
186 D3 Belver de Cinca Spain
163 D4 Belvès France
163 E5 Belvèze-du-Razès France
161 C4 Belvézet France
226 C4 Belvidere IL U.S.A.
234 C2 Belvidere NJ U.S.A.
147 B2 Belville Rep. of Ireland
183 F5 Belvís de la Jara Spain
85 F4 Belyando r. Qld Austr.
85 F4 Belyando Crossing Qld Austr.
120 D2 Belyayevka Rus. Fed.
Belyayevka Ukr. see Bilyayivka
121 G4 Belye Vody Kazakh.
84 B2 Belyuen N.T. Austr.
139 I4 Belyy Rus. Fed.
130 I2 Belyy, Ostrov i. Rus. Fed.
139 J5 Belyye Berega Rus. Fed.
139 K4 Belyye Stolby Rus. Fed.
139 K3 Belyy Gorodok Rus. Fed.
137 J2 Belyy Kolodez' Rus. Fed.
130 J4 Belyy Yar Rus. Fed.
158 C4 Belz France
136 C2 Belz Ukr.
175 L5 Bełżec Pol.
171 D3 Belzig Ger.
237 F5 Belzoni MS U.S.A.
175 K4 Bełżyce Pol.
213 □J3 Bemaraha, Plateau du Madag.
209 B6 Bembe Angola
207 F4 Bembèrèkè Benin
185 E3 Bembézar r. Spain
182 D2 Bembibre Castilla y León Spain
182 B1 Bembibre Galicia Spain
151 F4 Bembridge Isle of Wight, England U.K.
236 E2 Bemidji MN U.S.A.
237 F5 Bemis TN U.S.A.
164 E3 Bemmel Neth.
182 D3 Bemposta Bragança Port.
184 B1 Bemposta Santarém Port.
149 I3 Bempton East Riding of Yorkshire, England U.K.
206 D3 Béna Burkina
186 D2 Benabarre Spain
209 D6 Bena Dibele Dem. Rep. Congo
187 C5 Benaguasil Spain
185 H4 Benahadux Spain
185 E4 Benahavís Spain
204 D2 Benahmed Morocco
146 E4 Ben Aigan hill Scotland U.K.
185 E2 Benajarafe r. Spain
146 D5 Ben Alder mt. Scotland U.K.
83 F4 Benalla Vic. Austr.
185 F4 Benalmádena Spain
185 G3 Benalúa de Guadix Spain
185 G3 Benalúa de las Villas Spain
184 E4 Benalup de Sidonia Spain
185 F4 Benamargosa Spain
185 H3 Benamaurel Spain
185 F3 Benamejí Spain
185 F4 Benamocarra Spain
185 E4 Benaocaz Spain
185 E4 Benaoján Spain
Benares Uttar Prad. India see Varanasi
205 H1 Ben Arous Tunisia
189 B7 Ben Arous admin. div. Tunisia
187 C4 Benasal Spain
187 C6 Benasau Spain
186 D2 Benasque Spain
162 C2 Benassay France
176 D1 Benátky nad Jizerou Czech Rep.
184 B2 Benavente Port.
182 E2 Benavente Spain
252 D3 Benavides Bol.
182 E2 Benavides de Orbigo Spain
184 C1 Benavila Port.
146 E4 Ben Avon mt. Scotland U.K.
147 B3 Benbaun hill Rep. of Ireland
146 A4 Benbecula i. Scotland U.K.
147 C2 Benbulben hill Rep. of Ireland
147 E2 Benburb Northern Ireland U.K.
147 B3 Benbury hill Rep. of Ireland
184 C2 Bencatel Port.
109 G1 Bencha Jiangsu China
Bencheng Hebei China see Luannan
146 E5 Ben Chonzie hill Scotland U.K.
147 B3 Bencorr hill Rep. of Ireland
146 C5 Ben Cruachan mt. Scotland U.K.
87 C6 Bencubbin W.A. Austr.
238 B2 Bend OR U.S.A.
215 F4 Bendearg mt. S. Africa
209 C5 Bendela Dem. Rep. Congo
83 G2 Bendemeer N.S.W. Austr.
Bender Moldova see Tighina
210 F2 Bender-Bayla Somalia
226 D3 Benderville WI U.S.A.
Bendery Moldova see Tighina
168 E2 Bendestorf Ger.
83 F4 Bendigo Vic. Austr.
83 G4 Bendoc Vic. Austr.
169 C5 Bendorf Ger.
Bendzin Pol. see Będzin
138 D3 Bēne Latvia
164 E3 Beneden-Leeuwen Neth.
225 J2 Benedict, Mount hill Nfld. Can.
233 □I2 Benedicta ME U.S.A.
173 F4 Benediktbeuren Ger.
173 F4 Benediktenwand mt. Ger.
184 B1 Benedita Port.
254 E3 Beneditinos Brazil
254 D3 Benedito Leite Brazil
182 E3 Benegiles Spain
163 B5 Bénéjacq France
187 C6 Benejama Spain
187 C6 Benejúzar Spain
151 H3 Benenden Kent, England U.K.
213 □J4 Benenitra Madag.
176 D2 Benešov Czech Rep.
179 F2 Benešov nad Černou Czech Rep.
176 D1 Benešov nad Ploučnicí Czech Rep.
163 A5 Bénesse-Maremne France
195 F4 Benestare Italy
157 G4 Bénestroff France
162 B2 Benet France
192 B4 Benetutti Sardegna Italy
190 C4 Bene Vagienna Italy
162 D2 Bénévent-l'Abbaye France
193 G3 Benevento Italy
193 G3 Benevento prov. Campania Italy
Beneventum Italy see Benevento
232 D4 Benezette PA U.S.A.
157 H4 Benfeld France
234 A2 Benfer PA U.S.A.
184 B1 Benfica do Ribatejo Port.
107 H5 Beng r. China
96 C3 Beng, Nam r. Laos
Benga i. Fiji see Beqa
113 G8 Bengal, Bay of sea Indian Ocean
207 I6 Bengbis Cameroon
109 F1 Bengbu Anhui China
146 B4 Ben Geary hill Scotland U.K.
Benghazi Libya see Banghāzī
94 C2 Bengkalis Sumatera Indon.
94 C3 Bengkulu Sumatera Indon.
94 C3 Bengkulu prov. Indon.
209 B7 Bengo prov. Angola
147 B3 Bengorm hill Rep. of Ireland
142 E2 Bengtsfors Sweden
209 B8 Benguela Angola
209 B8 Benguela prov. Angola
204 D2 Benguerir Morocco
203 F2 Benha Egypt
146 D3 Ben Hee hill Scotland U.K.
146 B5 Ben Hiant hill Scotland U.K.
146 D3 Ben Hope hill Scotland U.K.
146 D3 Ben Horn hill Scotland U.K.
252 D3 Beni dept Bol.
252 D2 Beni r. Bol.
208 F4 Beni Dem. Rep. Congo
204 E3 Beni-Abbès Alg.
183 F1 Benia de Onís Spain
187 C6 Beniarrés Spain
180 D5 Beni Boufrah Morocco
186 D4 Benicarló Spain
187 D4 Benicasim Spain
240 F2 Benicia CA U.S.A.
187 C6 Benidorm Spain
187 C6 Beniel Spain
187 C5 Benifaió Spain
186 D4 Benifallet Spain
187 C6 Benifallim Spain
Benifayo Spain see Benifaió
181 F3 Benigánim Spain
204 E2 Beni Guil reg. Morocco
187 C6 Benilloba Spain
203 F2 Benî Mazâr Egypt
204 D2 Beni Mellal Morocco
207 F4 Benin country Africa
207 G5 Benin r. Nigeria
207 F5 Benin, Bight of g. Africa
207 G5 Benin City Nigeria
205 E3 Beni-Ounif Alg.
205 E2 Beni-Saf Alg.
210 B2 Benishangul admin. reg. Eth.
207 I4 Benisheikh Nigeria
187 D6 Benissa Spain
186 D3 Benissanet Spain
203 F2 Beni Suef Egypt
126 C5 Beni Suef governorate Egypt
187 D6 Benitachell Spain
114 C2 Benithora r. India
Benito r. Equat. Guinea see Mbini
261 H5 Benito Juárez Arg.
241 J5 Benito Juárez Mex.

245 H4 Benito Juárez Mex.
245 F2 Benito Juárez Mex.
245 G5 Benito Juárez, Presa resr Mex.
92 B2 Benito Soliven Phil.
185 H3 Benitalón Spain
185 I2 Benizar y la Tercia Spain
250 D6 Benjamim Constant Brazil
237 D5 Benjamin TX U.S.A.
242 C2 Benjamin Hill Mex.
236 C3 Benkelman NE U.S.A.
190 E1 Benken Switz.
146 D3 Ben Klibreck hill Scotland U.K.
188 E3 Benkovac Croatia
179 H4 Benkovski Bulg.
146 D5 Ben Lawers mt. Scotland U.K.
146 D5 Ben Ledi hill Scotland U.K.
150 C1 Benllech Isle of Anglesey, Wales U.K.
187 D4 Benlloch Spain
83 G2 Ben Lomond mt. N.S.W. Austr.
148 G5 Ben Lomond hill Scotland U.K.
240 F3 Ben Lomond CA U.S.A.
146 D3 Ben Loyal hill Scotland U.K.
146 D5 Ben Lui mt. Scotland U.K.
215 F4 Ben Macdhui mt. Lesotho
144 F3 Ben Macdui mt. Scotland U.K.
189 A7 Ben Mahdi Alg.
84 D3 Benmara N.T. Austr.
81 C5 Ben More mt. South I. N.Z.
146 B5 Ben More mt. Scotland U.K.
146 D5 Ben More mt. Scotland U.K.
81 C6 Benmore, Lake South I. N.Z.
146 D3 Ben More Assynt hill Scotland U.K.
81 C6 Benmore Peak South I. N.Z.
171 C4 Benndorf Ger.
164 D2 Benneckenstein (Harz) Ger.
169 F4 Bennekom Neth.
164 E2 Bennekom Neth.
222 C3 Bennett B.C. Can.
226 B2 Bennett WI U.S.A.
147 D4 Bennettsbridge Rep. of Ireland
231 E5 Bennettsville SC U.S.A.
146 C5 Ben Nevis mt. Scotland U.K.
80 E3 Benneydale North I. N.Z.
233 H3 Bennington NH U.S.A.
233 G3 Bennington VT U.S.A.
167 E3 Bennstedt Ger.
171 C4 Bennungen Ger.
158 B4 Bénodet France
81 B6 Ben Ohau Range mts South I. N.Z.
215 G2 Benoni S. Africa
207 I4 Bénoué r. Cameroon
208 C2 Bénoy Chad
182 C4 Benquerença Port.
163 B5 Benquet France
146 E4 Ben Rinnes hill Scotland U.K.
143 B3 Bensafrim Port.
171 D3 Bensdorf Ger.
169 F5 Benshausen Ger.
172 C2 Bensheim Ger.
204 D2 Ben Slimane Morocco
151 F3 Benson Oxfordshire, England U.K.
241 L6 Benson AZ U.S.A.
236 E2 Benson MN U.S.A.
206 C5 Bensonville Liberia
232 C5 Bens Run WV U.S.A.
146 C5 Ben Starav mt. Scotland U.K.
122 D5 Bent Iran
164 F2 Bentelo Neth.
206 B4 Benti Guinea
209 B8 Bentiaba Angola
180 E5 Ben Tieb Morocco
84 D3 Bentinck Island Qld Austr.
97 B5 Bentinck Island Myanmar
146 E5 Ben Tirran hill Scotland U.K.
208 F2 Bentiu Sudan
128 B3 Bent Jbail Lebanon
222 H4 Bentley Alta Can.
149 H4 Bentley South Yorkshire, England U.K.
232 C4 Bentleyville PA U.S.A.
253 F4 Bento Gomes r. Brazil
233 □J2 Benton N.B. Can.
237 E5 Benton AR U.S.A.
240 H3 Benton CA U.S.A.
236 F4 Benton IL U.S.A.
237 F4 Benton KY U.S.A.
237 E5 Benton LA U.S.A.
234 B1 Benton PA U.S.A.
234 C5 Benton TN U.S.A.
Bentong Malaysia see Bentung
226 D4 Benton Harbor MI U.S.A.
237 E4 Bentonville AR U.S.A.
232 B5 Bentonville OH U.S.A.
97 D5 Bên Tre Vietnam
94 C2 Bentung Malaysia
170 D1 Bentwisch Ger.
170 E2 Bentzin Ger.
207 G5 Benue r. Nigeria
207 H5 Benue state Nigeria
94 C2 Benum, Gunung mt. Malaysia
177 I3 Beňuš Slovakia
146 D5 Ben Vorlich hill Argyll and Bute, Scotland U.K.
146 D5 Ben Vorlich hill Perth and Kinross/Stirling, Scotland U.K.
147 B3 Benwee hill Rep. of Ireland
232 C4 Benwood WV U.S.A.
146 D4 Ben Wyvis mt. Scotland U.K.
80 H1 Benxi Liaoning China
114 E4 Beograd Srbija Yugo.
116 E4 Beohari Madh. Prad. India
206 D5 Béoumi Côte d'Ivoire
94 C4 Bepagut, Gunung r. Indon.
108 C3 Bepan Jiang r. Guizhou China
103 E7 Beppu Japan
79 □7a Bequ i. Fiji
247 □3 Bequia i. St Vincent
254 D2 Bequimão Brazil
117 G4 Bera Bangl.
261 G3 Berabevú Arg.
116 C4 Bera r. India
147 D2 Beragh Northern Ireland U.K.
213 □K2 Beramanja Madag.
196 D4 Berane Crna Gora Yugo.
183 H1 Beranga Spain
183 H1 Beranuy Spain
116 D3 Berasia Madh. Prad. India
94 B2 Berastagi Sumatera Indon.
198 A1 Berat Albania
94 C3 Beratus, Gunung mt. Indon.
173 F2 Beratzhausen Ger.
95 G2 Berau r. Indon.
91 H7 Berau, Teluk b. Indon.
261 H4 Berazategui Arg.
187 C3 Berbegal Spain
208 F3 Berber Sudan
210 E2 Berbera Somalia
208 B3 Berbérati C.A.R.
215 H2 Berbice r. Guyana
183 G1 Berbinzana Spain
183 C3 Bercedo Spain
177 I4 Bercel Hungary
155 I5 Bercenay-en-Othe France
183 E3 Bercero Spain
190 E4 Berceto Italy
173 J4 Berchem Belgium
192 D4 Berchidda Sardegna Italy
179 J2 Berching Ger.
107 F2 Berch Mongolia
173 G4 Berchtesgaden Ger.
173 H4 Berchtesgadener Alpen mts Ger.
185 G4 Bérchules Spain
182 D2 Bercianos del Páramo Spain
156 B2 Berck France
129 D3 Berd Armenia
137 I4 Berda r. Ukr.
159 C3 Berd'huis France
139 N7 Berdichev Ukr. see Berdychiv
131 N3 Berdigestyakh Rus. Fed.
130 J4 Berdsk Rus. Fed.
182 D1 Berducedo Spain
136 D5 Berdún Spain
137 I4 Berdyans'k Ukr.
232 A6 Berea KY U.S.A.
232 B5 Berea OH U.S.A.
150 C4 Bere Alston Devon, England U.K.
Béréby Côte d'Ivoire see Grand-Béréby

210 F2 Bereeda Somalia
150 C4 Bere Ferrers Devon, England U.K.
139 K1 Bereg Rus. Fed.
177 L3 Beregdaróc Hungary
Beregovo Ukr. see Berehove
190 E3 Bereguardo Italy
136 C3 Berehomet Ukr.
136 B3 Berehove Ukr.
139 H5 Berek Croatia
137 I3 Bereka r. Ukr.
137 I3 Bereka r. Ukr.
177 K4 Berekböszörmény Hungary
213 □J4 Bereketa Madag.
211 B6 Bereku Tanz.
206 E5 Berekum Ghana
177 H6 Beremend Hungary
139 L3 Berendeyevo Rus. Fed.
252 C4 Berenguela Bol.
203 G4 Berenice Egypt
Berenice Libya see Banghāzī
223 L4 Berens r. Man. Can.
213 □J4 Berenty Madag.
150 E4 Bere Regis Dorset, England U.K.
225 H4 Beresford N.B. Can.
236 D3 Beresford SD U.S.A.
136 C2 Berestechko Ukr.
197 H2 Bereşti Romania
137 H3 Berestivka Ukr.
137 H3 Berestova r. Ukr.
137 I4 Berestove Ukr.
137 H3 Berestoven'ka Ukr.
234 D3 Berestovets' Ukr.
136 C2 Berestyane Ukr.
137 G2 Bereza Belarus see Byaroza
137 F2 Berezan' r. Ukr.
137 F2 Berezanka Ukr.
137 G4 Bereznehuvate Ukr.
134 H3 Bereznik Arkhangel'skaya Oblast' Rus. Fed.
134 L4 Bereznik Rus. Fed.
136 D2 Bereznyky Ukr.
Berezov Rus. Fed. see Berezovo
134 L3 Berezovaya r. Rus. Fed.
136 D2 Berezovka Belarus see Byarozawka
100 C2 Berezovka Amurskaya Oblast' Rus. Fed.
120 D1 Berezovka Orenburgskaya Oblast' Rus. Fed.
134 L4 Berezovka Permskaya Oblast' Rus. Fed.
Berezovka Odes'ka Oblast' Ukr. see Berezivka
130 H3 Berezovo Rus. Fed.
136 E4 Berezovyy Rus. Fed.
136 E1 Berezyne Ukr.
172 D4 Berg Baden-Württemberg Ger.
171 C5 Berg Bayern Ger.
173 F4 Berg Bayern Ger.
169 F5 Berg Rheinland-Pfalz Ger.
165 F5 Berg Lux.
172 C3 Berg (Pfalz) Ger.
171 C4 Berga Sachsen-Anhalt Ger.
171 D5 Berga Thüringen Ger.
186 E2 Berga Spain
199 E2 Bergama Turkey
193 J2 Bergamo Italy
193 J2 Bergamo prov. Lombardia Italy
186 C4 Bergantes r. Spain
183 H1 Bergara Spain
173 F2 Bergatreute Ger.
150 C4 Berg bei Neumarkt in der Oberpfalz Ger.
179 E2 Berg bei Rohrbach Austria
141 L3 Bergby Sweden
170 C2 Berge Brandenburg Ger.
168 D4 Berge Niedersachsen Ger.
192 D4 Bergeggi Italy
170 E1 Berge Mecklenburg-Vorpommern Ger.
168 E3 Bergen Niedersachsen Ger.
164 D2 Bergen Neth.
142 A2 Bergen Norway
215 H2 Bergen S. Africa
232 E3 Bergen NY U.S.A.
168 F3 Bergen (Dumme) Ger.
235 G2 Bergen County county NJ U.S.A.
235 D2 Bergen op Zoom Neth.
164 D2 Bergen op Zoom Neth.
159 F5 Bergerac France
156 C4 Bergères-lès-Vertus France
263 B2 Bergerson, Mount Antarctica
160 C2 Bergesserin France
165 E3 Bergeyk Neth.
170 E3 Bergfelde Ger.
164 D2 Berghaupten Ger.
178 B3 Bergheim Austria
173 F3 Bergheim Ger.
183 G2 Berghülen Ger.
179 E2 Berg im Drautal Austria
169 C5 Bergisch Gladbach Ger.
173 F3 Bergkamen Ger.
173 H3 Bergkirchen Ger.
226 C2 Bergland MI U.S.A.
169 E4 Bergneustadt Ger.
141 L2 Bergnäsviken Sweden
169 C4 Bergneustadt Ger.
Bergoo Italy see Bergamo
161 D4 Bergonne France
232 C2 Bergoo WV U.S.A.
163 D4 Bergouey France
143 H2 Bergshamra Sweden
143 H2 Bergsjö Sweden
140 M2 Bergsviken Sweden
173 F2 Bergünberg? — Bergulen?
173 G2 Bergünde Ger.
183 G2 Bergüll
156 C2 Bergues France
162 F1 Bergum Neth.
184 B3 Bergün Switz.
215 G5 Bergville S. Africa
172 F2 Bergwitz Ger.
107 F2 Berh Mongolia
94 B4 Berhala, Selat sea chan. Indon.
117 G4 Berhampore W. Bengal India
197 H2 Berheci r. Romania
197 H4 Berhida Hungary
257 F2 Berilo Brazil
120 C4 Beringa, Ostrov i. Rus. Fed.
87 C5 Beringarra W.A. Austr.
165 E3 Beringe Neth.
184 C2 Beringel Port.
165 E3 Beringen Belgium
77 H2 Beringin Indon.
120 C4 Berehovsky Chukotskiy Avtonomnyy Okrug Rus. Fed.
220 A4 Bering Sea N. Pacific Ocean
220 B3 Bering Strait Rus. Fed./U.S.A.
151 F3 Berinsfield Oxfordshire, England U.K.

164 D3 Berkel Neth.
164 F2 Berkel r. Neth.
86 E2 Berkeley r. W.A. Austr.
150 D4 Berkeley Gloucestershire, England U.K.
240 F3 Berkeley CA U.S.A.
235 D2 Berkeley Heights NJ U.S.A.
232 D5 Berkeley Springs WV U.S.A.
168 F2 Berkenthin Ger.
151 G3 Berkhamsted Hertfordshire, England U.K.
164 E2 Berkhout Neth.
164 E1 Berkhout Neth.
262 U1 Berkner Island Antarctica
197 H4 Berkovitsa Bulg.
234 C2 Berks County county PA U.S.A.
233 G3 Berkshire Hills MA U.S.A.
151 F2 Berkswell West Midlands, England U.K.
164 F2 Berkel Belgium
165 D3 Berlaar Belgium
156 D2 Berlaimont France
222 G4 Berland r. Alta Can.
184 E2 Berlanga Spain
183 H3 Berlanga de Duero Spain
165 D3 Berlare Belgium
140 O1 Berlevåg Norway
167 E3 Berlicum Neth.
164 E1 Berlikum Neth.
170 E3 Berlin Ger.
171 E3 Berlin land Ger.
165 B4 Berlin CT U.S.A.
235 E2 Berlin MD U.S.A.
233 H3 Berlin NH U.S.A.
234 □H2 Berlin NH U.S.A.
234 D3 Berlin NJ U.S.A.
232 C4 Berlin OH U.S.A.
232 D5 Berlin PA U.S.A.
226 C4 Berlin WI U.S.A.
262 O1 Berlin, Mount Antarctica
169 F4 Berlingerode Ger.
81 C4 Berlins South I. N.Z.
234 C2 Berlinsville PA U.S.A.
196 E3 Berliste Romania
171 C4 Berlstedt Ger.
83 G4 Bermagui N.S.W. Austr.
172 D2 Bermatingen Ger.
122 D2 Berme Turkm.
243 G5 Bermejillo Mex.
260 D3 Bermejo r. Arg.
258 F2 Bermejo r. Arg./Bol.
252 D5 Bermejo Bol.
261 G6 Bermejo, Isla i. Arg.
183 H1 Bermeo Spain
182 D3 Bermillo de Sayago Spain
231 □ Bermuda terr. N. Atlantic Ocean
264 E4 Bermuda Rise sea feature N. Atlantic Ocean
190 C2 Bern canton Switz.
190 C2 Bern Switz.
163 C5 Bernac-Dessus France
239 F5 Bernalillo NM U.S.A.
256 C5 Bernardino de Campos Brazil
183 F3 Bernardos Spain
234 D3 Bernardsville NJ U.S.A.
176 D2 Bernartice Czech Rep.
261 F5 Bernasconi Arg.
172 C2 Bernau Baden-Württemberg Ger.
170 E3 Bernau Brandenburg Ger.
173 G4 Bernau am Chiemsee Ger.
156 C2 Bernaville France
159 G2 Bernay France
173 E4 Bernbeuren Ger.
171 C4 Bernburg (Saale) Ger.
179 H3 Berndorf Austria
169 H4 Berndorf Ger.
171 C4 Berne Ger.
Berne Switz. see Bern
226 E5 Berne IN U.S.A.
182 E2 Bernesga r. Spain
173 F2 Bernex France
159 F2 Bernay Ger.
129 B1 Berneck Switz.
173 J2 Berneck Ger.
151 I4 Berneval-le-Grand France
146 A5 Berneray i. Western Isles, Scotland U.K.
146 A5 Berneray i. Western Isles, Scotland U.K.
Berner Alpen mts Switz. see Berner Alpen
170 E3 Bernesga r. Spain
186 E2 Bernesga Spain
173 F2 Bernhardsthal Austria
173 □2 Bernhardswald Ger.
87 B5 Bernier Island W.A. Austr.
161 D3 Bernin France
183 H4 Berninches mt. Spain
183 H4 Berninches mt. Spain
204 D2 Bernisdale Highland, Scotland U.K.
157 J3 Bernissart Belgium
170 D2 Bernitt Ger.
170 E2 Bernkastel-Kues Ger.
168 E3 Bernos-Beaulac France
172 E3 Bernried Bayern Ger.
173 F3 Bernsdorf Ger.
235 F1 Bernstadt Sachsen Ger.
232 E4 Bernstadt KY U.S.A.
179 H3 Bernstein Austria
234 B4 Bernville PA U.S.A.
Beroea Greece see Veroia
Beroea Syria see Ḥalab
190 D1 Beroroha Madag.
176 D2 Beroun Czech Rep.
197 F5 Berovo Macedonia
199 □ Berrahal Alg.
189 A7 Berrahal Alg.
161 E5 Berre, Étang de lag. France
204 D2 Berrechid Morocco
82 F3 Berri S.A. Austr.
205 F2 Berriane Alg.
146 C3 Berriedale Highland, Scotland U.K.
146 E4 Berriedale Water r. Scotland U.K.
158 A5 Berrien France
83 F3 Berrigan N.S.W. Austr.
184 D4 Berrocal Spain
260 D3 Berrotarán Arg.
205 F1 Berrouaghia Alg.
150 D4 Berrow Somerset, England U.K.
116 C5 Berru r. India
120 C1 Berry-au-Bac France
155 D3 Berry Creek r. U.S.A.
246 D1 Berry Islands Bahamas
234 B2 Berryville PA U.S.A.
232 E5 Berryville VA U.S.A.
185 I4 Berja Spain
163 C4 Bersac-sur-Rivalier France
183 F2 Bershad' Ukr.
192 B3 Berson France
191 D4 Bersone Italy
246 D2 Betsy Bay Mayaguana
157 J5 Bertamirãns Spain
182 B2 Berthelsdorf mt. Austria
165 H2 Berthelming France
165 G2 Berthelsdorf Ger.
206 D4 Bertincourt France
191 H4 Bertinoro Italy
172 G2 Bertogne Belgium
143 H2 Bertoua Cameroon
190 E4 Bertrange Lux.
158 D3 Bertry France
199 A5 Beru atoll Gilbert Is Kiribati
150 D2 Berumbur Ger.
164 E1 Beruniy Uzbek.
120 D1 Berwald Brazil — Beruri Brazil
116 D5 Beruwala Sri Lanka
151 F2 Berwyn r. Wales, Scotland U.K.
146 F5 Berwick Vic. Austr.
150 C4 Berwick LA U.S.A.
234 B2 Berwick PA U.S.A.
149 F3 Berwick-upon-Tweed Northumberland, England U.K.

150 D2 Berwyn hills Wales U.K.
234 C2 Berwyn PA U.S.A.
137 G4 Beryslav Ukr.
Berytus Lebanon see Beirut
197 E3 Berzasca Romania
138 F3 Bērzaune Latvia
139 N1 Berže r. Lith.
176 G5 Berzence Hungary
185 L1 Berzocana Spain
157 E3 Berzé-le-Ville France
186 D2 Besalú Spain
160 B1 Besançon France
183 F2 Besande Spain
95 F3 Besar, Gunung mt. Indon.
94 C1 Besar, Gunung mt. Malaysia
183 F1 Besaya r. Spain
139 H5 Besbre r. France
160 B2 Besbre r. France
139 H5 Bescanó Spain
169 D5 Beselich-Obertiefenbach Ger.
127 F3 Beşiri Turkey
7 J6 Beskid Niski hills Pol.
175 I6 Beskid Żywiecki mts Pol.
Beskra Alg. see Biskra
129 D2 Beslan Rus. Fed.
197 F5 Besleţi Bulg.
194 F2 Besni Turkey
190 D3 Besozzo Italy
186 C2 Besparmak Dağları mts Cyprus see Pentadaktylos Range
149 H4 Bessacarr South Yorkshire, England U.K.
161 B5 Bessan France
208 B3 Bessaoua Chad
190 D2 Bessarabka Moldova see Basarabeasca
121 G4 Bessay-sur-Allier France
160 D3 Bessbrook Northern Ireland U.K.
161 E3 Besse France
160 A1 Besse-et-St-Anastaise France
161 C4 Bessèges France
231 C5 Bessemer AL U.S.A.
226 C2 Bessemer MI U.S.A.
232 C4 Bessemer PA U.S.A.
160 C3 Bessenay France
172 D2 Bessenbach Ger.
159 G4 Bessé-sur-Braye France
161 E5 Besse-sur-Issole France
163 D5 Bessières France
162 D2 Bessines-sur-Gartempe France
129 B1 Besskorbnaya Rus. Fed.
136 E3 Bessonovka Rus. Fed.
199 D3 Bessou, Mont de hill France
160 D1 Bèze France
120 C2 Bezau Austria
149 E3 Bezenği Rus. Fed.
177 J2 Bezenye Hungary
138 D3 Bezhanovo Bulg.
139 K3 Bezhetsk Rus. Fed.
139 K3 Bezhetskiy Verkh reg. Rus. Fed.
161 E5 Béziers France
184 D2 Bezledy Pol.
136 D1 Bibrka Ukr.
151 F3 Bibury Gloucestershire, England U.K.
161 C5 Bezouce France
177 L3 Bezvodne Slovakia
257 M4 Bicas Brazil
197 H2 Bicaz Maramureş Romania
197 H2 Bicaz Neamţ Romania
193 H3 Biccari Italy
226 C3 Bicesse? — Big Rapids MI U.S.A.
226 C3 Big r. U.S.A.
223 J4 Bichena Eth.
108 B3 Bicheno Chongqing China see Bishan
83 G5 Bicheno Tas. Austr.
100 D5 Bichevaya Rus. Fed.
207 H3 Bichi Nigeria
100 I1 Bichi r. Rus. Fed.
173 H3 Bichl Ger.
116 B3 Bichölim Goa India
140 L7 Bichvint'a Georgia
173 G3 Bickendorf Ger.
151 F2 Bickenhill West Midlands, England U.K.
84 D2 Bickerton Island N.T. Austr.
150 D4 Bickleigh Devon, England U.K.
150 C3 Bickleigh Devon, England U.K.
151 H3 Bicknacre Essex, England U.K.
241 J4 Bicknell UT U.S.A.
129 B2 Biço Azer.
208 B4 Bicuari, Parque Nacional do nat. park Angola
80 F7 Bida r. Kazakh. — Betpak-Dala plain Kazakh.
80 F7 Betroka Madag.
235 B2 Betsy Bay — Bidart France
114 B3 Bidasar Rajasthan India
173 H3 Bidburg Ger.
150 C4 Biddenden Kent, England U.K.
164 C2 Biddinghuizen Neth.
149 G4 Biddulph Staffordshire, England U.K.
150 C3 Bideford Devon, England U.K.
150 C3 Bideford Bay England U.K.
143 I7 Bidente r. Italy
121 E5 Bidford-on-Avon Warwickshire, England U.K.
122 D2 Bidkhan, Kūh-e mt. Iran
205 I5 Bidon 5 tourist site Alg.
163 B5 Bidos France
124 F3 Bidouze r. France
186 B2 Bidwell OH U.S.A.
169 D5 Bieber Ger.
172 D2 Biebesheim am Rhein Ger.
120 C2 Bieber Ger.
171 C6 Biedenkopf Ger.
190 C3 Biel Spain
167 C5 Biel Switz.
171 D4 Bieleboh hill Ger.
191 I5 Bielawa Pol.
171 K3 Bielawy Pol.
174 F2 Bielcza Pol.
175 J5 Bielec-Bala — Bielsko-Biała Pol.
172 D5 Biella Italy
143 I4 Biella prov. Piemonte Italy
186 D2 Bielsa Spain
171 I5 Bielsk Pol.
175 L3 Bielsk Podlaski Pol.
174 F4 Bielsko-Biała Pol.
174 E3 Bielsko-Biała prov. Pol.
169 F4 Bienenbüttel Ger.
97 D5 Biên Hòa Vietnam
190 D2 Bienne see Biel
117 J4 Bienne r. France
209 C8 Bié prov. Angola

161 E4 Beuil France
83 E3 Beulah Vic. Austr.
150 D2 Beulah Powys, Wales U.K.
226 D3 Beulah MI U.S.A.
236 C2 Beulah ND U.S.A.
151 H3 Beult r. England U.K.
169 F4 Beuningen Neth.
169 F4 Beuren Ger.
127 I3 Beurnik Pol.
157 E3 Beuville France
Beutheb Pol. see Bytom
160 C2 Beuvray, Mont hill France
160 B1 Beuvron r. France
159 H4 Beuvron r. France
156 C2 Beuvry France
159 G2 Beuzeville France
190 C2 Bex Switz.
151 I4 Bexbach Ger.
151 H4 Bexhill East Sussex, England U.K.
127 J6 Beşiri Turkey — Beypi Turkey
175 I6 Beşli Turkey
128 B3 Beyağaç Turkey
199 F3 Beyazköy Turkey
163 B3 Beyce Turkey see Orhaneli
199 F5 Beychac-et-Caillau France
199 G1 Beyciler Dölü Turkey
199 F2 Beydağ Turkey
199 G3 Beydağları mts Turkey
199 G3 Beyendorf Ger.
199 G3 Beykonak Turkey
199 E1 Beyköy Turkey
199 F1 Beyköy Turkey
206 C4 Beyla Guinea
161 B5 Beylagan Azer. see Beyləqan
199 G2 Beyləqan Azer.
199 G2 Beylikova Turkey
193 C2 Beyla Guinea
160 D1 Beynac-et-Cazenac France
162 D2 Beynat France
165 E4 Beyne-Heusay Belgium
120 C3 Beyneu Kazakh.
120 D3 Beyoba Manisa Turkey
199 E2 Beyoba Manisa Turkey
199 E2 Beyoneisu Retugan i. Japan
103 I8 Beyoneisu-retgan i. Japan
126 C3 Beypazarı Turkey
126 E3 Beypınarı Turkey
122 C5 Beypore India
Beyrouth Lebanon see Beirut
126 C3 Beyşehir Turkey
126 C3 Beyşehir Gölü l. Turkey
137 K4 Beysug Rus. Fed.
137 J5 Beysugskiy Liman lag. Rus. Fed.
127 F3 Beytüşşebap Turkey
161 F4 Bez r. France
199 E4 Bezas Spain
178 A3 Bezau Austria
203 F2 Biba Egypt
102 □2 Bibai Japan
209 B8 Bibala Angola
83 G4 Bibbenluke N.S.W. Austr.
191 L5 Bibbiena Italy
191 I5 Bibbona Italy
208 B3 Bibémi Cameroon
172 C3 Biberach Ger.
172 D3 Biberach an der Riß Ger.
173 F3 Biberist Ger.
173 F2 Bibert r. Ger.
129 E2 Bibiani Ghana
206 E5 Bibiani Ghana
191 H3 Bibione Italy
114 C2 Bibiyana r. Bangl.
172 C2 Biblos Lebanon see Jbail
136 C3 Bibrka Ukr.

116 B5 Bhogat Gujarat India
116 G5 Bhokardan Mahar. India
117 G5 Bhola Bangl.
116 D4 Bhogaon Uttar Prad. India
215 G4 Bhongweni S. Africa
116 B3 Bhopal Madh. Prad. India
114 D2 Bhopalpatnam Madh. Prad. India
114 B2 Bhor Mahar. India
116 D4 Bhrigukaccha Gujarat India see Bharuch
117 F5 Bhuban Orissa India
117 F5 Bhubaneshwar Orissa India
Bhubaneswar Orissa India see Bhubaneshwar
114 B3 Bhuj Gujarat India
96 B3 Bhumiphol Dam Thai.
215 H2 Bhungwa Mahar. India
116 C5 Bhusawal Mahar. India
117 G4 Bhutan country Asia
114 B4 Bhuvanagiri Tamil Nadu India
250 E5 Bia r. Ghana
209 E7 Bia, Monts mts Dem. Rep. Congo
96 C3 Bia, Phou mt. Laos
122 D5 Biabān mts Iran
174 F4 Biadki Pol.
190 E2 Biasca Switz.
165 I6 Biała r. Pol.
174 E3 Biała r. Pol.
174 G4 Biała-Parcela Pierwsza Pol.
175 K2 Biała Piska Pol.
175 L3 Biała Podlaska Pol.
175 I4 Biała Rawska Pol.
174 F2 Białe Błota Pol.
174 F4 Białka r. Pol.
175 I4 Białobrzegi Pol.
174 G5 Białobrzegi Pol.
174 F2 Białogard Pol.
175 L3 Białowieża Pol.
174 E2 Biały Bór Pol.
175 I6 Biały Dunajec Pol.
175 J3 Białystok Pol.
194 F5 Biancavilla Sicilia Italy
195 F4 Bianco Italy
190 D3 Bianco, Corno mt. Italy
Bianco, Monte mt. France/Italy see Mont Blanc
107 I5 Biandan Gazi r. mouth China
190 D3 Biandrate Italy
208 D3 Bianga C.A.R.
206 D5 Bianouan Côte d'Ivoire
160 E2 Bians-les-Usiers France
190 D3 Biandza Italy
107 K5 Bianzhuang Shandong China see Cangshan
92 D5 Biao Phil.
116 D5 Biaora Madh. Prad. India
122 C2 Bīārjmand Iran
122 C5 Biaro i. Indon.
163 A5 Biarritz France
163 A5 Biarritz airport France
162 A4 Biarrotte France
162 C3 Biars-sur-Cère France
163 A4 Bias France
163 C4 Bias Aquitaine France
160 D2 Biasca Switz.
191 J2 Biatorbágy Hungary
203 F2 Biba Egypt
102 □1 Biba Egypt

184 D2 Bienvenida hill Spain
251 H3 Bienvenue Fr. Guiana
209 B8 Bié Plateau Angola
177 H1 Bierawa Pol.
174 G5 Bierawka r. Pol.
85 F5 Bierbank Qld Austr.
125 E2 Bierdzany Pol.
174 C4 Biere Ger.
190 B2 Bière Switz.
184 D2 Bierge Spain
159 F4 Bierné France
163 D6 Biert France
174 F3 Biertowice Pol.
174 F4 Bieruń Pol.
174 E3 Bierutów Pol.
186 C2 Bierzwienna-Długa Pol.
175 H3 Bierzwnik Pol.
186 D2 Biescas Spain
186 C2 Biescas Spain
170 E3 Biesenthal Ger.
171 D4 Biesiekierz Pol.
215 E2 Biesiesvlei S. Africa
157 F4 Biesheim France
214 D4 Biespoort S. Africa
175 K6 Bieszczady mts Pol.
175 L5 Bieszczadzki Park Narodowy nat. park Pol.
172 D3 Bietigheim-Bissingen Ger.
172 D2 Bietikow Ger.
190 D3 Bietschhorn mt. Switz.
165 G5 Bièvre Belgium
157 H3 Bièvuzi Pol.
193 H3 Biferno r. Italy
208 A5 Bifoun Gabon
240 F2 Big r. CA U.S.A.
199 E1 Biga Turkey
199 F2 Bigadiç Turkey
261 G3 Bigand Arg.
163 B4 Biganos France
187 C4 Bigastro Spain
199 G2 Biga Yarımadası pen. Turkey
238 E2 Big Baldy Mountain MT U.S.A.
222 F5 Big Bar Creek B.C. Can.
226 D2 Big Bay MI U.S.A.
78 □3a Big Bay b. Vanuatu
226 D3 Big Bay de Noc b. MI U.S.A.
240 I4 Big Bear Lake CA U.S.A.
238 E2 Big Belt Mountains MT U.S.A.
215 H2 Big Bend Swaziland
237 F5 Big Black r. MS U.S.A.
236 D4 Big Blue r. NE U.S.A.
150 D2 Bigbury-on-Sea Devon, England U.K.
78 □3a Bigej i. Kwajalein Marshall Is
234 D3 Big Elk Creek r. MD U.S.A.
106 C2 Biger Nuur salt l. Mongolia
115 F5 Big Falls MN U.S.A.
226 A1 Big Fork r. MN U.S.A.
190 D3 Biasca Switz.
146 E6 Biggar South Lanarkshire, Scotland U.K.
215 G3 Biggarsberg S. Africa
86 □ Bigge Island W.A. Austr.
85 H5 Biggenden Qld Austr.
222 B3 Bigger, Mount B.C. Can.
78 □3a Biggarann r. Kwajalein Marshall Is
151 H3 Biggin Hill Greater London, England U.K.
151 G2 Biggleswade Bedfordshire, England U.K.
240 G2 Biggs CA U.S.A.
238 B2 Biggs OR U.S.A.
238 F2 Bighorn r. MT U.S.A.
238 F2 Bighorn r. Montana/Wyoming U.S.A.
238 F2 Bighorn Mountains WY U.S.A.
78 □3a Bigi i. Kwajalein Marshall Is
129 E3 Bigir Azer.
226 E3 Big Island VA U.S.A.
237 C6 Big Lake TX U.S.A.
173 E2 Bigbert r. Ger.
238 C1 Big Lost r. ID U.S.A.
238 E2 Big Muddy Creek r. MT U.S.A.
158 D2 Big Otter r. VA U.S.A.
223 G3 Big Pine CA U.S.A.
232 D6 Big Pine Peak CA U.S.A.
238 F2 Big Porcupine Creek r. MT U.S.A.
222 C3 Big Port Walter AK U.S.A.
226 C2 Big Rapids MI U.S.A.
223 H4 Big River Sask. Can.
222 G2 Big Salmon r. Y.T. Can.
222 C2 Big Salmon r. Y.T. Can.
238 C5 Big Sandy r. U.S.A.
236 D3 Big Sandy r. WY U.S.A.
236 D2 Big Sandy Creek r. CO U.S.A.
236 D3 Big Sioux r. SD U.S.A.
240 I2 Big Smokey Valley NV U.S.A.
237 C5 Big Spring TX U.S.A.
236 C3 Big Springs NE U.S.A.
237 C5 Big Sur CA U.S.A.
238 D2 Big Timber MT U.S.A.
223 L4 Big Trout Lake Ont. Can.
186 D2 Bigolaš Spain — Bigolaz? Spain
193 D2 Biguglia Corse France
222 H4 Big Valley Alta Can.
241 H5 Big Water UT U.S.A.
185 H2 Bigüézal Spain
97 B4 Bilauktaung Range mts Myanmar/Thai.

Bodrum to Boulemane

286

199 E3 Bodrum Turkey
140 K3 Bodsjö Sweden
140 M2 Bodträskfors Sweden
113 □1 Boduhali i. N. Male Maldives
177 J3 Bódva r. Hungary
177 J3 Bodva r. Slovakia
177 J3 Bódvaszilas Hungary
175 I3 Bodzanów Pol.
175 I5 Bodzentyn Pol.
163 C4 Boé France
165 D3 Boechout Belgium
183 F3 Boecillo Spain
183 F2 Boedo r. Spain
160 E2 Boëge France
214 D3 Boegoeberg S. Africa
164 E3 Boekel Neth.
165 C3 Boekhoute Belgium
160 C3 Boën France
208 D5 Boende Dem. Rep. Congo
214 C5 Boerboonfontein S. Africa
237 D6 Boerne TX U.S.A.
215 F5 Boesmans r. S. Africa
237 F6 Boeuf r. LA U.S.A.
182 D2 Boeza Spain
182 D2 Boeza r. Spain
256 C5 Bofete Brazil
206 B4 Boffa Guinea
161 C4 Boffres France
169 E4 Boffzen Ger.
142 C2 Bøfjell hill Norway
177 J4 Bogács Hungary
182 D4 Bogajo Spain
96 A3 Bogale Myanmar
96 A4 Bogale r. Myanmar
237 F6 Bogalusa LA U.S.A.
83 F2 Bogan r. N.S.W. Austr.
207 E3 Bogandé Burkina
83 F3 Bogan Gate N.S.W. Austr.
85 F4 Bogantungan Qld Austr.
185 H2 Bogarra Spain
196 D3 Bogatić Srbija Yugo.
134 J4 Bogatye Saby Rus. Fed.
174 C5 Bogatynia Pol.
126 D3 Boğazlıyan Turkey
111 D6 Bogcang Zangbo r. Xizang China
177 K6 Bogda Romania
110 E3 Bogda Feng mt. Xinjiang China
197 G4 Bogdan mt. Bulg.
197 G4 Bogdana Romania
197 F5 Bogdanci Macedonia
177 L4 Bogdand Romania
174 D3 Bogdaniec Pol.
Bogdanovka Georgia see Ninotsminda
120 C1 Bogdanovka Rus. Fed.
106 A3 Bogda Shan mts China
121 H1 Bogembay Kazakh.
173 G3 Bogen Ger.
140 L1 Bogen Norway
142 D4 Bogense Denmark
83 G2 Boggabilla Qld Austr.
83 G2 Boggabri N.S.W. Austr.
78 □3a Boggenatjen i. Kwajalein Marshall Is
147 B4 Boggeragh Mountains hills Rep. of Ireland
78 □3a Boggerik i. Kwajalein Marshall Is
87 C4 Boggola hill W.A. Austr.
247 □2 Boggy Peak hill Antigua Antigua and Barbuda
Boghari Alg. see Ksar el Boukhari
85 F4 Bogie r. Qld Austr.
146 F4 Bogie r. Scotland U.K.
190 E4 Bogliasco Italy
190 D2 Bognanco Italy
146 F4 Bogniebrae Aberdeenshire, Scotland U.K.
151 G4 Bognor Regis West Sussex, England U.K.
156 E3 Bogny-sur-Meuse France
207 I4 Bogo Cameroon
170 D1 Bogø Denmark
170 D1 Bogo i. Denmark
92 C4 Bogo Phil.
Bogodukhov Ukr. see Bohodukhiv
121 G1 Bogodukhovka Kazakh.
147 D3 Bog of Allen reg. Rep. of Ireland
121 G1 Bogolyubovo Kazakh.
139 I4 Bogolyubovo Smolenskaya Oblast' Rus. Fed.
139 M3 Bogolyubovo Vladimirskaya Oblast' Rus. Fed.
83 F4 Bogong, Mount Vic. Austr.
94 D4 Bogor Jawa Barat Indon.
175 J5 Bogoria Pol.
139 L5 Bogoroditsk Rus. Fed.
139 J5 Bogoroditskoye Rus. Fed.
134 H4 Bogorodsk Rus. Fed.
100 G1 Bogorodskoye Khabarovskiy Kray Rus. Fed.
134 J4 Bogorodskoye Kirovskaya Oblast' Rus. Fed.
250 C3 Bogotá Col.
177 K3 Bogota hill Slovakia
130 J4 Bogotol Rus. Fed.
134 I4 Bogovarovo Rus. Fed.
Bogoyavlenskoye Tambovskaya Oblast' Rus. Fed. see Pervomayskiy
117 G4 Bogra Bangl.
131 K4 Boguchany Rus. Fed.
135 H6 Boguchar Rus. Fed.
137 K3 Boguchar r. Rus. Fed.
175 J6 Boguchwała Pol.
206 B2 Bogué Maur.
237 F6 Bogue Chitto r. MS U.S.A.
Boguslav Ukr. see Bohuslav
174 E5 Boguszów-Gorce Pol.
246 □ Bog Walk Jamaica
177 H5 Bogyiszló Hungary
95 F2 Boh r. Indon.
107 H4 Bo Hai g. China
107 I4 Bohai Haixia sea chan. China
156 D3 Bohain-en-Vermandois France
107 H4 Bohai Wan b. China
158 B3 Bohars France
136 C3 Bohdan Ukr.
137 H4 Bohdanivka Ukr.
179 G2 Böheimkirchen Austria
176 D1 Bohemia reg. Czech Rep.
235 E2 Bohemia NY U.S.A.
86 E3 Bohemia Downs W.A. Austr.
Bohemian Forest mts Ger. see Böhmer Wald
147 C4 Boher Rep. of Ireland
148 B4 Boheraphuca Rep. of Ireland
207 F5 Bohicon Benin
179 E4 Bohinjska Bistrica Slovenia
179 E4 Bohinjsko jezero l. Slovenia
172 C2 Böhl Ger.
171 D4 Böhlen Ger.
171 D4 Böhlitz-Ehrenberg Ger.
215 G3 Bohlokong S. Africa
168 E3 Böhme Ger.
168 E3 Böhme r. Ger.
Böhmen reg. Czech Rep. see Bohemia
173 G2 Böhmer Wald mts Ger.
169 D3 Bohmte Ger.
170 D3 Böhne Ger.
137 H2 Bohodukhiv Ukr.
137 G3 Bohodukhivka Ukr.
92 C4 Bohol i. Phil.
147 B3 Bohola Rep. of Ireland
92 C4 Bohol Sea Phil.
92 B4 Bohol Strait Phil.
176 G5 Böhönye Hungary
179 G4 Bohor mt. Slovenia
136 C3 Bohorodchany Ukr.
183 E4 Bohoyo Spain
110 D3 Bohu Xinjiang China
177 H2 Bohumín Czech Rep.
176 G2 Bohuňovice Czech Rep.
136 F3 Bohuslav Ukr.
176 C2 Bohutín Czech Rep.
177 L4 Boianu Mare Romania
214 D3 Boichoko S. Africa
215 F2 Boikhutso S. Africa
86 D3 Boileau, Cape W.A. Austr.
234 A2 Boiling Springs PA U.S.A.
96 A2 Boinu r. Myanmar
254 F5 Boipeba, Ilha i. Brazil
182 B2 Boiro Spain
256 B3 Bois r. Brazil
156 C4 Boiscommun France
160 E2 Bois-d'Amont France
236 D2 Bois de Sioux r. MN U.S.A.
238 C3 Boise ID U.S.A.
238 C3 Boise r. ID U.S.A.
237 C4 Boise City OK U.S.A.
158 D3 Boisgervilly France
156 B3 Bois-Guillaume France
156 C4 Bois-le-Roi France
161 C5 Boisseron France
163 E4 Boisset France
161 C4 Boisset-et-Gaujac France
223 K5 Boissevain Man. Can.
163 E5 Boissezon France
191 H2 Boite r. Italy
215 E2 Boitumelong S. Africa
256 D5 Boituva Brazil
170 E2 Boitzenburg Ger.
162 C2 Boivre r. France
168 F2 Boize r. Ger.
168 F2 Boizenburg Ger.
174 D4 Bojadła Pol.
193 G3 Bojano Italy
175 J5 Bojanów Pol.
174 E4 Bojanowo Pol.
92 B2 Bojeador, Cape Phil.
177 H3 Bojná Slovakia
177 H3 Bojnice Slovakia
197 E4 Bojnik Srbija Yugo.
122 D2 Bojnūrd Iran
95 E4 Bojonegoro Jawa Timur Indon.
207 H5 Boju-Ega Nigeria
Bokaak atoll Marshall Is see Majuro
111 E4 Bokadaban Feng mt. Qinghai/Xinjiang China
117 H4 Bokajan Assam India
117 F5 Bokaro Bihar India
206 B4 Boké Guinea
168 D2 Bokel Ger.
214 B5 Bokfontein S. Africa
83 F2 Bokhara r. N.S.W. Austr.
207 H5 Bokito Cameroon
168 E1 Böklund Ger.
209 B6 Boko Congo
177 H4 Bokod Hungary
Bokombayevskoye Kyrg. see Bökönbaev
121 I4 Bökönbaev Kyrg.
Bokonbayevo Kyrg. see Bökönbaev
177 K4 Bököny Hungary
202 C6 Bokoro Chad
209 B6 Boko-Songho Congo
Bokovo-Antratsit Ukr. see Antratsyt
135 H6 Bokovskaya Rus. Fed.
215 G2 Boksburg S. Africa
139 I2 Boksitogorsk Rus. Fed.
214 C2 Bokspits S. Africa
100 F2 Boktor Rus. Fed.
208 D5 Bokungu Dem. Rep. Congo
Bokurdak Turkm. see Bakhardok
202 B6 Bol Chad
244 C3 Bola del Viejo, Cerro mt. Mex.
206 B4 Bolama Guinea-Bissau
123 F4 Bolan r. Pak.
208 E3 Bolanda, Jebel mt. Sudan
172 C2 Bolanden Ger.
160 E1 Bolandoz France
190 E4 Bolano Italy
244 B3 Bolaños r. Mex.
185 G2 Bolaños de Calatrava Spain
159 G2 Bolbec France
177 H5 Bölcske Hungary
122 B4 Boldajī Iran
170 E2 Boldekow Ger.
168 E1 Bolderslev Denmark
177 K3 Boldogkőváralja Hungary
149 H3 Boldon Tyne and Wear, England U.K.
151 F4 Boldre Hampshire, England U.K.
197 H3 Boldu Romania
122 D1 Boldumsaz Turkm.
177 K6 Boldur Romania
177 J3 Boldva Hungary
110 C2 Bole Xinjiang China
206 E4 Bole Ghana
186 C2 Bolea Spain
136 B3 Bolekhiv Ukr.
177 G3 Boleráz Slovakia
175 I5 Bolesław Pol.
174 D4 Bolesławiec Pol.
174 G4 Bolesławiec Pol.
174 C3 Boleszkowice Pol.
135 J5 Bolgar Respublika Tatarstan Rus. Fed.
206 E4 Bolgatanga Ghana
Bolgrad Ukr. see Bolhrad
136 E5 Bolhrad Ukr.
100 D3 Boli Heilong. China
140 M2 Boliden Sweden
Bolifuri i. S. Male Maldives see Bolifushi
113 □1 Bolifushi i. S. Male Maldives
175 I3 Bolimów Pol.
92 A2 Bolinao Phil.
197 G3 Bolintin-Vale Romania
250 C2 Bolívar dept Col.
252 A1 Bolívar Peru
237 E4 Bolivar MO U.S.A.
232 D3 Bolivar NY U.S.A.
237 F5 Bolivar TN U.S.A.
251 F3 Bolívar state Venez.
252 D4 Bolivia country S. America
197 E4 Boljevac Srbija Yugo.
128 A1 Bolkar Dağları mts Turkey
139 K5 Bolkhov Rus. Fed.
227 F1 Bolkow Ont. Can.
170 C1 Bölkow Ger.
174 E5 Bolków Pol.
172 D3 Boll Ger.
142 E3 Bollebygd Sweden
161 C4 Bollène France
190 C3 Bollengo Italy
190 C2 Bolligen Switz.
168 E1 Bollingstedt Ger.
149 G4 Bollington Cheshire, England U.K.
141 L3 Bollnäs Sweden
83 F2 Bollon Qld Austr.
142 E2 Bollsbyn Sweden
172 B4 Bollschweil Ger.
140 L3 Bollstabruk Sweden
166 E3 Bollstedt Ger.
184 D3 Bollullos Par del Condado Spain
157 H5 Bollwiller France
143 E3 Bolmen l. Sweden
151 G2 Bolnhurst Bedfordshire, England U.K.
129 D3 Bolnisi Georgia
208 C5 Bolobo Dem. Rep. Congo
92 B5 Bolod Islands Phil.
191 G4 Bologna Italy
191 G4 Bologna prov. Emilia-Romagna Italy
157 F4 Bologne France
250 C6 Bolognesi Loreto Peru
252 B2 Bolognesi Ucayali Peru
194 C5 Bolognetta Sicilia Italy
193 F2 Bolognola Italy
139 H3 Bologovo Rus. Fed.
139 J3 Bologoye Rus. Fed.
215 E3 Bolokanang S. Africa
139 K4 Bolokhovo Rus. Fed.
208 D4 Bolombo r. Dem. Rep. Congo
Bolon' Rus. Fed. see Achan
243 H4 Bolonchén de Rejón Mex.
207 H6 Bolondo Equat. Guinea
92 B5 Bolong Phil.
209 B7 Bolongongo Angola
192 A4 Bolotana Sardegna Italy
215 F4 Bolotwa S. Africa
96 D4 Bolovens, Phouphieng plat. Laos
117 F5 Bolpur W. Bengal India
129 F4 Bolqarçay r. Azer.
258 C3 Bolsa, Cerro mt. Arg.
192 D2 Bolsena Italy
192 D2 Bolsena, Lago di l. Italy
138 C4 Bol'shakovo Rus. Fed.
129 E1 Bol'shaya Areshevka Rus. Fed.
134 J4 Bol'shaya Atnya Rus. Fed.
137 J1 Bol'shaya Bereyka Rus. Fed.
120 B1 Bol'shaya Chernigovka Rus. Fed.
120 F1 Bol'shaya Churakovka Kazakh.
120 B1 Bol'shaya Glushitsa Rus. Fed.
134 F2 Bol'shaya Imandra, Ozero l. Rus. Fed.
137 I2 Bol'shaya Khalan' Rus. Fed.
134 I4 Bol'shaya Kokshaga r. Rus. Fed.
137 K1 Bol'shaya Lipovitsa Rus. Fed.
135 H7 Bol'shaya Martinovka Rus. Fed.
Bol'shaya Novoselka Ukr. see Velyka Novosilka
134 M1 Bol'shaya Oyu r. Rus. Fed.
134 M2 Bol'shaya Rogovaya r. Rus. Fed.
134 L2 Bol'shaya Synya r. Rus. Fed.
Bol'shaya Tsarevshchina Samarskaya Oblast' Rus. Fed. see Volzhskiy
134 K4 Bol'shaya Usa Rus. Fed.
139 I2 Bol'shaya Vishera Rus. Fed.
121 I2 Bol'shaya Vladimirovka Kazakh.
137 J2 Bol'she Bykovo Rus. Fed.
137 J4 Bol'shekrepinskaya Rus. Fed.
121 K2 Bol'shenarymskoye Kazakh.
139 J3 Bol'she-Ploskoye Rus. Fed.
137 I2 Bol'shetroitskoye Rus. Fed.
131 L2 Bol'shevik, Ostrov i. Severnaya Zemlya Rus. Fed.
134 K2 Bol'shezemel'skaya Tundra lowland Rus. Fed.
120 D3 Bol'shiye Barsuki, Peski des. Kazakh.
137 J4 Bol'shiye Saly Rus. Fed.
121 I4 Bol'shoy Aksu Kazakh.
131 Q3 Bol'shoy Aluy r. Rus. Fed.
131 R3 Bol'shoy Anyuy r. Rus. Fed.
131 M2 Bol'shoy Begichev, Ostrov i. Rus. Fed.
138 G1 Bol'shoy Berezovyy, Ostrov i. Rus. Fed.
121 J2 Bol'shoy Bukon' Kazakh.
137 I2 Bol'shoye Gorodishche Rus. Fed.
135 I5 Bol'shoye Ignatovo Rus. Fed.
134 I5 Bol'shoye Murashkino Rus. Fed.
139 J5 Bol'shoye Polpino Rus. Fed.
134 G4 Bol'shoye Selo Rus. Fed.
137 H2 Bol'shoye Soldatskoye Rus. Fed.
120 C2 Bol'shoy Ik r. Rus. Fed.
120 A2 Bol'shoy Irgiz r. Rus. Fed.
100 E4 Bol'shoy Kamen' Rus. Fed.
Bol'shoy Kavkaz mts Asia/Europe see Caucasus
139 L5 Bol'shoy Khomutets Rus. Fed.
134 L2 Bol'shoy Patok r. Rus. Fed.
131 O4 Bol'shoy Shantar, Ostrov i. Rus. Fed.
Bol'shoy Tokmak Kyrg. see Tokmak
Bol'shoy Tokmak Ukr. see Tokmak
139 H3 Bol'shoy Tuder r. Rus. Fed.
120 B2 Bol'shoy Uzen' r. Kazakh./Rus. Fed.
129 B1 Bol'shoy Zelenchuk r. Rus. Fed.
149 H4 Bolsover Derbyshire, England U.K.
164 E1 Bolsward Neth.
174 G1 Bolszewo Pol.
186 D2 Boltañá Spain
149 H3 Boltby North Yorkshire, England U.K.
190 C2 Boltigen Switz.
227 H4 Bolton Ont. Can.
92 C5 Bolton Phil.
149 G4 Bolton Greater Manchester, England U.K.
149 G3 Bolton-le-Sands Lancashire, England U.K.
137 H3 Boltyshka Ukr.
126 C2 Bolu Turkey
199 G1 Bolu prov. Turkey
140 □B2 Bolungarvík Iceland
111 F4 Boluntay Qinghai China
109 E4 Boluo Guangdong China
139 J5 Bolva r. Rus. Fed.
199 G2 Bolvadin Turkey
150 C4 Bolventor Cornwall, England U.K.
177 H6 Bóly Hungary
197 H4 Bolyarovo Bulg.
191 G2 Bolzano Italy
191 G2 Bolzano prov. Trentino - Alto Adige Italy
209 B6 Boma Dem. Rep. Congo
83 G3 Bomaderry N.S.W. Austr.
207 G5 Bomadi Nigeria
108 A2 Bomai Sichuan China
165 E4 Bomal Belgium
193 G2 Bomba Italy
83 G4 Bombala N.S.W. Austr.
184 A1 Bombarral Port.
Bombay Mahar. India see Mumbai
80 E2 Bombay North I. N.Z.
241 J5 Bombay Beach CA U.S.A.
91 H7 Bomberai, Semenanjung pen. Indon.
209 B5 Bombo r. Dem. Rep. Congo
257 E3 Bom Despacho Brazil
117 H4 Bomdila Arun. Prad. India
150 E2 Bomere Heath Shropshire, England U.K.
111 F6 Bomi Xizang China
254 G3 Bom Jardim Brazil
256 A2 Bom Jardim de Goiás Brazil
257 E4 Bom Jardim de Minas Brazil
254 D4 Bom Jesus Piauí Brazil
255 C9 Bom Jesus Rio Grande do Sul Brazil
254 E4 Bom Jesus da Gurgueia, Serra do hills Brazil
254 E5 Bom Jesus da Lapa Brazil
256 C3 Bom Jesus de Goiás Brazil
257 G4 Bom Jesus do Itabapoana Brazil
257 G4 Bom Jesus do Norte Brazil
168 E3 Bomlitz Ger.
142 A2 Bømlo i. Norway
208 E4 Bomokandi r. Dem. Rep. Congo
208 C4 Bomongo Dem. Rep. Congo
163 E6 Bompas France
194 C5 Bompensiere Sicilia Italy
194 D5 Bompietro Sicilia Italy
255 C8 Bom Retiro Brazil
257 E4 Bom Sucesso Minas Gerais Brazil
256 B5 Bom Sucesso Paraná Brazil
Bona Alg. see Annaba
160 B1 Bona France
122 A2 Bonāb Iran
163 C6 Bonac-Irazein France
190 E2 Bonaduz Switz.
232 E6 Bon Air VA U.S.A.
247 □8 Bonaire i. Neth. Antilles
83 H2 Bonalbo N.S.W. Austr.
195 F4 Bonamico r. Italy
242 □I6 Bonanza Nic.
184 D4 Bonanza Spain
246 E3 Bonao Dom. Rep.
86 E2 Bonaparte Archipelago is W.A. Austr.
183 E2 Boñar Spain
146 D4 Bonar Bridge Highland, Scotland U.K.
192 A4 Bonarcado Sardegna Italy
247 □7 Bonasse Trin. and Tob.
190 E4 Bonassola Italy
225 K3 Bonavista Nfld. Can.
160 D1 Bonboillon France
82 C2 Bon Bon S.A. Austr.
159 F3 Bonchamp-lès-Laval France
146 F6 Bonchester Bridge Scottish Borders, Scotland U.K.
190 C1 Boncourt Switz.
137 J3 Bondarevo Rus. Fed.
135 H5 Bondari Rus. Fed.
191 G4 Bondeno Italy
208 D4 Bondo Dem. Rep. Congo
92 B3 Bondoc Peninsula Phil.
172 C3 Bondorf Ger.
206 E4 Bondoukou Côte d'Ivoire
206 E4 Bondoukui Burkina
95 F4 Bondowoso Jawa Timur Indon.
231 E7 Bonds Cay i. Bahamas
226 C3 Bonduel WI U.S.A.
156 D2 Bondues France
Bondyuzhskiy Rus. Fed. see Mendeleyevsk
Bône Alg. see Annaba
93 B4 Bone, Teluk b. Indon.
168 F1 Bönebüttel Ger.
193 G3 Bonefro Italy
214 C4 Bonekraal S. Africa
169 C4 Bönen Ger.
163 C4 Bon-Encontre France
93 B4 Bonerate, Kepulauan is Indon.
146 E5 Bo'ness Falkirk, Scotland U.K.
236 D3 Bonesteel SD U.S.A.
187 B6 Bonete Spain
257 E4 Bonfim Brazil
256 A2 Bonfim r. Brazil
257 E2 Bonfinópolis de Minas Brazil
210 C3 Bonga Eth.
92 B3 Bongabong Phil.
117 G4 Bongaigaon Assam India
208 D4 Bongandanga Dem. Rep. Congo
214 D3 Bongani S. Africa
92 A5 Bongao Phil.
85 H5 Bongaree Qld Austr.
93 B3 Bongka r. Indon.
206 C5 Bong Mountains hills Liberia
209 B7 Bongo, Serra do mts Angola
213 □J3 Bongolava mts Madag.
208 B2 Bongor Chad
206 D5 Bongouanou Côte d'Ivoire
208 B5 Bongoville Gabon
97 E4 Bông Sơn Vietnam
237 D5 Bonham TX U.S.A.
140 L3 Bönhamn Sweden
206 E3 Boni Mali
183 I5 Boniches Spain
206 D4 Boniéredougou Côte d'Ivoire
174 G3 Boniewo Pol.
192 B3 Bonifacio Corse France
Bonifacio, Bocche di str. France/Italy see Bonifacio, Strait of
Bonifacio, Bouches de str. France/Italy see Bonifacio, Strait of
192 A3 Bonifacio, Strait of France/Italy
193 H5 Bonifati Italy
231 C6 Bonifay FL U.S.A.
190 C2 Bönigen Switz.
174 E1 Bonin Pol.
Bonin Islands N. Pacific Ocean see Ogasawara-shotō
231 D7 Bonita Springs FL U.S.A.
253 F5 Bonito Brazil
256 B2 Bonito r. Brazil
146 F6 Bonjedward Scottish Borders, Scotland U.K.
207 F3 Bonkoukou Niger
169 C5 Bonn Ger.
Bonna Ger. see Bonn
163 D5 Bonnac France
192 A4 Bonnanaro Sardegna Italy
162 D2 Bonnat France
160 C2 Bonnay France
172 C4 Bonndorf im Schwarzwald Ger.
161 D4 Bonne r. France
234 A3 Bonneauville PA U.S.A.
163 C5 Bonnefont France
238 C1 Bonners Ferry ID U.S.A.
159 G3 Bonnétable France
159 G5 Bonneuil-Matours France
156 B4 Bonneval Centre France
160 E3 Bonneval Rhône-Alpes France
161 F3 Bonneval-sur-Arc France
160 E2 Bonnevaux France
160 E2 Bonneville France
82 E4 Bonney, Lake S.A. Austr.
156 B3 Bonnières-sur-Seine France
87 C6 Bonnie Rock W.A. Austr.
161 D5 Bonnieux France
214 C5 Bonnievale S. Africa
172 D2 Bönnigheim Ger.
168 E2 Bönningstedt Ger.
163 B5 Bonnut France
207 G5 Bonny Nigeria
146 E5 Bonnybridge Falkirk, Scotland U.K.
215 G4 Bonny Ridge S. Africa
146 E6 Bonnyrigg Midlothian, Scotland U.K.
233 □J2 Bonny River N.B. Can.
160 A1 Bonny-sur-Loire France
223 I4 Bonnyville Alta Can.
158 D4 Bono France
192 B4 Bono Sardegna Italy
92 A4 Bonobono Phil.
97 D5 Bonom Mhai mt. Vietnam
Bononia Italy see Bologna
192 A4 Bonorva Sardegna Italy
206 E5 Bonoua Côte d'Ivoire
81 B6 Bonpland, Mount South I. N.Z.
240 I5 Bonsall CA U.S.A.
160 E2 Bons-en-Chablais France
83 G2 Bonshaw N.S.W. Austr.
160 C3 Bonson France
214 C5 Bontberg mt. S. Africa
206 B5 Bonthe Sierra Leone
92 B2 Bontoc Phil.
93 A4 Bontosunggu Sulawesi Selatan Indon.
215 G4 Bontrand S. Africa
215 E5 Bontrug S. Africa
177 G4 Bőny Hungary
177 H5 Bonyhád Hungary
84 B4 Bonython Range hills N.T. Austr.
143 H2 Boo Sweden
93 D3 Boo, Kepulauan is Irian Jaya Indon.
170 F2 Boock Ger.
82 C2 Bookabie S.A. Austr.
241 M2 Book Cliffs ridge UT U.S.A.
237 C4 Booker TX U.S.A.
206 C4 Boola Guinea
83 G2 Boolba Qld Austr.
82 D3 Booleroo Centre S.A. Austr.
147 D4 Booley Hills Rep. of Ireland
83 F3 Booligal N.S.W. Austr.
87 B5 Boologooro W.A. Austr.
83 G2 Boomi N.S.W. Austr.
226 E3 Boon MI U.S.A.
85 H5 Boonah Qld Austr.
239 F4 Boone CO U.S.A.
236 E3 Boone IA U.S.A.
231 D4 Boone NC U.S.A.
232 D6 Boones Mill VA U.S.A.
237 E5 Booneville AR U.S.A.
232 B6 Booneville KY U.S.A.
237 F5 Booneville MS U.S.A.
215 F1 Boons S. Africa
232 E5 Boonsboro MD U.S.A.
235 D2 Boonton NJ U.S.A.
106 C2 Böön Tsagaan Nuur salt l. Mongolia
240 F2 Boonville CA U.S.A.
230 C4 Boonville IN U.S.A.
236 E4 Boonville MO U.S.A.
233 F3 Boonville NY U.S.A.
252 D3 Boopi r. Bol.
210 D2 Boorama Somalia
83 F3 Booroorban N.S.W. Austr.
83 G3 Boorowa N.S.W. Austr.
83 E4 Boort Vic. Austr.
165 D4 Boortmeerbeek Belgium
156 B3 Boos France
173 E3 Boos Ger.
210 F2 Boosaaso Somalia
168 F1 Boostedt Ger.
233 □I3 Boothbay Harbor ME U.S.A.
263 D2 Boothby, Cape Antarctica
221 J3 Boothia, Gulf of Nunavut Can.
221 I2 Boothia Peninsula Nunavut Can.
149 F3 Bootle Cumbria, England U.K.
149 G4 Bootle Merseyside, England U.K.
208 A5 Booué Gabon
173 E3 Bopfingen Ger.
206 C5 Bopolu Liberia
169 C5 Boppard Ger.
258 G3 Boqueirão Brazil
254 D5 Boqueirão, Serra do hills Brazil
247 □1 Boquerón Puerto Rico
176 B2 Bor Czech Rep.
134 I4 Bor Rus. Fed.
210 A3 Bor Sudan
126 D3 Bor Turkey
197 F3 Bor Srbija Yugo.
129 F4 Boradigah Azer.
213 □K3 Boraha, Nosy i. Madag.
238 D2 Borah Peak ID U.S.A.
Boran Kazakh. see Buran
156 C3 Boran-sur-Oise France
Boraraigh i. Western Isles, Scotland U.K. see Boreray
142 E3 Borås Sweden
117 E5 Borasambar Orissa India
122 B4 Borāzjān Iran
251 G6 Borba Brazil
184 C2 Borba Port.
190 D4 Borbera r. Italy
92 C4 Borbon Phil.
190 D4 Borbore r. Italy
256 C4 Borborema Brazil
254 F3 Borborema, Planalto da plat. Brazil
197 G2 Borca Romania
Borchalo Georgia see Marneuli
169 D4 Borchen Ger.
263 K2 Borchgrevink Coast Antarctica
127 F2 Borçka Turkey
164 F2 Borculo Neth.
86 D3 Borda, Cape W.A. Austr.
256 D5 Borda da Mata Brazil
199 F3 Bor Dağı mt. Turkey
183 H3 Bordalba Spain
177 I5 Bordány Hungary
163 B4 Bordeaux France
116 D5 Bordehi Madh. Prad. India
184 B3 Bordeira Port.
168 D1 Bordelum Ger.
87 C7 Borden W.A. Austr.
225 I4 Borden P.E.I. Can.
221 G2 Borden Island N.W.T. Can.
221 J2 Borden Peninsula Nunavut Can.
234 D2 Bordentown NJ U.S.A.
163 C6 Bordères-Louron France
163 C5 Bordères-sur-l'Échez France
Borders admin. div. Scotland U.K. see Scottish Borders
82 E4 Bordertown S.A. Austr.
163 B5 Bordes Aquitaine France
163 C5 Bordes Midi-Pyrénées France
168 F1 Bordesholm Ger.
190 C5 Bordighera Italy
186 F2 Bordils Spain
194 B5 Bordino r. Sicilia Italy
205 G1 Bordj Bou Arréridj Alg.
186 C4 Bordón Spain
144 D1 Borðoy i. Faroe Is
121 H4 Bordu Kyrg.
Bordunskiy Kyrg. see Bordu
197 H3 Borduşani Romania
190 E4 Bore Italy
206 E3 Boré Mali
262 X2 Boreas Nunatak Antarctica
151 H3 Boreham Essex, England U.K.
151 G3 Borehamwood Hertfordshire, England U.K.
173 H2 Borek hill Czech Rep.
175 I5 Borek Pol.
174 F5 Borek Strzeliński Pol.
174 F4 Borek Wielkopolski Pol.
225 G1 Borel r. Que. Can.
146 E6 Boreland Dumfries and Galloway, Scotland U.K.
136 C2 Boremel' Ukr.
143 F2 Boren l. Sweden
143 F2 Borensberg Sweden
146 B4 Boreraig Highland, Scotland U.K.
146 A4 Boreray i. Western Isles, Scotland U.K.
146 □ Boreray i. Western Isles, Scotland U.K.
179 H2 Bořetice Czech Rep.
172 A2 Borg Ger.
Borgå Fin. see Porvoo
140 K2 Borgafjäll Sweden
140 □B2 Borgarnes Iceland
169 E4 Borgentreich Ger.
168 C3 Börger Ger.
164 F2 Borger Neth.
237 C5 Borger TX U.S.A.
187 G5 Borges r. Spain
190 D4 Borghetto di Borbera Italy
143 G3 Borgholm Kalmar Sweden
169 D3 Borgholzhausen Ger.
195 F4 Borgia Italy
146 D3 Borgie r. Scotland U.K.
165 E4 Borgloon Belgium
192 B2 Borgo Corse France
191 F5 Borgo a Mozzano Italy
190 D3 Borgo d'Ale Italy
191 F3 Borgoforte Italy
190 C3 Borgofranco d'Ivrea Italy
195 H2 Borgo Grappa Italy
190 D3 Borgo-lavezzaro Italy
190 D3 Borgomanero Italy
190 C5 Borgomaro Italy
190 C3 Borgone Susa Italy
190 E3 Borgonovo Val Tidone Italy
191 G4 Borgo Panigale airport Italy
193 F2 Borgorose Italy
190 C4 Borgo San Dalmazzo Italy
191 G5 Borgo San Lorenzo Italy
190 D3 Borgo San Martino Italy
190 D3 Borgosesia Italy
191 G4 Borgo Tossignano Italy
190 E4 Borgo Val di Taro Italy
191 G2 Borgo Valsugana Italy
193 F2 Borgo Velino Italy
190 D3 Borgo Vercelli Italy
170 E3 Borgsdorf Ger.
142 C1 Borgsjåbrotet mt. Norway
168 E1 Borgstedt Ger.
146 D7 Borgue Dumfries and Galloway, Scotland U.K.
116 D5 Bori Mahar. India
116 C5 Bori r. India
207 G5 Bori Nigeria
Börili Kazakh. see Burli
139 J5 Borilovo Rus. Fed.
234 B3 Boring MD U.S.A.
197 G5 Borino Bulg.
139 L5 Borinskoye Rus. Fed.
Borislav Ukr. see Boryslav
135 H6 Borisoglebsk Rus. Fed.
139 L3 Borisoglebskiy Rus. Fed.
Borisov Belarus see Barysaw
135 G6 Borisovka Rus. Fed.
139 K2 Borisovo-Sudskoye Rus. Fed.
Borispol' Ukr. see Boryspil'
213 □J2 Boriziny Madag.
188 F3 Borja mts Bos.-Herz.
250 B6 Borja Peru
183 I3 Borja Spain
183 H3 Borjabad Spain
Borjas Blancas Spain see Les Borges Blanques
129 C3 Borjomi Georgia
138 G4 Borkavichy Belarus
169 B4 Borken Ger.
169 E4 Borken (Hessen) Ger.
140 L1 Borkenes Norway
171 D3 Borkheide Ger.
175 K4 Borki Pol.
202 C5 Borkou-Ennedi-Tibesti pref. Chad
175 I4 Borkowice Pol.
168 B2 Borkum Ger.
168 B2 Borkum i. Ger.
143 F1 Borlänge Sweden
199 F2 Borlu Turkey
161 E5 Bormes-les-Mimosas France
190 D4 Bormida r. Italy
190 F2 Bormio Italy
171 C3 Born Ger.
171 D4 Borna Sachsen Ger.
171 E4 Borna Sachsen Ger.
170 D1 Born am Darß Ger.
169 F4 Born-Berge hill Ger.
164 E1 Borndiep sea chan. Neth.
160 E2 Borne r. France
164 F2 Borne Neth.
156 C3 Bornel France
165 D3 Bornem Belgium
90 D6 Borneo i. Asia
164 F2 Bornerbroek Neth.
160 E3 Bornes mts France
182 D3 Bornes Port.
182 C3 Bornes de Aguiar Port.
174 E2 Borne Sulinowo Pol.
169 B5 Bornheim Ger.
169 C5 Bornhofen Ger.
143 F4 Bornholm county Denmark
141 K5 Bornholm i. Denmark
168 F1 Bornhöved Ger.
169 C5 Bornich Ger.
207 I4 Borno state Nigeria
184 E4 Bornos Spain
183 H4 Bornova r. Spain
199 E2 Bornova Turkey
168 F2 Börnsen Ger.
171 C4 Bornstedt Ger.
183 I3 Borobia Spain
95 E4 Borobudur tourist site Indon.
177 L5 Borod Romania
137 H3 Borodayivka Ukr.
136 E4 Borodino Ukr.
138 G1 Borodinskoye Rus. Fed.
136 E2 Borodyanka Ukr.
131 O3 Borogontsy Rus. Fed.
110 C2 Borohoro Shan mts China
176 F1 Borohrádek Czech Rep.
139 L2 Borok Rus. Fed.
139 K3 Borok-Sulezhskiy Rus. Fed.
137 H2 Boromlya Ukr.
137 H2 Boromlya r. Ukr.
206 E4 Boromo Burkina
206 D3 Boron Mali
240 I4 Boron CA U.S.A.
92 C4 Borongan Phil.
174 G5 Boronów Pol.
192 A4 Borore Sardegna Italy
85 G5 Bororen Qld Austr.
174 G5 Boroszów Pol.
177 I5 Borota Hungary
206 D4 Borotou Côte d'Ivoire
149 H3 Boroughbridge North Yorkshire, England U.K.
151 H3 Borough Green Kent, England U.K.
137 I3 Borova Kharkivs'ka Oblast' Ukr.
136 F2 Borova Kyivs'ka Oblast' Ukr.
137 J3 Borova r. Ukr.
197 F4 Borovan Bulg.
176 D3 Borovany Czech Rep.
136 C2 Borove Rivnens'ka Oblast' Ukr.
136 D2 Borove Rivnens'ka Oblast' Ukr.
139 I2 Borovenka Rus. Fed.
139 I2 Borovichi Rus. Fed.
121 K1 Borovlyanka Rus. Fed.
179 F5 Borovnica Slovenia
188 G3 Borovo Selo Croatia
134 J4 Borovoy Kirovskaya Oblast' Rus. Fed.
134 F2 Borovoy Respublika Kareliya Rus. Fed.
134 K3 Borovoy Respublika Komi Rus. Fed.
121 G1 Borovoye Kazakh.
139 K4 Borovsk Rus. Fed.
120 F1 Borovskoy Kazakh.
175 J5 Borów Pol.
175 J5 Borowa Pol.
175 J4 Borowie Pol.
183 G4 Borox Spain
257 E3 Borrachudo r. Brazil
256 B5 Borrazópolis Brazil
143 F4 Borrby Sweden
170 D1 Borre Denmark
241 I5 Borrego Springs CA U.S.A.
170 D2 Borrentin Ger.
162 D4 Borrèze France
187 C4 Borriol Spain
147 E4 Borris Rep. of Ireland
147 D4 Borris-in-Ossory Rep. of Ireland
147 C4 Borrisokane Rep. of Ireland
84 D3 Borroloola N.T. Austr.
149 F3 Borrowdale Cumbria, England U.K.
177 K4 Borş Romania
140 J3 Børsa Norway
197 F2 Borşa Romania
197 G2 Borşa Romania
177 K3 Borša Slovakia
116 C5 Borsad Gujarat India
165 D3 Borsbeek Belgium
171 D4 Borsdorf Ger.
197 G2 Borsec Romania
198 A1 Borsh Albania
137 K2 Borshchevskiye Peski Rus. Fed.
136 E4 Borshchi Ukr.
136 D3 Borshchiv Ukr.
136 C3 Borshchivka Ukr.
107 F1 Borshchovochnyy Khrebet mts Rus. Fed.
175 M6 Borshchovychi Ukr.
127 G4 Borsippa tourist site Iraq
120 B1 Borskoye Rus. Fed.
Borský Jur Slovakia see Borský Svätý Jur
179 I2 Borský Svätý Jur Slovakia
177 K3 Borsod-Abaúj-Zemplén county Hungary
177 J3 Borsodbóta Hungary
177 J3 Borsodnádasd Hungary
177 J3 Borsodszentgyörgy Hungary
165 C3 Borssele Neth.
169 F3 Börßum Ger.
168 D3 Borstel Ger.
171 E5 Borstendorf Ger.
Bortala Xinjiang China see Bole
110 C2 Bortala He r. China
150 C2 Borth Ceredigion, Wales U.K.
192 A4 Bortigali Sardegna Italy
192 B4 Bortigiadas Sardegna Italy
162 E3 Bort-les-Orgues France
106 B2 Bor-Üdzüür Mongolia
122 B4 Borūjen Iran
122 B3 Borūjerd Iran
106 C3 Bor Ul Shan mts China
197 G4 Borushtitsa Bulg.
192 A4 Borutta Sardegna Italy
146 B4 Borve Highland, Scotland U.K.
136 B3 Borynya Ukr.
136 B3 Boryslav Ukr.
136 F2 Boryspil' Ukr.
174 G2 Bory Tucholskie for. Pol.
175 K4 Borzechów Pol.
174 F4 Borzęciczki Pol.
137 G2 Borzenka r. Ukr.
136 B3 Borzhava r. Ukr.
Borzhomi Georgia see Borjomi
137 G2 Borzna Ukr.
190 E4 Borzonasca Italy
177 H4 Börzsöny hills Hungary
107 H1 Borzya Rus. Fed.
107 G1 Borzya r. Rus. Fed.
174 F1 Borzytuchom Pol.
192 A4 Bosa Sardegna Italy
177 G3 Bošáca Slovakia
121 H3 Bosaga Kazakh.
Bosagha Kazakh. see Bosaga
Bosaginskiy Kazakh. see Bosaga
192 A4 Bosa Marina Sardegna Italy
197 H2 Bosanci Romania
188 F3 Bosanska Dubica Bos.-Herz.
188 F3 Bosanska Gradiška Bos.-Herz.
188 F3 Bosanska Kostajnica Bos.-Herz.
188 F3 Bosanska Krupa Bos.-Herz.
188 G3 Bosanski Brod Bos.-Herz.
188 F3 Bosanski Novi Bos.-Herz.
188 F3 Bosanski Petrovac Bos.-Herz.
188 G3 Bosanski Šamac Bos.-Herz.
188 F3 Bosansko Grahovo Bos.-Herz.
177 H3 Bošany Slovakia
176 G4 Bősárkány Hungary
168 F1 Bosau Ger.
215 F3 Bosberg mt. S. Africa
150 E2 Bosbury Herefordshire, England U.K.
150 C4 Boscastle Cornwall, England U.K.
233 H3 Boscawen NH U.S.A.
Boscawen Island Tonga see Niuatoputopu
193 E1 Bosco Italy
226 B4 Boscobel WI U.S.A.
191 G3 Bosco Chiesanuova Italy
190 D4 Bosco Marengo Italy
193 G4 Boscotrecase Italy
168 F1 Bösdorf Ger.
108 C4 Bose Guangxi China
168 C2 Bösel Ger.
151 G4 Bosham West Sussex, England U.K.
Boshchakul' Kazakh. see Bozshakol'
100 G2 Boshnyakovo Sakhalin Rus. Fed.
215 F1 Boshoek S. Africa
215 E3 Boshof S. Africa
197 F4 Bosilegrad Srbija Yugo.
Bosiljgrad Srbija Yugo. see Bosilegrad
172 C3 Bösingen Ger.
120 E1 Boskol' Kazakh.
164 D2 Boskoop Neth.
176 F2 Boskovice Czech Rep.
188 G3 Bosna r. Bos.-Herz.
197 H4 Bosna hills Bulg.
Bosna i Hercegovina country Europe see Bosnia-Herzegovina
Bosna Saray Bos.-Herz. see Sarajevo
Bosnia and Herzegovina, Federation of aut. div. Bos.-Herz. see Federacija Bosna i Hercegovina
188 F3 Bosnia-Herzegovina country Europe
208 C3 Bosobolo Dem. Rep. Congo
105 G3 Bōsō-hantō pen. Japan
Bosost Spain see Bòssost
179 H1 Bošovice Czech Rep.
215 F2 Bospoort S. Africa
Bosporus str. Turkey see İstanbul Boğazı
182 B1 Bosque Spain
208 C3 Bossangoa C.A.R.
141 K3 Bössbod Sweden
208 C3 Bossembélé C.A.R.
162 C4 Bosset France
214 C3 Bossiekom S. Africa
237 E5 Bossier City LA U.S.A.
206 D4 Bossora Burkina
186 D2 Bòssost Spain
215 F1 Bosspruit S. Africa
86 D3 Bossut, Cape W.A. Austr.
111 D4 Bostan Xinjiang China
122 A4 Bostān Iran
110 D3 Bosten Hu l. China
147 C3 Boston Rep. of Ireland
151 G2 Boston Lincolnshire, England U.K.
233 H3 Boston MA U.S.A.
82 C3 Boston Bay S.A. Austr.
227 H1 Boston Creek Ont. Can.
237 E5 Boston Mountains AR U.S.A.
149 H4 Boston Spa West Yorkshire, England U.K.
188 G3 Bosut r. Croatia
226 D5 Boswell IN U.S.A.
232 D4 Boswell PA U.S.A.
116 B5 Botad Gujarat India
206 C5 Botata Liberia
140 L3 Boteå Sweden
197 G3 Boteni Romania
151 I2 Botesdale Suffolk, England U.K.
212 E4 Boteti r. Botswana
135 D8 Botev mt. Bulg.
197 F4 Botevgrad Bulg.
215 F2 Bothaville S. Africa
168 E2 Bothel Ger.
149 F3 Bothel Cumbria, England U.K.
238 B2 Bothell WA U.S.A.
150 E4 Bothenhampton Dorset, England U.K.
141 L3 Bothnia, Gulf of Fin./Sweden
83 F5 Bothwell Tas. Austr.
227 G4 Bothwell Ont. Can.
182 C3 Boticas Port.
188 G4 Botin mt. Bos.-Herz.
179 G5 Botinec Stupnički Croatia
137 H4 Botiyeve Ukr.
177 L4 Botiz Romania
232 A4 Botkins OH U.S.A.
135 I6 Botkul', Ozero l. Kazakh./Rus. Fed.
129 E2 Botlikh Rus. Fed.
207 H6 Bot Makak Cameroon
136 E4 Botna r. Moldova
186 B3 Botorrita Spain
197 H2 Botoşani Romania
107 H4 Botou Hebei China
195 F4 Botricello Italy
206 D5 Botro Côte d'Ivoire
235 E1 Botsford CT U.S.A.
215 F3 Botshabelo S. Africa
140 M2 Botsmark Sweden
212 D5 Botswana country Africa
195 F3 Botte Donato, Monte mt. Italy
169 D4 Bottendorf (Burgwald) Ger.
168 F3 Bottendorf (Obernholz) Ger.
140 M2 Bottenviken g. Fin./Sweden
151 G2 Bottesford Leicestershire, England U.K.
149 I4 Bottesford North Lincolnshire, England U.K.
192 B4 Bottidda Sardegna Italy
236 C1 Bottineau ND U.S.A.
247 G3 Bottom Saba Neth. Antilles
169 B4 Bottrop Ger.
256 C5 Botucatu Brazil
257 F2 Botumirim Brazil
196 E5 Botun Macedonia
Botushany Moldova see Butuceni
225 K3 Botwood Nfld. Can.
172 B3 Bötzingen Ger.
206 D5 Bouaflé Côte d'Ivoire
156 B3 Bouafles France
206 D5 Bouaké Côte d'Ivoire
205 F2 Boualem Alg.
206 D4 Bouandougou Côte d'Ivoire
208 B3 Bouar C.A.R.
204 E2 Bouârfa Morocco
158 E4 Bouaye France
176 C2 Boubín mt. Czech Rep.
208 C3 Bouca C.A.R.
163 A5 Boucau France
84 C2 Boucaut Bay N.T. Austr.
161 D5 Bouc-Bel-Air France
159 F3 Boucé France
156 D2 Bouchain France
189 A7 Bouchegouf Alg.
159 F4 Bouchemaine France
Boucher, Île i. Î. Loyauté New Caledonia see Tiga
233 G2 Boucherville Que. Can.
161 D5 Bouches-du-Rhône dept Provence-Alpes-Côte-d'Azur France
227 J2 Bouchette Que. Can.
156 C3 Bouchoir France
225 H4 Bouctouche N.B. Can.
180 E5 Boudinar Morocco
190 B2 Boudry Switz.
156 D2 Boué France
217 □3b Bouéni Mayotte
209 B6 Bouenza admin. reg. Congo
209 B6 Bouenza r. Congo
159 F4 Bouessay France
159 H5 Bouesse France
205 G1 Bougaa Alg.
86 E2 Bougainville, Cape W.A. Austr.
91 L8 Bougainville Island P.N.G.
85 F2 Bougainville Reef Coral Sea Is Terr. Austr.
78 □6 Bougainville Strait Solomon Is
Bougie Alg. see Bejaïa
163 C4 Bouglon France
206 D4 Bougouni Mali
205 F2 Bougtob Alg.
158 E4 Bouguenais France
163 D5 Bouillac France
247 □2 Bouillante Guadeloupe
161 C5 Bouillargues France
165 E5 Bouillon Belgium
156 D4 Bouilly France
158 D5 Bouin France
205 F1 Bouira Alg.
204 C3 Bou Izakarn Morocco
160 E2 Boujailles France
161 B5 Boujan-sur-Libron France
204 B4 Boujdour Western Sahara
205 F2 Bou Kahil, Djebel mts Alg.
207 F4 Boukoumbé Benin
208 C2 Boukta Chad
157 G3 Boulay-Moselle France
162 C3 Boulazac France
161 C5 Boulbon France
87 D6 Boulder W.A. Austr.
238 F3 Boulder CO U.S.A.
238 D2 Boulder MT U.S.A.
241 L3 Boulder UT U.S.A.
241 J3 Boulder Canyon gorge NV U.S.A.
241 J4 Boulder City NV U.S.A.
204 D2 Boulemane Boulemane Morocco

Boulemane to **Brodheadsville** 287

204 D2 **Boulemane** *Boulemane* Morocco
241 I5 **Boulevard** *CA* U.S.A.
Boulhaut Morocco *see* **Ben Slimane**
84 D4 **Boulia** *Qld* Austr.
157 F3 **Bouligny** France
163 D5 **Bouloc** France
Boulogne France *see* **Boulogne-sur-Mer**
158 E4 **Boulogne** *r.* France
156 C4 **Boulogne-Billancourt** France
163 C5 **Boulogne-sur-Gesse** France
156 B2 **Boulogne-sur-Mer** France
159 G4 **Bouloire** France
208 E3 **Boulou** *r.* C.A.R.
77 G4 **Bouloupari** New Caledonia
161 E5 **Boulouris** France
206 E3 **Boulsa** Burkina
149 G4 **Boulsworth Hill** *hill England* U.K.
157 E3 **Boult-aux-Bois** France
156 E3 **Boulzicourt** France
204 D3 **Boumalne Dadès** Morocco
208 B5 **Boumango** Gabon
207 I6 **Boumba** *r.* Cameroon
208 B3 **Boumbé I** *r.* C.A.R.
205 F1 **Boumerdes** Alg.
186 E2 **Boumort** *mt.* Spain
186 E2 **Boumort, Serra del** *mts* Spain
206 E4 **Bouna** Côte d'Ivoire
204 E2 **Bou Naceur, Jbel** *mt.* Morocco
206 B2 **Boû Nâga** Maur.
233 □H2 **Boundary Mountains** *ME* U.S.A.
240 H3 **Boundary Peak** *NV* U.S.A.
234 D2 **Bound Brook** *NJ* U.S.A.
206 D4 **Boundiali** Côte d'Ivoire
208 B5 **Boundji** Congo
96 E3 **Boung** *r.* Vietnam
208 D3 **Boungou** *r.* C.A.R.
163 C4 **Bouniagues** France
206 B3 **Bounkiling** Senegal
238 E3 **Bountiful** *UT* U.S.A.
84 D3 **Bountiful Island** *Qld* Austr.
77 H6 **Bounty Islands** N.Z.
266 G9 **Bounty Trough** *sea feature* S. Pacific Ocean
261 G3 **Bouquet** Arg.
78 □5 **Bourail** New Caledonia
160 C2 **Bourbince** *r.* France
Bourbon *reg.* France *see* **Bourbonnais**
Bourbon *terr.* Indian Ocean *see* **Réunion**
160 B2 **Bourbon-Lancy** France
160 B2 **Bourbon-l'Archambault** France
160 A2 **Bourbonnais** *reg.* France
157 F5 **Bourbonne-les-Bains** France
156 C2 **Bourbourg** France
160 D3 **Bourbre** *r.* France
158 C3 **Bourbriac** France
162 A3 **Bourcefranc-le-Chapus** France
161 D4 **Bourdeaux** France
162 C3 **Bourdeilles** France
157 G4 **Bourdonnay** France
206 E2 **Bourem** Mali
162 C2 **Bouresse** France
162 B3 **Bourg** France
159 G2 **Bourg-Achard** France
162 D3 **Bourganeuf** France
161 C3 **Bourg-Argental** France
158 E4 **Bourgbarré** France
158 B3 **Bourg-Blanc** France
161 D3 **Bourg-de-Péage** France
160 C2 **Bourg-de-Thizy** France
163 C4 **Bourg-de-Visa** France
156 A3 **Bourg-Dun** France
160 D2 **Bourg-en-Bresse** France
162 E1 **Bourges** France
233 F2 **Bourget** *Ont.* Can.
160 D3 **Bourget, Lac du** *l.* France
156 D3 **Bourg-et-Comin** France
160 A3 **Bourg-Lastic** France
161 C4 **Bourg-lès-Valence** France
163 D6 **Bourg-Madame** France
227 J1 **Bourgmont** *Que.* Can.
159 F4 **Bourgneuf-en-Mauges** France
158 E4 **Bourgneuf-en-Retz** France
156 E3 **Bourgogne** France
156 E5 **Bourgogne** *admin. reg.* France
160 D3 **Bourgoin-Jallieu** France
161 C4 **Bourg-St-Andéol** France
163 D5 **Bourg-St-Bernard** France
160 E3 **Bourg-St-Maurice** France
159 G2 **Bourgtheroulde-Infreville** France
159 F2 **Bourguébus** France
159 G4 **Bourgueil** France
83 F2 **Bourke** *N.S.W.* Austr.
227 G1 **Bourkes** *Ont.* Can.
157 F4 **Bourmont** France
161 D3 **Bourne** *r.* France
151 G2 **Bourne** *Lincolnshire, England* U.K.
151 F4 **Bournemouth** *Bournemouth, England* U.K.
151 F4 **Bournemouth** *admin. div. England* U.K.
159 E5 **Bournezeau** France
161 B3 **Bournoncle-St-Pierre** France
182 B3 **Bouro** Port.
160 E1 **Bourogne** France
206 E4 **Bouroum-Bouroum** Burkina
207 I4 **Bourrah** Cameroon
163 C4 **Bourran** France
163 B4 **Bourriot-Bergonce** France
165 F5 **Bourscheid** Lux.
164 G1 **Bourtange** Neth.
159 G3 **Bourth** France
150 E3 **Bourton** *Dorset, England* U.K.
151 F3 **Bourton-on-the-Water** *Gloucestershire, England* U.K.
206 E3 **Bourzanga** Burkina
205 G2 **Bou Saâda** Alg.
189 B7 **Bou Salem** Tunisia
241 J5 **Bouse** *AZ* U.S.A.
162 E2 **Boussac** France
206 E3 **Boussé** Burkina
163 C5 **Boussens** France
160 D1 **Boussières** France
208 C2 **Bousso** Chad
156 E2 **Boussois** France
165 C4 **Boussu** Belgium
165 D4 **Boutersem** Belgium
206 B2 **Boutilimit** Maur.
162 B3 **Boutonne** *r.* France
156 B3 **Bouttencourt** France
Bouvet Island *terr.* S. Atlantic Ocean *see* **Bouvetøya**
264 J9 **Bouvetøya** *terr.* S. Atlantic Ocean
161 D4 **Bouvières** France
158 E4 **Bouvron** France
157 G4 **Bouxières-aux-Dames** France
157 H4 **Bouxwiller** France
156 E3 **Bouy** France
207 G3 **Bouza** Niger
159 H5 **Bouzanne** *r.* France
157 G3 **Bouzonville** France
156 E3 **Bouzy** France
195 E4 **Bova** Italy
195 F4 **Bovalino** Italy
195 E5 **Bova Marina** Italy
179 E4 **Bovec** Slovenia
182 C2 **Bóveda** Spain
183 G2 **Bóveda** Spain
190 F3 **Bovegno** Italy
169 E4 **Bovenden** Ger.
Boven Kapuas Mountains Indon./Malaysia *see* **Kapuas Hulu, Pegunungan**
164 E2 **Bovenkarspel** Neth.
164 F2 **Bovensmilde** Neth.
156 C3 **Boves** France
190 C4 **Boves** Italy
150 D4 **Bovey** *r. England* U.K.
226 A2 **Bovey** *MN* U.S.A.
150 D4 **Bovey Tracey** *Devon, England* U.K.
148 C3 **Boviel** *Northern Ireland* U.K.
165 E4 **Bovigny** Belgium
193 F3 **Boville Ernica** Italy
150 E4 **Bovington Camp** *Dorset, England* U.K.
193 H3 **Bovino** Italy
191 G3 **Bovolone** Italy
261 H2 **Bovril** Arg.
168 E1 **Bovrup** Denmark
137 G3 **Bovtyshka** Ukr.
86 F3 **Bow** *r. W.A.* Austr.
223 I5 **Bow** *r. Alta* Can.
Bowa *Sichuan* China *see* **Muli**
236 C1 **Bowbells** *ND* U.S.A.
149 H3 **Bowburn** *Durham, England* U.K.
232 D5 **Bowden** *WV* U.S.A.
Bowditch *atoll* Tokelau *see* **Fakaofo**
260 D4 **Bowen** Arg.
85 G4 **Bowen** *Qld* Austr.
85 F4 **Bowen** *r. Qld* Austr.
226 B5 **Bowen** *IL* U.S.A.
83 G4 **Bowen, Mount** *Vic.* Austr.
85 F4 **Bowen Downs** *Qld* Austr.
84 C1 **Bowen Strait** *N.T.* Austr.
85 G5 **Bowenville** *Qld* Austr.
234 C3 **Bowers Beach** *DE* U.S.A.
263 K2 **Bowers Mountains** Antarctica
266 G2 **Bowers Ridge** *sea feature* Bering Sea
149 G3 **Bowes** *Durham, England* U.K.
85 F4 **Bowie** *Qld* Austr.
241 M5 **Bowie** *AZ* U.S.A.
234 B4 **Bowie** *MD* U.S.A.
237 D5 **Bowie** *TX* U.S.A.
223 I5 **Bow Island** *Alta* Can.
122 A2 **Bowkan** Iran
149 G4 **Bowland, Forest of** *reg. England* U.K.
230 C4 **Bowling Green** *KY* U.S.A.
236 F4 **Bowling Green** *MO* U.S.A.
232 B4 **Bowling Green** *OH* U.S.A.
232 E5 **Bowling Green** *VA* U.S.A.
85 F3 **Bowling Green, Cape** *Qld* Austr.
85 F3 **Bowling Green Bay** *Qld* Austr.
236 C2 **Bowman** *ND* U.S.A.
222 F5 **Bowman, Mount** *B.C.* Can.
262 T2 **Bowman Coast** Antarctica
263 G2 **Bowman Island** Antarctica
262 T2 **Bowman Peninsula** Antarctica
234 B2 **Bowmansdale** *PA* U.S.A.
234 C2 **Bowmanstown** *PA* U.S.A.
234 B2 **Bowmansville** *PA* U.S.A.
227 H4 **Bowmanville** *Ont.* Can.
149 G2 **Bowmont Water** *r. England/Scotland* U.K.
146 B6 **Bowmore** *Argyll and Bute, Scotland* U.K.
149 F3 **Bowness-on-Solway** *Cumbria, England* U.K.
149 G3 **Bowness-on-Windermere** *Cumbria, England* U.K.
Bowo *Sichuan* China *see* **Bomai**
Bowo *Xizang* China *see* **Bomi**
83 H2 **Bowraville** *N.S.W.* Austr.
222 F4 **Bowron** *r. B.C.* Can.
150 E3 **Box** *Wiltshire, England* U.K.
172 D2 **Boxberg** *Baden-Württemberg* Ger.
171 F4 **Boxberg** *Sachsen* Ger.
171 E4 **Boxdorf** Ger.
236 C2 **Box Elder** *SD* U.S.A.
236 C2 **Box Elder** *r. SD* U.S.A.
143 F2 **Boxholm** Sweden
107 H4 **Boxing** *Shandong* China
164 E3 **Boxmeer** Neth.
164 E3 **Boxtel** Neth.
126 D2 **Boyabat** Turkey
250 C3 **Boyaca** *dept* Col.
197 H4 **Boyadzhik** Bulg.
199 F1 **Boyalıca** Turkey
Boyalık Turkey *see* **Çiçekdağı**
197 F4 **Boyana** *tourist site* Bulg.
109 F2 **Boyang** *Jiangxi* China
197 H4 **Boyanovo** Bulg.
87 B7 **Boyanup** *W.A.* Austr.
136 F2 **Boyarka** Ukr.
83 H2 **Boyd** *r. N.S.W.* Austr.
87 E5 **Boyd Lagoon** *salt flat W.A.* Austr.
232 D6 **Boydton** *VA* U.S.A.
236 E3 **Boyer** *r. IA* U.S.A.
234 C2 **Boyertown** *PA* U.S.A.
232 E6 **Boykins** *VA* U.S.A.
222 H4 **Boyle** *Alta* Can.
147 C3 **Boyle** Rep. of Ireland
85 G4 **Boyne** *r. Qld* Austr.
85 G5 **Boyne** *r. Qld* Austr.
147 E3 **Boyne** *r.* Rep. of Ireland
226 E3 **Boyne City** *MI* U.S.A.
156 C4 **Boynes** France
Boysun Uzbek. *see* **Baysun**
253 E5 **Boyuibe** Bol.
129 E3 **Böyük Dähnä** Azer.
122 A1 **Böyük Hinaldağ** *mt.* Azer.
129 E4 **Böyük İşıqlı Dağ** *mt.* Armenia
87 C7 **Boyup Brook** *W.A.* Austr.
199 G2 **Bozan** Turkey
129 B3 **Bozan Dağı** *mt.* Turkey
Bozashy Tübegi *pen.* Kazakh. *see* **Buzachi, Poluostrov**
199 F3 **Bozburun** Turkey
199 G3 **Bozburun Dağ** *mt.* Turkey
128 C1 **Bozdağ** *mt.* Turkey
199 E2 **Bozdağ** *mt.* Turkey
199 F2 **Boz Dağ** *mts* Turkey
Bozdag, Khrebet *hills* Azer. *see* **Bozdağ Silsiläsi**
199 E2 **Boz Dağları** *mts* Turkey
129 E3 **Bozdağ Silsiläsi** *hills* Azer.
129 C4 **Bozdağ Tepe** *mt.* Turkey
199 F3 **Bozdoğan** Turkey
151 G2 **Bozeat** *Northamptonshire, England* U.K.
161 E3 **Bozel** France
238 E2 **Bozeman** *MT* U.S.A.
Bozen Italy *see* **Bolzano**
175 H3 **Bożewo** Pol.
109 E1 **Bozhou** *Anhui* China
176 F3 **Božice** Czech Rep.
179 H5 **Božjakovina** Croatia
126 D3 **Bozkır** Turkey
Bozköl Kazakh. *see* **Boskol'**
199 F3 **Bozkurt** Turkey
Bozoglan *mts* Turkey *see* **Bolkar Dağları**
161 A4 **Bozouls** France
208 C3 **Bozoum** C.A.R.
126 E3 **Bozova** Turkey
197 F3 **Bozovici** Romania
122 A2 **Bozqūsh, Kūh-e** *mts* Iran
121 H2 **Bozshakol'** Kazakh.
199 G2 **Bozüyük** Turkey
128 A1 **Bozyazı** Turkey
190 F3 **Bozzolo** Italy
190 C4 **Bra** Italy
146 E5 **Braan** *r. Scotland* U.K.
143 F3 **Braås** Sweden
262 T2 **Brabant Island** Antarctica
165 D4 **Brabant Wallon** *prov.* Belgium
188 F4 **Brač** *i.* Croatia
146 B4 **Bracadale** *Highland, Scotland* U.K.
146 B4 **Bracadale, Loch** *b. Scotland* U.K.
Bracara Port. *see* **Braga**
192 E2 **Bracciano** Italy
192 E2 **Bracciano, Lago di** *l.* Italy
224 E4 **Bracebridge** *Ont.* Can.
149 I4 **Bracebridge Heath** *Lincolnshire, England* U.K.
162 B3 **Brach** France
169 C5 **Brachbach** Ger.
159 H4 **Bracieux** France
148 B4 **Brackagh** Rep. of Ireland
140 K3 **Bräcke** Sweden
168 F2 **Brackel** Ger.
172 D2 **Brackenheim** Ger.
237 C6 **Brackettville** *TX* U.S.A.
188 F4 **Bračkí Kanal** *sea chan.* Croatia
151 F2 **Brackley** *Northamptonshire, England* U.K.
147 D3 **Bracknagh** Rep. of Ireland
151 G3 **Bracknell** *Bracknell Forest, England* U.K.
151 G3 **Bracknell Forest** *admin. div. England* U.K.
253 G2 **Braço Norte** *r.* Brazil
197 F2 **Brad** Romania
193 I4 **Bradano** *r.* Italy
231 D7 **Bradenton** *FL* U.S.A.
227 H3 **Bradford** *Ont.* Can.
149 H4 **Bradford** *West Yorkshire, England* U.K.
232 A4 **Bradford** *OH* U.S.A.
232 D4 **Bradford** *PA* U.S.A.
233 G3 **Bradford** *VT* U.S.A.
234 B1 **Bradford County** *county PA* U.S.A.
234 C2 **Bradford Hills** *PA* U.S.A.
150 E3 **Bradford-on-Avon** *Wiltshire, England* U.K.
151 F4 **Brading** *Isle of Wight, England* U.K.
226 D5 **Bradley** *IL* U.S.A.
235 D2 **Bradley Beach** *NJ* U.S.A.
232 B4 **Bradner** *OH* U.S.A.
150 D4 **Bradninch** *Devon, England* U.K.
150 E4 **Bradpole** *Dorset, England* U.K.
149 G4 **Bradshaw** *Greater Manchester, England* U.K.
232 C6 **Bradshaw** *WV* U.S.A.
86 E2 **Bradshaw, Mount** *hill W.A.* Austr.
149 H4 **Bradwell** *Derbyshire, England* U.K.
151 I2 **Bradwell** *Norfolk, England* U.K.
151 H3 **Bradwell Waterside** *Essex, England* U.K.
237 D6 **Brady** *TX* U.S.A.
237 D6 **Brady Creek** *r. TX* U.S.A.
146 □G1 **Brae** *Shetland, Scotland* U.K.
146 D4 **Braeantra** *Highland, Scotland* U.K.
146 F5 **Braehead** *Angus, Scotland* U.K.
82 D3 **Braemar** *S.A.* Austr.
146 E4 **Braemar** *Aberdeenshire, Scotland* U.K.
194 D5 **Braemi** *r. Sicilia* Italy
182 B3 **Braga** Port.
182 B3 **Braga** *admin. dist.* Port.
261 G4 **Bragado** Arg.
254 D2 **Bragança** Brazil
182 D3 **Bragança** Port.
182 D3 **Bragança** *admin. dist.* Port.
256 D5 **Bragança Paulista** Brazil
226 A3 **Braham** *MN* U.S.A.
136 F2 **Brahin** Belarus
136 F2 **Brahinka** *r.* Belarus
168 F2 **Brahlstorf** Ger.
117 I4 **Brahmakund** *Arun. Prad.* India
117 G5 **Brahmanbaria** Bangl.
117 F5 **Brahmani** *r.* India
115 E2 **Brahmapur** *Orissa* India
111 E7 **Brahmaputra** *r.* China/India
alt. **Dihang (India),**
alt. **Yarlung Zangbo (China)**
83 G3 **Braidwood** *N.S.W.* Austr.
226 C5 **Braidwood** *IL* U.S.A.
197 H3 **Brăila** Romania
197 H3 **Brăilei, Insula Mare a** *i.* Romania
151 F2 **Brailsford** *Derbyshire, England* U.K.
156 D3 **Braine** France
165 D4 **Braine-l'Alleud** Belgium
165 D4 **Braine-le-Comte** Belgium
236 E2 **Brainerd** *MN* U.S.A.
159 G4 **Brain-sur-Allonnes** France
151 H3 **Braintree** *Essex, England* U.K.
149 F3 **Braithwaite** *Cumbria, England* U.K.
84 C1 **Braithwaite Point** *N.T.* Austr.
165 E4 **Braives** Belgium
213 F4 **Brak** *r. Northern* S. Africa
214 C5 **Brak** *r. W. Cape* S. Africa
168 D2 **Brake (Unterweser)** Ger.
165 C4 **Brakel** Belgium
169 E4 **Brakel** Ger.
164 E3 **Brakel** Neth.
206 B2 **Brâkna** *admin. reg.* Maur.
143 F3 **Bräkneån** *r.* Sweden
215 G2 **Brakpan** S. Africa
214 D4 **Brakpoort** S. Africa
215 F2 **Brakspruit** S. Africa
142 E2 **Brålanda** Sweden
174 F4 **Bralin** Pol.
190 E4 **Brallo di Pregola** Italy
222 F5 **Bralorne** *B.C.* Can.
163 E5 **Bram** France
161 E3 **Bramans** France
178 D3 **Bramberg am Wildkogel** Austria
82 C3 **Bramfield** *S.A.* Austr.
151 I2 **Bramford** *Suffolk, England* U.K.
116 D5 **Bramhapuri** *Mahar.* India
149 H4 **Bramley** *South Yorkshire, England* U.K.
142 C4 **Bramming** Denmark
224 E5 **Brampton** *Ont.* Can.
151 G2 **Brampton** *Cambridgeshire, England* U.K.
149 G3 **Brampton** *Cumbria, England* U.K.
151 I2 **Brampton** *Suffolk, England* U.K.
169 C3 **Bramsche** *Niedersachsen* Ger.
169 D3 **Bramsche** *Niedersachsen* Ger.
168 D2 **Bramstedt** Ger.
85 E2 **Bramwell** *Qld* Austr.
182 E1 **Braña Caballo** *mt.* Spain
171 E5 **Braňany** Czech Rep.
177 H3 **Branč** Slovakia
195 F5 **Brancaleone** Italy
151 H2 **Brancaster** *Norfolk, England* U.K.
225 K4 **Branch** *Nfld.* Can.
234 B2 **Branch Dale** *PA* U.S.A.
234 D1 **Branchville** *NJ* U.S.A.
253 E2 **Branco** *r. Mato Grosso* Brazil
251 F5 **Branco** *r. Roraima* Brazil
206 □ **Branco** *i.* Cape Verde
173 F2 **Brand** Ger.
247 □8 **Brandaris** *hill Bonaire* Neth. Antilles
212 B4 **Brandberg** *mt.* Namibia
141 L3 **Brändbo** Sweden
142 D1 **Brandbu** Norway
142 C4 **Brande** Denmark
168 E2 **Brande-Hörnerkirchen** Ger.
178 C3 **Brandenberg** Austria
171 D3 **Brandenburg** Ger.
171 E3 **Brandenburg** *land* Ger.
230 C4 **Brandenburg** *KY* U.S.A.
171 E5 **Brand-Erbisdorf** Ger.
149 I4 **Brandesburton** *East Riding of Yorkshire, England* U.K.
215 F3 **Brandfort** S. Africa
171 E4 **Brandis** *Brandenburg* Ger.
171 D4 **Brandis** *Sachsen* Ger.
214 B4 **Brandkop** S. Africa
179 G2 **Brand-Nagelberg** Austria
141 M3 **Brändö** *Åland* Fin.
192 B2 **Brando** *Corse* France
85 F3 **Brandon** *Qld* Austr.
223 L5 **Brandon** *Man.* Can.
147 A4 **Brandon** Rep. of Ireland
149 H3 **Brandon** *Durham, England* U.K.
151 H2 **Brandon** *Suffolk, England* U.K.
237 F5 **Brandon** *MS* U.S.A.
236 D3 **Brandon** *SD* U.S.A.
233 G3 **Brandon** *VT* U.S.A.
147 A4 **Brandon Bay** Rep. of Ireland
147 E4 **Brandon Hill** *hill* Rep. of Ireland
147 A4 **Brandon Mountain** *hill* Rep. of Ireland
234 B2 **Brandonville** *PA* U.S.A.
232 D5 **Brandonville** *WV* U.S.A.
170 E1 **Brandshagen** Ger.
234 A2 **Brandtsville** *PA* U.S.A.
214 C4 **Brandvlei** S. Africa
176 D1 **Brandýs nad Labem-Stará Boleslav** Czech Rep.
234 C3 **Brandywine Creek, East Branch** *r. PA* U.S.A.
234 C3 **Brandywine Creek, West Branch** *r. DE* U.S.A.
234 C2 **Brandywine Manor** *PA* U.S.A.
235 F1 **Branford** *CT* U.S.A.
231 D6 **Branford** *FL* U.S.A.
160 D2 **Branges** France
179 E5 **Branica** *r.* Slovenia
143 H4 **Braniewo** Pol.
177 L6 **Brănişca** Romania
156 D5 **Branlin** *r.* France
140 M2 **Brännberg** Sweden
163 B4 **Branne** France
173 G4 **Brannenburg** Ger.
183 F2 **Branõsera** Spain
262 T2 **Bransfield Strait** Antarctica
151 F4 **Bransgore** *Hampshire, England* U.K.
175 K3 **Brańsk** Pol.
237 C4 **Branson** *CO* U.S.A.
149 I4 **Branston** *Lincolnshire, England* U.K.
175 J3 **Brańszczyk** Pol.
95 F4 **Brantas** *r.* Indon.
224 D5 **Brantford** *Ont.* Can.
151 I3 **Brantham** *Suffolk, England* U.K.
177 G1 **Brantice** Czech Rep.
231 C6 **Brantley** *AL* U.S.A.
162 C3 **Brantôme** France
137 H2 **Brantsivka** Ukr.
226 B3 **Brantwood** *WI* U.S.A.
137 F2 **Branytsya** Ukr.
190 E2 **Branzi** Italy
183 G3 **Braojos** Spain
190 F3 **Braone** Italy
161 D5 **Bras** France
196 E4 **Brasaljce** *Kosovo, Srbija* Yugo.
225 I4 **Bras d'Or Lake** *N.S.* Can.
182 B4 **Brasfemes** Port.
Brasil *country* S. America *see* **Brazil**
257 G2 **Brasil, Planalto do** *plat.* Brazil
256 A4 **Brasilândia** Brazil
256 C1 **Brasilândia** Brazil
252 C2 **Brasileia** Brazil
256 D1 **Brasília** Brazil
257 E2 **Brasília de Minas** Brazil
138 E3 **Brasla** *r.* Latvia
Braslav Belarus *see* **Braslaw**
138 F4 **Braslaw** Belarus
197 G3 **Braşov** Romania
139 J5 **Brasovo** Rus. Fed.
257 F4 **Brás Pires** Brazil
207 G5 **Brass** Nigeria
163 E5 **Brassac** France
161 B3 **Brassac-les-Mines** France
165 D3 **Brasschaat** Belgium
95 G1 **Brassey, Banjaran** *mts Sabah* Malaysia
84 C4 **Brassey, Mount** *N.T.* Austr.
87 D5 **Brassey Range** *hills W.A.* Austr.
160 B1 **Brassy** France
142 D2 **Brastad** Sweden
173 H2 **Břasy** Czech Rep.
197 G4 **Bratan** *mt.* Bulg.
197 F2 **Bratca** Romania
176 G3 **Bratislava** Slovakia
176 G3 **Bratislavský Kraj** *admin. reg.* Slovakia
175 J5 **Bratkowice** Pol.
131 L4 **Bratsk** Rus. Fed.
137 F4 **Brats'ke** Ukr.
131 L4 **Bratskoye Vodokhranilishche** *resr* Rus. Fed.
136 E3 **Bratslav** Ukr.
233 G3 **Brattleboro** *VT* U.S.A.
142 E1 **Brattmon** Sweden
150 E3 **Bratton** *Wiltshire, England* U.K.
140 I3 **Brattvåg** Norway
188 G3 **Bratunac** Bos.-Herz.
169 C5 **Braubach** Ger.
162 B3 **Braud-et-St-Louis** France
257 F3 **Braúnas** Brazil
178 E2 **Braunau am Inn** Austria
172 A2 **Brauneberg** Ger.
169 D5 **Braunfels** Ger.
169 F4 **Braunlage** Ger.
172 C4 **Bräunlingen** Ger.
172 D2 **Braunsbach** Ger.
171 C4 **Braunsbedra** Ger.
169 F3 **Braunschweig** Ger.
169 E4 **Braunschweig** *admin. reg. Niedersachsen* Ger.
151 F2 **Braunston** *Northamptonshire, England* U.K.
151 F2 **Braunstone** *Leicestershire, England* U.K.
150 C3 **Braunton** *Devon, England* U.K.
215 F4 **Braunville** S. Africa
206 □ **Brava** *i.* Cape Verde
185 H3 **Bravatas** *r.* Spain
232 C5 **Brave** *PA* U.S.A.
136 E4 **Bravicea** Moldova
252 D4 **Bravo, Cerro** *mt.* Bol.
242 F3 **Bravo del Norte, Río** *r.* Mex./U.S.A.
alt. **Rio Grande**
241 J5 **Brawley** *CA* U.S.A.
147 E3 **Bray** Rep. of Ireland
214 D1 **Bray** S. Africa
151 G3 **Bray** *Windsor and Maidenhead, England* U.K.
150 D4 **Bray** *r. England* U.K.
156 C1 **Bray-Dunes** France
159 G4 **Braye** *r.* France
147 A5 **Bray Head** *hd* Rep. of Ireland
136 E3 **Brayiliv** Ukr.
156 D4 **Bray-sur-Seine** France
149 H4 **Brayton** *North Yorkshire, England* U.K.
185 F2 **Brazatortas** Spain
222 H4 **Brazeau** *r. Alta* Can.
222 G4 **Brazeau, Mount** *Alta* Can.
160 D1 **Brazey-en-Plaine** France
177 L5 **Brazii** Romania
254 C4 **Brazil** *country* S. America
230 C4 **Brazil** *IN* U.S.A.
264 H7 **Brazil Basin** *sea feature* S. Atlantic Ocean
237 E6 **Brazos** *r. TX* U.S.A.
209 B6 **Brazzaville** Congo
188 G3 **Brčko** Bos.-Herz.
174 G2 **Brda** *r.* Pol.
174 G3 **Brdów** Pol.
176 C2 **Brdy** *hills* Czech Rep.
Bré Rep. of Ireland *see* **Bray**
183 I3 **Brea** Spain
84 D4 **Breadalbane** *Qld* Austr.
146 D5 **Breadalbane** *reg. Scotland* U.K.
87 E5 **Breaden, Lake** *salt flat W.A.* Austr.
183 G4 **Brea de Tajo** Spain
215 F5 **Breakfast Vlei** S. Africa
85 H5 **Breaksea Spit** *Qld* Austr.
158 E3 **Bréal-sous-Montfort** France
150 E3 **Bream** *Gloucestershire, England* U.K.
80 E1 **Bream Bay** *North I.* N.Z.
149 G2 **Breamish** *r. England* U.K.
146 A3 **Breanais** *Western Isles, Scotland* U.K.
146 B3 **Breascleit** *Western Isles, Scotland* U.K.
151 F2 **Breaston** *Derbyshire, England* U.K.
159 G2 **Bréauté** France
197 G3 **Breaza** Romania
95 E4 **Brebes** *Jawa Tengah* Indon.
161 F5 **Brec d'Utelle** *mt.* France
158 E3 **Brécey** France
158 D4 **Brech** France
156 C3 **Brêche** *r.* France
150 C3 **Brechfa** *Carmarthenshire, Wales* U.K.
146 F5 **Brechin** *Angus, Scotland* U.K.
165 D3 **Brecht** Belgium
239 F4 **Breckenridge** *CO* U.S.A.
236 D2 **Breckenridge** *MN* U.S.A.
237 D5 **Breckenridge** *TX* U.S.A.
169 C4 **Breckerfeld** Ger.
151 H2 **Breckland** *lowland England* U.K.
259 B9 **Brecknock, Península** *pen.* Chile
232 C4 **Brecksville** *OH* U.S.A.
176 F3 **Břeclav** Czech Rep.
150 D3 **Brecon** *Powys, Wales* U.K.
150 D3 **Brecon Beacons** *reg. Wales* U.K.
150 D3 **Brecon Beacons National Park** *Wales* U.K.
164 D3 **Breda** Neth.
186 F3 **Breda** Spain
143 E3 **Bredaryd** Sweden
214 C6 **Bredasdorp** S. Africa
83 G3 **Bredbo** *N.S.W.* Austr.
168 C3 **Breddenberg** Ger.
170 D3 **Breddin** Ger.
168 E2 **Breddorf** Ger.
142 C4 **Brede** *r.* Denmark
151 H4 **Brede** *r. England* U.K.
165 B3 **Bredene** Belgium
170 E2 **Bredereiche** Ger.
150 E2 **Bredon** *Worcestershire, England* U.K.
168 D1 **Bredstedt** Ger.
140 L3 **Bredträsk** Sweden
140 K2 **Bredviken** Sweden
120 E1 **Bredy** Rus. Fed.
165 E3 **Bree** Belgium
214 C6 **Breede** *r.* S. Africa
170 C2 **Breese** Ger.
164 D2 **Breezand** Neth.
232 D5 **Breezewood** *PA* U.S.A.
172 C4 **Breg** *r.* Ger.
197 E5 **Bregalnica** *r.* Macedonia
179 G5 **Bregana** Croatia
191 G3 **Breganze** Italy
178 A3 **Bregenz** Austria
168 F1 **Bregninge** Denmark
197 F3 **Bregovo** Bulg.
191 F3 **Breguzzo** Italy
158 E3 **Bréhal** France
158 D3 **Bréhan** France
169 F4 **Brehme** Ger.
171 D4 **Brehna** Ger.
140 □A2 **Breiðafjörður** *b.* Iceland
157 H3 **Breidenbach** France
169 D5 **Breidenbach** Ger.
236 C2 **Breien** *ND* U.S.A.
168 E1 **Breiholz** Ger.
190 E2 **Breil** Switz.
161 F5 **Breil-sur-Roya** France
215 F4 **Breipaal** S. Africa
172 B3 **Breisach am Rhein** Ger.
190 C1 **Breitenbach** Switz.
169 E5 **Breitenbach am Herzberg** Ger.
178 C3 **Breitenbach am Inn** Austria
173 H3 **Breitenberg** Ger.
173 E3 **Breitenbrunn** *Bayern* Ger.
173 F2 **Breitenbrunn** *Bayern* Ger.
168 E2 **Breitenburg** Ger.
168 F2 **Breitenfelde** Ger.
171 C4 **Breitenhagen** Ger.
178 B3 **Breitenwang** Austria
169 F4 **Breitenworbis** Ger.
178 C3 **Breiter Grieskogel** *mt.* Austria
170 E2 **Breiter Luzinsee** *l.* Ger.
172 C4 **Breitnau** Ger.
169 D5 **Breitscheid** *Hessen* Ger.
169 C5 **Breitscheid** *Rheinland-Pfalz* Ger.
169 F5 **Breitungen** Ger.
140 M1 **Breivikbotn** Norway
254 C4 **Brejinho de Nazaré** Brazil
254 E2 **Brejo** Brazil
254 E4 **Brejo** *r.* Brazil
168 D1 **Breklum** Ger.
140 J3 **Brekstad** Norway
158 B3 **Brélès** France
190 E3 **Brembo** *r.* Italy
168 D2 **Bremen** Ger.
168 D2 **Bremen** *land* Ger.
231 C5 **Bremen** *GA* U.S.A.
226 D5 **Bremen** *IN* U.S.A.
232 B5 **Bremen** *OH* U.S.A.
87 C7 **Bremer Bay** *W.A.* Austr.
87 C7 **Bremer Bay** *b. W.A.* Austr.
168 D2 **Bremerhaven** Ger.
87 D7 **Bremer Range** *hills W.A.* Austr.
Bremersdorp Swaziland *see* **Manzini**
238 B2 **Bremerton** *WA* U.S.A.
168 E2 **Bremervörde** Ger.
190 D1 **Bremgarten** Switz.
169 C5 **Bremm** Ger.
142 A2 **Bremnes** Norway
162 A2 **Brem-sur-Mer** France
175 J5 **Breń** *r.* Pol.
216 □3d **Breña Alta** *La Palma* Canary Is
150 D3 **Brendon Hills** *England* U.K.
184 E3 **Brenes** Spain
237 D6 **Brenham** *TX* U.S.A.
184 C2 **Brenhas** *r.* Port.
174 G6 **Brenna** Pol.
160 D2 **Brenne** *r.* France
159 G4 **Brenne** *r.* France
191 G2 **Brennero** Italy
Brennero, Passo di *pass* Austria/Italy *see* **Brenner Pass**
Brennerpaß *pass* Austria/Italy *see* **Brenner Pass**
178 C4 **Brenner Pass** *pass* Austria/Italy
190 F3 **Breno** Italy
160 D2 **Brénod** France
163 D5 **Brens** France
172 C2 **Brensbach** Ger.
224 E4 **Brent** *Ont.* Can.
191 H3 **Brenta** *r.* Italy
191 F2 **Brenta, Gruppo di** *mts* Italy
150 E3 **Brent Knoll** *Somerset, England* U.K.
151 H3 **Brentwood** *Essex, England* U.K.
235 E2 **Brentwood** *NY* U.S.A.
173 E3 **Brenz** *r.* Ger.
191 F3 **Brenzone** Italy
190 F3 **Brescia** Italy
190 F3 **Brescia** *prov. Lombardia* Italy
165 C3 **Breskens** Neth.
Breslau Pol. *see* **Wrocław**
156 B2 **Bresle** *r.* France
156 C3 **Bresles** France
190 E3 **Bressana Bottarone** Italy
191 G2 **Bressanone** Italy
146 □G1 **Bressay** *i. Scotland* U.K.
163 D5 **Bressols** France
162 B2 **Bressuire** France
136 B1 **Brest** Belarus
158 B3 **Brest** France
179 G5 **Brestanica** Slovenia
179 G4 **Bresternica** Slovenia
Brest-Litovsk Belarus *see* **Brest**
Brest Oblast *admin. div.* Belarus *see* **Brestskaya Voblasts'**
197 E4 **Brestovac** *Srbija* Yugo.
177 K6 **Brestovăț** Romania
Brestskaya Oblast' *admin. div.* Belarus *see* **Brestskaya Voblasts'**
138 E5 **Brestskaya Voblasts'** *admin. div.* Belarus
158 D3 **Bretagne** *admin. reg.* France
163 C5 **Bretagne-d'Armagnac** France
250 C6 **Bretana** Peru
216 □1b **Bretanha** *São Miguel* Azores
197 H2 **Bretcu** Romania
158 E3 **Breteil** France
163 D4 **Bretenoux** France
159 G3 **Breteuil** *Haute-Normandie* France
156 C3 **Breteuil** *Picardie* France
158 E5 **Brétignolles-sur-Mer** France
156 C4 **Brétigny-sur-Orge** France
171 F4 **Bretnig** Ger.
182 E3 **Bretocino** Spain
222 H4 **Breton** *Alta* Can.
246 C2 **Breton, Cayo** *i.* Cuba
159 G3 **Bretoncelles** France
237 F6 **Breton Sound** *b. LA* U.S.A.
235 D2 **Breton Woods** *NJ* U.S.A.
172 C2 **Bretten** Ger.
150 E1 **Bretton** *Flintshire, Wales* U.K.
159 F2 **Brettville-sur-Laize** France
172 B2 **Bretzenheim** Ger.
172 D2 **Bretzfeld** Ger.
252 B2 **Breu** *r.* Brazil/Peru
172 D2 **Breuberg-Neustadt** Ger.
157 G5 **Breuches** France
157 G5 **Breuchin** *r.* France
164 E3 **Breugel** Neth.
190 C3 **Breuil-Cervinia** Italy
162 B3 **Breuil-Magné** France
156 B4 **Breuilpont** France
164 E2 **Breukelen** Neth.
169 E4 **Breuna** Ger.
157 F4 **Breuvannes-en-Bassigny** France
231 D5 **Brevard** *NC* U.S.A.
251 I5 **Breves** Brazil
142 C2 **Brevik** Norway
142 E2 **Breviken** Sweden
160 E2 **Brévon** *r.* France
169 E4 **Brevörde** Ger.
83 F2 **Brewarrina** *N.S.W.* Austr.
233 □I2 **Brewer** *ME* U.S.A.
206 C5 **Brewerville** Liberia
150 E2 **Brewood** *Staffordshire, England* U.K.
236 D3 **Brewster** *NE* U.S.A.
235 E1 **Brewster** *NY* U.S.A.
232 C4 **Brewster** *OH* U.S.A.
238 C1 **Brewster** *WA* U.S.A.
Brewster, Kap *c.* Greenland *see* **Kangikajik**
231 C6 **Brewton** *AL* U.S.A.
215 G2 **Breyten** S. Africa
139 K2 **Breytovo** Rus. Fed.
177 I2 **Breza** Slovakia
Brezhnev Rus. Fed. *see* **Naberezhnyye Chelny**
176 F3 **Březí** Czech Rep.
188 E3 **Brežice** Slovenia
179 H4 **Breznica** Croatia
176 C2 **Březnice** Czech Rep.
197 F4 **Breznik** Bulg.
197 F3 **Breznița-Motru** Romania
197 F5 **Breznitsa** Bulg.
171 E5 **Březno** Czech Rep.
177 I3 **Brezno** Slovakia
156 B4 **Brézolles** France
177 G2 **Březová** Czech Rep.
177 G3 **Brezová pod Bradlom** Slovakia
177 L3 **Brezovec** Slovakia
179 F4 **Brezovica** Slovenia
197 G4 **Brezovo** Bulg.
188 F3 **Brezovo Polje** *hill* Croatia
208 D3 **Bria** C.A.R.
162 D3 **Briance** *r.* France
161 E4 **Briançon** France
241 K3 **Brian Head** *mt. UT* U.S.A.
235 E1 **Briarcliff Manor** *NY* U.S.A.
160 A1 **Briare** France
163 D5 **Briatexte** France
195 F4 **Briatico** Italy
85 H5 **Bribie Island** *Qld* Austr.
161 F4 **Bric Bouchet** *mt.* France/Italy
136 D3 **Briceni** Moldova
161 E4 **Bric Froid** *mt.* France/Italy
Brichany Moldova *see* **Briceni**
190 C4 **Bricherasio** Italy
147 C3 **Brickeens** Rep. of Ireland
234 B2 **Brickerville** *PA* U.S.A.
234 D3 **Bricksboro** *NJ* U.S.A.
235 D2 **Brick Township** *NJ* U.S.A.
157 E4 **Bricon** France
158 E2 **Bricquebec** France
147 D4 **Bride** *r.* Rep. of Ireland
161 E3 **Brides-les-Bains** France
151 I3 **Bridge** *Kent, England* U.K.
235 F2 **Bridgehampton** *NY* U.S.A.
147 E4 **Bridgeland** Rep. of Ireland
226 D5 **Bridgeman** *MI* U.S.A.
147 D1 **Bridgend** Rep. of Ireland
146 F5 **Bridgend** *Angus, Scotland* U.K.
146 B6 **Bridgend** *Argyll and Bute, Scotland* U.K.
150 D3 **Bridgend** *Bridgend, Wales* U.K.
146 E4 **Bridgend** *Moray, Scotland* U.K.
150 D3 **Bridgend** *admin. div. Wales* U.K.
146 E5 **Bridge of Allan** *Stirling, Scotland* U.K.
146 D5 **Bridge of Balgie** *Perth and Kinross, Scotland* U.K.
146 E5 **Bridge of Cally** *Perth and Kinross, Scotland* U.K.
146 E5 **Bridge of Craigisla** *Angus, Scotland* U.K.
146 F4 **Bridge of Don** *Aberdeen, Scotland* U.K.
146 F5 **Bridge of Dun** *Angus, Scotland* U.K.
146 F5 **Bridge of Dye** *Aberdeenshire, Scotland* U.K.
146 E5 **Bridge of Earn** *Perth and Kinross, Scotland* U.K.
146 E3 **Bridge of Forss** *Highland, Scotland* U.K.
146 D5 **Bridge of Orchy** *Argyll and Bute, Scotland* U.K.
146 □G1 **Bridge of Walls** *Shetland, Scotland* U.K.
146 D6 **Bridge of Weir** *Renfrewshire, Scotland* U.K.
231 C5 **Bridgeport** *AL* U.S.A.
240 H2 **Bridgeport** *CA* U.S.A.
233 G4 **Bridgeport** *CT* U.S.A.
227 F4 **Bridgeport** *MI* U.S.A.
236 C3 **Bridgeport** *NE* U.S.A.
234 C2 **Bridgeport** *PA* U.S.A.
237 D5 **Bridgeport** *TX* U.S.A.
238 E2 **Bridger** *MT* U.S.A.
238 F3 **Bridger Peak** *WY* U.S.A.
234 C3 **Bridgeton** *NJ* U.S.A.
87 C7 **Bridgetown** *W.A.* Austr.
247 □4 **Bridgetown** Barbados
225 H4 **Bridgetown** *N.S.* Can.
147 E4 **Bridgetown** Rep. of Ireland
233 F5 **Bridgeville** *DE* U.S.A.
83 F5 **Bridgewater** *Tas.* Austr.
225 H4 **Bridgewater** *N.S.* Can.
233 H4 **Bridgewater** *MA* U.S.A.
233 □J1 **Bridgewater** *ME* U.S.A.
233 F3 **Bridgewater** *NY* U.S.A.
232 D5 **Bridgewater** *VA* U.S.A.
82 E4 **Bridgewater, Cape** *Vic.* Austr.
150 E2 **Bridgnorth** *Shropshire, England* U.K.
233 □H2 **Bridgton** *ME* U.S.A.
150 D3 **Bridgwater** *Somerset, England* U.K.
150 D3 **Bridgwater Bay** *England* U.K.
176 G2 **Břidličná** Czech Rep.
149 I3 **Bridlington** *East Riding of Yorkshire, England* U.K.
149 I3 **Bridlington Bay** *England* U.K.
83 F5 **Bridport** *Tas.* Austr.
150 E4 **Bridport** *Dorset, England* U.K.
162 C3 **Brie** France
156 C4 **Brie** *reg.* France
158 C3 **Briec** France
156 C4 **Brie-Comte-Robert** France
169 C5 **Briedel** Ger.
Brieg Pol. *see* **Brzeg**
164 D3 **Brielle** Neth.
156 E4 **Brienne-le-Château** France
160 C2 **Briennon** France
156 D4 **Brienon-sur-Armançon** France
190 D2 **Brienz** Switz.
193 H4 **Brienza** Italy
190 D2 **Brienzer Rothorn** *mt.* Switz.
190 C2 **Brienzer See** *l.* Switz.
234 A1 **Brier Mountain** *hill PA* U.S.A.
232 C5 **Briery Knob** *mt. WV* U.S.A.
171 F3 **Briescht** Ger.
170 D3 **Brieselang** Ger.
171 F3 **Briesen** Ger.
171 E4 **Brieske** Ger.
171 F3 **Brieskow-Finkenheerd** Ger.
171 F4 **Briesnig** Ger.
168 F2 **Brietlingen** Ger.
157 E3 **Brieuilles-sur-Bar** France
183 H2 **Brieva de Cameros** Spain
157 F3 **Briey** France
190 C2 **Brig** Switz.
172 C4 **Brigach** *r.* Ger.
235 D3 **Brigantine** *NJ* U.S.A.
149 I4 **Brigg** *North Lincolnshire, England* U.K.
238 F3 **Briggsdale** *CO* U.S.A.
226 C4 **Briggsville** *WI* U.S.A.
149 F3 **Brigham** *Cumbria, England* U.K.
238 D3 **Brigham City** *UT* U.S.A.
149 H4 **Brighouse** *West Yorkshire, England* U.K.
151 F4 **Brighstone** *Isle of Wight, England* U.K.
83 F4 **Bright** *Vic.* Austr.
151 I3 **Brightlingsea** *Essex, England* U.K.
227 I3 **Brighton** *Ont.* Can.
81 C6 **Brighton** *South I.* N.Z.
151 G4 **Brighton** *Brighton and Hove, England* U.K.
238 F4 **Brighton** *CO* U.S.A.
227 F4 **Brighton** *MI* U.S.A.
232 E3 **Brighton** *NY* U.S.A.
232 B5 **Brighton** *WV* U.S.A.
151 G4 **Brighton and Hove** *admin. div. England* U.K.
85 E4 **Brighton Downs** *Qld* Austr.
81 D4 **Brightwater** *South I.* N.Z.
160 C3 **Brignais** France
163 C5 **Brignemont** France
158 B3 **Brignogan-Plage** France
161 E5 **Brignoles** France
146 D5 **Brig o'Turk** *Stirling, Scotland* U.K.
151 G2 **Brigstock** *Northamptonshire, England* U.K.
183 H4 **Brihuega** Spain
206 A3 **Brikama** Gambia
226 C3 **Brillion** *WI* U.S.A.
157 F4 **Brillon-en-Barrois** France
169 D4 **Brilon** Ger.
149 H4 **Brimington** *Derbyshire, England* U.K.
226 E2 **Brimley** *MI* U.S.A.
226 B2 **Brimson** *MN* U.S.A.
247 □2 **Brimstone Hill Fortress National Park** St Kitts and Nevis
184 C2 **Brinches** Port.
182 D3 **Brincones** Spain
195 G2 **Brindisi** Italy
195 G2 **Brindisi** *prov. Puglia* Italy
193 H4 **Brindisi Montagna** Italy
82 C2 **Bring, Lake** *salt flat S.A.* Austr.
188 E3 **Brinje** Croatia
237 F5 **Brinkley** *AR* U.S.A.
261 F2 **Brinkmann** Arg.
168 C2 **Brinkum** *Niedersachsen* Ger.
168 D2 **Brinkum** *Niedersachsen* Ger.
82 D3 **Brinkworth** *S.A.* Austr.
160 B1 **Brinon-sur-Beuvron** France
159 I4 **Brinon-sur-Sauldre** France
149 H4 **Brinsley** *Nottinghamshire, England* U.K.
157 G4 **Brin-sur-Seille** France
149 H4 **Brinsworth** *South Yorkshire, England* U.K.
161 B4 **Brion** France
183 H2 **Briones** Spain
159 G2 **Brionne** France
161 B3 **Brioude** France
162 B2 **Brioux-sur-Boutonne** France
159 F3 **Briouze** France
225 G2 **Brisay** *Que.* Can.
85 H5 **Brisbane** *Qld* Austr.
191 G4 **Brisighella** Italy
159 F4 **Brissac-Quince** France
233 □J1 **Bristol** *N.B.* Can.
150 E3 **Bristol** *Bristol, England* U.K.
150 E3 **Bristol** *admin. div. England* U.K.
233 G4 **Bristol** *CT* U.S.A.
231 C6 **Bristol** *FL* U.S.A.
234 B4 **Bristol** *MD* U.S.A.
233 H3 **Bristol** *NH* U.S.A.
234 D2 **Bristol** *PA* U.S.A.
233 H4 **Bristol** *RI* U.S.A.
232 B6 **Bristol** *TN* U.S.A.
233 G2 **Bristol** *VT* U.S.A.
220 B4 **Bristol Bay** *AK* U.S.A.
150 C3 **Bristol Channel** *est. England* U.K.
241 I4 **Bristol Mountains** *CA* U.S.A.
151 I2 **Briston** *Norfolk, England* U.K.
237 D5 **Bristow** *OK* U.S.A.
150 E4 **Brit** *r. England* U.K.
Britannia Island *Î. Loyauté* New Caledonia *see* **Maré**
182 B3 **Britelo** Port.
262 S2 **British Antarctic Territory** Antarctica
222 F5 **British Columbia** *prov.* Can.
221 J1 **British Empire Range** *mts Nunavut* Can.
British Guiana *country* S. America *see* **Guyana**
British Honduras *country* Central America *see* **Belize**
88 C7 **British Indian Ocean Territory** *terr.* Indian Ocean
264 J6 **British Isles** N. Atlantic Ocean
British Solomon Islands *country* S. Pacific Ocean *see* **Solomon Islands**
179 F4 **Britof** Slovenia
Brito Godins Angola *see* **Kiwaba N'zogi**
215 F1 **Brits** S. Africa
214 D4 **Britstown** S. Africa
147 E3 **Brittas** Rep. of Ireland
147 E4 **Brittas Bay** Rep. of Ireland
146 B4 **Brittle, Loch** *b. Scotland* U.K.
236 D2 **Britton** *SD* U.S.A.
170 E3 **Britz** Ger.
162 D3 **Brive-la-Gaillarde** France
161 B3 **Brives-Charensac** France
183 G2 **Briviesca** Spain
158 E2 **Brix** France
178 D3 **Brixen im Thale** Austria
150 D4 **Brixham** *Torbay, England* U.K.
Brixia Italy *see* **Brescia**
178 C3 **Brixlegg** Austria
151 G2 **Brixworth** *Northamptonshire, England* U.K.
191 I3 **Brkini** *reg.* Slovenia
Brlik *Zhambylskaya Oblast'* Kazakh. *see* **Birlik**
121 H4 **Brlik** *Zhambylskaya Oblast'* Kazakh.
176 F2 **Brněnský kraj** *admin. reg.* Czech Rep.
171 F5 **Brniště** Czech Rep.
176 F2 **Brno** Czech Rep.
143 G2 **Bro** Sweden
Broach *Gujarat* India *see* **Bharuch**
231 D5 **Broad** *r. SC* U.S.A.
233 F3 **Broadalbin** *NY* U.S.A.
87 D6 **Broad Arrow** *W.A.* Austr.
224 E3 **Broadback** *r. Que.* Can.
146 B3 **Broad Bay** *Scotland* U.K.
150 D4 **Broadclyst** *Devon, England* U.K.
83 F4 **Broadford** *Vic.* Austr.
147 C4 **Broadford** *Clare* Rep. of Ireland
147 C4 **Broadford** *Limerick* Rep. of Ireland
146 C4 **Broadford** *Highland, Scotland* U.K.
147 B2 **Broad Haven** *b.* Rep. of Ireland
150 B3 **Broad Haven** *Pembrokeshire, Wales* U.K.
150 E2 **Broad Heath** *Worcestershire, England* U.K.
146 E6 **Broad Law** *hill Scotland* U.K.
150 E4 **Broadmayne** *Dorset, England* U.K.
84 C3 **Broadmere** *N.T.* Austr.
151 H4 **Broad Oak** *East Sussex, England* U.K.
85 G4 **Broad Sound** *sea chan. Qld* Austr.
85 G4 **Broad Sound Channel** *Qld* Austr.
85 G4 **Broadsound Range** *hills Qld* Austr.
151 I3 **Broadstairs** *Kent, England* U.K.
238 F2 **Broadus** *MT* U.S.A.
223 K5 **Broadview** *Sask.* Can.
83 H2 **Broadwater** *N.S.W.* Austr.
236 C3 **Broadwater** *NE* U.S.A.
147 E4 **Broadway** Rep. of Ireland
151 F2 **Broadway** *Worcestershire, England* U.K.
232 D5 **Broadway** *VA* U.S.A.
150 E4 **Broadwey** *Dorset, England* U.K.
150 E4 **Broadwindsor** *Dorset, England* U.K.
80 D1 **Broadwood** *North I.* N.Z.
168 E1 **Broager** Denmark
143 F3 **Broby** Sweden
190 C2 **Broc** Switz.
163 B4 **Brocas** France
138 D3 **Brocēni** Latvia
146 B4 **Brochel** *Highland, Scotland* U.K.
223 K3 **Brochet** *Man.* Can.
149 G4 **Brock** *r. England* U.K.
168 E2 **Brockel** *Niedersachsen* Ger.
168 F3 **Bröckel** Ger.
169 F4 **Brocken** *mt.* Ger.
151 F4 **Brockenhurst** *Hampshire, England* U.K.
86 C4 **Brockman, Mount** *W.A.* Austr.
232 E3 **Brockport** *NY* U.S.A.
232 D4 **Brockport** *PA* U.S.A.
233 H3 **Brockton** *MA* U.S.A.
234 B2 **Brockton** *PA* U.S.A.
169 D3 **Brockum** Ger.
224 F4 **Brockville** *Ont.* Can.
233 □J2 **Brockway** *N.B.* Can.
232 D4 **Brockway** *PA* U.S.A.
150 E3 **Brockworth** *Gloucestershire, England* U.K.
232 D3 **Brocton** *NY* U.S.A.
196 E5 **Brod** Macedonia
176 G2 **Brodek u Přerova** Czech Rep.
170 D1 **Broderstorf** Ger.
136 E3 **Brodets'ke** Ukr.
221 J2 **Brodeur Peninsula** *Nunavut* Can.
226 C4 **Brodhead** *WI* U.S.A.
234 C2 **Brodhead** *r. PA* U.S.A.
234 C2 **Brodheadsville** *PA* U.S.A.

146 C6	Brodick *North Ayrshire, Scotland* U.K.
232 D6	Brodnax VA U.S.A.
175 H2	Brodnica *Kujawsko-Pomorskie* Pol.
174 F4	Brodnica *Wielkopolskie* Pol.
176 G3	Brodské Slovakia
174 C4	Brody Pol.
136 C2	Brody Ukr.
215 E2	Broedersput S. Africa
164 F3	Broekhuizenvorst Neth.
215 E4	Broekpoort r. S. Africa
159 G2	Broglie France
169 C5	Brohl Ger.
170 E2	Brohm Ger.
160 D1	Broin France
174 D2	Brojce Pol.
175 J3	Brok Pol.
175 J3	Brok r. Pol.
168 E2	Brokdorf Ger.
142 C2	Brokefjell *mt.* Norway
87 C7	Broke Inlet *W.A.* Austr.
237 E4	Broken Arrow OK U.S.A.
83 G3	Broken Bay *N.S.W.* Austr.
236 D3	Broken Bow NE U.S.A.
237 E5	Broken Bow OK U.S.A.
232 E5	Brokenburg VA U.S.A.
223 L5	Brokenhead r. *Man.* Can.
82 E2	Broken Hill *N.S.W.* Austr.
	Broken Hill Zambia *see* Kabwe
265 K7	Broken Plateau *sea feature* Indian Ocean
251 H3	Brokopondo Suriname
	Brokopondo Stuwmeer resr Suriname *see* Professor van Blommestein Meer
168 E2	Brokstedt Ger.
194 D4	Brolo *Sicilia* Italy
173 E2	Brombachsee *l.* Ger.
	Bromberg Pol. *see* Bydgoszcz
168 F3	Brome Ger.
150 E2	Bromfield *Shropshire, England* U.K.
151 G2	Bromham *Bedfordshire, England* U.K.
150 E3	Bromham *Wiltshire, England* U.K.
151 G3	Bromley *Greater London, England* U.K.
161 A4	Brommat France
149 H3	Brompton *North Yorkshire, England* U.K.
149 H3	Brompton on Swale *North Yorkshire, England* U.K.
143 G3	Brömsebro Sweden
150 E2	Bromsgrove *Worcestershire, England* U.K.
169 D4	Bromskirchen Ger.
150 E2	Bromyard *Herefordshire, England* U.K.
160 C3	Bron France
150 D2	Bronaber *Gwynedd, Wales* U.K.
183 I4	Bronchales Spain
142 C3	Brønderslev Denmark
206 E3	Brong-Ahafo *admin. reg.* Ghana
190 E3	Broni Italy
215 G3	Bronkhorstspruit S. Africa
139 L4	Bronnitsy Rus. Fed.
140 K2	Brønnøysund Norway
231 D6	Bronson FL U.S.A.
226 E5	Bronson MI U.S.A.
194 D5	Bronte *Sicilia* Italy
235 G2	Bronte County *county* NY U.S.A.
136 D2	Bronyts'ka Huta Ukr.
190 E3	Bronzone, Monte *mt.* Italy
151 I2	Brooke *Norfolk, England* U.K.
232 E5	Brooke VA U.S.A.
147 D2	Brookeborough *Northern Ireland* U.K.
92 A4	Brooke's Point Phil.
235 I2	Brookfield CT U.S.A.
236 E4	Brookfield MO U.S.A.
226 C4	Brookfield WI U.S.A.
237 F6	Brookhaven MS U.S.A.
238 A3	Brookings OR U.S.A.
236 D3	Brookings SD U.S.A.
234 C3	Brookland Terrace DE U.S.A.
233 H3	Brookline MA U.S.A.
226 B5	Brooklyn IL U.S.A.
227 E4	Brooklyn MI U.S.A.
234 B3	Brooklyn Park MD U.S.A.
226 A3	Brooklyn Park MN U.S.A.
232 D6	Brookneal VA U.S.A.
226 A5	Brook Park MN U.S.A.
225 I5	Brooks *Alta* Can.
233 □12	Brooks ME U.S.A.
232 C6	Brooks WV U.S.A.
262 T2	Brooks, Cape Antarctica
222 C2	Brooks Brook *Y.T.* Can.
234 C3	Brookside DE U.S.A.
220 D3	Brooks Range *mts* AK U.S.A.
226 D5	Brookston IN U.S.A.
226 A2	Brookston MN U.S.A.
231 D6	Brooksville FL U.S.A.
232 A5	Brooksville KY U.S.A.
87 C7	Brookton *W.A.* Austr.
233 □J2	Brookton ME U.S.A.
230 C4	Brookville IN U.S.A.
232 D4	Brookville PA U.S.A.
146 C4	Broom, Loch *inlet Scotland* U.K.
86 D3	Broome *W.A.* Austr.
87 C7	Broomehill *W.A.* Austr.
147 E2	Broomfield *Rep. of Ireland* U.K.
151 H3	Broomfield *Essex, England* U.K.
150 D3	Broons France
161 A4	Broquiès France
146 E3	Brora *Highland, Scotland* U.K.
146 E3	Brora r. *Highland, Scotland* U.K.
143 F4	Brösarp Sweden
150 E2	Broseley *Shropshire, England* U.K.
136 C3	Broshniv-Osada Ukr.
147 B4	Brosna *Rep. of Ireland* U.K.
147 D3	Brosna r. *Rep. of Ireland* U.K.
162 B3	Brosse France
232 D6	Brosville VA U.S.A.
256 C5	Brotas Brazil
184 B2	Brotas Port.
254 E5	Brotas de Macaúbas Brazil
238 B3	Brothers OR U.S.A.
186 C2	Broto Spain
157 F4	Brottes France
149 I3	Brotton *Redcar and Cleveland, England* U.K.
156 B4	Brou France
149 G3	Brough *Cumbria, England* U.K.
149 I4	Brough *East Riding of Yorkshire, England* U.K.
146 E3	Brough *Highland, Scotland* U.K.
148 D4	Brough *Rep. of Ireland* U.K.
146 E2	Brough Head *Scotland* U.K.
147 D2	Broughshane *Northern Ireland* U.K.
150 E1	Broughton *Flintshire, Wales* U.K.
151 G2	Broughton *Northamptonshire, England* U.K.
149 I4	Broughton *North Lincolnshire, England* U.K.
146 F3	Broughton *Scottish Borders, Scotland* U.K.
151 F2	Broughton Astley *Leicestershire, England* U.K.
149 F3	Broughton in Furness *Cumbria, England* U.K.
146 F2	Broughton Island Nunavut Can. *see* Qikiqtarjuaq
	Broughtown *Orkney, Scotland* U.K.
176 F1	Broumov Czech Rep.
157 K4	Broussard France
161 A4	Brousse France
164 C3	Brouwershaven Neth.
136 F2	Brovary Ukr.
85 G5	Brovinia *Qld* Austr.
142 C3	Brovst Denmark
226 C5	Browerville MN U.S.A.
87 C6	Brown, Lake *salt flat W.A.* Austr.
82 D3	Brown, Mount *hill* S.A. Austr.
82 C3	Brown, Point S.A. Austr.
227 E4	Brown City MI U.S.A.
85 E3	Brown Creek r. *Qld* Austr.
85 D4	Brown Deer WI U.S.A.
149 G4	Brown Edge *Staffordshire, England* U.K.

87 E5	Browne Range *hills W.A.* Austr.
237 C5	Brownfield TX U.S.A.
151 F2	Brownhills *West Midlands, England* U.K.
238 D1	Browning MT U.S.A.
240 I4	Brownlee CA U.S.A.
226 A4	Brownsdale MN U.S.A.
234 D3	Browns Mills NJ U.S.A.
246 □	Brown's Town Jamaica
230 C4	Brownstown IN U.S.A.
232 B4	Brownsville PA U.S.A.
232 D7	Brownsville TN U.S.A.
237 D7	Brownsville TX U.S.A.
251 H3	Brownsweg Suriname
233 □12	Brownville ME U.S.A.
233 □12	Brownville Junction ME U.S.A.
237 D6	Brownwood TX U.S.A.
86 D2	Browse Island *W.A.* Austr.
146 E6	Broxburn *West Lothian, Scotland* U.K.
190 C2	Broye r. Switz.
156 B4	Broyes France
171 F5	Brozany Czech Rep.
182 D5	Brozas Spain
190 F3	Brozzo Italy
176 E2	Brtnice Czech Rep.
146 E5	Bruar Water r. *Scotland* U.K.
156 C2	Bruay-la-Bussière France
174 G3	Bruce MS U.S.A.
226 B3	Bruce r. *W.I.* Austr.
86 C4	Bruce, Mount *W.A.* Austr.
226 C2	Bruce Crossing MI U.S.A.
227 G3	Bruce Peninsula *Ont.* Can.
227 G3	Bruce Rock *W.A.* Austr.
161 F4	Bruche r. France
168 E3	Bruchhausen-Vilsen Ger.
169 D5	Bruchköbel Ger.
172 B2	Bruchmühlbach Ger.
172 C2	Bruchsal Ger.
169 D4	Bruchweiler-Bärenbach Ger.
179 H2	Bruck an der Leitha Austria
179 M3	Bruck an der Mur Austria
173 F3	Brückberg Ger.
172 B2	Brücken Ger.
173 E3	Brücken (Pfalz) Ger.
173 G2	Bruck in der Oberpfalz Ger.
179 F4	Brückl Austria
173 F4	Bruckmühl Ger.
195 I5	Bruculi *Sicilia* Italy
174 G3	Brudzeń Duży Pol.
174 D3	Brudzew Pol.
150 E3	Brue r. *England* U.K.
161 D5	Brue-Auriac France
170 C2	Brüel Ger.
159 I5	Bruère-Allichamps France
165 C4	Brugelette Belgium
	Bruges Belgium *see* Brugge
190 D1	Brugg Switz.
165 C3	Brugge Belgium
169 B4	Brüggen Ger.
169 B4	Brüggen Ger.
169 E4	Brüggen Ger.
191 H3	Brugnera Italy
163 D5	Bruguières France
140 I3	Bruhagen Norway
172 C2	Brühl Ger.
169 B5	Brühl Ger.
232 B5	Bruin KY U.S.A.
232 D4	Bruin PA U.S.A.
164 D3	Bruinisse Neth.
241 L2	Bruin Point *mt.* UT U.S.A.
212 C4	Brukkaros, Mount Namibia
222 G4	Brûlé *Alta* Can.
226 B2	Brule WI U.S.A.
159 F4	Brûlon France
165 D5	Brûly Belgium
255 D2	Brumadinho Brazil
254 E5	Brumado Brazil
157 H4	Brumath France
164 F2	Brummen Neth.
177 H2	Brumov-Bylnice Czech Rep.
177 G1	Brumovice Czech Rep.
141 J3	Brumunddal Norway
191 J2	Bruna r. Italy
147 E3	Brú Na Bóinne *tourist site Meath Rep. of Ireland*
170 C3	Brunau Ger.
151 I2	Brundall *Norfolk, England* U.K.
151 I2	Brundish *Suffolk, England* U.K.
	Brundisium Italy *see* Brindisi
238 D3	Bruneau r. ID U.S.A.
238 D3	Bruneau, East Fork r. *Idaho/Nevada* U.S.A.
238 D3	Bruneau, West Fork r. *Idaho/Nevada* U.S.A.
156 B3	Brunehamel France
95 F1	Brunei country Asia
	Brunei *see* Bandar Seri Begawan
95 F1	Brunei Bay Malaysia
183 J4	Brunete Spain
84 C3	Brunette Downs *N.T.* Austr.
140 K3	Brunflo Sweden
191 J2	Brunico Italy
163 D4	Bruniquel France
179 O4	Brunn Austria
	Brünn Czech Rep. *see* Brno
170 E2	Brunn Ger.
143 J2	Brunna Sweden
179 N6	Brunn am Gebirge Austria
190 D1	Brunnen Switz.
81 C5	Brunner, Lake South I. N.Z.
234 B2	Brunnerville PA U.S.A.
234 J4	Bruno Sask. Can.
226 A2	Bruno MN U.S.A.
168 E2	Brunsbüttel Ger.
165 E4	Brunssum Neth.
157 H5	Brunstatt Ger.
	Braunschweig
231 E5	Brunswick GA U.S.A.
232 E5	Brunswick MD U.S.A.
233 □13	Brunswick ME U.S.A.
236 E4	Brunswick MO U.S.A.
232 C4	Brunswick OH U.S.A.
259 C9	Brunswick, Peninsula de *pen.* Chile
86 E2	Brunswick Bay *W.A.* Austr.
83 H7	Brunswick Head *N.S.W.* Austr.
87 B7	Brunswick Junction *W.A.* Austr.
176 G2	Bruntál Czech Rep.
215 H3	Bruntville S. Africa
83 F5	Bruny Island *Tas.* Austr.
196 E4	Brus Srbija Yugo.
220 B3	Bruskasfo AK U.S.A.
214 D3	Brusands S. Africa
85 C6	Brushy Tableland *reg.* Qld Austr.
82 D3	Bruskleboo S.A. Austr.
146 F4	Buckburn *Aberdeen, Scotland* U.K.
234 C2	Bucks County *county* PA U.S.A.
241 M4	Buckskin Mountains AZ U.S.A.
241 G2	Bucks Mountain CA U.S.A.
233 □12	Bucksport ME U.S.A.
170 D2	Buckwitz Ger.
214 C3	Bucleuch S. Africa
220 B3	Bucobia r. Côte d'Ivoire

Būr Sudan Sudan see Port Sudan
82 E3 Burta N.S.W. Austr.
173 E3 Burtenbach Ger.
138 E3 Burtnieku ezers l. Latvia
151 F4 Burton Dorset, England U.K.
227 F4 Burton MI U.S.A.
150 E4 Burton Bradstock Dorset, England U.K.
149 G3 Burton-in-Kendal Cumbria, England U.K.
151 G2 Burton Latimer Northamptonshire, England U.K.
149 H3 Burton Leonard North Yorkshire, England U.K.
147 C2 Burtonport Rep. of Ireland
234 B3 Burtonsville MD U.S.A.
149 I4 Burton upon Stather North Lincolnshire, England U.K.
151 F2 Burton upon Trent Staffordshire, England U.K.
140 M2 Burträsk Sweden
233 □J1 Burts Corner N.B. Can.
83 E3 Burtundy N.S.W. Austr.
84 C4 Burt Well N.T. Austr.
93 C3 Buru i. Maluku Indon.
183 F5 Burujón Spain
137 H5 Burul'cha r. Ukr.
126 C5 Burullus, Bahra el lag. Egypt
Burullus, Lake lag. Egypt see Burullus, Bahra el
Burultokay Xinjiang China see Fuhai
211 A5 Burundi country Africa
Burunniy Rus. Fed. see Tsagan Aman
211 A5 Bururi Burundi
150 E2 Burwarton Shropshire, England U.K.
151 H4 Burwash East Sussex, England U.K.
222 B2 Burwash Landing Y.T. Can.
151 H2 Burwell Cambridgeshire, England U.K.
236 D3 Burwell NE U.S.A.
146 F3 Burwick Orkney, Scotland U.K.
149 G4 Bury Greater Manchester, England U.K.
Buryatia aut. rep. Rus. Fed. see Buryatiya, Respublika
106 G1 Buryatiya, Respublika aut. rep. Rus. Fed.
Buryatskaya Mongolskaya A.S.S.R. aut. rep. Rus. Fed. see Buryatiya, Respublika
137 G2 Buryn' Ukr.
151 H2 Bury St Edmunds Suffolk, England U.K.
174 G4 Burzenin Pol.
161 C4 Burzet France
192 A4 Busachi Sardegna Italy
190 D4 Busalla Italy
Busan S. Korea see Pusan
190 F4 Busana Italy
238 F2 Busby MT U.S.A.
190 C4 Busca Italy
179 H2 Buschberg hill Austria
170 D3 Buschow Ger.
168 E1 Busdorf Ger.
Buseire Syria see Al Buşayrah
194 B4 Buseto Palizzolo Sicilia Italy
148 C2 Bush r. Northern Ireland U.K.
136 E3 Busha Ukr.
136 D2 Bushcha Ukr.
128 D4 Büshehr Iran
122 B4 Büshehr prov. Iran
210 A5 Bushenyi Uganda
151 G3 Bushey Hertfordshire, England U.K.
Bushire Iran see Büshehr
234 C1 Bushkill PA U.S.A.
234 D1 Bush Kill r. PA U.S.A.
147 E1 Bushmills Northern Ireland U.K.
231 D6 Bushnell FL U.S.A.
226 B5 Bushnell IL U.S.A.
196 E5 Bushtricë Albania
210 D4 Busia Kenya
156 D2 Busigny France
177 I3 Bušince Slovakia
208 D4 Businga Dem. Rep. Congo
208 C5 Busira r. Dem. Rep. Congo
136 C3 Bus'k Ukr.
136 C1 Buskerud county Norway
175 I5 Busko-Zdrój Pol.
Buskul' Kazakh. see Boskol'
157 G5 Bussang France
87 B7 Busselton W.A. Austr.
193 H4 Bussento r. Italy
190 F3 Busseto Italy
162 C3 Bussière-Badil France
162 D2 Bussière-Dunoise France
162 D3 Bussière-Galant France
162 C2 Bussière-Poitevine France
190 B2 Bussigny Switz.
193 F2 Bussi sul Tirino Italy
171 C5 Büßleben Ger.
191 F3 Bussolengo Italy
190 C3 Bussoleno Italy
164 E2 Bussum Neth.
156 D4 Bussy-en-Othe France
160 C1 Bussy-le-Grand France
243 E3 Bustamante Mex.
197 G3 Buşteni Romania
261 G3 Bustinza Arg.
190 D3 Busto Arsizio Italy
92 A3 Busuanga Phil.
92 A3 Busuanga i. Phil.
168 D1 Büsum Ger.
191 I2 But r. Italy
208 E4 Buta Dem. Rep. Congo
210 C2 Butajīra Eth.
197 F4 Butan Bulg.
97 B6 Butang Group is Thai.
211 A5 Butare Rwanda
228 G6 Butaritari atoll Kiribati
146 C6 Bute i. Scotland U.K.
146 C6 Bute, Sound of sea chan. Scotland U.K.
197 H2 Butea Romania
222 D4 Butedale B.C. Can.
208 F4 Butembo Dem. Rep. Congo
177 L5 Buteni Romania
194 D5 Butera Sicilia Italy
165 F4 Bütgenbach Belgium
215 G3 Butha Buthe Lesotho
Butha Qi Nei Mongol China see Zalantun
96 A2 Buthidaung Myanmar
160 F3 Buthier di Valpelline r. Italy
255 C9 Butiá Brazil
210 A4 Butiaba Uganda
237 F5 Butler AL U.S.A.
231 C5 Butler GA U.S.A.
226 E5 Butler IN U.S.A.
232 A5 Butler KY U.S.A.
236 E4 Butler MO U.S.A.
235 D1 Butler NJ U.S.A.
232 D4 Butler PA U.S.A.
147 D2 Butlers Bridge Rep. of Ireland
93 B4 Buton i. Indon.
136 E4 Butor Moldova
137 I2 Butovo Rus. Fed.
170 D2 Bütow Ger.
182 D4 Butrera mt. Spain
198 B2 Butrintit, Liqeni i l. Albania
175 I2 Butryny Pol.
190 E1 Bütschwil Switz.
175 M4 Butsyn Ukr.
237 F5 Buttahatchee r. MS U.S.A.
238 D2 Butte MT U.S.A.
236 D3 Butte NE U.S.A.
172 C2 Büttelborn Ger.
171 C4 Buttelstedt Ger.
173 F2 Buttenheim Ger.
173 E3 Buttenwiesen Ger.
149 F3 Buttermere Cumbria, England U.K.
226 B2 Butternut WI U.S.A.
149 I3 Butterwick North Yorkshire, England U.K.
94 C1 Butterworth Malaysia
215 G5 Butterworth S. Africa
240 G2 Buttes, Sierra mt. CA U.S.A.
147 C4 Buttevant Rep. of Ireland
172 D2 Butthard Ger.
146 B3 Butt of Lewis hd Scotland U.K.
240 H4 Buttonwillow CA U.S.A.
171 C4 Buttstädt Ger.
169 F4 Buttstedt Ger.
87 D7 Butty Head hd W.A. Austr.
234 C2 Buttzville NJ U.S.A.
92 C4 Butuan Phil.
136 E4 Butuceni Moldova
108 B3 Butuo Sichuan China
135 H6 Buturlinovka Rus. Fed.
117 E4 Butwal Nepal
Butysh Rus. Fed. see Kama
169 D5 Butzbach Ger.
170 C2 Bützow Ger.
234 C2 Butztown PA U.S.A.
210 E4 Buulobarde Somalia
Buurakan r. Kyrg. see Burkan-Suu
211 D5 Buur Gaabo Somalia
210 E4 Buurhabaka Somalia
164 F2 Buurse Neth.
210 B4 Buvuma Island Uganda
128 B5 Buwāṭah, Jabal mt. Saudi Arabia
124 B2 Buwāṭah Saudi Arabia
117 F4 Buxar Bihar India
159 G5 Buxerolles France
173 F3 Buxheim Ger.
160 A2 Buxières-les-Mines France
151 H4 Buxted East Sussex, England U.K.
168 E2 Buxtehude Ger.
149 H4 Buxton Derbyshire, England U.K.
160 C2 Buxy France
134 H4 Buy Rus. Fed.
134 K4 Buy r. Rus. Fed.
106 C2 Buyant Bayanhongor Mongolia
106 A1 Buyant Bayan-Ölgiy Mongolia
107 F2 Buyant Hentiy Mongolia
106 C2 Buyant Gol r. Mongolia
106 C2 Buyant Gol r. Mongolia
107 F2 Buyant-Uhaa Mongolia
226 A1 Buyck MN U.S.A.
129 E2 Buynaksk Rus. Fed.
206 D5 Buyo Côte d'Ivoire
108 B4 Buyun Jiang r. Yunnan China
127 G3 Büyük Ağrı Dağı mt. Turkey
129 C3 Büyükçatak Turkey
199 F1 Büyükçekmece Turkey
199 G2 Büyükkabaca Turkey
199 G2 Büyükkarabağ Turkey
199 E1 Büyükkarıştıran Turkey
199 F3 Büyükkonak Turkey
199 E3 Büyükmenderes r. Turkey
199 F2 Büyükorhan Turkey
128 C1 Büyükşahinbey Turkey
199 G2 Büyükyenice Balıkesir Turkey
107 I3 Buyun Shan mt. Liaoning China
120 B3 Buzachi, Poluostrov pen. Kazakh.
162 D2 Buzançais France
157 E3 Buzancy France
197 H3 Buzău Romania
197 H3 Buzău r. Romania
197 H3 Buzău r. Romania
135 K5 Buzdyak Rus. Fed.
191 I3 Buzet Croatia
163 C4 Buzet-sur-Baïse France
162 C5 Buzet-sur-Tarn France
139 M4 Buzha r. Rus. Fed.
213 G3 Búzi Moz.
213 G3 Búzi r. Moz.
197 E3 Buziaş Romania
177 K3 Buzica Slovakia
Büzmeyin Turkm. see Byuzmeyin
129 G3 Buzovna Azer.
120 C1 Buzuluk Rus. Fed.
135 H6 Buzuluk r. Rus. Fed.
160 B5 Buzy France
233 H4 Buzzards Bay MA U.S.A.
Bwcle Flintshire, Wales U.K. see Buckley
114 B3 Byadgi Karnataka India
138 G4 Byahoml' Belarus
197 G4 Byala Ruse Bulg.
197 H4 Byala Varna Bulg.
199 E1 Byala Reka r. Bulg.
197 F4 Byala Slatina Bulg.
138 G5 Byalynichy Belarus
Byam Martin atoll Arch. des Tuamotu Fr. Polynesia see Ahunui
138 E5 Byarezina r. Belarus
138 F5 Byarezina r. Belarus
138 E5 Byaroza Belarus
138 E5 Byarozawka Belarus
175 K4 Bychawa Pol.
175 G4 Bycina Pol.
174 G4 Byczyna Pol.
174 G2 Bydgoszcz Pol.
138 E5 Byelaazyorsk Belarus
136 D2 Byelaazyorsk Belarus
139 H5 Byelitsk Belarus
Byelorussia country Europe see Belarus
175 N1 Byenyakoni Belarus
Byerastavitsa Belarus see Pahranichny
138 G5 Byerazino Belarus
238 F4 Byers CO U.S.A.
138 G4 Byeshankovichy Belarus
232 C5 Byesville OH U.S.A.
139 H5 Byesyedz' r. Belarus
85 G4 Byfield Qld Austr.
151 F2 Byfield Northamptonshire, England U.K.
151 G3 Byfleet Surrey, England U.K.
140 M2 Bygdeå Sweden
140 M2 Bygdsiljum Sweden
142 B2 Bygland Norway
171 F4 Byhleguhre Ger.
137 I3 Byk r. Ukr.
139 H5 Bykhaw Belarus
Bykhov Belarus see Bykhaw
136 D2 Bykivka Ukr.
142 B2 Bykle Norway
135 I6 Bykovo Rus. Fed.
135 I5 Bylas AZ U.S.A.
150 D1 Bylchau Conwy, Wales U.K.
150 B1 Bylderup-Bov Denmark
221 K2 Bylot Island Nunavut Can.
129 C2 Bylym Rus. Fed.
227 G3 Byng Inlet Ont. Can.
85 E3 Bynoe r. Qld Austr.
85 E3 Bynoe Harbour N.T. Austr.
107 H1 Byrka Rus. Fed.
137 G2 Byrlivka Ukr.
83 F2 Byrock N.S.W. Austr.
226 C4 Byron IL U.S.A.
233 □H2 Byron ME U.S.A.
232 B3 Byron MI U.S.A.
83 H2 Byron, Cape N.S.W. Austr.
83 H2 Byron Bay N.S.W. Austr.
Byron Island Gilbert Is Kiribati see Nikunau
131 K2 Byrranga, Gory mts Rus. Fed.
137 G1 Byrynne Ukr.
136 E2 Byshiv Ukr.
176 D1 Byšice Czech Rep.
140 M2 Byske Sweden
140 M2 Byskeälven r. Sweden
100 D1 Byssa r. Rus. Fed.
175 H6 Bystra Pol.
177 I2 Bystrá mt. Slovakia
176 F2 Bystré Czech Rep.
177 K2 Bystré Slovakia
177 H3 Bystričany Slovakia
177 H2 Bystřice Czech Rep.
176 G2 Bystřice Czech Rep.
176 E1 Bystřice r. Czech Rep.
176 F2 Bystřice nad Pernštejnem Czech Rep.
177 G2 Bystřice pod Hostýnem Czech Rep.
107 F1 Bystrinskiy Golets, Gora mt. Rus. Fed.
Bystrovka Kyrg. see Kemin
136 C3 Bystrytsya Ukr.
136 C3 Bystrytsya r. Ukr.
121 K1 Bystryy Istok Rus. Fed.
134 K5 Bystryy Tanyp r. Rus. Fed.
174 F5 Bystrzyca Pol.
174 E4 Bystrzyca r. Pol.
175 K4 Bystrzyca r. Pol.
174 F5 Bystrzyca Kłodzka Pol.
176 F1 Bystrzyckie, Góry mts Czech Rep./Pol.
137 G4 Bytantay r. Rus. Fed.
177 H2 Bytča Slovakia
174 D3 Bytnica Pol.
175 G4 Bytom Pol.
174 D4 Bytom Odrzański Pol.
139 J5 Bytosh' Rus. Fed.
143 G4 Bytów Pol.
211 A5 Byumba Rwanda
122 D2 Byuzmeyin Turkm.
143 G3 Byxelkrok Kalmar Sweden
Byzantium Turkey see İstanbul
176 G3 Bzenec Czech Rep.
129 B2 Bzip'i r. Georgia
129 B2 Bzip'is K'edi hills Georgia
175 I3 Bzura r. Pol.

C

96 D3 Ca, Sông r. Vietnam
253 F6 Caacupé Para.
253 F6 Caaguazú Para.
253 G6 Caaguazú, Cordillera de hills Para.
209 B8 Caála Angola
251 F5 Caapiranga Brazil
255 B7 Caarapó Brazil
253 F6 Caazapá Para.
252 A2 Cabaçal r. Brazil
246 C2 Cabaiguán Cuba
163 B6 Cabaliros, Pic de mt. France
252 B3 Caballas Peru
185 G3 Caballo mt. Spain
250 D5 Caballococha Peru
252 A2 Cabana Peru
165 C5 Cabanac France
163 B4 Cabanac-et-Villagrains France
252 C3 Cabanaconde Peru
182 B3 Cabana Maior Port.
182 D4 Cabañaquinta Spain
184 C3 Cabañas Port.
185 H3 Cabañas mt. Spain
182 E5 Cabañas del Castillo Spain
182 C4 Cabanas de Viriato Port.
182 D2 Cabañas Raras Spain
92 B3 Cabanatuan Phil.
163 D5 Cabanès hill France
187 D4 Cabanes Spain
161 C5 Cabannes France
225 G4 Cabano Que. Can.
188 E3 Čabar Croatia
165 E5 Cabasse France
186 D3 Cabassers Spain
182 C2 Cabe r. Spain
184 C3 Cabeça Gorda Port.
184 B2 Cabeção Port.
252 D1 Cabeceiras Brazil
182 C3 Cabeceiras de Basto Port.
184 C1 Cabeço de Vide Port.
182 C5 Cabeço Rainha mt. Port.
254 G3 Cabedelo Brazil
163 E6 Cabestany France
197 F2 Cabeşti Romania
182 D3 Cabeza de Framontanos Spain
185 E2 Cabeza del Buey Spain
182 D5 Cabeza del Caballo Spain
184 D2 Cabeza la Vaca Spain
183 G5 Cabezamesada Spain
182 E5 Cabezarados Spain
253 E4 Cabezas Bol.
183 E4 Cabezas del Villar Spain
247 □1 Cabezas de San Juan pt Puerto Rico
184 C3 Cabezas Rubias Spain
183 I3 Cabezón de Morés mt. Spain
187 B6 Cabezo de Torres Spain
185 G4 Cabezo Gordo hill Spain
183 E3 Cabezón Spain
183 F2 Cabezón de Cameros Spain
183 F1 Cabezón de la Sal Spain
183 F1 Cabezón de Liébana Spain
182 E4 Cabezuela del Valle Spain
261 G6 Cabildo Arg.
250 D2 Cabimas Venez.
209 B6 Cabinda Angola
209 B6 Cabinda prov. Angola
238 D1 Cabinet Mountains MT U.S.A.
Cabistra Turkey see Ereğli
226 B2 Cable WI U.S.A.
254 B3 Cabo Brazil
216 □1a Cabo da Praia Terceira Azores
213 H2 Cabo Delgado prov. Moz.
257 F5 Cabo Frio Brazil
183 H3 Cabolafuente Spain
85 E4 Caboolture Qld Austr.
242 B2 Caborca Mex.
225 I4 Cabot Strait Nfld./N.S. Can.
159 F2 Cabourg France
Cabo Verde country N. Atlantic Ocean see Cape Verde
206 □ Cabo Verde, Ilhas do is N. Atlantic Ocean
Cabo Yubi Morocco see Tarfaya
185 F3 Cabra Spain
185 F3 Cabra r. Spain
182 B3 Cabração Port.
186 E3 Cabra del Camp Spain
185 G3 Cabra del Santo Cristo Spain
187 C4 Cabra de Mora Spain
246 E3 Cabral Dom. Rep.
187 C5 Cabral, Serra do mts Brazil
192 A5 Cabras Sardegna Italy
185 F3 Cabras mt. Spain
192 A5 Cabras, Stagno di l. Sardegna Italy
129 E4 Cābrayıl Azer.
183 H3 Cabrejas, Sierra de mts Spain
183 H3 Cabrejas del Pinar Spain
184 B2 Cabrela Port.
184 B2 Cabrela r. Port.
246 E3 Cabrera Dom. Rep.
185 F5 Cabrera r. Spain
182 D2 Cabrera r. Spain
187 G3 Cabrera, Illa de i. Spain
163 F5 Cabrerets France
223 I5 Cabri Sask. Can.
183 I5 Cabriel r. Spain
161 D5 Cabriès-d'Aigues France
182 C4 Cabril Port.
182 D3 Cabrillanes Spain
182 D4 Cabrillas Spain
183 H4 Cabrillas r. Spain
246 E2 Cabrobó Brazil
253 E2 Cabugao Phil.
188 F4 Čabulja mt. Bos.-Herz.
184 F4 Cabuyaro Col.
182 D2 Caçador Brazil
255 C8 Caçador Brazil
Cacagoin Sichuan China see Qagca
245 E5 Cacahuatepec Mex.
196 E4 Čačak Srbija Yugo.
257 E5 Caçapava Brazil
255 B9 Caçapava do Sul Brazil
232 D5 Cacapon r. WV U.S.A.
255 B9 Caçarelhos Port.
250 C3 Cáceres Col.
194 C5 Caccamo Sicilia Italy
193 I3 Caccia, Monte hill Italy
195 F3 Caccuri Italy
182 C4 Cacém Port.
255 A9 Cacequi Brazil
253 F4 Cáceres Brazil
184 D1 Cáceres Spain
182 D5 Cáceres prov. Extremadura Spain
261 H5 Cachari Arg.
237 F4 Cache r. IL U.S.A.
206 A3 Cacheau r. Guinea-Bissau
222 F5 Cache Creek B.C. Can.
240 G2 Cache Creek r. CA U.S.A.
238 F3 Cache la Poudre r. CO U.S.A.
238 E3 Cache Peak ID U.S.A.
206 A3 Cacheu Guinea-Bissau
258 D2 Cachi Arg.
258 D2 Cachi, Nevados de mts Arg.
254 B4 Cachimbo, Serra do hills Brazil
209 D7 Cachimo Angola
258 C2 Cachina r. Chile
209 C8 Cachingues Angola
254 F5 Cachoeira Bahia Brazil
256 B3 Cachoeira Mato Grosso do Sul Brazil
256 B3 Cachoeira Alta Brazil
256 B2 Cachoeira de Goiás Brazil
254 C2 Cachoeira do Arari Brazil
257 E3 Cachoeira dos Macacos Brazil
255 B9 Cachoeira do Sul Brazil
257 E5 Cachoeira Paulista Brazil
257 F5 Cachoeiras de Macacu Brazil
257 G4 Cachoeiro de Itapemirim Brazil
184 C3 Cachopo Port.
177 G3 Čachtice Slovakia
182 B4 Cacia Port.
185 G3 Cacín Spain
185 F3 Cacín r. Spain
206 B4 Cacine Guinea-Bissau
209 C7 Cacolo Angola
244 B3 Cacoma, Sierra mts Mex.
209 B8 Caconda Angola
209 B6 Cacongo Angola
237 C4 Cactus TX U.S.A.
240 I3 Cactus Range mts NV U.S.A.
256 B3 Caçu Brazil
209 B7 Cacuaco Angola
209 C7 Caculama Angola
254 E5 Caculé Brazil
257 H2 Cacumba, Ilha i. Brazil
209 B7 Cacuso Angola
184 A1 Cadafais Port.
150 D2 Cadair Idris hills Wales U.K.
163 D5 Cadalen France
183 F4 Cadalso de los Vidrios Spain
148 B4 Cadamstown Rep. of Ireland
186 G2 Cadaqués Spain
184 A1 Cadaval Port.
177 H2 Čadca Slovakia
210 D2 Caddabassa i. Eth.
151 G3 Caddington Bedfordshire, England U.K.
191 F4 Cadelbosco di Sopra Italy
84 C2 Cadell r. N.T. Austr.
190 D2 Cadenazzo Switz.
168 E2 Cadenberge Ger.
161 D5 Cadenet France
190 E4 Cadeo Italy
243 E3 Cadereyta Nuevo León Mex.
245 E3 Cadereyta Querétaro Mex.
Cader Idris hills Wales U.K. see Cadair Idris
161 C4 Caderousse France
Cadí mt. Spain see Torre de Cadí
186 E2 Cadí, Túnel de tun. Spain
185 G4 Cádiar Spain
82 C2 Cadibarrawirracanna, Lake salt flat S.A. Austr.
92 B3 Cadig Mountains Phil.
227 H1 Cadillac Que. Can.
223 J5 Cadillac Sask. Can.
163 B4 Cadillac France
226 E3 Cadillac MI U.S.A.
129 C3 Çadır Dağı mt. Turkey
129 C2 Çadırkaya Turkey
92 B4 Cadiz Phil.
184 D4 Cádiz Spain
184 E4 Cádiz prov. Andalucía Spain
241 J4 Cadiz CA U.S.A.
230 C4 Cadiz KY U.S.A.
232 C4 Cadiz OH U.S.A.
184 C4 Cádiz, Golfo de g. Spain
173 E2 Cadolzburg Ger.
222 G4 Cadomin Alta Can.
191 G3 Cadoneghe Italy
226 B3 Cadott WI U.S.A.
222 G3 Cadotte r. Alta Can.
222 G3 Cadotte Lake Alta Can.
163 D5 Cadours France
87 C6 Cadoux W.A. Austr.
254 E4 Caém Brazil
159 F2 Caen France
159 F2 Caen, Plaine de plain France
150 D3 Caerau Cardiff, Wales U.K.
Caerdydd Cardiff, Wales U.K. see Cardiff
Caere Italy see Cerveteri
Caerffili Caerphilly, Wales U.K. see Caerphilly
Caerfyrddin Carmarthenshire, Wales U.K. see Carmarthen
150 D1 Caergwrle Flintshire, Wales U.K.
Caergybi Isle of Anglesey, Wales U.K. see Holyhead
150 D1 Caerhun Conwy, Wales U.K.
150 E3 Caerleon Newport, Wales U.K.
150 C1 Caernarfon Gwynedd, Wales U.K.
150 C1 Caernarfon Bay Wales U.K.
150 C1 Caernarfon Castle tourist site Wales U.K.
Caernarvon Gwynedd, Wales U.K. see Caernarfon
150 D3 Caerphilly Caerphilly, Wales U.K.
150 D3 Caerphilly admin. div. Wales U.K.
150 D2 Caersws Powys, Wales U.K.
150 E3 Caerwent Monmouthshire, Wales U.K.
Caesaraugusta Spain see Zaragoza
Caesarea Alg. see Cherchell
128 B3 Caesarea tourist site Israel
Caesarea Cappadociae Turkey see Kayseri
Caesarea Philippi Syria see Bāniyās
Caesarodunum France see Tours
Caesaromagus Essex, England U.K. see Chelmsford
257 F3 Caeté Brazil
252 C2 Caeté r. Brazil
254 E5 Caetité Brazil
190 C3 Cafasse Italy
258 D2 Cafayate Arg.
256 C4 Cafelândia Brazil
Caffa Ukr. see Feodosiya
251 G4 Cafuini r. Brazil
92 B2 Cagayan r. Phil.
92 C4 Cagayan de Oro Phil.
92 B4 Cagayan Islands Phil.
193 H4 Caggiano Italy
191 H5 Cagli Italy
192 B5 Cagliari Sardegna Italy
192 B5 Cagliari prov. Sardegna Italy
192 B5 Cagliari, Golfo di b. Sardegna Italy
163 E5 Cagnac-les-Mines France
193 H3 Cagnano Varano Italy
161 E5 Cagnes-sur-Mer France
250 C5 Caguán r. Col.
247 □1 Caguas Puerto Rico
147 B5 Caha hill Rep. of Ireland
231 C5 Cahaba r. AL U.S.A.
209 C8 Cahama Angola
147 B5 Caha Mountains hills Rep. of Ireland
147 C4 Caher Rep. of Ireland
147 A5 Cahermore Rep. of Ireland
147 A5 Cahersiveen Rep. of Ireland
147 D4 Cahir Rep. of Ireland
Cahirciveen Rep. of Ireland see Cahersiveen
234 D1 Cahoonzie NY U.S.A.
163 D4 Cahors France
250 B6 Cahuapanas Peru
136 E4 Cahul Moldova
163 D5 Cahuzac-sur-Vère France
213 G3 Caia Moz.
184 C2 Caia Port.
184 C1 Caia r. Port.
261 D4 Caia, Barragem do resr Port.
253 F3 Caiabis, Serra dos hills Brazil
256 B1 Caiapó r. Brazil
256 A2 Caiapó, Serra do mts Brazil
256 B2 Caiapônia Brazil
193 G3 Caiazzo Italy
246 C2 Caibarién Cuba
96 D2 Cai Bàu, Đao i. Vietnam
97 D5 Cai Be Vietnam
254 F3 Caicó Brazil
246 E2 Caicos Islands Turks and Caicos Is
246 D2 Caicos Passage Bahamas/Turks and Caicos Is
109 E2 Caidian Hubei China
Caidu Henan China see Shangcai
87 E7 Caiguna W.A. Austr.
108 D2 Caihua Hubei China
252 C3 Cailloma Peru
244 A2 Caimanero, Laguna del lag. Mex.
260 B2 Caimanes Chile
209 B8 Caimbambo Angola
183 I4 Caimodorro mt. Spain
136 E4 Căinar r. Moldova
209 B8 Cainde Angola
197 G3 Căineni Romania
241 L2 Caineville UT U.S.A.
108 B1 Cainnyigoin Sichuan China
182 B1 Caión Spain
161 C4 Cairanne France
262 W1 Caird Coast Antarctica
146 A4 Cairinis Western Isles, Scotland U.K.
146 C5 Cairnbaan Argyll and Bute, Scotland U.K.
146 D5 Cairndow Argyll and Bute, Scotland U.K.
146 E5 Cairneyhill Fife, Scotland U.K.
146 E4 Cairn Gorm mt. Scotland U.K.
146 E4 Cairngorm Mountains Scotland U.K.
146 C7 Cairnryan Dumfries and Galloway, Scotland U.K.
85 F3 Cairns Qld Austr.
146 D6 Cairnsmore of Carsphairn hill Scotland U.K.
146 D7 Cairnsmore of Fleet hill Scotland U.K.
146 E4 Cairn Toul mt. Scotland U.K.
203 F2 Cairo Egypt
231 C5 Cairo GA U.S.A.
237 F4 Cairo IL U.S.A.
193 F3 Cairo, Monte mt. Italy
190 D4 Cairo Montenotte Italy
Caisleán an Bharraigh Rep. of Ireland see Castlebar
161 C5 Caissargues France
146 C6 Caisteal Abhail hill Scotland U.K.
151 I2 Caister-on-Sea Norfolk, England U.K.
149 I4 Caistor Lincolnshire, England U.K.
183 H3 Caithness reg. Scotland U.K.
209 B8 Caitou Angola
209 C8 Caiundo Angola
83 F2 Caiwarro Qld Austr.
109 F3 Caixi Fujian China
Caiyuanzhen Zhejiang China see Shengsi
252 D5 Caiza Bol.
109 F2 Caizi Hu l. China
252 A1 Cajabamba Peru
252 A1 Cajamarca Peru
250 B6 Cajamarca dept Peru
254 D2 Cajapió Brazil
163 D4 Cajarc France
254 D2 Cajari Brazil
252 A2 Cajatambo Peru
254 F3 Cajàzeiras Brazil
196 D4 Ćajetina Srbija Yugo.
92 B3 Cajidiocan Phil.
177 H3 Čajkov Slovakia
188 G4 Čajniče Bos.-Herz.
260 B4 Cajón Chile
245 G5 Cajones r. Mex.
252 D4 Cajuata Bol.
256 D4 Cajuru Brazil
197 G2 Cajvana Romania
106 C4 Caka Qinghai China
177 H3 Čakajovce Slovakia
Caka'lho Xizang China see Yanjing
129 A4 Cakırkaş Turkey
129 C3 Çakmak Turkey
129 C3 Çakmak Dağı mts Turkey
188 F3 Čakovec Croatia
199 F2 Çal Turkey
Çal Turkey see Çukurca
215 F4 Cala S. Africa
184 D3 Cala Spain
184 D3 Cala r. Spain
207 H5 Calabar Nigeria
187 B7 Calabardina Spain
227 I3 Calabogie Ont. Can.
193 I6 Calabria admin. reg. Italy
186 D3 Calaceite Spain
165 F3 Calacuccia Corse France
185 G2 Cala d'Alcaufar Spain
186 □ Cala d'Or Spain
192 A3 Cala d'Oliva Sardegna Italy
187 G5 Cala d'Or Spain
186 □ Cala en Porter Spain
186 E3 Calaf Spain
187 F4 Calafat Romania
259 B8 Calafate Arg.
186 B3 Calafell Spain
187 G5 Cala Figuera Spain
197 H2 Calafindeşti Romania
193 H3 Calaggio r. Italy
192 B4 Cala Gonone Sardegna Italy
92 B3 Calagua Islands Phil.
Calagurris Spain see Calahorra
185 G4 Calahonda Spain
183 I2 Calahorra Spain
209 C9 Calai Angola
156 B2 Calais France
233 □J2 Calais ME U.S.A.
258 D2 Calalasteo, Sierra de mts Arg.
78 □3b Calalin i. Majuro Marshall Is
191 H2 Calalzo di Cadore Italy
252 C5 Calama Chile
190 D4 Calamandrana Italy
250 C2 Calamar Col.
92 A4 Calamian Group is Phil.
187 G5 Cala Millor Spain
186 B4 Calamocha Spain
184 D2 Calamonte Spain
187 G5 Cala Murada Spain
197 F3 Călan Romania
146 B3 Calanais Western Isles, Scotland U.K.
184 D3 Calañas Spain
190 E2 Calancasca r. Switz.
186 C4 Calanda Spain
213 B5 Calandula Angola
94 A1 Calang Sumatera Indon.
192 B4 Calangianus Sardegna Italy
195 E4 Calanna Italy
202 D2 Calanscio Sand Sea des. Libya
92 B3 Calapan Phil.
187 G5 Cala Rajada Spain
185 H3 Calar Alta mt. Spain
136 E4 Călăraşi Moldova
197 H3 Călăraşi Romania
186 □ Cala Santa Galdana Spain
194 D5 Calascibetta Sicilia Italy
195 D4 Calasetta Sardegna Italy
185 I2 Calasparra Spain
194 B5 Calatafimi Sicilia Italy
183 H3 Calatañazor Spain
184 B3 Cala Tarida Spain
183 I3 Calatayud Spain
183 I3 Calatorao Spain
171 E4 Calau Ger.
92 B3 Calauag Phil.
187 E6 Cala Vadella Spain
193 G3 Calavaveula hill Spain
92 B3 Calbayog Phil.
171 C4 Calbe (Saale) Ger.
169 F3 Calberlah Ger.
92 C4 Calbiga Phil.
252 C3 Calca Peru
136 F5 Calcaseu r. LA U.S.A.
192 A2 Calcatoggio Corse France
190 F5 Calci Italy
193 I4 Calciano Italy
190 D3 Calcinato Italy
190 E3 Calcio Italy
251 I4 Calçoene Brazil
117 G5 Calcutta W. Bengal India
197 G3 Căldăraru Romania
193 F1 Caldarola Italy
191 G2 Caldaro sulla Strada del Vino Italy
250 C3 Caldas dept Col.
184 A1 Caldas da Rainha Port.
Caldas de Mombuy Spain see Caldes de Montbui
184 B3 Caldas de Monchique Port.
182 B2 Caldas de Reis Spain
182 B3 Caldas de Vizela Port.
256 C2 Caldas Novas Brazil
149 F3 Caldbeck Cumbria, England U.K.
186 C2 Caldearenas Spain
151 G2 Caldecott Rutland, England U.K.
182 B3 Caldelas Port.
182 B3 Caldelas Taipas Port.
169 E4 Calden Ger.
222 G1 Calder r. N.W.T. Can.
258 C2 Caldera Chile
146 E6 Caldercruix North Lanarkshire, Scotland U.K.
183 I4 Calderesos, Sierra de mts Spain
85 F5 Caldervale Qld Austr.
186 F3 Caldes de Montbui Spain
186 F3 Caldes d'Estrac Spain
149 G3 Caldew r. England U.K.
150 C3 Caldey Island Wales U.K.
150 E3 Caldicot Monmouthshire, Wales U.K.
129 C4 Çaldıran Van Turkey
127 F3 Çaldıran Van Turkey
191 G3 Caldogno Italy
191 G2 Caldonazzo Italy
149 H3 Caldwell North Yorkshire, England U.K.
238 C3 Caldwell ID U.S.A.
237 D4 Caldwell KS U.S.A.
232 C5 Caldwell OH U.S.A.
237 D6 Caldwell TX U.S.A.
227 H4 Caledon Ont. Can.
215 F4 Caledon r. Lesotho/S. Africa
214 B6 Caledon S. Africa
148 C3 Caledon Northern Ireland U.K.
84 D2 Caledon Bay N.T. Austr.
225 H4 Caledonia N.S. Can.
227 H4 Caledonia Ont. Can.
Caledonia admin. div. U.K. see Scotland
226 E4 Caledonia MI U.S.A.
226 B4 Caledonia MN U.S.A.
232 E3 Caledonia NY U.S.A.
186 F3 Calella Spain
85 G4 Calen Qld Austr.
182 B3 Calendário Port.
192 A2 Calenzana Corse France
191 G5 Calenzano Italy
231 C5 Calera AL U.S.A.
184 D2 Calera de León Spain
183 E5 Calera y Chozas Spain
183 G3 Caleruega Spain
260 B4 Caletones Chile
260 E4 Caleufú Arg.
241 I5 Calexico CA U.S.A.
148 E3 Calf of Man i. Isle of Man
146 F2 Calfsound Orkney, Scotland U.K.
222 H5 Calgary Alta Can.
146 B5 Calgary Argyll and Bute, Scotland U.K.
216 □1c Calheta São Jorge Azores
184 □ Calheta Madeira
216 □1c Calheta de Nesquim Pico Azores
231 C5 Calhoun GA U.S.A.
230 C4 Calhoun KY U.S.A.
250 B4 Cali Col.
199 F1 Çalı Turkey
114 B4 Calicut Kerala India
241 J3 Caliente NV U.S.A.
236 E4 California MO U.S.A.
240 F1 California state U.S.A.
242 B2 California, Golfo de g. Mex.
186 D4 Cálig Spain
163 C4 Calignac France
129 F4 Cälilabad Azer.
258 D1 Calilegua Arg.
197 G3 Călimăneşti Romania
197 G2 Călimani, Munţii mts Romania
195 H2 Calimera Italy
260 C2 Calingasta Arg.
Caliniscu Moldova see Cupcina
241 J5 Calipatria CA U.S.A.
240 F2 Calistoga CA U.S.A.
193 H4 Calitri Italy
214 C5 Calitzdorp S. Africa
190 D4 Calizzano Italy
199 G3 Çalkaya Turkey
243 H4 Calkini Mex.
199 G2 Çalköy Turkey
82 E2 Callabonna, Lake salt flat S.A. Austr.
158 C3 Callac France
232 C6 Callaghan VA U.S.A.
240 I2 Callaghan, Mount NV U.S.A.
231 D6 Callahan FL U.S.A.
147 D4 Callan Rep. of Ireland
147 B3 Callan r. Northern Ireland U.K.
224 E4 Callander Ont. Can.
146 D5 Callander Stirling, Scotland U.K.
232 D6 Callands VA U.S.A.
92 B2 Callang Phil.
Callanish Western Isles, Scotland U.K. see Calanais
164 D2 Callantsoog Neth.
252 A3 Callao Peru
241 K2 Callao UT U.S.A.
161 E5 Callas France
184 E5 Callen France
156 E2 Callezuela Spain
161 E5 Callian France
190 D3 Calliano Italy
233 F4 Callicoon NY U.S.A.
85 G5 Callide Qld Austr.
222 H4 Calling Lake Alta Can.
150 C4 Callington Cornwall, England U.K.
85 G5 Calliope Qld Austr.
Callipolis Turkey see Gelibolu
187 C6 Callosa d'En Sarrià Spain
187 C6 Callosa de Segura Spain
227 G2 Callum Ont. Can.
85 E3 Callyharra Springs W.A. Austr.
222 H4 Calmar Alta Can.
226 B4 Calmar IA U.S.A.
197 G4 Călmăţui r. Romania
163 D5 Calmont Midi-Pyrénées France
163 D4 Calmont Midi-Pyrénées France
245 E3 Calnali Mex.
150 E3 Calne Wiltshire, England U.K.
197 G3 Călniştea r. Romania
190 E3 Calolziocorte Italy
183 I4 Calomarde Spain
186 G3 Calonge Spain
163 C4 Calonges France
156 C2 Calonne-Ricouart France
231 D7 Caloosahatchee r. FL U.S.A.
193 G3 Calore Italy
193 G3 Calore r. Italy
193 H4 Calore r. Italy
243 H4 Calotmul Mex.
85 H5 Caloundra Qld Austr.
177 G4 Čalovec Slovakia
Čalovo Slovakia see Veľký Meder
187 D6 Calpe Spain
245 E4 Calpulálpan Mex.
224 C3 Calstock Ont. Can.
194 C5 Caltabellotta Sicilia Italy
194 D5 Caltagirone Sicilia Italy
194 D5 Caltagirone r. Sicilia Italy
194 D5 Caltanissetta Sicilia Italy
194 D5 Caltanissetta prov. Sicilia Italy
194 C5 Caltavuturo Sicilia Italy
128 A1 Çaltıbozkır Turkey
129 C2 Çaltılıgaga Turkey
183 H3 Caltojar Spain
147 C3 Caltraghlea Rep. of Ireland
160 C3 Caluire-et-Cuire France
209 B7 Calulo Angola
226 C2 Calumet MI U.S.A.
226 A2 Calumet MN U.S.A.
209 D8 Calunda Angola
209 B8 Caluquembe Angola
190 C3 Caluso Italy
210 F2 Caluula Somalia
159 F2 Calvados dept Basse-Normandie France
182 B4 Calvão Port.
182 B3 Calvario Spain
182 E4 Calvarrasa de Abajo Spain
182 E4 Calvarrasa de Arriba Spain
193 H4 Calvello Italy
149 H4 Calver Derbyshire, England U.K.
147 E3 Calverstown Rep. of Ireland
84 D3 Calvert r. N.T. Austr.
84 D3 Calvert Hills N.T. Austr.
235 F2 Calverton NY U.S.A.
87 D4 Calvert Range hills W.A. Austr.
192 A2 Calvi Corse France
192 C1 Calvi, Monte hill Italy
187 F5 Calvià Spain
193 E2 Calvi dell'Umbria Italy
163 D4 Calvignac France
244 C3 Calvillo Mex.
146 E5 Calvine Perth and Kinross, Scotland U.K.
163 E4 Calvinet France
214 B4 Calvinia S. Africa
193 G3 Calvi Risorta Italy
161 C5 Calvisson France
182 E4 Calvitero mt. Spain
194 D6 Calvo, Monte hill Sicilia Italy
193 H3 Calvo, Monte mt. Italy
171 C3 Calvörde Ger.
182 C3 Calvos Spain
172 D3 Calw Ger.
185 G2 Calzada de Calatrava Spain
182 E3 Calzada de Valdunciel Spain
182 D4 Calzadilla Spain
151 H2 Cam r. England U.K.
209 B7 Camabatela Angola
254 F5 Camaçari Brazil
184 □ Camacha Madeira
224 E4 Camachigama r. Que. Can.
244 C1 Camacho Mex.
209 B8 Camacuio Angola
209 C8 Camacupa Angola
250 E2 Camaguán Venez.
246 C2 Camagüey Cuba
246 C2 Camagüey, Archipiélago de is Cuba
94 C1 Camah, Gunung mt. Malaysia
190 F5 Camaiore Italy
251 G6 Camaiú r. Brazil
246 C2 Camajuaní Cuba
Çamalan Turkey see Gülek
191 G5 Camaldoli Italy
183 F1 Camaleño Spain
254 F5 Camamu Brazil
252 B4 Camana Peru
252 B4 Camaná r. Peru
186 B4 Camañas Spain
209 D7 Camanongue Angola
255 B6 Camapuã Brazil
255 C9 Camaquã Brazil
255 C9 Camaquã r. Brazil
197 F2 Camăr Romania
184 □ Câmara de Lobos Madeira
253 F3 Camararé r. Brazil
186 D3 Camarasa Spain
183 F4 Camarena Spain
187 B4 Camarena r. Spain
187 B4 Camarena de la Sierra Spain
161 A5 Camarès France
161 C4 Camaret-sur-Aigues France
158 B3 Camaret-sur-Mer France
243 F3 Camargo Mex.
161 C5 Camargue reg. France
240 H4 Camarillo CA U.S.A.
182 A1 Camariñas Spain
186 D4 Camarles Spain
259 D7 Camarones, Bahía b. Arg.
147 E4 Camaross Rep. of Ireland
182 D2 Camarzana de Tera Spain
184 D3 Camas Spain
238 B2 Camas WA U.S.A.
238 D3 Camas r. ID U.S.A.
238 D3 Camas Creek r. ID U.S.A.
146 C5 Camasnacroise Highland, Scotland U.K.
194 C5 Camastra Sicilia Italy
97 D5 Ca Mau Vietnam
209 C7 Camaxilo Angola
182 B2 Cambados Spain
256 B5 Cambará Brazil
Cambay Gujarat India see Khambhat
Cambay, Gulf of India see Khambhat, Gulf of
256 B5 Cambé Brazil
151 G3 Camberley Surrey, England U.K.
163 B4 Cambes France
97 D4 Cambodia country Asia
163 A5 Cambo-les-Bains France
163 E5 Cambon France
255 C8 Camboriú Brazil
150 B4 Camborne Cornwall, England U.K.
234 B1 Cambra PA U.S.A.
82 D3 Cambrai S.A. Austr.
156 D2 Cambrai France
182 B1 Cambre Spain
159 G2 Cambremer France
182 C5 Cambres Port.
214 E5 Cambria S. Africa
Cambria admin. div. U.K. see Wales
240 G4 Cambria CA U.S.A.
150 D2 Cambrian Mountains hills Wales U.K.
224 D5 Cambridge Ont. Can.
246 □ Cambridge Jamaica
80 E2 Cambridge North I. N.Z.
151 H2 Cambridge Cambridgeshire, England U.K.
236 F3 Cambridge IL U.S.A.
233 H3 Cambridge MA U.S.A.
233 E5 Cambridge MD U.S.A.
226 A3 Cambridge MN U.S.A.
233 G3 Cambridge NY U.S.A.
232 C4 Cambridge OH U.S.A.
234 C2 Cambridge PA U.S.A.
233 G2 Cambridge VT U.S.A.
226 C4 Cambridge WI U.S.A.
221 H3 Cambridge Bay Nunavut Can.
86 F2 Cambridge Gulf W.A. Austr.
151 H2 Cambridgeshire admin. div. England U.K.
232 C4 Cambridge Springs PA U.S.A.
186 E3 Cambrils de Mar Spain
156 C2 Cambrin France
156 B2 Cambron France
170 C2 Cambs Ger.
256 D5 Cambuí Brazil
209 D6 Cambulo Angola
209 C7 Cambundi-Catembo Angola
257 E4 Cambuquira Brazil
171 C4 Camburg Ger.
250 A3 Cambutal, Cerro mt. Panama
83 G3 Camden N.S.W. Austr.
231 C5 Camden AL U.S.A.
237 E5 Camden AR U.S.A.
234 C3 Camden DE U.S.A.
233 □I2 Camden ME U.S.A.
231 E4 Camden NC U.S.A.
234 C3 Camden NJ U.S.A.
233 F3 Camden NY U.S.A.
232 A5 Camden OH U.S.A.
231 D5 Camden SC U.S.A.
237 F4 Camden TN U.S.A.
234 C3 Camden County county NJ U.S.A.
86 E2 Camden Sound sea chan. W.A. Austr.
236 E4 Camdenton MO U.S.A.
209 D7 Cameia Angola
150 C4 Camelford Cornwall, England U.K.
199 F3 Çameli Turkey
136 E3 Cameneca Moldova
191 I5 Camerano Italy
193 F1 Camerino Italy
Camerinum Italy see Camerino
241 L4 Cameron AZ U.S.A.
237 E6 Cameron LA U.S.A.
236 E4 Cameron MO U.S.A.
237 D6 Cameron TX U.S.A.
226 B3 Cameron WI U.S.A.
232 C5 Cameron WV U.S.A.
94 C1 Cameron Highlands Malaysia
94 C1 Cameron Highlands mts Malaysia
222 G3 Cameron Hills Y.T. Can.
81 A7 Cameron Mountains South I. N.Z.
240 G2 Cameron Park CA U.S.A.
207 I5 Cameroon country Africa
193 H4 Camerota Italy
Cameroun country Africa see Cameroon
207 H5 Cameroun, Mont vol. Cameroon
149 F3 Camerton Cumbria, England U.K.
251 I5 Cametá Brazil
84 B3 Camfield r. N.T. Austr.
199 E3 Çamiçi Muğla Turkey
193 F2 Camicia, Monte mt. Italy
92 B2 Camiguin i. Phil.
128 B1 Camili Turkey
92 B3 Camiling Phil.
231 C6 Camilla GA U.S.A.
168 F2 Camin Ger.
252 C4 Camiña Chile
182 B3 Caminha Port.
182 D4 Caminomorisco Spain
186 B4 Caminreal Spain
252 E5 Camiri Bol.
252 B2 Camisea r. Peru

209 D7 Camissombo Angola
128 D1 Çamlıdere Turkey
129 B3 Çamlıhemşin Turkey
129 B3 Çamlıkaya Turkey
87 C7 Camm, Lake salt flat W.A. Austr.
194 C5 Cammarata Sicilia Italy
194 C5 Cammarata, Monte mt. Sicilia Italy
171 D3 Cammer Ger.
170 D2 Cammin Ger.
Cammin Pol. see Kamień Pomorski
254 E2 Camocim Brazil
147 E4 Camolin Rep. of Ireland
156 C3 Camon France
190 F3 Camonica, Val val. Italy
84 D3 Camooweal Qld Austr.
185 F4 Camorro Alto mt. Spain
158 D4 Camors France
92 C4 Camotes Sea g. Phil.
244 B4 Camotlán de Miraflores Mex.
147 D2 Camowen r. Northern Ireland U.K.
147 B4 Camp Rep. of Ireland
193 H4 Campagna Italy
161 B4 Campagnac France
192 D2 Campagnatico Italy
163 B5 Campagne Aquitaine France
163 C4 Campagne Aquitaine France
156 B2 Campagne-lès-Hesdin France
261 H4 Campana Arg.
195 F3 Campana Italy
259 B8 Campana, Isla i. Chile
260 B4 Campanario mt. Arg./Chile
257 G3 Campanário Brazil
184 □ Campanario Madeira
184 E2 Campanario Spain
257 E4 Campanha Brazil
193 G3 Campania admin. reg. Italy
184 D4 Campano Spain
85 F4 Campaspe r. Qld Austr.
183 F3 Campaspero Spain
214 D3 Campbell S. Africa
240 G3 Campbell CA U.S.A.
232 C4 Campbell OH U.S.A.
84 B4 Campbell, Mount hill N.T. Austr.
224 E4 Campbellford Ont. Can.
232 B4 Campbell Hill hill OH U.S.A.
77 G6 Campbell Island N.Z.
266 G9 Campbell Plateau sea feature S. Pacific Ocean
86 E2 Campbell Range hills W.A. Austr.
222 E5 Campbell River B.C. Can.
227 I3 Campbells Bay Que. Can.
226 C4 Campbellsport WI U.S.A.
232 A5 Campbellstown OH U.S.A.
230 C4 Campbellsville KY U.S.A.
225 H4 Campbellton N.B. Can.
83 G3 Campbelltown N.S.W. Austr.
83 F5 Campbell Town Tas. Austr.
234 B2 Campbelltown PA U.S.A.
146 C6 Campbeltown Argyll and Bute, Scotland U.K.
158 E4 Campbon France
232 C6 Camp Creek WV U.S.A.
186 F2 Campdevànol Spain
182 C3 Campeã Port.
243 H5 Campeche Mex.
243 H5 Campeche state Mex.
245 H4 Campeche, Bahía de g. Mex.
246 C2 Campechuela Cuba
187 C6 Campello Spain
193 E2 Campello sul Clitunne Italy
182 B5 Campelo Port.
184 A1 Campelos Port.
158 D4 Campénéac France
197 F2 Câmpeni Romania
83 E4 Camperdown Vic. Austr.
215 H3 Camperdown S. Africa
190 D3 Campertogno Italy
256 D4 Campestre Brazil
161 B5 Campestre-et-Luc France
234 B2 Camp Hill PA U.S.A.
226 B3 Campia WI U.S.A.
197 F2 Câmpia Turzii Romania
191 G5 Campi Bisenzio Italy
192 A5 Campidano reg. Sardegna Italy
192 C1 Campiglia Marittima Italy
190 C3 Campiglia Soana Italy
147 E4 Campile Rep. of Ireland
184 B3 Campilhas r. Port.
183 I5 Campillo de Alto Buey Spain
185 G3 Campillo de Arenas Spain
183 I4 Campillo de Dueñas Spain
184 E2 Campillo de Llerena Spain
185 F3 Campillos Spain
183 I5 Campillos-Paravientos Spain
197 G3 Câmpina Romania
256 A6 Campina da Lagoa Brazil
254 G3 Campina Grande Brazil
256 C6 Campina Grande do Sul Brazil
256 D5 Campinas Brazil
256 C3 Campina Verde Brazil
184 C2 Campinho Port.
183 G3 Campisábalos Spain
195 H2 Campi Salentina Italy
192 B2 Campitello Corse France
193 F2 Campli Italy
207 H6 Campo Cameroon
Campo r. Cameroon see Ntem
213 H3 Campo Moz.
182 B3 Campo Port.
186 D2 Campo Spain
250 C4 Campoalegre Col.
254 E4 Campo Alegre de Lourdes Brazil
193 G3 Campobasso Italy
193 G3 Campobasso prov. Molise Italy
194 C5 Campobello di Licata Sicilia Italy
194 B5 Campobello di Mazara Sicilia Italy
257 E4 Campo Belo Brazil
255 C8 Campo Belo do Sul Brazil
182 B1 Campo da Feira Spain
191 G3 Campodarsego Italy
183 E1 Campo de Caso Spain
185 G1 Campo de Criptana Spain
192 A3 Campo dell'Oro airport Corse France
183 G3 Campo de San Pedro Spain
193 F3 Campodimele Italy
191 G2 Campo di Trens Italy
190 E2 Campodolcino Italy
255 B8 Campo Erê Brazil
194 C5 Campofelice di Roccella Sicilia Italy
256 C3 Campo Florido Brazil
191 I2 Campoformido Italy
254 E4 Campo Formoso Brazil
194 C5 Campofranco Sicilia Italy
184 D3 Campofrío Spain
258 E2 Campo Gallo Arg.
255 B7 Campo Grande Brazil
182 B2 Campo Lameiro Spain
256 C6 Campo Largo Brazil
193 F3 Campoli Appennino Italy
190 D4 Campo Ligure Italy
191 H3 Campolongo Maggiore Italy
184 E1 Campo Lugar Spain
254 E3 Campo Maior Brazil
184 C1 Campo Maior Port.
193 H3 Campomarino Molise Italy
195 G2 Campomarino Puglia Italy
190 D4 Campomorone Italy
256 A6 Campo Mourão Brazil
182 D2 Camponaraya Spain
255 B8 Campo Novo Brazil
193 I5 Campora San Giovanni Italy
183 G4 Campo Real Spain
194 C5 Camporeale Sicilia Italy
184 B3 Campo Redondo Port.
190 F4 Camporgiano Italy
190 C5 Camporosso Italy
187 B5 Camporrobles Spain
257 G4 Campos Brazil
182 C3 Campos Port.
256 D3 Campos Altos Brazil
191 G4 Camposanto Italy
254 D5 Campos Belos Brazil
187 G5 Campos del Puerto Spain
187 B6 Campos del Río Spain
257 E5 Campos do Jordão Brazil
257 E4 Campos Gerais Brazil
256 C5 Campos Novos Paulista Brazil
254 E3 Campos Sales Brazil
185 G3 Campotéjar Spain
190 D2 Campo Tencia mt. Switz.
193 F2 Campotosto Italy
193 F2 Campotosto, Lago di l. Italy
191 G2 Campo Tures Italy
236 F3 Camp Point IL U.S.A.
186 F2 Camprodon Spain
148 E1 Campsie Fells hills Scotland U.K.
161 E5 Camps-la-Source France
234 B4 Camp Springs MD U.S.A.
232 B6 Campton KY U.S.A.
146 F6 Camptown Scottish Borders, Scotland U.K.
234 B1 Camptown PA U.S.A.
197 G3 Câmpulung Romania
197 F2 Câmpulung la Tisa Romania
197 G2 Câmpulung Moldovenesc Romania
250 C5 Campuya r. Peru
241 L4 Camp Verde AZ U.S.A.
97 E5 Cam Ranh Vietnam
222 H4 Camrose Alta Can.
150 B3 Camrose Pembrokeshire, Wales U.K.
223 I3 Camsell Portage Sask. Can.
222 F2 Camsell Range mts N.W.T. Can.
191 G4 Camugnano Italy
Camulodunum Essex, England U.K. see Colchester
185 G1 Camuñas Spain
129 C3 Çamurlu Dağ mt. Turkey
128 C1 Çamuzkışlası Turkey
129 C3 Çamyazı Turkey
199 E1 Çan Turkey
177 K3 Čaňa Slovakia
257 F4 Canaã Brazil
225 H4 Canaan r. N.S. Can.
233 G3 Canaan CT U.S.A.
241 L3 Canaan Peak UT U.S.A.
254 B3 Cana Brava r. Brazil
257 H2 Cana Brava, Serra da hills Brazil
114 B3 Canacona Goa India
220 J5 Canada country N. America
187 C6 Cañada Spain
268 O1 Canada Basin sea feature Arctic Ocean
186 C4 Cañada de Benatanduz Spain
261 G3 Cañada de Gómez Arg.
185 I1 Cañada del Carrascal r. Spain
183 I5 Cañada del Hoyo Spain
185 E3 Cañada Rosal Spain
261 G3 Cañada Rosquin Arg.
234 C1 Canadensis PA U.S.A.
237 C5 Canadian TX U.S.A.
237 E5 Canadian r. U.S.A.
259 C7 Cañadon Grande, Sierra mts Arg.
233 F3 Canajoharie NY U.S.A.
199 E1 Çanakkale Turkey
199 E1 Çanakkale prov. Turkey
78 □5 Canala New Caledonia
192 B2 Canale-di-Verde Corse France
183 H4 Canalejas del Arroyo Spain
183 F3 Canalejas de Peñafiel Spain
222 H5 Canal Flats B.C. Can.
182 D4 Canalizo hill Spain
261 F3 Canals Arg.
163 D5 Canals France
187 C6 Canals Spain
191 G2 Canàl San Bovo Italy
232 B5 Canal Winchester OH U.S.A.
183 H4 Cañamares Spain
185 G2 Cañamares r. Spain
183 H4 Cañamares r. Spain
185 E1 Cañamero Spain
232 E3 Canandaigua NY U.S.A.
242 C2 Cananea Mex.
256 D6 Cananéia Brazil
250 D4 Canapiare, Cerro hill Col.
156 C2 Canaples France
256 C3 Canápolis Brazil
250 B5 Cañar Ecuador
250 B5 Cañar prov. Ecuador
254 B5 Canarana Brazil
192 B2 Canari Corse France
216 □3 Canarias, Islas is N. Atlantic Ocean
Canarias, Islas terr. N. Atlantic Ocean see Canary Islands
191 G4 Canaro Italy
216 □3 Canary Islands terr. N. Atlantic Ocean
182 C4 Canas de Senhorim Port.
232 E3 Canaseraga NY U.S.A.
233 F3 Canastota NY U.S.A.
256 D3 Canastra, Serra da mts Brazil
244 B1 Canatlán Mex.
182 D5 Cañaveral Spain
231 D6 Canaveral, Cape FL U.S.A.
184 D2 Cañaveral de León Spain
183 H4 Cañaveras Spain
183 H4 Cañaveruelas Spain
257 H1 Canavieiras Brazil
242 □J7 Cañazas Panama
191 G2 Canazei Italy
83 F2 Canbelego N.S.W. Austr.
83 G3 Canberra A.C.T. Austr.
238 B3 Canby CA U.S.A.
236 D2 Canby MN U.S.A.
158 E3 Cancale France
185 I2 Cancarix Spain
161 C3 Cance r. France
193 H4 Cancellara Italy
193 G3 Cancello ed Arnone Italy
156 B2 Canche r. France
250 C6 Canchyuaya, Cerros de hills Peru
186 C2 Cancias mt. Spain
163 C4 Cancon France
243 I4 Cancún Mex.
163 B6 Candanchú Spain
Çandar Turkey see Kastamonu
252 C4 Candarave Peru
199 E2 Çandarlı Turkey
182 E1 Candás Spain
186 D3 Candasnos Spain
159 E4 Candé France
257 E4 Candeias Brazil
252 E2 Candeias r. Brazil
193 H3 Candela Italy
237 C7 Candela r. Mex.
258 G2 Candelaria Misiones Arg.
260 E3 Candelaria San Luis Arg.
216 □1c Candelária Pico Azores
216 □1b Candelária São Miguel Azores
216 □3a Candelaria Tenerife Canary Is
243 H5 Candelaria Mex.
182 E4 Candelario Spain
182 E4 Candelario, Sierra de mts Spain
193 H3 Candelaro r. Italy
183 E4 Candeleda Spain
83 G4 Candelo N.S.W. Austr.
190 D3 Candelo Italy
182 B3 Candemil Port.
Candia Kriti Greece see Irakleio
190 D3 Candia Lomellina Italy
256 B6 Cândido de Abreu Brazil
254 D2 Cândido Mendes Brazil
256 B5 Cândido Mota Brazil
191 H5 Candigliano r. Italy
182 D2 Candín Spain
126 D2 Çandır Turkey
223 J4 Candle Lake Sask. Can.
235 E1 Candlewood Isle CT U.S.A.
235 E1 Candlewood Knolls CT U.S.A.
236 D1 Cando ND U.S.A.
92 B2 Candon Phil.
215 H2 Candover S. Africa
197 F3 Cândrelu, Vârful mt. Romania
86 B4 Cane r. W.A. Austr.
194 D5 Cane, Monte hill Sicilia Italy
Canea Kriti Greece see Chania
184 A2 Caneças Port.
182 B3 Canedo Port.
186 D2 Canejan Spain
163 B4 Canéjean France
260 B2 Canela Baja Chile
190 D4 Canelli Italy
261 I4 Canelones Uru.
261 J4 Canelones dept Uru.
192 E2 Canepina Italy
182 D1 Canero Spain
161 A5 Canet Languedoc-Roussillon France
161 B5 Canet Languedoc-Roussillon France
163 F6 Canet, Étang de lag. France
186 F3 Canet de Mar Spain
258 B5 Cañete Chile
183 I4 Cañete Spain
185 F3 Cañete de las Torres Spain
185 E4 Cañete la Real Spain
163 F6 Canet-en-Roussillon France
186 D4 Canet lo Roig Spain
163 F6 Canet-Plage France
237 E4 Caney KS U.S.A.
237 E4 Caney r. KS U.S.A.
186 C2 Canfranc-Estación Spain
252 B3 Cangallo Peru
209 C8 Cangamba Angola
209 C7 Cangandala Angola
182 B2 Cangas Spain
182 D1 Cangas del Narcea Spain
183 E1 Cangas de Onís Spain
209 B7 Cangola Angola
209 D8 Cangombe Angola
107 H5 Cangshan Shandong China
254 G3 Canguaretama Brazil
258 G3 Canguçu Brazil
258 G3 Canguçu, Serra do hills Brazil
107 H4 Cangzhou Hebei China
184 B2 Canha Port.
184 B2 Canha r. Port.
184 □ Canhas Madeira
184 B2 Canhestros Port.
163 D4 Caniac-du-Causse France
225 G2 Caniapiscau Que. Can.
225 G1 Caniapiscau r. Que. Can.
225 G2 Caniapiscau, Lac l. Que. Can.
Caniçado Moz. see Guija
184 □ Caniçal Madeira
194 C5 Canicattì Sicilia Italy
195 E5 Canicattini Bagni Sicilia Italy
184 □ Caniço Madeira
183 G3 Canicosa de la Sierra Spain
163 E6 Canigou, Pic du mt. France
185 H3 Caniles Spain
185 F4 Canillas de Aceituno Spain
186 E2 Canillo Andorra
222 F5 Canim Lake B.C. Can.
254 F3 Canindé Brazil
192 D2 Canino Italy
146 C3 Canisp hill Scotland U.K.
232 E3 Canisteo NY U.S.A.
232 E3 Canisteo r. NY U.S.A.
262 R2 Canisteo Peninsula Antarctica
158 E2 Canisy France
244 C2 Cañitas de Felipe Pescador Mex.
183 E3 Cañizal Spain
183 H4 Cañizares Spain
183 E3 Cañizo Spain
185 H3 Canjáyar Spain
239 F4 Canjilon NM U.S.A.
126 D2 Çankırı Turkey
211 A5 Cankuzo Burundi
92 B4 Canlaon Phil.
87 B6 Canna W.A. Austr.
195 F2 Canna r. Italy
146 B4 Canna i. Scotland U.K.
146 B4 Canna, Sound of sea chan. Scotland U.K.
114 B4 Cannanore Kerala India
114 B4 Cannanore Islands Lakshadweep India
193 E2 Cannara Italy
160 B2 Canne r. France
194 C5 Canne r. Sicilia Italy
190 D2 Cannero Riviera Italy
161 F5 Cannes France
194 D4 Canneto Isole Lipari Italy
192 C1 Canneto Toscana Italy
190 F3 Canneto sull'Oglio Italy
146 D4 Cannich Highland, Scotland U.K.
87 C6 Canning Hill hill W.A. Austr.
147 D3 Canningstown Rep. of Ireland
150 D3 Cannington Somerset, England U.K.
190 D2 Cannobio Italy
150 E2 Cannock Staffordshire, England U.K.
150 E2 Cannock Chase reg. England U.K.
226 A3 Cannon r. MN U.S.A.
236 C2 Cannonball r. ND U.S.A.
238 B2 Cannon Beach OR U.S.A.
235 E1 Cannondale CT U.S.A.
215 F5 Cannon Rocks S. Africa
232 B5 Cannonsburg KY U.S.A.
85 G4 Cannonvale Qld Austr.
83 G4 Cann River Vic. Austr.
184 C2 Cano Port.
250 A5 Canoa Ecuador
255 C9 Canoas Brazil
257 E3 Canoeiros Brazil
223 I4 Canoe Lake Sask. Can.
163 E6 Canohès France
255 C8 Canoinhas Brazil
195 F4 Canolo Italy
146 F6 Canonbie Dumfries and Galloway, Scotland U.K.
239 F4 Canon City CO U.S.A.
231 D6 Canoochia r. GA U.S.A.
85 G4 Canoona Qld Austr.
82 E3 Canopus S.A. Austr.
223 K5 Canora Sask. Can.
193 I3 Canosa di Puglia Italy
247 □3 Canouan i. St Vincent
83 G3 Canowindra N.S.W. Austr.
187 F5 Can Pastilla Spain
187 G5 Can Picafort Spain
183 H4 Canredondo Spain
193 G3 Cansano Italy
225 I4 Canso N.S. Can.
252 A2 Canta Peru
183 F1 Cantabria aut. comm. Spain
Cantabrian Mountains Spain see Cantábrica, Cordillera
Cantabrian Sea Spain see Cantábrico, Mar
182 F1 Cantábrica, Cordillera mts Spain
182 D1 Cantábrico, Mar sea Spain
191 G4 Cantagallo Italy
161 A3 Cantal dept Auvergne France
183 E3 Cantalapiedra Spain
183 G3 Cantalejo Spain
193 E2 Cantalice Italy
183 G3 Cantalojas Spain
183 E3 Cantalpino Spain
182 B4 Cantanhede Port.
186 C4 Cantavieja Spain
177 I6 Čantavir Vojvodina, Srbija Yugo.
156 B3 Canteleu France
163 A4 Canteloupe r. France
162 B3 Cantenac France
187 B7 Canteras Spain
185 H1 Canteras hill Spain
225 H4 Canterbury N.B. Can.
81 D5 Canterbury admin. reg. South I. N.Z.
151 I3 Canterbury Kent, England U.K.
81 C6 Canterbury Bight b. South I. N.Z.
81 C5 Canterbury Plains South I. N.Z.
97 D5 Cân Thơ Vietnam
191 H5 Cantiano Italy
240 I4 Cantil CA U.S.A.
92 C4 Cantilan Phil.
184 E3 Cantillana Spain
183 F3 Cantimpalos Spain
254 E4 Canto do Buriti Brazil
190 C3 Cantoira Italy
Canton Guangdong China see Guangzhou
150 D3 Canton Cardiff, Wales U.K.
231 C5 Canton GA U.S.A.
226 B5 Canton IL U.S.A.
236 F3 Canton MO U.S.A.
237 F5 Canton MS U.S.A.
234 C3 Canton NJ U.S.A.
233 F2 Canton NY U.S.A.
232 C4 Canton OH U.S.A.
227 I5 Canton PA U.S.A.
236 D3 Canton SD U.S.A.
237 E5 Canton TX U.S.A.
226 B3 Canton WI U.S.A.
Canton Island Phoenix Is Kiribati see Kanton
185 H3 Cantoria Spain
185 F1 Cantos Negros hill Spain
256 A6 Cantu r. Brazil
190 E3 Cantù Italy
256 B6 Cantu, Serra do hills Brazil
Cantuaria Kent, England U.K. see Canterbury
254 F4 Canudos Brazil
261 H4 Cañuelas Arg.
Canusium Italy see Canosa di Puglia
251 E6 Canutama Brazil
81 D4 Canvastown South I. N.Z.
151 H3 Canvey Island Essex, England U.K.
223 J4 Canwood Sask. Can.
213 G3 Canxixe Moz.
159 G2 Cany-Barville France
187 C5 Cànyoles r. Spain
222 B2 Canyon Y.T. Can.
237 C5 Canyon TX U.S.A.
238 C2 Canyon City OR U.S.A.
240 G2 Canyon Creek r. CA U.S.A.
240 G1 Canyondam CA U.S.A.
238 E2 Canyon Ferry Lake MT U.S.A.
222 E2 Canyon Ranges mts N.W.T. Can.
238 B3 Canyonville OR U.S.A.
209 D6 Canzar Angola
101 C4 Cao r. China
96 D2 Cao Băng Vietnam
Caocheng Shandong China see Caoxian
Caohe Hubei China see Qichun
110 D3 Caohu Xinjiang China
Caojiahe Hubei China see Qichun
108 A3 Caojian Yunnan China
146 B5 Caolas Argyll and Bute, Scotland U.K.
Caolas Scalpaigh Western Isles, Scotland U.K. see Kyles Scalpay
146 C6 Caolisport, Loch inlet Scotland U.K.
209 C7 Caombo Angola
97 E4 Cao Nguyên Đắc Lắc plat. Vietnam
191 G2 Caorame r. Italy
191 H3 Caorle Italy
107 G5 Caoxian Shandong China
Caozhou Shandong China see Heze
227 F4 Capac MI U.S.A.
193 H4 Capaccio Italy
194 C4 Capaci Sicilia Italy
209 D7 Capaia Angola
Çapakçur Turkey see Bingöl
192 D2 Capalbio Italy
177 L5 Căpâlna Romania
250 E3 Capanaparo r. Venez.
254 D2 Capanema Brazil
192 C2 Capanne, Monte mt. Italy
191 F5 Capannoli Italy
191 F5 Capannori Italy
256 C6 Capão Bonito Brazil
257 G4 Caparaó, Serra do mts Brazil
184 A2 Caparica Port.
250 D3 Caparo r. Venez.
182 B4 Caparrosa Port.
183 I2 Caparroso Spain
92 B3 Capas Phil.
197 F3 Căpăţânii, Munţii mts Romania
225 I4 Cap-aux-Meules Que. Can.
187 C5 Cap-Blanc Spain
163 A5 Capbreton France
225 H3 Cap-Chat Que. Can.
161 B5 Cap d'Agde France
186 □ Cap d'Artrutx Spain
225 F4 Cap-de-la-Madeleine Que. Can.
163 E4 Capdenac France
163 E4 Capdenac-Gare France
186 □ Cap d'En Font Spain
187 G5 Capdepera Spain
85 F4 Cape r. Qld Austr.
Cape Bald N.B. Can. see Cap-Pelé
83 G5 Cape Barren Island Tas. Austr.
264 J8 Cape Basin sea feature S. Atlantic Ocean
82 D3 Cape Borda S.A. Austr.
225 I4 Cape Breton Island N.S. Can.
225 K2 Cape Charles Nfld. Can.
233 E6 Cape Charles VA U.S.A.
206 E5 Cape Coast Ghana
Cape Coast Castle Ghana see Cape Coast
233 H4 Cape Cod Bay MA U.S.A.
231 D7 Cape Coral FL U.S.A.
84 C3 Cape Crawford N.T. Austr.
227 G3 Cape Croker Ont. Can.
221 K3 Cape Dorset Nunavut Can.
233 □H3 Cape Elizabeth ME U.S.A.
222 C3 Cape Fanshaw AK U.S.A.
231 E5 Cape Fear r. NC U.S.A.
225 I4 Cape George N.S. Can.
237 F4 Cape Girardeau MO U.S.A.
Cape Juby Morocco see Tarfaya
87 B7 Capel W.A. Austr.
151 H3 Capel Kent, England U.K.
151 G3 Capel Surrey, England U.K.
216 □1b Capelas São Miguel Azores
150 D1 Capel Curig Conwy, Wales U.K.
257 F2 Capelinha Brazil
85 G4 Capella Qld Austr.
164 D3 Capelle aan de IJssel Neth.
151 I3 Capel le Ferne Kent, England U.K.
165 F5 Capellen Lux.
216 □1c Capelo Faial Azores
209 B8 Capelongo Huíla Angola
Capelongo Huíla Angola see Kuvango
151 I2 Capel St Mary Suffolk, England U.K.
234 D4 Cape May NJ U.S.A.
234 D3 Cape May County county NJ U.S.A.
234 D3 Cape May Court House NJ U.S.A.
234 D4 Cape May Point NJ U.S.A.
209 C7 Capenda-Camulemba Angola
163 E5 Capendu France
225 H5 Cape Sable Island N.S. Can.
225 J3 Cape St George Nfld. Can.
161 B5 Capestang France
247 □2 Capesterre Guadeloupe
193 F2 Capestrano Italy
214 B5 Cape Town S. Africa
206 □ Cape Verde country N. Atlantic Ocean
264 G5 Cape Verde Basin sea feature N. Atlantic Ocean
264 G4 Cape Verde Plateau sea feature N. Atlantic Ocean
233 E2 Cape Vincent NY U.S.A.
225 H4 Cape Wolfe P.E.I. Can.
85 E2 Cape York Peninsula Qld Austr.
163 A4 Cap Ferret France
246 D3 Cap-Haïtien Haiti
185 G4 Capileira Spain
185 E2 Capilla Spain
244 C3 Capilla de Guadalupe Mex.
260 E2 Capilla del Monte Arg.
254 C2 Capim r. Brazil
182 C4 Capinha Port.
256 C3 Capinópolis Brazil
252 D4 Capinota Bol.
193 F3 Capistrello Italy
239 F5 Capitan NM U.S.A.
262 U2 Capitán Arturo Prat research stn Antarctica
261 G3 Capitán Bermudez Arg.
260 A6 Capitán Pastene Chile
261 H4 Capitán Sarmiento Arg.
257 F2 Capitão Enéas Brazil
234 C3 Capitol Park DE U.S.A.
256 B5 Capivara, Represa resr Brazil
256 D5 Capivari Brazil
254 F5 Capivari r. Bahia Brazil
256 D5 Capivari r. São Paulo Brazil
194 D5 Capizzi Sicilia Italy
177 L4 Căpleni Romania
188 F4 Čapljina Bos.-Herz.
186 E2 Cap Llitzet mt. Spain
213 G2 Capoche r. Moz./Zambia
192 D2 Capodimonte Italy
190 F2 Capo di Ponte Italy
193 G4 Capodochino airport Italy
194 D4 Capo d'Orlando Sicilia Italy
192 C2 Capoliveri Italy
191 G5 Capolona Italy
193 H4 Caposele Italy
192 A5 Capoterra Sardegna Italy
163 D6 Capoulet France
193 F2 Cappadocia Italy
147 C4 Cappagh Rep. of Ireland
147 C4 Cappamore Rep. of Ireland
147 C4 Cappawhite Rep. of Ireland
168 D2 Cappel Ger.
225 H4 Cap-Pelé N.B. Can.
193 G2 Cappelle sul Tavo Italy
168 D3 Cappeln (Oldenburg) Ger.
146 E6 Capplegill Dumfries and Galloway, Scotland U.K.
147 D4 Cappoquin Rep. of Ireland
193 G3 Capracotta Italy
192 B1 Capraia, Isola di i. Italy
192 B1 Capraia Isola Italy
192 E2 Capranica Italy
193 G4 Capri Italy
193 G4 Capri, Isola di i. Italy
193 G3 Capriati a Volturno Italy
85 G4 Capricorn, Cape Qld Austr.
85 G4 Capricorn Channel Qld Austr.
85 H4 Capricorn Group atolls Qld Austr.
190 E3 Caprino Bergamasco Italy
191 F3 Caprino Veronese Italy
212 D3 Caprivi admin. reg. Namibia
Capsa Tunisia see Gafsa
240 □D9 Captain Cook HI U.S.A.
163 B4 Captieux France
232 C5 Captina r. OH U.S.A.
193 G3 Capua Italy
244 D3 Capulín Mex.
209 B8 Capunda Cavilongo Angola
171 D3 Caputh Ger.
146 E5 Caputh Perth and Kinross, Scotland U.K.
163 C5 Capvern-les-Bains France
250 C4 Caqueta dept Col.
250 D5 Caquetá r. Col.
250 C3 Cáqueza Col.
183 G4 Carabaña Spain
252 C3 Carabaya, Cordillera de mts Peru
251 F5 Carabinani r. Brazil
250 E2 Carabobo state Venez.
197 G3 Caracal Romania
251 F4 Caracarai Brazil
250 E2 Caracas Venez.
253 F5 Caracol Mato Grosso do Sul Brazil
254 E4 Caracol Piauí Brazil
252 D4 Caracollo Bol.
185 F2 Caracuel de Calatrava Spain
92 C5 Caraga Phil.
83 F3 Caragabal N.S.W. Austr.
190 C4 Caraglio Italy
257 E5 Caraguatatuba Brazil
259 B5 Carahue Chile
257 G2 Caraí Brazil
147 F1 Cara Island Scotland U.K.
257 H2 Caraiva Brazil
251 I6 Carajás, Serra dos hills Brazil
Carales Sardegna Italy see Cagliari
Caralis Sardegna Italy see Cagliari
Caralps Spain see Queralbs
163 D5 Caraman France
193 G2 Caramanico Terme Italy
185 I3 Caramel r. Spain
92 B3 Caramoan Peninsula Phil.
182 B4 Caramulo Port.
182 B4 Caramulo mt. Port.
182 B4 Caramulo, Serra do mts Port.
253 F3 Caraná r. Brazil
252 D3 Caranavi Bol.
177 L5 Cărand Romania
257 F4 Carandaí Brazil
253 E5 Carandaiti Bol.
182 D1 Caranga Spain
257 F4 Carangola Brazil
182 B5 Caranguejeira Port.
197 F3 Caransebeş Romania
158 C3 Carantec France
250 C5 Cara Paraná r. Col.
193 H3 Carapelle Italy
193 H3 Carapelle r. Italy
193 H3 Carapellotto r. Italy
82 D3 Carappee Hill hill S.A. Austr.
225 H4 Caraquet N.B. Can.
250 A5 Caráquez Ecuador
250 C3 Carare r. Col.
190 E4 Carasco Italy
197 E3 Caraşova Romania
177 L4 Carastelec Romania
242 □J6 Caratasca Hond.
242 □J6 Caratasca, Laguna lag. Hond.
257 F3 Caratinga Brazil
250 D5 Caratué r. Col.
233 □I2 Caratunk ME U.S.A.
250 E6 Carauari Brazil
254 F3 Caraúbas Brazil
Caraúná mt. Brazil see Grande, Serra
185 I2 Caravaca de la Cruz Spain
190 E3 Caravaggio Italy
257 H2 Caravelas Brazil
252 B3 Caravelí Peru
182 E3 Carbajales de Alba Spain
182 B2 Carballeda de Avia Spain
182 B2 Carballiño Spain
182 B1 Carballo Galicia Spain
182 C2 Carballo Galicia Spain
182 D3 Carbellino Spain
223 L5 Carberry Man. Can.
242 C2 Carbó Mex.
194 B5 Carboi r. Sicilia Italy
163 B4 Carbon-Blanc France
234 C2 Carbon County county PA U.S.A.
239 F4 Carbondale CO U.S.A.
237 F4 Carbondale IL U.S.A.
234 C1 Carbondale PA U.S.A.
225 K4 Carbonear Nfld. Can.
183 H3 Carbonera de Frentes Spain
185 I4 Carboneras Spain
183 I5 Carboneras de Guadazaón Spain
183 F3 Carbonero El Mayor Spain
185 G2 Carboneros Spain
192 A5 Carbonia Sardegna Italy
191 H2 Carbonìn Italy
257 F2 Carbonita Brazil
163 D5 Carbonne France
146 B4 Carbost Highland, Scotland U.K.
146 B4 Carbost Highland, Scotland U.K.
147 E3 Carbury Rep. of Ireland
182 D4 Carcaboso Spain
185 F3 Carcabuey Spain
187 C5 Carcaixent Spain
222 G3 Carcajou Alta Can.
222 D1 Carcajou r. N.W.T. Can.
197 I3 Carcaliu Romania
162 A3 Carcans France
162 A3 Carcans-Plage France
182 D3 Carção Port.
92 B4 Carcar Phil.
261 G3 Carcaraña r. Arg.
190 D4 Carcare Italy
163 E5 Carcassonne France
183 I2 Carcastillo Spain
187 B5 Carcelén Spain
161 E5 Carcès France
185 G3 Carchelejo Spain
250 B4 Carchi prov. Ecuador
190 D3 Carcoforo Italy
149 H4 Carcroft South Yorkshire, England U.K.
222 C2 Carcross Y.T. Can.
163 D4 Cardaillac France
199 E1 Çardak anakkale Turkey
199 F3 Çardak Turkey
261 I4 Cardal Uru.
Cardamomes, Chaîne des mts Cambodia see Cardomom Range
114 C4 Cardamon Hills India
186 F3 Cardedeu Spain
192 B5 Cardedu Sardegna Italy
185 F2 Cardeña Spain
183 G2 Cardeñadijo Spain
246 B2 Cárdenas Cuba
245 E2 Cárdenas Mex.
243 G5 Cárdenas Mex.
183 I5 Cardenete Spain
183 F4 Cardeñosa Spain
195 E4 Cardeto Italy
Çardi Turkey see Harmancık
259 C8 Cardiel, Lago l. Arg.
150 D3 Cardiff Cardiff, Wales U.K.
150 D3 Cardiff admin. div. Wales U.K.
234 B3 Cardiff MD U.S.A.
150 D3 Cardiff International airport Wales U.K.
150 C2 Cardigan Ceredigion, Wales U.K.
150 C2 Cardigan Bay Wales U.K.
182 B5 Cardigos Port.
233 F2 Cardinal Ont. Can.
195 F4 Cardinale Italy
232 B4 Cardington OH U.S.A.
193 F3 Cardito Italy
96 C4 Cardomom Range mts Cambodia
216 □3b Cardón hill Fuerteventura Canary Is
242 B3 Cardón, Cerro hill Mex.
186 E3 Cardona Spain
261 I3 Cardona Uru.
245 E3 Cardonal Mex.
186 E3 Cardoner r. Spain
256 C4 Cardoso Brazil
256 D6 Cardoso, Ilha do i. Brazil
81 B6 Cardrona South I. N.Z.
81 B6 Cardrona, Mount South I. N.Z.
146 D6 Cardross Argyll and Bute, Scotland U.K.
222 H5 Cardston Alta Can.
85 F3 Cardwell Qld Austr.
257 E5 Careaçu Brazil
191 G3 Carega, Cima mt. Italy
197 F2 Carei Romania
177 L4 Careilor, Câmpia plain Romania
251 G5 Careiro Brazil
251 F5 Careiro do Castanho Brazil
260 B2 Carén Chile
183 I3 Carenas Spain
158 E2 Carentan France
158 D4 Carentoir France
183 F1 Cares r. Spain
232 B4 Carey OH U.S.A.
87 D6 Carey, Lake salt flat W.A. Austr.
87 B5 Carey Downs W.A. Austr.
217 □1 Cargados Carajos Islands Mauritius
146 E6 Cargenbridge Dumfries and Galloway, Scotland U.K.
192 A2 Cargèse Corse France
158 C3 Carhaix-Plouguer France
252 A2 Carhuamayo Peru
261 F5 Carhué Arg.
182 C4 Caria Port.
254 F4 Cariacá r. Brazil
257 G4 Cariacica Brazil
250 B6 Cariamanga Ecuador
209 B7 Cariango Angola
195 F3 Cariati Italy
246 B3 Caribbean Sea N. Atlantic Ocean
222 F4 Cariboo Mountains B.C. Can.
223 M3 Caribou r. Man. Can.
222 E2 Caribou r. N.W.T. Can.
233 □I1 Caribou ME U.S.A.
226 E2 Caribou Island Ont. Can.
222 H2 Caribou Islands N.W.T. Can.
224 B3 Caribou Lake Ont. Can.
222 H3 Caribou Mountains Alta Can.
242 D3 Carichic Mex.
92 C4 Carigara Phil.
157 F3 Carignan France
190 C4 Carignano Italy
83 F2 Carinda N.S.W. Austr.
186 B3 Cariñena Spain
254 E5 Carinhanha Brazil
254 E5 Carinhanha r. Brazil
194 C4 Carini Sicilia Italy
182 C1 Cariño Spain
193 F3 Carinola Italy
Carinthia land Austria see Kärnten
209 D8 Caripande Angola
251 F2 Caripe Venez.
251 F2 Caripito Venez.
254 E3 Cariris Novos, Serra dos hills Brazil
251 F2 Caris r. Venez.
190 D3 Carisio Italy
191 F2 Carisolo Italy
177 L6 Cârjiţi Romania
147 D2 Cark Mountain hill Rep. of Ireland
163 D5 Carla-Bayle France
Carlabhagh Western Isles, Scotland U.K. see Carloway
147 E2 Carland Northern Ireland U.K.
147 E3 Carlanstown Rep. of Ireland
193 G3 Carlantino Italy
161 A4 Carlat France
195 E5 Carlentini Sicilia Italy
187 C5 Carlet Spain
227 F4 Carleton MI U.S.A.
225 H4 Carleton, Mount hill N.B. Can.
224 E4 Carleton Place Ont. Can.
215 F2 Carletonville S. Africa
197 G2 Cârlibaba Romania
238 C3 Carlin NV U.S.A.
157 G3 Carling France
147 E2 Carlingford Rep. of Ireland
147 E2 Carlingford Lough inlet Rep. of Ireland/U.K.
236 F4 Carlinville IL U.S.A.
149 G3 Carlisle Cumbria, England U.K.
232 A5 Carlisle KY U.S.A.
233 F3 Carlisle NY U.S.A.
227 I5 Carlisle PA U.S.A.
215 F5 Carlisle Bridge S. Africa
87 E6 Carlisle Lakes salt flat W.A. Austr.
234 A2 Carlisle Springs PA U.S.A.
163 D6 Carlit, Pic mt. France
192 A5 Carloforte Sardegna Italy
195 F3 Carlopoli Italy
256 C5 Carlópolis Brazil
146 E6 Carlops Scottish Borders, Scotland U.K.
245 G4 Carlos A. Carrillo Mex.
261 G4 Carlos Casares Arg.
257 G2 Carlos Chagas Brazil
261 I3 Carlos Reyles Uru.
261 F4 Carlos Tejedor Arg.
168 F2 Carlow Ger.
147 E4 Carlow Rep. of Ireland
147 E4 Carlow county Rep. of Ireland
146 B3 Carloway Western Isles, Scotland U.K.
Carlsbad Czech Rep. see Karlovy Vary
240 I5 Carlsbad CA U.S.A.
239 F5 Carlsbad NM U.S.A.
237 C6 Carlsbad TX U.S.A.
172 C2 Carlsberg Ger.
265 H4 Carlsberg Ridge sea feature Indian Ocean
171 D5 Carlsfeld Ger.
215 E4 Carlton S. Africa
151 F2 Carlton Nottinghamshire, England U.K.
226 A2 Carlton MN U.S.A.
151 I2 Carlton Colville Suffolk, England U.K.
86 F2 Carlton Hill W.A. Austr.
149 H4 Carlton in Lindrick Nottinghamshire, England U.K.
146 E6 Carluke South Lanarkshire, Scotland U.K.
163 D4 Carlux France
223 K5 Carlyle Sask. Can.
236 F4 Carlyle IL U.S.A.
222 B2 Carmacks Y.T. Can.
190 C4 Carmagnola Italy
223 L5 Carman Man. Can.
Carmana Iran see Kermān
150 C3 Carmarthen Carmarthenshire, Wales U.K.
150 C3 Carmarthen Bay Wales U.K.
150 C3 Carmarthenshire admin. div. Wales U.K.
163 E4 Carmaux France
230 C4 Carmel IN U.S.A.
233 □I2 Carmel ME U.S.A.
233 G4 Carmel NY U.S.A.
128 B3 Carmel, Mount hill Israel
240 G3 Carmel-by-the-Sea CA U.S.A.
243 H5 Carmelita Guat.
261 H3 Carmelo Uru.
240 G3 Carmel Valley CA U.S.A.
261 G3 Carmen Arg.
250 C2 Carmen Col.
242 D2 Carmen r. Mex.
92 C4 Carmen Phil.
261 I3 Carmen Uru.
241 L6 Carmen AZ U.S.A.
183 F5 Carmena Spain
261 H4 Carmen de Areco Arg.
259 E6 Carmen de Patagones Arg.
182 E2 Cármenes Spain
236 F4 Carmi IL U.S.A.
195 H2 Carmiano Italy
240 G2 Carmichael CA U.S.A.
85 G4 Carmila Qld Austr.
257 F4 Carmo Brazil
257 E4 Carmo da Cachoeira Brazil
257 E5 Carmo de Minas Brazil
256 D3 Carmo do Paranaíba Brazil
87 C7 Carmody, Lake salt flat W.A. Austr.
Carmona Angola see Uíge
184 E3 Carmona Spain
184 D1 Carmonita Spain
257 E4 Carmópolis do Minas Brazil
146 F5 Carmyllie Angus, Scotland U.K.
158 C4 Carnac France
146 D4 Carn a'Chuilinn hill Scotland U.K.
147 E2 Carnagh Northern Ireland U.K.
87 B6 Carnamah W.A. Austr.
87 B5 Carnarvon W.A. Austr.
214 D4 Carnarvon S. Africa
87 D5 Carnarvon Range hills W.A. Austr.
85 G5 Carnarvon Range mts Qld Austr.
146 F5 Carnbee Fife, Scotland U.K.
146 D4 Carn Chuinneag hill Scotland U.K.
146 D4 Carn Dearg hill Highland, Scotland U.K.
146 D4 Carn Dearg hill Highland, Scotland U.K.
147 D1 Carndonagh Rep. of Ireland
147 E1 Carnduff Northern Ireland U.K.
146 E4 Carn Ealasaid hill Scotland U.K.
150 D1 Carnedd Llywelyn mt. Wales U.K.
150 D2 Carnedd y Filiast hill Wales U.K.
87 D5 Carnegie W.A. Austr.
87 D5 Carnegie, Lake salt flat W.A. Austr.
267 N6 Carnegie Ridge sea feature S. Pacific Ocean
146 C4 Carn Eighe mt. Scotland U.K.
146 E4 Carne na Loine hill Scotland U.K.
258 B5 Carnero, Bahía del b. Chile
82 C2 Carnes S.A. Austr.
231 D5 Carnesville GA U.S.A.
147 E4 Carnew Rep. of Ireland
226 D3 Carney MI U.S.A.
262 P2 Carney Island Antarctica
234 C3 Carneys Point NJ U.S.A.
146 F4 Carnferg hill Scotland U.K.
149 G3 Carnforth Lancashire, England U.K.
146 E4 Carn Glas-choire hill Scotland U.K.
115 G4 Car Nicobar i. Andaman & Nicobar Is India
156 D2 Carnières France
138 E3 Carnikava Latvia
147 F2 Carnlough Northern Ireland U.K.
146 E4 Carn Mor hill Scotland U.K.
147 C3 Carnmore Rep. of Ireland
150 D2 Carno Powys, Wales U.K.
146 D4 Carn Odhar hill Scotland U.K.
158 C3 Carnoët France
161 B5 Carnon-Plage France
208 B3 Carnot C.A.R.
76 D5 Carnot, Cape S.A. Austr.
182 A2 Carnota Spain
86 D3 Carnot Bay W.A. Austr.
161 E5 Carnoules France
146 F5 Carnoustie Angus, Scotland U.K.
161 D5 Carnoux-en-Provence France
147 E4 Carnsore Point Rep. of Ireland
148 C3 Carnteel Northern Ireland U.K.
146 E6 Carnwath South Lanarkshire, Scotland U.K.
227 F4 Caro MI U.S.A.
251 F4 Caroaebe r. Brazil
Caroch mt. Spain see El Caroche
85 H3 Carola Cay rf Coral Sea Is Terr. Austr.
231 D7 Carol City FL U.S.A.
193 I5 Carolei Italy
254 D3 Carolina Brazil
247 □1 Carolina Puerto Rico
215 H2 Carolina S. Africa
231 E5 Carolina Beach NC U.S.A.
222 H4 Caroline Alta Can.
234 C4 Caroline County county MD U.S.A.
267 I6 Caroline Island Kiribati
266 E5 Caroline Islands N. Pacific Ocean
81 A6 Caroline Peak South I. N.Z.
158 E3 Carolles France
214 A3 Carolusberg S. Africa
161 D4 Caromb France
190 E2 Carona Italy
251 F2 Caroní r. Venez.
194 D4 Caronia Sicilia Italy
250 D2 Carora Venez.
197 I3 C. A. Rosetti Romania
195 G2 Carosino Italy
195 G2 Carovigno Italy
193 G3 Carovilli Italy
227 I3 Carp Ont. Can.
190 E4 Carpaneto Piacentino Italy
192 E2 Carparola Italy
177 I2 Carpathian Mountains Europe
Carpaţii mts Europe see Carpathian Mountains
197 F3 Carpaţii Meridionali mts Romania
191 H5 Carpegna Italy
190 F3 Carpenedolo Italy
84 D2 Carpentaria, Gulf of N.T./Qld Austr.
85 F3 Carpentaria Downs Qld Austr.
161 D4 Carpentras France
191 F4 Carpi Italy
195 H2 Carpignano Salentino Italy
190 D3 Carpignano Sesia Italy
254 G3 Carpina Brazil
191 H5 Carpina r. Italy
177 L5 Cărpinet Romania
190 F4 Carpineti Italy
193 F3 Carpineto Romano Italy
196 E3 Cărpiniş Romania
193 H3 Carpino Italy
193 G3 Carpinone Italy
240 H4 Carpinteria CA U.S.A.
183 E3 Carpio Spain
236 C1 Carpio ND U.S.A.
159 F2 Carpiquet France
158 E4 Carquefou France
161 E5 Carqueiranne France
184 D1 Carquesa hill Spain
147 B3 Carra, Lough l. Rep. of Ireland
233 □H2 Carrabassett ME U.S.A.
231 C6 Carrabelle FL U.S.A.
147 C3 Carracastle Rep. of Ireland
182 D2 Carracedelo Spain
146 C6 Carradale Argyll and Bute, Scotland U.K.
Carraig na Siuire Rep. of Ireland see Carrick-on-Suir
250 C2 Carraipía Col.
182 B1 Carral Spain
147 B3 Carraloe Rep. of Ireland
147 B5 Carran hill Rep. of Ireland
183 G4 Carranque Spain
147 B5 Carrantuohill mt. Rep. of Ireland
184 B3 Carrapateira Port.
182 C4 Carrapichana Port.
190 F4 Carrara Italy
186 C4 Carrascal mt. Spain
182 E4 Carrascal del Obispo Spain
183 G3 Carrascal del Río Spain
183 H4 Carrascosa Spain
183 H4 Carrascosa del Campo Spain
83 F3 Carrathool N.S.W. Austr.
185 F4 Carratraca Spain
182 C3 Carrazeda de Ansiães Port.

182 C3 Carrazedo de Montenegro Port.
86 F3 Carr Boyd Range hills W.A. Austr.
146 E4 Carrbridge Highland, Scotland U.K.
182 B3 Carreço Port.
184 B1 Carregado Port.
182 C4 Carregal do Sal Port.
182 B5 Carregueiros Port.
182 B1 Carreira Spain
184 C3 Carreiros r. Port.
183 F1 Carreña de Cabrales Spain
260 C5 Carrero, Cerro mt. Arg.
163 B5 Carresse-Cassaber France
Carrhae Turkey see Harran
183 G1 Carriazo Spain
147 C2 Carrick Donegal Rep. of Ireland
147 E4 Carrick Wexford Rep. of Ireland
146 D6 Carrick reg. Scotland U.K.
147 D4 Carrickbeg Rep. of Ireland
147 D3 Carrickboy Rep. of Ireland
147 F2 Carrickfergus Northern Ireland U.K.
147 E3 Carrickmacross Rep. of Ireland
147 D2 Carrickmore Northern Ireland U.K.
147 C3 Carrick-on-Shannon Rep. of Ireland
147 D4 Carrick-on-Suir Rep. of Ireland
182 B5 Carriço Port.
82 D3 Carrieton S.A. Austr.
147 C5 Carrigaline Rep. of Ireland
147 D3 Carrigallen Rep. of Ireland
147 B5 Carriganimmy Rep. of Ireland
147 D2 Carrigans Rep. of Ireland
147 B4 Carrigkerry Rep. of Ireland
147 C5 Carrigtwohill Rep. of Ireland
242 E3 Carrillo Mex.
236 D2 Carrington ND U.S.A.
182 B1 Carrio Spain
183 F2 Carrion r. Spain
185 G1 Carrión de Calatrava Spain
184 D3 Carrión de los Céspedes Spain
183 F2 Carrión de los Condes Spain
261 G3 Carrizales Arg.
241 L4 Carrizo AZ U.S.A.
237 C4 Carrizo Creek r. TX U.S.A.
182 E2 Carrizo de la Ribera Spain
185 H2 Carrizosa Spain
237 D6 Carrizo Springs TX U.S.A.
239 F5 Carrizozo NM U.S.A.
185 H1 Carro hill Spain
236 E3 Carroll IA U.S.A.
234 A3 Carroll County county MD U.S.A.
237 F5 Carrollton AL U.S.A.
231 C5 Carrollton GA U.S.A.
236 F4 Carrollton IL U.S.A.
230 C4 Carrollton KY U.S.A.
236 E4 Carrollton MO U.S.A.
237 F5 Carrollton MS U.S.A.
232 C4 Carrollton OH U.S.A.
232 D4 Carrolltown PA U.S.A.
85 E3 Carron r. Qld Austr.
146 D4 Carron r. Highland, Scotland U.K.
146 C4 Carron, Loch inlet Scotland U.K.
146 E6 Carronbridge Dumfries and Galloway, Scotland U.K.
161 F5 Carros France
223 K4 Carrot r. Sask. Can.
223 K4 Carrot River Sask. Can.
159 F3 Carrouges France
147 D1 Carrowkeel Rep. of Ireland
147 C3 Carrowmore Rep. of Ireland
147 C2 Carrowneden Rep. of Ireland
232 E6 Carrsville VA U.S.A.
190 C4 Carrù Italy
237 F4 Carruthersville MO U.S.A.
147 F2 Carryduff Northern Ireland U.K.
161 D5 Carry-le-Rouet France
162 B3 Cars France
163 D4 Carsac-Aillac France
146 C5 Carsaig Argyll and Bute, Scotland U.K.
126 E2 Çarşamba Turkey
129 A3 Çarşıbaşı Turkey
193 F2 Carsoli Italy
86 E2 Carson r. W.A. Austr.
236 C2 Carson ND U.S.A.
240 H2 Carson r. NV U.S.A.
226 E4 Carson City MI U.S.A.
240 H2 Carson City NV U.S.A.
86 E2 Carson Escarpment W.A. Austr.
240 H2 Carson Lake NV U.S.A.
227 F4 Carsonville MI U.S.A.
160 F1 Carspach France
146 D6 Carsphairn Dumfries and Galloway, Scotland U.K.
146 E6 Carstairs South Lanarkshire, Scotland U.K.
Carstensz-top mt. Indon. see Jaya, Puncak
260 B3 Cartagena Chile
250 C2 Cartagena Col.
187 C7 Cartagena Spain
250 C3 Cartago Col.
242 □J7 Cartago Costa Rica
185 F4 Cártama Spain
184 B1 Cartaxo Port.
184 C3 Cartaya Spain
162 B3 Cartelègue France
85 E2 Carter, Mount hill Qld Austr.
158 E2 Carteret France
235 D2 Carteret NJ U.S.A.
Carteret Island Solomon Is see Malaita
231 C5 Cartersville GA U.S.A.
81 E4 Carterton North I. N.Z.
151 F3 Carterton Oxfordshire, England U.K.
183 F1 Cartes Spain
205 H1 Carthage tourist site Tunisia
226 B5 Carthage IL U.S.A.
237 E4 Carthage MO U.S.A.
231 B5 Carthage MS U.S.A.
231 E5 Carthage NC U.S.A.
233 F3 Carthage NY U.S.A.
231 C4 Carthage TN U.S.A.
237 E5 Carthage TX U.S.A.
Carthago tourist site Tunisia see Carthage
Carthago Nova Spain see Cartagena
227 G2 Cartier Ont. Can.
86 D2 Cartier Island Ashmore & Cartier Is Austr.
149 G3 Cartmel Cumbria, England U.K.
191 H5 Cartoceto Italy
223 L5 Cartwright Man. Can.
225 J2 Cartwright Nfld. Can.
254 G4 Caruarú Brazil
182 D2 Carucedo Spain
193 G3 Carunchio Italy
197 H2 Cărunta, Vârful mt. Romania
251 F2 Carúpano Venez.
254 D2 Carutapera Brazil
182 B5 Carvalhal Santarém Port.
184 B2 Carvalhal Setúbal Port.
182 C3 Carvalho de Egas Port.
232 B6 Carver KY U.S.A.
182 D3 Carviçais Port.
156 C2 Carvin France
184 A1 Carvoeira Port.
184 B3 Carvoeiro Port.
184 A1 Carvoeiro, Cabo c. Port.
85 F5 Carwell Qld Austr.
129 F3 Çarxı Azer.
231 E5 Cary NC U.S.A.
83 E2 Caryapundy Swamp Qld Austr.
232 A6 Caryville TN U.S.A.
226 B3 Caryville WI U.S.A.
185 I3 Casa Alta hill Spain
185 F4 Casabermeja Spain
258 D1 Casabindo, Cerro de mt. Arg.
260 B3 Casablanca Chile
204 D2 Casablanca Morocco
256 D4 Casa Branca Brazil
184 B2 Casa Branca Évora Port.
184 C2 Casa Branca Portalegre Port.
193 G3 Casacalenda Italy
242 C2 Casa de Janos Mex.
185 F2 Casa de Michos Spain
260 D6 Casa de Piedra, Embalse resr Arg.
193 G3 Casagiove Italy
192 A2 Casaglione Corse France
241 L5 Casa Grande AZ U.S.A.
195 H2 Casa l'Abate Italy
193 G2 Casalanguida Italy
183 H2 Casalarreina Spain
193 G2 Casalbordino Italy
193 H3 Casalbore Italy
193 H4 Casalbuono Italy
190 E3 Casalbuttano ed Uniti Italy
190 D4 Casàl Cermelli Italy
191 G4 Casalecchio di Reno Italy
190 D3 Casale Monferrato Italy
193 H4 Casaletto Spartano Italy
191 G4 Casalfiumanese Italy
191 F4 Casalgrande Italy
190 C4 Casalgrasso Italy
184 B1 Casalinho Port.
190 F4 Casalmaggiore Italy
193 H3 Casalnuovo Monterotaro Italy
190 E3 Casalpusterlengo Italy
193 H3 Casalvecchio di Puglia Italy
193 H4 Casàl Velino Italy
206 A3 Casamance r. Senegal
195 F2 Casamassima Italy
192 B2 Casamozza Corse France
250 D3 Casanare dept Col.
250 D3 Casanare r. Col.
185 F4 Casarabonela Spain
195 H2 Casarano Italy
182 D5 Casar de Cáceres Spain
182 D4 Casar de Palomero Spain
183 G3 Casarejos Spain
185 E4 Casares Spain
182 D4 Casares de las Hurdes Spain
185 F3 Casariche Spain
183 F4 Casarrubios del Monte Spain
191 H3 Casarsa della Delizia Italy
190 E4 Casarza Ligure Italy
187 B4 Casas Altas Spain
185 H1 Casas de Benítez Spain
185 E1 Casas de Don Pedro Spain
185 H1 Casas de Fernando Alonso Spain
185 H1 Casas de Haro Spain
187 B5 Casas de Juan Gil Spain
185 I1 Casas de Juan Núñez Spain
185 H2 Casas de Lázaro Spain
182 E4 Casas del Monte Spain
185 H1 Casas de los Pinos Spain
187 B6 Casas del Puerto Spain
182 D5 Casas de Millán Spain
187 B5 Casas de Ves Spain
242 D2 Casas Grandes Mex.
242 D2 Casas Grandes r. Mex.
185 I1 Casas-Ibáñez Spain
185 H1 Casasimarro Spain
184 C2 Casas Novas de Mares Port.
183 E3 Casasola de Arión Spain
182 E5 Casatejada Spain
190 E3 Casatenovo Italy
183 F4 Casavieja Spain
261 F5 Casbas Arg.
255 B9 Casca Brazil
87 D7 Cascade W.A. Austr.
81 B6 Cascade r. South I. N.Z.
236 F3 Cascade IA U.S.A.
238 C2 Cascade ID U.S.A.
238 E2 Cascade MT U.S.A.
228 B2 Cascade Range mts Can./U.S.A.
184 A2 Cascais Port.
242 □I7 Cascal, Paso del pass Nic.
183 I2 Cascante Spain
187 B4 Cascante del Río Spain
225 H3 Cascapédia r. Que. Can.
254 F3 Cascavel Ceará Brazil
256 A6 Cascavel Paraná Brazil
193 F2 Cascia Italy
191 F5 Casciana Terme Italy
190 F5 Cascina Italy
197 H3 Căscioarele Romania
226 D3 Casco WI U.S.A.
233 □I3 Casco Bay ME U.S.A.
184 B2 Casebres Port.
183 I2 Cáseda Spain
192 B5 Case della Marina Sardegna Italy
190 D3 Casei Gerola Italy
170 F2 Casekow Ger.
190 D4 Casella Italy
193 H4 Caselle in Pittari Italy
190 C3 Caselle Torinese Italy
195 F2 Case Perrone Italy
186 E2 Caserras Spain
193 G3 Caserta Italy
193 G3 Caserta prov. Campania Italy
184 B3 Casével Port.
227 F4 Caseville MI U.S.A.
263 H2 Casey research stn Antarctica
210 F2 Caseyr, Raas c. Somalia
147 D1 Cashel Donegal Rep. of Ireland
147 C3 Cashel Galway Rep. of Ireland
147 B3 Cashel Galway Rep. of Ireland
147 D4 Cashel Laois Rep. of Ireland
147 D4 Cashel Tipperary Rep. of Ireland
147 C3 Cashla Rep. of Ireland
147 A3 Cashleen Rep. of Ireland
85 G5 Cashmere Qld Austr.
226 B4 Cashton WI U.S.A.
92 B2 Casiguran Phil.
261 G3 Casilda Arg.
183 F4 Casillas Spain
182 D4 Casillas de Flores Spain
197 I3 Casimcea Romania
197 I3 Casimcea r. Romania
244 B4 Casimiro Castillo Mex.
257 F5 Casimiro de Abreu Brazil
190 F4 Casina Italy
83 H2 Casino N.S.W. Austr.
187 C5 Casinos Spain
176 E2 Čáslav Czech Rep.
252 A2 Casma Peru
Casnewydd Newport, Wales U.K. see Newport
226 E4 Casnovia MI U.S.A.
182 D2 Casoio r. Spain
190 F4 Casola in Lunigiana Italy
191 G4 Casola Valsenio Italy
191 G5 Casole d'Elsa Italy
193 G2 Casoli Italy
193 G4 Casoria Italy
186 C3 Caspe Spain
238 F3 Casper WY U.S.A.
226 C2 Caspian MI U.S.A.
Caspian Lowland Kazakh./Rus. Fed. see Prikaspiyskaya Nizmennost'
120 B3 Caspian Sea Asia/Europe
232 D5 Cass WV U.S.A.
227 F4 Cass r. MI U.S.A.
213 G2 Cassacatiza Moz.
232 D3 Cassadaga NY U.S.A.
186 F3 Cassà de la Selva Spain
163 C5 Cassagnabère-Tournas France
163 E4 Cassagnes-Bégonhès France
209 D7 Cassai Angola
209 D8 Cassamba Angola
163 E4 Cassaniouze France
193 I5 Cassano allo Ionio Italy
195 F2 Cassano delle Murge Italy
190 D3 Cassano Magnano Italy
190 D4 Cassano Spinola Italy
194 D5 Cassaro Sicilia Italy
227 F4 Cass City MI U.S.A.
156 C2 Cassel France
224 F4 Casselman Ont. Can.
236 D2 Casselton ND U.S.A.
163 C4 Casseneuil France
256 D4 Cássia Brazil
222 D3 Cassiar B.C. Can.
222 D3 Cassiar Mountains B.C. Can.
195 E6 Cassibile Sicilia Italy
195 E6 Cassibile r. Sicilia Italy
256 B3 Cassilândia Brazil
83 G3 Cassilis N.S.W. Austr.
190 D4 Cassine Italy
193 F3 Cassino Italy
161 D5 Cassis France
236 E2 Cass Lake MN U.S.A.
146 D4 Cassley r. Scotland U.K.
191 G3 Cassola Italy
209 B7 Cassongue Angola
226 D5 Cassopolis MI U.S.A.
161 A4 Cassuéjouls France
237 E4 Cassville MO U.S.A.
176 G3 Častá Slovakia
190 D3 Castagliona Olona Italy
191 G3 Castagnaro Italy
192 C1 Castagneto Carducci Italy
190 D4 Castagnole delle Lanze Italy
190 D4 Castagnole Monferrato Italy
187 C6 Castalla Spain
183 E5 Castañar de Ibor Spain
183 H2 Castañares de Rioja Spain
163 D5 Castanet-Tolosan France
254 D2 Castanhal Brazil
182 C4 Castanheira Port.
182 B4 Castanheira de Pêra Port.
260 C2 Castaño r. Arg.
190 D3 Castano Primo Italy
243 E3 Castaños Mex.
190 E2 Castasegna Switz.
190 E3 Casteggio Italy
183 I2 Castejón Spain
186 D3 Castejón del Puente Spain
186 C3 Castejón de Monegros Spain
186 D2 Castejón de Sos Spain
186 C3 Castejón de Valdejasa Spain
193 H3 Castèl Baronia Italy
191 I5 Castelbellino Italy
191 G4 Castèl Bolognese Italy
194 D5 Castelbuono Sicilia Italy
193 H4 Castelcivita Italy
194 C4 Casteldaccia Sicilia Italy
191 F3 Castèl d'Ario Italy
190 C4 Casteldelfino Italy
193 F2 Castèl del Monte Italy
192 D2 Castèl del Piano Italy
191 G4 Castèl del Rio Italy
194 D5 Castèl di Iudica Sicilia Italy
193 F2 Castèl di Lama Italy
194 D5 Castèl di Lucio Sicilia Italy
193 G3 Castèl di Sangro Italy
182 C4 Casteleiro Port.
191 I5 Castelfidardo Italy
191 F5 Castelfiorentino Italy
186 C3 Castelflorite Spain
191 G5 Castèl Focognano Italy
193 F3 Castelforte Italy
193 H4 Castelfranci Italy
191 G5 Castelfranco di Sopra Italy
191 F5 Castelfranco di Sotto Italy
191 G4 Castelfranco Emilia Italy
193 H3 Castelfranco in Miscano Italy
191 G3 Castelfranco Veneto Italy
193 G2 Castèl Frentano Italy
192 D2 Castèl Giorgio Italy
190 F3 Castèl Goffredo Italy
193 H4 Castelgrande Italy
163 C4 Casteljaloux France
173 E2 Castell Ger.
190 D4 Castell'Alfero Italy
193 F2 Castellalto Italy
194 B4 Castellammare, Golfo di b. Sicilia Italy
194 B4 Castellammare del Golfo Sicilia Italy
193 G4 Castellammare di Stabia Italy
190 C3 Castellamonte Italy
195 G2 Castellana Grotte Italy
161 E5 Castellane France
195 F2 Castellaneta Italy
195 F2 Castellaneta Marina Italy
185 H2 Castellanos mt. Spain
183 F2 Castellanos de Castro Spain
185 E4 Castellar de la Frontera Spain
183 I4 Castellar de la Muela Spain
186 E2 Castellar de la Ribera Spain
185 G2 Castellar de Santiago Spain
185 G2 Castellar de Santisteban Spain
190 E4 Castell'Arquato Italy
192 D2 Castell'Azzara Italy
190 D4 Castellazzo Bormida Italy
186 D3 Castelldans Spain
186 G3 Castell d'Aro Spain
186 D4 Castell de Cabres Spain
187 C6 Castell de Castells Spain
186 E3 Castelldefels Spain
185 G4 Castell de Ferro Spain
190 E3 Castelleone Italy
190 D3 Castelletto sopra Ticino Italy
186 F2 Castellfollit de la Roca Spain
186 C4 Castellfort Spain
261 I5 Castelli Buenos Aires Arg.
258 E2 Castelli Chaco Arg.
191 G5 Castellina in Chianti Italy
191 F5 Castellina Marittima Italy
193 F3 Castelliri Italy
Castell-nedd Neath Port Talbot, Wales U.K. see Neath
Castell Newydd Emlyn Ceredigion, Wales U.K. see Newcastle Emlyn
187 C5 Castellnovo Spain
191 G4 Castello d'Argile Italy
Castello de Ampurias Spain see Castellò d'Empúries
187 C5 Castelló de la Plana Spain
186 G2 Castellò d'Empúries Spain
187 C6 Castelló de Rugat Spain
190 D4 Castello di Annone Italy
187 C4 Castellón prov. Valencia Spain
Castellón de la Plana Spain see Castelló de la Plana
186 C4 Castellote Spain
191 G2 Castello Tesino Italy
186 D3 Castellserà Spain
186 F3 Castellterçol Spain
191 F3 Castellucchio Italy
193 H3 Castelluccio dei Sauri Italy
193 H4 Castelluccio Inferiore Italy
193 H3 Castellucio Valmaggiore Italy
194 D4 Castell'Umberto Sicilia Italy
194 B4 Castelluzzo Sicilia Italy
193 E3 Castèl Madama Italy
191 G4 Càstel Maggiore Italy
190 C4 Castelmagno Italy
191 G3 Castelmassa Italy
163 C4 Castelmoron-sur-Lot France
194 D1 Castel Morrone Italy
163 D5 Castelnau France
163 C5 Castelnau-Barbarens France
163 D5 Castelnaudary France
163 C5 Castelnau-d'Auzan France
163 C4 Castelnaud-de-Gratecambe France
163 E5 Castelnau-de-Brassac France
162 B3 Castelnau-de-Médoc France
163 D5 Castelnau-de-Montmiral France
163 D5 Castelnau d'Estréfonds France
161 B5 Castelnau-le-Lez France
163 C5 Castelnau-Magnoac France
163 D4 Castelnau-Montratier France
163 B5 Castelnau-Rivière-Basse France
191 F4 Castelnovo di Sotto Italy
190 F4 Castelnovo ne'Monti Italy
191 G5 Castelnuovo Berardenga Italy
193 H3 Castelnuovo della Daunia Italy
190 F4 Castelnuovo di Garfagnana Italy
192 C1 Castelnuovo di Val di Cecina Italy
190 C3 Castelnuovo Don Bosco Italy
190 D4 Castelnuovo Scrivia Italy
257 G4 Castelo Brazil
182 D4 Castelo Bom Port.
216 □1c Castelo Branco Faial Azores
182 D3 Castelo Branco Bragança Port.
182 C5 Castelo Branco Castelo Branco Port.
182 C4 Castelo Branco admin. dist. Port.
182 B5 Castelo de Bode, Barragem do resr Port.
182 B3 Castelo de Paiva Port.
184 C1 Castelo de Vide Port.
182 B3 Castelo do Neiva Port.
254 E3 Castelo do Piauí Brazil
182 B3 Castelões Port.
182 C3 Castelo Melhor Port.
182 D4 Castelo Mendo Port.
182 D4 Castelo Rodrigo Port.
191 I5 Castelplanio Italy
191 I5 Castelraimondo Italy
193 E2 Castèl Ritaldi Italy
191 G2 Castelrotto Italy
163 C4 Castelsagrat France
190 E3 Castèl San Giovanni Italy
191 G5 Castèl San Niccolò Italy
191 G4 Castèl San Pietro Terme Italy
193 F2 Castèl Sant'Angelo Italy
193 F2 Castelsantangelo sul Nera Italy
193 H4 Castelsaraceno Italy
192 A4 Castelsardo Sardegna Italy
163 D4 Castelsarrasin France
186 C4 Castelseras Spain
194 C5 Casteltermini Sicilia Italy
190 E3 Castelverde Italy
193 G3 Castelvetere in Val Fortore Italy
194 B5 Castelvetrano Sicilia Italy
190 E3 Castelvetro Placentino Italy
192 E2 Castèl Viscardo Italy
193 F3 Castèl Volturno Italy
191 G4 Castenaso Italy
163 C5 Castéra-Verduzan France
82 E4 Casterton Vic. Austr.
163 B5 Castetnau-Camblong France
163 A5 Castets France
192 B5 Castiadas Sardegna Italy
187 B4 Castielfabib Spain
186 C2 Castiello de Jaca Spain
192 B2 Castifao Corse France
190 F5 Castiglioncello Italy
191 G4 Castiglione dei Pepoli Italy
192 E1 Castiglione del Lago Italy
192 C2 Castiglione della Pescaia Italy
190 F3 Castiglione della Stiviere Italy
192 D1 Castiglione d'Orcia Italy
192 E2 Castiglione in Teverina Italy
193 G3 Castiglione Messer Marino Italy
191 G5 Castiglion Fiorentino Italy
193 F2 Castignano Italy
185 E1 Castilblanco Spain
184 E3 Castilblanco de los Arroyos Spain
232 D3 Castile NY U.S.A.
256 B4 Castilho Brazil
183 I2 Castiliscar Spain
250 A6 Castilla Peru
183 G5 Castilla - La Mancha aut. comm. Spain
183 F3 Castilla y León aut. comm. Spain
184 D3 Castilleja de la Cuesta Spain
185 H3 Castillejar Spain
183 E3 Castillejo hill Spain
182 D4 Castillejo de Martin Viejo Spain
183 G3 Castillejo de Mesleón Spain
183 G3 Castillejo de Robledo Spain
250 D2 Castilletes Col.
260 C3 Castillo, Cerro del mt. Arg.
259 C7 Castillo, Pampa del hills Arg.
183 F4 Castillo de Bayuela Spain
183 H5 Castillo de Garcimuñoz Spain
185 G3 Castillo de Locubín Spain
163 D6 Castillon-en-Couserans France
163 B4 Castillon-la-Bataille France
163 C4 Castillonnès France
186 B2 Castillo-Nuevo Spain
258 G4 Castillos Uru.
258 G4 Castillos, Lago de l. Uru.
183 H3 Castilruiz Spain
190 F3 Castione della Presolana Italy
178 E5 Castiòns di Strada Italy
147 B3 Castlebar Rep. of Ireland
146 A5 Castlebay Western Isles, Scotland U.K.
147 E3 Castlebellingham Rep. of Ireland
147 C3 Castleblakeney Rep. of Ireland
147 E2 Castleblayney Rep. of Ireland
151 F2 Castle Bromwich West Midlands, England U.K.
149 G3 Castle Carrock Cumbria, England U.K.
150 E3 Castle Cary Somerset, England U.K.
147 D4 Castlecomer Rep. of Ireland
147 C4 Castleconnell Rep. of Ireland
147 B2 Castleconor Rep. of Ireland
241 L2 Castle Dale UT U.S.A.
226 B2 Castle Danger MN U.S.A.
147 E2 Castledawson Northern Ireland U.K.
147 D2 Castlederg Northern Ireland U.K.
147 E4 Castledermot Rep. of Ireland
241 J5 Castle Dome Mountains AZ U.S.A.
151 F2 Castle Donington Leicestershire, England U.K.
146 E7 Castle Douglas Dumfries and Galloway, Scotland U.K.
147 E4 Castleellis Rep. of Ireland
147 D2 Castlefinn Rep. of Ireland
149 H4 Castleford West Yorkshire, England U.K.
147 C5 Castlefreke Rep. of Ireland
147 C2 Castlegal Rep. of Ireland
222 G5 Castlegar B.C. Can.
147 A4 Castlegregory Rep. of Ireland
147 B2 Castlehill Rep. of Ireland
246 D2 Castle Island Bahamas
147 B4 Castleisland Rep. of Ireland
148 B4 Castlejordan Rep. of Ireland
146 D7 Castle Kennedy Dumfries and Galloway, Scotland U.K.
147 C4 Castlelyons Rep. of Ireland
83 F4 Castlemaine Vic. Austr.
147 B4 Castlemaine Rep. of Ireland
150 B3 Castlemartin Pembrokeshire, Wales U.K.
147 C5 Castlemartyr Rep. of Ireland
222 H5 Castle Mountain Alta Can.
240 G4 Castle Mountain CA U.S.A.
81 F4 Castlepoint North I. N.Z.
147 D3 Castlepollard Rep. of Ireland
147 C3 Castlerea Rep. of Ireland
83 F2 Castlereagh r. N.S.W. Austr.
147 F2 Castlereagh Northern Ireland U.K.
147 E1 Castlerock Northern Ireland U.K.
239 F4 Castle Rock CO U.S.A.
238 B2 Castle Rock WA U.S.A.
147 E1 Castleroe Northern Ireland U.K.
149 H3 Castleside Durham, England U.K.
246 □ Castleton Jamaica
149 I3 Castleton North Yorkshire, England U.K.
233 G3 Castleton-On-Hudson NY U.S.A.
148 E3 Castletown Isle of Man
147 B3 Castletown Clare Rep. of Ireland
147 C5 Castletown Cork Rep. of Ireland
147 D4 Castletown Laois Rep. of Ireland
147 E3 Castletown Meath Rep. of Ireland
146 E3 Castletown Highland, Scotland U.K.
147 C4 Castletownroche Rep. of Ireland
147 B3 Castleville Rep. of Ireland
147 F2 Castlewellan Northern Ireland U.K.
223 I4 Castor Alta Can.
224 E2 Castor, Rivière du r. Que. Can.
237 E6 Castor Creek r. LA U.S.A.
Castra Regina Ger. see Regensburg
183 F2 Castrejón de la Peña Spain
182 C3 Castrelo do Val Spain
163 E5 Castres France
164 D2 Castricum Neth.
161 B5 Castries France
247 □3 Castries St Lucia
195 H3 Castrignano del Capo Italy
185 H3 Castril Spain
185 H3 Castril r. Spain
183 F3 Castrillo de Don Juan Spain
183 F3 Castrillo de Duero Spain
183 G3 Castrillo de la Reina Spain
183 G3 Castrillo de la Vega Spain
183 F2 Castrillo de Villavega Spain
183 F3 Castrillo Tejeriego Spain
256 C6 Castro Brazil
259 B6 Castro Chile
195 H2 Castro Italy
182 C2 Castro Spain
182 A1 Castro r. Spain
254 F5 Castro Alves Brazil
183 G1 Castrobarto Spain
182 E2 Castrocalbón Spain
182 C2 Castro Caldelas Spain
191 G4 Castrocaro Terme Italy
182 D2 Castrocontrigo Spain
182 C4 Castro Daire Port.
193 F3 Castro dei Volsci Italy
185 F3 Castro del Río Spain
182 C1 Castro de Ouro Spain
182 C1 Castro de Rei Spain
194 C5 Castrofilippo Sicilia Italy
182 E3 Castrogonzalo Spain
183 F2 Castrojeriz Spain
182 B2 Castro Laboreiro Port.
184 C3 Castro Marim Port.
183 F2 Castromocho Spain
183 E3 Castromonte Spain
182 E3 Castronuevo Spain
183 E3 Castronuño Spain
194 C5 Castronuovo di Sicilia Sicilia Italy
193 G3 Castropignano Italy
182 D2 Castropodame Spain
182 C1 Castropol Spain
169 C4 Castrop-Rauxel Ger.
195 E4 Castroreale Sicilia Italy
183 G1 Castro-Urdiales Spain
182 B2 Castrove hill Spain
184 B3 Castro Verde Port.
182 C1 Castroverde Spain
183 E3 Castroverde de Campos Spain
193 I5 Castrovillari Italy
240 G3 Castroville CA U.S.A.
252 B3 Castrovirreyna Peru
184 E2 Castuera Spain
106 A1 Cast Uul mt. Mongolia
86 E2 Casuarina, Mount hill W.A. Austr.
127 F3 Çat Turkey
209 C8 Catabola Angola
242 □I6 Catacamas Hond.
250 A6 Catacaos Peru
250 B6 Catacocha Ecuador
187 C5 Catadau Spain
257 F4 Cataguases Brazil
92 B3 Cataiñgan Phil.
127 F3 Çatak Turkey
256 D3 Catalão Brazil
199 F1 Çatalca Turkey
199 F1 Çatalca Yarımadası pen. Turkey
241 L5 Catalina AZ U.S.A.
Catalonia aut. comm. Spain see Cataluña
186 E3 Cataluña aut. comm. Spain
Catalunya aut. comm. Spain see Cataluña
126 D2 Çatalzeytin Turkey
258 D3 Catamarca Arg.
258 D2 Catamarca prov. Arg.
Catambia Moz. see Catandica
Catana Sicilia Italy see Catania
92 B3 Catanauan Phil.
213 G3 Catandica Moz.
92 C3 Catanduanes i. Phil.
256 C4 Catanduva Brazil
256 A6 Catanduvas Brazil
195 E5 Catania Sicilia Italy
194 D5 Catania prov. Sicilia Italy
195 E5 Catania, Golfo di g. Sicilia Italy
195 F4 Catanzaro Italy
195 F4 Catanzaro prov. Calabria Italy
195 F4 Catanzaro Marina Italy
226 B3 Cataract WI U.S.A.
254 F3 Catarina Brazil
237 D6 Catarina TX U.S.A.
92 C3 Catarman Phil.
187 C5 Catarroja Spain
234 C2 Catasauqua PA U.S.A.
82 C3 Catastrophe, Cape S.A. Austr.
226 B3 Catawba WI U.S.A.
231 D5 Catawba r. SC U.S.A.
227 I5 Catawissa PA U.S.A.
234 B2 Catawissa Creek r. PA U.S.A.
96 D2 Cat Ba, Đao i. Vietnam
92 C4 Catbalogan Phil.
246 C1 Cat Cays is Bahamas
92 C5 Cateel Phil.
245 G4 Catemaco Mex.
245 G4 Catemaco, Laguna l. Mex.
260 B3 Catemu Chile
194 D5 Catenanuova Sicilia Italy
209 B8 Catengue Angola
151 G3 Caterham Surrey, England U.K.
192 A2 Cateri Corse France
209 B7 Catete Angola
251 H6 Catete r. Brazil
83 G4 Cathcart N.S.W. Austr.
215 F5 Cathcart S. Africa
241 I5 Cathedral City CA U.S.A.
215 G3 Cathedral Peak Lesotho
147 A5 Catherdaniel Rep. of Ireland
231 C5 Catherine AL U.S.A.
241 K2 Catherine, Mount UT U.S.A.
240 G3 Catheys Valley CA U.S.A.
238 B2 Cathlamet WA U.S.A.
186 D4 Catí Spain
193 F2 Catignano Italy
206 B4 Catió Guinea-Bissau
246 D1 Cat Island Bahamas
182 C4 Cativelos Port.
232 B5 Catlettsburg KY U.S.A.
243 I4 Catoche, Cabo c. Mex.
182 B2 Catoira Spain
254 F3 Catolé do Rocha Brazil
149 G3 Caton Lancashire, England U.K.
195 E4 Catona r. Italy
234 B3 Catonsville MD U.S.A.
244 D2 Catorce Mex.
244 D2 Catorce, Sierra de mts Mex.
182 D2 Catoute mt. Spain
187 C6 Catral Spain
191 H5 Catria, Monte mt. Italy
260 D5 Catriel Arg.
261 F5 Catriló Arg.
251 F4 Catrimani r. Brazil
146 D6 Catrine East Ayrshire, Scotland U.K.
150 E2 Catshill Worcestershire, England U.K.
233 G3 Catskill NY U.S.A.
233 F3 Catskill Mountains NY U.S.A.
157 G3 Cattenom France
169 F5 Catterfeld Ger.
149 H3 Catterick North Yorkshire, England U.K.
149 H3 Catterick Camp North Yorkshire, England U.K.
146 F5 Catterline Aberdeenshire, Scotland U.K.
81 C6 Cattle Creek South I. N.Z.
191 H5 Cattolica Italy
194 C5 Cattolica Eraclea Sicilia Italy
213 G2 Catur Moz.
163 D4 Catus France
194 C5 Catuso, Monte mt. Sicilia Italy
177 L4 Căuaş Romania
254 C2 Cauaxi r. Brazil
92 B4 Cauayan Phil.
225 I1 Caubvick, Mount Nfld. Can.
250 B4 Cauca dept Col.
250 C2 Cauca r. Col.
254 F2 Caucaia Brazil
250 C3 Caucasia Col.
129 B2 Caucasus mts Asia/Europe
260 C2 Caucete Arg.
158 C4 Caudan France
162 C4 Caudau r. France
159 G2 Caudebec-en-Caux France
163 C4 Caudecoste France
187 C6 Caudete Spain
187 B5 Caudete de las Fuentes Spain
187 C5 Caudiel Spain
163 E6 Caudiès de-Fenouillèdes France
156 D2 Caudry France
163 D5 Caujac France
158 D3 Caulnes France
195 F4 Caulonia Italy
163 D4 Caumont Midi-Pyrénées France
163 D5 Caumont Midi-Pyrénées France
159 F2 Caumont-l'Éventé France
161 C5 Caumont-sur-Durance France
246 C2 Caunao r. Cuba
163 E5 Caunes-Minervois France
209 C7 Caungula Angola
260 A4 Cauquenes Chile
251 E3 Caura r. Venez.
251 F5 Caurés r. Brazil
192 A3 Cauro Corse France
225 H3 Causapscal Que. Can.
136 E4 Căuşeni Moldova
147 B4 Causeway Rep. of Ireland
147 E1 Causeway Head Northern Ireland U.K.
163 D4 Caussade France
252 D3 Cautário r. Brazil
163 B6 Cauterets France
246 C2 Cauto r. Cuba
129 F3 Cavad Azer.
193 G4 Cava de'Tirreni Italy
182 B3 Cávado r. Port.
190 D3 Cavaglià Italy
161 D5 Cavaillon France
161 E5 Cavalaire-sur-Mer France
254 D5 Cavalcante Brazil
184 B3 Cavaleiro Port.
191 G2 Cavalese Italy
236 D1 Cavalier ND U.S.A.
190 C4 Cavallermaggiore Italy
191 H3 Cavallino Italy
206 D5 Cavally r. Côte d'Ivoire
190 E3 Cava Manara Italy
147 D3 Cavan Rep. of Ireland
147 D3 Cavan county Rep. of Ireland
190 E2 Cavargna Italy
191 H3 Cavarzere Italy
191 I2 Cavazzo Carnico Italy
199 F2 Çavdarhisar Turkey
199 F3 Çavdır Turkey
81 C6 Cave South I. N.Z.
237 F4 Cave City AR U.S.A.
230 C4 Cave City KY U.S.A.
241 L5 Cave Creek AZ U.S.A.
191 I2 Cave del Predil Italy
161 C5 Caveirac France
87 F5 Cavenagh Range hills W.A. Austr.
83 E4 Cavendish Vic. Austr.
255 B9 Cavera, Serra do hills Brazil
256 A6 Cavernoso, Serra do mts Brazil
150 E2 Caverswall Staffordshire, England U.K.
182 C3 Cavês Port.
191 G4 Cavezzo Italy
251 I4 Caviana, Ilha i. Brazil
162 B3 Cavignac France
92 B3 Cavite Phil.
191 J3 Čavle Croatia
197 F2 Cavnic Romania
193 E3 Cavo, Monte hill Italy
195 F2 Cavone r. Italy
190 C4 Cavour Italy
226 C3 Cavour WI U.S.A.
191 F4 Cavriago Italy
191 G5 Cavriglia Italy
126 C3 Çavuşçu Turkey
199 G3 Çavuşköy Turkey
146 E4 Cawdor Highland, Scotland U.K.
83 E3 Cawndilla Lake imp. l. N.S.W. Austr.
Cawnpore Uttar Prad. India see Kanpur
149 H4 Cawood North Yorkshire, England U.K.
232 B6 Cawood KY U.S.A.
151 I2 Cawston Norfolk, England U.K.
257 E4 Caxambu Brazil
182 B5 Caxarias Port.
254 E3 Caxias Brazil
255 C9 Caxias do Sul Brazil
209 B7 Caxito Angola
251 I5 Caxiuana, Baía de l. Brazil
199 G2 Çay Turkey
129 C3 Çayarası Turkey
199 E2 Çaybaşı İzmir Turkey
Çaybaşı Turkey see Çayeli
231 D5 Cayce SC U.S.A.
126 D2 Çaycuma Turkey
127 F2 Çayeli Turkey
251 H3 Cayenne Fr. Guiana
156 B2 Cayeux-sur-Mer France
247 □1 Cayey Puerto Rico
126 D3 Çayhan Turkey
199 F3 Çayhisar Turkey
126 C2 Çayırhan Turkey
129 B4 Çayırlı Turkey
129 B3 Çaykara Turkey
163 D4 Caylus France
246 C3 Cayman Brac i. Cayman Is
246 B3 Cayman Islands terr. West Indies
264 D4 Cayman Trench sea feature Caribbean Sea
210 E2 Caynabo Somalia
150 E2 Caynham Shropshire, England U.K.
161 B4 Cayres France
246 B2 Cay Sal i. Bahamas
246 B2 Cay Sal Bank sea feature Bahamas
246 D2 Cay Santa Domingo i. Bahamas
149 I4 Caythorpe Lincolnshire, England U.K.
149 I3 Cayton North Yorkshire, England U.K.
240 G4 Cayucos CA U.S.A.
227 H4 Cayuga Ont. Can.
232 E3 Cayuga Heights NY U.S.A.
246 D2 Cay Verde i. Bahamas
209 D7 Cazage Angola
Cazaje Angola see Cazage
183 F4 Cazalegas Spain
184 E3 Cazalla de la Sierra Spain
163 D4 Cazals Midi-Pyrénées France
163 D4 Cazals Midi-Pyrénées France
197 H3 Căzănești Romania
163 B5 Cazaubon France
163 A4 Cazaux et de Sanguinet, Étang de l. France
233 F3 Cazenovia NY U.S.A.
163 D5 Cazères France
163 D4 Cazes-Mondenard France
163 E5 Cazilhac France
188 F3 Čazma Croatia
209 D7 Cazombo Angola
245 F3 Cazones Mex.
245 F3 Cazones r. Mex.
185 H3 Cazorla Spain
185 G3 Cazorla, Sierra de mts Spain
163 D4 Cazoulès France
213 G2 Cazula Moz.
183 F2 Cea Castilla y León Spain
182 C2 Cea Galicia Spain
183 E2 Cea r. Spain
Ceadâr-Lunga Moldova see Ciadîr-Lunga
Ceanannus Mór Meath Rep. of Ireland see Kells
146 A4 Ceann a'Bháigh Western Isles, Scotland U.K.
183 H1 Ceanuri Spain
Ceará Brazil see Fortaleza
254 F3 Ceará state Brazil
264 G6 Ceara Abyssal Plain sea feature S. Atlantic Ocean
146 B3 Cearsiadair Western Isles, Scotland U.K.
197 I3 Ceatalchioi Romania
Ceatharlach Rep. of Ireland see Carlow
159 F3 Ceaucé France
161 B3 Céaux-d'Allègre France
242 D3 Ceballos Mex.
128 A1 Cebireis Dağı mt. Turkey
182 C5 Cebolais de Cima Port.
183 F5 Cebolla Spain
244 B4 Ceboruco, Cerro mt. Mex.
244 B3 Ceboruco, Volcán vol. Mex.
177 I3 Čebovce Slovakia
183 F4 Cebreros Spain
92 B4 Cebu Phil.
92 B4 Cebu i. Phil.
193 F3 Ceccano Italy
177 H5 Cece Hungary
178 C4 Cece, Cima di mt. Italy
177 K3 Čečejovce Slovakia
176 E2 Čechtice Czech Rep.
177 H3 Čechynce Slovakia
226 C3 Cecil WI U.S.A.
234 C3 Cecil County county MD U.S.A.
85 G5 Cecil Plains Qld Austr.
87 D5 Cecil Rhodes, Mount hill W.A. Austr.
234 C3 Cecilton MD U.S.A.
191 F5 Cecina Italy
191 F5 Cecina r. Italy
195 F3 Cecita, Lago di l. Italy
182 D5 Ceclavín Spain
182 C3 Cedães Port.
226 E4 Cedar r. MI U.S.A.
236 C2 Cedar r. ND U.S.A.
236 D3 Cedar r. NE U.S.A.
214 B5 Cedarberg mts S. Africa
232 C6 Cedar Bluff VA U.S.A.
234 D3 Cedar Brook NJ U.S.A.
241 K3 Cedar City UT U.S.A.
239 F4 Cedaredge CO U.S.A.
236 E3 Cedar Falls IA U.S.A.
240 H3 Cedar Grove CA U.S.A.
226 D4 Cedar Grove WI U.S.A.
232 C5 Cedar Grove WV U.S.A.
223 K4 Cedar Lake Man. Can.
230 B3 Cedar Rapids IA U.S.A.
241 L3 Cedar Ridge AZ U.S.A.
226 D3 Cedar River MI U.S.A.
235 D3 Cedar Run NJ U.S.A.
227 F4 Cedar Springs Ont. Can.
226 E4 Cedar Springs MI U.S.A.
231 C5 Cedartown GA U.S.A.
215 G4 Cedarville S. Africa
226 C4 Cedarville IL U.S.A.
227 E3 Cedarville MI U.S.A.
232 B5 Cedarville OH U.S.A.
190 F2 Cedegolo Italy
182 B1 Cedeira Spain
182 B1 Cedeira hill Spain
183 F5 Cedena r. Spain
182 C5 Cedillo Spain
183 G4 Cedillo del Condado Spain
244 D2 Cedral Mex.
186 C4 Cedrillas Spain
192 B4 Cedrino r. Sardegna Italy
254 F3 Cedro Brazil
216 □1c Cedros Faial Azores
244 D1 Cedros Mex.
242 B2 Cedros, Isla i. Mex.
174 G1 Cedry Wielkie Pol.
82 C3 Ceduna S.A. Austr.
174 C3 Cedynia Pol.
182 A2 Cée Spain
210 E3 Ceelbuur Somalia
210 E2 Ceerigaabo Somalia
177 K5 Cefa Romania
194 D4 Cefalù Sicilia Italy
Cefn Bychan Caerphilly, Wales U.K. see Newbridge
150 D2 Cefn-mawr Wrexham, Wales U.K.
183 F3 Cega r. Spain
191 H3 Ceggia Italy
177 I4 Cegléd Hungary
177 I4 Ceglédbercel Hungary
195 G2 Ceglie Messapica Italy
175 J3 Cegłów Pol.
196 E5 Čegrane Macedonia
177 L4 Cehal Romania
185 I2 Cehegín Spain
108 C3 Ceheng Guizhou China
196 D4 Čehotina r. Yugo.
197 F2 Cehu Silvaniei Romania
247 □1 Ceiba Puerto Rico
177 L5 Ceica Romania
161 B5 Ceilhes-et-Rocozels France
Ceinewydd Ceredigion, Wales U.K. see New Quay
183 E2 Ceinos de Campos Spain
157 G4 Ceintrey France
182 B4 Ceira Port.
182 B4 Ceira r. Port.
176 F3 Čejč Czech Rep.
177 K3 Cejkov Slovakia
179 H2 Čejkovice Czech Rep.
174 G2 Cekcyn Pol.
126 D2 Çekerek Turkey
174 G4 Ceków-Kolonia Pol.
186 B4 Celadas Spain
94 C1 Celah, Gunung mt. Malaysia
176 D1 Čelákovice Czech Rep.
193 F2 Celano Italy
182 C2 Celanova Spain
244 D3 Celaya Mex.
147 E3 Celbridge Rep. of Ireland
163 D4 Célé r. France
Celebes i. Indon. see Sulawesi
93 B2 Celebes Sea Indon./Phil.
129 C4 Çelebibağı Turkey
182 B3 Celeiros Port.
250 B6 Celendín Peru
193 G3 Celenza Valfortore Italy
195 F3 Celico Italy
236 G3 Celina OH U.S.A.
231 C4 Celina TN U.S.A.
188 E2 Celje Slovenia
186 B4 Cella Spain
176 G4 Celldömölk Hungary
168 F3 Celle Ger.
192 D2 Cellere Italy
165 C4 Celles Belgium
163 D6 Celles France
162 B2 Celles-sur-Belle France
160 B3 Celles-sur-Durolle France
156 E4 Celles-sur-Ource France
159 H4 Cellettes France
191 H2 Cellina r. Italy
193 F2 Cellino Attanasio Italy
195 G2 Cellino San Marco Italy
193 F3 Cellole Italy
193 H3 Celone r. Italy
182 C4 Celorico da Beira Port.
182 C3 Celorico de Basto Port.
Celovec Austria see Klagenfurt
186 F2 Celrà Spain
145 D6 Celtic Sea Rep. of Ireland/U.K.
264 I2 Celtic Shelf sea feature N. Atlantic Ocean
199 G3 Çeltikçi Turkey
199 F1 Çeltikçi Turkey
129 C4 Çem r. Turkey
95 F2 Cemaru, Gunung mt. Indon.
191 G2 Cembra Italy
126 D2 Cemilbey Turkey
126 E3 Çemişgezek Turkey
150 D2 Cemmaes Powys, Wales U.K.
179 F4 Čemšeniška planina mt. Slovenia
163 D4 Cénac-et-St-Julien France
196 E2 Cenad Romania
191 G2 Cencenighe Agordino Italy
161 C4 Cendras France
162 C4 Cendrieux France
196 E3 Cenei Romania
191 G3 Ceneselli Italy
190 D4 Cengio Italy
183 H2 Cenicero Spain
183 F4 Ceniclentos Spain
185 I1 Cenizate Spain
190 F4 Ceno r. Italy
163 B4 Cenon France
196 E3 Čenta Vojvodina, Srbija Yugo.
190 C4 Centallo Italy
Centane S. Africa see Kentani
81 B6 Centaur Peak South I. N.Z.
Centellas Spain see Centelles
186 F3 Centelles Spain
260 C6 Centenario Arg.
256 B5 Centenário do Sul Brazil
213 F3 Centenary Zimbabwe
236 C2 Center ND U.S.A.
236 D3 Center NE U.S.A.
237 E6 Center TX U.S.A.
232 B4 Centerburg OH U.S.A.
235 E2 Centereach NY U.S.A.
235 F2 Center Moriches NY U.S.A.
233 □H3 Center Ossipee NH U.S.A.
231 C5 Center Point AL U.S.A.
235 E2 Centerport NY U.S.A.
234 C2 Center Square PA U.S.A.
234 C2 Center Valley PA U.S.A.
231 C5 Centerville AL U.S.A.
236 E3 Centerville IA U.S.A.
237 F4 Centerville MO U.S.A.
232 B5 Centerville OH U.S.A.
232 D4 Centerville PA U.S.A.
232 D4 Centerville PA U.S.A.
231 C5 Centerville TN U.S.A.
237 E6 Centerville TX U.S.A.
232 C5 Centerville WV U.S.A.
191 G4 Cento Italy
193 H4 Centola Italy
Centrafricaine, République country Africa see Central African Republic
212 E4 Central admin. dist. Botswana
254 E4 Central Brazil
206 E5 Central admin. reg. Ghana
210 C5 Central prov. Kenya
211 B8 Central admin. reg. Malawi
239 E5 Central NM U.S.A.
209 F8 Central prov. Zambia
252 D4 Central, Cordillera mts Bol.
250 B4 Central, Cordillera mts Col.
246 E3 Central, Cordillera mts Dom. Rep.
242 □J7 Central, Cordillera mts Panama

Column 1

252 A2 Central, Cordillera mts Peru
92 B2 Central, Cordillera mts Phil.
247 □¹ Central, Cordillera mts Puerto Rico
Central African Empire country Africa see Central African Republic
208 D3 Central African Republic country Africa
123 F4 Central Brahui Range mts Pak.
223 J5 Central Butte Sask. Can.
236 F3 Central City IA U.S.A.
236 D3 Central City NE U.S.A.
232 D4 Central City PA U.S.A.
257 G3 Central de Minas Brazil
233 H4 Central Falls RI U.S.A.
236 F4 Centralia IL U.S.A.
238 B2 Centralia WA U.S.A.
235 E2 Central Islip NY U.S.A.
123 F5 Central Makran Range mts Pak.
84 C4 Central Mount Stuart hill N.T. Austr.
84 B4 Central Mount Wedge N.T. Austr.
266 G5 Central Pacific Basin sea feature Pacific Ocean
Central Provinces state India see Madhya Pradesh
215 G3 Central Range mts Lesotho
91 J7 Central Range mts P.N.G.
Central Russian Upland hills Rus. Fed. see Sredne-Russkaya Vozvyshennost'
Central Siberian Plateau Rus. Fed. see Sredne-Sibirskoye Ploskogor'ye
233 E3 Central Square N.Y. U.S.A.
235 D1 Central Valley NY U.S.A.
207 H5 Central Village CT U.S.A.
241 J4 Centre prov. Cameroon
162 D1 Centre admin. reg. France
231 C5 Centre AL U.S.A.
234 B3 Centreville MD U.S.A.
226 E5 Centreville MI U.S.A.
232 E5 Centreville VA U.S.A.
192 B2 Centuri Corse France
215 G1 Centurion S. Africa
194 D5 Centuripe Sicilia Italy
231 C6 Century FL U.S.A.
109 D4 Cenxi Guangxi China
Ceos i. Greece see Kea
146 B3 Ceos Western Isles, Scotland U.K.
163 D4 Céou r. France
193 G2 Cepagatti Italy
Cephaloedium Sicilia Italy see Cefalù
Cephalonia i. Greece see Kefallonia
188 G3 Čepin Croatia
182 C4 Cepões Port.
241 J4 Cepoy France
194 D1 Ceppaloni Italy
193 F3 Ceprano Italy
95 E4 Cepu Jawa Tengah Indon.
196 D3 Cer hills Yugo.
Ceram i. Maluku Indon. see Seram
194 D3 Cerami Sicilia Italy
194 D5 Cerami r. Sicilia Italy
Ceram Sea Indon. see Seram Sea
190 D3 Cerano Italy
175 K3 Cerano Pol.
159 G4 Cérans-Foulletourte France
195 E4 Cerasi Italy
193 H4 Ceraso Italy
177 L6 Cerbǎl Romania
241 J4 Cerbère France
163 F6 Cerbère France
186 G2 Cerbère, Cap c. France/Spain
Cerbol r. Spain see Servol
184 B1 Cercal Lisboa Port.
184 B3 Cercal Setúbal Port.
184 B3 Cercal hill Port.
176 D2 Cerčany Czech Rep.
183 F4 Cercedilla Spain
182 B2 Cercedo Spain
193 G3 Cercemaggiore Italy
193 F2 Cerchio Italy
176 B2 Cerchov mt. Czech Rep.
160 B2 Cercy-la-Tour France
194 C5 Cerda Sicilia Italy
186 F3 Cerdanyola del Vallès Spain
182 C2 Cerdeira Port.
159 I4 Cerdon France
163 D4 Cère r. France
191 G3 Cerea Italy
223 I5 Cereal Alta Can.
177 I3 Cered Hungary
150 D2 Ceredigion admin. div. Wales U.K.
191 G3 Ceregnano Italy
174 F3 Cerekwica Pol.
158 E3 Cérences France
195 F3 Cerenzia Italy
261 G1 Ceres Arg.
254 C5 Ceres Brazil
190 C3 Ceres Italy
214 B5 Ceres S. Africa
240 G3 Ceres C.A.R.
190 C3 Ceresole Reale Italy
191 G3 Ceresone r. Italy
161 D5 Céreste France
163 E6 Céret France
250 C2 Cereté Col.
183 G3 Cerezo de Abajo Spain
183 G3 Cerezo de Arriba Spain
183 G2 Cerezo de Riotirón Spain
165 D4 Cerfontaine Belgium
177 K2 Čergov mts Slovakia
156 C3 Cergy France
171 G5 Cerhenice Czech Rep.
190 D4 Ceriale Italy
190 C3 Ceriana Italy
193 H3 Cerignola Italy
Cerigo i. Greece see Kythira
126 D3 Çerikli Turkey
160 A2 Cérilly France
156 D4 Cerisiers France
159 F2 Cerisy-la-Forêt France
158 E2 Cerisy-la-Salle France
159 F5 Cerizay France
119 J3 Cerkit mt. Slovenia
126 D2 Çerkeş Turkey
199 F1 Çerkezköy Turkey
199 E1 Çerkezmüsellim Turkey
179 F4 Cerklje Slovenia
188 E3 Cerknica Slovenia
188 E3 Cerkno Slovenia
129 C3 Çermə Turkey
197 J2 Cermei Romania
193 F2 Cermignano Italy
126 E3 Çermik Turkey
197 I3 Cerna r. Romania
197 J3 Cerna r. Romania
197 I3 Cerna r. Romania
197 G3 Cerna Romania
182 B5 Cernache do Bonjardim Port.
176 F2 Černá Hora Czech Rep.
176 C2 Černá Hora mt. Czech Rep.
197 H3 Cernavodă Romania
Cernăuți Chernivts'ka Oblast' see Chernivtsi
197 L1 Cernavodă Romania
157 H5 Cerny France
156 E3 Cernay-en-Dormois France
176 C1 Černčice Czech Rep.
183 G2 Cernégula Spain
179 H4 Cernelavci Slovenia
190 B1 Cernier Switz.
177 H2 Černík Slovakia
177 L2 Černín Slovakia
190 E3 Cernobbio Italy
176 E2 Černošín Czech Rep.
176 B2 Černošín Czech Rep.
176 D2 Černovice Czech Rep.
163 C4 Cernon r. France
256 C5 Cerqueira César Brazil
182 D4 Cerralbo Spain
243 F3 Cerralvo Mex.
191 H5 Cerreto d'Esi Italy
193 G3 Cerreto Sannita Italy
150 D1 Cerrigydrudion Conwy, Wales U.K.
196 D1 Cërrik Albania
258 D2 Cerrillos Arg.

Column 2

244 D2 Cerritos Mex.
193 G3 Cerro al Volturno Italy
256 C6 Cerro Azul Brazil
245 F3 Cerro Azul Mex.
252 A3 Cerro Azul Peru
258 C2 Cerro Bonete mt. Arg.
184 E3 Cerro del Hiero Spain
244 C4 Cerro de Ortega Mex.
252 A2 Cerro de Pasco Peru
185 G4 Cerrón mt. Spain
250 D2 Cerrón, Cerro mt. Venez.
260 C6 Cerros Colorados, Embalse resr Arg.
159 F4 Cersay France
193 I4 Cersosimo Italy
191 G5 Certaldo Italy
197 F3 Certeju de Sus Romania
190 E3 Certosa di Pavia Italy
190 C4 Certosa di Pesio Italy
183 C3 Cerva Port.
183 E5 Cervales mt. Spain
87 B6 Cervantes W.A. Austr.
259 B8 Cervantes, Cerro mt. Arg.
193 F3 Cervaro Italy
193 H3 Cervaro r. Italy
193 H4 Cervati, Monte mt. Italy
183 F2 Cervatos de la Cueza Spain
176 F1 Červená Voda Czech Rep.
197 G4 Cervenia Romania
176 G2 Červenka Czech Rep.
186 E3 Cervera Spain
186 D4 Cervera r. Spain
183 I3 Cervera de la Cañada Spain
183 H5 Cervera del Llano Spain
183 I2 Cervera de los Montes Spain
183 I2 Cervera del Río Alhama Spain
183 F2 Cervera de Pisuerga Spain
192 E3 Cerveteri Italy
191 H4 Cervia Italy
193 H4 Cervialto, Monte mt. Italy
191 H3 Cervignano del Friuli Italy
191 G2 Cervina, Punta mt. Italy
193 G3 Cervinara Italy
Cervino mt. Italy/Switz. see Matterhorn
190 C3 Cervo Italy
190 D5 Cervo Italy
182 C1 Cervo r. Italy
190 D3 Cervo Italy
182 C1 Cervo Spain
160 B1 Cervon France
193 I5 Cerzeto Italy
160 C3 Cesana r. France
250 C2 César dept Col.
250 C2 César r. Col.
194 D5 Cesarò Sicilia Italy
178 D5 Cesen, Monte mt. Italy
191 H4 Cesena Italy
191 H4 Cesenatico Italy
140 O4 Cēsis Latvia
138 E3 Cēsis Latvia
176 D1 Česká Kamenice Czech Rep.
176 D1 Česká Lípa Czech Rep.
176 F1 Česká Skalice Czech Rep.
177 I3 České Brezovo Slovakia
176 E2 České Budějovice Czech Rep.
179 F2 České Velenice Austria
176 D2 Českomoravská Vysočina hills Czech Rep.
176 D1 Český Brod Czech Rep.
176 F1 Český Dub Czech Rep.
176 D3 Český Krumlov Czech Rep.
176 B2 Český Les mts Czech Rep./Ger.
177 H2 Český Rudolec Czech Rep.
177 H2 Český Těšín Czech Rep.
241 J4 Cesme r. Croatia
199 J2 Çeşme Turkey
182 E4 Cespedosa Spain
161 A5 Cesse r. France
161 B5 Cessenon-sur-Orb France
160 D3 Cessnoy France
83 G3 Cessnock N.S.W. Austr.
158 E3 Cesson-Sévigné France
163 B4 Cestas France
206 C5 Cestos r. Liberia
132 B1 Cesvaine Latvia
138 F3 Cēsvaine Latvia
177 L4 Cetariu Romania
197 F3 Cetate Romania
Cetatea Albă see Bilhorod-Dnistrovs'kyy
188 F4 Cetina r. Croatia
183 I3 Cetina Spain
196 D4 Cetinje Crna Gora Yugo.
190 F2 Ceto Italy
159 G3 Ceton France
192 D2 Cetona Italy
193 H5 Cetraro Italy
161 D4 Cette-Eygun France
163 D6 Céu France
161 D4 Céüse, Montagne de mt. France
180 D5 Ceuta N. Africa
187 B6 Ceuta Spain
190 D4 Ceva Italy
77 H4 Ceva-i-Ra rf Fiji
191 F2 Cevedale, Monte mt. Italy
161 B5 Cévennes mts France
163 F3 Cevico de la Torre Spain
160 E3 Cevins France
190 C2 Cevio Switz.
129 B3 Cevizli Erzurum Turkey
128 C1 Cevizli Eskişehir Turkey
128 C1 Cevizli Gaziantep Turkey
199 L2 Cevizlik Turkey see Maçka
174 F1 Cewice Pol.
175 K5 Cewków Pol.
126 D3 Çeyhan Turkey
127 F3 Ceyhan r. Turkey
129 F3 Ceylanpınar Turkey
129 F3 Çeyldağ Azer.
Ceylon country Asia see Sri Lanka
129 F3 Ceyranbatan Azer.
161 D5 Ceyreste France
160 D2 Ceyzériat France
162 B3 Cèze r. France
173 G2 Cham r. Ger.
190 D1 Cham Switz.
122 B3 Cham, Kūh-e hill Iran
239 F4 Chama NM U.S.A.
211 B7 Chama Zambia
217 □3a Chamadani mt. Njazidja Comoros
212 B5 Chamais Bay Namibia
160 B3 Chamalières France
161 D4 Chamaloc France
97 C4 Chaman Pak.
97 C4 Chamao, Khao mt. Thai.
173 G2 Chamb r. Ger.
116 D2 Chamba Hima. Prad. India
211 C7 Chamba Tanz.
116 D3 Chambal r. India
129 D3 Chambarak Armenia
161 D3 Chambaran, Plateau de France

Column 3

226 A2 Chaffey WI U.S.A.
250 C4 Chafurray Col.
123 E4 Chagai Hills Afgh./Pak.
114 C3 Chagalamarri Andhra Prad. India
120 F3 Chagan Kzyl-Ordinskaya Oblast' Kazakh.
121 I2 Chagan Vostochnyy Kazakhstan Kazakh.
150 D4 Chagford Devon, England U.K.
122 B4 Chaghā Khūr mt. Iran
123 F3 Chaghcharān Afgh.
123 G1 Chaghla r. Kazakh.
160 C2 Chagny France
139 J2 Chagoda Rus. Fed.
139 J2 Chagoda r. Rus. Fed.
139 K2 Chagodoshcha r. Rus. Fed.
265 I5 Chagos Archipelago is B.I.O.T.
265 I5 Chagos-Laccadive Ridge sea feature Indian Ocean
265 I5 Chagos Trench sea feature Indian Ocean
120 B1 Chagra r. Rus. Fed.
Chagrayskoye Plato plat. Kazakh. see Shagyray, Plato
247 □7 Chaguanas Trin. and Tob.
250 E2 Chaguaramas Venez.
122 C1 Chagyllyshor, Vpadina depr. Turkm.
136 E5 Chaha r. Ukr.
122 B3 Chahār Maḩāll vä Bakhtīārī prov. Iran
122 C4 Chāh Ḩaqq Iran
123 G2 Chah-i-Ab Afgh.
245 G5 Chahuites Mex.
100 B4 Chai r. China
117 F5 Chaibasa Bihar India
Chaigoubu Hebei China see Huai'an
151 G4 Chailey East Sussex, England U.K.
162 D2 Chaillac France
159 F3 Chailland France
162 A2 Chaillé-les-Marais France
156 D4 Chailley France
160 C3 Chaillon Corse France
97 C4 Chai Nat Thai.
161 B3 Châine du Devès mts France
156 E4 Chaintrix-Bierges France
97 C4 Chai Si r. Thai.
259 B6 Chaitén Chile
94 Chai Wan H.K. China
110 D3 Chaiwopu Xinjiang China
97 B5 Chaiya r. Thai.
96 C2 Chaiyaphum Thai.
261 I2 Chajarí Arg.
117 F4 Chakai Bihar India
123 G4 Chakar r. Pak.
213 F3 Chakari Zimbabwe
211 C6 Chake Chake Tanz.
117 E4 Chakia Uttar Prad. India
123 H4 Chak Jhumra Pak.
117 F5 Chakradharpur Bihar India
117 F5 Chakradharpur Bihar India
129 B3 Ch'ak'vi Georgia
123 H3 Chakwal Pak.
252 B3 Chala Peru
161 E3 Chalabre France
Chaladidi Georgia see Sabazho
162 C3 Chalais France
160 D2 Chalamont France
123 F3 Chalap Dalan mts Afgh.
213 H3 Chalaua Moz.
242 □H6 Chalatenango El Salvador
111 C4 Chalchihuites Mex.
244 C2 Chalchihuites Mex.
245 F4 Chalco Mex.
154 K3 Chalco Mex.
151 F3 Chalgrove Oxfordshire, England U.K.
259 C8 Chalia r. Arg.
175 H3 Chalin Pol.
157 F5 Chalindrey France
109 E3 Chaling Hunan China
116 C5 Chalisgaon Mahar. India
114 C4 Chalisseri Kerala India
160 A2 Chalivoy-Milon France
159 G4 Chalkar, Ozero salt l. Kazakh.
198 C2 Chalkeia France
199 C4 Chalki i. Greece
198 C2 Chalkida Greece
198 C1 Chalkidona Kentriki Makedonia Greece
121 I4 Chalkudysu Kazakh.
114 C3 Chalkude Karnataka India
158 E5 Challans France
252 D4 Challapata Bol.
266 E5 Challenger Deep sea feature N. Pacific Ocean
86 Challenger France
158 C4 Challes-les-Eaux France
238 D3 Challis ID U.S.A.
237 F6 Chalmette LA U.S.A.
160 B2 Chalmoux France
252 C2 Chaloire r. France
117 G5 Chalonnes-sur-Loire France
156 E4 Châlons-en-Champagne France
Châlons-sur-Marne France see Châlons-en-Champagne
160 C2 Chalon-sur-Saône France
129 C2 Chaloyan Georgia
116 C1 Chalt Jammu and Kashmir
137 J4 Chaltyr' Rus. Fed.
215 F5 Chalumna S. Africa
122 B2 Chālūs Iran
122 B2 Chālūs, Rūd-e r. Iran
173 G2 Cham r. Ger.
190 D1 Cham Switz.
122 B3 Chama NM U.S.A.
122 B3 Chang'an Guangxi China see Rong'an
107 F5 Chang'an Shaanxi China
213 G5 Changane r. Moz.
213 G3 Changara Moz.
190 D1 Changbai Jilin China
101 C4 Changbai Shan mts China/N. Korea
101 C4 Changbai Shan mt. China/N. Korea

Column 4

161 D3 Chamechaude mt. France
173 G2 Chamerau Ger.
156 E5 Chamesson France
162 D3 Chameyrat France
260 D2 Chamical Arg.
129 B1 Chamlykskaya Rus. Fed.
210 C3 Ch'amo Hāyk' l. Eth.
190 C3 Chamois Italy
117 H4 Chamoli Uttar Prad. India see Gopeshwar
160 E3 Chamonix-Mont-Blanc France
Chamouchouane r. Que. Can. see Ashuapmushuan
160 E3 Chamouse, Montagne de mt. France
160 E3 Chamoux-sur-Gelon France
117 E5 Champa Madh. Prad. India
162 E3 Champagnac France
162 D3 Champagnac-de-Belair France
161 B3 Champagnac-le-Vieux France
222 B2 Champagne Y.T. Can.
159 G3 Champagne France
156 E4 Champagne-Ardenne admin. reg. France
215 G3 Champagne Castle mt. S. Africa
160 D3 Champagne-en-Valromey France
162 C3 Champagne-Mouton France
156 C3 Champagne-sur-Oise France
156 C4 Champagne-sur-Seine France
157 G5 Champagney France
160 D2 Champagnole France
86 E2 Champagny Islands W.A. Austr.
230 B3 Champaign IL U.S.A.
149 F2 Champany Falkirk, Scotland U.K.
260 C2 Champaqui, Cerro mt. Arg.
252 A2 Champara mt. Peru
97 D4 Champasak Laos
156 D4 Champaubert France
162 C3 Champcevinel France
225 J4 Champdeniers-St-Denis France
160 C1 Champ d'Oiseau France
145 H6 Champ du Feu mt. France
226 C2 Channing MI U.S.A.
156 E3 Champenoux France
157 G4 Champéry Switz.
97 C4 Champex Switz.
180 B2 Champey France
160 D2 Champforgeuil France
159 F3 Champgenéteux France
117 H5 Champhai Mizoram India
163 D3 Champier France
159 F4 Champigné France
160 B2 Champigneulles France
156 C3 Champignol-lez-Mondeville France
156 D4 Champigny France
222 H5 Champion Alta Can.
226 D2 Champion MI U.S.A.
233 G3 Champlain NY U.S.A.
224 F4 Champlain, Lake Can./U.S.A.
160 B1 Champlemy France
160 D1 Champlitte France
160 C2 Champoléon France
160 D3 Champoléon France
156 B3 Champoly France
245 H5 Champotón Mex.
156 B3 Champrond-en-Gâtine France
159 F3 Champsecret France
161 A3 Champs-sur-Tarentaine-Marchal France
156 C3 Champs-sur-Yonne France
161 D3 Champ-sur-Drac France
161 D4 Champtercier France
158 E4 Champtoceaux France
114 C4 Champua Orissa India
161 D3 Chamrajnagar Karnataka India
161 D3 Chamrousse France
184 B1 Chamusca Port.
135 I5 Chamzinka Rus. Fed.
97 C6 Chana Thai.
161 B4 Chana Thai.
Chanak Turkey see Çanakkale
243 G5 Chanal Mex.
260 C6 Chañar Arg.
258 C2 Chañaral Chile
122 D2 Chandak Iran
261 F3 Chañar Ladeado Arg.
251 C3 Chanaro, Cerro mt. Venez.
161 C3 Chanas France
136 C1 Chancha r. Belarus
252 C2 Chancay Peru
162 C3 Chanceaux France
159 G4 Chanceaux-sur-Choiselle France
162 C3 Chancelade France
182 B5 Chancelaria Port.
247 □² Chances Peak vol. Montserrat
260 A4 Chanco Chile
250 C3 Chanco Mahar. India see
220 D3 Chandalar r. AK U.S.A.
116 D3 Chandausi Uttar Prad. India
116 F5 Chandbali Orissa India
116 C4 Chanderi Madh. Prad. India
117 F5 Chandil Jhar India
225 H3 Chandler Que. Can.
241 L5 Chandler AZ U.S.A.
237 D5 Chandler OK U.S.A.
252 C2 Chandless r. Brazil
117 I5 Chandpur Bangl.
116 D3 Chandpur Uttar Prad. India
114 C2 Chandrapur Mahar. India
131 T3 Chandro Rus. Fed.
131 U3 Chandur Mahar. India
116 C5 Chandur India
114 C2 Chandvad Mahar. India
97 C4 Chanf Iran
97 C4 Chang, Ko i. Thai.

Column 5

101 C5 Changnyŏn N. Korea
116 D3 Ch'ang-pai Shan mts China/N. Korea see Changbai Shan
107 H3 Changping Beijing China
109 F2 Changpu Guizhou China
107 I4 Changqing Shandong China
108 C3 Changshu Jiangsu China
108 C2 Changshou Chongqing China
108 F3 Changshuijie Hunan China
108 F3 Changshui Jiangsu China
109 C6 Changsō S. Korea
109 F3 Changtai Fujian China
84 B2 Changtang Hunan China see Changde
109 F3 Changting Fujian China
100 D3 Changting Heilong. China
100 C4 Changtu Liaoning China
242 □J7 Changuinola Panama
101 D6 Ch'angwŏn S. Korea
107 E5 Changwu Shaanxi China
109 F2 Changxing China
107 G2 Changyang China
109 D2 Changyang Hubei China
107 H4 Changyi China
101 C5 Changyǒn N. Korea
Changyuan Chongqing China see Rongchang
162 C3 Changyuan Henan China
156 C3 Changzhi Shanxi China
107 G5 Changzhi Shanxi China
108 C3 Changzhou Jiangsu China
86 E2 Chañi, Nevado de mt. Arg.
198 D4 Chania Kriti Greece
162 B3 Chaniers France
198 C4 Chanion, Kolpos b. Kriti Greece
106 E5 Chankou Gansu China
252 A2 Champara mt. Peru
114 C3 Channapatna Karnataka India
158 D2 Channel Islands English Chan.
240 H5 Channel Islands U.S.A.
225 J4 Channel-Port-aux-Basques Nfld. Can.
246 □² Channel Rock i. Bahamas
145 H6 Channel Tunnel France/U.K.
226 C2 Channing MI U.S.A.
226 C2 Channing TX U.S.A.
237 C5 Channing TX U.S.A.
182 D2 Chantada Spain
161 F4 Chantemerle France
160 D3 Chantepie France
97 C4 Chanthaburi Thai.
156 C3 Chantilly France
162 A2 Chantonnay France
157 G4 Champigneulles France
160 E1 Chantraines France
159 F3 Chanu France
237 E4 Chanute KS U.S.A.
130 I4 Chany, Ozero salt l. Rus. Fed.
184 C3 Chanza r. Port./Spain
252 C2 Chao Peru
107 H4 Chaobai Xinhe r. China
109 F2 Chaohu Anhui China
109 F2 Chao Hu l. China
97 B3 Chao Phraya r. Thai.
107 I1 Chaor He r. China
107 I2 Chaor r. China
204 D2 Chaouèn Morocco
180 D5 Chaouèn prov. Morocco
156 E4 Chaource France
109 F4 Chaoyang Guangdong China see Jiayin
107 H4 Chaoyang Jilin China see Huinan
156 C3 Champs-sur-Yonne France
161 D3 Champ-sur-Drac France
222 H5 Champion Alta Can.
237 E4 Chanute KS U.S.A.
130 I4 Chany, Ozero salt l. Rus. Fed.
184 C3 Chanza r. Port./Spain
252 C2 Chao Peru
107 H4 Chaobai Xinhe r. China
109 F2 Chaohu Anhui China
253 G3 Chapada dos Guimarães Brazil
256 C5 Chapadão do Sul Brazil
254 E2 Chapadinha Brazil
244 C5 Chapala Mex.
244 C5 Chapala, Laguna de l. Mex.
260 C5 Chapalcó, Valle de val. Arg.
244 B3 Chapalilla Mex.
252 D3 Chapare r. Bol.
161 D3 Chapareillan France
250 C4 Chaparral Col.
137 H3 Chapayeve Ukr.
120 B2 Chapayevka r. Rus. Fed.
121 F1 Chapayevka Rus. Fed.
160 A3 Chapdes-Beaufort France
255 B8 Chapecó Brazil
255 B8 Chapecó r. Brazil
149 H4 Chapel-en-le-Frith Derbyshire, England U.K.
149 J4 Chapelfell Top hill England U.K.
231 E5 Chapel Hill NC U.S.A.
149 J4 Chapel-le-Dale England U.K.
247 □² Chapelton Jamaica
147 E5 Chapeltown Rep. of Ireland
149 H4 Chapeltown South Yorkshire, England U.K.
183 F4 Chapinería Spain
224 D4 Chapleau Ont. Can.
222 J5 Chaplin Sask. Can.
137 I5 Chaplynka Ukr.
137 G2 Chaplynivka Ukr.
137 K2 Chaplygin Rus. Fed.
137 G4 Chaplynka Ukr.
222 G5 Chapman, Mount B.C. Can.
232 D6 Chapmanville WV U.S.A.
232 E5 Chapmanville PA U.S.A.
255 E1 Chapada NY U.S.A.

Column 6

116 D4 Charkhari Uttar Prad. India
116 D3 Charkhi Dadri Haryana India
110 C3 Charkhlik Xinjiang China see Ruoqiang
151 F3 Charlbury Oxfordshire, England U.K.
215 G2 Charl Cilliers S. Africa
147 E2 Charlemont Northern Ireland U.K.
165 D4 Charleroi Belgium
225 G4 Charlesbourg Que. Can.
226 A4 Charles City IA U.S.A.
232 E6 Charles City VA U.S.A.
156 C3 Charles de Gaulle airport France
Charles Island Ecuador see Santa María, Isla
84 B2 Charles Point N.T. Austr.
233 E5 Charleston South I. N.Z.
237 E4 Charleston AR U.S.A.
237 F5 Charleston IL U.S.A.
226 B5 Charleston IA U.S.A.
236 F4 Charleston MO U.S.A.
237 F4 Charleston MS U.S.A.
235 C5 Charleston SC U.S.A.
241 J3 Charleston Peak NV U.S.A.
147 C3 Charlestown Rep. of Ireland
215 G2 Charlestown S. Africa
247 □² Charlestown St Kitts and Nevis
233 G3 Charlestown NH U.S.A.
233 H4 Charlestown RI U.S.A.
232 E5 Charles Town WV U.S.A.
157 G4 Charlestown of Aberlour Moray, Scotland U.K.
85 F5 Charleville Qld Austr.
147 C4 Charleville Rep. of Ireland see Rathluirc
156 E3 Charleville-Mézières France
231 E3 Charlevoix MI U.S.A.
222 F3 Charlie Lake B.C. Can.
160 C2 Charlieu France
226 E4 Charlotte MI U.S.A.
231 D5 Charlotte NC U.S.A.
247 F3 Charlotte Amalie Virgin Is (U.S.A.)
232 D6 Charlotte Court House VA U.S.A.
142 E2 Charlottenberg Sweden
232 D5 Charlottesville VA U.S.A.
225 I4 Charlottetown P.E.I. Can.
82 B4 Charlton Island i. Austr.
83 B7 Charlton Vic. Austr.
151 F5 Charlton Hampshire, England U.K.
150 E3 Charlton Wiltshire, England U.K.
150 E3 Charlton Kings Gloucestershire, England U.K.
151 G3 Charlwood Surrey, England U.K.
237 E4 Charly France
162 C3 Charmé France
157 G4 Charmes-sur-Rhône France
160 C2 Charmey Switz.
150 E4 Charminster Dorset, England U.K.
157 G4 Charmois-l'Orgueilleux France
150 E4 Charmouth Dorset, England U.K.
150 E4 Charmouth Dorset, England U.K.
160 C1 Charmes France
162 D2 Charmeil France
184 D2 Charneca France
139 H4 Charnitsa r. Belarus
86 E3 Charnley r. W.A. Austr.
156 D5 Charny France
157 F3 Charny-sur-Meuse France
156 D5 Charolles France
215 I5 Charost France
160 E1 Charquemont France
190 C2 Charrat Switz.
156 E5 Charrey-sur-Seine France
162 B2 Charroux France
156 B3 Chars France
123 G3 Charsadda Pak.
123 F2 Charshanga Turkm.
Charsk Kazakh. see Shar
175 H5 Charsterrs Pol.
232 B5 Charters KY U.S.A.
85 F4 Charters Towers Qld Austr.
156 C3 Chartres France
160 D3 Chartreuse, Massif de la France
156 C3 Chartreskoye Vodokhranilishche resr Kazakh./Uzbek.
190 C3 Charvensod Italy
160 E2 Charvonnex France
121 H3 Charyn r. Kazakh.
121 J2 Charyshskoye Rus. Fed.
174 F2 Charzykowy Pol.
175 F5 Chas India
180 F2 Chās mt. Port.
261 H4 Chascomús Arg.
222 G5 Chase B.C. Can.
234 B1 Chase MD U.S.A.
226 E4 Chase MI U.S.A.
232 D6 Chase City VA U.S.A.
138 G4 Chashniki Belarus
116 Q2 Chashma Barrage Pak.
127 H3 Chasiv Yar Ukr.
116 C1 Chaska MN U.S.A.
81 B7 Chaslands Mistake c. South I. N.Z.
101 C4 Chasŏng N. Korea
159 G5 Chasseneuil-du-Poitou France
162 C3 Chasseneuil-sur-Bonnieure France
156 E3 Chassenon France
161 B4 Chasseradès France
190 C3 Chasserand mt. Switz.
161 C4 Chasse-sur-Rhône France
162 C3 Chassezac r. France
157 F5 Chassigny-Aisey France
162 C3 Chassillé France
250 E2 Chassiron, Pointe de pt France
122 C2 Chāstab, Kūh-e mts Iran
165 D4 Chastre Belgium
116 D3 Chastyye Rus. Fed.
122 C2 Chāt Iran
160 D3 Chatang Xizang China see Zhanang
244 D2 Charcas Mex.
247 □³ Chateaubelair St Vincent
162 C2 Château-Arnoux France
162 C2 Chateaubernard France
158 D4 Châteaubourg France
158 E4 Châteaubriant France
162 D3 Château-Chinon France
158 E3 Château-d'Oex Switz.
158 E3 Château-du-Loir France
156 C3 Châteaudun France
233 G2 Chateaugay NY U.S.A.
159 F4 Château-Gontier France
156 B3 Châteaulandon France
160 C3 Château-la-Vallière France
160 C3 Châteaulin France
160 C2 Châteauneuf France
161 C5 Châteauneuf-de-Gadagne France
162 B3 Châteauneuf-de-Galaure France
156 C3 Châteauneuf-de-Randon France
158 D3 Châteauneuf-d'Ille-et-Vilaine France
156 B3 Châteauneuf-en-Thymerais France
162 D3 Châteauneuf-la-Forêt France
162 C3 Châteauneuf-la-Forêt France
161 D5 Châteauneuf-les-Martigues France

Column 7

162 B3 Châteauneuf-sur-Charente France
159 I5 Châteauneuf-sur-Cher France
156 C5 Châteauneuf-sur-Loire France
159 F4 Châteauneuf-sur-Sarthe France
160 B1 Châteauneuf-Val-de-Bargis France
162 D2 Châteauponsac France
161 D4 Châteauredon France
161 E4 Châteaurenard France
156 C5 Châteaurenard France
160 D2 Châteaurenard France
169 G4 Château-Renault France
161 E4 Châteauroux France
157 G4 Château-Salins France
157 E4 Château-Thierry France
161 B4 Châteauvillain France
222 G3 Chateh r. Alta Can.
160 E2 Châtel France
162 A2 Châtelaillon-Plage France
183 D8 Châtelaudren France
165 D4 Châtelet Belgium
160 C1 Châtel-Censoir France
165 D4 Châtelet Belgium
162 D2 Châtel-Gérard France
165 D4 Châtel-Montagne France
162 D2 Châtelperron France
160 B2 Châtel-St-Denis Switz.
157 F4 Châtel-sur-Moselle France
162 E2 Châtelus-Malvaleix France
157 F4 Châtenois France
156 C2 Châtenois-les-Forges France
160 C2 Châtenoy-le-Royal France
226 A4 Chatfield MN U.S.A.
232 B4 Chatfield OH U.S.A.
224 D5 Chatham N.B. Can.
224 D5 Chatham Ont. Can.
151 H3 Chatham Medway, England U.K.
222 C3 Chatham AK U.S.A.
233 I4 Chatham MA U.S.A.
235 D2 Chatham NJ U.S.A.
233 G3 Chatham NY U.S.A.
234 C3 Chatham PA U.S.A.
232 D6 Chatham VA U.S.A.
259 B8 Chatham, Isla i. Chile
Chatham Island i. Samoa see Savai'i
80 □ Chatham Islands N.Z.
266 H8 Chatham Rise sea feature S. Pacific Ocean
222 C3 Chatham Strait AK U.S.A.
165 D5 Châtillon Belgium
190 C3 Châtillon Belgium
161 D5 Châtillon-Coligny France
160 B2 Châtillon-en-Bazois France
160 D3 Châtillon-en-Diois France
160 D2 Châtillon-en-Michaille France
161 D3 Châtillon-la-Palud France
160 C2 Châtillon-sur-Chalaronne France
159 F3 Châtillon-sur-Colmont France
162 D2 Châtillon-sur-Indre France
160 A1 Châtillon-sur-Loire France
160 C2 Châtillon-sur-Marne France
159 F3 Châtillon-sur-Seine France
159 F5 Châtillon-sur-Thouet France
121 G4 Chatkal r. Kyrg.
121 G4 Chatkal mts Kyrg.
237 F6 Chatom AL U.S.A.
117 F4 Chatra Bihar India
84 E4 Chatsworth India see Sanvordem
227 H5 Chatsworth Ont. Can.
190 C2 Chatsworth IL U.S.A.
226 C3 Chatsworth IL U.S.A.
231 D5 Chatsworth GA U.S.A.
161 D3 Chatta France
151 H2 Chatteris Cambridgeshire, England U.K.
81 B6 Chatto Creek South I. N.Z.
149 H2 Chatton Northumberland, England U.K.
96 C4 Chatturat Thai.
161 D4 Chatuzange-le-Goubet France
234 C3 Chatwood PA U.S.A.
113 Chatyrkël', Ozero l. Kyrg. see Chatyr-Köl
121 H2 Chauchina Spain
185 I4 Chaudeny France
162 B4 Chaudes-Aigues France
165 D4 Chaudfontaine Belgium
97 D5 Châu Ðôc Vietnam
160 C2 Chaudron-en-Mauges France
160 C2 Chauffailles France
161 E4 Chauffayer France
161 D3 Chauhtan Rajasthan India
96 A2 Chauk Myanmar
116 E4 Chauk r. India
161 D3 Chaukhamba India see Badrinath Peaks
156 C3 Chaulnes France
160 D2 Chaumergy France
157 F4 Chaumont-en-Vexin France
157 F5 Chaumont-sur-Aire France
159 H4 Chaumont-Porcien France
157 F4 Chaumont-sur-Loire France
159 I4 Chaumont-sur-Loire France
162 A2 Chauny France
97 C5 Châu Phu Vietnam see Châu Ðôc
116 D5 Chaurai Madh. Prad. India
161 B2 Chauray France
160 A2 Chaussin France
122 C2 Chausu-yama mt. Japan
104 □3 Chausu-yama mt. Japan
121 H4 Chausy Belarus see Chavusy
138 H5 Chautauqua NY U.S.A.
233 I4 Chautay Kyrg.
162 C3 Chauvay Kyrg.
233 H4 Chauvigny France
162 C2 Chaux, Forêt de la France
158 E5 Chavagnes-en-Paillers France
114 D4 Chavakachcheri Sri Lanka
254 C2 Chaval Brazil
162 C3 Chavanay France
161 D3 Chavanges France
162 C3 Chavanac-Lafayette France
160 D3 Chavanoz France
123 A3 Chavār Iran
160 D3 Chavári Dytiki Ellas Greece see Kato Achaïa
197 G4 Chavari Greece
251 I5 Chaves Brazil
182 C3 Chaves Port.
123 H5 Chavusy Belarus
123 H5 Chawal r. Pak.
232 D5 Chazelles France
139 K2 Chayevo Rus. Fed.
134 K4 Chaykovskiy Rus. Fed.
163 C2 Chazay-d'Azergues France
162 C3 Chazelles France
162 C3 Chazelles-sur-Lyon France
233 G2 Chazy NY U.S.A.
149 G4 Cheadle Greater Manchester, England U.K.
151 F2 Cheadle Staffordshire, England U.K.
232 D5 Cheat r. WV U.S.A.
176 B1 Cheb Czech Rep.
226 D5 Chebanse IL U.S.A.
135 J5 Cheboksary Rus. Fed.
231 E3 Cheboygan MI U.S.A.
205 H5 Chebba Tunisia
134 H4 Chebsara Rus. Fed.
183 I4 Checa Spain
199 L2 Chechel'nyk Ukr.
129 E2 Chechersk Belarus
129 E2 Checheno-Ingushskaya A.S.S.R. aut. rep. Rus. Fed. see Chechenskaya Respublika
129 F2 Chechen', Ostrov i. Rus. Fed.
109 □ Chech'ŏn Taiwan
129 E2 Chechenskaya Respublika aut. rep. Rus. Fed.

Column 1

Chechnya *aut. rep.* Rus. Fed.
see Chechenskaya Respublika
101 D5 Chech'ŏn S. Korea
136 C3 Chechva *r.* Ukr.
175 I5 Chęciny Pol.
237 E5 Checotah *OK* U.S.A.
156 C5 Checy France
151 H2 Chedburgh *Suffolk,*
England U.K.
150 E3 Cheddar *Somerset,*
England U.K.
149 G4 Cheddleton *Staffordshire,*
England U.K.
96 A3 Cheduba Island Myanmar
157 E4 Chée *r.* France
147 E4 Cheekpoint *Rep. of Ireland*
232 D3 Cheektowaga *NY* U.S.A.
224 D3 Cheepash *r.* Ont. Can.
85 F5 Cheepie *Qld Austr.*
263 K2 Cheetham, Cape Antarctica
162 B2 Chef-Boutonne France
Chefoo *Shandong China see*
Yantai
220 B3 Chefornak *AK* U.S.A.
100 E2 Chegdomyn Rus. Fed.
Chegem 1 Rus. Fed.
see Chegem Pervyy
129 C2 Chegem *r.* Rus. Fed.
129 C2 Chegem Pervyy Rus. Fed.
204 D4 Chegga Maur.
213 F3 Chegutu Zimbabwe
238 B2 Chehalis *WA* U.S.A.
238 B2 Chehalis *r.* WA U.S.A.
127 G4 Chehariz *tourist site* Iraq
122 A3 Chehel Chashmeh, Küh-e
hill Iran
122 E4 Chehel Dokhtarän, Küh-e
mt. Iran
19B B1 Cheimaditis, Limni *l.* Greece
161 E5 Cheiron, Cime du *mt.* France
101 C6 Cheju S. Korea
101 C6 Cheju-do *i.* S. Korea
101 C6 Cheju-haehyŏp *sea chan.*
S. Korea
139 K4 Chekalin Rus. Fed.
134 K5 Chekan Rus. Fed.
Chek Chue *H.K. China see*
Stanley
139 K4 Chekhov *Moskovskaya Oblast'*
Rus. Fed.
100 G3 Chekhov *Sakhalin* Rus. Fed.
Chekiang *prov. China see*
Zhejiang
109 □ Chek Lap Kok *i.* H.K. China
134 H4 Chekshino Rus. Fed.
209 B9 Chela, Serra da *mts* Angola
63 C5 Chélan France
238 B2 Chelan *WA* U.S.A.
238 B1 Chelan, Lake *WA* U.S.A.
137 J4 Chelbas *r.* Rus. Fed.
137 J5 Chelbasskaya Rus. Fed.
184 A2 Cheleiros *r.* Port.
184 A2 Cheleiros *r.* Port.
122 C2 Cheleken Turkm.
184 C2 Cheles Spain
120 D3 Chelkar Kazakh.
187 C5 Chella Spain
175 L4 Chełm Pol.
175 H5 Chełmek Pol.
151 H3 Chelmer *r.* England U.K.
175 I6 Chełmiec Pol.
174 G2 Chełmno Pol.
174 G3 Chełmno Pol.
151 H3 Chelmondiston *Essex,*
England U.K.
233 H3 Chelmsford *MA* U.S.A.
174 G2 Chełmża Pol.
227 E4 Chelsea *MI* U.S.A.
233 G3 Chelsea *VT* U.S.A.
80 E4 Chelsea *North I.* N.Z.
150 E3 Cheltenham *Gloucestershire,*
England U.K.
234 C2 Cheltenham *PA* U.S.A.
187 C5 Chelva Spain
130 H4 Chelyabinsk Rus. Fed.
120 E1 Chelyabinskaya Oblast'
admin. div. Rus. Fed.
Chelyabinsk Oblast
admin. div. Rus. Fed. *see*
Chelyabinskaya Oblast'
232 C5 Chelyan *WV* U.S.A.
131 L2 Chelyuskin, Mys *c.* Rus. Fed.
204 C2 Chemaïa Morocco
243 I4 Chemax Mex.
159 F4 Chemazé France
213 G3 Chembe Zambia
209 F7 Chembe Zambia
136 D3 Chemerivtsi Ukr.
159 H4 Chéméry France
157 E3 Chéméry-sur-Bar France
162 B1 Chemillé France
160 D2 Chemin France
159 F4 Chemin-le-Gaudin France
Chemmis Egypt *see* Akhmîm
171 D5 Chemnitz Ger.
171 D5 Chemnitz *admin. reg.*
Sachsen Ger.
Chemulpo S. Korea *see*
Inch'ŏn
238 B3 Chemult *OR* U.S.A.
227 I5 Chemung *r.* NY U.S.A.
116 B3 Chemun *r.* India/Pak.
233 F3 Chenango *r.* NY U.S.A.
233 F3 Chenango Bridge *NY* U.S.A.
160 C2 Chénas France
210 C3 Ch'ench'a Eth.
Chendir *r. Turkm. see* Chandyr
160 D1 Chencecy-Buillon France
162 E2 Chenerailles France
114 D3 Chengalpattu *Tamil Nadu India*
114 C3 Chengam *Tamil Nadu India*
107 G4 Cheng'an *Hebei China*
108 D3 Chengbihe *Hunan China*
107 F5 Chengcheng *Shaanxi China*
Chengchow *Henan China see*
Zhengzhou
107 H3 Chengde *Hebei China*
108 D2 Chengdu *Sichuan China*
108 B3 Chengdu *Yunnan China*
109 F4 Chenggang *Guangdong China*
Chengjiang *Jiangxi China see*
Taihe
108 B3 Chengjiang *Yunnan China*
108 D2 Chengkou *Chongqing China*
108 D5 Chengmai *Hainan China*
Chengqiao *Shanghai China see*
Chongming
Chengshou *Sichuan China see*
Yingshan
Chengtu *Sichuan China see*
Chengdu
107 G5 Chengwu *Shandong China*
108 C1 Chengxian *Gansu China*
Chengxian *Guizhou China see*
Fuquan
Chengxiang *Chongqing China see*
Wuxi
Chengxiang *Jiangxi China see*
Quannan
Chengxiang *Sichuan China see*
Mianning
Chengxiang *Sichuan China see*
Qingshen
Chengyang *Shandong China*
see Juxian
Chengzhong *Guangxi China*
see Ningming
Chengzi *Yunnan China see*
Longchuan
157 G4 Cheniménil France
114 D3 Chennai *Tamil Nadu India*
226 C5 Chennai *Tamil Nadu India*
159 H4 Chenonceaux France
160 D1 Chenôve France
Chenstokhov Pol. *see*
Częstochowa
107 L1 Chentej Nuruu *mts* Mongolia
108 D3 Chenxi *Hunan China*
108 D5 Chenying *Jiangxi China see*
Wanning
109 E3 Chenzhou *Hunan China*
Cheom Ksan *Cambodia see*
Chôâm Khsant
197 G3 Chepelare Bulg.
250 B6 Chepén Peru

Column 2

260 D2 Chepes Arg.
137 I3 Chepil' Ukr.
242 □K7 Chepo Panama
150 E3 Chepstow *Monmouthshire,*
Wales U.K.
134 J4 Cheptsa *r.* Rus. Fed.
156 E4 Chepy France
159 I4 Cher *dept* Centre France
162 C1 Cher *r.* France
187 C5 Chera Spain
162 B3 Chérac France
160 D3 Chéran *r.* France
244 D4 Cherán Mex.
190 C4 Cherasco Italy
158 E4 Cherasse France
231 E5 Cheraw *SC* U.S.A.
158 E2 Cherbourg France
205 F1 Cherchell Alg.
Cherchen *Xinjiang China see*
Qiemo
135 J5 Cherdakly Rus. Fed.
134 L3 Cherdyn' Rus. Fed.
158 E4 Chère *r.* France
177 L4 Cherechiu Romania
129 D2 Cherek *r.* Rus. Fed.
134 K4 Cherekha *r.* Rus. Fed.
135 G6 Cheremisinovo Rus. Fed.
98 H1 Cheremkhovo Rus. Fed.
121 J1 Cheremnoye Rus. Fed.
100 E3 Cheremnyany Rus. Fed.
134 J4 Cheremukhovka Rus. Fed.
192 A4 Cheremule *Sardegna Italy*
130 J4 Cheremushskiy Rus. Fed.
Cherepkovo Moldova *see*
Ciripcău
139 K2 Cherepovets Rus. Fed.
134 I3 Cherepovo Rus. Fed.
205 E2 Chergui, Chott ech *imp. l.* Alg.
205 G2 Chéria Alg.
114 C2 Cherial *Andhra Prad.* India
190 E3 Cherio *r.* Italy
151 F3 Cheriton *Hampshire,*
England U.K.
233 G5 Cheriton *VA* U.S.A.
136 F3 Cherkas'ka Oblast'
admin. div. Ukr.
137 H3 Cherkas'ke Ukr.
137 I3 Cherkas'ke Ukr.
Cherkaskyy Ukr. *see* Cherkasy
Zymohir''ya
Cherkasskaya Oblast'
admin. div. Ukr. *see*
Cherkas'ka Oblast'
Cherkasskoye Ukr. *see* Cherkasy
137 G3 Cherkasy Ukr.
Cherkasy Oblast *admin. div.*
Ukr. *see* Cherkas'ka Oblast'
129 C1 Cherkessk Rus. Fed.
139 L3 Cherkutino Rus. Fed.
114 B3 Cherla *Andhra Prad.* India
121 H1 Cherlak Rus. Fed.
136 D3 Cherlenivka Ukr.
129 D2 Chermen Rus. Fed.
134 L4 Chermoz Rus. Fed.
139 K5 Chern' *r.* Rus. Fed.
139 K5 Chern' *r.* Rus. Fed.
121 G4 Chernak Kazakh.
139 L5 Chernava *Lipetskaya Oblast'*
Rus. Fed.
139 L5 Chernava *Ryazanskaya Oblast'*
Rus. Fed.
134 L1 Chernava *r.* Rus. Fed.
138 F2 Chernaya *r.* Rus. Fed.
137 K2 Chernaya Kalitva *r.* Rus. Fed.
134 J4 Chernaya Kholunitsa
Rus. Fed.
137 G2 Chernecha Sloboda Ukr.
Chernecho Moldova *see*
Şoldăneşti
137 H3 Cherneshchyna Ukr.
Chernigov Ukr. *see* Chernihiv
100 E3 Chernigovka Rus. Fed.
Chernigov Oblast *admin. div.*
Ukr. *see* Chernihivs'ka Oblast'
Chernigovskaya Rus. Fed.
129 A1 Chernigovskaya Rus. Fed.
Chernigovskoye Rus. Fed.
137 F2 Chernihiv Ukr.
Chernihiv Oblast *admin. div.*
Ukr. *see* Chernihivs'ka Oblast'
137 F2 Chernihivs'ka Oblast'
admin. div. Ukr.
Chernihivs'ka Oblast'
admin. div. Ukr.
197 G3 Cherni Vrükh *mt.* Bulg.
136 C3 Chernivtsi Ukr.
Chernivtsi 'ka Oblast' Ukr.
136 E3 Chernivtsi
Vinnyts'ka Oblast' Ukr.
Chernivtsi Oblast *admin. div.*
Ukr. *see* Chernivtsi 'ka Oblast'
136 C3 Cherniyiv Ukr.
Chernobyl' Ukr. *see* Chornobyl'
98 F1 Chernobrovkino Rus. Fed.
129 C1 Chernolesskoye Rus. Fed.
134 K3 Chernorechenskiy Rus. Fed.
121 J1 Chernoretskoye Kazakh.
135 I4 Chernovskoye Rus. Fed.
Chernovtsy Ukr. *see* Chernivtsi
Chernovtsy Oblast *admin. div.*
Ukr. *see* Chernivtsi 'ka Oblast'
Chernoye More *sea see* Black Sea
134 L4 Chernushka Rus. Fed.
136 E2 Chernyakhiv Ukr.
138 H1 Chernyakhovsk Rus. Fed.
135 G6 Chernyshevsk Rus. Fed.
99 K1 Chernyshevskiy Rus. Fed.
131 M3 Chernyshevskiy Rus. Fed.
135 H6 Chernyshkovskiy Rus. Fed.
137 L2 Chernyy Zemli *reg.*
Rus. Fed.
Chernyy Irtysh *r.*
China/Kazakh. *see* Ertix He
120 C2 Chernyy Otrog Rus. Fed.
134 F3 Chernyy Rynok Rus. Fed. *see*
Kochubey
135 I6 Chernyy Yar Rus. Fed.
236 E3 Cherokee *IA* U.S.A.
230 D4 Cherokee *OK* U.S.A.
231 D4 Cherokee *TN* U.S.A.
237 E4 Cherokees, Lake o' the
OK U.S.A.
246 □ Cherokee Sound *Gt Abaco*
Bahamas
156 D4 Chéroy France
260 A6 Cherquenco Chile
117 G4 Cherrapunji *Meghalaya* India
149 I4 Cherry Burton *East Riding of*
Yorkshire, England U.K.
236 C2 Cherry Creek *r.* SD U.S.A.
241 J1 Cherry Creek Mountains
NV U.S.A.
233 □J2 Cherryfield *ME* U.S.A.
234 C3 Cherry Hill *NJ* U.S.A.
77 G3 Cherry Island Solomon Is
227 I4 Cherry Valley *Ont.* Can.
149 I4 Cherry Willingham
Lincolnshire, England U.K.
131 R3 Cherskiy Rus. Fed.
Cherskiy Range *mts*
Rus. Fed. *see*
Cherskogo, Khrebet
107 F1 Cherskogo, Khrebet *mts*
Chitinskaya Oblast' Rus. Fed.
131 P3 Cherskogo, Khrebet *mts*
Respublika Sakha (Yakutiya)
Rus. Fed.
198 C1 Cherso *Kentriki Makedonia*
Greece
190 C4 Chersogno, Monte *mt.* Italy
186 C4 Chert Spain
225 □ Chertala *Kerala* India
194 D5 Chertala *Kerala* India
192 A4 Chiaramonti *Sardegna* Italy
191 I5 Chiaravalle Italy
195 M3 Chiaravalle Centrale Italy
190 E3 Chiari Italy

Column 3

151 G3 Chertsey *Surrey, England* U.K.
139 M4 Cherusti Rus. Fed.
162 D3 Cherveix-Cubas France
197 G4 Cherven Bryag Bulg.
129 D2 Cherves-Richemont France
129 D2 Chervlennaya Rus. Fed.
137 G3 Chervona Sloboda Ukr.
137 H2 Chervone *Sums'ka Oblast'* Ukr.
136 E3 Chervone
Zhytomyrs'ka Oblast' Ukr.
137 I4 Chervone Pole Ukr.
137 F2 Chervoni Partyzany Ukr.
Chervonoarmiys'k Ukr. *see*
Vil'nyans'k
Chervonoarmiys'k Ukr. *see*
Krasnoarmiys'k
Chervonoarmiys'k Ukr. *see*
Radyvyliv
136 E2 Chervonohrad Ukr.
137 H4 Chervonohvardiys'ke Ukr.
137 I3 Chervonooskil's'ke
Vodoskhovyshche *resr* Ukr.
226 D5 Chervonopartyzansk Ukr.
Chervonopartyzans'k Ukr.
137 J3 Chervonopartyzans'k Ukr.
137 G2 Chervonozavods'ke Ukr.
136 F4 Chervonoznam''yanka Ukr.
137 I3 Chervonyy Donets' Ukr.
137 G4 Chervonyy Mayak Ukr.
138 G5 Cheryan' Belarus
151 F3 Cherwell *r.* England U.K.
139 H5 Cherykaw Belarus
227 E4 Chesaning *MI* U.S.A.
233 E6 Chesapeake *VA* U.S.A.
234 B4 Chesapeake Bay
MD/VA U.S.A.
232 E5 Chesapeake Beach *MD* U.S.A.
234 C3 Chesapeake City *MD* U.S.A.
151 G3 Chesham *Buckinghamshire,*
England U.K.
149 G4 Cheshire *admin. div.*
England U.K.
235 F1 Cheshire *CT* U.S.A.
233 G3 Cheshire *MA* U.S.A.
149 G4 Cheshire Plain *England* U.K.
134 I2 Cheshskaya Guba *b.*
Rus. Fed.
151 G3 Cheshunt *Hertfordshire,*
England U.K.
150 E4 Chesil Beach *England* U.K.
234 D3 Chesilhurst *NJ* U.S.A.
227 G3 Chesley *Ont.* Can.
156 E5 Chesley France
120 E1 Chesma Rus. Fed.
Chesnokovka Rus. Fed. *see*
Novoaltaysk
156 D4 Chessy-les-Prés France
187 C5 Cheste Spain
225 H4 Chester *N.S.* Can.
149 G4 Chester *Cheshire, England* U.K.
240 G1 Chester *CA* U.S.A.
235 F1 Chester *CT* U.S.A.
226 E6 Chester *IL* U.S.A.
234 B4 Chester *MD* U.S.A.
238 F1 Chester *MT* U.S.A.
234 D2 Chester *NJ* U.S.A.
235 G1 Chester *NY* U.S.A.
232 C5 Chester *OH* U.S.A.
234 C3 Chester *PA* U.S.A.
231 D5 Chester *SC* U.S.A.
232 E6 Chester *VA* U.S.A.
234 B4 Chester *r.* MD U.S.A.
246 □ Chester Castle Jamaica
234 C2 Chester County *county*
PA U.S.A.
149 H4 Chesterfield *Derbyshire,*
England U.K.
235 F1 Chesterfield *CT* U.S.A.
231 D5 Chesterfield *MO* U.S.A.
231 D5 Chesterfield *SC* U.S.A.
232 E6 Chesterfield *VA* U.S.A.
77 F3 Chesterfield, Îles *is*
New Caledonia
223 N2 Chesterfield Inlet
Nunavut Can.
223 M2 Chesterfield Inlet *inlet*
Nunavut Can.
149 H3 Chester-le-Street *Durham,*
England U.K.
146 F6 Chesters *Scottish Borders,*
Scotland U.K.
234 B3 Chestertown *MD* U.S.A.
233 G3 Chestertown *NY* U.S.A.
233 F2 Chesterville *Ont.* Can.
234 C3 Chesterville *MD* U.S.A.
232 D4 Chestnut Ridge *PA* U.S.A.
225 I4 Chéticamp *N.S.* Can.
237 E4 Chetopa *KS* U.S.A.
243 H5 Chetumal Mex.
222 F4 Chetwynd *B.C.* Can.
136 C3 Chevanceaux France
235 I1 Chevanon France
241 E3 Chevelon Creek *r.* AZ U.S.A.
177 K6 Cheveresu Mare Romania
234 B4 Cheverly *MD* U.S.A.
160 D1 Chevigny-St-Sauveur France
157 F4 Chevillon France
81 D5 Cheviot *South I.* N.Z.
232 A5 Cheviot *OH* U.S.A.
149 G2 Cheviot Hills *England* U.K.
85 E5 Cheviot Range *hills Qld Austr.*
149 G2 Chevreaux *r.* Qld Austr.
131 G5 Chevreuse France
214 C4 Chew Bahir *salt l.* Eth.
238 C6 Chewelah *WA* U.S.A.
150 E3 Chew Magna *Bath and North*
East Somerset, England U.K.
237 D5 Cheyenne *OK* U.S.A.
236 C3 Cheyenne *WY* U.S.A.
236 C2 Cheyenne *r.* SD U.S.A.
236 C4 Cheyenne Wells *CO* U.S.A.
161 A3 Cheylade France
87 B7 Cheyne Bay *W.A. Austr.*
116 D4 Cheyyar *Tamil Nadu* India
114 D3 Cheyyur *r.* India
222 C4 Chezacut *B.C.* Can.
159 I5 Chézal-Benoît France
163 B6 Chèze France
116 B3 Chhabra *Rajasthan* India
116 A4 Chhapar *Rajasthan* India
117 G4 Chhapra *Bihar* India
116 D3 Chhata *Uttar Prad.* India
117 G4 Chhatak Bangl.
117 H4 Chhatarpur *Bihar* India
116 D4 Chhatarpur *Madh. Prad.* India
117 E5 Chhatrapur *Orissa* India
114 D2 Chhay Arèng, Stœng *r.*
Cambodia
116 D3 Chhibramau *Uttar Prad.* India
116 D5 Chhindwara *Madh. Prad.* India
116 D4 Chhipa Barod *Rajasthan* India
116 C4 Chhota Chhindwara
Madh. Prad. India
116 C5 Chhota Udepur *Gujarat* India
116 C5 Chhukhadan
Madh. Prad. India
117 H4 Chhukha Bhutan
257 H4 Chiador Brazil
109 G4 Chiai Taiwan
191 G3 Chiampo *r.* Italy
190 D2 Chiampo *r.* Italy
258 D3 Chiancito Arg.
209 B8 Chiange Angola
96 C3 Chiang Dao Thai.
96 C3 Chiang Khan Thai.
96 B3 Chiang Mai Thai.
96 B3 Chiang Rai Thai.
192 C7 Chiani *r.* Italy
191 F5 Chiani *r.* Italy
243 H3 Chiapa Mex.
232 C6 Chiloquin *OR* U.S.A.

Column 4

193 I4 Chiaromonte Italy
191 I2 Chiarso *r.* Italy
191 H5 Chiascio *r.* Italy
190 E3 Chiasso Italy
245 G4 Chiat'ura Georgia
245 E4 Chiaucatempan Mex.
245 E4 Chiautla Mex.
245 E4 Chiautzingo Mex.
73 C4 Chiavari Italy
190 E3 Chiavenna *r.* Italy
105 G3 Chiba Japan
105 G3 Chiba *pref.* Japan
213 G4 Chibabava Moz.
209 B8 Chibemba Angola
Chibi Hubei China *see* Chivi
209 B8 Chibia Angola
Chibizovka Rus. Fed. *see*
Zherdevka
213 G4 Chiboma Moz.
224 F3 Chibougamau *Que.* Can.
224 F3 Chibougamau *r.* Que. Can.
213 G5 Chiboto Moz.
209 B8 Chibwe Zambia
Chicacole *Andhra Prad.* India
see Srikakulam
226 D5 Chicago *IL* U.S.A.
226 D5 Chicago Heights *IL* U.S.A.
209 D6 Chicapa *r.* Angola
245 E2 Chicayán *r.* Mex.
225 H3 Chic-Chocs, Monts *mts*
Que. Can.
197 G3 Chicera Hamba *hill* Romania
221 B7 Chichagof *AK* U.S.A.
220 E4 Chichagof Island *AK* U.S.A.
123 F5 Chichak *r.* Pak.
204 C3 Chichaoua Morocco
252 D5 Chichas, Cordillera de
mts Bol.
159 F5 Chiché France
107 G3 Chicheng *Hebei China*
Chicheng *Sichuan China see*
Pengxi
243 H4 Chichén Itzá *tourist site* Mex.
151 G4 Chichester *West Sussex,*
England U.K.
86 C4 Chichester Range *mts*
W.A. Austr.
115 H3 Chichgarh *Mahar.* India
105 F3 Chichibu Japan
105 F3 Chichibu-gawa *r.* Japan
245 E5 Chichihualco Mex.
103 □1 Chichi-jima *i.* Japan
103 □1 Chichijima-rettō *is* Japan
116 D5 Chicholi *Madh. Prad.* India
232 E6 Chickahominy *r.* VA U.S.A.
231 C5 Chickamauga Lake *TN* U.S.A.
237 F6 Chickasawhay *r.* MS U.S.A.
237 D5 Chickasha *OK* U.S.A.
150 E4 Chickerell *Dorset, England* U.K.
184 D4 Chiclana de la Frontera Spain
250 B6 Chiclayo Peru
259 C6 Chico *r.* Buenos Aires Arg.
259 C6 Chico *r.* Chubut Arg.
259 C8 Chico *r.* Chubut Arg.
259 C7 Chico *r.* Santa Cruz Arg.
244 C2 Chico *r.* Mex.
240 G2 Chico *CA* U.S.A.
209 B8 Chicomba Angola
243 G6 Chicomucelo Mex.
217 □3b Chiconi Mayotte
211 B8 Chicono Moz.
245 E3 Chicontepec Mex.
245 I1 Chicopee *MA* U.S.A.
92 B2 Chico Sapocoy, Mount
Luzon Phil.
225 G3 Chicoutimi *Que.* Can.
225 G3 Chicoutimi *r.* Que. Can.
209 D9 Chicualacuala Moz.
114 C4 Chidambaram *Tamil Nadu* India
151 G3 Chiddingfold *Surrey,*
England U.K.
111 F6 Chido *Xizang* China
101 C5 Chido S. Korea
209 C9 Chiede Angola
231 D6 Chiefland *FL* U.S.A.
212 D3 Chiefs Island Botswana
173 G4 Chiemgauer Alpen *mts* Ger.
173 G4 Chieming Ger.
173 G4 Chiemsee *l.* Ger.
191 G2 Chienes Italy
209 F7 Chiengi Zambia
Chiengmai Thai. *see*
Chiang Mai
191 I5 Chienti *r.* Italy
157 F3 Chiers *r.* France
190 E2 Chiesa in Valmalenco Italy
177 L4 Chieşd Romania
191 I5 Chiese *r.* Italy
191 I5 Chieti *prov. Abruzzo* Italy
193 I2 Chieuti Italy
151 F3 Chieveley *West Berkshire,*
England U.K.
156 D3 Chièvres Belgium
107 H3 Chifeng *Nei Mongol China*
204 B5 Chiganak Kazakh.
105 F3 Chigasaki Japan
220 C4 Chignagak Volcano, Mount
AK U.S.A.
137 K2 Chigla *r.* Rus. Fed.
220 C4 Chignik *AK* U.S.A.
160 E2 Chignin France
250 B3 Chigorodó Col.
136 D1 Chigu Co *l.* China
251 H4 Chiguana Bol.
105 F3 Chigu Co *l.* China
245 E4 Chignahuapan Mex.
129 I1 Chikola *r.* Rus. Fed.
114 C2 Chikbalapur *Karnataka* India
114 C3 Chikhli *Mahar.* India
114 B2 Chikhli *Gujarat Karnataka* India
114 B2 Chikodi *Karnataka* India
116 D4 Chikodi Road *Karnataka* India
116 D5 Chikola *r.* India
106 E1 Chikoy *r.* Rus. Fed.
107 E1 Chikoy *r.* Rus. Fed.
114 B3 Chikumagawa *r.* Japan
105 F2 Chikumagawa *r.* Japan
105 F2 Chikuni Japan
211 B8 Chikwa Malawi
245 E2 Chila, Laguna *l.* Mex.
114 C3 Chilako *r.* B.C. Can.
114 C3 Chilamate *Karnataka* India
252 A1 Chilapa Mex.
245 E5 Chilapa Mex.
116 C2 Chilas Jammu and Kashmir
114 C3 Chilaw Sri Lanka
252 A3 Chilca Peru
187 D5 Chilches Spain
222 F3 Chilcotin *r.* B.C. Can.
85 G3 Chili, Sierra de *i.* Chile
151 F3 Childrey *Oxfordshire,*
England U.K.
237 D5 Childress *TX* U.S.A.
266 H3 Chinook Trough *sea feature*
N. Pacific Ocean

Column 5

198 C3 Chiliomodi Greece
222 C3 Chilkat *r.* Can./U.S.A.
222 F4 Chilko *r.* B.C. Can.
85 F3 Chillagoe *Qld Austr.*
260 A5 Chillán Chile
260 A5 Chillán, Nevado *mts* Chile
156 C4 Chilleurs-aux-Bois France
226 C5 Chillicothe *IL* U.S.A.
230 E4 Chillicothe *MO* U.S.A.
232 B5 Chillicothe *OH* U.S.A.
116 □ Chilling *Jammu and Kashmir*
222 F5 Chilliwack *B.C.* Can.
185 F2 Chillón Spain
185 G2 Chilluévar Spain
234 B4 Chilmark *MD* U.S.A.
122 C1 Chil''mämedkum, Peski *des.*
Turkm.
117 G4 Chilmari Bangl.
259 B6 Chiloé, Isla de *i.* Chile
259 B6 Chiloé, Isla Grande de *i.* Chile
see Chiloé, Isla de
209 F8 Chiloeches Spain
232 C6 Chiloquin *OR* U.S.A.
245 E5 Chilpancingo Mex.
232 B3 Chilson *MI* U.S.A.
209 D7 Chiluage Angola
209 F7 Chilubi Zambia
211 B7 Chilumba Malawi
109 G3 Chilung Taiwan
211 B7 Chilumba Tanz.
243 H6 Chimaltenango Guat.
213 G3 Chimanimani Zimbabwe
165 D4 Chimay Belgium
165 D4 Chimay, Bois de *for.* Belgium
260 B4 Chimbarongo Chile
260 C2 Chimbas Arg.
120 D4 Chimbay Uzbek.
252 A2 Chimbote Peru
Chimboy Uzbek. *see* Chimbay
151 G4 Chimeneas Spain
123 H4 Chiman Pak.
250 C2 Chimichagua Col.
120 E4 Chimion Uzbek.
Chimishliya Moldova *see*
Cimişlia
120 E4 Chimkent Kazakh. *see*
Shymkent
Chimkentskaya Oblast'
admin. div. Kazakh. *see*
Yuzhnyy Kazakhstan
213 G3 Chimoio Moz.
Chimorra *hill* Spain
260 D6 Chimpay Arg.
123 G2 Chimtargha, Qullai *mt.* Tajik.
Chimtorga, Gora *mt.* Tajik. *see*
Chimtargha, Qullai
197 K3 Chimsel Romania
123 H4 Chimshy Rus. Fed.
123 F5 Chin Pak.
233 F2 Chinabara *r.* Can.
96 A3 Chin *state* Myanmar
98 A4 China *country* Asia
243 F3 China Mex.
China, Republic of *country*
Asia *see* Taiwan
245 G5 Chinameca Mex.
243 H6 Chinandega de Gorostiza Mex.
190 C4 ChinasIa Italy
242 □I6 Chinandega Nic.
239 F6 Chinati Peak *TX* U.S.A.
121 G4 Chinaz Uzbek.
252 A3 Chincha Alta Peru
85 G5 Chinchilla *Qld Austr.*
185 I2 Chinchilla de Monte Aragón
Spain
114 C2 Chincholi *Karnataka* India
183 G4 Chinchón Spain
260 B3 Chinchorro, Banco
sea feature Mex.
260 B3 Chincolco Chile
233 F6 Chincoteague *VA* U.S.A.
233 F6 Chincoteague Bay
MD/VA U.S.A.
213 H3 Chinde Moz.
101 C6 Chindo S. Korea
101 C6 Chin-do *i.* S. Korea
160 D3 Chindrieux France
108 A1 Chindu *Qinghai China*
96 A2 Chindwin *r.* Myanmar
116 C2 Chinenn *Jammu and Kashmir*
Chinese Turkestan *aut. reg.*
China *see*
Xinjiang Uygur Zizhiqu
151 G3 Chingford *Greater London,*
England U.K.
101 C5 Chinghwa N. Korea
120 C2 Chingirlau Kazakh.
211 I2 Chingni *r.* Khrebet *mts*
Kazakh.
114 C3 Chingleput *Tamil Nadu* India
see Chengalpattu
209 E8 Chingola Zambia
209 B8 Chinguar Angola
204 B5 Chinguetti Maur.
101 C6 Chinhae S. Korea
213 F3 Chinhoyi Zimbabwe
123 H4 Chini *Hima. Prad.* India *see*
Kalpa
213 G3 Chiniak Bol.
123 H4 Chiniot Pak.
244 C3 Chinipas Mex.
101 D6 Chinju S. Korea
208 D3 Chinko *r.* C.A.R.
241 H4 Chinle *AZ* U.S.A.
109 F3 Chinmen Taiwan
109 G3 Chinmen Tao *i.* Taiwan
244 D3 Chinna Ganjam
Andhra Prad. India
114 C4 Chinnamanur *Tamil Nadu* India
114 C4 Chinnampo N. Korea *see*
Namp'o
114 C4 Chinna Salem *Tamil Nadu* India
151 G3 Chinnor *Oxfordshire,*
England U.K.
105 F3 Chino Japan
240 I4 Chino *CA* U.S.A.
87 C7 Chinocup, Lake *salt flat*
W.A. Austr.
162 C3 Chinon France
238 F3 Chinook *MT* U.S.A.

Column 6

151 H3 Chipping Ongar *Essex,*
England U.K.
150 E3 Chipping Sodbury *South*
Gloucestershire, England U.K.
190 C2 Chippis Switz.
243 J5 Chiprana Spain
197 F4 Chiprovtsi Bulg.
115 G2 Chipurupalle *Andhra Prad.*
India
115 D2 Chipurupalle *Andhra Prad.*
India
243 H6 Chiquimula Guat.
250 C3 Chiquinquirá Col.
261 G4 Chiquita, Mar *l.* Arg.
234 B4 Chiquita, Sierra *mts* Mex.
244 D4 Chiquito *r.* Mex.
253 E4 Chiquitos Jesuit Missions
tourist site Brazil
117 G4 Chir, *r.* Rus. Fed.
161 B4 Chirac France
211 B7 Chiradzulu Malawi
211 B8 Chiradzulu Malawi
129 F3 Chirakchuy *r.* Rus. Fed.
114 B4 Chirakkal *Kerala* India
114 D3 Chirala *Andhra Prad.* India
213 G3 Chiramba Moz.
111 A6 Chirawa *Rajasthan* India
121 G4 Chirchik Uzbek.
121 G4 Chirchik *r.* Uzbek.
250 E2 Chiripá *r.* Venez.
241 H6 Chiricahua Peak *AZ* U.S.A.
250 C2 Chiriguaná Col.
250 B6 Chiriiros Peru
242 □J7 Chiriqui, Golfo de *b.* Panama
242 □J7 Chiriquí, Laguna de *b.*
Panama
242 □J7 Chiriquí Grande Panama
101 C6 Chiri-san *mt.* S. Korea
185 H3 Chirivel Spain
129 D2 Chiri-Yurt Rus. Fed.
150 D2 Chirk *Wrexham, Wales* U.K.
146 F6 Chirnside *Scottish Borders,*
Scotland U.K.
217 □3b Chirongui Mayotte
160 C2 Chiroubles France
197 G4 Chirpan Bulg.
104 D3 Chiryū Japan
209 F8 Chisamba Zambia
209 E8 Chisasa Zambia
224 E2 Chisasibi *Que.* Can.
243 H6 Chisec Guat.
Chirovana *r.* China *see*
Chiseldon *Swindon,*
England U.K.
197 K3 Chiselet Romania
Chishima-retto *is* Rus. Fed.
see Kuril Islands
135 K5 Chishmy Rus. Fed.
231 C5 Chisholm *ME* U.S.A.
233 □J1 Chisholm *ME* U.S.A.
236 E2 Chisholm *MN* U.S.A.
123 H4 Chishtian Mandi Pak.
108 C3 Chishui *Guizhou China*
108 C2 Chishuihe China
Chisimaio Somalia *see*
Kismaayo
136 E4 Chişinău Moldova
177 L5 Chişindia Romania
197 L2 Chişineu-Criş Romania
177 I4 Chişlaz Romania
190 C4 Chisola *r.* Italy
134 J5 Chistopol' Rus. Fed.
121 F1 Chistopol'ye Kazakh.
Chistyakovo Ukr. *see* Torez
121 G1 Chistyakovskoye Kazakh.
252 D5 Chita Bol.
104 D4 Chita Japan
99 I1 Chita Rus. Fed.
104 D4 Chita-hantō *pen.* Japan
116 B4 Chitalwana *Rajasthan* India
Chita Oblast *admin. div.*
Rus. Fed. *see*
Chitinskaya Oblast'
209 B8 Chitato Angola
191 J5 Chitembo Angola
209 D8 Chitembo Angola
Chitinskaya Oblast'
admin. div. Rus. Fed.
211 B7 Chitipa Malawi
213 G3 Chitobe Moz.
209 D8 Chitokoloki Zambia
Chitor *Rajasthan* India *see*
Chittaurgarh
102 J2 Chitose Japan
114 C3 Chitradurga *Karnataka* India
123 H3 Chitrakut *Uttar Prad.* India
123 H3 Chitral Pak.
123 I3 Chitral *r.* Pak.
242 □J7 Chitré Panama
117 G5 Chittagong Bangl.
117 G5 Chittagong *admin. div.* Bangl.
117 F5 Chittaranjan *W. Bengal* India
117 G4 Chittaurgarh *Rajasthan* India
114 D3 Chittoor *Andhra Prad.* India
116 C4 Chittur *Kerala* India
213 F3 Chitungwiza Zimbabwe
213 F3 Chiuleni *r.* Moz.
190 G3 Chiuppano Italy
194 E2 Chiusa *r.* Italy
191 G1 Chiusa di Pesio Italy
194 D5 Chiusa Sclafani *Sicilia* Italy
190 D3 Chiusella *r.* Italy
190 D3 Chiusi Italy
191 G5 Chiusi della Verna Italy
191 G5 Chiusi, Lago di *l.* Italy
213 G2 Chiúta Moz.
187 C5 Chiva Spain
213 F3 Chivay Moz.
252 C4 Chivay Peru
258 D3 Chivilcoy Arg.
261 G4 Chivilcoy Arg.
190 D4 Chivasso Italy
251 E2 Chivor, Embalse de *resr* Col.
213 F3 Chivhu Zimbabwe
213 F3 Chivi Zimbabwe
120 B2 Chizha *r.* Rus. Fed.
190 B3 Chizé France
162 B2 Chizé France
101 C6 Ch'ŏa-do *i.* S. Korea
175 L2 Chizhёvka Rus. Fed.
176 F2 Chlebičov Czech Rep.
177 L2 Chlebnice Slovakia
175 K3 Chlewiska Pol.
174 D3 Chmielów Pol.
175 K6 Chlmec Slovakia
176 E1 Chlum Czech Rep.
176 D1 Chlumec nad Cidlinou
Czech Rep.
176 E2 Chlum u Třeboně Czech Rep.
175 I5 Chmielnik Pol.
177 H2 Chmielowice Pol.
121 K2 Choapa *r.* Chile
212 C3 Chobe admin. dist. Botswana
212 C3 Chobe *r.* Botswana/Namibia
191 F3 Chocianów Pol.
104 C2 Chōbagad *r.* India
246 □ Choapa *r.* Chile
215 G3 Choba S. Africa
232 C6 Christiania VA U.S.A.
142 C4 Christiansfeld Denmark

Column 7

151 H3 Chipping Ongar *Essex,*
England U.K.
150 E3 Chocholná-Velčice Slovakia
174 D4 Chocianów Pol.
174 D2 Chociw Pol.
250 B3 Chocó *dept* Col.
241 J5 Chocolate Mountains
AZ/CA U.S.A.
250 C3 Chocontá Col.
231 C6 Choctawhatchee *r.* FL U.S.A.
174 F4 Chocz Pol.
175 J4 Choczewo Pol.
114 C2 Chodavaram *Andhra Prad.*
India
175 H3 Chodecz Pol.
175 K4 Chodel Pol.
176 D1 Chodov Czech Rep.
176 C2 Chodová Planá Czech Rep.
175 K3 Chodów Pol.
174 E3 Chodzież Pol.
260 E6 Choele Choel Arg.
105 F3 Chōfu Japan
223 J4 Choiceland *Sask.* Can.
78 □6 Choiseul *i.* Solomon Is
259 F8 Choiseul Sound *sea chan.*
Falkland Is
160 E3 Choisy France
242 C3 Choix Mex.
174 F2 Chojna Pol.
175 I4 Chojnice Pol.
102 J4 Chōkai-san *vol.* Japan
210 C2 Ch'ok'ē Mountains Eth.
129 C2 Ch'okhatauri Georgia
121 H4 Chokpar Kazakh.
Chokue Moz. *see* Chókwé
131 P2 Chokurdakh Rus. Fed.
213 G5 Chókwé Moz.
240 G4 Cholame *CA* U.S.A.
240 G4 Cholame Creek *r.* CA U.S.A.
260 A1 Chola Shan *mts Sichuan China*
260 A6 Cholchol Chile
162 B1 Cholet France
242 □I6 Choloma Hond.
209 B8 Choma Zambia
101 C5 Chŏmch'ŏn S. Korea
161 B3 Chomérac France
161 C4 Chomérac France
Chomo *Xizang China see*
Yadong
111 F6 Chomo Ganggar *mt.* Xizang
China
117 G4 Chomo Lhari *mt.* Bhutan
116 C4 Chomun *Rajasthan* India
176 C1 Chomutov Czech Rep.
176 C1 Chomutovka *r.* Czech Rep.
131 L3 Chona *r.* Rus. Fed.
97 C4 Chon Buri Thai.
259 B6 Chonchi Chile
250 A5 Chone Ecuador
Chong'an *Fujian China see*
Wuyishan
101 C5 Chŏngjin N. Korea
101 D6 Ch'ŏngdo S. Korea
Chonggye *Xizang China see*
Qonggyai
103 D3 Chŏngju S. Korea
101 C5 Ch'ŏngjin N. Korea
101 C6 Ch'ŏngju S. Korea
101 C5 Chŏngju N. Korea
107 G3 Chongli *Hebei China*
Chonglong *Sichuan China see*
Zizhong
109 F2 Chongming *Shanghai China*
109 G2 Chongming Dao *i.* China
209 B8 Chongoroi Angola
101 C6 Chŏng'yŏng N. Korea
101 C6 Chŏngŭp S. Korea
108 C2 Chongqing *Chongqing China*
Chongqing *Jiangxi China*
109 C6 Chŏngŭp S. Korea
209 F8 Chongwe Zambia
108 D3 Chongyang *Hubei China*
109 E3 Chongyang Xi *r.* China
108 D3 Chongzhou *Sichuan China*
108 C3 Chongzuo *Guangxi China*
101 C6 Chŏnju S. Korea
109 □ Chonju S. Korea
184 D4 Chonos, Archipiélago de los
is Chile
246 □ Chonta Jamaica
215 I5 Chonta S. Africa
250 B4 Chontal *dept* Nic.
232 C6 Christiania VA U.S.A.
142 C4 Christiansfeld Denmark

Column 8

177 G3 Chocholná-Velčice Slovakia
174 D4 Chocianów Pol.
174 D2 Chociw Pol.
250 B3 Chocontá Col.
231 C6 Choctawhatchee *r.* FL U.S.A.
174 F1 Chocz Pol.
174 F1 Choczewo Pol.
114 C2 Chodavaram *Andhra Prad.*
India
175 H3 Chodecz Pol.
175 K4 Chodel Pol.
176 B1 Chodov Czech Rep.
176 C2 Chodová Planá Czech Rep.
175 K3 Chodów Pol.
174 E3 Chodzież Pol.
260 E6 Choele Choel Arg.
105 F3 Chōfu Japan
223 J4 Choiceland *Sask.* Can.
78 □6 Choiseul *i.* Solomon Is
259 F8 Choiseul Sound *sea chan.*
Falkland Is
160 E3 Choisy France
242 C3 Choix Mex.
174 F2 Chojna Pol.
175 I4 Chojnice Pol.
102 J4 Chōkai-san *vol.* Japan
210 C2 Ch'ok'ē Mountains Eth.
129 C2 Ch'okhatauri Georgia
121 H4 Chokpar Kazakh.
Chokue Moz. *see* Chókwé
131 P2 Chokurdakh Rus. Fed.
213 G5 Chókwé Moz.
240 G4 Cholame *CA* U.S.A.
240 G4 Cholame Creek *r.* CA U.S.A.
260 A1 Chola Shan *mts Sichuan China*
260 A6 Cholchol Chile
162 B1 Cholet France
242 □I6 Choloma Hond.
209 B8 Choma Zambia
101 C5 Chŏmch'ŏn S. Korea
161 B3 Chomérac France
111 F6 Chomo Ganggar *mt.* Xizang
China
117 G4 Chomo Lhari *mt.* Bhutan
116 C4 Chomun *Rajasthan* India
176 C1 Chomutov Czech Rep.
176 C1 Chomutovka *r.* Czech Rep.
131 L3 Chona *r.* Rus. Fed.
97 C4 Chon Buri Thai.
259 B6 Chonchi Chile
250 A5 Chone Ecuador
101 C5 Chŏngjin N. Korea
101 D6 Ch'ŏngdo S. Korea
103 D3 Chŏngju S. Korea
101 C5 Ch'ŏngjin N. Korea
101 C6 Ch'ŏngju S. Korea
101 C5 Chŏngju N. Korea
107 G3 Chongli *Hebei China*
109 F2 Chongming *Shanghai China*
109 G2 Chongming Dao *i.* China
209 B8 Chongoroi Angola
101 C6 Chŏng'yŏng N. Korea
108 C2 Chongqing *Chongqing China*
108 C2 Chongqing *mun.* China
109 E3 Chongqing *Jiangxi China*
101 C6 Chŏngŭp S. Korea
209 F8 Chongwe Zambia
108 D3 Chongyang *Hubei China*
109 E3 Chongyang Xi *r.* China
108 D3 Chongzhou *Sichuan China*
108 C3 Chongzuo *Guangxi China*
101 C6 Chŏnju S. Korea
109 □ Chonju S. Korea
184 D4 Chonos, Archipiélago de los
is Chile
246 □ Chonta Jamaica
215 I5 Chonta S. Africa
250 B4 Chontal *dept* Nic.
171 F4 Choo Phraw Hai Vietnam
255 B8 Chopimzinho Brazil
136 F2 Chopovychi Ukr.
233 F5 Choptank *r.* MD U.S.A.
198 D3 Chora *tourist site* Greece
199 I7 Chora *tourist site* Greece
149 G3 Chorley *Lancashire,*
England U.K.
151 G3 Chorleywood *Hertfordshire,*
England U.K.
137 L6 Chorna Ukr.
137 L6 Chorna *r.* Ukr.
177 K3 Chorna Tysa Ukr.
175 M5 Chorniyiv Ukr.
137 L3 Chornobay Ukr.
136 E1 Chornobyl' Ukr.
175 K4 Chornomors'ke Ukr.
136 D2 Chornomorske Ukr.
137 F3 Chornorudka Ukr.
137 J6 Chornorudka Ukr.
137 G3 Chornyy Tashlyk *r.* Ukr.
137 L4 Chorokh/Çoruh *r.*
Georgia/Turkey
174 F3 Choroszcz Pol.
255 B9 Chorozinho Brazil
232 C6 Chorrera, Punta *pt* Chile
174 E2 Chortkiv Ukr.
136 C4 Chortkiv Ukr.
101 C5 Ch'ŏrwon S. Korea
174 E4 Chorzele Pol.
175 I2 Chorzów Pol.
101 C4 Chosan N. Korea
105 G3 Chōshi Japan
259 D6 Choshuenco, Volcán *vol.* Chile
260 B6 Chos Malal Arg.
174 D2 Choszczno Pol.
174 C3 Choszczno Pol.
176 B1 Chotěboř Czech Rep.
176 D1 Chotěšov Czech Rep.
116 B3 Chotila *Gujarat* India
174 F3 Chotín Slovakia
177 J4 Chotoa-chandroudé *i.* Comoros
209 B9 Chouto Maur.
184 □ Chouto Port.
159 F2 Chouzy-sur-Cisse France
240 G2 Chowchilla *CA* U.S.A.
240 G2 Chowchilla *r.* CA U.S.A.
209 B8 Choya Arg.
258 D2 Choya Arg.
125 D3 Chozas de Abajo Spain
Chozas de la Sierra Spain *see*
Soto del Real
176 E2 Chrast *Pardubický kraj*
Czech Rep.
176 D1 Chrást *Plzeňský kraj*
Czech Rep.
176 E2 Chrastava Czech Rep.
177 K3 Chřibská Czech Rep.
176 □ Chřiby *hills* Czech Rep.
199 G5 Chrisman *IL* U.S.A.
81 E4 Chrissiesmeer S. Africa
215 J4 Christchurch *South I.* N.Z.
81 E5 Christchurch *Dorset,*
England U.K.
246 □ Christiana Jamaica
215 H2 Christiana S. Africa
Christiania Norway *see* Oslo
232 C6 Christiansburg *VA* U.S.A.
142 C4 Christiansfeld Denmark
Christianshåb Greenland *see*
Qasigiannguit

Column 1

247 F3 Christiansted Virgin Is. (U.S.A.)
226 B3 Christie WI U.S.A.
223 I3 Christina r. Alta Can.
81 B6 Christina, Mount South I. N.Z.
149 G4 Christleton Cheshire, England U.K.
86 E3 Christmas Creek W.A. Austr.
86 E3 Christmas Creek r. W.A. Austr.
86 ◻1 Christmas Island terr. Indian Ocean
149 H2 Christon Bank Northumberland, England U.K.
87 E5 Christopher, Lake salt flat W.A. Austr.
176 E2 Chrudim Czech Rep.
175 H3 Chrúslin Pol.
198 D1 Chrysoupoli Greece
148 E2 Chryston North Lanarkshire, Scotland U.K.
175 H5 Chrzanów Pol.
174 F4 Chrzastowa Wielka Pol.
174 G5 Chrząstowice Pol.
174 E3 Chrzypsko Wielkie Pol.
Chu Kazakh. see Shu
121 F3 Chu r. Kazakh.
117 G5 Chuadanga Bangl.
109 G2 Chuansha Shanghai China
108 A2 Chubalung Sichuan China
137 I4 Chubarivka Ukr. see Polohy
Chubartau Kazakh. see Barshatas
238 D3 Chubbuck ID U.S.A.
137 J4 Chuburka r. Rus. Fed.
121 G3 Chubynske Ukr.
259 D6 Chubut prov. Arg.
177 H2 Chuchelná Czech Rep.
135 H5 Chuchkovo Rus. Fed.
241 J5 Chuckwalla Mountains CA U.S.A.
242 ◻K7 Chucunaque r. Panama
150 D4 Chudleigh Devon, England U.K.
136 E2 Chudniv Ukr.
174 G5 Chudoba Pol.
139 H2 Chudovo Rus. Fed.
Chudskoye, Ozero l. Estonia/Rus. Fed. see Peipus, Lake
220 D3 Chugach Mountains AK U.S.A.
103 F6 Chūgoku-sanchi mts Japan
Chūgqênsumdo Qinghai China see Jigzhi
Chuguchak Xinjiang China see Tacheng
Chuguyev Ukr. see Chuhuyiv
100 E3 Chuguyevka Rus. Fed.
238 F3 Chugwater WY U.S.A.
Chuhai Guangdong China see Zhuhai
137 I3 Chuhuyiv Ukr.
121 H3 Chu-Iliyskiye Gory mts Kazakh.
108 A2 Chuka Xizang China
Chukai Malaysia see Cukai
Chukchi Peninsula Rus. Fed. see Chukotskiy Poluostrov
268 M1 Chukchi Plateau sea feature Arctic Ocean
220 A3 Chukchi Sea Rus. Fed./U.S.A.
134 H4 Chukhloma Rus. Fed.
131 T3 Chukotskiy Poluostrov pen. Rus. Fed.
137 G4 Chulakivka Ukr.
Chulakkurgan Kazakh. see Sholakkorgan
Chulaktau Kazakh. see Karatau
240 I5 Chula Vista CA U.S.A.
187 C5 Chulilla Spain
150 D4 Chulmleigh Devon, England U.K.
250 A6 Chulucanas Peru
123 I3 Chulung Pass Pak.
106 D1 Chuluut Gol r. Mongolia
130 J4 Chulym r. Rus. Fed.
110 D1 Chulyshman r. Rus. Fed.
252 C3 Chuma Bol.
137 H4 Chumaky Ukr.
258 D3 Chumbicha Arg.
108 A1 Chumda Qinghai China
197 G4 Chumerna mt. Bulg.
100 E1 Chumikan Rus. Fed.
129 D3 Ch'xumi Georgia
96 C3 Chum Phae Thai.
97 B5 Chumphon Thai.
96 C4 Chum Saeng Thai.
260 E2 Chuña Arg.
131 K4 Chuna r. Rus. Fed.
109 F2 Chun'an Zhejiang China
140 P2 Chuna-Tundra plain Rus. Fed.
101 C5 Ch'unch'ŏn S. Korea
121 I4 Chundzha Kazakh.
209 E8 Chunga Zambia
Chung-hua Jen-min Kung-ho-kuo country Asia see China
Chung-hua Min-kuo country Asia see Taiwan
101 C5 Ch'ungju S. Korea
Chungking Chongqing China see Chongqing
Ch'ungmu S. Korea see T'ongyŏng
101 C5 Ch'ŭngsan N. Korea
109 G4 Chungyang Shanmo mts Taiwan
100 D4 Chunhua Jilin China
243 H5 Chunhuhub Mex.
Chunxi Jiangsu China see Gaochun
131 K3 Chunya r. Rus. Fed.
211 B7 Chunya Tanz.
97 C3 Chuŏr Phnum Dângrêk mts Cambodia/Thai.
Chuosijia Sichuan China see Guanyinqiao
134 F2 Chupa Rus. Fed.
137 H2 Chupakhivka Ukr.
122 A2 Chûplū Iran
136 F3 Chupyra Ukr.
252 C5 Chuquicamata Chile
252 D5 Chuquisaca dept Bol.
Chuqung Qinghai China see Chindu
134 K4 Chur Rus. Fed.
190 C2 Chur Switz.
117 H4 Churachandpur Manipur India
131 O3 Churapcha Rus. Fed.
134 K5 Churbakovo Rus. Fed.
151 K2 Church End Essex, England U.K.
148 B3 Church Hill Rep. of Ireland
234 C3 Church Hill MD U.S.A.
232 B6 Church Hill TN U.S.A.
223 M3 Churchill Man. Can.
223 M3 Churchill r. Man. Can.
225 I2 Churchill r. Nfld. Can.
225 I2 Churchill Falls Nfld. Can.
263 K1 Churchill Mountains Antarctica
222 E3 Churchill Peak B.C. Can.
149 G4 Church Lawton Cheshire, England U.K.
236 D1 Churchs Ferry ND U.S.A.
150 E2 Church Stretton Shropshire, England U.K.
234 B4 Churchton MD U.S.A.
147 C5 Churchtown Cork Rep. of Ireland
234 C2 Churchtown PA U.S.A.
234 B3 Churchville MD U.S.A.
232 D5 Churchville VA U.S.A.
106 A1 Chureg-Tag, Gora mt. Rus. Fed.
117 F4 Churia Ghati Hills Nepal
252 A2 Churin Peru
129 E2 Churkey Rus. Fed.
129 E2 Churkeyskoye Vodokhranilishche resr Rus. Fed.
134 I4 Churov Rus. Fed.
137 G1 Churovichi Rus. Fed.
116 C3 Churu Rajasthan India
Churubay Nura Karagandinskaya Oblast' Kazakh. see Abay
226 D3 Churubusco IN U.S.A.
250 D2 Churuguara Venez.
190 E2 Churwalden Switz.
116 D2 Chushul Jammu and Kashmir

Column 2

241 M3 Chuska Mountains NM U.S.A.
134 L3 Chusovaya r. Rus. Fed.
134 L4 Chusovoy Rus. Fed.
Chust Ukr. see Khust
121 G4 Chust Uzbek.
225 G3 Chute-des-Passes Que. Can.
121 G2 Chute-Rouge Que. Can.
137 H3 Chutove Ukr.
109 ◻ Chuting Taiwan
78 ◻4a Chuuk is Micronesia
260 C6 Chuvashia aut. rep. Rus. Fed. see Chuvashskaya Respublika
Chuvashskaya A.S.S.R. aut. rep. Rus. Fed. see Chuvashskaya Respublika
135 I5 Chuvashskaya Respublika aut. rep. Rus. Fed.
108 B3 Chuxiong Yunnan China
121 H4 Chuy admin. div. Kyrg.
258 G3 Chuy Uru.
97 E4 Chuy Yang Sin mt. Vietnam Chuyang Sin Oblast' admin. div. Kyrg. see Chúy
160 C3 Chuzelles France
109 F1 Chuzhou Anhui China
176 D3 Chvalšiny Czech Rep.
127 G4 Chwârtâ Iraq
174 G1 Chwaszczyno Pol.
Chwilog Flintshire, Wales U.K. see Whitford
174 G6 Chybie Pol.
136 F4 Chychykliya r. Ukr.
121 G3 Chyganak Kazakh.
137 G3 Chyhyryn Ukr.
183 I2 Chymyshliya Moldova see Cimişlia
136 B3 Chynadiyeve Ukr.
175 J4 Chýňava Czech Rep.
175 J4 Chynów Pol.
211 C5 Chyulu Range mts Kenya
175 M6 Chyzhivka Ukr.
196 E3 Ciacova Romania
Ciadâr-Lunga Moldova see Ciadir-Lunga
136 E4 Ciadîr-Lunga Moldova
163 C5 Ciadoux France
193 H3 Ciagola, Monte mt. Italy
247 ◻ Ciales Puerto Rico
192 B3 Ciamannacce Corse France
95 E4 Ciamis Jawa Barat Indon.
193 E3 Ciampino Italy
193 E3 Ciampino airport Italy
232 B5 Cianciana Sicilia Italy
241 K2 Cianjur Jawa Barat Indon.
256 A5 Cianorte Brazil
161 F5 Cians r. France
174 F3 Ciasna Pol.
174 F3 Ciążeń Pol.
94 C4 Cibadak Jawa Barat Indon.
177 J5 Cibakháza Hungary
95 E4 Cibatu Jawa Barat Indon.
241 L4 Cibecue AZ U.S.A.
94 D4 Cibinong Jawa Barat Indon.
211 A5 Cibitoke Burundi
237 D6 Cibolo Creek r. TX U.S.A.
94 D4 Ciburi r. Indon.
242 C2 Cibuta, Sierra mt. Mex.
190 E4 Cicagna Italy
188 F4 Čićarija mts Croatia
193 G4 Cicciano Italy
126 D3 Çiçekdağı Turkey
128 B1 Çiçekli Turkey
129 F2 Çiçekli Turkey
193 H4 Cicerale Italy
226 D5 Cicero IL U.S.A.
254 F4 Cicero Dantas Brazil
175 L3 Ciche Woda r. Pol.
177 G3 Čičov Slovakia
183 I2 Cidacos r. Spain
126 D2 Cide Turkey
176 E1 Cidlina r. Czech Rep.
183 H3 Cidones Spain
247 ◻ Cidra Puerto Rico
175 I3 Ciechanów Pol.
175 K3 Ciechanowiec Pol.
174 G3 Ciechocinek Pol.
246 C2 Ciego de Ávila Cuba
175 I4 Cielądz Pol.
260 C4 Cielo, Cerro mt. Arg.
183 G4 Ciempozuelos Spain
246 B2 Cienfuegos Cuba
174 F4 Cienin Zaborny Pol.
175 J4 Ciepielów Pol.
175 J5 Ciepłowody Pol.
163 C6 Cier-de-Luchon France
174 F2 Cierznie Pol.
175 L5 Cieszanów Pol.
174 F2 Cieszków Pol.
174 G2 Cieszyn Pol.
174 E4 Cieszyn Wielkopolskie Pol.
163 C5 Cieutat France
163 D6 Cieux France
187 B6 Ciężkowice Pol.
128 B4 Çiftehan Turkey
199 F1 Çiftlik Turkey
199 G2 Çiftlikköy Turkey Kelkit
129 D3 Çiftlikköy Turkey
199 F1 Çiftlikköy Turkey
128 K3 Çiftlikköy Turkey
183 H4 Cifuentes Spain
177 H3 Cigale Hungary
177 K3 Cigánd Hungary
199 D3 Cigdem Turkey
183 G5 Cigales Spain
126 D3 Cihanbeyli Turkey
199 F2 Cihanbeyli Turkey
244 B4 Cihuatlán Mex.
185 F1 Cíjara, Embalse de resr Spain
177 J6 Cik r. Yugo.
134 Yunnan China see Gongshan
242 F3 Cikobia i. Fiji
85 ◻2 Cikobia i. Fiji
95 E4 Cilacap Jawa Tengah Indon.
127 F2 Çıldır Turkey
127 F2 Çıldır Gölü l. Turkey
94 D4 Ciledug Jawa Barat Indon.
109 D2 Cili Hunan China
197 G4 Cilieni Romania
199 G1 Çilimli Turkey
177 L4 Ciuhol Romania
136 D4 Ciulur r. Moldova
191 H2 Ciuluzetto Italy
92 B2 Claveria Phil.
224 D5 Clinton Ont. Can.
81 B7 Clinton South I. N.Z.
226 D3 Clinton IA U.S.A.
231 E5 Clinton KY U.S.A.
232 D4 Clinton LA U.S.A.
234 D3 Clinton MA U.S.A.
235 D5 Clinton MD U.S.A.
230 C4 Clinton MO U.S.A.
231 E5 Clinton MS U.S.A.
231 J2 Clinton NC U.S.A.
234 D2 Clinton NJ U.S.A.
233 H3 Clinton NY U.S.A.
231 J2 Clinton OK U.S.A.
231 E5 Clinton SC U.S.A.
232 C4 Clinton TN U.S.A.
231 I2 Clinton WI U.S.A.
222 H4 Clinton-Colden Lake N.W.T. Can.
226 C3 Clintonville WI U.S.A.
231 D6 Clio AL U.S.A.
232 C4 Clio MI U.S.A.
159 H5 Clion France
160 C2 Clion France
147 D4 Clisham hill Scotland U.K.
191 H2 Clisson France
237 E6 Clishall U.S.A.
150 D1 Clitheroe Lancashire, England U.K.
237 D5 Clive Alta Can.
81 B7 Clutha r. South I. N.Z.

Column 3 (Câmpulung Moldovenesc section)

241 M3 Cîmpulung Moldovenesc Romania see Câmpulung Moldovenesc
199 F1 Çınarcık Turkey
186 C3 Cinca r. Spain
186 D3 Cinca, Canal de r. Spain
188 F4 Cincar mt. Bos.-Herz.
236 G4 Cincinnati OH U.S.A.
226 A6 Cincinnatus NY U.S.A.
185 G1 Cinco Casas Spain
Cinco de Outubro Angola see Xá-Muteba
260 C6 Cinco Saltos Arg.
186 C4 Cinctorres Spain
197 G3 Cincu Romania
Cinderford Gloucestershire, England U.K.
199 F3 Çine Turkey
157 J2 Çiner r. Turkey
182 E2 Ciñera Spain
150 D1 Ciney Belgium
226 B2 Cinfães Port.
191 I5 Cingoli Italy
192 D2 Cinigiano Italy
192 B3 Ciniselo Balsamo Italy
194 C4 Cinisi Sicilia Italy
177 I3 Cinobaňa Slovakia
159 G4 Cinq-Mars-la-Pile France
195 F4 Cinquefrondi Italy
190 E4 Cinque Terre reg. Italy
245 H5 Cintalapa Mex.
163 D5 Cintegabelle France
161 D5 Cinto, Monte mt. France
157 F5 Cintrey France
183 I2 Cintruénigo Spain
215 G5 Cintsa S. Africa
256 B5 Cinzas r. Brazil
254 F4 Cipó Brazil
257 E3 Cipó r. Brazil
260 D6 Cipolletti Arg.
257 F4 Cipotânea Brazil
187 C4 Cirat Spain
192 B3 Cirbanal mt. Italy
193 G3 Circello Italy

255 G1 Cirebon Jawa Barat Indon.
151 F3 Cirencester Gloucestershire, England U.K.
Cirene tourist site Libya see Cyrene
157 E4 Cirey-sur-Blaise France
157 G4 Cirey-sur-Vezouze France
183 I3 Ciria Spain
190 C3 Ciriè Italy
193 I4 Cirigliano Italy
182 C3 Ciriñuela Spain
195 G3 Cirò Italy
195 G3 Cirò Marina Italy
163 B4 Ciron r. France
225 I1 Cirque Mountain Nfld. Can.
Cirta Alg. see Constantine
183 G5 Ciruelos Spain
190 D4 Ciry-le-Noble France
232 D4 Cisco IL U.S.A.
241 M2 Cisco UT U.S.A.
178 C4 Cismón r. Italy
175 K6 Cisna Pol.
183 C6 Cisnădie Romania
231 D2 Cisne r. Italy
191 H3 Cisón di Valmarino Italy
159 G5 Cissé France
161 E5 Cisterna di Latina Italy
195 G2 Cisternino Italy
183 E2 Cistierna Spain
246 D3 Citadelle Laferrière tourist site Haiti
191 H5 Citerna Italy
245 F5 Citlaltepec Mex.
Citlaltépetl vol. Mex. see Orizaba, Pico de
188 F4 Čitluk Bos.-Herz.
246 D3 Citou France
237 F6 Citronelle AL U.S.A.
214 B5 Citrusdal S. Africa
240 G2 Citrus Heights CA U.S.A.
191 G3 Cittadella Italy
192 D2 Città della Pieve Italy
191 H5 Città di Castello Italy
191 G5 Città di Torino airport Italy
192 E3 Cittaducale Italy
195 G5 Cittanova Italy
193 G2 Cittareale Italy
193 F3 Città Sant'Angelo Italy
193 D3 Cittiglio Italy
177 H3 Cívola Slovakia
231 C5 Ciudad Acuña Mex.
244 D3 Ciudad Altamirano Mex.
251 F2 Ciudad Bolívar Venez.
242 D2 Ciudad Camargo Mex.
242 C3 Ciudad Constitución Mex.
243 H6 Ciudad Cuauhtémoc Mex.
243 H5 Ciudad del Carmen Mex.
253 G3 Ciudad del Este Para.
242 D2 Ciudad Delicias Mex.
242 E2 Ciudad de Valles Mex.
251 F2 Ciudad Guayana Venez.
242 D4 Ciudad Guzmán Mex.
242 E3 Ciudad Hidalgo Mex.
245 F5 Ciudad Ixtepec Mex.
242 D3 Ciudad Juárez Mex.
242 E3 Ciudad Lerdo Mex.
245 E4 Ciudad López Mateos Mex.
256 B1 Ciudad Madero Mex.
245 F4 Ciudad Mante Mex.
244 D3 Ciudad Manuel Doblado Mex.
242 D2 Ciudad Mendoza Mex.
242 E2 Ciudad Mier Mex.
242 F3 Ciudad Obregón Mex.
185 G2 Ciudad Real Spain
185 G2 Ciudad Real prov. Castilla - La Mancha Spain
243 H5 Ciudad Río Bravo Mex.
182 E4 Ciudad Rodrigo Spain
245 F4 Ciudad Serdán Mex.
Ciudad Trujillo Dom. Rep. see Santo Domingo
242 D4 Ciudad Victoria Mex.
197 M3 Ciudanoviţa Romania
177 L4 Ciuhoi Romania
136 D4 Ciulur r. Moldova
177 K5 Ciumeghiu Romania
186 C3 Ciutadella de Menorca Spain
162 C2 Civaux France
191 H2 Civell mt. Italy
182 D4 Civetta, Monte mt. Italy
193 I3 Cividale del Friuli Italy
193 C3 Civita Castellana Italy
193 G2 Civita d'Antino Italy
191 I5 Civitanova Marche Italy
191 I5 Civitanova Alta Italy
193 E3 Civita Italy
193 F3 Civitavecchia Italy
191 G4 Civitella Casanova Italy
156 C4 Civitella d'Agliano Italy
191 G4 Civitella di Romagna Italy
193 E3 Civitella in Val di Chiana Italy
241 L5 Clanton AL U.S.A.
159 G4 Claypool AZ U.S.A.
151 I5 Clayton East Sussex, England U.K.

Column 4 (Clachan section)

146 B4 Clachan Highland, Scotland U.K. see
238 B2 Clackamas r. OR U.S.A.
146 E5 Clackmannanshire admin. div. Scotland U.K.
151 I3 Clacton-on-Sea Essex, England U.K.
146 C5 Cladich Argyll and Bute, Scotland U.K.
148 B3 Clady Northern Ireland U.K.
148 C3 Clady Northern Ireland U.K.
146 C5 Claggan Highland, Scotland U.K.
162 C2 Clain r. France
163 C4 Clairac France
223 H3 Claire, Lake Alta Can.
222 A4 Claire Lake SD U.S.A.
226 A3 Clair Lake SD U.S.A.
156 C3 Clairoix France
163 E4 Clairvaux-d'Aveyron France
160 D2 Clairvaux-les-Lacs France
162 C2 Claise r. France
161 D3 Claix France
160 D1 Clamecy France
147 C5 Clam Lake WI U.S.A.
148 B3 Clanabogan Northern Ireland U.K.
240 I2 Clan Alpine Mountains NV U.S.A.
81 C6 Clandeboye South I. N.Z.
147 E3 Clane Rep. of Ireland
151 F3 Clanfield Oxfordshire, England U.K.
161 F4 Clans France
231 C5 Clanton AL U.S.A.
214 B5 Clanwilliam S. Africa
214 B5 Clanwilliam S. Africa
146 C6 Claonaig Argyll and Bute, Scotland U.K.
151 G2 Clapham Bedfordshire, England U.K.
149 G3 Clapham North Yorkshire, England U.K.
261 H2 Clara Arg.
85 E3 Clara r. Qld Austr.
147 D3 Clara Rep. of Ireland
85 E3 Claraville Qld Austr.
149 I4 Clarborough Nottinghamshire, England U.K.
83 E3 Clare N.S.W. Austr.
82 D3 Clare S.A. Austr.
147 C4 Clare county Rep. of Ireland
149 D4 Clare r. Rep. of Ireland
151 H2 Clare Suffolk, England U.K.
226 E4 Clare MI U.S.A.
147 D3 Clarecastle Rep. of Ireland
147 C4 Clareen Rep. of Ireland
147 C3 Claregalway Rep. of Ireland
147 A3 Clare Island Rep. of Ireland
246 ◻ Claremont Jamaica
233 G3 Claremont NH U.S.A.
85 E2 Claremont Isles Qld Austr.
147 C3 Claremore OK U.S.A.
147 C3 Claremorris Rep. of Ireland
82 C2 Clarence r. N.S.W. Austr.
81 D5 Clarence r. South I. N.Z.
81 A6 Clarence, Mount South I. N.Z.
86 C3 Clarke Reef W.A. Austr.
160 C2 Clermain France
262 U2 Clarence Island Antarctica
84 B1 Clarence Strait N.T. Austr.
222 C3 Clarence Strait AK U.S.A.
246 C2 Clarence Town Bahamas
81 C7 Clarendon South I. N.Z.
237 F5 Clarendon AR U.S.A.
232 D4 Clarendon PA U.S.A.
237 C5 Clarendon TX U.S.A.
246 ◻ Clarendon parish Jamaica
246 ◻ Clarendon Park Jamaica
225 K3 Clarenville Nfld. Can.
223 G4 Claresholm Alta Can.
222 H5 Claret Languedoc-Roussillon France
161 D5 Claret Provence-Alpes-Côte-d'Azur France
187 C5 Clariano r. Spain
232 C4 Clarinda IA U.S.A.
232 C5 Clarington OH U.S.A.
232 D4 Clarion IA U.S.A.
232 D4 Clarion r. PA U.S.A.
246 □ Clarion Bank sea feature Bahamas
80 E2 Claris North I. N.Z.
236 D3 Clark SD U.S.A.
222 F1 Clark, Mount N.W.T. Can.
234 B2 Clark Creek r. PA U.S.A.
241 K4 Clarkdale AZ U.S.A.
85 F3 Clarke r. Qld Austr.
215 G4 Clarkebury S. Africa
84 B5 Clarke Range mts Qld Austr.
236 A5 Clarke River Qld Austr.
85 E3 Clarkes Creek r. Qld Austr.
225 K3 Clarke's Head Nfld. Can.
231 C5 Clarkesville GA U.S.A.
234 C2 Clarksburg MD U.S.A.
232 C5 Clarksburg WV U.S.A.
237 F5 Clarksdale MS U.S.A.
241 K2 Clarkson South I. N.Z.
226 D5 Clarks Junction South I. N.Z.
214 E5 Clarkson S. Africa
234 C1 Clarks Summit PA U.S.A.
232 C5 Clarkston WA U.S.A.
240 □ Clark's Town Jamaica
235 G1 Clarksville AR U.S.A.
231 C4 Clarksville IN U.S.A.
234 A2 Clarksville MD U.S.A.
234 B5 Clarksville TX U.S.A.
235 F1 Clarksville TX U.S.A.
256 B1 Claro r. Mato Grosso Brazil
255 B1 Claro r. Goiás Brazil
192 □ Claro Switz.
150 D2 Clashmore Highland, Scotland U.K.
146 C6 Clashnessie Highland, Scotland U.K.
238 B2 Clatskanie OR U.S.A.
146 E4 Clatt Aberdeenshire, Scotland U.K.
257 F2 Cláudio Brazil
147 D2 Claudy Northern Ireland U.K.
171 L4 Clausnitz Ger.
177 I3 Clausthal-Zellerfeld Ger.
92 B2 Claveria Phil.
146 D6 Clavering Essex, England U.K.
150 E2 Claverley Shropshire, England U.K.
161 J5 Clavier Belgium
165 E4 Claxton GA U.S.A.
162 C2 Clay r. France
231 D5 Clay WV U.S.A.
234 C2 Clay VA U.S.A.
236 E4 Clay Center KS U.S.A.
236 D3 Clay Center NE U.S.A.
231 C5 Clay City KY U.S.A.
231 C4 Clay City IL U.S.A.
151 G2 Claydon Oxon, England U.K.
163 C4 Claye-Souilly France
85 E3 Claymont OH U.S.A.
235 I2 Claypole Lincolnshire, England U.K.
241 L5 Claypool AZ U.S.A.
151 J5 Clay Springs AZ U.S.A.
151 I5 Clayton West Sussex, England U.K.
234 C3 Clayton DE U.S.A.
231 C5 Clayton GA U.S.A.
231 C5 Clayton NM U.S.A.
237 E5 Clayton OK U.S.A.
149 I4 Clayton-le-Moors Lancashire, England U.K.
80 B5 Cleadale Highland, Scotland U.K.

Column 5 (Cleadon section)

149 H3 Cleadon Tyne and Wear, England U.K.
147 B5 Cleady Rep. of Ireland
147 B5 Clear, Cape Rep. of Ireland
232 C5 Clearco WV U.S.A.
240 G1 Clear Creek Ont. Can.
241 L2 Clear Creek r. UT U.S.A.
241 L4 Clear Creek r. AZ U.S.A.
237 D5 Clear Creek r. WY U.S.A.
237 D5 Clear Fork Brazos r. TX U.S.A.
222 G3 Clear Hills Y.T. Can.
147 B5 Clear Island Rep. of Ireland
236 E3 Clear Lake IA U.S.A.
226 A3 Clear Lake SD U.S.A.
226 A3 Clear Lake SD U.S.A.
238 F2 Clearmont WY U.S.A.
232 E5 Clear Spring MD U.S.A.
223 I3 Clearwater B.C. Can.
222 H4 Clearwater r. Alberta/Saskatchewan Can.
231 C6 Clearwater r. FL U.S.A.
238 C2 Clearwater r. ID U.S.A.
236 D2 Clearwater r. MN U.S.A.
226 C3 Clearwater Lake WI U.S.A.
238 D2 Clearwater Mountains ID U.S.A.
149 F3 Cleator Moor Cumbria, England U.K.
147 D5 Cleburne TX U.S.A.
159 D5 Cléby France
159 F3 Céder France
150 E2 Cleehill Shropshire, England U.K.
238 B2 Cle Elum WA U.S.A.
149 I4 Cleethorpes North East Lincolnshire, England U.K.
157 F4 Clefmont France
158 C4 Cléguer France
158 C3 Cléguérec France
150 E2 Clehonger Herefordshire, England U.K.
197 G3 Clejani Romania
161 D4 Cleize France
165 E5 Clémency Lux.
256 B4 Clementina Brazil
231 D5 Clemson SC U.S.A.
232 C5 Clendenin WV U.S.A.
168 F3 Clenze Ger.
150 E2 Cleobury Mortimer Shropshire, England U.K.
156 B3 Cléon France
234 B2 Cleona PA U.S.A.
161 C4 Cléon-d'Andran France
92 A4 Cleopatra Needle mt. Palawan Phil.
159 G4 Clère-les-Pins France
156 B3 Clères France
156 E4 Clerf Lux. see Clervaux
257 H1 Clercy Que. Can.
161 C3 Clérieux France
81 A6 Clerke, Mount South I. N.Z.
86 C3 Clerke Reef W.A. Austr.
161 C3 Clermont Picardie France
163 D5 Clermont Midi-Pyrénées France
254 F3 Clermont Argus, Scotland U.K.
163 D5 Clermont FL U.S.A.
159 F4 Clermont-Créans France
162 C2 Clermont-de-Beauregard France
Clermont de Tonnère atoll Arch. des Tuamotu Fr. Polynesia see Reao
157 F3 Clermont-en-Argonne France
161 B3 Clermont-Ferrand France
161 B5 Clermont-l'Hérault France
165 E4 Clerval France
156 E4 Clervaux Lux.
165 F5 Clervé r. Lux.
196 C4 Cléry r. France
156 C2 Cléry-St-André France
82 D2 Cles S.A. Austr.
150 E3 Cleve S.A. Austr.
150 D5 Clevedon North Somerset, England U.K.
231 D5 Cleveland GA U.S.A.
237 F5 Cleveland MS U.S.A.
232 C4 Cleveland OH U.S.A.
231 C5 Cleveland TN U.S.A.
237 E6 Cleveland TX U.S.A.
235 I2 Cleveland UT U.S.A.
232 B6 Cleveland WI U.S.A.
85 F3 Cleveland, Cape Qld Austr.
238 D1 Cleveland, Mount MT U.S.A.
232 C4 Cleveland Heights OH U.S.A.
149 H3 Cleveland Hills England U.K.
146 C6 Cnoc Fraing hill Scotland U.K.
Cnossus tourist site Greece see Knossos
182 D1 Côa r. Port.
177 L5 Codru-Moma, Munţii mts Romania
150 E2 Codsall Staffordshire, England U.K.
237 E5 Cody r. WY U.S.A.
238 F2 Cody WY U.S.A.
232 B6 Coeburn VA U.S.A.
243 H6 Coega S. Africa
184 E3 Coelemu Chile
256 A5 Coelho Neto Brazil
254 E5 Coelho Neto Brazil
85 E2 Coen Qld Austr.
215 K1 Coenen S. Africa
164 D3 Coesfeld Ger.
109 C6 Coetivy i. Seychelles
214 E3 Coetzersdam S. Africa
238 C2 Coeur d'Alene ID U.S.A.
238 C2 Coeur d'Alene r. ID U.S.A.
164 F2 Coevorden Neth.
226 E5 Coffee Bay S. Africa
215 H6 Coffee Bay S. Africa
222 B2 Coffee Creek Y.T. Can.
237 F5 Coffeeville MS U.S.A.
237 E5 Coffeyville KS U.S.A.
82 B3 Coffin Bay S.A. Austr.
82 B3 Coffin Bay r. S.A. Austr.
83 C2 Coffs Harbour N.S.W. Austr.
215 F5 Cofimvaba S. Africa
245 F4 Cofre de Perote mt. Mex.
187 D5 Cofrentes Spain

Column 6 (Clogh section)

147 E4 Clogh Wexford Rep. of Ireland
147 E2 Clogh Northern Ireland U.K.
147 D2 Cloghan Donegal Rep. of Ireland
147 D3 Cloghan Offaly Rep. of Ireland
148 B4 Cloghan Westmeath Rep. of Ireland
147 C2 Cloghane Rep. of Ireland
147 C2 Cloghboy Rep. of Ireland
147 D4 Clogheen Rep. of Ireland
147 E2 Clogher Northern Ireland U.K.
147 E3 Clogherhead Rep. of Ireland
147 E1 Clogh Mills Northern Ireland U.K.
147 F2 Cloghy Northern Ireland U.K.
147 E3 Clohamon Rep. of Ireland
147 C3 Clonakenny Rep. of Ireland
147 C5 Clonakilty Rep. of Ireland
147 C5 Clonakilty Bay Rep. of Ireland
147 B4 Clonare Rep. of Ireland
148 B4 Clonaslee Rep. of Ireland
147 C3 Clonbern Rep. of Ireland
147 C4 Clonbur Rep. of Ireland
147 D4 Clondalkin Rep. of Ireland
147 E3 Clonee Rep. of Ireland
147 C4 Cloneen Rep. of Ireland
147 E4 Clonegal Rep. of Ireland
147 D4 Clonmany Rep. of Ireland
147 D4 Clonmel Rep. of Ireland
147 E4 Clonmellon Rep. of Ireland
147 E4 Clonmore Carlow Rep. of Ireland
147 D4 Clonmore Tipperary Rep. of Ireland
147 D3 Clonony Rep. of Ireland
147 C2 Clonoulty Rep. of Ireland
147 D4 Clonroche Rep. of Ireland
147 C2 Contarf Rep. of Ireland
147 D3 Clontibret Rep. of Ireland
147 D3 Clonygowan Rep. of Ireland
147 B4 Cloonacool Rep. of Ireland
147 B4 Cloonbannin Rep. of Ireland
147 B4 Cloonboo Rep. of Ireland
147 C3 Cloonagh Rep. of Ireland
147 C3 Cloonfad Roscommon Rep. of Ireland
147 C3 Cloonfad Roscommon Rep. of Ireland
147 C3 Cloonkeen Rep. of Ireland
147 C3 Cloontia Rep. of Ireland
222 E5 Clo-oose B.C. Can.
168 D3 Cloppenburg Ger.
226 A2 Cloquet r. MN U.S.A.
226 A2 Cloquet MN U.S.A.
258 F2 Clorinda Arg.
146 E6 Closeburn Dumfries and Galloway, Scotland U.K.
226 C1 Cloud Bay Ont. Can.
238 F2 Cloud Peak WY U.S.A.
81 B4 Cloudy Bay South I. N.Z.
162 C2 Clouère r. France
147 E2 Clough Northern Ireland U.K.
149 G4 Cloughton North Yorkshire, England U.K.
146 □3 Clousta Shetland, Scotland U.K.
224 F3 Clova Que. Can.
146 E5 Clova Angus, Scotland U.K.
150 C3 Clovelly Devon, England U.K.
146 F6 Clovenfords Scottish Borders, Scotland U.K.
241 K1 Clover UT U.S.A.
240 F3 Cloverdale CA U.S.A.
240 H3 Clovis CA U.S.A.
237 C5 Clovis NM U.S.A.
146 C5 Clovullin Highland, Scotland U.K.
149 H4 Clowne Derbyshire, England U.K.
156 B3 Cloyes-sur-le-Loir France
162 A2 Cloyne Ont. Can.
147 C5 Cloyne Rep. of Ireland
146 C4 Cluainie, Loch l. Scotland U.K.
221 J3 Cluff Lake Mine Sask. Can.
221 I3 Cluis France
197 K3 Cluj-Napoca Romania
161 E4 Clumanc France
150 D2 Clun Shropshire, England U.K.
150 D2 Clun r. England U.K.
146 D5 Clunes Highland, Scotland U.K.
82 D3 Cluny France
161 C2 Cluny France
190 E3 Clusone Italy
232 D6 Cluster Springs VA U.S.A.
81 B7 Clutha r. South I. N.Z.
87 E5 Clutterbuck Hills Hill W.A. Austr.
150 D2 Clun Bath and North East Somerset, England U.K.
150 C1 Clwydian Range hills Wales U.K.
150 D1 Clwyd Vale Rhondda Cynon Taff, Wales U.K.
231 D6 Clyde Alta Can.
81 B7 Clyde South I. N.Z.
146 D6 Clyde r. Scotland U.K.
222 H4 Clyde r. NV U.S.A.
146 D6 Clyde, Firth of est. Scotland U.K.
146 D6 Clydebank West Dunbartonshire, Scotland U.K.
221 L2 Clyde River Nunavut Can.
146 D1 Clydesdale val. Scotland U.K.
81 B7 Clydevale South I. N.Z.
226 C4 Clyman WI U.S.A.
150 C2 Clynderwen Carmarthenshire, Wales U.K.
150 C1 Clyro Powys, Wales U.K.
146 C6 Cnoc Moy hill Scotland U.K.

Column 7 (Coatesville section)

234 C3 Coatesville PA U.S.A.
225 U4 Coaticook Que. Can.
221 J3 Coats Island Nunavut Can.
262 V1 Coats Land reg. Antarctica
245 G4 Coatzacoalcos Mex.
245 G4 Coatzacoalcos r. Mex.
245 F5 Coatzintla Mex.
197 I3 Cobadin Romania
227 H2 Cobalt Ont. Can.
235 I1 Cobalt CT U.S.A.
243 H6 Cobán Guat.
245 G2 Cobanlağı Hatti Azer./Georgia
199 G2 Çobanlar Turkey
83 F2 Çobar N.S.W. Austr.
83 G4 Cobargo N.S.W. Austr.
84 D3 Cobb, Lake salt flat Qld U.K.
151 G3 Cobden Vic. Austr.
227 I3 Cobden Ont. Can.
147 C5 Cobh Rep. of Ireland
183 H4 Cobeja Spain
183 H4 Cobeta Spain
147 C5 Cóbh France see Koblenz
233 J3 Cobleskill NY U.S.A.
148 C4 Coblinstown Rep. of Ireland
224 E4 Cobo AK U.S.A.
260 D6 Cobourg Peninsula N.T. Austr.
227 G4 Cobourg Ont. Can.
87 C5 Cobra W.A. Austr.
83 F3 Cobram Vic. Austr.
184 C3 Cobres r. Port.
252 C4 Cobres Spain
254 C5 Cocachacra Peru
254 B2 Cocal Brazil
234 B2 Cocalico Creek r. PA U.S.A.
254 C5 Cocalinho Brazil
Cocanada Andhra Prad. India see Kakinada
252 D4 Cocapata Bol.
193 H4 Coccovello, Monte mt. Italy
252 D4 Cocentaina Spain
252 D4 Cochabamba Bol.
252 D4 Cochabamba dept Bol.
259 B6 Cochamó Chile
260 A5 Cocharcas Chile
169 C5 Cochem Ger.
114 Cochin Kerala India
241 M5 Cochise AZ U.S.A.
241 M5 Cochise Head mt. AZ U.S.A.
231 D5 Cochran GA U.S.A.
222 H5 Cochrane Alta Can.
224 D3 Cochrane Ont. Can.
223 I3 Cochrane r. Sask. Can.
259 B7 Cochrane Chile
223 I3 Cochranton PA U.S.A.
234 A2 Cochstedt Ger.
171 K4 Cochstedt Ger.
177 L5 Cociuba Mare Romania
82 C3 Cockaleechie S.A. Austr.
151 I4 Cock Bridge Aberdeenshire, Scotland U.K.
82 E3 Cockburn S.A. Austr.
246 D3 Cockburn Harbour Turks and Caicos Is
146 C5 Cockburnspath Scottish Borders, Scotland U.K.
246 C2 Cockburn Town San Salvador Bahamas
Cockburn Town Turks and Caicos Is see Grand Turk
149 H2 Cockenheugh hill England U.K.
146 F6 Cockenzie and Port Seton East Lothian, Scotland U.K.
149 G4 Cocker r. England U.K.
149 G4 Cockerham Lancashire, England U.K.
149 F3 Cockermouth Cumbria, England U.K.
149 H4 Cockett Swansea, Wales U.K.
150 D1 Cockeysville MD U.S.A.
234 B3 Cockfield Durham, England U.K.
234 B3 Cocklebiddy W.A. Austr.
215 E5 Cockscomb mt. S. Africa
254 C4 Coco r. Brazil
242 ◻J6 Coco r. Hond./Nic.
227 N5 Coco, Isla de i. N. Pacific Ocean
208 A4 Cocobeach Gabon
115 G3 Coconada Chile
241 K4 Coconino Plateau AZ U.S.A.
83 F3 Cocoparra Range hills N.S.W. Austr.
250 C3 Cocorná Col.
254 C5 Cocos Brazil
255 K4 Cocos Basin sea feature Indian Ocean
86 ◻1 Cocos Islands terr. Indian Ocean
267 N5 Cocos Ridge sea feature N. Pacific Ocean
244 C3 Cocula Mex.
163 C4 Cocumont France
252 C4 Cod, Cape MA U.S.A.
197 H2 Codăeşti Romania
251 F5 Codajás Brazil
149 H3 Codbeck r. England U.K.
151 I3 Coddenham Suffolk, England U.K.
149 I4 Coddington Nottinghamshire, England U.K.
234 J5 Coderre Sask. Can.
191 H3 Codevigo Italy
81 A7 Codfish Island Stewart I. N.Z.
192 B3 Codi, Monte mt. Sardegna Italy
252 C3 Codigoro Italy
197 G3 Codlea Romania
149 H4 Codnor Derbyshire, England U.K.
254 E3 Codó Brazil
190 E3 Codogno Italy
186 B1 Codos airport Spain
234 B3 Codorus PA U.S.A.
183 I3 Codos Spain
260 C3 Codrongianos Sardegna Italy
197 K3 Codrington, Mount Antarctica
191 H3 Codroipo Italy
177 L5 Codru-Moma, Munţii mts Romania

Cogo to Correntina
295

207 H6 Cogo Equat. Guinea
190 D4 Cogoleto Italy
161 E5 Cogolin France
183 G2 Cogollos Spain
183 F2 Cogollos r. Spain
185 G3 Cogollos Vega Spain
183 G4 Cogolludo Spain
182 C4 Cogula Port.
234 C3 Cohansey r. NJ U.S.A.
Čohkkiras Sweden see Jukkasjärvi
232 E3 Cohocton r. NY U.S.A.
233 G3 Cohoes NY U.S.A.
83 F3 Cohuna Vic. Austr.
242 □J8 Coiba, Isla i. Panama
262 T3 Coig r. Arg.
146 C3 Coigeach, Rubha pt Scotland U.K.
259 B7 Coihaique Chile
260 A5 Coihüe Chile
114 C4 Coimbatore Tamil Nadu India
182 B4 Coimbra Port.
182 B4 Coimbra admin. dist. Port.
185 F4 Coín Spain
156 D3 Coincy France
252 C4 Coipasa, Salar de salt flat Bol.
Coire Switz. see Chur
160 C3 Coise r. France
182 C4 Coja Port.
197 G3 Cojasca Romania
250 D2 Cojedes state Venez.
259 C7 Cojudo Blanco, Cerro mt. Arg.
177 J6 Čoka Vojvodina, Srbija Yugo.
238 E3 Cokeville WY U.S.A.
83 E4 Colac Vic. Austr.
81 A7 Colac South I. N.Z.
260 C1 Colangüil, Cordillera de mts Arg.
254 C2 Colares Brazil
257 G3 Colatina Brazil
163 C4 Colayrac-St-Cirq France
169 D5 Cölbe Ger.
Colbert Alg. see Aïn Oulmene
171 C3 Colbitz Ger.
191 H5 Colbordola Italy
227 I4 Colborne Ont. Can.
260 B4 Colbún Chile
236 C4 Colby KS U.S.A.
226 B3 Colby WI U.S.A.
252 B3 Colca r. Peru
197 H3 Colceag Romania
215 E5 Colchester S. Africa
151 H3 Colchester Essex, England U.K.
235 F1 Colchester CT U.S.A.
226 B5 Colchester IL U.S.A.
220 B4 Cold Bay AK U.S.A.
151 F4 Colden Common Hampshire, England U.K.
146 F6 Coldingham Scottish Borders, Scotland U.K.
171 D4 Colditz Ger.
223 I4 Cold Lake Alta Can.
234 D4 Cold Spring NJ U.S.A.
235 E1 Cold Spring NY U.S.A.
237 E6 Coldspring TX U.S.A.
240 I2 Cold Springs NV U.S.A.
222 G5 Coldstream B.C. Can.
81 C6 Coldstream South I. N.Z.
146 F6 Coldstream Scottish Borders, Scotland U.K.
227 H3 Coldwater Ont. Can.
237 D4 Coldwater KS U.S.A.
226 E5 Coldwater MI U.S.A.
237 F5 Coldwater r. MS U.S.A.
237 C4 Coldwater Creek r. OK U.S.A.
226 D1 Coldwell Ont. Can.
233 H2 Colebrook NH U.S.A.
215 G3 Coleford S. Africa
150 E3 Coleford Gloucestershire, England U.K.
150 E3 Coleford Somerset, England U.K.
85 E2 Coleman r. Qld Austr.
234 B3 Coleman MD U.S.A.
226 E4 Coleman MI U.S.A.
237 D6 Coleman TX U.S.A.
226 C3 Coleman WI U.S.A.
Çölemerik Turkey see Hakkârı
215 G3 Colenso S. Africa
197 G3 Colentina r. Romania
262 T2 Cole Peninsula Antarctica
82 E4 Coleraine Vic. Austr.
147 E1 Coleraine Northern Ireland U.K.
226 A2 Coleraine MN U.S.A.
81 C5 Coleridge, Lake South I. N.Z.
150 E3 Colerne Wiltshire, England U.K.
114 C4 Coleroon r. India
252 C4 Coles, Punta de pt Peru
83 G5 Coles Bay Tas. Austr.
215 E4 Colesberg S. Africa
151 F2 Coleshill Warwickshire, England U.K.
234 A3 Colesville MD U.S.A.
234 D1 Colesville NJ U.S.A.
223 I5 Coleville Sask. Can.
240 H2 Coleville CA U.S.A.
240 G2 Colfax CA U.S.A.
226 C5 Colfax IL U.S.A.
237 E6 Colfax LA U.S.A.
238 C2 Colfax WA U.S.A.
226 B3 Colfax WI U.S.A.
146 □H1 Colgrave Sound str. Scotland U.K.
259 C7 Colhué Huapí, Lago l. Arg.
197 G3 Colibași Romania
190 E2 Colico Italy
160 D2 Coligny France
215 F2 Coligny S. Africa
247 □2 Colihaut Dominica
164 C3 Colijnsplaat Neth.
244 C4 Colima Mex.
244 C4 Colima state Mex.
244 C4 Colima, Nevado de vol. Mex.
256 C4 Colina Brazil
260 B3 Colina Chile
254 D3 Colinas Brazil
183 G1 Colindres Spain
146 C6 Colintraive Argyll and Bute, Scotland U.K.
254 B5 Coliseu r. Brazil
146 B5 Coll i. Scotland U.K.
185 G3 Collado Bajo mt. Spain
183 G3 Collado Hermoso Spain
183 G4 Collado Villalba Spain
190 F4 Collagna Italy
193 D4 Collalto mt. Austria/Italy
182 E1 Collanzo Spain
83 G2 Collarenebri N.S.W. Austr.
193 F2 Collarmele Italy
193 E2 Collazzone Italy
193 F4 Collecchio Italy
190 F4 Colledara Italy
191 G5 Colle di Val d'Elsa Italy
213 F4 Colleen Dawn Zimbabwe
193 F3 Colleferro Italy
231 C5 College Park GA U.S.A.
237 D6 College Station TX U.S.A.
234 C2 Collegeville PA U.S.A.
190 C3 Collegno Italy
191 G2 Colle Isarco Italy
193 F3 Collelongo Italy
193 F3 Collepardo Italy
195 H2 Collepasso Italy
83 F2 Collerina N.S.W. Austr.
190 F5 Collesalvetti Italy
193 G3 Colle Sannita Italy
194 C5 Collesano Sicilia Italy
193 G3 Colletorto Italy
234 B1 Colley PA U.S.A.
193 H4 Colliano Italy
193 G3 Colli a Volturno Italy
83 G2 Collie N.S.W. Austr.
87 C7 Collie W.A. Austr.
86 E3 Collier Bay W.A. Austr.
87 C5 Collier Range hills W.A. Austr.
237 F5 Collierville TN U.S.A.
146 G4 Collieston Aberdeenshire, Scotland U.K.
146 E6 Collin Dumfries and Galloway, Scotland U.K.
192 A5 Collinas Sardegna Italy
158 D3 Collinée France
149 I4 Collingham Nottinghamshire, England U.K.
168 C2 Collinghorst (Rhauderfehn) Ger.
224 D4 Collingwood Ont. Can.
80 D4 Collingwood South I. N.Z.
235 D2 Collingwood Park NJ U.S.A.
237 F6 Collins MS U.S.A.
221 H2 Collinson Peninsula Nunavut Can.
85 F4 Collinsville Qld Austr.
231 C5 Collinsville AL U.S.A.
237 E4 Collinsville OK U.S.A.
232 D6 Collinsville VA U.S.A.
178 B5 Collio Italy
163 F6 Collioure France
260 A5 Collipulli Chile
171 E4 Collmberg hill Ger.
161 E5 Collobrières France
190 B2 Collombey Switz.
234 A1 Collomsville PA U.S.A.
147 E3 Collon Rep. of Ireland
160 D2 Collonges France
162 D3 Collonges-la-Rouge France
147 C2 Collooney Rep. of Ireland
157 H4 Colmar France
161 E4 Colmars France
173 E2 Colmberg Ger.
182 C4 Colmeal Port.
185 F4 Colmenar Spain
182 E4 Colmenar de Montemayor Spain
183 G4 Colmenar de Oreja Spain
183 G4 Colmenar Viejo Spain
160 B1 Colméry France
146 D6 Colmonell South Ayrshire, Scotland U.K.
151 F3 Coln r. England U.K.
146 E4 Colnabaichin Aberdeenshire, Scotland U.K.
151 G3 Colnbrook Windsor and Maidenhead, England U.K.
149 G4 Colne Lancashire, England U.K.
151 H3 Colne r. England U.K.
151 G3 Colney Heath Hertfordshire, England U.K.
168 D3 Colnrade Ger.
83 G3 Colo r. N.S.W. Austr.
195 F2 Colobraro Italy
191 G3 Cologna Veneta Italy
163 C5 Cologne France
Cologne Ger. see Köln
234 D3 Cologne NJ U.S.A.
226 D4 Coloma MI U.S.A.
226 C3 Coloma WI U.S.A.
Colomb-Béchar Alg. see Béchar
159 F2 Colombelles France
156 C4 Colombes France
157 F4 Colombey-les-Belles France
157 E4 Colombey-les Deux-Églises France
256 C4 Colômbia Brazil
250 C4 Colombia Col.
243 F3 Colombia Mex.
250 C4 Colombia country S. America
264 D5 Colombian Basin sea feature S. Atlantic Ocean
190 B2 Colombier Switz.
160 E3 Colombier, Mont mt. France
163 E4 Colombiès France
256 C6 Colombo Brazil
114 C5 Colombo Sri Lanka
227 H1 Colombourg Que. Can.
183 F1 Colombres Spain
185 G3 Colomera Spain
185 G3 Colomera r. Spain
186 F2 Colomers Spain
163 D5 Colomiers France
261 G3 Colón Buenos Aires Arg.
261 H3 Colón Entre Ríos Arg.
246 B2 Colón Cuba
244 D3 Colón Mex.
242 □K7 Colón Panama
226 E5 Colon MI U.S.A.
Colón, Archipiélago de is Pacific Ocean see Galápagos, Islas
82 C2 Colona S.A. Austr.
116 E4 Colonelganj Uttar Prad. India
246 D2 Colonel Hill Bahamas
258 E2 Colonia Arg.
91 I5 Colonia Yap Micronesia
261 I4 Colonia dept Uru.
235 D2 Colonia NJ U.S.A.
Colonia Agrippina Ger. see Köln
260 D4 Colonia Alvear Arg.
261 F5 Colonia Barón Arg.
260 E3 Colonia Biagorria Arg.
261 H3 Colonia Caseros Arg.
260 E6 Colonia Choele Choel, Isla i. Arg.
261 I4 Colonia del Sacramento Uru.
187 G5 Colònia de Sant Jordi Spain
187 G5 Colònia de Sant Pere Spain
258 E3 Colonia Dora Arg.
261 F4 Colonia Hilario Lagos Arg.
Colonia Julia Fenestris Italy see Fano
259 C7 Colonia Las Heras Arg.
232 E6 Colonial Heights VA U.S.A.
234 B2 Colonial Park PA U.S.A.
195 G3 Colonna, Capo c. Italy
193 F2 Colonnella Italy
267 M5 Colon Ridge sea feature Pacific Ocean
146 B5 Colonsay i. Scotland U.K.
260 F6 Colorado r. Arg.
258 D3 Colorado r. La Rioja Arg.
260 C2 Colorado r. San Juan Arg.
256 B5 Colorado Brazil
260 B4 Colorado r. Chile
245 F5 Colorado r. Mex.
242 B2 Colorado r. Mex./U.S.A.
237 D6 Colorado r. TX U.S.A.
241 M2 Colorado state U.S.A.
260 D2 Colorado, Cerro mt. Arg.
259 E5 Colorado, Delta del Río Arg.
241 K3 Colorado City AZ U.S.A.
237 C5 Colorado City TX U.S.A.
241 I5 Colorado Desert CA U.S.A.
241 M3 Colorado Plateau CO U.S.A.
258 C2 Colorados, Cerro mt. Arg.
239 F4 Colorado Springs CO U.S.A.
190 F4 Colorno Italy
184 B3 Colos Port.
Colossae Turkey see Honaz
161 D5 Colostre r. France
245 F6 Colotepec r. Mex.
244 C2 Colotlán Mex.
170 E2 Cölpin Ger.
252 D4 Colquechaca Bol.
146 E6 Colquhar Scottish Borders, Scotland U.K.
252 D4 Colquiri Bol.
231 C6 Colquitt GA U.S.A.
157 H4 Colroy-la-Grande France
232 B6 Colson KY U.S.A.
151 G2 Colsterworth Lincolnshire, England U.K.
238 F2 Colstrip MT U.S.A.
151 I2 Coltishall Norfolk, England U.K.
240 I4 Colton CA U.S.A.
233 F2 Colton NY U.S.A.
241 L2 Colton UT U.S.A.
235 D2 Colts Neck NJ U.S.A.
187 B7 Columbares hill Spain
235 F1 Columbia CT U.S.A.
230 C4 Columbia KY U.S.A.
237 E5 Columbia LA U.S.A.
234 B3 Columbia MD U.S.A.
236 E4 Columbia MO U.S.A.
237 F6 Columbia MS U.S.A.
231 E5 Columbia NC U.S.A.
234 C2 Columbia NJ U.S.A.
234 B2 Columbia PA U.S.A.
231 D5 Columbia SC U.S.A.
231 C5 Columbia TN U.S.A.
238 B2 Columbia r. WA U.S.A.
221 K1 Columbia, Cape Nunavut Can.
234 A4 Columbia, District of admin. dist. U.S.A.
222 G4 Columbia, Mount Alta/B.C. Can.
242 B2 Columbia, Sierra mts Mex.
230 C3 Columbia City IN U.S.A.
234 B1 Columbia County county PA U.S.A.
233 □J2 Columbia Falls ME U.S.A.
238 D1 Columbia Falls MT U.S.A.
222 F4 Columbia Mountains B.C. Can.
231 C5 Columbiana AL U.S.A.
232 C4 Columbiana OH U.S.A.
238 C2 Columbia Plateau U.S.A.
214 A5 Columbine, Cape S. Africa
231 C5 Columbus GA U.S.A.
230 C4 Columbus IN U.S.A.
237 E4 Columbus KS U.S.A.
237 F5 Columbus MS U.S.A.
238 E2 Columbus MT U.S.A.
231 D5 Columbus NC U.S.A.
236 D3 Columbus NE U.S.A.
234 D2 Columbus NJ U.S.A.
239 F6 Columbus NM U.S.A.
232 B5 Columbus OH U.S.A.
232 D4 Columbus PA U.S.A.
237 D6 Columbus TX U.S.A.
226 C4 Columbus WI U.S.A.
232 A4 Columbus Grove OH U.S.A.
257 F3 Coluna Brazil
183 E1 Colunga Spain
240 F2 Colusa CA U.S.A.
80 E2 Colville North I. N.Z.
238 C1 Colville WA U.S.A.
220 C2 Colville r. AK U.S.A.
80 E2 Colville, Cape North I. N.Z.
87 E6 Colville, Lake salt flat W.A. Austr.
80 E2 Colville Channel North I. N.Z.
220 F3 Colville Lake N.W.T. Can.
151 F2 Colwich Staffordshire, England U.K.
150 D1 Colwyn Bay Conwy, Wales U.K.
162 D3 Coly France
150 D4 Colyton Devon, England U.K.
191 H4 Comacchio Italy
191 H4 Comacchio, Valli di lag. Italy
111 E6 Comai Xizang China
244 C4 Comala Mex.
243 G5 Comalcalco Mex.
245 E3 Comales r. Mex.
197 H3 Comana Romania
237 D6 Comanche TX U.S.A.
262 U2 Comandante Ferraz research stn Antarctica
258 F2 Comandante Fontana Arg.
259 C8 Comandante Luis Piedra Buena Arg.
261 I6 Comandante Nicanor Otamendi Arg.
197 H2 Comănești Romania
186 E2 Coma Pedrosa, Pic de mt. Andorra
197 G3 Comarnic Romania
242 □I6 Comayagua Hond.
231 D5 Combahee r. SC U.S.A.
157 F5 Combeaufontaine France
160 E3 Combe de Savoie val. France
150 C3 Combe Martin Devon, England U.K.
147 F2 Comber Northern Ireland U.K.
227 I3 Combermere Ont. Can.
96 A3 Combermere Bay Myanmar
151 H2 Comberton Cambridgeshire, England U.K.
150 E4 Combe St Nicholas Somerset, England U.K.
165 E4 Comblain-au-Pont Belgium
160 C1 Comblanchien France
156 C2 Combles France
160 E3 Combloux France
190 F2 Combolo, Monte mt. Italy/Switz.
158 E3 Combourg France
158 B4 Combrit France
160 B3 Combronde France
260 E3 Comechingones, Sierra de mts Arg.
191 H2 Comeglians Italy
191 H2 Comèlico Superiore Italy
184 C1 Comenda Port.
256 C3 Comendador Gomes Brazil
257 G2 Comercinho Brazil
247 □1 Comerio Puerto Rico
191 H5 Comero, Monte mt. Italy
85 G4 Comet Qld Austr.
85 G4 Comet r. Qld Austr.
237 D6 Comfort TX U.S.A.
232 C5 Comfort WV U.S.A.
117 G5 Comilla Bangl.
183 F1 Comillas Spain
165 B4 Comines Belgium
Comino i. Malta see Kemmuna
Cominotto i. Malta see Kemmunett
194 D6 Comiso Sicilia Italy
245 G5 Comitancillo Mex.
243 G5 Comitán de Domínguez Mex.
194 C5 Comitini Sicilia Italy
177 J6 Comloșu Mare Romania
235 E2 Commack NY U.S.A.
227 H3 Commanda Ont. Can.
147 D2 Commeen Rep. of Ireland
160 D2 Commenailles France
163 B4 Commensacq France
160 A2 Commentry France
158 E5 Commequiers France
159 F3 Commer France
157 F4 Commercy France
214 B4 Commissioner's Salt Pan S. Africa
221 J3 Committee Bay Nunavut Can.
215 H2 Commondale S. Africa
Commonwealth Territory admin. div. Austr. see Jervis Bay Territory
190 E3 Como Italy
190 E3 Como prov. Lombardia Italy
190 E3 Como, Lago di l. Italy
Como, Lake Italy see Como, Lago di
245 G4 Comoapan Mex.
260 B3 Comodoro Arturo Merino Benitez airport Chile
259 D7 Comodoro Rivadavia Arg.
Comoé r. Côte d'Ivoire see Komoé
244 D3 Comonfort Mex.
Comores country Africa see Comoros
217 □3 Comoros country Africa
222 E5 Comox B.C. Can.
185 G4 Cómpeta Spain
190 E4 Compiano Italy
156 C3 Compiègne France
163 E4 Compolibat France
184 B2 Comporta Port.
244 B3 Compostela Mex.
92 C5 Compostela Phil.
162 D3 Compreignac France
256 D6 Comprida, Ilha i. Brazil
161 E5 Comps-sur-Artuby France
240 H5 Compton CA U.S.A.
226 C5 Compton IL U.S.A.
136 E4 Comrat Moldova
146 E5 Comrie Perth and Kinross, Scotland U.K.
237 C6 Comstock TX U.S.A.
193 F2 Comunanza Italy
194 D5 Comunelli r. Sicilia Italy
96 D3 Con, Sông r. Vietnam
111 E7 Cona Xizang China
191 H3 Cona Italy
128 C1 Çona Turkey
206 B4 Conakry Guinea
250 B5 Conambo r. Ecuador
83 F5 Conara Junction Tas. Austr.
192 B3 Conca Corse France
191 H5 Conca r. Italy
260 E3 Concarán Arg.
158 C4 Concarneau France
192 B4 Concas Sardegna Italy
254 F3 Conceição Brazil
256 E2 Conceição r. Brazil
184 C3 Conceição Port.
257 H3 Conceição da Barra Brazil
256 C3 Conceição das Alagoas Brazil
257 G5 Conceição de Macabu Brazil
254 C4 Conceição do Araguaia Brazil
254 F4 Conceição do Coité Brazil
257 F3 Conceição do Mato Dentro Brazil
257 E4 Conceição do Rio Verde Brazil
258 F3 Concepción Arg.
258 D2 Concepción Arg.
253 E4 Concepción Bol.
258 B5 Concepción Chile
244 D1 Concepción Mex.
242 B2 Concepción r. Mex.
242 □J7 Concepción Panama
253 F5 Concepción Para.
244 C4 Concepción de Buenos Aires Mex.
261 H3 Concepción del Uruguay Arg.
212 B4 Conception Bay Namibia
246 D2 Conception Island Bahamas
190 F3 Concesio Italy
213 F3 Concession Zimbabwe
183 G1 Concha Spain
256 C5 Conchas Brazil
239 F5 Conchas NM U.S.A.
156 A4 Conches-en-Ouche France
241 M4 Concho AZ U.S.A.
237 D6 Concho r. TX U.S.A.
242 D2 Conchos r. Chihuahua Mex.
243 F3 Conchos r. Nuevo León/Tamaulipas Mex.
260 B3 Concón Chile
240 F3 Concord CA U.S.A.
226 E4 Concord MI U.S.A.
231 D5 Concord NC U.S.A.
233 H3 Concord NH U.S.A.
232 E4 Concord PA U.S.A.
232 D6 Concord VA U.S.A.
233 H2 Concord VT U.S.A.
261 I2 Concordia Arg.
255 B8 Concórdia Brazil
244 A2 Concordiá Mex.
250 C6 Concordia Peru
214 A3 Concordia S. Africa
236 D4 Concordia KS U.S.A.
191 H3 Concordia Sagittaria Italy
123 H2 Concord Peak Afgh.
163 D4 Concorès France
163 D4 Concots France
260 B2 Concumén Chile
209 B7 Conda Angola
85 G5 Condamine Qld Austr.
85 G5 Condamine r. Qld Austr.
161 A3 Condat France
162 D3 Condat-sur-Vienne France
156 D3 Condé-en-Brie France
242 □I6 Condega Nic.
182 B4 Condeixa-a-Nova Port.
159 G3 Condé-sur-Huisne France
156 D2 Condé-sur-l'Escaut France
159 F3 Condé-sur-Noireau France
159 E2 Condé-sur-Vire France
255 E5 Condeúba Brazil
191 F3 Condino Italy
83 F3 Condobolin N.S.W. Austr.
195 E4 Condofuri Italy
163 C5 Condom France
238 B2 Condon OR U.S.A.
250 B6 Condor, Cordillera del mts Ecuador/Peru
190 C3 Condove Italy
150 E2 Condover Shropshire, England U.K.
231 C6 Conecuh r. AL U.S.A.
191 H3 Conegliano Italy
239 F4 Conejos CO U.S.A.
239 F4 Conejos r. Colorado/New Mexico U.S.A.
227 H5 Conemaugh r. PA U.S.A.
191 I5 Conero, Monte hill Italy
261 G3 Conesa Arg.
234 B3 Conestoga PA U.S.A.
234 B2 Conestoga Creek r. PA U.S.A.
232 C4 Conesville OH U.S.A.
234 B2 Conewago Creek r. PA U.S.A.
157 G5 Coney r. France
235 E2 Coney Island NY U.S.A.
157 F3 Conflans-en-Jarnisy France
157 G5 Conflans-sur-Lanterne France
193 I5 Conflenti Italy
91 L9 Conflict Group is P.N.G.
232 D5 Confluence PA U.S.A.
Confoederatio Helvetica country Europe see Switzerland
162 C2 Confolens France
241 K2 Confusion Range mts UT U.S.A.
253 F6 Confuso r. Para.
147 B3 Cong Rep. of Ireland
150 C4 Congdon's Shop Cornwall, England U.K.
Congdü Xizang China see Nyalam
109 E4 Conghua Guangdong China
108 D3 Congjiang Guizhou China
149 G4 Congleton Cheshire, England U.K.
208 B5 Congo country Africa
209 B6 Congo r. Congo/Dem. Rep. Congo
Congo (Brazzaville) country Africa see Congo
Congo (Kinshasa) country Africa see Congo, Democratic Republic of
208 D5 Congo, Democratic Republic of country Africa
Congo, Republic of country Africa see Congo
208 D5 Congo Basin Dem. Rep. Congo
264 J6 Congo Cone sea feature S. Atlantic Ocean
Congo Free State country Africa see Congo, Democratic Republic of
257 F4 Congonhas Brazil
256 B5 Congonhinhas Brazil
182 D2 Congosto Spain
183 F2 Congosto de Valdavia Spain
150 E3 Congresbury North Somerset, England U.K.
241 K4 Congress AZ U.S.A.
159 E4 Congrier France
243 H5 Conhuas Mex.
81 C6 Conical Peak hill South I. N.Z.
259 C6 Cónico, Cerro mt. Arg.
156 B4 Conie r. France
184 D4 Conil de la Frontera Spain
149 I4 Coningsby Lincolnshire, England U.K.
149 H4 Conisbrough South Yorkshire, England U.K.
84 C4 Coniston N.T. Austr.
224 D4 Coniston Ont. Can.
149 F3 Coniston Cumbria, England U.K.
85 F3 Conjuboy Qld Austr.
185 G4 Conjuros hill Spain
243 H4 Conkal Mex.
223 I4 Conklin Alta Can.
260 E3 Conlara r. Arg.
159 F3 Conlie France
160 D2 Conliège France
147 F2 Conlig Northern Ireland U.K.
224 E2 Conn r. Que. Can.
147 B2 Conn, Lough l. Rep. of Ireland
Connacht reg. Rep. of Ireland see Connaught
150 D1 Connah's Quay Flintshire, Wales U.K.
156 D4 Connantre France
227 G1 Connaught Ont. Can.
147 B3 Connaught reg. Rep. of Ireland
161 C4 Connaux France
232 C4 Conneaut OH U.S.A.
232 C4 Conneaut Lake PA U.S.A.
232 C4 Conneautville PA U.S.A.
235 F1 Connecticut r. CT U.S.A.
233 G4 Connecticut state U.S.A.
146 C5 Connel Argyll and Bute, Scotland U.K.
232 D4 Connellsville PA U.S.A.
85 E5 Connemara Qld Austr.
147 B3 Connemara reg. Rep. of Ireland
84 B5 Conner, Mount hill N.T. Austr.
159 G3 Connerré France
230 C4 Connersville IN U.S.A.
147 B4 Connolly Rep. of Ireland
222 C2 Connolly, Mount Y.T. Can.
146 B7 Connor Northern Ireland U.K.
85 G4 Connors Range hills Qld Austr.
83 F3 Conoble N.S.W. Austr.
234 B2 Conodoguinet Creek r. PA U.S.A.
250 C5 Cononaco r. Ecuador
146 D4 Conon Bridge Highland, Scotland U.K.
177 K5 Conop Romania
177 I6 Čonoplja Vojvodina, Srbija Yugo.
226 C2 Conover WI U.S.A.
170 E2 Conow Ger.
234 B3 Conowingo MD U.S.A.
163 E4 Conques France
163 E5 Conques-sur-Orbiel France
256 D3 Conquista Brazil
185 F2 Conquista Spain
238 E1 Conrad MT U.S.A.
264 L9 Conrad Rise sea feature Southern Ocean
237 E6 Conroe TX U.S.A.
191 G4 Consandolo Italy
261 H2 Conscripto Bernardi Arg.
165 F5 Consdorf Lux.
227 I3 Consecon Ont. Can.
257 F4 Conselheiro Lafaiete Brazil
257 G3 Conselheiro Pena Brazil
191 G4 Conselice Italy
187 F5 Consell Spain
157 F3 Consenvoye France
149 H3 Consett Durham, England U.K.
234 C2 Conshohocken PA U.S.A.
182 B2 Consistorio Spain
246 B2 Consolación del Sur Cuba
97 D5 Côn Sơn i. Vietnam
223 I4 Consort Alta Can.
Constance Ger. see Konstanz
Constance, Lake Ger./Switz. see Bodensee
184 B1 Constância Port.
197 I3 Constanța Romania
Constanța airport Romania see Kogălniceanu
186 E3 Constantí Spain
Constantia tourist site Cyprus see Salamis
Constantia Ger. see Konstanz
182 D3 Constantim Bragança Port.
182 C3 Constantim Vila Real Port.
184 E3 Constantina Spain
205 G1 Constantine Alg.
150 B4 Constantine Cornwall, England U.K.
226 E5 Constantine MI U.S.A.
Constantinople Turkey see İstanbul
183 F4 Constanzana Spain
260 A4 Constitución Chile
261 I2 Constitución Uru.
185 G1 Consuegra Spain
85 G5 Consuelo Qld Austr.
223 I5 Consul Sask. Can.
223 K1 Consul r. Nunavut Can.
238 D3 Contact NV U.S.A.
257 F4 Contagalo Brazil
257 E3 Contagem Brazil
252 B1 Contamana Peru
191 H3 Contarina Italy
254 F5 Contas r. Brazil
215 E3 Content S. Africa
194 C5 Contessa Entellina Sicilia Italy
190 C2 Conthey Switz.
193 E2 Contigliano Italy
146 D4 Contin Highland, Scotland U.K.
232 A4 Continental OH U.S.A.
163 A4 Contis-Plage France
233 H3 Contoocook r. NH U.S.A.
260 C6 Contralmirante Cordero Arg.
250 C3 Contratacion Col.
259 B8 Contreras, Isla i. Chile
162 D1 Contres France
157 F4 Contrexéville France
193 H4 Controne Italy
258 B5 Contulmo Chile
252 A1 Contumazá Peru
193 H4 Contursi Terme Italy
223 I1 Contwoyto Lake N.W.T./Nunavut Can.
156 C3 Conty France
237 F6 Convent LA U.S.A.
260 B4 Convento Viejo Chile
195 G2 Conversano Italy
232 A4 Convoy OH U.S.A.
215 E4 Conway S. Africa
Conway Conwy, Wales U.K. see Conwy
237 E5 Conway AR U.S.A.
232 A6 Conway KY U.S.A.
236 D1 Conway ND U.S.A.
233 □H3 Conway NH U.S.A.
231 E5 Conway SC U.S.A.
85 G4 Conway, Cape Qld Austr.
82 C2 Conway, Lake salt flat S.A. Austr.
237 D4 Conway Springs KS U.S.A.
150 D1 Conwy Conwy, Wales U.K.
150 D1 Conwy admin. div. Wales U.K.
150 D1 Conwy r. Wales U.K.
150 C1 Conwy Bay Wales U.K.
234 B2 Conyngham PA U.S.A.
82 C2 Coober Pedy S.A. Austr.
Cooch Behar W. Bengal India see Koch Bihar
85 G5 Coogoon r. Qld Austr.
82 B2 Cook S.A. Austr.
226 A2 Cook MN U.S.A.
222 B2 Cook, Mount Can./U.S.A.
Cook, Mount South I. N.Z. see Aoraki
Cook Atoll Kiribati see Tarawa
239 F5 Cookes Peak NM U.S.A.
231 C4 Cookeville TN U.S.A.
151 G3 Cookham Windsor and Maidenhead, England U.K.
215 E5 Cookhouse S. Africa
220 C3 Cook Inlet sea chan. AK U.S.A.
81 □2 Cook Islands S. Pacific Ocean
150 E2 Cookley Worcestershire, England U.K.
233 F3 Cooksburg NY U.S.A.
146 E4 Cook's Cairn hill Scotland U.K.
225 K3 Cook's Harbour Nfld. Can.
85 F2 Cooks Passage Qld Austr.
147 E2 Cookstown Northern Ireland U.K.
81 E4 Cook Strait South I. N.Z.
234 A3 Cooksville MD U.S.A.
85 F2 Cooktown Qld Austr.
147 C2 Coola Rep. of Ireland
83 F2 Coolabah N.S.W. Austr.
85 F5 Cooladdi Qld Austr.
83 G2 Coolah N.S.W. Austr.
83 F3 Coolamon N.S.W. Austr.
147 C2 Coolaney Rep. of Ireland
156 E4 Coole France
156 E4 Coole r. France
148 B4 Coole Rep. of Ireland
87 D6 Coolgardie W.A. Austr.
147 D4 Coolgrange Rep. of Ireland
147 E4 Coolgreany Rep. of Ireland
84 B2 Coolibah N.T. Austr.
241 L5 Coolidge AZ U.S.A.
87 B6 Coolimba W.A. Austr.
147 E3 Coolock Rep. of Ireland
147 D4 Coolroebeg Rep. of Ireland
85 H5 Coolum Beach Qld Austr.
83 G4 Cooma N.S.W. Austr.
147 A5 Coomacarrea hill Rep. of Ireland
82 E3 Coombah N.S.W. Austr.
150 C4 Coombe Cornwall, England U.K.
151 F3 Coombe Bissett Wiltshire, England U.K.
83 G2 Coonabarabran N.S.W. Austr.
82 D3 Coonalpyn S.A. Austr.
83 G2 Coonamble N.S.W. Austr.
87 D6 Coonana W.A. Austr.
82 E4 Coonawarra S.A. Austr.
82 C2 Coondambo S.A. Austr.
Coondapoor Karnataka India see Kundapura
86 C4 Coongan r. W.A. Austr.
85 F5 Coongoola Qld Austr.
226 A3 Coon Rapids MN U.S.A.
84 C2 Cooper r. N.T. Austr.
237 E5 Cooper TX U.S.A.
82 D2 Cooper Creek watercourse Qld/S.A. Austr.
232 B4 Cooperdale OH U.S.A.
83 H2 Coopernook N.S.W. Austr.
234 C2 Coopersburg PA U.S.A.
233 □I2 Coopers Mills ME U.S.A.
231 E7 Cooper's Town Bahamas
236 D2 Cooperstown ND U.S.A.
233 F3 Cooperstown NY U.S.A.
82 C2 Coorabie S.A. Austr.
87 C5 Coor-de-Wandy hill W.A. Austr.
87 C6 Coorow W.A. Austr.
85 H5 Cooroy Qld Austr.
231 C5 Coosa r. AL U.S.A.
238 A3 Coos Bay OR U.S.A.
83 G3 Cootamundra N.S.W. Austr.
147 D2 Cootehill Rep. of Ireland
114 D3 Cooum r. India
85 G5 Cooyar Qld Austr.
177 L5 Copăcel Romania
260 B5 Copahue, Volcán vol. Chile
243 G5 Copainalá Mex.
245 E5 Copala Mex.
245 E4 Copalillo Mex.
245 F6 Copalita r. Mex.
242 □H6 Copán tourist site Hond.
195 F4 Copanello Italy
236 C4 Cope CO U.S.A.
226 E3 Copemish MI U.S.A.
Copenhagen Denmark see København
195 H2 Copertino Italy
261 G6 Copetonas Arg.
96 D3 Cô Pi, Phou mt. Laos/Vietnam
235 E2 Copiague NY U.S.A.
258 C2 Copiapó Chile
258 C2 Copiapo, Volcán vol. Chile
146 F3 Copinsay i. Scotland U.K.
234 C2 Coplay PA U.S.A.
82 D2 Copley S.A. Austr.
149 H3 Copley Durham, England U.K.
149 H4 Copmanthorpe York, England U.K.
186 E3 Copons Spain
190 E3 Coppa r. Italy
191 G4 Copparo Italy
147 C5 Coppeen Rep. of Ireland
251 G3 Coppename r. Suriname
169 E3 Coppenbrügge Ger.
169 E4 Coppengrave Ger.
209 E8 Copperbelt prov. Zambia
224 D4 Copper Cliff Ont. Can.
85 E3 Copperfield r. Qld Austr.
226 D2 Copper Harbor MI U.S.A.
Coppermine Nunavut Can. see Kugluktuk
220 G3 Coppermine r. Nunavut Can.
214 D3 Copperton S. Africa
241 K1 Copperton UT U.S.A.
150 D4 Copplestone Devon, England U.K.
197 G2 Copșa Mică Romania
151 G3 Copthorne Surrey, England U.K.
151 F4 Copythorne Hampshire, England U.K.
111 D6 Coqên Xizang China
247 □1 Coqui Puerto Rico
Coquilhatville Dem. Rep. Congo see Mbandaka
Coquille i. Micronesia see Pikelot
238 A3 Coquille OR U.S.A.
244 C4 Coquimatlán Mex.
260 B1 Coquimbo Chile
260 B2 Coquimbo admin. reg. Chile
260 B1 Coquimbo, Bahía de b. Chile
222 F5 Coquitlam B.C. Can.
197 G4 Corabia Romania
257 E2 Coração de Jesus Brazil
195 F4 Corace r. Italy
Coracesium Turkey see Alanya
252 B3 Coracora Peru
83 H2 Coraki N.S.W. Austr.
87 B4 Coral Bay W.A. Austr.
79 □1a Coral Coast Fiji
221 J3 Coral Harbour Nunavut Can.
231 □2 Coral Heights Bahamas
78 □5 Coral Sea S. Pacific Ocean
266 F6 Coral Sea Basin S. Pacific Ocean
77 F3 Coral Sea Islands Territory terr. Austr.
147 D3 Coralstown Rep. of Ireland
235 E2 Coram NY U.S.A.
83 E4 Corangamite, Lake Vic. Austr.
232 C4 Coraopolis PA U.S.A.
129 F3 Corat Azer.
193 I3 Corato Italy
158 C3 Coray France
186 C4 Corbalán Spain
147 B2 Corbally Rep. of Ireland
156 C4 Corbeil-Essonnes France
156 C4 Corbeilles France
256 A6 Corbélia Brazil
160 D3 Corbelin France
157 G5 Corbenay France
156 D3 Corbeny France
186 D3 Corbera de Terra Alta Spain
156 C3 Corbie France
190 C2 Corbières Switz.
160 B1 Corbigny France
232 A6 Corbin KY U.S.A.
234 D3 Corbin City NJ U.S.A.
186 D3 Corbins Spain
191 H3 Corbola Italy
185 E3 Corbones r. Spain
149 G3 Corbridge Northumberland, England U.K.
197 I3 Corbu Romania
151 G2 Corby Northamptonshire, England U.K.
186 G3 Corçà Spain
Corcaigh Rep. of Ireland see Cork
160 D1 Corcelles-lès-Cîteaux France
193 E2 Corchiano Italy
193 E1 Corciano Italy
157 G4 Corcieux France
185 G1 Córcoles r. Spain
240 H3 Corcoran CA U.S.A.
158 E5 Corcoué-sur-Logne France
259 C6 Corcovado Arg.
259 B6 Corcovado, Golfo de sea chan. Chile
182 A2 Corcubión Spain
Corcyra i. Greece see Kerkyra
147 B4 Cordal Rep. of Ireland
85 H5 Cordalba Qld Austr.
257 F5 Cordeiro Brazil
231 D6 Cordele GA U.S.A.
240 F2 Cordelia CA U.S.A.
237 D5 Cordell OK U.S.A.
158 E4 Cordemais France
191 H3 Cordenòns Italy
163 D4 Cordes France
191 H2 Cordevole r. Italy
191 H3 Cordignano Italy
92 B4 Cordilleras Range mts Phil.
82 E1 Cordillo Downs S.A. Austr.
182 B4 Cordinhã Port.
257 E3 Cordisburgo Brazil
261 E2 Córdoba Arg.
261 F3 Córdoba prov. Arg.
250 C2 Córdoba dept Col.
245 F4 Córdoba Mex.
185 F3 Córdoba Spain
185 F2 Córdoba prov. Andalucía Spain
260 E3 Córdoba, Sierras de mts Arg.
184 D1 Cordobilla de Lácara Spain
252 B3 Cordova Peru
Cordova Spain see Córdoba
220 D3 Cordova AK U.S.A.
234 C4 Cordova MD U.S.A.
183 H2 Cordovín Spain
Corduba Spain see Córdoba
183 I4 Corduente Spain
254 E2 Coreaú Brazil
191 F4 Coreglia Antelminelli Italy
85 E3 Corella r. Qld Austr.
183 I2 Corella Spain
84 C3 Corella Lake salt flat N.T. Austr.
182 E3 Coreses Spain
150 E4 Corfe Castle Dorset, England U.K.
150 E4 Corfe Mullen Dorset, England U.K.
85 E4 Corfield Qld Austr.
193 F2 Corfinio Italy
232 D3 Corfu NY U.S.A.
182 C3 Corgo r. Port.
255 B6 Corguinho Brazil
193 E3 Cori Italy
182 D5 Coria Spain
184 D3 Coria del Río Spain
191 H5 Coriano Italy
254 D5 Coribe Brazil
83 G3 Coricudgy mt. N.S.W. Austr.
195 F3 Corigliano, Golfo di b. Italy
195 F3 Corigliano Calabro Italy
191 I5 Corinaldo Italy
85 G3 Coringa Islands Coral Sea Is Terr. Austr.
Corinium Gloucestershire, England U.K. see Cirencester
83 F5 Corinna Tas. Austr.
223 J5 Corinne Sask. Can.
Corinth Greece see Korinthos
237 F5 Corinth MS U.S.A.
233 G3 Corinth NY U.S.A.
Corinth, Gulf of sea chan. Greece see Korinthiakos Kolpos
Corinthus Greece see Korinthos
257 E3 Corinto Brazil
242 □I6 Corinto Nic.
185 E4 Coripe Spain
253 F4 Corixa Grande r. Bol./Brazil
253 F4 Corixinha r. Brazil
147 C5 Cork Rep. of Ireland
147 C4 Cork county Rep. of Ireland
158 C3 Corlay France
148 B4 Corlea Rep. of Ireland
147 B2 Corlee Rep. of Ireland
194 C5 Corleone Sicilia Italy
193 I4 Corleto Perticara Italy
199 E1 Çorlu Turkey
199 E1 Çorlu r. Turkey
160 C2 Cormatin France
159 G2 Cormeilles France
159 F2 Cormelles-le-Royal France
182 B1 Corme-Porto Spain
162 B3 Corme-Royal France
156 D3 Cormicy France
191 I3 Cormons Italy
156 E3 Cormontreuil France
191 I3 Cormor r. Italy
223 K4 Cormorant Man. Can.
193 H3 Cornacchia, Monte mt. Italy
147 D3 Cornafulla Rep. of Ireland
183 H2 Cornago Spain
147 B3 Cornamona Rep. of Ireland
190 E3 Cornaredo Italy
161 C4 Cornas France
168 D3 Cornau Ger.
169 E4 Cornberg Ger.
159 F4 Corné France
191 G2 Cornedo all'Isarco Italy
163 E6 Corneilla-del-Vercol France
215 G2 Cornelia S. Africa
256 B5 Cornélio Procópio Brazil
226 B3 Cornell WI U.S.A.
186 F3 Cornellá de Llobregat Spain
186 F2 Cornellà de Terri Spain
182 D1 Cornellana Spain
225 J3 Corner Brook Nfld. Can.
83 F4 Corner Inlet b. Vic. Austr.
185 I3 Corneros r. Spain
264 F3 Corner Seamounts sea feature N. Atlantic Ocean
136 E4 Cornești Moldova
Corneto Italy see Tarquinia
191 G3 Cornetto mt. Italy
232 B6 Cornettsville KY U.S.A.
177 L6 Cornetu, Vârful hill Romania
146 F4 Cornhill Aberdeenshire, Scotland U.K.
149 G2 Cornhill-on-Tweed Northumberland, England U.K.
149 G4 Cornholme West Yorkshire, England U.K.
197 H2 Corni Romania
192 C2 Cornia r. Italy
190 F4 Corniglio Italy
156 E3 Cornillet, Mont hill France
157 G5 Cornimont France
237 F4 Corning AR U.S.A.
240 F2 Corning CA U.S.A.
236 E3 Corning IA U.S.A.
232 E3 Corning NY U.S.A.
232 B5 Corning OH U.S.A.
Corn Islands is Nic. see Maíz, Islas del
193 E2 Corno r. Italy
193 F2 Corno, Monte mt. Italy
190 F2 Corno di Campo mt. Italy/Switz.
226 B2 Cornucopia WI U.S.A.
191 H3 Cornuda Italy
183 G2 Cornudilla Spain
161 B5 Cornus France
224 F4 Cornwall Ont. Can.
225 I4 Cornwall P.E.I. Can.
150 C4 Cornwall admin. div. England U.K.
235 D1 Cornwall NY U.S.A.
234 B2 Cornwall PA U.S.A.
221 I2 Cornwallis Island Nunavut Can.
221 I2 Cornwall Island Nunavut Can.
235 D1 Cornwall on Hudson NY U.S.A.
82 D3 Corny Point S.A. Austr.
250 D2 Coro Venez.
257 F3 Coroaci Brazil
254 D3 Coroatá Brazil
252 C4 Corocoro Bol.
251 F2 Corocoro, Isla i. Venez.
147 B4 Corofin Rep. of Ireland
80 E2 Coroglen North I. N.Z.
252 D4 Coroico Bol.
256 D3 Coromandel Brazil
80 E2 Coromandel North I. N.Z.
114 D4 Coromandel Coast India
80 E2 Coromandel Peninsula North I. N.Z.
80 E2 Coromandel Range hills North I. N.Z.
159 F4 Coron France
92 B3 Coron Phil.
184 B2 Corona r. Port.
183 I2 Corona mt. Spain
240 I5 Corona CA U.S.A.
239 F5 Corona NM U.S.A.
182 B3 Coronado Port.
240 I5 Coronado CA U.S.A.
242 □J7 Coronado, Bahiá de b. Costa Rica
223 I4 Coronation Alta Can.
220 G3 Coronation Gulf Nunavut Can.
262 U2 Coronation Island S. Orkney Is Atlantic Ocean
86 E2 Coronation Islands W.A. Austr.
261 G2 Coronda Arg.
261 G3 Coronel Bogada Arg.
261 H4 Coronel Brandsen Arg.
261 G6 Coronel Dorrego Arg.
257 F3 Coronel Fabriciano Brazil
258 D2 Coronel Moldes Arg.
257 F2 Coronel Murta Brazil
253 F6 Coronel Oviedo Para.
261 G5 Coronel Pringles Arg.
253 G5 Coronel Sapucaia Mato Grosso do Sul Brazil
253 G5 Coronel Sapucaia Mato Grosso do Sul Brazil
261 G5 Coronel Suárez Arg.
261 I5 Coronel Vidal Arg.
81 B6 Coronet Peak South I. N.Z.
198 B1 Çorovodë Albania
83 F3 Corowa N.S.W. Austr.
243 H5 Corozal Belize
247 □1 Corozal Puerto Rico
161 D4 Corps France
158 E4 Corps-Nuds France
258 G2 Corpus Arg.
237 D7 Corpus Christi TX U.S.A.
252 D4 Corque Bol.
259 B5 Corral Chile
182 E4 Corral mt. Spain
183 G5 Corral de Almaguer Spain
261 F3 Corral de Bustos Arg.
185 F2 Corral de Calatrava Spain
183 F5 Corral de Cantos mt. Spain
182 E3 Corrales Spain
244 D3 Corrales de Rábago Mex.
246 B2 Corralilla Cuba
240 G3 Corralitos CA U.S.A.
260 D2 Corralitos, Monte mt. Arg.
245 G4 Corral Nuevo Mex.
185 I2 Corral-Rubio Spain
87 B5 Corrandibby Range hills W.A. Austr.
213 H2 Corrane Moz.
192 B4 Corrasi, Punta mt. Sardegna Italy
147 B3 Corraun Peninsula Rep. of Ireland
157 G5 Corre France
146 F4 Correen Hills Scotland U.K.
191 F4 Correggio Italy
256 B2 Córrego do Ouro Brazil
257 F3 Córrego Novo Brazil
254 D4 Corrente Brazil
254 E5 Corrente r. Bahia Brazil
256 B3 Corrente r. Minas Gerais Brazil
257 F3 Corrente Grande r. Brazil
253 G4 Correntes r. Brazil
254 D5 Correntina Brazil
Correntina r. Brazil see Éguas

Corrèze to Culebra, Isla de

296

162 D3 Corrèze France
162 D3 Corrèze dept Limousin France
162 D3 Corrèze r. France
147 B3 Corrib, Lough l. Rep. of Ireland
191 I5 Corridonia Italy
146 C6 Corrie North Ayrshire, Scotland U.K.
258 F2 Corrientes Arg.
261 H1 Corrientes prov. Arg.
258 F3 Corrientes r. Arg.
250 C5 Corrientes r. Peru
244 B3 Corrientes, Cabo c. Mex.
237 E6 Corrigan TX U.S.A.
87 C7 Corrigin W.A. Austr.
151 H3 Corringham Thurrock, England U.K.
150 D2 Corris Gwynedd, Wales U.K.
156 D4 Corrobert France
232 D4 Corry PA U.S.A.
83 F4 Corryong Vic. Austr.
190 C4 Corsaglia r. Italy
195 H3 Corsano Italy
192 B2 Corse admin. reg. France
192 A2 Corse i. France
192 B1 Corse, Cap c. Corse France
192 A3 Corse-du-Sud dept Corse France
146 D6 Corserine hill Scotland U.K.
158 D3 Corseul France
150 E3 Corsham Wiltshire, England U.K.
Corsica i. France see Corse
237 D5 Corsicana TX U.S.A.
190 E3 Corsico Italy
146 E6 Corsock Dumfries and Galloway, Scotland U.K.
195 F4 Cortale Italy
244 D3 Cortazar Mex.
192 B2 Corte Corse France
184 D2 Corte de Peleas Spain
182 B2 Cortegada Spain
184 D3 Cortegana Spain
190 D4 Cortemilia Italy
190 F2 Corteno Golgi Italy
190 E3 Corteolona Italy
183 I3 Cortes Spain
Cortes, Sea of g. Mex. see California, Golfo de
186 C4 Cortes de Aragón Spain
185 H3 Cortes de Baza Spain
185 E4 Cortes de la Frontera Spain
187 C5 Cortes de Pallás Spain
239 E4 Cortez CO U.S.A.
241 I1 Cortez Mountains NV U.S.A.
184 B2 Corticadas do Lavre Port.
186 D3 Cortiella r. Spain
185 F1 Cortijo de Arriba Spain
245 E5 Cortijos r. Mex.
185 H2 Cortijos Nuevos Spain
191 H2 Cortina d'Ampezzo Italy
233 E3 Cortland NY U.S.A.
232 C4 Cortland OH U.S.A.
151 I2 Corton Suffolk, England U.K.
191 G5 Cortona Italy
206 B4 Corubal r. Guinea-Bissau
184 B2 Coruche Port.
Çoruh Turkey see Artvin
129 B3 Çoruh r. Turkey
127 F2 Çoruh r. Turkey
182 D2 Corullón Spain
126 D2 Çorum Turkey
253 F4 Corumbá Brazil
256 C3 Corumbá r. Brazil
256 C1 Corumbá de Goiás Brazil
256 C3 Corumbaíba Brazil
256 B5 Corumbataí r. Brazil
197 G2 Corund Romania
177 L4 Corund r. Romania
232 B3 Corunna Ont. Can.
Corunna Spain see A Coruña
227 E4 Corunna MI U.S.A.
254 F4 Coruripe Brazil
238 B2 Corvallis OR U.S.A.
191 G2 Corvara in Badia Italy
150 E2 Corve Dale val. England U.K.
187 B7 Corvera Spain
193 E3 Corvia, Colle hill Italy
216 □1 Corvo i. Azores
150 D2 Corwen Denbighshire, Wales U.K.
236 E3 Corydon IA U.S.A.
230 C4 Corydon IN U.S.A.
151 H3 Coryton Thurrock, England U.K.
232 D4 Coryville PA U.S.A.
Cos i. Greece see Kos
186 B4 Cosa Spain
244 A1 Cosalá Mex.
245 G4 Cosamaloapan Mex.
129 A3 Coşandere Turkey
151 F2 Cosby Leicestershire, England U.K.
193 E2 Coscerno, Monte mt. Italy
195 F3 Coscile r. Italy
245 F4 Coscomatepec Mex.
183 H3 Coscurita Spain
Cosentia Italy see Cosenza
193 I5 Cosenza Italy
193 I5 Cosenza prov. Calabria Italy
197 H3 Coşereni Romania
195 F3 Coserie r. Italy
146 E5 Coshieville Perth and Kinross, Scotland U.K.
232 C4 Coshocton OH U.S.A.
244 C2 Cosío Mex.
190 C4 Cosio di Arroscia Italy
183 G4 Coslada Spain
217 □2 Cosmolédo Atoll Seychelles
256 D5 Cosmópolis Brazil
160 A1 Cosne-Cours-sur-Loire France
160 A2 Cosne-d'Allier France
245 G5 Cosoleacaque Mex.
195 E4 Cosoleto Italy
260 E2 Cosquín Arg.
190 D3 Cossato Italy
171 E4 Cossebaude Ger.
159 F4 Cossé-le-Vivien France
192 A4 Cossoine Sardegna Italy
156 B5 Cosson r. France
190 B2 Cossonay Switz.
184 A2 Costa Bela coastal area Port.
187 C6 Costa Blanca coastal area Spain
186 G3 Costa Brava coastal area Spain
191 H5 Costacciaro Italy
197 H3 Costache Negri Romania
184 A2 Costa da Caparica Port.
184 B2 Costa da Galé coastal area Port.
184 C3 Costa de la Luz coastal area Spain
187 C5 Costa del Azahar coastal area Spain
185 E4 Costa del Sol coastal area Spain
242 □J6 Costa de Mosquitos coastal area Nic.
184 A2 Costa do Estoril coastal area Port.
186 F3 Costa Dorada coastal area Spain
184 A2 Costa do Sol coastal area Port.
252 D3 Costa Marques Brazil
256 A3 Costa Rica Brazil
246 A5 Costa Rica country Central America
242 D3 Costa Rica Mex.
182 D1 Costa Verde coastal area Spain
190 F3 Costa Volpino Italy
177 K6 Coşteiu Romania
147 B3 Costelloe Rep. of Ireland
Costermansville Dem. Rep. Congo see Bukavu
151 I2 Costessey Norfolk, England U.K.
136 D4 Costeşti Moldova
197 G3 Costeşti Romania
197 H2 Costeşti Romania
233 □I2 Costigan ME U.S.A.
190 D4 Costigliole d'Asti Italy
190 C4 Costigliole Saluzzo Italy
186 B3 Cosuenda Spain
197 F3 Coşuştea r. Romania
171 E4 Coswig Sachsen Ger.
171 D4 Coswig Sachsen-Anhalt Ger.
252 B3 Cotabambas Peru
92 C5 Cotabato Phil.
252 D4 Cotacajes r. Bol.
252 D5 Cotagaita Bol.
252 B3 Cotahuasi Peru
257 G3 Cotaxé r. Brazil
222 D3 Cote, Mount AK U.S.A.
236 D2 Coteau des Prairies slope SD U.S.A.
236 C1 Coteau du Missouri slope ND U.S.A.
236 C2 Coteau du Missouri slope SD U.S.A.
233 F2 Coteau Station Que. Can.
246 D3 Coteaux Haiti
156 D4 Côte Champenoise reg. France
163 A5 Côte d'Argent coastal area France
161 F5 Côte d'Azur airport France
161 F5 Côte d'Azur coastal area France
156 E4 Côte des Bars reg. France
206 D5 Côte d'Ivoire country Africa
156 E5 Côte-d'Or dept Bourgogne France
160 C2 Côte d'Or reg. France
Côte Française de Somalis country Africa see Djibouti
254 D4 Cotegipe Brazil
158 D3 Côtes-d'Armor dept Bretagne France
157 E3 Côtes de Meuse ridge France
157 F4 Côtes de Moselle hills France
Côtes-du-Nord dept Bretagne France see Côtes-d'Armor
163 F6 Côte Vermeille coastal area France
150 C3 Cothi r. Wales U.K.
252 D2 Coti r. Brazil
Cotiaeum Turkey see Kütahya
192 A3 Coti-Chiavari Corse France
186 D2 Cotiella mt. Spain
161 E5 Cotignac France
191 G4 Cotignola Italy
251 F4 Cotingo r. Brazil
136 E4 Cotiujeni Moldova
136 E4 Cotiujenii Mici Moldova
197 G3 Cotmeana r. Romania
207 F5 Cotonou Benin
250 B5 Cotopaxi prov. Ecuador
250 B5 Cotopaxi, Volcán vol. Ecuador
Cotovsc Moldova see Hînceşti
195 F3 Cotronei Italy
150 E3 Cotswold Hills England U.K.
238 B3 Cottage Grove OR U.S.A.
193 E2 Cottanello Italy
171 F4 Cottbus Ger.
114 D3 Cotteliar r. India
151 H2 Cottenham Cambridgeshire, England U.K.
151 G2 Cottesmore Rutland, England U.K.
161 E4 Cottian Alps mts France/Italy
251 H4 Cottica Suriname
Cottiennes, Alpes mts France/Italy see Cottian Alps
149 I4 Cottingham East Riding of Yorkshire, England U.K.
151 G2 Cottingham Northamptonshire, England U.K.
226 A2 Cotton MN U.S.A.
241 K4 Cottonwood AZ U.S.A.
240 F1 Cottonwood CA U.S.A.
238 C2 Cottonwood ID U.S.A.
236 D4 Cottonwood r. KS U.S.A.
236 E2 Cottonwood r. MN U.S.A.
236 D4 Cottonwood Falls KS U.S.A.
246 E3 Cotuí Dom. Rep.
237 D6 Cotulla TX U.S.A.
197 H1 Coţuşca Romania
161 B3 Coubon France
160 C2 Couches France
184 B2 Couço Port.
161 B4 Coucouron France
156 D3 Coucy-le-Château-Auffrique France
159 H4 Couddes France
156 C1 Coudekerque-Branche France
232 D4 Coudersport PA U.S.A.
82 D4 Couëdic, Cape de S.A. Austr.
158 E4 Couëron France
158 E3 Couesnon r. France
163 D6 Couflens France
163 D5 Coufouleux France
162 C2 Couhé France
163 E6 Couiza France
159 G3 Coulaines France
156 D5 Coulanges-la-Vineuse France
160 B1 Coulanges-lès-Nevers France
160 B1 Coulanges-sur-Yonne France
159 G3 Coulans-sur-Gée France
162 C3 Coulaures France
238 C2 Coulee City WA U.S.A.
238 C2 Coulee Dam WA U.S.A.
160 A2 Couleuvre France
159 I4 Coullons France
263 L2 Coulman Island Antarctica
156 E5 Coulmier-le-Sec France
156 B5 Coulmiers France
156 B2 Coulogne France
156 D3 Coulognes-Cohan France
162 C2 Coulombiers France
156 B4 Coulombs France
156 D4 Coulommiers France
161 C5 Coulon r. France
224 E4 Coulonge r. Que. Can.
162 B2 Coulonges-sur-l'Autize France
162 C3 Coulounieix-Chamiers France
146 D5 Coulport Argyll and Bute, Scotland U.K.
240 G3 Coulterville CA U.S.A.
238 C2 Council ID U.S.A.
236 E3 Council Bluffs IA U.S.A.
236 D4 Council Grove KS U.S.A.
151 F2 Countesthorpe Leicestershire, England U.K.
146 E5 Coupar Angus Perth and Kinross, Scotland U.K.
238 B1 Coupeville WA U.S.A.
161 A5 Coupiac France
159 F3 Couptrain France
182 B3 Coura Port.
251 G3 Courantyne r. Guyana
165 D4 Courcelles Belgium
233 □H2 Courcelles Que. Can.
157 G3 Courcelles-Chaussy France
157 G3 Courcelles-sur-Nied France
160 E1 Courchaton France
161 E3 Courchevel France
159 H4 Cour-Cheverny France
159 F3 Courcité France
162 B2 Courçon France
156 E3 Courcy France
182 C2 Courel, Serra do mts Spain
159 G3 Courgains France
156 D4 Courgenay France
190 C1 Courgenay Switz.
138 C4 Courland Lagoon b. Lith./Rus. Fed.
160 D2 Courlaoux France
159 F5 Courlay France
156 D4 Courlon-sur-Yonne France
190 B3 Courmayeur Italy
156 D3 Courmelles France
160 B3 Cournon-d'Auvergne France
161 B5 Cournonterral France
160 B3 Courpière France
190 C1 Courrendlin Switz.
163 C5 Courrensan France
156 C2 Courrières France
160 A1 Cours France
162 C3 Coursac France
161 B5 Coursan France
161 F5 Coursegoules France
159 F2 Courseulles-sur-Mer France
160 C2 Cours-la-Ville France
160 B1 Courson-les-Carrières France
190 C1 Court Switz.
156 B4 Courtalain France
190 C1 Courtelary Switz.
160 F1 Courtelevant France
222 E5 Courtenay B.C. Can.
156 D4 Courtenay France
161 C4 Courthézon France
156 E4 Courtisols France
232 E6 Courtland VA U.S.A.
147 C5 Courtmacsherry Rep. of Ireland
159 G3 Courtomer France
147 E4 Courtown Rep. of Ireland
Courtrai Belgium see Kortrijk
165 D4 Court-St-Etienne Belgium
156 B4 Courville-sur-Eure France
160 D2 Cousance France
157 F4 Cousances-les-Forges France
237 E5 Coushatta LA U.S.A.
160 B1 Cousin r. France
217 □2a Cousin i. Inner Islands Seychelles
162 D3 Coussac-Bonneval France
159 G5 Coussay-les-Bois France
156 E5 Coussegrey France
157 F4 Coussey France
161 D5 Coustellet France
163 E6 Coustouges France
158 E2 Coutances France
159 F3 Couterne France
Coutinho Moz. see Ulongue
257 F3 Couto de Magalhães de Minas Brazil
162 B3 Coutras France
223 I5 Coutts Alta Can.
162 C3 Couture r. France
247 □7 Couva Trin. and Tob.
190 B2 Couvet Switz.
165 D4 Couvin Belgium
156 D3 Couvron-et-Aumencourt France
163 C4 Couze r. France
163 C4 Couze-et-St-Front France
162 D3 Couzeix France
182 E4 Covacha del Losar mt. Spain
182 C2 Cova da Serpe, Sierra da mts Spain
183 H3 Covaleda Spain
183 G2 Covarrubias Spain
177 K5 Covăsinţ Romania
197 H3 Covasna Romania
146 C4 Cove Highland, Scotland U.K.
146 F4 Cove Bay Aberdeen, Scotland U.K.
241 K2 Cove Fort UT U.S.A.
182 B2 Covelo Spain
240 F2 Covelo CA U.S.A.
232 D5 Cove Mountains hills PA U.S.A.
252 D3 Covendo Bol.
151 F2 Coventry West Midlands, England U.K.
149 H3 Cover r. England U.K.
150 B4 Coverack Cornwall, England U.K.
241 K5 Covered Wells AZ U.S.A.
232 D6 Covesville VA U.S.A.
182 C4 Covilhã Port.
231 D5 Covington GA U.S.A.
230 C3 Covington IN U.S.A.
232 A5 Covington KY U.S.A.
237 F6 Covington LA U.S.A.
226 C2 Covington MI U.S.A.
232 A4 Covington OH U.S.A.
237 F5 Covington TN U.S.A.
232 C6 Covington VA U.S.A.
227 F2 Cow r. Ont. Can.
83 F3 Cowal, Lake dry lake N.S.W. Austr.
232 B5 Cowan KY U.S.A.
87 D6 Cowan, Lake salt flat W.A. Austr.
225 F4 Cowansville Que. Can.
151 G2 Cowbit Lincolnshire, England U.K.
150 D3 Cowbridge Vale of Glamorgan, Wales U.K.
87 C6 Cowcowing Lakes salt flat W.A. Austr.
146 E5 Cowdenbeath Fife, Scotland U.K.
82 D3 Cowell S.A. Austr.
232 C5 Cowen WV U.S.A.
83 F4 Cowes Vic. Austr.
151 F4 Cowes Isle of Wight, England U.K.
151 G4 Cowfold West Sussex, England U.K.
146 E5 Cowie Stirling, Scotland U.K.
85 F5 Cowley Qld Austr.
149 G4 Cowling North Yorkshire, England U.K.
238 B2 Cowlitz r. WA U.S.A.
232 D6 Cowpasture r. VA U.S.A.
83 G3 Cowra N.S.W. Austr.
149 G3 Cowshill Durham, England U.K.
84 C2 Cox r. N.T. Austr.
163 D5 Cox France
Coxen Hole Hond. see Roatán
151 H3 Coxheath Kent, England U.K.
149 H3 Coxhoe Durham, England U.K.
258 G3 Coxilha de Santana hills Brazil/Uru.
255 B9 Coxilha Grande hills Brazil
255 B6 Coxim Brazil
255 B6 Coxim r. Brazil
233 G3 Coxsackie NY U.S.A.
117 G5 Cox's Bazar Bangl.
149 H3 Coxwold North Yorkshire, England U.K.
260 B4 Coya Chile
206 B4 Coyah Guinea
150 D3 Coychurch Bridgend, Wales U.K.
146 D6 Coylton South Ayrshire, Scotland U.K.
146 E4 Coylumbridge Highland, Scotland U.K.
239 D6 Coyote r. Mex.
241 J5 Coyote Peak hill AZ U.S.A.
240 H3 Coyote Peak CA U.S.A.
244 A2 Coyotitán Mex.
244 D5 Coyuca de Benitez Mex.
244 D4 Coyuca de Catalán Mex.
236 D3 Cozad NE U.S.A.
185 G2 Cózar Spain
162 B3 Cozes France
197 G3 Cozia, Vârful mt. Romania
Cozie, Alpi mts France/Italy see Cottian Alps
243 I4 Cozumel Mex.
192 B3 Cozzano Corse France
193 I5 Cozzo del Pellegrino mt. Italy
148 C5 Craanford Rep. of Ireland
85 E1 Crab Island Qld Austr.
158 C4 Crach France
193 I4 Craco Italy
Cracovia Pol. see Kraków
85 G5 Cracow Qld Austr.
Cracow Pol. see Kraków
150 E2 Cradley Herefordshire, England U.K.
82 D2 Cradock S.A. Austr.
215 E5 Cradock S. Africa
80 E2 Cradock Channel North I. N.Z.
190 F3 Craffaro r. Italy
214 E2 Crafthole S. Africa
146 F5 Craichie Angus, Scotland U.K.
177 L4 Craidorolţ Romania
146 C4 Craig Highland, Scotland U.K.
222 C4 Craig AK U.S.A.
238 F3 Craig CO U.S.A.
146 C6 Craigandaive Argyll and Bute, Scotland U.K.
147 F2 Craigavad Northern Ireland U.K.
147 E2 Craigavon Northern Ireland U.K.
146 D6 Craigdarroch East Ayrshire, Scotland U.K.
83 F4 Craigieburn Vic. Austr.
81 C5 Craigieburn South I. N.Z.
146 C5 Craignure Argyll and Bute, Scotland U.K.
147 E2 Craigs Northern Ireland U.K.
232 D5 Craigsville VA U.S.A.
232 C5 Craigsville WV U.S.A.
146 F5 Crail Fife, Scotland U.K.
173 E2 Crailsheim Ger.
197 F3 Craiova Romania
177 K5 Craiva Romania
234 B3 Craley PA U.S.A.
156 D4 Cramant France
149 H2 Cramlington Northumberland, England U.K.
214 C2 Cramond S. Africa
163 D5 Crampagna France
148 B2 Crana r. Rep. of Ireland
149 G4 Cranage Cheshire, England U.K.
147 D2 Cranagh Northern Ireland U.K.
222 D4 Cranberry Junction B.C. Can.
234 D2 Cranberry Lake NJ U.S.A.
223 K4 Cranberry Portage Man. Can.
150 E4 Cranborne Chase for. England U.K.
83 F4 Cranbourne Vic. Austr.
87 C7 Cranbrook W.A. Austr.
222 H5 Cranbrook B.C. Can.
151 H3 Cranbrook Kent, England U.K.
235 D2 Cranbury NJ U.S.A.
226 C3 Crandon WI U.S.A.
238 C3 Crane OR U.S.A.
237 C6 Crane TX U.S.A.
226 A1 Crane Lake MN U.S.A.
151 G2 Cranfield Bedfordshire, England U.K.
148 B2 Cranford Rep. of Ireland
160 E3 Cran-Gevrier France
151 G3 Cranleigh Surrey, England U.K.
163 E4 Cransac France
146 F6 Cranshaws Scottish Borders, Scotland U.K.
146 D3 Cranstackie hill Scotland U.K.
232 B5 Cranston KY U.S.A.
233 H4 Cranston RI U.S.A.
149 I4 Cranwell Lincolnshire, England U.K.
Cranz Rus. Fed. see Zelenogradsk
159 F4 Craon France
156 D3 Craonne France
161 B3 Craponne-sur-Arzon France
262 P1 Crary Mountains Antarctica
146 D3 Crask Inn Highland, Scotland U.K.
197 F2 Crasna Romania
197 F2 Crasna r. Romania
136 E4 Crasnoe Moldova
254 E3 Crateús Brazil
146 E4 Crathie Aberdeenshire, Scotland U.K.
193 I5 Crati r. Italy
254 F3 Crato Brazil
184 C1 Crato Port.
147 C3 Craughwell Rep. of Ireland
190 D3 Cravagliana Italy
160 E1 Cravanche France
156 D5 Cravant France
253 F3 Cravari r. Brazil
150 E2 Craven Arms Shropshire, England U.K.
256 D4 Cravinhos Brazil
236 C3 Crawford NE U.S.A.
238 C1 Crawford Bay B.C. Can.
146 E6 Crawfordjohn South Lanarkshire, Scotland U.K.
81 C5 Crawford Range mts South I. N.Z.
230 C3 Crawfordsville IN U.S.A.
231 C6 Crawfordville FL U.S.A.
231 D5 Crawfordville GA U.S.A.
169 F5 Crawinkel Ger.
151 G3 Crawley West Sussex, England U.K.
238 E2 Crazy Mountains MT U.S.A.
146 A4 Creag Ghoraidh Western Isles, Scotland U.K.
146 D5 Creag Meagaidh mt. Scotland U.K.
158 E2 Créances France
160 C1 Créancey France
182 B2 Crecente Spain
160 C2 Crêches-sur-Saône France
156 B2 Crécy-en-Ponthieu France
156 C4 Crécy-la-Chapelle France
156 D3 Crécy-sur-Serre France
150 E2 Credenhill Herefordshire, England U.K.
150 D4 Crediton Devon, England U.K.
223 J3 Cree r. Sask. Can.
150 D3 Creech St Michael Somerset, England U.K.
239 F4 Creede CO U.S.A.
147 B4 Creegh Rep. of Ireland
242 D3 Creel Mex.
223 J3 Cree Lake Sask. Can.
227 G3 Creemore Ont. Can.
147 D1 Creeslough Rep. of Ireland
146 D7 Creetown Dumfries and Galloway, Scotland U.K.
147 B2 Creevagh Rep. of Ireland
147 D2 Creggan Northern Ireland U.K.
147 E2 Creggan Northern Ireland U.K.
147 B3 Cregganbaun Rep. of Ireland
147 C3 Creggs Rep. of Ireland
173 E2 Creglingen Ger.
157 G3 Créhange France
223 K4 Creighton Sask. Can.
215 G4 Creighton S. Africa
156 C3 Creil France
164 E2 Creil Neth.
161 B4 Creissels France
190 E3 Crema Italy
160 B3 Cremeaux France
183 E2 Crémenes Spain
160 D3 Crémieu France
169 F3 Cremlingen Ger.
222 H5 Cremona Alta Can.
190 F3 Cremona Italy
190 F3 Cremona prov. Lombardia Italy
156 E4 Creney-près-Troyes France
179 H4 Črenšovci Slovenia
163 B4 Créon France
157 F4 Crépey France
251 G6 Crepori r. Brazil
156 D3 Crépy France
156 C3 Crépy-en-Valois France
188 E3 Cres Croatia
188 E3 Cres i. Croatia
238 B3 Crescent OR U.S.A.
238 A3 Crescent City CA U.S.A.
231 D6 Crescent City FL U.S.A.
90 D3 Crescent Group is Paracel Is
83 H2 Crescent Head N.S.W. Austr.
190 D3 Crescentino Italy
241 M2 Crescent Junction UT U.S.A.
241 J4 Crescent Peak NV U.S.A.
240 I1 Crescent Valley NV U.S.A.
226 A4 Cresco IA U.S.A.
234 C1 Cresco PA U.S.A.
191 G4 Crespino Italy
261 G3 Crespo Arg.
183 F4 Crespos Spain
162 D3 Cressensac France
172 B4 Cressier Switz.
234 B2 Cressona PA U.S.A.
84 C3 Cresswell Downs N.T. Austr.
83 E4 Cressy Vic. Austr.
161 D4 Crest France
232 B4 Crestline OH U.S.A.
222 G5 Creston B.C. Can.
236 E3 Creston IA U.S.A.
238 F3 Creston WY U.S.A.
231 C6 Crestview FL U.S.A.
160 E3 Crest-Voland France
235 D3 Crestwood Village NJ U.S.A.
149 H4 Creswell Derbyshire, England U.K.
234 B3 Creswell PA U.S.A.
83 E4 Creswick Vic. Austr.
Creta i. Greece see Kriti
191 H2 Creta Forata, Monte mt. Italy
186 D4 Cretas Spain
160 D2 Crêt de la Neige mt. France
160 D3 Crêt de Pont mt. France
160 D2 Crêt des Eculaz mt. France
160 D2 Crêt du Nu mt. France
236 D3 Crete NE U.S.A.
156 C4 Créteil France
160 E1 Crêt Monniot mt. France
159 F2 Creully France
186 G2 Creus, Cap de c. Spain
162 E2 Creuse dept Limousin France
162 C1 Creuse r. France
173 F2 Creußen Ger.
173 F2 Creußen r. Ger.
157 G3 Creutzwald France
169 F4 Creuzburg Ger.
160 B2 Creuzier-le-Vieux France
191 G4 Crevalcore Italy
162 D2 Crevant France
157 G4 Crévéchamps France
156 C3 Crèvecœur-le-Grand France
187 C6 Crevillente Spain
149 G4 Crewe Cheshire, England U.K.
232 D6 Crewe VA U.S.A.
150 E4 Crewkerne Somerset, England U.K.
163 C4 Creysse France
216 □1c Criação Velha Pico Azores
146 D5 Crianlarich Stirling, Scotland U.K.
150 C2 Criccieth Gwynedd, Wales U.K.
255 C9 Criciúma Brazil
150 D3 Crickhowell Powys, Wales U.K.
151 F3 Cricklade Wiltshire, England U.K.
136 E4 Cricova Moldova
197 H3 Cricovu Sărat r. Romania
232 A4 Cridersville OH U.S.A.
146 E5 Crieff Perth and Kinross, Scotland U.K.
156 B2 Criel-sur-Mer France
146 E7 Criffell hill Scotland U.K.
149 H4 Crigglestone West Yorkshire, England U.K.
188 E3 Crikvenica Croatia
222 B3 Crillon, Mount AK U.S.A.
148 C3 Crilly Northern Ireland U.K.
Crimea pen. Ukr. see Kryms'kyy Pivostriv
Crimean Republic aut. rep. Ukr. see Krym, Respublika
171 D5 Crimmitschau Ger.
146 G4 Crimond Aberdeenshire, Scotland U.K.
146 C5 Crinan Argyll and Bute, Scotland U.K.
151 I2 Cringleford Norfolk, England U.K.
171 E4 Crinitz Ger.
239 F4 Cripple Creek CO U.S.A.
151 H4 Cripp's Corner East Sussex, England U.K.
159 G2 Criquetot-l'Esneval France
197 I3 Crişan Romania
233 F6 Crisfield MD U.S.A.
195 G2 Crispiano Italy
190 C4 Crissolo Italy
256 D2 Cristais, Serra dos mts Brazil
208 A4 Cristal, Monts de mts Equat. Guinea/Gabon
254 C4 Cristalândia Brazil
256 D2 Cristalina Brazil
Cristalino r. Brazil see Mariembero
253 G2 Cristalino r. Brazil
191 H2 Cristallo mt. Italy
256 C2 Cristianópolis Brazil
257 E5 Cristina Brazil
254 D4 Cristino Castro Brazil
177 L5 Criştioru de Jos Romania
182 E4 Cristóbal Spain
190 D4 Cristoforo Colombo airport Italy
197 G2 Cristuru Secuiesc Romania
197 E2 Crişul Alb r. Romania
197 E2 Crişul Negru r. Romania
197 E2 Crişul Repede r. Romania
197 E2 Crişurilor, Câmpia plain Romania
252 B3 Criterion mt. Peru
136 E4 Criuleni Moldova
170 C2 Crivitz Ger.
226 C3 Crivitz WI U.S.A.
254 C5 Crixás Brazil
254 C5 Crixás Açu r. Brazil
254 C5 Crixás Mirim r. Brazil
197 E5 Crna r. Macedonia
179 F4 Črna Slovenia
196 D4 Crna Glava mt. Yugo.
196 E4 Crna Gora mts Macedonia/Yugo.
196 D4 Crna Gora aut. rep. Yugo.
197 F4 Crna Trava Srbija Yugo.
196 E5 Crni Drim r. Macedonia
197 F4 Crni Timok r. Yugo.
188 E2 Črni vrh mt. Slovenia
188 E3 Črnomelj Slovenia
197 F4 Crnook mt. Yugo.
147 C2 Croagh Rep. of Ireland
147 C2 Croagheheen hill Rep. of Ireland
147 B3 Croagh Patrick hill Rep. of Ireland
188 E3 Croatia country Europe
195 F4 Crocchio r. Italy
195 F4 Crocco, Monte mt. Italy
191 G2 Croce, Monte mt. Italy
193 E2 Croce di Serra, Monte hill Italy
169 F5 Crock Ger.
95 F1 Crocker, Banjaran mts Malaysia
146 E6 Crocketford Dumfries and Galloway, Scotland U.K.
237 E6 Crockett TX U.S.A.
147 D2 Crockmore Rep. of Ireland
162 E3 Crocq France
191 H2 Croda dei Toni mt. Italy
191 H2 Croda Rossa mt. Italy
190 D2 Crodo Italy
150 D3 Croeserw Neath Port Talbot, Wales U.K.
150 B3 Croesgoch Pembrokeshire, Wales U.K.
149 H4 Crofton West Yorkshire, England U.K.
234 B3 Crofton MD U.S.A.
236 D3 Crofton NE U.S.A.
150 C3 Crofty Swansea, Wales U.K.
147 C3 Croghan Rep. of Ireland
233 F3 Croghan NY U.S.A.
149 G3 Croglin Cumbria, England U.K.
193 F2 Crognaleto Italy
146 D4 Croick Highland, Scotland U.K.
156 C2 Croisilles France
190 C3 Croix-Rousse mt. Italy
84 C1 Croker, Cape N.T. Austr.
84 C1 Croker Island N.T. Austr.
147 B4 Cromane Rep. of Ireland
146 D4 Cromarty Highland, Scotland U.K.
146 D4 Cromarty Firth est. Scotland U.K.
146 E4 Cromdale, Hills of Scotland U.K.
151 I2 Cromer Norfolk, England U.K.
150 E3 Cromhall South Gloucestershire, England U.K.
81 B6 Cromwell South I. N.Z.
235 F1 Cromwell CT U.S.A.
226 A2 Cromwell MN U.S.A.
81 C5 Cronadun South I. N.Z.
160 B2 Cronat France
161 B3 Cronce r. France
151 G3 Crondall Hampshire, England U.K.
149 H3 Crook Durham, England U.K.
238 B2 Crooked r. OR U.S.A.
246 D2 Crooked Island Bahamas
246 D2 Crooked Island Passage Bahamas
223 K4 Crooked River Sask. Can.
147 B5 Crookhaven Rep. of Ireland
236 D2 Crookston MN U.S.A.
147 C5 Crookstown Rep. of Ireland
232 B5 Crooksville OH U.S.A.
83 G3 Crookwell N.S.W. Austr.
147 C4 Croom Rep. of Ireland
195 F3 Cropalati Italy
195 F4 Cropani Italy
83 G2 Croppa Creek N.S.W. Austr.
85 E2 Crosbie r. Qld Austr.
146 B3 Crosbost Western Isles, Scotland U.K.
149 F4 Crosby Merseyside, England U.K.
149 I4 Crosby North Lincolnshire, England U.K.
236 E2 Crosby MN U.S.A.
236 C1 Crosby ND U.S.A.
149 G3 Crosby Ravensworth Cumbria, England U.K.
237 C5 Crosbyton TX U.S.A.
195 F3 Crosia Italy
207 H5 Cross r. Nigeria
158 D4 Crossac France
146 C6 Crossaig Argyll and Bute, Scotland U.K.
148 B4 Crossakeel Rep. of Ireland
149 F3 Crosscanonby Cumbria, England U.K.
231 D6 Cross City FL U.S.A.
233 □J1 Cross Creek N.B. Can.
147 D3 Crossdoney Rep. of Ireland
237 E5 Crossett AR U.S.A.
149 G3 Cross Fell hill England U.K.
222 H5 Crossfield Alta Can.
146 E6 Crossford South Lanarkshire, Scotland U.K.
147 F2 Crossgar Northern Ireland U.K.
147 E1 Crossgare Northern Ireland U.K.
150 D2 Crossgates Powys, Wales U.K.
146 D6 Crosshands East Ayrshire, Scotland U.K.
147 C5 Crosshaven Rep. of Ireland
146 D6 Crosshill South Ayrshire, Scotland U.K.
148 E2 Crosshouse East Ayrshire, Scotland U.K.
150 C2 Cross Inn Ceredigion, Wales U.K.
148 B4 Crosskeys Rep. of Ireland
147 E3 Cross Keys Rep. of Ireland
223 L4 Cross Lake Man. Can.
81 D5 Crossley, Mount South I. N.Z.
147 E2 Crossmaglen Northern Ireland U.K.
241 J4 Crossman Peak AZ U.S.A.
146 E7 Crossmichael Dumfries and Galloway, Scotland U.K.
147 B2 Crossmolina Rep. of Ireland
207 H5 Cross River state Nigeria
231 C5 Crossville TN U.S.A.
150 D2 Crossway Powys, Wales U.K.
191 F4 Crostolo r. Italy
149 G4 Croston Lancashire, England U.K.
227 F4 Croswell MI U.S.A.
Croton Italy see Crotone
195 G3 Crotone Italy
195 F3 Crotone prov. Calabria Italy
235 E1 Croton Falls NY U.S.A.
235 E1 Crotonville NY U.S.A.
161 E4 Crots France
171 D5 Crottendorf Ger.
151 H3 Crouch r. England U.K.
151 F3 Croughton Northamptonshire, England U.K.
162 C2 Croutelle France
156 D3 Crouy France
156 D3 Crouy-sur-Ourcq France
159 G4 Crouzilles France
147 C2 Crove Rep. of Ireland
222 E3 Crow r. B.C. Can.
238 F2 Crow Agency MT U.S.A.
151 H3 Crowborough East Sussex, England U.K.
238 F3 Crow Creek r. CO U.S.A.
237 D5 Crowell TX U.S.A.
150 E3 Crow Hill Herefordshire, England U.K.
151 G2 Crowland Lincolnshire, England U.K.
149 I4 Crowle North Lincolnshire, England U.K.
237 E6 Crowley LA U.S.A.
146 C4 Crowlin Islands Scotland U.K.
230 C3 Crown Point IN U.S.A.
239 E5 Crownpoint NM U.S.A.
233 G3 Crown Point NY U.S.A.
263 C2 Crown Prince Olav Coast Antarctica
262 W1 Crown Princess Martha Coast Antarctica
234 B3 Crownsville MD U.S.A.
85 H5 Crows Nest Qld Austr.
222 H5 Crowsnest Pass Alta Can.
151 G3 Crowthorne Bracknell Forest, England U.K.
236 E2 Crow Wing r. MN U.S.A.
146 D4 Croy Highland, Scotland U.K.
150 C3 Croyde Devon, England U.K.
85 E3 Croydon Qld Austr.
151 G3 Croydon Greater London, England U.K.
234 D2 Croydon PA U.S.A.
162 D2 Crozant France
232 D5 Crozet VA U.S.A.
265 H8 Crozet, Îles is Indian Ocean
217 □1 Crozet Basin sea feature Indian Ocean
265 G7 Crozet Plateau sea feature Indian Ocean
220 F2 Crozier Channel N.W.T. Can.
158 B3 Crozon France
161 C4 Cruas France
197 G2 Crucea Romania
252 C3 Crucero Peru
246 B2 Cruces Cuba
195 F3 Crucoli Italy
146 G4 Cruden Bay Aberdeenshire, Scotland U.K.
245 E1 Cruillas Mex.
146 B3 Crulabhig Western Isles, Scotland U.K.
159 G3 Crulai France
232 B6 Crum WV U.S.A.
150 D3 Crumlin Caerphilly, Wales U.K.
147 E2 Crumlin Northern Ireland U.K.
160 E2 Cruseilles France
147 C4 Crusheen Rep. of Ireland
157 F3 Crusnes France
157 F3 Crusnes r. France
245 F3 Crustepec, Cerro mt. Mex.
183 H5 Cruz mt. Spain
255 B9 Cruz Alta Brazil
260 E2 Cruz del Eje Arg.
257 E5 Cruzeiro Brazil
256 A5 Cruzeiro do Oeste Brazil
252 B1 Cruzeiro do Sul Acre Brazil
256 A5 Cruzeiro do Sul Paraná Brazil
262 O2 Cruzen Island Antarctica
245 E5 Cruz Grande Mex.
161 A5 Cruzy France
156 E5 Cruzy-le-Châtel France
196 D3 Crvenka Vojvodina, Srbija Yugo.
150 C3 Crymych Pembrokeshire, Wales U.K.
222 F4 Crysdale, Mount B.C. Can.
241 M3 Crystal NM U.S.A.
234 C3 Crystal Beach MD U.S.A.
82 D3 Crystal Brook S.A. Austr.
223 L5 Crystal City Man. Can.
236 F4 Crystal City MO U.S.A.
237 D6 Crystal City TX U.S.A.
226 C2 Crystal Falls MI U.S.A.
226 C4 Crystal Lake IL U.S.A.
231 D6 Crystal River FL U.S.A.
237 F6 Crystal Springs MS U.S.A.
177 J5 Csabacsűd Hungary
176 G4 Csabrendek Hungary
176 F5 Csákánydoroszló Hungary
177 H4 Csákvár Hungary
177 J5 Csanádapáca Hungary
177 J5 Csanádi-hát hills Hungary
177 J5 Csanádpalota Hungary
177 J5 Csanytelek Hungary
177 H4 Császár Hungary
177 I5 Császártöltés Hungary
177 H5 Csátalja Hungary
177 I5 Csávoly Hungary
177 I4 Csécse Hungary
177 I4 Csemő Hungary
177 I5 Csengele Hungary
177 L4 Csenger Hungary
177 J5 Csépa Hungary
176 F4 Csepreg Hungary
177 J3 Cserehát mts Hungary
177 I4 Cserhát hills Hungary
177 I4 Cserhátsurány Hungary
177 J5 Cserkeszőlő Hungary
177 J3 Csernely Hungary
176 G5 Cserszegtomaj Hungary
179 H4 Cserta r. Hungary
176 F5 Csesztreg Hungary
177 G4 Csetény Hungary
Csév Hungary see Piliscsév
177 I5 Csikéria Hungary
177 H4 Csókakő Hungary
177 K4 Csökmő Hungary
177 G5 Csököly Hungary
176 G5 Csokonyavisonta Hungary
177 J3 Csokvaomány Hungary
177 H4 Csolnok Hungary
177 I5 Csólyospálos Hungary
177 I4 Csömör Hungary
177 J5 Csongrád Hungary
177 J5 Csongrád county Hungary
177 G5 Csopak Hungary
177 H4 Csór Hungary
176 G4 Csorna Hungary
176 F5 Csörnyeföld Hungary
176 F5 Csörötnek Hungary
177 J5 Csorvás Hungary
177 H4 Csősz Hungary
177 G4 Csót Hungary
177 H4 Csóványos hill Hungary
176 G5 Csurgó Hungary
127 G4 Ctesiphon tourist site Iraq
182 D2 Cua r. Spain
182 E4 Cuacos de Yuste Spain
97 D5 Cu'a Đinh An r. mouth Vietnam
259 C7 Cuadrada, Sierra hills Arg.
182 E2 Cuadros Spain
245 E5 Cuajinicuilapa Mex.
182 C3 Cualedro Spain
213 H2 Cuamba Moz.
209 D9 Cuando r. Angola/Zambia
209 C8 Cuando Cubango prov. Angola
209 C9 Cuangar Angola
209 C7 Cuango Angola
209 C6 Cuango r. Angola/Dem. Rep. Congo
209 B7 Cuanza r. Angola
209 B7 Cuanza Norte prov. Angola
209 B7 Cuanza Sul prov. Angola
261 I2 Cuareim r. Uru.
261 I2 Cuaro r. Uru.
186 C3 Cuarte de Huerva Spain
261 F3 Cuarto r. Arg.
209 C9 Cuatir r. Angola
Cuatretonda Spain see Quatretonda
242 E3 Cuatro Ciénegas Mex.
252 E4 Cuatro Ojos Bol.
242 D2 Cuauhtémoc Mex.
244 C4 Cuauhtémoc Mex.
244 C1 Cuauhtémoc Mex.
245 E4 Cuautla Mex.
245 E4 Cuautlán Izcalli Mex.
184 C2 Cuba Port.
226 B5 Cuba IL U.S.A.
239 F4 Cuba NM U.S.A.
232 D3 Cuba NY U.S.A.
232 B5 Cuba OH U.S.A.
246 B2 Cuba country West Indies
241 K6 Cubabi, Cerro mt. Mex.
209 B8 Cubal Angola
209 B7 Cubal r. Angola
182 B2 Cubalhão Port.
209 D9 Cubango r. Angola/Namibia
256 D5 Cubatão Brazil
186 D3 Cubells Spain
223 J4 Cub Hills Sask. Can.
182 D1 Cubia r. Spain
185 G3 Cubillas r. Spain
183 G2 Cubillo r. Spain
162 C3 Cubjac France
187 B4 Cubla Spain
183 G2 Cubo de Bureba Spain
183 H3 Cubo de la Solana Spain
136 E4 Cubolta r. Moldova
126 D2 Çubuk Turkey
162 B4 Cubzac-les-Ponts France
186 B3 Cucalón Spain
259 B6 Cucao Chile
241 J5 Cucapa, Sierra mts Mex.
191 H5 Cucco, Monte mt. Italy
192 B4 Cuccuru su Pirastru hill Sardegna Italy
209 C8 Cuchi Angola
258 G4 Cuchilla Grande hills Uru.
261 I3 Cuchilla Grande Inferior hills Uru.
151 G3 Cuckfield West Sussex, England U.K.
151 H4 Cuckmere r. England U.K.
197 G2 Cucu, Vârful mt. Romania
250 E4 Cucuí Amazonas Brazil
209 C7 Cucumbi Angola
161 D5 Cucuron France
250 C3 Cúcuta Col.
186 C3 Cucutas hill Spain
197 H3 Cudalbi Romania
114 C4 Cuddalore Tamil Nadu India
114 C3 Cuddapah Andhra Prad. India
85 E5 Cuddapan, Lake salt flat Qld Austr.
234 D1 Cuddebackville NY U.S.A.
194 B5 Cuddia r. Sicilia Italy
149 G4 Cuddington Cheshire, England U.K.
128 D1 Cudi Dağı hill Turkey
182 D1 Cudillero Spain
163 B4 Cudos France
223 J4 Cudworth Sask. Can.
149 H4 Cudworth South Yorkshire, England U.K.
87 C5 Cue W.A. Austr.
209 C8 Cuebe r. Angola
209 D8 Cueio r. Angola
183 F3 Cuéllar Spain
209 C8 Cuemba Angola
250 B5 Cuenca Ecuador
92 B3 Cuenca Phil.
183 H4 Cuenca Spain
183 H5 Cuenca prov. Castilla - La Mancha Spain
183 H4 Cuenca, Serranía de mts Spain
183 E2 Cuenca de Campos Spain
244 D3 Cuerámaro Mex.
245 E4 Cuernavaca Mex.
237 D6 Cuero TX U.S.A.
161 E5 Cuers France
183 F5 Cuerva Spain
183 H4 Cuervo r. Spain
246 D2 Cueto Cuba
245 F3 Cuetzalán Mex.
259 C7 Cueva de las Manos tourist site Santa Cruz Arg.
187 D4 Cuevas r. Spain
185 F3 Cuevas Altas hill Spain
185 F3 Cuevas Bajas Spain
185 I3 Cuevas de Almanzora Spain
185 E4 Cuevas del Becerro Spain
185 H3 Cuevas del Campo Spain
183 G2 Cuevas de San Clemente Spain
187 D4 Cuevas de Vinromá Spain
186 B4 Cuevas Labradas Spain
252 E5 Cuevo Bol.
183 F2 Cueza r. Spain
151 G3 Cuffley Hertfordshire, England U.K.
158 E4 Cugand France
161 D5 Cuges-les-Pins France
197 F3 Cugir Romania
197 F3 Cugir r. Romania
192 A4 Cuglieri Sardegna Italy
163 D5 Cugnaux France
209 C6 Cugo r. Angola
158 E3 Cuguen France
253 F3 Cuiabá Brazil
253 F4 Cuiabá r. Brazil
245 F5 Cuicatlan Mex.
Cuihua Yunnan China see Daguan
Cuijiang Fujian China see Ninghua
164 E3 Cuijk Neth.
243 H6 Cuilapa Guat.
245 F5 Cuilapan Mex.
147 D2 Cuilcagh hill Rep. of Ireland/U.K.
146 B4 Cuillin Hills Scotland U.K.
146 B4 Cuillin Sound sea chan. Scotland U.K.
209 C7 Cuilo Angola
209 B6 Cuilo Pombo Angola
100 D3 Cuiluan Heilong. China
209 B6 Cuimba Angola
160 D2 Cuiseaux France
156 D3 Cuise-la-Motte France
160 C2 Cuisery France
257 G3 Cuité r. Brazil
245 F4 Cuitláhuac Mex.
209 D9 Cuito r. Angola
209 C8 Cuito Cuanavale Angola
244 D4 Cuitzeo, Laguna de l. Mex.
251 F5 Cuiuni r. Brazil
236 F4 Cuivre r. MO U.S.A.
197 F3 Cujmir Romania
94 C1 Cukai Malaysia
198 B2 Çukë Albania
129 C4 Çukurbağ Turkey
127 F3 Çukurca Turkey
129 A3 Çukurçayır Turkey
199 G2 Çukurhisar Eskişehir Turkey
128 B1 Çukurova plat. Turkey
136 E4 Cula r. Moldova
107 H4 Culai Shan mt. Shandong China
162 E2 Culan France
146 E4 Culardoch hill Scotland U.K.
92 B4 Culasi Phil.
238 F1 Culbertson MT U.S.A.
236 C3 Culbertson NE U.S.A.
146 D4 Culbokie Highland, Scotland U.K.
83 F3 Culcairn N.S.W. Austr.
177 M4 Culciu Romania
147 D1 Culdaff Rep. of Ireland
146 F4 Culdrain Aberdeenshire, Scotland U.K.
247 □1 Culebra, Isla de i. Puerto Rico

Culebras to **Dashköpri** 297

252 A2 **Culebras** Peru
247 □1 **Culebrinas** r. Puerto Rico
164 E3 **Culemborg** Neth.
129 D4 **Culfa** Azer.
242 D3 **Culiacán** Mex.
92 A4 **Culion** Phil.
92 A4 **Culion** i. Phil.
148 B3 **Culkey** Northern Ireland U.K.
187 C4 **Culla** Spain
148 B5 **Cullahill** Rep. of Ireland
185 H3 **Cullar** r. Spain
185 H3 **Cúllar-Baza** Spain
147 E2 **Cullaville** Northern Ireland U.K.
147 B2 **Culleens** Rep. of Ireland
146 F4 **Cullen** Moray, Scotland U.K.
237 E5 **Cullen** LA U.S.A.
85 E1 **Cullen Point** Qld Austr.
187 C5 **Cullera** Spain
146 D4 **Cullicudden** Highland, Scotland U.K.
147 B3 **Cullin** Rep. of Ireland
215 G1 **Cullinan** S. Africa
146 C5 **Cullipool** Argyll and Bute, Scotland U.K.
146 □G1 **Cullivoe** Shetland, Scotland U.K.
231 C5 **Cullman** AL U.S.A.
150 D4 **Cullompton** Devon, England U.K.
190 B2 **Cully** Switz.
147 E2 **Cullybackey** Northern Ireland U.K.
147 E2 **Cullyhanna** Northern Ireland U.K.
146 C3 **Cul Mor** hill Scotland U.K.
147 D1 **Culmore** Northern Ireland U.K.
150 D4 **Culmstock** Devon, England U.K.
146 C4 **Culnacraig** Highland, Scotland U.K.
146 B4 **Culnaknock** Highland, Scotland U.K.
160 D3 **Culoz** France
232 E5 **Culpeper** VA U.S.A.
250 □ **Culpepper, Isla** i. Islas Galápagos Ecuador
146 D4 **Culrain** Highland, Scotland U.K.
146 □G1 **Culswick** Shetland, Scotland U.K.
146 E6 **Culter Fell** hill Scotland U.K.
146 F4 **Cults** Aberdeen, Scotland U.K.
254 B4 **Culuene** r. Brazil
226 D5 **Culver** IN U.S.A.
87 E7 **Culver, Point** W.A. Austr.
81 D5 **Culverden** South I. N.Z.
146 D6 **Culzean Bay** Scotland U.K.
254 D2 **Cumã, Baía do** inlet Brazil
129 C4 **Cumaçay** Turkey
251 E2 **Cumaná** Venez.
199 G1 **Cumaova** Turkey
256 C3 **Cumari** Brazil
250 B4 **Cumbal, Nevado de** vol. Col.
232 B6 **Cumberland** KY U.S.A.
232 D5 **Cumberland** MD U.S.A.
232 C5 **Cumberland** OH U.S.A.
232 D6 **Cumberland** VA U.S.A.
226 A3 **Cumberland** WI U.S.A.
232 A6 **Cumberland** r. KY U.S.A.
259 □ **Cumberland Bay** S. Georgia
234 C3 **Cumberland County** county NJ U.S.A.
234 A2 **Cumberland County** county PA U.S.A.
223 K4 **Cumberland House** Sask. Can.
85 G4 **Cumberland Islands** Qld Austr.
232 B6 **Cumberland Mountain** mts KY/TN U.S.A.
221 L3 **Cumberland Peninsula** Nunavut Can.
231 C5 **Cumberland Plateau** Kentucky/Tennessee U.S.A.
221 L3 **Cumberland Sound** sea chan. Nunavut Can.
146 E6 **Cumbernauld** North Lanarkshire, Scotland U.K.
256 D5 **Cumbica** airport São Paulo Brazil
183 F5 **Cumbre Alta** mt. Spain
259 C7 **Cumbre Negro** mt. Arg.
184 D2 **Cumbres de San Bartolomé** Spain
184 D2 **Cumbres Mayores** Spain
149 F3 **Cumbria** admin. div. England U.K.
114 C3 **Cumbum** Andhra Prad. India
184 B3 **Cumeada** Port.
190 C4 **Cumiana** Italy
182 C3 **Cumieira** Port.
251 H5 **Cuminapanema** r. Brazil
146 F4 **Cuminestown** Aberdeenshire, Scotland U.K.
170 C2 **Cumlosen** Ger.
231 C5 **Cumming** GA U.S.A.
240 F2 **Cummings** CA U.S.A.
82 C3 **Cummins** S.A. Austr.
86 E3 **Cummins Range** hills W.A. Austr.
83 G3 **Cumnock** N.S.W. Austr.
146 D6 **Cumnock** East Ayrshire, Scotland U.K.
151 F3 **Cumnor** Oxfordshire, England U.K.
242 C2 **Cumpas** Mex.
260 B4 **Cumpeo** Chile
126 D3 **Çumra** Turkey
159 F4 **Cunault** France
260 A6 **Cunco** Chile
87 C6 **Cunderdin** W.A. Austr.
250 C3 **Cundinamarca** dept Col.
215 G3 **Cundycleugh** S. Africa
163 C4 **Cunegès** France
209 B9 **Cunene** prov. Angola
209 B9 **Cunene** r. Angola/Namibia alt. **Kunene**
190 C4 **Cuneo** Italy
190 C4 **Cuneo** prov. Piemonte Italy
171 F4 **Cunewalde** Ger.
156 E4 **Cunfin** France
82 C3 **Cungena** S.A. Austr.
97 E4 **Cung Son** Vietnam
126 E3 **Çüngüş** Turkey
257 E5 **Cunha** Brazil
182 C4 **Cunha** Port.
209 C8 **Cunhinga** Angola
136 E4 **Cunicea** Moldova
186 E3 **Cunit** Spain
160 B3 **Cunlhat** France
83 F2 **Cunnamulla** Qld Austr.
146 □G1 **Cunningsburgh** Shetland, Scotland U.K.
182 B2 **Cuntis** Spain
197 E3 **Cununa** mt. Romania
140 N1 **Čuokkarašša** mt. Norway
190 C3 **Cuorgnè** Italy
146 E5 **Cupar** Fife, Scotland U.K.
251 H5 **Cupari** r. Brazil
177 L4 **Cupari, Dealul** hill Romania
136 D3 **Cupcina** Moldova
193 G2 **Cupello** Italy
193 F1 **Cupra Marittima** Italy
191 I5 **Cupramontana** Italy
196 E4 **Ćuprija** Srbija Yugo.
242 C3 **Cupula, Pico** mt. Mex.
163 D5 **Cuq-Toulza** France
254 F4 **Curaçá** Brazil
250 D6 **Curaçá** r. Brazil
247 □10 **Curaçao** i. Neth. Antilles
260 B6 **Curacautín** Chile
260 E6 **Curacó** r. Arg.
258 B5 **Curanilahue** Chile
252 C2 **Curanja** r. Peru
250 C5 **Curaray** r. Ecuador
260 B6 **Curarrehue** Chile
177 L5 **Curățele** Romania
258 F3 **Curaya** r. Arg.
82 D2 **Curdlawidny Lagoon** salt flat S.A. Austr.
250 D5 **Curé** r. Col.
160 B1 **Cure** r. France
190 D3 **Cureggio** Italy
260 A4 **Curepto** Chile
160 C2 **Curgy** France
Curia Switz. see **Chur**
260 B4 **Curicó** Chile
250 E5 **Curicuriari, Serra** hill Brazil
250 E5 **Curieuriari** r. Brazil
254 D4 **Curimata** Brazil
195 F4 **Curinga** Italy
256 C6 **Curitiba** Brazil
255 C8 **Curitibanos** Brazil
256 B6 **Curiúva** Brazil
83 G2 **Curlewis** N.S.W. Austr.
82 D2 **Curnamona** S.A. Austr.
209 A8 **Curoca** r. Angola
190 D3 **Curone** r. Italy
191 F2 **Curon Venosta** Italy
182 C3 **Curopos** Port.
83 G2 **Currabubula** N.S.W. Austr.
147 E4 **Curracloe** Rep. of Ireland
147 E3 **Curragh** Rep. of Ireland
147 C3 **Curraghroe** Rep. of Ireland
147 C3 **Curragh West** Rep. of Ireland
147 C4 **Curraglass** Rep. of Ireland
184 □ **Curral das Freiras** Madeira
251 I5 **Curralinho** Brazil
227 F3 **Curran** MI U.S.A.
241 J2 **Currant** NV U.S.A.
83 F2 **Curranyalpa** N.S.W. Austr.
182 B2 **Currás** Spain
85 E5 **Currawilla** Qld Austr.
237 F4 **Current** r. MO U.S.A.
83 E4 **Currie** Tas. Austr.
241 J1 **Currie** NV U.S.A.
231 E4 **Currituck** NC U.S.A.
147 C3 **Curry** Rep. of Ireland
150 E3 **Curry Rivel** Somerset, England U.K.
195 H2 **Cursi** Italy
177 L6 **Curtea** Romania
197 G3 **Curtea de Argeș** Romania
196 E2 **Curtici** Romania
87 D6 **Curtin** W.A. Austr.
85 H5 **Curtis Channel** Qld Austr.
83 F4 **Curtis Group** is Tas. Austr.
85 G4 **Curtis Island** Qld Austr.
77 I5 **Curtis Island** N.Z.
177 L4 **Curtuișeni** Romania
251 H6 **Curuá** r. Brazil
251 I4 **Curuá, Ilha** i. Brazil
254 B3 **Curuaés** r. Brazil
251 H5 **Curuapanema** r. Brazil
251 H5 **Curuá Una** r. Brazil
254 D2 **Curuçá** Brazil
94 C3 **Curup** Sumatera Indon.
251 E4 **Curupira, Serra** mts Brazil/Venez.
253 E3 **Cururú** Bol.
253 F1 **Cururu** r. Brazil
254 D2 **Cururupu** Brazil
251 F3 **Curutú, Cerro** mt. Venez.
261 H1 **Curuzú Cuatiá** Arg.
257 E3 **Curvelo** Brazil
226 C2 **Curwood, Mount** hill MI U.S.A.
193 G3 **Cusano Mutri** Italy
252 C3 **Cusco** Peru
252 B3 **Cusco** dept Peru
147 E1 **Cushendall** Northern Ireland U.K.
147 E1 **Cushendun** Northern Ireland U.K.
148 B4 **Cushina** Rep. of Ireland
237 D4 **Cushing** OK U.S.A.
190 F4 **Cusna, Monte** mt. Italy
162 C3 **Cussac** France
162 B3 **Cussac-Fort-Médoc** France
161 B4 **Cussac-sur-Loire** France
160 B2 **Cusset** France
231 C5 **Cusseta** GA U.S.A.
160 C1 **Cussy-les-Forges** France
238 F2 **Custer** MT U.S.A.
236 C3 **Custer** SD U.S.A.
157 G4 **Custines** France
194 B4 **Custonaci** Sicilia Italy
238 D1 **Cut Bank** MT U.S.A.
238 D1 **Cut Bank Creek** r. MT U.S.A.
231 C6 **Cuthbert** GA U.S.A.
84 C2 **Cuthbertson Falls** N.T. Austr.
191 F4 **Cutigliano** Italy
240 H3 **Cutler** CA U.S.A.
233 □J2 **Cutler** ME U.S.A.
231 D7 **Cutler Ridge** FL U.S.A.
194 D5 **Cutò** r. Sicilia Italy
237 F6 **Cut Off** LA U.S.A.
260 C6 **Cutral-Co** Arg.
195 F3 **Cutro** Italy
195 H2 **Cutrofiano** Italy
83 F2 **Cuttaburra Creek** r. Qld Austr.
117 F5 **Cuttack** Orissa India
192 A3 **Cuttoli-Corticchiato** Corse France
244 D4 **Cutzamala** r. Mex.
209 B8 **Cuvelai** Angola
208 B5 **Cuvette** admin. reg. Congo
87 B5 **Cuvier, Cape** W.A. Austr.
163 E5 **Cuxac-Cabardès** France
161 A5 **Cuxac-d'Aude** France
129 F4 **Çuxanlı** Azer.
168 D2 **Cuxhaven** Ger.
232 C4 **Cuyahoga Falls** OH U.S.A.
240 H4 **Cuyama** CA U.S.A.
240 G4 **Cuyama** r. CA U.S.A.
92 B3 **Cuyapo** Phil.
92 B4 **Cuyo** Phil.
92 B4 **Cuyo East Passage** Phil.
92 B4 **Cuyo Islands** Phil.
92 B4 **Cuyo West Passage** Phil.
251 G3 **Cuyuni** r. Guyana
244 B4 **Cuyutlán** Mex.
162 D4 **Cuzance** France
Cuzco Peru see **Cusco**
185 F2 **Cuzna** r. Spain
163 C4 **Cuzorn** France
171 F5 **Cvikov** Czech Rep.
150 D3 **Cwm** Blaenau Gwent, Wales U.K.
150 D3 **Cwmafan** Neath Port Talbot, Wales U.K.
150 D2 **Cwmbach** Powys, Wales U.K.
150 D3 **Cwmbran** Torfaen, Wales U.K.
150 D3 **Cwmllynfell** Neath Port Talbot, Wales U.K.
211 A5 **Cyangugu** Rwanda
174 C3 **Cybinka** Pol.
Cyclades dept Greece see **Kyklades**
Cyclades is Greece see **Kyklades**
175 L4 **Cyców** Pol.
Cydonia Kriti Greece see **Chania**
Cydweli Carmarthenshire, Wales U.K. see **Kidwelly**
83 F5 **Cygnet** Tas. Austr.
232 B4 **Cygnet** OH U.S.A.
Cymru admin. div. U.K. see **Wales**
150 D2 **Cynghordy** Carmarthenshire, Wales U.K.
150 C3 **Cynin** r. Wales U.K.
232 A5 **Cynthiana** KY U.S.A.
150 C3 **Cynwyl Elfed** Carmarthenshire, Wales U.K.
223 I5 **Cypress Hills** Sask. Can.
128 A2 **Cyprus** country Asia
202 D3 **Cyrenaica** reg. Libya
202 D1 **Cyrene** tourist site Libya
156 D2 **Cysoing** France
Cythera i. Greece see **Kythira**
150 C3 **Cywyn** r. Wales U.K.
174 E3 **Czacz** Pol.
174 G4 **Czajków** Pol.
174 E2 **Czaplinek** Pol.
223 I4 **Czar** Alta Can.
175 J5 **Czarna** Podkarpackie Pol.
175 K5 **Czarna** Podkarpackie Pol.
175 H4 **Czarna** r. Pol.
175 H5 **Czarna** r. Pol.
175 J5 **Czarna** r. Pol.
175 L2 **Czarna Białostocka** Pol.
174 F1 **Czarna Dąbrówka** Pol.
175 K6 **Czarna Górna** Pol.
175 L2 **Czarna Hańcza** r. Pol.
175 I5 **Czarna Nida** r. Pol.
174 G3 **Czarna Struga** r. Pol.
174 G2 **Czarna Woda** Pol.
175 H5 **Czarnca** Pol.
174 E2 **Czarne** Pol.
175 J2 **Czarnia** Pol.
174 E3 **Czarnków** Pol.
174 G4 **Czarnożyły** Pol.
175 H6 **Czarny Dunajec** Pol.
177 I2 **Czarny Dunajec** r. Pol.
174 G4 **Czastary** Pol.
175 I6 **Czchów** Pol.
175 H6 **Czechowice-Dziedzice** Pol.
176 E2 **Czech Republic** country Europe
175 J4 **Czekarzewice** Pol.
175 K4 **Czemierniki** Pol.
174 E3 **Czempiń** Pol.
175 L3 **Czeremcha** Pol.
174 F4 **Czermin** Pol.
174 D4 **Czerna Mała** r. Pol.
174 D4 **Czerna Wielka** r. Pol.
174 F4 **Czernica** Pol.
174 E2 **Czernica** r. Pol.
175 I2 **Czernice Borowe** Pol.
174 F3 **Czerniejewo** Pol.
175 I4 **Czerniewice** Pol.
174 G3 **Czernikowo** Pol.
174 E4 **Czernina** Pol.
Czernowitz Chernivets'ka Oblast' Ukr. see **Chernivtsi**
174 F2 **Czersk** Pol.
174 D3 **Czerwieńsk** Pol.
175 J3 **Czerwin** Pol.
175 I3 **Czerwińsk nad Wisłą** Pol.
174 G5 **Czerwionka-Leszczyny** Pol.
174 E3 **Czerwonak** Pol.
171 G4 **Czerwona Woda** Pol.
175 J3 **Czerwonka Włościańska** Pol.
175 H4 **Czestków** Pol.
175 H5 **Częstochowa** Pol.
174 F4 **Czeszów** Pol.
174 E2 **Człopa** Pol.
174 F2 **Człuchów** Pol.
174 F3 **Czmoń** Pol.
171 F4 **Czorneboh** hill Ger.
175 I3 **Czosnów** Pol.
175 J6 **Czudec** Pol.
175 L3 **Czyże** Pol.
175 K3 **Czyżew-Osada** Pol.

D

96 D2 **Đa, Sông** r. Vietnam
169 C5 **Daaden** Ger.
107 J2 **Da'an** Jilin China
92 B4 **Daanbantayan** Phil.
164 F2 **Daarle** Neth.
128 B4 **Ḍabāb, Jabal aḍ** mt. Jordan
211 B7 **Dabaga** Tanz.
250 D2 **Dabajuro** Venez.
206 D4 **Dabakala** Côte d'Ivoire
107 H3 **Daban** Nei Mongol China
106 D4 **Daban Shan** mts China
108 B2 **Dabao** Sichuan China
177 I4 **Dabas** Hungary
108 D1 **Daba Shan** mts China
210 C1 **Dabat** Eth.
Dabba Sichuan China see **Daocheng**
250 B3 **Dabeiba** Col.
96 B3 **Dabein** Myanmar
170 C2 **Dabel** Ger.
116 C5 **Dabhoi** Gujarat India
114 B2 **Dabhol** Mahar. India
174 D3 **Dąbie** Pol.
174 G3 **Dąbie** Pol.
174 C2 **Dąbie, Jezioro** l. Pol.
109 E2 **Dabie Shan** mts China
143 G4 **Dąbki** Pol.
157 H4 **Dabo** France
116 D4 **Daboh** Madh. Prad. India
206 C4 **Dabola** Guinea
206 D5 **Dabou** Côte d'Ivoire
206 E4 **Daboya** Ghana
107 F4 **Dabqig** Nei Mongol China
116 D4 **Dabra** Madh. Prad. India
174 G3 **Dąbroszyn** Pol.
174 F3 **Dąbrowa** Kujawsko-Pormorskie Pol.
174 F5 **Dąbrowa** Opolskie Pol.
174 F5 **Dąbrowa** Opolskie Pol.
175 L2 **Dąbrowa Białostocka** Pol.
174 G3 **Dąbrowa Biskupia** Pol.
174 G2 **Dąbrowa Chełmińska** Pol.
175 H5 **Dąbrowa Górnicza** Pol.
175 I5 **Dąbrowa Tarnowska** Pol.
175 H3 **Dąbrowice** Pol.
174 D3 **Dąbrówka Wielkopolska** Pol.
175 I2 **Dąbrówno** Pol.
109 F3 **Dabu** Guangdong China
197 G4 **Dăbuleni** Romania
Dacca Bangl. see **Dhaka**
173 F3 **Dachau** Ger.
173 F3 **Dachauer Moos** marsh Ger.
106 D4 **Dachechang** Nei Mongol China
107 H3 **Dachengzi** Liaoning China
114 C2 **Dachepalle** Andhra Prad. India
175 L5 **Dachnów** Pol.
169 F4 **Dachrieden** Ger.
173 E2 **Dachsbach** Ger.
108 C2 **Dachuan** Sichuan China
176 E2 **Dačice** Czech Rep.
227 I3 **Dacre** Ont. Can.
149 G3 **Dacre** Cumbria, England U.K.
177 H4 **Dad** Hungary
129 B4 **Dadaş** Turkey
126 D2 **Daday** Turkey
210 D1 **Daddato** Djibouti
231 D6 **Dade City** FL U.S.A.
231 C5 **Dadeville** AL U.S.A.
Dadong Liaoning China see **Donggang**
163 D5 **Dadou** r. France
116 C5 **Dadra** Dadra India
Dadra Mahar. India see **Achalpur**
116 C5 **Dadra and Nagar Haveli** union terr. India
123 F5 **Dadu** Pak.
108 B2 **Dadu He** r. Sichuan China
97 D5 **Đa Dung** r. Vietnam
92 B3 **Daet** Phil.
108 C3 **Dafang** Guizhou China
109 G1 **Dafeng** Jiangsu China
117 H4 **Dafla Hills** India
198 C3 **Dafni** Dytiki Ellas Greece
223 M4 **Dafoe** r. Man. Can.
226 E2 **Dafter** MI U.S.A.
177 H4 **Dág** Hungary
116 C5 **Dag** Rajasthan India
199 G3 **Dağ** Antalya Turkey
210 D3 **Daga Medo** Eth.
206 B2 **Dagana** Senegal
183 G4 **Daganzo de Arriba** Spain
106 D5 **Dagcanglhamo** Gansu China
129 D3 **Dağ Cäyir** Azer.
129 C3 **Dağcı** Turkey
138 F3 **Dagda** Latvia
199 F2 **Dağdere** Manisa Turkey
Dage Hebei China see **Fengning**
168 D1 **Dagebüll** Ger.
Dagenraad atoll Arch. des Tuamotu Fr. Polynesia see **Manihi**
129 E2 **Dagestan, Respublika** aut. rep. Rus. Fed.
Dagestanskaya A.S.S.R. aut. rep. Rus. Fed. see **Dagestan, Respublika**
129 F2 **Dagestanskiye Ogni** Rus. Fed.
Dagezhen Hebei China see **Fengning**
215 E5 **Daggaboersnek** S. Africa
Daghestan aut. rep. Rus. Fed. see **Dagestan, Respublika**
163 D4 **Daglan** France
129 E4 **Dağlıq Qarabağ** aut. reg. Azer.
190 C1 **Dagmersellen** Switz.
Dagö i. Estonia see **Hiiumaa**
Dagon Myanmar see **Yangôn**
81 B6 **Dagon** mt. South I. N.Z.
129 C3 **Dağpınar** Turkey
111 D6 **Dagrag Zangbo** r. Xizang China
107 H4 **Dagu** Tianjin China
107 I4 **Dagu** r. China
108 B3 **Daguan** Yunnan China
100 D3 **Daguokui Shan** hill Heilong. China
92 B2 **Dagupan** Phil.
84 B3 **Daguragu** N.T. Austr.
Dagxoi Sichuan China see **Sowa**
Dagxoi Sichuan China see **Yidun**
111 E6 **Dagzê** Xizang China
124 B3 **Dahabān** Saudi Arabia
222 E2 **Dahadinni** r. N.W.T. Can.
Dahalach, Isole is Eritrea see **Dahlak Archipelago**
Dahana des. Saudi Arabia see **Ad Dahnā'**
114 B2 **Dahanu** Mahar. India
Dahe Guangxi China see **Ziyuan**
107 F3 **Dahei** r. China
100 D3 **Daheiding Shan** mt. China
106 B3 **Dahei Shan** mt. Xinjiang China
109 F3 **Daheng** Fujian China
Daheyan Xinjiang China see **Turpan Zhan**
100 E3 **Dahezhen** Heilong. China
107 H3 **Da Hinggan Ling** mts China
114 B2 **Dahivadi** Mahar. India
203 I6 **Dahlak Archipelago** is Eritrea
169 B5 **Dahlem** Ger.
171 E4 **Dahlen** Ger.
168 F2 **Dahlenburg** Ger.
171 E4 **Dahlener Heide** reg. Ger.
171 C3 **Dahlenwarsleben** Ger.
231 D5 **Dahlonega** GA U.S.A.
171 E3 **Dahlwitz-Hoppegarten** Ger.
205 H2 **Dahmani** Tunisia
171 E4 **Dahme** Brandenburg Ger.
170 C1 **Dahme** Schleswig-Holstein Ger.
171 E3 **Dahme** r. Ger.
172 B2 **Dahn** Ger.
116 C5 **Dahod** Gujarat India
Dahomey country Africa see **Benin**
Dahra Senegal see **Dara**
168 F3 **Dähre** Ger.
127 F3 **Dahūk** Iraq
127 F3 **Dahūk** governorate Iraq
125 E4 **Ḍaḥyah, Wādī** r. Yemen
105 E3 **Daibosatsu-rei** mt. Japan
107 H4 **Daicheng** Hebei China
Daido r. N. Korea see **Taedong-gang**
105 G2 **Daigo** Japan
78 □6 **Dai Island** Solomon Is
140 L2 **Daikanvik** Sweden
96 B3 **Daik-u** Myanmar
146 B3 **Dail Bho Thuath** Western Isles, Scotland U.K.
232 D5 **Dailey** WV U.S.A.
146 D6 **Dailly** South Ayrshire, Scotland U.K.
122 D3 **Daim** Iran
103 F5 **Daimanji-san** hill Japan
185 G1 **Daimiel** Spain
105 E3 **Daimugen-zan** mt. Japan
147 D3 **Daingean** Rep. of Ireland
237 E5 **Daingerfield** TX U.S.A.
104 C2 **Dainichiga-take** vol. Japan
104 C2 **Dainichi-gawa** r. Japan
104 C2 **Dainichi-zan** mt. Japan
108 A1 **Dainkog** Sichuan China
85 F3 **Daintree** Qld Austr.
156 C2 **Dainville** France
157 F4 **Dainville-Bertheléville** France
261 G5 **Daireaux** Arg.
Dairen Liaoning China see **Dalian**
146 F5 **Dairsie** Fife, Scotland U.K.
203 F3 **Dairût** Egypt
235 D1 **Dairyland** NY U.S.A.
226 A2 **Dairyland** WI U.S.A.
103 F6 **Dai-sen** vol. Japan
109 G2 **Daishan** Zhejiang China
104 B4 **Daitō** Japan
105 F2 **Daiya-gawa** r. Japan
Daiyue Shanxi China see **Shanyin**
109 F3 **Daiyun Shan** mts China
246 E3 **Dajabón** Dom. Rep.
84 D4 **Dajarra** Qld Austr.
Dajie Yunnan China see **Jiangchuan**
108 B2 **Dajin Chuan** r. Sichuan China
106 D4 **Dajing** Gansu China
106 B4 **Da Juh** Qinghai China
206 A3 **Dakar** Senegal
Dakhla Western Sahara see **Ad Dakhla**
203 F3 **Dakhla Oasis** Egypt
204 A5 **Dakhlet Nouâdhibou** admin. reg. Maur.
129 B1 **Dakhovskaya** Rus. Fed.
97 D4 **Đak Nghe** r. Vietnam
138 G5 **Dakol'ka** r. Belarus
116 C5 **Dakor** Gujarat India
207 G3 **Dakoro** Niger
236 E3 **Dakota City** IA U.S.A.
236 D3 **Dakota City** NE U.S.A.
196 E4 **Đakovica** Kosovo, Srbija Yugo.
188 G3 **Đakovo** Croatia
209 D7 **Dala** Angola
177 J5 **Đala** Vojvodina, Srbija Yugo.
178 B3 **Dalaas** Austria
206 B4 **Dalaba** Guinea
146 A4 **Dalabrog** Western Isles, Scotland U.K.
Dalad Qi Nei Mongol China see **Shulinzhao**
Dalai Jilin China see **Da'an**
106 D3 **Dalain Hob** Nei Mongol China
122 A3 **Dālā Khānī, Kūh-e** mt. Iran
122 B4 **Dālakī** Iran
122 B4 **Dalaki, Rūd-e** r. Iran
128 A5 **Dalal, Gebel** mt. Egypt
143 G1 **Dalälven** r. Sweden
199 F3 **Dalama** Aydın Turkey
107 G3 **Dalamamiao** Nei Mongol China
199 F3 **Dalaman** Turkey
199 F3 **Dalaman** r. Turkey
106 E3 **Dalandzadgad** Mongolia
92 B4 **Dalanganem Islands** Phil.
110 C3 **Dalaoba** Xinjiang China
Dalap-Uliga-Darrit Majuro Marshall Is see **Delap-Uliga-Djarrit**
143 F1 **Dalarna** county Sweden
141 K3 **Dalarna** reg. Sweden
97 E5 **Đa Lat** Vietnam
Dalatando Angola see **N'dalatando**
106 D3 **Dalay** Mongolia
146 E7 **Dalbeattie** Dumfries and Galloway, Scotland U.K.
85 F4 **Dalbeg** Qld Austr.
170 C2 **Dalberg-Wendelstorf** Ger.
226 A3 **Dalbo** MN U.S.A.
142 E2 **Dalbosjön** l. Sweden
85 G5 **Dalby** Qld Austr.
142 E4 **Dalby** Sweden
259 B6 **Dalcahue** Chile
142 A1 **Dale** Hordaland Norway
141 I3 **Dale** Sogn og Fjordane Norway
150 B3 **Dale** Pembrokeshire, Wales U.K.
232 E5 **Dale City** VA U.S.A.
169 B5 **Daleiden** Ger.
164 F2 **Dalen** Neth.
215 G2 **Daleside** S. Africa
175 I5 **Daleszyce** Pol.
231 C6 **Daleville** AL U.S.A.
234 C1 **Daleville** PA U.S.A.
141 K3 **Dalfors** Sweden
164 F2 **Dalfsen** Neth.
87 C5 **Dalgaranger, Mount** hill W.A. Austr.
83 G4 **Dalgety** N.S.W. Austr.
87 B5 **Dalgety** r. W.A. Austr.
146 E5 **Dalgety Bay** Fife, Scotland U.K.
151 H2 **Dalham** Suffolk, England U.K.
237 C4 **Dalhart** TX U.S.A.
225 H3 **Dalhousie** N.B. Can.
116 D2 **Dalhousie** Hima. Prad. India
107 F5 **Dali** Shaanxi China
108 B3 **Dali** Yunnan China
107 F4 **Dali** r. China
107 I4 **Dalian** Liaoning China
Daliang Guangdong China see **Shunde**
106 D4 **Daliang** Qinghai China
108 B2 **Daliang Shan** mts Sichuan China
185 H4 **Dalías** Spain
Daliburgh Western Isles, Scotland U.K. see **Dalabrog**
129 E4 **Dälidağ** mt. Azer.
175 H4 **Dalików** Pol.
129 E3 **Dälilär** Azer.
129 E3 **Dälimämmädli** Azer.
107 I3 **Dalin** Nei Mongol China
107 I3 **Daling** r. China
Dalinghe Liaoning China see **Linhai**
101 C4 **Dalizi** Jilin China
188 G3 **Dalj** Croatia
146 E6 **Dalkeith** Midlothian, Scotland U.K.
117 F4 **Dalkola** W. Bengal India
85 H5 **Dallarnil** Qld Austr.
146 E4 **Dallas** Moray, Scotland U.K.
238 B2 **Dallas** OR U.S.A.
234 C1 **Dallas** PA U.S.A.
237 D5 **Dallas** TX U.S.A.
226 B5 **Dallas City** IL U.S.A.
234 B3 **Dallastown** PA U.S.A.
Dalles City OR U.S.A. see **The Dalles**
170 E3 **Dallgow** Ger.
220 E4 **Dall Island** AK U.S.A.
210 D1 **Dallol** vol. Eth.
188 E3 **Dalmacija** reg. Croatia
146 D5 **Dalmally** Argyll and Bute, Scotland U.K.
116 E4 **Dalman** Uttar Prad. India
177 H5 **Dalmand** Hungary
Dalmatia reg. Croatia see **Dalmacija**
234 B2 **Dalmatia** PA U.S.A.
146 D6 **Dalmellington** East Ayrshire, Scotland U.K.
223 J4 **Dalmeny** Sask. Can.
190 E3 **Dalmine** Italy
146 D4 **Dalnavie** Highland, Scotland U.K.
100 E3 **Dal'negorsk** Rus. Fed.
100 E3 **Dal'nerechensk** Rus. Fed.
134 I5 **Dal'neye Konstantinovo** Rus. Fed.
Dalny Liaoning China see **Dalian**
206 D5 **Daloa** Côte d'Ivoire
85 G1 **Daloloia Group** is P.N.G.
108 C3 **Dalou Shan** mts China
171 D5 **Dalovice** Czech Rep.
146 D6 **Dalry** North Ayrshire, Scotland U.K.
146 D6 **Dalrymple** East Ayrshire, Scotland U.K.
85 F4 **Dalrymple, Lake** Qld Austr.
85 G4 **Dalrymple, Mount** Qld Austr.
138 D1 **Dalsbruk** Fin.
142 E2 **Dals Långed** Sweden
157 G3 **Dalstein** France
149 G3 **Dalston** Cumbria, England U.K.
117 F4 **Daltenganj** Bihar India
224 C3 **Dalton** Ont. Can.
215 H3 **Dalton** S. Africa
231 C5 **Dalton** GA U.S.A.
233 G3 **Dalton** MA U.S.A.
232 C4 **Dalton** OH U.S.A.
234 C1 **Dalton** PA U.S.A.
Daltonganj Bihar India see **Daltenganj**
149 F3 **Dalton-in-Furness** Cumbria, England U.K.
227 E1 **Dalton Mills** Ont. Can.
147 C4 **Dalua** r. Rep. of Ireland
94 C2 **Daludalu** Sumatera Indon.
161 E4 **Daluis** France
109 E4 **Daluo Shan** mt. Guangdong China
140 □C2 **Dalvík** Iceland
87 C6 **Dalwallinu** W.A. Austr.
146 D5 **Dalwhinnie** Highland, Scotland U.K.
84 B2 **Daly** r. N.T. Austr.
199 F3 **Dalyan** Turkey
240 F3 **Daly City** CA U.S.A.
84 B2 **Daly River** N.T. Austr.
147 C3 **Dalystown** Rep. of Ireland
84 C3 **Daly Waters** N.T. Austr.
136 B2 **Damachava** Belarus
207 H3 **Damagaram Takaya** Niger
129 C3 **Damal** Turkey
116 C5 **Daman** Daman India
116 B5 **Daman and Diu** union terr. India
138 E5 **Damanava** Belarus
122 B3 **Dāmaneh** Iran
203 F2 **Damanhûr** Egypt
Damão Daman India see **Daman**
122 B3 **Damaq** Iran
129 B3 **Damar** Turkey
208 C3 **Damara** C.A.R.
212 C4 **Damaraland** reg. Namibia
Damas Syria see **Damascus**
207 I3 **Damasak** Nigeria
157 G4 **Damas-aux-Bois** France
128 C3 **Damascus** Syria
232 E5 **Damascus** MD U.S.A.
234 C1 **Damascus** PA U.S.A.
232 C6 **Damascus** VA U.S.A.
174 F3 **Damasławek** Pol.
207 H4 **Damaturu** Nigeria
122 C3 **Damāvand** Iran
122 C3 **Damāvand, Qolleh-ye** mt. Iran
163 C4 **Damazan** France
209 B6 **Damba** Angola
157 H4 **Dambach-la-Ville** France
207 F4 **Dambai** Ghana
207 H3 **Dambatta** Nigeria
170 C2 **Dambeck** Ger.
207 I4 **Damboa** Nigeria
179 H1 **Dambořice** Czech Rep.
197 G3 **Dâmbovița** r. Romania
117 H4 **Damchara** Assam India
120 F2 **Damdy** Kustanayskaya Oblast' Kazakh.
157 G4 **Dameleviéres** France
246 D3 **Dame Marie** Haiti
151 F4 **Damerham** Hampshire, England U.K.
148 B5 **Damerstown** Rep. of Ireland
156 D3 **Damery** France
158 D4 **Damgan** France
122 C2 **Damghan** Iran
147 E1 **Damhead** Northern Ireland U.K.
163 D5 **Damiatte** France
Damietta Egypt see **Dumyât**
159 G3 **Damigny** France
107 G4 **Daming** Hebei China
108 D4 **Daming Shan** mt. Guangxi China
108 A1 **Damjong** Qinghai China
Dammam Saudi Arabia see **Ad Dammām**
156 B4 **Dammarie** France
190 D2 **Dammastock** mt. Switz.
165 C3 **Damme** Belgium
168 D3 **Damme** Ger.
174 F1 **Damnica** Pol.
174 F1 **Damno** Pol.
116 D5 **Damoh** Madh. Prad. India
206 E4 **Damongo** Ghana
128 B3 **Damour** Lebanon
168 E1 **Damp** Ger.
94 C2 **Dampar, Tasik** l. Malaysia
160 D1 **Damparis** France
86 C4 **Dampier** W.A. Austr.
86 C4 **Dampier Archipelago** is W.A. Austr.
160 D1 **Dampierre** France
156 C5 **Dampierre-en-Burly** France
160 E1 **Dampierre-sur-Linotte** France
160 D1 **Dampierre-sur-Salon** France
93 D3 **Dampir, Selat** sea chan. Irian Jaya Indon.
160 E1 **Damprichard** France
Damqoq Zangbo r. Xizang China see **Maquan He**
111 F5 **Dam Qu** r. Qinghai China
97 D5 **Dâmrei, Chuŏr Phnum** mts Cambodia
117 H3 **Damroh** Arun. Prad. India
171 D3 **Damsdorf** Ger.
170 C2 **Damshagen** Ger.
170 D1 **Damsholte** Denmark
190 B1 **Damvant** Switz.
156 B4 **Damville** France
157 F3 **Damvillers** France
164 F1 **Damwoude** Neth.
Damxoi Xizang China see **Comai**
111 E6 **Damxung** Xizang China
231 E4 **Dan** r. NC U.S.A.
240 H3 **Dana, Mount** CA U.S.A.
129 E3 **Danaçı** Azer.
185 G2 **Dañador** r. Spain
Danakil reg. Eritrea/Eth. see **Denakil**
206 C5 **Danané** Côte d'Ivoire
96 E3 **Đa Năng** Vietnam
106 B3 **Dananhu** Xinjiang China
92 C4 **Danao** Phil.
108 B2 **Danba** Sichuan China
234 C2 **Danboro** PA U.S.A.
151 H3 **Danbury** Essex, England U.K.
233 G4 **Danbury** CT U.S.A.
231 D4 **Danbury** NC U.S.A.
233 H3 **Danbury** NH U.S.A.
226 A2 **Danbury** WI U.S.A.
149 I3 **Danby** North Yorkshire, England U.K.
233 G3 **Danby** VT U.S.A.
109 E1 **Dancheng** Henan China
Dancheng Zhejiang China see **Xiangshan**
87 B6 **Dandaragan** W.A. Austr.
209 B7 **Dande** r. Angola
116 E3 **Dandel'dhura** Nepal
114 B3 **Dandeli** Karnataka India
149 F2 **Danderhall** Midlothian, Scotland U.K.
101 C4 **Dandong** Liaoning China
104 D3 **Dando-san** mt. Japan
231 D4 **Dandridge** TN U.S.A.
138 C4 **Danė** r. Lith.
149 G4 **Dane** r. England U.K.
151 H3 **Danehill** East Sussex, England U.K.
147 D3 **Danesfort** Rep. of Ireland
197 G4 **Daneți** Romania
Dänew Turkm. see **Dyanev**
108 D1 **Danfeng** Shaanxi China
Danfeng Yunnan China see **Shizong**
233 □J2 **Danforth** ME U.S.A.
Dangara Tajik. see **Danghara**
100 D3 **Dangbizhen** Rus. Fed.
106 E5 **Dangchang** Gansu China
Dangchengwan Gansu China see **Subei**
209 B6 **Dange** Angola
Danger Islands atoll Cook Is see **Pukapuka**
84 B1 **Danger Point** N.T. Austr.
214 B6 **Danger Point** S. Africa
162 C2 **Dangé-St-Romain** France
123 G2 **Danghara** Tajik.
106 B4 **Danghe Nanshan** mts China
210 C2 **Dangila** Eth.
Dangla Shan mts Xizang China see **Tanggula Shan**
117 H4 **Dangori** Assam India
111 E6 **Dangqên** Xizang China
243 H5 **Dangriga** Belize
107 H5 **Dangshan** Anhui China
109 F2 **Dangtu** Anhui China
207 G4 **Dan-Gulbi** Nigeria
210 B2 **Dangur** mt. Eth.
109 D2 **Dangyang** Hubei China
174 G5 **Daniec** Pol.
238 E3 **Daniel** WY U.S.A.
254 B5 **Daniel, Serra** hills Brazil
225 J3 **Daniel's Harbour** Nfld. Can.
214 D3 **Daniëlskuil** S. Africa
233 H4 **Danielson** CT U.S.A.
215 G2 **Danielsrus** S. Africa
231 D5 **Danielsville** GA U.S.A.
134 H4 **Danilov** Rus. Fed.
196 D4 **Danilovgrad** Crna Gora Yugo.
121 G1 **Danilovka** Kazakh.
135 I6 **Danilovka** Rus. Fed.
134 G4 **Danilovskaya Vozvyshennost'** hills Rus. Fed.
107 F4 **Daning** Shanxi China
129 F3 **Dänizkänarı** Azer.
Danjiang Guizhou China see **Leishan**
109 D1 **Danjiangkou** Hubei China
160 E1 **Danjoutin** France
125 G3 **Ḍank** Oman
124 C5 **Dankalia** prov. Eritrea
171 C4 **Dankerode** Ger.
169 F5 **Dankmarshausen** Ger.
139 L5 **Dankov** Rus. Fed.
121 I4 **Dankova, Pik** mt. Kyrg.
108 B2 **Danleng** Sichuan China
242 □I6 **Danlí** Hond.
221 P1 **Danmark Fjord** inlet Greenland
169 F3 **Danndorf** Ger.
168 G1 **Dannemare** Denmark
160 F1 **Dannemarie** France
233 G2 **Dannemora** NY U.S.A.
170 C2 **Dannenberg (Elbe)** Ger.
170 E2 **Dannenwalde** Ger.
80 F4 **Dannevirke** North I. N.Z.
168 E1 **Dannewerk** Ger.
215 H3 **Dannhauser** S. Africa
206 E4 **Dano** Burkina
Danshui Taiwan see **Tanshui**
232 E3 **Dansville** NY U.S.A.
116 C4 **Danta** Gujarat India
232 B6 **Dante** VA U.S.A.
114 D2 **Dantewara** Madh. Prad. India
Dantu Jiangsu China see **Zhenjiang**
197 I3 **Danube** r. Europe alt. **Donau (Austria/Germany)**, alt. **Duna (Hungary)**, alt. **Dunaj (Slovakia)**, alt. **Dunărea (Romania)**, alt. **Dunav (Yugoslavia)**
Danube Delta Romania see **Dunării, Delta**
96 A3 **Danubyu** Myanmar
237 E5 **Danville** AR U.S.A.
230 C3 **Danville** IL U.S.A.
230 C4 **Danville** IN U.S.A.
230 C4 **Danville** KY U.S.A.
232 B4 **Danville** OH U.S.A.
227 I5 **Danville** PA U.S.A.
232 D6 **Danville** VA U.S.A.
233 G2 **Danville** VT U.S.A.
Danxian Hainan China see **Danzhou**
109 F2 **Danyang** Jiangsu China
108 C3 **Danzhai** Guizhou China
108 D3 **Danzhou** Guangxi China
108 D5 **Danzhou** Hainan China
Danzhou Shaanxi China see **Yichuan**
Danzig Pol. see **Gdańsk**
Danzig, Gulf of Pol./Rus. Fed. see **Gdańsk, Gulf of**
92 B4 **Dao** Phil.
182 B4 **Dão** r. Port.
108 B2 **Daocheng** Sichuan China
Daojiang Hunan China see **Daoxian**
Daokou Henan China see **Huaxian**
159 F4 **Daon** France
108 D2 **Daoshiping** Hubei China
106 D4 **Daotanghe** Qinghai China
Dao Tay Sa is S. China Sea see **Paracel Islands**
Daoud Alg. see **Aïn Beïda**
206 E5 **Daoukro** Côte d'Ivoire
158 B3 **Daoulas** France
109 D3 **Daoxian** Hunan China
108 C2 **Daozhen** Guizhou China
92 C4 **Dapa** Phil.
207 F4 **Dapaong** Togo
117 I4 **Daphabum** mt. Arun. Prad. India
Daphnae tourist site Egypt see **Kawm Dafanah**
231 C6 **Daphne** AL U.S.A.
92 B4 **Dapiak, Mount** Mindanao Phil.
Dapingdi Sichuan China see **Yanbian**
92 B4 **Dapitan** Phil.
Dapu Guangxi China see **Liucheng**
126 C5 **Daqahlîya** governorate Egypt
111 F4 **Da Qaidam Zhen** Qinghai China
108 B3 **Daqiao** Yunnan China
100 C3 **Daqing** Heilong. China
107 I3 **Daqin Tal** Nei Mongol China
109 F3 **Daqiu** Fujian China
110 F3 **Daquan** Gansu China
106 B3 **Daquanwan** Xinjiang China
127 G4 **Dāqūq** Iraq
206 B3 **Dara** Senegal
128 C3 **Dar'ā** Syria
128 C3 **Dar'ā** governorate Syria
203 G3 **Dâra, Gebel** mt. Egypt
251 E5 **Daraá** r. Brazil
122 C4 **Dārāb** Iran
197 H1 **Darabani** Romania
92 B3 **Daraga** Phil.
138 G5 **Darahanava** Belarus
122 B3 **Dārān** Iran
97 E4 **Đa Răng, Sông** r. Vietnam
177 G6 **Darány** Hungary
99 J1 **Darasun** Rus. Fed.
Daraut-Kurgan Kyrg. see **Daroot-Korgan**
196 E4 **Đaravica** mt. Yugo.
203 G3 **Daraw** Egypt
207 H4 **Darazo** Nigeria
Darband Uzbek. see **Derbent**
122 D4 **Darband, Kūh-e** mt. Iran
138 C3 **Darbėnai** Lith.
180 D5 **Dar Ben Karricha el Behri** Morocco
117 F4 **Darbhanga** Bihar India
238 D2 **Darby** MT U.S.A.
234 C3 **Darby** PA U.S.A.
147 A4 **Darby's Bridge** Rep. of Ireland
108 A1 **Darcang** Sichuan China
189 C7 **Dar Chabanne** Tunisia
180 D5 **Dar Chaoui** Morocco
222 F5 **D'Arcy** B.C. Can.
188 G3 **Darda** Croatia
237 E5 **Dardanelle** AR U.S.A.
240 H2 **Dardanelle** CA U.S.A.
169 F4 **Dardesheim** Ger.
Dardo Sichuan China see **Kangding**
191 F2 **Darè** Italy
Dar el Beida Morocco see **Casablanca**
126 E3 **Darende** Turkey
211 C6 **Dar es Salaam** Tanz.
83 E3 **Dareton** N.S.W. Austr.
81 D5 **Darfield** South I. N.Z.
190 F3 **Darfo Boario Terme** Italy
123 E1 **Darganata** Turkm.
80 D1 **Dargaville** North I. N.Z.
175 J1 **Dargin, Jezioro** l. Pol.
83 F4 **Dargo** Vic. Austr.
207 F3 **Dargol** Niger
170 D2 **Dargun** Ger.
106 E1 **Darhan** Mongolia
Darhan Muminggan Lianheqi Nei Mongol China see **Bailingmiao**
199 F1 **Darıca** Turkey
199 G1 **Darıçayırı** Sakarya Turkey
199 F2 **Darıcı** Turkey
235 E1 **Darien** CT U.S.A.
231 D6 **Darien** GA U.S.A.
250 B2 **Darién, Golfo del** g. Col.
242 □K7 **Darién, Serranía del** mts Panama
129 A4 **Darıkent** Turkey
121 H2 **Dar'inskiy** Kazakh.
120 B2 **Dar'inskoye** Kazakh.
242 □I6 **Darío** Nic.
199 F3 **Darıveren** Denizli Turkey
Darīya Kazakh. see **Dar'inskiy**
Darjeeling W. Bengal India see **Darjiling**
117 G4 **Darjiling** W. Bengal India
87 C7 **Darkan** W.A. Austr.
82 D3 **Darke Peak** S.A. Austr.
147 E2 **Darkley** Northern Ireland U.K.
108 A1 **Darlag** Qinghai China
83 E3 **Darling** r. N.S.W. Austr.
214 B5 **Darling** S. Africa
85 G5 **Darling Downs** hills Qld Austr.
169 F4 **Darlingerode** Ger.
87 B7 **Darling Range** hills W.A. Austr.
149 H3 **Darlington** Darlington, England U.K.
149 H3 **Darlington** admin. div. England U.K.
234 B3 **Darlington** MD U.S.A.
231 E5 **Darlington** SC U.S.A.
226 B4 **Darlington** WI U.S.A.
83 F3 **Darlington Point** N.S.W. Austr.
87 D5 **Darlot, Lake** salt flat W.A. Austr.
143 G4 **Darłówko** Pol.
143 G4 **Darłowo** Pol.
197 H2 **Dărmănești** Romania
114 C2 **Darmaraopet** Andhra Prad. India
172 C2 **Darmstadt** Ger.
169 D6 **Darmstadt** admin. reg. Hessen Ger.
116 C5 **Darna** r. India
202 D1 **Darnah** Libya
215 H3 **Darnall** S. Africa
156 B3 **Darnétal** France
157 G4 **Darney** France
83 E3 **Darnick** N.S.W. Austr.
157 G4 **Darnieulles** France
186 F2 **Darnius** Spain
263 E2 **Darnley, Cape** Antarctica
186 G2 **Daró** r. Spain
183 I3 **Daroca** Spain
121 H5 **Daroot-Korgan** Kyrg.
134 I4 **Darovskoy** Rus. Fed.
182 B3 **Darque** Port.
146 F4 **Darra** Aberdeenshire, Scotland U.K.
147 B4 **Darragh** Rep. of Ireland
261 F5 **Darregueira** Arg.
122 D2 **Darreh Gaz** Iran
Darreh Gozaru r. Iran see **Gīzeh Rūd**
122 C4 **Darreh-ye Bāhābād** Iran
123 G3 **Darreh-ye Shekārī** r. Afgh.
123 G3 **Darreh-ye Shekārī** r. Afgh.
185 G3 **Darro** Spain
114 C3 **Darsi** Andhra Prad. India
170 D1 **Darß** pen. Ger.
150 D4 **Dart** r. England U.K.
128 C1 **Dār Ta'izzah** Syria
Dartang Xizang China see **Baqên**
151 H3 **Dartford** Kent, England U.K.
150 D4 **Dartington** Devon, England U.K.
150 D4 **Dartmeet** Devon, England U.K.
82 E4 **Dartmoor** Vic. Austr.
150 C4 **Dartmoor** hills England U.K.
150 D4 **Dartmoor National Park** England U.K.
225 I4 **Dartmouth** N.S. Can.
150 D4 **Dartmouth** Devon, England U.K.
85 F5 **Dartmouth, Lake** salt flat Qld Austr.
83 F4 **Dartmouth Reservoir** Vic. Austr.
149 H4 **Darton** South Yorkshire, England U.K.
91 J8 **Daru** P.N.G.
206 C5 **Daru** Sierra Leone
104 A3 **Daruga-mine** mt. Japan
188 F3 **Daruvar** Croatia
122 D1 **Darvaza** Turkm.
146 D6 **Darvel** East Ayrshire, Scotland U.K.
Darvi Hovd Mongolia see **Bulgan**
123 G2 **Darvoz, Qatorkŭhi** mts Tajik.
149 G4 **Darwen** Blackburn with Darwen, England U.K.
213 F3 **Darwendale** Zimbabwe
116 D5 **Darwha** Mahar. India
84 B2 **Darwin** N.T. Austr.
259 F8 **Darwin** Falkland Is
259 C9 **Darwin, Monte** mt. Chile
250 □ **Darwin, Volcán** vol. Islas Galápagos Ecuador
Darwin Island Islas Galápagos Ecuador see **Culpepper, Isla**
123 G4 **Darya Khan** Pak.
120 F3 **Dar'yalyktakyr, Ravnina** plain Kazakh.
202 D1 **Daryānah** Libya
Dar"yoi Amu r. Asia see **Amudar'ya**
Dar"yoi Sir r. Asia see **Syrdar'ya**
122 D4 **Dārzīn** Iran
116 B5 **Dasada** Gujarat India
107 G4 **Dasha** r. China
175 M6 **Dashava** Ukr.
107 G1 **Dashbalbar** Mongolia
Dashhowuz Turkm. see **Dashkhovuz**
107 I3 **Dashiqiao** Liaoning China
106 A3 **Dashitou** Xinjiang China
136 E3 **Dashiv** Ukr.
107 I2 **Dashizhai** Nei Mongol China
Dashkesan Azer. see **Daşkäsän**
122 D1 **Dashkhovuz** Turkm.
Dashkhovuz Oblast admin. div. Turkm. see **Dashkhovuzskaya Oblast'**
122 D1 **Dashkhovuzskaya Oblast'** admin. div. Turkm.
Dashköpri Turkm. see **Tashkepri**

Column 1

122 D2 Dasht Iran
123 E5 Dasht r. Pak.
122 C4 Dasht-e Palang r. Iran
176 E1 Dašice Czech Rep.
173 F3 Dasing Ger.
123 H3 Daska Pak.
129 E3 Daşkäsän Azer.
214 D5 Daşkö S. Africa
170 C1 Daskow Ger.
108 C3 Dasongshu Yunnan China
123 H2 Daspar mt. Pak.
207 F5 Dassa Benin
169 E4 Dassel Ger.
168 F2 Dassendorf Ger.
214 B5 Dassen Island S. Africa
168 F2 Dassow Ger.
129 E4 Dastakert Armenia
100 D4 Da Suifen He r. China
116 C3 Dasuya Punjab India
215 G2 Dasville S. Africa
175 H3 Daszyna Pol.
199 E3 Datça Turkey
102 J2 Date Japan
241 K5 Dateland AZ U.S.A.
116 C4 Datia Gujarat India
116 C4 Datha Madh. Prad. India
109 F3 Datian Fujian China
109 D4 Datian Ding mt. Guangdong China
239 F5 Datil NM U.S.A.
Datong Fujian China see Tong'an
100 C3 Datong Heilong. China
106 D4 Datong Qinghai China
107 G3 Datong Shanxi China
106 D4 Datong He r. China
106 C4 Datong Shan mts China
169 C4 Datteln Ger.
169 F4 Datterode (Ringgau) Ger.
92 C5 Datu Piang Phil.
123 G3 Daud Khel Pak.
117 F4 Daudnagar Bihar India
138 E4 Daugai Lith.
138 E3 Daugava r. Latvia
    alt. Zakhodnyaya Dzvina,
    alt. Zapadnaya Dvina,
    conv. Western Dvina
138 F4 Daugavpils Latvia
138 D3 Daugyvene r. Lith.
123 F2 Daulatabad Afgh.
117 G5 Daulatabad Bangl.
250 B5 Daule Ecuador
163 D5 Daumazan-sur-Arize France
159 F4 Daumeray France
169 B5 Daun Ger.
114 B2 Daund Mahar. India
96 A2 Daungyu r. Myanmar
223 K5 Dauphin Man. Can.
161 D5 Dauphin France
234 B2 Dauphin PA U.S.A.
234 B2 Dauphin County county PA U.S.A.
161 D4 Dauphiné, Alpes du mts France
207 H3 Daura Nigeria
87 B5 Daura Creek r. W.A. Austr.
107 H1 Dauriya Rus. Fed.
116 D4 Dausa Rajasthan India
169 D5 Dautphetal-Friedensdorf Ger.
169 D5 Dautphetal-Holzhausen Ger.
146 E4 Dava Moray, Scotland U.K.
129 F3 Däväçi Azer.
114 B3 Davangere Karnataka India
92 C5 Davao Phil.
92 C5 Davao Gulf Phil.
123 E5 Dāvar Panāh Iran
215 G2 Davel S. Africa
230 B3 Davenport IA U.S.A.
233 F3 Davenport NY U.S.A.
232 C4 Davenport WA U.S.A.
88 C5 Davenport Downs Qld Austr.
84 C4 Davenport Range hills N.T. Austr.
151 F2 Daventry Northamptonshire, England U.K.
215 G2 Daveyton S. Africa
161 C3 Davézieux France
242 □J7 David Panama
236 D3 David City NE U.S.A.
223 J5 Davidson Sask. Can.
84 B4 Davidson, Mount hill N.T. Austr.
234 B4 Davidsonville MD U.S.A.
82 B1 Davies, Mount S.A. Austr.
256 D3 Davinópolis Brazil
146 D4 Daviot Highland, Scotland U.K.
263 F2 Davis research stn Antarctica
86 D4 Davis r. W.A. Austr.
240 G2 Davis CA U.S.A.
232 D5 Davis WV U.S.A.
232 D5 Davis, Mount hill PA U.S.A.
241 J4 Davis Dam AZ U.S.A.
225 I2 Davis Inlet Nfld. Can.
227 F4 Davison MI U.S.A.
263 G2 Davis Sea Antarctica
221 M3 Davis Strait Can./Greenland
135 K5 Davlekanovo Rus. Fed.
198 C2 Davlia Greece
177 H5 Davod Hungary
195 F4 Davoli Italy
190 E2 Davos Switz.
199 E3 Davutlar Turkey
232 C4 Davy WV U.S.A.
136 D1 Davyd-Haradok Belarus
175 M6 Davyd Ukr.
137 G4 Davydiv Brid Ukr.
137 H4 Davydivka Ukr.
    Davydkovo Rus. Fed. see Tolbukhino
137 J2 Davydovka Rus. Fed.
107 I3 Dawa Liaoning China
    Dawahaidy atoll Arch. des Tuamotu Fr. Polynesia see Ravahere
210 D3 Dawa Wenz r. Eth.
111 D6 Dawaxung Xizang China
108 B2 Dawê Sichuan China
    Dawei Myanmar see Tavoy
    Dawei r. Myanmar see Tavoy
107 H5 Dawen r. China
150 D4 Dawlish Devon, England U.K.
96 B3 Dawna Range mts Myanmar/Thai.
125 F4 Dawqah Oman
124 D5 Dawrán Yemen
85 G4 Dawson r. Qld Austr.
220 E3 Dawson Y.T. Can.
231 C6 Dawson GA U.S.A.
236 D2 Dawson ND U.S.A.
259 C9 Dawson, Isla i. Chile
96 A3 Dawson, Mount B.C. Can.
222 F4 Dawson Creek B.C. Can.
222 A2 Dawson Range mts Y.T. Can.
222 E5 Dawsons Landing B.C. Can.
231 C6 Dawsonville GA U.S.A.
109 E2 Dawu Hubei China
    Dawu Qinghai China see Maqên
108 B2 Dawu Sichuan China
    Dawu Taiwan see Tawu
    Dawukou Ningxia China see Shizuishan
109 E2 Dawu Shan hill Hubei China
125 G3 Dawwah Oman
163 A5 Dax France
    Daxian Sichuan China see Dachuan
108 C4 Daxin Guangxi China
    Daxing Yunnan China see Ninglang
    Daxing Yunnan China see Wencheng
108 B2 Daxue Shan mts Sichuan China
    Daxue Zhejiang China see Liijing
107 I4 Dayang r. China
111 F7 Dayang r. China
107 J3 Dayangshu Nei Mongol China
108 B3 Dayao Yunnan China
109 E2 Dayao Hubei China
108 B2 Dayi Sichuan China
108 A3 Dayishan Jiangsu China see Guanyun
129 D2 Daykhokh, Gora mt. Rus. Fed.
83 F4 Daylesford Vic. Austr.
261 H2 Daymán r. Uru.
261 I2 Daymán, Cuchilla del hills Uru.

Column 2

108 D2 Dayong Hunan China
128 B3 Dayr Abū Sa'īd Jordan
127 F4 Dayr az Zawr Syria
128 C1 Dayr Ḥāfir Syria
223 H4 Daysland Alta Can.
226 A3 Dayton MN U.S.A.
232 A5 Dayton OH U.S.A.
231 C5 Dayton TN U.S.A.
237 E6 Dayton TX U.S.A.
232 D5 Dayton VA U.S.A.
238 C2 Dayton WA U.S.A.
231 D6 Daytona Beach FL U.S.A.
109 E3 Dayu Jiangxi China
238 D2 Dayu Ling mts China
107 H5 Da Yunhe canal China
238 C2 Dayville OR U.S.A.
103 E7 Dazaifu Japan
122 A2 Dazgir Iran
    Dazhe Guangdong China see Pingyuan
    Dazhongji Jiangsu China see Dafeng
108 C2 Dazhu Sichuan China
199 F3 Dazkırı Turkey
108 C2 Dazhou Chongqing China
108 C2 Dazu Rock Carvings tourist site Chongqing China
216 E4 De Aar S. Africa
147 E4 Dead r. Rep. of Ireland
233 □H2 Dead r. ME U.S.A.
226 D2 Dead r. MI U.S.A.
246 D2 Deadman's Cay Long I. Bahamas
241 J4 Dead Mountains NV U.S.A.
128 B4 Dead Sea salt l. Asia
236 C2 Deadwood SD U.S.A.
84 C2 Dead Adder Creek r. N.T. Austr.
84 B4 Deakin W.A. Austr.
151 I3 Deal Kent, England U.K.
235 D2 Deal NJ U.S.A.
215 E3 Dealesville S. Africa
222 E4 Dean r. B.C. Can.
150 E3 Dean, Forest of England U.K.
260 E2 Deán Funes Arg.
    Deanuvuotna inlet Norway see Tanafjorden
146 E5 Dean Water r. Scotland U.K.
227 F4 Dearborn MI U.S.A.
149 H4 Dearham Cumbria, England U.K.
149 H4 Dearne r. England U.K.
238 C2 Deary ID U.S.A.
222 D3 Dease r. B.C. Can.
222 D3 Dease Lake B.C. Can.
220 H3 Dease Strait Nunavut Can.
240 I3 Death Valley CA U.S.A.
240 I3 Death Valley depr. CA U.S.A.
241 I3 Death Valley Junction CA U.S.A.
159 G2 Deauville France
238 E2 Deaver WY U.S.A.
129 E3 Deavgay, Gora mt. Rus. Fed.
117 G5 Debagram W. Bengal India
137 J3 Debal'tseve Ukr.
    Debal'tsevo Ukr. see Debal'tseve
108 C2 Debao Guangxi China
196 E5 Debar Macedonia
210 C1 Debark Eth.
223 J4 Debden Sask. Can.
204 E2 Debdou Morocco
129 D3 Debed r. Armenia
151 I2 Debben r. England U.K.
151 I2 Debenham Suffolk, England U.K.
225 I4 Debert N.S. Can.
134 K4 Debesy Rus. Fed.
175 J5 Dębica Pol.
164 E2 De Bilt Neth.
131 Q3 Debin Rus. Fed.
175 J1 Dęblin Pol.
174 F1 Dębno Pol.
175 I6 Dębno Pol.
174 G3 Dębno Pol.
206 D3 Débo, Lac l. Mali
87 C6 Deborah East, Lake salt flat W.A. Austr.
87 C6 Deborah West, Lake salt flat W.A. Austr.
191 I3 Debrc Serbia
78 □b Deborzeczka Pol.
175 L4 Debrno Kloda Pol.
175 H2 Dębowa Kłoda Pol.
210 C2 Debre Birhan Eth.
227 K4 Debrecen Hungary
210 C2 Debre Markos Eth.
210 C2 Debre Sīna Eth.
196 E5 Debrešte Macedonia
210 C2 Debre Tabor Eth.
210 C3 Debre Werk' Eth.
210 C2 Debre Zeyit Eth.
174 F2 Debrzno Pol.
196 E4 Dečani Kosovo, Srbija Yugo.
231 C5 Decatur AL U.S.A.
231 C5 Decatur GA U.S.A.
230 D4 Decatur IL U.S.A.
230 D4 Decatur IN U.S.A.
226 E4 Decatur MI U.S.A.
237 F5 Decatur MS U.S.A.
231 C5 Decatur TN U.S.A.
237 D5 Decatur TX U.S.A.
231 C5 Decaturville TN U.S.A.
163 E4 Decazeville France
114 C2 Deccan plat. India
85 H5 Deception Bay Qld Austr.
    Deception Island Vanuatu see Moso
212 D4 Deception Pans salt pan Botswana
108 B3 Dechang Sichuan China
    Decheng Guangdong China see Dechang
177 G3 Dechtice Slovakia
192 A5 Decimomannu Sardegna Italy
192 A5 Decimoputzu Sardegna Italy
176 D1 Děčín Czech Rep.
160 C3 Décines-Charpieu France
158 B3 Decize France
238 F2 Decker MT U.S.A.
164 D1 De Cocksdorp Neth.
195 F3 Decollatura Italy
226 B3 Decorah IA U.S.A.
84 C1 De Courcy Head hd N.T. Austr.
177 H5 Decs Hungary
    Dedang Yunnan China see Yongde
197 F5 Dedaye Myanmar
151 F3 Deddington Oxfordshire, England U.K.
182 E5 Dedegül Dağları mts Turkey
179 H4 Dedeleben Ger.
169 F3 Dedelstorf Ger.
169 G3 Dedelow Ger.
169 E4 Dedemstorf Ger.
164 F2 Dedemsvaart Neth.
210 D2 Deder Eth.
177 J3 Dédestapolcány Hungary
151 H3 Dedham Essex, England U.K.
139 U6 Dedilovo Rus. Fed.
106 D1 Delger Mörön r. Mongolia
255 D4 Dedo de Deus mt. Brazil

Column 3

235 F1 Deep River CT U.S.A.
83 G2 Deepwater N.S.W. Austr.
234 C3 Deepwater r. CA U.S.A.
240 F2 Deer Creek r. CA U.S.A.
234 B3 Deer Creek r. MD U.S.A.
234 C3 Deerfield NJ U.S.A.
232 C3 Deerfield NY U.S.A.
210 E3 Deeri Somalia
87 F5 Deering, Mount W.A. Austr.
221 □I2 Deer Isle ME U.S.A.
223 M4 Deer Lake Nfld. Can.
223 M4 Deer Lake Ont. Can.
238 D2 Deer Lodge MT U.S.A.
235 E2 Deer Park NY U.S.A.
238 C2 Deer Park WA U.S.A.
    Deesa Gujarat India see Disa
238 D3 Deeth NV U.S.A.
171 D3 Deetz Ger.
137 J5 Defanovka Rus. Fed.
    Defeng Guizhou China see Liping
236 D3 Defiance OH U.S.A.
241 M4 Defiance Plateau AZ U.S.A.
231 C6 De Funiak Springs FL U.S.A.
163 D4 Dégagnac France
116 C4 Degana Rajasthan India
182 D2 Degaña Spain
191 H2 Degano r. Italy
197 F4 Deganwy Conwy, Wales U.K.
108 A2 Degê Sichuan China
184 C2 Degebe r. Port.
143 F4 Degeberga Sweden
210 D2 Degeh Bur Eth.
225 G4 Dégelis Que. Can.
207 G5 Degema Nigeria
143 F7 Degerfors Sweden
173 G3 Deggendorf Ger.
172 D3 Deggingen Ger.
123 H4 Degh r. Pak.
128 C1 Değirmenbaşı Turkey
199 F2 Değirmendere Turkey
199 E2 Değirmenlik Turkey
129 C3 Değirmenlidere Turkey
    Değirmenlik Cyprus see Kythrea
190 D4 Dego Italy
244 C3 Degollado Mex.
86 C4 De Grey W.A. Austr.
86 C4 De Grey r. W.A. Austr.
135 H6 Degtevo Rus. Fed.
165 C3 De Haan Belgium
203 I6 Dehalak Deset i. Eritrea
122 C4 Deh Bīd Iran
122 B4 Deh-Dasht Iran
122 B4 Deh-e Kohneh Iran
187 C7 Dehesa de Montejo Spain
183 F2 Dehesas de Guadix Spain
122 A3 Deh Golān Iran
122 A3 Dehlorān Iran
78 □4b Dehpohki r. Pohnpei Micronesia
    Dehqonobod Uzbek. see
116 D3 Dehra Dun Uttar Prad. India
117 F4 Dehri Bihar India
109 F3 Dehua Fujian China
100 C3 Dehui Jilin China
164 C3 Deidesheim Ger.
185 F5 Deifontes Spain
182 D3 Deilão Port.
173 F2 Deining Ger.
173 E3 Deiningen Ger.
126 D4 Deïr el Qamar Lebanon
    Deir-ez-Zor Syria see Dayr az Zawr
172 C3 Deißlingen Ger.
190 E4 Deiva Marina Italy
197 F2 Dej Romania
196 E5 Dejë, Mal mt. Albania
210 C2 Dejen Eth.
175 J1 Dejnany, Jezioro l. Pol.
    Deji Xizang China see Rinbung
108 D2 Dejiang Guizhou China
230 C3 De Kalb IL U.S.A.
237 F5 De Kalb MS U.S.A.
237 E6 De Kalb TX U.S.A.
231 G5 De Kalb Junction NY U.S.A.
191 J3 Dekani Slovenia
203 F4 Dekemhare Eritrea
78 □4b Deke Sokehs i. Pohnpei Micronesia
121 F5 Dekhkanabad Uzbek.
207 G5 Dekina Nigeria
165 D4 De Klinge Belgium
208 B3 Dékoa C.A.R.
164 F2 De Kooy Neth.
164 F2 De Krim Neth.
150 C4 Delabole Cornwall, England U.K.
261 G5 De la Garma Arg.
84 B2 Delamere r. N.T. Austr.
149 G4 Delamere Cheshire, England U.K.
234 D2 Delanco NJ U.S.A.
231 D6 De Land FL U.S.A.
240 H4 Delano CA U.S.A.
234 A2 Delano MN U.S.A.
241 K2 Delano Peak UT U.S.A.
78 □3b Delap i. Majuro Marshall Is
78 □3b Delap-Uliga-Djarrit Majuro Marshall Is
215 E2 Delareyville S. Africa
220 A4 Delarof Islands AK U.S.A.
226 C6 Delavan IL U.S.A.
226 C5 Delavan WI U.S.A.
232 B3 Delaware OH U.S.A.
236 E4 Delaware r. KS U.S.A.
234 C2 Delaware r. NJ/PA U.S.A.
233 F5 Delaware state U.S.A.
233 F4 Delaware, East Branch r. NY U.S.A.
233 F4 Delaware, West Branch r. NY U.S.A.
233 F5 Delaware Bay DE/NJ U.S.A.
234 C3 Delaware City DE U.S.A.
234 C2 Delaware County county PA U.S.A.
234 C2 Delaware Water Gap PA U.S.A.
225 G1 Delay r. Que. Can.
232 B6 Delbarton WV U.S.A.
226 B4 Delbonita Alta Can.
169 D3 Delbrück Ger.
169 D4 Delburne Alta Can.
260 E4 Del Campillo Arg.
197 F5 Delčevo Macedonia
164 F2 Delden Neth.
141 M3 Delet Teili r. Fin.
240 F2 Delevan r. CA U.S.A.
232 D3 Delevan NY U.S.A.
194 B8 Delfino I Sicilia Italy
194 E5 Delia Sicilia Italy
195 C5 Delianuova Italy
199 E3 Delice Turkey
121 F5 Delice r. Cork/Limerick Rep. of Ireland
247 □2 Delices Dominica
251 H3 Delices Fr. Guiana
194 D5 Delicato Italy
122 B3 Delijān Iran
186 D3 Delimeđe Italy
84 C1 Delissaville N.T. Can.
222 F1 Déline N.W.T. Can.
168 F2 Delingha Qinghai China
171 J5 Delingsdorf Ger.
223 J5 Delisle Sask. Can.
171 K4 Delitzsch Ger.
171 J3 Delitzsch Ger.
178 E4 Dellach Austria

Column 4

178 E4 Dellach im Drautal Austria
160 F1 Delle France
169 F3 Delligsen Ger.
190 F3 Dello Italy
236 D3 Dell Rapids SD U.S.A.
205 F1 Dellys Alg.
198 C2 Delphi tourist site Greece
230 C3 Delphi IN U.S.A.
232 A4 Delphos OH U.S.A.
214 E3 Delportshoop S. Africa
231 D7 Delray Beach FL U.S.A.
242 C2 Del Rio Mex.
237 C6 Del Rio TX U.S.A.
141 L3 Delsbo Sweden
207 G5 Delta state Nigeria
239 E4 Delta CO U.S.A.
232 A4 Delta OH U.S.A.
235 F3 Delta PA U.S.A.
241 K2 Delta UT U.S.A.
251 F2 Delta Amacuro state Venez.
85 E3 Delta Downs Qld Austr.
220 D3 Delta Junction AK U.S.A.
231 D6 Deltona FL U.S.A.
161 F4 Del Parrachée, Point France
87 B7 D'Entrecasteaux, Point W.A. Austr.
116 B5 Delvada Gujarat India
168 E1 Delve Ger.
147 D3 Delvin Rep. of Ireland
198 B2 Delvinë Albania
136 C3 Delyatyn Ukr.
120 C1 Dema r. Rus. Fed.
95 E4 Demak Jawa Tengah Indon.
157 F4 Demange-aux-Eaux France
    Demavend mt. Iran see Damāvand, Qolleh-ye
209 D6 Demba Dem. Rep. Congo
209 B7 Demba Chio Angola
118 A4 Dembava Lith.
210 B2 Dembech'a Eth.
198 D2 Dembeni Mayotte
211 B5 Dembeni Comoros
177 K3 Demecser Hungary
164 E2 De Meern Neth.
165 D3 Demen Ger.
165 D3 Demer r. Belgium
    Demerara Guyana see Georgetown
264 F5 Demerara Abyssal Plain sea feature N. Atlantic Ocean
137 H5 Demerdzhi mt. Ukr.
139 H4 Demidov Rus. Fed.
160 C2 Demigny France
239 F5 Deming NM U.S.A.
251 F4 Demini r. Brazil
251 F4 Demini, Serras do mts Brazil
199 E3 Demirci Turkey
129 A3 Demirci Turkey
129 C3 Demirkent Turkey
197 M5 Demirköy Turkey
199 F2 Demirtaş Turkey
129 A3 Demirözü Turkey
199 F1 Demirtaş Turkey
196 E5 Demir Hisar Macedonia
197 G5 Demir Kapija Macedonia
215 E5 Demistkraal S. Africa
170 E2 Demmin Ger.
190 C4 Demonte Italy
231 C5 Demopolis AL U.S.A.
230 C3 Demotte IN U.S.A.
94 C4 Dempo, Gunung vol. Indon.
87 D7 Dempster, Point W.A. Austr.
163 C5 Dému France
137 I3 Dem'yanivka Ukr.
    Dem'yanka Kustanayskaya Oblast' Kazakh. see Leninskoye
134 I3 Dem'yanovo Rus. Fed.
139 I3 Dem'yansk Rus. Fed.
136 C2 Demydiv Ukr.
136 C2 Demydivka Ukr.
136 F4 Demydove Ukr.
214 C4 De Naawte S. Africa
156 C2 Denain France
240 G3 Denair CA U.S.A.
203 I6 Denakil reg. Eritrea/Eth.
223 K4 Denare Beach Sask. Can.
121 F5 Denau Uzbek.
150 D1 Denbigh Denbighshire, Wales U.K.
150 D1 Denbighshire admin. div. Wales U.K.
164 D1 Den Bommel Neth.
    Den Bosch Neth. see 's-Hertogenbosch
164 D1 Den Burg Neth.
149 H4 Denby Dale West Yorkshire, England U.K.
96 C3 Den Chai Thai.
206 D2 Dendâra Maur.
165 D4 Dendermonde Belgium
165 D3 Den Dolder Neth.
165 C3 Dendre r. Belgium
214 F3 Dendron S. Africa
164 F3 Den Dungen Neth.
196 E4 Deneral Janković Kosovo, Srbija Yugo.
207 H3 Dengas Niger
207 G3 Denge Nigeria
107 G5 Dengfeng Henan China
207 H4 Dengi Nigeria
    Dengjiabu Jiangxi China see Yujiang
129 B2 Dengkagou China
    Dêngka Gansu China see Têwo
    Dêngkagoin Gansu China see Têwo
107 E3 Dengkou Nei Mongol China
111 F6 Dêngqên Xizang China
109 E4 Dengta Guangdong China
163 B5 Dengta Henan China
109 E1 Dengzhou Henan China
    Dengzhou Shandong China see Penglai
164 D1 Den Haag Neth. see 's-Gravenhage
86 F2 Denham W.A. Austr.
86 F2 Denham r. W.A. Austr.
233 H3 Denham NH U.S.A.
86 F2 Denham, Mount hill Jamaica
246 □ Denham Island Qld Austr.
151 G3 Denham Sound sea chan. W.A. Austr.
147 A7 Denham Bridge tourist site England U.K.
148 C2 Den Helder Neth.
147 D5 Denholm Scottish Borders, Scotland U.K.
149 H4 Denholme West Yorkshire, England U.K.
164 D1 Den Hoorn Neth.
82 C2 Denia Spain
83 B7 Denial Bay S.A. Austr.
82 C2 Deniliquin N.S.W. Austr.
238 D3 Denio NV U.S.A.
236 D3 Denison IA U.S.A.
237 D5 Denison TX U.S.A.
106 B2 Denison, Cape Antarctica
263 J2 Denison, Cape Antarctica

Column 5

86 F3 Denison Plains W.A. Austr.
    Denisovka Kazakh. see Ordzhonikidze
199 F3 Denizli Turkey
199 F3 Denizli prov. Turkey
161 E4 Denjuan, Sommet de mt. France
172 D3 Denkendorf Baden-Württemberg Ger.
173 F3 Denkendorf Bayern Ger.
172 C3 Denkingen Ger.
172 D4 Denkingen Baden-Württemberg Ger.
169 E4 Denklingen Ger.
169 F3 Denkte Ger.
188 F3 Dennis Croatia
169 F3 Denman N.S.W. Austr.
83 G3 Denman r. W.A. Austr.
226 D3 Denmark country Europe
226 D3 Denmark WI U.S.A.
86 F4 Denmark W.A. Austr.
    Denmark Fjord inlet Greenland see Danmark Fjord
221 P3 Denmark Strait Greenland/Iceland
173 F3 New Hampshire, England U.K.
151 I2 Dennington Suffolk, England U.K.
86 F4 Dennis, Lake salt flat W.A. Austr.
232 C4 Dennison OH U.S.A.
234 D3 Dennisville NJ U.S.A.
146 E5 Denny Falkirk, Scotland U.K.
164 E2 Den Oever Neth.
    Denov Uzbek. see Denau
95 F5 Denpasar Bali Indon.
170 E2 Densow Ger.
190 C2 Dent Blanche mt. Switz.
161 C4 Dent de Rez hill France
165 D4 Denthein am Forst Ger.
173 E2 Dentlein am Forst Ger.
149 G4 Denton Greater Manchester, England U.K.
234 C4 Denton MD U.S.A.
237 D5 Denton TX U.S.A.
84 C4 Dentrecasteaux Islands P.N.G.
188 F3 D'Entrecasteaux, Récifs rf New Caledonia
91 L8 D'Entrecasteaux Islands P.N.G.
190 B2 Dents du Midi mt. Switz.
151 H2 Denver Norfolk, England U.K.
238 F4 Denver CO U.S.A.
234 B2 Denver PA U.S.A.
170 E2 Denzlingen Ger.
116 D4 Deo Bihar India
116 D3 Deoband Uttar Prad. India
115 D2 Deobhog Madh. Prad. India
234 B2 Deodate PA U.S.A.
117 F5 Deogarh Rajasthan India
116 E5 Deogarh mt. Madh. Prad. India
115 E5 Deoghar Bihar India
162 D2 Deols France
116 D5 Deori Madh. Prad. India
117 F4 Deoria Uttar Prad. India
116 C2 Deosai, Plains of Jammu and Kashmir
100 C1 Dep r. Rus. Fed.
116 E5 Deopalpur Madh. Prad. India
165 B3 De Panne Belgium
225 H2 De Pas, Rivière r. Que. Can.
226 C3 De Pere WI U.S.A.
233 F3 Depew NY U.S.A.
159 E3 Deposit NY U.S.A.
227 I2 Depot-Forbes Que. Can.
227 I2 Depot-Rowanton Que. Can.
134 I4 Desnogorsk Rus. Fed.
259 C7 Desnudo, Cerro m. Arg.
226 B4 DeSoto WI U.S.A.
137 K4 Derecske Hungary
128 C1 Dereçti Turkey
177 J5 Derekegyháza Hungary
199 F3 Dereköy Turkey
199 F3 Dereköy Kütahya Turkey
173 F2 Derenburg Ger.
169 E4 Derental Ger.
177 J4 Derezuvate Ukr.
169 E4 Derg r. Rep. of Ireland/U.K.
173 E3 Dettingen an der Iller Ger.
170 D1 Dettmannsdorf Ger.
169 E2 Dettum Ger.
137 I2 Detva Slovakia

Column 6

203 H5 Derudeb Sudan
214 C6 De Rust S. Africa
199 F3 Deruta Italy
146 B5 Dervaig Argyll and Bute, Scotland U.K.
158 E4 Derval France
198 C2 Derveni Peloponnisos Greece
188 F3 Derventa Bos.-Herz.
83 F5 Derwent r. Tas. Austr.
151 F2 Derwent r. Derbyshire, England U.K.
149 I4 Derwent r. England U.K.
149 I3 Derwent Water l. England U.K.
139 J2 Derzha r. Rus. Fed.
139 I3 Derzhavino Rus. Fed.
121 F2 Derzhavinsk Kazakh.
    Derzhavinsk Kazakh. see Derzhavinsk
197 F4 Desa Romania
260 D4 Desaguadero r. Arg.
252 C4 Desaguadero r. Bol.
260 C4 Desague, Cerro m. Arg.
161 G3 Désaignes France
190 D3 Desana Italy
79 □3 Désappointement, Îles du is Arch. des Tuamotu Fr. Polynesia
237 F5 Des Arc AR U.S.A.
240 I2 Desatoya Mountains NV U.S.A.
227 F2 Desbarats Ont. Can.
151 G2 Desborough Northamptonshire, England U.K.
260 B4 Descabezado, Volcán mt. Chile
256 D4 Descalvado Brazil
182 D4 Descargamaría Spain
162 C2 Descartes France
223 K4 Deschambault Lake Sask. Can.
238 B2 Deschutes r. OR U.S.A.
210 C2 Desē Eth.
216 □3d Deseada vol. La Palma Canary Is
259 C7 Deseado Arg.
259 C7 Deseado r. Arg.
246 C3 Desembarco del Granma National Park tourist site Granma Cuba
242 B2 Desemboque Mex.
191 F3 Desenzano del Garda Italy
241 K2 Deseret UT U.S.A.
241 I3 Deseret Peak UT U.S.A.
227 I3 Deseronto Ont. Can.
184 □ Desertas, Ilhas is Madeira
184 □ Deserta Grande i. Madeira
241 J5 Desert Center CA U.S.A.
241 I5 Desert Hot Springs CA U.S.A.
160 A2 Desertines France
    Desertmartin Northern Ireland U.K.
241 L3 Desert View AZ U.S.A.
185 G2 Desesperada mt. Spain
161 B3 Desges France
161 E4 Deshaies i. Guadeloupe
232 B4 Deshler OH U.S.A.
250 A6 Desierto de Sechura des. Peru
116 C4 Deshnok Rajasthan India
177 L5 Dezna Romania
190 F3 Dezzo r. Italy
128 B4 Dhahab, Wādī adh r. Syria
124 D2 Dhahlān, Jabal hill Saudi Arabia
    Dhahran Saudi Arabia see Az Zahrān
198 B2 Deskati Greece
179 E4 Deskle Slovenia
236 D2 De Smet SD U.S.A.
237 C4 Des Moines NM U.S.A.
236 E3 Des Moines IA U.S.A.
236 E3 Des Moines r. IA U.S.A.
136 E3 Desna r. Rus. Fed./Ukr.
136 E2 Desna r. Rus. Fed./Ukr.
139 G1 Desna Rus. Fed.
159 G1 Desna Rus. Fed.
114 B2 Desna r. Romania
134 J4 Desnogorsk Rus. Fed.
259 B9 Desolación, Isla i. Chile
226 A6 DeSoto IL U.S.A.
215 E5 Despatch S. Africa
111 E6 Dêqên Xizang China see Dagzê
108 A2 Dêqên Sichuan China
109 D4 Deqing Guangdong China
109 D2 Deqing Zhejiang China
237 E5 De Queen AR U.S.A.
162 D3 De Quincy LA U.S.A.
156 A4 Der, Lac du l. France
123 G4 Dera Ghazi Khan Pak.
123 G4 Dera Ismail Khan Pak.
263 C2 Deram, Mount Antarctica
171 J3 Dessau Ger.
165 D4 Dessel Belgium
160 E1 Dessoubre r. France
165 D4 Destelbergen Belgium
227 H1 Destor Que. Can.
82 D3 D'Estrees Bay S.A. Austr.
192 C2 Destriana Spain
222 G2 Destruction Bay Y.T. Can.
188 F3 Desulo Sardegna Italy
174 D3 Deszczno Pol.
197 J5 Deta Romania
177 J5 Deszk Hungary
179 G3 Deutsch Evern Ger.
169 H2 Deutsch-Griffen Austria
178 F5 Deutschfeistritz Austria
178 E4 Deutsch-Griffen Austria
178 F5 Deutschkreutz Austria
179 J3 Deutsch Kaltenbrunn Austria
179 H3 Deutschlandsberg Austria
179 H2 Deutsch-Wagram Austria

Column 7

147 D4 Devil's Bit Mountain hill Rep. of Ireland
150 D2 Devil's Bridge Ceredigion, Wales U.K.
236 D1 Devils Lake ND U.S.A.
220 E4 Devil's Paw mt. AK U.S.A.
240 H3 Devil's Peak CA U.S.A.
246 D1 Devil's Point i. Cat I. Bahamas
222 C3 Devil's Thumb mt. Alaska/B.C. Can./U.S.A.
197 G5 Devin Bulg.
237 D6 Devine TX U.S.A.
137 J2 Devitsa r. Rus. Fed.
151 G5 Devizes Wiltshire, England U.K.
116 C4 Devli Rajasthan India
226 A1 Devlin Ont. Can.
197 H4 Devnya Bulg.
196 D5 Devoll r. Albania
175 □4 Devoluy mts France
227 F2 Devon Ont. Can.
215 G2 Devon S. Africa
150 D4 Devon admin. div. England U.K.
149 I4 Devon r. England U.K.
146 F5 Devon r. Scotland U.K.
83 F5 Devonport Tas. Austr.
240 I4 Devon Island Nunavut Can.
83 F5 Devonport Tas. Austr.
240 I4 Devore CA U.S.A.
261 F2 Devoto Arg.
199 G3 Devrek Turkey
135 F5 Devrekâni Turkey
199 F2 Devrek r. Turkey
114 B2 Devrukh Mahar. India
117 G4 Dewangang Bangl.
116 D5 Dewas Madh. Prad. India
215 F3 Dewetsdorp S. Africa
247 □1 Dewey Puerto Rico
164 F2 De Wijk Neth.
237 F5 De Witt AR U.S.A.
236 E3 De Witt IA U.S.A.
233 F3 DeWitt NY U.S.A.
149 H4 Dewsbury West Yorkshire, England U.K.
109 F2 Dexing Jiangxi China
233 □2 Dexter MI U.S.A.
227 F4 Dexter ME U.S.A.
235 A4 Dexter MN U.S.A.
237 F4 Dexter MO U.S.A.
237 C5 Dexter NM U.S.A.
233 E2 Dexter NY U.S.A.
232 C4 Dexterville WI U.S.A.
108 C2 Deyang Sichuan China
82 B2 Dey-Dey Lake salt flat S.A. Austr.
137 H2 Deykalivka Ukr.
143 I4 Deyma r. Rus. Fed.
122 B5 Deyyer Iran
122 B4 Dez r. Iran
122 B3 Deza Spain
182 B2 Deza r. Spain
222 B2 Dezadeash Y.T. Can.
122 B3 Dezfūl Iran
107 H4 Dezhou Shandong China
    Dezhou Sichuan China see Dechang
    Dêzhou Shāhpūr Iran see Marīvān
177 L5 Dezna Romania
190 F3 Dezzo r. Italy
128 B4 Dhahab, Wādī adh r. Syria
124 D2 Dhahlān, Jabal hill Saudi Arabia
    Dhahran Saudi Arabia see Az Zahrān
116 C5 Dhaka Bihar. Bangl.
117 G5 Dhaka admin. div. Bangl.
117 G5 Dhaleswari r. Bangl.
117 H4 Dhaleswari r. India
124 D5 Dhamār Yemen
124 B4 Dhamar governorate Yemen
116 E5 Dhamnod Madh. Prad. India
116 D3 Dhampur Uttar Prad. India
116 E5 Dhamtari Madh. Prad. India
116 C5 Dhanbad Bihar India
116 C5 Dhandhuka Gujarat India
116 E3 Dhang Range mts Nepal
117 F4 Dhankuta Nepal
116 C5 Dhar Madh. Prad. India
206 B2 Dhar Adrar hills Maur.
114 C4 Dharan Bazar Nepal
114 C4 Dharapuram Tamil Nadu India
116 B5 Dhari Gujarat India
114 C3 Dharmanagar Tripura India
114 C4 Dharmapuri Tamil Nadu India
114 C3 Dharmavaram Andhra Prad. India
117 E5 Dharmjaygarh Madh. Prad. India
206 D2 Dharmkot Punjab India
206 D2 Dhar Oualâta hills Maur.
206 C2 Dhar Tichît hills Maur.
114 C2 Dharur Mahar. India
114 B3 Dharwad Karnataka India
    Dharwar Karnataka India see Dharwad
116 C4 Dhasan r. India
117 H3 Dhaulagiri mt. Nepal
116 D4 Dhaulpur Rajasthan India
116 E4 Dhaurahra Uttar Prad. India
117 H4 Dhavla Greece see Davleia
117 H3 Dhawlagiri mt. Nepal see Dhaulagiri
128 A2 Dhebar Lake India
    Dhekelia Sovereign Base Area military base Cyprus
116 B5 Dhekiajuli Assam India
    Dhekiajuli India see Dhekiajuli
116 C5 Dhenkanal Orissa India
    Dheskáti Greece see Deskati
    Dhiakoftó Greece see Diakofto
128 B4 Dhíbān Jordan
    Dhidhima Greece see Didima
    Dhidhimótikhon Greece see Didymoteicho
113 □1 Dhiffushi i. N. Male Maldives
113 □1 Dhigufinolhu i. S. Male Maldives
124 D5 Dhi Na'im Yemen
127 G5 Dhī Qār governorate Iraq
198 D2 Dhodhekánisos is Greece see Dodekanisos
125 F4 Dhofar admin. reg. Oman see Zufār
116 C5 Dholera Gujarat India
198 C2 Dhomokós Greece see Domokos
114 C3 Dhone Andhra Prad. India
116 B5 Dhoraji Gujarat India
116 B5 Dhori Gujarat India
116 B5 Dhrangadhra Gujarat India
116 B5 Dhrol Gujarat India
172 A2 Dhron Ger.
    Dhrosia Greece see Drosia
116 E4 Dhubri Assam India
117 G4 Dhuburi Assam India
116 C5 Dhule Mahar. India
    Dhulia Mahar. India see Dhule
116 D5 Dhulian Madh. Prad. India
210 E2 Dhuudo Somalia
210 E3 Dhuuya Baan Saudi Arabia
210 E2 Dhytikí Ellás admin. reg. Greece see Dytiki Ellas
    Dhytikí Makedonía admin. reg. Greece see Dytiki Makedonia
198 B2 Dia i. Greece
161 F4 Diable, Cime mt. France
240 G3 Diablo, Mount CA U.S.A.
242 E2 Diablo, Picacho del mt. Mex.
241 H4 Diablo Range mts CA U.S.A.
211 C7 Diaca Moz.
206 B3 Diafarabé Mali
206 C3 Diaka r. Mali
206 C3 Diakon Mali
177 G3 Diakovce Slovakia
206 B3 Dialakoto Senegal
206 C3 Dialassagou Mali
261 E5 Diamante Arg.
260 C4 Diamante r. Arg.
193 H5 Diamante Italy

Diamante, Pampa del to Donskoye 299

260 C4 Diamante, Pampa del plain Arg.
85 D5 Diamantina watercourse Qld Austr.
257 F3 Diamantina Brazil
254 E5 Diamantina, Chapada plat. Brazil
265 K7 Diamantina Deep sea feature Indian Ocean
85 E4 Diamantina Lakes Qld Austr.
256 A2 Diamantino Mato Grosso Brazil
253 F3 Diamantino Mato Grosso Brazil
256 A2 Diamantino r. Brazil
117 G5 Diamond Harbour W. Bengal India
85 G3 Diamond Islets Coral Sea Is Terr. Austr.
241 J2 Diamond Peak NV U.S.A.
240 G2 Diamond Springs CA U.S.A.
238 E3 Diamondville WY U.S.A.
206 C3 Diamou Mali
206 B3 Diamounguél Senegal
109 D4 Dianbai Guangdong China
Dianbu Anhui China see Feidong
108 B3 Diancang Shan mt. Yunnan China
85 G2 Diane Bank sea feature Coral Sea Is Terr. Austr.
206 C3 Diangounté Kamara Mali
206 C5 Diani r. Guinea
108 C2 Dianjiang Chongqing China
190 D4 Diano d'Alba Italy
190 D5 Diano Marina Italy
254 D4 Dianópolis Brazil
206 D4 Dianra Côte d'Ivoire
Dianyang Yunnan China see Shidian
Diaobingshan Liaoning China see Tiefa
100 D3 Diaoling Heilong. China
207 F3 Diapaga Burkina
128 A2 Diarizos r. Cyprus
206 C4 Diatifèrè Guinea
198 C1 Diavata Kentriki Makedonia Greece
115 G3 Diavolo, Mount hill Andaman & Nicobar Is India
261 G3 Diaz Arg.
125 G2 Dibā al Ḥiṣn U.A.E.
125 G3 Ḍibab Oman
Dibang r. India see Dingba Qu
209 D6 Dibaya Dem. Rep. Congo
209 C6 Dibaya-Lubwe Dem. Rep. Congo
151 F4 Dibden Hampshire, England U.K.
199 F2 Dibek Dağı mt. Turkey
214 D2 Dibeng S. Africa
136 E2 Dibrova Kyivs'ka Oblast' Ukr.
136 D2 Dibrova Zhytomyrs'ka Oblast' Ukr.
117 H4 Dibrugarh Assam India
182 B2 Dices Spain
168 D3 Dickel Ger.
237 C5 Dickens TX U.S.A.
233 □I1 Dickey ME U.S.A.
236 C2 Dickinson ND U.S.A.
231 C4 Dickson TN U.S.A.
234 C1 Dickson City PA U.S.A.
140 □ Dickson Land reg. Svalbard
127 F3 Dicle r. Turkey alt. Dijlah, Nahr (Iraq/Syria), conv. Tigris
191 G5 Dicomano Italy
164 F3 Didam Neth.
151 F3 Didcot Oxfordshire, England U.K.
169 F3 Didderse Ger.
129 D2 Didi Borbalo, Mt'a Georgia
206 C3 Didiéni Mali
129 C2 Didi Jikhaishi Georgia
129 D3 Didi Lilo Georgia
198 C3 Didima Greece
136 E2 Didivshchyna Ukr.
222 H5 Didsbury Alta Can.
116 C4 Didwana Rajasthan India
213 □K3 Didy Madag.
199 E1 Didymoteicho Greece
138 F4 Didžiasalis Lith.
161 D4 Die France
215 H1 Die Berg mt. S. Africa
215 H1 Die Berg mt. S. Africa
169 C5 Dieblich Ger.
206 E4 Diébougou Burkina
172 C2 Dieburg Ger.
177 L5 Dieci Romania
Diedenhofen France see Thionville
173 E3 Diedorf Bayern Ger.
169 F4 Diedorf Thüringen Ger.
223 I5 Diefenbaker, Lake Sask. Can.
162 E3 Dièqe r. France
183 E4 Diego Alvaro Spain
259 B8 Diego de Almagro, Isla i. Chile
265 I5 Diego Garcia i. B.I.O.T.
247 □7 Diego Martin Trin. and Tob.
259 C9 Diego Ramirez, Islas is Chile
Diégo Suarez Madag. see Antsirañana
206 C5 Diéké Guinea
170 D2 Diekhof Ger.
169 E3 Diekholzen Ger.
165 F5 Diekirch Lux.
165 E5 Diekirch admin. dist. Lux.
190 D1 Dielsdorf Switz.
206 C3 Diéma Mali
206 A3 Diembéreng Senegal
169 E4 Diemel r. Ger.
164 D2 Diemen Neth.
160 D3 Diémoz France
172 C2 Dienheim Ger.
161 A3 Dienne France
138 E3 Dienvidsusēja r. Latvia
156 E4 Dienville France
169 D3 Diepenau Ger.
165 E4 Diepenbeek Belgium
164 F2 Diepenheim Neth.
164 F2 Diepenveen Neth.
168 D3 Diepholz Ger.
156 B3 Dieppe France
247 □2 Dieppe Bay Town St Kitts and Nevis
214 D4 Dieput S. Africa
169 C5 Dierdorf Ger.
164 F2 Dieren Neth.
237 E5 Dierks AR U.S.A.
106 E4 Di'er Nonchang Qu r. China
100 C3 Di'er Songhua Jiang r. China
168 F3 Diesdorf Ger.
171 D4 Dieskau Ger.
173 E2 Diespeck Ger.
164 E3 Diessen Neth.
173 F4 Dießen am Ammersee Ger.
190 D1 Diessenhofen Switz.
165 E4 Diest Belgium
179 F2 Dietachdorf Austria
173 E3 Dietenheim Ger.
173 E2 Dietenhofen Ger.
173 G3 Dietersburg Ger.
173 F2 Dietfurt an der Altmühl Ger.
190 D1 Dietikon Switz.
172 C3 Dietingen Ger.
179 F2 Dietmanns Niederösterreich Austria
179 G2 Dietmanns Niederösterreich Austria
173 E4 Dietmannsried Ger.
173 F4 Dietramszell Ger.
169 D5 Dietzenbach Ger.
169 D5 Dietzhölztal-Ewersbach Ger.
157 F3 Dieue-sur-Meuse France
161 D4 Dieulefit France
157 G4 Dieulouard France
157 G4 Dieuze France
164 F2 Diever Neth.
169 D5 Diez Ger.
185 G3 Diezma Spain
207 I3 Diffa Niger
207 I2 Diffa dept Niger
165 E5 Differdange Lux.
115 E2 Digapahandi Orissa India
117 H4 Digboi Assam India
225 H4 Digby N.S. Can.
141 K3 Digerbergen hill Sweden
142 E1 Digerberget hill Sweden
116 C4 Diggi Rajasthan India
129 D3 Dighomi Georgia
236 C4 Dighton KS U.S.A.
114 C2 Diglur Mahar. India
162 C3 Dignac France
191 H2 Dignano Italy
161 E4 Digne-les-Bains France
156 B4 Digny France
160 B2 Digoin France
191 H2 Digòn r. Italy
129 C3 Digor Turkey
129 D2 Digora Rus. Fed.
92 C5 Digos Phil.
116 D5 Digras Mahar. India
123 G5 Digri Pak.
91 I8 Digul r. Indon.
111 F7 Dihang r. India alt. Yarlung Zangbo (China), conv. Brahmaputra
175 M5 Dihtiv Ukr.
137 G2 Dihtyari Ukr.
210 D4 Diinsoor Somalia
127 G5 Dijlah, Nahr r. Iraq/Syria alt. Dicle (Turkey), conv. Tigris
165 D4 Dijle r. Belgium
160 D1 Dijon France
Dijon airport France see Longvic
140 L2 Dikanäs Sweden
116 C4 Diken Madh. Prad. India
210 D2 Dikhil Djibouti
117 H4 Dikho r. India
199 E2 Dikili Turkey
165 B4 Dikkebus Belgium
129 D2 Diklosmta mt. Rus. Fed.
129 C3 Dikmeköyü Turkey
206 D4 Dikodougou Côte d'Ivoire
114 B2 Diksal Mahar. India
165 B3 Diksmuide Belgium
130 J2 Dikson Rus. Fed.
207 I3 Dikwa Nigeria
210 C3 Dīla Eth.
185 G3 Dilar Spain
185 G3 Dilar r. Spain
122 D4 Dilaram Iran
165 D4 Dilbeek Belgium
129 B3 Dilek Dağı mt. Turkey
93 C5 Dili East Timor
129 D3 Dilijan Armenia
81 D5 Dilion Cone mt. South I. N.Z.
129 C3 Dilip'i Georgia
Dilizhan Armenia see Dilijan
169 D5 Dillenburg Ger.
237 D6 Dilley TX U.S.A.
206 D3 Dilli Mali
142 D2 Dilling Norway
203 F6 Dilling Sudan
172 A2 Dillingen (Saar) Ger.
173 E3 Dillingen an der Donau Ger.
220 C4 Dillingham AK U.S.A.
223 I4 Dillon Sask. Can.
223 I4 Dillon r. Alberta/Saskatchewan Can.
238 D2 Dillon MT U.S.A.
231 E5 Dillon SC U.S.A.
227 I5 Dillsburg PA U.S.A.
232 D6 Dillwyn VA U.S.A.
209 D7 Dilolo Dem. Rep. Congo
165 E3 Dilsen Belgium
127 G4 Diltāwa Iraq
207 I5 Dimako Cameroon
117 H4 Dimapur Nagaland India
191 F2 Dimaro Italy
244 A2 Dimas Mex.
Dimashq Syria see Damascus
128 C3 Dimashq governorate Syria
209 D6 Dimbelenge Dem. Rep. Congo
206 D5 Dimbokro Côte d'Ivoire
83 E4 Dimboola Vic. Austr.
85 F3 Dimbulah Qld Austr.
198 C2 Dimini Thessalia Greece
Dimitrov Ukr. see Dymytrov
197 G4 Dimitrovgrad Bulg.
135 J5 Dimitrovgrad Rus. Fed.
197 F4 Dimitrovgrad Srbija Yugo.
Dimitrovo Bulg. see Pernik
237 C5 Dimmitt TX U.S.A.
234 C1 Dimock PA U.S.A.
128 B4 Dīmona Israel
92 C4 Dinagat i. Phil.
117 G4 Dinajpur Bangl.
195 F4 Dinami Italy
158 D3 Dinan France
116 C2 Dinanagar Punjab India
165 D4 Dinant Belgium
117 F4 Dinapur Bihar India
199 G2 Dinar Turkey
122 B4 Dīnār, Kūh-e mt. Iran
188 F3 Dinara mt. Bos.-Herz.
188 F3 Dinara Planina mts Bos.-Herz./Croatia
158 D3 Dinard France
Dinaric Alps mts Bos.-Herz./Croatia see Dinara Planina
150 D3 Dinas Powys Vale of Glamorgan, Wales U.K.
Dinbych Denbighshire, Wales U.K. see Denbigh
Dinbych-y-Pysgod Pembrokeshire, Wales U.K. see Tenby
209 B8 Dinde Angola
203 G6 Dinder r. Sudan
124 A5 Dinder el Agaliyin r. Sudan
114 C2 Dindi r. India
114 C4 Dindigul Tamil Nadu India
207 H4 Dindima Nigeria
116 E5 Dindori Madh. Prad. India
116 C5 Dindori Mahar. India
158 B3 Dinéault France
199 G2 Dinek Eskişehir Turkey
126 D3 Dinek Konya Turkey
209 C6 Dinga Dem. Rep. Congo
123 H3 Dinga Pak.
108 D5 Ding'an Hainan China
117 H4 Dingba Qu r. India
107 E4 Dingbian Shaanxi China
109 E2 Dingbujie Anhui China
Dingcheng Hainan China see Ding'an
158 E3 Dingé France
169 F4 Dingelstädt Ger.
94 C3 Dingin, Bukit mt. Indon.
147 A4 Dingle Rep. of Ireland
147 A4 Dingle pen. Rep. of Ireland
147 A4 Dingle Bay Rep. of Ireland
234 D1 Dingmans Ferry PA U.S.A.
109 E3 Dingnan Jiangxi China
85 G4 Dingo Qld Austr.
173 G3 Dingolfing Ger.
Dingping Sichuan China see Linshui
92 B2 Dingras Phil.
107 G5 Dingtao Shandong China
206 C4 Dinguiraye Guinea
225 I4 Dingwall N.S. Can.
146 D4 Dingwall Highland, Scotland U.K.
106 E5 Dingxi Gansu China
Dingxian Hebei China see Dingzhou
107 G4 Dingxiang Shanxi China
106 C3 Dingxin Gansu China
107 G4 Dingxing Hebei China
109 F1 Dingyuan Anhui China
107 G4 Dingzhou Hebei China
110 F4 Dingzikou Qinghai China
117 G4 Dinhata W. Bengal India
96 D2 Dinh Lâp Vietnam
147 D4 Dinin r. Rep. of Ireland
164 F2 Dinkel r. Neth.
173 E2 Dinkelsbühl Ger.
173 E3 Dinkelscherben Ger.
168 D3 Dinklage Ger.
146 F4 Dinnet Aberdeenshire, Scotland U.K.
111 D6 Dinngyê Xizang China
149 H4 Dinnington South Yorkshire, England U.K.
241 M1 Dinosaur CO U.S.A.
137 J5 Dinskaya Rus. Fed.
169 B4 Dinslaken Ger.
164 D3 Dinteloord Neth.
164 E3 Dinther Neth.
240 H3 Dinuba CA U.S.A.
232 E6 Dinwiddie VA U.S.A.
164 F3 Dinxperlo Neth.
206 D3 Dioïla Mali
161 D4 Diois, Massif du mts France
206 C4 Dion r. Guinea
257 F3 Dionísio Brazil
255 B8 Dionísio Cerqueira Brazil
161 C5 Dions France
256 B2 Diorama Brazil
Dioscurias Georgia see Sokhumi
177 H4 Diósd Hungary
197 F2 Diosig Romania
177 I4 Diósjenő Hungary
Diospolis Magna tourist site Egypt see Thebes
160 B2 Diou France
206 A3 Diouloulou Senegal
207 F3 Dioundiou Niger
206 D3 Dioura Mali
206 A3 Diourbel Senegal
123 H4 Dipalpur Pak.
116 E3 Dipayal Nepal
117 H4 Diphu Assam India
193 I5 Dipignano Italy
Dipkarpaz Cyprus see Rizokarpason
123 G5 Diplo Pak.
92 B4 Dipolog Phil.
165 F5 Dippach Lux.
169 E5 Dipperz Ger.
171 E5 Dippoldiswalde Ger.
81 B6 Dipton South I. N.Z.
Dipu Zhejiang China see Anji
117 H4 Dirang Arun. Prad. India
206 E2 Diré Mali
85 E2 Direction, Cape Qld Austr.
210 D2 Dirē Dawa Eth.
242 □I7 Diriamba Nic.
209 D9 Dirico Angola
194 D5 Dirillo r. Sicilia Italy
158 B3 Dirinon France
87 B5 Dirk Hartog Island W.A. Austr.
164 D2 Dirkshorn Neth.
164 D3 Dirksland Neth.
173 E3 Dirlewang Ger.
172 C2 Dirmstein Ger.
83 G2 Dirranbandi Qld Austr.
149 G2 Dirrington Great Law hill Scotland U.K.
124 C4 Ḍirs Saudi Arabia
Dirschau Pol. see Tczew
241 L3 Dirty Devil r. UT U.S.A.
116 C4 Disa Gujarat India
117 H4 Disang r. India
262 T2 Disappointment, Cape Antarctica
259 □ Disappointment, Cape S. Georgia
87 D4 Disappointment, Lake salt flat W.A. Austr.
Disappointment Islands Arch. des Tuamotu Fr. Polynesia see Désappointement, Îles du
173 E3 Dischingen Ger.
82 E4 Discovery Bay Vic. Austr.
264 J8 Discovery Seamounts sea feature S. Atlantic Ocean
190 D2 Disentis Muster Switz.
190 E2 Disgrazia, Monte mt. Italy
203 G3 Dishna Egypt
Disko i. Greenland see Qeqertarsuaq
Disko Bugt b. Greenland see Qeqertarsuup Tunua
199 G2 Dişli Turkey
84 E3 Dismal Creek r. Qld Austr.
263 D2 Dismal Mountains Antarctica
156 C4 Disneyland Paris tourist site France
195 H2 Diso Italy
165 E4 Dison Belgium
112 H6 Dispur Assam India
232 E6 Disputanta VA U.S.A.
225 G4 Disraëli Que. Can.
151 I2 Diss Norfolk, England U.K.
159 G5 Dissay France
159 G4 Dissay-sous-Courcillon France
169 D3 Dissen am Teutoburger Wald Ger.
206 E4 Dissin Burkina
149 F3 Distington Cumbria, England U.K.
256 D1 Distrito Federal admin. dist. Brazil
245 E4 Distrito Federal admin. dist. Mex.
250 E2 Distrito Federal admin. dist. Venez.
126 C5 Disûq Egypt
171 C4 Ditfurt Ger.
214 D3 Ditloung S. Africa
194 E5 Dittaino r. Sicilia Italy
169 F5 Dittelbrunn Ger.
173 E2 Dittenheim Ger.
151 H3 Ditton Kent, England U.K.
172 D3 Ditzingen Ger.
116 B5 Diu Daman India
92 C4 Diuata Mountains Phil.
179 E5 Divača Slovenia
122 A3 Dīvān Darreh Iran
Divehi country Indian Ocean see Maldives
208 B5 Divénié Congo
190 D2 Diveria r. Italy
159 F2 Dives r. France
159 F2 Dives-sur-Mer France
135 H5 Diveyevo Rus. Fed.
Divichi Azer. see Däväçi
238 D2 Divide MT U.S.A.
234 C3 Dividing Creek NJ U.S.A.
195 E4 Divieto Sicilia Italy
177 I3 Divín Slovakia
177 H2 Divina Slovakia
257 F4 Divinésia Brazil
257 E4 Divinópolis Brazil
156 C2 Divion France
256 B2 Divisões, Serra das mts Brazil
Divisor, Sierra de mts Peru see Ultraoriental, Cordillera
135 H7 Divnoye Rus. Fed.
206 D5 Divo Côte d'Ivoire
160 E2 Divonne-les-Bains France
184 B2 Divor r. Port.
126 E3 Divriği Turkey
134 L4 Div'ya Rus. Fed.
Diwaniyah Iraq see Ad Dīwānīyah
206 E5 Dixcove Ghana
233 □H2 Dixfield ME U.S.A.
156 D4 Dixmont France
233 □I2 Dixmont ME U.S.A.
240 G2 Dixon CA U.S.A.
226 C5 Dixon IL U.S.A.
238 D2 Dixon MT U.S.A.
220 E4 Dixon Entrance sea chan. Can./U.S.A.
222 G3 Dixonville Alta Can.
233 H2 Dixville Que. Can.
127 F3 Diyadin Turkey
127 G4 Diyālá governorate Iraq
127 G4 Diyālá, Nahr r. Iraq
127 F3 Diyarbakır Turkey
116 B4 Diyodar Gujarat India
Dizak Iran see Dāvar Panāh
207 H6 Dizangué Cameroon
Dize Turkey see Yüksekova
232 B6 Dizney KY U.S.A.
156 D3 Dizy France
156 E3 Dizy-le-Gros France
207 I6 Dja r. Cameroon
202 B4 Djado, Plateau du Niger
Djakarta Indon. see Jakarta
Djakovica Kosovo, Srbija Yugo. see Đakovica
205 G2 Djamâa Alg.
208 B5 Djambala Congo
205 H4 Djanet Alg.
78 □3b Djarrit i. Majuro Marshall Is
Djarrit-Uliga-Dalap Majuro Marshall Is see Delap-Uliga-Djarrit
205 F4 Djebr mt. Alg.
202 C6 Djédaa Chad
205 F2 Djelfa Alg.
208 E3 Djéma C.A.R.
Djeneral Jankovič Kosovo, Srbija Yugo. see Đeneral Jankovič
206 D3 Djenné Mali
202 B6 Djermaya Chad
206 E3 Djibo Burkina
206 D4 Djiborosso Côte d'Ivoire
210 D2 Djibouti country Africa
210 D2 Djibouti Djibouti
Djidjelli Alg. see Jijel
206 C3 Djiguéni Maur.
207 I5 Djohong Cameroon
208 B4 Djoua r. Congo/Gabon
147 E3 Djouce Mountain hill Rep. of Ireland
207 F4 Djougou Benin
207 I6 Djoum Cameroon
143 F1 Djurås Sweden
116 C3 Dlairi Punjab India
177 K3 Dlhé Klčovo Slovakia
177 H2 Dlhé Pole Slovakia
176 G2 Dlouhá Loučka Czech Rep.
174 G5 Dłubnia r. Pol.
174 F4 Długołęka Pol.
175 K2 Długołęka Pol.
175 J3 Długosiodło Pol.
175 H4 Dłutów Pol.
120 B1 Dmitriyevka Samarskaya Oblast' Rus. Fed.
135 H5 Dmitriyevka Tambovskaya Oblast' Rus. Fed.
135 F5 Dmitriyev-L'govskiy Rus. Fed.
Dmitriyevsk Donets'ka Oblast' Ukr. see Makiyivka
139 K3 Dmitrov Rus. Fed.
139 L4 Dmitrovskiy Pogost Rus. Fed.
139 J5 Dmitrovsk-Orlovskiy Rus. Fed.
137 J1 Dmitryashevka Rus. Fed.
137 G2 Dmytrivka Chernihivs'ka Oblast' Ukr.
137 H4 Dmytrivka Dnipropetrovs'ka Oblast' Ukr.
137 I3 Dmytrivka Dnipropetrovs'ka Oblast' Ukr.
137 G3 Dmytrivka Kirovohrads'ka Oblast' Ukr.
137 F4 Dmytrivka Mykolayivs'ka Oblast' Ukr.
137 I4 Dmytrivka Zaporiz'ka Oblast' Ukr.
Dmytriyevs'k Donets'ka Oblast' Ukr. see Makiyivka
139 H4 Dnepr r. Rus. Fed. alt. Dnipro (Ukraine), alt. Dnyapro (Belarus), conv. Dnieper
Dneprodzerzhinsk Ukr. see Dniprodzerzhyns'k
Dnepropetrovsk Ukr. see Dnipropetrovs'k
Dnepropetrovskaya Oblast' admin. div. Ukr. see Dnipropetrovs'ka Oblast'
Dnepropetrovsk Oblast admin. div. Ukr. see Dnipropetrovs'ka Oblast'
Dneprorudnoye Ukr. see Dniprorudne
136 E4 Dnestrovsc Moldova
135 F7 Dnieper r. Europe alt. Dnepr (Rus. Fed.), alt. Dnipro (Ukraine), alt. Dnyapro (Belarus)
136 E3 Dniester r. Ukr. alt. Dnister (Ukraine), alt. Nistru (Moldova)
137 G4 Dnipro r. Ukr. alt. Dnepr (Rus. Fed.), alt. Dnyapro (Belarus), conv. Dnieper
137 H3 Dniprodzerzhyns'k Ukr.
137 G3 Dniprodzerzhyns'ke Vodoskhovyshche resr Ukr.
137 H3 Dnipropetrovs'k Ukr.
137 H3 Dnipropetrovs'ka Oblast' admin. div. Ukr.
Dnipropetrovsk Oblast admin. div. Ukr. see Dnipropetrovs'ka Oblast'
137 H4 Dniprorudne Ukr.
137 H4 Dniprovka Ukr.
137 H3 Dniprovs'ke Vodoskhovyshche resr Ukr.
137 G4 Dnipryany Ukr.
136 E3 Dnister r. Ukr. alt. Nistru (Moldova), conv. Dniester
136 F4 Dnistrov'ky Lyman l. Ukr.
138 G3 Dno Rus. Fed.
139 H5 Dnyapro r. Belarus alt. Dnepr (Rus. Fed.), alt. Dnipro (Ukraine), conv. Dnieper
213 G3 Doa Moz.
147 E2 Doagh Northern Ireland U.K.
225 H4 Doaktown N.B. Can.
213 □K2 Doany Madag.
163 B5 Doazit France
208 C2 Doba Chad
Doba Xizang China see Toiba
177 L4 Doba Romania
138 H5 Dobasna r. Belarus
170 D2 Dobbertin Ger.
191 H2 Dobbiaco Italy
227 G3 Dobbinton Ont. Can.
235 E1 Dobbs Ferry NY U.S.A.
175 I6 Dobczyce Pol.
138 D3 Dobele Latvia
171 E4 Döbeln Ger.
91 H7 Doberai, Jazirah pen. Indon.
Doberai Peninsula Indon. see Doberai, Jazirah
171 E4 Doberlug-Kirchhain Ger.
171 F4 Döbern Ger.
179 G2 Dobersberg Austria
168 F1 Dobersdorf Ger.
171 F4 Dobershau Ger.
174 D3 Dobiegniew Pol.
175 J4 Dobieszyn Pol.
179 G4 Dobl Austria
261 E5 Doblas Arg.
188 G3 Doboj Bos.-Herz.
122 C4 Do Borjī Iran
177 K5 Doboz Hungary
175 I6 Dobra Małopolskie Pol.
174 G4 Dobra Wielkopolskie Pol.
174 C2 Dobra Zachodniopomorskie Pol.
174 D2 Dobra Zachodniopomorskie Pol.
177 L6 Dobra Romania
171 C5 Döbraberg hill Ger.
177 I3 Dobrá Niva Slovakia
176 C2 Dobřany Czech Rep.
179 F2 Dobrá Voda Czech Rep.
174 G3 Dobre Kujawsko-Pomorskie Pol.
175 J3 Dobre Mazowieckie Pol.
137 G4 Dobre Ukr.
143 I4 Dobre Miasto Pol.
197 F2 Dobreşti Romania
197 H4 Dobrich Bulg.
135 H5 Dobrinka Rus. Fed.
176 D2 Dobříš Czech Rep.
171 D3 Dobritz Ger.
173 H2 Dobřív Czech Rep.
183 G2 Dobro Spain
174 G5 Dobrodzień Pol.
177 H5 Döbrököz Hungary
174 E5 Dobromierz Pol.
136 B3 Dobromyl' Ukr.
175 H4 Dobroń Pol.
177 L3 Dobron' Ukr.
176 E2 Dobronín Czech Rep.
137 I3 Dobropillya Ukr.
Dobropol'ye Ukr. see Dobropillya
175 L5 Dobrosyn Ukr.
174 F4 Dobroszyce Pol.
197 G3 Dobroteşti Romania
175 M5 Dobrotvir Ukr.
197 H2 Dobrovăţ Romania
171 F5 Dobrovice Czech Rep.
179 H4 Dobrovnik Slovenia
175 I5 Dobrowoda Pol.
139 L5 Dobroye Rus. Fed.
197 H4 Dobrudzhansko Plato plat. Bulg.
197 G3 Dobrun Romania
137 F1 Dobrush Belarus
176 F1 Dobruška Czech Rep.
134 L4 Dobryanka Rus. Fed.
137 F1 Dobryanka Ukr.
139 K4 Dobrynikha Rus. Fed.
175 I3 Dobrzankowo Pol.
174 D2 Dobrzany Pol.
174 F5 Dobrzeń Wielki Pol.
174 F4 Dobrzyca Pol.
174 E2 Dobrzyca r. Pol.
175 H3 Dobrzyków Pol.
175 H3 Dobrzyń nad Wisłą Pol.
177 J3 Dobšiná Slovakia
175 J1 Dobskie, Jezioro l. Pol.
81 C5 Dobson South I. N.Z.
81 B6 Dobson r. South I. N.Z.
231 D4 Dobson NC U.S.A.
150 C4 Dobwalls Cornwall, England U.K.
177 J5 Dóc Hungary
257 H3 Doce r. Espírito Santo Brazil
256 B3 Doce r. Goiás Brazil
146 D5 Dochart r. Scotland U.K.
146 D4 Dochgarroch Highland, Scotland U.K.
151 H2 Docking Norfolk, England U.K.
169 B5 Dockweiler Ger.
Doc Penfro Pembrokeshire, Wales U.K. see Pembroke Dock
244 D2 Doctor Arroyo Mex.
242 D2 Doctor Belisario Domínguez Mex.
87 E6 Doctor Hicks Range hills W.A. Austr.
244 D3 Doctor Mora Mex.
Doctor Petru Groza Romania see Ştei
114 C3 Dod Ballapur Karnataka India
151 H3 Doddinghurst Essex, England U.K.
149 G2 Doddington Northumberland, England U.K.
Dodecanese is Greece see Dodekanisos
199 E4 Dodekanisos is Greece
164 E3 Dodewaard Neth.
226 A3 Dodge Center MN U.S.A.
237 C4 Dodge City KS U.S.A.
226 B4 Dodgeville WI U.S.A.
191 G3 Dodici, Cima mt. Italy
211 B6 Dodoma Tanz.
211 B6 Dodoma admin. reg. Tanz.
223 I5 Dodsland Sask. Can.
232 B5 Dodsonville OH U.S.A.
164 F2 Doesburg Neth.
164 F3 Doetinchem Neth.
197 G3 Doftana r. Romania
224 B3 Dog r. Ont. Can.
111 E5 Dogai Coring salt l. China
111 E5 Dogaicoring Qangco salt l. China
199 E3 Doğanbey Turkey
199 E2 Doğanbey Turkey
199 G2 Doğançayır Eskişehir Turkey
126 E3 Doğanşehir Turkey
129 C4 Doğansu Turkey
222 F5 Dog Creek B.C. Can.
149 I4 Dogdyke Lincolnshire, England U.K.
199 G2 Döğer Turkey
172 C4 Dogern Ger.
224 B3 Dog Lake Ont. Can.
190 C4 Dogliani Italy
197 E3 Dognecea Romania
103 F5 Dōgo i. Japan
206 D4 Dogo Mali
207 G3 Dogondoutchi Niger
103 F6 Dōgo-yama mt. Japan
246 C1 Dog Rocks is Bahamas
127 G3 Doğubeyazıt Turkey
129 B3 Doğu Karadeniz Dağları mts Turkey
199 F3 Doğu Menteşe Dağları mts Turkey
111 D6 Dogxung Zangbo r. Xizang China
125 E2 Doha Qatar
Dohad Gujarat India see Dahod
171 C5 Döhlau Ger.
171 E5 Dohna Ger.
215 F5 Dohne S. Africa
168 C3 Dohren Ger.
111 C7 Dohrighat Uttar Prad. India
77 I4 Doi i. Fiji
111 E6 Doilungdêqên Xizang China
Doïranis, Limni l. Greece/Macedonia see Dojran, Lake
Doire Northern Ireland U.K. see Londonderry
96 B3 Doi Saket Thai.
117 F5 Doisanagar Bihar India
165 D4 Doische Belgium
256 C5 Dois Córregos Brazil
254 E4 Dois Irmãos, Serra dos hills Brazil
184 A1 Dois Portos Port.
176 G3 Dojč Slovakia
197 F5 Dojran, Lake Greece/Macedonia
Dojransko Ezero l. Greece/Macedonia see Dojran, Lake
205 G2 Dokhara, Dunes de des. Alg.
141 J3 Dokka Norway
140 M2 Dokkas Sweden
164 E1 Dokkum Neth.
164 E1 Dokkumer Ee r. Neth.
123 G5 Dokri Pak.
Dokshukino Rus. Fed. see Nartkala
138 F4 Dokshytsy Belarus
176 D1 Doksy Liberecký kraj Czech Rep.
171 F5 Doksy Středočeský kraj Czech Rep.
120 F2 Dokuchayevka Kazakh.
137 I4 Dokuchayevs'k Ukr.
199 G1 Dokurcun Sakarya Turkey
236 D2 Doland SD U.S.A.
150 D2 Dolanog Powys, Wales U.K.
241 J4 Dolan Springs AZ U.S.A.
259 D6 Dolavón Arg.
225 F3 Dolbeau Que. Can.
150 C2 Dolbenmaen Gwynedd, Wales U.K.
190 C5 Dolceacqua Italy
158 E3 Dol-de-Bretagne France
160 D1 Dole France
160 F3 Dolent, Mont mt. France/Italy
150 D2 Dolfor Powys, Wales U.K.
150 D1 Dolgarrog Conwy, Wales U.K.
150 D2 Dolgellau Gwynedd, Wales U.K.
170 E2 Dolgen Ger.
233 F3 Dolgeville NY U.S.A.
137 H2 Dolgiye Budy Rus. Fed.
175 I1 Dolgorukovo Kaliningradskaya Oblast' Rus. Fed.
139 L5 Dolgorukovo Lipetskaya Oblast' Rus. Fed.
135 G5 Dolgoye Rus. Fed.
197 H2 Dolhasca Romania
175 M5 Dołhobyczów Pol.
192 B5 Dolianova Sardegna Italy
174 D2 Dolice Pol.
Dolina Ukr. see Dolyna
129 C1 Dolinovka Rus. Fed.
100 G3 Dolinsk Sakhalin Rus. Fed.
Dolisie Congo see Loubomo
197 E4 Doljevac Srbija Yugo.
147 C4 Dolla Rep. of Ireland
146 E5 Dollar Clackmannanshire, Scotland U.K.
168 C2 Dollart Ger.
171 C3 Dolle Ger.
262 T2 Dolleman Island Antarctica
157 H5 Doller r. France
168 E2 Dollern Ger.
171 D4 Döllnitz Ger.
173 F3 Dollnstein Ger.
159 G3 Dollon France
169 F4 Döllstädt Ger.
169 F5 Dolmar hill Ger.
121 G1 Dolmatovo Kazakh.
197 G4 Dolna Lipnitska Bulg.
177 H3 Dolné Vestenice Slovakia
177 H2 Dolní Benešov Czech Rep.
171 F5 Dolní Beřkovice Czech Rep.
179 I2 Dolní Bojanovice Czech Rep.
176 E1 Dolní Bousov Czech Rep.
179 F1 Dolní Bukovsko Czech Rep.
197 H4 Dolni Chiflik Bulg.
197 G4 Dolni Dŭbnik Bulg.
179 H2 Dolní Dunajovice Czech Rep.
176 D3 Dolní Dvořiště Czech Rep.
176 F2 Dolní Kounice Czech Rep.
177 G3 Dolní Němčí Czech Rep.
176 D1 Dolní Podluží Czech Rep.
171 F5 Dolní Poustevna Czech Rep.
176 F2 Dolní Újezd Czech Rep.
176 B1 Dolní Žandov Czech Rep.
197 F4 Dolno Kamartsi Bulg.
197 G4 Dolno Levski Bulg.
174 E4 Dolnośląskie prov. Pol.
177 I2 Dolný Kubín Slovakia
Dolný Peter Slovakia see Svätý Peter
177 H3 Dolný Pial Slovakia
177 G4 Dolný Štál Slovakia
191 H3 Dolo Italy
190 F4 Dolo r. Italy
78 □4b Dolohmwar hill Pohnpei Micronesia
160 D3 Dolomieu France
Dolomites mts Italy see Dolomiti
191 G3 Dolomiti mts Italy
Dolonnur Nei Mongol China see Duolun
210 D3 Dolo Odo Eth.
261 I5 Dolores Arg.
243 H5 Dolores Guat.
242 C3 Dolores Mex.
187 C6 Dolores Spain
261 H3 Dolores Uru.
241 M2 Dolores r. CO U.S.A.
244 D3 Dolores Hidalgo Mex.
196 E3 Dolovo Vojvodina, Srbija Yugo.
220 G3 Dolphin and Union Strait Nunavut Can.
149 F2 Dolphinton South Lanarkshire, Scotland U.K.
178 D4 Dölsach Austria
174 F4 Dolsk Pol.
175 K3 Dołubowo Pol.
162 A3 Dolus-d'Oléron France
136 B3 Dolyna Ukr.
137 G3 Dolyns'ka Ukr.
137 I4 Dolzhanskaya Rus. Fed.
137 H2 Dolzhenkovo Rus. Fed.
91 I7 Dom, Gunung mt. Indon.
177 J3 Domaháza Hungary
199 F2 Domaniç Turkey
175 K3 Domanice Pol.
193 I5 Domanico Italy
175 H3 Domaniewice Łódzkie Pol.
175 I4 Domaniewice Mazowieckie Pol.
177 H2 Domaniža Slovakia
117 G4 Domar Bangl.
Domartang Xizang China see Banbar
156 C2 Domart-en-Ponthieu France
179 H4 Domašinec Croatia
177 J5 Domaszek Hungary
174 E5 Domaszków Pol.
174 F4 Domaszowice Pol.
190 E2 Domat Ems Switz.
156 D4 Domats France
176 B2 Domažlice Czech Rep.
111 F5 Domba Qinghai China
120 D2 Dombarovskiy Rus. Fed.
141 J3 Dombås Norway
157 F3 Dombasle-en-Argonne France
157 F4 Dombasle-en-Xaintois France
157 G4 Dombasle-sur-Meurthe France
129 B2 Dombay Rus. Fed.
213 G3 Dombe Moz.
209 B8 Dombe Grande Angola
177 K5 Dombegyház Hungary
177 H5 Dombóvár Hungary
177 K3 Dombrád Hungary
Dombrau Pol. see Dąbrowa Górnicza
190 B1 Dombresson Switz.
Dombrovitsa Rivnens'ka Oblast' Ukr. see Dubrovytsya
Dombrowa Pol. see Dąbrowa Górnicza
164 C3 Domburg Neth.
257 F3 Dom Cavati Brazil
Domda Qinghai China see Qingshuihe
160 A3 Dôme, Monts mts France
263 F1 Dome Argus ice feature Antarctica
263 H2 Dome Charlie ice feature Antarctica
Dome Circe ice feature Antarctica see Dome Charlie
222 F4 Dome Creek B.C. Can.
263 C2 Dome Fuji research stn Antarctica
178 D4 Domegge di Cadore Italy
138 D4 Domeikava Lith.
161 D3 Domène France
160 A2 Domérat France
241 J5 Dome Rock Mountains AZ U.S.A.
171 C3 Domersleben Ger.
86 F2 Domett, Cape W.A. Austr.
81 D4 Domett, Mount South I. N.Z.
157 F4 Domèvre-en-Haye France
157 G4 Domèvre-sur-Vezouze France
258 C3 Domeyko Chile
163 B5 Domezaine-Berraute France
255 B9 Dom Feliciano Brazil
159 F3 Domfront France
157 F4 Domgermain France
257 G4 Domingos Martins Brazil
182 C4 Dominguiso Port.
247 □2 Dominica country West Indies
242 □J7 Dominical Costa Rica
Dominicana, República country West Indies see Dominican Republic
246 E3 Dominican Republic country West Indies
247 □2 Dominica Passage Dominica/Guadeloupe
Dominique i. Fr. Polynesia see Hiva Oa
170 C2 Dömitz Ger.
257 F3 Dom Joaquim Brazil
157 E4 Dommartin-le-Franc France
156 E4 Dommartin-Varimont France
163 D4 Domme France
164 E3 Dommel r. Neth.
169 C5 Dommershausen Ger.
171 D4 Dommitzsch Ger.
197 G3 Domneşti Romania
197 G3 Domneşti Romania
170 C3 Dömnitz r. Ger.
210 E3 Domo Eth.
139 K4 Domodedovo Rus. Fed.
190 D2 Domodossola Italy
198 C2 Domokos Greece
217 □3 Domoni Comoros
156 C3 Domont France
177 H4 Dömös Hungary
157 G4 Dompaire France
157 F4 Dompcevrin France
255 B9 Dom Pedrito Brazil
254 D3 Dom Pedro Brazil
160 C2 Dompierre-les-Ormes France
160 B2 Dompierre-sur-Besbre France
162 A2 Dompierre-sur-Mer France
158 E5 Dompierre-sur-Yon France
95 G5 Dompu Sumbawa Indon.
157 F4 Domrémy-la-Pucelle France
177 I4 Dömsöd Hungary
170 C2 Domsühl Ger.
192 A6 Domus de Maria Sardegna Italy
192 A5 Domusnovas Sardegna Italy
260 B5 Domuyo, Volcán vol. Arg.
137 H4 Domuzla r. Ukr.
83 G2 Domville, Mount hill Qld Austr.
188 E2 Domžale Slovenia
85 G3 Don r. Qld Austr.
158 E4 Don r. France
114 C2 Don r. India
242 C3 Don Mex.
139 L5 Don r. Rus. Fed.
146 F4 Don r. Scotland U.K.
96 D4 Don, Xé r. Laos
147 E3 Donabate Rep. of Ireland
191 H3 Donada Italy
147 D2 Donagh Northern Ireland U.K.
147 F2 Donaghadee Northern Ireland U.K.
147 E2 Donaghcloney Northern Ireland U.K.
147 D4 Donaghmore Laois Rep. of Ireland
147 E3 Donaghmore Meath Rep. of Ireland
147 E2 Donaghmore Northern Ireland U.K.
83 E4 Donald Vic. Austr.
237 F6 Donaldsonville LA U.S.A.
258 C2 Donalnes, Cerro mt. Chile
231 C6 Donalsonville GA U.S.A.
184 D2 Don Álvaro Spain
185 F3 Doña Mencía Spain
147 E3 Donard Rep. of Ireland
260 B2 Doña Rosa, Cordillera mts Chile
244 B1 Donato Guerra Mex.
178 I2 Donau r. Austria/Ger. alt. Duna (Hungary), alt. Dunaj (Slovakia), alt. Dunărea (Romania), alt. Dunav (Yugoslavia), conv. Danube
172 C4 Donaueschingen Ger.
173 G2 Donaustauf Ger.
173 E3 Donauwörth Ger.
184 E2 Don Benito Spain
149 H4 Doncaster South Yorkshire, England U.K.
157 E3 Donchery France
209 B7 Dondo Angola
136 D3 Donduşeni Moldova
Dondyushany Moldova see Donduşeni
147 C2 Donegal Rep. of Ireland
147 C2 Donegal county Rep. of Ireland
147 C2 Donegal Bay Rep. of Ireland
Dönenbay Kazakh. see Dunenbay
137 J3 Donetsk Rus. Fed.
137 I4 Donets'k Ukr.
137 I3 Donets'ka Oblast' admin. div. Ukr.
Donetskaya Oblast' admin. div. Ukr. see Donets'ka Oblast'
137 I2 Donetskaya Seymitsa r. Rus. Fed.
Donetsko-Amrovsiyevka Ukr. see Amvrosiyivka
Donetsk Oblast admin. div. Ukr. see Donets'ka Oblast'
137 J3 Donets'kyy Ukr.
137 J3 Donets'kyy Kryazh hills Rus. Fed./Ukr.
207 H4 Donga r. Cameroon/Nigeria
207 H5 Donga Nigeria
109 D3 Dong'an Hunan China
87 B6 Dongara W.A. Austr.
116 E5 Dongargaon Madh. Prad. India
116 E5 Dongargarh Madh. Prad. India
110 F3 Dongbatu Gansu China
Dongbo Xizang China see Mêdog
Dongchuan Yunnan China see Yao'an
108 B3 Dongchuan Yunnan China
Dongcun Shandong China see Haiyang
Dongcun Shanxi China see Lanxian
107 H4 Dong'e Shandong China
164 D3 Dongen Neth.
158 D4 Donges France
108 D5 Dongfang Hainan China
100 E3 Dongfanghong Heilong. China
100 C4 Dongfeng Jilin China
93 A3 Donggala Sulawesi Tengah Indon.
101 C5 Donggang Liaoning China
Donggou Liaoning China see Donggang
109 E3 Donggu Jiangxi China
109 E4 Dongguan Guangdong China
96 D3 Đông Ha Vietnam
107 H5 Donghai Jiangsu China
Dong Hai sea N. Pacific Ocean see East China Sea
108 C2 Dong He r. China
96 D3 Đông Hôi Vietnam
109 E4 Dong Jiang r. China
100 D3 Dongjingcheng Heilong. China
108 D3 Dongkou Hunan China
108 C3 Donglan Guangxi China
106 D4 Dongle Gansu China
107 I3 Dongliao r. China
110 E4 Donglük Xinjiang China
Dongmen Guangxi China see Luocheng
107 G5 Dongming Shandong China
100 D3 Dongning Heilong. China
209 B8 Dongo Angola
190 E2 Dongo Italy
203 F5 Dongola Sudan
210 B3 Dongotona Mountains Sudan
208 C4 Dongou Congo
96 C3 Dong Phraya Fai mts Thai.
96 C4 Dong Phraya Yen esc. Thai.
109 E4 Dongping Guangdong China
Dongping Hunan China see Anhua
107 H5 Dongping Shandong China
107 H4 Dongping Hu l. China
Dongpo Sichuan China see Meishan
111 E6 Dongqiao Xizang China
109 F4 Dongshan Fujian China
Dongshan Jiangsu China see Jiangning
109 G2 Dongshan Jiangsu China
Dongshan Jiangxi China see Shangyou
109 E3 Dongshao Jiangxi China
107 F4 Dongsheng Nei Mongol China
Dongshuan Yunnan China see Tangdan
109 G1 Dongtai Jiangsu China
109 G1 Dongtai r. China
109 E2 Dongting Hu l. China
109 G3 Dongtou Zhejiang China
Dong Ujimqin Qi Nei Mongol China see Uliastai
Dongxiang Sichuan China see Xuanhan
108 C4 Dongxing Guangxi China
100 C3 Dongxing Heilong. China
109 G2 Dongyang Zhejiang China
107 H4 Dongying Shandong China
106 D4 Dongzhen Gansu China
109 F2 Dongzhi Anhui China
260 B4 Doñihue Chile
151 G2 Donington Lincolnshire, England U.K.
237 F4 Doniphan MO U.S.A.
196 E4 Donja Dubnica Kosovo, Srbija Yugo.
179 H4 Donja Dubrava Croatia
179 H4 Donja Konjšćina Croatia
179 G5 Donja Stubica Croatia
179 H4 Donja Višnjica Croatia
222 A2 Donjek r. Y.T. Can.
157 F4 Donjeux France
188 G3 Donji Miholjac Croatia
197 F3 Donji Milanovac Srbija Yugo.
188 F3 Donji Vakuf Bos.-Herz.
188 E3 Donji Zemunik Croatia
164 F1 Donkerbroek Neth.
215 E4 Donkerpoort S. Africa
140 K2 Dønna i. Norway
225 G4 Donnacona Que. Can.
194 D6 Donnalucata Sicilia Italy
190 C3 Donnas Italy
222 G4 Donnelly Alta Can.
80 D1 Donnellys Crossing North I. N.Z.
156 D4 Donnemarie-Dontilly France
179 F3 Donnersbach Austria
172 B2 Donnersberg hill Ger.
173 E2 Donnersdorf Ger.
150 E2 Donnington Telford and Wrekin, England U.K.
87 B7 Donnybrook W.A. Austr.
147 C4 Donohill Rep. of Ireland
157 H4 Donon mt. France
192 B5 Donori Sardegna Italy
186 B1 Donostia - San Sebastián Spain
147 C5 Donoughmore Rep. of Ireland
199 D3 Donoussa i. Greece
226 D5 Donovan IL U.S.A.
137 I4 Dons'ke Ukr.
137 K4 Donskoy Rostovskaya Oblast' Rus. Fed.
139 L5 Donskoy Tul'skaya Oblast' Rus. Fed.
139 L5 Donskoye Lipetskaya Oblast' Rus. Fed.
135 H7 Donskoye Stavropol'skiy Kray Rus. Fed.

Donskoye Belogor'ye to Duratón

300

137 J2 **Donskoye Belogor'ye** hills Rus. Fed.
92 B3 **Donsol** Phil.
96 B3 **Donthami** r. Myanmar
158 E3 **Donville-les-Bains** France
163 C4 **Donzac** France
172 D3 **Donzdorf** Ger.
162 D3 **Donzenac** France
161 C4 **Donzère** France
160 B1 **Donzy** France
147 A3 **Dooagh** Rep. of Ireland
147 C2 **Doocastle** Rep. of Ireland
147 A3 **Dooega** Rep. of Ireland
147 B3 **Dooghbeg** Rep. of Ireland
147 A2 **Doogort** Rep. of Ireland
147 B2 **Doohooma** Rep. of Ireland
148 B3 **Dooish** Northern Ireland U.K.
86 C4 **Dooleena** hill W.A. Austr.
84 D3 **Doomadgee** Qld Austr.
147 C4 **Doon** Rep. of Ireland
146 D6 **Doon** r. Scotland U.K.
146 D6 **Doon, Loch** l. Scotland U.K.
147 B4 **Doonaha** Rep. of Ireland
147 B4 **Doonbeg** Rep. of Ireland
147 B4 **Doonbeg** r. Rep. of Ireland
147 A3 **Doonloughan** Rep. of Ireland
147 A4 **Doonmanagh** Rep. of Ireland
164 E2 **Doorn** Neth.
164 E2 **Doornspijk** Neth.
226 D3 **Door Peninsula** WI U.S.A.
174 E3 **Dopiewo** Pol.
108 B2 **Do Qu** r. Sichuan China
237 C5 **Dora** NM U.S.A.
86 D4 **Dora, Lake** salt flat W.A. Austr.
190 D3 **Dora Baltea** r. Italy
160 E3 **Dora di Ferret** r. Italy
160 F3 **Dora di Veny** r. Italy
190 C3 **Dora Riparia** r. Italy
Dorbiljin Xinjiang China see **Emin**
Dorbod Heilong. China see **Taikang**
Dorbod Qi Nei Mongol China see **Ulan Hua**
196 E4 **Đorče Petrov** Macedonia
150 E4 **Dorchester** Dorset, England U.K.
234 D3 **Dorchester** NJ U.S.A.
156 C4 **Dordives** France
162 C3 **Dordogne** dept Aquitaine France
160 A3 **Dordogne** r. France
151 F2 **Dordon** Warwickshire, England U.K.
164 D3 **Dordrecht** Neth.
215 F4 **Dordrecht** S. Africa
160 B2 **Dore** r. France
160 A3 **Dore, Monts** mts France
223 J4 **Doré Lake** Sask. Can.
161 B3 **Dore-l'Église** France
178 A3 **Doren** Austria
169 E3 **Dörentrup** Ger.
146 D4 **Dores** Highland, Scotland U.K.
257 F3 **Dores de Guanhães** Brazil
257 E3 **Dores do Indaiá** Brazil
173 G3 **Dorfen** Ger.
178 E3 **Dorfgastein** Austria
168 E3 **Dorfmark** Ger.
170 C2 **Dorf Mecklenburg** Ger.
192 B4 **Dorgali** Sardegna Italy
106 B1 **Dörgön** Mongolia
177 K5 **Dorgoş** Romania
123 F4 **Dori** r. Afgh.
207 E3 **Dori** Burkina
214 B4 **Doring** r. S. Africa
214 B5 **Doring** r. S. Africa
214 B4 **Doringbaai** S. Africa
214 B4 **Doringbos** S. Africa
198 B3 **Dorio** Peloponnisos Greece
84 B2 **Dorisvale** N.T. Austr.
151 G3 **Dorking** Surrey, England U.K.
157 H4 **Dorlisheim** France
206 E5 **Dormaa-Ahenkro** Ghana
169 B4 **Dormagen** Ger.
177 J4 **Dormánd** Hungary
156 D3 **Dormans** France
190 D3 **Dormelletto** Italy
172 C3 **Dormettingen** Ger.
100 E3 **Dormidontovka** Rus. Fed.
114 D2 **Dornakal** Andhra Prad. India
179 G4 **Dornava** Slovenia
169 E4 **Dörnberg (Habichtswald)** Ger.
178 A3 **Dornbirn** Austria
171 C4 **Dornburg (Saale)** Ger.
169 D5 **Dornburg-Frickhofen** Ger.
168 E2 **Dornbusch** Ger.
169 F5 **Dorndorf** Ger.
171 C4 **Dorndorf-Steudnitz** Ger.
182 C3 **Dornelas** Port.
160 B2 **Dornes** France
169 E4 **Dörnhagen (Fuldabrück)** Ger.
172 C3 **Dornhan** Ger.
146 C4 **Dornie** Highland, Scotland U.K.
171 D3 **Dörnitz** Ger.
190 D3 **Dorno** Italy
146 D4 **Dornoch** Highland, Scotland U.K.
146 D4 **Dornoch Firth** est. Scotland U.K.
107 G1 **Dornod** prov. Mongolia
107 F2 **Dornogovĭ** prov. Mongolia
234 B2 **Dornsife** PA U.S.A.
172 D3 **Dornstadt** Ger.
172 C3 **Dornstetten** Ger.
168 C2 **Dornum** Ger.
168 C2 **Dornumersiel** Ger.
206 E2 **Doro** Mali
197 H3 **Dorobanţu** Romania
177 H4 **Dorog** Hungary
177 I4 **Dorogháza** Hungary
139 I4 **Dorogobuzh** Rus. Fed.
197 H2 **Dorohoi** Romania
175 L4 **Dorohusk** Pol.
139 K4 **Dorokhovo** Rus. Fed.
177 L4 **Dorolţ** Romania
137 F4 **Doroshivka** Ukr.
Dorostol Bulg. see **Silistra**
136 C2 **Dorosyni** Ukr.
140 L2 **Dorotea** Sweden
234 D3 **Dorothy** NJ U.S.A.
Dorpat Estonia see **Tartu**
168 C3 **Dörpen** Ger.
87 B5 **Dorre Island** W.A. Austr.
83 H2 **Dorrigo** N.S.W. Austr.
238 B3 **Dorris** CA U.S.A.
207 H5 **Dorsale Camerounaise** slope Cameroon/Nigeria
227 H3 **Dorset** Ont. Can.
150 E4 **Dorset** admin. div. England U.K.
232 C4 **Dorset** OH U.S.A.
169 F3 **Dorstadt** Ger.
169 B4 **Dorsten** Ger.
160 D2 **Dortan** France
169 C4 **Dortmund** Ger.
232 B6 **Dorton** KY U.S.A.
126 E3 **Dörtyol** Turkey
174 G4 **Doruchów** Pol.
129 C4 **Dorukdibi** Turkey
168 D2 **Dorum** Ger.
168 E3 **Dörverden** Ger.
Dorylaeum Turkey see **Eskişehir**
172 D2 **Dörzbach** Ger.
187 C5 **Dos Aguas** Spain
122 D4 **Do Sārī** Iran
183 G5 **Dosbarrios** Spain
241 M5 **Dos Cabezas Mountains** AZ U.S.A.
250 C6 **Dos de Mayo** Peru
199 G3 **Döşemealtı** Turkey
123 E3 **Doshakh, Koh-i-** mt. Afgh.
184 E3 **Dos Hermanas** Spain
243 H5 **Dos Lagunos** Guat.
96 D2 **Đo Son** Vietnam
240 G3 **Dos Palos** CA U.S.A.
197 G5 **Dospat** Bulg.
197 G5 **Dospat** r. Bulg.
185 H3 **Dos Picos** mt. Spain
170 D3 **Dosse** r. Ger.
172 C2 **Dossenheim** Ger.
208 C2 **Dosséo, Bahr** r. Chad
207 F3 **Dosso** Niger
207 F3 **Dosso** dept Niger
190 D2 **Dossola, Val** val. Italy
120 C3 **Dossor** Kazakh.
185 F2 **Dos Torres** Spain
121 J3 **Dostyk** Kazakh.
Dostyq Kazakh. see **Dostyk**
231 C6 **Dothan** AL U.S.A.
168 D3 **Dötlingen** Ger.
172 C3 **Dotternhausen** Ger.
190 D1 **Döttingen** Switz.
156 D2 **Douai** France
207 H5 **Douala** Cameroon
158 B3 **Douarnenez** France
85 H5 **Double Island Point** Qld Austr.
237 C5 **Double Mountain Fork** r. TX U.S.A.
240 H4 **Double Peak** CA U.S.A.
85 F3 **Double Point** Qld Austr.
231 C5 **Double Springs** AL U.S.A.
176 E2 **Doubrava** r. Czech Rep.
160 E2 **Doubs** France
160 E1 **Doubs** dept Franche-Comté France
160 D2 **Doubs** r. France/Switz.
86 E2 **Doubtful Bay** W.A. Austr.
87 C7 **Doubtful Island Bay** W.A. Austr.
81 A6 **Doubtful Sound** South I. N.Z.
81 A6 **Doubtful Sound** inlet South I. N.Z.
156 D5 **Douchy** France
156 D2 **Douchy-les-Mines** France
160 D2 **Doucier** France
159 G2 **Doudeville** France
162 B1 **Doué-la-Fontaine** France
206 E3 **Douentza** Mali
148 D2 **Dougarie** North Ayrshire, Scotland U.K.
205 H1 **Dougga** tourist site Tunisia
147 C2 **Dough Mountain** hill Rep. of Ireland
145 E4 **Douglas** Isle of Man
80 E3 **Douglas** North I. N.Z.
147 C5 **Douglas** Rep. of Ireland
214 D3 **Douglas** S. Africa
146 E6 **Douglas** South Lanarkshire, Scotland U.K.
222 C3 **Douglas** AK U.S.A.
241 M6 **Douglas** AZ U.S.A.
231 D6 **Douglas** GA U.S.A.
238 F3 **Douglas** WY U.S.A.
148 B3 **Douglas Bridge** Northern Ireland U.K.
241 M1 **Douglas Creek** r. CO U.S.A.
262 T2 **Douglas Range** mts Antarctica
234 C2 **Douglassville** PA U.S.A.
146 F5 **Douglastown** Angus, Scotland U.K.
231 C5 **Douglasville** GA U.S.A.
Douhudi Hubei China see **Gong'an**
157 F4 **Doulaincourt-Saucourt** France
Douliu Taiwan see **Touliu**
156 C2 **Doullens** France
207 F4 **Doumè** Benin
207 I5 **Doumé** Cameroon
207 I5 **Doumé** r. Cameroon
109 E4 **Doumen** Guangdong China
146 E2 **Dounby** Orkney, Scotland U.K.
146 D5 **Doune** Stirling, Scotland U.K.
146 D5 **Doune Hill** hill Scotland U.K.
207 F4 **Dounkassa** Benin
146 E3 **Dounreay** Highland, Scotland U.K.
176 C1 **Doupovské Hory** mts Czech Rep.
165 C4 **Dour** Belgium
256 C3 **Dourada, Cachoeira** waterfall Brazil
256 B2 **Dourada, Serra** hills Brazil
254 C5 **Dourada, Serra** mts Brazil
255 B7 **Dourados** Brazil
255 B7 **Dourados** r. Brazil
208 B2 **Dourbali** Chad
161 B4 **Dourbie** r. France
161 B4 **Dourbies** France
156 C4 **Dourdan** France
161 A4 **Dourdou** r. France
161 A5 **Dourdou** r. France
163 E5 **Dourgne** France
156 B2 **Douriez** France
182 B3 **Douro** r. Port. alt. **Duero (Spain)**
Doushi Hubei China see **Gong'an**
160 E3 **Doussard** France
256 A5 **Doutor Camargo** Brazil
160 E2 **Douvaine** France
158 E2 **Douve** r. France
159 F2 **Douvres-la-Délivrande** France
161 C3 **Doux** r. France
205 H2 **Douz** Tunisia
163 B5 **Douze** r. France
162 C3 **Douzillac** France
157 F3 **Douzy** France
191 G4 **Dovadola** Italy
136 E2 **Dovbysh** Ukr.
151 F2 **Dove** r. Derbyshire/Staffordshire, England U.K.
149 I3 **Dove** r. North Yorkshire, England U.K.
151 I2 **Dove** r. Suffolk, England U.K.
225 J2 **Dove Brook** Nfld. Can.
221 P2 **Dove Bugt** b. Greenland
241 M3 **Dove Creek** CO U.S.A.
83 F5 **Dover** Tas. Austr.
151 I3 **Dover** Kent, England U.K.
234 C3 **Dover** DE U.S.A.
233 □H3 **Dover** NH U.S.A.
234 D2 **Dover** NJ U.S.A.
232 C4 **Dover** OH U.S.A.
234 B3 **Dover** PA U.S.A.
231 C4 **Dover** TN U.S.A.
87 E7 **Dover, Point** W.A. Austr.
145 H6 **Dover, Strait of** France/U.K.
233 □I2 **Dover-Foxcroft** ME U.S.A.
151 F2 **Doveridge** Derbyshire, England U.K.
235 E1 **Dover Plains** NY U.S.A.
Dovey r. Wales U.K. see **Dyfi**
122 B4 **Doveyrīch, Rūd-e** r. Iran/Iraq
136 B3 **Dovhe** Ukr.
136 C2 **Dovhoshyyi** Ukr.
175 I1 **Dovinė** r. Lith.
141 J3 **Dovrefjell** mts Norway
137 H2 **Dovzhyk** Ukr.
Dow, Lake Botswana see **Xau, Lake**
211 B8 **Dowa** Malawi
226 D5 **Dowagiac** MI U.S.A.
146 E5 **Dowally** Perth and Kinross, Scotland U.K.
123 F2 **Dowlatābād** Afgh.
122 B4 **Dowlatābād** Iran
123 E2 **Dowlatābād** Iran
147 F2 **Down** county Northern Ireland U.K.
240 H5 **Downey** CA U.S.A.
151 H2 **Downham Market** Norfolk, England U.K.
240 G2 **Downieville** CA U.S.A.
226 A5 **Downing** MO U.S.A.
234 C2 **Downingtown** PA U.S.A.
147 F2 **Downpatrick** Northern Ireland U.K.
236 D4 **Downs** KS U.S.A.
233 F3 **Downsville** NY U.S.A.
226 B3 **Downsville** WI U.S.A.
151 F4 **Downton** Wiltshire, England U.K.
222 E4 **Downton, Mount** B.C. Can.
147 C2 **Dowra** Rep. of Ireland
122 B3 **Dow Rūd** Iran
122 A3 **Dow Sar** Iran
151 G2 **Dowsby** Lincolnshire, England U.K.
160 A2 **Doyet** France
240 G1 **Doyle** CA U.S.A.
225 J4 **Doyles** Nfld. Can.
234 C2 **Doylestown** PA U.S.A.
197 G4 **Doyrentsi** Bulg.
122 D5 **Dozdān** r. Iran
103 F5 **Dōzen** is Japan
216 □1a **Doze Ribeiras** Terceira Azores
159 F2 **Dozulé** France
137 G3 **Drabiv** Ukr.
137 F3 **Drabivka** Ukr.
161 D3 **Drac** r. France
256 B4 **Dracena** Brazil
197 E5 **Dračevo** Macedonia
171 F4 **Drachhausen** Ger.
173 H2 **Drachselsried** Ger.
164 F1 **Drachten** Neth.
174 G2 **Dragacz** Pol.
197 H3 **Dragalina** Romania
177 L5 **Drăgan** r. Romania
177 L5 **Drăgăneşti** Romania
197 G3 **Drăgăneşti-Olt** Romania
197 G3 **Drăgăneşti-Vlaşca** Romania
197 G3 **Drăgăşani** Romania
168 F2 **Drage** Ger.
177 L5 **Drăgeşti** Romania
214 D3 **Draghoender** S. Africa
197 F4 **Dragoman** Bulg.
Dragonera, Isla i. Spain see **Sa Dragonera**
193 G3 **Dragoni** Italy
247 □7 **Dragon's Mouths** str. Trin. and Tob./Venez.
241 L5 **Dragoon** AZ U.S.A.
142 E4 **Dragør** Denmark
197 H3 **Dragoş Vodă** Romania
141 M3 **Dragsfjärd** Fin.
161 E5 **Draguignan** France
197 H1 **Drăguşeni** Romania
197 H3 **Drăguşeni** Romania
176 G2 **Drahanovice** Czech Rep.
136 C1 **Drahichyn** Belarus
171 E4 **Drahnsdorf** Ger.
83 H2 **Drake** N.S.W. Austr.
236 C2 **Drake** ND U.S.A.
168 E3 **Drakenburg** Ger.
215 G3 **Drakensberg** mts Lesotho/S. Africa
213 F5 **Drakensberg** mts S. Africa
215 G3 **Drakensberg Garden** S. Africa
215 G4 **Draken's Rock** mt. S. Africa
264 E9 **Drake Passage** S. Atlantic Ocean
240 F3 **Drakes Bay** CA U.S.A.
129 D3 **Drakhtik** Armenia
136 E5 **Drakulya** r. Ukr.
198 D1 **Drama** Greece
142 D2 **Drammen** Norway
156 C4 **Drancy** France
97 D4 **Drang, Prêk** r. Cambodia
140 □B2 **Drangajökull** ice cap Iceland
147 D4 **Drangan** Rep. of Ireland
142 C2 **Drangedal** Norway
116 G4 **Drangme Chhu** r. Bhutan
168 D2 **Drangstedt** Ger.
160 E2 **Dranse** r. France
170 D2 **Dranse** Ger.
169 E4 **Dransfeld** Ger.
170 E1 **Dranske** Ger.
241 L1 **Draper** UT U.S.A.
222 B3 **Draper, Mount** AK U.S.A.
147 E2 **Draperstown** Northern Ireland U.K.
Drapsaca Afgh. see **Kondūz**
116 C2 **Dras** Jammu and Kashmir
179 H2 **Drasenhofen** Austria
179 H3 **Draßmarkt** Austria
178 F4 **Drau** r. Austria alt. **Drava (Croatia)**, alt. **Dráva (Hungary)**
188 G3 **Drava** r. Croatia/Slovenia alt. **Drau (Austria)**, alt. **Dráva (Hungary)**
188 G3 **Dráva** r. Hungary alt. **Drau (Austria)**, alt. **Drava (Croatia)**
177 G6 **Drávafok** Hungary
188 E2 **Dravinja** r. Slovenia
188 E2 **Dravograd** Slovenia
174 D3 **Drawa** r. Pol.
174 D2 **Drawno** Pol.
174 E3 **Drawsko** Pol.
174 D2 **Drawsko Pomorskie** Pol.
151 I2 **Drayton** Norfolk, England U.K.
151 F3 **Drayton** Oxfordshire, England U.K.
222 H4 **Drayton Valley** Alta Can.
175 J2 **Drążdżewo** Pol.
189 A7 **Dréa** Alg.
189 A7 **Dréan** Alg.
168 D3 **Drebber** Ger.
171 F4 **Drebkau** Ger.
160 C2 **Drée** r. France
147 B4 **Dreenagh** Rep. of Ireland
170 D3 **Dreetz** Ger.
150 C3 **Drefach** Carmarthenshire, Wales U.K.
177 I3 **Drégelypalánk** Hungary
146 D6 **Dreghorn** North Ayrshire, Scotland U.K.
169 D5 **Dreieich** Ger.
178 D3 **Dreiherrnspitze** mt. Austria
171 C3 **Dreileben** Ger.
172 A2 **Dreis** Ger.
172 B3 **Dreisam** r. Ger.
173 H3 **Dreisesselberg** mt. Ger.
169 E5 **Dreistelzberge** hill Ger.
173 F4 **Dreitorspitze** mt. Ger.
175 K4 **Drelów** Pol.
168 E1 **Drelsdorf** Ger.
149 G1 **Drem** East Lothian, Scotland U.K.
191 I2 **Drenchia** Italy
188 G3 **Drenovci** Croatia
198 B1 **Drenovë** Korçë Albania
197 F4 **Drenovets** Bulg.
170 E2 **Drense** Ger.
169 C4 **Drensteinfurt** Ger.
164 F2 **Drenthe** prov. Neth.
168 D3 **Drentwede** Ger.
198 C3 **Drepano** Peloponnisos Greece
227 F4 **Dresden** Ont. Can.
171 E4 **Dresden** Ger.
171 F4 **Dresden** admin. reg. Sachsen Ger.
237 F4 **Dresden** TN U.S.A.
164 E3 **Dreumel** Neth.
156 B4 **Dreux** France
177 G2 **Dřevnice** r. Czech Rep.
171 D3 **Drewitz** Ger.
174 G1 **Drewnica** Pol.
232 E6 **Drewryville** VA U.S.A.
234 C3 **Drexel Hill** PA U.S.A.
174 D3 **Drezdenko** Pol.
164 E2 **Driebergen** Neth.
183 G4 **Driebes** Spain
169 D5 **Driedorf** Ger.
177 K3 **Drienov** Slovakia
164 F1 **Driesum** Neth.
151 F3 **Driffield** Gloucestershire, England U.K.
234 C2 **Drifton** PA U.S.A.
232 D4 **Driftwood** PA U.S.A.
238 E3 **Driggs** ID U.S.A.
85 G5 **Drillham** Qld Austr.
137 F2 **Drimaylivka** Ukr.
147 D3 **Drimmo** Rep. of Ireland
146 C5 **Drimnin** Highland, Scotland U.K.
147 B5 **Drimoleague** Rep. of Ireland
196 D4 **Drin** r. Albania
188 G3 **Drina** r. Bos.-Herz./Yugo.
197 F3 **Drincea** r. Romania
196 E4 **Drini i Zi** r. Albania
196 D5 **Drinit, Gjiri i** b. Albania
198 B1 **Drino** r. Albania
232 B6 **Drip Rock** KY U.S.A.
147 C5 **Dripsey** Rep. of Ireland
262 O1 **Driscoll Island** Antarctica
Drissa Belarus see **Vyerkhnyadzvinsk**
179 F1 **Dříteň** Czech Rep.
176 F3 **Drnholec** Czech Rep.
188 F4 **Drniš** Croatia
179 H4 **Drnje** Croatia
191 F3 **Dro** Italy
142 D2 **Drøbak** Norway
197 F3 **Drobeta - Turnu Severin** Romania
161 C4 **Drobie** r. France
175 H3 **Drobin** Pol.
137 I3 **Drobysheve** Ukr.
177 L5 **Drocea, Vârful** hill Romania
136 D3 **Drochia** Moldova
168 E2 **Drochtersen** Ger.
164 F1 **Drogeham** Neth.
147 E3 **Drogheda** Rep. of Ireland
Drogichin Belarus see **Drahichyn**
Drogobych Ukr. see **Drohobych**
175 K3 **Drohiczyn** Pol.
136 B3 **Drohobych** Ukr.
Droichead Átha Rep. of Ireland see **Drogheda**
Droichead Nua Kildare Rep. of Ireland see **Newbridge**
150 E2 **Droitwich** Worcestershire, England U.K.
Drokiya Moldova see **Drochia**
169 C4 **Drolshagen** Ger.
147 C2 **Dromahair** Rep. of Ireland
83 F4 **Dromana** Vic. Austr.
147 E2 **Dromara** Northern Ireland U.K.
161 D4 **Drôme** dept Rhône-Alpes France
161 C4 **Drôme** r. France
159 F2 **Drôme** r. France
234 A2 **Dromgold** PA U.S.A.
147 E3 **Dromiskin** Rep. of Ireland
147 D3 **Dromod** Rep. of Ireland
147 D2 **Dromore** Northern Ireland U.K.
147 E2 **Dromore** Northern Ireland U.K.
147 C2 **Dromore West** Rep. of Ireland
190 C4 **Dronero** Italy
149 H4 **Dronfield** Derbyshire, England U.K.
146 D6 **Drongan** East Ayrshire, Scotland U.K.
165 C3 **Drongen** Belgium
162 B3 **Dronne** r. France
221 N3 **Dronning Ingrid Land** reg. Greenland
221 P2 **Dronning Louise Land** reg. Greenland
Dronning Maud Land reg. Antarctica see **Queen Maud Land**
164 E2 **Dronten** Neth.
164 D2 **Droogmakerij de Beemster** tourist site Neth.
163 B4 **Dropt** r. France
179 G2 **Drosendorf** Austria
123 G3 **Drosh** Pak.
198 C2 **Drosia** Greece
179 H2 **Drösing** Austria
156 B4 **Droué** France
107 G1 **Drovyanaya** Rus. Fed.
224 C3 **Drowning** r. Ont. Can.
171 D4 **Droyßig** Ger.
136 D2 **Drozdyn'** Ukr.
150 D2 **Druid** Denbighshire, Wales U.K.
148 D2 **Druimdrishaig** Argyll and Bute, Scotland U.K.
Druk-Yul country Asia see **Bhutan**
157 H4 **Drulingen** France
147 C4 **Drumandoora** Rep. of Ireland
147 D3 **Drumanespick** Rep. of Ireland
147 F2 **Drumaness** Northern Ireland U.K.
146 C3 **Drumbeg** Highland, Scotland U.K.
147 E2 **Drumbilla** Rep. of Ireland
147 D2 **Drumcard** Northern Ireland U.K.
148 E2 **Drumclog** South Lanarkshire, Scotland U.K.
147 E3 **Drumcondra** Rep. of Ireland
147 E3 **Drumconrath** Rep. of Ireland
147 D3 **Drumcree** Rep. of Ireland
147 D2 **Drumduff** Northern Ireland U.K.
160 D3 **Drumettaz-Clarafond** France
147 D1 **Drumfree** Rep. of Ireland
223 H5 **Drumheller** Alta Can.
147 C2 **Drumkeeran** Rep. of Ireland
148 B3 **Drumlea** Rep. of Ireland
147 D3 **Drumlish** Rep. of Ireland
146 F5 **Drumlithie** Aberdeenshire, Scotland U.K.
147 E4 **Drummin** Rep. of Ireland
Drummond atoll Gilbert Is Kiribati see **Tabiteuea**
238 D2 **Drummond** MT U.S.A.
226 B2 **Drummond** WI U.S.A.
Drummond Island Phoenix Is Kiribati see **McKean**
85 F5 **Drummond Range** hills Qld Austr.
225 F4 **Drummondville** Que. Can.
146 D7 **Drummore** Dumfries and Galloway, Scotland U.K.
147 D2 **Drumnacross** Rep. of Ireland
146 D4 **Drumnadrochit** Highland, Scotland U.K.
148 B3 **Drumnakilly** Northern Ireland U.K.
147 D2 **Drumquin** Northern Ireland U.K.
148 B4 **Drumraney** Rep. of Ireland
147 C2 **Drumshanbo** Rep. of Ireland
148 B4 **Drumsna** Rep. of Ireland
164 E3 **Drunen** Neth.
148 B3 **Drung** Rep. of Ireland
190 D1 **Drusberg** mt. Switz.
157 H4 **Drusenheim** France
Druskieniki Lith. see **Druskininkai**
138 E5 **Druskininkai** Lith.
164 E3 **Druten** Neth.
138 H5 **Druts'** r. Belarus
138 F4 **Druya** Belarus
160 B1 **Druyes-les-Belles-Fontaines** France
175 H4 **Drużbice** Pol.
Druzhba Kazakh. see **Dostyk**
137 G1 **Druzhba** Ukr.
137 H4 **Druzhbivka** Ukr.
137 I3 **Druzhkivka** Donets'ka Oblast' Ukr.
Druzhkovka Donets'ka Oblast' Ukr. see **Druzhkivka**
Druzhkovka Kharkivs'ka Oblast' Ukr. see **Lozova**
139 H2 **Druzhnaya Gorka** Rus. Fed.
177 K3 **Družstevná pri Hornáde** Slovakia
175 J4 **Drwalew** Pol.
175 G2 **Drwęca** r. Pol.
175 I5 **Drwinia** Pol.
84 C2 **Dry** r. N.T. Austr.
197 G4 **Dryanovo** Bulg.
137 J1 **Dryazgi** Rus. Fed.
139 H4 **Drybin** Belarus
150 E3 **Drybrook** Gloucestershire, England U.K.
237 C4 **Dry Cimarron** r. KS U.S.A.
224 A3 **Dryden** Ont. Can.
233 E3 **Dryden** NY U.S.A.
232 B6 **Dryden** VA U.S.A.
238 F3 **Dry Fork** r. WY U.S.A.
263 G2 **Drygalski Island** Antarctica
175 K2 **Drygały** Pol.
150 D2 **Drygarn Fawr** hill Wales U.K.
215 E2 **Dry Harts** r. S. Africa
241 J3 **Dry Lake** NV U.S.A.
146 D5 **Drymen** Stirling, Scotland U.K.
138 F4 **Drysa** r. Belarus
86 E2 **Drysdale** r. W.A. Austr.
84 C1 **Drysdale Island** N.T. Austr.
174 G3 **Drzewce** Pol.
175 I4 **Drzewica** Pol.
174 G2 **Drzycim** Pol.
207 H5 **Dschang** Cameroon
208 D4 **Dua** r. Dem. Rep. Congo
122 B3 **Dūāb** r. Iran
192 A4 **Dualchi** Sardegna Italy
108 D4 **Du'an** Guangxi China
Duancun Shanxi China see **Wuxiang**
217 □3b **Duangani** Mayotte
85 G4 **Duaringa** Qld Austr.
246 E3 **Duarte, Pico** mt. Dom. Rep.
256 C5 **Duartina** Brazil
182 D3 **Duas Igrejas** Port.
206 E5 **Duayaw-Nkwanta** Ghana
176 D1 **Dubá** Czech Rep.
124 A2 **Ḍubā** Saudi Arabia
125 F2 **Dubai** U.A.E.
240 F1 **Dubakella Mountain** CA U.S.A.
136 E4 **Dubăsari** Moldova
136 E4 **Dubău** Moldova
223 L2 **Dubawnt** r. Nunavut Can.
223 K2 **Dubawnt Lake** N.W.T./Nunavut Can.
Dubayy U.A.E. see **Dubai**
124 A2 **Dubbagh, Jabal ad** mt. Saudi Arabia
83 G3 **Dubbo** N.S.W. Austr.
206 D5 **Dube** r. Liberia
136 C2 **Dubechne** Ukr.
175 L4 **Dubeczno** Pol.
171 E4 **Duben** Brandenburg Ger.
171 D4 **Düben** Ger.
190 D1 **Dübendorf** Switz.
171 D4 **Dübener Heide** reg. Ger.
175 K1 **Dubeninki** Pol.
135 I5 **Dubenki** Rus. Fed.
Dubesar' Moldova see **Dubăsari**
171 E5 **Dubí** Czech Rep.
175 K6 **Dubiecko** Pol.
175 L4 **Dubienka** Pol.
196 D4 **Dubinës, Maja e** mt. Albania
190 E2 **Dubino** Italy
136 D3 **Dubivka** Ukr.
137 F3 **Dubiyivka** Ukr.
129 E2 **Dubki** Rus. Fed.
226 D1 **Dublin** Ont. Can.
147 E3 **Dublin** Rep. of Ireland
147 E3 **Dublin** county Rep. of Ireland
231 D5 **Dublin** GA U.S.A.
234 B3 **Dublin** MD U.S.A.
234 C2 **Dublin** PA U.S.A.
232 C6 **Dublin** VA U.S.A.
147 E3 **Dublin Bay** Rep. of Ireland
176 D2 **Dublovice** Czech Rep.
136 B3 **Dublyany** L'vivs'ka Oblast' Ukr.
136 C3 **Dublyany** L'vivs'ka Oblast' Ukr.
138 F3 **Dubna** r. Latvia
139 K3 **Dubna** Moskovskaya Oblast' Rus. Fed.
139 K4 **Dubna** Tul'skaya Oblast' Rus. Fed.
176 G3 **Dubňany** Czech Rep.
176 D3 **Dubné** Czech Rep.
177 H3 **Dubnica nad Váhom** Slovakia
136 C2 **Dubno** Ukr.
238 D2 **Dubois** ID U.S.A.
232 D4 **Du Bois** PA U.S.A.
238 E3 **Dubois** WY U.S.A.
Dubossary Moldova see **Dubăsari**
136 B3 **Dubove** Ukr.
177 J2 **Dubovica** Slovakia
139 L5 **Dubovka** Tul'skaya Oblast' Rus. Fed.
135 I6 **Dubovka** Volgogradskaya Oblast' Rus. Fed.
Dubovo Moldova see **Dubău**
139 M4 **Dubovoye, Ozero** l. Rus. Fed.
135 H7 **Dubovskoye** Rus. Fed.
137 G2 **Dubov"yazivka** Ukr.
129 F3 **Dübrar Dağı** mt. Azer.
179 H5 **Dubrava** Croatia
177 I2 **Dúbrava** Slovakia
179 G5 **Dubravica** Croatia
177 I3 **Dúbravy** Slovakia
206 B4 **Dubréka** Guinea
Dubris Kent, England U.K. see **Dover**
136 D2 **Dubrivka** Ukr.
139 L4 **Dubrovichi** Rus. Fed.
139 I5 **Dubrovka** Rus. Fed.
188 G4 **Dubrovnik** Croatia
121 G1 **Dubrovnoye** Kazakh.
175 L6 **Dubrovytsya** L'vivs'ka Oblast' Ukr.
136 D2 **Dubrovytsya** Rivnens'ka Oblast' Ukr.
139 H4 **Dubrowna** Belarus
121 J4 **Dubun** Kazakh.
230 B3 **Dubuque** IA U.S.A.
136 F3 **Dubynove** Ukr.
138 D4 **Dubysa** r. Lith.
79 □3 **Duc de Gloucester, Îles du** is Arch. des Tuamotu Fr. Polynesia
158 E3 **Ducey** France
109 F2 **Duchang** Jiangxi China
170 E2 **Ducherow** Ger.
241 L1 **Duchesne** UT U.S.A.
241 M1 **Duchesne** r. UT U.S.A.
84 D4 **Duchess** Qld Austr.
223 I5 **Duchess** Alta Can.
171 E5 **Duchov** Czech Rep.
85 E2 **Ducie** r. Qld Austr.
267 K7 **Ducie Island** Pitcairn Is
231 C4 **Duck** r. TN U.S.A.
223 K4 **Duck Bay** Man. Can.
86 C4 **Duck Creek** r. W.A. Austr.
151 H3 **Duck End** Essex, England U.K.
223 J4 **Duck Lake** Sask. Can.
241 J2 **Duckwater** NV U.S.A.
241 J2 **Duckwater Peak** NV U.S.A.
159 G2 **Duclair** France
97 E5 **Đưc Trong** Vietnam
250 C4 **Duda** r. Col.
177 G4 **Dudar** Hungary
137 G4 **Dudchany** Ukr.
149 G2 **Duddo** Northumberland, England U.K.
149 F3 **Duddon** r. England U.K.
165 F5 **Dudelange** Lux.
169 B6 **Dudeldorf** Ger.
169 F4 **Duderstadt** Ger.
196 E2 **Dudestii Vechi** Romania
117 E4 **Dudhi** Uttar Prad. India
177 H3 **Dudince** Slovakia
190 C2 **Düdingen** Switz.
130 J3 **Dudinka** Rus. Fed.
150 E2 **Dudley** West Midlands, England U.K.
241 L5 **Dudleyville** AZ U.S.A.
114 C2 **Dudna** r. India
139 J5 **Dudorovskiy** Rus. Fed.
116 C4 **Dudu** Rajasthan India
215 G2 **Duduza** S. Africa
188 F2 **Dudváh** r. Slovakia
146 F4 **Dudwick, Hill of** hill Scotland U.K.
206 D5 **Duékoué** Côte d'Ivoire
94 C3 **Duen, Bukit** vol. Indon.
183 F3 **Dueñas** Spain
254 C4 **Dueré** Brazil
182 E2 **Duerna** r. Spain
160 C3 **Duerne** France
182 D3 **Duero** r. Spain alt. **Douro (Portugal)**
191 G3 **Dueville** Italy
165 D3 **Duffel** Belgium
238 C3 **Duffer Peak** NV U.S.A.
151 F2 **Duffield** Derbyshire, England U.K.
232 B6 **Duffield** VA U.S.A.
78 □6 **Duff Islands** Solomon Is
146 E4 **Dufftown** Moray, Scotland U.K.
190 C3 **Dufourspitze** mt. Italy/Switz.
223 L5 **Dufrost** Man. Can.
121 F5 **Dugab** Uzbek.
84 E3 **Dugald** r. Qld Austr.
188 E3 **Duga Resa** Croatia
128 C5 **Dughdash** mts Saudi Arabia
Dughoba Uzbek. see **Dugab**
188 E3 **Dugi Otok** i. Croatia
188 F4 **Dugi Rat** Croatia
157 F3 **Dugny-sur-Meuse** France
188 F4 **Dugopolje** Croatia
188 F3 **Dugo Selo** Croatia
199 E1 **Düğüncübaşı** Turkey
241 K1 **Dugway** UT U.S.A.
108 D1 **Du He** r. China
163 B5 **Duhort-Bachen** France
202 C4 **Duhūn Tārsū** mts Chad/Libya
85 E2 **Duifken Point** Qld Austr.
169 E3 **Duingen** Ger.
191 I3 **Duino** Italy
169 B4 **Duisburg** Ger.
250 C3 **Duitama** Col.
164 F3 **Duiven** Neth.
213 F4 **Duiwelskloof** S. Africa
108 B2 **Dujiangyan** Sichuan China
127 G4 **Dukān Dam** Iraq
131 Q3 **Dukat** Rus. Fed.
197 F4 **Dukat** mt. Yugo.
215 F4 **Dukathole** S. Africa
198 A1 **Dukat i Ri** Albania
Duke of Clarence atoll Tokelau see **Nukunonu**
Duke of Gloucester Islands Arch. des Tuamotu Fr. Polynesia see **Duc de Gloucester, Îles du**
Duke of York atoll Tokelau see **Atafu**
125 E2 **Dukhān** Qatar
124 C2 **Dukhnah** Saudi Arabia
120 B1 **Dukhovnitskoye** Rus. Fed.
139 I4 **Dukhovshchina** Rus. Fed.
139 H4 **Dukhovshchinskaya Vozvyshennost'** hills Rus. Fed.
100 E2 **Duki** Rus. Fed.
100 E2 **Duki** r. Rus. Fed.
207 H4 **Dukku** Nigeria
175 J6 **Dukla** Pol.
Dukou Sichuan China see **Panzhihua**
138 F4 **Dūkštas** Lith.
212 E4 **Dukwe** Botswana
106 E1 **Dulaanhaan** Mongolia
237 F6 **Dulac** LA U.S.A.
106 C4 **Dulan** Qinghai China
Dulawan Phil. see **Datu Piang**
261 F2 **Dulce** r. Arg.
183 H4 **Dulce** r. Spain
239 F4 **Dulce** NM U.S.A.
242 □I6 **Dulce Nombre de Culmí** Hond.
107 G1 **Dul'durga** Rus. Fed.
147 E3 **Duleek** Rep. of Ireland
131 O3 **Dulgalakh** r. Rus. Fed.
197 H4 **Dŭlgopol** Bulg.
85 E1 **Dulhunty** r. Qld Austr.
95 F2 **Dulit, Pegunungan** mts Sarawak Malaysia
108 D3 **Duliu Jiang** r. China
117 H4 **Dullabchara** Assam India
151 H2 **Dullingham** Cambridgeshire, England U.K.
215 H1 **Dullstroom** S. Africa
169 C4 **Dülmen** Ger.
146 E4 **Dulnain** r. Scotland U.K.
146 E4 **Dulnain Bridge** Highland, Scotland U.K.
197 H4 **Dulovo** Bulg.
226 A2 **Duluth** MN U.S.A.
236 E2 **Duluth/Superior** airport MN U.S.A.
150 D3 **Dulverton** Somerset, England U.K.
139 M3 **Dulyapino** Rus. Fed.
128 C3 **Dūmā** Syria
92 B4 **Dumaguete** Phil.
94 C2 **Dumai** Sumatera Indon.
129 C3 **Dumanlı Dağı** mt. Turkey
129 B4 **Dumanlı Tepe** mt. Turkey
83 G2 **Dumaresq** r. N.S.W. Austr.
237 F5 **Dumas** AR U.S.A.
237 C5 **Dumas** TX U.S.A.
146 D6 **Dumbarton** West Dunbartonshire, Scotland U.K.
215 H2 **Dumbe** S. Africa
78 □5 **Dumbéa** New Caledonia
177 I3 **Ďumbier** mt. Slovakia
87 C7 **Dumbleyung** W.A. Austr.
87 C7 **Dumbleyung, Lake** salt flat W.A. Austr.
177 L6 **Dumbrava** Romania
197 G2 **Dumbrăveni** Romania
197 H3 **Dumbrăveni** Romania
197 G3 **Dumbrăviţa** Romania
177 K6 **Dumbrăviţa** Romania
182 A1 **Dumbría** Spain
117 H4 **Dum Duma** Assam India
197 H2 **Dumeşti** Romania
146 E6 **Dumfries** Dumfries and Galloway, Scotland U.K.
146 E6 **Dumfries and Galloway** admin. div. Scotland U.K.
139 J5 **Duminichi** Rus. Fed.
197 G2 **Dumitra** Romania
117 F4 **Dumka** Bihar India
129 B3 **Dumlu** Turkey
129 B3 **Dumlu Dağı** mt. Turkey
128 A1 **Dumlugöze** Turkey
199 F2 **Dumlupınar** Turkey
114 D2 **Dummagudem** Andhra Prad. India
170 D2 **Dummerstorf** Ger.
224 E4 **Dumoine** r. Que. Can.
263 J2 **Dumont d'Urville** research stn Antarctica
169 B5 **Dümpelfeld** Ger.
117 F4 **Dumraon** Bihar India
203 F2 **Dumyât** Egypt
126 C5 **Dumyât** governorate Egypt
163 D5 **Dun** France
169 F4 **Dün** ridge Ger.
188 G3 **Duna** r. Hungary alt. **Donau (Austria/Germany)**, alt. **Dunaj (Slovakia)**, alt. **Dunărea (Romania)**, alt. **Dunav (Yugoslavia)**, conv. **Danube**
177 H4 **Dunaalmás** Hungary
Dünaburg Latvia see **Daugavpils**
177 H5 **Dunaegyháza** Hungary
177 H5 **Dunafalva** Hungary
177 H5 **Dunaföldvár** Hungary
177 I4 **Dunaharaszti** Hungary
188 F2 **Dunaj** r. Slovakia alt. **Donau (Austria/Germany)**, alt. **Duna (Hungary)**, alt. **Dunărea (Romania)**, alt. **Dunav (Yugoslavia)**, conv. **Danube**
175 I5 **Dunajec** r. Pol.
176 G3 **Dunajská Lužná** Slovakia
177 G4 **Dunajská Streda** Slovakia
177 I4 **Dunakeszi** Hungary
176 G4 **Dunakiliti** Hungary
83 F5 **Dunalley** Tas. Austr.
Dunanbay Kazakh. see **Dunenbay**
177 I5 **Dunapataj** Hungary
197 I3 **Dunărea** r. Romania alt. **Donau (Austria/Germany)**, alt. **Duna (Hungary)**, alt. **Dunaj (Slovakia)**, alt. **Dunav (Yugoslavia)**, conv. **Danube**
197 I3 **Dunării, Delta** Romania
177 G4 **Dunaszeg** Hungary
177 H5 **Dunaszekcső** Hungary
177 H5 **Dunaszentgyörgy** Hungary
176 G4 **Dunasziget** Hungary
177 I5 **Dunatetétlen** Hungary
177 H5 **Dunaújváros** Hungary
197 H3 **Dunav** r. Yugo. alt. **Donau (Austria/Germany)**, alt. **Duna (Hungary)**, alt. **Dunaj (Slovakia)**, alt. **Dunărea (Romania)**, conv. **Danube**
177 I4 **Dunavarsány** Hungary
177 H5 **Dunavecse** Hungary
197 F4 **Dunavtsi** Bulg.
136 D3 **Dunayivtsi** Khmel'nyts'ka Oblast' Ukr.
136 D3 **Dunayivtsi** Khmel'nyts'ka Oblast' Ukr.
81 C6 **Dunback** South I. N.Z.
85 E3 **Dunbar** Qld Austr.
146 F5 **Dunbar** East Lothian, Scotland U.K.
232 D5 **Dunbar** PA U.S.A.
226 C3 **Dunbar** WI U.S.A.
232 C5 **Dunbar** WV U.S.A.
146 E3 **Dunbeath** Highland, Scotland U.K.
146 E5 **Dunblane** Stirling, Scotland U.K.
147 E3 **Dunboyne** Rep. of Ireland
222 F5 **Duncan** B.C. Can.
241 M5 **Duncan** AZ U.S.A.
237 D5 **Duncan** OK U.S.A.
147 E4 **Duncannon** Rep. of Ireland
227 I5 **Duncannon** PA U.S.A.
147 B4 **Duncannon Bridge** Rep. of Ireland
115 G4 **Duncan Passage** Andaman & Nicobar Is India
246 □ **Duncans** Jamaica
146 E3 **Duncansby Head** hd Scotland U.K.
246 D2 **Duncan Town** Bahamas
151 F2 **Dunchurch** Warwickshire, England U.K.
147 E4 **Duncormick** Rep. of Ireland
138 D3 **Dundaga** Latvia
146 C5 **Dun da Ghaoithe** hill Scotland U.K.
227 G3 **Dundalk** Ont. Can.
147 E2 **Dundalk** Rep. of Ireland
234 B3 **Dundalk** MD U.S.A.
147 E3 **Dundalk Bay** Rep. of Ireland
224 E5 **Dundas** Ont. Can.
87 D7 **Dundas, Lake** salt flat W.A. Austr.
84 B1 **Dundas Strait** N.T. Austr.
107 F2 **Dundbürd** Mongolia
Dún Dealgan Rep. of Ireland see **Dundalk**
215 H3 **Dundee** S. Africa
146 F5 **Dundee** Dundee, Scotland U.K.
146 F5 **Dundee** admin. div. Scotland U.K.
227 F5 **Dundee** MI U.S.A.
232 E3 **Dundee** NY U.S.A.
106 E2 **Dundgovĭ** prov. Mongolia
107 H3 **Dund Hot** Nei Mongol China
147 F2 **Dundonald** Northern Ireland U.K.
146 D6 **Dundonald** South Ayrshire, Scotland U.K.
85 F5 **Dundoo** Qld Austr.
146 D4 **Dundreggan** Highland, Scotland U.K.
146 E7 **Dundrennan** Dumfries and Galloway, Scotland U.K.
147 E3 **Dundrum** Dublin Rep. of Ireland
147 C4 **Dundrum** Tipperary Rep. of Ireland
147 F2 **Dundrum** Northern Ireland U.K.
147 F2 **Dundrum Bay** Northern Ireland U.K.
116 E4 **Dundwa Range** mts India/Nepal
146 E6 **Duneaton Water** r. Scotland U.K.
146 F4 **Dunecht** Aberdeenshire, Scotland U.K.
81 C6 **Dunedin** South I. N.Z.
231 D6 **Dunedin** FL U.S.A.
83 G3 **Dunedoo** N.S.W. Austr.
121 J2 **Dunenbay** Kazakh.
163 C4 **Dunes** France
148 B2 **Dunfanaghy** Rep. of Ireland
146 E5 **Dunfermline** Fife, Scotland U.K.
147 E2 **Dungannon** Northern Ireland U.K.
Dún Garbhán Waterford Rep. of Ireland see **Dungarvan**
116 C3 **Dungargarh** Rajasthan India
116 C5 **Dungarpur** Rajasthan India
147 D4 **Dungarvan** Kilkenny Rep. of Ireland
147 D4 **Dungarvan** Waterford Rep. of Ireland
151 H4 **Dungeness** hd England U.K.
169 C5 **Düngenheim** Ger.
147 E2 **Dungiven** Northern Ireland U.K.
147 C2 **Dungloe** Rep. of Ireland
83 G3 **Dungog** N.S.W. Austr.
147 C5 **Dungourney** Rep. of Ireland
208 F4 **Dungu** Dem. Rep. Congo
94 C1 **Dungun** Malaysia
149 I4 **Dunholme** Lincolnshire, England U.K.
Dunhou Jiangxi China see **Ji'an**
100 D4 **Dunhua** Jilin China
110 F3 **Dunhuang** Gansu China
161 C3 **Dunières** France
85 G5 **Dunkeld** Qld Austr.
83 E4 **Dunkeld** Vic. Austr.
146 E5 **Dunkeld** Perth and Kinross, Scotland U.K.
147 C3 **Dunkellin** r. Rep. of Ireland
179 G2 **Dunkelsteiner Wald** for. Austria
156 C1 **Dunkerque** France
147 D4 **Dunkerrin** Rep. of Ireland
150 D3 **Dunkery Beacon** hill England U.K.
147 C2 **Dunkineely** Rep. of Ireland
Dunkirk France see **Dunkerque**
151 H3 **Dunkirk** Kent, England U.K.
232 D3 **Dunkirk** NY U.S.A.
232 B4 **Dunkirk** OH U.S.A.
206 E5 **Dunkwa** Ghana
147 E3 **Dún Laoghaire** Rep. of Ireland
236 E3 **Dunlap** IA U.S.A.
226 E5 **Dunlap** IN U.S.A.
231 C5 **Dunlap** TN U.S.A.
147 E3 **Dunlavin** Rep. of Ireland
147 E3 **Dunleer** Rep. of Ireland
162 D2 **Dun-le-Palestel** France
160 C1 **Dun-les-Places** France
148 A2 **Dunlewy** Rep. of Ireland
146 D6 **Dunlop** East Ayrshire, Scotland U.K.
147 E1 **Dunloy** Northern Ireland U.K.
145 D4 **Dunluce** tourist site Northern Ireland U.K.
147 B5 **Dunmanus** Rep. of Ireland
147 B5 **Dunmanus Bay** Rep. of Ireland
147 B5 **Dunmanway** Rep. of Ireland
84 C3 **Dunmarra** N.T. Austr.
147 D4 **Dunmoon** Rep. of Ireland
147 C3 **Dunmore** Rep. of Ireland
234 C1 **Dunmore** PA U.S.A.
232 D5 **Dunmore** WV U.S.A.
147 E4 **Dunmore East** Rep. of Ireland
246 C1 **Dunmore Town** Eleuthera Bahamas
147 F2 **Dunmurry** Northern Ireland U.K.
231 E5 **Dunn** NC U.S.A.
147 D2 **Dunnamanagh** Northern Ireland U.K.
231 D6 **Dunnellon** FL U.S.A.
146 E3 **Dunnet** Highland, Scotland U.K.
146 E3 **Dunnet Head** hd Scotland U.K.
240 G2 **Dunnigan** CA U.S.A.
146 E5 **Dunning** Perth and Kinross, Scotland U.K.
236 C3 **Dunning** NE U.S.A.
172 C3 **Dunningen** Ger.
149 I4 **Dunnington** York, England U.K.
87 C5 **Dunns Range** hills W.A. Austr.
227 H4 **Dunnville** Ont. Can.
83 E4 **Dunolly** Vic. Austr.
146 D6 **Dunoon** Argyll and Bute, Scotland U.K.
147 A4 **Dunquin** Rep. of Ireland
146 E6 **Dun Rig** hill Scotland U.K.
146 F6 **Duns** Scottish Borders, Scotland U.K.
81 D5 **Dunsandel** South I. N.Z.
87 B7 **Dunsborough** W.A. Austr.
146 E6 **Dunscore** Dumfries and Galloway, Scotland U.K.
236 C1 **Dunseith** ND U.S.A.
168 D3 **Dünsen** Ger.
147 E3 **Dunshaughlin** Rep. of Ireland
238 B3 **Dunsmuir** CA U.S.A.
151 G3 **Dunstable** Bedfordshire, England U.K.
81 B6 **Dunstan Mountains** South I. N.Z.
150 D3 **Dunster** Somerset, England U.K.
160 A2 **Dun-sur-Auron** France
157 F3 **Dun-sur-Meuse** France
81 C6 **Duntroon** South I. N.Z.
168 C2 **Dunum** Ger.
148 E2 **Dunure** South Ayrshire, Scotland U.K.
150 C3 **Dunvant** Swansea, Wales U.K.
146 B4 **Dunvegan** Highland, Scotland U.K.
146 B4 **Dunvegan, Loch** b. Scotland U.K.
146 B4 **Dunvegan Head** hd Scotland U.K.
123 G4 **Dunyapur** Pak.
107 J1 **Duobukur** r. China
107 H3 **Duolun** Nei Mongol China
114 C3 **Dupadu** Andhra Prad. India
109 D3 **Dupang Ling** mts China
227 H1 **Duparquet** Que. Can.
Duperré Alg. see **Aïn Defla**
179 F4 **Duplica** Slovenia
197 F4 **Dupnitsa** Bulg.
236 C2 **Dupree** SD U.S.A.
86 B4 **Dupuy, Cape** W.A. Austr.
Duque de Bragança Angola see **Calandula**
257 F5 **Duque de Caxias** Brazil
259 B8 **Duque de York, Isla** i. Chile
226 A2 **Duquette** MN U.S.A.
230 B4 **Du Quoin** IL U.S.A.
210 C2 **Dura** r. Eth.
128 B4 **Dūrā** West Bank
191 H2 **Dura, Cima** mt. Italy
173 E4 **Durach** Ger.
76 C3 **Durack** r. W.A. Austr.
86 E3 **Durack Range** hills W.A. Austr.
Dura Europos Syria see **Aş Şālihīyah**
126 D2 **Durağan** Turkey
199 F2 **Durak** Turkey
183 H2 **Durana** Spain
163 C4 **Durance** France
161 C5 **Durance** r. France
227 F4 **Durand** MI U.S.A.
226 B3 **Durand** WI U.S.A.
185 F2 **Duranes** hill Spain
241 J5 **Durango** Baja California Norte Mex.
244 B1 **Durango** Durango Mex.
244 B1 **Durango** state Mex.
183 H1 **Durango** Spain
239 F4 **Durango** CO U.S.A.
244 B2 **Durango, Sierra de** mts Mex.
197 I4 **Durankulak** Bulg.
191 H2 **Duranno, Monte** mt. Italy
237 F5 **Durant** MS U.S.A.
237 D5 **Durant** OK U.S.A.
163 C4 **Duras** France
183 F3 **Duratón** r. Spain

163 D4 Duravel France
261 I3 Durazno Uru.
261 I3 Durazno dept Uru.
Durazzo Albania see Durrës
172 C3 Durbach Ger.
163 D5 Durban France
215 H3 Durban S. Africa
161 A6 Durban-Corbières France
214 B5 Durbanville S. Africa
172 C3 Dürbheim Ger.
232 D5 Durbin WV U.S.A.
157 G4 Durbion r. France
165 E4 Durbuy Belgium
185 G4 Dúrcal Spain
185 G4 Dúrcal r. Spain
177 H2 Ďurčiná Slovakia
160 A2 Durdat-Larequille France
159 G2 Durdent r. France
188 F2 Đurđevac Croatia
110 E2 Düre Xinjiang China
169 B5 Düren Ger.
122 D3 Düren Iran
161 B5 Durfort France
116 E5 Durg Madh. Prad. India
117 G4 Durgapur Bangl.
117 F5 Durgapur W. Bengal India
227 G3 Durham Ont. Can.
149 H3 Durham Durham, England U.K.
149 G3 Durham admin. div. England U.K.
240 G2 Durham CA U.S.A.
235 F1 Durham CT U.S.A.
231 E5 Durham NC U.S.A.
233 □H3 Durham NH U.S.A.
233 □J1 Durham Bridge N.B. Can.
85 E5 Durham Downs Qld Austr.
94 C2 Duri Sumatera Indon.
146 E6 Durisdeer Dumfries and Galloway, Scotland U.K.
Durlas Rep. of Ireland see Thurles
136 E4 Durleşti Moldova
156 D1 Durme r. Belgium
172 D3 Dürmentingen Ger.
172 C3 Durmersheim Ger.
196 D4 Durmitor mt. Yugo.
146 D3 Durness Highland, Scotland U.K.
179 H2 Dürnkrut Austria
Durocortorum France see Reims
85 G5 Durong South Qld Austr.
Durostorum Bulg. see Silistra
Durovernum Kent, England U.K. see Canterbury
196 D5 Durrës Albania
84 E5 Durrie Qld Austr.
173 E3 Dürrlauingen Ger.
171 F4 Dürröhrsdorf-Dittersbach Ger.
147 D4 Durrow Rep. of Ireland
173 E2 Dürrwangen Ger.
147 A5 Dursey Island Rep. of Ireland
150 E3 Dursley Gloucestershire, England U.K.
199 F2 Dursunbey Turkey
159 F4 Durtal France
Duru Guizhou China see Wuchuan
208 F4 Duru r. Dem. Rep. Congo
183 H3 Duruelo de la Sierra Spain
122 E3 Düruh Iran
210 E2 Durukhsi Somalia
128 C3 Durūz, Jabal ad mt. Syria
80 D4 D'Urville Island South I. N.Z.
234 C1 Duryea PA U.S.A.
146 □G1 Dury Voe inlet Scotland U.K.
138 E4 Dusetos Lith.
122 D2 Dushak Turkm.
108 C3 Dushan Guizhou China
123 G2 Dushanbe Tajik.
110 D2 Dushanzi Xinjiang China
129 D2 Dushet'i Georgia
227 I5 Dushore PA U.S.A.
138 D4 Dusia l. Lith.
177 H5 Dusnok Hungary
174 G2 Dusocin Pol.
86 F2 Dussejour, Cape W.A. Austr.
169 B4 Düsseldorf Ger.
169 B4 Düsseldorf admin. reg. Nordrhein-Westfalen Ger.
164 D3 Dussen Neth.
172 D3 Dußlingen Ger.
171 D4 Düßnitz Ger.
123 G2 Dusti Tajik.
121 G4 Dustlik Uzbek.
238 C2 Dusty WA U.S.A.
174 E3 Duszniki Pol.
174 E5 Duszniki-Zdrój Pol.
Dutch East Indies country Asia see Indonesia
234 E1 Dutchess County county NY U.S.A.
Dutch Guiana country S. America see Suriname
220 B4 Dutch Harbor AK U.S.A.
241 K1 Dutch Mountain UT U.S.A.
Dutch New Guinea prov. Indon. see Irian Jaya
Dutch West Indies terr. West Indies see Netherlands Antilles
179 E5 Dutovlje Slovenia
207 H4 Dutsan-Wai Nigeria
207 H4 Dutse Nigeria
207 G3 Dutsin-Ma Nigeria
85 E4 Dutton r. Qld Austr.
227 G4 Dutton Ont. Can.
238 E2 Dutton MT U.S.A.
82 D2 Dutton, Lake salt flat S.A. Austr.
241 K2 Dutton, Mount UT U.S.A.
223 J5 Duval Sask. Can.
134 L5 Duvan Rus. Fed.
137 J3 Duvanka r. Ukr.
Duvannyy Azer. see Qobustan
140 K3 Duved Sweden
246 E3 Duvergé Dom. Rep.
Duvno Bos.-Herz. see Tomislavgrad
127 G3 Duwin Iraq
108 C3 Duyun Guizhou China
199 G1 Düzce Turkey
129 D3 Düz Cırdaxan Azer.
Duzdab Iran see Zāhedān
129 A3 Düzköy Turkey
136 D1 Dvarets Belarus
197 G4 Dve Mogili Bulg.
Dvinsk Latvia see Daugavpils
134 G2 Dvinskaya Guba g. Rus. Fed.
139 H3 Dvin'ye, Ozero l. Rus. Fed.
136 D2 Dvirets' Ukr.
175 M5 Dvirtsi Ukr.
188 F3 Dvor Croatia
177 G2 Dvorce Czech Rep.
137 I3 Dvorichna Ukr.
177 H4 Dvory nad Žitavou Slovakia
176 E1 Dvůr Králové Czech Rep.
211 B8 Dwangwa Malawi
116 B5 Dwarka Gujarat India
212 E5 Dwarsberg S. Africa
87 C7 Dwellingup W.A. Austr.
215 H4 Dweshula S. Africa
226 C5 Dwight IL U.S.A.
175 J5 Dwikozy Pol.
164 F2 Dwingeloo Neth.
214 C5 Dwyka S. Africa
214 C5 Dwyka r. S. Africa
137 K3 D'yachenkovo Rus. Fed.
134 H4 D'yakonovo Rus. Fed.
137 J4 Dyakove Ukr.
148 C3 Dyan Northern Ireland U.K.
123 E2 Dyanev Turkm.
197 H4 Dyankovo Bulg.
139 J5 Dyat'kovo Rus. Fed.
234 C1 Dyberry PA U.S.A.
234 C1 Dyberry Creek r. PA U.S.A.
146 F4 Dyce Aberdeen, Scotland U.K.
175 K6 Dydnia Pol.
221 L3 Dyer, Cape Nunavut Can.
227 G3 Dyer Bay Ont. Can.
262 T2 Dyer Plateau Antarctica
237 F4 Dyersburg TN U.S.A.
81 E4 Dyeville North I. N.Z.
Dyffryn Isle of Anglesey, Wales U.K. see Valley
150 D2 Dyfi r. Wales U.K.
174 D1 Dygowo Pol.
167 H4 Dyje r. Austria/Czech Rep.
137 H3 Dykan'ka Ukr.
146 E4 Dyke Moray, Scotland U.K.
146 E5 Dykehead Angus, Scotland U.K.
129 C2 Dykh-Tau, Gora mt. Rus. Fed.
165 D4 Dyle r. Belgium
176 B2 Dyleň hill Czech Rep.
175 J2 Dylewo Pol.
175 H2 Dylewska Góra hill Pol.
129 E2 Dylym Rus. Fed.
151 H3 Dymchurch Kent, England U.K.
136 F2 Dymer Ukr.
150 E3 Dymock Gloucestershire, England U.K.
138 G1 Dymovka r. Rus. Fed.
137 I3 Dymytrov Ukr.
137 G3 Dymytrove Ukr.
142 C1 Dyna mt. Norway
83 F2 Dynevor Downs Qld Austr.
175 K6 Dynów Pol.
160 C2 Dyo France
215 G4 Dyoki S. Africa
Dyrrhachium Albania see Durrës
85 G4 Dysart Qld Austr.
150 D1 Dyserth Denbighshire, Wales U.K.
173 H2 Dyšina Czech Rep.
138 F4 Dysna r. Lith.
138 F4 Dysnų ežeras l. Lith.
214 D5 Dysselsdorp S. Africa
198 B2 Dytiki Ellas admin. reg. Greece
198 B1 Dytiki Makedonia admin. reg. Greece
197 H4 Dyulino Bulg.
129 E3 Dyul'tydag, Gora mt. Rus. Fed.
134 K5 Dyurtyuli Rus. Fed.
136 E5 Dyviziya Ukr.
175 I2 Dywity Pol.
106 D2 Dzaanhushuu Mongolia
106 C2 Dzag Gol r. Mongolia
217 □3b Dzaoudzi Mayotte
Dzaudzhikau Rus. Fed. see Vladikavkaz
106 B1 Dzavhan prov. Mongolia
106 B1 Dzavhan Gol r. Mongolia
176 C1 Džban mts Czech Rep.
106 D2 Dzegstey Mongolia
136 D3 Dzelentsi Ukr.
106 E1 Dzelter Mongolia
Dzerzhinsk Belarus see Dzyarzhynsk
134 H4 Dzerzhinsk Rus. Fed.
Dzerzhinskoye Kazakh. see Kabanbay
137 I3 Dzerzhyns'k Ukr.
136 D2 Dzerzhyns'k Ukr.
100 D1 Dzhagdy, Khrebet mts Rus. Fed.
Dzhaksy Kazakh. see Zhaksy
120 F3 Dzhalagash Kazakh.
Dzhalalabad Azer. see Cälilabad
Dzhalal-Abad Kyrg. see Jalal-Abad
Dzhalal-Abadskaya Oblast' admin. div. Kyrg. see Jalal-Abad
134 K5 Dzhalil' Rus. Fed.
100 B1 Dzhalinda Rus. Fed.
Dzhaltyr Kazakh. see Zhaltyr
Dzhambeyty Zapadnyy Kazakhstan Kazakh. see Zhympity
Dzhambul Zhambylskaya Oblast' Kazakh. see Taraz
Dzhambulskaya Oblast' admin. div. Kazakh. see Zhambylskaya Oblast'
Dzhandari Georgia see Jandari
122 C1 Dzhanga Turkm.
120 B2 Dzhangala Kazakh.
120 E4 Dzhangel'dy Uzbek.
Dzhankel'dy Uzbek. see Dzhangel'dy
137 H5 Dzhankoy Ukr.
121 I3 Dzhansugurov Kazakh.
120 A2 Dzhanybek Kazakh.
Dzhaparidze Georgia see Jap'aridze
Dzharkent Kazakh. see Zharkent
121 F5 Dzharkurgan Uzbek.
131 O3 Dzhebariki-Khaya Rus. Fed.
197 G5 Dzhebel Bulg.
122 C2 Dzhebel Turkm.
Dzhergalan Kyrg. see Jyrgalang
Dzhermuk Armenia see Jermuk
Dzhetygara Kazakh. see Zhitikara
120 F4 Dzhetymtau, Gory hills Uzbek.
Dzhetysay Kazakh. see Zhetysay
120 E5 Dzheykhun Turkm.
Dzhezdy Kazakh. see Zhezdy
Dzhezkazgan Karagandinskaya Oblast' Kazakh. see Zhezkazgan
106 E1 Dzhida Rus. Fed.
106 E1 Dzhida r. Rus. Fed.
106 D1 Dzhidinskiy, Khrebet mts Mongolia/Rus. Fed.
Dzhingil'dy Uzbek. see Dzhangel'dy
Dzhirgatal' Tajik. see Jirgatol
121 F4 Dzhizak Uzbek.
Dzhizak Oblast admin. div. Uzbek. see Dzhizakskaya Oblast'
121 F4 Dzhizakskaya Oblast' admin. div. Uzbek.
Dzhokhar Ghala Rus. Fed. see Groznyy
Dzhordzhiashvili Georgia see Jorjiashvili
135 G7 Dzhubga Rus. Fed.
131 O4 Dzhugdzhur, Khrebet mts Rus. Fed.
Dzhul'fa Azer. see Culfa
136 E3 Dzhulynka Ukr.
121 F5 Dzhuma Uzbek.
121 I3 Dzhungarskiy Alatau, Khrebet mts China/Kazakh.
129 E2 Dzhurmut r. Rus. Fed.
Dzhurun Kazakh. see Zhuryn
136 E3 Dzhuryn Ukr.
120 F3 Dzhusaly Kzyl-Ordinskaya Oblast' Kazakh.
175 K3 Dziadkowice Pol.
174 F4 Dziadowa Kłoda Pol.
175 H2 Działdówka r. Pol.
175 I2 Działdowo Pol.
175 I5 Działoszyce Pol.
174 G4 Działoszyn Pol.
175 H2 Działyń Pol.
243 H5 Dzibalchén Mex.
174 F1 Dziemiany Pol.
174 G5 Dziergowice Pol.
175 I3 Dzierzążnia Pol.
175 H2 Dzierzgoń Pol.
175 I2 Dzierzgowo Pol.
174 E5 Dzierżoniów Pol.
175 J1 Dzietrzychowo Pol.
174 F3 Dziewierzewo Pol.
243 H4 Dzilam de Bravo Mex.
138 G4 Dzisna Belarus
243 H4 Dzitás Mex.
138 E5 Dzitva r. Belarus
136 C2 Dzivin Belarus
174 C2 Dziwna r. Pol.
207 F5 Dzodze Ghana
107 E2 Dzogsool Mongolia
106 C1 Dzöölön Mongolia
129 D3 Dzoraget r. Armenia
Dzungarian Basin China see Junggar Pendi
106 B1 Dzur Mongolia
107 F2 Dzüünbayan Mongolia
106 E2 Dzuunmod Mongolia
106 B2 Dzüyl Mongolia
175 I2 Dźwierzuty Pol.
174 C1 Dzwinów Pol.
175 K5 Dzwola Pol.
175 H5 Dzwonowice Pol.
138 F5 Dzyaniskavichy Belarus
139 I5 Dzyarazhnya r. Belarus
138 F5 Dzyarzhynsk Belarus
138 E5 Dzyatlava Belarus
136 D1 Dzyatlavichy Belarus
138 F4 Dzyerkawshchyna Belarus

E

236 C4 Eads CO U.S.A.
241 M4 Eagar AZ U.S.A.
225 J2 Eagle r. Nfld. Can.
220 D3 Eagle AK U.S.A.
239 F4 Eagle CO U.S.A.
234 C2 Eagle PA U.S.A.
236 C2 Eagle Butte SD U.S.A.
238 C2 Eagle Cap mt. OR U.S.A.
240 I4 Eagle Crags mt. CA U.S.A.
223 J4 Eagle Creek r. Sask. Can.
233 □I1 Eagle Lake ME U.S.A.
241 J5 Eagle Mountain CA U.S.A.
226 B2 Eagle Mountain hill MN U.S.A.
237 C6 Eagle Pass TX U.S.A.
259 F9 Eagle Passage Falkland Is
239 F6 Eagle Peak TX U.S.A.
220 E3 Eagle Plain Y.T. Can.
226 C2 Eagle River MI U.S.A.
226 C3 Eagle River WI U.S.A.
232 D6 Eagle Rock VA U.S.A.
149 H3 Eaglescliffe Stockton-on-Tees, England U.K.
146 E6 Eaglesfield Dumfries and Galloway, Scotland U.K.
222 G4 Eaglesham Alta Can.
146 D6 Eaglesham East Renfrewshire, Scotland U.K.
241 K5 Eagle Tail Mountains AZ U.S.A.
234 C2 Eagleville PA U.S.A.
151 G3 Ealing Greater London, England U.K.
Eap i. Micronesia see Yap
87 D5 Earaheedy W.A. Austr.
149 G4 Earby Lancashire, England U.K.
150 D2 Eardisley Herefordshire, England U.K.
223 M5 Ear Falls Ont. Can.
151 H2 Earith Cambridgeshire, England U.K.
240 H4 Earlimart CA U.S.A.
81 A6 Earl Mountains South I. N.Z.
151 G2 Earls Barton Northamptonshire, England U.K.
151 H3 Earls Colne Essex, England U.K.
151 F2 Earl Shilton Leicestershire, England U.K.
146 D5 Earl's Seat hill Scotland U.K.
146 F6 Earlston Scottish Borders, Scotland U.K.
151 I2 Earl Stonham Suffolk, England U.K.
227 H2 Earlton Ont. Can.
146 E5 Earn r. Scotland U.K.
81 B6 Earnscleugh South I. N.Z.
81 B6 Earnslaw, Mount South I. N.Z.
241 J4 Earp CA U.S.A.
146 A5 Earsairidh Western Isles, Scotland U.K.
237 C5 Earth TX U.S.A.
146 C5 Easdale Argyll and Bute, Scotland U.K.
151 G4 Easebourne West Sussex, England U.K.
149 H3 Easington Durham, England U.K.
149 J4 Easington East Riding of Yorkshire, England U.K.
149 H3 Easingwold North Yorkshire, England U.K.
147 C2 Easky Rep. of Ireland
231 D5 Easley SC U.S.A.
87 D6 East, Mount hill W.A. Austr.
84 C2 East Alligator r. N.T. Austr.
263 H1 East Antarctica reg. Antarctica
233 F4 East Ararat PA U.S.A.
232 D3 East Aurora NY U.S.A.
146 D6 East Ayrshire admin. div. Scotland U.K.
84 B2 East Baines r. N.T. Austr.
234 C2 East Bangor PA U.S.A.
East Bengal country Asia see Bangladesh
151 I3 East Bergholt Suffolk, England U.K.
235 F1 East Berlin CT U.S.A.
234 B3 East Berlin PA U.S.A.
234 B1 East Berwick PA U.S.A.
81 E4 Eastbourne North I. N.Z.
151 H4 Eastbourne East Sussex, England U.K.
232 D4 East Brady PA U.S.A.
233 F4 East Branch NY U.S.A.
151 G2 East Bridgford Nottinghamshire, England U.K.
149 I4 Eastburn East Riding of Yorkshire, England U.K.
246 E2 East Caicos i. Turks and Caicos Is
80 G2 East Cape North I. N.Z.
241 L2 East Carbon City UT U.S.A.
266 E5 East Caroline Basin sea feature N. Pacific Ocean
226 D5 East Chicago IN U.S.A.
99 M5 East China Sea N. Pacific Ocean
80 E2 East Coast Bays North I. N.Z.
150 E4 East Coker Somerset, England U.K.
223 H5 East Coulee Alta Can.
151 H4 East Dean East Sussex, England U.K.
151 H2 East Dereham Norfolk, England U.K.
146 D6 East Dunbartonshire admin. div. Scotland U.K.
223 I5 Eastend Sask. Can.
87 B6 Easter Group is W.A. Austr.
Easter Island S. Pacific Ocean see Pascua, Isla de
206 E5 Eastern admin. reg. Ghana
210 C5 Eastern prov. Kenya
206 C4 Eastern prov. Sierra Leone
211 A8 Eastern prov. Zambia
215 F4 Eastern Cape prov. S. Africa
85 E4 Eastern Creek r. Qld Austr.
Eastern Desert Egypt see Şaḩara el Sharqîya
210 B3 Eastern Equatoria state Sudan
114 C4 Eastern Ghats mts India
Eastern Lesser Sunda Islands prov. Indon. see Nusa Tenggara Timur
Eastern Samoa terr. S. Pacific Ocean see American Samoa
Eastern Sayan Mountains Rus. Fed. see Vostochnyy Sayan
Eastern Taurus plat. Turkey see Güneydoğu Toroslar
Eastern Transvaal prov. S. Africa see Mpumalanga
146 □G1 Easter Quarff Shetland, Scotland U.K.
146 D4 Easter Ross reg. Scotland U.K.
223 L4 Easterville Man. Can.
259 F9 East Falkland i. Falkland Is
233 H4 East Falmouth MA U.S.A.
149 J4 East Fen reg. England U.K.
149 I3 Eastfield North Yorkshire, England U.K.
East Flanders prov. Belgium see Oost-Vlaanderen
East Frisian Islands Ger. see Ostfriesische Inseln
149 G3 Eastgate Durham, England U.K.
240 I2 Eastgate NV U.S.A.
236 D2 East Grand Forks MN U.S.A.
226 E4 East Grand Rapids MI U.S.A.
234 C2 East Greenville PA U.S.A.
151 G3 East Grinstead West Sussex, England U.K.
235 F1 East Haddam CT U.S.A.
235 F1 East Hampton CT U.S.A.
233 G3 Easthampton MA U.S.A.
235 F2 East Hampton NY U.S.A.
151 F3 East Hanney Oxfordshire, England U.K.
151 H2 East Harling Norfolk, England U.K.
235 F1 East Hartford CT U.S.A.
235 F1 East Haven CT U.S.A.
85 E3 East Haydon Qld Austr.
233 □I2 East Holden ME U.S.A.
151 G3 East Horsley Surrey, England U.K.
150 E3 East Huntspill Somerset, England U.K.
265 K6 East Indiaman Ridge sea feature Indian Ocean
233 G3 East Jamaica VT U.S.A.
226 E3 East Jordan MI U.S.A.
East Kazakhstan Oblast admin. div. Kazakh. see Vostochnyy Kazakhstan
149 J4 East Keal Lincolnshire, England U.K.
146 D6 East Kilbride South Lanarkshire, Scotland U.K.
226 D3 East Lake MI U.S.A.
237 D5 Eastland TX U.S.A.
226 E4 East Lansing MI U.S.A.
151 F4 Eastleigh Hampshire, England U.K.
232 B4 East Liberty OH U.S.A.
146 F6 East Linton East Lothian, Scotland U.K.
235 E1 East Litchfield CT U.S.A.
232 C4 East Liverpool OH U.S.A.
146 B3 East Loch Roag inlet Scotland U.K.
146 B4 East Loch Tarbert inlet Scotland U.K.
215 F5 East London S. Africa
233 G3 East Longmeadow MA U.S.A.
150 C4 East Looe Cornwall, England U.K.
146 F6 East Lothian admin. div. Scotland U.K.
235 F1 East Lyme CT U.S.A.
224 E2 Eastmain Que. Can.
224 E2 Eastmain r. Que. Can.
151 H3 East Malling Kent, England U.K.
233 G2 Eastman Que. Can.
231 D5 Eastman GA U.S.A.
266 F5 East Mariana Basin sea feature Pacific Ocean
149 I4 East Markham Nottinghamshire, England U.K.
85 F4 Eastmere Qld Austr.
233 G3 East Middlebury VT U.S.A.
151 F2 East Midlands airport England U.K.
233 □I2 East Millinocket ME U.S.A.
235 E1 East Morris CT U.S.A.
231 D7 East Naples FL U.S.A.
235 E2 East Northport NY U.S.A.
149 I4 Eastoft North Lincolnshire, England U.K.
150 E4 Easton Dorset, England U.K.
240 H3 Easton CA U.S.A.
235 E1 Easton CT U.S.A.
233 E5 Easton MD U.S.A.
234 C2 Easton PA U.S.A.
150 E3 Easton-in-Gordano North Somerset, England U.K.
235 D2 East Orange NJ U.S.A.
267 L8 East Pacific Ridge S. Pacific Ocean
267 L4 East Pacific Rise sea feature N. Pacific Ocean
East Pakistan country Asia see Bangladesh
232 C4 East Palestine OH U.S.A.
226 C5 East Peoria IL U.S.A.
234 B2 East Petersburg PA U.S.A.
233 □J2 Eastport ME U.S.A.
226 E3 Eastport MI U.S.A.
235 F2 Eastport NY U.S.A.
151 G4 East Preston West Sussex, England U.K.
234 B3 East Prospect PA U.S.A.
235 F2 East Quogue NY U.S.A.
240 I1 East Range mts NV U.S.A.
146 D6 East Renfrewshire admin. div. Scotland U.K.
East Retford Nottinghamshire, England U.K. see Retford
231 C5 East Ridge TN U.S.A.
149 I4 East Riding of Yorkshire admin. div. England U.K.
146 E7 Eastriggs Dumfries and Galloway, Scotland U.K.
151 I3 Eastry Kent, England U.K.
230 B4 East St Louis IL U.S.A.
East Sea N. Pacific Ocean see Japan, Sea of
235 E2 East Setauket NY U.S.A.
234 C1 East Side PA U.S.A.
240 H4 East Side Canal r. CA U.S.A.
83 G4 East Sister Island Tas. Austr.
234 C1 East Stroudsburg PA U.S.A.
151 H4 East Sussex admin. div. England U.K.
232 B2 East Tawas MI U.S.A.
93 C5 East Timor terr. Asia
117 F4 East Tons r. India
83 F2 East Toorale N.S.W. Austr.
226 C4 East Troy WI U.S.A.
241 L4 East Verde r. AZ U.S.A.
Eastview Ont. Can. see Vanier
233 F6 Eastville VA U.S.A.
240 H2 East Walker r. NV U.S.A.
151 G4 East Wittering West Sussex, England U.K.
149 H4 Eastwood Nottinghamshire, England U.K.
151 F3 East Woodhay Hampshire, England U.K.
227 H4 East York Ont. Can.
87 B7 Eaton W.A. Austr.
238 F3 Eaton CO U.S.A.
230 C4 Eaton OH U.S.A.
151 G3 Eaton Bray Bedfordshire, England U.K.
223 I5 Eatonia Sask. Can.
226 E4 Eaton Rapids MI U.S.A.
235 E2 Eatons Neck NY U.S.A.
151 G2 Eaton Socon Cambridgeshire, England U.K.
231 D5 Eatonton GA U.S.A.
235 D2 Eatontown NJ U.S.A.
233 □I1 Eatonville Que. Can.
238 B2 Eatonville WA U.S.A.
226 B3 Eau Claire WI U.S.A.
226 B3 Eau Claire r. WI U.S.A.
156 B3 Eaulne r. France
163 D5 Eaunes France
91 J5 Eauripik atoll Micronesia
266 E5 Eauripik Rise-New Guinea Rise sea feature N. Pacific Ocean
Eaurypyg atoll Micronesia see Eauripik
163 B6 Eaux-Bonnes France
163 C5 Eauze France
78 □3a Ebadon i. Kwajalein Marshall Is
85 E2 Ebagoola Qld Austr.
207 G4 Eban Nigeria
245 E2 Ebano Mex.
178 D3 Ebbs Austria
150 D3 Ebbw Vale Blaenau Gwent, Wales U.K.
207 H6 Ebebiyin Equat. Guinea
169 F4 Ebeleben Ger.
142 D3 Ebeltoft Denmark
178 C3 Eben am Achensee Austria
215 G5 Ebende S. Africa
179 E4 Ebene Reichenau Austria
179 H3 Ebenfurth Austria
179 E3 Eben im Pongau Austria
232 D4 Ebensburg PA U.S.A.
179 E3 Ebensee Austria
169 F5 Ebensfeld Ger.
179 F4 Ebenthal Austria
172 D4 Ebenweiler Ger.
179 H3 Eberau Austria
172 C2 Eberbach Ger.
169 F4 Ebergötzen Ger.
172 D3 Eberhardzell Ger.
173 F2 Ebermannsdorf Ger.
173 F2 Ebermannstadt Ger.
169 F5 Ebern Ger.
179 F4 Eberndorf Austria
171 E4 Ebersbach Sachsen Ger.
171 F4 Ebersbach Sachsen Ger.
172 D3 Ebersbach an der Fils Ger.
173 F3 Ebersberg Ger.
179 E2 Eberschwang Austria
179 G3 Ebersdorf Austria
168 E2 Ebersdorf Niedersachsen Ger.
171 C5 Ebersdorf Thüringen Ger.
157 H4 Ebersmunster France
179 F4 Eberstein Austria
170 E3 Eberswalde-Finow Ger.
234 C2 Ebervale PA U.S.A.
177 K4 Ebes Hungary
102 J2 Ebetsu Japan
78 □3a Ebeye Kwajalein Marshall Is
172 C3 Ebhausen Ger.
108 B2 Ebian Sichuan China
190 D1 Ebikon Switz.
105 F3 Ebina Japan
103 E7 Ebino Japan
Ebi Nor salt l. China see Ebinur Hu
110 C2 Ebinur Hu salt l. China
128 C2 Ebla tourist site Syria
190 E1 Ebnat-Kappel Switz.
209 B7 Ebo Angola
208 D4 Ebola r. Dem. Rep. Congo
193 H4 Eboli Italy
207 H6 Ebolowa Cameroon
207 H5 Ebonyi state Nigeria
173 E2 Ebrach Ger.
Ebre r. Spain see Ebro
179 H3 Ebreichsdorf Austria
160 B2 Ébreuil France
183 H3 Ebrillos r. Spain
172 B4 Ebringen Ger.
183 I4 Ebro r. Spain
183 G1 Ebro, Embalse del resr Spain
187 B4 Ebrón r. Spain
169 D5 Ebsdorfergrund-Dreihausen Ger.
169 D5 Ebsdorfergrund-Rauischholzhausen Ger.
168 F2 Ebstorf Ger.
Eburacum York, England U.K. see York
Eburodunum France see Embrun
Ebusus i. Spain see Eivissa
245 E4 Ecatepec Mex.
165 D4 Écaussinnes-d'Enghien Belgium
Ecbatana Iran see Hamadān
146 E6 Ecclefechan Dumfries and Galloway, Scotland U.K.
149 G4 Eccles Greater Manchester, England U.K.
146 F6 Eccles Scottish Borders, Scotland U.K.
232 C6 Eccles WV U.S.A.
149 H4 Ecclesfield South Yorkshire, England U.K.
150 E2 Eccleshall Staffordshire, England U.K.
149 G4 Eccleston Lancashire, England U.K.
199 E1 Eceabat Turkey
92 B2 Echague Phil.
190 B2 Echallens Switz.
246 B5 Echandi, Cerro mt. Costa Rica
183 I2 Echarri Spain
183 H2 Echarri-Aranaz Spain
159 G3 Échauffour France
205 F1 Ech Chélif Alg.
Echeng Hubei China see Ezhou
160 E1 Échenoz-la-Méline France
242 B2 Echeverria, Pico mt. Mex.
162 B3 Échillais France
198 B2 Echinades i. Greece
173 F3 Eching Bayern Ger.
173 G3 Eching Bayern Ger.
198 D1 Echinos Greece
162 B2 Échiré France
161 D3 Échirolles France
105 E3 Echizen-dake mt. Japan
Echmiadzin Armenia see Ejmiatsin
238 C2 Echo OR U.S.A.
83 F5 Echo, Lake Tas. Austr.
220 G3 Echo Bay N.W.T. Can.
224 C4 Echo Bay Ont. Can.
241 L3 Echo Cliffs esc. AZ U.S.A.
223 M4 Echoing r. Man./Ont. Can.
162 C3 Échourgnac France
179 G2 Echsenbach Austria
165 E3 Echt Neth.
146 F4 Echt Aberdeenshire, Scotland U.K.
169 F4 Echte Ger.
165 F5 Echternach Lux.
83 F4 Echuca Vic. Austr.
169 D5 Echzell Ger.
185 E3 Écija Spain
261 I4 Ecilda Paullier Uru.
148 E1 Eck, Loch l. Scotland U.K.
196 E3 Ečka Vojvodina, Srbija Yugo.
171 C4 Eckartsberga Ger.
157 H4 Eckbolsheim France
173 F2 Eckental Ger.
226 E2 Eckerman MI U.S.A.
168 E1 Eckernförde Ger.
141 L3 Eckerö Åland Fin.
173 F2 Eckersdorf Ger.
146 F6 Eckford Scottish Borders, Scotland U.K.
149 H4 Eckington Derbyshire, England U.K.
150 E2 Eckington Worcestershire, England U.K.
232 C6 Eckman WV U.S.A.
222 H4 Eckville Alta Can.
168 D2 Eckwarden (Butjadingen) Ger.
157 E4 Éclaron-Braucourt-Ste-Livière France
159 G4 Écommoy France
257 G3 Ecoporanga Brazil
156 B3 Écos France
159 F3 Écouché France
159 F4 Écouflant France
156 B3 Écouis France
157 F4 Écrouves France
177 G4 Écs Hungary
177 I4 Ecséd Hungary
177 I4 Ecseg Hungary
177 J4 Ecsegfalva Hungary
177 I4 Ecser Hungary
250 B5 Ecuador country S. America
162 D1 Écueillé France
160 C2 Écuisses France
156 E4 Écury-sur-Coole France
203 I6 Ed Eritrea
142 D2 Ed Sweden
223 I4 Edam Sask. Can.
164 E2 Edam Neth.
146 F2 Eday i. Scotland U.K.
203 F6 Ed Dair, Jebel mt. Sudan
210 B2 Ed Damazin Sudan
203 G5 Ed Damer Sudan
203 F5 Ed Debba Sudan
168 E2 Eddelak Ger.
171 C4 Edderitz Ger.
146 D4 Edderton Highland, Scotland U.K.
225 J3 Eddies Cove Nfld. Can.
203 G6 Ed Dueim Sudan
83 G5 Eddystone Point Tas. Austr.
237 F4 Eddyville KY U.S.A.
164 E2 Ede Neth.
207 G5 Ede Nigeria
207 H6 Edéa Cameroon
165 D3 Edegem Belgium
256 C2 Edéia Brazil
177 J3 Edelény Hungary
179 G3 Edelschrott Austria
169 F3 Edemissen Ger.
83 G4 Eden N.S.W. Austr.
148 D3 Eden Northern Ireland U.K.
149 F3 Eden r. England U.K.
232 D6 Eden NC U.S.A.
237 D6 Eden TX U.S.A.
238 E3 Eden WY U.S.A.
151 H3 Edenbridge Kent, England U.K.
215 E3 Edenburg S. Africa
81 B7 Edendale South I. N.Z.
215 H3 Edendale S. Africa
147 D3 Edenderry Rep. of Ireland
149 G4 Edenfield Lancashire, England U.K.
82 E4 Edenhope Vic. Austr.
172 C2 Edenkoben Ger.
226 A3 Eden Prairie MN U.S.A.
231 E4 Edenton NC U.S.A.
215 G2 Edenvale S. Africa
215 F2 Edenville S. Africa
169 E4 Eder r. Ger.
169 E4 Edermünde Ger.
147 D2 Ederny Northern Ireland U.K.
198 C1 Edessa Greece
Edessa Turkey see Şanlıurfa
140 K3 Edevik Sweden
168 C2 Edewecht Ger.
168 C2 Edewechterdamm Ger.
Edfu Egypt see Idfu
236 D3 Edgar NE U.S.A.
86 D4 Edgar, Mount hill W.A. Austr.
86 D3 Edgar Ranges hills W.A. Austr.
233 H4 Edgartown MA U.S.A.
80 F2 Edgecumbe North I. N.Z.
80 F3 Edgecumbe, Mount hill North I. N.Z.
Edgecumbe Island Solomon Is see Utupua
231 D5 Edgefield SC U.S.A.
Edge Island Svalbard see Edgeøya
236 D2 Edgeley ND U.S.A.
234 B3 Edgemere MD U.S.A.
236 C3 Edgemont SD U.S.A.
140 □ Edgeøya i. Svalbard
223 I4 Edgerton Alta Can.
232 A4 Edgerton OH U.S.A.
232 E6 Edgerton VA U.S.A.
226 C4 Edgerton WI U.S.A.
222 G5 Edgewood B.C. Can.
234 B3 Edgewood MD U.S.A.
234 B2 Edgewood PA U.S.A.
147 D3 Edgeworthstown Rep. of Ireland
78 □3a Edgigen i. Kwajalein Marshall Is
150 E2 Edgmond Telford and Wrekin, England U.K.
Édhessa Greece see Edessa
81 B6 Edievale South I. N.Z.
169 C5 Ediger-Eller Ger.
129 C3 Edik'ilisa Georgia
236 E3 Edina MO U.S.A.
232 C4 Edinboro PA U.S.A.
237 D7 Edinburg TX U.S.A.
232 D5 Edinburg VA U.S.A.
146 E6 Edinburgh Edinburgh, Scotland U.K.
146 E6 Edinburgh admin. div. Scotland U.K.
199 E1 Edincik Turkey
136 D3 Edineţ Moldova
172 C2 Edingen-Neckarhausen Ger.
126 B2 Edirne Turkey
199 E1 Edirne prov. Turkey
234 C2 Edison PA U.S.A.
129 D1 Edissiya Rus. Fed.
231 D5 Edisto r. SC U.S.A.
238 E2 Edith, Mount MT U.S.A.
82 D3 Edithburgh S.A. Austr.
222 G4 Edith Cavell, Mount Alta Can.
87 D5 Edith Withnell, Lake salt flat W.A. Austr.
87 D6 Edjudina W.A. Austr.
173 G3 Edling Ger.
149 H2 Edlingham Northumberland, England U.K.
179 H3 Edlitz Austria
237 D5 Edmond OK U.S.A.
238 B2 Edmonds WA U.S.A.
147 C3 Edmondstown Rep. of Ireland
85 F3 Edmonton Qld Austr.
222 H4 Edmonton Alta Can.
230 C4 Edmonton KY U.S.A.
226 E4 Edmore MI U.S.A.
236 D1 Edmore ND U.S.A.
149 H3 Edmundbyres Durham, England U.K.
225 G4 Edmundston N.B. Can.
237 D6 Edna TX U.S.A.
222 C4 Edna Bay AK U.S.A.
Edo Japan see Tōkyō
207 G5 Edo state Nigeria
105 F3 Edo-gawa r. Japan
190 F2 Edolo Italy
128 B4 Edom reg. Israel/Jordan
199 E2 Edremit Turkey
199 E2 Edremit Körfezi b. Turkey
106 C2 Edrengiyn Nuruu mts Mongolia
182 D3 Edrosa Port.
182 D3 Edroso Port.
143 H2 Edsbro Sweden
143 G2 Edsbruk Sweden
141 K3 Edsbyn Sweden
140 L3 Edsele Sweden
222 G4 Edson Alta Can.
260 E4 Eduardo Castex Arg.
222 D1 Eduni, Mount N.W.T. Can.
83 F3 Edward r. N.S.W. Austr.
85 E2 Edward r. Qld Austr.
208 F5 Edward, Lake Dem. Rep. Congo/Uganda
262 T1 Edward, Mount Antarctica
86 F4 Edward, Mount N.T. Austr.
Edwardesabad Pak. see Bannu
84 C2 Edward Island N.T. Austr.
233 F2 Edwards NY U.S.A.
237 C6 Edwards Plateau TX U.S.A.
236 F4 Edwardsville IL U.S.A.
262 N1 Edward VII Peninsula Antarctica
149 H4 Edwinstowe Nottinghamshire, England U.K.
222 D3 Edziza, Mount B.C. Can.
Edzo N.W.T. Can. see Rae-Edzo
164 F2 Eefde Neth.
165 C3 Eeklo Belgium
240 E1 Eel r. CA U.S.A.
240 F1 Eel, South Fork r. CA U.S.A.
164 F1 Eelde-Paterswolde Neth.
164 E2 Eem r. Neth.
164 E2 Eemnes Neth.
214 B5 Eendekuil S. Africa
164 F1 Eenrum Neth.
164 F2 Eerbeek Neth.
165 C3 Eernegem Belgium
165 E3 Eersel Neth.
Eesti country Europe see Estonia
78 □5 Éfaté i. Vanuatu
179 F2 Eferding Austria
Efes tourist site Turkey see Ephesus
173 F2 Effeltrich Ger.
226 A2 Effie MN U.S.A.
151 G3 Effingham Surrey, England U.K.
236 F4 Effingham IL U.S.A.
234 C2 Effort PA U.S.A.
190 D1 Effretikon Switz.
126 D2 Eflâni Turkey
172 B4 Efringen-Kirchen Ger.
Efsus Turkey see Afşin
197 F3 Eftimie Murgu Romania
107 F1 Eg Mongolia
183 I2 Ega r. Spain
241 J2 Egan Range mts NV U.S.A.
227 I3 Eganville Ont. Can.
187 C6 Egea hill Spain
Egedesminde Greenland see Aasiaat
171 C4 Egeln Ger.
173 F3 Egenhofen Ger.
171 D5 Eger r. Ger.
173 E3 Eger r. Ger.
177 J4 Eger Hungary
177 J4 Egerbakta Hungary
177 J3 Egercsehi Hungary
168 E1 Egernsund Denmark
142 B2 Egersund Norway
87 C5 Egerton, Mount hill W.A. Austr.
176 F5 Egervár Hungary
168 F2 Egestorf Ger.
178 A3 Egg Austria
168 E1 Eggebek Ger.
142 C2 Eggedøla r. Norway
169 D4 Eggegebirge hills Ger.
179 G2 Eggenburg Austria
173 G3 Eggenfelden Ger.
172 C2 Eggenstein-Leopoldshafen Ger.
168 C3 Eggermühlen Ger.
171 C4 Eggersdorf Ger.
179 G3 Eggersdorf bei Graz Austria
170 E3 Eggersdorf bei Strausberg Ger.
170 F2 Eggesin Ger.
226 D3 Egg Harbor WI U.S.A.
234 D3 Egg Harbor City NJ U.S.A.
172 C4 Eggingen Ger.
190 C2 Eggiwil Switz.
173 H3 Egglham Ger.
173 F2 Eggolsheim Ger.
173 G4 Eggstätt Ger.
151 G3 Egham Surrey, England U.K.
165 D4 Eghezée Belgium
Egiarreta Spain see Eguiarreta
146 F2 Egilsay i. Scotland U.K.
140 □D2 Egilsstaðir Iceland
Eğin Turkey see Kemaliye
86 C4 Eginbah W.A. Austr.
Egindibulaq Kazakh. see Yegindybulak
173 H3 Eging am See Ger.
199 G3 Eğirdir Turkey
199 G3 Eğirdir Gölü l. Turkey
106 D1 Egiyn Gol r. Mongolia
162 E3 Égletons France
173 F4 Egling Ger.
173 E3 Egling an der Paar Ger.
149 H2 Eglingham Northumberland, England U.K.
147 D1 Eglinton Northern Ireland U.K.
172 C4 Eglisau Switz.
148 C3 Eglish Northern Ireland U.K.
173 F2 Egloffstein Ger.
150 D2 Eglwys Fach Ceredigion, Wales U.K.
150 C2 Eglwyswrw Pembrokeshire, Wales U.K.
164 D2 Egmond aan Zee Neth.
164 D2 Egmond-Binnen Neth.
80 D3 Egmont, Cape North I. N.Z.
Egmont, Mount vol. North I. N.Z. see Taranaki, Mount
80 E3 Egmont Village North I. N.Z.
191 G2 Egna Italy
149 F3 Egremont Cumbria, England U.K.
199 F2 Eğrigöz Dağı mts Turkey
156 D4 Égriselles-le-Bocage France
149 I3 Egton North Yorkshire, England U.K.
142 C4 Egtved Denmark
254 D5 Éguas r. Brazil
183 I2 Eguiarreta Spain
161 D5 Éguilles France
156 E4 Éguilly-sous-Bois France
157 H4 Eguisheim France
162 D2 Éguzon-Chantôme France
131 T3 Egvekinot Rus. Fed.
177 J4 Egyek Hungary
179 H3 Egyházasfalu Hungary
177 H5 Egyházaskozár Hungary
176 F4 Egyházasrádóc Hungary
203 F2 Egypt country Africa
234 C2 Egypt PA U.S.A.
173 E2 Ehebach r. Ger.
173 F3 Ehekirchen Ger.
106 D4 Ehen Hudag Nei Mongol China
103 F7 Ehime pref. Japan
173 E2 Ehingen Ger.
172 D3 Ehingen (Donau) Ger.
171 C3 Ehle r. Ger.
169 E4 Ehlen (Habichtswald) Ger.
172 C3 Ehningen Ger.
168 F3 Ehra-Lessien Ger.
241 J5 Ehrenberg AZ U.S.A.
84 B4 Ehrenberg Range hills N.T. Austr.
169 F5 Ehrenberg-Wüstensachsen Ger.
168 D3 Ehrenburg Ger.
179 G4 Ehrenhausen Austria
169 D5 Ehringshausen Ger.
178 B3 Ehrwald Austria
79 □3 Eiao i. Fr. Polynesia
183 H1 Eibar Spain
173 E2 Eibelstadt Ger.
171 D5 Eibenstock Ger.
164 F2 Eibergen Neth.
179 G4 Eibiswald Austria
172 C2 Eich Ger.
173 F3 Eichenau Ger.
171 C3 Eichenbarleben Ger.
169 E5 Eichenberg hill Ger.
172 D2 Eichenbühl Ger.
173 G3 Eichendorf Ger.
169 E5 Eichenzell Ger.
179 G2 Eichgraben Austria
171 D5 Eichigt Ger.
173 F3 Eichstätt Ger.
172 B3 Eichstetten Ger.
171 E3 Eichwalde Ger.
171 C4 Eickendorf Ger.
168 F3 Eicklingen Ger.
140 I3 Eide Norway
168 D1 Eider r. Ger.
142 B1 Eidfjord Norway
140 J3 Eidsvåg Norway
85 G5 Eidsvold Qld Austr.
142 D1 Eidsvoll Norway
140 □ Eidsvollfjellet mt. Svalbard
169 B5 Eifel hills Ger.
172 C4 Eigeltingen Ger.
190 D2 Eiger mt. Switz.
142 A2 Eigerøya i. Norway
146 B5 Eigg i. Scotland U.K.
146 B5 Eigg, Sound of sea chan. Scotland U.K.
114 B5 Eight Degree Channel India/Maldives
262 R2 Eights Coast Antarctica
86 D3 Eighty Mile Beach W.A. Austr.
165 E4 Eijsden Neth.
142 A1 Eikelandsosen Norway
142 B2 Eiken Norway
146 C5 Eil, Loch inlet Scotland U.K.
Eilat Israel see Elat
83 F4 Eildon Vic. Austr.
83 F4 Eildon, Lake Vic. Austr.
171 D4 Eilenburg Ger.
171 C4 Eilenstedt Ger.
251 G4 Eilerts de Haan Gebergte mts Suriname
92 □ Eil Malk i. Palau
171 C3 Eilsleben Ger.
169 E3 Eime Ger.
169 E4 Eimen Ger.
Eimeo i. Fr. Polynesia see Moorea
168 F3 Eimke Ger.
146 B3 Einacleit Western Isles, Scotland U.K.
85 F3 Einasleigh Qld Austr.
85 E3 Einasleigh r. Qld Austr.
169 E4 Einbeck Ger.
165 E3 Eindhoven Neth.
171 C4 Eine r. Ger.
172 C2 Einhausen Ger.
146 D4 Einig r. Scotland U.K.
171 D5 Einsiedel Ger.
190 D1 Einsiedeln Switz.
157 G4 Einville-au-Jard France
Éire country Europe see Ireland, Republic of
264 G2 Eirik Ridge sea feature N. Atlantic Ocean
Eiriosgaigh i. Scotland U.K. see Eriskay
250 D6 Eiru r. Brazil
250 D6 Eirunepé Brazil
169 E4 Eisberg hill Ger.
165 F5 Eisch r. Lux.
165 E4 Eisden Belgium
169 F4 Eisdorf Ger.
173 G3 Eiselfing Ger.
169 F5 Eisenach Ger.
172 C4 Eisenbach (Hochschwarzwald) Ger.
171 C5 Eisenberg Ger.
172 C2 Eisenberg (Pfalz) Ger.
179 F3 Eisenerz Austria
Eisenhower, Mount Alta Can. see Castle Mountain
179 E4 Eisenhut mt. Austria
171 F3 Eisenhüttenstadt Ger.
179 F4 Eisenkappel Austria
179 H3 Eisenstadt Austria
169 F5 Eisfeld Ger.
146 C4 Eishort, Loch inlet Scotland U.K.
138 E4 Eišiškės Lith.
171 C4 Eisleben Lutherstadt Ger.
172 D3 Eislingen (Fils) Ger.
80 E2 Eistow North I. N.Z.
173 F3 Eitensheim Ger.
169 E5 Eiterfeld Ger.
169 C5 Eitorf Ger.
169 E3 Eitzum (Despetal) Ger.
141 I3 Eivinvik Norway
187 E6 Eivissa Spain
187 E5 Eivissa i. Spain
182 C2 Eixe, Serra do mts Spain
182 B4 Eixo Port.
182 B3 Eja Port.
186 B2 Ejea de los Caballeros Spain
213 □J5 Ejeda Madag.

Column 1

Ejin Horo Qi *Nei Mongol* China see Altan Shiret
Ejin Horo Qi *Nei Mongol* China see Dalain Hob
Ejmiadzin Armenia see Ejmiatsin
129 D3 Ejmiatsin Armenia
186 C4 Ejulve Spain
206 E5 Ejura Ghana
238 F2 Ekalaka *MT* U.S.A.
207 H5 Ekang Nigeria
215 G1 Ekangala S. Africa
141 N4 Ekenäs Fin.
142 E2 Ekenäs Sweden
165 D3 Ekeren Belgium
143 G2 Ekerö Sweden
207 G5 Eket Nigeria
80 E4 Eketahuna *North I.* N.Z.
Ekhinos Greece see Echinos
Ekhmim Egypt see Akhmim
121 H2 Ekibastuz Kazakh.
100 E1 Ekimchan Rus. Fed.
128 D1 Ekinyazı Turkey
207 G5 Ekiti *state* Nigeria
207 H5 Ekondo Titi Cameroon
140 F2 Ekostrovskaya Imandra, Ozero *l.* Rus. Fed.
207 G5 Ekpoma Nigeria
165 C3 Eksaarde Belgium
165 E3 Eksel Belgium
Eksere Turkey see Gündoğmuş
142 E1 Ekshärad Sweden
199 G3 Ekşili Turkey
143 F3 Eksjö Sweden
214 A3 Eksteenfontein S. Africa
140 L2 Ekträsk Sweden
224 D2 Ekwan *r.* Ont. Can.
96 B3 Ela Myanmar
El Aaiún Western Sahara see Laâyoune
244 C4 El Aguaje Mex.
198 D1 Elaiochori *Anatoliki Makedonia kai Thraki* Greece
187 F2 El Algar Spain
189 B7 El Alia Tunisia
184 C3 El Almendro Spain
185 H4 El Alquián Spain
220 A6 El Alto Peru
126 C5 El 'Amiriya Egypt
156 B4 Elancourt France
215 H1 Elands *r.* S. Africa
213 F5 Elands *r.* S. Africa
215 F5 Elandsberg *mt.* S. Africa
215 G1 Elandsdoorn S. Africa
215 E5 Elandsdrif S. Africa
215 H3 Elandskraal S. Africa
215 G3 Elandslaagte S. Africa
215 F1 Elandsputte S. Africa
150 D2 Elan Village *Powys, Wales* U.K.
Elar Armenia see Abovyan
184 E3 El Arahal Spain
El Araïche Morocco see Larache
242 B2 El Arco Mex.
183 E4 El Arenal *Castilla y León* Spain
El Arenal *Islas Baleares* Spain see S'Arenal
85 F3 El Arish *Qld* Austr.
203 G2 El 'Arish Egypt
205 G1 El Arrouch Alg.
203 F3 El Ashmûnein Egypt
198 C2 El Asnam Alg. see Ech Chélif
128 B5 El Astillero Spain
128 C5 Elat Israel
204 B5 El 'Aṭf *reg.* Western Sahara
198 B2 Elati *mt. Ionioi Nisoi* Greece
91 K5 Elato *atoll* Micronesia
126 E3 Elazığ Turkey
129 A4 Elazığ *prov.* Turkey
231 C6 Elba *AL* U.S.A.
192 C2 Elba, Isola d' *i.* Italy
128 A5 El Bahr El Ahmar *governorate* Egypt
185 H2 El Ballestero Spain
203 F3 El Balyana Egypt
100 F2 El'ban Rus. Fed.
250 C2 El Banco Col.
182 E4 El Barco de Ávila Spain
El Barco de Valdeorras Spain see O Barco
183 F4 El Barraco Spain
242 D2 El Barreal *salt l.* Mex.
244 C2 El Barril Mex.
196 E5 Elbasan Albania
126 D3 Elbaşı Turkey
205 F2 El Bayadh Alg.
168 E2 Elbe *r.* Ger. *alt.* Labe (Czech Rep.)
238 B2 Elbe *WA* U.S.A.
206 C2 'Elb el Fçâl *des.* Maur.
260 B3 El Bellota *airport Valparaíso* Chile
169 C3 Elbergen Ger.
183 G4 El Berrueco Spain
226 D3 Elberta *MI* U.S.A.
241 L2 Elberta *UT* U.S.A.
231 D5 Elberton *GA* U.S.A.
156 B3 Elbeuf France
128 C1 Elbeyli Turkey
244 D4 El Billete, Cerro *mt.* Mex.
Elbing Pol. see Elbląg
169 F4 Elbingerode (Harz) Ger.
126 E3 Elbistan Turkey
163 J3 Elbląg Pol.
242 □J6 El Bluff Nic.
182 D4 El Bodón Spain
El Bollo Spain see O Bolo
259 C6 El Bolsón Arg.
185 H2 El Bonillo Spain
185 E4 El Bosque Spain
El Boulaida Alg. see Blida
223 J5 Elbow *Sask.* Can.
231 E7 Elbow Cay *i.* Bahamas
236 D2 Elbow Lake *MN* U.S.A.
129 C2 El'brus Rus. Fed.
129 C2 Elbrus *mt.* Rus. Fed.
208 F3 El Buheyrat *state* Sudan
185 I2 El Buitre *mt.* Spain
185 F1 El Bullaque Spain
164 F3 Elburg Neth.
185 H4 El Burgo Spain
183 H2 Elburgo Spain
186 C3 El Burgo de Ebro Spain
183 G3 El Burgo de Osma Spain
183 E2 El Burgo Ranero Spain
Elburz Mountains Iran see Alborz, Reshteh-ye
183 I3 El Buste Spain
137 J4 El'buzd *r.* Rus. Fed.
182 D4 El Cabaco Spain
185 I3 El Cabildo y la Campana Spain
185 H4 El Cabo de Gata Spain
240 I5 El Cajon *CA* U.S.A.
251 F3 El Callao Venez.
El Caló Spain see Es Caló
245 D5 El Camotal, Sierra *mts* Mex.
183 E5 El Campillo de la Jara Spain
El Campo Spain see Campo Lugar
237 D6 El Campo *TX* U.S.A.
183 I4 El Campo de Peñaranda Spain
183 H5 El Cañavate Spain
237 C7 El Capulín *r.* Mex.
258 E2 El Carmen Bol.
252 E3 El Carmen Bol.
260 B5 El Carmen Chile
250 C3 El Carmen Ecuador
187 G2 El Caroche *mt.* Spain
185 F3 El Carpio Spain
183 F5 El Carpio de Tajo Spain
183 G4 El Casar Spain
183 F4 El Casar de Escalona Spain
187 C4 El Castellar Spain
184 D3 El Castillo de las Guardas Spain
243 G6 El Cebú, Cerro *mt.* Mex.
185 G2 El Centenillo Spain
241 J5 El Centro *CA* U.S.A.
253 E4 El Cerro Bol.
184 D3 El Cerro de Andévalo Spain
187 C6 El Cerro de la Sierra Spain
242 G3 El Chichonal *vol.* Mex.
84 C1 Elcho Island *N.T.* Austr.
183 H2 Elciego Spain

Column 2

El Coca Ecuador see Puerto Francisco de Orellana
185 F2 El Collado *hill* Spain
184 E3 El Conejo, Sierra *mts* Mex.
186 F3 El Congost *r.* Spain
184 E3 El Coronil Spain
245 G5 El Corte *r.* Mex.
246 B2 El Cotorro Cuba
245 G6 El Coyol Mex.
182 D4 El Cubo de Don Sancho Spain
182 E3 El Cubo de Tierra del Vino Spain
184 E2 El Cuervo Spain
187 C6 Elda Spain
210 B4 Eldama Ravine Kenya
170 C2 Elde *r.* Ger.
227 H2 Eldee Ont. Can.
226 C5 Eldena Ger.
226 C3 Eldena *IL* U.S.A.
140 □C3 Eldhraun *lava field* Iceland
250 C2 El Difícil Col.
131 O3 El'dikan Rus. Fed.
168 F3 Eldingen Ger.
El Djezaïr Alg. see Alger
236 E4 Eldon *MO* U.S.A.
234 D2 Eldora *NJ* U.S.A.
258 G2 Eldorado Brazil
242 D3 El Dorado Mex.
237 E5 El Dorado *AR* U.S.A.
237 D4 El Dorado *KS* U.S.A.
237 D4 Eldorado *TX* U.S.A.
241 J4 Eldorado Mountains *NV* U.S.A.
232 C5 Eleanor *WV* U.S.A.
241 J2 Electric Peak *MT* U.S.A.
198 C2 Elefsina Greece
232 D5 El Eglab *plat.* Alg.
138 D3 Eleja Latvia
185 H4 El Ejido Spain
177 K5 Elek *r.* Rus. Fed. see Ilek
234 C3 Elek Hungary
139 L4 Elektrénai Lith.
139 L4 Elektrogorsk Rus. Fed.
139 L4 Elektrostal' Rus. Fed.
207 G5 Elele Nigeria
210 B3 Elemi Triangle *terr.* Africa
197 G4 Elena Bulg.
169 F4 Elend Ger.
198 B2 Eleousa *Ipeiros* Greece
114 B2 Elephanta Caves *tourist site Mahar.* India
239 F5 Elephant Butte Reservoir *NM* U.S.A.
262 U2 Elephant Island Antarctica
183 H4 El Escorial Spain
197 F5 Eleshnitsa Bulg.
127 F3 Eleşkirt Turkey
187 F3 El Espinar Spain
188 H6 El Estor Guat.
187 C7 El Estrecho Spain
246 C1 El Estrecho *r.* Bahamas
226 B3 Eleva *WI* U.S.A.
171 F5 Elevtheroupoli Greece
221 H2 Elef Ringnes Island *Nunavut* Can.
128 C1 Elek Turkey
87 C7 Elleker *W.A.* Austr.
116 C3 Ellenabad *Haryana* India
173 E2 Ellenberg Ger.
232 C5 Ellenboro *WV* U.S.A.
233 G2 Ellenburg Depot *NY* U.S.A.
233 F5 Ellendale *DE* U.S.A.
236 D2 Ellendale *ND* U.S.A.
238 B3 Ellensburg *WA* U.S.A.
235 D1 Ellenville *NY* U.S.A.
244 B1 Elen, Cerro *mt.* Mex.
78 □3a Eller *i. Kwajalein Marshall Is*
184 D4 El León, Cerro *mt.* Mex.
168 E2 Ellerau Ger.
168 E2 Ellerbek Ger.
168 E2 Ellerhoop Ger.
81 D5 Ellesmere *South I.* N.Z.
150 E2 Ellesmere *Shropshire, England* U.K.
81 D5 Ellesmere, Lake *South I.* N.Z.
221 J2 Ellesmere Island *Nunavut* Can.
Ellesmere Port *Cheshire, England* U.K.
165 C4 Ellezelles Belgium
221 H3 Elliant France
Ellice *r. Nunavut* Can.
Ellice Island *atoll Tuvalu* see Funafuti
Ellice Islands *country* S. Pacific Ocean see Tuvalu
234 B3 Ellicott City *MD* U.S.A.
232 D3 Ellicottville *NY* U.S.A.
231 C5 Ellijay *GA* U.S.A.
244 B2 El Limón Mex.
245 E2 El Limón Mex.
173 E2 Ellingen Ger.
149 H2 Ellingham *Northumberland, England* U.K.
209 E3 Ellinikon Greece
226 B2 Ellington *WI* U.S.A.
84 C3 Elliot *N.T.* Austr.
215 F4 Elliot S. Africa
85 F3 Elliot, Mount *Qld* Austr.
214 G5 Elliotdale S. Africa
232 D2 Elliot Knob *mt. VA* U.S.A.
224 D4 Elliot Lake *Ont.* Can.
238 D3 Ellis *ID* U.S.A.
236 C4 Ellis *KS* U.S.A.
213 F3 Elliston *S. Austr.* Austr.
231 G5 Elliston *S.A.* Austr.
187 C5 El Saler Spain
115 M5 Ellisville *MS* U.S.A.
185 I2 El Llano Spain
182 C3 Elloboar Spain
244 C3 El Salado Mex.
245 D5 El Salto Durango Mex.
244 C3 El Salto *Jalisco* Mex.
243 H6 El Salvador *country* Central America
258 C2 El Salvador Chile
244 D1 El Salvador Mex.
92 C4 El Salvador Phil.
185 I3 Els Arcs Spain
227 F1 Elsas Ont. Can.
185 G4 El Saucejo Spain
182 D4 El Saugo Spain
242 D3 El Sauz Mex.
216 □3a El Sauzal *Tenerife Canary Is*
240 I6 El Sauzal Mex.
185 E4 Elsava *r.* Ger.
215 H1 Elsbethen Austria
178 E3 Elsdon *Northumberland, England* U.K.
169 H2 Elsdorf *Niedersachsen* Ger.
169 B5 Elsdorf *Nordrhein-Westfalen* Ger.
110 C2 Elm He *r.* China
197 H4 Elminska Planina *hills* Bulg.
128 C2 Elmirdağ Turkey
180 E2 Elmau Ger.
199 F2 Elmir Greece
83 F5 Elmore *Vic.* Austr.
232 A4 Elmira *N.Y.* Austr.

Column 3

204 C2 El Jadida Morocco
242 D3 El Jaralito Mex.
182 D4 Eljas Spain
205 H2 El Jem Tunisia
222 H5 Elk *r. B.C.* Can.
175 K2 Ełk Pol.
175 K2 Ełk *r.* Pol.
234 C3 Elk *r. PA* U.S.A.
231 C5 Elk *r. TN* U.S.A.
128 B2 El Kaa Lebanon see Qaa
236 F3 Elkader *IA* U.S.A.
205 H1 El Kala Alg.
138 E3 Elkas kalns *hill* Latvia
232 B6 Elkatawa *KY* U.S.A.
237 D6 Elk City *OK* U.S.A.
240 F2 Elk Creek *CA* U.S.A.
84 C4 Elkedra *N.T.* Austr.
204 D2 El Kelaâ des Srarhna Morocco
169 C5 Elkenroth Ger.
210 D3 Keré Eth.
222 H5 Elkford *B.C.* Can.
240 G2 Elk Grove *CA* U.S.A.
128 A3 El Khalil West Bank see Hebron
203 F5 El Khandaq Sudan
203 F3 El Khârga Egypt
230 C3 Elkhart *KS* U.S.A.
237 C4 Elkhart *IN* U.S.A.
237 C4 El Kharrûb *Sudan* see Khartoum
204 D5 El Khnâchich *esc.* Mali
226 C4 Elkhorn *WI* U.S.A.
236 D3 Elkhorn *r. NE* U.S.A.
236 D3 Elkhorn City *KY* U.S.A.
129 D2 El'khotovo Rus. Fed.
197 H4 Elkhovo Bulg.
128 B1 Elkilen Turkey see Beytüşşebap
231 D4 Elkin *NC* U.S.A.
232 D5 Elkins *WV* U.S.A.
234 C3 Elkins Park *PA* U.S.A.
224 D4 Elk Lake Ont. Can.
232 E4 Elkland *PA* U.S.A.
234 C3 Elk Mills *MD* U.S.A.
238 E3 Elk Mountain *WY* U.S.A.
238 D2 Elk Neck *MD* U.S.A.
223 I4 Elko *B.C.* Can.
238 D3 Elko *NV* U.S.A.
223 I4 Elk Point *Alta* Can.
236 D3 Elk Point *SD* U.S.A.
234 B3 Elkridge *MD* U.S.A.
226 A3 Elk River *MN* U.S.A.
241 M1 Elk Springs *CO* U.S.A.
230 C4 Elkton *KY* U.S.A.
234 C3 Elkton *MD* U.S.A.
234 D2 Elkton *VA* U.S.A.
232 C5 Elkview *WV* U.S.A.
184 E3 El Labrador, Cerro *mt.* Mex.
143 H1 Ellan Sweden
129 E3 Ellas country Europe see Greece
87 B5 Ellavalla *W.A.* Austr.
231 C5 Elleben *KY* U.S.A.
178 C3 Ellöbgen Austria
158 C4 Ellé *r.* France
171 D5 Ellefeld Ger.

Column 4

227 I4 Elmira *NY* U.S.A.
241 K5 El Mirador, Cerro *mt.* Mex.
245 F3 El Mirage *AZ* U.S.A.
183 G4 El Molar Spain
185 F1 El Molinillo Spain
185 H3 El Moral Spain
83 F4 Elmore *Vic.* Austr.
205 H4 El Mreïti Maur.
260 E3 El Morro *r.* Arg.
235 E1 Elmsford *NY* U.S.A.
168 E2 Elmshorn Ger.
172 B2 Elmstein Ger.
151 H2 Elmswell *Suffolk, England* U.K.
208 E2 El Muglad Sudan
187 B6 El Mugrón *mt.* Spain
227 H3 Elmvale Ont. Can.
226 A3 Elmwood *IL* U.S.A.
244 C4 El Naranjo *r.* Mex.
163 E6 Elne France
140 I3 Elnesvågen Norway
92 A4 El Nido Phil.
203 F6 El Obeid Sudan
184 D3 Elora *r.* Spain
158 B3 Elorn *r.* France
250 B5 El Oro *prov.* Ecuador
242 E3 El Oro Coahuila Mex.
244 D4 El Oro *México* Mex.
259 B3 El Orro Arg.
186 D2 Elortondo Arg.
183 I2 Elorz Spain
184 F4 El Oso Spain
177 H5 Előszállás Hungary
244 A2 Elota *r.* Mex.
205 G2 El Oued Alg.
260 C4 Eloxochitlán Mex.
241 L5 Eloy *AZ* U.S.A.
157 G4 Éloyes France
185 F4 El Palo Spain
250 D2 El Pao Venez.
242 □I6 El Paraíso Hond.
245 G5 El Paraíso Mex.
216 □3d El Paso *La Palma Canary Is*
226 C5 El Paso *IL* U.S.A.
239 F6 El Paso *TX* U.S.A.
185 H1 El Pedernoso Spain
245 E2 El Pedregoso *r.* Mex.
184 E3 El Pedroso Spain
183 F3 El Pedroso de la Armuña Spain
260 B3 El Peñón *mt.* Chile
230 C3 El Peral Spain
182 E3 El Perdigón Spain
187 C5 El Perelló Spain
186 E4 El Perelló Spain
168 E1 Elpersbüttel Ger.
147 C4 Elphin Rep. of Ireland
146 C3 Elphin *Highland, Scotland* U.K.
185 H1 El Picazo Spain
215 J1 El Pinell de Bray Spain
182 E3 El Piñero Spain
186 E3 El pla de Santa Maria Spain
260 B3 El Plomo, Nevado *mt.* Chile
186 C4 El Pobo Spain
185 I2 El Pobo de Dueñas Spain
187 C5 El Port Spain
187 D4 Eli Portal *CA* U.S.A.
186 G2 El Port de la Selva Spain
240 I5 El Porvenir *Baja California Norte* Mex.
242 D2 El Porvenir Mex.
242 □K7 El Porvenir Panama
184 D3 El Prat de Llobregat Spain
242 H6 El Progreso Guat.
123 G2 El Provencio Spain
215 I2 El Puente *r.* Arg.
183 E5 El Puerto de Arzobispo Spain
187 C7 El Puerto de Santa María Spain

Column 5

128 A5 El Suweis *governorate* Egypt
260 B3 El Tabo Chile
245 F3 El Tajín *tourist site* Mex.
205 H1 El Tarf Alg.
189 B7 El Tarf *prov.* Alg.
244 D4 El Tecolote, Cerro *mt.* Mex.
182 D2 El Teleno *mt.* Spain
245 G4 El Temascal Mex.
186 E3 El Morell Spain
260 E3 El Morro *mt.* Arg.
183 F4 El Tiemblo Spain
251 E2 El Tigre Venez.
128 C1 El Tittman Ger.
183 H5 El Toboso Spain
250 D2 El Tocuyo Venez.
147 C4 El'ton Rep. of Ireland
120 A2 El'ton Rus. Fed.
151 G2 Elton *Cambridgeshire, England* U.K.
149 G4 Elton *Cheshire, England* U.K.
238 E2 Eltopia *WA* U.S.A.
182 E4 El Torno Spain
261 G3 El Trébol Arg.
245 E5 El Treinta Mex.
185 F1 El Trincheto Spain
186 D2 El Triunfo Spain
184 D3 El Tumbalejo Spain
203 G2 El Tûr Egypt
186 D2 El Turbón *mt.* Spain
169 D5 Eltville am Rhein Ger.
203 G3 El Ugsur Egypt
114 D2 Eluru *Andhra Prad.* India
138 E4 Elva Estonia
146 E6 Elvanfoot *South Lanarkshire, Scotland* U.K.
Elvanli Turkey see Tömük
184 C2 Elvas Port.
158 D4 Elven France
186 E3 El Vendrell Spain
234 C2 Elverson *PA* U.S.A.
141 J3 Elverum Norway
250 C3 El Viejo *mt.* Col.
242 □I6 El Viejo Nic.
244 B3 El Vigía, Cerro *mt.* Mex.
149 I4 Elvington *York, England* U.K.
86 F3 Elvire *r. W.A.* Austr.
242 E3 El Vizcaíno Mex.
184 E3 El Viso del Alcor Spain
190 D3 Elvo *r.* Italy
126 B6 El Wâdî El Jadid *governorate* Egypt
230 C3 Elwood *IN* U.S.A.
230 C3 Elwood *NE* U.S.A.
236 D3 Elwood *NJ* U.S.A.
214 J4 Elwood *NJ* U.S.A.
169 F4 Elxleben Ger.
151 H2 Ely *Cambridgeshire, England* U.K.
150 D3 Ely *Cardiff, Wales* U.K.
226 B2 Ely *MN* U.S.A.
241 J2 Ely *NV* U.S.A.
232 B4 Elyria *OH* U.S.A.
185 F1 Elysburg *PA* U.S.A.
244 C3 Elz Ger.
172 B3 Elz *r.* Ger.
245 F5 El Zacatón, Cerro *mt.* Mex.
172 C3 Elzach Ger.
210 D4 Eltze Ger.
168 E3 Elze (Wedemark) Ger.
78 □3 Emaé *i.* Vanuatu
160 D1 Émagny France
169 C4 Emajõgi *r.* Estonia
122 D2 Emäm Qolī Iran
120 C2 Emāmrūd Iran
121 G2 Emām Şāḥeb Afgh.
143 G3 Emån *r.* Sweden
215 I2 Emangusi S. Africa
78 □5 Emao *i.* Vanuatu
120 C3 Emar Kazakh.
120 C3 Emba *r.* Kazakh.
215 G2 Embalenhle S. Africa
258 D1 Embarcación Arg.
223 I3 Embarras Portage *Alta* Can.
226 C4 Embarrass *MN* U.S.A.
128 B3 Embdi Somalia see Emba
203 F3 El Qasr Egypt
183 I4 Embid Spain
183 I3 Embid de Ariza Spain
149 H2 Embleton *Northumberland, England* U.K.
260 B1 Embi *i.* Chile
260 B3 El Quisco Chile
244 C4 El Rancho Mex.
183 H2 El Rasillo Spain
183 H4 El Real de la Jara Spain
183 H4 El Real de San Vicente Spain
243 G3 El Recuenco Spain
244 D3 El Refugio Mex.
237 D5 El Reno *OK* U.S.A.
203 G3 El Ridisíya Bahari Egypt
240 H4 Rio *CA* U.S.A.
244 A2 El Rincón Mex.
185 F1 Robledo Spain
185 G3 Rocío Spain
245 E2 El Romeral Spain
184 C3 El Rompido Spain
228 D5 Ronquillo Spain
223 I4 Rosario Sask. Can.
183 H5 El Royo Spain
244 C2 El Rucio Mex.
222 C2 Elsa *r.* Italy
191 I5 Elsa *r.* Italy
186 B2 El Sabinar *Aragón* Spain
185 H2 El Sabinar *Murcia* Spain
203 F2 El Saff Egypt
203 G3 El Sahuaro Mex.

Column 6

114 C3 Emmiganuru *Andhra Prad.* India
232 E5 Emmitsburg *MD* U.S.A.
234 B3 Emmorton *MD* U.S.A.
151 H2 Emneth *Norfolk, England* U.K.
223 M5 Emo Ont. Can.
177 J4 Emőd Hungary
Emona Slovenia see Ljubljana
237 E5 Emory *TX* U.S.A.
237 E5 Emory Peak *TX* U.S.A.
206 B4 Empada Guinea-Bissau
242 C3 Empalme Mex.
244 D3 Empalme Escobedo Mex.
181 E4 Empanadas *mt.* Spain
215 H3 Empangeni S. Africa
258 F2 Empedrado Arg.
260 A4 Empedrado Chile
164 E3 Empel Neth.
266 G2 Emperor Seamount Chain N. Pacific Ocean
266 G2 Emperor Trough *sea feature* N. Pacific Ocean
165 D4 Empfingen Ger.
226 D3 Empingham Reservoir *England* U.K. see Rutland Water
226 D3 Empoli Italy
191 F5 Empoli Italy
199 E3 Emponas *Notio Aigaio* Greece
199 D3 Emporeio Greece
236 D4 Emporia *KS* U.S.A.
232 D3 Emporia *VA* U.S.A.
223 I5 Empress *Alta* Can.
213 F3 Empress Mine Zimbabwe
165 E4 Emptinne Belgium
Empty Quarter *des.* Saudi Arabia see Rub' al Khālī
161 C3 Empurany France
168 C2 Ems *r.* Ger.
169 C3 Emsbüren Ger.
227 H3 Emsdale Ont. Can.
169 C3 Emsdetten Ger.
173 F2 Emskirchen Ger.
164 E2 Emst Neth.
168 D3 Emstek Ger.
151 G4 Emsworth *Hampshire, England* U.K.
215 H1 Emthonjeni S. Africa
168 D3 Emtinghausen Ger.
85 E3 Emu Creek *r. Qld* Austr.
138 F2 Emumägi *hill* Estonia
85 G4 Emu Park *Qld* Austr.
100 C1 Emur *r.* China
147 E2 Emyvale Rep. of Ireland
215 G2 Emzinoni S. Africa
104 D3 Ena Japan
140 N3 Enafors Sweden
250 D4 Enambú Col.
141 L3 Enånger Sweden
104 D3 Ena-san *mt.* Japan
255 B9 Encantadas, Serra das *hills* Brazil
245 H5 Encantado *r.* Mex.
92 B3 Encanto, Cape Phil.
244 C3 Encarnación Mex.
253 D6 Encarnación Para.
206 E5 Enchi Ghana
185 I1 Encina *r.* Spain
186 B3 Encinacorba Spain
237 D6 Encinal *TX* U.S.A.
185 G2 Encinas *r.* Spain
183 E4 Encinas de Abajo Spain
187 C4 Encinasola Spain
182 D4 Encinas Reales Spain
240 I6 Encinillas Mex.
240 I5 Encino *CA* U.S.A.
239 F5 Encino *NM* U.S.A.
215 H3 Enciso Spain
82 B3 Encounter Bay *S.A.* Austr.
78 □5 Encruzilhada Brazil
255 B9 Encruzilhada do Sul Brazil
210 B4 Encs Hungary
177 L4 Encsencs Hungary
222 E4 Endako *B.C.* Can.
94 C2 Endau r. Malaysia
85 E1 Endeavour Strait *Qld* Austr.
231 C6 Endeavour AL U.S.A.
231 C6 Endeavour AL U.S.A.
77 I2 Enderbury i. Kiribati
222 G5 Enderby *B.C.* Can.
Enderby *atoll Micronesia* see Puluwat
151 F2 Enderby *Leicestershire, England* U.K.
264 L9 Enderby Abyssal Plain *sea feature* Southern Ocean
220 C3 Endicott Mountains *AK* U.S.A.
263 D2 Enderby Land Antarctica
220 D2 Enderby *atoll* see Enderby Island
173 B3 Endingen Ger.
207 I6 Endom Cameroon
177 I3 Endrefalva Hungary
182 E4 Endrinal Spain
163 H6 Endoin, Pique d' *mt.* France
227 I4 Endwell *NY* U.S.A.
86 B7 Eneabba *W.A.* Austr.
142 D2 Enebakk Norway
191 I3 Enego Italy
113 J5 Enem Rus. Fed.
266 N. Pacific Ocean see Wake Atoll
210 D3 Enemek Turkey
210 D3 Emei Sichuan China see Emeishan
108 B2 Eneida Spain

Column 7

114 C3 Emmiganuru
215 F4 Encobo S. Africa
169 C3 Engden Ger.
232 B6 Eolia *KY* U.S.A.
Eooa *i. Tonga* see Eua
191 F5 Engelberg Switz.
173 H2 Engelhard *NC* U.S.A.
179 H2 Engelhartszell Austria
168 D2 Engel's Saratovskaya Oblast'
173 G3 Engelsberg Ger.
173 G3 Engelskirchen Ger.
173 G5 Engelsmanplaat *sea chan.* Neth.
261 G4 Emilio Ayarza Arg.
250 D3 Emilio Carranza Mex.
191 H4 Emilius, Monte *mt.* Italy
110 C2 Emin He *r.* China
197 H4 Eminska Planina *hills* Bulg.
141 J3 Engerdal Norway
199 F2 Enğişehir Turkey
172 C4 Engen Ger.
83 F5 Emo, Seb-Gonde Ger.
94 C2 Emmer-Compascuum Neth.
247 □2 English Harbour Town Antigua and Barbuda
235 G2 Enon Beach *NJ* U.S.A.
219 I5 Epila Spain
181 E2 Éphyra Greece
226 G3 Episkopi Cyprus

Column 8

215 D3 Enhlalakahle S. Africa
237 D4 Enid *OK* U.S.A.
78 □3b Enigu *i. Majuro Marshall Is*
172 D3 Eningen unter Achalm Ger.
198 C2 Enipefs *r.* Greece
102 J2 Eniwa Japan
185 H4 Enix Spain
214 E5 Enkeldoorn Zimbabwe see Chivhu
169 E2 Enkenbach Ger.
164 E2 Enkhuizen Neth.
172 B2 Enkirch Ger.
143 G2 Enköping Sweden
Enle *Yunnan* China see Zhenyuan
194 D5 Enna Sicilia Italy
194 D5 Enna *prov. Sicilia* Italy
203 F6 En Nahud Sudan
202 D5 Ennedi, Massif *mts* Chad
147 D3 Ennell, Lough *l.* Rep. of Ireland
169 C4 Ennepetal Ger.
215 F2 Ennerdale S. Africa
157 E4 Ennery France
246 C3 Ennery Haiti
160 B3 Ennezat France
83 F2 Enngonia *N.S.W.* Austr.
123 K3 Ennīhābād India
236 C2 Enning *SD* U.S.A.
147 D4 Ennis Rep. of Ireland
238 E3 Ennis *MT* U.S.A.
237 D5 Ennis *TX* U.S.A.
147 E4 Enniscorthy Rep. of Ireland
147 C5 Enniskean Rep. of Ireland
147 E3 Enniskerry Rep. of Ireland
147 D3 Enniskillen *Northern Ireland* U.K.
147 B4 Ennistymon Rep. of Ireland
78 □3a Enniwetak *i. Kwajalein Marshall Is*
128 B3 Enn Nâqoûra Lebanon
179 N3 Enns Austria
179 F2 Enns *r.* Austria
78 □3a Ennubirr *i. Kwajalein Marshall Is*
78 □3a Ennubuj *i. Kwajalein Marshall Is*
140 O3 Eno Fin.
214 K3 Enoch *UT* U.S.A.
234 B2 Enola *PA* U.S.A.
140 O3 Enonkoski Fin.
140 M1 Enontekiö Fin.
161 C5 Enoree *r. SC* U.S.A.
233 G2 Enosburg Falls *VT* U.S.A.
109 E4 Enping *Guangdong* China
92 B2 Enrile Phil.
246 E3 Enriquillo Dom. Rep.
164 E2 Ens Neth.
83 F4 Ensay *Vic.* Austr.
164 F2 Enschede Neth.
173 F2 Ensdorf Ger.
169 D4 Ense Ger.
261 I4 Ensenada Arg.
242 A2 Ensenada Baja California Norte Mex.
242 C4 Ensenada Baja California Sur Mex.
247 □1 Ensenada Puerto Rico
172 B2 Ensheim Ger.
108 D2 Enshi *Hubei* China
105 G4 Enshū-nada *g.* Japan
160 D3 Ensisheim France
147 F5 Ensley *AL* U.S.A.
231 F3 Enstone *Oxfordshire, England* U.K.
161 D5 Ensués-la-Redonne France
210 B4 Entebbe Uganda
146 E6 Enterkinfoot *Dumfries and Galloway, Scotland* U.K.
222 G2 Enterprise *N.W.T.* Can.
227 I3 Enterprise N.W.T. Can.
231 C6 Enterprise *AL* U.S.A.
238 C3 Enterprise *OR* U.S.A.
241 K3 Enterprise *UT* U.S.A.
95 F2 Entimau, Bukit *hill Sarawak* Malaysia
190 D5 Entlebuch Switz.
190 C4 Entracque Italy
184 B3 Entradas Port.
160 D3 Entraigues-sur-Sorgues France
160 B1 Entrains-sur-Nohain France
162 E3 Entrammes France
159 F4 Entrance *Alta* Can.
84 B2 Entrance Island *N.T.* Austr.
161 E4 Entraunes France
161 A4 Entraygues-sur-Truyère France
261 H3 Entre Rios *prov.* Arg.
252 D5 Entre Rios Bol.
254 F4 Entre Rios Brazil
257 F4 Entre Rios de Minas Brazil
158 B3 Entrevaux France
184 B1 Entroncamento Port.
215 H3 Entumeni S. Africa
207 G5 Enugu Nigeria
207 G5 Enugu *state* Nigeria
131 T3 Enurmino Rus. Fed.
182 C5 Envendos Port.
250 C2 Envermeu France
250 C3 Envigado Col.
252 C1 Envira Brazil
250 D5 Envira *r.* Brazil
177 H5 Enying Hungary
81 G5 Enys, Mount *South I.* N.Z.
172 D2 Enz *r.* Ger.
190 F4 Enzan Japan
105 H3 Enzan Japan
172 C2 Enzersdorf an der Fischa Austria
172 C3 Enzklösterle Ger.
147 C6 Eochaill Rep. of Ireland see Youghal
222 B6 Eolia *KY* U.S.A.
Europäisch Niklsrk?
161 C4 Épagny France
190 B2 Épalinges Switz.
245 F5 Epazoyucan Mex.
170 D5 Epe Ger.
207 F5 Epe Nigeria
164 F2 Epe Neth.
177 J5 Eperjes Hungary
156 C4 Épernay France
156 B4 Épernon France
199 E3 Ephesus *tourist site* Turkey
241 L2 Ephraim *UT* U.S.A.
234 B2 Ephrata *PA* U.S.A.
238 B2 Ephrata *WA* U.S.A.
78 □3a Épi *i.* Vanuatu
Epidamnus Albania see Durrës
198 B3 Epidavros *tourist site* Greece
185 D5 Épiéds-en-Beauce France
181 F4 Épila Spain
181 E2 Épinac France
157 G4 Épinal France
181 F2 Épiry France
198 A2 Epirus *admin. reg.* Greece see Ipeiros
160 B1 Épiry France
128 B2 Episkopi Cyprus
160 D1 Époisses France
160 C1 Époisses France
172 D2 Eppelborn Ger.
172 B2 Eppelborn Ger.
172 D1 Eppelheim Ger.
169 D4 Eppenbrunn Ger.
169 D5 Eppendorf Ger.
172 D1 Eppertshausen Ger.
149 F4 Epperstone *Notts, England* U.K.
151 G3 Epping *Essex, England* U.K.
233 J2 Epping *NH* U.S.A.
169 D5 Eppingen Ger.
169 D5 Eppishausen Ger.
151 G3 Eppynt, Mynydd *hills Wales* U.K.
151 G3 Epsom *Surrey, England* U.K.
161 C4 Epte *r.* France
161 D5 Épuisay France
149 I4 Epworth *North Lincolnshire, England* U.K.

Eqlīd to Falkenberg
303

122 C4 Eqlīd Iran
208 D4 Équateur admin. reg. Dem. Rep. Congo
207 H6 Equatorial Guinea country Africa
158 E2 Équerdreville-Hainneville France
191 F5 Era r. Italy
191 H3 Eraclea Italy
191 H3 Eraclea Mare Italy
186 B1 Eracurri mt. Spain
92 A4 Eran Phil.
183 H1 Erandio Spain
116 C5 Erandol Mahar. India
215 G1 Erasmia S. Africa
Erawadi r. Myanmar see Irrawaddy
190 E3 Erba Italy
203 H4 Erba, Jebel mt. Sudan
126 E2 Erbaa Turkey
172 D3 Erbach Baden-Württemberg Ger.
172 D2 Erbach Hessen Ger.
173 G2 Erbendorf Ger.
172 B2 Erbeskopf hill Ger.
190 D3 Erbognone r. Italy
158 E4 Erbray France
128 A2 Ercan airport Cyprus
163 D6 Ercé France
127 F3 Erçek Turkey
260 A6 Ercilla Chile
127 F3 Erciş Turkey
126 D3 Erciyes Dağı mt. Turkey
177 H4 Ercsi Hungary
177 H4 Érd Hungary
140 N1 Erdalsfjellet hill Norway
Erdaobaihe Jilin China see Baihe
106 B5 Erdaogou Qinghai China
100 C4 Erdao Jiang r. China
171 C4 Erdeborn Ger.
199 E1 Erdek Turkey
126 D3 Erdemli Turkey
106 C1 Erdenet Hövsgöl Mongolia
106 E1 Erdenet Orhon Mongolia
106 D2 Erdenetsogt Bayanhongor Mongolia
106 E3 Erdenetsogt Ömnögovĭ Mongolia
158 C4 Erdeven France
173 F3 Erding Ger.
171 E5 Erdmannsdorf Ger.
135 I7 Erdniyevskiy Rus. Fed.
158 E4 Erdre r. France
173 F3 Erdweg Ger.
256 A6 Eré, Campos hills Brazil
158 D3 Éréac France
251 E3 Erebato r. Venez.
263 L1 Erebus, Mount vol. Antarctica
127 G5 Erech tourist site Iraq
255 B8 Erechim Brazil
107 G1 Ereentsav Mongolia
126 D3 Ereğli Turkey
126 C2 Ereğli Turkey
Erego Moz. see Errego
194 D5 Erei, Monti mts Sicilia Italy
Erementaū Kazakh. see Yereymentau
110 D3 Erenhaberga Shan mts China
107 G3 Erenhot Nei Mongol China
196 E4 Erenik r. Yugo.
129 C4 Erentepe Turkey
122 D3 Eresk Iran
183 F3 Eresma r. Spain
199 D2 Eresos Voreio Aigaio Greece
198 C2 Eretria Greece
Erevan Armenia see Yerevan
168 E1 Erfde Ger.
204 D3 Erfoud Morocco
169 B5 Erftstadt Ger.
171 C5 Erfurt Ger.
127 E3 Ergani Turkey
204 D5 Erg Atouila des. Mali
204 D5 'Erg Chech des. Alg./Mali
205 H4 Erg d' Amer des. Alg.
202 C6 Erg du Djourab des. Chad
207 H2 Erg du Ténéré des. Niger
107 F3 Ergel Mongolia
199 E1 Ergene r. Turkey
173 E2 Ergersheim Ger.
204 E4 Erg labès des. Alg.
204 D4 Erg Iguidi des. Alg./Maur.
205 E5 'Erg I-n-Sâkâne des. Mali
205 G4 Erg Issaouane des. Alg.
138 E3 Ērgļi Latvia
173 G3 Ergolding Ger.
173 G3 Ergoldsbach Ger.
158 B3 Ergué-Gabéric France
208 B2 Erguig r. Chad
107 I1 Ergun Nei Mongol China
Ergun He r. China/Rus. Fed. see Argun'
Ergun Youqi Nei Mongol China see Ergun
173 G3 Erharting Ger.
182 E2 Eria r. Spain
146 D3 Eriboll Highland, Scotland U.K.
146 D3 Eriboll, Loch inlet Scotland U.K.
164 F2 Erica Neth.
194 B4 Erice Sicilia Italy
183 I2 Erice Spain
184 A2 Ericeira Port.
146 E5 Ericht r. Scotland U.K.
146 D5 Ericht, Loch l. Scotland U.K.
223 L5 Erickson Man. Can.
237 E4 Erie KS U.S.A.
232 C3 Erie PA U.S.A.
227 G4 Erie, Lake Can./U.S.A.
Erieddu i. N. Male Maldives see Eriyadhu
206 D2 'Erîgât des. Mali
130 D2 Erik Eriksenstretet sea chan. Svalbard
223 L5 Eriksdale Man. Can.
143 F3 Eriksmåla Sweden
185 E2 Erillas hill Spain
227 G4 Erin Ont. Can.
231 C4 Erin TN U.S.A.
173 H3 Ering Ger.
143 F3 Eringsboda Sweden
146 A4 Eriskay i. Scotland U.K.
172 D4 Eriskirch Ger.
151 H2 Eriswell Suffolk, England U.K.
190 C1 Eriswil Switz.
Erithraí Greece see Erythres
Erithropótamos r. Greece see Erydropotamos
203 H6 Eritrea country Africa
113 □1 Eriyadhu i. N. Male Maldives
Eriyadu i. N. Male Maldives see Eriyadhu
169 B4 Erkelenz Ger.
156 C2 Erkelsbrugge France
129 B1 Erken-Shakhar Rus. Fed.
173 E3 Erkheim Ger.
199 G2 Erkmen Afyon Turkey
171 E3 Erkner Ger.
178 D3 Erl Austria
186 C2 Erla Spain
190 C1 Erlach Switz.
173 F2 Erlangen Ger.
109 D1 Erlangping Henan China
173 H3 Erlau r. Ger.
179 G2 Erlauf Austria
179 G2 Erlauf r. Austria
171 D5 Erlbach Ger.
84 C5 Erldunda N.T. Austr.
172 D2 Erlenbach am Main Ger.
169 D5 Erlensee Ger.
190 D4 Erli Italy
100 D4 Erlong Shan mt. China
234 D4 Erma NJ U.S.A.
Ermak Pavlodarskaya Oblast' Kazakh. see Aksu
164 E2 Ermelo Neth.
182 C3 Ermelo Port.
215 G2 Ermelo S. Africa
126 D3 Ermenek Turkey
128 A1 Ermenek r. Turkey
182 B3 Ermesinde Port.
184 B2 Ermidas do Sado Port.
198 C3 Ermioni Greece
244 C2 Ermita de los Correas Mex.
156 C4 Ermont France
198 D3 Ermoupoli Notio Aigaio Greece
172 D3 Erms r. Ger.
171 C4 Ermsleben Ger.
183 H1 Ermua Spain
82 C1 Ernabella S.A. Austr.
114 C4 Ernakulam Kerala India
169 D5 Erndtebrück Ger.
147 C2 Erne r. Rep. of Ireland/U.K.
159 F3 Ernée France
159 F3 Ernée r. France
87 D5 Ernest Giles Range hills W.A. Austr.
179 H2 Ernstbrunn Austria
172 A2 Ernz Noire r. Lux.
114 C4 Erode Tamil Nadu India
78 □3b Eroj i. Majuro Marshall Is
173 E3 Erolzheim Ger.
85 E5 Eromanga Qld Austr.
212 B4 Erongo admin. reg. Namibia
164 E3 Erp Neth.
177 K4 Érpatak Hungary
169 C5 Erpel Ger.
106 B3 Erpu Xinjiang China
Erqu Shaanxi China see Zhouzhi
165 D4 Erquelinnes Belgium
158 D3 Erquy France
87 B5 Errabiddy Hills W.A. Austr.
204 D3 Er Rachidia Morocco
203 F6 Er Rahad Sudan
146 B5 Erraid i. Scotland U.K.
204 E3 Er Raoui des. Alg.
186 B1 Errazu Spain
213 H3 Errego Moz.
147 C1 Errigal hill Rep. of Ireland
147 D4 Errill Rep. of Ireland
170 C1 Errindlev Denmark
190 D4 Erro r. Italy
186 B2 Erro r. Spain
146 E5 Errochty Water r. Scotland U.K.
146 D4 Errogie Highland, Scotland U.K.
233 □H2 Errol NH U.S.A.
78 □5 Erromango i. Vanuatu
Erronan i. Vanuatu see Futuna
210 B2 Er Roseires Sudan
177 H5 Érsekcsanád Hungary
198 B1 Ersekë Albania
177 I3 Érsekvadkert Hungary
169 F4 Ershausen Ger.
Ersis Turkey see Kılıçkaya
236 D2 Erskine MN U.S.A.
157 H4 Erstein France
190 D2 Erstfeld Switz.
210 D1 Erta Ale vol. Eth.
106 A2 Ertai Xinjiang China
135 H6 Ertil' Rus. Fed.
172 D3 Ertingen Ger.
Ertis Kazakh. see Irtyshsk
Ertis r. Kazakh./Rus. Fed. see Irtysh
110 D1 Ertix He r. China/Kazakh.
191 H2 Erto Italy
78 □3a Eru i. Kwajalein Marshall Is
82 D2 Erudina S.A. Austr.
207 G4 Erufu Nigeria
127 F3 Eruh Turkey
192 A4 Erula Sardegna Italy
207 F5 Eruwa Nigeria
258 G4 Erval Brazil
257 F4 Ervália Brazil
159 F4 Erve r. France
182 C3 Ervedosa do Douro Port.
184 B3 Ervidel Port.
156 C2 Ervillers France
182 C3 Ervões Port.
156 D4 Ervy-le-Châtel France
231 D4 Erwin TN U.S.A.
169 D4 Erwitte Ger.
170 C3 Erxleben Sachsen-Anhalt Ger.
171 C3 Erxleben Sachsen-Anhalt Ger.
199 E1 Erydropotamos r. Greece
198 B3 Erymanthos r. Greece
198 C2 Erythres Greece
108 A3 Eryuan Yunnan China
196 D5 Erzen r. Albania
Erzerum Turkey see Erzurum
171 E5 Erzgebirge mts Czech Rep./Ger.
100 C2 Erzhan Heilong. China
172 C2 Erzhausen Ger.
106 B1 Erzin Rus. Fed.
126 E3 Erzin Turkey
126 E3 Erzincan Turkey
129 A4 Erzincan prov. Turkey
127 F3 Erzurum Turkey
129 B3 Erzurum prov. Turkey
191 H5 Esanatoglia Italy
195 G3 Esaro r. Italy
193 I5 Esaro r. Italy
102 J4 Esashi Japan
142 C4 Esbjerg Denmark
142 C4 Esbjerg airport Denmark
156 C4 Esbly France
Esbo Fin. see Espoo
254 G4 Escada Brazil
182 C2 Escairón Spain
92 B4 Escalante Phil.
183 G1 Escalante Spain
241 L3 Escalante UT U.S.A.
241 L3 Escalante r. UT U.S.A.
241 K3 Escalante Desert UT U.S.A.
192 B5 Escalaplano Sardegna Italy
182 D4 Escalhão Port.
163 A5 Escaliers, Pic des mt. France
186 E2 Escaló Spain
187 E6 Es Caló Spain
242 D3 Escalón Mex.
240 G3 Escalon CA U.S.A.
183 F4 Escalona Spain
183 F3 Escalona del Prado Spain
182 C5 Escalos de Baixo Port.
182 C5 Escalos de Cima Port.
183 H3 Escalote r. Spain
231 C6 Escambia r. FL U.S.A.
183 H4 Escamilla Spain
226 D3 Escanaba MI U.S.A.
161 B5 Escandorgue ridge France
185 F3 Escañuela Spain
243 H5 Escárcega Mex.
183 G4 Escariche Spain
182 C4 Escarigo Port.
186 B2 Escaroz Spain
163 D5 Escatalens France
186 C3 Escatrón Spain
156 D2 Escaudain France
165 C4 Escaut r. Belgium
164 E3 Esch Neth.
173 E4 Eschach r. Ger.
157 H4 Eschau France
172 D2 Eschau Ger.
169 D5 Eschborn Ger.
168 B3 Esche Ger.
168 F2 Escheburg Ger.
168 F3 Eschede Ger.
190 D1 Eschenbach Switz.
173 F2 Eschenbach in der Oberpfalz Ger.
169 D5 Eschenburg-Eibelshausen Ger.
169 E4 Eschenstruth (Helsa) Ger.
169 E4 Eschershausen Ger.
178 C4 Eschio r. Italy
173 G2 Eschlkam Ger.
190 C2 Escholzmatt Switz.
165 E5 Esch-sur-Alzette Lux.
165 E5 Esch-sur-Sûre Lux.
169 F4 Eschwege Ger.
169 B5 Eschweiler Ger.
247 E3 Escocesa, Bahía b. Dom. Rep.
252 C3 Escoma Bol.
187 C7 Escombreras Spain
237 C6 Escondido r. Mex.
242 □J6 Escondido r. Nic.
240 I5 Escondido CA U.S.A.
187 F5 Escorca Spain
186 C4 Escorihuela Spain
163 A5 Escos France
163 E6 Escouloubre France
163 A4 Escource France
163 A4 Escource r. France
161 E5 Escragnolles France
186 C4 Escucha Spain
241 M5 Escudilla mt. AZ U.S.A.
244 B2 Escuinapa Mex.
243 H6 Escuintla Guat.
243 G6 Escuintla Mex.
250 D2 Escuque Venez.
184 E1 Escurial Spain
186 C3 Escuriza r. Spain
160 B2 Escurolles France
256 D2 Escurso r. Brazil
182 B2 Escusa Spain
183 F4 Escusa mt. Spain
185 G3 Escúzar Spain
207 H6 Eséka Cameroon
131 O3 Ese-Khayya Rus. Fed.
199 F3 Eşen Turkey
199 F3 Eşen r. Turkey
199 F1 Esence Turkey
129 A4 Esence Dağları mts Turkey
129 D4 Eşengöl Dağı mt. Iran/Turkey
122 C2 Esenguly Turkm.
199 F1 Esenköy Turkey
128 B1 Esenpınar Turkey
168 C2 Esens Ger.
199 F1 Esenyurt Turkey
186 D2 Ésera r. Spain
122 B3 Eşfahān Iran
122 C3 Eşfahān prov. Iran
122 D2 Esfarayen, Reshteh-ye mts Iran
182 B2 Esfarrapada Spain
182 C2 Esgos Spain
183 F3 Esgueva r. Spain
183 F3 Esguevillas de Esgueva Spain
108 B3 Eshan Yunnan China
151 G3 Esher Surrey, England U.K.
129 B2 Eshera Georgia
215 H3 Eshowe S. Africa
213 F4 Esigodini Zimbabwe
215 I3 Esikhawini S. Africa
Esil Kazakh. see Yesil'
Esil r. Kazakh./Rus. Fed. see Ishim
191 I5 Esino r. Italy
129 B3 Esirçölü Tepe mt. Turkey
215 H2 eSizameleni S. Africa
85 H5 Esk Qld Austr.
83 F5 Esk r. Tas. Austr.
149 F3 Esk r. Cumbria, England U.K.
149 F3 Esk r. England/Scotland U.K.
80 F3 Eskdale North I. N.Z.
146 E6 Eskdalemuir Dumfries and Galloway, Scotland U.K.
225 H2 Esker Nfld. Can.
137 I3 Eskhar Ukr.
140 □D2 Eskifjörður Iceland
199 F2 Eski Gediz Turkey
170 C1 Eskilstrup Denmark
143 G2 Eskilstuna Sweden
220 E3 Eskimo Lakes N.W.T. Can.
Eskimo Point Nunavut Can. see Arviat
127 F3 Eski Mosul Iraq
121 H4 Eski-Nookat Kyrg.
126 D2 Eskipazar Turkey
199 G2 Eskişehir Turkey
199 G2 Eskişehir prov. Turkey
183 D3 Esla r. Spain
Esla, Embalse de resr Spain see Ricobayo, Embalse de
122 A3 Eslāmābād-e Gharb Iran
173 G2 Eslarn Ger.
183 I2 Eslava Spain
199 F3 Esler Dağı mt. Turkey
169 D4 Eslohe (Sauerland) Ger.
142 E4 Eslöv Sweden
199 F2 Eşme Turkey
129 C3 Eşmeçayır Turkey
260 B3 Esmeralda Chile
246 C2 Esmeralda Cuba
259 B8 Esmeralda, Isla i. Chile
257 E3 Esmeraldas Brazil
250 B4 Esmeraldas Ecuador
250 B4 Esmeraldas prov. Ecuador
252 D3 Esmeraldo r. Bol.
186 □ Es Migjorn Gran Spain
232 D6 Esmont VA U.S.A.
182 B4 Esmoriz Port.
156 D2 Esnes France
165 E4 Esneux Belgium
187 C5 Espadàn mt. Spain
182 D2 Espadañedo Spain
122 E5 Espakeh Iran
Espalha r. Brazil see São Francisco
161 A4 Espalion France
161 B3 Espaly-St-Marcel France
España country Europe see Spain
227 G2 Espanola Ont. Can.
239 F4 Espanola NM U.S.A.
250 □ Española, Isla i. Islas Galápagos Ecuador
184 D2 Esparragalejo Spain
185 E2 Esparragosa Spain
186 E3 Esparraguera Spain
161 D5 Esparron France
242 □I6 Esparta Hond.
240 F2 Esparto CA U.S.A.
186 B2 Esparza de Salazar Spain
121 H4 Espe Kazakh.
182 D4 Espeja Spain
183 G3 Espeja de San Marcelino Spain
185 F3 Espejo Spain
183 G3 Espejón Spain
164 E2 Espel Neth.
163 A5 Espelette France
169 D3 Espelkamp Ger.
169 E4 Espenau Ger.
184 E4 Espera Spain
184 C1 Esperança Port.
256 B6 Esperança, Serra de mts Brazil
87 D7 Esperance W.A. Austr.
87 D7 Esperance Bay W.A. Austr.
254 D3 Esperantinópolis Brazil
262 U2 Esperanza research stn Antarctica
261 G2 Esperanza Arg.
245 F4 Esperanza Puebla Mex.
242 C3 Esperanza Sonora Mex.
252 C2 Esperanza Peru
92 C4 Esperanza Phil.
247 □1 Esperanza Puerto Rico
163 E6 Espéraza France
193 F3 Esperia Italy
163 E6 Espezel France
184 A2 Espichel, Cabo c. Port.
185 F2 Espiel Spain
255 C8 Espigão, Serra do mts Brazil
183 F2 Espigüete mt. Spain
183 F1 Espinama Spain
161 E4 Espinasses France
243 E3 Espinazo Mex.
245 G5 Espinazo del Diablo, Sierra mts Mex.
257 F2 Espinhaço, Serra do mts Brazil
182 B4 Espinhal Port.
184 C2 Espinheira hill Port.
182 B3 Espinho Port.
255 B9 Espinilho, Serra do hills Brazil
183 F1 Espinilla Spain
255 E5 Espinosa Brazil
183 G3 Espinosa de Cerrato Spain
183 G4 Espinosa de Henares Spain
183 G1 Espinosa de los Monteros Spain
183 F5 Espinoso del Rey Spain
163 E6 Espira-de-l'Agly France
Espirito Santo Brazil see Vila Velha
257 G3 Espírito Santo state Brazil
184 C3 Espírito Santo Port.
92 B2 Espiritu Phil.
78 □5 Espíritu Santo i. Vanuatu
243 I5 Espíritu Santo, Bahía del b. Mex.
243 H4 Espita Mex.
182 B5 Espite Port.
254 F4 Esplanada Brazil
183 H4 Esplegares Spain
186 F3 Esplugues de Llobregat Spain
186 D3 Esplús Spain
186 G2 Espolla Spain
161 B5 Espondeilham France
186 F2 Esponellà Spain
141 N3 Espoo Fin.
187 F5 Esporles Spain
182 B3 Esposende Port.
186 E2 Espot Spain
160 E1 Esprels France
185 I3 Espuña mt. Spain
213 G4 Espungabera Moz.
234 B1 Espy PA U.S.A.
259 C6 Esquel Arg.
222 F5 Esquimalt B.C. Can.
261 H2 Esquina Arg.
243 H6 Esquipulas Guat.
183 G4 Esquivias Spain
140 M2 Esrange Sweden
204 C3 Essaouira Morocco
159 G3 Essay France
207 H5 Essé Cameroon
168 E3 Essel Ger.
204 C4 Es Semara Western Sahara
165 D3 Essen Belgium
169 C4 Essen Ger.
168 C3 Essen (Oldenburg) Ger.
173 G3 Essenbach Ger.
87 D5 Essendon, Mount hill W.A. Austr.
160 E1 Essert France
227 F4 Essex Ont. Can.
151 H3 Essex admin. div. England U.K.
241 J4 Essex CA U.S.A.
235 F1 Essex CT U.S.A.
233 H3 Essex MA U.S.A.
234 B3 Essex MD U.S.A.
233 G2 Essex NY U.S.A.
235 D2 Essex County county NJ U.S.A.
233 G2 Essex Junction VT U.S.A.
Essexvale Zimbabwe see Esigodini
227 F4 Essexville MI U.S.A.
173 E3 Essingen Ger.
150 E2 Essington Staffordshire, England U.K.
172 D3 Esslingen am Neckar Ger.
131 Q4 Esso Rus. Fed.
156 D3 Essômes-sur-Marne France
156 C4 Essonne dept Île-de-France France
156 C4 Essonne r. France
156 E4 Essoyes France
207 H5 Essu Cameroon
138 F2 Essu Estonia
203 G6 Es Suki Sudan
207 I5 Est prov. Cameroon
182 C1 Estaca de Bares, Punta da pt Spain
241 J5 Estación Coahuila Mex.
185 G2 Estación de Baeza Spain
186 D2 Estadilla Spain
163 E6 Estagel France
122 C4 Eşţahbān Iran
161 A4 Estaing France
227 G2 Estaire Ont. Can.
156 C2 Estaires France
254 F4 Estância Brazil
239 F5 Estancia NM U.S.A.
122 E4 Estand, Kūh-e mt. Iran
163 B5 Estang France
187 F5 Estanyol de Mitjorn Spain
182 B4 Estarreja Port.
186 C2 Estarrón r. Spain
186 E2 Estats, Pic d' mt. France/Spain
190 B2 Estavayer-le-Lac Switz.
215 G3 Estcourt S. Africa
168 E2 Este r. Ger.
191 G3 Este Italy
247 □1 Este, Punta pt Puerto Rico
186 C3 Esteban hill Spain
170 C3 Estedt Ger.
182 B3 Estela Port.
242 □I6 Estelí Nic.
183 H2 Estella Spain
234 D3 Estell Manor NJ U.S.A.
184 D1 Estena hill Spain
185 F1 Estena r. Spain
173 E2 Estenfeld Ger.
185 F3 Estepa Spain
183 G2 Estepar Spain
185 E4 Estepona Spain
185 F2 Esteras r. Spain
183 H3 Esteras de Medinaceli Spain
186 C4 Estercuel Spain
161 E5 Esterel reg. France
163 A5 Estérençuby France
173 F4 Estergebirge mts Ger.
223 K5 Esterhazy Sask. Can.
156 D4 Esternay France
179 E2 Esternberg Austria
240 G4 Estero Bay CA U.S.A.
190 C5 Esteron r. Italy
186 E2 Esterri d'Aneu Spain
168 C3 Esterwegen Ger.
238 F3 Estes Park CO U.S.A.
250 A1 Este Sudeste, Cayos del is Col.
223 K5 Estevan Sask. Can.
236 E3 Estherville IA U.S.A.
161 C3 Estiavreilles France
231 D5 Estill SC U.S.A.
163 C4 Estillac France
165 D4 Estinnes-au-Mont Belgium
156 D4 Estissac France
257 D5 Estiva Brazil
254 D3 Estiva r. Brazil
160 A2 Estivareilles France
187 C5 Estivella Spain
184 C3 Estói Port.
184 B3 Estômbar Port.
223 I5 Eston Sask. Can.
149 H3 Eston Redcar and Cleveland, England U.K.
138 E2 Estonia country Europe
Estonskaya S.S.R. country Europe see Estonia
168 E2 Estorf Niedersachsen Ger.
168 E3 Estorf Niedersachsen Ger.
184 A2 Estoril Port.
161 E5 Estoublon France
160 C3 Estrablin France
156 C3 Estrées-St-Denis France
182 C5 Estreito Port.
184 □ Estreito da Calheta Madeira
184 C2 Estrela Port.
182 C4 Estrela, Serra da mts Port.
257 E3 Estrela do Indaiá Brazil
256 D3 Estrela do Sul Brazil
185 G2 Estrella mt. Spain
241 K5 Estrella, Sierra mts AZ U.S.A.
183 G4 Estremera Spain
184 C2 Estremoz Port.
183 H3 Estriégala Spain
163 B5 Estrigon r. France
254 C4 Estrondo, Serra hills Brazil
208 A4 Estuaire prov. Gabon
122 B3 Estūh Iran
Esu Cameroon see Essu
159 G4 Esvres France
177 K4 Esztár Hungary
177 H4 Esztergom Hungary
158 D3 Étables-sur-Mer France
82 D2 Etadunna S.A. Austr.
162 C3 Étagnac France
116 D4 Etah Uttar Prad. India
157 F3 Étain France
160 B1 Étais-la-Sauvin France
160 C1 Étalante France
165 E5 Étalle Belgium
225 J3 Etamamiou Que. Can.
156 C4 Étampes France
82 D1 Etamunbanie, Lake salt flat S.A. Austr.
160 C2 Étang-sur-Arroux France
156 B2 Étaples France
162 A3 Étaules France
162 B3 Étauliers France
116 D4 Etawah Rajasthan India
116 D4 Etawah Uttar Prad. India
78 □3a Etcharai i. Kwajalein Marshall Is
242 C3 Etchojoa Mex.
158 C4 Étel France
141 N3 Etelä-Suomi prov. Fin.
160 E1 Éternoz France
215 H2 eThandakukhanya S. Africa
165 E5 Ethe Belgium
223 K5 Ethelbert Man. Can.
86 D4 Ethel Creek W.A. Austr.
85 E2 Ethel Creek r. Qld Austr.
214 D3 E'Thembini S. Africa
85 E3 Etheridge r. Qld Austr.
210 C3 Ethiopia country Africa
199 E2 Etili Turkey
126 D3 Etimesğut Turkey
160 D2 Étival France
157 G4 Étival-Clairefontaine France
146 C5 Etive, Loch inlet Scotland U.K.
156 E5 Étivey France
245 F5 Etla Mex.
141 J3 Etna r. Norway
195 E5 Etna, Monte vol. Sicilia Italy
Etna, Mount vol. Sicilia Italy see Etna, Monte
142 A2 Etne Norway
227 H4 Etobicoke Ont. Can.
156 D4 Étoges France
161 C4 Étoile-sur-Rhône France
85 G4 Eton Qld Austr.
151 G3 Eton Windsor and Maidenhead, England U.K.
Etorofu-tō i. Kuril'skiye O-va Rus. Fed. see Iturup, Ostrov
212 C3 Etosha Pan salt pan Namibia
208 B4 Etoumbi Congo
235 D2 Etra NJ U.S.A.
156 C4 Étréchy France
Etrek r. Iran/Turkm. see Atrek
156 B3 Étrépagny France
159 G2 Étretat France
156 D3 Étreux France
197 G4 Etropole Bulg.
190 C3 Etroubles Italy
163 B6 Etsaut France
165 F5 Ettelbruck Lux.
78 □4a Etten i. Chuuk Micronesia
78 □4a Etten i. Chuuk Micronesia
172 B3 Ettenheim Ger.
164 D3 Etten-Leur Neth.
146 D4 Etteridge Highland, Scotland U.K.
171 C4 Ettersburg Ger.
151 F2 Ettington Warwickshire, England U.K.
172 C3 Ettlingen Ger.
146 E6 Ettrick Scottish Borders, Scotland U.K.
149 G2 Ettrickbridge Scottish Borders, Scotland U.K.
146 E6 Ettrick Forest reg. Scotland U.K.
146 F6 Ettrick Water r. Scotland U.K.
169 C5 Ettringen Ger.
114 C4 Ettumanur Kerala India
160 D1 Étuz France
151 F2 Etwall Derbyshire, England U.K.
186 B1 Etxalar Spain
Etxarri Spain see Echarri
Etxarri-Aranatz Spain see Echarri-Aranaz
244 B3 Etzatlán Mex.
223 I5 Etzicom Coulee r. Alta Can.
156 B2 Eu France
79 □2a Eua i. Tonga
83 F3 Euabalong N.S.W. Austr.
172 D2 Eubigheim Ger.
Euboea i. Greece see Evvoia
87 F6 Eucla W.A. Austr.
232 C4 Euclid OH U.S.A.
254 F4 Euclides da Cunha Brazil
256 A5 Euclides da Cunha Paulista Brazil
83 G4 Eucumbene, Lake N.S.W. Austr.
237 F5 Eudora AR U.S.A.
82 D3 Eudunda S.A. Austr.
169 F5 Euerbach Ger.
169 F5 Euerdorf Ger.
231 C6 Eufaula AL U.S.A.
237 E5 Eufaula OK U.S.A.
237 E5 Eufaula Lake resr OK U.S.A.
178 E3 Eugendorf Austria
238 B2 Eugene OR U.S.A.
253 F2 Eugênia r. Brazil
163 B5 Eugénie-les-Bains France
83 G3 Eugowra N.S.W. Austr.
183 H2 Eulate Spain
83 F2 Eulo Qld Austr.
182 C1 Eume r. Spain
85 G4 Eungella Qld Austr.
237 E6 Eunice LA U.S.A.
237 C5 Eunice NM U.S.A.
165 F4 Eupen Belgium
171 D4 Euper Ger.
118 D2 Euphrates r. Asia alt. Al Furāt (Iraq/Syria), alt. Fırat (Turkey)
237 F5 Eupora MS U.S.A.
141 M3 Eura Fin.
141 M3 Eurajoki Fin.
173 F3 Eurasburg Bayern Ger.
173 F4 Eurasburg Bayern Ger.
179 F2 Euratsfeld Austria
156 B3 Eure dept Haute-Normandie France
156 B3 Eure r. France
156 B4 Eure-et-Loir dept Centre France
238 A3 Eureka CA U.S.A.
237 D4 Eureka KS U.S.A.
238 D1 Eureka MT U.S.A.
241 J2 Eureka NV U.S.A.
232 B5 Eureka OH U.S.A.
236 D2 Eureka SD U.S.A.
241 K2 Eureka UT U.S.A.
221 J2 Eureka Sound sea chan. Nunavut Can.
237 E4 Eureka Springs AR U.S.A.
240 I3 Eureka Valley CA U.S.A.
83 E2 Euriowie N.S.W. Austr.
83 F4 Euroa Vic. Austr.
85 G5 Eurombah Qld Austr.
85 G5 Eurombah Creek r. Qld Austr.
201 H6 Europa, Île i. Indian Ocean
183 E1 Europa, Picos de mts Spain
132 Europe continent
164 D3 Europoort reg. Neth.
157 F4 Eurville-Bienville France
169 B5 Euskirchen Ger.
169 E5 Eußenheim Ger.
231 D6 Eustis FL U.S.A.
83 E3 Euston N.S.W. Austr.
231 C5 Eutaw AL U.S.A.
168 F1 Eutin Ger.
172 C3 Eutingen im Gäu Ger.
171 D4 Eutzsch Ger.
157 F4 Euville France
84 C3 Eva Downs N.T. Austr.
190 C3 Evançon r. Italy
215 G2 Evander S. Africa
236 B4 Evans, Mount CO U.S.A.
222 H4 Evansburg Alta Can.
232 C4 Evans City PA U.S.A.
234 B1 Evans Falls PA U.S.A.
221 J3 Evans Strait Nunavut Can.
226 D4 Evanston IL U.S.A.
238 E3 Evanston WY U.S.A.
224 D4 Evansville Ont. Can.
230 C4 Evansville IN U.S.A.
226 C4 Evansville WI U.S.A.
238 F3 Evansville WY U.S.A.
237 D6 Evant TX U.S.A.
146 D4 Evanton Highland, Scotland U.K.
Eva Perón Arg. see La Plata
Eva Perón prov. Arg. see La Pampa
226 E4 Evart MI U.S.A.
215 F2 Evaton S. Africa
160 A2 Évaux-les-Bains France
122 C5 Evaz Iran
129 D4 Evci Turkey
199 F2 Evciler Turkey
128 B1 Evcili Turkey
226 A2 Eveleth MN U.S.A.
237 F4 Evening Shade AR U.S.A.
151 F3 Evenlode r. England U.K.
131 Q3 Evensk Rus. Fed.
140 L1 Evenskjær Norway
82 C2 Everard, Lake salt flat S.A. Austr.
84 C4 Everard, Mount N.T. Austr.
82 C1 Everard, Mount S.A. Austr.
82 C1 Everard Range hills S.A. Austr.
150 E3 Evercreech Somerset, England U.K.
164 E3 Everdingen Neth.
Everek Turkey see Develi
117 F4 Everest, Mount China/Nepal
233 □J1 Everett N.B. Can.
232 D4 Everett PA U.S.A.
238 B2 Everett WA U.S.A.
165 C3 Evergem Belgium
231 D7 Everglades swamp FL U.S.A.
231 D7 Everglades City FL U.S.A.
231 C6 Evergreen AL U.S.A.
228 D7 Everman, Volcán vol. Mex.
238 B1 Everson WA U.S.A.
251 G3 Everton Guyana
141 K3 Evertsberg Sweden
85 E4 Evesham Qld Austr.
151 F2 Evesham Worcestershire, England U.K.
151 F2 Evesham, Vale of val. England U.K.
169 F3 Evessen Ger.
160 E2 Évian-les-Bains France
140 M3 Evijärvi Fin.
207 H6 Evinayong Equat. Guinea
232 D6 Evington VA U.S.A.
198 B2 Evinos r. Greece
192 A2 Evisa Corse France
142 B2 Evje Norway
190 C2 Evolène Switz.
184 C2 Évora Port.
184 C2 Évora admin. dist. Port.
184 C2 Évora-Monte Port.
198 C1 Evosmo Greece
122 A2 Evowghlī Iran
158 E3 Évran France
159 E4 Èvre r. France
159 F2 Évrecy France
156 B3 Évreux France
159 F3 Évron France
199 E1 Evros r. Greece/Turkey
198 C3 Evrotas r. Greece
156 C4 Évry France
198 D2 Evvoia i. Greece
198 C1 Evzonoi Kentriki Makedonia Greece
240 □ Ewa HI U.S.A.
240 □ Ewa Beach HI U.S.A.
85 F3 Ewan Qld Austr.
246 □ Ewarton Jamaica
210 D4 Ewaso Ngiro r. Kenya
214 D2 Ewbank S. Africa
146 C4 Ewe, Loch b. Scotland U.K.
151 G3 Ewell Surrey, England U.K.
226 C2 Ewen MI U.S.A.
Ewenkizu Zizhiqi Nei Mongol China see Bayan Tohoi
151 G3 Ewhurst Surrey, England U.K.
234 D2 Ewing NJ U.S.A.
262 T2 Ewing Island Antarctica
208 B5 Ewo Congo
198 C3 Examilia Peloponnisos Greece
215 F3 Excelsior S. Africa
240 H2 Excelsior Mountain CA U.S.A.
240 H2 Excelsior Mountains NV U.S.A.
236 E4 Excelsior Springs MO U.S.A.
234 B1 Exchange PA U.S.A.
162 D3 Excideuil France
150 D4 Exe r. England U.K.
150 D3 Exebridge Somerset, England U.K.
262 P1 Executive Committee Range mts Antarctica
226 B3 Exeland WI U.S.A.
83 G3 Exeter N.S.W. Austr.
227 G4 Exeter Ont. Can.
150 D4 Exeter Devon, England U.K.
240 H3 Exeter CA U.S.A.
233 □H3 Exeter NH U.S.A.
161 E3 Exilles Italy
164 F2 Exloo Neth.
159 G3 Exmes France
150 D4 Exminster Devon, England U.K.
150 D3 Exmoor hills England U.K.
150 D3 Exmoor National Park England U.K.
233 F6 Exmore VA U.S.A.
86 B4 Exmouth W.A. Austr.
150 D4 Exmouth Devon, England U.K.
83 G2 Exmouth, Mount N.S.W. Austr.
86 B4 Exmouth Gulf W.A. Austr.
265 L6 Exmouth Plateau sea feature Indian Ocean
85 G5 Expedition Range mts Qld Austr.
225 K3 Exploits r. Nfld. Can.
222 H5 Exshaw Alta Can.
234 C2 Exton PA U.S.A.
245 E3 Extoraz r. Mex.
182 G5 Extremadura aut. comm. Spain
207 I4 Extrême-Nord prov. Cameroon
182 B3 Extremo Port.
246 C1 Exuma Cays is Bahamas
246 D1 Exuma Sound sea chan. Bahamas
135 G7 Eya r. Rus. Fed.
149 H4 Eyam Derbyshire, England U.K.
211 B5 Eyasi, Lake salt l. Tanz.
Eyawadi r. Myanmar see Irrawaddy
161 D3 Eybens France
162 D3 Eyburie France
163 D6 Eycheil France
142 C2 Eydehavn Norway
168 D3 Eydelstedt Ger.
151 G2 Eye Peterborough, England U.K.
151 I2 Eye Suffolk, England U.K.
134 M2 Eyelenoborsk Rus. Fed.
146 F6 Eyemouth Scottish Borders, Scotland U.K.
146 B3 Eye Peninsula Scotland U.K.
147 B5 Eyeries Rep. of Ireland
161 D4 Eygues r. France
161 D4 Eyguians France
161 D5 Eyguières France
162 E3 Eygurande France
162 C3 Eygurande-et-Gardedeuil France
140 □C3 Eyjafjallajökull ice cap Iceland
140 □C2 Eyjafjörður inlet Iceland
210 F3 Eyl Somalia
Eylau Rus. Fed. see Bagrationovsk
163 C4 Eymet France
199 F3 Eymir Turkey
162 D3 Eymoutiers France
151 H3 Eynsford Kent, England U.K.
151 F3 Eynsham Oxfordshire, England U.K.
161 C5 Eyragues France
162 B3 Eyrans France
163 A4 Eyre r. France
82 D2 Eyre, Lake salt flat S.A. Austr.
147 C3 Eyrecourt Rep. of Ireland
84 D5 Eyre Creek watercourse Qld Austr.
162 D3 Eyrein France
81 B6 Eyre Mountains South I. N.Z.
81 B6 Eyre Peak South I. N.Z.
82 C3 Eyre Peninsula S.A. Austr.
161 C4 Eyrieux r. France
163 B4 Eysines France
168 E3 Eystrup Ger.
130 A3 Eysturoy i. Faroe Is
144 D1 Eysturoy i. Faroe Is
151 I3 Eythorne Kent, England U.K.
207 H5 Eyumojok Cameroon
122 C3 Eyvānaki Iran
160 C3 Eyzin-Pinet France
215 H3 Ezakheni S. Africa
215 G2 eZamokuhle S. Africa
183 H2 Ezcaray Spain
186 B1 Ezcurra Spain
161 F5 Èze France
232 B6 Ezel KY U.S.A.
215 G2 Ezenzeleni S. Africa
260 C6 Ezequiel Ramos Mexía, Embalse resr Arg.
109 E2 Ezhou Hubei China
134 J3 Ezhva Respublika Komi Rus. Fed.
199 F2 Eziler Denizli Turkey
199 E2 Ezine Turkey
126 E2 Ezinepazar Turkey
Ezo i. Japan see Hokkaidō
128 A2 Ezousa r. Cyprus
127 G5 Ezra's Tomb tourist site Iraq
156 B4 Ézy-sur-Eure France

F

114 B5 Faadhippolhu Atoll Maldives
113 D10 Faadhippolhu Atoll Maldives
210 D4 Faafxadhuun Somalia
Faarava atoll Arch. des Tuamotu Fr. Polynesia see Fakarava
186 D3 Fabara Spain
163 D5 Fabas France
239 F6 Fabens TX U.S.A.
182 D2 Fabero Spain
177 L4 Fábiánháza Hungary
175 H3 Fabianki Pol.
177 J5 Fábiánsebestyén Hungary
142 D4 Fåborg Denmark
177 I3 Fabova hoľa mt. Slovakia
161 B5 Fabrègues France
191 H5 Fabriano Italy
193 E2 Fabrica di Roma Italy
185 H2 Fábricas de San Juan de Alcaraz Spain
195 F4 Fabrizia Italy
192 E2 Fabro Italy
250 C3 Facatativá Col.
182 B3 Facha Port.
184 E4 Facinas Spain
85 G4 Facing Island Qld Austr.
234 C1 Factoryville PA U.S.A.
184 C1 Fadagosa Port.
207 F3 Fada-Ngourma Burkina
177 H5 Fadd Hungary
205 H4 Fadnoun, Plateau du Alg.
191 I2 Faedis Italy
191 G4 Faenza Italy
Færoerne terr. N. Atlantic Ocean see Faroe Islands
Faeroes terr. N. Atlantic Ocean see Faroe Islands
Faesulae Italy see Fiesole
192 D2 Faete, Monte hill Italy
208 C3 Fafa r. C.A.R.
182 B3 Fafe Port.
191 I2 Fagagna Italy
197 G3 Făgăraş Romania
Fagatau atoll Arch. des Tuamotu Fr. Polynesia see Fangatau
78 □2 Fagatogo American Samoa
141 J3 Fagernes Norway
143 F2 Fagersta Sweden
197 F3 Făget Romania
193 I5 Fagnano Castello Italy
165 D4 Fagne reg. Belgium
156 E4 Fagnières France
206 D2 Faguibine, Lac l. Mali
148 B2 Fahan Rep. of Ireland
168 E1 Fahrdorf Ger.
168 F2 Fahrenkrug Ger.
173 F3 Fahrenzhausen Ger.
171 E3 Fahrland Ger.
125 G3 Fahūd, Jabal hill Oman
216 □1c Faial i. Azores
184 □ Faial Madeira
216 □1c Faial, Canal do sea chan. Azores
193 G3 Faicchio Italy
78 □4a Faichuk is Chuuk Micronesia
169 C5 Faid Ger.
190 D2 Faido Switz.
182 D3 Failde Port.
165 E4 Faimes Belgium
160 C1 Fain-lès-Montbard France
157 F4 Fains-Véel France
220 D3 Fairbanks AK U.S.A.
232 A5 Fairborn OH U.S.A.
236 D3 Fairbury NE U.S.A.
226 B3 Fairchild WI U.S.A.
81 B7 Fairfax South I. N.Z.
232 E5 Fairfax VA U.S.A.
233 G2 Fairfax VT U.S.A.
81 C6 Fairfield South I. N.Z.
240 F2 Fairfield CA U.S.A.
235 E1 Fairfield CT U.S.A.
236 F3 Fairfield IA U.S.A.
238 D3 Fairfield ID U.S.A.
236 F4 Fairfield IL U.S.A.
232 A5 Fairfield OH U.S.A.
237 D6 Fairfield TX U.S.A.
241 K1 Fairfield UT U.S.A.
232 D6 Fairfield VA U.S.A.
235 E1 Fairfield County county CT U.S.A.
151 F3 Fairford Gloucestershire, England U.K.
227 F4 Fairgrove MI U.S.A.
233 H4 Fairhaven MA U.S.A.
235 D2 Fair Haven NJ U.S.A.
233 G3 Fair Haven VT U.S.A.
234 C3 Fair Hill MD U.S.A.
146 □G2 Fair Isle i. Scotland U.K.
235 D2 Fair Lawn NJ U.S.A.
234 B3 Fairlee MD U.S.A.
233 G3 Fairlee VT U.S.A.
234 D2 Fairless Hills PA U.S.A.
81 C6 Fairlie South I. N.Z.
146 D6 Fairlie North Ayrshire, Scotland U.K.
85 F2 Fairlight Qld Austr.
151 H4 Fairlight East Sussex, England U.K.
236 E3 Fairmont MN U.S.A.
232 C5 Fairmont WV U.S.A.
222 H5 Fairmont Hot Springs B.C. Can.
151 F4 Fair Oak Hampshire, England U.K.
237 F5 Fair Oaks AR U.S.A.
226 D4 Fair Plain MI U.S.A.
239 F4 Fairplay CO U.S.A.
226 D3 Fairport MI U.S.A.
234 C3 Fairton NJ U.S.A.
85 F2 Fairview Qld Austr.
222 G3 Fairview Alta Can.
226 B5 Fairview IL U.S.A.
232 B5 Fairview KY U.S.A.
227 E3 Fairview MI U.S.A.
235 D2 Fairview NJ U.S.A.
235 E1 Fairview NY U.S.A.
237 D4 Fairview OK U.S.A.
232 C3 Fairview PA U.S.A.
241 L2 Fairview UT U.S.A.
226 B4 Fairview WI U.S.A.
234 C3 Fairville PA U.S.A.
220 E4 Fairweather, Mount Alaska/B.C. Can./U.S.A.
148 B3 Fairy Water r. Northern Ireland U.K.
91 J5 Fais i. Micronesia
123 H4 Faisalabad Pak.
156 E3 Faissault France
236 C2 Faith SD U.S.A.
193 G4 Faito, Monte mt. Italy
Faizabad Afgh. see Feyzābād
116 E4 Faizabad Uttar Prad. India
184 □ Fajã da Ovelha Madeira
216 □1b Fajã de Cima São Miguel Azores
182 C4 Fajão Port.
184 B2 Fajarda Port.
247 □1 Fajardo Puerto Rico
175 K4 Fajsławice Pol.
177 H5 Fajsz Hungary
81 □1 Fakaofo atoll Tokelau
Fakaofu atoll Tokelau see Fakaofo
79 □3 Fakarava atoll Arch. des Tuamotu Fr. Polynesia
134 K4 Fakel Rus. Fed.
151 H2 Fakenham Norfolk, England U.K.
140 K3 Fåker Sweden
117 G4 Fakiragram Assam India
197 H4 Fakiyska Reka r. Bulg.
142 E4 Fakse Denmark
142 E4 Fakse Bugt b. Denmark
107 I3 Faku Liaoning China
150 C4 Fal r. England U.K.
206 C4 Falaba Sierra Leone
182 C1 Faladoira, Serra da mts Spain
207 F3 Falagountou Burkina
159 F3 Falaise France
117 G4 Falakata W. Bengal India
96 A2 Falam Myanmar
122 B3 Falavarjan Iran
191 G2 Falcade Italy
147 C1 Falcarragh Rep. of Ireland
183 I2 Falces Spain
197 I2 Fălciu Romania
157 G3 Falck France
191 G5 Falco, Monte mt. Italy
250 D2 Falcón state Venez.
194 D5 Falconara Sicilia Italy
193 I5 Falconara Albanese Italy
191 I5 Falconara Marittima Italy
195 E4 Falcone Sicilia Italy
Falcon Island Tonga see Fonuafo'ou
223 M5 Falcon Lake Man. Can.
243 F3 Falcon Lake l. Mex./U.S.A.
206 B3 Falémé r. Mali/Senegal
134 J4 Falenki Rus. Fed.
193 E2 Faleria Italy
Falerii Italy see Civita Castellana
193 I5 Falerna Italy
193 F1 Falerone Italy
Faleshty Moldova see Făleşti
136 D4 Făleşti Moldova
237 D7 Falfurrias TX U.S.A.
222 G4 Falher Alta Can.
169 F4 Falken Ger.
173 G2 Falkenberg Bayern Ger.
173 G3 Falkenberg Bayern Ger.
170 E3 Falkenberg Brandenburg Ger.
171 E4 Falkenberg Brandenburg Ger.
142 E3 Falkenberg Sweden

Column 1

170 D2 Falkenhagen Ger.
171 D4 Falkenhain Ger.
170 E3 Falkensee Ger.
173 G2 Falkenstein Bayern Ger.
171 D4 Falkenstein Sachsen Ger.
170 E3 Falkenthal Ger.
146 E5 Falkirk Falkirk, Scotland U.K.
146 E6 Falkirk admin. div.
 Scotland U.K.
146 E5 Falkland Fife, Scotland U.K.
264 F9 Falkland Escarpment
 sea feature S. Atlantic Ocean
259 F8 Falkland Islands terr.
 S. Atlantic Ocean
264 F9 Falkland Plateau sea feature
 S. Atlantic Ocean
259 E9 Falkland Sound sea chan.
 Falkland Is
142 E2 Falköping Sweden
175 I4 Fałków Pol.
237 E4 Fall r. KS U.S.A.
232 B6 Fall Branch TN U.S.A.
240 I5 Fallbrook CA U.S.A.
226 B3 Fall Creek WI U.S.A.
190 C3 Fallère, Monte mt. Italy
158 E5 Falleron France
140 M2 Fällfors Sweden
262 T2 Fallières Coast Antarctica
146 E5 Fallin Stirling, Scotland U.K.
168 E3 Fallingbostel Ger.
147 A2 Fallmore Rep. of Ireland
215 F5 Fallodon S. Africa
240 H2 Fallon NV U.S.A.
233 H4 Fall River MA U.S.A.
234 C1 Falls PA U.S.A.
234 A4 Falls Church VA U.S.A.
236 E3 Falls City NE U.S.A.
232 D4 Falls Creek PA U.S.A.
234 D2 Fallsington PA U.S.A.
234 B3 Fallston MD U.S.A.
190 D2 Falmenta Italy
246 □ Falmouth Jamaica
150 B4 Falmouth Cornwall,
 England U.K.
232 A5 Falmouth KY U.S.A.
233 H4 Falmouth MA U.S.A.
233 □H3 Falmouth ME U.S.A.
234 B2 Falmouth MI U.S.A.
232 E5 Falmouth VA U.S.A.
150 B4 Falmouth Bay England U.K.
247 □² Falmouth Harbour
 Antigua and Barbuda
206 D3 Falo Mali
206 D3 Falou Mali
261 F6 Falsa, Bahía b. Arg.
225 G1 False r. Que. Can.
214 B6 False Bay S. Africa
220 B4 False Pass AK U.S.A.
117 F5 False Point India
186 D3 Falset Spain
259 C9 Falso Cabo de Hornos c. Chile
142 D4 Falster i. Denmark
149 G2 Falstone Northumberland,
 England U.K.
197 H2 Fălticeni Romania
143 F1 Falun Sweden
93 D3 Fam, Kepulauan is
 Irian Jaya Indon.
 Famagusta Cyprus see
 Ammochostos
 Famagusta Bay Cyprus see
 Ammochostos Bay
182 C4 Famalicão Port.
258 D3 Famatina Arg.
258 C3 Famatina, Sierra de mts Arg.
158 F5 Fambach Ger.
157 G3 Fameck France
122 B3 Famenin Iran
165 D4 Famenne val. Belgium
87 D5 Fame Range hills W.A. Austr.
86 E4 Family Well W.A. Austr.
206 D3 Fana Mali
78 □4a Fanaik i. Chuuk Micronesia
78 □4a Fanan i. Chuuk Micronesia
191 F4 Fanano Italy
78 □4a Fanapanges i. Chuuk
 Micronesia
109 F2 Fanchang Anhui China
213 □J4 Fandriana Madag.
147 E3 Fane r. Rep. of Ireland
96 B3 Fang Thai.
79 □³ Fangataufa atoll Arch. des
 Tuamotu Fr. Polynesia
79 □³ Fangataufa atoll Arch. des
 Tuamotu Fr. Polynesia
 Fangcheng Guangxi China see
 Fangchenggang
109 F2 Fangcheng Henan China
108 D4 Fangchenggang Guangxi China
108 D2 Fangdou Shan mts China
109 G4 Fangliao Taiwan
192 A2 Fango r. Corse France
109 D1 Fangshan Taiwan
100 D3 Fangxian Hubei China
100 D3 Fangzheng Heilong. China
196 D5 Fani i Vogël r. Albania
138 F5 Fanipal' Belarus
163 E5 Fanjeaux France
108 D2 Fankuai Sichuan China
 Fankuaidian Sichuan China see
 Fankuai
109 □ Fanling H.K. China
186 C2 Fanlo Spain
147 E2 Fannich, Loch l. Scotland U.K.
140 J3 Fannrem Norway
122 D5 Fannūj Iran
142 C4 Fanø i. Denmark
191 I5 Fano Italy
142 C4 Fanø Bugt b. Denmark
78 □¹a Fanos i. Tonga see
 Fonualei
109 F2 Fanshan Anhui China
109 G3 Fanshan Zhejiang China
107 Q4 Fanshi Shanxi China
96 C2 Fan Si Pan mt. Vietnam
177 K5 Fântâna Rece hill Romania
177 K5 Fântânele Romania
 Fanum Fortunae Italy see
 Fano
107 G5 Fanxian Henan China
182 B3 Fão Port.
206 C3 Farab Mali
 Farab-Pristan' Turkm. see
 Deheyhouk
208 E4 Faradje Dem. Rep. Congo
 Faradofay Madag. see
 Tôlañaro
213 □J4 Farafangana Madag.
206 B3 Farafenni Gambia
193 G2 Fara Filiorum Petri Italy
202 F3 Farâfra Oasis Egypt
123 E3 Farah Afgh.
123 E3 Farah prov. Afgh.
123 □K2 Farahalana Madag.
193 □ Fara in Sabina Italy
91 K3 Farallon de Medinilla i.
 N. Mariana Is
91 J2 Farallon de Pajaros vol.
 N. Mariana Is
182 E3 Faramontanos de Tábara
 Spain
206 C4 Faranah Guinea
197 H2 Faraoani Romania
123 F2 Farap Turkm.
124 C4 Fararah Oman
124 C4 Farasān, Jazā'ir is
 Saudi Arabia
193 G2 Fara San Martino Italy
186 B2 Farasdues Spain
213 □J3 Faratsiho Madag.
147 G5 Farchant Ger.
165 D4 Farciennes Belgium
177 L6 Fârdea Romania
145 E7 Fardes r. Spain
147 D3 Fardrum Rep. of Ireland
151 F4 Farebersviller France
151 F4 Fareham Hampshire,
 England U.K.
156 D4 Faremoutiers France
 Farewell, Cape Greenland see
 Nunap Isua
80 □ Farewell, Cape South I. N.Z.
80 □ Farewell Spit South I. N.Z.
193 E2 Farfa r. Italy
142 E2 Färgelanda Sweden

Column 2

 Farghona Uzbek. see Fergana
 Farghona Wiloyati admin. div.
 Uzbek. see
 Ferganskaya Oblast'
231 D6 Fargo GA U.S.A.
236 D2 Fargo ND U.S.A.
163 C4 Fargues France
168 E1 Fargues-sur-Ourbise France
236 E2 Faribault MN U.S.A.
116 D3 Faridabad Haryana India
116 C3 Faridkot Punjab India
117 G5 Faridpur Bangl.
116 D3 Faridpur Uttar Prad. India
122 D2 Fārīq Iran
141 K3 Färila Sweden
206 B3 Farim Guinea-Bissau
151 F3 Faringdon Oxfordshire,
 England U.K.
149 G4 Farington Lancashire,
 England U.K.
122 A1 Fariz r. Brazil
190 F4 Farini Italy
182 D3 Fariza de Sayago Spain
143 G3 Färjestaden Kalmar Sweden
198 C2 Farkadhon Greece
123 G2 Farkhar Afgh.
123 G2 Farkhato Afgh.
231 E4 Farkwa Tanz.
85 G4 Farleigh Qld Austr.
151 F3 Farleigh Wallop Hampshire,
 England U.K.
186 C3 Farlete Spain
192 D1 Farma r. Italy
199 E3 Farmakonisi i. Greece
150 E3 Farmborough Bath and North
 East Somerset, England U.K.
226 C5 Farmer City IL U.S.A.
237 E5 Farmerville LA U.S.A.
235 D3 Farmingdale NJ U.S.A.
222 F4 Farmington B.C. Can.
235 F1 Farmington CT U.S.A.
234 C4 Farmington DE U.S.A.
226 B5 Farmington IL U.S.A.
233 □H2 Farmington ME U.S.A.
237 F4 Farmington MO U.S.A.
233 □H3 Farmington NH U.S.A.
239 E4 Farmington NM U.S.A.
238 E3 Farmington UT U.S.A.
232 B3 Farmington Hills MI U.S.A.
235 E2 Farmingville NY U.S.A.
177 I4 Farmos Hungary
222 E4 Far Mountain B.C. Can.
232 D6 Farmville VA U.S.A.
177 H3 Fárna Slovakia
151 G3 Farnborough Hampshire,
 England U.K.
149 I4 Farndon Cheshire, England U.K.
149 H2 Farndon Nottinghamshire,
 England U.K.
149 H2 Farne Islands England U.K.
192 D2 Farnese Italy
233 G2 Farnham Que. Can.
151 G3 Farnham Surrey, England U.K.
232 E6 Farnham VA U.S.A.
87 E5 Farnham, Lake salt flat
 W.A. Austr.
222 G5 Farnham, Mount B.C. Can.
151 G3 Farnham Royal
 Buckinghamshire, England U.K.
171 C4 Farnstädt Ger.
149 G4 Farnworth Greater Manchester,
 England U.K.
251 G5 Faro Brazil
207 I4 Faro r. Cameroon
184 C3 Faro Port.
184 C3 Faro admin. dist. Port.
182 C2 Faro mt. Spain
143 H3 Fårö Gotland Sweden
182 C2 Faro, Serra do mts Spain
144 D1 Faroe Islands terr.
 N. Atlantic Ocean
190 C3 Faroma, Monte mt. Italy
143 H3 Fårösund Gotland Sweden
217 □² Farquhar Atoll Seychelles
217 □² Farquhar Islands Seychelles
87 D5 Farquharson Tableland hills
 W.A. Austr.
146 D4 Farr Highland, Scotland U.K.
191 H2 Farra d'Alpago Italy
232 E4 Farrandsville PA U.S.A.
147 B4 Farranfore Rep. of Ireland
146 D4 Farrar r. Scotland U.K.
124 C4 Farräsh, Jabal az hill
 Saudi Arabia
122 C4 Farrāshband Iran
122 C3 Farrokhī Iran
122 D3 Farrokhkhord Uttar Prad. India
122 C4 Färs prov. Iran
129 B1 Fars r. Rus. Fed.
122 C3 Farsakh Iran
198 C2 Farsala Greece
198 C2 Farsaliotis r. Greece
122 D3 Farsj, Jazireh-ye i. Iran
143 C3 Farsø Denmark
238 E3 Farson WY U.S.A.
142 B2 Farsund Norway
197 H3 Fârțâneşti Romania
256 D2 Fartura r. Brazil
255 B8 Fartura, Serra da mts Brazil
142 C3 Fårvang Denmark
142 C3 Farvel, Kap c. Greenland see
 Nunap Isua
226 E4 Farwell MI U.S.A.
237 C5 Farwell TX U.S.A.
123 F2 Fāryāb prov. Afgh.
171 C5 Feilitzsch Ger.
160 E3 Feillens France
164 B2 Feio r. Brazil see Aguapeí
174 J4 Feira Zambia see Luangwa
195 J3 Feira de Santana Brazil
182 C1 Feira de Monte Spain
128 B5 Feirāni, Gebel mt. Egypt
160 E3 Feissons-sur-Isère France
216 □3a Fasnia Tenerife Canary Is
168 F3 Fassberg Ger.
136 E2 Fastiv Ukr.
 Fastov Ukr. see Fastiv
208 F4 Fataki Dem. Rep. Congo
109 H5 Fate, Monte delle mt. Italy
116 C3 Fatehabad Haryana India
116 D4 Fatehgarh Madh. Prad. India
116 D4 Fatehgarh Rajasthan India
116 C4 Fatehpur Rajasthan India
116 E4 Fatehpur Uttar Prad. India
182 C4 Fatehpur Sikri Uttar Prad. India
178 S. Africa
193 H1 Fatezh Rus. Fed.
206 A3 Fatick Senegal
182 B5 Fátima Port.
 Fattoilep atoll Micronesia see
 Faraulep
177 H4 Fatuhiva i. Fr. Polynesia see
 Fatu Hiva
79 □³ Fatu Hiva i. Fr. Polynesia
78 □6 Fauabu Malaita Solomon Is
157 H5 Faucogney-et-la-Mer France
161 B5 Faugères France
147 D1 Faughan r.
 Northern Ireland U.K.
190 F5 Fauglia Italy
163 C4 Faulquemont France
172 D2 Faulbach Ger.
177 J1 Faulenrost Ger.
236 D2 Faulkton SD U.S.A.
113 □11 Faulhorn mt. Switz.
150 D2 Faulhouse West Lothian,
 Scotland U.K.

Column 3

160 E3 Faverges France
157 G5 Faverney France
161 B4 Faverolles France
151 H3 Faversham Kent, England U.K.
157 F4 Favières France
195 □8 Favignana Sicilia Italy
195 B5 Favignana, Isola i. Sicilia Italy
222 H4 Fawcett Alta Can.
151 F4 Fawley Hampshire,
 England U.K.
234 B2 Fawn r. Ont. Can.
234 A4 Fawn Grove PA U.S.A.
215 H3 Fawnleas S. Africa
124 C2 Fawwārah Saudi Arabia
140 □B2 Faxaflói b. Iceland
140 L3 Faxälven r. Sweden
234 B1 Faxon PA U.S.A.
202 C5 Faya Chad
78 □3 Fayaoué i. Loyauté
 New Caledonia
156 C5 Fay-aux-Loges France
163 D4 Fayelles France
158 F4 Fayence France
161 E5 Fayence France
231 D4 Fayette AL U.S.A.
226 D3 Fayette MI U.S.A.
236 E4 Fayette MO U.S.A.
237 F6 Fayette MS U.S.A.
231 C4 Fayetteville AR U.S.A.
231 C5 Fayetteville GA U.S.A.
231 D5 Fayetteville NC U.S.A.
233 E3 Fayetteville NY U.S.A.
232 B5 Fayetteville TN U.S.A.
232 C5 Fayetteville TN U.S.A.
232 C5 Fayetteville WV U.S.A.
127 H5 Faylakah i. Kuwait
157 F5 Fayl-la-Forêt France
157 G5 Faymont France
186 D3 Fayón Spain
91 G5 Fay-sur-Lignon France
91 I4 Fayu i. Micronesia
121 G4 Fazao i. Chuuk Micronesia
151 F2 Fazeley Staffordshire,
 England U.K.
116 C3 Fazilka Punjab India
125 E2 Fazrān, Jabal hill Saudi Arabia
204 B5 Fdérik Maur.
147 B4 Feale r. Rep. of Ireland
146 C4 Fearnmore Highland,
 Scotland U.K.
163 D5 Féas France
234 C2 Feasterville PA U.S.A.
240 G2 Feather r. CA U.S.A.
240 G2 Feather, North Fork r.
 CA U.S.A.
81 E4 Featherston North I. N.Z.
150 E2 Featherstone Staffordshire,
 England U.K.
149 H4 Featherstone West Yorkshire,
 England U.K.
159 H2 Fécamp France
192 D1 Feccia r. Italy
157 H4 Fecht r. France
188 G3 Federacija Bosna i
 Hercegovina aut. div.
 Bos.-Herz.
261 I2 Federación Arg.
261 H2 Federal Arg.
207 G4 Federal Capital Territory
 admin. div. Nigeria
 Federal District admin. dist.
 Brazil see Distrito Federal
 Federal District admin. dist.
 Mex. see Distrito Federal
 Federal District admin. dist.
 Venez. see Distrito Federal
233 F5 Federalsburg MD U.S.A.
 Federated Malay States
 country Asia see Malaysia
144 J1 Fedorov Kazakhstan
137 H4 Fedorivka Ukr.
 Fedorovka Zapadnyy Kazakhstan
 Kazakh. see Larochette
120 E1 Fedorovka Kustanayskaya
 Oblast' Kazakh.
121 I1 Fedorovka Pavlodarskaya
 Oblast' Kazakh.
120 B2 Fedorovka Respublika
 Bashkortostan Rus. Fed.
120 C1 Fedorovka Samarskaya Oblast'
 Rus. Fed.
135 I6 Fedorovka Saratovskaya Oblast'
 Rus. Fed.
137 J3 Fedorovskaya Rus. Fed.
146 D4 Feehlin r. Scotland U.K.
147 D2 Feeny Northern Ireland U.K.
78 □4a Fefan i. Chuuk Micronesia
176 F2 Fegrác France
177 J4 Fegyvernek Hungary
177 L4 Fehérgyarmat Hungary
175 K5 Fehér-Körös r. Hungary
109 G2 Fehérvárcsurgó Hungary
170 C1 Fehmarn i. Ger.
 Fehmarn Belt str.
 Denmark/Ger. see Femer Bælt
170 D3 Fehrbellin Ger.
173 O3 Fehring Austria
257 G4 Feia, Lagoa lag. Brazil
 Feicheng Shandong China see
 Feixian
109 F2 Feidong Anhui China
156 D2 Feignies France
252 C2 Feijó Brazil
172 B2 Feilbingert Ger.
80 E4 Feilding North I. N.Z.
171 C5 Feilitzsch Ger.
192 D3 Feinstein Italy
162 A3 Feins France
217 J3 Feira Bangl.
161 H2 Feixi Anhui China
109 F2 Feixian Shandong China
107 Q4 Feixiang Hebei China
142 D4 Fejø i. Denmark
177 H4 Fejér county Hungary
126 D3 Feke Turkey
177 K5 Fekete-Körös r. Hungary
149 H2 Felanitx Spain
177 L6 Felchow Ger.
169 J3 Feld am See Austria
179 G4 Feldbach France
160 F1 Feldberg Ger.
172 C2 Feldberg mt. Ger.
146 B6 Feolin Ferry Argyll and Bute,
 Scotland U.K.
147 C4 Feonanagh Rep. of Ireland
78 □6 Fera i. Solomon Is
 Fera Greece see Feres
194 B5 Ficarazzi Sicilia Italy
194 C5 Ficarolo Italy
210 D2 Fiché Eth.
173 F7 Fichtelberg Ger.
173 F6 Fichtelberg hills Ger.
172 F2 Fichtelgeb r. Ger.
172 D2 Fichtenberg Ger.
172 D3 Fichtenberg Ger.
146 D4 Feshiebridge Highland,
 Scotland U.K.
236 D2 Fessenden ND U.S.A.
157 H5 Fessenheim France
156 D3 Festieux France
216 □3e Feteira Faial Azores
216 □3b Feteira São Miguel Azores
177 H2 Feteşti Romania
173 F7 Feteşti-Gară Romania
147 D4 Fethard Tipperary
 Rep. of Ireland
147 E4 Fethard Wexford
 Rep. of Ireland
 Fethiye Malatya Turkey see
 Yazıhan
199 F3 Fethiye Muğla Turkey
199 F3 Fethiye Körfezi b. Turkey
177 I5 Fetomb Hungary
158 □ Fetlar i. dept Bretagne France
 Fettercairn Aberdeenshire,
 Scotland U.K.
173 F7 Feucht Ger.
173 E6 Feuchtwangen Ger.
163 C4 Feugarolles France
225 G1 Feuilles, Rivière aux r.
 Que. Can.
82 C2 Finke, Mount N.T. Austr.
179 H3 Finkenberg Austria
168 E3 Finkenstein Austria
234 B3 Finksburg MD U.S.A.
126 E3 Finland country Europe
226 C2 Finland MN U.S.A.
143 N4 Finland, Gulf of Europe
222 E3 Finlay r. B.C. Can.
222 E3 Finlay Forks B.C. Can.
83 I5 Finley N.S.W. Austr.
226 D3 Finley ND U.S.A.
147 D3 Finn r. Rep. of Ireland
143 F2 Finnborka Sweden
171 C4 Finne ridge Ger.
143 H1 Finnea Sweden
85 F2 Finnerodja Sweden
85 F2 Finnigan, Mount Qld Austr.
151 G2 Finningham Suffolk,
 England U.K.
149 I4 Finningley South Yorkshire,
 England U.K.
141 M5 Finno Finland
191 H2 Finnis, Cape S.A. Austr.
82 B4 Finnis, Cape S.A. Austr.
84 □1 Finniss r. N.T. Austr.
90 E4 Finschhafen P.N.G.
140 N1 Finnmark admin. reg. Norway
140 M1 Finnmarksvidda reg. Norway
193 E1 Finnsnes Norway
172 D2 Finnwil Ger.
173 F3 Finnwil Ger.

Column 4

146 E6 Fell, Loch hill Scotland U.K.
191 I2 Fella r. Italy
172 D3 Fellbach Ger.
162 E3 Felletin France
149 H3 Felling Tyne and Wear,
 England U.K.
246 □ Fellowship Jamaica
232 D5 Fellowsville WV U.S.A.
168 F1 Felm Ger.
177 K5 Felnac Romania
 Fels Lux. see Larochette
169 E4 Felsberg Ger.
 Felsina Italy see Bologna
177 K3 Felsőcsatár Hungary
177 I4 Felsőlajos Hungary
177 I4 Felsőnyék Hungary
177 O6 Felsőszentmárton Hungary
177 J4 Felsőtárkány Hungary
179 H4 Felső-Válicka r. Hungary
177 J3 Felsőzsolca Hungary
168 E1 Felsted Denmark
151 H3 Felsted Essex, England U.K.
149 H2 Feltham Northumberland,
 England U.K.
234 C3 Felton DE U.S.A.
234 A3 Felton PA U.S.A.
191 G2 Feltre Italy
151 H2 Feltwell Norfolk, England U.K.
193 F2 Fema, Monte mt. Italy
254 D5 Femeas r. Brazil
168 F1 Femer Bælt str. Denmark/Ger.
216 □3a Femés hill Lanzarote Canary Is
195 F3 Femminamorta, Monte
 mt. Italy
142 D4 Femø i. Denmark
107 F5 Femr r. China
147 E4 Fenagh Carlow Rep. of Ireland
148 B3 Fenagh Leitrim Rep. of Ireland
216 □3b Fenais da Ajuda São Miguel
 Azores
160 D1 Fenay France
163 D5 Fendeille France
216 Fenelon Falls Ont. Can.
78 □4a Feneppi i. Chuuk Micronesia
 Fénérive Madag. see
 Fenoarivo Atsinanana
161 F4 Fenestrelle Italy
157 H4 Fénétrange France
157 I4 Feneu France
136 F2 Fenevychi Ukr.
199 D1 Fengari mt. Anatoliki Makedonia
 kai Thraki Greece
 Fengcheng Fujian China see
 Anxi
 Fengcheng Fujian China see
 Lianjiang
107 R4 Fengcheng Liaoning China
109 G2 Fengchuan Jiangxi China see
 Fengxin
108 C2 Fengdu Chongqing China
109 G4 Fenggang Guizhou China
109 G4 Fenggang Jiangxi China see
 Yihuang
109 G3 Fenghua Zhejiang China
108 D3 Fenghuang Hunan China
 Fengjiaba Sichuan China see
 Wangcang
108 C2 Fengjie Chongqing China
109 F2 Fengkai Guangdong China
109 G4 Fenglin Taiwan
107 R4 Fengning Shaanxi China
 Qishan
107 H3 Fengnan Hebei China
107 H3 Fengning Hebei China
107 H3 Fengqi Shaanxi China see
 Luochuan
109 F2 Fengqing Yunnan China
108 A3 Fengqing Henan China
107 G5 Fengqiu Henan China
107 H3 Fengrun Hebei China
108 C3 Fengshan Guangxi China
109 G4 Fengshan Hubei China see
 Luotian
108 C3 Fengshan Guangxi China see
 Fengjia
109 F1 Fengtai Anhui China
109 E2 Fengwei Yunnan China
 Zhenkang
107 H5 Fengxian Jiangsu China
109 G3 Fengxian Shaanxi China
109 G2 Fengxiang Shanghai China
109 G3 Fengxiang Heilong. China see
 Luobei
107 G5 Fengyang Yunnan China
 Lincang
109 F2 Fengxin Jiangxi China
109 F1 Fengyang Anhui China
109 E2 Fengyi Guizhou China see
 Zhen'gan
109 G2 Fengyi Sichuan China see
 Maoxian
109 F2 Fengyüan Taiwan
109 G3 Fengzhen Nei Mongol China
177 I2 Feni Bangl.
163 C4 Fenioux France
190 C3 Feni Italy
147 B4 Fenit Rep. of Ireland
150 C2 Feniton Devon, England U.K.
117 G5 Fenny r. Bangl./India
117 L4 Fenny Bentley
 England U.K.
216 □4 Fenoarivo Madag.
213 □J3 Fenoarivo Atsinanana Madag.
163 D3 Fenouillet France
180 C1 Fenstanton Cambridgeshire,
 England U.K.
126 E3 Fevzipaşa Turkey
227 E4 Fenton MI U.S.A.
81 □1 Fenua Loa i. Tokelau
81 □1 Fenua Ura atoll Arch. de la
 Société Fr. Polynesia see
 Manuae
146 D6 Fenwick East Ayrshire,
 Scotland U.K.
149 H2 Fenwick Northumberland,
 England U.K.
232 C5 Fenwick WV U.S.A.
109 F2 Fenyang Shanxi China
213 □J4 Fenyi Jiangxi China
208 B2 Fenyang Chad
190 C3 Fiano Italy
193 E2 Fiano Romano Italy
191 I5 Fiastra r. Italy
146 B6 Fiave Italy
184 B3 Ficalho hill Port.
194 A5 Ficarazzi Sicilia Italy
194 C5 Ficarolo Italy
210 D2 Fiché Eth.
173 F7 Fichtelberg Ger.
173 F6 Fichtelberg hills Ger.
172 F2 Fichtelgeb r. Ger.
172 D2 Fichtenberg Ger.
172 D3 Fichtenberg Ger.

Column 5

206 D4 Ferkessédougou Côte d'Ivoire
194 D5 Ferla Sicilia Italy
179 N4 Ferlach Austria
147 D2 Fermanagh county Northern
 Ireland U.K.
182 B4 Fermil Port.
182 B4 Fermentelos Port.
191 H5 Fermignano Italy
193 F1 Fermo Italy
225 H2 Fermont Que. Can.
182 D3 Fermoselle Spain
191 G5 Fermoy Rep. of Ireland
191 G5 Fermoy Rep. of Ireland
135 G1 Fernández Spain
184 B2 Fernancaballero Spain
250 □ Fernandina, Isla i. Islas
 Galápagos Ecuador
231 D6 Fernandina Beach FL U.S.A.
264 G6 Fernando de Noronha i. Brazil
256 B4 Fernandópolis Brazil
 Fernando Poó i. Equat. Guinea
 see Bioco
185 F3 Fernán Núñez Spain
213 J2 Fernão Veloso Moz.
234 D1 Ferndale NY U.S.A.
234 D1 Ferndale NY U.S.A.
238 B1 Ferndale WA U.S.A.
179 E4 Ferndorf Austria
151 F4 Ferndown Dorset, England U.K.
146 E4 Ferness Highland,
 Scotland U.K.
160 E2 Ferney-Voltaire France
80 F3 Fernhill North I. N.Z.
150 E2 Fernhill Heath Worcestershire,
 England U.K.
151 G3 Fernhurst West Sussex,
 England U.K.
142 D4 Fern i. Denmark
107 F5 Fern r. China
147 C4 Fenagh Carlow Rep. of Ireland
222 H5 Fernie B.C. Can.
179 G4 Fernitz Austria
238 C2 Fernley NV U.S.A.
234 C1 Fernridge PA U.S.A.
147 D3 Ferns Rep. of Ireland
226 C2 Fernwood ID U.S.A.
195 F4 Feroleto Antico Italy
78 □4a Ferozepore Punjab India see
 Firozpur
161 G5 Ferrals-les-Corbières France
195 F2 Ferrandina Italy
191 G4 Ferrara Italy
191 G4 Ferrara prov. Emilia-Romagna
 Italy
191 H4 Ferrarese r. Italy
193 E2 Ferreira Spain
193 E2 Ferreira Spain
184 B2 Ferreira do Alentejo Port.
182 B5 Ferreira do Zêzere Port.
251 H4 Ferreira-Gomes Brazil
184 A1 Ferrel Port.
250 B6 Ferreñafe Peru
182 D3 Ferreras de Abajo Spain
182 D3 Ferreras de Arriba Spain
190 C4 Ferrere Italy
186 B3 Ferreries Spain
186 B3 Ferreruela de Huerva Spain
182 D3 Ferreruela de Tábara Spain
160 F1 Ferrette France
261 E2 Ferreyra Arg.
237 F6 Ferriday LA U.S.A.
156 E2 Ferrière-la-Grande France
165 D4 Ferrières Belgium
156 C4 Ferrières France
161 B3 Ferrières-St-Mary France
160 D3 Ferrières-sur-Ariège France
84 B2 Ferro r. Sicilia Italy
195 F3 Ferro r. Italy
182 B1 Ferrol Spain
241 C2 Ferron UT U.S.A.
257 F3 Ferros Brazil
195 F4 Ferru, Monte hill Sardegna Italy
190 C4 Ferru VA U.S.A.
147 E4 Ferrycarrig Rep. of Ireland
146 F5 Ferryden Angus, Scotland U.K.
149 H3 Ferryhill Durham, England U.K.
225 K4 Fincastle VA U.S.A.
 Ferryville Tunisia see
 Menzel Bourguiba
172 A2 Ferschweiler Ger.
120 D1 Fershampenuaz Rus. Fed.
179 H3 Fertő l. Austria/Hungary
179 H3 Fertő l. Austria/Hungary
232 D1 Fertília Sardegna Italy
179 H3 Fertőd Austria
176 F1 Fertőszéplak Hungary
182 B2 Fervença Port.
164 E1 Ferwerd Neth.
159 K4 Ferwoda Rus. Fed.
204 D2 Fès Morocco
209 C6 Feshi Dem. Rep. Congo
146 D4 Feshiebridge Highland,
 Scotland U.K.
236 D2 Fessenden ND U.S.A.
157 H5 Fessenheim France
156 D3 Festieux France
216 □3e Feteira Faial Azores
216 □3b Feteira São Miguel Azores
177 H2 Feteşti Romania
173 F7 Feteşti-Gară Romania
147 D4 Fethard Tipperary Rep. of Ireland
147 E4 Fethard Wexford
 Rep. of Ireland
 Fethiye Malatya Turkey see
 Yazıhan
199 F3 Fethiye Muğla Turkey
199 F3 Fethiye Körfezi b. Turkey
177 I5 Fetomb Hungary
146 □1 Fetlar i. Scotland U.K.
158 □ Fetlar i. dept Bretagne France
146 F5 Fettercairn Aberdeenshire,
 Scotland U.K.
173 F7 Feucht Ger.
173 E6 Feuchtwangen Ger.
163 C4 Feugarolles France
225 G1 Feuilles, Rivière aux r.
 Que. Can.
84 C5 Finke watercourse N.T. Austr.
84 C5 Finke S.A. Austr.
82 C2 Finke, Mount N.T. Austr.
84 B2 Finke Bay N.T. Austr.
84 C5 Finke Gorge National Park
 N.T. Austr.
179 H3 Finkenberg Austria
168 E3 Finkenstein Austria
234 B3 Finksburg MD U.S.A.
126 E3 Finland country Europe
226 C2 Finland MN U.S.A.
143 N4 Finland, Gulf of Europe
222 E3 Finlay r. B.C. Can.
222 E3 Finlay Forks B.C. Can.
83 I5 Finley N.S.W. Austr.
226 D3 Finley ND U.S.A.
147 D3 Finn r. Rep. of Ireland
143 F2 Finnborka Sweden
171 C4 Finne ridge Ger.
143 H1 Finnea Sweden
85 F2 Finnerodja Sweden
85 F2 Finnigan, Mount Qld Austr.
151 G2 Finningham Suffolk,
 England U.K.
149 I4 Finningley South Yorkshire,
 England U.K.

Column 6

146 F5 Fife admin. div. Scotland U.K.
226 E3 Fife Lake MI U.S.A.
146 F5 Fife Ness Scotland U.K.
83 I7 Fifield N.S.W. Austr.
226 B3 Fifield WI U.S.A.
203 G5 Fifth Cataract rapids Sudan
222 H3 Fifth Meridian Alta Can.
161 E5 Figanières France
192 A2 Figarella r. Corse France
192 B3 Figari Corse France
227 F3 Figline Ont. Can.
190 E3 Figino Valdarno Italy
184 B2 Figueira r. Port.
191 G4 Figueira da Foz Port.
182 A4 Figueira de Castelo Rodrigo
 Port.
261 G3 Figueira de los Caballeiros Port.
256 B2 Figueira e Barros Port.
184 C1 Figueiredo de Alva Port.
184 C1 Figueiró r. Port.
184 C1 Figueiró da Granja Port.
184 C1 Figueiró dos Vinhos Port.
182 D3 Figueres Spain
186 F2 Figueres Spain
182 D3 Figueruela de Arriba Spain
204 D2 Figuig Morocco
205 E2 Figuig Morocco
207 I4 Figuil Cameroon
213 □J3 Fihaonana Madag.
91 □ rary is S. Pacific Ocean
85 F2 Firth Shetland, Scotland U.K.
 Firuzabad Balúchestán va
 Sistán Iran see Räsk
122 C4 Firūzābād Iran
122 D2 Firūzeh Iran
122 D2 Firūzkūh Iran
122 D2 Firyuza Turkm.
186 C2 Fiscal Spain
173 E3 Fischach Ger.
179 M2 Fischamend Markt Austria
179 G3 Fischbach Austria
172 B2 Fischbach Ger.
173 E7 Fischbachau Ger.
172 B2 Fischbach bei Dahn Ger.
170 D3 Fischbeck Ger.
113 E3 Fischen im Allgäu Ger.
212 C6 Fish watercourse Namibia
214 B5 Fish r. S. Africa
149 H3 Fishburn Durham, England U.K.
82 B2 Fisher r. S.A. Austr.
223 J5 Fisher r. Man. Can.
223 J4 Fisher River Man. Can.
232 D5 Fisher Strait Nunavut Can.
150 C3 Fishguard Pembrokeshire,
 Wales U.K.
150 C3 Fishguard Bay Wales U.K.
233 G5 Fishing Creek MD U.S.A.
233 G4 Fishing Creek r. NY U.S.A.
235 E2 Fishkill NY U.S.A.
235 E1 Fishkill Creek r. NY U.S.A.
151 I2 Fishtoft Lincolnshire, England U.K.
141 I3 Fiskå Norway
262 C1 Fiske, Cape Antarctica
156 C3 Fismes France
194 D5 Fisterra Spain
182 A2 Fisterra, Cabo c. Spain
233 H3 Fitchburg MA U.S.A.
226 C4 Fitchburg WI U.S.A.
235 F1 Fitchville CT U.S.A.
232 B4 Fitchville OH U.S.A.
183 I2 Fitero Spain
146 □2 Fitful Head hd Scotland U.K.
142 A2 Fitjar Norway
198 C2 Fitia Greece see Fyteies
78 □1b Fito, Mount vol. Samoa
163 B5 Fitou France
252 E2 Fitzcarrald Peru
190 D3 Fitzgerald Alta Can.
231 D6 Fitzgerald GA U.S.A.
194 B5 Fitz-James France
84 D2 Fitzmaurice r. N.T. Austr.
185 H3 Fitzroy r. W.A. Austr.
86 D3 Fitzroy r. W.A. Austr.
259 B8 Fitz Roy, Cerro mt. Arg.
86 E4 Fitzroy Crossing W.A. Austr.
84 □1 Fiumana r. Italy
193 H3 Fiumarella r. Italy
 Fiume Croatia see Rijeka
193 I5 Fiumefreddo Bruzio Italy
195 □6 Fiumefreddo di Sicilia
 Italy
191 I1 Fiume Veneto Italy
195 D5 Fiumicino Italy
192 B3 Fium'Orbo r. Corse France
146 C5 Fiunary Highland, Scotland U.K.
199 G3 Five Fingers Strait see
193 H3 Five Forks South I. N.Z.
238 D4 Five Points CA U.S.A.
81 B6 Five Rivers South I. N.Z.
240 F3 Fivizzano Italy
161 B5 Fix-St-Geneys France
209 F6 Fizi Dem. Rep. Congo
204 D2 Fizuli Azer. see Füzuli
140 I2 Fjällåsjöåns Sweden
143 I5 Fjällbacka Sweden
141 Q2 Fjällnäs Sweden
206 E4 Fjärdhundra reg. Sweden
142 F1 Fjell Norway
161 B5 Fjerritslev Denmark
204 D2 Fkih Ben Salah Morocco
142 C1 Flå Norway
179 E4 Flachau Austria
173 F4 Flachslanden Ger.
168 G2 Flachsmeer Ger.
146 □2 Fladdabister Shetland,
 Scotland U.K.
142 C3 Fladsá r. Denmark
169 K2 Fladungen Ger.
163 A5 Flagnac France
241 E4 Flagstaff S. Africa
241 □4 Flagstaff AZ U.S.A.
233 □J2 Flagstaff Lake ME U.S.A.
234 B2 Flagtown NJ U.S.A.
220 B4 Flaherty Island Nunavut Can.
143 H1 Flakaberg Sweden
178 B1 Flamanville France
197 M1 Flămânzi Romania
226 B3 Flambeau r. WI U.S.A.
149 J3 Flamborough East Riding of
 Yorkshire, England U.K.
149 J3 Flamborough Head hd
 England U.K.
246 □ Flanders, Isla i. Chile
216 □3b Flamengos Faial Azores
186 D2 Flamicell r. Spain
 Flaming hills Ger.
223 M2 Flaming hills Can.
235 G4 Flanders NY U.S.A.
235 F2 Flanders Lake hills Ger.
156 C2 Flandre reg. France
224 D3 Flandre NY U.S.A.
236 D2 Flandreau SD U.S.A.
140 N2 Flåsjön l. Sweden
161 C5 Flassans-sur-Issole France
222 F2 Flat r. N.W.T. Can.
226 E4 Flat r. MI U.S.A.
149 I4 Flatbrookville NJ U.S.A.
140 □C2 Flateyjarskvísl r. Iceland
236 D2 Flathead r. MT U.S.A.
81 A6 Flathead Lake MT U.S.A.
227 K4 Flat Island S. China Sea
232 B5 Flat Lick KY U.S.A.
81 F1 Flat Mountain South I. N.Z.
146 C5 Flatnitz Austria
142 C3 Flat Top mt. U.S.A.
232 C6 Flatwoods KY U.S.A.
232 C5 Flatwoods WV U.S.A.
142 C2 Flekkefjord Norway
142 C2 Flekkerøy i. Norway

Flémalle to Freyburg (Unstrut) 305

165 E4 Flémalle Belgium
232 B5 Flemingsburg KY U.S.A.
234 D2 Flemington NJ U.S.A.
264 G2 Flemish Cap sea feature N. Atlantic Ocean
151 H2 Flempton Suffolk, England U.K.
143 G2 Flen Sweden
168 E1 Flensborg Fjord inlet Denmark/Ger.
168 E1 Flensburg Ger.
Flensburger Förde inlet Denmark/Ger. see Flensborg Fjord
165 E4 Fléron Belgium
159 F3 Flers France
227 G3 Flesherton Ont. Can.
170 C3 Flessau Ger.
262 S2 Fletcher Peninsula Antarctica
163 C5 Fleurance France
225 J3 Fleur de Lys Nfld. Can.
162 C2 Fleuré France
160 C2 Fleurie France
190 B2 Fleurier Switz.
165 D4 Fleurus Belgium
161 B5 Fleury France
156 B5 Fleury-les-Aubrais France
156 B3 Fleury-sur-Andelle France
159 F2 Fleury-sur-Orne France
157 F3 Fléville-Lixières France
164 E2 Flevoland prov. Neth.
150 C4 Flexbury Cornwall, England U.K.
169 E5 Flieden Ger.
178 B3 Fließ Austria
149 F3 Flimby Cumbria, England U.K.
190 E2 Flims Switz.
151 H3 Flimwell East Sussex, England U.K.
85 E3 Flinders r. Qld Austr.
87 B7 Flinders Bay W.A. Austr.
85 F2 Flinders Group is Qld Austr.
82 C3 Flinders Island S.A. Austr.
83 G4 Flinders Island Tas. Austr.
85 G3 Flinders Passage Qld Austr.
82 D3 Flinders Ranges mts S.A. Austr.
85 G3 Flinders Reefs Coral Sea Is Terr. Austr.
156 D2 Flines-lez-Raches France
223 K4 Flin Flon Man. Can.
150 D1 Flint Flintshire, Wales U.K.
227 F4 Flint MI U.S.A.
231 C6 Flint r. GA U.S.A.
227 F4 Flint r. MI U.S.A.
168 F1 Flintbek Ger.
267 I6 Flint Island Kiribati
85 G5 Flinton Qld Austr.
150 D1 Flintshire admin. div. Wales U.K.
232 D5 Flintstone MD U.S.A.
157 F4 Flirey France
142 E1 Flisa Norway
141 K3 Flisa r. Norway
142 B2 Fliseggi mt. Norway
151 G2 Flitwick Bedfordshire, England U.K.
186 D3 Flix Spain
156 C2 Flixecourt France
156 E3 Flize France
142 E3 Floda Sweden
149 G2 Flodden Northumberland, England U.K.
156 D5 Flogny-la-Chapelle France
171 E5 Flöha Ger.
171 E5 Flöha r. Ger.
157 E3 Floing France
163 B4 Floirac France
262 P1 Flood Range mts Antarctica
226 A2 Floodwood MN U.S.A.
149 G3 Flookburgh Cumbria, England U.K.
84 B2 Flora r. N.T. Austr.
226 D5 Flora IN U.S.A.
161 B4 Florac France
231 C6 Florala AL U.S.A.
157 G3 Florange France
85 F3 Flora Reef Coral Sea Is Terr. Austr.
84 D3 Floraville Qld Austr.
165 D4 Floreffe Belgium
227 F4 Florence Ont. Can.
Florence Italy see Firenze
231 C5 Florence AL U.S.A.
241 L5 Florence AZ U.S.A.
239 F4 Florence CO U.S.A.
236 D4 Florence KS U.S.A.
234 D2 Florence NJ U.S.A.
238 A3 Florence OR U.S.A.
231 E5 Florence SC U.S.A.
226 C3 Florence WI U.S.A.
241 L5 Florence Junction AZ U.S.A.
233 □J1 Florenceville N.B. Can.
250 C4 Florencia Col.
261 I3 Florencio Sánchez Uru.
165 D4 Florennes Belgium
161 B5 Florensac France
Florentia Italy see Firenze
165 E5 Florenville Belgium
261 H4 Flores r. Arg.
216 □1 Flores i. Azores
254 F3 Flores Pernambuco Brazil
254 E3 Flores Piauí Brazil
243 H5 Flores Guat.
93 B5 Flores i. Indon.
261 I3 Flores dept Uru.
183 E4 Flores de Ávila Spain
254 D5 Flores de Goiás Brazil
Floreshty Moldova see Florești
93 A4 Flores Sea Indon.
254 F4 Floresta Brazil
194 D5 Floresta Sicilia Italy
136 E4 Florești Moldova
256 B5 Florestópolis Brazil
237 D6 Floresville TX U.S.A.
235 D2 Florham Park NJ U.S.A.
254 E3 Floriano Brazil
255 C8 Florianópolis Brazil
252 E4 Florida Bol.
260 A5 Florida Chile
246 C2 Florida Cuba
247 □1 Florida Puerto Rico
261 I4 Florida Uru.
261 I4 Florida dept Uru.
235 D1 Florida NY U.S.A.
231 D6 Florida state U.S.A.
231 D7 Florida, Straits of Bahamas/U.S.A.
231 D7 Florida Bay FL U.S.A.
182 E3 Florida de Liébana Spain
78 □6 Florida Islands Solomon Is
231 D7 Florida Keys is FL U.S.A.
256 B4 Flórida Paulista Brazil
195 E5 Floridia Sicilia Italy
237 B7 Florido r. Mex.
197 F2 Florii, Vârful hill Romania
240 G2 Florin CA U.S.A.
198 B1 Florina Greece
192 A4 Florinas Sardegna Italy
256 B5 Florínia Brazil
236 F4 Florissant MO U.S.A.
141 I3 Florø Norway
169 E5 Flörsbach Ger.
169 D5 Flörsheim am Main Ger.
172 C2 Flörsheim-Dalsheim Ger.
169 D5 Florstadt Ger.
173 G2 Floß Ger.
173 G2 Flossenbürg Ger.
146 E3 Flotta i. Scotland U.K.
163 E5 Floure France
226 A4 Floyd IA U.S.A.
232 C6 Floyd VA U.S.A.
241 K4 Floyd, Mount AZ U.S.A.
237 C5 Floydada TX U.S.A.
178 B4 Fluchthorn mt. Austria/Switz.
190 D2 Flüelen Switz.
190 D2 Flühli Switz.
186 C3 Flúmen r. Spain
192 B5 Flumendosa r. Sardegna Italy
193 H3 Flumeri Italy
160 E3 Flumet France
192 B4 Flumineddu r. Sardegna Italy
192 B5 Flumineddu r. Sardegna Italy
192 A5 Fluminimaggiore Sardegna Italy
190 E1 Flums Switz.
Flushing Neth. see Vlissingen
232 B3 Flushing MI U.S.A.
232 C4 Flushing OH U.S.A.
192 A4 Flussio Sardegna Italy
186 G2 Fluvià r. Spain
91 J8 Fly r. P.N.G.
262 R2 Flying Fish, Cape Antarctica
86 □1 Flying Fish Cove Christmas I.
84 C2 Flying Fox Creek r. N.T. Austr.
79 □2 Foa i. Tonga
223 K5 Foam Lake Sask. Can.
190 D3 Fobello Italy
188 G4 Foča Bos.-Herz.
199 E2 Foça Turkey
165 E4 Focant Belgium
191 H3 Focce dell'Adige r. mouth Italy
146 E4 Fochabers Moray, Scotland U.K.
215 F2 Fochville S. Africa
168 E1 Fockbek Ger.
197 H3 Focșani Romania
197 H2 Focuri Romania
159 I4 Foëcy France
84 D2 Foelsche r. N.T. Austr.
109 E4 Fogang Guangdong China
84 B2 Fog Bay N.T. Austr.
234 C2 Fogelsville PA U.S.A.
193 H3 Foggia Italy
193 H3 Foggia prov. Puglia Italy
191 H5 Foglia r. Italy
141 M3 Föglö Åland Fin.
206 □ Fogo i. Cape Verde
121 G4 Fogoleva Kazakh.
179 F3 Fohnsdorf Austria
168 D1 Föhr i. Ger.
171 D3 Fohrde Ger.
172 A2 Föhren Ger.
184 B3 Fóia hill Port.
191 G5 Foiano della Chiana Italy
177 L4 Foieni Romania
147 A5 Foilclough hill Rep. of Ireland
146 D3 Foinaven hill Scotland U.K.
163 D6 Foix France
186 E3 Foix r. Spain
139 J5 Fokino Rus. Fed.
207 G4 Fokku Nigeria
177 H5 Foktő Hungary
142 B1 Folarskarnuten mt. Norway
140 K2 Folda sea chan. Norway
177 J5 Földeák Hungary
177 K4 Földes Hungary
140 J2 Foldfjorden sea chan. Norway
198 D3 Folegandros i. Greece
231 C6 Foley AL U.S.A.
236 E2 Foley MN U.S.A.
224 D3 Foleyet Ont. Can.
85 G4 Foleyvale Qld Austr.
Folgares Angola see Capelongo
191 G3 Folgaria Italy
263 H2 Folger, Cape Antarctica
182 C2 Folgoso de Courel Spain
182 D2 Folgoso de la Ribera Spain
193 F2 Folignano Italy
193 E2 Foligno Italy
151 I3 Folkestone Kent, England U.K.
151 G2 Folkingham Lincolnshire, England U.K.
231 D6 Folkston GA U.S.A.
141 J3 Folldal Norway
191 H3 Follina Italy
140 K3 Föllinge Sweden
192 C2 Follonica Italy
150 C4 Folly Gate Devon, England U.K.
157 G3 Folschviller France
232 C5 Folsom WV U.S.A.
217 □3 Fomboni Comoros
246 C2 Fómento Cuba
135 H7 Fomin Rus. Fed.
134 H5 Fominki Rus. Fed.
134 H4 Fominskoye Rus. Fed.
183 G2 Foncea hill Spain
233 F3 Fonda NY U.S.A.
223 J3 Fond-du-Lac Sask. Can.
223 J3 Fond du Lac r. Sask. Can.
226 C4 Fond du Lac WI U.S.A.
232 B6 Fonde KY U.S.A.
182 B3 Fondevila Spain
193 F3 Fondi Italy
185 H4 Fondón Spain
185 G3 Fonelas Spain
186 B3 Fonfría Spain
182 D3 Fonfría Spain
206 C4 Fon Going ridge Guinea
192 B4 Fonni Sardegna Italy
163 C4 Fonroque France
Fonsagrada Spain see A Fonsagrada
250 C2 Fonseca Col.
163 D5 Fonsorbes France
157 G5 Fontaine Franche-Comté France
161 D3 Fontaine Rhône-Alpes France
156 C4 Fontainebleau France
160 D1 Fontaine-Française France
156 B3 Fontaine-le-Bourg France
159 G2 Fontaine-le-Dun France
160 D1 Fontaine-lès-Dijon France
157 G5 Fontaine-lès-Luxeuil France
165 D4 Fontaine-l'Évêque Belgium
160 C2 Fontaines Bourgogne France
156 D5 Fontaines Bourgogne France
161 F4 Fontan France
234 B2 Fontana PA U.S.A.
183 G4 Fontanar Spain
185 F1 Fontanarejo Spain
190 F4 Fontanellato Italy
193 F3 Fontanelle r. Italy
161 C5 Fontanès France
225 G2 Fontanges Que. Can.
190 E4 Fontanigorda Italy
161 B3 Fontannes France
185 F2 Fontanosas Spain
222 F3 Fontas B.C. Can.
222 F3 Fontas r. B.C. Can.
Font Blanca, Pic de mt. France/Spain see Port, Pic du
251 E5 Fonte Boa Brazil
193 F2 Fontecchio Italy
193 F2 Fontecellese, Monte mt. Italy
216 □1a Fonte do Bastardo Terceira Azores
207 H5 Fontem Cameroon
162 B2 Fontenay-le-Comte France
156 C4 Fontenay-Trésigny France
160 B1 Fontenoy France
157 G5 Fontenoy-le-Château France
157 F4 Fontenoy-sur-Moselle France
182 B5 Fontes Port.
159 G4 Fontevraud-l'Abbaye France
159 G5 Fontgombault France
191 G3 Fonti, Cima mt. Italy
216 □1a Fontinhas Terceira Azores
183 F4 Fontiveros Spain
157 F3 Fontoy France
163 E6 Font-Romeu-Odeillo-Via France
147 E3 Fontstown Rep. of Ireland
140 □D2 Fontur pt Iceland
161 C5 Fontvieille France
79 □2 Fonuafo'ou i. Tonga
Fonuafu'u i. Tonga see Fonuafo'ou
77 I3 Fonualei i. Tonga
78 □4a Fonuchu i. Chuuk Micronesia
177 G5 Fonyód Hungary
186 D2 Fonz Spain
191 G2 Fonzaso Italy
Foochow Fujian China see Fuzhou
227 H3 Foot's Bay Ont. Can.
108 D1 Foping Shaanxi China
190 E2 Foppolo Italy
193 E2 Forano Italy
122 C3 Forat Iran
Foraulep atoll Micronesia see Faraulep
157 G3 Forbach France
172 C3 Forbach Ger.
83 G3 Forbes N.S.W. Austr.
222 G4 Forbes, Mount Alta Can.
81 A6 Forbes, Mount South I. N.Z.
117 F4 Forbesganj Bihar India
161 E5 Forcalcueiret France
186 C4 Forcall Spain
161 D5 Forcalquier France
182 B2 Forcarei Spain
Forcary Spain see Forcarei
193 F2 Force Italy
172 B3 Forchheim Baden-Württemberg Ger.
173 F2 Forchheim Bayern Ger.
172 D2 Forchtenberg Ger.
179 H3 Forchtenstein Austria
225 H1 Ford r. Que. Can.
146 C5 Ford Argyll and Bute, Scotland U.K.
149 G2 Ford Northumberland, England U.K.
226 D3 Ford r. MI U.S.A.
84 B2 Ford, Cape N.T. Austr.
240 H4 Ford City CA U.S.A.
232 D4 Ford City PA U.S.A.
141 I3 Førde Norway
80 E3 Fordell North I. N.Z.
171 C4 Förderstedt Ger.
151 H2 Fordham Cambridgeshire, England U.K.
151 F4 Fordingbridge Hampshire, England U.K.
192 A5 Fordongianus Sardegna Italy
146 F5 Fordoun Aberdeenshire, Scotland U.K.
262 O1 Ford Range mts Antarctica
235 D2 Fords NJ U.S.A.
83 F2 Fords Bridge N.S.W. Austr.
147 E3 Fordstown Rep. of Ireland
146 F4 Fordyce Aberdeenshire, Scotland U.K.
237 E5 Fordyce AR U.S.A.
206 B4 Forécariah Guinea
221 O3 Forel, Mont mt. Greenland
151 F4 Foreland hd England U.K.
237 E5 Foreman AR U.S.A.
223 I5 Foremost Alta Can.
193 H4 Forenza Italy
222 E4 Foresight Mountain B.C. Can.
224 D5 Forest Ont. Can.
237 F5 Forest MS U.S.A.
232 B4 Forest OH U.S.A.
232 D6 Forest VA U.S.A.
223 H4 Forestburg Alta Can.
234 D1 Forestburg NY U.S.A.
234 C1 Forest City PA U.S.A.
85 E3 Forest Creek r. Qld Austr.
83 F3 Forest Hill N.S.W. Austr.
85 F5 Forest Hill Qld Austr.
240 G2 Foresthill CA U.S.A.
83 G5 Forestier Peninsula Tas. Austr.
226 C3 Forest Junction WI U.S.A.
226 A3 Forest Lake MN U.S.A.
241 L4 Forest Lakes AZ U.S.A.
231 C5 Forest Park GA U.S.A.
240 G2 Forest Ranch CA U.S.A.
151 H3 Forest Row East Sussex, England U.K.
225 G3 Forestville Que. Can.
240 F2 Forestville CA U.S.A.
234 B4 Forestville MD U.S.A.
227 F4 Forestville MI U.S.A.
232 D3 Forestville NY U.S.A.
142 A2 Føresvik Norway
160 B3 Forez, Monts du mts France
160 B3 Forez, Plaine du plain France
146 F5 Forfar Angus, Scotland U.K.
237 C4 Forgan OK U.S.A.
156 B3 Forges-les-Eaux France
173 E4 Forggensee l. Ger.
146 E4 Forgie Moray, Scotland U.K.
193 G4 Forino Italy
193 F4 Forio Italy
171 C5 Föritz Ger.
182 B3 Forjães Port.
234 B3 Fork MD U.S.A.
237 F5 Forked Deer r. TN U.S.A.
233 F5 Forked River NJ U.S.A.
147 E2 Forkhill Northern Ireland U.K.
238 A2 Forks WA U.S.A.
234 B1 Forkston PA U.S.A.
234 B1 Forksville PA U.S.A.
232 D6 Fork Union VA U.S.A.
191 H4 Forlì Italy
191 H5 Forlì prov. Emilia-Romagna Italy
191 H4 Forlimpopoli Italy
236 D2 Forman ND U.S.A.
190 D2 Formazza Italy
149 F4 Formby Merseyside, England U.K.
187 E6 Formentera i. Spain
187 G5 Formentor, Cap de c. Spain
156 B3 Formerie France
Former Yugoslav Republic of Macedonia country Europe see Macedonia
193 F3 Formia Italy
187 C4 Formiche Alto Spain
193 G3 Formicola Italy
257 E4 Formiga Brazil
191 F4 Formigine Italy
191 G4 Formignana Italy
163 E6 Formiguères France
258 F2 Formosa Arg.
258 F2 Formosa prov. Arg.
Formosa country Asia see Taiwan
255 D5 Formosa Brazil
253 G3 Formosa, Serra hills Brazil
254 D4 Formosa do Rio Preto Brazil
Formosa Strait China/Taiwan see Taiwan Strait
182 B4 Formoselha Port.
254 D5 Formoso Minas Gerais Brazil
254 C4 Formoso Tocantins Brazil
254 D5 Formoso r. Bahia Brazil
256 A3 Formoso r. Goiás Brazil
254 C4 Formoso r. Tocantins Brazil
147 B3 Formoyle Rep. of Ireland
192 A3 Fornelli Sardegna Italy
186 □ Fornells Spain
186 F3 Fornells de la Selva Spain
191 H2 Forni Avoltri Italy
191 H2 Forni di Sopra Italy
191 H2 Forni di Sotto Italy
190 C3 Forno Alpi Graie Italy
178 D4 Forno di Zoldo Italy
182 D3 Fornos Port.
182 C4 Fornos de Algodres Port.
190 F4 Fornovo di Taro Italy
193 G2 Foro r. Italy
140 J3 Forolshogna mt. Norway
137 G5 Foros Ukr.
184 B2 Foros de Vale Figueira Port.
184 B1 Foros do Arrão Port.
Føroyar terr. N. Atlantic Ocean see Faroe Islands
177 I5 Forráskút Hungary
146 E4 Forres Moray, Scotland U.K.
87 F6 Forrest W.A. Austr.
86 F2 Forrest r. W.A. Austr.
226 C5 Forrest IL U.S.A.
262 U1 Forrestal Range mts Antarctica
237 F5 Forrest City AR U.S.A.
87 F6 Forrest Lakes salt flat W.A. Austr.
226 C4 Forreston IL U.S.A.
Forrest River Mission W.A. Austr. see Oombulgurri
177 K3 Forró Hungary
162 B2 Fors France
142 B2 Forsand Norway
85 E3 Forsayth Qld Austr.
150 E2 Forsbrook Staffordshire, England U.K.
142 E2 Forshaga Sweden
146 E3 Forsinard Highland, Scotland U.K.
140 L2 Forsnäs Sweden
141 M3 Forssa Fin.
172 C2 Forst Baden-Württemberg Ger.
171 F4 Forst Brandenburg Ger.
83 H3 Forster N.S.W. Austr.
173 F3 Forstern Ger.
173 F3 Forstinning Ger.
231 D5 Forsyth GA U.S.A.
237 E4 Forsyth MO U.S.A.
238 F2 Forsyth MT U.S.A.
227 I1 Forsythe Que. Can.
84 D3 Forsyth Islands Qld Austr.
85 E4 Forsyth Range hills Qld Austr.
123 H4 Fort Abbas Pak.
224 D2 Fort Albany Ont. Can.
252 D2 Fortaleza Bol.
254 F2 Fortaleza Brazil
186 C4 Fortanete Spain
Fort Archambault Chad see Sarh
232 D5 Fort Ashby WV U.S.A.
222 H4 Fort Assiniboine Alta Can.
226 C4 Fort Atkinson WI U.S.A.
146 D4 Fort Augustus Highland, Scotland U.K.
222 E4 Fort Babine B.C. Can.
215 F5 Fort Beaufort S. Africa
238 E2 Fort Benton MT U.S.A.
223 J4 Fort Black Sask. Can.
Fort Brabant N.W.T. Can. see Tuktoyaktuk
240 F2 Fort Bragg CA U.S.A.
Fort Carillon NY U.S.A. see Ticonderoga
Fort Carnot Madag. see Ikongo
Fort Charlet Alg. see Djanet
Fort Chimo Que. Can. see Kuujjuaq
223 I3 Fort Chipewyan Alta Can.
238 F3 Fort Collins CO U.S.A.
85 E4 Fort Constantine Qld Austr.
224 E4 Fort-Coulonge Que. Can.
233 F2 Fort Covington NY U.S.A.
Fort Crampel C.A.R. see Kaga Bandoro
Fort-Dauphin Madag. see Tôlañaro
237 C6 Fort Davis TX U.S.A.
247 □3 Fort-de-France Martinique
Fort de Kock Sumatera Indon. see Bukittinggi
Fort de Polignac Alg. see Illizi
231 C5 Fort Deposit AL U.S.A.
236 E3 Fort Dodge IA U.S.A.
215 G4 Fort Donald S. Africa
241 M1 Fort Duchesne UT U.S.A.
182 B2 Forte Spain
192 A4 Forte, Monte hill Sardegna Italy
233 G3 Fort Edward NY U.S.A.
227 H4 Fort Erie Ont. Can.
86 C4 Fortescue r. W.A. Austr.
234 C3 Fortescue NJ U.S.A.
191 G2 Fortezza Italy
192 C2 Fortezza, Monte della hill Italy
233 □J1 Fort Fairfield ME U.S.A.
Fort Foureau Cameroon see Kousséri
226 A1 Fort Frances Ont. Can.
Fort Franklin N.W.T. Can. see Déline
231 C6 Fort Gaines GA U.S.A.
239 F4 Fort Garland CO U.S.A.
232 B5 Fort Gay WV U.S.A.
Fort George Que. Can. see Chisasibi
220 F3 Fort Good Hope N.W.T. Can.
Fort Gouraud Maur. see Fdérik
146 E6 Forth South Lanarkshire, Scotland U.K.
144 F3 Forth r. Scotland U.K.
146 E5 Forth, Firth of est. Scotland U.K.
Fort Hall Kenya see Muranga
239 F6 Fort Hancock TX U.S.A.
215 F5 Fort Hare S. Africa
241 J2 Fortification Range mts NV U.S.A.
245 F4 Fortín Mex.
253 E5 Fortín Ávalos Sánchez Para.
253 F5 Fortín Carlos Antonio López Para.
253 F5 Fortín Coronel Bogado Para.
253 E5 Fortín Coronel Eugenio Garay Para.
146 D5 Fortingall Perth and Kinross, Scotland U.K.
253 E5 Fortín General Mendoza Para.
253 E5 Fortín Hernandarías Para.
253 E5 Fortín Infante Rivarola Para.
253 F5 Fortín Juan de Zalazar Para.
253 F5 Fortín Presidente Ayala Para.
253 E5 Fortín Teniente Juan Echauri López Para.
184 C1 Fortios Port.
Fort Jameson Zambia see Chipata
Fort Johnston Malawi see Mangochi
233 □I1 Fort Kent ME U.S.A.
238 B3 Fort Klamath OR U.S.A.
Fort Lamy Chad see Ndjamena
Fort Laperrine Alg. see Tamanrasset
238 F3 Fort Laramie WY U.S.A.
231 D7 Fort Lauderdale FL U.S.A.
235 E2 Fort Lee NJ U.S.A.
222 F2 Fort Liard N.W.T. Can.
246 E3 Fort Liberté Haiti
232 E5 Fort Loudon PA U.S.A.
223 I3 Fort Mackay Alta Can.
222 H5 Fort Macleod Alta Can.
226 B5 Fort Madison IA U.S.A.
156 B2 Fort-Mahon-Plage France
Fort Manning Malawi see Mchinji
226 B3 Fort McCoy WI U.S.A.
223 I3 Fort McMurray Alta Can.
220 E3 Fort McPherson N.W.T. Can.
235 E1 Fort Montgomery NY U.S.A.
236 C3 Fort Morgan CO U.S.A.
215 H3 Fort Mtombeni S. Africa
231 D7 Fort Myers FL U.S.A.
222 F3 Fort Nelson B.C. Can.
222 F3 Fort Nelson r. B.C. Can.
Fort Norman N.W.T. Can. see Tulít'a
Fort Orange NY U.S.A. see Albany
193 H3 Fortore r. Italy
231 C5 Fort Payne AL U.S.A.
238 F1 Fort Peck MT U.S.A.
238 F2 Fort Peck Reservoir MT U.S.A.
231 D7 Fort Pierce FL U.S.A.
236 C2 Fort Pierre SD U.S.A.
210 A4 Fort Portal Uganda
222 G2 Fort Providence N.W.T. Can.
223 K5 Fort Qu'Appelle Sask. Can.
Fort Randall AK U.S.A. see Cold Bay
232 A4 Fort Recovery OH U.S.A.
222 H2 Fort Resolution N.W.T. Can.
213 F3 Fort Rixon Zimbabwe
81 B7 Fortrose South I. N.Z.
146 D4 Fortrose Highland, Scotland U.K.
Fort Rosebery Zambia see Mansa
Fort Rousset Congo see Owando
Fort Rupert Que. Can. see Waskaganish
222 E4 Fort St James B.C. Can.
222 F3 Fort St John B.C. Can.
Fort Sandeman Pak. see Zhob
222 H4 Fort Saskatchewan Alta Can.
237 E4 Fort Scott KS U.S.A.
224 C1 Fort Severn Ont. Can.
120 B3 Fort-Shevchenko Kazakh.
222 F2 Fort Simpson N.W.T. Can.
223 H2 Fort Smith N.W.T. Can.
237 E5 Fort Smith AR U.S.A.
238 F2 Fort Smith MT U.S.A.
237 C6 Fort Stockton TX U.S.A.
239 F5 Fort Sumner NM U.S.A.
237 D4 Fort Supply OK U.S.A.
241 M5 Fort Thomas AZ U.S.A.
Fort Trinquet Maur. see Bîr Mogreïn
187 B6 Fortuna Spain
238 A3 Fortuna CA U.S.A.
236 C1 Fortuna ND U.S.A.
225 K4 Fortune Bay Nfld. Can.
150 E4 Fortuneswell Dorset, England U.K.
231 D5 Fort Valley GA U.S.A.
222 G3 Fort Vermilion Alta Can.
Fort Victoria Zimbabwe see Masvingo
Fort Walton FL U.S.A. see Fort Walton Beach
231 C6 Fort Walton Beach FL U.S.A.
Fort Ware B.C. Can. see Ware
234 C2 Fort Washington PA U.S.A.
230 C3 Fort Wayne IN U.S.A.
251 G3 Fort Wellington Guyana
146 C5 Fort William Highland, Scotland U.K.
239 E5 Fort Wingate NM U.S.A.
237 D5 Fort Worth TX U.S.A.
236 C2 Fort Yates ND U.S.A.
234 C1 Forty Fort PA U.S.A.
Forty-Second Hill S. Africa see 42nd Hill
220 D3 Fort Yukon AK U.S.A.
Forum Iulii France see Fréjus
122 C5 Forūr, Jazīreh-ye i. Iran
140 K2 Forvik Norway
195 E5 Forza d'Agrò Sicilia Italy
163 C6 Fos France
190 F4 Fosdinovo Italy
109 E4 Foshan Guangdong China
141 K3 Foskvallen Sweden
140 J3 Fosna pen. Norway
206 E5 Foso Ghana
193 G2 Fossacesia Italy
178 D5 Fossalta di Portogruaro Italy
190 C4 Fossano Italy
191 H5 Fossato di Vico Italy
162 C3 Fossemagne France
165 D4 Fosses-la-Ville Belgium
160 D2 Fossiat France
238 B2 Fossil OR U.S.A.
86 E3 Fossil Downs W.A. Austr.
191 H5 Fossombrone Italy
161 C5 Fos-sur-Mer France
83 F4 Foster Vic. Austr.
232 A5 Foster KY U.S.A.
222 C3 Foster, Mount Alaska/B.C. Can./U.S.A.
221 P2 Foster Bugt b. Greenland
234 D1 Fosterdale NY U.S.A.
233 □J2 Fosterville N.B. Can.
232 B4 Fostoria OH U.S.A.
177 I4 Fót Hungary
213 □J5 Fotadrevo Madag.
149 I4 Fotherby Lincolnshire, England U.K.
Fotuna i. Vanuatu see Futuna
156 B3 Foucarmont France
160 D1 Foucherans France
158 B4 Fouesnant France
157 F4 Foug France
208 A5 Fougamou Gabon
158 E3 Fougères France
157 G5 Fougerolles France
159 F3 Fougerolles-du-Plessis France
156 C3 Fouilloy France
146 □F1 Foula i. Scotland U.K.
157 F4 Foulain France
206 B3 Foulamôri Guinea
163 C4 Foulayronnes France
146 F6 Foulden Scottish Borders, Scotland U.K.
208 A5 Foulenzem Gabon
147 E4 Foulkesmill Rep. of Ireland
149 G4 Foulridge Lancashire, England U.K.
81 C4 Foulwind, Cape South I. N.Z.
207 H5 Foumban Cameroon
207 H5 Foumbot Cameroon
217 □3a Foumbouni Njazidja Comoros
204 D3 Foum Zguid Morocco
206 A3 Foundiougne Senegal
232 B6 Fount KY U.S.A.
226 A4 Fountain MN U.S.A.
147 B4 Fountain Cross Rep. of Ireland
241 L2 Fountain Green UT U.S.A.
234 C2 Fountain Hill PA U.S.A.
149 H3 Fountains Abbey tourist site England U.K.
184 C3 Foupana r. Port.
162 A3 Fouras France
163 C5 Fourcès France
160 B1 Fourchambault France
157 F4 Fourches, Mont des hill France
240 I4 Four Corners CA U.S.A.
151 H3 Four Elms Kent, England U.K.
215 G3 Fouriesburg S. Africa
151 F3 Four Marks Hampshire, England U.K.
156 E2 Fourmies France
161 B4 Fournels France
199 E3 Fournoi Greece
199 E3 Fournoi i. Greece
151 H4 Four Oaks East Sussex, England U.K.
161 C5 Fourques Languedoc-Roussillon France
163 E6 Fourques Languedoc-Roussillon France
163 C4 Fourques-sur-Garonne France
160 B2 Fours France
203 G5 Fourth Cataract rapids Sudan
206 B4 Fouta Djallon reg. Guinea
81 A7 Foveaux Strait South I. N.Z.
234 B3 Fowbelsburg MD U.S.A.
150 C4 Fowey Cornwall, England U.K.
150 C4 Fowey r. England U.K.
231 E7 Fowl Cay i. Bahamas
240 H3 Fowler CA U.S.A.
239 F4 Fowler CO U.S.A.
230 C3 Fowler IN U.S.A.
226 E4 Fowler MI U.S.A.
82 C2 Fowlers Bay S.A. Austr.
82 C3 Fowlers Bay b. S.A. Austr.
227 E4 Fowlerville MI U.S.A.
127 H3 Fowman Iran
150 E2 Fownhope Herefordshire, England U.K.
222 E3 Fox r. B.C. Can.
223 M3 Fox r. Man. Can.
226 C5 Fox r. IL U.S.A.
226 C4 Fox r. WI U.S.A.
182 B1 Foxas Spain
85 F4 Fox Creek r. Qld Austr.
222 G4 Fox Creek Alta Can.
221 K3 Foxe Basin g. Nunavut Can.
221 J3 Foxe Channel Nunavut Can.
221 K3 Foxe Peninsula Nunavut Can.
147 B3 Foxford Rep. of Ireland
81 C5 Fox Glacier South I. N.Z.
220 B4 Fox Islands AK U.S.A.
222 H3 Fox Lake Alta Can.
226 C4 Fox Lake IL U.S.A.
222 C2 Fox Mountain Y.T. Can.
238 F3 Foxpark WY U.S.A.
80 E4 Foxton North I. N.Z.
80 E4 Foxton Beach North I. N.Z.
223 I5 Fox Valley Sask. Can.
146 D4 Foyers Highland, Scotland U.K.
148 B4 Foygh Rep. of Ireland
147 D2 Foyle r. Rep. of Ireland/U.K.
147 D1 Foyle, Lough b. Rep. of Ireland/U.K.
147 B4 Foynes Rep. of Ireland
184 B1 Foz Port.
182 C1 Foz Spain
184 A1 Foz do Arelho Port.
209 A9 Foz do Cunene Angola
255 B8 Foz do Iguaçu Brazil
182 C5 Foz Giraldo Port.
190 C4 Frabosa Soprana Italy
175 L2 Frącki Pol.
227 I5 Frackville PA U.S.A.
182 E4 Frades de la Sierra Spain
186 D3 Fraga Spain
195 G2 Fragagnano Italy
179 F2 Fraham Austria
258 G4 Fraile Muerto Uru.
185 G3 Frailes Spain
165 D4 Fraire Belgium
160 D1 Fraisans France
161 A5 Fraisse-sur-Agout France
157 H4 Fraize France
262 Q1 Frakes, Mount Antarctica
165 C4 Frameries Belgium
151 H4 Framfield East Sussex, England U.K.
233 H3 Framingham MA U.S.A.
151 I2 Framlingham Suffolk, England U.K.
143 G1 Främlingshem Sweden
169 E5 Frammersbach Ger.
263 E2 Framnes Mountains Antarctica
263 D2 Fram Peak Antarctica
175 K5 Frampol Pol.
151 G2 Frampton Lincolnshire, England U.K.
150 E3 Frampton on Severn Gloucestershire, England U.K.
256 D4 Franca Brazil
193 G2 Francavilla al Mare Italy
195 E5 Francavilla di Sicilia Sicilia Italy
195 G2 Francavilla Fontana Italy
193 I4 Francavilla in Sinni Italy
154 F3 France country Europe
82 E4 Frances S.A. Austr.
222 D2 Frances r. Y.T. Can.
163 C4 Francescas France
222 D2 Frances Lake Y.T. Can.
226 D5 Francesville IN U.S.A.
208 B5 Franceville Gabon
157 G5 Franche-Comté admin. reg. France
223 K5 Francis Sask. Can.
Francis atoll Gilbert Is Kiribati see Beru
Francisco de Orellana Ecuador see Puerto Francisco de Orellana
250 C5 Francisco de Orellana Peru
242 E3 Francisco I. Madero Mex.
244 B1 Francisco I. Madero Mex.
244 B3 Francisco I. Madero Mex.
257 F2 Francisco Sá Brazil
242 A1 Francisco Zarco Mex.
213 E4 Francistown Botswana
182 C3 Franco Port.
256 D5 Franco da Rocha Brazil
194 D5 Francofonte Sicilia Italy
225 J4 Francois Nfld. Can.
186 E3 Francolí r. Spain
234 A4 Franconia VA U.S.A.
165 E4 Francorchamps Belgium
163 D4 Francoulès France
238 E3 Francs Peak WY U.S.A.
164 E1 Franeker Neth.
160 D2 Frangy France
169 D4 Frankenau Ger.
171 E5 Frankenberg Ger.
169 D4 Frankenberg (Eder) Ger.
179 E2 Frankenburg am Hausruck Austria
179 G3 Frankenfels Austria
169 F5 Frankenhain Ger.
169 F5 Frankenheim Ger.
179 E3 Frankenmarkt Austria
227 F4 Frankenmuth MI U.S.A.
172 C2 Frankenthal (Pfalz) Ger.
171 C5 Frankenwald mts Ger.
246 □ Frankfield Jamaica
227 I3 Frankford Ont. Can.
215 G2 Frankfort S. Africa
230 C3 Frankfort IN U.S.A.
230 C4 Frankfort KY U.S.A.
226 D3 Frankfort MI U.S.A.
232 B5 Frankfort OH U.S.A.
169 D5 Frankfurt am Main Ger.
171 F3 Frankfurt an der Oder Ger.
173 E3 Fränkische Alb hills Ger.
173 F2 Fränkische Rezat r. Ger.
169 E5 Fränkische Saale r. Ger.
173 F2 Fränkische Schweiz reg. Ger.
87 C7 Frankland r. W.A. Austr.
83 F4 Frankland, Cape Tas. Austr.
150 E2 Frankley Worcestershire, England U.K.
215 G4 Franklin S. Africa
241 M5 Franklin AZ U.S.A.
231 C5 Franklin GA U.S.A.
230 C4 Franklin IN U.S.A.
230 C4 Franklin KY U.S.A.
237 F6 Franklin LA U.S.A.
233 H3 Franklin MA U.S.A.
233 □I2 Franklin ME U.S.A.
231 D5 Franklin NC U.S.A.
236 D3 Franklin NE U.S.A.
233 H3 Franklin NH U.S.A.
234 D1 Franklin NJ U.S.A.
232 A5 Franklin OH U.S.A.
232 D4 Franklin PA U.S.A.
231 C5 Franklin TN U.S.A.
237 D6 Franklin TX U.S.A.
232 E6 Franklin VA U.S.A.
226 C4 Franklin WI U.S.A.
232 D5 Franklin WV U.S.A.
234 A2 Franklinburg PA U.S.A.
228 C1 Franklin D. Roosevelt Lake WA U.S.A.
232 B5 Franklin Furnace OH U.S.A.
226 C5 Franklin Grove IL U.S.A.
82 D3 Franklin Harbor b. S.A. Austr.
263 L1 Franklin Island Antarctica
222 F2 Franklin Mountains N.W.T. Can.
81 A6 Franklin Mountains South I. N.Z.
234 D2 Franklin Park NJ U.S.A.
83 F5 Franklin Sound sea chan. Tas. Austr.
235 E2 Franklin Square NY U.S.A.
221 I2 Franklin Strait Nunavut Can.
237 F6 Franklinton LA U.S.A.
234 C3 Franklinville NJ U.S.A.
232 D3 Franklinville NY U.S.A.
175 I1 Frankowo Pol.
140 K3 Frankrike Sweden
83 F4 Frankston Vic. Austr.
81 B6 Frankton South I. N.Z.
160 D1 Franois France
214 D3 Fransenhof S. Africa
141 L3 Fränsta Sweden
176 B1 Františkovy Lázně Czech Rep.
224 C3 Franz Ont. Can.
170 D1 Franzburg Ger.
81 C5 Franz Josef Glacier South I. N.Z.
Franz Josef Land is Rus. Fed. see Zemlya Frantsa-Iosifa
173 F3 Franz Josef Strauss airport Ger.
194 D5 Frasca, Monte hill Sicilia Italy
193 E3 Frascati Italy
193 I5 Frascineto Italy
173 G4 Frasdorf Ger.
86 D3 Fraser r. W.A. Austr.
222 F5 Fraser r. B.C. Can.
225 I1 Fraser r. Nfld. Can.
87 C5 Fraser, Mount hill W.A. Austr.
214 C4 Fraserburg S. Africa
146 F4 Fraserburgh Aberdeenshire, Scotland U.K.
224 D3 Fraserdale Ont. Can.
85 H5 Fraser Island Qld Austr.
87 B4 Fraser Island W.A. Austr.
222 E4 Fraser Lake B.C. Can.
222 E4 Fraser Plateau B.C. Can.
87 D7 Fraser Range W.A. Austr.
87 D7 Fraser Range hills W.A. Austr.
80 F3 Frasertown North I. N.Z.
160 E2 Frasne France
165 C4 Frasnes-lez-Buissenal Belgium
165 D4 Frasnes-lez-Gosselies Belgium
191 F4 Frassinoro Italy
193 G3 Frasso Telesino Italy
178 A3 Frastanz Austria
182 C5 Fratel Port.
194 D4 Fratello r. Sicilia Italy
226 E2 Frater Ont. Can.
197 G4 Frătești Romania
191 G3 Fratta r. Italy
191 G3 Fratta Polesine Italy
193 E2 Fratta Todina Italy
190 C1 Fraubrunnen Switz.
173 H3 Frauenau Ger.
190 D1 Frauenfeld Switz.
179 H3 Frauenkirchen Austria
171 E5 Frauenstein Ger.
179 G4 Frauental an der Laßnitz Austria
169 F5 Frauenwald Ger.
173 F3 Fraunberg Ger.
171 D5 Fraureuth Ger.
261 H3 Fray Bentos Uru.
261 G3 Fray Luis Beltrán Arg.
258 G4 Fray Marcos Uru.
163 D4 Frayssinet-le-Gélat France
234 C2 Frazer PA U.S.A.
232 B4 Frazeysburg OH U.S.A.
240 H4 Frazier Park CA U.S.A.
182 B3 Freamunde Port.
197 I3 Frecăței Romania
161 B5 Frech, Mont mt. France
182 C3 Frechas Port.
169 B5 Frechen Ger.
183 F2 Frechilla Spain
149 G4 Freckleton Lancashire, England U.K.
169 E4 Freden (Leine) Ger.
168 E2 Fredenbeck Ger.
226 E3 Frederic MI U.S.A.
226 A3 Frederic WI U.S.A.
234 C3 Frederica DE U.S.A.
142 C4 Fredericia Denmark
87 C5 Frederick r. W.A. Austr.
232 E5 Frederick MD U.S.A.
237 D5 Frederick OK U.S.A.
226 A4 Fredericksburg IA U.S.A.
234 B2 Fredericksburg PA U.S.A.
237 D6 Fredericksburg TX U.S.A.
232 E5 Fredericksburg VA U.S.A.
237 F4 Fredericktown MO U.S.A.
232 B4 Fredericktown OH U.S.A.
225 H4 Fredericton N.B. Can.
233 □J2 Fredericton Junction N.B. Can.
142 E4 Frederiksborg county Denmark
Frederikshåb Greenland see Paamiut
142 D3 Frederikshavn Denmark
142 E4 Frederikssund Denmark
247 F3 Frederiksted Virgin Is (U.S.A.)
142 E4 Frederiksværk Denmark
170 E3 Fredersdorf Ger.
241 K3 Fredonia AZ U.S.A.
237 E4 Fredonia KS U.S.A.
232 D3 Fredonia NY U.S.A.
232 C4 Fredonia PA U.S.A.
226 D4 Fredonia WI U.S.A.
140 L2 Fredrika Sweden
143 F1 Fredriksberg Sweden
Fredrikshamn Fin. see Hamina
142 D2 Fredrikstad Norway
Fredriksvern Norway see Stavern
175 K6 Fredropol Pol.
234 B2 Freeburg PA U.S.A.
233 F4 Freehold NJ U.S.A.
234 C1 Freeland PA U.S.A.
82 D3 Freeling S.A. Austr.
84 C4 Freeling, Mount hill N.T. Austr.
82 D2 Freeling Heights hill S.A. Austr.
240 H2 Freel Peak CA U.S.A.
236 D3 Freeman SD U.S.A.
234 C2 Freemansburg PA U.S.A.
231 C6 Freeport FL U.S.A.
226 C4 Freeport IL U.S.A.
233 □H3 Freeport ME U.S.A.
235 E2 Freeport NY U.S.A.
232 D4 Freeport PA U.S.A.
237 E6 Freeport TX U.S.A.
231 E7 Freeport City Bahamas
237 D7 Freer TX U.S.A.
226 D3 Freesoil MI U.S.A.
215 F3 Free State prov. S. Africa
206 B4 Freetown Sierra Leone
235 F2 Freetown NY U.S.A.
235 D2 Freewood Acres NJ U.S.A.
217 □2a Frégate i. Inner Islands Seychelles
184 D2 Fregenal de la Sierra Spain
192 E3 Fregene Italy
186 D4 Freginals Spain
82 C1 Fregon S.A. Austr.
158 D3 Fréhel France
171 E5 Freiberg Ger.
171 D4 Freiberger Mulde r. Ger.
172 C4 Freiburg admin. reg. Baden-Württemberg Ger.
Freiburg Switz. see Fribourg
168 E2 Freiburg (Elbe) Ger.
172 B3 Freiburg im Breisgau Ger.
169 E5 Freiensteinau Ger.
168 E1 Freienwill Ger.
257 G2 Frei Gonzaga Brazil
173 F2 Freihung Ger.
257 G3 Frei Inocêncio Brazil
185 H3 Freila Spain
173 G4 Freilassing Ger.
172 C2 Freinsheim Ger.
260 A6 Freire Chile
172 B2 Freisen Ger.
173 F3 Freising Ger.
161 E4 Freissinières France
179 F2 Freistadt Austria
157 G3 Freistroff France
171 E5 Freital Ger.
182 C4 Freixedas Port.
182 B5 Freixianda Port.
182 C3 Freixiel Port.
182 C4 Freixiosa Port.
182 B3 Freixo Port.
182 D3 Freixo de Espada à Cinta Port.
163 E5 Fréjairolles France
161 E5 Fréjus France
161 E5 Fréjus, Golfe de b. France
161 E3 Fréjus Tunnel France/Italy
142 A1 Frekhaug Norway
169 F3 Frellstedt Ger.
87 B7 Fremantle W.A. Austr.
173 E3 Fremdingen Ger.
150 C3 Fremington Devon, England U.K.
240 G3 Fremont CA U.S.A.
226 E5 Fremont IN U.S.A.
226 E4 Fremont MI U.S.A.
236 D3 Fremont NE U.S.A.
232 B4 Fremont OH U.S.A.
226 C3 Fremont WI U.S.A.
241 L2 Fremont r. UT U.S.A.
241 L2 Fremont Junction UT U.S.A.
232 B6 Frenchburg KY U.S.A.
246 D2 French Cay i. Turks and Caicos Is
French Congo country Africa see Congo
232 D4 French Creek r. PA U.S.A.
251 H4 French Guiana terr. S. America
French Guinea country Africa see Guinea
83 F4 French Island Vic. Austr.
238 F1 Frenchman r. MT U.S.A.
233 □I2 Frenchman Bay ME U.S.A.
236 C3 Frenchman Creek r. NE U.S.A.
81 D4 French Pass South I. N.Z.
79 □3 French Polynesia terr. S. Pacific Ocean
French Somaliland country Africa see Djibouti
73 G6 French Southern and Antarctic Lands terr. Indian Ocean
French Sudan country Africa see Mali
French Territory of the Afars and Issas country Africa see Djibouti
234 C2 Frenchtown NJ U.S.A.
233 □I1 Frenchville ME U.S.A.
156 B2 Frencq France
205 F2 Frenda Alg.
156 B3 Freneuse France
173 E2 Frensdorf Ger.
151 G3 Frensham Surrey, England U.K.
177 H2 Frenštát pod Radhoštěm Czech Rep.
193 G3 Frentani, Monti dei mts Italy
215 G3 Frere S. Africa
169 C3 Freren Ger.
179 E4 Fresach Austria
193 G3 Fresagrandinaria Italy
251 I6 Fresco r. Brazil
206 D5 Fresco Côte d'Ivoire
263 K2 Freshfield, Cape Antarctica
147 D4 Freshford Rep. of Ireland
151 F4 Freshwater Isle of Wight, England U.K.
150 C3 Freshwater East Pembrokeshire, Wales U.K.
156 B4 Fresnay-l'Evêque France
159 G3 Fresnay-sur-Sarthe France
185 G2 Fresnedas r. Spain
185 F2 Fresnedillas hill Spain
160 D1 Fresne-St-Mamès France
157 F3 Fresnes-en-Woëvre France
157 F5 Fresnes-sur-Apance France
156 D2 Fresnes-sur-Escaut France
244 C2 Fresnillo Mex.
240 H3 Fresno CA U.S.A.
240 G3 Fresno r. CA U.S.A.
182 E4 Fresno Alhándiga Spain
182 E3 Fresno de la Ribera Spain
182 E3 Fresno de Sayago Spain
183 E3 Fresno el Viejo Spain
156 B3 Fresnoy-Folny France
156 D3 Fresnoy-le-Grand France
156 B2 Fressenneville France
157 G5 Fresse-sur-Moselle France
151 I2 Fressingfield Suffolk, England U.K.
141 I3 Fresvikbreen glacier Norway
146 E3 Freswick Highland, Scotland U.K.
160 D1 Fretigney-et-Velloreille France
172 D2 Freudenberg Baden-Württemberg Ger.
173 F2 Freudenberg Bayern Ger.
169 C5 Freudenberg Nordrhein-Westfalen Ger.
172 A2 Freudenburg Ger.
172 C3 Freudenstadt Ger.
156 C2 Frévent France
232 D3 Frewsburg NY U.S.A.
171 C4 Freyburg (Unstrut) Ger.

Garopaba to Giza

307

255 C9 **Garopaba** Brazil
116 C4 **Garoth** *Madh. Prad.* India
206 E2 **Garou, Lac** *l.* Mali
207 I4 **Garoua** Cameroon
207 I5 **Garoua Boulai** Cameroon
143 F2 **Garphyttan** Sweden
Garqêntang *Xizang* China *see* **Sog**
182 E2 **Garrafe de Torio** Spain
163 A6 **Garralda** Spain
147 B5 **Garrane** Rep. of Ireland
183 H3 **Garray** Spain
168 D3 **Garrel** Ger.
226 E5 **Garrett** *IN* U.S.A.
147 C2 **Garrison** *Northern Ireland* U.K.
232 B5 **Garrison** *KY* U.S.A.
236 E2 **Garrison** *MN* U.S.A.
236 C2 **Garrison** *ND* U.S.A.
235 E1 **Garrison** *NY* U.S.A.
147 E3 **Garristown** Rep. of Ireland
129 C3 **Garrnarrich** Armenia
147 F1 **Garronpoint** *Northern Ireland* U.K.
182 D5 **Garrovillas** Spain
185 I3 **Garrucha** Spain
146 D4 **Garry** *r. Scotland* U.K.
146 D4 **Garry, Loch** *l. Highland, Scotland* U.K.
122 D2 **Garrygala** Turkm.
146 B3 **Garrynahine** *Western Isles, Scotland* U.K.
215 F4 **Garryowen** S. Africa
147 C5 **Garryvoe** Rep. of Ireland
173 G3 **Gars am Inn** Ger.
179 G2 **Gars am Kamp** Austria
149 G3 **Garsdale Head** *Cumbria, England* U.K.
143 F4 **Gärsnäs** Sweden
149 G4 **Garstang** *Lancashire, England* U.K.
168 F2 **Garstedt** Ger.
179 F2 **Garsten** Austria
81 B6 **Garston** *South I.* N.Z.
Gartar *Sichuan* China *see* **Qianning**
162 C2 **Gartempe** *r.* France
150 D2 **Garth** *Powys, Wales* U.K.
150 D2 **Garthmyl** *Powys, Wales* U.K.
146 D5 **Gartocharn** *West Dunbartonshire, Scotland* U.K.
Gartog *Xizang* China *see* **Markam**
170 C2 **Gartow** Ger.
172 C3 **Gärtringen** Ger.
170 F2 **Gartz** Ger.
95 D4 **Garut** *Jawa Barat* Indon.
147 D3 **Garvagh** Rep. of Ireland
147 E2 **Garvagh** *Northern Ireland* U.K.
147 D2 **Garvaghy** *Northern Ireland* U.K.
146 F6 **Garvald** *East Lothian, Scotland* U.K.
146 D4 **Garvamore** *Highland, Scotland* U.K.
184 B3 **Garvão** Port.
146 B5 **Garvard** *Argyll and Bute, Scotland* U.K.
146 D4 **Garve** *Highland, Scotland* U.K.
81 B6 **Garvie Mountains** *South I.* N.Z.
117 E4 **Garwa** *Bihar* India
175 J4 **Garwolin** Pol.
230 C3 **Gary** *IN* U.S.A.
232 C6 **Gary** *WV* U.S.A.
108 A2 **Garyi** *Sichuan* China
103 F6 **Garyū-zan** *mt.* Japan
170 E1 **Garz** Ger.
258 E3 **Garza** Arg.
111 B5 **Gar Zangbo** *r.* China
108 A2 **Garzê** *Sichuan* China
250 C4 **Garzón** Col.
Gasan-Kuli Turkm. *see* **Esenguly**
174 F3 **Gąsawa** Pol.
178 B4 **Gaschurn** Austria
171 D4 **Gaschwitz** Ger.
163 B5 **Gascogne** *reg.* France
154 C5 **Gascogne, Golfe de** *g.* France/Spain
236 F4 **Gasconade** *r. MO* U.S.A.
Gascony *reg.* France *see* **Gascogne**
Gascony, Gulf of France/Spain *see* **Gascogne, Golfe de**
87 B5 **Gascoyne** *r. W.A.* Austr.
87 C5 **Gascoyne, Mount** *hill W.A.* Austr.
87 B5 **Gascoyne Junction** *W.A.* Austr.
183 H4 **Gascueña** Spain
Gascuña, Golfo de *g.* France/Spain *see* **Gascogne, Golfe de**
113 □1 **Gasfinolhu** *i. N. Male* Maldives
124 B5 **Gash and Setit** *prov.* Eritrea
116 D2 **Gasherbrum** *mt.* Jammu and Kashmir
123 E5 **Gasht** Iran
207 H3 **Gashua** Nigeria
175 K2 **Gąski** Pol.
156 B3 **Gasny** France
175 I3 **Gąsocin** Pol.
246 C2 **Gaspar** Cuba
94 D3 **Gaspar, Selat** *sea chan.* Indon.
225 H3 **Gaspé** *Que.* Can.
225 H3 **Gaspé, Péninsule de** *pen. Que.* Can.
195 F4 **Gasperina** Italy
179 E2 **Gaspoltshofen** Austria
206 E3 **Gassan** Burkina
102 J4 **Gassan** *vol.* Japan
206 B3 **Gassane** Senegal
232 C5 **Gassaway** *WV* U.S.A.
164 F2 **Gasselte** Neth.
164 F2 **Gasselternijveen** Neth.
161 E5 **Gassin** France
207 H4 **Gassol** Nigeria
241 J3 **Gass Peak** *NV* U.S.A.
Gasteiz Spain *see* **Vitoria-Gasteiz**
100 G2 **Gastello** *Sakhalin* Rus. Fed.
179 G2 **Gastern** Austria
163 A4 **Gastes** France
232 E6 **Gaston** *NC* U.S.A.
231 D5 **Gastonia** *NC* U.S.A.
198 B3 **Gastouni** Greece
182 D4 **Gata** Spain
185 H4 **Gata, Cabo de** *c.* Spain
182 D4 **Gata, Sierra de** *mts* Spain
187 D6 **Gata de Gorgos** Spain
222 E3 **Gataga** *r. B.C.* Can.
196 E3 **Gătaia** Romania
139 H2 **Gatchina** Rus. Fed.
232 B6 **Gate City** *VA* U.S.A.
146 D7 **Gatehouse of Fleet** *Dumfries and Galloway, Scotland* U.K.
177 I5 **Gátér** Hungary
171 C4 **Gatersleben** Ger.
149 H3 **Gateshead** *Tyne and Wear, England* U.K.
231 E4 **Gatesville** *NC* U.S.A.
237 D6 **Gatesville** *TX* U.S.A.
241 M2 **Gateway** *CO* U.S.A.
224 F4 **Gatineau** *Que.* Can.
224 F4 **Gatineau** *r. Que.* Can.
185 F2 **Gato** *r.* Spain
Gatong *Xizang* China *see* **Jomda**
Gatooma Zimbabwe *see* **Kadoma**
187 C5 **Gátova** Spain
179 H2 **Gattendorf** Austria
191 H4 **Gatteo a Mare** Italy
161 F5 **Gattières** France
190 D3 **Gattinara** Italy
85 H5 **Gatton** *Qld* Austr.
242 □J7 **Gatún, Lago** *l.* Panama
122 B3 **Gatvand** Iran
151 G3 **Gatwick** *airport England* U.K.
79 □1 **Gau** *i.* Fiji
172 C2 **Gau-Algesheim** Ger.
156 D3 **Gauchy** France
185 E4 **Gaucín** Spain
123 E4 **Gaud-i-Zirreh** *depr.* Afgh.
Gauhati *Assam* India *see* **Guwahati**
138 E3 **Gauja** *r.* Latvia
138 E4 **Gauja** *r.* Lith.
172 D2 **Gaukönigshofen** Ger.
Gaul *country* Europe *see* **France**
184 □ **Gaula** Madeira
140 J3 **Gaula** *r.* Norway
232 C5 **Gauley Bridge** *WV* U.S.A.
172 C2 **Gau-Odernheim** Ger.
141 I3 **Gaupne** Norway
Gaurdak Turkm. *see* **Govurdak**
116 E5 **Gaurella** *Madh. Prad.* India
114 C3 **Gauribidanur** *Karnataka* India
117 G5 **Gaurnadi** Bangl.
142 C2 **Gausta** *mt.* Norway
215 G2 **Gauteng** *prov.* S. Africa
173 F3 **Gauting** Ger.
186 C3 **Gautizalema** *r.* Spain
186 F3 **Gavà** Spain
190 F3 **Gavardo** Italy
163 B6 **Gavarnie** France
Gavarr Armenia *see* **Kamo**
123 E5 **Gavāter** Iran
177 K3 **Gávavencsellő** Hungary
122 C5 **Gāvbandī** Iran
122 C5 **Gāvbūs, Kūh-e** *mts* Iran
163 A5 **Gave** *r.* France
182 B2 **Gave** Port.
163 B5 **Gave d'Arrens** *r.* France
163 B5 **Gave d'Aspe** *r.* France
163 A5 **Gave d'Oloron** *r.* France
163 B5 **Gave d'Ossau** *r.* France
122 A3 **Gāveh Rūd** *r.* Iran
165 C4 **Gavere** Belgium
190 D4 **Gavi** Italy
255 E5 **Gavião** *r.* Brazil
184 C1 **Gavião** Port.
190 D3 **Gavirate** Italy
143 G1 **Gävle** Sweden
143 F1 **Gävleborg** *county* Sweden
143 G1 **Gävlebukten** *b.* Sweden
192 B4 **Gavoi** *Sardegna* Italy
192 C2 **Gavorrano** Italy
158 E3 **Gavray** France
135 H5 **Gavrilovka Vtoraya** Rus. Fed.
139 M3 **Gavrilov Posad** Rus. Fed.
139 L3 **Gavrilov-Yam** Rus. Fed.
117 F4 **Gawan** *Bihar* India
179 H2 **Gaweinstal** Austria
116 D5 **Gawilgarh Hills** India
82 D3 **Gawler** *S.A.* Austr.
82 C3 **Gawler Ranges** *hills S.A.* Austr.
175 K1 **Gawliki Wielkie** Pol.
174 D4 **Gaworzyce** Pol.
149 G4 **Gawsworth** *Cheshire, England* U.K.
149 G3 **Gawthrop** *Cumbria, England* U.K.
207 G4 **Gawu** Nigeria
120 D2 **Gay** Rus. Fed.
226 C2 **Gay** *MI* U.S.A.
100 D4 **Gaya** *r.* China
117 F4 **Gaya** *Bihar* India
207 F4 **Gaya** Niger
Gayá *r.* Spain *see* **Gaià**
148 B4 **Gaybrook** Rep. of Ireland
204 C4 **G'Aydat al Jhoucha** *ridge* Western Sahara
137 I5 **Gayduk** Rus. Fed.
207 F3 **Gayéri** Burkina
226 E3 **Gaylord** *MI* U.S.A.
236 E2 **Gaylord** *MN* U.S.A.
85 G5 **Gayndah** *Qld* Austr.
134 K3 **Gayny** Rus. Fed.
Gaysin Ukr. *see* **Haysyn**
151 H2 **Gayton** *Norfolk, England* U.K.
134 G4 **Gayutino** Rus. Fed.
Gayvoron Ukr. *see* **Hayvoron**
128 B4 **Gaza** *terr.* Asia
128 B4 **Gaza** Gaza
213 G4 **Gaza** *prov.* Moz.
123 E1 **Gaz-Achak** Turkm.
121 G4 **Gazalkent** Uzbek.
122 C2 **Gazandzhyk** Turkm.
207 I4 **Gazawa** Cameroon
126 E3 **Gaziantep** Turkey
128 C1 **Gaziantep** *prov.* Turkey
Gazibenli Turkey *see* **Yahyalı**
129 C3 **Gaziler** Turkey
Gazimağusa Cyprus *see* **Ammochostos**
100 B1 **Gazimur** *r.* Rus. Fed.
100 A2 **Gazimurskiy Khrebet** *mts* Rus. Fed.
126 D3 **Gazipaşa** Turkey
120 E4 **Gazli** Uzbek.
Gazojak Turkm. *see* **Gaz-Achak**
183 I2 **Gazolaz** Spain
191 F3 **Gazoldo degli Ippoliti** Italy
191 G3 **Gazzo Veronese** Italy
191 F3 **Gazzuolo** Italy
206 D5 **Gbaaka** Liberia
206 B5 **Gbangbatok** Sierra Leone
206 C5 **Gbarnga** Liberia
206 C5 **Gbatala** Liberia
177 H4 **Gbelce** Slovakia
176 G3 **Gbely** Slovakia
207 F4 **Gbéroubouè** Benin
207 H5 **Gboko** Nigeria
143 H4 **Gdańsk** Pol.
175 H1 **Gdańsk, Gulf of** Pol./Rus. Fed.
Gdańska, Zatoka *g.* Pol./Rus. Fed. *see* **Gdańsk, Gulf of**
Gdingen Pol. *see* **Gdynia**
138 F2 **Gdov** Rus. Fed.
175 I6 **Gdów** Pol.
143 H4 **Gdynia** Pol.
146 D4 **Geal Charn** *hill Highland, Scotland* U.K.
146 E4 **Geal Charn** *hill Highland, Scotland* U.K.
163 E6 **Géant, Pic du** *mt.* France
238 B3 **Gearhart Mountain** *OR* U.S.A.
Gearraidh na h-Aibhne *Western Isles, Scotland* U.K. *see* **Garrynahine**
148 B4 **Geashill** Rep. of Ireland
163 B5 **Geaune** France
169 F4 **Gebesee** Ger.
169 C5 **Gebhardshain** Ger.
199 G3 **Gebiz** Turkey
210 C2 **Gebre Guracha** Eth.
199 F1 **Gebze** Turkey
Gecheng *Chongqing* China *see* **Chengkou**
172 C3 **Gechingen** Ger.
94 C3 **Gedang, Gunung** *mt.* Indon.
138 E4 **Gedanonių kalnas** *hill* Lith.
203 G6 **Gedaref** Sudan
203 G6 **Gedaref** *state* Sudan
151 G2 **Geddington** *Northamptonshire, England* U.K.
177 H5 **Géderlak** Hungary
169 E5 **Gedern** Ger.
165 D5 **Gedinne** Belgium
199 F2 **Gediz** Turkey
199 E2 **Gediz** *r.* Turkey
151 H2 **Gedney Drove End** *Lincolnshire, England* U.K.
210 D4 **Gedo** *admin. reg.* Somalia
163 C6 **Gèdre** France
142 D4 **Gedser** Denmark
142 C3 **Gedsted** Denmark
Gedzheti Georgia *see* **Gejet'i**
165 E3 **Geel** Belgium
83 F4 **Geelong** *Vic.* Austr.
87 B6 **Geelvink Channel** *W.A.* Austr.
165 E4 **Geer** *r.* Belgium
164 D3 **Geertruidenberg** Neth.
168 C3 **Geeste** Ger.
168 D2 **Geeste** *r.* Ger.
164 F2 **Geesteren** Neth.
170 C3 **Geestgottberg** Ger.
168 F2 **Geesthacht** Ger.
165 E4 **Geetbets** Belgium
171 C5 **Gefell** Ger.
210 C2 **Gefersa** Eth.
164 E3 **Geffen** Neth.
171 C5 **Gefrees** Ger.
138 C4 **Gėgė** *r.* Lith.
Gegechkori Georgia *see* **Martvili**
177 K3 **Gégény** Hungary
129 D3 **Geghadir** Armenia
129 D3 **Geghama Lerrnashght'a** *mts* Armenia
111 C5 **Gê'gyai** *Xizang* China
78 □3a **Gehh** *i. Kwajalein* Marshall Is
168 D3 **Gehrde** Ger.
169 E3 **Gehrden** Ger.
171 C5 **Gehren** Ger.
109 F2 **Ge Hu** *l.* China
207 H3 **Geidam** Nigeria
172 D2 **Geiersberg** *hill* Ger.
173 G2 **Geiersthal** Ger.
234 C2 **Geigertown** *PA* U.S.A.
223 K3 **Geikie** *r. Sask.* Can.
85 E2 **Geikie Range** *hills Qld* Austr.
169 B5 **Geilenkirchen** Ger.
142 C1 **Geilo** Norway
169 E5 **Geisa** Ger.
169 E5 **Geiselbach** Ger.
173 G3 **Geiselhöring** Ger.
173 E2 **Geiselwind** Ger.
173 F3 **Geisenfeld** Ger.
173 G3 **Geisenhausen** Ger.
172 B2 **Geisenheim** Ger.
171 E5 **Geising** Ger.
172 C4 **Geisingen** Ger.
169 F4 **Geisleden** Ger.
172 C3 **Geislingen** Ger.
172 D3 **Geislingen an der Steige** Ger.
169 F4 **Geismar** Ger.
157 H4 **Geispolsheim** France
178 D3 **Geißstein** *mt.* Austria
179 G3 **Geistthal** Austria
211 B5 **Geita** Tanz.
171 D4 **Geithain** Ger.
140 K2 **Geittind** *mt.* Norway
129 C2 **Gejet'i** Georgia
108 B4 **Gejiu** *Yunnan* China
122 D2 **Gekdepe** Turkm.
210 A3 **Gel** *r.* Sudan
194 D5 **Gela** *Sicilia* Italy
194 D5 **Gela** *r. Sicilia* Italy
194 D5 **Gela, Golfo di** *g. Sicilia* Italy
111 E5 **Geladaindong** *mt. Qinghai* China
210 E3 **Geladī** Eth.
211 C5 **Gelai** *vol.* Tanz.
161 F4 **Gélas, Cime du** *mt.* France/Italy
170 D1 **Gelbensande** Ger.
173 E2 **Gelchsheim** Ger.
164 F2 **Gelderland** *prov.* Neth.
164 E3 **Geldermalsen** Neth.
169 B4 **Geldern** Ger.
169 F5 **Geldersheim** Ger.
165 E3 **Geldrop** Neth.
165 E4 **Geleen** Neth.
199 E2 **Gelembe** Turkey
210 D2 **Gelemso** Eth.
171 D5 **Gelenau** Ger.
199 G2 **Gelendost** Turkey
135 G7 **Gelendzhik** Rus. Fed.
117 G4 **Gelephu** Bhutan
199 E1 **Gelibolu** Turkey
199 E1 **Gelibolu Yarımadası** *pen.* Turkey
199 G2 **Gelincik Dağı** *mt.* Turkey
163 C4 **Gelise** *r.* France
176 F5 **Gellénháza** Hungary
150 D3 **Gelligaer** *Caerphilly, Wales* U.K.
78 □3a **Gellinam** *i. Kwajalein* Marshall Is
169 E5 **Gelnhausen** Ger.
177 J3 **Gelnica** Slovakia
163 B5 **Gelos** France
163 B5 **Geloux** *r.* France
142 C4 **Gels** *r.* Denmark
186 C3 **Gelsa** Spain
176 F5 **Gelse** Hungary
169 C4 **Gelsenkirchen** Ger.
173 F3 **Geltendorf** Ger.
168 E1 **Gelting** Ger.
171 D3 **Geltow** Ger.
165 D4 **Gembloux** Belgium
207 H5 **Gembu** Nigeria
160 D1 **Gemeaux** France
208 C4 **Gemena** Dem. Rep. Congo
161 D5 **Gémenos** France
126 E3 **Gemerek** Turkey
177 J3 **Gemerská Hôrka** Slovakia
177 J3 **Gemerská Poloma** Slovakia
164 E3 **Gemert** Neth.
199 F3 **Gemiş** Turkey
199 F1 **Gemlik** Turkey
172 C2 **Gemmingen** Ger.
191 I2 **Gemona del Friuli** Italy
162 B3 **Gémozac** France
203 G3 **Gemsa** Egypt
212 D5 **Gemsbok National Park** Botswana
214 E1 **Gemsbokvlakte** S. Africa
172 B2 **Gemünden** Ger.
169 D5 **Gemünden (Wohra)** Ger.
169 E5 **Gemünden am Main** Ger.
107 H1 **Gen** *r.* China
185 E4 **Genal** *r.* Spain
210 D3 **Genalē Wenz** *r.* Eth.
165 D4 **Genappe** Belgium
185 H2 **Génave** Spain
193 E3 **Genazzano** Italy
129 B4 **Genç** Turkey
162 C2 **Gençay** France
176 F4 **Gencsapáti** Hungary
124 B5 **Gendoa** *r.* Eth.
160 D1 **Gendrey** France
164 F3 **Gendringen** Neth.
164 E3 **Gendt** Neth.
160 C2 **Génelard** France
164 F2 **Genemuiden** Neth.
260 E5 **General Acha** Arg.
261 G5 **General Alvear** *Buenos Aires* Arg.
260 D4 **General Alvear** *Mendoza* Arg.
261 G4 **General Arenales** Arg.
253 F6 **General Artigas** Para.
261 H4 **General Belgrano** Arg.
General Belgrano II *research stn* Antarctica *see* **Belgrano II**
262 U2 **General Bernardo O'Higgins** *research stn* Antarctica
261 F3 **General Cabrera** Arg.
261 H2 **General Campos** Arg.
256 A1 **General Carneiro** Brazil
259 B7 **General Carrera, Lago** *l.* Arg./Chile
261 F6 **General Daniel Cerri** Arg.
261 F3 **General Deheza** Arg.
General Freire Angola *see* **Muxaluando**
261 H3 **General Galarza** Arg.
260 C3 **General Gutiérrez** Arg.
258 F2 **General José de San Martín** Arg.
261 I5 **General Juan Madariaga** Arg.
252 C4 **General Lagos** Chile
261 H4 **General Las Heras** Arg.
261 I5 **General Lavalle** Arg.
261 F4 **General Levalle** Arg.
92 C4 **General Luna** Phil.
92 C4 **General MacArthur** Phil.
General Machado Angola *see* **Camacupa**
258 D2 **General Martín Miguel de Güemes** Arg.
261 F4 **General Pico** Arg.
261 G4 **General Pinto** Arg.
261 I5 **General Pirán** Arg.
260 D6 **General Roca** Arg.
261 H4 **General Rodriguez** Arg.
261 G3 **General Rojo** Arg.
253 E4 **General Saavedra** Bol.
256 B4 **General Salgado** Brazil
General San Martín *research stn* Antarctica *see* **San Martín**
261 H4 **General San Martín** Arg.
261 F5 **General San Martín** Arg.
92 C5 **General Santos** Phil.
244 C1 **General Simón Bolívar** Mex.
243 F3 **General Terán** Mex.
197 I4 **General Toshevo** Bulg.
261 F4 **General Villegas** Arg.
232 E4 **Genesee** *PA* U.S.A.
232 E3 **Genesee** *r. NY* U.S.A.
232 E3 **Geneseo** *NY* U.S.A.
182 D1 **Genestoso** Spain
210 C2 **Genet** Eth.
158 E3 **Genêts** France
215 F2 **Geneva** S. Africa
Geneva Switz. *see* **Genève**
231 C6 **Geneva** *AL* U.S.A.
226 C5 **Geneva** *IL* U.S.A.
236 D3 **Geneva** *NE* U.S.A.
232 E3 **Geneva** *NY* U.S.A.
232 C4 **Geneva** *OH* U.S.A.
Geneva, Lake France/Switz. *see* **Léman, Lac**
190 B2 **Genève** Switz.
160 E2 **Genève** *canton* Switz.
183 H2 **Genevilla** Spain
160 E2 **Genevois** *mts* France
Genf Switz. *see* **Genève**
191 H5 **Genga** Italy
108 B1 **Gengda** *Sichuan* China
172 C3 **Gengenbach** Ger.
109 E4 **Genglou** *Guangdong* China
108 A4 **Gengma** *Yunnan* China
Gengqing *Sichuan* China *see* **Dêgê**
Gengxuan *Yunnan* China *see* **Gengma**
210 B3 **Geni** *r.* Sudan
Genichesk Ukr. *see* **Heniches'k**
185 E3 **Genil** *r.* Spain
198 D1 **Genisea** Greece
163 B4 **Génissac** France
165 E4 **Genk** Belgium
160 D1 **Genlis** France
192 B5 **Gennargentu, Monti del** *mts Sardegna* Italy
192 B5 **Genn'Argiolas, Monte** *hill Sardegna* Italy
164 E3 **Gennep** Neth.
162 B1 **Gennes** France
83 G4 **Genoa** *Vic.* Austr.
Genoa Italy *see* **Genova**
226 C4 **Genoa** *IL* U.S.A.
161 B4 **Génolhac** France
192 B5 **Genoni** *Sardegna* Italy
162 D2 **Genouillac** France
162 C2 **Genouillé** France
159 H4 **Genouilly** France
190 D4 **Genova** Italy
190 E4 **Genova** *prov. Liguria* Italy
190 D4 **Genova, Golfo di** *g.* Italy
187 C6 **Genovés** Spain
250 □ **Genovesa, Isla** *i. Islas Galápagos* Ecuador
163 C4 **Gensac** France
165 C3 **Gent** Belgium
171 D3 **Genthin** Ger.
254 E4 **Gentio do Ouro** Brazil
162 E3 **Gentioux, Plateau de** France
162 D3 **Gentioux-Pigerolles** France
Genua Italy *see* **Genova**
193 I4 **Genzano di Lucania** Italy
193 E3 **Genzano di Roma** Italy
197 F2 **Geoagiu** *r.* Romania
87 B7 **Geographe Bay** *W.A.* Austr.
87 B5 **Geographe Channel** *W.A.* Austr.
Geok-Tepe Turkm. *see* **Gekdepe**
86 C4 **George** *r. W.A.* Austr.
225 H1 **George** *r. Que.* Can.
214 D5 **George** S. Africa
83 G3 **George, Lake** *N.S.W.* Austr.
82 D4 **George, Lake** *S.A.* Austr.
86 D4 **George, Lake** *salt flat W.A.* Austr.
210 A4 **George, Lake** Uganda
233 G3 **George, Lake** *NY* U.S.A.
84 B4 **George Gills Range** *mts N.T.* Austr.
150 C3 **Georgeham** *Devon, England* U.K.
George Land *i. Zemlya Frantsa-Iosifa* Rus. Fed. *see* **Zemlya Georga**
173 G2 **Georgenberg** Ger.
173 F2 **Georgensgmünd** Ger.
233 G3 **Georges Mills** *NH* U.S.A.
85 E3 **Georgetown** *Qld* Austr.
83 F5 **George Town** *Tas.* Austr.
246 D2 **George Town** *Gt Exuma* Bahamas
224 E5 **Georgetown** *Ont.* Can.
246 B3 **George Town** Cayman Is
206 B3 **Georgetown** Gambia
251 G3 **Georgetown** Guyana
94 C1 **George Town** Malaysia
235 E1 **Georgetown** *CT* U.S.A.
233 F5 **Georgetown** *DE* U.S.A.
231 C6 **Georgetown** *GA* U.S.A.
230 C4 **Georgetown** *KY* U.S.A.
232 B5 **Georgetown** *OH* U.S.A.
231 E5 **Georgetown** *SC* U.S.A.
237 D6 **Georgetown** *TX* U.S.A.
262 T2 **George VI Sound** *sea chan.* Antarctica
263 K2 **George V Land** *reg.* Antarctica
237 D6 **George West** *TX* U.S.A.
129 C3 **Georgia** *country* Asia
231 D5 **Georgia** *state* U.S.A.
222 E5 **Georgia, Strait of** *B.C.* Can.
231 C6 **Georgiana** *AL* U.S.A.
224 D4 **Georgian Bay** *Ont.* Can.
Georgi Traykov Bulg. *see* **Dolni Chiflik**
Georgiu-Dezh Rus. Fed. *see* **Liski**
120 D2 **Georgiyevka** *Aktyubinskaya Oblast'* Kazakh.
121 J2 **Georgiyevka** *Vostochnyy Kazakhstan* Kazakh.
Georgiyevka *Zhambylskaya Oblast'* Kazakh. *see* **Korday**
129 C1 **Georgiyevsk** Rus. Fed.
134 I4 **Georgiyevskoye** *Kostromskaya Oblast'* Rus. Fed.
129 A1 **Georgiyevskoye** *Krasnodarskiy Kray* Rus. Fed.
168 C3 **Georgsdorf** Ger.
168 C2 **Georgsheil** Ger.
169 D3 **Georgsmarienhütte** Ger.
Georg von Neumayer *research stn* Antarctica *see* **Neumayer**
163 B5 **Ger** *Aquitaine* France
159 F3 **Ger** *Basse-Normandie* France
186 E2 **Ger** Spain
171 D5 **Gera** Ger.
165 C4 **Geraardsbergen** Belgium
169 F5 **Geraberg** Ger.
172 D2 **Gerabronn** Ger.
195 F4 **Gerace** Italy
195 F4 **Gerace** *r.* Italy
194 D5 **Geraci Siculo** *Sicilia* Italy
147 B5 **Gerahies** Rep. of Ireland
198 C1 **Gerakarou** Greece
198 C3 **Geraki** Greece
256 B6 **Geral, Serra** *mts* Brazil
254 D4 **Geral de Goiás, Serra** *hills* Brazil
81 C6 **Geraldine** *South I.* N.Z.
254 D5 **Geral do Paraná, Serra** *hills* Brazil
87 B6 **Geraldton** *W.A.* Austr.
157 G4 **Gérardmer** France
179 G2 **Geras** Austria
179 H2 **Gerasdorf bei Wien** Austria
122 C5 **Gerāsh** Iran
156 E4 **Géraudot** France
240 F1 **Gerber** *CA* U.S.A.
157 G4 **Gerbéviller** France
161 C4 **Gerbier de Jonc** *mt.* France
171 C4 **Gerbstedt** Ger.
176 G4 **Gérce** Hungary
172 D2 **Gerchsheim** Ger.
127 F3 **Gercüş** Turkey
168 F3 **Gerdau** Ger.
215 F2 **Gerdau** S. Africa
Gerdauen *Kaliningradskaya Oblast'* Rus. Fed. *see* **Zheleznodorozhnyy**
126 D2 **Gerede** Turkey
126 D2 **Gerede** *r.* Turkey
184 D3 **Gerena** Spain
177 J5 **Gerendás** Hungary
182 B3 **Gerês, Serra do** *mts* Port.
177 H5 **Geresdlak** Hungary
123 F4 **Gereshk** Afgh.
178 D2 **Geretsberg** Austria
173 F4 **Geretsried** Ger.
185 H3 **Gérgal** Spain
129 E2 **Gergebil'** Rus. Fed.
192 B5 **Gergei** *Sardegna* Italy
177 K3 **Gergely-hegy** *hill* Hungary
160 C2 **Gergy** France
173 E2 **Gerhardshofen** Ger.
122 D3 **Gerīmenj** Iran
183 F5 **Gerindote** Spain
236 C3 **Gering** *NE* U.S.A.
171 D4 **Geringswalde** Ger.
177 J4 **Gerje** *r.* Hungary
177 H5 **Gerjen** Hungary
238 C3 **Gerlach** *NV* U.S.A.
177 J2 **Gerlachovský štít** *mt.* Slovakia
172 D3 **Gerlingen** Ger.
261 F4 **Germania** Arg.
Germania *country* Europe *see* **Germany**
Germanicea Turkey *see* **Kahramanmaraş**
222 E4 **Germansen Landing** *B.C.* Can.
German South-West Africa *country* Africa *see* **Namibia**
232 E5 **Germantown** *MD* U.S.A.
232 A5 **Germantown** *OH* U.S.A.
237 F5 **Germantown** *TN* U.S.A.
226 C4 **Germantown** *WI* U.S.A.
166 E3 **Germany** *country* Europe
173 E4 **Germaringen** Ger.
157 F4 **Germay** France
199 E3 **Germencik** Turkey
173 F3 **Germering** Ger.
172 C2 **Germersheim** Ger.
156 C5 **Germigny-des-Prés** France
183 H1 **Gernika-Lumo** Spain
171 C4 **Gernrode** *Sachsen-Anhalt* Ger.
169 F4 **Gernrode** *Thüringen* Ger.
172 C3 **Gernsbach** Ger.
172 C2 **Gernsheim** Ger.
190 E2 **Gerola Alta** Italy
171 C5 **Geroldsgrün** Ger.
173 F3 **Gerolsbach** Ger.
169 B5 **Gerolstein** Ger.
173 E2 **Gerolzhofen** Ger.
Gerona Spain *see* **Girona**
198 D4 **Geropotamos** *r. Kriti* Greece
191 J3 **Gerovo** Croatia
165 D4 **Gerpinnes** Belgium
151 G3 **Gerrards Cross** *Buckinghamshire, England* U.K.
192 B5 **Gerrei** *reg. Sardegna* Italy
Gerri Spain *see* **Guerri de la Sal**
163 C5 **Gers** *dept Midi-Pyrénées* France
163 C4 **Gers** *r.* France
190 D2 **Gersau** Switz.
169 E5 **Gersfeld (Rhön)** Ger.
172 B2 **Gersheim** Ger.
114 B3 **Gersoppa** *Karnataka* India
171 E4 **Gerste** *r.* Ger.
168 C3 **Gersten** Ger.
173 E3 **Gerstetten** Ger.
157 H4 **Gerstheim** France
173 E3 **Gersthofen** Ger.
169 F5 **Gerstungen** Ger.
170 E2 **Gerswalde** Ger.
161 D4 **Gervanne** *r.* France
171 C3 **Gerwisch** Ger.
Géryville Alg. *see* **El Bayadh**
160 B3 **Gerzat** France
111 D5 **Gêrzê** *Xizang* China
126 D2 **Gerze** Turkey
173 G3 **Gerzen** Ger.
169 C4 **Gescher** Ger.
179 H3 **Geschriebenstein** *hill* Austria
169 F5 **Geschwenda** Ger.
169 D4 **Geseke** Ger.
192 B5 **Gesico** *Sardegna* Italy
Gesoriacum France *see* **Boulogne-sur-Mer**
157 E3 **Gespunsart** France
173 E3 **Gessertshausen** Ger.
190 C4 **Gesso** *r.* Italy
187 C5 **Gestalgar** Spain
159 E4 **Gesté** France
192 B5 **Gesturi** *Sardegna* Italy
193 H3 **Gesualdo** Italy
165 E4 **Gesves** Belgium
177 K5 **Geszt** Hungary
177 K4 **Geszteréd** Hungary
141 L3 **Geta** *Åland* Fin.
183 G4 **Getafe** Spain
165 E4 **Gete** *r.* Belgium
197 F3 **Getic, Podișul** *plat.* Romania
158 E4 **Gétigné** France
129 D3 **Getik** *r.* Armenia
168 E1 **Gettorf** Ger.
234 A3 **Gettysburg** *PA* U.S.A.
236 D2 **Gettysburg** *SD* U.S.A.
108 C3 **Getu He** *r.* China
256 C4 **Getulina** Brazil
262 P2 **Getz Ice Shelf** Antarctica
165 E4 **Geul** *r.* Neth.
94 B2 **Geumapang** *r.* Indon.
94 B1 **Geureudong, Gunung** *vol.* Indon.
83 G3 **Geurie** *N.S.W.* Austr.
127 F3 **Gevaş** Turkey
169 C4 **Gevelsberg** Ger.
158 E3 **Gévezé** France
197 F5 **Gevgelija** Macedonia
184 C1 **Gévora** *r.* Spain
114 B2 **Gevrai** *Mahar.* India
160 C1 **Gevrey-Chambertin** France
160 E2 **Gex** France
Gexianzhuang *Hebei* China *see* **Qinghe**
183 H1 **Gexto** Spain
Gey Iran *see* **Nīkshahr**
171 D5 **Geyer** Ger.
199 E2 **Geyikli** Turkey
215 E2 **Geysdorp** S. Africa
240 F2 **Geyserville** *CA* U.S.A.
199 G1 **Geyve** Turkey
256 C2 **Gezarina** Brazil
198 B1 **Gezavesh** Albania
179 G2 **Gföhl** Austria
214 D2 **Ghaap Plateau** S. Africa
127 F4 **Ghadaf, Wādī al** *watercourse* Iraq
Ghadamés Libya *see* **Ghadāmis**
202 A2 **Ghadāmis** Libya
122 C2 **Ghaem Shahr** Iran
117 F4 **Ghaghara** *r.* India
78 □6 **Ghaghe** *i.* Solomon Is
117 F5 **Ghaghra** *Bihar* India
120 E2 **Ghalkarteniz, Solonchak** *salt marsh* Kazakh.
Ghallaorol Uzbek. *see* **Gallyaaral**
206 E4 **Ghana** *country* Africa
116 C4 **Ghanliala** *Rajasthan* India
116 B5 **Ghantwar** *Gujarat* India
212 D4 **Ghanzi** Botswana
212 D4 **Ghanzi** *admin. dist.* Botswana
Ghap'an Armenia *see* **Kapan**
124 C3 **Gharāmīl, Jabal al** *hill* Saudi Arabia
126 C5 **Gharbîya** *governorate* Egypt
205 F2 **Ghardaïa** Alg.
189 B7 **Ghardimaou** Tunisia
117 E5 **Gharghoda** *Madh. Prad.* India
203 G2 **Ghârib, Gebel** *mt.* Egypt
123 G2 **Gharm** Tajik.
125 G4 **Gharm, Wādī** *r.* Oman
123 F5 **Gharo** Pak.
202 B1 **Gharyān** Libya
202 A3 **Ghāt** Libya
116 E4 **Ghatampur** *Uttar Prad.* India
117 F5 **Ghatgan** *Orissa* India
116 C5 **Ghatol** *Rajasthan* India
117 F5 **Ghatsila** *Bihar* India
123 G4 **Ghauspur** Pak.
Għawdex *i.* Malta *see* **Gozo**
202 C6 **Ghazal, Bahr el** *watercourse* Chad
208 F2 **Ghazal, Bahr el** *r.* Sudan
Ghazalkent Uzbek. *see* **Gazalkent**
204 E2 **Ghazaouet** Alg.
116 D3 **Ghaziabad** *Uttar Prad.* India
117 E4 **Ghazipur** *Uttar Prad.* India
Ghazna Afgh. *see* **Ghaznī**
123 G3 **Ghaznī** Afgh.
123 F3 **Ghaznī** *prov.* Afgh.
123 F3 **Ghazni** *r.* Afgh.
124 C2 **Ghazzālah** Saudi Arabia
190 F3 **Ghedi** Italy
197 F3 **Ghelari** Romania
197 H3 **Ghelința** Romania
Ghent Belgium *see* **Gent**
232 C6 **Ghent** *WV* U.S.A.
Gheorghe Gheorghiu-Dej Romania *see* **Onești**
197 H3 **Gheorghe Lazăr** Romania
197 G2 **Gheorgheni** Romania
114 B2 **Gherdi** *Mahar.* India
197 F2 **Gherla** Romania
190 D3 **Ghiffa** Italy
Ghijduwon Uzbek. *see* **Gizhduvan**
192 A4 **Ghilarza** *Sardegna* Italy
177 K5 **Ghioroc** Romania
197 F3 **Ghioroiu** Romania
177 K6 **Ghiroda** Romania
165 C4 **Ghislenghien** Belgium
192 B2 **Ghisonaccia** *Corse* France
192 B2 **Ghisoni** *Corse* France
116 C1 **Ghizar** Jammu and Kashmir
177 K6 **Ghizela** Romania
78 □6 **Ghizunabeana Islands** Solomon Is
114 B2 **Ghod** *Mahar.* India
114 B2 **Ghod** *r.* India
116 C5 **Gholvad** *Mahar.* India
123 G3 **Ghorband** *r.* Afgh.
116 B4 **Ghotaru** *Rajasthan* India
123 G5 **Ghotki** Pak.
123 F3 **Ghowr** *prov.* Afgh.
117 F4 **Ghuari** *r.* India
Ghudamis Libya *see* **Ghadāmis**
114 C2 **Ghugus** *Mahar.* India
Ghukasyan Armenia *see* **Ashots'k'**
128 C4 **Ghurayfah** *hill* Saudi Arabia
123 E3 **Ghurian** Afgh.
124 D2 **Ghurrab, Jabal** *hill* Saudi Arabia
124 C3 **Ghurūb, Jabal** *hill* Saudi Arabia
202 C2 **Ghuzayyil, Sabkhat** *salt marsh* Libya
Ghuzor Uzbek. *see* **Guzar**
156 C1 **Ghyvelde** France
97 D5 **Gia Đinh** Vietnam
135 H7 **Giaginskaya** Rus. Fed.
128 A2 **Gialias** *r.* Cyprus
96 D3 **Giang** *r.* Vietnam
198 C1 **Giannitsa** Greece
192 D2 **Giannutri, Isola di** *i.* Italy
193 E2 **Giano dell'Umbria** Italy
215 G3 **Giant's Castle** *mt.* S. Africa
147 E1 **Giant's Causeway** *lava field Northern Ireland* U.K.
235 F1 **Giant's Neck** *CT* U.S.A.
95 F5 **Gianyar** *Bali* Indon.
195 E5 **Giardini-Naxos** *Sicilia* Italy
196 E3 **Giarmata** Romania
194 D5 **Giarratana** *Sicilia* Italy
195 E5 **Giarre** *Sicilia* Italy
162 E3 **Giat** France
192 A4 **Giave** *Sardegna* Italy
190 C3 **Giaveno** Italy
190 C3 **Giavino, Monte** *mt.* Italy
192 A5 **Giba** *Sardegna* Italy
184 E4 **Gibalbín** *hill* Spain
246 C2 **Gibara** Cuba
184 E3 **Gibarrayo** *hill* Spain
86 E2 **Gibb** *r. W.A.* Austr.
236 D3 **Gibbon** *NE* U.S.A.
238 D2 **Gibbonsville** *ID* U.S.A.
86 E3 **Gibb River** *W.A.* Austr.
234 D3 **Gibbsboro** *NJ* U.S.A.
234 C3 **Gibbstown** *NJ* U.S.A.
194 B5 **Gibellina Nuova** *Sicilia* Italy
212 C5 **Gibeon** Namibia
159 F2 **Giberville** France
162 A2 **Giboule** *r.* France
184 D3 **Gibraleón** Spain
185 E4 **Gibraltar** Europe
185 □ **Gibraltar, Bay of** Gibraltar/Spain
184 E4 **Gibraltar, Campo de** *reg.* Spain
204 D2 **Gibraltar, Strait of** Morocco/Spain
87 D7 **Gibson** *W.A.* Austr.
231 D5 **Gibson** *GA* U.S.A.
226 C5 **Gibson City** *IL* U.S.A.
87 D5 **Gibson Desert** *W.A.* Austr.
234 B3 **Gibson Island** *MD* U.S.A.
222 F5 **Gibsons** *B.C.* Can.
175 L1 **Giby** Pol.
129 F3 **Gicăki Dağı** *mt.* Azer.
106 B2 **Gichgeniyn Nuruu** *mts* Mongolia
210 B2 **Gidda** Eth.
114 C3 **Giddalur** *Andhra Prad.* India
203 G2 **Gîddi, Gebel el** *hill* Egypt
237 D6 **Giddings** *TX* U.S.A.
Giddi Pass *hill* Egypt *see* **Gîddi, Gebel el**
140 L3 **Gideälven** *r.* Sweden
175 H5 **Gidle** Pol.
210 C3 **Gīdolē** Eth.
172 D2 **Giebelstadt** Ger.
169 F4 **Gieboldehausen** Ger.
175 H4 **Gieczno** Pol.
168 F1 **Giekau** Ger.
164 E1 **Giekerk** Neth.
167 K3 **Giełczew** *r.* Pol.
175 I4 **Gielniów** Pol.
170 D2 **Gielow** Ger.
156 C5 **Gien** France
173 E3 **Giengen an der Brenz** Ger.
161 D3 **Gières** France
165 D3 **Gierle** Belgium
171 C4 **Giersleben** Ger.
169 F4 **Gierstädt** Ger.
175 I2 **Gierzwałd** Pol.
169 E4 **Gieselwerder (Oberweser)** Ger.
169 D5 **Gießen** Ger.
169 D5 **Gießen** *admin. reg. Hessen* Ger.
164 F1 **Gieten** Neth.
175 I2 **Gietrzwałd** Pol.
159 H4 **Gièvres** France
122 D2 **Gīfan** Iran
149 G2 **Gifford** *East Lothian, Scotland* U.K.
163 E4 **Giffou** *r.* France
160 E2 **Giffre** *r.* France
169 F3 **Gifhorn** Ger.
222 H4 **Gift Lake** *Alta* Can.
104 C3 **Gifu** Japan
104 C3 **Gifu** *pref.* Japan
135 H7 **Gigant** Rus. Fed.
242 C3 **Giganta, Cerro** *mt.* Mex.
250 C4 **Gigante** Col.
185 I3 **Gigante** *mt.* Spain
161 B5 **Gigean** France
146 C6 **Gigha** *i. Scotland* U.K.
146 C6 **Gigha, Sound of** *sea chan. Scotland* U.K.
197 F4 **Gighera** Romania
192 C2 **Giglio, Isola del** *i.* Italy
192 C2 **Giglio Castello** Italy
161 B5 **Gignac** *Languedoc-Roussillon* France
161 D5 **Gignac** *Provence-Alpes-Côte-d'Azur* France
190 C3 **Gignod** Italy
161 D4 **Gigondas** France
182 E1 **Gijón** Spain
163 E5 **Gijou** *r.* France
211 A5 **Gikongoro** Rwanda
241 J5 **Gila** *r. AZ* U.S.A.
241 K5 **Gila Bend** *AZ* U.S.A.
241 K5 **Gila Bend Mountains** *AZ* U.S.A.
241 J5 **Gila Mountains** *AZ* U.S.A.
122 B2 **Gīlān** *prov.* Iran
122 A3 **Gīlān-e Gharb** Iran
197 F2 **Gilău** Romania
129 F3 **Giläzi** Azer.
149 I4 **Gilberdyke** *East Riding of Yorkshire, England* U.K.
85 E3 **Gilbert** *r. Qld* Austr.
241 L5 **Gilbert** *AZ* U.S.A.
226 A2 **Gilbert** *MN* U.S.A.
232 C6 **Gilbert** *WV* U.S.A.
Gilbert Islands *country* Pacific Ocean *see* **Kiribati**
234 B2 **Gilberton** *PA* U.S.A.
85 E3 **Gilbert Range** *mts Qld* Austr.
266 G6 **Gilbert Ridge** *sea feature* Pacific Ocean
85 E3 **Gilbert River** *Qld* Austr.
234 C2 **Gilbertsville** *PA* U.S.A.
232 B4 **Gilboa** *OH* U.S.A.
254 D4 **Gilbués** Brazil
173 F3 **Gilching** Ger.
238 E1 **Gildford** *MT* U.S.A.
213 H3 **Gilé** Moz.
185 F3 **Gilena** Spain
87 C6 **Giles, Lake** *salt flat W.A.* Austr.
84 B3 **Giles Creek** *r. N.T.* Austr.
87 F5 **Giles Meteorological Station** *W.A.* Austr.
84 B4 **Giles Range** *mts N.T.* Austr.
161 F5 **Gilette** France
202 E4 **Gilf Kebir Plateau** Egypt
147 E2 **Gilford** *Northern Ireland* U.K.
83 G2 **Gilgai** *N.S.W.* Austr.
83 G2 **Gilgandra** *N.S.W.* Austr.
83 G2 **Gil Gil Creek** *r. N.S.W.* Austr.
116 C2 **Gilgit** Jammu and Kashmir
116 C2 **Gilgit** *r.* Jammu and Kashmir
83 F3 **Gilgunnia** *N.S.W.* Austr.
95 F5 **Gilimanuk** *Bali* Indon.
Gilindire Turkey *see* **Aydıncık**
147 C2 **Gill, Lough** *l.* Rep. of Ireland
223 M3 **Gillam** *Man.* Can.
149 I3 **Gillamoor** *North Yorkshire, England* U.K.
142 E3 **Gilleleje** Denmark
87 E5 **Gillen, Lake** *salt flat W.A.* Austr.
169 B5 **Gillenfeld** Ger.
82 D3 **Gilles, Lake** *salt flat S.A.* Austr.
232 E4 **Gillett** *PA* U.S.A.
226 C3 **Gillett** *WI* U.S.A.
238 F2 **Gillette** *WY* U.S.A.
140 K3 **Gillhov** Sweden
85 E4 **Gilliat** *Qld* Austr.
85 E4 **Gilliat** *r. Qld* Austr.
150 E3 **Gillingham** *Dorset, England* U.K.
151 H3 **Gillingham** *Medway, England* U.K.
149 H3 **Gilling West** *North Yorkshire, England* U.K.
146 E3 **Gills** *Highland, Scotland* U.K.
226 D3 **Gills Rock** *WI* U.S.A.
160 E3 **Gilly-sur-Isère** France
160 B2 **Gilly-sur-Loire** France
235 F1 **Gilman** *CT* U.S.A.
226 D5 **Gilman** *IL* U.S.A.
226 B3 **Gilman** *WI* U.S.A.
237 E5 **Gilmer** *TX* U.S.A.
146 E5 **Gilmerton** *Perth and Kinross, Scotland* U.K.
197 F3 **Gilort** *r.* Romania
240 G3 **Gilroy** *CA* U.S.A.
169 E5 **Gilserberg** Ger.
149 G3 **Gilsland** *Northumberland, England* U.K.
146 F6 **Gilston** *Scottish Borders, Scotland* U.K.
168 E3 **Gilten** Ger.
91 J8 **Giluwe, Mount** P.N.G.
150 D3 **Gilwern** *Monmouthshire, Wales* U.K.
164 D3 **Gilze** Neth.
210 B2 **Gīmbī** Eth.
247 □3 **Gimie, Mount** *vol.* St Lucia
195 F4 **Gimigliano** Italy
223 L5 **Gimli** *Man.* Can.
143 H1 **Gimo** Sweden
163 D5 **Gimone** *r.* France
163 C5 **Gimont** France
160 B2 **Gimouille** France
161 D5 **Ginasservis** France
203 H6 **Ginda** Eritrea
85 G4 **Gindie** *Qld* Austr.
252 D3 **Ginebra, Laguna** *l.* Bol.
128 A5 **Gineina, Râs el** *mt.* Egypt
161 A5 **Ginestas** France
216 □1b **Ginetes** *São Miguel* Azores
114 D5 **Gin Ganga** *r.* Sri Lanka
114 C3 **Gingee** *Tamil Nadu* India
165 E4 **Gingelom** Belgium
172 D3 **Gingen an der Fils** Ger.
85 G5 **Gin Gin** *Qld* Austr.
87 B6 **Gingin** *W.A.* Austr.
215 H3 **Gingindlovu** S. Africa
92 C4 **Gingoog** Phil.
170 E1 **Gingst** Ger.
210 D3 **Gīnīr** Eth.
138 D4 **Ginkūnai** Lith.
163 E6 **Ginoles** France
195 F2 **Ginosa** Italy
195 E4 **Ginostra** *Isole Lipari* Italy
Ginzo de Limia Spain *see* **Xinzo de Limia**
184 C3 **Giões** Port.
198 D4 **Giofyros** *r. Kriti* Greece
193 H4 **Gioi** Italy
195 E4 **Gioia, Golfo di** *b.* Italy
193 F3 **Gioia dei Marsi** Italy
195 F2 **Gioia del Colle** Italy
193 G3 **Gioia Sannitica** Italy
195 E4 **Gioia Tauro** Italy
195 F4 **Gioiosa Ionica** Italy
194 D4 **Gioiosa Marea** *Sicilia* Italy
190 D2 **Giornico** Switz.
198 D2 **Gioura** *i.* Greece
193 F2 **Giovenco** *r.* Italy
191 F2 **Gioveretto** *mt.* Italy
191 G5 **Giovi, Monte** *hill* Italy
193 I3 **Giovinazzo** Italy
224 F2 **Gipouloux** *r. Que.* Can.
83 F4 **Gippsland** *reg. Vic.* Austr.
113 □1 **Giraavaru** *i. N. Male* Maldives
116 B4 **Girab** *Rajasthan* India
177 K2 **Giraltovce** Slovakia
157 G4 **Girancourt** France
122 D4 **Gīrān Rīg** *mt.* Iran
116 D5 **Girar** *Mahar.* India
237 E4 **Girard** *KS* U.S.A.
232 C4 **Girard** *OH* U.S.A.
232 C3 **Girard** *PA* U.S.A.
234 B2 **Girardville** *PA* U.S.A.
192 B5 **Girasole** *Sardegna* Italy
Giravaru *i. N. Male* Maldives *see* **Giraavaru**
123 F5 **Girdar Dhor** *r.* Pak.
123 E4 **Girdi** Iran
207 I4 **Girei** Nigeria
126 E2 **Giresun** Turkey
203 F3 **Girga** Egypt
Girgenti *Sicilia* Italy *see* **Agrigento**
208 C4 **Giri** *r.* Dem. Rep. Congo
117 F4 **Giridih** *Bihar* India
195 F4 **Girifalco** Italy
83 F2 **Girilambone** *N.S.W.* Austr.
177 K4 **Girișu de Criș** Romania
136 D4 **Gîrla Mare** *r.* Moldova
116 C5 **Girna** *r.* India
Girne Cyprus *see* **Keryneia**
177 K6 **Giroc** Romania
169 C5 **Girod** Ger.
157 G5 **Giromagny** France
250 B5 **Girón** Ecuador
Giron Sweden *see* **Kiruna**
186 F3 **Girona** Spain
186 F2 **Girona** *prov. Cataluña* Spain
163 B4 **Gironde** *dept Aquitaine* France
162 B3 **Gironde** *est.* France
163 B4 **Gironde-sur-Dropt** France
186 E2 **Gironella** Spain
163 D5 **Girou** *r.* France
163 D5 **Giroussens** France
151 H2 **Girton** *Cambridgeshire, England* U.K.
255 B9 **Giruá** Brazil
146 D6 **Girvan** *South Ayrshire, Scotland* U.K.
134 F3 **Girvas** Rus. Fed.
80 G3 **Gisborne** *North I.* N.Z.
80 G3 **Gisborne** *admin. reg. North I.* N.Z.
149 G4 **Gisburn** *Lancashire, England* U.K.
222 F4 **Giscome** *B.C.* Can.
211 A5 **Gisenyi** Rwanda
142 E3 **Gislaved** Sweden
156 B3 **Gisors** France
Gissar Tajik. *see* **Hisor**
123 F2 **Gissar Range** *mts* Tajik./Uzbek.
Gissarskiy Khrebet *mts* Tajik./Uzbek. *see* **Gissar Range**
193 G2 **Gissi** Italy
165 B3 **Gistel** Belgium
190 D2 **Giswil** Switz.
211 A5 **Gitarama** Rwanda
211 A5 **Gitega** Burundi
169 F4 **Gittelde** Ger.
Giuba *r.* Somalia *see* **Jubba**
197 F3 **Giubega** Romania
190 E2 **Giubiasco** Switz.
191 F3 **Giudicarie, Valli** *val.* Italy
193 G4 **Giugliano in Campania** Italy
193 F3 **Giuliano di Roma** Italy
193 F2 **Giulianova** Italy
190 F4 **Giuncugnano** Italy
197 G2 **Giurgeului, Munții** *mts* Romania
197 G4 **Giurgiu** Romania
122 D2 **Givar** Iran
142 C4 **Give** Denmark
156 B3 **Giverny** France
157 E2 **Givet** France
160 C3 **Givors** France
165 D4 **Givry** Belgium
160 C2 **Givry** France
157 E4 **Givry-en-Argonne** France
213 F4 **Giyani** S. Africa
210 C2 **Giyon** Eth.
Giza Egypt *see* **El Gîza**

174 F3	Gizałki Pol.
126 C5	Giza Pyramids *tourist site* Egypt
122 A3	Gizeh Rüd *r.* Iran
129 D2	Gizel' Rus. Fed.
159 G4	Gizeux France
120 F4	Gizhduvan Uzbek.
193 F2	Gizio *r.* Italy
78 ⃞6	Gizo *New Georgia Is* Solomon Is
78 ⃞6	Gizo *i. New Georgia Is* Solomon Is
175 J1	Giżycko Pol.
193 I6	Gizzeria Italy
196 E4	Gjalicë e Lumës, Mal *mt.* Albania
142 C2	Gjerstad Norway
198 B1	Gjirokastër Albania
129 I3	Gjoa Haven *Nunavut* Can.
141 J3	Gjøvik Norway
198 A1	Gjuhëzës, Kepi *i pt* Albania
225 J4	Glace Bay *N.S.* Can.
190 D1	Glacier, Monte *mt.* Italy
222 C3	Glacier Bay *AK* U.S.A.
238 B1	Glacier Peak *vol. WA* U.S.A.
169 D3	Gladbeck Ger.
169 D5	Gladenbach Ger.
232 C6	Glade Spring *VA* U.S.A.
140 J2	Gladstad Norway
85 C4	Gladstone *Qld* Austr.
82 D3	Gladstone *S.A.* Austr.
83 G5	Gladstone *Tas.* Austr.
223 L5	Gladstone *Man.* Can.
81 E4	Gladstone *North I.* N.Z.
226 D3	Gladstone *MI* U.S.A.
232 D6	Gladstone *VA* U.S.A.
226 E4	Gladwin *MI* U.S.A.
232 D6	Gladys *VA* U.S.A.
198 D1	Glafki *Anatoliki Makedonia kai Thraki* Greece
160 E1	Glainans France
146 E5	Glamis *Angus, Scotland* U.K.
241 J5	Glamis *CA* U.S.A.
188 F3	Glamoč Bos.-Herz.
179 F4	Glan *r.* Austria
172 B2	Glan *r.* Ger.
92 C5	Glan Phil.
150 D3	Glanaman *Carmarthenshire, Wales* U.K.
147 B4	Glanaruddery Mountains *hills* Rep. of Ireland
161 D4	Glandage France
162 D3	Glandon France
161 E3	Glandon *r.* France
169 D3	Glandorf Ger.
162 C3	Glane *r.* France
169 C3	Glane *r.* Ger.
179 F4	Glaneregg Austria
164 F2	Glanerbrug Neth.
147 C5	Glanmire Rep. of Ireland
227 G4	Glanworth *Ont.* Can.
190 D2	Glarner Alpen *mts* Switz.
147 E2	Glarryford *Northern Ireland* U.K.
190 E1	Glarus Switz.
190 D1	Glarus *canton* Switz.
146 D3	Glas Bheinn *hill Scotland* U.K.
150 D2	Glasbury *Powys, Wales* U.K.
236 D4	Glasco *KS* U.S.A.
226 C5	Glasford *IL* U.S.A.
146 D6	Glasgow *Glasgow, Scotland* U.K.
146 D6	Glasgow *admin. div. Scotland* U.K.
234 C3	Glasgow *DE* U.S.A.
230 C4	Glasgow *KY* U.S.A.
238 F1	Glasgow *MT* U.S.A.
232 D6	Glasgow *VA* U.S.A.
171 E5	Glashütte Ger.
173 F2	Glashütten Ger.
169 D5	Glashütten Ger.
147 E2	Glaslough Rep. of Ireland
223 I4	Glaslyn *Sask.* Can.
146 E5	Glas Maol *mt. Scotland* U.K.
147 D3	Glassan Rep. of Ireland
234 C3	Glassboro *NJ* U.S.A.
148 E2	Glassford *South Lanarkshire, Scotland* U.K.
240 H3	Glass Mountain *CA* U.S.A.
149 F3	Glasson *Cumbria, England* U.K.
150 E3	Glastonbury *Somerset, England* U.K.
235 F1	Glastonbury *CT* U.S.A.
146 E5	Glas Tulaichean *mt.*
190 D1	Glatt *r.* Switz.
171 E4	Glaubitz Ger.
171 D5	Glauchau Ger.
197 G3	Glavacioc *r.* Romania
197 H2	Glavan Bulg.
197 H2	Glăvăneşti Romania
197 H4	Glavinitsa Bulg.
196 E4	Glavnik *Kosovo, Srbija* Yugo.
232 D2	Glazoué Benin
134 K4	Glazov Rus. Fed.
139 K5	Glazunovka Rus. Fed.
226 D3	Gleason *WI* U.S.A.
222 H5	Gleichen *Alta* Can.
171 C4	Gleina Ger.
179 G3	Gleisdorf Austria
	Gleiwitz Pol. *see* Gliwice
160 D3	Gleizé France
151 H2	Glemsford *Suffolk, England* U.K.
140 K3	Glen Sweden
233 CH2	Glen *NH* U.S.A.
146 C4	Glen Affric *val. Scotland* U.K.
227 G2	Glen Afton *Ont.* Can.
80 E2	Glen Afton *North I.* N.Z.
232 E6	Glen Allen *VA* U.S.A.
147 C3	Glenamaddy Rep. of Ireland
147 B2	Glenamoy Rep. of Ireland
147 B2	Glenamoy *r.* Rep. of Ireland
226 E3	Glen Arbor *MI* U.S.A.
147 E1	Glenariff *Northern Ireland* U.K.
147 F2	Glenarm *Northern Ireland* U.K.
147 D3	Glen Artney *val. Scotland* U.K.
146 E4	Glen Avon *val. Scotland* U.K.
81 C6	Glenavy *South I.* N.Z.
147 E2	Glenavy *Northern Ireland* U.K.
146 C5	Glenbeg *Highland, Scotland* U.K.
147 B4	Glenbeigh Rep. of Ireland
223 I5	Glenboro *Man.* Can.
146 E6	Glenbrack *Scottish Borders, Scotland* U.K.
146 B4	Glenbrittle *Highland, Scotland* U.K.
234 C1	Glenburn *PA* U.S.A.
234 B3	Glen Burnie *MD* U.S.A.
146 C4	Glen Cannich *val. Scotland* U.K.
241 L3	Glen Canyon *gorge UT* U.S.A.
146 E6	Glencaple *Dumfries and Galloway, Scotland* U.K.
146 E5	Glencarse *Perth and Kinross, Scotland* U.K.
146 D3	Glen Cassley *val. Scotland* U.K.
146 C5	Glen Clova *val. Scotland* U.K.
224 D5	Glencoe S. Africa
215 H3	Glencoe S. Africa
236 E3	Glencoe *MN* U.S.A.
146 C5	Glen Coe *val. Scotland* U.K.
147 C2	Glencolumbkille Rep. of Ireland
215 E5	Glenconnor S. Africa
235 E2	Glen Cove *NY* U.S.A.
147 E3	Glencullen Rep. of Ireland
227 E2	Glendale *Ont.* Can.
241 K5	Glendale *AZ* U.S.A.
240 H4	Glendale *CA* U.S.A.
241 K3	Glendale *UT* U.S.A.
82 C2	Glendambo *S.A.* Austr.
146 C5	Glendaruel *val. Scotland* U.K.
147 E4	Glen Dee *val. Scotland* U.K.
85 G4	Glenden *Qld* Austr.
258 F2	Glendo *WY* U.S.A.
223 I4	Glendon *Alta* Can.
234 C2	Glendon *PA* U.S.A.
147 D2	Glenduff Rep. of Ireland
146 E1	Glenealy Rep. of Ireland
146 B6	Gleneagles *Perth and Kinross, Scotland* U.K.

82 E4	Glenelg *r. Vic.* Austr.
146 C4	Glenelg *Highland, Scotland* U.K.
146 E5	Glenfarg *Perth and Kinross, Scotland* U.K.
147 D2	Glenfarne Rep. of Ireland
81 B7	Glen Feshie *val. Scotland* U.K.
151 F2	Glenfield *Leicester, England* U.K.
234 D2	Glen Gardner *NJ* U.S.A.
147 B5	Glengarriff Rep. of Ireland
146 C4	Glen Garry *val. Highland, Scotland* U.K.
146 D5	Glen Garry *val. Perth and Kinross, Scotland* U.K.
87 C5	Glengarry Range *hills W.A.* Austr.
148 B3	Glengavlen Rep. of Ireland
84 D5	Glengyle *Qld* Austr.
81 B7	Glenham *South I.* N.Z.
147 D1	Glenhead *Northern Ireland* U.K.
84 C4	Glen Helen *N.T.* Austr.
83 G2	Glen Innes *N.S.W.* Austr.
146 F4	Glenkindie *Aberdeenshire, Scotland* U.K.
146 D7	Glenluce *Dumfries and Galloway, Scotland* U.K.
146 C4	Glen Lyon *val. Scotland* U.K.
234 B1	Glen Lyon *PA* U.S.A.
222 C2	Glenlyon Peak *Y.T.* Can.
80 E2	Glen Massey *North I.* N.Z.
83 G1	Glenmoore *N.S.W.* Austr.
84 D4	Glen More *val. Scotland* U.K.
85 G5	Glenmorgan *Qld* Austr.
146 E5	Glen Muick *val. Scotland* U.K.
80 E2	Glen Murray *North I.* N.Z.
240 F2	Glenn *CA* U.S.A.
241 L6	Glenn, Mount *AZ* U.S.A.
147 B3	Glennagevlagh Rep. of Ireland
220 D3	Glennallen *AK* U.S.A.
146 C5	Glen Nevis *val. Scotland* U.K.
233 G3	Glens *NM* U.S.A.
234 D1	Glen Spey *PA* U.S.A.
147 C2	Glenties Rep. of Ireland
147 D1	Glentogher Rep. of Ireland
81 C7	Glen Tromie *val. Scotland* U.K.
146 D6	Glentunnel *South I.* N.Z.
232 C3	Glenville *WV* U.S.A.
226 C1	Glenwater *Ont.* Can.
232 D6	Glen Wilton *VA* U.S.A.
237 E6	Glen Wilton *VA* U.S.A.
240 ⃞D9	Glenwood *HI* U.S.A.
236 E3	Glenwood *IA* U.S.A.
236 F4	Glenwood *MN* U.S.A.
235 D1	Glenwood *NJ* U.S.A.
239 E5	Glenwood *NM* U.S.A.
241 L2	Glenwood *UT* U.S.A.
232 B5	Glenwood *WV* U.S.A.
226 A3	Glenwood *WI* U.S.A.
239 F4	Glenwood Springs *CO* U.S.A.
160 E1	Glère France
171 D4	Glesien Ger.
146 ⃞G1	Gletness *Shetland, Scotland* U.K.
	Glevum *Gloucestershire, England* U.K. *see* Gloucester
170 D1	Glewitz Ger.
226 B2	Glidden *WI* U.S.A.
171 F3	Glienicke Ger.
147 B4	Glin Rep. of Ireland
188 F3	Glina *r. Bos.-Herz./Croatia
188 F2	Glina Croatia
168 F2	Glinde Ger.
171 D3	Glindow Ger.
139 J5	Glinishchevo Rus. Fed.
136 D4	Glinjeni Moldova
139 I4	Glinka Rus. Fed.
175 I3	Glinojeck Pol.
151 G3	Glinton *Peterborough, England* U.K.
141 J3	Glittertinden *mt.* Norway
174 G5	Gliwice Pol.
179 F4	Globasnitz Austria
241 L5	Globe *AZ* U.S.A.
197 L6	Glodea, Vârful *hill* Romania
197 H3	Glodeanu-Sărat Romania
136 D4	Glodeni Moldova
197 G2	Glodeni Romania
179 F4	Glödnitz Austria
197 G3	Glodyany Moldova *see* Glodeni
174 F4	Głogów Pol. *see* Głogów
179 G3	Gloggnitz Austria
190 E2	Glogn *r.* Switz.
196 E4	Glogovac *Kosovo, Srbija* Yugo.
174 E4	Głogówek Pol.
175 J5	Głogów Małopolski Pol.
174 G2	Głogowo Pol.
140 K2	Glomfjord Norway
179 G2	Glöfritz an der Wild Austria
143 J4	Glomma *r.* Norway
173 F3	Glonn *r.* Ger.
173 F3	Glonn *r.* Ger.
178 B4	Glonn *r.* Austria
254 F4	Glória do Ribatejo Port.
184 B1	Glória do Ribatejo Port.
217 ⃞2	Glorieuses, Îles *is* Indian Ocean
	Glorioso Islands Indian Ocean *see* Glorieuses, Îles
159 G3	Glos-la-Ferrière France
198 D2	Glossa *Thessalia* Greece
149 H4	Glossop *Derbyshire, England* U.K.
171 E4	Glöthe Ger.
135 I5	Glotovka Rus. Fed.
83 G2	Gloucester *Qld* Austr.
150 E3	Gloucester *Gloucestershire, England* U.K.
233 H3	Gloucester *MA* U.S.A.
254 C3	Gloucester *VA* U.S.A.
150 E3	Gloucester, Vale of *val.* England U.K.
234 C3	Gloucester City *NJ* U.S.A.
234 C3	Gloucester County *county NJ* U.S.A.
85 G4	Gloucester Island *Qld* Austr.
232 E6	Gloucester Point *VA* U.S.A.
150 E3	Gloucestershire *admin. div.* England U.K.
147 C3	Glounthaune Rep. of Ireland
233 F3	Gloversville *NY* U.S.A.
225 K4	Glovertown *Nfld.* Can.
175 J4	Głowaczów Pol.
170 F2	Glöwen Ger.
175 H4	Głowno Pol.
129 B4	Gojra Pak.
123 H4	Gojra Pak.
175 H4	Głogói Pol.
114 B2	Gokak *Karnataka* India
128 D1	Gökay *r.* Turkey
129 C1	Gökbel *dağı* Turkey
129 A3	Gökçedere Turkey
199 E3	Gökçedağ Turkey
199 E2	Gökçen Turkey
129 B4	Gökçeören Turkey
199 F2	Gökçeören Turkey
128 A1	Gökçekaya Turkey
128 A1	Gökçekaya Turkey
199 E2	Gökçeyazı Turkey
129 B4	Gökdağ Turkey
128 A1	Gökdere *r.* Turkey
120 F4	Gökdepe Turkm. *see* Gekdepe
199 E3	Gökeören Turkey
126 D3	Gökırmak *r.* Turkey
129 B4	Gökova *Muğla* Turkey
199 F3	Gökova *Muğla* Turkey
199 E3	Gökova Körfezi *b.* Turkey

142 C3	Glyngøre Denmark
147 F2	Glynn *Northern Ireland* U.K.
126 E3	Göksun Turkey
126 D3	Göksu Nehri *r.* Turkey
128 A1	Göktepe Turkey
176 G5	Gola Croatia
117 F5	Gola *Bihar* India
116 E3	Gola *Uttar Prad.* India
175 J4	Gołąb Pol.
188 A3	Golada *Spain see A* Golada
117 H4	Golaghat *Assam* India
179 E5	Golak *mt.* Slovenia
117 G4	Golakganj *Assam* India
128 B3	Golan *hills* Syria
175 K4	Gołańcz Pol.
124 D4	Golbāf Iran
126 E3	Gölbaşı Turkey
199 F3	Gölbent *Muğla* Turkey
157 G4	Golbey France
114 C2	Golconda *Andhra Prad.* India
237 F4	Golconda *IL* U.S.A.
238 D3	Golconda *NV* U.S.A.
199 E2	Gölcük Turkey
199 F1	Gölcük Turkey
199 F2	Gölcük *r.* Turkey
178 E2	Golčův Jeníkov Czech Rep.
175 H5	Gołcza Pol.
174 C2	Golczewo Pol.
232 E4	Gold *PA* U.S.A.
172 D4	Goldach Switz.
175 K1	Goldap Pol.
173 J1	Goldapa *r.* Pol.
169 E5	Goldbach Ger.
238 D3	Gold Beach *OR* U.S.A.
170 D3	Goldbeck Ger.
170 C3	Goldberg Ger.
150 E3	Goldcliff *Newport, Wales* U.K.
	Gold Coast *country* Africa *see* Ghana
83 H2	Gold Coast *Qld* Austr.
206 E5	Gold Coast *coastal area* Ghana
179 E4	Goldeck *mt.* Austria
168 E1	Goldelund Ger.
222 G5	Golden *B.C.* Can.
147 D4	Golden Rep. of Ireland
80 D4	Golden Bay *South I.* N.Z.
183 D4	Goldendale *WA* U.S.A.
179 E2	Gölblers *hill* Austria
81 D6	Golden Downs *South I.* N.Z.
246 ⃞	Golden Grove Jamaica
222 E5	Golden Hinde *mt. B.C.* Can.
237 F6	Golden Meadow *LA* U.S.A.
151 G3	Golden Point *Hampshire, England* U.K.
223 I5	Golden Prairie *Sask.* Can.
168 D3	Goldenstedt Ger.
119 L2	Golden Throne *mt. Jammu and* Kashmir
147 C4	Golden Vale *lowland* Rep. of Ireland
215 G5	Golden Valley S. Africa
150 E2	Golden Valley *val. England* U.K.
243 F3	Golden Valley Zimbabwe
211 K5	Gonbad-e Kāvūs Iran
187 D6	Gongola *r.* Nigeria
233 G4	Gorham *NH* U.S.A.
129 D1	Gori Georgia
196 D4	Gorica *Crna Gora* Yugo.
179 H4	Goričan Croatia
164 D3	Gorinchem Neth.
151 F3	Goring *Oxfordshire, England* U.K.
191 H4	Gorino Italy
129 E4	Goris Armenia
173 E4	Goritsa Ger.
139 K3	Goritsy Rus. Fed.
170 E2	Göritz Ger.
191 I3	Gorizia Italy
191 I3	Gorizia *prov. Friuli - Venezia Giulia* Italy
139 L3	Gorka Italy
129 D1	Gor'kaya Balka *r.* Rus. Fed.

123 E5	Gokprosh Hills Pak.
129 C4	Göksu *r.* Turkey
177 K3	Gönc Hungary
182 C4	Gonçalo Port.
161 D2	Goncelin France
182 D2	Gonda *Uttar Prad.* India
116 B5	Gondal *Gujarat* India
250 C5	Gonder Eth.
182 B3	Gondar Eth. *see* Gonder
182 B3	Gondar *Braga* Port.
182 B2	Gondar *Porto* Port.
210 C1	Gonder Eth.
169 D5	Gondershausen Ger.
169 E4	Gondesende Port.
116 E5	Gondia *Mahar.* India
182 B3	Gondomar Port.
182 B2	Gondomar Port.
169 C5	Gondorf Ger.
182 B3	Gondriz Port.
157 F4	Gondrecourt-le-Château France
157 F4	Gondreville France
163 C5	Gondrin France
199 E1	Gönen Turkey
199 E1	Gönen Turkey
199 E1	Gönen *r.* Turkey
161 E5	Gonfaron France
159 G2	Gonfreville-l'Orcher France
109 E2	Gong'an *Hubei* China
	Gongbalou *Xizang* China *see* Gamba
111 H6	Gongcheng *Guangxi* China
108 D3	Gonggar *Xizang* China
108 B2	Gongga Shan *mt. Sichuan* China
106 D4	Gonghe *Qinghai* China
	Gonghe *Yunnan* China *see* Mouding
	Gongjiang *Jiangxi* China *see* Yudu
110 C3	Gongliu *Xinjiang* China
207 I4	Gongola *r.* Nigeria
83 F2	Gongolgon *N.S.W.* Austr.
106 C3	Gongpoquan *Gansu* China
108 C3	Gongquan *Sichuan* China
	Gongxian
108 A3	Gongshan *Yunnan* China
	Gongtang *Xizang* China *see* Damxung
108 B3	Gongwang Shan *mts Yunnan* China
	Gongxian *Henan* China *see* Gongyi
108 C2	Gongxian *Sichuan* China
107 G5	Gongyi *Henan* China
100 C4	Gongzhuling *Jilin* China
192 B5	Goni *Sardegna* Italy
175 K2	Goniądz Pol.
109 J2	Gonj *Xizang* China
192 A5	Gonnesa *Sardegna* Italy
198 C2	Gonnoi Greece
192 A5	Gonnosfanadiga *Sardegna* Italy
192 A5	Gonnosnò *Sardegna* Italy
160 E1	Gonsans France
215 G5	Gonubie S. Africa
199 G2	Gönyü Turkey
177 H4	Gonzaga Italy
245 E2	Gonzáles Mex.
192 A5	Gonzales *r. Sicilia* Italy
237 D6	Gonzales *TX* U.S.A.
261 H4	González Moreno Arg.
244 C2	González Ortega Mex.
232 E6	Goochland *VA* U.S.A.
232 D6	Goode *VA* U.S.A.
263 I2	Goodenough, Cape Antarctica

177 K3	Gönc Hungary
81 B7	Gore *South I.* N.Z.
232 D5	Gore *VA* U.S.A.
227 F3	Gore Bay *Ont.* Can.
146 E6	Gorebridge *Midlothian, Scotland* U.K.
199 E2	Göreli Rus. Fed.
139 K4	Gorelki Rus. Fed.
129 C3	Gorelovka Georgia
135 H5	Goreloye Rus. Fed.
147 E4	Gorey Rep. of Ireland
122 C2	Gorgān Iran
122 C2	Gorgān, Rüd-e *r.* Iran
122 C2	Gorgan Bay Iran
	Gorgany *mts* Ukr. *see* Horhany
86 C4	Gorge Range *hills W.A.* Austr.
85 F3	Gorge Range *mts Qld* Austr.
81 B7	Gorge Road *South I.* N.Z.
176 G5	Görgeteg Hungary
193 I4	Gorgoglione Italy
206 B2	Gorgol *admin. reg.* Maur.
176 F5	Gősfai Hegy *hill* Hungary
191 D3	Gorgona, Isola di *i.* Italy
190 E3	Gorgonzola Italy
210 C1	Gorgora Eth.
207 H3	Goro3ram Nigeria
187 D6	Gorgos *r.* Spain
233 H2	Gorham *NH* U.S.A.
171 C4	Görzig Ger.
171 D3	Görzke Ger.
175 H4	Gorzkowice Pol.
175 L5	Gorzków-Osada Pol.
174 F2	Górzno Pol.
174 C4	Górów Śląski Pol.
174 D3	Górów Wielkopolski Pol.
174 G3	Górzyca Pol.
175 J5	Gorzyce *Podkarpackie* Pol.
175 J5	Gorzyce *Podkarpackie* Pol.
174 G6	Gorzyce *Śląskie* Pol.
	Gosaisthan *mt. Xizang* China *see* Xixabangma Feng
191 G2	Gosaldo Italy
179 E3	Gosau Austria
151 G2	Gosberton *Lincolnshire, England* U.K.
174 D1	Gościno Pol.
174 D4	Gościszów Pol.
179 G4	Gosdorf Austria
104 B4	Gose Japan
173 D6	Goseck Ger.
176 F5	Gősfai Hegy *hill* Hungary
151 F5	Gosfield *Essex, England* U.K.
149 E3	Gosforth *Cumbria, England* U.K.
149 F2	Gosforth *Tyne and Wear, England* U.K.
173 E4	Goslar Ger.
169 F4	Goslar Ger.
175 H4	Gośliche Pol.
158 E3	Gosné France
188 E3	Gospić Croatia
151 F4	Gosport *Hampshire, England* U.K.
206 A3	Gossas Senegal
190 E1	Gossau *Sankt Gallen* Switz.
172 C4	Gossau *Zürich* Switz.
207 E3	Gossendorf Austria
206 E3	Gossi Mali
171 D5	Gößnitz Ger.
179 F2	Gößweinstein Ger.
173 I5	Gostagayevskaya Rus. Fed.
137 I2	Gostishchevo Rus. Fed.
196 E5	Gostivar Macedonia
179 E2	Göstling an der Ybbs Austria
174 F2	Gostycyn Pol.
175 H4	Gostyń Pol.
175 J3	Gostynin Pol.
108 A1	Gosu *Sichuan* China
142 J3	Gota Sweden
143 I4	Gøtaälven *r.* Sweden
143 J3	Götaland *reg.* Sweden
142 I3	Göteborg Sweden
142 I3	Göteborg-Landvetter *airport* Sweden
105 E3	Gotemba Japan
143 F6	Götene Sweden
	Gotenhafen Pol. *see* Gdynia
169 F5	Gotha Ger.
151 F2	Gotham *Nottinghamshire, England* U.K.
	Gothem *Gotland* Sweden
143 H3	Gothem *i. Gotland* Sweden
	Gothenburg Sweden *see* Göteborg
236 C3	Gothenburg *NE* U.S.A.
207 F3	Gothèye Niger
143 H3	Gotland *county* Sweden
143 H3	Gotland *i.* Sweden
197 K3	Gotse Delchev Bulg.
143 H2	Gotska Sandön *i.* Sweden
143 H3	Gotska Sandön *i.* Sweden
104 B5	Gotō Japan
104 A5	Gotō-rettō *is* Japan
198 C3	Gotsis Japan
172 E3	Gottero, Monte *mt.* Italy
173 G3	Gotteszell Ger.
169 E4	Gottfrieding Ger.
173 G3	Göttingen Ger.
169 D4	Gottmadingen Ger.
140 L3	Gottne Sweden
222 F5	Gott Peak *B.C.* Can.
	Gottwaldow Czech Rep. *see* Zlín
110 C1	Goturdepe Turkm. *see* Koturdepe
179 H2	Götzendorf an der Leitha Austria
157 G3	Götzis Austria
158 D2	Gouarec France
214 B5	Gouda Neth.
161 C4	Goudargues France
260 C4	Goudge Arg.
151 H3	Goudhurst *Kent, England* U.K.
207 H3	Goudoumaria Niger
226 E1	Goudreau *Ont.* Can.
206 C4	Gouéké Guinea
158 B3	Gouesnou France
158 D3	Gouet *r.* France
264 I8	Gough Island S. Atlantic Ocean
160 E1	Gouhenans France
224 F3	Gouin, Réservoir *resr Que.* Can.
161 A4	Goul *r.* France
226 E2	Goulais River *Ont.* Can.
83 G5	Goulburn *N.S.W.* Austr.
84 C1	Goulburn Islands *N.T.* Austr.
83 F4	Goulburn *r. Vic.* Austr.
87 C5	Gould, Mount *hill W.A.* Austr.
226 E2	Gould City *MI* U.S.A.
262 O2	Gould Coast Antarctica
234 C1	Gouldsboro *PA* U.S.A.
207 I3	Goulféy Cameroon
	Goulou *atoll* Micronesia *see* Ngulu
161 D5	Goult France
206 D3	Goumbou Mali
198 C1	Goumenissa Greece
160 E1	Goumois France
207 H4	Gouna Cameroon
206 E2	Goundam Mali
208 C2	Goundi Chad
206 A3	Gouraye Maur.
163 A5	Gourbera France
160 C2	Gourdon-Polignac France
163 D4	Gourdon *Midi-Pyrénées* France
161 C5	Gourdon *Provence-Alpes-Côte-d'Azur* France
146 F5	Gourdon *Aberdeenshire, Scotland* U.K.
207 H3	Gouré Niger
163 B6	Gourette France
156 E3	Gourgançon France
158 D3	Gourin France
214 C6	Gourits *r.* S. Africa
206 E2	Gourma-Rharous Mali
163 E5	Gourmay-en-Bray France
204 B3	Goûr Oulad Ahmed *reg.* Mali
156 C3	Goussainville France
167 C3	Gout-Rossignol France
164 B5	Goutum Neth.
257 F3	Gouvéa Brazil
182 C4	Gouveia Port.
233 F2	Gouverneur *NY* U.S.A.
165 C5	Gouvy Belgium
159 G4	Gouzeaucourt France
162 D2	Gouzon France
224 E4	Gove Port.
236 C4	Gove *KS* U.S.A.
177 F4	Govedartsi Bulg.
172 C2	Govenlea
84 D2	Gove Peninsula *N.T.* Austr.
129 C1	Govi, Hora
129 C1	Goyachevodsky
92 C1	Governor Generoso Phil.
246 C1	Governor's Harbour Eleuthera Bahamas
106 B2	Govĭ-Altay *prov.* Mongolia

Column 1

106 C2 Govĭ Altayn Nuruu *mts* Mongolia
116 E4 Govindgarh *Madh. Prad.* India
123 F2 Govurdak Turkm.
81 D4 Gowanbridge *South I.* N.Z.
232 D3 Gowanda *NY* U.S.A.
85 F5 Gowan Range *hills Qld* Austr.
175 I4 Gowarczów Pol.
234 B2 Gowen City *PA* U.S.A.
150 C3 Gower *pen. Wales* U.K.
227 G2 Gowganda *Ont.* Can.
174 F1 Gowidlino Pol.
174 C2 Gowienica *r.* Pol.
147 D3 Gowna, Lough *l.* Rep. of Ireland
175 J3 Goworowo Pol.
147 D4 Gowran Rep. of Ireland
Govurdak Turkm. see Govurdak
149 G4 Gowy *r. England* U.K.
149 I4 Goxhill *North Lincolnshire, England* U.K.
258 F3 Goya Arg.
247 □² Goyave Guadeloupe
129 E3 Göyçay Azer.
129 E3 Göyçay *r.* Azer.
84 C2 Goyder *r. N.T.* Austr.
84 C5 Goyder watercourse *N.T.* Austr.
82 D1 Goyder Lagoon *salt flat S.A.* Austr.
Goymatdag *hills* Turkm. see Koymatdag, Gory
199 G3 Göynük Turkey
127 F3 Göynük Turkey
199 G1 Göynük Turkey
199 I1 Göynük *r.* Turkey
199 F2 Göynükbelen Turkey
102 J4 Goyō-zan *mt.* Japan
202 D6 Goz-Beïda Chad
128 B1 Gözcüler Turkey
175 J4 Gózd Pol.
174 D4 Gozdnica Pol.
126 E3 Gözene Turkey
113 G4 Gozha Co *salt l.* China
195 □ Gozo *i.* Malta
190 D3 Gozzano Italy
214 E5 Graaf-Reinet S. Africa
214 B5 Graafwater S. Africa
173 G4 Graben-Neudorf Ger.
173 G4 Grabenstätt Ger.
169 F5 Grabfeld *plain* Ger.
175 G4 Grabia *r.* Pol.
175 H4 Grabica Pol.
206 D5 Grabo Côte d'Ivoire
214 B6 Grabouw S. Africa
197 F3 Grabovica *Srbija* Yugo.
121 H1 Grabovo Kazakh.
170 C2 Grabow *Mecklenburg-Vorpommern* Ger.
171 C3 Grabow *Sachsen-Anhalt* Ger.
175 H3 Grabów Pol.
143 G4 Grabow *r.* Pol.
170 D2 Grabowhöfe Ger.
175 L5 Grabowiec *Lubelskie* Pol.
175 J4 Grabowiec *Mazowieckie* Pol.
175 J4 Grabów nad Pilicą Pol.
174 G4 Grabów nad Prosną Pol.
174 F2 Grabowno Pol.
174 F4 Grabowno Wielkie Pol.
175 K2 Grabowo *Podlaskie* Pol.
175 K1 Grabowo *Warmińsko-Mazurskie* Pol.
190 E1 Grabs Switz.
188 E3 Gračac Croatia
188 G3 Gračanica Bos.-Herz.
162 D1 Graçay France
87 C7 Grace, Lake *salt flat W.A.* Austr.
224 E4 Gracefield *Que.* Can.
165 E4 Grâce-Hollogne Belgium
85 G4 Gracemere *Qld* Austr.
158 C3 Grâces France
139 M5 Grachevka *Lipetskaya Oblast'* Rus. Fed.
120 C1 Grachevka *Orenburgskaya Oblast'* Rus. Fed.
121 I2 Grachi Kazakh.
245 E2 Graciano Sánchez Mex.
242 □H6 Gracias Hond.
216 □³ᵃ Graciosa *i.* Azores
216 □³ᵃ Graciosa *i. Canary Is*
188 G3 Gradačac Bos.-Herz.
191 H5 Gradara Italy
254 C4 Gradaús, Serra dos *hills* Brazil
183 E2 Gradefes Spain
197 H4 Gradets Bulg.
163 B4 Gradignan France
197 H4 Gradishte *mt.* Bulg.
Gradiška Bos.-Herz. see Bosanska Gradiška
188 G3 Gradiška Croatia
197 H3 Grădiştea Romania
191 I3 Grado Italy
182 D1 Grado Spain
236 D2 Grady *NM* U.S.A.
146 E3 Graemsay *i.* Scotland U.K.
185 G3 Graena Spain
173 F3 Gräfelfing Ger.
173 F2 Gräfenberg Ger.
169 E5 Gräfendorf Ger.
179 D3 Grafendorf bei Hartberg Austria
171 D4 Gräfenhainichen Ger.
172 C4 Grafenhausen Ger.
169 F4 Gräfenroda Ger.
179 F4 Grafenstein Austria
171 C5 Gräfenthal Ger.
169 E4 Gräfentonna Ger.
173 F2 Grafenwöhr Ger.
192 E2 Graffignano Italy
169 F3 Grafhorst Ger.
171 C5 Gräfinau-Angstedt Ger.
173 F3 Grafing bei München Ger.
142 C1 Gráfjäll *mt.* Norway
173 F3 Grafrath Ger.
140 K3 Gräftåvälen Sweden
83 H2 Grafton *N.S.W.* Austr.
236 D1 Grafton *ND* U.S.A.
232 B4 Grafton *OH* U.S.A.
236 C4 Grafton *WV* U.S.A.
232 C5 Grafton *WV* U.S.A.
235 F3 Grafton, Cape *Qld* Austr.
241 J2 Grafton, Mount *NV* U.S.A.
85 F3 Grafton Passage *Qld* Austr.
142 C1 Grågalten *hill* Norway
193 J2 Gragnano Italy
231 E4 Graham *NC* U.S.A.
237 D5 Graham *TX* U.S.A.
241 M5 Graham, Mount *AZ* U.S.A.
Graham Bell Island *Zemlya Frantsa-Iosifa* Rus. Fed.
222 C4 Graham Island *B.C.* Can.
221 I2 Graham Island *Nunavut* Can.
262 U2 Graham Land *reg.* Antarctica
215 F5 Grahamstown S. Africa
Grahovo Bos.-Herz. see Bosansko Grahovo
C6 Graigue Rep. of Ireland
147 C4 Graiguenamanagh Rep. of Ireland
151 H3 Grain *Medway, England* U.K.
151 H3 Grain, Isle of *pen. England* U.K.
173 F4 Grainau Ger.
173 H3 Grainet Ger.
161 A4 Graissac France
161 B5 Graissessac France
183 I3 Graja de Iniesta Spain
183 D2 Grajal de Campos Spain
254 D3 Grajaú Brazil
254 D2 Grajaú *r.* Brazil
175 K2 Grajewo Pol.
134 J4 Grakhovo Rus. Fed.
197 F4 Gramada *mt.* Yugo.
163 B4 Gramastetten Austria
163 D4 Gramat France
163 C4 Gramat, Causse de *hills* France
197 H4 Gramatikovo Bulg.
179 F3 Gramatneusiedl Austria
161 D5 Grambois France
170 F2 Grambow Ger.

Column 2

170 C2 Gramkow Ger.
170 D1 Grammendorf Ger.
194 D5 Grammichele *Sicilia* Italy
Grammont Belgium see Geraardsbergen
190 C5 Grammont, Mont *mt.* Italy
198 B1 Grámmos *mt.* Greece
232 D4 Grampian *PA* U.S.A.
146 D5 Grampian Mountains *Scotland* U.K.
83 B4 Grampians, The *mts Vic.* Austr.
150 C4 Grampound *Cornwall, England* U.K.
164 F2 Gramsbergen Neth.
196 E5 Gramsh Albania
170 F2 Gramzow Ger.
Gran Hungary see Esztergom
190 C4 Grana *r.* Italy
190 D3 Grana *r.* Italy
214 B4 Granaatboskolk S. Africa
147 E3 Granabeg Rep. of Ireland
250 C4 Granada Col.
242 □J7 Granada Nic.
185 G3 Granada Spain
185 G3 Granada *prov. Andalucía* Spain
236 C4 Granada CO U.S.A.
216 □³ᵃ Granadilla de Abona *Tenerife Canary Is*
184 C3 Granado *hill* Spain
147 D3 Granard Rep. of Ireland
191 L4 Granarolo dell'Emilia Italy
178 D3 Granatspitze *mt.* Austria
183 G3 Granátula de Calatrava Spain
259 D7 Gran Bajo *depr.* Arg.
260 D6 Gran Bajo Salitroso *salt flat* Arg.
226 A3 Grandy *MN* U.S.A.
161 C4 Grane France
186 C3 Grañén Spain
260 B4 Graneros Chile
147 E3 Grange *Louth* Rep. of Ireland
147 C2 Grange *Sligo* Rep. of Ireland
147 D5 Grange *Waterford* Rep. of Ireland
160 E2 Grange, Mont de *mt.* France
233 G3 Grangebellow Rep. of Ireland
147 E4 Grangeford Rep. of Ireland
146 E5 Grange Hill Jamaica
146 E5 Grangemouth *Falkirk, Scotland* U.K.
149 G3 Grange-over-Sands *Cumbria, England* U.K.
238 E3 Granger *WY* U.S.A.
143 F4 Grängesberg Sweden
157 G4 Granges-sur-Vologne France
150 D3 Grangetown *Cardiff, Wales* U.K.
238 C2 Grangeville *ID* U.S.A.
170 M2 Granholt Sweden
161 D3 Granier, Mont *mt.* France
222 E4 Granisle *B.C.* Can.
234 B3 Granite *MD* U.S.A.
236 F4 Granite City *IL* U.S.A.
234 D1 Granite Falls *MN* U.S.A.
240 I1 Granite Mountain *AK* U.S.A.
241 J4 Granite Mountains *CA* U.S.A.
241 J5 Granite Mountains *CA* U.S.A.
238 E2 Granite Peak *MT* U.S.A.
241 K1 Granite Peak *UT* U.S.A.
159 E2 Granites *i.* Turks and Caicos Is
121 H4 Granitogorsk Kazakh.
194 B5 Granitola, Capo *c. Sicilia* Italy
194 B5 Granitola-Torretta *Sicilia* Italy
81 C4 Granity *South I.* N.Z.
254 C2 Granja Brazil
184 C2 Granja Port.
182 E3 Granja de Moreruela Spain
184 E2 Granja de Torrehermosa Spain
182 B4 Grão de Ulmeiro Port.
259 D7 Gran Laguna Salada *l.* Arg.
143 F2 Gränna Sweden
186 F3 Granollers Spain
174 F3 Granowo Pol.
252 B2 Gran Pajonal *plain* Peru
190 C3 Gran Paradiso *mt.* Italy
178 C4 Gran Pilastro *mt.* Austria/Italy
Gran San Bernardo, Colle del *pass* Italy/Switz. see Great St Bernard Pass
193 F2 Gran Sasso d'Italia *mts* Italy
171 D4 Granschütz Ger.
170 E2 Gransee Ger.
148 C3 Gransha *Northern Ireland* U.K.
236 C3 Grant *NE* U.S.A.
240 H2 Grant, Mount *NV* U.S.A.
240 D2 Grant, Mount *NV* U.S.A.
236 E3 Grant City *MO* U.S.A.
151 G2 Grantham *Lincolnshire, England* U.K.
234 B2 Grantham *PA* U.S.A.
262 P2 Grant Island Antarctica
146 E4 Granton *N.T.* Austr.
226 B3 Granton *WI* U.S.A.
146 E4 Grantown-on-Spey *Highland, Scotland* U.K.
226 D5 Grant Park *IL* U.S.A.
239 I2 Grant Range *mts NV* U.S.A.
226 A3 Grantsburg *WI* U.S.A.
146 F6 Grantshouse *Scottish Borders, Scotland* U.K.
239 I3 Grants Pass *OR* U.S.A.
232 C5 Grantsville *WV* U.S.A.
234 B2 Grantville *PA* U.S.A.
222 B2 Granville *Y.T.* Can.
158 E3 Granville France
241 M5 Granville *AZ* U.S.A.
233 G3 Granville *IL* U.S.A.
233 J1 Granville *NY* U.S.A.
232 B5 Granville *OH* U.S.A.
142 B1 Granvin Norway
170 C2 Granzin Ger.
257 F2 Grão Mogol Brazil
191 G3 Grappa, Monte *mt.* Italy
223 I1 Gras, Lac de *l. N.W.T.* Can.
163 B2 Grasberg Ger.
213 F5 Grasberg S. Africa
142 E1 Graselsberg Ger.
149 F3 Grasmere *Cumbria, England* U.K.
149 F3 Grasonville *MD* U.S.A.
234 D1 Grass *r. Man.* Can.
191 J3 Grassano Italy
173 I4 Grassau Italy
161 E5 Grasse France
232 D4 Grassflat *PA* U.S.A.
149 G3 Grassington *North Yorkshire, England* U.K.
156 C2 Grassy *r.* France
156 C2 Grass Valley *CA* U.S.A.
240 B2 Grass Valley *Oreg.* Austr.
236 D2 Grassy Butte *ND* U.S.A.
246 C2 Grassy Creek *r.* Andros Bahamas
168 E1 Gråsten Denmark
226 D3 Grástorp Sweden
163 D5 Gratentour France
217 □¹ᵇ Gratia *i.* Mauritius
217 □¹ᵇ Gratien *r.* Austria
179 F3 Gratkorn Austria
194 C5 Grattieri *Sicilia* Italy
179 F3 Gratwein Austria
190 C2 Graubünden *canton* Switz.
190 D2 Graun, Pol. see Grudziąż
237 F6 Grauer Kopf *hill* Ger.
163 D5 Graulhet France
171 E4 Graupa Ger.
186 D2 Graus Spain
183 I2 Grávalos Spain
254 B3 Gravatá Brazil
140 N1 Gravdal Norway
161 C4 Grand-Lieu, Lac de *l.* France
164 E4 Grave Neth.
190 E2 Gravedona Italy
237 H2 Gravelbourg Sask. Can.
156 C2 Gravelines France
194 C5 Gravina di Catania *Sicilia* Italy
158 D3 Gravenoire *France*
224 E4 Gravenhurst *Ont.* Can.
83 C3 Gravesend *N.S.W.* Austr.

Column 3

161 D3 Grand Pic de Belledonne *mt.* France
226 C2 Grand Portage *MN* U.S.A.
157 E3 Grandpré France
156 C4 Grandpuits-Bailly-Carrois France
223 I4 Grand Rapids *Man.* Can.
226 E4 Grand Rapids *MI* U.S.A.
226 A2 Grand Rapids *MN* U.S.A.
78 □⁵ Grand Récif de Cook *rf* New Caledonia
161 E4 Grand Rhône *r.* France
161 B4 Grandrieu France
160 C2 Grandris France
161 E3 Grand Roc Noir *mt.* France
Grand St Bernard, Col du *pass* Italy/Switz. see Great St Bernard Pass
251 H3 Grand Santi Fr. Guiana
190 B2 Grandson Switz.
238 E3 Grand Teton *mt. WY* U.S.A.
226 E3 Grand Traverse Bay *MI* U.S.A.
246 E2 Grand Turk Turks and Caicos Is
246 E2 Grand Turk *i.* Turks and Caicos Is
160 E1 Grandvelle-et-le-Perrenot France
226 B2 Grand View *MI* U.S.A.
160 E1 Grandvillars France
226 E4 Grandville *MI* U.S.A.
157 G4 Grandvilliers France
156 B3 Grandvilliers France
241 J4 Grand Wash Cliffs *mts AZ* U.S.A.
161 C4 Grane France
186 C3 Grañén Spain
147 E3 Grange *Louth* Rep. of Ireland
246 C1 Grange Bahamas
80 E2 Great Barrier Island *North I.* N.Z.
85 F1 Great Barrier Reef *Qld* Austr.
233 G3 Great Barrington *MA* U.S.A.
151 H2 Great Barton *Suffolk, England* U.K.
241 I2 Great Basin *NV* U.S.A.
222 F1 Great Bear *r. N.W.T.* Can.
222 G1 Great Bear Lake *N.W.T.* Can.
Great Belt *sea chan.* Denmark see Store Bælt
236 D4 Great Bend *KS* U.S.A.
233 F4 Great Bend *PA* U.S.A.
151 I3 Great Bentley *Essex, England* U.K.
146 B3 Great Bernera *i.* Scotland U.K.
151 H2 Great Bircham *Norfolk, England* U.K.
147 A4 Great Blasket Island *i.* Rep. of Ireland
149 H3 Great Broughton *North Yorkshire, England* U.K.
149 F3 Great Clifton *Cumbria, England* U.K.
97 A4 Great Coco Island Cocos Is
151 H2 Great Cornard *Suffolk, England* U.K.
148 E2 Great Cumbrae *i.* Scotland U.K.
76 E5 Great Dividing Range *mts* Austr.
149 I3 Great Dodd *hill* England U.K.
149 I3 Great Driffield *East Riding of Yorkshire, England* U.K.
227 F3 Great Duck Island *Ont.* Can.
151 H3 Great Dunmow *Essex, England* U.K.
Great Eastern Erg *des.* Alg. see Grand Erg Oriental
83 G4 Great Eccleston *Lancashire, England* U.K.
151 H2 Great Egg Harbor *r. NJ* U.S.A.
147 D2 Greatacombe
Northern Ireland U.K.
230 C4 Greencastle *IN* U.S.A.
232 E5 Greencastle *PA* U.S.A.
246 C1 Green Cay *i.* Bahamas
231 D6 Green Cove Springs *FL* U.S.A.
234 D3 Green Creek *NJ* U.S.A.
169 E4 Greene Ger.
226 A4 Greene *IA* U.S.A.
233 F2 Greene *NY* U.S.A.
231 E4 Greeneville *TN* U.S.A.
240 O3 Greenfield *CA* U.S.A.
236 D4 Greenfield *IA* U.S.A.
230 C4 Greenfield *IN* U.S.A.
233 I2 Greenfield *MA* U.S.A.
236 F4 Greenfield *MO* U.S.A.
232 B5 Greenfield *OH* U.S.A.
226 C5 Greenfield *WI* U.S.A.
235 I1 Greenfield Park *NY* U.S.A.
148 F2 Greengairs *North Lanarkshire, Scotland* U.K.
151 F3 Greenham *West Berkshire, England* U.K.
234 B3 Green Haven *MD* U.S.A.
87 B6 Green Head *W.A.* Austr.
87 B6 Green Head *hd W.A.* Austr.
149 G3 Greenhead *Northumberland, England* U.K.
150 E2 Greenhanwood *Shropshire, England* U.K.
84 C1 Greenhills *N.T.* Austr.
81 B7 Greenhills *South I.* N.Z.
147 E3 Greystones Rep. of Ireland
149 H4 Greyton S. Africa
151 F2 Greywall *North I.* N.Z.
223 J4 Green Lake Sask. Can.
226 C5 Green Lake *WI* U.S.A.
221 N2 Greenland *terr.* N. America
226 C2 Greenland *MI* U.S.A.
268 X2 Greenland Basin *sea feature* Arctic Ocean
218 G1 Greenland Sea Greenland/Svalbard
215 G5 Great Kei *r.* S. Africa
85 G4 Great Keppel Island *Qld* Austr.
146 F6 Greenlaw Scottish Borders, Scotland U.K.
151 G2 Great Linford *Milton Keynes, England* U.K.
83 C2 Greenly Island *S.A.* Austr.
234 B3 Greenmount *MD* U.S.A.
214 D5 Great Lane *r.* S. Africa
146 E6 Greenock *Inverclyde, Scotland* U.K.
148 E2 Greenodd *Cumbria, England* U.K.
232 A5 Great Miami *r. OH* U.S.A.
151 G3 Great Missenden *Buckinghamshire, England* U.K.
233 G4 Great Neck *NY* U.S.A.
235 F3 Great Nicobar *i. Andaman & Nicobar Is* India
150 D1 Great Ormes Head *hd* Wales U.K.
235 I1 Greenport *NY* U.S.A.
233 G4 Greenport *NY* U.S.A.
151 H2 Great Ouse *r. England* U.K.
85 F3 Great Oyster Bay *Tas.* Austr.
87 B7 Great Palm Island *Qld* Austr.
221 K3 Great Plain of the Koukdjuak *Nunavut* Can.
236 C3 Great Plains *KS* U.S.A.
226 C3 Great Ponton *Lincolnshire, England* U.K.
Great Rann of Kachchh *marsh* India see Rann of Kachchh
150 D2 Great Rhos *hill* Wales U.K.
211 B7 Great Rift Valley Africa
160 F3 Great St Bernard Pass Italy/Switz.
231 E7 Great Sale Cay *i.* Bahamas
149 G3 Great Salkeld *Cumbria, England* U.K.
238 D4 Great Salt Lake *UT* U.S.A.
241 K1 Great Salt Lake Desert *UT* U.S.A.
222 E4 Great Salt Pond *l.* St Kitts and Nevis
151 H2 Great Sampford *Essex, England* U.K.
77 E5 Great Sandy Desert *W.A.* Austr.
Great Sandy Island *Qld* Austr. see Fraser Island
151 H2 Great Shelford *Cambridgeshire, England* U.K.

Column 4

151 H3 Gravesend *Kent, England* U.K.
237 E4 Gravette *AR* U.S.A.
156 B3 Gravigny France
193 I4 Gravina *r.* Italy
192 A3 Gravina in Puglia Italy
193 I4 Gravina di Matera *r.* Italy
161 D1 Gray France
231 D5 Gray *GA* U.S.A.
232 A6 Gray *KY* U.S.A.
233 □H3 Gray *ME* U.S.A.
232 B6 Gray *TN* U.S.A.
162 A3 Grayan-et-l'Hôpital France
162 A3 Grayback Mountain *OR* U.S.A.
238 B3 Grayling *AK* U.S.A.
222 E3 Grayling *r. B.C.* Can.
231 G3 Grayling *r.* U.S.A.
149 G3 Grayrigg *Cumbria, England* U.K.
151 H3 Grays *Thurrock, England* U.K.
151 G3 Grayshott *Hampshire, England* U.K.
232 B5 Grayson *KY* U.S.A.
230 D4 Grayson *KY* U.S.A.
137 H2 Grayvoron Rus. Fed.
179 G3 Graz Austria
161 C3 Grazac France
185 E4 Grazalema Spain
175 H2 Grażawy Pol.
197 F4 Grdelica *Srbija* Yugo.
186 B4 Grea de Albarracín Spain
163 D4 Gréalou France
147 A4 Great Australian Bight *g.* Austr.
149 H3 Great Ayton *North Yorkshire, England* U.K.
151 H3 Great Baddow *Essex, England* U.K.
246 C1 Great Banks *sea feature* Bahamas
80 E2 Great Barrier Island *North I.* N.Z.
222 H2 Great Slave Lake *N.W.T.* Can.
231 C5 Great Smoky Mountains *N. Carolina/Tennessee* U.S.A.
222 E3 Great Snow Mountain *B.C.* Can.
151 I3 Great Stour *r. England* U.K.
148 C4 Great Sugar Loaf *hill* Rep. of Ireland
150 C4 Great Torrington *Devon, England* U.K.
87 F6 Great Victoria Desert *W.A.* Austr.
162 A3 Grayan-et-l'Africa see Usutu
151 H3 Great Wakering *Essex, England* U.K.
262 U2 Great Wall research stn Antarctica
149 I4 Great Wall tourist site China
151 H3 Great Waltham *Essex, England* U.K.
Great Western Erg *des.* Alg.
235 D1 Greenwood Lake *NY* U.S.A.
83 F5 Great Western Tiers *mts Tas.* Austr.
149 H3 Great Whernside *hill England* U.K.
214 B5 Great Winterhoek *mt.* S. Africa
150 E2 Great Wyrley *Staffordshire, England* U.K.
151 I2 Great Yarmouth *Norfolk, England* U.K.
151 H2 Great Yeldham *Essex, England* U.K.
246 □ Great Abaco *i.* Bahamas
76 C5 Great Australian Bight *g.* Austr.
Great Zab *r.* Iraq see Zāb al Kabīr, Nahr az
213 F4 Great Zimbabwe National Monument *tourist site* Zimbabwe
142 D2 Grebbestad Sweden
169 E5 Grebenau Ger.
169 E5 Grebenhain Ger.
Grebenkovskiy Ukr. see Hrebinka
129 E2 Grebenskaya Rus. Fed.
Grebenski Rus. Fed. see Grebenskaya
169 E4 Grebenstein Ger.
175 J3 Grębków Pol.
174 E4 Grębocice Pol.
174 G2 Grebocin Pol.
175 J5 Grębów Pol.
193 E2 Grecci Italy
193 H3 Greci Italy
197 I3 Greci, Vârful *hill* Romania
189 D5 Greco, Monte *mt.* Italy
173 F2 Greding Ger.
182 E4 Gredos, Sierra de *mts* Spain
Greece *country* Europe
233 E3 Greece *NY* U.S.A.
236 B3 Greeley *CO* U.S.A.
234 E1 Greeley *PA* U.S.A.
168 F1 Greely Center *NE* U.S.A.
221 J1 Greely Fiord *inlet* Can.
130 H1 Green-Bell, Ostrov *i. Zemlya Frantsa-Iosifa* Rus. Fed.
229 M1 Green *r. N.B.* Can.
230 C4 Green *r. KY* U.S.A.
236 C2 Green *r. WY* U.S.A.
241 M2 Green *r. WY* U.S.A.
226 C3 Green Bay *WI* U.S.A.
226 D3 Green Bay *b. WI* U.S.A.
160 C5 Green Bay *b. WI* U.S.A.
169 G3 Greenbrier *r. WV* U.S.A.
232 C6 Greenbrier *r. WV* U.S.A.
83 G4 Green Cape *N.S.W.* Austr.
231 E7 Greencastle Bahamas
147 E1 Greencastle Rep. of Ireland
147 D2 Greencastle

Column 5

222 H2 Great Slave Lake *N.W.T.* Can.
231 C5 Great Smoky Mountains *N. Carolina/Tennessee* U.S.A.
237 D5 Greenville *TX* U.S.A.
232 D5 Greenville *WV* U.S.A.
150 C3 Greenway *Pembrokeshire, Wales* U.K.
193 Greenwich *atoll* Micronesia see Kapingamarangi
151 G3 Greenwich *Greater London, England* U.K.
233 C3 Greenwich *CT* U.S.A.
234 C3 Greenwich *NJ* U.S.A.
233 G3 Greenwich *NY* U.S.A.
232 B4 Greenwich *OH* U.S.A.
237 E5 Greenwood *AR* U.S.A.
234 D3 Greenwood *DE* U.S.A.
230 C4 Greenwood *IN* U.S.A.
231 D5 Greenwood *MS* U.S.A.
231 D5 Greenwood *SC* U.S.A.
235 D1 Greenwood Lake *NY* U.S.A.
226 C2 Greetsiel (Krummhörn) Ger.
168 C2 Greetsiel (Krummhörn) Ger.
250 D6 Gregório *r.* Brazil
84 D3 Gregory *r. Qld* Austr.
227 F3 Gregory *SD* U.S.A.
236 D3 Gregory *SD* U.S.A.
82 D2 Gregory, Lake *salt flat S.A.* Austr.
86 E4 Gregory, Lake *salt flat W.A.* Austr.
87 C5 Gregory, Lake *salt flat W.A.* Austr.
86 C4 Gregory Downs *Qld* Austr.
85 E3 Gregory Range *hills Qld* Austr.
86 D4 Gregory Range *hills W.A.* Austr.
178 E4 Greifenburg Austria
171 E4 Greifendorf Ger.
190 D1 Greifensee *l.* Switz.
169 D5 Greifenstein Ger.
170 E1 Greifswald Ger.
170 E1 Greifswalder Bodden *b.* Ger.
169 E4 Greilenau Ger.
171 D5 Greiz Ger.
168 F1 Gremersdorf Ger.
134 G1 Gremikha Rus. Fed.
134 L4 Gremyachinsk Rus. Fed.
137 J2 Gremyach'ye Rus. Fed.
142 D3 Grena Denmark
237 F5 Grenada *i.* U.S.A.
247 □⁵ Grenada *country* West Indies
163 B5 Grenade-sur-l'Adour France
157 F5 Grenant France
190 C1 Grenchen Switz.
85 H5 Grenfell *N.S.W.* Austr.
223 K5 Grenfell Sask. Can.
161 D3 Grenoble France
247 □⁵ Grenville Grenada
85 E1 Grenville, Cape *Qld* Austr.
79 Grenville, Cape Fiji see Rotuma
172 G4 Grenzach-Wyhlen Ger.
161 D5 Gréoux-les-Bains France
170 D1 Gresenhorst Ger.
161 C4 Gresse *r.* France
168 F2 Gresse Ger.
161 D4 Gresse-en-Vercors France
179 G2 Gressoney-la-Trinite Italy
179 G3 Gresten Austria
160 D5 Grésy-sur-Aix France
160 D5 Grésy-sur-Isère France
149 G3 Greta *r. England* U.K.
192 D2 Greta *r.* Italy
148 F5 Gretna *Dumfries and Galloway, Scotland* U.K.
235 G1 Gretna *LA* U.S.A.
232 D6 Gretna *VA* U.S.A.
173 E2 Grettstadt Ger.
169 F4 Grebenstein Ger.
157 F4 Greux France
191 G5 Greve *r.* Italy
191 G5 Greve in Chianti Italy
164 C3 Grevelingen *sea chan.* Neth.
168 F2 Greven *Mecklenburg-Vorpommern* Ger.
169 C3 Greven *Nordrhein-Westfalen* Ger.
198 B1 Grevena Greece
165 F3 Grevenbicht Neth.
164 D4 Grevenbroich Ger.
165 F5 Grevenmacher Lux.
Greven *admin. dist.* Lux.
170 C2 Grevesmühlen Ger.
225 J4 Grey *r. Nfld.* Can.
81 C5 Grey *r.* N.Z.
81 C5 Grey, Cape *N.T.* Austr.
147 F2 Greyabbey
Northern Ireland U.K.
238 E2 Greybull *WY* U.S.A.
222 C2 Grey Hunter Peak *Y.T.* Can.
215 G2 Greylingstad S. Africa
233 I2 Greylock, Mount *MA* U.S.A.
81 C5 Greymouth *South I.* N.Z.
87 B5 Greys Plains *W.A.* Austr.
215 K2 Greystone Florida
147 E3 Greystones Rep. of Ireland
214 B6 Greyton S. Africa
151 F2 Greywell *North I.* N.Z.
215 H3 Greytown S. Africa
242 □J7 Grez-Doiceau Belgium
165 E4 Grez-en-Bouère France
191 G3 Grezzana Italy
146 A2 Grias *Western Isles, Scotland* U.K.
135 H6 Gribanovskiy Rus. Fed.
208 B3 Gribingui *r.* C.A.R.
240 C2 Gridley *CA* U.S.A.
226 C5 Gridley *IL* U.S.A.
191 J3 Grieg Ger.
157 H4 Gries France
178 D5 Gries am Brenner Austria
173 H3 Griesbach im Rottal Ger.
173 G2 Griesheim Austria
173 G2 Griesstätt Ger.
169 F4 Griffen Austria
231 C5 Griffin *GA* U.S.A.
85 I5 Griffith *N.S.W.* Austr.
224 F4 Griffith *Ont.* Can.
232 C5 Griffithsville *WV* U.S.A.
235 G4 Grigan *i.* N. Marianas Is see Agrihan
192 A5 Grighini, Monte *hill Sardegna* Italy
190 D2 Grigioni *canton* Switz. see Graubünden
169 G2 Grigiškės Lith.
181 Grignan France
190 D3 Grignano Italy
191 G3 Grigno Italy
191 G3 Grigno *r.* Italy
161 D3 Grigny France
153 E7 Grigoriopol Moldova
191 G3 Grigota Spain
164 F1 Grijpskerk Neth.
208 B3 Grijó Port.
83 F5 Grim, Cape Austr.
193 I5 Grimaldi Italy
192 C4 Grimaud France
168 E5 Grimma Ger.
170 E4 Grimmelshausen Ger.
134 D4 Grimmen Ger.
170 D1 Grimmenstein Austria
173 G2 Grimminger *r.* Ger.
191 G1 Grigno Italy
191 G1 Grigno *r.* Italy
170 D1 Grimma Ger.
169 H2 Grimmen Ger.
161 D5 Grimnitzsee *l.* Ger.
164 A2 Grina *r.* Neth.

Column 6

236 G3 Greenville *OH* U.S.A.
232 C4 Greenville *PA* U.S.A.
231 D5 Greenville *SC* U.S.A.
237 D5 Greenville *TX* U.S.A.
232 D5 Greenville *WV* U.S.A.
231 E5 Greenwood *SC* U.S.A.
85 F5 Gregory, Lake *salt flat W.A.* Austr.
222 H2 Great Slave Lake
129 E2 Grebenskaya Rus. Fed.
169 F4 Greifenberg (Meinhard) Ger.
169 E5 Grebenhain Ger.
170 E1 Greifswalder Bodden *b.* Ger.
169 E4 Greifenstein Ger.
170 E1 Greifswald Ger.
179 G3 Grein Austria
178 D4 Greiz Ger.
171 C3 Greiz Ger.
168 F1 Gremersdorf Ger.
134 G1 Gremikha Rus. Fed.
134 L4 Gremyachinsk Rus. Fed.
223 G3 Grenada *MS* U.S.A.
237 F5 Grenada Italy
247 □⁵ Grenada country West Indies
163 B5 Grenade-sur-l'Adour France
157 F5 Grenant France
190 C1 Grenchen Switz.
85 H5 Grenfell *N.S.W.* Austr.
161 D3 Grenoble France
247 □⁵ Grenville Grenada
85 E1 Grenville, Cape *Qld* Austr.
172 G4 Grenzach-Wyhlen Ger.
161 D5 Gréoux-les-Bains France
170 D1 Gresenhorst Ger.
161 C4 Gresse *r.* France
238 B2 Gretna *r.* Italy
234 B3 Greenbelt *MD* U.S.A.
226 C3 Greenbush *WI* U.S.A.
191 G5 Greve *r.* Italy
191 G5 Greve in Chianti Italy
164 C3 Grevelingen *sea chan.* Neth.
168 F2 Greven *Mecklenburg-Vorpommern* Ger.
169 C3 Greven *Nordrhein-Westfalen* Ger.
198 B1 Grevena Greece
165 F3 Grevenbicht Neth.
164 D4 Grevenbroich Ger.
165 F5 Grevenmacher Lux.
Grevenmacher *admin. dist.* Lux.
170 C2 Grevesmühlen Ger.
225 J4 Grey *r. Nfld.* Can.
81 C5 Grey *r.* N.Z.
81 C5 Grey, Cape *N.T.* Austr.
147 F2 Greyabbey *Northern Ireland* U.K.
238 E2 Greybull *WY* U.S.A.
222 C2 Grey Hunter Peak *Y.T.* Can.
215 G2 Greylingstad S. Africa
233 I2 Greylock, Mount *MA* U.S.A.
81 C5 Greymouth *South I.* N.Z.
87 B5 Greys Plains *W.A.* Austr.
215 H3 Greystones Rep. of Ireland
147 E3 Greystones Rep. of Ireland
214 B6 Greyton S. Africa
215 G4 Greytown S. Africa
191 G3 Grezzana Italy
254 C2 Gronelândia Namibia
212 C3 Grootfontein Namibia
135 H6 Gribanovskiy Rus. Fed.
208 B3 Gribingui *r.* C.A.R.
240 C2 Gridley *CA* U.S.A.
226 C5 Gridley *IL* U.S.A.
169 G2 Gries France
178 C5 Gries am Brenner Austria
173 H3 Griesbach im Rottal Ger.
161 E5 Grimaud France
168 E5 Grimma Ger.
170 E4 Grimmen Ger.
169 H2 Grimmen Ger.

Column 7

141 J3 Grindaheim Norway
140 □B3 Grindavík Iceland
190 D2 Grindelwald Switz.
142 C4 Grindsted Denmark
227 F3 Grind Stone City *MI* U.S.A.
197 H3 Grindu *Ialomiţa* Romania
197 J2 Grindu *Tulcea* Romania
197 H2 Grindu *r.* Romania
139 I5 Grinevo Rus. Fed.
149 I4 Gringley on the Hill *Nottinghamshire, England* U.K.
236 E3 Grinnell *IA* U.S.A.
183 E3 Griñón Spain
178 B3 Grins Austria
197 G2 Grinţieş Romania
188 E2 Grintovec *mt.* Slovenia
178 C3 Grinzens Austria
183 I3 Grio *r.* Spain
Griomasaigh *i. Scotland* U.K. see Grimsay
215 G4 Griqualand East *reg.* S. Africa
214 D3 Griqualand West *reg.* S. Africa
214 D3 Griquatown S. Africa
Grischun *canton* Switz. see Graubünden
221 J2 Grise Fiord *Nunavut* Can.
186 B3 Grisén Spain
Grishino Ukr. see
191 G3 Grisignano di Zocco Italy
156 B2 Gris Nez, Cap *c.* France
193 H5 Grisolia Italy
163 D5 Grisolles France
Grisons *canton* Switz. see Graubünden
143 K3 Grisslehamn Sweden
146 F3 Gritley *Orkney, Scotland* U.K.
137 J5 Grivenskaya Rus. Fed.
149 F3 Grizebeck *Cumbria, England* U.K.
222 F1 Grizzly Bear Mountain *hill N.W.T.* Can.
188 F3 Grmeč *mts* Bos.-Herz.
165 D3 Grobbendonk Belgium
173 F3 Gröbenzell Ger.
174 D4 Gröbers Ger.
138 C3 Grobiņa Latvia
215 G1 Groblersdal S. Africa
214 D3 Groblershoop S. Africa
179 E3 Gröbming Austria
171 C4 Gröbzig Ger.
197 G4 Grocka *Srbija* Yugo.
175 I5 Gródek Pol.
100 D3 Grodekovo Rus. Fed.
175 L2 Gródek Pol.
178 B5 Gröden Ger.
178 E3 Grödig Austria
175 I2 Gróditz Ger.
171 E4 Gröditz Ger.
174 F5 Grodków Pol.
Grodno Belarus see Hrodna
Grodnenskaya Oblast' *admin. div.* Belarus see Hrodzyenskaya Voblasts'
Grodnenskaya *admin. div.* Belarus see Hrodzyenskaya Voblasts'
Grodzyenskaya
Grodzisk Pol.
175 H2 Grodziczno Pol.
174 G3 Grodzisk Pol.
175 K3 Grodzisk Pol.
174 E4 Grodzisk Mazowiecki Pol.
174 F3 Grodzisk Wielkopolski Pol.
164 F2 Groenlo Neth.
215 H2 Groenvlei S. Africa
237 D6 Groesbeck *TX* U.S.A.
164 E3 Groesbeek Neth.
85 F4 Groganville *Qld* Austr.
169 E3 Grohnde (Emmerthal) Ger.
177 L6 Grohot, Vârful *hill* Romania
171 D4 Groitzsch Ger.
158 C2 Groix France
158 C2 Groix, Île de *i.* France
175 J2 Grójec Pol.
175 J2 Grójec Pol.
174 D4 Grom Pol.
174 D4 Gromadka Pol.
189 C7 Grombalia Tunisia
168 F1 Grömitz Ger.
175 I6 Gromnik Pol.
190 D3 Gromo Italy
171 H3 Grønå *r.* Denmark
168 F3 Grønau (Leine) Ger.
169 C3 Gronau (Westfalen) Ger.
160 C3 Grône *r.* Italy
169 C3 Gronau Italy
168 F3 Grönenbach Ger.
140 K2 Grong Norway
171 C4 Gröningen Ger.
164 F1 Groningen prov. Neth.
251 H3 Groningen Suriname
Groningen *terr.* N. America see Greenland
175 H1 Gronowo Markusy Pol.
143 F3 Grönskåra Sweden
222 C2 Groomsport
Northern Ireland U.K.
175 J2 Groombridge
222 G5 Groot *r. W. Cape* S. Africa
214 E5 Groot *r. E. Cape* S. Africa
214 E5 Groot *r. W. Cape* S. Africa
214 E5 Groot-Aar Pan *salt pan* S. Africa
215 G4 Groot Brak *r.* S. Africa
214 E5 Groot Brakrivier S. Africa
215 F4 Grootdraaidam *dam* S. Africa
214 E5 Grootdrink S. Africa
85 E2 Groote Eylandt *i. N.T.* Austr.
212 C3 Grootfontein Namibia
214 D5 Grootkolk Namibia
214 C4 Groot Karas Berg *plat.* Namibia
213 F4 Groot Letaba *r.* S. Africa
214 E5 Groot Marico S. Africa
214 E5 Groot Swartberge *mts* S. Africa
215 G2 Grootvlei S. Africa
215 F5 Groot Winterberg *mt.* S. Africa
190 D3 Gropello Cairoli Italy
163 D4 Grospierres France
161 D5 Grosbeliard *hill* France
Grosbois-en-Montagne France
190 E2 Groscavallo Italy
190 F2 Grosio Italy
247 □³ Grosle Ise St Lucia
159 I5 Gros-Morne Martinique
160 C2 Grosne *r.* France
247 □³ Gros Piton *mt.* St Lucia
176 I3 Grosotto Italy

Column 8

141 J3 Grindaheim Norway
168 F2 Groß Ammensleben Ger.
165 E4 Grossalmerode Ger.
173 G2 Großbartloff Ger.
171 B4 Großbeeren Ger.
169 F4 Groß Berßen Ger.
172 C2 Groß-Bieberau Ger.
169 E5 Großbodungen Ger.
171 F5 Großbothen Ger.
169 H2 Großbothen Ger.
175 G5 Großbreitenbach Ger.
169 H2 Groß Breitenbach (Burgwedel) Ger.
169 G3 Großburschla Ger.
169 F4 Groß Döln Ger.
173 G3 Großdubrau Ger.
174 D5 Große Laaber *r.* Ger.
171 D4 Große Lauter *r.* Ger.
169 C3 Groß Elbe (Elbe) Ger.
172 D2 Grosselfingen Ger.
170 E3 Grossenaspe Ger.
170 F3 Großenbrode Ger.
169 F4 Großenehrich Ger.
169 E4 Groß Engersdorf Austria
170 E3 Großenhain Ger.
169 G4 Großenlüder Ger.
169 D4 Grossenmoor Ger.
171 C5 Großenstein Ger.
169 E4 Großenwiehe Ger.
179 H2 Groß-Enzersdorf Austria

Großer Arber to Haar
310

173 H2 Großer Arber mt. Ger.
169 F5 Großer Beerberg hill Ger.
179 F3 Grosser Bösenstein mt. Austria
169 F5 Großer Breitenberg hill Ger.
179 F3 Grosser Buchstein mt. Austria
172 B2 Großer Eyberg hill Ger.
169 F5 Großer Gleichberg hill Ger.
171 D5 Großer Kornberg hill Ger.
170 E2 Großer Landgraben r. Ger.
178 C3 Grosser Löffler mt. Austria
171 E4 Große Röder r. Ger.
176 C2 Großer Osser mt. Czech Rep./Ger.
168 F1 Großer Plöner See l. Ger.
179 F3 Grosser Priel mt. Austria
173 H3 Großer Rachel mt. Ger.
171 E3 Großer Selchower See l. Ger.
179 E4 Grosser Speikkofel mt. Austria
179 F4 Grosser Speikkogel mt. Austria
168 C2 Großes Meer l. Ger.
178 D3 Großes Wiesbachhorn mt. Austria
192 D2 Grosseto Italy
192 D2 Grosseto prov. Toscana Italy
192 A3 Grosseto-Prugna Corse France
173 G3 Große Vils r. Ger.
170 E2 Groß Fredenwalde Ger.
169 F4 Großfurra Ger.
170 C3 Groß Garz Ger.
172 C2 Groß-Gerau Ger.
179 F2 Groß-Gerungs Austria
169 E3 Groß Giesen Ger.
171 E3 Groß Glienicke Ger.
178 D3 Großglockner mt. Austria
173 G4 Großgmain Ger.
170 C2 Groß Godems Ger.
179 G2 Großgöttfritz Austria
168 F2 Groß Grönau Ger.
173 E2 Großhabersdorf Ger.
168 F2 Großhansdorf Ger.
179 H2 Großharras Austria
169 F3 Groß Heere (Heere) Ger.
171 F5 Großhennersdorf Ger.
171 C4 Großheringen Ger.
168 C3 Groß-Hesepe Ger.
172 D2 Großheubach Ger.
168 D3 Groß Ippener Ger.
173 G4 Großkarolinenfeld Ger.
171 C4 Großkayna Ger.
170 E1 Groß Kiesow Ger.
179 G4 Großklein Austria
171 D4 Großkorbetha Ger.
171 E3 Groß Köris Ger.
171 F4 Großkoschen Ger.
171 D3 Groß Kreutz Ger.
179 H2 Großkrut Austria
168 F1 Groß Kummerfeld Ger.
170 C2 Groß Laasch Ger.
169 F3 Groß Lafferde (Lahstedt) Ger.
173 E2 Großlangheim Ger.
171 D4 Großlehna Ger.
171 F3 Groß Leine Ger.
171 F3 Groß Leuthen Ger.
171 F3 Groß Lindow Ger.
169 B5 Großlittgen Ger.
169 F4 Großlohra Ger.
171 E4 Großmehlen Ger.
173 F3 Großmehring Ger.
170 E2 Groß Miltzow Ger.
170 D1 Groß Mohrdorf Ger.
171 C4 Großmonra Ger.
171 C4 Groß Mühlingen Ger.
171 E4 Großnaundorf Ger.
171 D4 Groß Naundorf Ger.
170 E2 Groß Nemerow Ger.
168 F3 Groß Oesingen Ger.
171 E5 Großolbersdorf Ger.
171 C4 Großörner Ger.
171 F4 Groß Oßnig Ger.
172 D2 Großostheim Ger.
179 H3 Großpetersdorf Austria
170 D2 Groß Plasten Ger.
171 C4 Groß Quenstedt Ger.
179 F3 Großraming Austria
171 F4 Großräschen Ger.
172 D2 Großrinderfeld Ger.
172 C2 Groß-Rohrheim Ger.
171 F4 Großröhrsdorf Ger.
171 C4 Groß Rosenburg Ger.
172 A2 Großrosseln Ger.
171 C4 Großrudestedt Ger.
179 H2 Großrußbach Austria
179 G4 Groß St Florian Austria
171 F4 Groß Särchen Ger.
171 F4 Groß Schacksdorf Ger.
171 E5 Großschirma Ger.
179 F2 Großschönau Austria
171 F5 Großschönau Ger.
170 E3 Groß Schönebeck Ger.
170 C3 Groß Schwechten Ger.
171 F4 Großschweidnitz Ger.
169 F3 Groß Schwülper (Schwülper) Ger.
179 G2 Groß-Siegharts Austria
168 E1 Großsolt Ger.
168 C3 Groß Stavern Ger.
171 D4 Großsteinberg Ger.
170 C2 Groß Stieten Ger.
171 D4 Großtreben Ger.
169 F3 Groß Twülpstedt Ger.
172 C2 Groß-Umstadt Ger.
178 D3 Großvenediger mt. Austria
172 D2 Großwallstadt Ger.
190 D1 Grosswangen Switz.
170 C2 Groß Warnow Ger.
169 F4 Großwechsungen Ger.
179 G2 Großweikersdorf Austria
170 D2 Groß Welle Ger.
168 E1 Groß Wittensee Ger.
170 D2 Groß Wokern Ger.
170 D3 Großwudicke Ger.
170 D2 Groß Wüstenfelde Ger.
170 E3 Groß Ziethen Ger.
172 C2 Groß-Zimmern Ger.
157 G4 Grostenquin France
188 E3 Grosuplje Slovenia
263 L1 Grosvenor Mountains Antarctica
238 E3 Gros Ventre Range mts WY U.S.A.
165 D3 Grote Nete r. Belgium
235 F1 Groton CT U.S.A.
233 E3 Groton NY U.S.A.
236 D2 Groton SD U.S.A.
193 E3 Grottaferrata Italy
195 G2 Grottaglie Italy
193 F2 Grottammare Italy
193 F1 Grottazzolina Italy
194 C5 Grotte Sicilia Italy
192 D2 Grotte di Castro Italy
195 F4 Grotteria Italy
232 D5 Grottoes VA U.S.A.
195 F2 Grottole Italy
222 G4 Grouard Mission Alta Can.
206 E5 Groumania Côte d'Ivoire
224 D3 Groundhog r. Ont. Can.
164 E1 Grouw Neth.
237 E4 Grove OK U.S.A.
232 B5 Grove City OH U.S.A.
232 C4 Grove City PA U.S.A.
231 C6 Grove Hill AL U.S.A.
141 K3 Grövelsjön Sweden
263 F2 Grove Mountains Antarctica
234 B1 Grover PA U.S.A.
240 G4 Grover Beach CA U.S.A.
233 H2 Groveton NH U.S.A.
237 E6 Groveton TX U.S.A.
234 D2 Groveville NJ U.S.A.
241 K5 Growler Mountains AZ U.S.A.
197 H4 Grozd'ovo Bulg.
129 D2 Groznyy Rus. Fed.
171 C5 Grub am Forst Ger.
142 B2 Grubbåfjellet mt. Norway
165 F3 Grubbenvorst Neth.
170 C1 Grube Ger.
188 F3 Grubišno Polje Croatia
174 G2 Gruczno Pol.
Grudovo Bulg. see Sredets
175 I2 Grudusk Pol.
174 G2 Grudziądz Pol.
190 D4 Grue r. Italy
157 G4 Gruey-lès-Surance France
190 C3 Grugliasco Italy
146 B6 Gruinart, Loch inlet Scotland U.K.
161 B5 Gruissan France
182 D1 Grullos Spain
197 H2 Grumăzeşti Romania
171 E4 Grumbach Ger.
193 H4 Grumento Nova Italy
195 F1 Grumo Appula Italy
142 E2 Grums Sweden
171 D5 Grüna Ger.
179 G2 Grünau Austria
179 E3 Grünau Austria
179 G3 Grünbach am Schneeberg Austria
169 D5 Grünberg Ger.
Grünberg Pol. see Zielona Góra
179 F3 Grünburg Austria
141 K3 Grundagssätern Sweden
141 K3 Grundforsen Sweden
179 E3 Grundlsee l. Austria
140 L3 Grundsuna Sweden
232 B6 Grundy VA U.S.A.
236 E3 Grundy Center IA U.S.A.
170 E3 Grüneberg Ger.
168 E2 Grünendeich Ger.
171 E4 Grünewald Ger.
171 E4 Grünewalde Ger.
171 E3 Grünheide Ger.
172 D4 Grünkraut Ger.
171 F3 Grunow Ger.
172 D2 Grünsfeld Ger.
172 C2 Grünstadt Ger.
160 B2 Grury France
174 G2 Gruta Pol.
146 □G2 Grutness Shetland, Scotland U.K.
237 C4 Gruver TX U.S.A.
190 C2 Gruyères Switz.
138 D3 Gruzdžiai Lith.
Gruzinskaya S.S.R. country Asia see Georgia
139 L5 Gryazi Rus. Fed.
139 L4 Gryaznoye Rus. Fed.
134 H4 Gryazovets Rus. Fed.
175 I6 Grybów Pol.
174 D2 Gryfice Pol.
174 C2 Gryfino Pol.
174 D4 Gryfów Śląski Pol.
174 F3 Grylewo Pol.
140 L1 Gryllefjord Norway
142 A2 Grytenuten hill Norway
143 G1 Gryttjom Sweden
259 □ Grytviken S. Georgia
175 I2 Gryźliny Pol.
174 G3 Grzegorzew Pol.
174 E2 Grzmiąca Pol.
174 G3 Grzymiszew Pol.
174 G2 Grzywna Pol.
179 E3 Gschwandt Austria
172 D3 Gschwend Ger.
190 C2 Gstaad Switz.
173 G4 Gstadt am Chiemsee Ger.
190 C2 Gsteig Switz.
117 F5 Gua Bihar India
191 G3 Guà r. Italy
242 □J7 Guabito Panama
246 C2 Guacanayabo, Golfo de b. Cuba
247 F5 Guacara Venez.
250 D3 Guacharía r. Col.
258 D2 Guachipas Arg.
257 G4 Guaçuí Brazil
185 G3 Guadahortuna Spain
185 H3 Guadahortuna r. Spain
184 D3 Guadaira r. Spain
184 E3 Guadairilla r. Spain
184 D2 Guadajira r. Spain
184 E3 Guadajoz Spain
185 F3 Guadajoz r. Spain
244 C3 Guadalajara Mex.
183 G4 Guadalajara Spain
183 H4 Guadalajara prov. Castilla - La Mancha Spain
187 B4 Guadalaviar r. Spain
184 E3 Guadalbacar r. Spain
185 G3 Guadalbullón r. Spain
78 □6 Guadalcanal i. Solomon Is
184 E2 Guadalcanal Spain
185 F3 Guadalcázar Spain
184 E2 Guadalefra r. Spain
185 G2 Guadalén r. Spain
185 H3 Guadalentín r. Spain
185 I3 Guadalentín r. Spain
184 D4 Guadalete r. Spain
185 F4 Guadalhorce r. Spain
185 G3 Guadalimar r. Spain
185 E3 Guadalmazán r. Spain
185 H2 Guadalmena r. Spain
185 F2 Guadalmez Spain
185 F2 Guadalmez r. Spain
186 C3 Guadalope r. Spain
185 D4 Guadalquivir r. Spain
216 □1c Guadalupe Graciosa Azores
254 E3 Guadalupe Brazil
245 E5 Guadalupe Guerrero Mex.
243 E3 Guadalupe Nuevo León Mex.
245 F4 Guadalupe Puebla Mex.
244 C2 Guadalupe Zacatecas Mex.
242 A2 Guadalupe i. Mex.
250 B6 Guadalupe Peru
185 E1 Guadalupe Spain
241 L5 Guadalupe AZ U.S.A.
240 G4 Guadalupe CA U.S.A.
237 D6 Guadalupe r. TX U.S.A.
237 D6 Guadalupe r. TX U.S.A.
184 E1 Guadalupe, Sierra de mts Spain
244 B1 Guadalupe Aguilera Mex.
239 F6 Guadalupe Bravos Mex.
237 B6 Guadalupe Peak TX U.S.A.
241 J5 Guadalupe Victoria Baja California Norte Mex.
244 B1 Guadalupe Victoria Durango Mex.
185 E3 Guadalvacarejo r. Spain
183 H4 Guadamajud r. Spain
185 E2 Guadamatilla r. Spain
184 E2 Guadamez r. Spain
183 F5 Guadamur Spain
183 F4 Guadarrama Spain
183 F5 Guadarrama r. Spain
183 F4 Guadarrama, Sierra de mts Spain
183 I5 Guadazaón r. Spain
247 □2 Guadeloupe terr. West Indies
247 □2 Guadeloupe Passage Caribbean Sea
184 D4 Guadiamar r. Spain
185 C3 Guadiana r. Port./Spain
185 G3 Guadiana Menor r. Spain
185 E4 Guadiaro r. Spain
185 E3 Guadiato r. Spain
183 H4 Guadiela r. Spain
183 E4 Guadiervas r. Spain
185 G3 Guadix Spain
259 B6 Guafo, Isla i. Chile
92 B3 Guagua Phil.
255 C9 Guaíba Brazil
250 B4 Guaillabamba r. Ecuador
246 C2 Guáimaro Cuba
250 D4 Guainia dept Col.
250 E4 Guainía r. Col./Venez.
251 F3 Guaiquinima, Cerro mt. Venez.
255 B8 Guaíra Brazil
256 C4 Guaira São Paulo Brazil
256 A5 Guairaçá Brazil
259 B6 Guaitecas, Islas is Chile
252 D2 Guajará Mirim Brazil
183 F5 Guajaraz r. Spain
185 G4 Guájar-Faraguit Spain
252 D1 Guajarraã Brazil
247 □1 Guajataca r. Puerto Rico
242 E3 Guaje, Llano de plain Mex.
250 C2 Guajira dept Col.
250 B5 Gualaceo Ecuador
240 F2 Gualala CA U.S.A.
243 H6 Gualán Guat.
250 B5 Gualaquiza Ecuador
193 E2 Gualdo Cattaneo Italy
191 H5 Gualdo Tadino Italy
261 H3 Gualeguay Arg.
261 H3 Gualeguay r. Arg.
261 H3 Gualeguaychu Arg.
259 D6 Gualicho, Salina salt flat Arg.
252 C4 Guallatiri vol. Chile
244 C2 Gualterio Mex.
191 F4 Gualtieri Italy
91 J4 Guam terr. N. Pacific Ocean
259 B7 Guamblin, Isla i. Chile
261 F5 Guamini Arg.
246 C2 Guamo Cuba
251 E3 Guampí, Sierra de mts Venez.
242 C3 Guamúchil Mex.
107 H4 Gu'an Hebei China
107 H5 Guan r. China
246 B2 Guanabacoa Cuba
242 □I7 Guanacaste, Cordillera de mts Costa Rica
242 D3 Guanacevi Mex.
261 F5 Guanaco, Cerro hill Arg.
246 A2 Guanahacabibes, Península de pen. Cuba
242 □I5 Guanaja Hond.
246 B2 Guanajay Cuba
244 D3 Guanajuato Mex.
244 D3 Guanajuato state Mex.
244 D3 Guanajuato, Sierra de mts Mex.
254 E5 Guanambi Brazil
250 B7 Guañape, Islas de is Peru
250 D2 Guanare Venez.
250 E2 Guanare Viejo r. Venez.
250 D2 Guanarito Venez.
250 D2 Guanarito r. Venez.
252 D3 Guanay Bol.
107 F4 Guandi Shan mt. Shanxi China
257 G3 Guandu r. Brazil
109 E3 Guandu Guangdong China
246 A2 Guane Cuba
108 C2 Guang'an Sichuan China
109 F3 Guangchang Jiangxi China
109 F2 Guangde Anhui China
109 E4 Guangdong prov. China
109 F2 Guangfeng Jiangxi China
109 E4 Guanghai Guangdong China
108 C2 Guanghan Sichuan China
Guanghua Hubei China see Laohekou
107 G4 Guangling Shanxi China
108 B3 Guangmao Shan mt. Yunnan China
Guangming Sichuan China see Xide
109 F2 Guangming Ding mt. Anhui China
108 C3 Guangnan Yunnan China
109 E4 Guangning Guangdong China
Guangning Liaoning China see Beining
107 H4 Guangrao Shandong China
109 E2 Guangshan Henan China
109 E2 Guangshui Hubei China
Guangxi aut. reg. China see Guangxi Zhuangzu Zizhiqu
108 D4 Guangxi Zhuangzu Zizhiqu aut. reg. China
108 C1 Guangyuan Sichuan China
109 F3 Guangze Fujian China
109 E4 Guangzhou Guangdong China
107 G4 Guangzong Hebei China
257 F3 Guanhães Brazil
257 F3 Guanhães r. Brazil
107 H5 Guanhe Kou r. mouth China
247 □1 Guánica Puerto Rico
251 F2 Guanipa r. Venez.
108 C3 Guanling Guizhou China
108 D2 Guanmian Shan mts China
108 D1 Guanpo Henan China
Guansuo Guizhou China see Guanling
260 B1 Guanta Chile
251 E2 Guanta Venez.
246 D2 Guantánamo Cuba
246 D3 Guantánamo Bay Naval Base military base Cuba
107 G4 Guantao Hebei China
Guanxian Sichuan China see Dujiangyan
109 D3 Guanyang Guangxi China
108 B2 Guanyinqiao Sichuan China
107 H5 Guanyun Jiangsu China
Guapay r. Santa Cruz Bol. see Grande
257 E4 Guapé Brazil
250 B4 Guapí Col.
256 C6 Guapiara Brazil
242 □J7 Guápiles Costa Rica
252 D3 Guaporé r. Bol./Brazil
255 C9 Guaporé Brazil
Guaporé state Brazil see Rondônia
252 C4 Guaqui Bol.
256 D4 Guará Brazil
254 D5 Guará r. Brazil
186 C2 Guara, Sierra de mts Spain
254 G3 Guarabira Brazil
257 F4 Guaraciaba Brazil
250 B5 Guaranda Ecuador
257 F4 Guarani Brazil
256 A6 Guaraniaçu Brazil
256 C4 Guarantã Brazil
257 G4 Guarapari Brazil
256 B6 Guarapuava Brazil
256 C6 Guaraqueçaba Brazil
256 B4 Guararapes Brazil
257 H2 Guaratinga Brazil
257 E5 Guaratinguetá Brazil
255 C8 Guaratuba Brazil
252 C3 Guarayos Bol.
193 F3 Guarcino Italy
182 C4 Guarda Port.
182 C4 Guarda admin. dist. Port.
Guardafui, Cape Somalia see Caseyr, Raas
185 H3 Guardal r. Spain
187 C6 Guardamar del Segura Spain
256 D2 Guarda Mor Brazil
195 F4 Guardavalle Italy
193 G2 Guardiagrele Italy
193 I4 Guardia Perticara Italy
193 I5 Guardia Piemontese Italy
193 G3 Guardia Sanframondi Italy
185 H4 Guardias Viejas Spain
186 E2 Guardiola de Bergueda Spain
183 F2 Guardo Spain
182 D3 Guardramiro Spain
182 C5 Guardunha, Serra de mts Port.
184 D2 Guareña Spain
183 E3 Guareña r. Spain
186 C2 Guarga r. Spain
253 E1 Guariba r. Brazil
250 E2 Guárico state Venez.
185 F4 Guaro Spain
185 G2 Guarrizas r. Spain
250 D3 Guarrojo r. Col.
185 G2 Guarromán Spain
256 D5 Guarujá Brazil
256 D5 Guarulhos Brazil
246 E5 Guasare r. Venez.
242 C3 Guasave Mex.
192 B5 Guasila Sardegna Italy
191 F4 Guastalla Italy
Guastatoya Guat. see El Progreso
117 G5 Guasuba r. India
243 H6 Guatemala country Central America
243 H6 Guatemala Guat.
267 M5 Guatemala Basin sea feature Pacific Ocean
Guatemala City Guat. see Guatemala
261 F3 Guatimozin Arg.
261 F5 Guatrache Arg.
250 D4 Guaviare dept Col.
250 E3 Guaviare r. Col.
256 D4 Guaxupé Brazil
246 C2 Guayabal Cuba
260 D2 Guayaguas, Sierra da mts Arg.
245 F2 Guayalejo r. Mex.
247 □1 Guayama Puerto Rico
247 □1 Guayanilla Puerto Rico
250 E3 Guayapo, Serranía mts Venez.
250 B5 Guayaquil Ecuador
250 A5 Guayaquil, Golfo de g. Ecuador
252 D2 Guayaramerín Bol.
250 A5 Guayas prov. Ecuador
242 C3 Guaymas Mex.
247 □1 Guaynabo Puerto Rico
261 H2 Guayquiraró r. Arg.
243 H6 Guazacapán Guat.
210 B2 Guba Eth.
120 D4 Gubadag Turkm.
134 L4 Gubakha Rus. Fed.
92 C3 Gubat Phil.
148 B3 Gubaveeny Rep. of Ireland
114 C3 Gubbi Karnataka India
191 H5 Gubbio Italy
129 E2 Gubden Rus. Fed.
171 F4 Guben Ger.
197 G4 Gŭbene Bulg.
175 J1 Guber r. Pol.
174 C4 Gubin Pol.
207 I3 Gubio Nigeria
135 G6 Gubkin Rus. Fed.
107 G4 Gucheng Hebei China
109 D1 Gucheng Hubei China
114 C4 Gudalur Tamil Nadu India
129 D2 Gudamaqris K'edi hills Georgia
186 C4 Gudar Spain
115 D2 Gudari Orissa India
129 B2 Gudaut'a Georgia
141 J3 Gudbrandsdalen val. Norway
142 D3 Gudenå r. Denmark
169 E4 Gudensberg Ger.
129 E2 Gudermes Rus. Fed.
168 E1 Guderup Denmark
143 F4 Gudhjem Bornholm Denmark
207 H4 Gudi Nigeria
114 D2 Gudivada Andhra Prad. India
114 C3 Gudiyattam Tamil Nadu India
142 D4 Gudme Denmark
157 F4 Gudmont-Villiers France
100 D4 Gudong r. China
168 F2 Gudow Ger.
123 E5 Gudri r. Pak.
126 D2 Güdül Turkey
114 C3 Gudur Andhra Prad. India
114 C3 Gudur Andhra Prad. India
100 E2 Gudzhal r. Rus. Fed.
225 G1 Guè, Rivière du r. Que. Can.
157 H5 Guebwiller France
206 C4 Guéckédou Guinea
158 D4 Guégon France
185 G3 Güéjar-Sierra Spain
204 C5 Guelb er Rîchât hill Maur.
208 B2 Guélengdeng Chad
205 G1 Guelma Alg.
189 A7 Guelma prov. Alg.
204 C3 Guelmine Morocco
224 D5 Guelph Ont. Can.
157 H4 Guémar France
158 E4 Guémené-Penfao France
158 C3 Guémené-sur-Scorff France
245 E2 Guémez Mex.
157 G3 Guénange France
207 F4 Guéné Benin
183 G1 Güeñes Spain
158 E4 Guenrouet France
206 B3 Guènt Paté Senegal
158 D4 Guer France
208 C2 Guéra pref. Chad
208 C2 Guéra, Massif du mts Chad
158 D4 Guérande France
205 G2 Guerara Alg.
204 E2 Guercif Morocco
202 D6 Guéréda Chad
162 D2 Guéret France
160 B1 Guérigny France
207 F4 Guérin-Kouka Togo
240 F2 Guerneville CA U.S.A.
Guernica Spain see Gernika-Lumo
158 D2 Guernsey terr. Channel Is
238 F3 Guernsey WY U.S.A.
206 C2 Guérou Maur.
184 C3 Guerreiros do Rio Port.
237 C6 Guerrero Coahuila Mex.
243 F3 Guerrero Tamaulipas Mex.
244 D5 Guerrero state Mex.
184 D2 Guerrero r. Spain
242 B3 Guerrero Negro Mex.
163 C6 Guerreys, Pic de mt. France
186 E2 Guerri de la Sal Spain
186 B2 Güesa Spain
163 A5 Guéthary France
160 C2 Gueugnon France
206 D5 Guéyo Côte d'Ivoire
Gufeng Fujian China see Pingnan
Gufu Hubei China see Xingshan
129 D3 Gugark' Armenia
210 C3 Gugē mt. Eth.
78 □3a Gugegwe i. Kwajalein Marshall Is
172 C2 Güglingen Ger.
193 G3 Guglionesi Italy
91 K3 Guguan i. N. Mariana Is
109 F2 Guhe Anhui China
122 D5 Gūh Kūh mt. Iran
170 D2 Gühlen-Glienicke Ger.
Guhuai Henan China see Pingyu
182 B5 Guia Port.
216 □3a Guía de Isora Tenerife Canary Is
182 D2 Guiana mt. Spain
264 F5 Guiana Basin sea feature N. Atlantic Ocean
250 E3 Guiana Highlands mts S. America
206 D5 Guibéroua Côte d'Ivoire
156 B4 Guichainville France
158 E4 Guichen France
82 D4 Guichen Bay S.A. Austr.
109 F2 Guichi Anhui China
245 G5 Guichicovi Mex.
261 I3 Guichón Uru.
158 C3 Guiclan France
207 G3 Guidan-Roumji Niger
208 C2 Guidari Chad
106 D5 Guide Qinghai China
158 C4 Guidel France
149 H2 Guide Post Northumberland, England U.K.
207 I4 Guider Cameroon
207 I4 Guidiguis Cameroon
206 B3 Guidimaka admin. reg. Maur.
108 C3 Guiding Guizhou China
191 F3 Guidizzolo Italy
109 E3 Guidong Hunan China
193 E3 Guidonia-Montecelio Italy
257 F4 Guidoval Brazil
206 B2 Guier, Lac de l. Senegal
160 D3 Guiers r. France
208 A5 Guietsou Gabon
108 D4 Guigang Guangxi China
191 F4 Guiglia Italy
206 D5 Guiglo Côte d'Ivoire
158 E4 Guignen France
156 C4 Guignes France
156 D3 Guignicourt France
213 G5 Guija Moz.
108 D4 Gui Jiang r. China
109 G2 Guiji Shan mts China
182 D4 Guijo de Coria Spain
182 D4 Guijo de Galisteo Spain
182 D4 Guijo de Granadilla Spain
182 E4 Guijuelo Spain
161 E4 Guil r. France
151 G3 Guildford Surrey, England U.K.
233 H2 Guildhall VT U.S.A.
146 E5 Guildtown Perth and Kinross, Scotland U.K.
158 B3 Guilers France
235 F1 Guilford CT U.S.A.
233 □I2 Guilford ME U.S.A.
161 C4 Guilherand France
Guilherme Capelo Angola see Cacongo
182 B3 Guilhofrei Port.
108 D3 Guilin Guangxi China
161 E4 Guillaumes France
184 D3 Guillena Spain
161 E4 Guillestre France
158 D3 Guilliers France
160 C1 Guillon France
163 B4 Guillos France
158 B4 Guilvinec France
216 □3a Güímar Tenerife Canary Is
254 D2 Guimarães Brazil
182 B3 Guimarães Port.
92 B4 Guimaras i. Phil.
107 H5 Guimeng Ding mt. Shandong China
207 F4 Guinagourou Benin
106 D5 Guinan Qinghai China
92 C4 Guindulman Phil.
206 C4 Guinea country Africa
207 G6 Guinea, Gulf of Africa
264 I5 Guinea Basin sea feature N. Atlantic Ocean
206 B4 Guinea-Bissau country Africa
Guinea-Conakry country Africa see Guinea
Guinea Ecuatorial country Africa see Equatorial Guinea
Guiné-Bissau country Africa see Guinea-Bissau
Guinée country Africa see Guinea
206 C4 Guinée-Forestière admin. reg. Guinea
206 B4 Guinée-Maritime admin. reg. Guinea
246 B2 Güines Cuba
156 B2 Guînes France
158 C3 Guingamp France
206 B3 Guinguinéo Senegal
158 B3 Guipavas France
108 D4 Guiping Guangxi China
158 E4 Guipry France
186 A1 Guipúzcoa prov. País Vasco Spain
246 B2 Güira de Melena Cuba
255 B6 Guiratinga Brazil
251 I3 Guisanbourg Fr. Guiana
183 E4 Guisando Spain
161 E4 Guisane r. France
149 H3 Guisborough Redcar and Cleveland, England U.K.
156 D3 Guiscard France
158 C3 Guiscriff France
156 D3 Guise France
149 H4 Guiseley West Yorkshire, England U.K.
Guishan Yunnan China see Xinping
158 B3 Guissény France
186 E3 Guissona Spain
151 H2 Guist Norfolk, England U.K.
182 C1 Guitiriz Spain
162 B3 Guîtres France
206 D5 Guitri Côte d'Ivoire
92 C4 Guiuan Phil.
140 N1 Guivi hill Fin.
Guixi Chongqing China see Dianjiang
108 C3 Guiyang Guizhou China
109 E3 Guiyang Hunan China
109 E3 Guiyang Hunan China
108 C3 Guizhou prov. China
109 D4 Guizi Guangdong China
163 A4 Gujan-Mestras France
116 C5 Gujarat state India
123 H3 Gujar Khan Pak.
207 H4 Gujba Nigeria
Gujerat state India see Gujarat
123 H3 Gujranwala Pak.
123 H3 Gujrat Pak.
129 D3 Gukarrich Armenia
Gukasyan Armenia see Ashots'k'
109 F3 Gukou Fujian China
135 G6 Gukovo Rus. Fed.
116 D2 Gulabgarh Jammu and Kashmir
120 D4 Gulabie Uzbek.
106 D4 Gulang Gansu China
83 G2 Gulargambone N.S.W. Austr.
199 E2 Gülbahçe Turkey
121 G4 Gul'bakhor Uzbek.
114 C2 Gulbarga Karnataka India
138 F3 Gulbene Latvia
Gul'cha Kyrg. see Gülchö
121 H4 Gülchö Kyrg.
129 B3 Gül dağı mt. Turkey
170 C1 Guldborg Denmark
126 D3 Gülek Turkey
Gulf of Chihli China see Bo Hai
237 F6 Gulfport MS U.S.A.
231 C6 Gulf Shores AL U.S.A.
83 G3 Gulgong N.S.W. Austr.
113 □1 Gulhi i. S. Male Maldives
100 B1 Gulian Heilong. China
108 C3 Gulin Sichuan China
121 G4 Gulistan Uzbek.
Guliston Uzbek. see Gulistan
170 C2 Gülitz Ger.
107 I1 Guliya Shan mt. Nei Mongol China
Gulja Xinjiang China see Yining
135 H7 Gul'kevichi Rus. Fed.
224 B3 Gull r. Ont. Can.
148 C3 Gulladuff Northern Ireland U.K.
146 F5 Gullane East Lothian, Scotland U.K.
223 I5 Gull Lake Sask. Can.
143 F2 Gullspång Sweden
199 F2 Güllü Uşak Turkey
199 E3 Güllübahçe Turkey
129 E3 Güllük Azer.
199 E3 Güllük Turkey
199 E3 Güllük Körfezi b. Turkey
116 C2 Gulmarg Jammu and Kashmir
126 D3 Gülnar Turkey
165 E4 Gulpen Neth.
170 D3 Gülper See l. Ger.
199 E2 Gülpınar Turkey
129 B2 Gulrip'shi Georgia
126 D3 Gülşehir Turkey
121 H3 Gul'shad Kazakh.
170 E2 Gültz Ger.
Gulü Henan China see Xincai
210 B4 Gulu Uganda
197 G4 Gŭlŭbovo Bulg.
85 G5 Guluguba Qld Austr.
207 I4 Gulumba Gana Nigeria
84 D1 Guluwuru Island N.T. Austr.
146 C5 Gulvain hill Scotland U.K.
211 C6 Gulwe Tanz.
197 G4 Gulyantsi Bulg.
170 D2 Gülzow Ger.
168 F2 Gülzow Ger.
Guma Xinjiang China see Pishan
123 G4 Gumal r. Pak.
212 D3 Gumare Botswana
Gumbinnen Rus. Fed. see Gusev
210 A3 Gumbiri mt. Sudan
122 C2 Gumdag Turkm.
207 H3 Gumel Nigeria
Gümgüm Turkey see Varto
183 G3 Gumiel de Hizán Spain
183 G3 Gumiel de Mercado Spain
117 F5 Gumla Bihar India
105 E2 Gumma pref. Japan
169 C4 Gummersbach Ger.
94 B1 Gumpang r. Indon.
169 F5 Gumpelstadt Ger.
170 D3 Gumtow Ger.
126 E2 Gümüşhane Turkey
129 A3 Gümüşhane prov. Turkey
199 E2 Gümüşsuyu Turkey
199 F1 Gümüşyaka Turkey
116 D4 Guna Madh. Prad. India
Gunan Chongqing China see Qijiang
177 I6 Gunaroš Vojvodina, Srbija Yugo.
210 C2 Guna Terara mt. Eth.
83 F3 Gunbar N.S.W. Austr.
123 G2 Gund r. Tajik.
83 G3 Gundagai N.S.W. Austr.
172 B3 Gundelfingen Ger.
173 E3 Gundelfingen an der Donau Ger.
172 D2 Gundelsheim Baden-Württemberg Ger.
173 E2 Gundelsheim Bayern Ger.
114 C3 Gunderi Karnataka India
157 H4 Gundershoffen France
114 D3 Gundlakamma r. India
114 C4 Gundlupet Karnataka India
126 D3 Gündoğmuş Turkey
Gundorovka Rus. Fed. see Donetsk
199 G2 Gündüzler Turkey
129 C4 Gündüzü Turkey
199 F2 Güneşli Turkey
199 F2 Güney Turkey
199 F2 Güney Turkey
126 E3 Güneydoğu Toroslar plat. Turkey
199 G2 Güneyköy Afyon Turkey
129 B3 Güneysu Turkey
128 A1 Güneyyurt Turkey
209 C6 Gungu Dem. Rep. Congo
209 B8 Gungue Angola
129 E2 Gunib Rus. Fed.
223 L4 Gunisao r. Man. Can.
188 G3 Gunja Croatia
206 A3 Gunjur Gambia
199 F2 Günlüce Turkey
Gunma pref. Japan see Gumma
140 L2 Gunnarn Sweden
140 M2 Gunnarsbyn Sweden
85 F3 Gunnawarra Qld Austr.
221 P3 Gunnbjørn Fjeld nunatak Greenland
83 G2 Gunnedah N.S.W. Austr.
149 I4 Gunness North Lincolnshire, England U.K.
83 G3 Gunning N.S.W. Austr.
150 C4 Gunnislake Cornwall, England U.K.
239 F4 Gunnison CO U.S.A.
241 L2 Gunnison UT U.S.A.
239 E4 Gunnison r. CO U.S.A.
241 L2 Gunnison Reservoir UT U.S.A.
84 B2 Gunn Point N.T. Austr.
84 D3 Gunpowder Creek r. Qld Austr.
234 B3 Gunpowder Falls r. MD U.S.A.
Güns Hungary see Kőszeg
114 C2 Gun Sangari Mahar. India
179 E2 Gunskirchen Austria
171 C4 Günstedt Ger.
Gunt r. Tajik. see Gund
114 C3 Guntakal Andhra Prad. India
169 F4 Güntersberge Ger.
172 C2 Guntersblum Ger.
179 H2 Guntersdorf Austria
172 D2 Güntersleben Ger.
231 C5 Guntersville AL U.S.A.
182 C2 Guntin de Pallares Spain
179 H2 Guntramsdorf Austria
114 D2 Guntur Andhra Prad. India
84 D3 Gununa Qld Austr.
94 B2 Gunungsitoli Indon.
94 B2 Gunungtua Sumatera Indon.
115 D2 Gunupur Orissa India
126 C3 Günyüzü Turkey
173 E3 Günz r. Ger.
Gunza Angola see Porto Amboim
173 E3 Günzburg Ger.
173 E2 Gunzenhausen Ger.
106 E4 Guochengyi Gansu China
109 E1 Guo He r. China
109 F1 Guo He r. China
Guoluezhen Henan China see Lingbao
109 F1 Guoyang Anhui China
Guozhen Shaanxi China see Baoji
116 C1 Gupis Jammu and Kashmir
197 H3 Gura Caliţei Romania
Guradu i. S. Male Maldives see Guraidhu
136 E4 Gura Galbenei Moldova
177 L5 Gurahonţ Romania
197 G2 Gura Humorului Romania
113 □1 Guraidhu i. S. Male Maldives
116 C2 Gurais Jammu and Kashmir
207 G4 Gurara r. Nigeria
177 L6 Gurasada Romania
197 G3 Gura Şuţii Romania
197 H3 Gura Teghii Romania
208 E4 Gurba r. Dem. Rep. Congo
107 G3 Gurban Obo Nei Mongol China
110 D2 Gurbantünggüt Shamo des. China
129 D4 Gürbulak Turkey
116 C2 Gurdaspur Punjab India
122 E5 Gurdim Iran
237 E5 Gurdon AR U.S.A.
Gurdzhaani Georgia see Gurjaani
199 E2 Güre Turkey
199 F2 Güre Turkey
Gurgan Iran see Gorgān
116 D3 Gurgaon Haryana India
202 E6 Gurgei, Jebel mt. Sudan
197 G2 Gurghiu r. Romania
197 G2 Gurghiului, Munţii mts Romania
254 E3 Gurgueia r. Brazil
116 B4 Gurha Rajasthan India
251 F3 Guri, Embalse de resr Venez.
256 C3 Gurinhatã Brazil
129 D3 Gurjaani Georgia
179 F4 Gurk Austria
179 F4 Gurk r. Austria
Gurlan Uzbek. see Gurlen
120 E4 Gurlen Uzbek.
114 C2 Gurmatkal Karnataka India
226 D4 Gurnee IL U.S.A.
150 D3 Gurnos Powys, Wales U.K.
213 G3 Guro Moz.
127 F3 Gürpınar Turkey
114 C3 Gurramkonda Andhra Prad. India
186 C2 Gurrea de Gállego Spain
199 F1 Gürsu Bursa Turkey
Gu-ru i. S. Male Maldives see Gulhi
Guru i. S. Male Maldives see Gulhi
213 H2 Gurué Moz.
126 E3 Gürün Turkey
251 I5 Gurupá Brazil
251 I5 Gurupa, Ilha Grande de i. Brazil
254 C4 Gurupi Brazil
254 C3 Gurupi, Serra do hills Brazil
116 C4 Guru Sikhar mt. Rajasthan India
213 F3 Guruve Zimbabwe
Guruwe Zimbabwe see Guruve
114 C2 Guruzala Andhra Prad. India
106 D3 Gurvan Sayan Uul mts Mongolia
Gur'yev Kazakh. see Atyrau
138 C4 Gur'yevsk Rus. Fed.
Gur'yevskaya Oblast' admin. div. Kazakh. see Atyrauskaya Oblast'
139 M4 Gus' r. Rus. Fed.
207 G3 Gusau Nigeria
170 C2 Gusborn Ger.
171 C3 Güsen Ger.
138 D4 Gusev Rus. Fed.
139 M4 Gusevskiy Rus. Fed.
101 B5 Gushan Liaoning China
123 E3 Gushgy Turkm.
123 E2 Gushgy r. Turkm.
109 E1 Gushi Henan China
207 E4 Gushiegu Ghana
102 □1 Gushikawa Japan
196 D4 Gusinje Crna Gora Yugo.
139 H4 Gusino Rus. Fed.
106 E1 Gusinoozersk Respublika Buryatiya Rus. Fed.
117 F5 Guskara W. Bengal India
139 M4 Gus'-Khrustal'nyy Rus. Fed.
170 F3 Gusow Ger.
192 A5 Guspini Sardegna Italy
190 F3 Gussago Italy
179 H3 Güssing Austria
190 F3 Gussola Italy
179 G3 Gußwerk Austria
140 □ Gustav Adolf Land reg. Svalbard
247 G3 Gustavia St Barthélémy West Indies
237 D7 Gustavo Díaz Ordaz Mex.
245 G5 Gustavo Diaz Ordaz Veracruz Mex.
143 H2 Gustavsberg Sweden
220 E4 Gustavus AK U.S.A.
140 □ Gustav V Land reg. Svalbard
171 C4 Güsten Ger.
172 A2 Gusterath Ger.
240 G3 Gustine CA U.S.A.
170 D2 Güstrow Ger.
102 □1 Gusukube Japan
172 C3 Gutach (Schwarzwaldbahn) Ger.
197 F2 Gutâiului, Munţii mts Romania
179 F2 Gutau Austria
146 □G1 Gutcher Shetland, Scotland U.K.
179 G3 Gutenstein Austria
171 E3 Güterfelde Ger.
171 C4 Güterglück Ger.
169 D4 Gütersloh Ger.
241 M5 Guthrie AZ U.S.A.
230 C4 Guthrie KY U.S.A.
237 D5 Guthrie OK U.S.A.
237 C5 Guthrie TX U.S.A.
236 E3 Guthrie Center IA U.S.A.
234 C2 Guthriesville PA U.S.A.
109 F3 Gutian Fujian China
109 F3 Gutian Fujian China
252 E4 Gutiérrez Bol.
245 H4 Gutiérrez Gómez Mex.
Guting Shandong China see Yutai
129 E3 Guton, Gora mt. Azer./Rus. Fed.
176 F5 Gutorfölde Hungary
170 D2 Gutow Ger.
190 D2 Guttannen Switz.
179 F4 Guttaring Austria
236 F3 Guttenberg IA U.S.A.
213 F3 Gutu Zimbabwe
170 E2 Gützkow Ger.
129 B4 Güveçli Turkey
140 L2 Guvertfjället mts Sweden
117 G4 Guwahati Assam India
127 F3 Guwēr Iraq
Guwlumayak Turkm. see Kuuli-Mayak
169 E4 Guxhagen Ger.
109 E3 Guxian Jiangxi China
251 G3 Guyana country S. America
Guyane Française terr. S. America see French Guiana
Guyang Hunan China see Guzhang
107 F3 Guyang Nei Mongol China
160 C2 Guye r. France
Guyi Guangxi China see Sanjiang
237 C4 Guymon OK U.S.A.
122 C4 Gūyom Iran
Guyong Fujian China see Jiangle
83 G2 Guyra N.S.W. Austr.
225 I4 Guysborough N.S. Can.
107 G3 Guyuan Hebei China
106 E5 Guyuan Ningxia China
121 F5 Guzar Uzbek.
129 F3 Güzdäk Azer.
128 B1 Güzeloluk Turkey
Güzelyurt Cyprus see Morfou
108 D2 Guzhang Hunan China
109 F1 Guzhen Anhui China
Guzhou Guizhou China see Rongjiang
242 D2 Guzmán, Lago de l. Mex.
138 C4 Gvardeysk Rus. Fed.
Gvardeyskoye Rus. Fed. see Elin-Yurt
137 K2 Gvazda Rus. Fed.
83 G2 Gwabegar N.S.W. Austr.
207 G4 Gwada Nigeria
207 G3 Gwadabawa Nigeria
123 E5 Gwadar Pak.
123 E5 Gwadar West Bay Pak.
Gwador Pak. see Gwadar
116 D4 Gwalior Madh. Prad. India
213 F4 Gwanda Zimbabwe
207 G4 Gwarzo Nigeria
150 D3 Gwaun-Cae-Gurwen Neath Port Talbot, Wales U.K.
213 E3 Gwayi r. Zimbabwe
174 E2 Gwda r. Pol.
147 C2 Gweebarra Bay Rep. of Ireland
147 C1 Gweedore Rep. of Ireland
Gwelo Zimbabwe see Gweru
213 F3 Gweru Zimbabwe
212 E4 Gweta Botswana
226 D2 Gwinn MI U.S.A.
236 D2 Gwinner ND U.S.A.
150 B4 Gwithian Cornwall, England U.K.
207 I4 Gwoza Nigeria
83 G2 Gwydir r. N.S.W. Austr.
150 C1 Gwynedd admin. div. Wales U.K.
150 D1 Gwytherin Conwy, Wales U.K.
160 D1 Gy France
111 F6 Gyaca Xizang China
Gya'gya Xizang China see Saga
Gyaijêpozhanggê Qinghai China see Zhidoi
111 F6 Gyai Qu r. Xizang China
108 A1 Gyairong Qinghai China
Gyaisi Sichuan China see Jiulong
177 I4 Gyál Hungary
199 E3 Gyali i. Greece
Gyamotang Xizang China see Dêngqên
Gyandzha Azer. see Gäncä
Gyangkar Xizang China see Dinngyê
111 D6 Gyangrang Xizang China
Gyangtse Xizang China see Gyangzê
111 E6 Gyangzê Xizang China
106 C5 Gyaring Qinghai China
111 E6 Gyaring Co l. China
106 C5 Gyaring Hu l. Qinghai China
176 G4 Gyarmat Hungary
198 D3 Gyaros i. Greece
Gyaurs Turkm. see Sakhra
Gydan, Khrebet mts Rus. Fed. see Kolymskiy, Khrebet
130 I2 Gydanskiy Poluostrov pen. Rus. Fed.
Gyêgu Qinghai China see Yushu
176 G5 Gyékényes Hungary
177 H4 Gyermely Hungary
156 E4 Gyé-sur-Seine France
Gyêwa Xizang China see Zabqung
168 E2 Gyhum Ger.
Gyigang Xizang China see Zayü
111 F6 Gyimda Xizang China
111 D6 Gyirong Xizang China
108 A2 Gyitang Xizang China
Gyixong Xizang China see Gonggar
111 F5 Gyiza Qinghai China
142 D4 Gyldenløveshøj hill Denmark
147 C5 Gyleen Rep. of Ireland
140 M2 Gyljen Sweden
85 H5 Gympie Qld Austr.
96 A3 Gyobingauk Myanmar
105 F2 Gyōda Japan
177 J5 Gyomaendrőd Hungary
177 G4 Gyömöre Hungary
177 I4 Gyömrő Hungary
177 I4 Gyöngyös Hungary
176 F4 Gyöngyös r. Hungary
177 G6 Gyöngyös r. Romania
177 I4 Gyöngyöshalász Hungary
177 I4 Gyöngyöspata Hungary
177 H5 Gyönk Hungary
177 G4 Győr Hungary
176 G4 Győr-Moson-Sopron county Hungary
177 G4 Győrság Hungary
Győrszentmárton Hungary see Pannonhalma
177 L4 Győrtelek Hungary
177 G4 Győrújbarát Hungary
177 G4 Győrújfalu Hungary
223 L5 Gypsumville Man. Can.
198 C3 Gytheio Greece
177 K5 Gyula Hungary
Gyulafehérvár Romania see Alba Iulia
177 L3 Gyulaháza Hungary
177 H5 Gyulaj Hungary
129 F3 Gyul'gerychay r. Rus. Fed.
Gyümai Qinghai China see Darlag
129 C3 Gyumri Armenia
197 H5 Gyurgen Bair hill Turkey
122 D2 Gyzylarbat Turkm.
139 J4 Gzhat' r. Rus. Fed.
Gzhatsk Rus. Fed. see Gagarin
175 I3 Gzy Pol.

H

117 G4 Ha Bhutan
138 E2 Haabneeme Estonia
165 D4 Haacht Belgium
179 F2 Haag Austria
179 E2 Haag am Hausruck Austria
173 F3 Haag an der Amper Ger.
173 G3 Haag in Oberbayern Ger.
140 □ Haakon VII Land reg. Svalbard
164 F2 Haaksbergen Neth.
165 D4 Haaltert Belgium
106 B1 Haanhöhiy Uul mts Mongolia
79 □2 Ha'ano i. Tonga
79 □2 Ha'apai Group is Tonga
134 D3 Haapajärvi Fin.
140 N2 Haapavesi Fin.
138 D2 Haapsalu Estonia
173 F3 Haar Ger.

Ha 'Arava to Hase
311

Ha 'Arava watercourse Israel/Jordan see 'Arabah, Wādī al
173 H3 Haarbach Ger.
172 B2 Haardt hills Ger.
172 B2 Haardtkopf hill Ger.
164 D2 Haarlem Neth.
214 D5 Haarlem S. Africa
169 C4 Haarstrang ridge Ger.
81 B5 Haast South I. N.Z.
81 B5 Haast r. South I. N.Z.
84 B4 Haast Bluff N.T. Austr.
81 B6 Haast Range mts South I. N.Z.
164 D3 Haastrecht Neth.
123 F5 Hab r. Pak.
173 F4 Habach Ger.
110 D1 Habahe Xinjiang China
Habai Group is Tonga see Ha'apai Group
Habana Cuba see La Habana
173 G1 Habartov Czech Rep.
163 B5 Habas France
222 G3 Habay Alta Can.
165 E5 Habay-la-Neuve Belgium
124 D5 Ḩabbān Yemen
127 F4 Ḩabbānīyah, Hawr al l. Iraq
124 C4 Ḩabhab ash Shaykh, Ḩarrāt lava field Saudi Arabia
178 C3 Habicht mt. Austria
117 G4 Habiganj Bangl.
104 B4 Habikino Japan
128 B4 Ḩabīs, Wādī al r. Jordan
143 F3 Habo Sweden
177 I2 Habovka Slovakia
117 G5 Habra W. Bengal India
176 E2 Habry Czech Rep.
157 H5 Habsheim France
125 E4 Ḩabshīyah, Jabal mts Yemen
169 C5 Hachenburg Ger.
105 E2 Hachibuse-yama mt. Japan
104 D2 Hachimori-yama mt. Japan
102 J3 Hachinohe Japan
105 F3 Hachiōji Japan
199 F2 Hacıbekir Turkey
126 D3 Hacıbektaş Turkey
129 C4 Hacıhalit Turkey
Hacıköy Turkey see Çekerek
183 G3 Hacinas Spain
128 C1 Hacıpaşa Turkey
129 F4 Hacıqahramanlı Azer.
129 F3 Hacı Zeynalabdin Azer.
82 D2 Hack, Mount S.A. Austr.
241 K4 Hackberry AZ U.S.A.
172 B2 Hackenheim Ger.
235 D2 Hackensack NJ U.S.A.
232 C5 Hacker Valley WV U.S.A.
147 E4 Hacketstown Rep. of Ireland
234 D2 Hackettstown NJ U.S.A.
151 G2 Hackleton Northamptonshire, England U.K.
151 I3 Hacklinge Kent, England U.K.
149 I3 Hackness North Yorkshire, England U.K.
234 C3 Hack Point MD U.S.A.
213 G4 Hacufera Moz.
175 J6 Haczów Pol.
125 E3 Hadabat al Budū plain Saudi Arabia
114 B3 Hadagalli Karnataka India
169 D5 Hadamar Ger.
123 F4 Hada Mountains Afgh.
124 C3 Ḩaḑan, Ḩarrat lava field Saudi Arabia
105 F3 Hadano Japan
151 G3 Haddenham Buckinghamshire, England U.K.
146 F6 Haddington East Lothian, Scotland U.K.
151 I2 Haddiscoe Norfolk, England U.K.
234 C3 Haddonfield NJ U.S.A.
207 H3 Hadejia Nigeria
142 D1 Hadeland reg. Norway
128 B3 Ḩadera Israel
128 B3 Ḩadera r. Israel
142 C4 Haderslev Denmark
142 C3 Haderup Denmark
114 C2 Hadgaon Mahar. India
124 C3 Ḩādhah Saudi Arabia
125 E3 Ḩādh Banī Zaynān des. Saudi Arabia
113 D11 Hadhdhunmathi Atoll Maldives
Hadhramaut reg. Yemen see Ḩaḑramawt
125 F5 Hadīboh Suquṭrā Yemen
111 D4 Hadilik Xinjiang China
126 D3 Hadım Turkey
202 D5 Hadjer Momou mt. Chad
151 H2 Hadleigh Suffolk, England U.K.
150 E2 Hadley Telford and Wrekin, England U.K.
221 H2 Hadley Bay Nunavut Can.
235 F1 Hadlyme CT U.S.A.
171 C4 Hadmersleben Ger.
157 G4 Hadol France
125 E4 Ḩaḑramawt governorate Yemen
125 D5 Ḩaḑramawt reg. Yemen
Hadranum Sicilia Italy see Adrano
179 H2 Hadres Austria
Hadria Italy see Adria
149 G2 Hadrian's Wall tourist site England U.K.
Hadrumetum Tunisia see Sousse
129 E4 Hadrut Azer.
140 K1 Hadseløy i. Norway
142 D3 Hadsten Denmark
142 D3 Hadsund Denmark
137 G2 Hadyach Ukr.
102 □2 Haebaru Japan
261 I3 Haedo, Cuchilla de hills Uru.
101 C5 Haeju N. Korea
101 C5 Haeju-man b. N. Korea
165 E3 Haelen Neth.
240 □B7 Haena HI U.S.A.
101 C6 Haenam S. Korea
124 D1 Ḩafar al Bāṭin Saudi Arabia
223 J4 Hafford Sask. Can.
126 E3 Hafik Turkey
124 B2 Hafirat al 'Aydā Saudi Arabia
124 D2 Hafirat Nasah Saudi Arabia
125 F3 Ḩafīt Oman
125 F2 Ḩafīt, Jabal mt. U.A.E.
123 H3 Hafizabad Pak.
117 H4 Haflong Assam India
140 □B2 Hafnarfjörður Iceland
179 G2 Hafnerbach Austria
129 F4 Haftoni Azer.
140 □B2 Hafursfjörður b. Iceland
Haga Myanmar see Haka
203 G6 Hag Abdullah Sudan
215 G5 Haga-Haga S. Africa
179 H5 Haganj Croatia
227 G2 Hagar Ont. Can.
114 C3 Hagari r. India
203 H5 Hagar Nish Plateau Eritrea
78 □1 Hagåtña Guam
143 G3 Hagbyån r. Sweden
168 C2 Hage Ger.
171 D3 Hagelberg hill Ger.
169 C4 Hagen Ger.
91 J8 Hagen, Mount P.N.G.
169 C3 Hagen am Teutoburger Wald Ger.
172 C2 Hagenbach Ger.
169 E3 Hagenburg Ger.
168 D2 Hagen im Bremischen Ger.
170 C2 Hagenow Ger.
222 E4 Hagensborg B.C. Can.
171 F4 Hagenwerder Ger.
210 C2 Hägere Hiywet Eth.
210 C3 Hägere Selam Eth.
232 B6 Hagerhill KY U.S.A.
232 E5 Hagerstown MD U.S.A.
163 B5 Hagetaubin France
163 B5 Hagetmau France
143 E1 Hagfors Sweden
140 K3 Häggenås Sweden
238 D2 Haggin, Mount MT U.S.A.
140 K3 Häggsjön Sweden
140 K3 Häggsjövik Sweden
103 E6 Hagi Japan
96 D2 Ha Giang Vietnam
97 E4 Ha Giao, Sông r. Vietnam
150 E2 Hagley Herefordshire, England U.K.
150 E2 Hagley Worcestershire, England U.K.
HaGolan hills Syria see Golan
157 G3 Hagondange France
147 B4 Hag's Head hd Rep. of Ireland
233 G3 Hague NY U.S.A.
157 H4 Haguenau France
217 □3a Hahaïa Njazidja Comoros
103 □3 Hahajima-rettō is Japan
169 F4 Hahausen Ger.
173 F2 Hahnbach Ger.
172 C2 Hähnlein Ger.
169 D5 Hahnstätten Ger.
176 F5 Hahót Hungary
107 H4 Hai r. China
211 C5 Hai Tanz.
109 G1 Hai'an Jiangsu China
172 D2 Haibach Bayern Ger.
173 G2 Haibach Bayern Ger.
105 E4 Haibara Japan
Haicheng Guangdong China see Haifeng
107 I3 Haicheng Liaoning China
Haicheng Ningxia China see Haiyuan
116 E4 Haidargarh Uttar Prad. India
173 G2 Haidenaab r. Ger.
179 F2 Haidershofen Austria
173 H3 Haidmühle Ger.
96 D2 Hai Dương Vietnam
Haifa Israel see Ḩefa
128 B3 Haifa, Bay of Israel
109 E4 Haifeng Guangdong China
87 E6 Haig W.A. Austr.
169 D5 Haiger Ger.
172 C3 Haigerloch Ger.
Haikakan country Asia see Armenia
Haikang Guangdong China see Leizhou
108 D4 Haikou Hainan China
124 C2 Ḩā'il Saudi Arabia
124 C2 Ḩā'il prov. Saudi Arabia
117 H4 Hailakandi Assam India
107 H1 Hailar Nei Mongol China
107 H1 Hailar r. China
238 D3 Hailey ID U.S.A.
224 E4 Haileybury Ont. Can.
100 D3 Hailin Heilong. China
Hailong Jilin China see Meihekou
151 H4 Hailsham East Sussex, England U.K.
100 C3 Hailun Heilong. China
140 N2 Hailuoto Fin.
109 G2 Haimen Jiangsu China
173 F3 Haimhausen Ger.
178 B3 Haiming Austria
173 G3 Haiming Ger.
169 F5 Haina Ger.
169 D4 Haina (Kloster) Ger.
108 D5 Hainan i. China
99 I8 Hainan prov. China
Hainan Strait China see Qiongzhou Haixia
165 D4 Hainaut prov. Belgium
179 H2 Hainburg an der Donau Austria
206 C5 Haindi Liberia
220 E4 Haines AK U.S.A.
231 D6 Haines City FL U.S.A.
222 B2 Haines Junction Y.T. Can.
234 D3 Hainesport NJ U.S.A.
222 B2 Haines Road Can./U.S.A.
179 G2 Hainfeld Austria
169 F4 Hainich ridge Ger.
171 E5 Hainichen Ger.
169 F4 Hainleite ridge Ger.
Haiphong Vietnam see Hai Phong
96 D2 Hai Phong Vietnam
100 E3 Haiqing Heilong. China
106 D3 Hairhan Namag Nei Mongol China
157 F4 Haironville France
172 C3 Haiterbach Ger.
246 D3 Haiti country West Indies
179 G2 Haitzendorf Austria
106 D4 Haiyan Qinghai China
109 G2 Haiyan Zhejiang China
Haiyang Anhui China see Xiuning
107 I4 Haiyang Shandong China
Haiyou Zhejiang China see Sanmen
106 E4 Haiyuan Ningxia China
107 H5 Haizhou Wan b. China
122 C3 Hāj Ali Qoli, Kavīr-e salt l. Iran
177 K4 Hajdú-Bihar county Hungary
177 K4 Hajdúböszörmény Hungary
177 K4 Hajdúdorog Hungary
177 K4 Hajdúhadház Hungary
177 K4 Hajdúnánás Hungary
177 K4 Hajdúsámson Hungary
177 K4 Hajdúszoboszló Hungary
177 K4 Hajdúszovát Hungary
125 F5 Ḩajhir mt. Suquṭrā Yemen
117 F4 Hajipur Bihar India
125 E2 Hajir reg. Saudi Arabia
124 C5 Ḩajjah Yemen
124 C4 Ḩajjah governorate Yemen
122 C4 Ḩājjīābād Iran
122 C4 Ḩājjīābād Iran
177 H4 Hajmáskér Hungary
175 L3 Hajnówka Pol.
117 G4 Hajo Assam India
177 I5 Hajós Hungary
124 C3 Ḩajrah Saudi Arabia
177 G3 Hájske Slovakia
96 A2 Haka Myanmar
240 □D9 Hakalau HI U.S.A.
129 E4 Häkäri r. Azer.
103 I5 Hakase-yama mt. Japan
81 C6 Hakataramea South I. N.Z.
81 C5 Hakatere South I. N.Z.
Hakatere r. South I. N.Z. see Ashburton
259 C6 Hakelhuincul, Altiplanicie de plat. Arg.
Hakha Myanmar see Haka
128 B4 Hakippa, Har hill Israel
127 F3 Hakkârı Turkey
140 M2 Hakkas Sweden
104 B4 Hakken-zan mt. Japan
102 J3 Hakkōda-san mt. Japan
105 E4 Hakkō-san hill Japan
102 K1 Hako-dake mt. Japan
102 J3 Hakodate Japan
212 C4 Hakos Mountains Namibia
129 B4 Haksever Turkey
104 C2 Hakui Japan
104 C2 Haku-san vol. Japan
Hal Belgium see Halle
123 G5 Hala Pak.
128 B4 Ḩalā', Jabal al mt. Jordan
128 C1 Ḩalab Syria
128 C1 Ḩalab governorate Syria
124 D3 Ḩalabān Saudi Arabia
127 G4 Halabja Iraq
Halach Turkm. see Khalach
243 H4 Halachó Mex.
100 C3 Halahai Jilin China
136 D3 Halahora de Sus Moldova
203 G4 Halaib Triangle terr. Egypt/Sudan
128 A4 Halâl, Gebel hill Egypt
125 G4 Ḩalānīyāt, Juzur al is Oman
176 G4 Halászi Hungary
197 H2 Hălăuceşti Romania
143 F2 Hålaveden hills Sweden
240 □C8 Halawa HI U.S.A.
128 C2 Halba Lebanon
106 C1 Halban Hövsgöl Mongolia
171 E3 Halbe Ger.
179 G4 Halbenrain Austria
171 C4 Halberstadt Ger.
150 D4 Halberton Devon, England U.K.
173 E4 Halblech Ger.
179 H3 Halbturn Austria
92 B3 Halcon, Mount Mindoro Phil.
215 G4 Halcyon Drift S. Africa
142 D2 Halden Norway
171 C3 Haldensleben Ger.
173 E4 Haldenwang Ger.
117 G5 Haldi r. W. Bengal India
117 G5 Haldia W. Bengal India
117 G4 Haldibari W. Bengal India
116 D3 Haldwani Uttar Prad. India
149 G4 Hale Greater Manchester, England U.K.
227 F3 Hale MI U.S.A.
87 C5 Hale, Mount hill W.A. Austr.
129 C3 Halefoğlu Turkey
122 C5 Hāleh Iran
240 □ Haleiwa HI U.S.A.
165 E4 Halen Belgium
177 H2 Halenkov Czech Rep.
Haleparki Deresi r. Syria/Turkey see Quwayq, Nahr
151 I2 Hales Norfolk, England U.K.
150 E2 Halesowen West Midlands, England U.K.
151 I2 Halesworth Suffolk, England U.K.
234 B3 Halethorpe MD U.S.A.
149 G4 Halewood Merseyside, England U.K.
231 C5 Haleyville AL U.S.A.
206 E5 Half Assini Ghana
126 E3 Halfeti Turkey
173 G4 Halfing Ger.
81 B7 Halfmoon Bay Stewart I. N.Z.
240 F3 Half Moon Bay CA U.S.A.
82 C2 Half Moon Lake salt flat S.A. Austr.
222 F3 Halfway r. B.C. Can.
232 E5 Halfway MD U.S.A.
164 D2 Halfweg Neth.
214 C4 Halfweg S. Africa
142 E1 Halgån r. Sweden
107 H2 Halhgol Mongolia
227 H3 Haliburton Ont. Can.
224 E4 Haliburton Highlands hills Ont. Can.
177 I3 Halič Slovakia
Halicarnassus Turkey see Bodrum
225 I4 Halifax N.S. Can.
149 H4 Halifax West Yorkshire, England U.K.
231 E4 Halifax NC U.S.A.
234 B2 Halifax PA U.S.A.
232 D6 Halifax VA U.S.A.
85 F3 Halifax, Mount Qld Austr.
85 F3 Halifax Bay Qld Austr.
138 D1 Halikko Fin.
129 B4 Halilçavuş Turkey
128 C2 Ḩalīmah mt. Lebanon/Syria
82 B2 Halinor Lake salt flat S.A. Austr.
Haliut Nei Mongol China see Urad Zhongqi
114 B3 Haliyal Karnataka India
146 E3 Halkirk Highland, Scotland U.K.
150 D1 Halkyn Flintshire, Wales U.K.
Hall atoll Gilbert Is Kiribati see Maiana
143 H3 Hall Gotland Sweden
148 E2 Hall East Renfrewshire, Scotland U.K.
234 B4 Hall MD U.S.A.
140 L3 Hälla Sweden
144 F2 Halladale r. Scotland U.K.
234 B2 Hallam PA U.S.A.
142 E3 Halland county Sweden
151 H4 Halland East Sussex, England U.K.
142 E3 Hallandsåsen hills Sweden
101 C6 Halla-san mt. S. Korea
221 J3 Hall Beach Nunavut Can.
173 F3 Hallbergmoos Ger.
165 D3 Halle Antwerpen Belgium
165 D4 Halle Vlaams Brabant Belgium
169 E4 Halle Ger.
171 C4 Halle admin. reg. Sachsen-Anhalt Ger.
171 C4 Halle (Saale) Ger.
169 D3 Halle (Westfalen) Ger.
143 F2 Hällefors Sweden
143 G2 Hälleforsnäs Sweden
178 E3 Hallein Austria
140 K3 Hallen Jämtland Sweden
143 G1 Hållen Uppsala Sweden
169 D4 Hallenberg Ger.
156 B3 Hallencourt France
171 C4 Halle-Neustadt Ger.
173 E2 Hallerndorf Ger.
263 L2 Hallett, Cape Antarctica
237 D6 Hallettsville TX U.S.A.
142 D2 Hälleviksstrand Sweden
262 W1 Halley research stn Antarctica
262 X2 Hallgreen, Mount Antarctica
236 C2 Halliday ND U.S.A.
168 D1 Halligen is Ger.
142 C1 Hallingdal val. Norway
142 C2 Hallingdalselva r. Norway
143 G3 Hallingeberg Sweden
178 C3 Hall in Tirol Austria
266 F5 Hall Islands Micronesia
138 E2 Halliste r. Estonia
140 L2 Hällnäs Sweden
236 D1 Hallock MN U.S.A.
150 E2 Hallow Worcestershire, England U.K.
221 L3 Hall Peninsula Nunavut Can.
86 E2 Hall Point W.A. Austr.
234 B1 Halls PA U.S.A.
143 F2 Hallsberg Sweden
86 E3 Halls Creek W.A. Austr.
227 H3 Halls Lake Ont. Can.
173 E2 Hallstadt Ger.
179 E3 Hallstatt Austria
179 E3 Hallstätter See l. Austria
143 H1 Hallstavik Sweden
233 F4 Hallstead PA U.S.A.
147 E3 Halltown Rep. of Ireland
165 C4 Halluin Belgium
164 E1 Hallum Neth.
140 L2 Hällvik Sweden
140 K3 Hallviken Sweden
190 D1 Hallwiler See l. Switz.
150 C4 Hallworthy Cornwall, England U.K.
177 L5 Hălmăgel Romania
177 L5 Hălmagiu Romania
93 D2 Halmahera i. Maluku Indon.
93 D3 Halmahera Sea Maluku Indon.
177 L4 Halmăşd Romania
197 F2 Halmeu Romania
142 E3 Halmstad Sweden
116 C5 Halol Gujarat India
188 E2 Haloze reg. Slovenia
142 D3 Hals Denmark
195 □ Hal Saflieni Hypogeum tourist site Malta
171 E5 Halsbrücke Ger.
169 C5 Halsenbach Ger.
Hälsingborg Sweden see Helsingborg
151 H3 Halstead Essex, England U.K.
168 E2 Halstenbek Ger.
164 D3 Halsteren Neth.
157 G3 Halstroff France
140 N3 Halsua Fin.
106 B4 Haltang r. China
169 C4 Haltern Ger.
151 G3 Halton Buckinghamshire, England U.K.
149 G3 Halton Lancashire, England U.K.
149 G4 Halton admin. div. England U.K.
149 G3 Halton Gill North Yorkshire, England U.K.
149 G3 Haltwhistle Northumberland, England U.K.
116 B5 Halvad Gujarat India
169 C4 Halver Ger.
150 D4 Halwell Devon, England U.K.
136 C3 Halych Ukr.
137 G2 Halytsya Ukr.
176 B2 Halže Czech Rep.
156 D3 Ham France
146 □F1 Ham Shetland, Scotland U.K.
103 F6 Hamada Japan
204 D5 Ḩamâda Çafia des. Mali
204 D4 Ḩamada ed Douakel plat. Alg.
204 D5 Ḩamâda El Ḩaricha des. Mali
122 B3 Hamadān Iran
122 B3 Hamadān prov. Iran
202 B3 Ḩamādat Murzuq plat. Libya
204 D3 Ḩamada Tounassine des. Alg.
204 E3 Hamaguir Alg.
128 C2 Ḩamāh Syria
128 C2 Ḩamāh governorate Syria
105 D4 Hamakita Japan
217 □3a Hamalengo mt. Njazidja Comoros
104 D4 Hamamatsu Japan
104 D4 Hamana-ko l. Japan
184 E2 Hamapega hill Spain
141 J3 Hamar Norway
140 K1 Hamarøy Norway
140 K1 Hamarøy i. Norway
124 B5 Hamasien prov. Eritrea
203 G3 Hamâta, Gebel mt. Egypt
157 H3 Hambach France
114 D5 Hambantota Sri Lanka
168 F2 Hamberge Ger.
168 D2 Hambergen Ger.
151 G3 Hambleden Buckinghamshire, England U.K.
151 F4 Hamble-le-Rice Hampshire, England U.K.
149 G4 Hambleton Lancashire, England U.K.
232 D5 Hambleton WV U.S.A.
149 H3 Hambleton Hills England U.K.
172 C2 Hambrücken Ger.
168 E3 Hambühren Ger.
168 E2 Hamburg Ger.
168 E2 Hamburg land Ger.
215 F5 Hamburg S. Africa
237 F5 Hamburg AR U.S.A.
235 F1 Hamburg CT U.S.A.
236 E3 Hamburg IA U.S.A.
234 D1 Hamburg NJ U.S.A.
232 D3 Hamburg NY U.S.A.
234 C2 Hamburg PA U.S.A.
142 D2 Hamburgsund Sweden
158 E3 Hambye France
124 C4 Ḩamḑah Saudi Arabia
207 F3 Hamdallay Niger
124 C4 Ḩamdānah Saudi Arabia
233 G4 Hamden CT U.S.A.
199 E2 Hamdibey Turkey
128 B1 Hamdili Turkey
168 E1 Hamdorf Ger.
141 M3 Hämeenkangas moorland Fin.
138 E1 Hämeenkoski Etelä-Suomi Fin.
141 M3 Hämeenkoski Länsi-Suomi Fin.
141 M3 Hämeenkyrö Fin.
141 N3 Hämeenlinna Fin.
HaMelaḩ, Yam salt l. Asia see Dead Sea
168 E3 Hämelhausen Ger.
87 B5 Hamelin W.A. Austr.
87 B7 Hamelin, Cape W.A. Austr.
87 B5 Hamelin Pool b. W.A. Austr.
169 E3 Hameln Ger.
171 C3 Hamersleben Ger.
86 C4 Hamersley W.A. Austr.
87 C6 Hamersley Lakes salt flat W.A. Austr.
86 C4 Hamersley Range mts W.A. Austr.
170 C3 Hämerten Ger.
101 C5 Hamhŭng N. Korea
106 B3 Hami Xinjiang China
122 B4 Ḩamīd Iran
199 E1 Hamidiye Turkey
84 E4 Hamilton Qld Austr.
84 C5 Hamilton S.A. Austr.
231 □1 Hamilton Bermuda
224 E5 Hamilton Ont. Can.
Hamilton r. Nfld. Can. see Churchill
80 E2 Hamilton North I. N.Z.
146 D6 Hamilton South Lanarkshire, Scotland U.K.
231 C5 Hamilton AL U.S.A.
231 C5 Hamilton GA U.S.A.
226 B5 Hamilton IL U.S.A.
238 D2 Hamilton MT U.S.A.
235 D2 Hamilton NJ U.S.A.
233 F3 Hamilton NY U.S.A.
232 A5 Hamilton OH U.S.A.
237 D6 Hamilton TX U.S.A.
240 G3 Hamilton, Mount CA U.S.A.
241 J2 Hamilton, Mount NV U.S.A.
81 B6 Hamilton Burn South I. N.Z.
240 F2 Hamilton City CA U.S.A.
84 C4 Hamilton Downs N.T. Austr.
225 J2 Hamilton Inlet Nfld. Can.
233 F3 Hamilton Mountain hill NY U.S.A.
148 C3 Hamilton's Bawn Northern Ireland U.K.
141 N3 Hamina Fin.
116 D3 Hamirpur Hima. Prad. India
116 E4 Hamirpur Uttar Prad. India
Hamitabat Turkey see Isparta
231 E5 Hamlet NC U.S.A.
82 D3 Hamley Bridge S.A. Austr.
234 C1 Hamlin PA U.S.A.
237 C5 Hamlin TX U.S.A.
232 B5 Hamlin WV U.S.A.
169 C4 Hamm Nordrhein-Westfalen Ger.
172 C2 Hamm Rheinland-Pfalz Ger.
169 C5 Hamm (Sieg) Ger.
204 C3 Hammada du Drâa plat. Alg.
202 A2 Hammādat Tingharat des. Libya
168 E2 Hammah Ger.
127 F3 Ḩammām al 'Alīl Iraq
181 F5 Hammam Boughrara Alg.
189 C7 Hammamet Tunisia
205 H1 Hammamet, Golfe de g. Tunisia
189 C7 Hammam-Lif Tunisia
215 G1 Hammanskraal S. Africa
127 G5 Ḩammār, Hawr al imp. l. Iraq
141 L3 Hammarland Åland Fin.
215 H3 Hammarsdale S. Africa
140 L3 Hammarstrand Sweden
165 D3 Hamme Belgium
142 C3 Hammel Denmark
169 E5 Hammelburg Ger.
170 E2 Hammelspring Ger.
165 D4 Hamme-Mille Belgium
171 D5 Hammerbrücke Ger.
140 K3 Hammerdal Sweden
140 M1 Hammerfest Norway
151 F2 Hammerwich Staffordshire, England U.K.
169 B4 Hamminkeln Ger.
82 D3 Hammond S.A. Austr.
230 C3 Hammond IN U.S.A.
237 F6 Hammond LA U.S.A.
238 F2 Hammond MT U.S.A.
227 E3 Hammond Bay MI U.S.A.
232 E3 Hammondsport NY U.S.A.
234 D3 Hammonton NJ U.S.A.
146 □G1 Hamnavoe Shetland, Scotland U.K.
146 □G1 Hamnavoe Shetland, Scotland U.K.
146 □G1 Hamnavoe Shetland, Scotland U.K.
165 E4 Hamoir Belgium
165 E4 Hamois Belgium
165 E3 Hamont Belgium
234 C3 Hamorton PA U.S.A.
81 C6 Hampden South I. N.Z.
233 □I2 Hampden Highlands ME U.S.A.
232 D6 Hampden Sydney VA U.S.A.
114 C3 Hampi Karnataka India
140 M2 Håmpjåkk Sweden
157 G4 Hampont France
151 F4 Hampreston Dorset, England U.K.
151 F3 Hampshire admin. div. England U.K.
234 B3 Hampstead MD U.S.A.
225 H4 Hampton N.B. Can.
237 E5 Hampton AR U.S.A.
236 E3 Hampton IA U.S.A.
233 □H3 Hampton NH U.S.A.
234 D2 Hampton NJ U.S.A.
231 D5 Hampton SC U.S.A.
233 E6 Hampton VA U.S.A.
235 F2 Hampton Bays NY U.S.A.
87 E7 Hampton Tableland reg. W.A. Austr.
195 □ Hamrun Malta
238 E3 Hams Fork r. WY U.S.A.
157 G3 Ham-sous-Varsberg France
151 H3 Hamstreet Kent, England U.K.
165 D4 Ham-sur-Heure Belgium
97 D5 Ham Tân Vietnam
122 D5 Hāmūn-e Jaz Mūrīān salt marsh Iran
123 E4 Hāmūn Helmand salt flat Afgh./Iran
123 F4 Hamun-i-Lora dry lake Pak.
123 E4 Hamun-i-Mashkel salt flat Pak.
127 F3 Hamur Turkey
105 F3 Hamura Japan
Hamwic Southampton, England U.K. see Southampton
Hamza Uzbek. see Khamza
128 A1 Hamzalar Turkey
176 G2 Haná r. Czech Rep.
240 □C8 Hana HI U.S.A.
246 B2 Hanábana r. Cuba
129 C3 Hanak Turkey
Hanakpınar Turkey see Çınar
124 B2 Ḩanalc Saudi Arabia
240 □B7 Hanalei HI U.S.A.
102 J4 Hanamaki Japan
240 □B8 Hanamaulu HI U.S.A.
211 B6 Hanang mt. Tanz.
Hananui hill Stewart I. N.Z. see Anglem, Mount
240 □B8 Hanapepe HI U.S.A.
169 D5 Hanau Ger.
Hânceşti Moldova see Hînceşti
107 F5 Hancheng Shaanxi China
156 B4 Hanches France
109 E2 Hanchuan Hubei China
232 D5 Hancock MD U.S.A.
226 C2 Hancock MI U.S.A.
233 F4 Hancock NY U.S.A.
234 C3 Hancocks Bridge NJ U.S.A.
104 C4 Handa Japan
146 C3 Handa Island Scotland U.K.
107 G4 Handan Hebei China
168 E2 Handeloh Ger.
211 C6 Handeni Tanz.
168 E1 Handewitt Ger.
Handian Shanxi China see Changzhi
177 H3 Handlová Slovakia
168 F2 Handorf Ger.
168 C3 Handrup Ger.
105 F3 Haneda airport Japan
HaNegev des. Israel see Negev
168 E1 Hanerau-Hademarschen Ger.
Hanfeng Chongqing China see Kaixian
240 H3 Hanford CA U.S.A.
114 B3 Hangal Karnataka India
101 C5 Han-gang r. S. Korea
106 C1 Hangayn Nuruu mts Mongolia
Hangchow Zhejiang China see Hangzhou
Hangchuan Fujian China see Guangze
171 E3 Hangelsberg Ger.
Hanggin Houqi Nei Mongol China see Xamba
Hanggin Qi Nei Mongol China see Xin
Hangö Fin. see Hanko
107 H4 Hangu Tianjin China
123 G3 Hangu Pak.
109 G2 Hangzhou Zhejiang China
109 G2 Hangzhou Wan b. China
150 E3 Hanham South Gloucestershire, England U.K.
127 F3 Hani Turkey
125 E2 Ḩanīdh Saudi Arabia
199 F1 Hanife r. Turkey
177 K3 Haniska Slovakia
Hanjia Chongqing China see Pengshui
Hanjiang Jiangsu China see Yangzhou
109 F4 Han Jiang r. China
106 E4 Hanjiaoshui Ningxia China
140 N3 Hankasalmi Fin.
168 F3 Hankensbüttel Ger.
215 E5 Hankey S. Africa
141 M4 Hanko Fin.
199 G2 Hanköy Turkey
241 L2 Hanksville UT U.S.A.
116 D2 Hanle Jammu and Kashmir
223 J5 Hanley Sask. Can.
150 E2 Hanley Castle Worcestershire, England U.K.
81 D5 Hanmer Springs South I. N.Z.
85 F2 Hann r. Qld Austr.
86 E3 Hann r. W.A. Austr.
86 E2 Hann, Mount hill W.A. Austr.
223 I5 Hanna Alta Can.
175 L4 Hanna Pol.
241 M5 Hannagan Meadow AZ U.S.A.
236 F4 Hannibal MO U.S.A.
232 E3 Hannibal NY U.S.A.
232 C5 Hannibal OH U.S.A.
137 G3 Hannivka Ukr.
105 F3 Hannō Japan
157 F3 Hannonville-sous-les-Côtes France
169 E3 Hannover Ger.
169 E3 Hannover admin. reg. Niedersachsen Ger.
169 E4 Hannoversch Münden Ger.
84 C4 Hann Range mts N.T. Austr.
165 E4 Hannut Belgium
143 F4 Hanöbukten b. Sweden
Hanoi Vietnam see Ha Nôi
96 D2 Ha Nôi Vietnam
224 D4 Hanover Ont. Can.
Hanover Ger. see Hannover
246 □ Hanover parish Jamaica
214 E4 Hanover S. Africa
235 F1 Hanover CT U.S.A.
233 G3 Hanover NH U.S.A.
232 B4 Hanover OH U.S.A.
234 B3 Hanover PA U.S.A.
232 E6 Hanover VA U.S.A.
259 B8 Hanover, Isla i. Chile
234 B2 Hanoverdale PA U.S.A.
214 E4 Hanover Road S. Africa
176 G4 Hanság hill Hungary
165 C3 Hansbeke Belgium
263 D2 Hansen Mountains Antarctica
170 C2 Hanshagen Ger.
109 D2 Hanshou Hunan China
109 E2 Han Shui r. China
116 D3 Hansi Haryana India
151 G2 Hanslope Milton Keynes, England U.K.
140 L1 Hansnes Norway
82 D2 Hanson, Lake salt flat S.A. Austr.
232 B6 Hansonville VA U.S.A.
168 F2 Hanstedt Niedersachsen Ger.
168 F2 Hanstedt Niedersachsen Ger.
142 C3 Hanstholm Denmark
107 H2 Han Sum Nei Mongol China
157 G4 Han-sur-Nied France
Hantengri Feng mt. Kazakh./Kyrg. see Khan-Tengri, Pik
177 H5 Hantos Hungary
138 F5 Hantsavichy Belarus
116 E4 Hanumana Madh. Prad. India
116 C3 Hanumangarh Rajasthan India
177 K2 Hanušovce nad Topľou Slovakia
176 F1 Hanušovice Czech Rep.
106 D1 Hanuy Gol r. Mongolia
158 B3 Hanvec France
83 F3 Hanwwod N.S.W. Austr.
Hanyang Hubei China see Caidian
108 D1 Hanyin Shaanxi China
105 F2 Hanyū Japan
Hanyuan Gansu China see Xihe
108 B2 Hanyuan Sichuan China
108 C1 Hanzhong Shaanxi China
79 □3 Hao atoll Arch. des Tuamotu Fr. Polynesia
Haomen Qinghai China see Menyuan
117 G5 Haora W. Bengal India
185 E5 Haouz, Jebel el hill Morocco
140 N2 Haparanda Sweden
165 E3 Hapert Neth.
117 H4 Hapoli Arun. Prad. India
173 F2 Happburg Ger.
151 I2 Happisburgh Norfolk, England U.K.
241 L4 Happy Jack AZ U.S.A.
225 I2 Happy Valley - Goose Bay Nfld. Can.
164 E3 Haps Neth.
101 D4 Hapsu N. Korea
116 D3 Hapur Uttar Prad. India
126 D5 Ḩaql Saudi Arabia
210 D2 Hara Alol mt. Djibouti
124 C4 Ḩaraḑ Yemen
128 B5 Ḩarad, Jabal al mt. Jordan
124 D3 Ḩaradah Saudi Arabia
125 E2 Ḩaraḑh Saudi Arabia
138 G4 Haradok Belarus
138 G4 Haradotskaye Wzvyshsha hills Belarus
140 M2 Harads Sweden
138 F5 Haradzishcha Belarus
138 F5 Haradzyeya Belarus
117 E4 Haraiya Uttar Prad. India
124 C4 Ḩarajā Saudi Arabia
102 J5 Haramachi Japan
116 C2 Haramukh mt. Jammu and Kashmir
Haran Turkey see Harran
138 G4 Harany Belarus
123 H4 Harappa Road Pak.
213 F3 Harare Zimbabwe
215 E3 Ha Rasebi S. Africa
125 F4 Ḩarāsīs, Jiddat al des. Oman
175 K5 Harasiuki Pol.
122 C4 Harāt Iran
208 D2 Haraze-Mangueigne Chad
169 E4 Harbarnsen Ger.
206 C5 Harbel Liberia
100 C3 Harbin Heilong. China
171 C3 Harbke Ger.
151 I3 Harbledown Kent, England U.K.
123 F4 Harboi Hills Pak.
156 C3 Harbonnières France
227 F4 Harbor Beach MI U.S.A.
226 E3 Harbor Springs MI U.S.A.
225 K4 Harbour Breton Nfld. Can.
173 E3 Harburg (Schwaben) Ger.
151 F2 Harbury Warwickshire, England U.K.
241 K5 Harcuvar Mountains AZ U.S.A.
178 A3 Hard Austria
125 E4 Ḩarḑah, Wādī r. Yemen
116 D5 Harda Khas Madh. Prad. India
142 B1 Hardanger reg. Norway
142 A2 Hardangerfjorden sea chan. Norway
212 C5 Hardap admin. reg. Namibia
212 C5 Hardap Dam Namibia
141 I3 Hardbakke Norway
231 D5 Hardeeville SC U.S.A.
179 G2 Hardegg Austria
169 E4 Hardegsen Ger.
156 B2 Hardelot-Plage France
95 F1 Harden, Bukit mt. Indon.
164 F2 Hardenberg Neth.
164 E2 Harderwijk Neth.
87 C4 Hardey r. W.A. Austr.
172 D2 Hardheim Ger.
236 F4 Hardin IL U.S.A.
238 F2 Hardin MT U.S.A.
86 C4 Harding r. W.A. Austr.
215 G4 Harding S. Africa
234 D3 Harding Lakes NJ U.S.A.
87 C5 Harding Range hills W.A. Austr.
151 G2 Hardingstone Northamptonshire, England U.K.
164 D3 Hardinxveld-Giessendam Neth.
223 I4 Hardisty Alta Can.
116 E4 Hardoi Uttar Prad. India
172 C3 Hardt Ger.
Hardwar Uttar Prad. India see Haridwar
231 D5 Hardwick GA U.S.A.
233 G2 Hardwick VT U.S.A.
234 C1 Hardwood Ridge PA U.S.A.
237 F4 Hardy AR U.S.A.
Hardy, Mount North I. N.Z. see Rangipoua
225 K3 Hare Bay Nfld. Can.
151 G3 Harefield Greater London, England U.K.
149 F2 Hare Hill hill Scotland U.K.
140 I3 Hareid Norway
165 C4 Harelbeke Belgium
164 F1 Haren Neth.
168 C3 Haren (Ems) Ger.
210 D2 Härer Eth.
151 H3 Hare Street Hertfordshire, England U.K.
149 H4 Harewood West Yorkshire, England U.K.
128 B3 Harf el Mreffi mt. Lebanon
159 G2 Harfleur France
234 B3 Harford County county MD U.S.A.
107 H1 Hargant Nei Mongol China
Hargeisa Somalia see Hargeysa
172 B2 Hargesheim Ger.
210 E2 Hargeysa Somalia
197 G2 Harghita, Munţii mts Romania
197 G2 Harghita-Mădăraş, Vârful mt. Romania
203 H6 Hargigo Eritrea
165 E4 Hargimont Belgium
157 E2 Hargnies France
106 C4 Har Hu l. Qinghai China
216 □3c Haría Lanzarote Canary Is
124 D5 Ḩarīb Yemen
116 D3 Haridwar Uttar Prad. India
128 B4 Harif, Har mt. Israel
114 B3 Harihar Karnataka India
81 C5 Harihari South I. N.Z.
114 B3 Hariharpur Karnataka India
116 B5 Harij Gujarat India
138 D2 Hari kurk sea chan. Estonia
128 C1 Ḩārim Syria
104 A4 Harima-nada b. Japan
117 G5 Haringhat r. Bangl.
164 D3 Haringvliet est. Neth.
104 D2 Harinoki-dake mt. Japan
114 C4 Haripad Kerala India
123 H3 Haripur Pak.
128 C3 Ḩarīr, Wādī adh r. Syria
123 E2 Hari Rūd r. Afgh./Iran
141 K3 Härjåsjön Sweden
141 M3 Harjavalta Fin.
141 K3 Härjedalen reg. Sweden
176 F4 Harka Hungary
177 I5 Harkakötöny Hungary
140 K3 Hårkan r. Sweden
177 H6 Harkány Hungary
236 E3 Harlan IA U.S.A.
232 B6 Harlan KY U.S.A.
197 H2 Hârlău Romania
150 C2 Harlech Gwynedd, Wales U.K.
238 E1 Harlem MT U.S.A.
151 I2 Harleston Norfolk, England U.K.
234 C2 Harleysville PA U.S.A.
164 E1 Harlingen Neth.
237 D7 Harlingen TX U.S.A.
151 G3 Harlington Bedfordshire, England U.K.
151 H3 Harlow Essex, England U.K.
238 E2 Harlowton MT U.S.A.
156 D3 Harly France
232 D5 Harman WV U.S.A.
199 F2 Harmancık Turkey
199 F3 Harmanlı Turkey
179 H2 Harmannsdorf Austria
234 B3 Harmans MD U.S.A.
164 D2 Harmelen Neth.
233 □I2 Harmony ME U.S.A.
226 A4 Harmony MN U.S.A.
234 C2 Harmony NJ U.S.A.
168 F1 Harmsdorf Schleswig-Holstein Ger.
168 F2 Harmsdorf Schleswig-Holstein Ger.
114 C3 Harnahalli Karnataka India
114 B2 Harnai Mahar. India
123 F4 Harnai Pak.
156 C2 Harnes France
238 C3 Harney Basin OR U.S.A.
140 L3 Härnösand Sweden
106 B1 Har Nuur l. Mongolia
183 H2 Haro Spain
232 B6 Harold KY U.S.A.
146 □H1 Haroldswick Shetland, Scotland U.K.
157 G4 Haroué France
114 B3 Harpanahalli Karnataka India
151 G3 Harpenden Hertfordshire, England U.K.
206 D5 Harper Liberia
237 D4 Harper KS U.S.A.
222 H3 Harper Creek r. Alta Can.
232 E5 Harpers Ferry WV U.S.A.
151 G2 Harpole Northamptonshire, England U.K.
168 D3 Harpstedt Ger.
Harqin Qi Nei Mongol China see Jinshan
Harqin Zuoqi Mongolzu Zizhixian Liaoning China see Dachengzi
241 K5 Harquahala Mountains AZ U.S.A.
116 D5 Harrai Madh. Prad. India
128 D1 Harran Turkey
124 C3 Ḩarrāt Kishb lava field Saudi Arabia
146 E2 Harray, Loch of l. Scotland U.K.
224 E3 Harricanaw r. Ont./Que. Can.
146 E5 Harrietfield Perth and Kinross, Scotland U.K.
151 H3 Harrietsham Kent, England U.K.
235 D1 Harriman NY U.S.A.
83 H2 Harrington N.S.W. Austr.
234 C4 Harrington DE U.S.A.
233 □J2 Harrington ME U.S.A.
225 J3 Harrington Harbour Que. Can.
146 B4 Harris reg. Scotland U.K.
82 C2 Harris, Lake salt flat S.A. Austr.
84 B5 Harris, Mount N.T. Austr.
146 A4 Harris, Sound of sea chan. Scotland U.K.
215 F2 Harrisburg S. Africa
237 F5 Harrisburg AR U.S.A.
237 F4 Harrisburg IL U.S.A.
236 C3 Harrisburg NE U.S.A.
232 B5 Harrisburg OH U.S.A.
227 I5 Harrisburg PA U.S.A.
168 E1 Harrislee Ger.
87 C7 Harrismith W.A. Austr.
215 G3 Harrismith S. Africa
81 B6 Harris Mountains South I. N.Z.
237 E4 Harrison AR U.S.A.
226 E3 Harrison MI U.S.A.
236 C3 Harrison NE U.S.A.
235 E2 Harrison NY U.S.A.
237 F6 Harrisonburg LA U.S.A.
232 D5 Harrisonburg VA U.S.A.
234 B3 Harrisonville MD U.S.A.
236 E4 Harrisonville MO U.S.A.
227 G4 Harriston Ont. Can.
227 F3 Harrisville MI U.S.A.
233 F2 Harrisville NY U.S.A.
232 C5 Harrisville WV U.S.A.
Harrodsville North I. N.Z. see Otorohanga
149 H4 Harrogate North Yorkshire, England U.K.
232 B6 Harrogate TN U.S.A.
227 I3 Harrowsmith Ont. Can.
141 K3 Harsa Sweden
106 C5 Har Sai Shan mt. Qinghai China
177 J4 Harsány Hungary
168 E2 Harsefeld Ger.
197 G3 Hârseşti Romania
169 D4 Harsewinkel Ger.
122 A3 Harsīn Iran
126 E2 Harşit r. Turkey
171 C4 Harsleben Ger.
197 H3 Hârşova Romania
140 L2 Harsprånget Sweden
140 L1 Harstad Norway
151 H2 Harston Cambridgeshire, England U.K.
116 D5 Harsud Madh. Prad. India
169 E3 Harsum Ger.
220 E3 Hart r. Y.T. Can.
226 D4 Hart MI U.S.A.
82 D2 Hart, Lake salt flat S.A. Austr.
86 E3 Hart, Mount hill W.A. Austr.
177 I5 Harta Hungary
107 I3 Hartao Liaoning China
215 F2 Hartbeesfontein S. Africa
215 F1 Hartbeespoort S. Africa
179 G3 Hartberg Austria
142 B1 Harteigan mt. Norway
168 F2 Hartenholm Ger.
156 D3 Hartennes-et-Taux France
171 D5 Hartenstein Ger.
149 G3 Harter Fell hill England U.K.
151 H3 Hartfield East Sussex, England U.K.
206 C5 Hartford Liberia
233 G4 Hartford CT U.S.A.
230 C4 Hartford KY U.S.A.
226 D4 Hartford MI U.S.A.
236 D3 Hartford SD U.S.A.
226 C4 Hartford WI U.S.A.
230 C3 Hartford City IN U.S.A.
171 D4 Hartha Ger.
172 C2 Harthausen Ger.
172 B4 Hartheim Ger.
149 F2 Harthill North Lanarkshire, Scotland U.K.
197 G3 Hârtibaciu r. Romania
178 C3 Hart im Zillertal Austria
236 D3 Hartington NE U.S.A.
179 E2 Hartkirchen Austria
225 H4 Hartland N.B. Can.
150 C4 Hartland Devon, England U.K.
233 □I2 Hartland ME U.S.A.
150 C3 Hartland Point England U.K.
150 E2 Hartlebury Worcestershire, England U.K.
149 H3 Hartlepool Hartlepool, England U.K.
149 H3 Hartlepool admin. div. England U.K.
234 A2 Hartleton PA U.S.A.
151 H3 Hartley Kent, England U.K.
237 C5 Hartley TX U.S.A.
Hartley Zimbabwe see Chegutu
222 D4 Hartley Bay B.C. Can.
151 G3 Hartley Wintney Hampshire, England U.K.
234 C3 Hartly DE U.S.A.
173 H2 Hartmanice Czech Rep.
171 C5 Hartmannsdorf Ger.
141 N3 Hartola Fin.
214 E3 Harts r. S. Africa
235 E1 Hartsdale NY U.S.A.
231 C5 Hartselle AL U.S.A.
173 E3 Härtsfeld hills Ger.
151 F2 Hartshill Warwickshire, England U.K.
151 F2 Hartshorne Derbyshire, England U.K.
237 E5 Hartshorne OK U.S.A.
84 C4 Harts Range N.T. Austr.
84 C4 Harts Range mts N.T. Austr.
231 D5 Hartsville SC U.S.A.
231 C4 Hartsville TN U.S.A.
215 E2 Hartswater S. Africa
237 E4 Hartville MO U.S.A.
232 C4 Hartville OH U.S.A.
151 G2 Hartwell Northamptonshire, England U.K.
231 D5 Hartwell GA U.S.A.
231 D5 Hartwell Reservoir Georgia/S. Carolina U.S.A.
114 C3 Harur Tamil Nadu India
106 B2 Har Us Nuur l. Mongolia
106 B1 Har Us Nuur salt l. Mongolia
106 E1 Haruuhin Gol r. Mongolia
226 C4 Harvard IL U.S.A.
239 F4 Harvard, Mount CO U.S.A.
87 B7 Harvey W.A. Austr.
225 H4 Harvey N.B. Can.
226 D2 Harvey MI U.S.A.
236 C2 Harvey ND U.S.A.
234 B1 Harveys Lake PA U.S.A.
151 F2 Harvington Worcestershire, England U.K.
151 F3 Harwell Oxfordshire, England U.K.
151 I3 Harwich Essex, England U.K.
233 H4 Harwich Port MA U.S.A.
235 E1 Harwington CT U.S.A.
83 H2 Harwood N.S.W. Austr.
149 H4 Harworth Nottinghamshire, England U.K.
116 D3 Haryana state India
136 D1 Haryn' r. Belarus
Haryn' r. Ukr. see Horyn'
169 F4 Harz hills Ger.
171 C4 Harzgerode Ger.
129 B3 Hasan Dağı mt. Turkey
126 D3 Hasan Dağı mts Turkey
Hasan Guli Turkm. see Esenguly
127 F3 Hasankeyf Turkey
122 D5 Ḩasan Langī Iran
114 C2 Hasanparti Andhra Prad. India
199 F3 Hasanpaşa Burdur Turkey
122 A2 Ḩasan Sālārān Iran
114 C4 Hasanur Tamil Nadu India
128 B3 Hasbaïya Lebanon
126 D4 Hasbani r. Lebanon
126 D3 Hasbek Turkey
169 C3 Hasbergen Ger.
146 □H1 Hascosay i. Scotland U.K.
116 E5 Hasdo r. Madh. Prad. India
169 C3 Hase r. Ger.

Heyin to Hornád
313

Heyin Qinghai China see Guide
171 E4 Heynitz Ger.
160 D3 Heyrieux France
149 G3 Heysham Lancashire, England U.K.
215 H2 Heyshope Dam S. Africa
165 E3 Heythuysen Neth.
109 E4 Heyuan Guangdong China
82 E4 Heywood Vic. Austr.
149 G4 Heywood Greater Manchester, England U.K.
226 C5 Heyworth IL U.S.A.
107 G5 Heze Shandong China
108 C3 Hezhang Guizhou China
106 D5 Hezheng Gansu China
106 D5 Hezuozhen Gansu China
231 D7 Hialeah FL U.S.A.
Hiau i. Fr. Polynesia see Eiao
231 D5 Hiawassee GA U.S.A.
236 E4 Hiawatha KS U.S.A.
149 I4 Hibaldstow North Lincolnshire, England U.K.
215 H4 Hibberdene S. Africa
226 A2 Hibbing MN U.S.A.
83 F5 Hibbs, Point Tas. Austr.
86 D2 Hibernia Reef Ashmore & Cartier Is Austr.
237 F4 Hickman KY U.S.A.
231 D5 Hickory NC U.S.A.
234 C3 Hickory Hill PA U.S.A.
80 G2 Hicks Bay North I. N.Z.
235 E2 Hicksville NY U.S.A.
232 A4 Hicksville OH U.S.A.
237 D5 Hico TX U.S.A.
104 D3 Hida-gawa r. Japan
104 B5 Hidaka-gawa r. Japan
102 K2 Hidaka-sanmyaku mts Japan
104 C2 Hida-kōchi plat. Japan
243 F3 Hidalgo Coahuila Mex.
244 B1 Hidalgo Durango Mex.
245 E1 Hidalgo Tamaulipas Mex.
245 E3 Hidalgo state Mex.
242 D3 Hidalgo del Parral Mex.
177 H5 Hidas Hungary
104 D2 Hida-sanmyaku mts Japan
177 K3 Hidasnémeti Hungary
169 D3 Hiddenhausen Ger.
170 E1 Hiddensee Ger.
170 E1 Hiddensee i. Ger.
85 F3 Hidden Valley Qld Austr.
128 B1 Hıdırlı Turkey
197 F2 Hidişelu de Sus Romania
142 B2 Hidra i. Norway
256 C2 Hidrolândia Brazil
254 C5 Hidrolina Brazil
179 F3 Hieflau Austria
183 H3 Hiendelaencina Spain
78 □5 Hienghène New Caledonia
159 F4 Hière r. France
Hierosolyma Israel/West Bank see Jerusalem
183 G4 Hierro, Cabeza de mt. Spain
162 B3 Hiersac France
103 F6 Higashi-Hiroshima Japan
105 F2 Higashi-matsuyama Japan
105 F3 Higashimurayama Japan
102 J4 Higashine Japan
104 B4 Higashi-ōsaka Japan
103 D7 Higashi-suidō sea chan. Japan
105 D2 Higashi-yama mt. Japan
235 F1 Higganum CT U.S.A.
237 C4 Higgins TX U.S.A.
233 F3 Higgins Bay NY U.S.A.
214 D3 Higg's Hope S. Africa
151 H3 Higham Kent, England U.K.
151 G2 Higham Ferrers Northamptonshire, England U.K.
150 C4 Highampton Devon, England U.K.
High Atlas mts Morocco see Haut Atlas
149 G3 High Bentham North Yorkshire, England U.K.
146 D6 High Blantyre South Lanarkshire, Scotland U.K.
150 E3 Highbridge Somerset, England U.K.
234 D2 High Bridge NJ U.S.A.
151 F3 Highclere Hampshire, England U.K.
238 B3 High Desert OR U.S.A.
149 H3 High Etherley Durham, England U.K.
215 H4 Highflats S. Africa
151 H3 High Garrett Essex, England U.K.
246 □ Highgate Jamaica
151 H3 High Halden Kent, England U.K.
149 I3 High Hawsker North Yorkshire, England U.K.
149 G3 High Hesket Cumbria, England U.K.
237 E6 High Island TX U.S.A.
146 D4 Highland admin. div. Scotland U.K.
240 I4 Highland CA U.S.A.
234 B3 Highland MD U.S.A.
226 B2 Highland MN U.S.A.
235 E1 Highland NY U.S.A.
226 B4 Highland WI U.S.A.
234 B4 Highland Beach MD U.S.A.
235 E1 Highland Falls NY U.S.A.
234 D1 Highland Lake NY U.S.A.
235 D1 Highland Lakes NJ U.S.A.
226 D4 Highland Park IL U.S.A.
232 B3 Highland Park MI U.S.A.
235 D2 Highland Park NJ U.S.A.
240 H2 Highland Peak CA U.S.A.
241 J3 Highland Peak NV U.S.A.
235 E2 Highlands NJ U.S.A.
232 E6 Highland Springs VA U.S.A.
149 G4 High Legh Cheshire, England U.K.
222 G3 High Level Alta Can.
150 E2 Highley Shropshire, England U.K.
149 F3 High Lorton Cumbria, England U.K.
236 D2 Highmore SD U.S.A.
150 E3 Highnam Gloucestershire, England U.K.
149 H4 High Peak hill England U.K.
231 E5 High Point NC U.S.A.
234 D1 High Point hill NJ U.S.A.
222 G4 High Prairie Alta Can.
222 H5 High River Alta Can.
231 E7 High Rock Bahamas
83 F5 High Rocky Point Tas. Austr.
149 G3 High Seat hill England U.K.
231 D6 High Springs FL U.S.A.
High Tatras mts Pol./Slovakia see Tatry
235 D2 Hightstown NJ U.S.A.
151 F3 Highworth Swindon, England U.K.
151 G3 High Wycombe Buckinghamshire, England U.K.
242 D3 Higuera de Abuya Mex.
185 G3 Higuera de Arjona Spain
184 E2 Higuera de la Serena Spain
184 D3 Higuera de la Sierra Spain
184 D2 Higuera de Vargas Spain
184 D2 Higuera la Real Spain
247 □1 Higüero, Punta pt Puerto Rico
187 B6 Higueruela Spain
187 C5 Higueruelas Spain
247 E3 Higüey Dom. Rep.
105 F3 Higuri-gawa r. Japan
77 I3 Hihifo Tonga
210 E3 Hiiraan admin. reg. Somalia
138 D2 Hiiumaa i. Estonia
186 C3 Híjar Spain
94 C3 Hijau, Gunung mt. Indon.
124 B2 Hijaz reg. Saudi Arabia
105 E3 Hijiri-dake mt. Japan
92 C5 Hijo Phil.
183 H1 Hijuela r. Spain
105 E2 Hikabo-yama mt. Japan
103 E7 Hikari Japan
104 B5 Hiki-gawa r. Japan
241 J3 Hiko NV U.S.A.
104 C3 Hikone Japan
103 E7 Hiko-san mt. Japan
80 E1 Hikurangi North I. N.Z.
80 G2 Hikurangi mt. North I. N.Z.
129 F3 Hil Azer.
263 K1 Hilary Coast Antarctica
171 E5 Hilbersdorf Ger.
169 D5 Hilchenbach Ger.
241 K3 Hildale UT U.S.A.
169 F5 Hildburghausen Ger.
169 B4 Hilden Ger.
151 H3 Hildenborough Kent, England U.K.
169 F5 Hilders Ger.
149 I3 Hilderthorpe East Riding of Yorkshire, England U.K.
169 E3 Hildesheim Ger.
151 H2 Hilgay Norfolk, England U.K.
168 E3 Hilgermissen Ger.
173 F3 Hilgertshausen Ger.
117 G4 Hili Bangl.
168 C3 Hilkenbrook Ger.
87 B6 Hill r. W.A. Austr.
247 □4 Hillaby, Mount hill Barbados
Hillah Iraq see Al Ḩillah
214 C5 Hillandale S. Africa
232 B4 Hillard OH U.S.A.
236 D4 Hill City KS U.S.A.
236 C3 Hill City SD U.S.A.
241 M2 Hill Creek r. UT U.S.A.
234 B4 Hillcrest Heights MD U.S.A.
169 D3 Hille Ger.
164 D2 Hillegom Neth.
83 G3 Hill End N.S.W. Austr.
142 E4 Hillerød Denmark
81 D4 Hillersden South I. N.Z.
169 F3 Hillerse Ger.
143 E3 Hillerstorp Sweden
169 B5 Hillesheim Ger.
85 F3 Hillgrove Qld Austr.
227 F3 Hillman MI U.S.A.
87 C6 Hillman, Lake salt flat W.A. Austr.
236 F4 Hillsboro IL U.S.A.
236 F4 Hillsboro MO U.S.A.
236 D2 Hillsboro ND U.S.A.
233 H3 Hillsboro NH U.S.A.
239 F5 Hillsboro NM U.S.A.
232 B5 Hillsboro OH U.S.A.
238 B2 Hillsboro OR U.S.A.
237 D5 Hillsboro TX U.S.A.
226 B4 Hillsboro WI U.S.A.
247 □3 Hillsborough Grenada
147 E2 Hillsborough Northern Ireland U.K.
231 E4 Hillsborough NC U.S.A.
85 G4 Hillsborough, Cape Qld Austr.
169 C5 Hillscheid Ger.
226 E5 Hillsdale MI U.S.A.
233 G3 Hillsdale NY U.S.A.
227 I5 Hillsgrove PA U.S.A.
86 C4 Hillside W.A. Austr.
146 F5 Hillside Angus, Scotland U.K.
146 □G1 Hillside Shetland, Scotland U.K.
235 D2 Hillside NJ U.S.A.
224 C3 Hillsport Ont. Can.
83 F3 Hillston N.S.W. Austr.
232 C6 Hillsville VA U.S.A.
146 □G1 Hillswick Shetland, Scotland U.K.
147 E2 Hilltown Northern Ireland U.K.
240 □D9 Hilo HI U.S.A.
150 E3 Hilperton Wiltshire, England U.K.
173 F2 Hilpoltstein Ger.
157 H4 Hilsenheim France
169 D3 Hilter am Teutoburger Wald Ger.
84 D4 Hilton Qld Austr.
215 H3 Hilton S. Africa
151 F2 Hilton Derbyshire, England U.K.
232 E3 Hilton NY U.S.A.
227 F2 Hilton Beach Ont. Can.
231 D5 Hilton Head Island SC U.S.A.
173 F2 Hiltpoltstein Ger.
126 E3 Hilvan Turkey
164 E3 Hilvarenbeek Neth.
164 E2 Hilversum Neth.
172 C4 Hilzingen Ger.
116 D3 Himachal Pradesh state India
124 C2 Ḩimā Ḑarīyah, Jabal mt. Saudi Arabia
116 D2 Himalaya mts Asia
140 M2 Himanka Fin.
198 A1 Himarë Albania
80 E4 Himatangi North I. N.Z.
80 E4 Himatangi Beach North I. N.Z.
116 C5 Himatnagar Gujarat India
179 H2 Himberg Austria
168 F2 Himbergen Ger.
105 D1 Hime-gawa r. Japan
103 G6 Himeji Japan
102 J4 Himekami-dake mt. Japan
177 H5 Himesháza Hungary
215 G3 Himeville S. Africa
104 C2 Himi Japan
113 □1 Himmafushi i. N. Male Maldives
179 F4 Himmelberg Austria
142 C3 Himmelbjerget hill Denmark
168 E2 Himmelpforten Ger.
124 B5 Himora Eth.
128 C2 Ḩimş Syria
128 D2 Ḩimş governorate Syria
81 E4 Hinakura North I. N.Z.
92 C4 Hinatuan Phil.
136 E4 Hînceşti Moldova
246 D3 Hinche Haiti
85 F3 Hinchinbrook Island Qld Austr.
151 F2 Hinckley Leicestershire, England U.K.
226 C5 Hinckley IL U.S.A.
233 □I2 Hinckley ME U.S.A.
226 A2 Hinckley MN U.S.A.
241 K2 Hinckley UT U.S.A.
209 B6 Hinda Congo
111 B6 Hindan r. India
129 E3 Hindarx Azer.
116 D4 Hindaun Rajasthan India
173 E4 Hindelang Ger.
170 C3 Hindenburg Ger.
Hindenburg Pol. see Zabrze
149 I3 Hinderwell North Yorkshire, England U.K.
151 G3 Hindhead Surrey, England U.K.
149 G4 Hindley Greater Manchester, England U.K.
232 B6 Hindman KY U.S.A.
83 E4 Hindmarsh, Lake dry lake Vic. Austr.
117 F5 Hindola Orissa India
116 C4 Hindoli Rajasthan India
150 E3 Hindon Wiltshire, England U.K.
116 D5 Hindoria Madh. Prad. India
114 C3 Hindri r. India
81 C6 Hinds South I. N.Z.
142 D4 Hindsholm pen. Denmark
123 F3 Hindu Kush mts Afgh./Pak.
114 C3 Hindupur Andhra Prad. India
222 G3 Hines Creek Alta Can.
231 D6 Hinesville GA U.S.A.
116 D5 Hinganghat Mahar. India
151 H2 Hingham Norfolk, England U.K.
123 F5 Hingol r. Pak.
Hingol r. Pak. see Girdar Dhor
127 F3 Hınıs Turkey
234 B2 Hinkletown PA U.S.A.
140 □ Hinlopenstretet str. Svalbard
140 K1 Hinnøya i. Norway
105 F3 Hino Japan
92 B4 Hinobaan Phil.
104 C2 Hino-gawa r. Japan
104 C3 Hino-gawa r. Japan
182 D5 Hinojal Spain
184 D2 Hinojales Spain
185 H3 Hinojares Spain
185 F2 Hinojasas de Calatrava Spain
183 H3 Hinojedo mt. Spain
261 G5 Hinojo Arg.
184 D3 Hinojos Spain
183 I3 Hinojosa Spain
182 D4 Hinojosa de Duero Spain
186 C4 Hinojosa de Jarque Spain
185 E2 Hinojosa del Duque Spain
180 D2 Hinojosa de San Vicente Spain
233 G3 Hinsdale NH U.S.A.
168 C2 Hinte Ger.
178 C3 Hinteres Sonnenwendjoch mt. Austria
171 F5 Hinterhermsdorf Ger.
169 F5 Hinternah Ger.
190 E2 Hinterrhein Switz.
190 E2 Hinterrhein r. Switz.
173 H3 Hinterschmiding Ger.
170 F2 Hintersee Ger.
172 B2 Hinterweidenthal Ger.
172 C4 Hinterzarten Ger.
Hinthada Myanmar see Henzada
220 G4 Hinton Alta Can.
237 D5 Hinton OK U.S.A.
232 C6 Hinton WV U.S.A.
80 E2 Hinuera North I. N.Z.
190 D1 Hinwil Switz.
163 B5 Hinx France
Hiort i. Western Isles, Scotland U.K. see Hirta
178 C3 Hippach Austria
164 D2 Hippolytushoef Neth.
Hipponium Italy see Vibo Valentia
Hippo Regius Alg. see Annaba
Hippo Zarytus Tunisia see Bizerte
168 D2 Hipstedt Ger.
127 G3 Hirabit Dağ mt. Turkey
103 D7 Hirado Japan
150 D1 Hiraethog, Mynydd hills Wales U.K.
105 F1 Hiraga-take mt. Japan
104 B4 Hirakata Japan
117 E5 Hirakud Reservoir India
102 □1 Hirara Japan
103 F6 Hirata Japan
105 F3 Hiratsuka Japan
114 B3 Hirekerur Karnataka India
206 D5 Hiré-Watta Côte d'Ivoire
114 C3 Hiriyur Karnataka India
Hîrlău Romania see Hârlău
210 D2 Hīrna Eth.
137 I3 Hirnyk Donets'ka Oblast' Ukr.
175 M5 Hirnyk L'vivs'ka Oblast' Ukr.
102 J3 Hirosaki Japan
103 F6 Hiroshima Japan
103 F6 Hiroshima airport Japan
103 F6 Hiroshima pref. Japan
172 C3 Hirrlingen Ger.
173 F2 Hirschaid Ger.
173 F2 Hirschau Ger.
171 C5 Hirschberg Ger.
173 F4 Hirschberg mt. Ger.
Hirschberg Pol. see Jelenia Góra
173 G3 Hirschenstn mt. Ger.
171 E4 Hirschfeld Ger.
171 F5 Hirschfelde Ger.
172 C2 Hirschhorn (Neckar) Ger.
160 F1 Hirsingue France
137 H4 Hirsivka Ukr.
137 J3 Hirs'ke Ukr.
136 F3 Hirs'kyy Tikych r. Ukr.
156 E3 Hirson France
Hîrşova Romania see Hârşova
146 □ Hirta i. Western Isles, Scotland U.K.
179 H3 Hirtenberg Austria
142 C3 Hirtshals Denmark
105 F3 Hiruga-take mt. Japan
150 D3 Hirwaun Rhondda Cynon Taff, Wales U.K.
169 E5 Hirzenhain Ger.
104 C4 Hisai Japan
116 C3 Hisar Haryana India
199 F2 Hisarcık Turkey
Hisarköy Turkey see Domaniç
126 D2 Hisarönü Turkey
199 E3 Hisarönü Körfezi b. Turkey
123 G2 Hisor Tajik.
Hisor Tizmasi mts Tajik./Uzbek. see Gissar Range
Hispalis Spain see Sevilla
Hispania country Europe see Spain
246 D2 Hispaniola i. Caribbean Sea
Hissar Haryana India see Hisar
117 F4 Hisua Bihar India
127 F4 Hīt Iraq
103 E7 Hita Japan
183 G4 Hita Spain
105 G2 Hitachi Japan
105 G2 Hitachinaka Japan
105 G2 Hitachi-ōta Japan
113 □2 Hitaddu Addu Atoll Maldives
113 □2 Hitaddu i. Addu Atoll Maldives
151 G3 Hitchin Hertfordshire, England U.K.
Hithadhoo i. Addu Atoll Maldives see Hitaddu
103 E7 Hitoyoshi Japan
140 J3 Hitra i. Norway
178 A3 Hittisau Austria
170 C2 Hitzacker Ger.
179 G3 Hitzendorf Austria
173 F3 Hitzhofen Ger.
168 E2 Hitzhusen Ger.
190 D1 Hitzkirch Switz.
78 □5 Hiu i. Vanuatu
105 F2 Hiuchiga-take vol. Japan
79 □3 Hiva Oa i. Fr. Polynesia
222 F4 Hixon B.C. Can.
85 H4 Hixson Cay rf Qld Austr.
226 B3 Hixton WI U.S.A.
175 L5 Hiyche Ukr.
127 F3 Hizan Bitlis Turkey
142 D3 Hjallerup Denmark
143 F2 Hjälmaren l. Sweden
142 C2 Hjartdøld r. Norway
142 B2 Hjelmeland Norway
143 F2 Hjo Sweden
168 E1 Hjordkær Denmark
142 D3 Hjørring Denmark
142 D3 Hjuvik Sweden
96 B2 Hka, Nam r. Myanmar
96 B1 Hkakabo Razi mt. Myanmar
96 B2 Hkok r. Myanmar
96 B1 Hkring Bum mt. Myanmar
215 H3 Hlabisa S. Africa
96 B3 Hlaing r. Myanmar
Hlako Kangri mt. Xizang China see Lhagoi Kangri
215 H2 Hlatikulu Swaziland
176 F5 Hlebine Croatia
96 B3 Hlegu Myanmar
136 F2 Hlevakha Ukr.
136 E4 Hlinaia Moldova
177 H3 Hliník nad Hronom Slovakia
177 K3 Hlinné Slovakia
176 E2 Hlinsko Czech Rep.
197 H2 Hlipiceni Romania
191 J4 Hlm hill Croatia
137 G3 Hlobyne Ukr.
215 F3 Hlohlowane S. Africa
176 F3 Hlohovec Czech Rep.
177 G3 Hlohovec Slovakia
215 G3 Hlotse Lesotho
176 G2 Hlubočky Czech Rep.
176 D2 Hluboká nad Vltavou Czech Rep.
177 H2 Hlučín Czech Rep.
215 I3 Hluhluwe S. Africa
177 G3 Hluk Czech Rep.
137 G2 Hlukhiv Ukr.
136 E3 Hlukhivtsi Ukr.
138 G5 Hlusha Belarus
138 G5 Hlusk Belarus
136 C3 Hlyboka Ukr.
138 F4 Hlybokaye Belarus
136 D2 Hlynne Ukr.
137 G3 Hlyns'k Ukr.
136 C3 Hlynyany Ukr.
177 J2 Hniezdné Slovakia
177 J3 Hnilec r. Slovakia
136 E3 Hnivan' Ukr.
175 M6 Hnizdychiv Ukr.
136 C3 Hnizna r. Ukr.
177 I3 Hnúšťa Slovakia
136 C3 Hnyla Lypa r. Ukr.
137 I2 Hnylytsya Ukr.
136 F3 Hnylyy Tikych r. Ukr.
137 F4 Hnylyy Yelanets' r. Ukr.
207 F5 Ho Ghana
96 D2 Hoa Binh Vietnam
96 C2 Hoang Liên Son mts Vietnam
Hoang Sa is S. China Sea see Paracel Islands
83 F5 Hobart Tas. Austr.
237 D5 Hobart OK U.S.A.
237 C5 Hobbs NM U.S.A.
262 P1 Hobbs Coast Antarctica
129 B4 Höbek Dağı mt. Turkey
231 D7 Hobe Sound FL U.S.A.
215 F3 Hobhouse S. Africa
235 D2 Hoboken NJ U.S.A.
110 D2 Hoboksar Xinjiang China
177 G5 Hobol Hungary
142 D2 Hobøl Norway
107 G3 Hobor Nei Mongol China
Hobot Xar Qi Nei Mongol China see Xin Bulag
142 C3 Hobro Denmark
165 E5 Hobscheid Lux.
143 H3 Hoburg Gotland Sweden
210 F3 Hobyo Somalia
199 F2 Hocalar Turkey
178 D3 Hocharn mt. Austria
172 D2 Höchberg Ger.
179 F2 Hochbira hill Austria
168 E1 Hochdonn Ger.
172 D3 Hochdorf Ger.
190 D1 Hochdorf Switz.
172 C4 Höchenschwand Ger.
Hochfeiler mt. Austria/Italy see Gran Pilastro
179 E3 Hochfeind mt. Austria
157 H4 Hochfelden France
Hochgall mt. Austria/Italy see Collalto
173 G4 Hochgern mt. Ger.
179 E3 Hochgolling mt. Austria
169 F5 Höchheim Ger.
169 D5 Hochheim am Main Ger.
97 D5 Hô Chi Minh Vietnam
Ho Chi Minh City Vietnam see Hô Chi Minh
173 G4 Hochkalter mt. Ger.
178 E3 Hochkönig mt. Austria
179 F4 Hochobir mt. Austria
179 G3 Hochschwab mt. Austria
179 F3 Hochschwab mts Austria
172 B2 Hochspeyer Ger.
172 C2 Hochstadt (Pfalz) Ger.
173 E2 Höchstadt an der Aisch Ger.
173 E3 Höchstädt an der Donau Ger.
172 B2 Hochstetten-Dhaun Ger.
172 C2 Höchst im Odenwald Ger.
179 F3 Hochtor mt. Austria
178 C3 Hochunnutz mt. Austria
190 E2 Hochwang mt. Switz.
Hochwilde mt. Austria/Italy see L'Altissima
172 C2 Hockenheim Ger.
232 C5 Hocking r. OH U.S.A.
151 H3 Hockley Essex, England U.K.
151 F2 Hockley Heath West Midlands, England U.K.
175 K6 Hoczew Pol.
175 K6 Hoczewka r. Pol.
116 D4 Hodal Haryana India
177 L4 Hodász Hungary
104 C2 Hōdatsu-san hill Japan
210 F2 Hodda mt. Somalia
149 G4 Hodder r. England U.K.
151 G3 Hoddesdon Hertfordshire, England U.K.
Hodeidah Yemen see Al Ḩudaydah
177 J3 Hodejov Slovakia
168 E3 Hodenhagen Ger.
232 C5 Hodgesville WV U.S.A.
84 C2 Hodgson Downs N.T. Austr.
206 D2 Hodh Ech Chargui admin. reg. Maur.
206 C2 Hodh El Gharbi admin. reg. Maur.
177 J5 Hódmezővásárhely Hungary
205 G2 Hodna, Chott el salt l. Alg.
150 E2 Hodnet Shropshire, England U.K.
177 M4 Hodod Romania
179 H2 Hodonice Czech Rep.
176 G3 Hodonín Czech Rep.
197 G2 Hodoşa Romania
106 C1 Hödrögö Mongolia
215 G3 Hodsons Peak Lesotho
165 C3 Hoek Neth.
164 D3 Hoek van Holland Neth.
157 H4 Hœnheim France
165 E4 Hoensbroek Neth.
157 H4 Hœrdt France
100 D4 Hoeryŏng N. Korea
165 E4 Hoeselt Belgium
164 E2 Hoevelaken Neth.
164 D3 Hoeven Neth.
101 C5 Hoeyang N. Korea
171 C5 Hof Bayern Ger.
169 D5 Hof Rheinland-Pfalz Ger.
179 H3 Hof am Leithaberge Austria
178 E3 Hof bei Salzburg Austria
169 E5 Hofbieber Ger.
178 B3 Höfen Austria
168 F3 Höfer Ger.
233 G3 Hoffman Mountain NY U.S.A.
246 C1 Hoffman's Cay i. Bahamas
169 E4 Hofgeismar Ger.
169 D5 Hofheim am Taunus Ger.
169 F5 Hofheim in Unterfranken Ger.
173 H3 Hofkirchen Ger.
215 E4 Hofmeyr S. Africa
140 □D2 Höfn Iceland
143 G1 Hofors Sweden
140 □C2 Hofsjökull ice cap Iceland
103 E6 Hōfu Japan
Hofūf Saudi Arabia see Al Hufūf
142 E3 Höganäs Sweden
83 F4 Hogan Group is Tas. Austr.
233 F2 Hogansburg NY U.S.A.
85 F5 Hoganthulla Creek r. Qld Austr.
84 D4 Hogarth, Mount hill N.T. Austr.
222 C2 Hogg, Mount Y.T. Can.
205 G5 Hoggar plat. Alg.
143 G3 Högsby Sweden
143 F2 Högsjö Sweden
141 I3 Høgste Breakulen mt. Norway
149 J4 Hogsthorpe Lincolnshire, England U.K.
177 H5 Hőgyész Hungary
238 A2 Hoh r. WA U.S.A.
172 B3 Hohberg Ger.
171 D4 Hohburg Ger.
179 E4 Hohe Leier mt. Austria
178 E4 Hohe Leiten mt. Austria
173 E3 Hohen-Altheim Ger.
168 E2 Hohenaspe Ger.
173 H3 Hohenau Ger.
179 H2 Hohenau an der March Austria
179 G3 Hohenberg Austria
171 F4 Hohenbocka Ger.
179 H4 Hohenbrugg-Weinberg Austria
173 F3 Hohenbrunn Ger.
171 E4 Hohenbucko Ger.
173 F2 Hohenburg Ger.
171 C3 Hohendodeleben Ger.
170 E1 Hohendorf Ger.
169 F4 Hohenebra Ger.
179 G2 Hoheneich Austria
178 A3 Hohenems Austria
173 F2 Hohenfels Ger.
173 E4 Hohenfurch Ger.
170 D3 Hohengöhren Ger.
169 F3 Hohenhameln Ger.
173 F3 Hohenkammer Ger.
168 C2 Hohenkirchen Ger.
171 E4 Hohenleipisch Ger.
171 D5 Hohenleuben Ger.
173 F3 Hohenlinden Ger.
168 E2 Hohenlockstedt Ger.
172 D2 Hohenloher Ebene plain Ger.
170 E2 Hohenmocker Ger.
171 D4 Hohenmölsen Ger.
170 D3 Hohennauen Ger.
170 E3 Hohen Neuendorf Berlin Ger.
179 F3 Hohe Nock mt. Austria
169 E5 Hohenroda-Ransbach Ger.
169 F5 Hohenroth Ger.
170 F3 Hohensaaten Ger.
Hohensalza Pol. see Inowrocław
171 D3 Hohenseeden Ger.
171 D5 Hohenstein-Ernstthal Ger.
172 D3 Hohentengen Ger.
172 C4 Hohentengen am Hochrhein Ger.
173 G3 Hohenthann Ger.
171 D4 Hohenthurm Ger.
231 C5 Hohenwald TN U.S.A.
170 D2 Hohen Wangelin Ger.
173 F3 Hohenwart Ger.
173 G2 Hohenwarth Ger.
168 E1 Hohenwestedt Ger.
170 C3 Hohenwulsch Ger.
179 E2 Hohenzell Austria
179 E3 Hoher Dachstein mt. Austria
Hoh Ereg Nei Mongol China see Wuchuan
178 E3 Hoher Göll mt. Austria/Ger.
169 E5 Hohe Rhön mts Ger.
178 B3 Hoher Ifen mt. Austria/Ger.
178 D3 Hohe Salve mt. Austria
169 E4 Hohes Gras hill Ger.
169 F4 Hohes Kreuz Ger.
178 D3 Hohe Tauern mts Austria
165 F4 Hohe Venn moorland Belgium
190 C2 Hohgant mt. Switz.
Hohhot Nei Mongol China see Huhhot
172 C3 Hohloh hill Ger.
169 C5 Höhn Ger.
168 E1 Hohn Schleswig-Holstein Ger.
168 F3 Hohne Ger.
157 H4 Hohneck mt. France
168 F2 Hohnstorf (Elbe) Ger.
207 F5 Hohoe Ghana
137 G3 Hoholeve Ukr.
137 F2 Hoholiv Ukr.
137 H4 Hoholivka Ukr.
168 F1 Hohwacht (Ostsee) Ger.
111 E5 Hoh Xil Shan mts China
96 E4 Hôi An Vietnam
210 A4 Hoima Uganda
168 F2 Hoisdorf Ger.
236 D4 Hoisington KS U.S.A.
106 C4 Hoit Taria Qinghai China
117 H4 Hojai Assam India
Hojambaz Turkm. see Khodzhambaz
168 D1 Højer Denmark
103 F7 Hōjo Japan
96 C2 Hok r. Myanmar
143 E3 Hökensås hills Sweden
80 D1 Hokianga Harbour North I. N.Z.
105 G2 Hōki-gawa r. Japan
80 E4 Hokio Beach North I. N.Z.
81 C5 Hokitika South I. N.Z.
100 G4 Hokkaidō i. Japan
102 K2 Hokkaidō pref. Japan
142 C2 Hokksund Norway
122 D2 Hokmābād Iran
81 B7 Hokonui South I. N.Z.
81 B6 Hokonui Hills South I. N.Z.
129 D3 Hoktemberyan Armenia
105 E1 Hokura-gawa r. Japan
142 C1 Hol Buskerud Norway
140 L1 Hol Nordland Norway
177 J3 Hoľa mt. Slovakia
114 C3 Holalkere Karnataka India
137 G4 Hola Prystan' Ukr.
142 D4 Holbæk Denmark
215 H2 Holbank S. Africa
151 H2 Holbeach Lincolnshire, England U.K.
222 D5 Holberg B.C. Can.
168 E1 Holbøl Denmark
85 G3 Holborne Island Qld Austr.
83 F3 Holbrook N.S.W. Austr.
151 I3 Holbrook Suffolk, England U.K.
241 L4 Holbrook AZ U.S.A.
235 E2 Holbrook NY U.S.A.
226 B3 Holcombe WI U.S.A.
223 H4 Holden Alta Can.
149 G4 Holden Lancashire, England U.K.
241 K2 Holden UT U.S.A.
237 D5 Holdenville OK U.S.A.
149 I4 Holderness pen. England U.K.
168 D3 Holdorf Ger.
236 D3 Holdrege NE U.S.A.
168 G1 Holeby Denmark
114 C3 Hole Narsipur Karnataka India
177 G2 Holešov Czech Rep.
232 A4 Holgate OH U.S.A.
182 D5 Holguera Spain
246 C2 Holguín Cuba
176 G3 Holíč Slovakia
176 E1 Holice Czech Rep.
137 G2 Holinka Ukr.
141 K3 Höljes Sweden
179 H2 Hollabrunn Austria
169 C3 Hollage (Wallenhorst) Ger.
Holland country Europe see Netherlands
226 D4 Holland MI U.S.A.
232 D3 Holland NY U.S.A.
232 B4 Holland OH U.S.A.
237 F5 Hollandale MS U.S.A.
Hollandia Irian Jaya Indon. see Jayapura
151 I3 Holland-on-Sea Essex, England U.K.
164 F2 Hollandscheveld Neth.
146 F2 Hollandstoun Scotland U.K.
165 E5 Hollange Belgium
169 F3 Holle Ger.
171 C4 Holleben Ger.
173 F3 Hollenbach Ger.
168 F2 Hollenbek Ger.
179 G4 Hollenegg Austria
168 E2 Hollenstedt Ger.
179 F3 Hollenstein an der Ybbs Austria
232 D3 Holley NY U.S.A.
173 F2 Hollfeld Ger.
262 T2 Hollick-Kenyon Peninsula Antarctica
262 Q1 Hollick-Kenyon Plateau Antarctica
232 D4 Hollidaysburg PA U.S.A.
168 E1 Hollingstedt Ger.
151 H4 Hollington East Sussex, England U.K.
149 H4 Hollingworth Greater Manchester, England U.K.
222 C4 Hollis AK U.S.A.
237 D5 Hollis OK U.S.A.
240 G3 Hollister CA U.S.A.
177 K3 Hollóháza Hungary
141 N3 Hollola Fin.
164 E1 Hollum Neth.
227 F4 Holly MI U.S.A.
148 E2 Hollybush East Ayrshire, Scotland U.K.
150 E2 Hollybush Worcestershire, England U.K.
81 A6 Hollyford r. South I. N.Z.
235 D3 Holly Park NJ U.S.A.
237 F5 Holly Springs MS U.S.A.
147 E3 Hollywood Rep. of Ireland
231 D7 Hollywood FL U.S.A.
168 E2 Holm Ger.
136 E4 Hol'ma Ukr.
220 G2 Holman N.W.T. Can.
235 D2 Holmdel NJ U.S.A.
215 G2 Holmdene S. Africa
149 I4 Holme-on-Spalding-Moor East Riding of Yorkshire, England U.K.
235 E1 Holmes NY U.S.A.
149 G4 Holmes Chapel Cheshire, England U.K.
149 H4 Holmesfield Derbyshire, England U.K.
85 F3 Holmes Reef Coral Sea Is Terr. Austr.
142 D2 Holmestrand Norway
232 C4 Holmesville OH U.S.A.
149 H4 Holmfirth West Yorkshire, England U.K.
Holmgard Rus. Fed. see Velikiy Novgorod
140 M3 Holmsund Sweden
141 L3 Holmsveden Sweden
136 C2 Holoby Ukr.
177 L5 Holod Romania
197 F2 Holod r. Romania
136 C3 Holohory hills Ukr.
128 B3 Holon Israel
86 E2 Holothuria Banks rf W.A. Austr.
173 H2 Holoubkov Czech Rep.
136 F3 Holovanivs'k Ukr.
136 B3 Holovets'ko Ukr.
137 G3 Holovkivka Ukr.
175 M4 Holovne Ukr.
136 E2 Holovyne Ukr.
85 E2 Holroyd r. Qld Austr.
142 E3 Holsljunga Sweden
215 G2 Holspruit r. S. Africa
168 D2 Holste Ger.
142 C3 Holstebro Denmark
142 C4 Holsted Denmark
190 C1 Hölstein Switz.
236 E3 Holstein IA U.S.A.
Holsteinsborg Greenland see Sisimiut
232 B6 Holston r. TN U.S.A.
150 C4 Holsworthy Devon, England U.K.
151 I2 Holt Norfolk, England U.K.
150 E3 Holt Wiltshire, England U.K.
150 E1 Holt Wrexham, Wales U.K.
226 E4 Holt MI U.S.A.
164 F2 Holten Neth.
168 C2 Holtgast Ger.
170 C2 Holthusen Ger.
168 C2 Holtland Ger.
236 E4 Holton KS U.S.A.
226 D4 Holton MI U.S.A.
149 I4 Holton le Clay Lincolnshire, England U.K.
168 C2 Holtrop (Großefehn) Ger.
168 E1 Holtsee Ger.
241 J5 Holtville CA U.S.A.
234 B3 Holtwood PA U.S.A.
240 □D9 Holualoa HI U.S.A.
137 H3 Holubivka Ukr.
164 E1 Holwerd Neth.
164 F1 Holwierde Neth.
147 D4 Holycross Rep. of Ireland
220 C3 Holy Cross AK U.S.A.
239 F4 Holy Cross, Mount of the CO U.S.A.
150 C1 Holyhead Isle of Anglesey, Wales U.K.
150 C1 Holyhead Bay Wales U.K.
149 H2 Holy Island England U.K.
146 C6 Holy Island Scotland U.K.
150 C1 Holy Island Wales U.K.
236 C3 Holyoke CO U.S.A.
233 G3 Holyoke MA U.S.A.
Holy See Europe see Vatican City
150 D1 Holywell Flintshire, Wales U.K.
147 D2 Holywell Northern Ireland U.K.
146 E6 Holywood Dumfries and Galloway, Scotland U.K.
147 F2 Holywood Northern Ireland U.K.
169 C5 Holzappel Ger.
171 E4 Holzdorf Ger.
169 E4 Holzen Ger.
172 D3 Holzgerlingen Ger.
171 D4 Holzhausen Ger.
169 C5 Holzhausen an der Haide Ger.
173 E3 Holzheim Bayern Ger.
173 E3 Holzheim Bayern Ger.
173 E3 Holzheim Bayern Ger.
169 D5 Holzheim Hessen Ger.
173 F4 Holzkirchen Ger.
169 E4 Holzminden Ger.
169 F4 Holzthaleben Ger.
171 D4 Holzweißig Ger.
169 C4 Holzwickede Ger.
210 B5 Homa Bay Kenya
96 A1 Homalin Myanmar
222 E5 Homathko r. B.C. Can.
Homāyūnshahr Iran see Khomeynīshahr
169 E4 Homberg (Efze) Ger.
169 D5 Homberg (Ohm) Ger.
156 C3 Hombleux France
206 E3 Hombori Mali
157 G3 Hombourg-Budange France
157 G3 Hombourg-Haut France
172 B2 Homburg Ger.
221 L3 Home Bay Nunavut Can.
157 F3 Homécourt France
85 F3 Home Hill Qld Austr.
86 □2 Home Island Cocos Is
182 B3 Homem r. Port.
220 C4 Homer AK U.S.A.
231 D5 Homer GA U.S.A.
237 E5 Homer LA U.S.A.
226 E4 Homer MI U.S.A.
233 E3 Homer NY U.S.A.
232 D4 Homer City PA U.S.A.
151 I2 Homersfield Suffolk, England U.K.
231 D6 Homerville GA U.S.A.
85 F4 Homestead Qld Austr.
231 D7 Homestead FL U.S.A.
234 C2 Hometown PA U.S.A.
234 C3 Homeville PA U.S.A.
81 E4 Homewood North I. N.Z.
231 C5 Homewood AL U.S.A.
140 J3 Hommelvik Norway
114 C2 Homnabad Karnataka India
197 H2 Homocea Romania
177 I5 Homokmégy Hungary
177 G5 Homokszentgyörgy Hungary
177 M4 Homoroade Romania
177 L3 Homorod r. Romania
Homs Libya see Al Khums
Homs Syria see Ḩimş
137 F1 Homyel' Belarus
Homyel Oblast admin. div. Belarus see Homyel'skaya Voblasts'
139 G5 Homyel'skaya Voblasts' admin. div. Belarus
232 C6 Honaker VA U.S.A.
Honan prov. China see Henan
240 □D9 Honaunau HI U.S.A.
114 C3 Honavalli Karnataka India
114 B3 Honavar Karnataka India
199 F3 Honaz Turkey
136 F2 Honcharivs'ke Ukr.
250 C3 Honda Col.
117 F5 Honda Orissa India
117 F5 Hondapa Orissa India
186 B1 Hondarribia Spain
214 E4 Hondeblaf r. S. Africa
214 A4 Hondeklipbaai S. Africa
243 H5 Hondo r. Belize/Mex.
103 E7 Hondo Japan
239 F5 Hondo NM U.S.A.
237 D6 Hondo TX U.S.A.
239 F5 Hondo r. NM U.S.A.
187 C6 Hondón de las Nieves Spain
187 C6 Hondón de los Frailes Spain
156 C2 Hondschoote France
246 A4 Honduras country Central America
242 □I5 Honduras, Gulf of Belize/Hond.
190 C3 Hône Italy
142 D1 Hønefoss Norway
232 E3 Honeoye Falls NY U.S.A.
234 C1 Honesdale PA U.S.A.
234 C2 Honey Brook PA U.S.A.
159 G2 Honfleur France
96 D2 Hong, Mouths of the Vietnam
96 D2 Hông, Sông r. Vietnam
109 E2 Hong'an Hubei China
101 C5 Hongch'ŏn S. Korea
96 D2 Hông Gai Vietnam
110 E4 Honggouzi Qinghai China
96 D1 Hongguo Guizhou China
109 E4 Honghai Wan b. China
108 B4 Honghe Yunnan China
109 E1 Hong He r. China
109 E2 Honghu Hubei China
Hongjialou Shandong China see Licheng
108 D3 Hongjiang Hunan China
Hongjiang Sichuan China see Wangcang
109 □ Hong Kong H.K. China
109 E4 Hong Kong special admin. reg. China
107 F4 Hongliu r. China
Hongliuwan Gansu China see Aksay
110 F3 Hongliuyuan Gansu China
97 D5 Hông Ngư Vietnam
Hongqiao Hunan China see Qidong
109 G2 Hongqiao airport China
Hongqizhen Hainan China see Tongshi
108 A2 Hongshan Yunnan China
108 D4 Hongshui He r. China
107 F4 Hongtong Shanxi China
225 H3 Honguedo, Détroit d' sea chan. Que. Can.
Hongwansi Gansu China see Sunan
101 C4 Hongwŏn N. Korea
108 B1 Hongyuan Sichuan China
109 F1 Hongze Jiangsu China
109 F1 Hongze Hu l. China
78 □6 Honiara Guadalcanal Solomon Is
150 D4 Honiton Devon, England U.K.
102 J4 Honjō Japan
105 F2 Honjō Japan
141 M3 Honkajoki Fin.
149 H4 Honley West Yorkshire, England U.K.
114 B3 Honnali Karnataka India
140 N1 Honningsvåg Norway
240 □D8 Honokaa HI U.S.A.
240 □C8 Honokahua HI U.S.A.
80 F2 Honokawa mt. North I. N.Z.
240 □ Honolulu HI U.S.A.
240 □ Honolulu County county HI U.S.A.
240 □D9 Honomu HI U.S.A.
226 D3 Honor MI U.S.A.
240 □ Honouliuli HI U.S.A.
174 B3 Hönow Ger.
183 H5 Honrubia Spain
183 G3 Honrubia de la Cuesta Spain
103 F6 Honshū i. Japan
183 H5 Hontacillas Spain
183 F3 Hontalbilla Spain
183 H5 Hontanaya Spain
163 B5 Hontanx France
177 H3 Hontianske Nemce Slovakia
183 G2 Hontoria de la Cantera Spain
183 G3 Hontoria del Pinar Spain
183 G3 Hontoria de Valdearados Spain
240 □D9 Honuapo HI U.S.A.
114 B2 Honwad Karnataka India
151 H3 Hoo Medway, England U.K.
238 B2 Hood, Mount vol. OR U.S.A.
222 C3 Hood Bay AK U.S.A.
Hood Island Islas Galápagos Ecuador see Española, Isla
87 C7 Hood Point W.A. Austr.
238 B2 Hood River OR U.S.A.
164 D2 Hoofddorp Neth.
168 D1 Hooge Ger.
165 D3 Hoogerheide Neth.
164 F2 Hoogersmilde Neth.
164 F2 Hoogeveen Neth.
164 F1 Hoogezand-Sappemeer Neth.
164 D3 Hooge Zwaluwe Neth.
164 F2 Hooghalen Neth.
Hooghly r. mouth India see Hugli
164 E2 Hoogkarspel Neth.
164 F3 Hoog-Keppel Neth.
164 F1 Hoogkerk Neth.
164 E2 Hoogland Neth.
168 B3 Hoogstede Ger.
165 D3 Hoogstraten Belgium
164 D3 Hoogvliet Neth.
149 I4 Hook East Riding of Yorkshire, England U.K.
151 G3 Hook Hampshire, England U.K.
237 C4 Hooker OK U.S.A.
151 F3 Hook Norton Oxfordshire, England U.K.
Hook of Holland Neth. see Hoek van Holland
85 H5 Hook Point Qld Austr.
85 G3 Hook Reef Qld Austr.
168 D2 Hooksiel Ger.
240 □C8 Hoolehua HI U.S.A.
220 E4 Hoonah AK U.S.A.
220 B3 Hooper Bay AK U.S.A.
226 D5 Hoopeston IL U.S.A.
215 E2 Hoopstad S. Africa
142 E4 Höör Sweden
164 E2 Hoorn Neth.
77 I3 Hoorn, Îles de is Wallis and Futuna Is
164 D3 Hoornaar Neth.
105 E3 Hōō-san mt. Japan
233 G3 Hoosick NY U.S.A.
241 J3 Hoover Dam AZ/NV U.S.A.
106 D2 Höövör Mongolia
140 □B2 Hóp lag. Iceland
127 F2 Hopa Turkey
234 D2 Hopatcong NJ U.S.A.
234 C1 Hop Bottom PA U.S.A.
222 F5 Hope B.C. Can.
81 D4 Hope South I. N.Z.
81 D5 Hope r. South I. N.Z.
150 D1 Hope Flintshire, Wales U.K.
237 E5 Hope AR U.S.A.
234 D2 Hope NJ U.S.A.
82 D2 Hope, Lake salt flat S.A. Austr.
87 D7 Hope, Lake salt flat W.A. Austr.
146 D3 Hope, Loch l. Scotland U.K.
246 □ Hope Bay Jamaica
225 I2 Hopedale Nfld. Can.
237 F6 Hopedale LA U.S.A.
214 B5 Hopefield S. Africa
Hopei prov. China see Hebei
243 H5 Hopelchén Mex.
146 E4 Hopeman Moray, Scotland U.K.
140 □ Hopen i. Svalbard
Hopes Advance Bay Que. Can. see Aupaluk
83 E3 Hopetoun Vic. Austr.
87 D7 Hopetoun W.A. Austr.
214 E3 Hopetown S. Africa
85 F2 Hope Vale Qld Austr.
233 H4 Hope Valley RI U.S.A.
234 D2 Hopewell NJ U.S.A.
232 E6 Hopewell VA U.S.A.
235 E1 Hopewell Junction NY U.S.A.
178 D3 Hopfgarten im Brixental Austria
83 E4 Hopkins r. Vic. Austr.
87 F5 Hopkins, Lake salt flat W.A. Austr.
230 C4 Hopkinsville KY U.S.A.
235 G1 Hopkinton RI U.S.A.
240 F2 Hopland CA U.S.A.
172 B2 Hoppstädten Ger.
169 C3 Hopsten Ger.
151 I2 Hopton Norfolk, England U.K.
151 H2 Hopton Suffolk, England U.K.
150 E2 Hoptonheath Shropshire, England U.K.
238 B2 Hoquiam WA U.S.A.
106 D5 Hor Qinghai China
136 F2 Hora Ukr.
129 E4 Horadiz Azer.
104 D4 Hōraiji-san hill Japan
151 H4 Horam East Sussex, England U.K.
127 F2 Horasan Turkey
176 C2 Horažďovice Czech Rep.
172 C3 Horb am Neckar Ger.
170 D1 Horbelev Denmark
151 G2 Horbling Lincolnshire, England U.K.
157 H4 Horbourg-Wihr France
178 A3 Hörbranz Austria
143 E4 Hörby Sweden
183 E3 Horcajo de las Torres Spain
185 F1 Horcajo de los Montes Spain
183 H5 Horcajo de Santiago Spain
183 E4 Horcajo Medianero Spain
183 G4 Horche Spain
185 F2 Horcón hill Spain
258 D2 Horcones r. Arg.
142 B1 Hordaland county Norway
169 F4 Hörden Ger.
151 F4 Hordle Hampshire, England U.K.
150 C2 Horeb Ceredigion, Wales U.K.
80 D1 Horeke North I. N.Z.
197 F3 Horezu Romania
173 E3 Horgau Ger.
190 D1 Horgen Switz.
172 D4 Horgenzell Ger.
106 C1 Horgo Mongolia
196 D2 Horgoš Vojvodina, Srbija Yugo.
136 B3 Horhany mts Ukr.
106 E3 Hörh Uul mts Mongolia
197 I3 Horia Romania
176 E1 Hořice Czech Rep.
226 C4 Horicon WI U.S.A.
107 F3 Horinger Nei Mongol China
179 H3 Horitschon Austria
106 D2 Horiult Mongolia
266 H7 Horizon Deep sea feature S. Pacific Ocean
171 F4 Horka Ger.
139 H4 Horki Belarus
151 G3 Horley Surrey, England U.K.
262 Q1 Horlick Mountains Antarctica
171 E4 Hörlitz Ger.
137 J3 Horlivka Ukr.
122 E4 Hormak Iran
247 □1 Hormigueros Puerto Rico
183 H2 Hormilla Spain
122 D5 Hormoz i. Iran
122 C5 Hormoz, Kūh-e mt. Iran
122 D5 Hormozgan prov. Iran
122 C5 Hormūd-e Bāgh Iran
122 D5 Hormuz, Strait of Iran/Oman
179 G2 Horn Austria
222 G2 Horn r. N.W.T. Can.
140 □B2 Horn c. Iceland
Horn, Cape Chile see Hornos, Cabo de
184 D2 Hornachos Spain
185 E3 Hornachuelos Spain
Hornád r. Hungary/Slovakia see Hernád

Ibie to 'Irq Subay 315

161 C4 Ibie r. France
104 C3 Ibi-gawa r. Japan
254 F4 Ibimirim Brazil
208 F4 Ibina r. Dem. Rep. Congo
256 B5 Ibiporã Brazil
256 C4 Ibirá Brazil
257 G3 Ibiraçu Brazil
254 E5 Ibitiara Brazil
256 C4 Ibitinga Brazil
256 D5 Ibiúna Brazil
Ibiza Spain see Eivissa
Ibiza i. Spain see Eivissa
194 D5 Iblei, Monti mts Sicilia Italy
163 B5 Ibos France
254 E5 Ibotirama Brazil
208 A5 Iboundji Gabon
208 A5 Iboundji, Mont hill Gabon
125 G3 Ibrā' Oman
Ibrala Turkey see Yeşildere
135 I5 Ibresi Rus. Fed.
125 G3 Ibrī Oman
185 G2 Ibros Spain
151 F2 Ibstock Leicestershire, England U.K.
104 C3 Ibuki-yama mt. Japan
103 E8 Ibusuki Japan
250 E5 Içá r. Brazil
252 B3 Ica Peru
252 B3 Ica dept Peru
250 E4 Içana r. Brazil
Icaria i. Greece see Ikaria
254 D2 Icatu Brazil
241 J3 Iceberg Canyon gorge NV U.S.A.
126 D3 İçel İçel Turkey
128 A1 İçel prov. Turkey
221 Q3 Iceland country Europe
264 H2 Iceland Basin sea feature N. Atlantic Ocean
264 I1 Icelandic Plateau sea feature N. Atlantic Ocean
256 C4 Icem Brazil
117 F4 Ichak Bihar India
114 B2 Ichalkaranji Mahar. India
115 E2 Ichchapuram Andhra Prad. India
173 E3 Ichenhausen Ger.
172 B3 Ichenheim Ger.
105 G3 Ichihara Japan
105 F3 Ichikawa Japan
104 A4 Ichi-kawa r. Japan
105 E3 Ichikawadaimon Japan
252 D4 Ichilo r. Bol.
104 C3 Ichinomiya Aichi Japan
104 D4 Ichinomiya Aichi Japan
102 J4 Ichinoseki Japan
131 Q4 Ichinskiy, Vulkan vol. Rus. Fed.
Ichkeria aut. rep. Rus. Fed. see Chechenskaya Respublika
137 G2 Ichnya Ukr.
101 C5 Ich'ŏn N. Korea
101 C5 Ich'ŏn S. Korea
165 C3 Ichtegem Belgium
169 F5 Ichtershausen Ger.
199 F2 İcikler Turkey
173 F4 Icking Ger.
151 H4 Icklesham East Sussex, England U.K.
151 H2 Icklingham Suffolk, England U.K.
199 F3 İçmeler Turkey
254 F3 Icó Brazil
216 □3a Icod de Los Vinos Tenerife Canary Is
257 G4 Iconha Brazil
Iconium Turkey see Konya
Icosium Alg. see Alger
Iculisma France see Angoulême
İd Turkey see Narman
81 C6 Ida, Mount South I. N.Z.
237 E5 Idabel OK U.S.A.
236 E3 Ida Grove IA U.S.A.
207 G5 Idah Nigeria
238 D2 Idaho state U.S.A.
238 D3 Idaho City ID U.S.A.
238 D3 Idaho Falls ID U.S.A.
238 B2 Idanha OR U.S.A.
182 C5 Idanha-a-Nova Port.
116 C5 Idar Gujarat India
172 B2 Idar-Oberstein Ger.
81 B6 Ida Valley South I. N.Z.
142 D2 Idefjorden inlet Norway/Sweden
170 C3 Iden Ger.
106 C1 Ider Mongolia
106 D1 Ideriyn Gol r. Mongolia
170 C1 Idestrup Denmark
203 G3 Idfu Egypt
202 A3 Idhān Awbārī des. Libya
202 B3 Idhān Murzūq des. Libya
Idhra i. Greece see Ydra
Idi Amin Dada, Lake Dem. Rep. Congo/Uganda see Edward, Lake
186 A1 Idiazabal Spain
191 G4 Idice r. Italy
209 C6 Idiofa Dem. Rep. Congo
220 C3 Iditarod AK U.S.A.
140 M1 Idivuoma Sweden
203 F2 Idku Egypt
149 I4 Idle r. England U.K.
128 C2 Idlib Syria
128 C2 Idlib governorate Syria
151 F3 Idmiston Wiltshire, England U.K.
183 I2 Idocin Spain
177 J6 Iđoš Vojvodina, Srbija Yugo.
Idra i. Greece see Ydra
84 C5 Idracowra N.T. Austr.
141 K3 Idre Sweden
188 E2 Idrija Slovenia
188 D2 Idrijca r. Slovenia
138 G3 Idritsa Rus. Fed.
190 F3 Idro Italy
163 B5 Idron-Ousse-Sendets France
168 E1 Idstedt Ger.
169 D5 Idstein Ger.
114 C4 Idukki Kerala India
215 G5 Idutywa S. Africa
240 I5 Idyllwild CA U.S.A.
Idzhevan Armenia see Ijevan
102 □2 Ie Japan
138 E3 Iecava Latvia
138 D3 Iecava r. Latvia
102 □2 Ie-jima i. Japan
256 B5 Iepê Brazil
165 B4 Ieper Belgium
197 F2 Ier r. Romania
199 D4 Ierapetra Kriti Greece
211 C7 Ifakara Tanz.
91 J5 Ifalik atoll Micronesia
Ifaluk atoll Micronesia see Ifalik
213 □J4 Ifanadiana Madag.
213 □J4 Ifanirea Madag.
207 G5 Ife Nigeria
202 C6 Ifenat Chad
207 H2 Iferouâne Niger
205 G4 Ifetesene mt. Alg.
173 F4 Iffeldorf Ger.
158 D3 Iffendic France
172 C3 Iffezheim Ger.
85 E3 Iffley Qld Austr.
207 F2 Ifôghas, Adrar des hills Mali
207 G5 Ifon Nigeria
82 C2 Ifould Lake salt flat S.A. Austr.
204 D2 Ifrane Morocco
159 F2 Ifs France
169 F4 Ifta Ger.
179 F5 Ig Slovenia
207 G4 Igabi Nigeria
177 G5 Igal Hungary
196 D4 Igalo Crna Gora Yugo.
95 E2 Igan r. Sarawak Malaysia
210 B4 Iganga Uganda
177 H5 Igar Hungary
256 D4 Igarapava Brazil
254 D2 Igarape Açú Brazil
254 D3 Igarapé Grande Brazil
254 C2 Igarapé Miri Brazil
256 D5 Igaratá Brazil
130 J3 Igarka Rus. Fed.
253 G6 Igatimí Para.
114 B2 Igatpuri Mahar. India
207 G4 Igbeti Nigeria
207 F4 Igboho Nigeria
207 H5 Igbor Nigeria
127 G3 Iğdır Turkey
129 D4 Iğdır prov. Turkey
159 G3 Igé France
183 H2 Igea Spain
172 A2 Igel Ger.
173 F2 Igensdorf Ger.
172 D2 Igersheim Ger.
172 C2 Iggelheim Ger.
173 H3 Iggensbach Ger.
141 L3 Iggesund Sweden
197 F2 Ighiu Romania
190 E2 Igis Switz.
192 A5 Iglesias Sardegna Italy
192 A5 Iglesiente reg. Sardegna Italy
204 E3 Igli Alg.
173 E3 Igling Ger.
134 L5 Iglino Rus. Fed.
221 J3 Igloolik Nunavut Can.
Igluligaarjuk Nunavut Can. see Chesterfield Inlet
128 A5 'Igma, Gebel el plat. Egypt
224 B3 Ignace Ont. Can.
244 B1 Ignacio Allende Mex.
245 G4 Ignacio de la Llave Mex.
242 D2 Ignacio Zaragosa Mex.
138 F4 Ignalina Lith.
126 B2 İğneada Turkey
177 L5 Ignești Romania
157 G4 Igney France
160 D1 Ignon r. France
134 H4 Igodovo Rus. Fed.
211 A6 Igombe r. Tanz.
139 I4 Igorevskaya Rus. Fed.
160 C1 Igornay France
183 H1 Igorre Spain
198 B2 Igoumenitsa Greece
134 K4 Igra Rus. Fed.
182 B2 Igrexa Spain
182 B2 Igrexario Spain
186 C2 Igriés Spain
130 H3 Igrim Rus. Fed.
255 B8 Iguaçu r. Brazil
255 E5 Iguaí Brazil
250 C4 Iguaje, Mesa de hills Col.
245 E4 Iguala Mex.
186 E3 Igualada Spain
185 E4 Igualeja Spain
256 D6 Iguape Brazil
256 B5 Iguaraçu Brazil
257 E4 Iguarapé Brazil
257 E4 Iguatama Brazil
255 B7 Iguatemi Brazil
255 B7 Iguatemi r. Brazil
254 F3 Iguatu Brazil
182 D2 Igueña Spain
160 C2 Iguerande France
211 B6 Igunga Tanz.
207 G5 Iguobazuwa Nigeria
Iguvium Italy see Gubbio
213 □K2 Iharaña Madag.
176 G5 Iharosberény Hungary
114 B5 Ihavandhippolhu Atoll Maldives
107 E3 Ihbulag Mongolia
102 □1 Iheya-jima i. Japan
106 E2 Ihhayrhan Mongolia
207 G5 Ihiala Nigeria
177 J2 Ihľany Slovakia
168 C2 Ihlowerhörn (Ihlow) Ger.
136 E2 Ihnatpil' Ukr.
163 A5 Iholdy France
213 □J4 Ihosy Madag.
168 C2 Ihrhove Ger.
172 B3 Ihringen Ger.
173 F3 Ihrlerstein Ger.
199 G2 İhsaniye Turkey
106 E1 Ihsuuj Mongolia
107 I3 Ih Tal Nei Mongol China
105 D3 Iida Japan
102 I5 Iide-san mt. Japan
140 N2 Iijoki r. Fin.
140 N3 Iisalmi Fin.
138 F1 Iitti Fin.
105 E2 Iiyama Japan
103 E7 Iizuka Japan
207 F5 Ijebu-Ode Nigeria
129 D3 Ijevan Armenia
164 E1 IJlst Neth.
164 D2 IJmuiden Neth.
204 D5 Ijoubbâne des. Mali
164 E2 IJssel r. Neth.
164 E2 IJsselmeer l. Neth.
164 E2 IJsselmuiden Neth.
164 E2 IJsselstein Neth.
255 B9 Ijuí Brazil
253 G6 Ijuí r. Brazil
165 C3 IJzendijke Neth.
165 B3 IJzer r. Belgium alt. Yser (France)
Ikaahuk N.W.T. Can. see Sachs Harbour
141 M3 Ikaalinen Fin.
215 F1 Ikageleng S. Africa
215 F2 Ikageng S. Africa
213 □J3 Ikahavo hill Madag.
213 □J4 Ikalamavony Madag.
81 C5 Ikamatua South I. N.Z.
207 H5 Ikang Nigeria
207 H4 Ikara Nigeria
207 G5 Ikare Nigeria
199 E3 Ikaria i. Greece
104 B4 Ikaruga Japan
142 C3 Ikast Denmark
81 C6 Ikawai South I. N.Z.
80 F3 Ikawhenua Range mts North I. N.Z.
104 B3 Ikeda Japan
104 C4 Ikegoya-yama mt. Japan
207 F5 Ikeja Nigeria
208 D5 Ikela Dem. Rep. Congo
208 C4 Ikelemba r. Dem. Rep. Congo
207 G5 Ikem Nigeria
207 G5 Ikere Nigeria
Ikerre Nigeria see Ikere
176 F4 Ikervár Hungary
197 F4 Ikhtiman Bulg.
215 E3 Ikhutseng S. Africa
103 D7 Iki i. Japan
128 D1 İkiağiz Turkey
135 I7 Iki-Burul Rus. Fed.
207 G5 Ikire Nigeria
129 B3 İkizdere Turkey
207 H5 Ikom Nigeria
104 B4 Ikoma Japan
213 □J4 Ikongo Madag.
217 □3a Ikoni Njazidja Comoros
129 B1 Ikon-Khalk Rus. Fed.
213 □J3 Ikopa r. Madag.
137 J2 Ikorets r. Rus. Fed.
207 F5 Ikorodu Nigeria
207 G5 Ikot Ekpene Nigeria
205 H4 Ikouhaouene, Adrar mt. Alg.
177 G4 Ikrény Hungary
101 C6 Iksan S. Korea
211 B6 Ikungi Tanz.
211 B6 Ikungu Tanz.
136 C2 Ikva r. Ukr.
207 G4 Ila Nigeria
92 B2 Ilagan Phil.
114 C4 Ilaiyankudi Tamil Nadu India
213 □K3 Ilaka Atsinanana Madag.
122 A3 Īlām Iran
122 A3 Īlām prov. Iran
117 F4 Ilam Nepal
109 G3 Ilan Taiwan
174 C3 Ilanka r. Pol.
190 E2 Ilanz Switz.
137 H3 Ilarionove Ukr.
207 F5 Ilaro Nigeria
252 C4 Ilave Peru
175 H2 Iława Pol.
207 G5 Ilawe-Ekiti Nigeria
122 D4 Ilazārān, Kūh-e mt. Iran
106 C2 Il Bogd Uul mts Mongolia
192 B5 Ilbono Sardegna Italy
150 E4 Ilchester Somerset, England U.K.
Ile r. China/Kazakh. see Ili
223 J4 Île-à-la-Crosse Sask. Can.
209 D6 Ilebo Dem. Rep. Congo
156 C4 Île-de-France admin. reg. France
211 B7 Ileje Tanz.
120 C2 Ilek Kazakh.
120 C2 Ilek r. Rus. Fed.
137 H2 Ilek-Pen'kovka Rus. Fed.
147 B5 Ilen r. Rep. of Ireland
Ilerda prov. Cataluña Spain see Lérida
Île Royale i. N.S. Can. see Cape Breton Island
207 G5 Ilesa Nigeria
Ilesha Nigeria see Ilesa
207 F4 Ilesha Ibariba Nigeria
134 J5 Ilet' r. Rus. Fed.
134 H3 Ileza Rus. Fed.
169 F4 Ilfeld Ger.
223 M3 Ilford Man. Can.
151 H3 Ilford Greater London, England U.K.
85 F4 Ilfracombe Qld Austr.
150 C3 Ilfracombe Devon, England U.K.
126 D2 Ilgaz Turkey
126 C3 Ilgın Turkey
257 E5 Ilhabela Brazil
257 E5 Ilha Grande, Baía da b. Brazil
255 B7 Ilha Grande, Represa resr Brazil
256 B4 Ilha Solteíra, Represa resr Brazil
182 B4 Ílhavo Port.
255 F5 Ilhéus Brazil
121 I3 Ili r. China/Kazakh.
Ili Kazakh. see Kapchagay
197 F3 Ilia Romania
220 C4 Iliamna Lake AK U.S.A.
126 E3 İliç Turkey
129 B4 Ilıca Turkey
129 B4 Ilıca Turkey
121 G4 Il'ich Kazakh.
Il'ichevsk Azer. see Şärur
Il'ichevsk Ukr. see Illichivs'k
Ilici Spain see Elche
92 C4 Iligan Phil.
92 C4 Iligan Bay Phil.
Ili He r. China/Kazakh. see Ili
188 G4 Ilijaš Bos.-Herz.
221 P2 Ilimananngip Nunaa i. Greenland
131 L3 Ilimpeya r. Rus. Fed.
120 D2 Il'inka Kazakh.
121 K2 Il'inka Rus. Fed.
139 H4 Il'ino Rus. Fed.
134 K4 Il'inskiy Rus. Fed.
139 I1 Il'inskiy Rus. Fed.
100 G3 Il'inskiy Sakhalin Rus. Fed.
134 I3 Il'insko-Podomskoye Rus. Fed.
137 J4 Il'inskoye Rus. Fed.
139 J5 Il'inskoye Rus. Fed.
139 K3 Il'inskoye Rus. Fed.
139 L3 Il'inskoye Rus. Fed.
139 L3 Il'inskoye-Khovanskoye Rus. Fed.
Il'intsy Ukr. see Illintsi
233 F3 Ilion NY U.S.A.
188 E3 Ilirska Bistrica Slovenia
Ilium tourist site Turkey see Truva
138 F4 Iliya r. Belarus
Iliysk Kazakh. see Kapchagay
177 L3 Ilk Hungary
114 C3 Ilkal Karnataka India
151 F2 Ilkeston Derbyshire, England U.K.
149 H4 Ilkley West Yorkshire, England U.K.
157 H4 Ill r. France
183 H4 Illana Spain
92 B5 Illana Bay Phil.
260 B2 Illapel Chile
260 B2 Illapel r. Chile
185 H4 Illar Spain
191 G3 Illasi r. Italy
163 B4 Illats France
82 C1 Illbillee, Mount hill S.A. Austr.
158 E3 Ille r. France
158 E3 Ille-et-Vilaine dept Bretagne France
207 G3 Illéla Niger
207 G3 Illela Nigeria
173 D3 Iller r. Ger.
173 E3 Illerrieden Ger.
173 E3 Illertissen Ger.
183 G4 Illescas Spain
163 E6 Ille-sur-Têt France
136 F4 Illichivs'k Ukr.
156 B4 Illiers-Combray France
252 D4 Illimani, Nevado de mt. Bol.
172 C3 Illingen Baden-Württemberg Ger.
172 B2 Illingen Saarland Ger.
136 F4 Illinka Ukr.
226 B5 Illinois r. IL U.S.A.
236 F4 Illinois state U.S.A.
136 E3 Illintsi Ukr.
205 H4 Illizi Alg.
157 H4 Illkirch-Graffenstaden France
172 D4 Illmensee Ger.
179 H3 Illmitz Austria
185 G3 Íllora Spain
192 A4 Illorai Sardegna Italy
173 F2 Illschwang Ger.
183 I3 Illueca Spain
157 H5 Illzach France
171 C4 Ilm r. Ger.
173 F3 Ilm r. Ger.
87 E6 Ilma, Lake salt flat W.A. Austr.
124 D4 'Ilmān, Jabal al hill Saudi Arabia
139 H2 Il'men', Ozero l. Rus. Fed.
169 F5 Ilmenau Ger.
168 F2 Ilmenau r. Ger.
150 E4 Ilminster Somerset, England U.K.
136 B3 Il'nytsya Ukr.
252 C4 Ilo Peru
207 G5 Ilobu Nigeria
92 B4 Iloilo Phil.
140 O3 Ilomantsi Fin.
207 G4 Ilorin Nigeria
188 F3 Ilova r. Croatia
135 I6 Ilovatka Rus. Fed.
137 J4 Ilovays'k Ukr.
197 F5 Ilovica Macedonia
137 J2 Ilovka Rus. Fed.
135 H6 Ilovlya Rus. Fed.
135 H6 Ilovlya r. Rus. Fed.
175 I3 Iłów Pol.
174 D4 Iłowa Pol.
175 I2 Iłowo Osada Pol.
164 D2 Ilpendam Neth.
131 R3 Il'pyrskiy Rus. Fed.
Il'pyrskoye Rus. Fed. see Il'pyrskiy
141 L3 Ilsbo Sweden
169 F3 Ilse r. Ger.
169 F3 Ilsede Ger.
169 F4 Ilsenburg (Harz) Ger.
172 D2 Ilsfeld Ger.
172 D2 Ilshofen Ger.
150 D4 Ilsington Devon, England U.K.
137 J5 Il'skiy Rus. Fed.
138 F4 Ilūkste Latvia
221 M3 Ilulissat Greenland
Ilva i. Italy see Elba, Isola d'
138 F4 Il'ya Belarus
Il'yaly Turkm. see Yylanly
134 L3 Ilych r. Rus. Fed.
179 G3 Ilz Austria
173 H3 Ilz r. Ger.
175 J4 Iłża Pol.
175 J4 Iłżanka r. Pol.
103 F6 Imabari Japan
102 J3 Imabetsu Japan
251 G5 Imabú r. Brazil
105 F2 Imaichi Japan
213 H2 Imala Moz.
127 G5 Imām al Ḩamzah Iraq
126 D3 İmamoğlu Turkey
Iman Rus. Fed. see Dal'nerechensk
100 E3 Iman r. Rus. Fed.
121 G1 Imantau, Ozero l. Kazakh.
103 D7 Imari Japan
206 E3 Imasgo Burkina
Imassogo Burkina see Imasgo
251 F3 Imataca, Serranía de mts Venez.
141 O3 Imatra Fin.
250 B4 Imbabura prov. Ecuador
255 C9 Imbituba Brazil
256 B6 Imbituva Brazil
177 H4 Imeľ Slovakia
imeni 26 Bakinskikh Komissarov Azer. see 26 Bakı Komissarı
122 C2 imeni 26 Bakinskikh Komissarov Turkm.
134 H4 imeni Babushkina Rus. Fed.
123 E2 imeni C. A. Niyazova Turkm.
imeni Chapayevka Turkm. see imeni C. A. Niyazova
131 P3 imeni Gastello Rus. Fed.
imeni G. I. Petrovskogo Cherkas'ka Oblast' Ukr. see Horodyshche
139 M3 imeni Gor'kogo Rus. Fed.
imeni G. Ya. Sedova Ukr. see Syedove
137 H2 imeni Karla Libknekhta Rus. Fed.
imeni Khamzy Khakikmzade Uzbek. see Khamza
imeni Kirova Kazakh. see Kopbirlik
imeni Kirova Donets'ka Oblast' Ukr. see Kirove
imeni Kirova Donets'ka Oblast' Ukr. see Kirovs'k
imeni L. M. Kaganovicha Ukr. see Popasna
134 I4 imeni M. I. Kalinina Rus. Fed.
imeni Petra Stuchki Latvia see Aizkraukle
100 F1 imeni Poliny Osipenko Rus. Fed.
139 K2 imeni Zhelyabova Rus. Fed.
137 H3 Imeny Lenina, Ozero l. Ukr.
191 G2 Imèr Italy
194 D5 Imera r. Sicilia Italy
251 E4 Imeri, Serra mts Brazil
210 D3 Īmī Eth.
204 C3 Imi-n-Tanoute Morocco
204 B4 Imirikliy Labyad reg. Western Sahara
Imishli Azer. see İmişli
129 F4 İmişli Azer.
101 C5 Imjin-gang r. N. Korea/S. Korea
227 F4 Imlay City MI U.S.A.
169 F5 Immelborn Ger.
172 C4 Immendingen Ger.
169 E4 Immenhausen Ger.
173 F2 Immenreuth Ger.
172 D4 Immenstaad am Bodensee Ger.
173 E4 Immenstadt im Allgäu Ger.
149 I4 Immingham North East Lincolnshire, England U.K.
231 D7 Immokalee FL U.S.A.
207 G5 Imo state Nigeria
191 G4 Imola Italy
188 F4 Imotski Croatia
215 G3 Impendle S. Africa
254 D3 Imperatriz Brazil
190 D5 Imperia Italy
190 C4 Imperia prov. Liguria Italy
260 A6 Imperial r. Chile
252 A3 Imperial Peru
241 J5 Imperial CA U.S.A.
236 C3 Imperial NE U.S.A.
240 I5 Imperial Beach CA U.S.A.
86 C3 Imperieuse Reef W.A. Austr.
208 C4 Impfondo Congo
117 H4 Imphal Manipur India
160 B2 Imphy France
151 H2 Impington Cambridgeshire, England U.K.
191 G5 Impruneta Italy
177 I5 Imrehegy Hungary
199 D1 İmroz anakkale Turkey
İmroz i. Turkey see Gökçeada
İmrun Turkey see Pütürge
101 C6 Imsil S. Korea
178 B3 Imst Austria
242 C2 Imuris Mex.
180 E5 Imzouren Morocco
100 E2 In r. Rus. Fed.
105 D3 Ina Japan
174 C2 Ina r. Pol.
92 A4 Inagauan Phil.
104 B4 Ina-gawa r. Japan
147 B4 Inagh Rep. of Ireland
105 F3 Inagi Japan
254 F4 Inajá Brazil
253 H2 Inaja r. Brazil
252 C3 Inambari Peru
252 C3 Inambari r. Peru
177 K3 Ináncs Hungary
215 H3 Inanda S. Africa
81 C4 Inangahua Junction South I. N.Z.
252 C2 Iñapari Peru
140 N1 Inari Fin.
140 N1 Inarijärvi l. Fin.
140 N1 Inarijoki r. Fin./Norway
252 D2 Inauini r. Brazil
103 J5 Inawashiro-ko l. Japan
104 C3 Inazawa Japan
187 F5 Inca Spain
199 F3 İnceler Turkey
147 B4 Inch Kerry Rep. of Ireland
147 E4 Inch Wexford Rep. of Ireland
146 F5 Inchbare Angus, Scotland U.K.
81 C5 Inchbonnie South I. N.Z.
122 D2 Īncheh Iran
173 F3 Inchenhofen Ger.
156 B2 Incheville France
147 B5 Inchigeelagh Rep. of Ireland
210 C3 Inch'īnī Terara mt. Eth.
146 D6 Inchinnan Renfrewshire, Scotland U.K.
204 B5 Inchiri admin. reg. Maur.
101 C5 Inch'ŏn S. Korea
213 G3 Inchope Moz.
146 E5 Inchture Perth and Kinross, Scotland U.K.
183 G2 Incinillas Spain
Incio Spain see A Cruz de Incio
Incirli Sakarya Turkey see Karasu
213 G5 Incomati r. Moz.
165 D4 Incourt Belgium
192 B3 Incudine, Monte mt. France
138 E3 Inčukalns Latvia
146 B6 Indaal, Loch b. Scotland U.K.
257 E3 Indaiá r. Brazil
256 A3 Indaiá Grande r. Brazil
256 D5 Indaiatuba Brazil
140 L3 Indalsälven r. Sweden
141 I3 Indalstø Norway
244 D4 Indaparapeo Mex.
116 D4 Indargarh Madh. Prad. India
116 D4 Indargarh Rajasthan India
210 C1 Inda Silasē Eth.
242 D3 Indé Mex.
Indefatigable Island Islas Galápagos Ecuador see Santa Cruz, Isla
240 H3 Independence CA U.S.A.
236 F3 Independence IA U.S.A.
237 E4 Independence KS U.S.A.
230 C4 Independence KY U.S.A.
226 A2 Independence MN U.S.A.
236 E4 Independence MO U.S.A.
232 C6 Independence VA U.S.A.
226 B3 Independence WI U.S.A.
238 C3 Independence Mountains NV U.S.A.
252 D4 Independencia Bol.
254 E3 Independência Brazil
245 F3 Independencia Mex.
197 H3 Independenţa Romania
197 I4 Independenţa Romania
197 H3 Independenţa Romania
107 I2 Inder Nei Mongol China
120 B2 Inderborskiy Kazakh.
114 C2 Indi Karnataka India
113 H6 India country Asia
226 D2 Indian r. MI U.S.A.
232 D4 Indiana PA U.S.A.
230 C3 Indiana state U.S.A.
264 P9 Indian-Antarctic Basin sea feature Southern Ocean
265 L8 Indian-Antarctic Ridge sea feature Southern Ocean
230 C4 Indianapolis IN U.S.A.
222 G3 Indian Cabins Alta Can.
Indian Desert India/Pak. see Thar Desert
232 B6 Indian Fields KY U.S.A.
225 J2 Indian Harbour Nfld. Can.
223 K5 Indian Head Sask. Can.
233 F3 Indian Lake NY U.S.A.
235 F1 Indian Neck CT U.S.A.
213 □G5 Indian Ocean OCEAN
236 E3 Indianola IA U.S.A.
237 F5 Indianola MS U.S.A.
256 D3 Indianópolis Brazil
241 K2 Indian Peak UT U.S.A.
226 E3 Indian River MI U.S.A.
241 J3 Indian Springs NV U.S.A.
241 L4 Indian Wells AZ U.S.A.
256 B2 Indiara Brazil
254 F4 Indiaroba Brazil
247 □1 Indiera Alta Puerto Rico
131 P2 Indigirka r. Rus. Fed.
196 E3 Inđija Vojvodina, Srbija Yugo.
242 □J7 Indio r. Nic.
241 I5 Indio CA U.S.A.
261 G6 Indio Rico Arg.
78 □6 Indispensable Strait Solomon Is
137 H5 Indol r. Ukr.
139 K1 Indomanka r. Rus. Fed.
90 D7 Indonesia country Asia
116 C5 Indore Madh. Prad. India
94 C3 Indragiri r. Indon.
95 E4 Indramayu Jawa Barat Indon.
Indrapura, Gunung vol. Indon. see Kerinci, Gunung
115 D2 Indravati r. India
159 H5 Indre dept Centre France
162 C1 Indre r. France
159 G4 Indre-et-Loire dept Centre France
82 C1 Indulkana S.A. Austr.
Indur Andhra Prad. India see Nizamabad
114 C2 Indurti Andhra Prad. India
116 E2 Indus r. China/Pak. alt. Shiquan He (China)
123 F5 Indus, Mouths of the Pak.
265 I3 Indus Cone sea feature Indian Ocean
215 F4 Indwe S. Africa
215 F5 Indwe r. S. Africa
197 H4 Indzhe Voyvoda Bulg.
126 D2 İnebolu Turkey
199 F1 İnegöl Turkey
93 B5 Inerie vol. Flores Indon.
197 E2 Ineu Arad Romania
177 L4 Ineu Bihor Romania
Inevi Turkey see Cihanbeyli
232 B6 Inez KY U.S.A.
204 C3 Inezgane Morocco
214 C6 Infanta, Cape S. Africa
Infantes Spain see Villanueva de los Infantes
245 G5 Inferior, Laguna lag. Mex.
253 E2 Infernao, Cachoeira waterfall Brazil
244 D4 Infiernillo, Presa resr Mex.
183 E1 Infiesto Spain
96 C2 Ing, Mae Nam r. Thai.
209 B6 Inga Dem. Rep. Congo
141 N3 Ingå Fin.
207 G2 Ingal Niger
240 G2 Ingalls, Mount CA U.S.A.
151 H3 Ingatestone Essex, England U.K.
172 D2 Ingelfingen Ger.
172 C2 Ingelheim am Rhein Ger.
165 C4 Ingelmunster Belgium
143 F3 Ingelstad Sweden
208 C5 Ingende Dem. Rep. Congo
258 E1 Ingeniero Guillermo Nueva Juárez Arg.
260 D6 Ingeniero Huergo Arg.
259 C6 Ingeniero Jacobacci Arg.
260 E4 Ingeniero Luiggi Arg.
261 H4 Ingeniero Maschwitz Arg.
261 H4 Ingeniero Otamendi Arg.
222 E3 Ingenika r. B.C. Can.
216 □3f Ingenio Gran Canaria Canary Is
252 B3 Ingenio r. Peru
224 D5 Ingersoll Ont. Can.
106 D1 Ingettolgoy Mongolia
85 F3 Ingham Qld Austr.
120 F5 Ingichka Uzbek.
183 H2 Inglares r. Spain
149 G3 Ingleborough hill England U.K.
149 H3 Ingleton Durham, England U.K.
149 G3 Ingleton North Yorkshire, England U.K.
149 G4 Inglewhite Lancashire, England U.K.
83 G2 Inglewood Qld Austr.
83 E4 Inglewood Vic. Austr.
80 E3 Inglewood North I. N.Z.
240 H5 Inglewood CA U.S.A.
149 G3 Inglewood Forest England U.K.
84 D2 Inglis Island N.T. Austr.
107 G1 Ingoda r. Rus. Fed.
96 B1 Ingoka Pum mt. Myanmar
172 D3 Ingoldingen Ger.
149 J4 Ingoldmells Lincolnshire, England U.K.
173 F3 Ingolstadt Ger.
82 C2 Ingomar S.A. Austr.
238 F2 Ingomar MT U.S.A.
225 I4 Ingonish N.S. Can.
117 G4 Ingraj Bazar W. Bengal India
146 G6 Ingram Northumberland, England U.K.
232 D6 Ingram VA U.S.A.
226 B3 Ingram WI U.S.A.
159 F4 Ingrandes Pays de la Loire France
159 G5 Ingrandes Poitou-Charentes France
252 E5 Ingre Bol.
156 B5 Ingré France
263 F2 Ingrid Christensen Coast Antarctica
158 C4 Inguiniel France
Ingul r. Ukr. see Inhul
Ingulets Ukr. see Inhulets'
Ingushetia aut. rep. Rus. Fed. see Ingushskaya Respublika
129 D2 Ingushskaya Respublika aut. rep. Rus. Fed.
215 I2 Ingwavuma S. Africa
Ingwavuma r. Swaziland see Ngwavuma
157 H4 Ingwiller France
213 G4 Inhambane Moz.
213 G4 Inhambane prov. Moz.
254 F4 Inhambupe Brazil
213 G3 Inhaminga Moz.
257 F3 Inhapim Brazil
213 G4 Inhassoro Moz.
205 F5 I-n-Hihaou, Adrar hills Alg.
199 G1 İnhisar Turkey
137 F4 Inhul r. Ukr.
137 G4 Inhulets' Ukr.
137 G4 Inhulets' r. Ukr.
256 C2 Inhumas Brazil
93 B5 Inielika vol. Flores Indon.
185 I1 Iniesta Spain
257 E3 Inimutaba Brazil
138 C1 Iniö Fin.
250 E4 Inírida r. Col.
Inis Rep. of Ireland see Ennis
Inis Córthaidh Rep. of Ireland see Enniscorthy
147 A3 Inishark i. Rep. of Ireland
147 A3 Inishbofin i. Rep. of Ireland
147 B3 Inisheer i. Rep. of Ireland
147 B3 Inishmaan i. Rep. of Ireland
147 B3 Inishmore i. Rep. of Ireland
147 C2 Inishmurray i. Rep. of Ireland
147 D1 Inishowen pen. Rep. of Ireland
147 E1 Inishowen Head hd Rep. of Ireland
147 D1 Inishtrahull i. Rep. of Ireland
147 D1 Inishtrahull Sound sea chan. Rep. of Ireland
147 A3 Inishturk i. Rep. of Ireland
107 H2 Injgan Sum Nei Mongol China
210 C2 Injibara Eth.
85 G5 Injune Qld Austr.
120 F3 Inkardar'ya Kazakh.
151 F2 Inkberrow Worcestershire, England U.K.
176 G5 Inke Hungary
85 E3 Inkerman Qld Austr.
137 G5 Inkerman Ukr.
222 C3 Inklin B.C. Can.
222 C3 Inklin r. B.C. Can.
81 D5 Inland Kaikoura Range mts South I. N.Z.
Inland Sea Japan see Seto-naikai
233 F3 Inlet NY U.S.A.
173 E5 Inn r. Europe
103 E7 Innai Japan
82 E1 Innamincka S.A. Austr.
140 K2 Inndyr Norway
146 D6 Innellan Argyll and Bute, Scotland U.K.
217 □2a Inner Islands Seychelles
146 E6 Innerleithen Scottish Borders, Scotland U.K.
173 H3 Innernzell Ger.
146 C4 Inner Sound sea chan. Scotland U.K.
190 D2 Innertkirchen Switz.
173 F3 Inning am Ammersee Ger.
85 F3 Innisfail Qld Austr.
222 H4 Innisfail Alta Can.
147 C5 Innishannon Rep. of Ireland
147 E2 Inniskeen Rep. of Ireland
100 D2 Innokent'yevka Rus. Fed.
103 F6 Innoshima Japan
178 C3 Innsbruck Austria
191 G1 Innsbruck airport Austria
224 E1 Innuksuak r. Que. Can.
147 A5 Inny r. Kerry Rep. of Ireland
147 D3 Inny r. Longford/Westmeath Rep. of Ireland
256 B3 Inocência Brazil
208 C5 Inongo Dem. Rep. Congo
199 G2 İnönü Turkey
Inoucdjouac Que. Can. see Inukjuak
177 H3 Inovec mt. Slovakia
175 I4 Inowłódz Pol.
174 G3 Inowrocław Pol.
129 C1 Inozemtsevo Rus. Fed.
252 D4 Inquisivi Bol.
190 C1 Ins Switz.
205 F4 In Salah Alg.
135 I5 Insar Rus. Fed.
146 F4 Insch Aberdeenshire, Scotland U.K.
87 B5 Inscription, Cape W.A. Austr.
96 B3 Insein Myanmar
174 D2 Ińsko Pol.
157 G4 Insming France
Insterburg Rus. Fed. see Chernyakhovsk
129 E3 İnstitut Azer.
138 C4 Instruch r. Rus. Fed.
197 H3 Însurăţei Romania
213 E3 Insuza r. Zimbabwe
134 M2 Inta Rus. Fed.
261 F4 Intendente Alvear Arg.
199 E1 İntepe Turkey
Interamna Italy see Teramo
190 C2 Interlaken Switz.
226 A1 International Falls MN U.S.A.
197 H3 Întorsura Buzăului Romania
190 E3 Introbio Italy
250 C5 Intutu Peru
224 E1 Inukjuak Que. Can.
220 E3 Inuvik N.W.T. Can.
252 B2 Inuya r. Peru
104 C3 Inuyama Japan
134 L4 In'va r. Rus. Fed.
147 C2 Inver Rep. of Ireland
146 C4 Inveralligin Highland, Scotland U.K.
146 G4 Inverallochy Aberdeenshire, Scotland U.K.
147 B3 Inveran Rep. of Ireland
146 C5 Inveraray Argyll and Bute, Scotland U.K.
146 F5 Inverarity Angus, Scotland U.K.
146 D5 Inverarnan Argyll and Bute, Scotland U.K.
146 F5 Inverbervie Aberdeenshire, Scotland U.K.
81 B7 Invercargill South I. N.Z.
146 D6 Inverclyde admin. div. Scotland U.K.
83 G2 Inverell N.S.W. Austr.
146 E5 Inverey Aberdeenshire, Scotland U.K.
146 D4 Invergarry Highland, Scotland U.K.
146 D4 Invergordon Highland, Scotland U.K.
146 C5 Inverinan Argyll and Bute, Scotland U.K.
146 F5 Inverkeilor Angus, Scotland U.K.
146 E5 Inverkeithing Fife, Scotland U.K.
146 C3 Inverkirkaig Highland, Scotland U.K.
146 C4 Inverlael Highland, Scotland U.K.
85 E3 Inverleigh Qld Austr.
223 K5 Invermay Sask. Can.
146 D4 Invermoriston Highland, Scotland U.K.
225 I4 Inverness N.S. Can.
146 D4 Inverness Highland, Scotland U.K.
240 F2 Inverness CA U.S.A.
231 D6 Inverness FL U.S.A.
146 C5 Invernoaden Argyll and Bute, Scotland U.K.
146 D5 Inversnaid Stirling, Scotland U.K.
146 F4 Inverurie Aberdeenshire, Scotland U.K.
84 B3 Inverway N.T. Austr.
97 B4 Investigator Channel Myanmar
82 C3 Investigator Group is S.A. Austr.
265 K5 Investigator Ridge sea feature Indian Ocean
82 D3 Investigator Strait S.A. Austr.
232 D5 Inwood WV U.S.A.
215 G4 Inxu r. S. Africa
Inyanga Zimbabwe see Nyanga
213 G3 Inyangani mt. Zimbabwe
Inyati Zimbabwe see Nyathi
Inyazura Zimbabwe see Nyazura
240 I4 Inyokern CA U.S.A.
240 H3 Inyo Mountains CA U.S.A.
211 B6 Inyonga Tanz.
135 I5 Inza Rus. Fed.
173 G4 Inzell Ger.
120 D1 Inzer Rus. Fed.
134 L5 Inzer r. Rus. Fed.
135 H5 Inzhavino Rus. Fed.
178 C3 Inzing Austria
158 C4 Inzinzac-Lochrist France
198 B2 Ioannina Greece
198 B2 Ioanninon, Limni l. Greece
191 I2 Iôf di Montasio mt. Italy
103 □3 Iō-jima i. Japan
134 G2 Iokanga r. Rus. Fed.
237 E4 Iola KS U.S.A.
234 B1 Iola PA U.S.A.
226 C3 Iola WI U.S.A.
Iolotan' Turkm. see Yeloten
209 B9 Iona Angola
225 I4 Iona N.S. Can.
146 B5 Iona i. Scotland U.K.
146 B5 Iona Abbey tourist site Scotland U.K.
240 I2 Ione NV U.S.A.
238 C1 Ione WA U.S.A.
197 G3 Ioneşti Romania
226 E4 Ionia MI U.S.A.
Ionian Islands Greece see Ionioi Nisoi
198 A2 Ionian Sea Greece/Italy
Ionio prov. Puglia Italy see Taranto
198 A2 Ionioi Nisoi is Greece
Iori r. Azer. see Qabırrı
129 E3 Iori r. Georgia
198 D3 Ios Greece
199 D3 Ios i. Greece
Iō-tō i. Japan see Iō-jima
102 □1 Iō-Tori-jima i. Japan
206 A2 Iouîk Maur.
236 F3 Iowa r. IA U.S.A.
236 E3 Iowa state U.S.A.
236 F3 Iowa City IA U.S.A.
236 E3 Iowa Falls IA U.S.A.
104 C2 Iō-zan hill Japan
136 E1 Ipa r. Belarus
256 C2 Ipameri Brazil
257 G3 Ipanema Brazil
254 F4 Ipanema r. Brazil
252 B2 Iparía Peru
257 F3 Ipatinga Brazil
135 H7 Ipatovo Rus. Fed.
256 C5 Ipauçu Brazil
226 B5 Ipava IL U.S.A.
198 B2 Ipeiros admin. reg. Greece
177 H4 Ipeľ r. Slovakia
177 I3 Ipeľ r. Slovakia
215 E2 Ipelegeng S. Africa
177 H4 Ipeľská pahorkatina mts Slovakia
173 E2 Iphofen Ger.
256 C3 Ipiaçu Brazil
250 B4 Ipiales Col.
254 F5 Ipiaú Brazil
254 F5 Ipirá Brazil
256 B6 Ipiranga Brazil
Ípiros admin. reg. Greece see Ipeiros
78 □4a Ipis i. Chuuk Micronesia
252 B1 Ipixuna Brazil
252 B1 Ipixuna r. Amazonas Brazil
251 F6 Ipixuna r. Amazonas Brazil
94 C1 Ipoh Malaysia
177 H4 Ipoly r. Hungary/Slovakia
215 E3 Ipopeng S. Africa
256 B2 Iporá Brazil
256 C6 Iporanga Brazil
194 D6 Ippari r. Sicilia Italy
173 E2 Ippesheim Ger.
150 D4 Ipplepen Devon, England U.K.
208 D3 Ippy C.A.R.
199 E1 İpsala Turkey
173 E2 Ipsheim Ger.
149 H4 Ipstones Staffordshire, England U.K.
85 H5 Ipswich Qld Austr.
151 I2 Ipswich Suffolk, England U.K.
236 D2 Ipswich SD U.S.A.
254 E3 Ipu Brazil
256 C4 Ipuã Brazil
254 E3 Ipueiras Brazil
256 D5 Ipuiúna Brazil
254 E4 Ipupiara Brazil
139 H5 Iput' r. Rus. Fed.
137 F1 Iputs' r. Belarus
221 L3 Iqaluit Nunavut Can.
111 F4 Iqe He r. China
253 F3 Iquê r. Brazil
252 C5 Iquique Chile
Iquiri r. Brazil see Ituxi
250 C5 Iquitos Peru
102 □1 Irabu-jima i. Japan
251 H3 Iracoubo Fr. Guiana
104 C4 Irago-suidō str. Japan
255 B8 Irai Brazil
198 C1 Irakleia Greece
199 D3 Irakleia i. Greece
198 D4 Irakleio Kriti Greece
198 D4 Irakleiou, Kolpos b. Kriti Greece
Iráklia i. Greece see Irakleia
Iraklion Kriti Greece see Irakleio
254 E5 Iramaia Brazil
122 C4 Iran country Asia
95 F2 Iran, Pegunungan mts Indon.
156 D5 Irancy France
122 A2 Īrānshāh Iran
122 E5 Īrānshahr Iran
244 D3 Irapuato Mex.
127 F4 Iraq country Asia
205 G4 Irarrarene reg. Alg.
233 G2 Irasville VT U.S.A.
251 H5 Iratapuru r. Brazil
256 B6 Irati Brazil
183 I2 Irati r. Spain
177 K5 Iratoşu Romania
134 K2 Irayel' Rus. Fed.
242 □J7 Irazu, Volcán vol. Costa Rica
138 D3 Irbe r. Latvia
Irbes šaurums sea chan. Estonia/Latvia see Irbe Strait
138 D3 Irbe Strait Estonia/Latvia
Irbe väin sea chan. Estonia/Latvia see Irbe Strait
128 B3 Irbid Jordan
Irbil Iraq see Arbīl
130 H4 Irbit Rus. Fed.
151 G2 Irchester Northamptonshire, England U.K.
179 F3 Irdning Austria
137 F3 Irdyn' Ukr.
254 E4 Irecê Brazil
177 H5 Iregszemcse Hungary
183 H2 Iregua r. Spain
147 D3 Ireland, Republic of country Europe
235 D1 Ireland Corners NY U.S.A.
147 E3 Ireland's Eye i. Rep. of Ireland
134 L4 Iren' r. Rus. Fed.
81 A6 Irene, Mount South I. N.Z.
251 G4 Ireng r. Guyana/Venez.
256 A6 Iretama Brazil
129 D1 Irgakly Rus. Fed.
129 D3 Irganch'ai Georgia
199 F2 Irgıllı Turkey
120 E2 Irgiz Kazakh.
120 E2 Irgiz r. Kazakh.
192 B4 Irgoli Sardegna Italy
204 C3 Irherm Morocco
204 D3 Irhil M'Goun mt. Morocco
Iri S. Korea see Iksan
Irian Barat prov. Indon. see Irian Jaya
93 D3 Irian Jaya prov. Indon.
91 I7 Irian Jaya reg. Indon.
202 D6 Iriba Chad
251 G4 Iricoumé, Serra hills Brazil
122 A2 Īrī Dāgh mt. Iran
196 D3 Irig Vojvodina, Srbija Yugo.
92 B3 Iriga Phil.
160 C3 Irigny France
120 D2 Iriklinskiy Rus. Fed.
211 B6 Iringa Tanz.
211 B7 Iringa admin. reg. Tanz.
114 C4 Irinjalakuda Kerala India
102 □1 Iriomote-jima i. Japan
251 H5 Iriri r. Brazil
254 B4 Iriri Novo r. Brazil
Irish Free State country Europe see Ireland, Republic of
145 E5 Irish Sea Rep. of Ireland/U.K.
163 A5 Irissarry France
254 D2 Irituia Brazil
182 B2 Irixo Spain
137 J5 Irkliyevskaya Rus. Fed.
137 G3 Irkliyiv Ukr.
98 H1 Irkutsk Rus. Fed.
98 H1 Irkutskaya Oblast' admin. div. Rus. Fed.
Irkutsk Oblast admin. div. Rus. Fed. see Irkutskaya Oblast'
173 G3 Irlbach Ger.
223 I4 Irma Alta Can.
226 C3 Irma WI U.S.A.
126 D3 Irmak Turkey
264 G2 Irminger Basin sea feature N. Atlantic Ocean
194 D6 Irminio r. Sicilia Italy
231 D5 Irmo SC U.S.A.
164 E1 Irnsum Neth.
208 C2 Iro, Lac l. Chad
158 E3 Irodouër France
158 B3 Iroise, Mer d' g. France
82 D3 Iron Baron S.A. Austr.
227 F2 Iron Bridge Ont. Can.
150 E2 Ironbridge Telford and Wrekin, England U.K.
232 E3 Irondequoit NY U.S.A.
226 A2 Iron Junction MN U.S.A.
82 D3 Iron Knob S.A. Austr.
226 C3 Iron Mountain MI U.S.A.
241 K3 Iron Mountain mt. UT U.S.A.
147 C2 Iron Mountains hills Rep. of Ireland
226 C2 Iron River MI U.S.A.
226 B2 Iron River WI U.S.A.
237 F4 Ironton MO U.S.A.
232 B5 Ironton OH U.S.A.
226 B2 Ironwood MI U.S.A.
233 F2 Iroquois Ont. Can.
226 D5 Iroquois r. IN U.S.A.
224 D3 Iroquois Falls Ont. Can.
92 C3 Irosin Phil.
Irpen' Ukr. see Irpin'
136 F2 Irpin' Ukr.
136 F2 Irpin' r. Ukr.
125 D2 'Irq al Ḩarūrī des. Saudi Arabia
124 C2 Irq al Mazhūr des. Saudi Arabia
124 D2 'Irq ath Thāmām des. Saudi Arabia
124 D2 'Irq Banbān des. Saudi Arabia
125 D2 'Irq Jahām des. Saudi Arabia
124 C3 'Irq Subay des. Saudi Arabia

Column 1

96 A3 Irrawaddy admin. div. Myanmar
96 A4 Irrawaddy r. Myanmar
96 A4 Irrawaddy, Mouths of the Myanmar
172 A2 Irrel Ger.
122 C1 Irsarybaba, Gory hills Turkm.
122 A2 Irsch Ger.
178 E4 Irschen Austria
173 F4 Irschenberg Ger.
173 E4 Irsee Ger.
136 E2 Irsha r. Ukr.
136 B3 Irshava Ukr.
193 I4 Irsina Italy
143 G2 Irsta Sweden
149 G3 Irthing r. England U.K.
151 G2 Irthlingborough Northamptonshire, England U.K.
121 H1 Irtysh r. Kazakh./Rus. Fed.
121 H1 Irtyshsk Kazakh.
Irtyshskoye Kazakh. see Irtyshsk
183 H4 Irueste Spain
105 F3 Iruma Japan
105 F3 Iruma-gawa r. Japan
208 F4 Irumu Dem. Rep. Congo
186 B1 Irún Spain
Iruña Spain see Pamplona
252 D4 Irupana Bol.
186 B1 Irurita Spain
183 I2 Irurozqui Spain
Irurtzun Spain see Irurzun
183 I2 Irurzun Spain
146 D6 Irvine North Ayrshire, Scotland U.K.
240 I5 Irvine CA U.S.A.
232 B6 Irvine KY U.S.A.
85 F3 Irvinebank Qld Austr.
146 D6 Irvine Bay Scotland U.K.
147 D2 Irvinestown Northern Ireland U.K.
237 D5 Irving TX U.S.A.
87 B6 Irwin r. W.A. Austr.
231 D5 Irwinton GA U.S.A.
171 C3 Irxleben Ger.
207 G3 Isa Nigeria
85 G4 Isaac r. Qld Austr.
186 C2 Isaba Spain
236 C2 Isabel SD U.S.A.
92 B4 Isabela Negros Phil.
92 B5 Isabela Phil.
247 □ Isabela Puerto Rico
250 □ Isabela, Isla i. Islas Galápagos Ecuador
242 □I6 Isabela, Cordillera mts Nic.
226 B2 Isabella MN U.S.A.
86 E4 Isabella, Lake salt flat W.A. Austr.
247 □ Isabel Segunda Puerto Rico
186 D2 Isábena r. Spain
199 F3 Isabey Turkey
129 C4 Isabey Dağı mt. Turkey
158 D4 Isac r. France
197 I3 Isaccea Romania
140 □B2 Ísafjarðardjúp est. Iceland
140 □B2 Ísafjörður Iceland
116 D4 Isagarh Madh. Prad. India
103 F7 Isahaya Japan
123 G3 Isá Khel Pak.
134 H2 Isakogorka Rus. Fed.
192 B4 Isalle r. Sardegna Italy
197 F3 Isalniţa Romania
250 D4 Isana r. Col.
207 G4 Isanlu Nigeria
205 G4 Isaouane-n-Tifernine des. Alg.
173 G3 Isar r. Ger.
191 G2 Isarco r. Italy
177 I4 Isaszeg Hungary
156 C2 Isbergues France
146 □H1 Isbister Shetland, Scotland U.K.
146 □H1 Isbister Shetland, Scotland U.K.
Isca Newport, Wales U.K. see Caerleon
183 F3 Íscar Spain
199 G2 İscehisar Turkey
157 F4 Isches France
178 B3 Ischgl Austria
193 H4 Ischia Italy
193 F4 Ischia, Isola d' i. Italy
193 H3 Ischitella Italy
86 E3 Ischl r. W.A. Austr.
156 C5 Isdes France
104 C4 Ise Japan
142 D4 Isefjord b. Denmark
105 F3 Isehara Japan
178 D4 Isel r. Austria
173 G3 Isen r. Ger.
173 G3 Isen r. Ger.
157 F4 Is-en-Bassigny France
134 K4 Isenbayevo Rus. Fed.
169 F3 Isenbüttel Ger.
190 F3 Iseo Italy
190 F3 Iseo, Lago d' l. Italy
161 D3 Isère dept Rhône-Alpes France
161 C4 Isère r. France
169 C4 Iserlohn Ger.
169 E3 Isernhagen Ger.
193 G3 Isernia Italy
193 G3 Isernia prov. Molise Italy
105 F2 Isesaki Japan
104 C4 Ise-wan b. Japan
207 F5 Iseyin Nigeria
Isfahan Iran see Eşfahān
121 G5 Isfana Tajik.
123 G1 Isfara Tajik.
140 □ Isfjorden inlet Svalbard
139 I2 Ishcherskaya Rus. Fed.
134 L3 Isherim, Gora mt. Rus. Fed.
251 G4 Isherton Guyana
134 J5 Isheyevka Rus. Fed.
102 □1 Ishigaki-jima i. Japan
102 J2 Ishikari-gawa r. Japan
102 J2 Ishikari-wan b. Japan
104 C2 Ishikawa pref. Japan
121 G1 Ishim r. Kazakh./Rus. Fed.
130 H4 Ishim Rus. Fed.
120 D1 Ishimbay Rus. Fed.
102 J4 Ishinomaki Japan
102 G2 Ishioka Japan
103 F7 Ishizuchi-san mt. Japan
123 G2 Ishkoshim Tajik.
116 C1 Ishkuman Jammu and Kashmir
139 L3 Ishnya Rus. Fed.
226 D2 Ishpeming MI U.S.A.
135 H5 Ishtikhon Uzbek.
Ishtykhan
121 F5 Ishtykhan Uzbek.
117 G4 Ishurdi Bangl.
252 D3 Isiboro r. Bol.
159 E3 Isigny-le-Buat France
159 E2 Isigny-sur-Mer France
199 F2 Işıklar Turkey
199 F2 Işıklı Turkey
192 B5 İsili Sardegna Italy
130 I4 Isil'kul' Rus. Fed.
250 B5 Isinliví Ecuador
215 H3 Isipingo S. Africa
208 E4 Isiro Dem. Rep. Congo
85 F5 Isisford Qld Austr.
179 F5 Iška r. Slovenia
132 E3 Iskateley Rus. Fed.
128 E3 İskenderun Turkey
128 E3 İskenderun Körfezi b. Turkey
126 D2 İskilip Turkey
Iski-Naukat Kyrg. see Eski-Naukat
130 J4 Iskitim Rus. Fed.
137 G3 Iskra Bulg.
137 H3 Iskra Poltavs'ka Oblast' Ukr.
Kirovohrads'ka Oblast' Ukr.
137 G4 Iskra Poltavs'ka Oblast' Ukr.
197 G4 Iskŭr r. Bulg.
208 D3 Iskushuban Somalia
222 D3 Iskut r. B.C. Can.
245 G4 Isla Mex.
146 E5 Isla r. Angus/Perth and Kinross, Scotland U.K.
184 C3 Isla Canela Spain
184 C3 Isla Cristina Spain
186 B3 Islallana Spain
129 B3 İslâhiye Turkey
Islamabad Jammu and Kashmir see Anantnag
123 H3 Islamabad Pak.
184 D3 Isla Mayor marsh Spain
184 D3 Isla Menor marsh Spain
123 G5 Islamkot Pak.
231 D7 Islamorada FL U.S.A.
117 F4 Islampur Bihar India
222 F2 Island r. N.W.T. Can.

Column 2

Ísland country Europe see Iceland
233 □I1 Island Falls ME U.S.A.
82 D2 Island Lagoon salt flat S.A. Austr.
223 M4 Island Lake Man. Can.
223 M4 Island Lake l. Man. Can.
238 E2 Island Park ID U.S.A.
233 H2 Island Pond VT U.S.A.
80 E1 Islands, Bay of North I. N.Z.
181 H3 Islas Baleares aut. comm. Spain
261 F3 Isla Verde Arg.
146 B6 Islay i. Scotland U.K.
146 B6 Islay, Sound of sea chan. Scotland U.K.
197 G4 Islaz Romania
162 D3 Isle France
162 B4 Isle r. France
151 H2 Isleham Cambridgeshire, England U.K.
150 C1 Isle of Anglesey admin. div. Wales U.K.
148 E3 Isle of Man i. Irish Sea
146 D7 Isle of Whithorn Dumfries and Galloway, Scotland U.K.
151 F4 Isle of Wight admin. div. England U.K.
232 E6 Isle of Wight VA U.S.A.
156 E3 Isle-sur-Suippe France
Isle, L' see Izmayil
203 G2 Ismâ'ilîya Egypt
128 A4 Ismâ'ilîya governorate Egypt
Ismailly Azer. see İsmayıllı
173 F3 Ismaning Ger.
129 F3 İsmayıllı Azer.
203 G3 Isna Egypt
182 C5 Isna Port.
146 □ Isnello Sicilia Italy
173 E4 Isny im Allgäu Ger.
213 □J4 Isoanala Madag.
141 M3 Isojoki Fin.
211 B7 Isoka Zambia
140 M3 Isokyrö Fin.
161 F4 Isola 2000 France
192 B2 Isolaccio-di-Fiumorbo Corse France
193 F2 Isola del Gran Sasso d'Italia Italy
191 G3 Isola della Scala Italy
194 C4 Isola delle Femmine Sicilia Italy
193 F3 Isola del Liri Italy
195 G4 Isola di Capo Rizzuto Italy
190 D4 Isola del Cantone Italy
186 E2 Isona Spain
191 J3 Isonzo r. Italy
213 □J4 Isorana Madag.
199 G3 Isparta Turkey
199 G3 Isparta prov. Turkey
197 N4 Isperikh Bulg.
146 □ Ispica Sicilia Italy
127 F2 İspir Turkey
Ispisar Tajik. see Khüjand
163 A5 Ispoure France
190 D3 Ispra Italy
129 B1 İspravnaya Rus. Fed.
172 C3 Ispringen Ger.
128 B3 Israel country Asia
256 B2 Israelândia Brazil
87 D7 Israelite Bay W.A. Austr.
Israʾil country Asia see Israel
135 I5 Issa Rus. Fed.
138 G3 Issa r. Rus. Fed.
207 H5 Issanguele Cameroon
251 G3 Issano Guyana
161 C4 Issarlès France
169 B4 Isselburg Ger.
169 H5 Issenheim France
206 D5 Issia Côte d'Ivoire
163 C3 Issigeac France
190 C3 Issime Italy
185 I2 Isso Spain
190 C3 Issogne Italy
160 B3 Issoire France
161 E3 Issole r. France
162 D2 Issoudun France
169 B4 Issum Ger.
211 B6 Issuna Tanz.
160 D1 Is-sur-Tille France
Issyk-Kul' Kyrg. see Balykchy
Issyk-Kul', Ozero salt l. Kyrg. see Ysyk-Köl
Issyk-Kul admin. div. Kyrg. see Ysyk-Köl
Issyk-Kul'skaya Oblast' admin. div. Kyrg. see Ysyk-Köl
160 B2 Issy-l'Évêque France
191 J4 Ista r. Croatia
191 J5 Ista r. Croatia
139 K5 Ista r. Rus. Fed.
254 D5 İstabulat tourist site Iraq
177 J3 Istállós-kő hill Hungary
185 F4 Istán Spain
199 F1 İstanbul Turkey
199 F1 İstanbul prov. Turkey
199 F1 İstanbul Boğazı str. Turkey
151 I3 Istead Rise Kent, England U.K.
174 G6 Istebné Slovakia
177 I2 Istebné Slovakia
176 F5 Isten dombja hill Hungary
122 B3 İştgāh-e Eznā Iran
198 C2 Istiaia Greece
123 H2 İstik r. Tajik.
129 D4 İstisu Azer.
250 B3 İstmina Col.
105 G4 Istochnoye Rus. Fed.
196 H4 Istok Kosovo, Srbija Yugo.
139 K4 Istra Rus. Fed.
191 C5 Istres France
Istria pen. Croatia see Istra
197 I3 Istria Romania
197 I3 Istriţa, Dealul hill Romania
163 A5 Isturits France
Itypia country Africa see Ethiopia
169 F6 Itz r. Ger.
168 E2 Itzehoe Ger.
168 F2 Itzstedt Ger.
194 D5 Iudica, Monte hill Sicilia Italy
237 F5 Iuka MS U.S.A.
131 T3 Iul'tin Rus. Fed.
213 H2 Iuluti Moz.
257 G4 Iúna Brazil
254 F4 Ivaí Brazil
256 A5 Ivaí r. Brazil
213 □J4 Ivakoany mt. Madag.
140 N1 Ivalo Fin.
140 N1 Ivalojoki r. Fin.
176 F4 Iván Hungary
171 L6 Ivana Belarus
176 D2 Ivančena Czech Rep.
138 E5 Ivanava Belarus
120 B1 Ivanivka
177 L1 Ivangorod Rus. Fed.
138 F2 Ivangorod Rus. Fed.
125 D3 Ivangrad Crna Gora Yugo. see Berane

Column 3

254 G3 Itamaracá, Ilha de i. Brazil
257 H2 Itamaraju Brazil
257 F2 Itamarandiba Brazil
257 G3 Itambacuri Brazil
257 G3 Itambacuri r. Brazil
257 G3 Itambé Brazil
257 F3 Itambé, Pico de mt. Brazil
104 B4 Itami Japan
104 □1 Itami airport Japan
112 H6 Itanagar Arun. Prad. India
254 D5 Itanguari r. Brazil
256 D6 Itanhaém Brazil
257 E5 Itanhandu Brazil
251 F6 Itanhauã r. Brazil
257 G2 Itanhém Brazil
257 G2 Itanhém r. Brazil
257 H1 Itanhomi Brazil
251 H4 Itany r. Fr. Guiana/Suriname
257 G2 Itaóbim Brazil
257 F4 Itaocara Brazil
254 C5 Itapaci Brazil
254 F2 Itapagé Brazil
257 E6 Itapecerica Brazil
257 G4 Itapemirim Brazil
254 C5 Itaperuna Brazil
256 C5 Itapetinga Brazil
256 C5 Itapetininga Brazil
254 F4 Itapeva Brazil
251 F3 Itapi r. Brazil
254 E4 Itapicuru Brazil
254 D3 Itapicuru, Serra de hills Brazil
254 D2 Itapicuru Mirim Brazil
254 D2 Itapicuru Mirim r. Brazil
254 F2 Itapipoca Brazil
256 D5 Itapira Brazil
256 B3 Itapiranga Brazil
256 B1 Itapirapuã Brazil
251 G5 Itapiúna Brazil
256 C4 Itápolis Brazil
254 F3 Itaporanga Paraíba Brazil
256 C5 Itaporanga São Paulo Brazil
254 E5 Itapuá Brazil
255 C9 Itapuã Brazil
255 C5 Itapuranga Brazil
253 G3 Itaquaquecetuba Brazil
255 A9 Itaquí Brazil
257 G3 Itarana Brazil
257 G1 Itarantim Brazil
256 C6 Itararé Brazil
256 C6 Itararé r. Brazil
116 D5 Itarsi Madh. Prad. India
140 D3 Itä-Suomi prov. Fin.
260 C3 Itata r. Chile
256 D5 Itatiba Brazil
256 B3 Itatinga Brazil
256 C5 Itauçu Brazil
256 E3 Itaueira r. Brazil
257 E4 Itaúna Brazil
257 H3 Itaúnas r. Brazil
198 C2 Itea Greece
162 C2 Iteu France
162 C2 Iteuil France
209 E8 Itezhi-Tezhi Dam Zambia
198 D2 Ithaca Ionioi Nisoi Greece see Ithaki
226 E4 Ithaca MI U.S.A.
232 E3 Ithaca NY U.S.A.
198 B2 Ithaki Greece
198 B2 Ithaki i. Greece
169 E3 Ith Hils ridge Ger.
210 C3 Iti r. Dem. Rep. Congo
257 G2 Itinga Brazil
255 B6 Itiquira Brazil
254 F3 Itiquira r. Brazil
256 D4 Itirapina Brazil
254 F4 Itiúba Brazil
254 F4 Itiúba, Serra de hills Brazil
258 E1 Itiyura r. Brazil
117 H4 Itkhari Bihar India
105 F4 Itō Japan
213 □2 Itoculo Moz.
105 D1 Itoigawa Japan
156 F3 Iton r. France
213 □J4 Itongafeno mt. Madag.
Itum-Kale
211 B7 Itungi Port Malawi
251 H3 Ituni Guyana
257 F4 Itupiranga Brazil
256 B3 Iturama Brazil
256 B3 Iturbe Para.
243 H6 Iturbide Campeche Mex.
245 E1 Iturbide Nuevo León Mex.
208 E4 Ituri r. Dem. Rep. Congo
99 Q3 Iturup, Ostrov i. Kuril'skiye O-va Rus. Fed.
257 E4 Itutinga Brazil
177 H4 Ituverava Brazil
252 D2 Ituxi r. Brazil
258 F2 Ituzaingó Arg.
168 D2 Itzehoe Ger.
256 A5 Iuiú Brazil

Column 4

139 K3 Ivan'kovskoye Vodokhranilishche resr Rus. Fed.
100 E2 Ivankovtsy Rus. Fed.
136 C3 Ivano-Frankivs'k Ivano-Frankivs'ka Oblast' admin. div. Ukr.
136 C3 Ivano-Frankivs'ka Oblast' admin. div. Ukr.
Ivano-Frankivs'k Oblast' admin. div. Ukr. see Ivano-Frankivs'ka Oblast'
136 B3 Ivano-Frankove Ukr.
Ivano-Frankovsk Ukr. see Ivano-Frankivs'k
Ivano-Frankovskaya Oblast' admin. div. Ukr. see Ivano-Frankivs'ka Oblast'
136 E3 Ivanopil' Ukr.
Ivanovka Kazakh. see Kokzhayyk
100 C2 Ivanovka Amurskaya Oblast' Rus. Fed.
120 C1 Ivanovka Orenburgskaya Oblast' Rus. Fed.
Ivanovka Belarus see Ivanava
197 G4 Ivanovo tourist site Bulg.
139 M3 Ivanovo Ivanovskaya Oblast' Rus. Fed.
139 K2 Ivanovo Tverskaya Oblast' Rus. Fed.
Ivanovo Oblast admin. div. Rus. Fed. see Ivanovskaya Oblast'
197 J5 Ivanovskaya Oblast' admin. div. Rus. Fed.
139 M3 Ivanovskaya Oblast' admin. div. Rus. Fed.
121 J2 Ivanovskiy Khrebet mts Kazakh.
137 H2 Ivanovskoye Kurskaya Oblast' Rus. Fed.
139 L3 Ivanovskoye Yaroslavskaya Oblast' Rus. Fed.
188 E2 Ivančica mts Croatia
197 H4 Ivanski Bulg.
120 B1 Ivanteyevka Rus. Fed.
136 C2 Ivanychi Ukr.
137 G2 Ivanytsya Ukr.
138 E5 Ivatsevichy Belarus
197 H5 Ivaylovgrad Bulg.
134 M3 Ivdel' Rus. Fed.
151 L3 Iver Buckinghamshire, England U.K.
147 B5 Iveragh Pen. Rep. of Ireland
140 □ Iversenfjellet hill Svalbard
197 H3 Iveşti Romania
197 I3 Iveşti Romania
207 H5 Ivindo r. Gabon
208 B5 Ivindo r. Gabon
151 L3 Ivinghoe Buckinghamshire, England U.K.
255 B7 Ivinheima Brazil
254 A5 Ivinheima r. Brazil
139 J1 Ivinskiy Razliv resr Rus. Fed.
188 E3 Iviza i. Spain see Eivissa
186 J2 Ivnya Rus. Fed.
213 □J4 Ivohibe Madag.
256 B2 Ivolândia Brazil
232 E6 Ivor VA U.S.A.
Ivory Coast country Africa see Côte d'Ivoire
139 G5 Ivot Rus. Fed.
190 C3 Ivrea Italy
190 C3 Ivrea Italy
129 D3 Ivris Zegani plat. Georgia
156 B4 Ivry-la-Bataille France
157 D2 Ivry-sur-Seine France
221 K3 Ivugivik Que. Can. see Ivujivik
221 K3 Ivujivik Que. Can.
138 F5 Ivyanyets Belarus
150 D3 Ivybridge Devon, England U.K.
232 C5 Ivydale WV U.S.A.
151 H3 Iwade Kent, England U.K.
105 F2 Iwai Japan
105 G1 Iwaki Japan
102 J3 Iwaki-san vol. Japan
103 F6 Iwakuni Japan
102 J4 Iwakura Japan
102 J2 Iwamizawa Japan
105 F3 Iwasawa Japan
105 J2 Iwashiro Japan
102 J4 Iwatate Japan
105 D4 Iwata Japan
102 J4 Iwate pref. Japan
102 J4 Iwate-san vol. Japan
207 F4 Iwatsuki Japan
116 C5 Iwo Nigeria
207 G5 Iwo Nigeria
Iwo Jima i. Japan see Iō-jima
138 B5 Iwye Belarus
245 E5 Ixhuatepec Mex.
245 G5 Ixhuatlán Mex.
245 F4 Ixhuatlán Mex.
252 C3 Ixiamas Bol.
245 E3 Iximquilpán Mex.
231 G2 Ixopo S. Africa
245 G5 Ixtacomitán Mex.
244 D3 Ixtapa de Azaba Spain
245 F5 Ixtepec Mex.
120 D2 Ixtepec Mex.
211 B7 Ixtepec Mex.
243 J5 Ixtlahuacán de los Reyes Mex.
244 D2 Ixtlán del Río Mex.
244 D3 Ixtlán Guerrero Mex.
244 B3 Ixtlán Jalisco Mex.
245 E4 Ixtapan de la Sal Mex.
244 B3 Ixtlán Mex.
244 B3 Ixtlán Mex.
231 D6 Ixworth Suffolk, England U.K.
98 G1 Iya r. Rus. Fed.
211 B7 Iyayi Turkey
129 B3 İyidere Turkey
İyirmi Altı Bakı Komissarı see 26 Bakı Komissarı
208 E4 Iyuri r. Dem. Rep. Congo
103 F7 Iyo Japan
103 F7 Iyomishima Japan
177 H4 Iz i. Croatia
243 H6 Izabal, Lago de l. Guat.
245 E3 Izalco vol. Mex.
243 H6 Izalde r. Spain
102 J2 Izari-dake mt. Japan
183 I2 Izarra Spain
197 G3 Izbăşeşti hill Romania
129 E2 Izberbash Rus. Fed.
175 L5 Izbica Kujawska Pol.
131 K3 Izbica Kujawska Pol.
213 H2 Izeda Port.
165 C4 Izegem Belgium
165 C4 Izel Belgium
213 □4 Izena-jima i. Japan
160 D2 Izernore France
161 D3 Izeron France
134 K4 Izhevsk Rus. Fed.
134 K2 Izhma Respublika Komi Rus. Fed.
134 K2 Izhma r. Rus. Fed.
134 K2 Izhma Respublika Komi Rus. Fed. see Sosnogorsk
125 G3 Izki Oman
124 □ Izkí Oman see Izmayil
136 C3 Izmayil Ukr.
199 E2 İzmir Turkey
199 E2 İzmir prov. Turkey
199 F2 İzmit Turkey see Kocaeli
199 F1 İzmit Körfezi b. Turkey
184 C... Izmorene Morocco
185 F3 Iznájar Spain
185 F1 Iznalloz Spain
199 F1 İznik Turkey
199 F1 İznik Gölü l. Turkey
216 □3c Iznoski Rus. Fed.
137 J3 Iznoski Rus. Fed.
135 H7 Izobil'nyy Rus. Fed.
196 F3 Izola Slovenia
137 M2 Izoplit Rus. Fed.
196 G3 Izvanku Ukr.
128 C3 Izra' Syria

Column 5

245 E4 Iztaccíhuatl, Volcán vol. Mex.
197 G5 Iztochni Rodopi mts Bulg.
245 E4 Izúcar de Matamoros Mex.
103 E7 Izu-hantō pen. Japan
104 E1 Izumi Kagoshima Japan
104 B4 Izumi Osaka Japan
104 B3 Izumiōtsu Japan
104 B3 Izumisano Japan
104 B4 Izumisano Japan
105 F3 Izumo Japan
266 E3 Izu-Ogasawara Trench sea feature N. Pacific Ocean
105 F4 Izu-shotō is Japan
Izu-tobu vol. Japan see Amagi-san
100 D2 Izvestkovy Rus. Fed.
197 G3 Izvoarele Giurgiu Romania
197 G3 Izvoarele Olt Romania
197 H3 Izvoarele Prahova Romania
197 G3 Izvoru Romania
136 D2 Izyaslav Ukr.
134 L2 Iz"yayu Rus. Fed.
137 I3 Izyum Ukr.

J

141 N3 Jaala Fin.
193 J4 Jabaga
188 J4 Jabalanac Croatia
123 G3 Jabal as Sirāj Afgh.
185 F2 Jabalón r. Spain
185 F2 Jabaloyas Spain
116 D5 Jabalpur Madh. Prad. India
185 D1 Jabalquinto Spain
124 C4 Jabbana Fara Islands Saudi Arabia
165 C3 Jabbeke Belgium
128 C3 Jabbūl, Sabkhat al salt flat Syria
170 D2 Jabel r. Ger.
84 C2 Jabiru N.T. Austr.
128 B2 Jablah Syria
188 F3 Jablanica Bos.-Herz.
197 H4 Jablanica r. Yugo.
120 B1 Jablanica r. Yugo.
176 L1 Jablonec nad Nisou Czech Rep.
176 Q3 Jablonica Slovakia
175 H6 Jabłonka Pol.
175 K3 Jabłonna Lacka Pol.
174 K4 Jabłonna Pierwsza Pol.
176 D1 Jablonné v Podještědí Czech Rep.
175 H2 Jabłonowo Pomorskie Pol.
176 F3 Jablůnka Czech Rep.
177 H2 Jablunkov Czech Rep.
254 C4 Jaboatão Brazil
256 C4 Jaboticabal Brazil
257 F3 Jaboticatubas Brazil
161 C1 Jabron r. France
193 E3 Jabuka Vojvodina, Srbija Yugo.
186 C2 Jaca Spain
245 E3 Jacala Mex.
251 H4 Jacaré r. Brazil
256 D3 Jacaré r. Brazil
255 B5 Jacarezinho Brazil
255 C5 Jacaraú Brazil
257 E5 Jacareí Brazil
254 D4 Jacaré r. Brazil
254 D5 Jacaré r. Brazil
257 F3 Jaceaba Brazil
260 D3 Jáchal r. Arg.
173 F2 Jachen r. Ger.
176 F4 Jachenau Ger.
176 B1 Jáchymov Czech Rep.
255 B5 Jaciara Brazil
257 D2 Jacinto Brazil
261 F6 Jacinto Arauz Arg.
259 D2 Jacinto Machado Brazil
252 D2 Jaciparaná r. Brazil
82 F2 Jack r. N.T. Austr.
226 D1 Jack Fish r. Ont. Can.
233 □I2 Jackman ME U.S.A.
231 G2 Jacksboro TN U.S.A.
237 D5 Jacksboro TX U.S.A.
231 C6 Jackson AL U.S.A.
240 I2 Jackson CA U.S.A.
232 A6 Jackson KY U.S.A.
237 C5 Jackson MI U.S.A.
238 C6 Jackson MN U.S.A.
237 F5 Jackson MO U.S.A.
237 F5 Jackson MS U.S.A.
237 F4 Jackson NC U.S.A.
237 C5 Jackson OH U.S.A.
231 D5 Jackson TN U.S.A.
237 C5 Jackson WI U.S.A.
238 E3 Jackson WY U.S.A.
262 T2 Jackson, Mount Antarctica
81 B5 Jackson Bay South I. N.Z.
81 B5 Jackson Bay b. South I. N.Z.
81 B5 Jackson Head pt South I. N.Z.
226 D3 Jacksonport WI U.S.A.
81 C5 Jacksons South I. N.Z.
225 J3 Jackson's Arm Nfld. Can.
231 G3 Jacksonville AL U.S.A.
237 G5 Jacksonville AR U.S.A.
231 D6 Jacksonville FL U.S.A.
236 E4 Jacksonville IL U.S.A.
231 E5 Jacksonville NC U.S.A.
237 E6 Jacksonville TX U.S.A.
231 D6 Jacksonville Beach FL U.S.A.
246 D3 Jacmel Haiti
123 G4 Jacobabad Pak.
254 E4 Jacobina Brazil
241 X3 Jacob Lake AZ U.S.A.
215 E3 Jacobsdal S. Africa
226 A2 Jacobson MN U.S.A.
224 E3 Jacques-Cartier, Détroit de sea chan. Que. Can.
225 H3 Jacques Cartier, Mont mt. Que. Can.
225 H3 Jacques Cartier Passage Que. Can.
121 H4 Jacquet River N.B. Can.
256 A3 Jacuba r. Brazil
255 C9 Jacuí r. Brazil
256 C3 Jacuípe r. Brazil
250 D4 Jacumã Brazil
254 D3 Jacunda Brazil
251 H5 Jacundá r. Brazil
255 B9 Jacutinga Minas Gerais Brazil
251 I5 Jacutinga r. Brazil
257 E5 Jacutinga Minas Gerais Brazil
165 C4 Jade r. Ger.
N. Dakota/S. Dakota U.S.A.

Column 6

215 E3 Jagersfontein S. Africa
114 D2 Jaggayyapeta Andhra Prad. India
122 D5 Jaghin Iran
196 E4 Jagodina Srbija Yugo.
Jagsamka Sichuan China see Luding
172 D2 Jagst r. Ger.
172 D2 Jagsthausen Ger.
173 E2 Jagstzell Ger.
114 C1 Jagtial Andhra Prad. India
142 C3 Jaguapitã Brazil
258 G4 Jaguarão r. Brazil/Uru.
258 G4 Jaguarão Uru.
254 E4 Jaguarari Brazil
254 F3 Jaguaretama Brazil
256 C6 Jaguariaíva Brazil
254 F3 Jaguaribe Brazil
254 F3 Jaguaribe r. Brazil
254 F5 Jaguaripe Brazil
254 F4 Jaguaruana Brazil
246 B2 Jagüey Grande Cuba
117 F4 Jahanabad Bihar India
122 B2 Jahān Dāgh mt. Iran
84 B1 Jahleel, Point N.T. Austr.
171 K4 Jahna r. Ger.
171 F3 Jahnsfelde Ger.
122 C4 Jahrom Iran
207 H3 Jahun Nigeria
254 E3 Jaicós Brazil
114 B2 Jaigarh Mahar. India
Jailolo Gilolo i. Maluku Indon. see Halmahera
106 D5 Jainca Qinghai China
117 H4 Jaintiapur Bangl.
116 C4 Jaipur Rajasthan India
117 G4 Jaipurhat Bangl.
116 E4 Jais Uttar Prad. India
116 B4 Jaisalmer Rajasthan India
116 E5 Jaisinghnagar Madh. Prad. India
116 C4 Jaitaran Rajasthan India
116 D5 Jaitgarh hill Mahar. India
116 D4 Jaitpur Uttar Prad. India
188 F3 Jajce Bos.-Herz.
Jajpur state India see Orissa
176 F4 Ják Hungary
128 B2 Jabbah Syria
177 I5 Jakabszállás Hungary
94 D4 Jakarta Indon.
222 G2 Jakes Corner Y.T. Can.
116 B3 Jakham r. Afgh.
140 L2 Jäkkvik Sweden
116 C3 Jakhal Haryana India
140 M3 Jakobstad Fin.
179 H5 Jakovlje Croatia
175 I3 Jaktorów Pol.
177 J2 Jakubany Slovakia
176 F3 Jakubov Slovakia
196 E5 Jakupica mts Macedonia
237 C5 Jal NM U.S.A.
244 B3 Jala Mex.
124 D2 Jalājil Saudi Arabia
123 G3 Jalālabad Afgh.
116 D3 Jalalabad Punjab India
116 D4 Jalalabad Uttar Prad. India
123 H3 Jalal-Abad Kyrg.
121 H4 Jalal-Abad admin. div. Kyrg. see Jalal-Abad
116 C5 Jalalpur Gujarat India
116 E4 Jalalpur Uttar Prad. India
123 I3 Jalalpur Pirwala Pak.
116 C5 Jalandhar Punjab India
114 B1 Jaldrug Karnataka India
256 B4 Jales Brazil
116 E4 Jalesar Uttar Prad. India
117 G5 Jaleswar Orissa India
116 D5 Jalgaon Mahar. India
165 F6 Jalhay Belgium
127 G5 Jālībah Iraq
160 B2 Jaligny-sur-Besbre France
207 H4 Jalingo Nigeria
244 B3 Jalisco state Mex.
159 F4 Jallais France
114 B2 Jalna Mahar. India
186 B3 Jalón r. Spain
116 B4 Jalor Rajasthan India
244 C3 Jalostotitlán Mex.
245 E3 Jalpa Guat.
84 C2 Jalboi r. N.T. Austr.
244 D2 Jalpa de Díaz Mex.
245 F4 Jalpa Enríquez Mex.
245 E3 Jalpa del Marqués Mex.
245 E3 Jalpan Mex.
117 G4 Jalpaiguri W. Bengal India
245 E3 Jalpa Mex.
207 H4 Jalula Iraq see Jalawlā'
122 E3 Jām r. Iran
246 D3 Jamaica Cuba
246 D3 Jamaica country West Indies
246 D3 Jamaica Channel Haiti/Jamaica
225 H3 Jacques Cartier, Mont Que. Can.
117 G4 Jamalpur Bangl.
117 F4 Jamalpur Bihar India
255 B6 Jamanxim r. Brazil
162 A2 Jard-sur-Mer France
94 □ Jambi Sumatera Indon.
94 C3 Jambi prov. Indon.
116 E5 Jambo Rajasthan India
161 E5 Jamboaye r. Indon.
94 B1 Jamboaye r. Indon.
114 C2 Jamekunte Andhra Prad. India
170 C2 Jamel Ger.
237 E5 Jamena r. MO U.S.A.

Column 7

175 H2 Jamielnik Pol.
141 M3 Jämijärvi Fin.
185 G3 Jamilena Spain
234 C2 Jamison PA U.S.A.
114 B3 Jamkhandi Karnataka India
114 B2 Jamkhed Mahar. India
114 C3 Jammalamadugu Andhra Prad. India
142 C3 Jammerbugten b. Denmark
116 C2 Jammu Jammu and Kashmir
116 D2 Jammu and Kashmir terr. Asia
116 B5 Jamnagar Gujarat India
116 D4 Jamner Mahar. India
116 C4 Jamni r. India
165 E5 Jamoigne Belgium
94 D4 Jampang Kulon Jawa Barat Indon.
123 G4 Jampur Pak.
141 N3 Jämsä Fin.
141 N3 Jämsänkoski Fin.
117 F5 Jamshedpur Jharkhand India
117 G5 Jamtara Jharkhand India
140 K3 Jämtland county Sweden
117 F4 Jamui Bihar India
95 G2 Jamuk, Gunung mt. Indon.
117 G4 Jamuna r. Bangl.
196 E3 Jamu Mare Romania
111 H3 Jamuna r. India
182 C2 Jamuz r. Spain
210 E4 Janaale Somalia
141 N3 Janakkala Fin.
116 C4 Janakpur Madh. Prad. India
114 C2 Janakpur Nepal
251 I4 Janaúba Brazil
177 L3 Jánd Hungary
256 D3 Jandaia Brazil
256 B5 Jandaia do Sul Brazil
122 D3 Jandaq Iran
173 H3 Jandelsbrunn Ger.
216 □3b Jandía hill Fuerteventura Canary Is
216 □3b Jandía, Península de pen. Fuerteventura Canary Is
116 C3 Jandiala Punjab India
250 D5 Jandiatuba r. Brazil
85 G5 Jandowae Qld Austr.
185 F2 Jándula r. Spain
185 I2 Jandulilla r. Spain
240 G1 Janesville CA U.S.A.
226 C4 Janesville WI U.S.A.
122 D3 Jangal Iran
114 C2 Jangaon Andhra Prad. India
Jangeldi Uzbek. see Dzhangel'dy
117 G4 Jangipur W. Bengal India
111 J3 Jangngam Xizang China
Jangngai Zangbo r. Xizang China
111 D5 Jangngai Zangbo r. Xizang China
171 E2 Jänickendorf Ger.
174 G3 Janikowo Pol.
256 A6 Janiópolis Brazil
188 E3 Janja Bos.-Herz.
188 E3 Janja r. Bos.-Herz.
179 J6 Janjevo Kosovo, Srbija Yugo.
177 L4 Jánkmajtis Hungary
196 E4 Jankov Kamen mt. Yugo.
175 J3 Janków Pol.
175 J3 Janów Pol.
175 J3 Janowiec Pol.
175 J2 Janowiec Kościelny Pol.
175 J3 Janowiec Wielkopolski Pol.
175 K5 Janów Lubelski Pol.
175 I2 Janów Podlaski Pol.
83 Q Bay Sask. Can.
171 H4 Jänschwalde Ger.
214 E5 Jansenville S. Africa
255 D5 Januária Brazil
128 A5 Janūb Sînî' governorate Egypt
159 F4 Janville France
114 C2 Janwada Karnataka India
158 B3 Janzé France
116 C5 Janzar mt. Pak.
158 E4 Janzé France
114 C2 Janzé France
256 B4 Jaora Madh. Prad. India
102 D2 Japan country Asia
101 N... Japan, Sea of N. Pacific Ocean
266 E3 Japan Basin sea feature Sea of Japan
266 F2 Japan Trench sea feature N. Pacific Ocean
129 E3 Jap'aridze Georgia
117 H4 Japauli Mount Nagaland India
181 I3 Jaraba Spain
246 E3 Jarabacoa Dom. Rep.
160 E3 Jarahueca Cuba
254 D2 Jaramana Syria
254 D2 Jaramataia Brazil
182 D4 Jarandilla de la Vera Spain
245 E4 Jarara r. Mex.
251 H5 Jaraqui r. Brazil
129 D1 Jarash Jordan
143 G1 Järbo Sweden
Jardboesville MD U.S.A. see Lexington Park
Jar-bulak Kazakh. see Kabanbay
175 L5 Jarczów Pol.
116 D3 Jardim Ceará Brazil
255 A5 Jardim Mato Grosso do Sul Brazil
185 H3 Jardín r. Spain
162 A2 Jard-sur-Mer France
108 A... Jargalang Arhangay Mongolia
108 A2 Jargalant Bayanhongor Mongolia
106 A2 Jargalant Bayan-Ölgiy Mongolia
107 G2 Jargalant Dornod Mongolia
106 C2 Jargalant Govĭ-Altay Mongolia
Jargalant Hovd Mongolia see Hovd
106 E2 Jargalant Töv Mongolia
106 B2 Jargalant Hayrhan mt. Mongolia
107 F2 Jargalthaan Mongolia
251 G5 Jari r. Brazil
251 I5 Jari r. Brazil
174 E2 Jarocin Wielkopolskie Pol.
175 K5 Jarocin Pol.
176 E2 Jaroměř Czech Rep.
176 E2 Jaroměřice nad Rokytnou Czech Rep.
175 K5 Jarosław Pol.
176 E3 Jaroslavice Czech Rep.
140 K... Järpen Sweden
176 F2 Jarošov nad Nežárkou Czech Rep.
175 I2 Järpås Sweden
179 J5 Jarovnice Slovakia
140 K3 Järpsund-Wedjeg Ger.
121 G1 Jarqůrghon Uzbek. see Dzharkurgan
84 C4 Jarra Jarra Range hills W.A. Austr.
241 X3 Jarratt VA U.S.A.
234 D2 Jarrettsville MD U.S.A.
149 P4 Jarrow Tyne and Wear, England U.K.
106 E4 Jartai Nei Mongol China

Column 8

175 H2 Jamielnik Pol.
141 M3 Jämijärvi Fin.
185 G3 Jamilena Spain
234 C2 Jamison PA U.S.A.
114 B3 Jamkhandi Karnataka India
114 B2 Jamkhed Mahar. India
114 C3 Jammalamadugu Andhra Prad. India
142 C3 Jammerbugten b. Denmark
116 C2 Jammu Jammu and Kashmir
116 D2 Jammu and Kashmir terr. Asia
116 B5 Jamnagar Gujarat India
116 D4 Jamner Mahar. India
116 C4 Jamni r. India
165 E5 Jamoigne Belgium
94 D4 Jampang Kulon Jawa Barat Indon.
123 G4 Jampur Pak.
141 N3 Jämsä Fin.
141 N3 Jämsänkoski Fin.
117 F5 Jamshedpur Jharkhand India
117 G5 Jamtara Jharkhand India
140 K3 Jämtland county Sweden
117 F4 Jamui Bihar India
95 G2 Jamuk, Gunung mt. Indon.
117 G4 Jamuna r. Bangl.
196 E3 Jamu Mare Romania
111 H3 Jamuna r. India
182 C2 Jamuz r. Spain
210 E4 Janaale Somalia
141 N3 Janakkala Fin.
116 C4 Janakpur Madh. Prad. India
114 C2 Janakpur Nepal
251 I4 Janaúba Brazil
177 L3 Jánd Hungary
256 D3 Jandaia Brazil
256 B5 Jandaia do Sul Brazil
122 D3 Jandaq Iran
173 H3 Jandelsbrunn Ger.
216 □3b Jandía hill Fuerteventura Canary Is
216 □3b Jandía, Península de pen. Fuerteventura Canary Is
116 C3 Jandiala Punjab India
250 D5 Jandiatuba r. Brazil
85 G5 Jandowae Qld Austr.
185 F2 Jándula r. Spain
185 I2 Jandulilla r. Spain
240 G1 Janesville CA U.S.A.
226 C4 Janesville WI U.S.A.
122 D3 Jangal Iran
114 C2 Jangaon Andhra Prad. India
108 A... Jargalang Mongolia
108 A2 Jargalant Bayanhongor Mongolia
106 A2 Jargalant Bayan-Ölgiy Mongolia
107 G2 Jargalant Dornod Mongolia
106 C2 Jargalant Govĭ-Altay Mongolia
253 E2 Jarú Brazil

178 D3 Kaprun Austria
210 B4 Kapsabet Kenya
101 D4 Kapsan N. Korea
139 I2 Kapsha r. Rus. Fed.
Kapsukas Lith. see Marijampolė
117 H5 Kaptai Bangl.
107 H1 Kaptsegaytuy Rus. Fed.
136 E1 Kaptsevichy Belarus
95 E3 Kapuas r. Indon.
95 F3 Kapuas r. Indon.
95 F2 Kapuas Hulu, Pegunungan mts Indon./Malaysia
82 D3 Kapunda S.A. Austr.
116 C4 Kapuriya Rajasthan India
116 C3 Kapurthala Punjab India
177 K2 Kapušany Slovakia
224 D3 Kapuskasing Ont. Can.
224 D3 Kapuskasing r. Ont. Can.
135 I6 Kapustin Yar Rus. Fed.
137 F2 Kapustyntsi Kyivs'ka Oblast' Ukr.
137 H2 Kapustyntsi Sums'ka Oblast' Ukr.
209 F7 Kaputa Zambia
83 G2 Kaputar mt. N.S.W. Austr.
176 G4 Kapuvár Hungary
Kapydzhik, Gora mt. Armenia/Azer. see Qazangödağ
138 F5 Kapyl' Belarus
101 C5 Kap'yŏng S. Korea
111 F6 Ka Qu r. Xizang China
116 E4 Kara Uttar Prad. India
134 N1 Kara r. Rus. Fed.
207 F4 Kara Togo
199 F1 Kara r. Turkey
127 F3 Kara r. Turkey
199 E2 Karaağaç Balıkesir Turkey
126 D3 Karaali Turkey
Karaaul Vostochnyy Kazakhstan Kazakh. see Karaul
121 H4 Kara-Balta Kyrg.
139 L3 Karabanovo Rus. Fed.
121 H2 Karabas Kazakh.
Karabekaul Turkm. see Garabekevyul
129 B4 Karabey Turkey
199 E1 Karabiga Turkey
123 E2 Karabil', Vozvyshennost' hills Turkm.
129 B4 Karaboğa Dağları mts Turkey
122 C1 Kara-Bogaz-Gol, Proliv sea chan. Turkm.
122 C1 Kara-Bogaz-Gol, Zaliv b. Turkm.
Karaboynak Turkm. see Atayab
129 E2 Karabudakhkent Rus. Fed.
126 D2 Karabük Turkey
121 I3 Karabulak Almatinskaya Oblast' Kazakh.
121 K3 Karabulak Vostochnyy Kazakhstan Kazakh.
129 D2 Karabulak Rus. Fed.
121 H2 Karabulakskaya Kazakh.
Karabura Xinjiang China see Yumin
199 F2 Karaburç İzmir Turkey
199 E2 Karaburun Turkey
120 E2 Karabutak Kazakh.
199 F1 Karacabey Turkey
199 E1 Karacakılavuz Turkey
126 C2 Karacaköy Turkey
127 E3 Karacalı Dağ mt. Turkey
128 A1 Karaçal Tepe mt. Turkey
199 F3 Karacasu Turkey
Karachay-Cherkess Republic aut. rep. Rus. Fed. see Karachayevo-Cherkesskaya Respublika
Karachayevo-Cherkesskaya A.S.S.R. aut. rep. Rus. Fed. see Karachayevo-Cherkesskaya Respublika
129 B2 Karachayevo-Cherkesskaya Respublika aut. rep. Rus. Fed.
129 B2 Karachayevsk Rus. Fed.
139 J5 Karachev Rus. Fed.
123 F5 Karachi Pak.
127 F3 Karaçoban Turkey
199 F3 Karaçulha Turkey
Karacurun Turkey see Hilvan
177 G5 Karád Hungary
114 B2 Karad Mahar. India
128 D1 Kara Dağ hill Turkey
199 E1 Kara Dağ hill Turkey
199 F1 Kara Dağ hills Turkey
126 D3 Kara Dağ mt. Turkey
121 H4 Kara-Darya r. Kyrg.
Kara-Dar'ya Uzbek. see Payshanba
Kara Deniz sea Asia/Europe see Black Sea
206 E4 Karaga Ghana
121 H2 Karaganda Kazakh.
121 H2 Karagandinskaya Oblast' admin. div. Kazakh.
129 D1 Karagas Rus. Fed.
121 I3 Karagash Kazakh.
134 K4 Karagay Rus. Fed.
121 H2 Karagayly Kazakh.
131 R4 Karaginskiy, Ostrov i. Rus. Fed.
120 B4 Karagiye, Vpadina depr. Kazakh.
129 B4 Karagöl Dağları mts Turkey
211 A5 Karagwe Tanz.
197 H5 Karahalil Turkey
199 F2 Karahallı Turkey
126 D3 Karahasanlı Turkey
199 F3 Karahisar Turkey
134 L5 Karaidel' Rus. Fed.
114 C4 Karaikal Pondicherry India
114 C4 Karaikkudi Tamil Nadu India
121 K3 Kara Irtysh r. Kazakh.
126 D3 Karaisalı Turkey
122 B3 Karaj Iran
Karak Jordan see Al Karak
Kara-Kala Turkm. see Garrygala
Karakalli Turkey see Özalp
120 D4 Karakalpakistan, Respublika aut. rep. Uzbek.
120 D3 Karakalpakiya Uzbek.
Karakalpakskaya Respublika aut. rep. Uzbek. see Karakalpakistan, Respublika
Karakalpakstan aut. rep. Uzbek. see Karakalpakistan, Respublika
120 F4 Karakatinskaya, Vpadina depr. Uzbek.
Karakax Xinjiang China see Moyu
111 C4 Karakax He r. China
111 C5 Karakax Shan mts Xinjiang China
129 C4 Karakaya r. Turkey
129 B4 Karakaya Tepe mt. Turkey
126 E3 Karakeçi Turkey
126 D3 Karakeçili Turkey
93 C1 Karakelong i. Indon.
Karaklis Armenia see Vanadzor
127 F3 Karakoçan Turkey
121 G1 Karakoga Kazakh.
120 C2 Karakol' Kazakh.
121 H4 Kara-Köl Kyrg.
121 I4 Karakol Kyrg.
Karaköprü Turkey see Karaçoban
123 H2 Karakoram mts Asia
116 D2 Karakoram Pass China/Jammu and Kashmir
210 C2 Kara K'orē Eth.
206 B3 Karakoro r. Mali/Maur.
Karaköse Turkey see Ağrı
128 B1 Karaköse Turkey
129 E2 Karakoysu r. Rus. Fed.
129 D4 Karakoyunlu Turkey
Karakubbud Ukr. see Komsomol's'ke
Kara-Kuga Kazakh. see Karakoga
Kara Kul' Kyrg. see Kara-Köl
120 E5 Karakul' Bukharskaya Oblast' Uzbek.
120 E5 Karakul' Bukharskaya Oblast' Uzbek.
Karakul', Ozero l. Tajik. see Qarokŭl
Kara-Kul'dzha Kyrg. see Kara-Kulja
134 K4 Karakulino Rus. Fed.
121 H4 Kara-Kulja Kyrg.
120 E1 Karakul'skoye Rus. Fed.
120 C3 Karakum, Peski des. Kazakh.
Karakum Desert Turkm. see Karakumy, Peski
123 E2 Karakumskiy Kanal canal Turkm.
122 E2 Karakumy, Peski des. Turkm.
127 F2 Karakurt Kars Turkey
199 E2 Karakurt Manisa Turkey
199 G2 Karakuş Dağı ridge Turkey
87 C5 Karalundi W.A. Austr.
93 A3 Karama r. Indon.
199 F2 Karaman Balıkesir Turkey
126 D3 Karaman Karaman Turkey
128 A1 Karaman prov. Turkey
199 F3 Karamanlı Turkey
110 D2 Karamay Xinjiang China
81 D4 Karamea South I. N.Z.
81 D4 Karamea r. South I. N.Z.
81 C4 Karamea Bight b. South I. N.Z.
199 G2 Karamıkkaracaören Turkey
111 D4 Karamiran Xinjiang China
111 D4 Karamiran He r. China
131 Q3 Karamken Rus. Fed.
199 F1 Karamürsel Turkey
138 G3 Karamyshevo Rus. Fed.
123 G2 Karan r. Afgh.
Karan state Myanmar see Kayin
177 I3 Karancsalja Hungary
177 I3 Karancskeszi Hungary
177 I3 Karancsság Hungary
206 A3 Karang Senegal
81 B5 Karangarua South I. N.Z.
95 F5 Karangasem Bali Indon.
95 E5 Karangbolong, Tanjung pt Indon.
93 C2 Karangetang vol. Indon.
208 B4 Karangoua r. Congo
116 D5 Karanja Mahar. India
114 C2 Karanja r. India
117 F5 Karanjia Orissa India
116 C3 Karanpura Rajasthan India
121 I1 Karaoba Kazakh.
199 E3 Karaova Turkey
121 H3 Karaoy Almatinskaya Oblast' Kazakh.
121 H3 Karaoy Almatinskaya Oblast' Kazakh.
197 H4 Karapelit Bulg.
126 D3 Karapınar Turkey
199 F2 Karapürçek Turkey
199 G1 Karapürçek Turkey
212 C5 Karas admin. reg. Namibia
214 A2 Karas mts Namibia
126 C2 Karaşar Turkey
111 C4 Karasay Xinjiang China
212 C6 Karasburg Namibia
Kara Sea Rus. Fed. see Karskoye More
139 L3 Karash Rus. Fed.
121 H2 Karashoky Kazakh.
188 G3 Karašica r. Croatia
177 H6 Karasica r. Hungary/Romania
137 H5 Karasivka r. Ukr.
140 N1 Kárášjohka Norway
140 N1 Kárášjohka r. Norway
Karasjok Norway see Kárášjohka
Karasjokka r. Norway see Kárášjohka
121 G1 Karasor, Ozero l. Kazakh.
Kara Strait Rus. Fed. see Karskiye Vorota, Proliv
120 E2 Karasu Kustanayskaya Oblast' Kazakh.
120 F1 Karasu Kustanayskaya Oblast' Kazakh.
121 H1 Karasu r. Kazakh.
128 C1 Karasu r. Syria/Turkey
Karasu Bitlis Turkey see Hizan
199 G1 Karasu Sakarya Turkey
127 F3 Karasu r. Turkey
Karasubazar Ukr. see Bilohirs'k
105 F2 Karasu-gawa r. Japan
121 I1 Karasuk Rus. Fed.
136 E5 Karasulak r. Ukr.
121 H4 Kara-Suu Kyrg.
136 C2 Karasyn Ukr.
122 E3 Karāt Iran
129 E2 Karata Rus. Fed.
121 K3 Karatan Kazakh.
126 D3 Karataş Turkey
128 C1 Karataş Turkey
199 F2 Karataş Manisa Turkey
121 G4 Karatau Kazakh.
121 F3 Karatau, Khrebet mts Kazakh.
114 C4 Karativu i. Sri Lanka
120 C2 Karatobe Kazakh.
120 D2 Karatogay Kazakh.
121 I3 Karatol r. Kazakh.
120 C3 Karaton Kazakh.
140 L2 Karats Sweden
103 D7 Karatsu Japan
106 A2 Karatünggü Xinjiang China
120 F2 Kara-Turgey r. Kazakh.
121 I2 Karaul Vostochnyy Kazakhstan Kazakh.
120 F5 Karaulbazar Uzbek.
116 D4 Karauli Rajasthan India
Karaulkel'dy Kazakh. see Bayganin
127 F2 Karaurgan Turkey
120 D4 Karauzyak Uzbek.
Karavan Kyrg. see Kerben
196 D5 Karavastasë, Gjiri i b. Albania
139 M3 Karavayevo Rus. Fed.
94 D4 Karawang Jawa Barat Indon.
Karaxahar r. China see Kaidu He
129 C4 Karayazı Turkey
128 C1 Karayılan Turkey
121 G2 Karazhal Kazakh.
120 D4 Karazhar Uzbek.
127 G4 Karbalā' Iraq
127 F4 Karbalā' governorate Iraq
169 D5 Karben Ger.
170 D2 Karbow-Vietlübbe Ger.
121 H2 Karbushevka Kazakh.
168 E1 Karby Ger.
177 J4 Karcag Hungary
177 K3 Karcsa Hungary
175 J3 Karczew Pol.
175 K4 Karczmiska Pol.
197 I4 Kardam Bulg.
199 E3 Kardamaina Notio Aigaio Greece
179 F1 Kardašova Řečice Czech Rep.
Kardeljevo Croatia see Ploče
169 C5 Karden Ger.
Kardhaámaina Notio Aigaio Greece see Kardamaina
Kardhítsa Greece see Karditsa
140 M2 Kardis Sweden
198 B2 Karditsa Greece
138 D2 Kärdla Estonia
177 J5 Kardos Hungary
179 H3 Kardos-ér r. Hungary
177 J5 Kardoskút Hungary
139 I4 Kardymovo Rus. Fed.
129 D2 Kardzhin Rus. Fed.
215 F3 Karee S. Africa
214 C4 Kareeberge mts S. Africa
214 E5 Kareedouw S. Africa
180 D5 Kareha, Jebel mt. Morocco
203 F5 Kareima Sudan
129 C3 K'areli Georgia
116 D5 Kareli Madh. Prad. India
Karelia aut. rep. Rus. Fed. see Kareliya, Respublika
138 F5 Karelichy Belarus
134 F3 Kareliya, Respublika aut. rep. Rus. Fed.
Karel'skaya A.S.S.R. aut. rep. Rus. Fed. see Kareliya, Respublika
134 F2 Karel'skiy Bereg coastal area Rus. Fed.
211 B6 Karema Dodoma Tanz.
211 A6 Karema Rukwa Tanz.
Karen state Myanmar see Kayin
99 K1 Karenga r. Rus. Fed.
116 D4 Karera Madh. Prad. India
140 M1 Karesuando Sweden
122 E5 Kārevāndar Iran
120 C2 Kargala Rus. Fed.
129 E2 Kargalinskaya Rus. Fed.
Kargalinski Rus. Fed. see Kargalinskaya
120 D2 Kargalinskoye Kazakh.
127 F3 Kargapazarı Dağları mts Turkey
Karghalik Xinjiang China see Yecheng
126 D2 Kargı Turkey
116 D2 Kargil Jammu and Kashmir
Kargilik Xinjiang China see Yecheng
128 B1 Kargıpınarı Turkey
134 G3 Kargopol' Rus. Fed.
174 D3 Kargowa Pol.
116 D4 Karhal Uttar Prad. India
143 G1 Karholmsbruk Sweden
207 H4 Kari Nigeria
204 D2 Karia Ba Mohammed Morocco
137 K1 Karian Rus. Fed.
213 F3 Kariba Zimbabwe
209 E9 Kariba, Lake resr Zambia/Zimbabwe
209 F9 Kariba Dam Zambia/Zimbabwe
102 I2 Kariba-yama vol. Japan
212 B4 Karibib Namibia
214 D5 Kariega r. S. Africa
80 D1 Karikari, Cape North I. N.Z.
95 E3 Karimata i. Indon.
95 E3 Karimata, Pulau-pulau is Indon.
95 E3 Karimata, Selat str. Indon.
117 H4 Karimganj Assam India
114 C2 Karimnagar Andhra Prad. India
95 E4 Karimunjawa, Pulau-pulau is Indon.
210 E2 Karin Somalia
141 M3 Karinainen Fin.
199 F3 Karınçalı Dağı mts Turkey
141 K3 Käringsjön Sweden
215 H1 Karino S. Africa
80 E2 Karioi hill North I. N.Z.
141 M3 Karis Fin.
211 A5 Karisimbi, Mont vol. Rwanda
Káristos Greece see Karystos
198 C1 Karitsa Greece
104 C4 Kariya Japan
Karjaa Fin. see Karis
138 D1 Karjalohja Fin.
116 C5 Karjan Gujarat India
114 B2 Karjat Mahar. India
117 F5 Karkai r. Bihar India
114 B3 Karkal Karnataka India
114 B2 Karkamb Mahar. India
214 A4 Karkams S. Africa
121 H2 Karkaralinsk Kazakh.
92 C5 Karkaralong, Kepulauan is Indon.
122 A4 Karkheh, Rūdkhāneh-ye r. Iran
137 G5 Karkinits'ka Zatoka g. Ukr.
141 N3 Karkkila Fin.
141 N3 Kärkölä Fin.
138 E2 Karksi-Nuia Estonia
106 B3 Karlik Shan mt. Xinjiang China
174 D1 Karlino Pol.
127 F3 Karlıova Turkey
137 H3 Karlivka Ukr.
129 C4 Karlıyayla Turkey
123 H2 Karl Marks, Qullai mt. Tajik.
Karl-Marx-Stadt Ger. see Chemnitz
Karlo-Libknekhtovsk Ukr. see Soledar
188 E3 Karlovac Croatia
176 B1 Karlovarský kraj admin. reg. Czech Rep.
176 G1 Karlovice Czech Rep.
Karlovka Ukr. see Karlivka
197 G4 Karlovo Bulg.
176 B1 Karlovy Vary Czech Rep.
172 C3 Karlsbad Ger.
141 K3 Karlsberg Sweden
143 F2 Karlsborg Sweden
170 E2 Karlsburg Ger.
Karlsburg Romania see Alba Iulia
172 C2 Karlsdorf-Neuthard Ger.
173 F3 Karlsfeld Ger.
170 E1 Karlshagen Ger.
143 F3 Karlshamn Sweden
168 E2 Karlshöfen Ger.
173 F3 Karlshuld Ger.
143 F2 Karlskoga Sweden
173 F3 Karlskron Ger.
143 F3 Karlskrona Sweden
172 C2 Karlsruhe Ger.
172 C3 Karlsruhe admin. reg. Baden-Württemberg Ger.
142 E2 Karlstad Sweden
236 D1 Karlstad MN U.S.A.
172 D2 Karlstadt Ger.
169 E5 Karlstein am Main Ger.
179 G2 Karlstein an der Thaya Austria
179 G2 Karlstetten Austria
220 C4 Karluk AK U.S.A.
139 H5 Karma Belarus
207 F3 Karma Niger
114 B2 Karmala Mahar. India
139 J4 Karmanovo Rus. Fed.
140 L2 Karmas Sweden
Karmir Armenia see Chambarak
Karmona Spain see Córdoba
142 A2 Karmøy i. Norway
120 F5 Karnabchul', Step' plain Uzbek.
117 H5 Karnafuli Reservoir Bangl.
116 D3 Karnal Haryana India
116 E3 Karnali r. Nepal
117 G5 Karnaphuli r. Bangl.
116 D3 Karnaprayag Uttar Prad. India
114 B3 Karnataka state India
137 H3 Karnaukhivka Ukr.
237 D6 Karnes City TX U.S.A.
174 D1 Karnice Pol.
175 I3 Karniewo Pol.
178 D4 Karnische Alpen mts Austria
197 H4 Karnobat Bulg.
179 E4 Kärnten land Austria
213 F3 Karoi Zimbabwe
191 I3 Karojba Croatia
177 H2 Karolinka Czech Rep.
117 H4 Karong Manipur India
211 B7 Karonga Malawi
87 D6 Karonie W.A. Austr.
214 D5 Karoo National Park S. Africa
82 D3 Karoonda S.A. Austr.
123 G4 Karor Pak.
Káros i. Greece see Keros
199 E1 Karotis Greece
198 A2 Karousades Ionioi Nisoi Greece
170 D2 Karow Mecklenburg-Vorpommern Ger.
171 D3 Karow Sachsen-Anhalt Ger.
174 D5 Karpacz Pol.
128 B2 Karpasia pen. Cyprus
Karpas Peninsula Cyprus see Karpasia
199 E4 Karpathos Notio Aigaio Greece
199 E4 Karpathos i. Greece
199 E3 Karpathou, Steno sea chan. Greece
Karpaty mts Europe see Carpathian Mountains
198 B2 Karpenisi Greece
Karpilovka Homyel'skaya Voblasts' Belarus see Aktsyabrski
134 M4 Karpinsk Rus. Fed.
134 I2 Karpogory Rus. Fed.
199 E3 Karpuzlu Aydın Turkey
199 E1 Karpuzlu Edirne Turkey
136 F2 Karpylivka Chernihivs'ka Oblast' Ukr.
137 G2 Karpylivka Chernihivs'ka Oblast' Ukr.
136 D2 Karpylivka Rivnens'ka Oblast' Ukr.
86 C4 Karratha W.A. Austr.
170 C2 Karrenzin Ger.
215 F4 Karringmelkspruit S. Africa
Karroo plat. S. Africa see Great Karoo
123 E3 Karrukh Afgh.
127 F2 Kars Turkey
129 C3 Kars prov. Turkey
129 C3 Kars r. Turkey
121 F3 Karsakpay Kazakh.
140 N3 Kärsämäki Fin.
138 F3 Kārsava Latvia
171 C4 Karsdorf Ger.
120 F5 Karshi Uzbek.
120 F5 Karshinskaya Step' plain Uzbek.
129 B3 Karşıköy Turkey
174 F2 Karsin Pol.
199 F1 Karşıyaka Turkey
199 E2 Karşıyaka Turkey
117 G4 Karsiyang W. Bengal India
130 G3 Karskiye Vorota, Proliv str. Rus. Fed.
130 I2 Karskoye More sea Rus. Fed.
170 C2 Karstädt Ger.
170 C2 Karstädt Ger.
134 D3 Karstula Fin.
135 I5 Karsun Rus. Fed.
177 I4 Kartal Hungary
199 F1 Kartal Turkey
217 □3a Kartala vol. Njazidja Comoros
120 E1 Kartaly Rus. Fed.
116 C3 Kartarpur Punjab India
138 C4 Kartena Lith.
232 D4 Karthaus PA U.S.A.
129 D2 K'art'lis K'edi hills Georgia
Kartsa Rus. Fed. see Oktyabr'skoye
140 N3 Karttula Fin.
143 H4 Kartuzy Pol.
209 F8 Karubwe Zambia
102 J3 Karumai Japan
85 E3 Karumba Qld Austr.
122 B4 Karun, Kūh-e hill Iran
122 B4 Kārūn, Rūd-e r. Iran
114 C4 Karunagapalli Kerala India
140 M2 Karungi Sweden
86 E3 Karunjie W.A. Austr.
142 C3 Karup Denmark
142 C3 Karup r. Denmark
114 C4 Karur Tamil Nadu India
211 A5 Karuzi Burundi
114 C3 Karvetnagar Andhra Prad. India
141 M3 Karvia Fin.
177 H2 Karviná Czech Rep.
136 E2 Karvynivka Ukr.
114 B3 Karwar Karnataka India
116 E4 Karwi Uttar Prad. India
175 J2 Karwica Pol.
170 C2 Karwitz Ger.
198 B2 Karya Ionioi Nisoi Greece
Karyagino Azer. see Füzuli
99 J1 Karymskoye Rus. Fed.
120 C4 Karynzharyk, Peski des. Kazakh.
198 D2 Karystos Greece
199 F3 Kaş Turkey
114 B2 Kasa Mahar. India
Kasaba Turkey see Turgutlu
224 B2 Kasabonika Ont. Can.
104 D2 Kasaga-dake mt. Japan
104 D3 Kasagi-yama mt. Japan
209 C5 Kasai r. Dem. Rep. Congo
104 A4 Kasai Japan
209 D6 Kasai, Plateau du Dem. Rep. Congo
209 D6 Kasai Occidental admin. reg. Dem. Rep. Congo
209 E6 Kasai Oriental admin. reg. Dem. Rep. Congo
209 D7 Kasaji Dem. Rep. Congo
105 G2 Kasama Japan
211 A7 Kasama Zambia
104 C3 Kasamatsu Japan
120 F5 Kasan Uzbek.
212 E3 Kasane Botswana
211 A7 Kasanga Tanz.
209 B6 Kasangulu Dem. Rep. Congo
121 G4 Kasansay Uzbek.
114 B3 Kasaragod Kerala India
138 D2 Kasari r. Estonia
104 C4 Kasatori-yama hill Japan
223 K2 Kasba Lake Can.
204 D2 Kasba Tadla Morocco
103 E8 Kaseda Japan
176 C2 Kasejovice Czech Rep.
209 E8 Kasempa Zambia
171 C5 Kasendorf Ger.
209 F7 Kasenga Dem. Rep. Congo
210 A4 Kasese Uganda
Kasevo Rus. Fed. see Neftekamsk
116 D4 Kasganj Uttar Prad. India
Kasha Xizang China see Gonjo
224 B3 Kashabowie Ont. Can.
122 B3 Kāshān Iran
135 H6 Kashary Rus. Fed.
224 D2 Kashechewan Ont. Can.
Kashgar Xinjiang China see Kashi
110 B4 Kashi Xinjiang China
104 B4 Kashiba Japan
104 B4 Kashihara Japan
105 G3 Kashima Ibaraki Japan
103 E7 Kashima Saga Japan
105 G2 Kashima-nada b. Japan
104 D2 Kashimayaria-dake mt. Japan
139 K3 Kashin Rus. Fed.
139 K3 Kashinka r. Rus. Fed.
116 D3 Kashipur Uttar Prad. India
139 L4 Kashira Rus. Fed.
139 L4 Kashirka r. Rus. Fed.
137 J2 Kashirskoye Rus. Fed.
209 F8 Kashitu Zambia
105 F3 Kashiwa Japan
104 B4 Kashiwara Japan
103 I5 Kashiwazaki Japan
121 F5 Kashkadar'inskaya Oblast' admin. div. Uzbek.
123 F2 Kashkadar'ya r. Uzbek.
Kashkadarya Oblast admin. div. Uzbek. see Kashkadar'inskaya Oblast'
129 C2 Kashkhatau Kabardino-Balkarskaya Respublika Rus. Fed.
137 I4 Kashlahach r. Ukr.
122 D3 Kāshmar Iran
Kashmir terr. Asia see Jammu and Kashmir
116 C2 Kashmir, Vale of val. India
123 G4 Kashmor Pak.
209 E6 Kashyukulu Dem. Rep. Congo
Kasi Uttar Prad. India see Varanasi
117 E4 Kasia Uttar Prad. India
199 G3 Kasımlar Turkey
135 H5 Kasimov Rus. Fed.
179 H5 Kašina Croatia
177 I5 Kaskantyú Hungary
236 F4 Kaskaskia r. IL U.S.A.
223 N3 Kaskattama r. Man. Can.
121 I4 Kaskelen Kazakh.
141 M3 Kaskinen Fin.
Kas Klong i. Cambodia see Kŏng, Kaôh
Kaskö Fin. see Kaskinen
222 G5 Kaslo B.C. Can.
139 J4 Kasnya r. Rus. Fed.
209 E6 Kasongo Dem. Rep. Congo
209 C6 Kasongo-Lunda Dem. Rep. Congo
199 E4 Kasos i. Greece
176 C2 Kašperské Hory Czech Rep.
129 D3 Kaspi Georgia
Kaspīy Mangy Oypaty lowland Kazakh./Rus. Fed. see Prikaspiyskaya Nizmennost'
129 E2 Kaspiysk Rus. Fed.
Kaspiyskiy Rus. Fed. see Lagan'
Kaspiyskoye More sea Asia/Europe see Caspian Sea
139 H4 Kasplya Rus. Fed.
139 H4 Kasplya r. Rus. Fed.
116 C5 Kasrawad Madh. Prad. India
Kasrik Turkey see Gürpınar
129 E3 Kasristsqali Georgia
Kassa Slovakia see Košice
138 D2 Kassaare laht b. Estonia
203 H6 Kassala Sudan
203 G6 Kassala state Sudan
198 C1 Kassandra pen. Greece
198 C1 Kassandras, Kolpos b. Greece
198 C1 Kassandreia Greece
168 F1 Kasseedorf Ger.
169 E4 Kassel Ger.
169 E4 Kassel admin. reg. Hessen Ger.
205 H2 Kasserine Tunisia
226 A3 Kasson MN U.S.A.
126 D2 Kastamonu Turkey
169 C5 Kastellaun Ger.
198 C4 Kastelli Kriti Greece
199 D4 Kastelli Kriti Greece
Kastéllion Kriti Greece see Kastelli
Kastellorizon i. Greece see Megisti
165 D3 Kasterlee Belgium
173 F2 Kastl Bayern Ger.
173 G3 Kastl Bayern Ger.
168 F2 Kastorf Ger.
198 B1 Kastoria Greece
198 B1 Kastorias, Limni l. Greece
135 G6 Kastornoye Rus. Fed.
139 I5 Kastsyukovichy Belarus
139 H5 Kastsyukowka Belarus
104 C3 Kasugai Japan
105 F3 Kasukabe Japan
215 F5 Kasuka Road S. Africa
211 A6 Kasulu Tanz.
105 G2 Kasumiga-ura l. Japan
129 F3 Kasumkent Rus. Fed.
211 B8 Kasungu Malawi
123 H4 Kasur Pak.
177 J5 Kaszaper Hungary
207 H3 Katagum Nigeria
233 □I2 Katahdin, Mount ME U.S.A.
116 D2 Kataklik Jammu and Kashmir
210 B4 Katakwi Uganda
209 D6 Katanda Dem. Rep. Congo
209 E7 Katanga admin. reg. Dem. Rep. Congo
116 D5 Katangi Madh. Prad. India
116 D5 Katangi Madh. Prad. India
100 G2 Katangli Sakhalin Rus. Fed.
87 C7 Katanning W.A. Austr.
104 B4 Katano Japan
122 B2 Kata Pusht Iran
105 F2 Katashina-gawa r. Japan
198 B3 Katastari Ionioi Nisoi Greece
211 A6 Katavi National Park Tanz.
115 G5 Katchall i. Andaman & Nicobar Is India
207 F4 Katchamba Togo
209 C8 Katchiungo Angola
209 E6 Katea Dem. Rep. Congo
198 C1 Katerini Greece
136 F3 Katerynopil' Ukr.
147 E2 Katesbridge Northern Ireland U.K.
211 B6 Katesh Tanz.
220 E4 Kate's Needle mt. Alaska/B.C. Can./U.S.A.
211 B8 Katete Zambia
129 E3 Katex Azer.
117 E5 Katghora Madh. Prad. India
96 B1 Katha Myanmar
203 G2 Katherîna, Gebel mt. Egypt
84 C2 Katherine N.T. Austr.
84 B2 Katherine r. N.T. Austr.
116 C5 Kathi Mahar. India
116 B5 Kathiawar pen. Gujarat India
128 A4 Kathîb el Henu hill Egypt
215 G2 Kathlehong S. Africa
171 F4 Kathlow Ger.
117 F4 Kathmandu Nepal
214 D2 Kathu S. Africa
116 C2 Kathua Jammu and Kashmir
206 C3 Kati Mali
95 F2 Katibas r. Sarawak Malaysia
177 K4 Kati-ér r. Hungary
117 F4 Katihar Bihar India
80 E2 Katikati North I. N.Z.
215 F5 Kati-Kati S. Africa
212 E3 Katima Mulilo Namibia
206 D4 Katiola Côte d'Ivoire
Kā Tiritiri o te Moana mts South I. N.Z. see Southern Alps
136 E5 Katlabukh, Ozero l. Ukr.
169 F4 Katlenburg-Lindau Ger.
177 G3 Kátlovce Slovakia
111 D4 Katma Xinjiang China
Katmandu Nepal see Kathmandu
198 B2 Kato Achaïa Greece
198 B2 Katochi Greece
198 C3 Kato Doliana Peloponnisos Greece
198 B3 Kato Figaleia Greece
198 C3 Kato Glykovrysi Greece
116 D5 Katol Mahar. India
235 E1 Katonah NY U.S.A.
209 F8 Katondwe Zambia
198 C1 Kato Nevrokopi Greece
210 A4 Katonga r. Uganda
121 K2 Katon-Karagay Kazakh.
Katonqaraghay Kazakh. see Katon-Karagay
83 G3 Katoomba N.S.W. Austr.
93 B3 Katoposa, Gunung mt. Indon.
116 C5 Katosan Gujarat India
198 C2 Kato Tithorea Greece
Kåtotjåkka mt. Sweden see Godučohkka
176 C2 Katovice Czech Rep.
175 H5 Katowice Pol.
117 G5 Katoya W. Bengal India
116 C5 Katpur Gujarat India
199 F3 Katrancık Dağı mts Turkey
146 D5 Katrine, Loch l. Scotland U.K.
143 G2 Katrineholm Sweden
179 F2 Katsdorf Austria
198 B2 Katsikas Greece
207 G3 Katsina Nigeria
207 G4 Katsina state Nigeria
207 H5 Katsina-Ala Nigeria
105 F3 Katsura-gawa r. Japan
104 B4 Katsuragi-san hill Japan
105 G3 Katsuura Japan
104 C2 Katsuyama Japan
121 F5 Kattakurgan Uzbek.
86 E4 Kattamudda Well W.A. Austr.
Kattaqŭrghon Uzbek. see Kattakurgan
123 F3 Kattasang Hills Afgh.
142 D3 Kattegat str. Denmark/Sweden
140 L2 Kattisavan Sweden
Kattowitz Pol. see Katowice
114 C4 Kattuputtur Tamil Nadu India
211 B7 Katumbi Malawi
110 D1 Katun' r. Rus. Fed.
134 I4 Katunino Rus. Fed.
110 D1 Katunskiy Khrebet mts Rus. Fed.
Katwa W. Bengal India see Katoya
164 D2 Katwijk aan Zee Neth.
175 J2 Kąty Pol.
Katyk Ukr. see Shakhtars'k
177 I5 Katymár Hungary
174 E4 Kąty Wrocławskie Pol.
173 G2 Katzbach r. Ger.
179 H3 Katzelsdorf Austria
172 D2 Katzenbuckel hill Ger.
169 C5 Katzenelnbogen Ger.
171 C5 Katzhütte Ger.
172 B2 Katzweiler Ger.
240 □B7 Kauai i. HI U.S.A.
240 □B8 Kauai Channel HI U.S.A.
169 C5 Kaub Ger.
173 E4 Kaufbeuren Ger.
173 E3 Kaufering Ger.
237 D5 Kaufman TX U.S.A.
169 E4 Kaufungen Ger.
141 M3 Kauhajoki Fin.
140 M3 Kauhava Fin.
226 C3 Kaukauna WI U.S.A.
96 B1 Kaukkwè Hills Myanmar
240 □B8 Kaulakahi Channel HI U.S.A.
165 E3 Kaulille Belgium
171 C5 Kaulsdorf Ger.
80 E4 Kaumai North I. N.Z.
225 I1 Kaumajet Mountains Nfld. Can.
240 □B8 Kaumakani HI U.S.A.
240 □C8 Kaumalapau HI U.S.A.
240 □C8 Kaunakakai HI U.S.A.
138 D4 Kaunas Lith.
234 D1 Kauneonga Lake NY U.S.A.
117 G4 Kaunia Bangl.
140 M2 Kaunisvaara Sweden
138 E4 Kauno marios l. Lith.
81 C5 Kaupiri South I. N.Z.
240 □C8 Kaupo HI U.S.A.
207 G3 Kaura-Namoda Nigeria
Kaushany Moldova see Căuşeni
140 M3 Kaustinen Fin.
165 F5 Kautenbach Lux.
140 M1 Kautokeino Norway
179 G2 Kautzen Austria
197 F5 Kavadarci Macedonia
196 D5 Kavajë Albania
199 E1 Kavak Çanakkale Turkey
126 E2 Kavak Samsun Turkey
199 E2 Kavak Dağı hill Turkey
199 F2 Kavaklıdere Turkey
199 F3 Kavaklıdere Turkey
198 D1 Kavala Greece
100 E3 Kavalerovo Rus. Fed.
114 D3 Kavali Andhra Prad. India
114 C4 Kavalpatnam Tamil Nadu India
122 C4 Kavār Iran
114 B4 Kavaratti Lakshadweep India
197 I4 Kavarna Bulg.
138 E4 Kavarskas Lith.
170 D2 Kavelstorf Ger.
206 B4 Kavendou, Mont mt. Guinea
114 C4 Kaveri r. India
114 C3 Kaveripatnam Tamil Nadu India
116 C5 Kavi Gujarat India
91 L7 Kavieng New Ireland P.N.G.
122 C3 Kavīr, Dasht-e des. Iran
122 C4 Kavīr-e Abarkuh des. Iran
122 D3 Kavīr-i-Namak salt flat Iran
129 C1 Kavkazskiy Rus. Fed.
175 L6 Kavs'ke Ukr.
251 H3 Kaw Fr. Guiana
104 C1 Kawachi-dake hill Japan
104 B4 Kawachi-nagano Japan
105 F3 Kawagoe Japan
105 F3 Kawaguchi Japan
240 □D8 Kawaihae HI U.S.A.
240 □B7 Kawaikini, Mount HI U.S.A.
240 □ Kawailoa Beach HI U.S.A.
80 E1 Kawakawa North I. N.Z.
209 F7 Kawambwa Zambia
104 B3 Kawanishi Japan
105 F2 Kawarazawa-gawa r. Japan
116 E5 Kawardha Madh. Prad. India
105 F3 Kawasaki Japan
225 H2 Kawawachikamach Que. Can.
80 F3 Kaweka mt. North I. N.Z.
80 F3 Kaweka Range mts North I. N.Z.
226 B1 Kawene Ont. Can.
80 F3 Kawerau North I. N.Z.
80 E3 Kawhia North I. N.Z.
80 E3 Kawhia Harbour North I. N.Z.
241 I3 Kawich Peak NV U.S.A.
241 I3 Kawich Range mts NV U.S.A.
96 B3 Kawkareik Myanmar
96 A2 Kawlin Myanmar
128 A4 Kawm Dafanah tourist site Egypt
Kawthoolei state Myanmar see Kayin
Kawthule state Myanmar see Kayin
Kaxgar Xinjiang China see Kashi
110 B4 Kaxgar He r. China
110 C3 Kax He r. China
111 C4 Kaxtax Shan mts China
206 E3 Kaya Burkina
129 C3 Kayaaltı Turkey
199 E2 Kayacı Dağı hill Turkey
126 E3 Kayadibi Turkey
105 E3 Kayaga-take mt. Japan
96 B3 Kayah state Myanmar
129 E2 Kayakent Rus. Fed.
211 A7 Kayambi Zambia
95 E3 Kayan r. Indon.
95 G2 Kayan r. Indon.
96 B3 Kayan Myanmar
211 A5 Kayanaza Burundi
92 □ Kayangel atoll Palau
114 C4 Kayankulam Kerala India
114 C2 Kayar Mahar. India
93 C2 Kayasa Halmahera Indon.
129 D1 Kayasula Rus. Fed.
238 F3 Kaycee WY U.S.A.
Kaydanovo Belarus see Dzyarzhynsk
241 L3 Kayenta AZ U.S.A.
209 B6 Kayes Congo
206 C3 Kayes Mali
206 C3 Kayes admin. reg. Mali
120 F2 Kayga Kazakh.
Kaygy Kazakh. see Kayga
96 B3 Kayin state Myanmar
165 F5 Kayl Lux.
199 F2 Kaymakçı İzmir Turkey
121 H1 Kaymanachikha Kazakh.
199 G2 Kaymaz Turkey
171 D5 Kayna Ger.
121 I2 Kaynar Kazakh.
126 E3 Kaynar Turkey
199 G1 Kaynarca Turkey
197 H5 Kaynarlı r. Turkey
199 G1 Kaynaşlı Turkey
Kayrakkum Tajik. see Qayroqqum
Kayrakkumskoye Vodokhranilishche resr Tajik. see Obanbori Qayroqqum
121 H2 Kayrakty Kazakh.
126 D3 Kayseri Turkey
157 H4 Kaysersberg France
94 D3 Kayuagung Sumatera Indon.
130 J3 Kayyerkan Rus. Fed.
121 H4 Kayyngdy Kyrg.
139 L5 Kazachka Rus. Fed.
131 O2 Kazach'ye Rus. Fed.
Kazakh Azer. see Qazax
Kazakhskaya S.S.R. country Asia see Kazakhstan
121 G2 Kazakhskiy Melkosopochnik plain Kazakh.
120 C4 Kazakhskiy Zaliv b. Kazakh.
120 J2 Kazakhstan country Asia
Kazakhstan Kazakh. see Aksay
139 L5 Kazaki Rus. Fed.
Kazakstan country Asia see Kazakhstan
120 E3 Kazalinsk Kazakh.
223 M2 Kazan r. Nunavut Can.
134 J5 Kazan' Rus. Fed.
129 C4 Kazan Turkey
126 D3 Kazancı Turkey
Kazandzhik Turkm. see Gazandzhyk
198 B2 Kazanje, Mal mt. Albania
134 J5 Kazanka r. Rus. Fed.
137 G4 Kazanka Ukr.
128 B1 Kazanlı Turkey
197 G4 Kazanlŭk Bulg.
139 L5 Kazanovka Rus. Fed.
175 J4 Kazanów Pol.
103 □3 Kazan-rettō is N. Pacific Ocean
135 H6 Kazanskaya Rus. Fed.
Kazatin Ukr. see Kozyatyn
120 D2 Kazatskiy Kazakh.
210 C1 Kaza Wenz r. Eth.
Kazbegi Georgia see Qazbegi
129 D2 Kazbek mt. Georgia/Rus. Fed.
199 E2 Kaz Dağı mts Turkey
122 B4 Kāzerūn Iran
121 G1 Kazgorodok Kazakh.
134 J3 Kazhim Rus. Fed.
123 E5 Kazhmak r. Pak.
Kazi Magomed Azer. see Qazımämmäd
175 I5 Kazimierza Wielka Pol.
174 G3 Kazimierz Biskupi Pol.
175 J4 Kazimierz Dolne Pol.
177 J3 Kazincbarcika Hungary
137 I2 Kazinka Belgorodskaya Oblast' Rus. Fed.
139 L5 Kazinka Lipetskaya Oblast' Rus. Fed.
139 L5 Kazinka Ryazanskaya Oblast' Rus. Fed.
137 K2 Kazinka Voronezhskaya Oblast' Rus. Fed.
138 E5 Kazlowshchyna Belarus
138 D4 Kazlų Rūda Lith.
174 E3 Kaźmierz Pol.
176 C2 Kaznějov Czech Rep.
105 F2 Kazo Japan
120 B2 Kaztalovka Kazakh.
209 D6 Kazumba Dem. Rep. Congo
209 E9 Kazungula Zambia
102 J3 Kazuno Japan
122 D2 Kazy Turkm.
121 G4 Kazygurt Yuzhnyy Kazakhstan Kazakh.
130 H3 Kazym r. Rus. Fed.
196 D4 Kçirë Albania
174 F3 Kcynia Pol.
176 C2 Kdyně Czech Rep.
198 D3 Kea i. Greece
240 □D9 Keaau HI U.S.A.
147 E2 Keady Northern Ireland U.K.
146 B5 Keal, Loch na b. Scotland U.K.
240 □C8 Kealaikahiki Channel HI U.S.A.
240 □D9 Kealakekua HI U.S.A.
240 □D9 Kealia HI U.S.A.
147 B5 Kealkill Rep. of Ireland
241 L4 Keams Canyon AZ U.S.A.
Kéamu i. Vanuatu see Anatom
235 D2 Keansburg NJ U.S.A.
147 F2 Kearney Northern Ireland U.K.
236 D3 Kearney NE U.S.A.
232 E5 Kearneysville WV U.S.A.
241 L5 Kearny AZ U.S.A.
235 D2 Kearny NJ U.S.A.
215 H3 Keate's Drift S. Africa
240 □D9 Keauhou HI U.S.A.
240 □C8 Keawakapu HI U.S.A.
126 E3 Keban Turkey
126 E3 Keban Barajı resr Turkey
207 F3 Kebbi state Nigeria
206 A3 Kébémèr Senegal
207 I4 Kébi r. Cameroon
205 H2 Kebili Tunisia
128 B2 Kebīr, Nahr al r. Lebanon/Syria
140 L2 Kebnekaise mt. Sweden
146 B3 Kebock Head hd Scotland U.K.
210 E3 K'ebrī Dehar Eth.
95 E4 Kebumen Jawa Tengah Indon.
177 I5 Kecel Hungary
210 C3 K'ech'a Terara mt. Eth.
222 E3 Kechika r. B.C. Can.
199 G3 Keçiborlu Turkey
177 I5 Kecskemét Hungary
94 C1 Kedah state Malaysia
138 D4 Kėdainiai Lith.
Kedairu Passage Fiji see Kadavu Passage
111 B6 Kedarnath Peak Uttar Prad. India
225 H4 Kedgwick N.B. Can.
109 E2 Kedian Hubei China
151 H2 Kedington Suffolk, England U.K.
95 F4 Kediri Jawa Timur Indon.
100 C3 Kedong Heilong. China
206 B3 Kédougou Senegal
134 K2 Kedva r. Rus. Fed.
174 G5 Kędzierzyn-Koźle Pol.
149 I4 Keelby Lincolnshire, England U.K.
222 E1 Keele r. Y.T. Can.
149 G4 Keele Staffordshire, England U.K.
222 D2 Keele Peak Y.T. Can.
240 I3 Keeler CA U.S.A.
Keeling Islands terr. Indian Ocean see Cocos Islands
Keelung Taiwan see Chilung
146 F5 Keen, Mount hill Scotland U.K.
147 D3 Keenagh Rep. of Ireland
240 H4 Keene CA U.S.A.
233 G3 Keene NH U.S.A.
232 C4 Keene OH U.S.A.
84 B2 Keep r. N.T. Austr.
165 D4 Keerbergen Belgium
215 F3 Keeromsberg mt. Free State S. Africa
214 B5 Keeromsberg mt. W. Cape S. Africa
85 E2 Keer-weer, Cape Qld Austr.
212 C5 Keetmanshoop Namibia
223 M5 Keewatin Ont. Can.
226 A2 Keewatin MN U.S.A.
Kefallinia i. Greece see Kefallonia
198 B2 Kefallonia i. Greece
199 E3 Kefalos Notio Aigaio Greece
Kefe Ukr. see Feodosiya
169 E5 Kefenrod Ger.
179 F2 Kefermarkt Austria
207 G4 Keffi Nigeria
199 G1 Kefken Kocaeli Turkey
140 □B2 Keflavík Iceland
114 D5 Kegalla Sri Lanka
Kegayli Uzbek. see Kegeyli
121 I4 Kegen Kazakh.
120 D4 Kegeyli Uzbek.
222 G3 Keg River Alta Can.
135 I7 Kegul'ta Rus. Fed.
138 E3 Ķegums Latvia
151 F2 Kegworth Leicestershire, England U.K.
172 B3 Kehl Ger.
165 F5 Kehlen Lux.
138 E2 Kehra Estonia
169 C5 Kehrig Ger.
138 E2 Kehtna Estonia
137 H3 Kehychivka Ukr.
241 K3 Keibab Plateau AZ U.S.A.
149 H4 Keighley West Yorkshire, England U.K.
138 E2 Keila Estonia
138 E2 Keila r. Estonia
214 C3 Keimoes S. Africa
215 G5 Kei Mouth S. Africa
215 F5 Kei Road S. Africa
215 F5 Keiskama r. S. Africa
215 F5 Keiskammahoek S. Africa
146 E3 Keiss Highland, Scotland U.K.
207 G3 Keïta Niger
208 C2 Kéita, Bahr r. Chad
140 N3 Keitele Fin.
140 N3 Keitele l. Fin.
82 E4 Keith S.A. Austr.
146 F4 Keith Moray, Scotland U.K.
84 B1 Keith, Cape N.T. Austr.
222 F1 Keith Arm b. N.W.T. Can.
222 F4 Keithley Creek B.C. Can.
104 D2 Kekachi-yama mt. Japan
240 □B8 Kekaha HI U.S.A.
138 E3 Ķekava Latvia
177 L3 Kékcse Hungary
81 D5 Kekerengu South I. N.Z.
177 J4 Kékes mt. Hungary
116 C4 Kekri Rajasthan India
Këk-Tash Kyrg. see Kök-Tash
210 E3 K'elafo Eth.
114 B5 Kelai atoll Maldives
107 F4 Kelan Shanxi China
94 C2 Kelang Malaysia
94 C1 Kelantan r. Malaysia
94 C1 Kelantan state Malaysia
93 A4 Kelara r. Indon.
122 B2 Kelārdasht Iran
169 B5 Kelberg Ger.
171 C4 Kelbra (Kyffhäuser) Ger.
177 G2 Kelč Czech Rep.
198 B1 Këlcyrë Albania
129 C3 Kel Dağı mt. Turkey
177 I5 Kelebia Hungary
199 F3 Kelekçi Turkey
199 F2 Keles Turkey
121 G4 Keles Uzbek.
173 F3 Kelheim Ger.
205 H1 Kelibia Tunisia
123 F2 Kelif Turkm.
123 E2 Kelifskiy Uzboy marsh Turkm.
169 D5 Kelkheim (Taunus) Ger.
126 E2 Kelkit Turkey
126 E2 Kelkit r. Turkey
172 A2 Kell Ger.
81 A6 Kellard, Mount South I. N.Z.
146 E4 Kellas Moray, Scotland U.K.
138 F2 Kellavere hill Estonia
208 B5 Kéllé Congo
170 C1 Kellenhusen Ger.
87 C6 Kellerberrin W.A. Austr.
121 G1 Kellerovka Kazakh.
223 K5 Kelliher Sask. Can.
168 E2 Kellinghusen Ger.
173 E3 Kellmünz an der Iller Ger.
238 C2 Kellogg ID U.S.A.
147 A5 Kells Kerry Rep. of Ireland
147 D4 Kells Kilkenny Rep. of Ireland
147 E3 Kells Meath Rep. of Ireland
147 E2 Kells Northern Ireland U.K.
147 E2 Kells r. Northern Ireland U.K.
147 C3 Kellysgrove Rep. of Ireland
138 D4 Kelmė Lith.
136 D3 Kel'mentsi Ukr.
165 F4 Kelmis Belgium
208 B2 Kelo Chad
78 □6 Keloma i. Solomon Is
222 G5 Kelowna B.C. Can.
149 G4 Kelsall Cheshire, England U.K.
226 A2 Kelsey MN U.S.A.
240 F2 Kelseyville CA U.S.A.
81 B6 Kelso South I. N.Z.

Kilmaurs to **Koartac** 321

148 E2 **Kilmaurs** East Ayrshire, Scotland U.K.
148 C4 **Kilmeague** Rep. of Ireland
147 B3 **Kilmeena** Rep. of Ireland
146 C5 **Kilmelford** Argyll and Bute, Scotland U.K.
134 J4 **Kil'mez'** Rus. Fed.
134 J4 **Kil'mez'** r. Rus. Fed.
150 D4 **Kilmington** Devon, England U.K.
147 C5 **Kilmona** Rep. of Ireland
83 F4 **Kilmore** Vic. Austr.
147 C4 **Kilmore** Clare Rep. of Ireland
147 E4 **Kilmore** Wexford Rep. of Ireland
147 E4 **Kilmore Quay** Rep. of Ireland
147 B4 **Kilmorna** Rep. of Ireland
146 C6 **Kilmory** Argyll and Bute, Scotland U.K.
146 B4 **Kilmory** Highland, Scotland U.K.
147 C4 **Kilmurry** Rep. of Ireland
148 C5 **Kilmyshall** Rep. of Ireland
147 D3 **Kilnaleck** Rep. of Ireland
147 E4 **Kilnamanagh** Rep. of Ireland
146 B5 **Kilninian** Argyll and Bute, Scotland U.K.
146 C5 **Kilninver** Argyll and Bute, Scotland U.K.
147 C3 **Kilnock** Rep. of Ireland
146 B5 **Kiloran** Argyll and Bute, Scotland U.K.
211 C6 **Kilosa** Tanz.
147 E4 **Kilquiggin** Rep. of Ireland
147 E2 **Kilrea** Northern Ireland U.K.
147 C2 **Kilrean** Rep. of Ireland
147 C3 **Kilreekill** Rep. of Ireland
147 B3 **Kilronan** Rep. of Ireland
147 D2 **Kilross** Donegal Rep. of Ireland
147 C4 **Kilross** Tipperary Rep. of Ireland
147 B4 **Kilrush** Rep. of Ireland
147 C3 **Kilsallagh** Rep. of Ireland
148 C4 **Kilsaran** Rep. of Ireland
147 E3 **Kilskeer** Rep. of Ireland
148 B3 **Kilskeery** Northern Ireland U.K.
146 D6 **Kilsyth** North Lanarkshire, Scotland U.K.
147 C3 **Kiltartan** Rep. of Ireland
147 E4 **Kiltealy** Rep. of Ireland
148 C4 **Kilteel** Rep. of Ireland
147 C3 **Kiltimagh** Rep. of Ireland
147 E4 **Kiltogan** Rep. of Ireland
147 C3 **Kiltoom** Rep. of Ireland
147 C3 **Kiltullagh** Rep. of Ireland
137 I4 **Kil'tychchya** r. Ukr.
148 A3 **Kiltyclogher** Rep. of Ireland
209 F7 **Kilwa** Dem. Rep. Congo
211 C7 **Kilwa Kivinje** Tanz.
211 C7 **Kilwa Masoko** Tanz.
147 F2 **Kilwaughter** Northern Ireland U.K.
146 D6 **Kilwinning** North Ayrshire, Scotland U.K.
147 C4 **Kilworth** Rep. of Ireland
Kilyazi Azer. see **Giläzi**
116 C5 **Kim** r. India
237 C4 **Kim** CO U.S.A.
211 C7 **Kimambi** Tanz.
82 D3 **Kimba** S.A. Austr.
236 C3 **Kimball** NE U.S.A.
232 B4 **Kimball** OH U.S.A.
91 L8 **Kimbe** New Britain P.N.G.
222 H5 **Kimberley** B.C. Can.
215 E3 **Kimberley** S. Africa
151 I2 **Kimberley** Norfolk, England U.K.
86 E3 **Kimberley Downs** W.A. Austr.
86 E3 **Kimberley Plateau** W.A. Austr.
87 C5 **Kimberley Range** hills W.A. Austr.
234 C2 **Kimberton** PA U.S.A.
151 G2 **Kimbolton** Cambridgeshire, England U.K.
101 D4 **Kimch'aek** N. Korea
101 D5 **Kimch'ŏn** S. Korea
101 D6 **Kimhae** S. Korea
Kími Greece see **Kymi**
141 M3 **Kimito** Fin.
105 F3 **Kimitsu** Japan
101 C6 **Kimje** S. Korea
221 L3 **Kimmirut** Nunavut Can.
198 D3 **Kimolos** i. Greece
209 B6 **Kimongo** Congo
139 L5 **Kimovsk** Tul'skaya Oblast' Rus. Fed.
206 D3 **Kimparana** Mali
232 B6 **Kimper** KY U.S.A.
209 B6 **Kimpese** Dem. Rep. Congo
102 I4 **Kimpoku-san** mt. Japan
151 G3 **Kimpton** Hertfordshire, England U.K.
139 K3 **Kimry** Rus. Fed.
222 E4 **Kimsquit** B.C. Can.
143 F2 **Kimstad** Sweden
209 B6 **Kimvula** Dem. Rep. Congo
95 G1 **Kinabalu, Gunung** mt. Sabah Malaysia
95 G1 **Kinabatangan** r. Sabah Malaysia
211 C6 **Kinango** Kenya
199 E3 **Kinaros** i. Greece
175 M6 **Kinashiv** Ukr.
222 G4 **Kinbasket Lake** B.C. Can.
146 E3 **Kinbrace** Highland, Scotland U.K.
223 J5 **Kincaid** Sask. Can.
224 D4 **Kincardine** Ont. Can.
149 F1 **Kincardine** Fife, Scotland U.K.
146 F4 **Kincardine O'Neil** Aberdeenshire, Scotland U.K.
96 B1 **Kinchang** Myanmar
222 D4 **Kincolith** B.C. Can.
146 E4 **Kincraig** Highland, Scotland U.K.
177 H4 **Kincses** Hungary
209 E7 **Kinda** Dem. Rep. Congo
209 B5 **Kindamba** Congo
96 A2 **Kindat** Myanmar
179 G3 **Kindberg** Austria
227 F4 **Kinde** MI U.S.A.
171 C4 **Kindelbrück** Ger.
237 E6 **Kinder** LA U.S.A.
169 C5 **Kinderbeuern** Ger.
164 D3 **Kinderdijk** Neth.
149 H4 **Kinder Scout** hill England U.K.
223 I5 **Kindersley** Sask. Can.
206 B4 **Kindia** Guinea
173 F3 **Kinding** Ger.
172 B2 **Kindsbach** Ger.
209 E5 **Kindu** Dem. Rep. Congo
135 J5 **Kinel'** Rus. Fed.
120 B1 **Kinel'-Cherkasy** Rus. Fed.
134 H4 **Kineshma** Rus. Fed.
151 F3 **Kineton** Gloucestershire, England U.K.
84 C1 **King** r. N.T. Austr.
84 C2 **King** r. N.T. Austr.
86 F2 **King** r. W.A. Austr.
87 D5 **King, Lake** salt flat W.A. Austr.
232 E6 **King and QueenCourthouse** VA U.S.A.
85 G5 **Kingaroy** Qld Austr.
147 C2 **Kingarrow** Rep. of Ireland
146 C6 **Kingarth** Argyll and Bute, Scotland U.K.
240 G3 **King City** CA U.S.A.
222 E5 **Kingcome** r. B.C. Can.
86 E2 **King Edward** r. W.A. Austr.
157 H5 **Kingersheim** France
233 □H2 **Kingfield** ME U.S.A.
237 D5 **Kingfisher** OK U.S.A.
232 E5 **King George** VA U.S.A.
259 E8 **King George Bay** Falkland Is
262 U2 **King George Island** Antarctica
King George Islands Arch. des Tuamotu Fr. Polynesia see **Roi Georges, Îles du**
87 C7 **King George Sound** b. W.A. Austr.
86 D4 **King Hill** hill W.A. Austr.
146 E5 **Kinghorn** Fife, Scotland U.K.
146 C4 **Kingie** r. Scotland U.K.
138 G2 **Kingisepp** Rus. Fed.
83 E4 **King Island** Tas. Austr.
King Island Myanmar see **Kadan Kyun**
Kingisseppa Estonia see **Kuressaare**
227 H1 **King Kirkland** Ont. Can.
263 F2 **King Leopold and Queen Astrid Coast** Antarctica
86 E3 **King Leopold Ranges** hills W.A. Austr.
241 J4 **Kingman** AZ U.S.A.
237 D4 **Kingman** KS U.S.A.
233 □I2 **Kingman** ME U.S.A.
75 I3 **Kingman Reef** N. Pacific Ocean
222 D3 **King Mountain** B.C. Can.
237 C6 **King Mountain** hill TX U.S.A.
234 C2 **King of Prussia** PA U.S.A.
82 C2 **Kingoonya** S.A. Austr.
262 S1 **King Peak** Antarctica
262 R2 **King Peninsula** Antarctica
147 D4 **Kings** r. Rep. of Ireland
240 G3 **Kings** r. CA U.S.A.
238 C3 **Kings** r. NV U.S.A.
146 F5 **Kingsbarns** Fife, Scotland U.K.
150 D4 **Kingsbridge** Devon, England U.K.
240 H3 **Kingsburg** CA U.S.A.
151 F2 **Kingsbury** Warwickshire, England U.K.
150 E4 **Kingsbury Episcopi** Somerset, England U.K.
84 B5 **Kings Canyon** N.T. Austr.
151 F3 **Kingsclere** Hampshire, England U.K.
82 D3 **Kingscote** S.A. Austr.
235 E2 **Kings County** county NY U.S.A.
147 E3 **Kingscourt** Rep. of Ireland
151 I3 **Kingsdown** Kent, England U.K.
80 E2 **Kingseat** North I. N.Z.
262 U2 **King Sejong** research stn Antarctica
226 C3 **Kingsford** MI U.S.A.
146 D5 **Kingshouse** Stirling, Scotland U.K.
150 D4 **Kingskerswell** Devon, England U.K.
231 D6 **Kingsland** GA U.S.A.
226 E5 **Kingsland** IN U.S.A.
151 G3 **Kings Langley** Hertfordshire, England U.K.
215 H2 **Kingsley** S. Africa
149 H4 **Kingsley** Staffordshire, England U.K.
226 E3 **Kingsley** MI U.S.A.
151 H2 **King's Lynn** Norfolk, England U.K.
77 H2 **Kingsmill Group** is Gilbert Is Kiribati
151 H3 **Kingsnorth** Kent, England U.K.
86 D3 **King Sound** b. W.A. Austr.
235 E2 **Kings Park** NY U.S.A.
238 E3 **Kings Peak** UT U.S.A.
232 B6 **Kingsport** TN U.S.A.
151 F2 **King's Sutton** Northamptonshire, England U.K.
150 D4 **Kingsteignton** Devon, England U.K.
150 E3 **Kingsthorne** Herefordshire, England U.K.
83 F5 **Kingston** Tas. Austr.
224 E4 **Kingston** Ont. Can.
246 □ **Kingston** Jamaica
81 B6 **Kingston** South I. N.Z.
146 E4 **Kingston** Moray, Scotland U.K.
233 H4 **Kingston** MA U.S.A.
236 E4 **Kingston** MO U.S.A.
233 F4 **Kingston** NY U.S.A.
232 B5 **Kingston** OH U.S.A.
234 C1 **Kingston** PA U.S.A.
231 C5 **Kingston** TN U.S.A.
232 C6 **Kingston** WV U.S.A.
151 F3 **Kingston Bagpuize** Oxfordshire, England U.K.
150 E2 **Kingstone** Herefordshire, England U.K.
241 J4 **Kingston Peak** CA U.S.A.
150 E3 **Kingston Seymour** North Somerset, England U.K.
82 D4 **Kingston South East** S.A. Austr.
149 I4 **Kingston upon Hull** Kingston upon Hull, England U.K.
149 I4 **Kingston upon Hull** admin. div. England U.K.
151 G3 **Kingston upon Thames** Greater London, England U.K.
247 □3 **Kingstown** St Vincent
231 E5 **Kingstree** SC U.S.A.
234 B3 **Kingsville** MD U.S.A.
237 D7 **Kingsville** TX U.S.A.
150 D4 **Kingswear** Devon, England U.K.
150 E3 **Kingswood** South Gloucestershire, England U.K.
151 G3 **Kingswood** Surrey, England U.K.
151 F3 **King's Worthy** Hampshire, England U.K.
150 D2 **Kington** Herefordshire, England U.K.
209 C6 **Kingungi** Dem. Rep. Congo
225 I1 **Kingurutik** r. Nfld. Can.
146 D4 **Kingussie** Highland, Scotland U.K.
232 E6 **King William** VA U.S.A.
221 I3 **King William Island** Nunavut Can.
Kingwilliamstown Rep. of Ireland see **Ballydesmond**
215 F5 **King William's Town** S. Africa
237 E6 **Kingwood** TX U.S.A.
232 D5 **Kingwood** WV U.S.A.
209 F7 **Kiniama** Dem. Rep. Congo
199 F3 **Kınık** Turkey
199 E2 **Kınık** Turkey
215 G4 **Kinirapoort** S. Africa
223 J4 **Kinistino** Sask. Can.
137 H4 **Kinka** r. Ukr.
209 B6 **Kinkala** Congo
80 E3 **Kinleith** North I. N.Z.
81 B6 **Kinloch** South I. N.Z.
146 B4 **Kinloch** Highland, Scotland U.K.
146 C3 **Kinlochbervie** Highland, Scotland U.K.
146 C5 **Kinlocheil** Highland, Scotland U.K.
146 C4 **Kinlochewe** Highland, Scotland U.K.
146 C4 **Kinloch Hourn** Highland, Scotland U.K.
146 D5 **Kinlochleven** Highland, Scotland U.K.
146 D5 **Kinloch Rannoch** Perth and Kinross, Scotland U.K.
146 E4 **Kinloss** Moray, Scotland U.K.
147 C2 **Kinlough** Rep. of Ireland
150 D1 **Kinmel Bay** Conwy, Wales U.K.
Kinmen Taiwan see **Chinmen**
227 H3 **Kinmount** Ont. Can.
142 E3 **Kinna** Sweden
147 B3 **Kinnadoohy** Rep. of Ireland
81 B5 **Kinnaird, Mount** South I. N.Z.
114 D2 **Kinnarasani** r. India
147 D3 **Kinnegad** Rep. of Ireland
235 D1 **Kinnelon** NJ U.S.A.
Kinneret, Yam l. Israel see **Tiberias, Lake**
147 D3 **Kinnitty** Rep. of Ireland
114 D4 **Kinniyai** Sri Lanka
140 N3 **Kinnula** Fin.
224 D2 **Kinoje** r. Ont. Can.
104 B4 **Kino-kawa** r. Japan
223 K3 **Kinoosao** Sask. Can.
Kinpoku-san mt. Japan see **Kimpoku-san**
165 E3 **Kinrooi** Belgium
215 G2 **Kinross** S. Africa
146 E5 **Kinross** Perth and Kinross, Scotland U.K.
147 C5 **Kinsale** Rep. of Ireland
232 E5 **Kinsale** VA U.S.A.
142 B1 **Kinsarvik** Norway
209 B6 **Kinshasa** Dem. Rep. Congo
209 C6 **Kinshasa** admin. reg. Dem. Rep. Congo
137 I4 **Kins'ki Rozdory** Ukr.
237 D4 **Kinsley** KS U.S.A.
232 C4 **Kinsman** OH U.S.A.
231 E5 **Kinston** NC U.S.A.
138 C4 **Kintai** Lith.
206 E4 **Kintampo** Ghana
151 F3 **Kintbury** West Berkshire, England U.K.
234 C2 **Kintersville** PA U.S.A.
84 B4 **Kintore** N.T. Austr.
146 F4 **Kintore** Aberdeenshire, Scotland U.K.
82 B1 **Kintore, Mount** S.A. Austr.
86 F4 **Kintore Range** hills N.T. Austr.
146 B6 **Kintour** Argyll and Bute, Scotland U.K.
146 C6 **Kintyre** pen. Scotland U.K.
96 A2 **Kinu** Myanmar
105 G3 **Kinu-gawa** r. Japan
105 F2 **Kinunuma-yama** mt. Japan
224 D2 **Kinushseo** r. Ont. Can.
222 H4 **Kinuso** Alta Can.
147 C3 **Kinvara** Rep. of Ireland
147 B3 **Kinvarra** Rep. of Ireland
150 E2 **Kinver** Staffordshire, England U.K.
114 C2 **Kinwat** Mahar. India
211 B6 **Kinyangiri** Tanz.
210 B4 **Kinyeti** mt. Sudan
172 B3 **Kinzig** r. Ger.
169 D5 **Kinzig** r. Ger.
211 B6 **Kiomboi** Tanz.
129 C2 **Kion-Khokh, Gora** mt. Rus. Fed.
227 H2 **Kiosk** Ont. Can.
239 F4 **Kiowa** CO U.S.A.
237 D4 **Kiowa** KS U.S.A.
238 F3 **Kiowa Creek** r. CO U.S.A.
240 □C8 **Kipahulu** HI U.S.A.
Kiparissía Greece see **Kyparissia**
134 G4 **Kipelovo** Rus. Fed.
138 G2 **Kipen'** Rus. Fed.
211 B7 **Kipengere Range** mts Tanz.
173 F3 **Kipfenberg** Ger.
211 A6 **Kipili** Tanz.
223 K5 **Kipling** Sask. Can.
Kipling Station Sask. Can. see **Kipling**
149 H4 **Kippax** West Yorkshire, England U.K.
190 C2 **Kippel** Switz.
146 D5 **Kippen** Stirling, Scotland U.K.
172 B3 **Kippenheim** Ger.
147 E3 **Kippure** hill Rep. of Ireland
121 J1 **Kiprino** Rus. Fed.
134 I4 **Kipshenga** Rus. Fed.
137 F2 **Kipti** Ukr.
233 F6 **Kiptopeke** VA U.S.A.
Kipungo Angola see **Quipungo**
209 E7 **Kipushi** Dem. Rep. Congo
209 F8 **Kipushia** Dem. Rep. Congo
117 E4 **Kirakat** Uttar Prad. India
78 □6 **Kirakira** San Cristobal Solomon Is
177 J3 **Királd** Hungary
177 G5 **Királyegyháza** Hungary
177 J5 **Királyhegyes** Hungary
199 E2 **Kiran Dağları** hills Turkey
114 D2 **Kirandul** Madh. Prad. India
206 C3 **Kirané** Mali
128 A1 **Kıravga** Turkey
138 G5 **Kirawsk** Belarus
199 F2 **Kiraz** Turkey
237 E6 **Kirbyville** TX U.S.A.
173 G4 **Kirchanschöring** Ger.
172 C2 **Kirchardt** Ger.
178 E4 **Kirchbach** Austria
179 G4 **Kirchbach in Steiermark** Austria
173 H3 **Kirchberg** Bayern Ger.
171 D5 **Kirchberg** Sachsen Ger.
190 C1 **Kirchberg** Bern Switz.
190 E1 **Kirchberg** Sankt Gallen Switz.
172 B2 **Kirchberg (Hunsrück)** Ger.
179 G2 **Kirchberg am Wagram** Austria
179 G2 **Kirchberg am Walde** Austria
179 G3 **Kirchberg am Wechsel** Austria
173 E3 **Kirchberg an der Iller** Ger.
172 D2 **Kirchberg an der Jagst** Ger.
179 G2 **Kirchberg an der Pielach** Austria
179 G4 **Kirchberg an der Raab** Austria
178 D3 **Kirchberg in Tirol** Austria
178 D3 **Kirchbichl** Austria
169 E4 **Kirchbrak** Ger.
170 C2 **Kirchdorf** Mecklenburg-Vorpommern Ger.
168 D3 **Kirchdorf** Niedersachsen Ger.
173 G3 **Kirchdorf am Inn** Ger.
173 F3 **Kirchdorf an der Amper** Ger.
179 F3 **Kirchdorf an der Krems** Austria
173 H3 **Kirchdorf im Wald** Ger.
178 D3 **Kirchdorf in Tirol** Austria
173 F2 **Kirchehrenbach** Ger.
169 C5 **Kirchen (Sieg)** Ger.
171 C5 **Kirchenlamitz** Ger.
173 F2 **Kirchenpingarten** Ger.
173 F2 **Kirchensittenbach** Ger.
172 D3 **Kirchentellinsfurt** Ger.
173 F2 **Kirchenthumbach** Ger.
169 D5 **Kirchhain** Ger.
169 F4 **Kirchheilingen** Ger.
172 D2 **Kirchheim** Bayern Ger.
169 E5 **Kirchheim** Hessen Ger.
172 D2 **Kirchheim am Neckar** Ger.
173 F3 **Kirchheim bei München** Ger.
172 C2 **Kirchheim-Bolanden** Ger.
173 E3 **Kirchheim in Schwaben** Ger.
172 D3 **Kirchheim unter Teck** Ger.
169 D4 **Kirchhundem** Ger.
170 C2 **Kirch Jesar** Ger.
169 F5 **Kirchlauter** Ger.
168 E3 **Kirchlinteln** Ger.
170 C2 **Kirch Mulsow** Ger.
169 E3 **Kirchohsen (Emmerthal)** Ger.
173 G3 **Kirchroth** Ger.
179 H3 **Kirchschlag in der Buckligen Welt** Austria
168 D3 **Kirchseelte** Ger.
168 E2 **Kirchtimke** Ger.
168 E2 **Kirchwalsede** Ger.
173 G3 **Kirchweidach** Ger.
168 D2 **Kirchwistedt** Ger.
169 F4 **Kirchworbis** Ger.
172 B4 **Kirchzarten** Ger.
172 D2 **Kirchzell** Ger.
129 C3 **Kırdamı** Turkey
131 L4 **Kirensk** Rus. Fed.
139 K5 **Kireyevsk** Rus. Fed.
Kirghizia country Asia see **Kyrgyzstan**
121 H4 **Kirghiz Range** mts Asia
120 C1 **Kirgiz-Miyaki** Rus. Fed.
Kirgizskaya S.S.R. country Asia see **Kyrgyzstan**
Kirgizskiy Khrebet mts Asia see **Kirghiz Range**
Kirgizstan country Asia see **Kyrgyzstan**
Kíria Greece see **Kyria**
Kiriákion Greece see **Kyriaki**
77 J2 **Kiribati** country Pacific Ocean
105 E2 **Kiriga-mine** mt. Japan
126 E3 **Kırıkhan** Turkey
126 D3 **Kırıkkale** Turkey
106 A2 **Kirikkuduk** Xinjiang China
80 E1 **Kirikopuni** North I. N.Z.
139 L2 **Kirillov** Rus. Fed.
Kirin Jilin China see **Jilin**
Kirin prov. China see **Jilin**
210 C5 **Kirinyaga** mt. Kenya
139 I2 **Kirishi** Rus. Fed.
103 E8 **Kirishima-yama** vol. Japan
267 I5 **Kiritimati** i. Kiribati
199 G2 **Kırka** Turkey
199 E2 **Kırkağaç** Turkey
146 E7 **Kirkbean** Dumfries and Galloway, Scotland U.K.
149 F3 **Kirkbride** Cumbria, England U.K.
122 A2 **Kirk Bulāg Dāgi** mt. Iran
149 H4 **Kirkburton** West Yorkshire, England U.K.
149 G4 **Kirkby** Merseyside, England U.K.
149 H4 **Kirkby in Ashfield** Nottinghamshire, England U.K.
149 G3 **Kirkby Lonsdale** Cumbria, England U.K.
149 H3 **Kirkby Malzeard** North Yorkshire, England U.K.
149 I3 **Kirkbymoorside** North Yorkshire, England U.K.
149 G3 **Kirkby Stephen** Cumbria, England U.K.
149 G3 **Kirkby Thore** Cumbria, England U.K.
146 E5 **Kirkcaldy** Fife, Scotland U.K.
146 C7 **Kirkcolm** Dumfries and Galloway, Scotland U.K.
146 E6 **Kirkconnel** Dumfries and Galloway, Scotland U.K.
146 D7 **Kirkcowan** Dumfries and Galloway, Scotland U.K.
147 F2 **Kirkcubbin** Northern Ireland U.K.
146 D7 **Kirkcudbright** Dumfries and Galloway, Scotland U.K.
148 E3 **Kirkcudbright Bay** Scotland U.K.
172 B2 **Kirkel-Neuhäusel** Ger.
142 E1 **Kirkenær** Norway
140 O1 **Kirkenes** Norway
227 H3 **Kirkfield** Ont. Can.
149 G4 **Kirkham** Lancashire, England U.K.
146 D7 **Kirkinner** Dumfries and Galloway, Scotland U.K.
146 D6 **Kirkintilloch** East Dunbartonshire, Scotland U.K.
141 N3 **Kirkkonummi** Fin.
241 K4 **Kirkland** AZ U.S.A.
226 C4 **Kirkland** IL U.S.A.
224 D3 **Kirkland Lake** Ont. Can.
129 A4 **Kırklar Dağı** mt. Turkey
129 B3 **Kırklar Dağı** mt. Turkey
126 B2 **Kırklareli** Turkey
199 E1 **Kırklareli** prov. Turkey
149 H3 **Kirklevington** Stockton-on-Tees, England U.K.
146 E6 **Kirkliston** Edinburgh, Scotland U.K.
81 C6 **Kirkliston Range** mts South I. N.Z.
148 E3 **Kirk Michael** Isle of Man
146 E5 **Kirkmichael** Perth and Kinross, Scotland U.K.
146 D6 **Kirkmichael** South Ayrshire, Scotland U.K.
146 E6 **Kirkmuirhill** South Lanarkshire, Scotland U.K.
149 G3 **Kirkoswald** Cumbria, England U.K.
146 D6 **Kirkoswald** South Ayrshire, Scotland U.K.
197 G5 **Kirkovo** Bulg.
129 B4 **Kırköy** Turkey
263 L1 **Kirkpatrick, Mount** Antarctica
146 E6 **Kirkpatrick-Fleming** Dumfries and Galloway, Scotland U.K.
149 H4 **Kirk Sandall** South Yorkshire, England U.K.
236 E3 **Kirksville** MO U.S.A.
148 D1 **Kirkton** Argyll and Bute, Scotland U.K.
146 F4 **Kirkton of Durris** Aberdeenshire, Scotland U.K.
146 F5 **Kirkton of Menmuir** Angus, Scotland U.K.
146 F4 **Kirktown of Auchterless** Aberdeenshire, Scotland U.K.
146 F4 **Kirktown of Deskford** Moray, Scotland U.K.
127 G4 **Kirkūk** Iraq
146 F3 **Kirkwall** Orkney, Scotland U.K.
215 E5 **Kirkwood** S. Africa
234 C3 **Kirkwood** DE U.S.A.
234 B3 **Kirkwood** PA U.S.A.
149 G2 **Kirk Yetholm** Scottish Borders, Scotland U.K.
Kirman Iran see **Kermān**
126 C2 **Kırmır** r. Turkey
129 A4 **Kırmızıköprü** Turkey
172 B2 **Kirn** Ger.
Kırobası Turkey see **Mağara**
Kīrov Kazakh. see **Balpyk Bi**
Kirov Kyrg. see **Kyzyl-Adyr**
139 J4 **Kirov** Kaluzhskaya Oblast' Rus. Fed.
134 J4 **Kirov** Kirovskaya Oblast' Rus. Fed.
Kirova, Zaliv b. Azer. see **Qızılağac Körfäzi**
Kirovabad Azer. see **Gäncä**
Kirovabad Tajik. see **Panj**
Kirovakan Armenia see **Vanadzor**
137 I3 **Kirove** Donets'ka Oblast' Ukr.
137 G3 **Kirove** Kirovohrads'ka Oblast' Ukr.
137 H4 **Kirove** Zaporiz'ka Oblast' Ukr.
120 C2 **Kirovo** Kazakh.
Kirovo Donets'ka Oblast' Ukr. see **Kirove**
Kirovo Kirovohrads'ka Oblast' Ukr. see **Kirovohrad**
Kirovo Uzbek. see **Besharyk**
Kirov Oblast admin. div. Rus. Fed. see **Kirovskaya Oblast'**
134 J4 **Kirovo-Chepetsk** Rus. Fed.
Kirovo-Chepetskiy Rus. Fed. see **Kirovo-Chepetsk**
Kirovograd Kirovohrads'ka Oblast' Ukr. see **Kirovohrad**
Kirovograd Oblast admin. div. Ukr. see **Kirovohrads'ka Oblast'**
Kirovogradskaya Oblast' admin. div. Ukr. see **Kirovohrads'ka Oblast'**
137 G3 **Kirovohrad** Kirovohrads'ka Oblast' Ukr.
Kirovohrad Oblast admin. div. Ukr. see **Kirovohrads'ka Oblast'**
136 G3 **Kirovohrads'ka Oblast'** admin. div. Ukr.
129 F4 **Kirovsk** Azer.
139 H2 **Kirovsk** Leningradskaya Oblast' Rus. Fed.
134 F2 **Kirovsk** Murmanskaya Oblast' Rus. Fed.
Kirovsk Turkm. see **Babadaykhan**
137 I3 **Kirovs'k** Donets'ka Oblast' Ukr.
137 J3 **Kirovs'k** Ukr.
137 K4 **Kirovskaya** Rus. Fed.
134 J4 **Kirovskaya Oblast'** admin. div. Rus. Fed.
137 H3 **Kirovs'ke** Dnipropetrovs'ka Oblast' Ukr.
137 J3 **Kirovs'ke** Donets'ka Oblast' Ukr.
137 H5 **Kirovs'ke** Respublika Krym Ukr.
Kirovskiy Kazakh. see **Balpyk Bi**
137 I2 **Kirovskiy** Kurskaya Oblast' Rus. Fed.
100 E3 **Kirovskiy** Primorskiy Kray Rus. Fed.
Kirovskoye Kyrg. see **Kyzyl-Adyr**
Kirovskoye Dnipropetrovs'ka Oblast' Ukr. see **Kirovs'ke**
Kirovskoye Donets'ka Oblast' Ukr. see **Kirovs'ke**
Kirovskoye Respublika Krym Ukr. see **Kirovs'ke**
Kırpaşa pen. Cyprus see **Karpasia**
137 J5 **Kirpili** r. Rus. Fed.
137 J5 **Kirpil'skaya** Rus. Fed.
146 E5 **Kirriemuir** Angus, Scotland U.K.
134 K4 **Kirs** Rus. Fed.
135 H5 **Kirsanov** Rus. Fed.
172 B2 **Kirschweiler** Ger.
126 D3 **Kırşehir** Turkey
175 L1 **Kirsna** r. Lith.
207 F3 **Kirtachi** Niger
123 F5 **Kirthar Range** mts Pak.
151 F3 **Kirtlington** Oxfordshire, England U.K.
151 G2 **Kirton** Lincolnshire, England U.K.
151 I2 **Kirton** Suffolk, England U.K.
149 I4 **Kirton in Lindsey** North Lincolnshire, England U.K.
169 E5 **Kirtorf** Ger.
129 C2 **Kirts'khi** Georgia
140 M2 **Kiruna** Sweden
211 A5 **Kirundo** Burundi
262 X2 **Kirwan Escarpment** Antarctica
135 I5 **Kirya** Rus. Fed.
105 F2 **Kiryū** Japan
139 L3 **Kirzhach** Rus. Fed.
143 F3 **Kisa** Sweden
211 C6 **Kisaki** Tanz.
208 E4 **Kisangani** Dem. Rep. Congo
211 C6 **Kisangire** Tanz.
177 L3 **Kisar** Hungary
94 B2 **Kisaran** Sumatera Indon.
211 C6 **Kisarawe** Tanz.
105 F3 **Kisarazu** Japan
128 D1 **Kısas** Turkey
177 H4 **Kisbér** Hungary
98 E1 **Kiselevsk** Rus. Fed.
188 G4 **Kiseljak** Bos.-Herz.
139 I1 **Kisel'nya** Rus. Fed.
177 J3 **Kisgyőr** Hungary
117 F4 **Kishanganj** Bihar India
116 B4 **Kishangarh** Rajasthan India
116 C4 **Kishangarh** Rajasthan India
116 C2 **Kishen Ganga** r. India/Pak.
104 B4 **Kishi-gawa** r. Japan
Kishinev Moldova see **Chişinău**
Kishiözen r. Kazakh./Rus. Fed. see **Malyy Uzen'**
104 B4 **Kishiwada** Japan
121 H1 **Kishkenekol'** Kazakh.
117 G4 **Kishorganj** Bangl.
146 C4 **Kishorn, Loch** inlet Scotland U.K.
116 C2 **Kishtwar** Jammu and Kashmir
207 F4 **Kisi** Nigeria
175 H2 **Kisielice** Pol.
175 K2 **Kisielnica** Pol.
211 B6 **Kisigo** r. Tanz.
210 B5 **Kisii** Kenya
211 C6 **Kisiju** Tanz.
129 C3 **Kısır Dağı** mt. Turkey
220 A4 **Kiska Island** AK U.S.A.
141 M3 **Kisko** Fin.
177 J4 **Kisköre** Hungary
177 I5 **Kiskőrös** Hungary
177 I5 **Kiskunfélegyháza** Hungary
177 I5 **Kiskunhalas** Hungary
177 I4 **Kiskunlacháza** Hungary
177 I5 **Kiskunmajsa** Hungary
177 H5 **Kisláng** Hungary
177 K4 **Kisléta** Hungary
177 G4 **Kislőd** Hungary
129 C2 **Kislovodsk** Rus. Fed.
137 J4 **Kislyakovskaya** Rus. Fed.
210 D5 **Kismaayo** Somalia
177 K4 **Kismarja** Hungary
Kismayu Somalia see **Kismaayo**
104 C3 **Kiso-gawa** r. Japan
105 E3 **Kiso-gawa** r. Japan
211 A5 **Kisoro** Uganda
105 D3 **Kiso-sanmyaku** mts Japan
179 F4 **Kisovec** Slovenia
222 E4 **Kispiox** B.C. Can.
222 E4 **Kispiox** r. B.C. Can.
Kisseraing Island Myanmar see **Kanmaw Kyun**
206 C4 **Kissidougou** Guinea
231 D6 **Kissimmee** FL U.S.A.
231 D7 **Kissimmee** r. FL U.S.A.
173 E3 **Kissing** Ger.
172 D4 **Kißlegg** Ger.
202 E4 **Kissu, Jebel** mt. Sudan
177 I5 **Kisszállás** Hungary
172 D2 **Kist** Ger.
188 E4 **Kistanje** Croatia
177 I5 **Kistelek** Hungary
135 H5 **Kistendey** Rus. Fed.
Kistna r. India see **Krishna**
177 J3 **Kistokaj** Hungary
177 J4 **Kisújszállás** Hungary
103 F6 **Kisuki** Japan
210 B5 **Kisumu** Kenya
177 L3 **Kisvárda** Hungary
Kisykkamys Kazakh. see **Dzhangala**
174 F3 **Kiszkowo** Pol.
177 J5 **Kiszombor** Hungary
210 A3 **Kit** r. Sudan
206 C3 **Kita** Mali
121 F5 **Kitab** Uzbek.
104 C3 **Kitagata** Japan
105 G2 **Kitaibaraki** Japan
103 □3 **Kita-Iō-jima** vol. Kazan-rettō Japan
104 A4 **Kitajima** Japan
102 J4 **Kitakami** Japan
102 J4 **Kitakami-gawa** r. Japan
102 I5 **Kitakata** Japan
103 E7 **Kita-Kyūshū** Japan
210 B4 **Kitale** Kenya
102 K2 **Kitami** Japan
102 K1 **Kitami-sanchi** mts Japan
105 F2 **Kitamoto** Japan
104 B5 **Kitayama-gawa** r. Japan
236 C4 **Kit Carson** CO U.S.A.
224 D5 **Kitchener** Ont. Can.
224 E3 **Kitchigama** r. Que. Can.
140 O3 **Kitee** Fin.
210 B4 **Kitgum** Uganda
Kíthira i. Greece see **Kythira**
Kíthnos i. Greece see **Kythnos**
222 D4 **Kitimat** B.C. Can.
140 N2 **Kitinen** r. Fin.
222 D4 **Kitkatla** B.C. Can.
Kitob Uzbek. see **Kitab**
139 M3 **Kitovo** Rus. Fed.
222 D4 **Kitsault** B.C. Can.
223 I4 **Kitscoty** Alta Can.
136 C3 **Kitsman'** Ukr.
103 E7 **Kitsuki** Japan
232 D4 **Kittanning** PA U.S.A.
234 D2 **Kittatinny Mountains** hills NJ U.S.A.
233 □H3 **Kittery** ME U.S.A.
140 N2 **Kittilä** Fin.
105 G1 **Kittoya-yama** hill Fukushima Japan
179 I2 **Kittsee** Austria
114 B3 **Kittur** Karnataka India
231 F4 **Kitty Hawk** NC U.S.A.
211 C5 **Kitui** Kenya
211 C5 **Kitumbeine** vol. Tanz.
211 B6 **Kitunda** Tanz.
222 D4 **Kitwanga** B.C. Can.
209 F8 **Kitwe** Zambia
178 D3 **Kitzbühel** Austria
178 D3 **Kitzbüheler Alpen** mts Austria
178 D3 **Kitzbüheler Horn** mt. Austria
179 G4 **Kitzeck im Sausal** Austria
171 D4 **Kitzen** Ger.
173 E2 **Kitzingen** Ger.
171 D4 **Kitzscher** Ger.
178 D3 **Kitzsteinhorn** mt. Austria
175 H5 **Kiucze** Pol.
141 M3 **Kiukainen** Fin.
91 J8 **Kiunga** P.N.G.
140 N3 **Kiuruvesi** Fin.
140 N2 **Kivalo** ridge Fin.
198 C3 **Kiveri** Greece
139 K3 **Kiverichi** Rus. Fed.
136 C2 **Kivertsi** Ukr.
140 N3 **Kivijärvi** Fin.
143 F4 **Kivik** Sweden
138 F2 **Kiviõli** Estonia
137 I3 **Kivsharivka** Ukr.
208 F5 **Kivu, Lake** Dem. Rep. Congo/Rwanda
209 C7 **Kiwaba N'zogi** Angola
175 I1 **Kiwity** Pol.
Kiyev Ukr. see **Kyiv**
121 G2 **Kiyevka** Kazakh.
Kiyevskaya Oblast' admin. div. Ukr. see **Kyivs'ka Oblast'**
139 K4 **Kiyevskiy** Rus. Fed.
Kiyevskoye Vodokhranilishche resr Ukr. see **Kyyivs'ke Vodoskhovyshche**
197 I5 **Kıyıköy** Turkey
121 F2 **Kiyma** Kazakh.
105 G3 **Kiyosumi-yama** hill Japan
105 E1 **Kiyotsu-gawa** r. Japan
134 L4 **Kizel** Rus. Fed.
134 I3 **Kizema** Rus. Fed.
134 F3 **Kizhi, Ostrov** i. Rus. Fed.
199 G2 **Kızık** Afyon Turkey
128 A1 **Kızılalan** Turkey
199 F3 **Kızılcadağ** Turkey
199 F3 **Kızılca Dağ** mt. Turkey
126 D2 **Kızılcahamam** Turkey
199 G2 **Kızılcaören** Turkey
199 F2 **Kızılca-söğüt** Turkey
129 C4 **Kızılcaziyaret Dağı** mt. Turkey
128 B1 **Kızıldağ** mt. Turkey
128 A1 **Kızıldağ** mt. Turkey
126 E3 **Kızıl Dağı** mt. Turkey
126 D2 **Kızılırmak** Turkey
126 D2 **Kızılırmak** r. Turkey
199 G3 **Kızılkaya** Turkey
199 G2 **Kızılören** Turkey
126 D3 **Kızılören** Turkey
120 D1 **Kizil'skoye** Rus. Fed.
127 F3 **Kızıltepe** Turkey
128 A1 **Kızılyaka** Turkey
199 F3 **Kızılyaka** Turkey
129 E2 **Kizil"yurt** Rus. Fed.
128 B1 **Kızkalesi** Turkey
129 E2 **Kizlyar** Respublika Dagestan Rus. Fed.
129 D2 **Kizlyar** Respublika Severnaya Osetiya Rus. Fed.
134 J4 **Kizner** Rus. Fed.
104 B4 **Kizu-gawa** r. Japan
Kizyl-Arbat Turkm. see **Gyzylarbat**
123 F2 **Kizylayak** Turkm.
142 C3 **Kjellerup** Denmark
140 N1 **Kjøllefjord** Norway
140 L1 **Kjøpsvik** Norway
214 D5 **Klaarstroom** S. Africa
164 D3 **Klaaswaal** Neth.
176 C2 **Klabava** r. Czech Rep.
143 E1 **Klacken** hill Sweden
177 H3 **Kľačno** Slovakia
188 G3 **Kladanj** Bos.-Herz.
170 C3 **Kläden** Ger.
176 D1 **Kladno** Czech Rep.
197 F3 **Kladovo** Srbija Yugo.
176 B2 **Kladruby** Czech Rep.
179 F4 **Klagenfurt** Austria
191 J2 **Klagenfurt** airport Austria
241 M4 **Klagetoh** AZ U.S.A.
138 C4 **Klaipėda** Lith.
175 I6 **Kłaj** Pol.
177 H3 **Kľak** mt. Slovakia
177 I2 **Kľak** mt. Slovakia
Klaksvig Faroe Is see **Klaksvík**
144 D1 **Klaksvík** Faroe Is
238 A3 **Klamath** CA U.S.A.
238 A3 **Klamath** r. CA U.S.A.
238 B3 **Klamath Falls** OR U.S.A.
238 B3 **Klamath Mountains** CA U.S.A.
191 J3 **Klana** Croatia
Klang Malaysia see **Kelang**
168 D1 **Klanxbüll** Ger.
222 D3 **Klappan** r. B.C. Can.
142 E2 **Klarälven** r. Sweden
140 L3 **Klärke** Sweden
177 H3 **Klasov** Slovakia
142 E2 **Klässbol** Sweden
176 C1 **Klášterec nad Ohří** Czech Rep.
95 E4 **Klaten** Jawa Tengah Indon.
176 C2 **Klatovy** Czech Rep.
179 F3 **Klaus an der Pyhrnbahn** Austria
171 E3 **Klausdorf** Brandenburg Ger.
170 E1 **Klausdorf** Mecklenburg-Vorpommern Ger.
168 F1 **Klausdorf** Schleswig-Holstein Ger.
172 A2 **Klausen** Ger.
179 H2 **Klausen Leopoldsdorf** Austria
136 F2 **Klavdiyevo-Tarasove** Ukr.
214 B4 **Klawer** S. Africa
220 E4 **Klawock** AK U.S.A.
164 F2 **Klazienaveen** Neth.
206 C5 **Kle** Liberia
179 E4 **Kleblach-Lind** Austria
234 C2 **Klecknersville** PA U.S.A.
174 F3 **Kłecko** Pol.
174 G3 **Kleczew** Pol.
222 E5 **Kleena Kleene** B.C. Can.
214 C3 **Kleinbegin** S. Africa
168 C3 **Klein Berßen** Ger.
172 B2 **Kleinblittersdorf** Ger.
170 E2 **Klein Bünzow** Ger.
247 □10 **Klein Curaçao** i. Neth. Antilles
214 B4 **Klein Doring** r. S. Africa
171 E4 **Kleine Elster** r. Ger.
140 J3 **Kleinegga** mt. Norway
173 G3 **Kleine Laaber** r. Ger.
173 F3 **Kleine Paar** r. Ger.
170 E1 **Kleiner Jasmunder Bodden** b. Ger.
178 C3 **Kleiner Solstein** mt. Austria
171 F4 **Kleine Spree** r. Ger.
173 G3 **Kleine Vils** r. Ger.
234 B2 **Kleinfeltersville** PA U.S.A.
172 D2 **Kleinheubach** Ger.
171 C4 **Kleinjena** Ger.
171 D3 **Klein Kreutz** Ger.
171 E3 **Kleinmachnow** Ger.
214 B6 **Kleinmond** S. Africa
168 E2 **Klein Nordende** Ger.
172 D1 **Kleinostheim** Ger.
171 C4 **Kleinpaschleben** Ger.
172 D2 **Kleinrinderfeld** Ger.
214 C5 **Klein Roggeveldberge** mts S. Africa
168 F2 **Klein Rönnau** Ger.
179 F4 **Klein Sankt Paul** Austria
214 A3 **Kleinsee** S. Africa
214 C5 **Klein Swartberg** mt. S. Africa
215 F3 **Klein-Vet** r. S. Africa
172 D2 **Kleinwallstadt** Ger.
171 C3 **Klein Wanzleben** Ger.
169 F3 **Kleinwinnigstedt (Winnigstedt)** Ger.
198 C3 **Kleitoria** Greece
175 L3 **Klejniki** Pol.
188 F3 **Klekovača** mt. Bos.-Herz.
136 E3 **Klembivka** Ukr.
222 D4 **Klemtu** B.C. Can.
176 B2 **Klenčí pod Čerchovem** Czech Rep.
174 D4 **Klenica** Pol.
177 I3 **Klenovec** Slovakia
176 G2 **Klenovice na Hané** Czech Rep.
177 I3 **Klenovský Vepor** mt. Slovakia
175 L2 **Kleosin** Pol.
175 L2 **Klepacze** Pol.
137 K2 **Klepovka** Rus. Fed.
142 A2 **Kleppe** Norway
142 A1 **Kleppestø** Norway
174 D3 **Klępsk** Pol.
215 F2 **Klerksdorp** S. Africa
215 F2 **Klerkskraal** S. Africa
136 D2 **Klesiv** Ukr.
175 L3 **Kleszczele** Pol.
174 F3 **Kleszczewo** Pol.
175 H4 **Kleszczów** Pol.
139 I5 **Kletnya** Rus. Fed.
Kletsk Belarus see **Klyetsk**
135 H6 **Kletskaya** Rus. Fed.
Kletskiy Rus. Fed. see **Kletskaya**
171 E4 **Klettwitz** Ger.
136 C2 **Klevan'** Ukr.
169 B4 **Kleve** Ger.
137 G2 **Kleven'** r. Rus. Fed.
138 G5 **Klichaw** Belarus
107 H1 **Klichka** Rus. Fed.
171 D4 **Klieken** Ger.
215 E5 **Klienpoort** S. Africa
170 D3 **Klietz** Ger.
139 H5 **Klimavichy** Belarus
197 H4 **Kliment** Bulg.
177 H2 **Klimkovice** Czech Rep.
134 J4 **Klimkovka** Rus. Fed.
175 I5 **Klimontów** Pol.
175 J5 **Klimontów** Pol.
Klimovichi Belarus see **Klimavichy**
135 F5 **Klimovo** Rus. Fed.
139 K4 **Klimovsk** Rus. Fed.
140 K2 **Klimpfjäll** Sweden
139 K3 **Klin** Rus. Fed.
177 I2 **Klin** Slovakia
196 E4 **Klina** Kosovo, Srbija Yugo.
222 E5 **Klinaklini** r. B.C. Can.
92 C5 **Kling** Phil.
171 E5 **Klingenberg** Ger.
172 D2 **Klingenberg am Main** Ger.
171 D5 **Klingenthal** Ger.
234 B2 **Klingerstown** PA U.S.A.
95 E2 **Klingkang, Banjaran** mts Indon./Malaysia
170 D2 **Klink** Ger.
176 C1 **Klínovec** mt. Czech Rep.
139 K3 **Klinsko-Dmitrovskaya Gryada** ridge Rus. Fed.
143 H3 **Klintehamn** Gotland Sweden
120 B2 **Klintsovka** Rus. Fed.
139 I5 **Klintsy** Rus. Fed.
215 G2 **Klip** r. S. Africa
214 B6 **Klipdale** S. Africa
215 E5 **Klipfontein** S. Africa
168 E1 **Kliplev** Denmark
142 E3 **Klippan** Sweden
214 E5 **Klipplaat** S. Africa
214 B4 **Kliprand** S. Africa
215 H1 **Klipskool** S. Africa
188 F4 **Klis** Croatia
197 F4 **Klisura** Srbija Yugo.
142 C3 **Klitmøller** Denmark
Klitória Greece see **Kleitoria**
171 F4 **Klitten** Ger.
168 D1 **Klixbüll** Ger.
177 I6 **Kljajićevo** Vojvodina, Srbija Yugo.
188 F3 **Ključ** Bos.-Herz.
176 F3 **Klobouky** Czech Rep.
174 G5 **Kłobuck** Pol.
179 G4 **Klöch** Austria
175 J4 **Kłoczew** Pol.
170 G3 **Kłodawa** Pol.
174 G3 **Kłodawa** Pol.
174 E5 **Kłodzko** Pol.
142 D1 **Kløfta** Norway
175 H5 **Kłomnice** Pol.
174 G4 **Klonowa** Pol.
138 E2 **Klooga** Estonia
164 F2 **Kloosterhaar** Neth.
165 D3 **Kloosterzande** Neth.
177 J3 **Kloptaň** mt. Slovakia
179 H5 **Kloštar Ivanić** Croatia
176 G6 **Kloštar Podravski** Croatia
170 E3 **Klosterfelde** Ger.
171 C4 **Klosterhäseler** Ger.
173 E3 **Klosterlechfeld** Ger.
171 C4 **Klostermansfeld** Ger.
179 H2 **Klosterneuburg** Austria
190 E2 **Klosters** Switz.
171 F4 **Klosterwasser** r. Ger.
171 E3 **Kloster Zinna** Ger.
172 C4 **Kloten** Switz.
169 C5 **Klotten** Ger.
170 C3 **Klötze (Altmark)** Ger.
222 B2 **Kluane** r. Y.T. Can.
Kluang Malaysia see **Keluang**
174 G5 **Kluczbork** Pol.
175 H5 **Kluczewsko** Pol.
Klukhori Rus. Fed. see **Karachayevsk**
175 H4 **Kluki** Pol.
175 K3 **Klukowo** Pol.
220 E4 **Klukwan** AK U.S.A.
164 D3 **Klundert** Neth.
95 F5 **Klungkung** Bali Indon.
123 G5 **Klupro** Pak.
168 C3 **Kluse** Ger.
175 K2 **Klusy** Pol.
170 C2 **Klütz** Ger.
175 I4 **Klwów** Pol.
138 G5 **Klyava** r. Belarus
135 K5 **Klyavlino** Rus. Fed.
139 M3 **Klyaz'ma** r. Rus. Fed.
138 F5 **Klyetsk** Belarus
137 H3 **Klymivka** Ukr.
137 G2 **Klyshky** Ukr.
131 R4 **Klyuchevskaya, Sopka** vol. Rus. Fed.
121 I1 **Klyuchi** Altayskiy Kray Rus. Fed.
131 R4 **Klyuchi** Kamchatskaya Oblast' Rus. Fed.
78 □6 **Kmagha** Sta Isabel Solomon Is
215 F4 **Knapdaar** S. Africa
81 B7 **Knapdale** South I. N.Z.
146 C6 **Knapdale** reg. Scotland U.K.
226 B3 **Knapp Mound** hill WI U.S.A.
142 E3 **Knäred** Sweden
149 H3 **Knaresborough** North Yorkshire, England U.K.
143 F1 **Knästen** hill Sweden
149 H3 **Knayton** North Yorkshire, England U.K.
151 G3 **Knebworth** Hertfordshire, England U.K.
168 F3 **Knesebeck** Ger.
165 C3 **Knesselare** Belgium
169 F6 **Knetzgau** Ger.
188 G3 **Kneževi Vinogradi** Croatia
177 H6 **Kneževo** Croatia
197 G4 **Knezha** Bulg.
171 G5 **Kněžmost** Czech Rep.
196 E4 **Knić** Srbija Yugo.
236 C2 **Knife** r. ND U.S.A.
226 B2 **Knife River** MN U.S.A.
150 D2 **Knighton** Powys, Wales U.K.
240 G2 **Knights Landing** CA U.S.A.
188 F3 **Knin** Croatia
143 F3 **Knislinge** Sweden
179 F3 **Knittelfeld** Austria
172 C2 **Knittlingen** Ger.
143 G2 **Knivsta** Sweden
176 D3 **Knížecí stolec** mt. Czech Rep.
197 G5 **Knizhovnik** Bulg.
197 F4 **Knjaževac** Srbija Yugo.
87 B6 **Knobby Head** hd W.A. Austr.
Knob Lake Nfld. Can. see **Schefferville**
86 F2 **Knob Peak** hill W.A. Austr.
147 B4 **Knock** Clare Rep. of Ireland
147 C3 **Knock** Mayo Rep. of Ireland
146 C5 **Knock** Argyll and Bute, Scotland U.K.
147 B5 **Knockaboy** hill Rep. of Ireland
147 B4 **Knockacummer** hill Rep. of Ireland
147 C2 **Knockalongy** hill Rep. of Ireland
147 B4 **Knockalough** Rep. of Ireland
148 C5 **Knockananna** Rep. of Ireland
148 C5 **Knockanarrigan** Rep. of Ireland
146 E4 **Knockandhu** Moray, Scotland U.K.
147 B4 **Knockanefune** hill Rep. of Ireland
146 D4 **Knockban** Highland, Scotland U.K.
147 E4 **Knockbrandon** Rep. of Ireland
147 E3 **Knockbridge** Rep. of Ireland
147 D4 **Knockbrit** Rep. of Ireland
147 C3 **Knockcroghery** Rep. of Ireland
146 F4 **Knock Hill** hill Scotland U.K.
147 C3 **Knock International** airport Rep. of Ireland
147 E1 **Knocklayd** hill Northern Ireland U.K.
147 C4 **Knocklong** Rep. of Ireland
147 C4 **Knockmealdown Mountains** hills Rep. of Ireland
147 B2 **Knockmore** Rep. of Ireland
147 C3 **Knockmoyle** Rep. of Ireland
147 B4 **Knocknaboul** Rep. of Ireland
148 C2 **Knocknacarry** Northern Ireland U.K.
147 B4 **Knocknagree** Rep. of Ireland
147 C4 **Knocknaskagh** hill Rep. of Ireland
147 C5 **Knockraha** Rep. of Ireland
147 C5 **Knocks** Rep. of Ireland
165 C3 **Knokke-Heist** Belgium
170 E2 **Knorrendorf** Ger.
198 D4 **Knosos** tourist site Greece
Knossós tourist site Greece see **Knosos**
149 H4 **Knottingley** West Yorkshire, England U.K.
151 F2 **Knowle** West Midlands, England U.K.
262 T2 **Knowles, Cape** Antarctica
233 □I1 **Knowles Corner** ME U.S.A.
233 G2 **Knowlton** Que. Can.
230 C3 **Knox** IN U.S.A.
232 D4 **Knox** PA U.S.A.
Knox Atoll Kiribati see **Tarawa**
226 A5 **Knox City** MO U.S.A.
263 G2 **Knox Coast** Antarctica
231 D5 **Knoxville** GA U.S.A.
236 E3 **Knoxville** IA U.S.A.
231 D5 **Knoxville** TN U.S.A.
146 C4 **Knoydart** mts Scotland U.K.
150 D2 **Knucklas** Powys, Wales U.K.
221 L2 **Knud Rasmussen Land** reg. Greenland
169 E4 **Knüllwald-Remsfeld** Ger.
174 G5 **Knurów** Pol.
149 G4 **Knutsford** Cheshire, England U.K.
134 I5 **Knyaginino** Rus. Fed.
138 F4 **Knyahinin** Belarus
137 G4 **Knyaze-Hryhorivka** Ukr.
175 M5 **Knyazhe** Ukr.
214 D6 **Knysna** S. Africa
175 K2 **Knyszyn** Pol.
100 F3 **Ko, Gora** mt. Rus. Fed.
208 F2 **Koalib, Jebel** mt. Sudan
211 C6 **Koani** Tanz.
Koartac Que. Can. see **Quaqtaq**

94 D3	Koba Indon.
179 E4	Kobarid Slovenia
103 E8	Kobayashi Japan
104 B4	Kobe Japan
137 H3	Kobelyaky Ukr.
142 E4	København Denmark
142 E4	København mun. Denmark
206 C3	Kobenni Maur.
179 F3	Kobero Japan
179 H3	Kobersdorf Austria
175 H4	Kobiele Wielkie Pol.
174 E5	Kobierzyce Pol.
114 G5	Kobiór Pol.
102 D1	Kōbi-shō i. Japan
169 C5	Koblenz Ger.
169 C5	Koblenz admin. reg. Rheinland-Pfalz Ger.
137 F4	Kobleve Ukr.
210 C7	Kobo Eth.
210 A4	Koboko Uganda
139 K2	Kobra Rus. Fed.
134 J4	Kobra Rus. Fed.
91 H8	Kobroör i. Indon.
170 C2	Kobrow Ger.
136 C1	Kobryn Belarus
129 B3	K'obulet'i Georgia
105 E3	Kobushiga-take mt. Japan
131 N3	Kobyay Rus. Fed.
174 F4	Kobyla Góra Pol.
174 C2	Kobylanka Pol.
136 C3	Kobylets'ka Polyana Ukr.
176 F3	Kobylí Czech Rep.
174 F4	Kobylin Pol.
175 K2	Kobylin-Borzymy Pol.
174 F1	Kobyłka Pol.
178 I3	Kobyłnica Pol.
199 F1	Kocaafşar r. Turkey
199 G1	Kocaali Turkey
199 G3	Kocaalilar Turkey
199 F2	Kocaavşar Turkey
199 F3	Kocabaş Denizli Turkey
199 F2	Koca Dağ mt. Turkey
199 F1	Kocaeli Turkey
199 F1	Kocaeli prov. Turkey
199 F1	Kocaeli Yarımadası pen. Turkey
129 C3	Kocaköy Turkey
197 F5	Kočani Macedonia
129 C4	Kocapınar Turkey
199 E3	Kocarlı Turkey
129 C4	Kocasu r. Turkey
199 F1	Kocasu r. Turkey
129 C1	Koçatepe Turkey
128 C1	Koçbaşı Tepe mt. Turkey
196 D3	Kočeljevo Srbija Yugo.
188 E3	Kočevje Slovenia
100 C3	Koch'ang S. Korea
174 G5	Kochanowice Pol.
117 U4	Koch Bihar W. Bengal India
173 F4	Kochel am See Ger.
173 F4	Kochelsee l. Ger.
172 D2	Kocher r. Ger.
137 H2	Kocherezhky Ukr.
197 F4	Kocherinovo Bulg.
136 E2	Kocheriv Ukr.
137 I2	Kochetovka Rus. Fed.
134 K4	Kochevo Rus. Fed.
	Kochi Kerala India see Cochin
103 F7	Kōchi Japan
103 F7	Kōchi pref. Japan
120 E1	Kochkar' Kyrg.
121 H4	Kochkor Kyrg.
	Kochkorka Kyrg. see Kochkor
135 I5	Kochkurovo Rus. Fed.
129 E1	Kochubey Rus. Fed.
129 B1	Kochubeyevskoye Rus. Fed.
198 D2	Kochylas hill Sterea Ellas Greece
175 K4	Kock Pol.
129 D3	Koçkıran Turkey
129 C3	Koçköyü Turkey
170 C3	Köckte Ger.
177 G3	Kočovce Slovakia
177 H4	Kocs Hungary
177 H5	Kocsola Hungary
174 F2	Koczała Pol.
114 B3	Kod Karnataka India
114 C4	Kodaikanal Tamil Nadu India
105 F3	Kodaira Japan
102 D1	Kodaka-jima i. Japan
136 F2	Kodaky Ukr.
115 E2	Kodala Orissa India
117 F4	Kodarma Bihar India
175 L4	Kodeń Pol.
171 F4	Kodersdorf Ger.
220 C4	Kodiak AK U.S.A.
220 C4	Kodiak Island AK U.S.A.
116 B5	Kodinar Gujarat India
134 G3	Kodino Rus. Fed.
138 C1	Kodisjoki Fin.
171 C5	Köditz Ger.
114 C4	Kodiyakkarai Tamil Nadu India
176 G4	Kodó r. Hungary
102 J3	Kodomari Japan
129 B2	Kodori r. Georgia
129 B2	Kodoris K'edi hills Georgia
136 E2	Kodra Ukr.
175 H4	Kodrąb Pol.
114 C3	Kodumuru Andhra Prad. India
136 E3	Kodyma Ukr.
136 F3	Kodyma r. Ukr.
197 G5	Kodzhaele mt. Bulg./Greece
214 D3	Koegas S. Africa
214 C3	Koegrabie S. Africa
164 F2	Koekange Neth.
165 B3	Koekelare Belgium
214 B4	Koekenaap S. Africa
212 C5	Koës Namibia
165 C3	Koewacht Neth.
241 K5	Kofa Mountains AZ U.S.A.
123 G2	Kofarnihon Tajik.
123 G2	Kofarnihon r. Tajik.
197 H5	Kofçaz Turkey
173 G3	Köfering Ger.
215 E3	Koffiefontein S. Africa
128 A1	Kofinas, Oros mt. Kriti Greece
179 G3	Köflach Austria
206 E5	Koforidua Ghana
105 E3	Kōfu Japan
105 F2	Koga Japan
197 I3	Kogălniceanu airport Romania
230 F4	Kogaluk r. Nfld. Can.
224 E1	Kogaluk r. Nfld. Can.
85 G5	Kogan Qld Austr.
105 F3	Koganei Japan
142 E4	Køge Denmark
142 E4	Køge Bugt b. Denmark
134 L3	Kogel' r. Rus. Fed.
207 G4	Kogi state Nigeria
123 G3	Kogon Uzbek. see Kagan
138 E2	Kohat Estonia
117 H4	Kohima Nagaland India
78 □4	Kohinggo i. New Georgia Is Solomon Is
122 B4	Kohkīlūyeh va Būyer Ahmadī prov. Iran
173 G2	Kohlberg Ger.
168 D2	Köhlen Ger.
266 R2	Kohler Range mts Antarctica
241 L4	Kohls Ranch AZ U.S.A.
138 F2	Kohtla-Järve Estonia
80 E2	Kohukohunui hill North I. N.Z.
84 C6	Kohunlich mt. South I. N.Z.
136 E5	Kohyl'nyk r. Ukr.
222 A2	Koidern Y.T. Can.
222 A2	Koidern Mountain Y.T. Can.
206 C4	Koidu Sierra Leone
	Sefadu
214 A4	Koingnaas S. Africa
114 C2	Koilkonda Andhra Prad. India
217 □3a	Koimbani Njazidja Comoros
134 J3	Koin r. Rus. Fed.
127 G3	Koi Sanjaq Iraq
140 O3	Koitere l. Fin.
105 F3	Koito-gawa r. Japan
101 D6	Kŏje-do i. S. Korea
176 G2	Kojetín Czech Rep.
87 C7	Kojonup W.A. Austr.
129 D3	Kojori Georgia
95 K4	Kok r. Thai.
171 H4	Koka Hungary
233 □12	Kokadjo ME U.S.A.

105 G3	Kokai-gawa r. Japan
120 F2	Kokalat Kazakh.
	Kokand Uzbek. see Pakhtaabad
141 M4	Kökar Åland Fin.
138 C2	Kokarsfjärden b. Fin.
81 C5	Kokatahi South I. N.Z.
177 I3	Kokava nad Rimavicou Slovakia
123 G2	Kokcha r. Afgh.
	Kokchetav Kazakh. see Kokshetau
141 M3	Kokemäki Fin.
138 G4	Kokhanava Belarus
139 M3	Kokhma Rus. Fed.
206 B3	Koki Senegal
121 H4	Kök-Janggak Kyrg.
140 N3	Kokkola Fin.
138 E3	Koknese Latvia
207 G4	Koko Nigeria
206 C3	Kokofata Mali
206 D5	Kokolo-Pozo Côte d'Ivoire
230 D3	Komoko IN U.S.A.
139 J5	Kokoreva Rus. Fed.
206 B4	Kokou mt. Guinea
121 J2	Kokpekti Kazakh.
179 F4	Kokra r. Slovenia
179 F4	Kokrica Slovenia
101 C5	Koksan N. Korea
121 G4	Koksaray Kazakh.
	Kokshaal-Tau, Khrebet mts China/Kyrg. see Kakshal-Too
134 I4	Koksharka Rus. Fed.
121 G1	Kokshetau Kazakh.
165 B3	Koksijde Belgium
225 G1	Koksoak r. Que. Can.
215 G4	Kokstad S. Africa
121 I3	Koksu Almatinskaya Oblast' Kazakh.
121 G4	Koksu Yuzhnyy Kazakhstan Kazakh.
121 G3	Koktal Kazakh.
121 H4	Kök-Tash Kyrg.
121 I3	Koktebek Kazakh.
	Koktokay Xinjiang China see Fuyun
103 E8	Kokubu Japan
105 E3	Kokushiga-take mt. Japan
	Kok-Yangak Kyrg. see Kök-Janggak
121 J2	Kokzhayyk Kazakh.
140 P1	Kola r. Rus. Fed.
117 F5	Kolabira Orissa India
123 F5	Kolachi r. Afgh.
175 H4	Kolacin Pol.
174 L5	Kolacze Pol.
174 E2	Kołaczkowo Pol.
175 J6	Kołaczyce Pol.
116 C2	Kolaghat W. Bengal India
	Kolahoi mt. Jammu and Kashmir
206 C4	Kolahun Liberia
93 B4	Kolaka Sulawesi Tenggara Indon.
175 K2	Kolaki Kościelne Pol.
92 B4	Kolamandugu Phil.
97 B6	Ko Lanta Thai.
114 C3	Kolar Karnataka India
114 D2	Kolar Madh. Prad. India
114 C3	Kolaras Rajasthan India
	Kolar Gold Fields Karnataka India see Kolar
140 M2	Kolari Fin.
	Kolarovgrad Bulg. see Shumen
177 G4	Kolárovo Slovakia
140 M3	Kolåsen Sweden
196 D4	Kolašin Crna Gora Yugo.
116 C4	Kolayat Rajasthan India
143 G2	Kolbäck Sweden
170 F2	Kolbacz Pol.
174 G2	Kolbaskowo Pol.
	Kolberg Pol. see Kołobrzeg
168 E2	Kolbermoor Ger.
175 J3	Kolbiel Pol.
142 D2	Kolbotn Norway
175 J5	Kołbuszowa Pol.
139 L3	Kol'chugino Rus. Fed.
137 G5	Kol'chyne Ukr.
174 F1	Kolczygłowy Pol.
206 B3	Kolda Senegal
142 E4	Kolding Denmark
240 □8	Kolekole mt. HI U.S.A.
240 □G1	Kolekole Kauai HI U.S.A.
142 M2	Koler Sweden
168 E4	Kölleda Hungary
171 J1	Koluguev, Ostrov i. Rus. Fed.
117 F5	Kolhan r. Bihar India
116 G4	Kolhapur Mahar. India
114 N3	Kolho Fin.
113 D11	Kolhumadulu Atoll Maldives
206 B3	Koliba r. Guinea/Guinea-Bissau
	Kolikata W. Bengal India see Calcutta
168 E1	Kolima r. Fin.
171 N1	Kolín Czech Rep.
176 C2	Kolindský Czech Rep.
210 C5	K'olito Eth.
206 E5	Koliu r. Côte d'Ivoire
209 B5	Kom Ombo Egypt
208 C2	Komono Congo
91 I8	Komoran i. Indon.
174 E3	Komorniki Pol.
177 I3	Komorovce Slovakia
105 E2	Komoro Japan
197 H4	Komotini Greece
177 I5	Kompelje Pol.
177 I5	Kömpöc Hungary
	Kompong Cham Cambodia see Kâmpóng Cham
	Kompong Chhnang Cambodia see Kâmpóng Chhnang
	Kompong Kleang Cambodia see Kâmpóng Khleăng
	Kompong Som Cambodia see Sihanoukville
	Kompong Speu Cambodia see Kâmpóng Spoe
	Kompong Thom Cambodia see Kâmpóng Thum
198 B2	Kompoti Greece
174 F5	Kompráchcice Pol.
	Komrat Moldova see Comrat
214 C5	Komsberg mts S. Africa
214 C5	Komsberg mts S. Africa
	Komsomol Kazakh. see Komsomolets
	Komsomolets Turkm. see Komsomol'skiy
120 E1	Komsomolets, Ostrov i. Rus. Fed.
131 K1	Komsomolets, Ostrov i. Severnaya Zemlya Rus. Fed.
139 M3	Komsomol'sk Rus. Fed.
139 M3	Komsomol'sk Ukr.
137 G2	Komsomol's'k Ukr.
176 B2	Komsomol'skiy Rus. Fed. Yugorsk
	Komsomol'skiy Rus. Fed. see Komsomol'sk
131 J3	Komsomol'skiy Rus. Fed.
135 I6	Komsomol'skiy Respublika Mordoviya Rus. Fed.
121 H3	Komsomol'skiy Rus. Fed.
129 E1	Komsomol'skoye Rus. Fed.
137 H2	Komsomol'skoye Ukr.
137 I5	Komysh-Zorya Ukr.
137 H4	Komyshuvate Ukr.
137 H3	Komyshuvakha Ukr.
137 G3	Komyshuvakha Ukr.
137 H4	Komyshuvakha Ukr.
141 U1	Komysh-Zorya Ukr.
115 D2	Konada Andhra Prad. India

130 J4	Kolpashevo Rus. Fed.
139 H2	Kolpino Rus. Fed.
135 G5	Kolpny Rus. Fed.
178 C3	Kolsass Austria
121 H4	Kol'shat Kazakh.
139 M3	Kolva r. Rus. Fed.
134 F2	Kol'skiy Poluostrov pen.
143 F2	Kolsva Sweden
141 K3	Kölsvallen Sweden
177 H3	Kolta Slovakia
120 B1	Koltubanovskiy Rus. Fed.
196 E3	Kolubara r. Yugo.
145 B6	Koluba Turkey see Kahta
203 I6	Koluli Eritrea
175 H4	Koluszki Pol.
120 D2	Koluton Kazakh.
135 G5	Kolva r. Rus. Fed.
134 L3	Kolva r. Rus. Fed.
140 J2	Kolvereid Norway
134 F2	Kolvitskoye, Ozero l. Rus. Fed.
209 E7	Kolwezi Dem. Rep. Congo
114 B2	Kolya r. Indon.
131 R3	Kolybel'skoye Rus. Fed.
131 R3	Kolyma r. Rus. Fed.
	Kolyma Lowland Rus. Fed. see Kolymskaya Nizmennost'
	Kolyma Range mts Rus. Fed. see Kolymskiy, Khrebet
131 Q3	Kolymskaya Nizmennost' lowland Rus. Fed.
131 R3	Kolymskiy, Khrebet mts Rus. Fed.
131 P3	Kolyuchaya Vodokhranilische resr Rus. Fed.
131 T3	Kolyuchinskaya Guba b. Rus. Fed.
121 J2	Kolyvan' Rus. Fed.
177 K4	Komádi Hungary
105 F3	Komae Japan
105 D3	Komagane Japan
105 E2	Komaga-take mt. Japan
102 J2	Komaga-take vol. Japan
214 A3	Komaggas S. Africa
214 A3	Komaggas Mountains S. Africa
103 C3	Komaki Japan
175 K6	Komańcza Pol.
100 F2	Komarnaya, Gora mt. Rus. Fed.
131 R4	Komarichi Rus. Fed.
196 C4	Komarna r. Yugo.
177 H4	Komárno Slovakia
138 B3	Komárno Ukr.
177 H4	Komárom Hungary
177 H4	Komárom-Esztergom county Hungary
176 C2	Komárov Czech Rep.
136 C2	Komarove Ukr.
138 G1	Komarovo Rus. Fed.
175 K4	Komarówka Podlaska Pol.
139 N4	Komarov Osada Pol.
215 H1	Komati r. Swaziland
215 H1	Komatipoort S. Africa
104 C2	Komatsu Japan
104 A4	Komatsushima Japan
212 C3	Kombat Namibia
206 E3	Kombissiri Burkina
	Kombóti Greece see Kompoti
114 C3	Konice Czech Rep.
175 H5	Koniecpol Pol.
172 D2	Königsbronn Ger.
	Königsberg Rus. Fed. see Kaliningrad
169 F5	Königsberg in Bayern Ger.
173 J6	Königsbronn Ger.
171 E4	Königsbrück Ger.
173 G3	Königsbrunn Ger.
171 C5	Königsee Ger.
172 C3	Königsfeld im Schwarzwald Ger.
171 J3	Königsgraben r. Ger.
178 D3	Königsleiten Austria
171 C4	Königshütte Pol. see Chorzów
169 I3	Königslutter am Elm Ger.
173 H3	Königsmoos Ger.
173 F2	Königssee l. Ger.
173 F2	Königstein Ger.
171 E5	Königswalde Ger.
179 E2	Königswartha Ger.
179 N4	Königswiesen Austria
169 C5	Königswinter Ger.
173 F6	Königs Wusterhausen Ger.
174 G3	Konin Pol.
100 F1	Konin r. Rus. Fed.
198 B1	Konitsa Greece
172 C4	Königsbach-Stein Ger.
190 C2	Koniz Switz.
188 F2	Konj mt. Bos.-Herz.
188 F2	Konjic Bos.-Herz.
188 F3	Konjuh mts Bos.-Herz.
139 P4	Konkolovka Rus. Fed.
139 L5	Kon-Kolodez' Rus. Fed.
206 B3	Konna Mali
232 C6	Konnarock VA U.S.A.
171 C4	Könnern Ger.
171 D5	Könnersreuth Ger.
140 N3	Konnevesi Fin.
137 F3	Kononcha Ukr.
206 E4	Konongo Ghana
100 K3	Konoplyane Ukr.
134 H3	Konosha Rus. Fed.
105 F2	Kōnosu Japan
137 G2	Konotop Ukr.
110 D3	Konqi He r. China
175 H3	Końskie Pol.
175 H5	Konradsreuth Ger.
175 J3	Konskowola Pol.
210 D3	Konso Eth.
167 K3	Końskowola Pol.
210 D3	Konso Eth.
	Konstantinograd Ukr. see Krasnohrad
100 C2	Konstantinovka Rus. Fed.
	Konstantinovka Donets'ka Oblast' Ukr. see Kostyantynivka
	Konstantinovka Kharkivs'ka Oblast' Ukr. see Kostyantynivka
	Konstantinovka Zaporiz'ka Oblast' Ukr. see Kostyantynivka
139 L3	Konstantinovo Rus. Fed.
135 H7	Konstantinovsk Rus. Fed.
172 E6	Konstanz Ger.
207 G4	Kontagora Nigeria
140 O3	Kontiomäki Fin.
140 P2	Kontiolahti Fin.
121 H2	Kon Tum Vietnam
97 E4	Kontum, Plateau du Vietnam
121 G1	Konyrat Kazakh.
121 J1	Konyratskiy Rus. Fed.
129 D2	Konyrolen Kazakh.
126 D3	Konya Turkey
199 I2	Konya prov. Turkey
199 I2	Konya Ovası plain Turkey
110 E3	Konya Xinjiang China
120 E3	Konyrat Kazakh.
121 J1	Konyrolen Kazakh.
121 H3	Konyrat Karagandinskaya Oblast' Kazakh.
135 K5	Konzhakovskiy Kamen', Gora mt. Rus. Fed.
87 D6	Kookynie W.A. Austr.
107 B3	Koolan Island W.A. Austr.
126 B3	Kooline W.A. Austr.
84 D5	Kooloonong, Lake salt flat Qld Austr.

129 C4	Konakkuran Turkey
139 K3	Konakovo Rus. Fed.
104 C3	Kōnan Japan
101 B4	Konar pro. Afgh.
123 G3	Konar r. Afgh.
	Konarka Orissa India see Konarka
115 E2	Konarka r. Turkey
175 K2	Konarzyce Pol.
174 F2	Konarzyny Pol.
116 D4	Konch Uttar Prad. India
139 J2	Konchezero Rus. Fed.
134 F3	Konchezero Rus. Fed.
136 C1	Konchtys Belarus
114 D2	Kondagaon Madh. Prad. India
199 E3	Köndälänçay r. Azer.
114 C2	Kondapalle Andhra Prad. India
114 D2	Kondavid Andhra Prad. India
87 C7	Kondinin W.A. Austr.
	Kondinskoye Khanty-Mansiyskiy Avtonomnyy Okrug Rus. Fed. see Oktyabr'skoye
130 H3	Kondinskoye Khanty-Mansiyskiy Avtonomnyy Okrug Rus. Fed.
211 B6	Kondoa Tanz.
135 I5	Kondol' Rus. Fed.
129 D3	Kondoli Georgia
134 F3	Kondopoga Rus. Fed.
177 J5	Kondoros Hungary
139 J4	Kondrovo Rus. Fed.
123 G2	Kondūz Afgh.
123 G2	Kondūz prov. Afgh.
78 □5	Koné New Caledonia
197 F5	Konečka Planina mts Macedonia
	Köneürgench Turkm. see Keneurgench
206 D4	Kong Côte d'Ivoire
97 C5	Kŏng, Kaôh i. Cambodia
97 D5	Kŏng, Tônlé r. Cambodia
96 D4	Kong, Xé r. Laos
221 O3	Kong Christian IX Land reg. Greenland
221 P2	Kong Christian X Land reg. Greenland
142 C4	Kongeå r. Denmark
	Kongelab atoll Marshall Is see Rongelap
142 E4	Kongens Lyngby Denmark
221 M3	Kong Frederik IX Land reg. Greenland
221 P2	Kong Frederik VIII Land reg. Greenland
221 N3	Kong Frederik VI Kyst coastal area Greenland
221 P2	Kong Karls Land is Svalbard
95 G2	Kong Kaÿ hill Indon.
95 G2	Kongkandi mt. Indon.
104 D2	Kongdko-san mt. Japan
209 E6	Kongolo Dem. Rep. Congo
221 P2	Kong Oscars Fjord inlet Greenland
206 E3	Kongoussi Burkina
142 C2	Kongsberg Norway
140 □	Kongsoya i. Svalbard
142 E1	Kongsvinger Norway
110 A4	Kongur Shan mt. Xinjiang China
211 C6	Kongwa Tanz.
221 P2	Kong Wilhelm Land reg. Greenland
116 E4	Kora Uttar Prad. India
196 E5	Korab mts Albania/Macedonia
210 E3	K'orahē Eth.
110 C3	Koramlik Xinjiang China
188 E3	Korana r. Bos.-Herz./Croatia
114 C3	Korangal Andhra Prad. India
115 D2	Koraput Orissa India
	Korat Thai. see Nakhon Ratchasima
114 C2	Koratla Andhra Prad. India
115 D2	Korba Madh. Prad. India
169 D4	Korbach Ger.
173 G2	Korbußli Georgia
94 C1	Korbu, Gunung mt. Malaysia
198 B1	Korçë Albania
171 I5	Korchino Rus. Fed.
130 D3	Korchivka Ukr.
198 C2	Korchyk r. Ukr.
188 F4	Korčula Croatia
188 F4	Korčula i. Croatia
188 F4	Korčulanski Kanal sea chan. Croatia
175 K3	Korczew Pol.
175 J6	Korczyna Pol.
121 H4	Korday Zhambylskaya Oblast' Kazakh.
172 A2	Kordel Ger.
136 E3	Kordelivka Ukr.
122 D3	Kordestān prov. Iran
123 H4	Kord Khvord Iran
122 C2	Kord Kūy Iran
134 I4	Kordon Rus. Fed.
101 C5	Korea, North country Asia
101 C5	Korea, South country Asia
101 C5	Korea Bay g. China/N. Korea
101 D6	Korea Strait Japan/S. Korea
114 B2	Koregaon Mahar. India
137 H2	Koreiz Ukr.
210 C1	Korem Eth.
137 I2	Korenovsk Rus. Fed.
135 G7	Korenovsk Rus. Fed.
	Korenovskaya Rus. Fed. see Korenovsk
206 D3	Koréra-Koré Mali
136 D2	Korets' Ukr.
171 K5	Korf Rus. Fed.
174 F5	Korfantów Pol.
199 F1	Körfez Turkey
262 T1	Korff Ice Rise Antarctica
127 F2	Korfovskiy Rus. Fed.
110 C3	Korgas Xinjiang China
142 N2	Korgen Norway
199 G2	Korgun Turkey
206 D4	Korhogo Côte d'Ivoire
205 C5	Koribundu Sierra Leone
116 B5	Kori Creek inlet Gujarat India
175 G5	Konradsreuth Ger.
214 C5	Koringplaas S. Africa
80 E3	Koriniti North I. N.Z.
198 C2	Korinthiakos Kolpos sea chan. Greece
198 C2	Korinthos Greece
177 G4	Köris-hegy hill Hungary
196 E4	Koritnik mt. Yugo. see Korçë
103 J5	Kōriyama Japan
122 D2	Korkai Iran
199 F1	Korkuteli Turkey
110 D3	Korla Xinjiang China
188 F2	Körle Ger.
169 J4	Körmend Hungary
175 L6	Kornat i. Croatia
188 F3	Kornati i. Croatia
	Korneuburg Austria
121 H2	Korneyevka Karagandinskaya Oblast' Kazakh.
120 D1	Korneyevka Severnyy Kazakhstan Kazakh.
121 J1	Korneyevka Rus. Fed.
139 L1	Kornilovo Rus. Fed.
136 D3	Kornin Ukr.
171 F1	Kornisi Georgia
129 C1	Kornwestheim Ger.
174 D3	Kórnik Pol.
176 F1	Korno Ukr.
204 F6	Koro Côte d'Ivoire
79 □7	Koro i. Fiji
206 E3	Koro Mali
203 G6	Koro Sudan
135 G6	Korocha Rus. Fed.
214 C5	Korocha r. Rus. Fed.
126 D3	Köroğlu Dağları mts Turkey
126 C2	Köroğlu Tepesi mt. Turkey
211 C6	Korogwe Tanz.
84 D5	Koroit Vic. Austr.

82 D2	Koolkootinnie, Lake salt flat S.A. Austr.
82 D3	Koolunga S.A. Austr.
87 C6	Koolyanobbing W.A. Austr.
83 F3	Koondrook Vic. Austr.
82 C2	Koonibba S.A. Austr.
214 C2	Koopan-Suid S. Africa
83 G3	Koorawatha N.S.W. Austr.
87 C6	Koorda W.A. Austr.
86 B4	Koordarrie W.A. Austr.
241 L2	Koosharem UT U.S.A.
238 C2	Kooskia ID U.S.A.
222 G5	Kootenay r. B.C. Can.
222 G5	Kootenay Bay B.C. Can.
222 G5	Kootenay Lake B.C. Can.
83 G2	Kootingal N.S.W. Austr.
214 C4	Kootjieskolk S. Africa
164 E2	Kootwijkerbroek Neth.
135 G6	Kopa Kazakh.
121 I2	Kopa r. Kazakh.
129 C4	Kopal Turkey
137 H4	Kopani Ukr.
135 I7	Kopanovka Rus. Fed.
137 F3	Kopanskaya Rus. Fed.
137 H4	Kopani Ukr.
114 B2	Kopargaon Mahar. India
136 D3	Kopayhorod Ukr.
121 I3	Kopbirlik Kazakh.
176 G3	Kopčany Slovakia
188 D3	Koper Slovenia
142 C2	Kopervik Norway
122 D2	Kopet-Dag, Khrebet mts Iran/Turkm.
	Kopet-Dag, Khrebet mts Iran/Turkm. see Kopet Dag
176 F4	Kópháza Hungary
174 F5	Kopice Pol.
176 E1	Kopidno Czech Rep.
143 G2	Köping Sweden
196 D4	Koplik Albania
140 L3	Köpmanholmen Sweden
114 B3	Koppa Karnataka India
114 B3	Koppal Karnataka India
142 E1	Koppang Norway
190 D2	Kopparberg r. Romania
143 F2	Kopparberg Sweden
	Kopparberg county Sweden see Dalarna
164 C3	Kopparberg Neth.
203 F5	Köppeli hill Ger.
100 C2	Koppi r. Rus. Fed.
215 F2	Koppies S. Africa
214 C2	Koppieskraal Pan salt pan S. Africa
178 E3	Koppl Austria
188 F2	Koprivnica Croatia
126 C3	Köprü r. Turkey
199 F2	Köprübaşı Manisa Turkey
129 B3	Köprübaşı Trabzon Turkey
129 B4	Köprübaşı Turkey
175 J3	Köprülü Turkey
199 J5	Koprzywnica Pol.
175 J5	Koprzywnica r. Pol.
134 I3	Kopshor r. Rus. Fed.
135 S6	Kopstal Lux.
165 F5	Kopustin Belarus
138 E2	Kõpu r. Estonia
80 E2	Kopu North I. N.Z.
80 F3	Kopuawhara North I. N.Z.
136 C3	Kopychyntsi Ukr.
136 C3	Kopyl' Belarus see Kapyl'
116 E4	Kora Uttar Prad. India
196 E5	Korab mts Albania/Macedonia
139 M5	Korablino Rus. Fed.
210 E3	K'orahē Eth.
114 A2	Korak r. India
188 F2	Korana r. Bos.-Herz./Croatia
114 C3	Korangal Andhra Prad. India
115 D2	Koraput Orissa India
116 E4	Korar Madh. Prad. India
95 B2	Kota Samarahan Sarawak Malaysia
94 C3	Kota Tinggi Malaysia
117 G5	Kotchandpur Bangl.
232 C2	Kotch r. B.C. Can.
123 G5	Kot Diji Pak.
116 D3	Kotdwara Uttar Prad. India
175 K5	Kotegara Hungary
197 J4	Kotel Bulg.
135 I4	Kotel'nich Rus. Fed.
135 H7	Kotel'nikovo Rus. Fed.
131 O2	Kotel'nyy, Ostrov i. Novosibirskiye O-va Rus. Fed.
170 E2	Kotelow Ger.
137 H2	Kotel'va Ukr.
80 F3	Kotemaori North I. N.Z.
115 D2	Kotgarh India
116 B2	Kotgarh Hima. Prad. India
115 D2	Kothagudem Andhra Prad. India see Kottagudem
171 C4	Köthen (Anhalt) Ger.
116 E3	Kothi Madh. Prad. India
206 B3	Kotiari Naoudé Senegal
210 B4	Kotido Uganda
141 N3	Kotka Fin.
116 C3	Kot Kapura Punjab India
174 E4	Kotla Pol.
134 I3	Kotlas Rus. Fed.
134 I3	Kotlas Rus. Fed.
220 B3	Kotlik AK U.S.A.
174 F4	Kotlin Pol.
175 J5	Kotlina Sandomierska basin Pol.
188 E2	Kotly Rus. Fed.
207 G4	Koton-Karifi Nigeria
196 D4	Kotor Crna Gora Yugo.
179 H4	Kotoriba Croatia
207 G3	Kotorkoshi Nigeria
139 L3	Kotoros'l r. Rus. Fed.
188 F3	Kotor Varoš Bos.-Herz.
137 H3	Kotovka Ukr.
135 I6	Kotovo Rus. Fed.
	Kotovsk Moldova see Hînceşti
135 H5	Kotovsk Rus. Fed.
136 E4	Kotovs'k Ukr.
116 D4	Kot Putli Rajasthan India
138 E5	Kotra r. Belarus
114 D2	Kotri r. India
123 G5	Kotri Pak.
178 E5	Kötschach Austria
114 C2	Kottagudem Andhra Prad. India
114 C4	Kottayam Kerala India
114 C4	Kottayam Pondicherry India
114 C3	Kotte Sri Lanka see Sri Jayewardenepura Kotte
169 C5	Kottenheim Ger.
178 G5	Köttmannsdorf Austria
179 F3	Köttmannsdorf Austria
208 D3	Kotto r. C.A.R.
114 C3	Kotturu Karnataka India
79 □7a	Kotu Group i.s Tonga
122 C2	Koturdepe Turkm.
131 L2	Kotuy r. Rus. Fed.
220 B3	Kotzebue AK U.S.A.
220 B3	Kotzebue Sound sea chan. AK U.S.A.
214 A3	Kotzehoop S. Africa
214 A4	Kotzesrus S. Africa
172 G2	Kötzting Ger.
208 D3	Kouango C.A.R.
166 A3	Koudekerke Neth.
206 D3	Koudougou Burkina
199 H5	Koufalia Greece
214 D5	Koukonis i. Greece
214 D5	Kouga r. S. Africa
214 D5	Kougaberge mts S. Africa
206 D5	Kouibli Côte d'Ivoire
208 A3	Kouilou r. Congo
208 B3	Kouka Burkina
206 C4	Koukourou r. C.A.R.
208 D3	Koukourou r. C.A.R.
208 B3	Koulamoutou Gabon
206 D3	Koulikoro Mali
206 C3	Koulikoro admin. reg. Mali
207 H4	Kouloum Cameroon
208 C3	Kouma r. C.A.R.
78 □5	Koumac New Caledonia
85 G4	Koumala Qld Austr.
206 B3	Koumbia Guinea
208 B3	Koumbala Guinea
206 C3	Koumra Chad
206 D3	Koundâra Guinea
206 B3	Koundian Guinea
206 C3	Koungheul Senegal
217 □3a	Kouni Mayotte
206 C3	Kounradskiy Karagandinskaya Oblast' Kazakh.
121 H3	Kounradskiy Karagandinskaya Oblast' Kazakh. see Konyrat
206 B3	Kounsitel Guinea
237 E6	Kountze TX U.S.A.
214 C5	Koup S. Africa
206 C3	Koupéla Burkina
217 □3a	Kouqian Jilin China see Yongji
206 C3	Kourani Njazidja Comoros
176 D2	Kourim Czech Rep.
251 H3	Kourou Fr. Guiana
206 C4	Kouroussa Guinea
206 B3	Kousséri Cameroon
207 F4	Koussountou Togo
206 D4	Koutiala Mali
198 D7	Koutsopodi Peloponnisos Greece
141 N3	Kouvola Fin.
208 C5	Kouyou r. Congo

196 E3 Kovačica Vojvodina, Srbija Yugo.
177 H5 Kővágószőlős Hungary
136 F3 Kovalivka Ukr.
134 B2 Kovallberget Sweden
177 H3 Kovarce Slovakia
176 C1 Kovářská Czech Rep.
137 F2 Kovchyn Ukr.
140 O2 Kovdor Rus. Fed.
136 C2 Kovel' Ukr.
134 H4 Kovernino Rus. Fed.
139 H5 Kovili Vojvodina, Srbija Yugo.
134 C4 Kovilpatti Tamil Nadu India
196 E3 Kovin Vojvodina, Srbija Yugo.
       Kovno Lith. see Kaunas
134 J2 Kovriga, Gora hill Rus. Fed.
139 M3 Kovrov Rus. Fed.
137 J3 Kovsharivka Ukr.
137 H3 Kow"yahy Ukr.
135 H5 Kovylkino Rus. Fed.
139 K1 Kovzhskoye, Ozero l. Rus. Fed.
175 K1 Kowal Pol.
174 G4 Kowale Pol.
175 K1 Kowale Oleckie Pol.
174 G4 Kowale-Pańskie Pol.
85 E2 Kowanyama Qld Austr.
174 D5 Kowary Pol.
81 C5 Kowhitirangi South I. N.Z.
175 I4 Kowiesy Pol.
109 □ Kowloon H.K. China
109 □ Kowloon Peninsula H.K. China
206 C5 Koyama Guinea
199 F3 Köyceğiz Turkey
133 J3 Koygorodok Rus. Fed.
122 C1 Koymatdag, Gory hills Turkm.
197 G4 Koynare Bulg.
134 L3 Koyp, Gora mt. Rus. Fed.
124 □ Koyukuk r. AK U.S.A.
126 E2 Koyulhisar Turkey
207 I4 Koza Cameroon
134 G4 Koza Rus. Fed.
137 I2 Kozacha Lopan' Ukr.
       Kozağacı Turkey see Günyüzü
126 D3 Kozan Turkey
198 B1 Kozani Greece
188 F3 Kozara mts Bos.-Herz.
177 H5 Kozármisleny Hungary
137 F2 Kozarn Ukr.
177 H3 Kozárovce Slovakia
       Kozarska Dubica Bos.-Herz. see Bosanska Dubica
137 G4 Kozats'ke Ukr.
137 I3 Kozats'ke Ukr.
137 F2 Kozelets' Ukr.
133 J4 Kozel'shchyna Ukr.
135 J4 Kozel'sk Rus. Fed.
120 E3 Kozhabakhy Kazakh.
136 E3 Kozhanka Ukr.
134 L3 Kozhim-Iz, Gora mt. Rus. Fed.
136 D3 Kozhukivtsi Ukr.
134 L2 Kozhva Rus. Fed.
134 L2 Kozhva r. Rus. Fed.
134 L2 Kozhym r. Rus. Fed.
175 H5 Koziegłowy Pol.
175 C2 Kozielice Pol.
137 H2 Kozienice Pol.
137 H2 Kozin Ukr.
197 F4 Kozloduy Bulg.
177 H2 Kozlovice Czech Rep.
       Kozlovka Chuvashskaya Respublika Rus. Fed.
135 I5 Kozlovka Respublika Mordoviya Rus. Fed.
135 H6 Kozlovka Voronezhskaya Oblast' Rus. Fed.
137 K2 Kozlovka Voronezhskaya Oblast' Rus. Fed.
139 K3 Kozlovo Rus. Fed.
175 I5 Kozłów Pol.
137 I3 Kozłów Biskupi Pol.
175 I2 Kozłowo Pol.
126 C2 Kozlu Turkey
199 G3 Kozluca Turkey
188 G3 Kozluk Bos.-Herz.
174 F4 Koźmin Pol.
175 H5 Koźmin Rus. Fed.
136 I4 Koz"modem"yansk Rus. Fed.
121 G4 Kozmoldak Kazakh.
197 F4 Koznitsa mt. Bulg.
136 C3 Kozova Ukr.
137 J3 Kozshchyszcznya Pol.
138 D4 Koźuchów Pol.
177 F5 Kožuf mts Greece/Macedonia
136 E3 Kozyatyn Ukr.
137 G2 Kozylivka Ukr.
136 F2 Kozyn Kyiv's'ka Oblast' Ukr.
136 C3 Kozyn L'viv's'ka Oblast' Ukr.
199 E1 Kozyörük Turkey
137 F4 Kozyrka Ukr.
207 F5 Kpalimé Togo
207 E4 Kpandae Ghana
207 F5 Kpedze Ghana
97 B5 Kra, Isthmus of Thai.
215 F4 Kraai r. S. Africa
214 E3 Kraankuil S. Africa
165 D3 Krabbendijke Neth.
97 B7 Krabi Thai.
95 B5 Kra Buri Thai.
97 D4 Krâchéh Cambodia
141 M3 Kräckelbäcken Sweden
170 F2 Krackow Ger.
171 C5 Kraftsdorf Ger.
95 E4 Kragan Jawa Tengah Indon.
142 C2 Kragerø Norway
164 E2 Kraggenburg Neth.
196 E3 Kragujevac Srbija Yugo.
163 I4 Kraiburg am Inn Ger.
173 F3 Krähberg mt. Germany
173 F3 Krailling Ger.
174 F2 Krajenka Pol.
94 D4 Krakatau i. Indon.
       Krakau Pol. see Kraków
136 B3 Krakovets' Ukr.
175 H5 Kraków Pol.
226 C3 Krakow WI U.S.A.
170 D2 Krakow am See Ger.
170 D2 Krakower See l. Ger.
175 G4 Krakowsko-Częstochowska, Wyżyna plat. Pol.
97 B5 Kra Lenya r. Myanmar
95 F5 Králíky Czech Rep.
188 E3 Kraljevica Croatia
196 E4 Kraljevo Srbija Yugo.
177 G3 Kráľova, Vodná nádrž resr Slovakia
177 J3 Kráľova hoľa mt. Slovakia
177 G3 Kráľová nad Váhom Slovakia
177 G3 Kráľov Brod Slovakia
176 E1 Královéhradecký kraj admin. reg. Czech Rep.
176 D2 Králův Dvůr Czech Rep.
175 J3 Kramarzyny Pol.
137 I2 Kramators'k Ukr.
141 M3 Kramfors Sweden
164 D3 Krammer est. Neth.
178 C3 Kramsach Austria
175 K6 Kramsk Pol.
169 B4 Kranenburg Ger.
198 C2 Kranidi Greece
191 J1 Kranj Slovenia
179 L4 Kranjska Gora Slovenia
215 F3 Kransfontein S. Africa
215 H3 Kranskop S. Africa
173 F3 Kranzberg Ger.
188 F3 Krapanj Croatia
188 E2 Krapina Croatia
188 E2 Krapinske Toplice Croatia
175 K6 Krasiczyn Pol.
       Krasiliv Ukr. see Krasyliv
       Krasiliv Chernihivs'ka Oblast' Ukr. see Krasylivka
       Krasiliv Zhytomyrs'ka Oblast' Ukr. see Krasylivka
175 L6 Krasiv Ukr.

136 C3 Krasiyiv Ukr.
100 D4 Kraskino Rus. Fed.
138 F4 Krāslava Latvia
176 B1 Kraslice Czech Rep.
136 C3 Krasna r. Ukr.
171 I4 Krásná Lípa Czech Rep.
139 H5 Krasnapollye Belarus
135 I4 Krasna Polyana Rus. Fed.
136 F3 Krasna Slobidka Ukr.
138 E5 Krasnasyel'ski Belarus
139 H5 Krasnaya Gora Rus. Fed.
134 H4 Krasnaya Gorbatka Rus. Fed.
121 H2 Krasnaya Polyana Kazakh.
129 B2 Krasnaya Polyana Rus. Fed.
138 F5 Krasnaya Slabada Belarus
137 H2 Krasnaya Yaruga Rus. Fed.
139 K5 Krasnaya Zarya Rus. Fed.
175 I3 Krasne Mazowieckie Pol.
175 K5 Krasne Podkarpackie Pol.
137 F2 Krasne Chernihivs'ka Oblast' Ukr.
137 G2 Krasne Chernihivs'ka Oblast' Ukr.
136 C3 Krasne Ivano-Frankivs'ka Oblast' Ukr.
137 G4 Krasne Khersons'ka Oblast' Ukr.
175 I1 Krasne L'viv's'ka Oblast' Ukr.
136 D3 Krasne Ternopils'ka Oblast' Ukr.
136 E2 Krasne Vinnyts'ka Oblast' Ukr.
175 L5 Krasnik Pol.
175 K5 Krásník Pol.
136 E4 Krasni Okny Ukr.
       Krasnoarmeysk Kazakh. see Tayynsha
139 L3 Krasnoarmeysk Moskovskaya Oblast' Rus. Fed.
135 I6 Krasnoarmeysk Saratovskaya Oblast' Rus. Fed.
       Krasnoarmeysk Ukr. see Krasnoarmiys'k
       Krasnoarmeyskaya Rus. Fed. see Poltavskaya
131 S3 Krasnoarmeyskiy Chukotskiy Avtonomnyy Okrug Rus. Fed.
135 H7 Krasnoarmeyskiy Rostovskaya Oblast' Rus. Fed.
       Krasnoarmeyskoye Rus. Fed. see Urus-Martan
137 I3 Krasnoarmiys'k Ukr.
134 I3 Krasnoborsk Rus. Fed.
175 L5 Krasnobród Pol.
135 G7 Krasnodar Rus. Fed.
       Krasnodar Kray admin. div. Rus. Fed. see Krasnodarskiy Kray
129 A1 Krasnodarskiy Kray admin. div. Rus. Fed.
137 J3 Krasnodon Luhans'ka Oblast' Ukr.
137 J3 Krasnodon Luhans'ka Oblast' Ukr.
139 H2 Krasnofarfornyy Rus. Fed.
       Krasnogorka Kazakh. see Ul'ken Sulutar
138 G3 Krasnogorodsk Rus. Fed.
139 K4 Krasnogorsk Moskovskaya Oblast' Rus. Fed.
100 G2 Krasnogorsk Sakhalin ... Rus. Fed.
121 K1 Krasnogorskoye Altayskiy Kray Rus. Fed.
134 K4 Krasnogorskoye Udmurtskaya Respublika Rus. Fed.
       Krasnograd Ukr. see Krasnohrad
       Krasnogvardeysk Uzbek. see Bulungur
139 M3 Krasnogvardeyskiy Rus. Fed.
137 J2 Krasnogvardeyskoye Belgorodskaya Oblast' Rus. Fed.
       Krasnogvardeyskoye Respublika Adygeya Rus. Fed. see Krasnogvardeyskoye
135 H7 Krasnogvardeyskoye Stavropol'skiy Kray Rus. Fed.
139 I3 Krasnohorivka Ukr.
138 E2 Krasnohrad Ukr.
136 D3 Krasnohorka Ukr.
137 J5 Krasnohvardiys'ke Ukr.
139 K5 Krasnolesnyy Rus. Fed.
175 I5 Krasnoles'ye Rus. Fed.
175 H5 Krasnopavlivka Ukr.
107 H1 Krasnoperekops'k Ukr.
134 K4 Krasnopil'ya Rus. Fed.
120 C2 Krasnopillya Ukr.
121 K1 Krasnorechenskiy Rus. Fed.
135 G6 Krasnorechenskoye Ukr.
137 H2 Krasnorichens'ke Ukr.
130 J3 Krasnosel'kup Rus. Fed.
121 J2 Krasnoshchekovo Rus. Fed.
114 D3 Krasnosielc Pol.
136 E3 Krasnosilka Vinnyts'ka Oblast' Ukr.
136 D3 Krasnosilka Zhytomyrs'ka Oblast' Ukr.
135 H5 Krasnosłobodsk Rus. Fed.
57 K1 Krasnoslobodsk Rus. Fed.
134 L4 Krasnotur'insk Rus. Fed.
120 D1 Krasnousol'skiy Rus. Fed.
134 L3 Krasnovishersk Rus. Fed.
       Krasnovodsk Turkm. see Turkmenbashi
       Krasnovodskaya Oblast' admin. div. Turkm. see Balkanskaya Oblast'
122 C2 Krasnovodskiy Zaliv b. Turkm.
122 C1 Krasnovodskoye Plato plat. Turkm.
122 G4 Krasnoyar Kazakh.
131 K4 Krasnoyarovo Rus. Fed.
120 D2 Krasnoyarsk Rus. Fed.
98 F1 Krasnoyarskiy Kray admin. div. Rus. Fed.
137 J2 Krasnoyarskoye Belgorodskaya Oblast' Rus. Fed.
139 I5 Krasnoye Belgorodskaya Oblast' Rus. Fed.
136 I4 Krasnoye Bryanskaya Oblast' Rus. Fed.
134 I4 Krasnoye Kirovskaya Oblast' Rus. Fed.
137 J4 Krasnoye Krasnodarskiy Kray Rus. Fed.
120 B1 Krasnoye Lipetskaya Oblast' Rus. Fed.
135 L5 Krasnoye Respublika Kalmykiya - Khalm'g-Tangch Rus. Fed.
164 D3 Krammer est. Neth.
178 C3 Kramsch Austria
169 B4 Kramsk Pol.
131 S3 Krasnoye, Ozero l. Rus. Fed.
139 M4 Krasnoye-na-Volge Rus. Fed.
174 F5 Krasnoye Plamya Rus. Fed.
137 I2 Krasnoye Znamya Rus. Fed.
136 F3 Krasnoyil's'k Ukr.
139 L3 Krasnozatonskiy Rus. Fed.
138 D4 Krasnoznamensk Rus. Fed.
121 G2 Krasnoznamenskoye Kazakh.
137 G2 Krasnoznam"yanka Ukr.
175 L2 Krasnyborki Pol.
175 L5 Krasnystaw Pol.
215 L6 Krolpa Ger.
139 J6 Krasnyye Chikoy Rus. Fed.
174 F1 Krasnyye Okny Ukr.
206 D5 Krasnyye Plamya Rus. Fed.
143 K6 Krasnyy Bor Rus. Fed.
135 K4 Krasnyye Barrikady Rus. Fed.
176 J5 Krasnyy Kholm Rus. Fed.
177 H3 Krasnyy Tkachi Rus. Fed.
175 L3 Krasnyy Kamyshanik Rus. Fed.
       Rus. Fed. see Komsomol'skiy

139 K2 Krasnyy Kholm Rus. Fed.
120 A2 Krasnyy Kut Rus. Fed.
137 J2 Krasnyy Liman Rus. Fed.
139 H3 Krasnyy Luch Rus. Fed.
137 J3 Krasnyy Luch Ukr.
137 I3 Krasnyy Lyman Ukr.
139 M3 Krasnyy Oktyabr' Rus. Fed.
137 K4 Krasnyy Sulin Rus. Fed.
135 I6 Krasnyy Tekstil'shchik Rus. Fed.
121 G1 Krasnyy Kazakh.
120 B3 Krasnyy Yar Astrakhanskaya Oblast' Rus. Fed.
120 B1 Krasnyy Yar Samarskaya Oblast' Rus. Fed.
135 I6 Krasnyy Yar Volgogradskaya Oblast' Rus. Fed.
175 I5 Krasocin Pol.
136 E2 Krasyatychi Ukr.
136 D3 Krasyliv Ukr.
137 F2 Krasylivka Chernihivs'ka Oblast' Ukr.
136 E2 Krasylivka Zhytomyrs'ka Oblast' Ukr.
174 G4 Kraszewice Pol.
175 I1 Kraszewo Pol.
177 L3 Kraszna r. Hungary
197 F4 Kratie Cambodia
174 F4 Kratovo Macedonia
175 H3 Kratoszewice Pol.
138 F4 Krauja Latvia
262 X2 Kraul Mountains Antarctica
171 F4 Krauschwitz Ger.
172 D2 Krausnick Ger.
       Krávanh, Chuŏr Phnum mts Cambodia see Cardomom Range
177 H2 Kravaře Czech Rep.
129 F2 Kraynovka Rus. Fed.
198 B4 Kreba-Neudorf Ger.
169 F4 Krebeck Ger.
139 H2 Krechevitsy Rus. Fed.
169 B5 Kreekrak Neth.
169 E4 Kreiensen Ger.
164 E2 Kreileroord Neth.
173 F3 Kreßberg Ger.
135 E4 Krekenava Lith.
198 B2 Kremaston, Techniti Limni resr Greece
188 E3 Kremen mt. Croatia
215 F2 Krugersdorp S. Africa
129 C1 Krugloye ozero, Gora mt. Rus. Fed.
       Kruglyakova Ch. Rus. Fed. see Oktyabr'skiy
138 G4 Kruhlaye Belarus
94 C4 Krui Sumatera Indon.
214 C5 Kruidfontein S. Africa
165 I4 Kruiningen Neth.
215 G6 Kruisfontein S. Africa
164 C4 Kruishoutem Belgium
196 D5 Krujë Albania
175 L6 Krukenychi Ukr.
175 J2 Krukowo Pol.
174 F3 Krukrauta mt. Yugo.
130 F3 Kruchovo r. Rus. Fed.
170 C3 Krüden Ger.
169 C5 Kruft Ger.

139 J5 Kromy Rus. Fed.
171 C5 Kronach Ger.
172 C2 Kronau Ger.
169 D5 Kronberg im Taunus Ger.
142 C2 Kronfjell hill Norway
97 C5 Krŏng Kaôh Kŏng Cambodia
143 P3 Kronoberg county Sweden
139 M3 Kronoby Fin.
131 R4 Kronotskiy Zaliv b. Rus. Fed.
221 P1 Kronprins Christian Land reg. Greenland
221 O3 Kronprins Frederik Bjerge nunataks Greenland
168 D2 Kronprinzenkoog Ger.
168 F1 Kronshagen Ger.
138 G2 Kronshtadt Rus. Fed.
       Kronstadt Romania see Braşov
       Kronstadt Rus. Fed. see Kronshtadt
179 F2 Kronstorf Austria
215 F2 Kroonstad S. Africa
170 C1 Kröpelin Ger.
135 H5 Kropotkin Rus. Fed.
174 C4 Kropp Ger.
169 C4 Kroppenstedt Ger.
171 D4 Kropstädt Ger.
175 I6 Krościenko nad Dunajcem Pol.
240 □C8 Krøderen Norway
174 F4 Kroślin Pol.
174 F4 Krośniewice Pol.
175 J6 Krosno Pol.
174 D4 Krosno Odrzańskie Pol.
175 C1 Krossen r. Ger.
101 C4 Krotoszyce Pol.
174 F4 Krotoszyn Pol.
179 G3 Krottendorf Austria
237 F6 Krotz Springs LA U.S.A.
94 C2 Krouna Czech Rep.
198 D4 Krousonas Kriti Greece
172 B2 Krüv Ger.
95 E4 Kroya Jawa Tengah Indon.
191 J3 Kršan Croatia
188 E3 Krško Slovenia
174 F3 Krstaca mt. Yugo.
174 F3 Kruchowo Pol.
170 C3 Krüden Ger.
169 C5 Kruft Ger.
215 H1 Kruger National Park S. Africa
215 F2 Krugersdorp S. Africa
129 C1 Kruglolake Rus. Fed.
       Kruglyakova Rus. Fed. see Oktyabr'skiy
138 G4 Kruhlaye Belarus
94 C4 Krui Sumatera Indon.
214 C5 Kruidfontein S. Africa
165 I4 Kruiningen Neth.
215 G6 Kruisfontein S. Africa
164 C4 Kruishoutem Belgium
196 D5 Krujë Albania
102 □ Kruino-shima i. Japan
178 E3 Kruml Austria
179 H2 Krumpa (Geiseltal) Ger.
179 F4 Krumpendorf am Wörther See Austria
173 F4 Krün Ger.
       Krungkao Thai. see Ayutthaya
       Krung Thep Thai. see Bangkok
128 A2 Krupa r. Lith.
       Krupa Bos.-Herz. see Bosanska Krupa
       Krupa na Uni Bos.-Herz. see Bosanska Krupa
196 D3 Krupanj Srbija Yugo.
175 L4 Krupe Pol.
177 I3 Krupina Slovakia
177 I3 Krupinská Planina plat. Pol.
176 C1 Krupka Czech Rep.
138 G2 Krupki Belarus
137 H3 Krupodernytsi Ukr.
168 E1 Kruså Denmark
196 E5 Kruševac Srbija Yugo.
196 D5 Kruševo Macedonia
176 B1 Krušné Hory mts Czech Rep.
177 H3 Krušovica Slovakia
177 J2 Kruszwica Pomorskie Pol.
175 H5 Kruszyna Pomorskie Pol.
137 J2 Kruszyna Sląskie Pol.
215 G2 Kriel S. Africa
170 E2 Krien Ger.
198 B2 Kriens Switz.
153 I4 Krievkalns hill Latvia
198 B2 Krikelos Greece
196 E4 Krikovo Moldova see Cricova
179 F5 Krim i. Slovenia
208 B2 Krim-Krim Chad
264 H4 Krim mt. Germany
176 E1 Křimec Czech Rep.
198 D1 Krinides Greece
       Kripka r. Rus. Fed./Ukr. see Krepkaya
171 F3 Krippenstein mt. Austria
114 D3 Krishna r. India
114 C3 Krishna, Mouths of the India
114 C3 Krishnagiri Tamil Nadu India
117 G4 Krishnai r. India
114 C3 Krishnanagar W. Bengal India
117 G4 Krishnarajasagara Karnataka India
143 O3 Kristdala Sweden
129 C1 Kristiania Norway see Oslo
145 M4 Kristiansand Norway
135 G7 Kristiansand Sweden
140 I3 Kristiansund Norway
       Kristiinankaupunki Fin. see Kristinestad
143 F2 Kristinehamn Sweden
141 M3 Kristinestad Fin.
175 I6 Kristinopol' Ukr. see Chervonohrad
198 D1 Kriti i. Greece
137 H3 Kriti i. Greece
175 L2 Krivaja r. Yugo.
215 F4 Kritzmow Ger.
       Kriulyany Moldova see Criuleni
139 L4 Kriusha Rus. Fed.
174 C4 Krivaja r. Yugo.
131 M4 Krivaja r. Yugo.
139 L4 Krivandino Rus. Fed.
174 G4 Kriva Palanka Macedonia
174 F4 Kriva Reka r. Macedonia
196 E5 Krivoklátská Vrchovina hills Czech Rep.
139 L5 Krivorojskoye Rus. Fed.
135 H6 Krivov'ye Rus. Fed.
137 H4 Krivoy Rog Ukr. see Kryvyy Rih
137 J2 Kriżanov Czech Rep.
188 F3 Krizevci Croatia
175 H3 Krk Croatia
188 E3 Krk i. Croatia
174 E4 Krka r. Croatia
136 F2 Krka r. Slovenia
175 H2 Krkonoše mts Czech Rep.
175 L3 Krnov Czech Rep.
139 L3 Krobia Pol.
174 G4 Kroczyce Pol.
206 D5 Krogis Ger.
206 B4 Krohnwodoke Liberia
207 F2 Krokfjord Norway
206 F3 Krokeaí Greece see Krokees
141 N4 Krokek Sweden
143 H4 Krokowa Pol.
174 E4 Krokstadøra Norway
137 G2 Kroletevo Pol.
175 I2 Królewska Huta Pol. see Chorzów
121 G2 Królowa Most Pol.
175 L2 Królowy Most Pol.
215 I6 Krom r. S. Africa
174 G4 Kroma r. Rus. Fed.
204 D2 Kromčlad S. Africa
136 F2 Kroměříž Czech Rep.
175 H2 Krommenie Neth.
177 H3 Krompachy Slovakia
171 C5 Kromsdorf Ger.

139 J5 Kromy Rus. Fed.
175 I5 Książ Wielki Pol.
174 F3 Książ Wielkopolski Pol.
175 K5 Księżpol Pol.
122 C1 Kskyrbulak Yuzhnyy, Gora hill Turkm.
205 E2 Ksour, Monts des mts Alg.
205 E2 Ksour, Monts des mts Tunisia
205 H2 Ksour Essaf Tunisia
134 I4 Kstovo Rus. Fed.
125 D2 Kü', Jabal al hill Saudi Arabia
95 F1 Kuala Belait Brunei
168 D2 Kuala Dungun Malaysia see Dungun
120 D1 Kuala Kangsar Malaysia
95 F3 Kuala Kerai Malaysia
94 C1 Kuala Kinabatangan r. mouth Sabah Malaysia
95 C1 Kuala Kubu Baharu Malaysia
94 C1 Kuala Lipis Malaysia
94 C2 Kuala Lumpur Malaysia
95 F3 Kualapembuang Kalimantan Tengah Indon.
94 C2 Kuala Pilah Malaysia
240 □C8 Kuaiqaq HI U.S.A.
174 F4 Krösslin Pol.
175 H5 Krosno Pol.
174 J6 Krosno Odrzańskie Pol.
175 C1 Krossen r. Ger.
101 C4 Kuancheng Hebei China
101 C4 Kuandian Liaoning China
131 B2 Kuanguyuan Yunnan China see Yiliang
109 G4 Kuanshan Taiwan
94 C2 Kuantan Malaysia
80 E2 Kuaotunu North I. N.Z.
129 C2 Kuba Azer. see Quba
129 C2 Kuba Rus. Fed.
129 E2 Kubachi Rus. Fed.
129 B1 Kuban' r. Rus. Fed.
129 A1 Kubanskaya Rus. Fed.
127 E2 Kübär Dayr az Zawr Syria
127 E4 Kubär Dayr az Zawr Syria
170 C3 Kriden Ger.
140 L3 Kubbe Sweden
215 H1 Kübékháza Hungary
215 F2 Kubenskoye, Ozero l. Rus. Fed.
134 G4 Kuberle Rostovskaya Oblast' Rus. Fed. see Krasnoarmeyskiy
190 E2 Kubinka Rus. Fed.
125 J2 Kublych r. Ukr.
136 J3 Kubrat Bulg.
139 L1 Kubrinsk Rus. Fed.
197 E3 Kučevo Srbija Yugo.
175 I4 Kucha r. India
172 B2 Kuchaman Rajasthan India
179 I4 Kuchera Rajasthan India
172 G3 Kuchen Ger.
125 J2 Kucheryavka Ukr.
94 E4 Kuching Sarawak Malaysia
102 □ Kuchino-shima i. Japan
178 E4 Kuchl Austria
172 C3 Kuchurhan r. Ukr.
214 E4 Kücük Ağrı Dağı mt. Turkey
199 G3 Küçükbahçe Turkey
199 E3 Küçükköy Turkey
199 G2 Küçükköy Turkey
174 F4 Küçükkuyu anakkale Turkey
199 E3 Küçükmenderes r. Turkey
199 G3 Küçükmenderes r. Turkey
199 F5 Küçükköy Turkey
196 D3 Kuczbork-Osada Pol.
175 L4 Kuda Gujarat India
114 B2 Kudachi Karnataka India
113 □ Kuda Finolhu i. S. Male Maldives
113 □ Kudahalani i. N. Male Maldives
103 E7 Kudamatsu Japan
114 D3 Kudara-Somon Rus. Fed.
168 F2 Kudarebe Ger.
189 G5 Kudat Sabah Malaysia
138 C4 Kudirkos Naumiestis Lith.
114 E4 Kudligi Karnataka India
215 J2 Kudowa-Zdrój Pol.
103 E2 Kudremukh, mt. Karnataka India
98 F4 Kudus Jawa Tengah Indon.
134 G4 Kudymkar r. Japan
215 I3 Kufstein Austria
121 J3 Kugaly Kazakh.
134 I4 Kugesi Rus. Fed.
208 B2 Kuh, Ras-al- hill Latvia
198 B2 Kühbonán Iran
196 E5 Kühbonán Iran
176 B1 Kühdamm Austria
177 H3 Kufelde Ger.
175 H2 Küh-e Piryakh mt. Tajik.
171 C5 Pir'yakh, Qatorkühi

138 D4 Kulautuva Lith.
137 H2 Kul'baki Rus. Fed.
138 C3 Kuldīga Latvia
109 D2 Kuldja Xinjiang China see Yining
100 D2 Kulebaki Rus. Fed.
199 G3 Kuleshovka Rus. Fed.
116 B5 Kuleshovka Rus. Fed.
175 K2 Kulesze Pol.
116 E3 Kulesze Kościelne Pol.
177 J4 Kulgera N.T. Austr.
120 D1 Kulgunino Rus. Fed.
129 E2 Kuli Rus. Fed.
134 K4 Kuligi Rus. Fed.
134 I3 Kuli Keral Malaysia
139 L3 Kulikovo Arkhangel'skaya Oblast' Rus. Fed.
139 J5 Kulikovo Lipetskaya Oblast' Rus. Fed.
94 C1 Kulim Malaysia
87 C7 Kulin W.A. Austr.
114 C4 Kulittalai Tamil Nadu India
85 L2 Kulja W.A. Austr.
120 E4 Kulkuduk Uzbek.
141 M3 Kullaa Fin.
169 F4 Küllstedt Ger.
116 D3 Kullu Hima. Prad. India
171 C5 Kulmain Ger.
171 C5 Kulmbach Ger.
123 D2 Kūlob Tajik.
139 I2 Kuloino Rus. Fed.
134 H3 Kuloy Rus. Fed.
134 H2 Kuloy r. Rus. Fed.
127 F3 Kulp Turkey
182 D3 Kulpara S.A. Austr.
234 B2 Kulpmont PA U.S.A.
120 C3 Kul'sary Kazakh.
172 D2 Külsheim Ger.
199 G3 Kulube Tepe mt. Turkey
120 D2 Kulunda r. Rus. Fed.
121 I1 Kulunda Rus. Fed.
121 I1 Kulundinskaya Step' plain Kazakh./Rus. Fed.
121 I1 Kulundinskoye, Ozero salt l. Rus. Fed.
83 B3 Kulwin Vic. Austr.
123 D2 Kulyab Tajik. see Kūlob
136 C3 Kulykiv Ukr.
136 G4 Kulykivka Ukr.
137 F2 Kulykivka Ukr.
140 O2 Kuma r. Rus. Fed.
105 F2 Kumagaya Japan
95 E4 Kumai, Teluk b. Indon.
120 D2 Kumak r. Rus. Fed.
103 E7 Kumamoto Japan
104 D7 Kumamoto Daği mts Turkey
103 E7 Kumamoto pref. Japan
104 C5 Kumano Japan
197 E4 Kumanovo Macedonia
81 C5 Kumara South I. N.Z.
81 C5 Kumara Junction South I. N.Z.
117 G5 Kumarkhali Bangl.
206 E5 Kumasi Ghana
215 G4 Ku-Mayima S. Africa
116 C4 Kumayri Armenia see Gyumri
207 H5 Kumba Nigeria
199 E1 Kumbağ Turkey
114 C4 Kumbakonam Tamil Nadu India
179 J3 Kumberg Austria
199 G2 Kümbet Turkey
116 C4 Kümbet Turkey
170 F2 Kümmel Ger.
207 H5 Kumbo Nigeria
138 D4 Kumbri Latvia
124 D3 Kum-Dag Turkm. see Gumdag
118 C3 Kumdah Saudi Arabia
199 G2 Kumeny Ridge
134 J4 Kumeny Rus. Fed.
101 C6 Kŭm-gang r. S. Korea
101 E5 Kŭm-gang r. S. Korea
103 D6 Kume-jima i. Japan
101 C5 Kŭmho-gang r. S. Korea
101 B5 Kumi S. Korea
170 D2 Kumkale Turkey
143 N3 Kumla Sweden
207 H3 Kumligge Åland Fin.
171 D5 Kumluca Turkey
168 F2 Kummer Ger.
170 D2 Kummerower See l. Ger.
170 D2 Kummersdorf-Alexanderdorf Ger.
171 I4 Kümmersbruck Ger.
207 H4 Kumo Nigeria
96 B1 Kumon Range mts Myanmar
105 G3 Kumotori-yama mt. Japan
123 C4 Kumphawapi Thai.
140 N2 Kumputunturi hill Fin.
117 E5 Kumshum Bangl.
87 B7 Kumunagg Well W.A. Austr.
123 G3 Kunar r. Afgh.
100 H3 Kunashir, Ostrov i. Rus. Fed.
       Kunashirskiy Proliv sea chan. Japan/Rus. Fed. see Nemuro-kaikyō
116 D4 Kunbaja Hungary
177 I5 Kunbaracs Hungary
129 D1 Kun'bator Rus. Fed.
174 G4 Kujakowice Dolne Pol.
117 F6 Kujang Orissa India
101 C5 Kujang N. Korea
174 G2 Kujawsko-Pomorskie prov. Pol.
102 □ Kuji Japan
105 G2 Kuji-gawa r. Japan
105 G3 Kujikuri Japan
105 G3 Kujikuri-hama coastal area Japan
196 E4 Kukës Albania
123 H2 Kuki Japan
105 F2 Kukinō r. Japan
179 H3 Kukmirn Austria
174 G3 Kukobzko Pol.
240 □C8 Kukuihaele HI U.S.A.
227 F1 Kukukus Lake Ont. Can.
100 □ Kukushya Gunung vol. Indon.
       Kül'yab Tajik. see Kūlob
138 C3 Kunda Estonia
172 C3 Kuntar Prad. India
116 E3 Kunda r. India
116 E4 Kunda-dia-Baze Angola
95 H3 Kundat Sabah Malaysia
116 D4 Kundgol Karnataka India
137 H4 Kundian Pak.
135 I2 Kundrag r. Afgh. cond.
124 E2 Kubräl, Kühl-e hill Iran
122 B2 Kukälak Pak.
209 B9 Kunene admin. reg. Namibia
212 B3 Kunene r. Angola/Namibia alt. Cunene
203 H2 Kunes Norway
140 O1 Kunes Chang Xinjiang China
135 H6 Künes He r. Xinjiang Xinyuan
175 L2 Kungala N.S.W. Austr.
179 H3 Kunkmírn Austria
179 H3 Kumkînôn Pol.
179 H3 Kunda r. India

114 D2 Kunigal Karnataka India
104 C2 Kunimi-dake mt. Japan
103 E7 Kunimi-dake mt. Japan
177 G2 Kunin Czech Rep.
174 G5 Kuniów Pol.
117 F5 Kunjabar Orissa India
234 C2 Kunkletown PA U.S.A.
116 B5 Kunlavav Gujarat India
117 G4 Kunlui r. India/Nepal
108 B1 Kunming Yunnan China
116 D4 Kuno r. India
176 C2 Kunovice Czech Rep.
175 J5 Kunów Pol.
177 I4 Kunpeszér Hungary
170 D3 Kunrau Ger.
101 C6 Kunsan S. Korea
109 G2 Kunshan Jiangsu China
171 H4 Kunszállás Hungary
177 I4 Kunszentmárton Hungary
177 I4 Kunszentmiklós Hungary
86 F2 Kununurra W.A. Austr.
223 L2 Kunwak r. Nunavut Can.
175 H4 Kuńkowce Pol.
139 H3 Kun'ya r. Rus. Fed.
       Kunya Henan China see Yexian
       Kunyang Yunnan China see Jinning
       Kunyang Zhejiang China see Pingyang
       Kunya-Urgench Turkm. see Keneurgench
137 I3 Kun"ye Ukr.
176 E2 Kunžak Czech Rep.
169 E5 Künzell Ger.
172 D2 Künzelsau Ger.
171 C4 Künzels-Berg hill Ger.
178 D3 Künzing Ger.
109 G2 Kuocang Shan mts China
140 N3 Kuopio Fin.
141 N3 Kuorevesi Fin.
174 F5 Kup Pol.
188 F3 Kupa r. Croatia/Slovenia
93 B5 Kupang Timor Indon.
139 I3 Kupanskoye Rus. Fed.
117 F5 Kupari Orissa India
137 I2 Kupchino Moldova see Cupcina
171 C5 Kupferberg Ger.
172 D2 Kupferzell Ger.
172 B1 Kupino Rus. Fed.
138 F4 Kupiškis Lith.
191 J3 Kupjak Croatia
172 F2 Küplü Turkey
172 E2 Kuppenheim Ger.
222 C3 Kupreanof AK U.S.A.
220 E4 Kupreanof Island AK U.S.A.
171 C5 Küps Ger.
116 C2 Kupwara Jammu and Kashmir
137 I2 Kup"yans'k Ukr.
137 I2 Kup"yans'k-Uzlovyy Ukr.
136 C3 Kupychiv Ukr.
110 C3 Kuqa Xinjiang China
129 E3 Kür r. Azer.
129 F4 Kür r. Georgia
100 D2 Kur r. Rus. Fed.
129 E4 Kura r. Azer.
129 F4 Kura r. Azer./Georgia
85 D5 Kuraburu r. W.A. Austr.
121 H1 Kuragino Rus. Fed.
207 H4 Kuragwi Nigeria
104 C2 Kurai-yama mt. Japan
129 E3 Kürkçay r. Azer.
134 L5 Kurakh Rus. Fed.
137 I4 Kurakhove Ukr.
       Kurakhovo Rus. Fed. see Kurakhove
       Kurakhovstroy Ukr. see Kurakhove
       Kura kurk sea chan. Estonia/Latvia see Irbe Strait
104 D5 Kurama-yama hill Japan
85 E7 Kuranda Qld Austr.
120 D2 Kurashasykiy Kazakh.
103 F6 Kurashiki Japan
116 E5 Kurasia Madh. Prad. India
84 B4 Kura Soak well W.A. Austr.
103 F6 Kurayoshi Japan
106 F4 Kurayskiy Khrebet mts Rus. Fed.
139 H5 Kurba r. Rus. Fed.
199 F1 Kurban Daği mt. Turkey
137 I3 Kurbatovo Rus. Fed.
121 H2 Kurchaly Kazakh.
135 G6 Kurchatov Rus. Fed.
135 G6 Kurchatov Kazakh.
177 H5 Kurd Hungary
129 F3 Kürdämir Azer.
121 G2 Kurday Kazakh.
197 H4 Kürdzhali Bulg.
197 H4 Kürdzhinovo Bulg.
103 F6 Kure Japan
199 D2 Küre Turkey
118 G1 Küre Dağları mts Turkey
174 G4 Kurejka r. Rus. Fed.
138 D2 Kuressaare Estonia
266 E2 Kuril Basin sea feature Sea of Okhotsk
196 D4 Kurilo, Mal mt. Albania
99 Q2 Kuril'sk Rus. Fed.
       Kuril'skiye O-va Rus. Fed. see Kuril'skiye Ostrova
       Kuril'skiye Ostrova i. Rus. Fed. see Kuril Islands
266 E3 Kuril Trench sea feature N. Pacific Ocean
176 F2 Kuřim Czech Rep.
120 E1 Kurinskaya Rus. Fed.
139 M4 Kurkachi Rus. Fed.
177 J5 Kurkçü Turkey see Sankavak
121 G3 Kurgaldzhino Kazakh.
140 M3 Kurikka Fin.
102 J4 Kurikoma-yama vol. Japan
266 D2 Kuril Basin sea feature Sea of Okhotsk
196 D4 Kurile, Mal mt. Albania
99 Q2 Kuril'sk Rus. Fed.
       Kuril'skiye Ostrova i. Rus. Fed. see Kuril Islands
266 E3 Kuril Trench sea feature N. Pacific Ocean
176 F2 Kuřim Czech Rep.
139 M4 Kurkachi Rus. Fed.
210 B2 Kurmuk Sudan
172 E3 Kürnach Ger.
114 C3 Kurnool Andhra Prad. India
104 B3 Kurobe Japan
103 G1 Kurobe-gawa r. Japan
104 B3 Kurohone Japan
102 □ Kuroishi Japan
102 J4 Kuroiso Japan
104 B3 Kurokawa Japan
105 G2 Kuroo-shima i. Japan
103 E7 Kuroshio-machi Japan
104 B3 Kuroso-yama mt. Japan
175 L4 Kurów Pol.
137 H4 Kurovskoye Rus. Fed.

L

109 F1 Lai'an Anhui China
Laibach Slovenia see Ljubljana
108 D4 Laibin Guangxi China
172 D3 Laichingen Ger.
146 C4 Laide Highland, Scotland U.K.
85 H5 Laidley Qld Austr.
146 D5 Laide, Loch l. Scotland U.K.
240 □C8 Laie HI U.S.A.
108 D2 Laifeng Hubei China
156 E3 Laifour France
159 G3 L'Aigle France
183 F4 La Iglesuela Spain
186 C4 La Iglesuela del Cid Spain
156 E5 Laignes France
190 D5 Laigueglia Italy
162 A2 L'Aiguillon-sur-Mer France
140 M3 Laihia Fin.
129 C2 Laila, Mt'a Georgia
156 B5 Lailly-en-Val France
157 H4 Laimont France
190 E3 Lainate Italy
214 C5 Laingsburg S. Africa
227 F4 Laingsburg MI U.S.A.
140 M2 Lainioälven r. Sweden
179 Q2 Lainsitz r. Austria
232 A5 Lair KY U.S.A.
207 H2 L'Aïr, Massif de mts Niger
234 B1 Lairdsville PA U.S.A.
146 D3 Lairg Highland, Scotland U.K.
185 H3 La Iruela Spain
94 C3 Lais Sumatera Indon.
92 C5 Lais Phil.
246 B2 La Isabela Cuba
140 L2 Laisälven r. Sweden
134 J5 Laishevo Rus. Fed.
216 □3a La Isleta pen. Gran Canaria Canary Is
161 A4 Laissac France
140 L2 Laisvall Sweden
141 M3 Laitila Fin.
141 T6 Lait'uri Georgia
191 G2 Laives Italy
107 H4 Laiwu Shandong China
107 I4 Laixi Shandong China
107 I4 Laiyang Shandong China
107 G4 Laiyuan Hebei China
159 F2 Laize r. France
107 H4 Laizhou Shandong China
107 H4 Laizhou Wan b. China
159 F2 Laizon r. France
260 B1 Laja, Laguna de l. Chile
84 B3 Lajamanu N.T. Austr.
162 A2 La Jana Spain
162 A2 La Jarrie France
191 F5 Lajatico Italy
161 E4 La Javie France
255 B9 Lajeado Brazil
254 F4 Lajedo Brazil
256 D6 Lajes dos Santos i. Brazil
182 D4 Lajeosa Guarda Port.
182 C4 Lajeosa Viseu Port.
182 C4 Lajeosa do Mondego Port.
216 □1a Lajes Terceira Azores
255 C8 Lajes Brazil
257 G4 Lajes do Pico Pico Azores
196 E3 Lajkovac Srbija Yugo.
240 H4 La Jolla Peak hill CA U.S.A.
162 D2 La Jonchère-St-Maurice France
186 F2 La Jonquera Spain
177 H5 Lajoskomárom Hungary
177 I4 Lajosmizse Hungary
160 D2 La Joux, Forêt de for. France
242 D3 La Joya Chihuahua Mex.
252 C4 La Joya Durango Mex.
252 C4 La Joya Peru
176 G4 Lajta r. Austria/Hungary
159 F4 La Jumellière France
La Junquera Spain see La Jonquera
236 C4 La Junta CO U.S.A.
246 B2 La Juventud, Isla de i. Cuba
116 B5 Lakadiya Gujarat India
124 C4 Lakathah Saudi Arabia
213 □K3 Lakato Madag.
140 M2 Lakaträsk Sweden
232 B6 Lake KY U.S.A.
238 F2 Lake WY U.S.A.
80 E4 Lake Alice North I. N.Z.
236 D3 Lake Andes SD U.S.A.
234 C1 Lake Ariel PA U.S.A.
237 E6 Lake Arthur LA U.S.A.
116 B5 Lalpur Gujarat India
83 E4 Lake Bolac Vic. Austr.
231 D6 Lake Butler FL U.S.A.
83 F3 Lake Cargelligo N.S.W. Austr.
235 E1 Lake Carmel NY U.S.A.
237 E6 Lake Charles LA U.S.A.
239 F4 Lake City AR U.S.A.
231 D6 Lake City FL U.S.A.
236 E3 Lake City IA U.S.A.
231 D6 Lake City IA U.S.A.
226 E3 Lake City MI U.S.A.
226 A3 Lake City MN U.S.A.
235 C4 Lake City PA U.S.A.
233 F7 Lake City SC U.S.A.
81 C5 Lake Clear NY U.S.A.
222 E5 Lake Coleridge South I. N.Z.
137 J4 Lake Cowichan B.C. Can.
149 F3 Lakedemonovka Rus. Fed.
Lake District National Park England U.K.
81 E4 Lake Ferry North I. N.Z.
85 F2 Lakefield Qld Austr.
224 E4 Lakefield Ont. Can.
241 M1 Lake Fork r. CO U.S.A.
237 E6 Lake Geneva WI U.S.A.
233 G3 Lake George NY U.S.A.
87 C7 Lake Grace W.A. Austr.
Lake Harbour Nunavut Can. see Kimmirut
241 J4 Lake Havasu City AZ U.S.A.
235 D2 Lake Hiawatha NJ U.S.A.
234 D2 Lake Hopatcong NJ U.S.A.
235 D2 Lakehurst NJ U.S.A.
240 H4 Lake Isabella CA U.S.A.
237 E6 Lake Jackson TX U.S.A.
81 B6 Lake King W.A. Austr.
87 C7 Lake King W.A. Austr.
231 D7 Lakeland FL U.S.A.
231 D6 Lakeland GA U.S.A.
234 D2 Lake Lenape NJ U.S.A.
226 C2 Lake Linden MI U.S.A.
222 G5 Lake Louise Alta Can.
211 B5 Lake Manyara National Park Tanz.
236 E3 Lake Mills IA U.S.A.
84 D4 Lake Nash N.T. Austr.
151 H2 Lakenheath Suffolk, England U.K.
238 B2 Lake Oswego OR U.S.A.
81 B5 Lake Paringa South I. N.Z.
234 D3 Lake Pine NJ U.S.A.
231 D7 Lake Placid FL U.S.A.
233 G2 Lake Placid NY U.S.A.
233 F3 Lake Pleasant NY U.S.A.
240 F2 Lakeport CA U.S.A.
227 F4 Lakeport MI U.S.A.
237 F5 Lake Providence LA U.S.A.
81 C6 Lake Pukaki South I. N.Z.
240 H1 Lake Range mts NV U.S.A.
83 F6 Lake River Ont. Can.
224 D2 Lake Riviera NJ U.S.A.
227 H3 Lake St Peter Ont. Can.
83 G4 Lakes Entrance Vic. Austr.
240 H3 Lakeshore CA U.S.A.
236 B6 Lake Shore MD U.S.A.
240 I5 Lakeside AZ U.S.A.
235 I1 Lakeside CA U.S.A.
235 D1 Lakeside NJ U.S.A.
235 E2 Lake Success NY U.S.A.
234 B4 Lake Tabourie N.S.W. Austr.
81 C6 Lake Tekapo South I. N.Z.
232 D5 Lake Telemark NJ U.S.A.
232 D3 Lake View OH U.S.A.
238 E3 Lakeview OR U.S.A.
238 D2 Lakeview OR U.S.A.
234 D1 Lake Village AR U.S.A.
240 I5 Lakeville MN U.S.A.
231 D7 Lake Wales FL U.S.A.
235 D2 Lakewood CO U.S.A.
234 D1 Lakewood NJ U.S.A.
235 D2 Lakewood OH U.S.A.
232 E3 Lakewood OH U.S.A.
236 C5 Lakewood OH U.S.A.
116 D4 Lakhdenpokh'ya Rus. Fed.
116 C4 Lakheri Rajasthan India
116 D4 Lakhimpur Uttar Prad. India
117 H4 Lakhipur Assam India
Lakhisarai Bihar India see
Luckeesarai

128 B4 Lakhish r. Israel
116 B5 Lakhnadon Madh. Prad. India
116 B5 Lakhpat Gujarat India
116 B5 Lakhtar Gujarat India
139 H5 Lakhva r. Belarus
236 C4 Lakin KS U.S.A.
139 L3 Lakinsk Rus. Fed.
Lakinskiy Rus. Fed. see Lakinsk
177 I5 Lakitelek Hungary
224 D2 Lakitusaki r. Ont. Can.
129 D2 Lakkha-Nevre Rus. Fed.
123 G3 Lakki Pak.
198 C3 Lakonikos Kolpos b. Greece
175 H2 Łąkorz Pol.
206 D5 Lakota Côte d'Ivoire
236 D1 Lakota ND U.S.A.
140 N1 Laksefjorden sea chan. Norway
140 N1 Laksely Norway
Lakshadweep is India see Laccadive Islands
114 B4 Laksham Bangl.
117 G5 Laksham Bangl.
114 C2 Lakshettipet Andhra Prad. India
114 B3 Lakshmeshwar Karnataka India
Lakshmikantapur India see Lacunza
92 B5 Lala Phil.
261 F3 La Laguna Arg.
242 C4 La Laguna, Picacho de mt. Mex.
260 A5 La Laja Chile
244 D3 La Laja r. Mex.
123 H3 Lala Musa Pak.
245 G5 Lalana r. Mex.
185 I3 La Lantejuela Spain
184 D2 La Lapa Spain
213 F3 Lalapanzi Zimbabwe
197 H5 Lalapaşa Turkey
213 H2 Lalaua Moz.
186 D3 L'Albagés Spain
161 F3 L'Albaron mt. France
163 D4 Lalbenque France
137 C5 L'Alcúdia Spain
160 E3 La Léchère France
85 G4 Laleham Qld Austr.
122 D4 Lāleh Zār, Kūh-e mt. Iran
170 D2 Lalendorf Ger.
150 D3 Laleston Bridgend, Wales U.K.
161 C4 Lalevade-d'Ardèche France
117 F4 Lalganj Bihar India
114 C4 Lalgudi Tamil Nadu India
122 B3 Lālī Iran
210 C1 Lalibela Eth.
250 A5 La Libertad Ecuador
243 H6 La Libertad El Salvador
243 H5 La Libertad Guat.
252 A2 La Libertad dept Peru
260 B3 La Ligua Chile
260 B3 La Ligua, Bahía de b. Chile
Laligyugh Armenia see Vazashen
100 C3 Lalin Heilong. China
100 C3 Lalin r. China
182 B2 Lalín Spain
163 C4 Lalinde France
185 E4 La Línea de la Concepción Spain
116 D4 Lalitpur Uttar Prad. India
116 D4 Lalitpur Nepal see Patan
161 A5 La Livinière France
161 D4 Lalley France
92 B2 Lal-Lo Phil.
117 G4 Lalmanirhat Bangl.
Lalmikur Uzbek. see Lyal'mikar
223 I3 La Loche Sask. Can.
160 B2 La Loire et de l'Allier, Plaines de plain France
200 E5 La Loma Negra, Planicie de plain Arg.
161 C5 La Londe-les-Maures France
163 C5 Lalouvesc France
156 B4 La Loupe France
163 D4 La Louvière Belgium
177 L3 Lalove Ukr.
160 D1 La Loye France
161 E3 L'Alpe-d'Huez France
116 B5 Lalpur Gujarat India
134 I3 Lal'sk Rus. Fed.
116 C4 Lalsot Rajasthan India
178 C4 L'Altissima mt. Austria/Italy
186 C3 Lalueza Spain
185 E3 La Luisiana Spain
171 F4 Lalvariswalde Ger.
150 C2 Lampeter Ceredigion, Wales U.K.
234 B3 Lampeter PA U.S.A.
96 B3 Lamphun Thai.
97 C4 Lam Plai Mat r. Thai.
151 G2 Lamport Northamptonshire, England U.K.
178 D3 Lamprechtshausen Austria
94 D4 Lampung prov. Indon.
174 F4 Lamsfeld-Groß Liebitz Ger.
116 E5 Lamta Madh. Prad. India
211 B5 Lamu Kenya
183 H3 La Mudarra Spain
183 H2 La Muela hill Spain
187 C3 La Muela hill Spain
161 D4 La Mure France
163 B4 Lamure-sur-Azergues France
194 C5 Lana Qld Austr.
191 G2 Lana r. Italy
240 □C8 Lanai i. HI U.S.A.
240 □C8 Lanai City HI U.S.A.
186 C3 Lanaja Spain
165 E4 Lanaken Belgium
92 C5 Lanao, Lake l. Phil.
226 C4 Lanark Ont. Can.
146 F5 Lanark South Lanarkshire, Scotland U.K.

156 D2 Lambres-lez-Douai France
190 E3 Lambro r. Italy
172 C2 Lambsheim Ger.
96 C4 Lam Chi r. Thai.
97 C4 Lam Chi r. Thai.
238 F2 Lame Deer MT U.S.A.
236 C3 Lamego Port.
161 E3 La Meije mt. France
158 E4 La Meilleraye-de-Bretagne France
182 C4 Lameiras Port.
247 □2 Lamentin Guadeloupe
258 D3 La Merced Arg.
252 B2 La Merced Peru
173 E3 Lamerdingen Ger.
82 E1 Lameroo S.A. Austr.
193 F3 La Merta mt. Italy
240 I5 La Mesa CA U.S.A.
237 C5 La Mesa TX U.S.A.
149 H3 Lamesley Tyne and Wear, England U.K.
186 D4 L'Ametlla de Mar Spain
182 B2 Lamezia Italy
204 A5 Lamhar Touil, Sabkhet imp. l. Western Sahara
198 C2 Lamia Greece
159 G3 La Milesse France
226 C4 Laming r. Austria
122 B2 Lamir Iran
244 C4 La Mira Mex.
242 C4 La Mirada CA U.S.A.
242 C2 La Misa r. Mex.
92 B5 Lamitan Phil.
146 D6 Lamlash North Ayrshire, Scotland U.K.
109 □ Lamma Island H.K. China
215 G1 Lammerkop S. Africa
146 F6 Lammer Law hill Scotland U.K.
81 B6 Lammerlaw Range mts South I. N.Z.
81 B6 Lammerlaw Top mt. South I. N.Z.
146 F6 Lammermuir Hills Scotland U.K.
143 F3 Lammhult Sweden
141 N3 Lammi Fin.
138 F2 Lammijärvi lake channel Estonia/Rus. Fed.
226 C5 La Moille IL U.S.A.
233 G2 Lamoille r. VT U.S.A.
226 B5 La Moine r. IL U.S.A.
185 H4 La Mojonera Spain
161 E5 La Môle France
226 C4 Lamon Italy
92 B3 Lamon Bay Phil.
191 H4 Lamone r. Italy
95 I4 Lamongan Jawa Timur Indon.
163 C6 La Mongie France
236 E3 Lamoni r. IA U.S.A.
160 B3 La Monnerie-le-Montel France
240 H4 Lamont CA U.S.A.
238 F1 Lamont WY U.S.A.
194 D5 La Montagna hill Sicilia Italy
163 G4 Lamontélarié France
156 C3 Lamonzie-St-Martin France
163 C4 Lamorlaye France
161 B4 Lamothe France
163 D4 La Mothe-Achard France
163 D3 La Mothe-Capdeville France
163 C4 La Mothe-Cassel France
163 C4 La Mothe-Landerron France
162 B2 La Mothe-St-Héray France
91 K5 Lamotrek atoll Micronesia
227 H1 La Motte France
159 I4 La Motte France
159 I4 La Motte-Beuvron France
161 D4 La Motte-Chalancon France
161 D4 La Motte-d'Aveillans France
161 D4 La Motte-du-Caire France
163 C4 La Motte-Servolex France
236 D2 La Moure ND U.S.A.
260 B3 Lampa Chile
252 C3 Lampa Peru
96 B3 Lampang Thai.
96 C3 Lam Pao Reservoir Thai.
168 L1 Langballig Ger.
214 D3 Langberg mts S. Africa
236 D1 Langdon ND U.S.A.
173 H2 Langdorf Ger.
161 B3 Langeac France
162 C1 Langeais France
214 B5 Langebaan S. Africa
170 D1 Langeballe Denmark
169 F5 Langeberg S. Africa
169 G3 LangegFeld Ger.
214 E4 Langeberg mts S. Africa
142 D2 Langeland i. Denmark
142 D2 Langelands Bælt str. Denmark
141 N3 Längelmäki Fin.
169 F4 Langelsheim Ger.
169 F4 Langen Hessen Ger.
172 F3 Langenaltheim Ger.
169 D5 Langen Niedersachsen Ger.
173 F3 Langenargen Ger.
169 D5 Langenau Ger.
169 D4 Langenaubach Ger.
173 F2 Langenbach Ger.
169 E4 Langenbernsdorf Ger.
223 K5 Langenburg Sask. Can.
169 C5 Langeneichstädt Ger.
169 D4 Langeneß i. Ger.
171 D5 Langeln Ger.
179 K3 Langenlois Austria
169 K2 Langenloisheim Ger.
173 H3 Langenmosen Ger.
171 F4 Langennaundorf Ger.
169 C4 Langenneufnach Ger.
171 E4 Langenpreising Ger.
158 D3 Langenselbold Ger.
173 G2 Langenstein Austria
169 F4 Langenwang Austria
179 L4 Langenweddingen Ger.
171 F5 Langenzenn Ger.
173 F2 Langeoog Ger.
179 K2 Langeoog i. Ger.

158 C3 Landeleau France
165 H1 Landen Belgium
238 F2 Lander WY U.S.A.
96 C4 Lam Chi r. Thai.
158 B3 Landerneau France
157 H4 Landersheim France
163 B5 Landes dept Aquitaine France
168 E3 Landes reg. France
158 B4 Landes de Lanvaux reg. France
158 D3 Landes du Mené reg. France
187 E3 Landeta Arg.
187 B5 Landete Spain
157 F5 Landévant France
158 B3 Landévennec France
94 C3 Landgraaf Neth.
94 C3 Landik, Gunung mt. Indon.
161 A6 Landinier Neth.
190 C1 Landino r. France
163 B4 Landis France
223 I4 Landis Sask. Can.
182 E3 Landisville PA U.S.A.
149 I3 Landkirchen auf Fehmarn Ger.
140 K3 Landögssjön l. Sweden
226 C2 Land O' Lakes WI U.S.A.
237 D6 Landolfshausen Ger.
140 K3 Landön Sweden
97 C5 Landor W. Austr.
150 D3 Landore Swansea, Wales U.K.
161 B4 Landos France
190 E2 Landquart Switz.
156 D2 Landrecies France
156 E5 Landres France
157 I5 Landres-et-St-Georges France
227 I1 Landrienne Que. Can.
182 C1 Landrove r. Spain see Landro
231 D5 Landrum SC U.S.A.
160 E3 Landry France
171 D4 Landsberg Ger.
173 I3 Landsberg am Lech Ger.
81 B5 Landsborough r. South I. N.Z.
169 B6 Landscheid Ger.
150 □ Land's End pt England U.K.
142 E1 Landskrona Sweden
164 D2 Landsmeer Neth.
172 B2 Landstuhl Ger.
158 B3 Landudec France
197 I5 La Nedei mt. Romania
147 D3 Lanesborough Rep. of Ireland
158 C4 Lanester France
231 C5 Lanett AL U.S.A.
159 G3 La Neuve-Lyre France
190 C1 La Neuveville Switz.
157 I5 La Neuville-au-Pont France
157 I5 Laneuville-sur-Meuse France
108 D2 Lanfeng Henan China see
Lankao
96 B1 Lang, Nam r. Myanmar
142 C3 Langå Denmark
96 C2 Langa Spain
96 B2 Langa r. Vietnam
129 F3 Längäbän Azer.
129 F4 Länkäran r. Azer.
252 C3 Lanlacuni Bajo Peru
161 A4 Lanloup France
142 C3 Lanmeur France
142 C3 Lannemezan France
163 D5 Lannemezan, Plateau de France
159 J3 Lannepax France
156 C4 Lannilis France
158 C3 Lannion France
158 C3 Lannion, Baie de b. France
224 F4 L'Annonciation Que. Can.
156 D2 Lannoy France
161 A3 Lanobre France
92 B2 La Nocle-Maulaix France
163 A4 Lanoraia Spain
235 I3 Lanoka Harbour NJ U.S.A.
244 C4 La Noria Mex.
108 A3 Lanping Yunnan China
161 A4 Lans, Montagne de mts France
161 C5 Lansargues France
234 D3 Lansdale PA U.S.A.
234 C3 Lansdowne MD U.S.A.
224 F4 Lansdowne Ont. Can.
226 C2 L'Anse MI U.S.A.
170 D2 Lansen Ger.
225 G2 L'Anse-St-Jean Que. Can.
234 C2 Lansford PA U.S.A.
222 C2 Lansing r. Y.T. Can.
226 B4 Lansing IA U.S.A.
226 A4 Lansing MN U.S.A.
140 M3 Länsi-Suomi prov. Fin.
140 M2 Lansjärv Sweden
176 F2 Lanškroun Czech Rep.
161 D4 Lansmant France
183 G3 Lanta r. Spain
187 F3 Lantadilla Spain
109 □ Lantau Island H.K. China
157 G5 Lantautière r. France
107 H3 Lantian Shaanxi China
160 C2 Lanton France
163 A4 Lantosque France
160 D1 Lanty France
170 C2 Lanu France
179 K2 Lanu Austria
161 B4 Lanuéjouls France
161 B4 Lanuéjols France
192 A4 La Nurra reg. Sardegna Italy
261 H4 Lanús Arg.
192 B5 Lanusei Sardegna Italy
92 C4 Lanuza Phil.
158 D3 Lanvallay France
158 D3 Lanvéoc France
158 B3 Lanvollon France
100 C3 Lanxi Heilong. China
109 F2 Lanxi Zhejiang China
107 I4 Lanxian Shanxi China
190 C1 Lanzo Torinese Italy
193 J5 Lao r. Italy
96 C2 Lao, Mae r. Thai.
96 D2 Laoag Phil.
92 B2 Laoang Phil.
108 A4 Laobie Shan mts Yunnan China
108 D4 Laobukou Guangxi China
96 D2 Lao Cai Vietnam
108 D2 Laohekou Hubei China
107 I3 Laohutun Liaoning China
107 I4 Laojie Yunnan China
Laojunmiao Gansu China see
Yumen
107 I4 Laokai Jilin China
107 I4 Langkang i. Malaysia
93 C4 Langkesi, Kepulauan is Indon.
97 B5 Lang Kha Toek, Khao mt. Thai.
214 C5 Langklip S. Africa
95 J3 Langkon Sabah Malaysia
224 C3 Langlade Que. Can.
227 I1 Langlade France
159 I4 Langley KY U.S.A.
232 B6 Langley WA U.S.A.
232 B6 Langley WA U.S.A.
85 F4 Langlo Crossing Qld Austr.
255 A5 La Oroya Peru
184 C6 L'Arboç Spain
172 C2 Langnau Switz.
168 G1 Langø Denmark
161 B5 Langogne France
163 B4 Langoiran France
163 B4 Langon France
96 C3 Langong, Xé r. Laos
158 B3 Langonnet France
140 K1 Langøya i. Norway
150 C2 Langport Somerset, England U.K.
109 F3 Langqi Fujian China
173 G2 Langquaid Ger.
157 F5 Langres France
157 F5 Langres, Plateau de France
94 B1 Langsa Sumatera Indon.
179 F2 Langschlag Austria
140 J3 Långsele Sweden
107 F3 Langshan Nei Mongol China
107 E3 Lang Shan mts China
143 G3 Långshyttan Sweden
96 D2 Lang Son Vietnam
149 Q5 Langstrothdale Chase hills England U.K.
172 A2 Langsur Ger.
207 H4 Langtang Nigeria
117 F3 Langtang National Park Nepal
149 I3 Langthwaite North Yorkshire, England U.K.
140 L2 Långträsk Sweden
237 C6 Langtry TX U.S.A.
161 A6 Languedoc-Roussillon admin. reg. France
158 D3 Langueux France
161 C4 Languidic France
183 G3 Languilla Spain
169 F4 Langula Ger.
134 C2 Långvattnet Sweden
141 I3 Långvinds bruk Sweden
168 D2 Langwarden (Butjadingen) Ger.
149 F5 Langwathby Cumbria, England U.K.
168 E3 Langwedel Niedersachsen Ger.
168 E1 Langwedel Schleswig-Holstein Ger.
173 E3 Langweid am Lech Ger.
107 I4 Langya Shan mt. Hebei China
108 C2 Langzhong Sichuan China
182 B3 Lanheses Port.
158 B3 Lanhouarneau France
192 C2 Laniel Que. Can.
175 H3 Łanięta Pol.
223 J5 Lanigan Sask. Can.
259 C5 Lanin, Volcán vol. Arg./Chile
150 C4 Lanivet Cornwall, England U.K.
136 D3 Lanivtsi Ukr.
95 L2 Lanjak, Bukit mt. Sarawak Malaysia
185 H4 Lanjarón Spain
150 B4 Lanjarón Spain
92 B7 Lanping Phil.
141 N3 Lanojärvi Fin.
141 N3 Lapinlahti Fin.
194 C5 La Pizzuta mt. Sicilia Italy
237 F6 Laplace LA U.S.A.
96 C3 Lap Lae Thai.

100 D4 Laotieshan Shuidao sea chan. China see Bohai Haixia
101 C4 Laotougou Jilin China
100 D4 Laotuding Shan hill Liaoning China
206 B4 Laou, Oued r. Morocco
206 B4 Laoudi-Ba Côte d'Ivoire
100 D4 Laoye Ling mts China
255 G2 Laozi Brazil
185 I3 La Paca Spain
207 F4 La Pacaudière France
207 G4 Lapai Nigeria
160 B2 Lapalisse France
162 A2 La Pallice France
216 □3h La Palma i. Canary Is
250 C2 La Palma Col.
242 □K7 La Palma Panama
187 C4 La Palma Spain
244 L5 La Palma AZ U.S.A.
184 D3 La Palma del Condado Spain
161 A4 La Palme France
258 G4 La Paloma Uru.
161 E5 La Palud-sur-Verdon France
161 E5 La Palud-sur-Verdon France
260 C2 La Pampa prov. Arg.
175 I6 Lapanów Pol.
240 G4 La Panza Range mts CA U.S.A.
261 F2 La Para Arg.
184 D2 La Parra Spain
183 H5 La Parra de Las Vegas Spain
183 H5 La Parrilla hill Spain
182 B5 Lapas Port.
261 G3 La Paz Entre Ríos Arg.
258 D3 La Paz Mendoza Arg.
252 C4 La Paz Bol.
252 C4 La Paz dept Bol.
242 □I6 La Paz Hond.
244 B3 La Paz Mex.
261 I4 La Paz Uru.
226 D5 Lapaz IN U.S.A.
250 D5 La Pedrera Col.
227 F4 Lapeer MI U.S.A.
190 D2 La Pellerine France
184 D2 La Peña de Francia, Sierra de mts Spain
159 F4 La Penne France
161 D5 La Penne-sur-Huveaune France
183 H4 La Peraleja Spain
242 D2 La Perla Mex.
102 J1 La Pérouse Strait Japan/Rus. Fed.
245 H4 La Pesca Mex.
161 C4 La Pesga Mex.
158 B3 La Petite-Pierre France
163 C4 La Peza Spain
158 C3 Lapford Devon, England U.K.
244 C3 La Piedad Mex.
238 D3 La Pine OR U.S.A.
92 C3 Lapinig Phil.
92 B4 La Pinilla Spain
141 N3 Lapinjärvi Fin.
141 N3 Lapinlahti Fin.
194 C5 La Pizzuta mt. Sicilia Italy
237 F6 Laplace LA U.S.A.
96 C3 Lap Lae Thai.
96 C3 La Plaine-sur-Mer France
236 D2 La Plant SD U.S.A.
261 I4 La Plata Arg.
232 C5 La Plata MD U.S.A.
236 E4 La Plata MO U.S.A.
261 I4 La Plata, Río de sea chan. Arg./Uru.
182 D1 La Plaza Spain
162 E3 Lapleau France
163 C4 Laplume France
186 C2 Lapmežciems Latvia
186 F2 La Pobla de Lillet Spain
186 D3 La Pobla de Segur Spain
182 B2 La Pola de Gordón Spain
159 F3 La Pommeraye France
192 B2 La Porta Corse France
107 F4 Laporte PA U.S.A.
234 B2 Laporte PA U.S.A.
226 D5 Laporte IN U.S.A.
186 D3 La Portella Spain
182 B2 La Portera Spain
93 A4 Laposo, Bukit mt. Indon.
159 F3 La Pouèze France
157 H4 Lapoutroie France
196 C3 Lapovo Srbija Yugo.
250 C2 La Poyata Col.
142 C3 Lapp Sweden
141 O3 Lappajärvi Fin.
141 O3 Lappajärvi l. Fin.
141 O3 Lappeenranta Fin.
140 M3 Lappeenranta Fin.
140 L2 Lappi Fin.
140 M2 Lappi prov. Fin.
140 M1 Lapland reg. Europe
141 O3 Lappträsk Sweden
233 Q2 La Prairie Que. Can.
190 C1 La Preste France
261 G4 Laprida Arg.
163 C4 La Proveda de Soria Spain
237 D6 La Pryor TX U.S.A.
199 I1 Lapseki Turkey
182 C2 Lapte r. Spain
182 C2 Laptevo Rus. Fed. see Yasnogorsk
131 N2 Laptev Sea Rus. Fed.
140 M3 Lapua Fin.
140 M3 Lapuanjoki r. Fin.
92 B4 Lapu-Lapu Phil.
258 C3 La Puebla Spain see Sa Pobla
185 H4 La Puebla de Almoradiel Spain
185 I2 La Puebla de Cazalla Spain
185 G3 La Puebla de Híjar Spain
185 H3 La Puebla de los Infantes Spain
184 D4 La Puebla del Río Spain
183 H2 La Puebla de Montalbán Spain
183 F3 La Puebla de Valdavia Spain
183 J3 La Puebla de Valverde Spain
183 F5 La Pueblanueva Spain
100 C3 Lapugnacia Indon.
160 C2 La Puerta Arg.
185 H2 La Puerta de Segura Spain
177 L6 Lăpugiu de Jos Romania
92 B4 Lapu-Lapu Phil.
258 C3 La Punilla, Cordillera de mts Chile
190 D2 La Punt Switz.
250 A4 La Puntilla pt Ecuador
216 □3c Lanzarote i. Canary Is
179 H3 Lanzenkirchen Austria
171 D6 Lanzhou Czech Rep.
107 I3 Lanzhou Gansu China
196 D4 Lanziging Jilin China
190 C1 Lanzo Torinese Italy

143 H3 Lärbro Gotland Sweden
163 A5 Larceveau-Arros-Cibits France
159 E3 Larchamp France
156 C4 Larchant France
161 C6 Larche Limousin France
162 D3 Larche Provence-Alpes-Côte-d'Azur France
235 E2 Larchmont NY U.S.A.
227 G2 Larchwood Ont. Can.
191 F3 Lardaro Italy
165 D5 L'Ardenne, Plateau de Belgium
227 H1 Larder Lake Ont. Can.
182 C5 Lardosa Port.
183 G1 Laredo Spain
237 D7 Laredo TX U.S.A.
161 A5 La Redorte France
259 B9 La Reina Adelaida, Archipiélago de is Chile
227 H1 La Reine Que. Can.
164 F2 Laren Gelderland Neth.
164 E2 Laren Noord-Holland Neth.
163 A4 La Réole France
147 C2 Largan Rep. of Ireland
Largeau Chad see Faya
161 C4 Largentière France
161 E4 L'Argentière-la-Bessée France
231 F2 Largo FL U.S.A.
183 F5 Largoward Fife, Scotland U.K.
146 D6 Largs North Ayrshire, Scotland U.K.
186 D4 La Rhune hill Spain
191 F5 Lari Italy
205 H1 L'Ariana Tunisia
189 C7 L'Ariana admin. div. Tunisia
93 A3 Lariang r. Indon.
183 H3 La Riba de Escalote Spain
161 C3 La Ricamarie France
184 D3 Larimore ND U.S.A.
184 D3 La Rinconada Spain
193 G3 Larino Italy
258 D3 La Rioja Arg.
260 D1 La Rioja prov. Arg.
183 H2 La Rioja aut. comm. Spain
198 C2 Larisa Greece
Larissa Greece see Larisa
163 D4 Larkenall South Lanarkshire, Scotland U.K.
146 E6 Larkhall South Lanarkshire, Scotland U.K.
225 J2 Lark Harbour Nfld. Can.
151 F5 Larkhill Wiltshire, England U.K.
123 E3 Lar Koh mt. Afgh.
150 □ Lark Passage Qld Austr.
151 H2 Larling Norfolk, England U.K.
160 E2 Larmont r. France/Switz.
161 C4 Larmont-Plage France
Larnaca Cyprus see Larnaka
128 A2 Larnaka Cyprus
147 F2 Larne Northern Ireland U.K.
236 D4 Larned KS U.S.A.
147 F2 Larne Lough inlet Northern Ireland U.K.
182 D1 La Robla Spain
184 D1 La Roca de la Sierra Spain
190 C2 La Roche Switz.
158 A4 La Rochebeaucourt-et-Argentine France
162 C3 La Roche-Bernard France
163 C4 La Roche-Canillac France
162 C3 La Roche-Chalais France
162 A2 La Roche-de-Rame France
158 C3 La Roche-Derrien France
163 C4 La Roche-des-Arnauds France
165 E4 La Roche-en-Ardenne Belgium
162 C3 La Rochefoucauld France
162 A2 La Roche-Guyon France
162 A2 La Rochelle France
159 F4 La Roche-Posay France
160 D2 La Rochepot France
163 C4 Laroche-St-Cydroine France
158 E4 La Roche-sur-Foron France
158 E4 La Roche-sur-Yon France
162 A2 La Roche-Vineuse France
165 E4 La Rochette France
185 H1 La Roda Spain
185 H3 La Roda de Andalucía Spain
247 K5 La Romana Dom. Rep.
223 I4 La Romana Sask. Can.
161 E4 La Romieu France
223 J4 La Ronge, Lac l. Sask. Can.
162 E4 Laroquebrou France
161 C5 La Roquebrussanne France
161 C5 La Roque-d'Anthéron France
161 E4 Laroque-Timbaut France
161 E4 La Roque-Ste-Marguerite France
243 E3 La Rosa Mex.
244 E3 La Rosita Mex.
182 C1 Larouco, Serra do mts Spain
161 A4 La Rouquette France
183 I2 Larraga Spain
161 C6 Larrainzar Spain
183 I2 Larrasoaña Spain
163 A5 Larrazet France
163 A5 Larressingle France
86 C3 Larrey Point W.A. Austr.
84 D3 Larrimah N.T. Austr.
183 H2 Larroque France
163 A5 Larroque France
263 C2 Lars Christensen Coast Antarctica
Larsmo Fin. see Luoto
140 I3 Larsnes Norway
156 B2 L'Artois, Collines de hills France
161 A5 La Rúa Spain see A Rúa
163 B5 Laruns France
162 D3 Laruscade France
142 B2 Larvik Norway
137 I4 Laryne Ukr.
161 B4 Larzac, Causse du plat. France
191 F5 Lasà Italy
252 B2 La Sabana Arg.
245 E2 Las Adjuntas, Presa de resr Mex.
241 M2 La Sal UT U.S.A.
252 B2 La Sal, Cerros de mts Peru
258 C2 La Salina salt pan Arg.
241 M2 La Sal Junction UT U.S.A.
160 B2 La Salle Que. Can.
161 E4 La Salle France
190 C2 La Salle Italy
226 C5 La Salle IL U.S.A.
161 C6 Las Salinas del Janubio Spain
243 E2 Las Cabezas de San Juan Spain
260 D4 Las Cabras Chile
185 I2 Las Bela Pak.
142 B2 Lásby Denmark
142 C2 Las Berlanas Spain
243 F2 Las Cabezas de San Juan Spain
260 D4 Las Cabras Chile
242 C3 Las Animas Mex.
204 A5 Las and Somalia see Lascaanood
190 C2 La Sarine r. Switz.
190 C2 La Sarraz Switz.
161 E4 Lasarte-Oria Spain
261 F4 Las Asequias Arg.
163 B4 La Sauvetat France
160 E4 La Sauvetat-du-Drop France
163 A5 La Sauvetat-Peyralès France
163 B4 La Sauvetat-sur-Agout France
236 C4 Las Animas CO U.S.A.
190 C2 Lascano Uru.
183 C3 Las Arenas Spain
161 C2 La Sarine r. Switz.
244 E3 Las Asequias Arg.
254 C4 La Sauvetat France
163 A5 La Sauvete Hill France
247 L4 Las Aves, Islas is West Indies
245 G4 La Savane Hault.
143 G2 Lasberg Austria
244 A4 Las Bela Pak.
142 C3 Lásby Denmark
142 C2 Las Berlanas Spain
243 F2 Las Cabezas de San Juan Spain
260 C2 Las Cabras Chile
185 I2 Las Cañadas vol. crater Tenerife Canary Is
194 C3 Las Casas Sicilia Italy
187 D3 Las Casas Spain
260 C2 Las Casuarinas Arg.

135 G7 Leningradskaya Rus. Fed.
139 I2 Leningradskaya Oblast' admin. div. Rus. Fed.
131 S3 Leningradskiy Rus. Fed.
Leningradskiy Tajik. see Leninabad
137 F2 Leninivka Ukr.
129 E2 Leninkent Rus. Fed.
Lenino Respublika Krym Ukr. see Lenine
123 G2 Leninobod Tajik. see Khŭjand
Leninobod admin. div. Tajik. see Leninobod
Leninobod Uzbek. see Leninabad
121 J2 Leninogorsk Kazakh. see Leninogorsk
135 K5 Leninogorsk Rus. Fed.
121 H5 Lenin Peak Kyrg./Tajik.
121 G4 Leninpol' Kyrg.
135 I6 Leninsk Rus. Fed.
Leninsk Turkm. see Akdepe
Leninsk Uzb. see Asaka
137 H4 Lenins'ke Ukr.
137 H5 Lenins'ke Ukr.
120 D2 Leninskiy Kazakh.
139 K4 Leninskiy Rus. Fed.
130 J4 Leninsk-Kuznetskiy Rus. Fed.
120 F1 Leninskoye Kustanayskaya Oblast' Kazakh.
Leninskoye Yuzhnyy Kazakhstan Kazakh. see Kazygurt
120 B2 Leninskoye Zapadnyy Kazakhstan Kazakh. see Leninskoye
134 I4 Leninskoye Kirovskaya Oblast' Rus. Fed.
100 E3 Leninskoye Yevreyskaya Avtonomnaya Oblast' Rus. Fed.
163 B4 Le Nizan France
190 C2 Lenk Switz.
136 D3 Lenkivtsi Ukr.
Lenkoran' Azer. see Länkäran
86 E3 Lennard r. W.A. Austr.
169 E4 Lenne Ger.
169 C4 Lenne r. Ger.
169 C4 Lennestadt Ger.
172 D3 Lenningen Ger.
259 D9 Lennox, Isla i. Chile
146 D6 Lennoxtown East Dunbartonshire, Scotland U.K.
190 F3 Leno Italy
231 D5 Lenoir NC U.S.A.
231 C5 Lenoir City TN U.S.A.
190 B1 Le Noirmont Switz.
193 F3 Lenola Italy
232 B6 Lenore WV U.S.A.
156 D2 Le Nouvion-en-Thiérache France
233 G3 Lenox MA U.S.A.
165 C4 Lens Belgium
156 C2 Lens France
158 F1 Lensahn Ger.
131 M3 Lensk Rus. Fed.
160 D2 Lent France
164 E3 Lent Neth.
129 C2 Lentekhi Georgia
162 C2 Lenthöhren Ger.
176 F5 Lenti Hungary
191 H2 Lential Italy
173 F3 Lenting Ger.
195 E5 Lentini Sicilia Italy
195 E5 Lentini r. Sicilia Italy
Lentvaras Lith. see Lentvaris
138 E4 Lentvaris Lith.
139 K2 Lent'yevo Rus. Fed.
240 I4 Lenwood CA U.S.A.
190 D1 Lenzburg Switz.
170 C2 Lenzen Ger.
179 E3 Lenzing Austria
172 C4 Lenzkirch Ger.
206 E4 Léo Burkina
191 F4 Leo r. Italy
179 G3 Leoben Austria
179 H2 Leobendorf Austria
179 H3 Leobersdorf Austria
Leodhais, Eilean i. Scotland U.K. see Lewis, Isle of
246 D3 Léogane Haiti
178 D3 Leogang Austria
163 B4 Léognan France
236 D2 Leola SD U.S.A.
150 E2 Leominster Herefordshire, England U.K.
233 H3 Leominster MA U.S.A.
163 A5 León France
244 D3 León Mex.
242 I16 León Nic.
182 E2 León Spain
182 E2 León prov. Castilla y León Spain
236 E3 León IL U.S.A.
237 D6 León r. TX U.S.A.
182 D2 León, Montes de mts Spain
237 D5 Leonard TX U.S.A.
193 E3 Leonardo da Vinci airport Italy
232 E5 Leonardtown MD U.S.A.
212 C4 Leonardville Namibia
172 D3 Leonberg Ger.
161 D4 Léoncel France
Leontari
179 F2 Leonding Austria
165 B4 Leone, Monte mt. Italy/Switz.
261 F3 Leones Arg.
193 E2 Leonessa Italy
194 D5 Leonforte Sicilia Italy
83 F4 Leongatha Vic. Austr.
161 C4 Leoni, Monte hill Italy
198 C2 Leonidi Greece
100 G2 Leonidovo Sakhalin Rus. Fed.
87 D6 Leonora W.A. Austr.
198 C2 Leontari Greece
86 E3 Leopold r. W.A. Austr.
232 C5 Leopold OH U.S.A.
86 E3 Leopold Downs W.A. Austr.
Léopold II, Lac l. Dem. Rep. Congo see Mai-Ndombe, Lac
257 F4 Leopoldina Brazil
256 C2 Leopoldo de Bulhões Brazil
165 E3 Leopoldsburg Belgium
179 H2 Leopoldsdorf im Marchfelde Austria
170 E2 Leopoldshagen Ger.
169 D3 Leopoldshöhe Ger.
Léopoldville Dem. Rep. Congo see Kinshasa
236 C1 Leoti KS U.S.A.
136 E4 Leova Moldova
223 J4 Leoville Sask. Can.
Leova Moldova see Leova
158 C4 Le Palais France
162 D3 Le Palais-sur-Vienne France
158 E4 Le Pallet France
156 C2 Le Parcq France
163 C4 Le Passage France
161 C3 Le Pavillon-Ste-Julie France
144 C2 Lepe Spain
161 C3 Le Péage-de-Roussillon France
162 C2 Le Pêchereau France
Lepel' Belarus see Lyepyel'
158 E4 Le Pellerin France
163 D6 Le Périer France
163 E6 Le Perthus France
159 E3 Le Pertre France
215 E4 Lephoi S. Africa
162 B3 Le Pian-Médoc France
159 G3 Le Pin-au-Haras France
156 E4 L'Épine France
161 D4 L'Épine France
163 G2 Le Pin-la-Garenne France
162 C3 Le Pizou France
156 C3 Le Plan France
156 D2 Le Plessis-Belleville France
134 M3 Lep'lya r. Rus. Fed.
164 D4 Le Poët France
188 F2 Lepoglava Croatia
159 H5 Le Poinçonnet France
158 E5 Le Poiré-sur-Vie France
158 E5 Le Pont-de-Beauvoisin France
163 D6 Le Pont-de-Claix France
158 B4 Le Pont-de-Monvert France
156 C2 Le Pontet France
190 D2 Lepontine, Alpi mts Italy/Switz.
195 G3 Leporano Italy
163 A4 Le Porge France

163 A4 Le Porge-Océan France
156 B2 Le Portel France
196 K4 Leposavić Kosovo, Srbija Yugo.
161 B5 Le Pouget France
158 C4 Le Pouldu France
160 B2 Le Pouliguen France
161 C4 Le Pouzin France
140 N3 Leppävesi Fin.
140 N3 Leppävirta Fin.
161 E5 Le Pradet France
Lepsa r. Kazakh. see Lepsy
Lepsa Kazakh. see Lepsy
177 H4 Lepsény Hungary
Lepsi Kazakh. see Lepsinsk
121 J3 Lepsinsk Kazakh.
121 I3 Lepsy r. Kazakh.
121 J3 Lepsy Kazakh.
202 B1 Leptis Magna tourist site Libya
198 C1 Leptokarya Greece
156 B4 Le Puiset France
161 B3 Le-Puy-en-Velay France
159 F4 Le Puy-Notre-Dame France
158 E5 Le Puy-St-Réparade France
206 B2 Leqqebba Maur.
156 D2 Le Quesnoy France
206 D4 Léraba r. Burkina/Côte d'Ivoire
156 C4 Le Raincy France
226 C5 Le Roy IL U.S.A.
163 D6 Lercara Friddi Sicilia Italy
245 G4 Lerdo Mex.
208 B2 Léré Chad
163 H4 Léré Mali
206 D3 Lère Nigeria
207 H4 Lere Nigeria
158 D3 Le Relecq-Kerhuon France
182 B2 Lérez r. Spain
158 E3 Le Rheu France
250 D5 Lérida Col.
Lérida Spain see Lleida
Lérida prov. Cataluña Spain see Lleida
129 F4 Lerik Azer.
183 I2 Lerik Spain
243 H5 Lerma Mex.
244 C3 Lerma r. Mex.
183 G2 Lerma Spain
245 E4 Lerma de Vilada Mex.
163 B4 Lerm-et Musset France
129 C1 Lermontov Rus. Fed.
100 E3 Lermontovka Rus. Fed.
Lermontovskiy Rus. Fed. see Lermontov
192 C3 Lerno, Monte mt. Sardegna Italy
160 E3 Le Roignais mt. France
199 E3 Leros i. Greece
163 E4 Le Rouget France
157 F4 Lérouville France
226 C5 Le Roy IL U.S.A.
155 C4 Le Roy MN U.S.A.
232 E3 Le Roy NY U.S.A.
234 B1 Leroy PA U.S.A.
161 B4 Le Rozier France
157 G4 Lerrain France
164 C2 Lerrnec r. Italy
142 E3 Lerum Sweden
160 E1 Le Russey France
146 □G1 Lerwick Shetland, Scotland U.K.
163 B6 Lés Spain
190 D3 Lesa Italy
160 D3 Les Abrets France
247 □2 Les Abymes Guadeloupe
186 B1 Lesaca Spain
161 E5 Les Adrets-de-l'Estérel France
186 F3 Les Agudes mt. Spain
247 □2 Les St-Esprit Martinique
160 A1 Les Aix-d'Angillon France
160 A3 Les Ancizes-Comps France
186 B3 Les Andelys France
161 C5 Les Angles Languedoc-Roussillon France
163 E6 Les Angles Languedoc-Roussillon France
159 G3 Le Sap France
161 E5 Les Arcs Provence-Alpes-Côte-d'Azur France
160 E3 Les Arcs Rhône-Alpes France
159 F5 Les Aubiers France
161 E4 Le Sauze-Super-Sauze France
186 D3 Les Avellanes Spain
160 B4 Les Avenières France
161 B4 Les Bondons France
156 C5 Les Bordes France
186 D3 Les Bordes-sur-Arize France
186 D3 Les Borges Blanques Spain
186 D3 Les Borges del Camp Spain
199 D2 Lesbos i. Greece see Lesvos
175 K4 Leszkowice Pol.
173 I4 Leszno Mazowieckie Pol.
174 E4 Leszno Wielkopolskie Pol.
173 I4 Leszno Górne Pol.
161 D3 Le Taillefer mt. France
186 C2 Le Taillon mt. France
143 F2 Le Tallud France
161 C4 Le Tanneur mt. France
177 K4 Létavértes Hungary
151 I2 Letchworth Hertfordshire, England U.K.
163 A4 Le Teich France
161 C4 Le Teil France
161 C5 Le Teilleul France
161 E5 Le Télégraphe hill France
176 F5 Letenye Hungary
116 D4 Leteri Madh. Prad. India
215 F1 Lethabile S. Africa
96 A2 Letha Range mts Myanmar
222 H5 Lethbridge Alta Can.
225 H5 Lethbridge Nfld. Can.
168 D2 Lethe r. Ger.
159 G3 Le Theil France
158 E4 Le-Theil-de-Bretagne France
251 G4 Lethem Guyana
151 I2 Letheringsett Norfolk, England U.K.
150 B3 Le Thillot France
157 G4 Le Tholy France
161 E5 Le Thoronet France
93 C5 Leti, Kepulauan is Maluku Indon.
250 D6 Leticia Col.
107 H4 Leting Hebei China
193 □3 Letino Italy
214 D5 Letjiesbos S. Africa
177 H4 Letkés Hungary
214 E4 Letlhakane Botswana
215 E1 Letlhakeng Botswana
191 H2 Le Tofane mt. Italy
195 E5 Letojanni Sicilia Italy
179 H1 Letonice Czech Rep.
156 B2 Le Touquet-Paris-Plage France
161 C4 Le Tour d'Arre hill France
161 D4 Le Touvet France
176 F2 Letovice Czech Rep.
96 A3 Letpadan Myanmar
96 A2 Letpan Myanmar
157 G4 Le Trayon Switz.
161 A4 Le Truel France
141 R3 Letsbo Sweden
170 D3 Letschin Ger.
201 F2 Letsopa S. Africa
147 H2 Letter Donegal, Northern Ireland U.K.
147 H3 Lettercallow Rep. of Ireland
147 B3 Letterfrack Rep. of Ireland
147 C2 Letterkenny Rep. of Ireland
147 D3 Letterston Pembrokeshire, Wales U.K.
161 B4 Letur Spain
183 Q2 Letux Spain
136 D3 Letychiv Ukr.
107 L1 Letzlingen Ger.
172 C2 Leu Romania
114 D2 Léua Angola
171 E4 Leubingen Ger.
163 E6 Leucate France
163 F6 Leucate, Étang de lag. France

158 E5 Les Lucs-sur-Boulogne France
146 E6 Lesmahagow South Lanarkshire, Scotland U.K.
160 D1 Les Maillys France
160 E3 Les Marches France
160 B3 Les Martres-de-Veyre France
161 B5 Les Matelles France
156 E3 Les Mazures France
225 H3 Les Méchins Que. Can.
161 D4 Les Mées France
158 C4 Les Menuires France
158 D3 Les Minquiers is Channel Is
156 E4 Les Monges mt. France
156 E4 Lesmont France
156 C4 Les Mureaux France
177 G2 Lešná Czech Rep.
174 G5 Lésna r. Pol.
174 C5 Lešná Czech Rep.
174 G5 Lésnica Pol.
156 E4 Les Noës-près-Troyes France
234 K4 Lesnoy Kirovskaya Oblast' Rus. Fed.
139 M4 Lesnoy Ryazanskaya Oblast' Rus. Fed.
139 J2 Lesnoye Rus. Fed.
134 K4 Lesnyye Polyany Rus. Fed.
100 G2 Lesogorsk Sakhalin Rus. Fed.
138 G1 Lesogorskiy Rus. Fed.
161 C4 Les Ollières-sur-Eyrieux France
100 E3 Lesopil'noye Rus. Fed.
161 E4 Les Orres France
131 K4 Lesosibirsk Rus. Fed.
215 G3 Lesotho country Africa
215 G3 Lesotho Highlands Water Scheme Lesotho
100 E3 Lesozavodsk Rus. Fed.
162 B3 Lesparre-Médoc France
156 B2 Les Peintures France
161 D5 Les Pennes-Mirabeau France
163 A5 Lesperon France
161 B5 Les Petites-Loges France
197 F2 Lespezi mt. Romania
158 D2 Les Pieux France
161 B5 Lespignan France
186 D4 L'Espina mt. Spain
163 E5 Lespinassière France
163 A5 L'Espluga Calba Spain
160 E2 Les Planches-en-Montagne France
186 E3 L'Espluga Calba Spain
186 E3 L'Espluga de Francolí Spain
182 B1 Les Ponts-de-Cé France
190 B1 Les Ponts-de-Martel Switz.
186 F2 Les Preses Spain
163 C5 Lespugue France
156 C5 Les Riceys France
161 E4 Les Rosiers France
159 G2 Les Rousses France
162 A3 Les Sables-d'Olonne France
161 C4 Les Salles-du-Gardon France
158 E4 Lessay France
165 D4 Lesse r. Belgium
247 F4 Lesser Antilles is Caribbean Sea
Lesser Caucasus mts Asia see Malyy Kavkaz
116 D3 Lesser Himalaya mts India/Nepal
80 E4 Lesser Slave Lake Alta Can.
225 G4 Lesser Slave Lake Alta Can.
199 E3 Levitha i. Greece
Lesser Khingan Mountains China see Xiao Hinggan Ling
234 D2 Levittown NY U.S.A.
234 D2 Levittown PA U.S.A.
158 E3 Le-Vivier-sur-Mer France
197 H5 Levka Bulg.
Levkás i. Greece see Lefkada
Levkímmi Ionioi Nisoi Greece see Lefkimmi
177 J2 Levoča Slovakia
177 J2 Levočské vrchy mts Slovakia
162 D2 Levroux France
197 G4 Levski Bulg. see Karlovo
139 L5 Lev Tolstoy Rus. Fed.
79 □1a Leruka Fiji
96 B3 Lewe Myanmar
151 H4 Lewes East Sussex, England U.K.
233 F5 Lewes DE U.S.A.
174 F5 Lewen Brzeski Pol.
241 M3 Lewis CO U.S.A.
237 D4 Lewis KS U.S.A.
238 B2 Lewis r. WA U.S.A.
146 B3 Lewis, Isle of i. Scotland U.K.
234 A2 Lewis, Lake salt flat N.T. Austr.
234 B2 Lewisberry PA U.S.A.
232 A5 Lewisburg OH U.S.A.
227 I5 Lewisburg PA U.S.A.
231 C5 Lewisburg TN U.S.A.
232 C6 Lewisburg WV U.S.A.
222 D3 Lewis Cass, Mount Alaska/B.C. Can./U.S.A.
225 J3 Lewis Hills hill Nfld. Can.
81 D5 Lewis Pass South I. N.Z.
225 K3 Lewisporte Nfld. Can.
86 F4 Lewis Range hills W.A. Austr.
238 D1 Lewis Range mts MT U.S.A.
231 C5 Lewis Smith, Lake AL U.S.A.
238 C2 Lewiston ID U.S.A.
233 H2 Lewiston ME U.S.A.
236 E2 Lewiston MN U.S.A.
227 F4 Lewiston NY U.S.A.
232 D4 Lewistown IL U.S.A.
238 E3 Lewistown MT U.S.A.
234 B2 Lewistown PA U.S.A.
232 C5 Lewisville AR U.S.A.
232 C5 Lewisville OH U.S.A.
232 C5 Lewisville TX U.S.A.
149 J4 Leyburn North Yorkshire, England U.K.
164 E2 Leyden Neth. see Leiden
108 C3 Leye Guangxi China
122 A2 Leyla Dāgh mt. Iran
149 G4 Leyland Lancashire, England U.K.
163 D4 Leyme France
151 I3 Leysdown-on-Sea Kent, England U.K.
190 C2 Leysin Switz.
92 C4 Leyte i. Phil.
92 C4 Leyte r. Phil.
92 C4 Leyte Gulf Phil.
190 C2 Leytron Switz.
176 G2 Lež r. Czech Rep.
175 I5 Leżajsk Pol.
199 D4 Lezan France
163 C4 Lézardrieux France
247 □2 Lézat-sur-Lèze France
163 C4 Lezay France
174 G4 Leznik Czech Rep.
192 B2 Lezhë Albania
108 C2 Lezhi Sichuan China
139 H3 Lezhnevo Rus. Fed.
163 A5 Lézignan-Corbières France
161 C5 Lézignan France
155 E1 Lezuza Spain
183 Q3 Lezuza r. Spain
192 A2 Librazhdit Albania
174 G3 Lgota Wielka Pol.
139 L6 L'gov Rus. Fed.
111 D6 Lhagoi Kangri mt. Xizang China
115 F3 Lharidon, Moray, Scotland U.K.
111 F6 Lhari Xizang China
111 F6 Lharigarbo Xizang China see Amdo
111 E6 Lhasa Xizang China

146 F5 Leuchars Fife, Scotland U.K.
173 G2 Leuchtenberg Ger.
170 E3 Leuenberg Ger.
157 E5 Leuglay France
190 C2 Leuk Switz.
Lefkada Ionioi Nisoi Greece
190 C2 Leukerbad Switz.
146 B3 Leumrabhagh Western Isles, Scotland U.K.
169 D5 Leun Ger.
241 L4 Leupp AZ U.S.A.
85 G4 Leura Qld Austr.
164 E2 Leusden Neth.
94 B2 Leuser, Gunung mt. Indon.
178 C3 Leutasch Austria
173 G2 Leuterschach Ger.
169 C5 Leutesdorf Ger.
173 E4 Leutkirch im Allgäu Ger.
165 D4 Leuven Belgium
165 C4 Leuze-en-Hainaut Belgium
186 E5 Le Val Spain
161 C5 Le Val d'Ajol France
163 D3 Lhuis France
159 F3 L'Huisserie France
156 E4 Leuhtre France
111 F6 Lhünzê Xizang China
111 F6 Lhünzhub Xizang China
96 B3 Li, Mae r. Thai.
192 A2 Liamone r. Corse France
247 □2 Liamuiga, Mount vol. St Kitts and Nevis
109 F3 Liancheng Fujian China
Liancheng Guizhou China see Qinglong
Liancheng Yunnan China see Guangnan
156 C3 Liancourt France
100 D5 Liancourt Rocks i. N. Pacific Ocean
156 B2 Liane r. France
Lianfeng Fujian China see Liancheng
92 C4 Liangag Phil.
111 E6 Liangag Hu l. China
108 C3 Liangcheng Nei Mongol China
108 C1 Liangdang Gansu China
108 C1 Liangfeng Guangxi China
108 A3 Lianghe Yunnan China
Lianghekou Gansu China see Youyu
108 B2 Lianghekou Sichuan China
191 K6 Liangjiayoufang Shanxi China see Youyu
108 C2 Liangping Chongqing China
95 F7 Liangpran, Bukit mt. Indon.
Liangshan Chongqing China see Liangping
96 B1 Liang Shan mt. Myanmar
108 C3 Liangshi Hunan China see Shaodong
94 C2 Liang Timur, Gunung mt. Malaysia
108 B3 Liangwang Shan mts Yunnan China
108 C2 Liangzhou Gansu China see Wuwei
109 E2 Lianhe Chongqing China see Qianjiang
109 I3 Lianhua Jiangxi China
109 F3 Lianjiang Fujian China
108 C2 Lianjiang Guangdong China
108 C3 Lianjiang Jiangxi China see Xingguo
109 E3 Liannan Guangdong China
108 D3 Lianping Guangdong China
108 B3 Lianran Yunnan China see Anning
109 E3 Lianshan Guangdong China
107 I3 Lianshan Liaoning China
Lianshan Liaoning China see Nanchang
109 D2 Liantuo Hubei China
Lianxian Guangdong China see Lianzhou
109 D2 Lianyin Heilong. China
107 H5 Lianyuan Hunan China
109 F3 Lianyungang Jiangsu China
109 E3 Lianzhou Guangxi China see Hepu
100 B3 Lianzhushan Heilong. China
107 I3 Liao r. China
107 I3 Liaocheng Shandong China
107 I3 Liaodong Bandao pen. China
107 I3 Liaodong Wan b. China
107 I3 Liaodunzhan Xinjiang China
107 I3 Liaoning prov. China
107 I4 Liaoyang Liaoning China
100 A4 Liaoyuan Jilin China
107 I3 Liaozhong Liaoning China
198 D2 Liapades Ionioi Nisoi Greece
123 G3 Liaqatabad Pak.
222 F2 Liard r. Can.
222 F2 Liard Highway N.W.T. Can.
222 E2 Liard Plateau B.C. Can.
222 E3 Liard River B.C. Can.
156 E3 Liart France
146 E4 Liathach mt. Scotland U.K.
143 P3 Liatorp Sweden
124 C5 Liban country Asia see Lebanon
176 F1 Libáň Czech Rep.
123 I3 Liban, Jebel mts Lebanon
250 C3 Libano Col.
Libau Latvia see Liepāja
146 E6 Libberton South Lanarkshire, Scotland U.K.
176 C1 Libčeves Czech Rep.
171 F5 Libčice nad Vltavou Czech Rep.
208 C4 Libenge Dem. Rep. Congo
175 I2 Liberadz Pol.
237 C4 Liberal KS U.S.A.
257 F5 Liberdade Brazil
252 C1 Liberdade r. Amazonas Brazil
254 B4 Liberdade r. Mato Grosso Brazil
176 E1 Liberec Czech Rep.
176 F1 Liberecký kraj admin. reg. Czech Rep.
206 C4 Liberia country Africa
242 D7 Liberia Costa Rica
247 □ Liberta Antigua and Barbuda
261 H4 Libertad Arg.
258 D3 Libertador General San Martín Arg.
215 H3 Libertas S. Africa
230 C4 Liberty IN U.S.A.
230 C4 Liberty KY U.S.A.
233 G5 Liberty ME U.S.A.
232 C5 Liberty MO U.S.A.
233 K2 Liberty NY U.S.A.
232 A5 Liberty OH U.S.A.
237 E6 Liberty TX U.S.A.
232 C6 Liberty Center OH U.S.A.
232 C5 Libertyville IL U.S.A.
176 C1 Libětice Czech Rep.
259 C6 Libíšek Czech Rep.
82 B2 Libig Guangxi China
171 D6 Libochovice Czech Rep.
108 B2 Libo Guizhou China
176 C2 Libobo Czech Rep.
195 H5 Libode S. Africa
192 B3 Libohovë Albania
108 B3 Libourne France
169 G4 Libreville Gabon
209 A5 Libreville Gabon
202 A2 Librilla Spain
202 A2 Libya country Africa
202 B2 Libyan Desert Egypt/Libya
202 D2 Libyan Plateau Egypt
260 A4 Licantén Chile

122 B4 Likak Iran
209 E7 Likasi Dem. Rep. Congo
208 C4 Likati Dem. Rep. Congo
222 F4 Likely B.C. Can.
Likhachevo Ukr. see Pervomays'kyy
Likhachvov Ukr. see Pervomays'kyy
139 J3 Likhoslavl' Rus. Fed.
137 K3 Likhovskoy Rus. Fed.
139 L4 Likino-Dulevo Rus. Fed.
116 B3 Likma Madh. Prad. India
208 C4 Likouala admin. reg. Congo
208 C5 Likouala r. Congo
208 C5 Likouala aux Herbes r. Congo
134 H4 Likurga Rus. Fed.
159 G4 L'Île-Bouchard France
174 G5 L'Île-Rousse Corse France
168 D2 Lilienfeld Austria
168 D2 Lilienthal Ger.
108 D2 Liling Hunan China
138 F1 Liljendal Fin.
179 G3 Lilla Edet Sweden
140 M2 Lilla Luleälven r. Sweden
140 L2 Lillbäcken hill Sweden
165 B4 Lille Belgium
156 D2 Lille France
156 D2 Lille Bælt sea chan. Denmark
159 E4 Lillebonne France
141 H3 Lillehammer Norway
156 C2 Lillers France
142 C2 Lillesand Norway
150 F3 Lilleshall Telford and Wrekin, England U.K.
142 D2 Lillestrøm Norway
226 B4 Lilley MI U.S.A.
87 C5 Lillian, Point hill W.A. Austr.
146 F6 Lilliesleaf Scottish Borders, Scotland U.K.
231 D5 Lillington NC U.S.A.
183 G5 Lillo Spain
222 F5 Lillooet B.C. Can.
222 F5 Lillooet r. B.C. Can.
222 F5 Lillooet Range mts B.C. Can.
211 C6 Lilongwe Malawi
211 B8 Lilongwe Malawi
92 B4 Liloy Phil.
226 C3 Lily WI U.S.A.
82 D3 Lilydale S.A. Austr.
83 I4 Lilydale Tas. Austr.
196 D4 Lim r. Yugo.
261 H4 Lima Arg.
191 F4 Lima r. Italy
253 F5 Lima Para.
252 A3 Lima Peru
226 C5 Lima dept Peru
226 C5 Lima IL U.S.A.
236 E3 Lima MT U.S.A.
232 A4 Lima OH U.S.A.
134 C4 Lima Duarte Brazil
257 F3 Lima r. Italy
120 A3 Limah Oman
178 F2 Limanu Rus. Fed.
178 D4 Limana Italy
261 H4 Limache Chile
252 A2 Limajo r. Peru
222 B2 Liard r. Can.
260 B2 Limanes r. Arg.
252 D2 Limanton Mex.
79 □2 Limassol Cyprus see Lemesos
147 I2 Limavady Northern Ireland U.K.
260 D6 Limay r. Arg.
156 D3 Limay France
172 D2 Limbach Baden-Württemberg Ger.
172 A2 Limbach Saarland Ger.
171 D5 Limbach Sachsen Ger.
171 D6 Limbach-Oberfrohna Ger.
195 L4 Limbadi Italy
95 F1 Limbang r. Sarawak Malaysia
252 □ Limbani Latvia
116 B3 Limbazi Latvia
207 H5 Limbdi Gujarat India
211 B8 Limbe Cameroon
211 B8 Limbe Malawi
93 B2 Limbo r. Sulawesi Utara Indon.
213 H3 Limbo Moz.
84 B3 Limbri N.T. Austr.
165 E3 Limburg prov. Belgium
164 E3 Limburg prov. Neth.
169 D5 Limburg an der Lahn Ger.
172 C2 Limburgerhof Ger.
214 D3 Lime Acres S. Africa
81 B7 Limehills South I. N.Z.
256 C3 Limeira Brazil
147 D5 Limerick Rep. of Ireland
147 C4 Limerick county Rep. of Ireland
233 A1 Limestone ME U.S.A.
147 A2 Limfjorden sea chan. Denmark
182 B3 Limia r. Spain
199 D4 Limin Chersonisou Kriti Greece
140 N2 Liminka Fin.
233 □H3 Limingmon Norway
160 J5 Limmared Sweden
140 N2 Limmka r. Fin.
164 D2 Limmen Neth.
84 C2 Limmen Bight b. N.T. Austr.
84 C2 Limmen Bight River r. N.T. Austr.
198 D2 Limni Greece
199 E2 Limnos i. Greece
160 D4 Limoges France
233 □H2 Limoges Ont. Can.
162 D3 Limoges France
242 D7 Limón Hond.
250 A4 Limón Costa Rica
244 D4 Limón Mex.
190 A3 Limone Piemonte Italy
191 F3 Limone sul Garda Italy
160 B3 Limonest France
161 C5 Limousin reg. France
162 D3 Limousin, Monts du hills France
160 D5 Limousin, Plateaux du hills France
161 C5 Limoux France
160 □ Limoges r. Senegal?
215 I2 Limpopo prov. S. Africa
215 I1 Limpopo r. S. Africa/Zimbabwe
214 D4 Limpopo prov. S. Africa
108 A2 Lin Guangxi China
209 C6 Linakhamari Rus. Fed.
140 Q1 Linakhamari Rus. Fed.
109 F2 Lin'an Zhejiang China
92 A3 Linapacan Strait Phil.
260 B4 Linares Chile
244 E3 Linares Mex.
183 F5 Linares Spain
187 F3 Linares de Mora Spain
182 E3 Linares de Riofrío Spain
192 A2 Linas, Monte mt. Sardegna Italy
95 G5 Linau Balui plat. Sarawak Malaysia
108 B3 Lincang Yunnan China
165 E4 Lincent Belgium
Lincheng Hainan China see Lingao
Lincheng Hunan China see Huitong
109 □7 Lincoln Arg.
261 F3 Lincoln Arg.
81 D5 Lincoln South I. N.Z.
149 H4 Lincoln Lincolnshire, England U.K.
240 B2 Lincoln CA U.S.A.
236 F3 Lincoln IL U.S.A.
233 □H2 Lincoln ME U.S.A.
227 F4 Lincoln MI U.S.A.
236 D3 Lincoln NE U.S.A.
233 G3 Lincoln NH U.S.A.

Lincoln to Loison
328

234 B2 Lincoln PA U.S.A.
238 A2 Lincoln City OR U.S.A.
232 B4 Lincoln Park MI U.S.A.
221 N1 Lincoln Sea Can./Greenland
149 I4 Lincolnshire admin. div. England U.K.
149 I4 Lincolnshire Wolds hills England U.K.
231 D5 Lincolnton GA U.S.A.
234 C3 Lincoln University PA U.S.A.
235 D2 Lincroft NJ U.S.A.
254 E5 Linda, Serra hills Brazil
171 D3 Lindau Sachsen-Anhalt Ger.
168 E1 Lindau Schleswig-Holstein Ger.
172 D4 Lindau (Bodensee) Ger.
164 E2 Linde r. Neth.
168 F1 Lindelse Denmark
85 G4 Lindeman Group is Qld Austr.
222 H5 Linden Alta Can.
169 D5 Linden Hessen Ger.
168 E1 Linden Schleswig-Holstein Ger.
251 G3 Linden Guyana
231 C5 Linden AL U.S.A.
240 G2 Linden CA U.S.A.
232 B3 Linden MI U.S.A.
235 D2 Linden NJ U.S.A.
231 C5 Linden TN U.S.A.
237 E5 Linden TX U.S.A.
170 D2 Lindenberg Brandenburg Ger.
170 E3 Lindenberg Brandenburg Ger.
171 F3 Lindenberg Brandenburg Ger.
172 D4 Lindenberg im Allgäu Ger.
172 C2 Lindenfels Ger.
226 A2 Linden Grove MN U.S.A.
234 D3 Lindenwold NJ U.S.A.
168 C3 Lindern (Oldenburg) Ger.
143 F2 Lindesberg Sweden
142 B2 Lindesnes c. Norway
168 E1 Lindewitt Ger.
151 G3 Lindfield West Sussex, England U.K.
169 E3 Lindhorst Ger.
208 E4 Lindi r. Dem. Rep. Congo
211 C7 Lindi Tanz.
211 C7 Lindi admin. reg. Tanz.
107 J2 Lindian Heilong. China
Lindisfarne i. England U.K. see Holy Island
81 B6 Lindis Peak South I. N.Z.
169 C4 Lindlar Ger.
215 F2 Lindley S. Africa
256 D5 Lindóia Brazil
142 E3 Lindome Sweden
107 H3 Lindong Nei Mongol China
182 B3 Lindoso Port.
170 D3 Lindow Ger.
157 G4 Lindre, Étang de l. France
233 □J1 Lindsay N.B. Can.
224 E4 Lindsay Ont. Can.
240 H3 Lindsay CA U.S.A.
238 F2 Lindsay MT U.S.A.
87 D5 Lindsay Gordon Lagoon salt flat W.A. Austr.
236 D4 Lindsborg KS U.S.A.
143 G3 Lindsdal Sweden
232 C6 Lindside WV U.S.A.
170 C3 Lindstedt Ger.
Lindum Lincolnshire, England U.K. see Lincoln
168 E3 Lindwedel Ger.
176 C2 Líně Czech Rep.
234 B3 Lineboro MD U.S.A.
266 I5 Line Islands S. Pacific Ocean
234 C2 Line Lexington PA U.S.A.
107 F4 Linfen Shanxi China
234 C2 Linfield PA U.S.A.
151 H3 Linford Thurrock, England U.K.
146 C4 Ling r. Scotland U.K.
114 D2 Lingamparti Andhra Prad. India
108 D5 Lingao Hainan China
161 B4 Lingas, Montagne du mt. France
92 B2 Lingayen Phil.
92 B2 Lingayen Gulf Phil.
107 F5 Lingbao Henan China
109 F1 Lingbi Anhui China
Lingcheng Guangxi China see Lingshan
Lingcheng Hainan China see Lingshui
Lingcheng Shandong China see Lingxian
108 D3 Lingchuan Guangxi China
107 G5 Lingchuan Shanxi China
215 F5 Lingelethu S. Africa
215 E5 Lingelihle S. Africa
168 C3 Lingen (Ems) Ger.
178 A3 Lingenau Austria
172 C2 Lingenfeld Ger.
151 G3 Lingfield Surrey, England U.K.
94 D3 Lingga i. Indon.
94 D3 Lingga, Kepulauan is Indon.
92 C5 Lingig Phil.
238 F3 Lingle WY U.S.A.
234 B2 Linglestown PA U.S.A.
84 D3 Lingnoonganee Island Qld Austr.
157 H4 Lingolsheim France
107 G4 Lingqiu Shanxi China
108 D4 Lingshan Guangxi China
107 F4 Lingshi Shanxi China
108 D5 Lingshui Hainan China
114 C2 Lingsugur Karnataka India
107 E5 Lingtai Gansu China
195 E5 Linguaglossa Sicilia Italy
206 B3 Linguère Senegal
108 D3 Lingui Guangxi China
192 B2 Linguizzetta Corse France
151 I2 Lingwood Norfolk, England U.K.
Lingxi Hunan China see Yongshun
Lingxian Hunan China see Yanling
107 H4 Lingxian Shandong China
109 E2 Lingxiang Hubei China
107 H3 Lingyuan Liaoning China
108 C3 Lingyun Guangxi China
111 B5 Lingzi Thang Plains l. Aksai Chin
107 I3 Linhai Liaoning China
109 G2 Linhai Zhejiang China
257 G3 Linhares Brazil
182 C4 Linhares Port.
107 E3 Linhe Nei Mongol China
174 F1 Linia Pol.
81 B6 Linidis Valley South I. N.Z.
233 □H1 Linière Que. Can.
174 G1 Liniewo Pol.
Linjiang Fujian China see Shanghang
101 C4 Linjiang Jilin China
172 C2 Linkenheim-Hochstetten Ger.
143 F2 Linköping Sweden
100 D3 Linkou Heilong. China
146 E3 Linksness Orkney, Scotland U.K.
138 D3 Linkuva Lith.
109 D2 Linli Hunan China
146 E6 Linlithgow West Lothian, Scotland U.K.
107 G4 Linlü Shan mt. Henan China
Linmingguan Hebei China see Yongnian
236 F4 Linn MO U.S.A.
237 D7 Linn TX U.S.A.
240 F1 Linn, Mount CA U.S.A.
142 D2 Linnekleppen hill Norway
233 □J1 Linneus ME U.S.A.
146 C5 Linnhe, Loch inlet Scotland U.K.
169 B5 Linnich Ger.
189 D8 Linosa, Isola di i. Sicilia Italy
138 E5 Linova Belarus
170 D2 Linow Ger.
107 G4 Linqing Shandong China
Linru Henan China see Ruzhou
256 C4 Lins Brazil
168 E3 Linsburg Ger.
108 C2 Linshui Sichuan China
246 □ Linstead Jamaica
213 □J5 Linta r. Madag.
106 D5 Lintan Gansu China
106 D5 Lintao Gansu China
190 E1 Linth r. Switz.
190 E2 Linthal Switz.
171 D3 Linthe Ger.
234 B3 Linthicum Heights MD U.S.A.
168 D2 Lintig Ger.
80 E4 Linton North I. N.Z.
151 H2 Linton Cambridgeshire, England U.K.
236 C2 Linton ND U.S.A.
107 F5 Lintong Shaanxi China
170 D3 Linum Ger.
234 D3 Linwood NJ U.S.A.
109 E3 Linwu Hunan China
163 A5 Linxe France
107 H3 Linxi Nei Mongol China
106 D5 Linxia Gansu China
Linxian Henan China see Linzhou
107 F4 Linxian Shanxi China
109 E2 Linxiang Hunan China
212 E3 Linyanti r. Botswana/Namibia
212 D3 Linyanti Swamp Namibia
107 H4 Linyi Shandong China
107 H5 Linyi Shandong China
107 F5 Linyi Shanxi China
109 E1 Linying Henan China
186 D3 Linyola Spain
179 F2 Linz Austria
169 C5 Linz am Rhein Ger.
106 D4 Linze Gansu China
107 G4 Linzhou Henan China
186 B2 Linzoáin Spain
136 C2 Lioboml' Ukr.
213 H2 Lioma Moz.
161 B6 Lion, Golfe du g. France
246 □ Lionel Town Jamaica
193 H4 Lioni Italy
Lions, Gulf of France see Lion, Golfe du
222 F5 Lions Bay B.C. Can.
227 G3 Lion's Head Ont. Can.
159 F2 Lion-sur-Mer France
163 C4 Liorac-sur-Louyre France
202 B6 Lioua Chad
92 B3 Lipa Phil.
175 I2 Lipa Pol.
177 J2 Lipany Slovakia
194 D4 Lipari Isole Lipari Italy
194 D4 Lipari, Isola i. Isole Lipari Italy
194 D4 Lipari, Isole is Italy
136 D3 Lipcani Moldova
175 H4 Lipce Reymontowskie Pol.
140 O3 Liperi Fin.
139 L5 Lipetsk Rus. Fed.
139 L5 Lipetskaya Oblast' admin. div. Rus. Fed.
Lipetsk Oblast admin. div. Rus. Fed. see Lipetskaya Oblast'
252 D5 Lipez, Cordillera de mts Bol.
151 G3 Liphook Hampshire, England U.K.
174 C2 Lipiany Pol.
139 K1 Lipin Bor Rus. Fed.
108 D3 Liping Guizhou China
175 J6 Lipinki Pol.
174 D4 Lipinki Łużyckie Pol.
174 F2 Lipka Pol.
Lipkany Moldova see Lipcani
139 K5 Lipki Rus. Fed.
174 D3 Lipki Wielkie Pol.
196 E4 Lipljan Kosovo, Srbija Yugo.
139 I2 Lipnaya Gorka Rus. Fed.
175 H2 Lipnica Kujawsko-Pomorskie Pol.
174 F2 Lipnica Pomorskie Pol.
175 J5 Lipnik Pol.
175 H6 Lipnika Wielka Pol.
177 G2 Lipník nad Bečvou Czech Rep.
175 H3 Lipno Kujawsko-Pomorskie Pol.
174 E4 Lipno Wielkopolskie Pol.
163 B4 Liposthey France
197 E2 Lipova Romania
177 L6 Lipovei, Dealurile hills Romania
135 I6 Lipovka Volgogradskaya Oblast' Rus. Fed.
137 K2 Lipovka Voronezhskaya Oblast' Rus. Fed.
197 F3 Lipovu Romania
175 J2 Lipowiec Pol.
169 B4 Lippe r. Ger.
164 F1 Lippenhuizen Neth.
169 E4 Lippoldsberg (Wahlsburg) Ger.
169 D4 Lippstadt Ger.
237 C4 Lipscomb TX U.S.A.
175 L2 Lipsk Pol.
175 J4 Lipsko Pol.
Lipsoí i. Greece see Leipsoi
177 G2 Liptál Czech Rep.
207 F3 Liptougou Burkina
177 I2 Liptovská Kokava Slovakia
177 I2 Liptovská Mara, Vodná nádrž resr Slovakia
177 I3 Liptovská Osada Slovakia
177 J3 Liptovská Teplička Slovakia
177 I2 Liptovský Hrádok Slovakia
177 I2 Liptovský Mikuláš Slovakia
83 F4 Liptrap, Cape Vic. Austr.
108 D3 Lipu Guangxi China
195 G3 Lipuda r. Italy
174 F1 Lipusz Pol.
210 B4 Lira Uganda
159 E4 Liré France
193 F3 Liri r. Italy
210 A2 Liri, Jebel el mt. Sudan
190 E2 Liro r. Italy
196 E5 Lis Albania
197 G3 Lisa Romania
147 C3 Lisacul Rep. of Ireland
120 E1 Lisakovsk Kazakh.
208 D4 Lisala Dem. Rep. Congo
213 □J4 L'Isalo, Massif de mts Madag.
148 D3 Lisbane Northern Ireland U.K.
147 D2 Lisbellaw Northern Ireland U.K.
184 A2 Lisboa Port.
184 A1 Lisboa admin. dist. Port.
Lisbon Port. see Lisboa
226 C5 Lisbon IL U.S.A.
234 A3 Lisbon MD U.S.A.
233 □H2 Lisbon ME U.S.A.
236 D2 Lisbon ND U.S.A.
233 H2 Lisbon NH U.S.A.
232 C4 Lisbon OH U.S.A.
233 □H3 Lisbon Falls ME U.S.A.
147 E2 Lisburn Northern Ireland U.K.
147 B4 Liscannor Rep. of Ireland
147 B4 Liscannor Bay Rep. of Ireland
147 B3 Liscarney Rep. of Ireland
147 C4 Liscarroll Rep. of Ireland
192 B3 Liscia r. Sardegna Italy
192 B4 Liscoi r. Sardegna Italy
147 B3 Lisdoonvarna Rep. of Ireland
147 D3 Lisduff Rep. of Ireland
197 F5 Lisec mt. Macedonia
142 D3 Liseleje Denmark
147 C4 Lisgarode Rep. of Ireland
147 C5 Lisgoold Rep. of Ireland
Lishan Shaanxi China see Lintong
109 G3 Lishan Taiwan
136 E2 Lishchyn Ukr.
108 B3 Lishe Jiang r. Yunnan China
Lishi Jiangxi China see Dingnan
107 F4 Lishi Shanxi China
100 C4 Lishu Jilin China
109 F2 Lishui Jiangsu China
109 F2 Lishui Zhejiang China
108 D2 Li Shui r. China
175 J5 Lisia Góra Pol.
75 H2 Lisianski Island HI U.S.A.
Lisichansk Ukr. see Lysychans'k
174 F5 Lisięcice Pol.
159 G2 Lisieux France
139 H1 Lisiy Nos Rus. Fed.
150 C4 Liskeard Cornwall, England U.K.
135 G6 Liski Rus. Fed.
177 I2 Lisková Slovakia
162 C3 Lisle France
147 E2 Lislea Northern Ireland U.K.
156 C3 L'Isle-Adam France
160 D3 L'Isle-d'Abeau France
163 C5 L'Isle-de-Noé France
162 C3 L'Isle-d'Espagnac France
163 C5 L'Isle-en-Dodon France
163 D5 L'Isle-Jourdain France
162 C2 L'Isle-Jourdain France
161 D5 L'Isle-sur-la-Sorgue France
160 E1 L'Isle-sur-le-Doubs France
160 C1 L'Isle-sur-Serein France
163 D5 Lisle-sur-Tarn France
83 H2 Lismore N.S.W. Austr.
81 C5 Lismore South I. N.Z.
147 D4 Lismore Rep. of Ireland
146 C5 Lismore i. Scotland U.K.
147 C4 Lisnagry Rep. of Ireland
147 D4 Lisnakill Rep. of Ireland
147 E2 Lisnamuck Northern Ireland U.K.
147 D2 Lisnarrick Northern Ireland U.K.
147 D2 Lisnaskea Northern Ireland U.K.
136 E4 Lisne Ukr.
160 D1 Lison r. France
176 D2 Lišov Czech Rep.
147 C5 Lispatrick Rep. of Ireland
147 A4 Lispole Rep. of Ireland
147 D4 Lisronagh Rep. of Ireland
148 B4 Lisryan Rep. of Ireland
128 D4 Liss mt. Saudi Arabia
151 G3 Liss Hampshire, England U.K.
Lissa Croatia see Vis
Lissa Wielkopolskie Pol. see Leszno
163 D4 Lissac-et-Mouret France
148 C3 Lissan Northern Ireland U.K.
164 D2 Lisse Neth.
147 B4 Lisselton Rep. of Ireland
169 B5 Lissendorf Ger.
142 E1 Lisskogsbrändan Sweden
190 E3 Lissone Italy
147 B4 Lissycasey Rep. of Ireland
168 D1 List Ger.
142 B2 Lista pen. Norway
143 F4 Listed Bornholm Denmark
263 K1 Lister, Mount Antarctica
147 D4 Listerlin Rep. of Ireland
148 D3 Listooder Northern Ireland U.K.
224 D5 Listowel Ont. Can.
147 B4 Listowel Rep. of Ireland
85 F5 Listowel Downs Qld Austr.
162 B3 Listrac-Médoc France
121 K2 Listvyaga, Khrebet mts Kazakh./Rus. Fed.
174 G4 Liswarta r. Pol.
150 E3 Liswerry Newport, Wales U.K.
175 H5 Liszki Pol.
174 F2 Liszkowo Pol.
140 K3 Lit Sweden
108 D4 Litang Guangxi China
108 B2 Litang Sichuan China
108 B2 Litang Qu r. Sichuan China
251 H4 Litani r. Fr. Guiana/Suriname
128 B3 Līṭānī r. Lebanon
176 D2 Litavka r. Czech Rep.
240 G1 Litchfield CA U.S.A.
235 E1 Litchfield CT U.S.A.
236 F4 Litchfield IL U.S.A.
226 E4 Litchfield MI U.S.A.
236 E2 Litchfield MN U.S.A.
232 B4 Litchfield OH U.S.A.
234 E1 Litchfield County county CT U.S.A.
177 G4 Litér Hungary
163 A4 Lit-et-Mixe France
164 E3 Lith Neth.
149 G4 Litherland Merseyside, England U.K.
83 G3 Lithgow N.S.W. Austr.
138 D4 Lithuania country Europe
188 E2 Litija Slovenia
227 I5 Lititz PA U.S.A.
177 I3 Litke Hungary
198 C1 Litochoro Greece
176 D1 Litoměřice Czech Rep.
176 F2 Litomyšl Czech Rep.
184 B1 Litoral reg. Port.
176 G2 Litovel Czech Rep.
100 E2 Litovko Rus. Fed.
Litovskaya S.S.R. country Europe see Lithuania
179 G2 Litschau Austria
190 D1 Littau Switz.
237 E6 Little r. LA U.S.A.
237 E5 Little r. OK U.S.A.
237 D6 Little r. TX U.S.A.
231 E7 Little Abaco i. Bahamas
224 D3 Little Abitibi r. Ont. Can.
Little Aden Yemen see 'Adan as Sughra
115 G4 Little Andaman i. Andaman & Nicobar Is India
Little Ararat mt. Turkey see Küçük Ağrı Dağı
236 D4 Little Arkansas r. KS U.S.A.
231 E7 Little Bahama Bank sea feature Bahamas
80 E2 Little Barrier i. North I. N.Z.
Little Belt sea chan. Denmark see Lille Bælt
238 E2 Little Belt Mountains MT U.S.A.
238 F2 Little Bighorn r. MT U.S.A.
Little Bitter Lake Egypt see Murrat el Sughra, Buheirat
236 D4 Little Blue r. KS U.S.A.
149 G4 Littleborough Greater Manchester, England U.K.
222 H5 Little Bow r. Alta Can.
222 H3 Little Buffalo r. N.W.T. Can.
246 B3 Little Cayman i. Cayman Is
223 M3 Little Churchill r. Man. Can.
151 I3 Little Clacton Essex, England U.K.
97 A4 Little Coco Island Cocos Is
241 L3 Little Colorado r. AZ U.S.A.
151 H4 Little Common East Sussex, England U.K.
234 C3 Little Creek DE U.S.A.
241 K3 Little Creek Peak UT U.S.A.
148 E2 Little Cumbrae i. Scotland U.K.
224 D4 Little Current Ont. Can.
224 C3 Little Current r. Ont. Can.
150 D4 Little Dart r. England U.K.
150 E3 Littledean Gloucestershire, England U.K.
151 H2 Little Downham Cambridgeshire, England U.K.
246 D2 Little Exuma i. Bahamas
236 E2 Little Falls MN U.S.A.
233 F3 Little Falls NY U.S.A.
146 D4 Littleferry Highland, Scotland U.K.
241 K3 Littlefield AZ U.S.A.
237 C5 Littlefield TX U.S.A.
215 F5 Little Fish r. S. Africa
226 A1 Little Fork MN U.S.A.
226 A1 Little Fork r. MN U.S.A.
222 F5 Little Fort B.C. Can.
Little Ganges atoll Cook Is see Rakahanga
234 C2 Little Gap PA U.S.A.
223 M4 Little Grand Rapids Man. Can.
151 G4 Littlehampton West Sussex, England U.K.
246 D2 Little Inagua Island Bahamas
232 C5 Little Kanawha r. WV U.S.A.
214 C5 Little Karoo plat. S. Africa
240 I4 Little Lake CA U.S.A.
146 C4 Little Loch Broom inlet Scotland U.K.
225 I3 Little Mecatina r. Newfoundland/Québec Can.
232 A5 Little Miami r. OH U.S.A.
146 E4 Littlemill Highland, Scotland U.K.
146 A4 Little Minch sea chan. Scotland U.K.
151 G3 Little Missenden Buckinghamshire, England U.K.
236 C2 Little Missouri r. ND U.S.A.
151 F3 Littlemore Oxfordshire, England U.K.
232 C5 Little Muskingum r. OH U.S.A.
115 G5 Little Nicobar i. Andaman & Nicobar Is India
151 I3 Little Oakley Essex, England U.K.
215 G1 Little Olifants r. S. Africa
151 H2 Little Ouse r. England U.K.
226 D1 Little Pic r. Ont. Can.
234 A1 Little Pine Creek r. PA U.S.A.
234 A3 Little Pipe Creek r. MD U.S.A.
151 H2 Littleport Cambridgeshire, England U.K.
238 F2 Little Powder r. MT U.S.A.
222 D2 Little Rancheria r. B.C. Can.
116 B5 Little Rann marsh Gujarat India
237 F5 Little Red r. AR U.S.A.
222 H3 Little Red River Alta Can.
81 D5 Little River South I. N.Z.
231 E5 Little River SC U.S.A.
237 E5 Little Rock AR U.S.A.
240 I4 Littlerock CA U.S.A.
87 C4 Little Sandy Desert W.A. Austr.
246 D1 Little San Salvador i. Bahamas
236 D3 Little Sioux r. IA U.S.A.
222 G4 Little Smoky Alta Can.
222 G4 Little Smoky r. Alta Can.
238 E3 Little Snake r. CO U.S.A.
151 H4 Littlestone-on-Sea Kent, England U.K.
234 A3 Littlestown PA U.S.A.
247 □5 Little Tobago i. Trin. and Tob.
148 B5 Littleton Rep. of Ireland
151 F3 Littleton Hampshire, England U.K.
226 B5 Littleton IL U.S.A.
233 H2 Littleton NH U.S.A.
232 C5 Littleton WV U.S.A.
226 E3 Little Traverse Bay MI U.S.A.
232 D3 Little Valley NY U.S.A.
236 F4 Little Wabash r. IL U.S.A.
81 D4 Little Wanganui South I. N.Z.
236 C3 Little White r. SD U.S.A.
237 D5 Little Wichita r. TX U.S.A.
238 E3 Little Wind r. WY U.S.A.
238 D3 Little Wood r. ID U.S.A.
Little Zab r. Iraq see Zāb aş Şaghīr, Nahr az
143 J1 Littoinen Fin.
207 H5 Littoral prov. Cameroon
211 B8 Litunde Moz.
176 C1 Litvínov Czech Rep.
136 E3 Lityn Ukr.
173 F2 Litzendorf Ger.
107 H3 Liu r. China
107 I3 Liu r. China
108 C1 Liuba Shaanxi China
96 E1 Liucheng Guangxi China
109 F2 Liucheng Zhejiang China
108 C3 Liuchong He r. Guizhou China
Liuchow Guangxi China see Liuzhou
107 I3 Liugu r. China
100 C4 Liuhe Jilin China
109 D2 Liujiachang Hubei China
108 D3 Liujiang Guangxi China
Liujiaxia Gansu China see Yongjing
Liulin Gansu China see Jonê
Liupai Guangxi China see Tian'e
106 E5 Liupan Shan mts China
Liupanshui Guizhou China see Lupanshui
213 H2 Liupo Moz.
106 B3 Liushuquan Xinjiang China
209 D8 Liuwa Plain Zambia
109 E2 Liuyang Hunan China
109 E2 Liuyang He r. China
Liuzhangzhen Shanxi China see Yuanqu
108 D3 Liuzhou Guangxi China
177 K5 Livada Arad Romania
197 F2 Livada Satu Mare Romania
198 C1 Livadi Thessalia Greece
198 C1 Livadia Kentriki Makedonia Greece
100 E4 Livadiya Rus. Fed.
198 C2 Livanates Greece
138 F3 Līvāni Latvia
188 F3 Livanjsko Polje plain Bos.-Herz.
159 G2 Livarot France
138 D3 Livbērze Latvia
137 J2 Livenka Rus. Fed.
191 H3 Livenza r. Italy
240 G2 Live Oak CA U.S.A.
231 D6 Live Oak FL U.S.A.
157 G4 Liverdun France
86 E3 Liveringa W.A. Austr.
240 G3 Livermore CA U.S.A.
239 F6 Livermore, Mount TX U.S.A.
233 □H2 Livermore Falls ME U.S.A.
163 D4 Livernon France
83 G3 Liverpool N.S.W. Austr.
84 C2 Liverpool r. N.T. Austr.
225 H4 Liverpool N.S. Can.
149 G4 Liverpool Merseyside, England U.K.
233 E3 Liverpool NY U.S.A.
234 B2 Liverpool PA U.S.A.
149 F4 Liverpool Bay England U.K.
83 G2 Liverpool Plains N.S.W. Austr.
83 G2 Liverpool Range mts N.S.W. Austr.
149 H4 Liversedge West Yorkshire, England U.K.
190 F2 Livigno Italy
243 H6 Livingston Guat.
146 E6 Livingston West Lothian, Scotland U.K.
237 F5 Livingston AL U.S.A.
240 G3 Livingston CA U.S.A.
232 A6 Livingston KY U.S.A.
237 F6 Livingston LA U.S.A.
238 E2 Livingston MT U.S.A.
235 D2 Livingston NJ U.S.A.
237 E6 Livingston TX U.S.A.
237 E6 Livingston, Lake TX U.S.A.
209 E9 Livingstone Zambia
211 B7 Livingstone Mountains Tanz.
211 B7 Livingstonia Malawi
262 T2 Livingston Island Antarctica
233 F4 Livingston Manor NY U.S.A.
81 B6 Livingston Mountains South I. N.Z.
188 F4 Livno Bos.-Herz.
139 K5 Livny Rus. Fed.
140 O2 Livo r. Fin.
227 F4 Livonia MI U.S.A.
232 E3 Livonia NY U.S.A.
190 F5 Livorno Italy
190 F5 Livorno prov. Toscana Italy
190 D3 Livorno Ferraris Italy
160 B3 Livradois, Monts du mts France
216 □1b Livramento São Miguel Azores
254 E5 Livramento do Brumado Brazil
161 C4 Livron-sur-Drôme France
175 J3 Liw Pol.
125 G2 Liwā Oman
211 C7 Liwale Tanz.
175 J3 Liwiec r. Pol.
211 B8 Liwonde Malawi
Liwu Hebei China see Lixian
106 E5 Lixian Gansu China
107 G4 Lixian Hebei China
109 D2 Lixian Hunan China
108 B2 Lixian Sichuan China
109 F1 Lixin Anhui China
157 G3 Lixing-lès-St-Avold France
198 B2 Lixouri Ionioi Nisoi Greece
Lixus Morocco see Larache
198 B1 Liyadero Dytiki Makedonia Greece
109 F2 Liyang Jiangsu China
Liyuan Hunan China see Sangzhi
182 B5 Liz r. Port.
150 B5 Lizard Cornwall, England U.K.
254 D4 Lizarda Brazil
85 F2 Lizard Island Qld Austr.
150 B5 Lizard Point England U.K.
Lizarra Spain see Estella
183 H2 Lizarraga Spain
232 C5 Lizemores WV U.S.A.
137 J2 Lizinovka Rus. Fed.
108 B2 Liziping Sichuan China
162 C3 Lizonne r. France
156 D3 Lizy-sur-Ourcq France
195 H2 Lizzanello Italy
195 G2 Lizzano Italy
196 E3 Ljig Srbija Yugo.
142 B2 Ljomsnuten mt. Norway
188 F3 Ljubija Bos.-Herz.
196 D4 Ljubišnja mts Yugo.
188 E2 Ljubljana Slovenia
179 F4 Ljubljana airport Slovenia
179 F4 Ljubljanica r. Slovenia
196 D3 Ljubovija Srbija Yugo.
188 F4 Ljubuški Bos.-Herz.
143 H3 Ljugarn Gotland Sweden
140 L3 Ljungå Sweden
141 L3 Ljungan r. Sweden
141 L3 Ljungaverk Sweden
143 E3 Ljungby Sweden
143 G3 Ljungbyån r. Sweden
140 K3 Ljungdalen Sweden
143 F2 Ljungsbro Sweden
142 D2 Ljungskile Sweden
141 L3 Ljusdal Sweden
143 F2 Ljusfallshammar Sweden
142 E1 Ljusnan r. Sweden
141 L3 Ljusnan r. Sweden
141 L3 Ljusne Sweden
188 F2 Ljutomer Slovenia
186 F3 Llagostera Spain
260 B6 Llaima, Volcán vol. Chile
261 G2 Llambí Campbell Arg.
150 C2 Llanaelhaearn Gwynedd, Wales U.K.
150 D2 Llanarmon Dyffryn Ceiriog Wrexham, Wales U.K.
150 C2 Llanarth Ceredigion, Wales U.K.
150 C3 Llanarthney Carmarthenshire, Wales U.K.
150 D1 Llanasa Flintshire, Wales U.K.
150 C2 Llanbadarn Fawr Ceredigion, Wales U.K.
150 C1 Llanbadrig Isle of Anglesey, Wales U.K.
Llanbedr Ceredigion, Wales U.K. see Lampeter
150 C2 Llanbedr Gwynedd, Wales U.K.
150 C2 Llanbedrog Gwynedd, Wales U.K.
150 C1 Llanberis Gwynedd, Wales U.K.
150 D2 Llanbister Powys, Wales U.K.
150 D2 Llanbrynmair Powys, Wales U.K.
186 G2 Llançà Spain
260 C4 Llancanelo, Salina salt flat Arg.
150 C2 Llandanwg Gwynedd, Wales U.K.
150 C3 Llanddarog Carmarthenshire, Wales U.K.
150 C1 Llanddeiniolen Gwynedd, Wales U.K.
150 D2 Llandderfel Gwynedd, Wales U.K.
150 C3 Llanddowror Carmarthenshire, Wales U.K.
150 D3 Llandeilo Carmarthenshire, Wales U.K.
150 E3 Llandinabo Herefordshire, England U.K.
150 D2 Llandinam Powys, Wales U.K.
150 C3 Llandissilio Pembrokeshire, Wales U.K.
150 D3 Llandovery Carmarthenshire, Wales U.K.
150 D2 Llandrillo Denbighshire, Wales U.K.
150 D2 Llandrindod Wells Powys, Wales U.K.
150 D1 Llandudno Conwy, Wales U.K.
150 C1 Llandwrog Gwynedd, Wales U.K.
150 C3 Llandybie Carmarthenshire, Wales U.K.
150 C2 Llandysul Ceredigion, Wales U.K.
150 C3 Llanegwad Carmarthenshire, Wales U.K.
150 C1 Llaneilian Isle of Anglesey, Wales U.K.
150 C3 Llanelli Carmarthenshire, Wales U.K.
150 D2 Llanelltyd Gwynedd, Wales U.K.
150 D3 Llanelly Monmouthshire, Wales U.K.
Llanelwy Denbighshire, Wales U.K. see St Asaph
150 C1 Llanerchymedd Isle of Anglesey, Wales U.K.
183 F1 Llanes Spain
150 C1 Llanfaelog Isle of Anglesey, Wales U.K.
150 D2 Llanfair Caereinion Powys, Wales U.K.
150 D1 Llanfairfechan Conwy, Wales U.K.
150 C1 Llanfairpwllgwyngyll Isle of Anglesey, Wales U.K.
150 D1 Llanfair Talhaiarn Conwy, Wales U.K.
150 C1 Llanfair-yn-Neubwll Isle of Anglesey, Wales U.K.
150 C2 Llanfarian Ceredigion, Wales U.K.
150 C2 Llanfihangel-ar-Arth Carmarthenshire, Wales U.K.
150 D2 Llanfyllin Powys, Wales U.K.
150 D1 Llanfynydd Flintshire, Wales U.K.
150 D2 Llangadfan Powys, Wales U.K.
150 D3 Llangadog Carmarthenshire, Wales U.K.
150 C1 Llangefni Isle of Anglesey, Wales U.K.
150 C2 Llangeler Carmarthenshire, Wales U.K.
150 C2 Llangelynin Gwynedd, Wales U.K.
150 C3 Llangendeirne Carmarthenshire, Wales U.K.
150 D1 Llangernyw Conwy, Wales U.K.
150 C1 Llangoed Isle of Anglesey, Wales U.K.
150 D2 Llangollen Denbighshire, Wales U.K.
150 C2 Llangranog Ceredigion, Wales U.K.
150 C1 Llangristiolus Isle of Anglesey, Wales U.K.
150 C3 Llangunnor Carmarthenshire, Wales U.K.
150 D2 Llangurig Powys, Wales U.K.
150 C3 Llangwm Pembrokeshire, Wales U.K.
150 D3 Llangynidr Powys, Wales U.K.
150 D3 Llanharan Rhondda Cynon Taff, Wales U.K.
150 D2 Llanidloes Powys, Wales U.K.
150 C2 Llanilar Ceredigion, Wales U.K.
150 D3 Llanishen Cardiff, Wales U.K.
150 D2 Llanllwchaiarn Powys, Wales U.K.
150 C1 Llanllyfni Gwynedd, Wales U.K.
150 C3 Llannon Carmarthenshire, Wales U.K.
150 C2 Llannor Wales U.K.
242 C2 Llano Mex.
237 D6 Llano TX U.S.A.
237 D6 Llano r. TX U.S.A.
237 C5 Llano Estacado plain New Mexico/Texas U.S.A.
150 C2 Llanon Ceredigion, Wales U.K.
250 D3 Llanos plain Col./Venez.
259 B6 Llanquihue, Lago l. Chile
150 D2 Llanrhaeadr-ym-Mochnant Powys, Wales U.K.
150 C3 Llanrhidian Swansea, Wales U.K.
150 C2 Llanrhystud Ceredigion, Wales U.K.
150 C1 Llanrug Gwynedd, Wales U.K.
150 D3 Llanrumney Cardiff, Wales U.K.
150 D1 Llanrwst Conwy, Wales U.K.
Llansá Spain see Llançà
150 D1 Llansannffraid Glan Conwy Conwy, Wales U.K.
150 D1 Llansannan Conwy, Wales U.K.
150 C2 Llansawel Carmarthenshire, Wales U.K.
Llansteffan Carmarthenshire, Wales U.K. see Llanstephan
150 C3 Llanstephan Carmarthenshire, Wales U.K.
150 D3 Llanthony Monmouthshire, Wales U.K.
150 D3 Llantilio Pertholey Monmouthshire, Wales U.K.
150 E3 Llantrisant Monmouthshire, Wales U.K.
150 D3 Llantrisant Rhondda Cynon Taff, Wales U.K.
150 D3 Llantwit Major Vale of Glamorgan, Wales U.K.
150 D2 Llanuwchllyn Gwynedd, Wales U.K.
150 D2 Llanwddyn Powys, Wales U.K.
150 C2 Llanwenog Ceredigion, Wales U.K.
150 C1 Llanwnda Gwynedd, Wales U.K.
150 D2 Llanwnog Powys, Wales U.K.
150 D3 Llanwrda Carmarthenshire, Wales U.K.
150 D2 Llanwrtyd Wells Powys, Wales U.K.
150 C2 Llanybydder Carmarthenshire, Wales U.K.
Llanymddyfri Carmarthenshire, Wales U.K. see Llandovery
150 C1 Llanynghenedl Isle of Anglesey, Wales U.K.
150 C2 Llanystumdwy Gwynedd, Wales U.K.
186 D3 Llardecans Spain
252 A2 Llata Peru
187 C5 Llaurí Spain
186 E2 Llavorsí Spain
150 D1 Llay Wrexham, Wales U.K.
260 B3 Llay-Llay Chile
150 D2 Lledrod Ceredigion, Wales U.K.
186 D3 Lleida Spain
186 E2 Lleida prov. Cataluña Spain
184 D2 Llera Spain
245 E2 Llera de Canales Mex.
184 D2 Llerena Spain
150 C2 Lleyn Peninsula Wales U.K.
252 C4 Llica Bol.
187 C5 Lliria Spain
186 E2 Llívia Spain
186 E3 Llobregat r. Spain
186 E3 Llobregós r. Spain
183 H1 Llodio Spain
260 B3 Llolleo Chile
186 E3 Llorenç del Penedès Spain
186 F3 Lloret de Mar Spain
187 C5 Llosa de Ranes Spain
187 F5 Lloseta Spain
85 E2 Lloyd Bay Qld Austr.
222 E3 Lloyd George, Mount B.C. Can.
235 E2 Lloyd Harbor NY U.S.A.
223 I4 Lloydminster Alta Can.
187 G5 Llubí Spain
Lluchmayor Spain see Llucmajor
187 F5 Llucmajor Spain
252 C6 Llullaillaco, Volcán vol. Chile
150 D2 Llyswen Powys, Wales U.K.
174 G2 Lniano Pol.
165 B4 Lo Belgium
96 D2 Lô r. China/Vietnam
Lo i. Vanuatu see Loh
252 C5 Loa r. Chile
241 L2 Loa UT U.S.A.
95 G3 Loakulu Kalimantan Timur Indon.
256 A3 Loanda Brazil
146 E6 Loanhead Midlothian, Scotland U.K.
190 D4 Loano Italy
146 D6 Loans South Ayrshire, Scotland U.K.
186 C2 Loarre Spain
92 C4 Loay Phil.
139 J3 Lob' r. Rus. Fed.
175 M5 Lobachivka Ukr.
134 J4 Loban' r. Rus. Fed.
139 L5 Lobanovo Rus. Fed.
185 F3 Lobatejo mt. Spain
212 E5 Lobatse Botswana
171 F4 Löbau Ger.
208 C3 Lobaye pref. C.A.R.
208 C4 Lobaye r. C.A.R.
161 F4 Lobbie, Cima delle mt. Italy
171 C4 Löbejün Ger.
171 D4 Löbenberg hill Ger.
186 B2 Lobera de Onsella Spain
261 H6 Loberia Arg.
174 D2 Łobez Pol.
78 □3b Lobikaere i. Majuro Marshall Is
164 F3 Lobith Neth.
209 B8 Lobito Angola
250 A6 Lobitos Peru
170 D1 Löbnitz Ger.
171 D4 Löbnitz Ger.
139 K3 Lobnya Rus. Fed.
180 C3 Lobón Spain
261 H4 Lobos Arg.
216 □3b Lobos i. Canary Is
185 H3 Lobos mt. Spain
250 A6 Lobos de Afuera, Islas is Peru
250 A6 Lobos de Tierra, Isla i. Peru
Lobositz Czech Rep. see Lovosice
137 H3 Loboykivka Ukr.
171 D4 Lobstädt Ger.
171 D3 Loburg Ger.
81 D5 Loburn South I. N.Z.
174 F2 Łobżenica Pol.
190 C3 Locana Italy
190 D2 Locarno Switz.
169 E3 Loccum (Rehburg-Loccum) Ger.
192 B5 Loceri Sardegna Italy
146 D5 Lochaber mts Scotland U.K.
146 C5 Lochailort Highland, Scotland U.K.
146 C5 Lochaline Highland, Scotland U.K.
227 E1 Lochalsh Ont. Can.
146 C7 Lochans Dumfries and Galloway, Scotland U.K.
146 E6 Locharbriggs Dumfries and Galloway, Scotland U.K.
178 A3 Lochau Austria
146 C5 Lochawe Argyll and Bute, Scotland U.K.
146 D5 Lochay r. Scotland U.K.
Loch Baghasdail Western Isles, Scotland U.K. see Lochboisdale
146 A4 Lochboisdale Western Isles, Scotland U.K.
146 C5 Lochbuie Argyll and Bute, Scotland U.K.
146 C4 Lochcarron Highland, Scotland U.K.
146 C5 Lochdon Argyll and Bute, Scotland U.K.
146 D5 Lochearnhead Stirling, Scotland U.K.
164 F2 Lochem Neth.
178 E2 Lochen Austria
146 D4 Lochend Highland, Scotland U.K.
162 C1 Loches France
Loch Garman Rep. of Ireland see Wexford
146 E5 Lochgelly Fife, Scotland U.K.
146 C5 Lochgilphead Argyll and Bute, Scotland U.K.
146 D5 Lochgoilhead Argyll and Bute, Scotland U.K.
81 B7 Lochiel South I. N.Z.
215 H2 Lochiel S. Africa
146 C3 Lochinver Highland, Scotland U.K.
146 E6 Lochmaben Dumfries and Galloway, Scotland U.K.
146 A4 Lochmaddy Western Isles, Scotland U.K.
146 E5 Lochnagar mt. Scotland U.K.
Loch nam Madadh Western Isles, Scotland U.K. see Lochmaddy
176 C2 Lochovice Czech Rep.
175 J3 Łochów Pol.
146 C6 Lochranza North Ayrshire, Scotland U.K.
165 C3 Lochristi Belgium
238 D2 Lochsa r. ID U.S.A.
146 A4 Loch Sgioport Western Isles, Scotland U.K.
146 D6 Lochwinnoch Renfrewshire, Scotland U.K.
146 D5 Lochy, Loch l. Scotland U.K.
82 C3 Lock S.A. Austr.
232 B5 Lockbourne OH U.S.A.
232 E3 Locke NY U.S.A.
240 G2 Lockeford CA U.S.A.
179 H3 Lockenhaus Austria
146 E6 Lockerbie Dumfries and Galloway, Scotland U.K.
86 B4 Locker Point W.A. Austr.
83 F3 Lockhart N.S.W. Austr.
237 D6 Lockhart TX U.S.A.
85 E2 Lockhart River Qld Austr.
232 E4 Lock Haven PA U.S.A.
150 E3 Locking North Somerset, England U.K.
170 F2 Löcknitz Ger.
170 C2 Löcknitz r. Ger.
232 D3 Lockport NY U.S.A.
151 F4 Locks Heath Hampshire, England U.K.
149 I3 Lockton North Yorkshire, England U.K.
158 C4 Locmaria France
158 B3 Locmaria-Plouzané France
158 D4 Locmariaquer France
158 D4 Locminé France
158 C4 Locmiquélic France
97 D5 Lôc Ninh Vietnam
158 C4 Locoal-Mendon France
193 H3 Locone r. Italy
195 G2 Locorotondo Italy
158 C3 Locquirec France
195 F4 Locri Italy
158 B3 Locronan France
158 B4 Loctudy France
192 B4 Loculi Sardegna Italy
252 C4 Locumba r. Peru
235 D2 Locust NJ U.S.A.
235 E2 Locust Valley NY U.S.A.
128 B4 Lod Israel
171 C4 Lödderitz Ger.
170 F1 Loddin Ger.
150 D4 Loddiswell Devon, England U.K.
83 E3 Loddon r. Vic. Austr.
151 I2 Loddon Norfolk, England U.K.
192 B4 Lodè Sardegna Italy
138 E3 Lode Latvia
176 D1 Loděnice Czech Rep.
171 C4 Lodersleben Ger.
161 B5 Lodève France
139 I1 Lodeynoye Pole Rus. Fed.
222 B3 Lodge, Mount Alaska/B.C. Can./U.S.A.
223 I5 Lodge Creek r. Can./U.S.A.
238 F2 Lodge Grass MT U.S.A.
236 C3 Lodgepole Creek r. WY U.S.A.
116 D5 Lodhikheda Madh. Prad. India
123 G4 Lodhran Pak.
190 E3 Lodi Italy
190 E3 Lodi prov. Lombardia Italy
240 G2 Lodi CA U.S.A.
235 D2 Lodi NJ U.S.A.
232 B4 Lodi OH U.S.A.
226 C4 Lodi WI U.S.A.
140 K2 Løding Norway
140 K1 Lødingen Norway
190 E3 Lodi Vecchio Italy
209 D5 Lodja Dem. Rep. Congo
Lodomeria Rus. Fed. see Vladimir
183 H2 Lodosa Spain
116 B5 Lodrani Gujarat India
210 B4 Lodwar Kenya
175 H6 Łodygowice Pol.
175 H4 Łódź Pol.
175 H4 Łódzkie prov. Pol.
183 G4 Loeches Spain
96 C3 Loei Thai.
164 F2 Loenen Gelderland Neth.
164 E2 Loenen Utrecht Neth.
215 E5 Loerie S. Africa
214 B4 Loeriesfontein S. Africa
169 C5 Löf Ger.
178 D3 Lofer Austria
172 C4 Löffingen Ger.
140 K1 Lofoten is Norway
141 K3 Lofsdalen Sweden
215 E4 Lofter S. Africa
149 I3 Loftus Redcar and Cleveland, England U.K.
87 C5 Lofty Range hills W.A. Austr.
135 H6 Log Rus. Fed.
207 F3 Loga Niger
214 E1 Logageng S. Africa
146 D6 Logan East Ayrshire, Scotland U.K.
236 E3 Logan IA U.S.A.
237 C5 Logan NM U.S.A.
232 B5 Logan OH U.S.A.
238 E3 Logan UT U.S.A.
232 C6 Logan WV U.S.A.
222 A2 Logan, Mount Y.T. Can.
238 B1 Logan, Mount WA U.S.A.
85 F4 Logan Creek r. Qld Austr.
236 D3 Logan Creek r. NE U.S.A.
241 J3 Logandale NV U.S.A.
222 F5 Logan Lake B.C. Can.
222 D2 Logan Mountains N.W.T./Y.T. Can.
230 C3 Logansport IN U.S.A.
237 E6 Logansport LA U.S.A.
234 B3 Loganville PA U.S.A.
188 E3 Logatec Slovenia
140 L2 Lögda Sweden
140 L3 Lögdeälven r. Sweden
209 B6 Loge r. Angola
150 E2 Loggerheads Staffordshire, England U.K.
142 B2 Logna r. Norway
158 E4 Logne r. France
208 B1 Logone r. Africa
207 I4 Logone Birni Cameroon
208 B2 Logone Occidental pref. Chad
208 C2 Logone Oriental pref. Chad
206 D5 Logoualé Côte d'Ivoire
197 F3 Logrești Romania
156 B4 Logron France
183 H2 Logroño Spain
185 E1 Logrosán Spain
142 C3 Løgstør Denmark
192 A4 Logudoro reg. Sardegna Italy
142 C4 Løgumkloster Denmark
78 □5 Loh i. Vanuatu
142 D4 Lohals Denmark
117 F5 Lohardaga Bihar India
116 C3 Loharu Haryana India
214 D3 Lohatlha S. Africa
116 C4 Lohawat Rajasthan India
173 H2 Lohberg Ger.
158 E4 Lohéac France
168 E1 Lohe-Rickelshof Ger.
169 E4 Lohfelden Ger.
Lohifushi i. N. Male Maldives see Lhohifushi
Lohil r. China/India see Zayü Qu
141 N3 Lohja Fin.
169 C5 Lohmar Ger.
170 E1 Lohme Ger.
170 D2 Lohmen Mecklenburg-Vorpommern Ger.
171 F5 Lohmen Sachsen Ger.
169 D5 Löhnberg Ger.
169 D3 Löhne Ger.
168 D3 Lohne (Oldenburg) Ger.
179 E2 Lohnsburg am Kobernaußerwald Austria
172 D2 Lohr r. Ger.
169 D5 Lohra Ger.
172 D2 Lohr am Main Ger.
171 F4 Lohsa Ger.
140 M2 Lohtaja Fin.
96 C2 Loi, Nam r. Myanmar
191 G4 Loiano Italy
173 G3 Loiching Ger.
159 F4 Loigné-sur-Mayenne France
156 B4 Loigny-la-Bataille France
96 B3 Loikaw Myanmar
96 B3 Loi Lan mt. Myanmar/Thai.
208 D5 Loile r. Dem. Rep. Congo
141 M3 Loimaa Fin.
138 D1 Loimaan kunta Fin.
138 D1 Loimijoki r. Fin.
156 C4 Loing r. France
96 B1 Loipyet Hills Myanmar
156 B5 Loir r. France
159 G4 Loir, Les Vaux du val. France
159 F4 Loiré France
160 C3 Loire dept Rhône-Alpes France
159 D4 Loire r. France
156 B5 Loire, Val de val. France
158 D4 Loire-Atlantique dept Pays de la Loire France
Loire-Inférieure dept Pays de la Loire France see Loire-Atlantique
160 C3 Loire-sur-Rhône France
156 C5 Loiret dept Centre France
156 B5 Loiret r. France
156 B5 Loir-et-Cher dept Centre France
192 B4 Loiri-Porto San Paolo Sardegna Italy
159 F3 Loiron France
173 F4 Loisach r. Ger.
96 B2 Loi Sang mt. Myanmar
160 C3 Loise r. France
157 F3 Loison r. France

Loi Song to Lugdunum

329

96 B2 **Loi Song** mt. Myanmar
156 E4 **Loisy-sur-Marne** France
211 B5 **Loita Plains** Kenya
170 E2 **Loitz** Ger.
182 C3 **Loivos** Port.
182 C3 **Loivos do Monte** Port.
247 □1 **Loiza Aldea** Puerto Rico
250 B6 **Loja** Ecuador
250 B6 **Loja** prov. Ecuador
185 F3 **Loja** Spain
177 H3 **Lok** Slovakia
136 C2 **Lokachi** Ukr.
95 G1 **Lokan** r. Sabah Malaysia
179 E5 **Lokavec** Slovenia
129 F3 **Lökbatan** Azer.
177 I2 **Lokca** Slovakia
134 J3 **Lokchim** r. Rus. Fed.
165 D3 **Lokeren** Belgium
176 B1 **Loket** Czech Rep.
212 D5 **Lokgwabe** Botswana
137 G2 **Lokhvytsya** Ukr.
93 B3 **Lokilalaki, Gunung** mt. Indon.
142 C3 **Løkken** Denmark
140 J3 **Løkken** Norway
139 H3 **Loknya** Rus. Fed.
136 C2 **Loknytsya** Ukr.
207 G5 **Lokoja** Nigeria
208 C5 **Lokolo** r. Dem. Rep. Congo
208 C5 **Lokoro** r. Dem. Rep. Congo
208 C4 **Lokosafa** C.A.R.
177 K5 **Lőkösháza** Hungary
207 F5 **Lokossa** Benin
139 J5 **Lokot'** Rus. Fed.
138 E2 **Loksa** Estonia
209 B8 **Lola** Angola
206 C5 **Lola** Guinea
240 G2 **Lola, Mount** CA U.S.A.
136 C3 **Lolishniy Shepit** Ukr.
142 D4 **Lolland** i. Denmark
169 D5 **Lollar** Ger.
187 C6 **L'Ollería** Spain
211 B5 **Lollondo** Tanz.
238 D2 **Lolo** MT U.S.A.
93 C2 **Loloda Utara, Kepulauan** is Maluku Indon.
207 H6 **Lolodorf** Cameroon
260 B4 **Lolol** Chile
214 D2 **Lolwane** S. Africa
197 F4 **Lom** Bulg.
197 F4 **Lom** r. Bulg.
171 E5 **Lom** Czech Rep.
141 J3 **Lom** Norway
139 L3 **Lom** Rus. Fed.
241 M2 **Loma** CO U.S.A.
245 G4 **Loma Bonita** Mex.
260 C5 **Loma del Jaguel Moro** mt. Arg.
208 D4 **Lomako** r. Dem. Rep. Congo
240 I4 **Loma Linda** CA U.S.A.
209 E4 **Lomami** r. Dem. Rep. Congo
206 C4 **Loma Mountains** Sierra Leone
261 G5 **Loma Negra** Arg.
252 B3 **Lomas** Peru
262 T3 **Lomas, Bahía de** b. Chile
261 H4 **Lomas de Zamora** Arg.
Lomati r. S. Africa see **Mlumati**
175 L4 **Łomazy** Pol.
209 D8 **Lomba** r. Angola
216 □1b **Lomba da Fazenda** São Miguel Azores
216 □1b **Lomba da Maia** São Miguel Azores
251 H4 **Lombarda, Serra** hills Brazil
190 E3 **Lombardia** admin. reg. Italy
86 D3 **Lombardina** W.A. Austr.
163 E5 **Lombers** France
163 C5 **Lombez** France
95 G5 **Lombok** Lombok Indon.
95 G5 **Lombok** i. Indon.
95 F5 **Lombok, Selat** sea chan. Indon.
159 G3 **Lombron** France
207 F5 **Lomé** Togo
208 D5 **Lomela** r. Dem. Rep. Congo
190 D3 **Lomello** Italy
175 I3 **Łomianki** Pol.
207 I6 **Lomié** Cameroon
226 C4 **Lomira** WI U.S.A.
171 E4 **Lommatzsch** Ger.
156 C2 **Lomme** France
165 E3 **Lommel** Belgium
174 D3 **Łomnica** Pol.
176 F2 **Lomnice** Czech Rep.
176 D2 **Lomnice** r. Czech Rep.
179 F1 **Lomnice nad Lužnicí** Czech Rep.
176 E1 **Lomnice nad Popelkou** Czech Rep.
177 I2 **Lomno** mt. Slovakia
225 J3 **Lomond** Nfld. Can.
146 D5 **Lomond, Loch** l. Scotland U.K.
268 M1 **Lomonosov Ridge** sea feature Arctic Ocean
160 E1 **Lomont** hills France
138 G2 **Lomoriosov** Rus. Fed.
134 H2 **Lomovoye** Rus. Fed.
Lomphat Cambodia see **Lumphăt**
93 A4 **Lompobattang, Gunung** mt. Indon.
240 G4 **Lompoc** CA U.S.A.
96 C3 **Lom Sak** Thai.
140 L2 **Lomsjö** Sweden
175 K2 **Łomża** Pol.
114 C2 **Lonar** Mahar. India
190 F3 **Lonato** Italy
114 B2 **Lonavale** Mahar. India
176 G6 **Lončarica** Croatia
260 A6 **Loncoche** Chile
260 B6 **Loncopue** Arg.
117 G5 **Londa** Bangl.
114 B3 **Londa** Karnataka India
191 G5 **Londa** Italy
165 D4 **Londerzeel** Belgium
156 B3 **Londinières** France
Londinium Greater London, England U.K. see **London**
100 E2 **Londoko** Rus. Fed.
224 D5 **London** Ont. Can.
151 G3 **London** Greater London, England U.K.
232 A6 **London** KY U.S.A.
232 B5 **London** OH U.S.A.
152 **London area map** U.K.
151 H3 **London City** airport England U.K.
147 D2 **Londonderry** Northern Ireland U.K.
147 E2 **Londonderry** county Northern Ireland U.K.
233 G3 **Londonderry** VT U.S.A.
86 E2 **Londonderry, Cape** W.A. Austr.
259 C9 **Londonderry, Isla** i. Chile
258 D2 **Londres** Arg.
256 B5 **Londrina** Brazil
209 B8 **Londuimbali** Angola
235 E2 **Lonelyville** NY U.S.A.
240 H3 **Lone Pine** CA U.S.A.
156 B2 **Long** France
96 B3 **Long** Thai.
146 D5 **Long, Loch** inlet Argyll and Bute, Scotland U.K.
163 C6 **Long, Pic** mt. France
209 C8 **Longa** Angola
209 B7 **Longa** r. Bengo/Cuanza Sul Angola
209 C9 **Longa** r. Cuando Cubango Angola
198 B3 **Longa** Greece
131 S2 **Longa, Proliv** sea chan. Rus. Fed.
163 D5 **Longages** France
108 C4 **Long'an** Guangxi China
Long'an Sichuan China see **Pingwu**
191 G3 **Longare** Italy
186 B3 **Longares** Spain
191 H2 **Longarone** Italy
150 E3 **Long Ashton** North Somerset, England U.K.
260 B4 **Longaví** Chile
260 B4 **Longaví** r. Chile
260 B5 **Longaví, Nevado de** mt. Chile
81 C6 **Longbeach** South I. N.Z.
240 H5 **Long Beach** CA U.S.A.
235 E2 **Long Beach** NY U.S.A.
238 A2 **Long Beach** WA U.S.A.
151 G2 **Long Bennington** Lincolnshire, England U.K.
149 H2 **Longbenton** Tyne and Wear, England U.K.
233 G4 **Long Branch** NJ U.S.A.
150 E3 **Longbridge Deverill** Wiltshire, England U.K.
109 E3 **Longbu** Jiangxi China
151 F2 **Long Buckby** Northamptonshire, England U.K.
80 E4 **Longburn** North I. N.Z.
246 D2 **Long Cay** i. Bahamas
108 C2 **Longchang** Sichuan China
160 D2 **Longchaumois** France
Longcheng Anhui China see **Xiaoxian**
Longcheng Guangdong China see **Longmen**
Longcheng Jiangxi China see **Pengze**
Longcheng Yunnan China see **Chenggong**
109 E3 **Longchuan** Guangdong China
108 A3 **Longchuan** Yunnan China
Longchuan Yunnan China see **Nanhua**
108 A4 **Longchuan Jiang** r. China
151 F3 **Long Compton** Warwickshire, England U.K.
223 K5 **Long Creek** r. Sask. Can.
238 C2 **Long Creek** OR U.S.A.
151 F3 **Long Crendon** Buckinghamshire, England U.K.
151 F2 **Longdon** Staffordshire, England U.K.
151 F2 **Long Eaton** Derbyshire, England U.K.
160 D1 **Longecourt-en-Plaine** France
157 F4 **Longeville-en-Barrois** France
157 G3 **Longeville-lès-St-Avold** France
162 A2 **Longeville-sur-Mer** France
81 D5 **Longfellow, Mount** South I. N.Z.
147 D3 **Longford** Rep. of Ireland
147 D3 **Longford** county Rep. of Ireland
146 E5 **Longforgan** Perth and Kinross, Scotland U.K.
149 H2 **Longframlington** Northumberland, England U.K.
Longgang Chongqing China see **Dazu**
109 E4 **Longgang** Guangdong China
95 G2 **Longgi** r. Indon.
151 F3 **Long Hanborough** Oxfordshire, England U.K.
150 E3 **Longhope** Gloucestershire, England U.K.
146 E3 **Longhope** Orkney, Scotland U.K.
149 H2 **Longhorsley** Northumberland, England U.K.
149 H2 **Longhoughton** Northumberland, England U.K.
107 H3 **Longhua** Hebei China
109 D3 **Longhui** Hunan China
263 K1 **Longhurst, Mount** Antarctica
194 D4 **Longi** Sicilia Italy
262 U2 **Longing, Cape** Antarctica
95 F3 **Longiram** Kalimantan Timur Indon.
85 G4 **Long Island** Qld Austr.
246 D2 **Long Island** Bahamas
233 G4 **Long Island** NY U.S.A.
233 G4 **Long Island Sound** sea chan. CT/NY U.S.A.
151 F2 **Long Itchington** Warwickshire, England U.K.
107 I2 **Longjiang** Heilong. China
108 D3 **Long Jiang** r. China
Longjin Fujian China see **Qingliu**
Longjin Jiangxi China see **Anyi**
Longjuzhai Shaanxi China see **Danfeng**
107 I4 **Longkou** Shandong China
224 C3 **Longlac** Ont. Can.
233 F3 **Long Lake** NY U.S.A.
214 E3 **Longlands** S. Africa
151 F2 **Long Lawford** Warwickshire, England U.K.
108 C3 **Longli** Guizhou China
165 E5 **Longlier** Belgium
108 C3 **Longlin** Guangxi China
108 A3 **Longling** Yunnan China
146 F4 **Longmanhill** Aberdeenshire, Scotland U.K.
233 G3 **Longmeadow** MA U.S.A.
151 H2 **Long Melford** Suffolk, England U.K.
109 E4 **Longmen** Guangdong China
108 C1 **Longmen Shan** mts Sichuan China
108 C4 **Longming** Guangxi China
238 F3 **Longmont** CO U.S.A.
146 E4 **Longmorn** Moray, Scotland U.K.
109 E3 **Longnan** Jiangxi China
146 F6 **Longniddry** East Lothian, Scotland U.K.
159 G3 **Longny-au-Perche** France
193 I5 **Longobardi** Italy
195 F3 **Longobucco** Italy
184 C1 **Longomel** Port.
209 B8 **Longonjo** Angola
182 B2 **Longos Vales** Port.
260 B3 **Longotoma** Chile
Longping Guizhou China see **Luodian**
224 D5 **Long Point** Ont. Can.
227 G4 **Long Point Bay** Ont. Can.
234 D3 **Longport** NJ U.S.A.
236 E2 **Long Prairie** MN U.S.A.
156 B2 **Longpré-les-Corps-Saints** France
149 G3 **Long Preston** North Yorkshire, England U.K.
Longquan Guizhou China see **Fenggang**
Longquan Guizhou China see **Danzhai**
Longquan Yunnan China see **Yimen**
109 F2 **Longquan** Zhejiang China
109 G2 **Longquan Xi** r. China
225 J3 **Long Range Mountains** Nfld. Can.
225 J4 **Long Range Mountains** Nfld. Can.
162 B2 **Longré** France
85 F4 **Longreach** Qld Austr.
86 E2 **Long Reef** W.A. Austr.
108 B1 **Longriba** Sichuan China
149 G4 **Longridge** Lancashire, England U.K.
182 C4 **Longroiva** Port.
Longshan Guizhou China see **Longli**
108 D2 **Longshan** Hunan China
Longshan Yunnan China see **Longling**
108 D3 **Longsheng** Guangxi China
106 D4 **Longshou Shan** mts China
238 F3 **Longs Peak** CO U.S.A.
151 I2 **Long Stratton** Norfolk, England U.K.
151 H2 **Long Sutton** Lincolnshire, England U.K.
150 E3 **Long Sutton** Somerset, England U.K.
109 D2 **Longtian** Hunan China
85 F4 **Longton** Qld Austr.
149 G4 **Longton** Lancashire, England U.K.
150 E2 **Longton** Stoke-on-Trent, England U.K.
149 G2 **Longtown** Cumbria, England U.K.
156 C3 **Longueau** France
162 B1 **Longué-Jumelles** France
156 C2 **Longuenesse** France
225 H3 **Longue-Pointe** Que. Can.
233 G2 **Longueuil** Que. Can.
156 D4 **Longueville** France
156 B3 **Longueville-sur-Scie** France
157 F3 **Longuyon** France
240 F2 **Longvale** CA U.S.A.
241 L4 **Long Valley** AZ U.S.A.
234 D2 **Long Valley** NJ U.S.A.
160 D1 **Longvic** France
160 D1 **Longvic** airport France
222 H5 **Longview** Alta Can.
237 E5 **Longview** TX U.S.A.
238 B2 **Longview** WA U.S.A.
148 C4 **Longwood** Rep. of Ireland
157 F3 **Longwy** France
106 E5 **Longxi** Gansu China
Longxian Guangdong China see **Wengyuan**
106 E5 **Longxian** Shaanxi China
109 F3 **Longxi Shan** mt. Fujian China
Longxun Fujian China see **Dehua**
97 D5 **Long Xuyên** Vietnam
109 F3 **Longyan** Fujian China
107 G4 **Longyao** Hebei China
140 □ **Longyearbyen** Svalbard
100 C2 **Longzhen** Heilong. China
108 C4 **Longzhou** Guangxi China
Longzhouping Hubei China see **Changyang**
191 G3 **Lonigo** Italy
168 C3 **Löningen** Ger.
188 F3 **Lonja** r. Croatia
188 F3 **Lonjsko Polje** plain Croatia
159 F3 **Lonlay-l'Abbaye** France
164 F2 **Lonneker** Neth.
156 E3 **Lonny** France
237 F5 **Lonoke** AR U.S.A.
260 B6 **Lonquimay, Volcán** vol. Chile
163 B5 **Lons** France
143 F3 **Lönsboda** Sweden
140 K2 **Lønsdalen** val. Norway
160 D2 **Lons-le-Saunier** France
142 C3 **Lønstrup** Denmark
255 B7 **Lontra** r. Mato Grosso do Sul Brazil
254 C3 **Lontra** r. Tocantins Brazil
260 B4 **Lontué** Chile
165 F4 **Lontzen** Belgium
177 L3 **Lónya** Hungary
138 E2 **Loo** Estonia
92 B3 **Looc** Phil.
Loochoo Islands Japan see **Nansei-shotō**
226 E4 **Looking Glass** r. MI U.S.A.
240 H3 **Lookout Mountain** CA U.S.A.
85 F2 **Lookout Point** Qld Austr.
87 C7 **Lookout Point** W.A. Austr.
211 B5 **Loolmalasin** vol. crater Tanz.
86 E3 **Looma** W.A. Austr.
224 B3 **Loon** Ont. Can.
222 H3 **Loon** r. Alta Can.
87 E6 **Loongana** W.A. Austr.
223 I4 **Loon Lake** Sask. Can.
164 E3 **Loon op Zand** Neth.
156 C2 **Loon-Plage** France
147 B4 **Loop Head** hd Rep. of Ireland
156 D2 **Loos** France
179 G2 **Loosdorf** Austria
151 H3 **Loose** Kent, England U.K.
111 C4 **Lop** Xinjiang China
137 I3 **Lopan** r. Ukr.
139 J5 **Lopandino** Rus. Fed.
191 J4 **Lopar** Croatia
213 □J4 **Lopary** Madag.
Lopasnya Moskovskaya Oblast' Rus. Fed. see **Chekhov**
139 K4 **Lopasnya** r. Rus. Fed.
129 E2 **Lopatin** Rus. Fed.
100 G2 **Lopatina, Gora** mt. Sakhalin Rus. Fed.
120 A1 **Lopatino** Rus. Fed.
139 L4 **Lopatinskiy** Rus. Fed.
136 D3 **Lopatnic** Moldova
136 C2 **Lopatyn** Ukr.
139 I5 **Lopazna** Rus. Fed.
97 C4 **Lop Buri** Thai.
151 F3 **Lopcombe Corner** Wiltshire, England U.K.
158 B3 **Loperhet** France
78 □5 **Lopévi** i. Vanuatu
92 B3 **Lopez** Phil.
234 B1 **Lopez** PA U.S.A.
175 L4 **Łopiennik Górny** Pol.
192 A2 **Lopigna** Corse France
164 D3 **Lopik** Neth.
Lopnur Xinjiang China see **Yuli**
110 E3 **Lop Nur** salt l. China
208 C4 **Lopori** r. Dem. Rep. Congo
164 F1 **Loppersum** Neth.
140 M1 **Lopphavet** b. Norway
141 N3 **Loppi** Fin.
175 I5 **Łopuszno** Pol.
182 C2 **Lor** r. Spain
123 F4 **Lora** r. Afgh.
184 E3 **Lora del Río** Spain
232 B4 **Lorain** OH U.S.A.
226 B5 **Loraine** IL U.S.A.
123 G4 **Loralai** Pak.
123 G4 **Loralai** r. Pak.
183 G4 **Loranca de Tajuña** Spain
234 C2 **Lorane** PA U.S.A.
185 I3 **Lorca** Spain
172 D3 **Lorch** Baden-Württemberg Ger.
169 C5 **Lorch** Hessen Ger.
187 C6 **Lorcha** Spain
182 B3 **Lordelo** Port.
Lord Hood atoll Arch. des Tuamotu Fr. Polynesia see **Marutea**
Lord Howe Atoll Solomon Is see **Ontong Java Atoll**
82 □2 **Lord Howe Island** Austr.
266 F7 **Lord Howe Rise** sea feature S. Pacific Ocean
182 C4 **Lordosa** Port.
239 E5 **Lordsburg** NM U.S.A.
234 C1 **Lords Valley** PA U.S.A.
257 E5 **Lorena** Brazil
91 K7 **Lorengau** Admiralty Is P.N.G.
91 I8 **Lorentz** r. Indon.
245 F2 **Lorenzo del Real** Mex.
191 H3 **Loreo** Italy
122 B3 **Lorestān** prov. Iran
258 F2 **Loreto** Arg.
254 D3 **Loreto** Brazil
191 I5 **Loreto** Italy
242 C3 **Loreto** Mex.
253 F5 **Loreto** Para.
250 C5 **Loreto** dept Peru
92 C4 **Loreto** Phil.
193 F2 **Loreto Aprutino** Italy
226 B3 **Loretta** WI U.S.A.
161 E5 **Lorgues** France
210 C4 **Lorian Swamp** Kenya
250 C2 **Lorica** Col.
158 C4 **Lorient** France
182 C4 **Loriga** Port.
162 B3 **Lorignac** France
233 F2 **L'Orignal** Ont. Can.
187 C5 **Loriguilla** Spain
221 I3 **Lorillard** r. Nunavut Can.
177 I4 **Lőrinci** Hungary
238 F1 **Loring** MT U.S.A.
161 C4 **Loriol-sur-Drôme** France
160 B1 **Lormes** France
116 E5 **Lormi** Madh. Prad. India
163 B4 **Lormont** France
146 C5 **Lorn, Firth of** est. Scotland U.K.
85 F5 **Lorne** Qld Austr.
83 E4 **Lorne** Vic. Austr.
111 F6 **Loro** r. China
191 G5 **Loro Ciuffenna** Italy
206 E4 **Loropéni** Burkina
193 F1 **Loro Piceno** Italy
163 D5 **Lorp-Sentaraille** France
157 G4 **Lorquin** France
172 B4 **Lörrach** Ger.
157 G4 **Lorrain, Plateau** France
84 D3 **Lorraine** Qld Austr.
157 G4 **Lorraine** admin. reg. France
157 F4 **Lorraine, Plaine** plain France
156 C4 **Lorrez-le-Bocage-Préaux** France
156 C5 **Lorris** France
172 C2 **Lorsch** Ger.
87 D7 **Lort** r. W.A. Austr.
141 L3 **Lörudden** Sweden
168 C3 **Lorup** Ger.
206 B4 **Los, Îles de** is Guinea
183 G2 **Losa** r. Spain
182 D3 **Losacino** Spain
187 C5 **Losa del Obispo** Spain
116 C4 **Losal** Rajasthan India
242 E3 **Los Alamítos, Sierra de** mt. Mex.
240 G4 **Los Alamos** CA U.S.A.
239 F5 **Los Alamos** NM U.S.A.
187 C7 **Los Alcázares** Spain
187 B7 **Los Algezares** Spain
245 F4 **Los Altos** Mex.
260 B3 **Los Andes** Chile
260 A5 **Los Angeles** Chile
240 H4 **Los Angeles** CA U.S.A.
259 C7 **Los Antiguos** Arg.
246 B2 **Los Arabos** Cuba
183 H2 **Los Arcos** Spain
187 C6 **Los Arenales del Sol** Spain
183 H4 **Losares** mt. Spain
245 E5 **Los Arroyos** Mex.
240 G3 **Los Banos** CA U.S.A.
185 H2 **Los Barreros** mt. Spain
184 E4 **Los Barrios** Spain
182 E2 **Los Barrios de Luna** Spain
187 C7 **Los Belones** Spain
242 D2 **Los Caballos Mesteños, Llano de** plain Mex.
246 B2 **Los Canarreos, Archipiélago de** is Cuba
187 B7 **Los Cantareros** Spain
242 □I7 **Los Chiles** Costa Rica
259 B7 **Los Chonos, Archipiélago de** is Chile
260 E3 **Los Condores** Arg.
240 I5 **Los Coronados, Islas** is Mex.
183 F1 **Los Corrales de Buelna** Spain
186 B3 **Loscos** Spain
252 D3 **Los Cusis** Bol.
252 A6 **Los Desventurados, Islas de** is S. Pacific Ocean
Los Difuntios, Lago de l. Uru. see **Negra, Lago**
187 B7 **Los Dolores** Spain
259 D9 **Los Estados, Isla de** i. Arg.
135 H6 **Losevo** Rus. Fed.
185 I3 **Los Gallardos** Spain
245 E3 **Los Gatos** r. Mex.
240 G3 **Los Gatos** CA U.S.A.
260 E2 **Los Gigantes, Cerro** mt. Arg.
172 A2 **Losheim** Ger.
183 H5 **Los Hinojosos** Spain
175 K3 **Łosice** Pol.
188 E3 **Lošinj** i. Croatia
175 L3 **Łosinka** Pol.
246 C2 **Los Jardines de la Reina, Archipiélago de** is Cuba
258 E3 **Los Juríes** Arg.
215 G3 **Loskop** S. Africa
259 B5 **Los Lagos** Chile
259 B6 **Los Lagos** admin. reg. Chile
Loslau Pol. see **Wodzisław Śląski**
260 A6 **Los Laureles** Chile
260 D2 **Los Llanos, Sierra de** mts Arg.
216 □3d **Los Llanos de Aridane** La Palma Canary Is
239 F5 **Los Lunas** NM U.S.A.
187 B7 **Los Maldonados** Spain
187 B7 **Los Martinez** Spain
259 C6 **Los Menucos** Arg.
242 C3 **Los Mochis** Mex.
184 E3 **Los Molares** Spain
183 F4 **Los Molinos** Spain
240 F1 **Los Molinos** CA U.S.A.
260 B2 **Los Molles** r. Chile
242 □J7 **Los Mosquitos, Golfo de** b. Panama
245 F4 **Los Naranjos** Mex.
183 F5 **Los Navalmorales** Spain
183 F5 **Los Navalucillos** Spain
190 D2 **Losone** Switz.
175 I6 **Łososina Dolna** Pol.
246 B2 **Los Palacios** Cuba
184 E3 **Los Palacios y Villafranca** Spain
183 G1 **Los Pandos** Spain
260 C3 **Los Paramillos, Sierra de** mts Arg.
93 C5 **Lospatos** East Timor
260 C2 **Los Patos, Río de** r. Arg.
185 E2 **Los Pedroches** plat. Spain
187 B5 **Los Pedrones** Spain
185 G2 **Los Pozuelos de Calatrava** Spain
183 H3 **Los Rábanos** Spain
258 D2 **Los Ralos** Arg.
216 □3a **Los Realejos** Tenerife Canary Is
244 A1 **Los Remedios** r. Mex.
244 C4 **Los Reyes** Mex.
259 E6 **Los Riachos, Islas de** is Arg.
250 B5 **Los Ríos** prov. Ecuador
250 E2 **Los Roques, Islas** is Venez.
185 H3 **Los Royos** Spain
171 C4 **Lossa** r. Ger.
171 C4 **Lossa (Finne)** Ger.
182 E4 **Los Santos** Spain
184 D2 **Los Santos de Maimona** Spain
216 □3d **Los Sauces** La Palma Canary Is
260 A5 **Los Sauces** Chile
172 C3 **Loßburg** Ger.
163 B4 **Losse** France
164 F2 **Losser** Neth.
146 E4 **Lossie** r. Scotland U.K.
146 E4 **Lossiemouth** Moray, Scotland U.K.
216 □3a **Los Silos** Tenerife Canary Is
171 D5 **Lößnitz** Ger.
190 E2 **Lostallo** Switz.
250 D2 **Los Taques** Venez.
171 C3 **Lostau** Ger.
232 B6 **Lost Creek** KY U.S.A.
258 E3 **Los Telares** Arg.
244 C4 **Los Tepames** Mex.
250 E2 **Los Teques** Venez.
251 F2 **Los Testigos** is Venez.
240 H4 **Lost Hills** CA U.S.A.
149 G4 **Lostock Gralam** Cheshire, England U.K.
183 F1 **Los Tojos** Spain
185 F1 **Los Torneros, Sierra de** mts Spain
150 C4 **Lostwithiel** Cornwall, England U.K.
185 G3 **Los Villares** Spain
260 B2 **Los Vilos** Chile
183 G5 **Los Yébenes** Spain
137 F2 **Losynivka** Ukr.
163 D4 **Lot** dept Midi-Pyrénées France
161 A4 **Lot** r. France
258 B5 **Lota** Chile
141 J3 **Løten** Norway
163 C4 **Lot-et-Garonne** dept Aquitaine France
122 D2 **Lotfābād** Turkm.
146 F2 **Loth** Orkney, Scotland U.K.
215 H2 **Lothair** S. Africa
146 E3 **Lothmore** Highland, Scotland U.K.
210 B3 **Lotikipi Plain** Kenya
208 C5 **Lotoi** r. Dem. Rep. Congo
139 J3 **Lotoshino** Rus. Fed.
137 G4 **Lotskyne** Ukr.
Lot's Wife i. Japan see **Sōfu-gan**
140 O1 **Lotta** r. Fin./Rus. Fed. alt. **Lutto**
169 C3 **Lotte** Ger.
172 C4 **Lottstetten** Ger.
210 B3 **Lotuke** mt. Sudan
192 B5 **Lotzorai** Sardegna Italy
159 F4 **Louailles** France
96 C2 **Louang Namtha** Laos
96 C3 **Louangphrabang** Laos
108 B5 **Louang Phrabang Range** mts Laos/Thai.
158 C3 **Louannec** France
158 C3 **Louargat** France
209 B6 **Loubomo** Congo
171 G5 **Loučeň** Czech Rep.
176 C1 **Loučná** hill Czech Rep.
176 D3 **Loučovice** Czech Rep.
158 D3 **Loudéac** France
161 B3 **Loudes** France
109 D3 **Loudi** Hunan China
209 B6 **Loudima** Congo
231 C5 **Loudon** TN U.S.A.
232 B4 **Loudonville** OH U.S.A.
162 C1 **Loudun** France
159 F4 **Loué** France
160 D1 **Loue** r. France
209 B5 **Louéssé** r. Congo
206 A3 **Louga** Senegal
163 D5 **Louge** r. France
147 C1 **Loughanure** Rep. of Ireland
151 F2 **Loughborough** Leicestershire, England U.K.
147 E2 **Loughbrickland** Northern Ireland U.K.
147 B4 **Lougher** Rep. of Ireland
147 E2 **Loughgall** Northern Ireland U.K.
147 D3 **Lough Gowna** Rep. of Ireland
147 F2 **Loughlinisland** Northern Ireland U.K.
147 D4 **Loughmoe** Rep. of Ireland
150 C3 **Loughor** Swansea, Wales U.K.
150 C3 **Loughor** r. Wales U.K.
147 C3 **Loughrea** Rep. of Ireland
147 C2 **Loughros More Bay** Rep. of Ireland
151 H3 **Loughton** Essex, England U.K.
163 C4 **Lougratte** France
160 D2 **Louhans** France
232 B5 **Louisa** KY U.S.A.
232 E5 **Louisa** VA U.S.A.
225 J4 **Louisbourg** N.S. Can.
Louisburg N.S. Can. see **Louisbourg**
231 E4 **Louisburg** NC U.S.A.
Louis-Gentil Morocco see **Youssoufia**
91 L9 **Louisiade Archipelago** is P.N.G.
236 F4 **Louisiana** MO U.S.A.
237 F6 **Louisiana** state U.S.A.
213 F4 **Louis Trichardt** S. Africa
214 C3 **Louisvale** S. Africa
231 D5 **Louisville** GA U.S.A.
236 F4 **Louisville** IL U.S.A.
230 C4 **Louisville** KY U.S.A.
237 F5 **Louisville** MS U.S.A.
232 C4 **Louisville** OH U.S.A.
266 H8 **Louisville Ridge** sea feature S. Pacific Ocean
134 F2 **Loukhi** Rus. Fed.
208 C5 **Loukoléla** Congo
160 E1 **Loulans** France
162 B2 **Loulay** France
184 B3 **Loulé** Port.
206 D4 **Loulouni** Mali
207 H5 **Loum** Cameroon
176 C1 **Louny** Czech Rep.
161 F5 **Loup** r. France
236 D3 **Loup** r. NE U.S.A.
236 D3 **Loup City** NE U.S.A.
225 J3 **Lourdes** Nfld. Can.
163 B5 **Lourdes** France
226 A4 **Lourdes** IA U.S.A.
162 D2 **Lourdoueix-St-Pierre** France
Lourenço Marques Moz. see **Maputo**
184 A2 **Loures** Port.
182 B4 **Louriçal** Port.
184 A1 **Lourinhã** Port.
161 D5 **Lourmarin** France
198 B2 **Louros** Ipeiros Greece
182 B4 **Lourosa** Port.
156 C5 **Loury** France
182 B4 **Lousã** Port.
184 A2 **Lousa** Lisboa Port.
182 B4 **Lousã, Serra da** mts Port.
182 B3 **Lousada** Port.
214 D5 **Louterwater** S. Africa
83 F2 **Louth** N.S.W. Austr.
147 E3 **Louth** Rep. of Ireland
147 E3 **Louth** county Rep. of Ireland
149 I4 **Louth** Lincolnshire, England U.K.
198 C2 **Loutra Aidipsou** Greece
198 C3 **Loutraki** Greece
198 C1 **Loutros** Kentriki Makedonia Greece
Louvain Belgium see **Leuven**
165 E4 **Louveigné** Belgium
159 F3 **Louverné** France
163 B5 **Louvie-Juzon** France
156 B3 **Louviers** France
158 E3 **Louvigné-de-Bais** France
159 E3 **Louvigné-du-Désert** France
156 C3 **Louvres** France
156 D2 **Louvroil** France
214 E2 **Louwna** S. Africa
215 H2 **Louwsburg** S. Africa
156 E4 **Louze** France
140 M2 **Lövånger** Sweden
177 H4 **Lovasberény** Hungary
176 F5 **Lovászi** Hungary
177 G4 **Lovászpatona** Hungary
139 H2 **Lovat'** r. Rus. Fed.
140 K3 **Lövberga** Sweden
196 D3 **Lovćenac** Vojvodina, Srbija Yugo.
197 G4 **Lovech** Bulg.
238 F3 **Loveland** CO U.S.A.
233 □H2 **Lovell** ME U.S.A.
238 E2 **Lovell** WY U.S.A.
Lovello, Monte mt. Austria see **Grosser Löffler**
81 B7 **Lovells Flat** South I. N.Z.
240 H1 **Lovelock** NV U.S.A.
234 B1 **Lovelton** PA U.S.A.
165 C3 **Lovendegem** Belgium
190 F3 **Lovere** Italy
190 F2 **Lovero** Italy
232 C6 **Lovers' Leap** mt. VA U.S.A.
226 C4 **Loves Park** IL U.S.A.
141 N3 **Loviisa** Fin.
140 M2 **Lovikka** Sweden
232 D6 **Lovingston** VA U.S.A.
237 C5 **Lovington** NM U.S.A.
177 I3 **Lovinobaňa** Slovakia
141 K3 **Lövnäsvallen** Sweden
176 F4 **Lövő** Hungary
171 F5 **Lovosice** Czech Rep.
134 F1 **Lovozero** Rus. Fed.
188 E3 **Lovran** Croatia
179 G4 **Lovrenc** Slovenia
196 E3 **Lovrin** Romania
143 F1 **Lövsjön** Sweden
209 D6 **Lóvua** Lunda Norte Angola
209 D7 **Lôvua** Moxico Angola
227 J3 **Low** Que. Can.
208 E5 **Lowa** r. Dem. Rep. Congo
149 H4 **Lowdham** Nottinghamshire, England U.K.
226 D5 **Lowell** IN U.S.A.
233 H3 **Lowell** MA U.S.A.
226 E4 **Lowell** MI U.S.A.
238 B3 **Lowell** OR U.S.A.
233 G2 **Lowell** VT U.S.A.
233 □H2 **Lowelltown** ME U.S.A.
170 E3 **Löwenberg** Ger.
172 D2 **Löwenstein** Ger.
222 G5 **Lower Arrow Lake** B.C. Can.
Lower Austria land Austria see **Niederösterreich**
147 E2 **Lower Ballinderry** Northern Ireland U.K.
151 G3 **Lower Beeding** West Sussex, England U.K.
Lower California pen. Mex. see **Baja California**
150 E3 **Lower Cam** Gloucestershire, England U.K.
146 C4 **Lower Diabaig** Highland, Scotland U.K.
241 K4 **Lower Granite Gorge** AZ U.S.A.
81 E4 **Lower Hutt** North I. N.Z.
146 B5 **Lower Kilchattan** Argyll and Bute, Scotland U.K.
146 B6 **Lower Killeyan** Argyll and Bute, Scotland U.K.
222 C2 **Lower Laberge** Y.T. Can.
240 F2 **Lower Lake** CA U.S.A.
215 G3 **Lower Loteni** S. Africa
147 D2 **Lower Lough Erne** l. Northern Ireland U.K.
215 G4 **Lower Pitseng** S. Africa
222 D3 **Lower Post** B.C. Can.
215 H1 **Lower Sabie** S. Africa
Lower Saxony land Ger. see **Niedersachsen**
Lower Tunguska r. Rus. Fed. see **Nizhnyaya Tunguska**
151 I2 **Lowestoft** Suffolk, England U.K.
123 G3 **Lowgar** prov. Afgh.
149 H2 **Lowick** Northumberland, England U.K.
175 H3 **Łowicz** Pol.
Low Island Kiribati see **Starbuck Island**
232 D6 **Lowmoor** VA U.S.A.
83 F5 **Low Rocky Point** Tas. Austr.
151 I2 **Low Street** Norfolk, England U.K.
232 C5 **Lowsville** WV U.S.A.
146 E6 **Lowther Hills** Scotland U.K.
233 F3 **Lowville** NY U.S.A.
168 D2 **Loxstedt** Ger.
82 E3 **Loxton** S.A. Austr.
214 D4 **Loxton** S. Africa
146 D3 **Loyal, Loch** l. Scotland U.K.
227 I5 **Loyalsock Creek** r. PA U.S.A.
240 G2 **Loyalton** CA U.S.A.
234 B2 **Loyalton** PA U.S.A.
Loyalty Islands New Caledonia see **Loyauté, Îles**
Loyang Henan China see **Luoyang**
78 □5 **Loyauté, Îles** is New Caledonia
226 B4 **Loyd** WI U.S.A.
160 D3 **Loyettes** France
Loyev Belarus see **Loyew**
136 F2 **Loyew** Belarus
146 C4 **Loyne, Loch** l. Scotland U.K.
134 K4 **Loyno** Rus. Fed.
140 K2 **Løypskardtinden** mt. Norway
161 B4 **Lozère** dept Languedoc-Roussillon France
161 B4 **Lozère, Mont** mt. France
196 D3 **Loznica** Srbija Yugo.
197 H4 **Loznitsa** Bulg.
137 J3 **Lozno-Oleksandrivka** Ukr.
137 I2 **Loznoye** Rus. Fed.
176 G3 **Lozorno** Slovakia
137 H3 **Lozova** Kharkivs'ka Oblast' Ukr.
137 I3 **Lozova** Kharkivs'ka Oblast' Ukr.
Lozovaya Kazakh. see **Lozovoye**
Lozovaya Kharkivs'ka Oblast' Ukr. see **Lozova**
136 D3 **Lozove** Ukr.
137 I3 **Lozoven'ka** Ukr.
196 E3 **Lozovik** Srbija Yugo.
121 I1 **Lozovoye** Kazakh.
137 K2 **Lozovoye** Rus. Fed.
183 G4 **Lozoya** Spain
183 G4 **Lozoya** r. Spain
183 G4 **Lozoyuela** Spain
137 H4 **Lozuvatka** r. Ukr.
134 M3 **Loz'va** r. Rus. Fed.
191 H2 **Lozzo di Cadore** Italy
107 F4 **Lu** r. China
209 D7 **Luacano** Angola
209 D6 **Luachimo** r. Angola/Dem. Rep. Congo
208 C4 **Lua Dekere** r. Dem. Rep. Congo
213 H3 **Luala** r. Moz.
240 □ **Lualualei** HI U.S.A.
209 E8 **Luampa** r. Zambia
109 F2 **Lu'an** Anhui China
109 D1 **Luanchuan** Henan China
182 E1 **Luanco** Spain
209 B7 **Luanda** Angola
209 B7 **Luanda** prov. Angola
209 C7 **Luando** Angola
209 C7 **Luando** r. Angola
97 B5 **Luang, Khao** mt. Thai.
209 D8 **Luanginga** r. Zambia
78 □6 **Luangiua** i. Solomon Is
Luang Nam Tha Laos see **Louang Namtha**
Luang Prabang Laos see **Louangphrabang**
209 D8 **Luanguinga** r. Angola
209 F8 **Luangwa** Zambia
211 A8 **Luangwa** r. Zambia
106 B5 **Luanhaizi** Qinghai China
107 H4 **Luan He** r. China
107 H4 **Luannan** Hebei China
107 H3 **Luanping** Hebei China
209 F8 **Luanshya** Zambia
107 H4 **Luanxian** Hebei China
209 F7 **Luanza** Dem. Rep. Congo
Luanzhou Hebei China see **Luanxian**
Luao Angola see **Luau**
209 F7 **Luapula** prov. Zambia
182 D1 **Luarca** Spain
209 D7 **Luashi** Dem. Rep. Congo
211 C8 **Luatize** r. Moz.
209 D7 **Luau** Angola
207 H6 **Luba** Equat. Guinea
175 L5 **Lubaczów** Pol.
175 K5 **Lubaczówka** r. Pol.
209 C7 **Lubalo** Angola
174 D4 **Lubań** Pol.
138 F3 **Lubāna** Latvia
138 F3 **Lubānas ezers** l. Latvia
92 B3 **Lubang** Phil.
92 B3 **Lubang** i. Phil.
92 A3 **Lubang Islands** Phil.
209 B8 **Lubango** Angola
209 E6 **Lubao** Dem. Rep. Congo
171 D3 **Lübars** Ger.
175 K4 **Lubartów** Pol.
174 E3 **Lubasz** Pol.
175 H2 **Lubawa** Pol.
174 E5 **Lubawka** Pol.
169 D3 **Lübbecke** Ger.
165 D4 **Lubbeek** Belgium
171 E4 **Lübben** Ger.
171 E4 **Lübbenau** Ger.
237 C5 **Lubbock** TX U.S.A.
170 C3 **Lübbow** Ger.
233 □J2 **Lubec** ME U.S.A.
168 F2 **Lübeck** Ger.
232 C5 **Lubeck** WV U.S.A.
168 F1 **Lübecker Bucht** b. Ger.
209 E6 **Lubefu** Dem. Rep. Congo
107 I2 **Lubei** Nei Mongol China
177 I2 **Ľubeľa** Slovakia
175 K4 **Lubelska, Wyżyna** hills Pol.
175 K4 **Lubelskie** prov. Pol.
Lüben Dolnośląskie Pol. see **Lubin**
176 C1 **Lubenec** Czech Rep.
175 J6 **Lubenia** Pol.
177 J3 **Lubeník** Slovakia
120 C2 **Lubenka** Kazakh.
161 D5 **Lubéron, Montagne du** ridge France
162 D3 **Lubersac** France
170 C2 **Lübesse** Ger.
182 D2 **Lubián** Spain
174 G2 **Łubianka** Pol.
174 E4 **Lubiąż** Pol.
177 J2 **Ľubica** r. Slovakia
174 G2 **Lubichowo** Pol.
174 G2 **Lubicz Dolny** Pol.
175 H6 **Lubień** Pol.
175 G3 **Lubienka** r. Pol.
175 H3 **Lubień Kujawski** Pol.
174 G2 **Lubiewo** Pol.
174 E4 **Lubin** Dolnośląskie Pol.
167 H3 **Lubiń** Pol.
174 C3 **Lubiszyn** Pol.
175 K4 **Lublin** Pol.
174 G5 **Lubliniec** Pol.
170 E1 **Lubmin** Ger.
Lubnān country Asia see **Lebanon**
174 F2 **Lubnia** Pol.
174 G5 **Łubniany** Pol.
174 G4 **Łubnice** Pol.
175 J5 **Łubnice** Pol.
174 D3 **Lubniewice** Pol.
175 H3 **Łubno** Pol.
174 F1 **Łubno** Pol.
137 G2 **Lubny** Ukr.
215 H2 **Lubombo** admin. dist. Swaziland
175 I1 **Lubomino** Pol.
174 E3 **Luboń** Pol.
177 K2 **Ľubotice** Slovakia
177 J2 **Ľubotín** Slovakia
170 C2 **Lübow** Ger.
175 H2 **Lubowidz** Pol.
174 F3 **Łubowo** Pol.
174 G3 **Lubraniec** Pol.
185 H3 **Lubrín** Spain
174 D3 **Lubrza** Lubuskie Pol.
174 F5 **Lubrza** Opolskie Pol.
174 C4 **Lubsko** Pol.
170 C2 **Lübstorf** Ger.
174 G3 **Lubstów** Pol.
174 F5 **Lubsza** Pol.
174 C4 **Lubsza** r. Pol.
170 C2 **Lübtheen** Ger.
92 B2 **Lubuagan** Phil.
209 E7 **Lubudi** Dem. Rep. Congo
209 E7 **Lubudi** r. Dem. Rep. Congo
94 C3 **Lubuklinggau** Sumatera Indon.
94 B2 **Lubukpakam** Sumatera Indon.
94 C2 **Lubuksikaping** Sumatera Indon.
209 E7 **Lubumbashi** Dem. Rep. Congo
209 E8 **Lubungu** Zambia
174 D3 **Lubuskie** prov. Pol.
208 E5 **Lubutu** r. Dem. Rep. Congo
209 F7 **Lubwe** Zambia
176 B1 **Luby** Czech Rep.
175 L5 **Lubycza Królewska** Pol.
170 D2 **Lübz** Ger.
161 B4 **Luc** Languedoc-Roussillon France
163 E4 **Luc** Midi-Pyrénées France
185 H3 **Lucainena de las Torres** Spain
209 B7 **Lucala** Angola
227 G4 **Lucan** Ont. Can.
147 E3 **Lucan** Rep. of Ireland
196 E4 **Lučani** Srbija Yugo.
222 A2 **Lucania, Mount** Y.T. Can.
111 F4 **Lücaoshan** Qinghai China
209 D7 **Lucapa** Angola
185 H3 **Lúcar** Spain
185 H3 **Lúcar** mt. Spain
261 H2 **Lucas** r. Arg.
253 G3 **Lucas** Brazil
261 H3 **Lucas González** Arg.
232 B5 **Lucasville** OH U.S.A.
231 E7 **Lucaya** Bahamas
159 H4 **Luçay-le-Mâle** France
190 F5 **Lucca** Italy
190 F5 **Lucca** prov. Toscana Italy
236 D2 **Lucca** ND U.S.A.
194 C5 **Lucca Sicula** Sicilia Italy
192 B2 **Lucciana** Corse France
156 B4 **Lucé** France
246 □ **Lucea** Jamaica
146 D7 **Luce Bay** Scotland U.K.
237 F6 **Lucedale** MS U.S.A.
256 B4 **Lucélia** Brazil
92 B3 **Lucena** Phil.
185 F3 **Lucena** Spain
187 C4 **Lucena** r. Spain
186 B3 **Lucena de Jalón** Spain
187 C4 **Lucena del Cid** Spain
160 B2 **Lucenay-lès-Aix** France
160 C1 **Lucenay-l'Évêque** France
161 D4 **Luc-en-Diois** France
177 I3 **Lučenec** Slovakia
186 B3 **Luceni** Spain
193 H3 **Lucera** Italy
161 F5 **Lucéram** France
252 C3 **Lucerna** Peru
Lucerne Switz. see **Luzern**
240 F2 **Lucerne** CA U.S.A.
240 I4 **Lucerne Valley** CA U.S.A.
157 F4 **Lucey** France
177 I3 **Lucfalva** Hungary
100 E3 **Luchegorsk** Rus. Fed.
Lucheng Guangxi China see **Luchuan**
107 G4 **Lucheng** Shanxi China
Lucheng Sichuan China see **Kangding**
159 G4 **Luché-Pringé** France
211 C7 **Lucheringo** r. Moz.
156 C2 **Lucheux** France
139 L3 **Luchki** Rus. Fed.
139 H4 **Luchosa** r. Belarus
170 C3 **Lüchow** Ger.
108 D4 **Luchuan** Guangxi China
108 B4 **Lüchun** Yunnan China
156 C3 **Luchy** France
185 F2 **Luciana** Spain
175 H4 **Luciąża** r. Pol.
175 H3 **Lucień** Pol.
191 G5 **Lucignano** Italy
188 D3 **Lucija** Slovenia
182 D2 **Lucillo de Somoza** Spain
85 F3 **Lucinda** Qld Austr.
82 E4 **Lucindale** S.A. Austr.
93 C4 **Lucipara, Kepulauan** is Maluku Indon.
209 B8 **Lucira** Angola
193 G3 **Lucito** Italy
197 H3 **Luciu** Romania
Łuck Ukr. see **Luts'k**
226 A3 **Luck** WI U.S.A.
171 D4 **Lucka** Ger.
171 E4 **Luckau** Ger.
117 F4 **Luckeesarai** Bihar India
171 E3 **Luckenwalde** Ger.
215 E3 **Luckhoff** S. Africa
227 G4 **Lucknow** Ont. Can.
116 E4 **Lucknow** Uttar Prad. India
170 C3 **Lückstedt** Ger.
191 G2 **Luco, Monte** mt. Italy
193 F3 **Luco dei Marsi** Italy
162 A2 **Luçon** France
108 D2 **Lücongpo** Hubei China
163 B5 **Lucq-de-Béarn** France
159 F2 **Luc-sur-Mer** France
209 B6 **Lucunga** Angola
209 D8 **Lucusse** Angola
84 D4 **Lucy Creek** N.T. Austr.
160 B1 **Lucy-le-Bois** France
Lüda Liaoning China see **Dalian**
146 A4 **Ludag** Western Isles, Scotland U.K.
197 H4 **Luda Kamchiya** r. Bulg.
188 F2 **Ludbreg** Croatia
169 C4 **Lüdenscheid** Ger.
168 F3 **Lüder** Ger.
171 C3 **Lüderitz** Ger.
212 B5 **Lüderitz** Namibia
168 F2 **Lüdersdorf** Ger.
178 A3 **Ludesch** Austria
211 B7 **Ludewa** Tanz.
151 F3 **Ludgershall** Wiltshire, England U.K.
150 B4 **Ludgvan** Cornwall, England U.K.
116 C3 **Ludhiana** Punjab India
108 B3 **Ludian** Yunnan China
108 B2 **Luding** Sichuan China
169 C4 **Lüdinghausen** Ger.
226 D4 **Ludington** MI U.S.A.
235 E1 **Ludingtonville** NY U.S.A.
150 E2 **Ludlow** Shropshire, England U.K.
241 I4 **Ludlow** CA U.S.A.
233 G3 **Ludlow** VT U.S.A.
179 F4 **Ludmannsdorf** Austria
197 H4 **Ludogorsko Plato** plat. Bulg.
162 B4 **Ludon-Médoc** France
231 D6 **Ludowici** GA U.S.A.
157 G4 **Ludres** France
197 G2 **Luduş** Romania
143 F1 **Ludvika** Sweden
169 E5 **Ludwigsau-Friedlos** Ger.
172 D3 **Ludwigsburg** Ger.
171 G4 **Ludwigsdorf** Ger.
171 E3 **Ludwigsfelde** Ger.
172 D4 **Ludwigshafen** Ger.
172 C2 **Ludwigshafen am Rhein** Ger.
170 C2 **Ludwigslust** Ger.
Ludwigsort Rus. Fed. see **Ladushkin**
171 C5 **Ludwigsstadt** Ger.
175 K4 **Ludwin** Pol.
138 F3 **Ludza** Latvia
163 B4 **Lüe** France
209 D6 **Luebo** Dem. Rep. Congo
209 E5 **Lueki** r. Dem. Rep. Congo
182 D3 **Luelmo** Spain
209 C7 **Luena** Angola
209 E7 **Luena** Dem. Rep. Congo
209 F7 **Luena** Zambia
209 D8 **Luena** r. Zambia
209 D8 **Luena Flats** plain Zambia
209 D9 **Luengue** r. Angola
213 G3 **Luenha** r. Moz./Zimbabwe
169 E4 **Lüerdissen** Ger.
186 B2 **Luesia** Spain
108 C1 **Lüeyang** Shaanxi China
109 E4 **Lufeng** Guangdong China
Lufeng Hunan China see **Xupu**
108 B3 **Lufeng** Yunnan China
209 E7 **Lufira** r. Dem. Rep. Congo
237 E6 **Lufkin** TX U.S.A.
Lufu Yunnan China see **Lunan**
211 A7 **Lufubu** r. Zambia
196 E3 **Lug** r. Yugo.
138 G2 **Luga** Rus. Fed.
138 G2 **Luga** r. Rus. Fed.
190 D2 **Lugano** Switz.
190 D3 **Lugano, Lago di** l. Italy/Switz.
Lugano, Lake Italy/Switz. see **Lugano, Lago di**
Lugansk Ukr. see **Luhans'k**
Luganskaya Oblast' admin. div. Ukr. see **Luhans'ka Oblast'**
Lugansk Oblast admin. div. Ukr. see **Luhans'ka Oblast'**
78 □5 **Luganville** Vanuatu
177 L4 **Lugaşu de Jos** Romania
171 D5 **Lugau** Ger.
169 E4 **Lügde** Ger.
Lugdunum France see **Lyon**

Lugela to Mağara Dağı

330

213 H3 Lugela Moz.
213 H3 Lugela r. Moz.
213 H1 Lugenda r. Moz.
150 E2 Lugg r. Wales U.K.
81 B6 Luggate South I. N.Z.
111 E6 Luggudontsen mt. Xizang China
163 B4 Luglon France
193 E2 Lugnano in Teverina Italy
160 C2 Lugny France
160 C2 Lugny-lès-Charolles France
191 G4 Lugo Italy
182 C1 Lugo Spain
182 C2 Lugo prov. Galicia Spain
192 B2 Lugo-di-Nazza Corse France
197 E3 Lugoj Romania
182 E1 Lugones Spain
162 B4 Lugon-et-l'Île-du-Carnay France
163 B4 Lugos France
139 K3 Lugovaya Rus. Fed.
Lugovaya Proleyka Volgogradskaya Oblast' Rus. Fed. see Primorsk
121 H4 Lugovoy Kazakh.
121 H4 Lugovoye Kazakh.
160 E2 Lugrin France
185 G3 Lugros Spain
136 C2 Luha r. Ukr.
177 G2 Luhačovice Czech Rep.
137 J3 Luhan' r. Ukr.
137 J3 Luhanchyk r. Ukr.
141 N3 Luhanka Fin.
137 J3 Luhans'k Ukr.
137 J3 Luhans'ka Oblast' admin. div. Ukr.
Luhansk Oblast admin. div. Ukr. see Luhans'ka Oblast'
169 E3 Luhden Ger.
109 F1 Luhe Jiangsu China
168 F2 Luhe r. Ger.
173 G2 Luhe-Wildenau Ger.
107 H2 Luhin Sum Nei Mongol China
Luhit r. China/India see Zayü Qu
96 A1 Luhit r. India
170 E1 Lühmannsdorf Ger.
Luhua Sichuan China see Heishui
108 B2 Luhuo Sichuan China
136 E2 Luhyny Ukr.
209 D7 Luia Angola
209 D6 Luia r. Angola
213 G3 Luia r. Moz.
209 D9 Luiana Angola
209 D9 Luiana r. Angola
197 H3 Luica Romania
146 D4 Luichart, Loch l. Scotland U.K.
Luichow Peninsula China see Leizhou Bandao
Luik Belgium see Liège
208 D5 Luilaka r. Dem. Rep. Congo
Luimbale Angola see Londuimbali
Luimneach Rep. of Ireland see Limerick
146 C5 Luing i. Scotland U.K.
190 D3 Luino Italy
182 C2 Luintra Spain
209 D8 Luio r. Angola
140 N2 Luiro r. Fin.
156 B4 Luisant France
254 E2 Luís Correia Brazil
241 I5 Luís Echeverría Álvarez Mex.
254 F3 Luís Gomes Brazil
209 E7 Luishia Dem. Rep. Congo
242 D2 Luis L. León, Presa resr Mex.
244 C2 Luis Moya Mex.
262 V1 Luitpold Coast Antarctica
209 D6 Luiza Dem. Rep. Congo
209 E6 Luizi Dem. Rep. Congo
261 H4 Luján Arg.
261 H4 Lujan r. Arg.
260 C3 Luján de Cuyo Arg.
109 F2 Lujiang Anhui China
137 G2 Luka Ukr.
177 G3 Lukáčovce Slovakia
176 F4 Lukácsháza Hungary
209 B6 Lukala Dem. Rep. Congo
209 E8 Lukanga Swamps Zambia
Lukapa Angola see Lucapa
188 G3 Lukavac Bos.-Herz.
175 L5 Łukawiec Pol.
87 C5 Luke, Mount hill W.A. Austr.
209 C5 Lukenie r. Dem. Rep. Congo
147 D4 Lukeswell Rep. of Ireland
241 K6 Lukeville AZ U.S.A.
134 H4 Lukh Rus. Fed.
134 H4 Lukh r. Rus. Fed.
139 L4 Lukhovitsy Rus. Fed.
197 G5 Lŭki Bulg.
136 C2 Lukiv Ukr.
109 □ Luk Keng H.K. China
208 C5 Lukolela Dem. Rep. Congo
Lukou Hunan China see Zhuzhou
188 G3 Lukovac r. Bos.-Herz.
198 A2 Lukovë Albania
197 G4 Lukovit Bulg.
139 J3 Lukovnikovo Rus. Fed.
175 K4 Łuków Pol.
175 K3 Łukowisko Pol.
135 I5 Lukoyanov Rus. Fed.
138 D4 Lukšiai Lith.
209 E6 Lukuga r. Dem. Rep. Congo
209 B6 Lukula Dem. Rep. Congo
211 C7 Lukuledi Tanz.
209 D8 Lukulu Zambia
209 F8 Lukusashi r. Zambia
136 B3 Luky Ukr.
209 D5 Lula r. Dem. Rep. Congo
192 B4 Lula Sardegna Italy
140 M2 Luleå Sweden
140 M2 Luleälven r. Sweden
199 E1 Lüleburgaz Turkey
258 D2 Lules Arg.
108 B3 Luliang Yunnan China
107 F4 Lüliang Shan mts China
237 D6 Luling TX U.S.A.
147 E3 Lullymore Rep. of Ireland
107 H4 Lulong Hebei China
208 C4 Lulonga r. Dem. Rep. Congo
208 D4 Lulu r. Dem. Rep. Congo
Luluabourg Dem. Rep. Congo see Kananga
111 D6 Lülung Xizang China
87 C5 Lulworth, Mount hill W.A. Austr.
111 D6 Lumachomo Xizang China
260 A6 Lumaco Chile
95 F5 Lumajang Jawa Timur Indon.
111 C5 Lumajangdong Co salt l. China
Lumbala Moxico Angola see Lumbala Kaquengue
Lumbala Moxico Angola see Lumbala N'guimbo
209 D8 Lumbala Kaquengue Angola
209 D8 Lumbala N'guimbo Angola
209 D9 Lumbe r. Zambia
231 E5 Lumber r. SC U.S.A.
231 E5 Lumberton NC U.S.A.
183 I2 Lumbier Spain
213 I2 Lumbo Moz.
182 D4 Lumbrales Spain
183 H2 Lumbreras Spain
156 C2 Lumbres France
117 H4 Lumding Assam India
211 B7 Lumecha Tanz.
190 F3 Lumezzane Italy
140 N2 Lumijoki Fin.
197 I3 Lumina Romania
257 E4 Luminárias Brazil
192 A2 Lumio Corse France
143 H3 Lummelunda Gotland Sweden
165 E4 Lummen Belgium
141 M3 Lumparland Åland Fin.
146 F4 Lumphanan Aberdeenshire, Scotland U.K.
97 D4 Lumphăt Cambodia
186 B3 Lumpiaque Spain
231 C5 Lumpkin GA U.S.A.
223 J5 Lumsden Sask. Can.
81 B6 Lumsden South I. N.Z.
95 F3 Lumut, Gunung mt. Indon.
106 E2 Lün Mongolia
92 B2 Luna Phil.
186 C2 Luna Spain
184 E4 Luna hill Spain
182 E2 Luna r. Spain
241 M5 Luna NM U.S.A.
156 C4 Lunain r. France
192 A5 Lunamatrona Sardegna Italy
108 B3 Lunan Yunnan China
227 F5 Luna Pier MI U.S.A.
161 B5 Lunas France
116 C5 Lunavada Gujarat India
124 B2 Lunayyir, Ḥarrāt lava field Saudi Arabia
177 L5 Lunca Bihor Romania
197 G4 Lunca Teleorman Romania
197 G2 Lunca Bradului Romania
177 L6 Lunca Cernii de Jos Romania
197 G2 Lunca Ilvei Romania
146 E5 Luncarty Perth and Kinross, Scotland U.K.
197 G3 Luncavăț r. Romania
177 L5 Luncoiu de Jos Romania
142 E4 Lund Sweden
241 J2 Lund NV U.S.A.
241 K2 Lund UT U.S.A.
209 C7 Lunda Norte prov. Angola
223 L5 Lundar Man. Can.
209 D7 Lunda Sul prov. Angola
211 B8 Lundazi Zambia
222 H5 Lundbreck Alta Can.
168 F1 Lundby Denmark
142 C4 Lunde Denmark
168 E1 Lunden Ger.
Lundi r. Zimbabwe see Runde
146 F5 Lundin Links Fife, Scotland U.K.
226 C3 Lunds WI U.S.A.
150 C3 Lundy Island England U.K.
168 D2 Lune r. Ger.
149 G3 Lune r. England U.K.
169 B5 Lünebach Ger.
215 H2 Luneberg S. Africa
168 F2 Lüneburg Ger.
168 E2 Lüneburg admin. reg. Niedersachsen Ger.
161 C5 Lunel France
161 F3 Lunella, Punta mt. Italy
161 C5 Lunel-Viel France
169 C4 Lünen Ger.
232 D6 Lunenburg VA U.S.A.
159 I5 Lunery France
168 D2 Lunestedt Ger.
157 G4 Lunéville France
213 I2 Lunga Moz.
209 E8 Lunga r. Zambia
190 D2 Lungern Switz.
111 C6 Lunggar Xizang China
206 B4 Lungi Sierra Leone
Lungleh Mizoram India see Lunglei
117 H5 Lunglei Mizoram India
111 D6 Lungmari mt. Xizang China
147 E4 Lungnaquilla Mountain hill Rep. of Ireland
193 I5 Lungro Italy
209 D8 Lungué-Bungo r. Angola
209 D8 Lungwebungu r. Zambia
116 B4 Luni r. India
123 G4 Luni r. Pak.
Luninets Belarus see Luninyets
240 H2 Luning NV U.S.A.
135 I5 Lunino Rus. Fed.
136 D1 Luninyets Belarus
163 D5 L'Union France
116 C3 Lunkaransar Rajasthan India
116 C3 Lunkha Rajasthan India
123 H2 Lunkho mt. Afgh./Pak.
146 □G1 Lunna Ness hd Scotland U.K.
169 C3 Lünne Ger.
170 F3 Lunow Ger.
206 B4 Lunsar Sierra Leone
209 F8 Lunsemfwa r. Zambia
213 F5 Lunsklip S. Africa
110 D3 Luntai Xinjiang China
164 E2 Lunteren Neth.
198 B1 Lunxhërisë, Mali i ridge Albania
171 D5 Lunzenau Ger.
107 G5 Luo r. Henan China
107 F5 Luo r. Shaanxi China
100 D3 Luobei Heilong. China
110 E4 Luobuzhuang Xinjiang China
Luocheng Fujian China see Hui'an
106 C4 Luocheng Gansu China
108 D3 Luocheng Guangxi China
107 F5 Luochuan Shaanxi China
108 C3 Luodian Guizhou China
109 D4 Luoding Guangdong China
192 B3 Luogosanto Sardegna Italy
109 E1 Luohe Henan China
108 D4 Luo Jiang r. China
107 F5 Luonan Shaanxi China
107 F5 Luoning Henan China
108 C3 Luoping Yunnan China
141 N3 Luopioinen Fin.
109 E1 Luoshan Henan China
109 E2 Luotian Hubei China
140 M3 Luoto Fin.
Luoxiong Yunnan China see Luoping
Luoyang Guangdong China see Boluo
107 G5 Luoyang Henan China
Luoyang Zhejiang China see Taishun
109 F3 Luoyuan Fujian China
209 B6 Luozi Dem. Rep. Congo
100 D4 Luozigou Jilin China
211 B7 Lupa Market Tanz.
213 E3 Lupane Zimbabwe
108 C3 Lupanshui Guizhou China
95 E2 Lupar r. Sarawak Malaysia
143 G4 Łupawa r. Pol.
173 F2 Lupburg Ger.
184 C1 Lupe r. Port.
197 G2 Lupeni Harghita Romania
197 F3 Lupeni Hunedoara Romania
246 E3 Luperón Dom. Rep.
172 C3 Lupfen hill Ger.
163 C5 Lupiac France
211 B7 Lupilichi Moz.
186 C2 Lupiñén Spain
185 G3 Lupión Spain
209 C8 Lupire Angola
175 K6 Łupków Pol.
191 J3 Lupoglav Croatia
92 C5 Lupon Phil.
171 D4 Luppa Ger.
157 G4 Luppy France
241 M4 Lupton AZ U.S.A.
134 K3 Lup'ya r. Rus. Fed.
Luqiao Sichuan China see Luding
106 D5 Luqu Gansu China
Lu Qu r. China see Tao He
107 G4 Luquan Hebei China
108 B3 Luquan Yunnan China
185 F3 Luque Spain
209 C7 Luquembo Angola
247 □1 Luquillo Puerto Rico
192 B4 Luras Sardegna Italy
226 B5 Luray MO U.S.A.
232 D5 Luray VA U.S.A.
163 B5 Lurbe-St-Christau France
160 A2 Lurcy-Lévis France
157 G5 Lure France
161 D4 Lure, Montagne de mt. France
161 D4 Lure, Sommet de mt. France
211 C8 Lureco r. Moz.
209 C7 Luremo Angola
147 E2 Lurgan Northern Ireland U.K.
192 B2 Luri Corse France
210 A3 Luri r. Sudan
252 D4 Luribay Bol.
252 A3 Lurín Peru
Luring Xizang China see Gêrzê
213 I2 Lúrio Moz.
213 I2 Lurio r. Moz.
140 K2 Lurøy Norway
161 D5 Lurs France
159 I4 Lury-sur-Arnon France
209 F8 Lusaka Zambia
209 F8 Lusaka prov. Zambia
209 D6 Lusambo Dem. Rep. Congo
209 E6 Lusangi Dem. Rep. Congo
194 D2 Lusciano Italy
223 I4 Luseland Sask. Can.
190 C4 Luserna San Giovanni Italy
86 E3 Lush, Mount hill W.A. Austr.
108 B2 Lushan Sichuan China
Lushar Qinghai China see Huangzhong
107 F5 Lushi Henan China
196 D5 Lushnjë Albania
211 C6 Lushoto Tanz.
108 A3 Lushui Yunnan China
107 I4 Lushunkou Liaoning China
109 G1 Lüsi Jiangsu China
95 E4 Lusi r. Indon.
162 C2 Lusignan France
160 B2 Lusigny France
156 E4 Lusigny-sur-Barse France
215 G4 Lusikisiki S. Africa
147 E3 Lusk Rep. of Ireland
238 F3 Lusk WY U.S.A.
161 D4 Lus-la-Croix-Haute France
Luso Angola see Luena
182 B4 Luso Port.
146 D5 Luss Argyll and Bute, Scotland U.K.
162 B4 Lussac France
162 C2 Lussac-les-Châteaux France
162 D2 Lussac-les-Églises France
148 D2 Lussa Loch l. Scotland U.K.
161 C4 Lussan France
168 F3 Lüßberg hill Ger.
170 D2 Lüssow Ger.
146 B4 Lusta Highland, Scotland U.K.
172 C2 Lustadt Ger.
190 E1 Lustenau Austria
215 H2 Lusushwana r. Swaziland
Lusutufu r. Africa see Usutu
175 H3 Luszyn Pol.
Lut, Bahrat salt l. Asia see Dead Sea
122 D4 Lut, Dasht-e des. Iran
191 G2 Lutago Italy
Lutai Tianjin China see Ninghe
168 F2 Lütau Ger.
256 B5 Lutécia Brazil
Lutetia France see Paris
122 D4 Lūt-e Zangī Aḥmad des. Iran
226 E3 Luther MI U.S.A.
232 D4 Luthersburg PA U.S.A.
171 D4 Lutherstadt Wittenberg Ger.
176 G2 Lutín Czech Rep.
168 F1 Lütjenburg Ger.
168 F2 Lütjensee Ger.
175 H3 Lutocin Pol.
175 H4 Lutomiersk Pol.
151 G3 Luton Luton, England U.K.
151 G3 Luton admin. div. England U.K.
95 F1 Lutong Sarawak Malaysia
213 F3 Lutope r. Zimbabwe
175 K6 Lutowiska Pol.
175 I1 Lutry Pol.
223 I2 Łutselk'e N.W.T. Can.
136 C2 Luts'k Ukr.
169 F4 Lutter am Barenberge Ger.
157 H5 Lutterbach France
151 F2 Lutterworth Leicestershire, England U.K.
214 D5 Luttig S. Africa
140 O1 Lutto r. Fin./Rus. Fed. alt. Lotta
209 D8 Lutuai Angola
137 J3 Lutuhyne Ukr.
174 G4 Lututów Pol.
174 F3 Lutynia r. Pol.
231 D6 Lutz FL U.S.A.
171 D4 Lützen Ger.
169 C5 Lutzerath Ger.
173 E3 Lutzingen Ger.
170 C2 Lützow Ger.
214 C3 Lutzputs S. Africa
171 D4 Lützschena Ger.
214 B4 Lutzville S. Africa
141 N3 Luumäki Fin.
210 D4 Luuq Somalia
231 C6 Luverne AL U.S.A.
236 D3 Luverne MN U.S.A.
141 M3 Luvia Fin.
209 E6 Luvua r. Dem. Rep. Congo
209 D8 Luvuei Angola
213 F4 Luvuvhu r. S. Africa
211 C7 Luwegu r. Tanz.
210 B4 Luwero Uganda
209 F7 Luwingu Zambia
93 B3 Luwuk Sulawesi Tengah Indon.
160 D1 Lux France
165 E4 Luxembourg prov. Belgium
165 F5 Luxembourg country Europe
165 F5 Luxembourg Lux.
165 F5 Luxembourg admin. dist. Lux.
Luxemburg country Europe see Luxembourg
226 D3 Luxemburg WI U.S.A.
163 A5 Luxe-Sumberraute France
157 G5 Luxeuil-les-Bains France
163 B4 Luxey France
108 D2 Luxi Hunan China
108 A3 Luxi Yunnan China
108 B3 Luxi Yunnan China
108 C2 Luxian Sichuan China
215 E4 Luxolweni S. Africa
Luxor Egypt see El Uqşur
150 C4 Luxulyan Cornwall, England U.K.
163 A5 Luy r. France
Luyang Sichuan China see Lushan
163 B5 Luy de Béarn r. France
163 B5 Luy de France r. France
182 D2 Luyego de Somoza Spain
109 E1 Luyi Henan China
165 E3 Luyksgestel Neth.
159 G4 Luynes France
Luyuan Shaanxi China see Gaoling
216 □1c Luz Graciosa Azores
257 E3 Luz Brazil
184 C2 Luz Évora Port.
184 B3 Luz Faro Port.
184 C3 Luz Faro Port.
182 D3 Luz hill Port.
134 I3 Luza Rus. Fed.
134 I3 Luza r. Rus. Fed.
134 L2 Luza r. Rus. Fed.
183 H4 Luzaga Spain
156 C3 Luzarches France
163 B6 Luz-Ardiden France
176 F2 Luže Czech Rep.
163 D4 Luzech France
176 D1 Lužec nad Vltavou Czech Rep.
190 D1 Luzern Switz.
190 D1 Luzern canton Switz.
234 C1 Luzerne PA U.S.A.
234 B1 Luzerne County county PA U.S.A.
139 K4 Luzha r. Rus. Fed.
108 D3 Luzhai Guangxi China
Luzhang Yunnan China see Lushui
108 C3 Luzhi Guizhou China
108 C2 Luzhou Sichuan China
184 B3 Luzianes Port.
256 D2 Luziânia Brazil
176 D1 Lužické Hory mts Czech Rep.
254 E2 Luzilândia Brazil
174 G1 Luzino Pol.
183 F1 Luzmela Spain
176 C1 Lužná Czech Rep.
175 J6 Łużna Pol.
176 D2 Lužnice r. Czech Rep.
92 B3 Luzon i. Phil.
183 H3 Luzón Spain
92 B1 Luzon Strait Phil.
163 C6 Luz-St-Sauveur France
160 B2 Luzy France
174 G4 Łużyca r. Pol.
191 F4 Luzzara Italy
193 I5 Luzzi Italy
136 D1 L'va r. Ukr.
136 C3 L'viv Ukr.
Lviv Oblast admin. div. Ukr. see L'vivs'ka Oblast'
136 C2 L'vivs'ka Oblast' admin. div. Ukr.
L'vov Ukr. see L'viv
Lvov Oblast admin. div. Ukr. see L'vivs'ka Oblast'
L'vovskaya Oblast' admin. div. Ukr. see L'vivs'ka Oblast'
139 K4 L'vovskiy Rus. Fed.
Lwów Ukr. see L'viv
174 E3 Lwówek Pol.
174 D4 Lwówek Śląski Pol.
136 D3 Lyadova r. Ukr.
138 G2 Lyady Rus. Fed.
138 F5 Lyakhavichy Belarus
Lyakhovichi Belarus see Lyakhavichy
131 P2 Lyakhovskiye Ostrova is Novosibirskiye O-va Rus. Fed.
81 A6 Lyall, Mount South I. N.Z.
Lyallpur Pak. see Faisalabad
121 F5 Lyal'mikar Uzbek.
135 I5 Lyambir' Rus. Fed.
134 L4 Lyamino Rus. Fed.
Lyangar Kashkadar'inskaya Oblast' Uzbek. see Langar
121 F4 Lyangar Navoiyskaya Oblast' Uzbek.
134 M3 Lyapin r. Rus. Fed.
137 G3 Lyashivka Ukr.
141 O3 Lyaskelya Rus. Fed.
197 G4 Lyaskovets Bulg.
138 E5 Lyasnaya Belarus
138 D5 Lyasnaya r. Belarus
175 L3 Lyasnaya Lyevaya r. Belarus
177 L3 Lybokhora Ukr.
146 E3 Lybster Highland, Scotland U.K.
175 M4 Lybytiv Ukr.
170 E2 Lychen Ger.
137 H3 Lychkove Ukr.
139 I3 Lychkovo Rus. Fed.
Lyck Pol. see Ełk
140 L2 Lycksele Sweden
234 A1 Lycoming County county PA U.S.A.
234 A1 Lycoming Creek r. PA U.S.A.
Lycopolis Egypt see Asyût
151 H4 Lydd Kent, England U.K.
Lydda Israel see Lod
262 W2 Lyddan Island Antarctica
213 F5 Lydenburg S. Africa
150 C4 Lydford Devon, England U.K.
150 E3 Lydney Gloucestershire, England U.K.
175 I3 Łydynia r. Pol.
138 E5 Lyebyada r. Belarus
136 E2 Lyel'chytsy Belarus
240 H3 Lyell, Mount CA U.S.A.
84 B4 Lyell Brown, Mount hill N.T. Austr.
81 D4 Lyell Range mts South I. N.Z.
138 G4 Lyepyel' Belarus
198 C3 Lygourio Greece
137 I3 Lyhivka Ukr.
227 I5 Lykens PA U.S.A.
137 F2 Lykhachiv Ukr.
137 G3 Lykhivka Ukr.
139 I2 Lykoshino Rus. Fed.
214 E2 Lykso S. Africa
226 A4 Lyle MN U.S.A.
136 E5 Lyman Ukr.
238 E3 Lyman WY U.S.A.
137 I3 Lyman, Ozero l. Ukr.
136 E4 Lymans'ke Ukr.
150 E4 Lyme Bay England U.K.
150 E4 Lyme Regis Dorset, England U.K.
151 I3 Lyminge Kent, England U.K.
151 F4 Lymington Hampshire, England U.K.
149 G4 Lymm Warrington, England U.K.
151 I3 Lympne Kent, England U.K.
150 D4 Lympstone Devon, England U.K.
143 I4 Łyna r. Pol.
232 B6 Lynch KY U.S.A.
231 C5 Lynchburg TN U.S.A.
232 D6 Lynchburg VA U.S.A.
231 E5 Lynches r. SC U.S.A.
232 D6 Lynch Station VA U.S.A.
233 □H2 Lynchville ME U.S.A.
85 E3 Lynd r. Qld Austr.
238 B1 Lynden WA U.S.A.
85 F3 Lyndhurst Qld Austr.
82 D2 Lyndhurst S.A. Austr.
151 F4 Lyndhurst Hampshire, England U.K.
87 B4 Lyndon W.A. Austr.
87 B4 Lyndon r. W.A. Austr.
236 E4 Lyndon KS U.S.A.
226 C4 Lyndon Station WI U.S.A.
232 D3 Lyndonville NY U.S.A.
233 G2 Lyndonville VT U.S.A.
149 F3 Lyne r. England U.K.
151 F3 Lyneham Wiltshire, England U.K.
149 H2 Lynemouth Northumberland, England U.K.
146 E3 Lyness Orkney, Scotland U.K.
142 B2 Lyngdal Norway
140 M1 Lyngen sea chan. Norway
140 M1 Lyngseidet Norway
150 C4 Lynher r. England U.K.
86 D2 Lynher Reef W.A. Austr.
150 D3 Lynmouth Devon, England U.K.
Lynn Norfolk, England U.K. see King's Lynn
233 H3 Lynn MA U.S.A.
241 K2 Lynndyl UT U.S.A.
231 C6 Lynn Haven FL U.S.A.
223 K3 Lynn Lake Man. Can.
137 H2 Lynove Ukr.
137 G2 Lynovytsya Ukr.
87 B6 Lynton W.A. Austr.
150 D3 Lynton Devon, England U.K.
138 F4 Lyntupy Belarus
223 J2 Lynx Lake N.W.T. Can.
226 B4 Lynxville WI U.S.A.
160 C3 Lyon France
Lyon airport France see Satolas
146 E5 Lyon r. Scotland U.K.
146 D5 Lyon, Loch l. Scotland U.K.
233 G2 Lyon Mountain NY U.S.A.
160 C3 Lyonnais, Monts du hills France
82 C2 Lyons S.A. Austr.
87 B5 Lyons r. W.A. Austr.
Lyons France see Lyon
231 D5 Lyons GA U.S.A.
236 D4 Lyons KS U.S.A.
232 E3 Lyons NY U.S.A.
233 F3 Lyons Falls NY U.S.A.
156 B3 Lyons-la-Forêt France
235 E1 Lyons Plain CT U.S.A.
234 C2 Lyon Station PA U.S.A.
139 H4 Lyozna Belarus
136 C2 Lypa r. Ukr.
136 E2 Lypnyky Ukr.
137 G2 Lypova Dolyna Ukr.
136 E3 Lypovets' Ukr.
137 I2 Lyptsi Ukr.
156 D2 Lys r. France
190 C3 Lys r. Italy
168 F1 Lysabild Denmark
177 H2 Lysá Hora mt. Czech Rep.
137 F3 Lysa Hora Ukr.
171 F5 Lysá nad Labem Czech Rep.
177 H2 Lysá pod Makytou Slovakia
175 J2 Łyse Pol.
142 B2 Lysekammen mt. Norway
142 D2 Lysekil Sweden
175 I5 Łysica hill Pol.
176 F2 Lysice Czech Rep.
198 B2 Lysimachia, Limni l. Greece
174 G5 Lyski Pol.
134 I4 Lyskovo Rus. Fed.
137 J4 Lysogorka Rus. Fed.
174 G2 Łysomice Pol.
190 C1 Lyss Switz.
142 D3 Lystrup Denmark
134 L4 Lys'va Rus. Fed.
142 E1 Lysvik Sweden
136 F3 Lysyanka Ukr.
137 J3 Lysychans'k Ukr.
135 I6 Lysyye Gory Rus. Fed.
175 H4 Łyszkowice Pol.
150 E4 Lytchett Matravers Dorset, England U.K.
150 E4 Lytchett Minster Dorset, England U.K.
146 E3 Lyth Highland, Scotland U.K.
149 F4 Lytham St Anne's Lancashire, England U.K.
139 K4 Lytkarino Rus. Fed.
175 M5 Lytovezh Ukr.
81 D5 Lyttelton South I. N.Z.
81 D5 Lyttelton Harbour South I. N.Z.
222 F5 Lytton B.C. Can.
138 G5 Lyuban' Belarus
139 H2 Lyuban' Rus. Fed.
136 D3 Lyubar Ukr.
136 F4 Lyubashivka Ukr.
137 H1 Lyubazh Rus. Fed.
138 F5 Lyubcha Belarus
136 F2 Lyubech Ukr.
139 K4 Lyubertsy Rus. Fed.
136 C2 Lyubeshiv Ukr.
134 H4 Lyubim Rus. Fed.
197 H5 Lyubimets Bulg.
137 H2 Lyubimovka Rus. Fed.
138 E5 Lyubishchytsy Belarus
139 J2 Lyubitovo Rus. Fed.
175 I1 Lyublino Rus. Fed.
175 M4 Lyublynets' Ukr.
139 J5 Lyubokhna Rus. Fed.
175 M4 Lyubokhyny Ukr.
137 H2 Lyubostan' Rus. Fed.
Lyubotin Ukr. see Lyubotyn
137 H3 Lyubotyn Ukr.
137 I4 Lyubymivka Ukr.
175 L6 Lyubyntsi Ukr.
139 I2 Lyubytino Rus. Fed.
139 J5 Lyudinovo Rus. Fed.
197 H4 Lyulyakovo Bulg.
134 I4 Lyunda r. Rus. Fed.
138 F5 Lyusina Belarus
134 L2 Lyzha r. Rus. Fed.
138 G3 Lža r. Latvia
138 G3 Lzha r. Rus. Fed.

M

96 B2 Ma r. Myanmar
96 C2 Ma, Nam r. Laos
96 D3 Ma, Sông r. Vietnam
113 □1 Maabadi i. N. Male Maldives
Maafushi i. S. Male Maldives see Mafushi
240 □C8 Maalaea HI U.S.A.
114 B5 Maalhosmadulu Atoll Maldives
147 B3 Maam Rep. of Ireland
Maamakundhoo i. N. Male Maldives see Makunudhoo
209 E9 Maamba Zambia
147 B3 Maam Cross Rep. of Ireland
207 H6 Ma'an Cameroon
128 B4 Ma'an Jordan
140 N3 Maaninka Fin.
109 F2 Ma'anshan Anhui China
106 D1 Maanyt Bulgan Mongolia
107 E2 Maanyt Töv Mongolia
138 E2 Maardu Estonia
165 E3 Maarheeze Neth.
Maarianhamina Åland Fin. see Mariehamn
164 E2 Maarn Neth.
128 C2 Ma'arrat an Nu'mān Syria
164 E2 Maarssen Neth.
164 E2 Maarssenbroek Neth.
164 E2 Maartensdijk Neth.
164 D3 Maas r. Neth. alt. Meuse (Belgium/France)
147 C2 Maas Rep. of Ireland
165 E3 Maasbracht Neth.
165 F3 Maasbree Neth.
164 D3 Maasdam Neth.
165 E3 Maaseik Belgium
92 C4 Maasin Phil.
164 D3 Maasland Neth.
165 E4 Maasmechelen Belgium
164 D3 Maassluis Neth.
165 E4 Maastricht Neth.
83 F5 Maatsuyker Group is Tas. Austr.
Maba Guangdong China see Qujiang
109 F1 Maba Jiangsu China
215 F1 Mabaalstad North West S. Africa
215 F1 Mabaalstad North West S. Africa
92 B3 Mabalacat Phil.
208 A5 Mabanda Gabon
124 D5 Ma'bar Yemen
251 G2 Mabaruma Guyana
Mabating Yunnan China see Hongshan
82 C2 Mabel Creek S.A. Austr.
86 E3 Mabel Downs W.A. Austr.
224 B3 Mabella Ont. Can.
227 I3 Maberly Ont. Can.
108 B2 Mabian Sichuan China
149 J4 Mablethorpe Lincolnshire, England U.K.
160 C2 Mably France
215 G1 Mabopane S. Africa
225 I4 Mabou N.S. Can.
128 B4 Mabrak, Jabal mt. Jordan
214 E1 Mabule Botswana
212 D5 Mabutsane Botswana
259 B7 Macá, Monte mt. Chile
261 F5 Macachín Arg.
87 C5 Macadam Plains W.A. Austr.
84 B2 Macadam Range hills N.T. Austr.
257 G5 Macaé Brazil
185 H3 Macael Spain
254 G3 Macaíba Brazil
254 E5 Macajuba Brazil
211 B8 Macaloge Moz.
224 E3 Macamic Que. Can.
Macan, Kepulauan atolls Indon. see Taka'Bonerate, Kepulauan
186 F2 Maçanet de Cabrenys Spain
Macao Macau China see Macau
182 C5 Mação Port.
251 I4 Macapá Brazil
Macar Turkey see Gebiz
250 B6 Macará Ecuador
255 E5 Macarani Brazil
250 C4 Macarena, Cordillera mts Col.
251 F2 Macareo, Caño r. Venez.
83 E4 Macarthur Vic. Austr.
250 B5 Macas Ecuador
182 D3 Maçãs r. Port./Spain
Macassar Sulawesi Selatan Indon. see Ujung Pandang
Macassar Strait Indon. see Makassar Strait
187 C5 Macastre Spain
254 F3 Macau Brazil
109 E4 Macau Macau China
162 B3 Macau France
252 C2 Macauã r. Brazil
254 E5 Macaúbas Brazil
77 I5 Macauley Island N.Z.
190 D2 Maccagno Italy
213 G5 Maccaretane Moz.
195 E5 Macchia r. Sicilia Italy
193 G3 Macchiagodena Italy
231 D6 Macclenny FL U.S.A.
149 G4 Macclesfield Cheshire, England U.K.
224 B3 Macdiarmid Ont. Can.
86 F4 Macdonald, Lake salt flat W.A. Austr.
84 B4 Macdonnell Ranges mts N.T. Austr.
146 F4 Macduff Aberdeenshire, Scotland U.K.
177 K5 Macea Romania
182 C2 Maceda Spain
182 D3 Macedo de Cavaleiros Port.
Macedon country Europe see Macedonia
197 E5 Macedonia country Europe
235 E1 Macedonia CT U.S.A.
254 G4 Maceió Brazil
182 C4 Maceira Guarda Port.
182 B5 Maceira Leiria Port.
206 C4 Macenta Guinea
191 I5 Macerata Italy
191 I5 Macerata prov. Marche Italy
191 H5 Macerata Feltria Italy
82 D3 Macfarlane, Lake salt flat S.A. Austr.
147 B5 Macgillycuddy's Reeks mts Rep. of Ireland
148 C3 MacGregor's Corner Northern Ireland U.K.
123 F4 Mach Pak.
257 G2 Machacalis Brazil
252 D4 Machacamarca Bol.
250 B5 Machachi Ecuador
253 E2 Machadinho r. Brazil
257 E4 Machado Brazil
215 H1 Machadodorp S. Africa
184 C2 Machados Port.
211 C5 Machakos Kenya
250 B5 Machala Ecuador
260 B4 Machali Chile
Machali Qinghai China see Madoi
213 G4 Machanga Moz.
253 E5 Macharetí Bol.
210 B2 Machar Marshes Sudan
84 D5 Machattie, Lake salt flat Qld Austr.
156 E3 Machault France
Machaze Moz. see Chitobe
158 E5 Machecoul France
165 D4 Machelen Belgium
150 D3 Machen Caerphilly, Wales U.K.
109 E2 Macheng Hubei China
157 G3 Macheren France
114 C2 Macherla Andhra Prad. India
171 D4 Machern Ger.
185 F1 Machero mt. Spain
226 C4 Machesney Park IL U.S.A.
116 D3 Machhiwara Punjab India
116 E4 Machhlishahr Uttar Prad. India
233 □J2 Machias ME U.S.A.
232 D3 Machias NY U.S.A.
233 □I1 Machias r. ME U.S.A.
184 □ Machico Madeira
105 F3 Machida Japan
114 D2 Machilipatnam Andhra Prad. India
211 B8 Machinga Malawi
250 C2 Machiques Venez.
146 B6 Machir Bay Scotland U.K.
Machiwara Punjab India see Machhiwara
245 H4 Machona, Laguna lag. Mex.
146 C6 Machrihanish Argyll and Bute, Scotland U.K.
137 H3 Machukhy Ukr.
252 B3 Machupicchu tourist site Peru
252 D3 Machupo r. Bol.
150 D2 Machynlleth Powys, Wales U.K.
213 G5 Macia Moz.
Macias Nguema i. Equat. Guinea see Bioco
175 J4 Maciejowice Pol.
261 G3 Maciel Arg.
197 I3 Măcin Romania
192 B2 Macinaggio Corse France
83 G2 Macintyre r. N.S.W. Austr.
83 G2 Macintyre Brook r. Qld Austr.
252 B3 Macizo de Tocate mts Peru
241 M2 Mack CO U.S.A.
129 A3 Maçka Turkey
85 G4 Mackay Qld Austr.
223 I3 MacKay r. Alta Can.
238 D2 Mackay ID U.S.A.
86 F4 Mackay, Lake salt flat W.A. Austr.
223 I2 MacKay Lake N.W.T. Can.
262 O1 Mackay Mountains Antarctica
172 B2 Mackenbach Ger.
169 F4 Mackenrode Ger.
85 G4 Mackenzie r. Qld Austr.
222 F4 Mackenzie B.C. Can.
226 C1 Mackenzie Ont. Can.
222 E1 Mackenzie r. N.W.T. Can.
Mackenzie Guyana see Linden
Mackenzie atoll Micronesia see Ulithi
220 E3 Mackenzie Bay Y.T. Can.
222 G2 Mackenzie Highway N.W.T. Can.
221 G2 Mackenzie King Island N.W.T. Can.
222 C1 Mackenzie Mountains N.W.T./Y.T. Can.
Mackillop, Lake salt flat Qld Austr. see Yamma Yamma, Lake
226 E3 Mackinac Island MI U.S.A.
226 C5 Mackinaw r. IL U.S.A.
226 E3 Mackinaw City MI U.S.A.
223 I4 Macklin Sask. Can.
83 H2 Macksville N.S.W. Austr.
83 H2 Maclean N.S.W. Austr.
215 F5 Macleantown S. Africa
215 G4 Maclear S. Africa
83 H2 Macleay r. N.S.W. Austr.
MacLeod Alta Can. see Fort Macleod
87 B5 MacLeod, Lake imp. l. W.A. Austr.
222 C2 Macmillan r. Y.T. Can.
209 C6 Macocola Angola
226 B5 Macomb IL U.S.A.
192 A4 Macomer Sardegna Italy
211 D8 Macomia Moz.
160 C2 Mâcon France
231 D5 Macon GA U.S.A.
236 E4 Macon MO U.S.A.
237 F5 Macon MS U.S.A.
232 B5 Macon OH U.S.A.
237 F6 Macon, Bayou r. LA U.S.A.
235 D1 Macopin NJ U.S.A.
213 G3 Macossa Moz.
183 E4 Macotera Spain
213 G4 Macovane Moz.
Macpherson Robertson Land reg. Antarctica see Mac. Robertson Land
83 F2 Macquarie r. N.S.W. Austr.
83 F5 Macquarie r. Tas. Austr.
83 G3 Macquarie, Lake b. N.S.W. Austr.
83 F5 Macquarie Harbour Tas. Austr.
82 □3 Macquarie Island S. Pacific Ocean
83 F2 Macquarie Marshes N.S.W. Austr.
83 G3 Macquarie Mountain N.S.W. Austr.
266 F9 Macquarie Ridge sea feature S. Pacific Ocean
81 C6 Macraes Flat South I. N.Z.
263 E2 Mac. Robertson Land reg. Antarctica
147 C5 Macroom Rep. of Ireland
243 H5 Mactún Mex.
190 C3 Macugnaga Italy
196 E5 Macukull Albania
82 C1 Macumba S.A. Austr.
234 C2 Macungie PA U.S.A.
254 F4 Macururé Brazil
252 C3 Macusani Peru
243 G5 Macuspana Mex.
233 □I2 Macwahoc ME U.S.A.
177 K3 Mád Hungary
128 B4 Mādabā Jordan
215 H2 Madadeni S. Africa
213 □ Madagascar i. Africa
265 H6 Madagascar Basin sea feature Indian Ocean
265 G7 Madagascar Ridge sea feature Indian Ocean
207 I4 Madagli Nigeria
124 B2 Madā'in Şāliḥ Saudi Arabia
216 □1c Madalena Pico Azores
254 F3 Madalena Brazil
197 G5 Madan Bulg.
114 C3 Madanapalle Andhra Prad. India
91 K8 Madang P.N.G.
116 D4 Madaora Uttar Prad. India
207 G3 Madaoua Niger
177 I5 Madaras Hungary
197 E2 Mădăraș Romania
117 G5 Madaripur Bangl.
207 G3 Madarounfa Niger
227 I3 Madawaska Ont. Can.
224 E4 Madawaska r. Ont. Can.
233 □I1 Madawaska ME U.S.A.
96 B2 Madaya Myanmar
192 B5 Maddalena Spiaggia Sardegna Italy
193 G3 Maddaloni Italy
114 D2 Madded Madh. Prad. India
114 C3 Maddur Karnataka India
164 D3 Made Neth.
251 G5 Madeira r. Brazil
184 □ Madeira terr. N. Atlantic Ocean
184 □ Madeira, Arquipélago da is N. Atlantic Ocean
Madeira, Arquipélago da terr. N. Atlantic Ocean see Madeira
184 □ Madeira, Ilha da i. Madeira
Madeira Islands N. Atlantic Ocean see Madeira, Arquipélago da
253 E2 Madeirinha r. Brazil
150 E2 Madeley Staffordshire, England U.K.
150 E2 Madeley Telford and Wrekin, England U.K.
236 E2 Madelia MN U.S.A.
126 E3 Maden Turkey
242 C2 Madera Mex.
185 H2 Madera r. Spain
240 G3 Madera CA U.S.A.
183 F3 Maderano r. Spain
178 B3 Madererspitze mt. Austria
183 G3 Maderuelo Spain
114 B3 Madgaon Goa India
116 B5 Madhavpur Gujarat India
117 F4 Madhepura Bihar India
111 C7 Madhoganj Uttar Prad. India
117 F4 Madhubani Bihar India
114 C3 Madhugiri Karnataka India
116 D5 Madhya Pradesh state India
95 F2 Madi, Dataran Tinggi plat. Indon.
215 E2 Madibogo S. Africa
82 D2 Madigan Gulf salt flat S.A. Austr.
114 B3 Madikeri Karnataka India
237 D5 Madill OK U.S.A.
209 B6 Madimba Dem. Rep. Congo
206 D4 Madinani Côte d'Ivoire
124 D5 Madīnat ash Sha'b Yemen
128 D2 Madīnat ath Thawrah Syria
157 F4 Madine, Lac de l. France
209 A6 Madingo-Kayes Congo
209 B6 Madingou Congo
252 D3 Madini r. Bol.
163 B5 Madiran France
213 □J3 Madirovalo Madag.
231 C5 Madison AL U.S.A.
235 F1 Madison CT U.S.A.
231 D6 Madison FL U.S.A.
231 D5 Madison GA U.S.A.
230 C4 Madison IN U.S.A.
233 □I2 Madison ME U.S.A.
236 D2 Madison MN U.S.A.
236 D3 Madison NE U.S.A.
235 D2 Madison NJ U.S.A.
232 C4 Madison OH U.S.A.
236 D2 Madison SD U.S.A.
232 D5 Madison VA U.S.A.
226 C4 Madison WI U.S.A.
232 C5 Madison WV U.S.A.
238 E2 Madison r. MT U.S.A.
232 D6 Madison Heights VA U.S.A.
230 C4 Madisonville KY U.S.A.
231 C5 Madisonville TN U.S.A.
237 E6 Madisonville TX U.S.A.
95 E4 Madiun Jawa Timur Indon.
150 E2 Madley Herefordshire, England U.K.
87 D5 Madley, Mount hill W.A. Austr.
224 E4 Madoc Ont. Can.
177 H5 Madocsa Hungary
106 C5 Madoi Qinghai China
157 G4 Madon r. France
138 F3 Madona Latvia
194 C5 Madonie mts Sicilia Italy
234 B3 Madonna MD U.S.A.
191 F2 Madonna di Campiglio Italy
199 E2 Madra Dağı mts Turkey
124 B3 Madrakah Saudi Arabia
Madras Tamil Nadu India see Chennai
Madras state India see Tamil Nadu
238 B2 Madras OR U.S.A.
245 F1 Madre, Laguna lag. Mex.
237 D7 Madre, Laguna lag. TX U.S.A.
245 H5 Madre, Sierra mts Mex.
92 B2 Madre, Sierra mt. Phil.
Madre de Chiapas, Sierra mts Mex. see Madre, Sierra
257 E4 Madre de Deus de Minas Brazil
252 C2 Madre de Dios dept Peru
259 B8 Madre de Dios, Isla i. Chile
244 D4 Madre del Sur, Sierra mts Mex.
244 B1 Madre Occidental, Sierra mts Mex.
244 D1 Madre Oriental, Sierra mts Mex.
163 E6 Madrès, Pic de mt. France
92 C4 Madrid Phil.
183 G4 Madrid Spain
183 G4 Madrid aut. comm. Spain
92 B4 Madridejos Phil.
185 G1 Madridejos Spain
183 F3 Madrigal de las Altas Torres Spain
183 E4 Madrigal de la Vera Spain
183 G2 Madrigal del Monte Spain
184 E1 Madrigalejo Spain
185 I1 Madrigueras Spain
178 A4 Madrisahorn mt. Austria/Switz.
150 □ Madron Cornwall, England U.K.
184 E1 Madroñera Spain
185 I2 Madroño mt. Spain
246 B2 Madruga Cuba
113 □1 Madu i. S. Male Maldives
209 B6 Maduda Dem. Rep. Congo
115 D2 Madugula Andhra Prad. India
87 E6 Madura W.A. Austr.
95 F4 Madura i. Indon.
95 F4 Madura, Selat sea chan. Indon.
114 C4 Madurai Tamil Nadu India
114 C3 Madurantakam Tamil Nadu India
122 C4 Madvār, Kūh-e mt. Iran
116 E4 Madwas Madh. Prad. India
129 E2 Madzhalis Rus. Fed.
197 G5 Madzharovo Bulg.
213 F3 Madziwa Mine Zimbabwe
191 H2 Maè r. Italy
Maé i. Vanuatu see Émaé
105 F2 Maebashi Japan
96 B3 Mae Hong Son Thai.
158 C3 Maël-Carhaix France
142 C2 Mælefjell mt. Norway
186 D3 Maella Spain
183 F4 Maello Spain
150 C3 Maenclochog Pembrokeshire, Wales U.K.
150 D2 Maentwrog Gwynedd, Wales U.K.
193 F3 Maenza Italy
96 B3 Mae Ramat Thai.
96 B3 Mae Rim Thai.
197 F2 Măerişte Romania
96 B3 Mae Sariang Thai.
146 E3 Maes Howe tourist site Scotland U.K.
96 B3 Mae Sot Thai.
150 D3 Maesteg Bridgend, Wales U.K.
246 C3 Maestra, Sierra mts Cuba
185 E3 Maestre hill Spain
183 H2 Maestu Spain
96 B3 Mae Suai Thai.
213 □J3 Maevatanana Madag.
78 □5 Maéwo i. Vanuatu
223 K4 Mafeking Man. Can.
Mafeking S. Africa see Mafikeng
215 F3 Mafeteng Lesotho
83 F4 Maffra Vic. Austr.
211 C7 Mafia Channel Tanz.
211 C6 Mafia Island Tanz.
215 E1 Mafikeng S. Africa
211 B7 Mafinga Tanz.
255 C8 Mafra Brazil
184 A2 Mafra Port.
Mafraq Jordan see Al Mafraq
113 □1 Mafushi i. S. Male Maldives
215 H4 Magabeni S. Africa
184 E2 Magacela hill Spain
131 Q4 Magadan Rus. Fed.
161 B5 Magalas France
215 F1 Magaliesberg mts S. Africa
215 F1 Magaliesburg S. Africa
Magallanes Chile see Punta Arenas
92 B3 Magallanes Phil.
259 C9 Magallanes, Estrecho de sea chan. Chile
259 B9 Magallanes y Antártica Chilena admin. reg. Chile
183 I3 Magallón Spain
187 F5 Magalluf Spain
183 H3 Magaña Spain
147 E4 Maganey Rep. of Ireland
250 C2 Magangue Col.
126 D3 Mağara Turkey
129 C3 Mağara tourist site Turkey
128 A1 Mağara Dağı mt. Turkey

Mağarali to Mangoky
331

128 D1 Mağarali Turkey
129 F3 Magaramkent Rus. Fed.
207 H3 Magaria Niger
Magas Iran see Zābolī
92 B2 Magat r. Phil.
183 F3 Magaz Spain
237 E5 Magazine Mountain hill AR U.S.A.
194 C5 Magazzolo r. Sicilia Italy
206 C4 Magburaka Sierra Leone
100 C1 Magdagachi Rus. Fed.
171 C5 Magdala Ger.
261 I4 Magdalena Arg.
252 D3 Magdalena Bol.
250 C2 Magdalena dept Col.
250 C2 Magdalena r. Col.
242 C2 Magdalena Mex.
242 C2 Magdalena r. Mex.
239 F5 Magdalena NM U.S.A.
259 B7 Magdalena, Isla i. Chile
245 F4 Magdalena Cuayucatepec Mex.
Magdalena Island Fr. Polynesia see Fatu Hiva
95 G1 Magdalene, Gunung mt. Sabah Malaysia
171 C3 Magdeburg Ger.
171 C3 Magdeburg admin. reg. Sachsen-Anhalt Ger.
171 D3 Magdeburgerforth Ger.
85 G3 Magdelaine Cays atoll Coral Sea Is Terr. Austr.
237 F6 Magee MS U.S.A.
95 E4 Magelang Jawa Tengah Indon.
Magellan, Strait of Chile see Magallanes, Estrecho de
266 E4 Magellan Seamounts sea feature N. Pacific Ocean
190 D3 Magenta Italy
87 C7 Magenta, Lake salt flat W.A. Austr.
140 N1 Magerøya i. Norway
163 A5 Magescq France
177 L4 Măgeşti Romania
190 D2 Maggia Switz.
190 D2 Maggia r. Switz.
261 F3 Maggiolo Arg.
190 E4 Maggiorasca, Monte mt. Italy
190 D3 Maggiore, Lago l. Italy
Maggiore, Lake Italy see Maggiore, Lago
192 B4 Maggiore, Monte hill Sardegna Italy
193 G3 Maggiore, Monte mt. Italy
246 □ Maggotty Jamaica
203 F2 Maghâgha Egypt
128 B5 Maghā'ir Shu'ayb tourist site Saudi Arabia
206 B3 Maghama Maur.
147 B5 Maghanlawaun Rep. of Ireland
128 A4 Maghâra, Gebel hill Egypt
147 C2 Maghera Rep. of Ireland
147 E2 Maghera Northern Ireland U.K.
147 E2 Magherafelt Northern Ireland U.K.
148 C3 Magheralin Northern Ireland U.K.
147 D2 Magheramason Northern Ireland U.K.
147 E2 Maghery Northern Ireland U.K.
204 E2 Maghnia Alg.
149 G4 Maghull Merseyside, England U.K.
148 C2 Magilligan Northern Ireland U.K.
185 G3 Mágina mt. Spain
192 E1 Magione Italy
195 F3 Magisano Italy
Magitang Qinghai China see Jainca
188 G3 Maglaj Bos.-Herz.
160 E2 Magland France
197 F3 Maglavit Romania
193 F2 Magliano de'Marsi Italy
192 D2 Magliano in Toscana Italy
193 E2 Magliano Sabina Italy
195 H2 Maglie Italy
177 I4 Maglód Hungary
241 L5 Magma AZ U.S.A.
162 D2 Magnac-Laval France
162 C3 Magnac-sur-Touvre France
194 B6 Magna Grande hill Italy
195 E5 Magna Grande mt. Sicilia Italy
162 B2 Magné France
85 F3 Magnetic Island Qld Austr.
85 F3 Magnetic Passage Qld Austr.
134 F1 Magnetity Rus. Fed.
157 G4 Magnières France
139 J5 Magnitnyy Rus. Fed.
120 D1 Magnitogorsk Rus. Fed.
237 E5 Magnolia AR U.S.A.
234 C3 Magnolia DE U.S.A.
234 B3 Magnolia MD U.S.A.
237 F6 Magnolia MS U.S.A.
175 J4 Magnuszew Pol.
160 B2 Magny-Cours France
156 B3 Magny-en-Vexin France
100 G1 Mago Rus. Fed.
177 H5 Mágocs Hungary
177 J5 Mágocs-ér r. Hungary
213 F2 Màgoé Moz.
225 F4 Magog Que. Can.
192 A4 Magomadas Sardegna Italy
Magosa Cyprus see Ammochostos
209 E8 Magoye Zambia
245 F3 Magozal Mex.
225 H3 Magpie Que. Can.
224 C4 Magpie r. Ont. Can.
225 H3 Magpie r. Que. Can.
225 H3 Magpie-Ouest r. Que. Can.
190 E4 Magra r. Italy
222 H5 Magrath Alta Can.
187 C5 Magre r. Spain
240 I3 Magruder Mountain NV U.S.A.
206 B2 Magṭa' Laḥjar Maur.
211 B5 Magu Tanz.
108 C4 Maguan Yunnan China
213 G5 Magude Moz.
215 H2 Magudu S. Africa
182 C3 Magueija Port.
184 E2 Maguilla Spain
147 D2 Maguiresbridge Northern Ireland U.K.
207 I3 Magumeri Nigeria
233 □J2 Magundy N.B. Can.
117 G5 Magura Bangl.
177 H3 Magura mt. Slovakia
136 D4 Măgura, Dealul hill Moldova
197 F2 Măgura Mare, Vârful hill Romania
197 F3 Măgurii, Vârful mt. Romania
215 F5 Magwali S. Africa
Magway Myanmar see Magwe
Magway admin. div. Myanmar see Magwe
96 A2 Magwe Myanmar
96 A2 Magwe admin. div. Myanmar
177 K4 Magy Hungary
177 G5 Magyaratád Hungary
177 H6 Magyarbóly Hungary
Magyarkanizsa Vojvodina, Srbija Yugo. see Kanjiža
Magyar Köztársaság country Europe see Hungary
177 H5 Magyarszék Hungary
122 A2 Mahābād Iran
114 B2 Mahabaleshwar Mahar. India
116 F4 Mahabharat Range mts Nepal
213 □J4 Mahabo Madag.
114 B2 Mahad Mahar. India
210 E4 Mahaddayweyne Somalia
116 D5 Mahadeo Hills Madh. Prad. India
114 D2 Mahadeopur Andhra Prad. India
232 D4 Mahaffey PA U.S.A.
251 G3 Mahaicony Guyana
213 □J2 Mahajamba r. Madag.
116 C3 Mahajan Rajasthan India
213 □J2 Mahajanga Madag.
213 □J3 Mahajanga prov. Madag.
95 G3 Mahakam r. Indon.
213 E4 Mahalapye Botswana
211 A6 Mahale Mountain National Park Tanz.
213 □K2 Mahalevona Madag.
122 B3 Mahallāt Iran
116 D3 Maham Haryana India
122 D4 Māhān Iran
117 F5 Mahanadi r. India
213 □K3 Mahanoro Madag.
234 B2 Mahanoy City PA U.S.A.
234 B2 Mahanoy Creek r. PA U.S.A.
234 B2 Mahantango Creek r. PA U.S.A.
117 F4 Maharajganj Bihar India
116 E4 Maharajganj Uttar Prad. India
116 D4 Maharajpur Madh. Prad. India
114 B2 Maharashtra state India
122 C4 Mahārlū, Daryācheh-ye salt l. Iran
96 C3 Maha Sarakham Thai.
128 C4 Maḥaṭṭat Ḍab'ah Jordan
247 □2 Mahault, Baie b. Guadeloupe
213 □J2 Mahavavy r. Madag.
114 D4 Mahaweli Ganga r. Sri Lanka
213 □J3 Mahazoma Madag.
114 D2 Mahbubabad Andhra Prad. India
114 C2 Mahbubnagar Andhra Prad. India
124 C3 Mahd adh Dhahab Saudi Arabia
125 F2 Maḥḍah Oman
137 H3 Mahdalynivka Ukr.
205 F2 Mahdia Alg.
251 G3 Mahdia Guyana
205 H2 Mahdia Tunisia
114 B4 Mahe Pondicherry India
217 □2b Mahé i. Inner Islands Seychelles
217 □1b Mahébourg Mauritius
116 D3 Mahendragarh Haryana India
115 E2 Mahendragiri mt. Orissa India
211 C7 Mahenge Tanz.
81 C6 Maheno South I. N.Z.
175 L5 Maheriv Ukr.
116 C5 Mahesana Gujarat India
116 C5 Maheshwar Madh. Prad. India
125 F5 Maḥfirhīn Suquṭrā Yemen
116 D4 Mahgawan Madh. Prad. India
116 C5 Mahi r. Rajasthan India
80 F3 Mahia North I. N.Z.
80 F3 Mahia Peninsula North I. N.Z.
182 D3 Mahíde Spain
78 □6 Mahige Island Solomon Is
139 H5 Mahilyow Belarus
Mahilyow Oblast admin. div. Belarus see Mahilyowskaya Voblasts'
139 H5 Mahilyowskaya Voblasts' admin. div. Belarus
114 B2 Mahim Mahar. India
206 C3 Mahina Mali
140 K2 Mahkene mt. Sweden
215 H3 Mahlabatini S. Africa
96 A2 Mahlaing Myanmar
215 H2 Mahlangasi S. Africa
215 F3 Mahlatswetsa S. Africa
172 B3 Mahlberg Ger.
171 E3 Mahlow Ger.
170 C3 Mahlsdorf Ger.
171 C3 Mahlwinkel Ger.
116 E4 Mahmudabad Uttar Prad. India
122 C2 Mahmudabad Iran
123 G3 Maḥmūd-e 'Erāqī Afgh.
197 I3 Mahmudia Romania
199 E2 Mahmudiye anakkale Turkey
199 G2 Mahmudiye Eskişehir Turkey
128 A1 Mahmutlar Turkey
199 F1 Mahmutşevketpaşa Turkey
236 D2 Mahnomen MN U.S.A.
116 D4 Mahoba Uttar Prad. India
80 E3 Mahoenui North I. N.Z.
116 E4 Maholi Uttar Prad. India
186 □ Mahón Spain
225 H4 Mahone Bay N.S. Can.
235 E1 Mahopac NY U.S.A.
185 I1 Mahora Spain
206 D3 Mahou Mali
125 E4 Mahrāt, Wādī r. Yemen
116 D4 Mahrauni Uttar Prad. India
173 G2 Mähring Ger.
122 E3 Māhrūd Iran
Mahsana Gujarat India see Mahesana
111 F4 Mahuanggou Qinghai China
240 □D8 Mahukona HI U.S.A.
117 H4 Mahur Assam India
114 C2 Mahur Mahar. India
207 G4 Mahuta Nigeria
211 C7 Mahuta Tanz.
116 B5 Mahuva Gujarat India
116 D4 Mahwa Rajasthan India
197 H5 Mahya Dağı mt. Turkey
Mai i. Vanuatu see Émaé
78 □2 Maia American Samoa
216 □1b Maia São Miguel Azores
182 B3 Maia Port.
Maiaia Moz. see Nacala
186 D3 Maials Spain
77 H1 Maiana atoll Gilbert Is Kiribati
117 H4 Maibang Assam India
250 C2 Maicao Col.
224 E3 Maicasagi r. Que. Can.
224 E3 Maicasagi, Lac l. Que. Can.
160 E1 Maîche France
251 F6 Maici r. Brazil
251 H5 Maicuru r. Brazil
195 F4 Maida Italy
150 E3 Maiden Bradley Wiltshire, England U.K.
234 C2 Maiden Creek r. PA U.S.A.
151 G3 Maidenhead Windsor and Maidenhead, England U.K.
150 E4 Maiden Newton Dorset, England U.K.
226 A3 Maiden Rock WI U.S.A.
146 D6 Maidens South Ayrshire, Scotland U.K.
223 I4 Maidstone Sask. Can.
151 H3 Maidstone Kent, England U.K.
207 I4 Maiduguri Nigeria
190 E1 Maienfeld Switz.
195 F4 Maierato Italy
173 E4 Maierhöfen Ger.
197 G2 Maieru Romania
187 C6 Maigmó mt. Spain
156 C3 Maignelay-Montigny France
210 C3 Mai Gudo mt. Eth.
147 C4 Maigue r. Rep. of Ireland
116 E4 Maihar Madh. Prad. India
80 E3 Maihiihi North I. N.Z.
117 G5 Maijdi Bangl.
108 C1 Maiji Shan mt. Gansu China
116 E5 Maikala Range hills Madh. Prad. India
172 C2 Maikammer Ger.
208 E4 Maiko r. Dem. Rep. Congo
117 E5 Mailan Hill mt. Madh. Prad. India
116 E3 Mailani Uttar Prad. India
240 □ Maili HI U.S.A.
163 B4 Maillas France
156 B4 Maillebois France
162 B2 Maillezais France
160 B1 Mailly-la-Ville France
156 E4 Mailly-le-Camp France
156 C2 Mailly-Maillet France
123 H4 Mailsi Pak.
169 D5 Main r. Ger.
124 D4 Ma'īn tourist site Yemen
117 G4 Mainaguri W. Bengal India
172 D2 Mainaschaff Ger.
173 E2 Mainbernheim Ger.
225 K3 Main Brook Nfld. Can.
173 F3 Mainburg Ger.
114 C2 Maindargi Mahar. India
208 C5 Mai-Ndombe, Lac l. Dem. Rep. Congo
227 I4 Main Duck Island Ont. Can.
159 F4 Maine r. France
233 □I2 Maine state U.S.A.
233 □I3 Maine, Gulf of U.S.A.
159 F4 Maine-et-Loire dept Pays de la Loire France
250 C5 Mainé Hanari, Cerro hill Col.
207 I3 Maïné-Soroa Niger
96 B1 Maingkwan Myanmar
147 E3 Mainham Rep. of Ireland
172 D2 Mainhardt Ger.
92 C4 Mainit Phil.
108 A2 Mainkung Xizang China
146 E2 Mainland i. Orkney, Scotland U.K.
146 □G1 Mainland i. Shetland, Scotland U.K.
171 C5 Mainleus Ger.
111 F6 Mainling Xizang China
84 C2 Mainoru N.T. Austr.
84 C2 Mainoru r. N.T. Austr.
117 E5 Mainpat reg. Madh. Prad. India
116 D4 Mainpuri Uttar Prad. India
162 E2 Mainsat France
156 B4 Maintenon France
213 □J3 Maintirano Madag.
156 B4 Mainvilliers France
169 D5 Mainz Ger.
206 □ Maio i. Cape Verde
191 I5 Maiolati Spontini Italy
184 B1 Maior r. Port.
182 B4 Maiorca Port.
182 B5 Maiorga Port.
194 D2 Maiori Italy
260 B3 Maipó r. Chile
260 C4 Maipó, Volcán vol. Chile
261 I5 Maipú Arg.
260 C3 Maipú Arg.
260 B3 Maipú Chile
250 E2 Maiquetía Venez.
111 D6 Maiqu Zangbo r. Xizang China
190 C4 Maira r. Italy
184 E3 Mairena del Alcor Spain
254 E4 Mairi Brazil
256 D5 Mairiporã Brazil
256 C2 Mairipotaba Brazil
173 F3 Maisach Ger.
173 F3 Maisach r. Ger.
178 D3 Maishofen Austria
246 D2 Maisí Cuba
138 E4 Maišiagala Lith.
156 C4 Maisons-Laffitte France
179 G2 Maissau Austria
156 C4 Maisse France
165 E5 Maissin Belgium
Maitea i. Arch. de la Société Fr. Polynesia see Mehetia
173 G3 Maitenbeth Ger.
213 E4 Maitengwe Botswana
117 F5 Maithon Bihar India
83 G3 Maitland N.S.W. Austr.
82 D3 Maitland S.A. Austr.
86 C4 Maitland r. W.A. Austr.
95 G1 Maitland, Banjaran mts Sabah Malaysia
87 D5 Maitland, Lake salt flat W.A. Austr.
263 A2 Maitri research stn Antarctica
Maiwo i. Vanuatu see Maéwo
84 C2 Maiwok r. N.T. Austr.
84 B3 Maiyu, Mount hill N.T. Austr.
242 □J6 Maíz, Islas del is Nic.
111 E6 Maizhokunggar Xizang China
156 D4 Maizières-la-Grande-Paroisse France
157 G3 Maizières-lès-Metz France
104 B3 Maizuru Japan
184 E4 Majaceite r. Spain
183 G4 Majadahonda Spain
182 E5 Majadas de Tiétar Spain
196 D4 Maja Jezercë mt. Albania
114 C2 Majalgaon Mahar. India
251 F4 Majari r. Brazil
125 E5 Majdaḥah Yemen
175 J5 Majdan Królewski Pol.
175 L5 Majdan Niepryski Pol.
197 E3 Majdanpek Srbija Yugo.
257 F5 Majé Brazil
93 A3 Majene Sulawesi Selatan Indon.
188 G3 Majevica mts Bos.-Herz.
116 E4 Majhgawan Madh. Prad. India
116 D5 Majholi Madh. Prad. India
107 H4 Majia r. China
109 D4 Majiang Guangxi China
108 C3 Majiang Guizhou China
Majōl country N. Pacific Ocean see Marshall Islands
Majorca i. Spain see Mallorca
Mājro atoll Marshall Is see Majuro
177 H6 Majs Hungary
117 H4 Majuli Island India
Majunga Madag. see Mahajanga
78 □3b Majuro atoll Marshall Is
215 F3 Majwemasweu S. Africa
206 B3 Maka Senegal
209 B5 Makabana Congo
177 H4 Makád Hungary
240 □ Makaha HI U.S.A.
207 H6 Makak Cameroon
93 A3 Makale Sulawesi Selatan Indon.
117 F4 Makalu mt. China/Nepal
211 A6 Makamba Burundi
121 J3 Makanchi Kazakh.
211 B8 Makanjila Malawi
211 C6 Makanya Tanz.
208 C4 Makanza Dem. Rep. Congo
81 B7 Makarewa South I. N.Z.
207 I3 Makari Cameroon
Makari Mountain National Park Tanz. see Mahale Mountain National Park
136 E2 Makariv Ukr.
81 B6 Makarora r. South I. N.Z.
100 G2 Makarov Sakhalin Rus. Fed.
268 M1 Makarov Basin sea feature Arctic Ocean
136 B3 Makarove Ukr.
135 H5 Makarovo Rus. Fed.
188 F4 Makarska Croatia
134 J4 Makar'ye Rus. Fed.
134 H4 Makar'yev Rus. Fed.
Makassar Sulawesi Selatan Indon. see Ujung Pandang
93 A3 Makassar Strait Indon.
120 C3 Makat Kazakh.
215 I2 Makatini Flats lowland S. Africa
240 □C8 Makawao HI U.S.A.
213 □J4 Makay, Massif du mts Madag.
Makedonija country Europe see Macedonia
215 F3 Makeleketla S. Africa
79 □3 Makemo atoll Arch. des Tuamotu Fr. Polynesia
206 B4 Makeni Sierra Leone
211 B7 Makete Tanz.
Makeyevka Donets'ka Oblast' Ukr. see Makiyivka
212 E4 Makgadikgadi salt pan Botswana
129 E2 Makhachkala Rus. Fed.
215 F4 Makhaleng r. Lesotho
120 B3 Makhambet Kazakh.
124 C2 Makhāmīr, Jabal al hill Saudi Arabia
Makharadze Georgia see Ozurget'i
215 G3 Makheka mt. Lesotho
128 D2 Makhfar al Ḥammām Syria
129 D1 Makhmud-Mekteb Rus. Fed.
127 F4 Makhmūr Iraq
121 G1 Makhorovka Kazakh.
114 C2 Makhtal Andhra Prad. India
125 E4 Makhyah, Wādī r. Yemen
93 C2 Makian vol. Maluku Indon.
105 E2 Makihata-yama mt. Japan
81 C6 Makikihi South I. N.Z.
Makima atoll Arch. des Tuamotu Fr. Polynesia see Makemo
Makin atoll Kiribati see Butaritari
121 G1 Makinsk Kazakh.
Makira i. Solomon Is see San Cristobal
136 D3 Makiv Ukr.
137 F2 Makiyivka Chernihivs'ka Oblast' Ukr.
137 I3 Makiyivka Donets'ka Oblast' Ukr.
Makkah Saudi Arabia see Mecca
124 C3 Makkah prov. Saudi Arabia
225 J2 Makkovik Nfld. Can.
164 E1 Makkum Neth.
177 J5 Makó Hungary
251 G4 Makoa, Serra hills Brazil
79 □1 Makogai i. Fiji
208 B4 Makokou Gabon
215 F2 Makokskraal S. Africa
211 C7 Makonde Plateau Tanz.
Makongai i. Fiji see Makogai
211 B7 Makongolosi Tanz.
212 D5 Makopong Botswana
80 F4 Makotuku North I. N.Z.
208 B5 Makoua Congo
177 H2 Makov Slovakia
188 E3 Makovnik mt. Croatia
175 I4 Maków Pol.
174 F2 Mąkowarsko Pol.
175 J3 Maków Mazowiecki Pol.
175 H6 Maków Podhalański Pol.
198 C2 Makrakomi Greece
116 C4 Makrana Rajasthan India
Makran Coast Range mts Pak. see Talar-i-Band
198 D3 Makronisi i. Greece
198 C1 Makrygialos Kentriki Makedonia Greece
139 J3 Maksatikha Rus. Fed.
116 D5 Maksi Madh. Prad. India
100 F3 Maksimovka Rus. Fed.
116 D5 Maksudangarh Madh. Prad. India
174 G2 Maksymilianowo Pol.
122 A2 Mākū Iran
117 H4 Makum Assam India
211 B7 Makumbako Tanz.
209 D6 Makumbi Dem. Rep. Congo
Makundu i. N. Male Maldives see Makunudhoo
211 C6 Makunduchi Tanz.
109 F4 Makung Taiwan
211 C7 Makunguwiro Tanz.
113 □1 Makunudhoo i. N. Male Maldives
103 E8 Makurazaki Japan
207 H5 Makurdi Nigeria
80 E4 Makuri North I. N.Z.
215 E2 Makwassie S. Africa
117 G4 Mal W. Bengal India
252 A3 Mala Peru
Mala Rep. of Ireland see Mallow
Mala i. Solomon Is see Malaita
185 G3 Malá Spain
140 L2 Malå Sweden
92 C5 Malabang Phil.
114 B3 Malabar Coast India
137 H4 Mala Bilozerka Ukr.
207 H6 Malabo Equat. Guinea
177 I5 Mala Bosna Vojvodina, Srbija Yugo.
92 A4 Malabuñgan Phil.
Malaca Spain see Málaga
257 F2 Malacacheta Brazil
Malacca Malaysia see Melaka
Malacca state Malaysia see Melaka
94 B1 Malacca, Strait of Indon./Malaysia
176 G3 Malacky Slovakia
238 D3 Malad r. ID U.S.A.
238 D3 Malad City ID U.S.A.
137 G2 Mala Divytsya Ukr.
138 F4 Maladzyechna Belarus
177 H2 Malá Fatra mts Slovakia
185 F4 Málaga Spain
185 F4 Málaga prov. Andalucía Spain
234 C3 Malaga NJ U.S.A.
239 F5 Malaga NM U.S.A.
232 C5 Malaga OH U.S.A.
211 A6 Malagarasi r. Burundi/Tanz.
211 A6 Malagarasi Tanz.
185 G1 Malagón Spain
184 C3 Malagon r. Spain
147 E3 Malahide Rep. of Ireland
213 □J4 Malaimbandy Madag.
174 D2 Mała Ina r. Pol.
78 □6 Malaita i. Solomon Is
95 G5 Malaka mt. Sumbawa Indon.
210 A2 Malakal Sudan
114 D2 Malakanagiri Orissa India
188 E3 Mala Kapela mts Croatia
188 E3 Mala Kladuša Bos.-Herz.
78 □6 Malakobi Island Solomon Is
78 □5 Malakula i. Vanuatu
123 H3 Malakwal Pak.
191 G4 Malalbergo Italy
137 G4 Mala Lepetykha Ukr.
93 B3 Malamala Sulawesi Tenggara Indon.
191 H3 Malamocco Italy
136 C2 Mala Moshchanytsya Ukr.
157 F3 Malancourt France
95 F4 Malang Jawa Timur Indon.
Malange Angola see Malanje
209 C7 Malanje Angola
209 C7 Malanje prov. Angola
174 G4 Malanów Pol.
158 D4 Malansac France
207 F4 Malanville Benin
260 D2 Malanzán, Sierra de mts Arg.
137 H3 Mala Pereshchepyna Ukr.
114 C4 Malappuram Kerala India
143 G2 Mälaren l. Sweden
260 C4 Malargüe Arg.
224 E3 Malartic Que. Can.
136 C2 Malaryta Belarus
176 E1 Malá Skála Czech Rep.
222 E5 Malaspina Strait B.C. Can.
179 H4 Mala Subotica Croatia
137 H3 Mala Ternivka r. Ukr.
126 E3 Malatya Turkey
161 D4 Malaucène France
156 B3 Malaunay France
163 B5 Malaussanne France
116 C3 Malaut Punjab India
114 C3 Malavalli Karnataka India
136 F3 Mala Vil'shanka Ukr.
137 F3 Mala Vyska Ukr.
207 H3 Malawa Niger
174 F3 Mała Wełna r. Pol.
211 B7 Malawi country Africa
Malawi, Lake Africa see Nyasa, Lake
140 M3 Malax Fin.
Malaya pen. Malaysia see Malaysia, Semenanjung
129 E1 Malaya Areshevka Rus. Fed.
134 K2 Malaya Pera Rus. Fed.
139 I2 Malaya Vishera Rus. Fed.
92 C4 Malaybalay Phil.
122 B3 Malāyer Iran
156 D4 Malay-le-Grand France
85 G3 Malay Reef Coral Sea Is Terr. Austr.
94 C1 Malaysia country Asia
94 C2 Malaysia, Semenanjung pen. Malaysia
127 F3 Malazgirt Turkey
225 G4 Malbaie r. Que. Can.
207 G3 Malbaza Niger
84 E4 Malbon Qld Austr.
175 H1 Malbork Pol.
172 A2 Malborn Ger.
161 B4 Malbouzon France
160 E2 Malbuisson France
182 C4 Malcata, Serra de mts Port.
191 F3 Malcesine Italy
137 K3 Mal'chevskaya Rus. Fed.
170 D2 Malchin Ger.
170 D2 Malchiner See l. Ger.
170 D2 Malchow Ger.
177 K3 Malčice Slovakia
184 E2 Malcocinado Spain
87 D6 Malcolm W.A. Austr.
87 D7 Malcolm, Point W.A. Austr.
177 K2 Malcov Slovakia
174 E4 Malczyce Pol.
165 C3 Maldegem Belgium
164 E3 Malden Neth.
237 F4 Malden MO U.S.A.
267 I6 Malden Island Kiribati
186 D2 Malditos, Montes mts Spain
113 D10 Maldives country Indian Ocean
83 F4 Maldon Vic. Austr.
151 H3 Maldon Essex, England U.K.
258 G4 Maldonado Uru.
175 H2 Małdyty Pol.
217 □3a Male Njazidja Comoros
191 F2 Malè Italy
113 □1 Male N. Male Maldives
113 □1 Male Atoll Maldives
215 E3 Malebogo S. Africa
174 E1 Malechowo Pol.
114 C2 Malegaon Mahar. India
116 C5 Malegaon Mahar. India
183 I3 Maleján Spain
176 G3 Malé Karpaty hills Slovakia
122 E4 Malek Sīāh, Kūh-e mt. Afgh.
209 B6 Malele Dem. Rep. Congo
213 H2 Malema Moz.
161 D4 Malemort-du-Comtat France
162 D3 Malemort-sur-Corrèze France
168 F1 Malente Ger.
215 G1 Maleoskop S. Africa
143 F3 Måleràs Sweden
116 C3 Maler Kotla Punjab India
190 D2 Malesco Italy
197 F5 Maleševske Planine mts Bulg./Macedonia
156 C4 Malesherbes France
198 C2 Malesina Greece
158 D4 Malestroit France
107 F1 Maleta Rus. Fed.
194 D5 Maletto Sicilia Italy
139 L5 Malevka Rus. Fed.
194 D4 Malfa Isole Lipari Italy
214 C6 Malgas S. Africa
173 G3 Malgersdorf Ger.
129 D2 Malgobek Rus. Fed.
140 L2 Malgomaj l. Sweden
186 F3 Malgrat de Mar Spain
254 E5 Malhada Brazil
182 D3 Malhadas Port.
124 D2 Malham Saudi Arabia
116 C4 Malhargarh Madh. Prad. India
238 C2 Malheur r. OR U.S.A.
206 D3 Mali country Africa
206 B3 Mali Guinea
199 D4 Malia Kriti Greece
107 E5 Malian r. China
215 G3 Malibamatso r. Lesotho
240 H4 Malibu CA U.S.A.
159 F4 Malicorne-sur-Sarthe France
156 D5 Maligny France
111 C7 Malihabad Uttar Prad. India
96 B1 Mali Hka r. Myanmar
177 I6 Mali Iđoš Vojvodina, Srbija Yugo.
161 E4 Malijai France
123 E4 Malik Naro mt. Pak.
97 B4 Mali Kyun i. Myanmar
93 B3 Malili Sulawesi Selatan Indon.
143 F3 Målilla Sweden
188 E3 Mali Lošinj Croatia
209 F6 Malimba, Monts mts Dem. Rep. Congo
175 L6 Mali Mokryany Ukr.
147 D1 Malin Rep. of Ireland
Malin Ukr. see Malyn
147 C2 Malin Beg Rep. of Ireland
211 D5 Malindi Kenya
177 I3 Málinec Slovakia
Malines Belgium see Mechelen
208 B5 Malinga Gabon
147 D1 Malin Head hd Rep. of Ireland
197 H2 Mălini Romania
147 C2 Malin More Rep. of Ireland
139 L4 Malino Rus. Fed.
93 B2 Malino, Gunung mt. Indon.
100 E3 Malinovka r. Rus. Fed.
121 I2 Malinovoye Ozero Altayskiy Kray Rus. Fed.
191 J3 Malinska Croatia
211 C7 Malinyi Tanz.
108 C4 Malipo Yunnan China
198 B1 Maliq Albania
188 E3 Mali Raginac mt. Croatia
92 C5 Malita Phil.
92 C4 Malitbog Phil.
116 B5 Maliya Gujarat India
137 G4 Maliyivka Ukr.
196 D3 Mali Zvornik Srbija Yugo.
129 C2 Malka Rus. Fed.
129 D2 Malka r. Rus. Fed.
114 B2 Malkapur Mahar. India
116 D5 Malkapur Mahar. India
199 E1 Malkara Turkey
138 F5 Mal'kavichy Belarus
175 K3 Małkinia Górna Pol.
197 H5 Malko Tŭrnovo Bulg.
83 G4 Mallacoota Vic. Austr.
83 G4 Mallacoota Inlet b. Vic. Austr.
146 C5 Mallaig Highland, Scotland U.K.
203 F3 Mallawi Egypt
140 M1 Mållejus hill Norway
161 D5 Mallemort France
183 I3 Mallén Spain
170 C2 Mallentin Ger.
190 E2 Mallero r. Italy
173 G3 Mallersdorf Ger.
191 F2 Malles Venosta Italy
255 C8 Mallet Brazil
Mallia Kriti Greece see Malia
170 C2 Malliß Ger.
260 B4 Malloa Chile
187 F5 Mallorca i. Spain
147 C4 Mallow Rep. of Ireland
86 E4 Mallowa Well W.A. Austr.
150 D2 Mallwyd Gwynedd, Wales U.K.
140 J2 Malm Norway
123 E3 Malman Rūd r. Afgh.
140 M2 Malmberget Sweden
165 F4 Malmédy Belgium
214 B5 Malmesbury S. Africa
150 E3 Malmesbury Wiltshire, England U.K.
143 G2 Malmköping Sweden
142 E4 Malmö Sweden
142 E4 Malmö-Sturup airport Sweden
143 F2 Malmslätt Sweden
134 J4 Malmyzh Rus. Fed.
190 D3 Malnate Italy
191 G3 Malo Italy
78 □5 Malo i. Vanuatu
139 K5 Maloarkhangel'sk Rus. Fed.
196 E3 Malo Crniće Srbija Yugo.
175 I5 Małogoszcz Pol.
92 B3 Malolos Phil.
174 D4 Małomice Pol.
137 I3 Malomykhaylivka Ukr.
183 I3 Malón Spain
190 C3 Malone r. Italy
233 F2 Malone NY U.S.A.
108 B3 Malong Yunnan China
209 D7 Malonga Dem. Rep. Congo
190 F2 Malonno Italy
176 D3 Malonty Czech Rep.
175 I5 Małopolska, Wyżyna hills Pol.
175 I6 Małopolskie prov. Pol.
Malorita Belarus see Malaryta
134 G3 Maloshuyka Rus. Fed.
197 F3 Malovăț Romania
Malovata Moldova see Molovata
141 I3 Måløy Norway
139 K4 Maloyaroslavets Rus. Fed.
139 K2 Maloye Borisovo Rus. Fed.
175 I1 Maloye-Lugovoye Rus. Fed.
134 J2 Malozemel'skaya Tundra lowland Rus. Fed.
182 D4 Malpartida Port.
184 D1 Malpartida de Cáceres Spain
184 E2 Malpartida de la Serena Spain
182 D5 Malpartida de Plasencia Spain
149 G4 Malpas Cheshire, England U.K.
150 D3 Malpas Newport, Wales U.K.
216 □3e Malpaso mt. El Hierro Canary Is
267 N5 Malpelo, Isla de i. N. Pacific Ocean
182 B1 Malpica Spain
183 F5 Malpica de Tajo Spain
182 C5 Malpica do Tejo Port.
138 E3 Mālpils Latvia
114 C2 Malprabha r. India
116 C4 Malpura Rajasthan India
172 C3 Malsch Ger.
176 D3 Malše r. Czech Rep.
169 E4 Malsfeld Ger.
114 B2 Malsiras Mahar. India
179 E4 Malta Austria
189 E8 Malta country Europe
138 F3 Malta Latvia
138 F3 Malta r. Latvia
195 □ Malta i. Malta
182 C4 Malta Port.
238 D3 Malta ID U.S.A.
238 F1 Malta MT U.S.A.
212 C5 Maltahöhe Namibia
207 I3 Maltam Cameroon
149 H4 Maltby South Yorkshire, England U.K.
149 J4 Maltby le Marsh Lincolnshire, England U.K.
172 B3 Malterdingen Ger.
172 C4 Malters Switz.
149 I3 Malton North Yorkshire, England U.K.
183 I3 Maluenda Spain
Malukken is Indon. see Maluku
93 C3 Maluku is Indon.
93 D3 Maluku prov. Indon.
93 C2 Maluku, Kepulauan is Indon.
197 F2 Malului, Vârful hill Romania
207 G4 Malumfashi Nigeria
143 E1 Malung Sweden
175 H5 Maluszyn Pol.
215 G3 Maluti Mountains Lesotho
183 E3 Malva Spain
190 D2 Malvaglia Switz.
114 B2 Malvan Mahar. India
184 A2 Malveira Port.
Malvern Worcestershire, England U.K. see Great Malvern
237 E5 Malvern AR U.S.A.
232 C4 Malvern OH U.S.A.
150 E2 Malvern Link Worcestershire, England U.K.
Malvinas, Islas terr. S. Atlantic Ocean see Falkland Islands
171 F4 Malxe r. Ger.
177 H4 Malý Dunaj r. Slovakia
177 K3 Malý Horeš Slovakia
177 J3 Mályi Hungary
131 M3 Malykay Rus. Fed.
136 E2 Malyn Ukr.
137 I3 Malynivka Ukr.
136 D2 Malyns'k Ukr.
175 K2 Mały Płock Pol.
131 R3 Malyy Anyuy r. Rus. Fed.
177 L3 Malyy Bereznyy Ukr.
135 I7 Malyye Derbety Rus. Fed.
Malyye Kotyuzhany Moldova see Cotiujenii Mici
135 J5 Malyy Irgiz r. Rus. Fed.
129 C3 Malyy Kavkaz mts Asia
107 E1 Malyy Kunaley Rus. Fed.
136 D2 Malyy Stydyn Ukr.
120 B2 Malyy Uzen' r. Kazakh./Rus. Fed.
129 B1 Malyy Zelenchuk r. Rus. Fed.
131 P3 Mama r. Rus. Fed.
134 J5 Mamadysh Rus. Fed.
215 G2 Mamafubedu S. Africa
215 F3 Mamahabane S. Africa
79 □1 Mamanuca-i-Cake Group is Fiji
Mamanutha-i-Thake Group is Fiji see Mamanuca-i-Cake Group
80 D1 Mamaranui North I. N.Z.
235 E2 Mamaroneck NY U.S.A.
93 A3 Mamasa Sulawesi Selatan Indon.
254 D5 Mambai Brazil
92 C4 Mambajao Phil.
208 C4 Mambéré r. C.A.R.
208 B3 Mambéré-Kadéï pref. C.A.R.
208 C4 Mambili r. Congo
206 B4 Mambolo Sierra Leone
256 A6 Mamborê Brazil
183 G3 Mambrilla de Castejón Spain
92 B3 Mamburao Phil.
129 F2 Mamedkala Rus. Fed.
215 G1 Mamelodi S. Africa
159 G3 Mamers France
207 H5 Mamfé Cameroon
250 E5 Mamirauá, Reserve de Desenvolvimento Sustentável nature res. Brazil
160 E1 Mamirolle France
121 G1 Mamlyutka Kazakh.
173 F3 Mammendorf Ger.
173 G3 Mamming Ger.
195 F4 Mammola Italy
241 L5 Mammoth AZ U.S.A.
240 H3 Mammoth Lakes CA U.S.A.
192 B4 Mamoiada Sardegna Italy
192 B4 Mamone Sardegna Italy
138 B4 Mamonovo Rus. Fed.
121 J1 Mamontovo Rus. Fed.
234 D3 Mamora NJ U.S.A.
252 D2 Mamoré r. Bol./Brazil
206 B4 Mamou Guinea
217 □3b Mamoudzou Mayotte
Mamoutsou Mayotte see Mamoudzou
213 □J3 Mampikony Madag.
206 E5 Mampong Ghana
214 B5 Mamre S. Africa
175 J1 Mamry, Jezioro l. Pol.
93 A3 Mamuju Sulawesi Selatan Indon.
122 B3 Māmūnīyeh Iran
196 D5 Mamuras Albania
102 J4 Mamurogawa Japan
Mamutzu Mayotte see Mamoudzou
206 D5 Man Côte d'Ivoire
114 B2 Man r. India
232 C6 Man WV U.S.A.
251 H3 Mana Fr. Guiana
177 H3 Maňa Slovakia
240 □B7 Mana HI U.S.A.
250 B5 Manabí prov. Ecuador
250 C3 Manacacias r. Col.
251 F5 Manacapuru Brazil
187 G5 Manacor Spain
216 □1c Manadas São Jorge Azores
93 C2 Manado Sulawesi Utara Indon.
165 D4 Manage Belgium
242 □I6 Managua Nic.
242 □I6 Managua, Lago de l. Nic.
125 G3 Manaḥ Oman
80 E3 Manaia North I. N.Z.
213 □J4 Manakara Madag.
80 E4 Manakau North I. N.Z.
81 D5 Manakau mt. South I. N.Z.
124 C5 Manākhah Yemen
116 D2 Manali Hima. Prad. India
Manama Bahrain see Al Manāmah
114 C4 Manamadurai Tamil Nadu India
213 □J3 Manambaho r. Madag.
213 □J4 Manambondro Madag.
114 C4 Manamelkudi Tamil Nadu India
251 F2 Manamo, Caño r. Venez.
213 □J4 Mananantañana r. Madag.
213 □J4 Mananara r. Madag.
213 □K3 Mananara Avaratra Madag.
83 E3 Manangatang Vic. Austr.
84 D3 Manangoora N.T. Austr.
213 □K4 Mananjary Madag.
206 D4 Manankoro Mali
206 C3 Manantali, Lac de l. Mali
114 C4 Manantavadi Kerala India
78 □6 Manaoba Island Solomon Is
81 A6 Manapouri South I. N.Z.
81 A6 Manapouri, Lake South I. N.Z.
114 C4 Manapparai Tamil Nadu India
213 □J3 Manarantsandry Madag.
183 H1 Mañaria Spain
110 D2 Manas Xinjiang China
117 G4 Manas r. India
142 E1 Månäs Sweden
121 G4 Manas, Gora mt. Uzbek.
116 C4 Manasa Madh. Prad. India
110 D2 Manas He r. China
110 D2 Manas Hu l. China
129 E2 Manaskent Rus. Fed.
117 F3 Manaslu mt. Nepal
235 D2 Manasquan NJ U.S.A.
235 D2 Manasquan r. NJ U.S.A.
232 E5 Manassas VA U.S.A.
Manastir Macedonia see Bitola
177 L6 Mănăștiur Romania
247 □1 Manatí Puerto Rico
247 □1 Manati, Río Grande de r. Puerto Rico
Man-aung Kyun i. Myanmar see Cheduba Island
251 F5 Manaus Brazil
126 C3 Manavgat Turkey
226 C3 Manawa WI U.S.A.
116 C5 Manawar Madh. Prad. India
80 E2 Manawaru North I. N.Z.
80 E4 Manawatu r. North I. N.Z.
80 E3 Manawatu-Wanganui admin. reg. North I. N.Z.
92 C5 Manay Phil.
117 F5 Manbazar W. Bengal India
128 C1 Manbij Syria
149 J4 Manby Lincolnshire, England U.K.
226 E3 Mancelona MI U.S.A.
183 E4 Mancera de Abajo Spain
114 B2 Manchar Mahar. India
185 G3 Mancha Real Spain
158 E3 Manche dept Basse-Normandie France
246 □ Manchester parish Jamaica
149 G4 Manchester Greater Manchester, England U.K.
233 G4 Manchester CT U.S.A.
236 F3 Manchester IA U.S.A.
232 B6 Manchester KY U.S.A.
234 B3 Manchester MD U.S.A.
227 E4 Manchester MI U.S.A.
233 H3 Manchester NH U.S.A.
232 B5 Manchester OH U.S.A.
234 B2 Manchester PA U.S.A.
231 C5 Manchester TN U.S.A.
233 G3 Manchester VT U.S.A.
173 F3 Manching Ger.
246 □ Manchioneal Jamaica
184 D2 Manchita Spain
192 D2 Manciano Italy
163 C5 Manciet France
199 E2 Mancınık Dağı mts Turkey
239 E4 Mancos CO U.S.A.
241 M3 Mancos r. CO U.S.A.
122 B4 Mand, Rūd-e r. Iran
208 E2 Manda, Jebel mt. Sudan
213 □J4 Mandabe Madag.
256 A5 Mandaguaçu Brazil
256 B5 Mandaguari Brazil
116 B5 Mandal Gujarat India
116 C4 Mandal Rajasthan India
106 D1 Mandal Mongolia
142 B2 Mandal Norway
91 J7 Mandala, Puncak mt. Indon.
96 B2 Mandalay Myanmar
96 A2 Mandalay admin. div. Myanmar
Mandale Myanmar see Mandalay
Mandale admin. div. Myanmar see Mandalay
116 C4 Mandalgarh Rajasthan India
106 E2 Mandalgovĭ Mongolia
142 B2 Mandalselva r. Norway
107 G3 Mandalt Nei Mongol China
236 C2 Mandan ND U.S.A.
195 E4 Mandanici Sicilia Italy
92 B3 Mandaon Phil.
114 C4 Mandapam Tamil Nadu India
192 B5 Mandas Sardegna Italy
195 F3 Mandatoriccio Italy
116 B5 Mandav Hills Gujarat India
123 H4 Mandawa Rajasthan India
183 H4 Mandayona Spain
160 C2 Mandé, Mont de hill France
Mandeghughusu i. New Georgia Is Solomon Is see Simbo
172 B2 Mandelbachtal-Ormesheim Ger.
161 E5 Mandelieu-la-Napoule France
190 E3 Mandello del Lario Italy
182 B1 Mandeo r. Spain
210 D4 Mandera Kenya
241 K2 Manderfield UT U.S.A.
169 B5 Manderscheid Ger.
160 E1 Mandeure France
246 □ Mandeville Jamaica
81 B6 Mandeville South I. N.Z.
116 B4 Mandha Rajasthan India
Mandhoúdhíon Greece see Mantoudi
116 D3 Mandi Hima. Prad. India
206 D3 Mandiakui Mali
206 C4 Mandiana Guinea
123 H4 Mandi Burewala Pak.
Mandidzuzure Zimbabwe see Chimanimani
213 G3 Mandié Moz.
213 G2 Mandimba Moz.
208 A5 Mandji Gabon
116 E5 Mandla Madh. Prad. India
177 L3 Mándok Hungary
116 C4 Mandor Rajasthan India
86 D3 Mandora W.A. Austr.
84 B2 Mandorah N.T. Austr.
213 □J3 Mandoro Madag.
207 F4 Mandouri Togo
198 C2 Mandra Greece
213 □J5 Mandrare r. Madag.
Mandrenska r. Bulg. see Sredetska Reka
157 F4 Mandres-en-Barrois France
213 □K2 Mandritsara Madag.
213 □J4 Mandrosonoro Madag.
116 C4 Mandsaur Madh. Prad. India
161 C5 Manduel France
87 B7 Mandurah W.A. Austr.
195 G2 Manduria Italy
116 B5 Mandvi Gujarat India
116 C5 Mandvi Gujarat India
114 C3 Mandya Karnataka India
163 C5 Mane Midi-Pyrénées France
161 D5 Mane Provence-Alpes-Côte-d'Azur France
142 C2 Måne r. Norway
151 H2 Manea Cambridgeshire, England U.K.
169 F5 Manebach Ger.
116 B5 Manekwara Gujarat India
122 D2 Maneli Iran
116 E5 Manendragarh Madh. Prad. India
117 F4 Maner Bihar India
114 C2 Maner r. India
190 F3 Manerbio Italy
183 I2 Mañeru Spain
122 A3 Manesht Kūh mt. Iran
197 G3 Măneşti Romania
176 C2 Manětín Czech Rep.
136 C2 Manevychi Ukr.
203 F3 Manfalût Egypt
193 H3 Manfredonia Italy
193 I3 Manfredonia, Golfo di g. Italy
254 E5 Manga Brazil
206 E4 Manga Burkina
254 D4 Mangabeiras, Serra das hills Brazil
209 C6 Mangai Dem. Rep. Congo
81 □2 Mangaia i. Cook Is
80 E3 Mangakino North I. N.Z.
114 D2 Mangalagiri Andhra Prad. India
117 H4 Mangaldai Assam India
197 I4 Mangalia Romania
202 C6 Mangalmé Chad
114 B3 Mangalore Karnataka India
114 B2 Mangalvedha Mahar. India
81 D5 Mangamaunu South I. N.Z.
80 E3 Mangamingi North I. N.Z.
80 D1 Mangamuka North I. N.Z.
182 E3 Manganeses de la Lampreana Spain
182 E2 Manganeses de la Polvorosa Spain
80 D1 Manganui r. North I. N.Z.
114 B2 Mangaon Mahar. India
114 D2 Mangapet Andhra Prad. India
80 D4 Mangarakau South I. N.Z.
257 E5 Mangaratiba Brazil
79 □3 Mangareva i. Arch. des Tuamotu Fr. Polynesia
Mangareva Islands Arch. des Tuamotu Fr. Polynesia see Gambier, Îles
80 E4 Mangatainoka North I. N.Z.
80 E2 Mangatawhiri North I. N.Z.
215 F3 Mangaung S. Africa
116 E4 Mangawan Madh. Prad. India
80 E3 Mangaweka North I. N.Z.
80 F3 Mangaweka mt. North I. N.Z.
80 E2 Mangawhai North I. N.Z.
Mangde Chhu r. Bhutan see Trongsa Chhu
Ma'ngê Gansu China see Luqu
Mangea i. Cook Is see Mangaia
141 I3 Manger Norway
147 B5 Mangerton Mountain hill Rep. of Ireland
173 G4 Mangfall r. Ger.
173 F4 Mangfallgebirge mts Ger.
95 E3 Manggar Indon.
Mangghyshlaq Kazakh. see Mangistau
Mangghystaū Kazakh. see Mangistau
Mangghystaū Oblysy admin. div. Kazakh. see Mangistauskaya Oblast'
Mangghyt Uzbek. see Mangit
Manghit Uzbek. see Mangit
157 F3 Mangiennes France
120 B4 Mangistau Kazakh.
120 B3 Mangistau, Gory hills Kazakh.
120 C4 Mangistauskaya Oblast' admin. div. Kazakh.
120 E4 Mangit Uzbek.
95 F3 Mangkutup r. Indon.
129 D3 Manglisi Georgia
111 E4 Mangnai Qinghai China
211 B8 Mangochi Malawi
206 D4 Mangodara Burkina
213 □I4 Mangoky r. Toliara Madag.
213 □J4 Mangoky r. Toliara Madag.

332
Mangole to Marston Moretaine

93 C3 Mangole i. Indon.
114 B2 Mangoli Karnataka India
213 □I4 Mangolovolo Madag.
80 D1 Mangonui North I. N.Z.
213 □K3 Mangoro r. Madag.
150 E3 Mangotsfield South Gloucestershire, England U.K.
Mangqystaū Shyghanaghy b. Kazakh. see Mangyshlakskiy Zaliv
Mangra Qinghai China see Guinan
116 B5 Mangral Gujarat India
116 D4 Mangrol Rajasthan India
231 E7 Mangrove Cay i. Bahamas
116 D5 Mangrul Mahar. India
Mangshi Yunnan China see Luxi
182 C4 Mangualde Port.
258 G4 Mangueira, Lago l. Brazil
255 B8 Mangueirinha Brazil
205 H5 Manguéni, Plateau du Niger
100 B2 Mangui Nei Mongol China
Mangula Zimbabwe see Mhangura
242 □I6 Mangulile Hond.
237 D5 Mangum OK U.S.A.
254 D2 Mangunça, Ilha i. Brazil
107 G1 Mangut Rus. Fed.
Mangyshlak Kazakh. see Mangistau
120 B3 Mangyshlak, Poluostrov pen. Kazakh.
Mangyshlak Oblast admin. div. Kazakh. see Mangistauskaya Oblast'
Mangyshlakskaya Oblast' admin. div. Kazakh. see Mangistauskaya Oblast'
120 B3 Mangyshlakskiy Zaliv b. Kazakh.
Manhan Mongolia see Tögrög
179 G2 Manhartsberg hill Austria
236 D4 Manhattan KS U.S.A.
240 H5 Manhattan Beach CA U.S.A.
165 E4 Manhay Belgium
234 B2 Manheim PA U.S.A.
213 G5 Manhica Moz.
257 F4 Manhuaçu Brazil
257 G3 Manhuaçu r. Brazil
157 F3 Manhuelles France
257 G4 Manhumirim Brazil
250 C3 Mani Col.
198 C3 Mani pen. Greece
207 G3 Mani Nigeria
213 □J3 Mania r. Madag.
194 D5 Maniace Sicilia Italy
191 H2 Maniago Italy
198 B1 Maniakoi Greece
213 G3 Manica Moz.
213 G3 Manica prov. Moz.
213 G3 Manicaland prov. Zimbabwe
251 F6 Manicoré Brazil
251 F6 Manicoré r. Brazil
225 G3 Manicouagan Que. Can.
225 G3 Manicouagan r. Que. Can.
225 G3 Manicouagan, Réservoir resr Que. Can.
225 G3 Manic Trois, Réservoir resr Que. Can.
208 E5 Maniema admin. reg. Dem. Rep. Congo
125 E2 Manīfah Saudi Arabia
108 A2 Maniganggo Sichuan China
223 L5 Manigotagan Man. Can.
117 F4 Manihari Bihar India
79 □3 Manihi atoll Arch. des Tuamotu Fr. Polynesia
81 □2 Manihiki atoll Cook Is
221 M3 Maniitsoq Greenland
123 F5 Maniji r. Pak.
117 H5 Manikchhari Bangl.
117 G5 Manikganj Bangl.
Manikgarh Mahar. India see Rajura
116 E4 Manikpur Uttar Prad. India
92 B3 Manila Phil.
238 E3 Manila UT U.S.A.
92 B3 Manila Bay Phil.
83 G3 Manildra N.S.W. Austr.
83 G2 Manilla N.S.W. Austr.
185 E4 Manilva Spain
131 R3 Manily Rus. Fed.
84 C2 Maningrida N.T. Austr.
Manipur Manipur India see Imphal
117 H4 Manipur state India
96 A2 Manipur r. India/Myanmar
199 E2 Manisa Turkey
199 F2 Manisa prov. Turkey
187 C5 Manises Spain
254 B4 Manissauá Missu r. Brazil
226 D3 Manistee MI U.S.A.
226 D3 Manistee r. MI U.S.A.
226 D3 Manistique MI U.S.A.
223 L4 Manitoba prov. Can.
223 L5 Manitoba, Lake Man. Can.
223 L5 Manitou Man. Can.
225 H3 Manitou r. Que. Can.
232 E3 Manitou Beach NY U.S.A.
223 M5 Manitou Falls Ont. Can.
224 D4 Manitoulin Island Ont. Can.
224 C3 Manitouwadge Ont. Can.
227 G3 Manitowaning Ont. Can.
226 C2 Manitowish Waters WI U.S.A.
226 D3 Manitowoc WI U.S.A.
224 F4 Maniwaki Que. Can.
113 □1 Maniyafushi i. S. Male Maldives
250 C3 Manizales Col.
213 □J4 Manja Madag.
213 G5 Manjacaze Moz.
213 □J3 Manjak Madag.
114 B3 Manjarabad Karnataka India
114 C4 Manjeri Kerala India
101 C4 Man Jiang r. China
122 B2 Manjil Iran
87 C7 Manjimup W.A. Austr.
207 H5 Manjo Cameroon
114 C2 Manjra r. India
179 G2 Mank Austria
117 G4 Mankachar Assam India
Mankanza Dem. Rep. Congo see Makanza
236 D4 Mankato KS U.S.A.
236 E2 Mankato MN U.S.A.
136 F3 Man'kivka Ukr.
137 J3 Man'kivka Ukr.
136 E3 Man'kivka Ukr.
206 D4 Mankono Côte d'Ivoire
223 J5 Mankota Sask. Can.
160 C1 Manlay France
186 F3 Manlleu Spain
236 E3 Manly IA U.S.A.
116 C5 Manmad Mahar. India
84 C2 Mann r. N.T. Austr.
78 □3a Mann i. Kwajalein Marshall Is
84 B5 Mann, Mount N.T. Austr.
94 C4 Manna Sumatera Indon.
82 D3 Mannahill S.A. Austr.
114 C4 Mannar Sri Lanka
114 C4 Mannar, Gulf of India/Sri Lanka
114 C4 Mannargudi Tamil Nadu India
172 C4 Männedorf Switz.
179 H3 Mannersdorf am Leithagebirge Austria
179 H3 Mannersdorf an der Rabnitz Austria
114 D3 Manneru r. India
172 C2 Mannheim Ger.
Mannicolo Islands Solomon Is see Vanikoro Islands
222 G3 Manning Alta Can.
236 C2 Manning ND U.S.A.
231 D5 Manning SC U.S.A.
78 □6 Manning Strait Solomon Is
232 C5 Mannington WV U.S.A.
151 I3 Manningtree Essex, England U.K.
190 C2 Männlifluh mt. Switz.
84 B5 Mann Ranges mts S.A. Austr.
233 E3 Mannsville NY U.S.A.
192 A4 Mannu r. Sardegna Italy
192 A5 Mannu r. Sardegna Italy
192 B4 Mannu r. Sardegna Italy
192 B5 Mannu r. Sardegna Italy
192 A4 Mannu, Monte hill Sardegna Italy
223 I4 Mannville Alta Can.
206 C5 Mano r. Liberia/Sierra Leone
206 B5 Mano Sierra Leone
Man-of-War Rocks is HI U.S.A. see Gardner Pinnacles
111 B7 Manoharpur Rajasthan India
116 D4 Manohar Thana Rajasthan India
220 C4 Manokotak AK U.S.A.
186 G2 Manol r. Spain
197 H2 Manoleasa Romania
213 □K3 Manompana Madag.
209 E6 Manono Dem. Rep. Congo
150 C3 Manorbier Pembrokeshire, Wales U.K.
235 E2 Manorhaven NY U.S.A.
206 C5 Mano River Liberia
235 F2 Manorville NY U.S.A.
161 D5 Manosque France
174 E1 Manowo Pol.
101 C4 Manp'o N. Korea
116 C5 Manpur Madh. Prad. India
77 I2 Manra i. Phoenix Is Kiribati
186 E3 Manresa Spain
116 C5 Mansa Gujarat India
116 C3 Mansa Punjab India
209 F7 Mansa Zambia
206 B3 Mansabá Guinea-Bissau
206 B3 Mansa Konko Gambia
170 F3 Manschnow Ger.
123 H3 Mansehra Pak.
221 K3 Mansel Island Nunavut Can.
140 O2 Mansel'kya ridge Fin./Rus. Fed.
171 C4 Mansfeld Ger.
83 F4 Mansfield Vic. Austr.
149 H4 Mansfield Nottinghamshire, England U.K.
237 E5 Mansfield AR U.S.A.
237 E5 Mansfield LA U.S.A.
233 H3 Mansfield MA U.S.A.
232 B4 Mansfield OH U.S.A.
232 E4 Mansfield PA U.S.A.
233 G2 Mansfield, Mount VT U.S.A.
235 F1 Mansfield Center CT U.S.A.
149 H4 Mansfield Woodhouse Nottinghamshire, England U.K.
254 E4 Mansidão Brazil
183 H2 Mansilla Spain
183 E2 Mansilla de las Mulas Spain
162 C3 Mansle France
Manso r. Tocantins Brazil see Mortes, Rio das
192 A2 Manso Corse France
206 E5 Manso-Nkwanta Ghana
163 C4 Mansonville France
182 B4 Mansores Port.
150 E4 Manston Dorset, England U.K.
127 H5 Manşūrī Iran
126 D3 Mansurlu Turkey
250 A5 Manta Ecuador
92 A4 Mantalingajan, Mount Palawan Phil.
252 B3 Mantaro r. Peru
240 G3 Manteca CA U.S.A.
182 C4 Manteigas Port.
173 G2 Mantel Ger.
257 G3 Mantena Brazil
226 D5 Manteno IL U.S.A.
231 F5 Manteo NC U.S.A.
165 F5 Manternach Lux.
156 B4 Mantes-la-Jolie France
156 B4 Mantes-la-Ville France
114 C2 Manthani Andhra Prad. India
159 G4 Manthelan France
241 L2 Manti UT U.S.A.
257 D5 Mantiqueira, Serra da mts Brazil
160 D1 Mantoche France
235 D2 Mantoloking NJ U.S.A.
226 E3 Manton MI U.S.A.
198 C2 Mantoudi Greece
191 F3 Mantova Italy
191 F3 Mantova prov. Lombardia Italy
141 N3 Mäntsälä Fin.
141 N3 Mänttä Fin.
246 A2 Mantua Cuba
Mantua Italy see Mantova
234 C3 Mantua NJ U.S.A.
232 C4 Mantua OH U.S.A.
85 F5 Mantuan Downs Qld Austr.
134 I4 Manturovo Kostromskaya Oblast' Rus. Fed.
137 I2 Manturovo Kurskaya Oblast' Rus. Fed.
141 N3 Mäntyharju Fin.
Manu r. Bol. see Mapiri
252 C3 Manú r. Peru
81 □2 Manuae i. Cook Is
79 □3 Manuae atoll Arch. de la Société Fr. Polynesia
78 □2 Manua Islands American Samoa
215 G5 Manubi S. Africa
187 C5 Manuel Spain
254 C4 Manuel Alves r. Brazil
261 I4 Manuel J. Cobo Arg.
261 G3 Manuel Ocampo Arg.
256 B6 Manuel Ribas Brazil
259 B9 Manuel Rodriguez, Isla i. Chile
252 C2 Manuel Urbano Brazil
254 E5 Manuel Vitorino Brazil
122 D5 Manūjān Iran
92 B4 Manukan Phil.
80 E2 Manukau North I. N.Z.
80 E2 Manukau Harbour North I. N.Z.
147 B3 Manulla Rep. of Ireland
252 D2 Manupari r. Bol.
252 D2 Manurimi r. Bol.
252 D2 Manuripi r. Bol.
80 F3 Manutuke North I. N.Z.
114 C3 Manvi Karnataka India
234 D2 Manville NJ U.S.A.
114 C2 Manwat Mahar. India
237 E6 Many LA U.S.A.
213 F2 Manyame r. Moz./Zimbabwe
211 B5 Manyara, Lake salt l. Tanz.
199 E1 Manyas Turkey
197 F4 Manyashki Vrŭkh hill Bulg.
215 F3 Manyatseng S. Africa
223 I5 Manyberries Alta Can.
137 K4 Manychskaya Rus. Fed.
241 M3 Many Farms AZ U.S.A.
136 D3 Manykivtsi Ukr.
211 B6 Manyoni Tanz.
85 G5 Many Peaks Qld Austr.
87 C7 Many Peaks, Mount hill W.A. Austr.
162 C3 Manzac-sur-Vern France
128 A4 Manzala, Bahra el lag. Egypt
Manzala, Lake lag. Egypt see Manzala, Bahra el
182 D3 Manzanal de Arriba Spain
182 D2 Manzanal del Puerto Spain
185 G1 Manzanares Spain
183 G4 Manzanares r. Spain
183 G4 Manzanares el Real Spain
182 C2 Manzaneda Spain
182 C2 Manzaneda, Cabeza de mt. Spain
183 G2 Manzanedo Spain
183 G5 Manzaneque Spain
187 C4 Manzanera Spain
246 C2 Manzanillo Cuba
244 B4 Manzanillo Mex.
191 I3 Manzano Italy
209 F6 Manzanza Dem. Rep. Congo
122 B3 Manzariyeh Iran
160 A3 Manzat France
107 H1 Manzhouli Nei Mongol China
192 E2 Manziana Italy
160 C2 Manziat France
215 H2 Manzini Swaziland
215 H2 Manzini admin. dist. Swaziland
Manzovka Rus. Fed. see Sibirtsevo
202 B6 Mao Chad
246 E3 Mao Dom. Rep.
Maó Spain see Mahón
Mao, Nam r. Myanmar see Shweli
108 C3 Maoba Guizhou China
108 D2 Maoba Hubei China
109 E2 Maocifan Hubei China
108 B1 Mao'ergai Sichuan China
91 I7 Maoke, Pegunungan mts Indon.
215 F2 Maokeng S. Africa
101 B4 Maokui Shan mt. Liaoning China
106 D4 Maomao Shan mt. Gansu China
108 D4 Maoming Guangdong China
108 B3 Maotou Shan mt. Yunnan China
Maowen Sichuan China see Maoxian
108 B2 Maoxian Sichuan China
93 B3 Mapane Sulawesi Tengah Indon.
209 E9 Mapanza Zambia
243 G6 Mapastepec Mex.
215 E4 Maphodi S. Africa
91 I8 Mapi r. Indon.
250 E3 Mapiche, Serranía mts Venez.
242 E3 Mapimí Mex.
242 D3 Mapimí, Bolsón de des. Mex.
252 C3 Mapiri Bol.
252 D2 Mapiri r. Bol.
250 C4 Mapirpán Col.
80 E3 Mapiu North I. N.Z.
236 E3 Maple r. IA U.S.A.
226 E4 Maple r. MI U.S.A.
236 D2 Maple r. ND U.S.A.
236 D2 Maple r. ND U.S.A.
223 I5 Maple Creek Sask. Can.
241 M5 Maple Peak AZ U.S.A.
236 E3 Mapleton IA U.S.A.
241 L1 Mapleton UT U.S.A.
226 D3 Maplewood WI U.S.A.
266 G4 Mapmakers Seamounts sea feature N. Pacific Ocean
85 E1 Mapoon Qld Austr.
215 F3 Mapoteng Lesotho
114 B3 Mapuca Goa India
251 G5 Mapuera r. Brazil
215 H3 Mapumulo S. Africa
213 G5 Maputo Moz.
213 G5 Maputo prov. Moz.
213 G5 Maputo r. Moz./S. Africa
215 F3 Maputsoe Lesotho
Maqanshy Kazakh. see Makanchi
Maqat Kazakh. see Makat
106 D5 Maqên Qinghai China
106 C5 Maqên Gangri mt. Qinghai China
128 B5 Maqla, Jabal al mt. Saudi Arabia
204 C5 Maqṭeïr reg. Maur.
108 B1 Maqu Gansu China
Ma Qu r. China see Huang He
111 D6 Maquan He r. Xizang China
183 F4 Maqueda Spain
209 B6 Maquela do Zombo Angola
259 C6 Maquinchao Arg.
236 F3 Maquoketa IA U.S.A.
236 F3 Maquoketa r. IA U.S.A.
142 C2 Mår r. Norway
123 F5 Mar r. Pak.
182 B3 Mar Port.
257 F5 Mar, Serra do mts Brazil
256 C6 Mar, Serra do mts Paraná Brazil
257 E5 Mar, Serra do mts Rio de Janeiro/São Paulo Brazil
255 C9 Mar, Serra do mts Rio Grande do Sul/Santa Catarina Brazil
251 G3 Mara Guyana
117 E5 Mara Madh. Prad. India
192 A4 Mara Sardegna Italy
211 B5 Mara admin. reg. Tanz.
246 E5 Mara Venez.
251 E5 Maraã Brazil
254 C3 Maraba Brazil
256 B5 Marabá Paulista Brazil
157 F5 Marac France
251 I5 Maracá r. Brazil
251 F4 Maracá, Ilha i. Brazil
251 I4 Maracá, Ilha de i. Brazil
256 B5 Maracaí Brazil
250 D2 Maracaibo Venez.
250 D2 Maracaibo, Lago de l. Venez.
Maracaibo, Lake Venez. see Maracaibo, Lago de
253 G5 Maracaju Brazil
253 G5 Maracaju, Serra de hills Brazil
192 B5 Maracalagonis Sardegna Italy
254 D2 Maracanã Brazil
251 H5 Maracanaquará, Planalto plat. Brazil
Maracanda Uzbek. see Samarkand
254 E5 Maracás Brazil
254 E5 Maracás, Chapada de hills Brazil
250 E2 Maracay Venez.
Maradhoo i. Addu Atoll Maldives see Maradu
207 G3 Maradi Niger
207 G3 Maradi dept Niger
113 □2 Maradu i. Addu Atoll Maldives
129 F3 Maraga Rus. Fed.
122 A2 Marāgheh Iran
254 G4 Maragogi Brazil
92 B3 Maragondon Phil.
124 D2 Marah Saudi Arabia
251 E4 Marahuaca, Cerro mt. Venez.
158 D5 Marais breton marsh France
236 E4 Marais des Cygnes r. KS U.S.A.
254 C2 Marajó, Baía de est. Brazil
251 I5 Marajó, Ilha de i. Brazil
77 H1 Marakei atoll Gilbert Is Kiribati
Maraki atoll Gilbert Is Kiribati see Marakei
114 C3 Marakkanam Tamil Nadu India
Maralaba i. Vanuatu see Mere Lava
210 C4 Maralal Kenya
Maralbashi Xinjiang China see Bachu
129 C3 Maralik Armenia
82 B2 Maralinga S.A. Austr.
Maralwexi Xinjiang China see Bachu
78 □6 Maramasike i. Solomon Is
Maramba Zambia see Livingstone
262 U2 Marambio research stn Antarctica
197 G2 Maramureşului, Munţii mts Romania
123 F4 Maran mt. Pak.
122 A3 Marāna Iraq
241 L5 Marana AZ U.S.A.
183 H3 Maranchón Spain
122 A2 Marand Iran
Marandellas Zimbabwe see Marondera
191 F4 Maranello Italy
157 G3 Marange-Silvange France
254 F2 Maranguape Brazil
254 C5 Maranhão r. Brazil
254 D3 Maranhão state Brazil
184 C1 Maranhão Port.
184 C1 Maranhão, Barragem do resr Port.
191 G4 Marano Italy
191 I3 Marano, Laguna di lag. Italy
85 G5 Maranoa r. Qld Austr.
194 D2 Marano di Napoli Italy
250 C6 Marañón r. Peru
191 F4 Marano sul Panaro Italy
162 B2 Marans France
157 E4 Maranville France
182 C3 Marão mt. Port.
182 B3 Marão, Serra do mts Port.
206 D5 Maraoué r. Côte d'Ivoire
78 □6 Marapa i. Solomon Is
254 D2 Marapanim Brazil
81 A6 Mararoa r. South I. N.Z.
Maraş Cyprus see Varosia
Maraş Turkey see Kahramanmaraş
197 H3 Mărăşeşti Romania
197 H3 Mărăşu Romania
193 H5 Maratea Italy
184 B2 Marateca Port.
199 E3 Marathokampos Voreio Aigaio Greece
224 C3 Marathon Ont. Can.
Marathón Greece see Marathonas
231 D7 Marathon FL U.S.A.
233 E3 Marathon NY U.S.A.
237 C6 Marathon TX U.S.A.
226 C3 Marathon WI U.S.A.
198 C2 Marathonas Greece
251 E5 Marauiá r. Brazil
161 B5 Maraussan France
202 D1 Marāwah Libya
92 C4 Marawi Phil.
156 D4 Maraye-en-Othe France
129 F3 Märäzä Azer.
150 B4 Marazion Cornwall, England U.K.
171 E4 Marbach Ger.
190 C2 Marbach Switz.
172 D3 Marbach am Neckar Ger.
185 F4 Marbella Spain
185 F4 Marbella, Ensenada de b. Spain
86 C4 Marble Bar W.A. Austr.
241 L3 Marble Canyon AZ U.S.A.
213 F5 Marble Hall S. Africa
237 F4 Marble Hill MO U.S.A.
160 D2 Marboz France
215 H4 Marburg S. Africa
Marburg Slovenia see Maribor
169 D5 Marburg an der Lahn Ger.
177 L4 Marca Romania
176 G4 Marcal r. Hungary
176 G5 Marcali Hungary
176 G4 Marcaltő Hungary
191 I4 Marčana Croatia
194 B5 Marcanzotta r. Sicilia Italy
252 C3 Marcapata Peru
191 F3 Marcaria Italy
261 G2 Marcelino Escalada Arg.
193 E2 Marcellina Italy
226 E4 Marcellus MI U.S.A.
233 E3 Marcellus NY U.S.A.
177 H4 Marcelová Slovakia
162 B3 Marcenais France
161 A3 Marcenat France
179 H2 March r. Austria alt. Morava (Europe)
151 H2 March Cambridgeshire, England U.K.
214 C3 Marchand S. Africa
82 D3 Marchant Hill hill S.A. Austr.
191 H5 Marche admin. reg. Italy
165 E4 Marche-en-Famenne Belgium
179 H2 Marchegg Austria
185 E3 Marchena Spain
250 □ Marchena, Isla i. Islas Galápagos Ecuador
156 B5 Marchenoir France
163 B4 Marcheprime France
156 D2 Marchiennes France
260 B4 Marchihue Chile
165 E4 Marchin Belgium
84 D1 Marchinbar Island N.T. Austr.
151 F2 Marchington Staffordshire, England U.K.
261 F2 Mar Chiquita, Lago l. Arg.
261 I5 Mar Chiquita, Lago l. Arg.
179 F2 Marchtrenk Austria
150 E1 Marchwiel Wrexham, Wales U.K.
137 H2 Marchykhyna Buda Ukr.
163 C5 Marciac France
192 C2 Marciana Italy
192 C2 Marciana Marina Italy
193 G3 Marcianise Italy
191 G5 Marciano della Chiana Italy
138 F3 Mārciena Latvia
160 C2 Marcigny France
163 D4 Marcilhac-sur-Célé France
162 B3 Marcillac France
162 E3 Marcillac-la-Croisille France
163 E4 Marcillac-Vallon France
160 A2 Marcillat-en-Combraille France
159 H4 Marcilly-en-Gault France
156 C5 Marcilly-en-Villette France
156 D4 Marcilly-le-Hayer France
156 B4 Marcilly-sur-Eure France
175 I6 Marcinkowice Pol.
174 E5 Marciszów Pol.
156 B2 Marck France
157 H4 Marckolsheim France
182 B3 Marco de Canaveses Port.
156 D2 Marcoing France
253 F2 Marcolino r. Brazil
191 H3 Marcòn Italy
252 B3 Marcona Peru
191 H3 Marco Polo airport Italy
261 F3 Marcos Juárez Arg.
261 H4 Marcos Paz Arg.
161 E4 Marcoux France
156 D2 Marcq-en-Barœul France
233 G2 Marcy, Mount NY U.S.A.
129 G3 Mărdăkan Azer.
123 H3 Mardan Pak.
136 E4 Mardarivka Ukr.
261 I5 Mar de Ajó Arg.
261 I5 Mar del Plata Arg.
150 E2 Marden Herefordshire, England U.K.
151 H3 Marden Kent, England U.K.
156 D3 Mardeuil France
86 B4 Mardie W.A. Austr.
127 F3 Mardın Turkey
140 L2 Mårdsele Sweden
140 M2 Mårdudden Sweden
106 D2 Mardzad Mongolia
160 C3 Mare r. France
78 □5 Maré i. Î. Loyauté New Caledonia
191 G2 Marebbe Italy
191 H4 Marecchia r. Italy
186 □ Mare de Déu del Toro hill Spain
146 C4 Maree, Loch l. Scotland U.K.
85 F3 Mareeba Qld Austr.
149 I4 Mareham le Fen Lincolnshire, England U.K.
192 C1 Maremma reg. Italy
206 C3 Maréna Mali
207 G2 Marendet Niger
236 E3 Marengo IA U.S.A.
226 C4 Marengo IL U.S.A.
226 B2 Marengo WI U.S.A.
226 C2 Marenisco MI U.S.A.
162 A3 Marennes France
195 F4 Marepotamo r. Italy
151 H4 Maresfield East Sussex, England U.K.
86 E2 Maret Islands W.A. Austr.
194 B5 Marettimo Sicilia Italy
194 B5 Marettimo, Isola i. Sicilia Italy
162 C3 Mareuil France
159 I5 Mareuil-sur-Arnon France
156 E3 Mareuil-sur-Ay France
162 A2 Mareuil-sur-Lay-Dissais France
139 I3 Marevo Rus. Fed.
160 D1 Marey-sur-Tille France
239 F6 Marfa TX U.S.A.
150 D3 Margam Neath Port Talbot, Wales U.K.
Marganets Kazakh. see Zhezdy
Marganets Ukr. see Marhanets'
Margao Goa India see Madgaon
86 E3 Margaret r. W.A. Austr.
86 C4 Margaret, Mount hill W.A. Austr.
222 E5 Margaret Bay B.C. Can.
87 B7 Margaret River W.A. Austr.
233 F3 Margaretville NY U.S.A.
251 F2 Margarita, Isla de i. Venez.
137 J4 Margaritovo Rus. Fed.
215 H4 Margate S. Africa
151 I3 Margate Kent, England U.K.
235 D3 Margate City NJ U.S.A.
197 F2 Mărgău Romania
162 B3 Margaux France
177 K3 Margecany Slovakia
156 E4 Margerie-Hancourt France
149 H4 Margery Hill hill England U.K.
172 D2 Margetshöchheim Ger.
117 H4 Margherita Assam India
193 I3 Margherita di Savoia Italy
208 F4 Margherita Peak Dem. Rep. Congo/Uganda
Marghilon Uzbek. see Margilan
197 F2 Marghita Romania
121 G4 Margilan Uzbek.
177 L6 Margina Romania
197 G2 Marginea Romania
156 C3 Margny-lès-Compiègne France
123 E4 Margo, Dasht-i des. Afgh.
190 C3 Margone Italy
174 F3 Margonin Pol.
92 B5 Margosatubig Phil.
165 E4 Margraten Neth.
222 F4 Marguerite B.C. Can.
Marguerite, Pic mt. Dem. Rep. Congo/Uganda see Margherita Peak
161 C5 Marguerittes France
157 F3 Margut France
127 G4 Marhaj Khalīl Iraq
151 H2 Marham Norfolk, England U.K.
127 F3 Marhan Dāgh hill Iraq
137 H4 Marhanets' Ukr.
205 E2 Marhoum Alg.
252 D1 Mari r. Brazil
255 B7 Maria r. Brazil
79 □3 Maria atoll Arch. des Tuamotu Fr. Polynesia
79 □3 Maria atoll Îs Australes Fr. Polynesia
185 H3 María Spain
179 G2 Maria Anzbach Austria
161 C4 Mariac France
252 C5 María Elena Chile
142 C3 Mariager Denmark
261 H5 María Ignacia Arg.
84 C2 Maria Island N.T. Austr.
83 G5 Maria Island Tas. Austr.
179 G3 Maria Lankowitz Austria
182 C4 Marialva Port.
85 G4 Marian Qld Austr.
257 F4 Mariana Brazil
183 H4 Mariana Spain
246 B2 Marianao Cuba
266 E4 Mariana Ridge sea feature N. Pacific Ocean
266 E5 Mariana Trench sea feature N. Pacific Ocean
117 H4 Mariani Assam India
Mariánica, Cordillera mts Spain see Morena, Sierra
237 F5 Marianna AR U.S.A.
231 C6 Marianna FL U.S.A.
143 F3 Mariannelund Sweden
190 E3 Mariano Comense Italy
258 F3 Mariano Loza Arg.
Mariano Machado Angola see Ganda
194 C5 Marianopoli Sicilia Italy
174 D2 Marianowo Pol.
176 B2 Mariánské Lázně Czech Rep.
179 E3 Mariapfarr Austria
250 D4 Mariapirí, Mesa de hills Col.
256 B4 Mariápolis Brazil
179 F4 Maria Rain Austria
238 E2 Marias r. MT U.S.A.
244 A3 Marías, Islas is Mex.
179 F4 Maria Saal Austria
261 G4 María Teresa Arg.
80 D1 Maria van Diemen, Cape North I. N.Z.
179 F4 Maria Wörth Austria
179 G3 Mariazell Austria
124 D5 Ma'rib Yemen
124 D5 Ma'rib governorate Yemen
226 D3 Maribel WI U.S.A.
142 D4 Maribo Denmark
188 E2 Maribor Slovenia
257 F5 Maricá Brazil
Marica r. Bulg. see Maritsa
247 □1 Maricao Puerto Rico
241 K5 Maricopa AZ U.S.A.
240 H4 Maricopa CA U.S.A.
241 K5 Maricopa Mountains AZ U.S.A.
Maricourt Que. Can. see Kangiqsujuaq
208 F3 Maridi Sudan
250 E5 Marié r. Brazil
262 P1 Marie Byrd Land reg. Antarctica
143 G2 Mariefred Sweden
247 □2 Marie-Galante i. Guadeloupe
141 L3 Mariehamn Åland Fin.
Mari El aut. rep. Rus. Fed. see Mariy El, Respublika
254 C5 Mariembero r. Brazil
165 D4 Mariembourg Belgium
Marienbad Czech Rep. see Mariánské Lázně
171 E5 Marienberg Ger.
Marienburg Pol. see Malbork
168 C2 Marienhafe Ger.
169 E3 Marienhagen Ger.
169 C4 Marienheide Ger.
169 F3 Mariental Ger.
212 C5 Mariental Namibia
232 D4 Marienville PA U.S.A.
Marienwerder Pol. see Kwidzyn
143 E2 Mariestad Sweden
224 E1 Mariet r. Que. Can.
231 C5 Marietta GA U.S.A.
232 C5 Marietta OH U.S.A.
237 D5 Marietta OK U.S.A.
234 B2 Marietta PA U.S.A.
233 G2 Marieville Que. Can.
207 G4 Mariga r. Nigeria
193 G4 Marigliano Italy
192 A2 Marignana Corse France
161 D5 Marignane France
159 G4 Marigné-Laillé France
160 E2 Marignier France
158 E2 Marigny France
156 D4 Marigny-le-Châtel France
160 B1 Marigny-l'Église France
247 □2 Marigot Dominica
247 G3 Marigot St Maarten West Indies
120 E1 Mariinskoye Rus. Fed.
138 D4 Marijampolė Lith.
215 F1 Marikana S. Africa
197 F5 Marikostinovo Bulg.
256 C5 Marília Brazil
86 C4 Marillana W.A. Austr.
256 A6 Mariluz Brazil
209 C7 Marimba Angola
182 B2 Marín Spain
240 G3 Marina CA U.S.A.
192 D2 Marina di Alberese Italy
195 F3 Marina di Amendolara Italy
192 A5 Marina di Arbus Sardegna Italy
193 H4 Marina di Camerota Italy
192 C2 Marina di Campo Italy
192 C1 Marina di Castagneto Donoratico Italy
190 F5 Marina di Cecina Italy
193 H3 Marina di Chieuti Italy
195 F2 Marina di Ginosa Italy
195 F4 Marina di Gioiosa Ionica Italy
192 C2 Marina di Grosseto Italy
195 H3 Marina di Leuca Italy
190 F4 Marina di Massa Italy
194 C5 Marina di Palma Sicilia Italy
195 G2 Marina di Pulsano Italy
194 D6 Marina di Ragusa Sicilia Italy
191 H4 Marina di Ravenna Italy
Mar'ina Gorka Belarus see Mar"ina Horka
138 G5 Mar"ina Horka Belarus
185 F3 Marinaleda Spain
193 F1 Marina Palmense Italy
191 H4 Marina Romea Italy
195 F3 Marina Schiavonea Italy
92 B3 Marinduque i. Phil.
227 F4 Marine City MI U.S.A.
194 B5 Marinella Sicilia Italy
194 C5 Marineo Sicilia Italy
156 B3 Marines France
187 C5 Marines Spain
226 D3 Marinette WI U.S.A.
256 B5 Maringá Brazil
208 C4 Maringa r. Dem. Rep. Congo
232 B4 Maringo OH U.S.A.
213 G3 Maringué Moz.
160 B3 Maringues France
182 B4 Marinha das Ondas Port.
182 B5 Marinha Grande Port.
184 B1 Marinhais Port.
182 B3 Marinhas Port.
191 J3 Marinići Croatia
129 C1 Mar'in Kolodtsy Rus. Fed.
193 E3 Marino Italy
Marino Alejandro Selkirk, Isla i. S. Pacific Ocean see Alejandro Selkirk, Isla
231 C5 Marion AL U.S.A.
237 F5 Marion AR U.S.A.
235 F1 Marion CT U.S.A.
237 F4 Marion IL U.S.A.
230 C3 Marion IN U.S.A.
236 D4 Marion KS U.S.A.
237 F4 Marion KY U.S.A.
226 E3 Marion MI U.S.A.
231 D5 Marion NC U.S.A.
232 B4 Marion OH U.S.A.
231 E5 Marion SC U.S.A.
232 C6 Marion VA U.S.A.
226 C3 Marion WI U.S.A.
82 D3 Marion Bay S.A. Austr.
84 D4 Marion Downs Qld Austr.
85 H3 Marion Reef Coral Sea Is Terr. Austr.
193 I3 Mariotto Italy
205 H5 Mariou, Adrar mt. Alg.
251 H4 Maripasoula Fr. Guiana
240 H3 Mariposa CA U.S.A.
240 G3 Mariposa r. CA U.S.A.
253 E5 Mariscal Estigarribia Para.
197 F2 Mărişel Romania
197 G2 Mărişelu Romania
161 E4 Maritime Alps mts France/Italy
Maritime Kray admin. div. Rus. Fed. see Primorskiy Kray
Maritsa Bulg. see Simeonovgrad
197 H5 Maritsa r. Bulg.
134 J4 Mari-Turek Rus. Fed.
137 I4 Mariupol' Ukr.
251 F2 Mariusa, Isla i. Venez.
127 G4 Marīvān Iran
134 J4 Mariy El, Respublika aut. rep. Rus. Fed.
Mariyskaya A.S.S.R. aut. rep. Rus. Fed. see Mariy El, Respublika
160 C2 Marizy France
183 G5 Marjaliza Spain
138 E2 Märjamaa Estonia
128 B3 Marjayoûn Lebanon
150 E3 Mark Somerset, England U.K.
210 E4 Marka Somalia
121 K2 Markakol', Ozero l. Kazakh.
206 D3 Markala Mali
108 A2 Markam Xizang China
129 D4 Mārkān Iran
114 C3 Markapur Andhra Prad. India
143 E3 Markaryd Sweden
122 B3 Markazī prov. Iran
227 G3 Markdale Ont. Can.
172 D4 Markdorf Ger.
164 F2 Markelo Neth.
213 F4 Marken S. Africa
164 E2 Markermeer l. Neth.
171 D5 Markersdorf bei Burgstädt Ger.
151 F2 Market Bosworth Leicestershire, England U.K.
151 G2 Market Deeping Lincolnshire, England U.K.
150 E2 Market Drayton Shropshire, England U.K.
151 G2 Market Harborough Leicestershire, England U.K.
147 E2 Markethill Northern Ireland U.K.
151 F3 Market Lavington Wiltshire, England U.K.
149 I4 Market Rasen Lincolnshire, England U.K.
149 H4 Market Warsop Nottinghamshire, England U.K.
149 I4 Market Weighton East Riding of Yorkshire, England U.K.
151 F2 Markfield Leicestershire, England U.K.
172 D3 Markgröningen Ger.
131 M3 Markha r. Rus. Fed.
224 E5 Markham Ont. Can.
263 K1 Markham, Mount Antarctica
121 H4 Markhamet Uzbek.
175 J3 Marki Pol.
137 J2 Marki Rus. Fed.
183 H1 Markina-Xemein Spain
146 E5 Markinch Fife, Scotland U.K.
171 E3 Märkisch Buchholz Ger.
110 B4 Markit Xinjiang China
140 M2 Markitta Sweden
137 J3 Markivka Ukr.
136 E3 Markivka r. Ukr.
171 D4 Markkleeberg Ger.
240 H2 Markleeville CA U.S.A.
232 D5 Markleysburg PA U.S.A.
173 G3 Marklkofen Ger.
168 E3 Marklohe Ger.
164 E2 Marknesse Neth.
171 D5 Markneukirchen Ger.
177 G4 Márkó Hungary
198 C3 Markopoulo Greece
208 C3 Markounda C.A.R.
179 H5 Markovac Trojstveni Croatia
131 S3 Markovo Chukotskiy Avtonomnyy Okrug Rus. Fed.
139 M3 Markovo Ivanovskaya Oblast' Rus. Fed.
137 H2 Markovo Kurskaya Oblast' Rus. Fed.
207 F3 Markoye Burkina
171 D4 Markranstädt Ger.
120 A2 Marks Rus. Fed.
237 F5 Marks MS U.S.A.
234 D2 Marksboro NJ U.S.A.
151 H3 Marks Tey Essex, England U.K.
169 F5 Marksuhl Ger.
237 E6 Marksville LA U.S.A.
179 H3 Markt Allhau Austria
173 E2 Marktbergel Ger.
173 E2 Markt Berolzheim Ger.
173 E2 Markt Bibart Ger.
173 E2 Marktbreit Ger.
173 E2 Markt Erlbach Ger.
179 G3 Markt Hartmannsdorf Austria
172 D2 Marktheidenfeld Ger.
173 F3 Markt Indersdorf Ger.
173 G3 Marktl Ger.
171 C5 Marktleugast Ger.
171 D5 Marktleuthen Ger.
173 E4 Marktoberdorf Ger.
173 E3 Marktoffingen Ger.
222 E5 Marktosis B.C. Can.
179 H3 Markt Piesting Austria
173 G1 Marktredwitz Ger.
173 E4 Markt Rettenbach Ger.
171 C5 Marktrodach Ger.
179 F2 Markt St Florian Austria
179 H3 Markt St Martin Austria
173 H4 Marktschellenberg Ger.
173 F3 Markt Schwaben Ger.
173 E2 Marktseft Ger.
173 E3 Markt Wald Ger.
175 K4 Markuszów Pol.
151 G3 Markyate Hertfordshire, England U.K.
169 C4 Marl Ger.
82 C1 Marla S.A. Austr.
87 C6 Marlandy Hill hill W.A. Austr.
234 C3 Marlboro NJ U.S.A.
235 D2 Marlboro NJ U.S.A.
235 E1 Marlboro NY U.S.A.
85 G4 Marlborough Qld Austr.
81 D4 Marlborough admin. reg. South I. N.Z.
151 F3 Marlborough Wiltshire, England U.K.
235 F1 Marlborough CT U.S.A.
233 H3 Marlborough MA U.S.A.
233 G3 Marlborough NH U.S.A.
151 F3 Marlborough Downs hills England U.K.
150 D4 Marldon Devon, England U.K.
156 D3 Marle France
191 G2 Marlengo Italy
157 H4 Marlenheim France
227 F4 Marlette MI U.S.A.
161 C3 Marlhes France
160 D2 Marlieux France
237 D6 Marlin TX U.S.A.
232 C5 Marlinton WV U.S.A.
171 C5 Marlishausen Ger.
83 G4 Marlo Vic. Austr.
170 D1 Marlow Ger.
151 G3 Marlow Buckinghamshire, England U.K.
234 D3 Marlton NJ U.S.A.
157 G3 Marly Lorraine France
156 D2 Marly Nord - Pas-de-Calais France
190 C2 Marly Switz.
156 C3 Marly-la-Ville France
114 B3 Marmagao Goa India
160 C2 Marmagne Bourgogne France
159 I4 Marmagne Centre France
163 C4 Marmande France
199 E1 Marmara Turkey
Marmara, Sea of g. Turkey see Marmara Denizi
199 E1 Marmara Adası i. Turkey
199 F1 Marmara Denizi g. Turkey
199 E1 Marmaraereğlisi Turkey
202 E2 Marmarica reg. Libya
199 F3 Marmaris Turkey
199 E2 Marmaro Voreio Aigaio Greece
236 C2 Marmarth ND U.S.A.
184 C2 Marmelar Port.
184 B1 Marmeleira Port.
184 B3 Marmelete Port.
251 F6 Marmelos r. Brazil
232 C5 Marmet WV U.S.A.
87 D6 Marmion, Lake salt l. W.A. Austr.
191 F3 Marmirolo Italy
191 G2 Marmolada mt. Italy
185 F2 Marmolejo Spain
190 C3 Marmore r. Italy
157 H4 Marmoutier France
160 D1 Marnay France
160 E2 Marnaz France
156 E3 Marne dept Champagne-Ardenne France
156 C4 Marne r. France
168 E2 Marne Ger.
157 F5 Marne, Source de la tourist site France
156 C4 Marne-la-Vallée France
129 D3 Marneuli Georgia
172 C2 Marnheim Ger.
150 E4 Marnhull Dorset, England U.K.
170 C2 Marnitz Ger.
83 E4 Marnoo Vic. Austr.
208 C2 Maro Chad
213 □K2 Maroambihy Madag.
213 □K2 Maroantsetra Madag.
257 H2 Maroba r. Brazil
194 D5 Maroglio r. Sicilia Italy
79 □3 Marokau atoll Arch. des Tuamotu Fr. Polynesia
80 E3 Marokopa North I. N.Z.
116 D2 Marol Jammu and Kashmir
213 □K4 Marolambo Madag.
169 F5 Maroldsweisach Ger.
159 G3 Marolles-les-Braults France
156 B3 Maromme France
213 □K2 Maromokotro mt. Madag.
213 F3 Marondera Zimbabwe
251 H3 Maroni r. Fr. Guiana
162 D3 Maronne r. France
85 H5 Maroochydore Qld Austr.
87 B4 Maroonah W.A. Austr.
239 F4 Maroon Peak CO U.S.A.
246 □ Maroon Town Jamaica
93 A4 Maros Sulawesi Selatan Indon.
93 A4 Maros r. Indon.
196 E2 Maros r. Romania
177 J5 Maros-Körös Köze plain Hungary
177 J5 Maroslele Hungary
191 G3 Marostica Italy
Marosvásárhely Romania see Târgu Mureş
79 □3 Marotiri is Îs Australes Fr. Polynesia
213 □K2 Marotolana Madag.
207 I4 Maroua Cameroon
158 D3 Maroué France
213 □J5 Marovato Madag.
213 □J3 Marovoay Mahajanga Madag.
213 □K3 Marovoay Toamasina Madag.
251 H3 Marowijne r. Suriname
172 B2 Marpingen Ger.
149 G4 Marple Greater Manchester, England U.K.
127 F4 Marqādah Syria
Marqakōl l. Kazakh. see Markakol', Ozero
108 B1 Mar Qu r. Sichuan China
215 F3 Marquard S. Africa
173 G4 Marquartstein Ger.
245 E5 Marquelia Mex.
Marquesas Islands Fr. Polynesia see Marquises, Îles
257 F5 Marquês de Valença Brazil
226 D2 Marquette MI U.S.A.
237 D6 Marquez TX U.S.A.
156 D2 Marquion France
156 B2 Marquise France
79 □3 Marquises, Îles is Fr. Polynesia
163 E6 Marquixanes France
83 E2 Marra N.S.W. Austr.
83 F2 Marra r. N.S.W. Austr.
202 E6 Marra, Jebel mt. Sudan
213 G5 Marracuene Moz.
191 G4 Marradi Italy
204 D3 Marrakech Morocco
Marrakesh Morocco see Marrakech
202 E6 Marra Plateau Sudan
83 F5 Marrawah Tas. Austr.
82 D2 Marree S.A. Austr.
237 F6 Marrero LA U.S.A.
213 G3 Marromeu Moz.
192 A5 Marrubiu Sardegna Italy
164 E1 Marrum Neth.
211 C8 Marrupa Moz.
82 C1 Marryat S.A. Austr.
161 A3 Mars r. France
232 C4 Mars PA U.S.A.
203 G3 Marsa Alam Egypt
202 C2 Marsa al Burayqah Libya
210 C4 Marsabit Kenya
160 B3 Marsac-en-Livradois France
158 E4 Marsac-sur-Don France
190 E4 Marsaglia Italy
157 G4 Marsal France
194 B5 Marsala Sicilia Italy
202 E2 Marsa Matrûh Egypt
160 C1 Marsannay-la-Côte France
161 C4 Marsanne France
206 B3 Marsassoum Senegal
195 □ Marsaxlokk Malta
169 D4 Marsberg Ger.
168 F2 Marschacht Ger.
193 E2 Marsciano Italy
83 F3 Marsden N.S.W. Austr.
223 I4 Marsden Sask. Can.
149 H4 Marsden West Yorkshire, England U.K.
164 D2 Marsdiep sea chan. Neth.
161 B5 Marseillan France
161 D5 Marseille France
Marseille airport France see Provence
156 B3 Marseille-en-Beauvaisis France
Marseilles France see Marseille
226 C5 Marseilles IL U.S.A.
140 K2 Marsfjället mt. Sweden
128 B5 Marshah, Jabal mt. Saudi Arabia
223 I4 Marshall Sask. Can.
237 E5 Marshall AR U.S.A.
230 C4 Marshall IL U.S.A.
226 E4 Marshall MI U.S.A.
236 E2 Marshall MN U.S.A.
236 E4 Marshall MO U.S.A.
231 D5 Marshall NC U.S.A.
237 E5 Marshall TX U.S.A.
232 E5 Marshall VA U.S.A.
266 F5 Marshall Islands country N. Pacific Ocean
234 C1 Marshalls Creek PA U.S.A.
234 C3 Marshallton DE U.S.A.
236 E3 Marshalltown IA U.S.A.
150 E3 Marshfield South Gloucestershire, England U.K.
237 E4 Marshfield MO U.S.A.
226 B3 Marshfield WI U.S.A.
231 E7 Marsh Harbour Bahamas
233 □J1 Mars Hill ME U.S.A.
222 C2 Marsh Lake Y.T. Can.
122 B2 Marshūn Iran
161 C5 Marsillargues France
238 C3 Marsing ID U.S.A.
149 H3 Marske-by-the-Sea Redcar and Cleveland, England U.K.
157 F3 Mars-la-Tour France
156 E4 Marson France
163 E5 Marssac-sur-Tarn France
143 G2 Märsta Sweden
142 D4 Marstal Denmark
190 E1 Märstetten Switz.
151 F3 Marston Oxfordshire, England U.K.
150 E4 Marston Magna Somerset, England U.K.
151 G2 Marston Moretaine Bedfordshire, England U.K.

Column 1

78 □3a Marsugalt i. Kwajalein Marshall Is
117 F4 Marsyangdi r. Nepal
234 C4 Marsyhope r. MD U.S.A.
192 D2 Marta Italy
192 D2 Marta r. Italy
86 B3 Martaban Myanmar
96 B3 Martaban, Gulf of Myanmar
195 H2 Martano Italy
193 E2 Martano, Monte mt. Italy
95 F3 Martapura Kalimantan Selatan Indon.
94 D4 Martapura Sumatera Indon.
207 I3 Marte Nigeria
162 D4 Martel France
232 B4 Martel OH U.S.A.
162 D4 Martel, Causse de hills France
162 E5 Martelange Belgium
191 H3 Martellago Italy
191 F2 Martello Italy
177 U5 Mártély Hungary
224 E4 Marten River Ont. Can.
224 E5 Martensville Sask. Can.
187 C5 Martes mt. France
168 F3 Martfeld Ger.
177 I4 Martfű Hungary
151 I2 Martham Norfolk, England U.K.
233 H4 Martha's Vineyard i. MA U.S.A.
187 D4 Marthon France
246 C2 Martí Cuba
182 D4 Martiago Spain
191 I2 Martignacco Italy
163 B4 Martignas-sur-Jalles France
159 F4 Martigné-Briand France
157 F4 Martigné-Ferchaud France
159 F3 Martigné-sur-Mayenne France
190 C2 Martigny Switz.
160 C2 Martigny-le-Comte France
157 F4 Martigny-les-Bains France
157 F4 Martigny-les-Gerbonvaux France
183 F4 Martiherrero Spain
185 E5 Martil Morocco
163 B4 Martillac France
184 C3 Martim Longo Port.
182 E1 Martimporra Spain
Martín Vaz, Ilhas is
S. Atlantic Ocean see
Martin Vas, Ilhas
222 F2 Martin r. N.W.T. Can.
177 H2 Martin Slovakia
186 C3 Martin r. Spain
236 C3 Martin SD U.S.A.
195 G2 Martina Franca Italy
81 E4 Martinborough North I. N.Z.
182 B5 Martinchel Port.
185 F3 Martín de la Jara Spain
179 E3 Martín de Yeltes Spain
193 E3 Martinengo Italy
186 E2 Martinet Spain
245 F3 Martínez Mex.
240 F2 Martínez CA U.S.A.
231 D5 Martínez GA U.S.A.
231 C4 Martínez Lake AZ U.S.A.
169 F4 Martinfeld Ger.
182 B5 Martingança Port.
257 E3 Martinho Campos Brazil
247 □2 Martinique terr. West Indies
247 □2 Martinique Passage Dominica/Martinique
183 F3 Martín Muñoz de las Posadas Spain
198 C2 Martino Greece
256 D5 Martinópolis Brazil
270 □ Martin Peninsula Antarctica
179 G2 Martinsberg Austria
232 B4 Martinsburg OH U.S.A.
232 D4 Martinsburg PA U.S.A.
232 E5 Martinsburg WV U.S.A.
232 E3 Martins Creek PA U.S.A.
234 C1 Martins Creek r. PA U.S.A.
232 C4 Martins Ferry OH U.S.A.
193 F2 Martinsicuro Italy
147 C4 Martinstown Rep. of Ireland
230 C4 Martinsville IN U.S.A.
232 D6 Martinsville VA U.S.A.
264 H7 Martin Vas, Ilhas is
S. Atlantic Ocean see
Martin Vaz, Ilhas
S. Atlantic Ocean see
Martin Vas, Ilhas
192 A4 Martis Sardegna Italy
159 H5 Martizay France
151 I2 Martlesham Suffolk, England U.K.
150 E2 Martley Worcestershire, England U.K.
150 E4 Martock Somerset, England U.K.
Martök Kazakh. see Martuk
80 E4 Marton North I. N.Z.
177 H4 Martonvásár Hungary
177 H4 Martorell Spain
183 G3 Martos Spain
163 D5 Martres-Tolosane France
141 M3 Marttila Fin.
120 D2 Martuk Kazakh.
129 C3 Martuni Armenia
132 C3 Martvili Georgia
137 G2 Martynivka Ukr.
136 E2 Martynovychi Ukr.
207 G3 Maru Nigeria
103 F6 Marugame Japan
163 E4 Marugán Spain
190 G2 Maruggio Italy
81 D4 Maruia r. South I. N.Z.
254 F4 Maruim Brazil
105 E2 Maruko Japan
63 G3 Marulan N.S.W. Austr.
261 F2 Marull Arg.
164 F1 Marum Neth.
78 □5 Marum, Mount vol. Vanuatu
122 B4 Mārūm r. Iran
104 C2 Maruoka Japan
175 J4 Maruszów Pol.
213 □K2 Marwanad India
223 I4 Marwayne Alta Can.
173 I3 Marxheim Ger.
Marxwalde Ger. see Neuhardenberg
172 C3 Marzell Ger.
84 B2 Mary r. Qld Austr.
85 H5 Mary r. Qld Austr.
86 E3 Mary r. Qld Austr.
122 E3 Mary Turkm.
171 M5 Mar"yanivka Ukr.
137 I4 Mar"yanivka Ukr.
136 D2 Mar"yanivka Ukr.
137 J5 Mar"yanskaya Rus. Fed.
Mary El, Respublika aut. rep. Rus. Fed. see Mariy El, Respublika
146 D4 Marybank Highland, Scotland U.K.
85 H5 Maryborough Qld Austr.
63 B4 Maryborough Vic. Austr.
214 D3 Marydale S. Africa
234 C3 Marydel MD U.S.A.
120 B1 Mar"yevka Rus. Fed.
146 □G1 Maryfield Shetland, Scotland U.K.
137 I4 Mar"yinka Ukr.
137 H4 Mar"yivka Ukr.
Maryino Rus. Fed. see Pristen'
146 F5 Marykirk Aberdeenshire, Scotland U.K.
234 B4 Maryland state U.S.A.
234 B3 Maryland admin. div. Turkm. see Maryyskaya Oblast'
149 F3 Maryport Cumbria, England U.K.
225 H2 Mary's Harbour Nfld. Can.
225 K2 Marysvale UT U.S.A.

Column 2

83 F4 Marysville Vic. Austr.
225 H4 Marysville N.B. Can.
240 G2 Marysville CA U.S.A.
236 D4 Marysville KS U.S.A.
227 F4 Marysville MI U.S.A.
232 B4 Marysville OH U.S.A.
234 B2 Marysville PA U.S.A.
238 B1 Marysville WA U.S.A.
84 C5 Maryvale N.T. Austr.
85 F3 Maryvale Qld Austr.
236 E3 Maryville MO U.S.A.
231 D5 Maryville TN U.S.A.
146 F4 Marywell Aberdeenshire, Scotland U.K.
122 E2 Maryyskaya Oblast' admin. div. Turkm.
191 G4 Marzabotto Italy
256 C2 Marzagão Brazil
171 D3 Marzahna Ger.
171 D3 Marzahne Ger.
195 E6 Marzamemi Sicilia Italy
158 D4 Marzan France
191 G4 Marzeno r. Italy
173 F3 Marzling Ger.
160 D2 Marzy France
183 G2 Masa Spain
242 □I7 Masachapa Nic.
128 B4 Masada tourist site Israel
Más Afuera i. S. Pacific Ocean see Alejandro Selkirk, Isla
122 C4 Masāhūn, Küh-e mt. Iran
211 B5 Masai Mara National Reserve nature res. Kenya
192 A5 Masainas Sardegna Italy
192 A5 Masainas Sardegna Italy
123 H2 Masai Steppe plain Tanz.
123 F4 Masak Pak.
210 A5 Masaka Uganda
215 F4 Masakhane S. Africa
187 C5 Masalavés Spain
129 F4 Masallı Azer.
93 B3 Masamba Sulawesi Selatan Indon.
93 B3 Masamba mt. Indon.
101 D6 Masan S. Korea
137 H5 Masandra Ukr.
211 C7 Masasi Tanz.
Más á Tierra i. S. Pacific Ocean see Robinson Crusoe, Isla
242 □I1 Masaya Nic.
242 □I6 Masaya, Volcán vol. Nic.
92 B3 Masbate i. Phil.
92 B3 Masbate i. Phil.
163 E5 Mas-Cabardès France
195 E5 Mascali Sicilia Italy
195 E5 Mascalucia Sicilia Italy
205 F2 Mascara Alg.
183 G5 Mascaraque Spain
265 H6 Mascarene Basin sea feature Indian Ocean
265 H5 Mascarene Plain sea feature Indian Ocean
265 H5 Mascarene Ridge sea feature Indian Ocean
182 C3 Mascarenhas Port.
260 D2 Mascasín, Salina de salt pan Arg.
193 H4 Maschito Italy
209 B6 Mascia Dem. Rep. Congo
244 B3 Mascota Mex.
230 F2 Mascouche Que. Can.
186 C2 Mascún r. Spain
186 D4 Mas de Barberans Spain
186 D4 Mas de las Matas Spain
183 H4 Masegosa Spain
185 H2 Masegoso Spain
183 H4 Masegoso de Tajuña Spain
172 D3 Maselheim Ger.
210 B4 Maseno Kenya
211 C6 Masera r. Italy
178 D5 Maserada sul Piave Italy
215 I3 Maseru Lesotho
157 G5 Masevaux France
141 I3 Masfjorden Norway
163 D5 Mas-Grenier France
213 F3 Mashava Zimbabwe
149 H3 Masham North Yorkshire, England U.K.
108 D4 Mashan Guangxi China
213 H4 Mashava Zimbabwe
116 D2 Mashhad Iran
Jammu and Kashmir
137 G1 Masheve Ukr.
116 C4 Mashi r. India
137 H3 Mashivka Ukr.
123 E5 Mashkel r. Pak.
123 E5 Māshkīd r. Iran
213 F3 Mashonaland Central prov. Zimbabwe
213 F3 Mashonaland East prov. Zimbabwe
213 F3 Mashonaland West prov. Zimbabwe
129 C3 Mashtagi Azer. see Maştağa
242 C3 Masiáca Mex.
215 F4 Masibambane S. Africa
182 B2 Maside Spain
215 F3 Masilo S. Africa
209 C6 Masi-Manimba Dem. Rep. Congo
210 A4 Masindi Uganda
92 A3 Masinloc Phil.
190 D2 Masino r. Italy
214 D4 Masinyusane S. Africa
Masira, Gulf of Oman see Maşīrah, Khalīj
125 G3 Maşīrah, Jazīrat i. Oman
125 G4 Maşīrah, Khalīj b. Oman
125 G4 Masira Island Oman see Maşīrah, Jazīrat
129 D2 Masis Armenia
252 B2 Masisea Peru
191 G4 Masi Torello Italy
93 D3 Masiwang r. Maluku Indon.
215 I3 Masjaing S. Africa
122 B4 Masjed Soleymān Iran
147 B3 Mask, Lough l. Rep. of Ireland
120 D1 Maskät Iran
163 B5 Masleacq France
177 K5 Maşloc Romania
137 I2 Maslova Pristan' Rus. Fed.
175 J4 Maslovka Pol.
197 K2 Maslovo Rus. Fed.
191 G5 Masma r. Spain
213 □J3 Masma'uh Yemen
191 G2 Maso r. Italy
213 □K2 Masoala, Tanjona c. Madag.
226 A1 Mason MI U.S.A.
226 D5 Mason OH U.S.A.
237 D6 Mason TX U.S.A.
226 B3 Mason WI U.S.A.
232 B5 Mason WV U.S.A.
87 C5 Mason, Lake salt flat W.A. Austr.
81 B7 Mason Bay South I. N.Z.
236 E3 Mason City IA U.S.A.
226 C5 Mason City IL U.S.A.
190 C4 Masone Italy
81 D5 Masons Flat South I. N.Z.
232 D5 Masontown WV U.S.A.
233 F6 Masonville NJ U.S.A.
125 H2 Maşqat Oman see Muscat
125 H2 Masqat governorate Oman
233 H3 Massa Italy

Column 3

203 H6 Massawa Eritrea
203 H5 Massawa Channel Eritrea
159 H4 Massay France
169 F5 Maßbach Ger.
171 F4 Massen Ger.
233 F2 Massena NY U.S.A.
208 C2 Massenya Chad
162 D3 Masseret France
195 G2 Masseria Risana hill Italy
222 C4 Masset B.C. Can.
163 C5 Masseube France
224 D4 Massey Ont. Can.
234 C3 Massey MD U.S.A.
161 B3 Massiac France
193 F3 Massico, Monte hill Italy
232 B5 Massieville OH U.S.A.
161 B3 Massif Central mts France
206 D4 Massiguí Mali
Massilia France see Marseille
232 C4 Massillon OH U.S.A.
190 D4 Massimino Italy
206 D3 Massina Mali
173 G3 Massing Ger.
90 C2 Massinga Moz.
257 C3 Massinga Brazil
156 C4 Massy France
129 F3 Maştağa Azer.
81 E4 Mastershausen Ger.
81 E4 Masterton N.I. N.Z.
235 F2 Mastic NY U.S.A.
235 F2 Mastic Beach NY U.S.A.
246 C1 Mastic Point Andros Bahamas
144 J1 Mastervik Norway
123 H2 Mastung Pak.
123 F4 Mastura Pak.
124 B3 Mastūrāh Saudi Arabia
138 E5 Masty Belarus
192 A5 Masua Sardegna Italy
103 E6 Masuda Japan
Masuda Gabon see Franceville
Masulipatam Andhra Prad. India see Machilipatnam
192 A5 Masullas Sardegna Italy
Masuna i. American Samoa see Tutuila
94 C3 Masurai, Bukit mt. Indon.
213 F4 Masvingo Zimbabwe
213 F4 Masvingo prov. Zimbabwe
211 B5 Maswe Tanz.
128 C2 Maşyāf Syria
136 B2 Masyevichy Belarus
174 F1 Maszewo Lubuskie Pol.
174 D2 Maszewo Zachodniopomorskie Pol.
196 D5 Mat r. Albania
80 G2 Mat, Nam r. Laos
251 E3 Mata, Serrania de mts Venez.
213 E3 Matabeleland North prov. Zimbabwe
213 F4 Matabeleland South prov. Zimbabwe
117 G4 Matabhanga W. Bengal India
183 G3 Matabuena Spain
184 D2 Matachel r. Spain
224 D4 Matachewan Ont. Can.
209 B6 Matadi Dem. Rep. Congo
175 I3 Matagalls mt. Spain
242 □I6 Matagalpa Nic.
224 E3 Matagami Que. Can.
224 E3 Matagami, Lac l. Que. Can.
237 D6 Matagorda TX U.S.A.
254 F4 Mata Grande Brazil
80 F3 Matahiwi North I. N.Z.
Mataigou Ningxia China see Taole
80 F2 Matakana Island North I. N.Z.
80 F2 Matakana Island North I. N.Z.
79 □7 Matakitaki South I. N.Z.
209 B8 Matala Angola
184 D3 Matalascañas Spain
114 C5 Matale Sri Lanka
183 H4 Matalebreras Spain
214 D3 Mataleng S. Africa
124 C2 Maţāli', Jabal hill Saudi Arabia
183 E2 Matallana de Valmadrigal Spain
206 B3 Matam Senegal
183 H3 Matamala de Almazán Spain
80 F2 Matamata North I. N.Z.
214 C1 Mata-Mata S. Africa
80 F4 Matamau North I. N.Z.
207 H3 Matamey Niger
234 D1 Matamoras PA U.S.A.
242 E3 Matamoros Coahuila Mex.
243 F3 Matamoros Tamaulipas Mex.
232 E3 Matamoros Spain
255 B5 Matan Mourisca Port.
211 C7 Matandu r. Tanz.
225 H3 Matane Que. Can.
213 □J4 Matanga North I. N.Z.
191 J3 Matangi Italy
209 C8 Matongo Angola
122 C4 Matun Afgh. see Khowst
192 A5 Maxia, Punta mt. Sardegna Italy
253 G4 Maturín Venez.
183 H3 Matute mt. Spain
213 □J3 Matuu Brazil
120 C1 Matveyevka Rus. Fed.
137 J4 Matveyev Kurgan Rus. Fed.
137 H4 Matviyivka Mykolayivs'ka Oblast' Ukr.
137 H4 Matviyivka Zaporiz'ka Oblast' Ukr.
215 F3 Matwabeng S. Africa
86 D3 Matyra r. Rus. Fed.
139 L5 Matyrskiy Rus. Fed.
139 L5 Matyrskoye Vodokhranilishche resr Rus. Fed.
186 B1 Maya Spain
116 D4 Mau Madh. Prad. India
116 D4 Mau Uttar Prad. India
117 E4 Mau Uttar Prad. India
186 B2 Maúa Moz.
116 E4 Mau Aimma Uttar Prad. India
186 D2 Maubermé, Pic de mt. France/Spain
156 E2 Maubert-Fontaine France
163 C5 Maubourguet France
96 A3 Maubin Myanmar
146 D5 Mauchline East Ayrshire, Scotland U.K.
146 F4 Maud Aberdeenshire, Scotland U.K.
87 B4 Maud, Point W.A. Austr.
116 E4 Maudaha Uttar Prad. India
80 E4 Maude N.S.W. Austr.
264 J10 Maud Seamount sea feature S. Atlantic Ocean
179 H2 Mauerbach Austria
178 E2 Mauerkirchen Austria
173 H4 Mauern Ger.
173 H4 Mauerstetten Ger.
251 G5 Maués r. Brazil
91 K2 Maugani Madh. Prad. India
91 I5 Maug Islands N. Mariana Is
172 C3 Maujenitz Ger.
81 □ Mauke i. Cook Is
172 D3 Maulbronn Ger.
154 D3 Maulburg Ger.
169 C5 Mauley Ger.
159 F3 Maulévrier France

Column 4

149 H4 Matlock Derbyshire, England U.K.
149 H4 Matlock Bath Derbyshire, England U.K.
215 F2 Matlwangthwang S. Africa
251 E3 Mato r. Venez.
251 E3 Mato, Cerro mt. Venez.
232 C6 Matoaka WV U.S.A.
213 F4 Matobo Hills Zimbabwe
256 A2 Mato Grosso state Brazil
254 B5 Mato Grosso, Planalto do plat. Brazil
256 A4 Mato Grosso do Sul state Brazil
Matopo Hills Zimbabwe see Matobo Hills
252 D3 Matos r. Bol.
182 B3 Matosinhos Port.
160 C2 Matour France
257 E3 Matozinhos Brazil
177 I4 Mátra mts Hungary
176 D2 Matrabalka Hungary
125 G3 Matrah Oman
177 I3 Mátraverenye Hungary
177 I4 Mátraverebély Hungary
178 D3 Matrei am Brenner Austria
178 D3 Matrei in Osttirol Austria
143 N1 Matrosovo Rus. Fed.
179 I3 Matrosberg mt. S. Africa
215 F1 Matrooster S. Africa
126 B5 Matrūh governorate Egypt
147 E3 Matry Rep. of Ireland
214 D3 Matsap S. Africa
213 □J4 Matsesta Rus. Fed.
104 B4 Matsubara Japan
105 F3 Matsuda Japan
105 F3 Matsudo Japan
104 C4 Matsue Japan
105 D2 Matsumae Japan
104 C4 Matsusaka Japan
109 G3 Matsu Tao i. Taiwan
103 D7 Matsuura Japan
103 F7 Matsuyama Japan
224 E3 Mattagami r. Que. Can.
157 G2 Mattaincourt France
261 E4 Mattaldi Arg.
224 E4 Mattawa Ont. Can.
233 □I2 Mattawamkeag ME U.S.A.
95 F2 Mawa, Bukit mt. Indon.
124 D3 Māwān, Khashm hill Saudi Arabia
179 H3 Mattersburg Austria
178 D3 Matterhorn mt. Italy/Switz.
179 F3 Mattersburg Austria
179 H3 Matterhorn mt. Italy/Switz.
143 N4 Mattmar Sweden
104 C2 Mattō Japan
226 C4 Mattoon IL U.S.A.
178 E1 Mattsee Austria
178 E1 Mattsee l. Austria
143 N4 Mattmar Sweden
140 M2 Mattsund Sweden
Matturai Sri Lanka see Matara
252 A2 Matucana Peru
114 C5 Matugama Sri Lanka
192 C8 Matxitxako, Cabo c. Spain
192 A5 Matzaccara Sardegna Italy
178 E2 Matzen Austria
178 E2 Matzersdorf Austria
263 E2 Mawson research stn Antarctica
263 E2 Mawson Coast Antarctica
97 B5 Maw Taung mt. Myanmar
124 C5 Mawza Yemen
236 C2 Max ND U.S.A.
236 C4 Maxaranny PA U.S.A.
158 D4 Maxent France
173 G2 Maxhütte-Haidhof Ger.
192 A5 Maxia, Punta mt. Sardegna Italy
261 G3 Máximo Paz Arg.
197 H3 Maxineni Romania
213 G4 Maxixe Moz.
140 M3 Maxmo Fin.
169 C5 Maxsain Ger.
224 D4 Maxville Ont. Can.
237 □I2 Maxwell N.T. Can.
88 E4 Maxwelton Qld Austr.
86 D3 May r. W.A. Austr.
146 F5 May, Isle of i. Scotland U.K.
131 Q3 Maya r. Rus. Fed.
186 B1 Maya Spain
135 H5 Maya Rus. Fed.

Column 5

237 F6 Maurepas, Lake LA U.S.A.
161 C5 Maures, Massif des hills France
252 C4 Mauri r. Bol.
163 B4 Mauriac Aquitaine France
162 E3 Mauriac Auvergne France
Maurice country Indian Ocean see Mauritius
234 C3 Maurice r. NJ U.S.A.
82 B2 Maurice, Lake salt flat S.A. Austr.
234 D3 Mauricetown NJ U.S.A.
217 □ Mauritania country Africa
204 C6 Mauritanie country Africa see Mauritania
217 □1b Mauritius country Indian Ocean
193 G3 Mauro, Monte mt. Italy
158 D3 Mauron France
182 C3 Mauros mt. Spain
163 B4 Maurs France
234 B2 Maury r. France
161 C5 Maussane-les-Alpilles France
226 B4 Mauston WI U.S.A.
179 G2 Mautern an der Donau Austria
179 G2 Mauterndorf Austria
179 F3 Mautern in Steiermark Austria
173 H3 Mauth Ger.
179 F2 Mauthausen Austria
178 E4 Mauthen Austria
157 F4 Mauti i. Cook Is see Mauke
161 C4 Mauves France
163 C5 Mauvezin France
162 B2 Mauzé-sur-le-Mignon France
251 E4 Mavaca r. Venez.
211 C8 Mavago Moz.
213 G4 Mavengue Angola
199 G3 Mavikent Turkey
209 D8 Mavinga Angola
232 B6 Mavisdale VA U.S.A.
213 G3 Mavita Moz.
193 F2 Mavone r. Italy
198 B1 Mavrodendri Dytiki Makedonia Greece
198 C1 Mavrothalassa Greece
215 F4 Mavuya S. Africa
95 F2 Mawa, Bukit mt. Indon.
124 D3 Māwān, Khashm hill Saudi Arabia
226 B4 Mauston WI U.S.A.
179 G2 Mautern an der Donau Austria
179 G2 Mauterndorf Austria
179 F3 Mautern in Steiermark Austria
150 B4 Mawnan Cornwall, England U.K.
117 G4 Mawphlang Meghalaya India
124 C3 Mawqaq Saudi Arabia
203 I6 Mawshij Yemen
263 E2 Mawson research stn Antarctica
263 E2 Mawson Coast Antarctica
263 K2 Mawson Escarpment Antarctica
263 K2 Mawson Peninsula Antarctica
97 B5 Maw Taung mt. Myanmar
124 C5 Mawza Yemen
124 D5 Māwiyah Yemen
128 B4 Mawjib, Wādī al r. Jordan
96 A2 Mawlaik Myanmar
Mawlamyaing Myanmar see Moulmein
Mawlamyine Myanmar see Moulmein
150 B4 Mawnan Cornwall, England U.K.
179 F3 Mazamet France
163 C5 Mazan France
121 I2 Mays Landing NJ U.S.A.
234 D3 Maysville KY U.S.A.
232 B5 Maysville KY U.S.A.
236 E4 Maysville MO U.S.A.
96 A2 Mayu r. Myanmar
209 A5 Mayumba Gabon
114 C4 Mayuram Tamil Nadu India
227 F4 Mayville MI U.S.A.
236 D2 Mayville ND U.S.A.
232 D3 Mayville NY U.S.A.
226 C4 Mayville WI U.S.A.
131 Q3 Mayya Rus. Fed.
261 F5 Maza Arg.
139 V2 Maza Rus. Fed.
209 D8 Mazabuka Zambia
198 C1 Mazaki Turkey see Kayseri
205 G3 Mazagan Morocco
251 H4 Mazagão Brazil
184 D3 Mazagón Spain
156 B3 Mazagran France
138 E3 Maza Jugla r. Latvia
182 B2 Mazaleón Spain
163 B5 Mazamet France
161 B3 Mazan France
192 B6 Mazara del Vallo Sicilia Italy
183 H2 Mazarambroz Spain
123 F2 Mazār-e Sharīf Afgh.
194 B4 Mazara r. Sicilia Italy
187 B7 Mazarete Spain
187 B7 Mazarete Spain
185 C5 Mazarrón, Golfo de b. Spain
185 C5 Mazarrón, Golfo de b. Spain
251 F3 Mazaruni r. Guyana
242 A6 Mazatán Mex.
242 D3 Mazatán Mex.
245 I4 Mazatenango Guat.
244 B2 Mazatlán Mex.
241 L4 Mazatzal Peak AZ U.S.A.
159 F4 Mazé France
138 G5 Mazyr Belarus

Column 6

208 B2 Mayo-Kébbi pref. Chad
208 B5 Mayoko Congo
Mayo Landing Y.T. Can. see Mayo
92 B3 Mayon vol. Luzon Phil.
183 H2 Mayor r. Spain
183 I2 Mayor r. Spain
Mayor, Puig mt. Spain see Puig Major
261 F6 Mayor Buratovich Arg.
183 E2 Mayorga Spain
253 E4 Mayor Pablo Lagerenza Para.
217 □ Mayotte terr. Africa
246 □ Pay Pen Jamaica
Mayqayyng Kazakh. see Maykayin
247 □ Mayreau i. St Vincent
161 C4 Mayres France
161 C3 Mayreville France
178 D3 Mayrhofen Austria
128 B4 Maysalūn Syria
127 G5 Maysān governorate Iraq
169 C5 Mayschoß Ger.
175 I1 Mayskiy Rus. Fed.
137 I2 Mayskiy Belgorodskaya Oblast' Rus. Fed.
129 D2 Mayskiy Kabardino-Balkarskaya Respublika Rus. Fed.
134 K4 Mayskiy Permskaya Oblast' Rus. Fed.
137 K4 Mayskiy Rostovskaya Oblast' Rus. Fed.
121 I2 Mayskoye Kazakh.
234 D3 Mays Landing NJ U.S.A.
232 B5 Maysville KY U.S.A.
236 E4 Maysville MO U.S.A.
96 A2 Mayu r. Myanmar
209 A5 Mayumba Gabon
114 C4 Mayuram Tamil Nadu India
227 F4 Mayville MI U.S.A.
236 D2 Mayville ND U.S.A.
232 D3 Mayville NY U.S.A.
226 C4 Mayville WI U.S.A.
131 Q3 Mayya Rus. Fed.
139 V2 Maza Rus. Fed.
96 B2 Mazup OR U.S.A.
238 F2 Mazama WA U.S.A.
135 H5 Mayachnyy Rus. Fed.
246 D2 Mayaguana i. Bahamas
247 □ Mayagüez Puerto Rico
207 G3 Mayahi Niger
120 C2 Mayak Tajik.
126 D5 Mayāhī Niger
247 □ Mayagüez Puerto Rico
207 G3 Mayahi Niger
121 G4 Mayak Kazakh.
137 I3 Mayaky Ukr.
209 B5 Mayama Congo
122 C2 Mayamey Iran
243 H5 Mayan Mountains Belize/Guat.
108 D3 Mayang Hunan China
121 H2 Mayaqum Kazakh.
Mayar hill Scotland U.K.
246 D2 Mayarí Cuba
104 J4 Maya-san hill Japan
247 □ Maya-san hill Japan
238 E3 Maybell CO U.S.A.
232 B5 Maybeury WV U.S.A.
146 D5 Mayboie South Ayrshire, Scotland U.K.
235 D1 Maybrook NY U.S.A.
210 C1 Maych'ew Eth.
123 G3 Maydā Shahr Afgh.
83 F5 Maydena Tas. Austr.
210 E2 Maydh Somalia
115 Maulburg Ger.
169 F3 Mayen Ger.
159 F3 Mayenne France
159 F3 Mayenne dept Pays de la Loire France
159 F3 Mayenne r. France
241 L4 Mayer AZ U.S.A.
111 H3 Mayêr Kangri mt. Xizang China
211 C7 Mayerswille MS U.S.A.
222 H4 Mayerthorpe Alta Can.
159 G4 Mayet France
124 D5 Mayfa'ah Yemen
81 N7 Mayfield N.I. N.Z.
234 C1 Mayfield PA U.S.A.
230 B5 Mayfield KY U.S.A.
231 E4 Mayfield NC U.S.A.
239 H2 Mayhill NM U.S.A.
137 I4 Mayi Mongolia
108 A2 Mayi r. Myanmar
213 J3 Mayili Zimbabwe
211 A5 Mayili Tanz.
108 D3 Mayili Zimbabwe
108 B2 Mazūp r. Myanmar

Column 7

215 I2 Mbuluzi r. Swaziland
225 H3 McAdam N.B. Can.
234 C2 McAdoo PA U.S.A.
234 D1 McAfee NJ U.S.A.
237 E5 McAlester OK U.S.A.
234 A2 McAlisterville PA U.S.A.
237 D7 McAllen TX U.S.A.
226 D3 McAllister WI U.S.A.
84 D2 McArthur r. N.T. Austr.
232 B5 McArthur OH U.S.A.
227 I3 McArthur Mills Ont. Can.
226 E3 McBain MI U.S.A.
222 F4 McBride B.C. Can.
238 D2 McCall ID U.S.A.
237 C6 McCamey TX U.S.A.
238 D3 McCammon ID U.S.A.
226 C3 McCaslin Mountain hill WI U.S.A.
263 K1 McClintock, Mount Antarctica
221 H2 McClintock Channel Nunavut Can.
86 C3 McClintock Range hills W.A. Austr.
84 C1 McCluer Island N.T. Austr.
232 B5 McClure PA U.S.A.
220 G2 McClure Strait N.W.T. Can.
236 C2 McClusky ND U.S.A.
237 F6 McComb MS U.S.A.
232 B5 McComb OH U.S.A.
234 C1 McConnellsburg PA U.S.A.
232 C5 McConnelsville OH U.S.A.
236 C4 McCook NE U.S.A.
231 D5 McCormick SC U.S.A.
226 C4 McCoy VA U.S.A.
232 C6 McCoy VA U.S.A.
224 C1 McCrea r. N.W.T. Can.
223 L5 McCreary Man. Can.
241 J4 McCullough Range mts NV U.S.A.
232 B4 McCutchenville OH U.S.A.
227 F4 McDame B.C. Can.
238 C3 McDermitt OR U.S.A.
232 B5 McDermott OH U.S.A.
265 I8 McDonald Islands Indian Ocean
238 D2 McDonald Peak MT U.S.A.
231 C5 McDonough GA U.S.A.
241 L5 McDowell Peak AZ U.S.A.
231 E4 McEwensville PA U.S.A.
240 H4 McFarland CA U.S.A.
226 C4 McFarland WI U.S.A.
223 J3 McFarlane, r. Sask. Can.
81 B5 McFarlane, Mount South I. N.Z.
241 J2 McGill NV U.S.A.
225 H4 McGivney N.B. Can.
220 C3 McGrath AK U.S.A.
222 F4 McGrath r. B.C. Can.
214 H6 McGregor r. B.C. Can.
226 B3 McGregor S. Africa
226 A2 McGregor IA U.S.A.
227 G2 McGregor Bay Ont. Can.
85 F5 McGregor Range mts Qld Austr.
236 C4 McGuire, Mount ID U.S.A.
129 D2 Mchadijvari Georgia
204 D4 Mcherrah reg. Alg.
211 C7 Mchinga Tanz.
211 B8 Mchinji Malawi
85 E2 McIlwraith Range hills Qld Austr.
236 C2 McIntosh SD U.S.A.
86 A4 McKay Range hills W.A. Austr.
77 I2 McKean i. Phoenix Is Kiribati
232 A6 McKee KY U.S.A.
234 D3 McKee NJ U.S.A.
234 C2 McKeesport PA U.S.A.
232 C4 McKees Rocks PA U.S.A.
232 C6 McKenney VA U.S.A.
231 I5 McKenzie TN U.S.A.
226 C3 McKenzie r. OR U.S.A.
214 G5 McKerrow S. Africa
236 E2 McKinley, Mount AK U.S.A.
237 D5 McKinney TX U.S.A.
240 H4 McKittrick CA U.S.A.
232 D6 McLaughlin SD U.S.A.
226 C5 McLean IL U.S.A.
234 A4 McLean VA U.S.A.
236 F4 McLeansboro IL U.S.A.
222 F4 McLennan Alta Can.
234 C4 McLeod r. B.C. Can.
222 H4 McLeod Lake B.C. Can.
238 B1 McMinnville OR U.S.A.
231 C5 McMinnville TN U.S.A.
263 L1 McMurdo research stn Antarctica
241 K2 McNary AZ U.S.A.
231 D5 McNaughton WI U.S.A.
226 C3 McNaughton Lake B.C. Can. see Kinbasket Lake
241 M6 McNeal AZ U.S.A.
234 C1 McPhadyen r. Nfld. Can.
236 D4 McPherson KS U.S.A.
83 H2 McPherson Range mts N.S.W. Austr.
222 B2 McQuesten r. Y.T. Can.
231 D5 McRae GA U.S.A.
223 A3 McRoberts KY U.S.A.
224 A3 McSherrystown PA U.S.A.
220 G3 McTavish Arm b. N.W.T. Can.
232 E4 McVeytown PA U.S.A.
222 F1 McVicar Arm b. N.W.T. Can.
214 C6 McWhorter WV U.S.A.
139 U2 Mda r. Rus. Fed.
215 F5 Mdantsane S. Africa
205 G1 M'Daourouch Alg.
217 □3 Mde Njaidja Comoros
180 D5 Mdiq Morocco
213 H3 Mead, Lake resr NV U.S.A.
212 C3 Meade r. AK U.S.A.
220 C2 Meade r. AK U.S.A.
87 B5 Meadow W.A. Austr.
236 C2 Meadow SD U.S.A.
241 K2 Meadow AZ U.S.A.
222 H4 Meadow Bridge WV U.S.A.
232 D4 Meadow Lake Sask. Can.
241 J3 Meadow Valley Wash r. NV U.S.A.
232 C6 Meadowview VA U.S.A.
232 D5 Meadville MS U.S.A.
227 F4 Meadville PA U.S.A.
102 L2 Meaken vol. Japan
146 D4 Mealasta Island Scotland U.K.
182 A4 Mealhada Port.
146 A3 Mealisval hill Scotland U.K.
146 D5 Meall Chuaich hill Scotland U.K.
146 E4 Meall Dubh hill Scotland U.K.
146 C3 Meall Fuar-mhonaidh hill Scotland U.K.
225 J3 Mealy Mountains Nfld. Can.
192 B5 Meana Sardo Sardegna Italy
85 G5 Meandarra Qld Austr.
222 F3 Meander River Alta Can.
150 F4 Meare Somerset, England U.K.
151 L2 Meare r. England U.K.
151 J2 Measham Leicestershire, England U.K.
147 E3 Meath county Rep. of Ireland
160 A2 Meaulne France
156 C3 Méaulte France
156 C3 Meaux France
205 H6 Meberia Alg.
217 □3 Mbabane Swaziland
213 H3 Mebu Arun. Prad. India

Column 8

209 B6 Mbakaou Cameroon
208 C3 Mbala Zambia
211 A7 Mbala Zambia
210 A4 Mbale Uganda
207 I6 Mbalmayo Cameroon
209 B6 Mbam r. Cameroon
209 D6 Mbandaka Dem. Rep. Congo
209 B6 Mbandjok Cameroon
209 B6 Mbang Cameroon
209 B6 Mbanga Cameroon
207 H6 Mbanga Cameroon
209 B6 M'banza Congo Angola
209 B6 Mbanza-Ngungu Dem. Rep. Congo
206 B3 Mbar Senegal
211 A6 Mbarara Uganda
207 I4 Mbari r. C.A.R.
211 A7 Mbati Zambia
211 A7 Mbati C.A.R.
78 □5 Mbava i. New Georgia Is Solomon Is
207 I6 Mbé Cameroon
211 C7 Mbemkuru r. Tanz.
149 C7 Mbengga i. Fiji see Beqa
232 C1 Mbengwi Cameroon
209 D5 Mbenji i. Equat. Guinea
100 D3 Mbéni Comoros
217 □3 Mbéni Comoros
213 F4 Mberengwa Zimbabwe
211 A7 Mbereshi Zambia
211 B7 Mbeya Tanz.
211 B7 Mbeya admin. reg. Tanz.
207 I5 Mbi r. C.A.R.
211 B5 Mbigou Gabon
207 I5 Mbinga Tanz.
211 C7 Mbini Equat. Guinea
209 D5 Mbini r. Equat. Guinea
211 A7 Mbizi Mountains Tanz.
211 A7 Mboki C.A.R.
207 I5 Mbomo Congo
209 B5 Mbomou pref. Congo
C.A.R./Dem. Rep. Congo
208 B2 Mbomou r. C.A.R./Dem. Rep. Congo
207 I6 Mborokua i. Solomon Is
206 A3 Mbouda Senegal
207 A3 Mbour Senegal
206 B3 Mbout Maur.
208 C4 Mbrès C.A.R.
196 C3 Mbrostar Albania
209 D6 Mbuji-Mayi Dem. Rep. Congo
169 A5 Mbulu Tanz.
102 B3 Mbulu Tanz.
232 C3 Mchère Fr.
209 B6 Mchedi Belgium
165 D4 Mchelen Neth.
78 □6 Mecherchar i. Palau see
Eil Malk
196 C3 Mecheria Albania
169 A5 Mechernich Ger.
135 I5 Mechetinskaya Rus. Fed.
202 B6 Mechiméré Chad
185 □ Mechta r. Bulg.
168 F2 Mechtersen Ger.

226 D4 Michigan, Lake MI/WI U.S.A.
230 C3 Michigan City IN U.S.A.
208 B2 Michika Nigeria
224 C4 Michipicoten Bay Ont. Can.
224 C4 Michipicoten River Ont. Can.
244 C4 Michoacán state Mex.
175 K4 Michów Pol.
135 H5 Michurinsk Rus. Fed.
149 I3 Mickleton Durham, England U.K.
151 F2 Mickleton Gloucestershire, England U.K.
242 □I6 Micoud r. Nic.
247 □³ Micoud St Lucia
266 E5 Micronesia is Pacific Ocean
91 L6 Micronesia, Federated States of country N. Pacific Ocean
197 F2 Micula Romania
223 K5 Midale Sask. Can.
264 F4 Mid-Atlantic Ridge sea feature Atlantic Ocean
264 H8 Mid-Atlantic Ridge sea feature S. Atlantic Ocean
146 F2 Midbea Orkney, Scotland U.K.
165 E3 Middelbeers Neth.
164 C3 Middelbeers Neth.
215 E4 Middelburg E. Cape S. Africa
215 G1 Middelburg Mpumalanga S. Africa
142 C4 Middelfart Denmark
164 D3 Middelharnis Neth.
165 B3 Middelkerke Belgium
214 C4 Middelpos S. Africa
164 C3 Middelstum Neth.
215 E5 Middelwit S. Africa
164 E2 Middenmeer Neth.
267 M5 Middle America Trench sea feature N. Pacific Ocean
115 G3 Middle Andaman i. Andaman & Nicobar Is India
Middle Atlas mts Morocco see Moyen Atlas
151 F3 Middle Barton Oxfordshire, England U.K.
225 J3 Middle Bay Que. Can.
234 C1 Middleboro MA U.S.A.
230 D4 Middlebourne WV U.S.A.
227 I5 Middleburg PA U.S.A.
232 E5 Middleburg VA U.S.A.
233 F3 Middleburgh NY U.S.A.
235 E1 Middlebury CT U.S.A.
226 E5 Middlebury IN U.S.A.
237 G2 Middlebury VT U.S.A.
237 C6 Middle Concho r. TX U.S.A.
85 G4 Middle Creek r. Qld Austr.
234 C1 Middle Creek r. PA U.S.A.
235 F1 Middlefield CT U.S.A.
235 F1 Middle Haddam CT U.S.A.
149 H3 Middleham North Yorkshire, England U.K.
235 D1 Middle Hope NY U.S.A.
235 F2 Middle Island NY U.S.A.
236 D3 Middle Loup r. NE U.S.A.
150 E4 Middlemarsh Dorset, England U.K.
85 G4 Middlemount Qld Austr.
232 B4 Middleport OH U.S.A.
232 B4 Middleport PA U.S.A.
236 E3 Middle Raccoon r. IA U.S.A.
149 I4 Middle Rasen Lincolnshire, England U.K.
234 B3 Middle River MD U.S.A.
232 B6 Middlesboro KY U.S.A.
149 H3 Middlesbrough Middlesbrough, England U.K.
149 H3 Middlesbrough admin. div. England U.K.
232 E3 Middlesex NY U.S.A.
234 A2 Middlesex PA U.S.A.
235 F1 Middlesex County county CT U.S.A.
235 D2 Middlesex County county NJ U.S.A.
149 H3 Middlesmoor North Yorkshire, England U.K.
85 E4 Middleton Qld Austr.
225 H4 Middleton N.S. Can.
215 E5 Middleton S. Africa
149 G4 Middleton Greater Manchester, England U.K.
151 H2 Middleton Norfolk, England U.K.
232 A3 Middleton WI U.S.A.
226 C4 Middleton WI U.S.A.
151 F2 Middleton Cheney Northamptonshire, England U.K.
149 G3 Middleton in Teesdale Durham, England U.K.
151 G4 Middleton-on-Sea West Sussex, England U.K.
149 I4 Middleton-on-the-Wolds East Riding of Yorkshire, England U.K.
77 F4 Middleton Reef Austr.
151 F3 Middleton Stoney Oxfordshire, England U.K.
147 E2 Middletown Northern Ireland U.K.
240 F2 Middletown CA U.S.A.
235 F1 Middletown CT U.S.A.
234 C3 Middletown DE U.S.A.
232 E5 Middletown MD U.S.A.
235 D2 Middletown NJ U.S.A.
232 A5 Middletown NY U.S.A.
227 I5 Middletown PA U.S.A.
232 D5 Middletown VA U.S.A.
226 E4 Middleville MI U.S.A.
233 F3 Middleville NY U.S.A.
149 G4 Middlewich Cheshire, England U.K.
81 B6 Mid Dome mt. South I. N.Z.
204 D2 Midelt Morocco
80 E3 Midhirst North I. N.Z.
151 G4 Midhurst West Sussex, England U.K.
124 C4 Midi Yemen
163 E5 Midi, Canal du France
163 C6 Midi de Bigorre, Pic du mt. France
163 B6 Midi d'Ossau, Pic du mt. France
265 J5 Mid-Indian Basin sea feature Indian Ocean
265 I6 Mid-Indian Ridge sea feature Indian Ocean
161 A4 Midi-Pyrénées admin. reg. France
224 E4 Midland Ont. Can.
241 J5 Midland MD U.S.A.
227 E4 Midland MI U.S.A.
236 C2 Midland SD U.S.A.
238 A3 Midland TX U.S.A.
215 H3 Midlands prov. Zimbabwe
147 C5 Midleton Rep. of Ireland
146 E6 Midlothian admin. div. Scotland U.K.
237 D5 Midlothian TX U.S.A.
232 E6 Midlothian VA U.S.A.
168 D2 Midlum Ger.
227 G3 Midmay Ont. Can.
213 □3 Midongy Atsimo Madag.
103 E7 Midori r. Japan
163 B5 Midouze r. France
266 F4 Mid-Pacific Mountains sea feature N. Pacific Ocean
215 G1 Midrand S. Africa
92 C5 Midsayap Phil.
150 E3 Midsomer Norton Bath and North East Somerset, England U.K.
140 I3 Midt Norway
145 Midu r. Nic.
113 □⁷ Midu i. Addu Atoll Maldives
238 C2 Midvale ID U.S.A.
241 L1 Midway UT U.S.A.
75 H2 Midway Islands N. Pacific Ocean
238 C3 Midway Well W.A. Austr.
238 F3 Midwest WY U.S.A.
239 D4 Midwest City OK U.S.A.
164 G1 Midwolda Neth.
127 F3 Midyat Turkey
127 F3 Midye Turkey see Kıyıköy

146 □G1 Mid Yell Shetland, Scotland U.K.
197 F4 Midzhur mt. Bulg./Yugo.
104 C4 Mie pref. Japan
175 I5 Miechów Pol.
171 L1 Miecza r. Pol.
178 C3 Mieders Austria
183 I3 Miedes Spain
175 I5 Miedziana Góra Pol.
174 D3 Miedzichowo Pol.
175 K3 Miedzna Mazowieckie Pol.
175 H6 Miedzna Pol.
174 G5 Miedzno Pol.
174 F4 Miedzyborz Pol.
174 D3 Miedzychód Pol.
174 D3 Miedzylesie Pol.
175 K4 Miedzyrzec Podlaski Pol.
174 C2 Miedzyrzecz Pol.
174 C2 Miedzyzdroje Pol.
141 N3 Miehikkälä Fin.
174 E4 Miejska-Górka Pol.
175 J4 Miejsce Piastowe Pol.
174 F4 Miejska-Górka Pol.
65 C5 Miélan France
161 D4 Miélandre, Montagne de mt. France
171 K5 Mielec Pol.
174 F3 Mieleszyn Pol.
168 F1 Miekendorf Ger.
175 L3 Mielnik Pol.
174 L1 Mielno Pol.
211 C7 Miemembe Tanz.
178 C3 Mieming Austria
175 I5 Mierzawa r. Pol.
143 H4 Mierzeja Helska pen. Pol.
143 H3 Mierzeja Wiślana spit Pol.
172 B2 Miesau Ger.
171 C4 Miesbach Ger.
174 F3 Mieścisko Pol.
172 B2 Miesenbach Ger.
210 D2 Mi'ēso Eth.
171 C3 Mieste Ger.
171 C3 Miesterhorst Ger.
174 C3 Mieszkowice Pol.
172 D3 Mietingen Ger.
141 M3 Mietoinen Fin.
160 E2 Mieussy France
182 D3 Mieza Spain
232 B4 Mifflin OH U.S.A.
227 I5 Mifflinburg PA U.S.A.
232 E4 Mifflintown PA U.S.A.
234 B1 Mifflinville PA U.S.A.
106 E5 Migang Shan mt. Gansu China
215 I2 Migdol S. Africa
166 E5 Migennes France
194 G4 Migliarino Italy
191 G5 Migliaro Italy
195 F2 Miglionico Italy
162 C2 Mignaloux-Beauvoir France
159 K4 Mignères France
192 D2 Mignone r. Italy
160 E2 Migovillard France
225 H3 Miguasha Park tourist site N.B. Can.
183 G5 Miguel Alemán Mex.
245 F4 Miguel Alemán, Presa resr Mex.
254 E3 Miguel Alves Brazil
244 C1 Miguel Auza Mex.
254 E4 Miguel Calmon Brazil
245 F5 Miguel de la Madrid, Presa resr Mex.
183 G5 Miguel Esteban Spain
257 F5 Miguel Pereira Brazil
261 F5 Miguel Riglos Arg.
185 G2 Miguelturra Spain
197 G3 Mihăieşti Romania
139 G1 Mihail Hungary
126 C3 Mihaliccik Turkey
126 G4 Mihály Hungary
103 F6 Mihara Japan
105 F4 Mihara-yama vol. Japan
117 F5 Mihijam Bihar India
169 K4 Mihla Ger.
183 H4 Mijares r. Spain
184 F3 Mijas Spain
185 H5 Mijas mt. Spain
164 D2 Mijdrecht Neth.
105 L1 Mijoux-take mt. Japan
160 E2 Mijoux France
102 J2 Mikasa Japan
136 D1 Mikashevichy Belarus
177 K4 Mikepércs Hungary
138 G4 Mikhanovichy Belarus
138 C2 Mikha Tskhakaia Georgia see Senaki
135 I1 Mikhaylov Rus. Fed. see Prozorovo
121 I1 Mikhaylovka Pavlodarskaya Oblast' Kazakh.
121 I2 Mikhaylovka Zhambylskaya Oblast' Kazakh. see Sarykemer
121 H1 Mikhaylovka Kurskaya Oblast' Rus. Fed.
100 E4 Mikhaylovka Primorskiy Kray Rus. Fed.
135 H6 Mikhaylovka Volgogradskaya Oblast' Rus. Fed.
197 F4 Mikhaylovo Bulg.
137 K3 Mikhaylovo-Aleksandrovsky Rus. Fed.
121 I2 Mikhaylovskiy Altayskiy Kray Rus. Fed.
121 I2 Mikhaylovskiy Altayskiy Kray Rus. Fed.
Mikhaylovskoye Rus. Fed. see Shpakovskoye
Malinovoye Ozero
117 H4 Miki Hills India
141 N3 Mikkeli Fin.
141 N3 Mikkelin mlk Fin.
222 H3 Mikkwa r. Alta Can.
159 G4 Mikkwa r.
175 J2 Mikolajki Pol.
175 H3 Mikolajki Pomorskie Pol.
175 G1 Mikolów Pol.
Mikonos i. Greece see Mykonos
137 G1 Mikoyan Armenia see Yeghegnadzor
147 G4 Mikre Bulg.
128 B2 Mikri Prespa, Limni l. Greece
138 G2 Mikropoli Greece
198 F4 Mikst r. Japan
176 F3 Mikulášovice Czech Rep.
176 D3 Mikulov Czech Rep.
176 D3 Mikulovice Czech Rep.
179 L4 Mikulstätten See l. Austria
226 B3 Mikulov WI U.S.A.
226 A1 Mikumi Tanz.
211 C6 Mikumi National Park Tanz.
134 J3 Mikun' Rus. Fed.
105 H3 Mikuni Japan
105 G3 Mikuni-sanmyaku mts Japan
105 H3 Mikuni-yama mt. Japan
194 B3 Milá Alg.
236 E2 Mikuni WI U.S.A.
114 B5 Miladhunmadulu Atoll Maldives
254 F3 Milagres Brazil

250 B5 Milagro Ecuador
183 I2 Milagro Spain
183 G3 Milagros Spain
175 I1 Milakowo Pol.
227 F4 Milan Italy see Milano
236 E3 Milan MN U.S.A.
232 B4 Milan OH U.S.A.
209 C7 Milando Angola
82 D3 Milang S.A. Austr.
213 G3 Milange Moz.
190 E3 Milano Italy
190 D3 Milano prov. Lombardia Italy
190 D3 Milano (Malpensa) airport Italy
191 H4 Milano Marittima Italy
Milanovce Slovakia see Velký Kýr
175 K4 Milanów Pol.
175 I3 Milanówek Pol.
234 C1 Milanville PA U.S.A.
197 G2 Milas Romania
199 E3 Milas Turkey
195 K4 Milazzo Sicilia Italy
236 D2 Milbank SD U.S.A.
150 E4 Milborne Port Somerset, England U.K.
150 E4 Milborne St Andrew Dorset, England U.K.
233 □J2 Milbridge ME U.S.A.
170 C3 Milde r. Ger.
151 H2 Mildenhall Suffolk, England U.K.
146 D6 Mildenhall Greater Manchester, England U.K.
82 D3 Mildura Vic. Austr.
111 D1 Mile Düzü lowland Azer.
100 B3 Mile r. China
210 D2 Milē Eth.
148 D3 Milebush Northern Ireland U.K.
151 H3 Mile End Essex, England U.K.
246 □ Mile Gully Jamaica
175 I1 Milejewo Pol.
175 K4 Milejów Pol.
194 C5 Milena Sicilia Italy
85 G5 Miles Qld Austr.
174 F3 Milesław Pol.
137 K5 Milevo Ukr.
238 F2 Miles City MT U.S.A.
176 C1 Milešovka mt Czech Rep.
147 C4 Milestone Rep. of Ireland
197 H2 Miletin r. Romania
195 F4 Mileto Italy
193 G3 Miletto, Monte mt. Italy
174 F4 Mileura W.A. Austr.
176 D3 Milevsko Czech Rep.
149 G2 Milfield Northumberland, England U.K.
184 B3 Milfontes Port.
83 B3 Milford Rep. of Ireland
147 D1 Milford Donegal Rep. of Ireland
151 G3 Milford Surrey, England U.K.
235 E1 Milford DE U.S.A.
226 D5 Milford IL U.S.A.
233 H3 Milford MA U.S.A.
234 B3 Milford MD U.S.A.
232 B4 Milford MI U.S.A.
233 □I2 Milford ME U.S.A.
236 D3 Milford NE U.S.A.
233 H3 Milford NH U.S.A.
235 D1 Milford NY U.S.A.
234 B1 Milford PA U.S.A.
233 G3 Milford VT U.S.A.
241 K2 Milford UT U.S.A.
232 E4 Milford VA U.S.A.
150 B4 Milford Haven Pembrokeshire, Wales U.K.
151 F4 Milford on Sea Hampshire, England U.K.
81 A6 Milford Sound South I. N.Z.
81 A6 Milford Sound inlet South I. N.Z.
234 C2 Milford Square PA U.S.A.
85 E3 Milgarra Qld Austr.
226 C5 Milgun W.A. Austr.
226 D4 Milh, Bahr al l. Iraq see Razazah, Buhayrat ar
182 D3 Milhão Port.
161 C5 Milhaud France
174 F4 Milicz Pol.
84 B1 Milikapiti N.T. Austr.
87 C6 Miling W.A. Austr.
84 C2 Milingimbi N.T. Austr.
192 A4 Milis Sardegna Italy
194 D6 Militello in Val di Catania Sicilia Italy
158 B3 Milizac France
238 F1 Milk r. MT U.S.A.
203 F5 Milk, Wadi el watercourse Sudan/Egypt
171 H4 Milkel Ger.
175 J2 Mitki Pol.
131 Q4 Mil'kovo Rus. Fed.
151 I4 Milkwood Pk River Alta Can.
164 E3 Mill Neth.
85 B7 Millaa Millaa Qld Austr.
226 A5 Millard MO U.S.A.
185 I4 Millares Spain
185 I4 Millau France
246 □ Millbank Cornwall, England U.K.
231 C5 Millbrook Ont. Can.
103 E7 Millbrook AL U.S.A.
84 C2 Millbrook NY U.S.A.
150 C4 Millbrook Cornwall, England U.K.
148 A6 Mill Buie hill Scotland U.K.
238 D2 Mill City OR U.S.A.
232 D1 Mill Creek r. CA U.S.A.
233 F1 Mill Creek r. PA U.S.A.
234 B3 Milldale CT U.S.A.
231 D5 Milledgeville GA U.S.A.
226 C5 Milledgeville IL U.S.A.
236 E2 Mille Lacs lakes MN U.S.A.
159 H4 Mille Lacs, Lac des l. Ont. Can.
231 D5 Millen GA U.S.A.
214 C5 Miller S. Africa
236 D2 Miller SD U.S.A.
223 M4 Miller Lake Ont. Can.
135 H6 Miller Peak AZ U.S.A.
232 E5 Millersburg OH U.S.A.
232 E4 Millersburg PA U.S.A.
227 J5 Millersburg PA U.S.A.
82 D1 Millers Creek S.A. Austr.
233 G3 Millers Creek KY U.S.A.
233 G3 Millers Falls MA U.S.A.
81 B6 Millers Flat South I. N.Z.
232 E4 Millerstown PA U.S.A.
234 A3 Millersville MD U.S.A.
234 B3 Millersville PA U.S.A.
232 A5 Millerton OH U.S.A.
183 D2 Millevaches, Plateau de France
147 E2 Millford Northern Ireland U.K.
182 F1 Mill Hall PA U.S.A.
141 N3 Millhill Fin.
141 N3 Millikin mlk Fin.
82 E4 Millicent S.A. Austr.
234 A1 Mill Island Antarctica
154 F4 Millington MD U.S.A.
234 A3 Millington TN U.S.A.
223 F5 Millinocket ME U.S.A.
232 D4 Millmerran Qld Austr.

147 B4 Milltown Kerry Rep. of Ireland
148 C4 Milltown Kildare Rep. of Ireland
146 F4 Milltown Aberdeenshire, Scotland U.K.
148 C3 Milltown Northern Ireland U.K.
238 D2 Milltown MT U.S.A.
226 A3 Milltown WI U.S.A.
147 B4 Milltown Malbay Rep. of Ireland
146 F4 Milltown of Rothiemay Moray, Scotland U.K.
85 E3 Milltown Qld Austr.
215 F1 Milvale S. Africa
240 F3 Mill Valley CA U.S.A.
233 □J1 Millville N.B. Can.
234 C3 Millville NJ U.S.A.
227 G5 Millville PA U.S.A.
234 B1 Millwood WV U.S.A.
237 E5 Millwood Lake AR U.S.A.
156 C4 Milly-la-Forêt France
160 C2 Milly-Lamartine France
151 F4 Milly W.A. Austr.
183 I3 Milmarcos Spain
170 E2 Milmersdorf Ger.
165 E4 Milmort Belgium
146 E5 Milnathort Perth and Kinross, Scotland U.K.
Milne Land i. Greenland see Ilimananngip Nunaa
146 D6 Milngavie East Dunbartonshire, Scotland U.K.
149 G4 Milnrow Greater Manchester, England U.K.
149 G4 Milnthorpe Cumbria, England U.K.
87 B6 Milo r. Guinea
206 C4 Milo Sicilia Italy
195 E5 Milo Sicilia Italy
233 □I2 Milo ME U.S.A.
100 E4 Milogradovo Rus. Fed.
240 □2 Miloli'i HI U.S.A.
175 □3 Miłomłyn Pol.
174 G1 Miłoradz Pol.
198 D3 Milos i. Greece
139 L5 Miloslavskoye Rus. Fed.
174 F5 Miłosław Pol.
137 F5 Milove Ukr.
171 F5 Milovice Czech Rep.
147 C4 Milestone Rep. of Ireland
197 H2 Milovw r. Romania
170 D2 Milow Mecklenburg-Vorpommern Ger.
170 E3 Milow Brandenburg Ger.
175 H6 Miłówka Pol.
83 E2 Milparinka N.S.W. Austr.
240 G3 Milpitas CA U.S.A.
232 E4 Milroy PA U.S.A.
173 G2 Miltach Ger.
172 D2 Miltenberg Ger.
83 □3 Milton N.S.W. Austr.
227 H4 Milton Ont. Can.
81 B7 Milton South I. N.Z.
146 D4 Milton Highland, Scotland U.K.
146 E5 Milton Perth and Kinross, Scotland U.K.
235 E1 Milton DE U.S.A.
231 C6 Milton FL U.S.A.
233 □H3 Milton NH U.S.A.
235 I1 Milton NY U.S.A.
234 B1 Milton PA U.S.A.
232 C3 Milton VT U.S.A.
235 C4 Milton VA U.S.A.
150 D4 Milton Abbot Devon, England U.K.
238 D2 Milton-Freewater OR U.S.A.
151 G2 Milton Keynes Milton Keynes, England U.K.
151 G2 Milton Keynes admin. div. England U.K.
170 F1 Miltzow Ger.
109 F3 Miluo Hunan China
227 G4 Milverton Ont. Can.
150 D3 Milverton Somerset, England U.K.
226 D4 Milwaukee WI U.S.A.
264 E4 Milwaukee Deep sea feature Caribbean Sea
120 E2 Mily Kazakh.
135 H6 Milyutinskaya Rus. Fed.
169 F5 Milz Ger.
163 B5 Mimbaste France
82 C1 Mimili S.A. Austr.
114 C4 Mimisal Tamil Nadu India
163 A4 Mimizan France
192 A4 Mimizan-Plage France
176 D1 Mimoň Czech Rep.
208 A5 Mimongo Gabon
257 G4 Mimoso do Sul Brazil
103 G6 Mimuro-yama mt. Japan
244 H2 Mina Mex.
252 C5 Mina, Nevado de mt. Peru
122 D5 Minab Iran
122 D5 Minab r. Iran
260 B2 Mina Clavero Arg.
104 C3 Minaker B.C. Can.
223 L4 Minago r. Man. Can.
103 D4 Mino-Mikawa-kōgen reg. Japan
Minahassa Peninsula Indon. see Minahasa, Semenanjung
125 F2 Mina Jebel Ali U.A.E.
Prophet River
223 M5 Minaki Ont. Can.
103 F7 Minamata Japan
84 C2 Minami Japan
104 D4 Minamiashigara Japan
103 E4 Minamiaki-gawa r. Japan
176 D1 Minamiata Japan
105 □3 Minami-Iō-jima vol. Kazan-rettō Japan

237 E5 Mineola TX U.S.A.
150 D1 Minera Wrexham, Wales U.K.
232 E5 Mineral VA U.S.A.
129 C1 Mineral'nyye Vody Rus. Fed.
226 B4 Mineral Point WI U.S.A.
237 D5 Mineral Wells TX U.S.A.
241 H2 Mineral Wells WV U.S.A.
191 G4 Minerbio Italy
234 B2 Minersville PA U.S.A.
241 K2 Minersville UT U.S.A.
Minerva atoll Arch. des Tuamotu Fr. Polynesia see Reao
232 C4 Minerva OH U.S.A.
215 F1 Minerva S. Africa
240 F1 Mill Valley CA U.S.A.
233 □J1 Millville N.B. Can.
161 A5 Minervois, Monts du hills France
172 C2 Minfeld Ger.
111 C4 Minfeng Xinjiang China
209 E7 Minga Dem. Rep. Congo
129 E3 Mingäçevir Azer.
129 E3 Mingäçevir Su Anbarı resr Azer.
208 D3 Mingala C.A.R.
225 H4 Mingan Que. Can.
225 H4 Mingan, Îles de la Que. Can.
82 E3 Mingary S.A. Austr.
Mingechaur Azer. see Mingäçevir
Mingechaurskoye Vodokhranilishche resr Azer. see Mingäçevir Su Anbarı
85 F3 Mingela Qld Austr.
87 B6 Mingenew W.A. Austr.
109 F3 Mingfeng Hubei China see Yuan'an
109 I1 Mingguang Henan China
109 F1 Mingguang Anhui China
96 A2 Mingin Myanmar
96 A2 Mingin Range mts Myanmar
121 H4 Ming-Kush Kyrg.
183 I5 Minglanilla Spain
232 C4 Mingo Junction OH U.S.A.
183 F4 Mingorria Spain
211 C7 Mingoyo Tanz.
Mingshan Chongqing China see Fengdu
108 B2 Mingshan Sichuan China
100 C3 Mingshui Heilong. China
146 A5 Mingulay i. Scotland U.K.
213 □2 Minguri Moz.
109 F3 Mingxi Fujian China
Mingxing Hebei China see Weixian
Mingzhou Shaanxi China see Suide
Minhe r. China see Jinxian
127 J3 Minhe Qinghai China
84 C1 Minhla Magwe Myanmar
96 A3 Minhla Pegu Myanmar
109 F3 Minhou Fujian China
158 B3 Miniac-Morvan France
114 B4 Minicoy i. India
87 C6 Minigwal, Lake salt flat W.A. Austr.
179 H4 Minihof-Liebau Austria
138 C4 Minija r. Lith.
87 B4 Minilya W.A. Austr.
87 B4 Minilya r. W.A. Austr.
233 G2 Minister OH U.S.A.
235 C4 Minister NY U.S.A.
232 C4 Minister VT U.S.A.
238 C4 Minister UT U.S.A.
232 A4 Minister VA U.S.A.
206 B2 Minier Mali
183 H3 Ministra mt. Spain
183 H3 Ministra, Sierra mts Spain
223 K4 Minitonas Man. Can.
82 C3 Minlaton S.A. Austr.
208 D4 Minna Bluff pt Antarctica
261 C3 Minna Nigeria
108 D2 Min Jiang r. Sichuan China
109 F3 Min Jiang r. Fujian China
84 C1 Minjilang N.T. Austr.
129 E4 Minkänd Azer.
Min-Kush Kyrg. see Ming-Kush
82 D3 Minlaton S.A. Austr.
104 D6 Minmi N.S.W. Austr.
207 I5 Minna Nigeria
235 I2 Minna-shima i. Japan
106 A4 Minneapolis KS U.S.A.
223 L5 Minnedosa Man. Can.
232 D5 Minnehaha Springs WV U.S.A.
237 D6 Minneola KS U.S.A.
236 E2 Minnesota r. MN U.S.A.
226 A2 Minnesota state U.S.A.
226 B1 Minnesota City MN U.S.A.
87 B4 Minnie Creek W.A. Austr.
146 D7 Minnigaff Dumfries and Galloway, Scotland U.K.
82 C2 Minnipa S.A. Austr.
104 C3 Mino Japan
182 B2 Miño r. Port./Spain
105 L2 Minobu-yama mt. Japan
103 D4 Minobu-sanchi mts Japan
104 D4 Minokamo Japan
103 D3 Mino-Mikawa-kōgen reg. Japan
226 D3 Minong WI U.S.A.
226 C5 Minonk IL U.S.A.
104 B4 Minoo Japan
Minorca i. Spain see Menorca
236 C1 Minot ND U.S.A.
106 D6 Minqin Gansu China
109 F3 Minqing Fujian China
234 C2 Minquadale DE U.S.A.
109 H1 Minquan Henan China
168 F2 Minsen Ger.
138 F5 Min Shan mts Sichuan China
138 F5 Minsk Belarus
138 F5 Minskaya Oblast' admin. div. Belarus see Minskaya Voblasts'
138 F5 Minskaya Voblasts' admin. div. Belarus
175 J3 Mińsk Mazowiecki Pol.

257 E2 Mirabela Brazil
161 D4 Mirabel-aux-Baronnies France
194 D5 Mirabella Imbaccari Sicilia Italy
257 F4 Miracema Brazil
254 C2 Miracema do Tocantins
254 C2 Miracema do Tocantins Brazil
Mirada Hills CA U.S.A. see La Mirada
182 B5 Mira de Aire Port.
257 F4 Miradouro Brazil
163 C5 Miradoux France
250 D3 Miraflores Col.
183 G4 Miraflores de la Sierra Spain
257 Mirai Brazil
114 B2 Miraj Mahar. India
261 I6 Miramar Buenos Aires Arg.
261 E4 Miramar Córdoba Arg.
191 H4 Miramare Italy
161 D5 Miramas France
162 B3 Mirambeau France
186 A2 Mirambel Spain
163 C4 Miramont-de-Guyenne France
163 B5 Miramont-Sensacq France
110 C4 Miran Xinjiang China
253 F5 Miranda Brazil
253 F5 Miranda r. Brazil
250 E2 Miranda Venez.
87 D5 Miranda, Lake salt flat W.A. Austr.
183 I2 Miranda de Arga Spain
182 E4 Miranda del Castañar Spain
182 D3 Miranda del Corvo Port.
182 C3 Miranda do Douro Port.
162 C4 Mirande France
182 D3 Mirandela Port.
182 E5 Mirandilla Spain
163 E4 Mirandol-Bourgnounac France
256 B4 Mirandópolis Brazil
191 H3 Mirano Italy
256 B5 Mirante, Serra do hills Brazil
256 B3 Mirante do Paranapanema Brazil
198 B3 Miras Albania
256 C4 Mirassol Brazil
182 D2 Miravalles mt. Spain
182 E5 Miravete mt. Spain
Mir-Bashir Azer. see Tärtär
125 F4 Mirbāt Oman
129 F4 Mircäl Azer.
175 L5 Mircze Pol.
161 I5 Mirebeau Bourgogne France
162 C2 Mirebeau Poitou-Charentes France
157 G4 Mirecourt France
163 D5 Miremont France
161 D5 Mirepoix France
161 B5 Mireval France
117 F4 Mirganj Bihar India
95 F1 Mirgorod Ukr. see Myrhorod
175 F3 Miri Sarawak Malaysia
207 H3 Miria Niger
114 C2 Miriälguda Andhra Prad. India
85 G5 Miriam Vale Qld Austr.
117 H4 Miri Hills India
258 G4 Mirim, Lago l. Brazil/Uru.
Mirim, Voreio Aigaio Greece see Myrina
179 H2 Mirna r. Croatia
179 G5 Mirna r. Slovenia
179 J5 Mirna Slovenia
263 D2 Mirny research stn Antarctica
131 M3 Mirnyy Arkhangel'skaya Oblast' Rus. Fed.
139 V6 Mirnyy Bryanskaya Oblast' Rus. Fed.
131 M3 Mirnyy Respublika Sakha (Yakutiya) Rus. Fed.
129 D1 Mirnyy Stavropol'skiy Kray Rus. Fed.
174 D4 Mirocin Górny Pol.
81 D5 Miromiro mt. South I. N.Z.
Mironovka Kharkivs'ka Oblast' Ukr. see Myronivka
Mironovka Kyivs'ka Oblast' Ukr.
179 H2 Miroslav Czech Rep.
176 C2 Mirošov Czech Rep.
174 D5 Mirostowice Dolne Pol.
174 D4 Mirow Brandenburg Ger.
170 D2 Mirow Ger.
123 F5 Mirpur Pak.
123 G5 Mirpur Batoro Pak.
123 G5 Mirpur Khas Pak.
123 F5 Mirpur Sakro Pak.
111 D3 Mirsali Xinjiang China
174 D5 Mirsk Pol.
85 E4 Mirtna Qld Austr.
198 D3 Mirtoan Sea Greece
198 D3 Mirtöö Pelagos sea Greece
183 F4 Mirueña de los Infanzones Spain
213 □2 Miryang S. Korea
Mirzachirik Uzbek. see Gulistan
117 E4 Mirzapur Uttar Prad. India
175 J4 Mirzec Pol.
195 □3 Misa r. Latvia
104 B4 Misaki Japan
191 H1 Misano Adriatico Italy
245 F4 Misantla Mex.
105 F4 Misato Japan
104 D3 Misawa Japan
122 Mizafe Nigeria
102 J3 Misawa Japan
177 K5 Mişca Romania
193 L3 Miscano r. Italy
224 E4 Mischenkov Ont. Can.
222 B3 Mishek-Sarines France
115 G5 Misha Andaman & Nicobar Is India
116 C3 Misgar Jammu and Kashmir
214 D5 Misgund S. Africa
115 F4 Mish, Kūh-e hill Iran
100 D3 Mishan Heilong. China
228 C2 Mishawaka IN U.S.A.
103 D5 Mishima Japan
105 F4 Mishima Japan
105 I2 Mishkino Rus. Fed.
117 H4 Mishmi Hills India
117 D4 Mishraq hill Jordan
235 H2 Mishicot WI U.S.A.
194 C4 Misilmeri Sicilia Italy
242 □ Miskito, Costa de coastal area Nic.
242 □ Miskitos, Cayos is Nic.
177 J3 Miskolc Hungary
179 □ Mismā, 'Irq al des. Saudi Arabia
124 C2 Mismā, Tall al hill Jordan
Mismiyah Syria see Musmiyeh
93 C6 Misool i. Indon.
128 A3 Misqah Saudi Arabia
195 I2 Missanello Italy
163 G3 Missillac France
235 J2 Missinaibi r. Ont. Can.
224 D3 Missinaibi Lake Ont. Can.
85 E3 Mission r. Qld Austr.

236 C3 Mission SD U.S.A.
237 D7 Mission TX U.S.A.
85 F3 Mission Beach Qld Austr.
240 I5 Mission Viejo CA U.S.A.
206 B3 Missira Senegal
224 C2 Missisa r. Ont. Can.
224 D4 Missisicabi r. Que. Can.
224 E5 Missisicabi Ont. Can.
224 E4 Mississauga Ont. Can.
237 F6 Mississippi r. U.S.A.
237 F6 Mississippi state U.S.A.
237 F6 Mississippi Delta LA U.S.A.
237 F6 Mississippi Sound sea chan. U.S.A.
Missolonghi Greece see Mesolongi
238 D2 Missoula MT U.S.A.
204 C2 Missour Morocco
236 F4 Missouri r. U.S.A.
236 E4 Missouri state U.S.A.
236 F4 Missouri Valley IA U.S.A.
84 B3 Mistake Creek N.T. Austr.
225 H3 Mistake Creek r. Qld Austr.
225 I3 Mistassibi r. Que. Can.
225 I3 Mistassini r. Que. Can.
225 I3 Mistassini Que. Can.
224 F3 Mistassini, Lac l. Que. Can.
179 H2 Mistelbach Austria
170 E5 Mistelgau Ger.
195 E5 Misterbianco Sicilia Italy
149 I4 Misterton Nottinghamshire, England U.K.
224 F3 Mistissini Que. Can.
137 G5 Mistky Ukr.
261 F2 Mistolar, Lago l. Arg.
179 H4 Mistras tourist site Greece
194 D5 Mistretta Sicilia Italy
191 H2 Misurata Libya see Mişrātah
102 J3 Misawa Japan
105 F3 Mitaka Japan
213 G2 Mitande Moz.
251 H4 Mitaraca hill Suriname
150 E3 Mitcheldean Gloucestershire, England U.K.
85 F3 Mitchell r. N.S.W. Austr.
85 E2 Mitchell r. N.W. Austr.
85 F2 Mitchell r. Qld Austr.
83 A7 Mitchell r. Vic. Austr.
227 G4 Mitchell Ont. Can.
238 C2 Mitchell OR U.S.A.
236 D3 Mitchell SD U.S.A.
231 D5 Mitchell, Mount NC U.S.A.
Mitchell Island Cook Is see Nassau
Mitchell Island Tuvalu see Nukulaelae
84 B1 Mitchell Point N.T. Austr.
232 C5 Mitchelltown PA U.S.A.
147 C4 Mitchelstown Rep. of Ireland
203 F2 Mît Ghamr Egypt
116 D5 Mithapur Gujarat India
123 H5 Mithi Tiwano Pak.
123 G5 Mithi Pak.
Mithimna Greece see Mithymna
199 G2 Mithymna Greece
81 □² Mitiaro i. Cook Is
80 D2 Mitito i. Cook Is see Mitiaro
Mitilini Voreio Aigaio Greece see Mytilini
80 D2 Mititai N.T. N.Z.
104 D4 Mito Aichi Japan
105 G2 Mito Ibaraki Japan
80 E4 Mitre mt. North I. N.Z.
77 H3 Mitre Island Solomon Is
81 A6 Mitre Peak South I. N.Z.
135 G6 Mitrofanovka Rus. Fed.
Mitrovica Kosovo, Srbija Yugo. see Kosovska Mitrovica
156 C4 Mitry-Mory France
217 □3a Mitsamiouli Njazidja Comoros
213 □3 Mitsinjo Madag.
217 □3a Mits'iwa Eritrea see Massawa
217 □3a Mitsoudjé Njazidja Comoros
103 I5 Mitsuke Japan
104 D2 Mitsumatarenge-dake mt. Japan
105 E3 Mitsutōge-yama mt. Japan
105 G3 Mittagong N.S.W. Austr.
83 I3 Mitta Mitta Vic. Austr.
178 D3 Mittelberg Austria
172 D3 Mittelbiberach Ger.
173 I3 Mittelfranken admin. reg. Bayern Ger.
171 C4 Mittelhausen Ger.
169 I5 Mittelkalbach Ger.
172 D3 Mittelsinn Ger.
173 F4 Mittelspitze mt. Ger.
169 F4 Mittenaar Ger.
171 E6 Mittenwalde Brandenburg Ger.
170 E4 Mittenwalde Brandenburg Ger.
173 I5 Mitterfels Ger.
157 G4 Mittersheim France
173 J3 Mitterskirchen Ger.
173 I5 Mitterteich Ger.
Mittimatalik Nunavut Can. see Pond Inlet
171 D5 Mittweida Ger.
250 D4 Mitú Col.
250 D4 Mitsuas Col.
209 C7 Mitumba, Chaîne des mts Dem. Rep. Congo
209 C6 Mitumba, Monts mts Dem. Rep. Congo
208 B4 Mitzic Gabon

105 F3 Miyake Japan
105 F3 Miyake-jima i. Japan
102 D4 Miyako Japan
103 D8 Miyakonojō Japan
100 B5 Miyaluo Sichuan China
Miyang Yunnan China see Mile
116 D5 Miyani Gujarat India
103 □3 Miyanoura-dake mt. Japan
104 D4 Miyazaki Japan
103 D8 Miyazaki pref. Japan
104 D4 Miyazu Japan
103 G6 Miyoshi Japan
210 B3 Mizan Teferi Eth.
Mizda Libya see Mizdah
205 H2 Mizdah Libya
147 B5 Mizen Head hd Cork Rep. of Ireland
147 F5 Mizen Head hd Wicklow Rep. of Ireland
136 B5 Mizhhir"ya Ukr.
107 H4 Mizhi Shaanxi China
197 M2 Mizil Romania
Mizo Hills state India see Mizoram
117 H5 Mizoram state India
Mizpe Ramon Israel
252 D4 Mizque Bol.
252 D4 Mizque r. Bol.
105 F2 Mizuho Japan
104 D3 Mizunami Japan
102 Mizusawa Japan
143 L2 Mjölby Sweden
142 Mjøndalen Norway
213 G3 Mjoia
215 I6 Mkambati S. Africa
211 C6 Mkata Tanz.
211 C6 Mkata Plain Tanz.

215 H2 Mkhondvo r. Swaziland
211 K2 Mkoani Tanz.
211 C6 Mkokotoni Tanz.
211 C6 Mkomazi Tanz.
209 F8 Mkushi Zambia
215 I2 Mkuze S. Africa
215 I2 Mkuze r. S. Africa
176 D1 Mladá Boleslav Czech Rep.
176 D2 Mladá Vožice Czech Rep.
176 E1 Mladé Buky Czech Rep.
196 E3 Mladenovac Srbija Yugo.
197 E4 Mlado Nagoričane Macedonia
211 A6 Mlala Hills Tanz.
215 I2 Mlawa r. Swaziland
196 E3 Mlava r. Yugo.
175 I2 Mława r. Pol.
175 I3 Mławka r. Pol.
217 □3b Mlima Bénara mt. Mayotte
217 □3b Mlima Choungui mt. Mayotte
188 F4 Mljet i. Croatia
188 F4 Mljetski Kanal sea chan. Croatia
137 I2 Mlodat' r. Rus. Fed.
175 I3 Mlodzieszyn Pol.
215 F4 Mlumati S. Africa
215 F4 Mlungisi S. Africa
175 H1 Mlynary Pol.
175 J3 Mlyniv Ukr.
175 I4 Mlyniv Ukr.
175 M6 Mlynys'ka Ukr.
215 E1 Mmabatho S. Africa
213 E4 Mmadinare Botswana
176 D2 Mnichovice Czech Rep.
176 D1 Mnichovo Hradiště Czech Rep.
175 I5 Mnichów Pol.
175 I4 Mniów Pol.
177 J3 Mníšek nad Hnilcom Slovakia
175 J4 Mniszew Pol.
175 I3 Mniszków Pol.
215 H2 Mnjoli Dam Swaziland
100 F1 Mnogovershinnyy Rus. Fed.
141 I3 Mo Norway
252 B1 Moa r. Brazil
246 D2 Moa Cuba
93 D5 Moa i. Maluku Indon.
241 M2 Moab UT U.S.A.
208 A5 Moabi Gabon
252 C1 Moaco r. Brazil
91 J9 Moa Island Qld Austr.
79 □1 Moala i. Fiji
213 G5 Moamba Moz.
81 C5 Moana South I. N.Z.
182 B2 Moaña Spain
208 B5 Moanda Gabon
241 J3 Moapa NV U.S.A.
147 D3 Moate Rep. of Ireland
213 G3 Moatize Moz.
209 F6 Moba Dem. Rep. Congo
105 G3 Mobara Japan
208 D3 Mobaye C.A.R.
Mobayembongo
Dem. Rep. Congo see
Mobayi-Mbongo
208 D3 Mobayi-Mbongo
Dem. Rep. Congo
149 G4 Mobberley Cheshire, England U.K.
236 E4 Moberly MO U.S.A.
222 F4 Moberly Lake B.C. Can.
226 E1 Mobert Ont. Can.
231 B6 Mobile AL U.S.A.
241 K5 Mobile AZ U.S.A.
237 F6 Mobile Bay AL U.S.A.
93 B3 Mobo Phil.
236 C2 Mobridge SD U.S.A.
Mobutu, Lake
Dem. Rep. Congo/Uganda see
Albert, Lake
Mobutu Sese Seko, Lake
Dem. Rep. Congo/Uganda see
Albert, Lake
246 E3 Moca Dom. Rep.
254 C2 Mocajuba Brazil
Moçambique country Africa see
Mozambique
213 I2 Moçambique Moz.
Moçâmedes Angola see
Namibe
234 B1 Mocanaqua PA U.S.A.
184 B1 Moçarria Port.
240 C3 Moccasin CA U.S.A.
232 B6 Moccasin Gap VA U.S.A.
183 G5 Mocejón Spain
177 G3 Močenok Slovakia
139 K4 Mocha r. Rep. of Ireland
Mocha Yemen see
Al Mukha
258 B5 Mocha, Isla i. Chile
183 I3 Mochales Spain
175 H3 Mochowo Pol.
213 E4 Mochudi Botswana
174 E3 Mochy Pol.
211 C7 Mocímboa da Praia Moz.
211 C7 Mocímboa do Rovuma Moz.
197 G2 Mociu Romania
171 C3 Möckern Ger.
172 D2 Möckmühl Ger.
177 H4 Mockrehna Ger.
231 D5 Mocksville NC U.S.A.
185 G3 Moclín Spain
185 F4 Moclinejo Spain
250 E5 Mocoa r. Brazil
250 B4 Mocoa Col.
256 D4 Mococa Brazil
261 I2 Mocoretá r. Arg.
242 D3 Mocorito Mex.
242 D2 Mocorito r. Mex.
244 D2 Moctezuma
San Luis Potosí Mex.
242 C2 Moctezuma Chihuahua Mex.
245 E3 Moctezuma r. Mex.
239 E6 Moctezuma Sonora Mex.
213 H3 Mocuba Moz.
214 D2 Mocuba S. Africa
109 L4 Mocun Guangdong China
161 D2 Modane France
116 C5 Modasa Gujarat India
165 E4 Modave Belgium
150 D4 Modbury Devon, England U.K.
205 E3 Modder r. S. Africa
215 E3 Modderr S. Africa
191 F4 Modena Italy
191 F4 Modena prov.
Emilia-Romagna Italy
235 D1 Modena NY U.S.A.
235 I3 Modena PA U.S.A.
241 K3 Modena UT U.S.A.
157 H4 Moder r. France
240 G3 Modesto CA U.S.A.
194 D6 Modica Sicilia Italy
175 K5 Modliborzyce Pol.
179 H2 Mödling Austria
175 I4 Modliszewice Pol.
192 A4 Modolo Sardegna Italy
107 F2 Modot Mongolia
176 G3 Modra Slovakia
188 G3 Modrič Bos.-Herz.
176 F2 Modřice Czech Rep.
179 F4 Mödringberg mt. Austria
177 J2 Modrý Kameň Slovakia
195 F1 Modugno Italy
83 F4 Moe Vic. Austr.
213 H3 Moebase Moz.
80 E1 Moehau hill North I. N.Z.
174 D2 Moehnau-sur-Mer France
150 D1 Moel Famau hill
Wales U.K.
150 C1 Moelfre Isle of Anglesey,
Wales U.K.
150 D2 Moel Sych hill Wales U.K.
141 J3 Moelv Norway
215 F3 Moeng S. Africa
Moen i. Chuuk Micronesia see
Weno
140 L1 Moen Norway
191 G2 Moena Italy
251 H3 Moengo Suriname
241 I3 Moenkopi AZ U.S.A.
241 L4 Moenkopi Wash r. AZ U.S.A.
165 C3 Moerbeke Belgium
80 E1 Moerewa North I. N.Z.
164 E3 Moergestel Neth.
165 C3 Moerkerke Belgium
Moero, Lake
Dem. Rep. Congo/Zambia see
Mweru, Lake
169 B4 Moers Ger.
190 E2 Moesa r. Switz.
214 D2 Moeswal S. Africa

78 □6 Moetambe, Mount Choiseul
Solomon Is
146 E6 Moffat Dumfries and Galloway,
Scotland U.K.
182 D3 Mofreita Port.
177 L4 Moftin Romania
116 C3 Moga Punjab India
Mogadiscio Somalia see
Muqdisho
Mogador Morocco see
Essaouira
182 D3 Mogadouro Port.
182 D3 Mogadouro, Serra de
mts Port.
213 F4 Mogalakwena r. S. Africa
114 D2 Mogalturru Andhra Prad. India
102 I4 Mogami-gawa r. Japan
216 □3a Mogán Gran Canaria
Canary Is
213 F5 Moganyaka S. Africa
96 B1 Mogaung Myanmar
147 C5 Mogeely Rep. of Ireland
170 D3 Mögeldin Denmark
168 D1 Mögeltønder Denmark
179 H4 Mogersdorf Austria
191 I2 Moggio Udinese Italy
172 D3 Mögglingen Ger.
175 I4 Mogielnica Pol.
175 I6 Mogielnica r. Pol.
256 D5 Mogi-Guaçu Brazil
196 E5 Mogila Macedonia
175 H6 Mogilany Pol.
Mogilev Belarus see Mahilyow
Mogilev Oblast admin. div.
Belarus see
Mahilyowskaya Voblasts'
Mogilev Podol'skiy Ukr. see
Mohyliv-Podil's'kyy
Mogilevskaya Oblast'
admin. div. Belarus see
Mahilyowskaya Voblasts'
174 E3 Mogilmica r. Pol.
175 H2 Mogilno Pol.
256 D5 Mogi-Mirim Brazil
213 I2 Mogincual Moz.
191 F4 Moglia Italy
191 I5 Mogliano Italy
191 H3 Mogliano Veneto Italy
172 D3 Möglingen Ger.
100 A1 Mogocha Rus. Fed.
139 K3 Mogocha r. Rus. Fed.
205 H1 Mogod mts Tunisia
212 E5 Mogoditshane Botswana
182 B4 Mogofores Port.
96 B2 Mogok Myanmar
241 L4 Mogollon Plateau AZ U.S.A.
185 G2 Mogón Spain
Mogontiacum Ger. see Mainz
192 A5 Mogorella Sardegna Italy
192 A5 Mogoro Sardegna Italy
192 A5 Mogoro r. Sardegna Italy
197 H2 Mogoşeşti Romania
175 I3 Mogowo Pol.
107 G1 Mogoytuy Rus. Fed.
208 B2 Mogroum Chad
184 D3 Moguer Spain
107 I2 Moguqi Nei Mongol China
215 F1 Mogwase S. Africa
107 G2 Mogyod Hungary
177 H6 Mogyoród Hungary
80 F3 Mohaka r. North I. N.Z.
116 E5 Mohala Madh. Prad. India
215 F4 Mohale's Hoek Lesotho
236 C1 Mohall ND U.S.A.
Mohammadabad Iran see
Darreh Gaz
205 F2 Mohammadia Alg.
116 E3 Mohan r. India/Nepal
116 D4 Mohana Madh. Prad. India
117 O4 Mohanganj Bangl.
185 I2 Moharque Spain
241 J4 Mohave r. AZ U.S.A.
226 C2 Mohawk MI U.S.A.
233 G3 Mohawk r. NY U.S.A.
241 K5 Mohawk Mountains AZ U.S.A.
163 A5 Mohéda France
163 A5 Mohèges-et-Haon France
163 A5 Mohières France
260 B4 Molina Chile
193 F2 Molina Aterno Italy
183 I4 Molina de Aragón Spain
187 B6 Molina de Segura Spain
193 F3 Molina di Ledro Italy
193 G3 Molinara Italy
182 D2 Molinaseca Spain
236 F3 Moline IL U.S.A.
237 H4 Moline KS U.S.A.
191 G4 Molinella Italy
160 B2 Molinet France
160 D2 Molinges France
185 H2 Molinicos Spain
191 J4 Molini di Tures Italy
234 B2 Molino FL U.S.A.
186 E3 Molino de Villobas Spain
186 C4 Molinos Spain
182 C3 Molins de Rei Spain
209 F7 Moliro Dem. Rep. Congo
193 G3 Molise admin. reg. Italy
193 H4 Moliterno Italy
171 L5 Moliviş r. Romania
171 D4 Mölkau Ger.
211 C4 Molkom Sweden
178 E1 Möll r. Austria
188 G3 Moll i. Bosanski Brod
122 B3 Molli Bodäjh Iran
129 F3 Mollakänd Azer.
142 C4 Mellebjerg hill Denmark
163 C4 Molledo Spain
117 H4 Moel Len mt. Nagaland India
170 E2 Mölkenbeck Ger.
87 C6 Mollen, Lake salt flat
W.A. Austr.
186 B3 Mollerussa Spain
160 B2 Mollies France
156 C3 Molliens-Dreuil France
185 F3 Mollina Spain
182 C3 Mollerussa Spain [variant]

161 F5 Monaco country Europe
264 H4 Monaco Basin sea feature
N. Atlantic Ocean
226 C3 Monico WI U.S.A.
161 D4 Monieux France
146 F5 Monifieth Angus, Scotland U.K.
148 B4 Monilea Rep. of Ireland
250 C3 Moniquirá Col.
161 B4 Monistrol-d'Allier France
186 E3 Monistrol de Montserrat
Spain
161 C3 Monistrol-sur-Loire France
240 I3 Monitor Mountain NV U.S.A.
240 I2 Monitor Range mts NV U.S.A.
257 E3 Mönkebo Sweden [Monjolos]
169 F1 Mönkeberg Ger.
211 B8 Monkey Bay Malawi
87 B5 Monkey Mia W.A. Austr.
175 K2 Moński r. Pol.
84 E5 Monkira Qld Austr.
150 C4 Monkokehampton Devon,
England U.K.
208 D5 Monkoto Dem. Rep. Congo
151 H2 Monks Eleigh Suffolk,
England U.K.
227 G4 Monkton Ont. Can.
234 D3 Monkton MD U.S.A.
187 C4 Monleón r. Spain
163 C5 Monléon-Magnoac France
150 D3 Monmouth
Wales U.K.
240 H3 Monmouth IL U.S.A.
236 F3 Monmouth IL U.S.A.
235 G2 Monmouth County county
NJ U.S.A.
Monmouthshire U.K. see
Monmouth
234 D2 Monmouth Junction NJ U.S.A.
136 C3 Monmouthshire Rus. Fed.
136 C3 Monmouthshire Ukr.
150 D3 Monmouthshire admin. div.
Wales U.K.

182 D4 Monforte de Lemos Spain
184 B2 Monfortinho Port.
184 B2 Monfurado hill Port.
256 D6 Mongaguá Brazil
191 F2 Monghidoro Italy
208 C4 Mongala r. Dem. Rep. Congo
117 G4 Mongar Bhutan
234 D1 Mongaup r. NY U.S.A.
234 D1 Mongaup Valley NY U.S.A.
208 F4 Mongbwalu Dem. Rep. Congo
96 D2 Mông Cai Vietnam
87 C6 Mongers Lake salt flat
W.A. Austr.
78 □6 Mongga New Georgia Is
Solomon Is
191 G4 Monghidoro Italy
Monghyr Bihar India see
Munger
202 C6 Mongo Chad
212 C6 Mongo hill Spain see Montgó
106 D2 Mongolia country Asia
Mongolküre Xinjiang China see
Zhaosu
Mongol Uls country Asia see
Mongolia
207 H6 Mongomo Equat. Guinea
86 E2 Mongona, Mount hill
W.A. Austr.
208 C3 Mongoumba C.A.R.
146 F5 Mongour hill U.K.
190 D3 Mongrando Italy
209 D8 Mongu Zambia
206 B2 Mönguel Maur.
191 H2 Monguelfo Italy
185 G3 Monachil Spain
185 G3 Monachil r. Spain
244 A6 Monach Islands Scotland U.K.
192 B3 Monacia-d'Aullène Corse
France

160 D3 Montalieu-Verceu France
162 A3 Montalivet-les-Bains France
194 C5 Montallegro Sicilia Italy
195 C4 Montalto mt. Italy
193 F7 Montalto delle Marche Italy
193 D7 Montalto di Castro Italy
192 D2 Montalto Marina Italy
193 I5 Montalto Uffugo Italy
182 C5 Montalvão Port.
240 H4 Montalvo CA U.S.A.
260 A3 Montalvo Chile
193 H3 Montamarta Spain
197 F4 Montana Bulg.
190 C2 Montana Switz.
238 E2 Montana state U.S.A.
Montaña Spain see
Puente de Montañana
242 □16 Montañas de Colón mts Hond.
194 C4 Montañas Spain [Montallegro]
242 D1 Montánchez, Sierra de
mts Spain
234 B2 Montandon PA U.S.A.
187 C4 Montanejos Spain
257 G3 Montanha Brazil
163 H4 Montanha Brazil
193 G3 Montaquila Italy
184 B1 Montargil Port.
156 C5 Montargis France
182 C3 Montastruc-la-Conseillère
France
156 C3 Montataire France
163 D4 Montauban France
158 D3 Montauban-de-Bretagne
France
163 E5 Montaud, Pic de mt. France
159 F3 Montaudin France
233 H4 Montauk NY U.S.A.
233 H4 Montauk Point NY U.S.A.
161 E5 Montauriol France
161 E5 Montauroux France
163 B5 Montaut Aquitaine France
163 B5 Montaut Aquitaine France
163 C6 Montaut Midi-Pyrénées France
163 C5 Montaut-les-Crénaux France
215 G3 Mont-aux-Sources mt.
Lesotho
163 C4 Montayral France
193 G3 Mazzaoli Italy
160 C1 Montbard France
160 D1 Montbarrey France
163 D5 Montbartier France
160 E1 Montbazens France
159 E4 Montbazon France
160 C1 Montbéliard France
160 E1 Montbenoît France
163 C5 Montbernard France
161 B4 Montbeton France
161 B5 Montblanc France
186 E3 Montblanc Spain
186 E3 Mont Blanc mt. France/Italy
161 D1 Montbozon France
163 B5 Montbrió del Camp Spain
160 B2 Montbrison France
162 D3 Montbron France
160 C1 Montbrun France
232 D4 Montcalm WV U.S.A.
156 B2 Montcaret France
160 C2 Montceau-les-Mines France
160 C2 Montcenis France
235 D2 Montclair NJ U.S.A.
156 B5 Montcresson France
163 D4 Montcuq France
156 D3 Montcy-Notre-Dame France
163 B5 Montdardier France
161 A5 Mont-Dauphin France
163 B5 Mont-de-Marsan France
156 C3 Montdidier France
232 A3 Monte Aff. France
261 I5 Monte, Lago del l. Arg.
163 H5 Montea mt. Italy
161 F5 Monteagudo Bol.
183 I5 Monteagudo de las Salinas
Spain
183 H3 Monteagudo de las Vicarías
Spain
260 A5 Monte Aguila Chile
245 F5 Monte Albán tourist site
Oaxaca Mex.
193 F1 Monte Alegre Brazil
256 B2 Monte Alegre Brazil
254 D2 Monte Alegre de Goiás Brazil
187 B6 Monte Alegre del Castillo
Spain
256 C3 Monte Alegre de Minas Brazil
254 C4 Monte Alto Brazil
256 C4 Monte Aprazivel Brazil
255 E5 Monte Azul Brazil
256 C3 Monte Azul Paulista Brazil
224 F4 Montebello Que. Can.
195 E5 Montebello Ionico Italy
88 B4 Montebello Islands W.A. Austr.
191 H3 Montebelluna Italy
158 B2 Montebourg France
190 E4 Montebruno Italy
161 F3 Monte Buey Arg.
191 H5 Monte Carlo Monaco
256 B2 Monte Carmelo Brazil
261 I2 Monte Caseros Arg.
163 D4 Montcassagne France
193 H1 Montecassiano Italy
190 D5 Montecastello di Vibio Italy
193 E7 Montecastrilli Italy
191 H5 Montecatini Terme Italy
191 F5 Montecatini Val di Cecina
Italy
193 E7 Montecchio Italy
190 F4 Montecchio Emilia Italy
193 F6 Montecchio Maggiore Italy
163 D5 Montech France
193 E7 Montechiaro d'Asti Italy
184 B3 Montechoro Port.
213 E4 Monte Christo S. Africa
161 G4 Montdragon Spain
250 C3 Monte Claro Port.
183 G3 Mónsul Spain
172 D3 Mönsheim Ger.
160 C2 Monsols France
163 D4 Monségur France
163 C5 Monségur France
163 D4 Monségur France

254 F3 Monteiro Brazil
185 K4 Montejaque Spain
185 G3 Montéjicar Spain
84 B3 Montejinnie N.T. Austr.
182 D3 Montejo de la Sierra Spain
191 C5 Montejo, Serra de del Port.
191 H5 Montelanico Italy
193 F3 Montelanico Italy
182 C5 Montelavar Port.
184 A2 Montelavar Port.
160 A3 Montel-de-Gelat France
193 H3 Monteleone di Puglia Italy
193 E7 Monteleone di Spoleto Italy
193 E2 Monteleone d'Orvieto Italy
192 A4 Monteleone Rocca Doria
Sardegna Italy
193 E2 Monteleone Sabino Italy
194 C4 Montelepre Sicilia Italy
192 D3 Montelibretti Italy
163 D4 Montélier France
161 C4 Montélimar France
253 F5 Monte Lindo r. Para.
184 A2 Montella Spain
193 H3 Montella Italy
226 C4 Montello WI U.S.A.
190 D5 Montels France
191 G5 Montelupo Fiorentino Italy
191 I5 Montelupone Italy
261 D5 Montemaggiore Belsito
Sicilia Italy
156 C4 Monte Maíz Arg.
193 H4 Montemarano Italy
191 I5 Montemarciano Italy
185 H2 Montemayor r. Spain
185 F3 Montemayor Spain
259 □7 Montemayor, Meseta de
plat. Arg.
183 F3 Montemayor de Pililla Spain
162 C3 Montemboeuf France
195 G2 Montemesola Italy
193 H3 Montemiletto Italy
184 D3 Montemolín Spain
193 F2 Montemonaco Italy
243 F3 Montemorelos Mex.
184 A2 Montemor-o-Novo Port.
184 A2 Montemor-o-Velho Port.
191 G5 Montemurlo Italy
193 I4 Montemurro Italy
159 F3 Montenay France
192 B3 Montende France
183 H2 Montenegro de Cameros
Spain
193 G3 Montenero di Bisaccia Italy
193 G2 Montenerodomo Italy
192 A5 Monteparano Italy
260 B2 Monte Patria Chile
247 E3 Monte Plata Dom. Rep.
191 I5 Monte Porzio Italy
193 F7 Monteprandone Italy
184 B2 Montepuez Moz.
213 I1 Montepuez r. Moz.
192 D1 Montepulciano Italy
258 E2 Monte Quemado Arg.
158 D2 Monterblanc France
191 H5 Monterchi Italy
182 B5 Monte Real Port.
193 F7 Montered Italy
156 C4 Monterenzio Italy
156 C4 Montereau-fault-Yonne France
156 C4 Monte Redondo Port.
182 B5 Monte Redondo Port.
193 G4 Monterenzio Italy
Monterey Nuevo León Mex.
232 C6 Monterey VA U.S.A.
240 B3 Monterey CA U.S.A.
240 B3 Monterey Bay CA U.S.A.
250 C2 Monteria Col.
191 G5 Monteriggioni Italy
252 D3 Monteros Bol.
250 C2 Monteroduni Italy
192 D2 Monte Romano Italy
191 G5 Monteroni d'Arbia Italy
195 H2 Monteroni di Lecce Italy
192 D2 Monterosi Italy
191 E5 Monterosso al Mare Italy
194 D5 Monterosso Almo Sicilia Italy
195 F4 Monterosso Calabro Italy
192 C1 Monterotondo Italy
191 F5 Monterotondo Marittimo Italy
243 E2 Monterrey Baja California Norte Mex.
243 E3 Monterrey Nuevo León Mex.
193 G3 Monterosso Italy
185 G2 Montes Altos Brazil
254 C4 Monte San Biagio Italy
193 F3 Monte San Giovanni
Campano Italy
238 D2 Montesano WA U.S.A.
195 H3 Montesano Salentino Italy
193 H4 Montesano sulla Marcellana
Italy
191 H5 Monte San Savino Italy
191 H5 Monte Santa Maria Tiberina
Italy
193 H4 Monte Sant'Angelo Italy
254 E3 Monte Santo Brazil
256 C2 Monte Santo de Minas Brazil
193 G3 Montesarchio Italy
195 F2 Montescaglioso Italy
257 E5 Montes Claros Brazil
183 F3 Montesclaros Spain
191 H4 Montese Italy
191 H5 Montesilvano Italy
193 G5 Montesquieu-Volvestre
France
163 C5 Montestruc-sur-Gers France
184 B3 Montes Velhos Port.
161 C4 Monteux France
194 A3 Montevago Sicilia Italy
194 A3 Montevecchio Sardegna Italy
261 G4 Monte Vera Arg.
191 H5 Monteverde Italy
261 I4 Montevideo Uru.
256 C3 Montevideo dept Uru.
236 E3 Montevideo MN U.S.A.
237 G4 Monte Vista CO U.S.A.
241 M3 Montezuma IA U.S.A.
237 F4 Montezuma KS U.S.A.
241 M3 Montezuma Creek UT U.S.A.
240 I3 Montezuma Peak NV U.S.A.
241 D4 Montezuma Peak NV U.S.A.
161 D2 Montfaucon Midi-Pyrénées
France
159 E4 Montfaucon Pays de la Loire
France
157 F3 Montfaucon-d'Argonne
France
161 C3 Montfaucon-en-Velay France
163 C5 Montferran-Savès France
163 C5 Montferrat France
161 D5 Montferrier France
164 D2 Montfoort Neth.
163 C5 Montfort Aquitaine France
158 D3 Montfort Bretagne France
163 B5 Montfort-en-Chalosse France
159 E4 Montfort-l'Amaury France
159 E3 Montfort-le-Gesnois France
158 D3 Montfort-sur-Risle France
161 B5 Montgaillard Midi-Pyrénées
France
161 C6 Montgaillard Midi-Pyrénées
France
161 D6 Montgaillard Midi-Pyrénées
France
161 E4 Montgenèvre France
163 C5 Montgesoye France
193 E7 Montgesty France
159 H5 Montgiscard France
159 G5 Montgó hill Spain
150 D2 Montgomery Powys,
Wales U.K.
231 C5 Montgomery AL U.S.A.
235 D1 Montgomery NY U.S.A.
234 B2 Montgomery PA U.S.A.
227 I5 Montgomery PA U.S.A.
232 C5 Montgomery WV U.S.A.

236 F4 Montgomery City MO U.S.A.
234 A3 Montgomery County county MD U.S.A.
234 C2 Montgomery County county PA U.S.A.
86 D2 Montgomery Islands W.A. Austr.
162 B3 Montguyon France
156 E3 Monthermé France
190 B2 Monthey Switz.
156 E3 Monthois France
157 F4 Monthureux-sur-Saône France
192 B4 Monti Sardegna Italy
191 H3 Monticano r. Italy
190 E3 Monticelli d'Ongina Italy
192 A2 Monticello Corse France
237 F5 Monticello AR U.S.A.
231 D6 Monticello FL U.S.A.
231 D5 Monticello GA U.S.A.
236 F3 Monticello IL U.S.A.
230 C3 Monticello IN U.S.A.
230 C4 Monticello KY U.S.A.
233 □J1 Monticello ME U.S.A.
236 E2 Monticello MN U.S.A.
236 F3 Monticello MO U.S.A.
237 F6 Monticello MS U.S.A.
234 D1 Monticello NY U.S.A.
241 M3 Monticello UT U.S.A.
226 C4 Monticello WI U.S.A.
190 F3 Montichiari Italy
192 D1 Monticiano Italy
185 H2 Montiel Spain
261 H2 Montiel, Cuchilla de hills Arg.
159 H5 Montierchaume France
156 E4 Montier-en-Der France
192 D1 Montieri Italy
157 F4 Montiers-sur-Saulx France
162 D3 Montignac France
165 D4 Montignies-le-Tilleul Belgium
190 F4 Montignoso Italy
157 G4 Montigny France
156 D5 Montigny-la-Resle France
157 G3 Montigny-lès-Metz France
160 D1 Montigny-Mornay-Villeneuve-sur-Vingeanne France
157 E5 Montigny-sur-Aube France
184 B2 Montijo Port.
184 D4 Montijo Spain
185 F3 Montilla Spain
185 G3 Montillana Spain
163 E4 Montirat France
256 B2 Montividiu Brazil
159 G2 Montivilliers France
185 G2 Montizón Spain
185 G2 Montizón r. Spain
163 F4 Montjaux France
159 F3 Montjean France
159 F4 Montjean-sur-Loire France
225 G3 Mont-Joli Que. Can.
190 C3 Montjovet Italy
163 E5 Montlaur France
224 F4 Mont-Laurier Que. Can.
156 C4 Montlhéry France
156 B3 Montlieu-la-Garde France
225 H3 Mont Louis Que. Can.
163 E6 Mont-Louis France
160 B3 Montluçon France
160 D3 Montluel France
221 K5 Montmagny Que. Can.
160 A2 Montmarault France
158 E3 Montmartin-sur-Mer France
157 F5 Montmédy France
163 E3 Montmélian France
160 C2 Montmerle-sur-Saône France
161 C4 Montmeyran France
161 E5 Montmeyan France
156 D4 Montmirail Champagne-Ardenne France
159 G3 Montmirail Pays de la Loire France
160 D1 Montmirey-le-Château France
162 C3 Montmoreau-St-Cybard France
226 D5 Montmorenci IN U.S.A.
230 G2 Montmorency Que. Can.
162 C2 Montmorillon France
161 D4 Montmorin France
160 D2 Montmorot France
157 D4 Montmort-Lucy France
186 F3 Montnegre de Llevant hill Spain
85 G5 Monto Qld Austr.
158 D4 Montoir-de-Bretagne France
159 G4 Montoire-sur-le-Loir France
158 D4 Montois slope France
161 C4 Montoison France
184 C2 Montoito Port.
163 E5 Montolieu France
183 I3 Montón Spain
191 H5 Montone Italy
191 H4 Montone r. Italy
193 E2 Montopoli di Sabina Italy
193 F2 Montorio al Vomano Italy
185 F2 Montoro Spain
185 G2 Montoro r. Spain
163 E5 Montory France
234 B1 Montour County county PA U.S.A.
232 E3 Montour Falls NY U.S.A.
159 F5 Montournais France
227 I5 Montoursville PA U.S.A.
246 □ Montpelier Jamaica
238 E3 Montpelier ID U.S.A.
226 F5 Montpelier IN U.S.A.
232 A4 Montpelier OH U.S.A.
233 G2 Montpelier VT U.S.A.
163 F5 Montpellier France
161 A4 Montpeyroux France
163 C4 Montpezat Aquitaine France
163 C5 Montpézat France
163 D4 Montpezat-de-Quercy France
161 C4 Montpezat-sous-Bauzon France
162 C3 Montpon-Ménestérol France
160 D2 Montpont-en-Bresse France
159 H4 Mont-près-Chambord France
Montreal Que. Can. see Montréal
224 F4 Montréal Que. Can.
224 C4 Montreal r. Ont. Can.
224 E4 Montreal r. Ont. Can.
160 C1 Montréal France
163 E5 Montréal France
163 C5 Montréal France
226 B2 Montreal WI U.S.A.
224 F4 Montréal-Dorval airport Que. Can.
160 D2 Montréal-la-Cluse France
219 H4 Montreal Lake Sask. Can.
224 F4 Montréal-Mirabel airport Que. Can.
224 C4 Montreal River Ont. Can.
163 E5 Montredon-Labessonnié France
161 C3 Montregard France
163 C5 Montréjeau France
159 H4 Montrésor France
192 A4 Montresta Sardegna Italy
160 D2 Montret France
156 C4 Montreuil Île-de-France France
156 B2 Montreuil Nord - Pas-de-Calais France
159 F4 Montreuil-Bellay France
159 F4 Montreuil-Juigné France
190 B2 Montreux Switz.
159 E4 Montrevault France
160 D2 Montrevel-en-Bresse France
159 H4 Montrichard France
163 D4 Montricoux France
160 E2 Montrond France
161 B4 Montrodat France
161 A5 Montredo mt. France
186 D3 Mont-roig del Camp Spain
160 D2 Montrond France
160 C3 Montrond-les-Bains France
146 F5 Montrose Angus, Scotland U.K.
239 F4 Montrose CO U.S.A.
227 F4 Montrose MI U.S.A.
235 E1 Montrose NY U.S.A.
234 C1 Montrose PA U.S.A.
232 C5 Montrose WV U.S.A.
232 E5 Montross VA U.S.A.
187 C5 Montroy Spain
160 E2 Montrozier France
162 C1 Monts France
156 B3 Mont-St-Aignan France
160 C1 Mont-St-Jean France
157 F3 Mont-St-Martin France
158 E3 Mont-St-Michel, Baie du b. France
156 D5 Mont-St-Sulpice France
160 C2 Mont-St-Vincent France
163 E4 Montsalvy France
186 D3 Montsant r. Spain
160 C1 Montsauche-les-Settons France
163 C5 Montsaunès France
163 D6 Montségur France
186 F3 Montseny Spain
247 □2 Montserrat terr. West Indies
159 G4 Montsoreau France
163 B5 Montsoué France
160 D2 Mont-sous-Vaudrey France
159 G5 Monts-sur-Guesnes France
Mont St Michel tourist site France see Le Mont-St-Michel
159 F3 Montsûrs France
156 E4 Montsuzain France
187 F5 Montuïri Spain
242 □J8 Montuosa, Isla i. Panama
185 F3 Monturque Spain
232 D6 Montvale VA U.S.A.
163 D4 Montvalent France
156 B3 Montville France
235 F1 Montville CT U.S.A.
165 E4 Montzen Belgium
157 F3 Montzéville France
241 L3 Monument Valley reg. AZ U.S.A.
215 F2 Monyakeng S. Africa
95 A2 Monywa Myanmar
190 E3 Monza Italy
209 E9 Monze Zambia
Monze, Cape pt Pak. see Muari, Ras
172 B2 Monzelfeld Ger.
172 B2 Monzingen Ger.
252 A2 Monzón Peru
186 D3 Monzón Spain
183 F2 Monzón de Campos Spain
235 F1 Moodus CT U.S.A.
215 H3 Mooi r. KwaZulu-Natal S. Africa
215 F2 Mooi r. North West S. Africa
215 H3 Mooirivier S. Africa
164 E3 Mook Neth.
212 E4 Mookane Botswana
82 D2 Moolawatana S.A. Austr.
82 E2 Moomba S.A. Austr.
82 C2 Moomin Creek r. N.S.W. Austr.
82 C2 Moonaree S.A. Austr.
83 G2 Moonbi Range mts N.S.W. Austr.
147 D4 Mooncoin Rep. of Ireland
84 E5 Moonda Lake salt flat Qld Austr.
147 E4 Moone Rep. of Ireland
85 G5 Moonie Qld Austr.
83 G2 Moonie r. N.S.W./Qld Austr.
82 D3 Moonta S.A. Austr.
85 D4 Moora W.A. Austr.
85 E5 Mooraberree Qld Austr.
171 C5 Moorbad Lobenstein Ger.
238 F2 Moorcroft WY U.S.A.
168 C2 Moordorf (Südbrookmerland) Ger.
164 D3 Moordrecht Neth.
87 B6 Moore r. W.A. Austr.
238 E2 Moore MT U.S.A.
87 C6 Moore, Lake salt flat W.A. Austr.
79 □3a Moorea i. Fr. Polynesia
232 D5 Moorefield WV U.S.A.
231 D7 Moore Haven FL U.S.A.
149 I4 Moorends South Yorkshire, England U.K.
173 F3 Moorenweis Ger.
85 G3 Moore Reef Coral Sea Is Terr. Austr.
234 B2 Mooresburg PA U.S.A.
246 C1 Moores Island Bahamas
233 □J2 Moores Mills N.B. Can.
234 D3 Moorestown NJ U.S.A.
246 □ Moore Town Jamaica
148 C3 Moorfields Northern Ireland U.K.
146 E6 Moorfoot Hills Scotland U.K.
236 D2 Moorhead MN U.S.A.
83 E3 Moornanyah Lake imp. l. N.S.W. Austr.
82 E3 Moorook S.A. Austr.
84 C1 Mooroongga Island N.T. Austr.
83 F4 Mooroopna Vic. Austr.
240 H4 Moorpark CA U.S.A.
214 B5 Moorreesburg S. Africa
165 D4 Moorslede Belgium
168 C2 Moorweg Ger.
172 C4 Moos Baden-Württemberg Ger.
173 G3 Moos Bayern Ger.
179 G2 Moosbach Ger.
173 F4 Moosburg Austria
173 F3 Moosburg an der Isar Ger.
224 D3 Moose r. Ont. Can.
224 D3 Moose Factory Ont. Can.
233 □I2 Moosehead Lake ME U.S.A.
223 J5 Moose Jaw Sask. Can.
223 J5 Moose Jaw r. Sask. Can.
226 A2 Moose Lake MN U.S.A.
223 K5 Moose Mountain Creek r. Sask. Can.
224 D3 Moose River Ont. Can.
233 H2 Mooselooke, Mount NH U.S.A.
173 F3 Moosinning Ger.
179 G4 Mooskirchen Austria
223 K5 Moosomin Sask. Can.
224 D3 Moosonee Ont. Can.
173 G3 Moosthenning Ger.
214 F4 Mopane S. Africa
213 G3 Mopeia Moz.
Mopelia atoll Arch. de la Société Fr. Polynesia see Maupihaa
212 E4 Mopipi Botswana
206 D3 Mopti Mali
206 E3 Mopti admin. reg. Mali
252 C4 Moquegua Peru
252 C4 Moquegua dept Peru
261 H4 Moquehuá Arg.
177 H4 Mór Hungary
207 G4 Mora Cameroon
184 B2 Mora Port.
183 G5 Mora Spain
141 K3 Mora Sweden
226 A3 Mora MN U.S.A.
239 F5 Mora NM U.S.A.
239 F5 Mora r. NM U.S.A.
260 B4 Mora, Cerro mt. Arg./Chile
196 D4 Morača r. Yugo.
138 F5 Morach r. Belarus
212 F4 Morad r. Pak.
116 D4 Moradabad Uttar Prad. India
254 F3 Morada Nova Brazil
257 E3 Morada Nova de Minas Brazil
186 D3 Móra d'Ebre Spain
187 C4 Mora de Rubielos Spain
183 G3 Moradillo de Roa Spain
213 □J3 Morafenobe Madag.
175 H2 Morąg Pol.
177 I5 Mórahalom Hungary
182 D3 Morais Port.
186 D3 Móra la Nova Spain
186 D3 Moral de Calatrava Spain
259 B7 Moraleda, Canal sea chan. Chile
185 G3 Moraleda de Zafayona Spain
184 D2 Moraleja Spain
182 E3 Moraleja del Vino Spain
183 F3 Moraleja de Sayago Spain
242 □H6 Morales Guat.
185 H4 Morales r. Spain
182 E3 Morales del Vino Spain
183 E3 Morales de Toro Spain
182 E3 Morales de Valverde Spain
182 D3 Moralina Spain
114 C2 Moram Mahar. India
213 □K3 Moramanga Madag.
226 E3 Moran MI U.S.A.
238 E3 Moran WY U.S.A.
85 G4 Moranbah Qld Austr.
Morang Nepal see Biratnagar
117 H4 Moranhat Assam India
193 I5 Morano Calabro Italy
190 D3 Morano sul Po Italy
246 □ Morant Bay Jamaica
114 C3 Morappur Tamil Nadu India
146 C5 Morar Highland, Scotland U.K.
146 C5 Morar hills Scotland U.K.
146 C5 Morar, Loch l. Scotland U.K.
142 E3 Morarp Sweden
182 D4 Morasverdes Spain
183 I3 Morata de Jalón Spain
183 G4 Morata de Tajuña Spain
185 I2 Moratalla Spain
114 C5 Moratuwa Sri Lanka
179 H2 Morava r. Europe alt. March (Austria)
179 H1 Moravany Czech Rep.
177 K3 Moravany Slovakia
213 □K2 Moravia Madag.
232 E3 Moravia NY U.S.A.
196 E4 Moravica r. Yugo.
197 E4 Moravica r. Yugo.
177 G2 Moravice r. Czech Rep.
177 H2 Morávka Czech Rep.
176 E3 Moravská Dyje r. Czech Rep.
179 I2 Moravská Nová Ves Czech Rep.
176 F2 Moravská Třebová Czech Rep.
176 E2 Moravské Budějovice Czech Rep.
177 H2 Moravskoslezský Beskydy mts Czech Rep.
176 G2 Moravský Beroun Czech Rep.
Moravský Ján Slovakia see Moravský Svätý Ján
176 G3 Moravský Písek Czech Rep.
176 G3 Moravský Svätý Ján Slovakia
87 B6 Morawa W.A. Austr.
175 I5 Morawica Pol.
146 E4 Moray admin. div. Scotland U.K.
85 F4 Moray Downs Qld Austr.
146 D4 Moray Firth b. Scotland U.K.
84 B2 Moray Range hills N.T. Austr.
172 B3 Morbach Ger.
190 E2 Morbegno Italy
116 B5 Morbi Gujarat India
160 E2 Morbier France
158 D4 Morbihan dept Bretagne France
179 H3 Mörbisch am See Austria
143 G3 Mörbylånga Kalmar Sweden
163 B4 Morcenx France
195 H3 Morciano di Leuca Italy
191 H5 Morciano di Romagna Italy
193 G3 Morcone Italy
100 B2 Mordaga Nei Mongol China
127 G3 Mor Dağı mt. Turkey
158 E3 Mordelles France
223 L5 Morden Man. Can.
199 E2 Mordoğan Turkey
Mordovia aut. rep. Rus. Fed. see Mordoviya, Respublika
135 I5 Mordoviya, Respublika aut. rep. Rus. Fed.
135 H5 Mordovo Rus. Fed.
Mordovskaya A.S.S.R. aut. rep. Rus. Fed. see Mordoviya, Respublika
139 L4 Mordves Rus. Fed.
Mordvinia aut. rep. Rus. Fed. see Mordoviya, Respublika
137 H4 Mordvynivka Ukr.
175 K3 Mordy Pol.
158 D4 Moréac France
156 D3 Moreanes Port.
236 C2 Moreau r. SD U.S.A.
236 C2 Moreau, South Fork r. SD U.S.A.
146 F6 Morebattle Scottish Borders, Scotland U.K.
146 G3 Morecambe Lancashire, England U.K.
149 F3 Morecambe Bay England U.K.
182 E1 Moreda Spain
183 H2 Moreda de Álava Spain
83 G2 Moree N.S.W. Austr.
156 B5 Morée France
232 B5 Morehead KY U.S.A.
231 E5 Morehead City NC U.S.A.
182 B3 Moreira do Rei Port.
116 D4 Morel r. India
190 D2 Mörel Switz.
244 D4 Morelia Mex.
85 E4 Morella Qld Austr.
187 C5 Morella Spain
194 D5 Morello r. Sicilia Italy
244 C2 Morelos Mex.
245 E4 Morelos state Mex.
116 D4 Morena Madh. Prad. India
184 D3 Morena, Sierra mts Spain
241 M5 Morenci AZ U.S.A.
226 E5 Morenci MI U.S.A.
197 G3 Moreni Romania
261 H4 Moreno Arg.
244 C2 Moreno Mex.
240 I5 Moreno Valley CA U.S.A.
182 H3 Morentín Spain
140 I3 Møre og Romsdal county Norway
253 F2 Morerú r. Brazil
182 E3 Moreruela de Tábara Spain
182 A2 Mores Sardegna Italy
149 F3 Moresby Cumbria, England U.K.
220 E4 Moresby, Mount B.C. Can.
222 C4 Moresby Island B.C. Can.
160 D3 Morestel France
85 H5 Moreton Bay Qld Austr.
150 D4 Moretonhampstead Devon, England U.K.
151 F3 Moreton-in-Marsh Gloucestershire, England U.K.
85 H5 Moreton Island Qld Austr.
150 E2 Moreton Say Shropshire, England U.K.
156 C4 Moret-sur-Loing France
190 C4 Moretta Italy
156 B3 Moreuil France
134 L1 Moreyu r. Rus. Fed.
160 E2 Morez France
150 C2 Morfa Nefyn Gwynedd, Wales U.K.
190 E4 Morfasso Italy
172 C2 Mörfelden Ger.
128 A2 Morfou Cyprus
128 A2 Morfou Bay Cyprus
140 N1 Morgam-Viibus hill Fin.
82 D3 Morgan S.A. Austr.
231 C6 Morgan GA U.S.A.
232 A5 Morgan KY U.S.A.
240 H3 Morgan, Mount CA U.S.A.
237 F6 Morgan City LA U.S.A.
230 C4 Morganfield KY U.S.A.
240 G3 Morgan Hill CA U.S.A.
231 D5 Morganton NC U.S.A.
230 C4 Morgantown KY U.S.A.
232 D5 Morgantown WV U.S.A.
235 D2 Morganville NJ U.S.A.
158 B3 Morgat France
215 G2 Morgenzon S. Africa
190 B2 Morges Switz.
190 C3 Morgex Italy
157 G4 Morhange France
117 F4 Morhar r. India
106 A3 Mori Xinjiang China
190 F3 Mori Italy
105 D4 Mori Japan
240 J2 Moriah, Mount NV U.S.A.
239 F5 Moriarty NM U.S.A.
83 F2 Moriarty's Range hills Qld Austr.
207 G4 Moribaya Guinea
149 F3 Moricambe Bay England U.K.
222 E4 Moricetown B.C. Can.
250 D4 Morichal Col.
193 E2 Moricone Italy
156 C4 Morienval France
104 B4 Moriguchi Japan
215 F4 Morija Lesotho
207 G3 Moriki Nigeria
185 F3 Moriles Spain
Morin Dawa Nei Mongol China see Nirji
169 E4 Moringen Ger.
193 F3 Morino Italy
139 H3 Morino Rus. Fed.
105 D4 Morioka Japan
197 H2 Moriṣca r. Romania
83 G3 Morisset N.S.W. Austr.
146 D4 Moriston r. Scotland U.K.
171 E4 Moritzburg Ger.
104 C3 Moriyama Japan
102 J4 Moriyoshi-zan vol. Japan
140 M2 Morjärv Sweden
123 E4 Morjen r. Pak.
134 J4 Morki Rus. Fed.
139 K3 Morkiny Gory Rus. Fed.
163 B5 Morlaàs France
158 C3 Morlaix France
183 C3 Morlanne France
165 D4 Morlanwelz Belgium
172 C2 Mörlenbach Ger.
222 H5 Morley Alta Can.
157 F4 Morley France
149 H4 Morley West Yorkshire, England U.K.
193 I5 Mormanno Italy
156 C4 Mormant France
161 D4 Mormoiron France
Mormugao Goa India see Marmagao
160 C3 Mornand France
160 C3 Mornant France
161 C4 Mornas France
247 □2 Morne-à-l'Eau Guadeloupe
247 □2 Morne Constant hill Guadeloupe
247 □2 Morne Diablotin vol. Dominica
247 □2 Morne Macaque vol. Dominica
190 D4 Mornese Italy
85 E5 Morney Qld Austr.
259 B8 Mornington, Isla i. Chile
264 D9 Mornington Abyssal Plain sea feature S. Atlantic Ocean
84 D3 Mornington Island Qld Austr.
198 B2 Mornos r. Greece
173 F3 Mörnsheim Ger.
123 F5 Moro Pak.
238 D2 Moro OR U.S.A.
204 D3 Morocco country Africa
226 D5 Morocco IN U.S.A.
136 C2 Morochne Ukr.
237 E5 Moro Creek r. AR U.S.A.
211 C6 Morogoro Tanz.
211 C7 Morogoro admin. reg. Tanz.
92 B5 Moro Gulf Phil.
215 F3 Morojaneng S. Africa
214 D2 Morokweng S. Africa
244 D3 Moroleón Mex.
193 F3 Morolo Italy
213 □I4 Morombe Madag.
246 C2 Morón Cuba
106 D1 Mörön Mongolia
190 C1 Moron mt. Switz.
250 B5 Morona Ecuador
250 B6 Morona r. Peru
250 B5 Morona-Santiago prov. Ecuador
213 □J4 Morondava Madag.
183 H3 Morón de Almazán Spain
185 E3 Morón de la Frontera Spain
206 D4 Morondo Côte d'Ivoire
240 I4 Morongo Valley CA U.S.A.
217 □3a Moroni Njazidja Comoros
241 L2 Moroni UT U.S.A.
106 B5 Moron Us He r. Qinghai China
183 I3 Moros Spain
183 I3 Moros r. Spain
192 B2 Morosaglia Corse France
93 D2 Morotai i. Maluku Indon.
210 B4 Moroto Uganda
210 B4 Moroto, Mount Uganda
103 E7 Morotsuka Japan
196 D3 Morović Vojvodina, Srbija Yugo.
247 □1 Morovis Puerto Rico
81 A6 Morowai South I. N.Z.
139 H2 Morozova Rus. Fed.
137 J2 Morozovka Rus. Fed.
135 H6 Morozovsk Rus. Fed.
190 C4 Morozzo Italy
254 E4 Morpara Brazil
227 G4 Morpeth Ont. Can.
149 H2 Morpeth Northumberland, England U.K.
Morphou Cyprus see Morfou
256 C6 Morretes Brazil
232 A6 Morrill KY U.S.A.
236 C3 Morrill NE U.S.A.
237 E5 Morrilton AR U.S.A.
222 H5 Morrin Alta Can.
256 C2 Morrinhos Brazil
80 E2 Morrinsville North I. N.Z.
223 L5 Morris Man. Can.
226 C5 Morris IL U.S.A.
236 E2 Morris MN U.S.A.
232 E4 Morris PA U.S.A.
233 F2 Morrisburg Ont. Can.
234 D2 Morris County county NJ U.S.A.
221 O1 Morris Jesup, Kap c. Greenland
261 F3 Morrison Arg.
226 C5 Morrison IL U.S.A.
81 C6 Morrisons South I. N.Z.
235 D2 Morris Plains NJ U.S.A.
234 B1 Morris Run PA U.S.A.
150 D3 Morriston Swansea, Wales U.K.
241 K5 Morristown AZ U.S.A.
235 D2 Morristown NJ U.S.A.
233 F2 Morristown NY U.S.A.
231 D4 Morristown TN U.S.A.
233 F3 Morrisville NY U.S.A.
235 D2 Morrisville PA U.S.A.
233 G2 Morrisville VT U.S.A.
192 B3 Morro, Monte hill Sardegna Italy
256 C4 Morro Agudo Brazil
240 G4 Morro Bay CA U.S.A.
185 F2 Morro del Águila hill Spain
252 B3 Morro do Chapéu Brazil
257 G4 Morro do Coco Brazil
258 C2 Morro do Sinal hills Brazil
253 G5 Morro Mazatán Mex.
193 F2 Morrone, Monte mt. Italy
252 D4 Morros Brazil
191 I5 Morrovalle Italy
213 G3 Morrumbala Moz.
169 C5 Morsbach Ger.
172 B3 Morsberg hill Ger.
172 G2 Morschen Ger.
223 J5 Morse Sask. Can.
237 C4 Morse TX U.S.A.
226 B2 Morse WI U.S.A.
263 I2 Morse, Cape Antarctica
135 H5 Morshanka Rus. Fed.
Morshansk Rus. Fed. see Morshanka
136 B3 Morshyn Ukr.
116 D5 Morsi Mahar. India
172 E4 Morsleben Ger.
168 E3 Morsum Ger.
157 G4 Mortagne r. France
159 G3 Mortagne-au-Perche France
162 B3 Mortagne-sur-Gironde France
159 F5 Mortagne-sur-Sèvre France
184 B2 Mortágua Port.
158 E3 Mortain France
190 D3 Mortara Italy
160 D1 Morte r. France
160 E1 Morteau France
158 D3 Morteaux-Couliboeuf France
159 F3 Mortefontaine France
191 I3 Mortegliano Italy
150 C3 Mortehoe Devon, England U.K.
195 E4 Mortelle Sicilia Italy
165 D3 Mortsel Belgium
261 G2 Morteros Arg.
257 E4 Mortes, Rio das r. Minas Gerais Brazil
254 C4 Mortes, Rio das r. Tocantins Brazil
215 F3 Mortimer S. Africa
151 F3 Mortimer West Berkshire, England U.K.
150 E2 Mortimer's Cross Herefordshire, England U.K.
223 J5 Mortlach Sask. Can.
82 E4 Mortlake Vic. Austr.
266 F5 Mortlock Islands Micronesia
Mortlock Islands P.N.G. see Takuu Islands
151 G2 Morton Lincolnshire, England U.K.
149 I4 Morton Lincolnshire, England U.K.
226 C5 Morton IL U.S.A.
237 C5 Morton TX U.S.A.
238 B2 Morton WA U.S.A.
226 C5 Morton Grove IL U.S.A.
159 G3 Mortrée France
178 D4 Mörtschach Austria
83 F3 Morundah N.S.W. Austr.
210 B4 Morungole mt. Uganda
Mururoa atoll Arch. des Tuamotu Fr. Polynesia see Mururoa
83 G3 Moruya N.S.W. Austr.
160 B1 Morvan hills France
85 F5 Morven Qld Austr.
81 C6 Morven South I. N.Z.
146 E4 Morven hill Aberdeenshire, Scotland U.K.
146 E3 Morven hill Highland, Scotland U.K.
146 C5 Morvern reg. Scotland U.K.
Morvi Gujarat India see Morbi
150 E2 Morville Shropshire, England U.K.
83 F4 Morwell Vic. Austr.
150 C4 Morwenstow Cornwall, England U.K.
174 C3 Moryń Pol.
174 G2 Morzeszczyn Pol.
172 E4 Morzine France
139 J4 Mosal'sk Rus. Fed.
136 D3 Moșana Moldova
172 D2 Mosbach Ger.
149 H4 Mosborough South Yorkshire, England U.K.
238 F2 Mosby MT U.S.A.
184 A2 Moscavide Port.
191 G5 Moscia r. Italy
193 F2 Mosciano Sant'Angelo Italy
Moscow Rus. Fed. see Moskva
238 C2 Moscow ID U.S.A.
234 C1 Moscow PA U.S.A.
Moscow Oblast admin. div. Rus. Fed. see Moskovskaya Oblast'
171 D5 Mosel Ger.
169 C5 Mosel r. Ger.
232 E6 Moseley VA U.S.A.
157 G3 Moselle dept Lorraine France
157 G3 Moselle r. France
171 C3 Möser Ger.
240 I1 Moses, Mount NV U.S.A.
238 C2 Moses Lake WA U.S.A.
212 E4 Mosetse Botswana
81 C6 Mosgiel South I. N.Z.
232 D4 Moshannon PA U.S.A.
139 J2 Moshenskoye Rus. Fed.
227 E1 Mosher Ont. Can.
207 G4 Moshi r. Nigeria
211 C5 Moshi Tanz.
137 F3 Moshny Ukr.
174 E3 Mosina Pol.
226 C3 Mosinee WI U.S.A.
215 E5 Mosita S. Africa
140 K2 Mosjøen Norway
140 K2 Moskenesøy i. Norway
140 K2 Moskenestraumen sea chan. Norway
140 M1 Moskkugáisi mt. Norway
175 H5 Moskorzew Pol.
140 L2 Moskosel Sweden
139 L4 Moskovskaya Oblast' admin. div. Rus. Fed.
Moskovskiy Uzbek. see Shakhrikhan
137 J2 Moskovskoye Rus. Fed.
139 K4 Moskva Rus. Fed.
139 L4 Moskva r. Rus. Fed.
123 G2 Moskva Tajik.
176 G6 Moslavina Podravska Croatia
197 H2 Moșna Romania
177 K6 Moșnița Nouă Romania
78 □5 Moso i. Vanuatu
191 G2 Moso in Passiria Italy
176 G4 Mosonmagyaróvár Hungary
176 G6 Mosor mts Croatia
177 H3 Mošovce Slovakia
137 I3 Mos'panove Ukr.
137 J4 Mospyne Ukr.
250 B4 Mosquera Col.
239 F5 Mosquero NM U.S.A.
187 C4 Mosqueruela Spain
182 D2 Moss Norway
208 C5 Mossaka Congo
Mossâmedes Angola see Namibe
256 B2 Mossâmedes Brazil
146 F4 Mossat Aberdeenshire, Scotland U.K.
81 B6 Mossburn South I. N.Z.
Mosselbaai S. Africa see Mossel Bay
214 D6 Mossel Bay S. Africa
208 B5 Mossendjo Congo
163 E6 Mosset France
83 F3 Mossgiel N.S.W. Austr.
215 G1 Mossiesdal S. Africa
172 D3 Mössingen Ger.
148 D3 Mossley Northern Ireland U.K.
85 F3 Mossman Qld Austr.
254 F3 Mossoró Brazil
147 E1 Moss-side Northern Ireland U.K.
146 E4 Mosstodloch Moray, Scotland U.K.
213 I2 Mossuril Moz.
83 G3 Moss Vale N.S.W. Austr.
223 K4 Mossy r. Sask. Can.
197 G5 Most Bulg.
176 C1 Most Czech Rep.
195 □ Mosta Malta
205 F2 Mostaganem Alg.
188 F4 Mostar Bos.-Herz.
255 C9 Mostardas Brazil
184 C3 Mosteiro Beja Port.
182 B3 Mosteiro Castelo Branco Port.
182 B2 Mosteiro Galicia Spain
182 C1 Mosteiros Galicia Spain
216 □1b Mosteiros São Miguel Azores
197 G3 Moșteni Romania
197 H3 Moștiștea r. Romania
175 I2 Mostkowo Pol.
183 G4 Móstoles Spain
223 I4 Mostoos Hills Sask. Can.
136 F4 Mostove Ukr.
129 B1 Mostovskoy Rus. Fed.
175 J3 Mostówka Pol.
Mosty Belarus see Masty
175 L4 Mosty Pol.
136 B3 Mostys'ka Ukr.
175 L6 Mostys'ka Druha Ukr.
Mosul Iraq see Al Mawşil
140 J3 Mosvik Norway
175 M4 Mosyr Ukr.
175 H4 Moszczenica Pol.
121 C2 Mot'a Eth.
78 □5 Mota i. Vanuatu
208 C4 Motaba r. Congo
185 H1 Mota del Cuervo Spain
183 E3 Mota del Marqués Spain
243 H6 Motagua r. Guat.
136 C1 Motal' Belarus
143 F3 Motala Sweden
78 □5 Mota Lava i. Vanuatu
174 F1 Motarzyno Pol.
197 H2 Moțca Romania
213 F5 Motetema S. Africa
116 D4 Moth Uttar Prad. India
146 E6 Motherwell North Lanarkshire, Scotland U.K.
214 D2 Mothibistat S. Africa
190 B2 Môtiers Switz.
190 B2 Môtiers Switz.
117 F4 Motihari Bihar India
185 I2 Motilla hill Spain
185 E2 Motilla del Palancar Spain
143 E5 Motjärnshyttan Sweden
101 B4 Motlan Ling hill Liaoning China
213 F4 Motloutse r. Botswana
102 □2 Motobu Japan
212 D5 Motokwe Botswana
213 I2 Motos Spain
140 P1 Motovskiy Zaliv sea chan. Rus. Fed.
243 G6 Motozintla Mex.
185 G4 Motril Spain
197 F3 Motru Romania
197 F3 Motru r. Romania
215 F1 Motshikiri S. Africa
214 E3 Motswedimosa S. Africa
236 C2 Mott ND U.S.A.
190 H3 Motta Montecorvino Italy
195 E4 Motta San Giovanni Italy
191 H3 Motta Visconti Italy
169 E5 Motten Ger.
173 E3 Möttingen Ger.
195 G2 Mottola Italy
81 D4 Motueka South I. N.Z.
81 □1 Motuiti i. Fr. Polynesia see Motu Iti
79 □3 Motu Iti i. Fr. Polynesia
81 D5 Motukarara South I. N.Z.
79 □3 Motukataia i. Tokelau
79 □3a Motu One atoll Arch. de la Société Fr. Polynesia
79 □3 Motu One i. Fr. Polynesia
81 D4 Motupiko South I. N.Z.
80 D4 Motupipi South I. N.Z.
80 D1 Motutangi North I. N.Z.
81 □3 Motutapu i. Rarotonga Cook Is
178 B3 Mötz Austria
142 D3 Mou Denmark
96 D3 Mouan, Nam r. Laos
207 H6 Mouanko Cameroon
161 E5 Mouans-Sartoux France
Mouaskar Alg. see Mascara
225 G3 Mouchalagane r. Que. Can.
159 E5 Mouchamps France
163 C5 Mouchan France
160 D2 Mouchard France
161 B4 Mouchet, Mont mt. France
246 E2 Mouchoir Bank sea feature Turks and Caicos Is
246 E2 Mouchoir Passage Turks and Caicos Is
182 C3 Mouçós Port.
108 B3 Mouding Yunnan China
206 B2 Moudjéria Maur.
190 B2 Moudon Switz.
161 F5 Mougins France
141 M3 Mouhijärvi Fin.
206 E4 Mouhoun r. Africa alt. Volta Noire, conv. Black Volta
208 A5 Mouila Gabon
159 F5 Mouilleron-en-Pareds France
83 F3 Moulamein N.S.W. Austr.
83 E3 Moulamein Creek r. N.S.W. Austr.
163 E4 Moularès France
Moulavibazar Bangl. see Maulvi Bazar
159 F3 Moulay France
247 □2 Moule Guadeloupe
209 A5 Moulengui Binza Gabon
163 C4 Mouleydier France
159 G4 Mouliherne France
163 D5 Moulin-Neuf France
160 B2 Moulins France
160 B2 Moulins-Engilbert France
159 G3 Moulins-la-Marche France
163 D6 Moulis France
162 B3 Moulis-en-Médoc France
162 C2 Moulismes France
163 B5 Moulle de Jaut, Pic du mt. France
96 B3 Moulmein Myanmar
96 A3 Moulmeingyun Myanmar
204 E2 Moulouya, Oued r. Morocco
151 G4 Moulsecoomb Brighton and Hove, England U.K.
159 F2 Moult France
151 G2 Moulton Lincolnshire, England U.K.
151 G2 Moulton Northamptonshire, England U.K.
151 H2 Moulton Suffolk, England U.K.
231 C5 Moulton AL U.S.A.
262 P1 Moulton, Mount Antarctica
233 H3 Moultonborough NH U.S.A.
231 D6 Moultrie GA U.S.A.
Moumolu-Naunitu i. Solomon Is see San Jorge
237 F4 Mound City IL U.S.A.
236 E4 Mound City KS U.S.A.
236 E3 Mound City MO U.S.A.
236 C2 Mound City SD U.S.A.
208 C2 Moundou Chad
232 C5 Moundsville WV U.S.A.
231 C5 Moundville AL U.S.A.
161 E4 Mounier, Mont mt. France
116 C4 Mount Abu Rajasthan India
231 C5 Mount Aetna PA U.S.A.
239 F5 Mountainair NM U.S.A.
150 D3 Mountain Ash Rhondda Cynon Taff, Wales U.K.
231 C5 Mountain Brook AL U.S.A.
232 C6 Mountain City TN U.S.A.
236 F4 Mountain Grove MO U.S.A.
237 E4 Mountain Home AR U.S.A.
238 D3 Mountain Home ID U.S.A.
234 C1 Mountainhome PA U.S.A.
241 L1 Mountain Home UT U.S.A.
226 A2 Mountain Iron MN U.S.A.
232 D5 Mountain Lake Park MD U.S.A.
235 D2 Mountain Lakes NJ U.S.A.
241 J4 Mountain Pass CA U.S.A.
234 C1 Mountain Top PA U.S.A.
237 E5 Mountain View AR U.S.A.
240 F3 Mountain View CA U.S.A.
240 □D9 Mountain View HI U.S.A.
220 B3 Mountain Village AK U.S.A.
234 A3 Mount Airy MD U.S.A.
232 C6 Mount Airy NC U.S.A.
235 D2 Mount Arlington NJ U.S.A.
87 C5 Mount Augustus W.A. Austr.
215 G4 Mount Ayliff S. Africa
236 E3 Mount Ayr IA U.S.A.
240 I4 Mount Baldy CA U.S.A.
82 D3 Mount Barker S.A. Austr.
87 C7 Mount Barker W.A. Austr.
86 E3 Mount Barnett W.A. Austr.
83 F4 Mount Beauty Vic. Austr.
147 C3 Mount Bellew Rep. of Ireland
146 E6 Mountbenger Scottish Borders, Scotland U.K.
80 E4 Mount Bruce North I. N.Z.
227 G4 Mount Brydges Ont. Can.
85 F3 Mount Carbine Qld Austr.
230 C4 Mount Carmel IL U.S.A.
234 B2 Mount Carmel PA U.S.A.
232 B6 Mount Carmel TN U.S.A.
241 K3 Mount Carmel Junction UT U.S.A.
226 C4 Mount Carroll IL U.S.A.
84 C5 Mount Cavenagh N.T. Austr.
147 C2 Mountcharles Rep. of Ireland
87 C5 Mount Clere W.A. Austr.
147 B4 Mountcollins Rep. of Ireland
81 C5 Mount Cook South I. N.Z.
85 F4 Mount Coolon Qld Austr.
213 F3 Mount Darwin Zimbabwe
233 □I2 Mount Desert Island ME U.S.A.
84 C4 Mount Denison N.T. Austr.
82 C2 Mount Eba S.A. Austr.
84 C5 Mount Ebenezer N.T. Austr.
222 C3 Mount Edgecumbe AK U.S.A.
237 D6 Mount Enterprise TX U.S.A.
226 E5 Mount Etna IN U.S.A.
148 B3 Mountfield Northern Ireland U.K.
215 G4 Mount Fletcher S. Africa
224 D5 Mount Forest Ont. Can.
215 G4 Mount Frere S. Africa
82 E4 Mount Gambier S.A. Austr.
85 F3 Mount Garnet Qld Austr.
232 B6 Mount Gay WV U.S.A.
232 B4 Mount Gilead OH U.S.A.
91 J8 Mount Hagen P.N.G.
148 B3 Mount Hamilton Northern Ireland U.K.
234 D3 Mount Holly NJ U.S.A.
234 A2 Mount Holly Springs PA U.S.A.
83 F3 Mount Hope N.S.W. Austr.
82 B3 Mount Hope S.A. Austr.
232 C6 Mount Hope WV U.S.A.
226 C4 Mount Horeb WI U.S.A.
86 E3 Mount House W.A. Austr.
85 E5 Mount Howitt Qld Austr.
81 C5 Mount Hutt South I. N.Z.
85 E4 Mount Ida AR U.S.A.
84 D4 Mount Isa Qld Austr.
232 D5 Mount Jackson VA U.S.A.
232 D4 Mount Jewett PA U.S.A.
147 D2 Mountjoy Northern Ireland U.K.
148 B3 Mountjoy Northern Ireland U.K.
234 B2 Mount Joy PA U.S.A.
87 D5 Mount Keith W.A. Austr.
210 C5 Mount Kenya National Park Kenya
235 E1 Mount Kisco NY U.S.A.
85 G4 Mount Larcom Qld Austr.
232 C4 Mount Lebanon PA U.S.A.
82 D3 Mount Lofty Range mts S.A. Austr.
227 G2 Mount MacDonald Ont. Can.
87 C6 Mount Magnet W.A. Austr.
83 E3 Mount Manara N.S.W. Austr.
80 F2 Mount Maunganui North I. N.Z.
147 D3 Mountmellick Rep. of Ireland
85 F3 Mount Molloy Qld Austr.
85 G4 Mount Morgan Qld Austr.
226 C4 Mount Morris IL U.S.A.
227 F4 Mount Morris MI U.S.A.
232 E3 Mount Morris NY U.S.A.
83 E2 Mount Murchison N.S.W. Austr.
232 C5 Mount Nebo WV U.S.A.
87 C4 Mount Newman W.A. Austr.
147 E2 Mount Norris Northern Ireland U.K.
147 D3 Mount Nugent Rep. of Ireland
232 A5 Mount Olivet KY U.S.A.
232 B5 Mount Orab OH U.S.A.
225 K4 Mount Pearl Nfld. Can.
234 C2 Mount Penn PA U.S.A.
85 G5 Mount Perry Qld Austr.
81 B6 Mount Pisa South I. N.Z.
82 D3 Mount Pleasant S.A. Austr.
225 H4 Mount Pleasant P.E.I. Can.
226 B5 Mount Pleasant IA U.S.A.
226 E4 Mount Pleasant MI U.S.A.
232 D4 Mount Pleasant PA U.S.A.
231 E5 Mount Pleasant SC U.S.A.
237 E5 Mount Pleasant TX U.S.A.
241 L2 Mount Pleasant UT U.S.A.
234 A2 Mount Pleasant Mills PA U.S.A.
234 C1 Mount Pocono PA U.S.A.
234 B4 Mount Rainier MD U.S.A.
147 D3 Mountrath Rep. of Ireland
81 D4 Mount Richmond Forest Park nature res. South I. N.Z.
214 E3 Mount Rupert S. Africa
234 D2 Mount Salem NJ U.S.A.
84 B3 Mount Sanford N.T. Austr.
150 B4 Mount's Bay England U.K.
147 C4 Mountshannon Rep. of Ireland
238 B3 Mount Shasta CA U.S.A.
81 C5 Mount Somers South I. N.Z.
151 F2 Mountsorrel Leicestershire, England U.K.
236 F4 Mount Sterling IL U.S.A.
232 B5 Mount Sterling KY U.S.A.
232 B5 Mount Sterling OH U.S.A.
214 E5 Mount Stewart S. Africa
232 D5 Mount Storm WV U.S.A.
85 F3 Mount Surprise Qld Austr.
84 C4 Mount Swan N.T. Austr.
147 C3 Mount Talbot Rep. of Ireland
232 E4 Mount Union PA U.S.A.
233 F3 Mount Upton NY U.S.A.
87 C5 Mount Vernon W.A. Austr.
237 F6 Mount Vernon AL U.S.A.
231 D5 Mount Vernon GA U.S.A.
236 F4 Mount Vernon IL U.S.A.
230 C4 Mount Vernon IN U.S.A.
232 A6 Mount Vernon KY U.S.A.
237 E4 Mount Vernon MO U.S.A.
235 E2 Mount Vernon NY U.S.A.
232 B4 Mount Vernon OH U.S.A.
237 E5 Mount Vernon TX U.S.A.
238 B1 Mount Vernon WA U.S.A.
234 B2 Mountville PA U.S.A.
84 C4 Mount Wedge N.T. Austr.
82 B3 Mount Wedge S.A. Austr.
82 C1 Mount Willoughby S.A. Austr.
234 B2 Mount Wolf PA U.S.A.
234 B4 Mount Zion MD U.S.A.
85 G5 Moura Qld Austr.
252 B1 Moura r. Brazil
184 C2 Moura Port.
184 C2 Mourão Port.
202 D5 Mourdi, Dépression du depr. Chad
206 D3 Mourdiah Mali
182 B3 Moure Port.
163 B5 Mourenx France
161 C5 Mouriès France
182 B4 Mourisca do Vouga Port.
182 B5 Mouriscas Port.
156 E3 Mourmelon-le-Grand France
148 B3 Mourne r. Northern Ireland U.K.
147 E2 Mourne Mountains hills Northern Ireland U.K.
161 E5 Mourre de Chanier mt. France
161 D5 Mourre Nègre mt. France
146 □G1 Mousa i. Scotland U.K.
165 D3 Mouscron Belgium
165 C4 Mouscron dept Belgium
208 C2 Mousgougou Chad
232 B6 Mousie KY U.S.A.
161 C5 Moussac France
161 A5 Moussan France
157 H4 Moussey France
202 C6 Moussoro Chad
163 E5 Moussoulens France
160 B1 Moussy France
158 C3 Moustéru France
163 B4 Moustey France
161 E5 Moustiers-Ste-Marie France
209 B5 Moutamba Congo
160 E2 Mouthe France
160 D2 Mouthier-en-Bresse France
160 E1 Mouthier-Haute-Pierre France
157 F3 Mouthiers-sur-Boëme France
232 C6 Mouth of Wilson VA U.S.A.
163 E6 Mouthoumet France
190 C1 Moutier Switz.
162 E2 Moutier-d'Ahun France
160 C3 Moutiers France
162 A2 Moutiers-les-Mauxfaits France
179 H1 Moutnice Czech Rep.
207 I4 Moutourwa Cameroon
156 B3 Moux France
160 C1 Moux-en-Morvan France
156 C3 Mouy France
205 F4 Mouydir, Monts du plat. Alg.
209 B5 Mouyondzi Congo
198 B2 Mouzaki Greece
202 B6 Mouzarak Chad
159 F5 Mouzay France
157 F3 Mouzon France
157 F4 Mouzon r. France
242 C2 Movas Mex.
197 H3 Movila Miresii Romania
197 G3 Movileni Romania
147 D1 Moville Rep. of Ireland
85 G5 Mowbullan, Mount Qld Austr.
146 F5 Mowtie Aberdeenshire, Scotland U.K.
232 B5 Moxahala OH U.S.A.
246 C1 Moxey Town Andros Bahamas
209 C8 Moxico prov. Angola
147 B2 Moy r. Rep. of Ireland
146 D4 Moy Highland, Scotland U.K.
147 C2 Moy Northern Ireland U.K.
216 □3f Moya Gran Canaria Canary Is
217 □3 Moya Comoros
187 B5 Moya Castilla - La Mancha Spain
Moya Cataluña Spain see Moià
206 B4 Moyamba Sierra Leone
147 A3 Moyard Rep. of Ireland
147 B3 Moycullen Rep. of Ireland
156 D3 Moy-de-l'Aisne France
204 D2 Moyen Atlas mts Morocco
208 C2 Moyen-Chari pref. Chad
Moyen Congo country Africa see Congo
215 F4 Moyeni Lesotho
157 G4 Moyenmoutier France
206 B4 Moyenne-Guinée admin. reg. Guinea
156 B2 Moyenneville France
208 A5 Moyen-Ogooué prov. Gabon
147 E3 Moyer hill Rep. of Ireland
157 G3 Moyeuvre-Grande France
147 E2 Moygashel Northern Ireland U.K.
147 B2 Moylaw Rep. of Ireland
148 B4 Moylett Rep. of Ireland
147 C3 Moylough Rep. of Ireland
147 E3 Moynalty Rep. of Ireland
Moynaq Uzbek. see Muynak
147 D3 Moyne Rep. of Ireland
210 A4 Moyo Uganda
250 B6 Moyobamba Peru
148 C3 Moyola r. Northern Ireland U.K.
211 A6 Moyowosi r. Tanz.
140 K1 Moysalen mt. Norway
202 C6 Moyto Chad
111 B4 Moyu Xinjiang China
147 E3 Moyvalley Rep. of Ireland
148 B3 Moyvore Rep. of Ireland
148 B4 Moyvoughly Rep. of Ireland
121 H3 Moyynkum Kazakh.
121 F3 Moyynkum, Peski des. Kazakh.
121 H3 Moyynty Kazakh.
160 B3 Mozac France
213 G4 Mozambique country Africa
213 H2 Mozambique Channel Africa
265 G6 Mozambique Ridge sea feature Indian Ocean
182 E4 Mozárbez Spain
129 D2 Mozdok Rus. Fed.
122 E2 Mozdūrān Iran
232 B6 Mozelle KY U.S.A.

Mozelos to Naga Hills

338

182 C4 **Mozelos** Port.
137 I3 **Mozh** *r.* Ukr.
138 G4 **Mozha** *r.* Belarus
139 K4 **Mozhaysk** Rus. Fed.
134 K4 **Mozhga** Rus. Fed.
108 A1 **Mozhong** *Qinghai* China
179 F4 **Mozirje** Slovenia
179 F4 **Mozirske Planine** *mts* Slovenia
137 G3 **Mozoliyivka** Ukr.
183 F3 **Mozoncillo** Spain
177 G5 **Mozsgó** Hungary
Mozyr' Belarus *see* **Mazyr**
206 A3 **Mpal** Senegal
211 A6 **Mpanda** Tanz.
215 H2 **Mpemvana** S. Africa
206 D3 **Mpessoba** Mali
215 G5 **Mpetu** S. Africa
210 B4 **Mpigi** Uganda
211 A7 **Mpika** Zambia
208 C3 **Mpoko** *r.* C.A.R.
215 H3 **Mpolweni** S. Africa
209 F7 **Mporokoso** Zambia
215 I3 **Mposa** S. Africa
208 C5 **Mpouya** Congo
211 A7 **Mpulungu** Zambia
215 H3 **Mpumalanga** S. Africa
215 G2 **Mpumalanga** *prov.* S. Africa
211 C6 **Mpwapwa** Tanz.
215 G4 **Mqanduli** S. Africa
Mqinvartsveri *mt.* Georgia/Rus. Fed. *see* **Kazbek**
175 J2 **Mrągowo** Pol.
173 G2 **Mrákov** Czech Rep.
135 L5 **Mrakovo** Rus. Fed.
Mrewa Zimbabwe *see* Murehwa
188 E3 **Mrežnica** *r.* Croatia
188 F3 **Mrkonjić-Grad** Bos.-Herz.
191 J3 **Mrkopalj** Croatia
174 F2 **Mrocza** Pol.
174 F4 **Mroczeń** Pol.
175 I4 **Mroczków** Pol.
175 H2 **Mroczno** Pol.
175 H4 **Mroga** *r.* Pol.
175 J3 **Mrozy** Pol.
137 F2 **Mryn** Ukr.
205 H2 **M'Saken** Tunisia
211 C6 **Msambweni** Kenya
211 C6 **Msata** Tanz.
174 E1 **Mścice** Pol.
176 D1 **Mšeno** Czech Rep.
138 G2 **Mshinskaya** Rus. Fed.
205 G2 **M'Sila** Alg.
139 J3 **Msta** Rus. Fed.
139 H2 **Msta** *r.* Rus. Fed.
Mstislavl' Belarus *see* Mstsislaw
175 H5 **Mstów** Pol.
139 H4 **Mstsislaw** Belarus
215 I2 **Msunduze** *r.* S. Africa
175 I6 **Mszana Dolna** Pol.
175 I4 **Mszczonów** Pol.
211 C7 **Mtama** Tanz.
210 B4 **Mtelo** Kenya
211 B6 **Mtera Reservoir** Tanz.
Mtoko Zimbabwe *see* **Mutoko**
215 H3 **Mtonjaneni** S. Africa
Mtorashanga Zimbabwe *see* Mutorashanga
217 □3b **Mtsamboro** Mayotte
217 □3b **Mtsangamouji** Mayotte
139 K5 **Mtsensk** Rus. Fed.
129 D3 **Mts'khet'a** Georgia
213 G6 **Mtubatuba** S. Africa
215 H3 **Mtunzini** S. Africa
211 D7 **Mtwara** Tanz.
211 C7 **Mtwara** *admin. reg.* Tanz.
96 A2 **Mu** *r.* Myanmar
184 B3 **Mu** *hill* Port.
211 C8 **Muaguide** Moz.
213 G2 **Mualadzi** Moz.
213 H3 **Mualama** Moz.
254 C2 **Muana** Brazil
209 B6 **Muanda** Dem. Rep. Congo
96 D3 **Muang Khammouan** Laos
97 D4 **Muang Không** Laos
96 D4 **Muang Khôngxédôn** Laos
97 B5 **Muang Luang** *r.* Thai.
96 C3 **Muang Pakxan** Laos
96 C3 **Muang Phôn-Hông** Laos
96 D4 **Muang Sam Sip** Thai.
96 C2 **Muang Sing** Laos
Muang Thai *country* Asia *see* Thailand
96 C3 **Muang Xaignabouri** Laos
213 G3 **Muanza** Moz.
94 C2 **Muar** Malaysia
94 C2 **Muar** *r.* Malaysia
94 C3 **Muarabeliti** *Sumatera* Indon.
94 C3 **Muarabungo** *Sumatera* Indon.
94 D4 **Muaradua** *Sumatera* Indon.
94 C3 **Muaraenim** *Sumatera* Indon.
94 C3 **Muaratebo** *Sumatera* Indon.
94 C3 **Muaratembesi** *Sumatera* Indon.
95 F3 **Muarateweh** *Kalimantan Tengah* Indon.
Muara Tuang *Sarawak* Malaysia *see* **Kota Samarahan**
123 F5 **Muari, Ras** *pt* Pak.
116 C3 **Muazzam** *Punjab* India
128 B5 **Mubārak, Jabal** *mt.* Jordan/Saudi Arabia
117 E4 **Mubarakpur** *Uttar Prad.* India
120 F5 **Mubarek** Uzbek.
210 A4 **Mubende** Uganda
207 I4 **Mubi** Nigeria
Muborak Uzbek. *see* **Mubarek**
209 B6 **Mucaba** Angola
251 F4 **Mucajaí** *r.* Brazil
251 F4 **Mucajaí, Serra do** *mts* Brazil
225 H1 **Mucalic** *r. Que.* Can.
213 F2 **Mucanha** *r.* Moz.
196 E4 **Mučanj** *mt.* Yugo.
86 D4 **Muccan** *W.A.* Austr.
193 F1 **Muccia** Italy
169 C5 **Much** Ger.
175 H6 **Mucharz** Pol.
87 B6 **Muchea** *W.A.* Austr.
171 C4 **Mücheln (Geiseltal)** Ger.
Mucheng *Henan* China *see* Wuzhi
211 A8 **Muchinga Escarpment** Zambia
253 E4 **Muchiri** Bol.
135 H6 **Muchkapskiy** Rus. Fed.
170 C2 **Muchow** Ger.
175 I6 **Muchówka** Pol.
108 B2 **Muchuan** *Sichuan* China
150 E2 **Much Wenlock** *Shropshire, England* U.K.
183 F3 **Mucientes** Spain
146 B5 **Muck** *i. Scotland* U.K.
171 F4 **Mücka** Ger.
85 G5 **Muckadilla** *Qld* Austr.
169 E5 **Mücke Große-Eichen** Ger.
169 E5 **Mücke-Nieder-Ohmen** Ger.
147 C1 **Muckish Mountain** *hill* Rep. of Ireland
146 □G1 **Muckle Roe** *i. Scotland* U.K.
250 D3 **Muco** *r.* Col.
211 D8 **Mucojo** Moz.
209 D7 **Muconda** Angola
195 F3 **Mucone** *r.* Italy
209 B9 **Mucope** Angola
177 H5 **Mucsi-hegy** *hill* Hungary
177 J3 **Múcsony** Hungary
213 H3 **Mucubela** Moz.
251 F5 **Mucucuaú** *r.* Brazil
251 E6 **Mucuim** *r.* Brazil
213 F3 **Mucumbura** Moz.
126 D3 **Mucur** Turkey
257 H3 **Mucuri** Brazil
257 H3 **Mucuri** *r.* Brazil
257 G3 **Mucurici** Brazil
216 □3b **Muda** *hill Fuerteventura* Canary Is
94 C1 **Muda** *r.* Malaysia
114 B3 **Mudabidri** *Karnataka* India
100 D3 **Mudanjiang** *Heilong.* China
100 D3 **Mudan Jiang** *r.* China
199 F1 **Mudanya** Turkey
172 D2 **Mudau** Ger.
128 C4 **Mudaysīsāt, Jabal al** *hill* Jordan
114 C2 **Muddebihal** *Karnataka* India
241 J3 **Muddy** *r. NV* U.S.A.
237 E5 **Muddy Boggy Creek** *r. OK* U.S.A.
234 B3 **Muddy Creek** *r. PA* U.S.A.
241 L2 **Muddy Creek** *r. UT* U.S.A.
241 J3 **Muddy Peak** *NV* U.S.A.
215 H3 **Muden** S. Africa
168 F3 **Müden (Aller)** Ger.
168 F3 **Müden (Örtze)** Ger.
169 C5 **Mudersbach** Ger.
114 C3 **Mudgal** *Karnataka* India
83 G3 **Mudgee** *N.S.W.* Austr.
114 B2 **Mudhol** *Karnataka* India
114 B3 **Mudigere** *Karnataka* India
223 J3 **Mudjatik** *r. Sask.* Can.
114 C2 **Mudkhed** *Mahar.* India
116 C3 **Mudki** *Punjab* India
96 B3 **Mudon** Myanmar
Mudraya *country* Africa *see* **Egypt**
210 E3 **Mudug** *admin. reg.* Somalia
199 G1 **Mudurnu** Turkey
199 G1 **Mudurnu** *r.* Turkey
134 G3 **Mud'yuga** Rus. Fed.
213 H2 **Muecate** Moz.
211 C7 **Mueda** Moz.
186 B3 **Muel** Spain
186 C4 **Muela de Arés** *mt.* Spain
183 G2 **Muela de Quintanilla** *hill* Spain
182 E3 **Muelas del Pan** Spain
86 E3 **Mueller Range** *hills W.A.* Austr.
245 G5 **Muerto, Mar** *lag.* Mex.
246 B1 **Muertos Cays** *is* Bahamas
147 D1 **Muff** Rep. of Ireland
203 G4 **Muftah** *well* Sudan
209 F8 **Mufulira** Zambia
209 E8 **Mufumbwe** Zambia
109 E2 **Mufu Shan** *mts* China
186 G2 **Muga** *r.* Spain
182 D3 **Muga de Sayago** Spain
129 F3 **Muğan** Azer.
129 F4 **Muğan Düzü** *lowland* Azer.
182 B1 **Mugardos** Spain
184 B1 **Muge** Port.
184 B1 **Muge** *r.* Port.
171 E4 **Mügeln** Ger.
171 E4 **Mügeln** Ger.
172 C3 **Muggensturm** Ger.
191 I3 **Muggia** Italy
Mughalbhin Pak. *see* **Jati**
117 E4 **Mughal Sarai** *Uttar Prad.* India
122 C3 **Mūghār** Iran
123 G2 **Mughsu** *r.* Tajik.
Mugia Spain *see* **Muxía**
209 F6 **Mugila, Monts** *mts* Dem. Rep. Congo
199 F3 **Muğla** Turkey
199 F3 **Muğla** *prov.* Turkey
120 D3 **Mugodzhary, Gory** *mts* Kazakh.
106 B5 **Mug Qu** *r. Qinghai* China
163 B5 **Mugron** France
211 C8 **Muguia** Moz.
116 E3 **Mugu Karnali** *r.* Nepal
211 B5 **Mugumu** Tanz.
106 A1 **Mugur-Aksy** Rus. Fed.
111 F5 **Mugxung** *Qinghai* China
Muhala *Xinjiang* China *see* Yutian
117 E4 **Muhammadabad** *Uttar Prad.* India
Muhammarah Iran *see* Khorramshahr
124 D3 **Muḩayriqah** Saudi Arabia
211 C6 **Muheza** Tanz.
172 C3 **Mühlacker** Ger.
171 D4 **Mühlanger** Ger.
170 E2 **Mühlbach** *r.* Ger.
171 E4 **Mühlberg** Ger.
169 F5 **Mühlberg** Ger.
173 G3 **Mühldorf am Inn** Ger.
179 F3 **Mühlen** Austria
170 D1 **Mühlen** *hill* Ger.
170 E3 **Mühlenbeck** Ger.
170 C2 **Mühlen-Eichsen** Ger.
172 C2 **Mühlhausen** Ger.
173 F2 **Mühlhausen** Ger.
169 F4 **Mühlhausen (Thüringen)** Ger.
169 D5 **Mühlheim am Main** Ger.
172 C3 **Mühlheim an der Donau** Ger.
263 A2 **Mühlig-Hofmann Mountains** Antarctica
172 D4 **Mühlingen** Ger.
171 C5 **Mühltroff** Ger.
140 N2 **Muhos** Fin.
128 C2 **Muḩradah** Syria
173 E2 **Muhr am See** Ger.
138 D2 **Muhu** *i.* Estonia
213 H2 **Muhula** Moz.
210 B3 **Mui** Eth.
164 E2 **Muiden** Neth.
156 B3 **Muids** France
209 D8 **Muié** Angola
Muineachán Rep. of Ireland *see* **Monaghan**
147 E4 **Muine Bheag** Rep. of Ireland
182 C3 **Muiños** Spain
226 E4 **Muir** *MI* U.S.A.
234 B2 **Muir** *PA* U.S.A.
146 F5 **Muirdrum** *Angus, Scotland* U.K.
146 E5 **Muirhead** *Angus, Scotland* U.K.
146 D6 **Muirkirk** *East Ayrshire, Scotland* U.K.
146 B3 **Muirneag** *hill Scotland* U.K.
146 F4 **Muir of Fowlis** *Aberdeenshire, Scotland* U.K.
146 D4 **Muir of Ord** *Highland, Scotland* U.K.
250 B4 **Muisne** Ecuador
213 H2 **Muite** Moz.
156 D3 **Muizon** France
95 F2 **Mujong** *r. Sarawak* Malaysia
101 C5 **Muju** S. Korea
Mukačevo Ukr. *see* **Mukacheve**
136 B3 **Mukacheve** Ukr.
Mukachevo Ukr. *see* Mukacheve
95 F2 **Mukah** *r. Sarawak* Malaysia
Mukalla Yemen *see* **Al Mukallā**
116 C4 **Mukandgarh** *Rajasthan* India
116 D4 **Mukandwara** *Rajasthan* India
102 J2 **Mu-kawa** *r.* Japan
96 D3 **Mukdahan** Thai.
Mukden *Liaoning* China *see* Shenyang
116 C3 **Mukerian** *Punjab* India
224 C2 **Muketei** *r. Ont.* Can.
175 M3 **Mukhavyets** *r.* Belarus
100 F2 **Mukhen** Rus. Fed.
107 F1 **Mukhorshibir'** Rus. Fed.
Mukhtuya Rus. Fed. *see* **Lensk**
87 C6 **Mukinbudin** *W.A.* Austr.
104 B4 **Mukō** Japan
94 C3 **Mukomuko** *Sumatera* Indon.
210 B4 **Mukono** Uganda
123 F2 **Mukry** Turkm.
Muksu *r.* Tajik. *see* **Mughsu**
116 B3 **Muktsar** *Punjab* India
209 F8 **Mukuku** Zambia
120 C3 **Mukur** *Atyrauskaya Oblast'* Kazakh.
121 J2 **Mukur** *Vostochnyy Kazakhstan* Kazakh.
223 L4 **Mukutawa** *r. Man.* Can.
226 C4 **Mukwonago** *WI* U.S.A.
116 D5 **Mul** *Mahar.* India
114 B2 **Mula** *r.* India
123 F4 **Mula** *r.* Pak.
187 B6 **Mula** Spain
185 I2 **Mula** *r.* Spain
113 D11 **Mulakatholhu Atoll** Maldives
Mulaku *atoll* Maldives *see* Mulakatholhu Atoll
100 D3 **Mulan** *Heilong.* China
92 B3 **Mulanay** Phil.
211 B8 **Mulanje** Malawi
213 G2 **Mulanje, Mount** Malawi
82 D2 **Mulapula, Lake** *salt flat S.A.* Austr.
190 E4 **Mulazzo** Italy
114 C3 **Mulbagal** *Karnataka* India
151 I2 **Mulbarton** *Norfolk, England* U.K.
116 D2 **Mulbekh** Jammu and Kashmir
146 E4 **Mulben** *Moray, Scotland* U.K.
237 E5 **Mulberry** *AR* U.S.A.
220 C3 **Mulchatna** *r. AK* U.S.A.
260 A5 **Mulchén** Chile
171 E5 **Mulda** Ger.
171 D4 **Mulde** *r.* Ger.
171 D4 **Muldenstein** Ger.
211 A5 **Muleba** Tanz.
238 F3 **Mule Creek** *WY* U.S.A.
242 B3 **Mulegé** Mex.
237 C5 **Muleshoe** *TX* U.S.A.
213 H3 **Mulevala** Moz.
172 D2 **Mulfingen** Ger.
86 C4 **Mulga Downs** *W.A.* Austr.
84 B5 **Mulga Park** *N.T.* Austr.
82 C2 **Mulgathing** *S.A.* Austr.
185 G3 **Mulhacén** *mt.* Spain
Mülhausen France *see* Mulhouse
169 B4 **Mülheim an der Ruhr** Ger.
169 C5 **Mülheim-Kärlich** Ger.
157 H5 **Mulhouse** France
108 B3 **Muli** *Sichuan* China
113 □2 **Mulikadu** *i. Addu Atoll* Maldives
100 D3 **Muling** *Heilong.* China
100 D3 **Muling** *Heilong.* China
100 E3 **Muling** *r.* China
146 C5 **Mull** *i. Scotland* U.K.
146 B5 **Mull, Sound of** *sea chan. Scotland* U.K.
122 B2 **Mulla Ali** Iran
148 C4 **Mullagh** *Cavan* Rep. of Ireland
147 B4 **Mullagh** *Clare* Rep. of Ireland
147 B3 **Mullagh** *Mayo* Rep. of Ireland
147 E3 **Mullagh** *Meath* Rep. of Ireland
147 B4 **Mullaghareirk** *hill* Rep. of Ireland
147 B4 **Mullaghareirk Mountains** *hills* Rep. of Ireland
147 D2 **Mullaghcarn** *hill Northern Ireland* U.K.
147 E3 **Mullaghcleevaun** *hill* Rep. of Ireland
147 D2 **Mullaghcloga** *hill Northern Ireland* U.K.
147 C2 **Mullaghmore** Rep. of Ireland
114 D4 **Mullaittivu** Sri Lanka
83 G2 **Mullaley** *N.S.W.* Austr.
147 E2 **Mullan** Rep. of Ireland
147 D2 **Mullan** *Northern Ireland* U.K.
146 C4 **Mullardoch, Loch** *l. Scotland* U.K.
147 F2 **Mullartown** *Northern Ireland* U.K.
236 C3 **Mullen** *NE* U.S.A.
83 F2 **Mullengudgery** *N.S.W.* Austr.
232 C6 **Mullens** *WV* U.S.A.
95 F2 **Muller, Pegunungan** *mts* Indon.
87 B6 **Mullewa** *W.A.* Austr.
172 B4 **Müllheim** Ger.
234 D3 **Mullica** *r. NJ* U.S.A.
234 C3 **Mullica Hill** *NJ* U.S.A.
147 D4 **Mullinavat** Rep. of Ireland
147 D3 **Mullingar** Rep. of Ireland
231 E5 **Mullins** *SC* U.S.A.
150 B4 **Mullion** *Cornwall, England* U.K.
83 G3 **Mullion Creek** *N.S.W.* Austr.
145 E4 **Mull of Galloway** *c. Scotland* U.K.
146 C6 **Mull of Kintyre** *hd Scotland* U.K.
146 B6 **Mull of Oa** *hd Scotland* U.K.
135 J5 **Mullovka** Rus. Fed.
171 F3 **Müllrose** Ger.
143 E3 **Mullsjö** Sweden
209 E9 **Mulobezi** Zambia
209 D9 **Mulonga Plain** Zambia
209 E6 **Mulongo** Dem. Rep. Congo
147 B3 **Mulrany** Rep. of Ireland
159 G4 **Mulsanne** France
116 D5 **Multai** *Madh. Prad.* India
123 G4 **Multan** Pak.
140 N3 **Multia** Fin.
95 F1 **Mulu, Gunung** *mt. Sarawak* Malaysia
114 C2 **Mulug** *Andhra Prad.* India
209 E7 **Mulumbe, Monts** *mts* Dem. Rep. Congo
122 E5 **Mūmān** Iran
114 B2 **Mumbai** *Mahar.* India
83 G3 **Mumbil** *N.S.W.* Austr.
209 B7 **Mumbondo** Angola
209 E8 **Mumbwa** Zambia
Muminabad Tajik. *see* Leningrad
Mŭ'minobod Tajik. *see* Leningrad
190 C1 **Mümliswil** Switz.
120 A3 **Mumra** Rus. Fed.
96 D4 **Mun, Mae Nam** *r.* Thai.
243 H4 **Muna** Mex.
131 N3 **Muna** *r.* Rus. Fed.
123 G5 **Munabao** Pak.
114 C2 **Munagala** *Andhra Prad.* India
103 E7 **Munakata** Japan
183 E4 **Muñana** Spain
120 C3 **Munayly** Kazakh.
120 C4 **Munayshy** Kazakh.
171 C5 **Münchberg** Ger.
171 F3 **Müncheberg** Ger.
173 F3 **München** Ger.
München *airport* Ger. *see* Franz Josef Strauss
171 C5 **Münchenbernsdorf** Ger.
190 C1 **Münchenbuchsee** Switz.
München-Gladbach Ger. *see* Mönchengladbach
169 D5 **Münchhausen** Ger.
222 E3 **Muncho Lake** *B.C.* Can.
101 C5 **Munch'ŏn** N. Korea
173 F3 **Münchsmünster** Ger.
173 E2 **Münchsteinach** Ger.
172 B2 **Münchweiler an der Rodalb** Ger.
190 E1 **Münchwilen** Switz.
230 C3 **Muncie** *IN* U.S.A.
84 D5 **Muncoonie West, Lake** *salt flat Qld* Austr.
227 I5 **Muncy** *PA* U.S.A.
234 B1 **Muncy Creek** *r. PA* U.S.A.
234 B1 **Muncy Valley** *PA* U.S.A.
183 H1 **Mundaka** Spain
207 H5 **Mundemba** Cameroon
178 E2 **Munderfing** Austria
172 D3 **Munderkingen** Ger.
151 I2 **Mundesley** *Norfolk, England* U.K.
151 H2 **Mundford** *Norfolk, England* U.K.
87 D4 **Mundiwindi** *W.A.* Austr.
85 E3 **Mundjura Creek** *r. Qld* Austr.
185 I2 **Mundo** *r.* Spain
157 H4 **Mundolshiem** France
254 E4 **Mundo Novo** Brazil
116 B5 **Mundra** *Gujarat* India
87 E6 **Mundrabilla** *W.A.* Austr.
241 L4 **Munds Park** *AZ* U.S.A.
85 G5 **Mundubbera** *Qld* Austr.
116 C4 **Mundwa** *Rajasthan* India
183 I3 **Munebrega** Spain
185 H1 **Munera** Spain
114 D2 **Muneru** *r.* India
230 C4 **Munfordville** *KY* U.S.A.
85 F5 **Mungallala** *Qld* Austr.
83 F2 **Mungallala Creek** *r. Qld* Austr.
85 F3 **Mungana** *Qld* Austr.
116 D4 **Mungaoli** *Madh. Prad.* India
213 G3 **Mungári** Moz.
116 E5 **Mungeli** *Madh. Prad.* India
117 F4 **Munger** *Bihar* India
227 F4 **Munger** *MI* U.S.A.
82 D2 **Mungeranie** *S.A.* Austr.
Mu Nggava *i.* Solomon Is *see* Rennell
183 H1 **Mungia** Spain
Mu Ngiki *i.* Solomon Is *see* Bellona
83 G2 **Mungindi** *N.S.W.* Austr.
117 G5 **Mungla** Bangl.
209 C7 **Mungo** Angola
147 C4 **Mungret** Rep. of Ireland
211 A7 **Mungwi** Zambia
101 C5 **Mun'gyŏng** S. Korea
209 B8 **Munhino** Angola
256 D5 **Munhoz** Brazil
Munich Ger. *see* **München**
183 E4 **Muñico** Spain
186 C3 **Muniesa** Spain
183 H2 **Munilla** Spain
226 D2 **Munising** *MI* U.S.A.
257 G4 **Muniz Freire** Brazil
Munkács Ukr. *see* **Mukacheve**
142 D2 **Munkedal** Sweden
140 K3 **Munkflohögen** Sweden
142 E2 **Munkfors** Sweden
106 D1 **Munku-Sardyk, Gora** *mt.* Mongolia/Rus. Fed.
165 C4 **Munkzwalm** Belgium
146 D4 **Munlochy** *Highland, Scotland* U.K.
169 F5 **Münnerstadt** Ger.
173 E3 **Munningen** Ger.
183 F4 **Muñogalindo** Spain
83 G5 **Munro, Mount** *Tas.* Austr.
117 G5 **Munshiganj** Bangl.
173 F4 **Münsing** Ger.
172 D3 **Münsingen** Ger.
190 C2 **Münsingen** Switz.
178 C3 **Münster** Austria
157 H4 **Munster** France
172 C2 **Münster** Ger.
168 F3 **Münster** Ger.
169 C4 **Münster** Ger.
169 C4 **Münster** *admin. reg. Nordrhein-Westfalen* Ger.
147 C4 **Munster** *reg.* Rep. of Ireland
190 D2 **Münster** Switz.
168 E2 **Münsterdorf** Ger.
173 E3 **Münsterhausen** Ger.
169 C5 **Münstermaifeld** Ger.
169 C3 **Münster-Osnabrück** *airport* Ger.
87 C6 **Muntadgin** *W.A.* Austr.
178 D3 **Muntanitz** *mt.* Austria
197 F2 **Muntele Mare, Vârful** *mt.* Romania
164 F1 **Muntendam** Neth.
197 H3 **Munteni** Romania
Munyal-Par *sea feature* India *see* **Bassas de Pedro Padua Bank**
213 F3 **Munyati** *r.* Zimbabwe
215 G4 **Munyu** S. Africa
169 D5 **Münzenberg** Ger.
179 E2 **Münzkirchen** Austria
140 M2 **Muodoslompolo** Sweden
140 M2 **Muonio** Fin.
140 M2 **Muonioälven** *r.* Fin./Sweden
140 M2 **Muonionalusta** Sweden
Muonionjoki *r.* Fin./Sweden *see* Muonioälven
190 D2 **Muotathal** Switz.
209 B9 **Mupa** Angola
213 F3 **Mupfure** *r.* Zimbabwe
107 I4 **Muping** *Shandong* China
124 D5 **Muqaybirah** Yemen
210 E4 **Muqdisho** Somalia
125 F4 **Muqshin, Wādī** *r.* Oman
129 F3 **Müqtādır** Azer.
257 G4 **Muqui** Brazil
Muqyr *Atyrauskaya Oblast'* Kazakh. *see* **Mukur**
179 H4 **Mur** *r.* Austria *alt.* **Mura (Croatia/Slovenia)**
179 H4 **Mura** *r.* Croatia/Slovenia *alt.* **Mur (Austria)**
173 G2 **Murach** *r.* Ger.
182 C5 **Muradal, Serra do** *mts* Port.
199 E2 **Muradiye** *Manisa* Turkey
127 F3 **Muradiye** *Van* Turkey
136 E3 **Murafa** *r.* Ukr.
102 I4 **Murakami** Japan
176 F5 **Murakeresztúr** Hungary
259 B8 **Murallón, Cerro** *mt.* Chile
211 A5 **Muramvya** Burundi
177 J3 **Muráň** Slovakia
177 J3 **Muráň** *r.* Slovakia
210 C5 **Muranga** Kenya
191 H3 **Murano** Italy
182 C1 **Muras** Spain
134 J4 **Murashi** Rus. Fed.
161 A5 **Murasson** France
176 F5 **Muraszemenye** Hungary
161 A3 **Murat** France
129 B4 **Murat** *r.* Turkey
127 E3 **Murat** *r.* Turkey
129 B4 **Muratgören** Turkey
199 E1 **Muratlı** Turkey
192 B2 **Murato** *Corse* France
161 A5 **Murat-sur-Vèbre** France
179 F3 **Murau** Austria
175 M3 **Murava** Belarus
192 B5 **Muravera** *Sardegna* Italy
102 J4 **Murayama** Japan
124 C2 **Murayr, Jabal** *hill* Saudi Arabia
190 D4 **Murazzano** Italy
157 H5 **Murbach** France
182 C3 **Murça** Port.
183 I2 **Murchante** Spain
170 E2 **Murchin** Ger.
83 F4 **Murchison** *Vic.* Austr.
87 B5 **Murchison** *watercourse W.A.* Austr.
81 D4 **Murchison** *South I.* N.Z.
263 L2 **Murchison, Mount** Antarctica
87 C5 **Murchison, Mount** *hill W.A.* Austr.
81 C5 **Murchison, Mount** *South I.* N.Z.
210 A4 **Murchison Falls National Park** Uganda
84 C4 **Murchison Range** *hills N.T.* Austr.
187 B7 **Murcia** Spain
185 I3 **Murcia** *aut. comm.* Spain
174 F3 **Murczyn** Pol.
161 A4 **Mur-de-Barrez** France
158 D3 **Mûr-de-Bretagne** France
234 C3 **Murderkill** *r. DE* U.S.A.
159 H4 **Mur-de-Sologne** France
236 C3 **Murdo** *SD* U.S.A.
225 H3 **Murdochville** *Que.* Can.
179 G4 **Mureck** Austria
199 E1 **Mürefte** Turkey
213 F3 **Murehwa** Zimbabwe
184 C2 **Mures** *r.* Port.
196 E2 **Mureş** *r.* Romania
163 D5 **Muret** France
Murewa Zimbabwe *see* Murehwa
140 K2 **Murfjället** *mt.* Norway
237 E5 **Murfreesboro** *AR* U.S.A.
231 E4 **Murfreesboro** *NC* U.S.A.
231 C5 **Murfreesboro** *TN* U.S.A.
172 C4 **Murg** Ger.
172 C3 **Murg** *r.* Ger.
123 H2 **Murgab** *r.* Tajik.
123 E2 **Murgap** Turkm.
123 E2 **Murgap** *r.* Turkm.
84 C1 **Murgenella Creek** *r. N.T.* Austr.
197 I2 **Murgeni** Romania
190 C1 **Murgenthal** Switz.
195 G2 **Murge Tarantine** *hills* Italy
123 E3 **Murghab** *r.* Afgh.
Murghob Turkm. *see* **Murgap**
Murghob *r.* Turkm. *see* **Murgap**
129 D3 **Murghuz Lerr** *mt.* Armenia
193 I4 **Murgia Sant'Elia** *hill* Italy
85 G5 **Murgon** *Qld* Austr.
87 C5 **Murgoo** *W.A.* Austr.
183 H2 **Murguía** Spain
129 B3 **Murgul** Turkey
106 C4 **Muri** *Qinghai* China
117 F5 **Muri** *Bihar* India
122 D2 **Mūrī** Iran
190 D1 **Muri** *Aargau* Switz.
190 C2 **Muri** *Bern* Switz.
95 E4 **Muria, Gunung** *mt.* Indon.
257 F4 **Muriaé** Brazil
182 D2 **Murias de Paredes** Spain
183 G1 **Muriedas** Spain
209 D7 **Muriege** Angola
102 K2 **Murii-dake** *mt.* Japan
226 C1 **Murillo** *Ont.* Can.
183 I2 **Murillo el Fruto** Spain
190 D3 **Murisengo** Italy
170 D2 **Müritz** *l.* Ger.
80 F3 **Muriwai** *North I.* N.Z.
140 M2 **Murjek** Sweden
148 B3 **Murley** *Northern Ireland* U.K.
192 D1 **Murlo** Italy
140 P1 **Murmansk** Rus. Fed.
140 P1 **Murmanskaya Oblast'** *admin. div.* Rus. Fed.
134 F1 **Murmanskiy Bereg** *coastal area* Rus. Fed.
Murmansk Oblast *admin. div.* Rus. Fed. *see* Murmanskaya Oblast'
140 P1 **Murmashi** Rus. Fed.
139 M4 **Murmino** Rus. Fed.
173 G4 **Murn** *r.* Ger.
173 F4 **Murnau am Staffelsee** Ger.
147 E4 **Murntown** Rep. of Ireland
182 B3 **Muro** Port.
187 G5 **Muro** Spain
187 G5 **Muro** *r.* Spain
187 C6 **Muro de Alcoy** Spain
160 A3 **Murol** France
195 H2 **Muro Leccese** Italy
193 H4 **Muro Lucano** Italy
134 H5 **Murom** Rus. Fed.
104 D2 **Muromagi-gawa** *r.* Japan
162 B2 **Muron** France
177 K5 **Murony** Hungary
102 J2 **Muroran** Japan
192 A4 **Muros** *Sardegna* Italy
182 D1 **Muros** *Asturias* Spain
182 A2 **Muros** *Galicia* Spain
103 G7 **Muroto** Japan
175 M5 **Murovane** Ukr.
136 D3 **Murovani Kurylivtsi** Ukr.
129 E3 **Murovdağ Silsiläsi** *hills* Azer.
174 F5 **Murów** Pol.
174 F3 **Murowana-Goślina** Pol.
238 C3 **Murphy** *ID* U.S.A.
231 D5 **Murphy** *NC* U.S.A.
240 G2 **Murphys** *CA* U.S.A.
83 F2 **Murra Murra** *Qld* Austr.
203 G2 **Murrat el Kubra, Buheirat** *l.* Egypt
128 A4 **Murrat el Sughra, Buheirat** *l.* Egypt
82 D3 **Murray** *r. S.A.* Austr.
87 B7 **Murray** *r. W.A.* Austr.
222 F3 **Murray** *r. B.C.* Can.
237 F4 **Murray** *KY* U.S.A.
91 J8 **Murray, Lake** P.N.G.
222 D2 **Murray, Mount** *Y.T.* Can.
82 D3 **Murray Bridge** *S.A.* Austr.
232 B5 **Murray City** *OH* U.S.A.
84 C4 **Murray Downs** *N.T.* Austr.
225 I4 **Murray Harbour** *P.E.I.* Can.
87 F5 **Murray Range** *hills W.A.* Austr.
214 D4 **Murraysburg** S. Africa
82 E3 **Murrayville** *Vic.* Austr.
123 H3 **Murree** Pak.
172 D3 **Murrhardt** Ger.
240 I5 **Murrieta** *CA* U.S.A.
83 G3 **Murringo** *N.S.W.* Austr.
147 B3 **Murrisk** *reg.* Rep. of Ireland
147 B3 **Murroogh** Rep. of Ireland
83 G3 **Murrumbateman** *N.S.W.* Austr.
83 E3 **Murrumbidgee** *r. N.S.W.* Austr.
213 H2 **Murrupula** Moz.
83 G2 **Murrurundi** *N.S.W.* Austr.
159 F4 **Mûrs-Erigné** France
117 G4 **Murshidabad** *W. Bengal* India
188 F2 **Murska Sobota** Slovenia
179 H4 **Mursko Središće** Croatia
116 D5 **Murtajapur** *Mahar.* India
185 G4 **Murtas** Spain
182 B4 **Murtede** Port.
190 C2 **Murten** Switz.
190 C2 **Murtensee** *l.* Switz.
188 E4 **Murter** Croatia
188 E4 **Murter** *i.* Croatia
83 E4 **Murtoa** *Vic.* Austr.
182 B4 **Murtosa** Port.
252 C2 **Muru** *r.* Brazil
114 B2 **Murud** *Mahar.* India
95 F2 **Murud, Gunung** *mt.* Indon.
183 H1 **Murueta** Spain
95 F3 **Murui** *r.* Indon.
95 F3 **Murung** *r.* Indon.
95 F3 **Murung** *r.* Indon.
120 F4 **Muruntau** Uzbek.
80 F3 **Murupara** *North I.* N.Z.
79 □3 **Mururoa** *atoll Arch. des Tuamotu* Fr. Polynesia
Murviedro Spain *see* **Sagunto**
161 B5 **Murviel-lès-Béziers** France
116 E5 **Murwara** *Madh. Prad.* India
83 H2 **Murwillumbah** *N.S.W.* Austr.
134 J4 **Murygino** Rus. Fed.
179 G3 **Mürz** *r.* Austria
202 B3 **Murzūq** Libya
174 D3 **Murzynowo** Pol.
179 G3 **Mürzzuschlag** Austria
127 F3 **Muş** Turkey
129 B4 **Muş** *prov.* Turkey
138 E3 **Mūša** *r.* Latvia/Lith.
124 A1 **Mûsa, Gebel** *mt.* Egypt
124 C5 **Musa Āli Terara** *vol.* Africa
117 F5 **Musabani** *Bihar* India
128 C1 **Musabeyli** Turkey
123 G4 **Musa Khel Bazar** Pak.
197 F4 **Musala** *mt.* Bulg.
128 B1 **Musalı** Turkey
101 D4 **Musan** N. Korea
125 G2 **Musandam** *admin. reg.* Oman
123 F3 **Musa Qala, Rūd-i** *r.* Afgh.
105 F3 **Musashino** Japan
Musay'īd Qatar *see* Umm Sa'id
124 D5 **Musaymir** Yemen
150 D4 **Musbury** *Devon, England* U.K.
125 G3 **Muscat** Oman
Muscat and Oman *country* Asia *see* **Oman**
236 F3 **Muscatine** *IA* U.S.A.
171 D4 **Muschwitz** Ger.
226 B4 **Muscoda** *WI* U.S.A.
234 C2 **Musconetcong** *r. NJ* U.S.A.
138 E4 **Musė** *r.* Lith.
192 A5 **Musei** *Sardegna* Italy
85 E2 **Musgrave** *Qld* Austr.
81 C5 **Musgrave, Mount** *South I.* N.Z.
225 K3 **Musgrave Harbour** *Nfld.* Can.
82 B1 **Musgrave Ranges** *mts S.A.* Austr.
209 C5 **Mushie** Dem. Rep. Congo
207 F5 **Mushin** Nigeria
137 G3 **Mushuryn Rig** Ukr.
114 C2 **Musi** *r.* India
94 D3 **Musi** *r.* Indon.
196 E5 **Musica** *mt.* Macedonia
241 K4 **Music Mountain** *AZ* U.S.A.
191 H3 **Musile di Piave** Italy
241 L2 **Musinia Peak** *UT* U.S.A.
222 F2 **Muskeg** *r. N.W.T.* Can.
233 H4 **Muskeget Channel** *MA* U.S.A.
226 D4 **Muskegon** *MI* U.S.A.
226 D4 **Muskegon** *r. MI* U.S.A.
226 D4 **Muskegon Heights** *MI* U.S.A.
222 G4 **Muskeg River** *Alta* Can.
232 C5 **Muskingum** *r. OH* U.S.A.
237 E5 **Muskogee** *OK* U.S.A.
227 H3 **Muskoka** *Ont.* Can.
222 F3 **Muskwa** *r. B.C.* Can.
Muslim-Croat Federation *aut. div.* Bos.-Herz. *see* **Federacija Bosna i Hercegovina**
134 K5 **Muslyumovo** Rus. Fed.
211 B5 **Musoma** Tanz.
191 I5 **Musone** *r.* Italy
225 I3 **Musquaro** *Que.* Can.
91 K7 **Mussau Island** P.N.G.
146 E6 **Musselburgh** *East Lothian, Scotland* U.K.
164 G2 **Musselkanaal** Neth.
238 F2 **Musselshell** *r. MT* U.S.A.
209 C7 **Mussende** Angola
209 B6 **Musserra** Angola
162 C3 **Mussidan** France
194 C5 **Mussomeli** *Sicilia* Italy
165 E5 **Musson** Belgium
116 D3 **Mussoorie** *Uttar Prad.* India
209 D8 **Mussuma** Angola
209 D8 **Mussuma** *r.* Angola
156 E5 **Mussy-sur-Seine** France
116 E4 **Mustafabad** *Uttar Prad.* India
199 F1 **Mustafakemalpaşa** Turkey
210 E3 **Mustahīl** Eth.
190 F2 **Müstair** Switz.
110 D2 **Mustau, Gora** *mt. Xinjiang* China
120 C2 **Mustayevo** Rus. Fed.
259 C7 **Musters, Lago** *l.* Arg.
247 □3 **Mustique** *i.* St Vincent
138 F3 **Mustjõgi** *r.* Estonia
138 E2 **Mustla** Estonia
138 F2 **Mustvee** Estonia
83 G3 **Muswellbrook** *N.S.W.* Austr.
175 I2 **Muszaki** Pol.
175 I6 **Muszyna** Pol.
203 F3 **Mut** Egypt
126 D3 **Mut** Turkey
179 G4 **Muta** Slovenia
209 E8 **Mutanda** Zambia
213 G3 **Mutare** Zimbabwe
124 D3 **Mutarjim, Khashm** *hill* Saudi Arabia
179 I2 **Mutěnice** Czech Rep.
146 E5 **Muthill** *Perth and Kinross, Scotland* U.K.
183 I2 **Mutilva Baja** Spain
Mutina Italy *see* **Modena**
93 C5 **Mutis, Gunung** *mt. Timor* Indon.
134 K2 **Mutnyy Materik** Rus. Fed.
213 G3 **Mutoko** Zimbabwe
82 E3 **Mutooroo** *S.A.* Austr.
213 F3 **Mutorashanga** Zimbabwe
193 G3 **Mutria, Monte** *mt.* Italy
217 □3 **Mutsamudu** Comoros
209 E7 **Mutshatsha** Dem. Rep. Congo
102 J3 **Mutsu** Japan
102 J3 **Mutsu-wan** *b.* Japan
85 F4 **Muttaburra** *Qld* Austr.
199 G2 **Muttalip** Turkey
178 B3 **Muttekopf** *mt.* Austria
190 C1 **Muttenz** Switz.
178 C3 **Mutters** Austria
172 C2 **Mutterstadt** Ger.
81 A7 **Muttonbird Islands** *Stewart I.* N.Z.
81 B7 **Muttonbird Islands** *Stewart I.* N.Z.
114 D3 **Muttukuru** *Andhra Prad.* India
114 C4 **Muttupet** *Tamil Nadu* India
213 H2 **Mutuali** Moz.
257 G3 **Mutum** Brazil
250 D6 **Mutum** *r.* Brazil
207 H4 **Mutum Biyu** Nigeria
254 C5 **Mutunópolis** Brazil
114 D4 **Mutur** Sri Lanka
187 C6 **Mutxamel** Spain
137 G2 **Mutyn** Ukr.
157 H4 **Mutzig** France
171 D4 **Mutzschen** Ger.
141 N3 **Muurame** Fin.
141 M3 **Muurla** Fin.
140 N2 **Muurola** Fin.
107 F4 **Mu Us Shamo** *des.* China
209 B7 **Muxaluando** Angola
129 E3 **Muxax** Azer.
Muxi *Sichuan* China *see* Muchuan
182 A1 **Muxía** Spain
209 B7 **Muxima** Angola
134 F3 **Muyezerskiy** Rus. Fed.
211 A5 **Muyinga** Burundi
120 D4 **Muynak** Uzbek.
Muynoq Uzbek. *see* **Muynak**
211 B7 **Muyombe** Zambia
207 H5 **Muyuka** Cameroon
209 E6 **Muyumba** Dem. Rep. Congo
121 G3 **Muyunkum, Peski** *des.* Kazakh.
121 H4 **Muyunkym** Kazakh.
108 D2 **Muyuping** *Hubei* China
123 H3 **Muzaffarabad** Pak.
123 G4 **Muzaffargarh** Pak.
116 D3 **Muzaffarnagar** *Uttar Prad.* India
117 F4 **Muzaffarpur** *Bihar* India
256 D4 **Muzambinho** Brazil
110 C3 **Muzat He** *r.* China
213 F2 **Muze** Moz.
158 D4 **Muzillac** France
250 C3 **Muzo** Col.
243 E3 **Múzquiz** Mex.
111 C5 **Muztag** *mt. Xinjiang* China
111 D4 **Muztag** *mt. Xinjiang* China
110 A4 **Muztagata** *mt. Xinjiang* China
Muztor Kyrg. *see* **Toktogul**
191 I3 **Muzzana del Turgnano** Italy
207 H6 **Mvangan** Cameroon
211 C6 **Mvomero** Tanz.
208 B4 **Mvoung** *r.* Gabon
217 □3a **Mvouni** *Njazidja* Comoros
209 B6 **Mvouti** Congo
213 F3 **Mvuma** Zimbabwe
217 □3 **Mwali** *i.* Comoros
211 C5 **Mwanga** Tanz.
211 B8 **Mwanza** Malawi
211 B5 **Mwanza** Tanz.
211 B5 **Mwanza** *admin. reg.* Tanz.
209 D6 **Mweka** Dem. Rep. Congo
209 F7 **Mwenda** Zambia
209 D6 **Mwene-Ditu** Dem. Rep. Congo
213 F4 **Mwenezi** Zimbabwe
213 F4 **Mwenezi** *r.* Zimbabwe
209 F7 **Mweru, Lake** Dem. Rep. Congo/Zambia
211 C7 **Mweru Plateau** Tanz.
209 E7 **Mwinilunga** Zambia
138 F4 **Myadzyel** Belarus
116 B4 **Myajlar** *Rajasthan* India
136 D2 **M"yakoty** Ukr.
96 A3 **Myanaung** Myanmar
96 A2 **Myanmar** *country* Asia
139 J4 **Myatlevo** Rus. Fed.
131 P3 **Myaundzha** Rus. Fed.
96 A3 **Myaungmya** Myanmar
146 E3 **Mybster** *Highland, Scotland* U.K.
198 C3 **Mycenae** *tourist site* Greece
Myeik Myanmar *see* **Mergui**
232 B5 **Myers** *KY* U.S.A.
234 B2 **Myerstown** *PA* U.S.A.
96 A2 **Myingyan** Myanmar
97 B4 **Myinmoletkat** *mt.* Myanmar
96 A2 **Myinmu** Myanmar
96 B1 **Myitkyina** Myanmar
96 B2 **Myittha** Myanmar
115 G1 **Myittha** *r.* Myanmar
177 G3 **Myjava** Slovakia
176 F3 **Myjava** *r.* Slovakia
137 G3 **Mykhaylivka** *Cherkas'ka Oblast'* Ukr.
137 I3 **Mykhaylivka** *Kharkivs'ka Oblast'* Ukr.
137 H3 **Mykhaylivka** *Poltavs'ka Oblast'* Ukr.
137 H4 **Mykhaylivka** *Zaporiz'ka Oblast'* Ukr.
137 H4 **Mykhaylivka** *Zaporiz'ka Oblast'* Ukr.
137 F2 **Mykhaylo-Kotsyubyns'ke** Ukr.
136 D2 **Mykhaylyuchka** Ukr.
136 B3 **Mykolayiv** *L'vivs'ka Oblast'* Ukr.
175 M5 **Mykolayiv** *L'vivs'ka Oblast'* Ukr.
137 G4 **Mykolayiv** *Mykolayivs'ka Oblast'* Ukr.
137 H4 **Mykolayivka** *Dnipropetrovs'ka Oblast'* Ukr.
137 I3 **Mykolayivka** *Dnipropetrovs'ka Oblast'* Ukr.
137 I3 **Mykolayivka** *Donets'ka Oblast'* Ukr.
137 H4 **Mykolayivka** *Khersons'ka Oblast'* Ukr.
136 F4 **Mykolayivka** *Odes'ka Oblast'* Ukr.
136 F5 **Mykolayivka** *Odes'ka Oblast'* Ukr.
137 I4 **Mykolayivka** *Zaporiz'ka Oblast'* Ukr.
136 E4 **Mykolayivka-Novorosiys'ka** Ukr.
Mykolayiv Oblast *admin. div.* Ukr. *see* **Mykolayivs'ka Oblast'**
137 G4 **Mykolayivs'ka Oblast'** *admin. div.* Ukr.
199 D3 **Mykonos** *Notio Aigaio* Greece
199 D3 **Mykonos** *i.* Greece
136 C3 **Mykulyntsi** Ukr.
134 J2 **Myla** *r.* Rus. Fed.
Mylae *Sicilia* Italy *see* **Milazzo**
Mylasa Turkey *see* **Milas**
171 D5 **Mylau** Ger.
138 F1 **Myllykoski** Fin.
150 B4 **Mylor** *Cornwall, England* U.K.
Mymensing Bangl. *see* Mymensingh
117 G4 **Mymensingh** Bangl.
138 C1 **Mynäjoki** *r.* Fin.
141 M3 **Mynämäki** Fin.
214 D4 **Mynfontein** S. Africa
105 E2 **Myōgi-san** *mt.* Japan
96 A2 **Myohaung** Myanmar
104 A4 **Myōken-yama** *hill* Japan
160 D1 **Myon** France
101 D4 **Myŏnggan** N. Korea
138 F4 **Myory** Belarus
103 J8 **Myozin-sho** *i.* Japan
140 □C3 **Mýrdalsjökull** *ice cap* Iceland
140 □C3 **Mýrdalssandur** *sand area* Iceland
140 K1 **Myre** Norway
140 M2 **Myrheden** Sweden
137 G3 **Myrhorod** Ukr.
198 D2 **Myrina** *Voreio Aigaio* Greece
137 G3 **Myrivs'ke** Ukr.
140 L1 **Myrlandshaugen** Norway
223 I4 **Myrnam** *Alta* Can.
137 I4 **Myrne** *Donets'ka Oblast'* Ukr.
137 G4 **Myrne** *Khersons'ka Oblast'* Ukr.
137 F2 **Myrne** *Kyivs'ka Oblast'* Ukr.
175 M5 **Myrne** *Volyns'ka Oblast'* Ukr.
137 H4 **Myrne** *Zaporiz'ka Oblast'* Ukr.
136 E4 **Myrnopillya** Ukr.
137 G5 **Myrnyy** Ukr.
137 I3 **Myronivka** *Kharkivs'ka Oblast'* Ukr.
136 F3 **Myronivka** *Kyivs'ka Oblast'* Ukr.
136 D2 **Myropil'** Ukr.
137 H2 **Myropillya** Ukr.
141 N3 **Myrskylä** Fin.
231 E5 **Myrtle Beach** *SC* U.S.A.
238 B3 **Myrtle Creek** *OR* U.S.A.
83 F4 **Myrtleford** *Vic.* Austr.
238 A3 **Myrtle Point** *OR* U.S.A.
121 G4 **Myrzakent** Kazakh.
142 D2 **Mysen** Norway
148 C5 **Myshall** Rep. of Ireland
138 E5 **Myshanka** *r.* Belarus
139 L3 **Myshkin** Rus. Fed.
Myshkino Rus. Fed. *see* Myshkin
137 I5 **Myskhako** Rus. Fed.
174 C3 **Myśla** *r.* Pol.
Mys Lazareva Rus. Fed. *see* Lazarev
175 H6 **Myślenice** Pol.
174 C3 **Myślibórz** Pol.
175 H2 **Myślice** Pol.
175 H5 **Mysłowice** Pol.
Myslowitz Pol. *see* **Mysłowice**
96 E4 **My Son** *tourist site* Vietnam
114 C3 **Mysore** *Karnataka* India
Mysore *state* India *see* Karnataka
Mysovsk Rus. Fed. *see* Babushkin
131 T3 **Mys Shmidta** Rus. Fed.
235 G1 **Mystic** *CT* U.S.A.
235 D3 **Mystic Islands** *NJ* U.S.A.
175 H1 **Myszewo** Pol.
175 H5 **Myszków** Pol.
175 J2 **Myszyneic** Pol.
134 H4 **Myt** Rus. Fed.
97 D5 **My Tho** Vietnam
Mytilene *i.* Greece *see* **Lesvos**
199 E2 **Mytilini** *Voreio Aigaio* Greece
199 E3 **Mytilinioi** *Voreio Aigaio* Greece
126 B3 **Mytilini Strait** Greece/Turkey
139 K4 **Mytishchi** Rus. Fed.
177 I3 **Mýtna** Slovakia
176 C2 **Mýto** Czech Rep.
241 L1 **Myton** *UT* U.S.A.
137 G3 **Mytrofanivka** Ukr.
140 □C2 **Mývatn** *l.* Iceland
140 □C2 **Mývatnsöræfi** *lava field* Iceland
136 C2 **Myzove** Ukr.
205 F2 **M'Zab Valley** *tourist site* Alg.
215 F4 **Mzamomhle** S. Africa
176 B2 **Mže** *r.* Czech Rep.
211 B7 **Mzimba** Malawi
213 F4 **Mzingwani** *r.* Zimbabwe
211 B7 **Mzuzu** Malawi
129 A2 **Mzymta** *r.* Rus. Fed.

N

96 C2 **Na, Nam** *r.* China/Vietnam
173 G2 **Naab** *r.* Ger.
164 D3 **Naaldwijk** Neth.
240 □D9 **Naalehu** *HI* U.S.A.
205 E2 **Naama** Alg.
141 M3 **Naantali** Fin.
164 E2 **Naarden** Neth.
179 F2 **Naarn im Machlande** Austria
147 E3 **Naas** Rep. of Ireland
214 A3 **Nababeep** S. Africa
Nabadwip *W. Bengal* India *see* Navadwip
182 B5 **Nabão** *r.* Port.
115 D2 **Nabarangapur** *Orissa* India
104 C4 **Nabari** Japan
104 C4 **Nabari-gawa** *r.* Japan
92 B4 **Nabas** Phil.
128 B3 **Nabatiyet et Tahta** Lebanon
87 D5 **Nabberu, Lake** *salt flat W.A.* Austr.
173 G2 **Nabburg** Ger.
211 C6 **Naberera** Tanz.
137 J2 **Naberezhnoye** Rus. Fed.
134 K5 **Naberezhnyye Chelny** Rus. Fed.
120 A2 **Naberezhnyy Uvekh** Rus. Fed.
205 H1 **Nabeul** Tunisia
189 C7 **Nabeul** *admin. div.* Tunisia
116 D3 **Nabha** *Punjab* India
129 E3 **Näbiağalı** Azer.
253 F5 **Nabileque** *r.* Brazil
117 F4 **Nabinagar** *Bihar* India
128 B3 **Nāblus** West Bank
206 E4 **Nabolo** Ghana
213 F5 **Naboomspruit** S. Africa
79 □1 **Nabouwalu** *Vanua Levu* Fiji
116 D2 **Nabra** *r.* India
177 L3 **Nábrád** Hungary
Nābulus West Bank *see* **Nāblus**
243 G5 **Nacajuca** Mex.
213 I2 **Nacala** Moz.
242 □I6 **Nacaome** Hond.
213 H2 **Nacaroa** Moz.
176 D2 **Načeradec** Czech Rep.
138 G4 **Nacha** *r.* Belarus
120 B3 **Nachalovo** Rus. Fed.
238 B2 **Naches** *WA* U.S.A.
211 C7 **Nachingwea** Tanz.
116 B4 **Nachna** *Rajasthan* India
176 F1 **Náchod** Czech Rep.
260 A5 **Nacimiento** Chile
185 H3 **Nacimiento** Spain
185 H4 **Nacimiento** *r.* Spain
170 D3 **Nackel** Ger.
172 C2 **Nackenheim** Ger.
237 E6 **Nacogdoches** *TX* U.S.A.
242 C2 **Nacozari de García** Mex.
175 I3 **Nacpolsk** Pol.
Nada *Hainan* China *see* Danzhou
222 C2 **Nadaleen** *r. Y.T.* Can.
176 F5 **Nádasd** Hungary
177 H4 **Nádasdladány** Hungary
116 D4 **Nadbai** *Rajasthan* India
151 F3 **Nadder** *r. England* U.K.
137 G4 **Naddnipryans'ke** Ukr.
Nådendal Fin. *see* **Naantali**
120 E1 **Nadezhdinka** Kazakh.
Nadezhdinskiy Kazakh. *see* Nadezhdinka
79 □1a **Nadi** *Viti Levu* Fiji
116 C5 **Nadiad** *Gujarat* India
196 E2 **Nădlac** Romania
204 E2 **Nador** Morocco
180 E5 **Nador** *prov.* Morocco
197 F3 **Nădrag** Romania
129 D2 **Nadterechnaya** Rus. Fed.
177 K4 **Nádudvar** Hungary
195 □ **Nadur** *Gozo* Malta
122 C3 **Nadūshan** Iran
136 C3 **Nadvirna** Ukr.
Nadvornaya Ukr. *see* **Nadvirna**
130 I3 **Nadym** Rus. Fed.
116 C4 **Naenwa** *Rajasthan* India
142 D4 **Næstved** Denmark
117 H5 **Naf** *r.* Bangl./Myanmar
128 B5 **Nafas, Râs el** *mt.* Egypt
190 E1 **Näfels** Switz.
149 I3 **Nafferton** *East Riding of Yorkshire, England* U.K.
128 B4 **Nafḥa, Har** *hill* Israel
198 B2 **Nafpaktos** Greece
198 C3 **Nafplio** Greece
Naft *r.* Iraq *see* **Āb Naft**
129 E3 **Naftalan** Azer.
124 D3 **Nafūd ad Daḩl** *des.* Saudi Arabia
124 C2 **Nafūd al 'Urayq** *des.* Saudi Arabia
124 D2 **Nafūd as Sirr** *des.* Saudi Arabia
124 C3 **Nafūd as Surrah** *des.* Saudi Arabia
124 D2 **Nafūd Qunayfidhah** *des.* Saudi Arabia
202 A2 **Nafūsah, Jabal** *hills* Libya
124 C2 **Nafy** Saudi Arabia
92 B3 **Naga** Phil.
224 C3 **Nagagami** *r. Ont.* Can.
104 C3 **Nagahama** Japan
117 H4 **Naga Hills** India

Naga Hills to Neftegorsk
339

Naga Hills state India see Nagaland
102 J4 Nagai Japan
105 E3 Nagaizumi Japan
117 H4 Nagaland state India
83 F4 Nagambie Vic. Austr.
105 E2 Nagano Japan
105 D2 Nagano pref. Japan
103 I5 Nagaoka Japan
117 H4 Nagaon Assam India
Nagapatam Tamil Nadu India see Nagappattinam
114 C4 Nagappattinam Tamil Nadu India
117 G4 Nagar r. Bangl./India
116 D2 Nagar Hima. Prad. India
114 B3 Nagar Karnataka India
116 D4 Nagar Rajasthan India
104 C3 Nagara-gawa r. Japan
114 D2 Nagaram Andhra Prad. India
105 F3 Nagareyama Japan
114 C2 Nagar Karnul Andhra Prad. India
242 □16 Nagarote Nic.
111 E6 Nagarzê Xizang China
103 D7 Nagasaki Japan
103 D7 Nagasaki pref. Japan
103 E6 Nagato Japan
116 C4 Nagaur Rajasthan India
115 D2 Nagavali r. India
116 C5 Nagda Madh. Prad. India
173 F2 Nagel Ger.
164 E2 Nagele Neth.
114 C4 Nagercoil Tamil Nadu India
203 G3 Nag' Hammâdi Egypt
116 D3 Nagina Uttar Prad. India
147 C4 Nagles Mountains hills Rep. of Ireland
175 I5 Nagłowice Pol.
116 E4 Nagod Madh. Prad. India
172 C3 Nagold Ger.
172 C3 Nagold r. Ger.
Nagong Chu r. China see Parlung Zangbo
183 I2 Nagore Spain
Nagorno-Karabakh aut. reg. Azer. see Dağlıq Qarabağ
Nagornyy Karabakh aut. reg. Azer. see Dağlıq Qarabağ
134 J4 Nagorsk Rus. Fed.
139 L3 Nagor'ye Rus. Fed.
191 F3 Nago-Torbole Italy
104 C3 Nagoya Japan
116 D5 Nagpur Mahar. India
111 F6 Nagqu Xizang China
111 F6 Nag Qu r. Xizang China
141 M3 Nagu Fin.
247 E3 Nagua Dom. Rep.
247 □1 Naguabo Puerto Rico
129 C1 Nagutskoye Rus. Fed.
176 G5 Nagyatád Hungary
177 G5 Nagybajom Hungary
177 J5 Nagybánhegyes Hungary
177 H5 Nagybaracska Hungary
Nagybecskerek Vojvodina, Srbija Yugo. see Zrenjanin
177 H5 Nagyberény Hungary
177 H5 Nagyberki Hungary
176 F4 Nagycenk Hungary
177 J4 Nagycsécs Hungary
177 K4 Nagycserkesz Hungary
177 L3 Nagydobos Hungary
177 H5 Nagydorog Hungary
177 L4 Nagyecsed Hungary
Nagyenyed Romania see Aiud
177 J4 Nagyfüged Hungary
177 K3 Nagyhalász Hungary
177 H6 Nagyharsány Hungary
177 K4 Nagyhegyes Hungary
177 H4 Nagyigmánd Hungary
177 J4 Nagyiván Hungary
177 K4 Nagykálló Hungary
177 K5 Nagykamarás Hungary
176 F5 Nagykanizsa Hungary
176 F5 Nagykapornak Hungary
177 H5 Nagykarácsony Hungary
177 I4 Nagykáta Hungary
177 K4 Nagykereki Hungary
177 H5 Nagykónyi Hungary
177 I4 Nagykőrös Hungary
177 H4 Nagykovácsi Hungary
177 J5 Nagylak Hungary
177 I3 Nagylóc Hungary
176 F4 Nagylózs Hungary
177 J5 Nagymágocs Hungary
177 H5 Nagymányok Hungary
177 H4 Nagymaros Hungary
177 K3 Nagy-Milic hill Hungary/Slovakia
177 H6 Nagynyárád Hungary
177 I4 Nagyoroszi Hungary
177 K4 Nagyrábé Hungary
176 G5 Nagyrécse Hungary
176 G4 Nagysimonyi Hungary
177 J5 Nagyszénás Hungary
177 G4 Nagyszentjános Hungary
177 H5 Nagyszokoly Hungary
177 I4 Nagytarcsa Hungary
177 J5 Nagytőke Hungary
Nagyvárad Romania see Oradea
177 L3 Nagyvarsány Hungary
177 G5 Nagyvázsony Hungary
177 H5 Nagyvenyim Hungary
102 □2 Naha Japan
116 D3 Nahan Hima. Prad. India
123 E5 Nahang r. Iran/Pak.
222 F2 Nahanni Butte N.W.T. Can.
222 F2 Nahanni Range mts N.W.T. Can.
128 B3 Nahariyya Israel
183 H4 Naharros Spain
122 B3 Nahāvand Iran
168 F2 Nahe Ger.
172 B2 Nahe r. Ger.
205 F4 N'Ahnet, Adrar mts Alg.
159 H4 Nahon r. France
124 B2 Nahr, Jabal hill Saudi Arabia
168 F2 Nahrendorf Ger.
244 D4 Nahuatzen Mex.
231 D6 Nahunta GA U.S.A.
92 B3 Naic Phil.
242 D3 Naica Mex.
117 G4 Naik Murad Bangl.
171 C5 Naila Ger.
163 D5 Nailloux France
150 E3 Nailsea North Somerset, England U.K.
150 E3 Nailsworth Gloucestershire, England U.K.
Naiman Qi Nei Mongol China see Daqin Tal
225 I1 Nain Nfld. Can.
116 E4 Naina Uttar Prad. India
116 D3 Naini Tal Uttar Prad. India
116 E5 Nainpur Madh. Prad. India
159 G5 Naintré France
79 □1 Nairai i. Fiji
146 E4 Nairn Highland, Scotland U.K.
146 E4 Nairn r. Scotland U.K.
227 G2 Nairn Centre Ont. Can.
211 C5 Nairobi Kenya
Naissus Srbija Yugo. see Niš
210 C5 Naivasha Kenya
157 F4 Naives-Rosières France
158 D4 Naizin France
100 C4 Naizishan Jilin China
163 D4 Najac France
122 B3 Najafābād Iran
246 C2 Najasa r. Cuba
124 C2 Najd reg. Saudi Arabia
183 H2 Nájera Spain
183 H2 Najerilla r. Spain
107 I1 Naji Nei Mongol China
116 D3 Najibabad Uttar Prad. India
183 H3 Nájima r. Spain
101 D4 Najin N. Korea
Najitun Nei Mongol China see Naji
125 E2 Najmah Saudi Arabia
124 D4 Najrān Saudi Arabia
124 D4 Najrān prov. Saudi Arabia
113 □1 Nakachchaafushi i. N. Male Maldives
105 G2 Naka-gawa r. Japan
103 G7 Naka-gawa r. Japan
102 □2 Nakagusuku Japan
Nakahchaafushi i. N. Male Maldives see Nakachchaafushi
103 E7 Nakama Japan
206 E4 Nakambé watercourse Burkina/Ghana
alt. Nakanbe,
alt. Volta Blanche,
conv. White Volta
103 F7 Nakamura Japan
Nakanbé watercourse Burkina/Ghana see White Volta
105 E2 Nakano Japan
102 □1 Nakano-shima i. Japan
105 F1 Nakano-take mt. Japan
211 C7 Nakapanya Tanz.
210 B4 Nakasongola Uganda
Nakatchafushi i. N. Male Maldives see Nakachchaafushi
102 K1 Nakatonbetsu-chō hill Japan
103 E7 Nakatsu Japan
104 D3 Nakatsugawa Japan
105 E2 Nakatsu-gawa r. Japan
113 □1 Nakatuku Fushi i. N. Male Maldives
203 H5 Nakfa Eritrea
Nakhichevan' Azer. see Naxçıvan
Nakhichevan' aut. reg. Azer. see Naxçıvan
100 E4 Nakhodka Rus. Fed.
117 H4 Nakhola Assam India
97 C4 Nakhon Nayok Thai.
97 C4 Nakhon Pathom Thai.
96 D3 Nakhon Phanom Thai.
97 C4 Nakhon Ratchasima Thai.
96 C4 Nakhon Sawan Thai.
97 B5 Nakhon Si Thammarat Thai.
Nakhrachi Khanty-Mansiyskiy Avtonomnyy Okrug Rus. Fed. see Kondinskoye
116 B5 Nakhtarana Gujarat India
224 C3 Nakina Ont. Can.
222 C3 Nakina r. B.C. Can.
129 C2 Nakip'u Georgia
174 F1 Nakla Pol.
176 G2 Náklo Czech Rep.
175 H5 Nakło Pol.
179 F4 Naklo Slovenia
174 F2 Nakło nad Notecią Pol.
220 C4 Naknek AK U.S.A.
116 C3 Nakodar Punjab India
175 J1 Nakomiady Pol.
211 B7 Nakonde Zambia
138 D3 Nākotne Latvia
177 J6 Nakovo Vojvodina, Srbija Yugo.
207 E4 Nakpanduri Ghana
142 D4 Nakskov Denmark
140 K3 Näkten l. Sweden
101 D6 Naktong-gang r. S. Korea
210 C5 Nakuru Kenya
222 G5 Nakusp B.C. Can.
123 F5 Nal r. Pak.
107 E2 Nalayh Mongolia
172 A2 Nalbach Ger.
117 G4 Nalbari Assam India
129 C2 Nal'chik Rus. Fed.
183 H2 Nalda Spain
114 C2 Naldurg Mahar. India
175 K4 Nałęczów Pol.
177 J3 Nálepkovo Slovakia
206 E4 Nalerigu Ghana
114 C2 Nalgonda Andhra Prad. India
117 F4 Nalhati W. Bengal India
117 G4 Nalitabari Bangl.
116 D5 Nalkhera Madh. Prad. India
114 C3 Nallamala Hills India
162 A2 Nalliers France
199 G1 Nallıhan Turkey
121 G1 Nalobino Kazakh.
209 D8 Nalolo Zambia
182 D1 Nalón r. Spain
202 A2 Nālūt Libya
176 C2 Nalžovské Hory Czech Rep.
213 G5 Namaacha Moz.
209 B9 Namacunde Angola
213 H3 Namacurra Moz.
215 G2 Namahadi S. Africa
114 C4 Namakkal Tamil Nadu India
122 D4 Namakzar-e Shadad salt flat Iran
121 G4 Namangan Uzbek.
Namangan Oblast admin. div. Uzbek. see Namanganskaya Oblast'
121 G4 Namanganskaya Oblast' admin. div. Uzbek.
Namangan Wiloyati admin. div. Uzbek. see Namanganskaya Oblast'
211 A6 Namanyere Tanz.
213 H2 Namapa Moz.
212 C5 Namaqualand reg. Namibia
214 A3 Namaqualand reg. S. Africa
213 H2 Namarrói Moz.
117 H4 Nambol Manipur India
172 B2 Namborn Ger.
85 H5 Nambour Qld Austr.
Nambouwalu Vanua Levu Fiji see Nabouwalu
183 G5 Nambroca Spain
83 H2 Nambucca Heads N.S.W. Austr.
Namcha Barwa mt. Xizang China see Namjagbarwa Feng
117 F4 Namche Bazar Nepal
101 C5 Namch'ŏn N. Korea
140 K2 Namdalen val. Norway
140 J2 Namdalseid Norway
96 D2 Nam Đinh Vietnam
226 B3 Namekagon r. WI U.S.A.
Namen Belgium see Namur
104 D2 Namerikawa Japan
176 F2 Náměšť nad Oslavou Czech Rep.
177 I2 Námestovo Slovakia
213 H2 Nametil Moz.
101 C5 Nam-gang r. N. Korea
101 C6 Namhae-do i. S. Korea
213 H2 Namialo Moz.
212 B5 Namib Desert Namibia
209 B8 Namibe Angola
209 B8 Namibe prov. Angola
212 B4 Namibia country Africa
264 J8 Namibia Abyssal Plain sea feature N. Atlantic Ocean
213 H3 Namidobe Moz.
214 B3 Namies S. Africa
122 B2 Namīn Iran
211 B8 Namitete Malawi
111 F6 Namjagbarwa Feng mt. Xizang China
Namka Xizang China see Doilungdêqên
96 B2 Namlang r. Myanmar
111 E6 Namling Xizang China
96 C3 Nam Ngum Reservoir Laos
83 G2 Namoi r. N.S.W. Austr.
91 K5 Namonuito atoll Micronesia
222 G3 Nampa Alta Can.
116 E3 Nampa mt. Nepal
238 C3 Nampa ID U.S.A.
206 D3 Nampala Mali
101 C5 Namp'o N. Korea
213 H2 Nampula Moz.
213 H2 Nampula prov. Moz.
96 C3 Nam Pung Reservoir Thai.
117 H4 Namrup Assam India
117 H4 Namsi Arun. Prad. India
140 J2 Namsos Norway
140 K2 Namsskogan Norway
131 N3 Namtsy Rus. Fed.
96 B2 Namtu Myanmar
222 E5 Namu B.C. Can.
Namuka i. Tonga see Nomuka
213 H2 Namuli, Monte mt. Moz.
213 H2 Namuno Moz.
165 D4 Namur Belgium
165 D4 Namur prov. Belgium
209 E8 Namwala Zambia
101 C6 Namwŏn S. Korea
90 D4 Namyit Island S. China Sea
174 F4 Namysłów Pol.
96 C3 Nan Thai.
96 C4 Nan, Mae Nam r. Thai.
208 B3 Nana r. C.A.R.
177 H4 Nána Slovakia
208 C3 Nana Barya r. C.A.R./Chad
208 C3 Nana-Grébizi pref. C.A.R.
222 F5 Nanaimo B.C. Can.
240 □ Nanakuli HI U.S.A.
208 B3 Nana-Mambéré pref. C.A.R.
109 F3 Nan'an Fujian China
85 H5 Nanango Qld Austr.
109 F4 Nan'ao Guangdong China
Nan'ao Jiangxi China see Dayu
104 C1 Nanao Japan
104 C2 Nanatsuka Japan
250 C5 Nanay r. Peru
Nanbai Guizhou China see Zunyi
Nanbin Chongqing China see Shizhu
108 C2 Nanbu Sichuan China
260 B4 Nancagua Chile
159 I4 Nançay France
100 D3 Nancha Heilong. China
109 E2 Nanchang Jiangxi China
109 E2 Nanchang Jiangxi China
Nanchangshan Shandong China see Changdao
109 F3 Nancheng Jiangxi China
245 G4 Nanchital Mex.
108 C2 Nanchong Sichuan China
108 C2 Nanchuan Chongqing China
183 H2 Nanclares de la Oca Spain
222 E4 Nancut B.C. Can.
157 G4 Nancy France
116 E3 Nanda Devi mt. Uttar Prad. India
116 E3 Nanda Kot mt. Uttar Prad. India
108 C3 Nandan Guangxi China
114 C2 Nanded Mahar. India
Nander Mahar. India see Nanded
83 G2 Nandewar Range mts N.S.W. Austr.
116 C5 Nandgaon Mahar. India
114 D2 Nandigama Andhra Prad. India
114 C3 Nandikotkur Andhra Prad. India
108 A4 Nanding He r. Yunnan China
116 C5 Nandod Gujarat India
165 E4 Nandrin Belgium
108 D4 Nandu Jiang r. China
116 D5 Nandura Mahar. India
116 C5 Nandurbar Mahar. India
114 C3 Nandyal Andhra Prad. India
197 H3 Nănești Romania
109 D4 Nanfeng Guangdong China
109 F3 Nanfeng Jiangxi China
111 F6 Nang Xizang China
211 C7 Nangade Moz.
207 I5 Nanga Eboko Cameroon
95 E3 Nangahpinoh Kalimantan Barat Indon.
84 C2 Nangalala N.T. Austr.
116 C2 Nanga Parbat mt. Jammu and Kashmir
123 G3 Nangarhār prov. Afgh.
95 E3 Nangatayap Kalimantan Barat Indon.
156 D4 Nangis France
101 C4 Nangnim N. Korea
101 C4 Nangnim-sanmaek mts N. Korea
107 G4 Nangong Hebei China
108 A1 Nangqên Qinghai China
211 C7 Nangulangwa Tanz.
114 C4 Nanguneri Tamil Nadu India
107 G4 Nanhe Hebei China
110 F4 Nanhu Gansu China
108 B3 Nanhua Yunnan China
109 G2 Nanhui Shanghai China
221 J2 Nanisivik Nunavut Can.
114 C3 Nanjangud Karnataka India
108 B3 Nanjian Yunnan China
108 C1 Nanjiang Sichuan China
Nanjie Guangdong China see Guangning
109 F3 Nanjing Fujian China
109 F1 Nanjing Jiangsu China
108 A4 Nanka Jiang r. Yunnan China
109 E3 Nankang Jiangxi China
Nankang Jiangxi China see Xingzi
Nanking Jiangsu China see Nanjing
103 F7 Nankoku Japan
209 C9 Nankova Angola
108 A4 Nanlan He r. Yunnan China
78 □4b Nanlaud hill Pohnpei Micronesia
107 G4 Nanle Henan China
108 A4 Nanlei He r. Yunnan China
109 F2 Nanling Anhui China
109 D3 Nan Ling mts China
108 D4 Nanliu Jiang r. China
Nanlong Sichuan China see Nanbu
Nanma Shandong China see Yiyuan
Nanmulingzue Xizang China see Namling
87 C5 Nannine W.A. Austr.
108 D4 Nanning Guangxi China
87 B7 Nannup W.A. Austr.
96 C3 Na Noi Thai.
221 N3 Nanortalik Greenland
Nanouki atoll Gilbert Is Kiribati see Nonouti
Nanouti atoll Gilbert Is Kiribati see Nonouti
108 C3 Nanpan Jiang r. China
116 E4 Nanpara Uttar Prad. India
107 H4 Nanpi Hebei China
107 I3 Nanpiao Liaoning China
109 F3 Nanping Fujian China
108 C1 Nanping Sichuan China
Nanpu Fujian China see Pucheng
109 F3 Nanpu Xi r. China
Nanqiao Shanghai China see Fengxian
183 F1 Nansa r. Spain
104 C4 Nansei Japan
102 □1 Nansei-shotō is Japan
268 B1 Nansen Basin sea feature Arctic Ocean
221 N1 Nansen Land reg. Greenland
221 I1 Nansen Sound sea chan. Nunavut Can.
90 E4 Nanshan Island S. China Sea
106 B3 Nanshankou Xinjiang China
Nansha Qundao is S. China Sea see Spratly Islands
211 B5 Nansio Tanz.
161 D5 Nans-les-Pins France
161 B4 Nant France
105 G2 Nantai-san hill Japan
105 F2 Nantai-san mt. Japan
150 D3 Nant Bran r. Wales U.K.
156 C4 Nanterre France
158 E4 Nantes France
162 A1 Nantes Atlantique airport France
156 C3 Nanteuil-le-Haudouin France
162 D2 Nantiat France
224 D5 Nanticoke Ont. Can.
233 F5 Nanticoke MD U.S.A.
234 B1 Nanticoke PA U.S.A.
233 F5 Nanticoke r. MD U.S.A.
104 C4 Nantō Japan
222 H5 Nanton Alta Can.
109 G1 Nantong Jiangsu China
109 G2 Nantong Jiangsu China
109 □ Nantou Guangdong China
109 G4 Nant'ou Taiwan
160 D2 Nantua France
233 H4 Nantucket MA U.S.A.
233 I4 Nantucket Island MA U.S.A.
233 H4 Nantucket Sound g. MA U.S.A.
211 C8 Nantulo Moz.
149 G4 Nantwich Cheshire, England U.K.
150 D3 Nantyglo Blaenau Gwent, Wales U.K.
232 D4 Nanty Glo PA U.S.A.
235 D1 Nanuet NY U.S.A.
Nanumaga i. Tuvalu see Nanumanga
77 H2 Nanumanga i. Tuvalu
77 H2 Nanumea i. Tuvalu
257 G2 Nanuque Brazil
93 C1 Nanusa, Kepulauan is Indon.
87 B4 Nanutarra Roadhouse W.A. Austr.
108 C2 Nanxi Sichuan China
109 E2 Nanxian Hunan China
109 E3 Nanxiong Guangdong China
109 G3 Nanyandang Shan mt. Zhejiang China
109 E1 Nanyang Henan China
102 J4 Nanyō Japan
210 C5 Nanyuki Kenya
107 J3 Nanzamu Liaoning China
109 D2 Nanzhang Hubei China
Nanzhao Fujian China see Zhao'an
109 E1 Nanzhao Henan China
108 C1 Nanzheng Shaanxi China
Nanzhou Hunan China see Nanxian
117 G4 Naogaon Bangl.
123 G5 Naokot Pak.
100 E3 Naoli r. China
122 E3 Naomid, Dasht-e des. Afgh./Iran
116 C2 Naoshera Jammu and Kashmir
198 C1 Naousa Kentriki Makedonia Greece
198 D3 Naousa Notio Aigaio Greece
240 F2 Napa CA U.S.A.
233 □J1 Napadogan N.B. Can.
213 H2 Napaha Moz.
220 C3 Napaimiut AK U.S.A.
210 B4 Napak mt. Uganda
220 G3 Napaktulik Lake Nunavut Can.
224 E4 Napanee Ont. Can.
235 D1 Napanoch NY U.S.A.
116 C4 Napasar Rajasthan India
220 B3 Napaskiak AK U.S.A.
226 C5 Naperville IL U.S.A.
190 C1 Napf mt. Switz.
80 F3 Napier North I. N.Z.
214 B6 Napier S. Africa
86 E2 Napier Broome Bay W.A. Austr.
263 D2 Napier Mountains Antarctica
84 C2 Napier Peninsula N.T. Austr.
86 E3 Napier Range hills W.A. Austr.
233 G2 Napierville Que. Can.
175 I2 Napiwoda Pol.
177 K4 Napkor Hungary
Naples Italy see Napoli
231 D7 Naples FL U.S.A.
233 □H3 Naples ME U.S.A.
232 E3 Naples NY U.S.A.
241 M1 Naples UT U.S.A.
108 C4 Napo Guangxi China
250 B5 Napo prov. Ecuador
250 C5 Napo r. Ecuador
194 B5 Napola Sicilia Italy
236 D2 Napoleon ND U.S.A.
232 A4 Napoleon OH U.S.A.
216 □2b Napoleon's Tomb tourist site St Helena
237 F6 Napoleonville LA U.S.A.
193 G4 Napoli Italy
193 G4 Napoli prov. Campania Italy
193 G4 Napoli, Golfo di b. Italy
261 F6 Naposta r. Arg.
226 E5 Nappanee IN U.S.A.
84 C4 Napperby N.T. Austr.
122 A2 Naqadeh Iran
128 A5 Naqb Malha mt. Egypt
124 D5 Naqūb Yemen
187 C5 Náquera Spain
104 B4 Nara Japan
104 B4 Nara pref. Japan
206 D3 Nara Mali
139 K4 Nara r. Rus. Fed.
138 F4 Narach Belarus
138 F4 Narach r. Belarus
82 E4 Naracoorte S.A. Austr.
83 F3 Naradhan N.S.W. Austr.
176 F4 Nárai Hungary
105 D2 Narai-gawa r. Japan
117 G5 Narail Bangl.
116 C4 Naraina Rajasthan India
107 G1 Naranbulag Dornod Mongolia
106 B1 Naranbulag Uvs Mongolia
250 B5 Naranjal Ecuador
247 □1 Naranjito Puerto Rico
245 F3 Naranjos Mex.
122 B3 Naraq Iran
115 E2 Narasannapeta Andhra Prad. India
114 D2 Narasapur Andhra Prad. India
114 D2 Narasaraopet Andhra Prad. India
105 G3 Narashino Japan
117 F5 Narasinghapur Orissa India
107 G1 Narasun Rus. Fed.
97 C6 Narathiwat Thai.
110 C3 Narat Shan mts China
237 C5 Nara Visa NM U.S.A.
117 G5 Narayanganj Bangl.
116 E5 Narayanganj Madh. Prad. India
114 B2 Narayangaon Mahar. India
114 C2 Narayanpet Andhra Prad. India
175 M6 Narayiv Ukr.
175 M6 Narayivka r. Ukr.
Narbada r. India see Narmada
150 C3 Narberth Pembrokeshire, Wales U.K.
Narbo France see Narbonne
192 A4 Narbolia Sardegna Italy
161 B5 Narbonne France
161 B5 Narbonne-Plage France
151 F2 Narborough Leicestershire, England U.K.
151 H2 Narborough Norfolk, England U.K.
Narborough Island Islas Galápagos Ecuador see Fernandina, Isla
192 A5 Narcao Sardegna Italy
182 D1 Narcea r. Spain
160 B1 Narcy France
122 C2 Nardin Iran
195 H2 Nardò Italy
123 G4 Narechi r. Pak.
114 B3 Naregal Karnataka India
87 C7 Narembeen W.A. Austr.
116 D3 Narendranagar Uttar Prad. India
264 E4 Nares Abyssal Plain sea feature S. Atlantic Ocean
264 E4 Nares Deep sea feature N. Atlantic Ocean
221 K2 Nares Strait Can./Greenland
87 E6 Naretha W.A. Austr.
175 L3 Narew Pol.
175 I3 Narew r. Pol.
175 L3 Narewka Pol.
175 L3 Narewka r. Pol.
123 F4 Nari r. Pak.
214 A4 Nariep S. Africa
129 F4 Närimanabad Azer.
129 F3 Närimankänd Azer.
120 A3 Narimanov Rus. Fed.
121 K2 Narimskiy Khrebet mts Kazakh.
126 E3 Narince Turkey
250 B4 Nariño dept Col.
105 G3 Narita Japan
105 G3 Narita airport Japan
140 M2 Narken Sweden
139 M4 Narma r. Rus. Fed.
116 C5 Narmada r. India
129 B3 Narman Turkey
116 D3 Narnaul Haryana India
193 E2 Narni Italy
Narnia Italy see Narni
194 C5 Naro Sicilia Italy
194 C5 Naro r. Sicilia Italy
134 M2 Narodnaya, Gora mt. Rus. Fed.
136 E2 Narodychi Ukr.
139 K4 Naro-Fominsk Rus. Fed.
211 B5 Narok Kenya
83 G4 Narooma N.S.W. Austr.
135 H5 Narovchat Rus. Fed.
136 E2 Narowlya Belarus
141 M3 Närpes Fin.
83 G2 Narrabri N.S.W. Austr.
233 H4 Narragansett Bay RI U.S.A.
83 F2 Narran r. N.S.W. Austr.
83 F3 Narrandera N.S.W. Austr.
83 F2 Narran Lake N.S.W. Austr.
87 C7 Narrogin W.A. Austr.
83 G3 Narromine N.S.W. Austr.
163 A5 Narrosse France
232 C6 Narrows VA U.S.A.
234 C1 Narrowsburg NY U.S.A.
114 C2 Narsapur Andhra Prad. India
221 N3 Narsaq Greenland
171 D4 Narsdorf Ger.
116 D5 Narsimhapur Madh. Prad. India
117 G5 Narsingdi Bangl.
116 D5 Narsinghgarh Madh. Prad. India
115 D2 Narsipatnam Andhra Prad. India
107 G3 Nart Nei Mongol China
106 E1 Nart Mongolia
179 H5 Narta Croatia
198 A1 Nartë Albania
129 C2 Nartkala Rus. Fed.
161 E5 Nartuby r. France
175 I3 Naruszewo Pol.
104 A4 Naruto Japan
138 G2 Narva Estonia
138 G2 Narva r. Estonia/Rus. Fed.
138 F2 Narva Bay Estonia/Rus. Fed.
92 B2 Narvacan Phil.
138 G2 Narva-Jõesuu Estonia
Narva laht b. Estonia/Rus. Fed. see Narva Bay
Narva Reservoir Estonia/Rus. Fed. see Narvskoye Vodokhranilishche
140 L1 Narvik Norway
Narvskiy Zaliv b. Estonia/Rus. Fed. see Narva Bay
138 G2 Narvskoye Vodokhranilishche resr Estonia/Rus. Fed.
116 D3 Narwana Haryana India
116 D4 Narwar Madh. Prad. India
84 C4 Narwietooma N.T. Austr.
134 K2 Nar'yan-Mar Rus. Fed.
121 H4 Naryn Kyrg.
121 H4 Naryn admin. div. Kyrg.
121 H4 Naryn r. Kyrg./Uzbek.
106 B1 Naryn Rus. Fed.
121 J4 Narynkol Kazakh.
Naryn Oblast admin. div. Kyrg. see Naryn
Narynqol Kazakh. see Narynkol
Narynskaya Oblast' admin. div. Kyrg. see Naryn
139 J5 Naryshkino Rus. Fed.
190 C4 Narzole Italy
140 L3 Näsåker Sweden
197 G2 Năsăud Romania
176 E2 Nasavrky Czech Rep.
161 B4 Nasbinals France
143 G3 Näsby Kalmar Sweden
81 C6 Naseby South I. N.Z.
116 C5 Nashik Mahar. India
226 A4 Nashua IA U.S.A.
233 H3 Nashua NH U.S.A.
237 E5 Nashville AR U.S.A.
231 D6 Nashville GA U.S.A.
236 F4 Nashville IL U.S.A.
231 E5 Nashville NC U.S.A.
232 B4 Nashville OH U.S.A.
234 B3 Nashville PA U.S.A.
231 C4 Nashville TN U.S.A.
226 A2 Nashwauk MN U.S.A.
188 G3 Našice Croatia
175 I3 Nasielsk Pol.
141 M3 Näsijärvi l. Fin.
Nasik Mahar. India see Nashik
Nasirabad Bangl. see Mymensingh
116 C4 Nasirabad Rajasthan India
123 G4 Nasirabad Pak.
225 I2 Naskaupi r. Nfld. Can.
117 F4 Nasmganj Bihar India
194 D4 Naso Sicilia Italy
194 D4 Naso r. Sicilia Italy
209 E7 Nasondoye Dem. Rep. Congo
226 B3 Nasonville WI U.S.A.
79 □1 Nasorolevu mt. Vanua Levu Fiji
Nasosnyy Azer. see Hacı Zeynalabdin
203 F2 Nasr Egypt
122 B3 Naşrābād Iran
122 D3 Naşrābād Iran
128 C3 Naşrānī, Jabal an mts Syria
Nasratabad Iran see Zābol
222 D4 Nass r. B.C. Can.
207 G4 Nassarawa Nigeria
207 H4 Nassarawa state Nigeria
85 E2 Nassau r. Qld Austr.
246 C1 Nassau Bahamas
81 □2 Nassau i. Cook Is
169 C5 Nassau Rheinland-Pfalz Ger.
171 E5 Nassau Sachsen Ger.
233 G3 Nassau NY U.S.A.
235 E2 Nassau County county NY U.S.A.
233 F6 Nassawadox VA U.S.A.
170 E3 Nassenheide Ger.
203 G4 Nasser, Lake resr Egypt
178 B3 Nassereith Austria
206 E4 Nassian Côte d'Ivoire
143 F3 Nässjö Sweden
165 E4 Nassogne Belgium
224 E1 Nastapoca r. Que. Can.
169 C5 Nastätten Ger.
138 E1 Nastola Fin.
105 F1 Nasu-dake vol. Japan
92 B3 Nasugbu Phil.
175 K4 Nasutów Pol.
139 H3 Nasva Rus. Fed.
139 H3 Nasva r. Rus. Fed.
141 L3 Nasviken Sweden
177 H4 Naszály Hungary
212 E4 Nata Botswana
254 G3 Natal Brazil
94 B2 Natal Sumatera Indon.
Natal prov. S. Africa see Kwazulu-Natal
265 G7 Natal Basin sea feature Indian Ocean
234 B2 Natalie PA U.S.A.
122 B3 Naţanz Iran
225 I3 Natashquan Que. Can.
225 I3 Natashquan r. Newfoundland/Québec Can.
81 □1 Na Taulaga i. Tokelau
237 F6 Natchez MS U.S.A.
237 E6 Natchitoches LA U.S.A.
149 G3 Nateby Cumbria, England U.K.
190 C2 Naters Switz.
83 F4 Nathalia Vic. Austr.
116 C3 Nathana Punjab India
84 C2 Nathan River N.T. Austr.
116 C4 Nathdwara Rajasthan India
140 □ Nathorst Land reg. Svalbard
207 F4 Natiaboani Burkina
240 I5 National City CA U.S.A.
80 E3 National Park North I. N.Z.
191 I3 Natisone r. Italy
207 F4 Natitingou Benin
257 G4 Natividade Rio de Janeiro Brazil
254 D4 Natividade Tocantins Brazil
222 D2 Natla r. N.W.T. Can.
96 A2 Natogyi Myanmar
117 G4 Nator Bangl.
102 J4 Natori Japan
211 C5 Natron, Lake salt l. Tanz.
105 G1 Natsui-gawa r. Japan
96 A3 Nattalin Myanmar
114 C4 Nattam Tamil Nadu India
96 B3 Nattaung mt. Myanmar
140 M2 Nattavaara Sweden
140 M2 Nattavaara by Sweden
179 E2 Natternback Austria
173 E3 Nattheim Ger.
137 I5 Natukhayevskaya Rus. Fed.
95 D1 Natuna, Kepulauan is Indon.
95 E1 Natuna Besar i. Indon.
232 D6 Natural Bridge VA U.S.A.
87 B7 Naturaliste, Cape W.A. Austr.
87 A5 Naturaliste Channel W.A. Austr.
265 L7 Naturaliste Plateau sea feature Indian Ocean
214 D5 Nature's Valley S. Africa
241 M2 Naturita CO U.S.A.
191 F2 Naturno Italy
Nau Tajik. see Nov
226 E2 Naubinway MI U.S.A.
163 E4 Naucelle France
162 E4 Naucelles France
178 B4 Nauders Austria
170 D3 Nauen Ger.
171 C4 Nauendorf Ger.
235 E1 Naugatuck CT U.S.A.
235 E1 Naugatuck r. CT U.S.A.
172 C2 Nauheim Ger.
162 A3 Naujac-sur-Mer France
92 B3 Naujan Phil.
138 D3 Naujoji Akmenė Lith.
116 C4 Naukh Rajasthan India
147 E3 Naul Rep. of Ireland
169 E4 Naumburg (Hessen) Ger.
171 C4 Naumburg (Saale) Ger.
171 E4 Naundorf Sachsen Ger.
171 E5 Naundorf Sachsen Ger.
169 C5 Nauroth Ger.
129 D2 Naurskaya Rus. Fed.
77 G2 Nauru i. Nauru
77 G2 Nauru country S. Pacific Ocean
123 G5 Naushahro Firoz Pak.
123 G5 Naushara Pak.
106 E1 Naushki Rus. Fed.
141 I3 Naustdal Norway
250 C6 Nauta Peru
Nautaca Uzbek. see Karshi
214 A2 Naute Dam Namibia
245 F3 Nautla Mex.
117 E4 Nautonwa Uttar Prad. India
226 B5 Nauvoo IL U.S.A.
208 E4 Nava r. Dem. Rep. Congo
183 E1 Nava Spain
Navabad Tajik. see Novobod
183 E4 Navacepeda de Tormes Spain
183 F4 Navacerreda Spain
185 G4 Navachica mt. Spain
182 E4 Navaconcejo Spain
183 F4 Nava de Arévalo Spain
183 F3 Nava de la Asunción Spain
183 E3 Nava del Rey Spain
183 E4 Nava de Sotrobal Spain
117 G5 Navadwip W. Bengal India
183 G3 Navafría Spain
183 F5 Navahermosa Spain
129 F3 Navahı Azer.
138 E5 Navahrudak Belarus
138 E5 Navahrudskaye Wzvyshsha hills Belarus
187 C5 Navajas Spain
239 F4 Navajo r. CO U.S.A.
241 L3 Navajo Mountain UT U.S.A.
183 E2 Navajos hill Spain
92 C4 Naval Phil.
186 D2 Naval Spain
183 F4 Navalagamella Spain
183 H3 Navalcaballo Spain
183 E4 Navalcán Spain
183 F4 Navalcarnero Spain
183 H3 Navalero Spain
183 F3 Navalmanzano Spain
183 F4 Navalmoral Spain
182 E5 Navalmoral de la Mata Spain
183 E4 Navalonguilla Spain
183 F4 Navalosa Spain
183 F4 Navalperal de Pinares Spain
185 F1 Navalpino Spain
183 F4 Navaluenga Spain
183 E5 Navalvillar de Ibor Spain
185 E1 Navalvillar de Pela Spain
183 F4 Navamorcuende Spain
147 E3 Navan Rep. of Ireland
Navangar Gujarat India see Jamnagar
138 G4 Navapolatsk Belarus
186 E3 Navarcles Spain
186 B2 Navardún Spain
131 S3 Navarin, Mys c. Rus. Fed.
259 D9 Navarino, Isla i. Chile
183 I2 Navarra aut. comm. Spain
83 E4 Navarre Vic. Austr.
Navarre aut. comm. Spain see Navarra
182 D4 Navarredonda de la Rinconada Spain
163 B5 Navarrenx France
187 C5 Navarrés Spain
183 H2 Navarrete Spain
261 H4 Navarro Arg.
240 F2 Navarro r. CA U.S.A.
186 E3 Navàs Spain
163 B6 Navasa Spain
185 F1 Navas de Estrena Spain
182 D5 Navas del Madroño Spain
183 F4 Navas del Rey Spain
183 F3 Navas de Oro Spain
185 G2 Navas de San Juan Spain
186 B2 Navaseués Spain
182 D4 Navasfrías Spain
134 H5 Navashino Rus. Fed.
237 D6 Navasota TX U.S.A.
237 D6 Navasota r. TX U.S.A.
246 D3 Navassa Island terr. West Indies
186 F2 Navata Spain
183 F4 Navatalgordo Spain
138 E5 Navayel'nya Belarus
190 F3 Nave Italy
184 B3 Nave Port.
182 C2 Navea r. Spain
182 D4 Nave de Haver Port.
148 C2 Nave Island Scotland U.K.
193 F2 Navelli Italy
160 E1 Navenne France
146 D3 Naver r. Scotland U.K.
146 D3 Naver, Loch l. Scotland U.K.
184 B3 Nave Redonda Port.
142 D2 Naverstad Sweden
162 D3 Naves France
186 E3 Navès Spain
139 K5 Navesnoye Rus. Fed.
138 E2 Navesti r. Estonia
185 E1 Navezuelas Spain
182 D1 Navia Spain
182 D1 Navia r. Spain
260 B3 Navidad Chile
237 D6 Navidad r. TX U.S.A.
247 E2 Navidad Bank sea feature Caribbean Sea
160 D2 Navilly France
255 B7 Naviraí Brazil
79 □1 Naviti i. Fiji
136 C2 Naviz Ukr.
139 J5 Navlya Rus. Fed.
139 J5 Navlya r. Rus. Fed.
197 I3 Năvodari Romania
120 F4 Navoi Uzbek.
120 E4 Navoiyskaya Oblast' admin. div. Uzbek.
242 C3 Navojoa Mex.
242 D3 Navolato Mex.
79 □1 Navotuvotu hill Vanua Levu Fiji
Navoy Oblast admin. div. Uzbek. see Navoiyskaya Oblast'
Návpaktos Greece see Nafpaktos
Návplion Greece see Nafplio
143 F3 Nävragöl Sweden
142 B2 Navrestad hill Norway
206 E4 Navrongo Ghana
Navşar Turkey see Şemdinli
116 C5 Navsari Gujarat India
116 C4 Nawa Rajasthan India
128 C3 Nawá Syria
117 G4 Nawabganj Bangl.
98 D6 Nawabganj Uttar Prad. India
111 C7 Nawabganj Uttar Prad. India
123 G5 Nawabshah Pak.
117 F4 Nawada Bihar India
116 C4 Nawalgarh Rajasthan India
111 B6 Nawashahr Punjab India
124 C3 Nawāṣīf, Ḥarrāt lava field Saudi Arabia
96 B2 Nawnghkio Myanmar
96 B2 Nawngleng Myanmar
Nawoiy Uzbek. see Navoi
Nawoiy Wiloyati admin. div. Uzbek. see Navoiyskaya Oblast'
175 I6 Nawojowa Pol.
129 D4 Naxçıvan Azer.
129 D4 Naxçıvan aut. reg. Azer.
129 D4 Naxçıvançay r. Azer.
108 C2 Naxi Sichuan China
199 D3 Naxos Notio Aigaio Greece
199 D3 Naxos i. Greece
250 B4 Naya Col.
117 F5 Nayagarh Orissa India
244 B2 Nayarit state Mex.
122 D3 Nāy Band, Kūh-e mt. Iran
163 B5 Nay-Bourdettes France
108 C3 Nayong Guizhou China
102 K1 Nayoro Japan
114 C3 Nayudupeta Andhra Prad. India
254 E3 Nazare Brazil
182 A5 Nazaré Port.
242 E3 Nazareno Mex.
114 C4 Nazareth Tamil Nadu India
128 B3 Nazareth Israel
234 C2 Nazareth PA U.S.A.
256 C2 Nazário Brazil
242 D3 Nazas Mex.
242 D3 Nazas r. Mex.
252 B3 Nazca Peru
267 N7 Nazca Ridge sea feature S. Pacific Ocean
102 □1 Naze Japan
151 H3 Nazeing Essex, England U.K.
159 G4 Nazelles-Négron France
122 A2 Nāzīk Iran
199 F3 Nazilli Turkey
127 E3 Nazımiye Turkey
Nazinon r. Burkina/Ghana see Red Volta
117 H4 Nazira Assam India
117 G5 Nazir Hat Bangl.
129 E3 Näzirli Azer.
139 H2 Naziya Rus. Fed.
222 F4 Nazko B.C. Can.
222 F4 Nazko r. B.C. Can.
122 A2 Nāzlū r. Iran
129 D2 Nazran' Rus. Fed.
210 C2 Nazrēt Eth.
125 G3 Nazwá Oman
130 I4 Nazyvayevsk Rus. Fed.
206 B2 Nbâk Maur.
215 E5 Ncanaha S. Africa
209 F7 Nchelenge Zambia
Ncheu Malawi see Ntcheu
212 D4 Ncojane Botswana
215 F4 Ncora S. Africa
207 H6 Ncue Equat. Guinea
211 B6 Ndala Tanz.
209 B7 N'dalatando Angola
207 F4 Ndali Benin
208 D2 Ndélé C.A.R.
207 I5 Ndélélé Cameroon
208 A5 Ndendé Gabon
Ndende i. Santa Cruz Is Solomon Is see Ndeni
78 □6 Ndeni i. Santa Cruz Is Solomon Is
207 H5 Ndikiniméki Cameroon
206 B3 Ndioum Guènt Senegal
202 B6 Ndjamena Chad
N'Djamena Chad see Ndjamena
208 D3 Ndji r. C.A.R.
207 H5 Ndjim r. Cameroon
208 A5 Ndjolé Gabon
Ndjouani i. Comoros see Nzwani
206 B3 Ndofane Senegal
Ndoi i. Fiji see Doi
209 F8 Ndola Zambia
206 D4 Ndorola Burkina
210 C4 Ndoto mt. Kenya
208 A5 Ndougou Gabon
78 □6 Ndovele New Georgia Is Solomon Is
Nduke i. New Georgia Is Solomon Is see Kolombangara
211 C7 Ndumbwe Tanz.
215 I2 Ndumu S. Africa
215 H3 Ndwedwe S. Africa
162 B3 Né r. France
163 C6 Né, Mont mt. France
198 D4 Nea Alikarnassos Kriti Greece
198 C2 Nea Anchialos Greece
198 C1 Nea Apollonia Greece
198 C2 Nea Artaki Greece
85 F5 Neabul Creek r. Qld Austr.
198 C3 Nea Epidavros Greece
147 E2 Neagh, Lough l. Northern Ireland U.K.
238 A1 Neah Bay WA U.S.A.
197 G3 Neajlov r. Romania
198 C1 Nea Kallikrateia Greece
198 D1 Nea Karvali Greece
147 B3 Neale Rep. of Ireland
84 B5 Neale, Lake salt flat N.T. Austr.
198 C2 Nea Liosia Greece
198 C2 Nea Makri Greece
198 C1 Nea Moudania Greece
197 H2 Neamţ r. Romania
198 D1 Nea Peramos Greece
198 B1 Neapoli Dytiki Makedonia Greece
199 D4 Neapoli Kriti Greece
198 C3 Neapoli Peloponnisos Greece
Neapolis Italy see Napoli
149 G3 Near Sawrey Cumbria, England U.K.
198 C1 Nea Santa Greece
150 D3 Neath Neath Port Talbot, Wales U.K.
150 D3 Neath r. Wales U.K.
150 D3 Neath Port Talbot admin. div. Wales U.K.
198 C1 Nea Zichni Greece
210 A4 Nebbi Uganda
168 D1 Nebel Ger.
173 E4 Nebelhorn mt. Ger.
110 C3 Nebesnaya, Gora mt. Xinjiang China
163 E6 Nébias France
83 F2 Nebine Creek r. Qld Austr.
122 C2 Nebitdag Turkm.
85 G4 Nebo Qld Austr.
241 L2 Nebo, Mount UT U.S.A.
139 I2 Nebolchi Rus. Fed.
171 C4 Nebra (Unstrut) Ger.
236 C3 Nebraska state U.S.A.
236 E3 Nebraska City NE U.S.A.
183 G3 Nebreda Spain
194 D5 Nebrodi, Monti mts Sicilia Italy
139 L3 Nebyloye Rus. Fed.
245 F3 Necaxa r. Mex.
226 B3 Necedah WI U.S.A.
176 E1 Nechanice Czech Rep.
137 F4 Nechayane Ukr.
237 E6 Neches r. TX U.S.A.
250 C2 Nechí r. Col.
185 G4 Nechite r. Spain
172 C2 Neckar r. Ger.
172 C2 Neckarbischofsheim Ger.
172 C2 Neckargemünd Ger.
172 C2 Neckarsteinach Ger.
172 D2 Neckarsulm Ger.
75 H2 Necker Island HI U.S.A.
261 H6 Necochea Arg.
250 B2 Necoclí Col.
151 H2 Necton Norfolk, England U.K.
182 B1 Neda Spain
136 F2 Nedanchychi Ukr.
198 B3 Nedas r. Greece
177 H2 Nedašov Czech Rep.
170 E2 Neddemin Ger.
197 G5 Nedelino Bulg.
188 F2 Nedelišće Croatia
Nederland country Europe see Netherlands
Nederlandse Antillen terr. West Indies see Netherlands Antilles
164 E2 Nederlangbroek Neth.
164 E3 Neder Rijn r. Neth.
170 C1 Neder Vindinge Denmark
165 E3 Nederweert Neth.
Nédha r. Greece see Nedas
171 D3 Nedlitz Ger.
136 D3 Nedoboyivtsi Ukr.
111 E6 Nêdong Xizang China
140 M1 Nedre Soppero Sweden
137 G2 Nedryhayliv Ukr.
142 A2 Nedstrandsfjorden sea chan. Norway
208 F4 Neduka r. Dem. Rep. Congo
176 F2 Nedvědice Czech Rep.
174 G5 Nędza Pol.
105 E2 Neeba-san mt. Japan
164 F2 Neede Neth.
233 H3 Needham MA U.S.A.
151 I2 Needham Market Suffolk, England U.K.
151 G2 Needingworth Cambridgeshire, England U.K.
241 J4 Needles CA U.S.A.
232 D5 Needmore PA U.S.A.
Neemuch Madh. Prad. India see Nimach
226 C3 Neenah WI U.S.A.
223 L5 Neepawa Man. Can.
165 F3 Neer Neth.
164 E3 Neerijnen Neth.
168 C2 Neermoor Ger.
165 E3 Neeroeteren Belgium
165 E3 Neerpelt Belgium
168 F2 Neetze Ger.
234 C2 Neffs PA U.S.A.
234 B2 Neffsville PA U.S.A.
205 G2 Nefta Tunisia
129 F4 Neftçala Azer.
129 G3 Neft Daşları Azer.
Neftechala Azer. see 26 Bakı Komissarı
Neftechala Azer. see Neftçala
129 A1 Neftegorsk Krasnodarskiy Kray Rus. Fed.
100 G1 Neftegorsk Sakhalin Rus. Fed.

Neftegorsk to Niagara-on-the-Lake

340

120 B1 Neftegorsk Samarskaya Oblast' Rus. Fed.
134 K4 Neftekamsk Rus. Fed.
129 D1 Neftekumsk Rus. Fed.
190 D1 Neftenbach Switz.
130 I3 Nefteyugansk Rus. Fed.
Neftezavodsk Turkm. see Seydi
Neftyanyye Kamni Azer. see Neft Daşları
150 C2 Nefyn Gwynedd, Wales U.K.
209 B6 Negage Angola
206 C3 Négala Mali
95 F5 Negara Bali Indon.
95 F3 Negara Kalimantan Selatan Indon.
95 F3 Negara r. Indon.
226 D2 Negaunee MI U.S.A.
210 C3 Negēlē Oromia Eth.
210 C3 Negēlē Oromia Eth.
94 C2 Negeri Sembilan state Malaysia
128 B4 Negev des. Israel
211 C7 Negomane Moz.
114 C5 Negombo Sri Lanka
197 F3 Negotin Srbija Yugo.
196 E5 Negotino Macedonia
197 F5 Negotino Macedonia
252 A2 Negra, Cordillera mts Peru
258 G4 Negra, Lago l. Uru.
250 A6 Negra, Punta pt Peru
257 F3 Negra, Serra mts Brazil
253 E3 Negra, Serranía de mts Bol.
191 F3 Negrar Italy
163 D6 Negre, Pic mt. Andorra
183 H3 Negredo Spain
182 B2 Negreira Spain
163 D4 Nègrepelisse France
197 H2 Negreşti Romania
197 F2 Negreşti-Oaş Romania
260 A5 Negrete Chile
84 B3 Negri r. N.T. Austr.
197 H2 Negri Romania
246 □ Negril Jamaica
Negri Sembilan state Malaysia see Negeri Sembilan
250 A6 Negritos Peru
260 E6 Negro r. Arg.
253 F4 Negro r. Brazil
253 F6 Negro r. Para.
251 G5 Negro r. S. America
182 D2 Negro r. Spain
261 H3 Negro r. Uru.
261 I3 Negro r. Paysandú/Río Negro Uru.
180 D5 Negro, Cabo c. Morocco
Negroponte i. Greece see Evvoia
92 B4 Negros i. Phil.
197 I4 Negru Vodă Romania
238 B2 Nehalem r. OR U.S.A.
122 B3 Nehavand Iran
122 E4 Nehbandān Iran
107 J1 Nehe Heilong. China
197 H3 Nehoiu Romania
209 C9 Nehone Angola
79 □2 Neiafu Vava'u Gp Tonga
246 E3 Neiba Dom. Rep.
157 H4 Neiderbronn-les-Bains France
157 G3 Neid Française r. France
108 C2 Neijiang Sichuan China
223 I4 Neilburg Sask. Can.
214 C3 Neilersdrif S. Africa
226 B3 Neillsville WI U.S.A.
107 D3 Nei Mongol Zizhiqu aut. reg. China
171 C4 Neinstedt Ger.
107 G4 Neiqiu Hebei China
171 F3 Neiße r. Ger./Pol.
250 C4 Neiva Col.
183 K2 Neiva r. Port.
190 D4 Neive Italy
109 D1 Neixiang Henan China
244 C4 Neixpa r. Mex.
Nejd reg. Saudi Arabia see Najd
176 B1 Nejdek Czech Rep.
122 C2 Neka Iran
122 C2 Nekā r. Iran
210 C2 Nek'emtē Eth.
135 H6 Nekhayevskaya Rus. Fed.
Nekhayevskiy Rus. Fed. see Nekhayevskaya
137 G2 Nekhayivka Ukr.
173 F4 Nekla Pol.
139 M4 Neklyudovo Rus. Fed.
136 E3 Nekrasove Ukr.
139 K3 Nekrasovskiy Rus. Fed.
139 M3 Nekrasovskoye Rus. Fed.
143 F4 Neksø Bornholm Denmark
183 G2 Nela r. Spain
114 C3 Nelamangala Karnataka India
182 C4 Nelas Port.
183 K2 Nelazskoye Rus. Fed.
85 E4 Nelia Qld Austr.
139 I3 Nelidovo Rus. Fed.
236 D3 Neligh NE U.S.A.
131 O4 Nel'kan Rus. Fed.
131 P3 Nel'kan Rus. Fed.
78 □3a Nell i. Kwajalein Marshall Is
227 G1 Nellie Lake Ont. Can.
173 D2 Nellingen Ger.
114 C3 Nellore Andhra Prad. India
261 G2 Nelson Arg.
222 G5 Nelson B.C. Can.
223 M3 Nelson r. Man. Can.
81 D4 Nelson South I. N.Z.
81 D4 Nelson admin. reg. South I. N.Z.
149 G4 Nelson Lancashire, England U.K.
241 K4 Nelson AZ U.S.A.
236 D3 Nelson NE U.S.A.
241 J4 Nelson NV U.S.A.
226 A3 Nelson WI U.S.A.
82 E4 Nelson, Cape Vic. Austr.
83 H3 Nelson Bay N.S.W. Austr.
81 C5 Nelson Creek South I. N.Z.
222 F3 Nelson Forks B.C. Can.
223 L4 Nelson House Man. Can.
233 F6 Nelsonia VA U.S.A.
235 E1 Nelsonville NY U.S.A.
214 D5 Nelspoort S. Africa
215 H1 Nelspruit S. Africa
134 K3 Nem r. Rus. Fed.
206 D2 Néma Maur.
134 J4 Nema Rus. Fed.
226 A2 Nemadji r. MN U.S.A.
Neman r. Belarus/Lith. see Nyoman
138 D4 Neman Rus. Fed.
138 D4 Neman r. Rus. Fed.
Nemausus France see Nîmes
207 G5 Nembe Nigeria
190 E3 Nembro Italy
177 I3 Nemce Slovakia
134 H4 Nemda r. Rus. Fed.
198 C3 Nemea Greece
227 F2 Nemegos Ont. Can.
138 E4 Nemenčinė Lith.
205 G2 Nementcha, Monts des mts Alg.
198 B1 Nëmerçkë, Mal ridge Albania
176 G4 Nemesszalók Hungary
176 G5 Nemesvid Hungary
177 H5 Németkér Hungary
Nemetocenna France see Arras
Nemirov Vinnyts'ka Oblast' Ukr. see Nemyriv
224 E3 Némiscau r. Que. Can.
136 F2 Nemishayeve Ukr.
107 J1 Nemor r. China
Nemours Alg. see Ghazaouet
156 C4 Nemours France
187 F3 Nemrut Dağı mt. Turkey
171 C4 Nemsdorf-Göhrendorf Ger.
177 H3 Nemšová Slovakia
100 E2 Nemta r. Rus. Fed.
138 C4 Nemunas r. Lith.
138 E3 Nemunėlis r. Lith.
102 I2 Nemuro Japan
102 L2 Nemuro-kaikyō sea chan. Japan/Rus. Fed.
136 B2 Nemyriv L'vivs'ka Oblast' Ukr.
136 E3 Nemyriv Vinnyts'ka Oblast' Ukr.
147 C4 Nenagh Rep. of Ireland
220 D3 Nenana AK U.S.A.
190 C2 Nendaz Switz.
151 H2 Nene r. England U.K.
Nenets Autonomous Okrug admin. div. Rus. Fed. see Nenetskiy Avtonomnyy Okrug
134 K2 Nenetskiy Avtonomnyy Okrug admin. div. Rus. Fed.
177 I3 Nenince Slovakia
107 J1 Nenjiang Heilong. China
107 J2 Nen Jiang r. China
168 C2 Nenndorf Ger.
170 D3 Nennhausen Ger.
173 F2 Nennslingen Ger.
169 E4 Nentershausen Hessen Ger.
169 C5 Nentershausen Rheinland-Pfalz Ger.
149 G3 Nenthead Cumbria, England U.K.
178 A3 Nenzing Austria
198 C1 Neo Agioneri Kentriki Makedonia Greece
78 □4a Neoch atoll Chuuk Micronesia
198 B2 Neochori Greece
198 D1 Neo Erasmio Anatoliki Makedonia kai Thraki Greece
104 C3 Neo-gawa r. Japan
199 E3 Neo Karlovasi Voreio Aigaio Greece
Neokhórion Greece see Neochori
241 L1 Neola UT U.S.A.
198 C2 Neo Monastiri Greece
192 A4 Neoneli Sardegna Italy
Néon Karlovásion Voreio Aigaio Greece see Neo Karlovasi
226 C3 Neopit WI U.S.A.
237 E4 Neosho MO U.S.A.
237 E4 Neosho r. KS U.S.A.
198 C1 Neos Marmaras Greece
174 E5 Néoules France
186 D2 Néouvielle, Pic de mt. France
116 E3 Nepal country Asia
116 E3 Nepalganj Nepal
116 D5 Nepanagar Madh. Prad. India
224 F4 Nepean Ont. Can.
241 L2 Nephi UT U.S.A.
147 B2 Nephin hill Rep. of Ireland
147 B2 Nephin Beg Range hills Rep. of Ireland
193 E2 Nepi Italy
221 L5 Nepisiguit r. N.B. Can.
176 C2 Nepomuk Czech Rep.
139 L5 Nepryadva r. Rus. Fed.
235 D2 Neptune NJ U.S.A.
82 D3 Neptune Islands S.A. Austr.
175 G3 Ner r. Pol.
193 E2 Nera r. Italy
163 C4 Nérac France
114 B2 Neral Mahar. India
85 H5 Nerang Qld Austr.
177 J6 Nerău Romania
138 E2 Neravai Lith.
174 D4 Nerchau Ger.
99 K1 Nerchinsk Rus. Fed.
100 A2 Nerchinskiy Zavod Rus. Fed.
163 E2 Nercillac France
192 B4 Nercone, Monte su mt. Sardegna Italy
162 B3 Néré France
197 H3 Nereju Romania
139 M3 Nerekhta Rus. Fed.
138 E3 Nereta Latvia
193 F2 Nereto Italy
188 F4 Neretva r. Bos.-Herz./Croatia
175 L4 Neretva r. Ukr.
188 F4 Neretvanski Kanal sea chan. Croatia
191 J4 Nerezine Croatia
116 D5 Neri Mahar. India
209 D8 Neriquinha Angola
138 D4 Neris r. Lith.
163 D2 Néris-les-Bains France
185 G4 Nerja Spain
139 M3 Nerl' Rus. Fed.
139 L3 Nerl' Rus. Fed.
139 K3 Nerl' r. Rus. Fed.
139 L3 Nero, Ozero l. Rus. Fed.
160 C3 Néronde France
160 A2 Nérondes France
256 C2 Nerópolis Brazil
169 B5 Neroth Ger.
134 L2 Neroyka, Gora mt. Rus. Fed.
116 D5 Ner Pinglai Mahar. India
184 F2 Nerpio Spain
162 C3 Nersac France
173 E3 Nersingen Ger.
136 F4 Nerubays'ke Ukr.
139 K5 Neruch' r. Rus. Fed.
139 I5 Nerussa r. Rus. Fed.
180 D3 Nerva Spain
191 H3 Nervesa della Battaglia Italy
160 C3 Nervieux France
183 H1 Nervión r. Spain
193 E2 Nery, Monte mt. Italy
131 N4 Neryungri Rus. Fed.
164 E1 Nes Neth.
134 I2 Nes' Rus. Fed.
134 I2 Nes' r. Rus. Fed.
142 C1 Nesbyen Norway
174 F4 Neschwitz Ger.
234 D3 Nesco NJ U.S.A.
234 B1 Nescopeck PA U.S.A.
234 B1 Nescopeck Creek r. PA U.S.A.
197 H4 Nesebŭr Bulg.
234 D2 Neshaminy Creek r. PA U.S.A.
140 □D2 Neskaupstaður Iceland
175 C3 Nesle France
177 H2 Nesluša Slovakia
140 K2 Nesna Norway
176 G2 Nesovice Czech Rep.
176 C4 Nesque r. France
234 C2 Nesquehoning PA U.S.A.
114 B2 Nesri Mahar. India
146 D4 Ness r. Scotland U.K.
146 D4 Ness, Loch l. Scotland U.K.
236 D4 Ness City KS U.S.A.
168 C2 Nesse Ger.
169 F5 Nesse r. Ger.
222 C3 Nesselrode, Mount Alaska/B.C. Can./U.S.A.
173 E4 Nesselwang Ger.
190 E1 Nesslau Switz.
163 C5 Neste r. France
138 D4 Nesterov Rus. Fed.
Nesterov Ukr. see Zhovkva
149 F4 Neston Cheshire, England U.K.
193 E2 Nestore r. Italy
191 H5 Nestore r. Italy
223 M5 Nestor Falls Ont. Can.
226 C2 Nestoria MI U.S.A.
198 D1 Nestos r. Greece
Nesvizh Belarus see Nyasvizh
128 B3 Netanya Israel
117 F5 Netarhat Bihar India
234 D2 Netcong NJ U.S.A.
169 E4 Nethe r. Ger.
164 E2 Netherlands country Europe
247 E4 Netherlands Antilles terr. West Indies
146 F4 Netherley Aberdeenshire, Scotland U.K.
150 D3 Nether Stowey Somerset, England U.K.
149 G2 Netherton Northumberland, England U.K.
146 E4 Nethy Bridge Highland, Scotland U.K.
213 H2 Netia Moz.
136 D2 Netishyn Ukr.
195 G3 Neto r. Italy
176 D2 Netolice Czech Rep.
170 D3 Netphen Ger.
169 F4 Netra (Ringgau) Ger.
117 G4 Netrakona Bangl.
116 C5 Netrang Gujarat India
190 E1 Netstal Switz.
157 E4 Nettancourt France
169 B5 Nettersheim Ger.
169 B4 Nettetal Ger.
221 K3 Nettilling Lake Nunavut Can.
149 I4 Nettleham Lincolnshire, England U.K.
193 E5 Nettuno Italy
171 D5 Netzschkau Ger.
173 G2 Neualbenreuth Ger.
169 D5 Neu-Anspach Ger.
210 B3 Neubari r. Sudan
168 E1 Neuberend Ger.
179 G3 Neuberg an der Mürz Austria
173 F3 Neubeuern Ger.
173 G3 Neubiberg Ger.
168 C3 Neuborger Ger.
170 E2 Neubrandenburg Ger.
168 D3 Neubruchhausen Ger.
172 D2 Neubrunn Ger.
170 C1 Neubukow Ger.
172 C3 Neubulach Ger.
173 H3 Neuburg am Inn Ger.
172 C3 Neuburg am Rhein Ger.
173 F3 Neuburg an der Donau Ger.
173 E3 Neuburg an der Kammel Ger.
170 C2 Neuburg-Steinhausen Ger.
171 E4 Neuburxdorf Ger.
190 B2 Neuchâtel Switz.
190 B1 Neuchâtel canton Switz.
190 B2 Neuchâtel, Lac de l. Switz.
168 F2 Neu Darchau Ger.
169 F5 Neudietendorf Ger.
179 H3 Neudorf Austria
171 D5 Neudorf Ger.
171 C5 Neudrossenfeld Ger.
172 C3 Neuenbürg Ger.
172 B4 Neuenburg am Rhein Ger.
173 E2 Neuendettelsau Ger.
170 F3 Neuenhagen Ger.
170 E3 Neuenhagen Berlin Ger.
169 B3 Neuenhaus Ger.
172 C4 Neuenhof Switz.
190 D1 Neuenkirch Switz.
170 E1 Neuenkirchen Mecklenburg-Vorpommern Ger.
170 E1 Neuenkirchen Mecklenburg-Vorpommern Ger.
168 D2 Neuenkirchen Niedersachsen Ger.
168 D2 Neuenkirchen Niedersachsen Ger.
168 D3 Neuenkirchen Niedersachsen Ger.
168 E2 Neuenkirchen Niedersachsen Ger.
169 C3 Neuenkirchen Niedersachsen Ger.
169 C3 Neuenkirchen Nordrhein-Westfalen Ger.
168 E1 Neuenkirchen Schleswig-Holstein Ger.
169 D3 Neuenkirchen (Oldenburg) Ger.
169 C5 Neuenkirchen-Seelscheid Ger.
169 C4 Neuenrade Ger.
172 D2 Neuenstadt am Kocher Ger.
172 D2 Neuenstein Ger.
168 D2 Neuenwalde Ger.
169 B5 Neuerburg Ger.
173 F3 Neufahrn bei Freising Ger.
173 G3 Neufahrn in Niederbayern Ger.
157 H4 Neuf-Brisach France
165 E5 Neufchâteau Belgium
157 F4 Neufchâteau France
156 B3 Neufchâtel-en-Bray France
159 G3 Neufchâtel-en-Saosnois France
156 B2 Neufchâtel-Hardelot France
156 E3 Neufchâtel-sur-Aisne France
168 E2 Neufeld Ger.
179 H3 Neufeld an der Leitha Austria
179 F2 Neufelden Austria
172 C3 Neuffen Ger.
157 F3 Neufmanil France
172 D3 Neufra Ger.
171 C4 Neugattersleben Ger.
171 F5 Neugersdorf Ger.
172 E2 Neuglobsow Ger.
170 D3 Neuhardenberg Ger.
168 C2 Neuharlingersiel Ger.
179 F4 Neuhaus Austria
168 F2 Neuhaus (Elbe) Ger.
168 E2 Neuhaus (Oste) Ger.
173 H3 Neuhaus am Inn Ger.
179 H4 Neuhaus am Klausenbach Austria
171 C5 Neuhaus am Rennweg Ger.
173 F2 Neuhaus an der Pegnitz Ger.
172 C3 Neuhausen Baden-Württemberg Ger.
171 E5 Neuhausen Sachsen Ger.
Neuhausen Rus. Fed. see Gur'yevsk
190 D1 Neuhausen Switz.
172 C4 Neuhausen ob Eck Ger.
171 C5 Neuhaus-Schierschnitz Ger.
169 E5 Neuhof Ger.
173 E2 Neuhof an der Zenn Ger.
179 F2 Neuhofen an der Krems Austria
179 F3 Neuhofen an der Ybbs Austria
159 G4 Neuillé-Pont-Pierre France
160 B1 Neuilly France
156 C3 Neuilly-en-Thelle France
160 B2 Neuilly-le-Réal France
157 E5 Neuilly-l'Évêque France
156 D3 Neuilly-St-Front France
156 C4 Neuilly-sur-Seine France
169 D5 Neu-Isenburg Ger.
170 D2 Neukalen Ger.
170 C2 Neu Kaliß Ger.
168 C2 Neukamperfehn Ger.
171 D4 Neukieritzsch Ger.
172 D4 Neukirch Baden-Württemberg Ger.
171 F4 Neukirch Sachsen Ger.
169 E5 Neukirchen Hessen Ger.
171 D5 Neukirchen Sachsen Ger.
171 D5 Neukirchen Sachsen Ger.
170 C1 Neukirchen Schleswig-Holstein Ger.
168 D1 Neukirchen Schleswig-Holstein Ger.
178 D3 Neukirchen am Großvenediger Austria
178 E2 Neukirchen an der Enknach Austria
179 E2 Neukirchen an der Vöckla Austria
173 G2 Neukirchen-Balbini Ger.
173 F2 Neukirchen bei Sulzbach-Rosenberg Ger.
173 H3 Neukirchen vorm Wald Ger.
170 C2 Neukloster Ger.
Neukuhren Kaliningradskaya Oblast' Rus. Fed. see Pionerskiy
168 C2 Neulehe Ger.
179 G2 Neulengbach Austria
173 E3 Neuler Ger.
170 F3 Neulewin Ger.
160 C3 Neulise France
186 F2 Neulós, Pic mt. Spain
171 E3 Neu Lübbenau Ger.
172 D2 Neumagen Ger.
171 D5 Neumark Sachsen Ger.
171 C4 Neumark Thüringen Ger.
179 F2 Neumarkt im Mühlkreis Austria
173 F2 Neumarkt in der Oberpfalz Ger.
179 F3 Neumarkt in Steiermark Austria
173 G3 Neumarkt-St Veit Ger.
262 X2 Neumayer research stn Antarctica
168 E1 Neumünster Ger.
96 D3 Neun, Nam r. Laos
173 G2 Neunburg vorm Wald Ger.
171 D5 Neundorf Ger.
159 H4 Neung-sur-Beuvron France
190 D1 Neunkirch Switz.
179 H3 Neunkirchen Austria
169 D5 Neunkirchen Nordrhein-Westfalen Ger.
172 B2 Neunkirchen Saarland Ger.
172 D2 Neunkirchen am Sand Ger.
172 C3 Neuötting Ger.
171 F4 Neupetershain Ger.
260 C6 Neuquén Arg.
260 C6 Neuquén prov. Arg.
260 D6 Neuquén r. Arg.
173 H3 Neureichenau Ger.
172 C3 Neuried Ger.
170 D3 Neuruppin Ger.
171 F4 Neusalza-Spremberg Ger.
Neu Sandez Pol. see Nowy Sącz
173 G3 Neusäß Ger.
173 H3 Neuschönau Ger.
231 E5 Neuse r. NC U.S.A.
171 D3 Neuseddin Ger.
179 H3 Neusiedl am See Austria
179 H3 Neusiedler See l. Austria/Hungary
173 F2 Neusorg Ger.
169 B4 Neuss Ger.
161 A3 Neussargues-Moissac France
172 C4 Neustadt Baden-Württemberg Ger.
170 D3 Neustadt Brandenburg Ger.
171 C5 Neustadt Thüringen Ger.
169 F4 Neustadt (Harz) Ger.
169 E5 Neustadt (Hessen) Ger.
169 C5 Neustadt (Wied) Ger.
173 F2 Neustadt am Kulm Ger.
169 F5 Neustadt am Rennsteig Ger.
169 E3 Neustadt am Rübenberge Ger.
173 E2 Neustadt an der Aisch Ger.
173 F3 Neustadt an der Donau Ger.
Neustadt an der Hardt Ger. see Neustadt an der Weinstraße
173 G2 Neustadt an der Waldnaab Ger.
172 C2 Neustadt an der Weinstraße Ger.
171 C5 Neustadt bei Coburg Ger.
170 C2 Neustadt-Glewe Ger.
168 F1 Neustadt in Holstein Ger.
171 F4 Neustadt in Sachsen Ger.
178 C3 Neustift im Stubaital Austria
170 E2 Neustrelitz Ger.
173 G3 Neutraubling Ger.
170 F3 Neutrebbin Ger.
173 E3 Neu-Ulm Ger.
161 A4 Neuvéglise France
157 G4 Neuves-Maisons France
162 C3 Neuvic Aquitaine France
162 E3 Neuvic Limousin France
156 C4 Neuville-aux-Bois France
159 G5 Neuville-de-Poitou France
160 D2 Neuville-les-Dames France
156 B3 Neuville-lès-Dieppe France
160 C3 Neuville-sur-Saône France
159 G3 Neuville-sur-Sarthe France
157 F3 Neuvilly-en-Argonne France
160 B2 Neuvy-Grandchamp France
159 G4 Neuvy-le-Roi France
159 I4 Neuvy-Pailloux France
159 H5 Neuvy-St-Sépulchre France
156 D4 Neuvy-Sautour France
159 I4 Neuvy-sur-Barangeon France
171 C3 Neuwegersleben Ger.
172 C3 Neuweiler Ger.
168 D1 Neuwerk i. Ger.
169 C5 Neuwied Ger.
168 F1 Neuwittenbek Ger.
168 E2 Neu Wulmstorf Ger.
171 D5 Neuwürschnitz Ger.
171 F4 Neu Zauche Ger.
168 E3 Neuzelle Ger.
171 F5 Neu Zittau Ger.
161 E3 Névache France
236 E3 Nevada IA U.S.A.
237 E4 Nevada MO U.S.A.
240 I2 Nevada state U.S.A.
258 C2 Nevada, Sierra mt. Arg.
185 G3 Nevada, Sierra mts Spain
240 G1 Nevada, Sierra mts CA U.S.A.
240 G2 Nevada City CA U.S.A.
260 C2 Nevado, Cerro mt. Arg.
260 C5 Nevado, Sierra del mts Arg.
245 E4 Nevado de Toluca, Volcán vol. Mex.
185 E2 Névalo r. Spain
114 B2 Nevasa Mahar. India
Nevdubstroy Leningradskaya Oblast' Rus. Fed. see Kirovsk
209 B8 Neve, Serra da mts Angola
176 D2 Neveklov Czech Rep.
138 G3 Nevel' Rus. Fed.
165 C3 Nevele Belgium
101 P3 Nevel'sk Sakhalin Rus. Fed.
183 I4 Nevera mt. Spain
120 A1 Neverkino Rus. Fed.
150 C2 Nevern Pembrokeshire, Wales U.K.
138 E4 Neveronys Lith.
160 B1 Nevers France
234 D1 Neversink r. NY U.S.A.
83 F2 Nevertire N.S.W. Austr.
257 F5 Neves Brazil
188 G4 Nevesinje Bos.-Herz.
162 G2 Névez France
138 D4 Nevėžis r. Lith.
161 A5 Névian France
195 H2 Neviano Italy
159 G2 Néville France
129 B1 Nevinnomyssk Rus. Fed.
247 □2 Nevis i. St Kitts and Nevis
146 C4 Nevis, Loch inlet Scotland U.K.
247 □2 Nevis Peak St Kitts and Nevis
126 D3 Nevşehir Turkey
241 J5 New r. CA U.S.A.
232 C6 New r. WV U.S.A.
146 E7 New Abbey Dumfries and Galloway, Scotland U.K.
146 F4 New Aberdour Aberdeenshire, Scotland U.K.
151 G3 New Addington Greater London, England U.K.
222 D4 New Aiyansh B.C. Can.
211 C7 Newala Tanz.
230 C4 New Albany IN U.S.A.
237 F5 New Albany MS U.S.A.
234 B1 New Albany PA U.S.A.
151 F3 New Alresford Hampshire, England U.K.
251 G3 New Amsterdam Guyana
83 F2 New Angledool N.S.W. Austr.
215 H3 Newark S. Africa
240 B3 Newark CA U.S.A.
234 C3 Newark DE U.S.A.
233 F4 Newark NJ U.S.A.
232 E3 Newark NY U.S.A.
232 B4 Newark OH U.S.A.
233 F4 Newark airport NJ U.S.A.
149 I4 Newark-on-Trent Nottinghamshire, England U.K.
227 I4 Newark Valley NY U.S.A.
151 H3 New Ash Green Kent, England U.K.
237 F6 New Augusta MS U.S.A.
226 E4 Newaygo MI U.S.A.
233 H4 New Bedford MA U.S.A.
238 B2 Newberg OR U.S.A.
233 F5 New Berlin NY U.S.A.
234 B2 New Berlin PA U.S.A.
234 C2 New Berlinville PA U.S.A.
231 E5 New Bern NC U.S.A.
226 E2 Newberry MI U.S.A.
231 D5 Newberry SC U.S.A.
240 I4 Newberry Springs CA U.S.A.
234 B2 New Bethlehem PA U.S.A.
149 H2 Newbiggin-by-the-Sea Northumberland, England U.K.
146 E6 Newbigging South Lanarkshire, Scotland U.K.
147 D2 Newbliss Rep. of Ireland
227 I5 New Bloomfield PA U.S.A.
224 E4 Newboro Ont. Can.
232 B5 New Boston OH U.S.A.
237 E5 New Boston TX U.S.A.
237 D6 New Braunfels TX U.S.A.
147 C3 Newbridge Galway Rep. of Ireland
147 E3 Newbridge Kildare Rep. of Ireland
147 C4 Newbridge Limerick Rep. of Ireland
150 D3 Newbridge Caerphilly, Wales U.K.
150 D2 Newbridge on Wye Powys, Wales U.K.
232 C4 New Brighton PA U.S.A.
91 K8 New Britain i. P.N.G.
235 F1 New Britain CT U.S.A.
234 C2 New Britain PA U.S.A.
266 F6 New Britain Trench sea feature Pacific Ocean
225 H4 New Brunswick prov. Can.
233 F4 New Brunswick NJ U.S.A.
226 D5 New Buffalo MI U.S.A.
234 B2 New Buffalo PA U.S.A.
147 D2 New Buildings Northern Ireland U.K.
232 E4 Newburg PA U.S.A.
227 I3 Newburgh Ont. Can.
146 F4 Newburgh Aberdeenshire, Scotland U.K.
146 E5 Newburgh Fife, Scotland U.K.
146 E6 Newburgh Scottish Borders, Scotland U.K.
233 F4 Newburgh NY U.S.A.
151 F3 Newbury West Berkshire, England U.K.
Newbury admin. div. England U.K. see West Berkshire
233 H3 Newburyport MA U.S.A.
207 G4 New Bussa Nigeria
149 G3 Newby Bridge Cumbria, England U.K.
146 F4 New Byth Aberdeenshire, Scotland U.K.
78 □5 New Caledonia terr. S. Pacific Ocean
266 F7 New Caledonia Trough sea feature Tasman Sea
235 E1 New Canaan CT U.S.A.
225 H3 New Carlisle Que. Can.
232 A5 New Carlisle OH U.S.A.
234 B4 New Carrollton MD U.S.A.
83 G3 Newcastle N.S.W. Austr.
225 H4 Newcastle N.B. Can.
224 E5 Newcastle Ont. Can.
246 □ Newcastle Jamaica
147 E3 Newcastle Dublin Rep. of Ireland
147 C3 Newcastle Galway Rep. of Ireland
147 D4 Newcastle Tipperary Rep. of Ireland
147 E3 Newcastle Wicklow Rep. of Ireland
215 G2 Newcastle S. Africa
147 F2 Newcastle Northern Ireland U.K.
150 D2 Newcastle Shropshire, England U.K.
240 G2 Newcastle CA U.S.A.
234 C3 New Castle DE U.S.A.
230 C4 New Castle IN U.S.A.
230 C4 New Castle KY U.S.A.
233 □I2 Newcastle ME U.S.A.
232 C4 New Castle PA U.S.A.
241 K3 Newcastle UT U.S.A.
232 C6 New Castle VA U.S.A.
238 F3 Newcastle WY U.S.A.
234 C3 New Castle County county DE U.S.A.
84 C3 Newcastle Creek r. N.T. Austr.
150 C2 Newcastle Emlyn Ceredigion, Wales U.K.
146 F6 Newcastleton Scottish Borders, Scotland U.K.
149 G4 Newcastle-under-Lyme Staffordshire, England U.K.
149 H3 Newcastle upon Tyne Tyne and Wear, England U.K.
84 C3 Newcastle Waters N.T. Austr.
147 B4 Newcastle West Rep. of Ireland
147 C5 Newcestown Rep. of Ireland
233 F6 New Church VA U.S.A.
Newchwang Liaoning China see Yingkou
235 E1 New City NY U.S.A.
234 B1 New Columbia PA U.S.A.
234 B1 New Columbus PA U.S.A.
241 M3 Newcomb NM U.S.A.
232 C4 Newcomerstown OH U.S.A.
232 C5 New Concord OH U.S.A.
234 B2 New Cumberland PA U.S.A.
146 D6 New Cumnock East Ayrshire, Scotland U.K.
146 F4 New Deer Aberdeenshire, Scotland U.K.
87 C7 Newdegate W.A. Austr.
116 D3 New Delhi Delhi India
233 □J1 New Denmark N.B. Can.
149 H4 New Earswick York, England U.K.
234 D2 New Egypt NJ U.S.A.
172 A2 Newel Ger.
85 F3 Newell Qld Austr.
236 C2 Newell SD U.S.A.
232 C4 Newell WV U.S.A.
87 E5 Newell, Lake salt flat W.A. Austr.
83 G2 New England Range mts N.S.W. Austr.
264 F3 New England Seamounts sea feature N. Atlantic Ocean
150 E3 Newent Gloucestershire, England U.K.
226 D4 New Era MI U.S.A.
232 D3 Newfane NY U.S.A.
233 G3 Newfane VT U.S.A.
234 C3 Newfield NJ U.S.A.
225 J3 Newfoundland i. Nfld. Can.
225 J2 Newfoundland prov. Can.
235 D1 Newfoundland NJ U.S.A.
234 C1 Newfoundland PA U.S.A.
238 D3 Newfoundland Evaporation Basin salt l. UT U.S.A.
234 B3 New Freedom PA U.S.A.
146 D6 New Galloway Dumfries and Galloway, Scotland U.K.
78 □6 New Georgia i. New Georgia Is Solomon Is
78 □6 New Georgia Islands Solomon Is
78 □6 New Georgia Sound sea chan. Solomon Is
226 C4 New Glarus WI U.S.A.
225 I4 New Glasgow N.S. Can.
147 E3 Newgrange Rep. of Ireland
145 D5 Newgrange Tomb tourist site Rep. of Ireland
235 D3 New Gretna NJ U.S.A.
91 J8 New Guinea i. Indon./P.N.G.
203 G6 New Halfa Sudan
240 H4 Newhall CA U.S.A.
235 E1 New Hamburg NY U.S.A.
233 H2 New Hampshire state U.S.A.
226 A4 New Hampton IA U.S.A.
235 D1 New Hampton NY U.S.A.
215 H3 New Hanover S. Africa
233 F3 New Hartford NY U.S.A.
151 H4 Newhaven East Sussex, England U.K.
233 G4 New Haven CT U.S.A.
226 A4 New Haven IA U.S.A.
226 E5 New Haven IN U.S.A.
227 F4 New Haven MI U.S.A.
232 C5 New Haven WV U.S.A.
235 F1 New Haven County county CT U.S.A.
222 E4 New Hazelton B.C. Can.
New Hebrides country S. Pacific Ocean see Vanuatu
266 G7 New Hebrides Trench sea feature Pacific Ocean
New Holland country Oceania see Australia
234 B2 New Holland PA U.S.A.
226 C4 New Holstein WI U.S.A.
234 D2 New Hope PA U.S.A.
237 F6 New Iberia LA U.S.A.
151 H4 Newick East Sussex, England U.K.
151 H3 Newington Kent, England U.K.
235 F1 Newington CT U.S.A.
148 B4 New Inn Cavan Rep. of Ireland
147 D3 New Inn Laois Rep. of Ireland
147 D4 Newinn Rep. of Ireland
91 L7 New Ireland i. P.N.G.
234 D3 New Jersey state U.S.A.
232 D4 New Kensington PA U.S.A.
232 E6 New Kent VA U.S.A.
147 C4 New Kildimo Rep. of Ireland
239 F5 Newkirk NM U.S.A.
237 D4 Newkirk OK U.S.A.
146 E6 New Lanark tourist site Scotland U.K.
231 D4 Newland NC U.S.A.
87 D6 Newland Range hills W.A. Austr.
146 F4 New Leeds Aberdeenshire, Scotland U.K.
232 B5 New Lexington OH U.S.A.
226 B4 New Lisbon WI U.S.A.
224 E4 New Liskeard Ont. Can.
233 G4 New London CT U.S.A.
232 B4 New London OH U.S.A.
226 C3 New London WI U.S.A.
235 F1 New London County county CT U.S.A.
146 D7 New Luce Dumfries and Galloway, Scotland U.K.
150 □ Newlyn Cornwall, England U.K.
146 F4 Newmachar Aberdeenshire, Scotland U.K.
237 F4 New Madrid MO U.S.A.
87 C4 Newman W.A. Austr.
80 E4 Newman North I. N.Z.
240 G3 Newman CA U.S.A.
262 O1 Newman Island Antarctica
234 B2 Newmanstown PA U.S.A.
224 E4 Newmarket Ont. Can.
246 □ Newmarket Jamaica
147 B4 Newmarket Cork Rep. of Ireland
147 D4 Newmarket Kilkenny Rep. of Ireland
151 H2 Newmarket Suffolk, England U.K.
146 B3 Newmarket Western Isles, Scotland U.K.
233 □H3 Newmarket NH U.S.A.
232 D5 New Market VA U.S.A.
147 C4 Newmarket-on-Fergus Rep. of Ireland
178 E3 Newmarkt am Wallersee Austria
232 C5 New Martinsville WV U.S.A.
238 C2 New Meadows ID U.S.A.
239 F5 New Mexico state U.S.A.
232 A5 New Miami OH U.S.A.
235 F1 New Milford CT U.S.A.
233 F4 New Milford PA U.S.A.
146 F4 Newmill Moray, Scotland U.K.
149 G4 New Mills Derbyshire, England U.K.
146 D6 Newmilns East Ayrshire, Scotland U.K.
151 F4 New Milton Hampshire, England U.K.
151 I3 New Mistley Essex, England U.K.
232 B5 New Moorefield OH U.S.A.
231 C5 Newnan GA U.S.A.
150 E3 Newnham Gloucestershire, England U.K.
87 C6 New Norcia W.A. Austr.
83 F5 New Norfolk Tas. Austr.
237 F6 New Orleans LA U.S.A.
234 A3 New Oxford PA U.S.A.
233 F4 New Paltz NY U.S.A.
226 E5 New Paris IN U.S.A.
232 A5 New Paris OH U.S.A.
232 C4 New Philadelphia OH U.S.A.
234 B2 New Philadelphia PA U.S.A.
146 F4 New Pitsligo Aberdeenshire, Scotland U.K.
80 E3 New Plymouth North I. N.Z.
150 C4 New Polzeath Cornwall, England U.K.
147 B3 Newport Mayo Rep. of Ireland
147 C4 Newport Tipperary Rep. of Ireland
151 H3 Newport Essex, England U.K.
146 E3 Newport Highland, Scotland U.K.
151 F4 Newport Isle of Wight, England U.K.
150 D3 Newport Newport, Wales U.K.
150 C2 Newport Pembrokeshire, Wales U.K.
150 E2 Newport Telford and Wrekin, England U.K.
150 E3 Newport admin. div. Wales U.K.
237 F5 Newport AR U.S.A.
234 C3 Newport DE U.S.A.
230 C4 Newport IN U.S.A.
233 □I2 Newport ME U.S.A.
227 F5 Newport MI U.S.A.
233 G3 Newport NH U.S.A.
234 C3 Newport NJ U.S.A.
238 A2 Newport OR U.S.A.
234 A2 Newport PA U.S.A.
233 H4 Newport RI U.S.A.
231 D5 Newport TN U.S.A.
233 G2 Newport VT U.S.A.
238 C1 Newport WA U.S.A.
150 C2 Newport Bay Wales U.K.
240 I5 Newport Beach CA U.S.A.
232 E6 Newport News VA U.S.A.
146 F5 Newport-on-Tay Fife, Scotland U.K.
151 G2 Newport Pagnell Milton Keynes, England U.K.
231 D6 New Port Richey FL U.S.A.
147 E2 Newport Trench Northern Ireland U.K.
235 E1 New Preston CT U.S.A.
246 C1 New Providence i. Bahamas
235 E2 New Providence NJ U.S.A.
234 B3 New Providence PA U.S.A.
150 C2 New Quay Ceredigion, Wales U.K.
150 B4 Newquay Cornwall, England U.K.
150 D2 New Radnor Powys, Wales U.K.
225 H3 New Richmond Que. Can.
232 A5 New Richmond OH U.S.A.
226 A3 New Richmond WI U.S.A.
234 C2 New Ringgold PA U.S.A.
241 K5 New River AZ U.S.A.
237 F6 New Roads LA U.S.A.
235 E2 New Rochelle NY U.S.A.
236 D2 New Rockford ND U.S.A.
151 H4 New Romney Kent, England U.K.
225 H4 New Ross N.S. Can.
147 E4 New Ross Rep. of Ireland
84 B3 Newry N.T. Austr.
147 E2 Newry Northern Ireland U.K.
226 B4 Newry WI U.S.A.
146 E5 New Scone Perth and Kinross, Scotland U.K.
New Siberia Islands Rus. Fed. see Novosibirskiye Ostrova
231 D6 New Smyrna Beach FL U.S.A.
83 F3 New South Wales state Austr.
232 D4 New Stanton PA U.S.A.
235 F1 New Suffolk NY U.S.A.
232 B6 New Tazewell TN U.S.A.
146 C5 Newton Argyll and Bute, Scotland U.K.
149 G4 Newton Lancashire, England U.K.
231 C6 Newton GA U.S.A.
236 E3 Newton IA U.S.A.
236 F4 Newton IL U.S.A.
236 D4 Newton KS U.S.A.
233 H3 Newton MA U.S.A.
237 F5 Newton MS U.S.A.
231 D5 Newton NC U.S.A.
234 D1 Newton NJ U.S.A.
237 E6 Newton TX U.S.A.
150 D4 Newton Abbot Devon, England U.K.
149 H3 Newton Aycliffe Durham, England U.K.
233 F2 Newton Falls NY U.S.A.
150 C4 Newton Ferrers Devon, England U.K.
146 F4 Newtonhill Aberdeenshire, Scotland U.K.
149 G4 Newton-le-Willows Merseyside, England U.K.
151 G3 Newton Longville Buckinghamshire, England U.K.
146 D6 Newton Mearns East Renfrewshire, Scotland U.K.
146 D4 Newtonmore Highland, Scotland U.K.
150 D4 Newton Poppleford Devon, England U.K.
150 D4 Newton St Cyres Devon, England U.K.
146 D7 Newton Stewart Dumfries and Galloway, Scotland U.K.
140 □ Newtontoppen mt. Svalbard
147 D4 Newtown Cork Rep. of Ireland
147 D4 Newtown Laois Rep. of Ireland
147 C3 Newtown Roscommon Rep. of Ireland
147 C4 Newtown Tipperary Rep. of Ireland
147 D4 Newtown Waterford Rep. of Ireland
150 E2 Newtown Herefordshire, England U.K.
150 D2 Newtown Powys, Wales U.K.
235 E1 Newtown CT U.S.A.
236 C1 New Town ND U.S.A.
232 B4 Newtown PA U.S.A.
234 D2 Newtown PA U.S.A.
147 F2 Newtownabbey Northern Ireland U.K.
147 F2 Newtownards Northern Ireland U.K.
Newtownbarry Rep. of Ireland see Bunclody
147 D2 Newtownbutler Northern Ireland U.K.
148 C3 Newtown Crommelin Northern Ireland U.K.
147 D2 Newtowncunningham Rep. of Ireland
147 D3 Newtown Forbes Rep. of Ireland
147 D2 Newtown Gore Rep. of Ireland
147 E2 Newtownhamilton Northern Ireland U.K.
147 D3 Newtownlow Rep. of Ireland
147 E3 Newtownmountkennedy Rep. of Ireland
146 F6 Newtown St Boswells Scottish Borders, Scotland U.K.
147 B4 Newtown Sandes Rep. of Ireland
234 C3 Newtown Square PA U.S.A.
147 D2 Newtownstewart Northern Ireland U.K.
150 D3 New Tredegar Caerphilly, Wales U.K.
234 C2 New Tripoli PA U.S.A.
146 E5 Newtyle Angus, Scotland U.K.
236 E2 New Ulm MN U.S.A.
232 B5 New Vienna OH U.S.A.
232 E4 Newville PA U.S.A.
233 □H2 New Vineyard ME U.S.A.
149 I4 New Waltham North East Lincolnshire, England U.K.
234 A3 New Windsor MD U.S.A.
235 D1 New Windsor NY U.S.A.
233 F3 New Woodstock NY U.S.A.
233 G4 New York NY U.S.A.
233 F3 New York state U.S.A.
235 E2 New York County county NY U.S.A.
80 New Zealand country Oceania
245 E4 Nexapa r. Mex.
162 D3 Nexon France
134 I4 Neya Rus. Fed.
134 H4 Neya r. Rus. Fed.
104 B4 Neyagawa Japan
122 D4 Ney Bīd Iran
150 C3 Neyland Pembrokeshire, Wales U.K.
122 C4 Neyrīz Iran
122 D2 Neyshābūr Iran
114 C4 Neyyattinkara Kerala India
245 E4 Nezahualcóyotl Mex.
245 H5 Nezahualcóyotl, Presa resr Mex.
176 G2 Nezamyslice Czech Rep.
176 D2 Nežárka r. Czech Rep.
137 I2 Nezhegol' r. Rus. Fed.
Nezhin Ukr. see Nizhyn
129 C1 Nezlobnaya Rus. Fed.
238 C2 Nezperce ID U.S.A.
177 I4 Nézsa Hungary
176 G2 Nezvěstice Czech Rep.
136 C3 Nezvys'ko Ukr.
95 E2 Ngabang Kalimantan Barat Indon.
209 C5 Ngabé Congo
97 B4 Nga Chong, Khao mt. Myanmar/Thai.
80 E1 Ngaiotonga North I. N.Z.
207 I3 Ngala Nigeria
208 C2 Ngama Chad
80 E3 Ngamatapouri North I. N.Z.
207 H5 Ngambé Cameroon
108 A2 Ngamda Xizang China
212 D3 Ngamiland admin. dist. Botswana
111 D6 Ngamring Xizang China
111 C6 Ngangla Ringco salt l. China
111 C5 Nganglong Kangri mt. Xizang China
111 C5 Nganglong Kangri mts Xizang China
111 D6 Ngangzê Co salt l. China
95 E4 Nganjuk Jawa Timur Indon.
108 C5 Ngan Sau, Sông r. Vietnam
96 B3 Ngao Thai.
207 I5 Ngaoundal Cameroon
207 I5 Ngaoundéré Cameroon
80 E3 Ngapuke North I. N.Z.
211 A5 Ngara Tanz.
Ngarrab Xizang China see Gyaca
80 E2 Ngaruawahia North I. N.Z.
80 F3 Ngaruroro r. North I. N.Z.
80 D1 Ngataki North I. N.Z.
80 F3 Ngatapa North I. N.Z.
80 E2 Ngatea North I. N.Z.
96 A3 Ngathainggyaung Myanmar
Ngawa Sichuan China see Aba
97 B4 Ngawan Chaung r. Myanmar
95 E4 Ngawi Jawa Timur Indon.
Ngcheangel atoll Palau see Kayangel
Ngeaur i. Palau see Angaur
91 I5 Ngeruangel i. Palau
Nggamea i. Fiji see Qamea
78 □6 Nggatokae i. New Georgia Is Solomon Is
78 □6 Nggela Sule i. Solomon Is
Nggelelevu i. Fiji see Qelelevu
212 D4 Nghabe r. Botswana
96 C3 Ngiap r. Laos
95 F4 Ngimbang Jawa Timur Indon.
Ngiva Angola see Ondjiva
96 D4 Ngoc Linh mt. Vietnam
207 I6 Ngoko r. Cameroon/Congo
209 E8 Ngoma Zambia
209 B6 Ngoma Tsé-Tsé Congo
215 H2 Ngome S. Africa
111 G6 Ngom Qu r. Qinghai China
80 F3 Ngongotaha North I. N.Z.
111 D5 Ngoqumaima Xizang China
106 C5 Ngoring Qinghai China
106 C5 Ngoring Hu l. Qinghai China
211 B5 Ngorongoro Conservation Area nature res. Tanz.
211 B5 Ngorongoro Crater Tanz.
207 H6 Ngoulemakong Cameroon
207 I6 Ngoumou Cameroon
208 A5 Ngounié prov. Gabon
208 A5 Ngounié r. Gabon
202 B6 Ngounsi Gabon
202 C6 Ngoura Chad
202 B6 Ngouri Chad
207 I3 Ngourti Niger
211 A5 Ngozi Burundi
215 G4 Ngqeleni S. Africa
215 G4 Ngqungqu S. Africa
207 I3 Nguigmi Niger
84 B1 Nguiu N.T. Austr.
84 C2 Ngukurr N.T. Austr.
91 I5 Ngulu atoll Micronesia
96 C3 Ngum, Nam r. Laos
78 □5 Nguna i. Vanuatu
Ngunza Angola see Sumbe
Ngunza-Kabolu Angola see Sumbe
207 H3 Nguru Nigeria
211 C6 Nguru Mountains Tanz.
212 E5 Ngwaketse admin. dist. Botswana
Ngwane country Africa see Swaziland
215 F2 Ngwathe S. Africa
215 I2 Ngwavuma r. Swaziland
215 H3 Ngwelezana S. Africa
215 H3 Ngwempisi r. S. Africa
209 E9 Ngwezi r. Zambia
213 G3 Nhamatanda Moz.
251 G5 Nhamundá Brazil
251 G5 Nhamundá r. Brazil
256 B4 Nhandeara Brazil
209 C7 N'harea Angola
97 E4 Nha Trang Vietnam
82 E4 Nhill Vic. Austr.
215 H2 Nhlangano Swaziland
215 H3 Nhlazatshe S. Africa
96 D2 Nho Quan Vietnam
Nhow i. Fiji see Gau
84 D2 Nhulunbuy N.T. Austr.
206 E5 Niablé Ghana
223 J4 Niacam Sask. Can.
206 E3 Niafounké Mali
226 D3 Niagara WI U.S.A.
224 E5 Niagara Falls Ont. Can.
232 D3 Niagara Falls NY U.S.A.
227 H4 Niagara-on-the-Lake Ont. Can.

Niagassola to North Rona 341

206 C3 Niagassola Guinea
206 C4 Niagouelé, Mont du hill Guinea
206 D4 Niakaramandougou Côte d'Ivoire
207 F3 Niamey Niger
206 D3 Niamina Mali
207 F4 Niamtougou Togo
Nianbai Qinghai China see Ledu
206 C4 Niandan r. Guinea
206 C4 Niandankoro Guinea
211 C6 Niangandu Tanz.
208 E4 Niangara Dem. Rep. Congo
206 E3 Niangay, Lac l. Mali
206 D4 Niangoloko Burkina
237 E4 Niangua r. MO U.S.A.
Niangxi Hunan China see Xinshao
206 D4 Niankorodougou Burkina
235 F1 Niantic CT U.S.A.
107 I2 Nianzishan Heilong. China
209 B5 Niari admin. reg. Congo
94 B2 Nias i. Indon.
213 H2 Niassa prov. Moz.
Niassa, Lago l. Africa see Nyasa, Lake
Niaur i. Palau see Angaur
163 D6 Niaux France
190 E4 Nibbiano Italy
86 E4 Nibil Well W.A. Austr.
129 E3 Nic Azer.
195 G3 Nicà r. Italy
138 C3 Nīca Latvia
Nicaea Turkey see İznik
246 A4 Nicaragua country Central America
242 □I7 Nicaragua, Lago de l. Nic.
Nicaragua, Lake Nic. see Nicaragua, Lago de
246 D2 Nicaro Cuba
195 F4 Nicastro Italy
161 F5 Nice France
Nice airport France see Côte d'Azur
240 F2 Nice CA U.S.A.
Nicephorium Syria see Ar Raqqah
231 C6 Niceville FL U.S.A.
190 C3 Nichelino Italy
103 E8 Nichinan Japan
117 E4 Nichlaul Uttar Prad. India
246 B2 Nicholas Channel Bahamas/Cuba
230 C4 Nicholasville KY U.S.A.
246 C1 Nicholl's Town Andros Bahamas
233 E3 Nichols NY U.S.A.
86 F3 Nicholson W.A. Austr.
84 D3 Nicholson r. Qld Austr.
227 F2 Nicholson Ont. Can.
234 C1 Nicholson PA U.S.A.
87 C5 Nicholson Range hills W.A. Austr.
233 F2 Nicholville NY U.S.A.
179 I3 Nickelsdorf Austria
232 B6 Nickelsville VA U.S.A.
115 G4 Nicobar Islands Andaman & Nicobar Is India
197 I3 Nicolae Bălcescu Romania
243 H5 Nicolás Bravo Mex.
245 E4 Nicolás Romero Mex.
240 G2 Nicolaus CA U.S.A.
195 E5 Nicolosi Sicilia Italy
Nicomedia Turkey see Kocaeli
Nicopolis Bulg. see Nikopol
Nicosia Cyprus see Lefkosia
194 D5 Nicosia Sicilia Italy
195 E4 Nicotera Italy
242 □I7 Nicoya Costa Rica
242 □I7 Nicoya, Península de pen. Costa Rica
233 □J1 Nictau N.B. Can.
197 I3 Niculiţel Romania
138 C4 Nida Lith.
175 I2 Nida r. Pol.
175 I5 Nida r. Pol.
114 D2 Nidadavole Andhra Prad. India
114 C2 Nidagunda Andhra Prad. India
190 C1 Nidau Switz.
149 H3 Nidd r. England U.K.
169 E5 Nidda Ger.
169 D5 Nidda r. Ger.
169 D5 Nidder r. Ger.
149 H3 Nidderdale val. England U.K.
142 C2 Nidelva r. Norway
190 D2 Nidwalden canton Switz.
197 E5 Nidže mt. Greece/Macedonia
175 I2 Nidzica Pol.
175 I5 Nidzica r. Pol.
164 F1 Niebert Neth.
184 D3 Niebla Spain
175 I3 Nieborów Pol.
168 D1 Niebüll Ger.
175 J6 Niebylec Pol.
174 F3 Niechanowo Pol.
175 H4 Niechcice Pol.
175 I2 Niechłonin Pol.
174 E4 Niechlów Pol.
157 G3 Nied r. France
157 G3 Nied Allemande r. France
169 E4 Niedenstein Ger.
173 G3 Niederaichbach Ger.
165 F5 Niederanven Lux.
169 E5 Niederaula Ger.
173 G3 Niederbayern admin. reg. Bayern Ger.
190 C1 Niederbipp Switz.
169 D5 Niederbrechen Ger.
172 C3 Niedereschach Ger.
179 E3 Niedere Tauern mts Austria
170 E3 Niederfinow Ger.
169 C5 Niederfischbach Ger.
169 E5 Nieder-Gemünden Ger.
171 D4 Niedergörsdorf Ger.
169 C5 Niederkassel Ger.
172 B2 Niederkirchen Ger.
169 B4 Niederkrüchten Ger.
168 C3 Niederlangen Ger.
171 E3 Niederlehme Ger.
171 C3 Niederndodeleben Ger.
178 D3 Niederndorf Austria
169 D5 Niederneisen Ger.
172 D2 Niedernhall Ger.
169 D5 Niedernhausen Ger.
178 D3 Niedernsill Austria
169 E3 Niedernwöhren Ger.
172 C2 Nieder-Olm Ger.
169 F4 Niederorschel Ger.
179 G2 Niederösterreich land Austria
169 E5 Nieder-Rodenbach Ger.
171 C4 Niederroßla Ger.
168 D3 Niedersachsen land Ger.
169 F4 Niedersachswerfen Ger.
169 D5 Niederselters Ger.
172 D2 Niederstetten Ger.
173 E3 Niederstotzingen Ger.
171 C4 Niedertrebra Ger.
190 E1 Niederurnen Switz.
173 G3 Niederviehbach Ger.
169 F5 Niederwerrn Ger.
171 E5 Niederwiesa Ger.
173 G3 Niederwinkling Ger.
172 B2 Niederwörresbach Ger.
169 C5 Niederzissen Ger.
175 K4 Niedrzwica Duża Pol.
175 K2 Niedźwiadna Pol.
175 I6 Niedźwiedź Pol.
207 H6 Niefang Equat. Guinea
172 C3 Niefern-Öschelbronn Ger.
175 J1 Niegocin, Jezioro l. Pol.
174 D4 Niegosławice Pol.
175 H5 Niegowa Pol.
171 C3 Niegripp Ger.
169 E4 Nieheim Ger.
164 F1 Niekerk Neth.
214 D3 Niekerkshoop S. Africa
175 I4 Niekłań Wielki Pol.
165 D3 Niel Belgium
175 L5 Nielisz Pol.
206 D4 Niellé Côte d'Ivoire
209 F6 Niemba Dem. Rep. Congo
171 D4 Niemberg Ger.
175 K4 Niemce Pol.
174 E5 Niemcza Pol.
171 D3 Niemegk Ger.
140 M2 Niemisel Sweden
174 F5 Niemodlin Pol.
174 G4 Niemysłów Pol.
206 D4 Niéna Mali
175 K5 Nienadówka Pol.
168 E1 Nienborstel Ger.
171 C4 Nienburg (Saale) Ger.
168 E3 Nienburg (Weser) Ger.
168 F3 Nienhagen Ger.
169 E3 Nienstädt Ger.
170 D1 Niepars Ger.
175 I5 Niepołomice Pol.
175 J3 Nieporęt Pol.
156 C2 Nieppe France
169 A4 Niers r. Ger.
172 C2 Nierstein Ger.
171 F4 Niesky Ger.
169 E4 Nieste Ger.
175 I4 Nieświń Pol.
174 G3 Nieszawa Pol.
175 J5 Nietulisko Duże Pol.
162 D3 Nieul France
162 A2 Nieul-le-Dolent France
162 A2 Nieul-sur-Mer France
251 H3 Nieuw Amsterdam Suriname
164 F3 Nieuw-Bergen Neth.
164 E2 Nieuwegein Neth.
164 D2 Nieuwe-Niedorp Neth.
164 F1 Nieuwe Pekela Neth.
164 D3 Nieuwerkerk Neth.
164 D3 Nieuwerkerk aan de IJssel Neth.
165 E4 Nieuwerkerken Belgium
164 G1 Nieuweschans Neth.
164 D3 Nieuwe-Tonge Neth.
164 F2 Nieuw-Heeten Neth.
164 D2 Nieuwkoop Neth.
164 F2 Nieuwlande Neth.
164 F2 Nieuwleusen Neth.
164 E2 Nieuw-Loosdrecht Neth.
164 E2 Nieuw-Milligen Neth.
165 D3 Nieuw-Namen Neth.
251 G3 Nieuw Nickerie Suriname
164 F1 Nieuwolda Neth.
214 B4 Nieuwoudtville S. Africa
165 B3 Nieuwpoort Belgium
164 D2 Nieuwveen Neth.
164 D2 Nieuw-Vennep Neth.
164 D3 Nieuw-Vossemeer Neth.
164 F2 Nieuw-Weerdinge Neth.
169 C5 Nievern Ger.
244 C2 Nieves Mex.
Nieves Galicia Spain see As Neves
160 B1 Nièvre dept Bourgogne France
160 B1 Nièvre r. France
160 B2 Nièvre de Champlemy r. France
175 K4 Niewęgłosz Pol.
126 D3 Niğde Turkey
215 G2 Nigel S. Africa
207 H2 Niger country Africa
207 G5 Niger r. Africa
207 G4 Niger state Nigeria
207 G5 Niger, Mouths of the Nigeria
206 C4 Niger, Source of the tourist site Guinea
264 J5 Niger Cone sea feature S. Atlantic Ocean
207 G4 Nigeria country Africa
146 D4 Nigg Bay Scotland U.K.
116 E3 Nighasan Uttar Prad. India
81 B6 Nightcaps South I. N.Z.
224 D3 Nighthawk Lake Ont. Can.
85 E2 Night Island Qld Austr.
182 B2 Nigrán Spain
198 C1 Nigrita Greece
244 D2 Nigromante Mex.
185 G4 Nigüelas Spain
138 E2 Nigula looduskaitseala nature res. Estonia
159 H5 Niherne France
Nihommatsu Japan see Nihonmatsu
Nihon country Asia see Japan
102 J5 Nihonmatsu Japan
102 I5 Niigata Japan
105 E1 Niigata pref. Japan
105 E2 Niigata-yake-yama vol. Japan
103 F7 Niihama Japan
240 □A8 Niihau i. HI U.S.A.
103 F6 Niimi Japan
102 I5 Niitsu Japan
185 H4 Níjar Spain
164 F2 Nijeveen Neth.
164 E2 Nijkerk Neth.
165 D3 Nijlen Belgium
164 E3 Nijmegen Neth.
164 F2 Nijverdal Neth.
198 C2 Nikaia Greece
140 O1 Nikel' Rus. Fed.
120 D2 Nikel'tau Kazakh.
121 J2 Nikitinka Kazakh.
137 J2 Nikitovka Rus. Fed.
140 L2 Nikkaluokta Sweden
207 F4 Nikki Benin
105 F2 Nikkō Japan
179 G3 Niklasdorf Austria
134 I4 Nikola Rus. Fed.
197 G4 Nikolaevo Bulg.
Nikolayev Mykolayivs'ka Oblast' Ukr. see Mykolayiv
121 F1 Nikolayevka Kazakh.
120 E1 Nikolayevka Chelyabinskaya Oblast' Rus. Fed.
100 E2 Nikolayevka Khabarovskiy Kray Rus. Fed.
137 J4 Nikolayevka Rostovskaya Oblast' Rus. Fed.
135 I5 Nikolayevka Ul'yanovskaya Oblast' Rus. Fed.
Nikolayev Oblast admin. div. Ukr. see Mykolayivs'ka Oblast'
135 I6 Nikolayevsk Rus. Fed.
Nikolayevskaya Oblast' admin. div. Ukr. see Mykolayivs'ka Oblast'
Nikolayevskiy Rus. Fed. see Nikolayevsk
100 G1 Nikolayevsk-na-Amure Rus. Fed.
Nikolayevskoye Respublika Adygeya Rus. Fed. see Krasnogvardeyskoye
135 I5 Nikol'sk Rus. Fed.
134 I4 Nikol'sk Rus. Fed.
Nikol'skaya Pestravka Rus. Fed. see Nikol'sk
Nikol'skiy Kazakh. see Satpayev
139 J1 Nikol'skiy Rus. Fed.
131 R4 Nikol'skoye Rus. Fed.
139 M3 Nikol'skoye Rus. Fed.
139 L5 Nikol'skoye Rus. Fed.
120 C1 Nikol'skoye Rus. Fed.
Nikol'skoye Rus. Fed. see Sheksna
139 K2 Nikol'skoye Rus. Fed.
197 G4 Nikopol Bulg.
137 H4 Nikopol' Ukr.
122 B2 Nīk Pey Iran
126 E2 Niksar Turkey
122 E5 Nīkshahr Iran
196 D4 Nikšić Crna Gora Yugo.
77 I2 Nikumaroro i. Phoenix Is Kiribati
77 H2 Nikunau i. Gilbert Is Kiribati
Nīl, Bahr el r. Africa see Nile
93 D4 Nila vol. Maluku Indon.
117 F5 Nilagiri Orissa India
114 C4 Nilakkottai Tamil Nadu India
114 C4 Nilambur Kerala India
241 J5 Niland CA U.S.A.
113 D11 Nilandhoo Atoll Maldives
114 C2 Nilanga Mahar. India
114 D4 Nilaveli Sri Lanka
203 F2 Nile r. Africa
203 G5 Nile state Sudan
226 D5 Niles MI U.S.A.
232 C4 Niles OH U.S.A.
114 B3 Nileswaram Kerala India
124 B5 Nili r. Eth.
140 M2 Nilivaara Sweden
110 C3 Nilka Xinjiang China
257 F5 Nilópolis Brazil
117 G4 Nilphamari Bangl.
140 O3 Nilsiä Fin.
199 F1 Nilüfer r. Turkey
157 G3 Nilvange France
142 C4 Nim Denmark
116 C4 Nimach Madh. Prad. India
116 C4 Nimaj Rajasthan India
100 E2 Niman r. Rus. Fed.
Nimba, Monts mts Africa see Nimba Mountains
116 C4 Nimbahera Rajasthan India
114 B2 Nimbal Karnataka India
206 C4 Nimba Mountains Africa
86 D4 Nimberra Well W.A. Austr.
Nimbhera Rajasthan India see Nimbahera
100 F1 Nimelen r. Rus. Fed.
161 C5 Nîmes France
191 I2 Nimis Italy
116 C4 Nimka Thana Rajasthan India
83 G4 Nimmitabel N.S.W. Austr.
222 E5 Nimpkish r. B.C. Can.
123 E4 Nīmrūz prov. Afgh.
116 D2 Nimu Jammu and Kashmir
Nimwegen Neth. see Nijmegen
78 □3a Ninai i. Kwajalein Marshall Is
127 F4 Nīnawá governorate Iraq
127 F3 Nīnawá tourist site Iraq
83 G2 Nindigully Qld Austr.
168 E1 Nindorf Ger.
114 B4 Nine Degree Channel India
Ninemile Bar Dumfries and Galloway, Scotland U.K. see Crocketford
83 E2 Nine Mile Lake salt flat N.S.W. Austr.
241 I2 Ninemile Peak NV U.S.A.
265 J7 Ninetyeast Ridge sea feature Indian Ocean
83 F4 Ninety Mile Beach Vic. Austr.
80 D1 Ninety Mile Beach North I. N.Z.
Nineveh tourist site Iraq see Nīnawá
151 H4 Ninfield East Sussex, England U.K.
100 D3 Ning'an Heilong. China
109 G2 Ningbo Zhejiang China
107 H3 Ningcheng Nei Mongol China
109 F3 Ningde Fujian China
109 E3 Ningdu Jiangxi China
Ning'er Yunnan China see Pu'er
109 F2 Ningguo Anhui China
109 G2 Ninghai Zhejiang China
107 H4 Ninghe Tianjin China
Ninghsia Hui Autonomous Region aut. reg. China see Ningxia Huizu Zizhiqu
109 F3 Ninghua Fujian China
207 H4 Ningi Nigeria
Ningjiang Jilin China see Songyuan
108 A2 Ningjing Shan mts Xizang China
108 B3 Ninglang Yunnan China
107 G5 Ningling Henan China
108 C4 Ningming Guangxi China
108 B3 Ningnan Sichuan China
108 C1 Ningqiang Shaanxi China
108 D1 Ningshan Shaanxi China
107 G4 Ningwu Shanxi China
Ningxia aut. reg. China see Ningxia Huizu Zizhiqu
106 E4 Ningxia Huizu Zizhiqu aut. reg. China
107 E5 Ningxian Gansu China
109 E2 Ningxiang Hunan China
107 H5 Ningyang Shandong China
109 D3 Ningyuan Hunan China
Ningzhou Yunnan China see Huaning
96 D2 Ninh Binh Vietnam
97 E4 Ninh Hoa Vietnam
260 A5 Ninhue Chile
91 J7 Ninigo Group is P.N.G.
102 J3 Ninohe Japan
129 C3 Ninotsminda Georgia
165 D4 Ninove Belgium
129 C1 Niny Rus. Fed.
253 G5 Nioaque Brazil
236 D3 Niobrara r. NE U.S.A.
208 C5 Nioki Dem. Rep. Congo
206 D3 Niono Mali
206 C3 Nioro Mali
206 B3 Nioro du Rip Senegal
162 B2 Niort France
114 B2 Nipani Karnataka India
260 A5 Ñipas Chile
223 J4 Nipawin Sask. Can.
116 C5 Niphad Mahar. India
224 B3 Nipigon Ont. Can.
236 F1 Nipigon r. Ont. Can.
224 B3 Nipigon, Lake Ont. Can.
227 H2 Nipissing Ont. Can.
224 E4 Nipissing, Lake Ont. Can.
240 G4 Nipomo CA U.S.A.
Nippon country Asia see Japan
Nippon Hai sea N. Pacific Ocean see Japan, Sea of
127 G4 Nippur tourist site Iraq
241 J4 Nipton CA U.S.A.
254 C5 Niquelândia Brazil
260 B5 Niquen Chile
246 C2 Niquero Cuba
122 A2 Nīr Iran
114 B2 Nira r. India
105 E3 Nirasaki Japan
260 A4 Nirivilo Chile
107 J1 Nirji Nei Mongol China
114 C2 Nirmal Andhra Prad. India
117 F4 Nirmali Bihar India
114 C2 Nirmal Range hills India
197 E4 Niš Srbija Yugo.
182 C5 Nisa Port.
182 C5 Nisa r. Port.
124 D5 Nişāb Yemen
197 E4 Nišava r. Yugo.
146 F6 Nisbet Scottish Borders, Scotland U.K.
194 D5 Niscemi Sicilia Italy
Nīshāpūr Iran see Neyshābūr
138 G4 Nishcha r. Belarus
102 L2 Nishibetsu-gawa r. Japan
104 B4 Nishinomiya Japan
102 □1 Nishino-omote Japan
103 □3 Nishino-shima vol. Japan
104 D4 Nishio Japan
103 D7 Nishi-Sonogi-hantō pen. Japan
104 A4 Nishiwaki Japan
254 G3 Nísia Floresta Brazil
Nisibis Turkey see Nusaybin
103 E7 Nisi-mera Japan
Nísiros i. Greece see Nisyros
233 G3 Niskayuna NY U.S.A.
224 B1 Niskibi r. Ont. Can.
175 K5 Nisko Pol.
222 B2 Nisling r. Y.T. Can.
165 D4 Nismes Belgium
165 D4 Nismes, Forêt de for. Belgium
136 E4 Nisporeni Moldova
142 E3 Nissan r. Sweden
161 B5 Nissan-lez-Enserune France
104 D3 Nisshin Japan
194 D5 Nissoria Sicilia Italy
142 C3 Nissum Bredning b. Denmark
164 E3 Nistelrode Neth.
136 F4 Nistru r. Moldova alt. Dnister (Ukraine), conv. Dniester
136 E4 Nistrului Inferior, Cîmpia lowland Moldova
222 C2 Nisutlin r. Y.T. Can.
199 E3 Nisyros i. Greece
103 F6 Nita Japan
225 G2 Nitchequon Que. Can.
Nitendi i. Santa Cruz Is Solomon Is see Ndeni
257 F5 Niterói Brazil
146 E6 Nith r. Scotland U.K.
146 E6 Nithsdale val. Scotland U.K.
177 H3 Nitra Slovakia
177 H4 Nitra r. Slovakia
177 H3 Nitrianske Pravno Slovakia
177 H3 Nitriansky Kraj admin. reg. Slovakia
232 C5 Nitro WV U.S.A.
156 D5 Nitry France
142 D1 Nittedal Norway
172 A2 Nittel Ger.
173 G2 Nittenau Ger.
173 F2 Nittendorf Ger.
Niua i. Vanuatu see Aniwa
77 I3 Niuafo'ou i. Tonga
Niuafu i. Tonga see Niuafo'ou
77 I3 Niuatoputopu i. Tonga
110 F4 Niubiziliang Qinghai China
81 □4 Niue terr. S. Pacific Ocean
Niujing Yunnan China see Binchuan
77 H3 Niulakita i. Tuvalu
108 B3 Niulan Jiang r. Yunnan China
240 □D8 Niulii HI U.S.A.
Niushan Jiangsu China see Donghai
77 H2 Niutao i. Tuvalu
109 F2 Niutoushan Anhui China
107 I3 Niuzhuang Liaoning China
140 N3 Nivala Fin.
163 A5 Nive r. France
85 F5 Nive Downs Qld Austr.
165 D4 Nivelles Belgium
175 I1 Nivenskoye Rus. Fed.
158 D4 Nivillac France
156 C3 Nivillers France
160 D3 Nivolas-Vermelle France
140 P2 Nivskiy Rus. Fed.
116 C4 Niwai Rajasthan India
116 D4 Niwari Madh. Prad. India
116 E5 Niwas Madh. Prad. India
175 J5 Niwiska Pol.
157 F3 Nixéville-Blercourt France
Nixia Sichuan China see Sêrxu
240 H2 Nixon NV U.S.A.
Niya Xinjiang China see Minfeng
111 C4 Niya He r. China
129 F3 Niyazoba Azer.
95 E2 Niyut, Gunung mt. Indon.
105 F3 Niza Japan
114 C2 Nizamabad Andhra Prad. India
114 D3 Nizampatnam Andhra Prad. India
176 D2 Nižbor Czech Rep.
134 I4 Nizhegorodskaya Oblast' admin. div. Rus. Fed.
131 L4 Nizhneangarsk Rus. Fed.
137 I5 Nizhnebakanskiy Rus. Fed.
135 G6 Nizhnedevitsk Rus. Fed.
121 K1 Nizhnekamenka Rus. Fed.
134 J5 Nizhnekamsk Rus. Fed.
134 K5 Nizhnekamskoye Vodokhranilishche resr Rus. Fed.
98 G1 Nizhneudinsk Rus. Fed.
130 I3 Nizhnevartovsk Rus. Fed.
Nizhnevolzhsk Rus. Fed. see Narimanov
131 O2 Nizhneyansk Rus. Fed.
134 L4 Nizhni Irginski Rus. Fed.
135 I6 Nizhniy Baskunchak Rus. Fed.
129 C2 Nizhniy Chegem Rus. Fed.
135 H6 Nizhniy Chir Rus. Fed.
129 E2 Nizhniy Dzhengutay Rus. Fed.
Nizhniye Kresty Rus. Fed. see Cherskiy
Nizhniye Ustriki Pol. see Ustrzyki Dolne
137 J2 Nizhniy Karabut Rus. Fed.
137 K2 Nizhniy Kislyay Rus. Fed.
129 D2 Nizhniy Kurp Rus. Fed.
135 H5 Nizhniy Lomov Rus. Fed.
137 K2 Nizhniy Mamon Rus. Fed.
134 H4 Nizhniy Novgorod Rus. Fed.
Nizhniy Novgorod Oblast admin. div. Rus. Fed. see Nizhegorodskaya Oblast'
134 K3 Nizhniy Odes Rus. Fed.
137 J2 Nizhniy Ol'shan Rus. Fed.
130 G4 Nizhniy Tagil Rus. Fed.
107 G1 Nizhniy Tsasuchey Rus. Fed.
134 I4 Nizhniy Yenangsk Rus. Fed.
134 K3 Nizhnyaya Omra Rus. Fed.
140 P2 Nizhnyaya Pirenga, Ozero l. Rus. Fed.
131 K4 Nizhnyaya Poyma Rus. Fed.
121 I1 Nizhnyaya Suyetka Rus. Fed.
131 J3 Nizhnyaya Tunguska r. Rus. Fed.
130 G4 Nizhnyaya Tura Rus. Fed.
137 J2 Nizhnyaya Veduga Rus. Fed.
137 F2 Nizhyn Ukr.
175 I3 Nizina reg. Pol.
126 E3 Nizip Turkey
177 K2 Nízke Beskydy hills Slovakia
177 I3 Nízke Tatry mts Slovakia
100 E4 Nizmennyy, Mys pt Rus. Fed.
177 J3 Nižná Slaná Slovakia
177 K3 Nižný Hrušov Slovakia
177 K3 Nižný Žipov Slovakia
Nizwā Oman see Nazwá
Nizza France see Nice
195 E5 Nizza di Sicilia Sicilia Italy
190 D4 Nizza Monferrato Italy
217 □3a Njazidja i. Comoros
196 D4 Njegoš mts Yugo.
211 C7 Njinjo Tanz.
191 J3 Njivice Croatia
209 E9 Njoko r. Zambia
211 B7 Njombe Tanz.
211 B6 Njombe r. Tanz.
78 □6 Njoroveto New Georgia Is Solomon Is
141 L3 Njurundabommen Sweden
141 L3 Njutånger Sweden
207 H5 Nkambe Cameroon
215 H3 Nkandla S. Africa
211 A6 Nkasi Tanz.
206 E5 Nkawkaw Ghana
211 B7 Nkhata Bay Malawi
211 B8 Nkhotakota Malawi
207 H5 Nkongsamba Cameroon
206 E5 Nkoranza Ghana
207 I5 Nkoteng Cameroon
215 F4 Nkululeko S. Africa
210 A4 Nkusi r. Uganda
215 H3 Nkwalini S. Africa
207 F4 Nkwanta Ghana
215 F5 Nkwenkwezi S. Africa
96 B1 Nmai Hka r. Myanmar
117 I4 Noa Dihing r. India
163 B4 Noaillan France
156 C3 Noailles France
163 A6 Noain Spain
117 G5 Noakhali Bangl.
191 H3 Noale Italy
185 G3 Noalejo Spain
117 F5 Noamundi Bihar India
190 C3 Noasca Italy
220 B3 Noatak r. AK U.S.A.
148 C4 Nobber Rep. of Ireland
103 E7 Nobeoka Japan
171 D5 Nobitz Ger.
183 G5 Noblejas Spain
230 C3 Noblesville IN U.S.A.
215 F4 Nobokwe S. Africa
102 J2 Noboribetsu Japan
253 F3 Nobres Brazil
85 E5 Noccundra Qld Austr.
159 G3 Nocé France
191 G2 Noce r. Italy
193 H5 Noce r. Italy
182 D2 Noceda Spain
193 G4 Nocera Inferiore Italy
193 I5 Nocera Terinese Italy
193 E1 Nocera Umbra Italy
190 F4 Noceto Italy
244 C3 Nochistlán Mex.
195 G2 Noci Italy
175 M1 Nočia r. Belarus/Lith.
195 H2 Nociglia Italy
85 E5 Nockatunga Qld Austr.
237 D5 Nocona TX U.S.A.
105 F3 Noda Japan
236 E4 Nodaway r. MO U.S.A.
142 B2 Nodeland Norway
160 E1 Nods France
163 D5 Noé France
224 D4 Noelville Ont. Can.
214 C2 Noenieput S. Africa
193 I4 Noepoli Italy
168 F1 Noer Ger.
261 F3 Noetinger Arg.
156 C2 Nœux-les-Mines France
183 F5 Noez Spain
183 F5 Noez, Pico de mt. Spain
183 G2 Nofuentes Spain
242 C2 Nogales Mex.
184 D2 Nogales Spain
239 E6 Nogales AZ U.S.A.
191 G3 Nogara Italy
163 B5 Nogaro France
174 H1 Nogat r. Pol.
103 E7 Nōgata Japan
Nogaysk Ukr. see Prymors'ke
129 E1 Nogayskaya Step' reg. Rus. Fed.
120 C2 Nogayty Kazakh.
157 F4 Nogent France
159 G3 Nogent-le-Bernard France
156 B4 Nogent-le-Roi France
159 G3 Nogent-le-Rotrou France
156 E4 Nogent-sur-Aube France
156 C4 Nogent-sur-Marne France
156 C3 Nogent-sur-Oise France
156 D4 Nogent-sur-Seine France
156 C5 Nogent-sur-Vernisson France
131 K3 Noginsk Evenkiyskiy Avtonomnyy Okrug Rus. Fed.
139 L4 Noginsk Moskovskaya Oblast' Rus. Fed.
100 G2 Nogliki Sakhalin Rus. Fed.
85 G5 Nogo r. Qld Austr.
85 G4 Nogoa r. Qld Austr.
104 C3 Nōgōhaku-san mt. Japan
261 H3 Nogoyá Arg.
261 H3 Nogoya r. Arg.
177 I4 Nógrád Hungary
177 I4 Nógrád county Hungary
183 H3 Nograles Spain
104 D2 Noguchigorō-dake mt. Japan
182 D3 Nogueira, Serra de mts Port.
183 I4 Noguera Spain
186 D2 Noguera de Tor r. Spain
186 D2 Noguera Pallaresa r. Spain
186 D3 Noguera Ribagorçana r. Spain
163 B5 Noguères France
187 C4 Nogueruelas Spain
160 A1 Nohain r. France
159 H5 Nohant-Vic France
116 C3 Nohar Rajasthan India
172 B2 Nohfelden Ger.
163 D5 Nohic France
182 B2 Noia Galicia Spain
195 F1 Noicattaro Italy
160 E1 Noidans-lès-Vesoul France
163 C5 Noilhan France
161 B4 Noir, Causse plat. France
227 I3 Noire r. Que. Can.
163 E5 Noire, Montagne mts France
158 C3 Noires, Montagnes hills France
160 B3 Noirétable France
158 D5 Noirmoutier, Île de i. France
158 D4 Noirmoutier-en-l'Île France
157 G3 Noisseville France
183 G1 Noja Spain
232 E5 Nokesville VA U.S.A.
116 C4 Nokha Rajasthan India
122 E5 Nokhowch, Kūh-e mt. Iran
141 M3 Nokia Fin.
Nökis Uzbek. see Nukus
223 J5 Nokomis Sask. Can.
202 B6 Nokou Chad
117 G4 Nokrek Peak Meghalaya India
142 E3 Nol Sweden
208 C4 Nola C.A.R.
194 D2 Nola Italy
160 C2 Nolay France
190 D4 Noli Italy
231 D4 Nolichuky r. TN U.S.A.
134 J4 Nolinsk Kirovskaya Oblast' Rus. Fed.
214 D5 Noll S. Africa
183 F4 Nombela Spain
220 B3 Nome AK U.S.A.
157 G4 Nomeny France
157 G4 Nomexy France
Nomoi Islands Micronesia see Mortlock Islands
215 F4 Nomonde S. Africa
78 □4a Nomoneas is Chuuk Micronesia
106 E1 Nomto Rus. Fed.
79 □2 Nomuka i. Tonga
79 □2 Nomuka Group is Tonga
91 L5 Nomwin atoll Micronesia
134 H4 Nomzha Rus. Fed.
223 I2 Nonacho Lake N.W.T. Can.
156 B4 Nonancourt France
159 G3 Nonant-le-Pin France
191 G4 Nonantola Italy
186 D3 Nonaspe Spain
215 H3 Nondweni S. Africa
156 C3 Nonette r. France
100 C3 Nong'an Jilin China
97 C4 Nong Hong Thai.
Nonghui Sichuan China see Guang'an
96 C3 Nong Khai Thai.
215 H2 Nongoma S. Africa
117 G4 Nongstoin Meghalaya India
161 C4 Nonières France
172 B3 Nonnenweier Ger.
Nonni r. China see Nen Jiang
82 D3 Nonning S.A. Austr.
172 A2 Nonnweiler Ger.
255 B8 Nonoai Brazil
242 D3 Nonoava Mex.
77 H2 Nonouti atoll Gilbert Is Kiribati
101 C5 Nonsan S. Korea
97 C4 Nonthaburi Thai.
162 C3 Nontron France
192 B2 Nonza Corse France
214 E4 Nonzwakazi S. Africa
138 F2 Nõo Estonia
87 C5 Nookawarra W.A. Austr.
82 D1 Noolyeanna Lake salt flat S.A. Austr.
84 B2 Noonamah N.T. Austr.
87 C6 Noondie, Lake salt flat W.A. Austr.
86 E3 Noonkanbah W.A. Austr.
164 F1 Noordbergum Neth.
164 C3 Noordbeveland i. Neth.
164 E3 Noord-Brabant prov. Neth.
164 F1 Noordbroek-Uiterburen Neth.
164 D2 Noord-Holland prov. Neth.
215 H1 Noordkaap S. Africa
214 B5 Noordkuil S. Africa
164 E2 Noordoost Polder Neth.
164 D2 Noordwijk aan Zee Neth.
164 D2 Noordwijk-Binnen Neth.
164 D2 Noordwijkerhout Neth.
164 F2 Noordwolde Neth.
141 M3 Noormarkku Fin.
220 B3 Noorvik AK U.S.A.
85 H5 Noosa Heads Qld Austr.
164 D2 Nootdorp Neth.
245 F5 Nopala Mex.
245 F4 Nopaltepec Mex.
209 B6 Nóqui Angola
193 G2 Nora r. Italy
100 D2 Nora r. Rus. Fed.
143 F2 Nora Sweden
192 A4 Noragugume Sardegna Italy
123 G2 Norak Tajik.
Norakert Armenia see Baghramyan
92 C5 Norala Phil.
224 E3 Noranda Que. Can.
Nor-Bayazet Armenia see Kamo
143 F1 Norberg Sweden
193 F2 Norcia Italy
233 □I2 Norcross ME U.S.A.
207 I4 Nord prov. Cameroon
156 D2 Nord dept Nord - Pas-de-Calais France
140 □ Nordaustlandet i. Svalbard
142 C4 Nordborg Denmark
142 D4 Nordby Denmark
168 C2 Norddeich Ger.
168 D1 Norddorf Ger.
222 G4 Nordegg Alta Can.
168 C2 Norden Ger.
173 E3 Nordendorf Ger.
168 D2 Nordenham Ger.
131 K2 Nordenshel'da, Arkhipelag is Rus. Fed.
222 B2 Nordenskiold r. Y.T. Can.
140 □ Nordenskiøld Land reg. Svalbard
Nordenskjold Archipelago is Rus. Fed. see Nordenshel'da, Arkhipelag
168 D1 Norder Hever sea chan. Ger.
168 C2 Norderney Ger.
168 C2 Norderney i. Ger.
168 D1 Norderoogsand i. Ger.
168 F2 Norderstedt Ger.
216 □1b Nordeste São Miguel Azores
216 □1b Nordestinho São Miguel Azores
141 I3 Nordfjord reg. Norway
141 I3 Nordfjordeid Norway
168 D1 Nordfriesische Inseln is Ger.
168 D1 Nordfriesland reg. Ger.
171 C3 Nordgermersleben Ger.
171 C5 Nordhalben Ger.
168 E1 Nordhastedt Ger.
169 F4 Nordhausen Ger.
172 D2 Nordheim Ger.
168 D2 Nordholz Ger.
169 C3 Nordhorn Ger.
142 A2 Nordhuglo Norway
142 C3 Nordjylland county Denmark
Nord Kap c. Iceland see Horn
140 N1 Nordkapp c. Norway
169 C4 Nordkirchen Ger.
208 F5 Nord-Kivu admin. reg. Dem. Rep. Congo
140 L1 Nord-Kvaløy i. Norway
140 N1 Nordkynhalvøya i. Norway
140 K2 Nordland county Norway
168 D2 Nordleda Ger.
140 K2 Nordli Norway
173 E3 Nördlingen Ger.
140 L3 Nordmaling Sweden
207 H5 Nord-Ouest prov. Cameroon
156 C2 Nord - Pas-de-Calais admin. reg. France
169 C4 Nordrhein-Westfalen land Ger.
169 E3 Nordstemmen Ger.
168 D1 Nordstrand i. Ger.
140 K2 Nord-Trøndelag county Norway
140 □C2 Norðurland eystra constituency Iceland
140 □B2 Norðurland vestra constituency Iceland
140 J3 Nordvika Norway
169 C3 Nordwalde Ger.
147 E4 Nore r. Rep. of Ireland
163 E5 Nore, Pic de mt. France
Noreg country Europe see Norway
138 D4 Noreikiškės Lith.
182 E1 Noreña Spain
142 C1 Noresund Norway
151 H2 Norfolk admin. div. England U.K.
236 D3 Norfolk NE U.S.A.
233 F2 Norfolk NY U.S.A.
233 E6 Norfolk VA U.S.A.
82 □1 Norfolk Island terr. S. Pacific Ocean
266 G7 Norfolk Island Ridge sea feature Tasman Sea
164 F1 Norg Neth.
Norge country Europe see Norway
149 G2 Norham Northumberland, England U.K.
142 B1 Norheimsund Norway
244 D2 Noria de Ángeles Mex.
104 D2 Norikura-dake vol. Japan
130 J3 Noril'sk Rus. Fed.
Norkyung Xizang China see Bainang
227 H3 Norland Ont. Can.
193 E3 Norma Italy
234 C3 Norma NJ U.S.A.
226 C5 Normal IL U.S.A.
85 E3 Norman r. Qld Austr.
237 D5 Norman OK U.S.A.
231 D5 Norman, Lake resr NC U.S.A.
85 F2 Normanby r. Qld Austr.
80 E3 Normanby North I. N.Z.
85 G4 Normanby Range hills Qld Austr.
Normandes, Îles is English Chan. see Channel Islands
251 G4 Normandia Brazil
159 F3 Normandie reg. France
159 F3 Normandie, Collines de hills France
215 G2 Normandien S. Africa
Normandy reg. France see Normandie
85 E3 Normanton Qld Austr.
149 H4 Normanton West Yorkshire, England U.K.
82 D3 Normanville S.A. Austr.
222 E1 Norman Wells N.W.T. Can.
227 H1 Normétal Que. Can.
87 C7 Nornalup W.A. Austr.
160 E1 Noroy-le-Bourg France
223 K5 Norquay Sask. Can.
140 M2 Norra Bredåker Sweden
140 M3 Norra Gloppet b. Fin.
140 K2 Norråker Sweden
140 M3 Norra Kvarken str. Fin./Sweden
140 L2 Norrbotten county Sweden
142 C3 Nørreå r. Denmark
142 D4 Nørre Alslev Denmark
168 G1 Nørreballe Denmark
142 D4 Nørre Lyndelse Denmark
142 C4 Nørre Nebel Denmark
156 C2 Norrent-Fontes France
142 C4 Nørre Snede Denmark
140 M2 Norrfjärden Sweden
143 F3 Norrhult-Klavreström Sweden
234 C2 Norristown PA U.S.A.
143 G2 Norrköping Sweden
141 L3 Norrsundet Sweden
143 H2 Norrtälje Sweden
87 D7 Norseman W.A. Austr.
80 F4 Norsewood North I. N.Z.
140 L2 Norsjö Sweden
100 D1 Norsk Rus. Fed.
251 I4 Norte, Canal do sea chan. Brazil
253 F2 Norte, Serra do hills Brazil
250 C2 Norte de Santander dept Col.
216 □1c Norte Grande São Jorge Azores
253 F3 Nortelândia Brazil
169 E4 Nörten-Hardenberg Ger.
216 □1c Norte Pequeno São Jorge Azores
263 L2 North, Cape Antarctica
233 G3 North Adams MA U.S.A.
149 H3 Northallerton North Yorkshire, England U.K.
87 C6 Northam W.A. Austr.
150 C3 Northam Devon, England U.K.
218 North America continent
233 □J2 North Amity ME U.S.A.
87 B6 Northampton W.A. Austr.
151 G2 Northampton Northamptonshire, England U.K.
233 G3 Northampton MA U.S.A.
234 C2 Northampton PA U.S.A.
234 C2 Northampton County county PA U.S.A.
85 F5 Northampton Downs Qld Austr.
151 G2 Northamptonshire admin. div. England U.K.
115 G3 North Andaman i. Andaman & Nicobar Is India
232 E6 North Anna r. VA U.S.A.
233 □I2 North Anson ME U.S.A.
265 L5 North Australian Basin sea feature Indian Ocean
146 D6 North Ayrshire admin. div. Scotland U.K.
151 F4 North Baddesley Hampshire, England U.K.
232 B4 North Baltimore OH U.S.A.
223 I4 North Battleford Sask. Can.
224 E4 North Bay Ont. Can.
224 E1 North Belcher Islands Nunavut Can.
238 A3 North Bend OR U.S.A.
232 E4 North Bend PA U.S.A.
233 G3 North Bennington VT U.S.A.
235 D2 North Bergen NJ U.S.A.
146 F5 North Berwick East Lothian, Scotland U.K.
233 □H3 North Berwick ME U.S.A.
North Borneo state Malaysia see Sabah
237 D6 North Bosque r. TX U.S.A.
83 F2 North Bourke N.S.W. Austr.
227 F4 North Branch MI U.S.A.
226 A3 North Branch MN U.S.A.
234 D2 North Branch NJ U.S.A.
235 F1 North Branford CT U.S.A.
246 E2 North Caicos i. Turks and Caicos Is
237 E5 North Canadian r. OK U.S.A.
North Cape c. Norway see Nordkapp
80 D1 North Cape c. North I. N.Z.
259 □ North Cape c. S. Georgia
226 C4 North Cape WI U.S.A.
234 D4 North Cape May NJ U.S.A.
231 E4 North Carolina state U.S.A.
234 C2 North Catasauqua PA U.S.A.
149 I4 North Cave East Riding of Yorkshire, England U.K.
224 D4 North Channel lake channel Ont. Can.
146 B6 North Channel Northern Ireland/Scotland U.K.
231 E5 North Charleston SC U.S.A.
150 E3 North Cheriton Somerset, England U.K.
87 C7 Northcliffe W.A. Austr.
232 D3 North Collins NY U.S.A.
237 C6 North Concho r. TX U.S.A.
233 □H2 North Conway NH U.S.A.
North Cousin Islet i. Inner Islands Seychelles see Cousin
222 F5 North Cowichan B.C. Can.
149 H3 North Cowton North Yorkshire, England U.K.
233 G3 North Creek NY U.S.A.
236 C2 North Dakota state U.S.A.
151 G3 North Downs hills England U.K.
149 I4 North Duffield North Yorkshire, England U.K.
213 E4 North East admin. dist. Botswana
234 C3 North East MD U.S.A.
232 D3 North East PA U.S.A.
85 H4 North East Cay rf Coral Sea Is Terr. Austr.
210 D4 North-Eastern prov. Kenya
North-East Frontier Agency state India see Arunachal Pradesh
149 I4 North East Lincolnshire admin. div. England U.K.
267 I4 Northeast Pacific Basin sea feature Pacific Ocean
246 C1 Northeast Providence Channel Bahamas
240 I4 North Edwards CA U.S.A.
169 E4 Northeim Ger.
151 H2 North Elmham Norfolk, England U.K.
206 E4 Northern admin. reg. Ghana
211 B7 Northern admin. reg. Malawi
213 F4 Northern prov. S. Africa
206 C4 Northern prov. Sierra Leone
203 F4 Northern state Sudan
209 F7 Northern prov. Zambia
Northern Aegean admin. reg. Greece see Voreio Aigaio
123 H2 Northern Areas admin. div. Pak.
208 E2 Northern Bahr el Ghazal state Sudan
214 B3 Northern Cape prov. S. Africa
81 □2 Northern Cook Islands Cook Is
202 E5 Northern Darfur state Sudan
Northern Donets r. Rus. Fed. see Severskiy Donets
Northern Dvina r. Rus. Fed. see Severnaya Dvina
147 E2 Northern Ireland prov. U.K.
203 F6 Northern Kordofan state Sudan
77 I3 Northern Lau Group is Fiji
91 J3 Northern Mariana Islands terr. N. Pacific Ocean
Northern Pindus Mountains Greece see Voreia Pindos
Northern Rhodesia country Africa see Zambia
Northern Sporades is Greece see Voreioi Sporades
84 C3 Northern Territory admin. div. Austr.
Northern Transvaal prov. S. Africa see Northern
146 F5 North Esk r. Angus, Scotland U.K.
146 E6 North Esk r. Midlothian/Scottish Borders, Scotland U.K.
236 F4 North Fabius r. MO U.S.A.
149 I4 North Ferriby East Riding of Yorkshire, England U.K.
233 G3 Northfield MA U.S.A.
226 A3 Northfield MN U.S.A.
234 D3 Northfield NJ U.S.A.
233 G2 Northfield VT U.S.A.
226 B3 Northfield WI U.S.A.
151 H3 Northfleet Kent, England U.K.
235 F1 Northford CT U.S.A.
151 I3 North Foreland c. England U.K.
240 H3 North Fork CA U.S.A.
235 F1 North Franklin CT U.S.A.
224 D3 North French r. Ont. Can.
North Frisian Islands Ger. see Nordfriesische Inseln
268 T1 North Geomagnetic Pole Arctic Ocean
149 I3 North Grimston North Yorkshire, England U.K.
235 F1 North Haven CT U.S.A.
233 □J2 North Head N.B. Can.
233 G2 North Hero VT U.S.A.
240 G2 North Highlands CA U.S.A.
233 G3 North Hudson NY U.S.A.
149 I4 North Hykeham Lincolnshire, England U.K.
151 G2 Northill Bedfordshire, England U.K.
84 D2 North Island N.T. Austr.
87 B6 North Island W.A. Austr.
80 D3 North Island N.Z.
241 L4 North Jadito Canyon gorge AZ U.S.A.
226 D5 North Judson IN U.S.A.
North Kazakhstan Oblast admin. div. Kazakh. see Severnyy Kazakhstan
85 F2 North Kennedy r. Qld Austr.
146 D4 North Kessock Highland, Scotland U.K.
232 C4 North Kingsville OH U.S.A.
223 M3 North Knife r. Man. Can.
117 E4 North Koel r. Bihar India
241 L5 North Komelik AZ U.S.A.
117 H4 North Lakhimpur Assam India
146 E6 North Lanarkshire admin. div. Scotland U.K.
80 E1 Northland admin. reg. North I. N.Z.
North Land is Rus. Fed. see Severnaya Zemlya
241 J3 North Las Vegas NV U.S.A.
151 F3 Northleach Gloucestershire, England U.K.
226 D5 North Liberty IN U.S.A.
232 C4 North Lima OH U.S.A.
149 I4 North Lincolnshire admin. div. England U.K.
237 E5 North Little Rock AR U.S.A.
236 D3 North Loup r. NE U.S.A.
222 C2 North Macmillan r. Y.T. Can.
235 F1 North Madison CT U.S.A.
221 H2 North Magnetic Pole Nunavut Can.
113 □1 North Male Atoll Maldives
239 F4 North Mam Peak CO U.S.A.
226 E5 North Manchester IN U.S.A.
232 A5 North Middletown KY U.S.A.
150 D3 North Molton Devon, England U.K.
234 B1 North Mountain mts PA U.S.A.
86 B4 North Muiron Island W.A. Austr.
222 F2 North Nahanni r. N.W.T. Can.
227 G5 North Olmsted OH U.S.A.
236 E2 Northome MN U.S.A.
North Ossetia aut. rep. Rus. Fed. see Severnaya Osetiya, Respublika
240 H3 North Palisade mt. CA U.S.A.
236 C3 North Platte NE U.S.A.
236 C3 North Platte r. NE U.S.A.
87 B6 North Point W.A. Austr.
268 A1 North Pole Arctic Ocean
231 C5 Northport AL U.S.A.
231 D7 North Port FL U.S.A.
226 E3 Northport MI U.S.A.
149 F1 North Queensferry Fife, Scotland U.K.
North Rhine - Westphalia land Ger. see Nordrhein-Westfalen
241 K3 North Rim AZ U.S.A.
225 I4 North River Bridge N.S. Can.
146 □G1 North Roe Shetland, Scotland U.K.
North Rona i. Western Isles, Scotland U.K. see Rona

North Ronaldsay to Oakey

342

146 F2 **North Ronaldsay** *i.* Scotland U.K.
146 F2 **North Ronaldsay Firth** *sea chan.* Scotland U.K.
238 B2 **North Santiam** *r. OR* U.S.A.
222 J4 **North Saskatchewan** *r. Alberta/Saskatchewan* Can.
241 J2 **North Schell Peak** *NV* U.S.A.
144 H3 **North Sea** *sea* Europe
235 F2 **North Sea** *NY* U.S.A.
223 L3 **North Seal** *r. Man.* Can.
149 H2 **North Shields** *Tyne and Wear, England* U.K.
240 I2 **North Shoshone Peak** *NV* U.S.A.
North Siberian Lowland Rus. Fed. *see* **Severo-Sibirskaya Nizmennost'**
North Sinai *governorate* Egypt *see* **Shamâl Sînâ'**
220 D3 **North Slope** *plain AK* U.S.A.
149 J4 **North Somercotes** *Lincolnshire, England* U.K.
150 E3 **North Somerset** *admin. div. England* U.K.
147 B3 **North Sound** *sea chan.* Rep. of Ireland
85 H5 **North Stradbroke Island** *Qld* Austr.
233 H2 **North Stratford** *NH* U.S.A.
149 H2 **North Sunderland** *Northumberland, England* U.K.
80 E3 **North Taranaki Bight** *b. North I.* N.Z.
222 F5 **North Thompson** *r. B.C.* Can.
149 I4 **North Thoresby** *Lincolnshire, England* U.K.
151 F3 **North Tidworth** *Wiltshire, England* U.K.
146 A4 **Northton** *Western Isles, Scotland* U.K.
232 D3 **North Tonawanda** *NY* U.S.A.
233 G2 **North Troy** *VT* U.S.A.
233 H3 **North Truro** *MA* U.S.A.
149 G3 **North Tyne** *r. England* U.K.
146 G4 **North Ugie** *r. Scotland* U.K.
146 A4 **North Uist** *i. Scotland* U.K.
149 G2 **Northumberland** *admin. div. England* U.K.
234 B2 **Northumberland** *PA* U.S.A.
234 B2 **Northumberland County** *county PA* U.S.A.
85 G4 **Northumberland Isles** *Qld* Austr.
149 G2 **Northumberland National Park** *England* U.K.
225 H4 **Northumberland Strait** Can.
238 B3 **North Umpqua** *r. OR* U.S.A.
222 F5 **North Vancouver** *B.C.* Can.
233 F3 **Northville** *NY* U.S.A.
234 C2 **North Wales** *PA* U.S.A.
151 I2 **North Walsham** *Norfolk, England* U.K.
233 □H2 **North Waterford** *ME* U.S.A.
151 H3 **North Weald Bassett** *Essex, England* U.K.
215 E2 **North West** *prov.* S. Africa
264 F1 **North West Atlantic Mid-Ocean Channnel** *sea chan.* N. Atlantic Ocean
86 B4 **North West Cape** *W.A.* Austr.
235 F1 **North Westchester** *CT* U.S.A.
209 D8 **North-Western** *prov.* Zambia
123 G3 **North West Frontier** *prov.* Pak.
266 F3 **Northwest Pacific Basin** *sea feature* N. Pacific Ocean
246 C1 **Northwest Providence Channel** Bahamas
225 J2 **North West River** *Nfld.* Can.
222 J2 **Northwest Territories** *admin. div.* Can.
149 G4 **Northwich** *Cheshire, England* U.K.
237 D5 **North Wichita** *r. TX* U.S.A.
234 D3 **North Wildwood** *NJ* U.S.A.
235 F1 **North Windham** *CT* U.S.A.
233 □H3 **North Windham** *ME* U.S.A.
268 N1 **Northwind Ridge** *sea feature* Arctic Ocean
149 H4 **North Wingfield** *Derbyshire, England* U.K.
151 F4 **Northwood** *Isle of Wight, England* U.K.
236 E3 **Northwood** *IA* U.S.A.
236 D2 **Northwood** *ND* U.S.A.
233 H3 **Northwood** *NH* U.S.A.
226 B3 **Northwoods Beach** *WI* U.S.A.
227 H4 **North York** *Ont.* Can.
149 I3 **North York Moors** *moorland England* U.K.
149 I3 **North York Moors National Park** *England* U.K.
149 H3 **North Yorkshire** *admin. div. England* U.K.
168 C2 **Nortmoor** Ger.
225 H4 **Norton** *N.B.* Can.
149 I3 **Norton** *North Yorkshire, England* U.K.
151 H2 **Norton** *Suffolk, England* U.K.
236 D4 **Norton** *KS* U.S.A.
232 B6 **Norton** *VA* U.S.A.
233 H2 **Norton** *VT* U.S.A.
213 F3 **Norton** Zimbabwe
149 H5 **Norton Canes** *Staffordshire, England* U.K.
Norton de Matos Angola *see* **Balombo**
150 D3 **Norton Fitzwarren** *Somerset, England* U.K.
226 D4 **Norton Shores** *MI* U.S.A.
220 B3 **Norton Sound** *sea chan. AK* U.S.A.
168 E1 **Nortorf** Ger.
168 C3 **Nortrup** Ger.
158 E4 **Nort-sur-Erdre** France
262 X2 **Norvegia, Cape** Antarctica
235 E1 **Norwalk** *CT* U.S.A.
232 B4 **Norwalk** *OH* U.S.A.
226 B4 **Norwalk** *WI* U.S.A.
235 E1 **Norwalk** *r. CT* U.S.A.
141 J3 **Norway** *country* Europe
233 □H2 **Norway** *ME* U.S.A.
227 I3 **Norway Bay** *Que.* Can.
223 L4 **Norway House** *Man.* Can.
264 I1 **Norwegian Basin** *sea feature* N. Atlantic Ocean
221 I2 **Norwegian Bay** *Nunavut* Can.
264 J1 **Norwegian Sea** N. Atlantic Ocean
227 G4 **Norwich** *Ont.* Can.
151 I2 **Norwich** *Norfolk, England* U.K.
233 G4 **Norwich** *CT* U.S.A.
233 F3 **Norwich** *NY* U.S.A.
146 □H1 **Norwick** *Shetland, Scotland* U.K.
233 H3 **Norwood** *MA* U.S.A.
231 D5 **Norwood** *NC* U.S.A.
233 F2 **Norwood** *NY* U.S.A.
232 A5 **Norwood** *OH* U.S.A.
92 B3 **Norzagaray** Phil.
102 J3 **Noshiro** Japan
137 F2 **Nosivka** Ukr.
136 D3 **Noskivtsi** Ukr.
214 C1 **Nosop** *watercourse* Africa *alt.* **Nossob**
Nosovka Ukr. *see* **Nosivka**
122 D4 **Noşratābād** Iran
146 □G1 **Noss, Isle of** *i. Scotland* U.K.
142 E2 **Nossan** *r.* Sweden
184 B2 **Nossa Senhora da Boa Fé** Port.
184 C1 **Nossa Senhora da Graça de Póvoa e Meadas** Port.
184 C2 **Nossa Senhora da Graça do Divor** Port.
184 C2 **Nossa Senhora das Neves** Port.
184 B2 **Nossa Senhora da Torega** Port.
184 C2 **Nossa Senhora de Machede** Port.
253 F3 **Nossa Senhora do Livramento** Brazil
216 □1b **Nossa Senhora dos Remédios** *São Miguel* Azores
142 E2 **Nossebro** Sweden
171 E4 **Nossen** Ger.
170 D2 **Nossendorf** Ger.
170 D2 **Nossentiner Hütte** Ger.
214 C2 **Nossob** *watercourse* Africa *alt.* **Nosop**
214 C1 **Nossob Camp** S. Africa
206 D3 **Nossombougou** Mali
213 □K4 **Nosy Varika** Madag.
176 G4 **Noszlop** Hungary
177 J4 **Noszvaj** Hungary
140 O1 **Nota** *r.* Fin./Rus. Fed.
225 I1 **Notakwanon** *r. Nfld.* Can.
193 F2 **Notaresco** Italy
241 K2 **Notch Peak** *UT* U.S.A.
174 D3 **Noteć** *r.* Pol.
198 B2 **Notia Pindos** *mts* Greece
222 G3 **Notikewin** *r. Alta* Can.
177 I4 **Nőtincs** Hungary
198 E3 **Notio Aigaio** *admin. reg.* Greece
Nótion Aiyaíon *admin. reg.* Greece *see* **Notio Aigaio**
198 C2 **Notios Evvoïkos Kolpos** *sea chan.* Greece
195 E6 **Noto** *Sicilia* Italy
195 E6 **Noto, Golfo di** *g. Sicilia* Italy
142 C2 **Notodden** Norway
104 C1 **Noto-hantō** *pen.* Japan
102 L1 **Notoro-ko** *l.* Japan
179 F5 **Notranje Gorice** Slovenia
225 G4 **Notre Dame, Monts** *mts Que.* Can.
225 K3 **Notre Dame Bay** *Nfld.* Can.
159 G2 **Notre-Dame-de-Gravenchon** France
Notre-Dame-de-Koartac *Que.* Can. *see* **Quaqtaq**
227 J3 **Notre-Dame-de-la-Salette** *Que.* Can.
158 D5 **Notre-Dame-de-Monts** France
158 E5 **Notre-Dame-de-Riez** France
162 C3 **Notre-Dame-de-Sanilhac** France
233 □H2 **Notre-Dame-des-Bois** *Que.* Can.
159 G4 **Notre-Dame-d'Oé** France
227 J2 **Notre-Dame-du-Laus** *Que.* Can.
227 H2 **Notre-Dame-du-Nord** *Que.* Can.
179 E4 **Nötsch im Gailtal** Austria
207 F5 **Notsé** Togo
102 L2 **Notsuke-suidō** *sea chan.* Japan/Rus. Fed.
227 G3 **Nottawasaga Bay** *Ont.* Can.
224 E3 **Nottaway** *r. Que.* Can.
168 E2 **Nottensdorf** Ger.
151 F2 **Nottingham** *Nottingham, England* U.K.
151 F2 **Nottingham** *admin. div. England* U.K.
234 B3 **Nottingham** *PA* U.S.A.
215 H3 **Nottingham Road** S. Africa
149 I4 **Nottinghamshire** *admin. div. England* U.K.
232 D6 **Nottoway** *VA* U.S.A.
232 E6 **Nottoway** *r. VA* U.S.A.
169 C4 **Nottuln** Ger.
223 J5 **Notukeu Creek** *r. Sask.* Can.
204 A5 **Nouâdhibou** Maur.
206 B2 **Nouakchott** Maur.
206 A2 **Noûmghâr** Maur.
159 I4 **Nouan-le-Fuzelier** France
159 H4 **Nouans-les-Fontaines** France
157 F3 **Nouart** France
78 □5 **Nouméa** New Caledonia
207 H5 **Noun** *r.* Cameroon
206 E3 **Nouna** Burkina
215 E4 **Noupoort** S. Africa
Nouveau-Comptoir *Que.* Can. *see* **Wemindji**
Nouvelle Anvers Dem. Rep. Congo *see* **Makanza**
78 □5 **Nouvelle Calédonie** *i.* S. Pacific Ocean
Nouvelle Calédonie *terr.* S. Pacific Ocean *see* **New Caledonia**
Nouvelles Hébrides *country* S. Pacific Ocean *see* **Vanuatu**
156 B2 **Nouvion** France
158 E3 **Nouvoitou** France
159 G4 **Nouzilly** France
156 E3 **Nouzonville** France
123 G1 **Nov** Tajik.
176 F5 **Nova** Hungary
257 G4 **Nova Almeida** Brazil
254 C5 **Nova América** Brazil
256 A5 **Nova Andradina** Brazil
137 J3 **Nova Astrakhan'** Ukr.
256 C3 **Nova Aurora** Brazil
Novabad Tajik. *see* **Novobod**
Novabad Tajik. *see* **Novobod**
177 H3 **Nová Baňa** Slovakia
136 E2 **Nova Borova** Ukr.
176 E2 **Nová Bystřice** Czech Rep.
209 B6 **Nova Caipemba** Angola
256 A6 **Nova Cantu** Brazil
Nova Chaves Angola *see* **Muconda**
197 F3 **Novaci** Romania
196 E3 **Nova Crnja** *Vojvodina, Srbija* Yugo.
254 G3 **Nova Cruz** Brazil
177 H3 **Nová Dubnica** Slovakia
257 F3 **Nova Era** Brazil
Nova Esperança Angola *see* **Buengas**
256 A5 **Nova Esperança** Brazil
191 H5 **Novafeltria** Italy
Nova Freixa Moz. *see* **Cuamba**
257 F5 **Nova Friburgo** Brazil
Nova Gaia Angola *see* **Cambundi-Catembo**
Nova Goa *Goa* India *see* **Panaji**
213 G4 **Nova Golegã** Moz.
188 D3 **Nova Gorica** Slovenia
188 F3 **Nova Gradiška** Croatia
256 C4 **Nova Granada** Brazil
137 G3 **Nova Haleshchyna** Ukr.
257 F5 **Nova Iguaçu** Brazil
137 G4 **Nova Kakhovka** Ukr.
137 G4 **Nova Kam"yanka** Ukr.
177 H3 **Nováky** Slovakia
160 D3 **Novalaise** France
186 C2 **Novales** Spain
191 G2 **Nova Levante** Italy
257 F3 **Nova Lima** Brazil
Nova Lisboa Angola *see* **Huambo**
191 J4 **Novalja** Croatia
256 A5 **Nova Londrina** Brazil
177 J2 **Nová Ľubovňa** Slovakia
138 G4 **Novalukoml'** Belarus
213 G4 **Nova Mambone** Moz.
137 G4 **Nova Mayachka** Ukr.
137 F4 **Nova Odesa** Ukr.
176 E1 **Nová Paka** Czech Rep.
137 H3 **Nova Parafiyivka** Ukr.
196 E3 **Nova Pazova** *Vojvodina, Srbija* Yugo.
254 E4 **Nova Pilão Arcado** Brazil
256 D3 **Nova Ponte** Brazil
137 G3 **Nova Praha** Ukr.
190 D3 **Novara** Italy
190 D2 **Novara** *prov. Piemonte* Italy
195 E4 **Novara di Sicilia** *Sicilia* Italy
254 E4 **Nova Remanso** Brazil
256 D4 **Nova Resende** Brazil
171 D5 **Nová Role** Czech Rep.
254 D5 **Nova Roma** Brazil
254 E3 **Nova Russas** Brazil
225 H5 **Nova Scotia** *prov.* Can.
254 E4 **Nova Sento Sé** Brazil
257 E3 **Nova Serrana** Brazil
Nova Sintra Angola *see* **Catabola**
195 F2 **Nova Siri** Italy
137 H2 **Nova Sloboda** Ukr.
254 F4 **Nova Soure** Brazil
190 E2 **Novate Mezzola** Italy
240 F2 **Novato** *CA* U.S.A.
188 F3 **Nova Topola** Bos.-Herz.
134 I3 **Novator** Rus. Fed.
136 D3 **Nova Ushytsya** Ukr.
196 D4 **Nova Varoš** *Srbija* Yugo.
179 G1 **Nová Včelnice** Czech Rep.
257 G3 **Nova Venécia** Brazil
171 G5 **Nová Ves I** Czech Rep.
257 H2 **Nova Viçosa** Brazil
137 H3 **Nova Vodolaha** Ukr.
254 B5 **Nova Xavantino** Brazil
137 K2 **Novaya Chigla** Rus. Fed.
Novaya Kakhovka Ukr. *see* **Nova Kakhovka**
137 K2 **Novaya Kalitva** Rus. Fed.
120 B2 **Novaya Kazanka** Kazakh.
139 I1 **Novaya Ladoga** Rus. Fed.
Novaya Odessa Ukr. *see* **Nova Odesa**
Novaya Pismyanka Rus. Fed. *see* **Leninogorsk**
131 P2 **Novaya Sibir', Ostrov** *i. Novosibirskiye O-va* Rus. Fed.
137 J2 **Novaya Usman'** Rus. Fed.
Novaya Volodaga Ukr. *see* **Nova Vodolaha**
130 G2 **Novaya Zemlya** *is* Rus. Fed.
Novaya Zhizn *Lipetskaya Oblast'* Rus. Fed. *see* **Kazinka**
197 H4 **Nova Zagora** Bulg.
137 G4 **Nova Zbur"yivka** Ukr.
137 G3 **Nove** Ukr.
176 D3 **Nové Hrady** Czech Rep.
187 C6 **Novelda** Spain
191 F4 **Novellara** Italy
176 F1 **Nové Město nad Metuj** Czech Rep.
177 G3 **Nové Mesto nad Váhom** Slovakia
176 F2 **Nové Město na Moravé** Czech Rep.
175 K6 **Nove Misto** Ukr.
176 B6 **Noventa di Piave** Italy
191 G3 **Noventa Vicentina** Italy
161 C5 **Noves** France
183 F4 **Novés** Spain
171 D5 **Nové Sedlo** Czech Rep.
171 E5 **Nové Strašecí** Czech Rep.
177 H4 **Nové Zámky** Slovakia
Novgorod Rus. Fed. *see* **Velikiy Novgorod**
Novgorod Oblast *admin. div.* Rus. Fed. *see* **Novgorodskaya Oblast'**
Novgorod-Severskiy Ukr. *see* **Novhorod-Sivers'kyy**
139 I2 **Novgorodskaya Oblast'** *admin. div.* Rus. Fed.
Novgorod-Volynskiy Ukr. *see* **Novohrad-Volyns'kyy**
Novgradets Bulg. *see* **Suvorovo**
137 G3 **Novhorodka** Ukr.
137 G2 **Novhorod-Sivers'kyy** Ukr.
137 I3 **Novhorods'ke** Ukr.
227 F4 **Novi** *MI* U.S.A.
196 E3 **Novi Bečej** *Vojvodina, Srbija* Yugo.
136 E2 **Novi Bilokorovychi** Ukr.
137 F2 **Novi Borovychi** Ukr.
136 C2 **Novi Chervyshcha** Ukr.
121 J1 **Novichikha** Rus. Fed.
191 F4 **Novi di Modena** Italy
183 H3 **Noviergas** Spain
Novi Grad Bos.-Herz. *see* **Bosanski Novi**
191 I3 **Novigrad** Croatia
176 F5 **Novigrad Podravski** Croatia
197 F4 **Novi Iskŭr** Bulg.
177 J5 **Novi Kneževac** *Vojvodina, Srbija* Yugo.
100 G3 **Novikovo** *Sakhalin* Rus. Fed.
196 E3 **Novi Kozarci** *Vojvodina, Srbija* Yugo.
Novi Kritsim Bulg. *see* **Stamboliyski**
190 D4 **Novi Ligure** Italy
160 E1 **Novillars** France
165 D4 **Noville** Belgium
244 B2 **Novillero** Mex.
188 F2 **Novi Marof** Croatia
137 G2 **Novi Mlyny** Ukr.
156 E3 **Novion-Porcien** France
197 H4 **Novi Pazar** Bulg.
196 E4 **Novi Pazar** *Srbija* Yugo.
196 D3 **Novi Sad** *Vojvodina, Srbija* Yugo.
137 H3 **Novi Sanzhary** Ukr.
175 M6 **Novi Strilyshcha** Ukr.
188 F3 **Novi Travnik** Bos.-Herz.
188 E3 **Novi Vinodolski** Croatia
139 M3 **Novki** Rus. Fed.
100 G3 **Novoaleksandropov** *Sakhalin* Rus. Fed.
137 J2 **Novoaleksandrovka** Rus. Fed.
135 H7 **Novoaleksandrovsk** Rus. Fed.
Novoalekseyevka Kazakh. *see* **Khobda**
98 D1 **Novoaltaysk** Rus. Fed.
137 J4 **Novoamvrosiyivs'ke** Ukr.
135 H6 **Novoanninskiy** Rus. Fed.
251 F6 **Novo Aripuanã** Brazil
136 F3 **Novoarkhanhel's'k** Ukr.
137 J3 **Novoaydar** Ukr.
137 J4 **Novoazovs'k** Ukr.
137 J4 **Novobataysk** Rus. Fed.
137 J3 **Novobelaya** Rus. Fed.
196 E3 **Novo Beograd** *Srbija* Yugo.
137 J5 **Novobeysugskaya** Rus. Fed.
137 J3 **Novobila** Ukr.
123 G2 **Novobod** Tajik.
123 G2 **Novobod** Tajik.
Novobogatīnsk Kazakh. *see* **Novobogatinskoye**
120 B3 **Novobogatinskoye** Kazakh.
137 H4 **Novobohdanivka** Ukr.
137 J3 **Novoborove** Ukr.
100 D2 **Novobureyskiy** Rus. Fed.
134 I4 **Novocheboksarsk** Rus. Fed.
135 J5 **Novocheremshansk** Rus. Fed.
135 H7 **Novocherkassk** Rus. Fed.
257 G2 **Novo Cruzeiro** Brazil
137 H4 **Novodanylivka** Ukr.
137 J4 **Novoderevyankovskaya** Rus. Fed.
136 D3 **Novodnistrovs'k** Ukr.
121 H2 **Novodolinka** Kazakh.
137 I3 **Novodonets'ke** Ukr.
137 J3 **Novodruzhes'k** Ukr.
139 J4 **Novodugino** Rus. Fed.
134 H2 **Novodvinsk** *Arkhangel'skaya Oblast'* Rus. Fed.
Novoekonomicheskoye Ukr. *see* **Dymytrov**
136 E3 **Novofastiv** Ukr.
137 F4 **Novofedorivka** Ukr.
Novogroznenskiy Rus. Fed. *see* **Oyskhara**
Novogrudok Belarus *see* **Navahrudak**
139 K4 **Novogurovskiy** Rus. Fed.
255 C9 **Novo Hamburgo** Brazil
137 H4 **Novohorivka** Ukr.
256 C4 **Novo Horizonte** Brazil
137 G4 **Novohradivka** Ukr.
176 D3 **Novohradské Hory** *mts* Czech Rep.
136 D2 **Novohrad-Volyns'kyy** Ukr.
137 I3 **Novohrodivka** Ukr.
137 H4 **Novohryhorivka** Ukr.
137 H4 **Novoivanivka** Ukr.
129 D3 **Novoivanovka** Azer.
120 D1 **Novokaolinovyy** Rus. Fed.
129 E2 **Novokayakent** Rus. Fed.
Novokazalinsk Kazakh. *see* **Ayteke Bi**
135 H6 **Novokhopersk** Rus. Fed.
100 D2 **Novokiyevskiy Uval** Rus. Fed.
137 F4 **Novokostyantynivka** Ukr.
137 F3 **Novokrasne** Ukr.
137 J3 **Novokrasnyanka** Ukr.
135 H7 **Novokubansk** Rus. Fed.
Novokubanskiy Rus. Fed. *see* **Novokubansk**
120 B1 **Novokuybyshevsk** Rus. Fed.
130 J4 **Novokuznetsk** Rus. Fed.
137 G4 **Novokyyivka** Ukr.
129 E2 **Novolakskoye** Rus. Fed.
263 A2 **Novolazarevskaya** *research stn* Antarctica
137 J5 **Novoleushkovskaya** Rus. Fed.
Novolukoml' Belarus *see* **Novalukoml'**
139 L5 **Novol'vovsk** Rus. Fed.
137 J5 **Novomalorossiyskaya** Rus. Fed.
121 H2 **Novomarkovka** Kazakh.
137 H3 **Novomar"yivka** Ukr.
137 K2 **Novomelovatka** Rus. Fed.
188 E3 **Novo Mesto** Slovenia
139 L4 **Novomichurinsk** Rus. Fed.
135 G7 **Novomikhaylovskiy** Rus. Fed.
196 E3 **Novo Miloševo** *Vojvodina, Srbija* Yugo.
137 J4 **Novominskaya** Rus. Fed.
Novomirgorod Ukr. *see* **Novomyrhorod**
139 L4 **Novomoskovsk** Rus. Fed.
137 H3 **Novomoskovs'k** Ukr.
137 H4 **Novomykhaylivka** Ukr.
137 J3 **Novomykil's'ke** Ukr.
137 H3 **Novomykolayivka** *Dnipropetrovs'ka Oblast'* Ukr.
137 G4 **Novomykolayivka** *Khersons'ka Oblast'* Ukr.
137 H4 **Novomykolayivka** *Khersons'ka Oblast'* Ukr.
137 H4 **Novomykolayivka** *Zaporiz'ka Oblast'* Ukr.
137 F3 **Novomyrhorod** Ukr.
137 G4 **Novonatalivka** Ukr.
Novonazyvayevka Rus. Fed. *see* **Nazyvayevsk**
121 G4 **Novonikolayevka** Kazakh.
Novonikolayevsk Rus. Fed. *see* **Novosibirsk**
137 J5 **Novonikolayevskaya** Rus. Fed.
135 H6 **Novonikolayevskiy** Rus. Fed.
137 H4 **Novooleksandrivka** Ukr.
137 H4 **Novooleksiyivka** Ukr.
251 G5 **Novo Olinda do Norte** Brazil
177 I6 **Novo Orahovo** *Vojvodina, Srbija* Yugo.
254 E3 **Novo Oriente** Brazil
120 D2 **Novoorsk** Rus. Fed.
137 G2 **Novoorzhyts'ke** Ukr.
137 G5 **Novoozerne** Ukr.
136 E2 **Novoozeryanka** Ukr.
254 E3 **Novo Parnarama** Brazil
Novopashiyskiy *Permskaya Oblast'* Rus. Fed. *see* **Gornozavodsk**
137 I3 **Novopavlivka** *Dnipropetrovs'ka Oblast'* Ukr.
136 F4 **Novopavlivka** *Mykolayivs'ka Oblast'* Ukr.
107 F1 **Novopavlovka** Rus. Fed.
129 C2 **Novopavlovsk** Rus. Fed.
Novopavlovskaya Rus. Fed. *see* **Novopavlovsk**
137 H3 **Novopetrivka** Ukr.
137 H3 **Novopidkryazh** Ukr.
120 F1 **Novopokrovka** *Kustanayskaya Oblast'* Kazakh.
121 F1 **Novopokrovka** *Severnyy Kazakhstan* Kazakh.
121 J2 **Novopokrovka** *Vostochnyy Kazakhstan* Kazakh.
100 E3 **Novopokrovka** *Primorskiy Kray* Rus. Fed.
137 K1 **Novopokrovka** *Tambovskaya Oblast'* Rus. Fed.
137 H3 **Novopokrovka** Ukr.
135 H7 **Novopokrovskaya** Rus. Fed.
Novopolotsk Belarus *see* **Navapolatsk**
137 G4 **Novopoltavka** *Mykolayivs'ka Oblast'* Ukr.
137 I4 **Novopoltavka** *Zaporiz'ka Oblast'* Ukr.
137 J3 **Novopskov** Ukr.
Novo Redondo Angola *see* **Sumbe**
120 B2 **Novorepnoye** Rus. Fed.
135 G7 **Novorossiysk** Rus. Fed.
Novorossiyskiy Kazakh. *see* **Novorossiyskoye**
120 D2 **Novorossiyskoye** Kazakh.
137 J5 **Novorozhdestvenskaya** Rus. Fed.
121 F1 **Novorybinka** Kazakh.
138 G3 **Novorzhev** Rus. Fed.
136 E4 **Novosamarka** Ukr.
129 D3 **Novosaratovka** Azer.
171 E5 **Novosedlice** Czech Rep.
176 F3 **Novosedly** Czech Rep.
129 C1 **Novoselitskoye** Rus. Fed.
136 E4 **Novoselivka** Ukr.
137 G5 **Novoselivs'ke** Ukr.
197 F5 **Novo Selo** Macedonia
139 L3 **Novoselovo** Rus. Fed.
Novoselskoye Rus. Fed. *see* **Achkhoy-Martan**
138 G2 **Novosel'ye** Rus. Fed.
136 D3 **Novoselytsya** Ukr.
120 C1 **Novosergiyevka** Rus. Fed.
135 G7 **Novoshakhtinsk** Rus. Fed.
100 E3 **Novoshakhtinskiy** Rus. Fed.
137 J4 **Novoshcherbinovskaya** Rus. Fed.
135 J5 **Novosheshminsk** Rus. Fed.
130 J4 **Novosibirsk** Rus. Fed.
131 P2 **Novosibirskiye Ostrova** *is* Rus. Fed.
139 K5 **Novosil'** Rus. Fed.
137 J2 **Novosil'skoye** Rus. Fed.
137 G4 **Novosofiyivka** Ukr.
139 H3 **Novosokol'niki** Rus. Fed.
120 A1 **Novospasskoye** Rus. Fed.
137 J3 **Novosvitlivka** Ukr.
177 I2 **Novoť** Slovakia
137 J5 **Novotitarovskaya** Rus. Fed.
120 D2 **Novotroitsk** Rus. Fed.
Novotroitskoye Kazakh. *see* **Tole Bi**
137 I4 **Novotroyits'ke** Ukr.
137 H4 **Novotroyits'ke** Ukr.
137 H4 **Novotroyits'ke** Ukr.
Novoukrainka *Kirovohrads'ka Oblast'* Ukr. *see* **Novoukrayinka**
Novoukrainka *Rivnens'ka Oblast'* Ukr. *see* **Novoukrayinka**
137 F3 **Novoukrayinka** *Kirovohrads'ka Oblast'* Ukr.
136 C2 **Novoukrayinka** *Rivnens'ka Oblast'* Ukr.
120 D2 **Novoural'sk** Rus. Fed.
120 B2 **Novouzensk** Rus. Fed.
121 H1 **Novovarshavka** Rus. Fed.
137 H4 **Novovasylivka** *Zaporiz'ka Oblast'* Ukr.
137 I4 **Novovasylivka** *Zaporiz'ka Oblast'* Ukr.
136 C2 **Novovolyns'k** Ukr.
135 G6 **Novovoronezh** Rus. Fed.
Novovoronezhskiy Rus. Fed. *see* **Novovoronezh**
137 G4 **Novovorontsovka** Ukr.
137 G4 **Novovoskresens'ke** Ukr.
121 I4 **Novovoznesenovka** Kyrg.
137 H3 **Novov"yazivs'ke** Ukr.
136 B3 **Novoyavorivs'ke** Ukr.
139 L5 **Novoye Dubovoye** Rus. Fed.
121 J2 **Novoyegor'yevskoye** Rus. Fed.
139 M3 **Novoye Leushino** Rus. Fed.
139 K3 **Novozavidovskiy** Rus. Fed.
136 E3 **Novozhyvotiv** Ukr.
139 H5 **Novozybkov** Rus. Fed.
188 F3 **Novska** Croatia
176 D1 **Nový Bor** Czech Rep.
176 E1 **Nový Bydžov** Czech Rep.
156 E3 **Novy-Chevrières** France
Novyj Cholmogory Rus. Fed. *see* **Arkhangel'sk**
Novyj Holmogory Rus. Fed. *see* **Arkhangel'sk**
177 G2 **Nový Jičín** Czech Rep.
176 G2 **Nový Malín** Czech Rep.
Novyy Afon Georgia *see* **Akhali Ap'oni**
134 K2 **Novyy Bor** Rus. Fed.
Novyy Bug Ukr. *see* **Novyy Buh**
137 G4 **Novyy Buh** Ukr.
137 F2 **Novyy Bykiv** Ukr.
Novyy Donbass Ukr. *see* **Dymytrov**
Novyye Aneny Moldova *see* **Anenii Noi**
Novyye Belokorovichi Ukr. *see* **Novi Bilokorovychi**
120 A1 **Novyye Burasy** Rus. Fed.
Novyye Petushki Rus. Fed. *see* **Petushki**
Novyy Kholmogory Rus. Fed. *see* **Arkhangel'sk**
Novyy Margelan Uzbek. *see* **Fergana**
137 H3 **Novyy Merchyk** Ukr.
139 L3 **Novyy Nekouz** Rus. Fed.
135 G6 **Novyy Oskol** Rus. Fed.
136 C3 **Novyy Rozdil** Ukr.
137 G3 **Novyystarodub** Ukr.
137 J4 **Novyy Svit** *Donets'ka Oblast'* Ukr.
137 H5 **Novyy Svit** *Respublika Krym* Ukr.
129 E2 **Novyy Terek** *r.* Rus. Fed.
134 J4 **Novyy Tor'yal** Rus. Fed.
130 I3 **Novyy Urengoy** Rus. Fed.
100 E2 **Novyy Urgal** Rus. Fed.
Novyy Uzen' Kazakh. *see* **Zhanaozen**
175 M5 **Novyy Vytkiv** Ukr.
175 M6 **Novyy Yarychiv** Ukr.
134 K5 **Novyy Zay** Rus. Fed.
176 G3 **Nový Život** Slovakia
175 H4 **Nowa Brzeźnica** Pol.
175 L2 **Nowa Chodorówka** Pol.
175 J5 **Nowa Dęba** Pol.
174 G1 **Nowa Karczma** Pol.
174 E5 **Nowa Ruda** Pol.
175 K5 **Nowa Sarzyna** Pol.
175 J5 **Nowa Słupia** Pol.
174 D4 **Nowa Sól** Pol.
237 E4 **Nowata** *OK* U.S.A.
175 K2 **Nowa Wieś Ełcka** Pol.
174 F1 **Nowa Wieś Lęborskie** Pol.
174 G3 **Nowa Wieś Wielka** Pol.
175 J4 **Nowa Wola Gołębiowska** Pol.
122 B2 **Nowdī** Iran
174 G2 **Nowe** Pol.
175 I5 **Nowe Brzesko** Pol.
174 D4 **Nowe Miasteczko** Pol.
175 I3 **Nowe Miasto** Pol.
175 H2 **Nowe Miasto Lubawskie** Pol.
175 I4 **Nowe Miasto nad Pilicą** Pol.
147 B5 **Nowen Hill** *hill* Rep. of Ireland
175 H3 **Nowe Ostrowy** Pol.
175 K3 **Nowe Piekuty** Pol.
174 F4 **Nowe Skalmierzyce** Pol.
174 C2 **Nowe Warpno** Pol.
Nowgong *Assam* India *see* **Nagaon**
116 D4 **Nowgong** *Madh. Prad.* India
175 K2 **Nowinka** Pol.
122 C2 **Now Kharegan** Iran
175 K4 **Nowodwór** Pol.
174 D2 **Nowogard** Pol.
175 J2 **Nowogród** Pol.
174 D4 **Nowogród Bobrzański** Pol.
174 D3 **Nowogródek Pomorski** Pol.
174 D4 **Nowogrodziec** Pol.
238 F2 **Nowood** *r. WY* U.S.A.
Noworadomsk Pol. *see* **Radomsko**
175 L3 **Nowosady** Pol.
175 K6 **Nowosielce** Pol.
175 K5 **Nowosielec** Pol.
175 H4 **Nowosolna** Pol.
83 G3 **Nowra** *N.S.W.* Austr.
122 B2 **Now Shahr** Iran
123 H3 **Nowshera** Pak.
175 K3 **Nowy Bartków** Pol.
175 H3 **Nowy Duninów** Pol.
174 F2 **Nowy Dwór** Pol.
175 L2 **Nowy Dwór** Pol.
143 H4 **Nowy Dwór Gdański** Pol.
175 I3 **Nowy Dwór Mazowiecki** Pol.
175 I5 **Nowy Korczyn** Pol.
175 L5 **Nowy Lubliniec** Pol.
175 I6 **Nowy Sącz** Pol.
143 H4 **Nowy Staw** Pol.
175 I6 **Nowy Targ** Pol.
174 E3 **Nowy Tomyśl** Pol.
175 J6 **Nowy Żmigród** Pol.
227 I5 **Noxen** *PA* U.S.A.
96 D3 **Noy, Xé** *r.* Laos
Noya *Cataluña* Spain *see* **L'Anoia**
Noya *Galicia* Spain *see* **Noia**
130 I3 **Noyabr'sk** Rus. Fed.
158 D4 **Noyal-Muzillac** France
158 D4 **Noyalo** France
158 D3 **Noyal-Pontivy** France
159 G4 **Noyant** France
159 F4 **Noyant-la-Plaine** France
161 D3 **Noyarey** France
129 D3 **Noyemberyan** Armenia
159 F4 **Noyen-sur-Sarthe** France
156 D5 **Noyers** France
159 H4 **Noyers-sur-Cher** France
161 D4 **Noyers-sur-Jabron** France
114 C4 **Noyil** *r.* India
156 C3 **Noyon** France
158 E4 **Nozay** France
175 K6 **Nozdrzec** Pol.
160 E2 **Nozeroy** France
129 E2 **Nozhay-Yurt** Rus. Fed.
215 E4 **Nozizwe** S. Africa
178 B5 **Nozza** *r.* Italy
210 B4 **Npitamaiong** *mt.* Kenya
215 H4 **Nqabeni** S. Africa
215 F5 **Nqamakwe** S. Africa
215 H3 **Nqutu** S. Africa
211 A8 **Nsalamu** Zambia
211 B8 **Nsanje** Malawi
206 E5 **Nsawam** Ghana
207 H6 **Nsoc** Equat. Guinea
209 F7 **Nsombo** Zambia
207 G5 **Nsukka** Nigeria
209 E8 **Ntambu** Zambia
208 C5 **Ntandembele** Dem. Rep. Congo
211 B8 **Ntcheu** Malawi
211 B8 **Ntchisi** Malawi
207 H6 **Ntem** *r.* Cameroon
215 F2 **Ntha** S. Africa
215 G2 **Nthorwane** S. Africa
215 G4 **Ntibane** S. Africa
208 A4 **Ntoum** Gabon
217 □3a **Ntsamouéni** *Njazidja* Comoros
217 □3a **Ntsoudjini** *Njazidja* Comoros
207 H5 **Ntui** Cameroon
211 A5 **Ntungamo** Uganda
212 E4 **Ntwetwe Pan** *salt pan* Botswana
215 G4 **Ntywenka** S. Africa
159 F4 **Nuaillé** France
162 B2 **Nuaillé-d'Aunis** France
Nuanetsi *r.* Zimbabwe *see* **Mwenezi**
234 C1 **Nuangola** *PA* U.S.A.
203 F4 **Nuba, Lake** *resr* Sudan
210 A2 **Nuba Mountains** Sudan
168 E1 **Nübbel** Ger.
245 F5 **Nube Flan, Cerro** *mt.* Mex.
168 E1 **Nübel** Ger.
203 G4 **Nubian Desert** Sudan
140 M1 **Nubivarri** *hill* Norway
260 A5 **Ñuble** *r.* Chile
182 E1 **Nubledo** Spain
197 F2 **Nucet** Romania
241 M2 **Nucla** *CO* U.S.A.
171 D4 **Nudersdorf** Ger.
169 F5 **Nüdlingen** Ger.
139 K3 **Nudol'** Rus. Fed.
175 M4 **Nudyzhe** Ukr.
237 D7 **Nueces** *r. TX* U.S.A.
159 F5 **Nueil-sur-Argent** France
223 L2 **Nueltin Lake** *Man./Nunavut* Can.
165 E3 **Nuenen** Neth.
186 C2 **Nueno** Spain
187 E6 **Nuestra Señora del Pilar** Spain
183 F1 **Nueva** Spain
259 D9 **Nueva, Isla** *i.* Chile
250 C6 **Nueva Alejandría** Peru
242 □H6 **Nueva Arcadia** Hond.
185 F3 **Nueva-Carteya** Spain
237 D7 **Nueva Ciudad Guerrero** Mex.
251 E2 **Nueva Esparta** *state* Venez.
253 F5 **Nueva Germania** Para.
246 B2 **Nueva Gerona** Cuba
261 I4 **Nueva Helvecia** Uru.
260 A6 **Nueva Imperial** Chile
244 C4 **Nueva Italia de Ruiz** Mex.
184 D4 **Nueva Jarilla** Spain
250 B4 **Nueva Loja** Ecuador
242 □H6 **Nueva Ocotepeque** Hond.
261 H3 **Nueva Palmira** Uru.
243 E3 **Nueva Rosita** Mex.
243 H6 **Nueva San Salvador** El Salvador
245 E1 **Nueva Villa de Padilla** Mex.
Nueve de Julio Arg. *see* **9 de Julio**
246 C2 **Nuevitas** Cuba
243 H4 **Nuevo, Cayo** *i.* Mex.
261 I3 **Nuevo Berlín** Uru.
242 D2 **Nuevo Casas Grandes** Mex.
242 D3 **Nuevo Ideal** Mex.
243 F3 **Nuevo Laredo** Mex.
241 J5 **Nuevo León** Mex.
244 E1 **Nuevo León** *state* Mex.
106 B1 **Nuga** Mongolia
210 F2 **Nugaal** *admin. reg.* Somalia
85 G5 **Nuga Nuga, Lake** *Qld* Austr.
81 B7 **Nugget Point** *South I.* N.Z.
192 B4 **Nughedu di San Nicolò** *Sardegna* Italy
139 K5 **Nugr'** *r.* Rus. Fed.
203 G3 **Nugrus, Gebel** *mt.* Egypt
114 C3 **Nugu** *r.* India
123 E5 **Nuh, Ras** *pt* Pak.
80 F3 **Nuhaka** *North I.* N.Z.
199 G2 **Nuhköy** Turkey
77 H2 **Nui** *i.* Tuvalu
Nui Con Voi *r.* Vietnam *see* **Hông, Sông**
159 F4 **Nuillé-sur-Vicoin** France
96 D4 **Nui Ti On** *mt.* Vietnam
156 E5 **Nuits** France
160 C1 **Nuits-St-Georges** France
108 A3 **Nu Jiang** *r.* China
Nu Jiang *r.* Myanmar *see* **Salween**
82 C3 **Nukey Bluff** *hill S.A.* Austr.
Nukha Azer. *see* **Şäki**
79 □2a **Nuku'alofa** *Tongatapu* Tonga
77 H2 **Nukufetau** *i.* Tuvalu
Nukuhiva *i.* Fr. Polynesia *see* **Nuku Hiva**
79 □3 **Nuku Hiva** *i.* Fr. Polynesia
77 H2 **Nukulaelae** *i.* Tuvalu
Nukulailai *i.* Tuvalu *see* **Nukulaelae**
Nukunau *i. Gilbert Is* Kiribati *see* **Nikunau**
Nukunono *atoll* Tokelau *see* **Nukunonu**
81 □1 **Nukunonu** *atoll* Tokelau
120 D4 **Nukus** Uzbek.
164 E3 **Nuland** Neth.
220 C3 **Nulato** *AK* U.S.A.
192 B4 **Nule** *Sardegna* Italy
187 C5 **Nules** Spain
86 D4 **Nullagine** *W.A.* Austr.
86 D4 **Nullagine** *r. W.A.* Austr.
82 B2 **Nullarbor** *S.A.* Austr.
82 B2 **Nullarbor Plain** *S.A.* Austr.
107 H3 **Nulu'erhu Shan** *mts* China
192 A4 **Nulvi** *Sardegna* Italy
83 F2 **Numalla, Lake** *salt flat Qld* Austr.
207 I4 **Numan** Nigeria
191 I5 **Numana** Italy
92 C4 **Numancia** Phil.
164 D3 **Numansdorp** Neth.
105 F2 **Numata** Japan
105 E3 **Numazu** Japan
215 H1 **Numbi Gate** S. Africa
84 C2 **Numbulwar** *N.T.* Austr.
142 C1 **Numedal** *val.* Norway
100 C3 **Numin** *r.* China
141 M3 **Nummi** Fin.
83 F4 **Numurkah** *Vic.* Austr.
221 N3 **Nunap Isua** *c.* Greenland
224 E1 **Nunavik** *reg.* Can.
223 L2 **Nunavut** *admin. div.* Can.
250 C3 **Nunchía** Col.
171 E4 **Nünchritz** Ger.
232 E3 **Nunda** *NY* U.S.A.
83 G2 **Nundle** *N.S.W.* Austr.
151 F2 **Nuneaton** *Warwickshire, England* U.K.
87 C6 **Nungarin** *W.A.* Austr.
107 H2 **Nungnain Sum** *Nei Mongol* China
213 H2 **Nungo** Moz.
220 B4 **Nunivak Island** *AK* U.S.A.
117 F5 **Nunkapasi** *Orissa* India
172 A2 **Nunkirchen** Ger.
116 D2 **Nunkun** *mt.* Jammu and Kashmir
131 T3 **Nunligran** Rus. Fed.
252 C3 **Nuñoa** Peru
182 D4 **Nuñomoral** Spain
171 E3 **Nunsdorf** Ger.
164 E2 **Nunspeet** Neth.
Nuojiang *Sichuan* China *see* **Tongjiang**
107 J1 **Nuomin** *r.* China
192 B4 **Nuoro** *Sardegna* Italy
192 B4 **Nuoro** *prov. Sardegna* Italy
78 □6 **Nupani** *i. Santa Cruz Is* Solomon Is
124 C2 **Nuqrah** Saudi Arabia
250 B3 **Nuquí** Col.
122 C2 **Nur** *r.* Iran
175 K3 **Nur** Pol.
121 G2 **Nura** *r.* Kazakh.
122 B4 **Nūrābād** Iran
192 B5 **Nuragus** *Sardegna* Italy
Nurakita *i.* Tuvalu *see* **Niulakita**
192 B5 **Nurallao** *Sardegna* Italy
192 B5 **Nuraminis** *Sardegna* Italy
120 F4 **Nurata** Uzbek.
121 F4 **Nuratau, Khrebet** *mts* Uzbek.
128 C1 **Nurdağı** Turkey
126 D3 **Nur Dağları** *mts* Turkey
190 E3 **Nure** *r.* Italy
192 A5 **Nureci** *Sardegna* Italy
Nurek Tajik. *see* **Norak**
Nurek Reservoir *l.* Tajik. *see* **Obanbori Norak**
Nurekskoye Vodokhranilishche *l.* Tajik. *see* **Obanbori Norak**
Nuremberg Ger. *see* **Nürnberg**
234 B2 **Nuremberg** *PA* U.S.A.
242 C2 **Nuri** Mex.
203 G5 **Nuri** Sudan
193 F2 **Nuria, Monte** *mt.* Italy
116 D2 **Nurla** Jammu and Kashmir
135 J5 **Nurlat** Rus. Fed.
134 J5 **Nurlaty** Rus. Fed.
140 O3 **Nurmes** Fin.
141 N3 **Nurmijärvi** Fin.
140 M3 **Nurmo** Fin.
173 F2 **Nürnberg** Ger.
148 C5 **Nurney** *Carlow* Rep. of Ireland
148 C4 **Nurney** *Kildare* Rep. of Ireland
Nurota Uzbek. *see* **Nurata**
123 G4 **Nurpur** Pak.
82 B2 **Nurrai Lakes** *salt flat S.A.* Austr.
192 B5 **Nurri** *Sardegna* Italy
83 F2 **Nurri, Mount** *hill N.S.W.* Austr.
140 K2 **Nursfjellet** *mt.* Norway
Nursia Italy *see* **Norcia**
172 D3 **Nürtingen** Ger.
175 K3 **Nurzec** *r.* Pol.
175 L3 **Nurzec-Stacja** Pol.
190 C3 **Nus** Italy
95 G5 **Nusa Tenggara Barat** *prov.* Indon.
93 B5 **Nusa Tenggara Timur** *prov.* Indon.
127 F3 **Nusaybin** Turkey
193 H4 **Nusco** Italy
93 D3 **Nusela, Kepulauan** *is Irian Jaya* Indon.
197 F2 **Nuşfalău** Romania
108 A3 **Nu Shan** *mts* China
123 F4 **Nushki** Pak.
172 C3 **Nusplingen** Ger.
179 F3 **Nußbach** Austria
173 G4 **Nußdorf** Ger.
173 G4 **Nußdorf am Inn** Ger.
178 D4 **Nußdorf-Debant** Austria
168 F2 **Nusse** Ger.
225 I1 **Nutak** *Nfld.* Can.
165 E4 **Nuth** Neth.
171 E3 **Nuthe** *r.* Ger.
151 G3 **Nuthurst** *West Sussex, England* U.K.
235 D2 **Nutley** *NJ* U.S.A.
241 M5 **Nutrioso** *AZ* U.S.A.
147 E2 **Nutt's Corner** *Northern Ireland* U.K.
84 C2 **Nutwood Downs** *N.T.* Austr.
221 M3 **Nuuk** Greenland
221 M2 **Nuussuaq** *pen.* Greenland
125 F2 **Nuway** Oman
214 B4 **Nuwerus** S. Africa
214 C5 **Nuweveldberge** *mts* S. Africa
192 A5 **Nuxis** *Sardegna* Italy
175 M4 **Nuyno** Ukr.
87 C7 **Nuyts, Point** *W.A.* Austr.
82 C3 **Nuyts Archipelago** *is S.A.* Austr.
178 A3 **Nüziders** Austria
114 D2 **Nuzvid** *Andhra Prad.* India
207 H5 **Nwa** Cameroon
212 E3 **Nxai Pan National Park** Botswana
95 F2 **Nyaän, Bukit** *hill* Indon.
87 C7 **Nyabing** *W.A.* Austr.
233 G4 **Nyack** *NY* U.S.A.
130 H3 **Nyagan'** Rus. Fed.
Nyagquka *Sichuan* China *see* **Yajiang**
Nyagrong *Sichuan* China *see* **Xinlong**
83 E3 **Nyah West** *Vic.* Austr.
111 E6 **Nyainqêntanglha Feng** *mt. Xizang* China
111 E6 **Nyainqêntanglha Shan** *mts Xizang* China
111 F5 **Nyainrong** *Xizang* China
215 F2 **Nyakallong** S. Africa
140 L3 **Nyåker** Sweden
Nyakh Rus. Fed. *see* **Nyagan'**
206 E5 **Nyakrom** Ghana
202 E6 **Nyala** Sudan
111 D6 **Nyalam** *Xizang* China
213 F3 **Nyamandhiovu** Zimbabwe
211 C7 **Nyamtumbo** Tanz.
Nyande Zimbabwe *see* **Masvingo**
134 H3 **Nyandoma** Rus. Fed.
134 G3 **Nyandomskiy Vozvyshennost'** *hills* Rus. Fed.
208 A5 **Nyanga** Congo
209 A5 **Nyanga** *prov.* Gabon
213 G3 **Nyanga** Zimbabwe
111 E6 **Nyang Qu** *r.* China
111 F6 **Nyang Qu** *r.* China
206 E4 **Nyankpala** Ghana
211 A5 **Nyanza** Rwanda
211 A6 **Nyanza-Lac** Burundi
95 G2 **Nyapa, Gunung** *mt.* Indon.
116 D3 **Nyar** *r.* India
176 G4 **Nyárád** Hungary
222 H2 **Nyarling** *r. N.W.T.* Can.
177 I5 **Nyárlőrinc** Hungary
177 I4 **Nyársapát** Hungary
211 A5 **Nyarugumba** Rwanda
211 B7 **Nyasa, Lake** Africa
Nyasaland *country* Africa *see* **Malawi**
138 F5 **Nyasvizh** Belarus
213 F3 **Nyathi** Zimbabwe
96 B3 **Nyaunglebin** Myanmar
96 A2 **Nyaungu** Myanmar
134 M3 **Nyays** *r.* Rus. Fed.
213 G3 **Nyazura** Zimbabwe
142 D4 **Nyborg** Denmark
140 O1 **Nyborg** Norway
140 M2 **Nyborg** Sweden
143 F3 **Nybro** Sweden
177 H2 **Nýdek** Czech Rep.
221 M1 **Nyeboe Land** *reg.* Greenland
138 F5 **Nyeharelaye** Belarus
111 E6 **Nyêmo** *Xizang* China
Nyenchen Tanglha Range *mts Xizang* China *see* **Nyainqêntanglha Shan**
210 C5 **Nyeri** Kenya
140 □ **Ny-Friesland** *reg.* Svalbard
143 F1 **Nyhammar** Sweden
111 D6 **Nyima** *Xizang* China
211 A8 **Nyimba** Zambia
111 F6 **Nyingchi** *Xizang* China
Nyinma *Gansu* China *see* **Maqu**
177 L4 **Nyírábrány** Hungary
177 K4 **Nyíracsád** Hungary
176 G4 **Nyirád** Hungary
177 K4 **Nyíradony** Hungary
177 L4 **Nyírbátor** Hungary
177 L4 **Nyírbéltek** Hungary
177 L4 **Nyírbogát** Hungary
177 K3 **Nyírbogdány** Hungary
177 L4 **Nyírcsászári** Hungary
177 K4 **Nyíregyháza** Hungary
177 K4 **Nyírgelse** Hungary
211 C5 **Nyiri Desert** Kenya
177 L4 **Nyírlugos** Hungary
177 K4 **Nyírmártonfalva** Hungary
177 K4 **Nyírmihálydi** Hungary
177 K3 **Nyírtelek** Hungary
177 K3 **Nyírtét** Hungary
177 K3 **Nyírtura** Hungary
210 C4 **Nyiru, Mount** Kenya
177 L4 **Nyírvasvári** Hungary
140 M3 **Nykarleby** Fin.
142 D4 **Nykøbing** Denmark
142 C3 **Nykøbing Mors** Denmark
142 D4 **Nykøbing Sjælland** Denmark
143 G2 **Nyköping** Sweden
143 F2 **Nykroppa** Sweden
143 G2 **Nykvarn** Sweden
134 B3 **Nyland** Sweden
213 F5 **Nylstroom** S. Africa
83 F3 **Nymagee** *N.S.W.* Austr.
83 H2 **Nymboida** *N.S.W.* Austr.
176 E1 **Nymburk** Czech Rep.
142 C4 **Nymindegab** Denmark
143 G2 **Nynäshamn** Sweden
83 F2 **Nyngan** *N.S.W.* Austr.
105 F2 **Nyohō-san** *mt.* Japan
159 F4 **Nyoiseau** France
215 G5 **Nyokana** S. Africa
138 D5 **Nyoman** *r.* Belarus/Lith.
138 E5 **Nyomanskaya Nizina** *lowland* Belarus
190 B2 **Nyon** Switz.
207 H6 **Nyong** *r.* Cameroon
161 D4 **Nyons** France
170 C1 **Nyråd** Denmark
176 C2 **Nýřany** Czech Rep.
134 L3 **Nyrob** Rus. Fed.
176 C2 **Nýrsko** Czech Rep.
174 F5 **Nysa** Pol.
174 F5 **Nysa Kłodzka** *r.* Pol.
Nysa Łużycka *r.* Ger./Pol. *see* **Neiße**
142 E2 **Nysäter** Sweden
140 K3 **Nysätern** Sweden
238 C3 **Nyssa** *OR* U.S.A.
Nystad Fin. *see* **Uusikaupunki**
142 D4 **Nysted** Denmark
105 E3 **Nyūgasa-yama** *mt.* Japan
134 I3 **Nyuksenitsa** Rus. Fed.
177 G4 **Nyúl** Hungary
209 F6 **Nyunzu** Dem. Rep. Congo
131 M3 **Nyurba** Rus. Fed.
129 E4 **Nyuvadi** Armenia
134 J3 **Nyuvchim** Rus. Fed.
131 M3 **Nyuya** Rus. Fed.
131 M3 **Nyuya** *r.* Rus. Fed.
175 M5 **Nyvytsi** Ukr.
136 B3 **Nyzhankovychi** Ukr.
137 H4 **Nyzhni Sirohozy** Ukr.
137 H4 **Nyzhni Torhayi** Ukr.
136 B3 **Nyzhni Vorota** Ukr.
136 B3 **Nyzhniy Bystryy** Ukr.
137 J3 **Nyzhniy Nahol'chyk** Ukr.
137 H5 **Nyzhn'ohirs'kyy** Ukr.
137 J3 **Nyzhnya Dubanka** Ukr.
137 H2 **Nyzhnya Syrovatka** Ukr.
137 H3 **Nyzhnya Tersa** *r.* Ukr.
177 M2 **Nyzhnya Vysots'ke** Ukr.
177 L2 **Nyzhnya Yablun'ka** Ukr.
137 H2 **Nyzy** Ukr.
209 A5 **Nzambi** Congo
208 F3 **Nzara** Sudan
206 C4 **Nzébéla** Guinea
211 B6 **Nzega** Tanz.
206 C5 **Nzérékoré** Guinea
209 B6 **N'zeto** Angola
206 D5 **Nzi** *r.* Côte d'Ivoire
206 D5 **Nzo** *r.* Côte d'Ivoire
210 B4 **Nzoia** *r.* Kenya
208 F4 **Nzoro** *r.* Dem. Rep. Congo
217 □3 **Nzwani** *i.* Comoros

O

236 D3 **Oacoma** *SD* U.S.A.
151 F2 **Oadby** *Leicestershire, England* U.K.
236 C2 **Oahe, Lake** *SD* U.S.A.
240 □ **Oahu** *i. HI* U.S.A.
Oaitupu *i.* Tuvalu *see* **Vaitupu**
82 E3 **Oakbank** *S.A.* Austr.
233 H4 **Oak Bluffs** *MA* U.S.A.
241 K2 **Oak City** *UT* U.S.A.
226 D4 **Oak Creek** *WI* U.S.A.
240 G3 **Oakdale** *CA* U.S.A.
235 F1 **Oakdale** *CT* U.S.A.
237 E6 **Oakdale** *LA* U.S.A.
235 E2 **Oakdale** *NY* U.S.A.
150 E2 **Oakengates** *Telford and Wrekin, England* U.K.
236 D2 **Oakes** *ND* U.S.A.
85 G5 **Oakey** *Qld* Austr.

Oakfield to **Omagh**

343

232 D3 **Oakfield** NY U.S.A.
234 D2 **Oakford** PA U.S.A.
237 F5 **Oak Grove** LA U.S.A.
226 E3 **Oak Grove** MI U.S.A.
151 G2 **Oakham** Rutland, England U.K.
232 B4 **Oak Harbor** OH U.S.A.
238 B1 **Oak Harbor** WA U.S.A.
232 B5 **Oak Hill** OH U.S.A.
232 C6 **Oak Hill** WV U.S.A.
240 H3 **Oakhurst** CA U.S.A.
235 D2 **Oakhurst** NJ U.S.A.
240 G4 **Oak Knolls** CA U.S.A.
240 F3 **Oakland** CA U.S.A.
232 D5 **Oakland** MD U.S.A.
233 □I2 **Oakland** ME U.S.A.
236 D3 **Oakland** NE U.S.A.
235 D1 **Oakland** NJ U.S.A.
238 B3 **Oakland** OR U.S.A.
240 F3 **Oakland** airport CA U.S.A.
230 C4 **Oakland City** IN U.S.A.
83 F3 **Oaklands** N.S.W. Austr.
226 D5 **Oak Lawn** IL U.S.A.
151 G2 **Oakley** Bedfordshire, England U.K.
151 F3 **Oakley** Buckinghamshire, England U.K.
146 E5 **Oakley** Fife, Scotland U.K.
151 F3 **Oakley** Hampshire, England U.K.
236 C4 **Oakley** KS U.S.A.
227 E4 **Oakley** MI U.S.A.
232 D4 **Oakmont** PA U.S.A.
86 D4 **Oakover** r. W.A. Austr.
226 D5 **Oak Park** IL U.S.A.
235 D1 **Oak Ridge** NJ U.S.A.
238 B3 **Oakridge** OR U.S.A.
231 C4 **Oak Ridge** TN U.S.A.
234 C2 **Oaks** PA U.S.A.
234 D3 **Oak Shade** NJ U.S.A.
80 D3 **Oakura** North I. N.Z.
82 E3 **Oakvale** S.A. Austr.
240 H4 **Oak View** CA U.S.A.
224 E5 **Oakville** Ont. Can.
235 E1 **Oakville** CT U.S.A.
232 A4 **Oakwood** OH U.S.A.
232 A5 **Oakwood** OH U.S.A.
234 C3 **Oakwood Beach** NJ U.S.A.
81 C6 **Oamaru** South I. N.Z.
80 D3 **Oaonui** North I. N.Z.
81 D5 **Oaro** South I. N.Z.
105 F2 **Ōashi-gawa** r. Japan
240 I3 **Oasis** CA U.S.A.
238 D3 **Oasis** NV U.S.A.
197 F1 **Oașului, Munții** mts Romania
Oates Coast reg. Antarctica see **Oates Land**
263 K2 **Oates Land** reg. Antarctica
83 F5 **Oatlands** Tas. Austr.
214 E5 **Oatlands** S. Africa
245 F5 **Oaxaca** Mex.
245 F5 **Oaxaca** state Mex.
121 J1 **Ob'** r. Rus. Fed.
Ob, Gulf of sea chan. Rus. Fed. see **Obskaya Guba**
224 C3 **Oba** Ont. Can.
Oba i. Vanuatu see **Aoba**
Obaghan r. Kazakh. see **Ubagan**
104 B4 **Obako-dake** mt. Japan
128 A1 **Obaköy** Turkey
138 G4 **Obal'** Belarus
207 H5 **Obala** Cameroon
104 B3 **Obama** Japan
207 H5 **Oban** Nigeria
146 C5 **Oban** Argyll and Bute, Scotland U.K.
102 J4 **Obanazawa** Japan
123 G2 **Obanbori Norak** l. Tajik.
123 G1 **Obanbori Qayroqqum** resr Tajik.
207 H5 **Oban Hills** mt. Nigeria
182 D2 **O Barco** Spain
183 G2 **Obarenes, Montes** mts Spain
197 H2 **Obârșeni, Dealul** hill Romania
Obbia Somalia see **Hobyo**
140 M3 **Obbola** Sweden
197 G2 **Obcina Feredeului** ridge Romania
197 G2 **Obcina Mare** ridge Romania
197 G2 **Obcina Mestecănișului** ridge Romania
179 F3 **Obdach** Austria
164 D2 **Obdam** Neth.
Obdorsk Rus. Fed. see **Salekhard**
176 C2 **Obecnice** Czech Rep.
Óbecse Vojvodina, Srbija Yugo. see **Bečej**
222 G4 **Obed** Alta Can.
185 F2 **Obejo** Spain
129 A3 **Öbektaş** Turkey
138 E4 **Obeliai** Lith.
81 B6 **Obelisk** mt. South I. N.Z.
258 G2 **Oberá** Arg.
179 G3 **Oberaich** Austria
178 E3 **Oberalm** Austria
190 D2 **Oberalpstock** mt. Switz.
173 F4 **Oberammergau** Ger.
173 E2 **Oberasbach** Ger.
173 F4 **Oberau** Ger.
173 G4 **Oberaudorf** Ger.
169 E5 **Oberaula** Ger.
173 F4 **Oberbayern** admin. reg. Bayern Ger.
172 C2 **Oberderdingen** Ger.
173 F3 **Oberding** Ger.
169 F4 **Oberdorla** Ger.
178 D4 **Oberdrauburg** Austria
190 E1 **Oberegg** Switz.
169 F5 **Oberelsbach** Ger.
190 D1 **Oberentfelden** Switz.
172 D4 **Oberessendorf** Ger.
169 C5 **Oberfell** Ger.
171 C5 **Oberfranken** admin. reg. Bayern Ger.
169 F3 **Oberg (Lahstedt)** Ger.
190 C1 **Obergösgen** Switz.
179 G2 **Ober-Grafendorf** Austria
173 F3 **Obergriesbach** Ger.
173 E4 **Obergünzburg** Ger.
171 F4 **Obergurig** Ger.
179 G4 **Oberhaag** Austria
173 F3 **Oberhaching** Ger.
173 E2 **Oberhaid** Ger.
172 C3 **Oberharmersbach** Ger.
173 F3 **Oberhausen** Bayern Ger.
169 B4 **Oberhausen** Nordrhein-Westfalen Ger.
169 F5 **Oberhof** Ger.
190 C2 **Oberhofen** Switz.
178 C3 **Oberhofen im Inntal** Austria
157 H4 **Oberhoffen-sur-Moder** France
172 C3 **Oberkirch** Ger.
173 E3 **Oberkochen** Ger.
171 C5 **Oberkotzau** Ger.
168 C3 **Oberlangen** Ger.
171 F4 **Oberlichtenau** Ger.
178 D4 **Oberlienz** Austria
236 C4 **Oberlin** KS U.S.A.
237 E6 **Oberlin** LA U.S.A.
232 B4 **Oberlin** OH U.S.A.
172 D3 **Obermarchtal** Ger.
169 F5 **Obermaßfeld-Grimmenthal** Ger.
172 B2 **Obermoschel** Ger.
157 H4 **Obernai** France
179 E2 **Obernberg am Inn** Austria
172 D2 **Obernburg am Main** Ger.
173 E3 **Oberndorf am Lech** Ger.
172 C3 **Oberndorf am Neckar** Ger.
179 G2 **Oberndorf an der Melk** Austria
178 D3 **Oberndorf bei Salzburg** Austria
179 F2 **Oberneukirchen** Austria
169 F4 **Obernfeld** Ger.
172 C3 **Obernheim** Ger.
172 B2 **Obernheim-Kirchenarnbach** Ger.
169 E3 **Obernkirchen** Ger.
173 H3 **Obernzell** Ger.
173 E2 **Obernzenn** Ger.
171 F5 **Oberoderwitz** Ger.
172 C2 **Ober-Olm** Ger.
83 G3 **Oberon** N.S.W. Austr.
173 E4 **Oberostendorf** Ger.
179 E2 **Oberösterreich** land Austria
173 F2 **Oberpfalz** admin. reg. Bayern Ger.
173 G2 **Oberpfälzer Wald** mts Ger.
173 F3 **Oberpframmern** Ger.
179 H3 **Oberpullendorf** Austria
172 C2 **Ober-Ramstadt** Ger.
172 D4 **Oberreute** Ger.
172 B4 **Oberried** Ger.
173 E3 **Oberrieden** Ger.
190 E1 **Oberriet** Switz.
171 C4 **Oberröblingen** Ger.
172 C2 **Ober-Roden** Ger.
171 C4 **Oberroßla** Ger.
172 D2 **Oberrot** Ger.
172 B3 **Oberrotweil** Ger.
173 F3 **Oberschleißheim** Ger.
173 G3 **Oberschneiding** Ger.
171 E5 **Oberschöna** Ger.
179 H3 **Oberschützen** Austria
179 H2 **Obersiebenbrunn** Austria
190 D1 **Obersiggenthal** Switz.
169 E5 **Obersinn** Ger.
172 D2 **Obersontheim** Ger.
169 F4 **Oberspier** Ger.
172 D3 **Oberstadion** Ger.
173 E4 **Oberstaufen** Ger.
173 E4 **Oberstdorf** Ger.
172 D2 **Oberstenfeld** Ger.
173 G3 **Obertaufkirchen** Ger.
172 D4 **Oberteuringen** Ger.
172 B2 **Oberthal** Ger.
169 E5 **Oberthulba** Ger.
173 G3 **Obertraubling** Ger.
173 F2 **Obertrubach** Ger.
178 E3 **Obertrum am See** Austria
169 D5 **Obertshausen** Ger.
136 C3 **Obertyn** Ukr.
170 E2 **Oberueckersee** l. Ger.
169 D5 **Oberursel (Taunus)** Ger.
178 E4 **Obervellach** Austria
173 G2 **Oberviechtach** Ger.
190 D2 **Oberwald** Switz.
169 E4 **Oberwälder Land** reg. Ger.
179 H3 **Oberwaltersdorf** Austria
179 H3 **Oberwart** Austria
169 C5 **Oberwesel** Ger.
179 G2 **Oberwölbling** Austria
172 C3 **Oberwolfach** Ger.
179 F3 **Oberwölz** Austria
137 H2 **Obesta** r. Rus. Fed.
171 C4 **Obhausen** Ger.
93 C3 **Obi** i. Maluku Indon.
207 H4 **Obi** Nigeria
93 C3 **Obi, Kepulauan** is Maluku Indon.
251 H5 **Óbidos** Brazil
184 A1 **Óbidos** Port.
123 G2 **Obigarm** Tajik.
102 K2 **Obihiro** Japan
196 E4 **Obilić** Kosovo, Srbija Yugo.
135 I7 **Obil'noye** Rus. Fed.
173 G3 **Obing** Ger.
237 F4 **Obion** r. TN U.S.A.
250 D2 **Obispos** Venez.
261 F2 **Obispo Trejo** Arg.
105 F3 **Obitsu-gawa** r. Japan
162 D3 **Objat** France
174 F1 **Objazda** Pol.
175 M4 **Oblapy** Ukr.
179 E3 **Öblarn** Austria
135 H6 **Oblivskaya** Rus. Fed.
100 D2 **Obluch'ye** Rus. Fed.
139 K4 **Obninsk** Rus. Fed.
208 E3 **Obo** C.A.R.
214 C2 **Obobogorap** S. Africa
210 D2 **Obock** Djibouti
136 E3 **Obodivka** Ukr.
207 G5 **Obolo** Nigeria
182 C2 **O Bolo** Spain
137 G3 **Obolon'** Ukr.
186 C4 **Obón** Spain
95 F1 **Obong, Gunung** mt. Sarawak Malaysia
174 E3 **Oborniki** Pol.
174 E4 **Oborniki Śląskie** Pol.
135 G6 **Oboyan'** Rus. Fed.
134 H3 **Obozerskiy** Rus. Fed.
117 E4 **Obra** Uttar Prad. India
174 D3 **Obra** r. Pol.
196 E3 **Obrenovac** Srbija Yugo.
238 B3 **O'Brien** OR U.S.A.
172 D2 **Obrigheim** Ger.
172 C2 **Obrigheim (Pfalz)** Ger.
Obringa r. Switz. see **Aare**
176 C1 **Obrnice** Czech Rep.
197 I4 **Obrochishte** Bulg.
174 G3 **Obrowo** Pol.
126 D3 **Obruk** Turkey
175 J3 **Obryte** Pol.
174 E3 **Obrzycko** Pol.
82 C2 **Observatory Hill** hill S.A. Austr.
139 I4 **Obsha** r. Rus. Fed.
120 B2 **Obshchiy Syrt** hills Rus. Fed.
130 I3 **Obskaya Guba** sea chan. Rus. Fed.
175 K5 **Obsza** Pol.
137 G2 **Obtove** Ukr.
104 C3 **Ōbu** Japan
206 E5 **Obuasi** Ghana
207 H5 **Obubra** Nigeria
188 G3 **Obudovac** Bos.-Herz.
207 H5 **Obudu** Nigeria
136 F2 **Obukhiv** Ukr.
Obukhov Ukr. see **Obukhiv**
139 L4 **Obukhovo** Rus. Fed.
134 K4 **Obva** r. Rus. Fed.
190 D2 **Obwalden** canton Switz.
134 J3 **Ob"yachevo** Rus. Fed.
182 C1 **O Cádabo** Spain
231 D6 **Ocala** FL U.S.A.
242 E3 **Ocampo** Coahuila Mex.
244 D3 **Ocampo** Guanajuato Mex.
245 E2 **Ocampo** Tamaulipas Mex.
250 C2 **Ocaña** Col.
192 A3 **Ocana** Corse France
183 G5 **Ocaña** Spain
182 B2 **O Castelo** Spain
182 B2 **O Castro** Spain
191 G4 **Occhiobello** Italy
193 G3 **Occhito, Lago di** l. Italy
252 C4 **Occidental, Cordillera** mts Chile
250 B4 **Occidental, Cordillera** mts Col.
252 C4 **Occidental, Cordillera** mts Peru
190 D3 **Occimiano** Italy
232 E5 **Occoquan** VA U.S.A.
232 C6 **Oceana** WV U.S.A.
235 E2 **Ocean Beach** NY U.S.A.
233 F5 **Ocean City** MD U.S.A.
234 D3 **Ocean City** NJ U.S.A.
235 D3 **Ocean County** county NJ U.S.A.
222 E4 **Ocean Falls** B.C. Can.
235 D3 **Ocean Gate** NJ U.S.A.
235 D2 **Ocean Grove** NJ U.S.A.
Ocean Island Kiribati see **Banaba**
Ocean Island atoll HI U.S.A. see **Kure Atoll**
240 G4 **Oceano** CA U.S.A.
246 C1 **Oceans Cay** i. Bahamas
240 I5 **Oceanside** CA U.S.A.
237 F6 **Ocean Springs** MS U.S.A.
234 D3 **Ocean View** NJ U.S.A.
235 D3 **Oceanville** NJ U.S.A.
183 G3 **Ocejón** mt. Spain
78 □4a **Ocha** i. Chuuk Micronesia
186 B2 **Ochagavía** Spain
137 F4 **Ochakiv** Ukr.
129 B2 **Och'amch'ire** Georgia
134 K4 **Ocher** Rus. Fed.
136 E3 **Ocheretnya** Ukr.
137 H4 **Ocheretuvate** Ukr.
157 F4 **Ochey** France
146 E5 **Ochil Hills** Scotland U.K.
146 D6 **Ochiltree** East Ayrshire, Scotland U.K.
231 C6 **Ochlockonee** r. GA U.S.A.
175 H3 **Ochnia** r. Pol.
168 C2 **Ocholt** Ger.
246 □ **Ocho Rios** Jamaica
Ochrida, Lake Albania/Macedonia see **Ohrid, Lake**
173 E2 **Ochsenfurt** Ger.
172 D3 **Ochsenhausen** Ger.
169 C5 **Ochtendung** Ger.
198 D2 **Ochthonia** Greece
171 C3 **Ochtmersleben** Ger.
169 C3 **Ochtrup** Ger.
231 D6 **Ocilla** GA U.S.A.
141 L3 **Ockelbo** Sweden
168 D1 **Ockholm** Ger.
146 C5 **Ockle** Highland, Scotland U.K.
197 G2 **Ocland** Romania
231 D6 **Ocmulgee** r. GA U.S.A.
197 F2 **Ocna Mureș** Romania
197 G3 **Ocna Sibiului** Romania
136 D3 **Ocnița** Moldova
197 G2 **Ocolașul Mare, Vârful** mt. Romania
252 B4 **Ocoña** Peru
85 E4 **O'Connell Creek** r. Qld Austr.
226 C4 **Oconomowoc** WI U.S.A.
226 D3 **Oconto** WI U.S.A.
226 C3 **Oconto Falls** WI U.S.A.
182 B2 **O Convento** Spain
182 C2 **O Corgo** Spain
243 G6 **Ocos** Guat.
243 G5 **Ocosingo** Mex.
242 □I6 **Ocotal** Nic.
244 C3 **Ocotlán** Mex.
177 I3 **Očová** Slovakia
243 G5 **Ocozocoautla** Mex.
182 C5 **Ocreza** r. Port.
177 I4 **Ócsa** Hungary
177 H5 **Öcsény** Hungary
177 J5 **Öcsöd** Hungary
158 E2 **Octeville** France
159 G2 **Octeville-sur-Mer** France
October Revolution Island Severnaya Zemlya Rus. Fed. see **Oktyabr'skoy Revolyutsii, Ostrov**
234 B3 **Octoraro Creek** r. MD U.S.A.
242 □J8 **Ocú** Panama
213 H2 **Ocua** Moz.
245 E4 **Ocuilan de Arteaga** Mex.
252 D4 **Ocurí** Bol.
174 G2 **Ocypel** Pol.
206 E5 **Oda** Ghana
103 F6 **Ōda** Japan
203 H4 **Oda, Jebel** mt. Sudan
128 C1 **Odabaşı** Turkey
140 □C2 **Ódáðahraun** lava field Iceland
101 D4 **Ŏdaejin** N. Korea
104 C4 **Ōdaigahara-zan** mt. Japan
226 B2 **Odanah** WI U.S.A.
102 J3 **Ōdate** Japan
105 F3 **Odawara** Japan
142 B1 **Odda** Norway
142 D4 **Odder** Denmark
146 □H1 **Oddsta** Shetland, Scotland U.K.
184 C2 **Odearce** r. Port.
184 B3 **Odeceixe** Port.
223 L3 **Odei** r. Man. Can.
184 C3 **Odeleite** Port.
184 C3 **Odeleite** r. Port.
226 C5 **Odell** IL U.S.A.
184 B3 **Odelouca** r. Port.
173 F3 **Odelzhausen** Ger.
237 D7 **Odem** TX U.S.A.
184 B3 **Odemira** Port.
199 E2 **Ödemiş** Turkey
186 E3 **Odena** Spain
Ödenburg Hungary see **Sopron**
215 F2 **Odendaalsrus** S. Africa
143 F2 **Odensbacken** Sweden
142 D4 **Odense** Denmark
234 B3 **Odenton** MD U.S.A.
172 C2 **Odenwald** reg. Ger.
174 G6 **Oder** r. Ger. alt. **Odra (Poland)**
169 E4 **Oder** r. Ger./Pol.
170 F3 **Oderberg** Ger.
170 F1 **Oderbucht** b. Ger.
170 F2 **Oderhaff** b. Ger.
171 E3 **Oderin** Ger.
172 B2 **Odernheim am Glan** Ger.
191 H3 **Oderzo** Italy
136 F4 **Odesa** Ukr.
143 F2 **Ödeshog** Sweden
136 E4 **Odes'ka Oblast'** admin. div. Ukr.
Odessa Ukr. see **Odesa**
234 C3 **Odessa** DE U.S.A.
237 C6 **Odessa** TX U.S.A.
238 C2 **Odessa** WA U.S.A.
Odessa Oblast admin. div. Ukr. see **Odes'ka Oblast'**
Odesskaya Oblast' admin. div. Ukr. see **Odes'ka Oblast'**
121 H1 **Odesskoye** Rus. Fed.
Odessus Bulg. see **Varna**
158 B4 **Odet** r. France
184 B3 **Odiáxere** Port.
184 D3 **Odiel** r. Spain
206 D4 **Odienné** Côte d'Ivoire
151 G3 **Odiham** Hampshire, England U.K.
164 E2 **Odijk** Neth.
139 K4 **Odintsovo** Rus. Fed.
184 B2 **Odivelas** Beja Port.
184 A2 **Odivelas** Lisboa Port.
184 B2 **Odivelas** r. Port.
197 H3 **Odobești** Romania
197 H3 **Odobeștilor, Măgura** hill Romania
174 F4 **Odolanów** Pol.
171 F5 **Odolena Voda** Czech Rep.
159 F2 **Odon** r. France
183 I4 **Odón** Spain
164 F2 **Odoorn** Neth.
197 G2 **Odorheiu Secuiesc** Romania
139 K5 **Odoyev** Rus. Fed.
174 G6 **Odra** r. Pol. alt. **Oder (Germany)**
183 F2 **Odra** r. Spain
137 H4 **Odradivka** Ukr.
177 G2 **Odry** Czech Rep.
175 I4 **Odrzywół** Pol.
196 D3 **Odžaci** Vojvodina, Srbija Yugo.
213 G3 **Odzi** r. Zimbabwe
Oea Libya see **Tripoli**
169 F3 **Oebisfelde** Ger.
169 E4 **Oedelsheim (Oberweser)** Ger.
171 E5 **Oederan** Ger.
168 E2 **Oederquart** Ger.
163 A5 **Œeyreluy** France
164 E3 **Oeffelt** Neth.
164 D2 **Oegstgeest** Neth.
254 E3 **Oeiras** Brazil
184 A2 **Oeiras** Port.
184 C3 **Oeiras** r. Port.
169 D4 **Oelde** Ger.
168 E2 **Oelixdorf** Ger.
236 C3 **Oelrichs** SD U.S.A.
171 D5 **Oelsnitz** Sachsen Ger.
171 D5 **Oelsnitz** Sachsen Ger.
236 F3 **Oelwein** IA U.S.A.
164 F2 **Oene** Neth.
84 C2 **Oenpelli** N.T. Austr.
190 C1 **Oensingen** Switz.
168 E2 **Oerel** Ger.
168 F2 **Oering** Ger.
169 F5 **Oerlenbach** Ger.
169 D4 **Oerlinghausen** Ger.
Oesel i. Estonia see **Hiiumaa**
165 E5 **Oesling** hills Lux.
165 D3 **Oesterdam** barrage Neth.
171 C5 **Oettersdorf** Ger.
173 E3 **Oettingen in Bayern** Ger.
178 B3 **Oetz** Austria
168 F2 **Oetzen** Ger.
168 E1 **Oeversee** Ger.
104 B3 **Ōe-yama** hill Japan
127 F2 **Of** Turkey
238 F2 **O'Fallon** r. MT U.S.A.
193 I3 **Ofanto** r. Italy
193 F2 **Ofena** Italy
207 G4 **Offa** Nigeria
147 D3 **Offaly** county Rep. of Ireland
190 E3 **Offanengo** Italy
157 G5 **Offemont** France
169 D5 **Offenbach am Main** Ger.
172 C2 **Offenbach an der Queich** Ger.
173 G3 **Offenberg** Ger.
172 B3 **Offenburg** Ger.
140 K3 **Offerdal** Sweden
193 F2 **Offida** Italy
173 E3 **Offingen** Ger.
156 B3 **Offranville** France
140 L1 **Ofotfjorden** sea chan. Norway
172 D3 **Ofterdingen** Ger.
78 □2 **Ofu** i. American Samoa
102 J4 **Ōfunato** Japan
95 F2 **Oga** r. Indon.
102 I4 **Oga** Japan
105 F1 **Oga-dake** mt. Japan
210 E3 **Ogadēn** reg. Eth.
104 C3 **Ōgaki** Japan
236 C3 **Ogallala** NE U.S.A.
94 D3 **Ogan** r. Indon.
103 □3 **Ogasawara-shotō** is N. Pacific Ocean
105 E2 **Ōga-tō** mt. Japan
105 F2 **Ogawa** Japan
102 J3 **Ogawara-ko** l. Japan
Ogbomosho Nigeria see **Ogbomoso**
207 G4 **Ogbomoso** Nigeria
236 E3 **Ogden** IA U.S.A.
238 E3 **Ogden** UT U.S.A.
222 C3 **Ogden, Mount** B.C. Can.
234 D1 **Ogdensburg** NJ U.S.A.
233 F2 **Ogdensburg** NY U.S.A.
231 D6 **Ogeechee** r. GA U.S.A.
226 B3 **Ogema** WI U.S.A.
168 C2 **Ogenbargen** Ger.
156 E4 **Oger** France
163 B5 **Ogeu-les-Bains** France
157 G4 **Ogéviller** France
190 E3 **Oggiono** Italy
78 □6 **Ogho** Choiseul Solomon Is
224 C4 **Ogidaki** Ont. Can.
220 E3 **Ogilvie** r. Y.T. Can.
220 D3 **Ogilvie Mountains** Y.T. Can.
129 C4 **Oğlaksuyu** Turkey
122 C2 **Oglanly** Turkm.
192 B2 **Ogliastro** Corse France
190 F3 **Oglio** r. Italy
85 G4 **Ogmore** Qld Austr.
150 D3 **Ogmore** Vale of Glamorgan, Wales U.K.
150 D3 **Ogmore Vale** Bridgend, Wales U.K.
160 D1 **Ognon** r. France
Oğnut Turkey see **Göynük**
93 B2 **Ogoamas, Gunung** mt. Indon.
207 H5 **Ogoja** Nigeria
224 C3 **Ogoki** r. Ont. Can.
224 C3 **Ogoki Lake** Ont. Can.
208 A5 **Ogooué** r. Gabon
208 B5 **Ogooué-Ivindo** prov. Gabon
208 B5 **Ogooué-Lolo** prov. Gabon
208 A5 **Ogooué-Maritime** prov. Gabon
197 F4 **Ogosta** r. Bulg.
207 F5 **Ogou** r. Togo
87 C6 **O'Grady, Lake** salt flat W.A. Austr.
197 F5 **Ogražden** mts Bulg./Macedonia
Ograzhden mts Bulg./Macedonia see **Ogražden**
138 E3 **Ogre** Latvia
138 E3 **Ogre** r. Latvia
175 J3 **Ogrodniki** Pol.
175 H5 **Ogrodzieniec** Pol.
171 F4 **Ogrosen** Ger.
182 B2 **O Grove** Spain
139 L3 **Ogudnevo** Rus. Fed.
188 E3 **Ogulin** Croatia
207 F5 **Ogun** state Nigeria
233 □H3 **Ogunquit** ME U.S.A.
129 E3 **Oğuz** Azer.
177 K6 **Ohaba Lungă** Romania
207 G5 **Ohafia** Nigeria
81 A6 **Ohai** South I. N.Z.
80 E3 **Ohakune** North I. N.Z.
185 H3 **Ohanes** Spain
212 C3 **Ohangwena** admin. reg. Namibia
226 D5 **O'Hare** airport IL U.S.A.
80 E4 **Ohau** North I. N.Z.
81 C6 **Ohau** r. South I. N.Z.
80 E2 **Ohaupo** North I. N.Z.
Ohcejohka Fin. see **Utsjoki**
168 C2 **Ohe** r. Ger.
173 H3 **Ohe** r. Ger.
Ohétéroah i. Îs Australes Fr. Polynesia see **Rurutu**
165 E4 **Ohey** Belgium
260 B4 **O'Higgins** admin. reg. Chile
259 B8 **O'Higgins, Lago** l. Chile
80 E2 **Ohinewai** North I. N.Z.
226 C5 **Ohio** IL U.S.A.
236 F4 **Ohio** r. Ohio/West Virginia U.S.A.
232 B4 **Ohio** state U.S.A.
232 A4 **Ohio City** OH U.S.A.
262 Q1 **Ohio Range** mts Antarctica
235 D1 **Ohioville** NY U.S.A.
105 E3 **Ōhito** Japan
137 H3 **Ohiyivka** Ukr.
172 B3 **Ohlsbach** Ger.
179 E3 **Ohlsdorf** Austria
173 F4 **Ohlstadt** Ger.
169 D5 **Ohm** r. Ger.
138 F2 **Õhne** r. Estonia
169 C3 **Ohne** Ger.
172 C4 **Öhningen** Ger.
79 □2 **'Ohonua** Tonga
80 F2 **Ohope** North I. N.Z.
177 G3 **Ohrady** Slovakia
169 F5 **Ohrdruf** Ger.
176 D1 **Ohře** r. Czech Rep.
171 C3 **Ohre** r. Ger.
196 E5 **Ohrid** Macedonia
196 E5 **Ohrid, Lake** Albania/Macedonia
Ohridsko Ezero l. Albania/Macedonia see **Ohrid, Lake**
213 F5 **Ohrigstad** S. Africa
172 D2 **Öhringen** Ger.
Ohrit, Liqeni i l. Albania/Macedonia see **Ohrid, Lake**
169 F3 **Ohrum** Ger.
80 E3 **Ohura** North I. N.Z.
182 B4 **Oiã** Port.
251 I4 **Oiapoque** Brazil
251 I3 **Oiapoque** r. Brazil/Fr. Guiana
186 B1 **Oiartzun** Spain
146 D4 **Oich** r. Scotland U.K.
113 □1 **Oidhuni** i. S. Male Maldives
104 B3 **Ōi-gawa** r. Japan
105 E4 **Ōi-gawa** r. Japan
156 C2 **Oignies** France
160 D2 **Oignin** r. France
164 E3 **Oijen** Neth.
Oik Kazakh. see **Uyuk**
232 D4 **Oil City** PA U.S.A.
240 H4 **Oildale** CA U.S.A.
147 E4 **Oilgate** Rep. of Ireland
147 C2 **Oily** r. Rep. of Ireland
182 C3 **Oímbra** Spain
108 A2 **Oi Qu** r. Xizang China
102 J3 **Oirase-gawa** r. Japan
159 F5 **Oiron** France
164 E3 **Oirschot** Neth.
156 C3 **Oise** dept Picardie France
156 C4 **Oise** r. France
160 D1 **Oiselay-et-Grachaux** France
156 B3 **Oisemont** France
159 F3 **Oisseau** France
156 B3 **Oissel** France
164 E3 **Oisterwijk** Neth.
103 E7 **Ōita** Japan
103 E7 **Ōita** pref. Japan
182 B2 **Oitavén** r. Spain
198 C2 **Oiti** mt. Greece
197 H2 **Oituz** r. Romania
159 I4 **Oizon** France
104 C2 **Oizuruga-dake** mt. Japan
240 H4 **Ojai** CA U.S.A.
185 G2 **Ojailén** r. Spain
Ojalava i. Samoa see **Upolu**
138 F2 **Ojamaa** r. Estonia
141 K3 **Öje** Sweden
185 F4 **Ojén** Spain
104 B4 **Ōji** Japan
242 D2 **Ojinaga** Mex.
245 F4 **Ojitlán** Mex.
105 E1 **Ojiya** Japan
207 G5 **Ojobo** Nigeria
244 C2 **Ojocaliente** Mex.
239 F4 **Ojo Caliente** NM U.S.A.
258 C2 **Ojos del Salado, Nevado** mt. Arg./Chile
183 I4 **Ojos Negros** Spain
175 I3 **Ojrzeń** Pol.
207 H5 **Oju** Nigeria
141 K3 **Öjung** Sweden
207 G5 **Oka** Nigeria
139 M4 **Oka** r. Rus. Fed.
212 C4 **Okahandja** Namibia
Okahu b. South I. N.Z. see **Jackson Bay**
80 E3 **Okahukura** North I. N.Z.
80 D1 **Okaihau** North I. N.Z.
81 D5 **Okains Bay** Canterbury N.Z.
207 F4 **Okaka** Nigeria
212 C4 **Okakarara** Namibia
225 I1 **Okak Islands** Nfld. Can.
175 H2 **Okalewo** Pol.
222 G5 **Okanagan Falls** B.C. Can.
222 G5 **Okanagan Lake** B.C. Can.
238 C1 **Okanogan** WA U.S.A.
238 C1 **Okanogan** r. WA U.S.A.
177 K5 **Okány** Hungary
123 H4 **Okara** Pak.
80 D3 **Okato** North I. N.Z.
212 D3 **Okavango** r. Botswana/Namibia
212 C3 **Okavango** admin. reg. Namibia
212 D3 **Okavango Delta** swamp Botswana
103 E7 **Ōkawa** Japan
105 E2 **Okaya** Japan
103 F6 **Okayama** Japan
103 F6 **Okayama** pref. Japan
104 D4 **Okazaki** Japan
129 B3 **Okçular Dağı** mt. Turkey
231 D7 **Okeechobee** FL U.S.A.
231 D7 **Okeechobee, Lake** FL U.S.A.
237 D4 **Okeene** OK U.S.A.
105 F2 **Okegawa** Japan
150 C4 **Okehampton** Devon, England U.K.
207 F4 **Oke-Iho** Nigeria
237 D5 **Okemah** OK U.S.A.
150 C4 **Okement** r. England U.K.
207 G5 **Okene** Nigeria
169 F3 **Oker** r. Ger.
116 B5 **Okha** Gujarat India
100 G1 **Okha** Sakhalin Rus. Fed.
Okhadunga Nepal see **Okhaldhunga**
117 F4 **Okhaldhunga** Nepal
134 K4 **Okhansk** Rus. Fed.
131 P4 **Okhotka** r. Rus. Fed.
131 P4 **Okhotsk** Rus. Fed.
102 L1 **Okhotsk, Sea of** Japan/Rus. Fed.
Okhotskoye More sea Japan/Rus. Fed. see **Okhotsk, Sea of**
137 H4 **Okhrimivka** Ukr.
Okhthoniá Greece see **Ochthonia**
137 H2 **Okhtyrka** Ukr.
139 I3 **Okhvat** Rus. Fed.
214 A3 **Okiep** S. Africa
102 □2 **Okinawa** Japan
102 □2 **Okinawa** i. Japan
102 □1 **Okinawa** pref. Japan
Okinawa-guntō is Japan see **Okinawa-shotō**
102 □1 **Okinawa-shotō** is Japan
102 □1 **Okinoerabu-jima** i. Japan
103 F5 **Oki-shotō** is Japan
207 G5 **Okitipupa** Nigeria
96 A3 **Okkan** Myanmar
237 D5 **Oklahoma** state U.S.A.
237 D5 **Oklahoma City** OK U.S.A.
231 D6 **Oklawaha** r. FL U.S.A.
237 D5 **Okmulgee** OK U.S.A.
177 L3 **Okna** r. Slovakia
Oknitsa Moldova see **Ocnița**
177 G4 **Okoč** Slovakia
207 H5 **Okola** Cameroon
237 F5 **Okolona** MS U.S.A.
232 A4 **Okolona** OH U.S.A.
208 B5 **Okondja** Gabon
174 E2 **Okonek** Pol.
175 L4 **Okopy** Pol.
177 G6 **Okor** r. Hungary
222 H5 **Okotoks** Alta Can.
139 I4 **Okovskiy Les** for. Rus. Fed.
208 B5 **Okoyo** Congo
121 J3 **Okpety, Gora** mt. Kazakh.
176 E2 **Okříšky** Czech Rep.
176 E2 **Okrouhlice** Czech Rep.
175 K4 **Okrzeja** Pol.
175 I5 **Oksa** Pol.
142 C4 **Oksbøl** Denmark
140 M1 **Øksfjord** Norway
134 G3 **Oksovskiy** Rus. Fed.
140 K2 **Oksskolten** mt. Norway
123 H2 **Oksu** r. Tajik.
Oktemberyan Armenia see **Hoktemberyan**
96 B3 **Oktwin** Myanmar
Oktyabr' Kazakh. see **Kandyagash**
121 I4 **Oktyabr'** Kazakh.
139 K3 **Oktyabr'** Rus. Fed.
Oktyabr'sk Kazakh. see **Kandyagash**
120 B1 **Oktyabr'sk** Rus. Fed.
Oktyabr'skaya Belarus see **Aktsyabrskaya**
137 J4 **Oktyabr'skaya** Rus. Fed.
Oktyabr'skiy Homyel'skaya Voblasts' Belarus see **Aktsyabrski**
Oktyabr'skiy Vitsyebskaya Voblasts' Belarus see **Aktsyabrski**
120 E1 **Oktyabr'skiy** Kazakh.
100 D1 **Oktyabr'skiy** Rus. Fed.
134 H3 **Oktyabr'skiy** Rus. Fed.
137 I2 **Oktyabr'skiy** Rus. Fed.
139 M3 **Oktyabr'skiy** Rus. Fed.
131 Q4 **Oktyabr'skiy** Rus. Fed.
137 J5 **Oktyabr'skiy** Rus. Fed.
Oktyabr'skiy Rus. Fed. see **Takhtamukay**
135 K5 **Oktyabr'skiy** Rus. Fed.
137 J4 **Oktyabr'skiy** Rus. Fed.
139 L4 **Oktyabr'skiy** Rus. Fed.
139 L5 **Oktyabr'skiy** Rus. Fed.
134 L4 **Oktyabr'skiy** Rus. Fed.
135 H7 **Oktyabr'skiy** Rus. Fed.
120 F1 **Oktyabr'skoye** Kazakh.
120 E1 **Oktyabr'skoye** Rus. Fed.
130 H3 **Oktyabr'skoye** Khanty-Mansiyskiy Avtonomnyy Okrug Rus. Fed.
139 L5 **Oktyabr'skoye** Rus. Fed.
120 C1 **Oktyabr'skoye** Rus. Fed.
129 D2 **Oktyabr'skoye** Rus. Fed.
131 K2 **Oktyabr'skoy Revolyutsii, Ostrov** i. Severnaya Zemlya Rus. Fed.
122 D1 **Oktyah'sk** Turkm.
188 F3 **Okučani** Croatia
103 E7 **Ōkuchi** Japan
139 I2 **Okulovka** Rus. Fed.
129 B2 **Ok'umi** Georgia
Okureshi Georgia see **Oqureshi**
81 B5 **Okuru** South I. N.Z.
104 D3 **Oku-sangai-dake** mt. Japan
102 I2 **Okushiri-tō** i. Japan
207 F4 **Okuta** Nigeria
131 Q4 **Ola** Rus. Fed.
237 E5 **Ola** AR U.S.A.
140 □B2 **Ólafsvík** Iceland
186 B2 **Olague** Spain
113 □1 **Olahali** i. N. Male Maldives
138 D3 **Olaine** Latvia
114 C3 **Olakkur** Tamil Nadu India
182 B5 **Olalhas** Port.
161 E4 **Olan, Pic d'** mt. France
240 H3 **Olancha** CA U.S.A.
240 H3 **Olancha Peak** CA U.S.A.
242 □I6 **Olanchito** Hond.
143 G3 **Öland** i. Sweden
161 A5 **Olargues** France
177 K5 **Olari** Romania
82 E3 **Olary** S.A. Austr.
177 K3 **Olaszliszka** Hungary
236 E4 **Olathe** KS U.S.A.
114 C4 **Olavakod** Kerala India
261 G5 **Olavarría** Arg.
183 I2 **Olave** Spain
140 □ **Olav V Land** reg. Svalbard
174 F5 **Oława** Pol.
183 H2 **Olazagutía** Spain
187 C4 **Olba** Spain
179 H3 **Olbendorf** Austria
171 E5 **Olbernhau** Ger.
171 F5 **Olbersdorf** Ger.
171 C4 **Olbersleben** Ger.
192 B4 **Olbia** Sardegna Italy
175 K5 **Olbięcin** Pol.
176 D2 **Olbramovice** Czech Rep.
177 K5 **Olcea** Romania
129 C3 **Ölçek** Turkey
173 F3 **Olching** Ger.
232 D3 **Olcott** NY U.S.A.
129 C3 **Ölçülü** Turkey
246 C2 **Old Bahama Channel** Bahamas/Cuba
151 F3 **Old Basing** Hampshire, England U.K.
114 D2 **Old Bastar** Madh. Prad. India
235 D2 **Old Bridge** NJ U.S.A.
150 E2 **Oldbury** West Midlands, England U.K.
147 D3 **Oldcastle** Rep. of Ireland
86 E3 **Old Cherrabun** W.A. Austr.
150 D1 **Old Colwyn** Conwy, Wales U.K.
85 E4 **Old Cork** Qld Austr.
220 E3 **Old Crow** Y.T. Can.
146 D6 **Old Dailly** South Ayrshire, Scotland U.K.
164 F2 **Oldeberkoop** Neth.
164 E1 **Oldeboorn** Neth.
164 E2 **Oldebroek** Neth.
164 F1 **Oldehove** Neth.
164 E2 **Oldemarkt** Neth.
168 D2 **Oldenbrok** Ger.
168 D2 **Oldenburg** Ger.
168 F1 **Oldenburg in Holstein** Ger.
168 E2 **Oldendorf** Ger.
168 F2 **Oldendorf (Luhe)** Ger.
168 D1 **Oldenswort** Ger.
164 F2 **Oldenzaal** Neth.
140 M1 **Olderdalen** Norway
151 I3 **Old Felixstowe** Suffolk, England U.K.
87 D7 **Oldfield** r. W.A. Austr.
233 F3 **Old Forge** NY U.S.A.
234 C1 **Old Forge** PA U.S.A.
232 B4 **Old Fort** OH U.S.A.
87 C5 **Old Gidgee** W.A. Austr.
149 G4 **Oldham** Greater Manchester, England U.K.
246 □ **Old Harbour** Jamaica
246 □ **Old Harbour Bay** Jamaica
147 C5 **Old Head of Kinsale** hd Rep. of Ireland
171 C4 **Oldisleben** Ger.
150 E3 **Oldland** South Gloucestershire, England U.K.
149 J4 **Old Leake** Lincolnshire, England U.K.
235 F1 **Old Lyme** CT U.S.A.
220 G5 **Oldman** r. Alta Can.
234 C3 **Oldman's Creek** r. NJ U.S.A.
146 F4 **Oldmeldrum** Aberdeenshire, Scotland U.K.
209 F8 **Old Mkushi** Zambia
215 G4 **Old Morley** S. Africa
235 G1 **Old Mystic** CT U.S.A.
233 □H3 **Old Orchard Beach** ME U.S.A.
225 K4 **Old Perlican** Nfld. Can.
240 H4 **Old River** CA U.S.A.
147 E4 **Old Ross** Rep. of Ireland
222 H5 **Olds** Alta Can.
235 F1 **Old Saybrook** CT U.S.A.
233 □H2 **Old Speck Mountain** ME U.S.A.
168 D1 **Oldsum** Ger.
147 E3 **Oldtown** Rep. of Ireland
149 G3 **Old Town** Cumbria, England U.K.
232 B5 **Oldtown** KY U.S.A.
233 □I2 **Old Town** ME U.S.A.
211 B5 **Olduvai Gorge** tourist site Tanz.
232 C4 **Old Washington** OH U.S.A.
234 D2 **Oldwick** NJ U.S.A.
241 J4 **Old Woman Mountains** CA U.S.A.
106 D1 **Öldziyt** Mongolia
232 D3 **Olean** NY U.S.A.
175 K1 **Olecko** Pol.
182 C5 **Oledo** Port.
190 D3 **Oleggio** Italy
182 C5 **Oleiros** Port.
131 N3 **Olekma** r. Rus. Fed.
131 N3 **Olekminsk** Rus. Fed.
137 G2 **Oleksandrivka** Chernihivs'ka Oblast' Ukr.
137 I3 **Oleksandrivka** Donets'ka Oblast' Ukr.
137 G3 **Oleksandrivka** Kirovohrads'ka Oblast' Ukr.
137 F4 **Oleksandrivka** Mykolayivs'ka Oblast' Ukr.
137 H4 **Oleksandrivka** Zaporiz'ka Oblast' Ukr.
Oleksandrivs'k Ukr. see **Zaporizhzhya**
137 G3 **Oleksandriya** Kirovohrads'ka Oblast' Ukr.
136 D2 **Oleksandriya** Rivnens'ka Oblast' Ukr.
137 I3 **Oleksiyevo-Druzhkivka** Ukr.
137 J3 **Oleksiyivka** Ukr.
165 D3 **Olen** Belgium
142 A2 **Ølen** Norway
134 F1 **Olenegorsk** Rus. Fed.
131 M3 **Olenek** Rus. Fed.
131 M2 **Olenek** r. Rus. Fed.
Ölengti r. Kazakh. see **Olenti**
139 I3 **Olenino** Rus. Fed.
137 I4 **Olenivka** Ukr.
Olenivs'ki Kar"yery Ukr. see **Dokuchayevs'k**
120 C2 **Olenti** r. Kazakh.
121 H1 **Olenti** r. Kazakh.
107 G1 **Olentuy** Rus. Fed.
Olenya Rus. Fed. see **Olenegorsk**
162 A3 **Oléron, Île d'** i. France
186 E3 **Olesa de Montserrat** Spain
Oleshky Ukr. see **Tsyurupyns'k**
137 F2 **Oleshnya** Chernihivs'ka Oblast' Ukr.
137 H2 **Oleshnya** Sums'ka Oblast' Ukr.
136 C3 **Oles'ko** Ukr.
174 F4 **Oleśnica** Pol.
175 J5 **Oleśnica** Pol.
175 I5 **Olesno** Małopolskie Pol.
174 G5 **Olesno** Opolskie Pol.
175 L5 **Oleszyce** Pol.
192 B2 **Oletta** Corse France
163 E6 **Olette** France
95 G5 **Olet Tongo** mt. Sumbawa Indon.
136 D2 **Olevs'k** Ukr.
234 C2 **Oley** PA U.S.A.
169 C4 **Olfen** Ger.
140 K2 **Ølfjellet** mt. Norway
100 E4 **Ol'ga** Rus. Fed.
224 E3 **Olga, Lac** l. Que. Can.
84 B5 **Olga, Mount** N.T. Austr.
140 □ **Olgastretet** str. Svalbard
190 E3 **Olginate** Italy
137 J5 **Ol'ginskaya** Rus. Fed.
137 J4 **Ol'ginskaya** Rus. Fed.
Olginskoye Rus. Fed. see **Kochubeyevskoye**
106 A1 **Ölgiy** Mongolia
146 E3 **Olgrinmore** Highland, Scotland U.K.
184 A1 **Olhalvo** Port.
184 C3 **Olhão** Port.
184 A1 **Olho Marinho** Port.
113 □1 **Olhuveli** i. S. Male Maldives
84 B5 **Olia Chain** mts N.T. Austr.
186 E2 **Oliana** Spain
183 G5 **Olías del Rey** Spain
188 E3 **Olib** i. Croatia
192 B4 **Oliena** Sardegna Italy
192 B4 **Oliena** r. Sardegna Italy
186 C3 **Oliete** Spain
212 C5 **Olifants** watercourse Namibia
214 B4 **Olifants** r. W. Cape S. Africa
214 C5 **Olifants** r. W. Cape S. Africa
213 F4 **Olifants** r. S. Africa
214 D2 **Olifantshoek** S. Africa
214 B5 **Olifantsrivierberge** mts S. Africa
193 G4 **Oligastro Marina** Italy
91 K5 **Olimarao** atoll Micronesia
Olimbos hill Cyprus see **Olympos**
Olimbos mt. Greece see **Olympos**
256 C4 **Olímpia** Brazil
245 E5 **Olinalá** Mex.
85 F1 **Olinda Entrance** sea chan. Qld Austr.
213 H3 **Olinga** Moz.
141 K3 **Olingsjövallen** Sweden
85 E4 **Olio** Qld Austr.
186 E3 **Oliola** Spain
Öli Qoltyq Sory dry lake Kazakh. see **Sor Mertvyy Kultuk**
Olisipo Port. see **Lisboa**
183 I2 **Olite** Spain
261 F3 **Oliva** Arg.
193 I5 **Oliva** r. Italy
187 C6 **Oliva** Spain
184 D2 **Oliva** hill Spain
258 C3 **Oliva, Cordillera de** mts Arg./Chile
184 D2 **Oliva de la Frontera** Spain
184 D2 **Oliva de Mérida** Spain
182 B3 **Olival** Port.
260 C2 **Olivares, Cerro de** mt. Arg./Chile
183 H5 **Olivares de Júcar** Spain
232 B5 **Olive Hill** KY U.S.A.
240 G2 **Olivehurst** CA U.S.A.
257 E4 **Oliveira** Brazil
182 B4 **Oliveira de Azeméis** Port.
182 B4 **Oliveira de Frades** Port.
182 B4 **Oliveira do Bairro** Port.
182 C4 **Oliveira do Conde** Port.
182 B3 **Oliveira do Douro** Port.
182 C4 **Oliveira do Hospital** Port.
254 E5 **Oliveira dos Brejinhos** Brazil
Olivença Moz. see **Lupilichi**
Olivença-a-Nova Angola see **Capunda Cavilongo**
193 H3 **Olivento** r. Italy
184 C2 **Olivenza** r. Port./Spain
184 C2 **Olivenza** Spain
222 G5 **Oliver** B.C. Can.
195 E4 **Oliveri** Sicilia Italy
261 G3 **Oliveros** Arg.
156 B5 **Olivet** France
226 E4 **Olivet** MI U.S.A.
236 D3 **Olivet** SD U.S.A.
193 H4 **Oliveto Citra** Italy
193 I4 **Oliveto Lucano** Italy
236 E2 **Olivia** MN U.S.A.
81 B6 **Olivine Range** mts South I. N.Z.
190 D2 **Olivone** Switz.
136 C3 **Oliyiv** Ukr.
177 K3 **Olka** r. Slovakia
210 C5 **Ol Kalou** Kenya
Ölkeyek r. Kazakh. see **Ul'kayak**
135 G6 **Ol'khovatka** Rus. Fed.
135 I6 **Ol'khovka** Rus. Fed.
175 H5 **Olkusz** Pol.
146 □G1 **Ollaberry** Shetland, Scotland U.K.
252 C3 **Ollachea** Peru
192 B5 **Olla stu** r. Sardegna Italy
149 H4 **Ollerton** Nottinghamshire, England U.K.
160 B3 **Olliergues** France
161 D5 **Ollioules** France
260 B2 **Ollita, Cordillera de** mts Arg./Chile
260 B2 **Ollitas** mt. Arg.
183 I2 **Ollo** Spain
192 B4 **Ollolai** Sardegna Italy
208 B5 **Ollombo** Congo
190 B2 **Ollon** Switz.
Olmaliq Uzbek. see **Almalyk**
183 G3 **Olmedilla de Roa** Spain
192 A4 **Olmedo** Sardegna Italy
183 F3 **Olmedo** Spain
192 B2 **Olmeta-di-Tuda** Corse France
192 A3 **Olmeto** Corse France
250 B6 **Olmos** Peru
183 F2 **Olmos de Ojeda** Spain
Olmütz Czech Rep. see **Olomouc**
151 G2 **Olney** Milton Keynes, England U.K.
236 F4 **Olney** IL U.S.A.
234 A3 **Olney** MD U.S.A.
237 D5 **Olney** TX U.S.A.
187 C5 **Olocau** Spain
186 C4 **Olocau del Rey** Spain
100 A2 **Olochi** Rus. Fed.
143 F3 **Olofström** Sweden
121 F1 **Ol'oinka** Kazakh.
225 I3 **Olomane** r. Que. Can.
176 G2 **Olomouc** Czech Rep.
176 G2 **Olomoucký kraj** admin. reg. Czech Rep.
190 E3 **Olona** r. Italy
139 I1 **Olonets** Rus. Fed.
139 I1 **Olonetskaya Vozvyshennost'** hills Rus. Fed.
92 B3 **Olongapo** Phil.
139 I1 **Olonka** r. Rus. Fed.
162 A2 **Olonne-sur-Mer** France
161 A5 **Olonzac** France
163 B5 **Oloron-Ste-Marie** France
78 □2 **Olosega** i. American Samoa
Olosenga i. American Samoa see **Swains Island**
186 F2 **Olot** Spain
Olot Uzbek. see **Alat**
171 D5 **Oloví** Czech Rep.
188 G3 **Olovo** Bos.-Herz.
107 G1 **Olovyannaya** Rus. Fed.
240 □C8 **Olowalu** HI U.S.A.
Oloy, Qatorkŭhi mts Asia see **Alai Range**
116 C5 **Olpad** Gujarat India
169 C4 **Olpe** Ger.
178 C3 **Olperer** mt. Austria
138 G5 **Ol'sa** r. Belarus
176 F2 **Olšany** Czech Rep.
176 G2 **Olšany u Prostějova** Czech Rep.
142 E2 **Olsätter** Sweden
177 G2 **Olšava** r. Czech Rep.
177 K3 **Olšava** r. Slovakia
169 D4 **Olsberg** Ger.
177 H2 **Olše** r. Czech Rep.
137 I2 **Ol'shanka** Rus. Fed.
137 F4 **Ol'shans'ke** Ukr.
164 F2 **Olst** Neth.
175 K3 **Olszanka** Mazowieckie Pol.
174 F5 **Olszanka** Opolskie Pol.
175 K6 **Olszany** Pol.
175 J2 **Olszewka** Pol.
175 J2 **Olszewo-Borki** Pol.
174 G3 **Olszówka** Pol.
175 H5 **Olsztyn** Śląskie Pol.
175 I2 **Olsztyn** Warmińsko-Mazurskie Pol.
175 I2 **Olsztynek** Pol.
175 L3 **Olszyn** Pol.
174 D4 **Olszyna** Pol.
197 G4 **Olt** r. Romania
260 D2 **Olta** Arg.
259 C6 **Olte, Sierra de** mts Arg.
190 C1 **Olten** Switz.
197 H3 **Oltenița** Romania
197 G3 **Olteț** r. Romania
197 H3 **Oltina** Romania
Oltinkŭl Uzbek. see **Altynkul'**
123 G1 **Oltintopkan** Tajik.
127 F2 **Oltu** Turkey
129 B3 **Oltu** r. Turkey
113 □1 **Olugiri** i. N. Male Maldives
129 C3 **Oluklu** Turkey
185 H3 **Olula del Río** Spain
129 C3 **Olur** Turkey
183 I3 **Ólvega** Spain
186 D2 **Olvena** Spain
185 E4 **Olvera** Spain
150 E3 **Olveston** South Gloucestershire, England U.K.
Ol'viopol' Ukr. see **Pervomays'k**
136 C2 **Olyka** Ukr.
139 L5 **Olym** r. Rus. Fed.
Olymbos hill Cyprus see **Olympos**
198 B3 **Olympia** tourist site Greece
238 B2 **Olympia** WA U.S.A.
128 A2 **Olympos** hill Cyprus
198 C1 **Olympos** mt. Greece
199 G3 **Olympos** tourist site Turkey
Olympus, Mount Greece see **Olympos**
238 B2 **Olympus, Mount** WA U.S.A.
137 J2 **Olymskiy** Rus. Fed.
234 C1 **Olyphant** PA U.S.A.
137 F2 **Olyshivka** Ukr.
131 R3 **Olyutorskiy** Rus. Fed.
131 R4 **Olyutorskiy Zaliv** b. Rus. Fed.
192 B4 **Olzai** Sardegna Italy
Olzheras Kemerovskaya Oblast' Rus. Fed. see **Mezhdurechensk**
111 C5 **Oma** Xizang China
134 I2 **Oma** r. Rus. Fed.
105 D2 **Ōmachi** Japan
102 J4 **Ōmagari** Japan
147 D2 **Omagh** Northern Ireland U.K.

Ōta to Panabá
345

105 F2 Ōta Japan
184 B1 Ota Port.
184 B1 Ota r. Port.
81 B6 Otago admin. reg. South I. N.Z.
81 C6 Otago Peninsula South I. N.Z.
Otahiti i. Fr. Polynesia see Tahiti
80 E3 Otairi North I. N.Z.
102 □1 O-take vol. Nansei-shotō Japan
102 □1 O-take vol. Nansei-shotō Japan
105 F3 Ōtake-san mt. Japan
80 E4 Otaki North I. N.Z.
81 B6 Otama South I. N.Z.
80 F3 Otamauri North I. N.Z.
121 H4 Otar Kazakh.
102 J2 Otaru Japan
176 G2 Otaslavice Czech Rep.
81 B7 Otatara South I. N.Z.
245 F4 Otatitlán Mex.
81 A7 Otautau South I. N.Z.
176 D2 Otava r. Czech Rep.
141 N3 Otava Fin.
250 B4 Otavalo Ecuador
212 C3 Otavi Namibia
105 G2 Ōtawara Japan
209 B9 Otchinjau Angola
Otdia atoll Marshall Is see Wotje
183 I2 Oteiza Spain
81 C6 Otekaieke South I. N.Z.
197 F3 Oțelu Roșu Romania
81 C6 Otematata South I. N.Z.
128 C1 Ötençay Turkey
138 F2 Otepää Estonia
138 F2 Otepää kõrgustik hills Estonia
140 L1 Oteren Norway
182 D3 Otero de Bodas Spain
183 F4 Otero de Herreros Spain
239 E7 Oteros r. Mex.
198 B1 Oteševo Macedonia
175 I5 Otfinów Pol.
151 H3 Otford Kent, England U.K.
106 C2 Otgon Tenger Uul mt. Mongolia
157 F3 Othain r. France
156 D4 Othe, Forêt d' for. France
238 C2 Othello WA U.S.A.
207 F4 Oti r. Ghana/Togo
177 G2 Otice Czech Rep.
172 C3 Ötigheim Ger.
215 H3 Otimati S. Africa
244 B1 Otinapa Mex.
81 C5 Otira South I. N.Z.
236 C3 Otis CO U.S.A.
172 C3 Ötisheim Ger.
234 D1 Otisville NY U.S.A.
185 G4 Otívar Spain
212 C4 Otjiwarongo Namibia
212 C4 Otjozondjupa admin. reg. Namibia
151 I2 Otley Suffolk, England U.K.
149 H4 Otley West Yorkshire, England U.K.
129 A4 Otlukbeli Erzincan Turkey
129 A4 Otlukbeli Dağları mts Turkey
174 F5 Otmuchów Pol.
179 H1 Otnice Czech Rep.
102 J2 Otobe-dake mt. Japan
188 E3 Otočac Croatia
Otog Qi Nei Mongol China see Ulan
188 G3 Otok Croatia
188 F3 Otoka Bos.-Herz.
80 F3 Otoko North I. N.Z.
207 F4 Otola Benin
80 E1 Otonga North I. N.Z.
210 A2 Otoro, Jebel mt. Sudan
80 E3 Otorohanga North I. N.Z.
174 E3 Otorowo Pol.
224 B3 Otoskwin r. Ont. Can.
103 □3 Otōto-jima i. Japan
120 B3 Otpan, Gora hill Kazakh.
Otpor Rus. Fed. see Zabaykal'sk
142 C2 Otra r. Norway
139 K5 Otradinskiy Rus. Fed.
129 B1 Otradnaya Rus. Fed.
139 H2 Otradnoye Leningradskaya Oblast' Rus. Fed.
Otradnoye Samarskaya Oblast' Rus. Fed. see Otradnyy
120 B1 Otradnyy Samarskaya Oblast' Rus. Fed.
195 H2 Otranto Italy
195 H2 Otranto, Strait of Albania/Italy
193 E2 Otricoli Italy
Otrogovo Saratovskaya Oblast' Rus. Fed. see Stepnoye
177 G2 Otrokovice Czech Rep.
131 S3 Otrozhnyy Rus. Fed.
226 E4 Otsego MI U.S.A.
104 B3 Ōtsu Japan
105 E3 Ōtsuki Japan
141 J3 Otta Norway
192 B4 Ottana Sardegna Italy
157 G3 Ottange France
224 F4 Ottawa Ont. Can.
224 F4 Ottawa r. Ont./Que. Can. alt. Outaouais, Rivière des
226 C5 Ottawa IL U.S.A.
236 E4 Ottawa KS U.S.A.
232 A4 Ottawa OH U.S.A.
224 D1 Ottawa Islands Nunavut Can.
171 E4 Ottendorf-Okrilla Ger.
172 B3 Ottenheim Ger.
172 C3 Ottenhöfen im Schwarzwald Ger.
179 G2 Ottenschlag Austria
179 F2 Ottensheim Austria
169 E4 Ottenstein Ger.
168 E2 Otter Ger.
150 D4 Otter r. England U.K.
172 B2 Otterbach Ger.
172 B2 Otterberg Ger.
149 G2 Otterburn Northumberland, England U.K.
146 C5 Otter Ferry Argyll and Bute, Scotland U.K.
173 F4 Otterfing Ger.
164 E2 Otterlo Neth.
168 D2 Otterndorf Ger.
224 D3 Otter Rapids Ont. Can.
168 E2 Ottersberg Ger.
142 E2 Otterstad Sweden
172 C3 Ottersweier Ger.
146 □G1 Otterswick Shetland, Scotland U.K.
142 D4 Otterup Denmark
171 D4 Otterwisch Ger.
150 C4 Ottery r. England U.K.
150 D4 Ottery St Mary Devon, England U.K.
177 G4 Öttevény Hungary
165 D4 Ottignies Belgium
157 H5 Ottmarsheim France
179 E2 Ottnang am Hausruck Austria
173 E4 Ottobeuren Ger.
173 F3 Ottobrunn Ger.
177 I5 Öttömös Hungary
190 E4 Ottone Italy
215 E2 Ottosdal S. Africa
215 E1 Ottoshoop S. Africa
169 E5 Ottrau Ger.
236 E3 Ottumwa IA U.S.A.
172 B2 Ottweiler Ger.
207 G5 Otukpa Nigeria
207 H5 Otukpo Nigeria
245 E4 Otumba Mex.
250 B6 Otuzco Peru
Otvazhniy Rus. Fed. see Zhigulevsk
232 B5 Otway OH U.S.A.
83 E4 Otway, Cape Vic. Austr.
83 E4 Otway Range mts Vic. Austr.
175 J3 Otwock Pol.
183 H1 Otxandio Spain
174 D4 Otyń Pol.
136 C3 Otyniya Ukr.
173 G3 Otzing Ger.
178 B4 Ötztaler Alpen mts Austria
96 C2 Ou, Nam r. Laos
207 H3 Ouacha Niger
237 F6 Ouachita r. AR U.S.A.
237 E5 Ouachita Mountains Arkansas/Oklahoma U.S.A.
228 H4 Ouachita Mountains AR/OK U.S.A.
208 D2 Ouadda C.A.R.
202 D6 Ouaddaï pref. Chad
206 B2 Ouâd Nâga Maur.
206 E3 Ouagadougou Burkina
206 E3 Ouahigouya Burkina
Ouahran Alg. see Oran
208 D3 Ouaka pref. C.A.R.
208 C3 Ouaka r. C.A.R.
206 D2 Oualâta Maur.
207 F4 Oualé r. Burkina
206 C3 Oualia Mali
207 F3 Ouallam Niger
251 I3 Ouanary Fr. Guiana
208 D2 Ouanda-Djailé C.A.R.
208 D3 Ouango C.A.R.
206 D4 Ouangolodougou Côte d'Ivoire
160 B1 Ouanne France
156 C5 Ouanne r. France
251 H4 Ouaqui Fr. Guiana
208 E3 Ouara r. C.A.R.
207 F4 Ouargaye Burkina
205 G3 Ouargla Alg.
204 C3 Ouarkziz, Jbel ridge Alg./Morocco
Ouarogou Burkina see Ouargaye
156 B4 Ouarville France
204 D3 Ouarzazate Morocco
207 F3 Ouatagouna Mali
Oubangui r. C.A.R./Dem. Rep. Congo see Ubangi
182 B4 Ouca Port.
160 D1 Ouche r. France
156 B5 Oucques France
164 D3 Oud-Beijerland Neth.
164 C3 Ouddorp Neth.
164 F1 Oudega Neth.
164 E2 Oudehaske Neth.
164 E2 Oudemirdum Neth.
165 C4 Oudenaarde Belgium
164 D3 Oudenbosch Neth.
165 C3 Oudenburg Belgium
164 G1 Oude Pekela Neth.
164 D2 Oude Rijn r. Neth.
164 D2 Ouderkerk aan de Amstel Neth.
164 D1 Oudeschild Neth.
164 D3 Oude-Tonge Neth.
164 D2 Oudewater Neth.
164 D3 Oud-Gastel Neth.
158 E4 Oudon France
159 F4 Oudon r. France
214 D5 Oudtshoorn S. Africa
165 D3 Oud-Turnhout Belgium
165 C3 Oudzele Belgium
204 D2 Oued Zem Morocco
78 □5 Ouégoa New Caledonia
206 D4 Ouélésébougou Mali
207 F3 Ouella Niger
207 F5 Ouémé r. Benin
206 E4 Ouessa Burkina
158 A3 Ouessant, Île d' i. France
207 F4 Ouèssè Benin
208 C4 Ouésso Congo
207 H5 Ouest prov. Cameroon
204 D2 Ouezzane Morocco
165 E4 Ouffet Belgium
147 B3 Oughterard Rep. of Ireland
160 D1 Ougney France
104 A4 Ougo-gawa r. Japan
184 C1 Ouguela Port.
105 E2 Ougura-yama mt. Japan
208 C3 Ouham pref. C.A.R.
208 C2 Ouham r. C.A.R./Chad
208 C3 Ouham Pendé pref. C.A.R.
207 F5 Ouidah Benin
242 C3 Ouiriego Mex.
159 F2 Ouistreham France
204 E2 Oujda Morocco
206 B2 Oujeft Maur.
204 C3 Oulad Teïma Morocco
140 N2 Oulainen Fin.
156 D3 Oulchy-le-Château France
165 F4 Oulder Belgium
206 C3 Ould Yenjé Maur.
205 G2 Ouled Djellal Alg.
205 F2 Ouled Naïl, Monts des mts Alg.
160 C3 Oullins France
204 D2 Oulmès Morocco
151 I2 Oulton Suffolk, England U.K.
140 N2 Oulu Fin.
140 N2 Oulu prov. Fin.
140 N2 Oulujärvi l. Fin.
140 N2 Oulujoki r. Fin.
140 N2 Oulunsalo Fin.
190 B3 Oulx Italy
206 D5 Oumé Côte d'Ivoire
205 G2 Oum el Bouaghi Alg.
202 C6 Oum-Hadjer Chad
205 G4 Ounane, Djebel mt. Alg.
204 C3 Ounara Morocco
140 N2 Ounasjoki r. Fin.
151 G2 Oundle Northamptonshire, England U.K.
223 K5 Oungre Sask. Can.
165 E4 Oupeye Belgium
165 F5 Our r. Lux.
239 F4 Ouray CO U.S.A.
241 M1 Ouray UT U.S.A.
156 E4 Ource r. France
156 D3 Ourcq r. France
206 C4 Ouré Kaba Guinea
254 D2 Ourém Brazil
182 C2 Ourense Spain
182 C2 Ourense prov. Galicia Spain
254 E3 Ouricurí Brazil
256 C5 Ourinhos Brazil
184 B3 Ourique Port.
254 D4 Ouro r. Brazil
182 C1 Ouro r. Spain
257 F4 Ouro Branco Brazil
256 D5 Ouro Fino Brazil
182 C1 Ourol Spain
257 F4 Ouro Preto Brazil
160 B1 Ouroux-en-Morvan France
160 C2 Ouroux-sur-Saône France
165 E4 Ourthe r. Belgium
159 G2 Ourville-en-Caux France
151 H4 Ouse r. East Sussex, England U.K.
149 I4 Ouse r. England U.K.
163 D6 Oust France
158 D4 Oust r. France
184 B2 Outão Port.
224 F4 Outaouais, Rivière des r. Ont./Que. Can. alt. Ottawa
225 G3 Outardes r. Que. Can.
156 C4 Outarville France
204 E2 Outat Oulad el Haj Morocco
182 D3 Outeiro Bragança Port.
182 B3 Outeiro Viana do Castelo Port.
182 C1 Outeiro de Rei Spain
182 C3 Outeiro Seco Port.
214 D5 Outeniekwaberge mts S. Africa
146 A4 Outer Hebrides is Scotland U.K.
Outer Mongolia country Asia see Mongolia
240 H5 Outer Santa Barbara Channel CA U.S.A.
212 C4 Outjo Namibia
223 J5 Outlook Sask. Can.
134 E3 Outokumpu Fin.
182 C2 Outomuro Spain
81 C6 Outram South I. N.Z.
156 B2 Outreau France
146 □H1 Out Skerries is Scotland U.K.
151 H2 Outwell Norfolk, England U.K.
78 □5 Ouvéa i. Î. Loyauté New Caledonia
161 A5 Ouveillan France
161 C4 Ouvèze r. France
83 E3 Ouyen Vic. Austr.
151 G2 Ouzel r. England U.K.
156 B5 Ouzouer-le-Marché France
156 C5 Ouzouer-sur-Loire France
199 E1 Ova r. Turkey
192 B3 Ovace, Punta d' mt. Corse France
126 D3 Ovacık Turkey
126 E3 Ovacık Turkey
199 G3 Ovacık Dağı mt. Turkey
190 D4 Ovada Italy
199 E3 Ovaeymiri Turkey
199 F2 Ovakent İzmir Turkey
129 C4 Ovakışla Turkey
199 E3 Ovakışlacık Muğla Turkey
199 F3 Ovaköy Antalya Turkey
234 A1 Oval PA U.S.A.
79 □1a Ovalau i. Fiji
260 B2 Ovalle Chile
212 B3 Ovamboland reg. Namibia
208 B4 Ovan Gabon
182 B4 Ovar Port.
191 H2 Ovaro Italy
78 □6 Ovau i. Solomon Is
260 E3 Oveja mt. Arg.
168 D2 Ovelgönne Ger.
83 F4 Ovens r. Vic. Austr.
147 C5 Ovens Rep. of Ireland
169 C5 Overath Ger.
146 F2 Overbister Orkney, Scotland U.K.
164 G2 Overdinkel Neth.
140 J2 Overhalla Norway
165 D4 Overijse Belgium
164 F2 Overijssel prov. Neth.
140 M2 Överkalix Sweden
87 B5 Overlander Roadhouse W.A. Austr.
236 E4 Overland Park KS U.S.A.
234 B3 Overlea MD U.S.A.
164 E3 Overloon Neth.
260 B4 Overo, Volcán vol. Arg.
165 E3 Overpelt Belgium
151 F2 Overseal Derbyshire, England U.K.
151 F3 Overton Hampshire, England U.K.
150 E2 Overton Wrexham, Wales U.K.
241 J3 Overton NV U.S.A.
237 E5 Overton TX U.S.A.
140 M2 Övertorneå Sweden
146 E6 Overtown North Lanarkshire, Scotland U.K.
143 G3 Överum Sweden
140 K2 Överuman l. Sweden
164 D2 Overveen Neth.
151 F3 Over Wallop Hampshire, England U.K.
190 D2 Ovesca r. Italy
165 C3 Ovezande Neth.
236 C3 Ovid CO U.S.A.
226 E4 Ovid MI U.S.A.
232 E3 Ovid NY U.S.A.
136 F4 Ovidiopol' Ukr.
197 I3 Ovidiu Romania
182 E1 Oviedo Spain
182 D1 Oviedo prov. Asturias Spain
190 D4 Oviglio Italy
193 F2 Ovindoli Italy
139 K2 Ovinishchenskaya Vozvyshennost' hills Rus. Fed.
192 B4 Ovodda Sardegna Italy
Ovolau i. Fiji see Ovalau
107 G2 Ovoot Mongolia
106 D2 Övörhangay prov. Mongolia
141 I3 Øvre Årdal Norway
141 J3 Øvre Rendal Norway
140 M1 Övre Soppero Sweden
136 E2 Ovruch Ukr.
106 D2 Övt Mongolia
80 F4 Owahanga North I. N.Z.
81 B7 Owaka South I. N.Z.
226 B1 Owakonze Ont. Can.
208 B5 Owando Congo
Owa Rafa i. Solomon Is see Santa Ana
Owa Riki i. Solomon Is see Santa Catalina
104 C4 Owase Japan
237 E4 Owasso OK U.S.A.
236 E2 Owatonna MN U.S.A.
123 E3 Owbeh Afgh.
175 J4 Owczarnia Pol.
233 E3 Owego NY U.S.A.
147 D3 Owel, Lough l. Rep. of Ireland
172 D3 Owen Ger.
81 D4 Owen, Mount South I. N.Z.
207 G5 Owena Nigeria
147 C2 Owenbeg Rep. of Ireland
214 D3 Owendale S. Africa
147 B2 Owenduff r. Rep. of Ireland
210 B4 Owen Falls Dam Uganda
147 B2 Oweniny r. Rep. of Ireland
147 B2 Owenmore r. Rep. of Ireland
147 D2 Owenreagh r. Northern Ireland U.K.
81 D4 Owen River South I. N.Z.
240 I3 Owens r. CA U.S.A.
230 C4 Owensboro KY U.S.A.
224 D4 Owen Sound Ont. Can.
84 C4 Owen Springs N.T. Austr.
91 K8 Owen Stanley Range mts P.N.G.
236 F4 Owensville MO U.S.A.
232 A5 Owensville OH U.S.A.
230 C4 Owenton KY U.S.A.
207 G5 Owerri Nigeria
80 E3 Owhango North I. N.Z.
172 D4 Owingen Ger.
232 E5 Owings MD U.S.A.
234 B3 Owings Mills MD U.S.A.
232 B5 Owingsville KY U.S.A.
223 M3 Owl r. Man. Can.
238 E3 Owl Creek r. WY U.S.A.
233 □I2 Owls Head ME U.S.A.
Owminzatow Toghi hills Uzbek. see Auminzatau, Gory
207 G5 Owo Nigeria
227 E4 Owosso MI U.S.A.
168 E1 Owschlag Ger.
238 C3 Owyhee NV U.S.A.
238 C3 Owyhee r. OR U.S.A.
238 C3 Owyhee Mountains ID U.S.A.
238 C3 Owyhee North Fork r. ID U.S.A.
238 C3 Owyhee South Fork r. ID U.S.A.
252 B2 Oxapampa Peru
140 □C2 Öxarfjörður b. Iceland
223 K5 Oxbow Sask. Can.
236 C1 Ox Creek r. ND U.S.A.
143 G2 Oxelösund Sweden
149 H4 Oxenhope West Yorkshire, England U.K.
81 D5 Oxford South I. N.Z.
151 F3 Oxford Oxfordshire, England U.K.
235 E1 Oxford CT U.S.A.
233 H3 Oxford MA U.S.A.
233 □H2 Oxford ME U.S.A.
227 F4 Oxford MI U.S.A.
237 F5 Oxford MS U.S.A.
231 E4 Oxford NC U.S.A.
234 D2 Oxford NJ U.S.A.
233 F3 Oxford NY U.S.A.
232 A5 Oxford OH U.S.A.
234 C3 Oxford PA U.S.A.
226 C4 Oxford WI U.S.A.
85 G4 Oxford Downs Qld Austr.
223 M4 Oxford House Man. Can.
151 F3 Oxfordshire admin. div. England U.K.
142 E4 Oxie Sweden
243 H4 Oxkutzcab Mex.
83 F3 Oxley N.S.W. Austr.
83 G2 Oxleys Peak N.S.W. Austr.
Ox Mountains hills Rep. of Ireland see Slieve Gamph
240 H4 Oxnard CA U.S.A.
151 G3 Oxshott Surrey, England U.K.
151 H3 Oxted Surrey, England U.K.
146 F6 Oxton Scottish Borders, Scotland U.K.
227 H3 Oxtongue Lake Ont. Can.
Oxus r. Asia see Amudar'ya
198 D2 Oxylithos Greece
95 E2 Oya r. Sarawak Malaysia
140 K2 Øya Norway
104 C2 Oyabe Japan
104 D2 Oyabe-gawa r. Japan
105 F2 Oyama Japan
105 F3 Ō-yama mt. Japan
105 F4 Ō-yama vol. Japan
251 I3 Oyapock r. Brazil/Fr. Guiana
208 A4 Oyem Gabon
223 I5 Oyen Alta Can.
156 C2 Oye-Plage France
106 C1 Oygon Mongolia
146 D4 Oykel r. Scotland U.K.
146 D4 Oykel Bridge Highland, Scotland U.K.
173 E4 Oy-Mittelberg Ger.
208 B5 Oyo Congo
207 F5 Oyo Nigeria
207 F4 Oyo state Nigeria
252 A2 Oyón Peru
183 H2 Oyón Spain
160 D2 Oyonnax France
Oyoqquduq Uzbek. see Ayakkuduk
Oysangur Rus. Fed. see Oyskhara
129 E2 Oyskhara Rus. Fed.
214 E6 Oyster Bay S. Africa
235 E2 Oyster Bay NY U.S.A.
235 D3 Oyster Creek NJ U.S.A.
121 H4 Oytal Kazakh.
168 E2 Oyten Ger.
128 A1 Oyukludağı mt. Turkey
Oyyl Kazakh. see Uil
Oyyq Kazakh. see Uyuk
182 B1 Oza Spain
Ozaeta Spain see Ozeta
127 G3 Özalp Turkey
92 B4 Ozamiz Phil.
156 B4 Ozanne r. France
231 C6 Ozark AL U.S.A.
237 E5 Ozark AR U.S.A.
237 E4 Ozark MO U.S.A.
237 E4 Ozark Plateau MO U.S.A.
236 E4 Ozarks, Lake of the MO U.S.A.
175 J5 Ożarów Pol.
175 H5 Ożarowice Pol.
175 I3 Ożarów Mazowiecki Pol.
199 E3 Özbaşı Turkey
Ozbekiston country Asia see Uzbekistan
177 J3 Ózd Hungary
177 I3 Ožďany Slovakia
199 E3 Özdere Turkey
129 B4 Özdilek Turkey
Özen Kazakh. see Kyzylsay
139 J2 Ozerevo Rus. Fed.
136 E5 Ozerne Odes'ka Oblast' Ukr.
136 C2 Ozerne Volyns'ka Oblast' Ukr.
136 E2 Ozerne Zhytomyrs'ka Oblast' Ukr.
139 K4 Ozerninskoye Vodokhranilishche resr Rus. Fed.
131 Q4 Ozernovskiy Rus. Fed.
120 E1 Ozernoye Kustanayskaya Oblast' Kazakh.
120 B2 Ozernoye Rus. Fed.
Ozernyy Karagandinskaya Oblast' Kazakh. see Shashubay
Ozernyy Kustanayskaya Oblast' Kazakh. see Ozernoye
139 M3 Ozernyy Ivanovskaya Oblast' Rus. Fed.
120 E2 Ozernyy Orenburgskaya Oblast' Rus. Fed.
139 I4 Ozernyy Smolenskaya Oblast' Rus. Fed.
198 B2 Ozeros, Limni l. Greece
138 D4 Ozersk Rus. Fed.
100 G3 Ozerskiy Sakhalin Rus. Fed.
139 L4 Ozery Rus. Fed.
100 D2 Ozeryane Rus. Fed.
137 G2 Ozeryany Ukr.
183 H2 Ozeta Spain
121 H4 Özgön Kyrg.
139 L4 Ozherel'ye Rus. Fed.
131 Q3 Ozhogina r. Rus. Fed.
192 B4 Ozieri Sardegna Italy
174 G5 Ozimek Pol.
120 B2 Ozinki Rus. Fed.
156 C4 Ozoir-la-Ferrière France
138 D3 Ozolnieki Latvia
237 C6 Ozona TX U.S.A.
177 H5 Ozora Hungary
175 H4 Ozorków Pol.
207 G5 Ozoro Nigeria
103 F7 Ōzu Japan
245 E4 Ozumba de Alzate Mex.
129 C3 Ozurget'i Georgia
128 A1 Özyurt Dağı mts Turkey
175 M5 Ozyutychi Ukr.
191 G4 Ozzano dell'Emilia Italy
190 D3 Ozzano Monferrato Italy

P

206 E4 Pâ Burkina
165 E3 Paal Belgium
78 □5 Paama i. Vanuatu
221 N3 Paamiut Greenland
96 B3 Pa-an Myanmar
Paanopa i. Kiribati see Banaba
214 B5 Paarl S. Africa
78 □4a Paata i. Chuuk Micronesia
Paatsjoki r. Europe see Patsoyoki
240 □D8 Paauilo HI U.S.A.
Pabaigh i. Western Isles, Scotland U.K. see Pabbay
146 B3 Pabail Iarach Western Isles, Scotland U.K.
214 C3 Paballelo S. Africa
101 D4 P'abal-li N. Korea
146 A4 Pabbay i. Western Isles, Scotland U.K.
146 A5 Pabbay i. Western Isles, Scotland U.K.
244 C2 Pabeilón de Arteaga Mex.
175 H4 Pabianice Pol.
Pabianitz Pol. see Pabianice
192 A5 Pabillonis Sardegna Italy
245 E1 Pablillo r. Mex.
117 G4 Pabna Bangl.
179 F2 Pabneukirchen Austria
138 E4 Pabradė Lith.
123 F5 Pab Range mts Pak.
158 C3 Pabu France
252 D2 Pacaás, Serra dos hills Brazil
256 B4 Pacaembu Brazil
252 D2 Pacahuaras r. Bol.
254 F3 Pacajus Brazil
214 D6 Pacaltsdorp S. Africa
175 J5 Pacanów Pol.
Pacaraimã, Serra mts S. America see Pakaraima Mountains
250 B6 Pacasmayo Peru
254 F2 Pacatuba Brazil
250 C6 Pacaya r. Peru
243 H6 Pacaya, Volcán de vol. Guat.
158 E3 Pacé France
194 B5 Paceco Sicilia Italy
242 C2 Pacheco Mex.
135 H5 Pachelma Rus. Fed.
195 E6 Pachino Sicilia Italy
252 B2 Pachitea r. Peru
252 A1 Pachiza Peru
116 D5 Pachmarhi Madh. Prad. India
198 D1 Pachni Greece
116 D5 Pachor Madh. Prad. India
116 C5 Pachora Mahar. India
116 C4 Pachpadra Rajasthan India
245 E3 Pachuca Mex.
192 E1 Paciano Italy
240 F3 Pacifica CA U.S.A.
267 I9 Pacific-Antarctic Ridge sea feature Pacific Ocean
240 G3 Pacific Grove CA U.S.A.
266 Pacific Ocean
177 K3 Pácin Hungary
196 D3 Pačir Vojvodina, Srbija Yugo.
95 E5 Pacitan Jawa Timur Indon.
83 E2 Packsaddle N.S.W. Austr.
182 B3 Pacos de Ferreira Port.
176 E2 Pacov Czech Rep.
176 G5 Pacsa Hungary
257 E2 Pacuí r. Brazil
177 K2 Pacutová hill Slovakia
175 H3 Pacyna Pol.
156 B3 Pacy-sur-Eure France
174 F5 Paczków Pol.
92 C5 Padada Phil.
Padali Rus. Fed. see Amursk
116 C3 Padampur Rajasthan India
94 C3 Padang Sumatera Indon.
94 C3 Padangpanjang Sumatera Indon.
94 B2 Padangsidimpuan Sumatera Indon.
134 F3 Padany Rus. Fed.
95 F1 Padas r. Sabah Malaysia
141 N3 Padasjoki Fin.
122 B3 Padatha, Kūh-e mt. Iran
251 E5 Padauiri r. Brazil
168 E1 Padborg Denmark
151 G3 Padbury Buckinghamshire, England U.K.
252 D5 Padcaya Bol.
83 F3 Paddington N.S.W. Austr.
215 H4 Paddock S. Africa
151 H3 Paddock Wood Kent, England U.K.
177 J6 Padej Vojvodina, Srbija Yugo.
232 C5 Paden City WV U.S.A.
169 D4 Paderborn Ger.
184 B3 Paderne Faro Port.
182 B2 Paderne Viana do Castelo Port.
182 C2 Paderne de Allariz Spain
197 F3 Padeșu, Vârful mt. Romania
175 J5 Padew Narodowa Pol.
149 G4 Padiham Lancashire, England U.K.
252 D4 Padilla Bol.
197 H3 Padina Romania
196 E3 Padina Vojvodina, Srbija Yugo.
196 E3 Padinska Skela Srbija Yugo.
163 D4 Padirac France
Padma r. Bangl. see Ganges
114 C4 Padmanabhapuram Tamil Nadu India
116 E5 Padmapur Mahar. India
157 G4 Padoux France
191 G3 Padova Italy
191 G3 Padova prov. Veneto Italy
116 C5 Padra Gujarat India
117 F4 Padrauna Uttar Prad. India
184 D3 Padre Caro hill Spain
257 G2 Padre Paraíso Brazil
192 A4 Padria Sardegna Italy
192 A2 Padro, Monte mt. Corse France
182 B2 Padrón Spain
192 B4 Padru Sardegna Italy
150 C4 Padstow Cornwall, England U.K.
138 F4 Padsvillye Belarus
82 E4 Padthaway S.A. Austr.
115 D2 Padua Orissa India
Padua Italy see Padova
237 F4 Paducah KY U.S.A.
237 C5 Paducah TX U.S.A.
185 G3 Padul Spain
193 H4 Padula Italy
193 G3 Paduli Italy
116 D2 Padum Jammu and Kashmir
197 F2 Pădurea Craiului, Munții mts Romania
81 E4 Paekakariki North I. N.Z.
101 D4 Paekdu-san mt. China/N. Korea
81 B6 Paerau South I. N.Z.
80 E2 Paeroa North I. N.Z.
80 F3 Paeroa hill North I. N.Z.
190 C4 Paesana Italy
191 H3 Paese Italy
195 D2 Paestum tourist site Italy
92 B3 Paete Phil.
128 A2 Pafos Cyprus
128 A2 Pafos airport Cyprus
188 E3 Pag Croatia
188 E3 Pag i. Croatia
134 M2 Paga r. Rus. Fed.
95 D4 Pagadenbaru Jawa Barat Indon.
92 B5 Pagadian Phil.
Pagalu i. Equat. Guinea see Annobón
91 K3 Pagan i. N. Mariana Is
191 G2 Paganella mt. Italy
193 F2 Paganica Italy
192 D2 Paganico Italy
94 C3 Pagaralam Sumatera Indon.
198 C2 Pagasitikos Kolpos b. Greece
95 F3 Pagatan Kalimantan Selatan Indon.
241 L3 Page AZ U.S.A.
86 E3 Page, Mount hill W.A. Austr.
138 C4 Pagėgiai Lith.
259 □ Paget, Mount S. Georgia
85 H3 Paget Cay rf Coral Sea Is Terr. Austr.
151 G4 Pagham West Sussex, England U.K.
138 E4 Pagiriai Kėdainiai Lith.
138 E4 Pagiriai Vilnius Lith.
192 E2 Paglia r. Italy
193 G2 Paglieta Italy
157 G4 Pagny-sur-Moselle France
Pagon i. N. Mariana Is see Pagan
78 □2 Pago Pago American Samoa
239 F4 Pagosa Springs CO U.S.A.
207 F4 Pagouda Togo
Pagqên Qinghai China see Gadê
224 C3 Pagwachuan r. Ont. Can.
224 C3 Pagwa River Ont. Can.
240 □D9 Pahala HI U.S.A.
94 C2 Pahang r. Malaysia
94 C2 Pahang state Malaysia
117 G4 Paharpur tourist site Bangl.
123 G3 Paharpur Pak.
80 E4 Pahiatua North I. N.Z.
173 F4 Pähl Ger.
168 E1 Pahlen Ger.
116 C2 Pahlgam Jammu and Kashmir
240 □D9 Pahoa HI U.S.A.
231 D7 Pahokee FL U.S.A.
241 J3 Pahranagat Range mts NV U.S.A.
138 D5 Pahranichny Belarus
241 J3 Pahrump NV U.S.A.
116 D4 Pahuj r. India
240 I3 Pahute Mesa plat. NV U.S.A.
240 □C8 Paia HI U.S.A.
182 B4 Paião Port.
240 G3 Paicines CA U.S.A.
138 E2 Paide Estonia
150 D4 Paignton Torbay, England U.K.
80 E1 Paihia North I. N.Z.
250 B6 Paiján Peru
141 N3 Päijänne l. Fin.
207 G4 Paiko Nigeria
252 D4 Paila r. Bol.
260 A6 Pailahueque Chile
163 D5 Pailhès France
Pailing Zhejiang China see Chun'an
259 B6 Paillaco Chile
240 □C8 Pailolo Channel HI U.S.A.
158 D4 Paimbœuf France
141 M3 Paimio Fin.
158 C3 Paimpol France
158 D3 Paimpont France
94 C3 Painan Sumatera Indon.
114 C4 Painavu Kerala India
260 B3 Paine Chile
259 B8 Paine, Cerro mt. Chile
257 E3 Paineiras Brazil
226 C2 Painesdale MI U.S.A.
232 C4 Painesville OH U.S.A.
257 E4 Pains Brazil
150 E3 Painswick Gloucestershire, England U.K.
241 L3 Painted Desert AZ U.S.A.
173 F3 Painten Ger.
Paint Hills Que. Can. see Wemindji
237 D6 Paint Rock TX U.S.A.
232 B6 Paintsville KY U.S.A.
250 C3 Paipa Col.
116 E5 Pairi r. India
227 G3 Paisley Ont. Can.
146 D6 Paisley Renfrewshire, Scotland U.K.
183 H1 País Vasco aut. comm. Spain
78 □5 Païta New Caledonia
250 A6 Paita Peru
114 B2 Paithan Mahar. India
109 G2 Paitou Zhejiang China
182 B3 Paiva r. Port.
Paiva Couceiro Angola see Quipungo
109 E2 Paizhou Hubei China
140 M2 Pajala Sweden
250 A5 Pajan Ecuador
216 □3b Pájara Fuerteventura Canary Is
183 I5 Pajarón Spain
183 I5 Pajaroncillo Spain
174 G4 Pajęczno Pol.
176 F5 Páka Hungary
114 C3 Pakala Andhra Prad. India
Pakanbaru Sumatera Indon. see Pekanbaru
251 F4 Pakaraima Mountains S. America
117 F4 Pakaur Bihar India
80 D4 Pakawau South I. N.Z.
101 C5 Pakch'ŏn N. Korea
224 D4 Pakesley Ont. Can.
131 R3 Pakhachi Rus. Fed.
120 D2 Pakhar' Kazakh.
Pákhni Greece see Pachni
Pakhoi Guangxi China see Beihai
139 K4 Pakhomovo Rus. Fed.
121 H4 Pakhtaabad Uzbek.
123 F4 Pakistan country Asia
Paknampho Thai. see Nakhon Sawan
176 G5 Pakod Hungary
96 A2 Pakokku Myanmar
174 G3 Pakość Pol.
174 F4 Pakosław Pol.
188 E4 Pakoštane Croatia
80 D1 Pakotai North I. N.Z.
177 H4 Pákozd Hungary
123 H4 Pakpattan Pak.
97 C5 Pak Phanang Thai.
97 C6 Pak Phayun Thai.
188 F3 Pakra r. Croatia
188 F3 Pakrac Croatia
138 D4 Pakruojis Lith.
177 H5 Paks Hungary
Pakse Laos see Pakxé
109 □ Pak Tam Chung H.K. China
97 C4 Pak Thong Chai Thai.
123 G3 Paktīā prov. Afgh.
123 GH3 Paktīkā prov. Afgh.
95 F2 Paku r. Sarawak Malaysia
93 B3 Pakue Indon.
136 F2 Pakul' Ukr.
96 D4 Pakxé Laos
Pal Senegal see Mpal
208 B2 Pala Chad
94 D4 Palabuhanratu Jawa Barat Indon.
183 F3 Palacios de Goda Spain
183 G3 Palacios de la Sierra Spain
182 D2 Palacios del Sil Spain
182 D2 Palacios de Sanabria Spain
178 C4 Pala di San Martino mt. Italy
161 D3 Paladru, Lac de l. France
Palaestinia reg. Asia see Palestine
186 G3 Palafrugell Spain
195 F2 Palagianello Italy
195 G2 Palagiano Italy
194 D5 Palagonia Sicilia Italy
191 F5 Palaia Italy
198 C3 Palaia Fokaia Greece
198 C4 Palaiochora Kriti Greece
198 B2 Palairos Greece
156 C4 Palaiseau France
Palakkat Kerala India see Palghat
198 C2 Palamas Greece
186 G3 Palamós Spain
116 D2 Palam Pur Hima. Prad. India
116 C4 Palana Rajasthan India
131 Q4 Palana Rus. Fed.
92 B2 Palanan Phil.
187 C5 Palancia r. Spain
129 B4 Palandöken Dağları mts Turkey
116 E5 Palandur Mahar. India
138 C4 Palanga Lith.
122 E4 Palangān, Kūh-e mts Iran
161 A4 Palanges, Montagne des mts France
95 F3 Palangkaraya Kalimantan Tengah Indon.
114 C4 Palani Tamil Nadu India
116 C4 Palanpur Gujarat India
190 F4 Palanzano Italy
92 C3 Palapag Phil.
213 E4 Palapye Botswana
114 D3 Palar r. India
117 G4 Palasbari Assam India
182 C2 Palas de Rei Spain
138 G4 Palata r. Belarus
193 G3 Palata Italy
131 Q3 Palatka Rus. Fed.
231 D6 Palatka FL U.S.A.
192 B3 Palau Sardegna Italy
92 □ Palau country N. Pacific Ocean
92 A3 Palauig Phil.
91 H5 Palau Islands Palau
266 D5 Palau Trench sea feature N. Pacific Ocean
161 B5 Palavas-les-Flots France
97 B4 Palaw Myanmar
92 A4 Palawan i. Phil.
92 A4 Palawan Passage str. Phil.
266 C5 Palawan Trough sea feature N. Pacific Ocean
92 B3 Palayan Phil.
114 C4 Palayankottai Tamil Nadu India
183 F4 Palazuelos de Eresma Spain
194 C5 Palazzo Adriano Sicilia Italy
194 D5 Palazzolo Acreide Sicilia Italy
190 E3 Palazzolo sull'Oglio Italy
193 I4 Palazzo San Gervasio Italy
179 G4 Paldau Austria
138 E2 Paldiski Estonia
188 G4 Pale Bos.-Herz.
134 H4 Palekh Rus. Fed.
94 D3 Palembang Sumatera Indon.
259 C6 Palena Chile
193 G3 Palena Italy
183 F2 Palencia Spain
183 F2 Palencia prov. Castilla y León Spain
185 F3 Palenciana Spain
243 G5 Palenque Mex.
183 F2 Palenzuela Spain
194 C4 Palermo Sicilia Italy
194 C5 Palermo prov. Sicilia Italy
194 C4 Palermo, Golfo di b. Sicilia Italy
189 D6 Palermo Punta Raisi airport Sicilia Italy
128 B3 Palestine reg. Asia
237 E6 Palestine TX U.S.A.
193 E3 Palestrina Italy
177 H5 Pálfa Hungary
114 B2 Palghar Mahar. India
114 C4 Palghat Kerala India
87 B4 Palgrave, Mount hill W.A. Austr.
182 B4 Palhaça Port.
177 K3 Pálháza Hungary
255 C8 Palhoca Brazil
116 E5 Pali Madh. Prad. India
114 B2 Pali Mahar. India
116 C4 Pali Rajasthan India
193 F3 Paliano Italy
177 I5 Palić Vojvodina, Srbija Yugo.
78 □4b Palikir Pohnpei Micronesia
92 C5 Palimbang Phil.
160 C2 Palinges France
193 H4 Palinuro Italy
156 D4 Palis France
239 E4 Palisade CO U.S.A.
165 E5 Paliseul Belgium
116 B5 Palitana Gujarat India
138 D2 Palivere Estonia
195 F5 Palizzi Italy
140 L2 Palja hill Sweden
140 O2 Paljakka hill Fin.
141 N3 Pälkäne Fin.
114 C4 Palk Bay Sri Lanka
138 G3 Palkino Rus. Fed.
115 D2 Palkohda Andhra Prad. India
114 C3 Palkonda Range mts India
117 F5 Palkot Bihar India
177 H2 Palkovice Czech Rep.
114 C4 Palk Strait India/Sri Lanka
Palla Bianca mt. Austria/Italy see Weißkugel
114 C4 Palladani Tamil Nadu India
195 F3 Pallagorio Italy
252 B3 Pallapalla mt. Peru
184 D2 Pallarés Spain
186 E2 Pallaresa r. Spain
147 C4 Pallas Green Rep. of Ireland
147 C4 Pallaskenry Rep. of Ireland
120 A2 Pallasovka Rus. Fed.
114 D3 Pallavaram Tamil Nadu India
114 D2 Palleru r. India
173 G3 Palling Ger.
87 C7 Pallinup r. W.A. Austr.
210 B4 Pallisa Uganda
81 E4 Palliser, Cape North I. N.Z.
79 □3 Palliser, Îles is Arch. des Tuamotu Fr. Polynesia
81 E4 Palliser Bay North I. N.Z.
116 C3 Pallu Rajasthan India
158 E5 Palluau France
159 H5 Palluau-sur-Indre France
254 D5 Palma r. Brazil
211 D7 Palma Moz.
184 B2 Palma Port.
193 G4 Palma Campania Italy
185 E3 Palma del Río Spain
187 F5 Palma de Mallorca Spain
194 C5 Palma di Montechiaro Sicilia Italy
192 A4 Palmadula Sardegna Italy
114 C3 Palmaner Andhra Prad. India
191 I3 Palmanova Italy
187 F5 Palma Nova Spain
244 D2 Palma Pegada Mex.
244 D4 Palmar Chico Mex.
254 G4 Palmares Brazil
255 C9 Palmares do Sul Brazil
227 H1 Palmarolle Que. Can.
242 □J7 Palmar Sur Costa Rica
255 C8 Palmas Paraná Brazil
254 C4 Palmas Tocantins Brazil
246 D2 Palma Soriano Cuba
182 B4 Palmaz Port.
231 D7 Palm Bay FL U.S.A.
231 D6 Palm Coast FL U.S.A.
240 H4 Palmdale CA U.S.A.
241 I5 Palm Desert CA U.S.A.
256 C6 Palmeira Brazil
182 B3 Palmeira Port.
255 B8 Palmeira das Missões Brazil
254 F4 Palmeira dos Índios Brazil
254 E3 Palmeirais Brazil
254 D5 Palmeiras r. Brazil
256 C2 Palmeiras de Goiás Brazil
184 B2 Palmela Port.
262 T2 Palmer research stn Antarctica
85 E3 Palmer r. Qld Austr.
220 D3 Palmer AK U.S.A.
262 T2 Palmer Land reg. Antarctica
234 B4 Palmer Park MD U.S.A.
Palmerston N.T. Austr. see Darwin
84 B2 Palmerston N.T. Austr.
227 G4 Palmerston Ont. Can.
81 □2 Palmerston atoll Cook Is
81 C6 Palmerston South I. N.Z.
147 E3 Palmerston Rep. of Ireland
85 G4 Palmerston, Cape Qld Austr.
80 E4 Palmerston North North I. N.Z.
234 C2 Palmerton PA U.S.A.
85 F2 Palmerville Qld Austr.
231 D7 Palmetto FL U.S.A.
195 E4 Palmi Italy
245 E2 Palmillas Mex.
260 C3 Palmira Arg.
250 B4 Palmira Col.
246 B2 Palmira Cuba
256 A6 Palmital Paraná Brazil
256 B5 Palmital São Paulo Brazil
261 I3 Palmitas Uru.
Palmnicken Rus. Fed. see Yantarnyy
184 E4 Palmones r. Spain
177 I5 Pálmonostora Hungary
240 I5 Palm Springs CA U.S.A.
85 G5 Palm Tree Creek r. Qld Austr.
Palmyra Syria see Tadmur
236 F4 Palmyra MO U.S.A.
234 C2 Palmyra NJ U.S.A.
232 E3 Palmyra NY U.S.A.
227 I5 Palmyra PA U.S.A.
232 D6 Palmyra VA U.S.A.
75 I3 Palmyra Atoll N. Pacific Ocean
117 F5 Palmyras Point India
146 E7 Palnackie Dumfries and Galloway, Scotland U.K.
192 B3 Palneca Corse France
114 C4 Palni Hills India
92 C4 Palo Phil.
244 C3 Palo Alto Mex.
240 F3 Palo Alto CA U.S.A.
250 B3 Palo de las Letras Col.
195 F1 Palo del Colle Italy
252 C3 Palomani mt. Peru
186 C4 Palomar de Arroyos Spain
245 G5 Palomares Mex.
184 D3 Palomares del Río Spain
240 I5 Palomar Mountain CA U.S.A.
184 D2 Palomas Spain
193 G2 Palombaro Italy
194 E6 Palombieri r. Sicilia Italy
183 H4 Palomera Spain
186 B4 Palomera, Sierra mts Spain
183 H5 Palomeras del Campo Spain
184 D2 Palomilas r. Spain
193 H4 Palomonte Italy
191 G3 Palòn, Cima mt. Italy
114 D2 Paloncha Andhra Prad. India
237 D5 Palo Pinto TX U.S.A.
93 B3 Palopo Sulawesi Selatan Indon.
187 C7 Palos, Cabo de c. Spain
258 F2 Palo Santo Arg.
184 D3 Palos de la Frontera Spain
238 C2 Palouse r. WA U.S.A.
241 J5 Palo Verde CA U.S.A.
85 E5 Palparara Qld Austr.
186 G3 Pals Spain
116 C5 Palsana Gujarat India
140 N2 Paltamo Fin.
139 J5 Pal'tso Rus. Fed.
93 A3 Palu Sulawesi Tengah Indon.
93 A3 Palu r. Indon.
127 E3 Palu Turkey
92 B3 Paluan Phil.
195 F3 Paludi Italy
163 A5 Palue r. France
159 G2 Paluel France
191 I2 Paluzza Italy
123 F2 Pal'vart Turkm.
116 D3 Palwal Haryana India
Palwancha Andhra Prad. India see Paloncha
131 S3 Palyavaam r. Rus. Fed.
Palyeskaya Nizina marsh Belarus/Ukr. see Pripet Marshes
172 A2 Palzem Ger.
179 I2 Pama Austria
207 F4 Pama Burkina
208 C3 Pama r. C.A.R.
83 E3 Pamamaroo Lake N.S.W. Austr.
217 □3b Pamandzi Mayotte
95 D4 Pamanukan Jawa Barat Indon.
250 D5 Pamar Col.
129 D3 P'ambaki Lerrnashght'a mts Armenia
213 G4 Pambarra Moz.
83 G4 Pambula N.S.W. Austr.
179 G4 Pameče Slovenia
95 F4 Pamekasan Jawa Timur Indon.
95 D4 Pameungpeuk Jawa Barat Indon.
199 E2 Pamfylla Voreio Aigaio Greece
179 H3 Pamhagen Austria
174 E3 Pamiątkowo Pol.
114 C3 Pamidi Andhra Prad. India
163 D5 Pamiers France
123 H2 Pamir r. Afgh./Tajik.
121 H5 Pamir mts Asia
231 E5 Pamlico r. NC U.S.A.
231 E5 Pamlico Sound sea chan. NC U.S.A.
237 C5 Pampa TX U.S.A.
252 B3 Pampachiri Peru
258 E2 Pampa de Infierno Arg.
252 D4 Pampa Grande Bol.
93 B4 Pampanua Sulawesi Selatan Indon.
190 C4 Pamparato Italy
261 E5 Pampas reg. Arg.
252 B3 Pampas Peru
252 B3 Pampas r. Peru
163 E4 Pampelonne France
Pampeluna Spain see Pamplona
214 E2 Pampierstad S. Africa
182 B4 Pampilhosa Port.
182 C4 Pampilhosa da Serra Port.
183 G2 Pampliega Spain
232 D6 Pamplin VA U.S.A.
250 C3 Pamplona Col.
92 B4 Pamplona Phil.
183 I2 Pamplona Spain
170 C2 Pampow Ger.
162 B2 Pamproux France
199 E2 Pamukçu Turkey
199 G1 Pamukova Turkey
232 E6 Pamunkey r. VA U.S.A.
208 B5 Pana Gabon
236 F4 Pana IL U.S.A.
243 H4 Panabá Mex.

Panabo to Pedrouzos

346

92 C5 Panabo Phil.
241 J3 Panaca NV U.S.A.
197 G2 Panaci Romania
116 E5 Panagar Madh. Prad. India
114 C2 Panagiri Andhra Prad. India
197 G4 Panagyurishte Bulg.
198 B2 Panaitolio Greece
114 B3 Panaji Goa India
246 B5 Panama country Central America
242 □K7 Panamá Panama
242 □K7 Panamá, Bahía de b. Panama
242 □K8 Panamá, Golfo de g. Panama
Panamá, Gulf of Panama see Panamá, Golfo de
242 □K7 Panama Canal Panama
Panama City Panama see Panamá
231 C6 Panama City FL U.S.A.
240 I3 Panamint Range mts CA U.S.A.
240 I3 Panamint Valley CA U.S.A.
252 A2 Panao Peru
117 G4 Panar r. India
195 E4 Panarea, Isola i. Isole Lipari Italy
191 G4 Panaro r. Italy
95 F4 Panarukan Jawa Timur Indon.
163 C5 Panassac France
92 B4 Panay i. Phil.
92 B4 Panay Gulf Phil.
162 D3 Panazol France
215 H2 Panbult S. Africa
241 J2 Pancake Range mts NV U.S.A.
190 C4 Pancalieri Italy
257 G3 Pancas Brazil
196 E3 Pančevo Vojvodina, Srbija Yugo.
117 G4 Panchagarh Bangl.
137 F3 Pancheve Ukr.
109 G3 Panch'iao Taiwan
95 F2 Pancingapan, Bukit mt. Indon.
197 H3 Panciu Romania
183 G2 Pancorbo Spain
197 E2 Pâncota Romania
186 B4 Pancrudo Spain
186 B4 Pancrudo r. Spain
Pancsova Vojvodina, Srbija Yugo. see Pančevo
92 B4 Pandan Panay Phil.
92 C3 Pandan Phil.
116 E5 Pandaria Madh. Prad. India
114 C3 Pandavapura Karnataka India
94 D4 Pandeglang Jawa Barat Indon.
255 D5 Pandeiros r. Brazil
138 E3 Pandėlys Lith.
116 D5 Pandhana Madh. Prad. India
114 B2 Pandharpur Mahar. India
116 D5 Pandhurna Madh. Prad. India
82 D1 Pandie Pandie S.A. Austr.
190 E3 Pandino Italy
252 D2 Pando dept Bol.
261 J4 Pando Uru.
Pandokrátor hill Ionioi Nisoi Greece see Pantokratoras
232 B4 Pandora OH U.S.A.
85 F1 Pandora Entrance sea chan. Qld Austr.
142 C3 Pandrup Denmark
150 E3 Pandy Monmouthshire, Wales U.K.
177 G4 Pándzsa r. Hungary
Paneas Syria see Bāniyās
194 E5 Panebianco r. Sicilia Italy
253 E2 Panelas Brazil
183 F1 Panes Spain
138 E4 Panevėžys Lith.
Panfilov Kazakh. see Zharkent
135 H6 Panfilovo Rus. Fed.
137 F2 Panfyly Ukr.
100 C1 Pang r. China
96 B2 Pang, Nam r. Myanmar
79 □2 Pangai Tonga
114 C2 Pangal Andhra Prad. India
114 C2 Pangal Andhra Prad. India
95 E4 Pangandaran Jawa Barat Indon.
211 C6 Pangani Tanz.
211 C6 Pangani r. Tanz.
92 C3 Pañganiban Phil.
207 I5 Pangar r. Cameroon
151 F3 Pangbourne West Berkshire, England U.K.
157 G3 Pange France
78 □6 Panggoe Choiseul Solomon Is
123 H3 Pangi Range mts Pak.
93 A4 Pangkajene Sulawesi Selatan Indon.
95 E3 Pangkalanbuun Kalimantan Tengah Indon.
94 B1 Pangkalansusu Sumatera Indon.
94 C1 Pangkal Kalong Malaysia
94 D3 Pangkalpinang Indon.
223 J5 Pangman Sask. Can.
221 L3 Pangnirtung Nunavut Can.
209 B7 Pango Aluquém Angola
130 I3 Pangody Rus. Fed.
94 D4 Pangrango vol. Indon.
259 B5 Panguipulli Chile
241 K3 Panguitch UT U.S.A.
78 □6 Panguna P.N.G.
80 D1 Panguru North I. N.Z.
92 B5 Pangutaran Group is Phil.
237 C5 Panhandle TX U.S.A.
260 B4 Paniahue Chile
209 F6 Pania-Mwanga Dem. Rep. Congo
192 E1 Panicale Italy
78 □5 Panie, Mont mt. New Caledonia
260 B4 Panimávida Chile
116 C5 Pani Mines Gujarat India
135 H6 Panino Rus. Fed.
116 D3 Panipat Haryana India
160 C3 Panissières France
92 A4 Panitan Phil.
186 B3 Paniza Spain
139 H4 Panizowye Belarus
123 G2 Panj Tajik.
Panj r. Afgh./Tajik. see Pyandzh
123F2 Panjakent Tajik.
Panjang i. Cocos Is see West Island
94 D4 Panjang Sumatera Indon.
163 B5 Panjas France
123 F5 Panjgur Pak.
116 C5 Panjhra r. India
Panjim Goa India see Panaji
107 I3 Panjin Liaoning China
123 G3 Panjkora r. Pak.
123 G4 Panjnad r. Pak.
140 O3 Pankakoski Fin.
168 F1 Panker Ger.
174 G5 Panki Pol.
139 H2 Pankovka Rus. Fed.
207 H4 Pankshin Nigeria
Panlian Sichuan China see Miyi
Panlong Henan China see Queshan
98 D7 Panna Madh. Prad. India
86 C4 Pannawonica W.A. Austr.
156 C4 Pannes France
193 H3 Panni Italy
165 E3 Panningen Neth.
177 G4 Pannonhalma Hungary
123 G5 Pano Aqil Pak.
184 B3 Panóias Port.
Panoplis Egypt see Akhmîm
256 B4 Panorama Brazil
Panormus Sicilia Italy see Palermo
114 C4 Panruti Tamil Nadu India
171 F4 Panschwitz-Kuckau Ger.
Panshan Liaoning China see Panjin
100 C4 Panshi Jilin China
Panshui Guizhou China see Pu'an
151 H3 Pant r. England U.K.
94 C3 Pantaicermin, Gunung mt. Indon.
253 F4 Pantanal de São Lourenço marsh Brazil
253 F4 Pantanal do Taquarí marsh Brazil
241 L6 Pantano AZ U.S.A.
93 C5 Pantar i. Indon.
137 G3 Pantayivka Ukr.
Pantelaria Sicilia Italy see Pantelleria
137 I3 Panteleymonivka Ukr.
194 A6 Pantelleria Sicilia Italy
194 B6 Pantelleria, Isola di i. Sicilia Italy
245 F3 Pantepec r. Mex.
Panticapaeum Ukr. see Kerch
186 C2 Panticosa Spain
183 G4 Pantoja Spain
198 A2 Pantokratoras hill Ionioi Nisoi Greece
86 F3 Panton r. W.A. Austr.
186 D3 Pantorrillas hill Spain
92 C5 Pantukan Phil.
150 D2 Pant-y-dwr Powys, Wales U.K.
245 E2 Pánuco Mex.
245 F2 Pánuco r. Mex.
114 B2 Panvel Mahar. India
116 D4 Panwari Uttar Prad. India
108 C3 Panxian Guizhou China
109 E4 Panyu Guangdong China
137 I3 Panyutyne Ukr.
108 B3 Panzhihua Sichuan China
209 C6 Panzi Dem. Rep. Congo
243 H6 Panzos Guat.
251 E2 Pao r. Venez.
254 F4 Pão de Açúcar Brazil
193 I5 Paola Italy
236 E4 Paola KS U.S.A.
230 C4 Paoli IN U.S.A.
234 C2 Paoli PA U.S.A.
192 B3 Paoloni, Serra hill Sardegna Italy
239 F4 Paonia CO U.S.A.
208 C3 Paoua C.A.R.
121 G4 Pap Uzbek.
176 G4 Pápa Hungary
240 □D9 Papa HI U.S.A.
193 H4 Papa, Monte del mt. Italy
240 □D9 Papaaloa HI U.S.A.
198 C3 Papadianika Greece
Papagaio r. Brazil see Sauêruiná
257 E3 Papagaios Brazil
245 E5 Papagayo r. Mex.
114 C3 Papagni r. India
240 □D9 Papaikou HI U.S.A.
80 E2 Papakura North I. N.Z.
245 G4 Papaloapan r. Mex.
80 F2 Papamoa Beach North I. N.Z.
114 C4 Papanasam Tamil Nadu India
114 C4 Papanasam Tamil Nadu India
245 F3 Papantla Mex.
250 C6 Papa Playa Peru
115 D2 Paparhahandi Orissa India
80 E2 Paparoa North I. N.Z.
81 C5 Paparoa Range mts South I. N.Z.
193 H5 Papasidero Italy
146 □G1 Papa Stour i. Scotland U.K.
146 F2 Papa Stronsay i. Scotland U.K.
177 G4 Pápateszér Hungary
80 E2 Papatoetoe North I. N.Z.
81 B7 Papatowai South I. N.Z.
146 F2 Papa Westray i. Scotland U.K.
Papay i. Scotland U.K. see Papa Westray
79 □3a Papeete Tahiti Fr. Polynesia
168 C2 Papenburg Ger.
170 D1 Papendorf Ger.
214 B4 Papendorp S. Africa
164 D3 Papendrecht Neth.
Paphos Cyprus see Pafos
Paphus Cyprus see Pafos
239 F6 Papigochic r. Mex.
197 G5 Papikio mt. Bulg./Greece
138 D3 Papilė Lith.
236 D3 Papillion NE U.S.A.
177 L2 Papín Slovakia
233 F2 Papineauville Que. Can.
197 H4 Papiya hill Bulg.
177 H4 Papkeszi Hungary
174 G2 Papowo Biskupie Pol.
173 E3 Pappenheim Ger.
175 K3 Paprotnia Pol.
146 B6 Paps of Jura hills Scotland U.K.
91 J8 Papua, Gulf of P.N.G.
78 □6 Papua New Guinea country Oceania
260 B3 Papudo Chile
96 B3 Papun Myanmar
84 B4 Papunya N.T. Austr.
151 G2 Papworth Everard Cambridgeshire, England U.K.
150 C4 Par Cornwall, England U.K.
257 E3 Pará r. Brazil
251 I5 Pará state Brazil
135 H5 Para r. Rus. Fed.
254 C2 Pará, Rio do r. Brazil
87 C4 Paraburdoo W.A. Austr.
177 I2 Paráč mt. Slovakia
92 B3 Paracale Phil.
257 F5 Paracambi Brazil
256 D2 Paracatu Brazil
256 D2 Paracatu r. Minas Gerais Brazil
257 E2 Paracatu r. Minas Gerais Brazil
90 D3 Paracel Islands S. China Sea
82 D2 Parachilna S.A. Austr.
123 G3 Parachinar Pak.
244 C4 Paracho Mex.
196 E4 Paraćin Srbija Yugo.
244 D3 Parácuaro Mex.
183 I5 Paracuellos Spain
254 F2 Paracuru Brazil
177 J4 Parád Hungary
182 C4 Parada Port.
182 C2 Parada Spain
182 B4 Parada de Ester Port.
182 C3 Parada de Pinhão Port.
183 E3 Parada de Rubiales Spain
185 E3 Paradas Spain
182 C3 Paradela Vila Real Port.
182 C3 Paradela Viseu Port.
182 C2 Paradela Spain
182 C3 Paradela de Guiães Port.
257 E3 Pará de Minas Brazil
224 E3 Paradis Que. Can.
225 J2 Paradise r. Nfld. Can.
251 G3 Paradise Guyana
240 G2 Paradise CA U.S.A.
226 E2 Paradise MI U.S.A.
241 J3 Paradise NV U.S.A.
222 H2 Paradise Gardens N.W.T. Can.
223 I4 Paradise Hill Sask. Can.
240 I2 Paradise Peak NV U.S.A.
225 J2 Paradise River Nfld. Can.
241 L5 Paradise Valley AZ U.S.A.
238 C3 Paradise Valley NV U.S.A.
117 F5 Paradwip Orissa India
175 I4 Paradyż Pol.
Paraetonium Egypt see Marsa Matrûh
137 G2 Parafiyivka Ukr.
138 F4 Paraf"yanava Belarus
254 D2 Paragominas Brazil
237 F4 Paragould AR U.S.A.
253 E3 Paragua r. Bol.
Paragua i. Phil. see Palawan
251 F3 Paragua r. Venez.
257 E4 Paraguaçu Brazil
256 B5 Paraguaçu Paulista Brazil
253 F5 Paraguai r. Brazil
246 E4 Paraguaná, Península de pen. Venez.
253 F6 Paraguarí Para.
258 F2 Paraguay r. Arg./Para.
253 F5 Paraguay country S. America
254 G3 Paraíba r. Brazil
254 F3 Paraíba state Brazil
257 F5 Paraíba do Sul Brazil
257 G4 Paraíba do Sul r. Brazil
257 E5 Paraibuna Brazil
Parainen Fin. see Pargas
243 G5 Paraíso Mex.
254 C4 Paraíso do Norte Brazil
257 E5 Paraisópolis Brazil
140 M2 Parakka Sweden
207 F4 Parakou Benin
82 D2 Parakylia S.A. Austr.
115 E2 Paralakhemundi Orissa India
198 C2 Paralia Greece
Paramagudi Tamil Nadu India see Paramakkudi
114 C4 Paramakkudi Tamil Nadu India
251 H3 Paramaribo Suriname
158 E3 Paramé France
250 C3 Paramillo mt. Col.
182 D3 Parâmio Port.
254 E5 Paramirim Brazil
254 E4 Paramirim r. Brazil
182 C2 Páramo hill Spain
182 D2 Páramo del Sil Spain
252 A2 Paramonga Peru
182 B4 Paramos Port.
235 D2 Paramus NJ U.S.A.
131 Q4 Paramushir, Ostrov i. Kuril'skiye O-va Rus. Fed.
198 B2 Paramythia Greece
261 G2 Paraná Arg.
254 D5 Paranã Brazil
254 C5 Paraná r. Brazil
256 B6 Paraná state Brazil
261 H4 Paraná r. S. America
261 H4 Paraná, Delta del Arg.
255 C8 Paranaguá Brazil
256 B3 Paranaíba Brazil
256 B4 Paranaíba r. Brazil
261 H3 Paraná Ibicuy r. Arg.
256 B3 Paranaiguara Brazil
253 F2 Paranaita r. Brazil
256 A5 Paranapanema r. Brazil
256 B6 Paranapiacaba, Serra mts Brazil
256 A5 Paranavaí Brazil
92 B5 Parang Phil.
114 D4 Parangi Aru r. Sri Lanka
114 C4 Parangipettai Tamil Nadu India
197 F3 Parângul Mare, Vârful mt. Romania
182 C4 Paranhos Port.
116 C5 Parantij Gujarat India
257 E3 Paraopeba Brazil
257 E3 Paraopeba r. Brazil
185 G3 Parapanda mt. Spain
93 C2 Parapara Halmahera Indon.
127 G4 Pārapāra Iraq
81 E4 Paraparaumu North I. N.Z.
256 B4 Parapuã Brazil
250 E3 Paraque, Cerro mt. Venez.
257 E5 Parati Brazil
254 E5 Paratinga Brazil
82 D3 Paratoo S.A. Austr.
127 G4 Parāū, Kūh-e mt. Iraq
254 C3 Parauapebas r. Brazil
251 H5 Parauaquara, Serra hill Brazil
251 G6 Parauari r. Brazil
129 E2 Paraulozen' r. Rus. Fed.
256 B2 Paraúna Brazil
160 C2 Paray-le-Monial France
116 D4 Parbati r. India
117 G4 Parbatipur Bangl.
114 C2 Parbhani Mahar. India
149 G4 Parbold Lancashire, England U.K.
247 □1 Parcelas Martorell Puerto Rico
187 C6 Parcent Spain
159 F4 Parcé-sur-Sarthe France
171 D3 Parchen Ger.
170 C2 Parchim Ger.
226 E4 Parchment MI U.S.A.
177 K3 Parchovany Slovakia
174 F1 Parchowo Pol.
175 J2 Parciaki Pol.
162 C3 Parcoul France
175 K4 Parczew Pol.
184 C2 Pardais Port.
226 C4 Pardeeville WI U.S.A.
163 B5 Pardies France
182 B4 Pardilhó Port.
197 I3 Pardina Romania
256 A4 Pardo r. Mato Grosso do Sul Brazil
255 F5 Pardo r. Bahia Brazil
255 D5 Pardo r. Minas Gerais Brazil
256 C4 Pardo r. São Paulo Brazil
256 C6 Pardo r. São Paulo Brazil
86 C4 Pardoo W.A. Austr.
176 E1 Pardubice Czech Rep.
176 F2 Pardubický kraj admin. reg. Czech Rep.
95 F4 Pare Jawa Timur Indon.
138 E5 Parechcha Belarus
111 B5 Pare Chu r. China
253 F3 Parecis r. Brazil
253 E2 Parecis, Serra dos hills Brazil
182 B3 Paredes Port.
182 B3 Paredes de Coura Port.
183 F2 Paredes de Nava Spain
260 B4 Paredones Chile
183 H4 Pareja Spain
161 A4 Pareloup, Lac de l. France
78 □4a Parem i. Chuuk Micronesia
81 E4 Paremata North I. N.Z.
78 □4b Parempei i. Pohnpei Micronesia
162 B4 Parempuyre France
114 B2 Parenda Mahar. India
224 F4 Parent Que. Can.
195 F3 Parenti Italy
163 A4 Parentis-en-Born France
81 C6 Pareora South I. N.Z.
93 A4 Parepare Sulawesi Selatan Indon.
260 E4 Parera Arg.
186 F3 Parets del Vallès Spain
171 C3 Parey Ger.
134 H4 Parfen'yevo Rus. Fed.
139 H3 Parfino Rus. Fed.
198 B2 Parga Greece
141 M3 Pargas Fin.
195 E4 Parghelia Italy
114 C2 Pargi Andhra Prad. India
157 E4 Pargny-sur-Saulx France
139 H1 Pargolovo Rus. Fed.
247 □2 Parham Antigua and Barbuda
252 D4 Paria Bol.
241 L3 Paria r. AZ/UT U.S.A.
247 □7 Paria, Gulf of Trin. and Tob./Venez.
251 F2 Paria, Península de pen. Venez.
94 C3 Pariaman Sumatera Indon.
241 K3 Paria Plateau AZ U.S.A.
244 C4 Paricutín, Volcán vol. Mex.
159 G4 Parigné-l'Évêque France
177 H5 Pári-hegy hill Hungary
141 O3 Parikkala Fin.
Parima r. Brazil see Uatatás
251 E4 Parima, Serra mts Brazil
250 C6 Parinari Peru
250 A6 Pariñas, Punta pt Peru
82 E3 Paringa S.A. Austr.
178 A5 Parino r. Italy
251 G5 Parintins Brazil
227 G4 Paris Ont. Can.
156 C4 Paris France
237 E5 Paris AR U.S.A.
238 E3 Paris ID U.S.A.
230 C4 Paris IL U.S.A.
232 A5 Paris KY U.S.A.
233 □H2 Paris ME U.S.A.
236 E4 Paris MO U.S.A.
237 F4 Paris TN U.S.A.
237 E5 Paris TX U.S.A.
153 Paris area map France
233 E3 Parish NY U.S.A.
163 D4 Parisot Midi-Pyrénées France
163 D5 Parisot Midi-Pyrénées France
120 E1 Parizh Rus. Fed.
236 D1 Park r. ND U.S.A.
140 M2 Parkajoki Sweden
114 C2 Parkal Andhra Prad. India
141 M3 Parkano Fin.
121 G4 Parkent Uzbek.
241 J4 Parker AZ U.S.A.
236 B4 Parker CO U.S.A.
236 D3 Parker SD U.S.A.
87 C7 Parker Range hills W.A. Austr.
232 C5 Parkersburg WV U.S.A.
83 G3 Parkes N.S.W. Austr.
234 C3 Parkesburg PA U.S.A.
226 B3 Park Falls WI U.S.A.
226 D5 Park Forest IL U.S.A.
Parkhar Tajik. see Farkhor
227 G4 Parkhill Ont. Can.
137 H2 Parkhomivka Ukr.
227 F2 Parkinson Ont. Can.
232 C4 Parkman OH U.S.A.
147 B5 Parknasilla Rep. of Ireland
236 E2 Park Rapids MN U.S.A.
233 F6 Parksley VA U.S.A.
173 G2 Parkstein Ger.
173 G3 Parkstetten Ger.
236 D3 Parkston SD U.S.A.
222 E5 Parksville B.C. Can.
116 D2 Parkutta Jammu and Kashmir
238 D3 Park Valley UT U.S.A.
234 B3 Parkville MD U.S.A.
183 G4 Parla Spain
Parlakimedi Orissa India see Paralakhemundi
115 E2 Parla Kimedi Orissa India
163 E4 Parlan France
114 C2 Parli Vaijnath Mahar. India
108 A2 Parlung Zangbo r. China
190 F4 Parma Italy
190 F4 Parma prov. Emilia-Romagna Italy
190 F4 Parma r. Italy
134 L2 Parma Rus. Fed.
238 C3 Parma ID U.S.A.
226 E4 Parma MI U.S.A.
232 C4 Parma OH U.S.A.
163 A5 Parme airport France
254 D4 Parnaguá Brazil
254 E2 Parnaíba Brazil
254 B4 Parnaíba r. Brazil
254 D4 Parnaibinha r. Brazil
254 E3 Parnarama Brazil
198 C2 Parnassos mt. Greece
81 D5 Parnassus South I. N.Z.
82 D3 Parndana S.A. Austr.
179 H3 Parndorf Austria
114 B2 Parner Mahar. India
198 C3 Parnon mts Greece
138 E2 Pärnu Estonia
138 E2 Pärnu r. Estonia
138 E2 Pärnu-Jaagupi Estonia
117 G4 Paro Bhutan
81 C5 Paroa South I. N.Z.
138 E1 Parola Fin.
156 D4 Paron France
Parona Turkey see Fındık
123 E3 Paropamisus mts Afgh.
93 A3 Paroreang, Bukit mt. Indon.
198 D3 Paros Notio Aigaio Greece
198 D3 Paros i. Greece
214 B5 Parow S. Africa
241 K3 Parowan UT U.S.A.
161 E4 Parpaillon mts France
82 E3 Parrakie S.A. Austr.
260 B5 Parral Chile
237 B7 Parral r. Mex.
83 G3 Parramatta N.S.W. Austr.
242 E3 Parras Mex.
150 D3 Parrett r. England U.K.
183 E4 Parrillas Spain
226 C3 Parrish WI U.S.A.
242 □I7 Parrita Costa Rica
225 H4 Parrsboro N.S. Can.
221 G2 Parry Channel Nunavut Can.
Parry Island Cook Is see Mauke
221 G2 Parry Islands Nunavut Can.
86 B4 Parry Range hills W.A. Austr.
224 D4 Parry Sound Ont. Can.
234 C2 Parryville PA U.S.A.
Pars prov. Iran see Fārs
117 F4 Parsa Bihar India
Parsa prov. Iran see Fārs
129 E4 Pārsābād Iran
168 F3 Parsau Ger.
173 F2 Parsberg Ger.
178 B3 Parseierspitze mt. Austria
174 D1 Parsęta r. Pol.
236 C2 Parshall ND U.S.A.
235 D2 Parsippany NJ U.S.A.
241 J2 Parsnip Peak NV U.S.A.
237 E4 Parsons KS U.S.A.
232 D5 Parsons WV U.S.A.
170 F3 Parstein Ger.
170 E3 Parsteiner See l. Ger.
114 B2 Partabgarh Mahar. India
114 D2 Partabpur Madh. Prad. India
117 E5 Partabpur Madh. Prad. India
185 H3 Partaloa Spain
194 B5 Partanna Sicilia Italy
140 L2 Pårte mt. Sweden
169 E5 Partenstein Ger.
162 B2 Parthenay France
192 A2 Partinello Corse France
149 G4 Partington Greater Manchester, England U.K.
194 C4 Partinico Sicilia Italy
100 E4 Partizansk Rus. Fed.
177 I2 Partizánska Ľupča Slovakia
177 H3 Partizánske Slovakia
149 J4 Partney Lincolnshire, England U.K.
149 F3 Parton Cumbria, England U.K.
224 D3 Partridge r. Ont. Can.
147 B3 Partry Rep. of Ireland
129 C2 P'arts'khanaqanevi Georgia
137 H4 Partyzany Ukr.
251 H5 Paru r. Brazil
251 E3 Parú, Serranía mts Venez.
251 G5 Paru de Oeste r. Brazil
114 C4 Parur Kerala India
137 F4 Parutyne Ukr.
123 G3 Parvān prov. Afgh.
122 D3 Parvāreh Iran
115 D2 Parvatipuram Andhra Prad. India
116 C4 Parvatsar Rajasthan India
111 C6 Paryang Xizang China
138 G5 Parychy Belarus
143 F3 Påryd Sweden
215 F2 Parys S. Africa
175 J4 Parysów Pol.
175 H4 Parzęczew Pol.
183 G1 Pas r. Spain
240 H4 Pasadena CA U.S.A.
234 B3 Pasadena MD U.S.A.
237 E6 Pasadena TX U.S.A.
186 B1 Pasai Donibane Spain
250 B5 Pasaje Ecuador
96 C4 Pa Sak, Mae Nam r. Thai.
129 C3 Paşalı Turkey
116 E5 Pasan Madh. Prad. India
129 D2 P'asanauri Georgia
127 I5 Pasargadae tourist site Iran
224 F3 Pascagama r. Que. Can.
237 F6 Pascagoula MS U.S.A.
237 F6 Pascagoula r. MS U.S.A.
227 I1 Pascalis Que. Can.
197 H2 Paşcani Romania
179 F2 Pasching Austria
252 B2 Pasco dept Peru
238 C2 Pasco WA U.S.A.
233 H4 Pascoag RI U.S.A.
257 H2 Pascoal, Monte hill Brazil
85 E2 Pascoe r. Qld Austr.
84 D3 Pascoe Inlet Qld Austr.
248 C5 Pascua, Isla de i. S. Pacific Ocean
92 B3 Pascual Phil.
156 C2 Pas-de-Calais dept Nord - Pas-de-Calais France
Pas de Calais str. France/U.K. see Dover, Strait of
156 C2 Pas-en-Artois France
170 F2 Pasewalk Ger.
139 I1 Pasha Rus. Fed.
139 I1 Pasha r. Rus. Fed.
137 J5 Pashkovskiy Rus. Fed.
191 I2 Pasiàn di Prato Italy
178 D5 Pasiano di Pordenone Italy
175 J3 Pasieki Pol.
92 B3 Pasig Phil.
117 H3 Pasighat Arun. Prad. India
127 F3 Pasinler Turkey
95 F5 Pasirian Jawa Timur Indon.
94 C1 Pasir Mas Malaysia
94 C2 Pasirpangarayan Sumatera Indon.
94 C1 Pasir Putih Malaysia
93 B4 Pasitelu, Pulau-pulau is Indon.
143 G3 Påskallavik Sweden
177 H2 Paskov Czech Rep.
123 E5 Paskūh Iran
143 H4 Pasłęk Pol.
143 H4 Pasłęka r. Pol.
87 D7 Pasley, Cape W.A. Austr.
188 E4 Pašman i. Croatia
123 E5 Pasni Pak.
245 F4 Paso del Macho Mex.
261 I1 Paso de los Libres Arg.
261 I3 Paso de los Toros Uru.
245 F4 Paso de Ovejas Mex.
253 F6 Paso de Patria Para.
259 C7 Paso Río Mayo Arg.
240 G4 Paso Robles CA U.S.A.
223 K4 Pasquia Hills Sask. Can.
123 H3 Pasrur Pak.
233 □I2 Passadumkeag ME U.S.A.
254 E3 Passagem Franca Brazil
147 C5 Passage West Rep. of Ireland
235 D2 Passaic NJ U.S.A.
235 D2 Passaic r. NJ U.S.A.
235 D1 Passaic County county NJ U.S.A.
179 G3 Passail Austria
159 F3 Passais France
217 □3b Passamaïnti Mayotte
257 E5 Passa Quatro Brazil
257 E4 Passa Tempo Brazil
173 H3 Passau Ger.
157 G5 Passavant-la-Rochère France
92 B4 Passi Phil.
192 E1 Passignano sul Trasimeno Italy
191 G2 Passirio r. Italy
255 B9 Passo Fundo Brazil
255 B9 Passo Real, Barragem resr Brazil
256 D4 Passos Brazil
170 F2 Passow Ger.
160 E3 Passy France
138 F4 Pastavy Belarus
250 B5 Pastaza prov. Ecuador
250 B6 Pastaza r. Peru
261 F4 Pasteur Arg.
250 B4 Pasto Col.
241 M3 Pastora Peak AZ U.S.A.
182 C1 Pastoriza Spain
244 D3 Pastor Ortiz Mex.
254 D3 Pastos Bons Brazil
183 H4 Pastrana Spain
116 C1 Pasu Jammu and Kashmir
92 B2 Pasuquin Phil.
Pasur Turkey see Kulp
95 F4 Pasuruan Jawa Timur Indon.
138 E3 Pasvalys Lith.
Pasvikelva r. Europe see Patsoyoki
175 I2 Pasym Pol.
174 E4 Paszowice Pol.
177 I4 Pásztó Hungary
252 C3 Pata Bol.
177 G3 Pata Slovakia
241 L6 Patagonia AZ U.S.A.
182 B5 Pataias Port.
Pataliputra Bihar India see Patna
Patan Gujarat India see Somnath
116 C5 Patan Gujarat India
116 D5 Patan Madh. Prad. India
114 B2 Patan Mahar. India
117 F4 Patan Nepal
114 C2 Patancheru Andhra Prad. India
123 F5 Patandar, Koh-i- mt. Pak.
207 G5 Patani Nigeria
116 D5 Patan Saongi Mahar. India
234 B3 Patapsco r. MD U.S.A.
234 B3 Patapsco, South Branch r. MD U.S.A.
116 D3 Pataudi Haryana India
Patavium Italy see Padova
156 B4 Patay France
83 E3 Patchewollock Vic. Austr.
235 E2 Patchogue NY U.S.A.
150 E3 Patchway South Gloucestershire, England U.K.
80 E3 Patea North I. N.Z.
Patea inlet South I. N.Z. see Doubtful Sound
80 E3 Patea r. North I. N.Z.
149 H3 Pateley Bridge North Yorkshire, England U.K.
215 E5 Patensie S. Africa
179 E4 Patergassen Austria
187 C5 Paterna Spain
184 D3 Paterna del Campo Spain
184 E4 Paterna de Rivera Spain
179 E4 Paternion Austria
193 H4 Paterno Basilicata Italy
194 D5 Paternò Sicilia Italy
193 H4 Paternopoli Italy
214 A5 Paternoster S. Africa
173 G2 Patersdorf Ger.
83 G3 Paterson N.S.W. Austr.
83 F2 Paterson r. Qld Austr.
215 E5 Paterson S. Africa
233 F4 Paterson NJ U.S.A.
86 D4 Paterson Range hills W.A. Austr.
117 E5 Pathalgaon Madh. Prad. India
114 C4 Pathanamthitta Kerala India
116 C2 Pathankot Punjab India
116 D5 Patharia Madh. Prad. India
Pathein Myanmar see Bassein
97 B5 Pathiu Thai.
114 C2 Pathri Mahar. India
97 C4 Pathum Thani Thai.
250 E5 Pati r. Brazil
116 C5 Pati Madh. Prad. India
95 E4 Pati Jawa Tengah Indon.
250 B4 Patía r. Col.
116 D3 Patiala Punjab India
247 □1 Patillas Puerto Rico
252 A2 Pativilca r. Peru
96 A1 Pātkai Bum mts India/Myanmar
111 D4 Patkaklik Xinjiang China
199 F3 Patlangıç Turkey
199 E3 Patmos i. Greece
117 F4 Patna Bihar India
146 D6 Patna East Ayrshire, Scotland U.K.
117 E5 Patnagarh Orissa India
127 F3 Patnos Turkey
174 G4 Pątnów Pol.
259 B7 Pato, Cerro mt. Chile
255 B8 Pato Branco Brazil
114 B2 Patoda Mahar. India
230 C4 Patoka r. IN U.S.A.
131 M4 Patomskoye Nagor'ye mts Rus. Fed.
198 A1 Patos Albania
254 F3 Patos Brazil
255 C9 Patos, Lagoa dos l. Brazil
256 D3 Patos de Minas Brazil
260 D2 Patquía Arg.
198 B2 Patra Greece
Patrae Greece see Patra
Pátrai Greece see Patra
198 B2 Patraïkos Kolpos b. Greece
Patras Greece see Patra
117 F5 Patrasaer W. Bengal India
117 F5 Patratu Bihar India
116 B5 Patri Gujarat India
195 E4 Patri r. Sicilia Italy
81 D4 Patriarch, Mount South I. N.Z.
193 F3 Patrica Italy
84 B4 Patricia, Mount hill N.T. Austr.
259 B8 Patricio Lynch, Isla i. Chile
232 C6 Patrick Springs VA U.S.A.
147 C4 Patrickswell Rep. of Ireland
192 B2 Patrimonio Corse France
149 J4 Patrington East Riding of Yorkshire, England U.K.
256 D3 Patrocínio Brazil
177 K3 Pátroha Hungary
178 C3 Patscherkofel mt. Austria
134 E1 Patsoyoki r. Europe
192 B4 Pattada Sardegna Italy
114 B2 Pattadakal tourist site Karnataka India
114 C4 Pattanapuram Kerala India
97 C6 Pattani Thai.
97 C6 Pattani r. Thai.
97 C4 Pattaya Thai.
233 □I2 Patten ME U.S.A.
234 C2 Pattenburg NJ U.S.A.
169 E3 Pattensen Ger.
149 G3 Patterdale Cumbria, England U.K.
240 G3 Patterson CA U.S.A.
237 F6 Patterson LA U.S.A.
235 E1 Patterson NY U.S.A.
232 D5 Patterson r. WV U.S.A.
222 C1 Patterson, Mount Y.T. Can.
240 H3 Patterson Mountain CA U.S.A.
116 E4 Patti Uttar Prad. India
194 D4 Patti Sicilia Italy
140 N2 Pattijoki Fin.
114 C3 Pattikonda Andhra Prad. India
150 E2 Pattingham Staffordshire, England U.K.
114 C4 Pattukkottai Tamil Nadu India
222 D3 Pattullo, Mount B.C. Can.
254 F3 Patu Brazil
117 G5 Patuakhali Bangl.
223 J4 Patuanak Sask. Can.
242 □I6 Patuca r. Hond.
197 F3 Pătulele Romania
116 D5 Patur Mahar. India
165 C4 Pâturages Belgium
80 E3 Patutu mt. North I. N.Z.
232 E5 Patuxent r. MD U.S.A.
262 S1 Patuxent Range mts Antarctica
177 H4 Páty Hungary
244 D4 Pátzcuaro Mex.
244 D4 Patzcuaro, Laguna de l. Mex.
163 B5 Pau France
Pau airport France see Pyrénées
252 B3 Paucarbamba Peru
252 B2 Paucartambo Peru
Paucartambo r. Peru see Yavero
253 H1 Pau d'Arco r. Brazil
179 G2 Paudorf Austria
117 G4 Pauhunri mt. Sikkim China/India
163 C5 Pauilhac France
162 B3 Pauillac France
252 D1 Pauini Brazil
252 D1 Pauini r. Brazil
251 F5 Pauini r. Brazil
96 A2 Pauk Myanmar
182 C4 Paul Port.
191 I2 Paularo Italy
220 F3 Paulatuk N.W.T. Can.
241 K4 Paulden AZ U.S.A.
237 F5 Paulding MS U.S.A.
232 A4 Paulding OH U.S.A.
161 A3 Paulhac France
161 B4 Paulhac-en-Margeride France
161 B3 Paulhaguet France
161 B5 Paulhan France
256 B4 Paulicéia Brazil
192 A4 Paulilatino Sardegna Italy
170 D3 Paulinenaue Ger.
163 E5 Paulinet France
234 C2 Paulins Kill r. NJ U.S.A.
Paulis Dem. Rep. Congo see Isiro
197 E2 Păuliş Romania
254 G3 Paulista Brazil
254 E4 Paulistana Brazil
236 E3 Paullina IA U.S.A.
254 F4 Paulo Afonso Brazil
256 C4 Paulo de Faria Brazil
215 H2 Paulpietersburg S. Africa
186 D4 Paüls dels Ports Spain
237 D5 Pauls Valley OK U.S.A.
150 E3 Paulton Bath and North East Somerset, England U.K.
158 E5 Paulx France
Paum i. Vanuatu see Paama
Paumotu, Îles is Fr. Polynesia see Tuamotu, Archipel des
197 H2 Păuneşti Romania
96 A3 Paungde Myanmar
116 D5 Pauni Mahar. India
234 C1 Paupack PA U.S.A.
116 D3 Pauri Uttar Prad. India
171 D5 Pausa Ger.
250 D3 Pauto r. Col.
140 L2 Pauträsk Sweden
156 E3 Pauvres France
240 □C8 Pauwela HI U.S.A.
114 C3 Pavagada Karnataka India
257 G2 Pavão Brazil
122 A3 Pāveh Iran
139 L5 Pavelets Rus. Fed.
190 E3 Pavia Italy
190 E3 Pavia prov. Lombardia Italy
184 B2 Pavia Port.
182 B4 Pavia r. Port.
191 I3 Pavia di Udine Italy
187 C5 Pavías Spain
163 C5 Pavie France
232 D3 Pavilion NY U.S.A.
156 A3 Pavilly France
138 C3 Pāvilosta Latvia
134 I4 Pavino Rus. Fed.
138 D4 Pavištyčio kalnas hill Lith.
175 M4 Pavitstsye Belarus
197 G4 Pavlikeni Bulg.
136 E4 Pavlivka Odes'ka Oblast' Ukr.
137 H2 Pavlivka Sums'ka Oblast' Ukr.
136 C2 Pavlivka Volyns'ka Oblast' Ukr.
121 I1 Pavlodar Kazakh.
Pavlodar Oblast admin. div. Kazakh. see Pavlodarskaya Oblast'
Pavlodar Oblysy admin. div. Kazakh. see Pavlodarskaya Oblast'
121 I1 Pavlodarskaya Oblast' admin. div. Kazakh.
220 B4 Pavlof Volcano AK U.S.A.
Pavlograd Ukr. see Pavlohrad
121 H1 Pavlogradka Rus. Fed.
137 H3 Pavlohrad Ukr.
137 H4 Pavlopillya Ukr.
177 L3 Pavlovce nad Uhom Slovakia
121 H2 Pavlovka Akmolinskaya Oblast' Kazakh.
120 E1 Pavlovka Kustanayskaya Oblast' Kazakh.
134 L5 Pavlovka Respublika Bashkortostan Rus. Fed.
120 A1 Pavlovka Ul'yanovskaya Oblast' Rus. Fed.
134 H5 Pavlovo Rus. Fed.
121 J1 Pavlovsk Altayskiy Kray Rus. Fed.
139 H2 Pavlovsk Leningradskaya Oblast' Rus. Fed.
135 H6 Pavlovsk Voronezhskaya Oblast' Rus. Fed.
135 G7 Pavlovskaya Rus. Fed.
120 E1 Pavlovskiy Kazakh.
139 L4 Pavlovskiy Posad Rus. Fed.
137 G3 Pavlysh Ukr.
191 F4 Pavullo nel Frignano Italy
78 □6 Pavuvu i. Solomon Is
116 E4 Pawai Madh. Prad. India
95 E3 Pawan r. Indon.
80 D1 Pawarenga North I. N.Z.
116 E3 Pawayan Uttar Prad. India
235 G1 Pawcatuck CT U.S.A.
171 D3 Päwesin Ger.
237 D4 Pawhuska OK U.S.A.
235 E1 Pawling NY U.S.A.
174 F2 Pawłówek Pol.
174 G6 Pawłowice Pol.
174 E4 Pawłowice Pol.
174 G5 Pawłowiczki Pol.
96 B3 Pawn r. Myanmar
237 D4 Pawnee OK U.S.A.
236 D4 Pawnee r. KS U.S.A.
236 D3 Pawnee City NE U.S.A.
174 G5 Pawonków Pol.
226 E4 Paw Paw MI U.S.A.
232 D5 Paw Paw WV U.S.A.
233 H4 Pawtucket RI U.S.A.
182 C2 Paxaro mt. Spain
234 B2 Paxinos PA U.S.A.
198 B2 Paxoi i. Greece
220 D3 Paxson AK U.S.A.
146 F6 Paxton Scottish Borders, Scotland U.K.
226 C5 Paxton IL U.S.A.
236 C3 Paxton NE U.S.A.
234 B2 Paxtonia PA U.S.A.
234 A2 Paxtonville PA U.S.A.
94 C3 Payakumbuh Sumatera Indon.
114 B3 Payaswani r. India
179 G3 Payerbach Austria
190 B2 Payerne Switz.
238 C2 Payette ID U.S.A.
238 C2 Payette r. ID U.S.A.
134 M1 Pay-Khoy, Khrebet hills Rus. Fed.
184 C3 Paymogo Spain
Payne Que. Can. see Kangirsuk
232 A4 Payne OH U.S.A.
240 G1 Paynes Creek CA U.S.A.
87 C6 Payne's Find W.A. Austr.
83 F4 Paynesville Vic. Austr.
236 E2 Paynesville MN U.S.A.
163 D4 Payrac France
163 E5 Payrin-Augmontel France
261 H3 Paysandú Uru.
261 I3 Paysandú dept Uru.
162 A1 Pays de la Loire admin. reg. France
163 E6 Pays de Sault reg. France
121 F4 Payshanba Uzbek.
241 L4 Payson AZ U.S.A.
260 C5 Payún, Altiplanicie del plat. Arg.
260 C5 Payún, Cerro vol. Arg.
134 N2 Payyer, Gora mt. Rus. Fed.
162 D3 Payzac France
Payzawat Xinjiang China see Jiashi
254 C4 Paz, Rio da r. Brazil
127 F2 Pazar Turkey
126 E3 Pazarcık Turkey
197 G4 Pazardzhik Bulg.
199 E2 Pazarköy Turkey
199 F2 Pazarlar Turkey
199 F2 Pazaryeri Turkey
129 B3 Pazaryolu Turkey
250 D3 Paz de Ariporo Col.
250 C3 Paz de Rio Col.
188 D3 Pazin Croatia
163 E6 Paziols France
182 B1 Pazo de Irixoa Spain
182 B2 Pazos Spain
139 H2 Pchevzha r. Rus. Fed.
175 H6 Pcim Pol.
197 E5 Pčinja r. Macedonia
256 A5 Peabiru Brazil
236 D4 Peabody KS U.S.A.
233 H3 Peabody MA U.S.A.
222 I3 Peace r. Alta/B.C. Can.
231 D7 Peace r. FL U.S.A.
151 G4 Peacehaven East Sussex, England U.K.
223 H3 Peace Point Alta Can.
222 G3 Peace River Alta Can.
232 C6 Peach Creek WV U.S.A.
222 G5 Peachland B.C. Can.
241 K4 Peach Springs AZ U.S.A.
87 D7 Peak Charles hill W.A. Austr.
149 H4 Peak District National Park England U.K.
233 □I1 Peaked Mountain hill ME U.S.A.
83 G3 Peak Hill N.S.W. Austr.
87 C5 Peak Hill W.A. Austr.
240 H4 Peak Mountain CA U.S.A.
85 G4 Peak Range hills Qld Austr.
185 G3 Peal de Becerro Spain
241 M2 Peale, Mount UT U.S.A.
241 M6 Pearce AZ U.S.A.
84 B2 Pearce Point N.T. Austr.
232 C6 Pearisburg VA U.S.A.
226 C1 Pearl Ont. Can.
237 F6 Pearl r. MS U.S.A.
75 H1 Pearl and Hermes Atoll HI U.S.A.
240 □ Pearl City HI U.S.A.
Pearl River r. China see Zhu Jiang
235 D1 Pearl River NY U.S.A.
237 D6 Pearsall TX U.S.A.
231 D6 Pearson GA U.S.A.
226 C3 Pearson WI U.S.A.
82 C3 Pearson Islands S.A. Austr.
215 E5 Pearston S. Africa
221 I2 Peary Channel Nunavut Can.
221 O1 Peary Land reg. Greenland
237 D5 Pease r. TX U.S.A.
150 E3 Peasedown St John Bath and North East Somerset, England U.K.
158 D4 Péaule France
86 C4 Peawah r. W.A. Austr.
224 C2 Peawanuck Ont. Can.
213 H3 Pebane Moz.
250 D5 Pebas Peru
161 B3 Pébrac France
196 E4 Peć Kosovo, Srbija Yugo.
237 D6 Pecan Bayou r. TX U.S.A.
257 F3 Peçanha Brazil
237 E6 Pecan Island LA U.S.A.
256 C6 Peças, Ilha das i. Brazil
226 C4 Pecatonica IL U.S.A.
190 D2 Peccia Switz.
191 F5 Peccioli Italy
177 I4 Pécel Hungary
140 O1 Pecha r. Rus. Fed.
140 O1 Pechenga Rus. Fed.
140 O1 Pechenga r. Rus. Fed.
137 I3 Pechenihy Ukr.
137 I3 Pecheniz'ke Vodoskhovyshche resr Ukr.
139 L4 Pecherniki Rus. Fed.
139 I4 Pechersk Rus. Fed.
185 H4 Pechina Spain
134 L2 Pechora Rus. Fed.
134 K1 Pechora r. Rus. Fed.
Pechora Sea Rus. Fed. see Pechorskoye More
134 K1 Pechorskaya Guba b. Rus. Fed.
134 K1 Pechorskoye More sea Rus. Fed.
138 F3 Pechory Rus. Fed.
196 E2 Pecica Romania
197 I4 Pecineaga Romania
227 F4 Peck MI U.S.A.
234 C1 Pecks Pond PA U.S.A.
176 E1 Pečky Czech Rep.
174 E4 Pęcław Pol.
192 C2 Pecora r. Italy
237 C6 Pecos TX U.S.A.
237 C6 Pecos r. New Mexico/Texas U.S.A.
165 C4 Pecq Belgium
177 H5 Pécs Hungary
177 H5 Pécsvárad Hungary
174 G4 Pęczniew Pol.
193 F1 Pedaso Italy
114 C2 Peddavagu r. India
114 C2 Pedda Vagu r. India
83 F5 Pedder, Lake Tas. Austr.
215 F5 Peddie S. Africa
138 F3 Pededze r. Latvia
250 A4 Pedernales Ecuador
246 E3 Pedernales Haiti
239 F6 Pedernales Mex.
237 D6 Pedernales r. TX U.S.A.
251 F2 Pedernales Venez.
256 C5 Pederneiras Brazil
191 G3 Pederobba Italy
140 M3 Pedersöre Fin.
138 F2 Pedja r. Estonia
257 G1 Pedra Azul Brazil
206 □ Pedra Badejo São Tiago Cape Verde
182 B3 Pedrada mt. Port.
182 C2 Pedrafita do Cebreiro Spain
182 B3 Pedra Furada Port.
183 F3 Pedrajas de San Esteban Spain
187 C5 Pedralba Spain
182 D2 Pedralba de la Pradería Spain
254 C5 Pedra Preta, Serra da mts Brazil
254 B3 Pedras r. Amazonas Brazil
254 D5 Pedras r. Bahia Brazil
250 D2 Pedregal Venez.
187 D6 Pedreguer Spain
256 D4 Pedregulho Brazil
254 D3 Pedreiras Maranhão Brazil
256 D5 Pedreiras São Paulo Brazil
185 F3 Pedrera Spain
186 F3 Pedres hill Spain
242 E3 Pedriceña Mex.
234 C3 Pedricktown NJ U.S.A.
183 G3 Pedro r. Spain
185 F3 Pedro Abad Spain
254 C4 Pedro Afonso Brazil
254 F3 Pedro Avelino Brazil
246 C3 Pedro Bank sea feature Jamaica
256 D6 Pedro Barros Brazil
183 F4 Pedro Bernardo Spain
246 C3 Pedro Cays is Jamaica
185 F2 Pedroche Spain
250 D4 Pedro Chico Col.
252 C5 Pedro de Valdivia Chile
244 D3 Pedro Escobedo Mex.
184 C2 Pedrógão Port.
182 C4 Pedrógão Port.
182 B5 Pedrógão Port.
182 B5 Pedrógão Grande Port.
182 B5 Pedrógão Pequeno Port.
255 B6 Pedro Gomes Brazil
184 E1 Pedro Gómez mt. Spain
250 E4 Pedro II, Ilha reg. Brazil/Venez.
253 G5 Pedro Juan Caballero Para.
257 E3 Pedro Leopoldo Brazil
254 E3 Pedroll Brazil
185 G3 Pedro-Martínez Spain
185 H1 Pedro Muñoz Spain
258 G3 Pedro Osório Brazil
183 G1 Pedrosa Spain
183 F2 Pedrosa del Príncipe Spain
182 E4 Pedrosillo de los Aires Spain
182 B3 Pedroso Port.
183 H2 Pedroso Spain
256 D6 Pedro Toledo Brazil
163 D6 Pédrous, Pic mt. France
182 B2 Pedrouzos Spain

Pedruso, Monte to Phlox
347

192 A4 Pedruso, Monte hill Sardegna Italy
82 E3 Peebinga S.A. Austr.
146 E6 Peebles Scottish Borders, Scotland U.K.
232 B5 Peebles OH U.S.A.
86 B4 Peedamulla W.A. Austr.
231 E5 Pee Dee r. SC U.S.A.
233 G4 Peekskill NY U.S.A.
220 E3 Peel r. Y.T. Can.
148 E3 Peel Isle of Man
81 C5 Peel, Mount South I. N.Z.
87 B7 Peel Inlet W.A. Austr.
170 E2 Peene r. Ger.
170 E1 Peenemünde Ger.
165 E3 Peer Belgium
82 D1 Peera Peera Poolanna Lake salt flat S.A. Austr.
222 H3 Peerless Lake Alta Can.
222 G4 Peers Alta Can.
182 C4 Pega Port.
161 B5 Pégairolles-de-l'Escalette France
81 D5 Pegasus Bay South I. N.Z.
171 D4 Pegau Ger.
179 G3 Peggau Austria
190 D4 Pegli Italy
193 H4 Peglio r. Italy
173 F2 Pegnitz Ger.
173 E2 Pegnitz r. Ger.
184 B1 Pego Port.
187 C6 Pego Spain
184 B2 Pego do Altar, Barragem do resr Port.
184 B2 Pegões Port.
174 E4 Pęgów Pol.
96 B3 Pegu Myanmar
96 A3 Pegu admin. div. Myanmar
187 F5 Peguera Spain
96 A3 Pegu Yoma mts Myanmar
151 I3 Pegwell Bay England U.K.
199 E1 Pehlivanköy Turkey
207 F4 Péhonko Benin
116 D3 Pehowa Haryana India
261 G4 Pehuajó Arg.
109 G4 Peikang Taiwan
158 D4 Peillac France
161 F5 Peille France
146 B4 Peinchorran Highland, Scotland U.K.
169 F3 Peine Ger.
259 B8 Peineta, Cerro mt. Arg.
116 C5 Peint Mahar. India
191 F2 Peio Italy
161 D4 Peipin France
Peipsi järv l. Estonia/Rus. Fed. see Peipus, Lake
138 F2 Peipus, Lake Estonia/Rus. Fed.
161 F5 Peïra-Cava France
198 C3 Peiraias Greece
160 E3 Peisey-Nancroix France
Pei Shan mts China see Bei Shan
171 C4 Peißen Ger.
171 D4 Peißen Ger.
173 F4 Peißenberg Ger.
173 E4 Peiting Ger.
171 F4 Peitz Ger.
254 C5 Peixe Brazil
256 C2 Peixe r. Goiás Brazil
254 C5 Peixe r. Goiás Brazil
256 B4 Peixe r. São Paulo Brazil
256 A2 Peixe, Rio do r. Brazil
257 F5 Peixes r. Brazil
253 F2 Peixes r. Brazil
107 H5 Peixian Jiangsu China
Peixian Jiangsu China see Pizhou
256 D4 Peixoto, Represa resr Brazil
254 B4 Peixoto de Azevedo Brazil
253 G2 Peixoto de Azevedo r. Brazil
164 F1 Peize Neth.
Peje Kosovo, Srbija Yugo. see Peć
197 E3 Pek r. Yugo.
215 F3 Peka Lesotho
95 E4 Pekalongan Jawa Tengah Indon.
94 C2 Pekanbaru Sumatera Indon.
225 H2 Pékans, Rivière aux r. Que. Can.
207 F5 Peki Ghana
226 C5 Pekin IL U.S.A.
Peking Beijing China see Beijing
94 C2 Pelabuhan Kelang Malaysia
259 C7 Pelada, Pampa hills Arg.
187 B5 Pelado mt. Spain
189 D8 Pelagie, Isole is Sicilia Italy
191 G5 Pelago Italy
196 E5 Pelagonija plain Macedonia
183 F4 Pelahustán Spain
95 F3 Pelaihari Kalimantan Selatan Indon.
260 B4 Pelarco Chile
182 B5 Pelariga Port.
182 D4 Pelarrodríguez Spain
198 C2 Pelasgia Greece
Pelasyía Greece see Pelasgia
161 E4 Pelat, Mont mt. France
215 G3 Pelatsoeu mt. Lesotho
78 □6 Pelau i. Solomon Is
174 D2 Pełczyce Pol.
197 F3 Peleaga, Vârful mt. Romania
183 E3 Peleagonzalo Spain
247 □3 Pelée, Montagne vol. Martinique
224 D5 Pelee Island Ont. Can.
224 D5 Pelee Point Ont. Can.
92 □ Peleliu i. Palau
134 J3 Peles Rus. Fed.
176 E2 Pelhřimov Czech Rep.
220 E4 Pelican AK U.S.A.
85 E3 Pelican Creek r. Qld Austr.
226 C3 Pelican Lake WI U.S.A.
223 K4 Pelican Narrows Sask. Can.
185 G3 Peligros Spain
136 D4 Pelinia Moldova
161 D5 Pélissanne France
196 E5 Pelister mt. Macedonia
188 F4 Pelješac pen. Croatia
140 N2 Pelkosenniemi Fin.
214 B3 Pella S. Africa
226 A1 Pelland MN U.S.A.
195 E4 Pellaro Italy
231 C5 Pell City AL U.S.A.
261 F5 Pellegrini Arg.
260 D6 Pellegrini, Lago l. Arg.
190 E4 Pellegrino Parmense Italy
163 C4 Pellegrue France
177 H5 Pellérd Hungary
191 H3 Pellestrina Italy
159 H5 Pellevoisin France
190 C4 Pellice r. Italy
178 B4 Pellizzano Italy
140 M2 Pello Fin.
226 E3 Pellston MI U.S.A.
260 A4 Pelluhue Chile
168 D1 Pellworm i. Ger.
222 B2 Pelly r. Y.T. Can.
221 J3 Pelly Bay Nunavut Can.
222 B2 Pelly Crossing Y.T. Can.
222 C2 Pelly Mountains Y.T. Can.
169 B5 Pelm Ger.
178 D4 Pelmo, Monte mt. Italy
185 E1 Peloche Spain
Peloponnese admin. reg. Greece see Peloponnisos
Peloponnesus admin. reg. Greece see Peloponnisos
198 C3 Peloponnisos admin. reg. Greece
195 D5 Peloritani, Monti mts Sicilia Italy
258 G3 Pelotas Brazil
255 C8 Pelotas, Rio das r. Brazil
197 G4 Pelovo Bulg.
174 G2 Pelplin Pol.
151 F2 Pelsall West Midlands, England U.K.
87 B6 Pelsart Group is W.A. Austr.
170 E2 Pelsin Ger.
128 A4 Pelusium tourist site Egypt
Pelusium, Bay of Egypt see Tîna, Khalîg el
161 C3 Pélussin France
161 E4 Pelvoux France
161 E4 Pelvoux, Massif du mts France
161 E4 Pelvoux, Mont mt. France
177 J4 Pély Hungary
150 C4 Pelynt Cornwall, England U.K.
227 F2 Pemache r. Ont. Can.
95 E4 Pemalang Jawa Tengah Indon.
95 E2 Pemangkat Kalimantan Barat Indon.
94 B2 Pematangsiantar Sumatera Indon.
213 I2 Pemba Moz.
209 E9 Pemba Zambia
211 C6 Pemba Channel Tanz.
211 C6 Pemba Island Tanz.
211 C6 Pemba North admin. reg. Tanz.
211 C6 Pemba South admin. reg. Tanz.
87 B7 Pemberton W.A. Austr.
222 F5 Pemberton B.C. Can.
234 D3 Pemberton NJ U.S.A.
222 H4 Pembina r. Alta Can.
236 D1 Pembina ND U.S.A.
236 D1 Pembina r. ND U.S.A.
226 D3 Pembine WI U.S.A.
150 C3 Pembrey Carmarthenshire, Wales U.K.
150 E2 Pembridge Herefordshire, England U.K.
224 E4 Pembroke Ont. Can.
150 C3 Pembroke Pembrokeshire, Wales U.K.
231 D5 Pembroke GA U.S.A.
233 □J2 Pembroke ME U.S.A.
81 A6 Pembroke, Mount South I. N.Z.
150 C3 Pembroke Dock Pembrokeshire, Wales U.K.
231 D7 Pembroke Pines FL U.S.A.
150 C3 Pembrokeshire admin. div. Wales U.K.
150 B3 Pembrokeshire Coast National Park Wales U.K.
151 H3 Pembury Kent, England U.K.
260 B5 Pemehue, Cordillera de mts Chile
173 G2 Pemfling Ger.
260 A5 Pemuco Chile
114 B2 Pen Mahar. India
96 A2 Pen r. Myanmar
137 H2 Pena r. Rus. Fed.
183 G3 Peña Cabollera mt. Spain
185 G3 Peña Cambrón mt. Spain
183 H2 Peñacerrada Spain
183 F1 Peña Cerredo mt. Spain
186 C2 Peña Collarada mt. Spain
183 E2 Peña Corada mt. Spain
182 B4 Penacova Port.
182 D4 Peña de Francia mt. Spain
183 I2 Peña de Izaga mt. Spain
183 G1 Peña del Aro mt. Spain
186 C2 Peña de Oroel mt. Spain
182 B3 Penafiel Port.
183 F3 Peñafiel Spain
185 E3 Peñaflor Spain
183 F3 Peñaflor de Hornija Spain
187 C4 Peñagolosa mt. Spain
183 H1 Peña Gorbea mt. Spain
183 G1 Penagos Spain
183 F1 Peña Labra, Sierra de mts Spain
183 G4 Peñalara mt. Spain
186 C3 Peñalba Spain
182 D2 Peñalba de Santiago tourist site Spain
183 H4 Peñalén Spain
150 C3 Penally Pembrokeshire, Wales U.K.
185 E2 Peñalsordo Spain
182 C4 Penalva do Castelo Port.
182 C4 Penamacor Port.
Penambo Range mts Sarawak Malaysia see Tama Abu, Banjaran
182 D3 Peña Mira mt. Spain
182 D2 Peña Negra mt. Spain
245 E2 Peña Nevada, Cerro mt. Mex.
Penang state Malaysia see Pinang
256 B4 Penápolis Brazil
183 F1 Peña Prieta mt. Spain
183 E4 Peñaranda de Bracamonte Spain
183 G3 Peñaranda de Duero Spain
234 C2 Pen Argyl PA U.S.A.
83 E3 Penarie N.S.W. Austr.
186 C4 Peñarroya mt. Spain
185 E2 Peñarroya-Pueblonuevo Spain
185 H2 Peñarrubia Spain
150 D3 Penarth Vale of Glamorgan, Wales U.K.
182 E1 Peñas, Cabo de c. Spain
259 B7 Penas, Golfo de g. Chile
183 F1 Peña Santa mt. Spain
185 H2 Peñascosa Spain
185 I2 Peñas de San Pedro Spain
182 D1 Peña Treisa mt. Spain
182 E1 Peña Ubiña mt. Spain
182 E3 Peñausende Spain
184 D2 Peña Utrera hill Spain
150 C2 Penbryn Ceredigion, Wales U.K.
177 I4 Penc Hungary
150 C2 Pencader Carmarthenshire, Wales U.K.
146 F6 Pencaitland East Lothian, Scotland U.K.
116 D5 Pench r. India
Pencheng Jiangxi China see Ruichang
263 F2 Penck, Cape Antarctica
150 D3 Pencoed Bridgend, Wales U.K.
208 C3 Pendé r. C.A.R.
150 □ Pendeen Cornwall, England U.K.
206 B4 Pendembu Sierra Leone
236 D3 Pender NE U.S.A.
86 D3 Pender Bay W.A. Austr.
199 F1 Pendik Turkey
182 C4 Pendilhe Port.
150 C3 Pendine Carmarthenshire, Wales U.K.
149 G4 Pendle Hill hill England U.K.
238 C2 Pendleton OR U.S.A.
222 E4 Pendleton Bay B.C. Can.
94 C3 Pendopo Sumatera Indon.
238 C1 Pend Oreille r. WA U.S.A.
238 C1 Pend Oreille Lake ID U.S.A.
116 E5 Pendra Madh. Prad. India
114 B2 Penduv Mahar. India
Pendzhikent Tajik. see Panjakent
184 C3 Penedo Gordo Port.
182 C4 Penedono Port.
182 B4 Penela Port.
207 F4 Pénessoulou Benin
158 D4 Pénestin France
177 L4 Penészlek Hungary
227 H3 Penetanguishene Ont. Can.
232 D4 Penfield PA U.S.A.
Penfro Pembrokeshire, Wales U.K. see Pembroke
108 C2 Peng'an Sichuan China
114 C2 Penganga r. India
209 E6 Penge Dem. Rep. Congo
109 F4 P'enghu Ch'üntao is Taiwan
P'enghu Liehtao is Taiwan see P'enghu Ch'üntao
226 A2 Pengilly MN U.S.A.
107 I4 Penglai Shandong China
108 B2 Pengshan Sichuan China
108 D2 Pengshui Chongqing China
108 C2 Pengxi Sichuan China
Pengxian Sichuan China see Pengzhou
109 F2 Pengze Jiangxi China
108 B2 Pengzhou Sichuan China
255 C8 Penha Brazil
182 C4 Penha Garcia Port.
213 G3 Penhalonga Zimbabwe
182 B5 Penhascoso Port.
232 D6 Penhook VA U.S.A.
184 A1 Peniche Port.
146 E6 Penicuik Midlothian, Scotland U.K.
171 D5 Penig Ger.
134 F3 Peninga Rus. Fed.
Peninsular Malaysia Malaysia see Malaysia, Semenanjung
146 C6 Peninver Argyll and Bute, Scotland U.K.
187 D4 Peñíscola Spain
149 H4 Penistone South Yorkshire, England U.K.
254 D4 Penitente, Serra do hills Brazil
207 H5 Penja Cameroon
244 D3 Penjamo Mex.
127 G4 Pēnjwīn Iraq
149 G4 Penketh Warrington, England U.K.
150 E2 Penkridge Staffordshire, England U.K.
170 F2 Penkun Ger.
150 E2 Penley Wrexham, Wales U.K.
156 B3 Penly France
158 B4 Penmarch France
158 B4 Penmarch, Pointe de pt France
Penn PA U.S.A. see Penn Hills
193 E2 Penna in Teverina Italy
163 E5 Pennautier France
163 D4 Penne France
193 F2 Penne Italy
163 C4 Penne-d'Agenais France
263 L2 Pennell Coast Antarctica
114 D3 Penner r. India
82 D3 Penneshaw S.A. Austr.
233 □J2 Pennfield N.B. Can.
232 D4 Penn Hills PA U.S.A.
160 F3 Pennine, Alpi mts Italy/Switz.
Pennine Alps mts Italy/Switz. see Pennine, Alpi
149 G3 Pennines hills England U.K.
215 H4 Pennington S. Africa
234 D2 Pennington NJ U.S.A.
232 B6 Pennington Gap VA U.S.A.
193 E1 Pennino, Monte mt. Italy
232 C5 Pennsboro WV U.S.A.
234 C2 Pennsburg PA U.S.A.
234 A2 Penns Creek PA U.S.A.
234 B2 Penns Creek r. PA U.S.A.
234 C3 Penns Grove NJ U.S.A.
234 C3 Pennsville NJ U.S.A.
227 H5 Pennsylvania state U.S.A.
232 E3 Penn Yan NY U.S.A.
146 B5 Pennyghael Argyll and Bute, Scotland U.K.
221 L3 Penny Icecap Nunavut Can.
263 K1 Penny Point Antarctica
234 D3 Penny Pot NJ U.S.A.
139 I3 Peno Rus. Fed.
233 □I2 Penobscot r. ME U.S.A.
82 E4 Penola S.A. Austr.
242 D3 Peñón Blanco Mex.
82 C2 Penong S.A. Austr.
242 □J7 Penonomé Panama
150 C2 Penrhiw-pal Ceredigion, Wales U.K.
81 □2 Penrhyn atoll Cook Is
267 I6 Penrhyn Basin sea feature Pacific Ocean
150 D1 Penrhyn Bay Conwy, Wales U.K.
150 C2 Penrhyndeudraeth Gwynedd, Wales U.K.
83 G3 Penrith N.S.W. Austr.
149 G3 Penrith Cumbria, England U.K.
150 B4 Penryn Cornwall, England U.K.
231 C6 Pensacola FL U.S.A.
262 T1 Pensacola Mountains Antarctica
253 E3 Pensamiento Bol.
122 B2 Pensär Azer.
226 D3 Pensaukee WI U.S.A.
83 E4 Penshurst Vic. Austr.
150 C4 Pensilva Cornwall, England U.K.
128 A2 Pentadaktylos Range mts Cyprus
192 B2 Penta-di-Casinca Corse France
115 D2 Pentakota Andhra Prad. India
86 E2 Pentecost r. W.A. Austr.
78 □5 Pentecost Island Vanuatu
225 H3 Pentecôte r. Que. Can.
Pentecôte, Île i. Vanuatu see Pentecost Island
197 H3 Penteleu, Vârful mt. Romania
222 G5 Penticton B.C. Can.
150 C1 Pentir Gwynedd, Wales U.K.
85 F4 Pentland Qld Austr.
146 E3 Pentland Firth sea chan. Scotland U.K.
146 E6 Pentland Hills Scotland U.K.
173 G3 Pentling Ger.
150 C1 Pentraeth Isle of Anglesey, Wales U.K.
150 D1 Pentrefoelas Conwy, Wales U.K.
226 D4 Pentwater MI U.S.A.
114 C3 Penukonda Andhra Prad. India
158 C3 Penvénan France
96 B3 Penwegon Myanmar
149 G4 Penwortham Lancashire, England U.K.
137 H2 Peny Rus. Fed.
150 D2 Penybont Powys, Wales U.K.
Pen-y-Bont ar Ogwr Bridgend, Wales U.K. see Bridgend
150 D2 Pen-y-bont-fawr Powys, Wales U.K.
150 D3 Pen-y-fai Bridgend, Wales U.K.
150 D2 Penygadair hill Wales U.K.
149 G3 Pen-y-Ghent hill England U.K.
150 C1 Penygroes Gwynedd, Wales U.K.
93 C4 Penyu, Kepulauan is Maluku Indon.
150 D3 Penywaun Rhondda Cynon Taff, Wales U.K.
135 I5 Penza Rus. Fed.
150 □ Penzance Cornwall, England U.K.
Penza Oblast admin. div. Rus. Fed. see Penzenskaya Oblast'
173 F4 Penzberg Ger.
135 I5 Penzenskaya Oblast' admin. div. Rus. Fed.
131 R3 Penzhinskaya Guba b. Rus. Fed.
173 E3 Penzing Ger.
170 E2 Penzlin Ger.
161 E4 Péone France
238 E1 Peoples Creek r. MT U.S.A.
241 K5 Peoria AZ U.S.A.
226 C5 Peoria IL U.S.A.
226 C5 Peoria Heights IL U.S.A.
240 □D9 Pepeekeo HI U.S.A.
206 B4 Pepel Sierra Leone
170 C1 Pepelow Ger.
161 A5 Pépieux France
165 D4 Pepingen Belgium
165 E4 Pepinster Belgium
174 F4 Pępowo Pol.
215 G3 Pepworth S. Africa
196 D5 Përqin Albania
235 D2 Pequannock NJ U.S.A.
182 D2 Peque Spain
234 B3 Pequea PA U.S.A.
234 B3 Pequea Creek r. PA U.S.A.
234 C2 Pequest r. NJ U.S.A.
257 E3 Pequi Brazil
177 G4 Pér Hungary
184 B3 Pêra Port.
198 C2 Perachora Peloponnisos Greece
85 E2 Pera Head hd Qld Austr.
182 C5 Perais Port.
94 C1 Perak r. Malaysia
94 C1 Perak state Malaysia
186 G2 Peralada Spain
183 E5 Peraleda de la Mata Spain
184 E2 Peraleda del Zaucejo Spain
186 B4 Peralejos Spain
186 C4 Perales del Alfambra Spain
182 D4 Perales del Puerto Spain
183 I2 Peralta Spain
186 C3 Peralta de Alcofea Spain
186 D3 Peralta de la Sal Spain
186 C2 Peraltilla Spain
184 C3 Peralva Port.
183 H4 Peralveche Spain
198 D4 Perama Kriti Greece
114 C4 Perambalur Tamil Nadu India
186 E2 Peramola Spain
184 C3 Peramora r. Spain
178 D4 Perarolo di Cadore Italy
225 H3 Percé Que. Can.
159 G3 Perche, Collines du hills France
179 H2 Perchtoldsdorf Austria
86 E4 Percival Lakes salt flat W.A. Austr.
158 E3 Percy France
233 H2 Percy NH U.S.A.
85 G4 Percy Isles Qld Austr.
192 B5 Perdasdefogu Sardegna Italy
192 A5 Perdaxius Sardegna Italy
215 G2 Perdekop S. Africa
254 D4 Perdida r. Brazil
261 H5 Perdido r. Arg.
253 F5 Perdido r. Brazil
186 D2 Perdido, Monte mt. Spain
193 H4 Perdifumo Italy
186 C3 Perdiguera Spain
186 D2 Perdiguère, Pic mt. France/Spain
198 B2 Perdika Greece
234 B2 Perdix PA U.S.A.
256 D3 Perdizes Brazil
257 E4 Perdões Brazil
185 H3 Perea mt. Spain
136 D2 Perebrody Ukr.
136 B3 Perechyn Ukr.
182 D3 Peredo Port.
130 H3 Peregrebnoye Rus. Fed.
177 J5 Peregu Mare Romania
136 C3 Perehins'ke Ukr.
250 C3 Pereira Col.
256 B4 Pereira Barreto Brazil
Pereira de Eça Angola see Ondjiva
184 B3 Pereiras Port.
254 F3 Pereiro Brazil
180 C4 Pereiro Port.
182 C1 Pereiro Spain
182 C2 Pereiro de Aguiar Spain
183 I3 Perejiles r. Spain
139 H2 Perekhoda r. Rus. Fed.
137 G2 Perekopivka Ukr.
137 K2 Pereleshinskiy Rus. Fed.
120 B2 Perelyub Rus. Fed.
226 D4 Pere Marquette r. MI U.S.A.
120 B2 Peremetnoye Kazakh.
137 F2 Peremoha Ukr.
139 K4 Peremyshl' Rus. Fed.
136 C3 Peremyshlyany Ukr.
252 B2 Perené r. Peru
87 C6 Perenjori W.A. Austr.
182 E3 Pereruela Spain
136 E4 Peresecina Moldova
137 H3 Pereshchepyne Ukr.
139 L3 Pereslavl'-Zalesskiy Rus. Fed.
175 M5 Perespa Ukr.
179 H3 Pereszteg Hungary
191 G5 Peretola airport Italy
197 G3 Peretu Romania
137 J3 Pereval's'k Ukr.
137 G2 Perevid r. Ukr.
120 C2 Perevolotskiy Rus. Fed.
134 I5 Perevoz Rus. Fed.
100 E3 Pereyaslavka Rus. Fed.
Pereyaslav-Khmel'nitskiy Ukr. see Pereyaslav-Khmel'nyts'kyy
137 F2 Pereyaslav-Khmel'nyts'kyy Ukr.
261 G3 Pérez Arg.
192 A4 Perfugas Sardegna Italy
179 F2 Perg Austria
261 G3 Pergamino Arg.
191 G5 Pergine Valdarno Italy
191 G2 Pergine Valsugana Italy
191 H5 Pergola Italy
140 N3 Perho Fin.
196 E2 Periam Romania
185 F4 Periana Spain
244 C4 Peribán de Ramos Mex.
225 F3 Péribonca r. Que. Can.
258 D2 Perico Arg.
244 B2 Pericos Nayarit Mex.
242 D3 Pericos Sinaloa Mex.
241 L5 Peridot AZ U.S.A.
197 H2 Perieni Romania
158 E2 Périers France
162 A2 Périgny France
162 C3 Périgueux France
250 C2 Perija, Sierra de mts Venez.
182 E3 Perilla de Castro Spain
177 K3 Perín-Chym Slovakia
94 C1 Peringat Malaysia
197 I3 Periprava Romania
197 H3 Perișoru Romania
198 C2 Peristera i. Greece
198 C2 Peristerio Greece
129 A4 Peri Suyu r. Turkey
259 C7 Perito Moreno Arg.
114 C4 Perivar r. India
198 B2 Perivoli Ionioi Nisoi Greece
198 D4 Perivolia Kriti Greece
177 J4 Perje r. Hungary
234 C2 Perkasie PA U.S.A.
177 H4 Perkáta Hungary
234 C2 Perkiomen Creek r. PA U.S.A.
172 A2 Perl Ger.
242 □J6 Perlas, Laguna de lag. Nic.
242 □J6 Perlas, Punta de pt Nic.
173 G2 Perlbach r. Ger.
170 C2 Perleberg Ger.
175 K3 Perlejewo Pol.
173 H3 Perlesreut Ger.
137 J2 Perlevka Rus. Fed.
94 C1 Perlis state Malaysia
175 J1 Perły Pol.
134 L4 Perm' Rus. Fed.
134 I4 Permas Rus. Fed.
198 B1 Përmet Albania
Perm Oblast admin. div. Rus. Fed. see Permskaya Oblast'
134 L4 Permskaya Oblast' admin. div. Rus. Fed.
188 E3 Permuda i. Croatia
138 F1 Pernå Fin.
Pernambuco Brazil see Recife
254 F4 Pernambuco state Brazil
264 H6 Pernambuco Abyssal Plain sea feature S. Atlantic Ocean
160 C1 Pernand-Vergelesses France
176 C2 Pernarec Czech Rep.
82 D2 Pernatty Lagoon salt flat S.A. Austr.
179 G3 Pernegg an der Mur Austria
114 B3 Pernem Goa India
179 H2 Pernersdorf Austria
184 B1 Pernes Port.
161 D5 Pernes-les-Fontaines France
198 D1 Perni Greece
197 F4 Pernik Bulg.
141 M3 Perniö Fin.
179 G3 Pernitz Austria
Pernov Estonia see Pärnu
190 E3 Pero Italy
184 B2 Peroguarda Port.
161 B5 Pérols France
160 D2 Péron France
87 B5 Peron, Cape W.A. Austr.
87 B7 Peron, Point W.A. Austr.
84 B2 Peron Islands N.T. Austr.
160 D2 Péronnas France
156 C3 Péronne France
87 B5 Peron Peninsula W.A. Austr.
190 C4 Perosa Argentina Italy
245 F4 Perote Mex.
160 D3 Pérouges France
182 C4 Pero Viseu Port.
163 E6 Perpignan France
260 A6 Perquenco Chile
260 B4 Perquilauquén r. Chile
150 B4 Perranporth Cornwall, England U.K.
150 B4 Perranzabuloe Cornwall, England U.K.
160 C2 Perrecy-les-Forges France
Perrégaux Alg. see Mohammadia
160 C2 Perreux France
160 D2 Perrigny France
240 I5 Perris CA U.S.A.
157 F5 Perrogney-les-Fontaines France
154 C2 Perros-Guirec France
226 E2 Perry Ont. Can.
231 D6 Perry FL U.S.A.
231 D5 Perry GA U.S.A.
236 E3 Perry IA U.S.A.
233 □J2 Perry ME U.S.A.
227 E4 Perry MI U.S.A.
237 D4 Perry OK U.S.A.
234 A2 Perry County county PA U.S.A.
234 B3 Perry Hall MD U.S.A.
234 B3 Perryman MD U.S.A.
263 G2 Perrymennyy, Cape Antarctica
232 B4 Perrysburg OH U.S.A.
237 C4 Perryton TX U.S.A.
237 E5 Perryville AR U.S.A.
234 B3 Perryville MD U.S.A.
163 E4 Pers France
156 C3 Persan France
129 C2 P'ersat'i Georgia
179 G2 Persenbeug Austria
122 C4 Persepolis tourist site Iran
253 E3 Perseverancia Bol.
143 G2 Pershagen Sweden
Pershnotravnevoye Ukr. see Pershotravens'k
150 E2 Pershore Worcestershire, England U.K.
137 I3 Pershotravens'k Ukr.
137 I4 Pershotravneve Donets'ka Oblast' Ukr.
136 E2 Pershotravneve Zhytomyrs'ka Oblast' Ukr.
Pershotravnevoye Ukr. see Mokvyn
Persia country Asia see Iran
Persian Gulf Asia see The Gulf
Persis prov. Iran see Färs
143 G3 Persnäs Kalmar Sweden
142 E3 Perstorp Sweden
126 E3 Pertek Turkey
83 F5 Perth Tas. Austr.
87 B6 Perth W.A. Austr.
224 E4 Perth Ont. Can.
146 E5 Perth Perth and Kinross, Scotland U.K.
235 D2 Perth Amboy NJ U.S.A.
146 D5 Perth and Kinross admin. div. Scotland U.K.
225 H4 Perth-Andover N.B. Can.
265 L6 Perth Basin sea feature Indian Ocean
156 E3 Perthes Champagne-Ardenne France
156 C4 Perthes Île-de-France France
141 M3 Pertteli Fin.
161 D5 Pertuis France
162 A2 Pertuis Breton sea chan. France
162 A2 Pertuis d'Antioche sea chan. France
141 N3 Pertunmaa Fin.
186 C2 Pertusa Spain
192 B3 Pertusato, Capo c. Corse France
Peru atoll Gilbert Is Kiribati see Beru
252 B2 Peru country S. America
226 C5 Peru IL U.S.A.
230 C3 Peru IN U.S.A.
233 G2 Peru NY U.S.A.
267 M7 Peru Basin sea feature S. Pacific Ocean
171 E5 Peruc Czech Rep.
267 N6 Peru-Chile Trench sea feature S. Pacific Ocean
193 E1 Perugia Italy
191 H5 Perugia prov. Umbria Italy
258 F3 Perugorría Arg.
256 D6 Peruíbe Brazil
114 C3 Peruru Andhra Prad. India
197 G4 Perushtitsa Bulg.
Perusia Italy see Perugia
165 C4 Péruwelz Belgium
159 G3 Pervenchères France
165 B3 Pervijze Belgium
137 H1 Pervoavgustovskiy Rus. Fed.
136 E4 Pervomaisc Moldova
121 H4 Pervomay Kyrg.
135 H5 Pervomaysk Rus. Fed.
137 J3 Pervomays'k Ukr.
136 F3 Pervomays'k Ukr.
137 G4 Pervomays'ke Ukr.
137 G5 Pervomays'ke Ukr.
121 J2 Pervomayskiy Kazakh.
Pervomayskiy Kyrg. see Pervomay
Pervomayskiy Arkhangel'skaya Oblast' Rus. Fed. see Novodvinsk
120 C2 Pervomayskiy Orenburgskaya Oblast' Rus. Fed.
139 I4 Pervomayskiy Smolenskaya Oblast' Rus. Fed.
139 M5 Pervomayskiy Tambovskaya Oblast' Rus. Fed.
139 K4 Pervomayskiy Tul'skaya Oblast' Rus. Fed.
Pervomayskoye Kyrg. see Pervomay
137 I3 Pervomays'kyy Ukr.
165 D4 Perwez Belgium
139 J2 Pes' Rus. Fed.
139 J2 Pes' r. Rus. Fed.
191 G5 Pesa r. Italy
183 G2 Pesadas de Burgos Spain
95 E3 Pesaguan r. Indon.
191 H5 Pesaro Italy
191 H5 Pesaro e Urbino prov. Marche Italy
240 F3 Pescadero CA U.S.A.
Pescadores is Taiwan see P'enghu Ch'üntao
190 F5 Pescaglia Italy
191 F3 Pescantina Italy
193 G2 Pescara Italy
193 F2 Pescara prov. Abruzzo Italy
193 G2 Pescara r. Italy
197 E3 Pescari Romania
193 F3 Pescasseroli Italy
160 B3 Peschadoires France
135 H7 Peschanokopskoye Rus. Fed.
Peschanoye Rus. Fed. see Yashkul'
193 I3 Peschici Italy
191 F5 Pescia Italy
193 F2 Pescina Italy
193 G3 Pescocostanzo Italy
193 G3 Pescolanciano Italy
193 H4 Pescopagano Italy
193 G3 Pescopennataro Italy
193 F2 Pescorocchiano Italy
193 G3 Pesco Sannita Italy
242 □J8 Pesé Panama
190 B2 Peseux Switz.
134 I2 Pesha r. Rus. Fed.
123 G3 Peshawar Pak.
196 E5 Peshkopi Albania
137 J4 Peshkovo Rus. Fed.
197 G4 Peshtera Bulg.
226 D3 Peshtigo WI U.S.A.
226 D3 Peshtigo r. WI U.S.A.
190 C4 Pesio r. Italy
121 F1 Peski Kazakh.
139 L4 Peski Moskovskaya Oblast' Rus. Fed.
135 H6 Peski Voronezhskaya Oblast' Rus. Fed.
134 K4 Peskovka Rus. Fed.
160 D1 Pesmes France
188 E2 Pesnica Slovenia
139 L2 Pesochnoye Rus. Fed.
182 C3 Peso da Régua Port.
242 □I6 Pespire Hond.
254 F4 Pesqueira Brazil
183 F3 Pesquera de Duero Spain
163 B4 Pessac France
163 C5 Pessan France
164 F2 Pesse Neth.
170 D3 Pessin Ger.
177 I4 Pest county Hungary
139 J2 Pestovo Rus. Fed.
120 B1 Pestravka Rus. Fed.
134 H4 Pestyaki Rus. Fed.
183 F1 Pesués Spain
244 C5 Petacalco, Bahía de b. Mex.
193 G2 Petacciato Italy
128 B3 Petah Tiqwa Israel
141 N3 Petäjävesi Fin.
198 B3 Petalidi Greece
198 D2 Petalioi i. Greece
198 D2 Petalion, Kolpos sea chan. Greece
240 F2 Petaluma CA U.S.A.
165 E5 Pétange Lux.
250 E2 Petare Venez.
198 B2 Petas Greece
244 D5 Petatlán Mex.
211 A8 Petauke Zambia
227 I3 Petawawa Ont. Can.
179 H4 Peteranec Croatia
224 D3 Peterbell Ont. Can.
82 D3 Peterborough S.A. Austr.
83 E4 Peterborough Vic. Austr.
224 E4 Peterborough Ont. Can.
151 G2 Peterborough Peterborough, England U.K.
151 G2 Peterborough admin. div. England U.K.
233 H3 Peterborough NH U.S.A.
146 F4 Peterculter Aberdeen, Scotland U.K.
146 G4 Peterhead Aberdeenshire, Scotland U.K.
177 I4 Péteri Hungary
262 R2 Peter I Island Antarctica
Peter I Øy i. Antarctica see Peter I Island
149 H3 Peterlee Durham, England U.K.
221 P2 Petermann Bjerg nunatak Greenland
84 B5 Petermann Ranges mts N.T. Austr.
260 B4 Peteroa, Volcán vol. Chile
173 E2 Petersaurach Ger.
169 E5 Petersberg Ger.
215 E5 Petersburg S. Africa
220 E4 Petersburg AK U.S.A.
236 F4 Petersburg IL U.S.A.
230 C4 Petersburg IN U.S.A.
234 D3 Petersburg NJ U.S.A.
233 G3 Petersburg NY U.S.A.
232 C4 Petersburg OH U.S.A.
232 E6 Petersburg VA U.S.A.
232 D5 Petersburg WV U.S.A.
173 F3 Petersdorf Ger.
170 C1 Petersdorf auf Fehmarn Ger.
151 G3 Petersfield Hampshire, England U.K.
171 F3 Petershagen Brandenburg Ger.
169 D3 Petershagen Nordrhein-Westfalen Ger.
173 F3 Petershausen Ger.
232 C6 Peterstown WV U.S.A.
220 C3 Petersville AK U.S.A.
147 C3 Peterswell Rep. of Ireland
Pétervárad Vojvodina, Srbija Yugo. see Petrovaradin
177 J3 Pétervására Hungary
Peterwardein Vojvodina, Srbija Yugo. see Petrovaradin
114 B2 Peth Mahar. India
195 F3 Petilia Policastro Italy
186 B2 Petilla de Aragón Spain
182 C2 Petín Spain
Petit Atlas mts Morocco see Anti Atlas
225 H4 Petitcodiac N.B. Can.
159 H2 Petit-Couronne France
162 D2 Petite Creuse r. France
163 B4 Petite Leyre r. France
157 G3 Petite-Rosselle France
159 I4 Petite Sauldre r. France
217 □3b Petite Terre i. Mayotte
246 D3 Petit-Goâve Haiti
Petitjean Morocco see Sidi Kacem
159 E5 Petit Lay r. France
158 E4 Petit Maine r. France
158 E4 Petit-Mars France
Petit Mécatina r. Newfoundland/Québec Can. see Little Mecatina
157 G4 Petitmont France
156 D4 Petit Morin r. France
160 D2 Petit-Noir France
222 F2 Petitot r. Alta/B.C. Can.
161 C5 Petit Rhône r. France
171 E4 Petkus Ger.
116 C5 Petlad Gujarat India
245 F4 Petlalcingo Mex.
116 C5 Petlawad Madh. Prad. India
177 L3 Petneháza Hungary
243 H4 Peto Mex.
177 I4 Petőfibánya Hungary
177 I5 Petőfiszállás Hungary
260 B3 Petorca Chile
226 E3 Petoskey MI U.S.A.
128 B4 Petra tourist site Jordan
187 G5 Petra Spain
195 E4 Petrace r. Italy
194 D5 Petralia-Soprana Sicilia Italy
194 D5 Petralia-Sottana Sicilia Italy
262 P1 Petras, Mount Antarctica
227 I4 Petre, Point Ont. Can.
Petrel Spain see Petrer
193 F3 Petrella, Monte mt. Italy
193 F2 Petrella Salto Italy
193 G3 Petrella Tifernina Italy
187 C6 Petrer Spain
177 L4 Petrești Romania
192 A3 Petreto-Bicchisano Corse France
191 H5 Petriano Italy
197 F5 Petrich Bulg.
188 G3 Petrijevci Croatia
Petrikau Pol. see Piotrków Trybunalski
Petrikov Belarus see Pyetrykaw
197 F3 Petrila Romania
188 F3 Petrinja Croatia
177 L5 Petriș Romania
193 F1 Petritoli Italy
137 H4 Petrivka Khersons'ka Oblast' Ukr.
136 F4 Petrivka Odes'ka Oblast' Ukr.
137 I4 Petrivs'ke Ukr.
137 G3 Petrivtsi Ukr.
258 C3 Petro, Cerro de mt. Chile
Petroaleksandrovsk Uzbek. see Turtkul'
138 G2 Petrodvorets Rus. Fed.
Petrograd Rus. Fed. see Sankt-Peterburg
Petrokov Pol. see Piotrków Trybunalski
Petrokrepost' Rus. Fed. see Shlissel'burg
185 I2 Pétrola Spain
254 F4 Petrolândia Brazil
227 F4 Petrolia Ont. Can.
240 E1 Petrolia CA U.S.A.
254 E4 Petrolina Brazil
256 C2 Petrolina de Goiás Brazil
Petromaryevka Ukr. see Pervomays'k
198 B1 Petron, Limni l. Greece
195 F3 Petronà Italy
Petropavl Kazakh. see Petropavlovsk
137 I3 Petropavlivka Ukr.
121 J3 Petropavlovka Kazakh.
106 E1 Petropavlovka Respublika Buryatiya Rus. Fed.
135 H6 Petropavlovka Voronezhskaya Oblast' Rus. Fed.
121 G1 Petropavlovsk Kazakh.
Petropavlovsk Rus. Fed. see Petropavlovsk-Kamchatskiy
131 Q4 Petropavlovsk-Kamchatskiy Rus. Fed.
121 K1 Petropavlovskoye Rus. Fed.
257 F5 Petrópolis Brazil
197 F3 Petroșani Romania
194 B5 Petrosino Sicilia Italy
176 G3 Petrov Czech Rep.
Petrovac Bos.-Herz. see Bosanski Petrovac
196 E3 Petrovac Srbija Yugo.
177 K3 Petrovany Slovakia
196 D3 Petrovaradin Vojvodina, Srbija Yugo.
137 G3 Petrove Ukr.
176 D2 Petrovice Czech Rep.
121 G1 Petrovka Kazakh.
120 A1 Petrovsk Rus. Fed.
135 G7 Petrovskaya Rus. Fed.
137 J3 Petrovs'ke Ukr.
139 M3 Petrovskiy Rus. Fed.
Petrovskoye Stavropol'skiy Kray Rus. Fed. see Svetlograd
139 M5 Petrovskoye Tambovskaya Oblast' Rus. Fed.
139 L3 Petrovskoye Yaroslavskaya Oblast' Rus. Fed.
107 F1 Petrovsk-Zabaykal'skiy Rus. Fed.
135 I6 Petrov Val Rus. Fed.
134 F3 Petrozavodsk Rus. Fed.
197 G2 Petru Rareș Romania
215 E3 Petrusburg S. Africa
136 D4 Petrușeni Moldova
215 G2 Petrus Steyn S. Africa
214 E4 Petrusville S. Africa
177 H2 Petřvald Czech Rep.
137 H3 Petrykivka Ukr.
Petsamo Rus. Fed. see Pechenga
215 G2 Petsana S. Africa
Pettau Slovenia see Ptuj
164 D2 Petten Neth.
173 G2 Pettendorf Ger.
147 D2 Pettigo Northern Ireland U.K.
195 F3 Pettinascura, Monte mt. Italy
194 D5 Pettineo Sicilia Italy
173 G4 Petting Ger.
178 B3 Pettneu am Arlberg Austria
193 F3 Pettorano sul Gizio Italy
191 G2 Pettorina r. Italy
130 H4 Petukhovo Rus. Fed.
139 L4 Petushki Rus. Fed.
151 G4 Petworth West Sussex, England U.K.
178 D4 Petzeck mt. Austria
179 E2 Peuerbach Austria
94 B1 Peuetsagu, Gunung vol. Indon.
162 B3 Peujard France
260 B4 Peumo Chile
94 B1 Peureula Sumatera Indon.
131 S3 Pevek Rus. Fed.
151 H4 Pevensey East Sussex, England U.K.
190 C4 Peveragno Italy
151 F3 Pewsey Wiltshire, England U.K.
151 F3 Pewsey, Vale of val. England U.K.
168 C2 Pewsum (Krummhörn) Ger.
157 G4 Pexonne France
161 E5 Peymeinade France
161 B5 Peyne r. France
161 D5 Peynier France
161 D5 Peypin France
162 D3 Peyrat-le-Château France
163 A5 Peyrehorade France
161 B4 Peyreleau France
162 E3 Peyrelevade France
190 C5 Peyrevieille, Mont mt. Italy
161 A5 Peyriac-de-Mer France
163 E5 Peyriac-Minervois France
160 D3 Peyrieu France
161 D3 Peyrins France
161 D5 Peyrolles-en-Provence France
161 D4 Peyruis France
163 C5 Peyrusse-Grande France
163 E4 Peyrusse-le-Roc France
134 I2 Peza r. Rus. Fed.
161 B5 Pézenas France
174 D2 Pęzino Pol.
176 G3 Pezinok Slovakia
163 C4 Pezuls France
173 G3 Pfaffenberg Ger.
171 F3 Pfaffendorf Ger.
173 E3 Pfaffenhausen Ger.
173 F3 Pfaffenhofen an der Ilm Ger.
173 E3 Pfaffenhofen an der Roth Ger.
157 H4 Pfaffenhoffen France
172 B4 Pfaffenweiler Ger.
190 D1 Pfäffikon Schwyz Switz.
190 D1 Pfäffikon Zürich Switz.
173 G3 Pfaffing Ger.
172 B2 Pfälzer Wald hills Ger.
169 C5 Pfalzfeld Ger.
172 C3 Pfalzgrafenweiler Ger.
173 G3 Pfarrkirchen Ger.
169 F5 Pfarrweisach Ger.
178 E3 Pfarrwerfen Austria
173 G3 Pfatter Ger.
172 D2 Pfedelbach Ger.
173 F3 Pfeffenhausen Ger.
178 B3 Pflach Austria
178 C3 Pfons Austria
173 F3 Pförring Ger.
173 E4 Pforzen Ger.
172 C3 Pforzheim Ger.
173 G2 Pfreimd Ger.
173 G2 Pfreimd r. Ger.
172 D3 Pfronstetten Ger.
173 E4 Pfronten Ger.
172 D4 Pfullendorf Ger.
172 D3 Pfullingen Ger.
178 B4 Pfunds Austria
172 C2 Pfungstadt Ger.
190 D1 Pfyn Switz.
116 C3 Phagwara Punjab India
215 F3 Phahameng Free State S. Africa
213 F5 Phahameng Northern S. Africa
213 F4 Phalaborwa S. Africa
123 H3 Phalia Pak.
116 C4 Phalodi Rajasthan India
157 H4 Phalsbourg France
116 B4 Phalsund Rajasthan India
114 B2 Phaltan Mahar. India
117 G4 Phalut Peak India/Nepal
97 C5 Phangan, Ko i. Thai.
97 B5 Phangnga Thai.
97 E5 Phan Rang Vietnam
97 E5 Phan Ri Vietnam
97 E5 Phan Thiêt Vietnam
116 D4 Phaphund Uttar Prad. India
148 C2 Pharis Northern Ireland U.K.
96 D2 Phat Diêm Vietnam
97 C6 Phatthalung Thai.
96 B3 Phayao Thai.
117 H4 Phek Nagaland India
84 C2 Phelp r. N.T. Austr.
232 E3 Phelps NY U.S.A.
226 C2 Phelps WI U.S.A.
96 C3 Phen Thai.
232 D6 Phenix VA U.S.A.
231 C5 Phenix City AL U.S.A.
97 B4 Phet Buri Thai.
96 C3 Phetchabun Thai.
96 C3 Phichit Thai.
Philadelphia Jordan see 'Ammān
214 B5 Philadelphia S. Africa
Philadelphia Turkey see Alaşehir
237 F5 Philadelphia MS U.S.A.
233 F2 Philadelphia NY U.S.A.
234 C3 Philadelphia PA U.S.A.
234 C3 Philadelphia County county PA U.S.A.
203 G4 Philae tourist site Egypt
Philip atoll Arch. des Tuamotu Fr. Polynesia see Makemo
236 C2 Philip SD U.S.A.
Philip Atoll Micronesia see Sorol
Philippeville Alg. see Skikda
165 D4 Philippeville Belgium
232 C5 Philippi WV U.S.A.
84 D5 Philippi, Lake salt flat Qld Austr.
165 C3 Philippine Neth.
266 D4 Philippine Basin sea feature N. Pacific Ocean
92 B3 Philippines country Asia
90 F3 Philippine Sea N. Pacific Ocean
266 D4 Philippine Trench sea feature N. Pacific Ocean
215 E4 Philippolis S. Africa
215 E4 Philippolis Road S. Africa
Philippopolis Bulg. see Plovdiv
172 C2 Philippsburg Ger.
173 H3 Philippsreut Ger.
169 F5 Philippsthal (Werra) Ger.
247 G3 Philipsburg St Maarten Neth. Antilles
238 D2 Philipsburg MT U.S.A.
232 D4 Philipsburg PA U.S.A.
164 D3 Philipsdam barrage Neth.
220 D3 Philip Smith Mountains AK U.S.A.
214 E4 Philipstown S. Africa
83 F4 Phillip Island Vic. Austr.
87 D7 Phillips r. W.A. Austr.
233 □H2 Phillips ME U.S.A.
226 B3 Phillips WI U.S.A.
222 E5 Phillips Arm B.C. Can.
236 D4 Phillipsburg KS U.S.A.
234 C2 Phillipsburg NJ U.S.A.
82 C2 Phillipson, Lake salt flat S.A. Austr.
86 E3 Phillips Range hills W.A. Austr.
232 D4 Phillipston PA U.S.A.
233 G3 Philmont NY U.S.A.
Philomelium Turkey see Akşehir
96 D4 Phimun Mangsahan Thai.
215 F2 Phiritona S. Africa
96 C3 Phitsanulok Thai.
226 C3 Phlox WI U.S.A.

222 E5 Port McNeill B.C. Can.
225 H3 Port-Menier C. Can.
246 □ Port Morant Jamaica
246 □ Portmore Jamaica
91 K8 Port Moresby P.N.G.
158 B3 Port-Mort France
147 F2 Portmuck Northern Ireland U.K.
85 E1 Port Musgrave b. Qld Austr.
146 C5 Portnacroish Argyll and Bute, Scotland U.K.
146 B3 Portnaguran Western Isles, Scotland U.K.
146 B6 Portnahaven Argyll and Bute, Scotland U.K.
146 B4 Portnalong Highland, Scotland U.K.
Port nan Giùran Western Isles, Scotland U.K. see Portnaguran
146 A4 Port nan Long Western Isles, Scotland U.K.
158 A4 Port-Navalo France
237 D6 Port Neches TX U.S.A.
82 D3 Port Neill S.A. Austr.
246 D2 Port Nelson Rum Cay Bahamas
225 G3 Portneuf r. Que. Can.
238 D3 Portneuf r. ID U.S.A.
146 B3 Port Nis Western Isles, Scotland U.K.
82 D3 Port Noarlunga S.A. Austr.
214 A3 Port Nolloth S. Africa
147 C2 Portnoo Rep. of Ireland
147 C4 Port Norris NJ U.S.A.
Port-Nouveau-Québec Que. Can. see Kangiqsualujjuaq
254 E2 Porto Brazil
192 A2 Porto Corse France
182 B3 Porto Port.
182 B3 Porto admin. dist. Port.
182 D2 Porto Spain
255 C9 Porto Alegre Brazil
Porto Alexandre Angola see Tombua
184 B2 Porto Alto Port.
209 B7 Porto Amboim Angola
Porto Amélia Moz. see Pemba
192 C2 Porto Azzurro Italy
81 C6 Portobello South I. N.Z.
255 C8 Porto Belo Brazil
192 A5 Porto Botte Sardegna Italy
254 D4 Porto Cavo Brazil
192 B3 Porto Cervo Sardegna Italy
195 G2 Porto Cesareo Italy
187 G5 Porto Colom Spain
184 □ Porto Covo da Bandeira Port.
187 G5 Porto Cristo Spain
184 □ Porto da Cruz Madeira
254 F4 Porto da Fôlha Brazil
182 B5 Porto de Mós Port.
251 H5 Porto de Moz Brazil
182 C1 Porto de Barqueiro Spain
253 F2 Porto dos Gaúchos Óbidos Brazil
182 A2 Porto do Son Spain
194 C5 Porto Empedocle Sicilia Italy
192 D2 Porto Ercole Italy
253 F3 Porto Esperidião Brazil
256 D5 Porto Feliz Brazil
192 C2 Portoferraio Italy
256 D4 Porto Ferreira Brazil
190 E4 Portofino Italy
257 F4 Porto Firme Brazil
146 D5 Port of Menteith Stirling, Scotland U.K.
254 D3 Porto Franco Brazil
247 □7 Port of Spain Trin. and Tob.
191 H4 Porto Garibaldi Italy
182 C1 Portogruaro Italy
206 □ Porto Inglês Cape Verde
216 □1a Porto Judeu Terceira Azores
240 G2 Portola CA U.S.A.
194 D4 Porto Levante Isole Lipari Italy
190 E4 Porto Levante Veneto Italy
255 B8 Porto Lucena Brazil
191 G4 Portomaggiore Italy
182 C2 Portomarín Spain
184 □ Porto Moniz Madeira
253 F5 Porto Murtinho Brazil
254 E2 Porto Nacional Brazil
207 F5 Porto-Novo Benin
206 □ Porto Novo Cape Verde
Porto Novo Tamil Nadu India see Parangipettai
194 B5 Porto Palo Sicilia Italy
189 E7 Portopalo di Capo Passero Italy
192 A4 Porto Pino Sardegna Italy
256 A4 Porto Primavera, Represa resr Brazil
231 D6 Port Orange FL U.S.A.
238 B2 Port Orchard WA U.S.A.
191 I5 Porto Recanati Italy
238 A3 Port Orford OR U.S.A.
209 B6 Porto Rico Angola
192 B3 Porto Rotondo Sardegna Italy
191 I3 Portorož Slovenia
191 I5 Porto San Giorgio Italy
192 B4 Porto San Paolo Sardegna Italy
251 I5 Porto Santana Brazil
191 I5 Porto Sant'Elpidio Italy
184 □ Porto Santo Madeira
192 D2 Porto Santo Stefano Italy
192 A5 Portoscuso Sardegna Italy
257 H2 Porto Seguro Brazil
191 I5 Porto Tolle Italy
192 A4 Porto Torres Sardegna Italy
255 C8 Porto União Brazil
192 A6 Porto-Vecchio Corse France
252 E2 Porto Velho Brazil
190 E4 Portovenere Italy
250 A5 Portoviejo Ecuador
146 C7 Portpatrick Dumfries and Galloway, Scotland U.K.
234 C3 Port Penn DE U.S.A.
227 H3 Port Perry Ont. Can.
83 F4 Port Phillip Bay Vic. Austr.
82 D3 Port Pirie S.A. Austr.
Port Radium N.W.T. Can. see Echo Bay
147 C2 Portrane Rep. of Ireland
150 B4 Portreath Cornwall, England U.K.
146 B4 Portree Highland, Scotland U.K.
222 E5 Port Renfrew B.C. Can.
225 K3 Port Rexton Nfld. Can.
147 C4 Portroe Rep. of Ireland
84 C2 Port Roper r. N.T. Austr.
227 G4 Port Rowan Ont. Can.
246 □ Port Royal Jamaica
232 E2 Port Royal VA U.S.A.
147 E1 Portrush Northern Ireland U.K.
Port Said Egypt see Bûr Sa'îd
163 C4 Port-Ste-Marie France
231 C6 Port St Joe FL U.S.A.
215 G4 Port St Johns S. Africa
161 C5 Port-St-Louis-du-Rhône France
231 D7 Port Saint Lucie City FL U.S.A.
148 B3 Port St Mary Isle of Man
158 E4 Port-St-Père France
182 B5 Portsall France
147 D1 Portsalon Rep. of Ireland
179 F4 Pörtschach am Wörther See Austria
186 D4 Ports de Beseit mts Spain
227 H3 Port Severn Ont. Can.
215 H4 Port Shepstone S. Africa
Port Simpson B.C. Can. see Lax Kw'alaams
247 □ Portsmouth Dominica
151 F4 Portsmouth Portsmouth, England U.K.
151 F4 Portsmouth admin. div. England U.K.
233 □H3 Portsmouth NH U.S.A.
232 B5 Portsmouth OH U.S.A.
233 E6 Portsmouth VA U.S.A.
146 F4 Portsoy Aberdeenshire, Scotland U.K.
83 J3 Port Stephens b. N.S.W. Austr.
147 E1 Portstewart Northern Ireland U.K.
203 H5 Port Sudan Sudan

237 F6 Port Sulphur LA U.S.A.
157 G5 Port-sur-Saône France
Port Swettenham Malaysia see Pelabuhan Kelang
150 D3 Port Talbot Neath Port Talbot, Wales U.K.
238 B3 Port Townsend WA U.S.A.
234 B2 Port Trevorton PA U.S.A.
172 D2 Portugal country Europe
183 G1 Portugalete Spain
Portuguese Angola see Chitato
250 D2 Portuguesa state Venez.
Portuguese East Africa country Africa see Mozambique
Portuguese Guinea country Africa see Guinea-Bissau
Portuguese Timor terr. Asia see East Timor
Portuguese West Africa country Africa see Angola
147 C3 Portumna Rep. of Ireland
Portus Herculis Monoeci country Europe see Monaco
182 B3 Port-Vendres France
163 F6 Port-Vendres France
82 D3 Port Victoria S.A. Austr.
78 □1 Port Vila Vanuatu
82 D3 Port Vincent S.A. Austr.
140 P1 Port Vladimir Rus. Fed.
80 E2 Port Waikato North I. N.Z.
82 D3 Port Wakefield S.A. Austr.
86 E2 Port Warrender W.A. Austr.
235 E2 Port Washington NY U.S.A.
226 D4 Port Washington WI U.S.A.
146 D7 Port William Dumfries and Galloway, Scotland U.K.
226 B2 Port Wing WI U.S.A.
114 C3 Porumamilla Andhra Prad. India
246 □ Porus Jamaica
139 H3 Porus'ya r. Rus. Fed.
252 C2 Porvenir Pando Bol.
253 E3 Porvenir Santa Cruz Bol.
259 C9 Porvenir Chile
141 N3 Porvoo Fin.
138 E1 Porvoonjoki r. Fin.
101 C5 Poryŏng S. Korea
175 J3 Porządzie Pol.
185 F1 Porzuna Spain
192 B4 Posada Sardegna Italy
182 E1 Posada de Llanera Spain
183 F1 Posada de Valdeón Spain
182 D1 Posadas Spain
185 E3 Posadas Spain
137 G4 Posad-Pokrovs'ke Ukr.
190 F2 Poschiavo Switz.
Poseidonia tourist site Italy see Paestum
Posen Pol. see Poznań
227 F3 Posen MI U.S.A.
170 E1 Posești Rom.
186 D2 Posets mt. Spain
134 G4 Poshekhon'ye Rus. Fed.
Poshekhon'ye-Volodarsk Rus. Fed. see Poshekhon'ye
122 D4 Poshteh-ye Chaqvir hill Iran
122 B2 Posht Kūh mts Iran
122 B2 Posht Kūh hill Iran
137 G5 Poshtove Ukr.
178 C5 Posina r. Italy
173 G2 Pösing Ger.
140 Q2 Posio Fin.
193 G4 Positano Italy
Poskam Xinjiang China see Zepu
235 F1 Posnet CT U.S.A.
93 B3 Poso Sulawesi Tengah Indon.
93 B3 Poso r. Indon.
127 F2 Posof Turkey
250 A5 Posorja Ecuador
123 J1 Pospelikha Rus. Fed.
254 D5 Posse Brazil
171 E5 Possesse France
157 E4 Possession France
263 L2 Possession Islands Antarctica
175 J4 Pößneck Ger.
237 G5 Post TX U.S.A.
114 C2 Postavy Belarus see Pastavy
173 F2 Postbauer-Heng Ger.
215 E5 Poste-de-la-Baleine Que. Can. see Kuujjuarapik
165 F3 Posterholt Neth.
214 D3 Postmasburg S. Africa
178 E3 Postojna Slovenia
178 E3 Postojnska Jama Slovenia
175 J3 Postoliska Pol.
176 C1 Postoloprty Czech Rep.
174 C3 Postomia r. Pol.
179 H7 Postomino Pol.
225 J2 Postville Nfld. Can.
226 B4 Postville IA U.S.A.
137 F2 Postysheve Ukr. see Krasnoarmiys'k
188 F4 Posušje Bos.-Herz.
93 C5 Poŝwiętne Bos.-Herz.
192 A2 Poŝwiętne Pol.
175 J3 Poŝwiętne Pol.
141 M3 Pöytyä Fin.
183 D2 Poza de la Sal Spain
185 F3 Pozaldez Spain
196 H3 Požarevac Srbija Yugo.
245 I3 Poza Rica Mex.
177 K3 Požárovce Slovakia
188 F3 Požega Croatia
196 I4 Požega Srbija Yugo.
175 I1 Pozezdrze Pol.
135 H6 Pozhva Rus. Fed.
134 L4 Pozhva Rus. Fed.
177 G2 Pozlovice Czech Rep.
174 E3 Poznań Pol.
184 C4 Pozo Alcón Spain
183 E3 Pozoamargo Spain
182 D4 Pozo Cañada Spain
253 D5 Pozo Colorado Para.
185 F3 Pozo de Guadalajara Spain
258 E2 Pozo del Tigre Arg.
183 F3 Pozohondo Spain
184 C4 Pozo-Lorente Spain
185 E3 Pozondón Spain
185 G3 Pozuelo Spain
183 G3 Pozuelo de Alarcón Spain
186 D3 Pozuelo de Aragón Spain
182 E3 Pozuelo del Páramo Spain
185 E2 Pozuelo del Rey Spain
184 A2 Pozuelo de Calatrava Spain
185 F3 Pozuzo Peru
184 □ Pozza di Fasso Italy
194 D6 Pozzallo Sicilia Italy
191 F4 Pozzo Formigaro Italy
192 A4 Pozzomaggiore Sardegna Italy
92 B4 Pototan Phil.
252 C5 Poteirilos Chile
158 E3 Potrerillos Hond.
245 F3 Potrero del Llano Mex.
250 B6 Potro r. Peru
171 E3 Potsdam Ger.
233 F3 Potsdam NY U.S.A.
172 F2 Potsdam admin. div. Ger.
77 G1 Pott, Île r. New Caledonia
115 C2 Potti Czech Rep.
172 E1 Pottenstein Ger.
177 I3 Potterne Wiltshire, England U.K.
151 F2 Potters Bar Hertfordshire, England U.K.
240 F2 Potter Valley CA U.S.A.
232 A3 Potterville MI U.S.A.
250 B4 Pottman Col.

151 G2 Potton Bedfordshire, England U.K.
179 H3 Pöttsching Austria
234 B1 Potts Grove PA U.S.A.
234 C2 Pottstown PA U.S.A.
234 B2 Pottsville PA U.S.A.
137 J2 Potukhiv r. Rus. Fed.
175 I4 Potworów Pol.
158 E4 Pouancé France
222 F4 Pouce Coupe B.C. Can.
225 H4 Pouch Cove Nfld. Can.
233 G4 Poughkeepsie NY U.S.A.
235 E1 Poughquag NY U.S.A.
160 D1 Pougny France
160 D1 Pougues-les-Eaux France
160 D1 Pougy France
160 D1 Pouilly France
163 B5 Pouilly-en-Auxois France
160 C2 Pouilly-les-Nonains France
160 A1 Pouilly-sous-Charlieu France
160 A1 Pouilly-sur-Loire France
160 C2 Pouilly-sur-Saône France
159 H4 Poulaines France
158 B4 Pouldreuzic France
160 C2 Poule-les-Écharmeaux France
147 B5 Poulgorm Bridge Rep. of Ireland
159 H5 Pouligny-St-Pierre France
158 C3 Poullaouen France
147 D4 Poulnamucky Rep. of Ireland
233 G3 Poultney VT U.S.A.
149 G4 Poulton-le-Fylde Lancashire, England U.K.
207 H6 Pouma Cameroon
232 B6 Pound VA U.S.A.
214 E4 Poupan S. Africa
163 C5 Poupas France
161 D2 Poupet, Mont hill France
161 D5 Pourcieux France
80 F4 Pourerere North I. N.Z.
156 D5 Pourrain France
182 C4 Pourri, Mont mt. France
156 D5 Pourrières France
182 C4 Pousada Bol.
257 E5 Pouso Alegre Brazil
182 B5 Poussan France
161 B5 Poussan France
97 C4 Poŭthĭsăt Cambodia
80 C2 Pouto North I. N.Z.
157 G4 Pouxeux France
163 C5 Pouyastruc France
163 D5 Pouydesseaux France
163 D5 Pouy-de-Touges France
159 G4 Pouzauges France
159 G4 Pouzay France
139 K3 Povarovo Rus. Fed.
177 G3 Považská Bystrica Slovakia
177 G3 Považský Inovec mts Slovakia
139 J3 Poved' r. Rus. Fed.
185 H2 Povedilla Spain
185 H2 Povenets Rus. Fed.
80 F3 Poverty Bay North I. N.Z.
196 D3 Povlen mt. Yugo.
216 □1b Povoação São Miguel Azores
182 B3 Póvoa de Lanhoso Port.
182 B3 Póvoa de São Miguel Port.
184 C4 Póvoa de Varzim Port.
182 B3 Póvoa do Concelho Port.
191 I2 Povoletto Italy
135 H6 Povorino Rus. Fed.
136 C2 Povors'k Ukr.
171 F5 Povrly Czech Rep.
240 I5 Poway CA U.S.A.
149 D5 Powburn Northumberland, England U.K.
238 E2 Powder r. MT U.S.A.
238 C2 Powder r. OR U.S.A.
238 F3 Powder, South Fork r. WY U.S.A.
238 F3 Powder River WY U.S.A.
234 B1 Powell PA U.S.A.
238 E2 Powell WY U.S.A.
232 B6 Powell r. TN/VA U.S.A.
241 L3 Powell, Lake resr UT U.S.A.
197 F2 Powell Mountain WV U.S.A.
222 E5 Powell River B.C. Can.
226 D3 Powers MI U.S.A.
147 C3 Power's Cross Rep. of Ireland
237 F4 Powhatan AR U.S.A.
232 E1 Powhatan VA U.S.A.
237 C5 Powhatan Point OH U.S.A.
150 E2 Powick Worcestershire, England U.K.
174 F3 Powidz Pol.
146 F5 Powmill Perth and Kinross, Scotland U.K.
108 A1 Powŏn China
150 D2 Powys admin. div. Wales U.K.
255 B5 Poxoréu Brazil
78 □2 Poya New Caledonia
183 E3 Poyales del Hoyo Spain
109 F2 Poyang Jiangxi China see Boyang
109 F2 Poyang Hu l. China
100 D2 Poyarkovo Rus. Fed.
139 I4 Poyarkovo Rus. Fed.
131 I4 Poynton Cheshire, England U.K.
147 E2 Poyntz Pass Northern Ireland U.K.
185 H3 Poyo, Cerro mt. Spain
199 I2 Poyrazcik Izmir Turkey
179 H2 Poysdorf Austria
183 B3 Poza de la Sal Spain
183 E3 Poza de la Vega Spain
196 H3 Požarovac Srbija Yugo.
126 D2 Pozanti Turkey
177 K3 Pozba Slovakia
257 G2 Poté Brazil
237 E5 Poteau OK U.S.A.
114 C2 Potegaon Mahar. India
193 H4 Potenza Italy
193 H4 Potenza r. Italy
191 I5 Potenza Italy
193 H4 Potenza prov. Basilicata Italy
191 I5 Potenza Picena Italy
183 F1 Potes Spain

163 E6 Prades Languedoc-Roussillon France
163 D6 Prades Midi-Pyrénées France
161 A4 Prades-d'Aubrac France
163 D4 Pradilla Spain
257 H2 Prado Brazil
182 B3 Prado Port.
183 D2 Prado de la Guzpeña Spain
184 E4 Prado del Rey Spain
182 B4 Prado Port.
142 E4 Præsto Denmark
190 B3 Pragelato Italy
179 G4 Pragersko Slovenia
178 D3 Prägraten Austria
Prague Czech Rep. see Praha
176 D1 Praha Czech Rep.
176 D1 Praha admin. reg. Czech Rep.
176 D1 Praha hill Czech Rep.
170 E2 Prahova r. Rom.
197 H3 Prahova r. Rom.
216 □1a Praia Graciosa Azores
206 □ Praia São Tiago Cape Verde
184 H5 Praia a Mare Italy
184 B3 Praia da Barra Port.
184 B3 Praia da Rocha Port.
182 B4 Praia da Tocha Port.
182 B4 Praia de Esmoriz Port.
182 B4 Praia do Almoxarife Faial Azores
256 D6 Praia Grande Brazil
194 D2 Praiano Italy
184 B2 Praia do Sado Port.
216 □1a Prainha Pico Azores
85 H5 Prainha Qld Austr.
251 H5 Prainha Brazil
238 C2 Prairie City OR U.S.A.
162 C2 Prairie du Chien WI U.S.A.
237 C5 Prairie Dog Town Fork r. TX U.S.A.
226 B4 Prairie du Chien WI U.S.A.
223 K4 Prairie River Sask. Can.
97 C4 Prakhon Chai Thai.
177 J3 Prakovce Slovakia
161 E4 Pralognan-la-Vanoise France
179 F2 Pram r. Austria
179 F2 Pram r. Austria
198 B2 Pramanta Greece
179 F2 Prambachkirchen Austria
207 F5 Prampram Ghana
97 C4 Pran r. Thai.
97 C4 Prang Ghana
206 E5 Prang Ghana
176 C2 Přeštice Czech Rep.
150 E4 Preston Dorset, England U.K.
149 F4 Preston Lancashire, England U.K.
149 F4 Preston East Riding of Yorkshire, England U.K.
146 F6 Preston Scottish Borders, Scotland U.K.
231 C5 Preston GA U.S.A.
238 E3 Preston ID U.S.A.
233 F5 Preston MD U.S.A.
226 A4 Preston MN U.S.A.
236 E4 Preston MO U.S.A.
86 C3 Preston, Cape W.A. Austr.
149 F5 Prestonpans East Lothian, Scotland U.K.
232 B6 Prestonsburg KY U.S.A.
149 F5 Prestwich Greater Manchester, England U.K.
146 E5 Prestwick South Ayrshire, Scotland U.K.
150 D4 Princetown Devon, England U.K.

237 E5 Prescott AR U.S.A.
241 K4 Prescott AZ U.S.A.
226 A3 Prescott WI U.S.A.
241 K4 Prescott Valley AZ U.S.A.
150 C3 Preseli, Mynydd hills Wales U.K.
197 E4 Preševo Srbija Yugo.
236 D3 Presho SD U.S.A.
183 D2 Presicce Italy
258 F2 Presidencia Roca Arg.
258 F2 Presidencia Roque Sáenz Peña Arg.
256 C5 Presidente Alves Brazil
256 B5 Presidente Bernardes Brazil
258 F2 Presidente de la Plaza Arg.
258 D3 Presidente Dutra Brazil
262 U2 Presidente Eduardo Frei research stn Antarctica
256 A4 Presidente Epitácio Brazil
Presidente Juan Perón prov. Arg. see Chaco
257 D3 Presidente Juscelino Brazil
257 D3 Presidente Olegário Brazil
256 B4 Presidente Prudente Brazil
256 B4 Presidente Venceslau Brazil
244 A2 Presidio r. Mex.
237 B6 Presidio TX U.S.A.
97 A4 Presidio TX U.S.A.
Preslav Bulg. see Veliki Preslav
121 F2 Presnovka Kazakh.
177 K3 Prešov Slovakia
177 K3 Prešovský Kraj admin. reg. Slovakia
198 B1 Prespa, Lake Europe
Prespansko Ezero l. Europe see Prespa, Lake
Prespës, Liqeni i l. Europe see Prespa, Lake
233 □I1 Presque Isle MI U.S.A.
227 F2 Presque Isle WI U.S.A.
226 C2 Presque Isle WI U.S.A.
162 C2 Pressac France
173 F2 Pressath Ger.
179 H2 Pressbaum Austria
Pressburg Slovakia see Bratislava
171 D4 Presseck Ger.
171 D4 Pressel Ger.
171 D5 Pressig Ger.
171 D5 Prestbury Cheshire, England U.K.
149 G4 Prestbury Cheshire, England U.K.
150 E4 Prestbury Gloucestershire, England U.K.
206 E5 Prestea Ghana
150 D2 Presteigne Powys, Wales U.K.
176 C2 Přeštice Czech Rep.

163 E6 Prades Languedoc-Roussillon France
237 E5 Prescott AR U.S.A.
222 B2 Primrose r. Y.T. Can.
172 A2 Prims r. Ger.
223 J4 Prince Albert Sask. Can.
214 D5 Prince Albert S. Africa
263 K1 Prince Albert Mountains Antarctica
220 G2 Prince Albert National Park Sask. Can.
214 C5 Prince Albert Road S. Africa
220 G2 Prince Albert Sound sea chan. N.W.T. Can.
222 C5 Prince Alfred Hamlet S. Africa
254 F4 Proprià Brazil
192 A3 Propriano Corse France
120 F1 Prorva r. Rus. Fed.
176 F2 Proseč Czech Rep.
171 E4 Prösen Ger.
146 F5 Prosen Water r. Scotland U.K.
85 G4 Proserpine Qld Austr.
232 E5 Prince Frederick MD U.S.A.
86 E2 Prince Frederick Harbour W.A. Austr.
222 F4 Prince George B.C. Can.
234 B4 Prince George's County county MD U.S.A.
221 H2 Prince Gustaf Adolf Sea Nunavut Can.
263 C2 Prince Harald Coast Antarctica
85 G8 Prince Edward Islands Indian Ocean
199 D1 Prosotsani Greece
198 C1 Prosotsani Greece
233 F4 Prospect OH U.S.A.
238 B3 Prospect OR U.S.A.
232 C4 Prospect PA U.S.A.
235 G2 Prospect Plains NJ U.S.A.
92 C4 Prosperidad Phil.
147 C4 Prosperous Rep. of Ireland
238 C2 Prosser WA U.S.A.
176 G2 Prostějov Czech Rep.
175 K2 Prostki Pol.
85 H3 Proston Qld Austr.
137 H3 Prostyan Ukr.
214 C6 Proteem S. Africa
175 J5 Proszowice Pol.
175 I5 Proszówki Pol.
233 E5 Princess Anne MD U.S.A.
263 A2 Princess Astrid Coast Antarctica
176 D2 Protivín Czech Rep.
137 I5 Protoka r. Rus. Fed.
137 I3 Protopopivka Ukr.
136 F2 Protvino Ukr.
85 F2 Princess Charlotte Bay Qld Austr.
139 K4 Protva r. Rus. Fed.
139 K4 Protva r. Rus. Fed.
137 K4 Protva r. Rus. Fed.
170 E3 Protul Mol.
263 F2 Princess Elizabeth Land reg. Antarctica
197 I4 Provadiya Bulg.
86 E2 Princess May Range hills W.A. Austr.
184 B3 Provença Port.
161 D5 Provence airport France
81 A6 Princess Mountains South I. N.Z.
Provence-Alpes-Côte-d'Azur admin. reg. France
161 D5 Provence airport France
263 B2 Princess Ragnhild Coast Antarctica
157 H4 Provenchères-sur-Fave France
87 D5 Princess Range hills W.A. Austr.
222 D4 Princess Royal Island B.C. Can.
233 H4 Providence RI U.S.A.
81 A7 Providence, Cape South I. N.Z.
247 □7 Prince's Town Trin. and Tob.
217 □2 Providence Atoll Seychelles
151 F2 Princethorpe Warwickshire, England U.K.
246 B4 Providencia, Isla de i. Caribbean Sea
222 F5 Princeton B.C. Can.
240 F2 Princeton CA U.S.A.
226 C5 Princeton IL U.S.A.
253 E4 Providência, Serra de hills Brazil
226 A4 Princeton IA U.S.A.
232 D6 Princeton KY U.S.A.
246 D2 Providenciales Island Turks and Caicos Is
131 T3 Provideniya Rus. Fed.
233 G3 Princeton MN U.S.A.
234 C3 Princeton NJ U.S.A.
233 H3 Providential Channel Qld Austr.
230 C4 Princeton MO U.S.A.
234 D4 Princeton NJ U.S.A.
232 C5 Princeton WV U.S.A.
233 H3 Provincetown MA U.S.A.
156 D4 Provins France
234 C3 Princeton Junction NJ U.S.A.
241 L1 Provo UT U.S.A.
150 D4 Princetown Devon, England U.K.
241 L1 Provost Alta Can.
171 D4 Prinzendorf an der Zaya Austria
188 F3 Prozor Bos.-Herz.
222 E4 Prince William Sound b. Alaska
139 K2 Prozorovo Rus. Fed.
196 B3 Prrenjas Albania
169 J2 Prince William N.B. Can.
206 E5 Pru r. Ghana
207 G6 Príncipe i. São Tomé and Príncipe
134 K3 Prub r. Rus. Fed.
175 K6 Prudnik Pol.
256 B6 Prudentópolis Brazil
220 D2 Prudhoe AK U.S.A.
238 B2 Prineville OR U.S.A.
149 I4 Prudhoe Northumberland, England U.K.
164 D3 Prinsenbeek Neth.
Prins Harald Kyst coastal area Antarctica see Prince Harald Coast
220 D2 Prudhoe Bay AK U.S.A.
85 G4 Prudhoe Island Qld Austr.
174 F5 Prudnik Pol.
137 I2 Prykolotne Ukr.
137 I3 Prynada Ukr.
175 F5 Prünchow Czech Rep.
169 F5 Prüm r. Ger.
169 F5 Prüm Ger.
159 E4 Prunay France
197 G1 Prundeni Romania
197 G2 Prundu Bârgăului Romania
197 G2 Prundu Bârgăului Romania
192 B3 Prunelli-di-Fiumorbo Corse France
163 E4 Prunet France
161 E5 Prunières France
159 H4 Pruniers-en-Sologne France
172 G3 Prunn Ger.
179 J3 Prusa Turkey see Bursa
179 F3 Prušánky Czech Rep.
174 F4 Pruszcz Pol.
172 F4 Pruszcz Pol.
174 C2 Pruszcz Gdański Pol.
175 I3 Pruszków Pol.
170 E1 Prut r. Europe
175 I4 Prutz Austria
178 C2 Prutting Ger.
178 B3 Prvić i. Croatia
179 J4 Pruzhany Ukr. see Pruzhany
177 G5 Pružina Slovakia
175 J5 Prvačina Slovenia
197 J3 Prvić i. Croatia
85 G4 Pryamitsyno Rus. Fed.
175 F5 Pryazovs'ke Ukr. see Prymors'k

193 H3 Promontorio del Gargano plat. Italy
234 C1 Promino PA U.S.A.
169 B5 Pronsfeld Ger.
139 L4 Pronya r. Belarus
168 F2 Pronstorf Ger.
139 H5 Pronya r. Belarus
222 F3 Prophet r. B.C. Can.
222 F3 Prophet River B.C. Can.
226 C5 Prophetstown IL U.S.A.
192 A3 Propriano Corse France
120 F1 Prorva r. Rus. Fed.
176 F2 Proseč Czech Rep.
171 E4 Prösen Ger.
146 F5 Prosen Water r. Scotland U.K.
85 G4 Proserpine Qld Austr.
199 D1 Prosotsani Greece
233 F4 Prospect OH U.S.A.
238 B3 Prospect OR U.S.A.
232 C4 Prospect PA U.S.A.
235 G2 Prospect Plains NJ U.S.A.
92 C4 Prosperidad Phil.
147 C4 Prosperous Rep. of Ireland
238 C2 Prosser WA U.S.A.
176 G2 Prostějov Czech Rep.
175 K2 Prostki Pol.
85 H3 Proston Qld Austr.
137 H3 Prostyan Ukr.
214 C6 Proteem S. Africa
175 J5 Proszowice Pol.
175 I5 Proszówki Pol.
176 D2 Protivín Czech Rep.
137 I5 Protoka r. Rus. Fed.
137 I3 Protopopivka Ukr.
136 F2 Protvino Ukr.
139 K4 Protva r. Rus. Fed.
170 E3 Protul Mol.
197 I4 Provadiya Bulg.
184 B3 Provença Port.
161 D5 Provence airport France
Provence-Alpes-Côte-d'Azur admin. reg. France
157 H4 Provenchères-sur-Fave France
233 H4 Providence RI U.S.A.
81 A7 Providence, Cape South I. N.Z.
217 □2 Providence Atoll Seychelles
246 B4 Providencia, Isla de i. Caribbean Sea
253 E4 Providência, Serra de hills Brazil
246 D2 Providenciales Island Turks and Caicos Is
131 T3 Provideniya Rus. Fed.
233 H3 Providential Channel Qld Austr.
233 H3 Provincetown MA U.S.A.
156 D4 Provins France
241 L1 Provo UT U.S.A.
241 L1 Provost Alta Can.
188 F3 Prozor Bos.-Herz.
139 K2 Prozorovo Rus. Fed.
196 B3 Prrenjas Albania
206 E5 Pru r. Ghana
134 K3 Prub r. Rus. Fed.
175 K6 Prudnik Pol.
256 B6 Prudentópolis Brazil
220 D2 Prudhoe AK U.S.A.
149 I4 Prudhoe Northumberland, England U.K.
220 D2 Prudhoe Bay AK U.S.A.
85 G4 Prudhoe Island Qld Austr.
174 F5 Prudnik Pol.
137 I2 Prykolotne Ukr.
175 F5 Prünchow Czech Rep.
169 F5 Prüm r. Ger.
169 F5 Prüm Ger.
197 G1 Prundeni Romania
197 G2 Prundu Bârgăului Romania
192 B3 Prunelli-di-Fiumorbo Corse France
163 E4 Prunet France
161 E5 Prunières France
159 H4 Pruniers-en-Sologne France
172 G3 Prunn Ger.
179 F3 Prušánky Czech Rep.
174 C2 Pruszcz Gdański Pol.
175 I3 Pruszków Pol.
170 E1 Prut r. Europe
175 I4 Prutz Austria
178 C2 Prutting Ger.
178 B3 Prvić i. Croatia
137 H2 Pryamitsyno Rus. Fed.
Pryazovs'ke Ukr. see Prymors'k
175 K2 Przytyk Pol.

Column 1

174 G1 Przywidz Pol.
198 C2 Psachna Greece
Psakhná Greece see Psachna
199 D2 Psara r. Greece
129 B1 Psebay Rus. Fed.
129 D2 Psedakh Rus. Fed.
129 A1 Psekups r. Rus. Fed.
137 I2 Psel r. Rus. Fed./Ukr. see Ps'ol
199 E3 Pserimos i. Greece
137 J5 Pshada Rus. Fed.
129 A1 Pshekha r. Rus. Fed.
129 A1 Pshish r. Rus. Fed.
121 G4 Pskent Uzbek.
138 G3 Pskov Rus. Fed.
138 F2 Pskov, Lake Estonia/Rus. Fed.
138 G3 Pskova r. Rus. Fed.
Pskov Oblast admin. div. Rus. Fed. see Pskovskaya Oblast'
138 G3 Pskovskaya Oblast' admin. div. Rus. Fed. Estonia/Rus. Fed. Pskovskoye Ozero l. Pskov, Lake
137 H2 Ps'ol r. Rus. Fed./Ukr.
188 F3 Psunj mts Croatia
174 C3 Pszczew Pol.
174 G1 Pszczółki Pol.
174 G6 Pszczyna Pol.
139 L5 Ptan' r. Rus. Fed.
198 C2 Pteleos Thessalia Greece
198 B1 Ptolemaïda Greece
Ptolemaïs Israel see 'Akko
138 G5 Ptsich r. Belarus
188 E2 Ptuj Slovenia
179 G4 Ptujsko jezero l. Slovenia
136 C2 Ptycha Ukr.
107 E5 Pu r. China
94 C3 Pu r. Indon.
240 □9 Puako HI U.S.A.
261 F5 Puán Arg.
108 C3 Pu'an Guizhou China
Pu'an Sichuan China see Jiange
96 E2 Pubei Guangxi China
160 E2 Publier France
250 B6 Pucacaca Peru
250 C5 Pucacuro r. Peru
252 B2 Pucallpa Peru
252 C3 Pucará Peru
252 C4 Pucarani Bol.
Pucarevo Bos.-Herz. see Novi Travnik
250 D5 Puca Urco Peru
178 E3 Puch bei Hallein Austria
179 G3 Puchberg am Schneeberg Austria
109 F3 Pucheng Fujian China
107 F5 Pucheng Shaanxi China
134 H4 Puchezh Rus. Fed.
173 F3 Puchheim Ger.
101 C5 Puch'ŏn S. Korea
177 H2 Púchov Slovakia
197 G3 Pucioasa Romania
143 H4 Puck Pol.
147 C4 Pucka, Zatoka b. Pol.
87 C5 Puckaun Rep. of Ireland
Puckford, Mount hill W.A. Austr.
187 C5 Puçol Spain
260 B6 Pucón Chile
216 □3a Pūdanū Iran
140 N2 Pudasjärvi Fin.
150 E4 Puddletown Dorset, England U.K.
169 C5 Puderbach Ger.
225 A2 Pudimoe S. Africa
108 C3 Puding Guizhou China
109 G2 Pudong airport China
134 G3 Pudozh Rus. Fed.
149 H4 Pudsey West Yorkshire, England U.K.
Puducherry Pondicherry India see Pondicherry
114 C4 Pudukkottai Tamil Nadu India
245 F3 Puebllo Mex.
241 J5 Puebla Mex.
Puebla Baja California Norte Mex.
245 E4 Puebla Mex.
245 E4 Puebla state Mex.
186 C3 Puebla de Albortón Spain
185 E2 Puebla de Alcocer Spain
186 C3 Puebla de Alfindén Spain
183 H5 Puebla de Almenara Spain
183 G4 Puebla de Beleña Spain
186 D4 Puebla de Benifasar Spain
182 D2 Puebla de Brollón Spain
185 H3 Puebla de Don Fadrique Spain
185 F1 Puebla de Don Rodrigo Spain
184 C3 Puebla de Guzmán Spain
184 D2 Puebla de la Calzada Spain
184 D2 Puebla de la Reina Spain
182 D2 Puebla del Caramiñal Spain
183 E1 Puebla de Lillo Spain
184 D2 Puebla del Maestre Spain
185 H2 Puebla del Príncipe Spain
184 D2 Puebla del Prior Spain
184 D1 Puebla de Obando Spain
182 D2 Puebla de Sanabria Spain
184 D2 Puebla de Sancho Pérez Spain
Puebla de San Julián Spain see Puebla de San Xulián
187 B4 Puebla de San Miguel Spain
182 C2 Puebla de San Xulián Spain
182 D2 Puebla de Trives Spain
182 D4 Puebla de Yeltes Spain
Puebla de Zaragoza Puebla Mex. see Puebla
239 F4 Pueblo CO U.S.A.
261 H4 Pueblo Arrúa Arg.
261 F3 Pueblo Italiano Arg.
242 □I6 Pueblo Nuevo Nic.
245 F2 Pueblo Viejo, Laguna de lag. Mex.
242 □I6 Pueblo Yaqui Mex.
161 A4 Puech del Pal mt. France
163 E4 Puech de Rouet hill France
260 B3 Puente Alto Chile
Puenteareas Spain see Ponteareas
Puente Caldelas Spain see Ponte Caldelas
182 D2 Puente de Domingo Flórez Spain
185 H2 Puente de Génave Spain
245 E4 Puente de Ixtla Mex.
182 E4 Puente del Congosto Spain
182 D2 Puente de Montañana Spain
183 F1 Puente de San Miguel Spain
185 F3 Puente-Genil Spain
183 I2 Puente la Reina Spain
183 F1 Puentenansa Spain
Puentes de García Rodríguez Spain see As Pontes de García Rodríguez
250 D2 Puente Torres Venez.
183 G1 Puente Viesgo Spain
108 B4 Pu'er Yunnan China
252 C3 Puerto Acosta Bol.
253 E3 Puerto Aisén Chile
253 E3 Puerto Alegre Bol.
243 F6 Puerto América Peru
245 F6 Puerto Ángel Mex.
242 □J7 Puerto Antequera Para.
242 □J7 Puerto Arista Mex.
242 □J7 Puerto Armuelles Panama
250 B4 Puerto Asís Venez.
258 F2 Puerto Bermejo Arg.
242 □J6 Puerto Berrío Col.
242 □J6 Puerto Cabello Venez.
242 □J6 Puerto Cabezas Nic.
242 □J6 Puerto Cabo Gracias á Dios Nic.
250 C2 Puerto Carreño Col.
252 B6 Puerto Casado Para.
250 B2 Puerto Chicama Peru
252 C5 Puerto Cisnes Chile
253 E6 Puerto Córdoba Col.
242 □I6 Puerto Cortés Hond.
250 D2 Puerto Cortés Venez.
250 E4 Puerto Cumarebo Venez.
258 E4 Puerto de Béjar Spain

Column 2

Puerto de Cabras Fuerteventura Canary Is see Puerto del Rosario
216 □3a Puerto de la Cruz Tenerife Canary Is
Puerto de la Selva Spain see El Port de la Selva
216 □3d Puerto del Rosario Fuerteventura Canary Is
Puerto del Son Spain see Porto do Son
187 B7 Puerto de Mazarrón Spain
243 I4 Puerto de Morelos Mex.
Puerto de Pollensa Spain see Port de Pollença
185 E1 Puerto de San Vicente Spain
Puerto de Sóller Spain see Port de Sóller
245 F6 Puerto Escondido Mex.
252 C3 Puerto Francisco de Orellana Ecuador
253 E3 Puerto Frey Bol.
252 D4 Puerto Grether Bol.
252 B2 Puerto Heath Peru
250 E4 Puerto Inírida Col.
253 F4 Puerto Isabel Bol.
242 □I7 Puerto Jesús Costa Rica
243 I4 Puerto Juárez Mex.
247 F5 Puerto La Cruz Venez.
185 G1 Puerto Lápice Spain
186 D2 Puértolas Spain
242 □J6 Puerto Lempira Hond.
185 F2 Puertollano Spain
250 C3 Puerto López Col.
185 I3 Puerto Lumbreras Spain
243 G6 Puerto Madero Mex.
259 D6 Puerto Madryn Arg.
252 C3 Puerto Maldonado Peru
282 D4 Puerto Mamoré Bol.
246 C2 Puerto Manatí Cuba
250 A6 Puerto Máncora Peru
253 F5 Puerto María Auxiliadora Para.
Puerto México Mex. see Coatzacoalcos
253 F5 Puerto Mihanovich Para.
187 C4 Puertomingalvo Spain
259 B8 Puerto Montt Chile
242 □I6 Puerto Morazán Nic.
250 D3 Puerto Morín Peru
246 C2 Puerto Nare Cuba
250 E3 Puerto Nuevo Col.
252 D3 Puerto Pando Bol.
242 B2 Puerto Peñasco Mex.
253 F5 Puerto Pinasco Para.
250 C3 Puerto Pirtu Venez.
246 E3 Puerto Plata Dom. Rep.
213 I4 Puerto Portillo Peru
116 D3 Puerto Princesa Phil.
Puerto Presidente Stroessner Para. see Ciudad del Este
184 D4 Puerto Real Spain
258 G2 Puerto Rico Bol.
247 □1 Puerto Rico terr. West Indies
264 E4 Puerto Rico Trench sea feature Caribbean Sea
259 B5 Puerto Sama Cuba see Samá
242 □I6 Puerto Sandino Nic.
253 F5 Puerto Santa Cruz Arg.
253 E3 Puerto Sastre Para.
252 C3 Puerto Saucedo Bol.
Puertos de Beceite mts Spain see Ports de Beseit
182 D4 Puerto Seguro Spain
184 E4 Puerto Serrano Spain
250 D5 Puerto Socorro Peru
Puerto Somoza Nic. see Puerto Sandino
253 F4 Puerto Suárez Bol.
252 A2 Puerto Supe Peru
242 □H5 Puerto Tejada Col.
250 B5 Puerto Tunigrama Peru
244 B3 Puerto Vallarta Mex.
259 B6 Puerto Varas Chile
250 B2 Puerto Victoria Peru
253 E3 Puerto Villazon Bol.
247 □1 Punta Santiago Puerto Rico
116 C3 Pugal Rajasthan India
108 B3 Puge Sichuan China
161 E5 Puget-sur-Argens France
161 E5 Puget-Théniers France
161 E5 Puget-Ville France
234 C2 Pughtown PA U.S.A.
193 H3 Puglia admin. reg. Italy
162 E3 Puglia r. Italy
193 I3 Pugnochiuso Italy
130 I3 Pugor r. Rus. Fed.
116 E3 Pugwash N.S. Can.
80 F3 Puha r. N.Z.
122 C5 Pühäl-e Khamīr, Kūh-e mts Iran
197 F1 Puhja Estonia
197 F3 Pui Romania
H3 Puichéric France
227 H3 Puiești Romania
197 F5 Puig Spain
186 E2 Puigcerdà Spain
186 E2 Puig d'Arques hill Spain
181 H1 Puig de Comanegra mt. Spain
186 E2 Puig de les Morreres mt. Spain
187 G5 Puig de Sant Salvador hill Spain
187 F5 Puig des Galatzó mt. Spain
187 G2 Puig Major mt. Spain
182 E2 Puigmal mt. France/Spain
186 E2 Puig Pedrós mt. France/Spain
186 E3 Puig-reig Spain
186 D3 Puigverd de Lleida Spain
162 C5 Puimoisson France
163 E4 Puisieux France
156 C2 Puisieux France
161 E5 Puisseguin France
161 B5 Puisserguier France
221 F2 Puits r. France
161 C4 Puivert France
206 C3 Pujehun Sierra Leone
109 F2 Pujiang Zhejiang China
172 Pujo France
163 B4 Pujols Aquitaine France
163 B4 Pujols Aquitaine France
81 C4 Pukaki, Lake South I. N.Z.
177 H3 Pukanec Slovakia
81 □2 Pukapuka atoll Cook Is
79 □3 Pukapuka i. Arch. des Tuamotu Fr. Polynesia
79 □3 Pukarua atoll Arch. des Tuamotu Fr. Polynesia
226 E1 Pukaskwa r. Ont. Can.
101 C4 Pukch'ŏng N. Korea
101 B4 Pukč'ŏng N. Korea
196 G4 Pukë Albania
80 G2 Pukeamaru hill North I. N.Z.
80 B5 Pukeatua North I. N.Z.
80 E2 Pukehoi North I. N.Z.
80 E2 Pukekohe North I. N.Z.
80 E2 Pukekohe North I. N.Z.
81 B7 Pukerau South I. N.Z.
80 G4 Pukeroa North I. N.Z.
80 F4 Pukerua Bay North I. N.Z.
81 D5 Puketeraki Range mts South I. N.Z.
81 E4 Puketitiri North I. N.Z.
80 F2 Puketoetoe mt. North I. N.Z.
80 F4 Puketoi Range hills North I. N.Z.
141 N3 Pukkila Fin.
134 H3 Pukoksa Rus. Fed.
101 C4 Puksoozero S. Korea
139 H2 Pula Xizang China see Nyingchi

Column 3

188 D3 Pula Croatia
191 I4 Pula Sardegna Italy
192 B5 Pula Sardegna Italy
252 D5 Pulacayo Bol.
92 C5 Pulandian Liaoning China
91 K5 Pulap atoll Micronesia
252 C6 Pular, Cerro mt. Chile
233 E3 Pulaski NY U.S.A.
231 I5 Pulaski TN U.S.A.
232 C5 Pulaski VA U.S.A.
226 C3 Pulaski WI U.S.A.
91 I8 Pulau r. Indon.
Pulau Pinang state Malaysia see Pinang
175 J4 Pulawy Pol.
151 G4 Pulborough West Sussex, England U.K.
191 I2 Pulfero Italy
183 F5 Pulgar Spain
169 B4 Pulheim Ger.
114 D3 Pulicat Tamil Nadu India
114 D3 Pulicat Lake inlet India
160 C2 Puligny-Montrachet France
114 C3 Pulivendla Andhra Prad. India
179 G2 Pulkau Austria
141 P2 Pulkkila Fin.
173 F3 Pullach in Isartal Ger.
238 C2 Pullman WA U.S.A.
91 H6 Pulo Anna i. Palau
92 B2 Pulog, Mount Luzon Phil.
140 P1 Pulozero Rus. Fed.
185 J1 Pulpí Spain
195 G2 Pulsano Italy
171 E4 Pulsen Ger.
171 F4 Pulsnitz Ger.
174 E1 Pulsnitz r. Ger.
175 J3 Pułtusk Pol.
86 □7 Pulu Capelok i. Cocos Is
127 E3 Pülümür Turkey
86 □7 Pulu Pandang i. Cocos Is
91 K5 Pulusuk atoll Micronesia
91 K5 Puluwat atoll Micronesia
157 H5 Pulversheim France
211 B6 Puma Tanz.
260 B4 Pumanque Chile
Pumiao Guangxi China see Yongning
238 F2 Pumpkin Creek r. MT U.S.A.
150 D2 Pumsaint Carmarthenshire, Wales U.K.
250 A5 Puná, Isla i. Ecuador
258 D2 Puna de Atacama plat. Arg.
81 C5 Punakaiki South I. N.Z.
117 G4 Punakha Bhutan
240 □D9 Punalu'u HI U.S.A.
79 □3a Punaruu r. Tahiti Fr. Polynesia
191 J3 Punat Croatia
252 D4 Punata Bol.
223 F4 Punch Pak.
222 F4 Punch Jammu and Kashmir Can.
213 H4 Punda Maria S. Africa
116 D3 Pundri Haryana India
114 B2 Pune Maharashtra India
114 C3 Punganuru Andhra Prad. India
213 G3 Pungo Andongo Angola
101 D4 P'ungsan N. Korea
213 G3 Pungue r. Angola
191 F2 Puni r. Italy
208 E5 Punia Dem. Rep. Congo
109 F4 Puning Guangdong China
116 C3 Punjab state India
123 G4 Punjab prov. Pak.
141 Q3 Punkaharju Fin.
252 C2 Puno Peru
252 C3 Puno dept Peru
254 C2 Punta Ala Italy
261 F6 Punta Alta Arg.
259 C9 Punta Arenas Chile
192 B4 Punta Balestrieri mt. Sardegna Italy
252 C4 Punta de Bombón Peru
242 □H5 Punta Gorda Belize
216 □3c Puntagorda La Palma Canary Is
23 D7 Punta Gorda Fl. U.S.A.
191 J4 Punta Križa Croatia
216 □3d Puntallana La Palma Canary Is
192 A5 Punta Mumullonis mt. Sardegna Italy
242 □I7 Puntarenas Costa Rica
191 H3 Punta Sabbioni Italy
247 □1 Punta Santiago Puerto Rico
252 D5 Puntas Negras, Cerro mt. Chile
184 D3 Punto Umbría Italy
250 D2 Punto Fijo Venez.
186 C2 Puntón de Guara mt. Spain
232 D4 Punxsutawney PA U.S.A.
140 N2 Puolanka Fin.
140 M2 Puoltikasvaara Sweden
192 C3 Puglia i. Italy
102 Puqi Hubei China
252 B3 Puquio Peru
130 I3 Pur r. Rus. Fed.
116 E3 Puranpur Uttar Prad. India
91 J8 Purari r. P.N.G.
179 H3 Purbach am Neusiedler See Austria
95 E4 Purbalingga Jawa Tengah Indon.
150 E4 Purbeck, Isle of pen. England U.K.
237 D5 Purcell OK U.S.A.
222 G5 Purcell Mountains B.C. Can.
232 E5 Purcellville VA U.S.A.
185 H3 Purchena Spain
185 G3 Purchil Spain
244 C4 Purépero Mex.
151 H3 Purfleet Thurrock, England U.K.
237 C4 Purgatoire r. CO U.S.A.
173 F5 Pürgen Ger.
179 G2 Purgstall an der Erlauf Austria
211 A7 Puri Angola
115 E2 Puri Orissa India
244 B4 Purificación Mex.
245 E2 Purificación r. Mex.
150 D3 Puriton Somerset, England U.K.
179 H2 Purkersdorf Austria
151 G3 Purley Greater London, England U.K.
151 F3 Purley on Thames West Berkshire, England U.K.
164 D2 Purmerend Neth.
114 C2 Purna Mahar. India
114 C2 Purna r. Mahar. India
116 D5 Purna r. Mahar. India
114 C2 Purnabhaba r. India
117 F4 Purnia Bihar India see Purnia
82 B1 Purnululu National Park W.A. Austr.
117 F4 Purnea Bihar India see Purnia
259 B6 Purranque Chile
114 C2 Pursat Cambodia see Poŭthisat
151 F3 Purton Wiltshire, England U.K.
221 K3 Purtuniq Que. Can.
244 D4 Puruándiro Mex.
191 K3 Purukcahu Indon.
183 J3 Puruliya W. Bengal India
116 E4 Purullena Spain
117 F4 Purulia W. Bengal India
250 E5 Purus r. Brazil
183 J3 Purujosa Spain
237 E4 Purvis MS U.S.A.
197 G7 Pŭrvomai Bulg.
116 E4 Purwa Uttar Prad. India
94 D4 Purwakarta Jawa Barat Indon.
95 E4 Purwodadi Jawa Tengah Indon.
95 E4 Purwokerto Jawa Tengah Indon.
101 D4 Puryŏng N. Korea
115 E2 Pusad Mahar. India
183 F5 Pusanés Spain
172 D3 Puschwitz Ger.
101 C5 Pusan S. Korea
173 I4 Pusan'i Junction South I. N.Z.
243 G4 Pusilá Mex.
134 H4 Puschino Rus. Fed.
101 C5 Puškin Rus. Fed.
139 H2 Pushkar Azer. see Biläsuvar

Column 4

120 A2 Pushkino Rus. Fed.
100 G3 Pushkinskaya, Gora mt. Sakhalin Rus. Fed.
138 G3 Pushkinskiye Gory Rus. Fed.
186 C2 Pushkinyt mt. Spain
177 K4 Püski Estonia
138 F2 Püssi Estonia
177 H2 Pustá Polom Czech Rep.
191 G2 Pusteria, Val val. Italy
177 H3 Pusté Úľany Slovakia
196 D1 Pusti Lisac mt. Yugo.
176 G2 Pustiměř Czech Rep.
136 B3 Pustomyty Ukr.
138 G3 Pustoshka Rus. Fed.
136 F3 Pustovity Ukr.
117 G5 Pusur r. Bangl.
175 L2 Puszcza Augustowska for. Pol.
175 I4 Puszcza Mariańska Pol.
174 D3 Puszcza Natecka for. Pol.
177 G5 Puszczykowo Pol.
177 H1 Pusztakovácsi Hungary
177 H1 Pusztamérges Hungary
177 H1 Pusztamonostor Hungary
177 I5 Pusztaszer Hungary
177 H4 Pusztavacs Hungary
177 H4 Pusztavám Hungary
159 F3 Putanges-Pont-Écrepin France
80 E3 Putaruru North I. N.Z.
170 E1 Putbus Ger.
Puteoli Italy see Pozzuoli
80 F3 Putere North I. N.Z.
134 L2 Puteyets Rus. Fed.
Puthein Myanmar see Bassein
109 F3 Putian Fujian China
195 G2 Putifigari Sardegna Italy
114 C3 Putignano Italy
252 C5 Putilovo Rus. Fed.
252 C5 Putina Peru
114 C4 Puting China see De'an
245 F5 Putla Mex.
170 D2 Putlitz Ger.
197 H3 Putna r. Romania
233 H4 Putnam CT U.S.A.
235 I1 Putnam County county NY U.S.A.
235 E1 Putnam Valley NY U.S.A.
233 G3 Putney VT U.S.A.
177 J3 Putnok Hungary
131 K3 Putorana, Gory mts Rus. Fed.
94 C2 Putrajaya Malaysia
252 C4 Putre Chile
214 C3 Putsonderwater S. Africa
114 C4 Puttalam Sri Lanka
114 C4 Puttalam Lagoon Sri Lanka
165 D3 Putte Belgium
165 D3 Putte Neth.
157 F3 Puttelange-aux-Lacs France
164 J2 Puttgarden Ger.
170 C1 Puttgarden Ger.
172 A2 Püttlingen Ger.
114 B3 Puttur Karnataka India
260 B4 Putú Chile
250 C4 Putumayo r. Col.
250 C4 Putumayo dept Col.
91 J7 Putussibau Kalimantan Barat Indon.
126 E3 Pütürge Turkey
95 F2 Putussibau Kalimantan Barat Indon.
240 □D9 Puuanahulu HI U.S.A.
240 □2 Puuhonua HI U.S.A.
141 N3 Puula l. Fin.
141 O3 Puumala Fin.
165 D3 Puurs Belgium
240 □H4 Puuwai HI U.S.A.
221 K3 Puvurnituq Que. Can.
107 F4 Puxian Shanxi China
238 B2 Puyallup WA U.S.A.
107 G5 Puyang Henan China
Puyang Zhejiang China see Pujiang
163 D4 Puybrun France
163 D5 Puycasquier France
159 F5 Puy Crapaud hill France
160 B3 Puy-de-Dôme dept Auvergne France
160 A3 Puy de Dôme mt. France
163 D5 Puy de Faucher mt. France
161 D4 Puy de la Gagère mt. France
160 B3 Puy de Montoncel mt. France
160 A3 Puy de Sancy mt. France
162 D2 Puy des Trois-Cornes hill France
163 E5 Puygouzon France
161 A3 Puy Griou mt. France
160 B3 Puy-Guillaume France
163 C5 Puylaroque France
161 C4 Puylaurens France
163 D5 Puy-l'Évêque France
188 B3 Puy Mary mt. France
163 C5 Puymaurin France
163 C4 Puymirol France
161 D5 Puymoyen France
250 C5 Puyo Ecuador
163 B5 Puyôo France
161 E4 Puy-St-Vincent France
187 F4 Puzol Spain see Puçol
125 F4 Puzak, Ghubbat al b. Yemen
177 H4 Pzani entrés. Hungary
211 C6 Pweto Dem. Rep. Congo
150 C2 Pwllheli Gwynedd, Wales U.K.
134 F3 Pyal'ma Rus. Fed.
96 A4 Pyamalaw r. Myanmar
123 G2 Pyandzh Tajik.
Pyandzh r. Afgh./Tajik. see Panj
Pyandzh Khatlon Tajik. see Panj
123 G2 Pyanskiy Perevoz Rus. Fed. see Perevoz
140 O2 Pyaozero, Ozero l. Rus. Fed.
140 O2 Pyaozerskiy Rus. Fed.
96 A2 Pyapon Myanmar
130 J2 Pyasina r. Rus. Fed.
197 G4 Pyasŭchnik r. Bulg.
129 C1 Pyatigorsk Rus. Fed.
137 J4 Pyatykhatky Ukr. see P'yatykhatky
137 H4 Pyatikhatki Ukr.
139 H7 P'yatykhatka Ukr.
137 H5 P'yatykhatky Ukr.
129 B2 P'yatykhatka Ukr.
259 B6 Pyatyhory Ukr.
151 F3 Pychas Rus. Fed.
96 A3 Pyè Myanmar
136 D5 Pye, Mount hill South I. N.Z.
138 B5 Pyershamayski Belarus
96 A1 Pyeongyang N. Korea
125 E5 Pyhä r. Fin.
163 B2 Pyhäjärvi Fin.
141 M3 Pyhäjärvi Fin.
140 O3 Pyhäjärvi l. Fin.
141 O3 Pyhäjärvi l. Fin.
140 O3 Pyhäjoki Fin.
179 Pyhärranta Austria
141 M3 Pyhäntä Fin.
141 N3 Pyhäsalmi Fin.
141 N3 Pyhäselkä Fin.
141 N3 Pyhäselkä l. Fin.
179 Pyhra Austria
96 A1 Pyingaing Myanmar
96 B2 Pyinmana Myanmar
96 A2 Pyin-U-Lwin Myanmar
163 I2 Pylaia Greece
198 B3 Pylos Greece
198 B3 Pylkömmel Rus. Fed.
101 C5 P'yŏksŏng N. Korea
101 C5 P'yŏktong N. Korea
101 C5 P'yŏnggang N. Korea
101 C5 P'yŏngsan N. Korea
101 C5 P'yŏngt'aek S. Korea
101 C5 P'yŏngyang N. Korea
178 C2 Pyramidenspitze mt. Austria

Column 5

83 F4 Pyramid Hill Vic. Austr.
87 D7 Pyramid Lake salt flat W.A. Austr.
240 H1 Pyramid Lake NV U.S.A.
240 H2 Pyramid Range mts NV U.S.A.
173 F2 Pyrbaum Ger.
Pyrénées mts Europe see Pyrenees
186 F2 Pyrenees mts Europe
163 B5 Pyrénées airport France
163 B5 Pyrénées-Atlantiques dept Aquitaine France
163 E6 Pyrénées-Orientales dept Languedoc-Roussillon France
198 C2 Pyrgetos Greece
199 D2 Pyrgi Voreio Aigaio Greece
198 B3 Pyrgos Greece
136 E2 Pyrizhky Ukr.
137 G3 Pyrohy Ukr.
86 C4 Pyrton, Mount hill W.A. Austr.
175 I4 Pyrzyce Pol.
174 D2 Pyrzyn Pol.
137 H3 Pys'menne Ukr.
124 G4 Pyszna r. Pol.
175 K5 Pysznica Pol.
138 F3 Pytalovo Rus. Fed.
96 B3 Pyu Myanmar
199 E3 Pyxaria mt. Greece

Q

126 E4 Qaa Lebanon
129 E3 Qābälä Azer.
Qabanbay Kazakh. see Kabanbay
128 B3 Qabātiya West Bank
125 F4 Qabil Oman
129 E3 Qabirri r. Azer.
Qaba Xizang China see Xaitongmoin
Qabqa Qinghai China see Gonghe
125 H4 Qabr Hūd Oman
129 F3 Qabyrgha r. Kazakh. see Kabyrga
177 J3 Qacentina Alg. see Constantine
129 D3 Qach'aghani Georgia
215 G4 Qacha's Nek Lesotho
129 D2 Qäçräš Azer.
122 D2 Qād ebād Iran
124 B3 Qadimah Saudi Arabia
127 G4 Qādir Karam Iraq
125 F5 Qādub Suquţrā Yemen
122 B4 Qā'emiyeh Iran
198 B1 Qafzea Kolonjë Albania
107 H1 Qagan Nur Nei Mongol China
107 J3 Qagan Nur Nei Mongol China
107 H2 Qagan Nur Nei Mongol China
107 J3 Qagan Nur l. Nei Mongol China
107 J3 Qagan Teg Nei Mongol China
107 J3 Qagan Us Qinghai China see Dulan
106 C4 Qagan Us He r. China
108 A1 Qagca Sichuan China
Qagchêng Sichuan China see Xiangcheng
135 H5 Qaharyuyi Houqi Nei Mongol China see Bayan Qagan
136 C4 Qahar Youyi Qianqi Nei Mongol China see Togrog Ul
137 G2 Qahar Youyi Zhongqi Nei Mongol China see Hobor
170 C2 Qahar Youyi Zhongqi Nei Mongol China see Hobor
124 D4 Qahd, Wādī al hills Saudi Arabia
129 E4 Qahremānlū Azer.
Qahremānshahr Iran see Kermānshāh
165 D3 Qaidam r. China
240 □4 Qaidam Pendi basin China
221 K3 Qaisar r. Afgh.
123 F3 Qaisar, Koh-i- mt. Afgh.
195 □ Qala Gozo Malta
215 G2 Qalabotjha S. Af. al imp. l. China
203 G6 Qala'en Nahl Sudan
123 G2 Qalansiyah Suqutrā Yemen Gant'iadi
160 A3 Qalât Afgh.
163 D5 Qal'at al Hişn tourist site Syria
163 D5 Qal'at al Marqab tourist site Syria
163 D5 Qal'at al Mu'azzam Saudi Arabia
160 D5 Qal'at at Bishah Saudi Arabia
160 D2 Qal'at al Muqaybirah, Jabal mt. Syria
163 G5 Qal'at Şālih Iraq
161 E3 Qal'eh Dāgh mt. Iran
160 E3 Qal 'eh-ye Now Afgh.
163 E5 Qalhāt Oman
163 E5 Qalqilya West Bank
163 C5 Qalqutan Kazakh. see Koluton
160 C5 Qalyūb Qalyūbīya Egypt
221 M3 Qamanirjuaq Lake Can.
221 M3 Qamani'tuaq Nunavut Can. see Baker Lake
161 E4 Qamar, Ghubbat al b. Yemen
125 F4 Qamar, Jabal al mts Oman
125 F4 Qamashi Uzbek. see Kamashi
108 A2 Qamdo Xizang China
79 □1 Qamea i. Fiji
202 C2 Qaminis Libya
122 B3 Qamşar Iran
122 B3 Qamşar Iran
132 C2 Qamystybas Kazakh. see Kamyshybash
210 F2 Qandala Somalia
122 A2 Qandaranbash Kazakh.
Qandyaghash Kazakh. see Kandyagash
129 E4 Qapal Kazakh. see Kapal
122 C2 Qapan Iran
110 C3 Qapqal Xinjiang China

Column 6

83 F4 Pyramid Hill ...   *(continued — column 6)*
129 E4 Qarasu r. Azer.
Qarasü Kustanayskaya Oblast' Kazakh. see Karasu
133 F3 Qara Şū Chāy r. Syria/Turkey see Karasu
129 E4 Qara Tarai mt. Afgh.
186 F2 Qaratau Kazakh. see Karatau
163 B5 Qaratau Zhotasy mts Kazakh. see Karatau, Khrebet
163 B5 Qaratöbe Kazakh. see Karatobe
163 E6 Qaratoghay Kazakh. see Karatogay
198 C2 Qaraton Kazakh. see Karaton
199 D2 Qaraūyl Vostochnyy Kazakhstan Kazakh. see Karaul
198 B3 Qarayeri Azer.
136 E2 Qarazhal Kazakh. see Karazhal
137 G3 Qardho Somalia
86 C4 Qareh Chāy r. Iran
175 I4 Qareh Dāgh mt. Iran
174 D2 Qareh Dāsh, Küh-e mt. Iran
137 H3 Qareh Sū r. Iran
124 G4 Qareh Zīā' od Dīn Iran
175 K5 Qarhan Qinghai China
138 F3 Qarkilik Xinjiang China see Ruoqiang
124 D4 Qarnayt, Jabal hill Saudi Arabia
203 G2 Qarn el Kabsh, Gebel mt. Egypt
123 H2 Qārokūl l. Tajik.
110 D4 Qarqan Xinjiang China see Qiemo
110 D4 Qarqan He r. China
121 G4 Qarqaraly Kazakh. see Karkaralinsk
129 E4 Qarqaraçy r. Kazakh.
110 D3 Qarqi Xinjiang China
120 C5 Qārpi Iran
123 F2 Qarqin Afgh.
Qarshi Uzbek. see Karshi
Qarshi Obisli China see Qarghaly
129 D3 Qartaba Lebanon
127 H5 Qārūh, Jazirat i. Kuwait
125 D2 Qaryat al Ulyā Saudi Arabia
122 C2 Qāsam, Küh-e mt. Iran
128 B4 Qasa Murg mts Afgh.
123 E3 Qasba Z har Iraq
117 F4 Qashqadaryo r. Uzbek. see Kashkadar'ya
Qashqadaryo Wiloyati admin. div. Uzbek. see Kashkadar'inskaya Oblast'
221 M3 Qasigiannguit Greenland
129 E4 Qaskelen Kazakh. see Kaskelen
108 C3 Qasq Nei Mongol China
128 B4 Qasr ad Dayr, Jabal mt. Jordan
128 C2 Qasr al Hayr tourist site Syria
128 C4 Qasr 'Amrah tourist site Jordan
128 C4 Qasr Burqu' tourist site Jordan
122 E5 Qaşr-e-Qand Iran
203 E2 Qasr Farafra Egypt
124 B3 Qaşr Himām Saudi Arabia
125 F4 Qa'tabah Yemen
125 F3 Qatar country Asia
119 H5 Qatār, Jabal hill Oman
122 D2 Qatlish Iran
202 E2 Qattāra Depression Egypt
Qattāra, Râs esc. Egypt see Qattāra Depression
202 E2 Qattāra, Munkhafaḑ al depr. Egypt see Qattāra Depression
129 E3 Qax Azer.
122 D3 Qāyen Iran
Qayghy Kazakh. see Kayga
Qaydam Pendi basin China see Qaidam Pendi
123 F2 Qaisar r. Afgh.
123 F3 Qaisar, Koh-i- mt. Afgh.
195 □ Qala Gozo Malta
127 F4 Qayyārah Iraq
129 E4 Qazangöldağ mt. Armenia/Azer.
123 G2 Qazaq Shyghanaghy b. Kazakh. see Kazakhskiy Zaliv
Qazaqstan country Asia see Kazakhstan
129 D3 Qazax Azer.
122 D3 Qazbegi Georgia
129 D3 Qazi Ahmad Pak.
129 G2 Qazimämmäd Azer.
122 B2 Qazvin Iran
106 D2 Qeh Nei Mongol China
79 □1 Qelelevu i. Fiji
196 B3 Qelqëzës, Mali i mt. Albania
107 I4 Qena Egypt see Qena
203 G3 Qeqertarsuaq Greenland
221 M3 Qeqertarsuaq i. Greenland
221 M3 Qeqertarsuatsiaat Greenland
221 M3 Qeqertarsuup Tunua b. Greenland
122 D3 Qeshlāq Iran
122 D3 Qeshm Iran
122 D5 Qeshm i. Iran
122 D3 Qeydār Iran
122 C2 Qeys i. Iran
215 G4 Qezel Owzan, Rūdkhāneh-ye r. Iran
129 E3 Qezel Qeshlāq Iran

Column 7

129 E4 Qarasu r. Azer.
Qingcheng Gansu China see Qingyang
101 B4 Qingchengzi Liaoning China
108 C1 Qingchuan Sichuan China
107 I4 Qingdao Shandong China
100 C3 Qingdang Heilong. China
Qinggang Jiangsu China see Qinghe
108 D2 Qingguandu Hunan China
106 C4 Qinghai prov. China
106 C4 Qinghai Hu salt l. Qinghai China
106 C4 Qinghai Nanshan mts Qinghai China
106 C4 Qinghe Hebei China
106 A2 Qinghe Xinjiang China
107 F4 Qinghua Henan China see Bo'ai
Qingjian Shaanxi China see Huajiyin
108 D2 Qingjiang Jiangsu China see Huai'an
Qingjiang Jiangxi China see Zhangshu
108 C2 Qing Jiang r. China
108 C3 Qingkou Jiangsu China see Ganyu
109 F3 Qinglong Fujian China
108 C3 Qinglong Guizhou China
107 H3 Qinglong Hebei China
107 H2 Qinglong Hebei China see Wulong
109 G2 Qinglong Shanghai China see Xishui
108 C3 Qingping Sichuan China see Dedu
107 I6 Qingshan Heilong. China see Dedu
108 B2 Qingshen Sichuan China
106 D4 Qingshizui Qinghai China
106 E5 Qingshui Gansu China
107 F4 Qingshuihe Nei Mongol China
108 A1 Qingshuihe Qinghai China
107 F4 Qingtian Zhejiang China
107 H3 Qingtongxia Ningxia China
107 H4 Qingtu Hebei China
109 F2 Qingxu Shanxi China
107 F4 Qingyang Anhui China
107 G2 Qingyang Gansu China
108 D2 Qingyang Jiangsu China see Sihong
Qingyuan Gansu China see Weiyuan
109 F3 Qingyuan Guangdong China
108 C3 Qingyuan Guangxi China see Yizhou
Qingyuan Liaoning China see Qingyuan
109 F3 Qingyuan Zhejiang China
107 G4 Qingyuan Shanxi China see Qingxu
109 G2 Qingzhen Zhejiang China
107 H4 Qingzhou Hebei China see Qingxian
109 D2 Qingzhou Hubei China
107 H4 Qingzhou Shandong China
107 H4 Qinhuangdao Hebei China
108 C3 Qinjiang Jiangxi China see Shicheng
107 G5 Qin Ling mts China
107 G5 Qinting Shanxi China see Lianhua
109 F2 Qinxian Shanxi China
107 F4 Qinyang Henan China
108 D3 Qinzhou Guangxi China
108 D3 Qinzhou Hainan China
122 D3 Qionghai Hainan China
108 B3 Qiongjiexue Xizang China see Qonggyai
108 B2 Qionglai Sichuan China
108 B2 Qionglai Shan mts Sichuan China
108 D3 Qiongshan Hainan China see Hongyuan
108 D3 Qiongzhou Hainan China
108 D3 Qiongzhou Haixia str. China
122 D3 Qir Iran
111 C4 Qira Xinjiang China
129 F4 Qırmızı Bazar Azer.
129 E4 Qiryat Ata Israel
124 B3 Qiryat Shemona Israel
108 B3 Qishan Anhui China
128 B3 Qimen
107 F5 Qishon Shaanxi China
125 F5 Qishn Yemen
124 C3 Qishran i. Saudi Arabia
126 E5 Qitab ash Shāmah vol. crater Saudi Arabia
100 D3 Qitaihe Heilong. China
108 D4 Qitaihe Yunnan China
108 A2 Qitbit, Wādī r. Oman
100 C3 Qiubei Yunnan China
108 B3 Qiujin Jiangxi China
107 I4 Qixia Shandong China
107 G4 Qixian Henan China
100 D3 Qixing r. China
122 D3 Qiyang Hunan China
129 F4 Qizilağac Körfäzi b. Azer.
129 E3 Qızıldaş Azer.
215 F4 Qizilrabot Tajik. see Kyzylrabot
129 E3 Qoborto S. Africa
Qoghaly Kazakh. see Kugaly
129 E3 Qogir Feng mt. China/Jammu and Kashmir see K2
202 A2 Qojür Iran
215 G5 Qolora Mouth S. Africa
122 B3 Qom Iran
122 B3 Qom r. Iran
108 A2 Qomdo Xizang China
128 C2 Qomishēh Iran
108 B3 Qomolangma Feng mt. China/Nepal see Everest, Mount
111 E6 Qonaqkänd Azer.
107 I3 Qonggyai Xizang China
129 E4 Qonggyai Xizang China see Kungrad
Qongrat Karagandinskaya Oblast' Kazakh. see Kungrad
Qongyröleng Kazakh. see Konyrolen
Qonystanü Kazakh. see Konystanu
108 B3 Qoqek Xinjiang China see Tacheng
215 F4 Qoqodala S. Africa
Qoradaryo r. Kyrg. see Kara-Darya
Qoraghaty Kazakh. see Kuragaty
Qoraqalpoghiston Uzbek. see Karakalpakiya
Qoraqalpoghiston Respublikasi aut. rep. Uzbek. see Karakalpakistan, Respublika
128 C2 Qornet es Saouda mt. Lebanon
129 C2 Qornisi Georgia
Qorowulbozor Uzbek.
128 B2 Qaraoun, Lac de l. Lebanon
122 A3 Qorveh Iran
127 F3 Qosh Tepe Iraq
Qoshqar Köli l. Kazakh. see Koshkarkol'
Qostanay Kazakh. see Kostanay
Qostanay Oblysy admin. div. Kazakh. see Kustanayskaya Oblast'
122 C2 Qotbābād Iran
122 A2 Qotūr Iran
128 C2 Qoubaiyat Lebanon
129 D3 Qovlar Azer.

Quadrazais to Raslavice

352

182 D4 Quadrazais Port.
193 G3 Quadri Italy
146 E5 Quaich r. Scotland U.K.
240 I4 Quail Mountains CA U.S.A.
87 C7 Quairading W.A. Austr.
168 C3 Quakenbrück Ger.
235 F1 Quaker Hill CT U.S.A.
234 D2 Quakertown NJ U.S.A.
234 C2 Quakertown PA U.S.A.
234 B2 Qualake PA U.S.A.
193 G4 Qualiano Italy
83 E3 Quambatook Vic. Austr.
83 F2 Quambone N.S.W. Austr.
84 E4 Quamby Qld Austr.
237 D5 Quanah TX U.S.A.
107 F5 Quanbao Shan mt. Henan China
Quan Dao Hoang Sa is S. China Sea see Paracel Islands
Quan Dao Truong Sa is S. China Sea see Spratly Islands
96 E4 Quang Ngai Vietnam
96 D3 Quang Tri Vietnam
96 D2 Quang Yen Vietnam
109 E1 Quan He r. China
Quanjiang Jiangxi China see Suichuan
Quan Long Vietnam see Ca Mau
109 E3 Quannan Jiangxi China
Quan Phu Quoc i. Vietnam see Phu Quôc, Đao
109 F3 Quanshang Fujian China
150 D3 Quantock Hills England U.K.
Quanwan H.K. China see Tsuen Wan
109 F3 Quanzhou Fujian China
109 D3 Quanzhou Guangxi China
223 K5 Qu'Appelle Sask. Can.
223 K5 Qu'Appelle r. Man./Sask. Can.
221 L3 Quaqtaq Que. Can.
255 A9 Quaraí Brazil
261 I2 Quaraí r. Brazil
165 C4 Quaregnon Belgium
190 D4 Quargnento Italy
142 C4 Quarnbek Ger.
190 D3 Quarona Italy
191 F5 Quarrata Italy
160 B1 Quarré-les-Tombes France
81 B7 Quarry Hills South I. N.Z.
234 B3 Quarryville PA U.S.A.
184 B3 Quarteira Port.
187 C5 Quartell Spain
190 E1 Quarten Switz.
192 B5 Quartu Sant'Elena Sardegna Italy
241 I3 Quartzite Mountain NV U.S.A.
241 J5 Quartzsite AZ U.S.A.
124 D4 Quaryat al Faw tourist site Saudi Arabia
256 B5 Quatá Brazil
247 □3 Quatre, Isle á i. St Vincent
156 E3 Quatre-Champs France
187 C6 Quatretonda Spain
216 □1a Quatro Ribeiras Terceira Azores
129 F3 Quba Azer.
129 E4 Qubadlı Azer.
129 F3 Qubalıbalaoğlan Azer.
122 D2 Quchan Iran
215 H3 Qudeni S. Africa
129 F3 Qudıyalçay r. Azer.
83 G3 Queanbeyan A.C.T. Austr.
225 G4 Québec Que. Can.
225 F2 Québec prov. Can.
256 D3 Quebra Anzol r. Brazil
261 I3 Quebracho Uru.
247 □1 Quebradillas Puerto Rico
150 E3 Quedgeley Gloucestershire, England U.K.
171 C4 Quedlinburg Ger.
Queen Adelaide Islands Chile see La Reina Adelaida, Archipiélago de
128 B4 Queen Alia airport 'Ammān Jordan
234 C4 Queen Anne MD U.S.A.
234 B3 Queen Anne's County county MD U.S.A.
222 E5 Queen Bess, Mount B.C. Can.
151 H3 Queenborough Kent, England U.K.
222 C4 Queen Charlotte B.C. Can.
259 E8 Queen Charlotte Bay Falkland Is
222 C4 Queen Charlotte Islands B.C. Can.
222 D5 Queen Charlotte Sound sea chan. B.C. Can.
222 E5 Queen Charlotte Strait B.C. Can.
226 A5 Queen City MO U.S.A.
241 L5 Queen Creek AZ U.S.A.
221 H2 Queen Elizabeth Islands N.W.T./Nunavut Can.
263 K1 Queen Elizabeth Range mts Antarctica
263 C2 Queen Fabiola Mountains Antarctica
222 B2 Queen Mary, Mount Y.T. Can.
263 G2 Queen Mary Land reg. Antarctica
221 H3 Queen Maud Gulf Nunavut Can.
263 A2 Queen Maud Land reg. Antarctica
262 O1 Queen Maud Mountains Antarctica
215 H3 Queensburgh S. Africa
149 H4 Queensbury West Yorkshire, England U.K.
84 B2 Queens Channel N.T. Austr.
221 I2 Queens Channel Nunavut Can.
83 F4 Queenscliff Vic. Austr.
235 E2 Queens County county NY U.S.A.
85 F4 Queensland state Austr.
83 F5 Queenstown Tas. Austr.
81 B6 Queenstown South I. N.Z.
Queenstown Rep. of Ireland see Cóbh
215 F4 Queenstown S. Africa
234 B4 Queenstown MD U.S.A.
238 A2 Queets WA U.S.A.
261 H3 Queguay Grande r. Uru.
160 E3 Queige France
254 F4 Queimadas Brazil
182 C4 Queiriga Port.
256 B4 Queiroz Brazil
183 H2 Quel Spain
209 C7 Quela Angola
159 F4 Quelaines-St-Gault France
213 H3 Quelimane Moz.
244 A2 Quelite Mex.
260 A5 Quella Chile
171 D4 Quellendorf Ger.
259 B6 Quellón Chile
Quelpart Island S. Korea see Cheju-do
257 E5 Queluz Brazil
184 A2 Queluz Port.
183 G3 Quemada Spain
256 D6 Quemada Grande, Ilha i. Brazil
239 E5 Quemado NM U.S.A.
209 D8 Quembo r. Angola
259 B6 Quemchi Chile
Quemoy i. Taiwan see Chinmen Tao
261 F5 Quemú-Quemú Arg.
156 B2 Quend France
169 C3 Quendorf Ger.
171 C4 Quenstedt Ger.
185 G3 Quéntar Spain
234 B2 Quentin PA U.S.A.
114 B3 Quepem Goa India
Que Que Zimbabwe see Kwekwe
261 H6 Quequén Grande r. Arg.
186 F2 Queralbs Spain
190 F5 Quercianella Italy
184 C3 Querença Port.
256 A5 Queréncia do Norte Brazil
244 D4 Queréndaro Mex.
169 F3 Querenhorst Ger.
244 D3 Querétaro Mex.
245 E3 Querétaro state Mex.
171 C4 Querfurt Ger.
163 E6 Quérigut France
168 E1 Quern Ger.
169 D3 Quernheim Ger.
149 G3 Quernmore Lancashire, England U.K.
191 G3 Quero Italy
183 G5 Quero Spain
242 C2 Querobabi Mex.
186 E3 Querol Spain
158 E2 Querqueville France
156 C3 Querrieu France
157 G5 Quers France
187 C5 Quesa Spain
185 G3 Quesada Spain
185 G3 Quesada r. Spain
109 E1 Queshan Henan China
222 F4 Quesnel B.C. Can.
222 F4 Quesnel r. B.C. Can.
156 D2 Quesnoy-sur-Deûle France
158 D3 Quessoy France
156 D3 Quessy France
158 D4 Questembert France
252 D5 Quetena de Lipez r. Bol.
160 D1 Quetigny France
123 F4 Quetta Pak.
158 E2 Quettehou France
158 E3 Quettreville-sur-Sienne France
245 E5 Quetzala r. Mex.
260 B5 Queuco Chile
259 B5 Queule Chile
156 C3 Quevauvillers France
158 C4 Quéven France
158 D3 Quévert France
162 B3 Queyrac France
163 E4 Quézac France
243 H6 Quezaltenango Guat.
243 H6 Quezaltepeque El Salvador
92 B4 Quezon Negros Phil.
92 A4 Quezon Palawan Phil.
92 B3 Quezon City Phil.
107 H5 Qufu Shandong China
111 E6 Qugayatang Xizang China
182 B4 Quiaios Port.
209 B7 Quibala Angola
209 B7 Quibaxe Angola
250 B3 Quibdó Col.
158 C4 Quiberon France
158 C4 Quiberon, Baie de b. France
158 C4 Quiberon, Presqu'île de pen. France
168 E2 Quickborn Ger.
209 B7 Quiculungo Angola
157 H3 Quierschied Ger.
156 D3 Quierzy France
156 D2 Quiévrechain France
260 A5 Quilaco Chile
114 B4 Quilandi Kerala India
252 B4 Quilca Peru
209 B7 Quilenda Angola
209 B8 Quilengues Angola
190 D4 Quiliano Italy
260 B3 Quilimarí Chile
260 E2 Quilino Arg.
252 D4 Quillacollo Bol.
163 E6 Quillan France
260 A5 Quillon Chile
260 B3 Quillota Chile
261 H4 Quilmes Arg.
209 B7 Quilombo dos Dembos Angola
114 C4 Quilon Kerala India
85 F5 Quilpie Qld Austr.
260 B3 Quilpué Chile
213 H3 Quilua Moz.
209 C6 Quimbele Angola
252 D4 Quime Bol.
244 B2 Quimichis Mex.
258 E2 Quimilí Arg.
158 B4 Quimper France
158 C4 Quimperlé France
147 C4 Quin Rep. of Ireland
146 C3 Quinag hill Scotland U.K.
238 A2 Quinault r. WA U.S.A.
252 C3 Quince Mil Peru
190 C3 Quincinetto Italy
240 G2 Quincy CA U.S.A.
231 C6 Quincy FL U.S.A.
230 B4 Quincy IL U.S.A.
233 H3 Quincy MA U.S.A.
226 E5 Quincy MI U.S.A.
232 B4 Quincy OH U.S.A.
156 C4 Quincy-Voisins France
250 C3 Quindio dept Col.
260 E3 Quines Arg.
158 E2 Quinéville France
213 I2 Quinga Moz.
160 D1 Quingey France
220 B4 Quinhagak AK U.S.A.
206 B4 Quinhámel Guinea-Bissau
97 E4 Qui Nhon Vietnam
251 E3 Quinigua, Cerro mts Venez.
238 C3 Quinn r. NV U.S.A.
241 J3 Quinn Canyon Range mts NV U.S.A.
232 C6 Quinnimont WV U.S.A.
161 E5 Quinson France
160 A2 Quinssaines France
184 C3 Quintã hill Port.
184 B2 Quinta do Anjo Port.
256 B5 Quintana Brazil
184 E2 Quintana de la Serena Spain
182 D2 Quintana del Castillo Spain
183 G2 Quintana del Pino Spain
183 F2 Quintana del Puente Spain
183 E2 Quintana de Rueda Spain
183 G2 Quintanapalla Spain
183 G5 Quintanar de la Orden Spain
183 G3 Quintanar de la Sierra Spain
185 I1 Quintanar del Rey Spain
183 H3 Quintana Redonda Spain
243 H5 Quintana Roo state Mex.
182 D3 Quintanilha Port.
Quintanilla de Abajo Spain see Quintanilla de Omesimo
183 F3 Quintanilla de Omesimo Spain
182 B4 Quintãs Port.
161 C3 Quintenas France
236 C4 Quinter KS U.S.A.
260 B3 Quintero Chile
158 D3 Quintin France
260 E4 Quinto r. Arg.
186 C3 Quinto Spain
190 D2 Quinto Switz.
234 C3 Quinton NJ U.S.A.
209 B6 Quinzau Angola
211 D7 Quionga Moz.
254 G4 Quipapá Brazil
185 I2 Quipar r. Spain
209 B8 Quipungo Angola
252 D3 Quiquive r. Bol.
242 □H6 Quiriguá tourist site Guat.
260 A5 Quirihue Chile
209 C7 Quirima Angola
83 G2 Quirindi N.S.W. Austr.
256 B3 Quirinópolis Brazil
252 D4 Quiroga Bol.
244 D4 Quiroga Mex.
182 C2 Quiroga Spain
182 E2 Quiruelas de Vidriales Spain
183 F4 Quismondo Spain
161 C5 Quissac France
257 G5 Quissamã Brazil
211 D8 Quissanga Moz.
209 C7 Quitapa Angola
211 D7 Quiterajo Moz.
256 B4 Quitéria r. Brazil
Quitexe Angola see Dange
258 E2 Quitilipi Arg.
231 D6 Quitman GA U.S.A.
237 F5 Quitman MS U.S.A.
237 E5 Quitman TX U.S.A.
250 B5 Quito Ecuador
156 A3 Quittebeuf France
254 F3 Quixadá Brazil
213 I2 Quixaxe Moz.
254 F3 Quixeramobim Brazil
209 B7 Quixinge Angola
109 E3 Qujiang Guangdong China
Qujiang Sichuan China see Quxian
108 C2 Qu Jiang r. China
108 B3 Qujing Yunnan China
215 G5 Quko S. Africa
Quljuqtow Toghi hills Uzbek. see Kul'dzhuktau, Gory
Qulsary Kazakh. see Kul'sary
126 C5 Qulûsana Egypt
106 B5 Qumar He r. China
106 B5 Qumarheyan Qinghai China
106 B5 Qumarlêb Qinghai China
215 G4 Qumbu S. Africa
111 F6 Qumdo Xizang China
215 F5 Qumrha S. Africa
202 D2 Qunayyin, Sabkhat al salt marsh Libya
Qŭnghirot Uzbek. see Kungrad
108 A2 Qu'nyido Xizang China
223 M1 Quoich r. Nunavut Can.
146 C4 Quoich, Loch l. Scotland U.K.
147 F2 Quoile r. Northern Ireland U.K.
84 B2 Quoin Island N.T. Austr.
111 C5 Quong Muztag mt. Xinjiang/Xizang China
82 D3 Quorn S.A. Austr.
212 E4 Quoxo r. Botswana
Quqên Sichuan China see Jinchuan
Qŭqon Uzbek. see Kokand
125 G3 Qurayat Oman
128 C5 Qurayyah tourist site Saudi Arabia
123 G2 Qŭrghonteppa Tajik.
129 E3 Qurmuxçay r. Azer.
203 G3 Qus Egypt
129 F3 Qusar Azer.
129 F3 Qusarçay r. Azer.
125 E5 Quşay'ir Saudi Arabia
203 G3 Quseir Egypt
Qushan Sichuan China see Beichuan
122 A2 Qūshchī Iran
Qŭshkŭpir Uzbek. see Koshkupyr
Qŭshrabot Uzbek. see Koshrabad
Qusmuryn Kazakh. see Kushmurun
Qusmuryn Köli salt l. Kazakh. see Kushmurun, Ozero
111 F6 Qusum Xizang China
Quthing Lesotho see Moyeni
215 F4 Quthing r. Lesotho
124 C2 Quṭn, Jabal hill Saudi Arabia
124 C4 Qutū' Island Saudi Arabia
128 C2 Quwayq, Nahr r. Syria/Turkey
125 F4 Qū' Wishām reg. Oman
106 E4 Quwu Shan mts China
Quxar Xizang China see Lhazê
108 C2 Quxian Sichuan China
111 E6 Qüxü Xizang China
Quyang Hunan China see Jingzhou
Quyghan Kazakh. see Kuygan
227 I3 Quyon Que. Can.
129 E3 Quzanlı Azer.
107 G4 Quzhou Hebei China
109 F2 Quzhou Zhejiang China
107 E4 Quzi Gansu China
129 D3 Qvareli Georgia
129 C2 Qvirila r. Georgia
Qyteti Stalin Albania see Kuçovë
Qyzan Kazakh. see Kyzan
Qyzylaghash Kazakh. see Kyzylagash
Qyzylorda Kazakh. see Kyzylorda
Qyzylorda Oblysy admin. div. Kazakh. see Kzyl-Ordinskaya Oblast'
Qyzyltaū Kazakh. see Kyzyltau
Qyzyltū Kazakh. see Kishkenekol'
Qyzylzhar Kazakh. see Kyzylzhar

R

179 E2 Raab Austria
179 H4 Raab r. Austria
Raab Hungary see Győr
179 G2 Raabs an der Thaya Austria
140 N2 Raahe Fin.
140 O3 Rääkkylä Fin.
164 F2 Raalte Neth.
164 D3 Raamsdonksveer Neth.
124 C2 Ra'an, Khashm ar hill Saudi Arabia
146 B4 Raasay i. Scotland U.K.
146 B4 Raasay, Sound of sea chan. Scotland U.K.
138 E2 Raasiku Estonia
188 E3 Rab i. Croatia
176 G4 Rába r. Hungary
95 G5 Raba Sumbawa Indon.
175 I5 Raba r. Pol.
191 J3 Rabac Croatia
182 B4 Rabaçal Port.
182 C4 Rabaçal Port.
182 C3 Rabaçal r. Port./Spain
182 C1 Rábade Spain
177 L5 Răbăgani Romania
176 F4 Rábahidvég Hungary
203 G6 Rabak Sudan
176 G4 Rábakecöl Hungary
182 D3 Rabanales Spain
176 F4 Rábapaty Hungary
176 G4 Rábapordány Hungary
163 D5 Rabastens France
163 C5 Rabastens-de-Bigorre France
Rabat Gozo Malta see Victoria
195 □ Rabat Malta
204 D2 Rabat Morocco
91 L7 Rabaul New Britain P.N.G.
175 H6 Raba Wyżna Pol.
Rabbath Ammon Jordan see 'Ammān
191 H4 Rabbi r. Italy
191 F2 Rabbies r. Italy
222 E3 Rabbit r. B.C. Can.
84 B4 Rabbit Flat N.T. Austr.
222 F2 Rabbitskin r. N.W.T. Can.
177 G4 Rábca r. Hungary
177 I2 Rabča Slovakia
177 I2 Rabčice Slovakia
171 E5 Rabenau Ger.
179 G2 Rabenstein an der Pielach Austria
170 C2 Raben Steinfeld Ger.
79 □1 Rabi i. Fiji
124 B3 Rābigh Saudi Arabia
243 H6 Rabinal Guat.
174 D2 Rąbino Pol.
190 E2 Rabiusa r. Switz.
175 H6 Rabka Pol.
169 F3 Räbke Ger.
Rabkob Madh. Prad. India see Dharmjaygarh
117 G5 Rabnabad Islands Bangl.
Râbniţa Moldova see Rîbniţa
216 □1b Rabo de Peixe São Miguel Azores
122 D4 Rābor Iran
191 H3 Raboso r. Italy
204 B5 Rabt Sbayta des. Western Sahara
202 D3 Rabyānah, Ramlat des. Libya
196 E3 Rača Srbija Yugo.
195 H3 Racale Italy
177 H4 Rácalmás Hungary
194 C5 Racalmuto Sicilia Italy
193 I4 Racanello r. Italy
191 I2 Raccolana r. Italy
190 C4 Racconigi Italy
246 D2 Raccoon Cay i. Bahamas
234 C3 Raccoon Creek r. NJ U.S.A.
232 B5 Raccoon Creek r. OH U.S.A.
194 D4 Raccuia Sicilia Italy
179 G4 Rače Slovenia
225 K4 Race, Cape Nfld. Can.
237 F6 Raceland LA U.S.A.
128 B3 Rachaïya Lebanon
237 D7 Rachal TX U.S.A.
175 L5 Rachanie Pol.
157 F4 Rachecourt-sur-Marne France
241 J3 Rachel NV U.S.A.
97 D5 Rach Gia Vietnam
129 C2 Rachis K'edi hills Georgia
174 F2 Raciąż Pol.
175 I3 Raciąż Pol.
175 I3 Raciążnica r. Pol.
174 G5 Racibórz Pol.
175 I6 Raciechowice Pol.
226 D4 Racine WI U.S.A.
232 C5 Racine WV U.S.A.
197 G2 Răciu Romania
177 H4 Ráckeve Hungary
146 E3 Rackwick Orkney, Scotland U.K.
171 D4 Rackwitz Ger.
175 I5 Racławice Pol.
197 G2 Racoş Romania
197 H3 Racoviţa Romania
177 K6 Racoviţa Romania
175 K2 Raczki Podlaskie Pol.
175 I2 Rączki Pol.
124 D5 Radā' Yemen
260 A6 Radal Chile
138 F4 Radashkovichy Belarus
197 G2 Rădăuţi Romania
176 C2 Radbuza r. Czech Rep.
139 K3 Radchenko Rus. Fed.
137 K3 Radchenskoye Rus. Fed.
230 C4 Radcliff KY U.S.A.
149 G4 Radcliffe Greater Manchester, England U.K.
151 F2 Radcliffe on Trent Nottinghamshire, England U.K.
194 D5 Raddusa Sicilia Italy
142 D2 Rade Norway
171 E4 Radeberg Ger.
171 E4 Radebeul Ger.
171 E4 Radeburg Ger.
179 G4 Radeče Slovenia
171 D4 Radefeld Ger.
171 D4 Radegast Ger.
136 C2 Radekhiv Ukr.
179 H4 Radenci Slovenia
137 G4 Radens'k Ukr.
170 D3 Radensleben Ger.
179 E4 Radenthein Austria
169 C4 Radevormwald Ger.
174 D1 Radew r. Pol.
178 C3 Radfeld Austria
232 C6 Radford VA U.S.A.
84 B1 Radford Point N.T. Austr.
151 F2 Radford Semele Warwickshire, England U.K.
116 B5 Radhanpur Gujarat India
171 F4 Radibor Ger.
192 D2 Radicofani Italy
191 G5 Radicondoli Italy
193 H3 Radicosa r. Italy
171 D4 Radis Ger.
120 A1 Radishchevo Rus. Fed.
224 E2 Radisson Que. Can.
223 J4 Radisson Sask. Can.
226 B3 Radisson WI U.S.A.
139 J5 Raditsa-Krylovka Rus. Fed.
222 G5 Radium Hot Springs B.C. Can.
179 G4 Radizelj Slovenia
137 I2 Rad'kovka Rus. Fed.
174 E5 Radków Pol.
175 H5 Radków Pol.
151 G3 Radlett Hertfordshire, England U.K.
262 R1 Radlinski, Mount Antarctica
179 G4 Radlje ob Dravi Slovenia
175 I5 Radłów Pol.
174 G5 Radłów Pol.
197 G4 Radnevo Bulg.
176 C2 Radnice Czech Rep.
177 J6 Radojevo Vojvodina, Srbija Yugo.
172 C4 Radolfzell am Bodensee Ger.
175 J4 Radom Pol.
175 H2 Radomin Pol.
197 F4 Radomir Bulg.
197 F5 Radomir mt. Bulg./Greece
175 J4 Radomka r. Pol.
177 K2 Radomka r. Slovakia
137 G2 Radomka Ukr.
175 J4 Radomska, Równina plain Pol.
175 H4 Radomsko Pol.
136 E2 Radomyshl' Ukr.
175 J5 Radomyśl nad Sanem Pol.
175 J5 Radomyśl Wielki Pol.
176 C1 Radonice Czech Rep.
Radoshkovichi Belarus see Radashkovichy
177 G3 Radošina Slovakia
176 G3 Radošovce Slovakia
175 I4 Radoszyce Pol.
197 H5 Radovets Bulg.
197 F5 Radoviš Macedonia
139 L4 Radovitskiy Rus. Fed.
188 E2 Radovljica Slovenia
174 D2 Radowo Małe Pol.
144 J1 Radøy i. Norway
179 E3 Radstadt Austria
150 E3 Radstock Bath and North East Somerset, England U.K.
82 C3 Radstock, Cape S.A. Austr.
197 H2 Răducăneni Romania
136 F2 Radul' Ukr.
138 E4 Radun' Belarus
143 H4 Radunia r. Pol.
137 G4 Radushne Ukr.
138 D4 Radviliškis Lith.
124 B2 Radwá, Jabal mt. Saudi Arabia
174 D4 Radwanice Pol.
175 K6 Radymno Pol.
136 C2 Radyvyliv Ukr.
175 I3 Radzanów Pol.
175 I4 Radzice Duże Pol.
174 F2 Radzicz Pol.
175 J1 Radzieje Pol.
174 G3 Radziejów Pol.
175 I6 Radziejowa mt. Pol.
175 I3 Radziejowice Pol.
175 I5 Radziemice Pol.
175 K2 Radziłów Pol.
177 I3 Radzovce Slovakia
175 J3 Radzymin Pol.
174 G2 Radzyń Chełminski Pol.
175 K4 Radzyń Podlaski Pol.
116 E4 Rae Bareli Uttar Prad. India
222 G2 Rae-Edzo N.W.T. Can.
231 E5 Raeford NC U.S.A.
222 G1 Rae Lakes N.W.T. Can.
165 F4 Raeren Belgium
169 B4 Raesfeld Ger.
87 D6 Raeside, Lake salt flat W.A. Austr.
80 D1 Raetea hill North I. N.Z.
80 E3 Raetihi North I. N.Z.
127 E5 Rāf hill Saudi Arabia
260 A5 Rafael Chile
261 G2 Rafaela Arg.
246 D2 Rafael Freyre Cuba
245 F4 Rafael J Garcia Mex.
Rafaḩ Gaza see Rafiaḩ
208 D3 Rafaï C.A.R.
136 D2 Rafalivka Ukr.
187 C5 Rafelbunyol Spain
194 C5 Raffadali Sicilia Italy
146 E4 Rafford Moray, Scotland U.K.
147 F2 Raffrey Northern Ireland U.K.
127 F5 Rafḩā' Saudi Arabia
128 B4 Rafiaḩ Gaza
198 D2 Rafina Greece
147 C3 Raford r. Rep. of Ireland
122 C4 Rafsanjān Iran
238 D3 Raft r. Idaho/Nevada U.S.A.
183 E4 Rágama Spain
138 E3 Ragana Latvia
195 F3 Raganello r. Italy
92 C5 Ragang, Mount vol. Mindanao Phil.
92 B3 Ragay Gulf Phil.
170 D2 Rägelin Ger.
87 D7 Ragged, Mount hill W.A. Austr.
246 D2 Ragged Island Bahamas
116 D4 Raghogarh Madh. Prad. India
80 E2 Raglan North I. N.Z.
150 E3 Raglan Monmouthshire, Wales U.K.
179 G4 Ragnitz Austria
171 D3 Ragösen Ger.
225 G3 Ragueneau Que. Can.
171 D4 Raguhn Ger.
Ragusa Croatia see Dubrovnik
194 D6 Ragusa Sicilia Italy
194 D6 Ragusa prov. Sicilia Italy
117 H4 Raha Assam India
93 B4 Raha Sulawesi Tenggara Indon.
139 H5 Rahachow Belarus
203 G6 Rahad r. Sudan
Rahaeng Thai. see Tak
124 C3 Rahaţ, Ḩarrat lava field Saudi Arabia
116 D5 Rahatgaon Madh. Prad. India
169 D3 Rahden Ger.
114 B2 Rahimatpur Mahar. India
123 G4 Rahimyar Khan Pak.
157 G5 Rahin r. France
122 B3 Rāhjerd Iran
80 D3 Rahotu North I. N.Z.
260 B6 Rahue mt. Chile
114 B2 Rahuri Mahar. India
193 F2 Raiano Italy
79 □3 Raiatea i. Arch. de la Société Fr. Polynesia
114 C2 Raichur Karnataka India
117 G4 Raiganj W. Bengal India
117 E5 Raigarh Madh. Prad. India
114 D2 Raigarh Orissa India
116 C3 Raikot Punjab India
241 J2 Railroad Valley NV U.S.A.
117 G5 Raimangal r. Bangl.
173 E3 Rain Bayern Ger.
173 G3 Rain Bayern Ger.
179 F2 Rainbach im Mühlkreis Austria
83 E3 Rainbow Vic. Austr.
85 H5 Rainbow Beach Qld Austr.
222 G3 Rainbow Lake Alta Can.
85 F1 Raine Entrance sea chan. Qld Austr.
85 F1 Raine Island Qld Austr.
232 C6 Rainelle WV U.S.A.
149 G4 Rainford Merseyside, England U.K.
123 G4 Raini r. Pak.
238 B2 Rainier, Mount vol. WA U.S.A.
149 G4 Rainow Cheshire, England U.K.
149 H4 Rainworth Nottinghamshire, England U.K.
236 E1 Rainy r. MN U.S.A.
223 M5 Rainy Lake Ont. Can.
223 M5 Rainy River Ont. Can.
117 G5 Raipur Bangl.
116 E5 Raipur Madh. Prad. India
116 C4 Raipur Rajasthan India
117 F5 Raipur W. Bengal India
117 F5 Rairangpur Orissa India
78 □3b Rairik i. Majuro Marshall Is
182 C2 Rairiz de Veiga Spain
Rairoa atoll Arch. des Tuamotu Fr. Polynesia see Rangiroa
168 F1 Raisdorf Ger.
116 D5 Raisen Madh. Prad. India
116 C3 Raisinghnagar Rajasthan India
141 M3 Raisio Fin.
156 D2 Raismes France
116 D5 Raitalai Madh. Prad. India
173 F2 Raitenbuch Ger.
226 C1 Raith Ont. Can.
81 D4 Rai Valley South I. N.Z.
79 □3 Raivavae i. Îs Australes Fr. Polynesia
123 H4 Raiwind Pak.
138 F2 Raja Estonia
93 D3 Rajaampat, Kepulauan is Irian Jaya Indon.
94 D4 Rajabasa, Gunung vol. Indon.
117 F5 Rajagangapur Orissa India
114 D2 Rajahmundry Andhra Prad. India
116 C3 Rajaldesar Rajasthan India
138 E1 Rajamäki Fin.
114 C3 Rajampet Andhra Prad. India
95 E2 Rajang r. Sarawak Malaysia
123 G4 Rajanpur Pak.
114 C4 Rajapalaiyam Tamil Nadu India
114 B2 Rajapur Mahar. India
116 C4 Rajasthan state India
117 F4 Rajauli Bihar India
117 G5 Rajbari Bangl.
176 F2 Rájec Czech Rep.
177 H2 Rajec Slovakia
177 H2 Rajecká Lesná Slovakia
116 D4 Rajgarh Madh. Prad. India
114 B2 Rajgarh Mahar. India
116 C3 Rajgarh Rajasthan India
116 D4 Rajgarh Rajasthan India
117 F4 Rajgir Bihar India
175 K2 Rajgród Pol.
179 H1 Rajhrad Czech Rep.
176 F2 Rajhradice Czech Rep.
116 E5 Rajim Madh. Prad. India
197 E4 Rajince Srbija Yugo.
176 G3 Rajka Hungary
116 B5 Rajkot Gujarat India
117 F4 Rajmahal Bihar India
117 F4 Rajmahal Hills India
116 E5 Raj Nandgaon Madh. Prad. India
116 C5 Rajpipla Gujarat India
116 C5 Rajpur Madh. Prad. India
116 D3 Rajpura Punjab India
Rajputana Agency state India see Rajasthan
116 C4 Rajsamand Rajasthan India
117 G4 Rajshahi Bangl.
117 G4 Rajshahi admin. div. Bangl.
128 C1 Rājū Syria
116 B5 Rajula Gujarat India
116 D5 Rajur Mahar. India
114 C2 Rajura Mahar. India
Rajura Mahar. India see Ahmadpur
111 D6 Raka Xizang China
177 J3 Rakaca r. Hungary
81 □2 Rakahanga atoll Cook Is
Rakahuri r. South I. N.Z. see Ashley
210 A5 Rakai Uganda
81 D5 Rakaia South I. N.Z.
81 D5 Rakaia r. South I. N.Z.
177 K3 Rakamaz Hungary
125 E2 Rakan, Ra's pt Qatar
116 C1 Rakaposhi mt. Jammu and Kashmir
Raka Zangbo r. Xizang China see Dogxung Zangbo
81 A7 Rakeahua, Mount hill Stewart I. N.Z.
179 F5 Rakek Slovenia
Rakhaing state Myanmar see Arakan
Rakhine state Myanmar see Arakan
136 C3 Rakhiv Ukr.
137 G4 Rakhmanivka Ukr.
123 E5 Rakhshan r. Pak.
79 □1a Rakiraki Viti Levu Fiji
197 G4 Rakitnitsa r. Bulg.
135 F6 Rakitnoye Belgorodskaya Oblast' Rus. Fed.
100 E3 Rakitnoye Primorskiy Kray Rus. Fed.
Rakiura i. N.Z. see Stewart Island
138 F2 Rakke Estonia
142 D2 Rakkestad Norway
123 G4 Rakni r. Pak.
177 J4 Rákóczifalva Hungary
177 J4 Rákócziújfalu Hungary
174 E3 Rakoniewice Pol.
177 L3 Rakoshyn Ukr.
177 H2 Raková Slovakia
197 F4 Rakovitsa Bulg.
176 C1 Rakovnická Pahorkatina hills Czech Rep.
176 C1 Rakovník Czech Rep.
197 G4 Rakovski Bulg.
170 E1 Rakow Ger.
175 J5 Raków Pol.
175 K5 Rakszawa Pol.
138 F2 Rakvere Estonia
176 F3 Rakvice Czech Rep.
237 F5 Raleigh MS U.S.A.
231 E5 Raleigh NC U.S.A.
172 A2 Ralingen Ger.
226 D2 Ralph MI U.S.A.
223 I5 Ralston Alta Can.
227 I5 Ralston PA U.S.A.
113 □1 Raluara Giri i. N. Male Maldives
222 F2 Ram r. N.W.T. Can.
128 B3 Rama Israel
242 □I6 Rama Nic.
136 C2 Rama r. Ukr.
194 D5 Ramacca Sicilia Italy
260 B3 Ramada, Cerro de la mt. San Juan Arg.
225 I1 Ramah Nfld. Can.
183 G1 Ramales de la Victoria Spain
184 A1 Ramalhal Port.
254 D5 Ramalho, Serra do hills Brazil
128 B4 Ramallah West Bank
261 G3 Ramallo Arg.
114 C3 Ramanagaram Karnataka India
114 C4 Ramanathapuram Tamil Nadu India
117 E5 Ramanuj Ganj Madh. Prad. India
235 D2 Ramapo r. NJ U.S.A.
215 E1 Ramatlabama S. Africa
161 E5 Ramatuelle France
114 C2 Ramayampet Andhra Prad. India
140 K1 Ramberg Norway
157 G4 Rambervillers France
170 E1 Rambin Ger.
187 B6 Rambla del Judío r. Spain
187 B6 Rambla del Moro r. Spain
156 B4 Rambouillet France
156 B4 Rambouillet, Forêt de for. France
165 E5 Rambrouch Lux.
157 F4 Rambucourt France
114 B3 Ramdurg Karnataka India
150 C4 Rame Cornwall, England U.K.
147 D1 Ramelton Rep. of Ireland
139 L4 Ramenskoye Rus. Fed.
156 E4 Ramerupt France
81 C5 Rameses, Mount South I. N.Z.
139 K3 Rameshki Rus. Fed.
114 C4 Rameswaram Tamil Nadu India
111 B7 Ramganga r. India
117 G5 Ramgarh Bangl.
117 F5 Ramgarh Bihar India
116 B4 Ramgarh Rajasthan India
116 C4 Ramgarh Rajasthan India
116 D4 Ramgarh Rajasthan India
122 B4 Rāmhormoz Iran
165 D4 Ramillies Belgium
84 C2 Ramingining N.T. Austr.
179 E3 Ramingstein Austria
216 □1a Raminho Terceira Azores
182 C2 Ramirás Spain
Ramitan Uzbek. see Romitan
128 B4 Ramla Israel
125 F3 Ramlat al Ghāfah des. Saudi Arabia
125 G3 Ramlat al Wahībah des. Oman
125 F4 Ramlat Amilḩayt des. Oman
124 D4 Ramlat Dahm des. Saudi Arabia/Yemen
128 B5 Ramm, Jabal mts Jordan
172 B2 Rammelsbach Ger.
171 F4 Rammenau Ger.
173 E3 Rammingen Ger.
215 F2 Rammulotsi S. Africa
Ramnad Tamil Nadu India see Ramanathapuram
116 E4 Ramnagar Madh. Prad. India
116 D3 Ramnagar Uttar Prad. India
116 C2 Ramnagar Jammu and Kashmir
143 G2 Ramnäs Sweden
142 D2 Ramnes Norway
197 H3 Râmnicul Sărat r. Romania
197 H3 Râmnicu Sărat Romania
197 G3 Râmnicu Vâlcea Romania
213 E4 Ramokgwebane Botswana
137 J2 Ramon' Rus. Fed.
240 I5 Ramona CA U.S.A.
157 G5 Ramonchamp France
244 C1 Ramón Corona Mex.
163 D5 Ramonville-St-Agne France
227 G1 Ramore Ont. Can.
237 B7 Ramos r. Mex.
243 E3 Ramos Arizpe Mex.
190 F2 Ramosch Switz.
212 E5 Ramotswa Botswana
107 G1 Rampart of Genghis Khan tourist site Asia
149 F3 Rampside Cumbria, England U.K.
111 B6 Rampur Hima. Prad. India
116 D3 Rampur Uttar Prad. India
116 D3 Rampur Uttar Prad. India
116 C4 Rampura Madh. Prad. India
Rampur Boalia Bangl. see Rajshahi
117 F4 Rampur Hat W. Bengal India
96 A3 Ramree Island Myanmar
179 E3 Ramsau am Dachstein Austria
173 G4 Ramsau bei Berchtesgaden Ger.
178 C3 Ramsau im Zillertal Austria
143 F2 Ramsberg Sweden
149 G4 Ramsbottom Greater Manchester, England U.K.
151 F3 Ramsbury Wiltshire, England U.K.
140 L3 Ramsele Sweden
172 C4 Ramsen Switz.
227 F2 Ramsey Ont. Can.
148 E3 Ramsey Isle of Man
151 G2 Ramsey Cambridgeshire, England U.K.
235 D1 Ramsey NJ U.S.A.
148 E3 Ramsey Bay Isle of Man
150 B3 Ramsey Island Wales U.K.
151 G2 Ramsey St Mary's Cambridgeshire, England U.K.
215 H4 Ramsgate S. Africa
151 I3 Ramsgate Kent, England U.K.
117 G4 Ramshai Hat W. Bengal India
122 B4 Rāmshir Iran
117 H3 Ramsing mt. Arun. Prad. India
141 K3 Ramsjö Sweden
168 C2 Ramsloh (Saterland) Ger.
172 B2 Ramstein Ger.
116 D5 Ramtek Mahar. India
117 H5 Ramu Bangl.
91 J7 Ramu r. P.N.G.
140 K3 Ramundberget Sweden
140 L3 Ramvik Sweden
138 E4 Ramygala Lith.
250 D4 Rana, Cerro hill Col.
182 D1 Rañadoiro, Sierra de mts Spain
117 G5 Ranaghat W. Bengal India
Ranai i. HI U.S.A. see Lanai
116 C4 Rana Pratap Sagar resr India
116 C5 Ranapur Madh. Prad. India
142 D1 Rånåsfoss Norway
260 B4 Rancagua Chile
165 D4 Rance Belgium
158 D3 Rance r. France
161 A5 Rance r. France
256 B5 Rancharia Brazil
222 D2 Rancheria Y.T. Can.
222 D2 Rancheria r. Y.T. Can.
238 F2 Ranchester WY U.S.A.
117 F5 Ranchi Bihar India
240 G2 Rancho Cordova CA U.S.A.
261 H4 Ranchos Arg.
239 F4 Ranchos de Taos NM U.S.A.
259 B6 Ranco, Lago l. Chile
234 D3 Rancocas Creek, North Branch r. NJ U.S.A.
234 D3 Rancocas Woods NJ U.S.A.
83 F3 Rand N.S.W. Austr.
232 C5 Rand WV U.S.A.
215 H3 Randalhurst S. Africa
234 B3 Randallstown MD U.S.A.
147 E2 Randalstown Northern Ireland U.K.
160 B2 Randan France
194 D5 Randazzo Sicilia Italy
215 F2 Randburg S. Africa
179 F2 Randegg Austria
142 D3 Randers Denmark
172 D2 Randersacker Ger.
215 F2 Randfontein S. Africa
233 H3 Randolph MA U.S.A.
233 □I2 Randolph ME U.S.A.
232 D3 Randolph NY U.S.A.
238 E3 Randolph UT U.S.A.
233 G3 Randolph VT U.S.A.
159 G3 Randonnai France
170 F2 Randow r. Ger.
240 I4 Randsburg CA U.S.A.
141 K3 Randsjö Sweden
215 G2 Randvaal S. Africa
140 M2 Råneå Sweden
159 F3 Rânes France
81 C6 Ranfurly South I. N.Z.
117 H4 Ranga r. India
97 C6 Rangae Thai.
117 H5 Rangamati Bangl.
117 H4 Rangapara North Assam India
233 □H2 Rangeley ME U.S.A.
241 M1 Rangely CO U.S.A.
172 C3 Rangendingen Ger.
224 D4 Ranger Lake Ont. Can.
178 D4 Rangersdorf Austria
116 E5 Rangi Mahar. India
117 G4 Rangia Patharughat Assam India
Rangiauria i. Chatham Is S. Pacific Ocean see Pitt Island
81 D5 Rangiora South I. N.Z.
80 F2 Rangipoua mt. North I. N.Z.
79 □3 Rangiroa atoll Arch. des Tuamotu Fr. Polynesia
80 F3 Rangitaiki North I. N.Z.
80 F2 Rangitaiki r. North I. N.Z.
81 C6 Rangitata South I. N.Z.
81 C6 Rangitata r. South I. N.Z.
80 E4 Rangitikei r. North I. N.Z.
80 E3 Rangiwaea Junction North I. N.Z.
80 E3 Rangiwahia North I. N.Z.
94 D4 Rangkasbitung Jawa Barat Indon.
Rangke Sichuan China see Zamtang
Rangôn Myanmar see Yangôn
Rangôn admin. div. Myanmar see Yangôn
Rangoon Myanmar see Yangôn
Rangoon admin. div. Myanmar see Yangôn
96 B3 Rangoon r. Myanmar
117 G4 Rangpur Bangl.
94 C2 Rangsang i. Indon.
171 E3 Rangsdorf Ger.
182 C4 Ranhados Port.
116 C4 Rani Rajasthan India
116 C3 Rania Haryana India
114 B3 Ranibennur Karnataka India
226 A1 Ranier City MN U.S.A.
117 F5 Raniganj W. Bengal India
117 E5 Ranijula Peak Madh. Prad. India
116 D3 Ranikhet Uttar Prad. India
123 G5 Ranipur Pak.
171 C5 Ranis Ger.
116 C4 Raniwara Rajasthan India
175 J5 Ranizów Pol.
237 C6 Rankin TX U.S.A.
223 M2 Rankin Inlet Nunavut Can.
83 F3 Rankin's Springs N.S.W. Austr.
Rankovićevo Srbija Yugo. see Kraljevo
178 A3 Rankweil Austria
85 G5 Rannes Qld Austr.
120 C2 Ranneye Rus. Fed.
146 D5 Rannoch, Loch l. Scotland U.K.
146 D5 Rannoch Moor moorland Scotland U.K.
146 D5 Rannoch Station Perth and Kinross, Scotland U.K.
116 B4 Rann of Kachchh marsh India
207 H4 Rano Nigeria
78 □6 Rano, Mount New Georgia Is Solomon Is
213 □J3 Ranobe r. Madag.
213 □K3 Ranomafana Madag.
213 □J4 Ranomena Madag.
97 B5 Ranong Thai.
78 □6 Ranongga i. New Georgia Is Solomon Is
213 □J5 Ranopiso Madag.
97 C6 Ranot Thai.
139 M4 Ranova r. Rus. Fed.
116 B5 Ranpur Gujarat India
169 C5 Ransbach-Baumbach Ger.
142 E1 Ransby Sweden
149 H4 Ranskill Nottinghamshire, England U.K.
226 C5 Ransom IL U.S.A.
234 C1 Ransom PA U.S.A.
165 D3 Ranst Belgium
213 □K2 Rantabe Madag.
141 O3 Rantasalmi Fin.
95 F3 Rantau Kalimantan Selatan Indon.
94 C2 Rantau i. Indon.
94 B2 Rantauprapat Sumatera Indon.
93 B3 Rantemario, Gunung mt. Indon.
179 F3 Ranten Austria
93 A3 Rantepao Sulawesi Selatan Indon.
226 C5 Rantoul IL U.S.A.
168 E1 Rantrum Ger.
139 J3 Rantsevo Rus. Fed.
140 N2 Rantsila Fin.
168 D1 Rantum Ger.
140 N2 Ranua Fin.
142 C3 Ranum Denmark
196 D5 Ranxë Albania
127 G3 Rānya Iraq
96 D3 Rao Go mt. Laos/Vietnam
100 E3 Raohe Heilong. China
157 G4 Raon-l'Étape France
191 G3 Raossi Italy
77 I4 Raoul Island N.Z.
79 □3 Rapa i. Îs Australes Fr. Polynesia
140 L2 Rapaälven r. Sweden
Rapa-iti i. Îs Australes Fr. Polynesia see Rapa
190 E4 Rapallo Italy
116 B5 Rapar Gujarat India
116 D3 Rapar Punjab India
260 B3 Rapel r. Chile
148 B4 Rapemills Rep. of Ireland
147 D2 Raphoe Rep. of Ireland
232 E5 Rapidan r. VA U.S.A.
82 D3 Rapid Bay S.A. Austr.
236 C2 Rapid City SD U.S.A.
227 H2 Rapide-Deux Que. Can.
227 H2 Rapide-Sept Que. Can.
193 F3 Rapido r. Italy
226 D3 Rapid River MI U.S.A.
138 F2 Räpina Estonia
252 D2 Rapirrān r. Brazil
138 E2 Rapla Estonia
191 G5 Rapolano Terme Italy
193 H4 Rapolla Italy
184 B1 Raposa Port.
176 G1 Rapotín Czech Rep.
182 C4 Rapoula do Côa Port.
232 E6 Rappahannock r. VA U.S.A.
93 A3 Rappang Sulawesi Selatan Indon.
169 F4 Rappbodetalstausee resr Ger.
172 C4 Rapperswil Switz.
179 G2 Rappottenstein Austria
116 E4 Rapti r. India
252 D3 Rapulo r. Bol.
114 C3 Rapur Andhra Prad. India
116 B5 Rapur Gujarat India
Raqqa Syria see Ar Raqqah
233 F2 Raquette r. NY U.S.A.
84 D1 Raragala Island N.T. Austr.
156 C3 Raray France
234 D2 Raritan, South Branch r. NJ U.S.A.
79 □3 Raroia atoll Arch. des Tuamotu Fr. Polynesia
190 C2 Raron Switz.
81 □3 Rarotonga i. Cook Is
116 C4 Ras Rajasthan India
191 J3 Raša Croatia
188 E3 Raša r. Croatia
125 G4 Ra's ad Daqm Oman
125 G3 Ra's al Ḩadd Oman
125 F2 Ras al Khaimah U.A.E.
Ra's al Khaymah U.A.E. see Ras al Khaimah
124 C3 Raşan, Jabal hill Saudi Arabia
183 G4 Rascafría Spain
Râşcani Moldova see Rîşcani
171 D5 Raschau Ger.
210 C1 Ras Dashen mt. Eth.
169 E5 Rasdorf Ger.
138 D4 Raseiniai Lith.
206 D2 Râs el Mâ Mali
113 □1 Rasfaree i. N. Male Maldives
203 G2 Râs Ghârib Egypt
106 A2 Rashaant Bayan-Ölgiy Mongolia
106 E2 Rashaant Dundgovĭ Mongolia
210 A2 Rashad Sudan
147 E2 Rasharkin Northern Ireland U.K.
147 D2 Rashedoge Rep. of Ireland
203 F2 Rashîd Egypt
137 G2 Rashivka Ukr.
215 F1 Rashoop S. Africa
122 B2 Rasht Iran
196 E4 Rasina r. Yugo.
183 G1 Rasines Spain
141 K3 Råsjö Sweden
123 E5 Rāsk Balūchestān va Sīstān Iran
196 E4 Raška Srbija Yugo.
111 A4 Raskam mts China
123 F4 Ras Koh mt. Pak.
123 F4 Raskoh mts Pak.
177 H2 Raškovice Czech Rep.
177 K2 Raslavice Slovakia

Rasmussen Basin to Richwood
353

221 I3 **Rasmussen Basin** sea feature Nunavut Can.
197 G3 **Râşnov** Romania
206 □ **Raso** i. Cape Verde
254 F4 **Raso da Catarina** hills Brazil
87 E6 **Rason Lake** salt flat W.A. Austr.
138 G4 **Rasony** Belarus
197 H3 **Rasova** Romania
197 F4 **Rasovo** Bulg.
171 G5 **Raspenava** Czech Rep.
186 D3 **Rasquera** Spain
117 E4 **Rasra** Uttar Prad. India
124 B2 **Ra's Sāq, Jabal** hill Saudi Arabia
125 G3 **Ra's Şirāb** Oman
189 C7 **Rass Jebel** Tunisia
135 H5 **Rasskazovo** Rus. Fed.
197 F4 **Rast** Romania
139 H5 **Rasta** r. Belarus
125 E2 **Ras Tannūrah** Saudi Arabia
172 C3 **Rastatt** Ger.
168 C3 **Rastdorf** Ger.
142 C3 **Råsted** Denmark
168 D2 **Rastede** Ger.
171 C4 **Rastenberg** Ger.
179 G2 **Rastenfeld** Austria
178 C3 **Rastkogel** mt. Austria
Rastorguyevo Rus. Fed. see **Vidnoye**
170 C2 **Rastow** Ger.
183 E3 **Rasueros** Spain
174 F4 **Raszków** Pol.
137 I2 **Rat'** r. Rus. Fed.
80 E3 **Rata** North I. N.Z.
Ratae Leicester, England U.K. see **Leicester**
94 D4 **Ratai, Gunung** mt. Indon.
138 F5 **Ratamka** Belarus
215 G2 **Ratanda** S. Africa
116 C4 **Ratangarh** Madh. Prad. India
116 C3 **Ratangarh** Rajasthan India
116 C5 **Ratanpur** Gujarat India
116 E5 **Ratanpur** Madh. Prad. India
141 K3 **Rätansbyn** Sweden
97 B4 **Rat Buri** Thai.
139 L5 **Ratchino** Lipetskaya Oblast' Rus. Fed.
120 C1 **Ratchino** Orenburgskaya Oblast' Rus. Fed.
168 F2 **Ratekau** Ger.
214 B4 **Ratelfontein** S. Africa
182 B3 **Rates** Port.
116 D4 **Rath** Uttar Prad. India
148 B4 **Rath** Rep. of Ireland
147 E3 **Rathangan** Rep. of Ireland
147 C3 **Rathcabban** Rep. of Ireland
147 D3 **Rathconrath** Rep. of Ireland
147 C4 **Rathcool** Rep. of Ireland
147 E3 **Rathcoole** Rep. of Ireland
147 C4 **Rathcormack** Rep. of Ireland
148 C5 **Rathdangan** Rep. of Ireland
147 D4 **Rathdowney** Rep. of Ireland
147 E4 **Rathdrum** Rep. of Ireland
96 A2 **Rathedaung** Myanmar
170 D3 **Rathenow** Ger.
150 A1 **Rathfarnham** Rep. of Ireland
147 E2 **Rathfriland** Northern Ireland U.K.
146 E5 **Rathillet** Fife, Scotland U.K.
147 C4 **Rathkeale** Rep. of Ireland
147 D4 **Rathkeevin** Rep. of Ireland
147 B2 **Rathlackan** Rep. of Ireland
147 B2 **Rathlee** Rep. of Ireland
147 E1 **Rathlin Island** Northern Ireland U.K.
147 C4 **Rathluirc** Rep. of Ireland
147 E3 **Rathmolyon** Rep. of Ireland
147 B4 **Rathmore** Rep. of Ireland
147 D1 **Rathmullan** Rep. of Ireland
147 E4 **Rathnew** Rep. of Ireland
146 E6 **Ratho** Edinburgh, Scotland U.K.
147 D3 **Rathowen** Rep. of Ireland
Ratibor Pol. see **Racibórz**
169 B4 **Ratingen** Ger.
Ratisbon Ger. see **Regensburg**
188 E2 **Ratitovec** mt. Slovenia
116 C3 **Ratiya** Haryana India
177 K3 **Rátka** Hungary
116 C5 **Ratlam** Madh. Prad. India
114 B2 **Ratnagiri** Mahar. India
114 D5 **Ratnapura** Sri Lanka
136 C2 **Ratne** Ukr.
Ratno Ukr. see **Ratne**
148 C4 **Ratoath** Rep. of Ireland
123 G5 **Rato Dero** Pak.
239 F4 **Raton** NM U.S.A.
169 F5 **Rattelsdorf** Ger.
179 G3 **Ratten** Austria
146 E5 **Rattray** Perth and Kinross, Scotland U.K.
141 K3 **Rättvik** Sweden
222 C3 **Ratz, Mount** B.C. Can.
168 F2 **Ratzeburg** Ger.
168 F2 **Ratzeburger See** l. Ger.
171 C3 **Rätzlingen** Ger.
94 C2 **Raub** Malaysia
169 C5 **Raubach** Ger.
173 G4 **Raubling** Ger.
261 H5 **Rauch** Arg.
234 A1 **Rauchtown** PA U.S.A.
157 E3 **Raucourt-et-Flaba** France
140 N2 **Raudanjoki** r. Fin.
197 F3 **Râu de Mori** Romania
127 G5 **Raudhatain** Kuwait
138 E2 **Raudna** r. Estonia
138 D4 **Raudondvaris** Lith.
171 F3 **Rauen** Ger.
172 C2 **Rauenberg** Ger.
171 C5 **Rauenstein** Ger.
173 E2 **Rauhe Ebrach** r. Ger.
80 F2 **Raukokore** North I. N.Z.
80 G2 **Raukumara** mt. North I. N.Z.
80 F3 **Raukumara Range** mts North I. N.Z.
117 E5 **Raul** r. India
161 A4 **Raulhac** France
257 F4 **Raul Soares** Brazil
141 M3 **Rauma** Fin.
81 E4 **Raumati** North I. N.Z.
138 E3 **Rauna** Latvia
151 G2 **Raunds** Northamptonshire, England U.K.
80 E3 **Raurimu** North I. N.Z.
178 D3 **Rauris** Austria
117 F5 **Raurkela** Orissa India
Rauschen Kaliningradskaya Oblast' Rus. Fed. see **Svetlogorsk**
169 D5 **Rauschenberg** Ger.
102 L1 **Rausu-dake** mt. Japan
136 E4 **Răut** r. Moldova
191 H2 **Raut, Monte** mt. Italy
140 N3 **Rautalampi** Fin.
140 O3 **Rautavaara** Fin.
171 D5 **Rautenkranz** Ger.
141 O3 **Rautjärvi** Fin.
Rauza Mahar. India see **Khuldabad**
163 B4 **Rauzan** France
79 □3 **Ravahéré** atoll Arch. des Tuamotu Fr. Polynesia
238 D2 **Ravalli** MT U.S.A.
122 A3 **Ravānsar** Iran
194 C5 **Ravanusa** Sicilia Italy
122 D4 **Rāvar** Iran
136 B2 **Rava-Rus'ka** Ukr.
193 G4 **Ravello** Italy
165 D3 **Ravels** Belgium
179 G2 **Ravelsbach** Austria
143 F3 **Rävemåla** Sweden
233 G3 **Ravena** NY U.S.A.
149 F3 **Ravenglass** Cumbria, England U.K.
191 H4 **Ravenna** Italy
191 H4 **Ravenna** prov. Emilia-Romagna Italy
236 D3 **Ravenna** NE U.S.A.
232 C4 **Ravenna** OH U.S.A.
234 C2 **Raven Rock** NJ U.S.A.
172 D4 **Ravensburg** Ger.
148 C3 **Ravensdale** Rep. of Ireland
85 F3 **Ravenshoe** Qld Austr.
164 E3 **Ravenstein** Neth.
87 D7 **Ravensthorpe** W.A. Austr.
149 G3 **Ravenstonedale** Cumbria, England U.K.
85 F4 **Ravenswood** Qld Austr.
232 C5 **Ravenswood** WV U.S.A.
116 D5 **Raver** Mahar. India
123 G4 **Ravi** r. Pak.
156 E5 **Ravières** France
234 B2 **Ravine** PA U.S.A.
188 E3 **Ravna Gora** Croatia
188 F3 **Ravna Gora** hill Croatia
179 G4 **Ravne** Slovenia
179 F4 **Ravne na Koroškem** Slovenia
123 E2 **Ravnina** Turkm.
120 D4 **Ravshan** Uzbek.
168 E1 **Ravsted** Denmark
127 F4 **Rāwah** Iraq
77 I2 **Rawaki** i. Phoenix Is Kiribati
123 H3 **Rawala Kot** Pak.
123 H3 **Rawalpindi** Pak.
175 I4 **Rawa Mazowiecka** Pol.
127 G3 **Rawāndiz** Iraq
94 C3 **Rawas** r. Indon.
116 C3 **Rawatsar** Rajasthan India
149 I4 **Rawcliffe** East Riding of Yorkshire, England U.K.
149 H4 **Rawcliffe** York, England U.K.
124 D5 **Rawdah** Yemen
174 E4 **Rawicz** Pol.
175 I4 **Rawka** r. Pol.
87 E6 **Rawlinna** W.A. Austr.
238 F3 **Rawlins** WY U.S.A.
87 E5 **Rawlinson, Mount** hill W.A. Austr.
87 F5 **Rawlinson Range** hills W.A. Austr.
149 H4 **Rawmarsh** South Yorkshire, England U.K.
Rawnina Turkm. see **Ravnina**
261 G4 **Rawson** Buenos Aires Arg.
259 D6 **Rawson** Chubut Arg.
262 N1 **Rawson Mountains** Antarctica
214 B5 **Rawsonville** S. Africa
149 G4 **Rawtenstall** Lancashire, England U.K.
117 F4 **Raxaul** Bihar India
226 A1 **Ray** MN U.S.A.
95 E3 **Raya, Bukit** mt. Kalimantan Indon.
95 F3 **Raya, Bukit** mt. Kalimantan Indon.
114 C3 **Rayachoti** Andhra Prad. India
114 C3 **Rayadurg** Andhra Prad. India
115 D2 **Rayagarha** Orissa India
128 C3 **Rayak** Lebanon
100 D2 **Raychikhinsk** Rus. Fed.
139 K2 **Rayda** Rus. Fed.
124 D5 **Raydah** Yemen
122 D4 **Rāyen** Iran
240 H4 **Rayes Peak** CA U.S.A.
120 C1 **Rayevskiy** Rus. Fed.
137 F3 **Rayhorod** Ukr.
137 J3 **Rayhorodka** Ukr.
137 I3 **Rayhorodok** Ukr.
151 H3 **Rayleigh** Essex, England U.K.
222 H5 **Raymond** Alta Can.
233 H3 **Raymond** NH U.S.A.
238 B2 **Raymond** WA U.S.A.
83 G3 **Raymond Terrace** N.S.W. Austr.
237 D7 **Raymondville** TX U.S.A.
223 J5 **Raymore** Sask. Can.
117 F5 **Rayna** W. Bengal India
151 H3 **Rayne** Essex, England U.K.
161 E5 **Rayol-Canadel-sur-Mer** France
245 E3 **Rayón** Mex.
243 E3 **Rayones** Mex.
97 C4 **Rayong** Thai.
125 F4 **Raysūt** Oman
215 G1 **Rayton** S. Africa
237 F5 **Rayville** LA U.S.A.
124 B3 **Rayyis** Saudi Arabia
158 B3 **Raz, Pointe du** pt France
162 C3 **Razac-sur-l'Isle** France
115 D2 **Razam** Andhra Prad. India
122 B3 **Razan** Iran
197 E4 **Ražanj** Srbija Yugo.
127 F4 **Razāzah, Buḩayrat ar** l. Iraq
Razdan Armenia see **Hrazdan**
Razdel'naya Ukr. see **Rozdil'na**
100 D4 **Razdol'noye** Rus. Fed.
122 B3 **Razeh** Iran
162 D2 **Razès** France
197 H4 **Razgrad** Bulg.
111 E6 **Razhêng Zangbo** r. Xizang China
197 I3 **Razim, Lacul** lag. Romania
197 F5 **Razlog** Bulg.
138 F3 **Rāznas** l. Latvia
177 H3 **Ráztočno** Slovakia
137 I2 **Razumnoye** Rus. Fed.
Raz"yezd 3km Rus. Fed. see **Novyy Urgal**
162 A2 **Ré, Île de** i. France
150 E2 **Rea Brook** r. England U.K.
246 □ **Reading** Jamaica
151 G3 **Reading** Reading, England U.K.
151 G3 **Reading** admin. div. England U.K.
226 E5 **Reading** MI U.S.A.
232 A5 **Reading** OH U.S.A.
234 C2 **Reading** PA U.S.A.
234 D2 **Readington** NJ U.S.A.
233 G3 **Readsboro** VT U.S.A.
226 B4 **Readstown** WI U.S.A.
147 E3 **Reaghstown** Rep. of Ireland
215 F1 **Reagile** S. Africa
254 F4 **Real** r. Brazil
182 B1 **Real** Spain
260 D4 **Real de Padre** Arg.
195 G2 **Reale, Canale** r. Italy
185 E4 **Reales** mt. Spain
261 E4 **Realicó** Arg.
163 E5 **Réalmont** France
194 C5 **Realmonte** Sicilia Italy
163 D4 **Réalville** France
234 B2 **Reamstown** PA U.S.A.
97 C4 **Reăng Kesei** Cambodia
79 □3 **Reao** atoll Arch. des Tuamotu Fr. Polynesia
Reate Italy see **Rieti**
163 C4 **Réaup** France
234 D2 **Reaville** NJ U.S.A.
146 E3 **Reay** Highland, Scotland U.K.
156 D4 **Rebais** France
140 L1 **Rebbenesøy** i. Norway
87 D6 **Rebecca, Lake** salt flat W.A. Austr.
165 D4 **Rebecq** Belgium
163 B5 **Rébénacq** France
163 E6 **Rébenty** r. France
Rebiana Sand Sea des. Libya see **Rabyānah, Ramlat**
185 F2 **Rebollera** mt. Spain
183 G3 **Rebollo** Spain
183 H3 **Rebollosa de Jadraque** Spain
182 C3 **Rebordelo** Port.
182 B1 **Rebordelo** Spain
121 J1 **Rebrikha** Rus. Fed.
194 D1 **Recale** Italy
191 I5 **Recanati** Italy
197 E3 **Recaş** Romania
183 G4 **Recas** Spain
190 E4 **Recco** Italy
136 E4 **Recea** Moldova
147 B3 **Recess** Rep. of Ireland
157 E5 **Recey-sur-Ource** France
87 D7 **Recherche, Archipelago of the** is W.A. Austr.
157 G4 **Réchicourt-le-Château** France
Rechitsa Homyel'skaya Voblasts' Belarus see **Rechytsa**
170 D2 **Rechlin** Ger.
123 H4 **Rechna Doab** lowland Pak.
179 H3 **Rechnitz** Austria
165 F4 **Recht** Belgium
172 D2 **Rechtenbach** Ger.
168 C2 **Rechtsupweg** Ger.
136 D2 **Rechytsa** Brestskaya Voblasts' Belarus
136 F1 **Rechytsa** Homyel'skaya Voblasts' Belarus
179 G4 **Rečica** Slovenia
254 G4 **Recife** Brazil
169 C3 **Recke** Ger.
190 D2 **Reckingen** Switz.
169 C4 **Recklinghausen** Ger.
170 D1 **Recknitz** r. Ger.
191 G3 **Recoaro Terme** Italy
258 F3 **Reconquista** Arg.
161 D4 **Recoubeau-Jansac** France
161 A4 **Recoules-Prévinquières** France
257 F4 **Recreio** Brazil
258 D3 **Recreo** Catamarca Arg.
261 G2 **Recreo** Santa Fé Arg.
177 J4 **Recsk** Hungary
232 B5 **Rectorville** KY U.S.A.
183 H3 **Recuerda** Spain
174 D2 **Recz** Pol.
175 H4 **Reczno** Pol.
85 E3 **Red** r. Qld Austr.
222 E3 **Red** r. B.C. Can.
223 L5 **Red** r. Can./U.S.A.
237 F6 **Red** r. U.S.A.
237 D5 **Red, North Fork** r. OK U.S.A.
174 G1 **Reda** Pol.
174 G1 **Reda** r. Pol.
165 E5 **Redange** Lux.
235 D2 **Red Bank** NJ U.S.A.
231 C5 **Red Bank** TN U.S.A.
Red Basin Sichuan China see **Sichuan Pendi**
225 J3 **Red Bay** Nfld. Can.
87 C5 **Red Bluff** hill W.A. Austr.
240 F1 **Red Bluff** CA U.S.A.
151 G3 **Redbourn** Hertfordshire, England U.K.
241 K4 **Red Butte** mt. AZ U.S.A.
149 H3 **Redcar** Redcar and Cleveland, England U.K.
149 H3 **Redcar and Cleveland** admin. div. England U.K.
148 B2 **Redcastle** Rep. of Ireland
223 I5 **Redcliff** Alta Can.
226 B2 **Red Cliff** WI U.S.A.
213 F3 **Redcliff** Zimbabwe
150 E3 **Redcliff Bay** North Somerset, England U.K.
85 H5 **Redcliffe** Qld Austr.
87 D6 **Redcliffe, Mount** hill W.A. Austr.
83 E3 **Red Cliffs** Vic. Austr.
236 D3 **Red Cloud** NE U.S.A.
147 E4 **Redcross** Rep. of Ireland
222 H4 **Red Deer** Alta Can.
222 I5 **Red Deer** r. Alberta/Saskatchewan Can.
223 K4 **Red Deer** r. Man./Sask. Can.
170 C1 **Reddelich** Ger.
215 F3 **Reddersburg** S. Africa
238 B3 **Redding** CA U.S.A.
235 E1 **Redding** CT U.S.A.
235 E1 **Redding Ridge** CT U.S.A.
151 F2 **Redditch** Worcestershire, England U.K.
149 G2 **Rede** r. England U.K.
222 H3 **Red Earth Creek** Alta Can.
170 C2 **Redefin** Ger.
214 B5 **Redelinghuys** S. Africa
254 C3 **Redenção** Brazil
254 D4 **Redenção** Brazil
158 C4 **Rédéné** France
161 C5 **Redessan** France
205 H2 **Redeyef** Tunisia
236 D2 **Redfield** SD U.S.A.
146 F5 **Redford** Angus, Scotland U.K.
222 B2 **Red Granite Mountain** Y.T. Can.
82 D3 **Redhill** S.A. Austr.
151 G3 **Redhill** Surrey, England U.K.
234 C2 **Red Hill** PA U.S.A.
147 D2 **Redhills** Rep. of Ireland
237 D4 **Red Hills** KS U.S.A.
233 G4 **Red Hook** NY U.S.A.
176 F5 **Rédics** Hungary
157 H4 **Réding** France
Redingen Lux. see **Redange**
182 B4 **Redinha** Port.
230 C3 **Redkey** IN U.S.A.
139 K3 **Redkino** Rus. Fed.
222 G2 **Redknife** r. N.W.T. Can.
223 M5 **Red Lake** Ont. Can.
241 K4 **Red Lake** AZ U.S.A.
236 E2 **Red Lake** MN U.S.A.
236 D2 **Red Lake** r. MN U.S.A.
236 D2 **Red Lake Falls** MN U.S.A.
236 E1 **Red Lakes** MN U.S.A.
240 I4 **Redlands** CA U.S.A.
234 D3 **Red Lion** NJ U.S.A.
234 B3 **Red Lion** PA U.S.A.
238 E2 **Red Lodge** MT U.S.A.
151 F4 **Redlynch** Wiltshire, England U.K.
238 B2 **Redmond** OR U.S.A.
241 L2 **Redmond** UT U.S.A.
173 E2 **Rednitz** r. Ger.
173 F2 **Rednitzhembach** Ger.
236 E3 **Red Oak** IA U.S.A.
235 E1 **Red Oaks Mill** NY U.S.A.
158 D4 **Redon** France
182 B2 **Redondela** Spain
182 C3 **Redondelo** Port.
184 C2 **Redondo** Port.
240 H5 **Redondo Beach** CA U.S.A.
238 D2 **Red Peak** MT U.S.A.
146 C4 **Redpoint** Highland, Scotland U.K.
Red River r. Vietnam see **Hông, Sông**
Red River, Mouths of the Vietnam see **Hong, Mouths of the**
224 B3 **Red Rock** Ont. Can.
241 L5 **Red Rock** AZ U.S.A.
227 I5 **Red Rock** PA U.S.A.
238 D2 **Red Rock** r. MT U.S.A.
87 E7 **Red Rocks Point** W.A. Austr.
150 C3 **Red Roses** Carmarthenshire, Wales U.K.
150 B4 **Redruth** Cornwall, England U.K.
124 A2 **Red Sea** Africa/Asia
203 G5 **Red Sea** state Sudan
222 F4 **Redstone** B.C. Can.
222 E1 **Redstone** r. N.W.T. Can.
227 G1 **Redstone** r. Ont. Can.
206 E4 **Red Volta** r. Burkina/Ghana
238 F1 **Redwater** r. MT U.S.A.
240 F1 **Redway** CA U.S.A.
236 C3 **Red Willow Creek** r. NE U.S.A.
225 J2 **Red Wine** r. Nfld. Can.
226 A3 **Red Wing** MN U.S.A.
171 C5 **Redwitz an der Rodach** Ger.
240 F3 **Redwood City** CA U.S.A.
236 E2 **Redwood Falls** MN U.S.A.
240 F2 **Redwood Valley** CA U.S.A.
175 H5 **Rędziny** Pol.
147 D3 **Ree, Lough** l. Rep. of Ireland
226 E4 **Reed City** MI U.S.A.
240 H3 **Reedley** CA U.S.A.
226 C4 **Reedsburg** WI U.S.A.
238 A3 **Reedsport** OR U.S.A.
232 C5 **Reedsville** OH U.S.A.
232 E4 **Reedsville** PA U.S.A.
233 E6 **Reedville** VA U.S.A.
232 C5 **Reedy** WV U.S.A.
81 C5 **Reefton** South I. N.Z.
147 C4 **Reens** Rep. of Ireland
151 I2 **Reepham** Norfolk, England U.K.
169 B4 **Rees** Ger.
227 F4 **Reese** MI U.S.A.
240 I1 **Reese** r. NV U.S.A.
168 E2 **Reeßum** Ger.
170 C2 **Reetz** Brandenburg Ger.
171 D3 **Reetz** Brandenburg Ger.
164 D2 **Reeuwijksebrug** Neth.
126 E3 **Refahiye** Turkey
182 B3 **Refóios do Lima** Port.
237 F5 **Reform** AL U.S.A.
243 G5 **Reforma** Mex.
234 B3 **Refton** PA U.S.A.
237 D6 **Refugio** TX U.S.A.
174 D1 **Rega** r. Pol.
182 B3 **Regadas** Port.
194 D5 **Regalbuto** Sicilia Italy
186 C3 **Regallo** r. Spain
179 E3 **Regau** Austria
173 H3 **Regen** Ger.
173 G2 **Regen** r. Ger.
173 G2 **Regensburg** Ger.
190 D1 **Regensdorf** Switz.
173 G2 **Regenstauf** Ger.
256 B5 **Regente Feijó** Brazil
205 F4 **Reggane** Alg.
164 F2 **Regge** r. Neth.
191 G5 **Reggello** Italy
Reggio Calabria Italy see **Reggio di Calabria**
Reggio Emilia-Romagna Italy see **Reggio nell'Emilia**
195 E4 **Reggio di Calabria** Calabria Italy
195 F4 **Reggio di Calabria** prov. Calabria Italy
Reggio Emilia Emilia-Romagna Italy see **Reggio nell'Emilia**
191 F4 **Reggio nell'Emilia** Emilia-Romagna Italy
191 F4 **Reggio nell'Emilia** prov. Emilia-Romagna Italy
197 G2 **Reghin** Romania
186 A1 **Regil** Spain
175 I3 **Regimin** Pol.
223 J5 **Regina** Sask. Can.
251 H3 **Régina** Fr. Guiana
256 D6 **Registro** Brazil
Regium Lepidum Emilia-Romagna Italy see **Reggio nell'Emilia**
171 D5 **Regnitzlosau** Ger.
160 C3 **Régny** France
182 B2 **Reguengo** Spain
184 C2 **Reguengos de Monsaraz** Port.
158 D4 **Réguiny** France
171 D5 **Rehau** Ger.
169 E3 **Rehburg (Rehburg-Loccum)** Ger.
168 D3 **Rehden** Ger.
116 D5 **Rehli** Madh. Prad. India
173 E3 **Rehling** Ger.
172 A2 **Rehlingen-Siersburg** Ger.
171 E5 **Řehlovice** Czech Rep.
170 C2 **Rehna** Ger.
212 C4 **Rehoboth** Namibia
233 F5 **Rehoboth Bay** DE U.S.A.
233 F5 **Rehoboth Beach** DE U.S.A.
157 F3 **Réhon** France
128 B4 **Rehovot** Israel
Reïbell Alg. see **Ksar Chellala**
171 D4 **Reibitz** Ger.
173 E2 **Reiche Ebrach** r. Ger.
172 C2 **Reichelsheim (Odenwald)** Ger.
169 D5 **Reichelsheim (Wetterau)** Ger.
172 D4 **Reichenau** Ger.
179 G3 **Reichenau an der Rax** Austria
172 C2 **Reichenbach** Hessen Ger.
171 D5 **Reichenbach** Sachsen Ger.
190 C2 **Reichenbach** Switz.
171 F4 **Reichenbach (Oberlausitz)** Ger.
172 D2 **Reichenberg** Ger.
179 F3 **Reichenfels** Austria
169 F4 **Reichensachsen (Wehretal)** Ger.
173 F2 **Reichenschwand** Ger.
178 D3 **Reichenspitze** mt. Austria
179 F2 **Reichenthal** Austria
173 F3 **Reichertshausen** Ger.
173 G3 **Reichertsheim** Ger.
173 F3 **Reichertshofen** Ger.
173 E4 **Reichling** Ger.
171 C5 **Reichmannsdorf** Ger.
172 D2 **Reicholzheim** Ger.
179 F3 **Reichraming** Austria
157 H4 **Reichshoffen** France
157 H4 **Reichstett** France
87 F6 **Reid** W.A. Austr.
190 C1 **Reiden** Switz.
146 C4 **Reidh, Rubha** pt Scotland U.K.
231 D5 **Reidsville** GA U.S.A.
231 E4 **Reidsville** NC U.S.A.
182 D4 **Reigada** Port.
151 G3 **Reigate** Surrey, England U.K.
162 B3 **Reignac** France
160 E2 **Reignier** France
169 C5 **Reil** Ger.
241 L5 **Reiley Peak** AZ U.S.A.
163 D4 **Reilhaguet** France
172 C2 **Reilingen** Ger.
161 D5 **Reillanne** France
183 I5 **Reillo** Spain
156 E3 **Reims** France
184 E2 **Reina** Spain
190 D1 **Reinach** Aargau Switz.
190 C1 **Reinach** Basellland Switz.
142 B2 **Reinaknuten** hill Norway
168 F2 **Reinbek** Ger.
170 E1 **Reinberg** Ger.
223 K4 **Reindeer** r. Sask. Can.
223 K3 **Reindeer Lake** Man./Sask. Can.
140 K2 **Reine** Norway
232 C5 **Reinersville** OH U.S.A.
141 J3 **Reineskarvet** mt. Norway
168 F2 **Reinfeld (Holstein)** Ger.
80 D1 **Reinga, Cape** North I. N.Z.
172 C2 **Reinheim** Ger.
234 B2 **Reinholds** PA U.S.A.
183 F2 **Reinosa** Spain
160 C2 **Reins** r. France
171 D4 **Reinsdorf** Sachsen-Anhalt Ger.
171 C4 **Reinsdorf** Thüringen Ger.
172 A2 **Reinsfeld** Ger.
142 B2 **Reinsnosi** mt. Norway
140 □B2 **Reiphólsfjöll** hill Iceland
Reirson Island atoll Cook Is see **Rakahanga**
173 G3 **Reisbach** Ger.
173 G3 **Reischach** Ger.
140 N3 **Reisjärvi** Fin.
169 D5 **Reiskirchen** Ger.
234 B3 **Reisterstown** MD U.S.A.
194 D5 **Reitano** Sicilia Italy
164 F1 **Reitdiep** r. Neth.
173 G4 **Reit im Winkl** Ger.
215 G2 **Reitz** S. Africa
215 F2 **Reitzburg** S. Africa
138 E2 **Reiu** r. Estonia
214 E2 **Reivilo** S. Africa
143 F2 **Rejmyre** Sweden
175 L4 **Rejowiec** Pol.
175 L4 **Rejowiec Fabryczny** Pol.
179 H4 **Reka** Croatia
191 J3 **Reka** r. Slovenia
114 D2 **Rekapalle** Andhra Prad. India
169 C4 **Reken** Ger.
164 F2 **Rekken** Neth.
175 M5 **Reklynets'** Ukr.
196 E4 **Rekovac** Srbija Yugo.
175 M6 **Rekshyn** Ukr.
142 C1 **Reksjåeggi** mt. Norway
138 D4 **Rėkyvos ežeras** l. Lith.
223 I2 **Reliance** N.W.T. Can.
184 B3 **Relíquias** Port.
205 F2 **Relizane** Alg.
187 C6 **Relleu** Spain
115 D2 **Relli** Andhra Prad. India
168 E2 **Rellingen** Ger.
216 □1b **Relva** São Miguel Azores
177 I5 **Rém** Hungary
169 C5 **Remagen** Ger.
159 G3 **Rémalard** France
82 D3 **Remarkable, Mount** hill S.A. Austr.
95 E4 **Rembang** Jawa Tengah Indon.
157 F4 **Rembercourt-Sommaisne** France
171 C5 **Remda** Ger.
216 □1b **Remédios** São Miguel Azores
246 C2 **Remedios** Cuba
205 H3 **Remel el Abiod** des. Tunisia
168 C2 **Remels (Uplengen)** Ger.
236 E2 **Remer** MN U.S.A.
122 D5 **Remeshk** Iran
177 L5 **Remetea** Romania
177 K6 **Remetea Mare** Romania
197 F2 **Remeţi** Romania
179 H4 **Remetinec** Croatia
Remi France see **Reims**
165 F5 **Remich** Lux.
165 E4 **Remicourt** Belgium
157 E3 **Remilly-Aillicourt** France
232 E5 **Remington** VA U.S.A.
251 H3 **Rémire** Fr. Guiana
217 □2 **Rémire** i. Seychelles
157 G4 **Remiremont** France
169 F3 **Remlingen** Ger.
238 B1 **Remmel Mountain** WA U.S.A.
186 B3 **Remolinos** Spain
157 G4 **Remoncourt** France
135 H7 **Remontnoye** Rus. Fed.
165 E4 **Remouchamps** Belgium
161 C5 **Remoulins** France
170 D2 **Remplin** Ger.
171 C5 **Remptendorf** Ger.
172 D3 **Rems** r. Ger.
169 C4 **Remscheid** Ger.
178 B4 **Remulo** r. Italy
158 D4 **Remungol** France
226 E4 **Remus** MI U.S.A.
161 D4 **Rémuzat** France
141 J3 **Rena** Norway
141 J3 **Rena** r. Norway
184 E1 **Rena** Spain
227 F1 **Renabie** Ont. Can.
161 D3 **Renage** France
260 A5 **Renaico** Chile
160 B2 **Renaison** France
Renaix Belgium see **Ronse**
114 C2 **Renapur** Mahar. India
159 E4 **Renazé** France
172 C3 **Renchen** Ger.
Rende Yunnan China see **Xundian**
193 I5 **Rende** Italy
78 □6 **Rendova** i. New Georgia Is Solomon Is
168 E1 **Rendsburg** Ger.
183 G1 **Renedo** Cantabria Spain
183 F3 **Renedo** Castilla y León Spain
183 F2 **Renedo de la Vega** Spain
190 B2 **Renens** Switz.
164 C3 **Renesse** Neth.
225 K4 **Renews** Nfld. Can.
224 E4 **Renfrew** Ont. Can.
146 D6 **Renfrew** Renfrewshire, Scotland U.K.
146 D6 **Renfrewshire** admin. div. Scotland U.K.
94 C3 **Rengat** Sumatera Indon.
260 B4 **Rengo** Chile
169 C5 **Rengsdorf** Ger.
169 E4 **Rengshausen (Knüllwald)** Ger.
108 D1 **Ren He** r. China
109 E2 **Renheji** Henan China
Renhou Hebei China see **Tangxian**
109 E3 **Renhua** Guangdong China
108 C3 **Renhuai** Guizhou China
136 E5 **Reni** Ukr.
232 C6 **Renick** WV U.S.A.
114 C3 **Renigunta** Andhra Prad. India
146 B4 **Renish Point** Scotland U.K.
168 C3 **Renkenberge** Ger.
138 E1 **Renko** Fin.
164 E3 **Renkum** Neth.
Renland reg. Greenland see **Tuttut Nunaat**
82 E3 **Renmark** S.A. Austr.
194 D6 **Renna** r. Sicilia Italy
169 F3 **Rennau** Ger.
78 □6 **Rennell** i. Solomon Is
169 D5 **Rennerod** Ger.
84 C3 **Renner Springs** N.T. Austr.
173 F3 **Rennertshofen** Ger.
158 E3 **Rennes** France
158 E3 **Rennes, Bassin de** basin France
163 E6 **Rennes-les-Bains** France
142 A2 **Rennesøy** i. Norway
223 M5 **Rennie** Man. Can.
172 C3 **Renningen** Ger.
149 H2 **Rennington** Northumberland, England U.K.
179 E3 **Rennweg** Austria
191 H4 **Reno** r. Italy
226 B4 **Reno** MN U.S.A.
240 H2 **Reno** NV U.S.A.
191 G2 **Renòn** Italy
192 B2 **Rénoso, Monte** mt. Corse France
215 F2 **Renoster** r. S. Africa
214 D5 **Renosterkop** S. Africa
215 F2 **Renosterspruit** S. Africa
232 E4 **Renovo** PA U.S.A.
107 H4 **Renqiu** Hebei China
168 E1 **Rens** Denmark
108 C2 **Renshou** Sichuan China
174 F5 **Reńska Wieś** Pol.
174 G5 **Reńska Wieś** Pol.
230 C3 **Rensselaer** IN U.S.A.
233 G3 **Rensselaer** NY U.S.A.
164 E2 **Renswoude** Neth.
186 B1 **Rentería** Spain
140 L2 **Rentjärn** Sweden
238 B2 **Renton** WA U.S.A.
169 F5 **Rentweinsdorf** Ger.
117 E4 **Renukut** Uttar Prad. India
156 E3 **Renwez** France
81 D4 **Renwick** South I. N.Z.
139 K2 **Renya** r. Rus. Fed.
170 C2 **Renzow** Ger.
206 E3 **Réo** Burkina
176 F4 **Répce** r. Hungary
176 G4 **Répcelak** Hungary
213 G4 **Repembe** r. Moz.
175 K3 **Repki** Pol.
160 C2 **Replonges** France
140 N1 **Repokaira** reg. Fin.
80 F3 **Reporoa** North I. N.Z.
141 M3 **Reposaari** Fin.
170 D1 **Reppelin** Ger.
168 F2 **Reppenstedt** Ger.
232 B4 **Republic** OH U.S.A.
238 C1 **Republic** WA U.S.A.
236 D4 **Republican** r. NE U.S.A.
236 C3 **Republican, South Fork** r. NE U.S.A.
188 F3 **Republika Srpska** aut. div. Bos.-Herz.
85 G4 **Repulse Bay** b. Qld Austr.
221 J3 **Repulse Bay** Nunavut Can.
135 G6 **Rep'yevka** Rus. Fed.
182 D2 **Requejo** Spain
250 C6 **Requena** Peru
187 B5 **Requena** Spain
260 B4 **Requinoa** Chile
163 E4 **Réquista** France
254 E3 **Reriutaba** Brazil
127 F3 **Reşadiye** Turkey
Reşadiye Turkey see **Yeniçağa**
126 E2 **Reşadiye** Turkey
199 E3 **Reşadiye Yarımadası** pen. Turkey
94 D4 **Resag, Gunung** mt. Indon.
191 G3 **Resana** Italy
197 E3 **Resava** r. Yugo.
197 E3 **Resavica** Srbija Yugo.
146 F5 **Rescobie** Angus, Scotland U.K.
196 E5 **Resen** Macedonia
257 E5 **Resende** Brazil
182 C3 **Resende** Port.
256 B6 **Reserva** Brazil
239 E5 **Reserve** NM U.S.A.
139 K3 **Reshetnikovo** Rus. Fed.
137 H3 **Reshetylivka** Ukr.
109 D2 **Reshi** Hunan China
234 C1 **Resica Falls** PA U.S.A.
258 F2 **Resistencia** Arg.
197 E3 **Reşiţa** Romania
174 D2 **Resko** Pol.
221 I2 **Resolute Bay** Nunavut Can.
221 L3 **Resolution Island** Nunavut Can.
81 A6 **Resolution Island** South I. N.Z.
150 D3 **Resolven** Neath Port Talbot, Wales U.K.
183 G1 **Respaldiza** Spain
183 F2 **Respenda de la Peña** Spain
257 G3 **Resplendor** Brazil
139 J4 **Ressa** r. Rus. Fed.
215 H1 **Ressango Garcia** S. Africa
139 J5 **Resseta** r. Rus. Fed.
156 C3 **Ressons-sur-Matz** France
196 E5 **Restelica** Kosovo, Srbija Yugo.
233 □J1 **Restigouche** r. N.B. Can.
255 B9 **Restinga Seca** Brazil
Resülayn Turkey see **Ceylanpınar**
194 D5 **Resuttano** Sicilia Italy
137 G2 **Ret'** r. Ukr.
243 H6 **Retalhuleu** Guat.
184 E2 **Retamal** Spain
182 C5 **Retaxo** Port.
149 I4 **Retford** Nottinghamshire, England U.K.
156 E3 **Rethel** France
168 E3 **Rethem (Aller)** Ger.
Réthimnon Kriti Greece see **Rethymno**
156 C3 **Rethondes** France
198 D4 **Rethymno** Kriti Greece
165 E3 **Retie** Belgium
183 G4 **Retiendas** Spain
158 E4 **Retiers** France
184 D2 **Retín** r. Spain
260 B5 **Retiro** Chile
182 D4 **Retortillo** Spain
183 F2 **Retortillo** tourist site Spain
183 H3 **Retortillo de Soria** Spain
161 C3 **Retournac** France
85 E5 **Retreat** Qld Austr.
177 I4 **Rétság** Hungary
173 E4 **Rettenberg** Ger.
186 B4 **Retuerta** mt. Spain
185 F1 **Retuerta del Bullaque** Spain
179 G2 **Retz** Austria
171 D3 **Reuden** Sachsen-Anhalt Ger.
171 D4 **Reuden** Sachsen-Anhalt Ger.
159 I4 **Reuilly** France
217 □1c **Réunion** terr. Indian Ocean
169 F5 **Reurieth** Ger.
186 E3 **Reus** Spain
165 E3 **Reusel** Neth.
165 E3 **Reusel** r. Neth.
190 D1 **Reuss** r. Switz.
173 G3 **Reut** Ger.
Reut r. Moldova see **Răut**
137 H2 **Reut** r. Rus. Fed.
172 B3 **Reute** Ger.
136 D4 **Reuţel** Moldova
170 D2 **Reuterstadt Stavenhagen** Ger.
173 G2 **Reuth bei Erbendorf** Ger.
172 D3 **Reutlingen** Ger.
139 K4 **Reutov** Rus. Fed.
178 B3 **Reutte** Austria
165 F3 **Reuver** Neth.
Reval Estonia see **Tallinn**
134 F2 **Revda** Rus. Fed.
241 I3 **Reveille Peak** NV U.S.A.
Revel Estonia see **Tallinn**
163 E5 **Revel** France
117 F4 **Revelganj** Bihar India
190 C4 **Revello** Italy
222 G5 **Revelstoke** B.C. Can.
250 A6 **Reventazón** Peru
234 C2 **Revere** PA U.S.A.
160 D3 **Revermont** reg. France
161 D4 **Revest-du-Bion** France
177 G5 **Révfülöp** Hungary
197 H3 **Reviga** Romania
197 H3 **Reviga** r. Romania
157 E4 **Revigny-sur-Ornain** France
183 F2 **Revilla de Collazos** Spain
183 G2 **Revilla del Campo** Spain
228 D7 **Revillagigedo, Islas** is Mex.
220 E4 **Revillagigedo Island** AK U.S.A.
156 E3 **Revin** France
191 H3 **Revine-Lago** Italy
139 J5 **Revna** r. Rus. Fed.
176 D2 **Řevnice** Czech Rep.
176 C1 **Řevničov** Czech Rep.
191 G2 **Revò** Italy
185 H2 **Revolcadores** mt. Spain
Revolyutsii, Pik mt. Tajik. see **Revolyutsiya, Qullai**
123 H2 **Revolyutsiya, Qullai** mt. Tajik.
177 J3 **Revúca** Slovakia
213 G3 **Revuè** r. Moz.
139 K4 **Revyakino** Rus. Fed.
116 E4 **Rewa** Madh. Prad. India
81 E4 **Rewa** hill North I. N.Z.
174 D1 **Rewal** Pol.
116 D3 **Rewari** Haryana India
262 S2 **Rex, Mount** Antarctica
238 E3 **Rexburg** ID U.S.A.
225 H4 **Rexton** N.B. Can.
242 □K7 **Rey, Isla del** i. Panama
136 E2 **Reya** Ukr.
207 I4 **Rey Bouba** Cameroon
151 I2 **Reydon** Suffolk, England U.K.
252 D3 **Reyes** Bol.
240 F2 **Reyes, Point** CA U.S.A.
128 C1 **Reyhanlı** Turkey
140 □B3 **Reykjanes** constituency Iceland
264 G2 **Reykjanes Ridge** sea feature N. Atlantic Ocean
140 □B3 **Reykjanestá** pt Iceland
140 □B2 **Reykjavík** Iceland
84 B2 **Reynolds** r. N.T. Austr.
232 B5 **Reynoldsburg** OH U.S.A.
84 C4 **Reynolds Range** mts N.T. Austr.
243 F3 **Reynosa** Mex.
160 C3 **Reyrieux** France
160 C2 **Reyssouze** r. France
122 B3 **Rezā, Kūh-e** hill Iran
Rezā'īyeh Iran see **Orūmīyeh**
Rezā'īyeh, Daryācheh-ye salt l. Iran see **Orūmīyeh, Daryācheh-ye**
158 E4 **Rezé** France
138 F3 **Rēzekne** Latvia
138 F3 **Rēzekne** r. Latvia
176 G5 **Rezi** Hungary
136 E4 **Rezina** Moldova
188 E3 **Rezinjski vrh** mt. Slovenia
197 I5 **Rezovska Reka** r. Bulg./Turkey
Rezvāndeh Iran see **Rezvānshahr**
122 B2 **Rezvānshahr** Iran
190 F3 **Rezzato** Italy
190 C4 **Rezzo** Italy
190 E4 **Rezzoaglio** Italy
197 F3 **Rgotina** Srbija Yugo.
168 E2 **Rhade** Ger.
190 E1 **Rhätikon** mts Switz.
172 B2 **Rhaunen** Ger.
150 D2 **Rhayader** Powys, Wales U.K.
169 D4 **Rheda-Wiedenbrück** Ger.
169 B4 **Rhede** Ger.
168 C2 **Rhede (Ems)** Ger.
169 E3 **Rheden** Ger.
234 B2 **Rheems** PA U.S.A.
Rhegium Calabria Italy see **Reggio di Calabria**
150 C2 **Rheidol** r. Wales U.K.
Rheims France see **Reims**
172 A1 **Rhein** r. Ger. alt. **Rhin (France)**, conv. **Rhine**
172 B3 **Rheinau** Ger.
169 B5 **Rheinbach** Ger.
169 B4 **Rheinberg** Ger.
172 B2 **Rheinböllen** Ger.
169 C5 **Rheinbreitbach** Ger.
169 C5 **Rheinbrohl** Ger.
169 C3 **Rheine** Ger.
190 E1 **Rheineck** Switz.
190 C1 **Rheinfelden** Switz.
172 B4 **Rheinfelden (Baden)** Ger.
172 B2 **Rheinhessen-Pfalz** admin. reg. Rheinland-Pfalz Ger.
169 B5 **Rheinisches Schiefergebirge** hills Ger.
169 C6 **Rheinland-Pfalz** land Ger.
169 B4 **Rhein-Ruhr** airport Ger.
170 D2 **Rheinsberg** Ger.
172 C3 **Rheinstetten** Ger.
190 E2 **Rheinwaldhorn** mt. Switz.
172 C2 **Rheinzabern** Ger.
190 C3 **Rhêmes-Notre-Dame** Italy
190 C3 **Rhêmes-St-Georges** Italy
164 E3 **Rhenen** Neth.
169 C5 **Rhens** Ger.
146 D3 **Rhiconich** Highland, Scotland U.K.
160 F1 **Rhin** r. France alt. **Rhein (Germany)**, conv. **Rhine**
170 D2 **Rhin** r. Ger.
157 H4 **Rhinau** France
157 G1 **Rhine** r. France alt. **Rhein (Germany)**, alt. **Rhin (France)**
233 G4 **Rhinebeck** NY U.S.A.
226 C3 **Rhinelander** WI U.S.A.
Rhineland-Palatinate land Ger. see **Rheinland-Pfalz**
170 D3 **Rhinluch** marsh Ger.
146 D6 **Rhinns of Kells** hills Scotland U.K.
210 A4 **Rhino Camp** Uganda
170 D3 **Rhinow** Ger.
170 D3 **Rhinowes Berge** hills Ger.
165 D4 **Rhisnes** Belgium
190 E3 **Rho** Italy
147 D3 **Rhode** Rep. of Ireland
233 H4 **Rhode Island** state U.S.A.
169 E4 **Rhoden (Diemelstadt)** Ger.
Rhodes Notio Aigaio Greece see **Rodos**
Rhodes i. Greece see **Rodos**
Rhodesia country Africa see **Zimbabwe**
238 D2 **Rhodes Peak** ID U.S.A.
197 F5 **Rhodope Mountains** Bulg./Greece
Rhodus i. Greece see **Rodos**
169 E5 **Rhön** mts Ger.
150 D3 **Rhondda** reg. Wales U.K.
150 D3 **Rhondda Cynon Taff** admin. div. Wales U.K.
160 C3 **Rhône** dept Rhône-Alpes France
161 C5 **Rhône** r. France/Switz.
161 D3 **Rhône-Alpes** admin. reg. France
150 D3 **Rhoose** Vale of Glamorgan, Wales U.K.
173 G4 **Rhordorf** Ger.
150 D3 **Rhos** Neath Port Talbot, Wales U.K.
150 D1 **Rhosllanerchrugog** Wrexham, Wales U.K.
150 D1 **Rhôs-on-Sea** Conwy, Wales U.K.
150 C3 **Rhossili** Swansea, Wales U.K.
148 E1 **Rhu** Argyll and Bute, Scotland U.K.
150 D1 **Rhuddlan** Denbighshire, Wales U.K.
161 A3 **Rhue** r. France
169 F4 **Rhumspringe** Ger.
Rhuthun Denbighshire, Wales U.K. see **Ruthin**
Rhydaman Carmarthenshire, Wales U.K. see **Ammanford**
150 D1 **Rhyl** Denbighshire, Wales U.K.
150 D3 **Rhymney** Caerphilly, Wales U.K.
146 F4 **Rhynie** Aberdeenshire, Scotland U.K.
207 H6 **Riaba** Equat. Guinea
195 F4 **Riace** Italy
254 D3 **Riachão** Brazil
254 D4 **Riachão das Neves** Brazil
254 E5 **Riacho de Santana** Brazil
257 F1 **Riacho dos Machados** Brazil
183 G3 **Riaguas** r. Spain
158 E4 **Riaillé** France
182 B2 **Rial** Spain
186 E2 **Rialb de Noguera** Spain
255 C5 **Rialma** Brazil
Rialp Spain see **Rialb de Noguera**
240 I4 **Rialto** CA U.S.A.
Rianjo Spain see **Rianxo**
193 E2 **Riano** Italy
183 F2 **Riaño** Spain
253 H3 **Rianópolis** Brazil
161 D5 **Rians** France
183 G5 **Riansáres** r. Spain
158 C4 **Riantec** France
182 B2 **Rianxo** Spain
116 C2 **Riasi** Jammu and Kashmir
94 C2 **Riau** prov. Indon.
94 D2 **Riau, Kepulauan** is Indon.
190 C2 **Riaz** Switz.
183 G3 **Riaza** Spain
183 G3 **Riaza** r. Spain
183 G1 **Riba** Spain
182 B2 **Ribadavia** Spain
182 D2 **Ribadelago** Spain
182 C1 **Ribadeo** Spain
183 H4 **Riba de Saelices** Spain
183 E1 **Ribadesella** Spain
183 I2 **Ribaforada** Spain
183 H2 **Ribafrecha** Spain
186 D3 **Riba-roja d'Ebre** Spain
Ribas de Fresser Spain see **Ribes de Freser**
255 B7 **Ribas do Rio Pardo** Brazil
213 H2 **Ribáuè** Moz.
169 F3 **Ribbesbüttel** Ger.
149 G4 **Ribble** r. England U.K.
149 G3 **Ribblesdale** val. England U.K.
142 C4 **Ribe** Denmark
142 C4 **Ribe** county Denmark
157 H4 **Ribeauvillé** France
156 C3 **Ribécourt-Dreslincourt** France
256 C6 **Ribeira** Brazil
256 D6 **Ribeira** r. Brazil
184 □ **Ribeira Brava** Madeira
184 □ **Ribeira da Janela** Madeira
182 C3 **Ribeira de Pena** Port.
216 □1b **Ribeira Grande** São Miguel Azores
182 B3 **Ribeirão** Port.
256 C6 **Ribeirão Branco** Brazil
257 E3 **Ribeirão das Neves** Brazil
256 B5 **Ribeirão do Pinhal** Brazil
256 D4 **Ribeirão Preto** Brazil
216 □1c **Ribeiras** Pico Azores
216 □1c **Ribeira Seca** São Jorge Azores
216 □1b **Ribeira Seca** São Miguel Azores
216 □1c **Ribeirinha** Faial Azores
216 □1c **Ribeirinha** Pico Azores
216 □1a **Ribeirinha** Terceira Azores
156 D3 **Ribemont** France
194 C5 **Ribera** Sicilia Italy
162 C3 **Ribérac** France
184 D2 **Ribera del Fresno** Spain
252 D2 **Riberalta** Bol.
187 C4 **Ribesalbes** Spain
186 F2 **Ribes de Freser** Spain
161 D4 **Ribiers** France
177 L5 **Ribiţa** Romania
188 E3 **Ribnica** Slovenia
136 E4 **Rîbniţa** Moldova
170 D1 **Ribnitz-Damgarten** Ger.
197 F5 **Ribnovo** Bulg.
183 G3 **Ribota** Spain
195 E4 **Ricadi** Italy
179 H1 **Říčany** Czech Rep.
176 D2 **Říčany** Czech Rep.
149 I3 **Riccal** r. England U.K.
193 G3 **Riccia** Italy
191 H5 **Riccio** Italy
191 H4 **Riccione** Italy
190 E4 **Riccò del Golfo di Spezia** Italy
241 J4 **Rice** CA U.S.A.
232 D6 **Rice** VA U.S.A.
226 B3 **Rice Lake** WI U.S.A.
226 A4 **Riceville** IA U.S.A.
232 B6 **Riceville** KY U.S.A.
157 G4 **Richardménil** France
215 I3 **Richards Bay** S. Africa
223 I3 **Richardson** r. Alta Can.
220 E3 **Richardson Mountains** N.W.T. Can.
81 B6 **Richardson Mountains** South I. N.Z.
206 B2 **Richard Toll** Senegal
234 C2 **Richboro** PA U.S.A.
233 G2 **Richelieu** Que. Can.
162 C1 **Richelieu** France
234 A2 **Richfield** PA U.S.A.
241 K2 **Richfield** UT U.S.A.
233 F3 **Richfield Springs** NY U.S.A.
233 E3 **Richford** NY U.S.A.
233 G2 **Richford** VT U.S.A.
240 H4 **Richgrove** CA U.S.A.
147 E2 **Richhill** Northern Ireland U.K.
225 H4 **Richibucto** N.B. Can.
223 I4 **Rich Lake** Alta Can.
234 D3 **Richland** NJ U.S.A.
234 B2 **Richland** PA U.S.A.
238 C2 **Richland** WA U.S.A.
226 B4 **Richland Center** WI U.S.A.
232 C6 **Richlands** VA U.S.A.
234 C2 **Richlandtown** PA U.S.A.
83 G3 **Richmond** N.S.W. Austr.
85 E4 **Richmond** Qld Austr.
227 J3 **Richmond** Ont. Can.
225 F4 **Richmond** Que. Can.
81 D4 **Richmond** South I. N.Z.
215 H3 **Richmond** Kwazulu-Natal S. Africa
214 D4 **Richmond** N. Cape S. Africa
149 H3 **Richmond** North Yorkshire, England U.K.
240 F3 **Richmond** CA U.S.A.
226 C4 **Richmond** IL U.S.A.
230 C4 **Richmond** IN U.S.A.
232 A6 **Richmond** KY U.S.A.
233 □I2 **Richmond** ME U.S.A.
227 F4 **Richmond** MI U.S.A.
237 E6 **Richmond** TX U.S.A.
232 E6 **Richmond** VA U.S.A.
233 G2 **Richmond** VT U.S.A.
81 D4 **Richmond, Mount** South I. N.Z.
235 D2 **Richmond County** county NY U.S.A.
232 B5 **Richmond Dale** OH U.S.A.
224 E5 **Richmond Hill** Ont. Can.
231 D6 **Richmond Hill** GA U.S.A.
247 □3 **Richmond Peak** St Vincent
83 H2 **Richmond Range** hills N.S.W. Austr.
81 D4 **Richmond Range** mts South I. N.Z.
233 F3 **Richmondville** NY U.S.A.
170 D1 **Richtenberg** Ger.
172 C4 **Richterswil** Switz.
237 F6 **Richton** MS U.S.A.
240 G2 **Richvale** CA U.S.A.
232 B4 **Richwood** OH U.S.A.

Richwood to Ronuro
354

232 C5 Richwood WV U.S.A.
193 H4 Ricigliano Italy
172 B4 Rickenbach Ger.
151 H2 Rickinghall Suffolk, England U.K.
140 M2 Rickleån r. Sweden
168 F1 Rickling Ger.
151 G3 Rickmansworth Hertfordshire, England U.K.
183 I3 Ricla Spain
182 E3 Ricobayo, Embalse de resr Spain
Ricomagus France see Riom
177 K3 Ricse Hungary
263 E2 Riddell Nunataks nunataks Antarctica
Ridder Kazakh. see Leninogorsk
164 D3 Ridderkerk Neth.
190 C2 Riddes Switz.
232 D4 Riddlesburg PA U.S.A.
227 J3 Rideau r. Ont. Can.
234 B3 Riderwood MD U.S.A.
224 C3 Ridge r. Ont. Can.
235 F2 Ridge NY U.S.A.
240 I4 Ridgecrest CA U.S.A.
235 E1 Ridgefield CT U.S.A.
235 D2 Ridgefield NJ U.S.A.
237 F5 Ridgeland MS U.S.A.
231 D5 Ridgeland SC U.S.A.
226 B3 Ridgeland WI U.S.A.
234 C4 Ridgely MD U.S.A.
227 G4 Ridgetown Ont. Can.
226 B4 Ridgeway IA U.S.A.
235 D2 Ridgeway NJ U.S.A.
232 D6 Ridgeway VA U.S.A.
235 D2 Ridgewood NJ U.S.A.
232 D4 Ridgway PA U.S.A.
177 I6 Riđica Vojvodina, Srbija Yugo.
146 G7 Riding Mill Northumberland, England U.K.
86 C4 Ridley r. W.A. Austr.
215 F2 Riebeeckstad S. Africa
214 B5 Riebeek-Kasteel S. Africa
215 F5 Riebeek-Oos S. Africa
214 B5 Riebeek Wes S. Africa
158 C4 Riec-sur-Belon France
173 F3 Ried Ger.
190 D2 Ried Switz.
173 E4 Riedbergerhorn mt. Ger.
168 D3 Riede Ger.
173 F2 Rieden Ger.
173 F3 Riedenburg Ger.
173 G4 Riedering Ger.
179 E2 Ried im Innkreis Austria
178 B3 Ried im Oberinntal Austria
178 C3 Ried im Zillertal Austria
179 F2 Ried in der Riedmark Austria
157 H5 Riedisheim France
172 D3 Riedlingen Ger.
172 A2 Riegelsberg Ger.
179 G3 Riegersburg Austria
234 C2 Rieglelsville PA U.S.A.
182 E2 Riego de la Vega Spain
190 C1 Riehen Switz.
215 F1 Riekertsdam S. Africa
172 C4 Rielasingen-Worblingen Ger.
182 E2 Riello Spain
183 F5 Rielves Spain
165 E4 Riemst Belgium
169 E5 Rieneck Ger.
177 L5 Rieni Romania
191 G2 Rienza r. Italy
140 M1 Rieppesgai'sa mt. Norway
168 F1 Riepsdorf Ger.
186 E3 Riera de Rajadell r. Spain
171 E4 Riesa Ger.
259 B9 Riesco, Isla i. Chile
168 E1 Rieseby Ger.
194 D5 Riesi Sicilia Italy
169 D3 Rieste Ger.
171 C4 Riestedt Ger.
214 D3 Riet r. S. Africa
138 C4 Rietavas Lith.
169 D4 Rietberg Ger.
214 D5 Rietbron S. Africa
214 C2 Rietfontein S. Africa
170 F2 Rieth Ger.
165 E3 Riethoven Neth.
214 C6 Riethuiskraal S. Africa
193 E2 Rieti Italy
193 E2 Rieti prov. Lazio Italy
215 G2 Rietkuil S. Africa
214 B4 Rietpoort S. Africa
171 F4 Rietschen Ger.
215 H3 Rietvlei S. Africa
178 C3 Rietz Austria
163 D5 Rieumes France
163 E4 Rieupeyroux France
161 B4 Rieutort-de-Randon France
158 D4 Rieux Bretagne France
163 D5 Rieux Midi-Pyrénées France
163 E5 Rieux-Minervois France
161 E5 Riez France
128 C3 Rifā'ī, Tall mt. Jordan/Syria
256 D4 Rifaina Brazil
Rifeng Jiangxi China see Lichuan
178 E3 Rifflkopf mt. Austria
191 G2 Rifiano Italy
239 F4 Rifle CO U.S.A.
210 B4 Rift Valley prov. Kenya
111 F6 Riga Arun. Prad. India
138 E3 Rīga Latvia
138 D3 Riga, Gulf of Estonia/Latvia
207 G4 Rigacikun Nigeria
122 D4 Rīgān Iran
Rīgas jūras līcis b. Estonia/Latvia see Riga, Gulf of
233 F2 Rigaud Que. Can.
161 E5 Rigaud France
238 E3 Rigby ID U.S.A.
238 C2 Riggins ID U.S.A.
160 F2 Riggisberg Switz.
190 D1 Rigi mts Switz.
190 E3 Riglio r. Italy
163 E4 Rignac France
193 E2 Rignano Flaminio Italy
193 H3 Rignano Garganico Italy
191 G5 Rignano sull'Arno Italy
156 D4 Rigny-le-Ferron France
160 C2 Rigny-sur-Arroux France
159 G4 Rigny-Ussé France
225 J2 Rigolet Nfld. Can.
202 B6 Rig-Rig Chad
146 E6 Rigside South Lanarkshire, Scotland U.K.
183 I2 Riguel r. Spain
124 B4 Rīh, Gezirat er i. Sudan
113 □1 Rihiveli i. S. Male Maldives
Riia laht b. Estonia/Latvia see Riga, Gulf of
141 N3 Riihimäki Fin.
138 E2 Riisipere Estonia
207 G4 Rijau Nigeria
188 E3 Riječki Zaliv b. Croatia
188 E3 Rijeka Croatia
191 J3 Rijeka airport Croatia
164 D3 Rijen Neth.
165 D3 Rijkevorsel Belgium
164 D2 Rijnsaterwoude Neth.
164 D2 Rijnsburg Neth.
164 D3 Rijsbergen Neth.
164 F2 Rijssen Neth.
164 D2 Rijswijk Neth.
136 B3 Rika r. Ukr.
140 L1 Riksgränsen Sweden
102 J4 Rikuzen-takata Japan
197 F4 Rila Bulg.
197 F4 Rila mts Bulg.
238 C3 Riley OR U.S.A.
232 D5 Rileyville VA U.S.A.
162 D3 Rilhac-Rancon France
165 D3 Rilland Neth.
159 G4 Rillé France
160 C3 Rillieux-la-Pape France
241 L5 Rillito AZ U.S.A.
186 C4 Rillo Spain
183 I4 Rillo de Gallo Spain
156 E3 Rilly-la-Montagne France
79 □3 Rimatara i. Îs Australes Fr. Polynesia
Rimatera i. Îs Australes Fr. Polynesia see Rimatara
157 F4 Rimaucourt France
177 J3 Rimava r. Slovakia
177 J3 Rimavská Seč Slovakia
177 J3 Rimavská Sobota Slovakia
173 G2 Rimbach Bayern Ger.
172 C2 Rimbach Hessen Ger.
222 H4 Rimbey Alta Can.
143 H2 Rimbo Sweden
232 D4 Rimersburg PA U.S.A.
197 F2 Rimetea Romania
143 F2 Rimforsa Sweden
191 H4 Rimini Italy
191 H4 Rimini prov. Emilia-Romagna Italy
Rîmnicu Sărat Romania see Râmnicu Sărat
Rîmnicu Vîlcea Romania see Râmnicu Vâlcea
156 E3 Rimogne France
163 D6 Rimont France
225 G3 Rimouski Que. Can.
172 D2 Rimpar Ger.
173 G4 Rimsting Ger.
111 E6 Rinbung Xizang China
93 A5 Rinca i. Indon.
256 C4 Rincão Brazil
173 H3 Rinchnach Ger.
Rincon Morocco see Mdiq
247 □1 Rincón Puerto Rico
252 D6 Rincón, Cerro del mt. Chile
245 F4 Rinconada Mex.
260 C4 Rincón del Atuel Arg.
185 F4 Rincón de la Victoria Spain
261 I3 Rincón del Bonete, Lago Artificial de resr Uru.
244 C2 Rincón de Romos Mex.
183 I2 Rincón de Soto Spain
116 E4 Rind r. India
138 C3 Rinda r. Latvia
140 J3 Rindal Norway
198 D3 Rineia i. Greece
194 D4 Rinella Isole Lipari Italy
232 C6 Riner VA U.S.A.
83 F5 Ringarooma Bay Tas. Austr.
143 G2 Ringarum Sweden
116 C4 Ringas Rajasthan India
147 C5 Ringaskiddy Rep. of Ireland
142 D4 Ringe Denmark
168 B3 Ringe Ger.
141 J3 Ringebu Norway
190 E2 Ringelspitz mt. Switz.
170 E2 Ringenwalde Ger.
231 C5 Ringgold GA U.S.A.
207 H3 Ringim Nigeria
142 C3 Ringkøbing Denmark
142 C3 Ringkøbing county Denmark
142 C4 Ringkøbing Fjord lag. Denmark
151 I2 Ringland Norfolk, England U.K.
171 C4 Ringleben Ger.
151 H4 Ringmer East Sussex, England U.K.
234 D2 Ringoes NJ U.S.A.
148 C2 Ringsend Northern Ireland U.K.
142 D4 Ringsted Denmark
140 L1 Ringvassøy i. Norway
147 D4 Ringville Rep. of Ireland
151 F4 Ringwood Hampshire, England U.K.
233 F4 Ringwood NJ U.S.A.
Rinía i. Greece see Rineia
168 E1 Rinkenæs Denmark
146 E4 Rinloan Aberdeenshire, Scotland U.K.
178 C3 Rinn Austria
146 C7 Rinns of Galloway pen. Scotland U.K.
146 B6 Rinns of Islay pen. Scotland U.K.
256 B4 Rinópolis Brazil
169 E3 Rinteln Ger.
196 C3 Rinya r. Romania
226 C4 Rio WI U.S.A.
255 C8 Rio Azul Brazil
250 B5 Riobamba Ecuador
257 G3 Rio Bananal Brazil
239 F4 Rio Blanco CO U.S.A.
257 F5 Rio Bonito Brazil
252 D2 Rio Branco Brazil
Rio Branco state Brazil see Roraima
256 C6 Rio Branco do Sul Brazil
255 B7 Rio Brilhante Brazil
259 B6 Río Bueno Chile
246 □ Rio Bueno Jamaica
182 B3 Rio Caldo Port.
251 F2 Río Caribe Venez.
257 F4 Rio Casca Brazil
260 E2 Río Ceballos Arg.
257 E5 Rio Claro Rio de Janeiro Brazil
256 D5 Rio Claro São Paulo Brazil
247 □7 Rio Claro Trin. and Tob.
261 E6 Río Colorado Arg.
260 E3 Río Cuarto Arg.
257 F5 Rio de Janeiro Brazil
257 F4 Rio de Janeiro state Brazil
238 A3 Rio Dell CA U.S.A.
182 C4 Rio de Mel Port.
184 B3 Rio de Moinhos Beja Port.
184 C2 Rio de Moinhos Évora Port.
184 B2 Rio de Moinhos Setúbal Port.
182 D3 Rio de Onor Port.
204 A5 Río de Oro, Bahía de b. Western Sahara
187 B4 Ríodeva r. Spain
191 G2 Rio di Pusteria Italy
257 F4 Rio Doce Brazil
255 C8 Rio do Sul Brazil
182 C3 Rio Douro Port.
254 G4 Rio Formoso Brazil
183 F4 Riofrío Spain
182 D3 Riofrío de Aliste Spain
183 G3 Riofrío de Riaza Spain
259 C8 Río Gallegos Arg.
185 F4 Ríogordo Spain
259 D9 Río Grande Arg.
258 G4 Rio Grande Brazil
246 □ Rio Grande r. Jamaica
245 F6 Río Grande Mex.
244 C2 Río Grande Mex.
242 F3 Rio Grande r. Mex./U.S.A. alt. Bravo del Norte, Río
247 □1 Rio Grande Puerto Rico
234 D3 Rio Grande NJ U.S.A.
258 C2 Río Grande, Salar de salt flat Arg.
237 D7 Rio Grande City TX U.S.A.
254 F3 Rio Grande do Norte state Brazil
255 B9 Rio Grande do Sul state Brazil
264 G8 Rio Grande Rise sea feature S. Atlantic Ocean
250 C2 Ríohacha Col.
258 D2 Río Hondo, Embalse resr Arg.
250 B6 Rioja Peru
185 H4 Rioja Spain
243 H4 Río Lagartos Mex.
254 G4 Rio Largo Brazil
192 A5 Riola Sardo Sardegna Italy
182 D5 Riolobos Spain
191 G4 Riolo Terme Italy
161 A5 Riols France
160 B3 Riom France
190 E4 Riomaggiore Italy
184 B1 Rio Maior Port.
192 C2 Rio Marina Italy
182 B3 Rio Mau Port.
161 A3 Riom-ès-Montagnes France
246 □ Rio Minho r. Jamaica
163 B5 Rion-des-Landes France
260 D6 Río Negro prov. Arg.
255 C8 Rio Negro Brazil
259 B6 Río Negro Chile
261 I3 Río Negro dept Uru.
182 D2 Rionegro del Puente Spain
193 H4 Rionero in Vulture Italy
193 G3 Rionero Sannitico Italy
129 B2 Rioni r. Georgia
257 F4 Rio Novo Brazil
257 G4 Rio Novo do Sul Brazil
163 B4 Rions France
181 E3 Riópar Spain
255 E5 Rio Pardo de Minas Brazil
257 F4 Rio Pomba Brazil
257 F5 Rio Preto Brazil
256 D2 Rio Preto, Serra do hills Brazil
261 F2 Río Primero Arg.
239 F5 Rio Rancho NM U.S.A.
160 C2 Riorges France
241 L6 Rio Rico AZ U.S.A.
182 C3 Ríos Spain
182 E2 Rioseco de Tapia Spain
261 F2 Río Segundo Arg.
250 B3 Ríosucio Col.
254 G3 Rio Tinto Brazil
182 C3 Rio Torto Port.
92 A4 Rio Tuba Phil.
256 B2 Rio Verde Brazil
250 B4 Rioverde Ecuador
190 C4 Rioverde r. Italy
245 E3 Río Verde Mex.
255 B6 Rio Verde de Mato Grosso Brazil
257 F3 Rio Vermelho Brazil
240 G2 Rio Vista CA U.S.A.
160 E1 Rioz France
250 E5 Riozinho r. Amazonas Brazil
253 F4 Riozinho r. Mato Grosso do Sul Brazil
190 B3 Ripa r. Italy
196 E3 Ripanj Srbija Yugo.
191 F5 Riparbella Italy
193 F2 Ripatransone Italy
140 M2 Ripats Sweden
191 I5 Ripe Italy
193 F3 Ripi Italy
193 H4 Ripiti r. Italy
137 F2 Ripky Ukr.
149 H4 Ripley Derbyshire, England U.K.
149 H3 Ripley North Yorkshire, England U.K.
237 F5 Ripley MS U.S.A.
232 D3 Ripley NY U.S.A.
232 B5 Ripley OH U.S.A.
237 F5 Ripley TN U.S.A.
232 C5 Ripley WV U.S.A.
186 F2 Ripoll Spain
149 H3 Ripon North Yorkshire, England U.K.
240 G3 Ripon CA U.S.A.
226 C4 Ripon WI U.S.A.
195 E5 Riposto Sicilia Italy
150 E2 Ripple Worcestershire, England U.K.
149 H4 Ripponden West Yorkshire, England U.K.
164 E3 Rips Neth.
157 H4 Riquewihr France
123 H3 Risalpur Pak.
128 A4 Risân 'Aneiza hill Egypt
250 C3 Risaralda dept Col.
141 K3 Risarven Sweden
140 K2 Risbäck Sweden
150 D3 Risca Caerphilly, Wales U.K.
136 D4 Rîşcani Moldova
163 B5 Riscle France
260 C4 Risco Plateado mt. Arg.
140 K2 Risede Sweden
116 D3 Rishikesh Uttar Prad. India
100 G3 Rishiri-zan vol. Japan
128 B4 Rishon Le Ẓiyyon Israel
149 G4 Rishton Lancashire, England U.K.
230 C4 Rising Sun IN U.S.A.
234 B3 Rising Sun MD U.S.A.
159 G2 Risle r. France
Rîşnov Romania see Râşnov
237 E5 Rison AR U.S.A.
142 C2 Risør Norway
156 C4 Ris-Orangis France
160 E2 Risoux, Mont mt. France
172 D3 Riß r. Ger.
140 J3 Rissa Norway
160 E2 Risse r. France
80 F3 Rissington North I. N.Z.
141 N3 Ristiina Fin.
140 O2 Ristijärvi Fin.
168 D1 Risum-Lindholm Ger.
95 F2 Ritan r. Indon.
138 E3 Rītausma Latvia
214 E3 Ritchie S. Africa
115 G3 Ritchie's Archipelago is Andaman & Nicobar Is India
209 C9 Rito Angola
262 X2 Ritscher Upland mts Antarctica
140 L2 Ritsem Sweden
240 H3 Ritter, Mount CA U.S.A.
168 D2 Ritterhude Ger.
169 B5 Rittersdorf Ger.
171 D5 Rittersgrün Ger.
183 H3 Rituerto r. Spain
138 F3 Rītupe r. Latvia
238 C2 Ritzville WA U.S.A.
186 E3 Riudoms Spain
136 E3 Riv r. Ukr.
138 C3 Rīva r. Latvia
159 F2 Riva Bella France
261 F4 Rivadavia Buenos Aires Arg.
260 C3 Rivadavia Mendoza Arg.
191 F3 Riva del Garda Italy
178 B5 Riva di Solto Italy
191 H2 Riva di Tures Italy
140 □ Rivalensundet str. Svalbard
190 C5 Riva Ligure Italy
190 E4 Rivanazzano Italy
239 F6 Riva Palacio Mex.
190 D4 Rivardo Ligure Italy
190 C3 Rivarolo Canavese Italy
190 F3 Rivarolo Mantovano Italy
242 □I7 Rivas Nic.
183 G4 Rivas-Vaciamadrid Spain
160 C3 Rive-de-Gier France
162 A2 Rivedoux-Plage France
193 H4 Rivello Italy
261 F5 Rivera Arg.
255 B9 Rivera Uru.
206 C5 River Cess Liberia
240 H3 Riverdale CA U.S.A.
226 A3 River Falls WI U.S.A.
233 G4 Riverhead NY U.S.A.
223 J5 Riverhurst Sask. Can.
87 D6 Riverina W.A. Austr.
83 F3 Riverina reg. N.S.W. Austr.
207 G5 Rivers state Nigeria
81 B6 Riversdale South I. N.Z.
214 C6 Riversdale S. Africa
81 F4 Riversdale Beach North I. N.Z.
81 C6 Riverside South I. N.Z.
215 G4 Riverside S. Africa
240 I5 Riverside CA U.S.A.
234 D2 Riverside NJ U.S.A.
234 B2 Riverside PA U.S.A.
222 E5 Rivers Inlet B.C. Can.
84 D3 Riversleigh Qld Austr.
147 C2 Riverstown Sligo Rep. of Ireland
147 D3 Riverstown Tipperary Rep. of Ireland
223 L5 Riverton Man. Can.
81 B7 Riverton South I. N.Z.
214 E3 Riverton S. Africa
234 C2 Riverton NJ U.S.A.
241 L1 Riverton UT U.S.A.
232 D5 Riverton VA U.S.A.
238 E3 Riverton WY U.S.A.
225 H4 Riverview N.B. Can.
215 I3 River View S. Africa
235 D2 Riverwood NJ U.S.A.
156 C3 Rivery France
161 D3 Rives France
163 E6 Rivesaltes France
232 C5 Rivesville WV U.S.A.
234 B3 Riviera Beach MD U.S.A.
235 D2 Riviera Beach NJ U.S.A.
225 H3 Rivière-au-Renard Que. Can.
225 G4 Rivière Bleue Que. Can.
225 G4 Rivière-du-Loup Que. Can.
225 H3 Riviere-Pentecote Que. Can.
225 H3 Riviere-Pigou Que. Can.
247 □3 Rivière-Pilote Martinique
247 □3 Rivière-Salée Martinique
161 B4 Rivière-sur-Tarn France
214 B6 Riviersonderend S. Africa
191 I3 Rivignano Italy
137 F3 Rivne Kirovohrads'ka Oblast' Ukr.
136 D2 Rivne Rivnens'ka Oblast' Ukr.
136 D3 Rivne Vinnyts'ka Oblast' Ukr.
136 D2 Rivnens'ka Oblast' admin. div. Ukr.
Rivne Oblast admin. div. Ukr. see Rivnens'ka Oblast'
193 E2 Rivodutri Italy
190 C3 Rivoli Italy
215 H1 Rivulets S. Africa
209 D9 Rivungo Angola
81 D4 Riwaka South I. N.Z.
112 I5 Riwoqê Xizang China
165 D4 Rixensart Belgium
157 H5 Rixheim France
124 D2 Riyadh Saudi Arabia
92 B3 Rizal Phil.
127 F2 Rize Turkey
129 B3 Rize prov. Turkey
107 H5 Rizhao Shandong China
107 H5 Rizhao Shandong China
Rizokarpaso Cyprus see Rizokarpason
128 B2 Rizokarpason Cyprus
198 C2 Rizomylos Greece
192 A3 Rizzanese r. Corse France
195 E4 Rizziconi Italy
194 D5 Rizzuto r. Sicilia Italy
195 G4 Rizzuto, Capo c. Italy
142 C2 Rjukan Norway
142 B2 Rjuvbrokkene mt. Norway
206 B2 Rkîz Maur.
191 G4 Ro Italy
142 D1 Roa Norway
183 G3 Roa Spain
82 □2 Roach Island Lord Howe I. Austr.
151 G2 Roade Northamptonshire, England U.K.
147 B3 Roadford Rep. of Ireland
232 B5 Roads OH U.S.A.
146 E3 Roadside Highland, Scotland U.K.
247 F3 Road Town Virgin Is (U.K.)
163 B4 Roaillan France
140 J2 Roan Norway
241 M2 Roan Cliffs ridge UT U.S.A.
146 F6 Roan Fell hill Scotland U.K.
160 C2 Roannais reg. France
160 C2 Roanne France
231 C5 Roanoke AL U.S.A.
226 C5 Roanoke IL U.S.A.
232 D6 Roanoke VA U.S.A.
232 E6 Roanoke r. NC U.S.A.
231 E4 Roanoke Rapids NC U.S.A.
241 M2 Roan Plateau UT U.S.A.
234 B1 Roaring Branch PA U.S.A.
190 F2 Roasco r. Italy
242 □I5 Roatán Hond.
150 D3 Roath Cardiff, Wales U.K.
134 C3 Röbäck Sweden
123 E4 Robat r. Afgh.
122 D4 Robāţ Iran
122 C4 Robāţ-e Shahr-e Bābak Iran
122 D2 Robāţ-e Ţoroq Iran
122 B3 Robāţ Karīm Iran
222 G4 Robb Alta Can.
214 B5 Robben Island S. Africa
231 D5 Robbinsville NC U.S.A.
234 D2 Robbinsville NJ U.S.A.
190 D3 Robbio Italy
82 D4 Robe S.A. Austr.
86 B4 Robe r. W.A. Austr.
210 C3 Robē Eth.
147 B3 Robe r. Rep. of Ireland
82 E2 Robe, Mount hill N.S.W. Austr.
190 F3 Robecco d'Oglio Italy
170 D2 Röbel Ger.
157 F4 Robert-Espagne France
237 C6 Robert Lee TX U.S.A.
146 F6 Roberton Scottish Borders, Scotland U.K.
146 E6 Roberton South Lanarkshire, Scotland U.K.
238 D3 Roberts ID U.S.A.
83 H2 Roberts, Mount Qld Austr.
232 C5 Robertsburg WV U.S.A.
263 K2 Roberts Butte mt. Antarctica
241 I2 Roberts Creek Mountain NV U.S.A.
140 M2 Robertsfors Sweden
117 E4 Robertsganj Uttar Prad. India
85 E3 Robertson r. Qld Austr.
214 B5 Robertson S. Africa
262 U2 Robertson Island Antarctica
87 D4 Robertson Range hills W.A. Austr.
206 C5 Robertsport Liberia
82 D3 Robertstown S.A. Austr.
Robert Williams Angola see Caála
225 F3 Roberval Que. Can.
234 B2 Robesonia PA U.S.A.
161 C4 Robiac France
149 I3 Robin Hood's Bay North Yorkshire, England U.K.
84 D3 Robinson r. N.T. Austr.
86 E3 Robinson r. W.A. Austr.
222 C2 Robinson Y.T. Can.
230 C4 Robinson IL U.S.A.
232 A5 Robinson KY U.S.A.
85 G5 Robinson Creek r. Qld Austr.
252 □ Robinson Crusoe, Isla i. S. Pacific Ocean
87 C5 Robinson Range hills W.A. Austr.
84 D3 Robinson River N.T. Austr.
83 E3 Robinvale Vic. Austr.
161 D5 Robion France
185 H2 Robledo Spain
183 F4 Robledo de Chavela Spain
183 F5 Robledo del Mazo Spain
182 E5 Robledollano Spain
183 E2 Robles de la Valcueva Spain
250 C2 Robles La Paz Col.
223 K5 Roblin Man. Can.
171 C4 Röblingen am See Ger.
182 E4 Robliza de Cojos Spain
253 F4 Robore Bol.
183 G3 Robregordo Spain
186 C3 Robres Spain
183 H2 Robres del Castillo Spain
78 □6 Rob Roy i. Solomon Is
223 I5 Robsart Sask. Can.
222 G4 Robson, Mount B.C. Can.
237 D7 Robstown TX U.S.A.
237 C5 Roby TX U.S.A.
184 A2 Roca, Cabo da c. Port.
Roçadas Angola see Xangongo
186 E3 Rocafort de Queralt Spain
163 D4 Rocamadour France
250 □ Roca Redonda i. Islas Galápagos Ecuador
242 B3 Rocas Alijos is Mex.
195 H2 Roca Vecchia Italy
161 E5 Rocbaron France
190 F3 Roccabianca Italy
194 C5 Rocca Busambra mt. Sicilia Italy
193 H4 Roccadaspide Italy
193 F3 Rocca d'Evandro Italy
193 F2 Rocca di Cambio Italy
193 F2 Rocca di Mezzo Italy
195 F3 Rocca di Neto Italy
193 E3 Rocca di Papa Italy
190 E3 Roccafranca Italy
193 H4 Roccagloriosa Italy
195 F2 Rocca Imperiale Italy
190 C4 Rocca la Meia mt. Italy
192 D2 Roccalbegna Italy
195 E5 Roccalumera Sicilia Italy
193 G3 Roccamandolfi Italy
193 E3 Rocca Massima Italy
194 C5 Roccamena Sicilia Italy
193 F3 Roccamonfina Italy
193 G2 Roccamontepiano Italy
193 I4 Roccanova Italy
194 C5 Roccapalumba Sicilia Italy
193 F3 Rocca Pia Italy
193 G3 Roccaraso Italy
191 G4 Rocca San Casciano Italy
193 G2 Rocca San Giovanni Italy
193 F3 Roccasecca Italy
193 F3 Roccasecca dei Volsci Italy
193 E2 Rocca Sinibalda Italy
192 D1 Roccastrada Italy
190 C4 Roccavione Italy
195 F4 Roccella Ionica Italy
193 H3 Rocchetta Sant'Antonio Italy
186 F2 Roc de France mt. France/Spain
161 A5 Roc de Layre mt. France
161 A5 Roc de Montalet mt. France
160 E2 Roc d'Enfer mt. France
158 C3 Roc de Toullaëron hill France
151 F2 Rocester Staffordshire, England U.K.
258 G4 Rocha Uru.
149 G4 Rochdale Greater Manchester, England U.K.
150 C4 Roche Cornwall, England U.K.
161 E3 Roche Bernaude mt. France/Italy
161 E4 Rochebrune, Grand Pic de mt. France
162 C3 Rochechouart France
159 G4 Rochecorbon France
161 D3 Roche de Méaudre mt. France
162 D3 Roche de Vic hill France
255 B6 Rochedo Brazil
165 E4 Rochefort Belgium
162 B3 Rochefort France
158 D4 Rochefort-en-Terre France
160 A3 Rochefort-Montagne France
160 D1 Rochefort-sur-Nenon France
134 H3 Rochegda Rus. Fed.
161 C4 Rochegude France
165 E5 Rochehaut Belgium
161 C3 Roche-la-Molière France
160 E1 Roche-lez-Beaupré France
226 C5 Rochelle IL U.S.A.
161 C4 Rochemaure France
157 F4 Roches-Bettaincourt France
158 E5 Rocheservière France
83 F4 Rochester Vic. Austr.
151 H3 Rochester Medway, England U.K.
149 G2 Rochester Northumberland, England U.K.
230 C3 Rochester IN U.S.A.
227 F4 Rochester MI U.S.A.
226 A3 Rochester MN U.S.A.
233 □H3 Rochester NH U.S.A.
232 E3 Rochester NY U.S.A.
147 D4 Rochestown Rep. of Ireland
157 F5 Rochetaillée France
151 H3 Rochford Essex, England U.K.
147 D3 Rochfortbridge Rep. of Ireland
156 D2 Rochin France
171 D4 Rochlitz Ger.
158 C3 Roc'h Trévezel hill France
184 D3 Rociana del Condado Spain
184 D4 Rocina r. Spain
222 E2 Rock r. Y.T. Can.
150 E2 Rock Worcestershire, England U.K.
226 D2 Rock MI U.S.A.
236 D3 Rock r. IA U.S.A.
226 B5 Rock r. IL U.S.A.
144 □ Rockall i. N. Atlantic Ocean
264 H2 Rockall Bank sea feature N. Atlantic Ocean
81 B6 Rock and Pillar Range mts South I. N.Z.
164 D3 Rockanje Neth.
222 E5 Rock Bay B.C. Can.
146 E7 Rockcliffe Dumfries and Galloway, Scotland U.K.
147 D2 Rockcorry Rep. of Ireland
232 C4 Rock Creek OH U.S.A.
238 F1 Rock Creek r. MT U.S.A.
234 A3 Rock Creek r. PA U.S.A.
234 B3 Rockdale MD U.S.A.
237 D6 Rockdale TX U.S.A.
262 O1 Rockefeller Plateau Antarctica
169 D5 Rockenberg Ger.
172 B2 Rockenhausen Ger.
235 F1 Rockfall CT U.S.A.
231 C5 Rockford AL U.S.A.
226 C4 Rockford IL U.S.A.
226 E4 Rockford MI U.S.A.
232 A4 Rockford OH U.S.A.
223 J5 Rockglen Sask. Can.
234 B2 Rock Glen PA U.S.A.
234 B3 Rock Hall MD U.S.A.
85 G4 Rockhampton Qld Austr.
84 C3 Rockhampton Downs N.T. Austr.
226 C1 Rock Harbor MI U.S.A.
147 C4 Rockhill Rep. of Ireland
234 D1 Rock Hill NY U.S.A.
231 D5 Rock Hill SC U.S.A.
87 B7 Rockingham W.A. Austr.
151 G2 Rockingham Northamptonshire, England U.K.
231 E5 Rockingham NC U.S.A.
85 F3 Rockingham Bay Qld Austr.
151 G2 Rockingham Forest England U.K.
233 G2 Rock Island Que. Can.
236 F3 Rock Island IL U.S.A.
236 D1 Rocklake ND U.S.A.
233 F2 Rockland Ont. Can.
233 H3 Rockland MA U.S.A.
233 □I2 Rockland ME U.S.A.
226 C2 Rockland MI U.S.A.
235 D1 Rockland County county NY U.S.A.
87 C4 Rocklea W.A. Austr.
240 G2 Rocklin CA U.S.A.
171 D4 Röcknitz Ger.
241 M3 Rock Point AZ U.S.A.
230 C4 Rockport IN U.S.A.
233 H3 Rockport MA U.S.A.
237 D7 Rockport TX U.S.A.
238 B1 Rockport WA U.S.A.
232 C5 Rockport WV U.S.A.
236 D3 Rock Rapids IA U.S.A.
238 F3 Rock River WY U.S.A.
246 C1 Rock Sound Eleuthera Bahamas
238 F2 Rock Springs MT U.S.A.
237 C6 Rocksprings TX U.S.A.
238 E3 Rock Springs WY U.S.A.
251 G3 Rockstone Guyana
226 C4 Rockton IL U.S.A.
230 C4 Rockville IN U.S.A.
234 A3 Rockville MD U.S.A.
235 G1 Rockville RI U.S.A.
235 E2 Rockville Centre NY U.S.A.
237 D5 Rockwall TX U.S.A.
236 E3 Rockwell City IA U.S.A.
150 D4 Rockwell Green Somerset, England U.K.
233 □I2 Rockwood ME U.S.A.
227 F4 Rockwood MI U.S.A.
232 D5 Rockwood PA U.S.A.
222 H5 Rockyford Alta Can.
236 C4 Rocky Ford CO U.S.A.
87 C7 Rocky Gully W.A. Austr.
225 J3 Rocky Harbour Nfld. Can.
235 F1 Rocky Hill CT U.S.A.
232 B5 Rocky Hill OH U.S.A.
222 G3 Rocky Lane Alta Can.
231 E5 Rocky Mount NC U.S.A.
232 D6 Rocky Mount VA U.S.A.
222 H4 Rocky Mountain House Alta Can.
228 E2 Rocky Mountains CO U.S.A.
156 D3 Rocourt-St-Martin France
156 E3 Rocroi France
171 C5 Rodach r. Ger.
169 F5 Rodach r. Ger.
169 F5 Rodach bei Coburg Ger.
186 E3 Roda de Berà Spain
186 F3 Roda de Ter Spain
172 B2 Rodalben Ger.
168 E2 Rodau r. Ger.
142 C1 Rodberg Norway
150 E3 Rodborough Gloucestershire, England U.K.
168 G1 Rødby Denmark
142 D4 Rødbyhavn Denmark
225 K3 Roddickton Nfld. Can.
142 C4 Rødding Sønderjylland Denmark
142 C3 Rødding Viborg Denmark
215 G4 Rode S. Africa
143 F3 Rödeby Sweden
149 G4 Rode Heath Cheshire, England U.K.
182 C2 Rodeiro Spain
142 C4 Rødekro Denmark
146 B4 Rodel Western Isles, Scotland U.K.
186 C2 Rodellar Spain
161 A4 Rodelle France
164 F1 Roden Neth.
150 E2 Roden r. England U.K.
183 I4 Ródenas Spain
168 D2 Rodenkirchen (Stadland) Ger.
171 C5 Rödental Ger.
260 C2 Rodeo Arg.
242 D3 Rodeo Mex.
239 E6 Rodeo NM U.S.A.
87 C5 Roderick r. W.A. Austr.
168 E3 Rodewald Ger.
171 D5 Rodewisch Ger.
161 A4 Rodez France
169 D5 Rodheim-Bieber Ger.
Rodholívos Greece see Rodolivos
Rodhópolis Greece see Rodopoli
Ródhos i. Greece see Rodos
Rodi i. Greece see Rodos
179 E4 Rodica mt. Slovenia
193 H3 Rodi Garganico Italy
173 G2 Roding Ger.
121 J1 Rodino Rus. Fed.
137 J4 Rodionovo-Nesvetayskaya Rus. Fed.
143 G1 Rödjebro Sweden
171 D4 Rodleben Ger.
197 G2 Rodna Romania
197 G2 Rodnei, Munții mts Romania
80 E2 Rodney, Cape North I. N.Z.
150 E3 Rodney Stoke Somerset, England U.K.
234 C3 Rodney Village DE U.S.A.
Rodnichek Rus. Fed. see Rodnichok
135 H6 Rodnichok Rus. Fed.
137 G3 Rodnykivka Ukr.
120 D2 Rodnykovka Kazakh.
242 A2 Rodolfo Sanchez Toboada Mex.
198 C1 Rodolivos Greece
196 D5 Rodonit, Kepi i pt Albania
Rodopi Planina mts Bulg./Greece see Rhodope Mountains
198 C1 Rodopoli Greece
199 F3 Rodos Notio Aigaio Greece
199 F3 Rodos i. Greece
186 F3 Rodós mt. Spain
Rodosto Turkey see Tekirdağ
182 C1 Rodrigas Spain
217 □1a Rodrigues Island Mauritius
261 I4 Rodriguez Uru.
86 E2 Roe r. W.A. Austr.
148 C2 Roe r. Northern Ireland U.K.
234 D2 Roebling NJ U.S.A.
86 C4 Roebourne W.A. Austr.
86 D3 Roebuck Bay W.A. Austr.
213 F5 Roedtan S. Africa
191 G2 Roèn, Monte mt. Italy
87 E6 Roe Plains W.A. Austr.
165 E3 Roermond Neth.
165 B4 Roesbrugge-Haringe Belgium
165 C4 Roeselare Belgium
221 J3 Roes Welcome Sound sea chan. Nunavut Can.
169 B5 Roetgen Ger.
193 H4 Rofrano Italy
Rogachev Belarus see Rahachow
137 J2 Rogachevka Rus. Fed.
139 K3 Rogachevo Rus. Fed.
252 D3 Rogagua, Laguna l. Bol.
142 B2 Rogaland county Norway
188 E2 Rogaška Slatina Slovenia
174 F4 Rogaszyce Pol.
151 G3 Rogate West Sussex, England U.K.
179 G4 Rogatec Slovenia
188 G4 Rogatica Bos.-Herz.
Rogatin Ukr. see Rohatyn
171 C3 Rogätz Ger.
222 G5 Rogers B.C. Can.
237 E4 Rogers AR U.S.A.
232 C6 Rogers, Mount VA U.S.A.
227 F3 Rogers City MI U.S.A.
238 D3 Rogerson ID U.S.A.
232 B6 Rogersville TN U.S.A.
224 E2 Roggan r. Que. Can.
165 E3 Roggel Neth.
173 E3 Roggenburg Ger.
170 C2 Roggendorf Ger.
170 D2 Roggentin Ger.
267 N8 Roggeveen Basin sea feature S. Pacific Ocean
214 C5 Roggeveld plat. S. Africa
214 C5 Roggeveldberge esc. S. Africa
193 I5 Roggiano Gravina Italy
Roghadal Western Isles, Scotland U.K. see Rodel
195 E4 Roghudi Italy
184 B3 Rogil Port.
192 B2 Rogliano Corse France
195 F3 Rogliano Italy
191 F5 Roglio r. Italy
161 D5 Rognac France
140 K2 Rognan Norway
139 I5 Rognedino Rus. Fed.
161 D5 Rognes France
168 F2 Rögnitz r. Ger.
157 F4 Rognon r. France
161 C5 Rognonas France
190 B4 Rognosa, Punta mt. Italy
137 J2 Rogovatoye Rus. Fed.
137 J5 Rogovskaya Rus. Fed.
175 H4 Rogów Pol.
174 F3 Rogowo Kujawsko-Pomorskie Pol.
175 H3 Rogowo Kujawsko-Pomorskie Pol.
174 E4 Rogoźnica Pol.
175 K3 Rogoźniczka Pol.
174 G2 Rogóźno Pol.
174 F3 Rogoźno Pol.
141 L3 Rogsta Sweden
238 A3 Rogue r. OR U.S.A.
78 □3b Roguron i. Majuro Marshall Is
175 J3 Roguszyn Pol.
114 B2 Roha Mahar. India
136 D2 Rohachiv Ukr.
158 D3 Rohan France
137 I3 Rohan' Ukr.
176 G3 Rohatec Czech Rep.
136 C3 Rohatyn Ukr.
137 F2 Rohizky Ukr.
173 E3 Röhlingen Ger.
170 C2 Rohlsdorf Brandenburg Ger.
170 D2 Rohlsdorf Brandenburg Ger.
240 F2 Rohnert Park CA U.S.A.
177 L3 Rohod Hungary
176 G3 Rohovce Slovakia
179 H2 Rohrau Austria
173 F3 Rohrbach Ger.
179 E2 Rohrbach in Oberösterreich Austria
157 H3 Rohrbach-lès-Bitche France
170 C3 Rohrberg Ger.
123 G5 Rohri Pak.
173 F3 Rohr in Niederbayern Ger.
173 F3 Röhrmoos Ger.
173 H3 Röhrnbach Ger.
168 E3 Rohrsen Ger.
116 D3 Rohtak Haryana India
96 C3 Roi Et Thai.
161 C3 Roiffieux France
79 □3 Roi Georges, Îles du is Arch. des Tuamotu Fr. Polynesia
78 □3a Roi-Namur i. Kwajalein Marshall Is
141 N3 Roine l. Fin.
117 H3 Roing Arun. Prad. India
146 C5 Rois-Bheinn hill Scotland U.K.
156 D3 Roisel France
156 C4 Roissy-en-Brie France
183 F1 Roiz Spain
138 D3 Roja Latvia
187 C6 Rojales Spain
261 G4 Rojas Arg.
142 E1 Röjdåfors Sweden
174 G3 Rojewo Pol.
123 G4 Rojhan Pak.
247 □1 Rojo, Cabo Puerto Rico
247 □1 Rojo, Cabo c. Puerto Rico
252 D3 Rojo Aguado, Laguna l. Bol.
94 C2 Rokan r. Indon.
85 E2 Rokeby Qld Austr.
175 H4 Rokiciny Pol.
175 K6 Rokietnica Podkarpackie Pol.
174 E3 Rokietnica Wielkopolskie Pol.
138 E4 Rokiškis Lith.
175 L3 Rokitno Pol.
140 M2 Roknäs Sweden
177 H3 Rokoš mt. Slovakia
105 E2 Rokuriga-hara plain Japan
176 C2 Rokycany Czech Rep.
136 C2 Rokyni Ukr.
176 F2 Rokytná r. Czech Rep.
136 F3 Rokytne Kyivs'ka Oblast' Ukr.
136 D2 Rokytne Rivnens'ka Oblast' Ukr.
176 G2 Rokytnice Czech Rep.
111 E5 Rola Kangri mt. Xizang China
157 F5 Rolampont France
256 B5 Rolândia Brazil
261 G3 Roldan Arg.
164 F2 Rolde Neth.
253 E2 Rolim de Moura Brazil
241 K5 Roll AZ U.S.A.
236 F4 Rolla MO U.S.A.
236 D1 Rolla ND U.S.A.
142 C1 Rollag Norway
182 E4 Rollán Spain
190 B2 Rolle Switz.
151 I2 Rollesby Norfolk, England U.K.
85 G5 Rolleston Qld Austr.
81 D5 Rolleston South I. N.Z.
81 C5 Rolleston, Mount South I. N.Z.
81 C5 Rolleston Range mts South I. N.Z.
227 H2 Rollet Que. Can.
246 D2 Rolleville Gt Exuma Bahamas
237 F5 Rolling Fork MS U.S.A.
238 D2 Rollins MT U.S.A.
233 □H3 Rollinsford NH U.S.A.
206 E3 Rollo Burkina
227 I2 Rolphton Ont. Can.
162 C2 Rom France
170 C2 Rom Ger.
210 B4 Rom mt. Uganda
85 G5 Roma Qld Austr.
193 E3 Roma Italy
193 E2 Roma prov. Lazio Italy
215 F3 Roma Lesotho
197 H2 Roma Romania
143 H3 Roma Gotland Sweden
237 D7 Roma TX U.S.A.
190 D3 Romagnano Sesia Italy
158 E3 Romagné France
81 B7 Romahapa South I. N.Z.
225 I3 Romaine r. Que. Can.
190 B2 Romainmôtier Switz.
197 H2 Roman Romania
151 H3 Roman r. England U.K.
192 A4 Romana Sardegna Italy
197 F3 Română, Câmpia plain Romania
197 F3 Romanaţilor, Câmpia plain Romania
149 H3 Romanby North Yorkshire, England U.K.
161 D3 Romanche r. France
264 H6 Romanche Gap sea feature S. Atlantic Ocean
234 B4 Romancoke MD U.S.A.
160 C2 Romanèche-Thorins France
197 G2 Romania country Europe
183 H3 Romanillos de Atienza Spain
175 M6 Romaniv Ukr.
137 H5 Roman-Kosh mt. Ukr.
146 E6 Romannobridge Scottish Borders, Scotland U.K.
191 G3 Romano d'Ezzelino Italy
190 E3 Romano di Lombardia Italy
183 H4 Romanones Spain
Romanovka Moldova see Basarabeasca
99 J1 Romanovka Respublika Buryatiya Rus. Fed.
135 H6 Romanovka Saratovskaya Oblast' Rus. Fed.
121 J1 Romanovo Rus. Fed.
190 E1 Romanshorn Switz.
161 D3 Romans-sur-Isère France
158 E3 Romazy France
157 G3 Rombas France
195 F4 Rombiolo Italy
92 B3 Romblon Phil.
Rombo, Ilhéus do is Cape Verde see Secos, Ilhéus
Rome Italy see Roma
231 C5 Rome GA U.S.A.
226 C5 Rome IL U.S.A.
233 □I2 Rome ME U.S.A.
233 F3 Rome NY U.S.A.
160 C2 Rome Château, Mont de hill France
226 E5 Rome City IN U.S.A.
184 B1 Romeira Port.
137 G2 Romen r. Ukr.
239 F4 Romeo CO U.S.A.
227 F4 Romeo MI U.S.A.
172 D3 Römerstein hill Ger.
182 C3 Romeu Port.
151 H3 Romford Greater London, England U.K.
169 F5 Römhild Ger.
158 E3 Romillé France
156 B3 Romilly-sur-Andelle France
156 D4 Romilly-sur-Seine France
244 D3 Romita Mex.
120 F5 Romitan Uzbek.
169 B4 Rommerskirchen Ger.
232 D5 Romney WV U.S.A.
151 H3 Romney Marsh reg. England U.K.
137 G2 Romny Ukr.
142 C4 Rømø i. Denmark
137 G3 Romodan Ukr.
135 I5 Romodanovo Rus. Fed.
190 B2 Romont Switz.
78 □4a Romonum i. Chuuk Micronesia
162 D1 Romorantin-Lanthenay France
94 C2 Rompin r. Malaysia
169 E5 Romrod Ger.
151 F4 Romsey Hampshire, England U.K.
142 D2 Rømskog Norway
150 E2 Romsley Worcestershire, England U.K.
95 G5 Romu mt. Sumbawa Indon.
197 G2 Romuli Romania
227 F4 Romulus MI U.S.A.
114 B3 Ron Karnataka India
146 C4 Rona i. Highland, Scotland U.K.
146 C2 Rona i. Western Isles, Scotland U.K.
Ronaigh i. Scotland U.K. see Ronay
146 □G1 Ronas Hill hill Scotland U.K.
146 A4 Ronay i. Scotland U.K.
191 H3 Roncade Italy
256 A6 Roncador Brazil
254 B5 Roncador, Serra do hills Brazil
246 B4 Roncador Cay i. Caribbean Sea
78 □6 Roncador Reef Solomon Is
186 C2 Roncal Spain
178 C4 Roncegno Italy
162 A3 Ronce-les-Bains France
186 B1 Roncesvalles Spain
232 C6 Ronceverte WV U.S.A.
157 G5 Ronchamp France
191 I3 Ronchi dei Legionari Italy
192 E2 Ronciglione Italy
191 H4 Ronco r. Italy
190 C3 Ronco Canavese Italy
191 F3 Roncone Italy
190 D4 Ronco Scrivia Italy
156 D2 Roncq France
185 E4 Ronda Spain
185 E4 Ronda, Serranía de mts Spain
142 D3 Rønde Denmark
190 C3 Rondissone Italy
256 A5 Rondon Brazil
250 D3 Rondón Col.
252 E2 Rondônia state Brazil
255 B6 Rondonópolis Brazil
98 C4 Rondu Jammu and Kashmir
108 D3 Rong'an Guangxi China
108 A2 Rongbaca Sichuan China
108 C2 Rongchang Chongqing China
Rongcheng Anhui China see Qingyang
Rongcheng Guangxi China see Rongxian
Rongcheng Hubei China see Jianli
107 I4 Rongcheng Shandong China
111 E6 Rong Chu r. China
266 G6 Rongelap atoll Marshall Is
108 D3 Rongjiang Guizhou China
Rongjiang Jiangxi China see Nankang
108 D4 Rong Jiang r. China
Rongjiawan Hunan China see Yueyang
96 A2 Rongklang Range mts Myanmar
Rongmei Hubei China see Hefeng
108 D3 Rongshui Guangxi China
Rongwo Qinghai China see Tongren
108 D4 Rongxian Guangxi China
108 C2 Rongxian Sichuan China
Rongzhag Sichuan China see Danba
Rönlap atoll Marshall Is see Rongelap
143 F4 Rønne Bornholm Denmark
171 D5 Ronneburg Ger.
143 F3 Ronneby Sweden
262 S2 Ronne Entrance str. Antarctica
169 E3 Ronnenberg Ger.
140 K3 Rönnöfors Sweden
86 C4 Ronsard Island W.A. Austr.
173 E4 Ronsberg Ger.
165 C4 Ronse Belgium
169 E5 Ronshausen Ger.
254 B5 Ronuro r. Brazil

156 A3 Saâne r. France
122 C2 Saane r. Switz.
190 C2 Saanen Switz.
222 F5 Saar land Ger. see Saarland
172 A2 Saar r. Ger.
172 A2 Saarbrücken Ger.
172 A2 Saarburg Ger.
138 D2 Saaremaa i. Estonia
140 N2 Saarenkylä Fin.
141 D3 Saari Fin.
140 N3 Saarijärvi Fin.
172 A2 Saarland land Ger.
172 A2 Saarlouis Ger.
172 A2 Saarwellingen Ger.
190 E2 Saas Switz.
190 C2 Saas Fee Switz.
190 C2 Saas Grund Switz.
190 C2 Saastal val. Switz.
129 F4 Saatly Azer.
Saatly Azer. see Saatlı
261 F5 Saavedra Arg.
247 G5 Saba i. Neth. Antilles
128 C3 Sab' Ābār Syria
169 E4 Šabac Serbia Yugo.
196 D3 Šabac Srbija Yugo.
186 F3 Sabadell Spain
206 C4 Sabadou Baranama Guinea
104 C3 Sabae Japan
95 C1 Sabah state Malaysia
211 D5 Sabaki r. Kenya
93 A4 Sabalana, Kepulauan is Indon.
116 D4 Sabalgarh Madh. Prad. India
242 □I6 Sabamagrande Hond.
246 B2 Sabana, Archipiélago de is Cuba
247 K5 Sabana de la Mar Dom. Rep.
247 □1 Sabana Grande Puerto Rico
250 C2 Sabanalarga Col.
246 E3 Sabaneta Dom. Rep.
94 A1 Sabang Indon.
126 D2 Şabanözü Turkey
197 H2 Săbăoani Romania
257 F3 Sabará Brazil
163 D5 Sabari r. India
114 C2 Sabari r. India
128 B3 Sabastiya West Bank
193 G3 Sabato r. Italy
193 F3 Sabaudia Italy
252 C4 Sabaya Bol.
129 B2 Sabburlu Georgia
190 F4 Sabbioneta Italy
214 D4 Sabelo S. Africa
210 C4 Sabena Desert Kenya
183 E2 Sabero Spain
202 B3 Sabha Libya
116 B5 Sabhrai Gujarat India
116 D3 Sabi r. India
Sabi r. Moz./Zimbabwe see Save
215 I1 Sabie r. Moz./S. Africa
213 F5 Sabie S. Africa
138 D3 Sabile Latvia
232 B5 Sabina OH U.S.A.
186 C2 Sabiñánigo Spain
185 H4 Sabinar, Punta del mt. Spain
243 Sabinas Mex.
237 C7 Sabinas r. Coahuila Mex.
237 C7 Sabinas r. Nuevo León Mex.
243 E3 Sabinas Hidalgo Mex.
237 E6 Sabine r. Louisiana/Texas U.S.A.
140 Sabine Land reg. Svalbard
237 E6 Sabine Pass TX U.S.A.
193 E2 Sabini, Monti mts Italy
257 F3 Sabinópolis Brazil
177 K2 Sabinov Slovakia
185 G2 Sabiote Spain
129 F3 Sabir Azer.
129 F3 Sabirabad Azer.
92 B3 Sablayan Phil.
225 H5 Sable, Cape N.S. Can.
231 D7 Sable, Cape FL U.S.A.
78 □1 Sable, Île de i. New Caledonia
225 G2 Sable, Rivière du r. Que. Can.
225 J5 Sable Island N.S. Can.
227 G2 Sables, River aux r. Ont. Can.
158 D3 Sables-d'Or-les-Pins France
159 F4 Sablé-sur-Sarthe France
161 D4 Sablet France
161 C4 Sablières France
129 C1 Sablinskoye Rus. Fed.
161 G3 Sablons France
254 F3 Saboeiro Brazil
184 B3 Sabóia Port.
207 H3 Sabon Kafi Niger
182 C3 Sabor r. Port.
206 E3 Sabou Burkina
163 B4 Sabres France
263 H2 Sabrina Coast Antarctica
182 C3 Sabrosa Port.
129 D2 Sabue Georgia
182 C4 Sabugal Port.
184 B2 Sabugueiro Évora Port.
182 C4 Sabugueiro Guarda Port.
129 F3 Sabunçu Azer.
199 G2 Sabuncu Kütahya Turkey
105 G2 Saburyū-yama mt. Japan
124 C2 Sabyā Saudi Arabia
Sabzawar Afgh. see Shindand
122 D2 Sabzevār Iran
Sabzvārān Iran see Jiroft
197 G2 Saca, Vârful mt. Romania
187 F5 Sa Cabaneta Spain
252 C4 Sacaca Bol.
177 L4 Săcădat Romania
177 K6 Săcălaz Romania
233 F3 Sacandaga r. NY U.S.A.
187 C5 Sacañet Spain
223 N4 Sachigo r. Ont. Can.
116 C5 Sachin Gujarat India
129 C2 Sach'khere Georgia
101 D6 Sach'on S. Korea
190 D2 Sachseln Switz.
171 E4 Sachsen land Ger.
171 D3 Sachsen-Anhalt land Ger.
173 E2 Sachsen bei Ansbach Ger.
169 D4 Sachsenberg (Lichtenfels) Ger.
169 G5 Sachsenbrunn Ger.
179 E4 Sachsenburg Austria
169 E3 Sachsenhagen Ger.
169 E4 Sachsenhausen (Waldeck) Ger.
172 D3 Sachsenheim Ger.
220 F2 Sachs Harbour N.W.T. Can.
191 H3 Sacile Italy
Sacirsuyu r. Syria/Turkey see Sājūr, Nahr
233 F3 Sackets Harbor NY U.S.A.
169 D5 Sackpfeife hill Ger.
225 H4 Sackville N.B. Can.
233 □11 Saco ME U.S.A.
238 F1 Saco MT U.S.A.
177 K6 Sacoşu Turcesc Romania
186 D1 Sacramenia Spain
183 D3 Sacramento Spain
256 D3 Sacramento Brazil
240 G2 Sacramento CA U.S.A.
240 G2 Sacramento r. CA U.S.A.
252 A1 Sacramento, Pampa del plain Peru
239 F5 Sacramento Mountains NM U.S.A.
240 F1 Sacramento Valley CA U.S.A.
253 F3 Sacre r. Brazil
149 H3 Sacriston Durham, England U.K.
193 E3 Sacrofano Italy
197 F2 Săcueni Romania
177 L5 Săcuieu Romania
253 F1 Sacuriuiná r. Brazil
127 □3b Sada Spain
116 D4 Sadabad Uttar Prad. India

122 B4 Sa'dābād Iran
Sá da Bandeira Angola see Lubango
124 A6 Sada de Sangüesa Spain
124 C4 Şa'dah Yemen
124 C4 Şa'dah governorate Yemen
192 B5 Sadali Sardegna Italy
93 A3 Sadang r. Indon.
211 C6 Sadani Tanz.
97 C6 Sadao Thai.
125 E5 Sadārak Azer.
129 D4 Sādārak Azer.
114 C2 Sadaseopet Andhra Prad. India
146 C6 Saddell Argyll and Bute, Scotland U.K.
Saddleback hill England U.K. see Blencathra
237 D5 Saddleback Mesa mt. NM U.S.A.
85 F2 Saddle Hill hill Qld Austr.
81 D4 Saddle Island Vanuatu see Mota Lava
115 G3 Saddle Peak hill Andaman & Nicobar Is India
97 D5 Sa De Vietnam
125 F4 Sadh Oman
124 A3 Sadhaura Haryana India
123 G4 Sadiqabad Pak.
174 F2 Sadki Pol.
175 I4 Sadkowice Pol.
174 D2 Sadlinki Pol.
184 B2 Sado r. Port.
102 I5 Sadoga-shima i. Japan
127 G2 Sadon Rus. Fed.
95 E2 Sadong r. Sarawak Malaysia
192 B4 Sa Donna, Pico mt. Sardegna Italy
137 H5 Sadove Ukr.
135 I7 Sadovoye Respublika Kalmykiya - Khalm'g-Tangch Rus. Fed.
137 K2 Sadovoye Voronezhskaya Oblast' Rus. Fed.
175 J5 Sadowie Pol.
175 J3 Sadowne Pol.
187 F5 Sa Dragonera i. Spain
116 C4 Sadri Rajasthan India
234 G3 Sadsburyville PA U.S.A.
171 F5 Sádek Czech Rep.
116 C3 Sadulshahar Rajasthan India
142 D3 Sæby Denmark
168 D1 Sæd Denmark
232 C4 Saegertown PA U.S.A.
183 H5 Saelices Spain
183 H4 Saelices de Mayorga Spain
183 E2 Saelices del Rio Spain
183 E2 Saelices de Mayorga Spain
169 C3 Saerbeck Ger.
165 E5 Saeul Lux.
Safi Israel see Zefat
206 B3 Safané Burkina
184 C2 Safara Port.
Šafárikovo Slovakia see Tornal'a
123 G2 Safed Khirs mts Afgh.
123 F3 Safed Koh mts Afgh.
142 J3 Säffle Sweden
241 M5 Safford AZ U.S.A.
158 E4 Saffré France
151 H2 Saffron Walden Essex, England U.K.
Safi Jordan see Aş Şāfī
204 C2 Safi Morocco
122 D2 Safiabad Iran
122 B2 Safid r. Iran
122 E4 Safīdābeh Iran
122 C4 Safīdār, Kūh-e mt. Iran
122 B3 Safid Dasht Iran
Safid Kūh mts Afgh. see Paropamisus
123 Safīta Syria
134 F1 Safonovo Murmanskaya Oblast' Rus. Fed.
139 I4 Safonovo Smolenskaya Oblast' Rus. Fed.
121 Safrā' al 'Asyāh esc. Saudi Arabia
124 C2 Safrā' as Sark esc. Saudi Arabia
126 D2 Safranbolu Turkey
128 B2 Safwān Iraq
177 L4 Şag Romania
196 E3 Şag Romania
111 D6 Saga Xizang China
103 E7 Saga Japan
103 E7 Saga pref. Japan
111 I5 Saga Kazakh.
102 J4 Saga Japan
96 A2 Sagaing Myanmar
96 A2 Sagaing admin. div. Myanmar
192 A4 Sagama Sardegna Italy
105 G3 Sagamihara Japan
105 H3 Sagami-nada b. Japan
232 D4 Sagamore PA U.S.A.
207 F5 Sagamu Nigeria
97 A4 Saganthit Kyun i. Myanmar
104 C3 Sagara Japan
114 C2 Sagar Karnataka India
114 C2 Sagar Karnataka India
116 D5 Sagar Madh. Prad. India
170 E1 Sagard Ger.
123 G3 Sagaredzho Georgia see Sagarejo
117 G5 Sagar Island India
117 H4 Sagarmatha mt. China/Nepal see Everest, Mount
117 H4 Sagarmatha National Park Nepal
220 D2 Sagavanirktok r. AK U.S.A.
168 D3 Sage Ger.
238 B4 Sage Creek r. MT U.S.A.
238 E1 Sage Creek r. MT U.S.A.
143 F1 Sågen Sweden
147 I2 Saggart Rep. of Ireland
235 F2 Sag Harbor NY U.S.A.
Sagin Kazakh. see Sagiz
114 C3 Sagileru r. India
227 E4 Saginaw MI U.S.A.
227 E4 Saginaw Bay MI U.S.A.
199 D2 Sağırkaraağaç Turkey
192 B7 Sagittario r. Italy
120 C2 Sagiz Kazakh.
199 E1 Sağlamtaş Turkey
206 C5 Saglo Liberia
Saglouc Que. Can. see Salluit
182 D4 Sagnes Corse France
185 H4 Sagra mt. Spain
184 B3 Sagres Port.
226 D5 Sagres, Ponta de pt Port.

203 G3 Şahara el Sharqiya des. Egypt
Saharan Atlas mts Alg. see Atlas Saharien
116 D3 Saharanpur Uttar Prad. India
86 D1 Sahara Well W.A. Austr.
117 F4 Saharsa Bihar India
115 D4 Sahaswan Uttar Prad. India
122 C3 Sahat, Kūh-e hill Iran
150 C4 Sahatwar Uttar Prad. India
213 □K4 Sahavato Madag.
129 D4 Şahbaz Azer.
129 D3 Şahdağ Silsiläsi hills Azer.
124 B4 Sahel prov. Eritrea
117 F4 Sahibganj Bihar India
123 H4 Sahiwal Punjab Pak.
123 H4 Sahiwal Punjab Pak.
124 C3 Sahl Rakbah plain Saudi Arabia
125 G2 Şahm Oman
122 A3 Şahneh Iran
127 G5 Şahrā al Ḥijārah reg. Iraq
Şahu Qinghai China see Zadoi
242 C2 Sahuaripa Mex.
241 L6 Sahuarita AZ U.S.A.
244 C3 Sahuayo Mex.
185 D2 Sahún Spain
161 D4 Sahune France
133 Q3 Sahuteng Ukr.
129 B4 Sahvelet Dağları mts Turkey
177 H3 Sahy Slovakia
114 Sahyadri mts India see Western Ghats
114 Sahyadriparvat Range hills India
128 C2 Sahyūn tourist site Syria
116 E4 Sai r. India
97 C6 Sai Buri Thai.
97 C6 Sai Buri r. Thai.
205 F2 Saïda Alg.
128 Saïda Lebanon
94 C4 Sai Dao Tai, Khao mt. Thai.
181 E5 Saïdia Morocco
117 G4 Saidpur Uttar Prad. India
123 H3 Saidu Pak.
104 C2 Sai-gawa r. Japan
105 E2 Sai-gawa r. Japan
146 A4 Saighdinis Western Isles, Scotland U.K.
123 G3 Sa'īndezh Iran
123 G3 Sa'in Qal'eh Iran see Sa'īndezh
156 D3 Sains-Richaumont France
236 F4 Saint r. IL U.S.A.
146 F6 Saint Abbs Scottish Borders, Scotland U.K.
146 F6 St Abb's Head hd Scotland U.K.
161 G3 St-Acheul France
161 A5 St-Affrique France
163 H5 St-Affrique, Causse de plat. France
160 B2 St-Agnan France
161 G1 St-Agnan-en-Vercors France
162 B3 St-Agnant France
162 D2 St-Agnant-de-Versillat France
147 C2 St Agnes Cornwall, England U.K.
148 B3 St Agnes i. England U.K.
162 D2 St-Agrève France
160 C1 St-Aignan France
158 D2 St-Aignan-sur-Roë France
162 B3 St-Aigulin France
160 C2 St-Albain France
161 D3 St-Alban-d'Ay France
161 D3 St-Alban-Leysse France
225 K4 St Alban's Nfld. Can.
151 G3 St Albans Hertfordshire, England U.K.
233 G2 St Albans VT U.S.A.
232 C5 St Albans WV U.S.A.
150 E4 St Alban's Head hd England U.K.
161 B4 St-Alban-sur-Limagnole France
222 H4 St Albert Alta Can.
161 J4 St Aldhelm's Head hd England U.K. see St Alban's Head
159 F2 St-Amand France
161 G3 St-Amand-en-Puisaye France
156 D2 St-Amand-les-Eaux France
159 H4 St-Amand-Longpré France
160 B4 St-Amand-Montrond France
161 A4 St-Amand-sur-Fion France
156 E4 St-Amand-sur-Sèvre France
163 H6 St-Amans-des-Cots France
163 C5 St-Amans-Soult France
163 C5 St-Amant-de-Boixe France
160 B3 St-Amant-Roche-Savine France
161 B4 St-Amant-Tallende France
157 H5 St-Amarin France
225 G3 St-Ambroise Que. Can.
161 D2 St-Amour France
163 E6 St-Andiol France
161 F5 St-André France
Si-André, Cap pt Madag. see Vilanandro, Tanjona
162 B3 St-André-de-Corcy France
161 C4 St-André-de-Cruzières France
162 B4 St-André-de-Cubzac France
161 B5 St-André-de-l'Eure France
161 B5 St-André-de-Sangonis France
163 A5 St-André-de-Seignanx France
161 D3 St-André-de-Valborgne France
160 B1 St-André-en-Morvan France
160 D3 St-André-les-Alpes France
162 C3 St-André-les-Vergers France
246 □ St Andrew parish Jamaica
233 □J2 St Andrews N.B. Can.
81 C6 St Andrews South I. N.Z.
146 F3 St Andrews Fife, Scotland U.K.
158 D2 St Angel France
246 □ St Ann parish Jamaica
246 □ St Ann's Bay Jamaica
150 D3 St Ann's Head hd Wales U.K.
244 A4 St Ansgar IA U.S.A.
225 K3 St Anthony Nfld. Can.
146 C4 Saint Anthony ID U.S.A.
146 D3 St-Antonin-Noble-Val France
161 C4 St-Apollinaire France
159 G4 St-Août France
162 C3 St-Arcons-d'Allier France
83 E4 St Arnaud Vic. Austr.
81 D5 St Arnaud South I. N.Z.
81 D5 St Arnaud Range mts South I. N.Z.
156 B4 St-Arnoult-en-Yvelines France
159 H4 St Asaph Denbighshire, Wales U.K.
225 B5 St Asaph IL U.S.A.
158 E3 St-Aubin-d'Aubigné France

158 E3 St-Aubin-du-Cormier France
156 B3 St-Aubin-lès-Elbeuf France
159 F2 St-Aubin-sur-Mer France
225 J3 St Augustin Que. Can.
231 D6 St Augustine FL U.S.A.
225 J4 St-Augustin r. Newfoundland/Québec Can.
150 C4 St Austell Cornwall, England U.K.
150 C4 St Austell Bay England U.K.
158 D4 St-Avé France
161 B3 St-Avold France
157 G3 St-Avold France
156 B5 St-Ay France
123 H4 St-Aygulf France
160 D3 St-Baldoph France
159 I4 St-Barthélemy Switz.
163 D6 St-Barthélemy, Pic de mt. France
163 C4 St-Barthélemy-d'Agenais France
162 C3 St-Barthélemy-d'Anjou France
162 C3 St-Barthélemy-de-Bellegarde France
163 C4 St-Barthélemy-de-Vals France
81 B6 St Bathans South I. N.Z.
81 B6 St Bathans, Mount South I. N.Z.
161 B5 St-Bauzille-de-Putois France
157 G4 St-Béat France
161 B3 St-Beauzély France
149 I4 St Bees Cumbria, England U.K.
149 I3 St Bees Head hd England U.K.
160 B1 St-Benin-d'Azy France
163 E5 St-Benoît France
217 □ St-Benoît Réunion
163 E4 St-Benoît-de-Carmaux France
162 D2 St-Benoît-du-Sault France
156 C5 St-Benoît-sur-Loire France
81 D5 St Bernard mt. South I. N.Z.
160 D3 St-Béron France
159 F3 St-Berthevin France
160 D2 St-Bertrand-de-Comminges France
190 B3 St-Blaise Switz.
157 H4 St-Blaise-la-Roche France
161 D5 St-Blin-Semilly France
190 D2 St-Blasien Ger.
160 C2 St-Bonnet-de-Bellac France
160 C2 St-Bonnet-de-Joux France
161 C3 St-Bonnet-des-Bruyères France
161 E4 St-Bonnet-en-Champsaur France
161 C3 St-Bonnet-le-Château France
161 C3 St-Bonnet-le-Froid France
162 B3 St-Bonnet-sur-Gironde France
163 E6 St-Saillagouse-Llo France
161 C3 Saillans France
161 B4 St-Branchs France
161 B4 St-Branchs France
150 B3 St Brelade Channel Is
158 D3 St-Brévin-les-Pins France
158 D3 St-Briac-sur-Mer France
150 D3 St Briavels Gloucestershire, England U.K.
156 C3 St-Brice-Courcelles France
163 C4 St-Brice-en-Coglès France
150 D3 St Brides Pembrokeshire, Wales U.K.
150 D3 St Bride's Bay Wales U.K.
150 D3 St Brides Major Vale of Glamorgan, Wales U.K.
158 D3 St-Brieuc France
158 D3 St-Brieuc, Baie de b. France
156 C4 St-Bris-le-Vineux France
160 C1 St-Broing-les-Moines France
158 E3 St-Broladre France
150 □ St Buryan Cornwall, England U.K.
161 D3 St-Cairns France
160 B2 St-Cannat France
158 D3 St-Cast-le-Guildo France
224 E5 St Catharines Ont. Can.
246 □ St Catherine parish Jamaica
247 □5 St Catherine, Mount hill Grenada
225 K4 St Catherine's Nfld. Can.
151 F4 St Catherine's Point England U.K.
163 C6 St-Céré France
160 E2 St-Cergues France
162 E3 St-Cernin France
162 E3 St-Cernin France
161 G4 St-Chaffrey France
162 B4 St-Chamarand France
161 C3 St-Chamond France
161 C4 St-Chaptes France
227 G2 St Charles Ont. Can.
238 D3 St Charles ID U.S.A.
232 B4 St Charles MI U.S.A.
231 F5 St Charles MO U.S.A.
226 A5 St Charles MN U.S.A.
161 C3 St-Chef France
162 D2 St-Chély-d'Apcher France
163 A5 St-Chély-d'Aubrac France
163 B5 St-Chinian France
161 B5 St-Christol France
161 E4 St-Christol-lès-Alès France
162 B3 St-Christoly-de-Blaye France
162 B3 St-Christoly-Médoc France
193 G3 St-Christophe Italy
158 E5 St-Christophe-du-Ligneron France
159 H4 St-Christophe-en-Bazelle France
160 C2 St-Christophe-en-Brionnais France
St Christopher i. see St Kitts
St Christopher and Nevis country West Indies see St Kitts and Nevis
162 B3 St-Ciers-de-Canesse France
162 B3 St-Ciers-sur-Gironde France
163 B5 St-Circq-Chalosse France
163 E5 St-Cirgues-en-Montagne France
163 C5 St-Cirq-Lapopie France
234 D5 St Clair r. Can./U.S.A.
227 F4 St Clair MI U.S.A.
234 B4 St Clair PA U.S.A.
227 F4 St Clair, Lake Can./U.S.A.
231 F6 St Clairsville OH U.S.A.
156 B4 St-Clair-sur-Epte France
161 B4 St-Clair-sur-l'Elle France
232 C5 St Clairsville OH U.S.A.
162 C3 St-Clar France
160 D2 St-Claud France
162 D2 St-Claude France
150 □ St Clears Carmarthenshire, Wales U.K.
150 □ St Clement Channel Is
156 D4 St Clement Channel Is
157 G4 St-Clément France
161 F6 St-Clément-de-Rivière France
142 B4 St Cloud MN U.S.A.
161 □ St-Cloud France
236 E2 St Cloud MN U.S.A.
236 C2 St Coeur-de-Marie Que. Can.
147 E3 St Columb Major Cornwall, England U.K.
146 E4 St Combs Aberdeenshire, Scotland U.K.
161 D3 St-Constant France
161 C4 St-Cosme-en-Vairais France
162 C3 St-Crépin-di-Richemont France
221 L5 St Croix r. Can./U.S.A.
247 □3 St Croix i. Virgin Is (U.S.A.)
226 A3 St Croix r. MN U.S.A.
221 L5 St Croix Island Virgin Is (U.S.A.)
163 D4 St-Cyprien France
163 F6 St-Cyprien-Plage France
161 B5 St-Cyr-l'École France
156 C4 St-Cyr-sur-Mer France
161 D5 St-Cyr-sur-Morin France
161 E5 St-Dalmas-le-Selvage France
225 L5 St David AZ U.S.A.
226 B5 St David IL U.S.A.

150 B3 St David's Pembrokeshire, Wales U.K.
150 B3 St David's Head hd Wales U.K.
150 B4 St Day Cornwall, England U.K.
156 C4 St-Denis France
163 E5 St-Denis France
217 □ St-Denis Réunion
161 C4 St-Denis-d'Anjou France
159 F3 St-Denis-de-Gastines France
162 D2 St-Denis-de-Jouhet France
162 B2 St-Denis-d'Oléron France
159 F3 St-Denis-d'Orques France
160 D3 St-Denis-du-Sig Alg. see Sig
160 D2 St-Denis-lès-Bourg France
150 C4 St Dennis Cornwall, England U.K.
158 D3 St-Denoual France
160 C2 St-Désert France
161 D2 St-Didier-en-Velay France
160 C2 St-Didier-sur-Chalaronne France
160 B3 St-Didier-sur-Rochefort France
157 G4 St-Dié France
160 B3 St-Dier-d'Auvergne France
157 F4 St-Dizier France
162 D2 St-Dizier-Leyrenne France
150 C2 St Dogmaels Pembrokeshire, Wales U.K.
158 D4 St-Dolay France
158 E3 St-Dominec France
247 St-Domingue country West Indies see Haiti
161 C3 St-Doulchard France
159 G2 Ste-Adresse France
162 C4 Ste-Alvère France
223 L5 Sainte Anne Man. Can.
247 □7 Ste-Anne Guadeloupe
225 G4 Ste-Anne-de-Beaupré Que. Can.
233 □I1 Ste-Anne-de-Madawaska N.B. Can.
225 H3 Ste-Anne-de-Portneuf Que. Can.
225 H3 Ste-Anne-des-Monts Que. Can.
160 C1 Ste-Cécile-les-Vignes France
163 E6 Ste-Croix France
190 A2 Ste-Croix Switz.
161 E5 Ste-Croix, Lac de l. France
163 D5 Ste-Croix-Volvestre France
150 C4 Ste-Croix Cornwall, England U.K.
161 E4 Ste-Émélie-de-l'Énergie Que. Can.
163 B5 Ste-Engrâce France
161 D3 Ste-Eulalie France
160 B3 Ste-Eulalie-d'Olt France
161 A4 Ste-Eulalie-en-Born France
162 C3 Ste-Feyre France
162 B3 Ste-Florine France
162 B3 Ste-Fortunade France
163 D5 Ste-Foy-de-Peyrolières France
163 C4 Ste-Foy-l'Argentière France
160 C3 Ste-Foy-lès-Lyon France
163 C4 Ste-Foy-Tarentaise France
161 D3 Ste-Gauburge-Ste-Colombe France
161 B4 Ste-Gemme-la-Plaine France
156 C4 Ste-Geneviève France
236 F4 Ste-Geneviève MO U.S.A.
159 G2 Ste-Geneviève-sur-Argence France
161 D3 Ste-Égrève France
162 B4 Ste-Hermine France
233 □I1 Ste-Hermine France
163 C4 Ste-Léocadie France
159 G4 Ste-Lheure Que. Can.
224 E5 St Élias Mountains Y.T. Can.
251 H3 St Élie Fr. Guiana
161 A4 St Élias Mountains Y.T. Can.
222 A2 St Élias, Mount Can./U.S.A.
251 H3 St Élie Fr. Guiana
163 C4 Ste-Livrade-sur-Lot France
161 D3 Ste-Élix-le-Château France
163 C5 Ste-Élix-Theux France
246 □ St Elizabeth parish Jamaica
159 H4 Ste-Lizaigne France
160 A2 St-Éloy-les-Mines France
192 B3 Ste-Lucie-de-Tallano Corse France
247 St Marguerite i. see Marguerite, Île de
159 G3 Ste Marguerite r. Que. Can.
157 G4 Ste-Marie France
225 G4 Ste-Marie Martinique
247 □3 Ste-Marie, Cap c. Madag. see Vohimena, Tanjona
Sainte-Marie, Île i. Madag. see Boraha, Nosy
157 H4 Ste-Marie-aux-Mines France
161 C4 Ste-Maure-de-Peyriac France
162 C1 Ste-Maure-de-Touraine France
161 E5 Ste-Maxime France
157 H3 Ste-Menehould France
158 E2 Ste-Mère-Église France
161 E4 St-Christol France
146 D6 St-Gérand-le-Puy France
156 C4 St-Germain France
226 A3 St Germain WI U.S.A.
160 C2 St-Germain-Chassenay France
161 B4 St-Germain-de-Calberte France
159 G3 St-Germain-de-la-Coudre France
161 C3 St-Germain-des-Fossés France
160 C3 St-Germain-du-Bois France
159 G3 St-Germain-du-Corbeis France
160 C2 St-Germain-du-Plain France
162 C3 St-Germain-en-Laye France
162 C3 St-Germain-Laval France
162 B3 St-Germain-Lembron France
161 B3 St-Germain-les-Belles France
162 B3 St-Germain-Lespinasse France
160 B2 St-Germain-l'Herm France
163 A5 St-Germans Cornwall, England U.K.
150 C4 St Germans Cornwall, England U.K.
154 Sté-Esprit France
161 B3 Ste-Sabine France
156 A4 St-Geniès-de-Malgoirès France
163 E6 St-Geniès-des-Mourgues France
161 E4 St-Geniez France
151 □1 St Geniez-d'Olt France
163 E6 St-Génis-des-Fontaines France
160 C3 Ste-Croix-en-Plaine France
161 D3 Ste-Sigolène France
163 A5 Ste-Esteben France
163 B3 Ste-Estèphe France
163 B3 Ste-Estève France
159 I5 St-Suzanne France
150 C4 St Germer-de-Fly France
156 D3 St-Gervais France
161 C4 St-Gervais-d'Auvergne France
159 H4 St-Gervais-la-Forêt France
163 D6 St-Gervais-les-Bains France
159 G5 St-Gervais-sur-Mare France
161 B5 St-Géry France
163 D4 St-Ghislain Belgium
162 D2 St-Girons France
163 D6 St-Girons-Plage France
161 D5 St-Gobain France
162 B3 St-Gondon France
161 D3 St-Gorgon-Main France
158 B4 St-Guénolé France
156 C4 St-Haon-le-Châtel France
214 B5 St Helena i. S. Atlantic Ocean
216 □2 St Helena terr. S. Atlantic Ocean
240 A2 St Helena CA U.S.A.
214 C5 St Helena Bay S. Africa
214 B5 St Helena Bay b. S. Africa
247 □2 St Helen's Nfld. Can.
149 G4 St Helens Merseyside, England U.K.
149 G4 St Helens Merseyside, England U.K.
238 B2 St Helens OR U.S.A.
238 B2 St Helens, Mount vol. WA U.S.A.
83 G5 St Helens Point Tas. Austr.
158 D2 St Helier Channel Is

158 E4 St-Herblain France
163 E5 St-Héribert France
156 E3 St-Hilaire-au-Temple France
161 C4 St-Hilaire France
163 D5 St-Hilaire-de-Loulay France
161 C4 St-Hilaire-de-Lusignan France
158 E5 St-Hilaire-de-Riez France
162 B3 St-Hilaire-des-Loges France
157 G4 St-Hilaire-de-Villefranche France
159 I3 St-Hilaire-du-Harcouët France
161 D3 St-Hilaire-du-Rosier France
160 B2 St-Hilaire-Fontaine France
156 B3 St-Hilaire-le-Grand France
159 F4 St-Florent-le-Vieil France
157 H4 St-Florent-St-Florent France
117 H4 Sainthia W. Bengal India
161 A4 St-Honorat, Mont mt. France
161 B2 St-Honoré-les-Bains France
165 F3 St-Hubert Belgium
225 F4 St-Hyacinthe Que. Can.
226 C2 St Ignace MI U.S.A.
190 B1 St-Imier Switz.
150 C3 St Ishmael Carmarthenshire, Wales U.K.
161 D5 St-Ismier France
150 C4 St Ive Cornwall, England U.K.
151 G2 St Ives Cambridgeshire, England U.K.
150 □ St Ives Cornwall, England U.K.
161 A5 St-Izaire France
233 □I1 St-Jacques N.B. Can.
St Jacques, Cap Vietnam see Vung Tau
224 E3 St-Jacques-de-Dupuy Que. Can.
158 E3 St-Jacques-de-la-Lande France
158 D3 St-Jacut-de-la-Mer France
246 □ St James parish Jamaica
226 B2 St James MN U.S.A.
236 F4 St James MO U.S.A.
235 G2 St James NY U.S.A.
161 E4 St-Jean r. Que. Can.
251 H3 St-Jean r. Fr. Guiana
225 F3 St-Jean, Lac l. Que. Can.
158 D4 St-Jean-Brévelay France
161 E5 St-Jean-Cap-Ferrat France
128 Sainte-Jean-d'Acre Israel see 'Akko
162 C3 St-Jean-d'Angély France
159 I3 St-Jean-d'Assé France
160 D3 St-Jean-de-Bournay France
158 D3 St-Jean-de-Braye France
159 I5 St-Jean-de-Daye France
161 D3 St-Jean-de-la-Ruelle France
161 E4 St-Jean-de-Losne France
163 A5 St-Jean-de-Luz France
161 C4 St-Jean-de-Maurienne France
159 I5 St-Jean-de-Mauréjols-et-Avéjan France
161 E4 St-Jean-de-Maurienne France
158 D3 St-Jean-de-Monts France
161 C3 St-Jean-de-Muzols France
225 G4 St-Jean-de-Port-Joli Que. Can.
159 G5 St-Jean-des-Sauves France
225 I4 St-Jean-de-Sixt France
161 B5 St-Jean-de-Védas France
247 □6 St-Jean-Grenada France
163 B4 St-Jean-d'Illac France
161 D3 St-Jean-du-Bruel France
161 D5 St-Jean-du-Falga France
161 A4 St-Jean-du-Gard France
247 □3 St-Jean-en-Royans France
147 E5 St-Jean-Pied-de-Port France
161 B3 St-Jean-Poutge France
161 D3 St-Jean-Soleymieux France
159 F3 St-Jean-sur-Erve France
160 D2 St-Jean-sur-Reyssouze France
225 F4 St-Jean-sur-Richelieu Que. Can.
160 E2 St-Jeoire France
224 F4 St-Jérôme Que. Can.
159 I3 St-Jores-d'Ay France
159 I5 St-Jeures France
158 D3 St-Joachim France
238 D2 St Joe r. ID U.S.A.
225 H4 Saint John N.B. Can.
235 G3 St John Channel Is
206 C5 St John r. Liberia
236 D6 St John KS U.S.A.
233 □J2 St John r. ME U.S.A.
247 □3 St John i. Virgin Is (U.S.A.)
247 □3 St John's Antigua and Barbuda
225 K4 St John's Nfld. Can.
241 M5 St Johns AZ U.S.A.
226 E4 St Johns MI U.S.A.
231 D6 St Johns r. FL U.S.A.
233 J2 St Johnsbury VT U.S.A.
146 D6 St Johns's Town of Dalry Dumfries and Galloway, Scotland U.K.
233 F3 St Johnsville NY U.S.A.
165 D3 St-Joris Belgium
163 D5 St-Jory France
162 C3 St-Jory-de-Chalais France
225 G4 St-Joseph Martinique
227 F5 St Joseph MI U.S.A.
236 E4 St Joseph MO U.S.A.
227 F5 St Joseph r. MI U.S.A.
224 D5 St-Joseph, Lake Ont. Can.
St-Joseph-d'Alma Que. Can. see Alma
163 D3 St-Jouan-des-Guérets France
159 G2 St-Jouin-Bruneval France
159 F4 St-Jouin-de-Marnes France
163 A5 St-Jovite Que. Can.
156 C4 St-Juéry France
163 C5 St-Julien France
160 D2 St-Julien France
160 C2 St-Julien-Beychevelle France
161 D3 St-Julien-Boutières France
161 C4 St-Julien-de-Civry France
154 D3 St-Julien-de-Concelles France
158 E4 St-Julien-de-Vouvantes France
160 C2 St-Julien-du-Sault France
163 D3 St-Julien-du-Verdon France
161 D4 St-Julien-en-Beauchêne France
163 A5 St-Julien-en-Born France
161 D3 St-Julien-en-Genevois France
161 B3 St-Julien-en-Quint France
162 C2 St-Julien-l'Ars France
161 A5 St-Julien-les-Rosiers France
163 D5 St-Julien-les-Villas France
160 D2 St-Julien-sur-Reyssouze France
163 C5 St-Junien France
163 C4 St-Just France
150 □ St Just Cornwall, England U.K.
163 A5 St-Just-en-Chaussée France
160 C3 St-Just-en-Chevalet France
159 I5 St-Just-Ibarra France
162 C2 St-Justin France
161 C4 St-Just-Malmont France
163 B4 St-Just-St-Rambert France
150 B4 St Just in Roseland Cornwall, England U.K.
161 C4 St-Just-la-Pendue France
160 D2 St-Jean-Bonnefonds France
160 D2 St-Just-Sauvage France
150 □ St Keverne Cornwall, England U.K.
247 □3 St Kilda i. Scotland U.K.
146 □ St Kitts i. St Kitts and Nevis
247 □3 St Kitts and Nevis country West Indies
83 C5 St Lary France
163 C6 St-Lary-Soulan France

Column 1

156 C2 St-Laurent, Golfe du g. Que. Can. see St Lawrence, Gulf of
163 B5 St-Laurent-Blangy France
161 C5 St-Laurent-Bretagne France
161 C4 St-Laurent-d'Aigouze France
186 F2 St-Laurent-de-Carnols France
160 C3 St-Laurent-de-Chamousset France
161 A5 St-Laurent-de-Cerdans France
163 E6 St-Laurent-de-la-Cabrerisse France
163 C5 St-Laurent-de-la-Salanque France
251 H3 St-Laurent-du-Maroni Fr. Guiana
161 D3 St-Laurent-du-Pont France
161 F5 St-Laurent-du-Var France
161 E4 St-Laurent-du-Verdon France
159 G2 St-Laurent-en-Caux France
160 D2 St-Laurent-en-Grandvaux France
161 B4 St-Laurent-les-Bains France
162 B4 St-Laurent-Médoc France
156 B5 St-Laurent-Nouan France
162 C3 St-Laurent-sur-Gorre France
157 F3 St-Laurent-sur-Othain France
159 G5 St-Laurent-sur-Sèvre France
85 G4 St Lawrence Qld Austr.
225 K4 St Lawrence Nfld. Can.
225 G3 St Lawrence inlet Que. Can.
234 C2 St Lawrence S.A. U.S.A.
225 I3 St Lawrence, Gulf of Que. Can.
220 B3 St Lawrence Island AK U.S.A.
224 F4 St Lawrence Seaway sea chan. Can./U.S.A.
223 K5 St Lazare Man. Can.
165 E5 St-Léger Belgium
160 B1 St-Léger-de-Fougeret France
160 B2 St-Léger-des-Vignes France
156 B4 St-Léger-en-Yvelines France
160 C2 St-Léger-sous-Beuvray France
160 C2 St-Léger-sur-Dheune France
225 H4 St Léonard N.B. Can.
225 F4 St Léonard Que. Can.
157 G4 St-Léonard France
232 E5 St Leonard MD U.S.A.
162 D3 St-Léonard-de-Noblat France
151 F4 St Leonards Dorset, England U.K.
162 C3 St-Léon-sur-l'Isle France
156 C3 St-Leu-d'Esserent France
225 K2 St Lewis Nfld. Can.
225 J2 St Lewis r. Nfld. Can.
163 D5 St-Lizier France
159 E2 St-Lô France
163 A5 St-Lon-les-Mines France
160 D2 St-Lothian France
163 B4 St-Loubès France
160 F1 St-Louis France
247 □3 St-Louis Guadeloupe
206 A2 St Louis Senegal
226 E4 St Louis MI U.S.A.
236 F4 St Louis MO U.S.A.
226 A2 St Louis r. MN U.S.A.
246 □ St-Louis du Nord Haiti
161 B5 St-Loup, Pic hill France
160 C2 St-Loup-de-la-Salle France
156 B4 St-Loup-de-Naud France
159 F5 St-Loup-Lamairé France
157 G5 St-Loup-sur-Semouse France
156 B4 St-Lubin-des-Joncherets France
158 E4 St-Luce-sur-Loire France
247 □3 St Lucia country West Indies
215 I3 St Lucia, Lake S. Africa
215 I3 St Lucia Estuary S. Africa
St Luke's Island Myanmar see Zadetkale Kyun
158 D3 St-Lunaire France
160 D2 St-Lupicin France
158 D2 St-Lyé France
163 D5 St-Lys France
163 B4 St-Macaire France
162 B1 St-Macaire-en-Mauges France
163 B4 St-Magne France
146 □G3 St Magnus Bay Scotland U.K.
161 D5 St-Maime France
162 B2 St-Maixent-l'École France
158 B3 St-Malo France
158 B3 St-Malo, Golfe de g. France
158 E2 St-Malo-de-la-Lande France
161 C5 St-Mamet-du-Gard France
163 E4 St-Mamet-la-Salvetat France
161 D5 St-Mandrier-sur-Mer France
246 □ St Marc Haiti
160 C2 St-Marcel France
162 D2 St-Marcel France
156 B3 St-Marcel France
161 C4 St-Marcel-d'Ardèche France
161 C3 St-Marcel-lès-Annonay France
161 C3 St-Marcel-lès-Sauzet France
161 C3 St-Marcel-lès-Valence France
163 D3 St-Marcellin France
163 C5 St-Marcet France
156 C5 St-Marc-sur-Seine France
156 B4 St-Mards-en-Othe France
151 I3 St Margaret's at Cliffe Kent, England U.K.
146 F3 St Margaret's Hope Orkney, Scotland U.K.
238 C2 St Mark's ID U.S.A.
St Mark's S. Africa see Cofimvaba
215 F5 St Marks E. Cape S. Africa
163 E6 St-Marsal France
159 G4 St-Mars-d'Outillé France
159 F3 St-Mars-du-Désert France
158 E4 St-Mars-la-Brière France
158 E4 St-Mars-la-Jaille France
161 B4 St-Martial France
163 D4 St-Martial-de-Nabirat France
163 D4 St-Martial-de-Valette France
158 D2 St Martin Channel Is
158 D2 St Martin Channel Is
161 D5 St Martin France
247 □3 St Martin i. West Indies
156 B2 St-Martin-Boulogne France
163 A5 St-Martin-d'Ablois France
163 A5 St-Martin-d'Arrossa France
159 I4 St-Martin-d'Auxigny France
161 E3 St-Martin-de-Belleville France
161 C5 St-Martin-de-Castillon France
158 E3 St-Martin-de-Crau France
158 E3 St-Martin-de-Fugères France
161 E3 St-Martin-de-Landelles France
161 E3 St-Martin-de-Londres France
161 E4 St-Martin-d'Entraunes France
162 A2 St-Martin-de-Ré France
159 F2 St-Martin-des-Besaces France
158 E3 St-Martin-des-Champs France
158 E3 St-Martin-des-Champs France
163 A5 St-Martin-de-Seignanx France
161 C4 St-Martin-de-Valamas France
158 E3 St-Martin-de-Vérargues France
161 D3 St-Martin-d'Hères France
163 B5 St-Martin-d'Oney France
160 D2 St-Martin-du-Frêne France
163 D2 St-Martin-du-Mont France
161 C4 St-Martin-du-Var France
160 C2 St-Martin-en-Bresse France
160 D1 St-Martin-en-Haut France
161 B4 St-Martin-la-Plaine France
159 G4 St-Martin-le-Beau France
150 D2 St Martin's Shropshire, England U.K.
150 □ St Martin's i. England U.K.
156 D5 St-Martin-sur-Ouanne France
162 C3 St-Martin-Valmeroux France
161 F4 St-Martin-Vésubie France
156 C2 St-Martory France
222 H5 St Mary r. B.C. Can.
246 □ St Mary parish Jamaica
81 B6 St Mary, Mount South I. N.Z.
151 F3 St Mary Bourne Hampshire, England U.K.
151 H3 St Mary in the Marsh Kent, England U.K.
83 G5 St Mary Peak S.A. Austr.
83 G5 St Mary's Tas. Austr.
227 G4 St Mary's Ont. Can.

Column 2

146 F3 St Mary's Orkney, Scotland U.K.
150 □ St Mary's i. England U.K.
236 D4 Saint Marys KS U.S.A.
232 A4 St Marys OH U.S.A.
232 D4 St Marys PA U.S.A.
232 C5 St Marys WV U.S.A.
225 K3 St Mary's r. OH U.S.A.
225 K4 St Mary's Bay b. Nfld. Can.
151 H3 St Mary's Bay Kent, England U.K.
232 H5 St Marys City MD U.S.A.
227 H1 St-Mathieu France
162 A2 St-Mathieu France
158 B3 St-Mathieu, Pointe de pt France
162 A2 St-Mathurin France
220 A3 St Matthew Island AK U.S.A.
231 D5 Saint Matthews SC U.S.A.
156 C3 St-Maur-des-Fossés France
224 F4 St Maurice r. Que. Can.
190 B2 St-Maurice Switz.
160 C3 St-Maurice-de-Beynost France
161 C3 St-Maurice-de-Lignon France
162 C3 St-Maurice-des-Lions France
162 D2 St-Maurice-la-Souterraine France
161 C3 St-Maurice-l'Exil France
161 B5 St-Maurice-Navacelles France
163 C4 St-Maur-sur-le-Loir France
150 B4 St Mawes Cornwall, England U.K.
157 G4 St-Max France
156 C3 St-Maxent France
163 C5 St-Maximin France
161 D5 St-Maximin-la-Ste-Baume France
162 C3 St-Méard-de-Drône France
162 B3 St-Médard-de-Guizières France
163 B4 St-Médard-en-Jalles France
158 D3 St-Méen-le-Grand France
158 E3 St-Méloir-des-Ondes France
162 B3 St-Même-les-Carrières France
156 K4 St-Memmie France
157 E3 St-Menges France
160 B2 St-Menoux France
150 C4 St Merryn Cornwall, England U.K.
162 D3 St-Mesmin France
156 D4 St-Mesmin France
159 F5 St-Mesmin France
163 C4 St-Mézard France
233 E5 St Michaels MD U.S.A.
150 □ St Michael's Mount tourist site England U.K.
163 C5 St-Michel France
156 B3 St-Michel France
162 C3 St-Michel France
158 C3 St-Michel, Montagne hill France
158 B4 St-Michel-Chef-Chef France
163 B4 St-Michel-de-Castelnau France
161 E3 St-Michel-de-Maurienne France
224 F4 St-Michel-des-Saints Que. Can.
158 C3 St-Michel-en-Grève France
162 A2 St-Michel-en-l'Herm France
159 F5 St-Michel-Mont-Mercure France
157 F4 St-Michel-sur-Meurthe France
157 F4 St-Mihiel France
146 F5 St Monans Fife, Scotland U.K.
163 B4 St-Mont France
161 C4 St-Montant France
157 G4 St-Nabord France
233 G2 St-Rémi Que. Can.
160 C2 St-Rémy France
160 C2 St-Rémy France
161 E4 St-Rémy-de-Provence France
161 E4 St-Rémy-en-Bouzemont-St-Genest-et-Isson France
105 F3 St-Rémy-sur-Avre France
105 F2 St-Rémy-sur-Durolle France
104 B4 Saku Ōsaka Japan
103 F6 Saku Japan
127 H5 Sakākah Saudi Arabia
236 C2 Sakakawea, Lake ND U.S.A.
224 F2 Sakami Que. Can.
224 E2 Sakami r. Que. Can.
224 E2 Sakami Lake Que. Can.
209 F8 Sakania Dem. Rep. Congo
197 H5 Sakar mts Bulg.
123 E2 Sakar r. Turkm.
Sakartvelo country Asia see Georgia
199 Q1 Sakarya Turkey
199 Q1 Sakarya prov. Turkey
206 D5 Sakassou Côte d'Ivoire
102 I4 Sakata Japan
101 C4 Sakchu N. Korea
121 H2 Saken Seyfullin Kazakh.
207 F5 Sakété Benin
100 G2 Sakhalin i. Rus. Fed.
100 G2 Sakhalin Oblast admin. div. Rus. Fed. see Sakhalinskaya Oblast'
100 G1 Sakhalinskaya Oblast' admin. div. Rus. Fed.
100 G1 Sakhalinskiy Zaliv b. Sakhalin Rus. Fed.
215 H1 Sakharov S. Africa
215 H1 Sakhelwe S. Africa
215 G2 Sakhile S. Africa
232 C6 Sakhnivtsi Ukr.
124 C2 Sakhra Turkm.
129 E3 Sakht-Sar Iran
129 E3 Şäki Azer.
207 F4 Saki Nigeria
Saki Ukr. see Saky
138 T2 Sakiai Lith.
123 F4 Sakiet Sidi Youssef Tunisia
93 H2 Sakishima-shotō is Japan
114 B3 Sakleshpur Karnataka India
120 C2 Sakmara Rus. Fed.
116 C5 Sakoli Mahar. India
96 A1 Sakon Nakhon Thai.
233 H4 Sakonnet r. RI U.S.A.
123 G5 Sakrand Pak.
214 C4 Sakrivier S. Africa
120 E3 Saksaul'skiy Kazakh.

Column 3

158 E4 St-Philbert-de-Grand-Lieu France
161 D5 St-Pierre mt. France
160 F3 St-Pierre Italy
247 □3 St-Pierre Martinique
217 □1c St-Pierre Réunion
217 □2 St Pierre i. Seychelles
225 K4 St-Pierre
225 J4 St Pierre and Miquelon terr. N. America
160 E3 St-Pierre-d'Albigny France
161 E3 St-Pierre-d'Allevard France
163 B4 St-Pierre-d'Aurillac France
161 D3 St-Pierre-de-Chartreuse France
162 C3 St-Pierre-de-Chignac France
161 D5 St-Pierre-de-Côle France
161 B5 St-Pierre-de-la-Fage France
159 G3 St-Pierre-de-Maillé France
158 E3 St-Pierre-de-Plesguen France
162 C1 St-Pierre-des-Corps France
159 F4 St-Pierre-des-Échaubrognes France
159 F3 St-Pierre-des-Landes France
159 F3 St-Pierre-des-Nids France
161 C4 St-Pierre-de-Trivisy France
163 A5 St-Pierre-d'Irube France
162 A3 St-Pierre-d'Oléron France
159 F3 St-Pierre-du-Chemin France
163 B5 St-Pierre-du-Mont France
158 E2 St-Pierre-Église France
160 F2 St-Pierre-en-Faucigny France
159 G2 St-Pierre-en-Port France
162 B3 St-Pierre-la-Cour France
162 C3 St-Pierre-le-Moûtier France
156 B3 St-Pierre-lès-Elbeuf France
159 F5 St-Pierre-lès-Nemours France
163 A5 St-Pierre-Quiberon France
159 F2 St-Pierre-sur-Dives France
160 A3 St-Pierreville France
156 C2 St-Pol-de-Léon France
156 C2 St-Pol-sur-Mer France
156 C3 St-Pol-sur-Ternoise France
162 D4 St-Pompont France
161 E4 St-Pons France
161 A5 St-Pons-de-Thomières France
162 B3 St-Porchaire France
160 B2 St-Pourçain-sur-Sioule France
190 B2 St-Prex Switz.
162 D3 St-Priest France
160 A3 St-Priest-des-Champs France
162 B3 St-Priest-Laprugne France
162 C3 St-Priest-Taurion France
162 B3 St-Privat France
161 C4 St-Privat-d'Allier France
161 C4 St-Privat-des-Vieux France
160 C4 St-Prix France
163 D4 St-Projet France
233 □H1 St-Prosper Que. Can.
163 C5 St-Puy France
225 H4 St Quentin N.B. Can.
156 D3 St-Quentin France
161 D3 St-Quentin-la-Poterie France
161 D3 St-Quentin-sur-Isère France
157 H4 St-Quirin France
161 D3 St-Rambert-d'Albon France
160 D3 St-Rambert-en-Bugey France
161 E5 St-Raphaël France
163 D2 Saint Regis MT U.S.A.
233 F2 St Regis r. NY U.S.A.
233 F2 St Regis Falls NY U.S.A.
161 C4 St-Remèze France
233 G2 St-Rémi Que. Can.
160 C2 St-Rémy France
160 C2 St-Rémy France
161 E4 St-Rémy-de-Provence France
161 E4 St-Rémy-en-Bouzemont-St-Genest-et-Isson France
158 D3 St-Rémy-sur-Avre France
160 B4 St-Rémy-sur-Durolle France
158 D3 St-Réverien France
190 C3 St-Rhemy Italy
160 C2 St-Rigaud, Mont mt. France
156 B2 St-Riquier France
159 G2 St-Romain-de-Colbosc France
160 D3 St-Romain-de-Jalionas France
160 C3 St-Romain-le-Puy France
156 B4 St-Romain-sous-Versigny France
159 H4 St-Romain-sur-Cher France
161 C4 St-Romans France
156 B4 St-Rome-de-Cernon France
156 B4 St-Rome-de-Tarn France
199 Q3 Sakarya r. Turkey
199 Q1 Sakarya prov. Turkey
206 D5 Sakassou Côte d'Ivoire
102 I4 Sakata Japan
101 C4 Sakchu N. Korea
121 H2 Saken Seyfullin Kazakh.
207 F4 Saki Nigeria
138 D4 Šakiai Lith.
207 F4 Saki Nigeria
Saki Ukr. see Saky
121 J2 Saksaul'skoye Kazakh.
137 J4 Samara r. Ukr.

Column 4

160 D2 St-Trivier-de-Courtes France
160 C2 St-Trivier-sur-Moignans France
162 A3 St-Trojan-les-Bains France
St Trond Belgium see Sint Truiden
161 E5 St-Tropez France
163 D5 St-Urcisse France
161 C3 St-Urcize France
161 D3 St-Uze France
158 E2 St-Vaast-la-Hougue France
156 D4 St-Valérien France
159 G2 St-Valéry-en-Caux France
156 B2 St-Valéry-sur-Somme France
160 C2 St-Vallier France
161 C3 St-Vallier France
161 E5 St-Vallier-de-Thiey France
161 C3 St-Vallier-sur-Marne France
161 F2 St-Vaury France
161 E4 St-Véran France
161 C3 St-Victoret France
159 F2 St-Victor-la-Coste France
190 C3 St-Vincent Italy
236 D1 St Vincent MN U.S.A.
247 □3 St Vincent i. West Indies
83 F5 St Vincent, Cap pt Austr.
St Vincent, Cape Port. see São Vicente, Cabo de
82 D3 St Vincent, Gulf S.A. Austr.
247 □3 St Vincent and the Grenadines i. West Indies
162 C3 St-Vincent-de-Connezac France
163 B5 St-Vincent-de-Paul France
163 A5 St-Vincent-de-Tyrosse France
231 C6 St Vincent Island FL U.S.A.
161 E4 St-Vincent-les-Forts France
247 □3 St Vincent Passage St Lucia/St Vincent
160 D1 St-Vit France
163 C4 St-Vite France
162 A3 St-Vivien-de-Médoc France
223 I4 St Walburg Sask. Can.
227 G4 St Williams Ont. Can.
162 A2 St-Xandre France
160 C2 St-Yan France
163 B5 St-Ybars France
160 B2 St-Yorre France
162 D3 St-Yrieix-la-Perche France
162 C3 St-Yrieix-sur-Charente France
158 C4 St-Yvy France
163 C4 St-Zacharie France
156 B4 Sainville France
91 K3 Saipal mt. Nepal
252 A2 Saipan i. N. Mariana Is
158 E2 Saire r. France
93 D3 Saisai r. Papua N.G.
163 E5 Saissac France
105 E3 Saitama Japan
105 E3 Saitama pref. Japan
Saiteki Turkey see Kadınhanı
103 E7 Saito Japan
140 M1 Saivomuotka Sweden
123 E2 Saïx France
252 C4 Sajama, Nevado mt. Bol.
197 H4 Šajince Srbija Yugo.
124 D2 Sajir Saudi Arabia
175 J1 Sajna r. Pol.
177 J4 Sajó r. Hungary
177 J3 Sajóhídvég Hungary
177 J3 Sajókaza Hungary
177 J3 Sajópetri Hungary
177 J3 Sajószentpéter Hungary
177 J4 Sajószöged Hungary
177 J3 Sajóvámos Hungary
128 D7 Sājūr, Nahr r. Syria/Turkey
210 C2 Saka Eth.
105 E3 Sakado Japan
105 F2 Sakai Gunma Japan
104 B4 Sakai Ōsaka Japan
104 D3 Sakai Japan
103 F6 Sakaide Japan
127 H5 Sakākah Saudi Arabia
236 C2 Sakakawea, Lake ND U.S.A.
224 F2 Sakami Que. Can.
224 E2 Sakami r. Que. Can.
224 E2 Sakami Lake Que. Can.
209 F8 Sakania Dem. Rep. Congo
197 H5 Sakar mts Bulg.
123 E2 Sakar r. Turkm.
123 J2 Sakar-Chaga Turkm.
Sakartvelo country Asia see Georgia
199 Q1 Sakarya Turkey
199 Q1 Sakarya prov. Turkey
206 D5 Sakassou Côte d'Ivoire
102 I4 Sakata Japan
101 C4 Sakchu N. Korea
121 H2 Saken Seyfullin Kazakh.
92 A Keo r. Thai.
207 F5 Sakété Benin
100 G2 Sakhalin i. Rus. Fed.
100 G2 Sakhalin Oblast' admin. div. Rus. Fed.
Sakhalinskaya Oblast' admin. div. Rus. Fed. see Sakhalinskaya Zaliv b. Sakhalin Rus. Fed.
100 G1 Sakhalinskaya Zaliv b. Sakhalin Rus. Fed.

Column 5

246 C2 Salado r. Cuba
245 G3 Salado r. Hidalgo/México Mex.
245 F5 Salado r. Oaxaca/Puebla Mex.
243 F3 Salado r. Mex.
184 D4 Salado r. Andalucía Spain
184 E4 Salado r. Andalucía Spain
185 F3 Salado r. Andalucía Spain
185 F3 Salado r. Andalucía Spain
206 C4 Salaga Ghana
162 D3 Salagnac France
92 C2 Salagou, Lac du l. France
128 D3 Şalāḩ, Tall hill Jordan
92 C2 Şalāḩ ad Dīn governorate Iraq
127 G7 Salahuddin Iraq
161 C3 Salaise-sur-Sanne France
177 M4 Sălaj county Romania
206 D2 Salajwe Botswana
202 C2 Salal Chad
125 F4 Şalāl Oman
243 H6 Salamá Guat.
242 □I6 Salamá Hond.
244 D3 Salamanca Chile
184 E2 Salamanca Spain
184 D4 Salamanca prov. Spain
Salamanca Spain see Castilla y León
232 D3 Salamanca NY U.S.A.
208 D2 Salamat pref. Chad
208 C2 Salamat, Bahr r. Chad
122 A3 Salāmatābād Iran
198 C3 Salamina Greece
198 C3 Salamina i. Greece
128 A2 Salamis tourist site Cyprus
Salamis i. Greece see Salamina
128 C2 Salamiyah Syria
226 E5 Salamonie r. IN U.S.A.
117 F5 Salamoni r. India
193 I4 Salandra Italy
138 C3 Salantai Lith.
216 □1c Salão Faial Azores
194 B5 Salaparuta Sicilia Italy
93 F2 Salar Nei Mongol China
185 F3 Salar Spain
197 P2 Sălard Romania
186 D2 Salardú Spain
250 B6 Salas Peru
182 D1 Salas Spain
184 C2 Salas de los Infantes Spain
138 E3 Salaspils Latvia
163 C5 Salat r. France
95 F4 Salatiga Jawa Tengah Indon.
116 E3 Salawah India
134 K4 Salaush Rus. Fed.
197 Q2 Sălaţig Romania
165 E5 Salm r. Belgium
120 C1 Salavat Rus. Fed.
252 A2 Salaverry Peru
93 I3 Salawati i. Papua Jaya Indon.
116 E3 Salaya Gujarat India
93 I4 Salayar i. Indon.
267 L7 Sala y Gómez, Isla i. S. Pacific Ocean
Salazar Angola see N'dalatando
261 D5 Salazar Arg.
186 B2 Salazar r. Spain
190 B3 Salbertrand Italy
162 E1 Salbris France
252 B3 Salcantay, Cerro mt. Peru
246 C2 Salcedo Dom. Rep.
173 G3 Salching Ger.
138 E4 Šalčia r. Lith.
138 E4 Šalčininkai Lith.
197 H3 Sălcioara Romania
150 D4 Salcombe Devon, England U.K.
246 E2 Saldae Alg. see Bejaïa
183 Q2 Saldaña Spain
214 C5 Saldanha S. Africa
183 I4 Saldenburg Ger.
183 P4 Saldón Spain
261 D6 Saldungaray Arg.
191 F2 Saldura r. Italy
138 D2 Saldus Latvia
82 E5 Sale Vic. Austr.
86 E3 Sale r. W.A. Austr.
190 D4 Sale Italy
96 A2 Sale Dem. Rep. Congo
149 G4 Sale Greater Manchester, England U.K.
196 C3 Salehard Romania
Salehurst East Sussex, England U.K.
130 H3 Salekhard Rus. Fed.
172 D4 Salem Baden-Württemberg Ger.
168 F2 Salem Schleswig-Holstein Ger.
114 C3 Salem Tamil Nadu India
215 F5 Salem S. Africa
237 H4 Salem AR U.S.A.
236 F4 Salem IL U.S.A.
233 H3 Salem MA U.S.A.
233 H3 Salem MO U.S.A.
234 C2 Salem NJ U.S.A.
233 G3 Salem NY U.S.A.
232 C4 Salem OH U.S.A.
238 B3 Salem OR U.S.A.
234 C2 Salem SD U.S.A.
232 D5 Salem VA U.S.A.
234 C2 Salem WV U.S.A.
234 C2 Salem County county NJ U.S.A.
194 E5 Salemi Sicilia Italy
141 N3 Sälen Sweden
146 C1 Salen Argyll and Bute, Scotland U.K.
146 C4 Salen Highland, Scotland U.K.
193 I4 Salerno Italy
193 I4 Salerno prov. Campania Italy
193 I4 Salerno, Golfo di g. Italy
Salernum Italy see Salerno
162 E3 Salers France
256 D3 Salès Oliveira Brazil
257 E5 Salesópolis Brazil
156 C4 Salettes France
149 G4 Salford Greater Manchester, England U.K.
151 J2 Salford Surrey, England U.K.
193 H4 Salgado Brazil
254 D3 Salgado r. Brazil
177 I3 Salgótarján Hungary
254 E3 Salgueiro Brazil
182 C2 Salgueiro Brazil
182 D5 Salgueiro Port.
151 I2 Salhouse Norfolk, England U.K.
142 J1 Salhus Norway
137 H5 Salhyr r. Ukr.
139 T5 Sali Rus. Fed.
196 F4 Sali Croatia
124 D2 Sālifah Saudi Arabia
256 D5 Salicar Brazil
194 B5 Salici, Monte mt. Sicilia Italy
138 D5 Saliena Latvia
193 G3 Salies-de-Béarn France
163 A5 Salies-du-Salat France
163 C5 Saligné-Eyvigues France
257 E2 Salihli Turkey
139 P5 Salihorsk Belarus
206 B3 Salikénié Senegal
253 G3 Salimo Moz.
211 B8 Salima Malawi
254 F3 Salina i. Isole Lipari Italy
241 I2 Salina UT U.S.A.
245 G5 Salina Cruz Mex.
258 E3 Salina Chica Arg.
254 D3 Saladas Brazil
261 E4 Saladillo Arg.
261 E5 Saladillo r. Buenos Aires Arg.
261 D4 Saladillo r. Santa Fé Arg.
244 D3 Saladillo Mex.
261 E4 Salado r. Arg.
261 D5 Salado r. Santa Fé Arg.

Column 6

183 I2 Salinas de Pamplona Spain
183 F2 Salinas de Pisuerga Spain
186 D2 Salinas de Sín Spain
239 F5 Salinas Peak NM U.S.A.
161 C5 Salin-de-Giraud France
161 C4 Salindres France
149 F1 Saline Fife, Scotland U.K.
227 F4 Saline MI U.S.A.
237 E5 Saline r. AR U.S.A.
236 D4 Saline r. KS U.S.A.
193 F2 Saline di Volterra Italy
191 F5 Saline di Volterra Italy
127 F4 Şāliḩ Iraq
232 C4 Salineville OH U.S.A.
96 A2 Salingyi Myanmar
254 D2 Salinópolis Brazil
254 D2 Salinópolis Brazil
184 D2 Salir Port.
125 F4 Salīr Port.
184 C5 Salir do Mato Port.
151 F3 Salisbury Wiltshire, England U.K.
233 J2 Salisbury MD U.S.A.
231 D5 Salisbury NC U.S.A.
232 D5 Salisbury PA U.S.A.
Salisbury Zimbabwe see Harare
235 H1 Salisbury Mills NY U.S.A.
151 E3 Salisbury Plain England U.K.
197 P3 Săliște Romania
197 Q2 Săliștea de Sus Romania
194 C5 Salito r. Sicilia Italy
244 C2 Salitral de Carrera Mex.
254 C4 Salitre r. Brazil
254 D3 Salitre r. Brazil
122 C2 Sālmās Iran
177 H4 Salobra r. India
160 C3 Salette France
168 F2 Salettes France
163 B4 Salettes France
256 D3 Salles Oliveira Brazil
257 E5 Salles-Curan France
185 F3 Salles-d'Angles France
197 F4 Salles-la-Source France
163 B5 Salles-sur-l'Hers France
171 F4 Salgast Ger.
179 F7 Salighberg Austria
147 E3 Sallins Rep. of Ireland
261 F5 Salliqueló Arg.
237 E5 Sallisaw OK U.S.A.
221 K3 Salluit Que. Can.
128 C3 Salmā Syria
222 F4 Salmo B.C. Can.
238 D3 Salmon ID U.S.A.
235 F1 Salmon r. CT U.S.A.
238 D3 Salmon r. ID U.S.A.
222 G5 Salmon Arm B.C. Can.
238 D3 Salmon Falls Creek r. Idaho/Nevada U.S.A.
87 D7 Salmon Gums W.A. Austr.
Salmonhurst N.B. Can. see New Denmark
238 D2 Salmon River Mountains ID U.S.A.
183 P4 Salmoral Spain
172 F2 Salmtal Ger.
141 M3 Salo Fin.
191 D3 Salò Italy
185 F2 Salobre Spain
185 F2 Salobreña Spain
140 N2 Saloinen Fin.
241 K5 Salome AZ U.S.A.
156 C2 Salon France
116 F4 Salon r. France
116 F4 Salon Uttar Prad. India
161 D5 Salon-de-Provence France
208 D3 Salonga r. Dem. Rep. Congo
Salonica Greece see Thessaloniki
Saloniki Greece see Thessaloniki
196 C3 Salonta Romania
151 J2 Salop admin. div. England U.K. see Shropshire
182 C2 Salor r. Spain
186 D2 Saloria, Pic de mt. Spain
161 C4 Salornino Spain
160 C2 Salornay-sur-Guye France
191 F2 Salorno Italy
163 D5 Salou Spain
206 D4 Salou, Cap de c. Spain
215 F5 Salouël France
141 N3 Salpausselkä reg. Fin.
128 E2 Salqīn Syria
147 D3 Salruck Rep. of Ireland
260 C2 Salsacate Arg.
186 E4 Salsadella Spain
214 D2 Salses-le-Château France
193 F2 Salsk Rus. Fed.
194 C5 Salso r. Sicilia Italy
191 D4 Salsola r. Italy
193 H4 Salsomaggiore Terme Italy
Salt Jordan see As Salt
185 I3 Salt Spain
241 K5 Salt r. AZ U.S.A.
236 F4 Salt r. MO U.S.A.
232 C5 Salt r. WV U.S.A.
260 C2 Salta Arg.
260 C2 Salta prov. Arg.
150 C4 Saltash Cornwall, England U.K.
149 F3 Saltburn-by-the-Sea Redcar and Cleveland, England U.K.
146 E5 Saltcoats North Ayrshire, Scotland U.K.
147 E5 Saltee Islands Rep. of Ireland
184 D4 Salteras Spain
182 C3 Salto Port.
222 E5 Salter Bay B.C. Can.
140 N2 Saltfjorden sea chan. Norway
239 H2 Salt Flat TX U.S.A.
150 D2 Saltford Bath and North East Somerset, England U.K.
237 F5 Salt Fork r. KS U.S.A.
237 D4 Salt Fork Arkansas r. KS U.S.A.
237 D4 Salt Fork Brazos r. TX U.S.A.
237 D5 Salt Fork Red r. OK U.S.A.
240 D2 Salt Lake City UT U.S.A.
231 G5 Salt Lick WV U.S.A.
140 N3 Saltnäs Norway
214 D6 Salt River S. Africa
246 C2 Salt River Jamaica
151 F2 Saltney Flintshire, Wales U.K.
260 C5 Salto Arg.
256 C3 Salto Brazil
256 D2 Salto r. Brazil
258 F3 Salto Uru.
256 D5 Salto Brazil
260 C2 Salto da Divisa Brazil
243 F3 Salto de Agua Mex.
258 E2 Salto de las Rosas Arg.
253 F3 Salto del Guairá Para.
256 D4 Salto Grande Arg.
260 B2 Salto Grande Brazil
259 E2 Salton City CA U.S.A.
241 F5 Salton Sea salt l. CA U.S.A.

Column 7

115 D2 Salur Andhra Prad. India
190 D3 Salussola Italy
190 C4 Saluzzo Italy
183 I4 Salvacañete Spain
184 C3 Salvada Port.
254 F5 Salvada Port.
Salvador country Central America see El Salvador
182 C4 Salvador Port.
258 E1 Salvador Mazza Arg.
184 D2 Salvador Port.
254 C2 Salvaterra Brazil
182 D5 Salvaterra do Extremo Port.
244 D3 Salvatierra Mex.
183 H2 Salvatierra Spain
184 D2 Salvaterra de los Barros Spain
184 D1 Salvatierra de Santiago Spain
241 I2 Salvation Creek r. UT U.S.A.
195 H3 Salve Italy
125 E2 Salviac France
125 E2 Salwah Saudi Arabia
125 E2 Salwah, Dawhat b. Qatar/Saudi Arabia
96 B3 Salween r. China see Nu Jiang
129 C4 Salween r. Myanmar
129 F4 Salyan Azer.
Sal'yany Azer. see Salyan
232 B5 Salyersville KY U.S.A.
179 I3 Salza r. Austria
179 I3 Salza r. Austria/Ger.
179 I3 Salza-Basque resr Austria
169 J3 Salzbergen Ger.
178 I3 Salzburg Austria
178 I3 Salzburg land Austria
168 F2 Salzgitter Ger.
169 F3 Salzhemmendorf Ger.
169 D4 Salzkotten Ger.
171 G4 Salzmünde Ger.
170 C3 Salzwedel Ger.
116 B4 Sam Rajasthan India
96 D3 Sam, Khwae r. Laos/Vietnam
246 D2 Samá Cuba
174 E3 Sáma r. Pol.
125 G3 Samad Oman
163 B5 Samadet France
242 D2 Samalayuca Mex.
116 E3 Samales Group is Phil.
114 D2 Samalkot Andhra Prad. India
203 F2 Samālūṭ Egypt
247 E3 Samaná Dom. Rep.
116 D3 Samana Punjab India
246 D2 Samana Cay i. Bahamas
114 C3 Samanala mt. Sri Lanka see Sri Pada
126 E3 Samandağı Turkey
123 F2 Samangân prov. Afgh.
122 D6 Samani r. Iran
199 P3 Samanlı Dağları mts Turkey
203 F2 Samannûd Egypt
225 I2 Samaqua r. Que. Can.
Samar Kazakh. see Samarskoye
120 B1 Samara r. Rus. Fed.
137 H3 Samara r. Ukr.
Samarga Rus. Fed. see Sri Amba
Samara Oblast admin. div. Rus. Fed. see Samarskaya Oblast'
190 D3 Samarate Italy
190 B2 Samarga Rus. Fed.
95 G3 Samarinda Kalimantan Timur Indon.
100 B1 Samarka Rus. Fed.
121 F5 Samarkand Uzbek.
123 G2 Samarkand, Pik mt. Tajik.
Samarkand Uzbek. see Samarkandskaya Oblast'
208 D3 Samarkandskaya Oblast' admin. div. Uzbek. see Samarkand
197 E2 Samarobriva France see Amiens
Samarqand Uzbek. see Samarkand
123 G2 Samarqand, Qullai mt. Tajik.
121 F5 Samarqand Wiloyati admin. div. Uzbek. see Samarkandskaya Oblast'
127 G4 Sāmarrā' Iraq
92 C4 Samar Sea g. Phil.
120 B1 Samarskaya Oblast' admin. div. Rus. Fed.
121 J2 Samarskoye Kazakh.
137 J4 Samarskoye Rus. Fed.
136 C2 Samary Ukr.
123 F2 Samasata Pak.
192 C7 Samassi Sardegna Italy
117 F4 Samastipur Bihar India
163 C5 Samatan France
192 B3 Samatzai Sardegna Italy
129 F3 Şamaxı Azer.
209 E6 Samba Dem. Rep. Congo
182 D3 Samba Madag.
116 C2 Samba Jammu and Kashmir
209 B7 Samba Cajú Angola
182 D3 Sambade Port.
206 B3 Sambaíba Brazil
95 G3 Sambaliung mts Indon.
117 E5 Sambalpur Orissa India
95 E2 Sambas Kalimantan Barat Indon.
213 J3 Sambava Madag.
137 J4 Sambek Rostovskaya Oblast' Rus. Fed.
137 J4 Sambek Rostovskaya Oblast' Rus. Fed.
Sambe-san vol. Japan see Sanbe-san
116 D3 Sambhal Uttar Prad. India
116 C4 Sambhar Rajasthan India
116 C4 Sambhar Lake India
95 G4 Samboja Kalimantan Timur Indon.
Sambor Cambodia see Sambir
261 H4 Samborombón, Bahía b. Arg.
175 J6 Samborzec Pol.
165 E5 Sambre r. Belgium/France
191 H4 Sambuca di Sicilia
191 F4 Sambuca Pistoiese Italy
193 F4 Sambuco Italy
191 G6 Sambughetti, Monte mt. Sicilia Italy
101 D5 Samch'ŏk S. Korea
101 D5 Samch'ŏnp'o S. Korea
118 C3 Samdari India [Sam'ch'ŏn]
190 D3 Samedan Switz.
182 D4 Sameiro Port.
156 C3 Samer France
162 C3 Samerón Que. Can.
137 H4 Sames Spain
139 R6 Samet' Rus. Fed.
207 F2 Samfya Zambia
209 F7 Samfya Zambia
136 D4 Samhorodok Ukr.
Kyiv Ukr. see Samhorodok
136 E3 Samhorodok Vinnyts'ka Oblast' Ukr.

Column 8

115 D2 Salur Andhra Prad. India
126 D5 Samandağı Turkey
123 F2 Samangân prov. Afgh.
199 P3 Samanlı Dağları mts Turkey
203 F2 Samannûd Egypt
225 I2 Samaqua r. Que. Can.
252 A2 Samaipata Bol.
179 K5 Salza r. Austria
179 K4 Salza r. Austria/Ger.
169 K3 Salzbergen Ger.
178 H3 Salzburg Austria
168 F2 Salzgitter Ger.
169 F3 Salzhemmendorf Ger.
169 D4 Salzkotten Ger.
171 G4 Salzmünde Ger.
170 C3 Salzwedel Ger.
116 B4 Sam Rajasthan India
96 D3 Sam, Khwae r. Laos/Vietnam
246 D2 Samá Cuba
174 E3 Sáma r. Pol.
125 G3 Samad Oman
163 B5 Samadet France
242 D2 Samalayuca Mex.
92 C4 Samales Group is Phil.
114 D2 Samalkot Andhra Prad. India
203 F2 Samālūṭ Egypt
247 E3 Samaná Dom. Rep.
116 D3 Samana Punjab India
246 D2 Samana Cay i. Bahamas
Samanala mt. Sri Lanka see Sri Pada
126 E3 Samandağı Turkey
123 F2 Samangân prov. Afgh.
122 D6 Samani r. Iran
199 P3 Samanlı Dağları mts Turkey
203 F2 Samannûd Egypt
225 I2 Samaqua r. Que. Can.
Samar Kazakh. see Samarskoye
120 B1 Samara r. Rus. Fed.
137 H3 Samara r. Ukr.
190 D3 Samarate Italy
190 B2 Samarga Rus. Fed.
95 G3 Samarinda Kalimantan Timur Indon.
100 B1 Samarka Rus. Fed.
121 F5 Samarkand Uzbek.
123 G2 Samarkand, Pik mt. Tajik.
127 G4 Sāmarrā' Iraq
92 C4 Samar Sea g. Phil.
120 B1 Samarskaya Oblast' admin. div. Rus. Fed.
121 J2 Samarskoye Kazakh.
137 J4 Samarskoye Rus. Fed.
136 C2 Samary Ukr.
123 F2 Samasata Pak.
192 C7 Samassi Sardegna Italy
117 F4 Samastipur Bihar India
163 C5 Samatan France
192 B3 Samatzai Sardegna Italy
129 F3 Şamaxı Azer.
209 E6 Samba Dem. Rep. Congo
182 D3 Samba Madag.
116 C2 Samba Jammu and Kashmir
209 B7 Samba Cajú Angola
182 D3 Sambade Port.
206 B3 Sambaíba Brazil
95 G3 Sambaliung mts Indon.
117 E5 Sambalpur Orissa India
95 E2 Sambas Kalimantan Barat Indon.
213 J3 Sambava Madag.
137 J4 Sambek Rostovskaya Oblast' Rus. Fed.
137 J4 Sambek Rostovskaya Oblast' Rus. Fed.
Sambe-san vol. Japan see Sanbe-san
116 D3 Sambhal Uttar Prad. India
116 C4 Sambhar Rajasthan India
116 C4 Sambhar Lake India
95 G4 Samboja Kalimantan Timur Indon.
261 H4 Samborombón, Bahía b. Arg.
175 J6 Samborzec Pol.
165 E5 Sambre r. Belgium/France
191 H4 Sambuca di Sicilia
191 F4 Sambuca Pistoiese Italy
193 F4 Sambuco Italy
191 G6 Sambughetti, Monte mt. Sicilia Italy
101 D5 Samch'ŏk S. Korea
101 D5 Samch'ŏnp'o S. Korea
118 C3 Samdi Dag mt. Turkey
190 D3 Samedan Switz.
182 D4 Sameiro Port.
156 C3 Samer France
139 R6 Samet' Rus. Fed.
209 F7 Samfya Zambia
136 D4 Samhorodok Ukr.
136 E3 Samhorodok Vinnyts'ka Oblast' Ukr.
102 D1 Samhah i. Yemen
124 E4 Samīrah Saudi Arabia
182 D2 Samir de los Caños Spain
250 C6 Samiria r. Peru
129 D2 Samkhret' Oset'i aut. reg. Georgia

Column 1

129 E3 Şămkir Azer.
128 C1 Şamköy Turkey
199 E2 Şamlı Turkey
195 F2 Sammichele di Bari Italy
190 F2 Samnaun Switz.
San Neua Laos see Xam Hua
182 B2 Samo r. Spain
78 □² Samoa country S. Pacific Ocean
266 H7 Samoa Basin sea feature Pacific Ocean
Samoa i Sisifo country S. Pacific Ocean see Samoa
188 B3 Samobor Croatia
179 G5 Samoborska Gora hills Croatia
134 H3 Samoded Rus. Fed.
160 E2 Samoëns France
191 G4 Samoggia r. Italy
197 F4 Samokov Bulg.
190 E2 Samolaco Italy
136 D3 Samolusivkivtsi Ukr.
184 B2 Samora Correia Port.
176 G3 Samorín Slovakia
199 E3 Samos Voreio Aigaio Greece
199 E3 Samos i. Greece
182 C2 Samos Spain
Samothrace i. Greece see Samothraki
199 D1 Samothraki i. Greece
197 F4 Samovodene Bulg.
135 H6 Samoylovka Rus. Fed.
206 E5 Sampa Côte d'Ivoire
138 G2 Sampang Jawa Indon.
Samro, Ozero r. Rus. Fed. see
Samprong Cambodia see Phumi Sâmraông
111 C6 Samraong Xizang China
96 C2 Sam Sao, Phou mts Laos/Vietnam
142 D4 Samsø i. Denmark
142 D4 Samsø Bælt sea chan. Denmark
96 D3 Sâm Sơn Vietnam
177 L4 Şamşud Romania
126 E2 Samsun Turkey
171 C3 Samswegen Ger.
121 I4 Samsy Kazakh.
170 E1 Samtens Ger.
116 D4 Samthar Uttar Prad. India
129 C2 Samtredia Georgia
84 C3 Samuel, Mount hill N.T. Austr.
129 C2 Samughneo Sardegna Italy
97 C5 Samui, Ko i. Thai.
105 F3 Samukawa Japan
123 H4 Samundri Pak.
129 F3 Samur Azer.
129 F3 Samur r. Azer./Rus. Fed.
Samutlu Turkey see Temelli
97 C4 Samut Prakan Thai.
97 C4 Samut Sakhon Thai.
97 C4 Samut Songkhram Thai.
206 D3 San Mali
175 J5 San r. Pol.
97 D4 San, Tônlé r. Cambodia
188 F3 Sana r. Bos.-Herz.
124 D5 Şan'ā' Yemen
124 C5 Şan'ā' governorate Yemen
124 C5 Sanaag admin. reg. Somalia
183 I2 San Adrián Spain
262 X2 Sanae research stn Antarctica
207 H6 Sanaga r. Cameroon
San Agostin FL U.S.A. see St Augustine
260 E2 San Agustín Arg.
250 B4 San Agustín Col.
92 C5 San Agustín, Cape Phil.
183 G4 San Agustín de Guadalix Spain
146 B6 Sanaigmore Argyll and Bute, Scotland U.K.
124 D3 Sanām Saudi Arabia
182 B2 San Amaro Spain
252 A6 San Ambrosio i. S. Pacific Ocean
122 A3 Sanandaj Iran
206 D3 Sanando Mali
240 G2 San Andreas CA U.S.A.
177 K6 Sânandrei Romania
252 D3 San Andrés Bol.
250 C3 San Andrés Col.
92 C3 San Andrés Phil.
246 B4 San Andres, Isla de i. Caribbean Sea
261 H4 San Andrés de Giles Arg.
182 E2 San Andrés de Rabanedo Spain
244 C4 San Andrés Ixtlán Mex.
239 F5 San Andres Mountains NM U.S.A.
245 G4 San Andrés Tuxtla Mex.
237 C6 San Angelo TX U.S.A.
206 D3 Sanankoroba Mali
240 F3 San Anselmo CA U.S.A.
182 D1 San Antolín de Ibias Spain
182 B2 San Antonino Spain
258 D2 San Antonio Arg.
242 □H5 San Antonio Belize
252 D3 San Antonio Bol.
260 B3 San Antonio Chile
92 B3 San Antonio Phil.
187 B5 San Antonio Spain
239 F5 San Antonio NM U.S.A.
237 D6 San Antonio TX U.S.A.
240 G4 San Antonio r. CA U.S.A.
237 D6 San Antonio r. TX U.S.A.
240 I4 San Antonio, Mount CA U.S.A.
187 E6 San Antonio Abad Spain
261 H4 San Antonio de Areco Arg.
258 D2 San Antonio de los Cobres Arg.
242 □I6 San Antonio de Oriente Hond.
207 G7 San Antonio de Palé Equat. Guinea
259 D6 San Antonio Oeste Arg.
161 D5 Sanary-sur-Mer France
183 H2 San Asensio Spain
78 □⁴a Sanat i. Chuuk Micronesia
234 C2 Sanatoga PA U.S.A.
260 D2 San Agustín de Valle Fértil Arg.
237 E6 San Augustine TX U.S.A.
116 D5 Sanawad Madh. Prad. India
244 D2 San Bartolo Mex.
216 □3c San Bartolomé Lanzarote Canary Is
183 F5 San Bartolomé de las Abiertas Spain
184 C4 San Bartolomé de la Torre Spain
183 F4 San Bartolomé de Pinares Spain
216 □3a San Bartolomé de Tirajana Gran Canaria Canary Is
193 H3 San Bartolomeo in Galdo Italy
245 E3 San Bartolo Morelos Mex.
260 E3 San Basilio Arg.
192 B5 San Basilio Sardegna Italy
San Baudilio de Llobregat Spain see Sant Boi de Llobregat
193 F2 San Benedetto del Tronto Italy
191 F3 San Benedetto Po Italy
243 H5 San Benito Guat.
237 D7 San Benito TX U.S.A.
240 G3 San Benito r. CA U.S.A.
184 C3 San Benito de la Contienda Spain
240 G3 San Benito Mountain CA U.S.A.
240 I4 San Bernardino CA U.S.A.
190 E2 San Bernardino, Passo di pass Switz.

Column 2

241 I4 San Bernardino Mountains CA U.S.A.
260 B3 San Bernardo Chile
242 D3 San Bernardo Mex.
103 F6 Sanbe-san vol. Japan
191 H3 San Biagio di Callalta Italy
194 C5 San Biagio Platani Sicilia Italy
242 C3 San Blas Nayarit Mex.
242 C3 San Blas Sinaloa Mex.
242 □K7 San Blas, Archipiélago de is Panama
242 □K7 San Blas, Cordillera de mts Panama
191 G3 San Bonifacio Italy
252 D3 San Borja Bol.
236 E3 Sanborn IA U.S.A.
191 H2 San Candido Italy
186 C3 San Caprasio hill Spain
260 C3 San Carlos Mendoza Arg.
258 D2 San Carlos Salta Arg.
260 B5 San Carlos Chile
San Carlos Equat. Guinea see Luba
243 E2 San Carlos Coahuila Mex.
245 E1 San Carlos Tamaulipas Mex.
242 □I7 San Carlos Nic.
253 F5 San Carlos Para.
253 F5 San Carlos r. Para.
92 B3 San Carlos Luzon Phil.
92 B4 San Carlos Negros Phil.
258 G4 San Carlos Uru.
241 L5 San Carlos AZ U.S.A.
250 E3 San Carlos Apure Venez.
251 G2 San Carlos Centro Arg.
259 C6 San Carlos de Bariloche Arg.
261 G5 San Carlos de Bolívar Arg.
San Carlos de la Rápita Spain see Sant Carles de la Ràpita
185 G2 San Carlos del Valle Spain
250 D2 San Carlos del Zulia Venez.
261 G2 San Carlos Sur Arg.
192 D2 San Casciano dei Bagni Italy
191 D2 San Casciano in Val di Pesa Italy
195 H2 San Cataldo Puglia Italy
194 C5 San Cataldo Sicilia Italy
261 H6 San Cayetano Arg.
182 B3 San Cebrián de Castro Spain
187 F5 Sancellas Spain
San Celoni Spain see Sant Celoni
160 A1 Sancergues France
160 A1 Sancerre France
160 A1 Sancerrois, Collines du hills France
195 H2 San Cesario di Lecce Italy
160 E1 Sancey-le-Grand France
108 C3 Sancha He r. Guizhou China
156 B4 Sancheville France
244 □ Sánchez Magallanes Mex.
116 D5 Sanchi Madh. Prad. India
142 D2 Sanchidrián Spain
96 C2 San Chien Pau mt. Laos
193 I4 San Chirico Nuovo Italy
193 I4 San Chirico Raparo Italy
116 B4 Sanchor Rajasthan India
134 I4 Sanchursk Rus. Fed.
182 C2 San Cibrão das Viñas Spain
182 C2 San Cipirello Sicilia Italy
231 C5 Sandyville WV U.S.A.
193 G4 San Cipriano d'Aversa Italy
245 E3 San Ciro de Acosta Mex.
260 B4 San Clemente Chile
185 H1 San Clemente Spain
240 I5 San Clemente CA U.S.A.
261 I5 San Clemente del Tuyú Arg.
240 H5 San Clemente Island CA U.S.A.
182 C2 San Clodio Spain
160 A2 Sancoins France
258 F2 San Cosme Arg.
193 I4 San Cosmo Albanese Italy
191 I5 San Costanzo Italy
261 G2 San Cristóbal Bol.
252 D5 San Cristóbal Bol.
253 E3 San Cristóbal Bol.
246 E3 San Cristóbal Dom. Rep.
78 □⁶ San Cristóbal i. Solomon Is
223 □I2 San Cristóbal Venez.
250 □ San Cristóbal, Isla i. Islas Galápagos Ecuador
San Cristóbal, Volcán vol. Nic.
San Cristóbal de Cea Galicia Spain see Cea
216 □3a San Cristóbal de la Laguna Tenerife Canary Is
243 G5 San Cristóbal de las Casas Mex.
183 F3 San Cristóbal de la Vega Spain
193 H4 San Croce, Monte mt. Italy
261 F3 Sancti Spíritu Arg.
246 C2 Sancti Spíritus Cuba
182 D4 Sancti-Spíritus prov. Cuba
185 E2 Sancti-Spíritus Spain
157 F3 Sancy France
142 B2 Sand Norway
215 F3 Sand r. Free State S. Africa
213 F4 Sand r. Northern S. Africa
104 B4 Sanda Japan
146 C6 Sanda Island Scotland U.K.
95 □ Sandakan Sabah Malaysia
117 G4 Sandakphu Peak Sikkim India
213 F4 San Damian d'Asti Italy
169 F6 Sand am Main Ger.
141 I3 Sandane Norway
178 K4 Sandanski Bulg.
197 F5 Sandaohezi Xinjiang China see Shawan
206 B3 Sandaré Mali
260 B4 Sanday i. Scotland U.K.
146 F2 Sanday Sound sea chan. Scotland U.K.
172 D2 Sandbach Ger.
149 J4 Sandbach Cheshire, England U.K.
169 F5 Sandberg Ger.
214 B5 Sandberg S. Africa
168 G1 Sandby Denmark
140 K2 Sanddola r. Norway
168 D2 Sande Ger.
141 I3 Sande Sogn og Fjordane Norway
142 D1 Sande Vestfold Norway
142 B3 Sande Port.
142 D2 Sandefjord Norway
142 D2 Sandefjord (Torp) airport Norway
142 A2 Sandeid Norway
195 F3 San Demetrio Corone Italy
193 F3 San Demetrio ne' Vestini Italy
263 D2 Sandercock Nunataks nunataks Antarctica
241 M4 Sanders AZ U.S.A.
169 E4 Sandershausen (Niestetal) Ger.
171 C4 Sandersleben Ger.
237 C4 Sanderson TX U.S.A.
231 D5 Sandersville GA U.S.A.
245 F6 San Francisco Cozoaltepec Mex.
258 □ San Francisco del Chañar Arg.
260 D3 San Francisco del Monte de Oro Arg.
245 H5 San Francisco del Rincón Mex.
246 E3 San Francisco de Macorís Dom. Rep.
260 B3 San Francisco de Mostazal Chile
242 □ San Francisco de Paula, Cabo c. Arg.
242 □H5 San Francisco Gotera El Salvador
187 E6 San Francisco Javier Spain

Column 3

244 D3 San Diego Mex.
240 I5 San Diego CA U.S.A.
237 D7 San Diego TX U.S.A.
240 I5 San Diego, Sierra mts Mex.
199 G2 Sandıklı Turkey
118 Q3 Sandila Uttar Prad. India
156 C5 Sandillon France
87 B5 Sandiman, Mount hill W.A. Austr.
134 L2 Sandivey r. Rus. Fed.
170 E3 Sandkrug Ger.
224 C4 Sand Lake Ont. Can.
142 A2 Sandnes Norway
146 □G1 Sandness Shetland, Scotland U.K.
140 K2 Sandnessjøen Norway
Sando i. Faroe Is see Sandoy
207 G3 Sando Moz.
209 D7 Sandoa Dem. Rep. Congo
175 J5 Sandomierz Pol.
197 G2 Sândominic Romania
250 C4 Sandoná Col.
195 G2 San Donaci Italy
191 H3 San Donà di Piave Italy
195 H2 San Donato di Lecce Italy
191 G3 San Donato Milanese Italy
193 F3 San Donato Val di Comino Italy
177 J5 Sándorfalva Hungary
139 K2 Sandovo Rus. Fed.
263 G2 Sandow, Mount Antarctica
96 A3 Sandoway Myanmar
151 F4 Sandown Isle of Wight, England U.K.
173 G2 Sandoy i. Faroe Is
150 C4 Sandplace Cornwall, England U.K.
238 C1 Sandpoint ID U.S.A.
146 A5 Sandray i. Scotland U.K.
151 G3 Sandridge Hertfordshire, England U.K.
84 D5 Sand River Reservoir Swaziland
215 H2 Sandsele Sweden
149 I3 Sandsend North Yorkshire, England U.K.
222 B4 Sandspit Qld Austr.
237 D4 Sand Springs OK U.S.A.
215 F2 Sandspruit r. S. Africa
168 D2 Sandstedt Ger.
232 E6 Sandston VA U.S.A.
87 C5 Sandstone W.A. Austr.
236 E2 Sandstone MN U.S.A.
241 K5 Sand Tank Mountains AZ U.S.A.
215 G2 Sandton S. Africa
234 C4 Sandts Eddy PA U.S.A.
103 G3 Sandu Guizhou China
109 E3 Sandu Hunan China
114 C3 Sandur Karnataka India
142 D2 Sandvika Norway
143 G1 Sandviken Sweden
214 C5 Sandviakte S. Africa
151 I3 Sandwich Kent, England U.K.
233 H4 Sandwich MA U.S.A.
Sandwich Island Vanuatu see Éfaté
Sandwich Islands N. Pacific Ocean see Hawaiian Islands
117 G5 Sandwip Bangl.
151 G2 Sandy Bedfordshire, England U.K.
246 □ Sandy Bay Jamaica
87 D7 Sandy Bight b. W.A. Austr.
85 H5 Sandy Cape Qld Austr.
83 F5 Sandy Cape Tas. Austr.
232 B5 Sandy Hook KY U.S.A.
235 E1 Sandy Hook CT U.S.A.
232 B5 Sandy Hook KY U.S.A.
86 D2 Sandy Island W.A. Austr.
123 E2 Sandykachy Turkm.
Sandykgachy Turkm. see Sundukli, Peski
121 G5 Sandykly Gumy des. Turkm.
222 H4 Sandy Lake Alta Can.
223 M4 Sandy Lake Ont. Can.
250 □ Sandyville Ecuador
160 D2 Sâne r. France
165 E5 Sanem Lux.
183 G4 San Emiliano Spain
253 F4 San Estanislao Para.
245 F4 San Esteban Cuautempan Mex.
183 G3 San Esteban de Gormaz Spain
182 E4 San Esteban de la Sierra Spain
260 B5 San Fabián de Alico Chile
261 H4 San Felice a Cancello Italy
193 G3 San Felice Circeo Italy
182 D4 San Felices de los Gallegos Spain
191 G4 San Felice sul Panaro Italy
260 B3 San Felipe Chile
250 D2 San Felipe Baja California Norte Mex.
242 D3 San Felipe Chihuahua Mex.
239 F4 San Felipe Guanajuato Mex.
183 I4 San Felipe r. Spain
250 D2 San Felipe Venez.
San Feliú de Guíxols Spain see Sant Feliu de Guíxols
San Feliú de Pallarols Spain see Sant Feliu de Pallerols
San Feliú Sasserra Spain see Sant Feliu Sasserra
195 E4 San Ferdinando Italy
261 H4 San Ferdinando di Puglia Italy
261 H4 San Fernando Arg.
260 B3 San Fernando Chile
242 D2 San Fernando Baja California Norte Mex.
243 F3 San Fernando Tamaulipas Mex.
92 B2 San Fernando Luzon Phil.
92 B3 San Fernando Luzon Phil.
184 D4 San Fernando Spain
250 D2 San Fernando Trin. and Tob.
241 H5 San Fernando CA U.S.A.
250 E3 San Fernando de Apure Venez.
250 D3 San Fernando de Atabapo Venez.
183 G4 San Fernando de Henares Spain
193 I5 San Fili Italy
195 E4 San Filippo del Mela Italy
184 D2 Sanfins do Douro Port.
203 F2 Sanford r. W.A. Austr.
243 H5 Sanford FL U.S.A.
233 □H3 Sanford ME U.S.A.
231 E5 Sanford NC U.S.A.
226 E2 Sanford MI U.S.A.
224 D5 Sanford, Mount vol. AK U.S.A.
252 B2 San Francisco Arg.
247 □ San Francisco Arg.
183 G4 San Francisco Bol.
242 D2 San Francisco Mex.
239 E5 San Francisco r. NM U.S.A.
170 D1 San Francisco Phil.
240 D3 San Francisco CA U.S.A.
240 D3 San Francisco Bay inlet CA U.S.A.

Column 4

194 D4 San Fratello Sicilia Italy
250 B4 Sanfront Italy
250 B4 San Gabriel Ecuador
244 D4 San Gabriel Chilac Mex.
240 H4 San Gabriel Mountains CA U.S.A.
94 D3 Sangachaly Azer. see Sanqaçal
108 A2 Sangaigerong Sumatera Indon.
182 A2 Sanghalos Port.
252 A3 San Gallan, Isla i. Peru
114 B2 Sangam Andhra Prad. India
114 B2 Sangameshwar Mahar. India
114 B2 Sangamner Mahar. India
236 F3 Sangamon r. IL U.S.A.
78 □⁶ San Jorge i. Solomon Is
92 B3 Sangar Phil.
131 N3 Sangar Rus. Fed.
92 B3 Sangarcia Spain
206 B4 Sangaréa Guinea
114 C2 Sangareddi Andhra Prad. India
206 B4 Sangaredi Guinea
114 C2 Sangaria Rajasthan India
95 G3 Sangasanga Kalimantan Timur Indon.
156 B2 Sangatte France
192 A5 San Gavino Monreale Sardegna Italy
250 B5 San Gil Col.
106 B1 Sangin, Nagor'ye mts Rus. Fed.
195 □ San Ġiljan Malta
92 C4 San Gimignano Italy
183 I4 San Ginés mt. Spain
193 F1 San Ginesio Italy
193 I3 San Giorgio a Liri Italy
191 H2 San Giorgio della Richinvelda Italy
191 I3 San Giorgio di Nogaro Italy
193 F2 San Giorgio di Piano Italy
191 G3 San Giorgio Ionico Italy
195 G2 San Giorgio la Molara Italy
191 G3 San Giorgio Lucano Italy
193 I4 San Giorgio a Piro Italy
190 E3 San Giovanni Bianco Italy
193 G4 San Giovanni d'Asso Italy
194 C5 San Giovanni Gemini Sicilia Italy
193 I3 San Giovanni Incarico Italy
195 G2 San Giovanni in Croce Italy
193 F1 San Giovanni in Fiore Italy
191 G4 San Giovanni in Persiceto Italy
193 F2 San Giovanni Lupatoto Italy
193 H3 San Giovanni Rotondo Italy
192 A5 San Giovanni Suergiu Sardegna Italy
190 D2 San Giovanni Teatino Italy
193 G5 San Giovanni Valdarno Italy
116 C5 Sangir Mahar. India
93 C2 Sangir i. Indon.
93 C2 Sangir, Kepulauan is Indon.
93 C2 San Giuliano Terme Italy
194 C5 San Giuseppe Jato Sicilia Italy
194 D2 San Giuseppe Vesuviano Italy
195 □ San Ġiustino Italy
106 B2 Sangiyn Dalay Mongolia
101 D5 Sangju S. Korea
95 G2 Sangkarang, Kepulauan is Indon.
97 C4 Sângke, Stœng r. Cambodia
95 G2 Sangkulirang Kalimantan Timur Indon.
123 H4 Sangla Pak.
114 B2 Sangli Mahar. India
207 H6 Sangmélima Cameroon
116 D4 Sangod Rajasthan India
114 B2 Sangole Mahar. India
240 I4 San Gorgonio Mountain CA U.S.A.
190 D2 San Gottardo, Passo del pass Switz.
117 F5 Sangpi Sichuan China
117 F5 Sangu r. Bangl.
184 D2 San Gregorio Chile
92 B2 San Gu r. Xizang China
239 F4 San Gregorio de Cristo Range mts CO U.S.A.
261 F4 San Gregorio Chile
260 E3 San Gregorio Uru.
258 G4 San Gregorio de Polanca Uru.
193 H4 San Gregorio Magno Italy
193 F3 San Gregorio Matese Italy
183 G7 Sangre Grande Trin. and Tob.
114 F5 Sangri Xizang China
116 D3 Sangro r. Italy
117 G5 Sangu r. Bangl.
222 H4 Sangudo Alta Can.
255 F2 Sangue r. Brazil
172 C4 Sanguinet France
163 A4 Sanguinet France
191 G3 Sanguinetto Italy
181 F2 Sanguszi Hebei China see Wuqiao
108 D3 Sangzhi Xizang China
206 D4 Sanhala Côte d'Ivoire
206 D4 Sanho r. Nei Mongol China
107 I1 Sanhe Nei Mongol China
109 F2 Sanhezhen Anhui China
San Hilario Sacalm Spain see Sant Hilari Sacalm
182 B3 Sanhûri Egypt
243 H5 San Ignacio Belize
252 D3 San Ignacio Beni Bol.
252 D4 San Ignacio Santa Cruz Bol.
253 E3 San Ignacio Santa Cruz Bol.
253 E3 San Ignacio Para.
92 B3 Sanikiluaq Nunavut Can.
196 E2 Sânişlău Romania
170 D2 Sanitz Ger.
178 D4 Sanjai r. Bihar India
117 F5 Sanjai r. Bihar India
242 B3 San Javier Arg.
92 C5 San Javier Beni Bol.
253 E4 San Javier Santa Cruz Bol.
187 D7 San Javier Spain
260 B3 San Javier de Loncomilla Chile
123 G3 Sanjawi Pak.
260 B3 Sanjiang Guangdong China see Liannan
104 D3 Sanjiang Guizhou China
182 C2 Sanjiang Guizhou China see Jinping

Column 5

Sanjiaocheng Qinghai China see Haiyan
108 D2 Sanjiaoping Hunan China
109 G2 Sanjie Zhejiang China
103 I5 Sanjō Japan
240 G3 San Joaquin Bol.
253 F5 San Joaquin Bol.
92 C4 San Joaquin r. Peru
240 G3 San Joaquin CA U.S.A.
240 G3 San Joaquin Valley CA U.S.A.
237 C5 San Jon NM U.S.A.
92 B3 San Jorge Phil.
78 □⁶ San Jorge i. Solomon Is
259 E3 San Jorge Arg.
259 D7 San Jorge, Golfo de g. Arg.
San Jorge, Golfo de g. Spain see Sant Jordi, Golf de
243 H6 San José Costa Rica
243 H6 San Jose Guat.
92 B3 San Jose Luzon Phil.
92 B3 San Jose Mindoro Phil.
187 E6 San José Spain
261 I4 San José dept Uru.
261 I4 San José r. Uru.
261 I4 San José, Cuchilla de hills Uru.
261 I2 San Jose, Volcán vol. Chile
260 C3 San José de Bavicora Mex.
92 B4 San Jose de Buenavista Phil.
253 E4 San José de Chiquitos Bol.
261 H2 San José de Comondú Mex.
261 G3 San José de Feliciano Arg.
244 C2 San Jose de Gracia Mex.
242 B3 San José de Gracia Aguascalientes Mex.
242 B3 San José de Gracia Mex.
242 C2 San José de Gracia Mex.
242 D3 San José de Guaribe Venez.
261 F2 San José de Jáchal Arg.
242 B3 San Josède la Brecha Mex.
261 F2 San José de la Dormida Arg.
250 B5 San José de la Mariquina Chile
247 □ San José del Cabo Mex.
242 C4 San José del Guaviare Col.
246 E3 San José de Ocoa Dom. Rep.
239 E6 San José de Primas Mex.
244 D3 San José de Raíces Mex.
261 H2 San José Iturbide Mex.
250 C3 San José del Palmar Col.
261 G4 San José del Rincón Mex.
250 C3 San José del Palmar Col.
123 H4 Sanjawi Pak.
244 D5 San Jerónimo Mex.
108 □ San Jiang Guangdong China see
Sanjiang Guizhou China

Column 6

179 G3 Sankt Lorenzen im Mürztal Austria
179 F3 Sankt Lorenzen ob Murau Austria
179 F3 Sankt Marein im Mürztal Austria
179 F3 Sankt Margarethen im Rosental Austria
168 E2 Sankt Margarethen an der Raab Austria
179 F3 Sankt Margarethen bei Knittelfeld Austria
179 F3 Sankt Margarethen in Burgenland Austria
172 C3 Sankt Märgen Ger.
179 F3 Sankt Marein Austria
179 G3 Sankt Marienkirchen an der Polsenz Austria
179 F3 Sankt Martin Niederösterreich Austria
179 E3 Sankt Martin Salzburg Austria
179 H4 Sankt Martin an der Raab Austria
179 E3 Sankt Martin im Mühlkreis Austria
San Mateo Spain see Sant Mateu
179 F3 Sankt Michael im Burgenland Austria
179 F3 Sankt Michael im Lungau Austria
179 G3 Sankt Michael in Obersteiermark Austria
168 E2 Sankt Michaelisdonn Ger.
190 E2 Sankt Moritz Switz.
179 F3 Sankt Nikolai im Saustal Austria
139 H2 Sankt-Peterburg Rus. Fed.
179 F3 Sankt Oswald bei Freistadt Austria
173 H3 Sankt Oswald-Riedlhütte Ger.
179 F4 Sankt Pantaleon Austria
179 F3 Sankt Paul im Lavanttal Austria
179 F3 Sankt Peter am Hart Austria
179 F3 Sankt Peter am Ottersbach Austria
179 F3 Sankt Peter-Freienstein Austria
179 F3 Sankt Peter im Sulmtal Austria
179 F3 Sankt Peter in der Au Austria
168 D1 Sankt Peter-Ording Ger.
Sankt Petersburg Rus. Fed. see Sankt-Peterburg
179 G3 Sankt Pölten Austria
179 G3 Sankt Ruprecht an der Raab Austria
179 F3 Sankt Stefan Austria
179 F3 Sankt Stefan im Gailtal Austria
179 F3 Sankt Stefan im Rosental Austria
179 F3 Sankt Stefan ob Leoben Austria
179 F3 Sankt Stefan ob Stainz Austria
178 D3 Sankt Ulrich am Pillersee Austria
179 F3 Sankt Ulrich bei Steyr Austria
179 G3 Sankt Urban Austria
179 F3 Sankt Valentin Austria
179 F3 Sankt Veit am Vogau Austria
179 G2 Sankt Veit an der Glan Austria
179 G3 Sankt Veit an der Gölsen Austria
179 F3 Sankt Veit im Pongau Austria
172 B2 Sankt Wendel Ger.
173 G3 Sankt Wolfgang Ger.
173 F3 Sankt Wolfgang im Salzkammergut Austria
209 D6 Sankuru r. Dem. Rep. Congo
184 D3 San Lázaro Para.
191 F3 San Lazzaro di Savena Italy
191 H4 San Leandro CA U.S.A.
191 H4 San Leo Italy
194 C5 San Leonardo Sicilia Italy
183 G3 San Leonardo de Yagüe Spain
191 G2 San Leonardo in Passiria Italy
126 E3 Şanlıurfa Turkey
261 G3 San Lorenzo Santa Fé Arg.
261 G2 San Lorenzo Beni Bol.
252 D5 San Lorenzo Tarija Bol.
250 B4 San Lorenzo Ecuador
252 C3 San Lorenzo Peru
183 H2 San Lorenzo r. Spain
259 B7 San Lorenzo, Cerro mt. Arg./Chile
252 A2 San Lorenzo, Isla i. Peru
216 □³ San Lorenzo Island CA U.S.A.
260 C5 San Lorenzo al Mare Italy
185 G2 San Lorenzo de Calatrava Spain
183 F4 San Lorenzo de El Escorial Spain
183 H5 San Lorenzo de la Parrilla Spain
San Lorenzo de Morunys Spain see Sant Llorenç de Morunys
191 H5 San Lorenzo di Sebato Italy
191 H5 San Lorenzo in Campo Italy
195 F4 San Lucido Italy
252 D3 San Lucas Bol.
250 C3 San Lucas, Serranía de mts Col.
260 D3 San Luis Arg.
260 D3 San Luis prov. Arg.
243 H5 San Luis Cuba
242 D3 San Luis Guat.
242 □H6 San Luis Mex.
244 D2 San Luis Pajón Hond.
244 D2 San Luis Potosí Mex.
244 D2 San Luis Potosí state Mex.
239 F6 San Luis Río Colorado Mex.
240 H4 San Luis Obispo CA U.S.A.
183 H5 San Luis Obispo Bay CA U.S.A.

Column 7

177 K4 Sânmartin Romania
183 G4 San Martín Spain
259 B8 San Martín, Lago l. Arg./Chile
245 G4 San Martín, Volcán vol. Mex.
183 G4 San Martín de la Vega Spain
179 F4 San Martín de la Vega del Alberche Spain
259 C6 San Martín de los Andes Arg.
183 G4 San Martín del Pimpollar Spain
183 F5 San Martín de Montalbán Spain
183 G4 San Martín de Pusa Spain
183 I2 San Martín de Unx Spain
183 F4 San Martín de Valdeiglesias Spain
191 G3 San Martino Buon Albergo Italy
192 B2 San-Martino-di-Lota Corse France
191 G3 San Martino di Lupari Italy
191 G3 San Martino in Badia Italy
191 G2 San Martino in Passiria Italy
193 H3 San Martino in Pensilis Italy
San Mateo Spain see Sant Mateu
240 F3 San Mateo CA U.S.A.
186 C3 San Mateo de Gállego Spain
243 H6 San Mateo Ixtatán Guat.
253 F4 San Matías Bol.
259 D6 San Matías, Golfo g. Arg.
194 D5 San Mauro Castelverde Sicilia Italy
193 I4 San Mauro Forte Italy
191 H4 San Mauro Pascoli Italy
190 C3 San Mauro Torinese Italy
109 G2 Sanmen Zhejiang China
109 G2 Sanmen Wan b. China
107 F5 Sanmenxia Henan China
191 H3 San Michele al Tagliamento Italy
193 H4 San Michele Mondovì Italy
195 G2 San Michele Salentino Italy
258 B7 San Miguel r. Bol.
253 E4 San Miguel r. Bol.
242 □H6 San Miguel El Salvador
252 D4 San Miguel r. Bol.
92 B3 San Miguel Phil.
261 G3 San Miguel de Allende Mex.
183 G3 San Miguel de Arroyo Spain
183 G3 San Miguel de Bernuy Spain
242 C2 San Miguel de Cruces Mex.
r. Mex.
252 D3 San Miguel de Huachi Bol.
261 H4 San Miguel del Monte Arg.
187 C7 San Miguel de Salinas Spain
258 D2 San Miguel de Tucumán Arg.
254 C5 San Miguel do Araguaia Brazil
260 E3 San Miguel el Alto Arg.
92 A5 San Miguel Islands Phil.
242 □K7 San Miguelito Panama
245 F5 San Miguel Octopan Mex.
245 F5 San Miguel Sola de Vega Mex.
187 D4 San Millán Arg.
240 G4 San Miguel r. CA U.S.A.
239 F4 San Miguel r. CO U.S.A.
109 F3 Sanming Fujian China
191 F5 San Miniato Italy
175 J5 Sanniki r. Pol.
92 B3 San Narciso Phil.
190 D3 Sannazzaro de' Burgondi Italy
114 B3 Sanndraigh i. Scotland U.K. see Sandray
195 F2 Sannicandro di Bari Italy
195 H2 Sannicandro Garganico Italy
195 H2 Sannicola Italy
195 H3 San Nicola dell'Alto Italy
192 C4 San Nicola Chile
92 B3 San Nicolas Phil.
244 B4 San Nicolás r. Mex.
244 D2 San Nicolás de los Agustinos Mex.
261 G3 San Nicolás de los Arroyos Arg.
184 E2 San Nicolás del Puerto Spain
216 □³ San Nicolás de Tolentino Gran Canaria Canary Is
239 C5 San Nicolas Island CA U.S.A.
196 E2 Sânnicolau Mare Romania
192 A5 San Nicolò d'Arcidano Sardegna Italy
192 B5 San Nicolò Gerrei Sardegna Italy
215 I2 Sannieshof S. Africa
175 H2 Sanniki Pol.
193 G3 Sannio, Monti del mts Italy
206 C3 Sanniquellie Liberia
252 D5 Sanoago Côte d'Ivoire see Sandu
191 G2 San Pancrazio Italy
195 G2 San Pancrazio Salentino Italy
193 H3 San Paolo di Civitate Italy
261 G2 San Pedro Buenos Aires Arg.
260 C2 San Pedro Catamarca Arg.
258 D2 San Pedro Jujuy Arg.
260 D2 San Pedro Misiones Arg.
242 □H6 San Pedro Belize
253 E3 San Pedro Santa Cruz Bol.
206 B4 San Pedro Côte d'Ivoire
245 E3 San Pedro Mex.
239 E6 San Pedro r. Chihuahua Mex.
239 F6 San Pedro watercourse AZ U.S.A.
177 J5 Sânpetru Mare Romania

Column 8

177 K4 Sânmartin Romania
183 G4 San Martín Spain
245 G4 San Martín de la Vega Spain
183 G4 San Martín del Pimpollar Spain
191 G3 San Martino Buon Albergo Italy
192 B2 San-Martino-di-Lota Corse France
191 G3 San Martino di Lupari Italy
191 G3 San Martino in Badia Italy
191 G2 San Martino in Passiria Italy
193 H3 San Martino in Pensilis Italy
San Mateo Spain see Sant Mateu
240 F3 San Mateo CA U.S.A.
186 C3 San Mateo de Gállego Spain
243 H6 San Mateo Ixtatán Guat.
253 F4 San Matías Bol.
259 D6 San Matías, Golfo g. Arg.
194 D5 San Mauro Castelverde Sicilia Italy
193 I4 San Mauro Forte Italy
191 H4 San Mauro Pascoli Italy
190 C3 San Mauro Torinese Italy
109 G2 Sanmen Zhejiang China
109 G2 Sanmen Wan b. China
107 F5 Sanmenxia Henan China
191 H3 San Michele al Tagliamento Italy
193 H4 San Michele Mondovì Italy
195 G2 San Michele Salentino Italy
190 C4 San Michele Mondovì Italy
187 D4 San Millán mt. Spain
240 G4 San Miguel r. CA U.S.A.
239 F4 San Miguel r. CO U.S.A.
239 F6 San Miguel Channel CA U.S.A.
240 G4 San Miguel de Huai Mex.
261 H4 San Miguel del Monte Arg.
187 C7 San Miguel de Salinas Spain
258 D3 San Miguel de Tucumán Arg.
254 C5 San Miguel el Alto Arg.
92 A5 San Miguel Islands Phil.
242 □K7 San Miguelito Panama
245 F5 San Miguel Octopan Mex.
245 F5 San Miguel Sola de Vega Mex.
187 H4 San Millán Arg.
183 H2 San Millán de la Cogolla Spain
109 F3 Sanming Fujian China
191 F5 San Miniato Italy
175 J5 Sanniki r. Pol.
92 B3 San Narciso Phil.
190 D3 Sannazzaro de' Burgondi Italy
114 B3 Sanndraigh i. Scotland U.K. see Sandray
195 F2 Sannicandro di Bari Italy
195 H2 Sannicandro Garganico Italy
195 H2 Sannicola Italy
195 H3 San Nicola dell'Alto Italy
192 C4 San Nicola Chile
92 B3 San Nicolas Phil.
244 D2 San Nicolás de los Agustinos Mex.
261 G3 San Nicolás de los Arroyos Arg.
184 E2 San Nicolás del Puerto Spain
216 □³ San Nicolás de Tolentino Gran Canaria Canary Is
239 C5 San Nicolas Island CA U.S.A.
196 E2 Sânnicolau Mare Romania
252 D5 San Onofre Col.
191 H5 San Onofre Col.
252 B4 San Pablo Potosí Bol.
253 E3 San Pablo Santa Cruz Bol.
253 E3 San Pablo r. Bol.
245 E3 San Pablo Mex.
240 F3 San Pablo CA U.S.A.
San Pablo de Manta Ecuador see San Pancracio
191 G2 San Pancrazio Italy
195 G2 San Pancrazio Salentino Italy
193 H3 San Paolo di Civitate Italy
261 G2 San Pedro Buenos Aires Arg.
260 C2 San Pedro Catamarca Arg.
258 D2 San Pedro Jujuy Arg.
260 D2 San Pedro Misiones Arg.
242 □H6 San Pedro Belize
253 E3 San Pedro Santa Cruz Bol.
206 B4 San Pedro Côte d'Ivoire
245 E3 San Pedro Mex.
239 E6 San Pedro r. Chihuahua Mex.
239 F6 San Pedro watercourse AZ U.S.A.

Column 9

177 K4 Sânmartin Spain
259 B8 San Martín, Lago l. Arg./Chile
245 G4 San Martín, Volcán vol. Mex.
183 G4 San Martín de la Vega Spain
179 F4 San Martín de la Vega del Alberche Spain
259 C6 San Martín de los Andes Arg.
183 G4 San Martín del Pimpollar Spain
183 F5 San Martín de Montalbán Spain
183 I2 San Martín de Unx Spain
183 F4 San Martín de Valdeiglesias Spain
191 G3 San Martino Buon Albergo Italy
192 B2 San-Martino-di-Lota Corse France
191 G3 San Martino di Lupari Italy
191 G3 San Martino in Badia Italy
191 G2 San Martino in Passiria Italy
193 H3 San Martino in Pensilis Italy
240 F3 San Mateo CA U.S.A.
186 C3 San Mateo de Gállego Spain
243 H6 San Mateo Ixtatán Guat.
253 F4 San Matías Bol.
259 C6 San Matías, Golfo g. Arg.
194 D5 San Mauro Castelverde Sicilia Italy
193 I4 San Mauro Forte Italy
191 H4 San Mauro Pascoli Italy
190 C3 San Mauro Torinese Italy
109 G2 Sanmen Zhejiang China
109 G2 Sanmen Wan b. China
107 F5 Sanmenxia Henan China
191 H3 San Michele al Tagliamento Italy
193 H4 San Michele Mondovì Italy
195 G2 San Michele Salentino Italy
258 B7 San Miguel r. Spain
240 G4 San Miguel r. CA U.S.A.
239 F4 San Miguel r. CO U.S.A.
242 B1 San Miguel de Horcasitas r. Mex.
252 D3 San Miguel de Huachi Bol.
261 H4 San Miguel del Monte Arg.
187 C7 San Miguel de Salinas Spain
258 B3 San Miguel de Tucumán Arg.
254 C5 San Miguel do Araguaia Brazil
260 E3 San Miguel el Alto Arg.
92 A5 San Miguel Islands Phil.
242 □K7 San Miguelito Panama
245 F5 San Miguel Sola de Vega Mex.
187 D4 San Millán Arg.
183 H2 San Millán de la Cogolla Spain
109 F3 Sanming Fujian China
191 G2 San Miniato Italy
92 B3 San Narciso Phil.
190 D3 Sannazzaro de' Burgondi Italy
114 B3 Sanndraigh i. Scotland U.K. see Sandray
195 F2 Sannicandro di Bari Italy
195 H2 Sannicandro Garganico Italy
195 H2 Sannicola Italy
195 H3 San Nicola dell'Alto Italy
192 C4 San Nicolò France
192 B3 San Nicolas Chile
92 B3 San Nicolas Phil.
244 D2 San Nicolás de los Agustinos Mex.
261 G3 San Nicolás de los Arroyos Arg.
184 E2 San Nicolás del Puerto Spain
216 □³ San Nicolás de Tolentino Gran Canaria Canary Is
239 C5 San Nicolas Island CA U.S.A.
192 A5 San Nicolò d'Arcidano Sardegna Italy
192 B5 San Nicolò Gerrei Sardegna Italy
215 I2 Sannieshof S. Africa
192 C3 Sannio, Monti del mts Italy
206 C3 Sanniquellie Liberia
175 K6 Sanok Pol.
252 D5 Sanoto Col.
261 G3 San Onofre Col.
191 G2 San Pancracio Italy
195 G2 San Pancrazio Salentino Italy
193 H3 San Paolo di Civitate Italy
261 G2 San Pedro Buenos Aires Arg.
260 C2 San Pedro Catamarca Arg.
258 D2 San Pedro Córdoba Arg.
253 G3 San Pedro Jujuy Arg.
252 C3 San Pedro Misiones Arg.
242 □H6 San Pedro Belize
253 E3 San Pedro Santa Cruz Bol.
206 B4 San Pedro Côte d'Ivoire
244 B2 San Pedro Mex.
239 E6 San Pedro r. Chihuahua Mex.
253 F4 San Pedro Para.
187 C7 San Pedro r. Spain
239 F6 San Pedro watercourse AZ U.S.A.
184 C1 San Pedro, Sierra de mts Spain
245 G3 San Pedro Almoloyan Mex.
244 D3 San Pedro Apóstol Mex.
240 H5 San Pedro Carchá Guat.
239 C5 San Pedro Channel CA U.S.A.
250 D5 San Pedro de Atacama Chile
250 B6 San Pedro de Ceque Spain
244 D2 San Pedro de la Cueva Mex.
242 C2 San Pedro del Arroyo Spain
246 E3 San Pedro de las Colonias Mex.
250 B6 San Pedro de Latarce Spain
250 B6 San Pedro de Lloc Peru
187 D5 San Pedro del Paraná Para.
187 D5 San Pedro del Pinatar Spain
183 G3 San Pedro del Romeral Spain
247 D5 San Pedro de Macorís Dom. Rep.
242 C2 San Pedro de Rozados Spain
242 □H6 San Pedro el Saucito Mex.
253 E3 San Pedro Sula Hond.
177 J5 Sânpetru Mare Romania

San Piero a Sieve to Sardegna 359

191 G5 San Piero a Sieve Italy
195 D4 San Piero Patti Sicilia Italy
195 E4 San Pietro Isole Lipari Italy
192 A5 San Pietro, Isola di i. Sardegna Italy
178 D4 San Pietro di Cadore Italy
191 F3 San Pietro in Cariano Italy
191 G4 San Pietro in Casale Italy
195 H2 San Pietro Vernotico Italy
241 L2 San Pitch r. UT U.S.A.
190 F4 San Polo d'Enza Italy
191 G4 San Prospero Italy
129 F3 Sanqaçal Azer.
146 E6 Sanquhar Dumfries and Galloway, Scotland U.K.
186 D3 San Quilez mt. Spain
192 D1 San Quirico d'Orcia Italy
260 C4 San Rafael Arg.
253 E4 San Rafael Bol.
260 B4 San Rafael Chile
240 F3 San Rafael CA U.S.A.
241 L2 San Rafael r. UT U.S.A.
250 D2 San Rafael Venez.
San Rafael del Moján Venez. see San Rafael
242 □I6 San Rafael del Norte Nic.
186 D4 San Rafael del Río Spain
247 E3 San Rafael del Yuma Dom. Rep.
241 L2 San Rafael Knob mt. UT U.S.A.
240 G4 San Rafael Mountains CA U.S.A.
252 D3 San Ramón Bol.
261 J4 San Ramón Uru.
190 C5 San Remo Italy
235 E2 San Remo NY U.S.A.
182 C2 San Román Spain
183 F2 San Román de la Cuba Spain
183 F4 San Román de los Montes Spain
185 E4 San Roque Andalucía Spain
182 B1 San Roque Galicia Spain
182 B2 San Roque Galicia Spain
193 H4 San Rufo Italy
237 D6 San Saba TX U.S.A.
237 D6 San Saba r. TX U.S.A.
163 E4 Sansac-de-Marmiesse France
San Sadurniño Spain see Avenida do Marqués de Figueroa
245 F4 San Salavador el Seco Mex.
206 B4 Sansalé Guinea
261 H2 San Salvador Arg.
246 D1 San Salvador i. Bahamas
243 H6 San Salvador El Salvador
261 H3 San Salvador r. Uru.
250 □ San Salvador, Isla i. Islas Galápagos Ecuador
183 F2 San Salvador de Cantamunda Spain
258 D2 San Salvador de Jujuy Arg.
192 A5 San Salvatore Sardegna Italy
190 D4 San Salvatore Monferrato Italy
193 G3 San Salvatore Telesino Italy
193 G2 San Salvo Italy
207 F4 Sansanné-Mango Togo
247 □1 San Sebastián Puerto Rico
182 B2 San Sebastián hill Spain
259 C9 San Sebastián, Bahía de b. Arg.
216 □3a San Sebastián de la Gomera La Gomera Canary Is
183 G4 San Sebastián de los Reyes Spain
245 F4 San Sebastián Zinacatepec Mex.
190 F4 San Secondo Parmense Italy
191 H5 Sansepolcro Italy
192 D2 San Severa Italy
193 I4 San Severino Lucano Italy
191 I5 San Severino Marche Italy
193 H3 San Severo Italy
109 G3 Sansha Fujian China
241 M5 San Simon AZ U.S.A.
188 F3 Sanski Most Bos.-Herz.
183 H2 Sansol Spain
80 E4 Sanson North I. N.Z.
Sansoral Islands Palau see Sonsorol Islands
193 I5 San Sosti Italy
192 B5 San Sperate Sardegna Italy
195 F1 San Spirito Italy
247 □2 Sans Toucher mt. Guadeloupe
108 D3 Sansui Guizhou China
252 A2 Santa r. Peru
256 C4 Santa Adélia Brazil
193 G3 Santa Agata de'Goti Italy
195 F4 Santa Agata del Bianco Italy
193 H5 Santa Agata di Esaro Italy
184 D1 Santa Amalia Spain
258 D2 Santa Ana Arg.
252 D3 Santa Ana La Paz Bol.
253 E4 Santa Ana Santa Cruz Bol.
243 H6 Santa Ana El Salvador
245 E4 Santa Ana México Mex.
242 C2 Santa Ana Sonora Mex.
78 □6 Santa Ana i. Solomon Is
185 I2 Santa Ana Spain
183 F4 Santa Ana hill Spain
240 I5 Santa Ana CA U.S.A.
183 F5 Santa Ana de Pusa Spain
252 D3 Santa Ana de Yacuma Bol.
261 H3 Santa Anita Arg.
244 C3 Santa Anita Mex.
237 D6 Santa Anna TX U.S.A.
216 □1a Santa Bárbara Terceira Azores
257 F3 Santa Bárbara Brazil
260 A5 Santa Bárbara Chile
Santa Bárbara Cuba see La Demajagua
242 □H6 Santa Bárbara Hond.
242 D3 Santa Bárbara Mex.
186 D4 Santa Bárbara Spain
187 B6 Santa Bárbara mt. Spain
185 H3 Santa Bárbara mt. Spain
240 H4 Santa Barbara CA U.S.A.
257 H2 Santa Bárbara, Ilha i. Brazil
255 B7 Santa Bárbara, Serra de hills Brazil
240 G4 Santa Barbara Channel CA U.S.A.
184 C3 Santa Bárbara de Casa Spain
184 C3 Santa Bárbara de Padrões Port.
256 D5 Santa Bárbara d'Oeste Brazil
255 B9 Santa Barbara do Sul Brazil
240 H5 Santa Barbara Island CA U.S.A.
216 □3f Santa Brígida Gran Canaria Canary Is
183 I2 Santacara Spain
260 E3 Santa Catalina Arg.
78 □6 Santa Catalina i. Solomon Is
240 I5 Santa Catalina, Gulf of CA U.S.A.
182 B1 Santa Catalina de Armada Spain
240 H5 Santa Catalina Island CA U.S.A.
255 C8 Santa Catarina state Brazil
243 E3 Santa Catarina Mex.
245 E5 Santa Catarina r. Mex.
247 □10 Santa Catarina Curaçao Neth. Antilles
184 B2 Santa Catarina Port.
255 C8 Santa Catarina, Ilha de i. Brazil
195 F4 Santa Caterina dello Ionio Italy
192 A4 Santa Caterina di Pittinuri Sardegna Italy
194 D5 Santa Caterina Villarmosa Sicilia Italy
Santa Catharina Curaçao Neth. Antilles see Santa Catarina
195 H2 Santa Cesarea Terme Italy
186 C2 Santa Cilia de Jaca Spain
260 A5 Santa Clara Chile
250 D5 Santa Clara Col.
246 C2 Santa Clara Cuba
244 C1 Santa Clara Mex.
241 I6 Santa Clara r. Mex.
239 F6 Santa Clara r. Mex.
240 G3 Santa Clara CA U.S.A.
241 K3 Santa Clara UT U.S.A.
240 H4 Santa Clara r. CA U.S.A.
184 B3 Santa Clara, Barragem de resr Port.
252 □ Santa Clara, Isla i. S. Pacific Ocean
184 B3 Santa Clara-a-Nova Port.
184 B3 Santa Clara-a-Velha Port.
184 C3 Santa Clara de Louredo Port.
261 G2 Santa Clara de Saguier Arg.
240 H4 Santa Clarita CA U.S.A.
250 C5 Santa Clotilde Peru
186 F3 Santa Coloma de Farners Spain
186 F3 Santa Coloma de Gramenet Spain
186 E3 Santa Coloma de Queralt Spain
182 D2 Santa Colomba de Somoza Spain
183 E2 Santa Columba de Curueño Spain
Santa Comba Angola see Waku-Kungo
182 B4 Santa Comba Dão Port.
182 D3 Santa Comba de Rossas Port.
186 F3 Santa Cristina d'Arco Spain
182 E2 Santa Cristina de la Polvorosa Spain
194 D6 Santa Croce Camerina Sicilia Italy
193 G3 Santa Croce del Sannio Italy
193 H3 Santa Croce di Magliano Italy
191 F5 Santa Croce sull'Arno Italy
259 C8 Santa Cruz prov. Arg.
259 C8 Santa Cruz r. Arg.
253 E4 Santa Cruz Bol.
253 E4 Santa Cruz dept Bol.
257 G3 Santa Cruz Espírito Santo Brazil
251 H5 Santa Cruz Pará Brazil
254 G3 Santa Cruz Rio Grande do Norte Brazil
260 B4 Santa Cruz Chile
242 □I7 Santa Cruz Costa Rica
246 □ Santa Cruz Jamaica
184 □ Santa Cruz Madeira
250 C6 Santa Cruz Peru
92 A3 Santa Cruz Luzon Phil.
92 B2 Santa Cruz Luzon Phil.
92 B3 Santa Cruz Luzon Phil.
184 A1 Santa Cruz Port.
183 I3 Santa Cruz mt. Spain
240 F3 Santa Cruz CA U.S.A.
241 K5 Santa Cruz watercourse AZ U.S.A.
250 □ Santa Cruz, Isla i. Islas Galápagos Ecuador
243 H6 Santa Cruz Barillas Guat.
257 H2 Santa Cruz Cabrália Brazil
216 □1c Santa Cruz da Graciosa Graciosa Azores
256 D4 Santa Cruz das Palmeiras Brazil
182 B4 Santa Cruz da Tapa Port.
183 G1 Santa Cruz de Bezana Spain
183 H2 Santa Cruz de Campezo Spain
256 C2 Santa Cruz de Goiás Brazil
216 □3d Santa Cruz de la Palma La Palma Canary Is
163 B6 Santa Cruz de la Serós Spain
244 C3 Santa Cruz de las Flores Mex.
184 E1 Santa Cruz de la Sierra Spain
183 G5 Santa Cruz de la Zarza Spain
243 H6 Santa Cruz del Quiché Guat.
183 F4 Santa Cruz del Retamar Spain
246 C2 Santa Cruz del Sur Cuba
187 B5 Santa Cruz de Moya Spain
185 G2 Santa Cruz de Mudela Spain
216 □3a Santa Cruz de Tenerife Tenerife Canary Is
242 □I6 Santa Cruz de Yojoa Hond.
256 C5 Santa Cruz do Rio Pardo Brazil
255 B9 Santa Cruz do Sul Brazil
240 H4 Santa Cruz Island CA U.S.A.
78 □6 Santa Cruz Islands Solomon Is
192 A5 Santadi Sardegna Italy
193 H5 Santa Domenica Talao Italy
194 D5 Santa Domenica Vittoria Sicilia Italy
257 F3 Santa Efigênia de Minas Brazil
261 H2 Santa Elena Arg.
252 D5 Santa Elena Bol.
185 G2 Santa Elena Spain
182 E2 Santa Elena de Jamuz Spain
194 C5 Santa Elisabetta Sicilia Italy
185 F3 Santaella Spain
183 H2 Santa Engracia Spain
185 F2 Santa Eufemia Spain
193 I6 Santa Eufemia, Golfo di g. Italy
195 E4 Santa Eufemia d'Aspromonte Italy
182 B2 Santa Eugenia Spain
184 C1 Santa Eulália Port.
186 B4 Santa Eulalia Aragón Spain
182 E1 Santa Eulalia Asturias Spain
183 E1 Santa Eulalia Asturias Spain
187 E6 Santa Eulalia del Río Spain
182 C1 Santa Eulalia de Oscos Spain
186 F3 Santa Eulàlia de Riuprimer Spain
261 G2 Santa Fé Arg.
261 G2 Santa Fé prov. Arg.
246 B2 Santa Fé Cuba
92 B3 Santa Fe Phil.
185 G3 Santa Fe Spain
239 F5 Santa Fe NM U.S.A.
250 □ Santa Fé, Isla i. Islas Galápagos Ecuador
Santa Fé de Bogotá Col. see Bogotá
257 E2 Santa Fé de Minas Brazil
256 B4 Santa Fé do Sul Brazil
254 D4 Santa Filomena Brazil
192 D2 Santa Fiora Italy
194 D4 Sant'Agata di Militello Sicilia Italy
193 H3 Sant'Agata di Puglia Italy
191 H5 Sant'Agata Feltria Italy
192 A5 Santa Giusta Sardegna Italy
191 H2 Santa Giustina Italy
191 G4 Sant'Agostino Italy
254 D2 Santa Helena Brazil
256 B2 Santa Helena de Goiás Brazil
108 C2 Santai Sichuan China
110 C2 Santai Xinjiang China
108 B3 Santai Yunnan China
254 F5 Santa Inês Bahia Brazil
254 D2 Santa Inês Maranhão Brazil
259 B9 Santa Inés, Isla i. Chile
184 C3 Santa Iria Port.
260 D5 Santa Isabel La Pampa Arg.
261 G3 Santa Isabel Santa Fé Arg.
252 D5 Santa Isabel Bol.
250 B5 Santa Isabel Ecuador
Santa Isabel Equat. Guinea see Malabo
247 □1 Santa Isabel Puerto Rico
78 □6 Santa Isabel i. Solomon Is
254 E2 Santa Isabel, Ilha Grande de i. Brazil
242 B2 Santa Isabel, Sierra mts Mex.
252 B4 Santa Isabel de Sihuas Peru
256 A5 Santa Isabel do Ivaí Brazil
260 A5 Santa Juana Chile
256 D3 Santa Juliana Brazil
184 B1 Santa Justa Port.
191 H4 Sant'Alberto Italy
182 C3 Santalha Port.
186 D2 Santa Liestra y San Quílez Spain
116 B5 Santalpur Gujarat India
191 F5 Santa Luce Italy
Santa Lucía Cuba see Rafael Freyre
250 B5 Santa Lucía Ecuador
243 H6 Santa Lucia Guat.
192 B4 Santa Lucia Sardegna Italy
182 B2 Santa Lucía Spain
261 I4 Santa Lucía Uru.
261 I4 Santa Lucía r. Uru.
185 F3 Santa Lucía, Cerro de mt. Spain
195 E4 Santa Lucia del Mela Sicilia Italy
216 □3f Santa Lucía de Tirajana Gran Canaria Canary Is
240 G3 Santa Lucia Range mts CA U.S.A.
216 □1c Santa Luzia Pico Azores
254 D3 Santa Luzia Maranhão Brazil
254 F3 Santa Luzia Paraíba Brazil
206 □ Santa Luzia i. Cape Verde
184 B3 Santa Luzia Beja Port.
184 C3 Santa Luzia Faro Port.
261 F4 Santa Magdalena Arg.
187 D4 Santa Magdalena de Pulpís Spain
197 H2 Santa Mare Romania
186 E3 Santa Margarida de Montbui Spain
184 B2 Santa Margarida do Sádão Port.
187 G5 Santa Margarita Spain
240 G4 Santa Margarita CA U.S.A.
194 C5 Santa Margherita di Belice Sicilia Italy
190 E4 Santa Margherita Ligure Italy
258 D2 Santa María Arg.
216 □1 Santa Maria i. Azores
252 E3 Santa María Bol.
251 H5 Santa Maria Pará Brazil
255 B9 Santa Maria Rio Grande do Sul Brazil
258 G3 Santa Maria r. Brazil
206 □ Santa Maria Cape Verde
242 D2 Santa María r. Mex.
244 E3 Santa María r. Mex.
186 C2 Santa María Spain
187 C5 Santa María mt. Spain
184 D3 Santa María r. Spain
190 F2 Santa Maria Switz.
240 G4 Santa Maria CA U.S.A.
241 K4 Santa Maria r. AZ U.S.A.
184 C4 Santa Maria, Cabo de c. Port.
255 D5 Santa Maria, Chapadão de hills Brazil
258 B5 Santa María, Isla i. Chile
250 □ Santa María, Isla i. Islas Galápagos Ecuador
254 D5 Santa Maria, Serra de hills Brazil
245 E4 Santa María Ajoloapan Mex.
193 G3 Santa Maria Capua Vetere Italy
254 F4 Santa Maria da Boa Vista Brazil
182 B4 Santa Maria da Feira Port.
254 C4 Santa Maria das Barreiras Brazil
256 C5 Santa Maria da Serra Brazil
254 D5 Santa Maria da Vitória Brazil
183 G1 Santa María de Cayón Spain
216 □3f Santa María de Guía Gran Canaria Canary Is
183 H3 Santa María de Huertas Spain
251 E2 Santa María de Ipire Venez.
183 E4 Santa Maria del Berrocal Spain
183 G2 Santa María del Campo Spain
183 H5 Santa María del Campo Rus Spain
193 H5 Santa Maria del Cedro Italy
190 E4 Santa Maria della Versa Italy
242 D3 Santa María del Oro Mex.
244 B3 Santa María del Oro Nayarit Mex.
182 E2 Santa María del Páramo Spain
244 D3 Santa María del Río Mex.
183 H4 Santa María del Val Spain
185 I3 Santa María de Nieva Spain
193 G4 Santa Maria di Castellabate Italy
195 H3 Santa Maria di Leuca, Capo c. Italy
194 D5 Santa Maria di Licodia Sicilia Italy
192 B2 Santa-Maria-di-Lota Corse France
191 H3 Santa Maria di Sala Italy
257 G2 Santa Maria do Salto Brazil
257 F3 Santa Maria do Suaçuí Brazil
245 F6 Santa María Huatulco Mex.
78 □5 Santa María Island Vanuatu
183 F3 Santa María la Real de Nieva Spain
257 F4 Santa Maria Madalena Brazil
190 D2 Santa Maria Maggiore Italy
241 K4 Santa Maria Mountains AZ U.S.A.
192 B5 Santa Maria Navarrese Sardegna Italy
190 E2 Santa Maria Rezzonico Italy
192 A3 Santa-Maria-Siché Corse France
193 H4 Santa Marina Italy
182 E2 Santa Marina del Rey Spain
194 D4 Santa Marina Salina Isole Lipari Italy
192 D2 Santa Marinella Italy
250 C2 Santa Marta Col.
185 H1 Santa Marta Castilla - La Mancha Spain
184 D2 Santa Marta Extremadura Spain
Santa Marta, Serra de mts Brazil see Divisões, Serra das
182 E4 Santa Marta de Tormes Spain
245 G4 Santa Martha, Cerro mt. Mex.
Santa Maura i. Greece see Lefkada
192 A2 Sant'Ambroggio Corse France
240 H4 Santa Monica CA U.S.A.
239 D7 Santa Monica, Pico mt. Mex.
240 H5 Santa Monica Bay CA U.S.A.
254 E5 Santana Brazil
256 B3 Santana r. Brazil
184 □ Santana Madeira
182 B4 Santana Coimbra Port.
184 C2 Santana Évora Port.
184 A2 Santana Setúbal Port.
197 E2 Sântana Romania
255 B9 Santana da Boa Vista Brazil
184 B3 Santana da Serra Port.
184 C3 Santana de Cambas Port.
254 E2 Santana do Acarau Brazil
254 C4 Santana do Araguaia Brazil
184 B2 Santana do Campo Port.
254 F3 Santana do Cariri Brazil
255 B9 Santana do Livramento Brazil
184 B2 Santana do Mato Port.
194 D2 Sant'Anastasia Italy
193 E2 Sant'Anatolia di Narco Italy
250 B4 Santander Col.
250 C3 Santander dept Col.
183 G1 Santander Spain
183 F1 Santander prov. Cantabria Spain
195 G2 Sant'Andrea, Isola i. Italy
195 F4 Sant Andrea Apostolo dello Ionio Italy
192 B5 Sant'Andrea Frius Sardegna Italy
177 K4 Sântandrei Romania
240 G3 Santa Nella CA U.S.A.
195 F4 Sant'Angelo Italy
193 G3 Sant Angelo a Cupola Italy
191 H5 Sant'Angelo in Lizzola Italy
191 H5 Sant'Angelo in Vado Italy
190 E3 Sant'Angelo Lodigiano Italy
106 B2 Santanghu Xinjiang China
Santanilla, Islas is Caribbean Sea see Swan Islands
194 B5 Santa Ninfa Sicilia Italy
241 L5 Santan Mountain hill AZ U.S.A.
257 G5 Sant'Anna, Ilha de i. Brazil
192 A5 Sant'Anna Arresi Sardegna Italy
192 A5 Sant'Antioco Sardegna Italy
192 A5 Sant'Antioco, Isola di i. Sardegna Italy
192 B4 Sant'Antonio di Gallura Sardegna Italy
192 A5 Sant'Antonio di Santadi Sardegna Italy
Santañy Spain see Santanyí
187 G5 Santanyí Spain
183 F4 Santa Olalla Spain
182 D4 Santa Olalla hill Spain
186 E3 Santa Oliva Spain
184 D3 Santa Ollala del Cala Spain
186 F2 Santa Pau Spain
240 H4 Santa Paula CA U.S.A.
115 D2 Santapilly Andhra Prad. India
187 C6 Santa Pola Spain
187 C6 Santa Pola, Cabo de c. Spain
241 L2 Santaquin UT U.S.A.
254 E3 Santa Quitéria Brazil
182 C4 Santar Port.
193 I4 Sant Arcangelo Italy
191 H4 Santarcangelo di Romagna Italy
251 H5 Santarém Brazil
184 B1 Santarém Port.
184 B1 Santarém admin. dist. Port.
254 G3 Santa Rita Brazil
243 E3 Santa Rita Mex.
246 E5 Santa Rita Venez.
254 D4 Santa Rita de Cassia Brazil
256 A2 Santa Rita do Araguaia Brazil
257 E5 Santa Rita do Sapucaí Brazil
261 E5 Santa Rosa La Pampa Arg.
260 C3 Santa Rosa Mendoza Arg.
252 D3 Santa Rosa Bol.
255 B8 Santa Rosa Brazil
250 B5 Santa Rosa Ecuador
253 F6 Santa Rosa Para.
252 C3 Santa Rosa Peru
261 I4 Santa Rosa Uru.
240 F2 Santa Rosa CA U.S.A.
239 F5 Santa Rosa NM U.S.A.
242 □H6 Santa Rosa de Copán Hond.
253 E4 Santa Rosa de la Roca Bol.
260 E3 Santa Rosa del Conlara Arg.
253 E4 Santa Rosa del Palmar Bol.
261 F2 Santa Rosa del Río Primero Arg.
250 C3 Santa Rosa de Osos Col.
256 D4 Santa Rosa de Viterbo Brazil
240 G5 Santa Rosa Island CA U.S.A.
244 D3 Santa Rosa Jauregui Mex.
242 B3 Santa Rosalía Mex.
241 I5 Santa Rosa Mountains CA U.S.A.
238 C3 Santa Rosa Range mts NV U.S.A.
241 K5 Santa Rosa Wash watercourse AZ U.S.A.
195 F3 Santa Severina Italy
183 E2 Santas Martas Spain
191 G5 Santa Sofia Italy
184 B2 Santa Sofia Port.
184 C2 Santa Susana Évora Port.
184 B2 Santa Susana Setúbal Port.
258 E2 Santa Sylvina Arg.
261 G3 Santa Teresa Arg.
84 C5 Santa Teresa N.T. Austr.
257 G3 Santa Teresa Brazil
254 C4 Santa Teresa r. Brazil
182 E4 Santa Teresa, Embalse de resr Spain
192 B3 Santa Teresa di Gallura Sardegna Italy
195 E5 Santa Teresa di Riva Sicilia Italy
261 I5 Santa Teresita Arg.
177 L4 Santău Romania
216 □3a Santa Úrsula Tenerife Canary Is
195 E5 Santa Venerina Sicilia Italy
256 B3 Santa Vitória Brazil
184 B3 Santa Vitória Port.
184 C2 Santa Vitória do Ameixial Port.
258 G4 Santa Vitória do Palmar Brazil
192 B5 Santa Vittoria, Monte mt. Sardegna Italy
240 G4 Santa Ynez r. CA U.S.A.
Santa Ysabel i. Solomon Is see Santa Isabel
186 F3 Sant Benet mt. Spain
186 F3 Sant Boix de Llobregat Spain
186 D4 Sant Carles de la Ràpita Spain
186 F3 Sant Celoni Spain
186 F3 Sant Cugat del Vallès Spain
158 B3 Santec France
240 I5 Santee CA U.S.A.
231 E5 Santee r. SC U.S.A.
193 F2 Sant'Egidio alla Vibrata Italy
193 G3 Sant'Elia a Pianisi Italy
193 F3 Sant Elia Fiumerapido Italy
184 D3 San Telmo Spain
191 I5 Sant'Elpidio a Mare Italy
192 B4 San Teodoro Sardegna Italy
189 F5 Santeramo in Colle Italy
191 G4 Santerno r. Italy
183 F2 Santervás de la Vega Spain
186 E3 Santes Creus Spain
186 B1 Santesteban Spain
186 G3 Sant Feliu de Guíxols Spain
186 F2 Sant Feliu de Palterols Spain
186 F3 Sant Feliu Sasserra Spain
190 D3 Santhià Italy
186 F3 Sant Hilari Sacalm Spain
186 F2 Sant Hipòlit de Voltregà Spain
255 B9 Santiago Brazil
260 B3 Santiago Chile
260 B3 Santiago admin. reg. Chile
246 E3 Santiago Dom. Rep.
242 C4 Santiago Baja California Sur Mex.
244 B4 Santiago Colima Mex.
243 E3 Santiago Nuevo León Mex.
244 B1 Santiago r. Mex.
242 □J7 Santiago Panama
253 F6 Santiago Para.
252 B3 Santiago Peru
250 B6 Santiago r. Peru
92 B2 Santiago Phil.
242 □J7 Santiago, Cerro mt. Panama
244 B3 Santiago, Río Grande de r. Mex.
253 F4 Santiago, Sierra de hills Bol.
245 G5 Santiago Astata Mex.
182 C5 Santiago de Alcántara Spain
185 F3 Santiago de Calatrava Spain
250 B6 Santiago de Cao Peru
Santiago de Carbajo Spain see Santiago de Alcántara
182 B2 Santiago de Compostela Spain
246 D2 Santiago de Cuba Cuba
185 H2 Santiago de la Espada Spain
245 F3 Santiago de la Peña Mex.
187 C7 Santiago de la Ribera Spain
182 D5 Santiago del Campo Spain
258 D2 Santiago del Estero Arg.
261 F1 Santiago del Estero prov. Arg.
Santiago de los Caballeros Dom. Rep. see Santiago
216 □3a Santiago del Teide Tenerife Canary Is
252 C3 Santiago de Pacaguaras Bol.
184 B2 Santiago do Cacém Port.
184 B2 Santiago do Escoural Port.
244 B3 Santiago Ixcuintla Mex.
245 F5 Santiago Ixtayutla Mex.
240 I5 Santiago Peak CA U.S.A.
261 F2 Santiago Temple Arg.
245 G4 Santiago Tuxtla Mex.
261 I4 Santiago Vazquez Uru.
244 B1 Santiaguillo, Laguna de l. Mex.
182 E4 Santibáñez de Béjar Spain
183 F2 Santibáñez de la Peña Spain
182 E4 Santibáñez de la Sierra Spain
182 D2 Santibáñez de Vidriales Spain
182 D4 Santibáñez el Bajo Spain
183 G2 Santibáñez Zarzaguda Spain
190 F4 Sant'Ilario d'Enza Italy
183 F1 Santillana Spain
184 D3 Santiponce Spain
Santipur W. Bengal India see Shantipur
190 E1 Säntis mt. Switz.
185 G2 Santisteban del Puerto Spain
183 F3 Santiuste de San Juan Bautista Spain
182 E3 Santiz Spain
186 □ Sant Jaume del Mediterrani Spain
186 D4 Sant Jaume d'Enveja Spain
186 F2 Sant Joan de les Abadesses Spain
186 E3 Sant Joan de Vilatorrada Spain
186 □ Sant Joan Gran Spain
186 D4 Sant Jordi, Golf de g. Spain
186 E2 Sant Julià de Lòria Andorra
186 E2 Sant Llorenç de Morunys Spain
187 G5 Sant Llorenç des Cardassar Spain
Sant Lluís Spain see San Luis
186 E3 Sant Martí de Tous Spain
186 E3 Sant Martí Sarroca Spain
186 D4 Sant Mateu Spain
187 E5 Sant Miquel Spain
184 C2 Santo Aleixo Port.
184 C2 Santo Aleixo da Restauração Port.
216 □1c Santo Amaro Pico Azores
216 □1c Santo Amaro São Jorge Azores
254 F5 Santo Amaro Brazil
257 G4 Santo Amaro de Campos Brazil
256 B4 Santo Anastácio Brazil
256 A4 Santo Anastácio r. Brazil
256 D5 Santo André Brazil
184 B2 Santo André Port.
255 B9 Santo Angelo Brazil
216 □1c Santo Antão São Jorge Azores
206 □ Santo Antão i. Cape Verde
216 □1c Santo António Pico Azores
216 □1b Santo António São Miguel Azores
254 G3 Santo Antônio Brazil
257 F3 Santo Antônio r. Brazil
207 G6 Santo António São Tomé and Príncipe
256 B2 Santo Antônio da Barra Brazil
256 B5 Santo Antônio da Platina Brazil
254 F5 Santo Antônio de Jesus Brazil
253 F3 Santo Antônio de Leverger Brazil
257 F4 Santo Antônio de Pádua Brazil
257 E4 Santo Antônio do Amparo Brazil
250 E5 Santo Antônio do Içá Brazil
257 G2 Santo Antônio do Jacinto Brazil
257 E4 Santo Antônio do Monte Brazil
184 A2 Santo António dos Cavaleiros Port.
Santo António do Zaire Angola see Soyo
253 F4 Santo Corazón Bol.
260 B3 Santo Domingo Chile
246 B2 Santo Domingo Cuba
246 E3 Santo Domingo Dom. Rep.
242 B2 Santo Domingo Baja California Norte Mex.
245 G5 Santo Domingo Oaxaca Mex.
244 D2 Santo Domingo San Luis Potosí Mex.
245 F4 Santo Domingo r. Mex.
242 □I6 Santo Domingo Nic.
186 C2 Santo Domingo mt. Spain
Santo Domingo country West Indies see Dominican Republic
Santo Domingo de Garafía La Palma Canary Is see Garafía
183 H2 Santo Domingo de la Calzada Spain
183 G3 Santo Domingo de Silos Spain
239 F5 Santo Domingo Pueblo NM U.S.A.
245 G5 Santo Domingo Tehuantepec Mex.
184 C3 Santo Estêvão Port.
184 B2 Santo Estêvão Port.
80 E4 Santoft North I. N.Z.
257 E3 Santo Hipólito Brazil
256 B5 Santo Inácio Brazil
184 B2 Santo Isidro de Pegões Port.
187 B6 Santomera Spain
193 F2 Sant Omero Italy
183 G1 Santoña Spain
100 C4 Santong r. China
92 C4 Santo Niño i. Phil.
195 F4 Sant Onofrio Italy
194 D5 Santo Pietro Sicilia Italy
192 B2 Santo-Pietro-di-Tenda Corse France
192 B2 Santo-Pietro-di-Venaco Corse France
Santorini i. Greece see Thira
256 D5 Santos Brazil
257 F4 Santos Dumont Brazil
252 D2 Santos Mercado Bol.
264 F7 Santos Plateau sea feature S. Atlantic Ocean
190 D4 Santo Stefano Belbo Italy
191 H2 Santo Stefano di Cadore Italy
194 D4 Santo Stefano di Camastra Sicilia Italy
190 E4 Santo Stefano di Magra Italy
194 C5 Santo Stefano Quisquina Sicilia Italy
191 H3 Santo Stino di Livenza Italy
182 B3 Santo Tirso Port.
239 F6 Santo Tomás Mex.
242 □I6 Santo Tomás Nic.
252 B3 Santo Tomás Peru
258 F3 Santo Tomé Arg.
185 G2 Santo Tomé Spain
182 E3 Santovenia Spain
186 E3 Sant Pere de Ribes Spain
186 F2 Sant Pere de Torelló Spain
186 G2 Sant Pere Pescador Spain
164 D2 Santpoort Neth.
186 F2 Sant Privat d'en Bas Spain
186 E3 Sant Quintí de Mediona Spain
116 C5 Santrampur Gujarat India
187 F5 Sant Telm Spain
182 E1 Santullano de las Regueras Spain
192 A4 Santu Lussurgiu Sardegna Italy
Santurce Spain see Santurtzi
183 H2 Santurde Spain
183 G1 Santurtzi Spain
186 E3 Sant Vincenç de Castellet Spain
241 K3 Sanup Plateau AZ U.S.A.
259 B7 San Valentín, Cerro mt. Chile
178 D5 San Vendemiano Italy
192 A4 San Vero Milis Sardegna Italy
261 G2 San Vicente Arg.
260 B4 San Vicente Chile
242 □H6 San Vicente El Salvador
242 A2 San Vicente Mex.
92 B2 San Vicente Phil.
182 B2 San Vicente Spain
184 C1 San Vicente de Alcántara Spain
183 H2 San Vicente de Arana Spain
252 A3 San Vicente de Cañete Peru
San Vicente de Castellet Spain see Sant Vincenç de Castellet
183 F1 San Vicente de la Barquera Spain
183 H2 San Vicente de la Sonsierra Spain
187 C6 San Vicente del Raspeig Spain
183 F3 San Vicente de Palacio Spain
183 G1 San Vicente de Toranzo Spain
191 I5 San Vicino, Monte mt. Italy
160 C2 Sanvignes-les-Mines France
195 E4 San Vincenzo Isole Lipari Italy
192 C1 San Vincenzo Toscana Italy
182 D3 San Vitero Spain
192 B5 San Vito Sardegna Italy
194 B4 San Vito, Capo c. Sicilia Italy
191 H3 San Vito al Tagliamento Italy
193 G2 San Vito Chietino Italy
195 G2 San Vito dei Normanni Italy
191 H2 San Vito di Cadore Italy
194 B4 San Vito lo Capo Sicilia Italy
193 E3 San Vito Romano Italy
195 F4 San Vito sullo Ionio Italy
116 C5 Sanwer Madh. Prad. India
182 B2 Sanxenxo Spain
108 D5 Sanya Hainan China
213 F3 Sanyati r. Zimbabwe
107 F5 Sanyuan Shaanxi China
193 H4 Sanza Italy
209 C6 Sanza Pombo Angola
182 E3 Sanzoles Spain
96 C3 Sao, Phou mt. Laos
184 B3 São Barnabé Port.
216 □1a São Bartolomeu Terceira Azores
256 D2 São Bartolomeu r. Brazil
184 C1 São Bartolomeu Port.
184 B2 São Bartolomeu da Serra Port.
184 B3 São Bartolomeu de Messines Port.
254 E3 São Benedito Brazil
216 □1a São Bento Terceira Azores
254 D2 São Bento Brazil
256 B6 São Bento do Amparo Brazil
254 G3 São Bento do Norte Brazil
254 E2 São Bernardo Brazil
256 D5 São Bernardo do Campo Brazil
253 F7 São Borja Brazil
184 C3 São Brás Port.
184 C3 São Brás de Alportel Port.
184 B2 São Brás do Regedouro Port.
216 □1c São Caetano Pico Azores
255 B8 São Carlos Brazil
256 D5 São Carlos Brazil
182 C3 São Cosmado Port.
184 B2 São Cristóvão Port.
184 B2 São Cristóvão r. Port.
254 D5 São Desidério Brazil
254 D5 São Domingos Brazil
256 A4 São Domingos r. Brazil
256 B3 São Domingos r. Brazil
184 B3 São Domingos Port.
257 G3 São Domingos do Norte Brazil
184 B1 São Facundo Port.
257 E1 São Felipe, Serra de hills Brazil
254 F5 São Félix Brazil
254 C4 São Félix Brazil
251 I6 São Félix Brazil
182 B3 São Félix da Marinha Port.
257 G4 São Fidélis Brazil
206 □ São Filipe Cape Verde
257 E1 São Francisco Brazil
257 E1 São Francisco r. Brazil
252 D2 São Francisco r. Brazil
255 C8 São Francisco, Ilha de i. Brazil
184 B2 São Francisco da Serra Port.
255 B9 São Francisco de Assis Brazil
256 C1 São Francisco de Goiás Brazil
255 C9 São Francisco de Paula Brazil
256 C3 São Francisco de Sales Brazil
254 E3 São Francisco do Maranhão Brazil
255 C8 São Francisco do Sul Brazil
255 B9 São Gabriel Brazil
257 G3 São Gabriel da Palha Brazil
184 B2 São Geraldo Port.
257 F5 São Gonçalo Brazil
257 E3 São Gonçalo do Abaeté Brazil
257 E3 São Gonçalo do Pará Brazil
257 E4 São Gonçalo do Sapucaí Brazil
257 E3 São Gotardo Brazil
184 C2 São Gregório Port.
211 B7 Sao Hill Tanz.
182 B4 São Jacinto Port.
256 B5 São Jerônimo da Serra Brazil
216 □1c São João Pico Azores
254 D2 São João, Ilhas de is Brazil
253 E2 São João, Serra de hills Brazil
254 D5 São João da Aliança Brazil
257 G4 São João da Barra Brazil
256 D4 São João da Boa Vista Brazil
182 B4 São João da Madeira Port.
182 C3 São João da Pesqueira Port.
257 E1 São João da Ponte Brazil
256 B4 São João das Duas Pontas Brazil
257 E4 São João del Rei Brazil
257 F5 São João de Meriti Brazil
182 C4 São João de Tarouca Port.
254 C3 São João do Araguaia Brazil
256 A5 São João do Caiuá Brazil
182 B4 São João do Campo Port.
254 F3 São João do Cariri Brazil
255 E5 São João do Paraíso Brazil
254 E4 São João do Piauí Brazil
184 C3 São João dos Caldeireiros Port.
254 E3 São João dos Patos Brazil
257 F3 São João Evangelista Brazil
257 F4 São João Nepomuceno Brazil
255 C9 São Joaquim Brazil
256 D4 São Joaquim da Barra Brazil
216 □1c São Jorge i. Azores
184 □ São Jorge Madeira
216 □1c São Jorge, Canal de sea chan. Azores
São Jorge da Mina Ghana see Elmina
256 A5 São Jorge do Ivaí Brazil
255 C8 São José Brazil
256 D4 São José da Boa Vista Brazil
184 B1 São José da Lamarosa Port.
257 E5 São José do Barreiro Brazil
254 F3 São José do Belmonte Brazil
257 G4 São José do Calçado Brazil
257 G3 São José do Divino Brazil
254 F3 São José do Egito Brazil
257 F3 São José do Jacurí Brazil
258 G4 São José do Norte Brazil
254 E3 São José do Peixe Brazil
256 D4 São José do Rio Pardo Brazil
256 C4 São José do Rio Preto Brazil
257 E5 São José dos Campos Brazil
256 B4 São José dos Dourados r. Brazil
255 C8 São José dos Pinhais Brazil
182 C3 São Julião de Montenegro Port.
257 E5 São Lourenço Brazil
253 F4 São Lourenço r. Brazil
184 C2 São Lourenço de Mamporcão Port.
258 H3 São Lourenço do Sul Brazil
254 D2 São Luís Brazil
184 B3 São Luís Port.
256 B2 São Luís de Montes Belos Brazil
257 E5 São Luís do Paraitinga Brazil
254 G4 Saõ Luis do Quitunde Brazil
255 B9 São Luís Gonzaga Brazil
184 C1 São Mamede, Serra de mts Port.
184 B2 São Mamede do Sádão Port.
184 C2 São Manços Port.
256 C5 São Manuel Brazil
256 D3 São Marcos r. Brazil
184 C3 São Marcos da Ataboeira Port.
184 B3 São Marcos da Serra Port.
184 C2 São Marcos do Campo Port.
182 B4 São Martinho da Cortiça Port.
184 B3 São Martinho das Amoreiras Port.
182 D3 São Martinho de Angueira Port.
182 A5 São Martinho do Porto Port.
216 □1c São Mateus Pico Azores
216 □1a São Mateus Terceira Azores
257 H3 São Mateus Brazil
257 H3 São Mateus r. Brazil
255 C8 São Mateus do Sul Brazil
184 C2 São Matias Port.
216 □1b São Miguel i. Azores
256 D2 São Miguel r. Brazil
182 C5 São Miguel hill Port.
256 D5 São Miguel Arcanjo Brazil
182 C4 São Miguel de Acha Port.
184 C2 São Miguel de Machede Port.
184 B1 São Miguel de Rio Torto Port.
184 C3 São Miguel do Pinheiro Port.
254 E3 São Miguel do Tapuio Brazil
255 B9 São Miguel Jesuit Missions tourist site Brazil
191 H5 Saonda r. Italy
217 □3a Saondzou mt. Njazidja Comoros
160 E1 Saône France
157 G5 Saône r. France
160 C2 Saône-et-Loire dept Bourgogne France
São Nicolau Angola see Bentiaba
253 G7 São Nicolau Brazil
206 □ São Nicolau i. Cape Verde
256 D5 São Paulo Brazil
256 C5 São Paulo state Brazil
250 D5 São Paulo de Olivença Brazil
256 D5 São Pedro Brazil
257 F5 São Pedro da Aldeia Brazil
184 A1 São Pedro da Cadeira Port.
182 C3 São Pedro de Agostem Port.
182 A5 São Pedro de Muel Port.
184 C3 São Pedro de Solis Port.
184 C2 São Pedro do Corval Port.
256 B5 São Pedro do Ivaí Brazil
255 B9 São Pedro do Sul Brazil
182 B4 São Pedro do Sul Port.
264 H5 São Pedro e São Paulo is N. Atlantic Ocean
São Pires r. Brazil see Teles Pires
254 D3 São Raimundo das Mangabeiras Brazil
254 E4 São Raimundo Nonato Brazil
161 F5 Saorge France
257 E2 São Romão Brazil
184 C2 São Romão Port.
182 C4 São Romão Port.
184 B2 São Romão do Sado Port.
216 □1c São Roque Pico Azores
256 D5 São Roque Brazil
256 D4 São Roque de Minas Brazil
São Salvador Angola see M'banza Congo
São Salvador do Congo Angola see M'banza Congo
216 □1a São Sebastião Terceira Azores
253 I5 São Sebastião Brazil
257 E5 São Sebastião, Ilha do i. Brazil
256 B5 São Sebastião da Amoreira Brazil
251 I5 São Sebastião da Boa Vista Brazil
256 D4 São Sebastião do Paraíso Brazil
255 B9 São Sepé Brazil
182 B4 São Silvestre Port.
256 B3 São Simão Brazil
256 D4 São Simão Brazil
256 B3 São Simão, Barragem de resr Brazil
256 C3 São Simão, Represa de resr Brazil
93 C2 Sao-Siu Maluku Indon.
184 B3 São Teotónio Port.
257 E4 São Tiago Brazil
206 □ São Tiago i. Cape Verde
207 G6 São Tomé São Tomé and Príncipe
207 G6 São Tomé i. São Tomé and Príncipe
257 G5 São Tomé, Cabo de c. Brazil
207 G6 São Tomé, Pico de mt. São Tomé and Príncipe
207 G6 São Tomé and Príncipe country Africa
184 B2 São Torcato hill Port.
161 D4 Saou France
256 D5 São Vicente Brazil
206 □ São Vicente i. Cape Verde
184 □ São Vicente Madeira
184 C2 São Vicente Port.
182 C3 São Vicente Port.
184 B3 São Vicente, Cabo de c. Port.
182 C4 São Vicente da Beira Port.
254 D2 São Vicente Ferrer Brazil
177 K4 Sáp Hungary
Sápai Greece see Sapes
252 B3 Sapallanga Peru
199 G1 Sapanca Turkey
254 D4 Sapão r. Brazil
151 F2 Sapcote Leicestershire, England U.K.
207 G5 Sapele Nigeria
199 D1 Sapes Greece
199 F2 Şaphane Turkey
242 □K8 Sapo, Serranía del mts Panama
187 G5 Sa Pobla Spain
195 E4 Saponara Sicilia Italy
256 B5 Sapopema Brazil
138 D5 Sapotskin Belarus
206 E4 Sapouy Burkina
139 M5 Sapozhok Rus. Fed.
236 D3 Sappa Creek r. NE U.S.A.
191 H2 Sappada Italy
102 J2 Sapporo Japan
117 G5 Saptamukhi r. India
257 E4 Sapucai r. Minas Gerais Brazil
256 C4 Sapucai r. São Paulo Brazil
237 D4 Sapulpa OK U.S.A.
124 C2 Sāq, Jabal hill Saudi Arabia
122 A2 Saqqez Iran
117 G4 Sara Bangl.
122 A2 Sarā Iran
122 A2 Sarāb Iran
128 A5 Sarabît el Khâdim tourist site Egypt
97 C4 Sara Buri Thai.
195 F3 Saraceno r. Italy
179 H4 Saračinec Croatia
Saragossa Spain see Zaragoza
250 B5 Saraguro Ecuador
135 H5 Sarai Rus. Fed.
117 F5 Saraikela Bihar India
123 H4 Sarai Sidhu Pak.
188 G4 Sarajevo Bos.-Herz.
85 G4 Saraji Qld Austr.
123 E2 Sarakhs Turkm.
120 D2 Saraktash Rus. Fed.
237 F6 Saraland AL U.S.A.
120 C2 Saralzhin Kazakh.
117 H4 Saramati mt. India/Myanmar
163 C5 Saramon France
156 B5 Saran France
121 H2 Saran' Kazakh.
95 E3 Saran, Gunung mt. Indon.
233 G2 Saranac r. NY U.S.A.
233 F2 Saranac Lake NY U.S.A.
177 K4 Sáránd Hungary
198 B2 Sarandë Albania
256 B5 Sarandi Paraná Brazil
255 B8 Sarandi Rio Grande do Sul Brazil
Sarandib country Asia see Sri Lanka
258 G4 Sarandí del Yí Uru.
261 I3 Sarandí Grande Uru.
92 C5 Sarangani Islands Phil.
117 E5 Sarangarh Madh. Prad. India
116 D5 Sarangpur Madh. Prad. India
135 I5 Saransk Rus. Fed.
Sara-Ostrov Azer. see Närimanabad
207 H4 Sara Peak Nigeria
134 K4 Sarapul Rus. Fed.
231 D7 Sarasota FL U.S.A.
116 B5 Saraswati r. Gujarat India
136 E4 Sărata r. Moldova
197 H3 Sărata r. Romania
136 E4 Sarata Ukr.
136 E5 Sarata r. Ukr.
136 E4 Sărătenii Vechi Moldova
240 F3 Saratoga CA U.S.A.
238 F3 Saratoga WY U.S.A.
233 G3 Saratoga Springs NY U.S.A.
120 A2 Saratov Rus. Fed.
Saratov Oblast admin. div. Rus. Fed. see Saratovskaya Oblast'
129 A1 Saratovskaya Rus. Fed.
120 A2 Saratovskaya Oblast' admin. div. Rus. Fed.
120 A1 Saratovskoye Vodokhranilishche resr Rus. Fed.
123 E5 Saravan Iran
96 D4 Saravan Laos
97 B4 Sarawa r. Myanmar
95 E2 Sarawak state Malaysia
129 F3 Saray Azer.
126 B2 Saray Turkey
206 C3 Saraya Senegal
199 F2 Saraycık Turkey
199 F3 Sarayköy Turkey
199 E1 Saraylar Turkey
126 D3 Sarayönü Turkey
123 E5 Sarbāz Iran
123 E5 Sarbāz r. Iran
197 G3 Sârbeni Romania
177 L4 Sârbi Romania
122 D3 Sarbīsheh Iran
177 H5 Sárbogárd Hungary
106 A2 Sarbulak Xinjiang China
191 F3 Sarca r. Italy
178 B4 Sarca di Genova r. Italy
156 C4 Sarcelles France
122 B2 Sarcham Iran
129 D3 Sarch'apet Armenia
111 C6 Sarda r. India/Nepal
116 E3 Sarda r. Nepal
192 A5 Sardara Sardegna Italy
116 C5 Sardarpur Madh. Prad. India
116 C3 Sardarshahr Rajasthan India
122 A2 Sar Dasht Iran
122 B4 Sardasht Būshehr Iran
122 B3 Sardasht Khūzestān Iran
192 B4 Sardegna admin. reg. Italy
192 A4 Sardegna i. Italy

Seaman Range to Shafter 361

241 J3 Seaman Range mts NV U.S.A.
149 I3 Seamer North Yorkshire, England U.K.
148 E2 Seamill North Ayrshire, Scotland U.K.
182 B3 Seara Port.
241 J4 Searchlight NV U.S.A.
237 F5 Searcy AR U.S.A.
233 □I2 Searsport ME U.S.A.
149 F3 Seascale Cumbria, England U.K.
240 G3 Seaside CA U.S.A.
238 B2 Seaside OR U.S.A.
235 D3 Seaside Park NJ U.S.A.
149 F3 Seaton Cumbria, England U.K.
150 D4 Seaton Devon, England U.K.
149 H2 Seaton Delaval Northumberland, England U.K.
149 H2 Seaton Sluice Northumberland, England U.K.
238 B2 Seattle WA U.S.A.
222 B2 Seattle, Mount Can./U.S.A.
215 E6 Sea View S. Africa
151 F4 Seaview Isle of Wight, England U.K.
85 F3 Seaview Range mts Qld Austr.
234 D3 Seaville NJ U.S.A.
81 D5 Seaward Kaikoura Range mts South I. N.Z.
242 □I6 Sebaco Nic.
182 B4 Sebal Port.
Sebastea Turkey see Sivas
231 D7 Sebastian FL U.S.A.
261 F2 Sebastián Elcano Arg.
242 B2 Sebastián Vizcaíno, Bahía b. Mex.
233 □I2 Sebasticook r. ME U.S.A.
Sebastopol Ukr. see Sevastopol'
240 F2 Sebastopol CA U.S.A.
95 G1 Sebatik i. Indon.
95 E3 Sebayan, Bukit mt. Indon.
161 A4 Sébazac-Concourès France
207 F3 Sebba Burkina
142 C3 Sebbersund Denmark
205 E2 Sebdou Alg.
206 C3 Sébékoro Mali
126 C2 Seben Turkey
Sebenico Croatia see Šibenik
Sebennytos Egypt see Samannūd
197 F3 Sebeş Romania
197 F2 Sebeş r. Romania
177 J5 Sebes-Körös r. Hungary
227 F4 Sebewaing MI U.S.A.
138 G3 Sebezh Rus. Fed.
126 E2 Şebinkarahisar Turkey
197 F2 Sebiş Romania
139 K2 Sebla r. Rus. Fed.
94 C3 Seblat, Gunung mt. Indon.
171 F5 Sebnitz Ger.
233 □I2 Seboeis ME U.S.A.
232 E6 Sebrell VA U.S.A.
231 D7 Sebring FL U.S.A.
135 H6 Sebrovo Rus. Fed.
95 G3 Sebuku i. Indon.
95 G1 Sebuku r. Indon.
260 D5 Seca, Pampa plain Arg.
196 E3 Sečanj Vojvodina, Srbija Yugo.
182 B4 Secarias Port.
177 K6 Secaş Romania
197 F2 Secaş r. Romania
242 □J8 Secas, Islas is Panama
191 G3 Secchia r. Italy
175 H5 Secemin Pol.
222 F5 Sechelt B.C. Can.
135 I5 Sechenovo Rus. Fed.
250 A6 Sechura Peru
250 A6 Sechura, Bahía de b. Peru
172 D2 Seckach Ger.
179 F3 Seckau Austria
156 D2 Seclin France
186 D4 Seco r. Spain
207 F4 Second Cataract rapids Sudan
162 B2 Secondigny France
241 L4 Second Mesa AZ U.S.A.
234 B2 Second Mountain ridge PA U.S.A.
85 E2 Second Three Mile Opening sea chan. Qld Austr.
206 □ Secos, Ilhéus is Cape Verde
177 K3 Sečovce Slovakia
81 A6 Secretary Island South I. N.Z.
215 G2 Secunda S. Africa
114 C2 Secunderabad Andhra Prad. India
252 D3 Sécure r. Bol.
177 J5 Secusigiu Romania
138 E3 Seda Latvia
138 E3 Seda r. Latvia
138 D3 Seda Lith.
184 C1 Seda Port.
184 B2 Seda r. Port.
236 E4 Sedalia MO U.S.A.
114 C2 Sedam Karnataka India
82 D3 Sedan S.A. Austr.
157 E3 Sedan France
237 D4 Sedan KS U.S.A.
85 E3 Sedan Dip Qld Austr.
183 G2 Sedano Spain
149 G3 Sedbergh Cumbria, England U.K.
81 E4 Seddon South I. N.Z.
81 C4 Seddonville South I. N.Z.
122 C4 Sedeh Fārs Iran
122 D3 Sedeh Khorāsan Iran
161 D4 Séderon France
149 H3 Sedgefield Durham, England U.K.
223 I4 Sedgewick Alta Can.
150 E2 Sedgley West Midlands, England U.K.
233 □I2 Sedgwick ME U.S.A.
206 B3 Sédhiou Senegal
191 H2 Sedico Italy
192 A4 Sedilo Sardegna Italy
192 A4 Sedini Sardegna Italy
176 G6 Sedlarica Croatia
176 D2 Sedlčany Czech Rep.
176 D2 Sedlec Prčice Czech Rep.
Sedlets Pol. see Siedlce
177 K3 Sedlice Slovakia
171 F4 Sedlitz Ger.
171 F5 Sedlo hill Czech Rep.
136 C2 Sedlyshche Ukr.
241 L4 Sedona AZ U.S.A.
Sedovo Ukr. see Syedove
205 G1 Sédrata Alg.
190 E3 Sedrina Italy
138 D4 Šeduva Lith.
175 H4 Sędziejowice Pol.
174 G3 Sędzin Pol.
175 I5 Sędziszów Pol.
175 J5 Sędziszów Małopolski Pol.
178 B3 See Austria
159 E3 Sée r. France
172 C3 Seebach Baden-Württemberg Ger.
169 F5 Seebach Thüringen Ger.
170 F2 Seebad Ahlbeck Ger.
170 F2 Seebad Bansin Ger.
170 F2 Seebad Heringsdorf Ger.
169 F5 Seebergen Ger.
179 E4 Seeboden Austria
173 G4 Seebruck Ger.
169 F4 Seeburg Ger.
168 F1 Seedorf Schleswig-Holstein Ger.
168 F2 Seedorf Schleswig-Holstein Ger.
173 F3 Seefeld Bayern Ger.
170 E3 Seefeld Brandenburg Ger.
168 D2 Seefeld (Stadland) Ger.
178 C3 Seefeld in Tirol Austria
147 D4 Seefin hill Rep. of Ireland
173 E4 Seeg Ger.
171 D4 Seegrehna Ger.
170 E2 Seehausen Brandenburg Ger.
171 C3 Seehausen Sachsen-Anhalt Ger.
170 C3 Seehausen (Altmark) Ger.
173 F4 Seehausen am Staffelsee Ger.
172 C2 Seeheim-Jugenheim Ger.
178 E3 Seekirchen am Wallersee Austria
214 D5 Seekoegat S. Africa
215 E4 Seekoei r. S. Africa
172 B3 Seelbach Ger.
241 J5 Seeley CA U.S.A.
262 R1 Seelig, Mount Antarctica
171 D5 Seelingstädt Ger.
170 F3 Seelow Ger.
169 E3 Seelze Ger.
Seenu Atoll Maldives see Addu Atoll
173 G4 Seeon Ger.
190 D1 Seerücken val. Switz.
159 G3 Sées France
169 F4 Seesen Ger.
173 F4 Seeshaupt Ger.
168 F2 Seevetal Ger.
179 E3 Seewalchen am Attersee Austria
160 E3 Séez France
206 C4 Sefadu Sierra Leone
199 E2 Seferihisar Turkey
206 C3 Séféto Mali
122 B3 Sefid, Kūh-e mt. Iran
214 E4 Sefophe Botswana
204 D2 Sefrou Morocco
81 C5 Sefton, Mount South I. N.Z.
206 C3 Ségala Mali
141 J3 Segalstad Norway
95 G1 Segama r. Sabah Malaysia
95 G2 Segamat Malaysia
190 E5 Segangane Morocco
197 F3 Şegarcea Romania
207 F4 Ségbana Benin
176 G5 Segesd Hungary
134 F3 Segezha Rus. Fed.
192 D2 Seggiano Italy
158 C3 Séglien France
193 F3 Segni Italy
Segontia Gwynedd, Wales U.K. see Caernarfon
Segontium Gwynedd, Wales U.K. see Caernarfon
162 B3 Segonzac France
187 C5 Segorbe Spain
206 D3 Ségou Mali
206 D3 Ségou admin. reg. Mali
250 C3 Segovia Col.
Segovia r. Hond./Nic. see Coco
183 F4 Segovia Spain
183 F3 Segovia prov. Castilla y León Spain
134 F3 Segozerskoye, Ozero resr Rus. Fed.
159 F4 Segré France
186 D3 Segre r. Spain
159 G3 Ségrie France
206 D5 Séguéla Côte d'Ivoire
206 D5 Séguélon Côte d'Ivoire
206 E3 Séguénéga Burkina
261 G3 Seguí Arg.
237 D6 Seguin TX U.S.A.
261 F2 Segundo r. Arg.
161 A4 Ségur France
182 D5 Segura Port.
185 I2 Segura r. Spain
185 H3 Segura, Sierra de mts Spain
185 H2 Segura de la Sierra Spain
184 D2 Segura de León Spain
186 C4 Segura de los Baños Spain
183 E3 Segurilla Spain
212 D4 Sehithwa Botswana
169 F3 Sehlde Ger.
169 E3 Sehnde Ger.
116 D5 Sehore Madh. Prad. India
123 F5 Sehwan Pak.
162 C4 Seia Port.
236 C4 Seibert CO U.S.A.
158 E4 Seiche r. France
159 F4 Seiches-sur-le-Loir France
179 G3 Seiersberg Austria
142 D1 Seierstad Norway
171 F5 Seifhennersdorf Ger.
150 E2 Seighford Staffordshire, England U.K.
161 A4 Seigne, Mont mt. France
225 G3 Seignelay r. Que. Can.
156 D5 Seignelay France
190 B1 Seignelégier Switz.
163 A5 Seignosse France
96 A2 Seikpyu Myanmar
146 C5 Seil i. Scotland U.K.
140 M1 Seiland i. Norway
162 D3 Seilhac France
237 D4 Seiling OK U.S.A.
161 E5 Seillans France
160 C2 Seille r. France
157 G3 Seille r. France
165 E4 Seilles Belgium
138 D4 Šeimena r. Lith.
140 M3 Seinäjoki Fin.
224 B3 Seine r. Ont. Can.
156 A3 Seine r. France
159 F2 Seine, Baie de b. France
160 C1 Seine, Sources de la tourist site France
156 D4 Seine, Val de val. France
156 D4 Seine-et-Marne dept Île-de-France France
Seine-Inférieure dept Haute-Normandie France see Seine-Maritime
156 A3 Seine-Maritime dept Haute-Normandie France
159 I3 Seine-St-Denis dept France
197 F2 Seini Romania
173 E2 Seinsheim Ger.
186 D2 Seira Spain
163 C5 Seissan France
179 F2 Seitenstetten Austria
177 J5 Şeitin Romania
163 D6 Seix France
184 □ Seixal Madeira
184 A2 Seixal Port.
182 B3 Seixas Port.
184 B3 Seixe r. Port.
182 C4 Seixo da Beira Port.
142 D4 Sejerby Denmark
142 D4 Sejerø i. Denmark
142 D4 Sejerø Bugt b. Denmark
175 L1 Sejny Pol.
94 C3 Sekayu Sumatera Indon.
177 K3 Sekčov r. Slovakia
Seke Sichuan China see Sêrtar
209 B6 Seke-Banza Dem. Rep. Congo
104 C3 Seki Japan
199 F3 Seki Turkey
199 F3 Seki r. Turkey
102 □1 Sekibi-sho i. Japan
94 D4 Sekicau, Gunung vol. Indon.
104 C2 Sekidō-san hill Japan
206 E5 Sekondi Ghana
210 C1 Sek'ot'a Eth.
175 J6 Sękowa Pol.
Sekseuil Kazakh. see Saksaul'skiy
123 E4 Sekūheh Iran
Sela Rus. Fed. see Shali
94 C3 Selagan r. Indon.
238 B2 Selah WA U.S.A.
94 C2 Selangor state Malaysia
192 B5 Selargius Sardegna Italy
94 C2 Selatpanjang Sumatera Indon.
150 D2 Selattyn Shropshire, England U.K.
220 B3 Selawik AK U.S.A.
183 G1 Selaya Spain
171 D5 Selb Ger.
178 D3 Selbhorn mt. Austria
171 C5 Selbitz Ger.
140 J3 Selbu Norway
149 H4 Selby North Yorkshire, England U.K.
236 C2 Selby SD U.S.A.
233 F5 Selbyville DE U.S.A.
191 J3 Selce Croatia
199 E3 Selçuk Turkey
236 C4 Selden KS U.S.A.
220 C4 Seldovia AK U.S.A.
193 G4 Sele r. Italy
213 E4 Selebi-Phikwe Botswana
Selebi-Pikwe Botswana see Selebi-Phikwe
197 E5 Selečka Planina mts Macedonia
192 B5 Selegas Sardegna Italy
192 B4 S'Elema r. Sardegna Italy
100 D1 Selemdzha r. Rus. Fed.
199 F2 Selendi Turkey
106 E1 Selenduma Rus. Fed.
106 E1 Selenga r. Rus. Fed.
106 E1 Selenge prov. Mongolia
106 E1 Selenge Mörön r. Mongolia
198 A1 Selenicë Albania
168 F1 Selent Ger.
168 F1 Selenter See l. Ger.
157 H4 Sélestat France
121 H1 Seletinskoye Kazakh.
Selety r. Kazakh. see Sileti
Seletyteniz, Oz. salt l. Kazakh. see Siletiteniz, Ozero
Seleucia Turkey see Silifke
Seleucia Pieria Turkey see Samandağı
177 K5 Seleuș Romania
138 G1 Seleznevo Rus. Fed.
140 □B3 Selfoss Iceland
236 C2 Selfridge ND U.S.A.
206 B3 Sélibabi Maur.
Selidovo Ukr. see Selydove
169 D5 Seligenstadt Ger.
139 I3 Seliger, Ozero l. Rus. Fed.
241 K4 Seligman AZ U.S.A.
129 C3 Selim Turkey
203 F4 Selima Oasis Sudan
199 E3 Selimiye Turkey
206 C4 Sélingué, Lac de l. Mali
206 C3 Selinnkegni Mali
198 C2 Selinous r. Greece
234 B2 Selinsgrove PA U.S.A.
139 I3 Selishche Rus. Fed.
135 H5 Selishchi Rus. Fed.
120 A3 Selitrennoye Rus. Fed.
139 I3 Selizharovo Rus. Fed.
141 I3 Selje Norway
142 C2 Seljord Norway
171 C4 Selke r. Ger.
223 L5 Selkirk Man. Can.
146 F6 Selkirk Scottish Borders, Scotland U.K.
222 G4 Selkirk Mountains B.C. Can.
Selkovski Rus. Fed. see Shelkovskaya
187 C6 Sella Spain
183 E1 Sella r. Spain
149 F3 Sellafield Cumbria, England U.K.
146 □G1 Sellafirth Shetland, Scotland U.K.
193 E2 Sellano Italy
234 C2 Sellersville PA U.S.A.
162 D1 Selles-St-Denis France
159 H4 Selles-sur-Cher France
85 F4 Sellheim r. Qld Austr.
195 F4 Sellia Marina Italy
160 D2 Sellières France
151 H3 Sellindge Kent, England U.K.
164 G2 Sellingen Neth.
Sellore Island Myanmar see Saganthit Kyun
178 C3 Sellrain Austria
241 L6 Sells AZ U.S.A.
177 G6 Sellye Hungary
169 C4 Selm Ger.
231 C5 Selma AL U.S.A.
240 H3 Selma CA U.S.A.
237 F5 Selmer TN U.S.A.
184 C2 Selmes Port.
182 D2 Selmo r. Spain
168 F2 Selmsdorf Ger.
156 B5 Selommes France
95 G5 Selong Lombok Indon.
160 D1 Selongey France
161 E4 Selonnet France
215 G1 Selonsrivier S. Africa
206 C4 Selouma Guinea
222 C2 Selous, Mount Y.T. Can.
170 C2 Selow Ger.
122 E4 Selseleh-ye Pīr Shūrān mts Iran
151 G4 Selsey West Sussex, England U.K.
151 G4 Selsey Bill hd England U.K.
168 E2 Selsingen Ger.
169 C5 Selters (Westerwald) Ger.
139 J5 Sel'tso Rus. Fed.
134 K4 Selty Rus. Fed.
157 I4 Seltz France
Selukwe Zimbabwe see Shurugwi
159 E3 Sélune r. France
195 G2 Selva Italy
187 D4 Selva Spain
186 B2 Selva r. Spain
191 G2 Selva dei Molini Italy
191 G3 Selva di Progno Italy
178 C4 Selva di Val Gardena Italy
204 B3 Selvagens, Ilhas is Madeira
127 G3 Selvānā Iran
260 A6 Selva Obscura Chile
250 D6 Selvas reg. Brazil
191 G3 Selvazzano Dentro Italy
190 E3 Selvino Italy
238 D2 Selway r. ID U.S.A.
223 J2 Selwyn Lake N.W.T./Sask. Can.
222 D1 Selwyn Mountains N.W.T./Y.T. Can.
84 D4 Selwyn Range hills Qld Austr.
136 C4 Selyatyn Ukr.
137 I3 Selydove Ukr.
172 C2 Selz r. Ger.
179 F3 Selzthal Austria
163 E5 Sémalens France
198 A1 Seman r. Albania
95 E4 Semarang Jawa Tengah Indon.
161 B3 Sembadel France
95 G2 Sembakung r. Indon.
208 B4 Sembé Congo
159 G4 Semblançay France
190 C2 Sembrancher Switz.
127 G3 Şemdinli Turkey
163 C5 Séméac France
160 B2 Sémelay France
Semendire Srbija Yugo. see Smederevo
197 F3 Semenic, Vârful mt. Romania
137 G1 Semenivka Chernihivs'ka Oblast' Ukr.
137 I3 Semenivka Kharkivs'ka Oblast' Ukr.
137 F2 Semenivka Kyivs'ka Oblast' Ukr.
137 G3 Semenivka Poltavs'ka Oblast' Ukr.
120 C1 Semenkino Rus. Fed.
137 K2 Semeno-Aleksandrovka Rus. Fed.
134 I4 Semenov Rus. Fed.
Semenovka Chernihivs'ka Oblast' Ukr. see Semenivka
94 F5 Semeru, Gunung vol. Indon.
Semey Kazakh. see Semipalatinsk
124 B5 Semhar prov. Eritrea
137 J4 Semibalki Rus. Fed.
139 L3 Semibratovo Rus. Fed.
182 B4 Semide Port.
137 J2 Semidesyatnoye Rus. Fed.
134 H4 Semigorodnyaya Rus. Fed.
135 H7 Semikarakorsk Rus. Fed.
135 G6 Semiluki Rus. Fed.
176 E1 Semily Czech Rep.
193 F4 Seminara Italy
160 D2 Semine r. France
237 C5 Seminole TX U.S.A.
121 K2 Seminskiy Khrebet mts Rus. Fed.
120 F1 Semiozernoye Kazakh.
121 J2 Semipalatinsk Kazakh.
121 F1 Semipolka Kazakh.
92 B4 Semirara Islands Phil.
95 E2 Semitau Kalimantan Barat Indon.
121 I2 Semiyarka Kazakh.
121 H2 Semizbuga Kazakh.
Semizbughy Kazakh. see Semizbuga
139 L3 Semkhoz Rus. Fed.
Sem Kolodezey Respublika Krym Ukr. see Lenine
196 E2 Semlac Romania
139 I4 Semlevo Rus. Fed.
208 F4 Semliki r. Dem. Rep. Congo/Uganda
170 D1 Semlow Ger.
169 F3 Semmenstedt Ger.
122 C3 Semnān Iran
122 B3 Semnān prov. Iran
106 D4 Sêmnyi Qinghai China
165 D5 Semois r. Belgium
165 D5 Semois, Vallée de la val. Belgium/France
157 F4 Semoutiers-Montsaon France
190 D1 Sempach Switz.
179 E5 Šempeter Slovenia
192 D2 Semproniano Italy
173 F3 Sempt r. Ger.
179 G3 Semriach Austria
139 I5 Semtsy Rus. Fed.
160 C1 Semur-en-Auxois France
160 C2 Semur-en-Brionnais France
162 B3 Semussac France
Semyonovskoye Arkhangel'skaya Oblast' Rus. Fed. see Bereznik
Semyonovskoye Kostromskaya Oblast' Rus. Fed. see Ostrovskoye
97 D4 Sên, Stœng r. Cambodia
252 D2 Sena Bol.
177 K3 Seňa Slovakia
186 C3 Sena Spain
256 C2 Senador Canedo Brazil
254 F3 Senador Pompeu Brazil
203 H6 Senafe Eritrea
191 G2 Senaiga r. Italy
129 C2 Senaki Georgia
195 F4 Senales Italy
192 B4 Senalonga, Punta mt. Sardegna Italy
252 C2 Sena Madureira Brazil
209 D9 Senanga Zambia
156 B3 Senarpont France
161 D5 Sénas France
237 F5 Senatobia MS U.S.A.
Sencelles Spain see Sancellas
137 G2 Sencha Ukr.
179 F4 Šenčur Slovenia
103 E8 Sendai Kagoshima Japan
102 J4 Sendai Miyagi Japan
103 E8 Sendai-gawa r. Japan
215 F2 Sendelingsfontein S. Africa
173 E3 Senden Bayern Ger.
169 C4 Senden Nordrhein-Westfalen Ger.
169 C4 Sendenhorst Ger.
182 D3 Sendim Bragança Port.
182 B3 Sendim Porto Port.
Sêndo Xizang China see Chido
197 H3 Şendreni Romania
158 D4 Séné France
206 E5 Sene r. Ghana
176 G3 Senec Slovakia
226 C5 Seneca IL U.S.A.
236 D4 Seneca KS U.S.A.
238 C2 Seneca OR U.S.A.
232 D4 Seneca PA U.S.A.
232 D5 Seneca Rocks WV U.S.A.
165 D4 Seneffe Belgium
206 B3 Sénégal country Africa
206 A2 Sénégal r. Maur./Senegal
192 A4 Seneghe Sardegna Italy
215 F3 Senekal S. Africa
185 H3 Senés Spain
192 B4 Senes, Monte hill Sardegna Italy
226 E2 Seney MI U.S.A.
161 E5 Senez France
179 G2 Senftenberg Austria
171 F4 Senftenberg Ger.
211 B8 Senga Malawi
116 D4 Sengar r. India
172 D3 Sengenthal Ger.
211 B5 Sengerema Tanz.
256 C6 Sengés Brazil
135 J5 Sengiley Rus. Fed.
Sengirli, Mys pt Kazakh. see Syngyrli, Mys
163 C6 Sengouagnet France
259 C7 Senguerr r. Arg.
213 F3 Sengwa r. Zimbabwe
124 B5 Senhit prov. Eritrea
184 C1 Senhora do Rosário Port.
254 E4 Senhor do Bonfim Brazil
176 G3 Senica Slovakia
176 G2 Senice na Hané Czech Rep.
191 I5 Senigallia Italy
191 H4 Senio r. Italy
199 G2 Senirkent Turkey
192 A5 Senis Sardegna Italy
193 I4 Senise Italy
188 E3 Senj Croatia
140 L1 Senja i. Norway
104 B4 Senjōga-dake mt. Japan
105 E3 Senjōga-dake mt. Japan
127 F2 Şenkaya Turkey
206 C4 Senko Guinea
209 E9 Senkobo Zambia
137 I3 Sen'kove Ukr.
128 C1 Şenköy Turkey
116 D2 Senku Jammu and Kashmir
214 D1 Senlac S. Africa
100 D4 Senlin Shan mt. Jilin China
156 C3 Senlis France
97 D4 Senmonorom Cambodia
203 G6 Sennar Sudan
203 G6 Sennar state Sudan
192 A4 Sennariolo Sardegna Italy
160 C2 Sennecey-le-Grand France
160 D1 Sennecey-lès-Dijon France
150 □ Sennen Cornwall, England U.K.
224 E3 Senneterre Que. Can.
171 C4 Sennewitz Ger.
Senno Belarus see Syanno
105 E2 Sennokura-yama mt. Japan
192 A4 Sennori Sardegna Italy
190 E1 Sennwald Switz.
150 D3 Sennybridge Powys, Wales U.K.
156 B4 Senonches France
157 G4 Senones France
192 B3 Senorbì Sardegna Italy
163 D5 Senouillac France
161 B3 Senouire r. France
179 G4 Senovo Slovenia
215 F4 Senqu r. Lesotho
156 D4 Sens France
158 E3 Sens-de-Bretagne France
156 D2 Sensée r. France
242 □H6 Sensuntepeque El Salvador
196 E3 Senta Vojvodina, Srbija Yugo.
163 C6 Sentein France
163 D4 Sentenac-d'Oust France
186 D2 Senterada Spain
179 G4 Šentilj Slovenia
241 K5 Sentinel AZ U.S.A.
193 G3 Sentinella, Colle della hill Italy
222 F4 Sentinel Peak B.C. Can.
262 S1 Sentinel Range mts Antarctica
Sentinum Italy see Sassoferrato
179 G5 Šentjernej Slovenia
179 G4 Šentjur pri Celju Slovenia
94 □ Sentosa i. Sing.
157 E3 Senuc France
177 K4 Senyő Hungary
129 B3 Senyurt Erzurum Turkey
127 F3 Şenyurt Turkey
171 E3 Senzig Ger.
Seo de Urgell Spain see La Seu d'Urgell
190 D1 Seon Switz.
116 E5 Seonath r. India
116 D4 Seondha Madh. Prad. India
116 D5 Seoni Madh. Prad. India
116 D5 Seoni Chhapara Madh. Prad. India
116 D5 Seoni-Malwa Madh. Prad. India
Seoul S. Korea see Sŏul
163 C4 Séoune r. France
86 D4 Separation Well W.A. Austr.
122 A3 Separ Shāhābād Iran
252 D3 Sepatini r. Brazil
257 E5 Sepetiba, Baía de b. Brazil
91 J7 Sepik r. P.N.G.
95 F2 Seping r. Sarawak Malaysia
193 G3 Sepino Italy
101 C5 Sepo N. Korea
174 F2 Sępólno Krajeńskie Pol.
117 H4 Sepon Assam India
253 F3 Sepotuba r. Brazil
117 H4 Seppa Arun. Prad. India
160 F1 Seppois-le-Bas France
197 E2 Şepreuş Romania
161 D5 Septèmes-les-Vallons France
156 B4 Septeuil France
163 D4 Septfonds France
225 H3 Sept-Îles Que. Can.
160 D2 Septmoncel France
182 D3 Sepulcro-Hilario Spain
183 G3 Sepúlveda Spain
94 D4 Seputih r. Indon.
191 H2 Sequals Italy
231 C5 Sequatchie r. TN U.S.A.
182 D3 Sequeros Spain
183 E3 Sequillo r. Spain
124 B4 Serae prov. Eritrea
129 B3 Şerafettin Dağları mts Turkey
135 H6 Serafimovich Rus. Fed.
156 E3 Seraincourt France
165 E4 Seraing Belgium
Sêraitang Qinghai China see Baima
93 D3 Seram i. Maluku Indon.
93 D3 Seram Sea Indon.
160 D3 Séran r. France
94 D4 Serang Jawa Barat Indon.
161 E5 Séranon France
95 E2 Serasan, Selat sea chan. Indon.
190 F5 Seravezza Italy
128 A5 Serbâl, Gebel mt. Egypt
Serbia aut. rep. Yugo. see Srbija
136 D3 Serbynivtsi Ukr.
111 F6 Sêrca Xizang China
191 F5 Serchio r. Italy
192 B5 Serdiana Sardegna Italy
Serdica Bulg. see Sofiya
135 I5 Serdoba r. Rus. Fed.
135 I5 Serdobsk Rus. Fed.
121 J2 Serebryansk Kazakh.
139 L4 Serebryanyye Prudy Rus. Fed.
177 G3 Sereď Slovakia
139 M3 Sereda Rus. Fed.
139 J4 Seredeyskiy Rus. Fed.
138 G2 Seredka Rus. Fed.
136 F4 Seredniy Kuyal'nyk r. Ukr.
206 C4 Sérédou Guinea
137 H1 Seredyna-Buda Rus. Fed.
136 B3 Seredyne Ukr.
126 D3 Şereflikoçhisar Turkey
177 H4 Seregélyes Hungary
190 E3 Seregno Italy
162 D3 Séreilhac France
156 D5 Serein r. France
94 C2 Seremban Malaysia
211 B5 Serengeti National Park Tanz.
211 B5 Serengeti Plain Tanz.
209 F8 Serenje Zambia
158 D4 Sérent France
210 B4 Serere Uganda
136 C3 Seret r. Ukr.
134 H5 Serezha r. Rus. Fed.
139 H3 Serezha r. Rus. Fed.
178 B3 Serfaus Austria
134 L4 Ser'ga Rus. Fed.
134 I5 Sergach Rus. Fed.
107 F2 Sergelen Mongolia
197 H5 Sergen Turkey
121 G2 Sergeyevka Akmolinskaya Oblast' Kazakh.
121 F1 Sergeyevka Severnyy Kazakhstan Kazakh.
137 J2 Sergeyevka Rus. Fed.
156 D4 Sergines France
130 H3 Sergino Rus. Fed.
254 F4 Sergipe state Brazil
139 L3 Sergiyev Posad Rus. Fed.
135 J5 Sergiyevsk Rus. Fed.
Sergiyevskiy Rus. Fed. see Fakel
190 E3 Sergnano Italy
Sergo Ukr. see Stakhanov
129 E2 Sergokala Rus. Fed.
137 G2 Serhiyivka Chernihivs'ka Oblast' Ukr.
137 H4 Serhiyivka Khersons'ka Oblast' Ukr.
136 F4 Serhiyivka Odes'ka Oblast' Ukr.
95 F1 Seria Brunei
190 E3 Seriate Italy
156 B3 Sérifontaine France
198 D3 Serifos i. Greece
161 B5 Sérignan France
161 C4 Sérignan-du-Comtat France
225 G2 Sérigny r. Que. Can.
199 G3 Serik Turkey
190 E3 Serina Italy
213 □J3 Sèrinama Madag.
251 I6 Seringa, Serra da hills Brazil
86 D2 Seringapatam Reef W.A. Austr.
199 F3 Serinhisar Turkey
129 B4 Serinova Turkey
128 C1 Serinyol Turkey
190 E3 Serio r. Italy
Sêrkang Xizang China see Nyainrong
136 C2 Serkhiv Ukr.
205 G5 Serkout mt. Alg.
Serle atoll Arch. des Tuamotu Fr. Polynesia see Pukarua
156 C4 Sermaises France
157 E4 Sermaize-les-Bains France
192 B2 Sermano Corse France
197 F5 Sermenin Macedonia
191 G4 Sermide Italy
160 B2 Sermoise-sur-Loire France
193 F3 Sermoneta Italy
160 C2 Sermoyer France
182 C4 Sernancelhe Port.
177 L3 Serne r. Ukr.
175 K4 Serniki Pol.
171 D4 Serno Ger.
135 J5 Sernovodsk Rus. Fed.
134 J4 Sernur Rus. Fed.
136 D2 Sernyky Ukr.
174 G2 Serock Kujawsko-Pomorskie Pol.
175 J3 Serock Mazowieckie Pol.
261 G3 Serodino Arg.
185 H3 Serón Spain
183 H3 Serón de Nájima Spain
164 C3 Serooskerke Neth.
186 D3 Seròs Spain
130 H4 Serov Rus. Fed.
212 E4 Serowe Botswana
184 C3 Serpa Port.
Serpa Pinto Angola see Menongue
225 G3 Serpent r. Que. Can.
87 B7 Serpentine r. W.A. Austr.
82 B2 Serpentine Lakes salt flat S.A. Austr.
247 G5 Serpent's Mouth sea chan. Trin. and Tob./Venez.
182 B4 Serpins Port.
187 C6 Serpis r. Spain
136 E4 Serpneve Ukr.
139 K4 Serpukhov Rus. Fed.
157 F5 Serqueux France
159 G2 Serquigny France
257 G4 Serra Brazil
192 A4 Serra r. Sardegna Italy
187 C5 Serra Spain
193 H3 Serracapriola Italy
183 F3 Serrada Spain
191 I5 Serra de'Conti Italy
182 B2 Serra de Outes Spain
216 □1a Serra de Santa Barbara vol. Terceira Azores
194 C5 Serradifalco Sicilia Italy
192 A3 Serra-di-Ferro Corse France
182 D5 Serradilla Spain
182 D4 Serradilla del Arroyo Spain
257 G2 Serra dos Aimorés Brazil
256 D3 Serra do Salitre Brazil
Sérrai Greece see Serres
192 A5 Serramanna Sardegna Italy
191 F4 Serramazzoni Italy
256 D4 Serrana Brazil
246 C4 Serranilla Bank sea feature Caribbean Sea
183 F4 Serranillos Spain
256 A3 Serranópolis Brazil
190 D4 Serra Riccò Italy
195 F4 Serra San Bruno Italy
191 I5 Serra San Quirico Italy
254 F3 Serra Talhada Brazil
191 H5 Serravalle San Marino
193 E1 Serravalle di Chienti Italy
190 D4 Serravalle Scrivia Italy
156 D3 Serre r. France
193 H4 Serre Italy
161 E4 Serre-Chevalier France
182 E5 Serrejón Spain
192 A5 Serrenti Sardegna Italy
Serrera, Pic de la mt. Andorra see Serrère, Pic de
186 E2 Serrère, Pic de mt. Andorra
161 D4 Serres France
198 C1 Serres Greece
163 B5 Serres-Castet France
216 □1a Serreta Terceira Azores
192 B5 Serri Sardegna Italy
192 A2 Serriera Corse France
160 D3 Serrière-de-Briord France
161 C3 Serrières France
172 A2 Serrig Ger.
254 F4 Serrinha Brazil
254 F3 Serrita Brazil
257 F3 Sêrro Brazil
183 E4 Serrota mt. Spain
162 C3 Sers France
195 F3 Sersale Italy
182 B5 Sertã Port.
254 F4 Sertânia Brazil
256 B5 Sertanópolis Brazil
256 A3 Sertão de Camapuã reg. Brazil
256 D4 Sertãozinho Brazil
108 B1 Sêrtar Sichuan China
139 H1 Sertolovo Rus. Fed.
93 D4 Serua vol. Maluku Indon.
213 E4 Serule Botswana
95 F3 Seruyan r. Indon.
138 F4 Servach r. Belarus
157 G5 Servance France
161 B4 Serverette France
198 C1 Servia Greece
161 B5 Servian France
193 F1 Servigliano Italy
186 D4 Servol r. Spain
158 E3 Servon-sur-Vilaine France
160 E3 Servoz France
108 A1 Sêrxu Sichuan China
156 E3 Sery France
186 C3 Sesa Spain
95 G2 Sesayap r. Indon.
227 G1 Sesekinika Ont. Can.
Sesel country Indian Ocean see Seychelles
183 G4 Seseña Spain
212 B3 Sesfontein Namibia
114 C3 Seshachalam Hills India
209 E9 Sesheke Zambia
190 D3 Sesia r. Italy
184 A2 Sesimbra Port.
183 H2 Sesma Spain
209 D8 Sessa Angola
193 F3 Sessa Aurunca Italy
193 H4 Sessa Cilento Italy
187 G5 Ses Salines Spain
190 D3 Sessera r. Italy
169 F5 Seßlach Ger.
190 E4 Sesta Godano Italy
183 H1 Sestao Spain
191 H5 Sestino Italy
191 H2 Sesto Italy
191 H3 Sesto al Reghena Italy
190 D3 Sesto Calende Italy
193 G3 Sesto Campano Italy
191 G5 Sesto Fiorentino Italy
191 F4 Sestola Italy
190 E3 Sesto San Giovanni Italy
139 K3 Sestra r. Rus. Fed.
190 B4 Sestriere Italy
190 E4 Sestri Levante Italy
138 G1 Sestroretsk Rus. Fed.
188 E3 Sestrunj i. Croatia
192 B5 Sestu Sardegna Italy
138 D4 Šešupė r. Lith./Rus. Fed.
188 F3 Sesvete Croatia
186 D3 Set r. Spain
96 D4 Set, Phou mt. Laos
235 E2 Setauket NY U.S.A.
161 B5 Sète France
256 D6 Sete Barras Brazil
138 E4 Šetekšna r. Lith.
257 E3 Sete Lagoas Brazil
185 E4 Setenil Spain
140 L1 Setermoen Norway
142 B2 Setesdal val. Norway
102 □1 Seteuchi Japan
168 F2 Seth Ger.
Seti Georgia see Mestia
116 E3 Seti r. Nepal
117 F4 Seti r. Nepal
Setia Italy see Sezze
205 G1 Sétif Alg.
183 I4 Setiles Spain
203 G6 Setit r. Africa
104 D3 Seto Japan
103 F7 Seto-naikai sea Japan
191 G4 Setta r. Italy
204 D2 Settat Morocco
208 A5 Setté Cama Gabon
192 B5 Sette Fratelli, Monte dei mt. Sardegna Italy
190 D4 Settepani, Monte mt. Italy
190 C3 Settimo Torinese Italy
190 C3 Settimo Vittone Italy
149 G3 Settle North Yorkshire, England U.K.
84 D3 Settlement Creek r. Qld Austr.
216 □2c Settlement of Edinburgh Tristan da Cunha S. Atlantic Ocean
257 F2 Setúbal r. Brazil
184 B2 Setúbal Port.
184 B2 Setúbal admin. dist. Port.
184 A2 Setúbal, Baía de b. Port.
257 F2 Setubinha Brazil
Seu i. Vanuatu see Hiu
173 F2 Seubersdorf in der Oberpfalz Ger.
162 B3 Seudre r. France
162 B3 Seugne r. France
192 B5 Seui Sardegna Italy
157 F4 Seuil-d'Argonne France
223 M5 Seul, Lac l. Ont. Can.
169 F4 Seulingen Ger.
159 F2 Seulles r. France
192 B5 Seulo Sardegna Italy
160 D1 Seurre France
137 H1 Sev r. Rus. Fed.
186 F3 Seva Spain
129 D3 Sevan Armenia
Sevan, Lake Armenia see Sevana Lich
Sevan, Ozero l. Armenia see Sevana Lich
129 D3 Sevana Lich l. Armenia
137 G5 Sevastopol' Ukr.
149 I3 Seven r. England U.K.
Seven Islands Que. Can. see Sept-Îles
87 C4 Seven Mile Creek r. W.A. Austr.
215 H3 Sevenoaks S. Africa
151 H3 Sevenoaks Kent, England U.K.
150 D3 Seven Sisters Neath Port Talbot, Wales U.K.
85 G5 Seventeen Seventy Qld Austr.
Seventy Mile House B.C. Can. see 70 Mile House
165 F3 Sevenum Neth.
234 B3 Seven Valleys PA U.S.A.
182 C3 Sever Port.
161 B4 Sévérac-le-Château France
182 B4 Sever do Vouga Port.
139 L4 Severka r. Rus. Fed.
83 G2 Severn r. N.S.W. Austr.
224 C2 Severn r. Ont. Can.
81 D5 Severn mt. South I. N.Z.
214 D2 Severn S. Africa
150 E3 Severn r. England/Wales U.K.
234 B3 Severn MD U.S.A.
232 E6 Severn NC U.S.A.
234 B4 Severn r. MD U.S.A.
234 B3 Severna Park MD U.S.A.
134 H2 Severnaya Dvina r. Rus. Fed.
134 L3 Severnaya Mylva r. Rus. Fed.
129 D2 Severnaya Osetiya, Respublika aut. rep. Rus. Fed.
130 H3 Severnaya Sos'va r. Rus. Fed.
131 L1 Severnaya Zemlya is Rus. Fed.
150 E3 Severn Beach South Gloucestershire, England U.K.
135 K5 Severnoye Rus. Fed.
137 I2 Severnyy Belgorodskaya Oblast' Rus. Fed.
139 K3 Severnyy Moskovskaya Oblast' Rus. Fed.
134 N2 Severnyy Respublika Komi Rus. Fed.
175 H1 Severnyy, Mys pt Rus. Fed.
131 S3 Severnyy Anyuyskiy Khrebet mts Rus. Fed.
120 D3 Severnyy Chink Ustyurta esc. Kazakh.
121 G1 Severnyy Kazakhstan admin. div. Kazakh.
134 K4 Severnyy Kommunar Rus. Fed.
Severnyy Suchan Rus. Fed. see Uglekamensk
134 L3 Severnyy Ural mts Rus. Fed.
99 I1 Severobaykal'sk Rus. Fed.
131 M4 Severo-Baykalskoye Nagor'ye mts Rus. Fed.
110 D1 Severo-Chuyskiy Khrebet mts Rus. Fed.
Severodonetsk Ukr. see Syeverodonets'k
134 G2 Severodvinsk Arkhangel'skaya Oblast' Rus. Fed.
Severo-Kazakhstanskaya Oblast' admin. div. Kazakh. see Severnyy Kazakhstan
131 Q4 Severo-Kuril'sk Kuril'skiye O-va Rus. Fed.
140 P1 Severomorsk Rus. Fed.
134 G3 Severoonezhsk Rus. Fed.
Severo-Osetinskaya A.S.S.R. aut. rep. Rus. Fed. see Severnaya Osetiya, Respublika
131 L2 Severo-Sibirskaya Nizmennost' lowland Rus. Fed.
134 L3 Severoural'sk Rus. Fed.
131 K3 Severo-Yeniseyskiy Rus. Fed.
139 L4 Severo-Zadonsk Rus. Fed.
Seversk Ukr. see Sivers'k
135 G7 Severskaya Rus. Fed.
135 H7 Severskiy Donets r. Rus. Fed.
Severskiy Donets r. Ukr. see Sivers'kyy Donets'
158 E2 Sèves r. France
155 I4 Seveso Italy
190 E3 Seveso r. Italy
179 F1 Ševětín Czech Rep.
241 K2 Sevier UT U.S.A.
241 K2 Sevier r. UT U.S.A.
231 D5 Sevierville TN U.S.A.
158 D3 Sévignac France
163 B5 Sévignacq France
156 E3 Sévigny-Waleppe France
250 C3 Sevilla Col.
184 E3 Sevilla Spain
184 E3 Sevilla prov. Andalucía Spain
183 F4 Sevilla la Nueva Spain
Seville Spain see Sevilla
183 F5 Sevilleja de la Jara Spain
197 G4 Sevlievo Bulg.
Sevlyush Ukr. see Vynohradiv
188 E2 Sevnica Slovenia
196 D4 Sevojno Srbija Yugo.
162 A1 Sèvre Nantaise r. France
162 A2 Sèvre Niortaise r. France
160 E3 Sévrier France
160 D2 Sevron r. France
137 H1 Sevsk Rus. Fed.
114 B2 Sewand r. India
116 C3 Sewani Haryana India
220 D3 Seward AK U.S.A.
226 C4 Seward IL U.S.A.
236 D3 Seward NE U.S.A.
232 D4 Seward PA U.S.A.
262 T2 Seward Mountains Antarctica
220 B3 Seward Peninsula AK U.S.A.
260 B4 Sewell Chile
234 C3 Sewell NJ U.S.A.
222 C4 Sewell Inlet B.C. Can.
172 B3 Sexau Ger.
Sexi Spain see Almuñécar
222 G4 Sexsmith Alta Can.
242 D3 Sextín r. Mex.
123 E3 Seyah Band Koh mts Afgh.
243 H5 Seybaplaya Mex.
217 □2 Seychelles country Indian Ocean
163 C4 Seyches France
171 D4 Seyda Ger.
199 G2 Seydi r. Turkey
123 E2 Seydi Turkm.
126 C3 Seydişehir Turkey
158 E2 Seye r. France
Seyhan Turkey see Adana
126 D3 Seyhan r. Turkey
199 G2 Seyitgazi Turkey
199 F2 Seyitömer Turkey
137 I2 Seym Rus. Fed.
137 H2 Seym r. Rus. Fed./Ukr.
131 Q3 Seymchan Rus. Fed.
199 F1 Seymen Turkey
83 F4 Seymour Vic. Austr.
215 F5 Seymour S. Africa
235 E1 Seymour CT U.S.A.
230 C4 Seymour IN U.S.A.
237 D5 Seymour TX U.S.A.
84 C5 Seymour Range mts N.T. Austr.
161 E4 Seyne France
161 C4 Seynes France
160 E3 Seynod France
Seypan i. N. Mariana Is see Saipan
160 D3 Seyssel France
163 D5 Seysses France
160 C3 Seysseuel France
161 D3 Seyssins France
197 H5 Seytan r. Turkey
188 D3 Sežana Slovenia
156 D4 Sézanne France
215 H4 Sezela S. Africa
139 J4 Sezha r. Rus. Fed.
176 D2 Sezimovo Ústí Czech Rep.
193 F3 Sezze Italy
197 G3 Sfântu Gheorghe Romania
197 I3 Sfântu Gheorghe Romania
205 H2 Sfax Tunisia
198 C1 Sfendami Greece
198 C1 Sfikia, Limni resr Greece
Sfîntu Gheorghe Romania see Sfântu Gheorghe
Sgiersch Pol. see Zgierz
146 B3 Sgiogarstaigh Western Isles, Scotland U.K.
146 C4 Sgorr Ruadh hill Scotland U.K.
164 D3 's-Gravendeel Neth.
164 D2 's-Gravenhage Neth.
165 C3 's-Gravenpolder Neth.
165 E4 's-Gravenvoeren Belgium
164 D3 's-Gravenzande Neth.
193 F3 Sgurgola Italy
146 C4 Sgurr a'Chaorachain mt. Scotland U.K.
146 D4 Sgurr a'Choire Ghlais mt. Scotland U.K.
146 B4 Sgurr Alasdair hill Scotland U.K.
146 D4 Sgurr a'Mhuilinn hill Scotland U.K.
146 C5 Sgurr Dhomhnuill hill Scotland U.K.
146 C4 Sgurr Fhuaran mt. Scotland U.K.
146 C4 Sgurr Mor mt. Scotland U.K.
146 C4 Sgurr na Ciche mt. Scotland U.K.
107 G4 Sha r. China
107 F5 Shaanxi prov. China
Shaartuz Tajik. see Shahrtuz
Shaba admin. reg. Dem. Rep. Congo see Katanga
Shabani Zimbabwe see Zvishavane
Shabbaz Uzbek. see Beruni
210 E4 Shabeellaha Dhexe admin. reg. Somalia
210 D4 Shabeellaha Hoose admin. reg. Somalia
135 G7 Shabel'sk Rus. Fed.
122 A2 Shabestar Iran
197 I4 Shabla Bulg.
139 J5 Shablykino Rus. Fed.
208 E5 Shabunda Dem. Rep. Congo
124 D5 Shabwah Yemen
124 D5 Shabwah governorate Yemen
110 B4 Shache Xinjiang China
Shacheng Hebei China see Huailai
263 L1 Shackleton Coast Antarctica
262 V1 Shackleton Range mts Antarctica
123 F5 Shadadkot Pak.
108 D2 Shadaogou Hubei China
232 B5 Shade OH U.S.A.
122 B4 Shādegān Iran
234 C1 Shades Glen PA U.S.A.
130 H4 Shadrinsk Rus. Fed.
232 D5 Shadwell VA U.S.A.
238 B3 Shady Grove OR U.S.A.
234 B4 Shady Side MD U.S.A.
232 C6 Shady Spring WV U.S.A.
263 K2 Shafer Peak Antarctica
122 D2 Shafi'abad Iran
120 F4 Shafirkan Uzbek.
120 C1 Shafranovo Rus. Fed.
Shafrikan Uzbek. see Shafirkan
240 H4 Shafter CA U.S.A.

Shaftesbury to Sibsagar

362

150 E3 Shaftesbury Dorset, England U.K.
81 C6 Shag r. South I. N.Z.
224 C2 Shagamu r. Ont. Can.
Shagamu Nigeria see Sagamu
107 F4 Shagedu Nei Mongol China
220 C3 Shageluk AK U.S.A.
Shaghan Vostochnyy Kazakhstan Kazakh. see Chagan
Shaghyray Üstirti plat. Kazakh. see Shagyray, Plato
121 G1 Shaglyteniz, Ozero l. Kazakh.
249 G7 Shag Rocks is S. Georgia
120 D3 Shagyray, Plato plat. Kazakh.
114 C2 Shahabad Andhra Prad. India
116 D3 Shahabad Haryana India
114 C2 Shahabad Karnataka India
116 D3 Shahabad Rajasthan India
116 E4 Shahabad Uttar Prad. India
Shāhābād Iran see Showt
Shāhābād Iran see Eslāmābād-e Gharb
116 C5 Shahada Mahar. India
94 C2 Shah Alam Malaysia
114 B3 Shahapur Karnataka India
114 B2 Shahapur Mahar. India
128 C3 Shahbā' Syria
114 D2 Shahdād Iran
123 G5 Shahdadpur Pak.
116 E5 Shahdol Madh. Prad. India
Shahejie Jiangxi China see Jiujiang
Shahepu Gansu China see Linze
Shahezhen Gansu China see Linze
Shahezhen Jiangxi China see Jiujiang
123 F3 Shah Fuladi mt. Afgh.
117 E4 Shahganj Uttar Prad. India
116 D4 Shahgarh Madh. Prad. India
116 B4 Shahgarh Rajasthan India
202 D1 Shaḥḥāt Libya
Shāhīn Dezh Iran see Sa'īndezh
116 D4 Shahjahanpur Rajasthan India
116 D4 Shahjahanpur Uttar Prad. India
122 D2 Shāh Jehān, Kūh-e mts Iran
122 D4 Shāh Kūh mt. Iran
127 I4 Shahmīrzād Iran
114 C2 Shahpur Karnataka India
116 D5 Shahpur Madh. Prad. India
116 D5 Shahpur Madh. Prad. India
116 D5 Shahpur Madh. Prad. India
Shāhpūr Iran see Salmās
123 G4 Shahpur Balochistān Pak.
123 H3 Shahpur Punjab Pak.
123 G5 Shahpur Sindh Pak.
116 D5 Shahpura Madh. Prad. India
116 E5 Shahpura Madh. Prad. India
116 C4 Shahpura Rajasthan India
122 E3 Shāhrakht Iran
122 C4 Shahr-e Bābak Iran
122 B3 Shahr-e Kord Iran
Shahrezā Iran see Qomisheh
Shahrisabz Uzbek. see Shakhrisabz
123 G2 Shahriston Tajik.
122 B3 Shahr Rey Iran
123 G4 Shahr Sultan Pak.
123 G2 Shahrtuz Tajik.
Shāhrūd Iran see Emāmrūd
122 B2 Shāhrūd, Rūdkhāneh-ye r. Iran
122 D4 Shāh Savārān, Kūh-e mts Iran
121 F4 Shaidara, Step' plain Kazakh.
123 F3 Shaikh Husain mt. Pak.
128 B5 Sha'īra, Gebel mt. Egypt
125 E2 Shaj'ah, Jabal hill Saudi Arabia
116 D5 Shajapur Madh. Prad. India
104 B4 Shakaga-dake mt. Japan
215 H3 Shakaskraal S. Africa
215 H3 Shakaville S. Africa
212 D3 Shakawe Botswana
123 G2 Shakh Khatlon Tajik.
Shakhagach Azer. see Şahağac
Shakhbuz Azer. see Şahbuz
139 J3 Shakhovskaya Rus. Fed.
121 H4 Shakhrikhan Uzbek.
121 F5 Shakhrisabz Uzbek.
Shakhristan Tajik. see Shahriston
137 J3 Shakhtars'k Ukr.
Shakhtersk Ukr. see Shakhtars'k
Shakhterskoye Ukr. see Pershotravens'k
121 H2 Shakhtinsk Kazakh.
Shakhty Respublika Buryatiya Rus. Fed. see Gusinoozersk
135 H7 Shakhty Rostovskaya Oblast' Rus. Fed.
Shakhtyorsk Ukr. see Shakhtars'k
Shakhtyorskoye Ukr. see Pershotravens'k
134 I4 Shakhun'ya Rus. Fed.
Shaki Nigeria see Saki
236 E2 Shakopee MN U.S.A.
102 J2 Shakotan-hantō pen. Japan
109 E3 Shakou Guangdong China
210 C3 Shala Hāyk' l. Eth.
134 H3 Shalakusha Rus. Fed.
122 B3 Shālamzār Iran
129 E3 Shalbuzdag, Gora mt. Rus. Fed.
121 I2 Shalday Kazakh.
151 F4 Shalfleet Isle of Wight, England U.K.
151 G3 Shalford Surrey, England U.K.
121 G3 Shalginskiy Kazakh.
Shalgiya Kazakh. see Shalginskiy
129 D2 Shali Rus. Fed.
125 F4 Shalim Oman
Shaliuhe Qinghai China see Gangca
120 B2 Shalkar, Ozero salt l. Kazakh.
Shalqar Kazakh. see Chelkar
Shalqar Kōli salt l. Kazakh. see Shalkar, Ozero
Shalqīya Kazakh. see Shalginskiy
108 A2 Shaluli Shan mts Sichuan China
117 I3 Shaluni mt. Arun. Prad. India
134 L4 Shalya Rus. Fed.
137 H2 Shalyhyne Ukr.
119 H5 Shām, Jabal mt. Oman
211 B6 Shama r. Tanz.
128 A4 Shamâl Sînâ' governorate Egypt
134 L4 Shamary Rus. Fed.
124 C1 Shāmat al Akbād des. Saudi Arabia
223 M3 Shamattawa Man. Can.
224 C2 Shamattawa r. Ont. Can.
122 B3 Shambār Iran
210 C2 Shambu Eth.
116 C4 Shamgarh Madh. Prad. India
Shamgong Bhutan see Zhemgang
129 E2 Shamil'kala Respublika Dagestan Rus. Fed.
129 E2 Shamkhal Rus. Fed.
Shamkhor Azer. see Şämkir
234 B2 Shamokin PA U.S.A.
234 B2 Shamokin Dam PA U.S.A.
136 E3 Shamrayivka Ukr.
237 C5 Shamrock TX U.S.A.
213 F3 Shamva Zimbabwe
96 B2 Shan state Myanmar
Shancheng Fujian China see Nanjing
Shancheng Shandong China see Shanxian
106 D4 Shandan Gansu China
107 H3 Shandian r. China
122 D2 Shandiz Iran
107 H4 Shandong prov. China
107 I4 Shandong Bandao pen. China
137 F3 Shandra Ukr.
127 G4 Shandrūkh Iraq
234 C2 Shanesville PA U.S.A.
213 E3 Shangani r. Zimbabwe
109 E1 Shangcai Henan China
109 E2 Shangcheng Henan China
111 E6 Shang Chu r. China
Shangchuankou Qinghai China see Minhe
107 G3 Shangdu Nei Mongol China
100 D3 Shangganling Heilong. China
109 E2 Shanggao Jiangxi China
109 G2 Shanghai Shanghai China
109 G2 Shanghai mun. China
109 F3 Shanghang Fujian China
107 H4 Shanghe Shandong China
101 C4 Shanghekou Liaoning China
Shangji Henan China see Xichuan
Shangjie Yunnan China see Yangbi
108 D1 Shangjin Hubei China
107 I1 Shangkuli Nei Mongol China
108 D1 Shangnan Shaanxi China
Shangpai Anhui China see Feixi
Shangpai Yunnan China see Fugong
Shangpaihe Anhui China see Feixi
107 G5 Shangqiu Henan China
107 G5 Shangqiu Henan China
109 F2 Shangrao Jiangxi China
109 E1 Shangshui Henan China
108 D4 Shangsi Guangxi China
Shangtang Zhejiang China see Yongjia
109 E3 Shangyou Jiangxi China
109 G2 Shangyu Zhejiang China
100 C3 Shangzhi Heilong. China
108 D1 Shangzhou Shaanxi China
107 H3 Shanhaiguan Hebei China
Shanhe Gansu China see Zhengning
100 C3 Shanhetun Heilong. China
207 I4 Shani Nigeria
129 D2 Shani, Mt'a Georgia/Rus. Fed.
151 F4 Shanklin Isle of Wight, England U.K.
106 B3 Shankou Xinjiang China
80 E4 Shannon North I. N.Z.
147 C4 Shannon airport Rep. of Ireland
147 C4 Shannon est. Rep. of Ireland
147 C4 Shannon r. Rep. of Ireland
215 F3 Shannon S. Africa
226 C4 Shannon IL U.S.A.
147 B4 Shannon, Mouth of the Rep. of Ireland
221 Q2 Shannon Ø i. Greenland
96 B2 Shan Plateau Myanmar
106 A3 Shanshan Xinjiang China
106 A3 Shanshanzhan Xinjiang China
Shansi prov. China see Shanxi
131 O4 Shantarskiye Ostrova is Rus. Fed.
Shan Teng hill H.K. China see Victoria Peak
117 G5 Shantipur W. Bengal India
148 C3 Shantonagh Rep. of Ireland
109 F4 Shantou Guangdong China
Shantung prov. China see Shandong
147 C2 Shanvus Rep. of Ireland
109 E4 Shanwei Guangdong China
107 F4 Shanxi prov. China
107 H5 Shanxian Shandong China
139 J4 Shanya r. Rus. Fed.
108 D1 Shanyang Shaanxi China
107 G4 Shanyin Shanxi China
109 D3 Shaodong Hunan China
109 E3 Shaoguan Guangdong China
109 E3 Shaoshan Hunan China
109 F3 Shaowu Fujian China
109 G2 Shaoxing Zhejiang China
109 D3 Shaoyang Hunan China
109 D3 Shaoyang Hunan China
149 G3 Shap Cumbria, England U.K.
109 D4 Shapa Guangdong China
Shaping Sichuan China see Ebian
146 F2 Shapinsay i. Scotland U.K.
146 F2 Shapinsay Sound sea chan. Scotland U.K.
134 K2 Shapkina r. Rus. Fed.
137 G2 Shapovalivka Ukr.
110 E1 Shapshal'skiy Khrebet mts Rus. Fed.
124 D2 Shaqrā' Saudi Arabia
121 J2 Shar Kazakh.
124 A2 Shār, Jabal mt. Saudi Arabia
128 B4 Sharāh, Jibāl ash mts Jordan
107 E1 Sharalday Rus. Fed.
134 K5 Sharan Rus. Fed.
134 I4 Sharanga Rus. Fed.
138 E5 Sharashova Belarus
147 D3 Sharavogue Rep. of Ireland
Sharbaqty Kazakh. see Shcherbakty
121 J1 Sharchino Rus. Fed.
121 F4 Shardara Kazakh.
Shardara Bögeni resr Kazakh./Uzbek. see Chardarinskoye Vodokhranilishche
123 H3 Shardi Pak.
106 B2 Sharga Govĭ-Altay Mongolia
106 C1 Sharga Hövsgöl Mongolia
Shargorod Ukr. see Sharhorod
121 F5 Shargun' Uzbek.
136 E3 Sharhorod Ukr.
106 E2 Sharhulsan Mongolia
Shari r. Cameroon/Chad see Chari
102 L2 Shari-dake vol. Japan
137 H2 Sharivka Ukr.
125 F2 Sharjah U.A.E.
134 K4 Sharkan Rus. Fed.
138 F4 Sharkawshchyna Belarus
87 B5 Shark Bay W.A. Austr.
125 E5 Sharkhāt Yemen
85 F2 Shark Reef Coral Sea Is Terr. Austr.
235 D2 Shark River Hills NJ U.S.A.
120 C1 Sharlyk Rus. Fed.
203 G3 Sharm el Sheikh Egypt
129 D2 Sharo-Argun r. Rus. Fed.
232 C4 Sharon PA U.S.A.
226 C4 Sharon WI U.S.A.
128 B3 Sharon, Plain of Israel
236 C4 Sharon Springs KS U.S.A.
232 A5 Sharonville OH U.S.A.
87 D7 Sharpe, Lake salt flat W.A. Austr.
150 E3 Sharpness Gloucestershire, England U.K.
232 E5 Sharpsburg MD U.S.A.
232 C5 Sharpsburg OH U.S.A.
Sharqat Iraq see Ash Sharqāṭ
128 B3 Sharqī, Jabal ash mts Lebanon/Syria
126 C5 Sharqîya governorate Egypt
123 H4 Sharqpur Pak.
234 B2 Shartlesville PA U.S.A.
Sharur Azer. see Şärur
106 C2 Shar Us Gol r. Mongolia
134 I4 Shar'ya Rus. Fed.
139 I2 Shar'ya r. Rus. Fed.
207 G5 Shasha Nigeria
213 E4 Shashe Botswana
213 F4 Shashe r. Botswana/Zimbabwe
210 C3 Shashemenē Eth.
Shashi Hubei China see Jingsha
121 H3 Shashubay Karagandinskaya Oblast' Kazakh.
238 B3 Shasta, Mount vol. CA U.S.A.
139 I4 Shatalovo Rus. Fed.
Shatilki Belarus see Svyetlahorsk
109 □ Sha Tin H.K. China
135 I5 Shatki Rus. Fed.
127 G2 Shatoy Rus. Fed.
135 H5 Shatsk Rus. Fed.
136 B2 Shats'k Ukr.
122 B4 Shaṭṭ al 'Arab r. Iran/Iraq
127 G5 Shaṭṭ al Gharrāf r. Iraq
237 D4 Shattuck OK U.S.A.
139 L4 Shatura Rus. Fed.
139 L4 Shaturtorf Rus. Fed.
Shaubak Jordan see Ash Shawbak
Shaŭildir Kazakh. see Shaul'der
121 G4 Shaul'der Kazakh.
223 I5 Shaunavon Sask. Can.
232 D5 Shavers Fork r. WV U.S.A.
129 D2 Shavi Klde, Mt'a Georgia/Rus. Fed.
149 G4 Shavington Cheshire, England U.K.
86 C4 Shaw r. W.A. Austr.
149 G4 Shaw Greater Manchester, England U.K.
110 D2 Shawan Xinjiang China
234 B3 Shawan MD U.S.A.
235 D1 Shawangunk Kill r. NY U.S.A.
235 D1 Shawangunk Mountains hills NY U.S.A.
226 C3 Shawano WI U.S.A.
232 A5 Shawhan KY U.S.A.
237 D5 Shawnee OK U.S.A.
238 F3 Shawnee WY U.S.A.
232 C6 Shawsville VA U.S.A.
109 F3 Sha Xi r. China
109 F3 Shaxian Fujian China
121 G4 Shayan Kazakh.
109 E2 Shayang Hubei China
131 R3 Shayboveyem r. Rus. Fed.
86 D4 Shay Gap W.A. Austr.
127 G4 Shaykh Jūwī Iraq
127 G4 Shaykh Sa'd Iraq
137 I4 Shaytanka r. Ukr.
110 F4 Shazaoyuan Gansu China
124 C2 Shaẕāẕ, Jabal mt. Saudi Arabia
138 E5 Shchara r. Belarus
137 J3 Shchastya Ukr.
137 H5 Shchebetovka Ukr.
139 K4 Shchekino Rus. Fed.
136 D2 Shchekychyn Ukr.
139 L4 Shchelkovo Rus. Fed.
134 K2 Shchel'yayur Rus. Fed.
Shcherbakov Rus. Fed. see Rybinsk
121 I1 Shcherbakty Kazakh.
137 F4 Shcherbani Ukr.
Shcherbinovka Ukr. see Dzerzhyns'k
134 G4 Shchetinskoye Rus. Fed.
135 G6 Shchigry Rus. Fed.
137 H5 Shcholkine Ukr.
137 F2 Shchors Ukr.
137 H3 Shchors'k Ukr.
Shchuchin Belarus see Shchuchyn
121 G1 Shchuchinsk Kazakh.
137 K2 Shchuch'ye Rus. Fed.
138 E5 Shchuchyn Belarus
134 L2 Shchuger r. Rus. Fed.
136 B3 Shchyrets' Ukr.
121 K2 Shebalino Rus. Fed.
135 G6 Shebekino Rus. Fed.
123 F2 Sheberghān Afgh.
226 D4 Sheboygan WI U.S.A.
137 J5 Shebsh r. Rus. Fed.
207 H4 Shebshi Mountains Nigeria
100 G3 Shebunino Sakhalin Rus. Fed.
Shecheng Hebei China see Shexian
225 H4 Shediac N.B. Can.
222 E4 Shedin Peak B.C. Can.
129 B1 Shedok Rus. Fed.
147 D3 Sheelin, Lough l. Rep. of Ireland
215 H2 Sheepmoor S. Africa
241 J3 Sheep Peak NV U.S.A.
164 F3 's-Heerenberg Neth.
151 H3 Sheering Essex, England U.K.
151 H3 Sheerness Kent, England U.K.
225 I4 Sheet Harbour N.S. Can.
128 B3 Shefar'am Israel
81 D5 Sheffield South I. N.Z.
149 H4 Sheffield South Yorkshire, England U.K.
231 C5 Sheffield AL U.S.A.
226 C5 Sheffield IL U.S.A.
232 D4 Sheffield PA U.S.A.
237 C6 Sheffield TX U.S.A.
151 G2 Shefford Bedfordshire, England U.K.
116 D5 Shegaon Mahar. India
227 G3 Sheguiandah Ont. Can.
108 C2 Shehong Sichuan China
147 B5 Shehy Mountains hills Rep. of Ireland
Sheikh, Jebel esh mt. Lebanon/Syria see Hermon, Mount
Sheikh Othman Yemen see Ash Shaykh 'Uthman
224 C3 Shekak r. Ont. Can.
Shekhem West Bank see Nāblus
137 K1 Shekhman' Rus. Fed.
123 H4 Shekhupura Pak.
Sheki Azer. see Şäki
134 G4 Sheksna Rus. Fed.
134 G4 Sheksninskoye Vodokhranilishche resr Rus. Fed.
121 J1 Shelabolikha Rus. Fed.
232 B6 Shelbiana KY U.S.A.
236 E4 Shelbina MO U.S.A.
230 C4 Shelburn IN U.S.A.
225 H5 Shelburne N.S. Can.
227 G3 Shelburne Ont. Can.
85 E1 Shelburne Bay Qld Austr.
233 G3 Shelburne Falls MA U.S.A.
226 D4 Shelby MI U.S.A.
237 F5 Shelby MS U.S.A.
238 E1 Shelby MT U.S.A.
231 D5 Shelby NC U.S.A.
232 B4 Shelby OH U.S.A.
236 F4 Shelbyville IL U.S.A.
230 C4 Shelbyville IN U.S.A.
236 E4 Shelbyville MO U.S.A.
231 C5 Shelbyville TN U.S.A.
215 E5 Sheldon S. Africa
236 E3 Sheldon IA U.S.A.
226 D5 Sheldon IL U.S.A.
226 B3 Sheldon WI U.S.A.
233 G2 Sheldon Springs VT U.S.A.
225 H3 Sheldrake Que. Can.
Shelek Kazakh. see Chilik
136 F4 Shelekhove Ukr.
131 Q3 Shelikhova, Zaliv g. Rus. Fed.
220 C4 Shelikof Strait AK U.S.A.
129 E2 Shelkovskaya Rus. Fed.
238 F2 Shell WY U.S.A.
146 B3 Shell, Loch inlet Scotland U.K.
223 J4 Shellbrook Sask. Can.
238 D3 Shelley ID U.S.A.
83 G3 Shellharbour N.S.W. Austr.
223 J4 Shell Lake Sask. Can.
226 B3 Shell Lake WI U.S.A.
87 E6 Shell Lakes salt flat W.A. Austr.
240 F1 Shell Mountain CA U.S.A.
138 H2 Shelon' r. Rus. Fed.
Shelter Bay Que. Can. see Port-Cartier
235 F1 Shelter Island NY U.S.A.
235 F1 Shelter Island Heights NY U.S.A.
235 E1 Shelton CT U.S.A.
238 B2 Shelton WA U.S.A.
134 F3 Sheltozero Rus. Fed.
Shelyakino Belgorodskaya Oblast' Rus. Fed. see Sovetskoye
Shemakha Azer. see Şamaxı
207 H4 Shemankar r. Nigeria
129 C3 Shemok'medi Georgia
121 J2 Shemonaikha Kazakh.
134 J4 Shemordan Rus. Fed.
135 I5 Shemursha Rus. Fed.
135 I5 Shemysheyka Rus. Fed.
236 E3 Shenandoah IA U.S.A.
227 I5 Shenandoah PA U.S.A.
232 D5 Shenandoah VA U.S.A.
232 E5 Shenandoah r. VA U.S.A.
232 D5 Shenandoah Mountains VA/WV U.S.A.
120 E2 Shenbertal Kazakh.
107 G4 Shenchi Shanxi China
207 H4 Shendam Nigeria
203 G5 Shendi Sudan
100 E3 Shending Shan hill Heilong. China
121 G4 Shengel'di Kazakh.
196 D5 Shëngjin Albania
109 E2 Shengli Hubei China
Shengli Feng mt. China/Kyrg. see Jengish Chokusu
Shengrenjian Shanxi China see Pinglu
109 G2 Shengsi Zhejiang China
109 G2 Shengsi Liedao is China
Shengxian Zhejiang China see Shengzhou
109 G2 Shengzhou Zhejiang China
196 D5 Shënkoll Albania
134 H3 Shenkursk Rus. Fed.
107 F4 Shenmu Shaanxi China
108 D2 Shennongjia Hubei China
109 E1 Shenqiu Henan China
100 D3 Shenshu Heilong. China
Shensi prov. China see Shaanxi
151 F2 Shenstone Staffordshire, England U.K.
135 J5 Shentala Rus. Fed.
87 D6 Shenton, Mount hill W.A. Austr.
Shenxian Hebei China see Shenzhou
107 G4 Shenxian Shandong China
107 I3 Shenyang Liaoning China
109 E4 Shenzhen Guangdong China
107 G4 Shenzhou Hebei China
116 C4 Sheoganj Rajasthan India
116 D4 Sheopur Madh. Prad. India
262 P2 Shepard Island Antarctica
136 D2 Shepetivka Ukr.
Shepetovka Ukr. see Shepetivka
232 A3 Shepherd MI U.S.A.
78 □5 Shepherd Islands Vanuatu
83 F4 Shepparton Vic. Austr.
151 G3 Shepperton Surrey, England U.K.
151 H3 Sheppey, Isle of i. England U.K.
234 B2 Sheppton PA U.S.A.
151 F2 Shepshed Leicestershire, England U.K.
137 G1 Sheptaky Ukr.
150 E3 Shepton Mallet Somerset, England U.K.
137 H2 Sheptukhovka Rus. Fed.
109 E1 Sheqi Henan China
121 F5 Sherabad Uzbek.
215 E4 Sherborne S. Africa
150 E4 Sherborne Dorset, England U.K.
151 F3 Sherborne St John Hampshire, England U.K.
206 B5 Sherbro Island Sierra Leone
225 I4 Sherbrooke N.S. Can.
225 G4 Sherbrooke Que. Can.
149 H3 Sherburn Durham, England U.K.
233 F3 Sherburne NY U.S.A.
149 H4 Sherburn in Elmet North Yorkshire, England U.K.
147 E3 Shercock Rep. of Ireland
121 J2 Sherdoyak Kazakh.
151 G3 Shere Surrey, England U.K.
116 C4 Shergarh Rajasthan India
117 F4 Sherghati Bihar India
237 E5 Sheridan AR U.S.A.
238 F2 Sheridan WY U.S.A.
149 H3 Sheriff Hutton North Yorkshire, England U.K.
82 C3 Sheringa S.A. Austr.
151 I2 Sheringham Norfolk, England U.K.
130 H3 Sherkaly Rus. Fed.
147 B5 Sherkin Island Rep. of Ireland
86 C4 Sherlock r. W.A. Austr.
107 H1 Sherlovaya Gora Rus. Fed.
232 D3 Sherman NY U.S.A.
237 D5 Sherman TX U.S.A.
233 □I2 Sherman Mills ME U.S.A.
241 J1 Sherman Mountain NV U.S.A.
Sherobod Uzbek. see Sherabad
139 H4 Sherovichi Rus. Fed.
117 G4 Sherpur Dhaka Bangl.
117 G4 Sherpur Rajshahi Bangl.
223 K4 Sherridon Man. Can.
150 E3 Sherston Wiltshire, England U.K.
114 C4 Shertally Kerala India
164 E3 's-Hertogenbosch Neth.
232 A4 Sherwood OH U.S.A.
81 C5 Sherwood Downs South I. N.Z.
149 H4 Sherwood Forest reg. England U.K.
100 D2 Sheryshevo Rus. Fed.
227 F3 Sheshegwaning Ont. Can.
222 D3 Sheslay B.C. Can.
222 C3 Sheslay r. B.C. Can.
134 J4 Shestakovo Kirovskaya Oblast' Rus. Fed.
137 K2 Shestakovo Voronezhskaya Oblast' Rus. Fed.
139 L3 Shestikhino Rus. Fed.
137 G4 Shestirnya Ukr.
146 □H1 Shetland admin. div. Scotland U.K.
144 G1 Shetland is Scotland U.K.
120 C3 Shetpe Kazakh.
235 F1 Shetucket r. CT U.S.A.
109 □ Sheung Shui H.K. China
137 H3 Shevchenkivka Ukr.
Shevchenko Mangistauskaya Oblast' Kazakh. see Aktau
137 F3 Shevchenkove Cherkas'ka Oblast' Ukr.
137 I3 Shevchenkove Kharkivs'ka Oblast' Ukr.
137 G2 Shevchen Kove Ukr.
Shevchenkovo Ukr. see Dolyns'ka
114 B2 Shevgaon Mahar. India
100 E1 Shevli r. Rus. Fed.
210 B3 Shewa Gīmīra Eth.
109 F2 Shexian Anhui China
107 G4 Shexian Hebei China
109 G1 Sheyang Jiangsu China
134 H4 Sheybukhta Rus. Fed.
236 D2 Sheyenne ND U.S.A.
236 D2 Sheyenne r. ND U.S.A.
122 C5 Sheykh Sho'eyb i. Iran
146 B4 Shiant, Sound of str. Scotland U.K.
146 B4 Shiant Islands Scotland U.K.
227 F4 Shiawassee r. MI U.S.A.
125 E5 Shibām Yemen
102 I5 Shibata Japan
100 C1 Shibazhan Heilong. China
102 K1 Shibetsu Hokkaidō Japan
102 L2 Shibetsu Hokkaidō Japan
203 F2 Shibîn el Kôm Egypt
108 D3 Shibing Guizhou China
105 F2 Shibukawa Japan
105 F2 Shibutsu-san mt. Japan
Shicheng Fujian China see Zhouning
109 F3 Shicheng Jiangxi China
105 E3 Shichimen-zan mt. Japan
227 I5 Shickshinny PA U.S.A.
Shicun Shanxi China see Xiangfen
128 D4 Shidād al Mismā' hill Saudi Arabia
107 I4 Shidao Shandong China
121 H1 Shiderti r. Kazakh.
108 A3 Shidian Yunnan China
Shidongsi Gansu China see Gaolan
146 C5 Shiel, Loch l. Scotland U.K.
146 C4 Shiel Bridge Highland, Scotland U.K.
84 D2 Shield, Cape N.T. Austr.
146 C4 Shieldaig Highland, Scotland U.K.
149 F2 Shieldhill Falkirk, Scotland U.K.
Shīeli Kazakh. see Chiili
124 A1 Shifa, Jabal ash mts Saudi Arabia
108 C2 Shifang Sichuan China
150 E2 Shifnal Shropshire, England U.K.
104 B3 Shiga pref. Japan
104 C4 Shigaraki Japan
Shigatse Xizang China see Xigazê
114 B3 Shiggaon Karnataka India
110 F3 Shigong Gansu China
120 B1 Shigony Rus. Fed.
107 F3 Shiguai Nei Mongol China
Shiguaigou Nei Mongol China see Shiguai
125 F4 Shiḥan, Wādī r. Oman
110 D2 Shihezi Xinjiang China
Shihkiachwang Hebei China see Shijiazhuang
196 D5 Shijak Albania
Shijiao Guangdong China see Fogang
107 G4 Shijiazhuang Hebei China
Shijiusuo Shandong China see Rizhao
123 E4 Shikar r. Pak.
114 B3 Shikarpur Karnataka India
123 G5 Shikarpur Pak.
109 E3 Shikengkong mt. Guangdong China
120 A1 Shikhany Rus. Fed.
105 F3 Shiki Japan
116 D4 Shikohabad Uttar Prad. India
103 F7 Shikoku i. Japan
103 F7 Shikoku-sanchi mts Japan
99 Q3 Shikotan, Ostrov i. Kuril'skiye O-va Rus. Fed.
Shikotan-tō i. Kuril'skiye O-va Rus. Fed. see Shikotan, Ostrov
102 J2 Shikotsu vol. Japan
149 H2 Shilbottle Northumberland, England U.K.
120 D2 Shil'da Rus. Fed.
149 H3 Shildon Durham, England U.K.
134 I2 Shilega Rus. Fed.
117 G4 Shiliguri W. Bengal India
109 E2 Shilipu Hubei China
Shiliu Hainan China see Changjiang
116 D2 Shilla mt. Jammu and Kashmir
146 A4 Shillay i. Scotland U.K.
147 E4 Shillelagh Rep. of Ireland
227 G1 Shillington Ont. Can.
234 C2 Shillington PA U.S.A.
128 B3 Shillo r. Israel
117 G4 Shillong Meghalaya India
234 C3 Shiloh NJ U.S.A.
232 B4 Shiloh OH U.S.A.
107 F4 Shilou Shanxi China
135 H5 Shilovo Rus. Fed.
Shilüüstey Mongolia see Balgatay
104 C4 Shima Japan
103 E7 Shimabara Japan
105 E4 Shimada Japan
104 C4 Shima-hantō pen. Japan
103 F6 Shimane pref. Japan
103 F6 Shimane-hantō pen. Japan
100 C1 Shimanovsk Rus. Fed.
210 E2 Shimbiris mt. Somalia
109 D2 Shimen Hunan China
Shimen Yunnan China see Yunlong
108 B2 Shimian Sichuan China
105 E3 Shimizu Japan
116 D3 Shimla Hima. Prad. India
Shimminato Japan see Shinminato
105 E4 Shimoda Japan
105 F2 Shimodate Japan
114 B3 Shimoga Karnataka India
102 J3 Shimokita-hantō pen. Japan
211 C6 Shimoni Kenya
103 E7 Shimonoseki Japan
105 E2 Shimosuwa Japan
105 F2 Shimotsuma Japan
114 C3 Shimsha r. India
116 C1 Shimshal Jammu and Kashmir
139 H2 Shimsk Rus. Fed.
146 D3 Shin, Loch l. Scotland U.K.
Shināfīyah Iraq see Ash Shanāfīyah
108 D4 Shinan Guangxi China
123 E3 Shīndand Afgh.
151 G3 Shinfield Wokingham, England U.K.
232 D4 Shinglehouse PA U.S.A.
226 D2 Shingleton MI U.S.A.
121 J3 Shingozha Kazakh.
213 F4 Shingwedzi S. Africa
149 G4 Shining Tor hill England U.K.
227 G2 Shining Tree Ont. Can.
102 J4 Shinjō Japan
123 G3 Shinkai Hills Afgh.
104 D2 Shinminato Japan
103 E6 Shinnan-yō Japan
146 D3 Shinness Lodge Highland, Scotland U.K.
232 C5 Shinnston WV U.S.A.
147 D4 Shinrone Rep. of Ireland
104 D4 Shinshiro Japan
129 E4 Shinuhayr Armenia
211 B5 Shinyanga Tanz.
211 B5 Shinyanga admin. reg. Tanz.
102 J4 Shiogama Japan
105 D2 Shiojiri Japan
105 E3 Shiomi-dake mt. Japan
Shipai Anhui China see Huaining
233 F5 Ship Bottom NJ U.S.A.
246 C1 Ship Chan Cay i. Bahamas
108 B4 Shiping Yunnan China
151 G3 Shiplake Oxfordshire, England U.K.
149 H4 Shipley West Yorkshire, England U.K.
232 D6 Shipman VA U.S.A.
225 H4 Shippegan N.B. Can.
232 E4 Shippensburg PA U.S.A.
232 D4 Shippenville PA U.S.A.
241 M3 Shiprock NM U.S.A.
241 M3 Shiprock Peak NM U.S.A.
151 F2 Shipston on Stour Warwickshire, England U.K.
149 H3 Shipton North Yorkshire, England U.K.
150 E2 Shipton Shropshire, England U.K.
151 F3 Shipton-under-Wychwood Oxfordshire, England U.K.
Shipu Shaanxi China see Huanglong
109 G2 Shipu Zhejiang China
108 D3 Shiqian Guizhou China
Shiqiao Guangdong China see Panyu
Shiqizhen Guangdong China see Zhongshan
108 D1 Shiquan Shaanxi China
Shiquanhe Xizang China see Gar
Shiquanhe Xizang China see Gar
116 E2 Shiquan He r. China conv. Indus
124 C2 Shi'r, Jabal hill Saudi Arabia
146 C5 Shira r. Scotland U.K.
122 B2 Shīrābād Iran
104 C4 Shirai-san mt. Japan
105 G1 Shirakawa Japan
104 D2 Shirake-mine mt. Japan
104 D3 Shirakura-yama mt. Japan
104 B4 Shirama-yama hill Japan
105 E2 Shirane-san mt. Japan
105 E3 Shirane-san mt. Japan
105 F2 Shirane-san vol. Japan
262 O1 Shirase Coast Antarctica
122 C4 Shīrāz Iran
126 C5 Shirbîn Egypt
211 B8 Shire r. Malawi
149 H4 Shirebrook Derbyshire, England U.K.
107 G2 Shireet Mongolia
150 E3 Shirenewton Monmouthshire, Wales U.K.
102 L2 Shiretoko-hantō pen. Japan
121 G4 Shirin Uzbek.
123 F4 Shirinab r. Pak.
120 D3 Shirkala reg. Kazakh.
122 C4 Shīr Kūh mt. Iran
149 H4 Shirland Derbyshire, England U.K.
235 F2 Shirley NY U.S.A.
102 J5 Shiroishi Japan
105 D3 Shirokura-yama mt. Japan
102 I5 Shirone Japan
207 G4 Shiroro Reservoir Nigeria
104 D2 Shirouma-dake mt. Japan
116 C5 Shirpur Mahar. India
106 C3 Shirten Höloy Gobi des. China
122 D2 Shīrvān Iran
122 A1 Shirvanskaya Step' plain Azer.
106 A3 Shisanjianfang Xinjiang China
100 C2 Shisanzhan Heilong. China
215 H2 Shiselweni admin. dist. Swaziland
220 B4 Shishaldin Volcano AK U.S.A.
Shisha Pangma mt. Xizang China see Xixabangma Feng
Shishkaya Armenia see Gukarrich
109 E2 Shishou Hubei China
109 F2 Shitai Anhui China
109 E3 Shitan Guangdong China
109 G2 Shitang Zhejiang China
106 E4 Shitanjing Ningxia China
203 I1 Shithāthah Iraq
116 B4 Shiv Rajasthan India
131 R4 Shiveluch, Sopka vol. Rus. Fed.
116 D4 Shivpuri Madh. Prad. India
128 B4 Shivta tourist site Israel
241 K3 Shivwits UT U.S.A.
241 K3 Shivwits Plateau AZ U.S.A.
96 D2 Shiwan Dashan mts China
211 A7 Shiwa Ngandu Zambia
109 E3 Shixing Guangdong China
108 D1 Shiyan Hubei China
108 D2 Shizhu Chongqing China
Shizilu Shandong China see Junan
109 F2 Shizipu Anhui China
108 B3 Shizong Yunnan China
106 E4 Shizuishan Ningxia China
105 E4 Shizuoka Japan
105 E4 Shizuoka pref. Japan
196 E4 Shkëlzenit, Maja e mt. Albania
129 C2 Shkhara mt. Georgia/Rus. Fed.
136 B3 Shklo Ukr.
Shklov Belarus see Shklow
139 H4 Shklow Belarus
136 C2 Shklyn' Ukr.
196 D4 Shkodër Albania
Shkodrës, Liqeni i l. Albania/Yugo. see Scutari, Lake
196 D5 Shkumbin r. Albania
137 J4 Shkurinskaya Rus. Fed.
139 J3 Shlina r. Rus. Fed.
139 I3 Shlino, Ozero l. Rus. Fed.
139 H2 Shlissel'burg Rus. Fed.
100 G1 Shmidta, Poluostrov pen. Sakhalin Rus. Fed.
83 G3 Shoalhaven r. N.S.W. Austr.
223 K5 Shoal Lake Man. Can.
223 K4 Shoal Lake Sask. Can.
230 C4 Shoals IN U.S.A.
85 G4 Shoalwater Bay Qld Austr.
103 F6 Shōbara Japan
151 H3 Shoeburyness Southend, England U.K.
234 C2 Shoemakersville PA U.S.A.
Shofirkon Uzbek. see Shafirkan
104 D2 Shō-gawa r. Japan
Shoh Khatlon Tajik. see Shakh
234 D1 Shohola PA U.S.A.
102 J2 Shokanbetsu-dake mt. Japan
102 K1 Shokotsu-gawa r. Japan
Shokpar Kazakh. see Chokpar
139 K1 Shola r. Rus. Fed.
120 F2 Sholaksay Kazakh.
Sholapur Mahar. India see Solapur
Sholaqorghan Kazakh. see Shollakorgan
Sholaqsay Kazakh. see Sholaksay
121 G4 Shollakorgan Kazakh.
86 B4 Sholl Island W.A. Austr.
134 F2 Shomba r. Rus. Fed.
104 D2 Shōmyō-gawa r. Japan
146 C5 Shona, Eilean i. Scotland U.K.
264 J9 Shona Ridge sea feature S. Atlantic Ocean
Shonzha Kazakh. see Chundzha
139 L3 Shopsha Rus. Fed.
148 C3 Shoptown Northern Ireland U.K.
Shoqpar Kazakh. see Chokpar
114 C4 Shoranur Kerala India
114 C2 Shorapur Karnataka India
120 D4 Shor Barsa-Kel'mes salt marsh Uzbek.
235 D2 Shore Acres NJ U.S.A.
151 H3 Shoreham Kent, England U.K.
151 G4 Shoreham-by-Sea West Sussex, England U.K.
Shorghun Uzbek. see Shargun'
123 H4 Shorkot Pak.
Shornaq Kazakh. see Chernak
121 G2 Shortandy Kazakh.
78 □6 Shortland Island Solomon Is
78 □6 Shortland Islands Solomon Is
232 E3 Shortsville NY U.S.A.
139 K3 Shosha r. Rus. Fed.
241 I4 Shoshone CA U.S.A.
238 D3 Shoshone ID U.S.A.
238 E2 Shoshone r. WY U.S.A.
240 I2 Shoshone Mountains NV U.S.A.
241 I3 Shoshone Peak NV U.S.A.
212 E4 Shoshong Botswana
238 E3 Shoshoni WY U.S.A.
137 G2 Shostka Ukr.
137 G2 Shostka r. Ukr.
151 I3 Shotley Gate Suffolk, England U.K.
150 D1 Shotton Flintshire, Wales U.K.
146 E6 Shotts North Lanarkshire, Scotland U.K.
107 H4 Shouguang Shandong China
109 F1 Shouxian Anhui China
107 G4 Shouyang Shanxi China
108 D1 Shouyang Shan mt. Shaanxi China
241 L4 Show Low AZ U.S.A.
129 D4 Showt Iran
135 H7 Shpakovskoye Rus. Fed.
137 F3 Shpola Ukr.
136 E3 Shpykiv Ukr.
136 E2 Shpyli Ukr.
Shqipërisë, Republika e country Europe see Albania
137 G2 Shramkivka Ukr.
232 B4 Shreve OH U.S.A.
237 E5 Shreveport LA U.S.A.
150 E2 Shrewsbury Shropshire, England U.K.
235 D2 Shrewsbury NJ U.S.A.
234 B3 Shrewsbury PA U.S.A.
151 F3 Shrewton Wiltshire, England U.K.
148 D3 Shrigley Northern Ireland U.K.
114 B2 Shrigonda Mahar. India
Shri Lanka country Asia see Sri Lanka
116 B4 Shri Mohangarh Rajasthan India
117 G5 Shrirampur W. Bengal India
114 C3 Shrirangapattana Karnataka India
151 F3 Shrivenham Oxfordshire, England U.K.
150 E2 Shropshire admin. div. England U.K.
235 E1 Shrub Oak NY U.S.A.
Shtefan-Vode Moldova see Ștefan Vodă
196 E5 Shtërmen Albania
196 E4 Shtiqën Albania
107 H5 Shu r. China
121 H4 Shu Kazakh.
127 G5 Shu'aiba Iraq
108 B1 Shuajingsi Sichuan China
129 C3 Shuakhevi Georgia
108 B3 Shuangbai Yunnan China
Shuangcheng Fujian China see Zherong
100 C3 Shuangcheng Heilong. China
109 E2 Shuanghe Hubei China
108 C2 Shuanghechang Sichuan China
100 D2 Shuanghedagang Heilong. China
Shuanghuyu Shaanxi China see Zizhou
Shuangjiang Guizhou China see Jiangkou
Shuangjiang Hunan China see Tongdao
108 A4 Shuangjiang Yunnan China
Shuangjiang Yunnan China see Eshan
107 I3 Shuangliao Jilin China
109 D3 Shuangpai Hunan China
Shuangshipu Shaanxi China see Fengxian
100 C4 Shuangyang Jilin China
100 D3 Shuangyashan Heilong. China
Shuangzhong Jiangxi China see Hukou
125 E4 Shu'ayt, Wādī r. Yemen
120 D2 Shubarkuduk Kazakh.
120 D2 Shubarshi Kazakh.
118 C3 Shubrâ el Kheima Egypt
109 F2 Shucheng Anhui China
110 A4 Shufu Xinjiang China
117 H4 Shuganu Manipur India
139 J2 Shugozero Rus. Fed.
Shuicheng Guizhou China see Lupanshui
Shuiding Xinjiang China see Huocheng
Shuidong Guangdong China see Dianbai
Shuihu Anhui China see Changfeng
109 F3 Shuiji Fujian China
Shuiji Shandong China see Laixi
108 C1 Shuijing Sichuan China
109 E4 Shuikou Guangdong China
109 D3 Shuikou Hunan China
108 C4 Shuikouguan Guangxi China
109 E3 Shuikoushan Hunan China
Shuiluocheng Gansu China see Zhuanglang
108 B3 Shuituo He r. Sichuan China
Shuizhai Guangdong China see Wuhua
123 G4 Shujaabad Pak.
100 C3 Shulan Jilin China
110 B4 Shule Xinjiang China
106 B3 Shule He r. China
106 C4 Shule Nanshan mts China
137 K1 Shul'gino Rus. Fed.
137 J3 Shul'hynka Ukr.
107 F3 Shulinzhao Nei Mongol China
Shul'mak Tajik. see Novobod
Shulu Hebei China see Xinji
139 H2 Shum Rus. Fed.
220 B4 Shumagin Islands AK U.S.A.
137 I2 Shumakovo Rus. Fed.
120 D4 Shumanay Uzbek.
102 K1 Shumarinai-ko l. Japan
197 H4 Shumen Bulg.
134 I5 Shumerlya Rus. Fed.
130 H4 Shumikha Rus. Fed.
138 G4 Shumilina Belarus
136 D2 Shums'k Ukr.
139 I5 Shumyachi Rus. Fed.
121 H3 Shunak, Gora mt. Kazakh.
128 B4 Shūnat Nimrīn Jordan
109 E4 Shunde Guangdong China
139 M3 Shunga Rus. Fed.
220 C3 Shungnak AK U.S.A.
234 B1 Shunk PA U.S.A.
129 E2 Shunudag, Gora mt. Rus. Fed.
107 H3 Shunyi Beijing China
108 C4 Shuolong Guangxi China
Shuoxian Shanxi China see Shuozhou
107 G4 Shuozhou Shanxi China
124 D4 Shuqqat Najrān depr. Saudi Arabia
124 D5 Shuqrah Yemen
122 C4 Shūr r. Iran
122 C4 Shūr r. Iran
122 E3 Shūr r. Iran
122 E4 Shūr r. Iran
122 B3 Shūrāb Iran
122 B3 Shūr Āb Iran
122 C3 Shūrāb Iran
Shurab Tajik. see Shŭrob
121 F5 Shurchi Uzbek.
122 D4 Shūr Gaz Iran
134 J4 Shurma Rus. Fed.
123 G1 Shŭrob Tajik.
122 E4 Shūrū Iran
213 F3 Shurugwi Zimbabwe
127 G5 Shuruppak tourist site Iraq
122 E4 Shusf Iran
122 B3 Shūsh Iran
Shusha Azer. see Şuşa
198 A1 Shushicë r. Albania
122 B3 Shushtar Iran
137 H2 Shustovo Rus. Fed.
128 C4 Shuwaysh, Tall ash hill Jordan
139 M3 Shuya Ivanovskaya Oblast' Rus. Fed.
134 F3 Shuya Respublika Kareliya Rus. Fed.
107 H5 Shuyang Jiangsu China
134 H4 Shuyskoye Rus. Fed.
139 K4 Shvartsevskiy Rus. Fed.
96 A2 Shwebo Myanmar
96 A3 Shwedaung Myanmar
96 B3 Shwegyin Myanmar
96 A3 Shwelaung r. Myanmar
96 B2 Shweli r. Myanmar
96 B2 Shweudaung mt. Myanmar
136 D3 Shybena Ukr.
Shyghanaq Kazakh. see Chiganak
Shyghys Qazaqstan Oblysy admin. div. Kazakh. see Vostochnyy Kazakhstan
Shyghys-Qongyrat Kazakh. see Shygys Konyrat
121 H3 Shygys Konyrat Kazakh.
121 G4 Shymkent Kazakh.
Shynggyrlaū Kazakh. see Chingirlau
Shyngqozha Kazakh. see Shingozha
116 C2 Shyok r. India
116 D2 Shyok Jammu and Kashmir
137 I3 Shypuvate Ukr.
137 G4 Shyroke Dnipropetrovs'ka Oblast' Ukr.
137 H3 Shyroke Zaporiz'ka Oblast' Ukr.
137 F4 Shyrokolanivka Ukr.
136 F4 Shyryayeve Ukr.
137 H3 Shyshaky Ukr.
146 B3 Siabost Western Isles, Scotland U.K.
116 D2 Siachen Glacier Jammu and Kashmir
161 E5 Siagne r. France
123 E5 Siahan Range mts Pak.
122 A2 Sīah Chashmeh Iran
123 F3 Siah Koh mts Afgh.
94 C2 Siak r. Indon.
94 C2 Siak Sri Inderapura Sumatera Indon.
123 H3 Sialkot Pak.
Siam country Asia see Thailand
192 A5 Siamanna Sardegna Italy
Sian Shaanxi China see Xi'an
Sianhala Côte d'Ivoire see Sanhala
143 G4 Sianów Pol.
251 E4 Siapa r. Venez.
92 C4 Siargao i. Phil.
233 I4 Siasconset MA U.S.A.
92 B5 Siasi Phil.
198 B1 Siatista Greece
92 B4 Siaton Phil.
138 D4 Šiauliai Lith.
209 F9 Siavonga Zambia
Siazan' Azer. see Siyäzän
125 G3 Sīb Oman
246 C2 Sibanicú Cuba
195 F3 Sibari Italy
Sibati Xinjiang China see Xibet
92 B4 Sibay i. Phil.
120 D1 Sibay Rus. Fed.
215 I2 Sibayi, Lake S. Africa
263 L2 Sibbald, Cape Antarctica
169 E3 Sibbesse Ger.
141 N3 Sibbo Fin.
188 E4 Šibenik Croatia
71 G2 Siberia reg. Rus. Fed.
94 B3 Siberut i. Indon.
94 B3 Siberut, Selat sea chan. Indon.
123 F4 Sibi Pak.
210 C4 Sibiloi National Park Kenya
Sibir' reg. Rus. Fed. see Siberia
100 E3 Sibirtsevo Rus. Fed.
130 I2 Sibiryakova, Ostrov i. Rus. Fed.
209 B5 Sibiti Congo
197 G3 Sibiu Romania
151 H3 Sible Hedingham Essex, England U.K.
236 E3 Sibley IA U.S.A.
94 B2 Sibolga Sumatera Indon.
94 B2 Siborongborong Sumatera Indon.
215 H2 Sibowe r. Swaziland
117 H4 Sibsagar Assam India

Sibsey to Slavgorod

363

149 J4 **Sibsey** Lincolnshire, England U.K.
95 E2 **Sibu** Sarawak Malaysia
92 B5 **Sibuco** Phil.
92 B5 **Sibuguey** r. Phil.
92 B5 **Sibuguey Bay** Phil.
208 C3 **Sibut** C.A.R.
92 B3 **Sibuyan** i. Phil.
197 F2 **Sic** Romania
222 G5 **Sicamous** B.C. Can.
92 B2 **Sicapoo** mt. Luzon Phil.
252 D4 **Sicasica** Bol.
92 B4 **Sicayac** Phil.
Sicca Veneria Tunisia see Le Kef
Sicheng Guangxi China see Lingyun
97 B5 **Sichon** Thai.
108 B2 **Sichuan** prov. China
108 C2 **Sichuan Pendi** basin Sichuan China
194 D5 **Sicilia** admin. reg. Italy
194 D4 **Sicilia** i. Italy
194 B5 **Sicilian Channel** Italy/Tunisia
Sicily i. Italy see **Sicilia**
174 E4 **Siciny** Pol.
234 D3 **Sicklerville** NJ U.S.A.
169 F3 **Sickte** Ger.
252 C3 **Sicuani** Peru
177 K5 **Şicula** Romania
194 C5 **Şiculiana** Sicilia Italy
177 I3 **Šíd** Slovakia
196 D3 **Šid** Vojvodina, Srbija Yugo.
150 D4 **Sidbury** Devon, England U.K.
164 F1 **Siddeburen** Neth.
116 C5 **Siddhapur** Gujarat India
Siddharthanagar Nepal see Bhairawa
114 C2 **Siddipet** Andhra Prad. India
140 L3 **Sidensjö** Sweden
206 D4 **Sidéradougou** Burkina
195 F4 **Siderno** Italy
214 D5 **Sidesaviwa** S. Africa
150 D4 **Sidford** Devon, England U.K.
116 E4 **Sidhauli** Uttar Prad. India
116 E4 **Sidhi** Madh. Prad. India
Sidhirókastron Greece see Sidirokastro
Sidhpur Gujarat India see Siddhapur
205 F2 **Sidi Aïssa** Alg.
202 E2 **Sidi Barrani** Egypt
205 E2 **Sidi Bel Abbès** Alg.
204 C2 **Sidi Bennour** Morocco
Sidi Bou Sa'id Tunisia see Sidi Bouzid
205 H2 **Sidi Bouzid** Tunisia
204 C3 **Sidi Ifni** Morocco
204 D2 **Sidi Kacem** Morocco
94 B2 **Sidikalang** Sumatera Indon.
205 G2 **Sidi Khaled** Alg.
204 B5 **Sidi Mhamed** well Western Sahara
205 G2 **Sidi Okba** Alg.
198 C1 **Sidirokastro** Greece
204 C2 **Sidi-Smaïl** Morocco
146 E5 **Sidlaw Hills** Scotland U.K.
151 H4 **Sidley** East Sussex, England U.K.
262 P1 **Sidley, Mount** Antarctica
150 D4 **Sidmouth** Devon, England U.K.
85 E2 **Sidmouth, Cape** Qld Austr.
226 C2 **Sidnaw** MI U.S.A.
222 F5 **Sidney** B.C. Can.
236 E3 **Sidney** IA U.S.A.
238 F2 **Sidney** MT U.S.A.
236 C3 **Sidney** NE U.S.A.
233 F3 **Sidney** NY U.S.A.
232 A4 **Sidney** OH U.S.A.
231 D5 **Sidney Lanier, Lake** GA U.S.A.
214 E3 **Sidney-on-Vaal** S. Africa
206 D4 **Sido** Mali
95 F4 **Sidoarjo** Jawa Timur Indon.
163 E5 **Sidobre** reg. France
Sidon Lebanon see **Saïda**
134 H4 **Sidorovo** Rus. Fed.
175 I2 **Sidra** r. Pol.
255 B7 **Sidrolândia** Brazil
215 H2 **Sidvokodvo** Swaziland
215 G4 **Sidwadweni** S. Africa
121 G4 **Sidzhak** Uzbek.
175 F4 **Sidzina** Pol.
140 M1 **Siebejokka** r. Norway
164 F3 **Siebengewald** Neth.
171 E4 **Siebenlehn** Ger.
174 E5 **Siecieborzyce** Pol.
175 J4 **Sieciechów** Pol.
169 G3 **Siedenburg** Ger.
175 J5 **Siedlanka** Pol.
175 K3 **Siedlce** Pol.
174 E3 **Siedlec** Pol.
174 D4 **Siedlisko** Lubuskie Pol.
174 F4 **Siedlisko** Wielkopolskie Pol.
175 L4 **Siedliszcze** Lubelskie Pol.
175 L5 **Siedliszcze** Lubelskie Pol.
169 C5 **Sieg** r. Ger.
169 C5 **Siegburg** Ger.
169 D5 **Siegen** Ger.
173 F3 **Siegenburg** Ger.
179 H3 **Siegendorf im Burgenland** Austria
179 H3 **Sieggraben** Austria
179 H3 **Sieghartskirchen** Austria
173 G4 **Siegsdorf** Ger.
168 F2 **Siek** Ger.
171 G4 **Siekierczyn** Pol.
175 L4 **Sielec** Pol.
177 I3 **Sielnica** Slovakia
171 F4 **Sielow** Ger.
175 K4 **Siemianówka** Pol.
175 L3 **Siemianówka, Jezioro** l. Pol.
175 K3 **Siemiatycze** Pol.
175 K4 **Siemień** Pol.
174 G4 **Siemkowice** Pol.
97 C4 **Siĕmréab** Cambodia
Siem Reap Cambodia see **Siĕmréab**
174 D1 **Siemyśl** Pol.
Si'en Guangxi China see Huanjiang
191 G5 **Siena** Italy
191 G5 **Siena** prov. Toscana Italy
175 K5 **Sieniawa** Pol.
158 E2 **Sienne** r. France
175 J3 **Siennica** Pol.
175 J4 **Sienno** Pol.
175 H6 **Siepraw** Pol.
174 G4 **Sieradz** Pol.
174 G5 **Sieraków** Pol.
174 E3 **Sieraków** Pol.
175 H3 **Sierakówek** Pol.
174 F1 **Sierakowice** Pol.
157 G3 **Sierck-les-Bains** France
157 H5 **Sierentz** France
168 F1 **Sierksdorf** Ger.
179 H2 **Sierndorf** Austria
179 F2 **Sierning** Austria
174 F4 **Sieroszewice** Pol.
175 H3 **Sierpc** Pol.
175 H3 **Sierpienica** r. Pol.
239 F6 **Sierra Blanca** TX U.S.A.
261 G5 **Sierra Chica** Arg.
184 D1 **Sierra de Fuentes** Spain
Sierra del Gistral mts Spain see **Xistral, Serra do**
186 C2 **Sierra de Luna** Spain
185 F3 **Sierra de Yeguas** Spain
187 D4 **Sierra Engarcerán** Spain
259 D6 **Sierra Grande** Arg.
206 C4 **Sierra Leone** country Africa
264 H5 **Sierra Leone Basin** sea feature N. Atlantic Ocean
264 H5 **Sierra Leone Rise** sea feature N. Atlantic Ocean
240 G4 **Sierra Madre Mountains** CA U.S.A.
242 E3 **Sierra Mojada** Mex.
240 G2 **Sierraville** CA U.S.A.
241 L6 **Sierra Vista** AZ U.S.A.
190 C2 **Sierre** Switz.
185 H3 **Sierro** Spain
185 H3 **Sierro** r. Spain
171 C4 **Siersleben** Ger.
138 D4 **Siesartis** r. Lith.
138 E4 **Siesartis** r. Lith.
187 C5 **Siete Aguas** Spain
183 E3 **Siete Iglesias de Trabancos** Spain
170 D2 **Sietow** Ger.
197 G2 **Șieu** Romania
197 G2 **Șieu** r. Romania
191 G5 **Sieve** r. Italy
170 D3 **Sieversdorf** Ger.
168 E1 **Sieverstedt** Ger.
140 N3 **Sievi** Fin.
175 H5 **Siewierz** Pol.
108 C4 **Sifang Ling** mts China
206 D5 **Sifié** Côte d'Ivoire
198 D3 **Sifnos** i. Greece
205 E2 **Sig** Alg.
139 I3 **Sig, Ozero** l. Rus. Fed.
79 □1a **Sigatoka** Viti Levu Fiji
77 I3 **Sigave** Wallis and Futuna Is
161 A5 **Sigean** France
170 C2 **Siggelkow** Ger.
149 I4 **Sigglesthorne** East Riding of Yorkshire, England U.K.
221 M2 **Sigguup Nunaa** pen. Greenland
197 F2 **Sighetu Marmației** Romania
197 G2 **Sighișoara** Romania
191 H5 **Sigillo** Italy
114 D5 **Sigiriya** Sri Lanka
129 F3 **Sığırlı** Azer.
94 A1 **Sigli** Sumatera Indon.
140 □C2 **Siglufjörður** Iceland
92 B4 **Sigma** Phil.
172 D3 **Sigmaringen** Ger.
172 D3 **Sigmaringendorf** Ger.
179 G2 **Sigmundsherberg** Austria
191 G5 **Signa** Italy
173 G2 **Signalberg** hill Ger.
165 F4 **Signal de Botrange** hill Belgium
161 D5 **Signal de la Ste-Baume** mt. France
161 B4 **Signal de Mailhebiau** mt. France
161 B4 **Signal de Randon** mt. France
160 C3 **Signal de St-André** hill France
162 D2 **Signal de Sauvagnac** hill France
162 D3 **Signal du Pic** hill France
159 F3 **Signal du Viviers** hill France
241 J5 **Signal Peak** AZ U.S.A.
190 C2 **Signau** Switz.
161 D5 **Signes** France
156 E3 **Signy-l'Abbaye** France
156 E3 **Signy-le-Petit** France
215 G4 **Sigoga** S. Africa
162 B3 **Sigogne** France
163 C4 **Sigoulès** France
236 E3 **Sigourney** IA U.S.A.
264 C4 **Sigsbee Deep** sea feature G. of Mexico
143 G2 **Sigtuna** Sweden
243 I6 **Siguatepeque** Hond.
182 B2 **Sigüeiro** Spain
183 H3 **Sigüenza** Spain
163 D6 **Siguer** r. France
186 B2 **Sigües** Spain
206 C4 **Siguiri** Guinea
138 E3 **Sigulda** Latvia
241 L2 **Sigurd** UT U.S.A.
97 C5 **Sihanoukville** Cambodia
116 E5 **Sihawa** Madh. Prad. India
177 I2 **Sihelné** Slovakia
109 F1 **Sihong** Jiangsu China
116 E5 **Sihora** Madh. Prad. India
116 D5 **Sihora** Mahar. India
Sihou Shandong China see Changdao
252 A2 **Sihuas** Peru
109 E4 **Sihui** Guangdong China
141 M3 **Siikainen** Fin.
140 N2 **Siikajoki** Fin.
140 N2 **Siikajoki** r. Fin.
140 N3 **Siilinjärvi** Fin.
127 F3 **Siirt** Turkey
78 □4a **Siis** i. Chuuk Micronesia
Sijjak Uzbek. see **Sidzhak**
165 C3 **Sijsele** Belgium
94 C3 **Sijunjung** Sumatera Indon.
116 B5 **Sika** Gujarat India
Sikaka Saudi Arabia see Sakākah
116 D4 **Sikandra Rao** Uttar Prad. India
222 F3 **Sikanni Chief** B.C. Can.
222 F3 **Sikanni Chief** r. B.C. Can.
116 C4 **Sikar** Rajasthan India
123 G3 **Sikaram** mt. Afgh.
206 D4 **Sikasso** Mali
206 D4 **Sikasso** admin. reg. Mali
198 C1 **Sikea** Kentriki Makedonia Greece
Sikéa Greece see **Sykea**
177 H4 **Sikenica** r. Slovakia
237 F4 **Sikeston** MO U.S.A.
177 H5 **Sik-hegy** hill Hungary
100 E4 **Sikhote-Alin'** mts Rus. Fed.
198 D3 **Sikinos** i. Greece
188 G3 **Sikirevci** Croatia
117 G4 **Sikkim** state India
177 H6 **Siklós** Hungary
175 H3 **Sikórz** Pol.
140 L2 **Siksjö** Sweden
117 F4 **Sikta** Bihar India
Sikuaishi Liaoning China see Changhai
182 C2 **Sil** r. Spain
92 C4 **Silago** Phil.
138 D4 **Šilalė** Lith.
191 F2 **Silandro** Italy
192 A4 **Silanus** Sardegna Italy
244 D3 **Silao** Mex.
237 F6 **Silas** AL U.S.A.
94 A1 **Silawaih Agam** vol. Indon.
92 B4 **Silay** Phil.
188 E3 **Silba** i. Croatia
168 E2 **Silberberg** hill Ger.
168 E1 **Silberstedt** Ger.
117 H4 **Silchar** Assam India
191 H3 **Sile** r. Italy
199 F1 **Şile** Turkey
151 F2 **Sileby** Leicestershire, England U.K.
149 F3 **Silecroft** Cumbria, England U.K.
138 F4 **Silene** Latvia
190 D2 **Silenen** Switz.
165 D4 **Silenrieux** Belgium
231 E5 **Siler City** NC U.S.A.
114 D2 **Sileru** r. India
185 H2 **Siles** Spain
174 E4 **Silesia** reg. Europe
Sileti Kazakh. see **Seletinskoye**
121 H1 **Sileti** r. Kazakh.
121 H1 **Siletiteniz, Ozero** salt l. Kazakh.
158 C3 **Silfiac** France
Silgadi Nepal see **Silgarhi**
116 E3 **Silgarhi** Nepal
117 H4 **Silghat** Assam India
217 □2a **Silhouette** i. Inner Islands Seychelles
205 H1 **Siliana** Tunisia
189 B8 **Siliana** admin. div. Tunisia
126 D3 **Silifke** Turkey
192 A4 **Siligo** Sardegna Italy
Siliguri W. Bengal India see Shiliguri
177 K5 **Șilindia** Romania
111 E6 **Siling Co** salt l. China
116 D4 **Silipur** Madh. Prad. India
192 A5 **Siliqua** Sardegna Italy
192 A4 **Silis** r. Sardegna Italy
78 □2 **Silisili, Mount** Samoa
Silistat Turkey see **Bozkır**
197 G3 **Siliștea** Romania
197 G3 **Siliștea Nouă** Romania
197 H3 **Silistra** Bulg.
Silistria Bulg. see **Silistra**
199 F1 **Silivri** Turkey
142 C2 **Siljan** Norway
141 K3 **Siljan** l. Sweden
143 F1 **Siljansnäs** Sweden
142 C3 **Silkeborg** Denmark
85 F3 **Silkwood** Qld Austr.
234 B1 **Silkworth** PA U.S.A.
178 C3 **Sill** r. Austria
187 C5 **Silla** Spain
138 F2 **Sillamäe** Estonia
190 F4 **Sillano** Italy
161 E5 **Sillans-la-Cascade** France
191 G4 **Sillaro** r. Italy
126 D3 **Sille** Turkey
182 B2 **Silleda** Spain
159 F3 **Sillé-le-Guillaume** France
156 E3 **Sillery** France
117 F5 **Silli** Bihar India
178 D4 **Sillian** Austria
116 C5 **Sillod** Mahar. India
149 F3 **Silloth** Cumbria, England U.K.
237 E4 **Siloam Springs** AR U.S.A.
215 H2 **Silobela** S. Africa
184 D3 **Silos de Calañas** Spain
134 M2 **Silovayakha** r. Rus. Fed.
186 F3 **Sils** Spain
190 E2 **Sils** Switz.
237 E6 **Silsbee** TX U.S.A.
149 H4 **Silsden** West Yorkshire, England U.K.
169 F4 **Silstedt** Ger.
138 F1 **Siltakylä** Fin.
123 E5 **Sīlūp** r. Iran
138 C4 **Šilutė** Lith.
215 H3 **Silutshana** S. Africa
257 F5 **Silva Jardim** Brazil
127 F3 **Silvan** Turkey
256 C2 **Silvânia** Brazil
190 E2 **Silvaplana** Switz.
182 B3 **Silvares** Braga Port.
182 C4 **Silvares** Castelo Branco Port.
116 C5 **Silvassa** Dadra India
184 B2 **Silveiras** Port.
143 G3 **Silverån** r. Sweden
247 E2 **Silver Bank** sea feature Turks and Caicos Is
246 E2 **Silver Bank Passage** Turks and Caicos Is
226 B2 **Silver Bay** MN U.S.A.
222 B2 **Silver City** Y.T. Can.
239 E5 **Silver City** NM U.S.A.
240 H2 **Silver City** NV U.S.A.
232 D3 **Silver Creek** NY U.S.A.
241 L4 **Silver Creek** r. AZ U.S.A.
80 E2 **Silverdale** North I. N.Z.
149 G3 **Silverdale** Lancashire, England U.K.
234 C2 **Silverdale** PA U.S.A.
151 H3 **Silver End** Essex, England U.K.
80 E3 **Silverhope** North I. N.Z.
226 C1 **Silver Islet** Ont. Can.
238 B3 **Silver Lake** OR U.S.A.
226 C3 **Silver Lake** WI U.S.A.
147 C4 **Silvermine Mountains** hills Rep. of Ireland
147 C4 **Silvermines** Rep. of Ireland
240 I3 **Silver Peak Range** mts NV U.S.A.
234 B4 **Silver Spring** MD U.S.A.
240 H2 **Silver Springs** NV U.S.A.
151 F2 **Silverstone** Northamptonshire, England U.K.
214 D3 **Silver Streams** S. Africa
222 E5 **Silverthrone Mountain** B.C. Can.
238 B1 **Silvertip Mountain** B.C. Can.
82 E2 **Silverton** N.S.W. Austr.
222 G5 **Silverton** B.C. Can.
150 D4 **Silverton** Devon, England U.K.
239 F4 **Silverton** CO U.S.A.
235 D2 **Silverton** NJ U.S.A.
237 C5 **Silverton** TX U.S.A.
227 F3 **Silver Water** Ont. Can.
251 G5 **Silves** Brazil
184 B3 **Silves** Port.
193 G2 **Silvi** Italy
250 B4 **Silvia** Col.
238 C3 **Silvies** r. OR U.S.A.
243 H5 **Silvituc** Mex.
190 F2 **Silvretta Gruppe** mts Switz.
178 B4 **Silvrettahorn** mt. Austria
129 F3 **Şilyan** Azer.
178 B3 **Silz** Austria
134 L5 **Sim** Rus. Fed.
134 L5 **Sim** r. Rus. Fed.
217 □3 **Sima** Comoros
139 L3 **Sima** Rus. Fed.
192 A5 **Simala** Sardegna Italy
183 F3 **Simancas** Spain
177 K5 **Șimand** Romania
160 C2 **Simandre** France
136 E2 **Simanichy** Belarus
198 C1 **Simantra** Greece
108 B4 **Simao** Yunnan China
254 F4 **Simão Dias** Brazil
127 G4 **Şīmareh, Rūdkhāneh-ye** r. Iran
117 F4 **Simaria** Bihar India
116 E4 **Simaria** Madh. Prad. India
187 C5 **Simat de la Valdigna** Spain
199 F2 **Simav** Turkey
199 F2 **Simav Dağları** mts Turkey
192 A5 **Simaxis** Sardegna Italy
173 G3 **Simbach** Ger.
173 H3 **Simbach am Inn** Ger.
195 F4 **Simbario** Italy
Simbirsk Rus. Fed. see Ul'yanovsk
78 □6 **Simbo** i. New Georgia Is Solomon Is
193 F3 **Simbruini, Monti** mts Italy
224 D5 **Simcoe** Ont. Can.
224 E4 **Simcoe, Lake** Ont. Can.
117 F5 **Simdega** Bihar India
141 L3 **Simeå** Sweden
203 H6 **Simēn Mountains** Eth.
197 G4 **Simeonovgrad** Bulg.
195 F4 **Simeri** r. Italy
197 F3 **Simeria** Romania
195 F4 **Simeri-Crichi** Italy
194 E5 **Simeto** r. Sicilia Italy
94 B2 **Simeuluë** i. Indon.
137 H5 **Simferopol'** Ukr.
Sími i. Greece see **Symi**
177 L4 **Șimian** Romania
161 D5 **Simiane-la-Rotonde** France
178 B4 **Similaun** mt. Austria/Italy
177 J2 **Siminy** mt. Slovakia
197 F5 **Simitli** Bulg.
240 H4 **Simi Valley** CA U.S.A.
Simla Hima. Prad. India see Shimla
239 F4 **Simla** CO U.S.A.
142 E3 **Simlångsdalen** Sweden
197 F2 **Șimleu Silvaniei** Romania
190 C2 **Simme** r. Switz.
173 F2 **Simmelsdorf** Ger.
169 B5 **Simmerath** Ger.
172 B2 **Simmern (Hunsrück)** Ger.
237 F6 **Simmesport** LA U.S.A.
246 D2 **Simm's** Long I. Bahamas
238 E2 **Simms** MT U.S.A.
138 D4 **Simnas** Lith.
140 N2 **Simo** Fin.
222 G4 **Simonette** r. Alta Can.
223 K4 **Simonhouse** Man. Can.
177 K3 **Šimonka** mt. Slovakia
232 C4 **Simons** OH U.S.A.
150 D3 **Simonsbath** Somerset, England U.K.
168 D1 **Simonsberg** Ger.
214 B6 **Simon's Town** S. Africa
164 F1 **Simonszand** i. Neth.
177 H5 **Simontornya** Hungary
222 E5 **Simoom Sound** B.C. Can.
Simoon Sound B.C. Can. see Simoom Sound
163 C5 **Simorre** France
94 D3 **Simpang** Sumatera Indon.
165 E4 **Simpelveld** Neth.
254 E3 **Simplício Mendes** Brazil
190 D2 **Simplon** Switz.
190 D2 **Simplon Pass** Switz.
223 J5 **Simpson** Sask. Can.
238 E1 **Simpson** MT U.S.A.
234 C1 **Simpson** PA U.S.A.
84 D5 **Simpson Desert** N.T. Austr.
87 E5 **Simpson Hill** hill W.A. Austr.
240 I2 **Simpson Park Mountains** NV U.S.A.
234 B3 **Simpsonville** MD U.S.A.
231 D5 **Simpsonville** SC U.S.A.
143 F4 **Simrishamn** Sweden
131 Q5 **Simushir, Ostrov** i. Kuril'skiye O-va Rus. Fed.
114 B2 **Sina** r. India
Sīnā', Shibh Jazīrat pen. Egypt see **Sinai**
94 B2 **Sinabang** Indon.
179 G3 **Sinabelkirchen** Austria
94 B2 **Sinabung** vol. Indon.
203 G2 **Sinai** pen. Egypt
156 E3 **Sinai, Mont** hill France
197 G3 **Sinaia** Romania
Sinai al Janûbîya governorate Egypt see **Janûb Sînâ'**
Sinai ash Shamâlîya governorate Egypt see **Shamâl Sînâ'**
97 B4 **Si Nakarin Reservoir** Thai.
244 A2 **Sinaloa** state Mex.
191 G5 **Sinalunga** Italy
Sinancha Rus. Fed. see **Cheremshany**
101 C5 **Sinanju** N. Korea
198 A2 **Sinarades** Ionioi Nisoi Greece
187 B5 **Sinarcas** Spain
209 E9 **Sinazongwe** Zambia
96 A3 **Sinbaungwe** Myanmar
96 A2 **Sinbyugyun** Myanmar
126 E3 **Sincan** Turkey
199 G2 **Sincanlı** Turkey
250 C2 **Sincé** Col.
250 C2 **Sincelejo** Col.
156 D3 **Sinceny** France
Sinchu Taiwan see **T'aoyüan**
222 F4 **Sinclair Mills** B.C. Can.
146 E3 **Sinclair's Bay** Scotland U.K.
254 E5 **Sincora, Serra do** hills Brazil
116 D4 **Sind** r. India
Sind prov. Pak. see **Sindh**
100 F2 **Sinda** Rus. Fed.
142 D3 **Sindal** Denmark
92 B4 **Sindañgan** Phil.
94 D4 **Sindangbarang** Jawa Barat Indon.
208 A5 **Sindara** Gabon
116 B4 **Sindari** Rajasthan India
172 C3 **Sindelfingen** Ger.
114 C2 **Sindgi** Karnataka India
123 G5 **Sindh** prov. Pak.
114 C3 **Sindhnur** Karnataka India
Síndhos Greece see **Sindos**
117 F4 **Sindhuli Garhi** Nepal
Sindhulimadi Nepal see Sindhuli Garhi
138 E2 **Sindi** Estonia
116 D5 **Sindi** Mahar. India
192 A4 **Sindia** Sardegna Italy
199 F2 **Sındırgı** Turkey
114 C2 **Sindkhed** Mahar. India
116 C5 **Sindkheda** Mahar. India
Sîndominic Romania see Sândominic
134 J3 **Sindor** Rus. Fed.
198 C1 **Sindos** Greece
206 D4 **Sindou** Burkina
114 C2 **Sindphana** r. India
117 F5 **Sindri** Bihar India
123 G4 **Sind Sagar Doab** lowland Pak.
134 J4 **Sinegor'ye** Rus. Fed.
199 E1 **Sinekçi** Turkey
193 G2 **Sinello** r. Italy
Sinel'nikovo Ukr. see Synel'nykove
207 F4 **Sinendé** Benin
184 B3 **Sines** Port.
184 B3 **Sines, Cabo de** c. Port.
187 G5 **Sineu** Spain
139 J5 **Sinezerki** Rus. Fed.
206 D5 **Sinfra** Côte d'Ivoire
203 G6 **Singa** Sudan
116 E3 **Singahi** Uttar Prad. India
217 □3a **Singani** Njazidja Comoros
94 D2 **Singapore** country Asia
94 □ **Singapore** Sing.
94 □ **Singapore, Strait of** Indon./Sing.
Singapura country Asia see Singapore
Singapura Sing. see **Singapore**
95 F5 **Singaraja** Bali Indon.
114 D2 **Singareni** Andhra Prad. India
Singatoka Viti Levu Fiji see Sigatoka
Singave Wallis and Futuna Is see Sigave
97 C4 **Sing Buri** Thai.
172 C4 **Singen (Hohentwiel)** Ger.
Sîngeorgiu de Pădure Romania see Sângeorgiu de Pădure
Sîngeorz-Băi Romania see Sângeorz-Băi
136 E4 **Sîngera** Moldova
136 E4 **Sîngerei** Moldova
110 E3 **Singgimtay** Xinjiang China
227 G3 **Singhampton** Ont. Can.
169 C5 **Singhofen** Ger.
211 B6 **Singida** Tanz.
211 B6 **Singida** admin. reg. Tanz.
Singidunum Srbija Yugo. see Beograd
Singim Xinjiang China see Singgimtay
93 B4 **Singkang** Sulawesi Selatan Indon.
95 E2 **Singkawang** Kalimantan Barat Indon.
94 D3 **Singkep** i. Indon.
94 B2 **Singkil** Sumatera Indon.
83 G3 **Singleton** N.S.W. Austr.
84 C4 **Singleton** N.T. Austr.
84 B4 **Singleton, Mount** hill N.T. Austr.
87 C6 **Singleton, Mount** hill W.A. Austr.
116 C4 **Singoli** Madh. Prad. India
Singora Thai. see **Songkhla**
Sin'gosan N. Korea see **Kosan**
117 G4 **Singra** Assam India
96 A2 **Singu** Myanmar
245 E4 **Singuilucan** Mex.
197 G3 **Singureni** Romania
101 C5 **Sin'gye** N. Korea
124 D4 **Sinḩ, Jabal** hill Saudi Arabia
Sinhala country Asia see Sri Lanka
101 C4 **Sinhŭng** N. Korea
192 A5 **Sini** Sardegna Italy
178 C4 **Sinigo** r. Italy
92 B3 **Siniloan** Phil.
Sining Qinghai China see **Xining**
93 A3 **Sinio, Gunung** mt. Indon.
192 B4 **Siniscola** Sardegna Italy
197 G5 **Sini Vrŭkh** mt. Bulg.
137 J2 **Siniye Lipyagi** Rus. Fed.
120 E2 **Siniy-Shikhan** Rus. Fed.
188 F4 **Sinj** Croatia
93 B4 **Sinjai** Sulawesi Selatan Indon.
127 F3 **Sinjār** Iraq
127 F3 **Sinjār, Jabal** mt. Iraq
203 H5 **Sinkat** Sudan
Sinkiang aut. reg. China see **Xinjiang Uygur Zizhiqu**
Sinkiang Uighur Autonomous Region aut. reg. China see **Xinjiang Uygur Zizhiqu**
147 C3 **Sinking** r. Rep. of Ireland
232 B5 **Sinking Spring** OH U.S.A.
136 D1 **Sinkyevichy** Belarus
183 F3 **Sinlabajos** Spain
156 D2 **Sin-le-Noble** France
Sînmartin Romania see Sânmartin
169 D5 **Sinn** Ger.
169 E5 **Sinn** r. Ger.
192 B5 **Sinnai** Sardegna Italy
251 H3 **Sinnamary** Fr. Guiana
114 B2 **Sinnar** Mahar. India
128 A5 **Sinn Bishr, Gebel** hill Egypt
137 H2 **Sinne** Ukr.
Sinneh Iran see **Sanandaj**
232 D4 **Sinnemahoning** PA U.S.A.
193 I4 **Sinni** r. Italy
Sînnicolau Mare Romania see Sânnicolau Mare
Sinoia Zimbabwe see **Chinhoyi**
197 I3 **Sinoie, Lacul** lag. Romania
253 G2 **Sinop** Brazil
126 D2 **Sinop** Turkey
Sinope Turkey see **Sinop**
195 E4 **Sinopoli** Italy
101 C4 **Sinp'a** N. Korea
Sînpetru Mare Romania see Sânpetru Mare
101 D4 **Sinp'o** N. Korea
101 C5 **Sinp'yŏng** N. Korea
172 C4 **Sins** Switz.
101 C5 **Sinsang** N. Korea
172 C2 **Sinsheim** Ger.
95 E2 **Sintang** Kalimantan Barat Indon.
164 D3 **Sint Annaland** Neth.
164 E1 **Sint Annaparochie** Neth.
164 E3 **Sint Anthonis** Neth.
247 □10 **Sint Christoffelberg** hill Curaçao Neth. Antilles
177 K5 **Sintea Mare** Romania
177 L4 **Șinteu** Romania
165 D3 **Sint Gillis-Waas** Belgium
165 E3 **Sint Huibrechts-Lille** Belgium
164 E1 **Sint Jacobiparochie** Neth.
165 D3 **Sint Jansteen** Neth.
165 D3 **Sint Katelijne-Waver** Belgium
165 C3 **Sint Laureins** Belgium
165 D3 **Sint Lenaarts** Belgium
247 G3 **Sint Maarten** i. Neth. Antilles
164 D3 **Sint Maartensdijk** Neth.
165 C3 **Sint Margriete** Belgium
165 C4 **Sint Maria-Lierde** Belgium
165 C3 **Sint Martens-Latem** Belgium
247 □9 **Sint Nicolaas** Aruba
164 E2 **Sint Nicolaasga** Neth.
165 D3 **Sint Niklaas** Belgium
237 D6 **Sinton** TX U.S.A.
164 D2 **Sint Pancras** Neth.
164 D3 **Sint Philipsland** Neth.
165 D4 **Sint Pieters-Leeuw** Belgium
184 A2 **Sintra** Port.
191 G4 **Sintria** r. Italy
139 K3 **Sintsovo** Rus. Fed.
165 E4 **Sint Truiden** Belgium
165 F4 **Sint Vith** Belgium
250 C2 **Sinú** r. Col.
101 C4 **Sinŭiju** N. Korea
138 G3 **Sinyaya** r. Rus. Fed.
172 C3 **Sinzheim** Ger.
169 C5 **Sinzig** Ger.
173 G3 **Sinzing** Ger.
177 H5 **Sió** r. Romania
186 D3 **Sió** r. Spain
177 H5 **Sióagárd** Hungary
92 B5 **Siocon** Phil.
177 H5 **Siófok** Hungary
209 D9 **Sioma** Zambia
190 C2 **Sion** Switz.
146 C3 **Sionascaig, Loch** l. Scotland U.K.
147 D2 **Sion Mills** Northern Ireland U.K.
160 B2 **Sioule** r. France
236 D3 **Sioux Center** IA U.S.A.
236 D3 **Sioux City** IA U.S.A.
236 D3 **Sioux Falls** SD U.S.A.
224 B3 **Sioux Lookout** Ont. Can.
243 H6 **Sipacate** Guat.
92 B4 **Sipalay** Phil.
247 □7 **Siparia** Trin. and Tob.
Siphaqeni S. Africa see Flagstaff
100 C4 **Siping** Jilin China
223 L4 **Sipiwesk** Man. Can.
262 P2 **Siple, Mount** Antarctica
262 N1 **Siple Coast** Antarctica
262 P2 **Siple Island** Antarctica
Sipolilo Zimbabwe see **Guruve**
197 H2 **Șipote** Romania
188 F3 **Šipovo** Bos.-Herz.
172 D4 **Sipplingen** Ger.
237 F5 **Sipsey** r. AL U.S.A.
125 F5 **Siqirah** Suquṭrā Yemen
256 C5 **Siqueira Campos** Brazil
242 □I6 **Siquia** r. Nic.
92 B4 **Siquijor** Phil.
92 B4 **Siquijor** i. Phil.
123 G6 **Sir** r. Pak.
114 C3 **Sira** Karnataka India
142 B2 **Sira** r. Norway
161 E4 **Sirac** mt. France
97 C4 **Si Racha** Thai.
195 E5 **Siracusa** Sicilia Italy
195 E5 **Siracusa** prov. Sicilia Italy
117 G4 **Sirajganj** Bangl.
222 F4 **Sir Alexander, Mount** B.C. Can.
162 E4 **Siran** France
126 E2 **Şiran** Turkey
116 E4 **Sirathu** Uttar Prad. India
207 F3 **Sirba** r. Burkina/Niger
Sircilla Andhra Prad. India see Sirsilla
Sirdaryo r. Asia see **Syrdar'ya**
Sirdaryo Uzbek. see **Syrdar'ya**
Sirdaryo Wiloyati admin. div. Uzbek. see **Syrdar'inskaya Oblast'**
Sirdingka Xizang China see Lhari
210 C2 **Sīrē** Oromia Eth.
210 C2 **Sīrē** Oromia Eth.
84 D2 **Sir Edward Pellew Group** is N.T. Austr.
226 A3 **Siren** WI U.S.A.
193 F2 **Sirente, Monte** mt. Italy
197 H2 **Siret** Romania
197 I3 **Siret** r. Romania
Siret r. Ukr. see **Seret**
86 E2 **Sir Graham Moore Islands** W.A. Austr.
128 C4 **Sirḩān, Wādī as** watercourse Jordan/Saudi Arabia
116 D3 **Sirhind** Punjab India
197 E2 **Șiria** Romania
122 D5 **Sīrīk** Iran
142 C2 **Sirikjerka** hill Norway
Sirína i. Greece see **Syrna**
123 G4 **Siritoi** r. Pak.
222 E2 **Sir James MacBrien, Mount** N.W.T. Can.
122 C4 **Sīrjān** Kermān Iran
122 C4 **Sīrjān** salt flat Iran
116 D3 **Sirmaur** Hima. Prad. India
191 F3 **Sirmione** Italy
Sirmium Vojvodina, Srbija Yugo. see **Sremska Mitrovica**
116 E4 **Sirmour** Madh. Prad. India
Sirmur Hima. Prad. India see Sirmaur
190 E1 **Sirnach** Switz.
127 F3 **Şırnak** Turkey
179 F4 **Širnitz** Austria
160 E2 **Sirod** France
116 C4 **Sirohi** Rajasthan India
177 J4 **Sirok** Hungary
177 J2 **Široké** Slovakia
191 I5 **Sirolo** Italy
114 D2 **Sironcha** Mahar. India
116 D4 **Sironj** Madh. Prad. India
191 G2 **Siròr** Italy
Síros i. Greece see **Syros**
204 D3 **Siroua, Jbel** mt. Morocco
114 C2 **Sirpur** Andhra Prad. India
240 H4 **Sirretta Peak** CA U.S.A.
122 C5 **Sīrrī, Jazīreh-ye** i. Iran
116 C3 **Sirsa** Haryana India
222 G5 **Sir Sandford, Mount** B.C. Can.
114 B3 **Sirsi** Karnataka India
116 D3 **Sirsi** Uttar Prad. India
114 C2 **Sirsilla** Andhra Prad. India
Sirte Libya see **Surt**
Sirte, Gulf of Libya see **Surt, Khalīj**
82 B1 **Sir Thomas, Mount** hill S.A. Austr.
185 E2 **Siruela** Spain
114 C3 **Siruguppa** Karnataka India
239 E6 **Sirupa** r. Mex.
114 B2 **Sirur** Karnataka India
114 B2 **Sirur** Mahar. India
127 F3 **Şirvan** Turkey
129 E3 **Şirvan Düzü** lowland Azer.
129 F3 **Şirvanovka** Azer.
114 C3 **Sirvel** Andhra Prad. India
175 K1 **Širvinta** r. Lith.
138 E4 **Širvintos** Lith.
127 G4 **Sīrwān** r. Iraq
222 G4 **Sir Wilfrid Laurier, Mount** B.C. Can.
85 E2 **Sir William Thompson Range** hills Qld Austr.
122 D3 **Siryan** Iran
Sis Turkey see **Kozan**
188 F3 **Sisak** Croatia
96 D4 **Sisaket** Thai.
243 H4 **Sisal** Mex.
185 H1 **Sisante** Spain
Siscia Croatia see **Sisak**
192 B2 **Sisco** Corse France
214 D2 **Sishen** S. Africa
129 E4 **Sisian** Armenia
206 E4 **Sisili** r. Burkina/Ghana
221 M3 **Sisimiut** Greenland
97 C4 **Sisŏphŏn** Cambodia
240 G4 **Sisquoc** r. CA U.S.A.
190 C1 **Sissach** Switz.
236 D2 **Sisseton** SD U.S.A.
206 E4 **Sissili** r. Burkina
156 D3 **Sissonne** France
232 C5 **Sissonville** WV U.S.A.
177 K5 **Șiștarovăț** Romania
226 D3 **Sister Bay** WI U.S.A.
161 D4 **Sisteron** France
238 B2 **Sisters** OR U.S.A.
232 C5 **Sistersville** WV U.S.A.
193 F3 **Sisto** r. Italy
178 C3 **Sistrans** Austria
139 K2 **Sit'** r. Rus. Fed.
117 F4 **Sitamarhi** Bihar India
116 C5 **Sitamau** Madh. Prad. India
175 L5 **Sitaniec** Pol.
116 E4 **Sitapur** Uttar Prad. India
176 F2 **Šitbořice** Czech Rep.
199 E4 **Siteia** Kriti Greece
215 H2 **Siteki** Swaziland
186 E3 **Sitges** Spain
198 C1 **Sithonia** pen. Greece
Sitía Kriti Greece see **Siteia**
106 B3 **Sitian** Xinjiang China
108 C3 **Siting** Guizhou China
254 D5 **Sítio da Abadia** Brazil
254 E5 **Sítio do Mato** Brazil
111 D7 **Sitka** Bihar India
220 E4 **Sitka** AK U.S.A.
175 I5 **Sitkówka-Nowiny** Pol.
196 E4 **Sitnica** r. Yugo.
177 H3 **Sitno** mt. Slovakia
138 G3 **Sitnya** r. Rus. Fed.
202 E2 **Sitra** oasis Egypt
96 B3 **Sittang** r. Myanmar
165 E4 **Sittard** Neth.
Sittaung r. Myanmar see Sittang
168 E2 **Sittensen** Ger.
172 D4 **Sitter** r. Ger.
179 F4 **Sittersdorf** Austria
215 F5 **Sittingbourne** S. Africa
151 H3 **Sittingbourne** Kent, England U.K.
Sittoung r. Myanmar see Sittang
96 A2 **Sittwe** Myanmar
95 F4 **Situbondo** Jawa Timur Indon.
171 C5 **Sitzendorf** Ger.
179 G2 **Sitzendorf an der Schmida** Austria
171 D4 **Sitzenroda** Ger.
242 □I6 **Siuna** Nic.
141 N3 **Siuntio** Fin.
192 B5 **Siurgus Donigala** Sardegna Italy
117 F5 **Siuri** W. Bengal India
134 K4 **Siva** Rus. Fed.
177 I6 **Sivac** Vojvodina, Srbija Yugo.
114 C4 **Sivaganga** Tamil Nadu India
114 C4 **Sivakasi** Tamil Nadu India
100 C1 **Sivaki** Rus. Fed.
122 C4 **Sivand** Iran
126 E3 **Sivas** Turkey
199 F2 **Sivaslı** Turkey
206 B3 **Sivé** Maur.
126 E3 **Siverek** Turkey
137 J3 **Sivers'k** Ukr.
139 H2 **Siverskiy** Rus. Fed.
Sivers'kyy Donets' r. Rus. Fed. see **Severskiy Donets**
137 J3 **Sivers'kyy Donets'** r. Ukr.
175 M6 **Sivka-Voynylivs'ka** Ukr.
134 M2 **Sivomaskinskiy** Rus. Fed.
126 E3 **Sivrice** Turkey
126 C3 **Sivrihisar** Turkey
165 D4 **Sivry** Belgium
157 F3 **Sivry-sur-Meuse** France
215 G2 **Sivukile** S. Africa
202 E2 **Siwa** Egypt
116 D3 **Siwalik Range** mts India/Nepal
117 F4 **Siwan** Bihar India
116 C4 **Siwana** Rajasthan India
202 E2 **Siwa Oasis** Egypt
129 E3 **Şıxarx** Azer.
161 D5 **Six-Fours-les-Plages** France
109 F1 **Sixian** Anhui China
226 E4 **Six Lakes** MI U.S.A.
147 C4 **Sixmilebridge** Rep. of Ireland
147 D2 **Sixmilecross** Northern Ireland U.K.
160 E2 **Sixt-Fer-à-Cheval** France
215 G1 **Siyabuswa** S. Africa
Siyang Guangxi China see Shangsi
109 F1 **Siyang** Jiangsu China
215 G2 **Siyathemba** S. Africa
215 H1 **Siyathuthuka** S. Africa
129 F3 **Siyäzän** Azer.
107 F3 **Siyitang** Nei Mongol China
184 A1 **Sizandro** r. Port.
Siziwang Qi Nei Mongol China see **Ulan Hua**
158 B3 **Sizun** France
134 K2 **Sizyabsk** Rus. Fed.
142 D4 **Sjælland** i. Denmark
196 E4 **Sjenica** Srbija Yugo.
143 E4 **Sjöbo** Sweden
140 I3 **Sjøholt** Norway
140 K2 **Sjona** sea chan. Norway
140 K2 **Sjoutnäset** Sweden
140 L1 **Sjøvegan** Norway
140 M2 **Sjulsmark** Sweden
140 □ **Sjuøyane** is Svalbard
140 K3 **Skäckerfjällen** mts Sweden
137 G4 **Skadovs'k** Ukr.
142 D4 **Skælsør** Denmark
142 C4 **Skærbæk** Denmark
221 Q2 **Skærfjorden** inlet Greenland
140 □C3 **Skaftárós** r. mouth Iceland
140 □C2 **Skagafjörður** inlet Iceland
140 □B2 **Skagaheiði** reg. Iceland
142 D3 **Skagen** Denmark
143 F2 **Skagern** l. Sweden
142 C3 **Skagerrak** str. Denmark/Norway
238 B1 **Skagit** r. WA U.S.A.
222 F5 **Skagit Mountain** B.C. Can.
220 E4 **Skagway** AK U.S.A.
138 E4 **Skaidiškės** Lith.
146 E2 **Skaill** Orkney, Scotland U.K.
146 F3 **Skaill** Orkney, Scotland U.K.
199 E3 **Skala** Notio Aigaio Greece
198 C3 **Skala** Peloponnisos Greece
175 H5 **Skała** Pol.
140 L1 **Skaland** Norway
136 D3 **Skala-Podil's'ka** Ukr.
171 F5 **Skalice** Czech Rep.
129 B1 **Skalistyy Khrebet** reg. Rus. Fed.
177 H2 **Skalité** Slovakia
140 K2 **Skalmodal** Sweden
176 B1 **Skalná** Czech Rep.
142 C3 **Skals** r. Denmark
142 C3 **Skanderborg** Denmark
142 E4 **Skåne** county Sweden
232 E3 **Skaneateles** NY U.S.A.
140 L2 **Skansholm** Sweden
174 D3 **Skąpe** Pol.
142 E2 **Skara** Sweden
146 E2 **Skara Brae** tourist site Scotland U.K.
Skardarsko Jezero l. Albania/Yugo. see **Scutari, Lake**
85 E1 **Skardon** r. Qld Austr.
116 C2 **Skardu** Jammu and Kashmir
142 B2 **Skåreheia** mt. Norway
142 D3 **Skärhamn** Sweden
142 D1 **Skarnes** Norway
143 G1 **Skärplinge** Sweden
141 K3 **Skärsjövålen** Sweden
141 J3 **Skarstind** mt. Norway
174 G1 **Skarszewy** Pol.
141 J3 **Skarvedalseggen** mt. Norway
140 L2 **Skarvsjöby** Sweden
175 J4 **Skaryszew** Pol.
136 D3 **Skarzhyntsi** Ukr.
175 I4 **Skarżysko-Kamienna** Pol.
142 E1 **Skasberget** hill Norway
138 D4 **Skaudvilė** Lith.
140 M2 **Skaulo** Sweden
142 C3 **Skave** Denmark
146 □H1 **Skaw** Shetland, Scotland U.K.
175 H5 **Skawa** r. Pol.
175 H6 **Skawina** Pol.
143 H2 **Skebobruk** Sweden
143 F2 **Skeda udde** Sweden
222 D4 **Skeena** r. B.C. Can.
222 D3 **Skeena Mountains** B.C. Can.
149 J4 **Skegness** Lincolnshire, England U.K.
140 □C3 **Skeiðarársandur** sand area Iceland
146 □G1 **Skeld** Shetland, Scotland U.K.
168 E1 **Skelde** Denmark
140 M2 **Skellefteå** Sweden
140 M2 **Skellefteälven** r. Sweden
140 M2 **Skelleftebukten** b. Sweden
140 M2 **Skelleftehamn** Sweden
149 G4 **Skelmersdale** Lancashire, England U.K.
146 D6 **Skelmorlie** North Ayrshire, Scotland U.K.
149 I3 **Skelton** Redcar and Cleveland, England U.K.
150 E3 **Skenfrith** Monmouthshire, Wales U.K.
175 H3 **Skępe** Pol.
141 L3 **Skeppshamn** Sweden
214 D3 **Skerpioenpunt** S. Africa
146 D3 **Skerray** Highland, Scotland U.K.
147 E3 **Skerries** Rep. of Ireland
150 D3 **Sketty** Swansea, Wales U.K.
136 B3 **Skhidni Beskydy** mts Pol./Ukr.
136 B3 **Skhidni Karpaty** mts Ukr.
175 L6 **Skhidnytsya** Ukr.
Skhimatárion Greece see Schimatari
142 D2 **Ski** Norway
198 C2 **Skiathos** Greece
198 C2 **Skiathos** i. Greece
147 B5 **Skibbereen** Rep. of Ireland
138 E5 **Skidal'** Belarus
149 F3 **Skiddaw** hill England U.K.
222 D4 **Skidegate Mission** B.C. Can.
Skidel' Belarus see **Skidal'**
234 B3 **Skidmore** MD U.S.A.
142 C2 **Skien** Norway
175 L5 **Skierbieszów** Pol.
175 I4 **Skierniewice** Pol.
205 G1 **Skikda** Alg.
143 F2 **Skinnskatteberg** Sweden
116 D2 **Skio** Jammu and Kashmir
146 C6 **Skipness** Argyll and Bute, Scotland U.K.
234 C2 **Skippack** PA U.S.A.
149 I4 **Skipsea** East Riding of Yorkshire, England U.K.
214 C6 **Skipskop** S. Africa
83 E4 **Skipton** Vic. Austr.
149 G4 **Skipton** North Yorkshire, England U.K.
234 B4 **Skipton** MD U.S.A.
Skíros i. Greece see **Skyros**
142 C3 **Skive** Denmark
175 K3 **Skiwy Duże** Pol.
140 □C2 **Skjálfandafljót** r. Iceland
140 □C2 **Skjálfandi** b. Iceland
140 K2 **Skjelatinden** mt. Norway
142 D1 **Skjellinhovde** hill Norway
142 B1 **Skjemmene** mt. Norway
142 B2 **Skjerkeknuten** hill Norway
142 C4 **Skjern** Denmark
142 C4 **Skjern** r. Denmark
140 M1 **Skjervøy** Norway
Skobelev Uzbek. see **Fergana**
121 H5 **Skobeleva, Pik** mt. Kyrg.
179 E5 **Skocjanske Jame** tourist site Slovenia
174 G6 **Skoczów** Pol.
215 E6 **Skoenmakerskop** S. Africa
188 E2 **Škofja Loka** Slovenia
179 F5 **Škofljica** Slovenia
141 L3 **Skog** Sweden
143 F3 **Skoghult** Sweden
150 B3 **Skokholm Island** Wales U.K.
174 F3 **Skoki** Pol.
226 D4 **Skokie** IL U.S.A.
136 B3 **Skole** Ukr.
143 F2 **Sköllersta** Sweden
175 J6 **Skołyszyn** Pol.
150 B3 **Skomer Island** Wales U.K.
174 G4 **Skomlin** Pol.
215 F2 **Skoonspruit** r. S. Africa
198 C2 **Skopelos** Greece
198 C2 **Skopelos** i. Greece
198 D2 **Skopia** hill Voreio Aigaio Greece
139 L5 **Skopin** Rus. Fed.
196 E5 **Skopje** Macedonia
Skoplje Macedonia see **Skopje**
174 G2 **Skórcz** Pol.
135 G6 **Skorodnoye** Rus. Fed.
174 F5 **Skorogoszcz** Pol.
174 F5 **Skoroszyce** Pol.
144 J1 **Skorpa** i. Norway
142 C3 **Skørping** Denmark
175 K3 **Skórzec** Pol.
198 C1 **Skotoussa** Greece
142 E2 **Skotterud** Norway
198 C1 **Skoutari** Greece
199 E2 **Skoutaros** Voreio Aigaio Greece
143 E2 **Skövde** Sweden
100 B1 **Skovorodino** Rus. Fed.
233 □I2 **Skowhegan** ME U.S.A.
142 C2 **Skrimfjell** hill Norway
138 E3 **Skrīveri** Latvia
188 D2 **Škrlatica** mt. Slovenia
175 J2 **Skroda** r. Pol.
140 M2 **Skröven** Sweden
138 D3 **Skrunda** Latvia
175 H3 **Skrwa** r. Pol.
175 H2 **Skrwilno** Pol.
174 E2 **Skrzatusz** Pol.
175 G6 **Skrzyczne** mt. Pol.
175 I4 **Skrzyńsko** Pol.
175 J6 **Skrzyszów** Pol.
142 A2 **Skudeneshavn** Norway
144 D1 **Skúgvoy** i. Faroe Is
215 F1 **Skuinsdrif** S. Africa
222 C2 **Skukum, Mount** Y.T. Can.
213 F5 **Skukuza** S. Africa
241 I3 **Skull Peak** NV U.S.A.
241 K4 **Skull Valley** AZ U.S.A.
174 G3 **Skulsk** Pol.
143 G2 **Skultuna** Sweden
236 F3 **Skunk** r. IA U.S.A.
138 C3 **Skuodas** Lith.
139 K4 **Skuratovskiy** Rus. Fed.
142 E4 **Skurup** Sweden
197 F4 **Skŭt** r. Bulg.
143 G1 **Skutskär** Sweden
175 M6 **Skvaryava** Ukr.
136 E3 **Skvyra** Ukr.
174 D3 **Skwierzyna** Pol.
177 H3 **Skýcov** Slovakia
198 C1 **Skydra** Kentriki Makedonia Greece
146 B4 **Skye** i. Scotland U.K.
142 B2 **Skykula** hill Norway
198 D2 **Skyros** Sterea Ellas Greece
198 D2 **Skyros** i. Greece
234 C1 **Skytop** PA U.S.A.
262 S1 **Skytrain Ice Rise** Antarctica
175 I5 **Słaboszów** Pol.
234 B2 **Slabtown** PA U.S.A.
234 D2 **Slack Woods** NJ U.S.A.
Sládečkovce Slovakia see Močenok
144 D1 **Slættaratindur** hill Faroe Is
142 D4 **Slagelse** Denmark
164 F2 **Slagharen** Neth.
140 L2 **Slagnäs** Sweden
149 G4 **Slaidburn** Lancashire, England U.K.
146 E6 **Slamannan** Falkirk, Scotland U.K.
95 E4 **Slamet, Gunung** vol. Indon.
177 J3 **Slaná** r. Slovakia
147 E3 **Slane** Rep. of Ireland
177 K3 **Slanec** Slovakia
147 E4 **Slaney** r. Rep. of Ireland
197 G3 **Slănic** Romania
197 H3 **Slănic** r. Romania
197 H2 **Slănic Moldova** Romania
177 K3 **Slanské Vrchy** mts Slovakia
138 G2 **Slantsy** Rus. Fed.
176 D1 **Slaný** Czech Rep.
176 F2 **Šlapanice** Czech Rep.
85 F3 **Slashers Reefs** Qld Austr.
Śląsk reg. Europe see **Silesia**
175 G5 **Śląska, Wyżyna** hills Pol.
174 G5 **Śląskie** prov. Pol.
234 C2 **Slateford** PA U.S.A.
235 D1 **Slate Hill** NY U.S.A.
188 F3 **Slatina** Croatia
197 G3 **Slatina** Romania
177 I3 **Slatina** r. Slovakia
197 F3 **Slatina-Timiș** Romania
234 C2 **Slatington** PA U.S.A.
176 G2 **Slatinice** Czech Rep.
232 C5 **Slaty Fork** WV U.S.A.
137 I2 **Slatyne** Ukr.
222 H2 **Slave** r. Alta/N.W.T. Can.
207 F5 **Slave Coast** Africa
222 H4 **Slave Lake** Alta Can.
Slavgorod Belarus see Slawharad
121 I1 **Slavgorod** Rus. Fed.
Slavgorod Dnipropetrovs'ka Oblast' Ukr. see **Slavhorod**

Slavhorod to Soufrière
364

137 H3 Slavhorod Dnipropetrovs'ka Oblast' Ukr.
137 H2 Slavhorod Sums'ka Oblast' Ukr.
177 G2 Slavičín Czech Rep.
197 F4 Slavinja Srbija Yugo.
138 G3 Slavkovichi Rus. Fed.
176 B1 Slavkovský Les hill Czech Rep.
176 F2 Slavkov u Brna Czech Rep.
191 I3 Slavnik mt. Slovenia
176 E3 Slavonice Czech Rep.
Slavonska Požega Croatia see Požega
188 G3 Slavonski Brod Croatia
177 J3 Slavošovce Slovakia
138 C4 Slavsk Rus. Fed.
136 D2 Slavuta Ukr.
136 F2 Slavutych Ukr.
Slavyanka Kazakh. see Myrzakent
100 D4 Slavyanka Rus. Fed.
197 G4 Slavyanovo Bulg.
Slavyansk Ukr. see Slov"yans'k
Slavyanskaya Rus. Fed. see Slavyansk-na-Kubani
135 G7 Slavyansk-na-Kubani Rus. Fed.
174 E4 Sława Pol.
175 L4 Sławatycze Pol.
174 F2 Sławęcin Pol.
139 H5 Slawharad Belarus
143 G4 Sławno Pol.
174 D2 Sławoborze Pol.
236 E3 Slayton MN U.S.A.
149 I4 Slea r. England U.K.
149 I4 Sleaford Lincolnshire, England U.K.
82 C3 Sleaford Bay S.A. Austr.
146 C4 Sleat pen. Scotland U.K.
146 C4 Sleat, Sound of sea chan. Scotland U.K.
149 I3 Sledmere East Riding of Yorkshire, England U.K.
164 F2 Sleen Neth.
164 D3 Sleeuwijk Neth.
149 I3 Sleights North Yorkshire, England U.K.
95 E4 Sleman Indon.
175 H6 Ślemień Pol.
129 D2 Sleptsovskaya Rus. Fed.
174 G3 Ślesin Pol.
174 E5 Ślęża hill Pol.
174 E4 Ślęża r. Pol.
Slezsko reg. Europe see Silesia
177 I3 Sliač Slovakia
241 M2 Slick Rock CO U.S.A.
237 F6 Slidell LA U.S.A.
233 F4 Slide Mountain NY U.S.A.
141 J3 Slidre Norway
164 D3 Sliedrecht Neth.
195 □ Sliema Malta
147 A4 Slievanea hill Rep. of Ireland
147 D2 Slieve Anierin hill Rep. of Ireland
147 D4 Slieveardagh Hills Rep. of Ireland
147 C3 Slieve Aughty Mountains hills Rep. of Ireland
147 D2 Slieve Beagh hill Rep. of Ireland/U.K.
147 C4 Slieve Bernagh hills Rep. of Ireland
147 D4 Slieve Bloom Mountains hills Rep. of Ireland
147 B4 Slievecallan hill Rep. of Ireland
147 B2 Slieve Car hill Rep. of Ireland
147 F2 Slieve Donard hill Northern Ireland U.K.
147 C4 Slievefelim Mountains hills Rep. of Ireland
148 C3 Slieve Gallion hill Northern Ireland U.K.
147 B3 Slieve Gamph hills Rep. of Ireland
147 C4 Slievekimalta hill Rep. of Ireland
147 D2 Slievekirk hill Northern Ireland U.K.
147 A4 Slieve Mish Mountains hills Rep. of Ireland
147 A5 Slieve Miskish Mountains hills Rep. of Ireland
147 D2 Slievenakilla hill Rep. of Ireland
147 D4 Slievenamon hill Rep. of Ireland
148 B3 Slieve Rushen hill Northern Ireland U.K.
147 C2 Slieve Snaght hill Donegal Rep. of Ireland
147 D1 Slieve Snaght hill Donegal Rep. of Ireland
146 B4 Sligachan Highland, Scotland U.K.
Sligeach Rep. of Ireland see Sligo
147 C2 Sligo Rep. of Ireland
147 C2 Sligo county Rep. of Ireland
232 D4 Sligo PA U.S.A.
147 C2 Sligo Bay Rep. of Ireland
175 K2 Ślina r. Pol.
151 G3 Slinfold West Sussex, England U.K.
164 F2 Slinge r. Neth.
146 C4 Slioch hill Scotland U.K.
137 G3 Sliporid r. Ukr.
232 C4 Slippery Rock PA U.S.A.
143 H3 Slite Gotland Sweden
197 H4 Sliven Bulg.
197 F4 Slivnitsa Bulg.
197 H4 Slivo Pole Bulg.
174 G2 Śliwice Pol.
188 E3 Sljeme mt. Croatia
241 J4 Sloan NV U.S.A.
240 G2 Sloat CA U.S.A.
235 D1 Sloatsburg NY U.S.A.
136 E4 Slobidka Ukr.
Sloboda Respublika Komi Rus. Fed. see Ezhva
Sloboda Smolenskaya Oblast' Rus. Fed. see Przheval'skoye
135 H6 Sloboda Voronezhskaya Oblast' Rus. Fed.
137 G2 Sloboda Ukr.
134 J4 Slobodskoy Rus. Fed.
Slobodzeya Moldova see Slobozia
136 E4 Slobozia Moldova
197 H3 Slobozia Romania
197 H3 Slobozia Bradului Romania
222 G5 Slocan B.C. Can.
164 F1 Slochteren Neth.
175 I5 Słomniki Pol.
138 E5 Slonim Belarus
137 I2 Slonovka Rus. Fed.
174 C3 Słońsk Pol.
164 D2 Slootdorp Neth.
164 E2 Sloten Neth.
151 G3 Slough Slough, England U.K.
151 G3 Slough admin. div. England U.K.
176 F2 Sloupnice Czech Rep.
177 I3 Slovakia country Europe
136 E2 Slovechna r. Ukr.
136 E2 Slovechne Ukr.
188 E2 Slovenia country Europe
Slovenija country Europe see Slovenia
188 E2 Slovenj Gradec Slovenia
188 E2 Slovenska Bistrica Slovenia
177 J2 Slovenská Ves Slovakia
188 E2 Slovenske Gorice hills Slovenia
179 G4 Slovenske Konjice Slovenia
177 K3 Slovenské Nové Mesto Slovakia
177 I3 Slovenské Rudohorie mts Slovakia
Slovensko country Europe see Slovakia
177 J3 Slovenský kras mts Slovakia
177 J3 Slovinky Slovakia
175 M6 Slovita Ukr.
137 I3 Slov"yanka Ukr.
137 I3 Slov"yanohirs'k Ukr.
137 J3 Slov"yanoserbs'k Ukr.
137 I3 Slov"yans'k Ukr.
136 E2 Slovyechna r. Belarus
175 H4 Słowik Pol.
174 C3 Słubice Pol.
175 H3 Słubice Pol.
138 F5 Sluch r. Belarus
136 D2 Sluch r. Ukr.
191 F2 Sluderno Italy
134 J4 Sludka Rus. Fed.
165 C3 Sluis Neth.
165 C3 Sluiskil Neth.
176 D1 Šluknov Czech Rep.
176 G2 Slunečná hill Czech Rep.
188 E3 Slunj Croatia
174 F3 Słupca Pol.
175 J5 Słupcza Pol.
175 H4 Słupia Pol.
175 H5 Słupia Pol.
175 I4 Słupia Pol.
143 G4 Słupia r. Pol.
175 H3 Słupno Pol.
143 G4 Słupsk Pol.
140 L2 Slussfors Sweden
174 G4 Słuszków Pol.
138 F5 Slutsk Belarus
138 D4 Šlyna r. Lith.
98 H1 Slyudyanka Rus. Fed.
237 E5 Smackover AR U.S.A.
162 A2 Smagne r. France
146 F6 Smailholm Scottish Borders, Scotland U.K.
143 F3 Småland reg. Sweden
142 D4 Smålandsfarvandet sea chan. Denmark
142 E3 Smålandsstenar Sweden
151 F2 Smalley Derbyshire, England U.K.
225 H2 Smallwood Reservoir Nfld. Can.
138 G4 Smalyavichy Belarus
175 I4 Smardzewice Pol.
138 F4 Smarhon' Belarus
179 G4 Šmarje pri Jelšah Slovenia
179 G4 Šmartno Slovenia
162 C2 Smarves France
223 J4 Smeaton Sask. Can.
171 F5 Smečno Czech Rep.
176 D1 Smědá r. Czech Rep.
143 G3 Smedby Sweden
196 E3 Smederevo Srbija Yugo.
196 E3 Smederevska Palanka Srbija Yugo.
197 H3 Smeeni Romania
151 H3 Smeeth Kent, England U.K.
Smela Ukr. see Smila
232 D4 Smethport PA U.S.A.
151 F2 Smethwick West Midlands, England U.K.
174 G2 Smętowo Graniczne Pol.
176 E1 Smidary Czech Rep.
175 M4 Smidyn Ukr.
174 E3 Śmigiel Pol.
137 F3 Smila Ukr.
138 G5 Smilavichy Belarus
164 F2 Smilde Neth.
137 G2 Smile Ukr.
136 D2 Smilka r. Ukr.
138 E3 Smiltene Latvia
138 D3 Smiltiņu kalns hill Latvia
176 E1 Smiřice Czech Rep.
121 G1 Smirnovo Kazakh.
Smirnovskiy Kazakh. see Smirnovo
100 G2 Smirnykh Sakhalin Rus. Fed.
222 H4 Smith Alta Can.
238 E2 Smith r. MT U.S.A.
232 D6 Smith r. VA U.S.A.
220 F3 Smith Arm b. N.W.T. Can.
147 D2 Smithborough Rep. of Ireland
236 D4 Smith Center KS U.S.A.
222 E4 Smithers B.C. Can.
222 E4 Smithers Landing B.C. Can.
215 F4 Smithfield S. Africa
231 E5 Smithfield NC U.S.A.
238 E3 Smithfield UT U.S.A.
232 E6 Smithfield VA U.S.A.
262 Q1 Smith Glacier Antarctica
262 T2 Smith Island Antarctica
237 F4 Smithland KY U.S.A.
84 B1 Smith Point N.T. Austr.
222 E3 Smith River B.C. Can.
232 E5 Smithsburg MD U.S.A.
224 E4 Smiths Falls Ont. Can.
83 F5 Smithton Tas. Austr.
83 H2 Smithtown N.S.W. Austr.
235 E2 Smithtown NY U.S.A.
235 D3 Smithville NJ U.S.A.
237 E5 Smithville OK U.S.A.
231 C5 Smithville TN U.S.A.
232 C5 Smithville WV U.S.A.
214 E5 Smitskraal S. Africa
177 J3 Smižany Slovakia
140 □D2 Smjörfjöll mts Iceland
240 H1 Smoke Creek Desert NV U.S.A.
222 G3 Smoky r. Alta Can.
82 C3 Smoky Bay S.A. Austr.
82 C3 Smoky Bay b. S.A. Austr.
83 H2 Smoky Cape N.S.W. Austr.
224 D3 Smoky Falls Ont. Can.
236 D4 Smoky Hill r. KS U.S.A.
236 C4 Smoky Hill, North Fork r. KS U.S.A.
228 G3 Smoky Hills KS U.S.A.
223 H4 Smoky Lake Alta Can.
140 I3 Smøla i. Norway
174 F1 Smołdzino Pol.
120 B2 Smolenka Rus. Fed.
139 I4 Smolensk Rus. Fed.
139 I4 Smolenskaya Oblast' admin. div. Rus. Fed.
Smolensk Oblast admin. div. Rus. Fed. see Smolenskaya Oblast'
139 I4 Smolensko-Moskovskaya Vozvyshennost' hills Rus. Fed.
121 K1 Smolenskoye Rus. Fed.
Smolevichi Belarus see Smalyavichy
174 F4 Smolice Pol.
198 B1 Smolikas mt. Greece
137 F3 Smoline Ukr.
142 E2 Smolmark Sweden
177 J3 Smolník Slovakia
197 G5 Smolyan Bulg.
100 E4 Smolyoninovo Rus. Fed.
224 D3 Smooth Rock Falls Ont. Can.
Smorgon' Belarus see Smarhon'
139 I5 Smotrova Buda Rus. Fed.
136 D3 Smotrych Ukr.
176 G1 Smrk mt. Czech Rep.
171 G5 Smrk mt. Czech Rep.
137 F2 Smyach Ukr.
197 H4 Smyadovo Bulg.
142 E4 Smygehamn Sweden
136 C2 Smyha Ukr.
175 I4 Smyków Pol.
262 S2 Smyley Island Antarctica
Smyrna Turkey see İzmir
234 C3 Smyrna DE U.S.A.
231 C5 Smyrna GA U.S.A.
231 C5 Smyrna TN U.S.A.
234 C3 Smyrna r. DE U.S.A.
233 □I1 Smyrna Mills ME U.S.A.
Smyth Island atoll Marshall Is see Majuro
140 □D2 Snæfell mt. Iceland
148 E3 Snaefell hill Isle of Man
140 □B2 Snæfellsjökull ice cap Iceland
140 □B2 Snæfellsnes pen. Iceland
222 A2 Snag Y.T. Can.
149 I3 Snainton North Yorkshire, England U.K.
149 H4 Snaith East Riding of Yorkshire, England U.K.
236 C3 Snake r. NE U.S.A.
238 C2 Snake r. U.S.A.
84 B2 Snake Creek r. N.T. Austr.
241 J2 Snake Range mts NV U.S.A.
222 F3 Snake River B.C. Can.
238 D3 Snake River Plain ID U.S.A.
222 G2 Snare r. N.W.T. Can.
Snare Lakes N.W.T. Can. see Wekweti
77 G6 Snares Islands N.Z.
140 K2 Snåsa Norway
232 B6 Sneedville TN U.S.A.
164 E1 Sneek Neth.
147 B5 Sneem Rep. of Ireland
214 B5 Sneeuberg mt. S. Africa
214 E4 Sneeuberge mts S. Africa
Snegurovka Ukr. see Tetiyiv
240 G3 Snelling CA U.S.A.
151 H2 Snettisham Norfolk, England U.K.
139 K5 Snezhed' r. Rus. Fed.
130 J3 Snezhnogorsk Rus. Fed.
Snezhnoye Ukr. see Snizhne
176 E1 Sněžka mt. Czech Rep.
188 E3 Snežnik mt. Slovenia
175 J2 Śniadowo Pol.
175 J2 Śniardwy, Jezioro l. Pol.
Sniečkus Lith. see Visaginas
Snieżka mt. Czech Rep. see Sněžka
174 E5 Śnieżnik mt. Pol.
137 G4 Snihurivka Ukr.
177 L3 Snina Slovakia
151 F2 Snitterfield Warwickshire, England U.K.
137 G2 Snityn Ukr.
137 J3 Snizhne Ukr.
146 B4 Snizort, Loch b. Scotland U.K.
141 J3 Snøhetta mt. Norway
238 B2 Snohomish WA U.S.A.
142 B2 Snønuten mt. Norway
139 I5 Snopot' r. Rus. Fed.
137 F2 Snov r. Ukr.
137 I2 Snova r. Rus. Fed.
139 L5 Snova r. Rus. Fed.
Snovsk Ukr. see Shchors
138 F5 Snow Belarus
222 G5 Snowcrest Mountain B.C. Can.
81 B6 Snowdon mt. South I. N.Z.
150 C1 Snowdon mt. Wales U.K.
150 D2 Snowdonia National Park Wales U.K.
Snowdrift N.W.T. Can. see Łutselk'e
223 I2 Snowdrift r. N.W.T. Can.
241 L4 Snowflake AZ U.S.A.
233 F5 Snow Hill MD U.S.A.
231 E5 Snow Hill NC U.S.A.
223 K4 Snow Lake Man. Can.
82 D3 Snowtown S.A. Austr.
238 D3 Snowville UT U.S.A.
83 G4 Snowy r. N.S.W./Vic. Austr.
233 F3 Snowy Mountain NY U.S.A.
83 F4 Snowy Mountains N.S.W. Austr.
246 D2 Snug Corner Acklins I. Bahamas
225 K2 Snug Harbour Nfld. Can.
227 G3 Snug Harbour Ont. Can.
136 C3 Snyatyn Ukr.
237 D5 Snyder OK U.S.A.
237 C5 Snyder TX U.S.A.
234 A2 Snyder County county PA U.S.A.
234 C2 Snyders PA U.S.A.
136 E3 Snyvoda r. Ukr.
Soaigh i. Western Isles, Scotland U.K. see Soay
182 B3 Soajo Port.
81 A6 Soaker, Mount South I. N.Z.
213 □J3 Soalala Madag.
182 B3 Soalhães Port.
182 C4 Soalheira Port.
213 □J4 Soamanonga Madag.
190 C3 Soana r. Italy
213 □K3 Soanierana-Ivongo Madag.
191 H5 Soara r. Italy
191 G3 Soave Italy
213 □J3 Soavinandriana Madag.
146 B4 Soay i. Highland, Scotland U.K.
146 □ Soay i. Western Isles, Scotland U.K.
136 E3 Sob r. Ukr.
207 H4 Soba Nigeria
101 C6 Sobaek-sanmaek mts S. Korea
210 A2 Sobat r. Sudan
105 E3 Sobatsubu-yama mt. Japan
182 C2 Sober Spain
172 B2 Sobernheim Ger.
176 D2 Soběslav Czech Rep.
91 J7 Sobger r. Indon.
139 M4 Sobinka Rus. Fed.
139 L4 Sobolevo Rus. Fed.
175 J4 Sobolew Pol.
103 E7 Sobo-san mt. Japan
175 H3 Sobota Pol.
176 G1 Sobotín Czech Rep.
176 G3 Sobotište Slovakia
176 E1 Sobotka Czech Rep.
174 E5 Sobótka Pol.
175 J5 Sobótka Pol.
174 F4 Sobótka Pol.
174 G1 Sobowidz Pol.
182 D2 Sobradelo Spain
256 D1 Sobradinho Brazil
182 B1 Sobrado Galicia Spain
182 B2 Sobrado Galicia Spain
254 E2 Sobral Brazil
182 B4 Sobral Port.
184 C2 Sobral da Adiça Port.
184 A1 Sobral de Monte Agraço Port.
182 C4 Sobral do Campo Port.
177 L3 Sobrance Slovakia
182 B3 Sobreira Port.
182 C5 Sobreira Formosa Port.
168 F1 Søby Denmark
137 G2 Sobych Ukr.
Soča r. Italy see Isonzo
188 D3 Soča r. Slovenia
191 H2 Socchieve Italy
175 I3 Sochaczew Pol.
129 A2 Sochi Rus. Fed.
175 I3 Sochocin Pol.
101 C5 Sŏch'ŏn S. Korea
198 C1 Sochos Greece
Society Islands Fr. Polynesia see La Société, Archipel de
177 K5 Socodor Romania
196 E3 Socol Romania
177 L4 Socond Romania
Soconusco, Sierra de mts Mex. see Madre, Sierra
256 D5 Socorro Brazil
250 C3 Socorro Col.
239 F5 Socorro NM U.S.A.
228 D7 Socorro, Isla i. Mex.
250 B6 Socota Peru
Socotra i. Yemen see Suquṭrā
185 I2 Socovos Spain
97 D5 Soc Trăng Vietnam
185 H1 Socuéllamos Spain
140 N2 Sodankylä Fin.
111 B5 Soda Plains Aksai Chin
238 E3 Soda Springs ID U.S.A.
105 F3 Sodegaura Japan
143 G3 Söderåkra Sweden
143 F1 Söderbärke Sweden
143 H1 Söderboda Sweden
143 G1 Söderfors Sweden
141 L3 Söderhamn Sweden
143 G2 Söderköping Sweden
143 G2 Södermanland county Sweden
168 F2 Soderstorf Ger.
143 G2 Södertälje Sweden
203 F6 Sodiri Sudan
214 D4 Sodium S. Africa
210 C3 Sodo Eth.
140 M3 Södra Gloppet b. Fin.
141 L3 Södra Kvarken str. Fin./Sweden
143 F3 Södra Vi Sweden
232 E3 Sodus NY U.S.A.
214 A4 Soebatsfontein S. Africa
213 F4 Soekmekaar S. Africa
Soerabaia Jawa Timur Indon. see Surabaya
165 E3 Soerendonk Neth.
169 D4 Soest Ger.
164 E2 Soest Neth.
168 C2 Soeste r. Ger.
198 C2 Sofades Greece
83 G3 Sofala N.S.W. Austr.
213 G4 Sofala Moz.
213 G3 Sofala prov. Moz.
Sofia Bulg. see Sofiya
213 □J2 Sofia r. Madag.
198 C3 Sofiko Greece
197 F4 Sofiya Bulg.
Sofiyevka Ukr. see Vil'nyans'k
137 G3 Sofiyivka Ukr.
100 E1 Sofiysk Khabarovskiy Kray Rus. Fed.
100 F2 Sofiysk Khabarovskiy Kray Rus. Fed.
139 K3 Sofrino Rus. Fed.
177 K5 Şofronea Romania
128 A1 Softa Kalesi tourist site Turkey
103 J9 Sōfu-gan i. Japan
111 F6 Sog Xizang China
250 C3 Sogamoso Col.
129 A3 Soğanlı Dağları mts Turkey
110 D3 Sogat Xinjiang China
100 E2 Sogda Rus. Fed.
168 C3 Sögel Ger.
142 B2 Søgne Norway
141 I3 Sognefjorden inlet Norway
141 I3 Sogn og Fjordane county Norway
92 C4 Sogod Phil.
129 D4 Soğuksu Turkey
199 G1 Söğüt Turkey
199 F3 Söğüt Dağı mts Turkey
129 B4 Söğütlü Turkey
101 C6 Sŏgwip'o S. Korea
203 F3 Sohâg Egypt
116 D5 Sohagpur Madh. Prad. India
151 H2 Soham Cambridgeshire, England U.K.
123 G3 Sohan r. Pak.
Sohar Oman see Şuḥār
165 E4 Soheit-Tinlot Belgium
117 E5 Sohela Orissa India
171 F4 Sohland am Rotstein Ger.
169 F3 Söhlde Ger.
116 D3 Sohna Haryana India
97 B4 Sohng Gwe, Khao hill Myanmar/Thai.
172 B2 Sohren Ger.
156 E2 Soignes, Forêt de for. Belgium
165 D4 Soignies Belgium
108 A2 Soila Xizang China
177 L5 Şoimi Romania
160 D1 Soing France
159 H4 Soings-en-Sologne France
140 N3 Soini Fin.
157 E2 Soire-le-Château France
169 E5 Soisberg hill Ger.
156 D3 Soissons France
156 D4 Soizy-aux-Bois France
103 F6 Sōja Japan
116 C4 Sojat Rajasthan India
116 C4 Sojat Road Rajasthan India
175 K5 Sójkowa Pol.
179 H4 Söjtör Hungary
135 J5 Sok r. Rus. Fed.
105 F3 Sōka Japan
136 C2 Sokal' Ukr.
101 D5 Sokch'o S. Korea
199 E3 Söke Turkey
209 E7 Sokele Dem. Rep. Congo
107 F1 Sokhondo, Gora mt. Rus. Fed.
106 E1 Sokhor, Gora mt. Rus. Fed.
Sokhós Greece see Sochos
129 B2 Sokhumi Georgia
129 B2 Sokhumi-Babushara airport Georgia
Sokiryany Ukr. see Sokyryany
103 D6 Sŏkkuram Grotto tourist site S. Korea
197 E4 Sokobanja Srbija Yugo.
207 F4 Sokodé Togo
100 G3 Sokol Sakhalin Rus. Fed.
134 H4 Sokol Vologod. Obl. Rus. Fed.
188 G4 Sokolac Bos.-Herz.
175 L2 Sokolany Pol.
136 F3 Sokolivka Cherkas'ka Oblast' Ukr.
175 M5 Sokolivka L'vivs'ka Oblast' Ukr.
175 L2 Sokółka Pol.
175 K1 Sokółki Pol.
179 H1 Sokolnice Czech Rep.
139 L4 Sokol'niki Rus. Fed.
139 J3 Sokol'niki Rus. Fed.
206 D3 Sokolo Mali
137 H4 Sokolohirne Ukr.
176 B1 Sokolov Czech Rep.
137 H3 Sokolova Balka Ukr.
179 H4 Sokolovac Croatia
121 G1 Sokolovka Kazakh.
121 K1 Sokolovo Rus. Fed.
137 J4 Sokolovo-Kundryuchenskiy Rus. Fed.
175 K5 Sokołów Małopolski Pol.
175 K3 Sokołow Podlaski Pol.
134 H4 Sokol'skoye Rus. Fed.
175 K3 Sokoły Pol.
206 A3 Sokone Senegal
177 G4 Sokorópátka Hungary
140 O1 Sokosti hill Fin.
207 G3 Sokoto Nigeria
207 G4 Sokoto r. Nigeria
207 G3 Sokoto state Nigeria
206 C4 Sokourala Guinea
136 D3 Sokyryany Ukr.
175 K5 Sól Pol.
246 C2 Sola Cuba
175 H6 Soła r. Pol.
Sola i. Tonga see Ata
116 D3 Solan Hima. Prad. India
240 I5 Solana Beach CA U.S.A.
184 D2 Solana de los Barros Spain
185 F2 Solana del Pino Spain
183 F4 Solana de Rioalmar Spain
142 C1 Sølandsfjellet mt. Norway
92 B2 Solano Phil.
114 B2 Solapur Mahar. India
195 E5 Solarino Sicilia Italy
192 B3 Solaro Corse France
192 A5 Solarussa Sardegna Italy
146 A4 Solas Western Isles, Scotland U.K.
140 L3 Solberg Sweden
143 F3 Solberga Sweden
197 G2 Solca Romania
177 H3 Solčany Slovakia
191 F2 Solda Italy
191 F2 Solda r. Italy
136 E4 Şoldăneşti Moldova
129 C1 Soldato-Aleksandrovskoye Rus. Fed.
129 C2 Soldatskaya Rus. Fed.
178 C4 Sölden Austria
186 E2 Soldeu Andorra
233 □I1 Soldier Pond ME U.S.A.
220 C3 Soldotna AK U.S.A.
174 G2 Solec Kujawski Pol.
175 I5 Solec-Zdrój Pol.
246 D5 Soledad Col.
240 G3 Soledad CA U.S.A.
245 F4 Soledad de Doblado Mex.
244 D2 Soledad Diez Gutierrez Mex.
255 B9 Soledade Brazil
137 J3 Soledar Ukr.
192 B5 Soleminis Sardegna Italy
141 J3 Sølen mt. Norway
135 H7 Solenoye Rus. Fed.
192 B3 Solenzara Corse France
206 D3 Solenzo Burkina
191 G3 Solesino Italy
156 D2 Solesmes Nord - Pas-de-Calais France
159 F4 Solesmes Pays de la Loire France
195 H2 Soleto Italy
163 B4 Solférino France
191 F3 Solferino Italy
140 K2 Solfjellsjøen Norway
134 H3 Solginskiy Rus. Fed.
127 F3 Solhan Turkey
191 F4 Soliera Italy
134 H4 Soligalich Rus. Fed.
162 D3 Solignac France
190 E4 Solignano Italy
191 H3 Soligo r. Italy
Soligorsk Belarus see Salihorsk
151 F2 Solihull West Midlands, England U.K.
134 L4 Solikamsk Rus. Fed.
120 C2 Sol'-Iletsk Rus. Fed.
189 C7 Soliman Tunisia
175 K6 Solina Pol.
169 C4 Solingen Ger.
175 K6 Solinka r. Pol.
175 K6 Solińskie, Jezioro l. Pol.
250 C4 Solita Col.
81 A6 Solitary, Mount South I. N.Z.
186 E3 Solivella Spain
Sol-Karmala Rus. Fed. see Severnoye
178 D3 Söll Austria
192 A3 Sollacaro Corse France
142 E2 Sollebrunn Sweden
140 L3 Sollefteå Sweden
179 H3 Sollenau Austria
143 G2 Sollentuna Sweden
187 F5 Sóller Spain
141 K3 Sollerön Sweden
168 G1 Søllested Denmark
171 D4 Söllichau Ger.
161 E5 Solliès-Pont France
161 E5 Solliès-Ville France
169 E4 Solling hills Ger.
169 F3 Söllingen Ger.
169 F4 Sollstedt Ger.
169 D5 Solms Ger.
139 K3 Solnechnogorsk Rus. Fed.
100 F2 Solnechnyy Khabarovskiy Kray Rus. Fed.
Solnechnyy Khabarovskiy Kray Rus. Fed. see Gornyy
176 F1 Solnice Czech Rep.
137 I2 Solntsevo Rus. Fed.
93 B3 Solo r. Indon.
95 F4 Solo r. Indon.
136 D3 Solobkivtsi Ukr.
193 G4 Solofra Italy
94 C3 Solok Sumatera Indon.
136 C2 Solokiya r. Ukr.
243 H6 Sololá Guat.
129 D1 Solomenskoye Rus. Fed.
163 C5 Solomiac France
136 D3 Solomna Ukr.
241 M5 Solomon AZ U.S.A.
236 D4 Solomon r. KS U.S.A.
236 D4 Solomon, North Fork r. KS U.S.A.
236 D4 Solomon, South Fork r. KS U.S.A.
78 □6 Solomon Islands country S. Pacific Ocean
91 L8 Solomon Sea P.N.G./Solomon Is
107 I2 Solon Nei Mongol China
233 □I2 Solon ME U.S.A.
137 H4 Solona r. Ukr.
137 I3 Solona r. Ukr.
137 H3 Solone Ukr.
121 K2 Soloneshnoye Rus. Fed.
226 B2 Solon Springs WI U.S.A.
194 D1 Solopaca Italy
93 B5 Solor, Kepulauan is Indon.
183 G1 Solórzano Spain
183 F4 Solosancho Spain
139 L4 Solotcha Rus. Fed.
190 C1 Solothurn Switz.
190 C1 Solothurn canton Switz.
136 C3 Solotvyn Ukr.
134 F2 Solovetskiy Rus. Fed.
134 F2 Solovetskiye Ostrova is Rus. Fed.
134 I4 Solovetskoye Rus. Fed.
136 E2 Soloviyivka Ukr.
107 G1 Solov'yevsk Mongolia
100 C1 Solov'yevsk Rus. Fed.
186 E3 Solsona Spain
177 I5 Solt Hungary
188 F4 Šolta i. Croatia
122 D2 Soltānābād Iran
122 B3 Soltānābād Iran
129 E4 Soltanlı Azer.
168 E3 Soltau Ger.
168 F3 Soltendieck Ger.
121 K1 Solton Rus. Fed.
139 H2 Sol'tsy Rus. Fed.
Soltüstik Qazaqstan Oblysy admin. div. Kazakh. see Severnyy Kazakhstan
177 I5 Soltvadkert Hungary
177 I5 Soltzentimre Hungary
196 E5 Solunska Glava mt. Macedonia
160 C2 Solutré-Pouilly France
150 B3 Solva Pembrokeshire, Wales U.K.
150 B3 Solva r. Wales U.K.
240 G4 Solvang CA U.S.A.
233 E3 Solvay NY U.S.A.
143 F3 Sölvesborg Sweden
134 I3 Sol'vychegodsk Rus. Fed.
146 E7 Solway Firth est. Scotland U.K.
209 E8 Solwezi Zambia
102 J5 Sōma Japan
199 E2 Soma Turkey
156 D2 Somain France
210 D3 Somali admin. reg. Eth.
210 E4 Somalia country Africa
265 H5 Somali Basin sea feature Indian Ocean
Somali Republic country Africa see Somalia
207 E5 Somanya Ghana
95 G2 Sombang, Gunung mt. Indon.
177 H5 Somberek Hungary
160 C1 Sombernon France
209 D7 Sombo Angola
196 D3 Sombor Vojvodina, Srbija Yugo.
169 E5 Somborn Ger.
165 D4 Sombreffe Belgium
244 C2 Sombrerete Mex.
259 C9 Sombrero Chile
115 G5 Sombrero Channel Andaman & Nicobar Is India
197 F2 Şomcuţa Mare Romania
116 C4 Somdari Rajasthan India
234 C3 Somerdale NJ U.S.A.
165 E3 Someren Neth.
141 M3 Somero Fin.
150 E3 Somerset admin. div. England U.K.
230 C4 Somerset KY U.S.A.
233 H4 Somerset MA U.S.A.
226 E4 Somerset MI U.S.A.
232 B5 Somerset OH U.S.A.
232 D5 Somerset PA U.S.A.
234 D2 Somerset County county NJ U.S.A.
215 E5 Somerset East S. Africa
221 I2 Somerset Island Nunavut Can.
214 B6 Somerset West S. Africa
151 H2 Somersham Cambridgeshire, England U.K.
234 D3 Somers Point NJ U.S.A.
233 □H3 Somersworth NH U.S.A.
150 E3 Somerton Somerset, England U.K.
241 J5 Somerton AZ U.S.A.
138 F2 Sõmeru Estonia
234 D2 Somerville NJ U.S.A.
237 F5 Somerville TN U.S.A.
197 F2 Someş r. Romania
197 F2 Someşan, Podişul plat. Romania
197 F2 Someşu Cald r. Romania
197 F2 Someşul Mare r. Romania
197 F2 Someşului, Câmpia plain Romania
197 F2 Someşu Mic r. Romania
233 □I2 Somesville ME U.S.A.
175 J3 Somianka Pol.
139 J2 Somino Rus. Fed.
215 I3 Somkele S. Africa
176 G4 Somlóvásárhely Hungary
191 F3 Sommacampagna Italy
190 D3 Somma Lombardo Italy
190 C4 Sommariva del Bosco Italy
194 C5 Sommatino Sicilia Italy
156 C3 Somme dept Picardie France
160 B2 Somme r. France
165 A4 Somme r. France
157 F3 Sommedieue France
165 E4 Somme-Leuze Belgium
143 F2 Sommen Sweden
143 F2 Sommen l. Sweden
156 E3 Sommepy-Tahure France
171 C4 Sömmerda Ger.
170 E3 Sommerfeld Ger.
171 C3 Sommersdorf Ger.
156 E3 Somme-Soude r. France
156 E4 Sommesous France
156 E3 Somme-Suippe France
157 E4 Sommevoire France
161 C5 Sommières France
162 C2 Sommières-du-Clain France
116 B5 Somnath Gujarat India
176 G5 Somogy county Hungary
177 G5 Somogyapáti Hungary
177 G5 Somogyjád Hungary
177 G5 Somogysárd Hungary
176 G5 Somogyszentpál Hungary
176 G5 Somogyszob Hungary
226 C5 Somonauk IL U.S.A.
174 G1 Somonino Pol.
185 H3 Somontín Spain
79 □1 Somosomo Taveuni Fiji
242 □I6 Somotillo Nic.
242 □I6 Somoto Nic.
137 J2 Somovo Rus. Fed.
115 E2 Sompeta Andhra Prad. India
174 G3 Sompolno Pol.
151 G4 Sompting West Sussex, England U.K.
156 E4 Sompuis France
197 E3 Šomrda hill Yugo.
259 D6 Somuncurá, Mesa Volcánica de plat. Arg.
114 B3 Somvarpet Karnataka India
165 D4 Somzée Belgium
117 F4 Son r. India
164 E3 Son Neth.
142 D2 Son Norway
191 F3 Sona Italy
242 □J8 Soná Panama
175 I3 Sona r. Pol.
Sonag Qinghai China see Zêkog
117 H4 Sonai r. India
117 H4 Sonai r. India
117 E5 Sonakhan Madh. Prad. India
116 D5 Sonala Mahar. India
121 G2 Sonaly Kazakh.
117 F5 Sonamukhi W. Bengal India
117 E5 Sonapur Orissa India
117 H4 Sonari Assam India
190 C1 Sonceboz Switz.
101 C5 Sŏnch'ŏn N. Korea
183 G2 Soncillo Spain
190 E3 Soncino Italy
190 F2 Sondalo Italy
142 C4 Sønderå r. Denmark
142 C4 Sønderborg Denmark
142 C4 Sønderjylland county Denmark
142 C4 Sønder Omme Denmark
169 F4 Sondershausen Ger.
142 D4 Søndersø Denmark
142 C3 Sønderup Denmark
Søndre Strømfjord Greenland see Kangerlussuaq
190 E2 Sondrio Italy
190 E2 Sondrio prov. Lombardia Italy
187 C5 Soneja Spain
114 C2 Sonepet Mahar. India
234 B1 Sonestown PA U.S.A.
207 I4 Song Nigeria
116 B5 Songad Gujarat India
Songbai Hubei China see Shennongjia
109 E2 Songbu Hubei China
97 E4 Sông Cau Vietnam
Songcheng Fujian China see Xiapu
97 D5 Sông Co Chiên r. mouth Vietnam
211 B7 Songea Tanz.
156 B3 Songeons France
101 C4 Sŏnggan N. Korea
97 D5 Sông Ham Luông r. mouth Vietnam
100 E3 Songhua Jiang r. China
Songjiachuan Shaanxi China see Wubu
100 D4 Songjiang Jilin China
109 G2 Songjiang Shanghai China
101 C4 Songjianghe Jilin China
Sŏngjin N. Korea see Kimch'aek
108 C2 Songkan Guizhou China
97 C6 Songkhla Thai.
96 D3 Song Khram, Mae Nam r. Thai.
121 H4 Songköl l. Kyrg.
107 I2 Songling Nei Mongol China
107 H3 Song Ling mts China
Songmai Sichuan China see Dêrong
108 B3 Songming Yunnan China
101 C5 Sŏngnam S. Korea
101 C5 Songnim N. Korea
209 B6 Songo Angola
213 G2 Songo Moz.
Songololo Dem. Rep. Congo see Mbanza-Ngungu
209 B6 Songololo Dem. Rep. Congo
108 B1 Songpan Sichuan China
117 G4 Songsak Meghalaya India
101 C6 Sŏngsan S. Korea
Songshan Guizhou China see Ziyun
107 G5 Song Shan mt. Henan China
108 D2 Songtao Guizhou China
109 F3 Songxi Fujian China
107 G5 Songxian Henan China
Songyang Yunnan China see Songming
Songyuan Fujian China see Songxi
100 C3 Songyuan Jilin China
109 D2 Songzi Hubei China
117 E5 Sonhat Madh. Prad. India
Sonid Youqi Nei Mongol China see Saihan Tal
Sonid Zuoqi Nei Mongol China see Mandalt
182 C3 Sonim Port.
116 D3 Sonipat Haryana India
116 D5 Sonkach Madh. Prad. India
134 D3 Sonkajärvi Fin.
Sonkël', Ozero l. Kyrg. see Songköl
139 K3 Sonkovo Rus. Fed.
96 C2 Sơn La Vietnam
123 F5 Sonmiani Bay Pak.
178 D3 Sonnblick mt. Austria
171 C5 Sonneberg Ger.
169 F5 Sonneborn Ger.
171 C5 Sonnefeld Ger.
178 D3 Sonnenjoch mt. Austria
171 E4 Sonnewalde Ger.
151 G3 Sonning Common Oxfordshire, England U.K.
193 F3 Sonnino Italy
179 F3 Sonntagberg Austria
257 E2 Sono r. Minas Gerais Brazil
254 C4 Sono r. Tocantins Brazil
241 L6 Sonoita AZ U.S.A.
240 F2 Sonoma CA U.S.A.
215 F1 Sonop S. Africa
242 C2 Sonora r. Mex.
242 C2 Sonora state Mex.
240 G3 Sonora CA U.S.A.
237 C6 Sonora TX U.S.A.
240 H2 Sonora Peak CA U.S.A.
122 A3 Sonqor Iran
183 G5 Sonseca Spain
187 G5 Son Servera Spain
175 I3 Sońsk Pol.
250 C3 Sonsón Col.
243 H6 Sonsonate El Salvador
91 H5 Sonsorol Islands Palau
214 D2 Sonstraal S. Africa
96 D2 Sơn Tây Vietnam
173 E3 Sontheim Ger.
173 E3 Sontheim an der Brenz Ger.
173 E4 Sonthofen Ger.
169 E4 Sontra Ger.
215 G4 Sonwabile S. Africa
Soochow Jiangsu China see Suzhou
138 E2 Soodla r. Estonia
Soomaaliya country Africa see Somalia
163 A5 Soorts-Hossegor France
261 I2 Sopas r. Uru.
186 D2 Sopeira Spain
231 D5 Soperton GA U.S.A.
161 F5 Sophia-Antipolis France
196 E5 Sopište Macedonia
197 G4 Sopot Bulg.
143 H4 Sopot Pol.
196 E3 Sopot Srbija Yugo.
108 A5 Sop Prap Thai.
176 F4 Sopron Hungary
176 F4 Sopronkövesd Hungary
183 G1 Sopuerta Spain
116 C2 Sopur Jammu and Kashmir
93 C2 Soputan, Gunung vol. Indon.
78 □4a Sopweru i. Chuuk Micronesia
111 F5 Soq Qu r. Xizang China
163 E5 Sor r. France
184 B2 Sôr r. Port.
182 C1 Sor r. Spain
193 F3 Sora Italy
179 F4 Sora r. Slovenia
114 B3 Sorab Karnataka India
191 G2 Soraga Italy
190 F4 Soragna Italy
141 L3 Söråker Sweden
101 D5 Sŏrak-san mt. S. Korea
192 D2 Sorano Italy
191 H2 Sorapis mt. Italy
252 C3 Sorata Bol.
142 B2 Sør-Audnedal Norway
185 H3 Sorbas Spain
183 G4 Sorbe r. Spain
146 D7 Sorbie Dumfries and Galloway, Scotland U.K.
190 F4 Sorbolo Italy
157 F4 Sorcy-St-Martin France
163 A5 Sorde-l'Abbaye France
163 B4 Sore France
163 E6 Sorède France
221 K5 Sorel Que. Can.
83 F5 Sorell Tas. Austr.
128 B4 Soreq r. Israel
190 E3 Soresina Italy
163 E5 Sorèze France
169 F4 Sorge Ger.
168 E1 Sorge r. Ger.
162 C3 Sorges France
192 B4 Sorgono Sardegna Italy
161 C4 Sorgues France
161 A5 Sorgues r. France
128 B1 Sorgun İçel Turkey
126 D3 Sorgun Yozgat Turkey
128 B1 Sorgun r. Turkey
183 H3 Soria Spain
183 H3 Soria prov. Castilla y León Spain
261 H3 Soriano Uru.
261 I3 Soriano dept Uru.
195 F4 Soriano Calabro Italy
193 E2 Soriano nel Cimino Italy
182 E4 Sorihuela Spain
185 G2 Sorihuela del Gaudalimar Spain
94 B2 Sorikmarapi vol. Indon.
146 B5 Sorisdale Argyll and Bute, Scotland U.K.
140 □ Sørkapp Land reg. Svalbard
120 C3 Sor Kaydak dry lake Kazakh.
122 C3 Sorkh, Kūh-e mts Iran
122 C3 Sorkheh Iran
128 A1 Sorkun Turkey
175 J2 Sorkwity Pol.
140 K2 Sørland Norway
120 C3 Sor Mertvyy Kultuk dry lake Kazakh.
140 M3 Sörmjöle Sweden
156 E3 Sormonne r. France
148 E2 Sorn East Ayrshire, Scotland U.K.
162 E3 Sornac France
172 B4 Sorne r. Switz.
142 D4 Sorø Denmark
117 F5 Soro Orissa India
194 D5 Soro, Monte mt. Sicilia Italy
136 E3 Soroca Moldova
256 D5 Sorocaba Brazil
120 C1 Sorochinsk Rus. Fed.
Soroki Moldova see Soroca
121 K1 Sorokino Rus. Fed.
Sorokino Luhans'ka Oblast' Ukr. see Krasnodon
91 J5 Sorol atoll Micronesia
93 D3 Sorong Irian Jaya Indon.
138 G3 Sorot' r. Rus. Fed.
210 B4 Soroti Uganda
140 M1 Sørøya i. Norway
140 M1 Sørøysundet sea chan. Norway
Sorp Turkey see Reşadıye
192 A4 Sorradile Sardegna Italy
184 B1 Sorraia r. Port.
140 L1 Sørreisa Norway
193 G4 Sorrento Italy
140 N3 Sorsakoski Fin.
140 O2 Sorsatunturi hill Fin.
140 L2 Sorsele Sweden
192 A4 Sorso Sardegna Italy
92 C3 Sorsogon Phil.
186 E2 Sort Spain
141 O3 Sortavala Rus. Fed.
182 C4 Sortelha Port.
195 E5 Sortino Sicilia Italy
140 K1 Sortland Norway
140 J3 Sør-Trøndelag county Norway
143 G2 Sorunda Sweden
168 E1 Sörup Ger.
Sõrve väin sea chan. Estonia/Latvia see Irbe Strait
185 G4 Sorvilán Spain
163 C4 Sos France
101 C5 Sŏsan S. Korea
143 E3 Sösdala Sweden
186 B2 Sos del Rey Católico Spain
139 J4 Sosenskiy Rus. Fed.
186 D3 Soses Spain
215 G1 Soshanguve S. Africa
175 M4 Soshychne Ukr.
194 C5 Sosio r. Sicilia Italy
139 J5 Soskovo Rus. Fed.
177 H4 Sóskút Hungary
139 L5 Sosna r. Rus. Fed.
260 C4 Sosneado mt. Arg.
174 F4 Sośnie Pol.
136 C2 Sosnivka L'vivs'ka Oblast' Ukr.
137 G2 Sosnivka Sums'ka Oblast' Ukr.
136 C2 Sosnivka Ternopils'ka Oblast' Ukr.
174 F2 Sośno Pol.
134 K3 Sosnogorsk Respublika Komi Rus. Fed.
136 D2 Sosnove Ukr.
121 I2 Sosnovka Kazakh.
134 I3 Sosnovka Arkhangel'skaya Oblast' Rus. Fed.
135 H5 Sosnovka Tambovskaya Oblast' Rus. Fed.
139 K2 Sosnovka Vologod. Obl. Rus. Fed.
139 H1 Sosnovo Rus. Fed.
135 I5 Sosnovoborsk Rus. Fed.
99 J1 Sosnovo-Ozerskoye Rus. Fed.
134 F2 Sosnovyy Rus. Fed.
Sosnovyy Bor Belarus see Sasnovy Bor
138 G2 Sosnovyy Bor Rus. Fed.
175 L4 Sosnowica Pol.
175 H5 Sosnowiec Pol.
Sosnowitz Pol. see Sosnowiec
175 L4 Sosnówka Pol.
137 G2 Sosnytsya Ukr.
161 F5 Sospel France
163 C6 Sost France
179 G4 Šoštanj Slovenia
130 H4 Sos'va Rus. Fed.
137 J4 Sosyka r. Rus. Fed.
207 F4 Sota r. Benin
260 B2 Sotaquí Chile
252 D2 Sotério r. Brazil
184 D3 Sotiel Coronada Spain
184 E2 Sotillo r. Spain
183 F4 Sotillo de la Adrada Spain
183 H3 Sotillo del Rincón Spain
140 O2 Sotkamo Fin.
260 E2 Soto Arg.
182 D1 Soto Spain
182 E2 Soto de la Vega Spain
183 G4 Soto del Real Spain
182 E1 Soto de Ribera Spain
245 E2 Soto la Marina Mex.
245 F2 Soto La Marina r. Mex.
183 G2 Sotopalacios Spain
183 H4 Sotos Spain
182 D4 Sotoserrano Spain
207 F4 Sotouboua Togo
182 E2 Soto y Amio Spain
183 F1 Sotres Spain
183 F2 Sotresgudo Spain
182 E1 Sotrondio Spain
Sotsgorodok Donets'ka Oblast' Ukr. see Hirnyk
192 B3 Sotta Corse France
156 B3 Sotteville-lès-Rouen France
194 D5 Sotto di Troina r. Sicilia Italy
191 H3 Sottomarina Italy
168 E2 Sottrum Ger.
141 M3 Sottunga Åland Fin.
185 H1 Sotuélamos Spain
243 H4 Sotuta Mex.
156 E3 Souain-Perthes-lès-Hurlus France
163 E5 Soual France
208 B4 Souanké Congo
161 B5 Soubès France
206 D5 Soubré Côte d'Ivoire
156 D4 Soucy France
198 D4 Souda Kriti Greece
84 D4 Soudan N.T. Austr.
158 E4 Soudan France
234 C2 Souderton PA U.S.A.
Soúdha Kriti Greece see Souda
163 C5 Soueich France
163 D6 Soueix France
159 I4 Souesmes France
157 H4 Soufflenheim France
199 E1 Soufli Greece
247 □2 Soufrière vol. Guadeloupe
247 □3 Soufrière St Lucia

Soufrière to Stawell

365

247 □3 Soufrière vol. St Vincent
247 □2 Soufrière Hills Montserrat
206 B4 Souguéta Guinea
163 D4 Souillac France
157 F3 Souilly France
205 G1 Souk Ahras Alg.
189 A7 Souk Ahras prov. Alg.
204 D2 Souk el Arbaâ du Rharb Morocco
180 D5 Souk el Had el Rharbia Morocco
180 C5 Souk Khemis du Sahel Morocco
180 D5 Souk Tleta Taghramet Morocco
180 D5 Souk-Tnine-de-Sidi-el-Yamani Morocco
101 C5 Sŏul S. Korea
162 A3 Soulac-sur-Mer France
156 E4 Soulaines-Dhuys France
163 D6 Soulan France
163 E6 Soulatgé France
159 F3 Soulgé-sur-Ouette France
158 E5 Soullans France
158 E2 Soulles r. France
157 H4 Soultz-sous-Forêts France
165 E4 Soumagne Belgium
163 B5 Soumoulou France
235 F2 Sound Beach NY U.S.A.
223 I4 Sounding Creek r. Alta Can.
156 C4 Souppes-sur-Loing France
163 B5 Souprosse France
128 B3 Soûr Lebanon
159 F3 Sourdeval France
254 C2 Soure Brazil
182 B4 Soure Port.
223 K5 Souris Man. Can.
225 I4 Souris P.E.I. Can.
223 L5 Souris r. Sask. Can.
Souriya country Asia see Syria
163 E6 Sournia France
182 C4 Souro Pires Port.
198 C2 Sourpi Greece
156 B4 Sours France
162 C3 Sourzac France
254 F3 Sousa Brazil
182 B3 Sousa r. Port.
Sousa Lara Angola see Bocoio
163 E4 Sousceyrac France
184 C2 Sousel Port.
182 B4 Souselas Port.
79 □3 Sous le Vent, Îles is Arch. de la Société Fr. Polynesia
205 H2 Sousse Tunisia
163 A5 Soustons France
214 B4 Sout r. S. Africa
234 B4 South r. MD U.S.A.
South Africa country Africa see South Africa, Republic of
212 E6 South Africa, Republic of country Africa
84 C2 South Alligator r. N.T. Austr.
151 F2 Southam Warwickshire, England U.K.
235 D2 South Amboy NJ U.S.A.
248 South America continent
224 D4 Southampton Ont. Can.
151 F4 Southampton Southampton, England U.K.
151 F4 Southampton admin. div. England U.K.
233 G4 Southampton NY U.S.A.
223 O1 Southampton Island Nunavut Can.
151 F4 Southampton Water est. England U.K.
115 G4 South Andaman i. Andaman & Nicobar Is India
232 E6 South Anna r. VA U.S.A.
149 H4 South Anston South Yorkshire, England U.K.
235 D2 Southard NJ U.S.A.
82 C2 South Australia state Austr.
265 L7 South Australian Basin sea feature Indian Ocean
237 F5 Southaven MS U.S.A.
146 D6 South Ayrshire admin. div. Scotland U.K.
239 F5 South Baldy mt. NM U.S.A.
149 H3 South Bank Redcar and Cleveland, England U.K.
231 D7 South Bay FL U.S.A.
224 D4 South Baymouth Ont. Can.
230 C3 South Bend IN U.S.A.
238 B2 South Bend WA U.S.A.
151 H3 South Benfleet Essex, England U.K.
151 H3 Southborough Kent, England U.K.
232 D6 South Boston VA U.S.A.
150 D4 South Brent Devon, England U.K.
81 D5 Southbridge South I. N.Z.
233 G3 Southbridge MA U.S.A.
225 J3 South Brook Nfld. Can.
215 H4 Southbroom S. Africa
233 G2 South Burlington VT U.S.A.
81 C6 Southburn South I. N.Z.
235 E1 Southbury CT U.S.A.
234 C1 South Canaan PA U.S.A.
231 D5 South Carolina state U.S.A.
149 I4 South Cave East Riding of Yorkshire, England U.K.
151 F3 South Cerney Gloucestershire, England U.K.
150 E4 South Chard Somerset, England U.K.
232 B5 South Charleston OH U.S.A.
232 C5 South Charleston WV U.S.A.
90 E4 South China Sea N. Pacific Ocean
South Coast Town Qld Austr. see Gold Coast
236 C2 South Dakota state U.S.A.
146 F6 Southdean Scottish Borders, Scotland U.K.
233 G3 South Deerfield MA U.S.A.
234 D3 South Dennis NJ U.S.A.
151 G4 South Downs hills England U.K.
83 F5 South East Cape Tas. Austr.
265 J7 Southeast Indian Ridge sea feature Indian Ocean
87 D7 South East Isles W.A. Austr.
267 L10 Southeast Pacific Basin sea feature S. Pacific Ocean
234 D3 South Egg Harbor NJ U.S.A.
223 K3 Southend Sask. Can.
146 C6 Southend Argyll and Bute, Scotland U.K.
151 H3 Southend admin. div. England U.K.
151 H3 Southend-on-Sea Southend, England U.K.
210 C3 Southern admin. reg. Eth.
211 B8 Southern admin. reg. Malawi
206 B5 Southern prov. Sierra Leone
209 E9 Southern prov. Zambia
Southern Aegean admin. reg. Greece see Notio Aigaio
81 C5 Southern Alps mts South I. N.Z.
81 □2 Southern Cook Islands Cook Is
87 C6 Southern Cross W.A. Austr.
208 E2 Southern Darfur state Sudan
223 L3 Southern Indian Lake Man. Can.
208 F2 Southern Kordofan state Sudan
77 I3 Southern Lau Group is Fiji
262 R3 Southern Ocean OCEAN
231 E5 Southern Pines NC U.S.A.
Southern Rhodesia country Africa see Zimbabwe
146 D6 Southern Uplands hills Scotland U.K.
Southern Urals mts Rus. Fed. see Yuzhnyy Ural
151 H2 Southery Norfolk, England U.K.
146 F5 South Esk r. Angus, Scotland U.K.
86 E3 South Esk Tableland reg. W.A. Austr.
223 J5 Southey Sask. Can.
215 F4 Southeyville S. Africa
236 F4 South Fabius r. MO U.S.A.
232 B3 Southfield MI U.S.A.
235 D1 Southfields NY U.S.A.
266 G7 South Fiji Basin sea feature S. Pacific Ocean
151 I3 South Foreland pt England U.K.
240 F1 South Fork CA U.S.A.
239 F4 South Fork CO U.S.A.
232 D4 South Fork PA U.S.A.
222 E5 Southgate r. B.C. Can.
151 G3 Southgate Greater London, England U.K.
263 H1 South Geomagnetic Pole (1995) Antarctica
264 G9 South Georgia terr. S. Atlantic Ocean
249 G7 South Georgia and South Sandwich Islands terr. S. Atlantic Ocean
234 C1 South Gibson PA U.S.A.
226 C1 South Gillies Ont. Can.
235 F1 South Glastonbury CT U.S.A.
150 E3 South Gloucestershire admin. div. England U.K.
236 E4 South Grand r. MO U.S.A.
151 G4 South Harting West Sussex, England U.K.
226 D4 South Haven MI U.S.A.
80 E2 South Head North I. N.Z.
233 G2 South Hero VT U.S.A.
149 H3 South Hetton Durham, England U.K.
232 D6 South Hill VA U.S.A.
266 E3 South Honshu Ridge sea feature N. Pacific Ocean
223 L3 South Indian Lake Man. Can.
235 F1 Southington CT U.S.A.
86 □2 South Island Cocos Is
81 D6 South Island N.Z.
210 C4 South Island National Park Kenya
223 M5 South Junction Man. Can.
South Kazakhstan Oblast admin. div. Kazakh. see Yuzhnyy Kazakhstan
149 I4 South Kelsey Lincolnshire, England U.K.
149 H4 South Kirkby West Yorkshire, England U.K.
117 F5 South Koel r. Bihar India
240 G2 South Lake Tahoe CA U.S.A.
146 E6 South Lanarkshire admin. div. Scotland U.K.
81 A6 Southland admin. reg. South I. N.Z.
151 H2 South Lopham Norfolk, England U.K.
236 D3 South Loup r. NE U.S.A.
235 F1 South Lyme CT U.S.A.
222 C2 South Macmillan r. Y.T. Can.
263 J2 South Magnetic Pole (1995) Antarctica
113 □1 South Male Atoll Maldives
151 H3 Southminster Essex, England U.K.
150 D3 South Molton Devon, England U.K.
234 A3 South Mountains hills PA U.S.A.
86 B4 South Muiron Island W.A. Austr.
222 D1 South Nahanni r. N.W.T. Can.
146 □G1 South Nesting Bay Scotland U.K.
233 F3 South New Berlin NY U.S.A.
151 H3 South Ockendon Thurrock, England U.K.
235 F1 Southold NY U.S.A.
264 G10 South Orkney Islands S. Atlantic Ocean
South Ossetia aut. reg. Georgia see Samkhret' Oset'i
151 G3 South Oxhey Hertfordshire, England U.K.
233 □H2 South Paris ME U.S.A.
87 B5 South Passage W.A. Austr.
231 D6 South Patrick Shores FL U.S.A.
150 E4 South Petherton Somerset, England U.K.
235 D2 South Plainfield NJ U.S.A.
236 C3 South Platte r. CO U.S.A.
262 T1 South Pole Antarctica
224 D3 South Porcupine Ont. Can.
85 H5 Southport Qld Austr.
83 F5 Southport Tas. Austr.
149 F4 Southport Merseyside, England U.K.
235 E1 Southport CT U.S.A.
231 E5 Southport NC U.S.A.
227 I4 Southport NY U.S.A.
233 □H3 South Portland ME U.S.A.
149 F2 South Queensferry Edinburgh, Scotland U.K.
227 H3 South River Ont. Can.
South Rona i. Highland, Scotland U.K. see Rona
146 F3 South Ronaldsay i. Scotland U.K.
233 G3 South Royalton VT U.S.A.
226 A3 South Saint Paul MN U.S.A.
264 H9 South Sandwich Islands S. Atlantic Ocean
264 H9 South Sandwich Trench sea feature S. Atlantic Ocean
240 F3 South San Francisco CA U.S.A.
223 J4 South Saskatchewan r. Alberta/Saskatchewan Can.
223 L3 South Seal r. Man. Can.
262 U2 South Shetland Islands Antarctica
264 E10 South Shetland Trough sea feature S. Atlantic Ocean
149 H2 South Shields Tyne and Wear, England U.K.
South Sinai governorate Egypt see Janûb Sînâ'
149 I4 South Skirlaugh East Riding of Yorkshire, England U.K.
236 E3 South Skunk r. IA U.S.A.
266 F6 South Solomon Trench sea feature Pacific Ocean
234 C1 South Sterling PA U.S.A.
234 C2 South Tamaqua PA U.S.A.
80 E3 South Taranaki Bight b. North I. N.Z.
265 N8 South Tasman Rise sea feature Southern Ocean
241 L2 South Tent mt. UT U.S.A.
235 D3 South Toms River NJ U.S.A.
116 E4 South Tons r. India
241 L5 South Tucson AZ U.S.A.
149 G3 South Tyne r. England U.K.
South Tyrol prov. Trentino - Alto Adige Italy see Bolzano
146 A4 South Uist i. Scotland U.K.
238 B3 South Umpqua r. OR U.S.A.
146 E3 South Walls pen. Scotland U.K.
151 G3 Southwater West Sussex, England U.K.
149 I4 Southwell Nottinghamshire, England U.K.
84 D3 South Wellesley Islands Qld Austr.
South-West Africa country Africa see Namibia
83 F5 South West Cape Tas. Austr.
81 A7 South West Cape Stewart I. N.Z.
85 H4 South West Cay rf Coral Sea Is Terr. Austr.
233 □I2 Southwest Harbor ME U.S.A.
265 G7 Southwest Indian Ridge sea feature Indian Ocean
85 G3 South West Island Coral Sea Is Terr. Austr.
267 I8 Southwest Pacific Basin sea feature S. Pacific Ocean
Southwest Peru Ridge sea feature S. Pacific Ocean see Nazca Ridge
83 H2 South West Rocks N.S.W. Austr.
226 E5 South Whitley IN U.S.A.
237 D5 South Wichita r. TX U.S.A.
150 E3 Southwick Wiltshire, England U.K.
232 B6 South Williamson KY U.S.A.
227 I5 South Williamsport PA U.S.A.
233 □H3 South Windham ME U.S.A.
151 I2 Southwold Suffolk, England U.K.
151 H3 South Woodham Ferrers Essex, England U.K.
151 H2 South Wootton Norfolk, England U.K.
149 H4 South Yorkshire admin. div. England U.K.
232 B5 South Zanesville OH U.S.A.
182 D4 Souto Guarda Port.
182 B5 Souto Santarém Port.
182 C2 Souto Spain
182 C4 Souto da Casa Port.
215 F3 Soutpan S. Africa
213 F4 Soutpansberg mts S. Africa
204 B5 Souttouf, Adrar mts Western Sahara
160 B2 Souvigny France
142 B1 Sovarnuten mt. Norway
197 G2 Sovata Romania
197 H2 Soveja Romania
195 F4 Soverato Italy
192 B2 Soveria Corse France
195 F3 Soveria Mannelli Italy
123 G2 Sovet Tajik.
Sovetabad Uzbek. see Khanabad
Sovetashen Armenia see Zangakutan
138 C4 Sovetsk Kaliningradskaya Oblast' Rus. Fed.
134 J4 Sovetsk Kirovskaya Oblast' Rus. Fed.
139 K5 Sovetsk Tul'skaya Oblast' Rus. Fed.
129 B1 Sovetskaya Krasnodarskiy Kray Rus. Fed.
129 D1 Sovetskaya Stavropol'skiy Kray Rus. Fed.
100 G2 Sovetskaya Gavan' Rus. Fed.
130 H3 Sovetskiy Khanty-Mansiyskiy Avtonomnyy Okrug Rus. Fed.
138 G1 Sovetskiy Leningradskaya Oblast' Rus. Fed.
134 N2 Sovetskiy Respublika Komi Rus. Fed.
134 J4 Sovetskiy Respublika Mariy El Rus. Fed.
Sovetskiy Tajik. see Sovet
137 J2 Sovetskoye Belgorodskaya Oblast' Rus. Fed.
Sovetskoye Chechenskaya Respublika Rus. Fed. see Shatoy
Sovetskoye Kabardino-Balkarskaya Respublika Rus. Fed. see Kashkhatau
Sovetskoye Respublika Dagestan Rus. Fed. see Khebda
120 A2 Sovetskoye Saratovskaya Oblast' Rus. Fed.
Sovetskoye Stavropol'skiy Kray Rus. Fed. see Zelenokumsk
188 F4 Soviči Bos.-Herz.
191 G5 Sovicille Italy
137 H5 Sovyets'kyy Ukr.
212 E4 Sowa Botswana
108 A2 Sowa Sichuan China
212 E4 Sowa Pan salt pan Botswana
149 H3 Sowerby North Yorkshire, England U.K.
149 H4 Sowerby Bridge West Yorkshire, England U.K.
215 F2 Soweto S. Africa
Sōya-kaikyō str. Japan/Rus. Fed. see La Pérouse Strait
243 G5 Soyaló Mex.
134 H2 Soyana r. Rus. Fed.
162 C3 Soyaux France
160 E1 Soye France
173 G3 Soyen Ger.
Soylan Armenia see Vayk'
134 J2 Soyma r. Rus. Fed.
209 B6 Soyo Angola
161 C4 Soyons France
Sozaq Kazakh. see Suzak
139 H5 Sozh r. Europe
134 K4 Sozimskiy Rus. Fed.
197 H4 Sozopol Bulg.
165 E4 Spa Belgium
262 T2 Spaatz Island Antarctica
172 B2 Spabrücken Ger.
195 E4 Spadafora Sicilia Italy
168 C3 Spahnharrenstätte Ger.
172 C3 Spaichingen Ger.
180 E2 Spain country Europe
Spalato Croatia see Split
Spalatum Croatia see Split
82 D3 Spalding S.A. Austr.
151 G2 Spalding Lincolnshire, England U.K.
176 C2 Spálené Poříčí Czech Rep.
173 E2 Spalt Ger.
169 E4 Spangenberg Ger.
150 D3 Span Head hill England U.K.
225 K4 Spaniard's Bay Nfld. Can.
224 D4 Spanish Ont. Can.
224 D4 Spanish r. Ont. Can.
241 L1 Spanish Fork UT U.S.A.
Spanish Guinea country Africa see Equatorial Guinea
Spanish Netherlands country Europe see Belgium
145 C5 Spanish Point Rep. of Ireland
Spanish Sahara terr. Africa see Western Sahara
246 □ Spanish Town Jamaica
246 C1 Spanish Wells Eleuthera Bahamas
170 E2 Spantekow Ger.
194 B4 Sparagio, Monte mt. Sicilia Italy
193 G3 Sparanise Italy
240 H2 Sparks NV U.S.A.
232 B3 Sparlingville MI U.S.A.
234 D1 Sparrow Bush NY U.S.A.
Sparta Greece see Sparti
195 E4 Spartà Sicilia Italy
231 D5 Sparta GA U.S.A.
226 E4 Sparta MI U.S.A.
232 C6 Sparta NC U.S.A.
234 D1 Sparta NJ U.S.A.
231 C5 Sparta TN U.S.A.
226 B4 Sparta WI U.S.A.
231 D5 Spartanburg SC U.S.A.
232 D4 Spartansburg PA U.S.A.
198 C3 Sparti Greece
195 F5 Spartivento, Capo c. Italy
222 H5 Sparwood B.C. Can.
139 J4 Spas-Demensk Rus. Fed.
137 H3 Spas'ke Ukr.
139 M4 Spas-Klepiki Rus. Fed.
137 I3 Spas'ko-Mykhaylivka Ukr.
137 G3 Spasove Ukr.
100 E3 Spassk-Dal'niy Rus. Fed.
139 M4 Spassk-Ryazanskiy Rus. Fed.
169 C5 Spay Ger.
146 D5 Spean Bridge Highland, Scotland U.K.
236 C2 Spearfish SD U.S.A.
237 C4 Spearman TX U.S.A.
195 H3 Specchia Italy
233 F3 Speculator NY U.S.A.
151 F3 Speen West Berkshire, England U.K.
190 E1 Speer mt. Switz.
223 J4 Speers Sask. Can.
172 A2 Speicher Ger.
173 F2 Speichersdorf Ger.
247 □4 Speightstown Barbados
179 G3 Speikkogel mt. Austria
211 B5 Speke Gulf Tanz.
169 C3 Spelle Ger.
193 E2 Spello Italy
146 C5 Spelve, Loch inlet Scotland U.K.
Spence Bay Nunavut Can. see Taloyoak
236 E3 Spencer IA U.S.A.
238 D2 Spencer ID U.S.A.
230 C4 Spencer IN U.S.A.
233 H3 Spencer MA U.S.A.
236 D3 Spencer NE U.S.A.
227 I4 Spencer NY U.S.A.
232 C6 Spencer VA U.S.A.
232 C5 Spencer WV U.S.A.
82 D3 Spencer, Cape S.A. Austr.
212 B5 Spencer Bay Namibia
82 D3 Spencer Gulf est. S.A. Austr.
84 B2 Spencer Range hills N.T. Austr.
222 F5 Spences Bridge B.C. Can.
169 D3 Spenge Ger.
149 H3 Spennymoor Durham, England U.K.
81 D5 Spenser Mountains South I. N.Z.
198 C2 Spercheios r. Greece
171 E3 Sperenberg Ger.
Sperkhiós r. Greece see Spercheios
194 D5 Sperlinga Sicilia Italy
193 F3 Sperlonga Italy
197 G2 Spermezeu Romania
147 D2 Sperrin Mountains hills Northern Ireland U.K.
232 D5 Sperryville VA U.S.A.
169 E6 Spessart reg. Ger.
Spétsai i. Greece see Spetses
198 C3 Spetses Greece
198 C3 Spetses i. Greece
146 E4 Spey r. Scotland U.K.
146 E4 Spey Bay Moray, Scotland U.K.
172 C2 Speyer Ger.
158 C3 Spézet France
193 I5 Spezzano Albanese Italy
Spice Islands Indon. see Maluku
175 K4 Spiczyn Pol.
147 B3 Spiddal Rep. of Ireland
173 H3 Spiegelau Ger.
168 C2 Spiekeroog Ger.
168 C2 Spiekeroog i. Ger.
179 F3 Spielberg bei Knittelfeld Austria
179 G4 Spielfeld Austria
172 B2 Spiesen-Elversberg Ger.
190 C2 Spiez Switz.
190 D4 Spigno Monferrato Italy
193 F3 Spigno Saturnia Italy
164 F1 Spijk Neth.
164 D3 Spijkenisse Neth.
191 G4 Spilamberto Italy
191 H2 Spilimbergo Italy
195 E4 Spilinga Italy
149 J4 Spilsby Lincolnshire, England U.K.
193 I4 Spinazzola Italy
157 F3 Spincourt France
191 H3 Spinea Italy
193 F2 Spinetoli Italy
234 C2 Spinnerstown PA U.S.A.
193 H4 Spinoso Italy
177 L4 Spinuş Romania
236 E3 Spirit Lake IA U.S.A.
238 C1 Spirit Lake ID U.S.A.
223 J4 Spiritwood Sask. Can.
139 J3 Spirovo Rus. Fed.
176 G6 Špišić-Bukovica Croatia
177 J2 Spišská Belá Slovakia
177 J3 Spišská Nová Ves Slovakia
177 J2 Spišská Stará Ves Slovakia
177 J3 Spišské Podhradie Slovakia
177 J3 Spišské Vlachy Slovakia
177 J2 Spišský Štvrtok Slovakia
129 D3 Spitak Armenia
179 F3 Spital am Pyhrn Austria
179 G3 Spital am Semmering Austria
116 D3 Spiti r. India
86 C4 Spit Point W.A. Austr.
140 □ Spitsbergen i. Svalbard
214 D5 Spitskop mt. S. Africa
215 E4 Spitskopvlei S. Africa
179 E4 Spittal an der Drau Austria
146 E5 Spittal of Glenshee Perth and Kinross, Scotland U.K.
179 G2 Spitz Austria
Spitzbergen i. Svalbard see Spitsbergen
178 D4 Spitzkofel mt. Austria
190 E1 Spitzmeilen mt. Switz.
137 J3 Spivakivka Ukr.
151 I2 Spixworth Norfolk, England U.K.
142 C3 Spjald Denmark
188 F4 Split Croatia
223 L3 Split Lake Man. Can.
190 E2 Splügen Switz.
136 E3 Spodakhy Ukr.
179 F4 Spodnja Idrija Slovenia
179 G4 Spodnje Hoče Slovenia
168 F1 Spodsbjerg Denmark
149 H4 Spofforth North Yorkshire, England U.K.
238 C2 Spokane WA U.S.A.
238 C2 Spokane r. WA U.S.A.
129 B1 Spokoynaya Rus. Fed.
190 F2 Spöl r. Italy
Spoletium Italy see Spoleto
193 E2 Spoleto Italy
193 G2 Spoltore Italy
191 F2 Spondigna Italy
165 E4 Spontin Belgium
226 B5 Spoon r. IL U.S.A.
226 B3 Spooner WI U.S.A.
171 D4 Spora Ger.
170 C2 Spornitz Ger.
234 B2 Sporting Hill PA U.S.A.
190 D4 Spotorno Italy
235 D2 Spotswood NJ U.S.A.
232 E5 Spotsylvania VA U.S.A.
238 F2 Spotted Horse WY U.S.A.
227 F2 Spragge Ont. Can.
238 B3 Sprague r. OR U.S.A.
172 D3 Spraitbach Ger.
168 F3 Sprakensehl Ger.
222 F4 Spranger, Mount B.C. Can.
90 D5 Spratly Island S. China Sea
90 D5 Spratly Islands S. China Sea
238 C2 Spray OR U.S.A.
226 C3 Spread Eagle WI U.S.A.
188 G3 Spreča r. Bos.-Herz.
171 E3 Spree r. Ger.
171 E3 Spreenhagen Ger.
172 C4 Spreitenbach Switz.
171 F4 Spremberg Ger.
172 B2 Sprendlingen Ger.
191 H3 Spresiano Italy
190 E2 Spriana Italy
165 E4 Sprimont Belgium
237 E4 Spring r. MO U.S.A.
227 F3 Spring Bay Ont. Can.
214 A3 Springbok S. Africa
234 C2 Spring City PA U.S.A.
241 L2 Spring City UT U.S.A.
84 D3 Spring Creek r. N.T. Austr.
236 C3 Spring Creek r. NE U.S.A.
225 K3 Springdale Nfld. Can.
237 E4 Springdale AR U.S.A.
169 E3 Springe Ger.
239 F4 Springer NM U.S.A.
241 M4 Springerville AZ U.S.A.
81 C5 Springfield South I. N.Z.
147 D2 Springfield Northern Ireland U.K.
237 C4 Springfield CO U.S.A.
231 D5 Springfield GA U.S.A.
238 D3 Springfield ID U.S.A.
236 F4 Springfield IL U.S.A.
230 C4 Springfield KY U.S.A.
233 G3 Springfield MA U.S.A.
233 □I2 Springfield ME U.S.A.
236 E2 Springfield MN U.S.A.
237 E4 Springfield MO U.S.A.
232 B5 Springfield OH U.S.A.
238 B2 Springfield OR U.S.A.
234 C3 Springfield PA U.S.A.
231 C4 Springfield TN U.S.A.
233 G3 Springfield VT U.S.A.
232 D5 Springfield WV U.S.A.
215 E4 Springfontein S. Africa
251 G3 Spring Garden Guyana
235 D1 Spring Glen NY U.S.A.
234 B2 Spring Glen PA U.S.A.
241 L2 Spring Glen UT U.S.A.
226 B4 Spring Green WI U.S.A.
226 B4 Spring Grove MN U.S.A.
234 B3 Spring Grove PA U.S.A.
232 E6 Spring Grove VA U.S.A.
225 H4 Springhill N.S. Can.
231 D6 Spring Hill FL U.S.A.
146 E6 Springholm Dumfries and Galloway, Scotland U.K.
222 F5 Springhouse B.C. Can.
226 D4 Spring Lake MI U.S.A.
235 D2 Spring Lake Heights NJ U.S.A.
241 J3 Spring Mountains NV U.S.A.
226 E4 Springport MI U.S.A.
215 G2 Springs S. Africa
235 F1 Springs NY U.S.A.
81 D5 Springs Junction South I. N.Z.
85 G5 Springsure Qld Austr.
85 E4 Springvale Qld Austr.
215 F5 Spring Valley S. Africa
240 I5 Spring Valley CA U.S.A.
226 A4 Spring Valley MN U.S.A.
235 D1 Spring Valley NY U.S.A.
226 A3 Spring Valley WI U.S.A.
236 D3 Springview NE U.S.A.
240 H3 Springville CA U.S.A.
232 D3 Springville NY U.S.A.
234 C1 Springville PA U.S.A.
241 L1 Springville UT U.S.A.
232 E3 Springwater NY U.S.A.
149 I4 Sproatley East Riding of Yorkshire, England U.K.
169 C4 Sprockhövel Ger.
151 I2 Sprowston Norfolk, England U.K.
222 H4 Spruce Grove Alta Can.
232 D5 Spruce Knob mt. WV U.S.A.
241 M2 Spruce Mountain CO U.S.A.
241 J1 Spruce Mountain NV U.S.A.
164 D3 Sprundel Neth.
234 B3 Spry PA U.S.A.
149 J4 Spurn Head hd England U.K.
220 C5 Spurr, Mount vol. AK U.S.A.
222 F5 Spuzzum B.C. Can.
175 J2 Spychowo Pol.
222 F5 Squamish B.C. Can.
222 F5 Squamish r. B.C. Can.
191 G3 Squaranto r. Italy
195 F4 Squillace Italy
195 F4 Squillace, Golfo di g. Italy
195 H2 Squinzano Italy
232 C6 Squire WV U.S.A.
87 E5 Squires, Mount hill W.A. Austr.
95 E4 Sragen Jawa Tengah Indon.
196 E4 Srbica Kosovo, Srbija Yugo.
196 E4 Srbija aut. rep. Yugo.
Srbinje Bos.-Herz. see Foča
Srbobran Bos.-Herz. see Donji Vakuf
196 D3 Srbobran Vojvodina, Srbija Yugo.
197 H3 Srebărna tourist site Bulg.
188 G3 Srebrenica Bos.-Herz.
197 H4 Sredets Burgas Bulg.
Sredets Grad Sofiya Bulg. see Sofiya
197 H4 Sredetska Reka r. Bulg.
131 Q4 Sredinnyy Khrebet mts Rus. Fed.
179 H4 Središče Slovenia
197 H4 Sredishte Bulg.
197 F4 Sredna Gora mts Bulg.
100 C2 Srednebelaya Rus. Fed.
131 Q3 Srednekolymsk Rus. Fed.
139 K4 Sredne-Russkaya Vozvyshennost' hills Rus. Fed.
131 M3 Sredne-Sibirskoye Ploskogor'ye plat. Rus. Fed.
137 J2 Sredniy Ikorets Rus. Fed.
197 G4 Srednogorie Bulg.
135 I6 Srednyaya Akhtuba Rus. Fed.
174 F3 Śrem Pol.
196 D3 Sremska Mitrovica Vojvodina, Srbija Yugo.
97 D4 Srêpok, Tônlé r. Cambodia
99 K1 Sretensk Rus. Fed.
95 E2 Sri Aman Sarawak Malaysia
137 G2 Sribne Ukr.
114 D3 Sriharikota Island India
114 C5 Sri Jayewardenepura Kotte Sri Lanka
115 E2 Srikakulam Andhra Prad. India
114 C3 Sri Kalahasti Andhra Prad. India
114 D5 Sri Lanka country Asia
116 C4 Sri Madhopur Rajasthan India
117 G4 Srimangal Bangl.
116 D3 Srinagar Uttar Prad. India
116 C2 Srinagar Jammu and Kashmir
114 B3 Sringeri Karnataka India
114 D5 Sri Pada mt. Sri Lanka
114 C4 Srirangam Tamil Nadu India
114 C2 Srisailam Andhra Prad. India
114 C4 Srivaikuntam Tamil Nadu India
114 B2 Srivardhan Mahar. India
114 C4 Srivilliputtur Tamil Nadu India
188 F3 Srnetica mts Bos.-Herz.
188 G3 Srnice Bos.-Herz.
175 J1 Srockowo Pol.
174 E4 Środa Śląska Pol.
174 F3 Środa Wielkopolska Pol.
146 D4 Sron a'Choire Ghairbh hill Scotland U.K.
121 K1 Srostki Rus. Fed.
196 E3 Srpska Crnja Vojvodina, Srbija Yugo.
Srpska Kostajnica Bos.-Herz. see Bosanska Kostajnica
Srpski Brod Bos.-Herz. see Bosanski Brod
196 E3 Srpski Itebej Vojvodina, Srbija Yugo.
115 D2 Srungavarapukota Andhra Prad. India
139 L5 Sselki Rus. Fed.
214 C2 Staansaam S. Africa
85 E3 Staaten r. Qld Austr.
179 H2 Staatz Austria
165 D3 Stabroek Belgium
Stabroek Guyana see Georgetown
176 C2 Stachy Czech Rep.
146 C3 Stac Pollaidh hill Scotland U.K.
Stac Polly hill Scotland U.K. see Stac Pollaidh
226 A3 Stacy MN U.S.A.
226 A4 Stacyville IA U.S.A.
168 E2 Stade Ger.
173 G4 Stadelhorn mt. Ger.
165 C4 Staden Belgium
168 F3 Stadensen Ger.
151 F3 Stadhampton Oxfordshire, England U.K.
146 A4 Stadhlaigearraidh Western Isles, Scotland U.K.
179 E2 Stadl-Paura Austria
164 F2 Stadskanaal Neth.
169 E5 Stadtallendorf Ger.
173 E3 Stadtbergen Ger.
169 E3 Stadthagen Ger.
171 C5 Stadtilm Ger.
169 B5 Stadtkyll Ger.
169 F5 Stadtlauringen Ger.
169 F5 Stadtlengsfeld Ger.
169 B4 Stadtlohn Ger.
169 E4 Stadtoldendorf Ger.
172 D2 Stadtprozelten Ger.
171 C5 Stadtroda Ger.
179 H3 Stadtschlaining Austria
171 C5 Stadtsteinach Ger.
168 E1 Stadum Ger.
190 D1 Stäfa Switz.
146 B5 Staffa i. Scotland U.K.
171 C5 Staffelberg hill Ger.
157 H5 Staffelfelden France
169 F5 Staffelstein Ger.
168 D3 Staffhorst Ger.
146 B4 Staffin Highland, Scotland U.K.
191 I5 Staffolo Italy
190 E3 Staffora r. Italy
150 E2 Stafford Staffordshire, England U.K.
232 E5 Stafford VA U.S.A.
246 C1 Stafford Creek Andros Bahamas
150 E2 Staffordshire admin. div. England U.K.
215 G4 Stafford's Post S. Africa
233 G4 Stafford Springs CT U.S.A.
173 H2 Štáhlavy Czech Rep.
232 D4 Stahlstown PA U.S.A.
171 E3 Stahnsdorf Ger.
138 E3 Staicele Latvia
172 D3 Staig Ger.
193 H3 Staina r. Italy
179 F3 Stainach Austria
149 H3 Staindrop Durham, England U.K.
151 G3 Staines Surrey, England U.K.
149 G3 Stainforth North Yorkshire, England U.K.
149 H4 Stainforth South Yorkshire, England U.K.
149 I3 Staintondale North Yorkshire, England U.K.
157 F4 Stainville France
179 G4 Stainz Austria
195 F5 Staiti Italy
177 L3 Stakčín Slovakia
146 D6 Stake, Hill of hill Scotland U.K.
137 J3 Stakhanov Ukr.
Stakhanovo Rus. Fed. see Zhukovskiy
150 E4 Stalbridge Dorset, England U.K.
190 C2 Stalden Switz.
151 I2 Stalham Norfolk, England U.K.
Stalin Bulg. see Varna
222 E3 Stalin, Mount B.C. Can.
Stalinabad Tajik. see Dushanbe
Stalingrad Rus. Fed. see Volgograd
Stalingradskaya Oblast' admin. div. Rus. Fed. see Volgogradskaya Oblast'
Staliniri Georgia see Ts'khinvali
Stalino Ukr. see Donets'k
Stalino Uzbek. see Shakhrikhan
Stalinogorsk Rus. Fed. see Novomoskovsk
Stalinogród Pol. see Katowice
Stalinsk Rus. Fed. see Novokuznetsk
178 E4 Stall Austria
143 G2 Stallarholmen Sweden
179 G3 Stallhofen Austria
149 G3 Stalling Busk North Yorkshire, England U.K.
173 G2 Stallwang Ger.
175 K5 Stalowa Wola Pol.
197 H3 Stâlpu Romania
149 G4 Stalybridge Greater Manchester, England U.K.
197 G4 Stamboliyski Bulg.
85 E4 Stamford Qld Austr.
151 G2 Stamford Lincolnshire, England U.K.
233 G4 Stamford CT U.S.A.
233 F3 Stamford NY U.S.A.
237 D5 Stamford TX U.S.A.
149 I4 Stamford Bridge East Riding of Yorkshire, England U.K.
149 H2 Stamfordham Northumberland, England U.K.
171 C5 Stammbach Ger.
173 F3 Stammham Ger.
Stampalia i. Greece see Astypalaia
212 C5 Stampriet Namibia
178 B3 Stams Austria
173 G2 Stamsried Ger.
140 K1 Stamsund Norway
147 E3 Stamullen Rep. of Ireland
232 D5 Stanardsville VA U.S.A.
236 E3 Stanberry MO U.S.A.
222 H5 Standard Alta Can.
164 D3 Standdaarbuiten Neth.
215 G2 Standerton S. Africa
149 G4 Standish Greater Manchester, England U.K.
227 F4 Standish MI U.S.A.
151 H3 Standon Hertfordshire, England U.K.
148 F2 Stane North Lanarkshire, Scotland U.K.
197 G3 Stănești Romania
241 L5 Stanfield AZ U.S.A.
214 B6 Stanford S. Africa
230 C4 Stanford KY U.S.A.
238 E2 Stanford MT U.S.A.
151 H3 Stanford-le-Hope Thurrock, England U.K.
143 H3 Stånga Gotland Sweden
143 G3 Stångån r. Sweden
193 H4 St'Angelo a Fasanella Italy
193 H4 St'Angelo dei Lombardi Italy
140 O1 Stangenestind hill Norway
215 H3 Stanger S. Africa
151 H2 Stanhoe Norfolk, England U.K.
149 G3 Stanhope Durham, England U.K.
234 D2 Stanhope NJ U.S.A.
197 I2 Stănilești Romania
175 K4 Stanin Pol.
196 D3 Stanišić Vojvodina, Srbija Yugo.
Stanislav Ivano-Frankivs'ka Oblast' Ukr. see Ivano-Frankivs'k
137 G4 Stanislav Khersons'ka Oblast' Ukr.
175 M5 Stanislavchyk Ukr.
175 J3 Stanisławów Pol.
197 G2 Stânișoarei, Munții mts Romania
Stanke Dimitrov Bulg. see Dupnitsa
176 C2 Staňkov Czech Rep.
83 F5 Stanley Tas. Austr.
233 □J1 Stanley N.B. Can.
109 □ Stanley H.K. China
259 F8 Stanley Falkland Is
149 H3 Stanley Durham, England U.K.
146 E5 Stanley Perth and Kinross, Scotland U.K.
238 D2 Stanley ID U.S.A.
236 C1 Stanley ND U.S.A.
232 D5 Stanley VA U.S.A.
226 B3 Stanley WI U.S.A.
84 B4 Stanley, Mount hill N.T. Austr.
83 F5 Stanley, Mount hill Tas. Austr.
Stanley, Mount Dem. Rep. Congo/Uganda see Margherita Peak
Stanleyville Dem. Rep. Congo see Kisangani
Stann Creek Belize see Dangriga
149 H2 Stannington Northumberland, England U.K.
198 B2 Stanos Greece
139 L5 Stanovaya Ryasa r. Rus. Fed.
139 L5 Stanovoye Rus. Fed.
131 M4 Stanovoye Nagor'ye mts Rus. Fed.
131 N4 Stanovoy Khrebet mts Rus. Fed.
139 K5 Stanovoy Kolodez' Rus. Fed.
178 C3 Stans Austria
190 D2 Stans Switz.
82 D3 Stansbury S.A. Austr.
86 F4 Stansmore Range hills W.A. Austr.
151 H3 Stansted airport England U.K.
151 H3 Stansted Mountfitchet Essex, England U.K.
83 G2 Stanthorpe Qld Austr.
151 H2 Stanton Suffolk, England U.K.
234 C3 Stanton DE U.S.A.
232 B6 Stanton KY U.S.A.
226 E4 Stanton MI U.S.A.
236 C2 Stanton ND U.S.A.
236 D3 Stanton NE U.S.A.
237 C5 Stanton TX U.S.A.
139 K5 Stantsiya Skuratovo Rus. Fed.
Stantsiya-Yakkabag Uzbek. see Yakkabag
151 H3 Stanway Essex, England U.K.
137 J3 Stanychno-Luhans'ke Ukr.
179 G3 Stanz im Mürztal Austria
168 F2 Stapel Ger.
169 F4 Stapelburg Ger.
168 F2 Stapelfeld Ger.
164 F2 Staphorst Neth.
151 F2 Stapleford Nottinghamshire, England U.K.
151 H3 Staplehurst Kent, England U.K.
236 E2 Staples MN U.S.A.
236 C3 Stapleton NE U.S.A.
175 I4 Stąporków Pol.
85 F3 Star r. Qld Austr.
139 J5 Star' Rus. Fed.
137 F2 Stara Basan' Ukr.
177 H2 Stará Bystrica Slovakia
136 D2 Stara Chortoryya Ukr.
175 J4 Starachowice Pol.
176 D2 Stará Huť Czech Rep.
174 G2 Stara Kiszewa Pol.
175 K3 Stara Kornica Pol.
136 E2 Stara Kotel'nya Ukr.
174 E2 Stara Łubianka Pol.
177 J2 Stará Ľubovňa Slovakia
177 I6 Stara Moravica Vojvodina, Srbija Yugo.
176 E1 Stará Paka Czech Rep.
196 E3 Stara Pazova Vojvodina, Srbija Yugo.
197 F4 Stara Planina mts Bulg./Yugo.
179 H5 Stara Plošćica Croatia
175 K6 Stara Sil' Ukr.
177 G3 Stará Turá Slovakia
136 D3 Stara Ushytsya Ukr.
136 C2 Stara Vyzhivka Ukr.
175 K5 Stara Wieś Pol.
Staraya Barda Altayskiy Kray Rus. Fed. see Krasnogorskoye
137 K2 Staraya Chigla Rus. Fed.
137 J2 Staraya Kalitva Rus. Fed.
120 A1 Staraya Kulatka Rus. Fed.
120 A2 Staraya Poltavka Rus. Fed.
139 H3 Staraya Russa Rus. Fed.
139 H3 Staraya Toropa Rus. Fed.
135 J5 Staraya Tumba Rus. Fed.
197 G4 Stara Zagora Bulg.
136 C3 Stara Zhadova Ukr.
267 I6 Starbuck Island Kiribati
137 I4 Starchenkove Ukr.
197 H3 Starchiojd Romania
237 F5 Star City AR U.S.A.
226 D5 Star City IN U.S.A.
150 D4 Starcross Devon, England U.K.
174 G5 Stare Budkowice Pol.
179 G1 Stařeč Czech Rep.
174 C2 Stare Czarnowo Pol.
174 D2 Stare Dąbrowa Pol.
175 K2 Stare Dolistowo Pol.
175 K3 Stare Hołowczyce Pol.
171 F5 Staré Křečany Czech Rep.
174 D3 Stare Kurowo Pol.
176 F1 Staré Město Czech Rep.
174 G3 Stare Miasto Pol.
175 H1 Stare Pole Pol.
136 C3 Stare Selo Ukr.
174 E4 Stare Strącze Pol.
Stargard in Pommern Pol. see Stargard Szczeciński
174 D2 Stargard Szczeciński Pol.
175 M4 Stari Koshary Ukr.
136 F2 Stari Petrivtsi Ukr.
196 E4 Stari Ras and Sopoćani tourist site Yugo.
139 J3 Staritsa Rus. Fed.
231 D6 Starke FL U.S.A.
171 D5 Starkenberg Ger.
232 D6 Starkey VA U.S.A.
237 F5 Starkville MS U.S.A.
233 F2 Star Lake NY U.S.A.
173 F4 Starnberg Ger.
173 F4 Starnberger See l. Ger.
110 C1 Staroaleyskoye Rus. Fed.
Starobel'sk Ukr. see Starobil's'k
137 J4 Starobesheve Ukr.
137 J3 Starobil's'k Ukr.
137 H4 Starobohdanivka Ukr.
138 F5 Starobyn Belarus
137 J4 Staroderevyankovskaya Rus. Fed.
139 I5 Starodub Rus. Fed.
174 G2 Starogard Gdański Pol.
Starokonstantinov Ukr. see Starokostyantyniv
136 D3 Starokostyantyniv Ukr.
136 E4 Starokozache Ukr.
137 J5 Staroleushkovskaya Rus. Fed.
135 G7 Starominskaya Rus. Fed.
137 I4 Staromlynivka Ukr.
137 J5 Staronizhestebliyevskaya Rus. Fed.
197 H4 Staro Oryakhovo Bulg.
137 I2 Starooskol'skoye Vodokhranilishche resr Rus. Fed.
197 G4 Starosel Bulg.
197 H4 Staro Selo Bulg.
139 M5 Staroseslavino Rus. Fed.
135 G7 Staroshcherbinovskaya Rus. Fed.
120 D1 Starosubkhangulovo Rus. Fed.
137 I5 Starotitarovskaya Rus. Fed.
137 H3 Starovirivka Ukr.
175 H4 Starowa Góra Pol.
134 H4 Staroye Rus. Fed.
135 I5 Staroye Drozhzhanoye Rus. Fed.
139 K3 Staroye Melkovo Rus. Fed.
135 H5 Staroyur'yevo Rus. Fed.
139 L4 Starozhilovo Rus. Fed.
175 H3 Starożreby Pol.
240 H1 Star Peak NV U.S.A.
193 H4 St'Arsenio Italy
150 D4 Start Bay England U.K.
149 H3 Startforth Durham, England U.K.
Starve Island Kiribati see Starbuck Island
175 H2 Stary Dzierzgoń Pol.
177 L1 Stary Dzików Pol.
177 G2 Starý Jičín Czech Rep.
174 D4 Stary Kisielin Pol.
175 H3 Stary Kobrzyniec Pol.
175 K5 Stary Majdan Pol.
176 C2 Starý Plzenec Czech Rep.
175 I6 Stary Sącz Pol.
177 J2 Starý Smokovec Slovakia
175 J3 Stary Szelków Pol.
175 H2 Stary Targ Pol.
177 H3 Starý Tekov Slovakia
137 I2 Starytsya Ukr.
175 K4 Stary Uścimów Pol.
138 G5 Staryya Darohi Belarus
136 C2 Staryy Chortoryys'k Ukr.
Staryye Dorogi Belarus see Staryya Darohi
137 I4 Staryy Krym Donets'ka Oblast' Ukr.
137 H5 Staryy Krym Respublika Krym Ukr.
129 C2 Staryy Lesken Rus. Fed.
130 I3 Staryy Nadym Rus. Fed.
136 C3 Staryy Oleksynets' Ukr.
135 G6 Staryy Oskol Rus. Fed.
136 D3 Staryy Ostropil' Ukr.
Staryy Salavan Rus. Fed. see Novocheremshansk
137 I2 Staryy Saltiv Ukr.
136 B3 Staryy Sambir Ukr.
Staryy Sambor Ukr. see Staryy Sambir
129 E2 Staryy Terek r. Rus. Fed.
129 D2 Staryy Urukh Rus. Fed.
174 G1 Starzyno Pol.
171 C4 Staßfurt Ger.
175 J5 Staszów Pol.
232 E4 State College PA U.S.A.
237 F6 State Line MS U.S.A.
Staten Island Arg. see Los Estados, Isla de
235 D2 Staten Island NY U.S.A.
231 D6 Statenville GA U.S.A.
231 D5 Statesboro GA U.S.A.
231 D5 Statesville NC U.S.A.
142 C2 Stathelle Norway
235 D2 Statue of Liberty tourist site NJ U.S.A.
179 G2 Statzberg hill Austria
179 G2 Statzendorf Austria
136 E4 Stăuceni Moldova
171 E4 Stauchitz Ger.
172 B4 Staufen im Breisgau Ger.
173 E3 Staufersberg hill Ger.
150 E3 Staunton Gloucestershire, England U.K.
232 D5 Staunton VA U.S.A.
171 E4 Staupitz Ger.
142 A2 Stavanger Norway
81 C5 Staveley South I. N.Z.
149 H4 Staveley Derbyshire, England U.K.
165 E4 Stavelot Belgium
164 D3 Stavenisse Neth.
142 D2 Stavern Norway
197 G4 Stavertsi Bulg.
136 F4 Stavkove Ukr.
177 L3 Stavne Ukr.
164 E2 Stavoren Neth.
135 H7 Stavropol' Rus. Fed.
Stavropol Kray admin. div. Rus. Fed. see Stavropol'skiy Kray
Stavropol'-na-Volge Rus. Fed. see Tol'yatti
135 H7 Stavropol'skaya Vozvyshennost' hills Rus. Fed.
129 C1 Stavropol'skiy Kray admin. div. Rus. Fed.
198 C1 Stavros Kentriki Makedonia Greece
198 C1 Stavros Kentriki Makedonia Greece
198 D1 Stavroupoli Anatoliki Makedonia kai Thraki Greece
83 E4 Stawell Vic. Austr.

Şükürbäyli to Tadmur
367

129 E4 Şükürbäyli Azer.
257 F4 Sul, Pico do mt. Brazil
144 J1 Sula i. Norway
134 J2 Sula r. Rus. Fed.
137 G3 Sula r. Ukr.
93 C3 Sula, Kepulauan is Indon.
123 G4 Sulaiman Ranges mts Pak.
129 E2 Sulak Rus. Fed.
129 E2 Sulak r. Rus. Fed.
94 C3 Sulasih, Gunung vol. Indon.
92 C4 Sulat Phil.
93 B3 Sulawesi i. Indon.
93 A3 Sulawesi Selatan prov. Indon.
93 B3 Sulawesi Tengah prov. Indon.
93 B4 Sulawesi Tenggara prov. Indon.
93 C2 Sulawesi Utara prov. Indon.
127 G4 Sulaymān Beg Iraq
124 D3 Sulayyimah Saudi Arabia
Sulci Sardegna Italy see Sant'Antioco
Sulcis Sardegna Italy see Sant'Antioco
192 A5 Sulcis reg. Sardegna Italy
174 D3 Sulechów Pol.
174 D3 Sulęcin Pol.
174 F3 Sulęcinek Pol.
174 F1 Sulęczyno Pol.
122 B2 Suledeh Iran
207 G4 Suleja Nigeria
175 H4 Sulejów Pol.
175 J3 Sulejówek Pol.
175 H4 Sulejowskie, Jezioro l. Pol.
95 G2 Suleman, Teluk b. Indon.
192 B4 Su Lernu r. Sardegna Italy
126 E3 Süleymanlı Turkey
199 E2 Süleymanlı Manisa Turkey
174 D4 Sulików Pol.
206 C5 Sulima Sierra Leone
197 I3 Sulina Romania
168 D3 Sulingen Ger.
140 L2 Suliskongen mt. Norway
140 L2 Sulitjelma Norway
141 O3 Sulkava Fin.
175 H6 Sułkowice Pol.
129 E2 Sulla-Chubutla r. Rus. Fed.
250 A6 Sullana Peru
147 C5 Sullane r. Rep. of Ireland
199 F2 Süller Turkey
151 G4 Sullington West Sussex, England U.K.
236 F4 Sullivan IL U.S.A.
230 C4 Sullivan IN U.S.A.
236 F4 Sullivan MO U.S.A.
222 E5 Sullivan Bay B.C. Can.
234 D1 Sullivan County county NY U.S.A.
234 B1 Sullivan County county PA U.S.A.
Sullivan Island Myanmar see Lanbi Kyun
146 □G1 Sullom Voe inlet Scotland U.K.
233 □I1 Sully Que. Can.
160 C1 Sully France
150 D3 Sully Vale of Glamorgan, Wales U.K.
156 C5 Sully-sur-Loire France
179 G4 Sulm r. Austria
175 H4 Sulmierzyce Łódzkie Pol.
174 F4 Sulmierzyce Wielkopolskie Pol.
Sulmo Italy see Sulmona
193 F2 Sulmona Italy
158 D4 Sulniac France
197 H5 Süloğlu Turkey
175 H5 Sułoszowa Pol.
174 F4 Sułów Pol.
175 K5 Sułów Pol.
237 E6 Sulphur LA U.S.A.
237 D5 Sulphur OK U.S.A.
237 E5 Sulphur r. TX U.S.A.
237 E5 Sulphur Springs TX U.S.A.
224 D4 Sultan Ont. Can.
123 E4 Sultan, Koh-i- mts Pak.
Sultanabad Andhra Prad. India see Osmannagar
Sultanabad Iran see Arāk
199 F1 Sultanbeyli Turkey
199 G2 Sultandağı Turkey
126 D3 Sultanhanı Turkey
199 F3 Sultanhisar Turkey
199 E1 Sultaniça Turkey
Sultaniye Turkey see Karapınar
116 E4 Sultanpur Uttar Prad. India
129 C1 Sultanskoye Rus. Fed.
92 B5 Sulu Archipelago is Phil.
126 D3 Sülüklü Turkey
121 G5 Sülüktü Kyrg.
202 D1 Suluntah Libya
202 D2 Sulūq Libya
114 D3 Suluru Andhra Prad. India
266 C5 Sulu Sea N. Pacific Ocean
137 F2 Sulymivka Ukr.
Sulyukta Kyrg. see Sülüktü
178 A3 Sulz Austria
173 F2 Sulz r. Ger.
173 E2 Sulzach r. Ger.
172 C3 Sulz am Neckar Ger.
173 H3 Sulzbach r. Ger.
172 D2 Sulzbach am Main Ger.
172 D2 Sulzbach an der Murr Ger.
172 D3 Sulzbach-Laufen Ger.
173 F2 Sulzbach-Rosenberg Ger.
172 B2 Sulzbach/Saar Ger.
178 A3 Sulzberg Austria
173 E4 Sulzberg Ger.
172 B4 Sulzburg Ger.
169 F5 Sulzdorf an der Lederhecke Ger.
173 F3 Sulzemoos Ger.
172 C2 Sulzfeld Baden-Württemberg Ger.
169 F5 Sulzfeld Bayern Ger.
173 E2 Sulzheim Ger.
169 F5 Sulzthal Ger.
250 B5 Sumaco, Volcán vol. Ecuador
125 G3 Sumāil Oman
94 B2 Sumatera i. Indon.
94 C3 Sumatera Barat prov. Indon.
94 C3 Sumatera Selatan prov. Indon.
94 B2 Sumatera Utara prov. Indon.
Sumatra i. Indon. see Sumatera
176 C2 Šumava mts Czech Rep.
93 B5 Sumba i. Indon.
93 A5 Sumba, Selat sea chan. Indon.
122 C2 Sumbar r. Turkm.
93 A5 Sumbawa i. Indon.
95 G5 Sumbawabesar Sumbawa Indon.
211 A6 Sumbawanga Tanz.
252 C3 Sumbay Peru
209 B7 Sumbe Angola
186 B1 Sumbilla Spain
94 C3 Sumbing, Gunung vol. Indon.
146 □G2 Sumburgh Shetland, Scotland U.K.
146 □G2 Sumburgh Head hd Scotland U.K.
206 C5 Sumbuya Sierra Leone
108 B2 Sumdo Sichuan China
222 C3 Sumdum AK U.S.A.
222 C3 Sumdum, Mount AK U.S.A.
254 F3 Sumé Brazil
95 D4 Sumedang Jawa Barat Indon.
122 B2 Sume'eh Sarā Iran
176 G5 Sümeg Hungary
161 B5 Sumène France
95 F4 Sumenep Jawa Timur Indon.
116 C4 Sumerpur Rajasthan India
Sumgait Azer. see Sumqayıt
177 J3 Šumiac Slovakia
190 C1 Sumiswald Switz.
102 □1 Sumiyō Japan
127 F3 Summēl Iraq
224 B2 Summer Beaver Ont. Can.
149 H3 Summer Bridge North Yorkshire, England U.K.
225 K3 Summerford Nfld. Can.
147 E3 Summerhill Rep. of Ireland
146 C3 Summer Isles Scotland U.K.
222 G5 Summerland B.C. Can.
225 I4 Summerside P.E.I. Can.
232 C5 Summersville WV U.S.A.
231 C5 Summerville GA U.S.A.
231 D5 Summerville SC U.S.A.
80 F4 Summit hill North I. N.Z.
235 D2 Summit NJ U.S.A.
236 D2 Summit SD U.S.A.
234 C2 Summit Hill PA U.S.A.
222 E3 Summit Lake B.C. Can.
222 F4 Summit Lake B.C. Can.
241 I2 Summit Mountain NV U.S.A.
239 F4 Summit Peak CO U.S.A.
234 B2 Summit Station PA U.S.A.
81 D5 Sumner South I. N.Z.
237 F5 Sumner MS U.S.A.
81 D5 Sumner, Lake South I. N.Z.
103 I5 Sumon-dake mt. Japan
104 A4 Sumoto Japan
93 A4 Sumpangbinangae Sulawesi Selatan Indon.
176 F2 Šumperk Czech Rep.
Sumpu Japan see Shizuoka
129 F3 Sumqayıt Azer.
129 F3 Sumqayıt r. Azer.
121 G4 Sumsar Kyrg.
137 G2 Sums'ka Oblast' admin. div. Ukr.
Sumskaya Oblast' admin. div. Ukr. see Sums'ka Oblast'
134 F2 Sumskiy Posad Rus. Fed.
168 F2 Sumte Ger.
231 D5 Sumter SC U.S.A.
116 D2 Sumur Jammu and Kashmir
176 G2 Šumvald Czech Rep.
190 D2 Sumvitg Switz.
137 H2 Sumy Ukr.
Sumy Oblast admin. div. Ukr. see Sums'ka Oblast'
238 E2 Sun r. MT U.S.A.
134 J4 Suna Rus. Fed.
102 J2 Sunagawa Japan
116 C3 Sunam Punjab India
117 G4 Sunamganj Bangl.
106 C4 Sunan Gansu China
101 C5 Sunan N. Korea
146 C5 Sunart, Loch inlet Scotland U.K.
177 J2 Šuňava Slovakia
125 F3 Şunaynah Oman
238 E1 Sunburst MT U.S.A.
83 F4 Sunbury Vic. Austr.
151 G3 Sunbury Surrey, England U.K.
232 B4 Sunbury OH U.S.A.
227 I5 Sunbury PA U.S.A.
261 G2 Sunchales Arg.
173 G3 Sünching Ger.
253 E6 Suncho Corral Arg.
101 C5 Sunch'ŏn N. Korea
101 C6 Sunch'ŏn S. Korea
215 F1 Sun City S. Africa
241 K5 Sun City AZ U.S.A.
240 I5 Sun City CA U.S.A.
233 H3 Suncook NH U.S.A.
177 L5 Suncuiuş Romania
138 C1 Sund Åland Fin.
94 D4 Sunda, Selat str. Indon.
Sunda Kalapa Indon. see Jakarta
238 F2 Sundance WY U.S.A.
117 G5 Sundarbans reg. Bangl./India
117 F5 Sundargarh Orissa India
116 D3 Sundarnagar Hima. Prad. India
265 L4 Sunda Shelf sea feature Indian Ocean
Sunda Strait Indon. see Sunda, Selat
Sunda Trench sea feature Indian Ocean see Java Trench
214 E5 Sundays r. E. Cape S. Africa
215 H3 Sundays r. Kwazulu-Natal S. Africa
86 D3 Sunday Strait W.A. Austr.
142 A2 Sunde Norway
149 H3 Sunderland Tyne and Wear, England U.K.
169 D4 Sundern (Sauerland) Ger.
169 F4 Sundhausen Ger.
199 G2 Sündiken Dağları mts Turkey
222 H5 Sundre Alta Can.
224 E4 Sundridge Ont. Can.
142 C3 Sunds Denmark
141 L3 Sundsvall Sweden
129 F3 Sündü Azer.
123 E2 Sundukli, Peski des. Turkm.
215 H3 Sundumbili S. Africa
116 D4 Sunel Rajasthan India
211 C6 Sunga Tanz.
94 D3 Sungailiat Sumatera Indon.
94 C3 Sungaipenuh Sumatera Indon.
Sungari r. China see Songhua Jiang
94 C1 Sungei Petani Malaysia
93 A4 Sungguminasa Sulawesi Selatan Indon.
Sungkiang Shanghai China see Songjiang
213 G3 Sungo Moz.
Sungqu Sichuan China see Songpan
129 C3 Süngülü Turkey
197 H4 Sungurlare Bulg.
126 D2 Sungurlu Turkey
192 A4 Suni Sardegna Italy
188 F3 Sunja Croatia
121 H3 Sunkar, Gora mt. Kazakh.
117 G4 Sunkosh Chhu r. Bhutan
117F4 Sun Kosi r. Nepal
137 G3 Sunky Ukr.
169 F5 Sünna Ger.
140 J3 Sunndalsøra Norway
142 E2 Sunne Sweden
141 I3 Sunnfjord reg. Norway
151 G3 Sunninghill Windsor and Maidenhead, England U.K.
241 L2 Sunnyside UT U.S.A.
238 C2 Sunnyside WA U.S.A.
240 F3 Sunnyvale CA U.S.A.
226 C4 Sun Prairie WI U.S.A.
253 F4 Sunsas, Sierra de hills Bol.
240 □ Sunset Beach HI U.S.A.
222 G4 Sunset House Alta Can.
131 M3 Suntar Rus. Fed.
210 C2 Suntu Eth.
238 D3 Sun Valley ID U.S.A.
100 C2 Sunwu Heilong. China
206 E5 Sunyani Ghana
129 E2 Sunzha r. Rus. Fed.
140 N3 Suolahti Fin.
141 N3 Suomenniemi Fin.
226 C1 Suomi Ont. Can.
Suomi country Europe see Finland
138 D1 Suomusjärvi Fin.
140 O2 Suomussalmi Fin.
103 E7 Suō-nada b. Japan
140 N3 Suonenjoki Fin.
97 D5 Suŏng Cambodia
96 C3 Suong r. Laos
134 F3 Suoyarvi Rus. Fed.
Suozhen Shandong China see Huantai
114 B3 Supa Karnataka India
241 K3 Supai AZ U.S.A.
117 F4 Supaul Bihar India
163 C6 Superbagnères France
156 D4 Superbe r. France
160 A3 Superbesse France
161 D4 Superdévoluy France
121 F5 Superfosfatnyy Uzbek.
241 L5 Superior AZ U.S.A.
238 D2 Superior MT U.S.A.
236 D3 Superior NE U.S.A.
226 A2 Superior WI U.S.A.
245 G5 Superior, Laguna lag. Mex.
226 D2 Superior, Lake Can./U.S.A.
161 A3 Superlioran France
191 J4 Supertarska Draga Croatia
188 F4 Supetar Croatia
97 C4 Suphan Buri Thai.
127 F3 Süphan Dağı mt. Turkey
193 F3 Supino Italy
91 I7 Supiori i. Indon.
137 F3 Supiy r. Ukr.
177 L4 Suplacu de Barcău Romania
139 J5 Suponevo Rus. Fed.
169 F3 Süpplingen Ger.
175 L2 Supraśl Pol.
175 L2 Supraśl r. Pol.
129 B2 Sup'sa r. Georgia
101 C4 Supung N. Korea
177 L4 Supur Romania
124 D4 Sūq al Inān Yemen
127 G5 Sūq ash Shuyūkh Iraq
109 F1 Suqian Jiangsu China
124 B2 Sūq Suwayq Saudi Arabia
125 F5 Suquţrā i. Yemen
173 G4 Sur r. Ger.
206 E4 Sur r. Ghana
177 H4 Súr Hungary
125 G3 Şūr Oman
240 G3 Sur, Point CA U.S.A.
135 I5 Sura Rus. Fed.
120 A1 Sura r. Rus. Fed.
129 F3 Şuraabad Azer.
95 F4 Surabaya Jawa Timur Indon.
117 E5 Surajpur Madh. Prad. India
95 E4 Surakarta Jawa Tengah Indon.
197 G3 Şura Mare Romania
160 D2 Suran r. France
123 E5 Sūran Iran
128 C2 Şūrān Syria
177 H3 Šurany Slovakia
85 G5 Surat Qld Austr.
116 C5 Surat Gujarat India
116 C3 Suratgarh Rajasthan India
97 B5 Surat Thani Thai.
175 K3 Suraż Pol.
139 H4 Surazh Belarus
139 I5 Surazh Rus. Fed.
173 G4 Surberg Ger.
85 F4 Surbiton Qld Austr.
195 H2 Surbo Italy
127 G4 Sūrdāsh Iraq
197 H3 Surdila-Greci Romania
197 F2 Surduc Romania
197 F4 Surdulica Srbija Yugo.
172 A2 Sûre r. Ger./Lux.
116 B5 Surendranagar Gujarat India
240 G4 Surf CA U.S.A.
235 D3 Surf City NJ U.S.A.
151 G2 Surfleet Lincolnshire, England U.K.
116 C5 Surgana Mahar. India
162 B2 Surgères France
246 B2 Surgidero de Batabanó Cuba
130 I3 Surgut Rus. Fed.
164 F1 Surhuizum Neth.
Suri W. Bengal India see Siuri
186 E3 Súria Spain
114 C2 Suriapet Andhra Prad. India
190 C3 Surier Italy
92 C4 Surigao Phil.
92 C4 Surigao Strait Phil.
97 C4 Surin Thai.
Surinam country S. America see Suriname
251 G3 Suriname country S. America
251 H3 Suriname r. Suriname
122 C4 Suriyān Iran
127 I4 Surkhābād Iran
121 F5 Surkhandar'inskaya Oblast' admin. div. Uzbek.
121 F5 Surkhandar'ya r. Uzbek.
Surkhandarya Oblast admin. div. Uzbek. see Surkhandar'inskaya Oblast'
116 E3 Surkhet Nepal
123 G2 Surkhob r. Tajik.
Surkhondaryo r. Uzbek. see Surkhandar'ya
Surkhondaryo Wiloyati admin. div. Uzbek. see Surkhandar'inskaya Oblast'
156 D3 Surmelin r. France
127 F2 Sürmene Turkey
140 J3 Surnadalsøra Norway
197 G4 Sŭrnevo Bulg.
135 H6 Surovikino Rus. Fed.
222 C3 Surprise B.C. Can.
184 C1 Surrazala r. Port.
222 F5 Surrey B.C. Can.
151 G3 Surrey admin. div. England U.K.
190 D1 Sursee Switz.
137 H3 Surs'ko-Mykhaylivka Ukr.
135 I5 Surskoye Rus. Fed.
202 C2 Surt Libya
202 C2 Surt, Khalīj g. Libya
140 □B3 Surtsey i. Iceland
197 G3 Suru, Vârful mt. Romania
254 C2 Surubiú r. Brazil
126 E3 Sürüç Turkey
Surud Ad mt. Somalia see Shimbiris
105 E4 Suruga-wan b. Japan
94 C3 Surulangun Sumatera Indon.
251 F4 Surumú r. Brazil
92 C5 Surup Phil.
156 C3 Survilliers France
168 C3 Surwold Ger.
Suryapet Andhra Prad. India see Suriapet
160 C3 Sury-le-Comtal France
158 D4 Surzur France
129 E4 Şuşa Azer.
142 D4 Suså r. Denmark
190 C3 Susa Italy
190 B3 Susa, Valle di val. Italy
Susah Tunisia see Sousse
103 F7 Susaki Japan
Susamyr Kyrg. see Suusamyr
233 E6 Susan VA U.S.A.
122 B4 Süsangerd Iran
134 H4 Susanino Rus. Fed.
240 G1 Susanville CA U.S.A.
190 F2 Susch Switz.
136 D2 Suschany Ukr.
191 H3 Susegana Italy
126 E2 Suşehri Turkey
168 F1 Süsel Ger.
197 G4 Sushitsa Bulg.
107 F5 Sushui r. China
176 C2 Sušice Czech Rep.
175 L5 Susiec Pol.
116 D5 Susner Madh. Prad. India
105 E2 Susobana-gawa r. Japan
109 F2 Susong Anhui China
105 E3 Susono Japan
233 F4 Susquehanna PA U.S.A.
227 I5 Susquehanna r. PA U.S.A.
232 E4 Susquehanna, West Branch r. PA U.S.A.
172 D3 Süßen Ger.
225 H4 Sussex N.B. Can.
234 D1 Sussex NJ U.S.A.
232 E6 Sussex VA U.S.A.
234 D1 Sussex County county NJ U.S.A.
168 D3 Süstedt Ger.
165 E3 Susteren Neth.
191 G3 Sustinente Italy
168 C3 Sustrum Ger.
78 □6 Susubona Sta Isabel Solomon Is
78 □6 Susuka Choiseul Solomon Is
131 P3 Susuman Rus. Fed.
199 F2 Susurluk Turkey
129 C3 Susuz Turkey
138 D4 Šušvė r. Lith.
211 B5 Suswa, Mount Kenya
175 H2 Susz Pol.
106 B2 Sutay Uul mt. Mongolia
199 G3 Sütçüler Turkey
194 C5 Sutera Sicilia Italy
83 G3 Sutherland N.S.W. Austr.
214 C5 Sutherland S. Africa
146 D3 Sutherland reg. Scotland U.K.
236 C3 Sutherland NE U.S.A.
232 E6 Sutherland VA U.S.A.
87 E5 Sutherland Range hills W.A. Austr.
116 B3 Sutlej r. India/Pak.
128 A1 Sütlüce Turkey
197 H5 Sütlüce Turkey
192 E2 Sutri Italy
240 G2 Sutter CA U.S.A.
240 G2 Sutter Creek CA U.S.A.
151 G2 Sutterton Lincolnshire, England U.K.
233 G2 Sutton Que. Can.
224 D2 Sutton r. Ont. Can.
81 C6 Sutton South I. N.Z.
151 H2 Sutton Cambridgeshire, England U.K.
236 D3 Sutton NE U.S.A.
232 C5 Sutton WV U.S.A.
151 H2 Sutton Bridge Lincolnshire, England U.K.
151 F2 Sutton Coldfield West Midlands, England U.K.
151 F3 Sutton Courtenay Oxfordshire, England U.K.
149 H4 Sutton in Ashfield Nottinghamshire, England U.K.
149 H3 Sutton-on-the-Forest North Yorkshire, England U.K.
149 I4 Sutton on Trent Nottinghamshire, England U.K.
151 H3 Sutton Valence Kent, England U.K.
85 F4 Suttor r. Qld Austr.
100 E2 Sutyr' r. Rus. Fed.
136 E3 Sutysky Ukr.
107 E2 Suugant Mongolia
215 E4 Suurberg mt. S. Africa
215 E5 Suurberg mts S. Africa
214 C6 Suurbraak S. Africa
138 E2 Suure-Jaani Estonia
121 H4 Suusamyr Kyrg.
79 □1a Suva Viti Levu Fiji
Suvalki Pol. see Suwałki
196 E4 Suva Reka Kosovo, Srbija Yugo.
129 D4 Suveren Turkey
192 C1 Suvereto Italy
Suvorov atoll Cook Is see Suwarrow
136 E5 Suvorov Moldova
139 K4 Suvorov Rus. Fed.
137 G4 Suvorove Dnipropetrovs'ka Oblast' Ukr.
136 E5 Suvorove Odes'ka Oblast' Ukr.
197 H4 Suvorovo Bulg.
Suvorovo Moldova see Ştefan Vodă
129 C1 Suvorovskaya Rus. Fed.
105 E2 Suwa Japan
175 K1 Suwałki Pol.
96 C4 Suwannaphum Thai.
231 D6 Suwannee r. FL U.S.A.
102 □1 Suwanose-jima i. Japan
95 G2 Suwaran, Gunung mt. Indon.
81 □2 Suwarrow atoll Cook Is
128 B3 Suwaylih Jordan
127 G4 Suwayqīyah, Hawr as imp. l. Iraq
Suways, Khalīj as g. Egypt see Suez, Gulf of
Suweilih Jordan see Suwaylih
Suweis, Khalîg el g. Egypt see Suez, Gulf of
Suweis, Qanâ el canal Egypt see Suez Canal
101 C5 Suwŏn S. Korea
108 D4 Suxu Guangxi China
121 J2 Suykbulak Kazakh.
250 A6 Suyo Peru
Sūyqbulaq Kazakh. see Suykbulak
122 D5 Sūzā Iran
121 G3 Suzak Kazakh.
105 E2 Suzaka Japan
139 M3 Suzdal' Rus. Fed.
161 C4 Suze-la-Rousse France
137 H1 Suzemka Rus. Fed.
109 F1 Suzhou Anhui China
Suzhou Gansu China see Jiuquan
109 G2 Suzhou Jiangsu China
101 C4 Suzi r. China
103 H5 Suzu Japan
104 C4 Suzuka Japan
104 C4 Suzuka-gawa r. Japan
104 C4 Suzuka-sanmyaku mts Japan
191 F4 Suzzara Italy
141 K3 Svabensverk Sweden
140 N1 Særholthalvøya pen. Norway
140 □ Svalbard terr. Arctic Ocean
197 H4 Svalenik Bulg.
142 D4 Svallerup Denmark
136 B3 Svalyava Ukr.
143 H2 Svanberga Sweden
129 C2 Svanet'is K'edi hills Georgia
143 F3 Svängsta Sweden
140 M2 Svanstein Sweden
137 H2 Svapa r. Rus. Fed.
140 M2 Svappavaara Sweden
143 F1 Svärdsjö Sweden
142 C2 Svarstad Norway
138 E1 Svarta r. Fin.
143 F2 Svartå Sweden
143 F2 Svartälven r. Sweden
143 E1 Svartån r. Sweden
143 G2 Svartån r. Sweden
140 M2 Svartbyn Sweden
Svartenhuk Halvø pen. Greenland see Sigguup Nunaa
140 M2 Svartlä Sweden
136 D2 Svarytsevychi Ukr.
171 D5 Svatava Czech Rep.
144 J1 Svatjell hill Norway
179 I2 Svatobořice-Mistřín Czech Rep.
137 J3 Svatove Ukr.
176 G3 Svätý Jur Slovakia
177 H4 Svätý Peter Slovakia
97 D5 Svay Riĕng Cambodia
134 I4 Svecha Rus. Fed.
138 E4 Svėdasai Lith.
141 K3 Sveg Sweden
142 A2 Sveio Norway
138 C4 Švėkšna Lith.
141 I3 Svelgen Norway
140 J3 Svellingen Norway
137 H1 Sven' Rus. Fed.
138 E4 Švenčionėliai Lith.
138 F4 Švenčionys Lith.
142 D4 Svendborg Denmark
142 E3 Svenljunga Sweden
140 □ Svenskøya i. Svalbard
140 K3 Svenstavik Sweden
138 E4 Šventoji r. Lith.
Sverdlovsk Rus. Fed. see Yekaterinburg
137 J3 Sverdlovs'k Ukr.
120 F5 Sverdlovsk Uzbek.
134 M4 Sverdlovskaya Oblast' admin. div. Rus. Fed.
Sverdlovsk Oblast admin. div. Rus. Fed. see Sverdlovskaya Oblast'
221 I2 Sverdrup Islands Nunavut Can.
Sverige country Europe see Sweden
Švermovo Slovakia see Telgárt
137 G2 Svesa Ukr.
179 H4 Sveta Marija Croatia
138 D3 Švėtė r. Lith.
Sveti Ivan Zelina Croatia see Zelina
188 F4 Sveti Jure mt. Croatia
197 E5 Sveti Nikole Macedonia
176 G1 Světlá Hora Czech Rep.
176 E2 Světlá nad Sázavou Czech Rep.
100 F3 Svetlaya Rus. Fed.
100 G2 Svetlodarskoye Sakhalin Rus. Fed.
Svetlogorsk Belarus see Svyetlahorsk
138 C4 Svetlogorsk Kaliningradskaya Oblast' Rus. Fed.
130 J3 Svetlogorsk Krasnoyarskiy Kray Rus. Fed.
135 H7 Svetlograd Stavropol'skiy Kray Rus. Fed.
134 K4 Svetlopolyansk Rus. Fed.
Svetlovodsk Ukr. see Svitlovods'k
138 C4 Svetlyy Kaliningradskaya Oblast' Rus. Fed.
120 E2 Svetlyy Orenburgskaya Oblast' Rus. Fed.
135 I6 Svetlyy Yar Rus. Fed.
138 G1 Svetogorsk Leningradskaya Oblast' Rus. Fed.
Svetogorsk Respublika Dagestan Rus. Fed. see Shamil'kala
Svetozarevo Srbija Yugo. see Jagodina
196 D3 Svetozar Miletić Vojvodina, Srbija Yugo.
138 E3 Svētupe r. Latvia
140 □C2 Svíahnúkar vol. Iceland
136 C3 Svicha r. Ukr.
177 K2 Svidník Slovakia
176 C2 Švihov Czech Rep.
188 F4 Svilaja mts Croatia
196 E3 Svilajnac Srbija Yugo.
197 H5 Svilengrad Bulg.
197 F3 Svinecea Mare, Vârful mt. Romania
177 K2 Svinia Slovakia
177 H3 Svinná Slovakia
142 D4 Svinninge Denmark
138 F4 Svir Belarus
139 J1 Svir' r. Rus. Fed.
139 I1 Svirskaya Guba b. Rus. Fed.
139 I1 Svir'stroy Rus. Fed.
175 M6 Svirzh r. Ukr.
197 G4 Svishtov Bulg.
138 E5 Svislach Hrodzyenskaya Voblasts' Belarus
138 F5 Svislach Minskaya Voblasts' Belarus
175 M2 Svislach r. Belarus
138 D5 Svislach r. Belarus
138 G5 Svislach r. Belarus
Svisloch r. Belarus see Svislach
Svisloch r. Belarus see Svislach
Svisloch r. Belarus see Svislach
177 J2 Svit Slovakia
176 F3 Svitava r. Czech Rep.
176 F2 Svitavy Czech Rep.
137 J3 Svitlodars'k Ukr.
137 H3 Svitlohirs'ke Ukr.
137 G3 Svitlovods'k Ukr.
175 L4 Svityaz' Ukr.
Svizzera country Europe see Switzerland
137 I2 Svoboda Rus. Fed.
176 E1 Svoboda nad Úpou Czech Rep.
100 D2 Svobodnyy Rus. Fed.
129 C1 Svobody Rus. Fed.
197 F4 Svoge Bulg.
138 G4 Svol'nya r. Belarus
140 K1 Svolvær Norway
176 F2 Svratka Czech Rep.
176 F2 Svratka r. Czech Rep.
177 H2 Svrčinovec Slovakia
197 F4 Svrljig Srbija Yugo.
197 F4 Svrljiške Planine mts Yugo.
Svyatogorovskiy Rudnik Ukr. see Dobropillya
139 M4 Svyatoye, Ozero l. Rus. Fed.
138 G5 Svyetlahorsk Belarus
137 G1 Svyha r. Ukr.
136 C2 Svynya r. Ukr.
136 D2 Svyten'ka r. Ukr.
123 H3 Swabi Pak.
151 F2 Swadlincote Derbyshire, England U.K.
215 E5 Swaershoek S. Africa
151 H2 Swaffham Norfolk, England U.K.
85 H4 Swain Reefs Qld Austr.
231 D5 Swainsboro GA U.S.A.
77 I3 Swains Island American Samoa
212 B4 Swakopmund Namibia
149 H3 Swale r. England U.K.
78 □6 Swallow Islands Santa Cruz Is Solomon Is
165 F3 Swalmen Neth.
225 G1 Swampy r. Que. Can.
87 B6 Swan r. W.A. Austr.
223 K4 Swan r. Man./Sask. Can.
224 D2 Swan r. Ont. Can.
148 B5 Swan Rep. of Ireland
151 F4 Swanage Dorset, England U.K.
232 C5 Swandale WV U.S.A.
214 D5 Swanepoelspoort mt. S. Africa
83 E3 Swan Hill Vic. Austr.
222 H4 Swan Hills Alta Can.
246 B3 Swan Islands is Caribbean Sea
234 D1 Swan Lake NY U.S.A.
151 H3 Swanley Kent, England U.K.
147 D2 Swanlinbar Rep. of Ireland
81 D5 Swannanoa South I. N.Z.
231 E5 Swanquarter NC U.S.A.
82 D3 Swan Reach S.A. Austr.
223 K4 Swan River Man. Can.
226 A2 Swan River MN U.S.A.
148 C3 Swan's Cross Roads Rep. of Ireland
83 G5 Swansea Tas. Austr.
150 D3 Swansea Swansea, Wales U.K.
150 D3 Swansea admin. div. Wales U.K.
150 D3 Swansea Bay Wales U.K.
240 F3 Swanton CA U.S.A.
233 G2 Swanton VT U.S.A.
151 H2 Swanton Morley Norfolk, England U.K.
174 G1 Swarożyn Pol.
215 G4 Swartberg S. Africa
214 B6 Swartberg mt. S. Africa
214 A4 Swartdoorn r. S. Africa
234 C3 Swarthmore PA U.S.A.
215 F5 Swart Kei r. S. Africa
215 E5 Swartkops S. Africa
215 E5 Swartkops r. S. Africa
Swart Nossob watercourse Namibia see Black Nossob
215 F2 Swartplaas S. Africa
214 D3 Swartputs S. Africa
215 F1 Swartruggens S. Africa
234 D1 Swartswood NJ U.S.A.
215 H2 Swart Umfolozi S. Africa
227 F4 Swartz Creek MI U.S.A.
174 F3 Swarzędz Pol.
241 K2 Swasey Peak UT U.S.A.
227 G1 Swastika Ont. Can.
123 G3 Swat r. Pak.
234 B2 Swatara Creek r. PA U.S.A.
Swatow Guangdong China see Shantou
148 C3 Swatragh Northern Ireland U.K.
151 F4 Sway Hampshire, England U.K.
215 H2 Swaziland country Africa
141 K3 Sweden country Europe
234 C3 Swedesboro NJ U.S.A.
84 D3 Sweers Island Qld Austr.
232 D6 Sweet Briar VA U.S.A.
238 B2 Sweet Home OR U.S.A.
232 C6 Sweet Springs WV U.S.A.
234 B1 Sweet Valley PA U.S.A.
237 C5 Sweetwater TX U.S.A.
238 F3 Sweetwater r. WY U.S.A.
238 E3 Sweetwater Station WY U.S.A.
214 C6 Swellendam S. Africa
215 F4 Swempoort S. Africa
175 I2 Świątki Pol.
174 G1 Świbno Pol.
175 J3 Świder r. Pol.
174 E5 Świdnica Pol.
174 D4 Świdnica Pol.
175 K4 Świdnik Pol.
174 D2 Świdwin Pol.
174 E5 Świebodzice Pol.
174 D3 Świebodzin Pol.
174 G2 Świecie Pol.
174 E4 Święciechowa Pol.
175 H2 Świecie nad Osą Pol.
175 H2 Świedziebnia Pol.
174 G2 Świekatowo Pol.
174 D5 Świeradów-Zdrój Pol.
175 I3 Świercze Pol.
174 F5 Świerczów Pol.
174 G5 Świerklaniec Pol.
174 D4 Świerzawa Pol.
174 C2 Świerzno Pol.
174 E1 Świeszyno Pol.
175 J2 Świętajno Pol.
175 K1 Świętajno Pol.
175 I5 Świętokrzyskie prov. Pol.
175 I5 Świętokrzyskie, Góry hills Pol.
233 □H2 Swift r. ME U.S.A.
223 J5 Swift Current Sask. Can.
223 J5 Swiftcurrent Creek r. Sask. Can.
164 E2 Swifterbant Neth.
234 C1 Swiftwater PA U.S.A.
148 B3 Swilly r. Rep. of Ireland
147 D1 Swilly, Lough inlet Rep. of Ireland
151 F3 Swindon Swindon, England U.K.
151 F3 Swindon admin. div. England U.K.
149 I4 Swinefleet East Riding of Yorkshire, England U.K.
151 G2 Swineshead Lincolnshire, England U.K.
147 C3 Swinford Rep. of Ireland
174 G3 Świnice Warckie Pol.
175 H6 Świnna Pol.
174 C2 Świnoujście Pol.
146 F6 Swinton Scottish Borders, Scotland U.K.
149 H4 Swinton South Yorkshire, England U.K.
Swiss Confederation country Europe see Switzerland
Świstocz r. Belarus see Svislach
190 D2 Switzerland country Europe
147 E3 Swords Rep. of Ireland
85 E4 Swords Range hills Qld Austr.
174 F2 Swornegacie Pol.
234 C1 Swoyerville PA U.S.A.
134 F3 Syamozero, Ozero l. Rus. Fed.
134 H3 Syamzha Rus. Fed.
138 G4 Syanno Belarus
138 E5 Syaredneneмanskaya Nizina lowland Belarus/Lith.
138 F5 Syarhyeyevichy Belarus
139 I1 Syas' r. Rus. Fed.
139 I1 Syas'troy Rus. Fed.
134 I4 Syava Rus. Fed.
215 G1 Sybrandskraal S. Africa
226 C5 Sycamore IL U.S.A.
139 J4 Sychevka Rus. Fed.
139 K4 Sychevo Rus. Fed.
174 F4 Syców Pol.
Sydenham atoll Gilbert Is Kiribati see Nonouti
83 G3 Sydney N.S.W. Austr.
225 I4 Sydney N.S. Can.
84 D3 Sydney Island Qld Austr.
Sydney Island Phoenix Is Kiribati see Manra
225 I4 Sydney Mines N.S. Can.
Sydzhak Uzbek. see Sidzhak
137 J4 Syedove Ukr.
128 A1 Syedra tourist site Turkey
137 J3 Syeverne Ukr.
137 J3 Syeverodonets'k Ukr.
168 D3 Syke Ger.
198 C3 Sykea Greece
234 B3 Sykesville MD U.S.A.
232 D4 Sykesville PA U.S.A.
140 I3 Sykkylven Norway
134 J3 Syktyvkar Rus. Fed.
231 C5 Sylacauga AL U.S.A.
117 G4 Sylhet Bangl.
117 G4 Sylhet admin. div. Bangl.
168 D1 Sylt i. Ger.
168 D1 Sylt-Ost Ger.
134 L4 Sylva r. Rus. Fed.
231 D5 Sylva NC U.S.A.
87 C4 Sylvania W.A. Austr.
231 D5 Sylvania GA U.S.A.
232 B4 Sylvania OH U.S.A.
222 H4 Sylvan Lake Alta Can.
231 D6 Sylvester GA U.S.A.
84 C3 Sylvester, Lake salt flat N.T. Austr.
222 E3 Sylvia, Mount B.C. Can.
199 E3 Symi Greece
199 E3 Symi i. Greece
146 E6 Symington South Lanarkshire, Scotland U.K.
92 B3 Syndicate Phil.
137 H3 Synel'nykove Ukr.
127 I2 Syngyrli, Mys pt Kazakh.
137 H2 Synivka Ukr.
131 N4 Synnagyn, Khrebet mts Rus. Fed.
141 J3 Synnfjell mt. Norway
86 E3 Synnott, Mount hill W.A. Austr.
86 E3 Synnott Range hills W.A. Austr.
150 C2 Synod Inn Ceredigion, Wales U.K.
134 L2 Synya Rus. Fed.
134 N2 Synya r. Rus. Fed.
136 F3 Synytsya r. Ukr.
136 F3 Synyukha r. Ukr.
Synzhera Moldova see Sîngerei
Synzherey Moldova see Sîngerei
235 E2 Syosset NY U.S.A.
263 C2 Syowa research stn Antarctica
175 J2 Sypniewo Pol.
Syracusae Sicilia Italy see Siracusa
Syracuse Sicilia Italy see Siracusa
236 C4 Syracuse KS U.S.A.
233 E3 Syracuse NY U.S.A.
171 D5 Syrau Ger.
121 G4 Syrdar'inskaya Oblast' admin. div. Uzbek.
121 E3 Syrdar'ya r. Asia
121 G4 Syrdar'ya Uzbek.
Syrdarya Oblast admin. div. Uzbek. see Syrdar'inskaya Oblast'
Syrdaryinskiy Uzbek. see Syrdar'ya
173 E3 Syrgenstein Ger.
126 E4 Syria country Asia
96 B3 Syriam Myanmar
Syrian Desert Asia see Bādiyat ash Shām
199 E3 Syrna i. Greece
198 D3 Syros i. Greece
139 L5 Syrskiy Rus. Fed.
141 N3 Sysmä Fin.
134 J3 Sysola r. Rus. Fed.
151 F2 Syston Leicestershire, England U.K.
136 E3 Sytkivtsi Ukr.
134 J4 Syumsi Rus. Fed.
134 K5 Syun r. Rus. Fed.
100 G2 Syurkum Rus. Fed.
137 H5 Syvash, Zatoka lag. Ukr.
137 H4 Syvas'ke Ukr.
137 G5 Syzivka Ukr.
120 B1 Syzran' Rus. Fed.
177 H4 Szabadbattyán Hungary
177 H4 Szabadegyháza Hungary
Szabadka Vojvodina, Srbija Yugo. see Subotica
177 K5 Szabadkígyós Hungary
177 I5 Szabadszállás Hungary
177 L3 Szabolcs-Szatmár-Bereg county Hungary
174 G4 Szadek Pol.
175 I6 Szaflary Pol.
177 J4 Szajol Hungary
177 H5 Szakes Hungary
177 I5 Szakmár Hungary
177 H4 Szákszend Hungary
177 K3 Szalaszend Hungary
177 I5 Szalkszentmárton Hungary
177 J3 Szalonna Hungary
174 F2 Szamocin Pol.
177 L3 Szamos r. Hungary
177 L3 Szamosszeg Hungary
174 E3 Szamotuły Pol.
177 I5 Szank Hungary
176 G4 Szany Hungary
177 H4 Szár Hungary
177 J5 Szarvas Hungary
177 J4 Szászberek Hungary
177 H5 Szászvár Hungary
177 L3 Szatmárcseke Hungary
177 J5 Szatymaz Hungary
177 H4 Százhalombatta Hungary
174 D3 Szczaniec Pol.
175 K6 Szczawne Pol.
175 I6 Szczawnica Pol.
174 E5 Szczawno-Zdrój Pol.
175 K5 Szczebrzeszyn Pol.
174 C2 Szczecin Pol.
174 E2 Szczecinek Pol.
175 H5 Szczekociny Pol.
175 J2 Szczepankowo Pol.
175 H4 Szczerców Pol.
175 J5 Szczucin Pol.
175 K2 Szczuczyn Pol.
175 I1 Szczurkowo Pol.
175 I5 Szczurowa Pol.
175 H6 Szczyrk Pol.
174 E5 Szczytna Pol.
174 G4 Szczytniki Pol.
175 I2 Szczytno Pol.
Szechwan prov. China see Sichuan
177 I3 Szécsény Hungary
177 H5 Szederkény Hungary
177 H5 Szedres Hungary
177 J5 Szeged Hungary
177 K4 Szeghalom Hungary
177 J5 Szegvár Hungary
177 H4 Székesfehérvár Hungary
177 J5 Székkutas Hungary
177 H5 Szekszárd Hungary
174 G1 Szemud Pol.
177 I4 Szendehely Hungary
177 J3 Szendrő Hungary
177 J3 Szendrőlád Hungary
177 I4 Szentendre Hungary
177 J5 Szentes Hungary
176 F5 Szentgotthárd Hungary
177 J4 Szentistván Hungary
177 I5 Szentkirály Hungary
177 G5 Szentlászló Hungary
177 I4 Szentlőrinckáta Hungary
177 I4 Szentmártonkáta Hungary
177 G5 Szentőrinc Hungary
176 F4 Szentpéterfa Hungary
177 K4 Szentpéterszeg Hungary
176 F5 Szepetnek Hungary
175 K3 Szepietowo Pol.
177 H5 Szeremle Hungary
177 K3 Szerencs Hungary
177 K4 Szerep Hungary
175 J6 Szerzyny Pol.
175 K1 Szeska Góra hill Pol.
175 J2 Szestno Pol.
177 H4 Szigetbecse Hungary
177 H4 Szigethalom Hungary
177 I4 Szigetszentmiklós Hungary
177 H4 Szigetújfalu Hungary
177 G5 Szigetvár Hungary
176 G5 Szigliget Hungary
177 J4 Szihalom Hungary
177 J3 Szikszó Hungary
176 G4 Szil Hungary
177 J3 Szilvásvárad Hungary
174 F4 Szkaradowo Pol.
174 D5 Szklarska Poręba Pol.
174 E4 Szklary Górne Pol.
175 K6 Szkło r. Pol.
175 J2 Szkwa r. Pol.
174 E4 Szlichtyngowa Pol.
177 H4 Szob Hungary
177 J3 Szögliget Hungary
177 J4 Szolnok Hungary
177 G5 Szőlősgyörök Hungary
176 F4 Szombathely Hungary
177 J4 Szomolya Hungary
175 K5 Szówsko Pol.
174 D4 Szprotawa Pol.
174 D4 Szprotawa r. Pol.
175 I5 Szreniawa r. Pol.
176 E1 Szrenica mt. Czech Rep.
175 I2 Szreńsk Pol.
175 H2 Szropy Pol.
175 L2 Sztabin Pol.
Sztálinváros Hungary see Dunaújváros
175 H2 Sztum Pol.
175 H1 Sztutowo Pol.
174 F2 Szubin Pol.
177 I4 Szűcsi Hungary
175 L2 Szudziałowo Pol.
177 I3 Szügy Hungary
177 J3 Szuhogy Hungary
175 K3 Szulborze Wielkie Pol.
175 K3 Szumowa Pol.
177 I4 Szurdokpüspöki Hungary
175 I4 Szydłowiec Pol.
175 I2 Szydłowo Pol.
174 E2 Szydłowo Pol.
175 J2 Szymonka Pol.
174 F4 Szymonków Pol.
174 G4 Szynkielów Pol.
175 L1 Szypliszki Pol.

T

210 D2 Taagga Duudka reg. Somalia
81 □3 Taakoka i. Rarotonga Cook Is
177 H5 Tab Hungary
92 B3 Tabaco Phil.
124 C2 Tābah Saudi Arabia
177 H4 Tabajd Hungary
95 F5 Tabanan Bali Indon.
183 F2 Tabanera de Cerrato Spain
95 F2 Tabang r. Indon.
215 G4 Tabankulu S. Africa
Ţabaqah Syria see Madīnat ath Thawrah
247 □7 Tabaquite Trin. and Tob.
182 E3 Tábara Spain
169 F5 Tabarz Ger.
122 D3 Ţabas Khorāsan Iran
122 E3 Ţabas Khorāsan Iran
138 E2 Tabasalu Estonia
245 H4 Tabasco state Mex.
122 D4 Tabāsin Iran
122 B4 Tābask, Kūh-e mt. Iran
250 D6 Tabatinga Amazonas Brazil
256 C4 Tabatinga São Paulo Brazil
254 D4 Tabatinga, Serra da hills Brazil
92 B2 Tabayoo, Mount Luzon Phil.
177 I5 Tabdi Hungary
204 E3 Tabelbala Alg.
223 H5 Taber Alta Can.
205 G2 Taberdga Alg.
143 F3 Taberg hill Sweden
185 H3 Tabernas Spain
Tabernes de Valldigna Spain see Tavernes de la Valldigna
185 H3 Taberno Spain
96 B1 Tabet, Nam r. Myanmar
78 □3a Tabik i. Kwajalein Marshall Is
94 C3 Tabir r. Indon.
77 H2 Tabiteuea atoll Gilbert Is Kiribati
138 F2 Tabivere Estonia
92 B3 Tablas i. Phil.
92 B3 Tablas Strait Phil.
214 B5 Table Mountain hill S. Africa
207 F5 Tabligbo Togo
185 F2 Tablillas r. Spain
182 C2 Taboada Spain
251 F6 Tabocal r. Brazil
253 G4 Tabocó r. Brazil
176 D2 Tábor Czech Rep.
211 B6 Tabora Tanz.
211 B6 Tabora admin. reg. Tanz.
177 I4 Táborfalva Hungary
123 G1 Taboshar Tajik.
261 H2 Tabossi Arg.
146 B3 Tabost Western Isles, Scotland U.K.
206 D5 Tabou Côte d'Ivoire
122 A2 Tabrīz Iran
182 B4 Tábua Port.
182 C3 Tabuaço Port.
267 I5 Tabuaeran i. Kiribati
183 I3 Tabuenca Spain
124 B1 Tabūk Saudi Arabia
124 B1 Tabūk prov. Saudi Arabia
83 H2 Tabulam N.S.W. Austr.
121 I1 Tabuny Rus. Fed.
193 G3 Taburno, Monte mt. Italy
78 □5 Tabwémasana, Mount Vanuatu
143 H2 Täby Sweden
177 H4 Tác Hungary
251 H5 Tacaipu, Serra hills Brazil
244 D4 Tacámbaro Mex.
243 G6 Tacaná, Volcán de vol. Mex.
242 □K7 Tacarcuna, Cerro mt. Panama
179 F4 Tacen Slovenia
110 C2 Tacheng Xinjiang China
173 G3 Tacherting Ger.
222 E4 Tachie B.C. Can.
105 F3 Tachikawa Tōkyō Japan
102 I4 Tachikawa Yamagata Japan
250 C2 Táchira state Venez.
176 B2 Tachov Czech Rep.
195 F4 Tacina r. Italy
92 C4 Tacloban Phil.
252 C4 Tacna Peru
252 C4 Tacna dept Peru
241 K5 Tacna AZ U.S.A.
238 B2 Tacoma WA U.S.A.
226 B2 Taconite Harbor MN U.S.A.
258 E2 Taco Pozo Arg.
216 □3a Tacoronte Tenerife Canary Is
258 G3 Tacuarembó Uru.
261 J3 Tacuarembó dept Uru.
242 C2 Tacupeto Mex.
174 F4 Taczanów Drugi Pol.
103 I5 Tadami-gawa r. Japan
192 A4 Tadasuni Sardegna Italy
149 H4 Tadcaster North Yorkshire, England U.K.
205 F3 Tademaït, Plateau du Alg.
78 □5 Tadine Î. Loyauté New Caledonia
205 H4 Tadjentourt hill Alg.
Tadjikistan country Asia see Tajikistan
210 D2 Tadjoura Djibouti
210 D2 Tadjoura, Golfe de g. Djibouti
151 F3 Tadley Hampshire, England U.K.
128 D2 Tadmur Syria

Tadó to Tashkentskaya Oblast'

368

250 B3 Tadó Col.
225 G3 Tadoussac Que. Can.
114 C3 Tadpatri Andhra Prad. India
205 H4 Tadrart hills Alg.
202 A3 Tadrart Acacus tourist site Libya
114 C2 Tadwale Mahar. India
Tadzhikskaya S.S.R. country Asia see Tajikistan
138 D2 Taebla Estonia
Taech'ŏn S. Korea see Poryŏng
101 C5 Taedong-gang r. N. Korea
101 D6 Taegu S. Korea
101 C5 Taejŏn S. Korea
101 C6 Taejŏng S. Korea
101 D5 T'aepaek S. Korea
150 C3 Taf r. Wales U.K.
77 I3 Tafahi i. Tonga
183 I2 Tafalla Spain
215 E4 Tafelberg S. Africa
214 C5 Tafelberg mt. S. Africa
251 G4 Tafelberg mt. Suriname
190 C2 Tafers Switz.
150 D3 Taffs Well Cardiff, Wales U.K.
Tafila Jordan see Aţ Ţafīlah
206 D4 Tafiré Côte d'Ivoire
258 D2 Tafí Viejo Arg.
204 C3 Tafraoute Morocco
122 B3 Tafresh Iran
240 H4 Taft CA U.S.A.
123 E4 Taftān, Kūh-e mt. Iran
128 C2 Taftanāz Syria
234 C1 Tafton PA U.S.A.
186 F2 Taga mt. Spain
102 J4 Tagajō Japan
135 G7 Taganrog Rus. Fed.
137 J4 Taganrog, Gulf of Rus. Fed./Ukr.
Taganrogskiy Zaliv b. Rus. Fed./Ukr. see Taganrog, Gulf of
206 C2 Tagant admin. reg. Maur.
122 D2 Tagarev, Gora mt. Iran/Turkm.
103 E7 Tagawa Japan
135 I5 Tagay Rus. Fed.
92 B4 Tagbilaran Phil.
111 C5 Tagchagpu Ri mt. Xizang China
Tagdempt Alg. see Tiaret
190 C5 Taggia Italy
206 E3 Taghin-Dassouri Burkina
Ţâghira Moldova see Ţighira
222 C2 Tagish Y.T. Can.
193 F2 Tagliacozzo Italy
191 I3 Tagliamento r. Italy
192 B2 Taglio-Isolaccio Corse France
156 E3 Tagnon France
92 C4 Tagoloan r. Phil.
122 D1 Tagta Turkm.
123 E3 Tagtabazar Turkm.
256 C1 Taguatinga Minas Gerais Brazil
254 D5 Taguatinga Tocantins Brazil
92 B2 Tagudin Phil.
77 F3 Tagula Island P.N.G.
92 C5 Tagum Phil.
184 B1 Tagus r. Port./Spain alt. Tajo (Spain), alt. Tejo (Portugal)
107 J2 Taha Heilong. China
222 G5 Tahaetkun Mountain B.C. Can.
185 H3 Tahal Spain
94 C1 Tahan, Gunung mt. Malaysia
204 D3 Tahanaoute Morocco
79 □3 Tahanea atoll Arch. des Tuamotu Fr. Polynesia
Tahanroz'ka Zatoka b. Rus. Fed./Ukr. see Taganrog, Gulf of
205 G5 Tahat, Mont mt. Alg.
Tahaurawe i. HI U.S.A. see Kahoolawe
100 C1 Tahe Heilong. China
80 D1 Taheke North I. N.Z.
147 B5 Tahilla Rep. of Ireland
106 C2 Tahilt Mongolia
79 □3a Tahiti i. Fr. Polynesia
177 I4 Tahitótfalu Hungary
123 E4 Tahlab r. Iran/Pak.
123 E4 Tahlab, Dasht-i plain Pak.
237 E5 Tahlequah OK U.S.A.
222 D3 Tahltan B.C. Can.
240 G2 Tahoe City CA U.S.A.
240 G2 Tahoe Vista CA U.S.A.
237 C5 Tahoka TX U.S.A.
80 E3 Tahora North I. N.Z.
80 F3 Tahorakuri North I. N.Z.
207 G3 Tahoua Niger
207 G3 Tahoua dept Niger
122 D4 Tahrūd Iran
122 D4 Tahrūd r. Iran
222 E5 Tahsis B.C. Can.
203 F3 Tahta Egypt
199 F2 Tahtaköprü Bursa Turkey
199 G3 Tahtali Dağ mt. Turkey
222 E4 Tahtsa Peak B.C. Can.
252 D2 Tahuamanú r. Bol.
252 C2 Tahuamanú Peru
79 □3 Tahuata i. Fr. Polynesia
93 C2 Tahuna Sulawesi Utara Indon.
206 D5 Taï Côte d'Ivoire
107 I3 Tai'an Liaoning China
107 H4 Tai'an Shandong China
107 E5 Taibai Shaanxi China
108 C1 Taibai Shan mt. Shaanxi China
Taibei Taiwan see T'aipei
185 H2 Taibilla r. Spain
191 H2 Taibòn Agordino Italy
Taibus Qi Nei Mongol China see Baochang
109 G3 T'aichung Taiwan
Taidong Taiwan see T'aitung
81 C7 Taieri r. South I. N.Z.
81 C6 Taieri Ridge South I. N.Z.
Taigong Guizhou China see Taijiang
107 G4 Taigu Shanxi China
107 G4 Taihang Shan mts China
107 G4 Taihang Shan mts China
80 E3 Taihape North I. N.Z.
109 E1 Taihe Anhui China
109 E3 Taihe Jiangxi China
Taihe Sichuan China see Shehong
Taihezhen Sichuan China see Shehong
109 F2 Taihu Anhui China
108 D3 Taijiang Guizhou China
107 J2 Taikang Heilong. China
107 G5 Taikang Henan China
96 A3 Taikkyi Myanmar
104 B3 Taiko-yama hill Japan
107 I2 Tailai Heilong. China
82 D3 Tailem Bend S.A. Austr.
Tailuge Taiwan see T'ailuko
109 G3 T'ailuko Taiwan
206 E4 Tain r. Ghana
146 D4 Tain Highland, Scotland U.K.
109 G4 T'ainan Taiwan
160 B1 Taingy France
161 C3 Tain-l'Hermitage France
157 G4 Taintrux France
109 □ Tai O H.K. China
191 G2 Taio Italy
257 F1 Taiobeiras Brazil
80 D1 Taipa North I. N.Z.
141 O3 Taipalsaari Fin.
109 G3 T'aipei Taiwan
Taiping Guangdong China see Shixing
109 E4 Taiping Guangdong China
Taiping Guangxi China see Chongzuo
108 D4 Taiping Guangxi China
94 C1 Taiping Malaysia
107 I2 Taiping Ling mt. Nei Mongol China
109 □ Tai Po H.K. China
254 G3 Taipu Brazil
107 G5 Taiqian Henan China
102 □1 Taira-jima i. Japan
Tairbeart Western Isles, Scotland U.K. see Tarbert
80 E2 Tairua North I. N.Z.
122 A3 Tairuq Iran
94 C4 Tais Sumatera Indon.
102 K2 Taisetsu-zan mts Japan
105 F2 Taishaku-san mt. Japan
109 E4 Taishan Guangdong China
109 F3 Taishun Zhejiang China
179 E2 Taiskirchen im Innkreis Austria
156 E3 Taissy France
81 D5 Taitanu South I. N.Z.
259 B7 Taitao, Península de pen. Chile
210 B4 Taiti mt. Kenya
109 G4 T'aitung Taiwan
140 O2 Taivalkoski Fin.
140 N1 Taivaskero hill Fin.
141 M3 Taivassalo Fin.
109 G4 Taiwan country Asia
Taiwan Haixia str. China/Taiwan see Taiwan Strait
Taiwan Shan mts Taiwan see Chungyang Shanmo
109 F4 Taiwan Strait China/Taiwan
Taixian Jiangsu China see Jiangyan
109 G1 Taixing Jiangsu China
Taïyetos Óros mts Greece see Tavgetos
107 G4 Taiyuan Shanxi China
107 F4 Taiyue Shan mts China
160 C2 Taizé France
111 F6 Taizhao Xizang China
Taizhong Taiwan see T'aichung
109 F1 Taizhou Jiangsu China
109 G2 Taizhou Zhejiang China
109 G2 Taizhou Wan b. China
101 C4 Taizi r. China
124 C5 Ta'izz Yemen
124 C5 Ta'izz governorate Yemen
243 H6 Tajamulco, Volcán de vol. Guat.
95 D3 Tajem, Gunung hill Indon.
205 H2 Tajerouine Tunisia
123 G2 Tajikistan country Asia
104 D3 Tajimi Japan
116 D4 Taj Mahal tourist site Uttar Prad. India
180 C3 Tajo r. Spain alt. Tejo (Portugal), conv. Tagus
127 H4 Tajrīsh Iran
252 D5 Tajsara, Cordillera de mts Bol.
183 G4 Tajuña r. Spain
96 B3 Tak Thai.
122 A2 Takāb Iran
93 B4 Taka'Bonerate, Kepulauan atolls Indon.
176 G4 Takácsi Hungary
105 G2 Takahagi Japan
104 C4 Takahama Japan
104 D2 Takahara-gawa r. Japan
103 F6 Takahashi Japan
262 Q1 Takahe, Mount Antarctica
104 B4 Takaishi Japan
81 D4 Takaka South I. N.Z.
116 D5 Takal Madh. Prad. India
103 G6 Takamatsu Japan
104 C4 Takami-yama mt. Japan
104 D2 Takaoka Japan
80 F4 Takapau North I. N.Z.
80 G3 Takapau North I. N.Z.
80 E2 Takapuna North I. N.Z.
102 □1 Takara-jima i. Japan
104 A4 Takasago Japan
105 F2 Takasaki Japan
104 C2 Takashōzu-yama mt. Japan
105 E2 Takasuma-yama mt. Japan
105 G2 Takasuzu-san hill Ibaraki Japan
212 E5 Takatokwane Botswana
104 B4 Takatsuki Japan
103 F7 Takatsuki-yama mt. Japan
251 G4 Takatu r. Brazil/Guyana
104 D2 Takayama Japan
97 C6 Tak Bai Thai.
104 C3 Takefu Japan
103 F6 Takehara Japan
151 H3 Takeley Essex, England U.K.
94 B1 Takengon Sumatera Indon.
Takeo Cambodia see Takêv
103 E7 Takeo Japan
Take-shima i. N. Pacific Ocean see Liancourt Rocks
122 B2 Takestān Iran
103 E7 Taketa Japan
104 C4 Taketoyo Japan
97 D5 Takêv Cambodia
123 G2 Takhar prov. Afgh.
116 E5 Takhatpur Madh. Prad. India
181 G5 Takhemaret Alg.
Takhiatash Uzbek. see Gulabie
222 C2 Takhini r. Y.T. Can.
222 C2 Takhini Hotspring Y.T. Can.
96 C4 Ta Khli Thai.
97 D5 Ta Khmau Cambodia
135 H7 Takhta Rus. Fed.
Takhta Turkm. see Tagta
Takhta-Bazar Turkm. see Tagtabazar
121 F1 Takhtabrod Kazakh.
120 E4 Takhtakupyr Uzbek.
137 J5 Takhtamukay Rus. Fed.
Takhtamukayskiy Rus. Fed. see Takhtamukay
122 B3 Takht Apān, Kūh-e mt. Iran
127 I5 Takht-e Jamshīd tourist site Iran
123 G4 Takht-i-Sulaiman mt. Pak.
122 B2 Takht-i-Suleiman mt. Iran
207 H3 Takiéta Niger
Takijuq Lake Nunavut Can. see Napaktulik Lake
102 J2 Takikawa Japan
81 A6 Takitimu Mountains South I. N.Z.
129 F4 Täklä Azer.
222 E4 Takla Landing B.C. Can.
Takla Makan des. China see Taklimakan Shamo
Taklimakan Desert China see Taklimakan Shamo
110 C4 Taklimakan Shamo des. China
123 G2 Takob Tajik.
206 E5 Takoradi Ghana
111 F6 Takpa Shiri mt. Xizang China
177 I4 Taksony Hungary
177 K4 Takta r. Hungary
177 K3 Taktaharkány Hungary
177 K3 Taktakenéz Hungary
222 C3 Taku B.C. Can.
220 E4 Taku r. Can./U.S.A.
103 E7 Taku Japan
78 □6 Takuan, Mount P.N.G.
97 B5 Takua Pa Thai.
97 B5 Takua Thung Thai.
207 H5 Takum Nigeria
81 □2 Takutea i. Cook Is
78 □6 Takwa Malaita Solomon Is
116 C5 Tal Madh. Prad. India
244 C3 Tala Mex.
258 G4 Tala Uru.
138 G4 Talachyn Belarus
123 H3 Talagang Pak.
260 B3 Talagante Chile
187 E6 Talaiassa, Serra hill Spain
161 A5 Talairan France
162 A3 Talais France
116 C5 Talaja Gujarat India
100 E2 Talakan Rus. Fed.
116 B5 Talala Gujarat India
137 G2 Talalayivka Ukr.
242 □J7 Talamanca, Cordillera de mts Costa Rica
183 I3 Talamantes Spain
190 E2 Talamona Italy
192 D2 Talamone Italy
192 B4 Talana Sardegna Italy
100 D2 Talandzha Rus. Fed.
94 C3 Talang, Gunung vol. Indon.
94 D3 Talangbetutu Sumatera Indon.
160 D1 Talant France
117 H4 Talap Assam India
250 A6 Talara Peru
123 E5 Talar-i-Band mts Pak.
185 E1 Talarrubias Spain
121 G3 Talas r. Kazakh./Kyrg.
121 H4 Talas Kyrg.
121 G4 Talas admin. div. Kyrg.
121 G4 Talas Ala-Too mts Kyrg.
139 I4 Talashkino Rus. Fed.
Talas Oblast admin. div. Kyrg. see Talas
Talas Range mts Kyrg. see Talas Ala-Too
Talasskaya Oblast' admin. div. Kyrg. see Talas
Talasskiy Alatau, Khrebet mts Kyrg. see Talas Ala-Too
128 B4 Tal'at al Jamā'ah, Rujm mt. Jordan
207 G3 Talata-Mafara Nigeria
128 C2 Ţal 'at Mūsá mt. Lebanon/Syria
93 C1 Talaud, Kepulauan is Indon.
182 D5 Talaván Spain
183 F5 Talavera de la Reina Spain
184 D2 Talavera la Real Spain
84 E3 Talawanta Qld Austr.
131 Q3 Talaya Rus. Fed.
92 C5 Talayan Phil.
187 B7 Talayón hill Spain
182 E5 Talayuela Spain
187 B5 Talayuelas Spain
183 H5 Talayuelo mt. Spain
116 D4 Talbehat Uttar Prad. India
87 E5 Talbot, Mount hill W.A. Austr.
234 B4 Talbot County county MD U.S.A.
231 C5 Talbotton GA U.S.A.
83 G3 Talbragar r. N.S.W. Austr.
260 B4 Talca Chile
258 B5 Talcahuano Chile
117 F5 Talcher Orissa India
100 C1 Taldan Rus. Fed.
139 K3 Taldom Rus. Fed.
121 I3 Taldykorgan Kazakh.
Taldy-Kurgan Kazakh. see Taldykorgan
Taldyqorghan Kazakh. see Taldykorgan
Taldysu Kyrg. see Taldy-Suu
121 I4 Taldy-Suu Kyrg.
114 B2 Talegaon Mahar. India
114 C1 Talegaon Mahar. India
122 B3 Taleh Zang Iran
116 D5 Talen Madh. Prad. India
163 B4 Talence France
215 G5 Taleni S. Africa
158 E3 Talensac France
187 C5 Tales Spain
122 B2 Tālesh Gīlān Iran
Tālesh Gīlān Iran see Hashtpar
139 K2 Talets, Ozero l. Rus. Fed.
86 C4 Talga r. W.A. Austr.
121 I4 Talgar Kazakh.
121 I4 Talgar, Pik mt. Kazakh.
150 C2 Talgarreg Ceredigion, Wales U.K.
150 D3 Talgarth Powys, Wales U.K.
182 B4 Talhadas Port.
124 C4 Ţalḩah Saudi Arabia
82 C3 Talia S.A. Austr.
93 C3 Taliabu i. Indon.
161 E4 Taliard France
92 C4 Talibon Phil.
150 D2 Taliesin Ceredigion, Wales U.K.
184 C2 Táliga Spain
114 C2 Talikota Karnataka India
120 F5 Talimardzhan Uzbek.
129 C3 T'alin Armenia
204 D3 Taliouine Morocco
114 B3 Taliparamba Kerala India
92 B4 Talisay Phil.
92 C4 Talisayan Phil.
129 F4 Talış Dağları mts Azer./Iran
146 B4 Talisker Highland, Scotland U.K.
134 I4 Talitsa Rus. Fed.
137 K1 Talitskiy Chamlyk Rus. Fed.
95 G5 Taliwang Sumbawa Indon.
168 F2 Talkau Ger.
191 G5 Talla Italy
82 C2 Tallacootra, Lake salt flat S.A. Austr.
146 C4 Talladale Highland, Scotland U.K.
231 C5 Talladega AL U.S.A.
127 F3 Tall 'Afar Iraq
147 E3 Tallaght Rep. of Ireland
231 C6 Tallahassee FL U.S.A.
83 F4 Tallangatta Vic. Austr.
147 E3 Tallanstown Rep. of Ireland
231 C5 Tallapoosa r. AL U.S.A.
231 C5 Tallassee AL U.S.A.
127 F3 Tall Baydar Syria
163 A5 Taller France
87 B6 Tallering Peak hill W.A. Austr.
234 C3 Talleyville DE U.S.A.
138 E2 Tallinn Estonia
128 C2 Tall Kalakh Syria
127 F3 Tall Kayf Iraq
127 F3 Tall Kūjik Syria
232 C4 Tallmadge OH U.S.A.
160 E3 Talloires France
192 B2 Tallone Corse France
182 B2 Tallós Spain
147 C4 Tallow Rep. of Ireland
237 F5 Tallulah LA U.S.A.
Tallymerjen Uzbek. see Talimardzhan
197 G3 Tălmaciu Romania
234 B2 Talmage PA U.S.A.
160 D1 Talmay France
146 D3 Talmine Highland, Scotland U.K.
162 B3 Talmont France
162 A2 Talmont-St-Hilaire France
136 F3 Tal'ne Ukr.
Tal'noye Ukr. see Tal'ne
116 C5 Talod Gujarat India
116 C5 Taloda Mahar. India
208 F2 Talodi Sudan
237 D4 Taloga OK U.S.A.
123 F5 Taloi Range mts Pak.
123 G2 Tāloqān Afgh.
192 B4 Talora r. Sardegna Italy
263 K2 Talos Dome ice feature Antarctica
96 C2 Ta Loung San mt. Laos
137 G3 Talova Balka Ukr.
135 H6 Talovaya Rus. Fed.
129 E1 Talovka Rus. Fed.
221 I3 Taloyoak Nunavut Can.
244 B3 Talpa Mex.
195 G2 Talsano Italy
106 C2 Talshand Mongolia
138 D3 Talsi Latvia
258 C2 Taltal Chile
223 H2 Taltson r. N.W.T. Can.
94 B2 Talu Sumatera Indon.
93 B2 Taludaa Sulawesi Utara Indon.
191 G2 Talvera r. Italy
83 G2 Talwood Qld Austr.
135 H6 Taly Rus. Fed.
136 F3 Tal'yanky Ukr.
83 E3 Talyawalka r. N.S.W. Austr.
Talyshskiye Gory mts Azer./Iran see Talış Dağları
105 F3 Tama Japan
183 F1 Tama Spain
95 F2 Tama Abu, Banjaran mts Sarawak Malaysia
Tamabo Range mts Sarawak Malaysia see Tama Abu, Banjaran
105 F3 Tama-gawa r. Japan
102 □2 Tamagusuku Japan
96 B1 Tamai, Nam r. Myanmar
183 G3 Tamajón Spain
87 B5 Tamala W.A. Austr.
135 H5 Tamala Rus. Fed.
250 C2 Tamalameque Col.
206 E4 Tamale Ghana
182 D4 Tamames Spain
103 E7 Tamana Japan
77 H2 Tamana i. Gilbert Is Kiribati
204 C3 Tamanar Morocco
206 D3 Tamani Mali
103 F6 Tamano Japan
205 G5 Tamanrasset Alg.
234 C2 Tamaqua PA U.S.A.
117 F5 Tamar Bihar India
Tamar Syria see Tadmur
150 C4 Tamar r. England U.K.
186 D3 Tamarite de Litera Spain
252 C4 Tamarugal, Pampa de plain Chile
177 H5 Tamási Hungary
197 H2 Tamaşi Romania
Tamatave Madag. see Toamasina
245 E2 Tamaulipas state Mex.
245 E2 Tamaulipas, Sierra de mts Mex.
242 D3 Tamazula Durango Mex.
244 C4 Tamazula Jalisco Mex.
245 E3 Tamazunchale Mex.
210 B4 Tambach Kenya
169 F5 Tambach-Dietharz Ger.
206 B3 Tambacounda Senegal
104 B3 Tamba-kōchi plat. Japan
213 G3 Tambara Moz.
83 G2 Tambar Springs N.S.W. Austr.
256 D4 Tambau Brazil
207 G3 Tambawel Nigeria
94 D2 Tambelan, Kepulauan is Indon.
87 C7 Tambellup W.A. Austr.
260 C3 Tambillo, Cerro mt. Arg.
85 F5 Tambo Qld Austr.
83 F4 Tambo r. Vic. Austr.
252 C4 Tambo r. Peru
252 B3 Tambobamba Peru
252 A3 Tambo de Mora Peru
250 A6 Tambo Grande Peru
213 □I3 Tambohorano Madag.
252 C3 Tambopata r. Peru
95 G5 Tambora, Gunung vol. Sumbawa Indon.
254 E3 Tamboril Brazil
250 C5 Tamboryacu r. Peru
135 H5 Tambov Rus. Fed.
100 D2 Tambovka Rus. Fed.
Tambov Oblast admin. div. Rus. Fed. see Tambovskaya Oblast'
135 H5 Tambovskaya Oblast' admin. div. Rus. Fed.
182 B2 Tambre r. Spain
95 G1 Tambunan, Bukit hill Sabah Malaysia
208 E3 Tambura Sudan
95 G1 Tambuyukon, Gunung mt. Sabah Malaysia
206 C2 Tâmchekkeţ Maur.
120 D2 Tamdy Kazakh.
120 F4 Tamdybulak Uzbek.
120 F4 Tamdytau, Gory hills Uzbek.
250 D3 Tame Col.
182 B3 Tâmega r. Port.
Tamenghest Alg. see Tamanrasset
117 H4 Tamenglong Manipur India
Tamerlanovka Kazakh. see Temirlanovka
207 G2 Tamesna reg. Niger
207 H2 Tamgak, Adrar mt. Niger
206 B3 Tamguée, Massif du mt. Guinea
116 D5 Tamia Madh. Prad. India
245 F3 Tamiahua Mex.
245 F3 Tamiahua, Laguna de lag. Mex.
94 B1 Tamiang r. Indon.
114 C4 Tamil Nadu state India
234 C1 Tamiment PA U.S.A.
190 E2 Tamins Switz.
106 D2 Tamirin Gol r. Mongolia
196 E3 Tamiš r. Yugo.
254 B5 Tamitatoala r. Brazil
203 F2 Tâmîya Egypt
124 C2 Tamīyah, Jabal hill Saudi Arabia
204 E2 Tamlelt, Plaine de plain Morocco
117 F5 Tamluk W. Bengal India
172 D3 Tamm Ger.
193 G3 Tammaro r. Italy
223 K1 Tammarvi r. Nunavut Can.
138 D1 Tammela Fin.
168 D1 Tammensiel Ger.
Tammerfors Fin. see Tampere
Tammisaari Fin. see Ekenäs
196 E3 Tamnava r. Yugo.
160 B1 Tamnay-en-Bazois France
182 C1 Támoga r. Spain
231 D7 Tampa FL U.S.A.
231 D7 Tampa Bay FL U.S.A.
141 M3 Tampere Fin.
245 F2 Tampico Mex.
124 D3 Tamrah Saudi Arabia
138 F2 Tamsalu Estonia
250 C6 Tamshiyacu Peru
179 E3 Tamsweg Austria
245 E3 Tamuín Mex.
117 F4 Tamur r. Nepal
185 F2 Tamurejo Spain
83 G2 Tamworth N.S.W. Austr.
149 H5 Tamworth Staffordshire, England U.K.
Tana r. Fin./Norway see Tenojoki
210 D5 Tana r. Kenya
Tana Madag. see Antananarivo
Tana i. Vanuatu see Tanna
Tana, Lake Eth. see T'ana Hāyk'
103 G7 Tanabe Japan
256 C4 Tanabi Brazil
140 O1 Tana Bru Norway
140 O1 Tanafjorden inlet Norway
220 A4 Tanaga Island AK U.S.A.
193 H4 Tanagro r. Italy
210 C2 T'ana Hāyk' l. Eth.
95 G3 Tanahgrogot Kalimantan Timur Indon.
94 B3 Tanahmasa i. Indon.
116 E3 Tanakpur Uttar Prad. India
93 A3 Tanambung Sulawesi Selatan Indon.
84 B3 Tanami N.T. Austr.
84 B3 Tanami Desert N.T. Austr.
97 D5 Tân An Vietnam
220 C3 Tanana AK U.S.A.
Tananarive Madag. see Antananarivo
213 □I4 Tanandava Madag.
190 D3 Tanaro r. Italy
150 D2 Tanat r. Wales U.K.
92 C4 Tanauan Phil.
192 B4 Tanaunella Sardegna Italy
Tanba-kōchi plat. Japan see Tamba-kōchi
85 E5 Tanbar Qld Austr.
159 G2 Tancarville France
Tancheng Fujian China see Pingtan
107 H5 Tancheng Shandong China
101 D4 Tanch'ŏn N. Korea
244 C4 Tancítario, Cerro de mt. Mex.
245 H5 Tancochapa r. Mex.
206 E5 Tanda Côte d'Ivoire
116 D3 Tanda Uttar Prad. India
117 E4 Tanda Uttar Prad. India
141 K3 Tandådalen Sweden
92 C4 Tandag Phil.
197 H3 Ţăndărei Romania
209 C9 Tandaué Angola
173 F3 Tandern Ger.
116 D2 Tandi Hima. Prad. India
261 H5 Tandil Arg.
261 H5 Tandil, Sierra del hills Arg.
208 C2 Tandjilé pref. Chad
123 G5 Tando Adam Pak.
123 G5 Tando Alahyar Pak.
123 G5 Tando Bago Pak.
123 G5 Tando Muhammmad Khan Pak.
83 E3 Tandou Lake imp. l. N.S.W. Austr.
147 E2 Tandragee Northern Ireland U.K.
141 K3 Tandsjöborg Sweden
116 E5 Tandula r. India
114 C2 Tandur Andhra Prad. India
114 C2 Tandur Andhra Prad. India
80 F3 Taneatua North I. N.Z.
102 □1 Tanega-shima i. Japan
96 B3 Tanen Taunggyi mts Thai.
175 K5 Tanew r. Pol.
234 A3 Taneytown MD U.S.A.
205 E5 Tanezrouft reg. Alg./Mali
205 E5 Tanezrouft Tan-Ahenet reg. Alg.
128 D3 Ţanf, Jabal aţ hill Syria
148 B4 Tang Rep. of Ireland
107 F1 Tanga Rus. Fed.
211 C6 Tanga Tanz.
211 C6 Tanga admin. reg. Tanz.
80 E2 Tangaehe North I. N.Z.
117 G4 Tangail Bangl.
213 □J4 Tangainony Madag.
114 D5 Tangalla Sri Lanka
244 C4 Tangamandapio Mex.
244 C4 Tangancícuaro de Arista Mex.
Tanganyika country Africa see Tanzania
211 A6 Tanganyika, Lake Africa
122 C2 Tangar Iran
255 C8 Tangará Brazil
78 □6 Tangarare Guadalcanal Solomon Is
114 C4 Tangasseri Kerala India
108 B3 Tangdan Yunnan China
Tangdukou Hunan China see Shaoyang
122 C2 Tangeli Iran
263 D2 Tange Promontory hd Antarctica
204 D2 Tanger Morocco
180 D5 Tanger prov. Morocco
94 D4 Tangerang Jawa Barat Indon.
171 C3 Tangerhütte Ger.
170 C3 Tangermünde Ger.
108 B1 Tanggor Sichuan China
107 H4 Tanggu Tianjin China
Tanggulashan Qinghai China see Tuotuoheyan
111 E5 Tanggula Shan mt. Qinghai China
111 E5 Tanggula Shan mts Xizang China
109 E1 Tanghe Henan China
109 E1 Tang He r. China
123 G3 Tangi Pak.
Tangier Morocco see Tanger
80 E4 Tangimoana North I. N.Z.
93 B3 Tangkelemboko, Gunung mt. Indon.
94 D4 Tangkittebak, Gunung mt. Indon.
96 A1 Tangla Assam India
108 A1 Tanglag Qinghai China
111 F6 Tangmai Xizang China
85 F4 Tangorin Qld Austr.
111 D6 Tangra Yumco salt l. China
107 H4 Tangshan Hebei China
168 F2 Tangstedt Ger.
96 B2 Tangte mt. Myanmar
92 B4 Tangub Mindanao Phil.
92 B4 Tangub Negros Phil.
207 F4 Tanguieta Benin
108 D3 Tangwan Hunan China
100 D3 Tangwang r. China
100 D2 Tangwanghe Heilong. China
107 G4 Tangxian Hebei China
109 E2 Tangxianzhen Hubei China
108 D2 Tangyan He r. China
107 G5 Tangyin Henan China
100 D3 Tangyuan Heilong. China
254 E5 Tanhaçu Brazil
108 A2 Taniantaweng Shan mts Xizang China
105 E2 Tanigawa-dake mt. Japan
91 H8 Tanimbar, Kepulauan is Indon.
160 E2 Taninges France
Taninthari Myanmar see Tenasserim
Tanintharyi Myanmar see Tenasserim
Tanintharyi admin. div. Myanmar see Tenasserim
Taninthayi Myanmar see Tenasserim
Tanjah Morocco see Tanger
92 B4 Tanjay Phil.
Tanjore Tamil Nadu India see Thanjavur
95 F3 Tanjung Kalimantan Selatan Indon.
94 B2 Tanjungbalai Sumatera Indon.
94 D4 Tanjungkarang-Telukbetung Sumatera Indon.
95 D3 Tanjungpandan Indon.
94 D2 Tanjungpinang Indon.
94 B2 Tanjungpura Sumatera Indon.
94 D3 Tanjungraja Sumatera Indon.
95 G2 Tanjungredeb Kalimantan Timur Indon.
95 G2 Tanjungselor Kalimantan Timur Indon.
123 G3 Tank Pak.
116 B5 Tankara Gujarat India
116 C5 Tankhala Gujarat India
106 E1 Tankhoy Rus. Fed.
116 D2 Tankse Jammu and Kashmir
117 F4 Tankuhi Uttar Prad. India
214 B5 Tankwa r. S. Africa
156 E5 Tanlay France
96 A3 Tanlwe r. Myanmar
173 G3 Tann Ger.
169 F5 Tann (Rhon) Ger.
171 C5 Tanna Ger.
78 □5 Tanna i. Vanuatu
146 F5 Tannadice Angus, Scotland U.K.
141 K3 Tännäs Sweden
160 B1 Tannay Bourgogne France
157 E3 Tannay Champagne-Ardenne France
169 F4 Tanne Ger.
Tannenberg Pol. see Stębark
222 G5 Tanner, Mount B.C. Can.
161 E5 Tanneron France
234 C1 Tannersville PA U.S.A.
173 G2 Tännesberg Ger.
173 E3 Tannhausen Ger.
178 B3 Tannheim Austria
173 E4 Tannheim Ger.
142 D3 Tannis Bugt b. Denmark
Tannoa i. Vanuatu see Tongoa
171 C5 Tannroda Ger.
85 G4 Tannum Sands Qld Austr.
106 A1 Tannu-Ola, Khrebet mts Rus. Fed.
Tannu Tuva aut. rep. Rus. Fed. see Tyva, Respublika
92 B4 Tañon Strait Phil.
116 B4 Tanot Rajasthan India
207 H3 Tanout Niger
245 E3 Tanquian Mex.
117 E4 Tansen Nepal
109 G3 Tanshui Taiwan
206 D3 Tansilla Burkina
149 H4 Tansley Derbyshire, England U.K.
203 F2 Tanta Egypt
96 B3 Tantabin Myanmar
204 C3 Tan-Tan Morocco
82 E4 Tantanoola S.A. Austr.
157 G4 Tantonville France
170 F2 Tantow Ger.
245 E3 Tantoyuca Mex.
116 D4 Tantpur Uttar Prad. India
107 I2 Tantu Jilin China
128 B3 Tantura Israel
114 D2 Tanuku Andhra Prad. India
105 F2 Tanuma Japan
84 C3 Tanumbirini N.T. Austr.
142 D2 Tanumshede Sweden
176 E1 Tanvald Czech Rep.
96 E2 Tanxu Guangxi China
137 J3 Tanyushivka Ukr.
211 B6 Tanzania country Africa
222 D3 Tanzilla r. B.C. Can.
Tao'an Jilin China see Taonan
Taobh Tuath Western Isles, Scotland U.K. see Northton
Taocheng Fujian China see Yongchun
Taocheng Guangdong China see Daxin
107 I2 Tao'er r. China
106 D5 Tao He r. China
Taohong Hunan China see Longhui
Taohuaping Hunan China see Longhui
109 E2 Taojiang Hunan China
Taolanaro Madag. see Tôlañaro
106 E4 Taole Ningxia China
107 I2 Taonan Jilin China
195 E5 Taormina Sicilia Italy
239 F4 Taos NM U.S.A.
204 D2 Taounate Morocco
204 E2 Taourirt Morocco
109 F3 Taoxi Fujian China
Taoyang Gansu China see Lintao
109 D2 Taoyuan Hunan China
109 G3 T'aoyüan Taiwan
Taozhou Anhui China see Guangde
138 E2 Tapa Estonia
243 G6 Tapachula Mex.
251 H5 Tapajós r. Brazil
94 B2 Tapaktuan Sumatera Indon.
244 C4 Tapalpa Mex.
261 G5 Tapalqué Arg.
Tapan Turkey see Mansurlu
251 H3 Tapanahoni r. Suriname
245 G5 Tapanatepec Mex.
251 H5 Tapara, Serra do hills Brazil
251 E6 Tapauá Brazil
251 E6 Tapauá r. Brazil
81 D4 Tapawera South I. N.Z.
255 B9 Tapera Brazil
254 F5 Taperoá Brazil
255 C9 Tapes Brazil
206 C5 Tapeta Liberia
173 E3 Tapfheim Ger.
116 C5 Tapi r. India
182 D1 Tapia de Casariego Spain
Tapiau Rus. Fed. see Gvardeysk
250 C6 Tapiche r. Peru
177 J4 Tápió r. Hungary
177 I4 Tápióbicske Hungary
256 D2 Tapiocanga, Chapada do hills Brazil
177 I4 Tápiógyörgye Hungary
177 I4 Tápióság Hungary
177 I4 Tápiószecső Hungary
177 I4 Tápiószele Hungary
177 I4 Tápiószőlős Hungary
256 D3 Tapira Minas Gerais Brazil
256 A5 Tapira Paraná Brazil
256 D5 Tapiraí Brazil
253 H2 Tapirapé r. Brazil
251 E4 Tapirapecó, Sierra mts Brazil/Venez.
94 C1 Tapis mt. Malaysia
176 F4 Táplánszentkereszt Hungary
176 G5 Tapolca Hungary
146 F4 Tap o' Noth hill Scotland U.K.
232 E6 Tappahannock VA U.S.A.
116 D3 Tappal Uttar Prad. India
235 E1 Tappan NY U.S.A.
122 B3 Tappeh, Kūh-e hill Iran
129 E3 Tap Qaraqoyunlu Azer.
Taprobane country Asia see Sri Lanka
176 G5 Tapsony Hungary
81 D4 Tapuaenuku mt. South I. N.Z.
92 B5 Tapul Phil.
92 B5 Tapul Group is Phil.
94 B2 Tapulonanjing mt. Indon.
94 C2 Tapung r. Indon.
Taputeouea atoll Gilbert Is Kiribati see Tabiteuea
124 D5 Taqar mt. Yemen
127 G4 Taqtaq Iraq
255 C9 Taquara Brazil
256 A1 Taquaral, Serra do hills Brazil
253 F4 Taquarí r. Brazil
256 C4 Taquaritinga Brazil
256 C5 Taquarituba Brazil
256 A4 Taquaruçu r. Brazil
177 I4 Tar Hungary
147 D4 Tar r. Rep. of Ireland
85 G5 Tara Qld Austr.
196 D4 Tara r. Bos.-Herz./Yugo.
147 E3 Tara, Hill of hill Rep. of Ireland
207 H4 Taraba r. Nigeria
207 H4 Taraba state Nigeria
256 B5 Tarabaí Brazil
252 D4 Tarabuco Bol.
Ţarābulus Libya see Tripoli
183 G4 Taracena Spain
136 E5 Taraclia Moldova
80 F3 Taradale North I. N.Z.
161 E5 Taradeau France
Taraíra r. Brazil see Traíra
252 E5 Tarairí Bol.
95 G2 Tarakan Kalimantan Timur Indon.
199 G1 Taraklı Turkey
Tarakliya Moldova see Taraclia
83 G3 Taralga N.S.W. Austr.
102 □1 Tarama-jima i. Japan
182 C1 Taramundi Spain
116 D5 Tarana Madh. Prad. India
116 C3 Taranagar Rajasthan India
80 D3 Taranaki admin. reg. North I. N.Z.
80 E3 Taranaki, Mount vol. North I. N.Z.
183 G4 Tarancón Spain
114 C4 Tarangambadi Tamil Nadu India
211 C6 Tarangire National Park Tanz.
Tarangul l. Kazakh. see Tarankol', Ozero
121 G1 Tarankol', Ozero l. Kazakh.
120 E1 Taranovskoye Kazakh.
146 A4 Taransay i. Scotland U.K.
195 G2 Taranto Italy
195 G2 Taranto prov. Puglia Italy
195 G2 Taranto, Golfo di g. Italy
176 G5 Tarany Hungary
252 C4 Tarapacá admin. reg. Chile
250 D5 Tarapacá Col.
250 B6 Tarapoto Peru
160 C3 Tarare France
261 I4 Tarariras Uru.
81 E4 Tararua Range mts North I. N.Z.
Tarasaigh i. Scotland U.K. see Taransay
161 C5 Tarascon France
163 D6 Tarascon-sur-Ariège France
136 D3 Tarashany Ukr.
136 F3 Tarashcha Ukr.
122 D3 Tarasht Iran
137 G4 Tarasivka Khersons'ka Oblast' Ukr.
137 J3 Tarasivka Luhans'ka Oblast' Ukr.
135 H6 Tarasovskiy Rus. Fed.
205 H4 Tarat Alg.
252 C4 Tarata Peru
252 C2 Tarauacá Brazil
250 D6 Tarauacá r. Brazil
192 A3 Taravo r. Corse France
77 H1 Tarawa atoll Kiribati
80 F3 Tarawera North I. N.Z.
80 F3 Tarawera, Lake North I. N.Z.
80 F3 Tarawera, Mount North I. N.Z.
121 G4 Taraz Zhambylskaya Oblast' Kazakh.
183 I3 Tarazona Spain
185 I1 Tarazona de la Mancha Spain
121 J3 Tarbagatay Kazakh.
107 E1 Tarbagatay Rus. Fed.
121 J3 Tarbagatay, Khrebet mts Kazakh.
187 C6 Tárbena Spain
147 B4 Tarbert Rep. of Ireland
146 C6 Tarbert Argyll and Bute, Scotland U.K.
146 C6 Tarbert Argyll and Bute, Scotland U.K.
146 B4 Tarbert Western Isles, Scotland U.K.
146 B6 Tarbert, Loch inlet Scotland U.K.
163 C5 Tarbes France
146 D5 Tarbet Argyll and Bute, Scotland U.K.
146 D6 Tarbolton South Ayrshire, Scotland U.K.
231 E5 Tarboro NC U.S.A.
177 L5 Tărcaia Romania
177 K3 Tarcal Hungary
177 L4 Tarcea Romania
191 I2 Tarcento Italy
82 C2 Tarcoola S.A. Austr.
83 F2 Tarcoon N.S.W. Austr.
197 F3 Tarcului, Munţii mts Romania
83 F3 Tarcutta N.S.W. Austr.
175 I4 Tarczyn Pol.
158 E3 Tard r. France
183 G2 Tardajos Spain
183 H3 Tardelcuende Spain
162 E2 Tardes r. France
163 B5 Tardets-Sorholus France
186 C3 Tardienta Spain
162 C3 Tardoire r. France
100 F2 Tardoki-Yani, Gora mt. Rus. Fed.
83 H2 Taree N.S.W. Austr.
83 E2 Tarella N.S.W. Austr.
140 M2 Tärendö Sweden
Tarentum Italy see Taranto
244 D4 Taretán Mex.
124 C4 Ţarfā, Ra's aţ pt Saudi Arabia
204 B4 Tarfaya Morocco
146 F5 Tarfside Angus, Scotland U.K.
Targan Kazakh. see Targyn
163 B4 Targon France
197 G3 Târgovişte Romania
174 F3 Targowa Górka Pol.
197 H3 Târgu Bujor Romania
197 F3 Târgu Cărbuneşti Romania
197 H2 Târgu Frumos Romania
204 D2 Targuist Morocco
197 F3 Târgu Jiu Romania
197 F2 Târgu Lăpuş Romania
197 G2 Târgu Mureş Romania
197 H2 Târgu Neamţ Romania
197 H2 Târgu Ocna Romania
197 H2 Târgu Secuiesc Romania
121 J2 Targyn Kazakh.
122 A3 Tarhān Iran
177 K5 Tarhos Hungary
202 B1 Tarhūnah Libya
125 F2 Tarif U.A.E.
184 E4 Tarifa Spain
252 D5 Tarija Bol.
252 D5 Tarija dept Bol.
114 B3 Tarikere Karnataka India
91 I7 Tariku r. Indon.
125 E4 Tarīm Yemen
Tarim Basin China see Tarim Pendi
211 B5 Tarime Tanz.
110 D3 Tarim He r. China
110 D3 Tarim Liuchang Xinjiang China
244 D3 Tarimoro Mex.
110 C4 Tarim Pendi basin China
123 F3 Tarīn Kowt Afgh.
91 I7 Taritatu r. Indon.
177 H4 Tarján Hungary
215 E5 Tarka r. S. Africa
177 G4 Tárkány Hungary
215 F5 Tarkastad S. Africa
129 E2 Tarki Rus. Fed.
236 E3 Tarkio MO U.S.A.
130 I3 Tarko-Sale Rus. Fed.
206 E5 Tarkwa Ghana
92 B3 Tarlac Phil.
92 B2 Tarlac r. Phil.
149 G4 Tarleton Lancashire, England U.K.
232 B5 Tarlton OH U.S.A.
142 C4 Tarm Denmark
252 B2 Tarma Peru
168 E2 Tarmstedt Ger.
163 E5 Tarn dept Midi-Pyrénées France
161 A4 Tarn r. France
177 I4 Tarna r. Hungary
140 K2 Tärnaby Sweden
123 F4 Tarnak r. Afgh.
177 J3 Tarnalelesz Hungary
177 J4 Tarnaméra Hungary
177 J4 Tarnaőrs Hungary
177 J4 Tarnaszentmiklós Hungary
197 F2 Târnava Mare r. Romania
197 F2 Târnava Mică r. Romania
197 G2 Târnăveni Romania
175 K5 Tarnawa Duża Pol.
175 L5 Tarnawatka Pol.
163 D4 Tarn-et-Garonne dept Midi-Pyrénées France
175 K6 Tarnica mt. Pol.
175 J5 Tarnobrzeg Pol.
175 K5 Tarnogród Pol.
134 H3 Tarnogskiy Gorodok Rus. Fed.
177 H4 Tárnok Hungary
Tarnopol Ukr. see Ternopil'
163 A5 Tarnos France
175 L5 Tarnoszyn Pol.
177 K5 Târnova Romania
197 F3 Târnova Romania
170 D2 Tarnow Ger.
175 I5 Tarnów Pol.
175 J6 Tarnowiec Pol.
Tarnowitz Pol. see Tarnowskie Góry
174 E2 Tarnówka Pol.
174 E3 Tarnowo Podgórne Pol.
174 G5 Tarnów Opolski Pol.
174 G5 Tarnowskie Góry Pol.
190 F4 Taro r. Italy
137 H3 Taroms'ke Ukr.
163 B5 Taron-Sadirac-Viellenave France
85 G5 Taroom Qld Austr.
105 F2 Tarō-san mt. Japan
182 C3 Tarouca Port.
204 C3 Taroudannt Morocco
182 B3 Tarouquela Port.
168 E1 Tarp Ger.
177 L3 Tarpa Hungary
117 G5 Tarpasa Bangl.
84 D3 Tarpaulin Swamp N.T. Austr.
82 E4 Tarpeena S.A. Austr.
231 D6 Tarpon Springs FL U.S.A.
149 G4 Tarporley Cheshire, England U.K.
246 C1 Tarpum Bay Eleuthera Bahamas
192 D2 Tarquinia Italy
192 D2 Tarquinia Lido Italy
Tarquinii Italy see Tarquinia
84 C3 Tarrabool Lake salt flat N.T. Austr.
Tarracina Italy see Terracina
Tarraco Spain see Tarragona
186 E3 Tarragona Spain
186 D3 Tarragona prov. Cataluña Spain
83 F5 Tarraleah Tas. Austr.
83 F3 Tarran Hills hill N.S.W. Austr.
81 B6 Tarras South I. N.Z.
Tarrasa Spain see Terrassa
186 E3 Tàrrega Spain
146 E4 Tarrel Highland, Scotland U.K.
178 B3 Tarrenz Austria
182 B1 Tarrio Spain
186 E3 Tarroja de Segarra Spain
Tarrong Xizang China see Nyêmo
235 E1 Tarrytown NY U.S.A.
193 I5 Tarsia Italy
202 C4 Tarso Ahon mt. Chad
202 C4 Tarso Emissi mt. Chad
202 C4 Tarso Kobour mt. Chad
126 D3 Tarsus Turkey
128 B1 Tarsus r. Turkey
258 E1 Tartagal Salta Arg.
258 F3 Tartagal Santa Fé Arg.
175 M5 Tartakiv Ukr.
129 E3 Tärtär Azer.
129 E3 Tärtär r. Azer.
129 E3 Tärtär r. Azer.
191 H3 Tartaro r. Italy
163 B5 Tartas France
138 F2 Tartu Estonia
128 B2 Ţarţūs Syria
128 C2 Ţarţūs governorate Syria
104 C3 Tarui Japan
Tarumae-san vol. Japan see Shikotsu
257 G3 Tarumirim Brazil
103 E8 Tarumizu Japan
129 E1 Tarumovka Rus. Fed.
96 B1 Tarung Hka r. Myanmar
139 K4 Tarusa Rus. Fed.
139 K4 Tarusa r. Rus. Fed.
94 B2 Tarutung Sumatera Indon.
136 E4 Tarutyne Ukr.
146 F4 Tarves Aberdeenshire, Scotland U.K.
149 G4 Tarvin Cheshire, England U.K.
191 I2 Tarvisio Italy
Tarvisium Italy see Treviso
195 □ Tarxien Malta
122 D4 Tarz Iran
120 F3 Tasbuget Kazakh.
224 E3 Taschereau Que. Can.
222 F5 Taseko Mountain B.C. Can.
114 B2 Tasgaon Mahar. India
129 A3 Taşgeçit Turkey
137 H3 Tashan' r. Ukr.
Tashauz Turkm. see Dashkhovuz
Tashauzskaya Oblast' admin. div. Turkm. see Dashkhovuzskaya Oblast'
136 E5 Tashbunar r. Ukr.
Tashi Chho Bhutan see Thimphu
Tashigang Bhutan see Trashigang
Tashino Rus. Fed. see Pervomaysk
129 D3 Tashir Armenia
121 G4 Tashkent Uzbek.
Tashkent Oblast admin. div. Uzbek. see Tashkentskaya Oblast'
121 G4 Tashkentskaya Oblast' admin. div. Uzbek.

Tashkepri to Tha Bo 369

123 E2 Tashkepri Turkm.
121 H4 Tash-Kömür Kyrg.
Tash-Kumyr Kyrg. see Tash-Kömür
120 C2 Tashla Rus. Fed.
137 F3 Tashlyk Ukr.
Tāshqurghān Afgh. see Kholm
Tasiilaq Greenland see Ammassalik
95 E4 Tasikmalaya Jawa Barat Indon.
168 F1 Tåsinge i. Denmark
225 G1 Tasiujaq Que. Can.
140 K2 Tåsjö Sweden
128 A1 Taşkale Turkey
128 A1 Taşkent Turkey
207 H3 Tasker Niger
121 J3 Taskesken Kazakh.
129 B3 Taşkıran Turkey
126 D2 Taşköprü Turkey
127 F3 Taşlıçay Turkey
129 C3 Taşlıoğul Turkey
81 D4 Tasman South I. N.Z.
81 D4 Tasman admin. reg. South I. N.Z.
81 C6 Tasman r. South I. N.Z.
81 C5 Tasman, Mount South I. N.Z.
266 F8 Tasman Abyssal Plain sea feature Austr.
265 O7 Tasman Basin sea feature Tasman Sea
81 D4 Tasman Bay South I. N.Z.
83 F5 Tasman Head hd Tas. Austr.
83 F5 Tasmania state Austr.
81 D4 Tasman Mountains South I. N.Z.
83 G5 Tasman Peninsula Tas. Austr.
77 H6 Tasman Sea S. Pacific Ocean
197 F2 Tăşnad Romania
126 E2 Taşova Turkey
177 I4 Tass Hungary
148 C3 Tassagh Northern Ireland U.K.
207 G2 Tassara Niger
160 C1 Tasselot, Mont hill France
205 G5 Tassili du Hoggar plat. Alg.
205 G4 Tassili n'Ajjer plat. Alg.
160 C3 Tassin-la-Demi-Lune France
142 E4 Tåstrup Denmark
121 G3 Tasty Kazakh.
121 F2 Tasty-Taldy Kazakh.
222 C4 Tasu B.C. Can.
128 A1 Taşucu Turkey
177 G5 Taszár Hungary
177 H4 Tát Hungary
177 H4 Tata Hungary
204 D3 Tata Morocco
177 H4 Tatabánya Hungary
177 I5 Tataháza Hungary
245 G4 Tatahuicapan Mex.
225 I4 Tatamagouche N.S. Can.
93 C5 Tata Mailau, Gunung mt. East Timor
78 □6 Tatamba Sta Isabel Solomon Is
117 F5 Tatanagar Bihar India
205 H2 Tataouine Tunisia
136 E5 Tatarbunary Ukr.
138 G5 Tatarka Belarus
137 H3 Tatarka r. Ukr.
199 G2 Tatarlı Turkey
128 C1 Tatarlı Turkey
116 D4 Tatarpur Rajasthan India
130 I4 Tatarsk Rus. Fed.
Tatarskaya A.S.S.R. aut. rep. Rus. Fed. see Tatarstan, Respublika
100 G2 Tatarskiy Proliv str. Rus. Fed.
134 J5 Tatarstan, Respublika aut. rep. Rus. Fed.
Tatar Strait Rus. Fed. see Tatarskiy Proliv
177 I4 Tatárszentgyörgy Hungary
197 H2 Tătăruşi Romania
122 A2 Tatavi r. Iran
85 E3 Tate r. Qld Austr.
105 F2 Tatebayashi Japan
105 E2 Tateshina-yama mt. Japan
105 F4 Tateyama Chiba Japan
104 D2 Tateyama Toyama Japan
104 D2 Tate-yama vol. Japan
124 C4 Tathlīth Saudi Arabia
83 G4 Tathra N.S.W. Austr.
213 E4 Tati Botswana
168 D1 Tating Ger.
120 A2 Tatishchevo Rus. Fed.
96 B2 Tatkon Myanmar
222 E5 Tatla Lake B.C. Can.
222 E5 Tatlayoko Lake B.C. Can.
110 D4 Tatlikbulak Xinjiang China
Tatra Mountains Pol./Slovakia see Tatry
111 D4 Tatrang Xinjiang China
175 H6 Tatry mts Pol./Slovakia
222 B3 Tatshenshini r. B.C. Can.
135 H6 Tatsinskiy Rus. Fed.
103 G6 Tatsuno Hyōgo Japan
105 D3 Tatsuno Nagano Japan
123 F5 Tatta Pak.
149 I4 Tattershall Lincolnshire, England U.K.
121 H4 Tatti Kazakh.
Tatty Kazakh. see Tatti
80 E3 Tatu hill North I. N.Z.
256 D5 Tatuí Brazil
222 E4 Tatuk Mountain B.C. Can.
138 E3 Tatula r. Lith.
237 C5 Tatum NM U.S.A.
237 E5 Tatum TX U.S.A.
127 F3 Tatvan Turkey
78 □2 Tau i. American Samoa
142 A2 Tau Norway
254 E3 Taua Brazil
257 E5 Taubaté Brazil
171 E4 Taubenheim Ger.
172 D2 Tauber r. Ger.
172 D2 Tauberbischofsheim Ger.
171 D4 Taucha Ger.
171 F3 Tauche Ger.
120 B3 Tauchik Kazakh.
171 F4 Tauer Ger.
173 F3 Taufkirchen Bayern Ger.
173 G3 Taufkirchen Bayern Ger.
173 G3 Taufkirchen (Vils) Ger.
169 E5 Taufstein hill Ger.
80 F3 Tauhara mt. North I. N.Z.
80 E2 Tauhoa North I. N.Z.
251 G4 Tauini r. Brazil
121 H3 Taukum, Peski des. Kazakh.
158 C3 Taulé France
161 C4 Taulignan France
80 E3 Taumarunui North I. N.Z.
215 E2 Taung S. Africa
96 A2 Taungdwingyi Myanmar
96 B2 Taunggyi Myanmar
96 B3 Taungnyo Range mts Myanmar
96 A2 Taungtha Myanmar
96 A3 Taunqup Myanmar
123 G4 Taunsa Pak.
150 D3 Taunton Somerset, England U.K.
233 H4 Taunton MA U.S.A.
169 C5 Taunus hills Ger.
80 E2 Taupiri North I. N.Z.
179 F3 Tauplitz Austria
80 F3 Taupo North I. N.Z.
80 E3 Taupo, Lake North I. N.Z.
138 D4 Tauragė Lith.
138 C4 Tauralaukis Lith.
80 F2 Tauranga North I. N.Z.
Taurasia Italy see Torino
224 F4 Taureau, Réservoir resr Que. Can.
195 F4 Taurianova Italy
80 E1 Taurikura North I. N.Z.
162 D3 Taurion r. France
195 H3 Taurisano Italy
Tauriuiná r. Mato Grosso Brazil see Verde
80 D1 Tauroa Point North I. N.Z.
Taurus Mountains Turkey see Toros Dağları
Taūshyq Kazakh. see Tauchik
186 B3 Tauste Spain
177 K5 Tăuţ Romania
163 E6 Tautavel France
158 E2 Taute r. France
171 C5 Tautenhain Ger.
177 L4 Tăuteu Romania
77 F2 Tauu Islands P.N.G.
160 A3 Tauves France
80 G3 Tauwhareparae North I. N.Z.
131 Q4 Tauyskaya Guba g. Rus. Fed.
Tauz Azer. see Tovuz
192 A2 Tavaco Corse France
191 I2 Tavagnacco Italy
196 D2 Tavankut Vojvodina, Srbija Yugo.
190 C1 Tavannes Switz.
159 G4 Tavant France
231 D6 Tavares FL U.S.A.
191 G5 Tavarnelle Val di Pesa Italy
199 F3 Tavas Turkey
Tavastehus Fin. see Hämeenlinna
160 D1 Tavaux France
130 H4 Tavda Rus. Fed.
182 B4 Taveiro Port.
161 C4 Tavel France
140 M2 Tavelsjö Sweden
151 I2 Taverham Norfolk, England U.K.
195 F3 Taverna Italy
160 C1 Tavernay France
192 E1 Tavernelle Italy
161 E5 Tavernes France
187 C5 Tavernes de la Valldigna Spain
150 C3 Tavernspite Pembrokeshire, Wales U.K.
156 C3 Taverny France
190 E4 Taverone r. Italy
186 F3 Tavertet Spain
79 □1 Taveuni i. Fiji
198 C3 Tavgetos mts Greece
195 H3 Taviano Italy
192 B2 Tavignano r. Corse France
193 H3 Taviolere plain Italy
184 C3 Tavira Port.
184 C3 Tavira, Ilha de i. Port.
227 G4 Tavistock Ont. Can.
150 C4 Tavistock Devon, England U.K.
193 G2 Tavo r. Italy
182 C3 Távora r. Spain
97 B4 Tavoy Myanmar
97 B4 Tavoy b. Myanmar
Tavoy Island Myanmar see Mali Kyun
121 J2 Tavricheskoye Kazakh.
Tavrīl Kazakh. see Tavricheskoye
137 G4 Tavriys'k Ukr.
199 F2 Tavşanlı Turkey
79 □1 Tavuki Kadavu Fiji
191 H5 Tavullia Italy
129 D3 Tavush r. Armenia
150 C4 Tavy r. England U.K.
150 C3 Taw r. England U.K.
81 E4 Tawa North I. N.Z.
117 G4 Tawang Arun. Prad. India
104 B4 Tawaramoto Japan
227 F3 Tawas City MI U.S.A.
95 G1 Tawau Sabah Malaysia
Tawè Myanmar see Tavoy
150 D3 Tawe r. Wales U.K.
172 A2 Tawern Ger.
80 F3 Tawhiuau mt. North I. N.Z.
116 C2 Tawi r. India
109 G4 Tawu Taiwan
245 E4 Taxco Mex.
178 D3 Taxenbach Austria
111 A4 Taxkorgan Xinjiang China
222 C2 Tay r. Y.T. Can.
146 E5 Tay r. Scotland U.K.
146 E5 Tay, Firth of est. Scotland U.K.
87 D7 Tay, Lake salt flat W.A. Austr.
146 D5 Tay, Loch l. Scotland U.K.
252 A2 Tayabamba Peru
92 B3 Tayabas Bay Phil.
210 E3 Tayeeglow Somalia
130 J4 Tayga Rus. Fed.
146 C6 Tayinloan Argyll and Bute, Scotland U.K.
136 F4 Tayirove Ukr.
222 F3 Taylor B.C. Can.
241 L4 Taylor AZ U.S.A.
236 D3 Taylor NE U.S.A.
234 C1 Taylor PA U.S.A.
237 D6 Taylor TX U.S.A.
239 F4 Taylor r. CO U.S.A.
81 C5 Taylor, Mount South I. N.Z.
239 F5 Taylor, Mount NM U.S.A.
234 C3 Taylors Bridge DE U.S.A.
148 B4 Taylor's Cross Rep. of Ireland
230 C4 Taylorsville KY U.S.A.
234 A3 Taylorsville MD U.S.A.
231 D5 Taylorsville NC U.S.A.
235 D2 Taylortown NJ U.S.A.
236 F4 Taylorville IL U.S.A.
124 B2 Taymā' Saudi Arabia
233 □J1 Taymouth N.B. Can.
131 K3 Taymura r. Rus. Fed.
131 L2 Taymyr, Ozero l. Rus. Fed.
131 J2 Taymyr, Poluostrov pen. Rus. Fed.
Taymyr Peninsula Rus. Fed. see Taymyr, Poluostrov
97 D5 Tây Ninh Vietnam
146 C5 Taynuilt Argyll and Bute, Scotland U.K.
120 B2 Taypak Kazakh.
Taypaq Kazakh. see Taypak
146 F5 Tayport Fife, Scotland U.K.
131 K4 Tayshet Rus. Fed.
120 C2 Taysoygan, Peski des. Kazakh.
Tayspun tourist site Iraq see Ctesiphon
199 F2 Taytan Turkey
92 B3 Taytay Luzon Phil.
92 A4 Taytay Palawan Phil.
95 E4 Tayu Jawa Tengah Indon.
100 C2 Tayuan Heilong. China
148 D1 Tayvallich Argyll and Bute, Scotland U.K.
122 E3 Tayyebād Iran
121 G1 Tayynsha Kazakh.
130 I3 Taz r. Rus. Fed.
204 E2 Taza Morocco
Taza-Bazar Uzbek. see Shumanay
216 □3d Tazacorte La Palma Canary Is
129 E3 Täzäkänd Azer.
127 G4 Tāza Khurmātū Iraq
102 J4 Tazawa-ko l. Japan
122 A2 Tazeh Kand Azer.
129 E4 Tāzeh Kand-e Angūt Iran
204 D3 Tazenakht Morocco
232 B6 Tazewell TN U.S.A.
232 C6 Tazewell VA U.S.A.
223 I2 Tazin r. N.W.T./Sask. Can.
202 D3 Tazirbu Water Wells Field Libya
177 I5 Tázlár Hungary
197 H2 Tazlău Romania
197 H2 Tazlău r. Romania
183 E1 Tazones Spain
205 E5 Tazouikert hill Mali
130 I3 Tazovskiy Rus. Fed.
204 D3 Tazzarine Morocco
Tbessa Alg. see Tébessa
129 D3 T'bilisi Georgia
135 H7 Tbilisskaya Rus. Fed.
207 I5 Tchabal Gangdaba mt. Cameroon
207 I5 Tchabal Mbabo mt. Cameroon
Tchad country Africa see Chad
207 F4 Tchamba Togo
207 F4 Tchaourou Benin
207 F5 Tchetti Benin
208 A5 Tchibanga Gabon
202 B4 Tchigaï, Plateau du Niger
209 C8 Tchikala-Tcholohanga Angola
209 B8 Tchindjenje Angola
207 G3 Tchin-Tabaradene Niger
207 I4 Tcholliré Cameroon
143 H4 Tczew Pol.
97 D4 Te, Prêk r. Cambodia
250 E5 Tea r. Brazil
182 B2 Tea r. Spain
244 B2 Teacapán Mex.
87 D5 Teague, Lake salt flat W.A. Austr.
81 A6 Te Anau South I. N.Z.
81 A6 Te Anau, Lake South I. N.Z.
235 D2 Teaneck NJ U.S.A.
80 E3 Te Anga North I. N.Z.
193 G3 Teano Italy
Teanum Sidicinum Italy see Teano
243 G5 Teapa Mex.
80 G2 Te Araroa North I. N.Z.
196 E4 Tearce Macedonia
80 E2 Te Aroha North I. N.Z.
80 E2 Te Aroha, Mount hill North I. N.Z.
Teate Italy see Chieti
80 E3 Te Awamutu North I. N.Z.
185 F4 Teba Spain
183 H5 Tebar Spain
207 G3 Tébarat Niger
149 G3 Tebay Cumbria, England U.K.
129 B2 Teberda Rus. Fed.
129 B2 Teberda r. Rus. Fed.
205 H2 Tébessa Alg.
205 H2 Tébessa, Monts de mts Alg.
253 F6 Tebicuary r. Para.
94 B2 Tebingtinggi Sumatera Indon.
94 C3 Tebingtinggi Sumatera Indon.
94 C3 Tebo r. Indon.
189 B7 Tébourba Tunisia
189 B7 Téboursouk Tunisia
129 D2 Tebulos Mt'a Georgia/Rus. Fed.
244 C4 Tecalitlán Mex.
245 E4 Tecamac Mex.
245 F4 Tecamachalco Mex.
245 F4 Tecamachalco Nogales Mex.
242 A1 Tecate Mex.
128 B1 Tece Turkey
163 F6 Tech r. France
206 E5 Techiman Ghana
197 I3 Techirghiol Romania
259 C6 Tecka Arg.
259 C6 Tecka r. Arg.
142 E4 Teckomatorp Sweden
243 H4 Tecoh Mex.
245 F3 Tecolutla Mex.
244 C4 Tecomán Mex.
241 I4 Tecopa CA U.S.A.
242 C2 Tecoripa Mex.
244 D5 Técpan Mex.
244 D5 Tecpan r. Mex.
244 B2 Tecuala Mex.
197 H3 Tecuci Romania
227 F5 Tecumseh MI U.S.A.
236 D3 Tecumseh NE U.S.A.
104 C2 Tedori-gawa r. Japan
122 E2 Tedzhen Turkm.
123 E2 Tedzhen r. Turkm.
122 E2 Tedzhenstroy Turkm.
241 M3 Teec Nos Pos AZ U.S.A.
106 D1 Teel Mongolia
110 E1 Teeli Rus. Fed.
147 D2 Teemore Northern Ireland U.K.
147 A5 Teeranearagh Rep. of Ireland
149 H3 Tees r. England U.K.
149 G3 Teesdale val. England U.K.
149 H3 Teesside airport England U.K.
227 G3 Teeswater Ont. Can.
148 C4 Teevurcher Rep. of Ireland
81 □1 Te Fakanava i. Tokelau
251 E5 Tefé r. Brazil
251 E5 Tefé, Lago l. Brazil
205 G4 Tefedest mts Alg.
199 F3 Tefenni Turkey
95 E4 Tegal Jawa Tengah Indon.
170 E3 Tegel airport Ger.
165 F3 Tegelen Neth.
173 G2 Tegernheim Ger.
173 F4 Tegernsee Ger.
193 H4 Teggiano Italy
207 G4 Tegina Nigeria
177 K4 Téglás Hungary
190 F2 Teglio Italy
191 H2 Tegnàs r. Italy
78 □5 Tégua i. Vanuatu
242 □I6 Tegucigalpa Hond.
216 □3a Tegueste Tenerife Canary Is
216 □3c Teguise Lanzarote Canary Is
240 H4 Tehachapi CA U.S.A.
80 E2 Te Hana North I. N.Z.
80 F3 Te Hauke North I. N.Z.
Teheran Iran see Tehrān
206 E4 Téhini Côte d'Ivoire
122 B3 Tehrān Iran
122 B3 Tehrān prov. Iran
Tehri Madh. Prad. India see Tikamgarh
116 D3 Tehri Uttar Prad. India
245 F4 Tehuacán Mex.
245 G5 Tehuantepec r. Mex.
243 G6 Tehuantepec, Golfo de g. Mex.
Tehuantepec, Gulf of Mex. see Tehuantepec, Golfo de
245 G5 Tehuantepec, Istmo de isth. Mex.
267 M5 Tehuantepec Ridge sea feature N. Pacific Ocean
245 E4 Tehuitzingo Mex.
171 C4 Teicha Ger.
171 D5 Teichwolframsdorf Ger.
216 □3a Teide, Pico del vol. Tenerife Canary Is
150 C2 Teifi r. Wales U.K.
150 D4 Teign r. England U.K.
150 D4 Teignmouth Devon, England U.K.
158 E4 Teillay France
163 E5 Teillet France
173 G4 Teisendorf Ger.
173 H2 Teisnach Ger.
161 A4 Teissières-lès-Bouliès France
169 F4 Teistungen Ger.
211 C5 Teita Hills Kenya
245 F5 Teitipac Mex.
197 G3 Teiu Romania
197 F2 Teiuş Romania
254 F3 Teixeira Brazil
Teixeira da Silva Angola see Bailundo
Teixeira de Sousa Angola see Luau
257 F4 Teixeiras Brazil
256 B6 Teixeira Soares Brazil
182 B1 Teixeiro Spain
182 C4 Teixoso Port.
182 C3 Teja r. Port.
183 I4 Tejadillos Spain
183 H3 Tejado Spain
95 F5 Tejakula Bali Indon.
245 F4 Tejar Mex.
216 □3f Tejeda Gran Canaria Canary Is
182 E4 Tejeda de Tiétar Spain
Tejen Turkm. see Tedzhen
117 G5 Tejgaon Bangl.
184 B2 Tejo r. Port.
alt. Tajo (Spain), conv. Tagus
244 D4 Tejupilco Mex.
80 F2 Te Kaha North I. N.Z.
80 D1 Te Kao North I. N.Z.
81 C6 Tekapo r. South I. N.Z.
81 C5 Tekapo, Lake South I. N.Z.
117 F4 Tekari Bihar India
105 E3 Tekari-dake mt. Japan
80 E2 Te Kauwhata North I. N.Z.
243 H4 Tekax Mex.
121 G4 Teke Kazakh.
197 H5 Teke r. Turkey
121 H1 Teke, Ozero salt l. Kazakh.
128 B1 Tekebaşı Turkey
121 I3 Tekeli Kazakh.
110 C3 Tekes Xinjiang China
121 J4 Tekes Kazakh.
110 C3 Tekes He r. China
203 H6 Tekezē Wenz r. Eritrea/Eth.
111 C4 Tekiliktag mt. Xinjiang China
199 E1 Tekirdağ Turkey
199 E1 Tekirdağ prov. Turkey
199 G3 Tekirova Turkey
115 E2 Tekkali Andhra Prad. India
129 A3 Tekke Turkey
127 F3 Tekman Turkey
117 H5 Teknaf Bangl.
129 B3 Tekneciler Turkey
81 D5 Tekoa, Mount South I. N.Z.
226 E4 Tekonsha MI U.S.A.
80 D2 Te Kopuru North I. N.Z.
81 □3 Te Kou hill Rarotonga Cook Is
80 E2 Te Kowhai North I. N.Z.
128 D1 Tektek Dağlari hills Turkey
80 E3 Te Kuiti North I. N.Z.
117 E5 Tel r. India
242 □I6 Tela Hond.
81 □1 Te Lafu i. Tokelau
81 □1 Te Lafu i. Tokelau
205 E2 Télagh Alg.
175 K3 Telaki Pol.
Telanaipura Sumatera Indon. see Jambi
207 F2 Télataï Mali
175 L5 Telatyn Pol.
129 D3 T'elavi Georgia
128 B3 Tel Aviv-Yafo Israel
176 E2 Telč Czech Rep.
243 H4 Telchac Puerto Mex.
139 K5 Tel'ch'ye Rus. Fed.
197 G2 Telciu Romania
168 F2 Teldau Ger.
216 □3f Telde Gran Canaria Canary Is
208 D4 Tele r. Dem. Rep. Congo
206 E2 Télé, Lac l. Mali
197 G3 Teleajen r. Romania
196 D3 Telečka Vojvodina, Srbija Yugo.
222 D3 Telegraph Creek B.C. Can.
177 J5 Telekgerendás Hungary
Telekhany Belarus see Tsyelyakhany
256 B6 Telêmaco Borba Brazil
142 C2 Telemark county Norway
260 E5 Telén Arg.
95 G2 Telen r. Indon.
Teleneshty Moldova see Teleneşti
136 E4 Teleneşti Moldova
197 G4 Teleorman r. Romania
205 G4 Telertheba, Djebel mt. Alg.
240 I3 Telescope Peak CA U.S.A.
193 G3 Telese Italy
253 F1 Teles Pires r. Brazil
129 E2 Teletl' Rus. Fed.
86 D4 Telfer Mining Centre W.A. Austr.
150 E2 Telford Telford and Wrekin, England U.K.
234 C2 Telford PA U.S.A.
150 E2 Telford and Wrekin admin. div. England U.K.
178 C3 Telfs Austria
177 J3 Telgárt Slovakia
158 B3 Telgruc-sur-Mer France
169 C4 Telgte Ger.
182 C4 Telhado Port.
206 B4 Télimélé Guinea
245 F5 Telixtlahuaca Mex.
202 E6 Teljo, Jebel mt. Sudan
222 E4 Telkwa B.C. Can.
157 F3 Tellancourt France
194 E6 Tellaro r. Sicilia Italy
Tell Atlas mts Alg. see Atlas Tellien
220 B3 Teller AK U.S.A.
Tell es-Sultan West Bank see Jericho
114 B4 Tellicherry Pondicherry India
165 E4 Tellin Belgium
168 E1 Tellingstedt Ger.
129 B3 Telli Tepe mt. Turkey
136 F4 Tellodar Ukr.
127 G5 Telloh Iraq
239 F4 Telluride CO U.S.A.
137 J4 Tel'manove Ukr.
Tel'mansk Turkm. see Gubadag
128 B3 Tel Megiddo tourist site Israel
179 H1 Telnice Czech Rep.
159 G4 Teloché France
182 C3 Telões Port.
245 E4 Teloloapán Mex.
Telo Martius France see Toulon
81 □1 Te Loto i. Tokelau
134 L3 Tel'pos-Iz, Gora mt. Rus. Fed.
138 D4 Telšiai Lith.
192 B4 Telti Sardegna Italy
171 E3 Teltow Ger.
94 C1 Teluk Anson Malaysia
Telukbajur Sumatera Indon. see Telukbayur
94 C3 Telukbayur Sumatera Indon.
Telukbetung Sumatera Indon. see Tanjungkarang-Telukbetung
94 B2 Telukdalam Indon.
Teluk Intan Malaysia see Teluk Anson
207 F5 Tema Ghana
227 H2 Temagami Ont. Can.
81 □3 Te Manga hill Rarotonga Cook Is
95 E4 Temanggung Jawa Tengah Indon.
80 E3 Te Mapou hill North I. N.Z.
245 F4 Temascal Mex.
80 E2 Te Mata North I. N.Z.
79 □3 Tematangi atoll Arch. des Tuamotu Fr. Polynesia
243 H4 Temax Mex.
215 G1 Temba S. Africa
91 I7 Tembagapura Irian Jaya Indon.
215 I2 Tembe r. Moz.
131 K3 Tembenchi r. Rus. Fed.
94 C3 Tembesi r. Indon.
94 C3 Tembilahan Sumatera Indon.
215 G2 Tembisa S. Africa
183 G5 Tembleque Spain
209 C6 Tembo Aluma Angola
Tembué Moz. see Chifunde
215 G4 Tembuland reg. S. Africa
150 E2 Teme r. England U.K.
240 I5 Temecula CA U.S.A.
126 D3 Temelli Turkey
106 C1 Temenchula, Gora mt. Rus. Fed.
94 C1 Temengor, Tasik resr Malaysia
179 G5 Temenica r. Slovenia
196 D3 Temerin Vojvodina, Srbija Yugo.
94 C2 Temerloh Malaysia
94 C1 Temiang, Bukit mt. Malaysia
120 D2 Temir Aktyubinskaya Oblast' Kazakh.
Temir Yuzhnyy Kazakhstan Kazakh. see Tumur
Temirlan Kazakh. see Temirlanovka
121 G4 Temirlanovka Kazakh.
121 H2 Temirtau Kazakh.
225 F3 Témiscamie r. Que. Can.
224 E4 Temiscaming Que. Can.
139 J4 Temkino Rus. Fed.
83 F5 Temma Tas. Austr.
140 N2 Temmes Fin.
135 H5 Temnikov Rus. Fed.
192 A4 Temo r. Sardegna Italy
79 □3 Temoe atoll Arch. des Tuamotu Fr. Polynesia
83 F3 Temora N.S.W. Austr.
241 L5 Tempe AZ U.S.A.
84 C5 Tempe Downs N.T. Austr.
171 E3 Tempelhof airport Ger.
192 B4 Tempio Pausania Sardegna Italy
226 E3 Temple MI U.S.A.
234 C2 Temple PA U.S.A.
237 D6 Temple TX U.S.A.
150 C2 Temple Bar Ceredigion, Wales U.K.
147 C4 Templederry Rep. of Ireland
151 I3 Temple Ewell Kent, England U.K.
147 B4 Templeglentan Rep. of Ireland
147 D4 Templemore Rep. of Ireland
147 B5 Templenoe Rep. of Ireland
147 E2 Templepatrick Northern Ireland U.K.
149 G3 Temple Sowerby Cumbria, England U.K.
81 D5 Templeton South I. N.Z.
150 C3 Templeton Pembrokeshire, Wales U.K.
240 G4 Templeton CA U.S.A.
147 D4 Templetuohy Rep. of Ireland
156 D2 Templeuve France
170 E2 Templin Ger.
147 D2 Tempo Northern Ireland U.K.
245 E3 Tempoal Mex.
245 E3 Tempoal r. Mex.
209 C8 Tempué Angola
135 G7 Temryuk Rus. Fed.
135 G7 Temryukskiy Zaliv b. Rus. Fed.
165 D3 Temse Belgium
197 F4 Temska Srbija Yugo.
190 F2 Temù Italy
260 A6 Temuco Chile
81 C6 Temuka South I. N.Z.
Temuli Sichuan China see Butuo
78 □4b Temwen i. Pohnpei Micronesia
78 □4b Temwetemwensekir hill Pohnpei Micronesia
120 D1 Temyasovo Rus. Fed.
250 B5 Tena Ecuador
243 H4 Tenabo Mex.
240 I1 Tenabo, Mount NV U.S.A.
206 E3 Ténado Burkina
235 E2 Tenafly NJ U.S.A.
138 D1 Tenala Fin.
114 D2 Tenali Andhra Prad. India
228 G7 Tenancingo Mex.
245 E4 Tenango Mex.
79 □3 Tenarunga atoll Arch. des Tuamotu Fr. Polynesia
97 B4 Tenasserim Myanmar
97 B4 Tenasserim admin. div. Myanmar
97 B4 Tenasserim r. Myanmar
160 D3 Tenay France
164 F1 Ten Boer Neth.
150 E2 Tenbury Wells Worcestershire, England U.K.
150 C3 Tenby Pembrokeshire, Wales U.K.
227 F2 Tenby Bay Ont. Can.
161 C3 Tence France
210 D2 Tendaho Eth.
155 H4 Tende France
115 G4 Ten Degree Channel Andaman & Nicobar Is India
203 F6 Tendelti Sudan
206 B2 Te-n-Dghâmcha, Sebkhet salt marsh Maur.
183 H4 Tendilla Spain
102 J4 Tendō Japan
204 E2 Tendrara Morocco
190 B2 Tendre, Mont mt. Switz.
159 H5 Tendu France
116 D5 Tendukheda Madh. Prad. India
129 C4 Tendürek Dağı mt. Turkey
206 C4 Téné r. Guinea
206 D3 Ténenkou Mali
138 C4 Tenenys r. Lith.
207 H1 Ténéré du Tafassâsset des. Niger
216 □3a Tenerife i. Canary Is
205 F1 Ténès Alg.
197 H4 Tenevo Bulg.
96 B3 Teng, Nam r. Myanmar
95 G4 Tengah, Kepulauan is Indon.
Tengcheng Guangxi China see Tengxian
108 A3 Tengchong Yunnan China
120 C4 Tenge Kazakh.
177 H5 Tengelic Hungary
172 C4 Tengen Ger.
95 G3 Tenggarong Kalimantan Timur Indon.
106 E4 Tengger Shamo des. Nei Mongol China
121 G2 Tengiz, Ozero salt l. Kazakh.
206 D4 Tengréla Côte d'Ivoire
135 H5 Ten'gushevo Rus. Fed.
108 D4 Tengxian Guangxi China
Tengxian Shandong China see Tengzhou
107 H5 Tengzhou Shandong China
161 E4 Ténibre, Mont mt. France/Italy
Teniente Jubany research stn Antarctica see Jubany
231 D6 Tenille FL U.S.A.
172 B3 Teningen Ger.
206 A2 Te-n-Ioubrar, Sebkhet salt marsh Maur.
177 J4 Tenk Hungary
114 C4 Tenkasi Tamil Nadu India
209 E7 Tenke Dem. Rep. Congo
131 P2 Tenkeli Rus. Fed.
134 J5 Ten'ki Rus. Fed.
206 E4 Tenkodogo Burkina
87 D5 Ten Mile Lake salt flat W.A. Austr.
191 I5 Tenna r. Italy
84 C3 Tennant Creek N.T. Austr.
172 C3 Tennenbronn Ger.
235 D2 Tennent NJ U.S.A.
237 F4 Tennessee r. U.S.A.
232 A6 Tennessee state U.S.A.
165 E4 Tenneville Belgium
140 L1 Tennevoll Norway
140 K2 Tennholmfjorden sea chan. Norway
140 O2 Tenniöjoki r. Fin./Rus. Fed.
260 B4 Teno Chile
260 B4 Teno r. Chile
245 F4 Tenochtitlán Mex.
140 O1 Tenojoki r. Fin./Norway
243 H5 Tenosique Mex.
104 B4 Tenri Japan
105 D4 Tenryū Japan
105 D4 Tenryū-gawa r. Japan
238 F2 Ten Sleep WY U.S.A.
93 B3 Tenteno Sulawesi Tengah Indon.
151 H3 Tenterden Kent, England U.K.
83 H2 Tenterfield N.S.W. Austr.
93 B2 Tentolomatinan, Gunung mt. Indon.
184 D2 Tentudia mt. Spain
182 B4 Tentúgal Port.
158 E4 Tenu r. France
177 G4 Tényő Hungary
244 C3 Teocaltiche Mex.
245 F4 Teocelo Mex.
261 G4 Teodelina Arg.
256 A5 Teodoro Sampaio Brazil
260 A6 Teodoro Schmidt Chile
257 G2 Teófilo Otôni Brazil
136 D3 Teofipol' Ukr.
116 E4 Teonthar Madh. Prad. India
243 G5 Teopisca Mex.
193 H4 Teora Italy
245 E4 Teotihuacán tourist site Mex.
245 F5 Teotitlán del Valle Mex.
206 E5 Tepa Ghana
242 C2 Tepache Mex.
80 D1 Te Paki North I. N.Z.
244 C4 Tepalcatepec Mex.
244 C4 Tepalcatepec r. Mex.
245 E3 Tepatepec Mex.
244 C3 Tepatitlán Mex.
177 K4 Tépe Hungary
245 F4 Tepeaca Mex.
245 E4 Tepeapulco Mex.
199 F1 Tepecik Turkey
242 D3 Tepehuanes Mex.
245 E4 Tepeji Mex.
Tepeköy Turkey see Karakoçan
198 B1 Tepelenë Albania
245 F5 Tepelmeme de Morelos Mex.
176 B2 Tepelská Vrchovina hills Czech Rep.
251 F4 Tepequem, Serra mts Brazil
244 D3 Tepetates Mex.
244 B3 Tepic Mex.
81 C5 Te Pirita South I. N.Z.
176 B2 Teplá Czech Rep.
176 B1 Teplá r. Czech Rep.
176 C3 Teplá Vltava r. Czech Rep.
134 L4 Teplaya Gora Rus. Fed.
137 J3 Teple Ukr.
129 D2 Tepli, Gora mt. Rus. Fed.
176 C1 Teplice Czech Rep.
177 J3 Teplička Slovakia
139 L5 Teploye Lipetskaya Oblast' Rus. Fed.
139 K5 Teploye Tul'skaya Oblast' Rus. Fed.
136 E3 Teplyk Ukr.
245 E4 Tepoztlan Mex.
193 E3 Teppia r. Italy
80 F2 Te Puke North I. N.Z.
80 F2 Te Puna North I. N.Z.
244 C3 Tequila Mex.
244 C3 Tequila, Volcán de vol. Mex.
245 G5 Tequisistlán Mex.
245 G5 Tequisistlán r. Mex.
245 E3 Tequisquiapán Mex.
245 F4 Tequixquitla Mex.
245 F4 Tequixtépec Mex.
186 G2 Ter r. Spain
207 F3 Téra Niger
184 B2 Tera r. Port.
182 E3 Tera r. Spain
164 D2 Ter Aar Neth.
80 E2 Te Rahu North I. N.Z.
116 D2 Teram Kangri mt. China/Jammu and Kashmir
193 F2 Teramo Italy
193 F2 Teramo prov. Abruzzo Italy
83 E4 Terang Vic. Austr.
80 E2 Te Rapa North I. N.Z.
164 G2 Ter Apel Neth.
123 G4 Teratani r. Pak.
175 L5 Teratyn Pol.
81 E4 Terawhiti, Cape North I. N.Z.
164 F3 Terborg-Silvolde Neth.
139 L5 Terbuny Rus. Fed.
Tercan Erzincan Turkey see Otlukbeli
127 F3 Tercan Erzincan Turkey
216 □1a Terceira i. Azores
261 F3 Tercero r. Arg.
163 A5 Tercis-les-Bains France
190 E3 Terdoppio r. Italy
139 J5 Tereben' Rus. Fed.
177 L4 Terebeşti Romania
136 B3 Tereblya r. Ukr.
136 C3 Terebovlya Ukr.
197 F3 Teregova Romania
Terek r. Georgia see Tergi
129 D2 Terek Rus. Fed.
127 G2 Terek r. Rus. Fed.
106 B1 Tere-Khol' Rus. Fed.
129 D1 Terekli-Mekteb Rus. Fed.
121 G4 Terek-Say Kyrg.
110 D1 Terektinskiy Khrebet mts Rus. Fed.
121 K2 Terekty Vostochnyy Kazakhstan Kazakh.
177 J6 Teremia Mare Romania
184 C2 Terena Port.
135 J5 Teren'ga Rus. Fed.
94 C1 Terengganu r. Malaysia
94 C1 Terengganu state Malaysia
Terengözek Kazakh. see Terenozek
255 B7 Terenos Brazil
120 F3 Terenozek Kazakh.
120 D2 Terensay Rus. Fed.
147 E3 Terenure Rep. of Ireland
Teren-Uzyak Kazakh. see Terenozek
256 B6 Teresa Cristina Brazil
187 B5 Teresa de Cofrentes Spain
120 A2 Tereshka r. Rus. Fed.
175 I3 Teresin Pol.
254 E3 Teresina Brazil
250 D4 Teresita Col.
257 F5 Teresópolis Brazil
175 L3 Terespol Pol.
136 B3 Teresva Ukr.
136 B4 Teresva r. Ukr.
175 K5 Tereszpol-Zaorenda Pol.
176 D1 Terezín Czech Rep.
136 F3 Terezyne Ukr.
178 C3 Terfens Austria
184 C3 Terges r. Port.
Tergeste Italy see Trieste
129 D2 Tergi r. Georgia
156 D3 Tergnier France
191 H3 Tergola r. Italy
192 A4 Tergu Sardegna Italy
164 D3 Terheijden Neth.
134 F1 Teriberka Rus. Fed.
121 F2 Terisakkan r. Kazakh.
175 K6 Terka Pol.
191 G2 Terlano Italy
237 C6 Terlingua Creek r. TX U.S.A.
193 I3 Terlizzi Italy
203 I6 Terma, Ras pt Eritrea
136 E2 Termakhivka Ukr.
126 E2 Terme Turkey
193 H5 Terme Luigiane Italy
186 D3 Térmens Spain
163 E5 Termes France
121 F5 Termez Uzbek.
161 E3 Termignon France
87 D7 Termination Island W.A. Austr.
156 B4 Terminiers France
194 C5 Termini Imerese Sicilia Italy
194 C4 Termini Imerese, Golfo di b. Sicilia Italy
193 E2 Terminillo, Monte mt. Italy
243 H5 Términos, Laguna de lag. Mex.
207 H2 Termit, Massif de hill Niger
Termiz Uzbek. see Termez
193 G3 Termoli Italy
147 D1 Termon Rep. of Ireland
Termonde Belgium see Dendermonde
148 C4 Termonfeckin Rep. of Ireland
150 E2 Tern r. England U.K.
137 H2 Tern r. Ukr.
164 E1 Ternaard Neth.
93 C2 Ternate Maluku Indon.
179 F3 Ternberg Austria
165 C3 Terneuzen Neth.
100 F3 Terney Rus. Fed.
193 E2 Terni Italy
193 E2 Terni prov. Umbria Italy
160 C2 Ternin r. France
179 H3 Ternitz Austria
137 I3 Ternivka Dnipropetrovs'ka Oblast' Ukr.
137 G4 Ternivka Mykolayivs'ka Oblast' Ukr.
136 E3 Ternivka Vinnyts'ka Oblast' Ukr.
156 C2 Ternoise r. France
136 C3 Ternopil' Ukr.
Ternopil Oblast admin. div. Ukr. see Ternopils'ka Oblast'
136 C3 Ternopils'ka Oblast' admin. div. Ukr.
Ternopol' Ukr. see Ternopil'
Ternopol Oblast admin. div. Ukr. see Ternopils'ka Oblast'
Ternopol'skaya Oblast' admin. div. Ukr. see Ternopils'ka Oblast'
135 H6 Ternovka Rus. Fed.
Ternovka Dnipropetrovs'ka Oblast' Ukr. see Ternivka
137 I4 Ternuvate Ukr.
137 I3 Terny Donets'ka Oblast' Ukr.
137 G2 Terny Sums'ka Oblast' Ukr.
216 □3f Teror Gran Canaria Canary Is
82 D3 Terowie S.A. Austr.
100 G2 Terpeniya, Zaliv g. Sakhalin Rus. Fed.
232 D5 Terra Alta WV U.S.A.
240 H4 Terra Bella CA U.S.A.
256 A5 Terra Boa Brazil
257 F2 Terra Branca Brazil
222 D4 Terrace B.C. Can.
224 C3 Terrace Bay Ont. Can.
216 □1a Terra Chã Terceira Azores
193 F3 Terracina Italy
193 F3 Terracina, Golfo di b. Italy
Terradas Spain see Terrades
186 F2 Terrades Spain
214 D1 Terra Firma S. Africa
140 K2 Terråk Norway
192 A5 Terralba Sardegna Italy
195 F3 Terranova da Sibari Italy
193 I5 Terranova di Pollino Italy
191 G5 Terranuova Bracciolini Italy
256 A5 Terra Rica Brazil
182 B3 Terras do Bouro Port.
194 C4 Terrasini Sicilia Italy
186 F3 Terrassa Spain
162 D3 Terrasson-la-Villedieu France
163 C5 Terraube France
195 F3 Terravecchia Italy
Terre Adélie reg. Antarctica see Adélie Land
247 □2 Terre de Bas i. Guadeloupe
247 □2 Terre de Haut i. Guadeloupe
230 C4 Terre Haute IN U.S.A.
234 B2 Terre Hill PA U.S.A.
237 D5 Terrell TX U.S.A.
157 F5 Terre-Natale France
245 F4 Terrenate Mex.
225 K4 Terrenceville Nfld. Can.
160 C1 Terre Plaine plain France
Terres Australes et Antarctiques Françaises terr. Indian Ocean see French Southern and Antarctic Lands
191 F5 Terricciola Italy
183 I4 Terriente Spain
185 E4 Terril mt. Spain
148 B4 Terrin Rep. of Ireland
185 H2 Terrinches Spain
149 I3 Terrington North Yorkshire, England U.K.
151 H2 Terrington St Clement Norfolk, England U.K.
157 G5 Territoire de Belfort dept Franche-Comté France
163 D4 Terrou France
184 A2 Terrugem Lisboa Port.
184 C2 Terrugem Portalegre Port.
238 F2 Terry MT U.S.A.
235 E1 Terryville CT U.S.A.
235 E2 Terryville NY U.S.A.
135 I6 Tersa r. Rus. Fed.
Tersakkan r. Kazakh. see Terisakkan
164 E1 Terschelling i. Neth.
Terskey Alatau, Khrebet mts Kyrg. see Terskey Ala-Too
121 I4 Terskey Ala-Too mts Kyrg.
134 G2 Terskiy Bereg coastal area Rus. Fed.
137 H4 Tersyanka Ukr.
192 B5 Tertenia Sardegna Italy
Terter Azer. see Tärtär
156 D3 Tertry France
187 B4 Teruel Spain
183 4 Teruel prov. Aragón Spain
138 E1 Tervakoski Fin.
197 H4 Tervel Bulg.
159 F5 Terves France
140 N3 Tervo Fin.
140 N2 Tervola Fin.
139 K3 Teryayevo Rus. Fed.
177 H4 Tés Hungary
191 H2 Tesa r. Italy
188 F3 Tešanj Bos.-Herz.
163 D4 Tescou r. France
245 G4 Tesechoacán r. Mex.
177 G3 Tešedíkovo Slovakia
203 H6 Teseney Eritrea
191 G2 Tesero Italy
135 H5 Tesha r. Rus. Fed.
207 E5 Teshi Ghana
102 K2 Teshio-dake mt. Japan
102 J1 Teshio-gawa r. Japan
102 J1 Teshio-sanchi mts Japan
197 E4 Tešica Srbija Yugo.
191 G2 Tesimo Italy
191 G3 Tesina r. Italy
244 C3 Tesistán Mex.
106 B1 Tesiyn Gol r. Mongolia
188 F3 Teslić Bos.-Herz.
222 C2 Teslin Y.T. Can.
222 C2 Teslin r. Y.T. Can.
197 G3 Teslui r. Romania
182 E3 Teso Santo hill Spain
255 B6 Tesouro Brazil
139 H2 Tesovo-Netyl'skiy Rus. Fed.
139 H2 Tesovskiy Rus. Fed.
168 F2 Tespe Ger.
207 G3 Tessaoua Niger
159 F3 Tessé-la-Madeleine France
165 E3 Tessenderlo Belgium
170 D1 Tessin Ger.
Tessin canton Switz. see Ticino
162 B3 Tesson France
159 E3 Tessy-sur-Vire France
151 F4 Test r. England U.K.
193 I3 Testa del Gargano Italy
194 D6 Testa dell'Acqua Sicilia Italy
182 B2 Testeiro, Montes de mts Spain
165 D3 Testelt Belgium
183 G5 Testillos r. Spain
205 H1 Testour Tunisia
163 F6 Têt r. France
177 G4 Tét Hungary
225 H4 Tetagouche r. N.B. Can.
150 E3 Tetbury Gloucestershire, England U.K.
177 L4 Teţchea Romania
213 G3 Tete Moz.
213 G2 Tete prov. Moz.
161 E4 Tête de l'Enchastraye mt. France/Italy
161 E4 Tête de l'Estrop mt. France
161 E4 Tête de Soulaure mt. France
190 B4 Tête des Toillies mt. Italy
222 G4 Tête Jaune Cache B.C. Can.
80 F3 Te Teko North I. N.Z.
245 E4 Tetela de Volcán Mex.
78 □6 Tetepare i. New Georgia Is Solomon Is
164 D3 Teteringen Neth.
136 F2 Teteriv r. Ukr.
170 D2 Teterow Ger.
177 K4 Tetétlen Hungary
197 G4 Teteven Bulg.
149 I4 Tetford Lincolnshire, England U.K.
192 B4 Teti Sardegna Italy
Tetiyev Ukr. see Tetiyiv
136 E3 Tetiyiv Ukr.
137 H2 Tetkino Rus. Fed.
149 I4 Tetney Lincolnshire, England U.K.
238 E2 Teton r. MT U.S.A.
204 D2 Tétouan Morocco
180 D5 Tétouan prov. Morocco
196 E4 Tetovo Macedonia
116 B5 Tetpur Gujarat India
171 C5 Tettau Ger.
168 C2 Tettens Ger.
172 D4 Tettnang Ger.
Tetuán Morocco see Tétouan
79 □3a Tetufera mt. Tahiti Fr. Polynesia
Tetyukhe Rus. Fed. see Dal'negorsk
Tetyukhe-Pristan' Rus. Fed. see Rudnaya Pristan'
135 J5 Tetyushi Rus. Fed.
173 G2 Teublitz Ger.
171 D4 Teuchern Ger.
Teuchezhsk Rus. Fed. see Adygeysk
258 E2 Teuco r. Arg.
190 E1 Teufen Switz.
192 A6 Teulada Sardegna Italy
187 D6 Teulada Spain
244 C3 Teul de González Ortega Mex.
93 D4 Teun vol. Maluku Indon.
94 A1 Teunom r. Indon.
173 G2 Teunz Ger.
171 E3 Teupitz Ger.
171 C5 Teuschnitz Ger.
169 D3 Teutoburger Wald hills Ger.
171 C4 Teutschenthal Ger.
141 M3 Teuva Fin.
177 H5 Tevel Hungary
191 H5 Tevere r. Italy
193 E1 Teverone r. Italy
128 B3 Teverya Israel
81 B6 Teviot South I. N.Z.
215 E4 Teviot S. Africa
146 F6 Teviot r. Scotland U.K.
146 F6 Teviotdale val. Scotland U.K.
146 F6 Teviothead Scottish Borders, Scotland U.K.
81 A7 Te Waewae South I. N.Z.
81 A7 Te Waewae Bay South I. N.Z.
Te Waiponamu i. N.Z. see South Island
85 H5 Tewantin Qld Austr.
95 F3 Teweh r. Indon.
80 E3 Te Wera North I. N.Z.
80 F3 Te Wera North I. N.Z.
80 F3 Te Whaiti North I. N.Z.
81 E4 Te Wharau North I. N.Z.
150 E3 Tewkesbury Gloucestershire, England U.K.
138 E5 Tewli Belarus
106 D5 Têwo Gansu China
146 B6 Texa i. Scotland U.K.
237 E5 Texarkana AR U.S.A.
237 E5 Texarkana TX U.S.A.
83 G2 Texas Qld Austr.
237 D6 Texas state U.S.A.
237 E6 Texas City TX U.S.A.
245 E4 Texcoco Mex.
164 D1 Texel i. Neth.
237 C4 Texhoma OK U.S.A.
245 G5 Texistepec Mex.
245 E4 Texmelucan Mex.
237 D5 Texoma, Lake Oklahoma/Texas U.S.A.
215 F3 Teyateyaneng Lesotho
162 C3 Teyjat France
139 M3 Teykovo Rus. Fed.
151 H3 Teynham Kent, England U.K.
163 D4 Teyssieu France
160 C2 Teyssonne r. France
134 H4 Teza r. Rus. Fed.
215 I3 Teza S. Africa
245 F4 Teziutlán Mex.
245 F4 Tezonapa Mex.
245 E3 Tezontepec Mex.
117 H4 Tezpur Assam India
117 I4 Tezu Arun. Prad. India
96 C2 Tha, Nam r. Laos
223 M2 Tha-anne r. Nunavut Can.
215 G3 Thabana-Ntlenyana mt. Lesotho
215 F3 Thaba Nchu S. Africa
215 H2 Thabankulu mt. S. Africa
213 E6 Thaba Putsoa mt. Lesotho
215 F4 Thaba Putsoa mts S. Africa
215 G3 Thaba-Tseka Lesotho
213 E5 Thabazimbi S. Africa
96 C3 Tha Bo Laos

Thabong to Tkvarcheli
370

215 F2 **Thabong** S. Africa
161 E3 **Thabor, Mont** *mt.* France
96 A3 **Thade** *r.* Myanmar
124 D2 **Thādiq** Saudi Arabia
Tha Hin Thai. *see* **Lop Buri**
96 D2 **Thai Binh** Vietnam
96 C3 **Thailand** *country* Asia
97 C5 **Thailand, Gulf of** Asia
97 B5 **Thai Muang** Thai.
96 D2 **Thai Nguyên** Vietnam
125 E2 **Thaj** Saudi Arabia
117 G4 **Thakurgaon** Bangl.
116 E5 **Thakurtola** *Madh. Prad.* India
169 F5 **Thal** Ger.
123 G3 **Thal** Pak.
205 H2 **Thala** Tunisia
97 B5 **Thalang** Thai.
Thalassery *Pondicherry* India *see* **Tellicherry**
173 F2 **Thalbach** *r.* Ger.
123 G4 **Thal Desert** Pak.
171 C4 **Thale (Harz)** Ger.
172 B2 **Thaleischweiler-Fröschen** Ger.
97 C6 **Thale Luang** *lag.* Thai.
172 A2 **Thalfang** Ger.
178 E3 **Thalgau** Austria
171 D4 **Thalheim** Ger.
179 F2 **Thalheim bei Wels** Austria
Thaliparamba *Kerala* India *see* **Taliparamba**
83 G2 **Thallon** *Qld* Austr.
171 D4 **Thallwitz** Ger.
173 F2 **Thalmässing** *Bayern* Ger.
173 G3 **Thalmassing** *Bayern* Ger.
190 D1 **Thalwil** Switz.
212 E5 **Thamaga** Botswana
124 D5 **Thamar, Jabal** *mt.* Yemen
125 F4 **Thamarit** Oman
151 G3 **Thame** *Oxfordshire, England* U.K.
151 F3 **Thame** *r. England* U.K.
227 F4 **Thames** *r. Ont.* Can.
80 E2 **Thames** *North I.* N.Z.
151 H3 **Thames** *est. England* U.K.
151 H3 **Thames** *r. England* U.K.
235 F1 **Thames** *r. CT* U.S.A.
80 E2 **Thames, Firth of** *b. North I.* N.Z.
Thamesdown *admin. div. England* U.K. *see* **Swindon**
227 G4 **Thamesford** *Ont.* Can.
227 G4 **Thamesville** *Ont.* Can.
169 F4 **Thamsbrück** Ger.
125 E4 **Thamūd** Yemen
Thamugadi *tourist site* Alg. *see* **Timgad**
Thana *Mahar.* India *see* **Thane**
116 D4 **Thana Ghazi** *Rajasthan* India
96 B3 **Thanatpin** Myanmar
96 B4 **Thanbyuzayat** Myanmar
116 C5 **Thandla** *Madh. Prad.* India
Thandwè Myanmar *see* **Sandoway**
114 B2 **Thane** *Mahar.* India
151 I3 **Thanet, Isle of** *pen. England* U.K.
116 B5 **Thangadh** *Gujarat* India
83 D3 **Thangoo** *W.A.* Austr.
85 G5 **Thangool** *Qld* Austr.
96 D3 **Thanh Hoa** Vietnam
114 C4 **Thanjavur** *Tamil Nadu* India
Thanlwin *r.* Myanmar *see* **Salween**
157 H5 **Thann** France
173 E3 **Thannhausen** Ger.
123 F5 **Thano Bula Khan** Pak.
212 D3 **Thaoge** *r.* Botswana
157 G4 **Thaon-les-Vosges** France
97 B5 **Thap Put** Thai.
97 B5 **Thap Sakae** Thai.
116 B5 **Thara** *Gujarat* India
116 B4 **Tharad** *Gujarat* India
171 E5 **Tharandt** Ger.
164 E2 **'t Harde** Neth.
116 B4 **Thar Desert** India/Pak.
85 E5 **Thargomindah** *Qld* Austr.
96 A3 **Tharrawaddy** Myanmar
184 C3 **Tharsis** Spain
127 F4 **Tharthār, Buḥayrat ath** *l.* Iraq
125 F3 **Tharwānīyyah** U.A.E.
198 D1 **Thasos** *Anatoliki Makedonia kai Thraki* Greece
198 D1 **Thasos** *i.* Greece
151 F3 **Thatcham** *West Berkshire, England* U.K.
241 M5 **Thatcher** *AZ* U.S.A.
198 B1 **Thatë, Mali i** *mt.* Albania
96 D2 **Thât Khê** Vietnam
96 B3 **Thaton** Myanmar
161 B5 **Thau, Bassin de** *lag.* France
160 A2 **Thaumiers** France
96 A1 **Thaungdut** Myanmar
96 B3 **Thaungyin** *r.* Myanmar/Thai.
178 C3 **Thaur** Austria
96 D3 **Tha Uthen** Thai.
128 D6 **Thawr, Jabal** *mt.* Jordan
151 H3 **Thaxted** *Essex, England* U.K.
179 G2 **Thaya** Austria
179 G2 **Thaya** *r.* Austria/Czech Rep.
96 A3 **Thayetmyo** Myanmar
190 D1 **Thayngen** Switz.
96 B2 **Thazi** Myanmar
241 K5 **Theba** *AZ* U.S.A.
Thebae *tourist site* Egypt *see* **Thebes**
229 K6 **The Bahamas** *country* West Indies
203 G3 **Thebes** *tourist site* Egypt
Thebes Greece *see* **Thiva**
246 C1 **The Bluff** *Eleuthera* Bahamas
151 I2 **The Broads** *nat. park England* U.K.
149 G3 **The Calf** *hill England* U.K.
85 H1 **The Calvados Chain** *is* P.N.G.
149 F2 **The Cheviot** *hill England* U.K.
246 □ **The Cockpit Country** *hills* Jamaica
82 D3 **The Coorong** *inlet S.A.* Austr.
148 C4 **The Curragh** *lowland* Rep. of Ireland
238 B2 **The Dalles** *OR* U.S.A.
236 C3 **Thedford** *NE* U.S.A.
148 C3 **The Diamond** *Northern Ireland* U.K.
168 E3 **Thedinghausen** Ger.
84 D1 **The English Company's Islands** *N.T.* Austr.
83 G3 **The Entrance** *N.S.W.* Austr.
151 G2 **The Fens** *reg. England* U.K.
206 A3 **The Gambia** *country* Africa
146 D6 **The Glenkens** *val. Scotland* U.K.
84 B4 **The Granites** *hill N.T.* Austr.
205 F3 **The Great Oasis** Egypt
247 □3 **The Grenadines** *is* St Vincent
125 E1 **The Gulf** Asia
The Hague Neth. *see* **'s-Gravenhage**
147 E4 **The Harrow** Rep. of Ireland
215 G5 **The Haven** S. Africa
214 D4 **The Horseshoe** *mt.* S. Africa
81 C6 **The Hunters Hills** *South I.* N.Z.
159 I4 **Theillay** France
171 D4 **Theißen** Ger.
158 D4 **Theix** France
81 A6 **The Key** *South I.* N.Z.
223 L1 **Thelon** *r. N.W.T./Nunavut* Can.
151 F3 **The Long Mynd** *hills England* U.K.
148 C3 **The Loup** *Northern Ireland* U.K.
85 F3 **The Lynd Junction** *Qld* Austr.
146 D7 **The Machars** *reg. Scotland* U.K.
169 F5 **Themar** Ger.
214 E5 **Thembalesizwe** S. Africa
215 G2 **Thembalihle** S. Africa
146 B3 **The Minch** *sea chan. Scotland* U.K.
163 D4 **Theméricourt** France
150 D3 **The Mumbles** *Swansea, Wales* U.K.
159 H5 **Thenay** France
The Naze *c.* Norway *see* **Lindesnes**
151 F4 **The Needles** *stack England* U.K.
159 F5 **Thénezay** France
116 D5 **Theni** *Madh. Prad.* India
205 F2 **Theniet El Had** Alg.
162 D3 **Thenon** France
146 F2 **The North Sound** *sea chan. Scotland* U.K.
84 B4 **Theo, Mount** *hill N.T.* Austr.
146 B6 **The Oa** *pen. Scotland* U.K.
85 G5 **Theodore** *Qld* Austr.
223 K5 **Theodore** *Sask.* Can.
253 E1 **Theodore Roosevelt** *r.* Brazil
Theodosia Ukr. *see* **Feodosiya**
149 F3 **The Old Man of Coniston** *hill England* U.K.
159 I4 **Théols** *r.* France
161 E5 **Théoule-sur-Mer** France
147 B4 **The Paps** *hill* Rep. of Ireland
223 K4 **The Pas** *Man.* Can.
147 D4 **The Pike** Rep. of Ireland
Thera *i.* Greece *see* **Thira**
156 C3 **Thérain** *r.* France
81 B6 **The Remarkables** *mts South I.* N.Z.
169 F5 **Theres** Ger.
233 F2 **Theresa** *NY* U.S.A.
85 G4 **Theresa Creek** *r. Qld* Austr.
198 C1 **Thermaïkos Kolpos** *g.* Greece
198 C1 **Thermi** *Kentriki Makedonia* Greece
198 B2 **Thermo** Greece
Thérmon Greece *see* **Thermo**
238 E3 **Thermopolis** *WY* U.S.A.
83 F3 **The Rock** *N.S.W.* Austr.
185 □ **The Rock** *hill* Gibraltar
156 C2 **Thérouanne** France
86 □1 **The Settlement** Christmas I.
147 E2 **The Sheddings** *Northern Ireland* U.K.
The Slot *sea chan.* Solomon Is *see* **New Georgia Sound**
146 □F1 **The Sneug** *hill Scotland* U.K.
151 F4 **The Solent** *str. England* U.K.
198 B2 **Thesprotiko** Greece
198 B2 **Thessalia** *admin. reg.* Greece
224 D4 **Thessalon** *Ont.* Can.
Thessalonica Greece *see* **Thessaloniki**
198 C1 **Thessaloniki** Greece
Thessaly *admin. reg.* Greece *see* **Thessalia**
151 H3 **The Stocks** *Kent, England* U.K.
146 B4 **The Storr** *hill Scotland* U.K.
151 H2 **Thet** *r. England* U.K.
92 A4 **The Teeth** *mt. Palawan* Phil.
148 D3 **The Temple** *Northern Ireland* U.K.
87 D6 **The Terraces** *hills W.A.* Austr.
151 H2 **Thetford** *Norfolk, England* U.K.
225 G4 **Thetford Mines** *Que.* Can.
81 C5 **The Thumbs** *mt. South I.* N.Z.
96 A4 **Thetkethaung** *r.* Myanmar
96 B1 **The Triangle** *mts* Myanmar
146 D5 **The Trossachs** *hills Scotland* U.K.
82 C2 **The Twins** *S.A.* Austr.
96 D3 **Theun** *r.* Laos
215 F3 **Theunissen** S. Africa
165 E4 **Theux** Belgium
Theva-i-Ra *rf* Fiji *see* **Ceva-i-Ra**
247 G3 **The Valley** Anguilla
82 C3 **Thevenard** *S.A.* Austr.
86 B4 **Thevenard Island** *W.A.* Austr.
Theveste Alg. *see* **Tébessa**
151 H2 **The Wash** *b. England* U.K.
151 H3 **The Weald** *reg. England* U.K.
237 E6 **The Woodlands** *TX* U.S.A.
The Wrekin *admin. div. England* U.K. *see* **Telford and Wrekin**
163 B5 **Thèze** France
161 D4 **Thèze** France
Thiamis *r.* Greece *see* **Thyamis**
157 F4 **Thiaucourt-Regniéville** France
159 G2 **Thiberville** France
156 E4 **Thibie** France
237 F6 **Thibodaux** *LA* U.S.A.
223 L4 **Thicket Portage** *Man.* Can.
156 E4 **Thiéblemont-Farémont** France
236 D1 **Thief River Falls** *MN* U.S.A.
Thiel Neth. *see* **Tiel**
190 B2 **Thielle** *r.* Switz.
235 D1 **Thiells** *NY* U.S.A.
262 R1 **Thiel Mountains** Antarctica
238 B3 **Thielsen, Mount** *OR* U.S.A.
Thielt Belgium *see* **Tielt**
176 E3 **Thiene** Italy
173 E3 **Thierhaupten** Ger.
190 B2 **Thierrens** Switz.
160 B3 **Thiers** France
178 B3 **Thiersee** Austria
171 D5 **Thiersheim** Ger.
157 F3 **Thierville-sur-Meuse** France
206 A3 **Thiès** Senegal
192 A4 **Thiesi** *Sardegna* Italy
170 E1 **Thießow** Ger.
156 D4 **Thiézac** France
215 C5 **Thika** Kenya
Thikombia *i.* Fiji *see* **Cikobia**
114 B5 **Thiladhunmathee Atoll** Maldives
206 B3 **Thilogne** Senegal
Thimbu Bhutan *see* **Thimphu**
156 B4 **Thimert-Gâtelles** France
117 G4 **Thimphu** Bhutan
140 □B2 **Thingvallavatn (Þingvallavatn)** *l.* Iceland
140 □B2 **Thingvellir (Þingvellir)** Iceland
156 E3 **Thin-le-Moutier** France
78 □5 **Thio** New Caledonia
156 D3 **Thionville** France
199 D3 **Thira** Greece
199 D3 **Thira** *i.* Greece
203 F5 **Third Cataract** *rapids* Sudan
159 G3 **Thiron Gardais** France
156 B4 **Thironne** *r.* France
149 H3 **Thirsk** *North Yorkshire, England* U.K.
87 D7 **Thirsty, Mount** *hill W.A.* Austr.
Thiruvananthapuram *Kerala* India *see* **Trivandrum**
114 C4 **Thiruvarur** *Tamil Nadu* India
Thiruvattiyur *Tamil Nadu* India *see* **Tiruvottiyur**
160 E1 **Thise** France
142 C3 **Thisted** Denmark
140 □D2 **Thistilfjörður (Þistilfjörður)** *b.* Iceland
222 B2 **Thistle Creek** *Y.T.* Can.
82 D3 **Thistle Island** *S.A.* Austr.
198 C2 **Thiva** Greece
Thívai Greece *see* **Thiva**
156 B4 **Thivars** France
162 C3 **Thiviers** France
156 D3 **Thizy** France
140 □C2 **Thjórsá (Þjórsá)** *r.* Iceland
223 M2 **Thlewiaza** *r. Nunavut* Can.
223 I2 **Thoa** *r. N.W.T.* Can.
161 E4 **Thoard** France
96 B3 **Thoen** Thai.
96 C3 **Thoeng** Thai.
213 F4 **Thohoyandou** S. Africa
160 D2 **Thoirette** France
156 B4 **Thoiry** *Île-de-France* France
160 D2 **Thoiry** *Rhône-Alpes* France
160 C2 **Thoissey** France
160 C1 **Thoisy-la-Berchère** France
164 D3 **Tholen** Neth.
164 D3 **Tholen** *i.* Neth.
172 B2 **Tholey** Ger.
156 D4 **Tholon** *r.* France
87 C5 **Thomas** *r. W.A.* Austr.
84 D5 **Thomas, Lake** *salt flat S.A.* Austr.
168 F2 **Thomasburg** Ger.
240 I5 **Thomas Mountain** *CA* U.S.A.
235 E1 **Thomaston** *CT* U.S.A.
231 C5 **Thomaston** *GA* U.S.A.
233 □I2 **Thomaston** *ME* U.S.A.
233 □J2 **Thomaston Corner** *N.B.* Can.
147 D4 **Thomastown** Rep. of Ireland
231 C6 **Thomasville** *AL* U.S.A.
231 D6 **Thomasville** *GA* U.S.A.
231 D5 **Thomasville** *NC* U.S.A.
165 F4 **Thommen** Belgium
246 E3 **Thomonde** Haiti
223 L4 **Thompson** *Man.* Can.
222 F5 **Thompson** *r. B.C.* Can.
226 D3 **Thompson** *MI* U.S.A.
241 M2 **Thompson** *UT* U.S.A.
236 E3 **Thompson** *r. MO* U.S.A.
238 D2 **Thompson Falls** *MT* U.S.A.
239 F5 **Thompson Peak** *NM* U.S.A.
222 E5 **Thompson Sound** *B.C.* Can.
234 A2 **Thompsontown** *PA* U.S.A.
233 G4 **Thompsonville** *CT* U.S.A.
231 D5 **Thomson** *GA* U.S.A.
226 B5 **Thomson** *IL* U.S.A.
81 B6 **Thomson Mountains** *South I.* N.Z.
97 C4 **Thon Buri** Thai.
160 E3 **Thônes** France
96 B3 **Thongwa** Myanmar
157 F4 **Thonnance-lès-Joinville** France
160 E2 **Thonon-les-Bains** France
161 E4 **Thorame-Basse** France
161 E4 **Thorame-Haute** France
161 B4 **Thoras** France
163 E5 **Thoré** *r.* France
239 E5 **Thoreau** *NM* U.S.A.
159 G4 **Thoré-la-Rochette** France
161 E5 **Thorenc** France
160 E3 **Thorens-Glières** France
222 H4 **Thorhild** *Alta* Can.
156 D4 **Thorigny-sur-Oreuse** France
140 □C2 **Thórisvatn (Þórisvatn)** *l.* Iceland
179 G3 **Thörl** Austria
165 E3 **Thorn** Neth.
Thorn Pol. *see* **Toruń**
149 H3 **Thornaby-on-Tees** *Stockton-on-Tees, England* U.K.
226 E4 **Thornapple** *r. MI* U.S.A.
81 B7 **Thornbury** *South I.* N.Z.
150 E3 **Thornbury** *South Gloucestershire, England* U.K.
227 H2 **Thorne** *Ont.* Can.
149 I4 **Thorne** *South Yorkshire, England* U.K.
240 H2 **Thorne** *NV* U.S.A.
222 C4 **Thorne Bay** *AK* U.S.A.
151 G2 **Thorney** *Peterborough, England* U.K.
149 I4 **Thorngumbald** *East Riding of Yorkshire, England* U.K.
146 E6 **Thornhill** *Dumfries and Galloway, Scotland* U.K.
148 E1 **Thornhill** *Stirling, Scotland* U.K.
234 C3 **Thornhurst** *PA* U.S.A.
149 H3 **Thornley** *Durham, England* U.K.
146 E5 **Thornton** *Fife, Scotland* U.K.
149 G4 **Thornton** *Lancashire, England* U.K.
226 C3 **Thornton** *WI* U.S.A.
149 I3 **Thornton Dale** *North Yorkshire, England* U.K.
235 E1 **Thornwood** *NY* U.S.A.
227 H4 **Thorold** *Ont.* Can.
226 B3 **Thorp** *WI* U.S.A.
81 D4 **Thorpe** *South I.* N.Z.
151 I3 **Thorpe-le-Soken** *Essex, England* U.K.
151 I2 **Thorpe Market** *Norfolk, England* U.K.
151 I2 **Thorpeness** *Suffolk, England* U.K.
151 I2 **Thorpe St Andrew** *Norfolk, England* U.K.
222 H4 **Thorsby** *Alta* Can.
Thorshavn Faroe Is *see* **Tórshavn**
Thorshavnfjella *reg.* Antarctica *see* **Thorshavnheiane**
263 B2 **Thorshavnheiane** *reg.* Antarctica
140 □C2 **Thorvaldsfell (Þorvaldsfell)** *vol.* Iceland
215 F4 **Thota-ea-Moli** Lesotho
159 F4 **Thouarcé** France
158 E4 **Thouaré-sur-Loire** France
162 B2 **Thouars** France
117 H4 **Thoubal** *Manipur* India
162 B1 **Thouet** *r.* France
86 C4 **Thouin, Cape** *pt W.A.* Austr.
156 C3 **Thourotte** France
Thourout Belgium *see* **Torhout**
227 I3 **Thousand Islands** Can./U.S.A.
241 L2 **Thousand Lake Mountain** *UT* U.S.A.
240 H4 **Thousand Oaks** *CA* U.S.A.
241 I5 **Thousand Palms** *CA* U.S.A.
232 B6 **Thousandsticks** *KY* U.S.A.
198 D1 **Thrakiko Pelagos** *sea* Greece
151 G2 **Thrapston** *Northamptonshire, England* U.K.
83 G4 **Thredbo** *N.S.W.* Austr.
234 D2 **Three Bridges** *NJ* U.S.A.
238 E2 **Three Forks** *MT* U.S.A.
108 D2 **Three Gorges Project** *resr* China
83 F5 **Three Hummock Island** *Tas.* Austr.
80 D1 **Three Kings Islands** *North I.* N.Z.
226 C3 **Three Lakes** *WI* U.S.A.
226 D5 **Three Oaks** *MI* U.S.A.
241 L5 **Three Points** *AZ* U.S.A.
240 H3 **Three Rivers** *CA* U.S.A.
226 E5 **Three Rivers** *MI* U.S.A.
237 D6 **Three Rivers** *TX* U.S.A.
214 D4 **Three Sisters** S. Africa
238 B2 **Three Sisters** *mt. OR* U.S.A.
78 □6 **Three Sisters Islands** Solomon Is
87 B6 **Three Springs** *W.A.* Austr.
149 G3 **Threlkeld** *Cumbria, England* U.K.
149 G3 **Threshfield** *North Yorkshire, England* U.K.
Thrissur *Kerala* India *see* **Trichur**
237 D5 **Throckmorton** *TX* U.S.A.
234 C1 **Throop** *PA* U.S.A.
149 H2 **Thropton** *Northumberland, England* U.K.
87 E5 **Throssell, Lake** *salt flat W.A.* Austr.
86 D4 **Throssel Range** *hills W.A.* Austr.
146 E3 **Thrumster** *Highland, Scotland* U.K.
150 E3 **Thrupp** *Gloucestershire, England* U.K.
149 H4 **Thrybergh** *South Yorkshire, England* U.K.
97 D5 **Thu Dâu Môt** Vietnam
83 G3 **Thuddungra** *N.S.W.* Austr.
163 E6 **Thuès-entre-Valls** France
161 C4 **Thueyts** France
165 D4 **Thuin** Belgium
169 C3 **Thuine** Ger.
163 E6 **Thuir** France
128 D2 **Thulaythawāt Gharbī, Jabal** *hill* Syria
169 E5 **Thulba** *r.* Ger.
213 F4 **Thuli** *r.* Zimbabwe
Thulusdhoo *N. Male* Maldives *see* **Thulusdhu**
113 □1 **Thulusdhu** *N. Male* Maldives
171 D5 **Thum** Ger.
190 C2 **Thun** Switz.
85 E5 **Thunda** *Qld* Austr.
87 C6 **Thundelarra** *W.A.* Austr.
224 B3 **Thunder Bay** *Ont.* Can.
224 B3 **Thunder Bay** *b. Ont.* Can.
227 F3 **Thunder Bay** *b. MI* U.S.A.
223 J5 **Thunder Creek** *r. Sask.* Can.
246 B3 **Thunder Knoll** *sea feature* Caribbean Sea
151 H3 **Thundersley** *Essex, England* U.K.
190 C2 **Thuner See** *l.* Switz.
172 D2 **Thüngen** Ger.
172 D2 **Thüngersheim** Ger.
97 B5 **Thung Song** Thai.
97 B6 **Thung Wa** Thai.
157 H4 **Thur** *r.* France
190 D1 **Thur** *r.* Switz.
80 E4 **Thuraua** *North I.* N.Z.
149 H4 **Thurcroft** *South Yorkshire, England* U.K.
159 G5 **Thuré** France
160 B3 **Thuret** France
160 D2 **Thurey** France
190 E1 **Thurgau** *canton* Switz.
178 A3 **Thüringen** Austria
169 F4 **Thüringen** *land* Ger.
171 C4 **Thüringer Becken** *reg.* Ger.
169 F5 **Thüringer Wald** *mts* Ger.
Thuringia *land* Ger. *see* **Thüringen**
Thuringian Forest *mts* Ger. *see* **Thüringer Wald**
160 C3 **Thurins** France
170 D2 **Thürkow** Ger.
151 G2 **Thurlby** *Lincolnshire, England* U.K.
147 D4 **Thurles** Rep. of Ireland
171 D5 **Thurm** Ger.
173 H3 **Thurmansbang** Ger.
232 E5 **Thurmont** *MD* U.S.A.
171 C5 **Thurnau** Ger.
149 H4 **Thurnscoe** *South Yorkshire, England* U.K.
151 H3 **Thurrock** *admin. div. England* U.K.
149 F3 **Thursby** *Cumbria, England* U.K.
85 E1 **Thursday Island** *Qld* Austr.
233 F2 **Thurso** *Que.* Can.
146 E3 **Thurso** *Highland, Scotland* U.K.
146 E3 **Thurso** *r. Scotland* U.K.
151 H2 **Thurston** *Suffolk, England* U.K.
262 R2 **Thurston Island** Antarctica
Thurston Peninsula *i.* Antarctica *see* **Thurston Island**
151 I2 **Thurton** *Norfolk, England* U.K.
159 F3 **Thury-Harcourt** France
190 D1 **Thusis** Switz.
169 E3 **Thüster Berg** *hill* Ger.
160 D3 **Thusy** France
149 G3 **Thwaite** *North Yorkshire, England* U.K.
198 B2 **Thyamis** *r.* Greece
Thyatira Turkey *see* **Akhisar**
142 C3 **Thyborøn** Denmark
160 E2 **Thyez** France
85 E5 **Thylungra** *Qld* Austr.
211 B8 **Thyolo** Malawi
206 E4 **Thyou** *Boulkiemde* Burkina
Thyou *Yatenga* Burkina *see* **Tiou**
173 H3 **Thyrnau** Ger.
Thysville Dem. Rep. Congo *see* **Mbanza-Ngungu**
122 D5 **Tiāb** Iran
252 C4 **Tiahuanaco** Bol.
192 B4 **Tiana** *Sardegna* Italy
106 C3 **Tiancang** *Gansu* China
109 F1 **Tianchang** *Anhui* China
Tiancheng *Hubei* China *see* **Chongyang**
Tianchi *Sichuan* China *see* **Lezhi**
108 C4 **Tiandeng** *Guangxi* China
Tiandiba *Sichuan* China *see* **Jinyang**
108 C4 **Tiandong** *Guangxi* China
108 C3 **Tian'e** *Guangxi* China
129 D2 **T'ianet'i** Georgia
109 F2 **Tianfanjie** *Jiangxi* China
254 E2 **Tianguá** Brazil
107 H4 **Tianjin** *Tianjin* China
107 H4 **Tianjin** *mun.* China
106 C4 **Tianjun** *Qinghai* China
108 C3 **Tianlin** *Guangxi* China
109 E2 **Tianmen** *Hubei* China
100 D4 **Tianqiaoling** *Jilin* China
108 B2 **Tianquan** *Sichuan* China
107 I3 **Tianshan** *Nei Mongol* China
Tian Shan *mts* China/Kyrg. *see* **Tien Shan**
101 C4 **Tianshifu** *Liaoning* China
106 E5 **Tianshui** *Gansu* China
110 F3 **Tianshuijing** *Gansu* China
109 F2 **Tiantai** *Zhejiang* China
107 H3 **Tiantaiyong** *Nei Mongol* China
Tiantang *Anhui* China *see* **Yuexi**
108 C4 **Tianyang** *Guangxi* China
Tianyi *Nei Mongol* China *see* **Ningcheng**
Tianzhen *Shandong* China *see* **Gaoqing**
107 G3 **Tianzhen** *Shanxi* China
Tianzhou *Guangxi* China *see* **Tianyang**
106 D4 **Tianzhu** *Gansu* China
108 D3 **Tianzhu** *Guizhou* China
205 F2 **Tiaret** Alg.
85 H5 **Tiaro** *Qld* Austr.
216 □3c **Tías** *Lanzarote* Canary Is
206 D5 **Tiassalé** Côte d'Ivoire
256 B6 **Tibagi** Brazil
256 B5 **Tibagi** *r.* Brazil
Tibaji *r.* Brazil *see* **Tibagi**
127 F4 **Tibal, Wādī** *watercourse* Iraq
250 C3 **Tibaná** Col.
207 I5 **Tibati** Cameroon
123 G4 **Tibba** Pak.
146 E5 **Tibbermore** *Perth and Kinross, Scotland* U.K.
206 C4 **Tibé, Pic de** *mt.* Guinea
Tiber *r.* Italy *see* **Tevere**
Tiberias Israel *see* **Teverya**
128 B3 **Tiberias, Lake** Israel
202 C4 **Tibesti** *mts* Chad
Tibet, Plateau of *Xizang* China *see* **Qing Zang Gaoyuan**
187 C6 **Tibi** Spain
207 G3 **Tibiri** Niger
197 G2 **Țibleș, Vârful** *mt.* Romania
177 J4 **Tiboldaróc** Hungary
83 E2 **Tibooburra** *N.S.W.* Austr.
177 L4 **Tiborszállás** Hungary
117 E3 **Tibrikot** Nepal
143 F2 **Tibro** Sweden
149 H4 **Tibshelf** *Derbyshire, England* U.K.
Tibur Italy *see* **Tivoli**
242 B2 **Tiburón, Isla** *i.* Mex.
151 H3 **Ticehurst** *East Sussex, England* U.K.
197 H4 **Ticha** *r.* Bulg.
197 F4 **Tichak** *mt.* Bulg.
Tichau Pol. *see* **Tychy**
227 I3 **Tichborne** *Ont.* Can.
225 F3 **Tichégami** *r. Que.* Can.
206 C2 **Tichît** Maur.
190 E3 **Ticino** *r.* Italy/Switz.
190 D2 **Ticino** *canton* Switz.
Ticinum Italy *see* **Pavia**
149 H4 **Tickhill** *South Yorkshire, England* U.K.
197 F3 **Ticleni** Romania
233 G3 **Ticonderoga** *NY* U.S.A.
243 H4 **Ticul** Mex.
Ticumbia *i.* Fiji *see* **Cikobia**
143 E2 **Tidaholm** Sweden
143 F2 **Tidan** Sweden
143 E2 **Tidan** *r.* Sweden
168 F3 **Tiddische** Ger.
150 E3 **Tidenham** *Gloucestershire, England* U.K.
149 H4 **Tideswell** *Derbyshire, England* U.K.
205 F4 **Tidikelt, Plaine du** *plain* Alg.
234 D2 **Tidioute** *PA* U.S.A.
206 C2 **Tidjikja** Maur.
190 E3 **Tidone** *r.* Italy
163 A6 **Tiebas** Spain
206 D5 **Tiébissou** Côte d'Ivoire
183 E3 **Tiedra** Spain
107 I3 **Tiefa** *Liaoning* China
173 G2 **Tiefenbach** *Bayern* Ger.
173 G3 **Tiefenbach** *Bayern* Ger.
173 H3 **Tiefenbach** *Bayern* Ger.
172 C3 **Tiefenbronn** Ger.
190 E2 **Tiefencastel** Switz.
170 E3 **Tiefensee** Ger.
164 E3 **Tiel** Neth.
206 B3 **Tiel** Senegal
165 D3 **Tielen** Belgium
100 C3 **Tieli** *Heilong.* China
107 I3 **Tieling** *Liaoning* China
165 C4 **Tielt** Belgium
206 D4 **Tiémé** Côte d'Ivoire
165 D4 **Tienen** Belgium
172 C4 **Tiengen** Ger.
110 B3 **Tien Shan** *mts* China/Kyrg.
Tien Shan Oblast *admin. div.* Kyrg. *see* **Naryn**
Tientsin *Tianjin* China *see* **Tianjin**
Tientsin *mun.* China *see* **Tianjin**
191 F4 **Tiepido** *r.* Italy
159 F4 **Tiercé** France
215 F3 **Tierfontein** S. Africa
183 I3 **Tierga** Spain
143 G1 **Tierp** Sweden
258 C2 **Tierra Amarilla** Chile
239 F4 **Tierra Amarilla** *NM* U.S.A.
245 F4 **Tierra Blanca** Mex.
245 F5 **Tierra Colorada** Mex.
259 D9 **Tierra del Fuego** *prov.* Arg.
259 C9 **Tierra del Fuego, Isla Grande de** *i.* Arg./Chile
184 C3 **Tierra Llana de Huelva** *plain* Spain
183 I4 **Tierzo** Spain
185 E3 **Tiesa** *hill* Spain
179 G4 **Tieschen** Austria
182 E5 **Tiétar** *r.* Spain
183 E4 **Tiétar, Valle de** *val.* Spain
256 C5 **Tietê** Brazil
256 B4 **Tietê** *r.* Brazil
164 E1 **Tietjerk** Neth.
82 C1 **Tieyon** *S.A.* Austr.
159 E4 **Tiffauges** France
232 B4 **Tiffin** *OH* U.S.A.
Tiflis Georgia *see* **T'bilisi**
231 D6 **Tifton** *GA* U.S.A.
78 □5 **Tiga** *i. Î. Loyauté* New Caledonia
215 F2 **Tigane** S. Africa
197 G4 **Tigănești** Romania
94 C3 **Tigapuluh, Pegunungan** *mts* Indon.
136 E5 **Tigheciului, Dealurile** *hills* Moldova
136 E4 **Tighina** Moldova
136 D4 **Tighira** Moldova
146 C6 **Tighnabruaich** *Argyll and Bute, Scotland* U.K.
121 J2 **Tigiretskiy Khrebet** *mts* Kazakh./Rus. Fed.
117 F5 **Tigiria** *Orissa* India
191 F3 **Tignale** Italy
207 I5 **Tignère** Cameroon
160 E3 **Tignes** France
225 H4 **Tignish** *P.E.I.* Can.
139 H2 **Tigoda** *r.* Rus. Fed.
Tigranocerta Turkey *see* **Siirt**
210 C1 **Tigray** *admin. reg.* Eth.
261 H4 **Tigre** Arg.
250 C6 **Tigre** *r.* Ecuador/Peru
245 F2 **Tigre** *r.* Mex.
245 E2 **Tigre, Cerro del** *mt.* Mex.
260 C2 **Tigre, Sierra** *mts* Arg.
127 F3 **Tigris** *r.* Turkey *alt.* **Dicle (Turkey)**, *alt.* **Dijlah, Nahr (Iraq/Syria)**
206 B2 **Tiguent** Maur.
204 C4 **Tiguesmat** *hills* Maur.
207 G2 **Tiguidit, Falaise de** *esc.* Niger
156 C5 **Tigy** France
203 G2 **Tîh, Gebel el** *plat.* Egypt
124 C4 **Tihāmah** *reg.* Saudi Arabia
177 G5 **Tihany** Hungary
252 D3 **Tijamuchi** *r.* Bol.
116 D4 **Tijara** *Rajasthan* India
216 □3d **Tijarafe** *La Palma* Canary Is
164 E1 **Tijnje** Neth.
185 H3 **Tíjola** Spain
242 A1 **Tijuana** Mex.
255 C8 **Tijucas** Brazil
256 B3 **Tijuco** *r.* Brazil
Tika *i. Î. Loyauté* New Caledonia *see* **Tiga**
243 H5 **Tikal** *tourist site* Guat.
116 D4 **Tikamgarh** *Madh. Prad.* India
110 D3 **Tikanlik** *Xinjiang* China
137 J2 **Tikhaya Sosna** *r.* Rus. Fed.
Tikhero Greece *see* **Tykhero**
139 L2 **Tikhmenevo** Rus. Fed.
139 K4 **Tikhonova Pustyn'** Rus. Fed.
135 H7 **Tikhoretsk** Rus. Fed.
139 I2 **Tikhvin** Rus. Fed.
139 I2 **Tikhvinka** *r.* Rus. Fed.
139 I2 **Tikhvinskaya Gryada** *ridge* Rus. Fed.
267 K7 **Tiki Basin** *sea feature* Pacific Ocean
80 G2 **Tikitiki** *North I.* N.Z.
140 N3 **Tikkakoski** Fin.
138 E1 **Tikkurila** Fin.
80 F3 **Tikokino** *North I.* N.Z.
77 G3 **Tikopia** *i.* Solomon Is
127 F4 **Tikrīt** Iraq
131 N2 **Tiksi** Rus. Fed.
Tikumbia *i.* Fiji *see* **Cikobia**
215 E2 **Tikwana** S. Africa
116 E3 **Tila** *r.* Nepal
122 C2 **Tilavar** Iran
128 C1 **Tilbeşar Ovasi** *plain* Turkey
85 F5 **Tilbooroo** *Qld* Austr.
164 E3 **Tilburg** Neth.
227 F4 **Tilbury** *Ont.* Can.
151 H3 **Tilbury** *Thurrock, England* U.K.
258 D1 **Tilcara** Arg.
82 E2 **Tilcha** *S.A.* Austr.
160 D1 **Til-Châtel** France
237 D6 **Tilden** *TX* U.S.A.
197 F2 **Tileagd** Romania
151 F3 **Tilehurst** *Reading, England* U.K.
207 G3 **Tilemsès** Niger
207 F2 **Tilemsi, Vallée du** *watercourse* Mali
233 E5 **Tilghman** *MD* U.S.A.
163 B5 **Tilh** France
116 D4 **Tilhar** *Uttar Prad.* India
Tiligulo-Berezanka Ukr. *see* **Berezanka**
Tilimsen Alg. *see* **Tlemcen**
260 E3 **Tilisarao** Arg.
149 G2 **Till** *r. England* U.K.
207 F3 **Tillabéri** Niger
207 F3 **Tillabéri** *dept* Niger
163 C5 **Tillac** France
238 B2 **Tillamook** *OR* U.S.A.
160 D1 **Tille** *r.* France
171 C4 **Tilleda (Kyffhäuser)** Ger.
223 I5 **Tilley** *Alta* Can.
207 G2 **Tillia** Niger
146 E5 **Tillicoultry** *Clackmannanshire, Scotland* U.K.
156 B4 **Tillières-sur-Avre** France
156 E3 **Tilloy-et-Bellay** France
224 D5 **Tillsonburg** *Ont.* Can.
146 F4 **Tillyfourie** *Aberdeenshire, Scotland* U.K.
159 F2 **Tilly-sur-Seulles** France
Tilogne Senegal *see* **Thilogne**
199 E3 **Tilos** *i.* Greece
83 F2 **Tilpa** *N.S.W.* Austr.
138 F3 **Tilsa** *r.* Latvia
Tilsit *Kaliningradskaya Oblast'* Rus. Fed. *see* **Sovetsk**
149 G4 **Tilston** *Cheshire, England* U.K.
146 E5 **Tilt** *r. Scotland* U.K.
260 B3 **Tiltil** Chile
233 H3 **Tilton** *NH* U.S.A.
93 B3 **Tilu, Bukit** *mt.* Indon.
135 G6 **Tim** Rus. Fed.
137 I1 **Tim** *r.* Rus. Fed.
203 F3 **Tima** Egypt
148 B5 **Timahoe** Rep. of Ireland
253 F5 **Timane** *r.* Para.
216 □3c **Timanfaya** *hill Lanzarote* Canary Is
134 J2 **Timanskiy Kryazh** *ridge* Rus. Fed.
127 F3 **Timar** Turkey
81 C6 **Timaru** *South I.* N.Z.
120 B1 **Timashevo** Rus. Fed.
135 G7 **Timashevsk** Rus. Fed.
Timashevskaya Rus. Fed. *see* **Timashevsk**
191 I2 **Timau** Italy
Timbákion *Kriti* Greece *see* **Tympaki**
254 G3 **Timbaúba** Brazil
206 C2 **Timbedgha** Maur.
84 B2 **Timber Creek** *N.T.* Austr.
236 C2 **Timber Lake** *SD* U.S.A.
241 I3 **Timber Mountain** *NV* U.S.A.
232 D5 **Timberville** *VA* U.S.A.
250 B4 **Timbiquí** Col.
206 C4 **Timbo** Guinea
83 E4 **Timboon** *Vic.* Austr.
Timbuktu Mali *see* **Tombouctou**
179 E2 **Timelkam** Austria
206 E2 **Timétrine** *reg.* Mali
205 G2 **Timgad** *tourist site* Alg.
205 F3 **Timimoun** Alg.
121 F1 **Timiryazev** Kazakh.
121 F1 **Timiryazevo** Kazakh.
177 K6 **Timiș** *county* Romania
197 E3 **Timiș** *r.* Romania
196 E3 **Timișoara** Romania
196 E3 **Timișului, Câmpia** *plain* Romania
168 F2 **Timmendorfer Strand** Ger.
224 D3 **Timmins** *Ont.* Can.
226 B3 **Timms Hill** *hill WI* U.S.A.
Timoé *atoll Arch. des Tuamotu* Fr. Polynesia *see* **Temoe**
197 F3 **Timok** *r.* Yugo.
139 K2 **Timokhino** Rus. Fed.
147 C5 **Timoleague** Rep. of Ireland
254 E3 **Timon** Brazil
191 G2 **Timone** *r.* Italy
234 B3 **Timonium** *MD* U.S.A.
93 C5 **Timor** *i.* Indon.
76 C3 **Timor Sea** Austr./Indon.
Timor Timur *terr.* Asia *see* **East Timor**
257 F3 **Timóteo** Brazil
205 E3 **Timoudi** Alg.
87 D5 **Timperley Range** *hills W.A.* Austr.
141 L3 **Timrå** Sweden
151 E3 **Timsbury** *Bath and North East Somerset, England* U.K.
146 A3 **Timsgearraidh** *Western Isles, Scotland* U.K.
134 K3 **Timshor** *r.* Rus. Fed.
Timur *Yuzhnyy Kazakhstan* Kazakh. *see* **Temur**
116 D5 **Timurni Muafi** *Madh. Prad.* India
124 C2 **Tin, Jabal** *hill* Saudi Arabia
191 G2 **Tina** *r.* Italy
215 G4 **Tina** *r.* S. Africa
128 A4 **Tina, Khalîg el** *b.* Egypt
148 C5 **Tinahely** Rep. of Ireland
183 H4 **Tinajas** Spain
216 □3c **Tinajo** *Lanzarote* Canary Is
182 C5 **Tinalhas** Port.
177 K5 **Tinca** Romania
85 H5 **Tin Can Bay** *Qld* Austr.
159 F3 **Tinchebray** France
114 C3 **Tindivanam** *Tamil Nadu* India
204 C4 **Tindouf** Alg.
144 D1 **Tindur** *hill* Faroe Is
161 F5 **Tinée** *r.* France
182 D1 **Tineo** Spain
204 D3 **Tinerhir** Morocco
151 F3 **Tingewick** *Buckinghamshire, England* U.K.
94 D2 **Tinggi** *i.* Malaysia
206 C4 **Tingi Mountains** Sierra Leone
Tingis Morocco *see* **Tanger**
109 F3 **Ting Jiang** *r.* China
142 C4 **Tinglev** Denmark
Tingréla Côte d'Ivoire *see* **Tengréla**
143 F3 **Tingsryd** Sweden
143 H3 **Tingstäde** *Gotland* Sweden
244 C4 **Tinguindín** Mex.
260 B4 **Tinguiririca** Chile
260 B4 **Tinguiririca, Volcán** *vol.* Chile
142 B2 **Tingvatn** Norway
140 J3 **Tingvoll** Norway
146 E2 **Tingwall** *Orkney, Scotland* U.K.
146 □G1 **Tingwall** *Shetland, Scotland* U.K.
Tingzhou *Fujian* China *see* **Changting**
254 F5 **Tinharé, Ilha de** *i.* Brazil
182 C3 **Tinhela** *r.* Port.
91 K4 **Tinian** *i.* N. Mariana Is
Tini Heke *is* N.Z. *see* **Snares Islands**
80 F3 **Tiniroto** *North I.* N.Z.
188 G3 **Tinja** *r.* Bos.-Herz.
95 F1 **Tinjar** *r. Sarawak* Malaysia
206 C4 **Tinkisso** *r.* Guinea
137 G3 **Tin'ky** Ukr.
81 D5 **Tinline, Mount** *South I.* N.Z.
205 H5 **Ti-n-Merzouga** *des.* Alg.
142 C2 **Tinne** *r.* Norway
Tinnelvelly *Tamil Nadu* India *see* **Tirunelveli**
177 H4 **Tinnye** Hungary
258 D3 **Tinogasta** Arg.
198 D3 **Tinos** *Notio Aigaio* Greece
198 D3 **Tinos** *i.* Greece
185 F3 **Tiñosa** *mt.* Spain
183 F4 **Tiñosillos** Spain
156 D3 **Tinqueux** France
205 G3 **Tinrhert, Plateau du** Alg.
117 H4 **Tinsukia** *Assam* India
222 E4 **Tintagel** *B.C.* Can.
150 C4 **Tintagel** *Cornwall, England* U.K.
206 C2 **Țînțâne** Maur.
205 F4 **Tintejert, Adrar** *mt.* Alg.
158 E3 **Tinténiac** France
150 E3 **Tintern Parva** *Monmouthshire, Wales* U.K.
165 E5 **Tintigny** Belgium
258 E2 **Tintina** Arg.
82 E3 **Tintinara** *S.A.* Austr.
184 D3 **Tinto** *r.* Spain
149 F2 **Tinto** *hill Scotland* U.K.
81 F4 **Tinui** *North I.* N.Z.
236 C1 **Tioga** *ND* U.S.A.
234 B3 **Tioga** *PA* U.S.A.
232 E3 **Tioga** *r. PA* U.S.A.
234 A1 **Tioga County** *county PA* U.S.A.
94 D2 **Tioman** *i.* Malaysia
227 I1 **Tionaga** *Ont.* Can.
191 G3 **Tione** *r.* Italy
191 F2 **Tione di Trento** Italy
232 D4 **Tionesta** *PA* U.S.A.
206 C3 **Tioribougou** Mali
206 E3 **Tiou** Burkina
233 F3 **Tioughnioga** *r. NY* U.S.A.
205 F1 **Tipasa** Alg.
242 □16 **Tipitapa** Nic.
226 C3 **Tipler** *WI* U.S.A.
230 C3 **Tippecanoe** *r. IN* U.S.A.
147 C4 **Tipperary** Rep. of Ireland
147 D4 **Tipperary** *county* Rep. of Ireland
240 H3 **Tipton** *CA* U.S.A.
226 A5 **Tipton** *IA* U.S.A.
236 E4 **Tipton** *MO* U.S.A.
241 J4 **Tipton, Mount** *AZ* U.S.A.
237 F4 **Tiptonville** *TN* U.S.A.
224 C3 **Tip Top Hill** *hill Ont.* Can.
151 H3 **Tiptree** *Essex, England* U.K.
114 C3 **Tiptur** *Karnataka* India
252 C3 **Tipuani** Bol.
250 D4 **Tiquié** *r.* Brazil
243 H6 **Tiquisate** Guat.
254 D3 **Tiracambu, Serra do** *hills* Brazil
122 B3 **Tīrān** Iran
Tirana Albania *see* **Tiranë**
196 D5 **Tiranë** Albania
161 B3 **Tiranges** France
190 F2 **Tirano** Italy
117 H4 **Tirap** *Arun. Prad.* India
124 C2 **Tirāq, Jibāl al** *hills* Saudi Arabia
82 D1 **Tirari Desert** *S.A.* Austr.
136 E4 **Tiraspol** Moldova
80 E2 **Tirau** *North I.* N.Z.
80 F4 **Tiraumea** *North I.* N.Z.
199 E2 **Tire** Turkey
177 L? **Tiream** Romania
146 B5 **Tiree** *i. Scotland* U.K.
146 B3 **Tirga Mor** *hill Scotland* U.K.
183 H2 **Tirgo** Spain
Tîrgovişte Romania *see* **Târgovişte**
Tîrgu Bujor Romania *see* **Târgu Bujor**
Tîrgu Cărbuneşti Romania *see* **Târgu Cărbuneşti**
Tîrgu Frumos Romania *see* **Târgu Frumos**
Tîrgu Jiu Romania *see* **Târgu Jiu**
Tîrgu Lăpuş Romania *see* **Târgu Lăpuş**
Tîrgu Mureş Romania *see* **Târgu Mureş**
Tîrgu Neamţ Romania *see* **Târgu Neamţ**
Tîrgu Ocna Romania *see* **Târgu Ocna**
Tîrgu Secuiesc Romania *see* **Târgu Secuiesc**
123 G2 **Tirich Mir** *mt.* Pak.
185 H2 **Tiriez** Spain
186 D4 **Tirig** Spain
195 F4 **Tiriolo** Italy
204 C5 **Tiris Zemmour** *admin. reg.* Maur.
138 D3 **Tirkšliai** Lith.
Tirlemont Belgium *see* **Tienen**
120 D1 **Tirlyanskiy** Rus. Fed.
114 C2 **Tirna** *r.* India
Tîrnăveni Romania *see* **Târnăveni**
Tírnavos Greece *see* **Tyrnavos**
Tîrnova Romania *see* **Târnova**
185 E2 **Tiro** *hill* Spain
116 D5 **Tirodi** *Madh. Prad.* India
178 C3 **Tirol** *land* Austria
183 H2 **Tirón** *r.* Spain
80 E2 **Tironia** *North I.* N.Z.
257 E3 **Tiros** Brazil
171 D5 **Tirpersdorf** Ger.
190 F5 **Tirrenia** Italy
Tirreno, Mare *sea* France/Italy *see* **Tyrrhenian Sea**
173 G2 **Tirschenreuth** Ger.
192 A5 **Tirso** *r. Sardegna* Italy
142 D3 **Tirstrup** Denmark
185 F2 **Tirteafuera** Spain
185 F2 **Tirteafuera** *r.* Spain
114 B3 **Tirthahalli** *Karnataka* India
114 C4 **Tiruchchendur** *Tamil Nadu* India
114 C4 **Tiruchchirappalli** *Tamil Nadu* India
114 C4 **Tiruchengodu** *Tamil Nadu* India
114 C4 **Tirukkoyilur** *Tamil Nadu* India
114 C4 **Tirumangalam** *Tamil Nadu* India
114 C4 **Tirunelveli** *Tamil Nadu* India
252 B1 **Tiruntán** Peru
114 C3 **Tirupati** *Andhra Prad.* India
114 C3 **Tiruppattur** *Tamil Nadu* India
114 C4 **Tiruppattur** *Tamil Nadu* India
114 C4 **Tiruppur** *Tamil Nadu* India
114 C3 **Tiruttani** *Andhra Prad.* India
114 C4 **Tiruturaippundi** *Tamil Nadu* India
114 C3 **Tiruvallur** *Tamil Nadu* India
114 C3 **Tiruvannamalai** *Tamil Nadu* India
114 C3 **Tiruvettipuram** *Tamil Nadu* India
114 D3 **Tiruvottiyur** *Tamil Nadu* India
86 E4 **Tiru Well** *W.A.* Austr.
198 G3 **Tiryns** *tourist site* Greece
138 F3 **Tirza** *r.* Latvia
197 E4 **Tisa** *r.* Yugo. *alt.* **Tisza (Hungary)**, *alt.* **Tysa (Ukraine)**
114 C4 **Tisaiyanvilai** *Tamil Nadu* India
197 H3 **Tisău** Romania
150 E3 **Tisbury** *Wiltshire, England* U.K.
223 J4 **Tisdale** *Sask.* Can.
237 D5 **Tishomingo** *OK* U.S.A.
171 F5 **Tišice** Czech Rep.
205 H5 **Tiska, Mont** *mt.* Alg.
176 F2 **Tišnov** Czech Rep.
177 I3 **Tisovec** Slovakia
205 F2 **Tissemsilt** Alg.
192 A4 **Tissi** *Sardegna* Italy
117 G4 **Tista** *r.* India
177 J5 **Tisza** *r.* Hungary *alt.* **Tisa (Yugoslavia)**, *alt.* **Tysa (Ukraine)**
177 I5 **Tiszaalpár** Hungary
177 L3 **Tiszabecs** Hungary
177 L3 **Tiszabezdéd** Hungary
177 J4 **Tiszabő** Hungary
177 J5 **Tiszabura** Hungary
177 J4 **Tiszacsege** Hungary
177 K4 **Tiszaderzs** Hungary
177 K3 **Tiszadob** Hungary
177 K3 **Tiszaeszlár** Hungary
177 J5 **Tiszaföldvár** Hungary
177 J4 **Tiszafüred** Hungary
177 J4 **Tiszaigar** Hungary
177 J4 **Tiszajenő** Hungary
177 K3 **Tiszakarád** Hungary
177 J5 **Tiszakécske** Hungary
177 L3 **Tiszakerecseny** Hungary
177 J4 **Tiszakeszi** Hungary
177 K3 **Tiszalök** Hungary
177 K3 **Tiszalúc** Hungary
177 K3 **Tiszanagyfalu** Hungary
177 J4 **Tiszanána** Hungary
177 J4 **Tiszaörs** Hungary
177 J4 **Tiszapüspöki** Hungary
177 J4 **Tiszaroff** Hungary
177 J5 **Tiszasas** Hungary
177 L3 **Tiszaszentmárton** Hungary
177 J5 **Tiszasziget** Hungary
177 K3 **Tiszatelek** Hungary
177 J4 **Tiszatenyő** Hungary
177 J5 **Tiszaug** Hungary
177 K4 **Tiszaújváros** Hungary
177 K4 **Tiszavasvári** Hungary
117 H4 **Titabar** *Assam* India
187 B5 **Titaguas** Spain
263 K1 **Titan Dome** *ice feature* Antarctica
206 E3 **Titao** Burkina
198 D2 **Titarisios** *r.* Greece
131 N2 **Tit-Ary** Rus. Fed.
Titawin Morocco *see* **Tétouan**
206 B4 **Tite** Guinea-Bissau
196 E3 **Titel** *Vojvodina, Srbija* Yugo.
193 G3 **Titerno** *r.* Italy
123 H3 **Tithwal** Pak.
252 C3 **Titicaca, Lago** *l.* Bol./Peru
Titicaca, Lake Bol./Peru *see* **Titicaca, Lago**
235 E1 **Titicus** *CT* U.S.A.
172 C4 **Titisee** Ger.
Tititeа *mt. South I.* N.Z. *see* **Aspiring, Mount**
117 E5 **Titlagarh** *Orissa* India
190 D2 **Titlis** *mt.* Switz.
193 H6 **Tito** Italy
Titograd *Crna Gora* Yugo. *see* **Podgorica**
188 E3 **Titova Korenica** Croatia
Titova Mitrovica *Kosovo, Srbija* Yugo. *see* **Kosovska Mitrovica**
188 F3 **Titov Drvar** Bos.-Herz.
140 O1 **Titovka** *r.* Rus. Fed.
Titovo Užice *Srbija* Yugo. *see* **Užice**
Titovo Velenje Slovenia *see* **Velenje**
Titov Veles Macedonia *see* **Veles**
Titov Vrbas *Vojvodina, Srbija* Yugo. *see* **Vrbas**
84 C4 **Ti Tree** *N.T.* Austr.
227 F4 **Tittabawassee** *r. MI* U.S.A.
173 F3 **Titting** Ger.
173 H3 **Tittling** Ger.
173 G3 **Tittmoning** Ger.
197 G3 **Titu** Romania
183 G4 **Titulcia** Spain
231 D6 **Titusville** *FL* U.S.A.
232 D4 **Titusville** *PA* U.S.A.
146 B3 **Tiumpan Head** *hd Scotland* U.K.
116 C4 **Tivari** *Rajasthan* India
196 D4 **Tivat** *Crna Gora* Yugo.
186 D4 **Tivenys** Spain
227 G3 **Tiverton** *Ont.* Can.
150 D4 **Tiverton** *Devon, England* U.K.
Tivisa Spain *see* **Tivissa**
186 D3 **Tivissa** Spain
193 E3 **Tivoli** Italy
125 G3 **Tīwī** Oman
243 H4 **Tixkokob** Mex.
245 E5 **Tixtla** Mex.
210 C2 **Tiya** *tourist site* Eth.
244 C3 **Tizapán el Alto** Mex.
243 H4 **Tizimín** Mex.
205 G1 **Tizi Ouzou** Alg.
111 B4 **Tiznap He** *r.* China
204 C3 **Tiznit** Morocco
192 A3 **Tizzano** *Corse* France
143 F2 **Tjällmo** Sweden
140 L2 **Tjåmotis** Sweden
215 H1 **Tjaneni** Swaziland
140 L2 **Tjappsåive** Sweden
140 K2 **Tjärmyrberget** Sweden
140 M2 **Tjautas** Sweden
144 J1 **Tjeldstø** Norway
Tjirebon *Jawa Barat* Indon. *see* **Cirebon**
Tjolotjo Zimbabwe *see* **Tsholotsho**
142 D2 **Tjøme** Norway
142 D2 **Tjörn** *i.* Sweden
140 □C2 **Tjörnes** *pen.* Iceland
Tjumen' Rus. Fed. *see* **Tyumen'**
Tkibuli Georgia *see* **Tqibuli**
Tkvarcheli Georgia *see* **Tqvarch'eli**

245 F5	Tlacolula Mex.
245 G4	Tlacotalpán Mex.
245 G4	Tlacotenco Mex.
244 D5	Tlacotepec, Cerro mt. Mex.
245 E4	Tlahuapan Mex.
244 C3	Tlajomulco Mex.
245 F4	Tlalchichuca Mex.
245 E4	Tlalixcoyan Mex.
245 E4	Tlalmanalco Mex.
245 E4	Tlalnepantla Mex.
245 E4	Tlalpan Mex.
244 D4	Tlalpujahua Mex.
244 C3	Tlaltenango de Sánchez Román Mex.
245 E5	Tlapa Mex.
245 E4	Tlapacoyan Mex.
245 E4	Tlapanaloa r. Mex.
245 E4	Tlapehuala Mex.
244 C3	Tlaquepaque Mex.
245 E4	Tlaxcala Mex.
245 E4	Tlaxcala state Mex.
245 F5	Tlaxiaco Mex.
222 D4	Tlell B.C. Can.
205 E2	Tlemcen Alg.
174 G2	Tłeń Pol.
180 D5	Tleta Rissana Morocco
215 F2	Tlhabologang S. Africa
215 D3	Tlhakalatlou S. Africa
214 E2	Tlhakgameng S. Africa
215 G3	Tlholong S. Africa
177 H3	Tlmače Slovakia
212 E5	Tlokweng Botswana
175 H3	Tłuchowo Pol.
173 H2	Tlučná Czech Rep.
136 C3	Tlumach Ukr.
174 F6	Tlumačov Czech Rep.
175 J3	Tłuszcz Pol.
129 E2	Tłyarata Rus. Fed.
137 M5	Tłyustenkhabl' Rus. Fed.
139 J3	T'ma r. Rus. Fed.
204 B3	Tmeïmichât Maur.
97 D5	Tnaôt, Prêk r. Cambodia
136 D2	Tnya r. Ukr.
96 B3	To r. Myanmar
246 D2	Toa r. Cuba
64 C4	Toa Alta Puerto Rico
146 □G2	Toagel Mlungui Liancourt Rocks
247 □1	Toa Baja Puerto Rico
222 E3	Toad r. B.C. Can.
222 E3	Toad River B.C. Can.
177 I4	Tóalmás Hungary
213 □K3	Toamasina Madag.
213 □K3	Toamasina prov. Madag.
147 C5	Toames Rep. of Ireland
241 J1	Toana mts NV U.S.A.
131 C4	Toano Italy
232 E6	Toano VA U.S.A.
232 C6	Toast NC U.S.A.
80 F3	Toatoa North I. N.Z.
260 E5	Toay Arg.
108 A2	Toba Xizang China
169 F6	Toba Ger.
64 C4	Toba Japan
94 B2	Toba, Danau l. Indon.
	Toba, Lake Indon. see
	Toba, Danau
123 F4	Toba and Kakar Ranges mts Pak.
247 □1	Tobago i. Trin. and Tob.
213 F4	Tobane Botswana
185 □2	Tobarra Spain
123 H4	Toba Tek Singh Pak.
167 K3	Tobelbad Austria
147 E2	Tobermore Northern Ireland U.K.
84 D4	Tobermorey N.T. Austr.
85 E5	Tobermory Qld Austr.
224 D4	Tobermory Ont. Can.
146 B5	Tobermory Argyll and Bute, Scotland U.K.
146 C5	Toberonochy Argyll and Bute, Scotland U.K.
91 H6	Tobi i. Palau
254 F4	Tobías Barreto Brazil
88 E4	Tobin, Lake salt flat W.A. Austr.
240 I1	Tobin, Mount NV U.S.A.
225 H4	Tobique r. N.B. Can.
94 D3	Toboali Indon.
120 E1	Tobol Kazakh.
120 H1	Tobol r. Kazakh./Rus. Fed.
130 H4	Tobol'sk Rus. Fed.
78 □6	Tobona Island Solomon Is
92 B4	Toboso Phil.
	Tobruk Libya see Tubruq
234 C1	Tobyhanna PA U.S.A.
	Tobyl Kazakh. see Tobol
	Tobyl r. Kazakh./Rus. Fed. see Tobol
134 J2	Tobysh r. Rus. Fed.
252 A2	Tocache Nuevo Peru
162 D2	Tocane-St-Apre France
254 D3	Tocantinópolis Brazil
251 G6	Tocantins r. Pará Brazil
251 I5	Tocantins r. Brazil
254 C4	Tocantins state Brazil
231 D5	Toccoa GA U.S.A.
131 D2	Tocco da Casauria Italy
190 D3	Toce r. Italy
182 B4	Tocha Port.
123 G3	Tochi r. Pak.
105 F2	Tochigi Japan
105 F2	Tochigi pref. Japan
105 I5	Tochio Japan
142 D2	Töcksfors Sweden
185 □3	Tocón Spain
252 C5	Tocopilla Chile
252 □5	Tocopuri, Cerros de mts Bol./Chile
83 F7	Tocumwal N.S.W. Austr.
175 K3	Toczna r. Pol.
203 G3	Tôd Egypt
222 G5	Tod, Mount B.C. Can.
105 F3	Toda Japan
116 C5	Toda Bhim Rajasthan India
116 C4	Toda Rai Singh Rajasthan India
261 G4	Todd r. N.T. Austr.
84 C3	Todd r. N.T. Austr.
151 G3	Toddington Bedfordshire, England U.K.
151 F3	Toddington Gloucestershire, England U.K.
233 □J1	Todd Mountain hill N.B. Can.
87 C5	Todd Range hills W.A. Austr.
235 E1	Toddville NY U.S.A.
168 F2	Todesfelde Ger.
193 D2	Todi Italy
190 D2	Tödi mt. Switz.
149 G4	Todmorden West Yorkshire, England U.K.
257 G2	Todos os Santos r. Brazil
251 H5	Todos Santos Brazil
252 I5	Todos Santos r. Brazil
254 C4	Todos Santos state Brazil
172 B4	Todtmoos Ger.
172 B4	Todtnau Ger.
146 A4	Toe head hd Scotland U.K.
96 B4	Toe Jaga, Khao hill Thai.
182 C2	Toén Spain
222 H4	Tofield Alta Can.
222 E5	Tofino B.C. Can.
146 □G1	Toft Shetland, Scotland U.K.
146 □G1	Tofte MN U.S.A.
179 L2	Toga i. Tonga
232 D6	Toga VA U.S.A.
78 □6	Toga i. Vanuatu
105 G3	Tōgane Japan
210 D2	Togdheer admin. reg. Somalia
147 E3	Togher Cork Rep. of Ireland
147 D3	Togher Offaly Rep. of Ireland
220 B4	Togiak AK U.S.A.
95 G4	Togian, Kepulauan is Indon.
173 G3	Töging am Inn Ger.
207 F4	Togo country Africa
226 A2	Togo MN U.S.A.
111 K4	Tograsay He r. China
106 B2	Tögrög Mongolia
111 I2	Tögrög Nei Mongol China
149 H2	Togston Northumberland, England U.K.
107 F3	Togtoh Nei Mongol China
130 J4	Toguchin Rus. Fed.
134 J3	Tohana Haryana India
134 M1	Tohatchi NM U.S.A.
95 F2	Tohenbanu r. Sarawak Malaysia
140 O3	Tohmajärvi Fin.
140 N3	Toholampi Fin.

106 E3	Tohom Nei Mongol China
107 F2	Töhöm Mongolia
207 F5	Tohoun Togo
111 L6	Toiba r. Xizang China
141 N3	Toijala Fin.
190 D4	Toirano Italy
141 N3	Toivakka Fin.
240 I2	Toiyabe Range mts NV U.S.A.
	Tojikiston country Asia see Tajikistan
120 C1	Tojohira r. Japan
220 D3	Tok AK U.S.A.
102 K2	Tokachi-gawa r. Japan
104 C3	Tōkai Japan
177 K3	Tokaj Hungary
93 B3	Tokala, Gunung mt. Indon.
105 E1	Tōkamachi Japan
81 B7	Tokanui South I. N.Z.
203 H5	Tokar Sudan
81 C6	Tokarahi South I. N.Z.
135 H6	Tokarevka Rus. Fed.
175 I5	Tokarnia Pol.
102 □1	Tokashiki-jima i. Japan
126 E2	Tokat Turkey
80 D2	Tokatoka North I. N.Z.
137 K2	Tokava r. Ukr.
101 C5	Tŏkch'ŏn N. Korea
	Tokdo i. N. Pacific Ocean see Liancourt Rocks
81 □1	Tokelau terr. S. Pacific Ocean
	T'okhluja Armenia see Drakhtik
	Tokhtamysh Tajik. see Tükhtamish
104 D3	Toki Japan
104 C3	Toki-gawa r. Japan
	Tokkuztara Xinjiang China see
137 H4	Tokmachka r. Ukr.
137 H4	Tokmak Ukr.
	Tokmak Kyrg. see Tokmak
177 H4	Tokod Hungary
80 G3	Tokomaru Bay North I. N.Z.
80 C4	Tokon.ame Japan
80 E3	Tokoroa North I. N.Z.
102 L1	Tokoro-gawa r. Japan
105 F3	Tokorozawa Japan
206 C4	Tokounou Guinea
215 G2	Tokoza S. Africa
	Toksu Xinjiang China see Xinhe
110 E3	Toksun Xinjiang China
	Tok-tō i. N. Pacific Ocean see Liancourt Rocks
121 H4	Toktogul Kyrg.
	Toktogul'skoye Vodokhranilishche resr Kyrg. see Toktogul Suu Saktagychy
121 H4	Toktogul Suu Saktagychy resr Kyrg.
	Tokto-ri i. N. Pacific Ocean see Liancourt Rocks
77 I3	Tokū i. Tonga
102 □1	Tokunoshima Japan
102 □1	Toku-no-shima i. Japan
105 H3	Tokur Rus. Fed.
104 A4	Tokushima Japan
103 G7	Tokushima pref. Japan
103 E6	Tokuyama Japan
105 F3	Tōkyō Japan
105 F3	Tōkyō-wan b. Japan
78 □4a	Tol i. Chuuk Micronesia
80 G3	Tolaga Bay North I. N.Z.
213 □J3	Tôlañaro Madag.
258 D2	Tolar, Cerro mt. Arg.
146 B3	Tolastadh Ùr Western Isles, Scotland U.K.
183 F4	Tolbaños Spain
120 C1	Tolbazy Rus. Fed.
164 F1	Tolbert Neth.
106 A1	Tolbo Mongolia
	Tolbukhin Bulg. see Dobrich
139 M3	Tolbukhino Rus. Fed.
262 T1	Tolchin, Mount Antarctica
177 H5	Tolcsva Hungary
121 H4	Tole Bi Kazakh.
255 B8	Toledo Brazil
183 F5	Toledo Spain
183 F5	Toledo prov. Castilla-La Mancha Spain
236 E3	Toledo IA U.S.A.
230 C5	Toledo OH U.S.A.
232 B4	Toledo OH U.S.A.
238 B2	Toledo OR U.S.A.
183 F5	Toledo, Montes de mts Spain
237 E6	Toledo Bend Reservoir Louisiana/Texas U.S.A.
191 I5	Tolentino Italy
	Toletum Spain see Toledo
192 D2	Tolfa Italy
85 F7	Tolga Qld Austr.
141 J3	Tolga Norway
110 C2	Toli Xinjiang China
213 □I4	Toliara Madag.
213 □I4	Toliara prov. Madag.
250 C2	Tolima dept Col.
	Toling Xizang China see Zanda
93 B2	Tolitoli Sulawesi Tengah Indon.
168 E1	Tolk Ger.
143 H4	Tolkmicko Pol.
164 E2	Tollebeek Neth.
170 E2	Tollense r. Ger.
170 E2	Tollensesee l. Ger.
151 H3	Tollesbury Essex, England U.K.
151 H3	Tolleshunt D'Arcy Essex, England U.K.
241 K5	Tolleson AZ U.S.A.
	Tollimarjon Uzbek. see Talimardzhan
193 Q2	Tollo Italy
142 D2	Tollo Denmark
138 G2	Tolmachevo Rus. Fed.
191 I2	Tolmezzo Italy
188 D2	Tolmin Slovenia
177 H5	Tolna Hungary
177 H5	Tolna county Hungary
177 H5	Tolnai-hegyhát hills Hungary
177 I5	Tolnanémedi Hungary
242 □I6	Toloa Creek Hond.
	Tolochin Belarus see Talachyn
184 C1	Tolosa Spain
184 A1	Tolosa Port.
185 F4	Tolox Spain
227 F3	Tolsmaville Ont. Can.
146 B3	Tolsta Head hd Scotland U.K.
259 B5	Toltén Chile
259 B5	Toltén r. Chile
106 D1	Tölü Col.
250 E4	Toluca Mex.
186 D2	Tolva Spain
193 I4	Tolve Italy
191 J4	Tolve r. Italy
135 I5	Tol'yatti Rus. Fed.
137 J4	Tolybay Kazakh.
163 C4	Tolzac r. France
100 C2	Tom' r. Rus. Fed.
206 D3	Toma Burkina
226 B4	Tomah WI U.S.A.
226 B3	Tomahawk WI U.S.A.
102 J2	Tomakomai Japan
240 I2	Tomales CA U.S.A.
182 B3	Tomar Port.
228 □	Tomari Sakhalin Rus. Fed.
129 D2	Tomarovka Rus. Fed.
137 I2	Tomarovka Rus. Fed.
126 D3	Tomarza Turkey
251 H5	Tomás Barrón Bol.
136 D2	Tomashhorod Ukr.
	Tomashpil' Ukr. see
136 E3	Tomashpol' Ukr.
137 L1	Tomashuv Ukr.
175 H4	Tomashów Lubelski Pol.
175 I4	Tomaszów Mazowiecki Pol.
146 E4	Tomatin Highland, Scotland U.K.
244 B4	Tomatlán Mex.
252 D2	Tomave Bol.
256 C5	Tomazina Brazil
254 E4	Tombador, Serra do hills Bahia Brazil

253 F3	Tombador, Serra do hills Mato Grosso Brazil
163 C4	Tombebœuf France
231 AL A.L.A.	Tombigbee r. AL U.S.A.
215 G4	Tombo S. Africa
209 B6	Tombos Angola
257 F4	Tombos Brazil
206 E2	Tombouctou Mali
206 E2	Tombouctou admin. reg. Mali
241 L6	Tombstone AZ U.S.A.
209 A8	Tombua Angola
111 J1	Tom Burke S. Africa
142 D2	Tomdibulag Uzbek. see Tamdytau, Gory
139 K2	Tomdibulak Uzbek.
142 B2	Tomdtion Toghi hills Uzbek. see Jengish Chokusu
258 C6	Tomé Chile
143 E4	Tomelilla Sweden
185 Q1	Tomelloso Spain
121 F4	Tomenaryk Kazakh.
177 L5	Tomeşti Romania
177 L6	Tomeşti Romania
175 H6	Tomice Pol.
102 □1	Tomigusuku Japan
227 H2	Tomiko Ont. Can.
252 D4	Tomina Bol.
146 E4	Tomine r. Guinea
83 G3	Tomingley N.S.W. Austr.
93 B3	Tomini, Teluk g. Indon.
206 D3	Tominian Mali
146 E4	Tomintoul Moray, Scotland U.K.
105 E2	Tomioka Japan
188 F2	Tomislavgrad Bos.-Herz.
235 E1	Tomkins Cove NY U.S.A.
82 B1	Tomkinson Ranges mts S.A. Austr.
131 N4	Tommot Rus. Fed.
146 E4	Tomnavoulin Moray, Scotland U.K.
250 E3	Tomo r. Col.
198 B1	Tomorit, Maja e mt. Albania
111 E4	Tomorlog Qinghai China
107 G3	Tomortei Nei Mongol China
177 I5	Tompa Hungary
86 C4	Tom Price W.A. Austr.
235 D3	Toms r. NJ U.S.A.
130 J4	Tomsk Rus. Fed.
233 F5	Toms River NJ U.S.A.
128 B1	Tömük Turkey
102 K2	Tomuraushi-yama mt. Japan
	Tomur Feng mt. China/Kyrg. see Jengish Chokusu
129 D1	Tomuzlovka r. Rus. Fed.
220 D3	Tom White, Mount AK U.S.A.
186 F3	Tona Spain
102 □1	Tonaki-jima i. Japan
245 H5	Tonalá Mex.
244 C2	Tonalá Jalisco Mex.
84 C3	Tonami Japan
250 E5	Tonantins Brazil
192 B4	Tonara Sardegna Italy
238 C1	Tonasket WA U.S.A.
251 H3	Tonate Fr. Guiana
232 D3	Tonawanda NY U.S.A.
244 C4	Tonaya Mex.
	Tonb-e Bozorg, Jazireh-ye i. The Gulf see Greater Tunb
	Tonb-e Kúchek, Jazireh-ye i. The Gulf see Lesser Tunb
151 H3	Tonbridge Kent, England U.K.
182 B4	Tonda Port.
104 B4	Tondabayashi Japan
93 C2	Tondano Sulawesi Utara Indon.
182 B4	Tondela Port.
142 E4	Tønder Denmark
114 C4	Tondi Tamil Nadu India
150 E3	Tondu r. Wales U.K.
105 G3	Tone-gawa r. Japan
262 U1	Toney Mount Antarctica
191 G3	Tonezza del Cimone Italy
207 H5	Tonga Cameroon
215 H3	Tonga country S. Pacific Ocean
109 F3	Tong'an Fujian China
80 E3	Tongaporutu North I. N.Z.
80 □	Tongareva atoll Cook Is see
	Tongariro vol. North I. N.Z.
77 I3	Tongatapu i. Tonga
79 □2a	Tongatapu Group is Tonga
266 H7	Tonga Trench sea feature S. Pacific Ocean
109 E3	Tongbai Henan China
109 F2	Tongbai Shan mts China
109 F2	Tongcheng Anhui China
109 E2	Tongcheng Hubei China
	Tongcheng Shandong China see Dong'e
108 D3	Tongdao Hunan China
106 D5	Tongde Qinghai China
101 C5	Tongduch'ŏn S. Korea
165 F5	Tongeren Belgium
107 F5	Tonggu Jiangxi China
108 A2	Tonggu S. Korea
100 B3	Tonghai Yunnan China
100 D3	Tonghe Heilong. China
101 C4	Tonghua Jilin China
100 D3	Tonghua Jilin China
100 D3	Tongjiang Heilong. China
108 E2	Tongjiang Sichuan China
100 C3	Tongken r. China
96 C2	Tongking, Gulf of China/Vietnam
146 D7	Tongland Dumfries and Galloway, Scotland U.K.
	Tongle Guangxi China see Leye
107 I3	Tongliao Nei Mongol China
109 F2	Tongling Anhui China
109 F2	Tongling Anhui China
109 D3	Tonglu Zhejiang China
100 D3	Tongnae S. Korea
83 E2	Tongo N.S.W. Austr.
78 □5	Tongoa i. Vanuatu
213 □J4	Tongobory Madag.
260 B2	Tongoy, Bahía b. Chile
83 E2	Tongo Lake salt flat N.S.W. Austr.
260 B2	Tongoy Chile
	Tongquan Yunnan China see Malong
108 D3	Tongren Guizhou China
106 D5	Tongren Qinghai China
165 D5	Tongres Belgium see Tongeren
117 F4	Tongsa Bhutan see Trongsa
	Tongsa Bhutan see Trongsa
108 D3	Tongshi Hainan China
108 A1	Tongtian He r. China alt. Chang Jiang, alt. Jinsha Jiang, alt. Zhi Qu, conv. Yangtze, long Yangtze Kiang
146 D7	Tongue Highland, Scotland U.K.
238 F3	Tongue r. MT U.S.A.
	Tongue r. Ukr. see Arabats'ka Strilka, Kosa
246 E1	Tongue of the Ocean sea chan. Bahamas
106 E5	Tongwei Gansu China
107 H4	Tongxin Ningxia China
107 H4	Tongxiang Zhejiang China
106 E4	Tongxin Ningxia China
101 C4	Tongyu S. Korea
107 I2	Tongyu Jilin China
108 D2	Tongzi Guizhou China
108 □	Tongzhi Mongolia see Dzüyl
226 C5	Tonica IL U.S.A.
244 C4	Tonila Mex.
208 F3	Tonj Sudan
116 C4	Tonk Rajasthan India
122 B2	Tonkábon Iran
237 D4	Tonkawa OK U.S.A.
100 B3	Tonkina Rus. Fed.
96 C2	Tônlé Repou r. Laos
97 C5	Tônlé Sab l. Cambodia see
97 C4	Tônlé Sap l. Cambodia

150 D3	Tonna Neath Port Talbot, Wales U.K.
140 N2	Tonnio Fin.
177 M2	Tonjoš Vojvodina, Srbija Yugo.
190 E3	Tonno Italy
183 I4	Tonos Italy
183 I4	Tornos Spain
207 H4	Toro Nigeria
183 E3	Toro Spain
183 E3	Toro, Pico del mt. Mex.
183 E3	Torodi Niger
177 H4	Törökbálint Hungary
177 J4	Törökszentmiklós Hungary
224 E5	Toronto Ont. Can.
232 C4	Toronto OH U.S.A.
179 I3	Torony Hungary
139 H3	Toropatsa Rus. Fed.
139 H3	Toropets Rus. Fed.
210 B4	Tororo Uganda
126 D3	Toros Dağları mts Turkey
192 B4	Torpa Sardegna Italy
146 F4	Torphins Aberdeenshire, Scotland U.K.
150 C4	Torpoint Cornwall, England U.K.
83 F7	Torquay Vic. Austr.
150 D4	Torquay Torbay, England U.K.
183 I2	Torquemada Spain
147 E1	Torr Northern Ireland U.K.
185 G1	Torralba de Calatrava Spain
192 A4	Torralba Sardegna Italy
183 H4	Torralba Spain
183 H3	Torralba de Aragón Spain
183 I3	Torralba de El Burgo Spain
183 E5	Torralba de Oropesa Spain
183 I4	Torralba de los Sisones Spain
240 H5	Torrance CA U.S.A.
184 B2	Torrão Port.
191 E4	Torre mt. Port.
193 I4	Torre Annunziata Italy
193 I4	Torre Beretti e Castellaro Italy
187 L6	Torre Cardela Spain
183 I6	Torrecilla mt. Spain
183 I6	Torrecilla en Cameros Spain
183 I6	Torrecilla de la Jara Spain
183 I5	Torrecilla de la Orden Spain
183 I6	Torrecilla del Rebollar Spain
183 I6	Torrecillas en Cameros Spain
183 I3	Torrecilla de la Tiesa Spain
193 G3	Torrecuso Italy
193 I3	Torre del Greco Italy
196 D2	Torre del Mar Spain
186 E3	Torredembarra Spain
184 C1	Torre de Dom Chama Port.
185 I2	Torre de Juan Abad Spain
182 C3	Torre del Bierzo Spain
185 I2	Torre del Burgo Spain
193 I4	Torre del Campo Spain
193 I3	Torre del Greco Italy
191 E4	Torre de Miguel Sesmero Spain
182 C3	Torre de Moncorvo Port.
185 I2	Torre de' Passeri Italy
186 D2	Torre de' Picenardi Italy
184 D2	Torredonjimeno Spain
182 C2	Torre do Terrenho Port.
183 I2	Torregamones Spain
186 D2	Torregrossa Spain
193 I2	Torreiglesias Spain
183 G4	Torreira Port.
182 B2	Torrejoncillo Spain
183 G6	Torrejoncillo del Rey Spain
183 I3	Torrejón de Ardoz Spain
183 I4	Torrejón de la Calzada Spain
183 F6	Torrejón de Rubio Spain
183 I3	Torrelacárcel Spain
183 H6	Torrelaguna Spain
183 I3	Torrelapaja Spain
183 F1	Torrelavega Spain
183 I3	Torrellas Spain
186 E3	Torrelles de Foix Spain
182 C5	Torremaggiore Italy
183 I6	Torremanzanas Spain
183 F6	Torremayor Spain
183 I6	Torremegía Spain
163 G3	Torremocha Spain
185 I2	Torremocha Spain
185 G3	Torremolinos Spain
82 D2	Torrens, Lake salt flat S.A. Austr.
85 F7	Torrens Creek Qld Austr.
187 C5	Torrent Spain
187 D7	Torrente de Cinca Spain
185 L6	Torrenueva Spain
190 E6	Torre Nuovo Scalo Italy
242 E3	Torreón Mex.
184 D1	Torreorgaz Spain
187 C6	Torre Orsaia Italy
183 H5	Torre-Pacheco Spain
183 I5	Torreparedones hill Spain
190 C5	Torre Pellice Italy
184 C1	Torreperogil Spain
255 C9	Torres Brazil
182 C3	Torres Spain
244 E4	Torres Mex.
258 C2	Torres, Îles is Vanuatu
183 G3	Torres del Obispo Spain
182 D2	Torres Novas Port.
184 B1	Torres Strait Qld Austr.
182 B2	Torres Vedras Port.
187 F5	Torrevieja Spain
187 I3	Torri di Riubreós Spain
187 H2	Torrico, Monte mt. Italy
187 I3	Torrice Italy
185 G5	Torricella Italy
193 I3	Torricella in Sabina Italy
193 F2	Torricella Peligna Italy
193 F2	Torricella Sicura Italy
190 C3	Torricella Taverne Switz.
183 I3	Torrico Spain
184 D1	Torrico de San Pedro hill Spain
191 F3	Torri del Benaco Italy
190 C4	Torriglia Italy
193 I3	Torri in Sabina Italy
195 F2	Torrijo Spain
183 H5	Torrijos Spain
193 I3	Torrile Italy
146 C4	Torrin Highland, Scotland U.K.
235 I1	Torrington CT U.S.A.
238 F4	Torrington WY U.S.A.
256 D6	Torrinha Brazil
183 I4	Torrita di Siena Italy
187 B4	Tormón Spain
146 D6	Tormore North Ayrshire, Scotland U.K.
183 F4	Tornadizos de Ávila Spain
143 M1	Tornby Denmark
254 □	Torox Spain
143 N4	Torrubia del Campo Spain
183 I3	Torrubia de Soria Spain
183 G3	Torsa Chhu r. Bhutan
143 I4	Torne r. Europe
143 E2	Torsa Italy
140 L1	Torneå Fin. see Tornio
140 M2	Torneälven r. Sweden
168 J2	Tornesch Ger.
140 L2	Torneträsk Sweden
140 L1	Torneträsk l. Sweden
	Torngat, Monts mts Nfld./Que. Can. see Torngat Mountains
225 H1	Torngat Mountains Nfld./Que. Can.

196 D4	Tornik mt. Yugo.
140 N2	Tornio Fin.
177 M2	Tornjoš Vojvodina, Srbija Yugo.
190 E3	Torno Italy
183 I4	Tornos Italy
183 I4	Tornos Spain
207 H4	Toro Nigeria
183 E3	Toro Spain
207 F3	Torodi Niger
177 H4	Törökbálint Hungary
177 J4	Törökszentmiklós Hungary
224 E5	Toronto Ont. Can.
232 C4	Toronto OH U.S.A.
179 I3	Torony Hungary
139 H3	Toropatsa Rus. Fed.
139 H3	Toropets Rus. Fed.
210 B4	Tororo Uganda
126 D3	Toros Dağları mts Turkey
192 B4	Torpa Sardegna Italy
146 F4	Torphins Aberdeenshire, Scotland U.K.
150 C4	Torpoint Cornwall, England U.K.
83 F7	Torquay Vic. Austr.
150 D4	Torquay Torbay, England U.K.
183 I2	Torquemada Spain
147 E1	Torr Northern Ireland U.K.
185 G1	Torralba de Calatrava Spain
192 A4	Torralba Sardegna Italy
183 H4	Torralba Spain
183 H3	Torralba de Aragón Spain
183 I3	Torralba de El Burgo Spain
183 E5	Torralba de Oropesa Spain
183 I4	Torralba de los Sisones Spain
240 H5	Torrance CA U.S.A.
184 B2	Torrão Port.
191 E4	Torre mt. Port.
193 I4	Torre Annunziata Italy
193 I4	Torre Beretti e Castellaro Italy
187 L6	Torre Cardela Spain
183 I6	Torrecilla mt. Spain
183 I6	Torrecilla en Cameros Spain
183 I6	Torrecilla de la Jara Spain
183 I5	Torrecilla de la Orden Spain
183 I6	Torrecilla del Rebollar Spain
183 I3	Torrecilla de la Tiesa Spain
193 G3	Torrecuso Italy
193 I3	Torre del Greco Italy
196 D2	Torre del Mar Spain
186 E3	Torredembarra Spain
184 C1	Torre de Dom Chama Port.
185 I2	Torre de Juan Abad Spain
182 C3	Torre del Bierzo Spain
185 I2	Torre del Burgo Spain
193 I4	Torre del Campo Spain
193 I3	Torre del Greco Italy
191 E4	Torre de Miguel Sesmero Spain
182 C3	Torre de Moncorvo Port.
185 I2	Torre de' Passeri Italy
186 D2	Torre de' Picenardi Italy
184 D2	Torredonjimeno Spain
182 C2	Torre do Terrenho Port.
183 I2	Torregamones Spain
186 D2	Torregrossa Spain
193 I2	Torreiglesias Spain
183 G4	Torreira Port.
182 B2	Torrejoncillo Spain
183 G6	Torrejoncillo del Rey Spain
183 I3	Torrejón de Ardoz Spain
183 I4	Torrejón de la Calzada Spain
183 F6	Torrejón de Rubio Spain
183 I3	Torrelacárcel Spain
183 H6	Torrelaguna Spain
183 I3	Torrelapaja Spain
183 F1	Torrelavega Spain
183 I3	Torrellas Spain
186 E3	Torrelles de Foix Spain
182 C5	Torremaggiore Italy
183 I6	Torremanzanas Spain
183 F6	Torremayor Spain
183 I6	Torremegía Spain
163 G3	Torremocha Spain
185 I2	Torremocha Spain
185 G3	Torremolinos Spain
82 D2	Torrens, Lake salt flat S.A. Austr.
85 F7	Torrens Creek Qld Austr.
187 C5	Torrent Spain
187 D7	Torrente de Cinca Spain
185 L6	Torrenueva Spain
190 E6	Torre Nuovo Scalo Italy
242 E3	Torreón Mex.
184 D1	Torreorgaz Spain
187 C6	Torre Orsaia Italy
183 H5	Torre-Pacheco Spain
183 I5	Torreparedones hill Spain
190 C5	Torre Pellice Italy
184 C1	Torreperogil Spain
255 C9	Torres Brazil
182 C3	Torres Spain
244 E4	Torres Mex.
258 C2	Torres, Îles is Vanuatu
183 G3	Torres del Obispo Spain
182 D2	Torres Novas Port.
184 B1	Torres Strait Qld Austr.
182 B2	Torres Vedras Port.
187 F5	Torrevieja Spain
187 I3	Torri di Riubreós Spain
187 H2	Torrico, Monte mt. Italy
187 I3	Torrice Italy
185 G5	Torricella Italy
193 I3	Torricella in Sabina Italy
193 F2	Torricella Peligna Italy
193 F2	Torricella Sicura Italy
190 C3	Torricella Taverne Switz.
183 I3	Torrico Spain
184 D1	Torrico de San Pedro hill Spain
191 F3	Torri del Benaco Italy
190 C4	Torriglia Italy
193 I3	Torri in Sabina Italy
195 F2	Torrijo Spain
183 H5	Torrijos Spain
193 I3	Torrile Italy
146 C4	Torrin Highland, Scotland U.K.
235 I1	Torrington CT U.S.A.
238 F4	Torrington WY U.S.A.
256 D6	Torrinha Brazil
183 I4	Torrita di Siena Italy
187 B4	Tormón Spain
146 D6	Tormore North Ayrshire, Scotland U.K.
183 F4	Tornadizos de Ávila Spain
143 M1	Tornby Denmark
254 □	Torox Spain
143 N4	Torrubia del Campo Spain
183 I3	Torrubia de Soria Spain
183 G3	Torsa Chhu r. Bhutan
143 I4	Torsås Sweden
143 E2	Torsby Sweden
140 □	Tórshavn Faroe Is
143 I3	Törtel Hungary
241 L1	Tórtola i. Virgin Is (U.K.)
183 H3	Tórtoles de Esgueva Spain

234 B1	Towanda Creek r. PA U.S.A.
241 M3	Towaoc CO U.S.A.
151 G2	Towcester Northamptonshire, England U.K.
147 C5	Tower Rep. of Ireland
226 A2	Tower MN U.S.A.
234 B2	Tower City PA U.S.A.
81 A7	Tower Island Islas Galápagos Ecuador see Genovesa, Isla
81 A7	Tower Peak South I. N.Z.
149 I3	Tow Law Durham, England U.K.
234 D2	Town Bank NJ U.S.A.
236 C1	Towner ND U.S.A.
146 E7	Townhead of Greenlaw Dumfries and Galloway, Scotland U.K.
146 E5	Townhill Fife, Scotland U.K.
84 C2	Townn r. N.T. Austr.
237 K3	Townsend DE U.S.A.
233 I3	Townsend MA U.S.A.
238 E2	Townsend MT U.S.A.
85 G4	Townshend Island Qld Austr.
85 I3	Townsville Qld Austr.
93 B3	Towori, Teluk b. Indon.
234 B3	Towson MD U.S.A.
150 D1	Towyn Conwy, Wales U.K.
	Towyn Gwynedd, Wales U.K. see Tywyn
110 C3	Toxkan He r. China
240 H1	Toy NV U.S.A.
237 C6	Toyah TX U.S.A.
104 D2	Toyama Japan
104 C2	Toyama pref. Japan
104 C2	Toyama-wan b. Japan
104 C3	Toykut Ukr.
103 F7	Tōyo Japan
104 D3	Toyoake Japan
105 H2	Toyohashi Japan
104 D3	Toyokawa Japan
104 C2	Toyo-kawa r. Japan
104 A3	Toyonaka Japan
104 A3	Toyooka Japan
102 I5	Toyosaka Japan
105 D2	Toyoshina Japan
104 C3	Toyota Japan
140 M3	Töysä Fin.
121 G3	Toytepa Uzbek.
150 □	Tozal del Orri mt. Spain see Tossal de l'Orri
205 F2	Tozeur Tunisia
129 E3	Tozik Kangri mt. Xizang China see Almus
205 H2	Tozeur Tunisia
129 E3	Tpig Rus. Fed.
129 C2	Tqibuli Georgia
129 B2	Tqvarch'eli Georgia
182 C1	Trabada Spain
193 C5	Trabanca Spain
194 B6	Trabazos Spain
194 C5	Trabia Sicilia Italy
174 G1	Trąbki Wielkie Pol.
128 B2	Tråblous Lebanon
197 F5	Trabotivište Macedonia
127 E2	Trabzon Turkey
127 E2	Trabzon prov. Turkey
194 B6	Tracino Sicilia Italy
233 □J2	Tracy N.B. Can.
236 E3	Tracy CA U.S.A.
240 B3	Tracy CA U.S.A.
236 E2	Tracy MN U.S.A.
160 I4	Tracy-sur-Loire France
190 D3	Tradate Italy
169 I4	Traddelkopf hill Ger.
226 B2	Trade Lake WI U.S.A.
237 F4	Tradewater r. KY U.S.A.
284 B3	Trading r. Ont. Can.
140 K2	Trænfjorden sea chan. Norway
236 I3	Traer IA U.S.A.
184 C4	Trafalgar, Cabo c. Spain
175 F7	Trafik Mountain Y.T. Can.
193 I4	Tragacete Spain
185 H2	Tragoncillo mt. Spain
179 L4	Tragwein Austria
197 I4	Traian Romania
177 L6	Traian Vuia Romania
183 I8	Traiguén Chile
186 D3	Traiguera Spain
222 G5	Trail B.C. Can.
237 D5	Trail OK U.S.A.
173 F3	Train Ger.
161 F4	Trainel France
251 I4	Trainer PA U.S.A.
156 C3	Trainou France
254 F4	Traipu Brazil
255 B8	Traíra r. Brazil
254 F4	Traíras r. Brazil
179 K3	Traisen Austria
179 K3	Traisen r. Austria
179 J4	Traiskirchen Austria
179 M3	Traismauer Austria
173 G2	Traitsching Ger.
257 H3	Trajano de Morais Brazil
	Trajectum Neth. see Utrecht
214 C5	Traka r. S. Africa
138 L4	Trakai Lith.
147 H3	Tralee Rep. of Ireland
147 B4	Tralee Bay Rep. of Ireland
134 L1	Trá Lí Rep. of Ireland see Tralee
183 I4	Tramacastilla Spain
192 A1	Tramariglio Sardegna Italy
193 I4	Tramascastiel Spain
192 A1	Tramatza Sardegna Italy
191 I3	Tramazzo r. Italy
172 A4	Tramelan Switz.
192 A2	Tramezzo France
147 E4	Trá Mhór Rep. of Ireland see Tramore
232 E4	Trammel VA U.S.A.
191 H2	Tramonti di Sopra Italy
191 H2	Tramonti di Sotto Italy
147 D4	Tramore Rep. of Ireland
147 D4	Tramore Rep. of Ireland
193 □	Tramuntana, Serra de mts Spain
193 I4	Tramutola Italy
142 H2	Tranås Sweden
142 E2	Tranbjerg Denmark
142 E2	Tranebjerg Denmark
142 G2	Tranemo Sweden
147 I5	Tranent East Lothian, Scotland U.K.
96 B4	Trang Thai.
91 J8	Trangan i. Indon.
83 F3	Trangie N.S.W. Austr.
193 I3	Trani Italy
156 C4	Trannes France
258 C6	Tranqueras Uru.
259 C6	Tranqui, Isla i. Chile
260 D6	Tranquilla Chile
263 D2	Transantarctic Mountains Antarctica
223 H5	Trans Canada Highway Can.
	Transcarpathian Oblast admin. div. Ukr. see Zakarpats'ka Oblast'
223 J5	Transcona Man. Can.
161 G5	Trans-en-Provence France
245 H4	Transfiguración Mex.
197 G2	Transilvania reg. Romania
	Transilvaniei, Podişul plat. Romania
141 J3	Transtrand Sweden
	Transylvania reg. Romania
	Transylvanian Alps mts Romania see Carpaţii Meridionali
	Transylvanian Basin plat. Romania see Transilvaniei, Podişul
146 H3	Trantlemore Highland, Scotland U.K.
194 B8	Trapani Sicilia Italy
	Trapani prov. Sicilia Italy
127 D3	Trapezus Turkey see Trabzon
234 C4	Trappe PA U.S.A.
168 F1	Trappenkamp Ger.
238 D3	Trapper Peak MT U.S.A.
156 C2	Trappes France
255 C5	Trarego Italy
193 □	Traralgon Austr.
143 E4	Trarbach Ger.
206 B3	Trarza admin. reg. Maur.
193 □	Trasacco Italy
197 J3	Trascăului, Munţii mts Romania
117 G4	Trashigang Bhutan
190 □	Trasimeno, Lago l. Italy
182 □	Trasmiras Spain
192 D2	Trasubbie r. Italy

Trat to Turégano
372

97 C4 Trat Thai.
192 A5 Tratalias Sardegna Italy
179 F2 Traun Austria
179 F2 Traun r. Austria
173 G3 Traun r. Ger.
173 G4 Traunreut Ger.
179 E3 Traunsee l. Austria
179 G2 Traunstein Austria
173 G4 Traunstein Ger.
179 H2 Trautmannsdorf an der Leitha Austria
190 F3 Travagliato Italy
182 B4 Travanca do Mondego Port.
182 B4 Travassô Port.
182 C4 Travassós de Cima Port.
168 F2 Trave r. Ger.
83 E3 Travellers Lake imp. l. N.S.W. Austr.
168 F2 Travemünde Ger.
168 F2 Travenbrück Ger.
190 B2 Travers Switz.
81 D5 Travers, Mount South I. N.Z.
226 E3 Traverse City MI U.S.A.
190 F4 Traversetolo Italy
260 D4 Travesia Puntana des. Arg.
260 D3 Travesia Tunuyán des. Arg.
191 G2 Travignolo r. Italy
97 D5 Tra Vinh Vietnam
188 F3 Travnik Bos.-Herz.
192 B3 Travo r. Corse France
190 E4 Travo Italy
150 D2 Trawsfynydd Gwynedd, Wales U.K.
87 C6 Trayning W.A. Austr.
188 E2 Trbovlje Slovenia
147 B3 Trean Rep. of Ireland
246 □ Treasure Beach Jamaica
78 □6 Treasury Islands Solomon Is
177 G3 Trebatice Slovakia
171 F3 Trebatsch Ger.
190 E3 Trebbia r. Italy
171 E3 Trebbin Ger.
170 C3 Trebel Ger.
170 E2 Trebel r. Ger.
171 D4 Treben Ger.
176 C1 Třebenice Czech Rep.
170 E2 Trebenow Ger.
163 E5 Trèbes France
179 E4 Trebesing Austria
158 C3 Trébeurden France
176 E2 Třebíč Czech Rep.
188 G4 Trebinje Bos.-Herz.
195 F3 Trebisacce Italy
188 F4 Trebišnjica r. Bos.-Herz.
177 K3 Trebišov Slovakia
171 D4 Trebitz Ger.
188 F4 Trebižat r. Bos.-Herz.
Trebizond Turkey see Trabzon
188 E3 Trebnje Slovenia
182 C2 Trebolle Spain
176 D2 Třeboň Czech Rep.
85 F3 Trebonne Qld Austr.
158 B3 Tréboul France
171 D4 Trebsen Ger.
184 D4 Trebujena Spain
172 C2 Trebur Ger.
150 D3 Trecastle Powys, Wales U.K.
190 D3 Trecate Italy
193 H4 Trecchina Italy
191 G3 Trecenta Italy
150 D3 Tredegar Blaenau Gwent, Wales U.K.
151 F2 Tredington Warwickshire, England U.K.
191 G4 Tredozio Italy
148 B3 Treehoo Rep. of Ireland
168 E1 Treene r. Ger.
Trefaldwyn Powys, Wales U.K. see Montgomery
150 D2 Trefeglwys Powys, Wales U.K.
179 E4 Treffen Austria
158 B4 Treffiagat France
160 D2 Treffort-Cuisiat France
169 F4 Treffurt Ger.
Treffynnon Flintshire, Wales U.K. see Holywell
150 D1 Trefriw Conwy, Wales U.K.
Trefynwy Monmouthshire, Wales U.K. see Monmouth
150 D2 Tregaron Ceredigion, Wales U.K.
158 C3 Trégastel France
191 G3 Tregnago Italy
226 B3 Trego WI U.S.A.
150 C4 Tregony Cornwall, England U.K.
85 G3 Tregosse Islets and Reefs Coral Sea Is Terr. Austr.
260 A5 Treguaco Chile
158 D3 Trégueux France
158 C3 Tréguier France
158 C4 Trégunc France
150 D2 Tregynon Powys, Wales U.K.
140 L3 Trehörningsjö Sweden
168 E1 Treia Ger.
191 I5 Treia Italy
146 D5 Treig, Loch l. Scotland U.K.
162 D3 Treignac France
160 B1 Treigny France
Treinta de Agosto Arg. see 30 de Agosto
258 G4 Treinta y Tres Uru.
169 C5 Treis Ger.
246 □ Trelawney parish Jamaica
159 F4 Trélazé France
150 C3 Trelech Carmarthenshire, Wales U.K.
259 D6 Trelew Arg.
162 C3 Trélissac France
158 D3 Trélivan France
142 E4 Trelleborg Sweden
156 E2 Trélon France
197 F4 Trem mt. Yugo.
150 C2 Tremadog Gwynedd, Wales U.K.
150 C2 Tremadog Bay Wales U.K.
224 F4 Tremblant, Mont hill Que. Can.
158 E3 Tremblay France
156 B4 Tremblay-les-Villages France
182 D3 Tremedal de Tormes Spain
165 D4 Tremelo Belgium
159 F4 Trémentines France
184 B1 Tremês Port.
158 C4 Tréméven France
190 E3 Tremezzo Italy
193 H2 Tremiti, Isole is Italy
138 G5 Tremlya r. Belarus
163 C4 Trémolat France
227 I5 Tremont PA U.S.A.
238 D3 Tremonton UT U.S.A.
176 C2 Třemošná Czech Rep.
176 E2 Třemošnice Czech Rep.
161 A4 Trémouilles France
186 D2 Tremp Spain
226 B3 Trempealeau r. WI U.S.A.
168 F2 Tremsbüttel Ger.
150 B4 Trenance Cornwall, England U.K.
226 D2 Trenary MI U.S.A.
225 F4 Trenche r. Que. Can.
177 H3 Trenčianska Turná Slovakia
177 G3 Trenčianske Stankovce Slovakia
177 H3 Trenčianske Teplice Slovakia
177 H3 Trenčiansky Kraj admin. reg. Slovakia
177 H3 Trenčín Slovakia
169 E4 Trendelburg Ger.
261 E4 Trenel Arg.
95 E5 Trenggalek Jawa Timur Indon.
Trengganu state Malaysia see Terengganu
261 F4 Trenque Lauquén Arg.
163 B4 Trensacq France
170 E1 Trent Ger.
Trent Italy see Trento
149 I4 Trent r. Dorset, England U.K.
150 E4 Trent r. England U.K.
163 C4 Trentels France
191 G2 Trentino - Alto Adige admin. reg. Italy
191 G2 Trento Italy
191 G2 Trento prov. Trentino - Alto Adige Italy
193 G4 Trentola-Ducenta Italy
224 E4 Trenton Ont. Can.
231 D6 Trenton FL U.S.A.
231 C5 Trenton GA U.S.A.
236 E3 Trenton MO U.S.A.
231 E5 Trenton NC U.S.A.
236 C3 Trenton NE U.S.A.
234 D2 Trenton NJ U.S.A.
237 F5 Trenton TN U.S.A.
156 B4 Tréon France
150 D3 Treorchy Rhondda Cynon Taff, Wales U.K.
84 B1 Trepang Bay N.T. Austr.
225 K4 Trepassey Nfld. Can.
171 F3 Treppeln Ger.
160 D3 Trept France
195 H2 Trepuzzi Italy
192 D1 Trequanda Italy
190 D2 Tresa r. Italy
261 F4 Tres Algarrobas Arg.
190 E4 Tresana Italy
261 G6 Tres Arroyos Arg.
256 B6 Três Bicos Brazil
234 C2 Tresckow PA U.S.A.
161 D4 Trescléoux France
150 □ Tresco i. England U.K.
257 E4 Três Corações Brazil
190 E3 Trescore Balneario Italy
190 F2 Tresenda Italy
250 C4 Tres Esquinas Col.
Tres Forcas, Cabo c. Morocco see Trois Fourches, Cap des
146 B5 Treshnish Isles Scotland U.K.
191 G4 Tresigallo Italy
190 F2 Tre Signori, Corno dei mt. Italy
256 B4 Três Irmãos, Represa resr Brazil
258 E2 Tres Isletas Arg.
196 E4 Treska r. Macedonia
256 B4 Três Lagoas Brazil
261 F5 Tres Lomas Arg.
183 F1 Tres Mares, Pico mt. Spain
257 E3 Três Marias Brazil
257 E3 Três Marias, Represa resr Brazil
259 B7 Tres Montes, Península pen. Chile
192 A4 Tresnuraghes Sardegna Italy
183 G2 Trespaderne Spain
245 E5 Tres Palos Mex.
239 F6 Tres Picachos, Sierra mts Mex.
259 C6 Tres Picos mt. Arg.
243 G6 Tres Picos Mex.
261 G6 Tres Picos, Cerro mt. Arg.
245 H5 Tres Picos, Cerro mt. Mex.
239 F4 Tres Piedras NM U.S.A.
240 G3 Tres Pinos CA U.S.A.
257 E4 Três Pontas Brazil
256 C6 Três Pontões, Pico mt. Brazil
260 C3 Tres Porteñas Arg.
256 D3 Três Ranchos Brazil
257 F5 Três Rios Brazil
146 E5 Tressait Perth and Kinross, Scotland U.K.
160 D3 Tresserve France
176 E2 Třešť Czech Rep.
193 G3 Treste r. Italy
245 F4 Tres Valles Mex.
245 G4 Tres Zapotes tourist site Mex.
150 D3 Tretower Powys, Wales U.K.
161 D5 Trets France
173 E3 Treuchtlingen Ger.
171 D5 Treuen Ger.
171 D3 Treuenbrietzen Ger.
142 C2 Treungen Norway
158 D3 Trévé France
185 G4 Trevélez Spain
185 G4 Trevélez r. Spain
259 C6 Trevelín Arg.
157 F4 Tréveray France
161 B4 Trèves France
Treves Ger. see Trier
193 E2 Trevi Italy
183 G2 Treviana Spain
159 F2 Trévières France
190 E3 Treviglio Italy
192 E2 Trevignano Romano Italy
160 E1 Trévillers France
183 H2 Treviño Spain
191 H3 Treviso Italy
191 H3 Treviso airport Italy
191 H3 Treviso prov. Veneto Italy
182 C3 Trevões Port.
234 B2 Trevorton PA U.S.A.
234 D2 Trevose PA U.S.A.
150 B4 Trevose Head hd England U.K.
160 C3 Trévoux France
234 C2 Trexlertown PA U.S.A.
160 B2 Trézelles France
197 F4 Trgovište Srbija Yugo.
176 D3 Trhové Sviny Czech Rep.
177 K3 Trhovište Slovakia
83 F5 Triabunna Tas. Austr.
182 C2 Triacastela Spain
162 A2 Triaize France
84 D2 Trial Bay N.T. Austr.
129 D3 T'rialet'i Georgia
129 C3 T'rialet'is K'edi hills Georgia
Triánda Notio Aigaio Greece see Trianta
232 E5 Triangle VA U.S.A.
199 F3 Trianta Notio Aigaio Greece
123 G3 Tribal Areas admin. div. Pak.
177 H3 Tribeč mts Slovakia
158 E2 Tribehou France
172 C3 Triberg im Schwarzwald Ger.
100 G1 Tri Brata, Gora hill Sakhalin Rus. Fed.
170 D1 Tribsees Ger.
85 F3 Tribulation, Cape Qld Austr.
236 C4 Tribune KS U.S.A.
193 I4 Tricarico Italy
195 H3 Tricase Italy
191 I2 Tricesimo Italy
191 H2 Trichiana Italy
Trichinopoly Tamil Nadu India see Tiruchchirappalli
198 B2 Trichonida, Limni l. Greece
114 C4 Trichur Kerala India
156 C3 Tricot France
83 F3 Trida N.S.W. Austr.
Tridentum Italy see Trento
171 D5 Triebel r. Ger.
179 F3 Trieben Austria
171 D5 Triebes Ger.
156 B3 Trie-Château France
192 B4 Triei Sardegna Italy
172 C4 Triengen Switz.
172 A2 Trier Ger.
169 B5 Trier admin. reg. Rheinland-Pfalz Ger.
172 A2 Trierweiler Ger.
191 I3 Trieste Italy
191 I3 Trieste prov. Friuli - Venezia Giulia Italy
Trieste, Golfo di g. Europe see Trieste, Gulf of
188 D3 Trieste, Gulf of Europe
191 I3 Trieste-Ronchi dei Legionari airport Italy
163 C5 Trie-sur-Baïse France
157 F3 Trieux France
158 C3 Trieux r. France
173 H3 Triftern Ger.
184 C2 Trigaches Port.
161 E5 Trigance France
195 F1 Triggiano Italy
179 E4 Triglav mt. Slovenia
170 D2 Triglitz Ger.
158 D4 Trignac France
193 G2 Trigno r. Italy
216 □1c Trigo, Monte hill São Jorge Azores
156 C5 Triguères France
184 D3 Trigueros Spain
183 F3 Trigueros del Valle Spain
198 B2 Trikala Greece
Trikkala Greece see Trikala
91 I7 Trikora, Puncak mt. Indon.
198 C2 Trikorfa mt. Greece
188 F4 Trilj Croatia
147 D2 Trillick Northern Ireland U.K.
183 H4 Trillo Spain
156 C4 Trilport France
147 E3 Trim Rep. of Ireland
149 H3 Trimdon Durham, England U.K.
151 I3 Trimley St Mary Suffolk, England U.K.
190 E2 Trimmis Switz.
86 B4 Trimouille Island W.A. Austr.
150 C3 Trimsaran Carmarthenshire, Wales U.K.
114 D4 Trincomalee Sri Lanka
256 C2 Trindade Brazil
184 C3 Trindade Beja Port.
182 C3 Trindade Bragança Port.
264 H7 Trindade, Ilha da i. S. Atlantic Ocean
177 H2 Třinec Czech Rep.
151 G3 Tring Hertfordshire, England U.K.
198 B2 Tringia mt. Greece
252 D3 Trinidad Bol.
246 C2 Trinidad Cuba
245 G5 Trinidad r. Mex.
247 □7 Trinidad i. Trin. and Tob.
261 I3 Trinidad Uru.
239 F4 Trinidad CO U.S.A.
261 G6 Trinidad, Isla i. Arg.
247 G5 Trinidad and Tobago country West Indies
192 A4 Trinità d'Agultu Sardegna Italy
193 I3 Trinitapoli Italy
237 E6 Trinity TX U.S.A.
238 B3 Trinity r. CA U.S.A.
237 E6 Trinity r. TX U.S.A.
237 D5 Trinity, West Fork r. OK U.S.A.
85 F3 Trinity Bay Qld Austr.
225 K4 Trinity Bay Nfld. Can.
240 H1 Trinity Range mts NV U.S.A.
190 D3 Trino Italy
178 C3 Trins Austria
182 C4 Trinta Port.
232 B4 Trinway OH U.S.A.
170 D1 Trinwillershagen Ger.
183 F2 Triollo Spain
193 H3 Triolo r. Italy
195 F3 Trionto r. Italy
190 C5 Triora Italy
94 B2 Tripa r. Indon.
170 C2 Tripkau Ger.
198 C3 Tripoli Greece
Tripoli Lebanon see Trâblous
202 B1 Tripoli Libya
Trípolis Greece see Tripoli
Tripolis Lebanon see Trâblous
202 B2 Tripolitania reg. Libya
172 B2 Trippstadt Ger.
171 C5 Triptis Ger.
114 C4 Tripunittura Kerala India
117 G5 Tripura state India
178 B3 Trisanna r. Austria
178 D4 Tristach Austria
216 □2c Tristan da Cunha i. S. Atlantic Ocean
206 B4 Tristao, Îles is Guinea
178 E4 Tristenspitze mt. Austria
116 D3 Trisul mt. Uttar Prad. India
225 K3 Triton Nfld. Can.
168 F2 Trittau Ger.
172 A2 Trittenheim Ger.
254 F3 Triunfo Brazil
114 C4 Trivandrum Kerala India
193 G3 Trivento Italy
190 D3 Trivero Italy
190 D4 Triversa r. Italy
193 H4 Trivigno Italy
161 A3 Trizac France
177 G2 Trnava Czech Rep.
177 G3 Trnava Slovakia
177 H3 Trnavá Hora Slovakia
177 G3 Trnavský Kraj admin. reg. Slovakia
179 H4 Trnovec Bartolovečki Croatia
179 E5 Trnovski gozd mts Slovenia
159 F2 Troarn France
171 E4 Tröbitz Ger.
172 D3 Trochtelfingen Ger.
222 H5 Trochu Alta Can.
141 L3 Trödje Sweden
182 B3 Trofa Port.
179 G3 Trofaiach Austria
140 K2 Trofors Norway
188 F4 Trogir Croatia
178 E4 Trogkofel mt. Austria/Italy
188 F4 Troglav mt. Croatia
142 D2 Trøgstad Norway
193 H3 Troia Italy
184 B2 Tróia Port.
194 D5 Troina Sicilia Italy
194 D5 Troina r. Sicilia Italy
169 C5 Troisdorf Ger.
157 H4 Troisfontaines France
204 E2 Trois Fourches, Cap des c. Morocco
225 G3 Trois-Pistoles Que. Can.
165 E4 Trois-Ponts Belgium
225 F4 Trois-Rivières Que. Can.
247 □2 Trois-Rivières Guadeloupe
163 D6 Trois Seigneurs, Pic des mt. France
156 C3 Troissereux France
160 B2 Trois-Vèvres France
165 F4 Troisvierges Lux.
139 M4 Troitsa Rus. Fed.
120 E1 Troitsk Chelyabinskaya Oblast' Rus. Fed.
139 K4 Troitsk Moskovskaya Oblast' Rus. Fed.
137 I2 Troitskiy Belgorodskaya Oblast' Rus. Fed.
Troitskiy Moskovskaya Oblast' Rus. Fed. see Troitsk
134 L3 Troitsko-Pechorsk Rus. Fed.
121 K1 Troitskoye Altayskiy Kray Rus. Fed.
100 F2 Troitskoye Khabarovskiy Kray Rus. Fed.
120 C1 Troitskoye Orenburgskaya Oblast' Rus. Fed.
120 D1 Troitskoye Respublika Bashkortostan Rus. Fed.
135 I7 Troitskoye Respublika Kalmykiya - Khalm'g-Tangch Rus. Fed.
246 □ Troja Jamaica
174 G5 Troja r. Pol.
142 E2 Trollhättan Sweden
251 G5 Trombetas r. Brazil
217 □1 Tromelin, Île i. Indian Ocean
Tromelin Island Micronesia see Fais
190 D3 Tromello Italy
260 B5 Tromen, Volcán vol. Arg.
146 D4 Tromie r. Scotland U.K.
215 E4 Trompsburg S. Africa
140 L1 Troms county Norway
140 L1 Tromsø Norway
240 I4 Trona CA U.S.A.
259 C6 Tronador, Monte mt. Arg.
160 A2 Tronçais, Forêt de for. France
182 C3 Tronco Port.
244 C2 Troncoso Mex.
140 J3 Trondheim Norway
140 J3 Trondheimsfjorden sea chan. Norway
150 D4 Troney r. England U.K.
117 G4 Trongsa Bhutan
117 G4 Trongsa Chhu r. Bhutan
193 F2 Tronto r. Italy
157 F4 Tronville-en-Barrois France
190 D3 Tronzano Vercellese Italy
159 G4 Troo France
128 A2 Troödos, Mount Cyprus
128 A2 Troödos Mountains Cyprus
146 D6 Troon South Ayrshire, Scotland U.K.
198 B3 Tropaia Greece
251 G6 Tropas r. Brazil
195 E4 Tropea Italy
254 D5 Tropeiros, Serra dos hills Brazil
241 K3 Tropic UT U.S.A.
147 D2 Trory Northern Ireland U.K.
139 J5 Trosna Rus. Fed.
171 D4 Trossin Ger.
172 C3 Trossingen Ger.
139 I5 Trostan' Rus. Fed.
147 E1 Trostan hill Northern Ireland U.K.
173 F1 Tröstau Ger.
173 G3 Trostberg Ger.
137 H2 Trostyanets' Ukr.
136 E3 Trostyanets' Ukr.
136 C2 Trostyanets' Ukr.
146 B4 Trotternish hills Scotland U.K.
197 H2 Trotuş r. Romania
222 E3 Trout r. B.C. Can.
222 G2 Trout r. N.W.T. Can.
149 G3 Troutbeck Cumbria, England U.K.
227 H3 Trout Creek Ont. Can.
226 C2 Trout Creek MI U.S.A.
232 C6 Trout Dale VA U.S.A.
222 H3 Trout Lake Alta Can.
222 F2 Trout Lake N.W.T. Can.
222 F2 Trout Lake l. N.W.T. Can.
223 M5 Trout Lake l. Ont. Can.
226 E2 Trout Lake MI U.S.A.
225 J3 Trout River Nfld. Can.
227 I5 Trout Run PA U.S.A.
232 D6 Troutville VA U.S.A.
159 G2 Trouville-sur-Mer France
159 I4 Trouy France
182 B5 Troviscal Port.
150 E3 Trowbridge Wiltshire, England U.K.
83 F5 Trowutta Tas. Austr.
Troy tourist site Turkey see Truva
231 C6 Troy AL U.S.A.
236 E4 Troy KS U.S.A.
227 F4 Troy MI U.S.A.
236 F4 Troy MO U.S.A.
238 D1 Troy MT U.S.A.
231 E5 Troy NC U.S.A.
233 G3 Troy NH U.S.A.
233 G3 Troy NY U.S.A.
232 A4 Troy OH U.S.A.
227 I5 Troy PA U.S.A.
197 G4 Troyan Bulg.
136 E2 Troyaniv Ukr.
136 F3 Troyanka Ukr.
139 L5 Troyekurovo Lipetskaya Oblast' Rus. Fed.
139 L5 Troyekurovo Lipetskaya Oblast' Rus. Fed.
156 E4 Troyes France
137 J3 Troyits'ke Ukr.
136 F4 Troyits'ke Ukr.
137 G4 Troyits'ko-Safonove Ukr.
157 F3 Troyon France
241 J2 Troy Peak NV U.S.A.
176 G2 Tršice Czech Rep.
179 E5 Trstelj hill Slovenia
177 I2 Trstená Slovakia
196 E4 Trstenik Srbija Yugo.
177 G3 Trstice Slovakia
176 G3 Trstín Slovakia
84 D1 Truant Island N.T. Austr.
139 I5 Trubchevsk Rus. Fed.
139 L5 Trubetchino Rus. Fed.
182 E1 Trubia Spain
182 E1 Trubia r. Spain
137 F2 Trubizh r. Ukr.
161 B4 Truc de la Garde mt. France
Truc Giang Vietnam see Bên Tre
182 D2 Truchas Spain
157 H4 Truchtersheim France
Trucial Coast country Asia see United Arab Emirates
Trucial States country Asia see United Arab Emirates
240 G2 Truckee CA U.S.A.
120 A3 Trudfront Rus. Fed.
Trudovoy Kazakh. see Kuybyshevskiy
Trudovoy Rus. Fed. see Yusta
100 E4 Trudovoye Rus. Fed.
139 K5 Trudy r. Rus. Fed.
84 B4 Truer Range hills N.T. Austr.
184 D2 Trujillanos Spain
242 □I6 Trujillo Hond.
252 A2 Trujillo Peru
184 E1 Trujillo Spain
250 D2 Trujillo Venez.
250 D2 Trujillo state Venez.
Trujillo, Monte mt. Dom. Rep. see Duarte, Pico
247 □1 Trujillo Alto Puerto Rico
Truk is Micronesia see Chuuk
172 B2 Trulben Ger.
150 D4 Trull Somerset, England U.K.
237 F5 Trumann AR U.S.A.
232 E3 Trumansburg NY U.S.A.
235 E1 Trumbull CT U.S.A.
241 K3 Trumbull, Mount AZ U.S.A.
151 H2 Trumpington Cambridgeshire, England U.K.
197 F4 Trŭn Bulg.
159 G3 Trun France
190 D2 Trun Switz.
197 F4 Trŭna mt. Bulg.
83 F3 Trundle N.S.W. Austr.
Truong Sa is S. China Sea see Spratly Islands
225 I4 Truro N.S. Can.
150 B4 Truro Cornwall, England U.K.
95 F1 Trusan r. Sarawak Malaysia
197 H2 Truşeşti Romania
169 F5 Trusetal Ger.
196 D5 Trush Albania
137 G3 Trushivtsi Ukr.
136 B3 Truskavets' Ukr.
147 C2 Truskmore hill Rep. of Ireland
95 G1 Trus Madi, Gunung mt. Sabah Malaysia
197 G4 Trŭstenik Bulg.
222 F3 Trutch B.C. Can.
222 F3 Trutch Creek r. B.C. Can.
239 F5 Truth or Consequences NM U.S.A.
176 E1 Trutnov Czech Rep.
199 E2 Truva tourist site Turkey
161 A4 Truyère r. France
139 J2 Truzhenik Rus. Fed.
197 G4 Tryavna Bulg.
198 B2 Tryfos Dytiki Ellas Greece
168 F1 Tryggelev Denmark
175 K5 Tryńcza Pol.
236 C3 Tryon NE U.S.A.
141 K3 Trysil Norway
141 K3 Trysilelva r. Norway
141 K3 Trysilfjellet mt. Norway
138 D3 Tryškiai Lith.
188 E3 Tržac Bos.-Herz.
175 J3 Trzcianka Mazowieckie Pol.
174 E2 Trzcianka Wielkopolskie Pol.
175 K2 Trzcianne Pol.
174 D3 Trzciel Pol.
174 G4 Trzcinica Pol.
174 D1 Trzebiatów Pol.
174 C4 Trzebiel Pol.
174 F1 Trzebielino Pol.
175 K4 Trzebieszów Pol.
174 C2 Trzebież Pol.
175 H5 Trzebinia Pol.
174 F4 Trzebnica Pol.
175 K5 Trzebośnica r. Pol.
174 F3 Trzemeszno Pol.
175 L3 Trześcianka Pol.
175 J6 Trześniów Pol.
175 J5 Trześniówka r. Pol.
175 L5 Trzeszczany Pierwsze Pol.
188 E2 Tržič Slovenia
179 F4 Trzin Slovenia
174 C3 Trzrcińsko-Zdrój Pol.
175 H5 Trzyciąż Pol.
175 K5 Trzydnik Duży Pol.
106 A1 Tsagaannuur Bayan-Ölgiy Mongolia
107 H2 Tsagaannuur Dornod Mongolia
106 B2 Tsagaan Nuur salt l. Mongolia
Tsagaan-Uul Hövsgöl Mongolia see Sharga
135 I7 Tsagan Aman Rus. Fed.
135 I7 Tsagan-Nur Rus. Fed.
129 C2 Ts'ageri Georgia
Tsaidam Basin China see Qaidam Pendi
140 M1 Tsåktso mt. Sweden
129 C2 Tsalenjikha Georgia
140 K2 Tsangatjåkkå mt. Sweden
213 □J3 Tsaramandroso Madag.
213 □J3 Tsaratanana Madag.
213 □K2 Tsaratanana, Massif du mts Madag.
197 H4 Tsarevo Bulg.
Tsaribrod Srbija Yugo. see Dimitrovgrad
197 G4 Tsarimir Bulg.
Tsaritsyn Rus. Fed. see Volgograd
137 H3 Tsarychanka Ukr.
215 G4 Tsatsana mt. S. Africa
211 C5 Tsavo East National Park Kenya
211 C5 Tsavo West National Park Kenya
215 F4 Tsazo S. Africa
178 A3 Tschagguns Austria
171 F4 Tschernitz Ger.
106 B2 Tseel Mongolia
Tsefat Israel see Ẕefat
135 H7 Tselina Rus. Fed.
121 K1 Tselinnoye Rus. Fed.
120 E2 Tselinnyy Rus. Fed.
Tselinograd Kazakh. see Astana
Tselinogradskaya Oblast' admin. div. Kazakh. see Akmolinskaya Oblast'
Tsementnyy Rus. Fed. see Fokino
106 D1 Tsengel Mongolia
134 J4 Tsentral'nyy Rus. Fed.
Tsentral'nyy Rus. Fed. see Radovitskiy
139 L5 Tsentral'nyy Rus. Fed.
197 F4 Tserovo Bulg.
106 B2 Tsetsegnuur Mongolia
106 D2 Tsetserleg Arhangay Mongolia
Tsetserleg Hövsgöl Mongolia see Halban
207 F5 Tsévié Togo
212 D5 Tshabong Botswana
Tshad country Africa see Chad
209 B6 Tshela Dem. Rep. Congo
213 E4 Tshesebe Botswana
209 D6 Tshibala Dem. Rep. Congo
209 D6 Tshikapa Dem. Rep. Congo
209 D6 Tshikapa r. Dem. Rep. Congo
209 D6 Tshilenge Dem. Rep. Congo
209 D6 Tshimbulu Dem. Rep. Congo
215 F2 Tshing S. Africa
213 F4 Tshipise S. Africa
209 D6 Tshiumbe r. Angola/Dem. Rep. Congo
209 E6 Tshofa Dem. Rep. Congo
213 F5 Tshokwane S. Africa
213 E3 Tsholotsho Zimbabwe
212 D4 Tshootsha Botswana
208 D5 Tshuapa r. Dem. Rep. Congo
213 □J3 Tsiazonano mt. Madag.
197 F4 Tsibritsa r. Bulg.
220 E3 Tsiigehtchic N.W.T. Can.
134 J2 Tsil'ma r. Rus. Fed.
135 H7 Tsimlyansk Rus. Fed.
135 H7 Tsimlyanskoye Vodokhranilishche resr Rus. Fed.
Tsinan Shandong China see Jinan
214 D2 Tsineng S. Africa
Tsinghai prov. China see Qinghai
217 □3b Tsingoni Mayotte
Tsingtao Shandong China see Qingdao
Tsining Nei Mongol China see Jining
213 □J3 Tsinjomay mt. Madag.
213 □J5 Tsiombe Madag.
213 □J3 Tsiroanomandidy Madag.
Tsiteli Tskaro Georgia see Dedop'listsqaro
Tsitsihar Heilong. China see Qiqihar
222 E4 Tsitsutl Peak B.C. Can.
129 B2 Ts'ivi r. Georgia
129 D3 Ts'ivi, Mt'a Georgia
134 I5 Tsivil'sk Rus. Fed.
Tskhakaia Georgia see Senaki
Tskhaltubo Georgia see Tsqaltubo
129 C2 Ts'khinvali Georgia
129 D3 Ts'khneti Georgia
138 F5 Tsna r. Belarus
135 H5 Tsna r. Rus. Fed.
139 J3 Tsna r. Rus. Fed.
139 L4 Tsna r. Rus. Fed.
129 D3 Tsnori Georgia
212 D3 Tsodilo Hills Botswana
116 D2 Tsokr Chumo l. Jammu and Kashmir
215 G4 Tsolo S. Africa
215 F5 Tsomo S. Africa
215 F5 Tsomo r. S. Africa
116 D2 Tso Morari Lake Jammu and Kashmir
139 K5 Tson r. Rus. Fed.
Tsona Xizang China see Cona
199 D1 Tsopan hill Greece
198 B1 Tsotili Dytiki Makedonia Greece
129 D3 Tsovinar Armenia
129 C2 Tsqaltubo Georgia
104 C4 Tsu Japan
103 I5 Tsubame Japan
105 G2 Tsuchiura Japan
109 □ Tsuen Wan H.K. China
102 J3 Tsugarū-kaikyō str. Japan
Tsugaru Strait Japan see Tsugarū-kaikyō
105 G2 Tsukuba Japan
103 E7 Tsukumi Japan
106 E2 Tsul-Ulaan Mongolia
136 C2 Tsuman' Ukr.
212 C3 Tsumeb Namibia
212 D3 Tsumkwe Namibia
129 E2 Tsurib Rus. Fed.
105 E3 Tsuru Japan
104 C3 Tsuruga Japan
104 D2 Tsurugi-dake mt. Japan
103 G7 Tsurugi-san mt. Japan
Tsurukhaytuy Rus. Fed. see Priargunsk
102 I4 Tsuruoka Japan
104 C3 Tsushima Japan
Tsushima-kaikyō str. Japan/S. Korea see Korea Strait
103 G6 Tsuyama Japan
197 F5 Tsvetino Bulg.
137 F3 Tsvitkove Ukr.
137 G3 Tsvitne Ukr.
215 E3 Tswaraganang S. Africa
215 E2 Tswelelang S. Africa
136 E3 Tsybuliv Ukr.
138 E5 Tsyelyakhany Belarus
137 F1 Tsyerakhowka Belarus
Tsygira Moldova see Ţighira
175 N4 Tsyr r. Ukr.
137 G4 Tsyurupyns'k Ukr.
Tthenaagoo N.W.T. Can. see Nahanni Butte
182 C3 Tua r. Port.
80 E2 Tuakau North I. N.Z.
147 C3 Tuam Rep. of Ireland
81 D4 Tuamarina South I. N.Z.
147 C4 Tuamgraney Rep. of Ireland
79 □3 Tuamotu, Archipel des is Fr. Polynesia
Tuamotu Islands Fr. Polynesia see Tuamotu, Archipel des
81 B7 Tuapeka Mouth South I. N.Z.
129 A1 Tuapse Rus. Fed.
94 □ Tuas Sing.
81 A7 Tuatapere South I. N.Z.
146 B5 Tuath, Loch sea chan. Scotland U.K.
Tuath, Loch a' b. Scotland U.K. see Broad Bay
241 L3 Tuba City AZ U.S.A.
95 F4 Tuban Jawa Timur Indon.
255 C9 Tubarão Brazil
128 B3 Ţūbās West Bank
92 A4 Tubbataha Reefs Phil.
147 C2 Tubbercurry Rep. of Ireland
164 F2 Tubbergen Neth.
148 B5 Tubbrid Rep. of Ireland
183 G2 Tubilla del Agua Spain
172 D3 Tübingen Ger.
172 D3 Tübingen admin. reg. Baden-Württemberg Ger.
120 D1 Tubinskiy Rus. Fed.
165 D4 Tubize Belgium
206 C5 Tubmanburg Liberia
207 G4 Tubo r. Nigeria
92 B4 Tubod Phil.
190 F2 Tubre Italy
202 D1 Tubruq Libya
95 G2 Tubu r. Indon.
79 □3 Tubuai i. Îs Australes Fr. Polynesia
242 C2 Tubutama Mex.
238 C2 Tucannon r. WA U.S.A.
254 F4 Tucano Brazil
260 B5 Tucapel Chile
253 F4 Tucavaca Bol.
253 F4 Tucavaca r. Bol.
163 C6 Tuc de les Carants mt. Spain
163 E6 Tuchan France
170 D2 Tüchen Ger.
171 D3 Tuchheim Ger.
222 D2 Tuchitua Y.T. Can.
139 K4 Tuchkovo Rus. Fed.
171 E5 Tuchlovice Czech Rep.
222 F3 Tuchodi r. B.C. Can.
174 F2 Tuchola Pol.
174 F1 Tuchomie Pol.
175 J6 Tuchów Pol.
175 K4 Tuchowicz Pol.
136 D2 Tuchyn Ukr.
234 D3 Tuckahoe NJ U.S.A.
235 F2 Tuckahoe NY U.S.A.
234 D3 Tuckahoe r. NJ U.S.A.
234 C4 Tuckahoe Creek r. MD U.S.A.
87 C5 Tuckanarra W.A. Austr.
235 D3 Tuckerton NJ U.S.A.
234 C2 Tuckerton PA U.S.A.
Tucopia i. Solomon Is see Tikopia
157 F3 Tucquegnieux France
241 L5 Tucson AZ U.S.A.
241 L5 Tucson Mountains AZ U.S.A.
225 H1 Tuctuc r. Que. Can.
Tucumán Arg. see San Miguel de Tucumán
258 D2 Tucumán prov. Arg.
237 C5 Tucumcari NM U.S.A.
251 F2 Tucupita Venez.
251 I5 Tucuruí Brazil
251 I6 Tucuruí, Represa resr Brazil
175 L4 Tuczna Pol.
174 E2 Tuczno Pol.
142 D4 Tudeå r. Denmark
183 I2 Tudela Spain
183 F3 Tudela de Duero Spain
Tuder Italy see Todi
197 H2 Tudora Romania
197 H3 Tudor Vladimirescu Romania
139 I3 Tudovka r. Rus. Fed.
150 C2 Tudweiliog Gwynedd, Wales U.K.
187 B5 Tuejar Spain
182 C3 Tuela r. Port.
109 □ Tuen Mun H.K. China
191 G2 Tuenno Italy
117 H4 Tuensang Nagaland India
251 I5 Tueré r. Brazil
182 E2 Tuerto r. Spain
125 E2 Ţufayḩ Saudi Arabia
159 G3 Tuffé France
267 J2 Tufts Abyssal Plain sea feature N. Pacific Ocean
Tuga i. Vanuatu see Tégua
215 H3 Tugela r. S. Africa
215 H3 Tugela Ferry S. Africa
Tūghyl Kazakh. see Tugyl
108 B3 Tuguancun Yunnan China
92 B2 Tuguegarao Phil.
213 F4 Tugwi r. Zimbabwe
121 K3 Tugyl Kazakh.
107 H4 Tuhai r. China
182 B2 Tui Spain
252 D3 Tuichi r. Bol.
192 A5 Tuili Sardegna Italy
117 H5 Tuilianpui r. Bangl./India
216 □3b Tuineje Fuerteventura Canary Is
Tujiabu Jiangxi China see Yongxiu
120 D1 Tukan Rus. Fed.
93 B4 Tukangbesi, Kepulauan is Indon.
136 B3 Tukhol'ka Ukr.
123 H2 Tŭkhtamish Tajik.
80 F3 Tukituki r. North I. N.Z.
202 D1 Tūkrah Libya
220 E3 Tuktoyaktuk N.W.T. Can.
138 D3 Tukums Latvia
95 E3 Tukung, Bukit mt. Indon.
100 C1 Tukuringra, Khrebet mts Rus. Fed.
129 D1 Tukuy-Mekteb Rus. Fed.
211 B7 Tukuyu Tanz.
192 A4 Tula Sardegna Italy
245 E3 Tula Hidalgo Mex.
245 E2 Tula Tamaulipas Mex.
245 E3 Tula r. Mex.
139 K4 Tula Rus. Fed.
Tulach Mhór Rep. of Ireland see Tullamore
78 □6 Tulaghi Solomon Is
111 F4 Tulagt Ar Gol r. China
106 C4 Tulai Qinghai China
106 C4 Tulai Nanshan mts China
106 C4 Tulai Shan mts China
263 D2 Tula Mountains Antarctica
245 E3 Tulancingo Mex.
94 D4 Tulangbawang r. Indon.
Tula Oblast admin. div. Rus. Fed. see Tul'skaya Oblast'
240 H3 Tulare CA U.S.A.
239 F5 Tularosa NM U.S.A.
114 D2 Tulasi mt. Madh. Prad./Orissa India
168 F3 Tülau Ger.
175 I2 Tuławki Pol.
214 B5 Tulbagh S. Africa
179 H2 Tulbing Austria
177 K5 Tulca Romania
250 B4 Tulcán Ecuador
174 F3 Tulce Pol.
197 I3 Tulcea Romania
Tul'chin Ukr. see Tul'chyn
136 E3 Tul'chyn Ukr.
240 H3 Tule r. CA U.S.A.
Tuléar Madag. see Toliara
238 B3 Tulelake CA U.S.A.
161 C4 Tulette France
176 F5 Tulfás r. Hungary
178 C3 Tulfes Austria
197 G2 Tulgheş Romania
237 C5 Tulia TX U.S.A.
107 I1 Tulihe Nei Mongol China
174 G3 Tuliszków Pol.
222 E1 Tulít'a N.W.T. Can.
114 C2 Tuljapur Mahar. India
128 B3 Ţūlkarm West Bank
147 C4 Tulla Rep. of Ireland
147 C2 Tullaghan Rep. of Ireland
231 C5 Tullahoma TN U.S.A.
83 F3 Tullamore N.S.W. Austr.
147 D3 Tullamore Rep. of Ireland
148 B5 Tullaroan Rep. of Ireland
162 D3 Tulle France
83 F3 Tullibigeal N.S.W. Austr.
161 D3 Tullins France
179 H2 Tulln Austria
237 E6 Tullos LA U.S.A.
147 E4 Tullow Rep. of Ireland
85 F3 Tully Qld Austr.
147 D2 Tully Northern Ireland U.K.
147 D2 Tully Northern Ireland U.K.
147 E3 Tullyallen Rep. of Ireland
147 D2 Tullybrack hill Northern Ireland U.K.
147 E4 Tullycanna Rep. of Ireland
147 E2 Tullyhogue Northern Ireland U.K.
234 D2 Tullytown PA U.S.A.
147 D2 Tullyvin Rep. of Ireland
147 C2 Tullyvoos Rep. of Ireland
197 H3 Tulnici Romania
140 P1 Tuloma r. Rus. Fed.
175 I3 Tułowice Pol.
174 F5 Tułowice Pol.
237 E4 Tulsa OK U.S.A.
222 C3 Tulsequah B.C. Can.
116 E3 Tulsipur Nepal
147 C3 Tulsk Rep. of Ireland
139 K5 Tul'skaya Oblast' admin. div. Rus. Fed.
129 B1 Tul'skiy Rus. Fed.
121 H1 Tul'skoye Kazakh.
250 B3 Tuluá Col.
197 I3 Tuluceşti Romania
220 B3 Tuluksak AK U.S.A.
128 C3 Tulūl al Ashāqif hills Jordan
243 I4 Tulum tourist site Mex.
260 C2 Tulum, Valle de val. Arg.
98 H1 Tulun Rus. Fed.
95 E5 Tulungagung Jawa Timur Indon.
Tulusdu N. Male Maldives see Thulusdhu
251 F4 Tulu-Tuloi, Serra hills Brazil
210 B2 Tulu Welel mt. Eth.
134 K4 Tulva r. Rus. Fed.
137 G2 Tulyholove Ukr.
242 □I6 Tuma r. Nic.
139 M4 Tuma Rus. Fed.
250 B4 Tumaco Col.
215 F2 Tumahole S. Africa
111 E5 Tumain Xizang China
120 B3 Tumak Rus. Fed.
Tuman-gang r. Asia see Tumen Jiang
Tumannaya r. Asia see Tumen Jiang
134 F1 Tumannyy Rus. Fed.
139 J4 Tumanovo Rus. Fed.
131 S3 Tumanskiy Rus. Fed.
Tumasik Sing. see Singapore
251 G3 Tumatumari Guyana
143 G2 Tumba Sweden
92 C5 Tumbao Phil.
83 G3 Tumbarumba N.S.W. Austr.
250 A5 Tumbes Peru
250 A5 Tumbes dept Peru
222 F4 Tumbler Ridge B.C. Can.
82 D3 Tumby Bay S.A. Austr.
140 O2 Tumcha r. Fin./Rus. Fed.
Tumd Youqi Nei Mongol China see Salaqi
Tumd Zuoqi Nei Mongol China see Qasq
100 D4 Tumen Jilin China
108 D1 Tumen Shaanxi China
100 D4 Tumen Jiang r. Asia
251 F3 Tumereng Guyana
257 G3 Tumiritinga Brazil
114 C3 Tumkur Karnataka India
146 E5 Tummel, Loch l. Scotland U.K.
146 D5 Tummel Bridge Perth and Kinross, Scotland U.K.
202 B4 Tummo, Mountains of Libya/Niger
100 G2 Tumnin r. Rus. Fed.
97 C4 Tumpôr, Phnum mt. Cambodia
93 B3 Tumpu, Gunung mt. Indon.
93 B3 Tumputiga, Gunung mt. Indon.
116 D5 Tumsar Mahar. India
206 E4 Tumu Ghana
251 G4 Tumucumaque, Serra hills Brazil
115 D2 Tumudibandh Orissa India
182 D5 Tumuja r. Spain
252 D3 Tumupasa Bol.
121 G4 Tumur Yuzhnyy Kazakhstan Kazakh.
252 D5 Tumusla Bol.
83 G3 Tumut N.S.W. Austr.
134 K5 Tumutuk Rus. Fed.
110 C3 Tumxuk Xinjiang China
206 E4 Tuna Ghana
247 □1 Tuna, Punta pt Puerto Rico
143 F1 Tuna-Hästberg Sweden
247 □7 Tunapuna Trin. and Tob.
246 C2 Tunas de Zaza Cuba
Ţunb al Kubrá i. The Gulf see Greater Tunb
Ţunb aş Şughrá i. The Gulf see Lesser Tunb
151 H3 Tunbridge Wells, Royal Kent, England U.K.
199 F2 Tunçbilek Turkey
126 E3 Tunceli Turkey
129 A4 Tunceli prov. Turkey
108 D5 Tunchang Hainan China
129 C3 Tunçoluk Turkey
83 H3 Tuncurry N.S.W. Austr.
111 B7 Tundla Uttar Prad. India
211 B7 Tunduma Tanz.
207 H4 Tundun-Wada Nigeria
211 C7 Tunduru Tanz.
197 H5 Tundzha r. Bulg.
142 E4 Tune Denmark
Tunes Tunisia see Tunis
207 H4 Tunga Nigeria
146 B3 Tunga Western Isles, Scotland U.K.
114 C3 Tungabhadra r. India
92 B5 Tungawan Phil.
Tungdor Xizang China see Mainling
117 G5 Tungi Bangl.
140 □C2 Tungnaá r. Iceland
100 G1 Tungor Sakhalin Rus. Fed.
222 D2 Tungsten N.W.T. Can.
95 F2 Tungun, Bukit mt. Indon.
115 D2 Tuni Andhra Prad. India
237 F5 Tunica MS U.S.A.
172 C3 Tuningen Ger.
227 G1 Tunis Ont. Can.
205 H1 Tunis Tunisia
205 H1 Tunis, Golfe de g. Tunisia
205 H2 Tunisia country Africa
250 C3 Tunja Col.
234 C1 Tunkhannock PA U.S.A.
107 G4 Tunliu Shanxi China
226 B3 Tunnel City WI U.S.A.
232 D5 Tunnelton WV U.S.A.
139 M3 Tunoshna Rus. Fed.
151 I2 Tunstall Suffolk, England U.K.
173 G4 Tuntenhausen Ger.
225 H1 Tunulic r. Que. Can.
220 B3 Tununak AK U.S.A.
260 C3 Tunuyán Arg.
260 D4 Tunuyán r. Arg.
Tunxi Anhui China see Huangshan
177 L4 Tunyogmatolcs Hungary
Tuodian Yunnan China see Shuangbai
109 F1 Tuo He r. China
Tuojiang Hunan China see Fenghuang
Tuojiang Hunan China see Shuikou
108 C2 Tuo Jiang r. Sichuan China
240 G3 Tuolumne CA U.S.A.
240 G3 Tuolumne r. CA U.S.A.
240 H3 Tuolumne Meadows CA U.S.A.
192 D1 Tuoma r. Italy
108 C3 Tuoniang Jiang r. Guangxi China
Tuoputiereke Xinjiang China see Jeminay (Topterek)
191 H5 Tuoro sul Trasimeno Italy
111 F5 Tuotuo He r. China
106 B5 Tuotuoheyan Qinghai China
121 I4 Tüp Kyrg.
256 B4 Tupã Brazil
256 C3 Tupaciguara Brazil
Tupai i. Fr. Polynesia see Motu Iti
255 B9 Tupanciretã Brazil
237 F5 Tupelo MS U.S.A.
176 G2 Tupesy Czech Rep.
251 G5 Tupinambarama, Ilha i. Brazil
256 B4 Tupi Paulista Brazil
252 D5 Tupiza Bol.
174 C4 Tuplice Pol.
222 F4 Tupper B.C. Can.
233 F2 Tupper Lake NY U.S.A.
Tüpqaraghan Tübegi pen. Kazakh. see Mangyshlak, Poluostrov
260 C3 Tupungato Arg.
260 C3 Tupungato, Cerro mt. Arg./Chile
107 I2 Tuquan Nei Mongol China
250 B4 Túquerres Col.
197 F1 Tur r. Romania
111 D4 Tura Xinjiang China
177 I4 Tura Hungary
117 G4 Tura Meghalaya India
131 L3 Tura Rus. Fed.
124 C3 Turabah Saudi Arabia
251 E3 Turagua, Serranía mt. Venez.
80 E4 Turakina North I. N.Z.
80 E4 Turakina r. North I. N.Z.
100 D2 Turana, Khrebet mts Rus. Fed.
80 E3 Turangi North I. N.Z.
120 D5 Turan Lowland Asia
193 E2 Turano r. Italy
Turanskaya Nizmennost' lowland Asia see Turan Lowland
121 G4 Tura-Ryskulova Kazakh.
136 D1 Turaw Belarus
138 E2 Turba Estonia
250 C2 Turbaco Col.
175 I6 Turbacz mt. Pol.
123 E5 Turbat Pak.
190 D1 Turbenthal Switz.
244 D3 Turbio r. Mex.
136 E3 Turbiv Ukr.
250 B2 Turbo Col.
234 B1 Turbotville PA U.S.A.
178 E3 Türchlwand mt. Austria
182 E2 Turcia Spain
177 H3 Turčianske Teplice Slovakia
157 H4 Turckheim France
197 F2 Turda Romania
160 C3 Turdine r. France
87 C4 Turee Creek r. W.A. Austr.
183 F3 Turégano Spain

174 G3 Turek Pol.
138 E1 Turenki Fin.
174 E3 Turew Pol.
Turfan Xinjiang China see Turpan
Turfan Depression China see Turpan Pendi
121 H2 Turgay Akmolinskaya Oblast' Kazakh.
120 E2 Turgay Kustanayskaya Oblast' Kazakh.
120 E3 Turgay r. Kazakh.
120 E2 Turgayskaya Dolina val. Kazakh.
120 E2 Turgayskaya Stolovaya Strana reg. Kazakh.
106 A1 Türgen Uul mt. Mongolia
106 A1 Türgen Uul mt. Mongolia
224 E3 Turgeon r. Ont./Que. Can.
197 H4 Tŭrgovishte Bulg.
126 C3 Turgut Konya Turkey
199 F3 Turgut Muğla Turkey
199 E2 Turgutalp Turkey
199 E2 Turgutlu Turkey
199 E3 Turgutreis Turkey
126 E2 Turhal Turkey
138 E2 Türi Estonia
195 G2 Turi Italy
187 C5 Turia r. Spain
254 D2 Turiaçu Brazil
254 D2 Turiaçu r. Brazil
177 H2 Turie Slovakia
177 H3 Turiec r. Slovakia
223 H5 Turin Alta Can.
Turin Italy see Torino
130 H4 Turinsk Rus. Fed.
187 C5 Turís Spain
136 C2 Turiya r. Ukr.
136 C2 Turiys'k Ukr.
176 G5 Türje Hungary
99 I1 Turka Rus. Fed.
136 B3 Turka Ukr.
210 B4 Turkana, Lake salt l. Eth./Kenya
199 E1 Türkeli Turkey
173 F3 Türkenfeld Ger.
121 G4 Turkestan Kazakh.
123 F2 Turkestan Range mts Asia
177 J4 Túrkeve Hungary
126 D3 Turkey country Asia
232 B6 Turkey KY U.S.A.
236 F3 Turkey r. IA U.S.A.
86 F3 Turkey Creek W.A. Austr.
173 E3 Türkheim Ger.
135 H6 Turki Rus. Fed.
Türkistan Kazakh. see Turkestan
122 C1 Turkmenbashi Turkm.
199 G2 Türkmen Dağı mt. Turkey
123 E2 Turkmengala Turkm.
122 D1 Turkmenistan country Asia
Turkmeniya country Asia see Turkmenistan
Turkmen-Kala Turkm. see Turkmengala
Türkmenostan country Asia see Turkmenistan
Turkmenskaya S.S.R. country Asia see Turkmenistan
126 E3 Türkoğlu Turkey
246 E2 Turks and Caicos Islands terr. West Indies
246 E2 Turks Island Passage Turks and Caicos Is
246 E2 Turks Islands Turks and Caicos Is
141 M3 Turku Fin.
183 G5 Turleque Spain
240 G3 Turlock CA U.S.A.
147 B3 Turlough Clare Rep. of Ireland
147 B3 Turlough Mayo Rep. of Ireland
257 F2 Turmalina Brazil
222 E3 Turnagain r. B.C. Can.
80 F4 Turnagain, Cape North I. N.Z.
129 A3 Turnalı Turkey
177 J3 Turňa nad Bodvou Slovakia
179 G3 Turnau Austria
146 D6 Turnberry South Ayrshire, Scotland U.K.
81 B6 Turnbull, Mount South I. N.Z.
241 L5 Turnbull, Mount AZ U.S.A.
86 C4 Turner r. W.A. Austr.
227 F3 Turner MI U.S.A.
86 F3 Turner River W.A. Austr.
151 G3 Turners Hill West Sussex, England U.K.
206 B5 Turner's Peninsula Sierra Leone
222 H5 Turner Valley Alta Can.
165 D3 Turnhout Belgium
179 H4 Turnišče Slovenia
179 G3 Türnitz Austria
223 I3 Turnor Lake Sask. Can.
176 E1 Turnov Czech Rep.
Tŭrnovo Bulg. see Veliko Tŭrnovo
197 G4 Turnu Măgurele Romania
Turnu Severin Romania see Drobeta - Turnu Severin
175 K5 Turobin Pol.
83 G3 Turon r. N.S.W. Austr.
185 F4 Turón r. Spain
Turones France see Tours
188 E3 Turopolje plain Croatia
175 J2 Turośl Pol.
175 J2 Turośl Pol.
134 H4 Turovets Rus. Fed.
175 K4 Turów Pol.
110 E3 Turpan Xinjiang China
110 E3 Turpan Pendi depr. China
110 E3 Turpan Zhan Xinjiang China
184 B1 Turquel Port.
185 I3 Turre Spain
242 □J7 Turrialba Costa Rica
161 E4 Turriers France
146 F4 Turriff Aberdeenshire, Scotland U.K.
Turris Libisonis Sardegna Italy see Porto Torres
195 F2 Tursi Italy
197 F2 Turt Romania
120 E4 Turtkul' Uzbek.
223 I4 Turtleford Sask. Can.
85 G3 Turtle Island Coral Sea Is Terr. Austr.
Turtle Island Fiji see Vatoa
92 A5 Turtle Islands Phil.
206 B5 Turtle Islands Sierra Leone
226 A3 Turtle Lake WI U.S.A.
130 J3 Turukhansk Rus. Fed.
177 M4 Turulung Romania
251 G4 Turuna r. Brazil
136 F4 Turunchuk r. Ukr.
128 B1 Turunçlu Turkey
199 G3 Turunçova Turkey
114 C3 Turuvanur Karnataka India
256 B2 Turvelândia Brazil
255 C9 Turvo Brazil
256 B2 Turvo r. Goiás Brazil
256 C3 Turvo r. São Paulo Brazil
256 C5 Turvo r. São Paulo Brazil
177 L3 Tur"ya r. Ukr.
177 L3 Tur"ya-Bystra Ukr.
129 E3 Türyançay Azer.
129 E3 Türyançay r. Azer.
177 L3 Tur"ya-Polyana Ukr.
136 B3 Tur"ye Ukr.
177 L3 Tur"yi Remety Ukr.
136 C2 Turynka Ukr.
175 I2 Turza Wielka Pol.
177 H2 Turzovka Slovakia
122 D2 Ţūs Iran
185 H2 Tús r. Spain
194 D5 Tusa Sicilia Italy
194 D4 Tusa r. Sicilia Italy
241 K4 Tusayan AZ U.S.A.
231 C5 Tuscaloosa AL U.S.A.
192 D2 Tuscania Italy
Tuscany admin. reg. Italy see Toscana
232 C4 Tuscarawas r. OH U.S.A.
234 B2 Tuscarora PA U.S.A.
232 E4 Tuscarora Mountains hills PA U.S.A.
236 F4 Tuscola IL U.S.A.
237 D5 Tuscola TX U.S.A.
231 C5 Tuscumbia AL U.S.A.
236 E4 Tuscumbia MO U.S.A.
137 I2 Tuskar' r. Rus. Fed.
231 C5 Tuskegee AL U.S.A.
173 E3 Tussenhausen Ger.
232 D4 Tussey Mountains hills PA U.S.A.
173 G3 Tüßling Ger.
226 E3 Tustin MI U.S.A.
175 J5 Tuszów Narodowy Pol.
175 J5 Tuszyma Pol.
175 H4 Tuszyn Pol.
127 F3 Tutak Turkey
139 L3 Tutayev Rus. Fed.
151 F2 Tutbury Staffordshire, England U.K.
Tutera Spain see Tudela
114 C4 Tuticorin Tamil Nadu India
95 F2 Tutoh r. Sarawak Malaysia
95 F1 Tutong Brunei
197 H2 Tutova r. Romania
170 E2 Tutow Ger.
197 H3 Tutrakan Bulg.
150 E3 Tutshill Gloucestershire, England U.K.
234 D1 Tuttles Corner NJ U.S.A.
172 C4 Tuttlingen Ger.
221 P2 Tuttut Nunaat reg. Greenland
211 B6 Tutubu Tanz.
78 □2 Tutuila i. American Samoa
80 E1 Tutukaka North I. N.Z.
213 E4 Tutume Botswana
252 C4 Tutupaca, Volcán vol. Peru
81 E4 Tuturumuri North I. N.Z.
245 F5 Tututepec Mex.
173 F4 Tutzing Ger.
170 E2 Tützpatz Ger.
106 E1 Tuul Gol r. Mongolia
138 E1 Tuulos Fin.
101 C4 Tuun-bong mt. N. Korea
140 O3 Tuupovaara Fin.
140 O3 Tuusniemi Fin.
141 N3 Tuusula Fin.
Tuva aut. rep. Rus. Fed. see Tyva, Respublika
77 H2 Tuvalu country S. Pacific Ocean
77 I4 Tuvana-i-Colo i. Fiji
77 I4 Tuvana-i-Ra i. Fiji
Tuvana-i-Tholo i. Fiji see Tuvana-i-Colo
142 D3 Tuve Sweden
262 S2 Tuve, Mount Antarctica
Tuvinskaya A.S.S.R. aut. rep. Rus. Fed. see Tyva, Respublika
121 I4 Tuvuk Kazakh.
95 G2 Tuwau r. Indon.
124 D2 Tuwayq, Jabal hills Saudi Arabia
124 D3 Tuwayq, Jabal mts Saudi Arabia
128 B5 Ţuwayyil al Ḩājj mt. Jordan
128 C4 Ţuwayyil ash Shihāq mt. Jordan
124 B3 Tuwwal Saudi Arabia
235 D1 Tuxedo Park NY U.S.A.
178 C3 Tuxer Gebirge mts Austria
149 I4 Tuxford Nottinghamshire, England U.K.
244 C4 Tuxpan Jalisco Mex.
244 B3 Tuxpan Nayarit Mex.
245 F3 Tuxpan Veracruz Mex.
243 G5 Tuxtla Gutiérrez Mex.
Túy Spain see Tui
247 F5 Tuy r. Venez.
96 D2 Tuyên Quang Vietnam
97 E4 Tuy Hoa Vietnam
135 K5 Tuymazy Rus. Fed.
122 B3 Tūysarkān Iran
Tŭytepa Uzbek. see Toytepa
Tuz, Lake salt l. Turkey see Tuz Gölü
244 D4 Tuzantla r. Mex.
126 D3 Tuz Gölü salt l. Turkey
197 G4 Tŭzha Bulg.
134 I4 Tuzha Rus. Fed.
196 D4 Tuzi Crna Gora Yugo.
127 G4 Tuz Khurmātū Iraq
188 G3 Tuzla Bos.-Herz.
197 I3 Tuzla Romania
126 D3 Tuzla Turkey
127 F3 Tuzla r. Turkey
135 H7 Tuzlov r. Rus. Fed.
129 C3 Tuzluca Turkey
179 H4 Tužno Croatia
96 A1 Tuzu r. Myanmar
142 E3 Tvååker Sweden
140 L2 Tvärålund Sweden
176 F2 Tvarožná Czech Rep.
142 C2 Tvedestrand Norway
142 A1 Tveitakvitingen mt. Norway
139 J3 Tver' Rus. Fed.
Tver Oblast admin. div. Rus. Fed. see Tverskaya Oblast'
129 A1 Tverskaya Rus. Fed.
139 J3 Tverskaya Oblast' admin. div. Rus. Fed.
139 J3 Tvertsa r. Rus. Fed.
144 D1 Tvøroyri Faroe Is
179 H2 Tvrdonice Czech Rep.
177 I2 Tvrdošín Slovakia
197 G4 Tvŭrditsa Bulg.
240 G2 Twain Harte CA U.S.A.
174 F4 Twardogóra Pol.
146 E2 Twatt Orkney, Scotland U.K.
227 I3 Tweed Ont. Can.
149 G2 Tweed r. England/Scotland U.K.
146 E6 Tweeddale val. Scotland U.K.
164 F2 Tweede Exloërmond Neth.
83 H2 Tweed Heads N.S.W. Austr.
223 I4 Tweedie Alta Can.
149 G2 Tweedmouth Northumberland, England U.K.
146 E6 Tweedsmuir Scottish Borders, Scotland U.K.
214 B5 Tweefontein S. Africa
215 G2 Tweeling S. Africa
215 F3 Tweespruit S. Africa
164 F2 Twello Neth.
241 I4 Twentynine Palms CA U.S.A.
225 K3 Twillingate Nfld. Can.
240 G2 Twin Bridges CA U.S.A.
238 D2 Twin Bridges MT U.S.A.
225 H2 Twin Falls Nfld. Can.
238 D3 Twin Falls ID U.S.A.
86 E4 Twin Heads hill W.A. Austr.
234 D1 Twin Lakes PA U.S.A.
233 H2 Twin Mountain NH U.S.A.
240 G2 Twin Peak CA U.S.A.
87 C7 Twin Peaks hill W.A. Austr.
232 C4 Twinsburg OH U.S.A.
238 B1 Twisp WA U.S.A.
168 C3 Twist Ger.
169 D4 Twiste (Twistetal) Ger.
168 D3 Twistringen Ger.
222 D1 Twitya r. N.W.T. Can.
81 C6 Twizel South I. N.Z.
237 C4 Two Butte Creek r. CO U.S.A.
226 B2 Two Harbors MN U.S.A.
223 I4 Two Hills Alta Can.
148 B5 Twomileborris Rep. of Ireland
147 D3 Two Mile Bridge Rep. of Ireland
226 D3 Two Rivers WI U.S.A.
174 G5 Tworóg Pol.
151 F3 Twyford Hampshire, England U.K.
151 G3 Twyford Wokingham, England U.K.
146 D7 Twynholm Dumfries and Galloway, Scotland U.K.
Tyachev Ukr. see Tyachiv
136 B3 Tyachiv Ukr.
137 G4 Tyahynka Ukr.
Tyan' Shan' mts China/Kyrg. see Tien Shan
Tyanshanskaya Oblast' admin. div. Kyrg. see Naryn
96 A2 Tyao r. India/Myanmar
137 G3 Tyasmyn r. Ukr.
102 M1 Tyatya, Vulkan vol. Rus. Fed.
174 E2 Tychowo Pol.
174 G5 Tychy Pol.
175 K6 Tyczyn Pol.
140 J3 Tydal Norway
148 B3 Tydavnet Rep. of Ireland
Tyddewi Pembrokeshire, Wales U.K. see St David's
232 D5 Tygart Valley WV U.S.A.
100 C1 Tygda Rus. Fed.
100 C1 Tygda r. Rus. Fed.
147 E2 Tyholland Rep. of Ireland
199 E1 Tykhero Greece
137 G2 Tykhonovychi Ukr.
175 K2 Tykocin Pol.
175 J6 Tylawa Pol.
237 E5 Tyler TX U.S.A.
237 F6 Tylertown MS U.S.A.
136 F4 Tylihul r. Ukr.
100 G2 Tym' r. Sakhalin Rus. Fed.
175 I6 Tymbark Pol.
137 G3 Tymchenky Ukr.
137 J3 Tymonove Ukr.
137 H4 Tymoshivka Ukr.
100 G2 Tymovskoye Sakhalin Rus. Fed.
198 D4 Tympaki Kriti Greece
164 F1 Tynaarlo Neth.
148 C3 Tynan Northern Ireland U.K.
131 N4 Tynda Rus. Fed.
236 D3 Tyndall SD U.S.A.
Tyndinskiy Rus. Fed. see Tynda
146 D5 Tyndrum Stirling, Scotland U.K.
146 F5 Tyne r. Scotland U.K.
149 H3 Tyne and Wear admin. div. England U.K.
176 E1 Týnec nad Labem Czech Rep.
176 D2 Týnec nad Sázavou Czech Rep.
149 H2 Tynemouth Tyne and Wear, England U.K.
233 H3 Tyngsboro MA U.S.A.
143 E1 Tyngsjö Sweden
176 F1 Týniště nad Orlicí Czech Rep.
136 F3 Tynivka Ukr.
176 D2 Týn nad Vltavou Czech Rep.
136 D2 Tynne Ukr.
141 J3 Tynset Norway
Tyr Lebanon see Soûr
Tyras Ukr. see Bilhorod-Dnistrovs'kyy
175 K6 Tyrawa Wołoska Pol.
Tyre Lebanon see Soûr
262 S1 Tyree, Mount Antarctica
148 D3 Tyrella Northern Ireland U.K.
143 H2 Tyresö Sweden
173 G3 Tyrlaching Ger.
100 E2 Tyrma Rus. Fed.
100 D2 Tyrma r. Rus. Fed.
140 N2 Tyrnävä Fin.
198 C2 Tyrnavos Greece
129 C2 Tyrnyauz Rus. Fed.
Tyrol land Austria see Tirol
147 D2 Tyrone county Northern Ireland U.K.
239 E5 Tyrone NM U.S.A.
232 D4 Tyrone PA U.S.A.
83 E3 Tyrrell r. Vic. Austr.
83 E3 Tyrrell, Lake dry lake Vic. Austr.
147 D3 Tyrrellspass Rep. of Ireland
189 C5 Tyrrhenian Sea France/Italy
Tyrus Lebanon see Soûr
136 B3 Tysa r. Ukr. alt. Tisa (Yugoslavia), alt. Tisza (Hungary)
136 C3 Tysmenytsya Ukr.
142 A2 Tysnesøy i. Norway
142 A1 Tysse Norway
142 B1 Tyssedal Norway
175 L5 Tyszowce Pol.
150 D3 Tythegston Bridgend, Wales U.K.
138 D4 Tytuvėnai Lith.
129 E2 Tyube Rus. Fed.
129 G1 Tyub-Karagan, Poluostrov pen. Kazakh.
130 I4 Tyukalinsk Rus. Fed.
120 B3 Tyulen'i, Ostrova is Kazakh.
129 E1 Tyuleniy, Ostrov i. Rus. Fed.
120 D1 Tyul'gan Rus. Fed.
134 L4 Tyul'kino Rus. Fed.
130 H4 Tyumen' Rus. Fed.
Tyumen'-Aryk Kazakh. see Tomenaryk
121 J1 Tyumentsevo Rus. Fed.
131 N3 Tyung r. Rus. Fed.
Tyup Kyrg. see Tüp
106 C1 Tyva, Respublika aut. rep. Rus. Fed.
136 E3 Tyvriv Ukr.
174 C2 Tywa r. Pol.
150 C4 Tywardreath Cornwall, England U.K.
150 C3 Tywi r. Wales U.K.
150 C2 Tywyn Gwynedd, Wales U.K.
213 F4 Tzaneen S. Africa
243 H4 Tzucacab Mex.
164 E1 Tzummarum Neth.

U

Uaco Congo Angola see Waku-Kungo
79 □3 Ua Huka i. Fr. Polynesia
250 D4 Uainambi Brazil
Ualan atoll Micronesia see Kosrae
Ŭälīkhanov Kazakh. see Valikhanovo
79 □3 Ua Pou i. Fr. Polynesia
Ua Pu i. Fr. Polynesia see Ua Pou
251 E5 Uarini Brazil
87 B4 Uaroo W.A. Austr.
251 E3 Uasadi-jidi, Sierra mts Venez.
251 F4 Uatatás r. Brazil
251 G5 Uatumã r. Brazil
254 F4 Uauá Brazil
250 E5 Uaupés Brazil
250 E4 Uaupés r. Brazil
243 H5 Uaxactún Guat.
196 E3 Ub Srbija Yugo.
257 F4 Ubá Brazil
121 J2 Uba r. Kazakh.
169 B5 Übach-Palenberg Ger.
120 F1 Ubagan r. Kazakh.
257 E2 Ubaí Brazil
254 F5 Ubaitaba Brazil
124 C5 'Ubāl Yemen
120 C4 Ubal Karabaur hills Uzbek.
120 C4 Ubal Muzbel' hills Kazakh.
208 C5 Ubangi r. C.A.R./Dem. Rep. Congo
Ubangi-Shari country Africa see Central African Republic
257 F3 Ubaporanga Brazil
136 E1 Ubarts r. Belarus
250 C3 Ubate Col.
257 E5 Ubatuba Brazil
123 G4 Ubauro Pak.
161 E4 Ubaye r. France
103 E7 Ube Japan
185 G2 Úbeda Spain
256 D3 Uberaba Brazil
256 C4 Uberaba r. Brazil
172 A2 Überherrn Ger.
256 C3 Uberlândia Brazil
172 D4 Überlingen Ger.
173 G4 Übersee Ger.
183 H1 Ubidea Spain
256 A6 Ubiratâ Brazil
227 F4 Ubly MI U.S.A.
137 I2 Ublya r. Rus. Fed.
96 C3 Ubolratna Reservoir Thai.
215 I2 Ubombo S. Africa
96 D4 Ubon Ratchathani Thai.
136 D2 Ubort' r. Ukr.
161 E5 Ubraye France
185 E4 Ubrique Spain
172 C2 Ubstadt-Weiher Ger.
208 E5 Ubundu Dem. Rep. Congo
261 F3 Ucacha Arg.
129 E3 Ucar Azer.
252 B2 Ucayali dept Peru
250 C6 Ucayali r. Peru
192 A2 Ucciani Corse France
165 D4 Uccle Belgium
183 G4 Uceda Spain
161 C4 Ucel France
183 G3 Ucero Spain
183 G3 Ucero r. Spain
123 G4 Uch Pak.
182 B3 Ucha Port.
123 E2 Uch-Adzhi Turkm.
Üchajy Turkm. see Uch-Adzhi
122 B2 Üchān Iran
121 J3 Ucharal Kazakh.
161 C4 Uchaux France
105 E2 Uchimura-gawa r. Japan
104 C2 Uchinada Japan
102 J2 Uchiura-wan b. Japan
252 A2 Uchiza Peru
160 C2 Uchizy France
129 C2 Uchkeken Rus. Fed.
120 E4 Uchkuduk Uzbek.
121 F5 Uchkyay Uzbek.
Uchquduq Uzbek. see Uchkuduk
120 D4 Uchsay Uzbek.
Uchsoy Uzbek. see Uchsay
169 D3 Uchte Ger.
170 C3 Uchte r. Ger.
169 F5 Üchtelhausen Ger.
123 F5 Uchto r. Pak.
170 C3 Uchtspringe Ger.
131 O4 Uchur r. Rus. Fed.
183 F2 Ucieza r. Spain
157 G3 Uckange France
170 F1 Ückeritz Ger.
151 H4 Uckfield East Sussex, England U.K.
121 F4 Uckkulach Uzbek.
171 E4 Uckro Ger.
183 H5 Uclés Spain
222 E5 Ucluelet B.C. Can.
128 A1 Üçpınar Turkey
238 F2 Ucross WY U.S.A.
100 E1 Uda r. Rus. Fed.
137 I3 Uda r. Ukr.
129 D3 Udabno, Mt'a hill Georgia
135 I7 Udachnoye Rus. Fed.
131 M3 Udachnyy Rus. Fed.
114 C4 Udagamandalam Tamil Nadu India
116 C4 Udaipur Rajasthan India
116 C4 Udaipur Rajasthan India
117 G5 Udaipur Tripura India
116 D5 Udaipura Madh. Prad. India
175 L4 Udal r. Pol.
117 H4 Udalguri Assam India
174 E4 Udanin Pol.
117 E5 Udanti r. India/Myanmar
129 C1 Udarnyy Rus. Fed.
177 K3 Udava r. Slovakia
177 K3 Udavské Slovakia
137 G2 Uday r. Ukr.
114 C3 Udayagiri Andhra Prad. India
143 E1 Uddeholm Sweden
164 E2 Uddel Neth.
142 D2 Uddevalla Sweden
148 E2 Uddingston South Lanarkshire, Scotland U.K.
146 E6 Uddington South Lanarkshire, Scotland U.K.
140 L2 Uddjaure l. Sweden
129 C3 Ude Georgia
164 E3 Uden Neth.
164 E3 Udenhout Neth.
169 F4 Uder Ger.
178 C3 Uderns Austria
169 B5 Üdersdorf Ger.
114 C2 Udgir Mahar. India
Udhagamandalam Tamil Nadu India see Udagamandalam
116 C2 Udhampur Jammu and Kashmir
177 H2 Udiča Slovakia
134 I3 Udimskiy Rus. Fed.
191 I2 Udine Italy
191 H2 Udine prov. Friuli - Venezia Giulia Italy
Udmalaippettai Tamil Nadu India see Udumalaippettai
Udmurtia aut. rep. Rus. Fed. see Udmurtskaya Respublika
Udmurtskaya A.S.S.R. aut. rep. Rus. Fed. see Udmurtskaya Respublika
134 K4 Udmurtskaya Respublika aut. rep. Rus. Fed.
129 B1 Udobnaya Rus. Fed.
131 M4 Udokan, Khrebet mts Rus. Fed.
139 J3 Udomlya Rus. Fed.
96 C3 Udon Thani Thai.
174 F1 Udorpie Pol.
78 □4a Udot i. Chuuk Micronesia
175 L5 Udrycze Pol.
114 C4 Udumalaippettai Tamil Nadu India
114 B3 Udupi Karnataka India
137 I2 Udy Ukr.
Udzharma Georgia see Ujarma
Udzhary Azer. see Ucar
Uéa i. Î. Loyauté New Caledonia see Ouvéa
171 E4 Uebigau Ger.
170 F2 Uecker r. Ger.
170 F2 Ueckermünde Ger.
105 E2 Ueda Japan
173 E2 Uehlfeld Ger.
169 F3 Uehrde Ger.
93 B3 Uekuli Sulawesi Tengah Indon.
208 D3 Uele r. Dem. Rep. Congo
131 U3 Uelen Rus. Fed.
131 T3 Uel'kal' Rus. Fed.
169 B3 Uelsen Ger.
168 F3 Uelzen Ger.
104 C4 Ueno Japan
208 E4 Uere r. Dem. Rep. Congo
190 C2 Uetendorf Switz.
168 E2 Uetersen Ger.
172 D2 Uettingen Ger.
169 F3 Uetze Ger.
134 K5 Ufa Rus. Fed.
134 L5 Ufa r. Rus. Fed.
150 D4 Uffculme Devon, England U.K.
173 E2 Uffenheim Ger.
173 F4 Uffing am Staffelsee Ger.
193 H3 Ufita r. Italy
169 F4 Uftrungen Ger.
134 I3 Uftyuga r. Rus. Fed.
138 D3 Ugāle Latvia
211 A6 Ugalla r. Tanz.
210 B4 Uganda country Africa
188 F3 Ugar r. Bos.-Herz.
183 H1 Ugarana Spain
150 D4 Ugborough Devon, England U.K.
168 E1 Uge Denmark
195 H3 Ugento Italy
142 A1 Uggdal Norway
142 D3 Uggerby r. Denmark
195 H2 Uggiano la Chiesa Italy
207 G5 Ughelli Nigeria
215 G4 Ugie S. Africa
Ugi Island Solomon Is see Uki Island
185 G4 Ugíjar Spain
160 E3 Ugine France
100 G2 Uglegorsk Sakhalin Rus. Fed.
100 E4 Uglekamensk Rus. Fed.
134 L4 Ugleural'skiy Rus. Fed.
139 L3 Uglich Rus. Fed.
188 E3 Ugljan i. Croatia
139 I2 Uglovka Rus. Fed.
100 D2 Uglovoye Amurskaya Oblast' Rus. Fed.
100 E4 Uglovoye Primorskiy Kray Rus. Fed.
121 J2 Uglovskoye Rus. Fed.
177 G4 Ugod Hungary
Ugodskiy Zavod Rus. Fed. see Zhukovo
131 P3 Ugol'noye Rus. Fed.
Ugolnyy Chukotskiy Avtonomnyy Okrug Rus. Fed. see Beringovskiy
129 C2 Ugol'nyy Rus. Fed.
131 S3 Ugol'nyye Kopi Rus. Fed.
139 J4 Ugra Rus. Fed.
139 K4 Ugra r. Rus. Fed.
197 G4 Ugŭrchin Bulg.
130 I3 Ugut Rus. Fed.
177 K3 Uh r. Slovakia
Uharte-Arakil Spain see Huarte-Araquil
179 H2 Uherčice Czech Rep.
175 L4 Uherka r. Pol.
176 G2 Uherské Hradiště Czech Rep.
177 G2 Uherský Brod Czech Rep.
172 D3 Uhingen Ger.
176 C2 Úhlava r. Czech Rep.
172 D4 Uhldingen Ger.
176 E2 Uhlířské Janovica Czech Rep.
171 C5 Uhlstädt Ger.
136 B2 Uhniv Ukr.
232 C4 Uhrichsville OH U.S.A.
177 H3 Uhrovec Slovakia
137 H2 Uhroyidy Ukr.
171 C3 Uhrsleben Ger.
171 F4 Uhyst Ger.
254 E4 Uibaí Brazil
Uibhist a' Deas i. Scotland U.K. see South Uist
Uibhist a' Tuath i. Scotland U.K. see North Uist
171 C4 Uichteritz Ger.
146 B4 Uig Highland, Scotland U.K.
209 B6 Uíge Angola
209 B6 Uíge prov. Angola
101 C5 Ŭijŏngbu S. Korea
101 C4 Ŭiju N. Korea
120 C2 Uil Kazakh.
120 C2 Uil r. Kazakh.
129 C2 Uilpata, Gora mt. Rus. Fed.
140 O3 Uimaharju Fin.
241 K3 Uinkaret Plateau AZ U.S.A.
134 L4 Uinskoye Rus. Fed.
238 E3 Uinta r. CO U.S.A.
238 E3 Uinta Mountains UT U.S.A.
215 E5 Uitenhage S. Africa
164 D2 Uitgeest Neth.
164 D2 Uithoorn Neth.
164 F1 Uithuizen Neth.
164 F1 Uithuizermeeden Neth.
214 B3 Uitkyk S. Africa
214 C2 Uitsakpan salt pan S. Africa
214 B5 Uitspankraal S. Africa
177 J6 Uivar Romania
129 D3 Ujarma Georgia
175 H4 Ujazd Łódzkie Pol.
174 G5 Ujazd Opolskie Pol.
177 G2 Újezd Czech Rep.
176 F2 Újezd u Brna Czech Rep.
177 K4 Újfehértó Hungary
116 D4 Ujhani Uttar Prad. India
177 I4 Újhartyán Hungary
104 B4 Uji Japan
104 B4 Uji-gawa r. Japan
Ujiyamada Japan see Ise
116 C5 Ujjain Madh. Prad. India
177 L3 Ujkenéz Hungary
176 F4 Újkér Hungary
177 K5 Újkígyós Hungary
177 K4 Újléta Hungary
177 H6 Újpetre Hungary
174 E2 Ujście Pol.
175 H6 Ujsoły Pol.
177 K5 Újszalonta Hungary
177 J4 Újszász Hungary
177 J5 Újszentiván Hungary
177 K4 Újszentmargita Hungary
177 I4 Újszilvás Hungary
177 K4 Újtikos Hungary
176 F5 Újudvar Hungary
93 A4 Ujung Pandang Sulawesi Selatan Indon.
Újvidék Vojvodina, Srbija Yugo. see Novi Sad
207 G4 Ukata Nigeria
102 □1 Uke-jima i. Japan
127 F4 Ukhaydir tourist site Iraq
124 D4 Ukhdūd tourist site Saudi Arabia
135 H5 Ukholovo Rus. Fed.
175 M4 Ukhovets'k Ukr.
117 H4 Ukhrul Manipur India
Ukhta Respublika Kareliya Rus. Fed. see Kalevala
134 K3 Ukhta Respublika Komi Rus. Fed.
134 K3 Ukhta r. Rus. Fed.
83 H2 Uki N.S.W. Austr.
240 F2 Ukiah CA U.S.A.
238 C2 Ukiah OR U.S.A.
78 □6 Uki Island Solomon Is
174 D2 Ukleja r. Pol.
138 E4 Ukmergė Lith.
136 F3 Ukraine country Europe
121 J2 Ukrainka Vostochnyy Kazakhstan Kazakh.
121 J2 Ukrainka Vostochnyy Kazakhstan Kazakh.
Ukrainka Ukr. see Ukrayinka
Ukrainskaya S.S.R. country Europe see Ukraine
Ukrainskoye Ukr. see Ukrayins'ke
Ukrayina country Europe see Ukraine
136 F2 Ukrayinka Ukr.
137 G2 Ukrayins'ke Ukr.
188 F3 Ukrina r. Bos.-Herz.
209 B7 Uku Angola
209 B8 Ukuma Angola
111 B6 Ul r. India
138 G4 Ula Belarus
138 G4 Ula r. Belarus
175 M1 Ūla r. Lith.
199 F3 Ula Turkey
106 E2 Ulaanbaatar Mongolia
106 E2 Ulaanbaatar mun. Mongolia
107 F2 Ulaan-Ereg Mongolia
106 B1 Ulaangom Mongolia
106 E2 Ulaanhudag Mongolia
106 D2 Ulaan-Uul Mongolia
107 F2 Ulaan-Uul Mongolia
83 G3 Ulan N.S.W. Austr.
107 F4 Ulan Nei Mongol China
106 C4 Ulan Qinghai China
Ulan Bator Mongolia see Ulaanbaatar
121 G3 Ulanbel' Kazakh.
135 I7 Ulan Erge Respublika Kalmykiya - Khalm'g-Tangch Rus. Fed.
Ulanhad Nei Mongol China see Chifeng
107 I2 Ulanhot Nei Mongol China
107 F3 Ulan Hua Nei Mongol China
136 E3 Ulaniv Ukr.
135 I7 Ulan-Khol Rus. Fed.
175 K4 Ulan-Majorat Pol.
137 H2 Ulanove Ukr.
175 K5 Ulanów Pol.
106 D3 Ulan Tohoi Nei Mongol China
98 I1 Ulan-Ude Rus. Fed.
260 D2 Ulapes Arg.
126 E3 Ulaş Turkey
199 E1 Ulaş Turkey
192 B5 Ulassai Sardegna Italy
78 □6 Ulawa Island Solomon Is
121 J2 Ul'ba Kazakh.
Ülbi Kazakh. see Ul'ba
138 E3 Ulbroka Latvia
146 E3 Ulbster Highland, Scotland U.K.
149 I4 Ulceby North Lincolnshire, England U.K.
101 D5 Ulchin S. Korea
196 D5 Ulcinj Crna Gora Yugo.
214 E3 Ulco S. Africa
142 C4 Uldum Denmark
107 F1 Uldz Mongolia
107 G1 Uldz r. Mongolia
Uleåborg Fin. see Oulu
142 C2 Ulefoss Norway
185 H3 Uleila del Campo Spain
138 F2 Ülenurme Estonia
107 G1 Ulety Rus. Fed.
175 K4 Ułęż Pol.
142 C3 Ulfborg Denmark
Ulflingen Lux. see Troisvierges
164 F3 Ulft Neth.
107 H2 Ulgain Gol r. China
149 H2 Ulgham Northumberland, England U.K.
114 B2 Ulhasnagar Mahar. India
175 L5 Ulhówek Pol.
107 H2 Uliastai Nei Mongol China
106 C2 Uliastay Mongolia
Uliatea i. Arch. de la Société Fr. Polynesia see Raiatea
177 L3 Ulič Slovakia
165 D3 Ulicoten Neth.
Ulie atoll Micronesia see Woleai
78 □3b Uliga i. Majuro Marshall Is
208 E5 Ulindi r. Dem. Rep. Congo
134 F1 Ulita r. Rus. Fed.
91 I4 Ulithi atoll Micronesia
Uljanovsk Rus. Fed. see Ul'yanovsk
120 E2 Ul'kayak r. Kazakh.
Ülkenözen r. Kazakh./Rus. Fed. see Bol'shoy Uzen'
121 H4 Ul'ken Sulutar Kazakh.
Ülken Vladīmīrovka Kazakh. see Bol'shaya Vladimirovka
182 B2 Ulla r. Spain
83 G3 Ulladulla N.S.W. Austr.
146 C4 Ullapool Highland, Scotland U.K.
142 E3 Ullared Sweden
140 M2 Ullatti Sweden
186 D4 Ulldecona Spain
186 D3 Ulldemolins Spain
142 D4 Ullerslev Denmark
177 I5 Üllés Hungary
149 H4 Ulleskelf North Yorkshire, England U.K.
262 S1 Ullmer, Mount Antarctica
252 C4 Ulloma Bol.
140 L1 Ullsfjorden sea chan. Norway
129 F2 Ulluchay r. Rus. Fed.
101 D5 Ullŭng-do i. S. Korea
172 D3 Ulm Ger.
100 D2 Ul'ma r. Rus. Fed.
169 E5 Ulmbach Ger.
184 B1 Ulme r. Port.
169 B5 Ulmen Ger.
197 H3 Ulmeni Călăraşi Romania
197 F2 Ulmeni Maramureş Romania
188 G4 Ulog Bos.-Herz.
213 G2 Ulongue Moz.
82 D1 Uloowaranie, Lake salt flat S.A. Austr.
149 F3 Ulpha Cumbria, England U.K.
142 E3 Ulricehamn Sweden
179 E2 Ulrichsberg Austria
169 E5 Ulrichstein Ger.
164 F1 Ulrum Neth.
101 D6 Ulsan S. Korea
146 □G1 Ulsta Shetland, Scotland U.K.
142 D3 Ulsted Denmark
140 I3 Ulsteinvik Norway
147 D2 Ulster reg. Rep. of Ireland/U.K.
227 I5 Ulster PA U.S.A.
235 D1 Ulster County county NY U.S.A.
83 E3 Ultima Vic. Austr.
252 B1 Ultraoriental, Cordillera mts Peru
242 □I6 Ulua r. Hond.
129 B3 Ulubağ Turkey
199 F2 Ulubey Turkey
199 G2 Uluborlu Turkey
199 F1 Uludağ mt. Turkey
94 C2 Ulu Kali, Gunung mt. Malaysia
126 D3 Ulukışla Turkey
199 G2 Uluköy Turkey
215 H3 Ulundi S. Africa
110 D2 Ulungur He r. China
110 D2 Ulungur Hu l. China
240 □C8 Ulupalakua HI U.S.A.
Uluqsaqtuuq N.W.T. Can. see Holman
84 B5 Uluru hill N.T. Austr.
199 F2 Ulus Dağı mt. Turkey
Ulutau Kazakh. see Ulytau
121 F3 Ulutau, Gory mts Kazakh.
146 B5 Ulva i. Scotland U.K.
Ulvéah i. Vanuatu see Lopévi
142 A2 Ulvenåso mt. Norway
164 D3 Ulvenhout Neth.
149 F3 Ulverston Cumbria, England U.K.
83 F5 Ulverstone Tas. Austr.
142 B1 Ulvik Norway
141 L3 Ulvsjön Sweden
139 K2 Ul'yanikha Rus. Fed.
137 F4 Ulyanivka Mykolayivs'ka Oblast' Ukr.
137 H2 Ulyanivka Sums'ka Oblast' Ukr.
Ŭl'yanov Kazakh. see Ul'yanovskiy
139 H2 Ul'yanovka Rus. Fed.
136 F3 Ul'yanovka Ukr.
139 J5 Ul'yanovo Rus. Fed.
121 G4 Ul'yanovo Uzbek.
135 J5 Ul'yanovsk Rus. Fed.
135 I5 Ul'yanovskaya Oblast' admin. div. Rus. Fed.
121 H2 Ul'yanovskiy Kazakh.
Ulyanovsk Oblast admin. div. Rus. Fed. see Ul'yanovskaya Oblast'
Ul'yanovskoye Kazakh. see Ul'yanovskiy
107 H1 Ulyatuy Rus. Fed.
237 C4 Ulysses KS U.S.A.
232 B6 Ulysses KY U.S.A.
121 F2 Ulytau Kazakh.
120 E2 Uly-Zhylanshyk r. Kazakh.
183 I2 Ulzama r. Spain
100 B1 Uma Rus. Fed.
188 D3 Umag Croatia
252 D4 Umala Bol.
'Umān country Asia see Oman
243 H4 Umán Mex.
78 □4a Uman i. Chuuk Micronesia
136 F3 Uman' Ukr.
258 C3 Umango, Cerro mt. Arg.
116 E5 Umaria Madh. Prad. India
114 C2 Umarkhed Mahar. India
114 D2 Umarkot Orissa India
123 G5 Umarkot Pak.
82 D1 Umaroona, Lake salt flat S.A. Austr.
116 C5 Umarpada Gujarat India
238 C2 Umatilla OR U.S.A.
92 C4 Umayan r. Phil.
134 F2 Umba Murmanskaya Oblast' Rus. Fed.
84 D2 Umbakumba N.T. Austr.
84 C5 Umbeara N.T. Austr.
150 D4 Umberleigh Devon, England U.K.
191 H5 Umbertide Italy
81 B6 Umbrella Mountains South I. N.Z.
191 H5 Umbria admin. reg. Italy
195 F3 Umbriatico Italy
215 H3 Umdloti Beach S. Africa
213 F3 Ume r. Zimbabwe
140 M3 Umeå Sweden
140 M3 Umeälven r. Sweden
135 H5 Umet Rus. Fed.
215 I3 Umfolozi r. S. Africa
140 K2 Umfors Sweden
Umfuli r. Zimbabwe see Mupfure
215 H4 Umgababa S. Africa
215 H3 Umgeni r. S. Africa
125 D1 Umgharah Kuwait
215 H3 Umhali S. Africa
178 B3 Umhausen Austria
215 H3 Umhlanga S. Africa
182 B2 Umia r. Spain
105 D1 Umi-gawa r. Japan
240 □D9 Umikoa HI U.S.A.
220 H3 Umingmaktok Nunavut Can.
120 B4 Umirzak Kazakh.
224 E1 Umiujaq Que. Can.
172 B3 Umkirch Ger.
215 H4 Umkomaas S. Africa
215 H4 Umkomaas r. S. Africa
215 H3 Umlazi S. Africa
127 G5 Umma tourist site Iraq
128 B3 Umm ad Daraj, Jabal mt. Jordan
124 B3 Umm al Birak Saudi Arabia
128 B5 Umm al Hashīm, Jabal mt. Jordan
Umm al Qaywayn U.A.E. see Umm al Qaiwain
125 F2 Umm al Qaiwain U.A.E.
125 F3 Umm as Samīm salt flat Oman
125 E2 Umm Bāb Qatar
172 D3 Ummendorf Ger.
124 B2 Umm Lajj Saudi Arabia
128 B5 Umm Mafrûd, Gebel mt. Egypt
124 B3 Umm Mukhbār, Jabal hill Saudi Arabia
128 D5 Umm Nukhaylah hill Saudi Arabia
203 F6 Umm Ruwaba Sudan
202 E2 Umm Sa'ad Libya
125 E2 Umm Sa'id Qatar
128 B5 Umm Saysabān, Jabal mt. Jordan
128 A5 Umm Shomar, Gebel mt. Egypt
128 A5 Umm Tinâşşib, Gebel mt. Egypt
128 D4 Umm Wa'āl hill Saudi Arabia
128 A5 Umm Zanatir mt. Egypt
220 B4 Umnak Island AK U.S.A.
238 A3 Umpqua r. OR U.S.A.
199 G2 Umraniye Turkey
116 D5 Umred Mahar. India
114 B1 Umreth Gujarat India
Umtali Zimbabwe see Mutare
215 H4 Umtamvuna r. S. Africa
215 G4 Umtata S. Africa
215 G4 Umtata r. S. Africa
215 H4 Umtentweni S. Africa
207 G5 Umuahia Nigeria
256 A5 Umuarama Brazil
129 E3 Umudlu Azer.
129 B3 Umudum Turkey
199 E1 Umurbey Turkey
199 F2 Umurlar Turkey
80 E4 Umutoi North I. N.Z.
215 H3 Umvoti r. S. Africa
Umvuma Zimbabwe see Mvuma
215 G4 Umzimhlava r. S. Africa
215 G4 Umzimkulu S. Africa
215 H4 Umzimkulu r. S. Africa
215 G4 Umzimvubu r. S. Africa
Umzingwani r. Zimbabwe see Mzingwani
215 H4 Umzinto S. Africa
215 H4 Umzumbe S. Africa
188 F3 Una r. Bos.-Herz./Croatia
255 F5 Una Brazil
254 G4 Una r. Brazil
116 D3 Una Hima. Prad. India
183 I4 Uña Spain
81 D5 Una, Mount South I. N.Z.
128 C5 'Unāb, Jabal al hill Jordan
188 F3 Unac r. Bos.-Herz.
182 D2 Uña de Quintana Spain
233 F3 Unadilla NY U.S.A.
233 F3 Unadilla r. NY U.S.A.
256 D2 Unaí Brazil
220 B3 Unalakleet AK U.S.A.
220 B4 Unalaska AK U.S.A.
220 B4 Unalaska Island AK U.S.A.
211 B8 Unango Moz.
176 F3 Únanov Czech Rep.
146 C3 Unapool Highland, Scotland U.K.
136 F2 Unava r. Ukr.
124 C2 'Unayzah Saudi Arabia
126 E4 'Unayzah, Jabal hill Iraq
186 B2 Uncastillo Spain
116 E4 Unchahra Madh. Prad. India
241 M2 Uncompahgre Plateau CO U.S.A.
215 G3 Underberg S. Africa
83 E3 Underbool Vic. Austr.
140 K3 Undersåker Sweden
236 C2 Underwood ND U.S.A.
172 D3 Undingen Ger.
135 J5 Undory Rus. Fed.
163 A6 Undués de Lerda Spain
150 E3 Undy Monmouthshire, Wales U.K.
139 I5 Unecha Rus. Fed.
139 H5 Unecha r. Rus. Fed.
251 E5 Uneiuxi r. Brazil
83 F3 Ungarie N.S.W. Austr.
82 D3 Ungarra S.A. Austr.
Ungava, Baie d' b. Que. Can. see Ungava Bay
221 K3 Ungava, Péninsule d' pen. Que. Can.
225 H1 Ungava Bay Que. Can.
Ungava Peninsula Que. Can. see Ungava, Péninsule d'
Ungeny Moldova see Ungheni
173 E3 Ungerhausen Ger.
100 D4 Unggi N. Korea
136 D4 Ungheni Moldova
197 G2 Ungheni Romania
Unguja North admin. reg. Tanz. see Zanzibar North
Unguja South admin. reg. Tanz. see Zanzibar South
Unguja West admin. reg. Tanz. see Zanzibar West
197 G2 Ungurași Romania
122 D2 Unguz, Šolonchakovyye Vpadiny salt flat Turkm.
Üngüz Angyrsyndaky Garagum des. Turkm. see Zaunguzskiye Karakumy
Ungvár Ukr. see Uzhhorod
211 D5 Ungwana Bay Kenya
182 C4 Unhais da Serra Port.
182 C4 Unhais-o-Velho Port.
171 F5 Unhošť Czech Rep.
134 J4 Uni Rus. Fed.
254 E3 União Brazil
255 C8 União da Vitória Brazil
254 G4 União dos Palmares Brazil
116 D4 Uniara Rajasthan India
176 G2 Uničov Czech Rep.
174 G4 Uniejów Pol.
161 C3 Unieux France
188 E3 Unije i. Croatia
220 B4 Unimak Island AK U.S.A.
176 G3 Unín Slovakia
251 F5 Unini r. Brazil
252 B2 Unini Peru
260 E4 Unión Arg.
253 F6 Unión Para.
233 □I2 Union ME U.S.A.
236 F4 Union MO U.S.A.
235 D2 Union NJ U.S.A.
238 C2 Union OR U.S.A.
231 D5 Union SC U.S.A.
232 C6 Union WV U.S.A.
259 E5 Unión, Bahía b. Arg.
241 K4 Union, Mount AZ U.S.A.
235 D2 Union Beach NJ U.S.A.
234 A3 Union Bridge MD U.S.A.
232 A4 Union City OH U.S.A.
232 D4 Union City PA U.S.A.
237 F4 Union City TN U.S.A.
235 D2 Union County county NJ U.S.A.
234 A2 Union County county PA U.S.A.
214 D5 Uniondale S. Africa
234 C1 Union Dale PA U.S.A.
246 B2 Unión de Reyes Cuba
244 B4 Unión de Tula Mex.
147 B5 Unionhall Rep. of Ireland
245 G5 Unión Hidalgo Mex.
247 □3 Union Island St Vincent
231 C5 Union Springs AL U.S.A.
232 E3 Union Springs NY U.S.A.
231 C5 Uniontown AL U.S.A.
232 D5 Uniontown PA U.S.A.
235 F1 Unionville CT U.S.A.
227 F4 Unionville MI U.S.A.
236 E3 Unionville MO U.S.A.
240 H1 Unionville NV U.S.A.
234 D1 Unionville NY U.S.A.
234 C3 Unionville PA U.S.A.
232 E5 Unionville VA U.S.A.
174 G2 Unisław Pol.
125 F3 United Arab Emirates country Asia
United Arab Republic country Africa see Egypt
145 G4 United Kingdom country Europe
United Provinces state India see Uttar Pradesh
228 G3 United States of America country N. America
221 L1 United States Range mts Nunavut Can.
191 H4 Uniti r. Italy
223 I4 Unity Sask. Can.
238 C2 Unity OR U.S.A.
234 B1 Unityville PA U.S.A.
116 C5 Unjha Gujarat India
169 C5 Unkel Ger.
178 D3 Unken Austria
172 D3 Unlingen Ger.
169 C4 Unna Ger.
116 E4 Unnao Uttar Prad. India
169 C5 Unnau Ger.
101 C5 Ŭnp'a N. Korea
261 E2 Unquillo Arg.
101 C4 Unsan P'yŏngan-bukto N. Korea
101 C5 Ŭnsan P'yŏngan-namdo N. Korea
129 C4 Ünseli Turkey
146 □H1 Unst i. Scotland U.K.
149 H4 Unstone Derbyshire, England U.K.
171 C4 Unstrut r. Ger.
117 E4 Untari Bihar India
197 H2 Unţeni Romania
190 D1 Unterägeri Switz.
173 F4 Unterammergau Ger.
169 E5 Unterbreizbach Ger.
173 E4 Unterdießen Ger.
173 G3 Unterdietfurt Ger.

Column 1

169 E5 Unterfranken admin. reg. Bayern Ger.
173 H3 Untergriesbach Ger.
173 F3 Unterhaching Ger.
190 D1 Unter Inn Thal val. Austria
179 H4 Unterharm Austria
168 F3 Unterlüß Ger.
169 F5 Untermaßfeld Ger.
173 E3 Untermeitingen Ger.
169 F6 Untermerzbach Ger.
172 D2 Untermünkheim Ger.
173 G3 Unterneukirchen Ger.
173 E2 Unterpleichfeld Ger.
173 G3 Unterreit Ger.
190 D2 Unterschächen Switz.
190 D3 Unterschleißheim Ger.
173 E3 Unterschneidheim Ger.
169 F5 Untersiemau Ger.
171 C5 Untersteinach Ger.
173 E4 Unterthingau Ger.
179 F2 Unterueckersee l. Ger.
179 F2 Unterweißenbach Austria
171 C5 Unterweißenborn Ger.
173 G4 Unterwössen Ger.
129 E2 Untsukul' Rus. Fed.
251 E4 Unturán, Sierra de mts Venez.
222 D3 Unuk r. U.S.A./Can.
106 A5 Unuli Horog Qinghai China
156 B4 Unverre France
134 L3 Un'ya r. Rus. Fed.
134 I4 Unzha Rus. Fed.
183 I2 Unzue Spain
102 C1 Uotsuri-shima i. Japan
104 D2 Uozu Japan
176 E1 Upa r. Czech Rep.
139 K4 Upa r. Rus. Fed.
241 L1 Upalco UT U.S.A.
117 F5 Upar Ghat reg. Madh. Prad. India
151 F3 Upavon Wiltshire, England U.K.
221 M2 Upernavik Greenland
168 C2 Upgant-Schott Ger.
92 C5 Upi Phil.
250 C3 Upia r. Col.
176 F1 Upice Czech Rep.
214 C3 Upington S. Africa
141 N3 Upinniemi Fin.
240 I4 Upland CA U.S.A.
116 B5 Upleta Gujarat India
150 E4 Uplyme Devon, England U.K.
80 E3 Upokongaro North I. N.Z.
78 □2 Upolu i. Samoa
129 B1 Upornaya Rus. Fed.
232 B4 Upper Arlington OH U.S.A.
222 G5 Upper Arrow Lake B.C. Can.
    Upper Austria land Austria see Oberösterreich
234 C2 Upper Black Eddy PA U.S.A.
146 E3 Upper Camster Highland, Scotland U.K.
150 D2 Upper Chapel Powys, Wales U.K.
    Upper Chindwin Myanmar see Mawlaik
151 F3 Upper Clatford Hampshire, England U.K.
234 B3 Upper Crossroads MD U.S.A.
234 C3 Upper Darby PA U.S.A.
206 E4 Upper East admin. reg. Ghana
222 F4 Upper Fraser B.C. Can.
151 F3 Upper Heyford Oxfordshire, England U.K.
81 E4 Upper Hutt North I. N.Z.
226 B4 Upper Iowa r. IA U.S.A.
233 □J1 Upper Kent N.B. Can.
238 B3 Upper Klamath Lake OR U.S.A.
146 E4 Upper Knockando Moray, Scotland U.K.
147 E2 Upperlands Northern Ireland U.K.
222 D2 Upper Liard Y.T. Can.
147 D2 Upper Lough Erne l. Northern Ireland U.K.
234 B4 Upper Marlboro MD U.S.A.
210 B2 Upper Nile state Sudan
235 E1 Upper Nyack NY U.S.A.
232 B4 Upper Sandusky OH U.S.A.
    Upper Seal Lake Que. Can. see Iberville, Lac d'
81 D4 Upper Takaka South I. N.Z.
151 F2 Upper Tean Staffordshire, England U.K.
    Upper Tunguska r. Rus. Fed. see Angara
    Upper Volta country Africa see Burkina
114 B3 Uppinangadi Karnataka India
151 G2 Uppingham Rutland, England U.K.
    Uppland reg. Sweden
143 G2 Uppland Sweden
143 G3 Upplanda Sweden
143 G3 Upplands-Väsby Sweden
    Uppsala county Sweden
224 B3 Uppsala Ont. Can.
116 D2 Upshi Jammu and Kashmir
226 B2 Upson WI U.S.A.
85 F3 Upstart Bay Qld Austr.
150 E4 Upton Dorset, England U.K.
233 H3 Upton St Leonards Gloucestershire, England U.K.
150 E3 Upton upon Severn Worcestershire, England U.K.
80 E1 Upua r. Rus. Fed.
128 C2 'Uqayribāt Syria
124 C2 'Uqlat aş Şuqūr Saudi Arabia
    Uqturpan Xinjiang China see Wushi
127 C5 Ur tourist site Iraq
    Urad Qianqi Nei Mongol China see Xishanzui
107 F3 Urad Zhongqi Nei Mongol China
146 □G1 Urafirth Shetland, Scotland U.K.
190 D3 Urago d'Oglio Italy
140 P1 Ura-Guba Rus. Fed.
256 B5 Uraí Brazil
176 F4 Uraiújfalu Hungary
114 C4 Urakam Kerala India
83 H1 Ural hill N.S.W. Austr.
120 B3 Ural r. Kazakh./Rus. Fed.
83 G2 Uralla N.S.W. Austr.
    Ural Mountains Rus. Fed. see Ural'skiy Khrebet
120 B2 Ural'sk Kazakh.
    Ural'skaya Oblast' admin. div. Kazakh. see Zapadnyy Kazakhstan
    Ural'skiye Gory mts Rus. Fed. see Ural'skiy Khrebet
134 L2 Ural'skiy Khrebet mts Rus. Fed.
211 B6 Urambo Tanz.
114 B2 Uran Mahar. India
83 F3 Urana N.S.W. Austr.
83 F3 Urana, Lake N.S.W. Austr.
84 C2 Urandangi Qld Austr.
254 E5 Urandi Brazil
223 I3 Uranium City Sask. Can.
83 F3 Uranquity N.S.W. Austr.
84 C2 Urapunga N.T. Austr.
251 F4 Uraricoera Brazil
    Urartu country Asia see Armenia
192 A5 Uras Sardegna Italy
    Ura-Tyube Tajik. see Ŭroteppa
114 C2 Uravakonda Andhra Prad. India
241 M2 Uravan CO U.S.A.
105 F3 Urawa Japan
130 H3 Uray Rus. Fed.
105 F3 Urayasu Japan
125 E2 Uray'irah Saudi Arabia
124 D2 'Urayq ad Duḥūl des. Saudi Arabia
124 D2 'Urayq Şāqān des. Saudi Arabia
174 E4 Uraz Pol.
135 H5 Urazovo Rus. Fed.
169 C5 Urbach Ger.
236 F3 Urbana IL U.S.A.
226 E5 Urbana IL U.S.A.
232 B4 Urbana OH U.S.A.
191 H5 Urbania Italy
254 E2 Urbano Santos Brazil
169 C5 Urbar Ger.

Column 2

190 D4 Urbe Italy
183 G2 Urbel r. Spain
83 H2 Urbenville N.S.W. Austr.
172 C2 Urberach Ger.
191 H5 Urbino Italy
    Urbinum Italy see Urbino
183 H2 Urbión mt. Spain
191 I5 Urbisaglia Italy
160 B2 Urbise France
    Urbs Vetus Italy see Orvieto
176 G2 Urdce Czech Rep.
252 C3 Urcos Peru
163 A5 Urcuit France
185 G1 Urda Spain
261 G5 Urdampoleta Arg.
186 B1 Urdax Spain
    Ur'devarri hill Fin./Norway see Urtivaara
261 H3 Urdinarrain Arg.
134 J3 Urdoma Rus. Fed.
172 C4 Urdorf Switz.
156 D2 Urdos France
108 D2 Urad Tamir Gol r. Mongolia
183 H1 Urduña Spain
121 J3 Urdzhar Kazakh.
138 F5 Urechcha Belarus
197 H2 Urechești Romania
134 I4 Uren' Rus. Fed.
130 I3 Urengoy Rus. Fed.
142 B2 Urenosi mt. Norway
80 E3 Urenui North I. N.Z.
78 □5 Uréparapara i. Vanuatu
163 A5 Urepel France
164 F1 Uretarp Neth.
    Urfa Turkey see Şanlıurfa
169 B5 Urft r. Ger.
    Urga Mongolia see Ulaanbaatar
100 E2 Urga r. Rus. Fed.
    Urganch Uzbek. see Urgench
120 E4 Urgench Uzbek.
126 D3 Ürgüp Turkey
121 F5 Urgut Uzbek.
110 D2 Ürho Xinjiang China
192 A4 Uri Sardegna Italy
116 C2 Uri Jammu and Kashmir
190 D2 Uri canton Switz.
81 C5 Uriah, Mount South I. N.Z.
250 C2 Uribia Col.
163 A4 Urie r. Scotland U.K.
157 G4 Urimenil France
244 C4 Uripitijuata, Cerro mt. Mex.
239 F7 Urique r. Mex.
190 D1 Uri-Rotstock mt. Switz.
137 J1 Uritskaya Rus. Fed.
120 E2 Uril Wenz r. Eth.
199 F1 Urla Turkey
197 H3 Urlați Romania
147 D4 Urlingford Rep. of Ireland
107 E1 Urluk Rus. Fed.
134 I5 Urmary Rus. Fed.
176 D2 Úsov Czech Rep.
    Urmia Iran see Orūmīyeh
    Urmia, Lake salt l. Iran see Orūmīyeh, Daryācheh-ye
172 D3 Urmitz Ger.
149 G4 Urmston Greater Manchester, England U.K.
190 E1 Ürnäsch Switz.
186 A1 Urola r. Spain
207 G5 Uromi Nigeria
196 E4 Uroševac Kosovo, Srbija Yugo.
123 G2 Ŭroteppa Tajik.
137 H5 Urozhaynoye Rus. Fed.
184 C1 Urra Port.
186 C3 Urrea de Gaén Spain
162 E3 Urrea de Jalón Spain
163 A6 Urriés Spain
184 C1 Urros Port.
100 E2 Urrugne France
100 D4 Ursat'yevskaya Uzbek.
157 H2 Ursberg Ger.
173 E3 Ursensollen Ger.
139 M4 Urshel'skiy Rus. Fed.
245 E2 Úrsulo Galván Mex.
174 E3 Urszulin Pol.
190 C1 Urtenen Switz.
141 M1 Urtivaara hill Fin./Norway
242 C3 Uruáchic Mex.
254 C5 Uruaçu Brazil
253 H3 Uruana Brazil
239 C6 Uruapan Baja California Norte Mex.
244 C4 Uruapan Michoacán Mex.
252 B3 Urubamba Peru
251 F6 Urubaxi r. Brazil
251 G5 Urubu r. Brazil
256 B4 Urubupungá, Salto de waterfall Brazil
251 G5 Uruçara Brazil
251 F6 Uruçui Brazil
254 D4 Uruçuí, Serra do hills Brazil
254 D4 Urucuia r. Brazil
251 F6 Urucurituba Brazil
183 I3 Urueña Spain
255 S8 Uruguai r. Brazil
    alt. Uruguay (Arg./Uru.)
258 F3 Uruguaiana Brazil
261 R4 Uruguay country S. America
258 G4 Uruguay r. Arg./Uru. alt. Uruguai (Brazil)
    Uruk tourist site Iraq see Erech
92 □ Urukthapel i. Palau
110 D1 Ürümchi Xinjiang China see Ürümqi
110 D2 Ürümqi Xinjiang China
131 O3 Urup i. Kuril'skiye O-va Rus. Fed.
129 C2 Urup r. Rus. Fed.
131 M2 Urup r. Rus. Fed.
131 Q5 Urup, Ostrov i. Kuril'skiye O-va Rus. Fed.
253 E2 Urupá r. Brazil
256 C4 Urupês Brazil
138 E3 Urupskaya Krasnodarskiy Kray Rus. Fed. see Sovetskaya
124 D4 'Urūq al Awārik des. Saudi Arabia
125 F3 'Urūq ash Shaybah des. Saudi Arabia
134 J4 Urus-Martan Rus. Fed.
135 J5 Urussu Rus. Fed.
197 K3 Uruțău Romania
197 L4 Urziceni Satu Mare Romania
120 D4 Urziceni Ialomița Romania
134 J4 Urzhum Rus. Fed.
192 B4 Urzulei Sardegna Italy
160 B1 Urzy France
105 B7 Usa r. Japan
138 G1 Usa r. Belarus
103 B7 Usa Japan
80 E3 Uruti North I. N.Z.
211 A6 Uruwira Tanz.
129 C2 Urvan' Rus. Fed.
158 B2 Urville Nacqueville France
121 K2 Uryl' Kazakh.
102 □J2 Uryū-gawa r. Japan
100 B1 Uryumkan r. Rus. Fed.
135 I6 Uryupinsk Rus. Fed.

Column 3

134 L2 Usa r. Rus. Fed.
184 D2 Usagre Spain
199 F2 Uşak Turkey
199 F2 Uşak prov. Turkey
211 C6 Usakos Namibia
263 K2 Usarp Mountains Antarctica
259 F8 Usborne, Mount hill Falkland Is
196 E4 Ušče Srbija Yugo.
175 I6 Uścimów Pol.
175 J6 Uście Gorlickie Pol.
175 I5 Uście Solne Pol.
190 E4 Uscio Italy
170 E2 Usedom Ger.
170 E2 Usedom i. Ger.
87 B5 Useless Loop W.A. Austr.
192 A5 Usellus Sardegna Italy
138 G5 Usha r. Belarus
138 G5 Usha r. Belarus
    Ushachi Belarus see Ushachy
138 G4 Ushachy Belarus
121 J2 Ushanovo Kazakh.
    Ushant i. France see Ouessant, Île d'
138 G4 Ushachy Belarus
138 G5 Usha r. Belarus
138 D8 Ushibuka Japan
105 G2 Ushiku Japan
104 B5 Ushimado Japan
121 I3 Ushtobe Kazakh.
    Ush-Tyube Kazakh. see Ushtobe
259 C9 Ushuaia Arg.
136 D3 Ushya Ushya r. Ukr.
169 D5 Usingen Ger.
192 A4 Usini Sardegna Italy
134 L2 Usinsk Rus. Fed.
150 E3 Usk Monmouthshire, Wales U.K.
150 D3 Usk r. Wales U.K.
    Usk Uttar Prad. India see Uska
150 E3 Usk r. Wales U.K.
138 F5 Uskhodni Belarus
    Uskoplje Bos.-Herz. see Gornji Vakuf
199 F1 Üsküdar Turkey
197 H5 Üsküp Turkey
169 E4 Uslar Ger.
176 C2 Úslava r. Czech Rep.
139 L5 Usman' Rus. Fed.
139 L5 Usman' r. Rus. Fed.
121 F5 Usmat Uzbek.
    Usmet Uzbek. see Usmat
183 E5 Uso r. Spain
134 J3 Usogorsk Rus. Fed.
211 B6 Usoke Tanz.
134 I5 Usol'ye Rus. Fed.
98 H1 Usol'ye-Sibirskoye Rus. Fed.
176 D2 Úsov Czech Rep.
137 H1 Úsova Rus. Fed.
137 J1 Úsozha r. Rus. Fed.
137 I4 Úsozha r. Rus. Fed.
260 C3 Uspallata Arg.
121 I1 Uspenka Kazakh.
100 D2 Uspenka Kazakh.
134 I4 Uspenka Ukr.
100 E2 Ussuri r. Rus. Fed.
100 D4 Ussuriysk Rus. Fed.
134 I4 Usta r. Rus. Fed.
137 G2 Ust'-Abakanskoye Rus. Fed.
134 I3 Ust'-Alekseyevo Rus. Fed.
123 G4 Usta Muhammad Pak.
163 A5 Ustaritz France
215 H4 Ust'-Baïyk Rus. Fed.
106 B1 Ust'-Dzheguta Rus. Fed.
129 B1 Ust'-Dzheguta Rus. Fed.
    Ust'-Dzhegutinskaya Rus. Fed. see Ust'-Dzheguta
176 C1 Ústěk Czech Rep.
190 D1 Uster Switz.
194 C4 Ustica Sicilia Italy
194 C4 Ustica, Isola di i. Sicilia Italy
131 L4 Ust'-Ilimsk Rus. Fed.
131 L4 Ust'-Ilimskiy Vodokhranilishche resr Rus. Fed.
131 L4 Ust'-Ilimskiy
120 E1 Uy r. Rus. Fed.
98 H1 Ust'-Ordynskiy Rus. Fed.
98 H1 Ust'-Ordynskiy Buryatskiy Avtonomnyy Okrug admin. div. Rus. Fed.
163 D6 Ustou France
197 H4 Ustrem Bulg.
174 G6 Ustroń Pol.
175 K6 Ustrzyki Dolne Pol.
174 C4 Ustyluh Ukr.
100 B1 Usu Xinjiang China
134 J3 Ust'-Tsil'ma Rus. Fed.
134 K2 Ust'-Ulagan Rus. Fed.
100 E2 Ust'-Umalta Rus. Fed.
134 J3 Ust'-Usa Rus. Fed.
139 M3 Ust'-Vayen'ga Rus. Fed.
134 G4 Ust'ye r. Rus. Fed.
139 L3 Ust'ye Rus. Fed.
139 L5 Ust'ye-Kirovskoye Rus. Fed.
139 A4 Ustynivka Ukr.
110 D2 Ustyn Xinjiang China
136 C2 Ustyuzhna Rus. Fed.
110 D3 Usu Xinjiang China
103 B7 Usa Japan
103 C8 Usa Japan
242 □H6 Usulután El Salvador
243 G5 Usumacinta r. Guat./Mex.

Column 4

    Usumbura Burundi see Bujumbura

V

95 F2 Usun Apau, Dataran Tinggi plat. Sarawak Malaysia
175 H6 Usurbil Pol.
215 I2 Usutu r. Africa
139 H4 Usva r. Rus. Fed.
138 G4 Usvyaty Belarus
175 I5 Uszew Pol.
177 H5 Uszód Hungary
134 C2 Uszwica r. Pol.
192 A5 Uta Sardegna Italy
241 L2 Utah state U.S.A.
241 L2 Utah Lake U.S.A.
168 C2 Utarp Ger.
    Utashinai Kuril'skiye O-va Rus. Fed. see Yuzhno-Kuril'sk
125 C2 Utayyiq Saudi Arabia
186 C3 Utebo Spain
237 C5 Ute Creek r. NM U.S.A.
161 F5 Utelle France
209 D9 Utembo r. Angola
138 E4 Utena Lith.
149 I4 Utersum Ger.
211 C7 Utete Tanz.
138 I3 Uthai Thani Thai.
96 C4 Uthal Pak.
169 F4 Uthleben Ger.
168 D2 Uthlede Ger.
227 F4 Utica MI U.S.A.
237 F5 Utica MS U.S.A.
233 F3 Utica NY U.S.A.
232 B4 Utica OH U.S.A.
187 B5 Utiel Spain
242 □I5 Utila Hond.
254 E5 Utinga r. Brazil
215 E2 Utiwanang S. Africa
103 E7 Uto Japan
84 C4 Utopia N.T. Austr.
175 I3 Utrata r. Pol.
143 C5 Utraula Uttar Prad. India
184 E3 Utrecht S. Africa
184 E3 Utrecht prov. Neth.
184 E3 Utrecht S. Africa
184 E3 Utrera Spain
177 I6 Utrine Vojvodina, Srbija Yugo.
138 G3 Utroya r. Rus. Fed.
142 A2 Utsira Norway
140 N1 Utsjoki Fin.
105 D3 Utsugi-dake mt. Japan
105 F2 Utsunomiya Japan
135 I7 Utta r. Rus. Fed.
96 C3 Uttaradit Thai.
116 D3 Uttarkashi Uttar Prad. India
116 D4 Uttar Pradesh state India
178 D2 Uttendorf Oberösterreich Austria
178 B3 Uttendorf Salzburg Austria
173 F2 Uttenreuth Ger.
172 D3 Uttenweiler Ger.
168 G1 Utterslev Denmark
173 H3 Utting am Ammersee Ger.
151 F2 Uttoxeter Staffordshire, England U.K.
    Utu Xinjiang China see Miao'ergou
247 □I Utuado Puerto Rico
110 D2 Utubulak Xinjiang China
78 □6 Utupua i. Solomon Is
120 C2 Utva r. Kazakh.
170 E2 Utzedel Ger.
221 M2 Uummannaq Greenland
221 M2 Uummannaq c. Greenland see Nunap Isua
140 N3 Uusikaarlepyy Fin. see Nykarleby
141 M3 Uusikaupunki Fin.
106 D1 Üür Gol r. Mongolia
196 A1 Uvac r. Srbija Yugo.
237 D6 Uvalde TX U.S.A.
139 J5 Uvarovichy Belarus
135 H6 Uvarovo Rus. Fed.
159 F3 Uvéa i. Î. Loyauté
    New Caledonia see Ouvéa
120 E1 Uvel'ka r. Rus. Fed.
161 E4 Uvernet-Fours France
211 A6 Uvinza Tanz.
209 F5 Uvira Dem. Rep. Congo
139 M3 Uvod' r. Rus. Fed.
106 B1 Uvs prov. Mongolia
106 B1 Uvs Nuur salt l. Mongolia
103 F7 Uwajima Japan
124 B2 'Uwayrid, Harrat al lava field Saudi Arabia
202 E4 Uweinat, Jebel mt. Sudan
227 H3 Uxbridge Ont. Can.
151 G3 Uxbridge Greater London, England U.K.
160 D2 Uxeau France
169 B5 Uxheim Ger.
107 F4 Uxin Qi Nei Mongol China
163 D4 Uxmal tourist site Mex.
245 G5 Uxmal tourist site Mex.
120 D1 Uy r. Rus. Fed.
107 J2 Uyaly Kazakh.
106 D2 Uydzin Mongolia
106 B1 Üydzöö Gol r. China
120 E1 Uyskoye Rus. Fed.
96 A1 Uyu Chaung r. Myanmar
124 C2 'Uyun Saudi Arabia
252 D5 Uyuni, Salar de salt flat Bol.
252 D5 Uyuni Bol.
120 A1 Uza r. Rus. Fed.
121 G3 Uzayim, Nahr al r. Iraq
120 L2 Uzbekistan country Asia
    Uzbek S.S.R. country Asia see Uzbekistan
    Uzbekskaya S.S.R. country Asia see Uzbekistan
138 H5 Uzda Belarus
158 F3 Uzel France
121 I4 Uzen' Kazakh. see Kyzylsay
120 C2 Uzen' r. Kazakh.
158 D3 Uzerche France
161 F4 Uzès France
190 F2 Uzhhorod Ukr. see Uzhhorod
197 J2 Uzhcheny Romania
197 K1 Uzhhorod Ukr.
    Uzhhorod Ukr. see Uzhhorod
196 C3 Užice Srbija Yugo.
196 C3 Uzin Ukr.
139 L5 Uzlovaya Rus. Fed.
199 J3 Uzola r. Rus. Fed.
199 J4 Üzümlü Turkey
199 G5 Üzümlü Turkey
121 G5 Uzunada i. Turkey
121 I4 Uzunagach Almatinskaya Oblast' Kazakh.
121 I4 Uzunagach Almatinskaya Oblast' Kazakh.
110 D2 Uzunbulak Xinjiang China
128 A1 Uzunköprü Turkey
129 B5 Uzundere Turkey
129 E5 Uzungöl Turkey
243 G5 Uzynkaz Kazakh.

Column 5

113 □1 Vaadhu i. S. Male Maldives
113 □1 Vaagali i. S. Male Maldives
134 D3 Vaajakoski Fin.
215 D3 Vaal r. S. Africa
140 N2 Vaala Fin.
215 G2 Vaal Dam S. Africa
168 E2 Vaale Ger.
215 G1 Vaalplaas S. Africa
165 F4 Vaals Neth.
165 F4 Vaalserberg hill Neth.
213 F5 Vaalwater S. Africa
140 M3 Vaasa Fin.
164 F2 Vaassa Neth.
164 E2 Vaassen Neth.
113 □ Vaattaru i. N. Male Maldives
138 E4 Vaasenlaninkas Lith.
120 F4 Vabkent Uzbek.
139 I5 Vabich r. Belarus
161 F5 Vabre France
161 A5 Vabres-l'Abbaye France
177 I4 Vác Hungary
255 C9 Vacaré Brazil
257 F2 Vacacaí r. Brazil
255 B7 Vacaria Brazil
257 F2 Vacaria, Minas Gerais Brazil
255 B7 Vacaria, Mato Grosso do Sul Brazil
240 G2 Vacaville CA U.S.A.
161 C5 Vaccarès, Étang de lag. France
195 F3 Vaccarizzo Albanese Italy
169 F5 Vacha Ger.
134 H5 Vacha Rus. Fed.
177 I4 Vácharytán Hungary
160 E2 Vachères France
129 C2 Vachi Rus. Fed.
143 F3 Väckelsång Sweden
173 H2 Vacov Czech Rep.
161 C4 Vacqueyras France
161 I4 Vacquiers France
134 L5 Vad Rus. Fed.
135 H5 Vad r. Rus. Fed.
114 B2 Vada Mahar. India
138 D3 Vadakste r. Latvia/Lith.
196 D2 Vădastra Romania
142 C4 Vadeheavet sea chan. Denmark
197 H3 Vădeni Romania
136 E4 Vădeni, Dealul hill Moldova
105 F2 Vadinagu Japan
135 H1 Vadinsk Rus. Fed.
133 C6 Vadodara Gujarat India
140 O1 Vadsø Norway
142 F2 Vadstena Sweden
197 G2 Văduj Ukr.
173 F2 Vaduz Liechtenstein
170 D1 Væggerløse Denmark
142 K2 Værøy i. Norway
134 K2 Vaga r. Rus. Fed.
141 J3 Vågåmo Norway
188 E3 Vaganski Vrh mt. Croatia
144 D1 Vágar i. Faroe Is
144 D1 Vágar i. Faroe Is
115 I4 Vagaram Andhra Prad. India
143 F3 Vaggeryd Sweden
78 □6 Vagia Sterea Ellas Greece
199 I7 Vágia i. Italy
197 G3 Vagler Italy
199 I7 Vagli Sotto Italy
190 F4 Vagli Sotto Italy
143 G4 Vagnhärad Sweden
142 G3 Vägsele Sweden
140 L1 Vágsfjorden sea chan. Norway
177 H7 Vágur Slovakia
140 □ Vágur Faroe Is
139 B4 Vahivka Ukr.
141 N3 Vähäkyrö Fin.
169 G4 Vahlbruch Ger.
188 E3 Vaganski Vrm mt. Croatia
144 D1 Vágar i. Faroe Is
129 D1 Vahsel, Cape S. Georgia
141 M3 Vahto Fin.
77 H2 Vaiaku Tuvalu
184 E3 Vaiamonte Port.
191 G5 Vaiano Italy
140 F2 Vaida Estonia
237 F5 Vaiden MS U.S.A.
114 C4 Vaigai r. India
159 F3 Vaiges France
172 C3 Vaihingen an der Enz Ger.
114 C3 Vaijapur Mahar. India
114 C4 Vaikam Kerala India
160 B2 Vailly-sur-Aisne France
160 C2 Vailly-sur-Sauldre France
235 D1 Vails Gate NY U.S.A.
104 □ Vaimata Japan
138 C3 Väimela Estonia
79 □7a Vainağu i. Tuvalu
114 C3 Vairāgad Mahar. India
159 F4 Vair r. France
193 G4 Vairano Patenora Italy
193 E3 Vairano Scalo Italy
116 C3 Vairowal Punjab India
116 C3 Vais r. France
158 D3 Vaïssac France

Column 6

183 F2 Valdecebollas mt. Spain
183 I1 Valdecilla Spain
183 G1 Valdecuenca Spain
182 E5 Valdefuentes Spain
183 D1 Valdegeña Spain
183 E5 Valdelacasa Spain
183 E5 Valdelacasa de Tajo Spain
182 D4 Valdelamusa Spain
186 C4 Valdelinares Spain
183 E4 Valderas Spain
184 C4 Valdeobispo Spain
185 E2 Valdepeñas Spain
185 F3 Valdepeñas de Jaén Spain
183 E2 Valdepiélago Spain
183 E3 Valderaduey r. Spain
156 B4 Val-de-Reuil France
183 E5 Valdeverde Sicilia Italy
183 D4 Valderrobres Spain
184 D4 Valderrueda Spain
226 D3 Valders WI U.S.A.
261 G4 Valdés Arg.
259 E6 Valdés, Península pen. Arg.
183 F4 Val de Santo Domingo Spain
227 J3 Val-des-Bois Que. Can.
183 E5 Valdestillas Spain
186 D4 Valdetorres Spain
184 D5 Valdeverdeja Spain
183 E4 Valdevimbre Spain
250 B4 Valdez Ecuador
183 C2 Valdez AK U.S.A.
    Valdgeym Ukr. see Dobropillya
190 F2 Valditerro Italy
161 E3 Val d'Isère France
190 F2 Valdisotto Italy
259 B5 Valdivia Chile
250 C3 Valdivia Col.
162 C2 Valdivienne France
158 D2 Valdivienne France
190 F4 Val d'Ilzé France
191 G3 Valdobbiadene Italy
157 G3 Valdoie France
156 C3 Val-d'Oise dept Île-de-France France
161 E4 Val-d'Or Que. Can.
231 D6 Valdosta GA U.S.A.
141 I3 Valdres val. Norway
141 I3 Valdres val. Norway
169 D6 Valdrôme France
188 E3 Valdulce Ukr.
197 H3 Vălenii de Munte Romania
245 □ Valente Díaz y La Loma Mex.
160 E1 Valente Spain see Valencia
180 E2 Valentigney France
123 G2 Valentine NE U.S.A.
239 F6 Valentine TX U.S.A.
181 D5 Valenza Italy
163 G4 Valer Norway
250 D2 Valera Venez.
182 D1 Valera de Arriba Spain
161 C4 Valernes France
156 E3 Vales Mortos Port.
161 D4 Valeron Italy
197 F3 Valreuil France
177 H2 Valéa Spain
158 C3 Valga Spain see Ponte Valga
138 F3 Valga Estonia
190 D2 Valgrisenche Italy
245 □ Valguarnera Caropepe Sicilia Italy
235 E1 Valhalla NY U.S.A.
183 I4 Valhelmoso Port.
121 D6 Valier, Mont mt. France
177 L4 Vál Hungary
120 K3 Väladalen Sweden
193 I3 Valadares Port.
195 G2 Valadares mts Spain
150 D3 Vale of Glamorgan admin. div. Wales U.K.
142 D1 Vāler Norway
250 D2 Valera Venez.
177 I3 Vălpaz, Nahr al r. Iraq
177 K3 Valalaky Slovakia
197 F3 Válaliky Slovakia
197 F3 Vălani Romania
197 H3 Valea lui Mihai Romania
197 H3 Valea Lungă Romania
197 G3 Valea Lungă Romania
197 G3 Valea la Rosa Port.
190 F4 Vale das Mós Port.
184 B1 Vale de Açor Port.
184 C1 Vale de Açor Port.
184 C2 Vale de Cambra Port.
184 B1 Vale de Cavalos Port.
184 D2 Vale de Espinho Port.
184 B2 Vale de Estrela Port.
184 C1 Vale de Figueira Port.
184 B2 Vale de Guiso Port.
183 C4 Vale de Prazeres Port.
184 B2 Vale de Reis Port.
184 B1 Vale de Salgueiro Port.
184 C2 Vale de Santarém Port.
184 C2 Vale de Vargo Port.
184 C1 Vale do Pereiro Port.
184 C1 Vale do Peso Port.
184 C2 Vale das Mós Port.

Column 7

146 A4 Vallay i. Scotland U.K.
140 I3 Valldal Norway
187 C4 Vall d'Alba Spain
187 F5 Valldemossa Spain
181 E3 Valle de Uxó Spain
250 B4 Valle dept Col.
142 B2 Valle Norway
142 F1 Valle Italy
193 F2 Valle Castellana Italy
193 F3 Vallecorsa Italy
193 F2 Valle de la Serena Spain
244 D4 Valle de Bravo Mex.
184 D4 Valle de la Serena Spain
184 D2 Valle de Matamoros Mex.
184 D2 Valle de Santiago Mex.
191 H2 Valle di Cadore Italy
192 A4 Valledolmo Sicilia Italy
192 A4 Valledoria Sardegna Italy
250 C2 Valledupar Col.
217 □2a Vallée de Mai tourist site Seychelles
225 G4 Vallée-Jonction Que. Can.
260 C2 Valle Fértil, Sierra de mts Arg.
252 D4 Valle Grande Bol.
216 □3a Vallehermoso La Gomera Canary Is
243 F3 Valle Hermoso Mex.
160 D2 Valleiry France
240 F2 Vallejo CA U.S.A.
194 C5 Vallelunga Pratameno Sicilia Italy
190 E3 Valle Mosso Italy
140 L3 Vallen Sweden
245 F5 Valle Nacional Mex.
258 C3 Vallenar Chile
187 B4 Vallença Spain
156 C3 Vallendar France
142 D5 Vallensbæk Denmark
161 B4 Vallentuna Sweden
160 D2 Vallerauge France
192 A5 Valleraugue Sardegna Italy
193 A5 Vallerotonda Italy
216 □3a Vallero Gran Canaria Canary Is
158 E4 Vallet France
123 □ Valletta Malta
225 L5 Valley r. Man. Can.
143 H4 Valley Italy
150 C1 Valley Isle of Anglesey, Wales U.K.
240 I5 Valley Center CA U.S.A.
236 D2 Valley City ND U.S.A.
238 B3 Valley Falls OR U.S.A.
234 C2 Valley Forge PA U.S.A.
232 C5 Valley Head WV U.S.A.
147 E3 Valleymount Rep. of Ireland
203 E3 Valley of The Kings tourist site Egypt
240 G2 Valley Springs CA U.S.A.
230 C4 Valley Station KY U.S.A.
238 E2 Valley Stream NY U.S.A.
235 F1 Valley Stream NY U.S.A.
234 D4 Valley View Alta Can.
234 B3 Valley View PA U.S.A.
186 E3 Vallfogona de Riucorb Spain
162 E3 Valli Spain
193 H4 Vallmoll Spain
193 H4 Vallo della Lucania Italy
161 E3 Vallon-en-Sully France
190 B2 Vallorbe Switz.
160 E2 Vallorcine France
161 E4 Vallouise France
162 E3 Valls Spain
141 J3 Valls Sweden
190 E3 Valmadrera Italy
190 C3 Valmara Italy
223 J5 Val Marie Sask. Can.
    Valmaseda Spain see Balmaseda
185 F2 Valmayor r. Spain
138 E3 Valmiera Latvia
183 F4 Valmojado Spain
159 G2 Valmont France
193 E3 Valmontone Italy
191 G3 Valnera mt. Spain
183 G1 Valo Spain
156 E3 Valognes France
184 C1 Valongo Portalegre Port.
184 B1 Valongo Porto Port.
185 G4 Válor Spain
254 E3 Valória la Buena Spain
138 F1 Valozhyn Belarus
183 D3 Valpaços Port.
224 E3 Val-Paradis Que. Can.
117 B4 Valparai Tamil Nadu India
256 B4 Valparaíso Brazil
258 B4 Valparaíso admin. reg. Chile
244 C2 Valparaíso Mex.
243 I2 Valparaiso FL U.S.A.
230 C5 Valparaiso IN U.S.A.
258 B4 Valparaíso Chile
191 G3 Valperga Italy
188 F2 Valpovo Croatia
160 E2 Valras-Plage France
161 C4 Valréas France
183 C3 Valroquesta hill Spain
161 B5 Valros France
215 J1 Vals r. S. Africa
116 C5 Valsad Gujarat India
190 D3 Valsavarenche Italy
140 O3 Valsjöbyn Sweden
141 J3 Valsøyfjord Norway
135 G7 Val'skoye Rus. Fed.
190 E2 Valstagna Italy
160 C1 Val-Suzon France
141 H2 Val-Thorens France
184 B2 Valtiendas Spain
140 O3 Valtimo Fin.
165 F3 Valtournenche Italy
78 □ Valua i. Vanuatu see Mota Lava
183 □ Valuéjols France

Column 8

140 H3 Valldal Norway
187 C4 Vall d'Alba Spain
187 F5 Valldemossa Spain
181 E3 Valle de Uxó Spain
250 B4 Valle dept Col.
142 B2 Valle Norway
142 F1 Valle Italy
193 F2 Valle Castellana Italy
193 F3 Vallecorsa Italy
244 D4 Valle de Bravo Mex.
184 D4 Valle de la Serena Spain
184 D2 Valle de Matamoros Mex.
184 D2 Valle de Santiago Mex.
191 H2 Valle di Cadore Italy
192 A4 Valledolmo Sicilia Italy
192 A4 Valledoria Sardegna Italy
178 D1 Valley i. Man. Can.
173 F3 Valley Ger.
240 I5 Valley Center CA U.S.A.
236 D2 Valley City ND U.S.A.
238 B3 Valley Falls OR U.S.A.
234 C2 Valley Forge PA U.S.A.
232 C5 Valley Head WV U.S.A.
147 E3 Valleymount Rep. of Ireland
203 E3 Valley of The Kings tourist site Egypt
240 G2 Valley Springs CA U.S.A.
230 C4 Valley Station KY U.S.A.
235 F1 Valley Stream NY U.S.A.
234 D4 Valleyview Alta Can.
234 B3 Valley View PA U.S.A.
186 E3 Vallfogona de Riucorb Spain
162 E3 Valli Spain
193 H4 Vallmoll Spain
193 H4 Vallo della Lucania Italy
161 E3 Vallon-en-Sully France
190 B2 Vallorbe Switz.
160 E2 Vallorcine France
161 E4 Vallouise France
162 E3 Valls Spain
141 J3 Valls Sweden
190 E3 Valmadrera Italy
190 C3 Valmara Italy
223 J5 Val Marie Sask. Can.
185 F2 Valmayor r. Spain
138 E3 Valmiera Latvia
183 F4 Valmojado Spain
159 G2 Valmont France
193 E3 Valmontone Italy
191 G3 Valnera mt. Spain
183 G1 Valo Spain
156 E3 Valognes France
184 C1 Valongo Portalegre Port.
184 B1 Valongo Porto Port.
185 G4 Válor Spain
140 O3 Valøya Fin.
138 F2 Valozhyn Belarus
183 D3 Valpaços Port.
140 K2 Valsinni Italy
140 K2 Valsjöbyn Sweden
191 F1 Valstagna Italy
215 J3 Valspruit S. Africa
191 G3 Valstagna Italy
145 G3 Valsura r. India
160 C1 Val-Suzon France
184 E2 Valtiendas Spain
160 C1 Valtos Scotland U.K.
176 F3 Valtice Czech Rep.
142 D1 Valtimo Fin.
161 F5 Vamberk Czech Rep.
97 D5 Vam Co Đông r. Vietnam
97 D5 Vam Co Tay r. Vietnam
114 C3 Vammala Fin.
141 M3 Vammala Fin.
177 I4 Vámosgyörk Hungary
177 I4 Vámosmikola Hungary
177 K4 Vámospércs Hungary
177 I4 Vámosújfalu Hungary
115 I2 Vampula Fin.
116 B5 Vamsadhara r. India
129 C4 Van prov. Turkey
    Van, Lake salt l. Turkey see Van Gölü
142 D1 Vanävara Romania
176 F1 Vamberk Czech Rep.
129 C4 Vanavara Rus. Fed.

Van Buren to **Vetlanda** 375

237 E5 **Van Buren** AR U.S.A.
226 E5 **Van Buren** IN U.S.A.
233 □J1 **Van Buren** ME U.S.A.
237 F4 **Van Buren** MO U.S.A.
Van Buren OH U.S.A. see **Kettering**
233 □J2 **Vanceboro** ME U.S.A.
232 B5 **Vanceburg** KY U.S.A.
Vanch Tajik. see **Vanj**
Vanchskiy Khrebet mts Tajik. see **Vanj, Qatorkŭhi**
232 B6 **Vancleve** KY U.S.A.
235 E1 **Van Cortlandtville** NY U.S.A.
222 F5 **Vancouver** B.C. Can.
238 B2 **Vancouver** WA U.S.A.
87 C7 **Vancouver, Cape** W.A. Austr.
222 B2 **Vancouver, Mount** Can./U.S.A.
222 E5 **Vancouver Island** B.C. Can.
177 K4 **Váncsod** Hungary
Vanda Fin. see **Vantaa**
236 F4 **Vandalia** IL U.S.A.
232 A5 **Vandalia** OH U.S.A.
129 E3 **Vandam** Azer.
178 A3 **Vandans** Austria
114 C3 **Vandavasi** Tamil Nadu India
186 D3 **Vandellós** Spain
160 B2 **Vandenesse** France
160 C1 **Vandenesse-en-Auxois** France
215 F2 **Vanderbijlpark** S. Africa
226 E3 **Vanderbilt** MI U.S.A.
232 D4 **Vandergrift** PA U.S.A.
222 E4 **Vanderhoof** B.C. Can.
84 D2 **Vanderlin Island** N.T. Austr.
84 B1 **Van Diemen, Cape** N.T. Austr.
84 D3 **Van Diemen, Cape** Qld Austr.
84 C1 **Van Diemen Gulf** N.T. Austr.
Van Diemen's Land state Austr. see **Tasmania**
234 C1 **Vandling** PA U.S.A.
157 G4 **Vandœvre-lès-Nancy** France
191 G2 **Vandoies** Italy
138 E2 **Vändra** Estonia
193 G3 **Vandra** r. Italy
215 G2 **Vandyksdrif** S. Africa
Väner, Lake Sweden see **Vänern**
142 E2 **Vänern** l. Sweden
142 E2 **Vänersborg** Sweden
183 F2 **Vañes** Spain
262 T2 **Vang, Mount** Antarctica
211 C6 **Vanga** Kenya
213 □J4 **Vangaindrano** Madag.
138 E3 **Vangaži** Latvia
129 E3 **Vängli** Azer.
127 F3 **Van Gölü** salt l. Turkey
140 L1 **Vangsvik** Norway
223 J5 **Vanguard** Sask. Can.
78 □6 **Vangunu** i. New Georgia Is Solomon Is
78 □6 **Vangunu, Mount** New Georgia Is Solomon Is
239 F6 **Van Horn** TX U.S.A.
129 C2 **Vani** Georgia
224 F4 **Vanier** Ont. Can.
78 □6 **Vanikoro Islands** Solomon Is
190 C2 **Vanil Noir** mt. Switz.
91 J7 **Vanimo** P.N.G.
100 G2 **Vanino** Rus. Fed.
114 C3 **Vaniyambadi** Tamil Nadu India
123 G2 **Vanj** Tajik.
123 G2 **Vanj, Qatorkŭhi** mts Tajik.
140 L2 **Vänjaurträsk** Sweden
197 F3 **Vânju Mare** Romania
131 T3 **Vankarem** Rus. Fed.
233 F2 **Vankleek Hill** Ont. Can.
232 B4 **Vanlue** OH U.S.A.
140 □ **Van Mijenfjorden** inlet Svalbard
140 L1 **Vanna** i. Norway
140 L3 **Vännäs** Sweden
156 D4 **Vanne** r. France
158 D4 **Vannes** France
Vannovka Kazakh. see **Tura-Ryskulova**
140 L1 **Vanntindan** mt. Norway
191 G3 **Vanoi** r. Italy
215 G3 **Van Reenen** S. Africa
91 I7 **Van Rees, Pegunungan** mts Indon.
214 B4 **Vanrhynsdorp** S. Africa
85 E3 **Vanrook** Qld Austr.
85 E3 **Vanrook Creek** r. Qld Austr.
116 C5 **Vansada** Gujarat India
232 B6 **Vansant** VA U.S.A.
143 F1 **Vansbro** Sweden
142 B2 **Vanse** Norway
86 E2 **Vansittart Bay** W.A. Austr.
215 F3 **Vanstadensrus** S. Africa
141 N3 **Vantaa** Fin.
138 E1 **Vantaa** r. Fin.
87 D5 **Van Truer Tableland** reg. W.A. Austr.
215 H3 **Vant's Drift** S. Africa
77 I3 **Vanua Balavu** i. Fiji
78 □5 **Vanua Lava** i. Vanuatu
79 □1 **Vanua Levu** i. Fiji
Vanua Mbalavu i. Fiji see **Vanua Balavu**
78 □5 **Vanuatu** country S. Pacific Ocean
Vanua Valavo i. Fiji see **Vanua Balavu**
156 E5 **Vanvey** France
236 G3 **Van Wert** OH U.S.A.
214 C5 **Van Wyksdorp** S. Africa
214 C4 **Vanwyksvlei** S. Africa
177 I4 **Vanyarc** Hungary
190 D3 **Vanzone** Italy
214 D2 **Van Zylsrus** S. Africa
78 □5 **Vao** New Caledonia
163 D4 **Vaour** France
176 G1 **Vápenná** Czech Rep.
136 E3 **Vapnyarka** Ukr.
184 C3 **Vaqueiros** Port.
161 E5 **Var** dept Provence-Alpes-Côte-d'Azur France
161 F5 **Var** r. France
190 E4 **Vara** r. Italy
142 E2 **Vara** Sweden
114 C3 **Varada** r. India
185 H1 **Vara del Rey** Spain
246 B2 **Varadero** Cuba
159 E4 **Varades** France
177 L5 **Vărădia de Mureș** Romania
161 D5 **Varages** France
116 B5 **Varahi** Gujarat India
163 D4 **Varaire** France
190 C4 **Varaita** r. Italy
138 F3 **Varakļāni** Latvia
177 H5 **Varalja** Hungary
190 D3 **Varallo** Italy
122 B3 **Varāmīn** Iran
117 E4 **Varanasi** Uttar Prad. India
134 L1 **Varandey** Rus. Fed.
140 O1 **Varangerfjorden** sea chan. Norway
140 O1 **Varangerhalvøya** pen. Norway
193 H3 **Varano, Lago di** lag. Italy
190 E4 **Varano de'Melegari** Italy
138 F4 **Varapayeva** Belarus
185 F2 **Varas** r. Spain
188 F2 **Varaždin** Croatia
179 H4 **Varaždinske Toplice** Croatia
190 D4 **Varazze** Italy
142 E3 **Varberg** Sweden
177 J3 **Varbó** Hungary
161 D3 **Varces** France
177 L5 **Vârciorog** Romania
198 B2 **Varda** Greece
123 G3 **Vardak** prov. Afgh.
114 C2 **Vardannapet** Andhra Prad. India
196 F5 **Vardar** r. Macedonia
142 C4 **Varde** Denmark
142 C4 **Varde** r. Denmark
129 D3 **Vardenis** Armenia
129 D3 **Vardenisi Lerr** mt. Armenia
129 D4 **Vardenisi Lerrnashght'a** mts Armenia
129 D3 **Vardisubani** Georgia
141 M3 **Vårdö** Åland Fin.
140 O1 **Vardø** Norway
177 H5 **Várdomb** Hungary
138 D3 **Varduva** r. Lith.
139 L3 **Varegovo** Rus. Fed.
168 D2 **Varel** Ger.
206 A3 **Varela** Guinea-Bissau
138 E4 **Varėna** Lith.
138 E4 **Varėnė** r. Lith.
156 A3 **Varengeville-sur-Mer** France
137 I5 **Varenikovskaya** Rus. Fed.
156 B3 **Varenne** r. France
156 C5 **Varennes-Changy** France
157 F3 **Varennes-en-Argonne** France
160 D2 **Varennes-St-Sauveur** France
160 B2 **Varennes-sur-Allier** France
160 B1 **Varennes-Vauzelles** France
137 J4 **Varenovka** Rus. Fed.
188 G3 **Vareš** Bos.-Herz.
190 D3 **Varese** Italy
190 D3 **Varese** prov. Lombardia Italy
190 E4 **Varese Ligure** Italy
162 D3 **Varetz** France
100 E3 **Varfolomeyevka** Rus. Fed.
177 L5 **Vârfurașu, Vârful** mt. Romania
177 L5 **Vârfurile** Romania
142 E2 **Vårgårda** Sweden
254 F4 **Vargem** r. Brazil
257 G4 **Vargem Alta** Brazil
254 E2 **Vargem Grande** Brazil
256 D4 **Vargem Grande do Sul** Brazil
257 E4 **Varginha** Brazil
142 A2 **Varhaug** Norway
177 J5 **Variaș** Romania
163 D5 **Varilhes** France
177 H2 **Varín** Slovakia
Varkana Iran see **Gorgān**
140 N3 **Varkaus** Fin.
169 E4 **Varlosen (Niemetal)** Ger.
142 E2 **Värmland** county Sweden
142 E2 **Värmland** reg. Sweden
197 H4 **Varna** Bulg.
114 B2 **Varna** r. India
191 G2 **Varna** Italy
120 E1 **Varna** Rus. Fed.
143 F3 **Värnamo** Sweden
142 E1 **Värnäs** Sweden
134 I4 **Varnavino** Rus. Fed.
138 D4 **Varniai** Lith.
Várnjárg pen. Norway see **Varangerhalvøya**
176 D1 **Varnsdorf** Czech Rep.
231 D5 **Varnville** SC U.S.A.
177 I5 **Városföld** Hungary
Varosha Cyprus see **Varosia**
128 A2 **Varosia** Cyprus
188 F3 **Varoška Rijeka** Bos.-Herz.
177 G4 **Városlőd** Hungary
140 N3 **Varpaisjärvi** Fin.
177 H4 **Várpalota** Hungary
168 D3 **Varrel** Ger.
162 C3 **Vars** Poitou-Charentes France
161 E4 **Vars** Provence-Alpes-Côte-d'Azur France
197 G2 **Vârșag** Romania
199 G3 **Varsak** Turkey
196 E2 **Vârșand** Romania
177 I3 **Varsány** Hungary
190 E4 **Varsi** Italy
164 F3 **Varsseveld** Neth.
143 G2 **Vårsta** Sweden
Vartashen Azer. see **Oğuz**
142 D2 **Varteig** Norway
198 B3 **Vartholomio** Greece
127 F3 **Varto** Turkey
197 F3 **Vârtop** Romania
129 C2 **Varts'ikhe** Georgia
140 O3 **Värtsilä** Fin.
137 G2 **Varva** Ukr.
137 I2 **Varvarivka** Kharkivs'ka Oblast' Ukr.
136 D2 **Varvarivka** Khmel'nyts'ka Oblast' Ukr.
137 J2 **Varvarovka** Rus. Fed.
177 L3 **Vary** Ukr.
136 C2 **Varyazh** Ukr.
254 F3 **Várzea Alegre** Brazil
257 E2 **Várzea da Palma** Brazil
254 E3 **Várzea Grande** Brazil
190 E4 **Varzi** Italy
190 D2 **Varzo** Italy
160 B1 **Varzy** France
176 F4 **Vas** county Hungary
Vasa Fin. see **Vaasa**
254 F4 **Vasa Barris** r. Brazil
177 I4 **Vasad** Hungary
114 B2 **Vasai** Mahar. India
138 E2 **Vasalemma** Estonia
138 E2 **Vasalemma** r. Estonia
193 E2 **Vasanello** Italy
177 H5 **Vásárosdombó** Hungary
177 L3 **Vásárosnamény** Hungary
184 C3 **Vascão** r. Port.
197 F2 **Vașcău** Romania
134 I2 **Vashka** r. Rus. Fed.
136 C3 **Vashkivtsi** Ukr.
Vasht Iran see **Khāsh**
198 C1 **Vasilika** Greece
Vasilkov Ukr. see **Vasyl'kiv**
Vasilkovka Ukr. see **Vasyl'kivka**
134 I4 **Vasil'sursk** Rus. Fed.
136 E1 **Vasilyevichy** Belarus
135 H6 **Vasil'yevka** Rus. Fed.
139 J3 **Vasil'yevskiy Mokh** Rus. Fed.
136 E2 **Vas'kovychi** Ukr.
177 H5 **Vaskút** Hungary
162 B2 **Vasles** France
197 H2 **Vaslui** Romania
177 K3 **Vasmegyer** Hungary
227 F4 **Vassar** MI U.S.A.
141 K3 **Vassbo** Sweden
161 D4 **Vassieux-en-Vercors** France
162 D3 **Vassivière, Lac de** l. France
176 F4 **Vas-Soproni-síkság** hills Hungary
257 F5 **Vassouras** Brazil
159 F3 **Vassy** France
176 F4 **Vasszécseny** Hungary
Vastan Turkey see **Gevaș**
140 L3 **Västana** Sweden
138 D1 **Västanfjärd** Fin.
140 L2 **Västansjö** Sweden
143 G2 **Västerås** Sweden
140 K2 **Västerbotten** county Sweden
141 K3 **Västerdalälven** r. Sweden
140 L2 **Västerfjäll** Sweden
143 H2 **Västerhaninge** Sweden
140 L3 **Västernorrland** county Sweden
143 G3 **Västervik** Sweden
143 F2 **Västmanland** county Sweden
193 G2 **Vasto** Italy
168 F2 **Vastorf** Ger.
142 E2 **Västra Ämtervik** Sweden
142 E2 **Västra Götaland** county Sweden
140 M3 **Västra Kvarken** sea chan. Sweden
140 L2 **Västra Ormsjö** Sweden
176 F4 **Vasvár** Hungary
137 G3 **Vasylivka** Kirovohrads'ka Oblast' Ukr.
137 H2 **Vasylivka** Sums'ka Oblast' Ukr.
137 H4 **Vasylivka** Zaporiz'ka Oblast' Ukr.
136 F2 **Vasyl'kiv** Ukr.
137 I3 **Vasyl'kivka** Ukr.
175 M6 **Vasyuchyn** Ukr.
137 G3 **Vasyutyntsi** Ukr.
177 G4 **Vaszar** Hungary
177 L5 **Vața de Jos** Romania
162 D1 **Vatan** France
143 H3 **Väte** Gotland Sweden
Vaté i. Vanuatu see **Éfaté**
146 B4 **Vaternish Point** Scotland U.K.
146 A5 **Vatersay** i. Scotland U.K.
173 F3 **Vaterstetten** Ger.
Vathi Ionioi Nisoi Greece see **Ithaki**
Vathí Greece see **Vathy**
199 E3 **Vathy** Greece
193 E3 **Vatican City** Europe
195 E4 **Vaticano, Capo** c. Italy
Vaticano, Città del Europe see **Vatican City**
78 □6 **Vatilau** i. Solomon Is
Vatiu i. Cook Is see **Atiu**
140 □C2 **Vatnajökull** ice cap Iceland
140 I3 **Vatne** Norway
77 I3 **Vatoa** i. Fiji
213 □K3 **Vatomandry** Madag.
197 G2 **Vatra Dornei** Romania
177 J4 **Vatta** Hungary
Vätter, Lake Sweden see **Vättern**
143 F2 **Vättern** l. Sweden
143 G1 **Vattholma** Sweden
141 L3 **Vattrång** Sweden
79 □1a **Vatukoula** Viti Levu Fiji
79 □1 **Vatulele** i. Fiji
159 F2 **Vaubadon** France
157 F4 **Vaubecourt** France
156 D4 **Vauchassis** France
160 B1 **Vauclaix** France
161 D4 **Vaucluse** dept Provence-Alpes-Côte-d'Azur France
161 D5 **Vaucluse, Monts de** mts France
160 D1 **Vauconcourt-Nervezain** France
157 F4 **Vaucouleurs** France
190 B2 **Vaud** canton Switz.
157 G4 **Vaudémont** France
156 D4 **Vaudeurs** France
84 B4 **Vaughan Springs** N.T. Austr.
239 F5 **Vaughn** NM U.S.A.
160 C3 **Vaugneray** France
160 B1 **Vault-de-Lugny** France
160 C3 **Vaulx-en-Velin** France
160 D3 **Vaulx-Milieu** France
250 D4 **Vaupés** dept Col.
250 D4 **Vaupés** r. Col.
224 E2 **Vauquelin** r. Que. Can.
161 D5 **Vauvenargues** France
161 C5 **Vauvert** France
157 G5 **Vauvillers** France
157 F3 **Vaux-devant-Damloup** France
223 H5 **Vauxhall** Alta Can.
156 C4 **Vaux-le-Pénil** France
162 A3 **Vaux-sur-Mer** France
165 E5 **Vaux-sur-Sûre** Belgium
116 B4 **Vav** Gujarat India
213 □K3 **Vavatenina** Madag.
77 I3 **Vava'u** i. Tonga
79 □2 **Vava'u Group** is Tonga
157 F4 **Vavincourt** France
Vavitao i. Îs Australes Fr. Polynesia see **Raivavae**
206 D5 **Vavoua** Côte d'Ivoire
134 J4 **Vavozh** Rus. Fed.
114 D4 **Vavuniya** Sri Lanka
138 E5 **Vawkavysk** Belarus
138 E5 **Vawkavyskaye Wzvyshsha** hills Belarus
143 H2 **Vaxholm** Sweden
143 F3 **Växjö** Sweden
114 C3 **Vayalpad** Andhra Prad. India
Vayenga Rus. Fed. see **Severomorsk**
130 G2 **Vaygach, Ostrov** i. Rus. Fed.
114 C4 **Vayittiri** Kerala India
129 D4 **Vayk'** Armenia
162 D4 **Vayrac** France
162 C3 **Vayres** France
256 D2 **Vazante** Brazil
Vazáš Sweden see **Vittangi**
129 D3 **Vazashen** Armenia
177 I2 **Važec** Slovakia
139 J1 **Vazhinka** r. Rus. Fed.
129 D3 **Vaziani** Georgia
213 □J3 **Vazobe** mt. Madag.
139 J4 **Vazuza** r. Rus. Fed.
139 J4 **Vazuzskoye Vodokhranilishche** resr Rus. Fed.
176 D3 **Včelná** Czech Rep.
Veaikevárri Sweden see **Svappavaara**
160 C3 **Veauche** France
142 E4 **Veberöd** Sweden
140 M2 **Vebomark** Sweden
161 B4 **Vebron** France
190 F5 **Vecchiano** Italy
177 K3 **Vechec** Slovakia
169 F3 **Vechelde** Ger.
164 F2 **Vecht** r. Neth. alt. **Vechte (Germany)**
168 D3 **Vechta** Ger.
169 B3 **Vechte** r. Ger. alt. **Vecht (Neth.)**
182 E4 **Vecinos** Spain
169 F4 **Veckenstedt** Ger.
169 E4 **Veckerhagen (Reinhardshagen)** Ger.
177 I4 **Vecsés** Hungary
176 E2 **Vectec** hill Czech Rep.
138 E3 **Vecumnieki** Latvia
Vedana Rus. Fed. see **Vedeno**
114 C4 **Vedaranniyam** Tamil Nadu India
114 C4 **Vedasandur** Tamil Nadu India
142 E3 **Veddige** Sweden
197 G3 **Vedea** Argeș Romania
197 G4 **Vedea** Giurgiu Romania
197 G4 **Vedea** r. Romania
191 H3 **Vedelago** Italy
161 C5 **Vedène** France
129 E2 **Vedeno** Rus. Fed.
143 F2 **Vedevåg** Sweden
129 D4 **Vedi** Armenia
261 G4 **Vedia** Arg.
134 F3 **Vedlozero** Rus. Fed.
137 J3 **Vedmezha** r. Ukr.
182 B2 **Vedra** Spain
161 B3 **Védrines-St-Loup** France
136 F1 **Vedrych** r. Belarus
137 J2 **Veduga** r. Rus. Fed.
164 F1 **Veendam** Neth.
164 E2 **Veenendaal** Neth.
164 F1 **Veenhuizen** Neth.
168 C2 **Veenhusen** Ger.
164 F2 **Veenoord** Neth.
164 E1 **Veenwouden** Neth.
164 C3 **Veere** Neth.
168 E2 **Veerse** r. Ger.
140 K2 **Vefsnfjord** sea chan. Norway
140 J2 **Vega** i. Norway
237 C5 **Vega** TX U.S.A.
247 □1 **Vega Alta** Puerto Rico
247 □1 **Vega Baja** Puerto Rico
182 E2 **Vegacervera** Spain
182 D2 **Vega de Espinareda** Spain
182 C1 **Vegadeo** Spain
183 G1 **Vega de Pas** Spain
216 □3f **Vega de San Mateo** Gran Canaria Canary Is
182 E3 **Vega de Tirados** Spain
182 D2 **Vega de Valcarce** Spain
183 E3 **Vega de Valdetronco** Spain
183 G3 **Veganzones** Spain
182 D2 **Vegarienza** Spain
142 C2 **Vegarshei** Norway
183 E2 **Vegas del Condado** Spain
183 F4 **Vegas de Matute** Spain
164 E3 **Veghel** Neth.
195 G2 **Veglie** Italy
198 B1 **Vegoritis, Limni** l. Greece
159 F4 **Vègre** r. France
223 H4 **Vegreville** Alta Can.
252 A2 **Végueta** Peru
138 F1 **Vehkalahti** Fin.
170 D2 **Vehlow** Ger.
141 M3 **Vehmaa** Fin.
123 G4 **Vehoa** r. Pak.
159 G4 **Veigné** France
160 E2 **Veigy-Foncenex** France
169 F5 **Veilsdorf** Ger.
Veinticinco de Mayo Buenos Aires Arg. see **25 de Mayo**
Veinticinco de Mayo La Pampa Arg. see **25 de Mayo**
Veinticinco de Mayo Mendoza Arg. see **25 de Mayo**
Veinticinco de Mayo Uru. see **25 de Mayo**
184 C2 **Veiros** Port.
138 D4 **Veisiejis** Lith.
173 E2 **Veitsbronn** Ger.
179 G3 **Veitsch** Austria
179 G3 **Veitsch** mt. Austria
172 D2 **Veitshöchheim** Ger.
140 N2 **Veitsiluoto** Fin.
138 C4 **Veiviržas** r. Lith.
192 E2 **Vejano** Italy
142 C4 **Vejen** Denmark
184 E4 **Vejer de la Frontera** Spain
142 C4 **Vejle** Denmark
142 C4 **Vejle** county Denmark
173 H2 **Vejprnice** Czech Rep.
176 C1 **Vejprty** Czech Rep.
120 E5 **Vekil'bazar** Turkm.
116 C5 **Velachha** Gujarat India
183 F5 **Velada** Spain
188 F4 **Vela Luka** Croatia
183 H3 **Velamazán** Spain
216 □1c **Velas** São Jorge Azores
258 D3 **Velasco, Sierra de** mts Arg.
113 □1 **Velassary** i. S. Male Maldives
161 D5 **Velaux** France
258 G4 **Velázquez** Uru.
169 C4 **Velbert** Ger.
173 F2 **Velburg** Ger.
214 B5 **Velddrif** S. Africa
165 C3 **Veldegem** Belgium
173 F2 **Velden** Bayern Ger.
173 G3 **Velden** Bayern Ger.
165 F3 **Velden** Neth.
179 F4 **Velden am Wörther See** Austria
165 E3 **Veldhoven** Neth.
114 C3 **Veldurti** Andhra Prad. India
188 E3 **Velebit** mts Croatia
188 E3 **Velebitski Kanal** sea chan. Croatia
185 H3 **Velefique** Spain
197 H4 **Veleka** r. Bulg.
169 B4 **Velen** Ger.
177 H4 **Velence** Hungary
188 E2 **Velenje** Slovenia
197 E5 **Veles** Macedonia
196 D5 **Velës, Mali i** mt. Albania
176 D3 **Velešín** Czech Rep.
185 G3 **Veleta, Pico** mt. Spain
188 F4 **Velež** mts Bos.-Herz.
250 C3 **Vélez** Col.
185 H3 **Vélez-Blanco** Spain
185 G4 **Vélez de Benaudalla** Spain
185 F4 **Vélez-Málaga** Spain
185 H3 **Vélez-Rubio** Spain
170 D1 **Velgast** Ger.
256 D3 **Velhas** r. Minas Gerais Brazil
257 E2 **Velhas** r. Minas Gerais Brazil
Velibaba Turkey see **Aras**
135 I7 **Velichayevskoye** Rus. Fed.
136 C3 **Velika Berezovytsya** Ukr.
196 E4 **Velika Drenova** Srbija Yugo.
188 F3 **Velika Gorica** Croatia
136 C2 **Velika Hlusha** Ukr.
188 E3 **Velika Kapela** mts Croatia
188 E3 **Velika Kladuša** Bos.-Herz.
188 F3 **Velika Mlaka** Croatia
176 G6 **Velika Pisanica** Croatia
196 E3 **Velika Plana** Srbija Yugo.
179 F4 **Velika Rogatec** mt. Slovenia
134 J4 **Velikaya** Rus. Fed.
134 J4 **Velikaya** r. Rus. Fed.
131 S3 **Velikaya** r. Rus. Fed.
138 G3 **Velikaya** r. Rus. Fed.
134 F3 **Velikaya Guba** Rus. Fed.
100 F3 **Velikaya Kema** Rus. Fed.
Velikaya Novoselka Ukr. see **Velyka Novosilka**
188 F4 **Veliki Drvenik** i. Croatia
176 G6 **Veliki Grđevac** Croatia
196 E4 **Veliki Jastrebac** mts Yugo.
136 C3 **Veliki Kunynets'** Ukr.
197 H4 **Veliki Preslav** Bulg.
188 E3 **Veliki Risnjak** mt. Croatia
197 E4 **Veliki Šiljegovac** Srbija Yugo.
197 F4 **Veliki Strešer** mt. Yugo.
196 E3 **Veliki Šturac** mt. Yugo.
139 H3 **Velikiye Luki** Rus. Fed.
137 F2 **Velikiy Lystven** Ukr.
136 B3 **Velikiy Lyubin'** Ukr.
139 H2 **Velikiy Novgorod** Rus. Fed.
134 I3 **Velikiy Ustyug** Rus. Fed.
137 K2 **Velikoarkhangel'skoye** Rus. Fed.
139 M4 **Velikodvorskiy** Rus. Fed.
137 I2 **Velikomikhaylovka** Rus. Fed.
114 C3 **Velikonda Range** hills India
139 I3 **Velikooktyabr'skiy** Rus. Fed.
176 F6 **Veliko Trojstvo** Croatia
197 G4 **Veliko Tŭrnovo** Bulg.
129 C3 **Veliköy** Turkey
139 K2 **Velikoye** Vologod. Obl. Rus. Fed.
139 L3 **Velikoye** Yaroslavskaya Oblast' Rus. Fed.
139 M4 **Velikoye, Ozero** l. Rus. Fed.
186 D3 **Velilla de Cinca** Spain
186 C3 **Velilla de Ebro** Spain
Velilla de Guardo Spain see **Velilla del Río Carrión**
183 F2 **Velilla del Río Carrión** Spain
185 G3 **Velillas** r. Spain
188 E3 **Veli Lošinj** Croatia
196 D4 **Velimlje** Crna Gora Yugo.
163 C4 **Vélines** France
206 B3 **Vélingara** Senegal
197 G4 **Velingrad** Bulg.
193 E2 **Velino** r. Italy
193 F2 **Velino, Monte** mt. Italy
139 H4 **Velizh** Rus. Fed.
176 F2 **Velká Bíteš** Czech Rep.
176 D1 **Velká Dobrá** Czech Rep.
177 K2 **Veľká Domaša, Vodná nádrž** resr Slovakia
177 H3 **Veľká Fatra** mts Slovakia
176 G2 **Velká Haná** r. Czech Rep.
173 G2 **Velká Hleďsebe** Czech Rep.
177 G3 **Velká Javořina** hill Czech Rep./Slovakia
177 K2 **Veľká Javořina** mt. Slovakia
177 H3 **Veľká Lehota** Slovakia
177 H2 **Veľká Lúka** mt. Slovakia
177 H2 **Velká Polom** Czech Rep.
Veľká Rača mt. Pol./Slovakia see **Wielka Racza**
176 F3 **Velké Bílovice** Czech Rep.
171 F5 **Velké Březno** Czech Rep.
177 L3 **Veľké Kapušany** Slovakia
177 H2 **Velké Karlovice** Czech Rep.
179 I2 **Veľké Leváre** Slovakia
176 G1 **Velké Losiny** Czech Rep.
177 H3 **Veľké Lovce** Slovakia
177 H4 **Veľké Ludince** Slovakia
176 F2 **Velké Meziříčí** Czech Rep.
176 F3 **Velké Němčice** Czech Rep.
176 F3 **Velké Pavlovice** Czech Rep.
177 G3 **Veľké Rípňany** Slovakia
177 L3 **Veľké Trakany** Slovakia
177 H3 **Veľké Uherce** Slovakia
138 C1 **Velkua** Fin.
177 J3 **Veľký Blh** Slovakia
177 H3 **Veľký Ďur** Slovakia
177 H2 **Veľký Javorník** mt. Slovakia
177 I2 **Veľký Kriváň** mt. Slovakia
177 I3 **Veľký Krtíš** Slovakia
177 H3 **Veľký Kýr** Slovakia
177 G3 **Velký Lopeník** hill Czech Rep.
177 G4 **Veľký Meder** Slovakia
177 K2 **Veľký Šariš** Slovakia
177 H3 **Veľký Tribeč** hill Slovakia
176 G2 **Velký Týnec** Czech Rep.
176 B2 **Velký Zvon** hill Czech Rep.
179 F4 **Vellach** r. Austria
168 F2 **Vellahn** Ger.
78 □6 **Vella Lavella** i. New Georgia Is Solomon Is
114 C4 **Vellar** r. India
172 D2 **Vellberg** Ger.
193 E3 **Velletri** Italy
160 E1 **Vellevans** France
160 D1 **Vellexon-Queutrey-et-Vaudey** France
142 E4 **Vellinge** Sweden
183 H4 **Vellisca** Spain
169 E4 **Vellmar** Ger.
114 C3 **Vellore** Tamil Nadu India
186 D2 **Vellos** r. Spain
131 K3 **Vel'mo** r. Rus. Fed.
198 C3 **Velo** Peloponnisos Greece
157 F3 **Velosnes** France
165 E4 **Velp** r. Belgium
164 E3 **Velp** Neth.
169 F3 **Velpke** Ger.
134 H3 **Vel'sk** Rus. Fed.
Velsuna Italy see **Orvieto**
170 E3 **Velten** Ger.
169 F3 **Veltheim (Ohe)** Ger.
176 D1 **Veltrusy** Czech Rep.
191 G2 **Velturno** Italy
164 E2 **Veluwemeer** l. Neth.
236 C1 **Velva** ND U.S.A.
176 D1 **Velvary** Czech Rep.
198 C1 **Velvendos** Greece
139 I3 **Vel'ye, Ozero** l. Rus. Fed.
137 G3 **Velyka Andrusivka** Ukr.
137 I3 **Velyka Babka** Ukr.
137 G3 **Velyka Bahachka** Ukr.
137 H4 **Velyka Bilozerka** Ukr.
137 H4 **Velyka Bilozerka** r. Ukr.
137 G3 **Velyka Burimka** Ukr.
136 F2 **Velyka Dymerka** Ukr.
175 L6 **Velyka Horozhanna** Ukr.
136 E3 **Velyka Kisnytsya** Ukr.
137 I3 **Velyka Komyshuvakha** Ukr.
177 M3 **Velyka Kopanya** Ukr.
137 F4 **Velyka Korenykha** Ukr.
137 G4 **Velyka Kostromka** Ukr.
137 G4 **Velyka Lepetykha** Ukr.
136 E4 **Velyka Mykhaylivka** Ukr.
137 I4 **Velyka Novosilka** Ukr.
137 G4 **Velyka Oleksandrivka** Ukr.
137 H2 **Velyka Pysarivka** Ukr.
137 H3 **Velyka Rublivka** Ukr.
136 D2 **Velyka Tsvilya** Ukr.
137 F3 **Velyka Vys'** r. Ukr.
137 F3 **Velyka Vyska** Ukr.
137 H4 **Velyka Znam"yanka** Ukr.
177 L3 **Velyki Kom"yaty** Ukr.
137 G4 **Velyki Kopani** Ukr.
136 E3 **Velyki Korovyntsi** Ukr.
137 G3 **Velyki Krynky** Ukr.
177 L3 **Velyki Luchky** Ukr.
136 C2 **Velyki Mosty** Ukr.
137 G2 **Velyki Sorochyntsi** Ukr.
137 G3 **Velykiy Khutir** Ukr.
136 F4 **Velykiy Kuyal'nyk** r. Ukr.
137 G2 **Velykiy Sambir** Ukr.
136 F4 **Velykodolyns'ke** Ukr.
137 I4 **Velykomykhaylivka** Ukr.
137 H3 **Velykooleksandrivka** Ukr.
137 F4 **Velykoserbulivka** Ukr.
136 B3 **Velykyy Bereznyy** Ukr.
137 I2 **Velykyy Burluk** Ukr.
136 C4 **Velykyy Bychkiv** Ukr.
Velykyy Tokmak Ukr. see **Tokmak**
134 K3 **Vel'yu** r. Rus. Fed.
114 C2 **Vemalwada** Andhra Prad. India
264 J8 **Vema Seamount** sea feature S. Atlantic Ocean
265 I5 **Vema Trench** sea feature Indian Ocean
177 H5 **Véménd** Hungary
100 G3 **Vemor'ye** Sakhalin Rus. Fed.
114 C3 **Vempalle** Andhra Prad. India
192 B2 **Venaco** Corse France
245 E3 **Venados** r. Mex.
261 G3 **Venado Tuerto** Arg.
193 G3 **Venafro** Italy
251 F3 **Venamo** r. Guyana/Venez.
251 F3 **Venamo, Cerro** mt. Venez.
158 E5 **Venansault** France
160 C1 **Venarey-les-Laumes** France
190 C3 **Venaria** Italy
193 F2 **Venarotta** Italy
161 F4 **Venasca** Italy
161 F5 **Vence** France
256 C5 **Venceslau Bráz** Brazil
138 E4 **Venciūnai** Lith.
191 G3 **Venda, Monte** hill Italy
184 A2 **Venda do Pinheiro** Port.
257 G4 **Venda Nova** Brazil
182 C3 **Venda Nova, Barragem de** resr Port.
161 B5 **Vendargues** France
184 B2 **Vendas de Azeitão** Port.
184 B2 **Vendas Novas** Port.
160 B2 **Vendat** France
162 A3 **Vendays-Montalivet** France
158 E5 **Vendée** dept Pays de la Loire France
162 B2 **Vendée** r. France
157 H4 **Vendenheim** France
159 G5 **Vendeuvre-du-Poitou** France
156 E4 **Vendeuvre-sur-Barse** France
184 C2 **Vendinha** Port.
159 H5 **Vendœuvres** France
156 B5 **Vendôme** France
184 D2 **Vendoval** r. Spain
Vendrell Spain see **El Vendrell**
136 D3 **Vendychany** Ukr.
244 D2 **Venegas** Mex.
161 D5 **Venelles** France
163 E5 **Vénès** France
191 H3 **Veneta, Laguna** lag. Italy
Venetia Italy see **Venezia**
191 G3 **Veneto** admin. reg. Italy
139 L4 **Venev** Rus. Fed.
191 H3 **Venezia** Italy
191 H3 **Venezia** prov. Veneto Italy
Venezia, Golfo di g. Europe see **Venice, Gulf of**
251 E3 **Venezuela** country S. America
250 D2 **Venezuela, Golfo de** g. Venez.
264 E4 **Venezuelan Basin** sea feature S. Atlantic Ocean
114 B3 **Vengurla** Mahar. India
164 E2 **Venhuizen** Neth.
182 E3 **Venialbo** Spain
220 C4 **Veniaminof Volcano** AK U.S.A.
Venice Italy see **Venezia**
231 D7 **Venice** FL U.S.A.
237 F6 **Venice** LA U.S.A.
188 D3 **Venice, Gulf of** Europe
190 E2 **Venina** r. Italy
160 C3 **Vénissieux** France
156 D3 **Venizel** France
141 K3 **Venjan** Sweden
114 C3 **Venkatagiri** Andhra Prad. India
114 D2 **Venkatapuram** Andhra Prad. India
165 F3 **Venlo** Neth.
142 B2 **Vennesla** Norway
193 H4 **Venosa** Italy
193 H3 **Venosa** r. Italy
191 F2 **Venosta, Val** val. Italy
156 D5 **Venoy** France
164 E3 **Venray** Neth.
79 □3 **Vent, Îles du** is Arch. de la Société Fr. Polynesia
138 D3 **Venta** r. Latvia/Lith.
138 D3 **Venta** Lith.
161 D5 **Ventabren** France
161 F5 **Ventabren, Mont** mt. France
183 F3 **Venta de Baños** Spain
182 E1 **Venta de las Ranas** Spain
185 F2 **Venta del Charco** Spain
187 B5 **Venta del Moro** Spain
185 G2 **Venta de los Santos** Spain
182 D1 **Venta Nueva** Spain
185 G3 **Ventas de Huelma** Spain
185 F4 **Ventas de Zafarraya** Spain
161 D4 **Ventavon** France
215 F3 **Ventersburg** S. Africa
215 F2 **Ventersdorp** S. Africa
215 F2 **Venterskroon** S. Africa
215 E4 **Venterstad** S. Africa
161 B4 **Venteuges** France
190 C5 **Ventimiglia** Italy
192 B3 **Ventiseri** Corse France
259 C6 **Ventisquero** mt. Arg.
151 F4 **Ventnor** Isle of Wight, England U.K.
235 D3 **Ventnor City** NJ U.S.A.
193 F4 **Ventotene, Isola** i. Italy
161 D4 **Ventoux, Mont** mt. France
170 C2 **Ventschow** Ger.
138 C3 **Ventspils** Latvia
251 E3 **Ventuari** r. Venez.
240 H4 **Ventura** CA U.S.A.
83 F4 **Venus Bay** Vic. Austr.
Venusia Italy see **Venosa**
244 C4 **Venustiano** Mex.
245 F3 **Venustiano Carranza** Puebla Mex.
243 E3 **Venustiano Carranza, Presa** resr Mex.
192 B2 **Venzolasca** Corse France
191 I2 **Venzone** Italy
176 F4 **Vép** Hungary
137 H2 **Vepryk** Ukr.
139 J1 **Vepsovskaya Vozvyshennost'** hills Rus. Fed.
258 E3 **Vera** Arg.
185 I3 **Vera** Spain
256 C5 **Vera Cruz** Brazil
245 F4 **Veracruz** Mex.
Vera Cruz Mex. see **Veracruz**
245 F3 **Veracruz** state Mex.
184 C2 **Vera Cruz** Port.
234 C2 **Vera Cruz** PA U.S.A.
186 B1 **Vera de Bidasoa** Spain
186 C2 **Veral** r. Spain
255 C9 **Veranópolis** Brazil
116 B5 **Veraval** Gujarat India
136 C2 **Verba** Rivnens'ka Oblast' Ukr.
136 C2 **Verba** Volyns'ka Oblast' Ukr.
190 D3 **Verbania** Italy
235 E1 **Verbank** NY U.S.A.
190 D2 **Verbano-Cusio-Ossola** prov. Piemonte Italy
156 C3 **Verberie** France
193 H5 **Verbicaro** Italy
190 C2 **Verbier** Switz.
139 K3 **Verbilki** Rus. Fed.
137 G3 **Verblyuzhka** Ukr.
137 H4 **Verbove** Ukr.
136 C3 **Verbovets'** Ukr.
135 H5 **Verbovskiy** Rus. Fed.
190 E2 **Verceia** Italy
190 D3 **Vercelli** Italy
190 D3 **Vercelli** prov. Piemonte Italy
160 E1 **Vercel-Villedieu-le-Camp** France
170 D2 **Verchen** Ger.
161 D4 **Vercors** reg. France
Vercovicium tourist site England U.K. see **Housesteads**
179 F5 **Verd** Slovenia
139 M5 **Verda** r. Rus. Fed.
161 E4 **Verdaches** France
140 J3 **Verdalsøra** Norway
259 D6 **Verde** r. Arg.
256 B3 **Verde** r. Goiás Brazil
256 D3 **Verde** r. Goiás/Minas Gerais Brazil
256 B4 **Verde** r. Mato Grosso do Sul Brazil
256 B3 **Verde** r. Minas Gerais Brazil
256 C3 **Verde** r. Minas Gerais Brazil
257 E4 **Verde** r. Minas Gerais Brazil
254 E4 **Verde** r. Bahia Brazil
253 F3 **Verde** r. Mato Grosso Brazil
253 G2 **Verde** r. Mato Grosso Brazil
244 C3 **Verde** r. Aguascalientes/Jalisco Mex.
242 D3 **Verde** r. Chihuahua/Durango Mex.
245 E5 **Verde** r. Guerrero/Oaxaca Mex.
245 F6 **Verde** r. Oaxaca Mex.
245 E3 **Verde** r. San Luis Potosí Mex.
253 F5 **Verde** r. Para.
185 G3 **Verde** r. Spain
185 G4 **Verde** r. Spain
241 L5 **Verde** r. AZ U.S.A.
Verde, Cabo c. Senegal see **Vert, Cap**
261 F6 **Verde, Península** pen. Arg.
257 F1 **Verde Grande** r. Brazil
168 E3 **Verden (Aller)** Ger.
254 E5 **Verde Pequeno** r. Brazil
240 H2 **Verdi** NV U.S.A.
237 E5 **Verdigris** r. KS U.S.A.
198 B2 **Verdikoussa** Greece
256 B2 **Verdinho** r. Brazil
256 B3 **Verdinho, Serra do** mts Brazil
161 D5 **Verdon** r. France
182 B2 **Verdugo** r. Spain
157 F3 **Verdun** France
163 D5 **Verdun-sur-Garonne** France
160 D2 **Verdun-sur-le-Doubs** France
194 C5 **Verdura** r. Sicilia Italy
215 F2 **Vereeniging** S. Africa
137 G3 **Veremiyivka** Ukr.
215 G1 **Verena** S. Africa
177 I4 **Veresegyház** Hungary
134 K4 **Vereshchagino** Rus. Fed.
137 F2 **Veresoch** Ukr.
139 K3 **Verestovo, Ozero** l. Rus. Fed.
139 K4 **Vereya** Rus. Fed.
163 D4 **Verfeil** Midi-Pyrénées France
163 D5 **Verfeil** Midi-Pyrénées France
Vergara Spain see **Bergara**
258 G4 **Vergara** Uru.
191 G4 **Vergato** Italy
157 G4 **Vergaville** France
187 D6 **Vergel** Spain
214 E1 **Vergeleë** S. Africa
233 G2 **Vergennes** VT U.S.A.
186 G2 **Verges** Spain
161 C5 **Vergèze** France
191 H5 **Verghereto** Italy
156 D5 **Vergigny** France
198 C1 **Vergina** Greece
161 B3 **Vergongheon** France
162 C3 **Vergt** France
137 G3 **Verhuny** Cherkas'ka Oblast' Ukr.
137 G3 **Verhuny** Poltavs'ka Oblast' Ukr.
Véria Greece see **Veroia**
182 C3 **Verín** Spain
172 D3 **Veringenstadt** Ger.
Verin T'alin Armenia see **T'alin**
256 C3 **Veríssimo** Brazil
Veríssimo Sarmento Angola see **Camissombo**
215 F3 **Verkeerdevlei** S. Africa
137 H3 **Verkhivtseve** Ukr.
120 D1 **Verkhne-Avzyan** Rus. Fed.
137 I5 **Verkhnebakanskiy** Rus. Fed.
121 J2 **Verkhne-berezovskiy** Kazakh.
Verkhnedneprovsk Ukr. see **Verkhn'odniprovs'k**
139 I4 **Verkhnedneprovskiy** Rus. Fed.
130 J3 **Verkhneimbatsk** Rus. Fed.
134 L2 **Verkhnekolvinsk** Rus. Fed.
139 J4 **Verkhneruzskoye Vodokhranilishche** resr Rus. Fed.
134 I4 **Verkhnespasskoye** Rus. Fed.
140 O1 **Verkhnetulomskiy** Rus. Fed.
140 O1 **Verkhnetulomskoye Vodokhranilishche** resr Rus. Fed.
137 J2 **Verkhneturovo** Rus. Fed.
120 D1 **Verkhneural'sk** Rus. Fed.
131 N3 **Verkhnevilyuysk** Rus. Fed.
139 I3 **Verkhnevolzhskoye Vodokhranilishche** resr Rus. Fed.
134 K5 **Verkhneyarkeyevo** Rus. Fed.
131 Q3 **Verkhniy At-Uryakh** Rus. Fed.
135 I6 **Verkhniy Baskunchak** Rus. Fed.
137 I3 **Verkhniy Byshkyn** Ukr.
129 D2 **Verkhniye Achaluki** Rus. Fed.
Verkhniye Kholokhory Moldova see **Halahora de Sus**
129 D2 **Verkhniy Fiagdon** Rus. Fed.
Verkhniy Karabulag Georgia see **Zemo Qarabulakhi**
139 L5 **Verkhniy Lomovets** Rus. Fed.
135 H6 **Verkhniy Mamon** Rus. Fed.
Verkhniy Naur Rus. Fed. see **Lakkha-Nevre**
137 H4 **Verkhniy Rohachyk** Ukr.
107 F1 **Verkhniy Shergol'dzhin** Rus. Fed.
134 K4 **Verkhniy Tatyshly** Rus. Fed.
137 I4 **Verkhniytokmak** Ukr.
137 H3 **Verkhn'odniprovs'k** Ukr.
136 F3 **Verkhnyachka** Ukr.
175 M6 **Verkhnya Lypytsya** Ukr.
137 H2 **Verkhnya Syrovatka** Ukr.
137 H3 **Verkhnya Tersa** r. Ukr.
136 B3 **Verkhnya Vysots'ke** Ukr.
177 L3 **Verkhnya Vyznytsya** Ukr.
129 C2 **Verkhnyaya Balkariya** Rus. Fed.
177 L2 **Verkhnya Yablun'ka** Ukr.
137 I2 **Verkhnyaya Grayvoronka** Rus. Fed.
134 M2 **Verkhnyaya Inta** Rus. Fed.
135 G6 **Verkhnyaya Khava** Rus. Fed.
129 C2 **Verkhnyaya Mara** Rus. Fed.
131 K2 **Verkhnyaya Taymyra** r. Rus. Fed.
129 B2 **Verkhnyaya Teberda** Rus. Fed.
137 K2 **Verkhnyaya Tishanka** Rus. Fed.
137 K2 **Verkhnyaya Toyda** Rus. Fed.
134 I3 **Verkhnyaya Toyma** Rus. Fed.
139 K3 **Verkhnyaya Troitsa** Rus. Fed.
Verkhnyaya Tunguska r. Rus. Fed. see **Angara**
136 B3 **Verkhnye Syn'ovydne** Ukr.
134 J4 **Verkhoshizhem'ye** Rus. Fed.
139 N1 **Verkhovazh'ye** Rus. Fed.
Verkhovina Ukr. see **Verkhovyna**
139 K5 **Verkhov'ye** Rus. Fed.
136 C3 **Verkhovyna** Ukr.
131 N2 **Verkhoyanskiy Khrebet** mts Rus. Fed.
121 J2 **Verkhuba** Kazakh.
138 E4 **Verknė** r. Lith.
215 G2 **Verkykerskop** S. Africa
169 D4 **Verl** Ger.
165 E4 **Verlaine** Belgium
214 C6 **Vermaaklikheid** S. Africa
156 D3 **Vermand** France
256 B5 **Vermelha, Serra** hills Brazil
253 H3 **Vermelho** r. Mato Grosso Brazil
254 C3 **Vermelho** r. Pará Brazil
254 D3 **Vermelho** r. Tocantins Brazil
156 D5 **Vermenton** France
197 E3 **Vermeș** Romania
191 F2 **Vermiglio** Italy
223 I4 **Vermilion** Alta Can.
232 B4 **Vermilion** OH U.S.A.
226 C5 **Vermilion** r. IL U.S.A.
241 K3 **Vermilion Cliffs** esc. AZ U.S.A.
241 K3 **Vermilion Cliffs** esc. UT U.S.A.
226 A2 **Vermilion Range** hills MN U.S.A.
236 D3 **Vermillion** SD U.S.A.
236 D3 **Vermillion** r. SD U.S.A.
236 D3 **Vermillion, East Fork** r. SD U.S.A.
223 M5 **Vermillion Bay** Ont. Can.
230 F2 **Vermillon** r. Que. Can.
182 D4 **Vermiosa** Port.
182 B5 **Vermoil** Port.
233 G2 **Vermont** state U.S.A.
262 T2 **Vernadsky** research stn Antarctica
163 D6 **Vernajoul** France
238 E3 **Vernal** UT U.S.A.
190 C4 **Vernante** Italy
159 G4 **Vernantes** France
190 C2 **Vernayaz** Switz.
159 F4 **Vern-d'Anjou** France
224 D4 **Verner** Ont. Can.
176 D1 **Verneřice** Czech Rep.
163 D5 **Vernet** France
163 E6 **Vernet-les-Bains** France
159 G3 **Verneuil-sur-Avre** France
162 D3 **Verneuil-sur-Vienne** France
214 C3 **Verneuk Pan** salt pan S. Africa
190 B2 **Vernier** Switz.
191 G4 **Vernio** Italy
163 D5 **Verniolle** France
195 H2 **Vernole** Italy
222 G5 **Vernon** B.C. Can.
156 B3 **Vernon** France
237 F5 **Vernon** AL U.S.A.
230 C4 **Vernon** IN U.S.A.
235 D1 **Vernon** NJ U.S.A.
237 D5 **Vernon** TX U.S.A.
241 K1 **Vernon** UT U.S.A.
87 C5 **Vernon, Mount** hill W.A. Austr.
84 B2 **Vernon Islands** N.T. Austr.
156 B4 **Vernouillet** France
161 C4 **Vernoux-en-Vivarais** France
234 D2 **Vernoy** NJ U.S.A.
100 D2 **Vernoye** Rus. Fed.
158 E3 **Vern-sur-Seiche** France
157 G3 **Verny** France
Vernyy Kazakh. see **Almaty**
192 A2 **Vero** Corse France
186 D3 **Vero** r. Spain
231 D7 **Vero Beach** FL U.S.A.
177 I4 **Verőcemaros** Hungary
198 C1 **Veroia** Greece
190 F3 **Verolanuova** Italy
193 F3 **Veroli** Italy
156 D4 **Véron** France
191 F3 **Verona** Italy
191 G3 **Verona** prov. Veneto Italy
232 D5 **Verona** VA U.S.A.
226 C4 **Verona** WI U.S.A.
261 I4 **Verónica** Arg.
160 C2 **Verosvres** France
177 J4 **Verpelét** Hungary
235 E1 **Verplanck** NY U.S.A.
82 D3 **Verran** S.A. Austr.
190 C3 **Verres** Italy
162 C2 **Verrières** France
193 G3 **Verrino** r. Italy
190 D4 **Versa** r. Italy
190 E3 **Versa** r. Italy
191 I3 **Versa** r. Italy
156 C4 **Versailles** France
230 C4 **Versailles** IN U.S.A.
230 C4 **Versailles** KY U.S.A.
236 E4 **Versailles** MO U.S.A.
232 A4 **Versailles** OH U.S.A.
252 E3 **Versalles** Bol.
Versec Vojvodina, Srbija Yugo. see **Vršac**
138 E4 **Verseka** r. Lith.
160 D2 **Vers-en-Montage** France
169 D3 **Versmold** Ger.
190 B2 **Versoix** Switz.
161 A5 **Versols-et-Lapeyre** France
159 F2 **Verson** France
161 C5 **Vers-Pont-du-Gard** France
163 B4 **Vert** France
163 D4 **Vert** r. France
206 A3 **Vert, Cap** c. Senegal
160 B3 **Vertaizon** France
162 C3 **Verteillac** France
254 C4 **Vertentes** r. Brazil
177 H4 **Vértesacsa** Hungary
177 H4 **Vértesboglár** Hungary
163 C4 **Verteuil-d'Agenais** France
162 C3 **Verteuil-sur-Charente** France
162 B3 **Vertheuil** France
246 C2 **Vertientes** Cuba
137 F2 **Vertiyivka** Ukr.
156 B2 **Verton** France
191 F2 **Vertona, Cima** mt. Italy
158 E4 **Vertou** France
156 E4 **Vertus** France
191 H5 **Verucchio** Italy
215 H3 **Verulam** S. Africa
Verulamium Hertfordshire, England U.K. see **St Albans**
165 E4 **Verviers** Belgium
156 D3 **Vervins** France
Verwoerdburg S. Africa see **Centurion**
223 J5 **Verwood** Sask. Can.
151 F4 **Verwood** Dorset, England U.K.
Veryína Greece see **Vergina**
159 F4 **Verzée** r. France
156 E3 **Verzenay** France
195 F3 **Verzino** Italy
190 C4 **Verzuolo** Italy
156 E3 **Verzy** France
140 N3 **Vesanto** Fin.
192 B2 **Vescovato** Corse France
190 F3 **Vescovato** Italy
165 E4 **Vesdre** r. Belgium
176 G5 **Vése** Hungary
137 H4 **Vesele** Ukr.
197 G4 **Veselina** r. Bulg.
176 D2 **Veselí nad Lužnicí** Czech Rep.
176 G3 **Veselí nad Moravou** Czech Rep.
136 E2 **Veselivka** Ukr.
137 J4 **Veselo-Voznesenka** Rus. Fed.
121 J2 **Veseloyarsk** Rus. Fed.
137 J2 **Veseloye** Rus. Fed.
137 F2 **Veselynivka** Ukr.
137 F4 **Veselynove** Ukr.
135 H7 **Veselyy** Rus. Fed.
120 F1 **Veselyy Podol** Kazakh.
156 B4 **Vesgre** r. France
135 H6 **Veshenskaya** Rus. Fed.
190 D4 **Vesime** Italy
156 D3 **Vesle** r. France
134 K3 **Veslyana** r. Rus. Fed.
Vesontio France see **Besançon**
160 E1 **Vesoul** France
190 D3 **Vespolate** Italy
165 E3 **Vessem** Neth.
142 B2 **Vest-Agder** county Norway
140 K1 **Vesterålen** is Norway
140 K1 **Vesterålsfjorden** sea chan. Norway
168 G1 **Vesterby** Denmark
168 E1 **Vester Sottrup** Denmark
140 □B2 **Vestfirðir** constituency Iceland
142 C2 **Vestfjorddalen** val. Norway
140 K2 **Vestfjorden** sea chan. Norway
142 D2 **Vestfold** county Norway
263 F2 **Vestfold Hills** Antarctica
140 □ **Vestfonna** ice cap Svalbard
144 D1 **Vestmanna** Faroe Is
140 □B3 **Vestmannaeyjar** is Iceland
140 I3 **Vestnes** Norway
190 F3 **Vestone** Italy
142 D4 **Vestsjælland** county Denmark
140 □B2 **Vesturland** constituency Iceland
140 K1 **Vestvågøy** i. Norway
161 F5 **Vésubie** r. France
193 G4 **Vesuvio** vol. Italy
Vesuvius vol. Italy see **Vesuvio**
139 K2 **Ves'yegonsk** Rus. Fed.
176 G4 **Veszkény** Hungary
177 G4 **Veszprém** Hungary
176 G4 **Veszprém** county Hungary
177 G4 **Veszprémvarsány** Hungary
177 K5 **Vésztő** Hungary
215 E2 **Vet** r. S. Africa
79 □1 **Vetauua** i. Fiji
140 M3 **Veteli** Fin.
223 I4 **Veteran** Alta Can.
196 D3 **Veternik** Vojvodina, Srbija Yugo.
156 B3 **Vétheuil** France
177 L4 **Vetiș** Romania
143 F3 **Vetlanda** Sweden

134 I4 Vetluga Rus. Fed.
134 I4 Vetluga r. Rus. Fed.
130 F4 Vetluzhskiy Kostromskaya Oblast' Rus. Fed.
134 I4 Vetluzhskiy Nizhegorodskaya Oblast' Rus. Fed.
136 C2 Vetly Ukr.
139 I5 Vet'ma r. Rus. Fed.
197 H4 Vetovo Bulg.
192 E2 Vetralla Italy
197 H4 Vetren Bulg.
197 I2 Vetrişoaia Romania
176 D3 Větřní Czech Rep.
171 F4 Vetschau Ger.
140 M2 Vettasjärvi Sweden
169 C5 Vettelschoß Ger.
190 F4 Vetto Italy
193 F2 Vettore, Monte mt. Italy
159 G4 Veude r. France
159 G2 Veules-les-Roses France
159 G2 Veulettes-sur-Mer France
165 B3 Veurne Belgium
230 C4 Vevay IN U.S.A.
210 B3 Veveno r. Sudan
190 B2 Vevey Switz.
190 C2 Vex Switz.
135 G6 Veydelevka Rus. Fed.
160 C2 Veyle r. France
161 D4 Veynes France
160 B2 Veynon r. France
241 K3 Veyo UT U.S.A.
160 B3 Veyre-Monton France
160 E3 Veyrier-du-Lac France
122 B4 Veys Iran
138 C4 Vėžaičiai Lith.
160 B1 Vézelay France
157 G4 Vézelise France
161 C4 Vézénobres France
162 C4 Vézère r. France
197 G4 Vezhen mt. Bulg.
159 F4 Vezins France
161 A4 Vézins-de-Lévézou France
199 F1 Vezirhan Turkey
126 D2 Vezirköprü Turkey
157 G4 Vezouze r. France
190 F2 Vezza d'Oglio Italy
178 C4 Vezzana, Cima della mt. Italy
192 B2 Vezzani Corse France
191 G2 Vezzano Italy
206 C5 Via r. Liberia
252 C4 Viacha Bol.
191 F4 Viadana Italy
182 C3 Viade de Baixo Port.
161 F5 Vial, Mont mt. France
161 A4 Viala du Tarn France
Vialar Alg. see Tissemsilt
161 B4 Vialas France
261 G2 Viale Arg.
255 C9 Viamao Brazil
209 B7 Viana Angola
257 G4 Viana Espírito Santo Brazil
254 D2 Viana Maranhão Brazil
183 H2 Viana Spain
183 F3 Viana de Cega Spain
Viana del Bollo Spain see Viana do Bolo
184 C2 Viana do Alentejo Port.
182 C2 Viana do Bolo Spain
182 B3 Viana do Castelo Port.
182 B3 Viana do Castelo admin. dist. Port.
165 F5 Vianden Lux.
161 A5 Viane France
164 E3 Vianen Neth.
96 C3 Viangchan Laos
163 C4 Vianne France
182 B1 Viaño Pequeno Spain
256 C2 Vianópolis Brazil
185 H2 Vianos Spain
184 E3 Viar r. Spain
190 F5 Viareggio Italy
156 C3 Viarmes France
161 B5 Vias France
182 B3 Viatodos Port.
185 H4 Viator Spain
163 D4 Viaur r. France
163 E4 Viazac France
193 H4 Vibonati Italy
185 F3 Víboras r. Spain
142 C3 Viborg Denmark
142 C3 Viborg county Denmark
Viborg Rus. Fed. see Vyborg
195 F4 Vibo Valentia Italy
195 F4 Vibo Valentia prov. Calabria Italy
159 G3 Vibraye France
186 F3 Vic Spain
242 C3 Vicam Mex.
185 H4 Vícar Spain
194 C5 Vicari Sicilia Italy
148 B4 Vicarstown Rep. of Ireland
191 G5 Vicchio Italy
163 D6 Vicdessos France
163 D6 Vicdessos r. France
Viçe Turkey see Fındıklı
Vicecomodoro Marambio research stn Antarctica see Marambio
182 C1 Vicedo Spain
163 C5 Vic-en-Bigorre France
240 H5 Vicente, Point CA U.S.A.
242 A2 Vicente Guerrero Baja California Norte Mex.
245 H4 Vicente Guerrero Tabasco Mex.
245 E4 Vicente Guerrero Tlaxcala Mex.
245 F4 Vicente y Camalote Mex.
191 G3 Vicenza Italy
191 G3 Vicenza prov. Veneto Italy
163 C5 Vic-Fezensac France
Vich Spain see Vic
250 D3 Vichada dept Col.
250 E3 Vichada r. Col.
258 G3 Vichadero Uru.
134 H4 Vichuga Rus. Fed.
260 A4 Vichuquén Chile
160 B2 Vichy France
237 D4 Vici OK U.S.A.
186 C2 Vicién Spain
149 F3 Vickerstown Cumbria, England U.K.
241 K5 Vicksburg AZ U.S.A.
226 E4 Vicksburg MI U.S.A.
237 F5 Vicksburg MS U.S.A.
234 B2 Vicksburg PA U.S.A.
160 B3 Vic-le-Comte France
192 A2 Vico Corse France
192 E2 Vico, Lago di l. Italy
193 H3 Vico del Gargano Italy
193 G4 Vico Equense Italy
190 C4 Vicoforte Italy
193 F3 Vico nel Lazio Italy
254 F4 Viçosa Brazil
257 F4 Viçosa Brazil
193 E2 Vicovaro Italy
197 G2 Vicovu de Sus Romania
159 I5 Vicq-Exemplet France
162 D3 Vicq-sur-Breuilh France
156 D3 Vic-sur-Aisne France
161 A4 Vic-sur-Cère France
157 G4 Vic-sur-Seille France
263 C2 Victor, Mount Antarctica
168 C2 Victorbur (Südbrookmerland) Ger.
82 D3 Victor Harbor S.A. Austr.
261 G3 Victoria Arg.
261 H3 Victoria r. Arg.
84 B2 Victoria r. N.T. Austr.
83 F4 Victoria state Austr.
Victoria Cameroon see Limbe
222 F5 Victoria B.C. Can.
260 A6 Victoria Chile
247 □6 Victoria Grenada
242 □I6 Victoria Hond.
Victoria Malaysia see Labuan
195 □ Victoria Gozo Malta
92 B3 Victoria Phil.
197 H3 Victoria Brăila Romania
197 G3 Victoria Braşov Romania
217 □2b Victoria Mahé Seychelles
237 D6 Victoria TX U.S.A.
232 D6 Victoria VA U.S.A.
259 B7 Victoria, Isla i. Chile
82 E3 Victoria, Lake N.S.W. Austr.
Victoria, Mount Viti Levu Fiji see Tomanivi
96 A2 Victoria, Mount Myanmar
81 D5 Victoria, Mount South I. N.Z.
91 K8 Victoria, Mount P.N.G.
221 K2 Victoria and Albert Mountains Nunavut Can.
209 E9 Victoria Falls waterfall Zambia/Zimbabwe
212 E3 Victoria Falls Zimbabwe
220 H2 Victoria Island N.W.T./Nunavut Can.
263 K2 Victoria Land coastal area Antarctica
109 □ Victoria Peak hill H.K. China
81 D5 Victoria Range mts South I. N.Z.
84 B2 Victoria River N.T. Austr.
84 B3 Victoria River Downs N.T. Austr.
80 D1 Victoria Valley North I. N.Z.
225 G4 Victoriaville Que. Can.
214 D4 Victoria West S. Africa
260 E5 Victorica Arg.
240 I4 Victorville CA U.S.A.
177 K6 Victor Vlad Delamarina Romania
232 E3 Victory NY U.S.A.
84 C5 Victory Downs N.T. Austr.
260 B2 Vicuña Chile
260 E3 Vicuña Mackenna Arg.
182 C3 Vidago Port.
184 A1 Vidais Port.
237 F6 Vidalia LA U.S.A.
241 J4 Vidal Junction CA U.S.A.
186 B2 Vidángoz Spain
161 E5 Vidauban France
192 A4 Viddalba Sardegna Italy
142 C3 Videbæk Denmark
255 C8 Videira Brazil
261 G2 Videla Arg.
197 G3 Videle Romania
182 C4 Videmonte Port.
197 F4 Viden mt. Bulg.
175 K1 Vidgiriu kalnas hill Lith.
184 C2 Vidigueira Port.
197 G4 Vidima r. Bulg.
197 F4 Vidin Bulg.
177 I3 Vidiná Slovakia
116 D5 Vidisha Madh. Prad. India
146 □G1 Vidlin Shetland, Scotland U.K.
139 I1 Vidlitsa Rus. Fed.
176 G1 Vidnava Czech Rep.
139 K4 Vidnoye Rus. Fed.
161 C5 Vidourle r. France
188 F4 Vidova Gora hill Croatia
179 H4 Vidovec Croatia
177 L5 Vidra Romania
Vidreras Spain see Vidrieres
186 F3 Vidrieres Spain
140 M2 Vidsel Sweden
138 D4 Viduklė Lith.
188 G4 Viduša mts Bos.-Herz.
138 E3 Vidzemes centrālā augstiene hills Latvia
138 F4 Vidzy Belarus
158 E5 Vie r. France
159 F2 Vie r. France
173 G2 Viechtach Ger.
175 M1 Viečiūnai Lith.
215 G4 Viedgesville S. Africa
259 E6 Viedma Arg.
259 B8 Viedma, Lago l. Arg.
179 F2 Viehberg mt. Austria
158 E5 Vieillevigne France
182 B5 Vieira de Leiria Port.
182 B3 Vieira do Minho Port.
244 B2 Viejo r. Mex.
242 B2 Viejo, Cerro mt. Mex.
138 D3 Viekšniai Lith.
170 C2 Vielank Ger.
186 D2 Vielha Spain
163 B5 Viella France
Viella Spain see Vielha
163 C6 Vielle-Aure France
161 B3 Vielle-Brioude France
163 A5 Vielle-St-Girons France
163 E5 Vielmur-sur-Agout France
165 E4 Vielsalm Belgium
160 D1 Vielverge France
169 F4 Vienenburg Ger.
Vienna Austria see Wien
231 D5 Vienna GA U.S.A.
237 F4 Vienna IL U.S.A.
233 F5 Vienna MD U.S.A.
236 F4 Vienna MO U.S.A.
234 D2 Vienna NJ U.S.A.
232 C5 Vienna WV U.S.A.
160 C3 Vienne France
159 G5 Vienne dept Poitou-Charentes France
162 C1 Vienne r. France
157 E3 Vienne-le-Château France
Vientiane Laos see Viangchan
260 B5 Viento, Cordillera del mts Arg.
247 □1 Vieques i. Puerto Rico
157 E4 Vière r. France
170 F2 Viereck Ger.
140 N3 Vieremä Fin.
173 E2 Viereth-Trunstadt Ger.
173 F3 Vierkirchen Ger.
164 E3 Vierlingsbeek Neth.
169 F5 Viernau Ger.
172 C2 Viernheim Ger.
170 F2 Vierraden Ger.
169 B4 Viersen Ger.
159 F2 Vierville-sur-Mer France
190 D1 Vierwaldstätter See l. Switz.
162 E1 Vierzon France
242 E3 Viesca Mex.
170 D2 Viesecke Ger.
171 C5 Vieselbach Ger.
138 E3 Viesīte Latvia
193 I3 Vieste Italy
140 L2 Vietas Sweden
96 D3 Vietnam country Asia
Viet Nam country Asia see Vietnam
193 H4 Vietri di Potenza Italy
193 G4 Vietri sul Mare Italy
96 D2 Việt Tri Vietnam
163 A5 Vieux-Boucau-les-Bains France
247 □2 Vieux Bourg Guadeloupe
161 E4 Vieux Chaillol mt. France
160 E1 Vieux-Charmont France
156 D2 Vieux-Condé France
225 J3 Vieux-Fort Que. Can.
247 □3 Vieux Fort St Lucia
247 □2 Vieux Habitants Guadeloupe
138 E4 Vievis Lith.
148 E2 Viewpark North Lanarkshire, Scotland U.K.
161 D3 Vif France
138 E2 Vigala r. Estonia
92 B2 Vigan Phil.
191 G4 Vigarano Mainarda Italy
191 F3 Vigasio Italy
178 E3 Vigaun Austria
162 D3 Vigeois France
190 D3 Vigevano Italy
192 A3 Viggianello Corse France
193 I5 Viggianello Italy
193 H4 Viggiano Italy
190 D3 Viggiù Italy
254 C2 Vigia Brazil
184 B3 Vigia hill Port.
243 I5 Vigía Chico Mex.
177 I3 Vígľaš Slovakia
193 F3 Viglio, Monte mt. Italy
156 C2 Vignacourt France
190 D3 Vignale Monferrato Italy
193 E2 Vignanello Italy
163 B6 Vignemale mt. France
157 F4 Vigneulles-les-Hattonchâtel France
160 D2 Vignoble reg. France
191 G4 Vignola Italy
192 B3 Vignola r. Sardegna Italy
192 B3 Vignola Mare l'Agnata Sardegna Italy
157 F4 Vignory France
156 B3 Vigny France
182 B2 Vigo Spain
191 H2 Vigo di Cadore Italy
178 C4 Vigo di Fassa Italy
190 C4 Vigone Italy
191 G3 Vigonza Italy
191 F2 Vigo Rendena Italy
86 C4 Vigors, Mount W.A. Austr.
142 C3 Vigsø Bugt b. Denmark
190 D4 Viguzzolo Italy
157 G3 Vigy France
140 N2 Vihanti Fin.
123 H4 Vihari Pak.
162 B1 Vihiers France
177 L3 Vihorlat mt. Slovakia
177 K3 Vihorlatské vrchy mts Slovakia
138 D2 Vihterpalu r. Estonia
141 N3 Vihti Fin.
141 M3 Viiala Fin.
177 L4 Viile Satu Mare Romania
Viipuri Rus. Fed. see Vyborg
177 L4 Viişoara Romania
140 N3 Viitasaari Fin.
116 C3 Vijainagar Rajasthan India
116 C5 Vijapur Gujarat India
114 B2 Vijayadurg Mahar. India
Vijayanagar Karnataka India see Hampi
114 C4 Vijayapati Tamil Nadu India
114 D2 Vijayawada Andhra Prad. India
140 K2 Vik Norway
114 C2 Vikarabad Andhra Prad. India
143 G2 Vikbolandet pen. Sweden
142 A2 Vikedal Norway
142 C2 Vikersund Norway
142 A2 Vikevåg Norway
139 H4 Vikhra r. Rus. Fed.
197 F5 Vikhren mt. Bulg.
223 I4 Viking Alta Can.
140 J2 Vikna i. Norway
141 I3 Vikøyri Norway
Viktorovka Kazakh. see Taranovskoye
171 C4 Viktorshöhe hill Ger.
182 B3 Vila Spain
Vila Vanuatu see Port Vila
Vila Alferes Chamusca Moz. see Guija
184 C2 Vila Alva Port.
Vila Arriaga Angola see Bibala
250 D5 Vila Bittencourt Brazil
182 D4 Vila Boa Port.
184 C2 Vila Boim Port.
Vila Bugaço Angola see Camanongue
Vila Cabral Moz. see Lichinga
182 B3 Vila Caiz Port.
252 D4 Vilacaya Bol.
182 B3 Vila Chã Port.
182 C4 Vila Chã de Sá Port.
182 B3 Vila Chão do Marão Port.
Vila Coutinho Moz. see Ulongue
182 C4 Vila Cova à Coelheira Port.
182 B3 Vila Cova da Lixa Port.
186 E2 Vilada Spain
182 C1 Vila da Igrexa Spain
186 G2 Viladamat Spain
Vila da Ponte Angola see Kuvango
182 C3 Vila da Ponte Port.
216 □1a Vila da Praia da Vitória Terceira Azores
206 □ Vila da Ribeira Brava Cape Verde
Vila de Aljustrel Angola see Cangamba
Vila de Almoster Angola see Chiange
186 F3 Viladecans Spain
182 B2 Vila de Cruces Spain
Vila de João Belo Moz. see Xai-Xai
Vila de Junqueiro Moz. see Gurué
Vilademat Spain see Viladamat
182 B5 Vila de Rei Port.
206 □ Vila de Sal Rei Cape Verde
213 G3 Vila de Sena Moz.
Vila de Trego Morais Moz. see Chókwé
184 B3 Vila do Bispo Port.
182 B3 Vila do Conde Port.
206 □ Vila do Tarrafal São Tiago Cape Verde
186 F3 Viladrau Spain
184 C2 Vila Fernando Port.
216 □3a Vilaflor Tenerife Canary Is
182 C3 Vila Flor Port.
Vila Fontes Moz. see Caia
182 C4 Vila Franca das Naves Port.
186 E3 Vilafranca del Penedès Spain
184 B2 Vila Franca de Xira Port.
216 □1b Vila Franca do Campo São Miguel Azores
182 B2 Vilagarcía de Arousa Spain
Vila Gouveia Moz. see Catandica
158 D4 Vilaine r. France
186 G2 Vilajüiga Spain
138 F3 Viļaka Latvia
182 C1 Vilalba Spain
186 F2 Vilallonga Spain
Vila Luísa Moz. see Marracuene
Vila Marechal Carmona Angola see Uíge
182 C2 Vilamartín de Valdeorras Spain
187 C5 Vilamarxant Spain
260 A5 Vila Mercedes Chile
Vila Miranda Moz. see Macaloge
184 B1 Vila Moreira Port.
184 B3 Vilamoura Port.
213 □J3 Vilanandro, Tanjona pt Madag.
186 F2 Vilanant Spain
213 G4 Vilanculos Moz.
138 F3 Viļāni Latvia
184 A2 Vila Nogueira de Azeitão Port.
Vila Nova Angola see Tchikala-Tcholohanga
216 □1a Vila Nova Terceira Azores
184 B2 Vila Nova da Baronia Port.
187 D4 Vilanova d'Alcolea Spain
186 D3 Vilanova d'Aplicat Spain
182 B4 Vila Nova de Anços Port.
182 B2 Vilanova de Arousa Spain
Vilanova de Castelló Spain see Villanueva de Castellón
182 B3 Vila Nova de Cerveira Port.
182 B3 Vila Nova de Famalicão Port.
182 C3 Vila Nova de Foz Coa Port.
182 B3 Vila Nova de Gaia Port.
186 E3 Vilanova de l'Aguda Spain
182 C1 Vilanova de Lourenzá Spain
186 E3 Vilanova de Meià Spain
182 B5 Vila Nova de Ourém Port.
182 C4 Vila Nova de Paiva Port.
182 B4 Vila Nova de Poiares Port.
184 C3 Vila Nova de São Bento Port.
Vila Nova do Seles Angola see Uku
186 E3 Vilanova i la Geltrú Spain
206 □ Vila Nova Sintra Cape Verde
Vila Paiva de Andrada Moz. see Gorongosa
Vila Pery Moz. see Chimoio
182 C4 Vila Pouca da Beira Port.
182 C3 Vila Pouca de Aguiar Port.
182 B3 Vila Praia de Âncora Port.
182 C3 Vilarandelo Port.
182 C2 Vilarchao Spain
182 B3 Vilar da Veiga Port.
182 B3 Vilar de Andorinho Port.
182 C2 Vilar de Barrio Spain
182 C2 Vilar de Santos Spain
182 C3 Vilardevós Spain
182 C3 Vila Real Port.
182 C3 Vila Real admin. dist. Port.
187 C5 Vila-real de los Infantes Spain
184 C3 Vila Real de Santo António Port.
182 C3 Vilarelho da Raia Port.
182 D4 Vilar Formoso Port.
182 C3 Vilarinho da Castanheira Port.
182 B4 Vilarinho do Bairro Port.
182 C2 Vilariño de Conso Spain
186 E3 Vila-rodona Spain
184 C2 Vila Ruiva Port.
Vilas i. S. Male Maldives see Velassary
Vila Salazar Angola see N'dalatando
129 F4 Viläşçay r. Azer.
182 B3 Vila Seca Port.
186 E3 Vilaseca de Solcina Spain
Vila Teixeira de Sousa Angola see Luau
114 C4 Vilavankod Tamil Nadu India
257 G4 Vila Velha Brazil
182 C5 Vila Velha de Ródão Port.
182 B3 Vila Verde Braga Port.
182 B4 Vila Verde Coimbra Port.
182 C3 Vila Verde Vila Real Port.
182 C3 Vila Verde da Raia Port.
184 C3 Vila Verde de Ficalho Port.
184 C2 Vila Viçosa Port.
252 B3 Vilcabamba, Cordillera mts Peru
252 C3 Vilcanota, Cordillera de mts Peru
136 E2 Vil'cha Ukr.
185 G2 Vilches Spain
260 A6 Vilcun Chile
134 I3 Viled' r. Rus. Fed.
Vileyka Belarus see Vilyeyka
134 J3 Vil'gort Rus. Fed.
140 L2 Vilhelmina Sweden
253 E3 Vilhena Brazil
Viligili i. N. Male Maldives see Villingli
137 G5 Viline Ukr.
113 □1 Vilingli i. N. Male Maldives
138 E4 Viliya r. Belarus/Lith.
136 D2 Viliya r. Ukr.
138 E2 Viljandi Estonia
214 B6 Viljoenshof S. Africa
215 F2 Viljoenskroon S. Africa
138 D4 Vilkaviškis Lith.
137 J3 Vil'khova r. Ukr.
138 D4 Vilkija Lith.
252 D5 Villa Abecia Bol.
260 C2 Villa Aberastain Arg.
189 D5 Villa Adriana tourist site Italy
242 D2 Villa Ahumada Mex.
261 F6 Villa Alba Arg.
260 B4 Villa Alegre Chile
260 B3 Villa Alemana Chile
246 E3 Villa Altagracia Dom. Rep.
258 F3 Villa Ana Arg.
258 E2 Villa Angela Arg.
261 G3 Villa Angelica Arg.
244 D3 Villa Apaseo El Alto Mex.
261 F6 Villa Atlantica Arg.
260 D4 Villa Atuel Arg.
245 F3 Villa Ávila Camacho Mex.
245 G4 Villa Azueta Mex.
191 G3 Villa Bartolomea Italy
194 C4 Villabate Sicilia Italy
Villa Bens Morocco see Tarfaya
258 E2 Villa Berthet Arg.
184 C3 Villablanca Spain
182 D2 Villablino Spain
186 A1 Villabona Spain
183 E3 Villabrágima Spain
183 E3 Villabuena del Puente Spain
162 D3 Villac France
261 G4 Villa Cañás Arg.
183 G5 Villacañas Spain
190 F3 Villa Carcina Italy
186 □ Villacarlos Spain
260 E2 Villa Carlos Paz Arg.
185 G2 Villacarrillo Spain
195 G2 Villa Castelli Italy
183 F4 Villacastín Spain
179 E4 Villach Austria
192 A5 Villacidro Sardegna Italy
183 H3 Villaciervos Spain
Villa Cisneros Western Sahara see Ad Dakhla
Villa Cisneros, Ría de b. Western Sahara see Río de Oro, Bahía de
243 G6 Villa Comaltitlán Mex.
261 F2 Villa Concepción del Tío Arg.
183 G4 Villaconejos Spain
183 H4 Villaconejos de Trabaque Spain
261 G3 Villa Constitución Arg.
Villa Constitución Mex. see Ciudad Constitución
244 C3 Villa Corona Mex.
260 E2 Villa Cura Brochero Arg.
261 G3 Villada Arg.
183 F2 Villada Spain
190 E3 Villa d'Almè Italy
244 C4 Villa de Álvarez Mex.
244 C2 Villa de Cos Mex.
183 F4 Villa del Prado Spain
244 D3 Villa del Pueblito Mex.
185 F3 Villa del Río Spain
261 F2 Villa del Rosario Arg.
182 D3 Villadepera Spain
187 B5 Villa de Ves Spain
261 G3 Villa Diego Arg.
183 F2 Villadiego Spain
260 E2 Villa Dolores Arg.
261 H3 Villa Domínguez Arg.
191 G3 Villadose Italy
190 D2 Villadossola Italy
186 B3 Villadoz Spain
260 C6 Villa El Chocón Arg.
183 F2 Villaeles de Valdavia Spain
261 H3 Villa Elisa Arg.
261 G3 Villa Eloisa Arg.
244 D4 Villa Escalante Mex.
183 H5 Villaescusa de Haro Spain
183 G2 Villaescusa la Sombría Spain
182 E3 Villafáfila Spain
187 C4 Villafamés Spain
183 I3 Villafeliche Spain
243 G5 Villa Flores Mex.
183 E3 Villaflores Spain
253 F6 Villa Florida Para.
183 I2 Villafranca Spain
190 D4 Villafranca d'Asti Italy
187 G5 Villafranca de Bonany Spain
185 F3 Villafranca de Córdoba Spain
186 C3 Villafranca de Ebro Spain
182 D2 Villafranca del Bierzo Spain
186 B4 Villafranca del Campo Spain
186 C4 Villafranca del Cid Spain
184 D2 Villafranca de los Barros Spain
185 G1 Villafranca de los Caballeros Spain
Villafranca del Penedès Spain see Vilafranca del Penedès
191 F3 Villafranca di Verona Italy
190 E4 Villafranca in Lunigiana Italy
183 G2 Villafranca-Montes de Oca Spain
195 E4 Villafranca Tirrena Sicilia Italy
191 F3 Villafranca Veronese airport Italy
184 D3 Villafranco del Guadalquivir Spain
194 C5 Villafrati Sicilia Italy
183 E3 Villafrechos Spain
183 G3 Villafruela Spain
183 F3 Villafuerte Spain
Villagarcía de Arosa Spain see Vilagarcía de Arousa
183 E3 Villagarcía de Campos Spain
184 D2 Villagarcía de la Torre Spain
185 I1 Villagarcía del Llano Spain
261 I5 Villa Gesell Arg.
195 F3 Villagio Mancuso Italy
184 D2 Villagonzalo Spain
261 G3 Villa Governador Gálvez Arg.
245 E1 Villagrán Mex.
192 B5 Villagrande Strisaili Sardegna Italy
261 H2 Villaguay Arg.
258 F3 Villa Guillermina Arg.
185 F2 Villaharta Spain
253 F6 Villa Hayes Para.
243 G5 Villahermosa Mex.
185 H2 Villahermosa Spain
187 C4 Villahermosa del Río Spain
261 H2 Villa Hernandarias Arg.
183 F2 Villaherreros Spain
244 B3 Villa Hidalgo Nayarit Mex.
239 E6 Villa Hidalgo Mex.
183 G2 Villahizán Spain
183 G2 Villahoz Spain
260 E4 Villa Huidobro Arg.
156 E5 Villaines-en-Duesmois France
159 F3 Villaines-la-Juhel France
159 F4 Villaines-sous-Malicorne France
242 C3 Villa Insurgentes Mex.
261 F6 Villa Iris Arg.
187 C6 Villajoyosa Spain
244 B3 Villa Juárez Mex.
244 D2 Villa Juárez Mex.
191 G3 Villa Lagarina Italy
193 F3 Villalago Italy
183 E3 Villalar de los Comuneros Spain
193 F3 Villa Latina Italy
245 G4 Villa La Venta Mex.
245 F3 Villa Lázaro Cárdenas Mex.
194 C5 Villalba Sicilia Italy
247 □1 Villalba Puerto Rico
183 G3 Villalba de Duero Spain
183 F2 Villalba de Guardo Spain
184 D3 Villalba del Alcor Spain
183 H4 Villalba de la Sierra Spain
183 F3 Villalba de los Alcores Spain
184 D2 Villalba de los Barros Spain
183 H4 Villalba del Rey Spain
186 D3 Villalba dels Arcs Spain
183 H2 Villalba de Rioja Spain
182 D3 Villalcampo Spain
183 F2 Villalcázar de Sirga Spain
243 E3 Villaldama Mex.
183 I3 Villalengua Spain
185 H1 Villalgordo del Júcar Spain
183 H5 Villalgordo del Marquesado Spain
193 G3 Villa Literno Italy
183 E3 Villalobos Spain
183 E2 Villalón de Campos Spain
259 E5 Villálonga Arg.
187 C6 Villalonga Spain
183 E3 Villalpando Spain
185 I1 Villalpardo Spain
183 G4 Villaluenga de la Sagra Spain
183 F2 Villalumbroso Spain
185 I1 Villamalea Spain
182 E2 Villamañán Spain
182 E2 Villamandos Spain
185 H2 Villamanrique Spain
184 D3 Villamanrique de la Condesa Spain
183 F4 Villamanta Spain
192 A5 Villamar Sardegna Italy
Villamarchante Spain see Vilamarxant
261 F3 Villa María Arg.
261 G2 Villa María Arg.
261 H2 Villa María Grande Arg.
252 D5 Villa Martín Bol.
184 E4 Villamartín Spain
183 F2 Villamartín de Campos Spain
192 A5 Villamassargia Sardegna Italy
182 E4 Villamayor Spain
185 F2 Villamayor de Calatrava Spain
183 E3 Villamayor de Campos Spain
183 H5 Villamayor de Santiago Spain
183 F2 Villamayor de Treviño Spain
162 C3 Villamblard France
183 F2 Villamediana Spain
183 H2 Villamediana de Iregua Spain
182 D2 Villamejil Spain
184 E1 Villamesías Spain
182 D4 Villamiel Spain
190 F4 Villa Minozzo Italy
252 E5 Villa Montes Bol.
182 E3 Villamor de los Escuderos Spain
244 D3 Villa Morelos Mex.
183 G5 Villamuelas Spain
183 F3 Villamuriel de Cerrato Spain
163 B4 Villandraut France
195 G2 Villanova Italy
190 D4 Villanova d'Albenga Italy
190 C4 Villanova d'Asti Italy
193 H3 Villanova del Battista Italy
192 B5 Villanovafranca Sardegna Italy
192 A4 Villanova Monteleone Sardegna Italy
192 A5 Villanova Truschedu Sardegna Italy
192 B5 Villanova Tulo Sardegna Italy
190 E3 Villanterio Italy
186 C2 Villanúa Spain
183 F3 Villanubla Spain
261 F3 Villa Nueva Arg.
250 C2 Villanueva Col.
244 C2 Villanueva Mex.
Villanueva Spain see Vilanova de Lourenzá
183 H5 Villanueva de Alcardete Spain
Villanueva de Alcolea Spain see Vilanova d'Alcolea
183 H4 Villanueva de Alcorón Spain
185 F3 Villanueva de Algaidas Spain
183 G2 Villanueva de Argaño Spain
Villanueva de Arosa Spain see Vilanova de Arousa
183 G5 Villanueva de Bogas Spain
183 H2 Villanueva de Cameros Spain
187 C5 Villanueva de Castellón Spain
185 F2 Villanueva de Córdoba Spain
186 C3 Villanueva de Gállego Spain
183 F4 Villanueva de Gómez Spain
183 G4 Villanueva de la Cañada Spain
185 F4 Villanueva de la Concepción Spain
185 H2 Villanueva de la Fuente Spain
185 I1 Villanueva de la Jara Spain
185 G2 Villanueva de la Reina Spain
185 G2 Villanueva del Arzobispo Spain
184 C3 Villanueva de las Cruces Spain
184 E2 Villanueva de la Serena Spain
182 D4 Villanueva de la Sierra Spain
185 G3 Villanueva de las Torres Spain
183 E4 Villanueva de la Vera Spain
183 E3 Villanueva del Campo Spain
185 F2 Villanueva del Duque Spain
184 C2 Villanueva del Fresno Spain
184 C3 Villanueva de los Castillejos Spain
185 H2 Villanueva de los Infantes Spain
185 E2 Villanueva del Rey Spain
187 B6 Villanueva del Río Segura Spain
184 E3 Villanueva del Río y Minas Spain
185 F4 Villanueva del Rosario Spain
185 F3 Villanueva del Trabuco Spain
185 G2 Villanueva de San Carlos Spain
185 E3 Villanueva de San Juan Spain
185 F3 Villanueva de Tapia Spain
183 G2 Villanueva de Valdegovia Spain
Villanueva-y-Geltrú Spain see Vilanova i la Geltrú
183 F2 Villanuño de Valdavia Spain
177 H6 Villány Hungary
177 H6 Villányi-hegység ridge Hungary
258 F3 Villa Ocampo Arg.
242 D3 Villa Ocampo Mex.
258 E3 Villa Ojo de Agua Arg.
Villa O. Pereyra Mex. see Villa Orestes Pereyra
191 I3 Villa Opicina Italy
242 D3 Villa Orestes Pereyra Mex.
252 D4 Villa Oropeza Bol.
185 H2 Villapalacios Spain
192 A5 Villaperuccio Sardegna Italy
195 F3 Villapiana Italy
195 F3 Villapiana Lido Italy
191 G4 Villa Poma Italy
160 B2 Villapourçon France
260 B4 Villa Prat Chile
192 B5 Villaputzu Sardegna Italy
182 E2 Villaquejida Spain
182 E2 Villaquilambre Spain
252 D4 Villar Bol.
182 E3 Villaralbo Spain
185 F2 Villaralto Spain
261 G3 Villa Ramírez Arg.
183 G2 Villarcayo Spain
161 E3 Villar-d'Arêne France
161 D3 Villard-Bonnot France
161 D3 Villard-de-Lans France
185 I2 Villar de Chinchilla Spain
182 D4 Villar de Ciervo Spain
182 D3 Villardeciervos Spain
183 E3 Villardefrades Spain
187 C5 Villar del Arzobispo Spain
182 D4 Villar de la Yegua Spain
182 D3 Villar del Buey Spain
183 I4 Villar del Cobo Spain
183 I5 Villar del Humo Spain
182 D2 Villar de los Barrios Spain
186 B3 Villar de los Navarros Spain
183 E5 Villar del Pedroso Spain
184 D1 Villar del Rey Spain
183 I4 Villar del Salz Spain
183 H4 Villar de Olalla Spain
182 D3 Villar de Peralonso Spain
184 E1 Villar de Rena Spain
183 H2 Villar de Torre Spain
185 F3 Villardompardo Spain
Villareal Spain see Vila-real de los Infantes
Villareal de los Infantes Spain see Vila-real de los Infantes
261 F3 Villa Reducción Arg.
260 D6 Villa Regina Arg.
183 H5 Villarejo de Fuentes Spain
183 F5 Villarejo de Montalbán Spain
182 E2 Villarejo de Orbigo Spain
183 G4 Villarejo de Salvanés Spain
191 F2 Villa Rendena Italy
183 E2 Villarente Spain
182 E3 Villares de la Reina Spain
185 G3 Villargordo Spain
182 D3 Villarino de los Aires Spain
186 C4 Villarluengo Spain
194 D5 Villarosa Sicilia Italy
186 B4 Villarquemado Spain
183 F2 Villarramiel Spain
186 B3 Villarreal de Huerva Spain
260 A6 Villarrica Chile
253 F6 Villarrica Para.
260 A6 Villarrica, Lago l. Chile
182 E3 Villarrín de Campos Spain
185 H1 Villarrobledo Spain
185 H2 Villarrodrigo Spain
183 H2 Villarroya Spain
186 C4 Villarroya de los Pinares Spain
185 G1 Villarrubia de los Ojos Spain
183 G5 Villarrubia de Santiago Spain
183 H5 Villarrubio Spain
162 C3 Villars Aquitaine France
161 C3 Villars Rhône-Alpes France
161 E4 Villar-St-Pancrace France
183 H5 Villars del Saz Spain
160 E1 Villars-lès-Blamont France
160 D3 Villars-les-Dombes France
161 F5 Villars-sur-Var France
185 I1 Villarta Spain
185 F1 Villarta de los Montes Spain
185 G1 Villarta de San Juan Spain
234 D3 Villas NJ U.S.A.
192 B5 Villasalto Sardegna Italy
180 E1 Villasana de Mena Spain
183 F2 Villasandino Spain
195 E4 Villa San Giovanni Italy
261 H3 Villa San José Arg.
Villa Sanjurjo Morocco see Al Hoceima
258 D3 Villa San Martin Arg.
193 G3 Villa Santa Maria Italy
260 C2 Villa Santa Rosa Arg.
183 G1 Villasante de Montija Spain
191 H2 Villa Santina Italy
183 F2 Villasarracino Spain
163 E5 Villasavary France
183 H3 Villasayas Spain
182 D3 Villasbuenas Spain
182 D3 Villasdardo Spain
182 D2 Villaseca de Laciana Spain
183 G5 Villaseca de la Sagra Spain
182 D3 Villaseco de los Gamitos Spain
182 D3 Villaseco de los Reyes Spain
182 E3 Villaseco del Pan Spain
183 G5 Villasequilla de Yepes Spain
252 D4 Villa Serrano Bol.
192 B5 Villasimius Sardegna Italy
195 E5 Villasmundo Sicilia Italy
192 A5 Villasor Sardegna Italy
192 A5 Villaspeciosa Sardegna Italy
182 D4 Villasrubias Spain
187 B4 Villastar Spain
183 G2 Villasur de Herreros Spain
183 G5 Villatobas Spain
183 E4 Villatoro Spain
187 B5 Villatoya Spain
261 E2 Villa Tulumba Arg.
183 E2 Villaturiel Spain
183 F2 Villaumbrales Spain
258 C3 Villa Unión Arg.
243 E2 Villa Unión Mex.
244 B2 Villa Unión Mex.
244 A2 Villa Unión Mex.
192 A5 Villaurbana Sardegna Italy
260 E4 Villa Valeria Arg.
193 F3 Villavallelonga Italy
246 E3 Villa Vasquez Dom. Rep.
183 H2 Villavelayo Spain
192 A5 Villa Verde Sardegna Italy
185 H2 Villaverde de Guadalimar Spain
184 E3 Villaverde del Río Spain
187 A5 Villaverde y Pasaconsol Spain
190 D4 Villavernia Italy
250 C3 Villavicencio Col.
183 E1 Villaviciosa de Asturias Spain
185 E2 Villaviciosa de Córdoba Spain
183 G4 Villaviciosa de Odón Spain
187 C5 Villavieja Spain
183 G3 Villavieja del Lozoya Spain
182 D4 Villavieja de Yeltes Spain
252 D4 Villa Viscarra Bol.
183 F3 Villaviudas Spain
182 D1 Villayón Spain
183 F2 Villazanzo de Valderaduey Spain
252 D5 Villazon Bol.
157 H4 Villé France
160 D3 Villebois France
162 C3 Villebois-Lavalette France
163 D5 Villebrumier France
163 C5 Villecomtal-sur-Arros France
160 D1 Villecomte France
161 E5 Villecroze France
161 A5 Villedaigne France
244 D3 Ville de Reyes Mex.
159 E4 Villedieu-la-Blouère France
158 E3 Villedieu-les-Poêles France
159 H5 Villedieu-sur-Indre France
192 B2 Ville-di-Pietrabugno Corse France
159 G4 Villedômer France
156 D3 Ville-en-Tardenois France
162 C2 Villefagnan France
160 D3 Villefontaine France
161 B4 Villefort France
156 D5 Villefranche Bourgogne France
163 C5 Villefranche Midi-Pyrénées France
163 E5 Villefranche-d'Albigeois France
160 A2 Villefranche-d'Allier France
163 E6 Villefranche-de-Conflent France
163 D5 Villefranche-de-Lauragais France
162 C4 Villefranche-de-Lonchat France
161 A4 Villefranche-de-Panat France
163 E4 Villefranche-de-Rouergue France
163 D4 Villefranche-du-Périgord France
159 H4 Villefranche-sur-Cher France
161 F5 Villefranche-sur-Mer France
160 C3 Villefranche-sur-Saône France
163 A5 Villefranque France
183 F2 Villegas Spain
244 C2 Ville Juarez Mex.
187 B4 Villel Spain
161 D5 Villelaure France
156 C5 Villemandeur France
227 H2 Ville-Marie Que. Can.
Ville-Marie Que. Can. see Montréal
156 D4 Villemaur-sur-Vanne France
227 H1 Villemontel Que. Can.
156 E4 Villemorien France
163 E5 Villemoustaussou France
163 D5 Villemur-sur-Tarn France
187 C6 Villena Spain
156 D4 Villenauxe-la-Grande France
163 B4 Villenave-d'Ornon France
163 E4 Villeneuve Midi-Pyrénées France
161 D5 Villeneuve Provence-Alpes-Côte-d'Azur France
160 C2 Villeneuve Rhône-Alpes France
190 B2 Villeneuve Switz.
156 D4 Villeneuve-au-Chemin France
161 B3 Villeneuve-d'Allier France
156 D2 Villeneuve-d'Ascq France
161 C4 Villeneuve-de-Berg France
163 B5 Villeneuve-de-Marsan France
163 C5 Villeneuve-de-Rivière France
163 D6 Villeneuve-d'Olmes France
163 D5 Villeneuve-du-Paréage France
156 D4 Villeneuve-la-Guyard France
156 D4 Villeneuve-l'Archevêque France
161 C5 Villeneuve-lès-Avignon France
161 B5 Villeneuve-lès-Béziers France
161 B5 Villeneuve-lès-Maguelonne France
161 F5 Villeneuve-Loubet France
156 D3 Villeneuve-St-Germain France
160 B2 Villeneuve-sur-Allier France
163 C4 Villeneuve-sur-Lot France
156 D4 Villeneuve-sur-Yonne France
163 D5 Villeneuve-Tolosane France
163 D5 Villenouvelle France
163 E5 Villepinte France
237 E6 Ville Platte LA U.S.A.
159 G2 Villequier France
161 A4 Villercomtal France
163 C4 Villeréal France
160 C3 Villerest France
183 F3 Villerías Spain
161 A5 Villerouge-Termenès France
159 F2 Villers-Bocage France
156 C3 Villers-Bocage France
156 C3 Villers-Bretonneux France
156 C3 Villers-Carbonnel France
156 D3 Villers-Cotterêts France
156 A3 Villers-Écalles France
157 E3 Villers-en-Argonne France
160 E1 Villersexel France
160 D1 Villers-Farlay France
165 E4 Villers-le-Bouillet Belgium
160 E1 Villers-le-lac France
157 G4 Villers-lès-Nancy France
156 D2 Villers-Outréaux France
165 B5 Villers-St-Paul France
156 E3 Villers-Semeuse France
190 C2 Villers-sur-Glâne Switz.
159 F2 Villers-sur-Mer France
157 F3 Villers-sur-Meuse France
157 F3 Villerupt France
159 G2 Villerville France
156 E4 Villery France
156 E4 Villeseneux France
161 D4 Villes-sur-Auzon France
157 E3 Ville-sur-Tourbe France
193 F3 Villetta Barrea Italy
160 D3 Villette-d'Anthon France
160 C3 Villeurbanne France
161 B5 Villeveyrac France
161 C3 Villevocance France
260 C2 Villicun, Sierra mts Arg.
160 C2 Villié-Morgon France
215 G2 Villiers S. Africa
159 F4 Villiers-Charlemagne France
214 B5 Villiersdorp S. Africa
157 E4 Villiers-en-Lieu France
162 B2 Villiers-en-Plaine France
156 C3 Villiers-le-Bel France
157 F4 Villiers-le-Sec France
156 D5 Villiers-St-Benoît France
156 D4 Villiers-St-Georges France
147 D4 Villierstown Rep. of Ireland
160 D3 Villieu-Loyes-Mollon France
172 C3 Villingen Ger.
172 C3 Villingendorf Ger.
113 □1 Villingli i. N. Male Maldives
169 D5 Villmar Ger.
183 F2 Villoldo Spain
183 I5 Villora Spain
183 I5 Villora r. Spain
191 H3 Villorba Italy
183 E4 Villoria Spain
183 E3 Villoruela Spain
157 F4 Villotte-sur-Aire France
Villupuram Tamil Nadu India see Viluppuram
177 K3 Vilmány Hungary
223 I4 Vilna Alta Can.
Vilna Lith. see Vilnius
138 E4 Vilnius Lith.
137 H3 Vil'nohirs'k Ukr.
137 H4 Vil'nyans'k Ukr.
186 F3 Viloví d'Onyar Spain
141 N3 Vilppula Fin.
178 B3 Vils Austria
173 F2 Vils r. Ger.
173 H3 Vils r. Ger.
138 C2 Vilsandi i. Estonia
173 G3 Vilsbiburg Ger.
173 F2 Vilseck Ger.
137 F3 Vil'shana Ukr.
137 G2 Vil'shana Ukr.
137 I3 Vil'shana Ukr.
136 F3 Vil'shanka Ukr.
136 E3 Vil'shanka Ukr.
136 E2 Vil'shanka Ukr.
173 H3 Vilshofen Ger.
142 C3 Vilsund Vest Denmark
114 C4 Viluppuram Tamil Nadu India
182 D3 Vilvestre Spain
165 D4 Vilvoorde Belgium
138 F4 Vilyeyka Belarus
131 N3 Vilyuy r. Rus. Fed.
131 M3 Vilyuyskoye Vodokhranilishche resr Rus. Fed.
209 F8 Vimbe mt. Zambia
186 E3 Vimbodí Spain
184 A1 Vimeiro Port.
190 E3 Vimercate Italy
182 A1 Vimianzo Spain
184 C2 Vimieiro Port.
182 D3 Vimioso Port.
143 F3 Vimmerby Sweden
156 C5 Vimory France
159 G3 Vimoutiers France
140 M3 Vimpeli Fin.
176 C2 Vimperk Czech Rep.
207 I5 Vina r. Cameroon
240 F2 Vina CA U.S.A.
186 C3 Vinaceite Spain
260 B3 Viña del Mar Chile
190 C4 Vinadio Italy
186 D3 Vinaixa Spain
246 B2 Viñales Valley tourist site Pinar del Río Cuba
233 □I2 Vinalhaven ME U.S.A.
187 C6 Vinalopó r. Spain
171 F5 Vinařice Czech Rep.
78 □6 Vinarori, Mount New Georgia Is Solomon Is
186 D4 Vinaròs Spain
Vinaroz Spain see Vinaròs
161 B5 Vinassan France
161 D3 Vinay France
245 F3 Vinazco r. Mex.
163 E6 Vinça France
230 C4 Vincennes IN U.S.A.
234 D3 Vincentown NJ U.S.A.
250 B5 Vinces r. Ecuador
157 G4 Vincey France
193 G3 Vinchiaturo Italy
258 C3 Vinchina Arg.
252 B3 Vinchos Peru
191 F5 Vinci Italy
168 F1 Vindeballe Denmark
140 L3 Vindelälven r. Sweden
140 L2 Vindeln Sweden
142 C3 Vinderup Denmark
116 C5 Vindhya Range hills Madh. Prad. India
Vindobona Austria see Wien
186 D3 Vinebre Spain
234 C3 Vineland NJ U.S.A.
159 H4 Vineuil Centre France
159 H5 Vineuil Centre France
215 F4 Vineyard S. Africa
196 E2 Vinga Romania
196 E2 Vingăi, Câmpia plain Romania
143 F2 Vingåker Sweden
160 D1 Vingeanne r. France
163 E6 Vingrau France
96 D3 Vinh Vietnam
182 D3 Vinhais Port.
182 D3 Vinhas Port.
97 D5 Vinh Long Vietnam
96 D2 Vinh Yên Vietnam
179 H4 Vinica Croatia
197 F5 Vinica Macedonia
177 I3 Vinica Slovakia
176 G3 Viničné Slovakia
179 H1 Viničné Šumice Czech Rep.
183 H2 Viniegra de Arriba Spain
237 E4 Vinita OK U.S.A.
116 B5 Vinjhan Gujarat India
Vînju Mare Romania see Vânju Mare
136 D3 Vin'kivtsi Ukr.
188 G3 Vinkovci Croatia
Vinland i. Nfld. Can. see Newfoundland

Vinné to Wajima 377

177 K3 Vinné Slovakia
138 F2 Vinni Estonia
172 B2 Vinningen Ger.
Vinnitsa Ukr. see Vinnytsya
Vinnitsa Oblast admin. div. Ukr. see Vinnyts'ka Oblast'
Vinnitskaya Oblast' admin. div. Ukr. see Vinnyts'ka Oblast'
139 J1 Vinnitsy Rus. Fed.
136 D3 Vinnyts'ka Oblast' admin. div. Ukr.
136 E3 Vinnytsya Ukr.
Vinnytsya Oblast admin. div. Ukr. see Vinnyts'ka Oblast'
177 H3 Vinodol Slovakia
Vinogradov Ukr. see Vynohradiv
177 G3 Vinohrady nad Váhom Slovakia
161 D5 Vinon-sur-Verdon France
161 D4 Vinsobres France
262 S1 Vinson Massif mt. Antarctica
141 J3 Vinstra Norway
92 B2 Vintar Phil.
236 E3 Vinton IA U.S.A.
183 G4 Viñuelas Spain
183 H3 Vinuesa Spain
114 C2 Vinukonda Andhra Prad. India
209 B5 Vinza Congo
170 C3 Vinzelberg Ger.
168 E1 Viöl Ger.
160 C3 Violay France
161 C4 Violès France
Violeta Cuba see Primero de Enero
161 B5 Viols-le-Fort France
214 A3 Vioolsdrif S. Africa
156 C3 Viosne r. France
179 E5 Vipava Slovenia
179 E5 Vipava r. Slovenia
211 B8 Viphya Mountains Malawi
191 G2 Vipiteno Italy
170 D2 Vipperow Ger.
188 E3 Vir i. Croatia
179 F4 Vir Slovenia
92 C3 Virac Phil.
256 C4 Viradouro Brazil
116 C5 Viramgam Gujarat India
127 E3 Viranşehir Turkey
114 B3 Virarajendrapet Karnataka India
163 C4 Virazeil France
138 D3 Vircava r. Latvia/Lith.
86 C4 Virchow, Mount hill W.A. Austr.
223 K5 Virden Man. Can.
159 F3 Vire France
159 E2 Vire r. France
209 B8 Virei Angola
156 E2 Vireux-Molhain France
156 E2 Vireux-Wallerand France
156 E4 Virey-sous-Bar France
197 E2 Vîrful Highiş hill Romania
257 F2 Virgem da Lapa Brazil
178 D3 Virgen Austria
232 D6 Virgilina VA U.S.A.
241 J3 Virgin r. AZ U.S.A.
227 H1 Virginatown Ont. Can.
247 F3 Virgin Gorda i. Virgin Is (U.K.)
147 D3 Virginia Rep. of Ireland
215 F3 Virginia S. Africa
226 A2 Virginia MN U.S.A.
232 D6 Virginia state U.S.A.
233 F6 Virginia Beach VA U.S.A.
238 E2 Virginia City MT U.S.A.
240 H2 Virginia City NV U.S.A.
151 G3 Virginia Water Surrey, England U.K.
247 F3 Virgin Islands (U.K.) terr. West Indies
247 F3 Virgin Islands (U.S.A.) terr. West Indies
241 J3 Virgin Mountains AZ U.S.A.
257 F3 Virginópolis Brazil
160 D2 Viriat France
160 D3 Virieu France
160 D3 Virieu-le-Grand France
160 C3 Virigneux France
160 D3 Virignin France
161 D3 Viriville France
188 F2 Virje Croatia
138 E1 Virkkala Fin.
97 D4 Virôchey Cambodia
165 D4 Viroin r. Belgium
141 N3 Virolahti Fin.
226 B4 Viroqua WI U.S.A.
188 F3 Virovitica Croatia
141 M3 Virrat Fin.
143 F3 Virserum Sweden
165 E5 Virton Belgium
252 A2 Virú Peru
114 C4 Virudunagar Tamil Nadu India
138 D3 Virvytė r. Lith.
160 D2 Viry Franche-Comté France
160 E2 Viry Rhône-Alpes France
156 D3 Viry-Noureuil France
188 F4 Vis Croatia
188 F4 Vis i. Croatia
138 F4 Visaginas Lith.
Visakhapatnam Andhra Prad. India see Vishakhapatnam
240 H3 Visalia CA U.S.A.
161 C4 Visan France
197 H3 Vişani Romania
114 B2 Visapur Mahar. India
116 B5 Visavadar Gujarat India
92 B4 Visayan Sea Phil.
168 D3 Visbek Ger.
168 D1 Visby Denmark
143 H3 Visby Gotland Sweden
257 F4 Visconde do Rio Branco Brazil
221 G2 Viscount Melville Sound sea chan. N.W.T./Nunavut Can.
165 E4 Visé Belgium
188 G4 Višegrad Bos.-Herz.
191 H4 Viserba Italy
254 D2 Viseu Brazil
182 C4 Viseu Port.
182 C4 Viseu admin. dist. Port.
197 G2 Vişeu r. Romania
197 G2 Vişeu de Sus Romania
191 J3 Viševica mt. Croatia
115 D2 Vishakhapatnam Andhra Prad. India
197 H5 Vishegrad hill Bulg.
134 K3 Vishera r. Rus. Fed.
134 L4 Vishera r. Rus. Fed.
139 H2 Vishera r. Rus. Fed.
121 H2 Vishnevka Kazakh.
135 H5 Vishnevoye Rus. Fed.
Vishnevoye Dnipropetrovs'ka Oblast' Ukr. see Vyshneve
186 B4 Visiedo Spain
197 G3 Vişina Romania
143 F2 Visingsö i. Sweden
142 E3 Viskan r. Sweden
138 F3 Viški Latvia
188 F4 Viški Kanal sea chan. Croatia
143 F3 Vislanda Sweden
116 C5 Visnagar Gujarat India
171 G5 Višňová Czech Rep.
176 F3 Višňové Czech Rep.
177 H2 Višňové Slovakia
190 C4 Viso, Monte mt. Italy
185 G2 Viso del Marqués Spain
188 G4 Visoko Bos.-Herz.
190 D4 Visone Italy
177 J4 Visonta Hungary
190 C2 Visp Switz.
215 E4 Visrivier S. Africa
161 B3 Vissac-Auteyrac France
114 D2 Vissannapeta Andhra Prad. India
143 F3 Visselfjärda Sweden
168 E3 Visselhövede Ger.
193 F2 Visso Italy
190 C2 Vissoie Switz.
240 I5 Vista CA U.S.A.
235 E1 Vista NY U.S.A.
187 C4 Vistabella del Maestrazgo Spain
260 C3 Vista Flores Arg.
Vistula r. Pol. see Wisła
137 G4 Visun' r. Ukr.
177 J4 Visznek Hungary
197 G4 Vit r. Bulg.
250 E3 Vita r. Col.
194 B5 Vita Sicilia Italy
196 D4 Vitao mt. Yugo.
177 J3 Vít'az Slovakia
Vitebsk Belarus see Vitsyebsk
Vitebskaya Oblast' admin. div. Belarus see Vitsyebskaya Voblasts'
Vitebsk Oblast admin. div. Belarus see Vitsyebskaya Voblasts'
192 E2 Viterbo Italy
192 D2 Viterbo prov. Lazio Italy
157 G4 Viterne France
188 F3 Vitez Bos.-Herz.
252 D5 Vitichi Bol.
182 D3 Vitigudino Spain
79 □1a Viti Levu i. Fiji
99 K1 Vitim r. Rus. Fed.
99 J1 Vitimskoye Ploskogor'ye plat. Rus. Fed.
196 E4 Vitina Kosovo, Srbija Yugo.
179 G2 Vitis Austria
177 G2 Vítkov Czech Rep.
179 H3 Vitnyéd Hungary
197 E5 Vitolište Macedonia
196 E4 Vitomirica Kosovo, Srbija Yugo.
252 C4 Vitor Peru
252 B4 Vitor r. Peru
192 E2 Vitorchiano Italy
257 G4 Vitória Brazil
Vitoria Spain see Vitoria-Gasteiz
183 H2 Vitoria airport Spain
255 E5 Vitória da Conquista Brazil
183 H2 Vitoria-Gasteiz Spain
264 G7 Vitória Seamount sea feature S. Atlantic Ocean
195 G3 Vitravo r. Italy
158 E3 Vitré France
157 F5 Vitrey-sur-Mance France
161 D5 Vitrolles France
156 C2 Vitry-en-Artois France
156 E4 Vitry-en-Perthois France
156 E4 Vitry-la-Ville France
156 E4 Vitry-le-François France
160 B2 Vitry-sur-Loire France
156 C4 Vitry-sur-Seine France
136 E2 Vits' r. Belarus
139 H4 Vitsyebsk Belarus
138 G4 Vitsyebskaya Voblasts' admin. div. Belarus
140 M2 Vittangi Sweden
160 C1 Vitteaux France
157 F4 Vittel France
194 D6 Vittoria Sicilia Italy
191 H3 Vittorio Veneto Italy
193 G3 Vitulazio Italy
137 I5 Vityazevo Rus. Fed.
171 C4 Vitzenburg Ger.
187 C5 Viuda r. Spain
160 E2 Viuz-en-Sallaz France
161 C4 Vivarais, Monts du mts France
192 B2 Vivario Corse France
137 J3 Vivcharove Ukr.
182 C1 Viveiro Spain
186 C4 Vivel del Río Martín Spain
187 C5 Viver Spain
Vivero Spain see Viveiro
161 B3 Viverols France
185 H2 Viveros Spain
237 E5 Vivian LA U.S.A.
157 E3 Vivier-au-Court France
161 C4 Viviers France
163 E4 Viviez France
161 C5 Viv-le-Fesq France
213 F4 Vivo S. Africa
179 F4 Vivodnik mt. Slovenia
162 C2 Vivonne France
156 E5 Vix Bourgogne France
162 B2 Vix Pays de la Loire France
137 H3 Viys'kove Ukr.
136 D3 Viytivtsi Ukr.
Vizagapatam Andhra Prad. India see Vishakhapatnam
242 B3 Vizcaíno, Desierto de des. Mex.
242 B3 Vizcaíno, Sierra mts Mex.
183 H1 Vizcaya prov. País Vasco Spain
126 B2 Vize Turkey
160 C3 Vizézy r. France
134 I2 Vizhas r. Rus. Fed.
175 L6 Vizhomlya Ukr.
115 D2 Vizianagaram Andhra Prad. India
161 D3 Vizille France
134 J3 Vizinga Rus. Fed.
197 H3 Viziru Romania
177 G2 Vizovice Czech Rep.
177 I3 Vizslás Hungary
177 K3 Vizsoly Hungary
194 D5 Vizzini Sicilia Italy
198 A1 Vjosë r. Albania
165 D4 Vlaams Brabant prov. Belgium
164 D3 Vlaardingen Neth.
179 E1 Vlachovo Březí Czech Rep.
177 L5 Vlădeasa, Munţii mts Romania
197 F2 Vlădeasa, Vârful mt. Romania
197 F4 Vladičin Han Srbija Yugo.
129 D2 Vladikavkaz Rus. Fed.
139 M3 Vladimir Rus. Fed.
177 K5 Vladimirescu Romania
100 E4 Vladimiro-Aleksandrovskoye Rus. Fed.
Vladimir Oblast admin. div. Rus. Fed. see Vladimirskaya Oblast'
120 F1 Vladimirovka Kazakh.
129 D1 Vladimirovka Rus. Fed.
197 F4 Vladimirovo Bulg.
Vladimirovskiy Kazakh. see Vladimirovka
139 M4 Vladimirskaya Oblast' admin. div. Rus. Fed.
Vladimir-Volynskiy Ukr. see Volodymyr-Volyns'kyy
176 E2 Vladislav Czech Rep.
100 D4 Vladivostok Rus. Fed.
134 G4 Vladychnoye Rus. Fed.
164 G1 Vlagtwedde Neth.
197 G2 Vlăhiţa Romania
197 E4 Vlajna mt. Yugo.
188 G3 Vlasenica Bos.-Herz.
196 D3 Vlašić Planina mts Yugo.
176 D2 Vlašim Czech Rep.
137 G3 Vlasivka Ukr.
197 F4 Vlasotince Srbija Yugo.
Vlasova-Ayuta Rus. Fed. see Ayutinskiy
139 L4 Vlasovo Rus. Fed.
177 G3 Vlčany Slovakia
164 F2 Vledder Neth.
214 C5 Vleiland S. Africa
164 E2 Vleuten Neth.
164 D1 Vlieland i. Neth.
164 E3 Vlijmen Neth.
165 C3 Vlissingen Neth.
198 A1 Vlorë Albania
198 A1 Vlorës, Gjiri i b. Albania
169 D3 Vlotho Ger.
Vlotslavsk Pol. see Włocławek
176 D1 Vltava r. Czech Rep.
179 F4 Vnanje Gorice Slovenia
139 K2 Vnina r. Rus. Fed.
171 D4 Vockerode Ger.
179 E2 Vöcklabruck Austria
179 E2 Vöcklamarkt Austria
177 G3 Voderady Slovakia
191 J3 Vodice Istra Croatia
188 E4 Vodice Šibenik Croatia
134 G3 Vodlozero, Ozero l. Rus. Fed.
176 D2 Vodňany Czech Rep.
188 D3 Vodnjan Croatia
Vodopyanovo Lipetskaya Oblast' Rus. Fed. see Donskoye
146 □G1 Voe Shetland, Scotland U.K.
215 E5 Voël r. S. Africa
169 B4 Voerde (Niederrhein) Ger.
165 E4 Voerendaal Neth.
142 D3 Voerså Denmark
207 F5 Vogan Togo
164 D2 Vogelenzang Neth.
157 H4 Vogelgrun France
Vogelkop Peninsula Indon. see Doberai, Jazirah
207 H4 Vogel Peak Nigeria
170 E2 Vogelsang Ger.
169 D5 Vogelsberg hills Ger.
171 E3 Vogelsdorf Ger.
157 H4 Vogelsheim France
172 B2 Vogelweh Ger.
190 E4 Voghera Italy
191 G4 Voghiera Italy
129 E4 Voghji r. Armenia
188 G4 Vogošća Bos.-Herz.
172 D4 Vogt Ger.
173 G4 Vogtareuth Ger.
161 C4 Vogüé France
78 □5 Voh New Caledonia
173 F3 Vohburg an der Donau Ger.
Vohémar Madag. see Iharaña
173 G2 Vohenstrauß Ger.
Vohibinany Madag. see Ampasimanolotra
213 □J4 Vohilava Fianarantsoa Madag.
213 □K4 Vohilava Fianarantsoa Madag.
Vohimarina Madag. see Iharaña
213 □J5 Vohimena, Tanjona c. Madag.
213 □J4 Vohipeno Madag.
213 □K4 Vohitrandriana Madag.
169 D4 Vöhl Ger.
138 E2 Võhma Estonia
172 C3 Vöhrenbach Ger.
172 C3 Vöhringen Ger.
173 E3 Vöhringen Ger.
211 C5 Voi Kenya
157 F4 Void-Vacon France
171 C4 Voigtstedt Ger.
157 E4 Voillecomte France
197 F3 Voineasa Romania
197 H2 Voineşti Romania
206 C4 Voinjama Liberia
161 D3 Voiron France
156 B4 Voise r. France
160 D2 Voiteur France
179 G3 Voitsberg Austria
177 K3 Vojčice Slovakia
142 C4 Vojens Denmark
Vojnice Slovakia see Bátorove Kosihy
179 G4 Vojnik Slovenia
196 D3 Vojvodina prov. Yugo.
138 F2 Voka Estonia
177 H6 Vokány Hungary
134 I4 Vokhma Rus. Fed.
207 I4 Voko Cameroon
134 K3 Vol' r. Rus. Fed.
176 C3 Volary Czech Rep.
Volaterrae Italy see Volterra
238 F2 Volborg MT U.S.A.
258 D1 Volcán Arg.
252 D5 Volcán, Cerro vol. Bol.
260 B2 Volcán, Cerro del vol. Chile
261 H5 Volcán, Sierra del hills Arg.
Volcano Bay Japan see Uchiura-wan
240 □D9 Volcano House HI U.S.A.
Volcano Islands N. Pacific Ocean see Kazan-rettō
Volchansk Ukr. see Vovchans'k
139 H5 Volchas r. Belarus
121 J1 Volchikha Rus. Fed.
139 J3 Volchina r. Rus. Fed.
141 I3 Volda Norway
173 H2 Volduchy Czech Rep.
164 E2 Volendam Neth.
232 D6 Volens VA U.S.A.
139 L3 Volga Rus. Fed.
139 L3 Volga r. Rus. Fed.
Volga Upland hills Rus. Fed. see Privolzhskaya Vozvyshennost'
135 H7 Volgodonsk Rus. Fed.
135 I6 Volgograd Rus. Fed.
Volgograd Oblast admin. div. Rus. Fed. see Volgogradskaya Oblast'
135 I6 Volgogradskaya Oblast' admin. div. Rus. Fed.
135 I6 Volgogradskoye Vodokhranilishche resr Rus. Fed.
139 M3 Volgorechensk Rus. Fed.
Volhynia admin. div. Ukr. see Volyns'ka Oblast'
136 E4 Volintiri Moldova
173 E2 Volkach Ger.
173 E2 Volkach r. Ger.
179 F4 Völkermarkt Austria
172 C4 Volkertshausen Ger.
190 D1 Volketswil Switz.
139 I2 Volkhov Rus. Fed.
139 I1 Volkhov r. Rus. Fed.
139 I1 Volkhovskaya Guba b. Rus. Fed.
139 H2 Volkhovskiy Rus. Fed.
172 A2 Völklingen Ger.
169 E4 Volkmarsen Ger.
Volkovysk Belarus see Vawkavysk
Volkovyskiye Vysoty hills Belarus see Vawkavyskaye Wzvyshsha
215 G2 Volksrust S. Africa
171 C4 Volkstedt Ger.
168 C2 Völlen Ger.
164 E2 Vollenhove Neth.
168 D2 Vollersode Ger.
160 B3 Vollore-Montagne France
157 H3 Volmunster France
160 C1 Volnay France
Vol'nogorsk Ukr. see Vil'nohirs'k
100 D4 Vol'no-Nadezhdinskoye Rus. Fed.
137 I4 Volnovakha Ukr.
121 G1 Vol'noye Rus. Fed.
Vol'nyansk Ukr. see Vil'nyans'k
100 E2 Volochayevka-Vtoraya Rus. Fed.
Volochisk Ukr. see Volochys'k
136 D3 Volochys'k Ukr.
136 E3 Volodarka Ukr.
137 I4 Volodars'ke Ukr.
120 B3 Volodarskiy Rus. Fed.
Volodarskoye Kazakh. see Saumalkol'
136 E2 Volodars'k-Volyns'kyy Ukr.
136 D2 Volodymyrets' Ukr.
137 G4 Volodymyrivka Ukr.
136 C2 Volodymyr-Volyns'kyy Ukr.
134 G4 Vologda Rus. Fed.
Vologda Oblast admin. div. Rus. Fed. see Vologodskaya Oblast'
157 G4 Vologne r. France
139 M2 Vologodskaya Oblast' admin. div. Rus. Fed.
137 I3 Volokhiv Yar Ukr.
139 J3 Volokolamsk Rus. Fed.
135 G6 Volokonovka Rus. Fed.
161 E4 Volonne France
214 D3 Volop S. Africa
198 C2 Volos Greece
175 L6 Voloshcha Ukr.
137 J3 Voloshino Rus. Fed.
134 H3 Voloshka Rus. Fed.
137 I3 Volos'ka Balakliya Ukr.
137 I3 Volos'ka Balakliyka r. Ukr.
138 G2 Volosovo Rus. Fed.
177 L3 Volosyanka Ukr.
139 H3 Volot Rus. Fed.
137 J2 Volotovo Rus. Fed.
136 B3 Volovets' Ukr.
135 G5 Volovo Lipetskaya Oblast' Rus. Fed.
139 L5 Volovo Tul'skaya Oblast' Rus. Fed.
177 J3 Volovské vrchy mts Slovakia
Volozhin Belarus see Valozhyn
178 D5 Volpago del Mòntello Italy
190 D4 Volpedo Italy
190 C3 Volpiano Italy
171 C3 Völpke Ger.
178 C3 Völs Austria
170 E2 Völschow Ger.
192 D2 Volsini, Monti mts Italy
Volsinii Italy see Orvieto
120 A1 Vol'sk Rus. Fed.
214 D5 Volstruisleegte S. Africa
207 F5 Volta admin. reg. Ghana
207 F5 Volta r. Ghana
207 F5 Volta, Lake resr Ghana
Volta Blanche r. Africa see White Volta
86 E2 Voltaire, Cape W.A. Austr.
Volta Noire r. Africa see Black Volta
257 E5 Volta Redonda Brazil
Volta Rouge r. Burkina/Ghana see Nazinon
191 F5 Volterra Italy
169 C3 Voltlage Ger.
183 F3 Voltoya r. Spain
193 H3 Volturara Appula Italy
194 D2 Volturara Irpina Italy
193 H3 Volturino Italy
193 H4 Volturino, Monte mt. Italy
193 F3 Volturno r. Italy
204 D2 Volubilis tourist site Morocco
197 H3 Voluntari Romania
235 G1 Voluntown CT U.S.A.
198 C1 Volvi, Limni l. Greece
160 B3 Volvic France
161 D5 Volx France
137 J2 Volya Rus. Fed.
134 M3 Vol'ya r. Rus. Fed.
175 L6 Volya Arlamivs'ka Ukr.
176 C2 Volyně Czech Rep.
176 C2 Volyňka r. Czech Rep.
137 G2 Volynka Ukr.
Volyn Oblast admin. div. Ukr. see Volyns'ka Oblast'
136 C2 Volyns'ka Oblast' admin. div. Ukr.
Volynskaya Oblast' admin. div. Ukr. see Volyns'ka Oblast'
136 D3 Volytsya Ukr.
136 D3 Volytsya Druha Ukr.
134 J5 Volzhsk Rus. Fed.
120 B1 Volzhskiy Samarskaya Oblast' Rus. Fed.
135 I6 Volzhskiy Volgogradskaya Oblast' Rus. Fed.
193 G2 Vomano r. Italy
178 C3 Vomp Austria
78 □6 Vonavona i. New Georgia Is Solomon Is
223 J4 Vonda Sask. Can.
134 I4 Vondanka Rus. Fed.
213 □J4 Vondrozo Madag.
160 D1 Vonges France
198 B2 Vonitsa Greece
160 C2 Vonnas France
114 C3 Vontimitta Andhra Prad. India
176 G5 Vonyarcvashegy Hungary
164 D2 Voorburg Neth.
233 G3 Voorheesville NY U.S.A.
164 D2 Voorschoten Neth.
164 F2 Voorst Neth.
164 E2 Voorthuizen Neth.
138 D2 Voosi kurk sea chan. Estonia
139 I4 Vop' r. Rus. Fed.
140 □D2 Vopnafjörður b. Iceland
140 M3 Vörå Fin.
179 F3 Voralm mt. Austria
138 E4 Voranava Belarus
178 A3 Vorarlberg land Austria
179 E2 Vorchdorf Austria
164 F2 Vorden Neth.
179 F3 Vordernberg Austria
190 E1 Vorderrhein r. Switz.
142 D4 Vordingborg Denmark
169 F3 Vordorf Ger.
196 D5 Vorë Albania
198 B1 Voreia Pindos mts Greece
199 D2 Voreio Aigaio admin. reg. Greece
198 C2 Voreioi Sporades is Greece
198 C2 Voreios Evvoïkos Kolpos sea chan. Greece
161 D3 Voreppe France
161 B3 Vorey France
139 I5 Vorga Rus. Fed.
134 M2 Vorgashor Rus. Fed.
Voríai Sporádhes is Greece see Voreioi Sporades
Voría Píndhos mts Greece see Voreia Pindos
264 J1 Voring Plateau sea feature N. Atlantic Ocean
117 H3 Vorjing mt. Arun. Prad. India
134 N2 Vorkuta Rus. Fed.
142 D1 Vorma r. Norway
138 D2 Vormsi i. Estonia
139 L5 Vorob'yevka Rus. Fed.
135 H6 Vorob'yevka Rus. Fed.
130 J3 Vorogovo Rus. Fed.
136 C3 Vorokhta Ukr.
197 H2 Vorona Romania
135 H6 Vorona r. Rus. Fed.
135 G6 Voronezh Rus. Fed.
139 L5 Voronezh r. Rus. Fed.
Voronezh Oblast admin. div. Rus. Fed. see Voronezhskaya Oblast'
135 H6 Voronezhskaya Oblast' admin. div. Rus. Fed.
137 G2 Voronizh Ukr.
137 G2 Voron'ky Ukr.
136 D2 Voronky Rivnens'ka Oblast' Ukr.
139 I1 Voronov, Mys pt Rus. Fed.
139 K4 Voronovo Rus. Fed.
136 E3 Voronovytsya Ukr.
121 J2 Vorontsovka Kazakh.
135 H6 Vorontsovka Rus. Fed.
Vorontsovo-Aleksandrovskoye Stavropol'skiy Kray Rus. Fed. see Zelenokumsk
136 C3 Voronyaky hills Ukr.
134 H4 Voron'ye Rus. Fed.
Voroshilov Rus. Fed. see Ussuriysk
Voroshilovgrad Ukr. see Luhans'k
Voroshilovsk Rus. Fed. see Stavropol'
Voroshilovsk Ukr. see Alchevs'k
129 E4 Vorotan r. Iran
134 I4 Vorotynets Rus. Fed.
139 K4 Vorotynsk Rus. Fed.
129 C1 Vorovskolesskaya Rus. Fed.
137 H2 Vorozhba Sums'ka Oblast' Ukr.
137 H2 Vorozhba Sums'ka Oblast' Ukr.
263 B2 Vorposten Peak Antarctica
173 F2 Vorra Ger.
179 G3 Vorsau Austria
165 D3 Vorselaar Belgium
135 F6 Vorskla r. Rus. Fed.
137 H2 Vorsklitsa r. Rus. Fed./Ukr.
165 E3 Vorst Belgium
214 D1 Vorstershoop S. Africa
177 L5 Vorţa Romania
263 B2 Vørterkaka Nunatak mt. Antarctica
138 E2 Võrtsjärv l. Estonia
138 F3 Võru Estonia
168 E2 Vorwerk Ger.
139 J4 Vorya r. Rus. Fed.
136 F2 Vorzel' Ukr.
214 D4 Vosburg S. Africa
123 G2 Vose Tajik.
179 H2 Vösendorf Austria
157 G4 Vosges dept Lorraine France
157 G5 Vosges mts France
139 L3 Voshchazhnikovo Rus. Fed.
129 D3 Voskevan Armenia
139 L4 Voskresensk Rus. Fed.
137 G4 Voskresens'ke Ukr.
139 L5 Voskresenskoye Lipetskaya Oblast' Rus. Fed.
134 I4 Voskresenskoye Nizhegorodskaya Oblast' Rus. Fed.
120 D1 Voskresenskoye Respublika Bashkortostan Rus. Fed.
139 K4 Voskresenskoye Tul'skaya Oblast' Rus. Fed.
139 K2 Voskresenskoye Vologod. Obl. Rus. Fed.
160 C1 Vosne-Romanée France
141 I3 Voss Norway
165 D3 Vosselaar Belgium
Vostochno-Kazakhstanskaya Oblast' admin. div. Kazakh. see Vostochnyy Kazakhstan
Vostochno-Kounradskiy Kazakh. see Shygys Konyrat
100 G2 Vostochno-Sakhalinskiy Gory mts Sakhalin Rus. Fed.
134 K4 Vostochnyy Rus. Fed.
120 D4 Vostochnyy Chink Ustyurta esc. Uzbek.
121 K2 Vostochnyy Kazakhstan admin. div. Kazakh.
98 F1 Vostochnyy Sayan mts Rus. Fed.
100 E3 Vostok Primorskiy Kray Rus. Fed.
Vostok Sakhalin Rus. Fed. see Neftegorsk
176 D2 Votice Czech Rep.
134 K4 Votkinsk Rus. Fed.
134 K4 Votkinskoye Vodokhranilishche resr Rus. Fed.
142 C1 Votna r. Norway
256 D5 Votorantim Brazil
139 I4 Votrya r. Rus. Fed.
256 C4 Votuporanga Brazil
162 E2 Voueize r. France
Vouga Angola see Cunhinga
182 B4 Vouga r. Port.
160 C1 Vougeot France
162 B2 Vouillé France
162 C2 Vouillé France
198 C3 Voula Greece
156 E5 Voulaines-les-Templiers France
156 C4 Voulx France
162 C2 Vouneuil-sous-Biard France
159 G5 Vouneuil-sur-Vienne France
198 B1 Vourinos mt. Greece
160 B1 Voutenay-sur-Cure France
162 D3 Voutezac France
162 B2 Vouvant France
159 G4 Vouvray France
190 B2 Vouvry Switz.
182 B4 Vouzela Port.
156 E3 Vouziers France
156 C5 Vouzon France
137 H3 Vovcha r. Ukr.
137 I2 Vovcha r. Ukr.
137 I2 Vovchans'k Ukr.
137 G2 Vovchyk Ukr.
156 B4 Voves France
136 D3 Vovk r. Ukr.
136 D2 Vovkoshiv Ukr.
136 D3 Vovkovyntsi Ukr.
208 E3 Vovodo r. C.A.R.
141 K3 Voxna Sweden
141 L3 Voxnan r. Sweden
134 J4 Voya r. Rus. Fed.
137 F3 Voyevods'ke Ukr.
175 M6 Voynyliv Ukr.
Vöyri Fin. see Vörå
134 K3 Voyvozh Rus. Fed.
78 □6 Voza Choiseul Solomon Is
139 K3 Vozdvizhenskoye Rus. Fed.
139 L4 Vozha r. Rus. Fed.
134 G3 Vozhe, Ozero l. Rus. Fed.
134 H3 Vozhega Rus. Fed.
183 I3 Vozmediano Spain
121 G1 Voznesenka Kazakh.
137 F4 Voznesens'k Ukr.
129 D2 Voznesenskaya Ingushskaya Respublika Rus. Fed.
129 B1 Voznesenskaya Krasnodarskiy Kray Rus. Fed.
137 F4 Voznesens'ke Ukr.
135 H5 Voznesenskoye Rus. Fed.
139 M3 Voznesen'ye Rus. Fed.
139 J1 Voznesen'ye Rus. Fed.
137 G4 Vozsiyats'ke Ukr.
121 G1 Vozvyshenka Kazakh.
Vozvyshenskiy Kazakh. see Vozvyshenka
100 D2 Vozzhayevka Rus. Fed.
142 C3 Vrå Denmark
197 G4 Vrabevo Bulg.
177 H3 Vráble Slovakia
198 B3 Vrachionas hill Ionioi Nisoi Greece
198 B2 Vrachnaiika Greece
142 C2 Vrådal Norway
136 F4 Vradiyivka Ukr.
Vrakhiónas Óros hill Ionioi Nisoi Greece see Vrachionas
Vrakhnaíika Greece see Vrachnaiika
188 F4 Vran mt. Bos.-Herz.
197 H4 Vrana r. Bulg.
100 E4 Vrangel' Rus. Fed.
100 F1 Vrangelya, Mys pt Rus. Fed.
131 T2 Vrangelya, Ostrov i. Rus. Fed.
188 G3 Vranjak Bos.-Herz.
197 E4 Vranje Srbija Yugo.
197 F4 Vranjska Banja Srbija Yugo.
179 H2 Vranovice Czech Rep.
177 K3 Vranov nad Topľou Slovakia
196 E5 Vrapčište Macedonia
197 F4 Vratarnica Srbija Yugo.
197 F4 Vratsa Bulg.
188 F3 Vrbanja r. Bos.-Herz.
188 F3 Vrbas r. Bos.-Herz.
196 D3 Vrbas Vojvodina, Srbija Yugo.
176 G1 Vrbno pod Pradědem Czech Rep.
177 J2 Vrbov Slovakia
176 G3 Vrbovce Slovakia
177 G3 Vrbové Slovakia
188 F3 Vrbovec Croatia
188 E3 Vrbovsko Croatia
176 E1 Vrchlabí Czech Rep.
157 F4 Vrécourt France
215 G2 Vrede S. Africa
215 F2 Vredefort S. Africa
169 B3 Vreden Ger.
214 A5 Vredenburg S. Africa
214 B4 Vredendal S. Africa
251 G3 Vreed-en-Hoop Guyana
164 E2 Vreeland Neth.
168 C3 Vrees Ger.
182 C3 Vreia de Jales Port.
196 E4 Vrela Kosovo, Srbija Yugo.
179 F5 Vremščica mt. Slovenia
165 D5 Vresse Belgium
188 E3 Vrhnika Slovenia
114 C4 Vriddhachalam Tamil Nadu India
164 F1 Vries Neth.
164 F2 Vriezenveen Neth.
143 F3 Vrigstad Sweden
160 A1 Vrille r. France
111 B7 Vrindavan Uttar Prad. India
156 E3 Vrizy France
196 E4 Vrnjačka Banja Srbija Yugo.
156 B2 Vron France
164 F2 Vroomshoop Neth.
176 C1 Vroutek Czech Rep.
164 C3 Vrouwenpolder Neth.
196 D5 Vrrin Albania
196 E3 Vršac Vojvodina, Srbija Yugo.
191 I3 Vrsar Croatia
179 E5 Vrtojba Slovenia
215 E2 Vryburg S. Africa
215 H2 Vryheid S. Africa
173 H2 Všeruby Czech Rep.
171 F5 Všetaty Czech Rep.
177 G2 Vsetín Czech Rep.
139 H1 Vsevolozhsk Rus. Fed.
137 H3 Vshyva r. Ukr.
177 H3 Vtáčnik mt. Slovakia
177 H3 Vtáčnik mts Slovakia
160 D2 Vuache, Montagne de mt. France
79 □1 Vuaqava i. Fiji
197 G5 Vůcha r. Bulg.
188 G3 Vučica r. Croatia
196 E4 Vučitrn Kosovo, Srbija Yugo.
197 E4 Vučje Srbija Yugo.
164 E3 Vught Neth.
137 I4 Vuhledar Ukr.
137 J3 Vuhlehirs'k Ukr.
188 G3 Vuka r. Croatia
188 G3 Vukovar Croatia
134 L3 Vuktyl' Rus. Fed.
215 G2 Vukuzakhe S. Africa
222 H5 Vulcan Alta Can.
197 F3 Vulcan Romania
136 E5 Vulcăneşti Moldova
194 D4 Vulcano, Isola i. Isole Lipari Italy
197 F4 Vůlchedrům Bulg.
197 H4 Vůlchidol Bulg.
193 H3 Vulgano r. Italy
Vulkaneshty Moldova see Vulcăneşti
193 H4 Vulture, Monte mt. Italy
241 K5 Vulture Mountains AZ U.S.A.
97 D5 Vung Tau Vietnam
138 F1 Vuohijärvi Fin.
140 O2 Vuokatti Fin.
138 H1 Vuoksa r. Rus. Fed.
138 G1 Vuoksi r. Fin.
140 N2 Vuolijoki Fin.
140 M2 Vuollerim Sweden
197 H4 Vůrbitsa Bulg.
197 G3 Vurpăr Romania
197 F4 Vůrshets Bulg.
197 H2 Vutcani Romania
114 D2 Vuyyuru Andhra Prad. India
179 G4 Vuzenica Slovenia
136 C2 Vuzlove L'vivs'ka Oblast' Ukr.
136 B3 Vuzlove Zakarpats'ka Oblast' Ukr.
138 F4 Vuzlyanka r. Belarus
120 E1 Vvedenka Kazakh.
139 M3 Vveden'ye Rus. Fed.
211 B7 Vwawa Tanz.
175 M2 Vyalikaya Byerastavitsa Belarus
139 H2 Vyal'ye, Ozero l. Rus. Fed.
116 C5 Vyara Gujarat India
Vyarkhowye Belarus see Ruba
Vyatka Kirovskaya Oblast' Rus. Fed. see Kirov
134 J5 Vyatka r. Rus. Fed.
134 J4 Vyatskiye Polyany Rus. Fed.
100 E3 Vyazemskiy Rus. Fed.
139 J4 Vyaz'ma Rus. Fed.
139 I4 Vyaz'ma r. Rus. Fed.
134 H4 Vyazniki Rus. Fed.
120 A1 Vyazovka Saratovskaya Oblast' Rus. Fed.
135 H6 Vyazovka Volgogradskaya Oblast' Rus. Fed.
137 I2 Vyazovoye Rus. Fed.
138 G1 Vyborg Rus. Fed.
138 G1 Vyborgskiy Zaliv b. Rus. Fed.
134 I3 Vychegda r. Rus. Fed.
134 I3 Vychegodskiy Rus. Fed.
177 I2 Východná Slovakia
175 N4 Vyderta Ukr.
175 M4 Vydranytsya Ukr.
106 E1 Vydrino Rus. Fed.
175 M4 Vydrychi Ukr.
138 F4 Vyerkhnyadzvinsk Belarus
139 H5 Vyetka Belarus
138 G4 Vyetryna Belarus
139 J5 Vygonichi Rus. Fed.
134 F3 Vygozero, Ozero l. Rus. Fed.
177 H3 Vyhne Slovakia
135 H5 Vyksa Rus. Fed.
160 E1 Vy-lès-Lure France
136 E5 Vylkove Ukr.
136 B3 Vylok Ukr.
134 J3 Vym' r. Rus. Fed.
136 C3 Vynnyky Ukr.
136 B3 Vynohradiv Ukr.
137 F4 Vynohradne Ukr.
137 G4 Vynohradove Khersons'ka Oblast' Ukr.
137 G5 Vynohradove Respublika Krym Ukr.
139 I3 Vypolzovo Rus. Fed.
137 G2 Vyrishal'ne Ukr.
139 H2 Vyritsa Rus. Fed.
137 H2 Vyry Ukr.
135 G7 Vyselki Rus. Fed.
136 F2 Vyshcha Dubechnya Ukr.
137 I3 Vyshche Solone Ukr.
137 H4 Vyshchetarasivka Ukr.
139 M4 Vyshgorod Rus. Fed.
136 F2 Vyshhorod Ukr.
136 B3 Vyshka Ukr.
139 H5 Vyshkov Rus. Fed.
136 B3 Vyshkove Ukr.
137 G3 Vyshneve Dnipropetrovs'ka Oblast' Ukr.
136 F2 Vyshneve Kyivs'ka Oblast' Ukr.
139 J3 Vyshnevolotskaya Gryada ridge Rus. Fed.
139 J3 Vyshnevolotskoye Vodokhranilishche resr Rus. Fed.
137 I1 Vyshneye-Ol'shanoye Rus. Fed.
175 M4 Vyshniv Ukr.
136 C3 Vyshnivets' Ukr.
139 J3 Vyshniy-Volochek Rus. Fed.
136 B3 Vyshnya r. Ukr.
137 G3 Vyshnyaky Ukr.
176 G2 Vyškov Czech Rep.
176 D3 Vysoká mt. Czech Rep.
176 G3 Vysoká hill Slovakia
136 E2 Vysoka Pich Ukr.
176 F3 Vysoká pri Morave Slovakia
138 D5 Vysokaye Belarus
176 F2 Vysoké Mýto Czech Rep.
139 K4 Vysokinichi Rus. Fed.
137 H3 Vysokopillya Kharkivs'ka Oblast' Ukr.
137 G4 Vysokopillya Khersons'ka Oblast' Ukr.
139 K3 Vysokovsk Rus. Fed.
Vysokoye Belarus see Vysokaye
139 J3 Vysokoye Rus. Fed.
138 G1 Vysotsk Rus. Fed.
136 D2 Vysots'k Ukr.
179 F2 Vyšší Brod Czech Rep.
136 E2 Vystupovychi Ukr.
139 K1 Vytegra Rus. Fed.
134 I3 Vyya r. Rus. Fed.
136 C2 Vyzhivka r. Ukr.
136 C3 Vyzhnytsya Ukr.
138 E4 Vyžuona r. Lith.
175 I1 Vzmor'ye Rus. Fed.

W

206 E4 Wa Ghana
168 E1 Waabs Ger.
210 D4 Waajid Somalia
169 F4 Waake Ger.
173 F4 Waakirchen Ger.
173 E4 Waal Ger.
164 D3 Waal r. Neth.
165 E3 Waalre Neth.
164 E3 Waalwijk Neth.
164 D2 Waarland Neth.
165 C3 Waarschoot Belgium
165 D3 Waasmunster Belgium
91 J8 Wabag P.N.G.
224 B3 Wabakimi Lake Ont. Can.
222 H4 Wabamun Alta Can.
222 H3 Wabasca r. Alta Can.
222 H4 Wabasca-Desmarais Alta Can.
230 C3 Wabash IN U.S.A.
232 A4 Wabash OH U.S.A.
236 F4 Wabash r. IN U.S.A.
226 A3 Wabasha MN U.S.A.
224 C3 Wabassi r. Ont. Can.
210 D3 Wabē Gestro r. Eth.
210 D3 Wabē Mena r. Eth.
226 C3 Wabeno WI U.S.A.
169 E4 Wabern Ger.
210 E3 Wabē Shebelē Wenz r. Eth.
223 L4 Wabowden Man. Can.
174 G2 Wąbrzeźno Pol.
109 F1 Wabu Anhui China
225 H2 Wabush Nfld. Can.
231 E5 Waccamaw r. SC U.S.A.
233 F6 Wachapreague VA U.S.A.
172 C2 Wachenheim an der Weinstraße Ger.
170 D3 Wachow Ger.
165 C3 Wachtebeke Belgium
169 E5 Wächtersbach Ger.
168 E1 Wacken Ger.
173 G2 Wackersdorf Ger.
225 H3 Waco Que. Can.
237 D6 Waco TX U.S.A.
226 A3 Wacouta MN U.S.A.
202 E6 Wad Banda Sudan
202 B2 Waddān, Jabal hills Libya
164 D1 Waddeneilanden is Neth.
Wadden Islands Neth. see Waddeneilanden
164 D2 Waddenzee sea chan. Neth.
151 G3 Waddesdon Buckinghamshire, England U.K.
168 F2 Waddeweitz Ger.
82 D3 Waddikee S.A. Austr.
149 I4 Waddington Lincolnshire, England U.K.
222 E5 Waddington, Mount B.C. Can.
147 E4 Waddingtown Rep. of Ireland
164 D2 Waddinxveen Neth.
85 H5 Waddy Point Qld Austr.
150 C4 Wadebridge Cornwall, England U.K.
223 K5 Wadena Sask. Can.
236 E2 Wadena MN U.S.A.
190 D1 Wädenswil Switz.
172 A2 Wadern Ger.
169 D4 Wadersloh Ger.
231 D5 Wadesboro NC U.S.A.
84 B2 Wadeye N.T. Austr.
114 B2 Wadgaon Mahar. India
116 D5 Wadgaon Mahar. India
172 A2 Wadgassen Ger.
151 H3 Wadhurst East Sussex, England U.K.
116 B5 Wadhwan Gujarat India
Wadhwan Gujarat India see Surendranagar
114 C2 Wadi Karnataka India
109 E1 Wadian Henan China
128 B4 Wādī as Sīr Jordan
203 F4 Wadi Halfa Sudan
128 B4 Wādī Mūsá Jordan
234 D3 Wading r. NJ U.S.A.
235 F2 Wading River NY U.S.A.
175 H4 Wadlew Pol.
203 G6 Wad Medani Sudan
102 □1 Wadomari Japan
175 H6 Wadowice Pol.
175 J5 Wadowice Górne Pol.
240 H2 Wadsworth NV U.S.A.
232 C4 Wadsworth OH U.S.A.
Wadu i. S. Male Maldives see Vaadhu
214 C6 Waenhuiskrans S. Africa
262 P1 Waesche, Mount Antarctica
107 I4 Wafangdian Liaoning China
102 J4 Waga-gawa r. Japan
116 C3 Wagah Punjab India
174 G3 Waganiec Pol.
168 D3 Wagenfeld Ger.
168 F3 Wagenhoff Ger.
164 E3 Wageningen Neth.
251 G3 Wageningen Suriname
221 J3 Wager Bay Nunavut Can.
83 F3 Wagga Wagga N.S.W. Austr.
172 C2 Waghäusel Ger.
87 C7 Wagin W.A. Austr.
173 G4 Waging am See Ger.
173 G4 Waginger See l. Ger.
222 D4 Waglisla B.C. Can.
254 E5 Wagner Brazil
236 D3 Wagner SD U.S.A.
237 E4 Wagoner OK U.S.A.
239 F4 Wagon Mound NM U.S.A.
178 E3 Wagrain Austria
174 F3 Wągrowiec Pol.
123 H3 Wah Pak.
207 F5 Wahala Togo
208 F2 Wahda state Sudan
240 □ Wahiawa HI U.S.A.
169 E4 Wahlhausen Ger.
171 E4 Wahlsdorf Ger.
168 F2 Wahlstedt Ger.
236 D3 Wahoo NE U.S.A.
236 D2 Wahpeton ND U.S.A.
Wahran Alg. see Oran
168 F3 Wahrenholz Ger.
241 K2 Wah Wah Mountains UT U.S.A.
114 B2 Wai Mahar. India
240 □C8 Waiakoa HI U.S.A.
240 □B8 Waialeale, Mount HI U.S.A.
240 □ Waialee HI U.S.A.
240 □ Waialua HI U.S.A.
240 □ Waianae HI U.S.A.
80 G2 Waiapu r. North I. N.Z.
80 F4 Waiaruhe North I. N.Z.
81 D5 Waiau South I. N.Z.
80 F3 Waiau r. North I. N.Z.
81 A7 Waiau r. South I. N.Z.
81 D5 Waiau r. South I. N.Z.
172 D3 Waiblingen Ger.
172 C2 Waibstadt Ger.
173 G2 Waidhaus Ger.
173 F3 Waidhofen Ger.
179 G2 Waidhofen an der Thaya Austria
179 F3 Waidhofen an der Ybbs Austria
93 D3 Waigeo i. Irian Jaya Indon.
173 E2 Waigolshausen Ger.
81 C6 Waihao Downs South I. N.Z.
80 D1 Waiharara North I. N.Z.
80 E2 Waiharoa North I. N.Z.
80 E2 Waiheke Island North I. N.Z.
80 E2 Waihi North I. N.Z.
80 E2 Waihi Beach North I. N.Z.
80 E2 Waihou r. North I. N.Z.
80 F3 Waihua North I. N.Z.
81 B6 Waikaia South I. N.Z.
81 B6 Waikaia r. South I. N.Z.
81 B6 Waikaka South I. N.Z.
81 E4 Waikanae North I. N.Z.
240 □ Waikane HI U.S.A.
240 □C8 Waikapu HI U.S.A.
80 E2 Waikare, Lake North I. N.Z.
80 F3 Waikaremoana, Lake North I. N.Z.
80 E2 Waikaretu North I. N.Z.
81 D5 Waikari South I. N.Z.
80 E2 Waikato admin. reg. North I. N.Z.
80 E2 Waikato r. North I. N.Z.
81 B7 Waikawa South I. N.Z.
80 E3 Waikeria North I. N.Z.
82 D3 Waikerie S.A. Austr.
240 □D9 Waikii HI U.S.A.
80 F3 Waikirikiri North I. N.Z.
81 B7 Waikoikoi South I. N.Z.
80 F3 Waikokopa North I. N.Z.
81 C6 Waikouaiti South I. N.Z.
240 □B7 Wailua HI U.S.A.
240 □C8 Wailua HI U.S.A.
240 □C8 Wailuku HI U.S.A.
81 B7 Waimahake South I. N.Z.
81 D5 Waimakariri r. South I. N.Z.
80 F3 Waimana North I. N.Z.
240 □ Waimanalo HI U.S.A.
81 C4 Waimangaroa South I. N.Z.
80 F3 Waimarama North I. N.Z.
81 C4 Waimarie South I. N.Z.
81 C6 Waimate South I. N.Z.
80 D1 Waimatenui North I. N.Z.
80 E2 Waimauku North I. N.Z.
240 □B8 Waimea HI U.S.A.
240 □D8 Waimea HI U.S.A.
240 □ Waimea HI U.S.A.
165 F4 Waimes Belgium
173 E3 Wain Ger.
232 D3 Wainfleet Ont. Can.
149 J4 Wainfleet All Saints Lincolnshire, England U.K.
114 C2 Wainganga r. India
81 E4 Waingawa North I. N.Z.
150 C4 Wainhouse Corner Cornwall, England U.K.
223 I4 Wainwright Alta Can.
220 C2 Wainwright AK U.S.A.
80 F3 Waioeka r. North I. N.Z.
80 E1 Waiotira North I. N.Z.
80 E3 Waiouru North I. N.Z.
80 E2 Waipa r. North I. N.Z.
81 B7 Waipahi South I. N.Z.
240 □ Waipahu HI U.S.A.
80 F3 Waipaoa r. North I. N.Z.
81 D5 Waipara South I. N.Z.
80 F3 Waipawa North I. N.Z.
80 E2 Waipipi North I. N.Z.
80 E1 Waipu North I. N.Z.
80 F3 Waipukurau North I. N.Z.
80 F3 Wairakei North I. N.Z.
81 E4 Wairarapa, Lake North I. N.Z.
81 E4 Wairau r. South I. N.Z.
81 D4 Wairau Valley South I. N.Z.
80 F3 Wairoa North I. N.Z.
80 E2 Wairoa r. North I. N.Z.
80 F3 Wairoa r. North I. N.Z.
173 F2 Waischenfeld Ger.
109 F2 Waishe Zhejiang China
80 F3 Waitahanui North I. N.Z.
81 B6 Waitahuna South I. N.Z.
80 E2 Waitakaruru North I. N.Z.
81 C6 Waitaki South I. N.Z.
81 C6 Waitaki r. South I. N.Z.
80 □ Waitangi Chatham Is S. Pacific Ocean
81 C5 Waitangitaona r. South I. N.Z.
80 E3 Waitara North I. N.Z.
81 C6 Waitati South I. N.Z.
84 C4 Waite River N.T. Austr.
80 E2 Waitoa North I. N.Z.
80 E3 Waitomo Caves North I. N.Z.
80 E3 Waitotara North I. N.Z.
80 E3 Waitotari r. North I. N.Z.
238 C2 Waitsburg WA U.S.A.
80 E2 Waiuku North I. N.Z.
81 B7 Waiwera South South I. N.Z.
109 F3 Waiyang Fujian China
79 □1 Waiyevu Taveuni Fiji
179 E2 Waizenkirchen Austria
103 H5 Wajima Japan

210 D4 Wajir Kenya
81 D4 Wakapuaka South I. N.Z.
104 B3 Wakasa-wan b. Japan
81 B6 Wakatipu, Lake South I. N.Z.
223 J4 Wakaw Sask. Can.
79 □1 Wakaya i. Fiji
104 B4 Wakayama Japan
104 B5 Wakayama pref. Japan
75 F2 Wake Atoll N. Pacific Ocean
236 D4 WaKeeney KS U.S.A.
227 J3 Wakefield Que. Can.
246 □ Wakefield Jamaica
81 D4 Wakefield South I. N.Z.
149 H4 Wakefield West Yorkshire, England U.K.
226 C2 Wakefield MI U.S.A.
232 B5 Wakefield OH U.S.A.
234 B3 Wakefield PA U.S.A.
233 H4 Wakefield RI U.S.A.
232 E6 Wakefield VA U.S.A.
Wakeham Que. Can. see Kangiqsujuaq
Wake Island N. Pacific Ocean see Wake Atoll
96 A3 Wakema Myanmar
102 J1 Wakkanai Japan
215 H2 Wakkerstroom S. Africa
83 F3 Wakool N.S.W. Austr.
83 E3 Wakool r. N.S.W. Austr.
209 B7 Waku-Kungo Angola
224 D3 Wakwayowkastic r. Ont. Can.
114 C3 Walajapet Tamil Nadu India
171 C3 Walbeck Ger.
151 I2 Walberswick Suffolk, England U.K.
174 E5 Wałbrzych Pol.
169 E4 Walburg Ger.
83 G2 Walcha N.S.W. Austr.
173 F4 Walchensee l. Ger.
178 D3 Walchsee Austria
168 C3 Walchum Ger.
238 F3 Walcott WY U.S.A.
165 D4 Walcourt Belgium
174 E2 Wałcz Pol.
172 D4 Wald Baden-Württemberg Ger.
173 G2 Wald Bayern Ger.
172 C4 Wald Switz.
172 C3 Waldachtal Ger.
179 F2 Waldaist r. Austria
172 B2 Waldböckelheim Ger.
169 C5 Waldbreitbach Ger.
169 C5 Waldbröl Ger.
172 D2 Waldbrunn Ger.
169 D5 Waldbrunn-Lahr Ger.
172 D4 Waldburg Ger.
87 C5 Waldburg Range mts W.A. Austr.
171 E4 Walddrehna Ger.
169 E4 Waldeck Ger.
179 H3 Waldegg Austria
235 D1 Walden NY U.S.A.
172 D3 Waldenbuch Ger.
172 D2 Waldenburg Baden-Württemberg Ger.
171 D5 Waldenburg Sachsen Ger.
Waldenburg Pol. see Wałbrzych
190 C1 Waldenburg Switz.
173 G2 Walderbach Ger.
173 G2 Waldershof Ger.
151 H3 Walderslade Medway, England U.K.
172 B2 Waldfischbach-Burgalben Ger.
179 G2 Waldhausen Austria
179 F2 Waldhausen im Strudengau Austria
171 E4 Waldheim Ger.
179 F2 Walding Austria
169 E4 Waldkappel Ger.
172 B3 Waldkirch Ger.
173 H3 Waldkirchen Ger.
173 G3 Waldkraiburg Ger.
172 C2 Wald-Michelbach Ger.
172 B2 Waldmohr Ger.
173 G2 Waldmünchen Ger.
231 D6 Waldo FL U.S.A.
226 D4 Waldo WI U.S.A.
233 □I2 Waldoboro ME U.S.A.
150 C4 Waldon r. England U.K.
232 E5 Waldorf MD U.S.A.
174 G2 Wałdowo-Szlacheckie Pol.
238 A2 Waldport OR U.S.A.
172 A2 Waldrach Ger.
237 E5 Waldron AR U.S.A.
226 E5 Waldron MI U.S.A.
263 H2 Waldron, Cape Antarctica
171 D5 Waldsassen Ger.
172 C4 Waldshut Ger.
190 E1 Waldstatt Switz.
172 D3 Waldstetten Baden-Württemberg Ger.
173 E3 Waldstetten Bayern Ger.
173 G2 Waldthurn Ger.
87 C6 Walebing W.A. Austr.
108 B2 Walêg Sichuan China
190 E1 Walenstadt Switz.
150 D2 Wales admin. div. U.K.
206 E4 Walewale Ghana
165 F5 Walferdange Lux.
83 G2 Walgett N.S.W. Austr.
262 Q1 Walgreen Coast Antarctica
226 D4 Walhalla MI U.S.A.
236 D1 Walhalla ND U.S.A.
231 D5 Walhalla SC U.S.A.
87 B6 Walkaway W.A. Austr.
170 D2 Walkendorf Ger.
169 F4 Walkenried Ger.
84 C2 Walker r. N.T. Austr.
226 E4 Walker MI U.S.A.
236 E2 Walker MN U.S.A.
240 H2 Walker r. NV U.S.A.
231 E7 Walker Cay i. Bahamas
85 E3 Walker Creek r. Qld Austr.
240 H2 Walker Lake NV U.S.A.
262 R2 Walker Mountains Antarctica
232 E5 Walkersville MD U.S.A.
232 C5 Walkersville WV U.S.A.
227 G3 Walkerton Ont. Can.
226 D5 Walkerton IN U.S.A.
235 D1 Walker Valley NY U.S.A.
236 C2 Wall SD U.S.A.
87 C4 Wall, Mount hill W.A. Austr.
87 B6 Wallabi Group is W.A. Austr.
85 E2 Wallaby Island Qld Austr.
238 C2 Wallace ID U.S.A.
231 E5 Wallace NC U.S.A.
236 C3 Wallace NE U.S.A.
232 B6 Wallace VA U.S.A.
224 D5 Wallaceburg Ont. Can.
81 B7 Wallacetown South I. N.Z.
86 D3 Wallal Downs W.A. Austr.
87 C6 Wallambin, Lake salt flat W.A. Austr.
83 G2 Wallangarra Qld Austr.
82 D3 Wallaroo S.A. Austr.
149 F4 Wallasey Merseyside, England U.K.
85 G5 Wallaville Qld Austr.
238 C2 Walla Walla WA U.S.A.
172 C2 Walldorf Baden-Württemberg Ger.
172 C1 Walldorf Hessen Ger.
169 F5 Walldorf Thüringen Ger.
172 D2 Walldürn Ger.
214 A4 Wallekraal S. Africa
83 G3 Wallendbeen N.S.W. Austr.
171 C5 Wallenfels Ger.
190 E1 Wallensee l. Switz.
173 G3 Wallerfing Ger.
179 H3 Wallern im Burgenland Austria
173 G3 Wallersdorf Ger.
178 E3 Wallersee l. Austria
173 E3 Wallerstein Ger.
173 F4 Wallgau Ger.
173 E2 Wallhausen Baden-Württemberg Ger.
172 B2 Wallhausen Rheinland-Pfalz Ger.
80 F4 Wallingford North I. N.Z.
151 F3 Wallingford Oxfordshire, England U.K.
235 F1 Wallingford CT U.S.A.
233 G3 Wallingford VT U.S.A.
Wallis canton Switz. see Valais
77 I3 Wallis, Îles is Wallis and Futuna Is
77 I3 Wallis and Futuna Islands terr. S. Pacific Ocean
172 C4 Wallisellen Switz.
Wallis et Futuna, Îles terr. S. Pacific Ocean see Wallis and Futuna Islands
Wallis Islands Wallis and Futuna Is see Wallis, Îles
235 D1 Wallkill NY U.S.A.
235 E1 Wallkill r. NY U.S.A.
238 C2 Wallowa OR U.S.A.
238 C2 Wallowa Mountains OR U.S.A.
146 □G1 Walls Shetland, Scotland U.K.
168 E1 Wallsbüll Ger.
149 H3 Wallsend Tyne and Wear, England U.K.
170 C3 Wallstawe Ger.
169 D5 Walluf Ger.
238 C2 Wallula WA U.S.A.
85 G5 Wallumbilla Qld Austr.
151 I3 Walmer Kent, England U.K.
149 F3 Walney, Isle of i. England U.K.
226 C5 Walnut IL U.S.A.
232 E4 Walnut Bottom PA U.S.A.
240 F3 Walnut Creek CA U.S.A.
236 D4 Walnut Creek r. KS U.S.A.
240 G2 Walnut Grove CA U.S.A.
234 C2 Walnutport PA U.S.A.
237 F4 Walnut Ridge AR U.S.A.
173 F3 Walpertskirchen Ger.
87 C7 Walpole W.A. Austr.
233 G3 Walpole NH U.S.A.
78 □5 Walpole, Île i. New Caledonia
175 J2 Wałpusza r. Pol.
178 D3 Wals Austria
151 F2 Walsall West Midlands, England U.K.
173 E2 Walsdorf Ger.
239 F4 Walsenburg CO U.S.A.
85 E3 Walsh r. Qld Austr.
237 C4 Walsh CO U.S.A.
170 D3 Walsleben Ger.
151 H2 Walsoken Cambridgeshire, England U.K.
168 E3 Walsrode Ger.
175 H1 Wałsza r. Pol.
115 D2 Waltair Andhra Prad. India
173 E4 Waltenhofen Ger.
231 D5 Walterboro SC U.S.A.
237 D5 Walters OK U.S.A.
169 F5 Waltershausen Ger.
83 F2 Walter's Range hills Qld Austr.
237 F5 Walthall MS U.S.A.
227 I3 Waltham Que. Can.
149 I4 Waltham North East Lincolnshire, England U.K.
233 H3 Waltham MA U.S.A.
233 □I2 Waltham ME U.S.A.
151 H3 Waltham Abbey Essex, England U.K.
151 G2 Waltham on the Wolds Leicestershire, England U.K.
173 F3 Walting Ger.
226 D5 Walton IN U.S.A.
233 F3 Walton NY U.S.A.
232 C5 Walton WV U.S.A.
149 G4 Walton-le-Dale Lancashire, England U.K.
151 G3 Walton-on-Thames Surrey, England U.K.
151 I3 Walton-on-the-Naze Essex, England U.K.
Walvisbaai Namibia see Walvis Bay
212 B4 Walvis Bay Namibia
212 B4 Walvis Bay b. Namibia
264 I8 Walvis Ridge sea feature S. Atlantic Ocean
87 C6 Walyahmoing hill W.A. Austr.
208 E4 Wamba Dem. Rep. Congo
209 C5 Wamba r. Dem. Rep. Congo
207 H4 Wamba Nigeria
183 F3 Wamba Spain
236 D4 Wamego KS U.S.A.
211 C6 Wami r. Tanz.
238 F3 Wamsutter WY U.S.A.
83 F2 Wanaaring N.S.W. Austr.
81 B6 Wanaka South I. N.Z.
81 B6 Wanaka, Lake South I. N.Z.
235 D2 Wanamassa NJ U.S.A.
234 B1 Wanamie PA U.S.A.
109 E3 Wan'an Jiangxi China
235 D1 Wanaque NJ U.S.A.
82 E3 Wanbi S.A. Austr.
108 B3 Wanbi Yunnan China
231 F5 Wanchese NC U.S.A.
258 G2 Wanda Arg.
100 E3 Wanda Shan mts China
223 H4 Wandering River Alta Can.
169 F5 Wandersleben Ger.
168 E1 Wanderup Ger.
108 A3 Wanding Yunnan China
Wandingzhen Yunnan China see Wanding
Wandiwash Tamil Nadu India see Vandavasi
81 D5 Wandle Downs South I. N.Z.
170 E3 Wandlitz Ger.
85 G5 Wandoan Qld Austr.
151 G3 Wandsworth Greater London, England U.K.
179 G2 Wang Austria
96 B3 Wang, Mae Nam r. Thai.
80 E3 Wanganui North I. N.Z.
80 E3 Wanganui r. North I. N.Z.
81 C5 Wanganui r. South I. N.Z.
83 F4 Wangaratta Vic. Austr.
82 C3 Wangary S.A. Austr.
108 C1 Wangcang Sichuan China
109 E2 Wangcheng Hunan China
Wangda Xizang China see Zogang
107 G4 Wangdu Hebei China
117 G4 Wangdue Phodrang Bhutan
169 E4 Wangelnstedt Ger.
168 F1 Wangels Ger.
190 C1 Wangen Switz.
172 D4 Wangen im Allgäu Ger.
168 C2 Wangerooge Ger.
168 C2 Wangerooge i. Ger.
93 B5 Wanggamet, Gunung mt. Sumba Indon.
106 C4 Wang Gaxun Qinghai China
Wanggezhuang Shandong China see Jiaonan
190 D1 Wängi Switz.
109 F2 Wangjiang Anhui China
100 C3 Wangkui Heilong. China
Wang Mai Khon Thai. see Sawankhalok
108 D4 Wangmao Guangxi China
108 C3 Wangmo Guizhou China
Wangolodougou Côte d'Ivoire see Ouangolodougou
100 D4 Wangqing Jilin China
Wangying Jiangsu China see Huaiyin
108 C1 Wangziguan Gansu China
222 G4 Wanham Alta Can.
251 H3 Wanhatti Suriname
208 E4 Wanie-Rukula Dem. Rep. Congo
116 B5 Wankaner Gujarat India
168 F1 Wankendorf Ger.
Wankie Zimbabwe see Hwange
210 E4 Wanlaweyn Somalia
168 D2 Wanna Ger.
87 F6 Wanna Lakes salt flat W.A. Austr.
87 B6 Wanneroo W.A. Austr.
109 F2 Wannian Jiangxi China
108 D5 Wanning Hainan China
164 E3 Wanroij Neth.
107 F5 Wanrong Shanxi China
108 D3 Wanshan Guizhou China
171 C4 Wansleben am See Ger.
80 F4 Wanstead North I. N.Z.
151 F3 Wantage Oxfordshire, England U.K.
235 E2 Wantagh NY U.S.A.
227 G2 Wanup Ont. Can.
108 D2 Wanxian Chongqing China
108 D2 Wanxian Chongqing China
108 D1 Wanyuan Sichuan China
109 E2 Wanzai Jiangxi China
165 E4 Wanze Belgium
Wanzhi Anhui China see Wuhu
232 A4 Wapakoneta OH U.S.A.
164 F2 Wapenveld Neth.
175 H2 Wąpiersk Pol.
222 G4 Wapiti r. Alta Can.
175 I2 Waplewo Pol.
174 F3 Wapno Pol.
235 E1 Wappinger Creek r. NY U.S.A.
235 E1 Wappingers Falls NY U.S.A.
236 F3 Wapsipinicon r. IA U.S.A.
108 B1 Waqên Sichuan China
232 C6 War WV U.S.A.
208 F2 Warab Sudan
208 F2 Warab state Sudan
105 F3 Warabi Japan
123 F5 Warah Pak.
114 C2 Warangal Andhra Prad. India
116 E5 Waraseoni Madh. Prad. India
83 F5 Waratah Tas. Austr.
169 F3 Warberg Ger.
151 G2 Warboys Cambridgeshire, England U.K.
85 E5 Warbreccan Qld Austr.
222 H4 Warburg Alta Can.
169 E4 Warburg Ger.
83 F4 Warburton Vic. Austr.
87 E5 Warburton W.A. Austr.
82 D1 Warburton watercourse S.A. Austr.
215 H2 Warburton S. Africa
87 E5 Warburton Range hills W.A. Austr.
165 E4 Warche r. Belgium
149 G3 Warcop Cumbria, England U.K.
157 F3 Warcq France
81 E4 Ward South I. N.Z.
262 T2 Ward, Mount Antarctica
81 A6 Ward, Mount South I. N.Z.
81 B5 Ward, Mount South I. N.Z.
82 D3 Wardang Island S.A. Austr.
215 G2 Warden S. Africa
168 D2 Wardenburg Ger.
116 D5 Wardha Mahar. India
114 C2 Wardha r. India
146 E3 Ward Hill hill Scotland U.K.
151 F2 Wardington Oxfordshire, England U.K.
146 □G1 Ward of Bressay hill Scotland U.K.
170 D2 Wardow Ger.
149 G3 Ward's Stone hill England U.K.
222 E3 Ware B.C. Can.
151 G3 Ware Hertfordshire, England U.K.
233 G3 Ware MA U.S.A.
165 C4 Waregem Belgium
150 E4 Wareham Dorset, England U.K.
233 H4 Wareham MA U.S.A.
165 E4 Waremme Belgium
170 D2 Waren Ger.
169 C4 Warendorf Ger.
164 F1 Warffum Neth.
164 E1 Warga Neth.
Wargili i. S. Male Maldives see Vaagali
85 G4 Warginburra Peninsula Qld Austr.
Wargla Alg. see Ouargla
151 G3 Wargrave Wokingham, England U.K.
83 G2 Warialda N.S.W. Austr.
170 C2 Warin Ger.
96 D4 Warin Chamrap Thai.
147 E2 Waringstown Northern Ireland U.K.
149 G2 Wark Northumberland, England U.K.
175 J4 Warka Pol.
80 E2 Warkworth North I. N.Z.
149 H2 Warkworth Northumberland, England U.K.
Warli Sichuan China see Walêg
151 G3 Warlingham Surrey, England U.K.
156 C2 Warloy-Baillon France
174 G2 Warlubie Pol.
223 J4 Warman Sask. Can.
212 C6 Warmbad Namibia
173 F2 Warmensteinach Ger.
156 E3 Warmeriville France
143 I4 Warmia reg. Pol.
151 F2 Warmington Warwickshire, England U.K.
175 I2 Warmińsko-Mazurskie prov. Pol.
150 E3 Warminster Wiltshire, England U.K.
234 C2 Warminster PA U.S.A.
164 D2 Warmond Neth.
169 D3 Warmsen Ger.
241 I2 Warm Springs NV U.S.A.
232 D5 Warm Springs VA U.S.A.
214 C5 Warmwaterberg S. Africa
170 D1 Warnemünde Ger.
223 H5 Warner Alta Can.
233 H3 Warner NH U.S.A.
238 B3 Warner Mountains CA U.S.A.
231 D5 Warner Robins GA U.S.A.
240 I5 Warner Springs CA U.S.A.
253 E4 Warnes Bol.
165 B4 Warneton Belgium
173 F4 Warngau Ger.
151 G3 Warnham West Sussex, England U.K.
174 C2 Warnice Pol.
170 C2 Warnow Ger.
170 D1 Warnow r. Ger.
164 F2 Warnsveld Neth.
114 C2 Waronda Mahar. India
87 B7 Waroona W.A. Austr.
116 D5 Warora Mahar. India
168 E3 Warpe Ger.
85 G5 Warra Qld Austr.
83 E4 Warracknabeal Vic. Austr.
83 G3 Warragamba Reservoir N.S.W. Austr.
83 F4 Warragul Vic. Austr.
82 D2 Warrakalanna, Lake salt flat S.A. Austr.
82 C3 Warramboo S.A. Austr.
87 C6 Warramboo hill W.A. Austr.
83 F2 Warrambool r. N.S.W. Austr.
82 D1 Warrandirinna, Lake salt flat S.A. Austr.
83 F4 Warrandyte Vic. Austr.
86 D4 Warrawagine W.A. Austr.
83 F2 Warrego r. N.S.W./Qld Austr.
85 F5 Warrego Range hills Qld Austr.
83 F2 Warren N.S.W. Austr.
87 B7 Warren r. W.A. Austr.
227 G2 Warren Ont. Can.
237 E5 Warren AR U.S.A.
226 C4 Warren IL U.S.A.
226 E5 Warren IN U.S.A.
227 F4 Warren MI U.S.A.
236 D1 Warren MN U.S.A.
232 C4 Warren OH U.S.A.
232 D4 Warren PA U.S.A.
234 D2 Warren County county NJ U.S.A.
235 D3 Warren Grove NJ U.S.A.
Warren Hastings Island Palau see Merir
147 E2 Warrenpoint Northern Ireland U.K.
226 B3 Warrens WI U.S.A.
236 E4 Warrensburg MO U.S.A.
233 G3 Warrensburg NY U.S.A.
234 B1 Warrensville PA U.S.A.
215 E3 Warrenton S. Africa
231 D5 Warrenton GA U.S.A.
236 F4 Warrenton MO U.S.A.
231 E4 Warrenton NC U.S.A.
232 E5 Warrenton VA U.S.A.
207 G5 Warri Nigeria
87 C6 Warriedar hill W.A. Austr.
81 C6 Warrington South I. N.Z.
149 G4 Warrington Warrington, England U.K.
149 G4 Warrington admin. div. England U.K.
231 C6 Warrington FL U.S.A.
83 E4 Warrnambool Vic. Austr.
236 E1 Warroad MN U.S.A.
82 C3 Warrow S.A. Austr.
84 C1 Warruwi N.T. Austr.
Warsaw Pol. see Warszawa
226 B5 Warsaw IL U.S.A.
230 C3 Warsaw IN U.S.A.
230 C4 Warsaw KY U.S.A.
236 E4 Warsaw MO U.S.A.
232 D3 Warsaw NY U.S.A.
232 E6 Warsaw VA U.S.A.
179 F3 Warscheneck mt. Austria
210 E4 Warshiikh Somalia
168 C2 Warsingsfehn Ger.
149 H4 Warslow Staffordshire, England U.K.
169 D4 Warstein Ger.
175 J3 Warszawa Pol.
174 G4 Warta Pol.
174 C3 Warta r. Pol.
174 D4 Warta Bolesławiecka Pol.
179 F3 Wartberg an der Krems Austria
231 C4 Wartburg TN U.S.A.
171 B5 Wartburg Schloß tourist site Thüringen Ger.
173 F3 Wartenberg Ger.
169 E5 Wartenberg-Angersbach Ger.
172 D3 Warthausen Ger.
170 F2 Wartin Ger.
175 H4 Wartkowice Pol.
169 E5 Wartmannsroth Ger.
149 G3 Warton Lancashire, England U.K.
116 D5 Warud Mahar. India
83 H2 Warwick Qld Austr.
151 F2 Warwick Warwickshire, England U.K.
234 C3 Warwick MD U.S.A.
235 D1 Warwick NY U.S.A.
233 H4 Warwick RI U.S.A.
149 G3 Warwick Bridge Cumbria, England U.K.
84 D2 Warwick Channel N.T. Austr.
151 F2 Warwickshire admin. div. England U.K.
108 B2 Warzhong Sichuan China
222 H5 Wasa B.C. Can.
207 G4 Wasaga Nigeria
227 G3 Wasaga Beach Ont. Can.
241 L2 Wasatch Range mts UT U.S.A.
215 H3 Wasbank S. Africa
168 E1 Wasbek Ger.
146 E2 Wasbister Orkney, Scotland U.K.
169 F3 Wasbüttel Ger.
223 J5 Wascana Creek r. Sask. Can.
172 D3 Wäschenbeuren Ger.
240 H4 Wasco CA U.S.A.
226 B2 Wascott WI U.S.A.
236 E2 Waseca MN U.S.A.
175 J3 Wąsewo Pol.
226 C5 Washburn IL U.S.A.
233 □I1 Washburn ME U.S.A.
236 C2 Washburn ND U.S.A.
232 B6 Washburn TN U.S.A.
226 B2 Washburn WI U.S.A.
104 C3 Washiga-take mt. Japan
116 D5 Washim Mahar. India
225 F3 Washimeska r. Que. Can.
149 H3 Washington Tyne and Wear, England U.K.
235 E1 Washington CT U.S.A.
234 A4 Washington DC U.S.A.
231 D5 Washington GA U.S.A.
236 F3 Washington IA U.S.A.
226 C5 Washington IL U.S.A.
230 C4 Washington IN U.S.A.
236 D4 Washington KS U.S.A.
232 B5 Washington KY U.S.A.
231 E5 Washington NC U.S.A.
233 G3 Washington NH U.S.A.
234 D2 Washington NJ U.S.A.
232 C4 Washington PA U.S.A.
241 K3 Washington UT U.S.A.
232 D5 Washington VA U.S.A.
238 B2 Washington state U.S.A.
263 L2 Washington, Cape Antarctica
233 H2 Washington, Mount NH U.S.A.
232 B5 Washington Court House OH U.S.A.
234 D2 Washington Crossing NJ U.S.A.
235 E1 Washington Depot CT U.S.A.
234 A3 Washington Grove MD U.S.A.
226 D3 Washington Island WI U.S.A.
221 L2 Washington Land reg. Greenland
235 D1 Washingtonville NY U.S.A.
234 B1 Washingtonville PA U.S.A.
237 D5 Washita r. OK U.S.A.
238 C2 Washtucna WA U.S.A.
156 E3 Wasigny France
175 L2 Wasilków Pol.
220 D3 Wasilla AK U.S.A.
127 G4 Wāsiţ governorate Iraq
127 G4 Wasit tourist site Iraq
224 E3 Waskaganish Que. Can.
222 H4 Waskatenau Alta Can.
174 E4 Wąsosz Pol.
175 K2 Wąsosz Pol.
174 E3 Wąsowo Pol.
242 □I6 Waspán Nic.
164 D3 Waspik Neth.
149 H3 Wass North Yorkshire, England U.K.
206 B3 Wassadou Senegal
165 E4 Wasseiges Belgium
157 H4 Wasselonne France
190 D2 Wassen Switz.
164 D2 Wassenaar Neth.
169 B4 Wassenberg Ger.
173 E3 Wasseralfingen Ger.
173 G3 Wasserburg am Inn Ger.
169 E5 Wasserkuppe hill Ger.
169 F4 Wasserleben Ger.
172 A2 Wasserliesch Ger.
169 F5 Wasserlosen Ger.
173 E2 Wassertrüdingen Ger.
156 D2 Wassigny France
206 B4 Wassou Guinea
240 H2 Wassuk Range mts NV U.S.A.
157 E4 Wassy France
169 F5 Wasungen Ger.
93 B4 Watampone Sulawesi Selatan Indon.
93 A4 Watansoppeng Sulawesi Selatan Indon.
105 F2 Watarase-gawa r. Japan
232 B6 Watauga r. TN U.S.A.
150 D3 Watchet Somerset, England U.K.
149 G3 Watchgate Cumbria, England U.K.
Watenstadt-Salzgitter Ger. see Salzgitter
151 H2 Waterbeach Cambridgeshire, England U.K.
233 G4 Waterbury CT U.S.A.
233 G2 Waterbury VT U.S.A.
246 C2 Water Cays i. Bahamas
227 H4 Waterdown Ont. Can.
231 D5 Wateree r. SC U.S.A.
222 C4 Waterfall AK U.S.A.
147 D4 Waterford Rep. of Ireland
147 D4 Waterford county Rep. of Ireland
215 E5 Waterford S. Africa
240 G3 Waterford CA U.S.A.
235 F1 Waterford CT U.S.A.
232 D4 Waterford PA U.S.A.
234 D3 Waterford Works NJ U.S.A.
223 J4 Waterhen r. Sask. Can.
84 C2 Waterhouse r. N.T. Austr.
84 C5 Waterhouse Range mts N.T. Austr.
164 D2 Wateringen Neth.
165 C3 Waterland-Oudeman Belgium
84 B3 Waterloo N.T. Austr.
165 D4 Waterloo Belgium
224 D5 Waterloo Ont. Can.
206 B4 Waterloo Sierra Leone
236 E3 Waterloo IA U.S.A.
236 F4 Waterloo IL U.S.A.
234 B3 Waterloo MD U.S.A.
232 E3 Waterloo NY U.S.A.
226 C4 Waterloo WI U.S.A.
151 F4 Waterlooville Hampshire, England U.K.
226 C5 Waterman IL U.S.A.
235 F2 Watermill NY U.S.A.
149 F2 Water of Leith r. Scotland U.K.
146 D5 Water of Tulla r. Scotland U.K.
151 F2 Water Orton Warwickshire, England U.K.
213 F4 Waterpoort S. Africa
147 D2 Waterside Northern Ireland U.K.
226 C2 Watersmeet MI U.S.A.
222 H5 Waterton Park Alta Can.
235 E1 Watertown CT U.S.A.
233 F3 Watertown NY U.S.A.
236 D2 Watertown SD U.S.A.
226 C4 Watertown WI U.S.A.
215 G2 Waterval r. S. Africa
215 H1 Waterval-Boven S. Africa
82 D3 Watervale S.A. Austr.
237 F5 Water Valley MS U.S.A.
147 A5 Waterville Rep. of Ireland
233 □I2 Waterville ME U.S.A.
232 B4 Waterville OH U.S.A.
238 B2 Waterville WA U.S.A.
233 G3 Watervliet NY U.S.A.
95 E4 Wates Indon.
227 G4 Watford Ont. Can.
151 G3 Watford Hertfordshire, England U.K.
236 C2 Watford City ND U.S.A.
223 K3 Wathaman r. Sask. Can.
87 C6 Watheroo W.A. Austr.
222 G4 Watino Alta Can.
232 E3 Watkins Glen NY U.S.A.
231 D5 Watkinsville GA U.S.A.
Watling Island Bahamas see San Salvador
151 F3 Watlington Oxfordshire, England U.K.
237 D5 Watonga OK U.S.A.
93 D2 Watowato, Bukit mt. Halmahera Indon.
223 J5 Watrous Sask. Can.
239 F5 Watrous NM U.S.A.
208 F4 Watsa Dem. Rep. Congo
226 D5 Watseka IL U.S.A.
85 E2 Watson r. Qld Austr.
223 J4 Watson Sask. Can.
262 P1 Watson Escarpment Antarctica
222 D2 Watson Lake Y.T. Can.
234 B1 Watsontown PA U.S.A.
240 G3 Watsonville CA U.S.A.
87 E5 Watt, Mount hill W.A. Austr.
156 C2 Watten France
146 E3 Watten Highland, Scotland U.K.
168 F1 Wattenbek Ger.
178 C3 Wattens Austria
190 C2 Wattenwil Switz.
156 E2 Wattignies-la-Victoire France
147 D2 Wattlebridge Northern Ireland U.K.
170 D2 Wattmannshagen Ger.
151 H2 Watton Norfolk, England U.K.
151 G3 Watton-at-Stone Hertfordshire, England U.K.
156 D2 Wattrelos France
231 C5 Watts Bar Lake resr TN U.S.A.
232 D3 Wattsburg PA U.S.A.
190 E1 Wattwil Switz.
93 B3 Watuwila, Bukit mt. Indon.
169 D5 Watzenborn-Steinberg Ger.
208 E3 Wau Sudan
83 H2 Wauchope N.S.W. Austr.
84 C4 Wauchope N.T. Austr.
231 D7 Wauchula FL U.S.A.
93 A3 Waukara, Gunung mt. Indon.
86 D4 Waukarlycarly, Lake salt flat W.A. Austr.
226 C4 Waukau WI U.S.A.
226 D4 Waukegan IL U.S.A.
226 C4 Waukesha WI U.S.A.
226 B4 Waukon IA U.S.A.
226 C4 Waunakee WI U.S.A.
236 C3 Wauneta NE U.S.A.
226 C3 Waupaca WI U.S.A.
226 C4 Waupun WI U.S.A.
235 G1 Wauregan CT U.S.A.
237 D5 Waurika OK U.S.A.
226 C3 Wausau WI U.S.A.
226 D3 Wausaukee WI U.S.A.
232 A4 Wauseon OH U.S.A.
226 C3 Wautoma WI U.S.A.
84 B3 Wave Hill N.T. Austr.
151 I2 Waveney r. England U.K.
80 E3 Waverley North I. N.Z.
236 E3 Waverly IA U.S.A.
232 E3 Waverly NY U.S.A.
232 B5 Waverly OH U.S.A.
231 C4 Waverly TN U.S.A.
232 E6 Waverly VA U.S.A.
165 D4 Wavre Belgium
156 C2 Wavrin France
96 B3 Waw Myanmar
224 C4 Wawa Ont. Can.
207 G4 Wawa Nigeria
224 E3 Wawagosic r. Que. Can.
235 D1 Wawarsing NY U.S.A.
174 F5 Wąwelno Pol.
91 J8 Wawoi r. P.N.G.
175 K4 Wąwolnica Pol.
174 D3 Wawrów Pol.
175 I5 Wawrzeńczyce Pol.
237 D5 Waxahachie TX U.S.A.
169 B5 Waxweiler Ger.
110 D4 Waxxari Xinjiang China
87 D5 Way, Lake salt flat W.A. Austr.
79 □1a Waya i. Fiji
Wayaobu Shaanxi China see Zichang
231 D6 Waycross GA U.S.A.
232 B6 Wayland KY U.S.A.
226 E4 Wayland MI U.S.A.
226 B5 Wayland MO U.S.A.
232 E3 Wayland NY U.S.A.
227 F4 Wayne MI U.S.A.
236 D3 Wayne NE U.S.A.
235 D2 Wayne NJ U.S.A.
234 C2 Wayne PA U.S.A.
232 B5 Wayne WV U.S.A.
234 C1 Wayne County county PA U.S.A.
231 D5 Waynesboro GA U.S.A.
237 F6 Waynesboro MS U.S.A.
232 E5 Waynesboro PA U.S.A.
231 C5 Waynesboro TN U.S.A.
232 D5 Waynesboro VA U.S.A.
232 C5 Waynesburg PA U.S.A.
237 E4 Waynesville MO U.S.A.
231 D5 Waynesville NC U.S.A.
237 D4 Waynoka OK U.S.A.
207 I4 Waza Cameroon
156 D2 Waziers France
123 H3 Wazirabad Pak.
174 G2 Wda r. Pol.
Wdig Pembrokeshire, Wales U.K. see Goodwick
78 □5 We Î. Loyauté New Caledonia
149 H3 Wear r. England U.K.
233 H3 Weare NH U.S.A.
84 D3 Wearyan r. N.T. Austr.
85 F2 Weary Bay Qld Austr.
237 D5 Weatherford OK U.S.A.
237 D5 Weatherford TX U.S.A.
234 C2 Weatherly PA U.S.A.
149 G4 Weaverham Cheshire, England U.K.
238 B3 Weaverville CA U.S.A.
86 F4 Webb, Mount hill W.A. Austr.
224 D4 Webbwood Ont. Can.
224 C2 Webequie Ont. Can.
80 F4 Weber North I. N.Z.
238 D3 Weber r. UT U.S.A.
222 D4 Weber, Mount B.C. Can.
265 M5 Weber Basin sea feature Indon.
210 D4 Webi Shabeelle r. Somalia
233 H3 Webster MA U.S.A.
234 B3 Webster MD U.S.A.
236 D2 Webster SD U.S.A.
226 A3 Webster WI U.S.A.
236 E3 Webster City IA U.S.A.
232 C5 Webster Springs WV U.S.A.
165 D3 Wechelderzande Belgium
169 F5 Wechmar Ger.
222 H2 Wecho r. N.W.T. Can.
171 D4 Wechselburg Ger.
164 G1 Wedde Neth.
262 V2 Weddell Abyssal Plain sea feature Southern Ocean
259 E8 Weddell Island Falkland Is
83 E4 Wedderburn Vic. Austr.
81 C6 Wedderburn South I. N.Z.
168 E1 Weddingstedt Ger.
168 E2 Wedel (Holstein) Ger.
140 □ Wedel Jarlsberg Land reg. Svalbard
222 F5 Wedge Mountain B.C. Can.
150 E3 Wedmore Somerset, England U.K.
150 E2 Wednesbury West Midlands, England U.K.
231 C5 Wedowee AL U.S.A.
238 B3 Weed CA U.S.A.
168 F2 Weede Ger.
151 F2 Weedon Bec Northamptonshire, England U.K.
232 D4 Weedville PA U.S.A.
234 D3 Weekstown NJ U.S.A.
165 D3 Weelde Belgium
83 G2 Weemelah N.S.W. Austr.
215 H3 Weenen S. Africa
168 C2 Weener Ger.
178 C3 Weerberg Austria
164 F2 Weerselo Neth.
165 E3 Weert Neth.
168 E1 Wees Ger.
190 E1 Weesen Switz.
164 E2 Weesp Neth.
83 F3 Weethalle N.S.W. Austr.
83 G2 Wee Waa N.S.W. Austr.
169 B4 Weeze Ger.
171 C3 Weferlingen Ger.
169 B4 Wegberg Ger.
214 C3 Wegdraai S. Africa
171 C4 Wegeleben Ger.
171 C3 Wegenstedt Ger.
172 C4 Weggis Switz.
174 D4 Węgliniec Pol.
175 J1 Węgorzewo Pol.
174 D2 Węgorzyno Pol.
175 K3 Węgrów Pol.
175 I3 Węgrzynowo Pol.
173 H3 Wegscheid Ger.
168 D2 Wehdel Ger.
164 F1 Wehe-den Hoorn Neth.
164 F3 Wehl Neth.
Wehlau Rus. Fed. see Znamensk
172 B4 Wehr Ger.
168 D3 Wehrbleck Ger.
169 D5 Wehrheim Ger.
173 E3 Wehringen Ger.
107 G4 Wei r. Henan China
107 F5 Wei r. Shaanxi China
107 H4 Wei r. Shandong China
169 C5 Weibern Ger.
172 D2 Weibersbrunn Ger.
107 H3 Weichang Hebei China
173 F3 Weichering Ger.
173 F3 Weichs Ger.
171 D5 Weida Ger.
171 D5 Weida r. Ger.
173 E2 Weidenbach Ger.
173 F2 Weidenberg Ger.
173 G2 Weiden in der Oberpfalz Ger.
172 D3 Weidenstetten Ger.
172 B2 Weidenthal Ger.
173 G2 Weiding Ger.
Weidongmen Heilong. China see Qianjin
172 B2 Weiersbach Ger.
107 H4 Weifang Shandong China
171 F4 Weigersdorf Ger.
234 B3 Weiglestown PA U.S.A.
107 I4 Weihai Shandong China
173 E2 Weihenzell Ger.
173 G2 Weiherhammer Ger.
173 G3 Weihmichl Ger.
107 G5 Weihui Henan China
179 H2 Weikendorf Austria
172 D2 Weikersheim Ger.
173 E3 Weil Ger.
172 B4 Weil am Rhein Ger.
172 D2 Weilbach Ger.
169 D5 Weilburg Ger.
172 C3 Weil der Stadt Ger.
178 A3 Weiler Austria
172 D4 Weiler Ger.
172 B2 Weilerbach Ger.
169 B5 Weilerswist Ger.
172 C4 Weilheim Ger.
172 D3 Weilheim an der Teck Ger.
173 F4 Weilheim in Oberbayern Ger.
83 F2 Weilmoringle N.S.W. Austr.
169 D5 Weilmünster Ger.
171 C5 Weimar Ger.
169 E4 Weimar (Ahnatal) Ger.
107 F5 Weinan Shaanxi China
169 D5 Weinbach Ger.
171 E4 Weinböhla Ger.
190 E1 Weinfelden Switz.
172 D4 Weingarten Ger.
172 C2 Weingarten (Baden) Ger.
172 C2 Weinheim Ger.
108 C3 Weining Guizhou China
172 D2 Weinsberg Ger.
172 B2 Weinsheim Rheinland-Pfalz Ger.
169 B5 Weinsheim Rheinland-Pfalz Ger.
172 D3 Weinstadt Ger.
85 E2 Weipa Qld Austr.
Weiqu Shaanxi China see Chang'an
83 G2 Weir r. Qld Austr.
87 C5 Weiragoo Range hills W.A. Austr.
223 M3 Weir River Man. Can.
232 C4 Weirton WV U.S.A.
171 D5 Weischlitz Ger.
146 □G1 Weisdale Shetland, Scotland U.K.
170 C2 Weisen Ger.
173 E2 Weisendorf Ger.
238 C2 Weiser ID U.S.A.
238 C2 Weiser r. ID U.S.A.
107 H5 Weishan Shandong China
108 B3 Weishan Yunnan China
107 G5 Weishi Henan China
172 A2 Weiskirchen Ger.
171 C5 Weismain Ger.
173 F4 Weißach r. Ger.
171 C4 Weiße Elster r. Ger.
173 F2 Weiße Laber r. Ger.
178 B3 Weißenbach am Lech Austria
171 F4 Weißenberg Ger.
169 F4 Weißenborn Ger.
171 E5 Weißenborn Ger.
169 F4 Weißenborn-Lüderode Ger.
171 C5 Weißenbrunn Ger.
173 E2 Weißenburg in Bayern Ger.
171 C4 Weißenfels Ger.
173 E3 Weißenhorn Ger.
172 D4 Weißensberg Ger.
171 C4 Weißensee Ger.
171 C5 Weißenstadt Ger.
179 E4 Weißenstein Austria
169 C5 Weißenthurm Ger.
171 C5 Weißer Main r. Ger.
173 G2 Weißer Regen r. Ger.
171 F4 Weißer Schöps r. Ger.
190 C2 Weisshorn mt. Switz.
171 E4 Weißig Ger.
171 F4 Weißkeißel Ger.
179 F2 Weißkirchen an der Traun Austria
179 F3 Weißkirchen in Steiermark Austria
171 F4 Weißkollm Ger.
178 B4 Weißkugel mt. Austria/Italy
190 D2 Weissmies mt. Switz.
212 C5 Weissrand Mountains Namibia
171 F4 Weißwasser Ger.
179 F2 Weistrach Austria
165 F4 Weiswampach Lux.
172 B3 Weisweil Ger.
157 H4 Weitbruch France
169 C5 Weitefeld Ger.
179 G2 Weiten Austria
179 G4 Weitendorf Austria
170 E1 Weitenhagen Ger.
179 F4 Weitensfeld Austria
179 G2 Weitersfeld Austria
172 C2 Weiterstadt Ger.
164 G2 Weiteveen Neth.
173 E4 Weitnau Ger.
179 F2 Weitra Austria
169 F5 Weitramsdorf Ger.
171 E4 Weixdorf Ger.
108 A3 Weixi Yunnan China
107 G4 Weixian Hebei China
108 C3 Weixin Yunnan China
106 B3 Weiya Xinjiang China
106 E5 Weiyuan Gansu China
Weiyuan Qinghai China see Huzhu
Weiyuan Yunnan China see Jinggu
108 B4 Weiyuan Jiang r. Yunnan China
179 G3 Weiz Austria
Weizhou Sichuan China see Wenchuan
107 I3 Weizi Liaoning China
143 H4 Wejherowo Pol.
223 L4 Wekusko Man. Can.
222 H1 Wekweti N.W.T. Can.
175 H2 Wel r. Pol.
82 C1 Welbourn Hill S.A. Austr.
232 C6 Welch WV U.S.A.
233 □H2 Weld ME U.S.A.
87 D6 Weld, Mount hill W.A. Austr.
173 E3 Welden Ger.
210 C2 Weldiya Eth.
151 G2 Weldon Northamptonshire, England U.K.
87 C5 Weld Range hills W.A. Austr.
165 E4 Welkenraedt Belgium
210 C2 Welk'īt'ē Eth.
215 F2 Welkom S. Africa
164 F3 Well Neth.
227 H4 Welland Ont. Can.
151 G2 Welland r. England U.K.
227 H4 Welland Canal Ont. Can.
171 D4 Wellaune Ger.
168 E2 Welle Ger.
165 E4 Wellen Belgium
172 C3 Wellendingen Ger.
151 F2 Wellesbourne Warwickshire, England U.K.
227 G4 Wellesley Ont. Can.
84 D3 Wellesley Islands Qld Austr.
233 H4 Wellfleet MA U.S.A.
173 F3 Wellheim Ger.
165 E4 Wellin Belgium
169 C5 Welling Ger.
151 G2 Wellingborough Northamptonshire, England U.K.
83 G3 Wellington N.S.W. Austr.
82 D3 Wellington S.A. Austr.
227 I4 Wellington Ont. Can.
81 E4 Wellington North I. N.Z.
81 E4 Wellington admin. reg. North I. N.Z.
214 B5 Wellington S. Africa
150 D4 Wellington Somerset, England U.K.
150 E2 Wellington Telford and Wrekin, England U.K.
238 F3 Wellington CO U.S.A.
237 D4 Wellington KS U.S.A.
240 H2 Wellington NV U.S.A.
232 B4 Wellington OH U.S.A.
237 C5 Wellington TX U.S.A.
241 L2 Wellington UT U.S.A.
259 B8 Wellington, Isla i. Chile
147 E4 Wellington Bridge Rep. of Ireland
84 C2 Wellington Range hills N.T. Austr.
87 D5 Wellington Range hills W.A. Austr.
222 F4 Wells B.C. Can.
150 E3 Wells Somerset, England U.K.
238 D3 Wells NV U.S.A.
87 D5 Wells, Lake salt flat W.A. Austr.
232 E4 Wellsboro PA U.S.A.
232 C4 Wellsburg WV U.S.A.
80 E2 Wellsford North I. N.Z.
151 H2 Wells-next-the-Sea Norfolk, England U.K.
226 E3 Wellston MI U.S.A.
232 E3 Wellsville NY U.S.A.
232 C4 Wellsville OH U.S.A.
234 B2 Wellsville PA U.S.A.
241 J5 Wellton AZ U.S.A.
174 E3 Wełna r. Pol.
151 H2 Welney Norfolk, England U.K.
175 L4 Wełnianka r. Pol.
240 □D9 Weloka HI U.S.A.
179 F2 Wels Austria
172 A2 Welschbillig Ger.
170 F2 Welse r. Ger.
150 G3 Welsh Newton Herefordshire, England U.K.
150 D2 Welshpool Powys, Wales U.K.
171 E4 Welsickendorf Ger.
171 C4 Welsleben Ger.
149 I4 Welton Lincolnshire, England U.K.
169 C4 Welver Ger.
Welwitschia Namibia see Khorixas
151 G3 Welwyn Hertfordshire, England U.K.
151 G3 Welwyn Garden City Hertfordshire, England U.K.
172 D3 Welzheim Ger.
172 D3 Welzheimer Wald hills Ger.
171 F4 Welzow Ger.
150 E2 Wem Shropshire, England U.K.
150 D3 Wembdon Somerset, England U.K.
211 B6 Wembere r. Tanz.
215 G3 Wembesi S. Africa
222 G4 Wembley Alta Can.
173 E3 Wemding Ger.
164 D3 Wemeldinge Neth.
210 D3 Wemel Shet' r. Eth.
224 E2 Wemindji Que. Can.
146 D6 Wemyss Bay Inverclyde, Scotland U.K.
246 C1 Wemyss Bight Eleuthera Bahamas
107 H5 Wen r. China
251 F3 Wenamu r. Guyana/Venez.
238 B2 Wenatchee WA U.S.A.
238 B2 Wenatchee Mountains WA U.S.A.
108 D5 Wenchang Hainan China
Wenchang Sichuan China see Zitong
109 G3 Wencheng Zhejiang China
206 E5 Wenchi Ghana
210 C2 Wench'īt Shet' r. Eth.
Wenchow Zhejiang China see Wenzhou
108 B2 Wenchuan Sichuan China
169 F3 Wendeburg Ger.
172 C2 Wendelsheim Ger.
173 F2 Wendelstein Ger.
173 G4 Wendelstein mt. Ger.
169 C5 Wenden Ger.
Wenden Latvia see Cēsis
241 K5 Wenden AZ U.S.A.
107 I4 Wendeng Shandong China
151 H2 Wendens Ambo Essex, England U.K.
168 F2 Wendisch Evern Ger.
170 D2 Wendisch Priborn Ger.
171 F3 Wendisch Rietz Ger.
172 D3 Wendlingen am Neckar Ger.
210 C3 Wendo Eth.
206 B4 Wéndou Mbôrou Guinea
151 G3 Wendover Buckinghamshire, England U.K.
238 D3 Wendover UT U.S.A.
150 B4 Wendron Cornwall, England U.K.
165 C3 Wenduine Belgium
Wenfeng Jiangxi China see Yongfeng
190 C2 Wengen Switz.
169 C3 Wengsel (Isterberg) Ger.
108 A2 Wengshui Yunnan China
109 E3 Wengyuan Guangdong China
Wenhua Yunnan China see Weishan
Wenjiang Sichuan China see Gaoxian
109 E3 Wenjiashi Jiangxi China
Wenlan Yunnan China see Mengzi
Wenlin Sichuan China see Renshou
109 G2 Wenling Zhejiang China
85 E2 Wenlock r. Qld Austr.
150 E2 Wenlock Edge ridge England U.K.
250 □ Wenman, Isla i. Islas Galápagos Ecuador
169 D4 Wenne r. Ger.
169 E3 Wennigsen (Deister) Ger.
149 G3 Wenning r. England U.K.
168 D1 Wenningstedt Ger.
178 B3 Wenns Austria
78 □4a Weno Chuuk Micronesia
78 □4a Weno i. Chuuk Micronesia
226 C5 Wenona IL U.S.A.
233 F5 Wenona MD U.S.A.
Wenping Yunnan China see Ludian
108 D2 Wenquan Chongqing China
108 C2 Wenquan Guizhou China
Wenquan Hubei China see Yingshan
106 C5 Wenquan Qinghai China
110 C2 Wenquan Xinjiang China
109 E2 Wenquanzhen Hubei China
108 C4 Wenshan Yunnan China
108 C2 Wenshui Guizhou China
149 H3 Wensley North Yorkshire, England U.K.
149 G3 Wensleydale val. England U.K.
110 C3 Wensu Xinjiang China

Wensum to **Windischgarsten**
379

151 I2 **Wensum** r. England U.K.
149 I4 **Went** r. England U.K.
168 F2 **Wentorf** Ger.
168 F2 **Wentorf bei Hamburg** Ger.
83 E3 **Wentworth** N.S.W. Austr.
231 E4 **Wentworth** NC U.S.A.
233 H3 **Wentworth** NH U.S.A.
226 B2 **Wentworth** WI U.S.A.
107 F5 **Wenxi** Shanxi China
108 C1 **Wenxian** Gansu China
107 F4 **Wenyu** r. China
173 G2 **Wenzenbach** Ger.
109 G3 **Wenzhou** Zhejiang China
171 D3 **Wenzlow** Ger.
150 E2 **Weobley** Herefordshire, England U.K.
215 F3 **Wepener** S. Africa
165 D4 **Wépion** Belgium
116 D4 **Wer** Rajasthan India
172 D2 **Werbach** Ger.
170 E3 **Werbellin** Ger.
171 F4 **Werben** Ger.
170 C3 **Werben (Elbe)** Ger.
171 E4 **Werbig** Ger.
175 L5 **Werbkowice** Pol.
165 E4 **Werbomont** Belgium
212 D5 **Werda** Botswana
171 D5 **Werdau** Ger.
210 E3 **Werdër** Eth.
171 D3 **Werder** Brandenburg Ger.
170 E2 **Werder** Mecklenburg-Vorpommern Ger.
169 C4 **Werdohl** Ger.
168 C2 **Werdum** Ger.
151 H2 **Wereham** Norfolk, England U.K.
178 E3 **Werfen** Austria
169 C4 **Werl** Ger.
168 C3 **Werlte** Ger.
169 C4 **Wermelskirchen** Ger.
171 D4 **Wermsdorf** Ger.
169 E5 **Wern** r. Ger.
172 D3 **Wernau** Ger.
179 E4 **Wernberg** Austria
173 G2 **Wernberg-Köblitz** Ger.
179 G4 **Werndorf** Austria
169 C4 **Werne** Ger.
171 B5 **Werneck** Ger.
170 E3 **Werneuchen** Ger.
169 F4 **Wernigerode** Ger.
169 F5 **Wernshausen** Ger.
168 C3 **Werpeloh** Ger.
169 E4 **Werra** r. Ger.
169 D3 **Werre** r. Ger.
82 E3 **Werrimull** Vic. Austr.
83 G2 **Werris Creek** N.S.W. Austr.
173 E4 **Wertach** Ger.
173 E3 **Wertach** r. Ger.
172 D2 **Wertheim** Ger.
172 C4 **Werthenstein** Switz.
169 F4 **Werther** Ger.
169 D3 **Werther (Westfalen)** Ger.
173 E3 **Wertingen** Ger.
164 E2 **Wervershoof** Neth.
165 C4 **Wervik** Belgium
169 B4 **Wesel** Ger.
170 D2 **Wesenberg** Ger.
168 F3 **Wesendorf** Ger.
164 F2 **Wesepe** Neth.
169 D2 **Weser** r. Ger.
168 D2 **Weser** sea chan. Ger.
168 C3 **Weser-Ems** admin. reg. Niedersachsen Ger.
169 D3 **Wesergebirge** hills Ger.
236 C4 **Weskan** KS U.S.A.
237 D7 **Weslaco** TX U.S.A.
215 F5 **Wesley** S. Africa
233 □J2 **Wesley** ME U.S.A.
225 K3 **Wesleyville** Nfld. Can.
232 C3 **Wesleyville** PA U.S.A.
175 J3 **Wesoła** Pol.
84 D1 **Wessel, Cape** N.T. Austr.
168 D1 **Wesselburen** Ger.
169 B5 **Wesseling** Ger.
84 D1 **Wessel Islands** N.T. Austr.
168 E1 **Wesseln** Ger.
215 F2 **Wesselsbron** S. Africa
214 D2 **Wesselsvlei** S. Africa
215 G2 **Wesselton** S. Africa
165 E3 **Wessem** Neth.
236 D2 **Wessington Springs** SD U.S.A.
173 F3 **Weßling** Ger.
173 F4 **Wessobrunn** Ger.
234 B4 **West** r. MD U.S.A.
82 C3 **Westall, Point** S.A. Austr.
84 C2 **West Alligator** r. N.T. Austr.
226 C4 **West Allis** WI U.S.A.
262 P1 **West Antarctica** reg. Antarctica
235 D3 **West Atlantic City** NJ U.S.A.
149 H3 **West Auckland** Durham, England U.K.
265 K6 **West Australian Basin** sea feature Indian Ocean
235 E2 **West Babylon** NY U.S.A.
84 B2 **West Baines** r. N.T. Austr.
116 B5 **West Banas** r. India
128 B4 **West Bank** terr. Asia
225 J2 **West Bay** Nfld. Can.
246 B3 **West Bay** Cayman Is
226 C4 **West Bend** WI U.S.A.
117 F5 **West Bengal** state India
151 H3 **West Bergholt** Essex, England U.K.
151 F3 **West Berkshire** admin. div. England U.K.
234 D3 **West Berlin** NJ U.S.A.
232 B5 **Westboro** OH U.S.A.
227 E3 **West Branch** MI U.S.A.
151 F2 **West Bridgford** Nottinghamshire, England U.K.
151 F2 **West Bromwich** West Midlands, England U.K.
235 F1 **Westbrook** CT U.S.A.
233 □H3 **Westbrook** ME U.S.A.
234 D1 **Westbrookville** NY U.S.A.
233 H2 **West Burke** VT U.S.A.
83 F5 **Westbury** Tas. Austr.
150 E3 **Westbury** Wiltshire, England U.K.
226 B4 **Westby** WI U.S.A.
246 D2 **West Caicos** i. Turks and Caicos Is
146 E6 **West Calder** West Lothian, Scotland U.K.
234 B2 **West Cameron** PA U.S.A.
81 A6 **West Cape** South I. N.Z.
87 C7 **West Cape Howe** W.A. Austr.
234 D4 **West Cape May** NJ U.S.A.
266 E5 **West Caroline Basin** sea feature N. Pacific Ocean
234 C3 **West Chester** PA U.S.A.
235 E1 **Westchester County** county NY U.S.A.
239 F4 **Westcliffe** CO U.S.A.
81 C5 **West Coast** admin. reg. South I. N.Z.
150 E4 **West Coker** Somerset, England U.K.
226 A3 **West Concord** MN U.S.A.
151 G3 **Westcott** Surrey, England U.K.
235 D3 **West Creek** NJ U.S.A.
81 B6 **West Dome** mt. South I. N.Z.
165 C3 **Westdorpe** Neth.
227 F3 **West Duck Island** Ont. Can.
146 D6 **West Dunbartonshire** admin. div. Scotland U.K.
231 E7 **West End** Bahamas
233 F3 **West End** NY U.S.A.
165 B3 **Westende** Belgium
178 D3 **Westendorf** Austria
164 F2 **Westenholte** Neth.
168 E1 **Westensee** Ger.
168 F3 **Westerbeck (Sassenburg)** Ger.
214 D3 **Westerberg** S. Africa
164 F2 **Westerbork** Neth.
169 C5 **Westerburg** Ger.
146 E3 **Westerdale** Highland, Scotland U.K.
171 C4 **Westeregeln** Ger.
168 C2 **Westerende-Kirchloog (Ihlow)** Ger.
81 C5 **Westerfield** South I. N.Z.
151 G4 **Westergate** West Sussex, England U.K.
168 F2 **Westergellersen** Ger.
164 F2 **Westerhaar** Neth.
151 H3 **Westerham** Kent, England U.K.
171 C4 **Westerhausen** Ger.
172 D3 **Westerheim** Baden-Württemberg Ger.
173 E3 **Westerheim** Bayern Ger.
168 C2 **Westerholt** Ger.
168 E2 **Westerhorn** Ger.
165 E3 **Westerhoven** Neth.
168 D1 **Westerland** Ger.
165 D3 **Westerlo** Belgium
235 G1 **Westerly** RI U.S.A.
206 E5 **Western** admin. reg. Ghana
209 D8 **Western** prov. Zambia
206 B4 **Western Area** admin. div. Sierra Leone
87 D5 **Western Australia** state Austr.
208 E3 **Western Bahr el Ghazal** state Sudan
214 C5 **Western Cape** prov. S. Africa
202 D6 **Western Darfur** state Sudan
Western Dvina r. Europe see **Zapadnaya Dvina**
208 F3 **Western Equatoria** state Sudan
114 B3 **Western Ghats** mts India
146 B3 **Western Isles** admin. div. Scotland U.K.
208 F2 **Western Kordofan** state Sudan
Western Lesser Sunda Islands prov. Indon. see **Nusa Tenggara Barat**
83 F4 **Western Port** b. Vic. Austr.
Western Province prov. Zambia see **Copperbelt**
204 D3 **Western Sahara** terr. Africa
Western Samoa country S. Pacific Ocean see **Samoa**
Western Sayan Mountains reg. Rus. Fed. see **Zapadnyy Sayan**
168 E1 **Wester-Ohrstedt** Ger.
146 E6 **Wester Parkgate** Dumfries and Galloway, Scotland U.K.
146 C4 **Wester Ross** reg. Scotland U.K.
165 C3 **Westerschelde** est. Neth.
168 C2 **Westerstede** Ger.
172 D3 **Westerstetten** Ger.
232 B4 **Westerville** OH U.S.A.
164 E3 **Westervoort** Neth.
169 C5 **Westerwald** hills Ger.
171 E4 **Westewitz** Ger.
259 E8 **West Falkland** i. Falkland Is
236 D2 **West Fargo** ND U.S.A.
91 K5 **West Fayu** atoll Micronesia
149 I4 **West Fen** reg. Lincolnshire, England U.K.
151 H4 **Westfield** East Sussex, England U.K.
233 G3 **Westfield** MA U.S.A.
233 □J1 **Westfield** ME U.S.A.
235 D2 **Westfield** NJ U.S.A.
232 D3 **Westfield** NY U.S.A.
232 E4 **Westfield** PA U.S.A.
226 C4 **Westfield** WI U.S.A.
West Flanders prov. Belgium see **West-Vlaanderen**
233 □I2 **West Forks** ME U.S.A.
235 D2 **West Freehold** NJ U.S.A.
West Frisian Islands Neth. see **Waddeneilanden**
164 F1 **Westgat** sea chan. Neth.
85 F5 **Westgate** Qld Austr.
149 G3 **Westgate** Durham, England U.K.
238 D1 **West Glacier** MT U.S.A.
151 G4 **West Grinstead** West Sussex, England U.K.
234 C3 **West Grove** PA U.S.A.
151 F2 **West Haddon** Northamptonshire, England U.K.
232 B5 **West Hamlin** WV U.S.A.
235 F2 **Westhampton** NY U.S.A.
150 E3 **West Harptree** Bath and North East Somerset, England U.K.
235 F1 **West Hartford** CT U.S.A.
173 E3 **Westhausen** Ger.
235 F1 **West Haven** CT U.S.A.
235 E1 **West Haverstraw** NY U.S.A.
234 C2 **West Hazleton** PA U.S.A.
146 F4 **Westhill** Aberdeenshire, Scotland U.K.
172 C2 **Westhofen** Ger.
157 H4 **Westhoffen** France
236 C1 **Westhope** ND U.S.A.
263 F2 **West Ice Shelf** Antarctica
247 F2 **West Indies** N. America
146 □H1 **Westing** Shetland, Scotland U.K.
West Irian prov. Indon. see **Irian Jaya**
84 D2 **West Island** N.T. Austr.
86 □2 **West Island** Cocos Is
235 E2 **West Islip** NY U.S.A.
232 B5 **West Jefferson** OH U.S.A.
164 C3 **Westkapelle** Neth.
West Kazakhstan Oblast admin. div. Kazakh. see **Zapadnyy Kazakhstan**
146 D6 **West Kilbride** North Ayrshire, Scotland U.K.
233 H4 **West Kingston** RI U.S.A.
149 F4 **West Kirby** Merseyside, England U.K.
149 I3 **West Knapton** North Yorkshire, England U.K.
230 C3 **West Lafayette** IN U.S.A.
85 E4 **Westland** Qld Austr.
232 B3 **Westland** MI U.S.A.
78 □3b **West Landing** i. Majuro Marshall Is
151 F3 **West Lavington** Wiltshire, England U.K.
234 C2 **West Lawn** PA U.S.A.
215 F2 **Westleigh** S. Africa
151 I2 **Westleton** Suffolk, England U.K.
232 B6 **West Liberty** KY U.S.A.
232 B4 **West Liberty** OH U.S.A.
146 E6 **West Linton** Scottish Borders, Scotland U.K.
146 C6 **West Loch Tarbert** inlet Scotland U.K.
222 H4 **Westlock** Alta Can.
150 C4 **West Looe** Cornwall, England U.K.
224 D5 **West Lorne** Ont. Can.
146 E6 **West Lothian** admin. div. Scotland U.K.
150 E4 **West Lulworth** Dorset, England U.K.
209 E8 **West Lunga** r. Zambia
West Malaysia pen. Malaysia see **Malaysia, Semenanjung**
165 D3 **Westmalle** Belgium
151 H3 **West Malling** Kent, England U.K.
Westman Islands Iceland see **Vestmannaeyjar**
85 G5 **Westmar** Qld Austr.
266 E4 **West Mariana Basin** sea feature Pacific Ocean
147 D3 **Westmeath** county Rep. of Ireland
237 F5 **West Memphis** AR U.S.A.
151 F3 **West Meon** Hampshire, England U.K.
80 E3 **Westmere** North I. N.Z.
151 H3 **West Mersea** Essex, England U.K.
151 F2 **West Midlands** admin. div. England U.K.
235 D1 **West Milford** NJ U.S.A.
227 F5 **West Millgrove** OH U.S.A.
232 A5 **West Milton** OH U.S.A.
234 B1 **West Milton** PA U.S.A.
234 B3 **Westminster** MD U.S.A.
150 D3 **West Monkton** Somerset, England U.K.
237 E5 **West Monroe** LA U.S.A.
151 F4 **West Moors** Dorset, England U.K.
84 D3 **Westmoreland** Qld Austr.
236 D4 **Westmoreland** KS U.S.A.
246 □ **Westmorland** Jamaica
241 J5 **Westmorland** CA U.S.A.
234 B1 **West Nanticoke** PA U.S.A.
146 E2 **Westness** Orkney, Scotland U.K.
149 F3 **Westnewton** Cumbria, England U.K.
213 F4 **West Nicholson** Zimbabwe
237 D6 **West Nueces** r. TX U.S.A.
235 E1 **West Nyack** NY U.S.A.
81 C6 **Weston** South I. N.Z.
150 E4 **Weston** Dorset, England U.K.
150 E2 **Weston** Staffordshire, England U.K.
235 E1 **Weston** CT U.S.A.
232 B4 **Weston** OH U.S.A.
232 C5 **Weston** WV U.S.A.
215 F2 **Westonaria** S. Africa
150 E3 **Weston-super-Mare** North Somerset, England U.K.
150 E3 **Westonzoyland** Somerset, England U.K.
233 F5 **Westover** MD U.S.A.
231 D7 **West Palm Beach** FL U.S.A.
West Papua prov. Indon. see **Irian Jaya**
237 F4 **West Plains** MO U.S.A.
83 F5 **West Point** pt. Tas. Austr.
240 G2 **West Point** CA U.S.A.
226 D5 **Westpoint** IN U.S.A.
237 F5 **West Point** MS U.S.A.
236 D3 **West Point** NE U.S.A.
233 G4 **West Point** NY U.S.A.
232 C4 **West Point** OH U.S.A.
232 E6 **West Point** VA U.S.A.
231 C5 **West Point Lake** resr Alabama/Georgia U.S.A.
227 I3 **Westport** Ont. Can.
81 C4 **Westport** South I. N.Z.
147 B3 **Westport** Rep. of Ireland
240 F2 **Westport** CA U.S.A.
235 E1 **Westport** CT U.S.A.
233 G2 **Westport** NY U.S.A.
147 B3 **Westport Quay** Rep. of Ireland
149 H3 **West Rainton** Durham, England U.K.
223 K4 **Westray** Man. Can.
146 E2 **Westray** i. Scotland U.K.
146 E2 **Westray Firth** sea chan. Scotland U.K.
235 E1 **West Redding** CT U.S.A.
224 D4 **Westree** Ont. Can.
222 F4 **West Road** r. B.C. Can.
146 F6 **Westruther** Scottish Borders, Scotland U.K.
233 G3 **West Rutland** VT U.S.A.
240 G2 **West Sacramento** CA U.S.A.
232 B4 **West Salem** OH U.S.A.
227 H4 **West Seneca** NY U.S.A.
West Siberian Plain Rus. Fed. see **Zapadno-Sibirskaya Ravnina**
83 F4 **West Sister Island** Tas. Austr.
151 I2 **West Somerton** Norfolk, England U.K.
233 H2 **West Stewartstown** NH U.S.A.
151 G3 **West Sussex** admin. div. England U.K.
164 E1 **West-Terschelling** Neth.
233 G2 **West Topsham** VT U.S.A.
151 G4 **West Town** Hampshire, England U.K.
234 D1 **Westtown** NY U.S.A.
226 B4 **West Union** IA U.S.A.
232 B5 **West Union** OH U.S.A.
232 C5 **West Union** WV U.S.A.
238 E3 **West Valley City** UT U.S.A.
226 D5 **Westville** IN U.S.A.
237 E5 **Westville** OK U.S.A.
232 C5 **West Virginia** state U.S.A.
165 B4 **West-Vlaanderen** prov. Belgium
240 H2 **West Walker** r. NV U.S.A.
150 C3 **Westward Ho!** Devon, England U.K.
151 F4 **West Wellow** Hampshire, England U.K.
146 E5 **West Wemyss** Fife, Scotland U.K.
149 J5 **West Winch** Norfolk, England U.K.
85 G4 **Westwood** Qld Austr.
240 G1 **Westwood** CA U.S.A.
235 D2 **Westwood** NJ U.S.A.
83 F3 **West Wyalong** N.S.W. Austr.
151 G3 **West Wycombe** Buckinghamshire, England U.K.
146 □G1 **West Yell** Shetland, Scotland U.K.
238 E2 **West Yellowstone** MT U.S.A.
234 B3 **West York** PA U.S.A.
149 G4 **West Yorkshire** admin. div. England U.K.
164 D2 **Westzaan** Neth.
93 C4 **Wetar** i. Maluku Indon.
93 C5 **Wetar, Selat** sea chan. Indon.
222 H4 **Wetaskiwin** Alta Can.
211 C6 **Wete** Tanz.
171 C4 **Wethau** Ger.
149 G3 **Wetheral** Cumbria, England U.K.
149 H4 **Wetherby** West Yorkshire, England U.K.
235 F1 **Wethersfield** CT U.S.A.
175 K6 **Wetlina** Pol.
226 D2 **Wetmore** MI U.S.A.
168 D3 **Wetschen** Ger.
169 D5 **Wetter** r. Ger.
169 D5 **Wetter (Hessen)** Ger.
169 C4 **Wetter (Ruhr)** Ger.
165 C3 **Wetteren** Belgium
171 D4 **Wetterzeube** Ger.
171 C4 **Wettin** Ger.
190 D1 **Wettingen** Switz.
169 C3 **Wettringen** Ger.
168 C3 **Wettrup** Ger.
173 F3 **Wettstetten** Ger.
231 C5 **Wetumpka** AL U.S.A.
190 D1 **Wetzikon** Switz.
169 D5 **Wetzlar** Ger.
165 C4 **Wevelgem** Belgium
231 C6 **Wewahitchka** FL U.S.A.
91 J7 **Wewak** P.N.G.
168 E2 **Wewelsfleth** Ger.
237 D5 **Wewoka** OK U.S.A.
147 E4 **Wexford** Rep. of Ireland
147 E4 **Wexford** county Rep. of Ireland
147 E4 **Wexford Bay** Rep. of Ireland
223 J4 **Weyakwin** Sask. Can.
173 F4 **Weyarn** Ger.
226 C3 **Weyauwega** WI U.S.A.
151 G3 **Weybridge** Surrey, England U.K.
223 K5 **Weyburn** Sask. Can.
169 C5 **Weyerbusch** Ger.
179 F3 **Weyer Markt** Austria
157 H4 **Weyersheim** France
169 F3 **Weyhausen** Ger.
168 D3 **Weyhe** Ger.
225 H4 **Weymouth** N.S. Can.
150 E4 **Weymouth** Dorset, England U.K.
233 H3 **Weymouth** MA U.S.A.
234 D3 **Weymouth** NJ U.S.A.
85 E2 **Weymouth, Cape** Qld Austr.
164 F2 **Wezep** Neth.
80 F3 **Whakaki** North I. N.Z.
80 E3 **Whakamaru** North I. N.Z.
80 F3 **Whakapunake** hill North I. N.Z.
Whakaraupō inlet South I. N.Z. see **Lyttelton Harbour**
80 F2 **Whakatane** North I. N.Z.
Whakatipu Kā Tuka r. South I. N.Z. see **Hollyford**
83 G2 **Whalan Creek** r. N.S.W. Austr.
Whale r. Que. Can. see **La Baleine, Rivière à**
222 C3 **Whale Bay** AK U.S.A.
246 C1 **Whale Cay** i. Bahamas
223 M2 **Whale Cove** Nunavut Can.
222 C3 **Whale Pass** AK U.S.A.
149 H4 **Whaley Bridge** Derbyshire, England U.K.
232 E6 **Whaleyville** VA U.S.A.
146 □H1 **Whalsay** i. Scotland U.K.
149 H2 **Whalton** Northumberland, England U.K.
80 E4 **Whangaehu** r. North I. N.Z.
80 E2 **Whangamata** North I. N.Z.
81 D4 **Whangamoa** South I. N.Z.
80 E3 **Whangamomona** North I. N.Z.
80 E2 **Whangaparaoa** North I. N.Z.
80 G3 **Whangara** North I. N.Z.
80 E1 **Whangarei** North I. N.Z.
151 G2 **Whaplode** Lincolnshire, England U.K.
224 E2 **Whapmagoostui** Que. Can.
81 E4 **Wharanui** South I. N.Z.
81 F4 **Whareama** North I. N.Z.
149 H4 **Wharfe** r. England U.K.
227 F2 **Wharncliffe** Ont. Can.
232 C6 **Wharncliffe** WV U.S.A.
234 D2 **Wharton** NJ U.S.A.
237 D6 **Wharton** TX U.S.A.
81 C5 **Whataroa** South I. N.Z.
222 G2 **Wha Ti** N.W.T. Can.
146 D7 **Whauphill** Dumfries and Galloway, Scotland U.K.
240 G2 **Wheatland** CA U.S.A.
238 F3 **Wheatland** WY U.S.A.
227 F4 **Wheatley** Ont. Can.
226 C5 **Wheaton** IL U.S.A.
236 D2 **Wheaton** MN U.S.A.
150 E2 **Wheaton Aston** Staffordshire, England U.K.
234 A3 **Wheaton-Glenmont** MD U.S.A.
150 D3 **Wheddon Cross** Somerset, England U.K.
237 C5 **Wheeler** TX U.S.A.
226 B3 **Wheeler** WI U.S.A.
231 C5 **Wheeler Lake** resr AL U.S.A.
239 F4 **Wheeler Peak** NM U.S.A.
241 J2 **Wheeler Peak** NV U.S.A.
232 B5 **Wheelersburg** OH U.S.A.
240 H4 **Wheeler Springs** CA U.S.A.
232 C4 **Wheeling** WV U.S.A.
261 G3 **Wheelwright** Arg.
149 G3 **Whernside** hill England U.K.
151 F3 **Wherwell** Hampshire, England U.K.
149 H3 **Whickham** Tyne and Wear, England U.K.
150 D4 **Whiddon Down** Devon, England U.K.
147 B5 **Whiddy Island** Rep. of Ireland
86 C4 **Whim Creek** W.A. Austr.
150 D4 **Whimple** Devon, England U.K.
82 B1 **Whinham, Mount** S.A. Austr.
235 D2 **Whippany** NJ U.S.A.
240 F2 **Whispering Pines** CA U.S.A.
222 F5 **Whistler** B.C. Can.
225 K4 **Whitbourne** Nfld. Can.
146 E6 **Whitburn** West Lothian, Scotland U.K.
227 H4 **Whitby** Ont. Can.
149 I3 **Whitby** North Yorkshire, England U.K.
151 G3 **Whitchurch** Buckinghamshire, England U.K.
150 D3 **Whitchurch** Cardiff, Wales U.K.
151 F3 **Whitchurch** Hampshire, England U.K.
150 E2 **Whitchurch** Shropshire, England U.K.
227 H4 **Whitchurch-Stouffville** Ont. Can.
81 C5 **Whitcombe, Mount** South I. N.Z.
224 C3 **White** r. Ont. Can.
222 B2 **White** r. Can./U.S.A.
229 H4 **White** r. AR U.S.A.
237 F5 **White** r. AR U.S.A.
241 M1 **White** r. CO U.S.A.
230 C4 **White** r. IN U.S.A.
226 D4 **White** r. MI U.S.A.
241 J3 **White** r. NV U.S.A.
236 D3 **White** r. SD U.S.A.
233 G3 **White** r. VT U.S.A.
226 B2 **White** r. WI U.S.A.
230 C4 **White, East Fork** r. IN U.S.A.
84 B4 **White, Lake** salt flat N.T. Austr.
237 E4 **White, North Fork** r. MO U.S.A.
149 G2 **Whiteadder Water** r. Scotland U.K.
225 J3 **White Bay** Nfld. Can.
236 C2 **White Butte** mt. ND U.S.A.
241 L3 **White Canyon** UT U.S.A.
147 C5 **Whitechurch** Cork Rep. of Ireland
147 D4 **Whitechurch** Waterford Rep. of Ireland
83 E2 **White Cliffs** N.S.W. Austr.
226 E4 **White Cloud** MI U.S.A.
81 B6 **Whitecoomb** mt. South I. N.Z.
146 E6 **White Coomb** hill Scotland U.K.
222 H4 **Whitecourt** Alta Can.
146 E6 **Whitecraig** East Lothian, Scotland U.K.
147 E2 **Whitecross** Northern Ireland U.K.
234 B1 **White Deer** PA U.S.A.
233 G2 **Whiteface Mountain** NY U.S.A.
233 H2 **Whitefield** NH U.S.A.
227 G2 **Whitefish** Ont. Can.
222 E1 **Whitefish** r. N.W.T. Can.
238 D1 **Whitefish** MT U.S.A.
226 D3 **Whitefish** r. MI U.S.A.
226 D3 **Whitefish Bay** WI U.S.A.
223 J2 **Whitefish Lake** N.W.T. Can.
234 B3 **Whiteford** MD U.S.A.
147 C4 **Whitegate** Clare Rep. of Ireland
147 C5 **Whitegate** Cork Rep. of Ireland
147 B5 **White Hall** Rep. of Ireland
147 D4 **Whitehall** Rep. of Ireland
146 F2 **Whitehall** Orkney, Scotland U.K.
236 F4 **White Hall** IL U.S.A.
234 B3 **White Hall** MD U.S.A.
226 D4 **Whitehall** MI U.S.A.
238 D2 **Whitehall** MT U.S.A.
233 G3 **Whitehall** NY U.S.A.
232 B5 **Whitehall** OH U.S.A.
234 B1 **White Hall** PA U.S.A.
234 C2 **Whitehall** PA U.S.A.
226 B3 **Whitehall** WI U.S.A.
149 F3 **Whitehaven** Cumbria, England U.K.
234 C1 **White Haven** PA U.S.A.
147 F2 **Whitehead** Northern Ireland U.K.
225 I4 **White Hill** hill N.S. Can.
151 G3 **Whitehill** Hampshire, England U.K.
146 F4 **Whitehills** Aberdeenshire, Scotland U.K.
222 C2 **Whitehorse** Y.T. Can.
234 D2 **White Horse** NJ U.S.A.
151 F3 **White Horse, Vale of** val. England U.K.
234 D2 **Whitehouse** NJ U.S.A.
234 D2 **White House Station** NJ U.S.A.
263 D2 **White Island** Antarctica
215 F5 **White Kei** r. S. Africa
87 D5 **White Lake** salt flat W.A. Austr.
234 D1 **White Lake** NY U.S.A.
83 G5 **Whitemark** Tas. Austr.
234 C1 **White Mills** PA U.S.A.
240 H3 **White Mountain Peak** CA U.S.A.
233 H2 **White Mountains** NH U.S.A.
228 G1 **Whitemouth** r. Man. Can.
222 G3 **Whitemud** r. Alta Can.
203 G6 **White Nile** state Sudan
203 G6 **White Nile** r. Sudan/Uganda alt. **Abiad, Bahr el**, alt. **Jebel, Bahr el**
203 G6 **White Nile Dam** Sudan
212 C4 **White Nossob** watercourse Namibia
232 B6 **White Oak** KY U.S.A.
226 E5 **White Pigeon** MI U.S.A.
226 C2 **White Pine** MI U.S.A.
241 J2 **White Pine Range** mts NV U.S.A.
235 E1 **White Plains** NY U.S.A.
146 F4 **Whiterashes** Aberdeenshire, Scotland U.K.
224 C3 **White River** Ont. Can.
241 M5 **Whiteriver** AZ U.S.A.
236 C3 **White River** SD U.S.A.
233 G3 **White River Junction** VT U.S.A.
241 J2 **White River Valley** NV U.S.A.
241 J2 **White Rock Peak** NV U.S.A.
White Russia country Europe see **Belarus**
238 B2 **White Salmon** WA U.S.A.
222 H2 **Whitesand** r. Alta/N.W.T. Can.
223 K5 **Whitesand** r. Sask. Can.
234 D3 **Whitesboro** NJ U.S.A.
233 F3 **Whitesboro** NY U.S.A.
232 B6 **Whitesburg** KY U.S.A.
White Sea Rus. Fed. see **Beloye More**
233 E6 **White Stone** VA U.S.A.
238 E2 **White Sulphur Springs** MT U.S.A.
232 C6 **White Sulphur Springs** WV U.S.A.
234 C1 **Whites Valley** PA U.S.A.
232 C6 **Whitesville** WV U.S.A.
215 H3 **White Umfolozi** r. S. Africa
231 E5 **Whiteville** NC U.S.A.
206 E4 **White Volta** watercourse Burkina/Ghana alt. **Nakambé**, alt. **Nakanbe**, alt. **Volta Blanche**
206 E4 **White Volta** r. Ghana
240 I5 **White Water** CA U.S.A.
241 M2 **Whitewater** CO U.S.A.
226 C4 **Whitewater** WI U.S.A.
239 E5 **Whitewater Baldy** mt. NM U.S.A.
82 B2 **White Well** S.A. Austr.
236 C4 **White Woman Creek** r. KS U.S.A.
85 E4 **Whitewood** Qld Austr.
223 K5 **Whitewood** Sask. Can.
83 F4 **Whitfield** Vic. Austr.
151 I3 **Whitfield** Kent, England U.K.
150 D1 **Whitford** Flintshire, Wales U.K.
146 D7 **Whithorn** Dumfries and Galloway, Scotland U.K.
80 E2 **Whitianga** North I. N.Z.
233 □J2 **Whiting** ME U.S.A.
235 D3 **Whiting** NJ U.S.A.
226 C3 **Whiting** WI U.S.A.
146 C6 **Whiting Bay** North Ayrshire, Scotland U.K.
150 C3 **Whitland** Carmarthenshire, Wales U.K.
149 H2 **Whitley Bay** Tyne and Wear, England U.K.
231 C4 **Whitley City** KY U.S.A.
234 C3 **Whitman Square** NJ U.S.A.
231 D5 **Whitmire** SC U.S.A.
215 G4 **Whitmore** S. Africa
262 Q1 **Whitmore Mountains** Antarctica
151 F2 **Whitnash** Warwickshire, England U.K.
227 H3 **Whitney** Ont. Can.
240 H3 **Whitney, Mount** CA U.S.A.
233 F3 **Whitney Point** NY U.S.A.
150 C4 **Whitsand Bay** England U.K.
151 I3 **Whitstable** Kent, England U.K.
85 G4 **Whitsunday Group** is Qld Austr.
85 G4 **Whitsunday Island** Qld Austr.
85 G4 **Whitsunday Passage** Qld Austr.
Whitsun Island Vanuatu see **Pentecost Island**
227 F3 **Whittemore** MI U.S.A.
240 H5 **Whittier** CA U.S.A.
149 H2 **Whittingham** Northumberland, England U.K.
150 D2 **Whittington** Shropshire, England U.K.
83 F4 **Whittlesea** Vic. Austr.
215 F5 **Whittlesea** S. Africa
151 G2 **Whittlesey** Cambridgeshire, England U.K.
226 B3 **Whittlesey** WI U.S.A.
226 B2 **Whittlesey, Mount** hill WI U.S.A.
83 F3 **Whitton** N.S.W. Austr.
149 G4 **Whitworth** Lancashire, England U.K.
223 J2 **Wholdaia Lake** N.W.T. Can.
241 K5 **Why** AZ U.S.A.
82 D3 **Whyalla** S.A. Austr.
Whydah Benin see **Ouidah**
96 B3 **Wiang Pa Pao** Thai.
96 C3 **Wiang Sa** Thai.
175 K6 **Wiar** r. Pol.
175 J2 **Wiartel** Pol.
224 D4 **Wiarton** Ont. Can.
206 E4 **Wiasi** Ghana
174 F3 **Wiatrowo** Pol.
206 E5 **Wiawso** Ghana
146 A4 **Wiay** i. Scotland U.K.
174 F5 **Wiązów** Pol.
238 F2 **Wibaux** MT U.S.A.
165 C3 **Wichelen** Belgium
237 D4 **Wichita** KS U.S.A.
237 D5 **Wichita** r. TX U.S.A.
237 D5 **Wichita Falls** TX U.S.A.
237 D5 **Wichita Mountains** OK U.S.A.
146 E3 **Wick** Highland, Scotland U.K.
150 E3 **Wick** South Gloucestershire, England U.K.
150 D3 **Wick** Vale of Glamorgan, Wales U.K.
151 G4 **Wick** West Sussex, England U.K.
146 E3 **Wick** r. Scotland U.K.
169 C4 **Wickede** airport Ger.
169 C4 **Wickede (Ruhr)** Ger.
241 K5 **Wickenburg** AZ U.S.A.
87 C7 **Wickepin** W.A. Austr.
237 E5 **Wickes** AR U.S.A.
151 H3 **Wickford** Essex, England U.K.
86 C4 **Wickham** W.A. Austr.
84 B3 **Wickham** r. N.T. Austr.
151 F4 **Wickham** Hampshire, England U.K.
83 E4 **Wickham, Cape** Tas. Austr.
84 B3 **Wickham, Mount** hill N.T. Austr.
151 I2 **Wickham Market** Suffolk, England U.K.
237 F4 **Wickliffe** KY U.S.A.
147 E4 **Wicklow** Rep. of Ireland
147 E3 **Wicklow** county Rep. of Ireland
147 F4 **Wicklow Head** hd Rep. of Ireland
147 E4 **Wicklow Mountains** Rep. of Ireland
174 F1 **Wicko** Pol.
150 E3 **Wickwar** South Gloucestershire, England U.K.
234 B2 **Wiconisco** PA U.S.A.
234 B2 **Wiconisco Creek** r. PA U.S.A.
174 G4 **Widawa** Pol.
174 F4 **Widawa** r. Pol.
175 G4 **Widawka** r. Pol.
85 H5 **Wide Bay** Qld Austr.
150 D4 **Widecombe in the Moor** Devon, England U.K.
146 E2 **Wide Firth** sea chan. Scotland U.K.
263 B2 **Widerøe, Mount** Antarctica
151 H3 **Widford** Hertfordshire, England U.K.
87 D6 **Widgiemooltha** W.A. Austr.
93 D3 **Widi, Kepulauan** is Maluku Indon.
190 E1 **Widnau** Switz.
149 G4 **Widnes** Halton, England U.K.
174 C2 **Widuchowa** Pol.
174 F2 **Więcbork** Pol.
170 D1 **Wieck am Darß** Ger.
175 I2 **Wieczfnia Kościelna** Pol.
169 C5 **Wied** r. Ger.
169 F4 **Wieda** Ger.
171 D5 **Wiederau** Ger.
171 D4 **Wiederitzsch** Ger.
171 F4 **Wiednitz** Ger.
168 D2 **Wiefelstede** Ger.
171 C4 **Wiehe** Ger.
169 D3 **Wiehengebirge** hills Ger.
169 C5 **Wiehl** Ger.
170 E1 **Wiek** Ger.
174 G5 **Większyce** Pol.
175 I2 **Wielbark** Pol.
174 E3 **Wieleń** Pol.
173 F4 **Wielenbach** Ger.
175 H3 **Wielgie** Pol.
174 E3 **Wielichowo** Pol.
175 I6 **Wieliczka** Pol.
175 K2 **Wieliczki** Pol.
174 G2 **Wielka Nieszawka** Pol.
177 H2 **Wielka Racza** mt. Pol./Slovakia
175 K6 **Wielka Rawka** mt. Pol.
174 E5 **Wielka Sowa** mt. Pol.
175 L5 **Wielkie Oczy** Pol.
174 G1 **Wielki Klincz** Pol.
174 F3 **Wielkopolskie** prov. Pol.
175 J6 **Wielopole Skrzyńskie** Pol.
174 G5 **Wielowieś** Pol.
165 C4 **Wielsbeke** Belgium
174 G4 **Wieluń** Pol.
168 E2 **Wiemersdorf** Ger.
179 H2 **Wien** Austria
179 H2 **Wien** land Austria
179 H2 **Wiener Neudorf** Austria
179 H3 **Wiener Neustadt** Austria
168 F3 **Wienhausen** Ger.
175 I4 **Wieniawa** Pol.
174 G3 **Wieniec** Pol.
179 G2 **Wiensberg** mt. Austria
170 C3 **Wiepke** Ger.
175 H6 **Wieprz** Pol.
175 J4 **Wieprz** r. Pol.
143 G4 **Wieprza** r. Pol.
175 K3 **Wiercień Duży** Pol.
164 F2 **Wierden** Neth.
168 F3 **Wieren** Ger.
164 D2 **Wieringermeer Polder** Neth.
164 E2 **Wieringerwerf** Neth.
172 C3 **Wiernsheim** Ger.
174 G4 **Wieruszów** Pol.
175 L4 **Wierzbica** Lubelskie Pol.
175 J4 **Wierzbica** Mazowieckie Pol.
174 F4 **Wierzbica Górna** Pol.
174 G3 **Wierzbinek** Pol.
174 F5 **Wierzbnik** Pol.
175 L2 **Wierzchlesie** Pol.
174 G3 **Wierzchosławice** Pol.
175 I5 **Wierzchosławice** Pol.
174 E2 **Wierzchowo** Pol.
174 G1 **Wierzchucino** Pol.
174 G2 **Wierzyca** r. Pol.
179 G4 **Wies** Austria
173 E4 **Wies** Ger.
171 D5 **Wiesa** Ger.
173 G2 **Wiesau** Ger.
169 D5 **Wiesbaden** Ger.
172 B4 **Wiese** r. Ger.
179 G2 **Wieselburg** Austria
179 H3 **Wiesen** Austria
169 E5 **Wiesen** Ger.
190 E2 **Wiesen** Switz.
171 F3 **Wiesenau** Ger.
171 D3 **Wiesenburg** Ger.
173 G2 **Wiesenfelden** Ger.
172 D3 **Wiesensteig** Ger.
173 G2 **Wiesent** Ger.
173 F2 **Wiesent** r. Ger.
173 F2 **Wiesenthau** Ger.
173 E2 **Wiesentheid** Ger.
173 F2 **Wiesenttal** Ger.
178 C3 **Wiesing** Austria
168 E2 **Wiesle** r. Ger.
172 C2 **Wiesloch** Ger.
179 H3 **Wiesmath** Austria
168 C2 **Wiesmoor** Ger.
234 C2 **Wiessport** PA U.S.A.
168 C3 **Wietmarschen** Ger.
175 I5 **Wietrzychowice** Pol.
168 E3 **Wietze** Ger.
169 E3 **Wietze** r. Ger.
168 E3 **Wietzen** Ger.
168 E3 **Wietzendorf** Ger.
143 H4 **Wieżyca** hill Pol.
149 G4 **Wigan** Greater Manchester, England U.K.
173 E4 **Wiggensbach** Ger.
237 F6 **Wiggins** MS U.S.A.
145 G6 **Wight, Isle of** i. England U.K.
150 E2 **Wigmore** Herefordshire, England U.K.
151 F2 **Wigston** Leicestershire, England U.K.
149 F3 **Wigton** Cumbria, England U.K.
146 D7 **Wigtown** Dumfries and Galloway, Scotland U.K.
146 D7 **Wigtown Bay** Scotland U.K.
164 E3 **Wijchen** Neth.
140 □ **Wijdefjorden** inlet Svalbard
174 E4 **Wijewo** Pol.
164 F2 **Wijhe** Neth.
164 D2 **Wijk aan Zee** Neth.
164 E3 **Wijk bij Duurstede** Neth.
164 E3 **Wijk en Aalburg** Neth.
165 D3 **Wijnegem** Belgium
164 F1 **Wijnjewoude** Neth.
241 K4 **Wikieup** AZ U.S.A.
210 C1 **Wik'ro** Eth.
227 G3 **Wikwemikong** Ont. Can.
190 E1 **Wil** Switz.
175 H6 **Wilamowice** Pol.
236 D3 **Wilber** NE U.S.A.
81 C5 **Wilberforce** r. South I. N.Z.
84 D1 **Wilberforce, Cape** N.T. Austr.
238 C2 **Wilbur** WA U.S.A.
173 E2 **Wilburgstetten** Ger.
237 E5 **Wilburton** OK U.S.A.
83 E2 **Wilcannia** N.S.W. Austr.
232 D4 **Wilcox** PA U.S.A.
Wilczek Land i. Zemlya Frantsa-Iosifa Rus. Fed. see **Zemlya Vil'cheka**
175 H1 **Wilczęta** Pol.
174 G3 **Wilczogóra** Pol.
174 G3 **Wilczyn** Pol.
171 E3 **Wildau** Ger.
172 C3 **Wildbad im Schwarzwald** Ger.
172 C3 **Wildberg** Baden-Württemberg Ger.
170 D3 **Wildberg** Brandenburg Ger.
170 E2 **Wildberg** Mecklenburg-Vorpommern Ger.
240 I2 **Wildcat Peak** NV U.S.A.
215 G4 **Wild Coast** S. Africa
169 F5 **Wildeck-Obersuhl** Ger.
169 F5 **Wildeck-Richelsdorf** Ger.
169 F4 **Wildemann** Ger.
179 H2 **Wildendürnbach** Austria
171 D5 **Wildenfels** Ger.
214 D5 **Wilderness** S. Africa
232 E5 **Wilderness** VA U.S.A.
168 D3 **Wildeshausen** Ger.
169 E5 **Wildflecken** Ger.
226 C1 **Wild Goose** Ont. Can.
222 G4 **Wildhay** r. Alta Can.
190 C2 **Wildhorn** mt. Switz.
239 F6 **Wild Horse Draw** r. TX U.S.A.
236 C3 **Wild Horse Hill** mt. NE U.S.A.
179 G4 **Wildon** Austria
173 E4 **Wildpoldsried** Ger.
236 D2 **Wild Rice** r. MN U.S.A.
236 D2 **Wild Rice** r. ND U.S.A.
178 D3 **Wildseeloder** mt. Austria
178 D2 **Wildshut** Austria
178 B4 **Wildspitze** mt. Austria
222 H4 **Wildwood** Alta Can.
231 D6 **Wildwood** FL U.S.A.
234 D4 **Wildwood** NJ U.S.A.
234 D4 **Wildwood Crest** NJ U.S.A.
236 C4 **Wiley** CO U.S.A.
232 D5 **Wiley Ford** WV U.S.A.
175 J4 **Wilga** Pol.
175 J4 **Wilga** r. Pol.
215 G2 **Wilge** r. Free State S. Africa
215 G1 **Wilge** r. Gauteng/Mpumalanga S. Africa
82 C2 **Wilgena** S.A. Austr.
91 J8 **Wilhelm, Mount** P.N.G.
251 G4 **Wilhelmina Gebergte** mts Suriname
140 □ **Wilhelmøya** i. Svalbard
Wilhelm-Pieck-Stadt Ger. see **Guben**
179 G2 **Wilhelmsburg** Austria
170 E2 **Wilhelmsburg** Ger.
172 D4 **Wilhelmsdorf** Ger.
168 D2 **Wilhelmshaven** Ger.
171 C5 **Wilhelmsthal** Ger.
179 F2 **Wilhering** Austria
173 E2 **Wilhermsdorf** Ger.
113 □2 **Wilingili** i. Addu Atoll Maldives
171 D5 **Wilkau-Haßlau** Ger.
234 C1 **Wilkes-Barre** PA U.S.A.
231 D4 **Wilkesboro** NC U.S.A.
263 I2 **Wilkes Coast** Antarctica
263 I2 **Wilkes Land** reg. Antarctica
223 I4 **Wilkie** Sask. Can.
232 D4 **Wilkinsburg** PA U.S.A.
262 T2 **Wilkins Coast** Antarctica
82 C2 **Wilkinson Lakes** salt flat S.A. Austr.
147 E3 **Wilkinstown** Rep. of Ireland
175 K4 **Wilkołaz Pierwszy** Pol.
175 J4 **Wilków** Pol.
174 F4 **Wilków** Pol.
222 D3 **Will, Mount** B.C. Can.
238 B2 **Willamette** r. OR U.S.A.
150 D4 **Willand** Devon, England U.K.
239 F5 **Willard** NM U.S.A.
232 B4 **Willard** OH U.S.A.
233 F5 **Willards** MD U.S.A.
149 F4 **Willaston** Cheshire, England U.K.
241 M5 **Willcox** AZ U.S.A.
169 E4 **Willebadessen** Ger.
165 D3 **Willebroek** Belgium
164 D3 **Willemstad** Neth.
247 □10 **Willemstad** Curaçao Neth. Antilles
84 B2 **Willeroo** N.T. Austr.
223 I3 **William** r. Sask. Can.
83 E4 **William, Mount** Vic. Austr.
87 B4 **Williambury** W.A. Austr.
82 D2 **William Creek** S.A. Austr.
87 C7 **Williams** W.A. Austr.
85 E4 **Williams** r. Qld Austr.
87 C7 **Williams** r. W.A. Austr.
241 K4 **Williams** AZ U.S.A.
240 F2 **Williams** CA U.S.A.
236 E3 **Williamsburg** IA U.S.A.
232 A6 **Williamsburg** KY U.S.A.
226 E3 **Williamsburg** MI U.S.A.
232 A5 **Williamsburg** OH U.S.A.
232 D4 **Williamsburg** PA U.S.A.
232 E6 **Williamsburg** VA U.S.A.
246 C1 **Williams Island** Bahamas
222 F4 **Williams Lake** B.C. Can.
232 E3 **Williamson** NY U.S.A.
232 B6 **Williamson** WV U.S.A.
230 C3 **Williamsport** IN U.S.A.
232 B5 **Williamsport** OH U.S.A.
227 I5 **Williamsport** PA U.S.A.
227 E4 **Williamston** MI U.S.A.
231 E5 **Williamston** NC U.S.A.
233 G3 **Williamstown** MA U.S.A.
234 D3 **Williamstown** NJ U.S.A.
233 F3 **Williamstown** NY U.S.A.
234 B2 **Williamstown** PA U.S.A.
232 C5 **Williamstown** WV U.S.A.
169 B4 **Willich** Ger.
233 G4 **Willimantic** CT U.S.A.
235 F1 **Willimantic** r. CT U.S.A.
234 D2 **Willingboro** NJ U.S.A.
151 H4 **Willingdon** East Sussex, England U.K.
169 D4 **Willingen (Upland)** Ger.
151 H2 **Willingham** Cambridgeshire, England U.K.
Willingili i. N. Male Maldives see **Villingli**
Willingili i. N. Male Maldives see **Vilingli**
169 E5 **Willingshausen** Ger.
151 F2 **Willington** Derbyshire, England U.K.
190 D1 **Willisau** Switz.
85 G3 **Willis Group** atolls Coral Sea Is Terr. Austr.
259 □ **Willis Islands** S. Georgia
214 C4 **Williston** S. Africa
231 D6 **Williston** FL U.S.A.
236 C1 **Williston** ND U.S.A.
231 D5 **Williston** SC U.S.A.
222 F4 **Williston Lake** B.C. Can.
150 D3 **Williton** Somerset, England U.K.
240 F2 **Willits** CA U.S.A.
236 E2 **Willmar** MN U.S.A.
149 J4 **Willoughby** Lincolnshire, England U.K.
232 C4 **Willoughby** OH U.S.A.
233 G2 **Willoughby, Lake** VT U.S.A.
222 F4 **Willow** r. B.C. Can.
241 J4 **Willow Beach** AZ U.S.A.
223 J5 **Willow Bunch** Sask. Can.
222 H5 **Willow Creek** r. Alta Can.
238 B3 **Willow Creek** CA U.S.A.
238 B2 **Willow Creek** r. OR U.S.A.
241 M1 **Willow Creek** r. UT U.S.A.
234 C3 **Willow Grove** DE U.S.A.
234 C2 **Willow Grove** PA U.S.A.
232 E4 **Willow Hill** PA U.S.A.
222 F2 **Willowlake** r. N.W.T. Can.
214 D5 **Willowmore** S. Africa
84 C4 **Willowra** N.T. Austr.
240 F2 **Willows** CA U.S.A.
237 F4 **Willow Springs** MO U.S.A.
234 B3 **Willow Street** PA U.S.A.
215 G5 **Willowvale** S. Africa
86 F4 **Wills, Lake** salt flat W.A. Austr.
172 B3 **Willstätt** Ger.
82 D3 **Willunga** S.A. Austr.
231 C6 **Wilma** FL U.S.A.
170 E2 **Wilmersdorf** Brandenburg Ger.
171 F4 **Wilmersdorf** Brandenburg Ger.
82 D3 **Wilmington** S.A. Austr.
234 C3 **Wilmington** DE U.S.A.
231 E5 **Wilmington** NC U.S.A.
232 B5 **Wilmington** OH U.S.A.
233 G3 **Wilmington** VT U.S.A.
231 D5 **Wilmington Island** GA U.S.A.
149 G4 **Wilmslow** Cheshire, England U.K.
164 D2 **Wilnis** Neth.
Wilno Lith. see **Vilnius**
169 D5 **Wilnsdorf** Ger.
164 F2 **Wilp** Neth.
171 E4 **Wilsdruff** Ger.
168 E2 **Wilseder Berg** hill Ger.
170 E2 **Wilsickow** Ger.
86 F3 **Wilson** r. W.A. Austr.
Wilson atoll Micronesia see **Ifalik**
236 D4 **Wilson** KS U.S.A.
226 B4 **Wilson** MN U.S.A.
231 E5 **Wilson** NC U.S.A.
232 D3 **Wilson** NY U.S.A.
234 C2 **Wilson** PA U.S.A.
239 F4 **Wilson, Mount** CO U.S.A.
241 J2 **Wilson, Mount** NV U.S.A.
238 B2 **Wilson, Mount** OR U.S.A.
263 K2 **Wilson Hills** Antarctica
240 H3 **Wilsonia** CA U.S.A.
232 E6 **Wilsons** VA U.S.A.
83 F4 **Wilson's Promontory** pen. Vic. Austr.
168 E2 **Wilstedt** Ger.
168 E2 **Wilster** Ger.
168 B3 **Wilsum** Ger.
179 H2 **Wiltersdorf** Austria
171 F4 **Wilthen** Ger.
172 A2 **Wiltingen** Ger.
84 C2 **Wilton** r. N.T. Austr.
151 F3 **Wilton** Wiltshire, England U.K.
235 E1 **Wilton** CT U.S.A.
233 □H2 **Wilton** ME U.S.A.
236 C2 **Wilton** ND U.S.A.
233 H3 **Wilton** NH U.S.A.
150 F3 **Wiltshire** admin. div. England U.K.
165 E5 **Wiltz** Lux.
87 D5 **Wiluna** W.A. Austr.
80 F4 **Wimbledon** North I. N.Z.
151 H2 **Wimblington** Cambridgeshire, England U.K.
151 F4 **Wimborne Minster** Dorset, England U.K.
156 B2 **Wimereux** France
171 C4 **Wimmelburg** Ger.
83 E4 **Wimmera** r. Vic. Austr.
190 C2 **Wimmis** Switz.
179 H3 **Wimpassing** Austria
Wina r. Cameroon see **Vina**
230 C3 **Winamac** IN U.S.A.
215 F3 **Winburg** S. Africa
214 D2 **Wincanton** S. Africa
150 E3 **Wincanton** Somerset, England U.K.
151 F3 **Winchcombe** Gloucestershire, England U.K.
151 H4 **Winchelsea** East Sussex, England U.K.
233 G3 **Winchendon** MA U.S.A.
172 A2 **Wincheringen** Ger.
233 F2 **Winchester** Ont. Can.
81 C6 **Winchester** South I. N.Z.
151 F3 **Winchester** Hampshire, England U.K.
236 F4 **Winchester** IL U.S.A.
230 C3 **Winchester** IN U.S.A.
232 A6 **Winchester** KY U.S.A.
233 G3 **Winchester** NH U.S.A.
231 C5 **Winchester** TN U.S.A.
232 D5 **Winchester** VA U.S.A.
165 E4 **Wincrange** Lux.
220 E3 **Wind** r. Y.T. Can.
238 E3 **Wind** r. WY U.S.A.
175 J1 **Winda** Pol.
82 D2 **Windabout, Lake** salt flat S.A. Austr.
173 F3 **Windach** Ger.
Windau Latvia see **Ventspils**
232 D4 **Windber** PA U.S.A.
168 E1 **Windeby** Ger.
231 D5 **Winder** GA U.S.A.
149 G3 **Windermere** Cumbria, England U.K.
149 G3 **Windermere** l. England U.K.
172 B2 **Windesheim** Ger.
234 C2 **Windgap** PA U.S.A.
169 C5 **Windhagen** Ger.
222 C3 **Windham** AK U.S.A.
235 F1 **Windham** CT U.S.A.
232 C4 **Windham** OH U.S.A.
169 F4 **Windhausen** Ger.
212 C4 **Windhoek** Namibia
221 I4 **Windigo** r. Ont. Can.
179 G2 **Windigsteig** Austria
173 G2 **Windischeschenbach** Ger.
179 F3 **Windischgarsten** Austria

Windlestraw Law to Xinhua
380

146 F6 Windlestraw Law hill Scotland U.K.
148 C4 Windmill Rep. of Ireland
239 F5 Wind Mountain NM U.S.A.
236 E3 Windom MN U.S.A.
85 E5 Windorah Qld Austr.
173 H3 Windorf Ger.
241 M4 Window Rock AZ U.S.A.
232 C5 Wind Ridge PA U.S.A.
238 E3 Wind River Range mts WY U.S.A.
151 F3 Windrush r. England U.K.
173 E2 Windsbach Ger.
83 G3 Windsor N.S.W. Austr.
225 K3 Windsor Nfld. Can.
225 H4 Windsor N.S. Can.
224 D5 Windsor Ont. Can.
225 F4 Windsor Que. Can.
151 G3 Windsor Windsor and Maidenhead, England U.K.
233 G4 Windsor CT U.S.A.
231 E4 Windsor NC U.S.A.
234 D2 Windsor NJ U.S.A.
233 F3 Windsor NY U.S.A.
234 B3 Windsor PA U.S.A.
232 E6 Windsor VA U.S.A.
233 G3 Windsor VT U.S.A.
151 G3 Windsor and Maidenhead admin. div. England U.K.
233 G4 Windsor Locks CT U.S.A.
214 E3 Windsorton S. Africa
247 G4 Windward Islands Caribbean Sea
Windward Islands Arch. de la Société Fr. Polynesia see Vent, Îles du
246 D3 Windward Passage Cuba/Haiti
87 B7 Windy Harbour W.A. Austr.
231 C5 Winfield AL U.S.A.
237 D4 Winfield KS U.S.A.
232 C5 Winfield WV U.S.A.
150 E3 Winford North Somerset, England U.K.
151 G3 Wing Buckinghamshire, England U.K.
149 H3 Wingate Durham, England U.K.
84 B2 Wingate Mountains hills N.T. Austr.
235 E1 Wingdale NY U.S.A.
83 G2 Wingen N.S.W. Austr.
165 C3 Wingene Belgium
157 H4 Wingen-sur-Moder France
169 F4 Wingerode Ger.
83 H2 Wingham N.S.W. Austr.
224 D5 Wingham Ont. Can.
151 I3 Wingham Kent, England U.K.
156 C2 Wingles France
168 E2 Wingst Ger.
173 G3 Winhöring Ger.
86 D4 Winifred, Lake salt flat W.A. Austr.
261 E5 Winifreda Arg.
224 C2 Winisk Ont. Can.
224 C2 Winisk r. Ont. Can.
214 B5 Winkelhaaks r. S. Africa
173 F2 Winkelhaid Ger.
241 L5 Winkelman AZ U.S.A.
215 F2 Winkelpos S. Africa
168 D3 Winkelsett Ger.
151 G3 Winkfield Bracknell Forest, England U.K.
173 G2 Winklarn Ger.
150 D4 Winkleigh Devon, England U.K.
223 L5 Winkler Man. Can.
178 D4 Winklern Austria
179 F3 Winklern bei Oberwölz Austria
238 B2 Winlock WA U.S.A.
84 B5 Winnalls Ridge N.T. Austr.
206 E5 Winneba Ghana
236 E3 Winnebago MN U.S.A.
226 C3 Winneconne WI U.S.A.
238 C3 Winnemucca NV U.S.A.
172 D3 Winnenden Ger.
236 C3 Winner SD U.S.A.
151 G3 Winnersh Wokingham, England U.K.
168 E1 Winnert Ger.
238 E2 Winnett MT U.S.A.
237 E6 Winnfield LA U.S.A.
175 I3 Winnica Pol.
237 E6 Winnie TX U.S.A.
87 B4 Winning W.A. Austr.
169 C5 Winningen Rheinland-Pfalz Ger.
171 C4 Winningen Sachsen-Anhalt Ger.
223 L5 Winnipeg Man. Can.
223 L5 Winnipeg r. Man./Ont. Can.
223 L5 Winnipeg, Lake Man. Can.
223 L5 Winnipegosis Man. Can.
223 K4 Winnipegosis, Lake Man. Can.
237 F5 Winnsboro LA U.S.A.
231 D5 Winnsboro SC U.S.A.
237 E5 Winnsboro TX U.S.A.
172 B2 Winnweiler Ger.
241 L4 Winona AZ U.S.A.
226 C2 Winona MI U.S.A.
226 B3 Winona MN U.S.A.
237 F4 Winona MO U.S.A.
237 F5 Winona MS U.S.A.
233 G2 Winooski VT U.S.A.
233 G2 Winooski r. VT U.S.A.
164 G1 Winschoten Neth.
150 E3 Winscombe North Somerset, England U.K.
168 E3 Winsen (Aller) Ger.
168 F2 Winsen (Luhe) Ger.
149 G4 Winsford Cheshire, England U.K.
174 E4 Wińsko Pol.
150 E3 Winsley Wiltshire, England U.K.
151 G3 Winslow Buckinghamshire, England U.K.
241 L4 Winslow AZ U.S.A.
233 □I2 Winslow ME U.S.A.
234 D3 Winslow NJ U.S.A.
233 G4 Winsted CT U.S.A.
149 H3 Winston Durham, England U.K.
231 D4 Winston-Salem NC U.S.A.
164 E1 Winsum Friesland Neth.
164 F1 Winsum Groningen Neth.
226 B3 Winter WI U.S.A.
169 D4 Winterberg Ger.
215 F5 Winterberg mts S. Africa
150 E3 Winterbourne South Gloucestershire, England U.K.
150 E4 Winterbourne Abbas Dorset, England U.K.
170 C3 Winterfeld Ger.
233 □I2 Winter Harbor ME U.S.A.
231 D6 Winter Haven FL U.S.A.
172 D3 Winterlingen Ger.
231 D6 Winter Park FL U.S.A.
233 □I2 Winterport ME U.S.A.
240 G2 Winters CA U.S.A.
237 D6 Winters TX U.S.A.
171 D4 Wintersdorf Ger.
236 E3 Winterset IA U.S.A.
234 B3 Winters Run r. MD U.S.A.
234 B3 Winterstown PA U.S.A.
164 F3 Winterswijk Neth.
190 D1 Winterthur Switz.
215 G3 Winterton S. Africa
149 I4 Winterton North Lincolnshire, England U.K.
215 G1 Winterveld S. Africa
233 □I1 Winterville ME U.S.A.
235 F1 Winthrop CT U.S.A.
233 □I2 Winthrop ME U.S.A.
85 E4 Winton Qld Austr.
81 B7 Winton South I. N.Z.
149 G3 Winton Cumbria, England U.K.
231 E4 Winton NC U.S.A.
172 A2 Wintrich Ger.
157 H4 Wintzenheim France
151 G2 Winwick Cambridgeshire, England U.K.
169 E4 Winzenburg Ger.
179 H3 Winzendorf Austria
173 H3 Winzer Ger.
171 C4 Wipper r. Ger.
169 F4 Wipperdorf Ger.
169 C4 Wipperfürth Ger.
168 C3 Wippingen Ger.
171 C4 Wippra Kurort Ger.
168 C2 Wirdumer (Wirdum) Ger.
169 C5 Wirges Ger.
149 H4 Wirksworth Derbyshire, England U.K.
82 D3 Wirrabara S.A. Austr.
149 F4 Wirral pen. England U.K.
82 D2 Wirraminna S.A. Austr.
82 E4 Wirrega S.A. Austr.
82 C2 Wirrida, Lake salt flat S.A. Austr.
82 C3 Wirrulla S.A. Austr.
171 C5 Wirsberg Ger.
78 □4a Wisas i. Chuuk Micronesia
151 H2 Wisbech Cambridgeshire, England U.K.
233 □I2 Wiscasset ME U.S.A.
168 E2 Wischhafen Ger.
226 B4 Wisconsin r. WI U.S.A.
236 F2 Wisconsin state U.S.A.
226 C4 Wisconsin, Lake WI U.S.A.
226 C4 Wisconsin Dells WI U.S.A.
226 C3 Wisconsin Rapids WI U.S.A.
232 B6 Wise VA U.S.A.
146 E6 Wishaw North Lanarkshire, Scotland U.K.
236 D2 Wishek ND U.S.A.
210 F3 Wisil Dabarow Somalia
149 H3 Wiske r. England U.K.
175 I3 Wiskitki Pol.
174 G6 Wisła Pol.
143 H4 Wisła r. Pol.
175 I5 Wiślica Pol.
175 K5 Wisłok r. Pol.
175 J5 Wisłoka r. Pol.
170 C2 Wismar Ger.
237 F6 Wisner LA U.S.A.
175 K3 Wiśniew Pol.
175 I2 Wiśniewo Pol.
175 I6 Wiśniowa Pol.
156 B2 Wissant France
157 H3 Wissembourg France
169 C5 Wissen Ger.
150 E2 Wistanstow Shropshire, England U.K.
222 E4 Wistaria B.C. Can.
149 G4 Wistaston Cheshire, England U.K.
168 E2 Wistedt Ger.
175 K6 Wisznia r. Pol.
174 F4 Wisznia Mała Pol.
175 L4 Wisznice Pol.
215 G1 Witbank S. Africa
214 C2 Witdraai S. Africa
151 H3 Witham Essex, England U.K.
151 H2 Witham r. England U.K.
233 G2 Witherbee NY U.S.A.
150 D4 Witheridge Devon, England U.K.
149 J4 Withernsea East Riding of Yorkshire, England U.K.
231 D6 Withlacoochee r. FL U.S.A.
231 D6 Withlacoochee r. FL U.S.A.
215 G2 Witkoppies mt. S. Africa
174 F3 Witkowo Wielkopolskie Pol.
174 D2 Witkowo Zachodniopomorskie Pol.
151 G3 Witley Surrey, England U.K.
164 E1 Witmarsum Neth.
215 E5 Witmos S. Africa
215 G1 Witnek S. Africa
151 F3 Witney Oxfordshire, England U.K.
174 C3 Witnica Pol.
175 H3 Witonia Pol.
174 F2 Witosław Pol.
214 E3 Witput S. Africa
215 H1 Witrivier S. Africa
156 E3 Witry-lès-Reims France
168 D1 Wittdün Ger.
214 D5 Witteberg mt. E. Cape S. Africa
215 G3 Witteberg mt. Free State S. Africa
214 C5 Witteberge mts S. Africa
157 H5 Wittelsheim France
169 C4 Witten Ger.
172 D4 Wittenbach Switz.
Wittenberg Ger. see Lutherstadt Wittenberg
226 C3 Wittenberg WI U.S.A.
170 C3 Wittenberge Ger.
170 C2 Wittenburg Ger.
170 C2 Wittenförden Ger.
170 E1 Wittenhagen Ger.
157 H5 Wittenheim France
86 C4 Wittenoom W.A. Austr.
Wittenoom Gorge W.A. Austr. see Wittenoom
151 G2 Wittering Peterborough, England U.K.
171 D5 Wittgensdorf Ger.
95 G1 Witti, Banjaran mts Sabah Malaysia
173 G3 Wittibreut Ger.
171 F4 Wittichenau Ger.
172 D2 Wittighausen Ger.
168 F3 Wittingen Ger.
173 E3 Wittislingen Ger.
172 A2 Wittlich Ger.
234 B4 Wittman MD U.S.A.
169 F3 Wittmar Ger.
168 C2 Wittmund Ger.
149 H3 Witton Gilbert Durham, England U.K.
170 E1 Wittow pen. Ger.
170 D2 Wittstock Ger.
212 C4 Witvlei Namibia
215 F2 Witwatersberg mts S. Africa
215 F2 Witwatersrand mts S. Africa
169 E4 Witzenhausen Ger.
168 F2 Witzhave Ger.
170 C2 Witzin Ger.
168 D1 Witzwort Ger.
150 D3 Wiveliscombe Somerset, England U.K.
151 H3 Wivenhoe Essex, England U.K.
175 K1 Wiżajny Pol.
156 C2 Wizernes France
175 K2 Wizna Pol.
175 I3 Wkra r. Pol.
174 G3 Władysławów Pol.
143 H4 Władysławowo Pol.
174 D4 Wleń Pol.
175 H3 Włocławek Pol.
175 L4 Włodawa Pol.
175 L4 Włodawka r. Pol.
175 H5 Włodowice Pol.
174 F5 Włodzienin Pol.
175 H4 Włodzimierzów Pol.
174 E4 Włoszakowice Pol.
175 H5 Włoszczowa Pol.
170 C2 Wöbbelin Ger.
Wobkent Uzbek. see Vabkent
233 □H2 Woburn Que. Can.
151 G3 Woburn Bedfordshire, England U.K.
151 G2 Woburn Sands Milton Keynes, England U.K.
83 F4 Wodonga Vic. Austr.
175 J3 Wodynie Pol.
175 H4 Wodzierady Pol.
175 I5 Wodzisław Pol.
174 G5 Wodzisław Śląski Pol.
164 D2 Woerden Neth.
157 H4 Wœrth France
157 F3 Wœvre, Forêt de for. France
164 E2 Wognum Neth.
190 D1 Wohlen Aargau Switz.
190 C2 Wohlen Bern Switz.
171 C4 Wohlmirstedt Ger.
263 A2 Wohlthat Mountains Antarctica
168 F2 Wohltorf Ger.
169 D5 Wohra r. Ger.
168 E1 Wöhrden Ger.
175 K4 Wohyń Pol.
157 G3 Woippy France
175 J6 Wojaszówka Pol.
175 J5 Wojciechowice Pol.
175 K4 Wojcieszków Pol.
174 D5 Wojcieszów Pol.
174 G3 Wójcin Pol.
78 □3b Woje Majuro i. Majuro Marshall Is
Wōjjā atoll Marshall Is see Wotje
175 H5 Wojkowice Pol.
175 I6 Wojnicz Pol.
174 F2 Wojnowo Pol.
175 L5 Wojsławice Pol.
175 L5 Wojsławka r. Pol.
91 H8 Wokam i. Indon.
100 D3 Woken r. China
117 H4 Wokha Nagaland India
151 G3 Woking Surrey, England U.K.
151 G3 Wokingham Wokingham, England U.K.
151 G3 Wokingham admin. div. England U.K.
170 E2 Wokuhl Ger.
175 H3 Wola Pol.
175 J4 Wola Mysłowska Pol.
175 I4 Wolanów Pol.
175 L4 Wola Uhruska Pol.
175 I3 Wola Wierzbowska Pol.
175 H4 Wolbórz Pol.
175 H5 Wolbrom Pol.
235 F1 Wolcott CT U.S.A.
226 D5 Wolcott IN U.S.A.
232 E3 Wolcott NY U.S.A.
233 G2 Wolcott VT U.S.A.
226 E5 Wolcottville IN U.S.A.
174 G4 Wołczyn Pol.
170 E2 Woldegk Ger.
164 G1 Woldendorp Neth.
149 I3 Wold Newton East Riding of Yorkshire, England U.K.
Wolea atoll Micronesia see Woleai
91 J5 Woleai atoll Micronesia
208 A4 Woleu-Ntem prov. Gabon
222 C2 Wolf r. Y.T. Can.
237 F5 Wolf r. TN U.S.A.
226 C3 Wolf r. WI U.S.A.
250 □ Wolf, Volcán vol. Islas Galápagos Ecuador
172 C3 Wolfach Ger.
238 D2 Wolf Creek MT U.S.A.
238 B3 Wolf Creek OR U.S.A.
237 D4 Wolf Creek r. OK U.S.A.
233 □H3 Wolfeboro NH U.S.A.
172 D4 Wolfegg Ger.
171 D4 Wolfen Ger.
169 F3 Wolfenbüttel Ger.
169 D5 Wölfersheim Ger.
179 E3 Wolfgangsee l. Austria
169 E4 Wolfhagen Ger.
169 F5 Wölfis Ger.
Wolf Island Islas Galápagos Ecuador see Wenman, Isla
226 D4 Wolf Lake MI U.S.A.
179 G2 Wolfpassing Austria
238 F1 Wolf Point MT U.S.A.
173 E2 Wolframs-Eschenbach Ger.
173 F4 Wolfratshausen Ger.
179 F4 Wolfsberg Austria
169 F3 Wolfsburg Ger.
172 B2 Wolfstein Ger.
225 H4 Wolfville N.S. Can.
170 E1 Wolgast Ger.
190 D1 Wolhusen Switz.
175 L5 Wolica r. Pol.
174 C2 Wolin Pol.
174 C2 Wolin i. Pol.
175 H3 Wólka Pol.
175 K4 Wólka Pol.
175 L3 Wólka Dobryńska Pol.
171 E5 Wolkenstein Ger.
179 H2 Wolkersdorf Austria
169 F4 Wolkramshausen Ger.
151 G2 Wollaston Northamptonshire, England U.K.
259 D9 Wollaston, Islas is Chile
223 K3 Wollaston Lake Sask. Can.
223 K3 Wollaston Lake l. Sask. Can.
220 G3 Wollaston Peninsula N.W.T./Nunavut Can.
190 D1 Wollerau Switz.
83 G3 Wollongong N.S.W. Austr.
215 E2 Wolmaransstad S. Africa
171 C4 Wolmirsleben Ger.
171 C3 Wolmirstedt Ger.
173 F3 Wolnzach Ger.
175 J3 Wołomin Pol.
174 E4 Wołów Pol.
172 D2 Wolpertshausen Ger.
172 D4 Wolpertswende Ger.
169 E3 Wölpinghausen Ger.
169 F3 Wolsdorf Ger.
82 E4 Wolseley S.A. Austr.
214 B5 Wolseley S. Africa
236 D2 Wolsey SD U.S.A.
149 H3 Wolsingham Durham, England U.K.
151 F2 Wolston Warwickshire, England U.K.
174 E3 Wolsztyn Pol.
171 E3 Woltersdorf Brandenburg Ger.
171 E3 Woltersdorf Brandenburg Ger.
170 C3 Woltersdorf Niedersachsen Ger.
169 E4 Woltershausen Ger.
164 F2 Wolvega Neth.
150 E2 Wolverhampton West Midlands, England U.K.
226 E3 Wolverine MI U.S.A.
215 E5 Wolwefontein S. Africa
215 E3 Wolwespruit S. Africa
94 A1 Wolya r. Indon.
150 E2 Wombourne Staffordshire, England U.K.
149 H4 Wombwell South Yorkshire, England U.K.
234 B2 Womelsdorf PA U.S.A.
164 E1 Wommels Neth.
172 B2 Womrather Höhe hill Ger.
84 D3 Wonarah N.T. Austr.
85 G5 Wondai Qld Austr.
165 C3 Wondelgem Belgium
215 G1 Wonderfontein S. Africa
215 F2 Wonderkop S. Africa
215 F3 Wonderkop mt. S. Africa
215 F1 Wondermere S. Africa
173 G1 Wondreb r. Ger.
83 F2 Wongalarroo Lake salt l. N.S.W. Austr.
87 C6 Wongan Hills W.A. Austr.
117 G4 Wong Chhu r. Bhutan
109 □ Wong Chuk Hang H.K. China
109 □ Wong Leng hill H.K. China
101 C5 Wŏnju S. Korea
95 E4 Wonogiri Jawa Tengah Indon.
95 E4 Wonosari Indon.
95 E4 Wonosobo Jawa Tengah Indon.
222 F3 Wonowon B.C. Can.
101 C5 Wŏnsan N. Korea
173 F2 Wonsees Ger.
151 F3 Wonston Hampshire, England U.K.
83 F4 Wonthaggi Vic. Austr.
87 C5 Wonyulgunna, Mount hill W.A. Austr.
151 G3 Wooburn Buckinghamshire, England U.K.
82 D2 Woocalla S.A. Austr.
222 A2 Wood, Mount Y.T. Can.
84 D2 Woodah, Isle i. N.T. Austr.
231 D6 Woodbine GA U.S.A.
234 A3 Woodbine MD U.S.A.
234 D3 Woodbine NJ U.S.A.
226 C3 Woodboro WI U.S.A.
81 D4 Woodbourne South I. N.Z.
234 D1 Woodbourne NY U.S.A.
151 I2 Woodbridge Suffolk, England U.K.
235 E1 Woodbridge CT U.S.A.
235 D2 Woodbridge NJ U.S.A.
232 E5 Woodbridge VA U.S.A.
83 H2 Woodburn N.S.W. Austr.
226 E5 Woodburn IN U.S.A.
238 B2 Woodburn OR U.S.A.
235 E1 Woodbury CT U.S.A.
226 E4 Woodbury MI U.S.A.
234 C3 Woodbury NJ U.S.A.
234 C3 Woodbury Heights NJ U.S.A.
84 C3 Woodcock, Mount hill N.T. Austr.
151 F3 Woodcote Oxfordshire, England U.K.
83 H2 Woodenbong N.S.W. Austr.
147 E4 Woodenbridge Rep. of Ireland
83 F4 Woodend Vic. Austr.
81 B7 Woodend South I. N.Z.
81 D5 Woodend South I. N.Z.
147 C3 Woodford Rep. of Ireland
240 H2 Woodfords CA U.S.A.
149 I4 Woodhall Spa Lincolnshire, England U.K.
151 G4 Woodingdean Brighton and Hove, England U.K.
240 H3 Woodlake CA U.S.A.
240 G2 Woodland CA U.S.A.
233 □J2 Woodland ME U.S.A.
238 B2 Woodland WA U.S.A.
234 B4 Woodland Beach MD U.S.A.
239 F4 Woodland Park CO U.S.A.
94 □ Woodlands Sing.
91 L8 Woodlark Island P.N.G.
234 B3 Woodlawn MD U.S.A.
151 G3 Woodley Wokingham, England U.K.
234 C3 Woodlyn PA U.S.A.
149 I4 Woodmansey East Riding of Yorkshire, England U.K.
149 G4 Woodplumpton Lancashire, England U.K.
223 L5 Woodridge Man. Can.
234 D1 Woodridge NY U.S.A.
82 B1 Woodroffe, Mount S.A. Austr.
238 E3 Woodruff UT U.S.A.
226 C3 Woodruff WI U.S.A.
84 C3 Woods, Lake salt flat N.T. Austr.
228 H1 Woods, Lake of the Can./U.S.A.
232 C5 Woodsfield OH U.S.A.
233 H4 Woods Hole MA U.S.A.
83 F4 Woodside Vic. Austr.
234 C3 Woodside DE U.S.A.
83 G3 Woodstock N.S.W. Austr.
85 F3 Woodstock Qld Austr.
225 H4 Woodstock N.B. Can.
224 D5 Woodstock Ont. Can.
151 F3 Woodstock Oxfordshire, England U.K.
226 C4 Woodstock IL U.S.A.
232 D5 Woodstock VA U.S.A.
233 G3 Woodstock VT U.S.A.
147 D4 Woodstown Rep. of Ireland
234 C3 Woodstown NJ U.S.A.
233 G2 Woodsville NH U.S.A.
151 I2 Woodton Norfolk, England U.K.
147 E3 Woodtown Rep. of Ireland
227 H3 Woodville Ont. Can.
80 E4 Woodville North I. N.Z.
237 F6 Woodville MS U.S.A.
232 B4 Woodville OH U.S.A.
237 E6 Woodville TX U.S.A.
237 D4 Woodward OK U.S.A.
240 H4 Woody CA U.S.A.
150 E2 Woofferton Shropshire, England U.K.
150 E4 Wool Dorset, England U.K.
150 C3 Woolacombe Devon, England U.K.
84 C2 Woolen r. N.T. Austr.
149 G2 Wooler Northumberland, England U.K.
85 E4 Woolgar r. Qld Austr.
83 H2 Woolgoolga N.S.W. Austr.
83 H2 Wooli N.S.W. Austr.
84 C4 Woolla Downs N.T. Austr.
262 W1 Woollard, Mount Antarctica
82 D2 Wooltana S.A. Austr.
232 C6 Woolwine VA U.S.A.
87 D7 Woolyeenyer Hill hill W.A. Austr.
82 D2 Woomera S.A. Austr.
233 H3 Woonsocket RI U.S.A.
236 D2 Woonsocket SD U.S.A.
85 G5 Woorabinda Qld Austr.
87 B5 Wooramel r. W.A. Austr.
232 C4 Wooster OH U.S.A.
151 G2 Wootton Bedfordshire, England U.K.
151 F3 Wootton Bassett Wiltshire, England U.K.
210 D2 Woqooyi Galbeed admin. reg. Somalia
190 C2 Worb Switz.
85 E2 Worbody Point Qld Austr.
214 B5 Worcester S. Africa
150 E2 Worcester Worcestershire, England U.K.
233 H3 Worcester MA U.S.A.
233 F3 Worcester NY U.S.A.
150 E2 Worcestershire admin. div. England U.K.
179 H2 Wördern Austria
150 E2 Worfield Shropshire, England U.K.
178 D3 Wörgl Austria
173 E4 Woringen Ger.
149 F3 Workington Cumbria, England U.K.
149 H4 Worksop Nottinghamshire, England U.K.
164 E2 Workum Neth.
238 F2 Worland WY U.S.A.
171 D4 Wörlitz Ger.
165 F5 Wormeldange Lux.
164 D2 Wormer Neth.
156 C2 Wormhout France
146 F5 Wormit Fife, Scotland U.K.
172 C2 Worms Ger.
173 E3 Wörnitz r. Ger.
206 D4 Worofla Côte d'Ivoire
151 G3 Worplesdon Surrey, England U.K.
168 D2 Worpswede Ger.
172 C2 Wörrstadt Ger.
179 F3 Wörschach Austria
165 D3 Wortel Belgium
173 F3 Wörth Ger.
151 G3 Worth West Sussex, England U.K.
172 D2 Wörth am Main Ger.
172 C2 Wörth am Rhein Ger.
173 G2 Wörth an der Donau Ger.
173 G3 Wörth an der Isar Ger.
151 G4 Worthing West Sussex, England U.K.
236 E3 Worthington MN U.S.A.
232 B4 Worthington OH U.S.A.
234 B3 Worton MD U.S.A.
266 G6 Wotje atoll Marshall Is
150 E3 Wotton-under-Edge Gloucestershire, England U.K.
93 B3 Wotu Sulawesi Selatan Indon.
164 E2 Woudenberg Neth.
164 D3 Woudrichem Neth.
164 E2 Woudsend Neth.
151 G2 Woughton on the Green Milton Keynes, England U.K.
236 C3 Wounded Knee SD U.S.A.
207 H5 Wouri r. Cameroon
157 H3 Woustviller France
164 D3 Wouw Neth.
85 G4 Wowan Qld Austr.
93 B4 Wowoni i. Indon.
175 H5 Woźniki Pol.
149 I4 Wragby Lincolnshire, England U.K.
Wrangel Island Rus. Fed. see Vrangelya, Ostrov
220 E4 Wrangell AK U.S.A.
220 C4 Wrangell Mountains AK U.S.A.
149 J4 Wrangle Lincolnshire, England U.K.
146 C3 Wrath, Cape Scotland U.K.
236 C3 Wray CO U.S.A.
151 F2 Wreake r. England U.K.
Wrecsam Wrexham, Wales U.K. see Wrexham
174 G5 Wręczyca Wielka Pol.
170 D2 Wredenhagen Ger.
149 I3 Wrelton North Yorkshire, England U.K.
168 D2 Wremen Ger.
231 D5 Wrens GA U.S.A.
168 F3 Wrestedt Ger.
169 D4 Wrexen (Diemelstadt) Ger.
150 E1 Wrexham Wrexham, Wales U.K.
150 E1 Wrexham admin. div. Wales U.K.
81 B7 Wreys Bush South I. N.Z.
168 F2 Wriedel Ger.
170 F3 Wriezen Ger.
92 C4 Wright Phil.
238 F3 Wright WY U.S.A.
241 L6 Wrightson, Mount AZ U.S.A.
234 D2 Wrightstown PA U.S.A.
226 C3 Wrightstown WI U.S.A.
231 D5 Wrightsville GA U.S.A.
234 B2 Wrightsville PA U.S.A.
240 I4 Wrightwood CA U.S.A.
222 F2 Wrigley N.W.T. Can.
232 B5 Wrigley KY U.S.A.
150 E3 Wrington North Somerset, England U.K.
168 E2 Wrist Ger.
151 H3 Writtle Essex, England U.K.
174 G4 Wróblew Pol.
174 F4 Wrocław Pol.
168 E1 Wrohm Ger.
175 K1 Wronki Warmińsko-Mazurskie Pol.
174 E3 Wronki Wielkopolskie Pol.
175 K3 Wrotnów Pol.
151 F3 Wroughton Swindon, England U.K.
174 G3 Wrząielka Pol.
175 J4 Wrzelowiec Pol.
174 F1 Wrzeście Pol.
174 F3 Września Pol.
174 F3 Wrześnica r. Pol.
175 J5 Wschodnia r. Pol.
174 E4 Wschowa Pol.
Wu'an Fujian China see Changtai
107 G4 Wu'an Hebei China
87 C6 Wubin W.A. Austr.
107 F4 Wubu Shaanxi China
107 I2 Wuchagou Nei Mongol China
100 C3 Wuchang Heilong. China
109 E2 Wuchang Hubei China
109 F2 Wucheng Anhui China
Wuchow Guangxi China see Wuzhou
108 D4 Wuchuan Guangdong China
108 C2 Wuchuan Guizhou China
107 F3 Wuchuan Nei Mongol China
106 E4 Wuda Nei Mongol China
107 H3 Wudan Nei Mongol China
107 I4 Wudao Liaoning China
107 H4 Wudi Shandong China
207 H4 Wudil Nigeria
108 B3 Wuding Yunnan China
107 F4 Wuding r. China
82 C3 Wudinna S.A. Austr.
108 C1 Wudu Gansu China
108 D2 Wufeng Hubei China
Wufeng Yunnan China see Zhenxiong
108 D3 Wugang Hunan China
107 F5 Wugong Shaanxi China
106 E4 Wuhai Nei Mongol China
109 E2 Wuhan Hubei China
109 F1 Wuhe Anhui China
109 F2 Wuhu Anhui China
109 F2 Wuhu Anhui China
109 E4 Wuhua Guangdong China
109 G2 Wujiang Jiangsu China
108 C2 Wu Jiang r. China
Wujin Jiangsu China see Changzhou
Wujin Sichuan China see Xinjin
207 H5 Wukari Nigeria
171 C4 Wulfen Ger.
170 D2 Wulfersdorf Ger.
169 F5 Wülfershausen an der Saale Ger.
168 F2 Wulfsen Ger.
169 F4 Wulften Ger.
108 B2 Wulian Feng mts Yunnan China
108 B3 Wuliang Shan mts Yunnan China
108 D4 Wuli Jiang r. China
108 D2 Wuling Shan mts China
170 D3 Wulkau Ger.
179 H2 Wullersdorf Austria
108 C2 Wulong Chongqing China
107 I4 Wulong r. China
Wulongji Henan China see Huaibin
168 D2 Wulsbüttel Ger.
207 H5 Wum Cameroon
108 B3 Wumeng Shan mts Yunnan China
108 D4 Wuming Guangxi China
168 D2 Wümme r. Ger.
108 B2 Wungda Sichuan China
109 E2 Wuning Jiangxi China
169 D4 Wünnenberg Ger.
171 D5 Wünschendorf Ger.
171 E3 Wünsdorf Ger.
171 D5 Wunsiedel Ger.
169 E3 Wunstorf Ger.
96 A2 Wuntho Myanmar
109 F3 Wuping Fujian China
169 C4 Wuppertal Ger.
214 B5 Wuppertal S. Africa
107 F4 Wuqi Shaanxi China
107 G4 Wuqiang Hebei China
107 H4 Wuqiao Hebei China
107 H4 Wuqing Tianjin China
Wuquan Henan China see Wuyang
87 C6 Wuranga W.A. Austr.
173 F3 Würm r. Ger.
173 G3 Wurmannsquick Ger.
172 C3 Wurmlingen Ger.
207 G3 Wurno Nigeria
169 B5 Würselen Ger.
235 D1 Wurtsboro NY U.S.A.
171 C5 Wurzbach Ger.
172 D2 Würzburg Ger.
171 D4 Wurzen Ger.
108 D2 Wushan Chongqing China
106 E5 Wushan Gansu China
108 C2 Wusheng Sichuan China
109 F2 Wusheng Zhejiang China
110 B3 Wushi Xinjiang China
170 D3 Wust Ger.
169 E4 Wüstegarten hill Ger.
172 D2 Wüstenrot Ger.
170 D3 Wusterhausen Ger.
170 E1 Wusterhusen Ger.
170 D3 Wustermark Ger.
171 D3 Wusterwitz Ger.
169 F4 Wüstheuterode Ger.
170 D3 Wustrau-Altfriesack Ger.
170 D2 Wustrow Mecklenburg-Vorpommern Ger.
170 C3 Wustrow Niedersachsen Ger.
Wusuli Jiang r. Rus. Fed. see Ussuri
172 C4 Wutach r. Ger.
107 G4 Wutai Shanxi China
169 F5 Wutha Ger.
100 D3 Wutong r. China
110 E3 Wutonggou Xinjiang China
165 D3 Wuustwezel Belgium
109 F2 Wuwei Anhui China
106 D4 Wuwei Gansu China
108 D2 Wuxi Chongqing China
Wuxi Hunan China see Luxi
109 G2 Wuxi Jiangsu China
Wuxia Chongqing China see Wushan
107 G4 Wuxiang Shanxi China
Wuxing Zhejiang China see Huzhou
108 D4 Wuxu Guangxi China
108 D4 Wuxuan Guangxi China
109 E2 Wuxue Hubei China
Wuyang Guizhou China see Zhenyuan
109 E1 Wuyang Henan China
109 F2 Wuyi Zhejiang China
100 D2 Wuyiling Heilong. China
109 F3 Wuyishan Fujian China
109 F3 Wuyi Shan mts China
109 F3 Wuyi Shan tourist site Fujian China
109 F2 Wuyuan Jiangxi China
107 F3 Wuyuan Nei Mongol China
Wuyuan Zhejiang China see Haiyan
Wuyun Zhejiang China see Jinyun
107 F4 Wuzhai Shanxi China
109 D2 Wuzhen Hubei China
107 G5 Wuzhi Henan China
106 E4 Wuzhong Ningxia China
109 D4 Wuzhou Guangxi China
85 E3 Wyaaba Creek r. Qld Austr.
226 B5 Wyaconda r. MO U.S.A.
87 C6 Wyalkatchem W.A. Austr.
227 I5 Wyalusing PA U.S.A.
227 F4 Wyandotte MI U.S.A.
85 F5 Wyandra Qld Austr.
226 C5 Wyanet IL U.S.A.
83 F2 Wyara, Lake salt flat Qld Austr.
151 G2 Wyberton Lincolnshire, England U.K.
83 E4 Wycheproof Vic. Austr.
235 D1 Wyckoff NJ U.S.A.
175 K2 Wydminy Pol.
151 H3 Wye Kent, England U.K.
149 H4 Wye r. Derbyshire, England U.K.
150 E3 Wye r. England/Wales U.K.
87 C6 Wyemandoo hill W.A. Austr.
234 B4 Wye Mills MD U.S.A.
226 B3 Wyeville WI U.S.A.
177 I1 Wygoda Pol.
172 B3 Wyhl Ger.
171 D4 Wyhra r. Ger.
168 D1 Wyk auf Föhr Ger.
174 F3 Wylatowo Pol.
232 D6 Wylliesburg VA U.S.A.
87 C4 Wyloo W.A. Austr.
151 F3 Wylye Wiltshire, England U.K.
151 F3 Wylye r. England U.K.
168 C2 Wymeer Ger.
171 G4 Wymiarki Pol.
151 I2 Wymondham Norfolk, England U.K.
236 D3 Wymore NE U.S.A.
82 C2 Wynbring S.A. Austr.
86 F2 Wyndham W.A. Austr.
81 B7 Wyndham South I. N.Z.
83 F4 Wyndham-Werribee Vic. Austr.
237 F5 Wynne AR U.S.A.
83 F5 Wynyard Tas. Austr.
223 J5 Wynyard Sask. Can.
226 C4 Wyocena WI U.S.A.
82 B2 Wyola Lake salt flat S.A. Austr.
234 C3 Wyoming DE U.S.A.
226 C5 Wyoming IL U.S.A.
226 E4 Wyoming MI U.S.A.
238 F3 Wyoming state U.S.A.
234 B1 Wyoming County county PA U.S.A.
238 E3 Wyoming Peak WY U.S.A.
238 E3 Wyoming Range mts WY U.S.A.
234 C2 Wyomissing PA U.S.A.
83 G3 Wyong N.S.W. Austr.
84 D2 Wyonga r. N.T. Austr.
146 F2 Wyre i. Scotland U.K.
149 G4 Wyre r. England U.K.
175 L4 Wyryki-Połód Pol.
174 F2 Wyrzysk Pol.
175 I4 Wyśmierzyce Pol.
175 J6 Wysoka Podkarpackie Pol.
174 F2 Wysoka Wielkopolskie Pol.
174 D5 Wysoka Kopa mt. Pol.
175 K5 Wysokie Lubelskie Pol.
175 K2 Wysokie Warmińsko-Mazurskie Pol.
175 K3 Wysokie Mazowieckie Pol.
175 J6 Wysowa Pol.
227 I5 Wysox PA U.S.A.
175 K3 Wyszki Pol.
175 J3 Wyszków Pol.
175 I3 Wyszogród Pol.
151 F2 Wythall Worcestershire, England U.K.
232 C6 Wytheville VA U.S.A.
175 L4 Wytyczno Pol.
175 J4 Wyżnica r. Pol.

X

210 F2 Xaafun, Raas pt Somalia
210 F2 Xaafuun Somalia
129 E3 Xaçınçay r. Azer.
129 F3 Xaçmaz Azer.
195 □ Xagħra Gozo Malta
111 F6 Xagquka Xizang China
111 E6 Xainza Xizang China
111 E6 Xaitongmoin Xizang China
213 G5 Xai-Xai Moz.
243 H4 Xal, Cerro de hill Mex.
Xalapa Mex. see Jalapa Enríquez
182 A2 Xallas r. Spain
209 D9 Xamavera Angola
107 E3 Xamba Nei Mongol China
254 C3 Xambioá Brazil
256 A5 Xambrê Brazil
96 D2 Xam Hua Laos
209 C7 Xá-Muteba Angola
96 C3 Xan r. Laos
97 D4 Xan, Xé r. Vietnam
182 B1 Xanceda Spain
Xangda Qinghai China see Nangqên
209 B9 Xangongo Angola
96 D3 Xangxoy, Xé r. Laos
129 E4 Xankändi Azer.
129 E3 Xanlar Azer.
169 B4 Xanten Ger.
198 D1 Xanthi Greece
255 B8 Xanxerê Brazil
252 C2 Xapuri Brazil
252 C2 Xapuri r. Brazil
210 E3 Xarardheere Somalia
Xar Burd Nei Mongol China see Bayan Nuru
182 C2 Xares r. Spain
107 F3 Xar Moron r. China
107 I3 Xar Moron r. China
184 B2 Xarrama r. Port.
198 B2 Xarrë Albania
Xarsingma Xizang China see Yadong
209 C7 Xassengue Angola
129 D3 Xatınlı Azer.
187 C6 Xátiva Spain
212 E4 Xau, Lake Botswana
256 C5 Xavantes, Represa de resr Brazil
254 C5 Xavantes, Serra dos hills Brazil
97 D5 Xa Vo Đat Vietnam
110 C3 Xayar Xinjiang China
243 I4 X-Can Mex.
232 B5 Xenia OH U.S.A.
187 C5 Xeraco Spain
187 C5 Xeresa Spain
251 F5 Xeriuini r. Brazil
182 C1 Xermade Spain
Xero Potamos r. Cyprus see Xeros
128 A2 Xeros r. Cyprus
186 D4 Xerta Spain
157 G4 Xertigny France
195 □ Xewkija Gozo Malta
Xhora S. Africa see Elliotdale
212 E4 Xhumo Botswana
107 I3 Xi r. Liaoning China
107 H3 Xiabancheng Hebei China
100 C2 Xiabole Shan mt. China
100 D3 Xiachengzi Heilong. China
Xiacun Shandong China see Rushan
Xiaguan Yunnan China see Dali
106 D5 Xiahe Gansu China
109 E3 Xiajiang Jiangxi China
Xiajiang Xizang China see Qusum
107 H4 Xiajin Shandong China
109 F3 Xiamen Fujian China
107 F5 Xi'an Shaanxi China
109 E1 Xiancheng Henan China
108 D2 Xianfeng Hubei China
109 E1 Xiangcheng Henan China
108 A2 Xiangcheng Sichuan China
Xiangcheng Yunnan China see Xiangyun
109 E1 Xiangfan Hubei China
107 F5 Xiangfen Shanxi China
Xiangfeng Hubei China see Laifeng
Xianggang H.K. China see Hong Kong
Xianggang Tebie Xingzhengqu special admin. reg. China see Hong Kong
Xianghuang Qi Nei Mongol China see Xin Bulag
Xiangjiang Jiangxi China see Huichang
109 E2 Xiang Jiang r. China
96 C3 Xiangkhoang Laos
Xiangkou Chongqing China see Wulong
107 F5 Xiangning Shanxi China
111 B6 Xiangquan He r. China
106 C5 Xiangride Qinghai China
Xiangshan Yunnan China see Menghai
109 G2 Xiangshan Zhejiang China
107 H5 Xiangshui Jiangsu China
108 D3 Xiangshuiba Hunan China
109 E3 Xiangtan Hunan China
109 E3 Xiangxiang Hunan China
Xiangyang Hubei China see Xiangfan
109 E2 Xiangyin Hunan China
108 B3 Xiangyun Yunnan China
109 G2 Xianju Zhejiang China
109 E2 Xianning Hubei China
Xiannümiao Jiangsu China see Jiangdu
Xianshui Sichuan China see Dawu
108 B2 Xianshui He r. Sichuan China
109 E2 Xiantao Hubei China
109 F3 Xianxia Ling mts China
107 H4 Xianxian Hebei China
107 F5 Xianyang Shaanxi China
109 F3 Xianyou Fujian China
Xiaoba Ningxia China see Qingtongxia
109 E2 Xiaochang Hubei China
108 D4 Xiaodong Guangxi China
107 I1 Xiao'ergou Nei Mongol China
Xiaofan Hebei China see Wuqiang
109 E2 Xiaogan Hubei China
100 C2 Xiao Hinggan Ling mts China
108 B2 Xiaojin Sichuan China
109 F3 Xiaomei Zhejiang China
106 B5 Xiaonanchuan Qinghai China
111 F4 Xiao Qaidam Qinghai China
107 H4 Xiaoqing r. China
109 E3 Xiaosanjiang Guangdong China
109 G2 Xiaoshan Zhejiang China
108 A1 Xiao Surmang Qinghai China
109 F3 Xiaotao Fujian China
107 G4 Xiaowutai Shan mt. Hebei China
Xiaoxi Fujian China see Pinghe
107 H5 Xiaoxian Anhui China
108 B2 Xiaoxiang Ling mts Sichuan China
Xiaoyi Henan China see Gongyi
107 F4 Xiaoyi Shanxi China
109 G3 Xiapu Fujian China
Xiaqiong Sichuan China see Batang
107 F5 Xiaxian Shanxi China
Xiayanjing Xizang China see Yanjing
Xiayingpan Guizhou China see Lupanshui
Xiayingpan Guizhou China see Luzhi
Xiazhen Shandong China see Weishan
Xiazhuang Shandong China see Linshu
108 A2 Xibdê Sichuan China
110 E2 Xibet Xinjiang China
109 F3 Xibing Fujian China
Xibu Fujian China see Dongshan
108 B3 Xichang Sichuan China
Xicheng Hebei China see Yangyuan
108 C4 Xichou Yunnan China
109 D1 Xichuan Henan China
245 F4 Xico Mex.
245 E2 Xicohténcatl Mex.
245 F3 Xicotepec de Juárez Mex.
108 B2 Xide Sichuan China
Xidu Hunan China see Hengyang
250 E4 Xié r. Brazil
Xiejiaji Shandong China see Qingyun
109 D2 Xiemahe' Hubei China
Xieng Khouang Laos see Xiangkhoang
109 F1 Xifei He r. China
107 E5 Xifeng Gansu China
108 C3 Xifeng Guizhou China
100 C4 Xifeng Liaoning China
Xifengzhen Gansu China see Xifeng
111 E6 Xigazê Xizang China
108 C1 Xihan Shui r. Gansu China
108 C1 Xihe Gansu China
108 C2 Xi He r. Sichuan China
109 E1 Xihua Henan China
Xihuachi Gansu China see Heshui
106 E5 Xiji Ningxia China
109 E4 Xi Jiang r. Guangdong China
108 D4 Xijin Guangxi China
100 B1 Xikouzi Nei Mongol China
107 G3 Xil Nei Mongol China
Xilaganí Greece see Xylagani
107 I2 Xilaotou Shan mt. Nei Mongol China
107 I3 Xiliao r. China
Xiligou Qinghai China see Ulan
108 C3 Xilin Guangxi China
107 H3 Xilinhot Nei Mongol China
Xilinji Heilong. China see Mohe
129 F4 Xıllı Azer.
129 F3 Xilmilli Azer.
Xilókastron Greece see Xylokastro
Xilópolis Greece see Xylopoli
106 D3 Ximiao Nei Mongol China
107 F4 Xin Nei Mongol China
129 F3 Xınalıq Azer.
Xin'an Anhui China see Lai'an
Xin'an Hebei China see Anxin
107 G5 Xin'an Henan China
Xin Barag Youqi Nei Mongol China see Altan Emel
Xin Barag Zuoqi Nei Mongol China see Amgalang
101 C4 Xinbin Liaoning China
131 M5 Xin Bulag Nei Mongol China
109 E1 Xincai Henan China
Xinchang Jiangxi China see Yifeng
109 G2 Xinchang Zhejiang China
Xincheng Fujian China see Gutian
Xincheng Guangdong China see Xinxing
108 D3 Xincheng Guangxi China
106 E4 Xincheng Ningxia China
Xincheng Shanxi China see Yuanqu
Xincheng Sichuan China see Zhaojue
107 F4 Xinchengbu Shaanxi China
Xincun Yunnan China see Dongchuan
109 D4 Xindi Guangxi China
Xindi Hubei China see Honghu
109 D4 Xindu Guangxi China
Xindu Sichuan China see Luhuo
108 C2 Xindu Sichuan China
108 B2 Xinduqiao Sichuan China
109 E3 Xinfeng Guangdong China
109 E3 Xinfeng Jiangxi China
108 D3 Xing'an Guangxi China
109 E3 Xingan Jiangxi China
Xingba Xizang China see Lhünzê
Xingcheng Hebei China see Qianxi
107 I3 Xingcheng Liaoning China
Xingguo Gansu China see Qin'an
109 E3 Xingguo Jiangxi China
106 C5 Xinghai Qinghai China
109 F1 Xinghua Jiangsu China
100 E3 Xingkai Heilong. China
107 H3 Xinglong Hebei China
100 C2 Xinglong Heilong. China
100 C3 Xinglongzhen Heilong. China
109 E3 Xingning Guangdong China
109 E2 Xingou Hubei China
107 F5 Xingping Shaanxi China
108 C3 Xingren Guizhou China
Xingshan Guizhou China see Majiang
108 D2 Xingshan Hubei China
107 G4 Xingtai Hebei China
107 G4 Xingtang Hebei China
251 H5 Xingu r. Brazil
254 C3 Xinguara Brazil
108 C2 Xingwen Sichuan China
107 F4 Xingxian Shanxi China
106 B3 Xingxingxia Xinjiang China
107 G5 Xingyang Henan China
108 C3 Xingyi Guizhou China
109 F2 Xingzi Jiangxi China
107 G4 Xinhe Hebei China
110 C3 Xinhe Xinjiang China
107 G3 Xin Hot Nei Mongol China
Xinhua Guangdong China see Huadu
109 D3 Xinhua Hunan China
Xinhua Yunnan China see Qiaojia

Xinhua to Yongding
381

Xinhua Yunnan China see Funing
106 D4 Xinhuacun Gansu China
108 D3 Xinhuang Hunan China
107 H3 Xinhui Nei Mongol China
106 D4 Xining Qinghai China
107 G4 Xinji Hebei China
Xinji Henan China see Xinxian
109 E2 Xinjian Jiangxi China
107 F5 Xinjiang Shanxi China
Xinjiang aut. reg. China see Xinjiang Uygur Zizhiqu
109 F2 Xin Jiang r. China
Xinjiangkou Hubei China see Songzi
106 A3 Xinjiang Uygur Zizhiqu aut. reg. China
Xinjie Yunnan China see Yuanyang
Xinjin Liaoning China see Pulandian
108 B2 Xinjin Sichuan China
Xinjing Guangxi China see Jingxi
107 I3 Xinkai r. China
Xinling Hubei China see Badong
108 B2 Xinlong Sichuan China
107 G5 Xinmi Henan China
Xinmian Sichuan China see Shimian
107 I3 Xinmin Liaoning China
Xinning Gansu China see Ningxian
Xinning Guangxi China see Fusui
108 D3 Xinning Hunan China
Xinning Jiangxi China see Wuning
Xinning Sichuan China see Kaijiang
108 B3 Xinping Yunnan China
100 D2 Xinqing Heilong. China
109 F3 Xinquan Fujian China
Xinshan Jiangxi China see Anyuan
109 D3 Xinshao Hunan China
Xinshi Hubei China see Jingshan
Xinshiba Sichuan China see Ganluo
107 H5 Xintai Shandong China
109 E2 Xintanpu Hubei China
109 E3 Xintian Hunan China
109 E2 Xinxian Henan China
107 G5 Xinxiang Henan China
109 E4 Xinxing Guangdong China
109 E1 Xinyang Henan China
109 G1 Xinyang Gang r. China
109 E1 Xinye Henan China
107 H5 Xinye r. China
109 D4 Xinyi Guangdong China
107 H5 Xinyi Jiangsu China
Xinying Taiwan see Hsinying
109 E3 Xinyu Jiangxi China
Xinyuan Qinghai China see Tianjun
110 C3 Xinyuan Xinjiang China
107 I1 Xinzhangfang Nei Mongol China
107 G5 Xinzheng Henan China
Xinzhou Guangxi China see Longlin
Xinzhou Guizhou China see Huangping
109 E2 Xinzhou Hubei China
107 G4 Xinzhou Shanxi China
Xinzhu Taiwan see Hsinchu
182 C2 Xinzo de Limia Spain
Xiongshan Fujian China see Zhenghe
Xiongzhou Guangdong China see Nanxiong
252 D2 Xipamanu r. Bol./Brazil
109 D1 Xiping Henan China
109 E1 Xiping Henan China
106 D5 Xiqing Shan mts China
254 E4 Xique Xique Brazil
129 F3 Xırdalan Azer.
187 C5 Xirivella Spain
198 C2 Xiro hill Greece
199 E3 Xirokampo Greece
250 E6 Xiruá r. Brazil
Xisa Yunnan China see Xichou
107 F3 Xishanzui Nei Mongol China
Xisha Qundao is S. China Sea see Paracel Islands
108 C2 Xishui Guizhou China
109 E2 Xishui Hubei China
182 C1 Xistral, Serra do mts Spain
206 B4 Xitole Guinea-Bissau
Xiucaiwan Chongqing China see Fengdu
Xiugu Jiangxi China see Jinxi
Xi Ujimqin Qi Nei Mongol China see Bayan Ul Hot
109 F2 Xiuning Anhui China
108 D2 Xiushan Chongqing China
Xiushan Yunnan China see Tonghai
109 E2 Xiushui Jiangxi China
109 E2 Xiu Shui r. China
108 C3 Xiuwen Guizhou China
107 G5 Xiuwu Henan China
107 I3 Xiuyan Liaoning China
Xiuyan Shaanxi China see Qingjian
108 D4 Xiuying Hainan China
Xiwanzi Hebei China see Chongli
108 A1 Xiwu Qinghai China
111 D6 Xixabangma Feng mt. Xizang China
109 D1 Xixia Henan China
109 E1 Xixian Henan China
107 F4 Xixian Shanxi China
108 C1 Xixiang Shaanxi China
Xixón Spain see Gijón
107 G4 Xiyang Shanxi China
108 C3 Xiyang Jiang r. Yunnan China
Xizang aut. reg. China see Xizang Zizhiqu
Xizang Gaoyuan plat. Xizang China see Qing Zang Gaoyuan
108 A2 Xizang Zizhiqu aut. reg. China
129 F3 Xızı Azer.
210 E2 Xjis Somalia
129 E4 Xocalı Azer.
129 E4 Xocavänd Azer.
245 E3 Xochiatipan Mex.
245 E4 Xochicalco tourist site Mex.
245 E4 Xochimilco Mex.
245 E5 Xochistlahuaca Mex.
Xoi Xizang China see Qüxü
215 F5 Xolobe S. Africa
129 F4 Xol Qarabucaq Azer.
97 D5 Xom An Lôc Vietnam
97 D5 Xom Dưc Hanh Vietnam
245 E4 Xonacatlán Mex.
Xonrupt France see Xonrupt-Longemer
157 G4 Xonrupt-Longemer France
110 E4 Xorkol Xinjiang China
129 E3 Xosrov Azer.
182 C1 Xove Spain
Xuancheng Anhui China see Xuanzhou
108 D2 Xuan'en Hubei China
108 C2 Xuanhan Sichuan China
107 G3 Xuanhua Hebei China
97 D5 Xuân Lôc Vietnam
108 C3 Xuanwei Yunnan China
109 F2 Xuanzhou Anhui China
182 B2 Xubín Spain
109 E1 Xuchang Henan China
99 J5 Xuchang Henan China
Xucheng Guangdong China see Xuwen
129 F3 Xudat Azer.
210 D3 Xuddur Somalia
Xueba Xizang China see Sangri
Xuefeng Fujian China see Mingxi
108 D3 Xuefeng Shan mts China
107 F5 Xuehua Shan hill Shanxi China
108 A3 Xue Shan mts Yunnan China
107 H5 Xugou Jiangsu China
Xuguit Qi Nei Mongol China see Yakeshi
Xujiang Jiangxi China see Guangchang
Xulun Hobot Qagan Qi Nei Mongol China see Qagan Nur
Xulun Hoh Qi Nei Mongol China see Dund Hot
100 D2 Xun r. China
108 B3 Xundian Yunnan China
111 F6 Xung Qu r. Xizang China
108 D1 Xun He r. China
111 D6 Xungru Xizang China
100 C2 Xunhe Heilong. China
106 D5 Xunhua Qinghai China
108 D4 Xun Jiang r. China
100 D2 Xunke Heilong. China
182 C2 Xunqueira de Ambía Spain
109 E3 Xunwu Jiangxi China
107 G5 Xunxian Henan China
108 D1 Xunyang Shaanxi China
107 F5 Xunyi Shaanxi China
108 D3 Xupu Hunan China
107 G4 Xushui Hebei China
108 D4 Xuwen Guangdong China
Xuyang Sichuan China see Rongxian
109 F1 Xuyi Jiangsu China
108 C2 Xuyong Sichuan China
107 H5 Xuzhou Jiangsu China
199 D1 Xylagani Greece
198 C2 Xylokastro Greece
198 C1 Xylopoli Greece

Y

85 G4 Yaamba Qld Austr.
108 B2 Ya'an Sichuan China
83 E3 Yaapeet Vic. Austr.
Yabanabat Turkey see Kızılcahamam
207 H5 Yabassi Cameroon
78 □3a Yabbenohr i. Kwajalein Marshall Is
210 C3 Yabēlo Eth.
197 G4 Yablanitsa Bulg.
197 H4 Yablanovo Bulg.
137 J2 Yablochnoye Rus. Fed.
137 K1 Yablonovets Rus. Fed.
137 J5 Yablonovskiy Rus. Fed.
107 F1 Yablonovyy Khrebet mts Rus. Fed.
136 C3 Yabluniv Ukr.
137 F3 Yablunivka Ukr.
207 G3 Yabo Nigeria
106 D4 Yabrai Shan mts China
106 D4 Yabrai Yanchang Nei Mongol China
128 C3 Yabrūd Syria
247 □1 Yabucoa Puerto Rico
100 D3 Yabuli Heilong. China
136 E2 Yabunets' Ukr.
Yacha Hainan China see Baisha
108 D5 Yacheng Hainan China
108 C3 Yachi He r. China
105 G3 Yachiyo Chiba Japan
105 F2 Yachiyo Ibaraki Japan
83 F4 Yackandandah Vic. Austr.
252 E5 Yacuiba Bol.
114 C2 Yadgir Karnataka India
114 C3 Yadiki Andhra Prad. India
233 E5 Yadkin r. NC U.S.A.
231 D4 Yadkinville NC U.S.A.
111 E7 Yadong Xizang China
134 I5 Yadrin Rus. Fed.
79 □1 Yadua i. Fiji
Yafa Israel see Tel Aviv-Yafo
202 B1 Yafran Libya
206 E4 Yagaba Ghana
Yagaing state Myanmar see Arakan
199 E2 Yağcılı Turkey
Yağda Turkey see Erdemli
264 E9 Yaghan Basin sea feature S. Atlantic Ocean
128 B1 Yağızlar Turkey
129 C3 Yağlıca Dağı mt. Turkey
122 C2 Yagman Turkm.
129 C4 Yağmurlu r. Turkey
139 K2 Yagnitsa Rus. Fed.
197 G4 Yagoda Bulg.
120 A2 Yagodnaya Polyana Rus. Fed.
131 P3 Yagodnoye Rus. Fed.
Yagotin Ukr. see Yahotyn
207 I4 Yagoua Cameroon
111 C6 Yagra Xizang China
106 B5 Yagradagzê Shan mt. Qinghai China
246 C2 Yaguajay Cuba
Yaguarón r. Brazil/Uru. see Jaguarão
250 D5 Yaguas r. Peru
97 C6 Yaha Thai.
104 C4 Yahagi-gawa r. Japan
222 G5 Yahk B.C. Can.
136 E4 Yahorlyk r. Ukr.
137 F2 Yahotyn Ukr.
244 C3 Yahualica Mex.
118 D2 Yahyalı Turkey
97 B4 Yai, Khao hill Thai.
105 F2 Yaita Japan
216 □3c Yaiza Lanzarote Canary Is
105 E4 Yaizu Japan
108 B2 Yajiang Sichuan China
128 C1 Yakacık Turkey
128 B1 Yakapınar Turkey
104 D2 Yake-dake vol. Japan
107 I1 Yakeshi Nei Mongol China
136 D3 Yakhivtsi Ukr.
137 G2 Yakhnyky Ukr.
139 K3 Yakhroma Rus. Fed.
238 B2 Yakima WA U.S.A.
238 C2 Yakima r. WA U.S.A.
121 F5 Yakkabag Uzbek.
206 E3 Yako Burkina
197 F4 Yakoruda Bulg.
137 I3 Yakovenkove Ukr.
100 E3 Yakovlevka Rus. Fed.
137 I2 Yakovlevo Rus. Fed.
134 K4 Yakskur-Bod'ya Rus. Fed.
102 □1 Yaku-shima i. Japan
220 E4 Yakutat AK U.S.A.
131 N3 Yakutsk Rus. Fed.
137 H4 Yakymivka Ukr.
97 C6 Yala Thai.
199 F1 Yalakdere Turkey
129 F3 Yalama Azer.
128 A1 Yalan Dünya Mağarası tourist site Turkey
81 D5 Yaldhurst South I. N.Z.
222 F5 Yale B.C. Can.
227 F4 Yale MI U.S.A.
206 E3 Yalgo Burkina
87 C6 Yalgoo W.A. Austr.
199 E3 Yalıkavak Turkey
197 I5 Yalıköy Turkey
208 D3 Yalinga C.A.R.
138 G5 Yalizava Belarus
246 □ Yallahs Jamaica
85 F5 Yalleroi Qld Austr.
87 B7 Yallingup W.A. Austr.
83 F4 Yallourn Vic. Austr.
129 C3 Yalnızçam Dağları mts Turkey
237 F5 Yalobusha r. MS U.S.A.
Yalogo Burkina see Yalgo
208 C3 Yaloké C.A.R.
108 B3 Yalong Jiang r. Sichuan China
199 F1 Yalova Turkey
197 I5 Yalova prov. Turkey
Yaloven' Moldova see Ialoveni
136 E5 Yalpuh, Ozero l. Ukr.
Yalpukh r. Moldova see Ialpug
137 I4 Yalta Donets'ka Oblast' Ukr.
137 H5 Yalta Respublika Krym Ukr.
136 D3 Yaltushkiv Ukr.
107 I2 Yalu Jiang r. China
101 C4 Yalu Jiang r. China/N. Korea
130 H4 Yalutorovsk Rus. Fed.
199 G2 Yalvaç Turkey
Yama Ukr. see Sivers'k
103 E7 Yamaga Japan
102 J3 Yamagata Iwate Japan
102 J4 Yamagata Yamagata Japan
102 I4 Yamagata pref. Japan
103 E6 Yamaguchi Japan
103 E6 Yamaguchi pref. Japan
105 F3 Yamakita Japan
130 H2 Yamal, Poluostrov pen. Rus. Fed.
Yamal Peninsula Rus. Fed. see Yamal, Poluostrov
104 C2 Yamanaka Japan
105 E3 Yamanashi Japan
105 E3 Yamanashi pref. Japan
Yamankhalinka Kazakh. see Makhambet
105 E2 Yamanouchi Japan
107 F1 Yamarovka Rus. Fed.
105 F3 Yamato Kanagawa Japan
102 □1 Yamato Nansei-shotō Japan
104 B4 Yamato-kōriyama Japan
104 B4 Yamatotakada Japan
83 H2 Yamba N.S.W. Austr.
83 E4 Yambacoona Tas. Austr.
84 B2 Yambarran Range hills N.T. Austr.
208 B2 Yamba Tchangsou Chad
206 B4 Yambéring Guinea
250 D4 Yambi, Mesa de hills Col.
208 F3 Yambio Sudan
197 H4 Yambol Bulg.
250 B6 Yambrasbamba Peru
91 H8 Yamdena i. Indon.
103 E7 Yame Japan
96 B2 Yamethin Myanmar
105 G2 Yamizo-san mt. Japan
114 B2 Yamkanmardi Karnataka India
Yamkhad Syria see Ḥalab
138 G2 Yamm Rus. Fed.
85 E5 Yamma Yamma, Lake salt flat Qld Austr.
137 H2 Yamne Ukr.
206 D5 Yamoussoukro Côte d'Ivoire
137 F3 Yampil' Cherkas'ka Oblast' Ukr.
136 D3 Yampil' Khmel'nyts'ka Oblast' Ukr.
137 G2 Yampil' Sums'ka Oblast' Ukr.
136 E3 Yampil' Vinnyts'ka Oblast' Ukr.
Yampol' Cherkas'ka Oblast' Ukr. see Yampil'
Yampol' Khmel'nyts'ka Oblast' Ukr. see Yampil'
Yampol' Sums'ka Oblast' Ukr. see Yampil'
Yampol' Vinnyts'ka Oblast' Ukr. see Yampil'
116 E4 Yamuna r. India
116 D3 Yamunanagar Haryana India
111 E6 Yamzho Yumco l. China
107 F4 Yan r. China
207 H4 Yana Nigeria
131 O2 Yana r. Rus. Fed.
82 E4 Yanac Vic. Austr.
103 F7 Yanadani Japan
103 F7 Yanai Japan
114 D2 Yanam Andhra Prad. India
107 F4 Yan'an Shaanxi China
252 C3 Yanaoca Peru
Yanaon Andhra Prad. India see Yanam
134 K4 Yanaul Rus. Fed.
139 H4 Yanavichy Belarus
108 B3 Yanbian Sichuan China
124 B2 Yanbu' al Baḥr Saudi Arabia
124 B2 Yanbu' an Nakhl reg. Saudi Arabia
231 E4 Yanceyville NC U.S.A.
107 F4 Yanchang Shaanxi China
109 G1 Yancheng Jiangsu China
Yancheng Shandong China see Qihe
Yancheng Sichuan China see Jingyan
87 B6 Yanchep W.A. Austr.
107 E4 Yanchi Ningxia China
107 F4 Yanchuan Shaanxi China
137 I4 Yanchur r. Ukr.
83 F3 Yanco N.S.W. Austr.
83 F3 Yanco Creek r. N.S.W. Austr.
83 E2 Yanco Glen N.S.W. Austr.
Yandao Sichuan China see Yingjing
110 E4 Yandaxkak Xinjiang China
87 C5 Yandil W.A. Austr.
85 H5 Yandina Qld Austr.
96 A3 Yandoon Myanmar
Yandua i. Fiji see Yadua
106 B3 Yandun Xinjiang China
139 I1 Yanega Rus. Fed.
206 C4 Yanfolila Mali
107 G3 Yang r. China
208 E4 Yangambi Dem. Rep. Congo
111 F6 Ya'ngamdo Xizang China
111 F6 Ya'ngamdo Xizang China
206 D3 Yangasso Mali
111 E6 Yangbajain Xizang China
108 A3 Yangbi Yunnan China
Yangcheng Guangdong China see Yangshan
107 G5 Yangcheng Shanxi China
Yangchuan Guizhou China see Suiyang
109 D4 Yangchun Guangdong China
109 E4 Yangcun Guangdong China
Yangcun Tianjin China see Wuqing
101 C5 Yangdok N. Korea
107 G3 Yanggao Shanxi China
107 G4 Yanggu Shandong China
Yanghe Ningxia China see Yongning
120 E4 Yangiaryk Uzbek.
121 F4 Yangikishlak Uzbek.
120 F5 Yangi-Nishan Uzbek.
123 G2 Yangi Qal'eh Afgh.
120 F4 Yangirabad Uzbek.
121 G4 Yangiyul' Uzbek.
109 D4 Yangjiang Guangdong China
96 B3 Yangôn Myanmar
115 H2 Yangôn admin. div. Myanmar
109 D2 Yangping Hubei China
107 G4 Yangquan Shanxi China
109 E3 Yangshan Guangdong China
108 D3 Yangshuo Guangxi China
96 C3 Yang Talat Thai.
108 B3 Yangtouyan Yunnan China
108 A1 Yangtze r. China
alt. Chang Jiang,
alt. Jinsha Jiang,
alt. Tongtian He,
alt. Zhi Qu,
long Yangtze Kiang
Yangtze, Mouth of the China see Changjiang Kou
Yangtze Kiang r. China see Yangtze
183 H2 Yanguas Spain
109 D4 Yangxi Guangdong China
108 C1 Yangxian Shaanxi China
101 D5 Yangyang S. Korea
107 G3 Yangyuan Hebei China
109 F1 Yangzhou Jiangsu China
108 D2 Yanhe Guizhou China
82 C3 Yaninee, Lake salt flat S.A. Austr.
134 F3 Yanishpole Rus. Fed.
100 D4 Yanji Jilin China
107 G5 Yanjin Henan China
108 C2 Yanjin Yunnan China
Yanjing Sichuan China see Yanyuan
108 A2 Yanjing Xizang China
Yanjing Yunnan China see Yanjin
Yankou Sichuan China see Wusheng
236 D3 Yankton SD U.S.A.
129 C1 Yankul' Rus. Fed.
129 C1 Yankul' r. Rus. Fed.
107 G5 Yanling Henan China
109 E3 Yanling Hunan China
Yannina Greece see Ioannina
131 P2 Yano-Indigirskaya Nizmennost' lowland Rus. Fed.
114 D4 Yan Oya r. Sri Lanka
110 D3 Yanqi Xinjiang China
107 G3 Yanqing Beijing China
125 G3 Yanqul Oman
87 B4 Yanrey r. W.A. Austr.
107 H4 Yanshan Hebei China
109 F2 Yanshan Jiangxi China
108 C4 Yanshan Yunnan China
107 H3 Yan Shan mts China
107 G5 Yanshi Henan China
111 F5 Yanshiping Qinghai China
100 D3 Yanshou Heilong. China
131 O2 Yanskiy Zaliv g. Rus. Fed.
83 F2 Yantabulla N.S.W. Austr.
122 B2 Yantagh Iran
107 I4 Yantai Shandong China
259 B6 Yántales, Cerro mt. Chile
138 B4 Yantarnyy Rus. Fed.
235 F1 Yantic r. CT U.S.A.
108 C2 Yanting Sichuan China
100 C4 Yantongshan Jilin China
109 G2 Yantou Zhejiang China
197 G4 Yantra r. Bulg.
124 C3 Yanūfī, Jabal al hill Saudi Arabia
Yany-Kurgan Kazakh. see Zhanakorgan
108 B3 Yanyuan Sichuan China
107 H5 Yanzhou Shandong China
104 B4 Yao Japan
108 B3 Yao'an Yunnan China
Yaodu Anhui China see Dongzhi
109 F2 Yaoli Jiangxi China
207 H6 Yaoundé Cameroon
107 F5 Yaoxian Shaanxi China
107 F4 Yaozhen Shaanxi China
91 I5 Yap i. Micronesia
252 D3 Yapacani r. Bol.
258 F3 Yapeyú Arg.
235 F2 Yaphank NY U.S.A.
85 E3 Yappar r. Qld Austr.
151 G4 Yapton West Sussex, England U.K.
266 E5 Yap Trench sea feature N. Pacific Ocean
251 G4 Yapukarri Guyana
242 C3 Yaqui r. Mex.
134 K4 Yar Rus. Fed.
246 C2 Yara Cuba
250 D2 Yaracuy state Venez.
85 F5 Yaraka Qld Austr.
Yarangüme Turkey see Tavas
134 I4 Yaransk Rus. Fed.
82 C3 Yardea S.A. Austr.
129 F4 Yardımlı Azer.
234 D2 Yardley PA U.S.A.
234 D2 Yardville NJ U.S.A.
Yardymly Azer. see Yardımlı
151 I2 Yare r. England U.K.
134 K3 Yarega Rus. Fed.
136 C3 Yaremcha Ukr.
77 G2 Yaren Nauru
134 J3 Yarenga r. Rus. Fed.
134 J3 Yarensk Rus. Fed.
137 G3 Yares'ky Ukr.
Yargara Moldova see Iargara
250 C5 Yari r. Col.
104 D2 Yariga-take mt. Japan
124 D5 Yarīm Yemen
Yarımca Turkey see Körfez
247 E5 Yaritagua Venez.
Yarkand Xinjiang China see Shache
Yarkant Xinjiang China see Shache
111 B4 Yarkant He r. China
227 I3 Yarker Ont. Can.
123 H2 Yarkhun r. Pak.
87 F6 Yarle Lakes salt flat S.A. Austr.
197 F4 Yarlovo Bulg.
111 E7 Yarlung Zangbo r. China
alt. Dihang (India),
conv. Brahmaputra
149 H3 Yarm Stockton-on-Tees, England U.K.
136 D3 Yarmolyntsi Ukr.
225 H5 Yarmouth N.S. Can.
151 F4 Yarmouth Isle of Wight, England U.K.
Yarmouth Norfolk, England U.K. see Great Yarmouth
233 □H3 Yarmouth ME U.S.A.
128 B3 Yarmūk r. Asia
241 K4 Yarnell AZ U.S.A.
151 F3 Yarnton Oxfordshire, England U.K.
137 G2 Yaroshivka Ukr.
137 G2 Yaroslavets' Ukr.
139 L3 Yaroslavl' Rus. Fed.
Yaroslavl Oblast admin. div. Rus. Fed. see Yaroslavskaya Oblast'
129 B1 Yaroslavskaya Rus. Fed.
139 L3 Yaroslavskaya Oblast' admin. div. Rus. Fed.
100 E3 Yaroslavskiy Rus. Fed.
128 B3 Yarqon r. Israel
85 E2 Yarraden Qld Austr.
83 F4 Yarra Junction Vic. Austr.
86 B4 Yarraloola W.A. Austr.
83 F4 Yarram Vic. Austr.
85 G5 Yarraman Qld Austr.
83 F4 Yarrawonga Vic. Austr.
87 B6 Yarra Yarra Lakes salt flat W.A. Austr.
86 D4 Yarrie W.A. Austr.
85 F5 Yarronvale Qld Austr.
85 F4 Yarrowmere Qld Austr.
139 I4 Yartsevo Rus. Fed.
111 D6 Yaru r. China
250 C3 Yarumal Col.
108 A2 Yarwa Sichuan China
108 A2 Yarzhong Xizang China
Yaş Romania see Iaşi
115 E1 Yasai r. W. Bengal India
79 □1 Yasawa i. Fiji
79 □1 Yasawa Group is Fiji
136 C3 Yasen' Ukr.
137 J4 Yaseni r. Rus. Fed.
197 H4 Yasenkovo Bulg.
135 G7 Yasenskaya Rus. Fed.
135 H7 Yashalta Rus. Fed.
207 G3 Yashi Nigeria
207 F4 Yashikera Nigeria
135 K5 Yashkino Rus. Fed.
135 I7 Yashkul' Rus. Fed.
116 C1 Yasin Jammu and Kashmir
Yasinovataya Ukr. see Yasynuvata
136 C3 Yasinya Ukr.
197 H4 Yasna Polyana Bulg.
139 K4 Yasnogorsk Rus. Fed.
137 I3 Yasnohirka Ukr.
136 F2 Yasnohorodka Ukr.
120 D2 Yasnyy Rus. Fed.
96 D4 Yasothon Thai.
83 G3 Yass N.S.W. Austr.
83 G3 Yass r. N.S.W. Austr.
199 F3 Yassıhüyük Denizli Turkey
137 H2 Yastrubyne Ukr.
104 C3 Yasu Japan
103 F6 Yasugi Japan
122 B4 Yāsūj Iran
77 G3 Yasur vol. Vanuatu
136 D1 Yasyel'da r. Belarus
137 I3 Yasynuvata Ukr.
252 D2 Yata r. Bol.
208 D2 Yata r. C.A.R.
199 F3 Yatağan Turkey
211 C5 Yata Plateau Kenya
78 □5 Yaté New Caledonia
150 E3 Yate South Gloucestershire, England U.K.
151 G3 Yateley Hampshire, England U.K.
222 H2 Yates r. Alta/N.W.T. Can.
237 E4 Yates Center KS U.S.A.
Yatou Shandong China see Rongcheng
187 C5 Yatova Spain
136 F3 Yatran' r. Ukr.
105 E3 Yatsuga-take vol. Japan
103 E7 Yatsushiro Japan
103 E7 Yatsushiro-kai b. Japan
128 B4 Yaṭṭa West Bank
150 E3 Yatton North Somerset, England U.K.
252 B3 Yauca Peru
252 B3 Yauca r. Peru
247 □1 Yauco Puerto Rico
252 A2 Yauli Peru
250 D5 Yauna Maloca Col.
252 C3 Yauri Peru
245 E4 Yautepec Mex.
252 B3 Yauyos Peru
Yavan Tajik. see Yovon
250 D6 Yavari r. Brazil/Peru
alt. Javari
242 C3 Yávaros Mex.
116 D5 Yavatmal Mahar. India
252 B3 Yavero r. Peru
251 E3 Yaví, Cerro mt. Venez.
137 G4 Yavkyne Ukr.
121 G1 Yavlenka Kazakh.
175 L6 Yavora Ukr.
136 C3 Yavoriv Ivano-Frankivs'ka Oblast' Ukr.
136 B3 Yavoriv L'vivs'ka Oblast' Ukr.
140 O1 Yavr r. Fin./Rus. Fed.
128 C1 Yavuzlu Turkey
104 B4 Yawata Japan
103 F7 Yawatahama Japan
111 C4 Yawatongguz He r. China
111 C4 Yawatongguzlangar Xinjiang China
96 A2 Yaw Chaung r. Myanmar
243 H5 Yaxchilan tourist site Guat.
Yaxian Hainan China see Sanya
151 G2 Yaxley Cambridgeshire, England U.K.
129 B4 Yaygın Turkey
129 A4 Yaylabaşı Turkey
128 C2 Yayladağı Hatay Turkey
129 B4 Yayladere Turkey
129 C4 Yayladüzü Turkey
134 L4 Yayva Rus. Fed.
96 A2 Yazagyo Myanmar
122 C4 Yazd Iran
122 C4 Yazd prov. Iran
122 C4 Yazd-e Khvāst Iran
Yazgulemskiy Khrebet mts Tajik. see Yazgulom, Qatorkŭhi
123 G2 Yazgulom, Qatorkŭhi mts Tajik.
139 I2 Yazhelbitsy Rus. Fed.
126 E3 Yazıhan Malatya Turkey
199 F3 Yazıkent Turkey
199 G3 Yazır Turkey
237 F5 Yazoo r. MS U.S.A.
237 F5 Yazoo City MS U.S.A.
134 L3 Yaz'va r. Rus. Fed.
Y Bala Gwynedd, Wales U.K. see Bala
179 G2 Ybbs r. Austria
179 G2 Ybbs an der Donau Austria
179 F3 Ybbsitz Austria
253 F6 Ybycui Para.
163 B4 Ychoux France
162 E3 Ydes France
142 C4 Yding Skovhøj hill Denmark
198 C3 Ydra Greece
198 C3 Ydra i. Greece
Y Drenewydd Powys, Wales U.K. see Newtown
96 B4 Ye Myanmar
96 B4 Ye r. Myanmar
149 H4 Yeadon West Yorkshire, England U.K.
150 D4 Yealmpton Devon, England U.K.
Yebaishou Liaoning China see Jianping
121 G4 Yebekshi Kazakh.
183 H4 Yebra Spain
186 C2 Yebra de Basa Spain
111 B4 Yecheng Xinjiang China
187 B6 Yecla Spain
182 D4 Yecla de Yeltes Spain
242 C2 Yécora Mex.
114 C3 Yedatore Karnataka India
Yedintsy Moldova see Edineţ
129 B4 Yedisu Turkey
128 B2 Yeditepe Turkey
139 I3 Yedrovo Rus. Fed.
86 D3 Yeeda River W.A. Austr.
231 D7 Yeehaw Junction FL U.S.A.
82 C3 Yeelanna S.A. Austr.
139 J2 Yefimovskiy Rus. Fed.
139 L5 Yefremov Rus. Fed.
Yêgainnyin Qinghai China see Henan
129 D4 Yeghegis r. Armenia
129 D4 Yeghegnadzor Armenia
129 D3 Yeghvard Armenia
121 I2 Yegindybulak Kazakh.
135 H7 Yegorlyk r. Rus. Fed.
135 H7 Yegorlykskaya Rus. Fed.
139 L4 Yegor'yevsk Rus. Fed.
185 F2 Yeguas r. Spain
207 F4 Yégué Togo
210 A3 Yei r. Sudan
109 E2 Yeji Anhui China
206 E4 Yeji Ghana
Yejiaji Anhui China see Yeji
130 H4 Yekaterinburg Rus. Fed.
Yekaterinodar Rus. Fed. see Krasnodar
Yekaterinoslav Ukr. see Dnipropetrovs'k
100 D2 Yekaterinoslavka Rus. Fed.
137 J4 Yekaterinovka Rostovskaya Oblast' Rus. Fed.
135 I5 Yekaterinovka Saratovskaya Oblast' Rus. Fed.
Yekaterinovskaya Krasnodarskiy Kray Rus. Fed. see Krylovskaya
129 D2 Yekatorinogradskaya Rus. Fed.
Yekhegnadzor Armenia see Yeghegnadzor
139 I4 Yekimovichi Rus. Fed.
208 D4 Yekokora r. Dem. Rep. Congo
100 E2 Yelabuga Khabarovskiy Kray Rus. Fed.
134 J5 Yelabuga Respublika Tatarstan Rus. Fed.
135 H6 Yelan' Rus. Fed.
135 H6 Yelan' r. Rus. Fed.
135 H6 Yelan' r. Rus. Fed.
137 F4 Yelanets' Ukr.
83 G2 Yelarbon Qld Austr.
135 H5 Yelat'ma Rus. Fed.
199 F2 Yeleğen Turkey
Yelenovka Ukr. see Zoryns'k
Yelenovskiye Kar'yery Ukr. see Dokuchayevs'k
139 J5 Yelenskiy Rus. Fed.
139 L5 Yelets Rus. Fed.
134 N2 Yeletskiy Rus. Fed.
139 I2 Yeligovo Rus. Fed.
206 C3 Yélimané Mali
139 L4 Yelino Rus. Fed.
Yelizavetgrad Kirovohrads'ka Oblast' Ukr. see Kirovohrad
137 J4 Yelizavetovka Rostovskaya Oblast' Rus. Fed.
137 K2 Yelizavetovka Voronezhskaya Oblast' Rus. Fed.
131 Q4 Yelizovo Rus. Fed.
135 J5 Yelkhovka Rus. Fed.
146 □G1 Yell i. Scotland U.K.
114 D2 Yellandu Andhra Prad. India
114 B3 Yellapur Karnataka India
114 C2 Yellareddi Andhra Prad. India
226 B4 Yellow r. WI U.S.A.
87 C6 Yellowdine W.A. Austr.
234 D2 Yellow Frame NJ U.S.A.
234 C2 Yellow House PA U.S.A.
222 H2 Yellowknife N.W.T. Can.
222 H2 Yellowknife r. N.W.T. Can.
83 F3 Yellow Mountain hill N.S.W. Austr.
Yellow River r. China see Huang He
266 D3 Yellow Sea N. Pacific Ocean
232 B5 Yellow Springs OH U.S.A.
236 C2 Yellowstone r. MT U.S.A.
146 □G1 Yell Sound str. Scotland U.K.
237 E4 Yellville AR U.S.A.
238 B2 Yelm WA U.S.A.
185 H2 Yelmo mt. Spain
135 H5 Yel'niki Rus. Fed.
139 I4 Yel'nya Rus. Fed.
123 E2 Yeloten Turkm.
134 K4 Yelovo Rus. Fed.
129 D4 Yelp'in Armenia
136 E2 Yel'sk Belarus
182 D4 Yeltes r. Spain
242 □I6 Yelucá mt. Nic.
134 J3 Yelva r. Rus. Fed.
137 I4 Yelyseyivka Ukr.
137 G3 Yelyzavethradka Ukr.
106 C4 Yematan Qinghai China
183 I5 Yémeda Spain
124 D5 Yemen country Asia
136 D2 Yemil'chyne Ukr.
Yemişenbükü Turkey see Taşova
Yemmiganur Andhra Prad. India see Emmiganuru
134 H3 Yemtsa Rus. Fed.
134 J3 Yemva Respublika Komi Rus. Fed.
207 G5 Yenagoa Nigeria
137 J3 Yenakiyeve Ukr.
Yenakiyevo Ukr. see Yenakiyeve
96 A2 Yenangyaung Myanmar
96 D2 Yên Bai Vietnam
83 F3 Yenda N.S.W. Austr.
207 E4 Yendi Ghana
Yêndum Xizang China see Zhag'yab
208 D5 Yenge r. Dem. Rep. Congo
206 C4 Yengema Sierra Leone
110 B4 Yengisar Xinjiang China
110 D3 Yengisar Xinjiang China
129 B4 Yenibaşlar Turkey
135 F8 Yeniçağa Turkey
199 E2 Yenice anakkale Turkey
128 B1 Yenice İel Turkey
199 F1 Yeniceköy Bursa Turkey
126 D3 Yeniceoba Turkey
199 E1 Yeniçiftlik anakkale Turkey
199 E1 Yeniçiftlik Turkey
129 B4 Yenidal Turkey
199 F3 Yenidere r. Turkey
199 E2 Yenifoça Turkey
Yenıhan Turkey see Yıldızeli
199 E3 Yenihisar Turkey
Yenije-i-Vardar Greece see Giannitsa
129 F3 Yenikänd Azer.
199 E2 Yeniköy İzmir Turkey
199 F2 Yeniköy Turkey
199 F2 Yeniköy Turkey
199 E1 Yenimuhacirköy Edirne Turkey
199 F3 Yenipazar Aydın Turkey
199 G1 Yenipazar Bilecik Turkey
199 E2 Yenişakran Turkey
Yeniséa Greece see Genisea
Yenişehir Greece see Larisa
199 F1 Yenişehir Turkey
98 Yenisey r. Rus. Fed.
131 K4 Yeniseysk Rus. Fed.
131 K4 Yeniseyskiy Kryazh ridge Rus. Fed.
106 C5 Yeniugou Qinghai China
Yeniyol Turkey see Borçka
160 D3 Yenne France
135 I7 Yenotayevka Rus. Fed.
150 D4 Yeo r. England U.K.
116 C5 Yeola Mahar. India
87 E5 Yeo Lake salt flat W.A. Austr.
Yeotmal Mahar. India see Yavatmal
83 G3 Yeoval N.S.W. Austr.
150 E4 Yeovil Somerset, England U.K.
150 E3 Yeovilton Somerset, England U.K.
Yeo Yeo r. N.S.W. Austr. see Bland
183 G5 Yepes Spain
139 L5 Yepifan' Rus. Fed.
85 G4 Yeppoon Qld Austr.
Yerakaroú Greece see Gerakarou
135 H5 Yerakhtur Rus. Fed.
Yerákion Greece see Geraki
Yeraliyev Kazakh. see Kuryk
131 L3 Yerbogachen Rus. Fed.
114 C4 Yercaud Tamil Nadu India
121 H2 Yerementau, Gory hills Kazakh.
129 D3 Yerevan Armenia
121 H2 Yereymentau Kazakh.
114 C2 Yergara Karnataka India
135 I7 Yergeni hills Rus. Fed.
Yergoğu Romania see Giurgiu
Yeriḥo West Bank see Jericho
87 D6 Yerilla W.A. Austr.
240 H2 Yerington NV U.S.A.
199 F3 Yerkesik Muğla Turkey
128 A1 Yerköprü Mağarası tourist site Turkey
126 D3 Yerköy Turkey
114 B2 Yerla r. India
Yermak Pavlodarskaya Oblast' Kazakh. see Aksu
Yermentau Kazakh. see Yereymentau
135 H5 Yermish' Rus. Fed.
242 D3 Yermo Mex.
240 I4 Yermo CA U.S.A.
139 M3 Yermolino Rus. Fed.
100 B1 Yerofey Pavlovich Rus. Fed.
128 B4 Yeroham Israel
Yeropótamos r. Kriti Greece see Geropotamos
156 B4 Yerre r. France
156 C4 Yerres r. France
134 K2 Yersa r. Rus. Fed.
164 D3 Yerseke Neth.
139 I5 Yershichi Rus. Fed.
120 B2 Yershov Rus. Fed.
139 M1 Yertsevo Rus. Fed.
252 A2 Yerupaja mt. Peru
Yerushalayim Israel/West Bank see Jerusalem
120 A2 Yeruslan r. Rus. Fed.
159 G2 Yerville France
137 K2 Yeryshevka Rus. Fed.
Yerzhar Uzbek. see Gagarin
186 B2 Yesa Spain
Yeshera Georgia see Eshera
121 F2 Yesil' Kazakh.
128 C1 Yeşil Turkey
199 F3 Yeşildere Turkey
128 C1 Yeşildere Turkey
128 A1 Yeşildere Turkey
126 D3 Yeşilhisar Turkey
126 E2 Yeşilırmak r. Turkey
128 C1 Yeşilkent Turkey
199 F2 Yeşilköy Kütahya Turkey
199 F3 Yeşilova Turkey
Yeşilova Yozgat Turkey see Sorgun
199 G3 Yeşilyayla Turkey
199 F2 Yeşilyurt Manisa Turkey
199 F3 Yeşilyuva Turkey
146 E2 Yesnaby Orkney, Scotland U.K.
260 B4 Yeso, Cerro mt. Chile
129 C1 Yessentuki Rus. Fed.
129 C1 Yessentukskaya Rus. Fed.
131 L3 Yessey Rus. Fed.
185 H2 Yeste Spain
150 C4 Yes Tor hill England U.K.
185 H2 Yetas de Abajo Spain
Yêtatang Xizang China see Baqên
83 G2 Yetman N.S.W. Austr.
96 A2 Yeu Myanmar
158 D5 Yeu, Île d' i. France
Yevdokimovskoye Stavropol'skiy Kray Rus. Fed. see Krasnogvardeyskoye
Yevlakh Azer. see Yevlax
129 E3 Yevlax Azer.
137 G5 Yevpatoriya Ukr.
160 A1 Yèvre r. France
100 E2 Yevreyskaya Avtonomnaya Oblast' admin. div. Rus. Fed.
137 J3 Yevsuh r. Ukr.
109 E1 Yexian Henan China
Yexian Shandong China see Laizhou
121 I4 Yeygen'yevka Kazakh.
135 G7 Yeysk Rus. Fed.
137 J4 Yeyskoye Ukreplenie Rus. Fed.
110 D3 Yeyungou Xinjiang China
Yezhou Hubei China see Jianshi
134 I2 Yezhuga r. Rus. Fed.
Yezo i. Japan see Hokkaidō
138 G4 Yezyaryshcha Belarus
Y Fenni Monmouthshire, Wales U.K. see Abergavenny
158 D3 Yffiniac France
Y Fflint Flintshire, Wales U.K. see Flint
163 B5 Ygos-St-Saturnin France
160 A2 Ygrande France
107 G5 Yi r. Henan China
107 H5 Yi r. Shandong China
261 I3 Yí r. Uru.
Yialí i. Greece see Gyali
128 A4 Yi'allaq, Gebel mt. Egypt
Yialousa Cyprus see Aigialousa
100 C3 Yi'an Heilong. China
Yiannitsá Greece see Giannitsa
108 C2 Yibin Sichuan China
108 C2 Yibin Sichuan China
109 D2 Yichang Hubei China
109 E2 Yicheng Hubei China
107 F5 Yicheng Shanxi China
107 G5 Yichuan Henan China
107 F5 Yichuan Shaanxi China
100 D3 Yichun Heilong. China
109 E3 Yichun Jiangxi China
Yidu Shandong China see Qingzhou
108 A2 Yidun Sichuan China
109 E2 Yifeng Jiangxi China
Yiggêtang Qinghai China see Qumarlêb
199 G1 Yığılca Turkey
128 C1 Yiğityolu Turkey
109 F3 Yihuang Jiangxi China
Yijiang Jiangxi China see Yiyang
107 F5 Yijun Shaanxi China
107 J1 Yilaha Heilong. China
100 D3 Yilan Heilong. China
Yilan Taiwan see Ilan
129 B3 Yıldırım Turkey
126 B2 Yıldız Dağları mts Turkey
126 E3 Yıldızeli Turkey
108 B3 Yiliang Yunnan China
108 C3 Yiliang Yunnan China
87 C7 Yilliminning W.A. Austr.
100 C3 Yilong Heilong. China
108 C2 Yilong Sichuan China
Yilong Yunnan China see Shiping
107 H3 Yimatu r. China
96 C1 Yimen Yunnan China
100 D3 Yimianpo Heilong. China
107 H1 Yimin r. China
107 H5 Yinan Shandong China
Yincheng Jiangxi China see Dexing
106 E4 Yinchuan Ningxia China
87 D6 Yindarlgooda, Lake salt flat W.A. Austr.
109 E2 Yingcheng Hubei China
109 E3 Yingde Guangdong China
Yinggen Hainan China see Qiongzhong
109 F1 Ying He r. China
108 A3 Yingjiang Yunnan China
108 B2 Yingjing Sichuan China
Yingkou Liaoning China see Dashiqiao
107 I3 Yingkou Liaoning China
109 E2 Yingshan Hubei China
108 C2 Yingshan Sichuan China
109 F1 Yingshang Anhui China
109 F2 Yingtan Jiangxi China
Yingtaoyuan Henan China see Fanxian
207 H5 Yingui Cameroon
107 G4 Yingxian Shanxi China
Yining Jiangxi China see Xiushui
110 C3 Yining Xinjiang China
108 D3 Yinjiang Guizhou China
109 E3 Yinkeng Jiangxi China
100 C3 Yinma r. China
96 A2 Yinmabin Myanmar
107 F3 Yin Shan mts China
Yinxian Zhejiang China see Ningbo
Yiófiros r. Kriti Greece see Giofyros
111 F6 Yi'ong Zangbo r. Xizang China
Yioúra i. Greece see Gioura
108 B3 Yipinglang Yunnan China
199 G2 Yıprak Turkey
Yiquan Guizhou China see Meitan
257 E5 Yira Chapeu, Monte mt. Brazil
210 C3 Yirga Alem Eth.
210 C3 Yirga Ch'efē Eth.
84 D2 Yirrkala N.T. Austr.
Yirshi Nei Mongol China see Yirxie
107 H2 Yirxie Nei Mongol China
Yisa Yunnan China see Honghe
Yishan Guangxi China see Yizhou
Yishan Jiangsu China see Guanyun
107 H4 Yi Shan mt. Shandong China
107 H5 Yishui Shandong China
Yíthion Greece see Gytheio
Yitiaoshan Gansu China see Jingtai
100 C4 Yitong Jilin China
100 C3 Yitong r. China
96 B2 Yi Tu, Nam r. Myanmar
107 I1 Yitulihe Nei Mongol China
106 B3 Yiwanquan Xinjiang China
106 B3 Yiwu Xinjiang China
109 F2 Yixian Anhui China
107 G4 Yixian Hebei China
107 I3 Yixian Liaoning China
109 F2 Yixing Jiangsu China
107 H3 Yixun r. China
109 E2 Yiyang Hunan China
109 F2 Yiyang Jiangxi China
107 H4 Yiyuan Shandong China
109 E3 Yizhang Hunan China
109 F1 Yizheng Jiangsu China
108 D3 Yizhou Guangxi China
Yizhou Hebei China see Yixian
Yizhou Liaoning China see Yixian
Yizra'el country Asia see Israel
141 O3 Ylämaa Fin.
141 M3 Yläne Fin.
140 M3 Ylihärmä Fin.
140 N2 Yli-Ii Fin.
140 N2 Ylikiiminki Fin.
140 M3 Ylistaro Fin.
140 M2 Ylitornio Fin.
140 N2 Ylivieska Fin.
140 N2 Ylläs hill Fin.
150 D2 Y Llethr hill Wales U.K.
141 M3 Ylöjärvi Fin.
221 P2 Ymer Nunatak Greenland
156 B4 Ymonville France
131 O3 Ynykchanskiy Rus. Fed.
Ynys Môn i. Wales U.K. see Anglesey
237 D6 Yoakum TX U.S.A.
207 H4 Yobe state Nigeria
102 J2 Yobetsu-dake vol. Japan
104 B4 Yodo-gawa r. Japan
234 B3 Yoe PA U.S.A.
259 C9 Yogan, Cerro mt. Chile
95 E4 Yogyakarta Indon.
95 E5 Yogyakarta admin. dist. Indon.
102 J2 Yoichi-dake mt. Japan
242 □I6 Yojoa, Lago de l. Hond.
101 C5 Yŏju S. Korea
207 I6 Yokadouma Cameroon
104 C3 Yōkaichi Japan
105 G3 Yōkaichiba Japan
102 □1 Yokate-jima i. Japan
104 C4 Yokkaichi Japan
207 I5 Yoko Cameroon
105 F3 Yokohama Japan
105 F3 Yokosuka Japan
102 J4 Yokote Japan
102 J3 Yokotsu-dake mt. Japan
207 I4 Yola Nigeria
240 G2 Yolo CA U.S.A.
Yolöten Turkm. see Yeloten
96 C4 Yom, Mae Nam r. Thai.
105 G1 Yomogida-dake hill Fukushima Japan
206 C5 Yomou Guinea
129 A3 Yomra Turkey
162 A2 Yon r. France
103 F6 Yonago Japan
102 □1 Yonaguni-jima i. Japan
101 C5 Yŏnan N. Korea
102 J3 Yoneshiro-gawa r. Japan
105 E1 Yone-yama hill Japan
102 J5 Yonezawa Japan
82 D3 Yongala S.A. Austr.
101 C6 Yŏng-am S. Korea
Yong'an Chongqing China see Fengjie
109 F3 Yong'an Fujian China
Yongbei Yunnan China see Yongsheng
106 D4 Yongchang Gansu China
109 F1 Yongcheng Henan China
101 D6 Yŏngch'ŏn S. Korea
108 C2 Yongchuan Chongqing China
109 F3 Yongchun Fujian China
108 A3 Yongde Yunnan China
106 D4 Yongdeng Gansu China
109 F3 Yongding Fujian China
Yongding Yunnan China see Fumin

Z

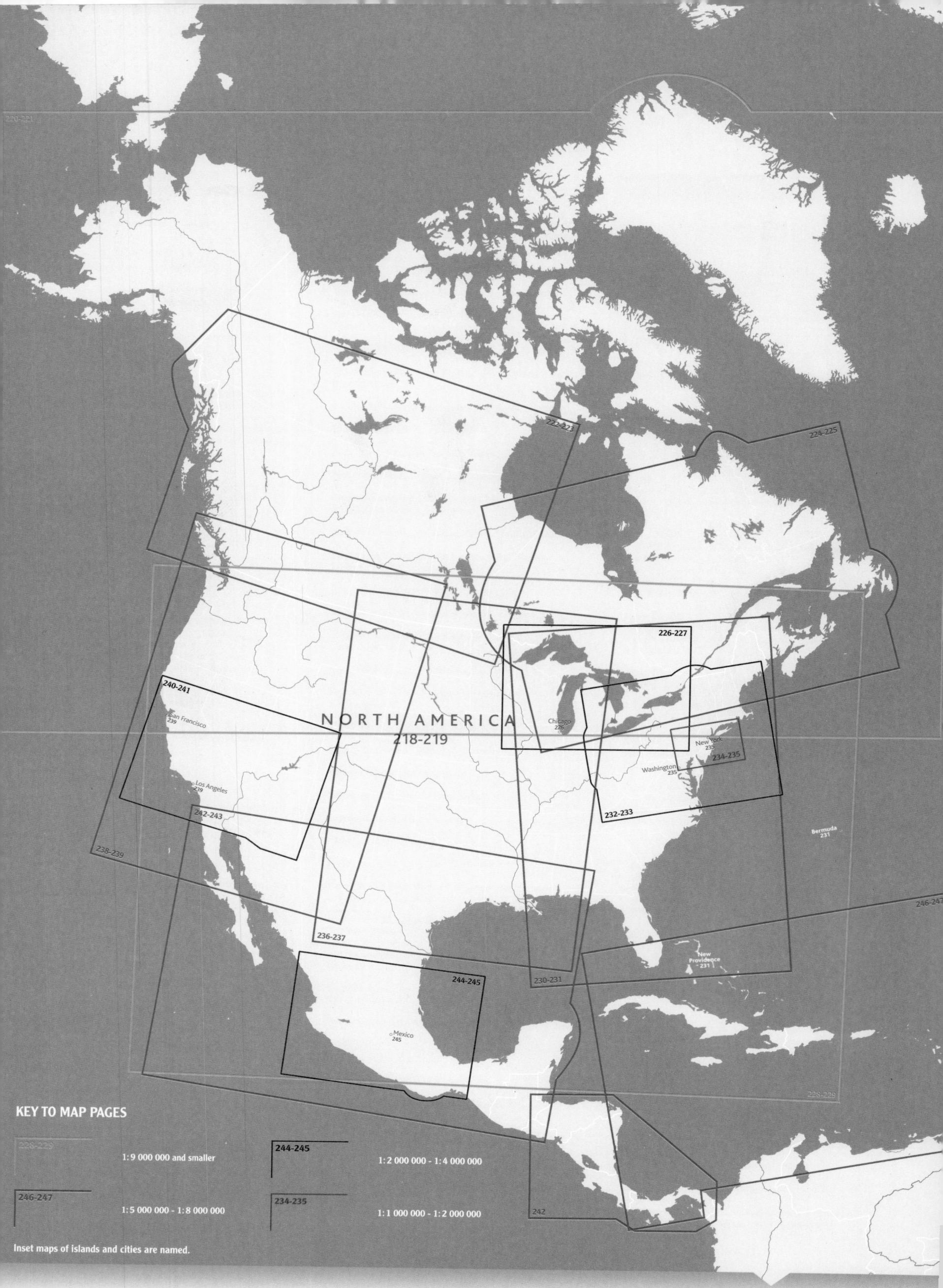

220-221

224-225

222-223

226-227

240-241

San Francisco
239

NORTH AMERICA
218-219

Chicago
226

New York
235

234-235

Washington
235

Los Angeles
239

242-243

232-233

238-239

Bermuda
231

246-247

236-237

244-245

230-231

New
Providence
231

228-229

Mexico
245

242

KEY TO MAP PAGES

228-229

1: 9 000 000 and smaller

244-245

1: 2 000 000 - 1: 4 000 000

246-247

1: 5 000 000 - 1: 8 000 000

234-235

1: 1 000 000 - 1: 2 000 000

Inset maps of islands and cities are named.